Drug Information Handbook

7th Edition | 1999-2000

lexi-comp

APhA

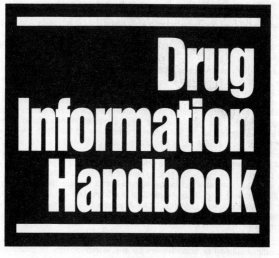

Drug Information Handbook

7ᵗʰ Edition ▌▌ **1999-2000**

Charles F. Lacy, RPh, PharmD
Drug Information Pharmacist
Cedars-Sinai Medical Center
Los Angeles, California

Lora L. Armstrong, RPh, BSPharm, BCPS
Director of Drug Information Services
The University of Chicago Hospitals
Chicago, Illinois

Morton P. Goldman, PharmD, BCPS
Assistant Director, Pharmacotherapy Services
Department of Pharmacy
Cleveland Clinic Foundation
Cleveland, Ohio

Leonard L. Lance, RPh, BSPharm
Pharmacist
Lexi-Comp, Inc.
Hudson, Ohio

LEXI-COMP INC

Hudson (Cleveland)

AMERICAN
PHARMACEUTICAL
ASSOCIATION APhA

This handbook is intended to serve the user as a handy quick reference and not as a complete drug information resource. It does not include information on every therapeutic agent available. The publication covers commonly used drugs and is specifically designed to present certain important aspects of drug data in a more concise format than is generally found in medical literature or product material supplied by manufacturers.

The nature of drug information is that it is constantly evolving because of ongoing research and clinical experience and is often subject to interpretation. While great care has been taken to ensure the accuracy of the information presented, the reader is advised that the authors, editors, reviewers, contributors, and publishers cannot be responsible for the continued currency of the information or for any errors, omissions, or the application of this information, or for any consequences arising therefrom. Therefore, the author(s) and/or the publisher shall have no liability to any person or entity with regard to claims, loss, or damage caused, or alleged to be caused, directly or indirectly, by the use of information contained herein. Because of the dynamic nature of drug information, readers are advised that decisions regarding drug therapy must be based on the independent judgment of the clinician, changing information about a drug (eg, as reflected in the literature and manufacturer's most current product (information), and changing medical practices. The editors are not responsible for any inaccuracy of quotation or for any false or misleading implication that may arise due to the text or formulas as used or due to the quotation of revisions no longer official.

The editors, authors, and contributors have written this book in their private capacities. No official support or endorsement by any federal agency or pharmaceutical company is intended or inferred.

The publishers have made every effort to trace the copyright holders for borrowed material. If they have inadvertently overlooked any, they will be pleased to make the necessary arrangements at the first opportunity.

If you have any suggestions or questions regarding any information presented in this handbook, please contact our drug information pharmacist at

1-800-837-LEXI (5394)

This manual was produced using the FormuLex™ Program — a complete publishing service of Lexi-Comp Inc.

Lexi-Comp Inc
1100 Terex Road
Hudson, Ohio 44236
(330) 650-6506

ISBN 0-916589-76-5 (North American Edition)
ISBN 0-916589-85-4 (International Edition)

TABLE OF CONTENTS

ABOUT THE AUTHORS

Charles F. Lacy, RPh, PharmD

Dr Lacy received his doctorate from the University of Southern California School of Pharmacy. With over 18 years of clinical experience at one of the nation's largest teaching hospitals, he has developed a reputation as an acknowledged expert in drug information and critical care drug therapy.

In his current capacity as Coordinator of Drug Information Services at Cedar-Sinai Health System in Los Angeles, Dr Lacy plays an active role in the education and training of the medical, pharmacy, and nursing staff. He coordinates the Drug Information Center, the Medical Center's Intern Pharmacist Clinical Training Program, the Department's Continuing Education Program for Pharmacists; maintains the Medical Center Formulary Program; and is editor of the Medical Center's *Drug Formulary Handbook* and the drug information newsletter *Prescription*.

Presently, Dr Lacy holds teaching affiliations with the University of Southern California School of Pharmacy, the University of California at San Francisco School of Pharmacy, the University of the Pacific School of Pharmacy, and the University of Alberta at Edmonton, School of Pharmacy and Health Sciences. Additionally, Dr Lacy is the current Director of the Center for International Health Care Practitioners at Western University of Health Sciences, where he plays a leading role in the advanced training of postgraduate pharmacists from areas throughout the Pacific rim, including Japan, Hong Kong, New Zealand, and Korea.

Dr Lacy is an active member of numerous professional associations including the American Society of Health-System Pharmacists (ASHP), the California Society of Hospital Pharmacists (CSHP), the American Society of Consultant Pharmacists (ASCP), and the American College of Clinical Pharmacy (ACCP).

Lora L. Armstrong, RPh, BSPharm, BCPS

Lora L. Armstrong received her bachelor's degree in pharmacy from Ferris State University. With over 17 years of clinical experience at one of the nation's most prominent teaching institutions, she has developed a reputation as an acknowledged expert in drug information. Her interests involve the areas of critical care, hematology, oncology, infectious disease, and pharmacokinetics. Ms. Armstrong is a Board Certified Pharmacotherapy Specialist (BCPS).

In her current capacity as Director of Drug Information at the University of Chicago Hospitals (UCH), Ms Armstrong plays an active role in the education and training of the medical, pharmacy, and nursing staff. She coordinates the Drug Information Center, the medical center's Adverse Drug Reaction Monitoring Program, and the department's Continuing Education Program for Pharmacists. She also maintains the hospital's strict formulary program and is editor of the *UCH Formulary of Accepted Drugs* and the drug information newsletter "Topics in Drug Therapy." Ms. Armstrong also serves on the Editorial Advisory Board of the *Journal of the American Pharmaceutical Association*.

Ms Armstrong is an active member of the American Society of Health-System Pharmacists (ASHP), the American Pharmaceutical Association (APhA), the American College of Clinical Pharmacy (ACCP), and the Society of Critical Care Medicine (SCCM). She is the APhA designated author for this handbook.

Morton P. Goldman, PharmD, BCPS

Dr Goldman received his bachelor's degree in pharmacy from the University of Pittsburgh, College of Pharmacy and his Doctor of Pharmacy degree from the University of Cincinnati, Division of Graduate Studies and Research. He completed his concurrent 2-year hospital pharmacy residency at the VA Medical Center in Cincinnati. Dr Goldman is presently the Assistant Director of Pharmacotherapy Services for the Department of Pharmacy at the Cleveland Clinic Foundation (CCF) after having spent over 3 years at CCF as an Infectious Disease pharmacist and 4 years as Clinical Manager. He holds faculty appointments from Case Western Reserve University, College of Medicine; The University of Toledo, College of Pharmacy; and The University of Cincinnati, College of Pharmacy. Dr Goldman is a board-certified Pharmacotherapy Specialist.

In his capacity as Assistant Director of Pharmacotherapy Services at CCF, Dr Goldman remains actively involved in patient care and clinical research with the Department of Infectious Disease, as well as the continuing education of the medical and pharmacy staff. He is an editor of CCF's *Guidelines for Antibiotic Use* and coordinates their annual Antimicrobial Review retreat. He is a member of the Pharmacy and Therapeutics Committee and many of its subcommittees. Dr Goldman has authored numerous journal articles and lectures locally and nationally on infectious diseases topics and current drug therapies. He is currently a reviewer for the *Annals of Pharmacotherapy* and the *Journal of the American Medical Association*, an editorial board member of the *Journal of Infectious Disease Pharmacotherapy*, and coauthor of the *Drug Information Handbook* and the *Drug Information Handbook for the Allied Health Professional* produced by Lexi-Comp, Inc. He also provides technical support to Lexi-Comp's Clinical Reference Library™ publications.

Dr Goldman is an active member of Cleveland's local clinical pharmacy society, the Ohio College of Clinical Pharmacy, the Society of Infectious Disease Pharmacists, the American College of Clinical Pharmacy, and the American Society of Health-Systems Pharmacy.

Leonard L. Lance, RPh, BSPharm

Leonard L. (Bud) Lance has been directly involved in the pharmaceutical industry since receiving his bachelor's degree in pharmacy from Ohio Northern University in 1970. Upon graduation from ONU, Mr Lance spent four years as a navy pharmacist in various military assignments and was instrumental in the development and operation of the first whole hospital I.V. admixture program in a military (Portsmouth Naval Hospital) facility.

After completing his military service, he entered the retail pharmacy field and has managed both an independent and a home I.V. franchise pharmacy operation. Since the late 1970s Mr Lance has focused much of his interest on using computers to improve pharmacy service and to advance the dissemination of drug information to practitioners and other health care professionals.

As a result of his strong publishing interest, he serves in the capacity of pharmacy editor and technical advisor as well as pharmacy (information) database coordinator for Lexi-Comp. Along with the *Drug Information Handbook for the Allied Health Professional* edition, he provides technical support to Lexi-Comp's *Pediatric Dosage Handbook, Laboratory Test Handbook, Diagnostic Procedure Handbook, Infectious Diseases Handbook, Poisoning & Toxicology Handbook*, and *Geriatric Dosage Handbook* publications. Mr Lance has also assisted approximately 120 major hospitals in producing their own formulary (pharmacy) publications through Lexi-Comp's custom publishing service.

Mr Lance is a member and past president (1984) of the Summit Pharmaceutical Association (SPA). He is also a member of the Ohio Pharmacists Association (OPA), the American Pharmaceutical Association (APhA), and the American Society of Health-System Pharmacists (ASHP).

EDITORIAL ADVISORY PANEL

Martin D. Higbee, PharmD
Associate Professor
Department of Pharmacy Practice
The University of Arizona
Tucson, Arizona

Jane Hurlburt Hodding, PharmD
Supervisor, Children's Pharmacy
Memorial Miller Children's Hospital
Long Beach, California

Rebecca T. Horvat, PhD
Assistant Professor of Pathology and Laboratory Medicine
University of Kansas Medical Center
Kansas City, Kansas

Carlos M. Isada, MD
Department of Infectious Disease
Cleveland Clinic Foundation
Cleveland, Ohio

David S. Jacobs, MD
President, Pathologists Chartered
Overland Park, Kansas

Bernard L. Kasten, Jr, MD
Vice-President/Medical Director
Corning Clinical Laboratories
Teteroboro, New Jersey

Polly E. Kintzel, PharmD
Clinical Pharmacy Specialist
Bone Marrow Transplantation, Detroit Medical Center
Harper Hospital
Detroit, Michigan

Donna M. Kraus, PharmD
Associate Professor of Pharmacy Practice
Departments of Pharmacy Practice and Pediatrics
Clinical Pharmacist
Pediatric Intensive Care Unit
University of Illinois at Chicago
Chicago, Illinois

Brenda R. Lance, RN, MSN
Nurse Coordinator
Ritzman Infusion Services
Akron, Ohio

Jerrold B. Leikin, MD
Associate Director
Emergency Services
Rush Presbyterian-St Luke's Medical Center
Chicago, Illinois

Timothy F. Meiller, DDS, PhD
Professor
Department of Oral Medicine and Diagnostic Sciences
Baltimore College of Dental Surgery
Professor of Oncology
Greenebaum Cancer Center
University of Maryland at Baltimore
Baltimore, Maryland

Eugene S. Olsowka, MD, PhD
Pathologist
Institute of Pathology PC
Saginaw, Michigan

Thomas E. Page, MA
Drug Recognition Expert and Instructor
Officer in Charge, DRE Unit
Los Angeles Police Department
Los Angeles, CA

Frank P. Paloucek, PharmD
Clinical Associate Professor
University of Illinois
Chicago, Illinois

EDITORIAL ADVISORY PANEL *(Continued)*

PREFACE

The volume and breadth of available literature on pharmacology, pharmacokinetics, drug therapy choices, adverse drug reactions, drug interactions, and medication usage guidelines is enormous and continues to grow at an explosive pace. In 1998, the FDA approved 31 molecular and nine biologic entities. The breadth of information provided regarding these new agents is also becoming more intense. This information is most useful when compiled into a logical guide that can be used by working healthcare practitioners. It is the goal of the authors of the *Drug Information Handbook* to provide this medical and pharmaceutical literature in a comprehensive, yet concise, compendium that is easy to use and practical to carry.

The authors have extensively researched the available literature, extracted the most valuable details and have arranged the information into this unified compendium. The information is presented in a concise manner designed to ensure consistent presentation of the information and to facilitate the practitioner's decisions regarding drug therapy. The format for this handbook was developed to lend itself for use by all practitioners and students involved in drug therapy, while paying particular attention to providing the newest, most pertinent, and most practical information available.

In this edition, in the interest of saving space, the <1% incidence in the adverse reactions field are strung and are no longer broken down into separate body systems. However, the foreign brand names are now in separate fields to accommodate the future addition of global brand names.

It is the hope of the authors of the *Drug Information Handbook* that our effort to provide you with this comprehensive collection of drug information in a portable and easy-to-use handbook will prove useful to you in your therapeutic decision making.

— Charles F. Lacy

ACKNOWLEDGMENTS

The *Drug Information Handbook* exists in its present form as the result of the concerted efforts of the following individuals: Robert D. Kerscher, publisher and president of Lexi-Comp Inc; Lynn D. Coppinger, managing editor; Barbara F. Kerscher, production manager; David C. Marcus, director of information systems; and Julian I. Graubart, American Pharmaceutical Association (APhA), Director of Books and Electronic Products.

Other members of the Lexi-Comp staff whose contributions deserve special mention include Diane M. Harbart, MT (ASCP), medical editor; Jeanne E. Wilson, production/systems liaison; Leslie J. Ruggles, Julie A. Katzen, Jennifer L. Rocky, Stacey L. Hurd, Kathleen E. Schleicher, and Linda L. Taylor, project managers; Alexandra J. Hart, composition specialist; Jackie L. Mizer, Ginger S. Conner, and Kathy Smith, production assistants; Tracey J. Reinecke, graphic designer; Cynthia A. Bell, CPhT; Edmund A. Harbart, vice-president, custom publishing division; Jack L. Stones, vice-president, reference publishing division; Jay L. Katzen, director of marketing and business development; Jerry M. Reeves, Marc L. Long, and Patrick T. Grubb, regional sales managers; Brad F. Bolinski, Kristin M. Thompson, Matthew C. Kerscher, Paul A. Rhine, Jason M. Buchwald, Tina L. Collins, Kelene A. Murphy, and Leslie G. Rodia, sales and marketing representatives; Kenneth J. Hughes, manager of authoring systems; Sean M. Conrad and James M. Stacey, system analysts; Thury L. O'Connor, vice-president of technology; David J. Wasserbauer, vice-president, finance and administration; Elizabeth M. Conlon and Rebecca A. Dryhurst, accounting; and Frederick C. Kerscher, fulfillment manager.

Much of the material contained in this book was a result of pharmacy contributors throughout the United States and Canada. Lexi-Comp has assisted many medical institutions to develop hospital-specific formulary manuals that contain clinical drug information as well as dosing. Working with these clinical pharmacists, hospital pharmacy and therapeutics committees, and hospital drug information centers, Lexi-Comp has developed an evolutionary drug database that reflects the practice of pharmacy in these major institutions.

In addition, the authors wish to thank their families, friends, and colleagues who supported them in their efforts to complete this handbook.

DESCRIPTION OF SECTIONS AND FIELDS USED IN THIS HANDBOOK

The *Drug Information Handbook, 7th Edition* is divided into four sections.

The first section is a compilation of introductory text pertinent to the use of this book.

The drug information section of the handbook, in which all drugs are listed alphabetically, details information pertinent to each drug. Extensive cross-referencing is provided by U.S. brand names, Canadian brand names, and synonyms. Many combination monographs have been added to this edition; however, they have been condensed with only brand names and forms available. For more information on these products, see the individual components.

The third section is an invaluable appendix which offers a compilation of tables, guidelines, nomograms, algorithms, and conversion information which can be helpful when considering patient care.

The last section of this handbook contains a Therapeutic Category & Key Word Index which lists all drugs in this handbook in their unique therapeutic class; also listed are controlled substances by their restriction class.

The **Alphabetical Listing of Drugs** is presented in a consistent format and provides the following fields of information:

Generic Name	U.S. adopted name
Pronunciation	Phonetic pronunciation guide
Related Information	Cross-reference to other pertinent drug information found elsewhere in this handbook
Brand Names	U.S. trade names (manufacturer-specific)
Canadian Brand Names	Trade names found in Canada
Synonyms	Other names or accepted abbreviations of the generic drug
Therapeutic Category	Unique systematic classification of medications
Use	Information pertaining to appropriate indications of the drug. Includes both FDA approved and non-FDA approved indications.
Restrictions	The controlled substance classification from the Drug Enforcement Agency (DEA). U.S. schedules are I-V. Schedules vary by country and sometimes state (ie, Massachusetts uses I-VI)
Pregnancy Risk Factor	Five categories established by the FDA to indicate the potential of a systemically absorbed drug for causing birth defects
Pregnancy/Breast-Feeding Implications	Information pertinent to or associated with the use of the drug as it relates to clinical effects on the fetus, breast-feeding/lactation, and clinical effects on the infant
Contraindications	Information pertaining to inappropriate use of the drug
Warnings/Precautions	Precautionary considerations, hazardous conditions related to use of the drug, and disease states or patient populations in which the drug should be cautiously used
Adverse Reactions	Side effects are grouped by percentage of incidence (if known) and/or body system; in the interest of saving space, <1% effects are grouped only by percentage
Overdosage/Toxicology	Comments and/or considerations are offered when appropriate and include signs/symptoms of excess drug and suggested management of the patient
Drug Interactions	If a drug has demonstrated involvement with cytochrome P-450 enzymes, the initial line of this field will identify the drug as an inhibitor, inducer, or substrate of specific isoenzymes (ie, CYP1A2). A summary of this information can also be found in a tabular format within the appendix section of this handbook. The remainder of the field presents a description of the interaction between the drug listed in the monograph and other drugs or drug classes. May include possible mechanisms and effect of combined therapy. May also include a strategy to manage the patient on combined therapy (ie, quinidine).

DESCRIPTION OF SECTIONS AND FIELDS USED IN THIS HANDBOOK *(Continued)*

Stability	Information regarding storage of product or steps for reconstitution. Provides the time and conditions for which a solution or mixture will maintain full potency. For example, some solutions may require refrigeration after reconstitution while stored at room temperature prior to preparation. Also includes compatibility information.
Mechanism of Action	How the drug works in the body to elicit a response
Pharmacodynamics/ Kinetics	The magnitude of a drug's effect depends on the drug concentration at the site of action. The pharmacodynamics are expressed in terms of onset of action and duration of action. Pharmacokinetics are expressed in terms of absorption, distribution (including appearance in breast milk and crossing of the placenta), protein binding, metabolism, bioavailability, half-life, time to peak serum concentration, and elimination.
Usual Dosage	The amount of the drug to be typically given or taken during therapy for children and adults; also includes any dosing adjustment/comments for renal impairment or hepatic impairment and other suggested dosing adjustments (eg, hematological toxicity)
Dietary Considerations	Information is offered, when appropriate, regarding food, nutrition, and/or alcohol
Administration	Information regarding the recommended final concentrations, rates of administration for parenteral drugs, or other guidelines when giving the medication
Monitoring Parameters	Laboratory tests and patient physical parameters that should be monitored for safety and efficacy of drug therapy
Reference Range	Therapeutic and toxic serum concentrations listed including peak and trough levels
Test Interactions	Listing of assay interferences when relevant; (B) = Blood; (S) = Serum; (U) = Urine
Patient Information	Specific information pertinent for the patient
Nursing Implications	Includes additional instructions for the administration of the drug and monitoring tips from the nursing perspective
Additional Information	Information about sodium content and/or pertinent information about specific brands
Dosage Forms	Information with regard to form, strength, and availability of the drug
Extemporaneous Preparations	Directions for preparing liquid formulations from solid drug products. May include stability information and references.

FDA PREGNANCY CATEGORIES

Throughout this book there is a field labeled Pregnancy Risk Factor (PRF) and the letter A, B, C, D or X immediately following which signifies a category. The FDA has established these five categories to indicate the potential of a systemically absorbed drug for causing birth defects. The key differentiation among the categories rests upon the reliability of documentation and the risk:benefit ratio. Pregnancy Category X is particularly notable in that if any data exists that may implicate a drug as a teratogen and the risk:benefit ratio is clearly negative, the drug is contraindicated during pregnancy.

These categories are summarized as follows:

A   Controlled studies in pregnant women fail to demonstrate a risk to the fetus in the first trimester with no evidence of risk in later trimesters. The possibility of fetal harm appears remote.

B   Either animal-reproduction studies have not demonstrated a fetal risk but there are no controlled studies in pregnant women, or animal-reproduction studies have shown an adverse effect (other than a decrease in fertility) that was not confirmed in controlled studies in women in the first trimester and there is no evidence of a risk in later trimesters.

C   Either studies in animals have revealed adverse effects on the fetus (teratogenic or embryocidal effects or other) and there are no controlled studies in women, or studies in women and animals are not available. Drugs should be given only if the potential benefits justify the potential risk to the fetus.

D   There is positive evidence of human fetal risk, but the benefits from use in pregnant women may be acceptable despite the risk (eg, if the drug is needed in a life-threatening situation or for a serious disease for which safer drugs cannot be used or are ineffective).

X   Studies in animals or human beings have demonstrated fetal abnormalities or there is evidence of fetal risk based on human experience, or both, and the risk of the use of the drug in pregnant women clearly outweighs any possible benefit. The drug is contraindicated in women who are or may become pregnant.

DRUGS IN PREGNANCY

Analgesics
Acceptable: Acetaminophen, meperidine, methadone
Controversial: Codeine, propoxyphene
Unacceptable: Nonsteroidal anti-inflammatory agents, salicylates, phenazopyridine

Antimicrobials
Acceptable: Penicillins, 1st and 2nd generation cephalosporins, erythromycin (base and EES), clotrimazole, miconazole, nystatin, isoniazid*, lindane, acyclovir, metronidazole
Controversial: 3rd generation cephalosporins, aminoglycosides, nitrofurantoin†
Unacceptable: Erythromycin estolate, chloramphenicol, sulfa, tetracyclines

ENT
Acceptable: Diphenhydramine*, dextromethorphan
Controversial: Pseudoephedrine
Unacceptable: Brompheniramine, cyproheptadine, dimenhydrinate

GI
Acceptable: Trimethobenzamide, antacids*, simethicone, other H_2-blockers, psyllium, bisacodyl, docusate
Controversial: Metoclopramide, prochlorperazine

Neurologic
Controversial: Phenytoin, phenobarbital
Unacceptable: Carbamazepine, valproic acid, ergotamine

Pulmonary
Acceptable: Theophylline, metaproterenol, terbutaline, inhaled steroids
Unacceptable: Epinephrine, oral steroids

Psych
Acceptable: Hydroxyzine*, lithium*, haloperidol
Controversial: Benzodiazepines, tricyclics, phenothiazines

Other
Acceptable: Heparin, insulin
Unacceptable: Warfarin, sulfonylureas

*Do not use in first trimester
†Do not use in third trimester

SAFE WRITING

Health professionals and their support personnel frequently produce handwritten copies of information they see in print; therefore, such information is subjected to even greater possibilities for error or misinterpretation on the part of others. Thus, particular care must be given to how drug names and strengths are expressed when creating written healthcare documents.

The following are a few examples of safe writing rules suggested by the Institute for Safe Medication Practices, Inc.*

1. There should be a space between a number and its units as it is easier to read. There should be no periods after the abbreviations mg or mL.

Correct	Incorrect
10 mg	10mg
100 mg	100mg

2. Never place a decimal and a zero after a whole number (2 mg is correct and 2.0 mg is **incorrect**). If the decimal point is not seen because it falls on a line or because individuals are working from copies where the decimal point is not seen, this causes a tenfold overdose.

3. Just the opposite is true for numbers less than one. Always place a zero before a naked decimal (0.5 mL is correct, .5 mL is **incorrect**).

4. Never abbreviate the word unit. The handwritten U or u, looks like a 0 (zero), and may cause a tenfold overdose error to be made.

5. IU is not a safe abbreviation for international units. The handwritten IU looks like IV. Write out international units or use int. units.

6. Q.D. is not a safe abbreviation for once daily, as when the Q is followed by a sloppy dot, it looks like QID which means four times daily.

7. O.D. is not a safe abbreviation for once daily, as it is properly interpreted as meaning "right eye" and has caused liquid medications such as saturated solution of potassium iodide and Lugol's solution to be administered incorrectly. There is no safe abbreviation for once daily. It must be written out in full.

8. Do not use chemical names such as 6-mercaptopurine or 6-thioguanine, as sixfold overdoses have been given when these were not recognized as chemical names. The proper names of these drugs are mercaptopurine or thioguanine.

9. Do not abbreviate drug names (5FC, 6MP, 5-ASA, MTX, HCTZ, CPZ, PBZ, etc) as they are misinterpreted and cause error.

10. Do not use the apothecary system or symbols.

11. Do not abbreviate microgram as µg; instead use mcg as there is less likelihood of misinterpretation.

12. When writing an outpatient prescription, write a complete prescription. A complete prescription can prevent the prescriber, the pharmacist, and/or the patient from making a mistake and can eliminate the need for further clarification. The legible prescriptions should contain:

   a. patient's full name

   b. for pediatric or geriatric patients: their age (or weight where applicable)

   c. drug name, dosage form and strength; if a drug is new or rarely prescribed, print this information

   d. number or amount to be dispensed

   e. complete instructions for the patient, including the purpose of the medication

   f. when there are recognized contraindications for a prescribed drug, indicate to the pharmacist that you are aware of this fact (ie, when prescribing a potassium salt for a patient receiving an ACE inhibitor, write "K serum level being monitored")

*From "Safe Writing" by Davis NM, PharmD and Cohen MR, MS, Lecturers and Consultants for Safe Medication Practices, 1143 Wright Drive, Huntington Valley, PA 19006. Phone: (215) 947-7566.

ALPHABETICAL LISTING OF DRUGS

♦ **A-200™ Shampoo [OTC]** *see Pyrethrins on page 996*

Abacavir (a BAK a veer)
Related Information
Antiretroviral Agents *on page 1306*
U.S. Brand Names Ziagen®
Therapeutic Category Antiretroviral Agent, Reverse Transcriptase Inhibitor; Reverse Transcriptase Inhibitor
Use Treatment of HIV infections in combination with other antiretroviral agents
Pregnancy Risk Factor C
Pregnancy/Breast-Feeding Implications
Clinical effects on the fetus: Administer during pregnancy only if benefits to mother outweigh risks to the fetus
Breast-feeding/lactation: HIV-infected mothers are discouraged from breast-feeding to decrease potential transmission of HIV
Health professional are encouraged to contact the antiretroviral pregnancy registry to monitor outcomes of pregnant women exposed to abacavir (1-800-258-4263)
Contraindications Prior hypersensitivity to abacavir (or carbovir) or any component of the formulation; do not rechallenge patients who have experienced hypersensitivity to abacavir
Warnings/Precautions Should always be used as a component of a multidrug regimen. Fatal hypersensitivity reactions have occurred. **Patients exhibiting symptoms of fever, skin rash, fatigue, and GI symptoms (eg, abdominal pain, nausea, vomiting) should discontinue therapy immediately and call for medical attention. Ziagen® SHOULD NOT be restarted because more severe symptoms may occur within hours, including LIFE-THREATENING HYPOTENSION AND DEATH. To report these events on abacavir hypersensitivity, a registry has been established (1-800-270-0425).** Use with caution in patients with hepatic dysfunction; prior liver disease, prolonged use, and obesity may be risk factors for development of lactic acidosis and severe hepatomegaly with steatosis.
Adverse Reactions Note: Hypersensitivity reactions, which may be fatal, occur in ~5% of patients (see Warnings). Symptoms may include anaphylaxis, fever, rash, fatigue, diarrhea, abdominal pain, nausea and vomiting. Less common symptoms may include edema, lethargy, malaise, myalgia, shortness of breath, mouth ulcerations, conjunctivitis, lymphadenopathy, hepatic failure and renal failure.

Rates of adverse reactions were defined during combination therapy with lamivudine. Adverse reaction rates attributable to abacavir alone are not available.

Adults:
Central nervous system: Insomnia (7%)
Gastrointestinal: Nausea (47%), vomiting (16%), diarrhea (12%), anorexia (11%), pancreatitis
Neuromuscular & skeletal: Weakness
Endocrine & metabolic: Hyperglycemia, hypertriglyceridemia (25%)
Miscellaneous: Elevated transaminases
Children:
Central nervous system: Fever (19%), headache (16%)
Dermatologic: Rash (11%)
Gastrointestinal: Nausea (38%), vomiting (38%), diarrhea (16%), anorexia (9%)
Stability Store at room temperature; do not freeze oral solution. Oral solution may be refrigerated.
Mechanism of Action Nucleoside reverse transcriptase inhibitor. Abacavir is a guanosine analogue which is phosphorylated to carbovir triphosphate which interferes with HIV viral RNA dependent DNA polymerase resulting in inhibition of viral replication.
Pharmacodynamics/Kinetics
Distribution: V_d: 0.86 L/kg
Protein binding 27% to 33%
Metabolism: Hepatic, via alcohol dehydrogenase and glucuronyl transferase to inactive carboxylate and glucuronide metabolites
Bioavailability: 83%
Half-life: 1.5 hours
Time to maximum peak: 0.7-1.7 hours
Elimination: Primarily in urine, as metabolites, (1.2% unchanged); fecal elimination accounted for only 16% of the total dose
Usual Dosage Oral:
Children: 3 months to 16 years: 8 mg/kg body weight twice daily (maximum 300 mg twice daily) in combination with other antiretroviral agents
Adults: 300 mg twice daily in combination with other antiretroviral agents
Administration May be taken with or without food.
Patient Information If you have experienced any of the following: fever, skin rash, fatigue, nausea, vomiting, diarrhea, abdominal pain, contact your physician IMMEDIATELY. If you are instructed to stop the medication, DO NOT TAKE THIS MEDICATION IN THE FUTURE.
Additional Information A medication guide is available and should be dispensed with each prescription or refill for abacavir. A warning card is also available and patients should be instructed to carry this card with them.
Dosage Forms
Solution, oral (strawberry-banana flavored): 20 mg/mL (240 mL)
Tablet: 300 mg

♦ **Abbokinase® Injection** *see Urokinase on page 1200*
♦ **Abbreviations and Measurements** *see page 1246*
♦ **ABCD** *see Amphotericin B Cholesteryl Sulfate Complex on page 73*

Abciximab (ab SIK si mab)

Related Information
Glycoprotein Antagonists *on page 1323*
U.S. Brand Names ReoPro®
Synonyms C7E3; 7E3
Therapeutic Category Non-nucleoside Reverse Transciptase Inhibitor (NNRTI); Platelet Aggregation Inhibitor
Use Adjunct to percutaneous transluminal coronary angioplasty or atherectomy (PTCA) for the prevention of acute cardiac ischemic complications in patients at high risk for abrupt closure of the treated coronary vessel. Use as an adjunct with heparin to prevent cardiac ischemic complications in patients with unstable angina not responding to conventional therapy when a percutaneous coronary intervention is scheduled within 24 hours.

Patients at high risk of closure or restenosis:
Acute evolving myocardial infarction (MI) within 12 hours of onset of symptoms requiring rescue PTCA
Early postinfarction angina or unstable angina with at least 2 episodes of angina associated with EKG changes during previous 24 hours
Non-Q-wave myocardial infarction
Clinical or angiographic characteristic indicating high risk (see "Characteristics of Type A, B, and C Lesions" below)
Unfavorable anatomy (ie, 2 or more type B lesions) **or**
One or more type B lesions with diabetes **or**
One or more type B lesions and a female and over the age of 65 **or**
One type C lesion
Thrombus score is based upon angiographic evidence

Characteristics of Type A, B, and C Lesions
Type A lesions (minimally complex)
Discrete (length <10 mm)
Concentric
Readily accessible
Nonangulated segment (<45°)
Smooth contour
Little or no calcification
Less than totally occlusive
Not ostial in location
No major side branch involvement
No thrombus
Type B lesions (moderately complex)
Tubular (length 10-20 mm)
Eccentric
Moderate tortuosity of proximal segment
Moderate angulated segment (>45°, <90°)
Irregular contour
Moderate or heavy calcification
Total occlusions <3 months old
Ostial in location
Bifurcation lesions requiring double lead wires
Some thrombus present
Type C lesions (severely complex)
Diffuse (length >20 mm)
Excessive tortuosity of proximal segment
Extremely angulated segments >90°
Total occlusions >3 months old and/or bridging collaterals
Inability to protect major side branches
Degenerated vein grafts with friable lesions

Pregnancy Risk Factor C
Pregnancy/Breast-Feeding Implications Clinical effects on the fetus: It is not known whether abciximab can cause fetal harm when administered to a pregnant woman or can affect reproduction capacity

Contraindications
Active internal hemorrhage or recent (within 6 weeks) clinically significant gastrointestinal or genitourinary bleeding
History of cerebrovascular accident within 2 years, or cerebrovascular accident with significant neurological deficit
Bleeding diathesis or administration of oral anticoagulants within 7 days unless prothrombin time (PT) is less than or equal to 1.2 times control PT value
Thrombocytopenia (<100,000 cells/μL)
Recent (within 6 weeks) major surgery or trauma
Intracranial tumor, arteriovenous malformation, or aneurysm
Severe uncontrolled hypertension
History of vasculitis
Use of dextran before PTCA or intent to use dextran during PTCA
Known hypersensitivity to abciximab or to murine proteins
(Continued)

Abciximab *(Continued)*

Warnings/Precautions Administration of abciximab is associated with a significantly increased frequency of major bleeding complications including retroperitoneal bleeding, spontaneous GI or GU bleeding and bleeding at the arterial access site

Clinical data indicate that the risk of major bleeding due to abciximab therapy may be elevated in the following settings:

Patients weighing <75 kilograms

Elderly patients (>65 years of age)

History of previous gastrointestinal disease

Recent thrombolytic therapy

Increased risk of hemorrhage during or following angioplasty is associated with the following factors; these risks may be additive to that associated with abciximab therapy:

Unsuccessful PTCA

PTCA procedure >70 minutes duration

PTCA performed within 12 hours of symptom onset for acute myocardial infarction

There is no data concerning the safety or efficacy of readministration of abciximab; administration of abciximab may result in human antichimeric antibody formation that can cause hypersensitivity reactions (including anaphylaxis), thrombocytopenia, or diminished efficacy. Anticoagulation, such as with heparin, may contribute to the risk of bleeding.

Adverse Reactions

>10%:

Cardiovascular: Hypotension

Central nervous system: Pain

Gastrointestinal: Nausea

Hematologic: Major bleeding episodes

1% to 10%:

Cardiovascular: Bradycardia, peripheral edema

Hematologic: Minor bleeding episodes, thrombocytopenia, anemia

Respiratory: Pleural effusion

Overdosage/Toxicology The antiplatelet effects can be quickly reversed with the administration of platelets

Drug Interactions Increased toxicity:

Bleeding: Heparin, other anticoagulants, thrombolytics, and antiplatelet drugs

Allergic reactions: Diagnostic or therapeutic monoclonal antibodies

Stability Vials should be stored at 2°C to 8°C, do not freeze; after admixture, the prepared solution is stable for 12 hours; abciximab should be administered in a separate intravenous line; no incompatibilities have been observed with glass bottles or PVC bags

Mechanism of Action Fab antibody fragment of the chimeric human-murine monoclonal antibody 7E3; this agent binds to platelets resulting in steric hindrance, thus inhibiting platelet aggregation

Pharmacodynamics/Kinetics Half-life: ~30 minutes

Usual Dosage I.V.: 0.25 mg/kg bolus administered 10-60 minutes before the start of intervention followed by an infusion of 0.125 mcg/kg/minute (to a maximum of 10 mcg/minute) for 12 hours

Patients with unstable angina not responding to conventional medical therapy and who are planning to undergo percutaneous coronary intervention within 24 hours may be treated with abciximab 0.25 mg/kg intravenous bolus followed by an 18- to 24-hour intravenous infusion of 10 mcg/minute, concluding 1 hour after the percutaneous coronary intervention

Administration Abciximab is intended for coadministration with aspirin postangioplasty and heparin infused and weight adjusted to maintain a therapeutic bleeding time (eg, ACT 300-500 seconds)

Bolus dose: Aseptically withdraw the necessary amount of abciximab (2 mg/mL) for the bolus dose through a 0.22-micron filter into a syringe; the bolus should be administered 10-60 minutes before the procedure

Continuous infusion: Aseptically withdraw 4.5 mL (9 mg) of abciximab for the infusion through a 0.22 micron filter into a syringe; inject this into 250 mL of NS or D_5W to make a solution with a final concentration of 35 mcg/mL. Infuse at a rate of 17 mL/hour (10 mcg/minute) for 12 hours via pump; **filter all infusions.**

Monitoring Parameters Prothrombin time, activated partial thromboplastin time, hemoglobin, hematocrit, platelet count, fibrinogen, fibrin split products, transfusion requirements, signs of hypersensitivity reactions, guaiac stools, and Hemastix® urine

Nursing Implications Do not shake the vial; maintain bleeding precautions, avoid unnecessary arterial and venous punctures, use saline or heparin lock for blood drawing, assess sheath insertion site and distal pulses of affected leg every 15 minutes for the first hour and then every 1 hour for the next 6 hours. Arterial access site care is important to prevent bleeding. Care should be taken when attempting vascular access that only the anterior wall of the femoral artery is punctured, avoiding a Seldinger (through and through) technique for obtaining sheath access. Femoral vein sheath placement should be avoided unless needed. While the vascular sheath is in place, patients should be maintained on complete bed rest with the head of the bed at a 30° angle and the affected limb restrained in a straight position.

Observe patient for mental status changes, hemorrhage, assess nose and mouth mucous membranes, puncture sites for oozing, ecchymosis and hematoma formation, and examine urine, stool and emesis for presence of occult or frank blood; gentle care should be provided when removing dressings.

Dosage Forms Injection: 2 mg/mL (5 mL)

♦ **Abelcet™ Injection** *see* Amphotericin B, Lipid Complex *on page 76*

♦ **Abenol®** *see* Acetaminophen *on page 19*

♦ **Abitrate®** *see* Clofibrate *on page 279*

♦ **ABLC** *see* Amphotericin B, Lipid Complex *on page 76*

♦ **Absorbine® Antifungal [OTC]** *see* Tolnaftate *on page 1159*

♦ **Absorbine® Antifungal Foot Powder [OTC]** *see* Miconazole *on page 775*

♦ **Absorbine® Jock Itch [OTC]** *see* Tolnaftate *on page 1159*

♦ **Absorbine Jr.® Antifungal [OTC]** *see* Tolnaftate *on page 1159*

Acarbose (AY car bose)

Related Information

Hypoglycemic Drugs, Comparison of Oral Agents *on page 1325*

U.S. Brand Names Precose®

Therapeutic Category Alpha-Glucosidase Inhibitor; Hypoglycemic Agent, Oral

Use

Monotherapy, as indicated as an adjunct to diet to lower blood glucose in patients with noninsulin-dependent diabetes mellitus (NIDDM) whose hyperglycemia cannot be managed on diet alone

Combination with a sulfonylurea, metformin, or insulin in patients with NIDDM when diet plus acarbose do not result in adequate glycemic control

Pregnancy Risk Factor B

Pregnancy/Breast-Feeding Implications Breast-feeding/lactation: It is not known whether acarbose is excreted in human milk

Contraindications Known hypersensitivity to the drug and in patients with diabetic ketoacidosis or cirrhosis; patients with inflammatory bowel disease, colonic ulceration, partial intestinal obstruction or in patients predisposed to intestinal obstruction; patients who have chronic intestinal diseases associated with marked disorders of digestion or absorption and in patients who have conditions that may deteriorate as a result of increased gas formation in the intestine

Warnings/Precautions Hypoglycemia: Acarbose may increase the hypoglycemic potential of sulfonylureas. Oral glucose (dextrose) should be used in the treatment of mild to moderate hypoglycemia. Severe hypoglycemia may require the use of either intravenous glucose infusion or glucagon injection.

Elevated serum transaminase levels: Treatment-emergent elevations of serum transaminases (AST and/or ALT) occurred in 15% of acarbose-treated patients in long-term studies. These serum transaminase elevations appear to be dose related. At doses >100 mg 3 times/day, the incidence of serum transaminase elevations greater than 3 times the upper limit of normal was 2-3 times higher in the acarbose group than in the placebo group. These elevations were asymptomatic, reversible, more common in females, and, in general, were not associated with other evidence of liver dysfunction.

When diabetic patients are exposed to stress such as fever, trauma, infection, or surgery, a temporary loss of control of blood glucose may occur. At such times, temporary insulin therapy may be necessary.

Adverse Reactions

>10%:

Gastrointestinal: Abdominal pain (21%) and diarrhea (33%) tend to return to pretreatment levels over time, and the frequency and intensity of flatulence (77%) tend to abate with time

Hepatic: Elevated liver transaminases

<1%: Sleepiness, headache, vertigo, erythema, urticaria, severe gastrointestinal distress, weakness

Overdosage/Toxicology An overdose will not result in hypoglycemia; an overdose may result in transient increases in flatulence, diarrhea, and abdominal discomfort which shortly subside

Drug Interactions Decreased effect: Thiazides and other diuretics, corticosteroids, phenothiazines, thyroid products, estrogens, oral contraceptives, phenytoin, nicotinic acid, sympathomimetics, calcium channel-blocking drugs, isoniazid, intestinal adsorbents (eg, charcoal), digestive enzyme preparations (eg, amylase, pancreatin)

Stability Store at <25°C (77°F) and protect from moisture

Mechanism of Action Competitive inhibitor of pancreatic α-amylase and intestinal brush border α-glucosidases, resulting in delayed hydrolysis of ingested complex carbohydrates and disaccharides and absorption of glucose; dose-dependent reduction in postprandial serum insulin and glucose peaks; inhibits the metabolism of sucrose to glucose and fructose

Pharmacodynamics/Kinetics

Absorption: <2% absorbed as active drug

Metabolism: Metabolized exclusively within the gastrointestinal tract, principally by intestinal bacteria and by digestive enzymes; ~34% of dose is metabolized, absorbed, and subsequently excreted in the urine; 13 metabolites have been identified

Bioavailability: Low systemic bioavailability of parent compound because acarbose acts locally within the gastrointestinal tract

Elimination: The fraction that is absorbed as intact drug is almost completely excreted by the kidney

(Continued)

Acarbose *(Continued)*

Usual Dosage Oral:

Adults: Dosage must be individualized on the basis of effectiveness and tolerance while not exceeding the maximum recommended dose

Initial dose: 25 mg 3 times/day with the first bite of each main meal

Maintenance dose: Should be adjusted at 4- to 8-week intervals based on 1-hour postprandial glucose levels and tolerance. Dosage may be increased from 25 mg 3 times/day to 50 mg 3 times/day. Some patients may benefit from increasing the dose to 100 mg 3 times/day.

Maintenance dose ranges: 50-100 mg 3 times/day.

Maximum dose:

≤60 kg: 50 mg 3 times/day

>60 kg: 100 mg 3 times/day

Patients receiving sulfonylureas: Acarbose given in combination with a sulfonylurea will cause a further lowering of blood glucose and may increase the hypoglycemic potential of the sulfonylurea. If hypoglycemia occurs, appropriate adjustments in the dosage of these agents should be made.

Dosing adjustment in renal impairment: Cl_{cr} <25 mL/minute: Peak plasma concentrations were 5 times higher and AUCs were 6 times larger than in volunteers with normal renal function; however, long term clinical trials in diabetic patients with significant renal dysfunction have not been conducted and treatment of these patients with acarbose is not recommended

Administration Should be administered with the first bite of each main meal

Monitoring Parameters Postprandial glucose, glycosylated hemoglobin levels, serum transaminase levels should be checked every 3 months during the first year of treatment and periodically thereafter

Patient Information Take acarbose 3 times/day at the start (with the first bite) of each main meal. It is important to continue to adhere to dietary instructions, a regular exercise program, and regular testing of urine and/or blood glucose.

The risk of hypoglycemia, its symptoms and treatment, and conditions that predispose to its development should be well understood by patients and responsible family members. A source of glucose (dextrose) should be readily available to treat symptoms of low blood glucose when taking acarbose in combination with a sulfonylurea or insulin. If side effects occur, they usually develop during the first few weeks of therapy and are most often mild to moderate gastrointestinal effects, such as flatulence, diarrhea, or abdominal discomfort and generally diminish in frequency and intensity with time.

Dosage Forms Tablet: 50 mg, 100 mg

♦ **Accolate®** *see Zafirlukast on page 1232*

♦ **Accupril®** *see Quinapril on page 1002*

♦ **Accutane®** *see Isotretinoin on page 640*

♦ **ACE** *see Captopril on page 185*

Acebutolol *(a se BYOO toe lole)*

Related Information

Beta-Blockers Comparison *on page 1311*

U.S. Brand Names Sectral®

Canadian Brand Names Monitan®; Rhotral

Synonyms Acebutolol Hydrochloride

Therapeutic Category Antihypertensive Agent; Beta-Adrenergic Blocker

Use Treatment of hypertension, ventricular arrhythmias, angina

Pregnancy Risk Factor B

Contraindications Hypersensitivity to beta-blocking agents, avoid use in uncompensated congestive heart failure; cardiogenic shock; bradycardia or heart block; sinus node dysfunction; A-V conduction abnormalities. Although acebutolol primarily blocks beta$_1$-receptors, high doses can result in beta$_2$-receptor blockage. Use with caution in bronchospastic lung disease and renal dysfunction (especially the elderly).

Warnings/Precautions Abrupt withdrawal of beta-blockers may result in an exaggerated cardiac beta-adrenergic responsiveness. Symptomatology has included reports of tachycardia, hypertension, ischemia, angina, myocardial infarction, and sudden death. It is recommended that patients be tapered gradually off of beta-blockers over a 2-week period rather than via abrupt discontinuation.

Adverse Reactions

>10%: Central nervous system: Fatigue

1% to 10%:

Cardiovascular: Chest pain, edema, bradycardia, hypotension

Central nervous system: Headache, dizziness, insomnia, depression, abnormal dreams

Dermatologic: Rash

Gastrointestinal: Constipation, diarrhea, dyspepsia, nausea, flatulence

Genitourinary: Polyuria

Neuromuscular & skeletal: Arthralgia, myalgia

Ocular: Abnormal vision

Respiratory: Dyspnea, rhinitis, cough

<1%: Ventricular arrhythmias, heart block, heart failure, facial edema, xerostomia, anorexia, impotence, urinary retention, cold extremities

Overdosage/Toxicology

Symptoms of intoxication include cardiac disturbances, CNS toxicity, bronchospasm, hypoglycemia, and hyperkalemia. The most common cardiac symptoms include hypotension and bradycardia; atrioventricular block, intraventricular conduction disturbances, cardiogenic shock, and asystole may occur with severe overdose, especially with membrane-depressant drugs (eg, propranolol); CNS effects include convulsions, coma, and respiratory arrest is commonly seen with propranolol and other membrane-depressant and lipid-soluble drugs

Treatment includes symptomatic treatment of seizures, hypotension, hyperkalemia and hypoglycemia; bradycardia and hypotension resistant to atropine, isoproterenol or pacing may respond to glucagon; wide QRS defects caused by the membrane-depressant poisoning may respond to hypertonic sodium bicarbonate; repeat-dose charcoal, hemoperfusion, or hemodialysis may be helpful.

Drug Interactions

Decreased effect of beta-blockers with aluminum salts, barbiturates, calcium salts, cholestyramine, colestipol, NSAIDs, penicillins (ampicillin), rifampin, salicylates, and sulfinpyrazone due to decreased bioavailability and plasma levels; decreased effect of sulfonylureas with beta-blockers

Increased effect/toxicity of beta-blockers with calcium blockers (diltiazem, felodipine, nicardipine), oral contraceptives, flecainide, haloperidol (propranolol, hypotensive effects), H₂-antagonists (metoprolol, propranolol only by cimetidine, possibly ranitidine), hydralazine (metoprolol, propranolol), loop diuretics (propranolol, not atenolol), MAO inhibitors (metoprolol, nadolol, bradycardia), phenothiazines (propranolol), propafenone (metoprolol, propranolol), quinidine (in extensive metabolizers), ciprofloxacin, thyroid hormones (metoprolol, propranolol, when hypothyroid patient is converted to euthyroid state)

Beta-blockers may increase the effect/toxicity of flecainide, haloperidol (hypotensive effects), hydralazine, phenothiazines, acetaminophen, anticoagulants (propranolol, warfarin), benzodiazepines (not atenolol), clonidine (hypertensive crisis after or during withdrawal of either agent), epinephrine (initial hypertensive episode followed by bradycardia), nifedipine and verapamil lidocaine, ergots (peripheral ischemia), prazosin (postural hypotension)

Beta-blockers may affect the action or levels of ethanol, disopyramide, nondepolarizing muscle relaxants and theophylline although the effects are difficult to predict

Stability Store at room temperature (~25°C/77°F); protect from light and dispense in a light-resistant, tight container

Mechanism of Action Competitively blocks beta₁-adrenergic receptors with little or no effect on beta₂-receptors except at high doses; exhibits membrane stabilizing and intrinsic sympathomimetic activity

Pharmacodynamics/Kinetics

Absorption: Oral: Well absorbed (40%)

Protein binding: 5% to 15%

Metabolism: Extensive first-pass

Half-life: 6-7 hours average

Time to peak: 2-4 hours

Elimination: ~55% of dose excreted via bile into feces and 35% excreted into urine

Usual Dosage Oral:

Adults:

Hypertension: 400-800 mg/day (larger doses may be divided); maximum: 1200 mg/day

Ventricular arrhythmias: Initial: 400 mg/day; maintenance: 600-1200 mg/day in divided doses

Elderly: Initial: 200-400 mg/day; dose reduction due to age related decrease in Cl_{cr} will be necessary; do not exceed 800 mg/day

Dosing adjustment in renal impairment:

Cl_{cr} 25-49 mL/minute/1.73 m²: Reduce dose by 50%

Cl_{cr} <25 mL/minute/1.73 m²: Reduce dose by 75%

Dosing adjustment in hepatic impairment: Use with caution

Administration To discontinue therapy, taper dose gradually

Monitoring Parameters Blood pressure, orthostatic hypotension, heart rate, CNS effects, EKG

Test Interactions ↑ triglycerides, potassium, uric acid, cholesterol (S), glucose; ↓ HDL, ↑ thyroxine (S)

Patient Information Do not discontinue abruptly; consult pharmacist or physician before taking with other adrenergic drugs (eg, cold medications); notify physician if CHF symptoms become worse or if other side effects occur; take at the same time each day; use with caution while driving or performing tasks requiring alertness; may mask signs of hypoglycemia in diabetics; may be taken without regard to meals

Dosage Forms Capsule, as hydrochloride: 200 mg, 400 mg

♦ **Acebutolol Hydrochloride** see Acebutolol on previous page

♦ **Acel-Imune®** see Diphtheria, Tetanus Toxoids, and Acellular Pertussis Vaccine on page 373

♦ **Aceon®** see Perindopril Erbumine on page 907

♦ **Acephen®** [OTC] see Acetaminophen on this page

♦ **Aceta®** [OTC] see Acetaminophen on this page

Acetaminophen (a seet a MIN oh fen)

Related Information

Acetaminophen Toxicity Nomogram on page 1493

(Continued)

Acetaminophen *(Continued)*

U.S. Brand Names Acephen® [OTC]; Aceta® [OTC]; Apacet® [OTC]; Arthritis Foundation® Pain Reliever, Aspirin Free [OTC]; Aspirin Free Anacin® Maximum Strength [OTC]; Children's Silapap® [OTC]; Feverall™ [OTC]; Feverall™ Sprinkle Caps [OTC]; Genapap® [OTC]; Halenol® Childrens [OTC]; Infants Feverall™ [OTC]; Infants' Silapap® [OTC]; Junior Strength Panadol® [OTC]; Liquiprin® [OTC]; Mapap® [OTC]; Maranox® [OTC]; Neopap® [OTC]; Panadol® [OTC]; Redutemp® [OTC]; Ridenol® [OTC]; Tempra® [OTC]; Tylenol® [OTC]; Tylenol® Extended Relief [OTC]; Uni-Ace® [OTC]

Canadian Brand Names Abenol®; A.F. Anacin®; Atasol®; Pediatrix; Tantaphen®

Synonyms APAP; N-Acetyl-P-Aminophenol; Paracetamol

Therapeutic Category Analgesic, Miscellaneous; Antipyretic

Use Treatment of mild to moderate pain and fever; does not have antirheumatic effects (analgesic)

Pregnancy Risk Factor B

Contraindications Patients with known G-6-PD deficiency; hypersensitivity to acetaminophen

Warnings/Precautions May cause severe hepatic toxicity on overdose; use with caution in patients with alcoholic liver disease; chronic daily dosing in adults of 5-8 g of acetaminophen over several weeks or 3-4 g/day of acetaminophen for 1 year have resulted in liver damage

Adverse Reactions Percentage unknown: May increase chloride, bilirubin, uric acid, glucose, ammonia, alkaline phosphatase; may decrease sodium, bicarbonate, calcium <1%: Rash, nausea, vomiting, blood dyscrasias (neutropenia, pancytopenia, leukopenia), anemia, analgesic nephropathy, nephrotoxicity with chronic overdose, hypersensitivity reactions (rare)

Overdosage/Toxicology Refer to the Acetaminophen Toxicity Nomogram *on page 1493* in the Appendix

Symptoms of overdose include hepatic necrosis, transient azotemia, renal tubular necrosis with acute toxicity, anemia, and GI disturbances with chronic toxicity.

Acetylcysteine 140 mg/kg orally (loading) followed by 70 mg/kg every 4 hours for 17 doses. Therapy should be initiated based upon laboratory analysis suggesting high probability of hepatotoxic potential. Activated charcoal is very effective at binding acetaminophen.

Drug Interactions CYP1A2 enzyme substrate (minor), CYP2E1 and 3A3/4 enzyme substrate

Decreased effect: Rifampin can interact to reduce the analgesic effectiveness of acetaminophen

Increased toxicity: Barbiturates, carbamazepine, hydantoins, sulfinpyrazone can increase the hepatotoxic potential of acetaminophen; chronic ethanol abuse increases risk for acetaminophen toxicity; effect of warfarin may be enhanced

Mechanism of Action Inhibits the synthesis of prostaglandins in the central nervous system and peripherally blocks pain impulse generation; produces antipyresis from inhibition of hypothalamic heat-regulating center

Pharmacodynamics/Kinetics

Protein binding: 20% to 50%

Metabolism: At normal therapeutic dosages, the parent compound is metabolized in the liver to sulfate and glucuronide metabolites, while a small amount is metabolized by microsomal mixed function oxidases to a highly reactive intermediate (acetylimidoquinone) which is conjugated with glutathione and inactivated; at toxic doses (as little as 4 g in a single day) glutathione conjugation becomes insufficient to meet the metabolic demand causing an increase in acetylimidoquinone concentration, which is thought to cause hepatic cell necrosis

Half-life:

Neonates: 2-5 hours

Adults: Normal renal function: 1-3 hours; End-stage renal disease: 1-3 hours

Time to peak serum concentration: Oral: 10-60 minutes after normal doses, may be delayed in acute overdoses

Usual Dosage Oral, rectal (if fever not controlled with acetaminophen alone, administer with full doses of aspirin on an every 4- to 6-hour schedule, if aspirin is not otherwise contraindicated):

Children <12 years: 10-15 mg/kg/dose every 4-6 hours as needed; do **not** exceed 5 doses (2.6 g) in 24 hours; alternatively, the following doses may be used. See table.

Acetaminophen Dosing

Age	Dosage (mg)	Age	Dosage (mg)
0-3 mo	40	4-5 y	240
4-11 mo	80	6-8 y	320
1-2 y	120	9-10 y	400
2-3 y	160	11 y	480

Adults: 325-650 mg every 4-6 hours or 1000 mg 3-4 times/day; do **not** exceed 4 g/day

Dosing interval in renal impairment:

Cl_{cr} 10-50 mL/minute: Administer every 6 hours

Cl_{cr} <10 mL/minute: Administer every 8 hours (metabolites accumulate)

Hemodialysis: Moderately dialyzable (20% to 50%)

Dosing adjustment/comments in hepatic impairment: Appears to be well tolerated in cirrhosis; serum levels may need monitoring with long-term use

Dietary Considerations

Food: May slightly delay absorption of extended-release preparations; rate of absorption may be decreased when given with food high in carbohydrates

Alcohol: Excessive intake of alcohol may increase the risk of acetaminophen-induced hepatotoxicity; avoid or limit alcohol intake

Monitoring Parameters Relief of pain or fever

Reference Range

Therapeutic concentration: 10-30 µg/mL

Toxic concentration: >200 µg/mL

Toxic concentration with probable hepatotoxicity: >200 µg/mL at 4 hours or 50 µg/mL at 12 hours

Nursing Implications

Suppositories: Do not freeze

Suspension, oral: Shake well before pouring a dose

Dosage Forms

Caplet: 160 mg, 325 mg, 500 mg

Caplet, extended: 650 mg

Capsule: 80 mg

Drops: 48 mg/mL (15 mL); 60 mg/0.6 mL (15 mL); 80 mg/0.8 mL (15 mL); 100 mg/mL (15 mL, 30 mL)

Elixir: 80 mg/5 mL, 120 mg/5 mL, 160 mg/5 mL, 167 mg/5 mL, 325 mg/5 mL

Liquid, oral: 160 mg/5 mL, 500 mg/15 mL

Solution: 100 mg/mL (15 mL); 120 mg/2.5 mL

Suppository, rectal: 80 mg, 120 mg, 125 mg, 300 mg, 325 mg, 650 mg

Suspension, oral: 160 mg/5 mL

Suspension, oral drops: 80 mg/0.8 mL

Tablet: 325 mg, 500 mg, 650 mg

Tablet, chewable: 80 mg, 160 mg

Acetaminophen and Codeine (a seet a MIN oh fen & KOE deen)

Related Information

Acetaminophen Toxicity Nomogram on page 1493

U.S. Brand Names Capital® and Codeine; Phenaphen® With Codeine; Tylenol® With Codeine

Canadian Brand Names Atasol® 8, 15, 30 With Caffeine; Empracet® 30, 60; Emtec-30®; Lenoltec No 1, 2, 3, 4; Novo-Gesic-C8; Novo-Gesic-C15; Novo-Gesic-C30

Synonyms Codeine and Acetaminophen

Therapeutic Category Analgesic, Narcotic

Use Relief of mild to moderate pain

Restrictions C-III; C-V

Pregnancy Risk Factor C

Contraindications Hypersensitivity to acetaminophen, codeine phosphate, or similar compounds

Warnings/Precautions Use with caution in patients with hypersensitivity reactions to other phenanthrene derivative opioid agonists (morphine, hydrocodone, hydromorphone, levorphanol, oxycodone, oxymorphone); tablets contain metabisulfite which may cause allergic reactions

Adverse Reactions

>10%:

Central nervous system: Lightheadedness, dizziness, sedation

Gastrointestinal: Nausea, vomiting

Respiratory: Shortness of breath

1% to 10%:

Central nervous system: Euphoria, dysphoria

Dermatologic: Pruritus

Gastrointestinal: Constipation, abdominal pain

Miscellaneous: Histamine release

<1%: Palpitations, hypotension, bradycardia, peripheral vasodilation, increased intracranial pressure, antidiuretic hormone release, biliary tract spasm, urinary retention, miosis, respiratory depression, physical and psychological dependence

Overdosage/Toxicology Refer to the Acetaminophen Toxicity Nomogram on page 1493 in the Appendix

Symptoms of overdose include hepatic necrosis, blood dyscrasias, respiratory depression

Acetylcysteine 140 mg/kg orally (loading) followed by 70 mg/kg every 4 hours for 17 doses; therapy should be initiated based upon laboratory analysis suggesting high probability of hepatotoxic potential

Naloxone 2 mg I.V. (0.01 mg/kg for children) with repeat administration as necessary up to a total of 10 mg; can also be used to reverse the toxic effects of the opiate. Activated charcoal is effective at binding certain chemicals, and this is especially true for acetaminophen.

Drug Interactions Increased toxicity: CNS depressants, phenothiazines, tricyclic antidepressants, guanabenz, MAO inhibitors (may also decrease blood pressure); effect of warfarin may be enhanced

Mechanism of Action Inhibits the synthesis of prostaglandins in the central nervous system and peripherally blocks pain impulse generation; produces antipyresis from inhibition of hypothalamic heat-regulating center; binds to opiate receptors in the CNS, (Continued)

Acetaminophen and Codeine *(Continued)*

causing inhibition of ascending pain pathways, altering the perception of and response to pain; causes cough supression by direct central action in the medulla; produces generalized CNS depression

Usual Dosage Doses should be adjusted according to severity of pain and response of the patient. Adult doses ≥60 mg codeine fail to give commensurate relief of pain but merely prolong analgesia and are associated with an appreciably increased incidence of side effects. Oral:

Children: Analgesic:
Codeine: 0.5-1 mg codeine/kg/dose every 4-6 hours
Acetaminophen: 10-15 mg/kg/dose every 4 hours up to a maximum of 2.6 g/24 hours for children <12 years
3-6 years: 5 mL 3-4 times/day as needed of elixir
7-12 years: 10 mL 3-4 times/day as needed of elixir
>12 years: 15 mL every 4 hours as needed of elixir

Adults:
Antitussive: Based on codeine (15-30 mg/dose) every 4-6 hours
Analgesic: Based on codeine (30-60 mg/dose) every 4-6 hours
1-2 tablets every 4 hours to a maximum of 12 tablets/24 hours

Dosing adjustment in renal impairment: Refer to individual monographs for Acetaminophen and Codeine

Monitoring Parameters Relief of pain, respiratory and mental status, blood pressure, bowel function

Patient Information May cause drowsiness; do not exceed recommended dose; do not take for more than 10 days without physician's advice

Nursing Implications Observe patient for excessive sedation, respiratory depression, constipation

Dosage Forms
Capsule:
#2: Acetaminophen 325 mg and codeine phosphate 15 mg (C-III)
#3: Acetaminophen 325 mg and codeine phosphate 30 mg (C-III)
#4: Acetaminophen 325 mg and codeine phosphate 60 mg (C-III)
Elixir: Acetaminophen 120 mg and codeine phosphate 12 mg per 5 mL with alcohol 7% (C-V)
Suspension, oral, alcohol free: Acetaminophen 120 mg and codeine phosphate 12 mg per 5 mL (C-V)
Tablet: Acetaminophen 500 mg and codeine phosphate 30 mg (C-III); acetaminophen 650 mg and codeine phosphate 30 mg (C-III)
Tablet:
#1: Acetaminophen 300 mg and codeine phosphate 7.5 mg (C-III)
#2: Acetaminophen 300 mg and codeine phosphate 15 mg (C-III)
#3: Acetaminophen 300 mg and codeine phosphate 30 mg (C-III)
#4: Acetaminophen 300 mg and codeine phosphate 60 mg (C-III)

♦ **Acetaminophen and Hydrocodone** *see* Hydrocodone and Acetaminophen *on page 575*

♦ **Acetaminophen and Oxycodone** *see* Oxycodone and Acetaminophen *on page 875*

Acetaminophen, Isometheptene, and Dichloralphenazone

(a seet a MIN oh fen, eye soe me THEP teen, & dye KLOR al FEN a zone)
U.S. Brand Names Isocom®; Isopap®; Midchlor®; Midrin®; Migratine®
Therapeutic Category Antimigraine Agent
Dosage Forms Capsule: Acetaminophen 326 mg, isometheptene mucate 65 mg, dichloralphenazone 100 mg

♦ **Acetaminophen Toxicity Nomogram** *see page 1493*

♦ **Acetasol® HC Otic** *see* Acetic Acid, Propylene Glycol Diacetate, and Hydrocortisone *on page 25*

♦ **Acetazolam®** *see* Acetazolamide *on this page*

Acetazolamide (a set a ZOLE a mide)

Related Information
Epilepsy Treatment *on page 1468*
Glaucoma Drug Therapy Comparison *on page 1322*
Sulfonamide Derivatives *on page 1337*
U.S. Brand Names Diamox®; Diamox Sequels®
Canadian Brand Names Acetazolam®; Apo®-Acetazolamide; Novo-Zolamide
Therapeutic Category Anticonvulsant; Carbonic Anhydrase Inhibitor; Diuretic, Carbonic Anhydrase Inhibitor
Use Lowers intraocular pressure to treat glaucoma, also as a diuretic, adjunct treatment of refractory seizures and acute altitude sickness; centrencephalic epilepsies (sustained release not recommended for anticonvulsant)
Pregnancy Risk Factor C
Pregnancy/Breast-Feeding Implications
Clinical effects on the fetus: Despite widespread usage, no reports linking the use of acetazolamide with congenital defects have been located
Breast-feeding/lactation: The American Academy of Pediatrics considers acetazolamide to be **compatible** with breast-feeding

Contraindications Hypersensitivity to sulfonamides or acetazolamide, patients with hepatic disease or insufficiency; patients with decreased sodium and/or potassium levels; patients with adrenocortical insufficiency, hyperchloremic acidosis, severe renal disease or dysfunction, or severe pulmonary obstruction; long-term use in noncongestive angle-closure glaucoma

Warnings/Precautions

Use in impaired hepatic function may result in coma; use with caution in patients with respiratory acidosis and diabetes mellitus; impairment of mental alertness and/or physical coordination may occur

I.M. administration is painful because of the alkaline pH of the drug

Drug may cause substantial increase in blood glucose in some diabetic patients; malaise and complaints of tiredness and myalgia are signs of excessive dosing and acidosis in the elderly

Adverse Reactions

>10%:
Central nervous system: Malaise
Gastrointestinal: Anorexia, diarrhea, metallic taste
Genitourinary: Polyuria
Neuromuscular & skeletal: Muscular weakness
1% to 10%: Central nervous system: Mental depression, drowsiness
<1%: Fever, fatigue, rash, hyperchloremic metabolic acidosis, hypokalemia, hyperglycemia, black stools, GI irritation, dryness of the mouth, dysuria, bone marrow suppression, blood dyscrasias, paresthesia, myopia, renal calculi

Overdosage/Toxicology

Symptoms of overdose include low blood sugar, tingling of lips and tongue, nausea, yawning, confusion, agitation, tachycardia, sweating, convulsions, stupor, and coma

Hypoglycemia should be managed with 50 mL I.V. dextrose 50% followed immediately with a continuous infusion of 10% dextrose in water (administer at a rate sufficient enough to approach a serum glucose level of 100 mg/dL). The use of corticosteroids to treat the hypoglycemia is controversial, however, the addition of 100 mg of hydrocortisone to the dextrose infusion may prove helpful.

Drug Interactions

Decreased effect: Increased lithium excretion and altered excretion of other drugs by alkalinization of urine (such as amphetamines, quinidine, procainamide, methenamine, phenobarbital, salicylates); primidone serum concentrations may be decreased

Increased toxicity: Cyclosporine trough concentrations may be increased resulting in possible nephrotoxicity and neurotoxicity; salicylate use may result in carbonic anhydrase inhibitor accumulation and toxicity including CNS depression and metabolic acidosis; digitalis toxicity may occur if hypokalemia is untreated

Stability

Reconstituted solution may be stored up to 12 hours at room temperature (15°C to 30°C) and for 3 days under refrigeration (2°C to 8°C)

Standard diluent: 500 mg/50 mL D_5W

Minimum volume: 50 mL D_5W

Stability of IVPB solution: 5 days at room temperature (25°C) and 44 days at refrigeration (5°C)

Reconstitute with at least 5 mL sterile water to provide a solution containing not more than 100 mg/mL; further dilution in 50 mL of either D_5W or NS for I.V. infusion administration

Mechanism of Action Reversible inhibition of the enzyme carbonic anhydrase resulting in reduction of hydrogen ion secretion at renal tubule and an increased renal excretion of sodium, potassium, bicarbonate, and water to decrease production of aqueous humor; also inhibits carbonic anhydrase in central nervous system to retard abnormal and excessive discharge from CNS neurons

Pharmacodynamics/Kinetics

Onset of action: Extended release capsule: 2 hours; I.V.: 2 minutes
Peak effect: Extended release capsule: 3-6 hours; Tablet: 1-4 hours; I.V.: 15 minutes
Duration: Extended release capsule: 18-24 hours; Tablet: 8-12 hours; I.V.: 4-5 hours
Distribution: Distributes into erythrocytes, kidneys; crosses blood-brain barrier; crosses placenta and distributes into milk to ~30% of plasma concentrations
Protein binding: 95%
Half-life: 2.4-5.8 hours
Elimination: 70% to 100% of I.V. or tablet dose is excreted unchanged in the urine within 24 hours

Usual Dosage Note: I.M. administration is not recommended because of pain secondary to the alkaline pH

Neonates and Infants: Hydrocephalus: To slow the progression of hydrocephalus in neonates and infants who may not be good candidates for surgery, acetazolamide I.V. or oral doses of 5 mg/kg/dose every 6 hours increased by 25 mg/kg/day to a maximum of 100 mg/kg/day, if tolerated, have been used. Furosemide was used in combination with acetazolamide.

Children:
Glaucoma:
Oral: 8-30 mg/kg/day or 300-900 mg/m²/day divided every 8 hours
I.M., I.V.: 20-40 mg/kg/24 hours divided every 6 hours, not to exceed 1 g/day
Edema: Oral, I.M., I.V.: 5 mg/kg or 150 mg/m² once every day
Epilepsy: Oral: 8-30 mg/kg/day in 1-4 divided doses, not to exceed 1 g/day; sustained release capsule is not recommended for treatment of epilepsy

(Continued)

Acetazolamide *(Continued)*

Adults:

Glaucoma:

Chronic simple (open-angle): Oral: 250 mg 1-4 times/day or 500 mg sustained release capsule twice daily

Secondary, acute (closed-angle): I.M., I.V.: 250-500 mg, may repeat in 2-4 hours to a maximum of 1 g/day

Edema: Oral, I.M., I.V.: 250-375 mg once daily

Epilepsy: Oral: 8-30 mg/kg/day in 1-4 divided doses; **sustained release capsule is not recommended for treatment of epilepsy**

Altitude sickness: Oral: 250 mg every 8-12 hours (or 500 mg extended release capsules every 12-24 hours)

Therapy should begin 24-48 hours before and continue during ascent and for at least 48 hours after arrival at the high altitude

Urine alkalinization: Oral: 5 mg/kg/dose repeated 2-3 times over 24 hours

Elderly: Oral: Initial: 250 mg twice daily; use lowest effective dose

Dosing adjustment in renal impairment:

Cl_{cr} 10-50 mL/minute: Administer every 12 hours

Cl_{cr} <10 mL/minute: Avoid use → ineffective

Hemodialysis: Moderately dialyzable (20% to 50%)

Peritoneal dialysis: Supplemental dose is not necessary

Administration

Oral: May cause an alteration in taste, especially carbonated beverages; short-acting tablets may be crushed and suspended in cherry or chocolate syrup to disguise the bitter taste of the drug, do not use fruit juices, alternatively submerge tablet in 10 mL of hot water and add 10 mL honey or syrup

I.V.: Recommended rate of administration: 100-500 mg/minute for I.V. push and 4-8 hours for I.V. infusions

Monitoring Parameters Intraocular pressure, potassium, serum bicarbonate; serum electrolytes, periodic CBC with differential

Test Interactions May cause false-positive results for urinary protein with Albustix®, Labstix®, Albutest®, Bumintest®

Patient Information Report numbness or tingling of extremities to physician; do not crush, chew, or swallow contents of long-acting capsule, but may be opened and sprinkled on soft food; ability to perform tasks requiring mental alertness and/or physical coordination may be impaired; take with food; drug may cause substantial increase in blood glucose in some diabetic patients

Additional Information Sodium content of 500 mg injection: 47.2 mg (2.05 mEq)

Dosage Forms

Capsule, sustained release: 500 mg

Injection: 500 mg

Tablet: 125 mg, 250 mg

Extemporaneous Preparations Tablets may be crushed and suspended in cherry, chocolate, raspberry, or other highly flavored carbohydrate syrup in concentrations of 25-100 mg/mL; simple suspensions are stable for 7 days. For solutions with longer stability, see references Parastampuria and Alexander.

Alexander KS, Haribhakti RP, and Parker GA, "Stability of Acetazolamide in Suspension Compounded From Tablets," *Am J Hosp Pharm*, 1991, 48(6):1241-4.

McEvoy G, ed, AHFS Drug Information 96, Bethesda, MD: American Society of Health System Pharmacists, 1996.

Parastampuria J and Gupta VD, "Development of Oral Liquid Dosage Forms of Acetazolamide," *J Pharm Sci*, 1990, 79:385-6.

Acetic Acid *(a SEE tik AS id)*

U.S. Brand Names Aci-jel®; VōSol®

Synonyms Ethanoic Acid

Therapeutic Category Antibacterial, Otic; Antibacterial, Topical

Use Irrigation of the bladder; treatment of superficial bacterial infections of the external auditory canal and vagina

Pregnancy Risk Factor C

Contraindications During transurethral procedures; hypersensitivity to drug or components

Warnings/Precautions Not for internal intake or I.V. infusion; topical use or irrigation use only; use of irrigation in patients with mucosal lesions of urinary bladder may cause irritation; systemic acidosis may result from absorption

Adverse Reactions <1%: Systemic acidosis, urologic pain, hematuria

Usual Dosage

Irrigation (note dosage of an irrigating solution depends on the capacity or surface area of the structure being irrigated):

For continuous irrigation of the urinary bladder with 0.25% acetic acid irrigation, the rate of administration will approximate the rate of urine flow; usually 500-1500 mL/24 hours

For periodic irrigation of an indwelling urinary catheter to maintain patency, about 50 mL of 0.25% acetic acid irrigation is required

Otic: Insert saturated wick; keep moist 24 hours; remove wick and instill 5 drops 3-4 times/day

Vaginal: One applicatorful every morning and evening

Nursing Implications For continuous or intermittent irrigation of the urinary bladder, urine pH should be checked at least 4 times/day and the irrigation rate adjusted to maintain a pH of 4.5-5

Dosage Forms
Jelly vaginal: 0.921% with oxyquinolone sulfate 0.025%, ricinoleic acid 0.7%, and glycerin 5% (85 g)
Solution:
Irrigation: 0.25% (1000 mL)
Otic: Acetic acid 2% in propylene glycol (15 mL, 30 mL, 60 mL)

Acetic Acid, Propylene Glycol Diacetate, and Hydrocortisone
(a SEE tik AS id, PRO pa leen GLY kole dye AS e tate, & hye droe KOR ti sone)
U.S. Brand Names Acetasol® HC Otic; VōSol® HC Otic
Therapeutic Category Antibiotic/Corticosteroid, Otic
Dosage Forms Solution, otic: Acetic acid 2%, propylene glycol diacetate 3%, and hydrocortisone 1% (10 mL)

Acetohexamide (a set oh HEKS a mide)
Related Information
Hypoglycemic Drugs, Comparison of Oral Agents *on page 1325*
Sulfonamide Derivatives *on page 1337*
U.S. Brand Names Dymelor®
Therapeutic Category Antidiabetic Agent, Oral; Hypoglycemic Agent, Oral; Sulfonylurea Agent
Use Adjunct to diet for the management of mild to moderately severe, stable, noninsulin-dependent (type II) diabetes mellitus
Pregnancy Risk Factor D
Contraindications Diabetes complicated by ketoacidosis, therapy of type I diabetes, hypersensitivity to sulfonylureas
Usual Dosage Adults: Oral (elderly patients may be more sensitive and should be started at a lower dosage initially):

Initial: 250 mg/day; increase in increments of 250-500 mg daily at intervals of 5-7 days up to 1.5 g/day. Patients on ≤1 g/day can be controlled with once daily administration. Patients receiving 1.5 g/day usually benefit from twice daily administration before the morning and evening meals. Doses >1.5 g daily are not recommended.
Dosing adjustment in renal impairment: Cl_{cr} <50 mL/minute: Acetohexamide is not recommended in patients with renal insufficiency due to the increased potential for developing hypoglycemia
Dosing adjustment in hepatic impairment: Initiate therapy at lower than recommended doses; further dosage adjustment may be necessary because acetohexamide is extensively metabolized but no specific guidelines are available
Additional Information Complete prescribing information for this medication should be consulted for additional detail
Dosage Forms Tablet: 250 mg, 500 mg

Acetophenazine (a set oh FEN a zeen)
Related Information
Antipsychotic Agents Comparison *on page 1305*
U.S. Brand Names Tindal®
Synonyms Acetophenazine Maleate
Therapeutic Category Antipsychotic Agent
Use Management of manifestations of psychotic disorders
Pregnancy Risk Factor C
Contraindications Blood dyscrasias and bone marrow suppression, patients in coma or brain damage, known hypersensitivity to acetophenazine
Usual Dosage Adults: Oral: 20 mg 3 times/day up to 60-120 mg/day
Hospitalized schizophrenic patients may require doses as high as 400-600 mg/day
Hemodialysis: Not dialyzable (0% to 5%)
Additional Information Complete prescribing information for this medication should be consulted for additional detail
Dosage Forms Tablet, as maleate: 20 mg

♦ **Acetophenazine Maleate** *see Acetophenazine on this page*
♦ **Acetoxymethylprogesterone** *see Medroxyprogesterone Acetate on page 721*

Acetylcholine (a se teel KOE leen)
Related Information
Glaucoma Drug Therapy Comparison *on page 1322*
U.S. Brand Names Miochol-E®
Synonyms Acetylcholine Chloride
Therapeutic Category Cholinergic Agent, Ophthalmic; Ophthalmic Agent, Miotic
Use Produces complete miosis in cataract surgery, keratoplasty, iridectomy and other anterior segment surgery where rapid miosis is required
Pregnancy Risk Factor C
Pregnancy/Breast-Feeding Implications Acetylcholine is used primarily in the eye and there are no reports of its use in pregnancy; because it is ionized at physiologic pH, transplacental passage would not be expected
(Continued)

Acetylcholine *(Continued)*

Contraindications Hypersensitivity to acetylcholine chloride and any components; acute iritis and acute inflammatory disease of the anterior chamber

Warnings/Precautions Systemic effects rarely occur but can cause problems for patients with acute cardiac failure, bronchial asthma, peptic ulcer, hyperthyroidism, GI spasm, urinary tract obstruction, and Parkinson's disease; open under aseptic conditions only

Adverse Reactions <1%: Bradycardia, hypotension, flushing, headache, altered distance vision, decreased night vision, transient lenticular opacities, dyspnea, diaphoresis

Overdosage/Toxicology Treatment includes flushing eyes with water or normal saline and supportive measures; if accidentally ingested, induce emesis or perform gastric lavage

Drug Interactions
Decreased effect possible with flurbiprofen and suprofen, ophthalmic
Increased effect may be prolonged or enhanced in patients receiving tacrine

Stability Prepare solution immediately before use and discard unused portion; acetylcholine solutions are unstable

Mechanism of Action Causes contraction of the sphincter muscles of the iris, resulting in miosis and contraction of the ciliary muscle, leading to accommodation spasm

Pharmacodynamics/Kinetics
Onset of miosis: Occurs promptly
Duration: ~10 minutes

Usual Dosage Adults: Intraocular: 0.5-2 mL of 1% injection (5-20 mg) instilled into anterior chamber before or after securing one or more sutures

Patient Information May sting on instillation; use caution while driving at night or performing hazardous tasks; do not touch dropper to eye

Nursing Implications Discard any solution that is not used; open under aseptic conditions only

Dosage Forms Powder, intraocular, as chloride: 1:100 [10 mg/mL] (2 mL, 15 mL)

♦ **Acetylcholine Chloride** *see Acetylcholine on previous page*

Acetylcysteine *(a se teel SIS teen)*

U.S. Brand Names Mucomyst®; Mucosil™

Synonyms Acetylcysteine Sodium; Mercapturic Acid; NAC; *N*-Acetylcysteine; *N*-Acetyl-L-cysteine

Therapeutic Category Antidote, Acetaminophen; Mucolytic Agent

Use Adjunctive mucolytic therapy in patients with abnormal or viscid mucous secretions in acute and chronic bronchopulmonary diseases; pulmonary complications of surgery and cystic fibrosis; diagnostic bronchial studies; antidote for acute acetaminophen toxicity

Pregnancy Risk Factor B

Pregnancy/Breast-Feeding Implications Clinical effects on the fetus: There are no adequate and well controlled studies in pregnant women; use if only clearly needed

Contraindications Known hypersensitivity to acetylcysteine

Warnings/Precautions Since increased bronchial secretions may develop after inhalation, percussion, postural drainage and suctioning should follow; if bronchospasm occurs, administer a bronchodilator; discontinue acetylcysteine if bronchospasm progresses

Adverse Reactions
>10%:
Gastrointestinal: Vomiting
Miscellaneous: Unpleasant odor during administration
1% to 10%:
Central nervous system: Drowsiness, chills
Gastrointestinal: Stomatitis, nausea
Local: Irritation
Respiratory: Bronchospasm, rhinorrhea, hemoptysis
Miscellaneous: Clamminess
<1%: Skin rash

Overdosage/Toxicology The treatment of acetylcysteine toxicity is usually aimed at reversing anaphylactoid symptoms or controlling nausea and vomiting. The use of epinephrine, antihistamines, and steroids may be beneficial.

Stability Store opened vials in the refrigerator, use within 96 hours; dilutions should be freshly prepared and used within 1 hour; light purple color of solution does **not** affect its mucolytic activity

Mechanism of Action Exerts mucolytic action through its free sulfhydryl group which opens up the disulfide bonds in the mucoproteins thus lowering mucous viscosity. The exact mechanism of action in acetaminophen toxicity is unknown; thought to act by providing substrate for conjugation with the toxic metabolite.

Pharmacodynamics/Kinetics
Oral:
Peak plasma levels: 1-2 hours
Distribution: 0.33-0.47 L/kg
Plasma protein binding: 50%
Onset of action: Inhalation: Mucus liquefaction occurs maximally within 5-10 minutes
Duration: Can persist for >1 hour
Half-life: Reduced acetylcysteine: 2 hours; Total acetylcysteine: 5.5 hours

Usual Dosage

Acetaminophen poisoning: Children and Adults: Oral: 140 mg/kg; followed by 17 doses of 70 mg/kg every 4 hours; repeat dose if emesis occurs within 1 hour of administration; therapy should continue until all doses are administered even though the acetaminophen plasma level has dropped below the toxic range

Inhalation: Acetylcysteine 10% and 20% solution (Mucomyst®) (dilute 20% solution with sodium chloride or sterile water for inhalation); 10% solution may be used undiluted

Infants: 1-2 mL of 20% solution or 2-4 mL 10% solution until nebulized given 3-4 times/day

Children: 3-5 mL of 20% solution or 6-10 mL of 10% solution until nebulized given 3-4 times/day

Adolescents: 5-10 mL of 10% to 20% solution until nebulized given 3-4 times/day

Note: Patients should receive an aerosolized bronchodilator 10-15 minutes prior to acetylcysteine

Meconium ileus equivalent: Children and Adults: 100-300 mL of 4% to 10% solution by irrigation or orally

Administration For treatment of acetaminophen overdosage, administer orally as a 5% solution

Dilute the 20% solution 1:3 with a cola, orange juice, or other soft drink

Use within 1 hour of preparation; unpleasant odor becomes less noticeable as treatment progresses

Reference Range Determine acetaminophen level as soon as possible, but no sooner than 4 hours after ingestion (to ensure peak levels have been obtained); administer for acetaminophen level >150 µg/mL; toxic concentration with probable hepatotoxicity: >200 µg/mL at 4 hours or 50 µg at 12 hours

Patient Information Clear airway by coughing deeply before aerosol treatment

Nursing Implications Assess patient for nausea, vomiting, and skin rash following oral administration for treatment of acetaminophen poisoning; intermittent aerosol treatments are commonly given when patient arises, before meals, and just before retiring at bedtime

Dosage Forms Solution, as sodium: 10% [100 mg/mL] (4 mL, 10 mL, 30 mL); 20% [200 mg/mL] (4 mL, 10 mL, 30 mL, 100 mL)

- ♦ **Acetylcysteine Sodium** see Acetylcysteine on previous page
- ♦ **Acetylsalicylic Acid** see Aspirin on page 102
- ♦ **Aches-N-Pain® [OTC]** see Ibuprofen on page 593
- ♦ **Achromycin® Ophthalmic** see Tetracycline on page 1122
- ♦ **Achromycin® Topical** see Tetracycline on page 1122
- ♦ **Aciclovir** see Acyclovir on next page
- ♦ **Acidulated Phosphate Fluoride** see Fluoride on page 498
- ♦ **Aci-jel®** see Acetic Acid on page 24
- ♦ **Aclovate® Topical** see Alclometasone on page 37

Acrivastine and Pseudoephedrine (AK ri vas teen & soo doe e FED rin)

Related Information

Pseudoephedrine on page 993

U.S. Brand Names Semprex®-D

Synonyms Pseudoephedrine and Acrivastine

Therapeutic Category Antihistamine, H₁ Blocker; Decongestant

Use Temporary relief of nasal congestion, decongest sinus openings, running nose, itching of nose or throat, and itchy, watery eyes due to hay fever or other upper respiratory allergies

Pregnancy Risk Factor B

Contraindications MAO inhibitor therapy within 14 days of initiating therapy, severe hypertension, severe coronary artery disease, hypersensitivity to pseudoephedrine, acrivastine (or other alkylamine antihistamines), or any component, renal impairment (Cl$_{cr}$ <48 mL/minute)

Warnings/Precautions Use with caution in patients >60 years of age; use with caution in patients with high blood pressure, ischemic heart disease, diabetes, increased intraocular pressure, GI or GU obstruction, asthma, thyroid disease, or prostatic hypertrophy; not recommended for use in children

Adverse Reactions

>10%: Central nervous system: Drowsiness, headache

1% to 10%:

Cardiovascular: Tachycardia, palpitations

Central nervous system: Nervousness, dizziness, insomnia, vertigo, lightheadedness, fatigue

Gastrointestinal: Nausea, vomiting, xerostomia, diarrhea

Genitourinary: Dysuria

Neuromuscular & skeletal: Weakness

Respiratory: Pharyngitis, cough increase

Miscellaneous: Diaphoresis

<1%: Dysmenorrhea, dyspepsia

Overdosage/Toxicology

Symptoms of overdose include trembling, tachycardia, stridor, loss of consciousness, and possible convulsions

There is no specific antidote for pseudoephedrine intoxication, and the bulk of the treatment is supportive. Hyperactivity and agitation usually respond to reduced

(Continued)

Acrivastine and Pseudoephedrine *(Continued)*

sensory input, however, with extreme agitation haloperidol (2-5 mg I.M. for adults) may be required.

Hyperthermia is best treated with external cooling measures, or when severe or unresponsive, muscle paralysis with pancuronium may be needed. Hypertension is usually transient and generally does not require treatment unless severe. For diastolic blood pressure >110 mm Hg, a nitroprusside infusion should be initiated. Seizures usually respond to diazepam I.V. and/or phenytoin maintenance regimens.

Drug Interactions
Decreased effect of guanethidine, reserpine, methyldopa, and beta-blockers
Increased toxicity with MAO inhibitors (hypertensive crisis), sympathomimetics, CNS depressants, alcohol (sedation)

Mechanism of Action Refer to Pseudoephedrine monograph; acrivastine is an analogue of triprolidine and it is considered to be relatively less sedating than traditional antihistamines; believed to involve competitive blockade of H_1-receptor sites resulting in the inability of histamine to combine with its receptor sites and exert its usual effects on target cells

Pharmacodynamics/Kinetics
Onset of action: Within 30 minutes
Absorption: Not affected by food
Protein binding: 50%
Metabolism: Hepatic to an active metabolite
Half-life: 1.4-2.5 hours
Elimination: Renal (65% eliminated unchanged)

Usual Dosage Adults: 1 capsule 3-4 times/day
Dosing comments in renal impairment: Do not use

Dosage Forms Capsule: Acrivastine 8 mg and pseudoephedrine hydrochloride 60 mg

Acyclovir *(ay SYE kloe veer)*

Related Information
Guidelines for the Prevention of Opportunistic Infections in Persons with HIV *on page 1388*
Treatment of Sexually Transmitted Diseases *on page 1429*

U.S. Brand Names Zovirax®
Canadian Brand Names Avirax™
Synonyms Aciclovir; ACV; Acycloguanosine
Therapeutic Category Antiviral Agent, Oral; Antiviral Agent, Parenteral; Antiviral Agent, Topical

Use Treatment of initial and prophylaxis of recurrent mucosal and cutaneous herpes simplex (HSV-1 and HSV-2) infections; herpes simplex encephalitis; herpes zoster; genital herpes infection; varicella-zoster infections in healthy, nonpregnant persons >13 years of age, children >12 months of age who have a chronic skin or lung disorder or are receiving long-term aspirin therapy, and immunocompromised patients; for herpes zoster, acyclovir should be started within 72 hours of the appearance of the rash to be effective; acyclovir will not prevent postherpetic neuralgias

Pregnancy Risk Factor C
Contraindications Hypersensitivity to acyclovir

Warnings/Precautions Use with caution in patients with pre-existing renal disease or in those receiving other nephrotoxic drugs concurrently; maintain adequate urine output during the first 2 hours after I.V. infusion; use with caution in patients with underlying neurologic abnormalities, serious hepatic or electrolyte abnormalities, or substantial hypoxia

Adverse Reactions
>10%: Local: Inflammation at injection site
1% to 10%:
  Central nervous system: Lethargy, dizziness, seizures, confusion, agitation, coma, headache
  Dermatologic: Rash
  Gastrointestinal: Nausea, vomiting
  Neuromuscular & skeletal: Tremor
  Renal: Impaired renal function
<1%: Mental depression, insomnia, anorexia, LFT elevation, sore throat, hallucinations, leukopenia, thrombocytopenia, anemia

Overdosage/Toxicology
Symptoms of overdose include seizures, somnolence, confusion, elevated serum creatinine, and renal failure
In the event of an overdose, sufficient urine flow must be maintained to avoid drug precipitation within the renal tubules. Hemodialysis has resulted in up to 60% reductions in serum acyclovir levels.

Drug Interactions Increased CNS side effects with zidovudine and probenecid

Stability Incompatible with blood products and protein-containing solutions; reconstituted solutions remain stable for 24 hours at room temperature; do not refrigerate reconstituted solutions as they may precipitate; in patients who require fluid restriction, a concentration of up to 10 mg/mL has been infused, however, concentrations >10 mg/mL (usual recommended concentration: <7 mg/mL in D_5W) increase the risk of phlebitis

Mechanism of Action Acyclovir is converted to acyclovir monophosphate by virus-specific thymidine kinase then further converted to acyclovir triphosphate by other cellular enzymes. Acyclovir triphosphate inhibits DNA synthesis and viral replication by competing with deoxyguanosine triphosphate for viral DNA polymerase and being incorporated into viral DNA.

Pharmacodynamics/Kinetics
Absorption: Oral: 15% to 30%; food does not appear to affect absorption
Distribution: Widely distributed throughout the body including brain, kidney, lungs, liver, spleen, muscle, uterus, vagina, and CSF
Protein binding: <30%
Metabolism: Small amount of hepatic metabolism
Half-life, terminal phase: Neonates: 4 hours; Children 1-12 years: 2-3 hours; Adults: 3 hours
Time to peak serum concentration: Oral: Within 1.5-2 hours; I.V.: Within 1 hour
Elimination: Primary route is the kidney (30% to 90% of a dose excreted unchanged); hemodialysis removes ~60% of the dose while removal by peritoneal dialysis is to a much lesser extent (supplemental dose recommended)

Usual Dosage
Dosing weight should be based on the smaller of lean body weight or total body weight
Treatment of herpes simplex virus infections: Children >12 years and Adults: I.V.:
  Mucocutaneous HSV or severe initial herpes genitalis infection: 750 mg/m²/day divided every 8 hours or 5 mg/kg/dose every 8 hours for 5-10 days
  HSV encephalitis: 1500 mg/m²/day divided every 8 hours or 10 mg/kg/dose for 10 days
Treatment of genital herpes simplex virus infections: Adults:
  Oral: 200 mg every 4 hours while awake (5 times/day) for 10 days if initial episode; for 5 days if recurrence (begin at earliest signs of disease)
  Topical: ½" ribbon of ointment for a 4" square surface area every 3 hours (6 times/day)
Treatment of varicella-zoster virus (chickenpox) infections:
  Oral:
    Children: 10-20 mg/kg/dose (up to 800 mg) 4 times/day for 5 days; begin treatment within the first 24 hours of rash onset
    Adults: 600-800 mg/dose every 4 hours while awake (5 times/day) for 7-10 days or 1000 mg every 6 hours for 5 days
  I.V.: Children and Adults: 1500 mg/m²/day divided every 8 hours or 10 mg/kg/dose every 8 hours for 7 days
Treatment of herpes zoster (shingles) infections:
  Oral:
    Children (immunocompromised): 250-600 mg/m²/dose 4-5 times/day for 7-10 days
    Adults (immunocompromised): 800 mg every 4 hours (5 times/day) for 7-10 days
  I.V.:
    Children and Adults (immunocompromised): 10 mg/kg/dose or 500 mg/m²/dose every 8 hours
    Older Adults (immunocompromised): 7.5 mg/kg/dose every 8 hours
    If nephrotoxicity occurs: 5 mg/kg/dose every 8 hours
Prophylaxis in immunocompromised patients:
  Varicella zoster or herpes zoster in HIV-positive patients: Adults: Oral: 400 mg every 4 hours (5 times/day) for 7-10 days
  Bone marrow transplant recipients: Children and Adults: I.V.:
    Allogeneic patients who are HSV seropositive: 150 mg/m²/dose (5 mg/kg) every 12 hours; with clinical symptoms of herpes simplex: 150 mg/m²/dose every 8 hours
(Continued)

Acyclovir *(Continued)*

Allogeneic patients who are CMV seropositive: 500 mg/m^2/dose (10 mg/kg) every 8 hours; for clinically symptomatic CMV infection, consider replacing acyclovir with ganciclovir

Chronic suppressive therapy for recurrent genital herpes simplex virus infections:
Adults: 200 mg 3-4 times/day or 400 mg twice daily for up to 12 months, followed by re-evaluation

Dosing adjustment in renal impairment:
Oral: HSV/varicella-zoster:
Cl_{cr} 10-25 mL/minute: Administer dose every 8 hours
Cl_{cr} <10 mL/minute: Administer dose every 12 hours
I.V.:
Cl_{cr} 25-50 mL/minute: 5-10 mg/kg/dose: Administer every 12 hours
Cl_{cr} 10-25 mL/minute: 5-10 mg/kg/dose: Administer every 24 hours
Cl_{cr} <10 mL/minute: 2.5-5 mg/kg/dose: Administer every 24 hours
Hemodialysis: Dialyzable (50% to 100%); administer dose postdialysis
Peritoneal dialysis: Dose as for Cl_{cr} <10 mL/minute
Continuous arteriovenous or venovenous hemofiltration (CAVH/CAVHD) effects: Dose as for Cl_{cr} <10 mL/minute

Administration Infuse over 1 hour; maintain adequate hydration of patient; check and rotate infusion sites for phlebitis

Monitoring Parameters Urinalysis, BUN, serum creatinine, liver enzymes, CBC

Patient Information Patients are contagious only when viral shedding is occurring; recurrences tend to appear within 3 months of original infection; acyclovir is **not** a cure; avoid sexual intercourse when lesions are present; may take with food

Nursing Implications Wear gloves when applying ointment for self-protection

Additional Information Sodium content of 1 g: 96.6 mg (4.2 mEq)

Dosage Forms
Capsule: 200 mg
Powder for Injection: 500 mg (10 mL); 1000 mg (20 mL)
Ointment, topical: 5% [50 mg/g] (3 g, 15 g)
Suspension, oral (banana flavor): 200 mg/5 mL
Tablet: 400 mg, 800 mg

♦ **Adagen™** *see* Pegademase Bovine *on page 889*
♦ **Adalat®** *see* Nifedipine *on page 838*
♦ **Adalat® CC** *see* Nifedipine *on page 838*
♦ **Adalat PA®** *see* Nifedipine *on page 838*
♦ **Adamantanamine Hydrochloride** *see* Amantadine *on page 51*

Adapalene *(a DAP a leen)*

U.S. Brand Names Differin®
Therapeutic Category Acne Products
Use Treatment of acne vulgaris
Pregnancy Risk Factor C
Pregnancy/Breast-Feeding Implications
Clinical effects on the fetus: No teratogenic effects were seen in rats at oral doses of adapalene 0.15-5 mg/kg/day
Breast feeding/lactation: There are no adequate and well controlled studies in pregnant women; it is not known whether adapalene is excreted in breast milk

Contraindications Hypersensitivity to adapalene or any of the components in the vehicle gel

Warnings/Precautions Use with caution in patients with eczema; avoid excessive exposure to sunlight and sunlamps; avoid contact with abraded skin, mucous membranes, eyes, mouth, angles of the nose

Certain cutaneous signs and symptoms such as erythema, dryness, scaling, burning or pruritus may occur during treatment; these are most likely to occur during the first 2-4 weeks and will usually lessen with continued use

Adverse Reactions
>10%: Dermatologic: Erythema, scaling, dryness, pruritus, burning, pruritus or burning immediately after application
≤1%: Skin irritation, stinging sunburn, acne flares

Overdosage/Toxicology
Toxic signs of an overdose commonly respond to drug discontinuation, and generally return to normal spontaneously within a few days to weeks
When confronted with signs of increased intracranial pressure, treatment with mannitol (0.25 g/kg I.V. up to 1 g/kg/dose repeated every 5 minutes as needed), dexamethasone (1.5 mg/kg I.V. load followed with 0.375 mg/kg every 6 hours for 5 days), and/or hyperventilation should be employed

Mechanism of Action Retinoid-like compound which is a modulator of cellular differentiation, keratinization and inflammatory processes, all of which represent important features in the pathology of acne vulgaris

Pharmacodynamics/Kinetics
Absorption: Topical: Minimum absorption occurs
Elimination: In bile

Usual Dosage Children >12 years and Adults: Topical: Apply once daily at bedtime; therapeutic results should be noticed after 8-12 weeks of treatment

Patient Information Thoroughly wash hands after applying; avoid hydration of skin immediately before application; minimize exposure to sunlight; avoid washing face more frequently than 2-3 times/day; if severe irritation occurs, discontinue medication temporarily and adjust dose when irritation subsides; avoid using topical preparations with high alcoholic content during treatment period; do not exceed prescribed dose

Nursing Implications Observe for signs of hypersensitivity, blistering, excessive dryness; do not apply to mucous membranes

Dosage Forms Gel, topical (alcohol free): 0.1% (15 g, 45 g)

♦ **Adapin® Oral** see Doxepin on page 392

♦ **Adderall®** see Dextroamphetamine and Amphetamine on page 344

♦ **Adeflor®** see Vitamins, Multiple on page 1226

♦ **Adenine Arabinoside** see Vidarabine on page 1217

♦ **Adenocard®** see Adenosine on this page

Adenosine (a DEN oh seen)

Related Information
Adult ACLS Algorithm, Tachycardia on page 1450
Antiarrhythmic Drugs Comparison on page 1297

U.S. Brand Names Adenocard®

Synonyms 9-Beta-D-ribofuranosyladenine

Therapeutic Category Antiarrhythmic Agent, Miscellaneous

Use Treatment of paroxysmal supraventricular tachycardia (PSVT) including that associated with accessory bypass tracts (Wolff-Parkinson-White syndrome); when clinically advisable, appropriate vagal maneuvers should be attempted prior to adenosine administration; not effective in atrial flutter, atrial fibrillation, or ventricular tachycardia; also used diagnostically as an adjunct to thallium-201 myocardial scintigraphy in patients unable to exercise adequately

Pregnancy Risk Factor C

Pregnancy/Breast-Feeding Implications Clinical effects on the fetus: Case reports (4) on administration during pregnancy have indicated no adverse effects on fetus or newborn attributable to adenosine

Contraindications Known hypersensitivity to adenosine; second or third degree A-V block or sick-sinus syndrome (except in patients with a functioning artificial pacemaker), atrial flutter, atrial fibrillation, and ventricular tachycardia (the drug is not effective in converting these arrhythmias to sinus rhythm)

Warnings/Precautions Patients with pre-existing S-A nodal dysfunction may experience prolonged sinus pauses after adenosine; there have been reports of atrial fibrillation/ flutter in patients with PSVT associated with accessory conduction pathways after adenosine; adenosine decreases conduction through the A-V node and may produce a short lasting first, second, or third degree heart block. Because of the very short half-life, the effects are generally self limiting. At the time of conversion to normal sinus rhythm, a variety of new rhythms may appear on the EKG.

A limited number of patients with asthma have received adenosine and have not experienced exacerbation of their asthma. Be alert to the possibility that adenosine could produce bronchoconstriction in patients with asthma.

Adverse Reactions
>10%:
Cardiovascular: Facial flushing (18%), palpitations, chest pain, hypotension
Central nervous system: Headache (18%), dizziness (12%)
Respiratory: Shortness of breath/dyspnea (12%)
Miscellaneous: Diaphoresis
1% to 10%:
Gastrointestinal: Nausea (3%)
Neuromuscular & skeletal: Paresthesia, numbness
Respiratory: Chest pressure (7%)
<1%: Lightheadedness, apprehension, intracranial pressure, metallic taste, tightness in throat, pressure in groin, neck and back pain, blurred vision, hyperventilation, burning sensation, heaviness in arms

Overdosage/Toxicology
Since half-life of adenosine is <10 seconds, any adverse effects are rapidly self-limiting. Intoxication is usually short-lived since the half-life of the drug is very short.
Treatment of prolonged effects requires individualization. Theophylline and other methylxanthines are competitive inhibitors of adenosine and may have a role in reversing its toxic effects.

Drug Interactions
Decreased effect: Methylxanthines antagonize effects
Increased effect: Dipyridamole potentiates effects of adenosine
Increased toxicity: Carbamazepine may increase heart block

Stability Do not refrigerate, precipitation may occur (may dissolve by warming to room temperature)

Mechanism of Action Slows conduction time through the A-V node, interrupting the re-entry pathways through the A-V node, restoring normal sinus rhythm

Pharmacodynamics/Kinetics
Onset: Clinical effects occur rapidly
Duration: Very brief
Metabolism: In the blood and tissue to inosine then to adenosine monophosphate (AMP) and hypoxanthine
(Continued)

Adenosine *(Continued)*

Half-life: <10 seconds, thus adverse effects are usually rapidly self-limiting

Usual Dosage Rapid I.V. push (over 1-2 seconds) via peripheral line:

Neonates: Initial dose: 0.05 mg/kg; if not effective within 2 minutes, increase dose by 0.05 mg/kg increments every 2 minutes to a maximum dose of 0.25 mg/kg or until termination of PSVT

Maximum single dose: 12 mg

Infants and Children: Pediatric advanced life support (PALS): Treatment of SVT: 0.1 mg/kg; if not effective, administer 0.2 mg/kg

Alternatively: Initial dose: 0.05 mg/kg; if not effective within 2 minutes, increase dose by 0.05 mg/kg increments every 2 minutes to a maximum dose of 0.25 mg/kg or until termination of PSVT; medium dose required: 0.15 mg/kg

Maximum single dose: 12 mg

Adults: 6 mg; if not effective within 1-2 minutes, 12 mg may be given; may repeat 12 mg bolus if needed

Maximum single dose: 12 mg

Hemodialysis: Significant drug removal is unlikely based on physiochemical characteristics

Peritoneal dialysis: Significant drug removal is unlikely based on physiochemical characteristics

Note: Patients who are receiving concomitant theophylline therapy may be less likely to respond to adenosine therapy

Note: Higher doses may be needed for administration via peripheral versus central vein

Administration For rapid bolus I.V. use only; administer I.V. push over 1-2 seconds at a peripheral I.V. site closest to patient; follow each bolus with normal saline flush. **Note:** Preliminary results in adults suggest adenosine may be administered via central line at lower doses (eg, adults initial dose: 3 mg)

Monitoring Parameters EKG monitoring, heart rate, blood pressure

Nursing Implications Be alert for possible exacerbation of asthma in asthmatic patients

Dosage Forms

Diagnostic use: 60 mg/20 mL and 90 mg/30 mL single-dose vials

Injection, preservative free: 3 mg/mL (2 mL)

- **Agrylin**® *see* Anagrelide *on page 84*
- **AHF** *see* Antihemophilic Factor (Human) *on page 88*
- **A-hydroCort**® *see* Hydrocortisone *on page 579*
- **Airet**® *see* Albuterol *on page 35*
- **Akarpine**® **Ophthalmic** *see* Pilocarpine *on page 927*
- **AKBeta**® *see* Levobunolol *on page 670*
- **AK-Chlor**® **Ophthalmic** *see* Chloramphenicol *on page 238*
- **AK-Cide**® **Ophthalmic** *see* Sulfacetamide Sodium and Prednisolone *on page 1091*
- **AK-Con**® *see* Naphazoline *on page 817*
- **AK-Dex**® *see* Dexamethasone *on page 337*
- **AK-Dilate**® **Ophthalmic Solution** *see* Phenylephrine *on page 918*
- **AK-Fluor** *see* Fluorescein Sodium *on page 497*
- **AK-Homatropine**® **Ophthalmic** *see* Homatropine *on page 569*
- **AK-NaCl**® **[OTC]** *see* Sodium Chloride *on page 1067*
- **AK-Nefrin**® **Ophthalmic Solution** *see* Phenylephrine *on page 918*
- **AK-Neo-Dex**® **Ophthalmic** *see* Neomycin and Dexamethasone *on page 825*
- **AK-Pentolate**® *see* Cyclopentolate *on page 304*
- **AK-Poly-Bac**® **Ophthalmic** *see* Bacitracin and Polymyxin B *on page 122*
- **AK-Pred**® **Ophthalmic** *see* Prednisolone *on page 961*
- **AKPro**® **Ophthalmic** *see* Dipivefrin *on page 376*
- **AK-Spore H.C.**® **Ophthalmic Ointment** *see* Bacitracin, Neomycin, Polymyxin B, and Hydrocortisone *on page 123*
- **AK-Spore H.C.**® **Ophthalmic Suspension** *see* Neomycin, Polymyxin B, and Hydrocortisone *on page 827*
- **AK-Spore H.C.**® **Otic** *see* Neomycin, Polymyxin B, and Hydrocortisone *on page 827*
- **AK-Spore**® **Ophthalmic Ointment** *see* Bacitracin, Neomycin, and Polymyxin B *on page 123*
- **AK-Spore**® **Ophthalmic Solution** *see* Neomycin, Polymyxin B, and Gramicidin *on page 826*
- **AK-Sulf**® **Ophthalmic** *see* Sulfacetamide Sodium *on page 1091*
- **AK-Taine**® *see* Proparacaine *on page 982*
- **AKTob**® **Ophthalmic** *see* Tobramycin *on page 1150*
- **AK-Tracin**® **Ophthalmic** *see* Bacitracin *on page 121*
- **AK-Trol**® *see* Neomycin, Polymyxin B, and Dexamethasone *on page 826*
- **Ala-Cort**® *see* Hydrocortisone *on page 579*
- **Ala-Scalp**® *see* Hydrocortisone *on page 579*
- **Alatrovafloxacin Mesylate** *see* Trovafloxacin *on page 1192*
- **Alba-Dex**® *see* Dexamethasone *on page 337*
- **Albalon**® **Liquifilm**® *see* Naphazoline *on page 817*

Albendazole (al BEN da zole)

U.S. Brand Names Albenza®

Therapeutic Category Anthelmintic

Use Treatment of parenchymal neurocysticercosis and cystic hydatid disease of the liver, lung, and peritoneum; albendazole has activity against *Ascaris lumbricoides* (roundworm), *Ancylostoma duodenal* and *Necator americanus* (hookworm), *Enterobius vermicularis* (pinworm), *Hymenolepis nana* and *Taenia* sp (tapeworms), *Opisthorchis sinensis* and *Opisthorchis viverrini* (liver flukes), *Strongyloides stercoralis* and *Trichuris trichiura* (whipworm); activity has also been shown against the liver fluke *Clonorchis sinensis*, *Giardia lamblia*, *Cysticercus cellulosae*, *Echinococcus granulosus*, *Echinococcus multilocularis*, and *Toxocara* sp.

Pregnancy Risk Factor C

Pregnancy/Breast-Feeding Implications Albendazole has been shown to be teratogenic in laboratory animals and should not be used during pregnancy, if at all possible

Contraindications Patients with hypersensitivity to albendazole or its components; pregnant women, if possible

Warnings/Precautions Discontinue therapy if LFT elevations are significant; may restart treatment when decreased to pretreatment values. Becoming pregnant within 1 month following therapy is not advised. Corticosteroids should be administered 1-2 days before albendazole therapy in patients with neurocysticercosis to minimize inflammatory reactions and steroid and anticonvulsant therapy should be used concurrently during the first week of therapy for neurocysticercosis to prevent cerebral hypertension. If retinal lesions exist in patients with neurocysticercosis, weigh risk of further retinal damage due to albendazole-induced changes to the retinal lesion vs benefit of disease treatment.

Adverse Reactions N = neurocysticercosis; H = hydatid disease
Central nervous system: Dizziness, vertigo, fever (≤1%); headache (11% - N; 1% - H); increased intracranial pressure
Dermatologic: Alopecia/rash/urticaria (<1%)
Gastrointestinal: Abdominal pain (6% - H, 0% - N); nausea/vomiting (3% to 6%)
Hematologic: Leukopenia (reversible) (<1%); granulocytopenia/agranulocytopenia/pancytopenia (rare)
Hepatic: Increased LFTs (~15% - H, <1% - N)
Miscellaneous: Allergic reactions (<1%)

Drug Interactions May inhibit CYP1A2 enzyme (mild)
Decreased effect: Carbamazepine may accelerate albendazole metabolism
(Continued)

33

Albendazole *(Continued)*

Increased effect: Dexamethasone increases plasma levels of albendazole metabolites; praziquantel may increase plasma concentrations of albendazole by 50%; albendazole inhibits hepatic cytochrome P-450 1A and may consequently interact by increasing the concentrations of many drugs which are metabolized by this route; food (especially fatty meals) increases the oral bioavailability by 4-5 times

Mechanism of Action Active metabolite, albendazole, causes selective degeneration of cytoplasmic microtubules in intestinal and tegmental cells of intestinal helminths and larvae; glycogen is depleted, glucose uptake and cholinesterase secretion are impaired, and desecratory substances accumulate intracellulary. ATP production decreases causing energy depletion, immobilization, and worm death.

Pharmacodynamics/Kinetics

Absorption: Oral absorption is poor (<5%); may increase up to 4-5 times when administered with a fatty meal

Distribution: Well distributed inside hydatid cysts; excellent CSF concentrations

Protein binding: 70%

Metabolism: Extensive first-pass metabolism; metabolic pathways include rapid sulfoxidation (major), hydrolysis, and oxidation

Half-life: 8-12 hours

Time to peak serum concentration: 2-2.4 hours

Elimination: Active and inactive metabolites excreted in urine

Usual Dosage Oral:

Neurocysticercosis:

<60 kg: 15 mg/kg/day in 2 divided doses (maximum: 800 mg/day) with meals for 8-30 days

≥60 kg: 400 mg twice daily for 8-30 days

Note: Give concurrent anticonvulsant and steroid therapy during first week

Hydatid:

<60 kg: 15 mg/kg/day in 2 divided doses with meals (maximum: 800 mg/day) for three 28-day cycles with 14-day drug-free interval in-between

≥60 kg: 400 mg twice daily for 3 cycles as above

Strongyloidiasis/tapeworm:

≤2 years: 200 mg/day for 3 days; may repeat in 3 weeks

>2 years and Adults: 400 mg/day for 3 days; may repeat in 3 weeks

Giardiasis: Adults: 400 mg/day for 3 days

Hookworm, pinworm, roundworm:

≤2 years: 200 mg as a single dose; may repeat in 3 weeks

>2 years and Adults: 400 mg as a single dose; may repeat in 3 weeks

Administration Give with meals; administer anticonvulsant and steroid therapy during first week of neurocysticercosis therapy

Monitoring Parameters Monitor fecal specimens for ova and parasites for 3 weeks after treatment; if positive, retreat; monitor LFTs, and clinical signs of hepatotoxicity; CBC at start of each 28-day cycle and every 2 weeks during therapy

Patient Information Take with a high fat diet

Dosage Forms Tablet: 200 mg

- ◆ **Albenza**® *see Albendazole on previous page*
- ◆ **Albert**® **Docusate** *see Docusate on page 384*
- ◆ **Albert**® **Glyburide** *see Glyburide on page 540*
- ◆ **Albert**® **Oxybutynin** *see Oxybutynin on page 873*
- ◆ **Albert**® **Pentoxifylline** *see Pentoxifylline on page 905*

Albumin *(al BYOO min)*

U.S. Brand Names Albuminar®; Albumisol®; Albunex®; Albutein®; Buminate®; Plasbumin®

Synonyms Albumin (Human); Normal Human Serum Albumin; Normal Serum Albumin (Human); Salt Poor Albumin; SPA

Therapeutic Category Blood Product Derivative; Plasma Volume Expander, Colloid

Use Plasma volume expansion and maintenance of cardiac output in the treatment of certain types of shock or impending shock; may be useful for burn patients, ARDS, and cardiopulmonary bypass; other uses considered by some investigators (but not proven) are retroperitoneal surgery, peritonitis, and ascites; unless the condition responsible for hypoproteinemia can be corrected, albumin can provide only symptomatic relief or supportive treatment; nutritional supplementation is not an appropriate indication for albumin

Pregnancy Risk Factor C

Contraindications Patients with severe anemia or cardiac failure, known hypersensitivity to albumin; avoid 25% concentration in preterm infants due to risk of idiopathic ventricular hypertrophy

Warnings/Precautions Use with caution in patients with hepatic or renal failure because of added protein load; rapid infusion of albumin solutions may cause vascular overload. All patients should be observed for signs of hypervolemia such as pulmonary edema. Use with caution in those patients for whom sodium restriction is necessary. Rapid infusion may cause hypotension.

Adverse Reactions 1% to 10%:

Cardiovascular: Precipitation of congestive heart failure or hypotension, tachycardia, hypervolemia

Central nervous system: Fever, chills

Dermatologic: Rash
Gastrointestinal: Nausea, vomiting
Respiratory: Pulmonary edema

Overdosage/Toxicology Symptoms of overdose include hypervolemia, congestive heart failure, pulmonary edema

Stability Do not use solution if it is turbid or contains a deposit; use within 4 hours after opening vial

Mechanism of Action Provides increase in intravascular oncotic pressure and causes mobilization of fluids from interstitial into intravascular space

Usual Dosage I.V.:

5% should be used in hypovolemic patients or intravascularly-depleted patients

25% should be used in patients in whom fluid and sodium intake must be minimized

Dose depends on condition of patient:

Children:

Emergency initial dose: 25 g

Nonemergencies: 25% to 50% of the adult dose

Adults: Usual dose: 25 g; no more than 250 g should be administered within 48 hours

Hypoproteinemia: 0.5-1 g/kg/dose; repeat every 1-2 days as calculated to replace ongoing losses

Hypovolemia: 0.5-1 g/kg/dose; repeat as needed; maximum dose: 6 g/kg/day

Administration Albumin administration must be completed within 6 hours after entering the 5% container, provided that administration is begun within 4 hours of entering the container; rapid infusion may cause vascular overload; albumin is best administered at a rate of 2-4 mL/minute; 25% albumin may be given at a rate of 1 mL/minute

Test Interactions ↑ alkaline phosphatase (S)

Additional Information Sodium content of 1 L: Both 5% and 25% albumin contain 130-160 mEq

Dosage Forms Injection, as human: 5% [50 mg/mL] (50 mL, 250 mL, 500 mL, 1000 mL); 25% [250 mg/mL] (10 mL, 20 mL, 50 mL, 100 mL)

- ♦ **Albuminar®** see Albumin on previous page
- ♦ **Albumin (Human)** see Albumin on previous page
- ♦ **Albumisol®** see Albumin on previous page
- ♦ **Albunex®** see Albumin on previous page
- ♦ **Albutein®** see Albumin on previous page

Albuterol (al BYOO ter ole)

Related Information

Bronchodilators, Comparison of Inhaled and Sympathomimetic on page 1314

U.S. Brand Names Airet®; Proventil®; Proventil® HFA; Ventolin®; Ventolin® Rotocaps®; Volmax®

Canadian Brand Names Apo®-Salvent; Novo-Salmol; Sabulin

Synonyms Salbutamol

Therapeutic Category Beta$_2$-Adrenergic Agonist Agent; Bronchodilator; Sympathomimetic

Use Bronchodilator in reversible airway obstruction due to asthma or COPD

Pregnancy Risk Factor C

Pregnancy/Breast-Feeding Implications

Clinical effects on the fetus: Crosses the placenta. Tocolytic effects, fetal tachycardia, fetal hypoglycemia secondary to maternal hyperglycemia with oral or intravenous routes reported. Available evidence suggests safe use during pregnancy.

Breast-feeding/lactation: No data on crossing into breast milk or clinical effects on the infant

Contraindications Hypersensitivity to albuterol, adrenergic amines or any ingredients

Warnings/Precautions Use with caution in patients with hyperthyroidism, diabetes mellitus, or sensitivity to sympathomimetic amines; cardiovascular disorders including coronary insufficiency or hypertension; excessive use may result in tolerance

Some adverse reactions may occur more frequently in children 2-5 years of age than in adults and older children

Because of its minimal effect on beta$_1$-receptors and its relatively long duration of action, albuterol is a rational choice in the elderly when a beta agonist is indicated. All patients should utilize a spacer device when using a metered dose inhaler. Oral use should be avoided in the elderly due to adverse effects.

Adverse Reactions

>10%:

Cardiovascular: Tachycardia, palpitations, pounding heartbeat

Gastrointestinal: GI upset, nausea

1% to 10%:

Cardiovascular: Flushing of face, hypertension or hypotension

Central nervous system: Nervousness, CNS stimulation, hyperactivity, insomnia, dizziness, lightheadedness, drowsiness, headache

Gastrointestinal: Xerostomia, heartburn, vomiting, unusual taste

Genitourinary: Dysuria

Neuromuscular & skeletal: Muscle cramping, tremor, weakness

Respiratory: Coughing

Miscellaneous: Diaphoresis (increased)

<1%: Chest pain, unusual pallor, loss of appetite, paradoxical bronchospasm

Overdosage/Toxicology

Symptoms of overdose include hypertension, tachycardia, angina, hypokalemia

(Continued)

Albuterol *(Continued)*

Hypokalemia and tachyarrhythmias: Prudent use of a cardioselective beta-adrenergic blocker (eg, atenolol or metoprolol); keep in mind the potential for induction of broncho-constriction in an asthmatic. Dialysis has not been shown to be of value in the treatment of an overdose with this agent.

Drug Interactions
Decreased effect: Beta-adrenergic blockers (eg, propranolol)

Increased therapeutic effect: Inhaled ipratropium may increase duration of bronchodilation, nifedipine may increase FEV-1

Increased toxicity: Cardiovascular effects are potentiated in patients also receiving MAO inhibitors, tricyclic antidepressants, sympathomimetic agents (eg, amphetamine, dopamine, dobutamine), inhaled anesthetics (eg, enflurane)

Mechanism of Action Relaxes bronchial smooth muscle by action on beta$_2$-receptors with little effect on heart rate

Pharmacodynamics/Kinetics
Peak effect: Oral: 2-3 hours; Nebulization/oral inhalation: Within 0.5-2 hours

Duration of action: Oral: 4-6 hours; Nebulization/oral inhalation: 3-4 hours

Metabolism: By the liver to an inactive sulfate, with 28% appearing in the urine as unchanged drug

Half-life: Inhalation: 3.8 hours; Oral: 3.7-5 hours

Elimination: 30% appears in urine as unchanged drug

Usual Dosage
Oral:

Children:

2-6 years: 0.1-0.2 mg/kg/dose 3 times/day; maximum dose not to exceed 12 mg/day (divided doses)

6-12 years: 2 mg/dose 3-4 times/day; maximum dose not to exceed 24 mg/day (divided doses)

Children >12 years and Adults: 2-4 mg/dose 3-4 times/day; maximum dose not to exceed 32 mg/day (divided doses)

Elderly: 2 mg 3-4 times/day; maximum: 8 mg 4 times/day

Inhalation MDI: 90 mcg/spray:

Children <12 years: 1-2 inhalations 4 times/day using a tube spacer

Children ≥12 years and Adults: 1-2 inhalations every 4-6 hours; maximum: 12 inhalations/day

Exercise-induced bronchospasm: 2 inhalations 15 minutes before exercising

Inhalation: Nebulization: 0.01-0.05 mL/kg of 0.5% solution every 4-6 hours; intensive care patients may require more frequent administration; minimum dose: 0.1 mL; maximum dose: 1 mL diluted in 1-2 mL normal saline; continuous nebulized albuterol at 0.3 mg/kg/hour has been used safely in the treatment of severe status asthmaticus in children; continuous nebulized doses of 3 mg/kg/hour ± 2.2 mg/kg/hour in children whose mean age was 20.7 months resulted in no cardiac toxicity; the optimal dosage for continuous nebulization remains to be determined.

Hemodialysis: Not removed

Peritoneal dialysis: Significant drug removal is unlikely based on physiochemical characteristics

Monitoring Parameters Heart rate, CNS stimulation, asthma symptoms, arterial or capillary blood gases (if patients condition warrants)

Test Interactions ↑ renin (S), ↑ aldosterone (S)

Patient Information Do not exceed recommended dosage; rinse mouth with water following each inhalation to help with dry throat and mouth; follow specific instructions accompanying inhaler; if more than one inhalation is necessary, wait at least 1 full minute between inhalations. May cause nervousness, restlessness, insomnia; if these effects continue after dosage reduction, notify physician; also notify physician if palpitations, tachycardia, chest pain, muscle tremors, dizziness, headache, flushing or if breathing difficulty persists.

Nursing Implications Before using, the inhaler must be shaken well; assess lung sounds, pulse, and blood pressure before administration and during peak of medication; observe patient for wheezing after administration, if this occurs, call physician

Dosage Forms
Aerosol: 90 mcg/dose (17 g) [200 doses]

Proventil®, Ventolin®: 90 mcg/dose (17 g) [200 doses]

Aerosol, chlorofluorocarbon free (Proventil® HFA): 90 mcg/dose (17 g)

Capsule for oral inhalation (Ventolin® Rotacaps®): 200 mcg [to be used with Rotahaler® inhalation device]

Solution, inhalation: 0.083% (3 mL); 0.5% (20 mL)

Airet®: 0.083%

Proventil®: 0.083% (3 mL); 0.5% (20 mL)

Ventolin®: 0.5% (20 mL)

Syrup, as sulfate: 2 mg/5 mL (480 mL)

Proventil®, Ventolin®: 2 mg/5 mL (480 mL)

Tablet, as sulfate: 2 mg, 4 mg

Proventil®, Ventolin®: 2 mg, 4 mg

Tablet, extended release:

Proventil® Repetabs®: 4 mg

Volmax®: 4 mg, 8 mg

♦ **Alcaine®** *see* Proparacaine *on page 982*

Alclometasone (al kloe MET a sone)

U.S. Brand Names Aclovate® Topical

Synonyms Alclometasone Dipropionate

Therapeutic Category Anti-inflammatory Agent; Corticosteroid, Topical (Low Potency)

Use Treats inflammation of corticosteroid-responsive dermatosis (low potency topical corticosteroid)

Pregnancy Risk Factor C

Contraindications Viral, fungal, or tubercular skin lesions, known hypersensitivity to alclometasone or any component

Warnings/Precautions Adverse systemic effects may occur when used on large areas of the body, denuded areas, for prolonged periods of time, with an occlusive dressing, and/or in infants or small children

Adverse Reactions
1% to 10%:
  Dermatologic: Itching, erythema, dryness papular rashes
  Local: Burning, irritation
<1%: Hypertrichosis, acneiform eruptions, hypopigmentation, perioral dermatitis, maceration of skin, skin atrophy, striae, miliaria

Overdosage/Toxicology Symptoms of overdose include cushingoid appearance (systemic), muscle weakness (systemic), osteoporosis (systemic) all with long-term use only. When consumed in excessive quantities for prolonged periods, systemic hypercorticism and adrenal suppression may occur; in those cases, discontinuation and withdrawal of the corticosteroid should be done judiciously.

Stability Store between 2°C and 30°C (36°F and 86°F)

Mechanism of Action Stimulates the synthesis of enzymes needed to decrease inflammation, suppress mitotic activity, and cause vasoconstriction

Usual Dosage Topical: Apply a thin film to the affected area 2-3 times/day

Patient Information Before applying, gently wash area to reduce risk of infection; apply a thin film to cleansed area and rub in gently and thoroughly until medication vanishes; avoid exposure to sunlight, severe sunburn may occur

Nursing Implications For external use only; do not use on open wounds; apply sparingly to occlusive dressings; should not be used in the presence of open or weeping lesions

Dosage Forms
Cream, as dipropionate: 0.05% (15 g, 45 g, 60 g)
Ointment, topical, as dipropionate: 0.05% (15 g, 45 g, 60 g)

♦ **Alclometasone Dipropionate** see Alclometasone on this page
♦ **Alconefrin® Nasal Solution [OTC]** see Phenylephrine on page 918
♦ **Aldactazide®** see Hydrochlorothiazide and Spironolactone on page 575
♦ **Aldactone®** see Spironolactone on page 1078
♦ **Aldara™** see Imiquimod on page 603

Aldesleukin (al des LOO kin)

Related Information
Cancer Chemotherapy Regimens on page 1263

U.S. Brand Names Proleukin®

Synonyms IL-2; Interleukin-2

Therapeutic Category Biological Response Modulator; Interleukin

Use Treatment of metastatic renal cell carcinoma; also, investigated in tumors known to have a response to immunotherapy, such as melanoma; has been used in conjunction with LAK cells, TIL cells, IL-1, and interferon

Pregnancy Risk Factor C

Contraindications Known history of hypersensitivity to interleukin-2 or any component; patients with an abnormal thallium stress test or pulmonary function test; patients who have had an organ allograft; retreatment in patients who have experienced sustained ventricular tachycardia (≥5 beats), cardiac rhythm disturbances not controlled or unresponsive to management, recurrent chest pain with EKG changes (consistent with angina or myocardial infarction), intubation required >72 hours, pericardial tamponade; renal dysfunction requiring dialysis >72 hours, coma or toxic psychosis lasting >48 hours, repetitive or difficult to control seizures, bowel ischemia/perforation, GI bleeding requiring surgery

Warnings/Precautions High-dose IL-2 therapy has been associated with capillary leak syndrome (CLS); CLS results in hypotension and reduced organ perfusion which may be severe and can result in death; therapy should be restricted to patients with normal cardiac and pulmonary functions as defined by thallium stress and formal pulmonary function testing; extreme caution should be used in patients with normal thallium stress tests and pulmonary functions tests who have a history of prior cardiac or pulmonary disease. Postnephrectomy patients must have a serum creatinine of ≤1.5 mg/dL prior to treatment.

Intensive aldesleukin treatment is associated with impaired neutrophil function (reduced chemotaxis) and with an increased risk of disseminated infection, including sepsis and bacterial endocarditis, in treated patients. Consequently, pre-existing bacterial infections should be adequately treated prior to initiation of therapy. Additionally, all patients with indwelling central lines should receive antibiotic prophylaxis effective against *S. aureus*. Antibiotic prophylaxis which has been associated with a reduced incidence of staphylococcal infections in aldesleukin studies includes the use of oxacillin, nafcillin, ciprofloxacin, or vancomycin.

(Continued)

Aldesleukin *(Continued)*

Standard prophylactic supportive care during high-dose IL-2 treatment includes acetaminophen to relieve constitutional symptoms and an H_2-antagonist to reduce the risk of GI ulceration and/or bleeding.

Adverse Reactions

>10%:

Cardiovascular: Sensory dysfunction, sinus tachycardia, arrhythmias, pulmonary congestion; hypotension (dose-limiting toxicity) which may require vasopressor support and hemodynamic changes resembling those seen in septic shock can be seen within 2 hours of administration; angina, acute myocardial infarction, SVT with hypotension has been reported, edema

Central nervous system: Dizziness, pain, fever, chills, cognitive changes, fatigue, malaise, disorientation, somnolence, paranoid delusion, and other behavioral changes; reversible and dose related; however, may continue to worsen for several days even after the infusion is stopped

Dermatologic: Pruritus, erythema, rash, dry skin, exfoliative dermatitis, macular erythema

Gastrointestinal: Nausea, vomiting, weight gain, diarrhea, stomatitis, anorexia, GI bleeding

Hematologic: Anemia, thrombocytopenia, leukopenia, eosinophilia, coagulation disorders

Hepatic: Elevated transaminase and alkaline phosphatase, jaundice

Neuromuscular & skeletal: Weakness, rigors which can be decreased or ameliorated with acetaminophen or a nonsteroidal agent and meperidine

Renal: Oliguria, anuria, proteinuria; renal failure (dose-limiting toxicity) manifested as oliguria noted within 24-48 hours of initiation of therapy; marked fluid retention, azotemia, and increased serum creatinine seen, which may return to baseline within 7 days of discontinuation of therapy; hypophosphatemia

Respiratory: Dyspnea, pulmonary edema

1% to 10%: Cardiovascular: Increase in vascular permeability: Capillary-leak syndrome manifested by severe peripheral edema, ascites, pulmonary infiltration, and pleural effusion; occurs in 2% to 4% of patients and is resolved after therapy ends

<1%: Congestive heart failure, coma, seizure, alopecia, hypercalcemia, hypocalcemia, hypomagnesemia, hypothyroidism, increased plasma levels of stress-related hormones, acidosis, pancreatitis, polyuria, arthritis, muscle spasm, allergic reactions

Overdosage/Toxicology

Side effects following the use of aldesleukin are dose related. Administration of more than the recommended dose has been associated with a more rapid onset of expected dose-limiting toxicities. Adverse reactions generally will reverse when the drug is stopped particularly because of its short serum half-life.

Provide supportive treatment of any continuing symptoms. Life-threatening toxicities have been ameliorated by the I.V. administration of dexamethasone, which may result in less of therapeutic effect of aldesleukin.

Drug Interactions

Decreased toxicity: Corticosteroids have been shown to decrease toxicity of IL-2, but have not been used since there is concern that they may decrease the efficacy of the lymphokine

Increased toxicity:

Aldesleukin may affect central nervous function; therefore, interactions could occur following concomitant administration of psychotropic drugs (eg, narcotics, analgesics, antiemetics, sedatives, tranquilizers)

Concomitant administration of drugs possessing nephrotoxic (eg, aminoglycosides, indomethacin), myelotoxic (eg, cytotoxic chemotherapy), cardiotoxic (eg, doxorubicin), or hepatotoxic (eg, methotrexate, asparaginase) effects with aldesleukin may ↑ toxicity in these organ systems; the safety and efficacy of aldesleukin in combination with chemotherapy agents has not been established

Beta-blockers and other antihypertensives may potentiate the hypotension seen with Proleukin®

Iodinated contrast media: Acute reactions including fever, chills, nausea, vomiting, pruritus, rash, diarrhea, hypotension, edema, and oliguria have occurred within hours of contrast infusion; this reaction may occur within 4 weeks or up to several months after IL-2 administration

Recommendations for IL-2 (Aldesleukin - Proleukin™) Dilutions in D_5W*

Concentration (mcg/mL)	Concentration (million units/mL)	Stability Recommendation
<60	<1	Human serum albumin must be added to bag **prior to addition** of IL-2; these solutions are stable for 6 days at room temperature.†
60-100	1-1.7	**These concentrations should not be utilized as they are unstable.**
100-500	1.7-8.4	These solutions are stable for 6 days at room temperature.†

*1.3 mg of IL-2 (aldesleukin - Proleukin™) is equivalent to 22 million units.

†Although stability is 6 days, IL-2 does not contain a preservative and 24-hour expiration dating should be used.

Volume of Human Serum Albumin to Be Added to IL-2 (Aldesleukin - Proleukin™) Infusions in D₅W

Volume of I.V. Diluent (mL)	Volume of 5% Human Serum Albumin to Be Added Prior to IL-2 Addition (mL)	Volume of 25% Human Serum Albumin to Be Added Prior to IL-2 Addition (mL)
50	1	0.2
100	2	0.4
150	3	0.6
200	4	0.8
250	5	1
500	10	2

Concentrations of IL-2 which fall into the unstable (60-100 mcg/mL **or** 1-1.7 microunits/mL) range require addition of human serum albumin (final human serum albumin concentration of 0.1%) as shown in the table

Stability

Store vials of lyophilized injection in a refrigerator at 2°C to 8°C (36°F to 46°F)

Reconstituted or diluted solution is stable for up to 48 hours at refrigerated and room temperatures 2°C to 25°C (36°F to 77°F); however, since this product contains no preservatives, the reconstituted and diluted solutions should be stored in the refrigerator

Compatible only with D₅W

Gently swirl, do not shake

Note: As with most biological proteins, solutions containing IL-2 should not be filtered; filtration will result in significant loss of bioactivity; see table.

Standard aldesleukin I.V. dilutions:

Dose/50-1000 mL D₅W

Concentrations <1,000,000 units/mL require the addition of human albumin to PVC bag prior to addition of IL-2

Stable for 48 hours at room temperature or refrigeration (2°C to 8°C); refrigeration is recommended due to lack of preservative

Incompatible with NS

Mechanism of Action IL-2 promotes proliferation, differentiation, and recruitment of T and B cells, natural killer (NK) cells, and thymocytes; IL-2 also causes cytolytic activity in a subset of lymphocytes and subsequent interactions between the immune system and malignant cells; IL-2 can stimulate lymphokine-activated killer (LAK) cells and tumor-infiltrating lymphocytes (TIL) cells. LAK cells (which are derived from lymphocytes from a patient and incubated in IL-2) have the ability to lyse cells which are resistant to NK cells; TIL cells (which are derived from cancerous tissue from a patient and incubated in IL-2) have been shown to be 50% more effective than LAK cells in experimental studies.

Pharmacodynamics/Kinetics

Absorption: Oral: Not absorbed

Distribution: V_d: Has been noted to be 4-7 L; primarily into the plasma and then into a second compartment, the lymphocytes themselves

Bioavailability: I.M.: 37%

Half-life: Initial: 6-13 minutes; Terminal: 20-120 minutes

Usual Dosage Refer to individual protocols; all orders must be written in million International units (million IU)

Adults: Metastatic renal cell carcinoma (RCC):

Treatment consists of two 5-day treatment cycles separated by a rest period. 600,000 units/kg (0.037 mg/kg)/dose administered every 8 hours by a 15-minute I.V. infusion for a total of 14 doses; following 9 days of rest, the schedule is repeated for another 14 doses, for a maximum of 28 doses per course

Dose modification: In high-dose therapy of RCC, see manufacturer's guidelines for holding and restarting therapy; hold or interrupt a dose - DO NOT DOSE REDUCE; or refer to specific protocol

Retreatment: Patients should be evaluated for response approximately 4 weeks after completion of a course of therapy and again immediately prior to the scheduled start of the next treatment course; additional courses of treatment may be given to patients only if there is some tumor shrinkage or stable disease following the last course and retreatment is not contraindicated. Each treatment course should be separated by a rest period of at least 7 weeks from the date of hospital discharge; tumors have continued to regress up to 12 months following the initiation of therapy

Investigational regimen: S.C.: 11 million Units (flat dose) daily x 4 days per week for 4 consecutive weeks; repeat every 6 weeks

Administration Administer in D₅W only; **incompatible** with sodium chloride solutions

Management of symptoms related to vascular leak syndrome:

If actual body weight increases >10% above baseline, or rales or rhonchi are audible:

Administer furosemide at dosage determined by patient response

Administer dopamine hydrochloride 2-4 mcg/kg/minute to maintain renal blood flow and urine output

If patient has dyspnea at rest: Administer supplemental oxygen by face mask

(Continued)

Aldesleukin *(Continued)*

If patient has severe respiratory distress: Intubate patient and provide mechanical ventilation; administer ranitidine (as the hydrochloride salt), 50 mg I.V. every 8-12 hours as prophylaxis against stress ulcers

Monitoring Parameters

The following clinical evaluations are recommended for all patients prior to beginning treatment and then daily during drug administration:

Standard hematologic tests including CBC, differential, and platelet counts

Blood chemistries including electrolytes, renal and hepatic function tests

Chest x-rays

Daily monitoring during therapy should include vital signs (temperature, pulse, blood pressure, and respiration rate) and weight; in a patient with a decreased blood pressure, especially <90 mm Hg, constant cardiac monitoring for rhythm should be conducted. If an abnormal complex or rhythm is seen, an EKG should be performed; vital signs in these hypotension patients should be taken hourly and central venous pressure (CVP) checked.

During treatment, pulmonary function should be monitored on a regular basis by clinical examination, assessment of vital signs and pulse oximetry. Patients with dyspnea or clinical signs of respiratory impairment (tachypnea or rales) should be further assessed with arterial blood gas determination. These tests are to be repeated as often as clinically indicated.

Cardiac function is assessed daily by clinical examination and assessment of vital signs. Patients with signs or symptoms of chest pain, murmurs, gallops, irregular rhythm or palpitations should be further assessed with an EKG examination and CPK evaluation. If there is evidence of cardiac ischemia or congestive heart failure, a repeat thallium study should be done.

Additional Information

1 Cetus Unit = 6 International units

1.1 mg = 18×10^6 International units (or 3×10^6 Cetus units)

1 Roche Unit (Teceleukin) = 3 International units

Reimbursement Hot Line: 1-800-775-7533

Professional services: 1-800-244-7668

Dosage Forms Powder for injection, lyophilized: 22×10^6 international units [18 million international units/mL = 1.1 mg/mL when reconstituted]

♦ **Aldoclor**® *see* Chlorothiazide and Methyldopa *on page 245*

♦ **Aldomet**® *see* Methyldopa *on page 758*

♦ **Aldoril**® *see* Methyldopa and Hydrochlorothiazide *on page 759*

Alendronate *(a LEN droe nate)*

U.S. Brand Names Fosamax®

Synonyms Alendronate Sodium

Therapeutic Category Bisphosphonate Derivative

Use Osteoporosis in postmenopausal women; Paget's disease of the bone

Pregnancy Risk Factor C

Contraindications Hypersensitivity to bisphosphonates or any component of the product; hypocalcemia; abnormalities of the esophagus which delay esophageal emptying such as stricture or achalasia; inability to stand or sit upright for at least 30 minutes

Warnings/Precautions Use caution in patients with renal impairment; concomitant hormone replacement therapy with alendronate for osteoporosis in postmenopausal women is not recommended; hypocalcemia must be corrected before therapy initiation with alendronate; ensure adequate calcium and vitamin D intake to provide for enhanced needs in patients with Paget's disease in whom the pretreatment rate of bone turnover may be greatly elevated.

Adverse Reactions

Note: Incidence of adverse effects increases significantly in patients treated for Paget's disease at 40 mg/day, mostly GI adverse effects

1% to 10%:

Central nervous system: Headache (2.6%); pain (4.1%)

Gastrointestinal: Flatulence (2.6%); acid regurgitation (2%); esophagitis ulcer (1.5%); dysphagia, abdominal distention (1%)

<1%: Rash, erythema (rare), gastritis (0.5%)

Overdosage/Toxicology

Symptoms of overdose include hypocalcemia, hypophosphatemia; upper GI adverse events (upset stomach, heartburn, esophagitis, gastritis or ulcer)

Treat with milk or antacids to bind alendronate; dialysis would not be beneficial

Mechanism of Action A bisphosphonate which inhibits bone resorption via actions on osteoclasts or on osteoclast precursors; decreases the rate of bone resorption direction, leading to an indirect decrease in bone formation

Pharmacodynamics/Kinetics

Absorption: Oral: Male: 0.6% given in a fasting state; Female: 0.7%

Protein binding: ~78%

Metabolism: Not metabolized

Bioavailability: Reduced up to 60% with food or drink

Half-life: Terminal: Exceeds 10 years; serum concentrations cleared >95% in 6 hours

Elimination: Renal with unabsorbed drug eliminated in feces

Usual Dosage Oral: Alendronate must be taken with plain water first thing in the morning and ≥30 minutes before the first food, beverage, or other medication of the day. Patients should be instructed to take alendronate with a full glass of water (6-8 oz) and not lie down for at least 30 minutes to improve alendronate absorption.

Adults: Patients with osteoporosis or Paget's disease should receive supplemental calcium and vitamin D if dietary intake is inadequate

Osteoporosis in postmenopausal women:
  Prophylaxis: 5 mg once daily
  Treatment: 10 mg once daily

Paget's disease of bone: 40 mg once daily for 6 months
  Retreatment: Relapses during the 12 months following therapy occurred in 9% of patients who responded to treatment. Specific retreatment data are not available. Retreatment with alendronate may be considered, following a 6-month post-treatment evaluation period, in patients who have relapsed based on increases in serum alkaline phosphatase, which should be measured periodically. Retreatment may also be considered in those who failed to normalize their serum alkaline phosphatase.

Elderly: No dosage adjustment is necessary

Dosage adjustment in renal impairment:
  Cl_{cr} 30-60 mL/minute: None necessary
  Cl_{cr} <35 mL/minute: Alendronate is not recommended due to lack of experience

Dosage adjustment in hepatic impairment: None necessary

Administration It is imperative to administer alendronate 30-60 minutes before the patient takes any food, drink, or other medications orally to avoid interference with absorption. The patient should take alendronate on an empty stomach with a full glass (8 oz) of **plain water** (not mineral water) and avoid lying down for 30 minutes after swallowing tablet to help delivery to stomach.

Monitoring Parameters Alkaline phosphatase should be periodically measured; serum calcium, phosphorus, and possibly potassium due to its drug class; use of absorptiometry may assist in noting benefit in osteoporosis; monitor pain and fracture rate

Reference Range Calcium (total): Adults: 9.0-11.0 mg/dL (2.05-2.54 mmol/L), may slightly decrease with aging; phosphorus: 2.5-4.5 mg/dL (0.81-1.45 mmol/L)

Patient Information Patients should be instructed that the expected benefits of alendronate may only be obtained when each tablet is taken with plain water the first thing in the morning and at least 30 minutes before the first food, beverage, or medication of the day. Also instruct them that waiting >30 minutes will improve alendronate absorption. Even dosing with orange juice or coffee markedly reduces the absorption of alendronate.

Instruct patients to take alendronate with a full glass of water (6-8 oz 180-240 mL) and not to lie down (stay fully upright sitting or standing) for at least 30 minutes following administration to facilitate delivery to the stomach and reduce the potential for esophageal irritation.

Patients should be instructed to take supplemental calcium and vitamin D if dietary intake is inadequate. Consider weight-bearing exercise along with the modification of certain behavioral factors, such as excessive cigarette smoking or alcohol consumption if these factors exist.

Dosage Forms Tablet, as sodium: 5 mg, 10 mg, 40 mg

♦ **Alendronate Sodium** see Alendronate on previous page
♦ **Alertec®** see Modafinil on page 791
♦ **Alesse™** see Ethinyl Estradiol and Levonorgestrel on page 449
♦ **Aleve® [OTC]** see Naproxen on page 818
♦ **Alfenta®** see Alfentanil on this page

Alfentanil (al FEN ta nil)

Related Information
  Narcotic Agonists Comparison on page 1328
U.S. Brand Names Alfenta®
Synonyms Alfentanil Hydrochloride
Therapeutic Category Analgesic, Narcotic
Use Analgesic adjunct given by continuous infusion or in incremental doses in maintenance of anesthesia with barbiturate or N_2O or a primary anesthetic agent for the induction of anesthesia in patients undergoing general surgery in which endotracheal intubation and mechanical ventilation are required
Restrictions C-II
Pregnancy Risk Factor C
Contraindications Hypersensitivity to alfentanil hydrochloride or narcotics; increased intracranial pressure, severe respiratory depression
Warnings/Precautions Drug dependence, head injury, acute asthma and respiratory conditions; hypotension has occurred in neonates with respiratory distress syndrome; use caution when administering to patients with bradyarrhythmias; rapid I.V. infusion may result in skeletal muscle and chest wall rigidity → impaired ventilation → respiratory distress/arrest; inject slowly over 3-5 minutes; nondepolarizing skeletal muscle relaxant may be required. Alfentanil may produce more hypotension compared to fentanyl, therefore, be sure to administer slowly and ensure patient has adequate hydration.
Adverse Reactions
  >10%:
    Cardiovascular: Bradycardia, peripheral vasodilation
    Central nervous system: Drowsiness, sedation, increased intracranial pressure
    Gastrointestinal: Nausea, vomiting, constipation
    Endocrine & metabolic: Antidiuretic hormone release
(Continued)

Alfentanil *(Continued)*

Ocular: Miosis

1% to 10%:

Cardiovascular: Cardiac arrhythmias, orthostatic hypotension

Central nervous system: Confusion, CNS depression

Ocular: Blurred vision

<1%: Convulsions, mental depression, paradoxical CNS excitation or delirium, dizziness, dysesthesia, rash, urticaria, itching, biliary tract spasm, urinary tract spasm, respiratory depression, bronchospasm, laryngospasm, physical and psychological dependence with prolonged use; cold, clammy skin

Overdosage/Toxicology

Symptoms of overdose include miosis, respiratory depression, seizures, CNS depression

Naloxone 2 mg I.V. (0.01 mg/kg for children) with repeat administration as necessary up to a total of 10 mg; may precipitate withdrawal

Drug Interactions CYP3A3/4 enzyme substrate

Decreased effect: Phenothiazines may antagonize the analgesic effect of opiate agonists

Increased effect: Dextroamphetamine may enhance the analgesic effect of morphine and other opiate agonists

Increased toxicity: CNS depressants (eg, benzodiazepines, barbiturates, phenothiazines, tricyclic antidepressants), erythromycin, reserpine, beta-blockers

Stability Dilute in D_5W, NS, or LR

Mechanism of Action Binds with stereospecific receptors at many sites within the CNS, increases pain threshold, alters pain perception, inhibits ascending pain pathways; is an ultra short-acting narcotic

Pharmacodynamics/Kinetics

Distribution: V_d: Newborns, premature: 1 L/kg; Children: 0.163-0.48 L/kg; Adults: 0.46 L/kg

Half-life, elimination: Newborns, premature: 5.33-8.75 hours; Children: 40-60 minutes; Adults: 83-97 minutes

Usual Dosage Doses should be titrated to appropriate effects; wide range of doses is dependent upon desired degree of analgesia/anesthesia

Children <12 years: Dose not established

Adults: Dose should be based on ideal body weight; see table.

Alfentanil

Indication	Approx Duration of Anesthesia (min)	Induction Period (Initial Dose) (mcg/kg)	Maintenance Period (Increments/ Infusion)	Total Dose (mcg/kg)	Effects
Incremental injection	≤30	8-20	3-5 mcg/kg or 0.5-1 mcg/kg/ min	8-40	Spontaneously breathing or assisted ventilation when required.
	30-60	20-50	5-15 mcg/kg	Up to 75	Assisted or controlled ventilation required. Attenuation of response to laryngoscopy and intubation.
Continuous infusion	>45	50-75	0.5-3 mcg/kg/ min average infusion rate 1-1.5 mcg/kg/min	Dependent on duration of procedure	Assisted or controlled ventilation required. Some attenuation of response to intubation and incision, with intraoperative stability.
Anesthetic induction	>45	130-245	0.5-1.5 mcg/kg/ min or general anesthetic	Dependent on duration of procedure	Assisted or controlled ventilation required. Administer slowly (over 3 minutes). Concentration of inhalation agents reduced by 30% to 50% for initial hour.

Monitoring Parameters Respiratory rate, blood pressure, heart rate

Reference Range 100-340 ng/mL (depending upon procedure)

Nursing Implications Monitor patient for CNS, respiratory depression, and urticaria

Dosage Forms Injection, preservative free, as hydrochloride: 500 mcg/mL (2 mL, 5 mL, 10 mL, 20 mL)

♦ **Alfentanil Hydrochloride** *see* Alfentanil *on previous page*

♦ **Alferon® N** *see* Interferon Alfa-n3 *on page 620*

Alglucerase *(al GLOO ser ase)*

U.S. Brand Names Ceredase®; Cerezyme®

Synonyms Glucocerebrosidase

Therapeutic Category Enzyme, Glucocerebrosidase

Use Orphan drug: Treatment of Gaucher's disease

Pregnancy Risk Factor C

Contraindications Hypersensitivity to any component

Warnings/Precautions Prepared from pooled human placental tissue that may contain the causative agents of some viral diseases

Adverse Reactions
>10%: Local: Discomfort, burning, and edema at the site of injection
<1%: Fever, chills, abdominal discomfort, nausea, vomiting

Overdosage/Toxicology No obvious toxicity was detected after single doses of up to 234 units/kg

Stability Refrigerate (4°C), do not shake

Mechanism of Action Glucocerebrosidase is an enzyme prepared from human placental tissue. Gaucher's disease is an inherited metabolic disorder caused by the defective activity of beta-glucosidase and the resultant accumulation of glucosyl cera-mide laden macrophages in the liver, bone, and spleen; acts by replacing the missing enzyme associated with Gaucher's disease.

Pharmacodynamics/Kinetics Half-life, elimination: ~4-20 minutes

Usual Dosage Usually administered as a 20-60 unit/kg I.V. infusion given with a frequency ranging from 3 times/week to once every 2 weeks

Administration Filter during administration

Patient Information Alglucerase should be stored under refrigeration (4°C), solutions should not be shaken

Dosage Forms Injection: 10 units/mL (5 mL); 80 units/mL (5 mL)

Alitretinoin (a li TRET i noyn)

U.S. Brand Names Panretin®

Therapeutic Category Antineoplastic Agent, Miscellaneous; Retinoic Acid Derivative

Use Topical treatment of cutaneous lesions in AIDS-related Kaposi's sarcoma; not indi-cated when systemic therapy for Kaposi's sarcoma is indicated

Pregnancy Risk Factor D

Pregnancy/Breast-Feeding Implications Potentially teratogenic and/or embryotoxic; limb, craniofacial, or skeletal defects have been observed in animal models. If used during pregnancy or if the patient becomes pregnant while using alitretinoin, the woman should be advised of potential harm to the fetus. Women of childbearing potential should avoid becoming pregnant. Excretion in human breast milk is unknown; women are advised to discontinue breast-feeding prior to using this medication.

Contraindications Hypersensitivity to alitretinoin, other retinoids, or any component of the formulation

Warnings/Precautions May cause fetal harm if absorbed by a woman who is pregnant. Patients with cutaneous T cell lymphoma have a high incidence of treatment-limiting adverse reactions. May be photosensitizing (based on experience with other retinoids); minimize sun or other UV exposure of treated areas. Do not use concurrently with topical products containing DEET (increased toxicity may result). Safety in pediatric patients or geriatric patients has not been established. Occlusive dressing should not be used.

Adverse Reactions
>10%:
Central nervous system: Pain (0% to 34%)
Dermatologic: Rash (25% to 77%), pruritus (8% to 11%)
Neuromuscular & skeletal: Paresthesia (3% to 22%)
5% to 10%:
Cardiovascular: Edema (3% to 8%)
Dermatologic: Exfoliative dermatitis (3% to 9%), skin disorder (0% to 8%)

Overdosage/Toxicology There has been no experience with human overdosage of alitretinoin, and overdose is unlikely following topical application; treatment is sympto-matic and supportive

Drug Interactions Increased toxicity of DEET may occur if products containing this compound are used concurrently with alitretinoin. Due to limited absorption after topical application, interaction with systemic medications is unlikely.

Stability Store at room temperature

Mechanism of Action Binds to retinoid receptors to inhibit growth of Kaposi's sarcoma

Pharmacodynamics/Kinetics Absorption: Indirect evidence suggests absorption after topical application is not extensive

Usual Dosage Topical: Apply gel twice daily to cutaneous Kaposi's sarcoma lesions

Administration Do not use occlusive dressings

Patient Information For external use only; avoid UV light exposure (sun or sunlamps) of treated areas

Dosage Forms Gel: 0.1%, 60 g tube

Allopurinol (al oh PURE i nole)

Related Information
Antacid Drug Interactions on page 1296
Desensitization Protocols on page 1347

U.S. Brand Names Zyloprim®

Canadian Brand Names Apo®-Allopurinol; Novo-Purol; Purinol®

Therapeutic Category Uricosuric Agent

Use Prevention of attack of gouty arthritis and nephropathy; also used to treat secondary hyperuricemia which may occur during treatment of tumors or leukemia, and to prevent recurrent calcium oxalate calculi

Pregnancy Risk Factor C

Pregnancy/Breast-Feeding Implications Clinical effects on the fetus: There are few reports describing the use of allopurinol during pregnancy; no adverse fetal outcomes attributable to allopurinol have been reported in humans

Contraindications Not to be used in pregnancy or lactation, or in patients with a previous severe allergy reaction to allopurinol or any component

Warnings/Precautions Do not use to treat asymptomatic hyperuricemia. Discontinue at first signs of rash; reduce dosage in renal insufficiency, reinstate with caution in patients who have had a previous mild allergic reaction, use with caution in children; monitor liver function and complete blood counts before initiating therapy and periodically during therapy, use with caution in patients taking diuretics concurrently.

Adverse Reactions
>10%: Dermatologic: Skin rash (usually maculopapular), exfoliative, urticarial or purpuric lesions, and Stevens-Johnson syndrome have been reported

1% to 10%:
Central nervous system: Drowsiness, chills, fever
Dermatologic: Alopecia
Gastrointestinal: Nausea, vomiting, diarrhea, abdominal pain, gastritis, dyspepsia
Hepatic: Increased alkaline phosphatase or AST/ALT, hepatomegaly, hyperbilirubinemia, and jaundice, hepatic necrosis has been reported

<1%: Vasculitis, headache, somnolence, toxic epidermal necrolysis, bone marrow suppression has been reported in patients receiving allopurinol with other myelosuppressive agents, thrombophlebitis, peripheral neuropathy, neuritis, paresthesia, cataracts, renal impairment, epistaxis, idiosyncratic reaction characterized by fever, chills, leukopenia, leukocytosis, eosinophilia, arthralgia, skin rash, pruritus

Overdosage/Toxicology
If significant amounts of allopurinol are thought to have been absorbed, it is a theoretical possibility that oxypurinol stones could be formed but no record of such occurrence in overdose exists

Alkalinization of the urine and forced diuresis can help prevent potential xanthine stone formation

Drug Interactions Hepatic enzyme inhibitor
Decreased effect: Alcohol decreases effectiveness
Increased toxicity:
Inhibits metabolism of azathioprine and mercaptopurine
Use with ampicillin or amoxicillin may increase the incidence of skin rash
Urinary acidification with large amounts of vitamin C may increase kidney stone formation
Thiazide diuretics enhance toxicity, monitor renal function
Allopurinol prolongs half-life of oral anticoagulants; allopurinol increases serum half-life of theophylline; allopurinol may compete for excretion in renal tubule with chlorpropamide and increases chlorpropamide's serum half-life

Mechanism of Action Allopurinol inhibits xanthine oxidase, the enzyme responsible for the conversion of hypoxanthine to xanthine to uric acid. Allopurinol is metabolized to oxypurinol which is also an inhibitor of xanthine oxidase; allopurinol acts on purine catabolism, reducing the production of uric acid without disrupting the biosynthesis of vital purines.

Pharmacodynamics/Kinetics
Decreases in serum uric acid occur in 1-2 days with nadir achieved in 1-2 weeks
Absorption:
Oral: ~80% of dose absorbed from GI tract; peak plasma concentrations are seen 30-120 minutes after administration
Rectal: Poor and erratic
Distribution: V_d ~1.6 L/kg; distributes into breast milk
Protein binding: <1%
Metabolism: ~75% metabolized to active metabolites, chiefly oxypurinol
Half-life:
Normal renal function:
Parent drug: 1-3 hours
Oxypurinol: 18-30 hours
End-stage renal disease: Half-life is prolonged
Elimination: Both allopurinol and oxypurinol are dialyzable; 10% may be eliminated by enterohepatic excretion; <10% excreted in urine unchanged; 45% to 65% excreted as oxypurinol

Usual Dosage Oral:
Children ≤10 years: 10 mg/kg/day in 2-3 divided doses **or** 200-300 mg/m²/day in 2-4 divided doses, maximum: 800 mg/24 hours

Alternative:
    <6 years: 150 mg/day in 3 divided doses
    6-10 years: 300 mg/day in 2-3 divided doses
Children >10 years and Adults: Daily doses >300 mg should be administered in divided doses
  Myeloproliferative neoplastic disorders: 600-800 mg/day in 2-3 divided doses for prevention of acute uric acid nephropathy for 2-3 days starting 1-2 days before chemotherapy
Gout:
    Mild: 200-300 mg/day
    Severe: 400-600 mg/day
Elderly: Initial: 100 mg/day, increase until desired uric acid level is obtained
Dosing adjustment in renal impairment: Must be adjusted due to accumulation of allopurinol and metabolites; removed by hemodialysis. See table.

Adult Maintenance Doses of Allopurinol*

Creatinine Clearance (mL/min)	Maintenance Dose of Allopurinol (mg)
140	400 qd
120	350 qd
100	300 qd
80	250 qd
60	200 qd
40	150 qd
20	100 qd
10	100 q2d
0	100 q3d

*This table is based on a standard maintenance dose of 300 mg of allopurinol per day for a patient with a creatinine clearance of 100 mL/min.

Hemodialysis: Administer dose posthemodialysis or administer 50% supplemental dose
Monitoring Parameters CBC, serum uric acid levels, I & O, hepatic and renal function, especially at start of therapy
Reference Range Uric acid, serum: An increase occurs during childhood
Adults:
    Male: 3.4-7 mg/dL or slightly more
    Female: 2.4-6 mg/dL or slightly more

Values >7 mg/dL are sometimes arbitrarily regarded as hyperuricemia, but there is no sharp line between normals on the one hand, and the serum uric acid of those with clinical gout. Normal ranges cannot be adjusted for purine ingestion, but high purine diet increases uric acid. Uric acid may be increased with body size, exercise, and stress.
Patient Information Take after meals with plenty of fluid (at least 10-12 glasses of fluids per day); discontinue the drug and contact physician at first sign of rash, painful urination, blood in urine, irritation of the eyes, or swelling of the lips or mouth; may cause drowsiness; alcohol decreases effectiveness
Dosage Forms Tablet: 100 mg, 300 mg
Extemporaneous Preparations Crush tablets to make a 5 mg/mL suspension in simple syrup; stable 14 days under refrigeration

Nahata MC and Hipple TF, *Pediatric Drug Formulations*, 1st ed, Harvey Whitney Books Co, 1990.

♦ **All-*trans*-Retinoic Acid** *see* Tretinoin, Oral *on page 1171*
♦ **Almora® (Gluconate)** *see* Magnesium Salts (Other) *on page 707*
♦ **Alomide® Ophthalmic** *see* Lodoxamide Tromethamine *on page 689*
♦ **Alor® 5/500** *see* Hydrocodone and Aspirin *on page 576*
♦ **Alora® Transdermal** *see* Estradiol *on page 433*
♦ **Alpha-Baclofen®** *see* Baclofen *on page 123*
♦ **Alphagan®** *see* Brimonidine *on page 154*
♦ **Alphamin®** *see* Hydroxocobalamin *on page 585*
♦ **AlphaNine® SD** *see* Factor IX Complex (Human) *on page 464*
♦ **Alpha-Tamoxifen®** *see* Tamoxifen *on page 1106*
♦ **Alphatrex®** *see* Betamethasone *on page 141*

Alprazolam (al PRAY zoe lam)

Related Information
  Benzodiazepines Comparison *on page 1310*
U.S. Brand Names Alprazolam Intensol®; Xanax®
Canadian Brand Names Apo®-Alpraz; Novo-Alprazol; Nu-Alprax
Therapeutic Category Antianxiety Agent; Benzodiazepine
Use Treatment of anxiety; adjunct in the treatment of depression; management of panic attacks
Restrictions C-IV
Pregnancy Risk Factor D
Contraindications Hypersensitivity to alprazolam or any component; there may be a cross-sensitivity with other benzodiazepines; severe uncontrolled pain, narrow-angle
(Continued)

Alprazolam *(Continued)*

glaucoma, severe respiratory depression, pre-existing CNS depression; not to be used in pregnancy or lactation

Warnings/Precautions Withdrawal symptoms including seizures have occurred 18 hours to 3 days after abrupt discontinuation; when discontinuing therapy, decrease daily dose by no more than 0.5 mg every 3 days; reduce dose in patients with significant hepatic disease. Not intended for management of anxieties and minor distresses associated with everyday life.

Adverse Reactions
>10%:
Cardiovascular: Tachycardia, chest pain
Central nervous system: Drowsiness, fatigue, ataxia, lightheadedness, memory impairment, insomnia, anxiety, depression, headache
Dermatologic: Rash
Endocrine & metabolic: Decreased libido
Gastrointestinal: Xerostomia, constipation, decreased salivation, nausea, vomiting, diarrhea, increased or decreased appetite
Neuromuscular & skeletal: Dysarthria
Ocular: Blurred vision
Miscellaneous: Diaphoresis
1% to 10%:
Cardiovascular: Syncope, hypotension
Central nervous system: Confusion, nervousness, dizziness, akathisia
Dermatologic: Dermatitis
Gastrointestinal: Weight gain or loss, increased salivation
Neuromuscular & skeletal: Rigidity, tremor, muscle cramps
Otic: Tinnitus
Respiratory: Nasal congestion, hyperventilation

Overdosage/Toxicology
Symptoms of overdose include somnolence, confusion, coma, and diminished reflexes
Treatment for benzodiazepine overdose is supportive. Rarely is mechanical ventilation required; flumazenil has been shown to selectively block the binding of benzodiazepines to CNS receptors, resulting in a reversal of benzodiazepine-induced sedation; however, its use may not alter the course of overdose.

Drug Interactions CYP3A3/4 enzyme substrate
Decreased therapeutic effect: Carbamazepine, disulfiram
Increased toxicity: Oral contraceptives, CNS depressants, cimetidine, lithium

Mechanism of Action Binds at stereospecific receptors at several sites within the central nervous system, including the limbic system, reticular formation; effects may be mediated through GABA

Pharmacodynamics/Kinetics
Distribution: V_d: 0.9-1.2 L/kg; distributes into breast milk
Protein binding: 80%
Metabolism: Extensive in the liver; major metabolite is inactive
Half-life: 12-15 hours
Time to peak serum concentration: Within 1-2 hours
Elimination: Excretion of metabolites and parent compound in urine

Usual Dosage Oral:
Children <18 years: Safety and dose have not been established
Adults:
Anxiety: Effective doses are 0.5-4 mg/day in divided doses; the manufacturer recommends starting at 0.25-0.5 mg 3 times/day; titrate dose upward; maximum: 4 mg/day
Depression: Average dose required: 2.5-3 mg/day in divided doses
Alcohol withdrawal: Usual dose: 2-2.5 mg/day in divided doses
Panic disorder: Many patients obtain relief at 2 mg/day, as much as 6 mg/day may be required
Dosing adjustment in hepatic impairment: Reduce dose by 50% to 60% or avoid in cirrhosis
Note: Treatment >4 months should be re-evaluated to determine the patient's need for the drug

Dietary Considerations Alcohol: May have additive CNS effects, avoid use

Monitoring Parameters Respiratory and cardiovascular status

Test Interactions ↑ alkaline phosphatase

Patient Information Avoid alcohol and other CNS depressants; avoid activities needing good psychomotor coordination until CNS effects are known; drug may cause physical or psychological dependence; avoid abrupt discontinuation after prolonged use

Nursing Implications Assist with ambulation during beginning therapy, raise bed rails and keep room partially illuminated at night; monitor for CNS respiratory depression

Dosage Forms
Solution, oral: 1 mg/mL (30 mL), 0.5 mg/5 mL (500 mL)
Tablet: 0.25 mg, 0.5 mg, 1 mg, 2 mg

♦ **Alprazolam Intensol®** *see Alprazolam on previous page*

Alprostadil *(al PROS ta dill)*

U.S. Brand Names Caverject® Injection; Edex™ Injection; Muse® Pellet; Prostin VR Pediatric® Injection

Synonyms PGE_1; Prostaglandin E_1

Therapeutic Category Prostaglandin

Use Temporary maintenance of patency of ductus arteriosus in neonates with ductal-dependent congenital heart disease until surgery can be performed. These defects include cyanotic (eg, pulmonary atresia, pulmonary stenosis, tricuspid atresia, Fallot's tetralogy, transposition of the great vessels) and acyanotic (eg, interruption of aortic arch, coarctation of aorta, hypoplastic left ventricle) heart disease; diagnosis and treatment of erectile dysfunction of vasculogenic, psychogenic, or neurogenic etiology; adjunct in the diagnosis of erectile dysfunction

Investigational: Treatment of pulmonary hypertension in infants and children with congenital heart defects with left-to-right shunts

Pregnancy Risk Factor X

Contraindications Hyaline membrane disease or persistent fetal circulation and when a dominant left-to-right shunt is present; respiratory distress syndrome; hypersensitivity to the drug or components; conditions predisposing patients to priapism (sickle cell anemia, multiple myeloma, leukemia); patients with anatomical deformation of the penis, penile implants; use in men for whom sexual activity is inadvisable or contraindicated; pregnancy

Warnings/Precautions Use cautiously in neonates with bleeding tendencies; apnea may occur in 10% to 12% of neonates with congenital heart defects, especially in those weighing <2 kg at birth; apnea usually appears during the first hour of drug infusion; priapism may occur; treat immediately to avoid penile tissue damage and permanent loss of potency; discontinue therapy if signs of penile fibrosis develop (penile angulation, cavernosal fibrosis, or Peyronie's disease). When used in erectile dysfunction (Muse®), syncope occurring within 1 hour of administration, has been reported; the potential for drug-drug interactions may occur when Muse® is prescribed concomitantly with antihypertensives; some lowering of blood pressure may occur without symptoms, and swelling of leg veins, leg pain, perineal pain, and rapid pulse have been reported in <2% of patients during in-clinic titration and home treatment.

Adverse Reactions

>10%:
Cardiovascular: Flushing
Central nervous system: Fever
Genitourinary: Penile pain
Respiratory: Apnea

1% to 10%:
Cardiovascular: Bradycardia, hypotension, hypertension, tachycardia, cardiac arrest, edema
Central nervous system: Seizures, headache, dizziness
Endocrine & metabolic: Hypokalemia
Gastrointestinal: Diarrhea
Genitourinary: Prolonged erection, penile fibrosis, penis disorder, penile rash, penile edema
Hematologic: Disseminated intravascular coagulation
Local: Injection site hematoma, injection site bruising
Neuromuscular & skeletal: Back pain
Respiratory: Upper respiratory infection, flu syndrome, sinusitis, nasal congestion, cough
Miscellaneous: Sepsis, localized pain in structures other than the injection site

<1%: Cerebral bleeding, congestive heart failure, second degree heart block, shock, supraventricular tachycardia, ventricular fibrillation, hyperemia, hyperirritability, hypothermia, jitteriness, lethargy, hypoglycemia, hyperkalemia, gastric regurgitation, anuria, balanitis, urethral bleeding, penile numbness, yeast infection, penile pruritus and erythema, abnormal ejaculation, anemia, bleeding, thrombocytopenia, hyperbilirubinemia, hyperextension of neck, stiffness, hematuria, bradypnea, bronchial wheezing, peritonitis, leg pain, perineal pain

Overdosage/Toxicology

Symptoms of overdose when treating patent ductus arteriosus include apnea, bradycardia, hypotension, and flushing

If hypotension or pyrexia occurs, the infusion rate should be reduced until the symptoms subside, while apnea or bradycardia requires drug discontinuation; if intracavernous overdose occurs, supervise until any systemic effects have resolved or until penile detumescence has occurred

Stability

Ductus arteriosus: Refrigerate ampuls; protect from freezing; prepare fresh solutions every 24 hours; **compatible** in D_5W, $D_{10}W$, and NS solutions

Erectile dysfunction: Refrigerate at 2°C to 8°C until dispensed; after dispensing, stable for up to 3 months at or below 25°C; do not freeze; use only the supplied diluent for reconstitution (ie, bacteriostatic/sterile water with benzyl alcohol 0.945%)

Mechanism of Action Causes vasodilation by means of direct effect on vascular and ductus arteriosus smooth muscle; relaxes trabecular smooth muscle by dilation of cavernosal arteries when injected along the penile shaft, allowing blood flow to and entrapment in the lacunar spaces of the penis (ie, corporeal veno-occlusive mechanism)

Pharmacodynamics/Kinetics

Distribution: Nonsignificant amounts distribute peripherally following penile injection
Protein binding, plasma: 81% to albumin
Metabolism: ~75% metabolized by oxidation in one pass through the lungs
Half-life: 5-10 minutes
Elimination: Metabolites excreted in urine (90% within 24 hours)
(Continued)

Alprostadil *(Continued)*

Usual Dosage

Patent ductus arteriosus (Prostin VR Pediatric®):

I.V. continuous infusion into a large vein, or alternatively through an umbilical artery catheter placed at the ductal opening: 0.05-0.1 mcg/kg/minute with therapeutic response, rate is reduced to lowest effective dosage; with unsatisfactory response, rate is increased gradually; maintenance: 0.01-0.4 mcg/kg/minute

PGE₁ is usually given at an infusion rate of 0.1 mcg/kg/minute, but it is often possible to reduce the dosage to $1/2$ or even $1/10$ without losing the therapeutic effect. The mixing schedule is shown in the table.

Alprostadil

Add 1 Ampul (500 mcg) to:	Concentration (mcg/mL)	Infusion Rate	
		mL/min/kg Needed to Infuse 0.1 mcg/kg/min	mL/kg/24 h
250 mL	2	0.05	72
100 mL	5	0.02	28.8
50 mL	10	0.01	14.4
25 mL	20	0.005	7.2

Therapeutic response is indicated by increased pH in those with acidosis or by an increase in oxygenation (pO₂) usually evident within 30 minutes

Erectile dysfunction

Caverject®, Edex®:

Vasculogenic, psychogenic, or mixed etiology: Individualize dose by careful titration; usual dose: 2.5-60 mcg (doses >60 mcg are not recommended); initiate dosage titration at 2.5 mcg, increasing by 2.5 mcg to a dose of 5 mcg and then in increments of 5-10 mcg depending on the erectile response until the dose produces an erection suitable for intercourse, not lasting >1 hour; if there is absolutely no response to initial 2.5 mcg dose, the second dose may increased to 7.5 mcg, followed by increments of 5-10 mcg

Neurogenic etiology (eg, spinal cord injury): Initiate dosage titration at 1.25 mcg, increasing to a doses of 2.5 mcg and then 5 mcg; increase further in increments 5 mcg until the dose is reached that produces an erection suitable for intercourse, not lasting >1 hour

Note: Patient must stay in the physician's office until complete detumescence occurs; if there is no response, then the next higher dose may be given within 1 hour; if there is still no response, a 1-day interval before giving the next dose is recommended; increasing the dose or concentration in the treatment of impotence results in increasing pain and discomfort

Muse® Pellet: Intraurethral: Administer as needed to achieve an erection; duration of action is about 30-60 minutes; use only two systems per 24-hour period

Monitoring Parameters Arterial pressure, respiratory rate, heart rate, temperature, degree of penile pain, length of erection, signs of infection

Patient Information Store in refrigerator; if self-injecting for the treatment of impotence, dilute with the supplied diluent and use immediately after diluting; see physician at least every 3 months to ensure proper technique and for dosage adjustment.

Alternate sides of the penis with each injection; do not inject more than 3 times/week, allowing at least 24 hours between each dose; dispose of the syringe, needle, and vial properly; discard single-use vials after each use; report moderate to severe penile pain or erections lasting >6 hours to a physician immediately; inform a physician as soon as possible if any new penile pain, nodules, hard tissue or signs of infection develop; the risk of transmission of blood-borne diseases is increased with use of alprostadil injections since a small amount of bleeding at the injection site is possible.

Do not share this medication or needles/syringes; do not drive or operate heavy machinery within 1 hour of administration

Nursing Implications

Ductus arteriosus: Monitor arterial pressure; assess all vital functions; apnea and bradycardia may indicate overdose, stop infusion if occurring; infuse for the shortest time and at the lowest dose that will produce the desired effects. Flushing is usually a result of catheter malposition; central line preferred for I.V. administration.

Erectile dysfunction: Use a $1/2$", 27- to 30-gauge needle; inject into the dorsolateral aspect of the proximal third of the penis, avoiding visible veins; alternate side of the penis for injections; if the patient is going to be self-injecting at home, carefully assess their aseptic technique for injection and knowledge of proper disposal of the syringe, needle and vial; observe for signs of infection, penile fibrosis, and significant pain or priapism

Dosage Forms

Injection:

Caverject®: 5 mcg, 10 mcg, 20 mcg

Edex® Injection: 5 mcg, 10 mcg, 20 mcg, 40 mcg

Prostin VR Pediatric®: 500 mcg/mL (1 mL)

Pellet, urethral: 125 mcg, 250 mcg, 500 mcg, 1000 mcg

♦ **Alrex**™ *see* Loteprednol *on page 698*

♦ **Altace**™ *see* Ramipril *on page 1009*

Alteplase (AL te plase)

U.S. Brand Names Activase®

Canadian Brand Names Lysatec-rt-PA®

Synonyms Alteplase, Recombinant; Alteplase, Tissue Plasminogen Activator, Recombinant; t-PA

Therapeutic Category Thrombolytic Agent

Use Management of acute myocardial infarction for the lysis of thrombi in coronary arteries; management of acute massive pulmonary embolism (PE) in adults

Acute myocardial infarction (AMI): Chest pain ≥20 minutes, ≤12-24 hours; S-T elevation ≥0.1 mV in at least two EKG leads

Acute pulmonary embolism (APE): Age ≤75 years: As soon as possible within 5 days of thrombotic event. Documented massive pulmonary embolism by pulmonary angiography or echocardiography or high probability lung scan with clinical shock.

Acute ischemic stroke (rule out hemorrhagic courses before administering)

Pregnancy Risk Factor C

Contraindications No central venous puncture (CVP line) or noncompressible arterial sticks. BP systolic ≥185, diastolic ≥110 unresponsive to nitrate or calcium antagonist; recent (within 1 month): cerebral-vascular accident, gastrointestinal bleeding, trauma or surgery, prolonged external cardiac massage; intracranial neoplasm, suspected aortic dissection, arteriovenous malformation or aneurysm, bleeding diathesis, hemostatic defects, seizure occurring at the time of stroke, suspicion of subarachnoid hemorrhage

Warnings/Precautions Doses >150 mg have been associated with an increase of intracranial hemorrhage; acute pericarditis, severe liver dysfunction, septic thrombophlebitis, patients receiving concurrent oral anticoagulants, advanced age

Adverse Reactions

1% to 10%:

Cardiovascular: Hypotension

Central nervous system: Fever

Dermatologic: Bruising

Gastrointestinal: GI hemorrhage, nausea, vomiting

Genitourinary: GU hemorrhage

<1%: Retroperitoneal hemorrhage, gingival hemorrhage, intracranial hemorrhage, rapid lysis of coronary artery thrombi by thrombolytic agents may be associated with reperfusion-related atrial and/or ventricular arrhythmias, epistaxis

Overdosage/Toxicology Increased incidence of intracranial bleeding

Drug Interactions Increased effect: Anticoagulants, aspirin, ticlopidine, dipyridamole, and heparin are at least additive

Stability The lyophilized product may be stored at room temperature (not to exceed 30°C/86°F), or under refrigeration; once reconstituted it must be used within 8 hours

Alteplase is **incompatible** with dobutamine, dopamine, heparin, and nitroglycerin infusions; physically **compatible** with lidocaine, metoprolol, and propranolol when administered via Y site; **compatible** with either D_5W or NS

Standard dose: 100 mg/100 mL 0.9% NaCl (total volume: 200 mL)

Mechanism of Action Initiates local fibrinolysis by binding to fibrin in a thrombus (clot) and converts entrapped plasminogen to plasmin

Pharmacodynamics/Kinetics Elimination: Cleared rapidly from circulating plasma at a rate of 550-650 mL/minute, primarily by the liver; >50% present in plasma is cleared within 5 minutes after the infusion has been terminated, and ~80% is cleared within 10 minutes

Usual Dosage

Coronary artery thrombi: I.V.: Front loading dose: Total dose is 100 mg over 1.5 hours (for patients who weigh <65 kg, use 1.25 mg/kg/total dose). Add this dose to a 100 mL bag of 0.9% sodium chloride for a total volume of 200 mL. Infuse 15 mg (30 mL) over 1-2 minutes; infuse 50 mg (100 mL) over 30 minutes. Begin heparin 5000-10,000 unit bolus followed by continuous infusion of 1000 units/hour. Infuse 35 mg/hour (70 mL) for next 2 hours.

Acute pulmonary embolism: 100 mg over 2 hours

Acute ischemic stroke: Doses should be given within the first 3 hours of the onset of symptoms. Load with 0.09 mg/kg as a bolus, followed by 0.81 mg/kg as a continuous infusion over 60 minutes; maximum total dose should not exceed 90 mg

Administration Do not use bacteriostatic water for reconstitution

Reference Range

Not routinely measured; literature supports therapeutic levels of 0.52-1.8 µg/mL

Fibrinogen: 200-400 mg/dL

Activated partial thromboplastin time (APTT): 22.5-38.7 seconds

Prothrombin time (PT): 10.9-12.2 seconds

Nursing Implications Assess for hemorrhage during first hour of treatment

Dosage Forms Powder for injection, lyophilized (recombinant): 20 mg [11.6 million units] (20 mL); 50 mg [29 million units] (50 mL); 100 mg [58 million units] (100 mL)

♦ **Alteplase, Recombinant** see Alteplase on this page

♦ **Alteplase, Tissue Plasminogen Activator, Recombinant** see Alteplase on this page

♦ **ALternaGEL® [OTC]** see Aluminum Hydroxide on next page

Altretamine (al TRET a meen)

Related Information
Toxicities of Chemotherapeutic Agents *on page 1288*
U.S. Brand Names Hexalen®
Synonyms Hexamethylmelamine
Therapeutic Category Antineoplastic Agent, Miscellaneous
Use Palliative treatment of persistent or recurrent ovarian cancer following first-line therapy with a cisplatin- or alkylating agent-based combination
Pregnancy Risk Factor D
Contraindications Hypersensitivity to altretamine, pre-existing severe bone marrow suppression or severe neurologic toxicity
Warnings/Precautions The U.S. Food and Drug Administration (FDA) currently recommends that procedures for proper handling and disposal of antineoplastic agents be considered. Peripheral blood counts and neurologic examinations should be done routinely before and after drug therapy. Use with caution in patients previously treated with other myelosuppressive drugs or with pre-existing neurotoxicity; use with caution in patients with renal or hepatic dysfunction; altretamine may be slightly mutagenic.
Adverse Reactions
>10%:
Central nervous system: Peripheral sensory neuropathy, neurotoxicity
Gastrointestinal: Nausea, vomiting
Hematologic: Anemia, thrombocytopenia, leukopenia
1% to 10%:
Central nervous system: Seizures
Gastrointestinal: Anorexia, diarrhea, stomach cramps
Hepatic: Increased alkaline phosphatase
<1%: Dizziness, depression, rash, alopecia, myelosuppression, hepatotoxicity, tremor
Overdosage/Toxicology
Symptoms of overdose include nausea, vomiting, peripheral neuropathy, severe bone marrow suppression
After decontamination, treatment is supportive
Drug Interactions
Decreased effect: Phenobarbital may increase metabolism of altretamine
Increased toxicity: May cause severe orthostatic hypotension when administered with MAO inhibitors; cimetidine may decrease metabolism of altretamine
Mechanism of Action Although altretamine clinical antitumor spectrum resembles that of alkylating agents, the drug has demonstrated activity in alkylator-resistant patients; probably requires hepatic microsomal mixed-function oxidase enzyme activation to become cytotoxic. The drug selectively inhibits the incorporation of radioactive thymidine and uridine into DNA and RNA, inhibiting DNA and RNA synthesis; metabolized to reactive intermediates which covalently bind to microsomal proteins and DNA. These reactive intermediates can spontaneously degrade to demethylated melamines and formaldehyde which are also cytotoxic.
Pharmacodynamics/Kinetics
Absorption: Oral: Well absorbed (75% to 89%)
Metabolism: Rapid and extensive demethylation in liver; high concentrations in liver and kidney, but low concentrations in other organs
Half-life: 13 hours
Peak plasma levels: 0.5-3 hours after dose
Elimination: In urine (<1% unchanged)
Usual Dosage Adults: Oral (refer to protocol): 4-12 mg/kg/day in 3-4 divided doses for 21-90 days
Alternatively: 240-320 mg/m^2/day in 3-4 divided doses for 21 days, repeated every 6 weeks
Alternatively: 260 mg/m^2/day for 14-21 days of a 28-day cycle in 4 divided doses
Temporarily discontinue (for ≥14 days) & subsequently restart at 200 mg/m^2/day if any of the following occurs:
if GI intolerance unresponsive to symptom measures
WBC <2000/mm^3
granulocyte count <1000/mm^3
platelet count <75,000/mm^3
progressive neurotoxicity
Administration Administer orally; administer total daily dose as 4 divided oral doses after meals and at bedtime
Patient Information Report any numbness or tingling in extremities to physician; nausea and vomiting may occur and even begin up to weeks after therapy is stopped
Dosage Forms Capsule: 50 mg

♦ **Alu-Cap® [OTC]** *see Aluminum Hydroxide on this page*

Aluminum Acetate and Acetic Acid
(a LOO mi num AS e tate & a SEE tik AS id)
U.S. Brand Names Otic Domeboro®
Therapeutic Category Otic Agent, Anti-infective
Dosage Forms Solution, otic: Aluminum acetate 10% and acetic acid 2% (60 mL)

Aluminum Hydroxide (a LOO mi num hye DROKS ide)
U.S. Brand Names ALternaGEL® [OTC]; Alu-Cap® [OTC]; Alu-Tab® [OTC]; Amphojel® [OTC]; Dialume® [OTC]; Nephrox Suspension [OTC]

Therapeutic Category Antidote, Hyperphosphatemia

Use Treatment of hyperacidity; hyperphosphatemia

Pregnancy Risk Factor C

Pregnancy/Breast-Feeding Implications

Clinical effects on the fetus: No data available; available evidence suggests safe use during pregnancy and breast-feeding

Breast-feeding/lactation: No data available

Contraindications Hypersensitivity to aluminum salts or drug components

Warnings/Precautions Hypophosphatemia may occur with prolonged administration or large doses; aluminum intoxication and osteomalacia may occur in patients with uremia. Use with caution in patients with congestive heart failure, renal failure, edema, cirrhosis, and low sodium diets, and patients who have recently suffered gastrointestinal hemorrhage; uremic patients not receiving dialysis may develop osteomalacia and osteoporosis due to phosphate depletion.

Elderly, due to disease and/or drug therapy, may be predisposed to constipation and fecal impaction. Careful evaluation of possible drug interactions must be done. When used as an antacid in ulcer treatment, consider buffer capacity (mEq/mL) to calculate dose; consider renal insufficiency as predisposition to aluminum toxicity.

Adverse Reactions

>10%: Gastrointestinal: Constipation, chalky taste, stomach cramps, fecal impaction

1% to 10%: Gastrointestinal: Nausea, vomiting, discoloration of feces (white speckles)

<1%: Hypophosphatemia, hypomagnesemia

Overdosage/Toxicology

Aluminum antacids may cause constipation, phosphate depletion, and bezoar or fecalith formation; in patients with renal failure, aluminum may accumulate to toxic levels

Deferoxamine, traditionally used as an iron chelator, has been shown to increase urinary aluminum output

Deferoxamine chelation of aluminum has resulted in improvements of clinical symptoms and bone histology; however, remains an experimental treatment for aluminum poisoning and has a significant potential for adverse effects

Drug Interactions Decreased effect: Tetracyclines, digoxin, indomethacin, or iron salts, isoniazid, allopurinol, benzodiazepines, corticosteroids, penicillamine, phenothiazines, ranitidine, ketoconazole, itraconazole

Usual Dosage Oral:

Peptic ulcer disease:

Children: 5-15 mL/dose every 3-6 hours or 1 and 3 hours after meals and at bedtime

Adults: 15-45 mL every 3-6 hours or 1 and 3 hours after meals and at bedtime

Prophylaxis against gastrointestinal bleeding:

Infants: 2-5 mL/dose every 1-2 hours

Children: 5-15 mL/dose every 1-2 hours

Adults: 30-60 mL/dose every hour

Titrate to maintain the gastric pH >5

Hyperphosphatemia:

Children: 50-150 mg/kg/24 hours in divided doses every 4-6 hours, titrate dosage to maintain serum phosphorus within normal range

Adults: 500-1800 mg, 3-6 times/day, between meals and at bedtime; best taken with a meal or within 20 minutes of a meal

Antacid: Adults: 30 mL 1 and 3 hours postprandial and at bedtime

Monitoring Parameters Monitor phosphorous levels periodically when patient is on chronic therapy

Test Interactions Decreases phosphorus, inorganic (S)

Patient Information Dilute dose in water or juice, shake well; chew tablets thoroughly before swallowing with water; do not take oral drugs within 1-2 hours of administration; notify physician if relief is not obtained or if there are any signs to suggest bleeding from the GI tract

Nursing Implications Used primarily as a phosphate binder; dose should be given within 20 minutes of a meal and followed with water

Dosage Forms

Capsule:

Alu-Cap®: 400 mg

Dialume®: 500 mg

Liquid: 600 mg/5 mL

ALternaGEL®: 600 mg/5 mL

Suspension, oral: 320 mg/5 mL; 450 mg/5 mL; 675 mg/5 mL

Amphojel®: 320 mg/5 mL

Tablet:

Amphojel®: 300 mg, 600 mg

Alu-Tab®: 500 mg

♦ **Aluminum Sucrose Sulfate, Basic** see Sucralfate on page 1088

♦ **Alupent®** see Metaproterenol on page 739

♦ **Alu-Tab® [OTC]** see Aluminum Hydroxide on previous page

Amantadine (a MAN ta deen)

Related Information

Community-Acquired Pneumonia in Adults on page 1419

Depression Disorders and Treatments on page 1465

Guidelines for the Prevention of Opportunistic Infections in Persons with HIV on page 1388

(Continued)

Amantadine *(Continued)*

Parkinson's Disease, Dosing of Drugs Used for Treatment of *on page 1336*

U.S. Brand Names Symadine®; Symmetrel®

Canadian Brand Names Endantadine®; PMS-Amantadine

Synonyms Adamantanamine Hydrochloride; Amantadine Hydrochloride

Therapeutic Category Anti-Parkinson's Agent; Antiviral Agent, Oral

Use Symptomatic and adjunct treatment of parkinsonism; prophylaxis and treatment of influenza A viral infection; treatment of drug-induced extrapyramidal symptoms

Pregnancy Risk Factor C

Contraindications Hypersensitivity to amantadine hydrochloride or any component

Warnings/Precautions Use with caution in patients with liver disease, a history of recurrent and eczematoid dermatitis, uncontrolled psychosis or severe psychoneurosis, seizures and in those receiving CNS stimulant drugs; reduce dose in renal disease; when treating Parkinson's disease, do not discontinue abruptly. In many patients, the therapeutic benefits of amantadine are limited to a few months. Elderly patients may be more susceptible to the CNS effects (using 2 divided daily doses may minimize this effect).

Adverse Reactions

1% to 10%:
  Cardiovascular: Orthostatic hypotension, peripheral edema
  Central nervous system: Insomnia, depression, anxiety, irritability, dizziness, hallucinations, headache
  Dermatologic: Livedo reticularis
  Gastrointestinal: Nausea, anorexia, constipation, xerostomia

<1%: Congestive heart failure, slurred speech, confusion, fatigue, rash, decreased libido, urinary retention, vomiting, weakness, visual disturbances, dyspnea

Overdosage/Toxicology

Symptoms of overdose include nausea, vomiting, slurred speech, blurred vision, lethargy, hallucinations, seizures, myoclonic jerking

Following GI decontamination, treatment should be directed at reducing the CNS stimulation and at maintaining cardiovascular function. Seizures can be treated with diazepam while a lidocaine infusion may be required for the cardiac dysrhythmias.

Drug Interactions

Increased effect: Drugs with anticholinergic or CNS stimulant activity
Increased toxicity/levels: Hydrochlorothiazide plus triamterene, amiloride

Stability Protect from freezing

Mechanism of Action As an antiviral, blocks the uncoating of influenza A virus preventing penetration of virus into host; antiparkinsonian activity may be due to its blocking the reuptake of dopamine into presynaptic neurons and causing direct stimulation of postsynaptic receptors

Pharmacodynamics/Kinetics

Onset of antidyskinetic action: Within 48 hours

Absorption: Well absorbed from GI tract

Distribution: To saliva, tear film, and nasal secretions; in animals, tissue (especially lung) concentrations higher than serum concentrations, crosses blood-brain barrier
  V_d: Normal: 4.4±0.2 L/kg; Renal failure: 5.1±0.2 L/kg

Protein binding:
  Normal renal function: ~67%
  Hemodialysis patients: ~59%

Metabolism: Not appreciable, small amounts of an acetyl metabolite identified

Half-life: 10-28 hours; Impaired renal function: 7-10 days

Time to peak: 1-4 hours

Elimination: 80% to 90% excreted unchanged in urine by glomerular filtration and tubular secretion

Usual Dosage

Children:
  1-9 years: (<45 kg): 5-9 mg/kg/day in 1-2 divided doses to a maximum of 150 mg/day
  10-12 years: 100-200 mg/day in 1-2 divided doses
  Prophylaxis: Administer for 10-21 days following exposure if the vaccine is concurrently given or for 90 days following exposure if the vaccine is unavailable or contraindicated and re-exposure is possible

Adults:
  Drug-induced extrapyramidal reactions: 100 mg twice daily; may increase to 300 mg/day, if needed
  Parkinson's disease: 100 mg twice daily as sole therapy; may increase to 400 mg/day if needed with close monitoring; initial dose: 100 mg/day if with other serious illness or with high doses of other anti-Parkinson drugs
  Influenza A viral infection: 200 mg/day in 1-2 divided doses
  Prophylaxis: Minimum 10-day course of therapy following exposure if the vaccine is concurrently given or for 90 days following exposure if the vaccine is unavailable or contraindicated and re-exposure is possible

Elderly patients should take the drug in 2 daily doses rather than a single dose to avoid adverse neurologic reactions; see Warnings/Precautions

Dosing interval in renal impairment:
  Cl_{cr} 50-60 mL/minute: Administer 200 mg alternating with 100 mg/day
  Cl_{cr} 30-50 mL/minute: Administer 100 mg/day
  Cl_{cr} 20-30 mL/minute: Administer 200 mg twice weekly
  Cl_{cr} 10-20 mL/minute: Administer 100 mg 3 times/week

Cl$_{cr}$ <10 mL/minute: Administer 200 mg alternating with 100 mg every 7 days

Hemodialysis: Slightly hemodialyzable (5% to 20%); no supplemental dose is needed

Peritoneal dialysis: No supplemental dose is needed

Continuous arteriovenous or venovenous hemofiltration (CAVH/CAVHD): No supplemental dose is needed

Monitoring Parameters Renal function, mental status, blood pressure

Patient Information Do not abruptly discontinue therapy, it may precipitate a parkinsonian crisis; may impair ability to perform activities requiring mental alertness or coordination; must take throughout flu season or for at least 10 days following vaccination for effective prophylaxis; take second dose of the day in early afternoon to decrease incidence of insomnia

Nursing Implications If insomnia occurs, the last daily dose should be given several hours before retiring; assess parkinsonian symptoms prior to and throughout course of therapy

Dosage Forms

Capsule, as hydrochloride: 100 mg

Syrup, as hydrochloride: 50 mg/5 mL (480 mL)

- ◆ **Amantadine Hydrochloride** *see* Amantadine *on page 51*
- ◆ **Amaphen®** *see* Butalbital Compound *on page 165*
- ◆ **Amaryl®** *see* Glimepiride *on page 537*
- ◆ **Ambenyl® Cough Syrup** *see* Bromodiphenhydramine and Codeine *on page 156*
- ◆ **Ambien™** *see* Zolpidem *on page 1241*
- ◆ **Ambi® Skin Tone [OTC]** *see* Hydroquinone *on page 584*
- ◆ **AmBisome®** *see* Amphotericin B, Liposomal *on page 77*

Amcinonide (am SIN oh nide)

Related Information

Corticosteroids Comparison *on page 1319*

U.S. Brand Names Cyclocort®

Therapeutic Category Anti-inflammatory Agent; Corticosteroid, Topical (High Potency)

Use Relief of the inflammatory and pruritic manifestations of corticosteroid-responsive dermatoses (high potency corticosteroid)

Pregnancy Risk Factor C

Contraindications Hypersensitivity to amcinonide or any component; use on the face, groin, or axilla

Warnings/Precautions Adverse systemic effects may occur when used on large areas of the body, denuded areas, for prolonged periods of time, with an occlusive dressing, and/or in infants or small children; occlusive dressings should not be used in presence of infection or weeping lesions

Adverse Reactions

1% to 10%:

Dermatologic: Itching, maceration of skin, skin atrophy, erythema, dryness, papular rashes

Local: Burning, irritation

<1%: Hypertrichosis, acneiform eruptions, hypopigmentation, perioral dermatitis, striae, miliaria

Overdosage/Toxicology Symptoms of overdose include cushingoid appearance (systemic), muscle weakness (systemic), osteoporosis (systemic) all with long-term use only. When consumed in excessive quantities for prolonged periods, systemic hypercorticism and adrenal suppression may occur; in those cases, discontinuation and withdrawal of the corticosteroid should be done judiciously.

Mechanism of Action Stimulates the synthesis of enzymes needed to decrease inflammation, suppress mitotic activity, and cause vasoconstriction

Pharmacodynamics/Kinetics

Absorption: Adequate through intact skin; increases with skin inflammation or occlusion

Metabolism: In the liver

Elimination: By the kidney and in bile

Usual Dosage Adults: Topical: Apply in a thin film 2-3 times/day

Patient Information Before applying, gently wash area to reduce risk of infection; apply a thin film to cleansed area and rub in gently and thoroughly until medication vanishes; avoid exposure to sunlight, severe sunburn may occur

Nursing Implications Assess for worsening of rash or fever

Dosage Forms

Cream: 0.1% (15 g, 30 g, 60 g)

Lotion: 0.1% (20 mL, 60 mL)

Ointment, topical: 0.1% (15 g, 30 g, 60 g)

- ◆ **Amcort®** *see* Triamcinolone *on page 1174*
- ◆ **Amen®** *see* Medroxyprogesterone Acetate *on page 721*
- ◆ **Amerge®** *see* Naratriptan *on page 819*
- ◆ **Americaine® [OTC]** *see* Benzocaine *on page 133*
- ◆ **A-methaPred® Injection** *see* Methylprednisolone *on page 762*
- ◆ **Amethocaine Hydrochloride** *see* Tetracaine *on page 1121*
- ◆ **Amethopterin** *see* Methotrexate *on page 751*
- ◆ **Ametop™** *see* Tetracaine *on page 1121*
- ◆ **Amfepramone** *see* Diethylpropion *on page 354*
- ◆ **Amgenal® Cough Syrup** *see* Bromodiphenhydramine and Codeine *on page 156*

♦ **Amicar®** see Aminocaproic Acid *on page 57*
♦ **Amidate®** see Etomidate *on page 459*

Amifostine (am i FOS teen)

U.S. Brand Names Ethyol®
Synonyms Ethiofos; Gammaphos
Therapeutic Category Antidote, Cisplatin
Use Reduces the cumulative renal toxicity associated with repeated administration of cisplatin in patients with advanced ovarian cancer or nonsmall cell lung cancer. In these settings, the clinical data do not suggest that the effectiveness of cisplatin-based chemotherapy regimens is altered by amifostine.
Pregnancy Risk Factor C
Contraindications Known hypersensitivity to aminothiol compounds or mannitol
Warnings/Precautions The U.S. Food and Drug Administration (FDA) currently recommends that procedures for proper handling and disposal of antineoplastic agents be considered

Limited data are currently available regarding the preservation of antitumor efficacy when amifostine is administered prior to cisplatin therapy in settings other than advanced ovarian cancer or nonsmall cell lung cancer. Amifostine should therefore not be used in patients receiving chemotherapy for other malignancies in which chemotherapy can produce a significant survival benefit or cure, except in the context of a clinical study.

Patients who are hypotensive or in a state of dehydration should not receive amifostine. Patients receiving antihypertensive therapy that cannot be stopped for 24 hours preceding amifostine treatment also should not receive amifostine. Patients should be adequately hydrated prior to amifostine infusion and kept in a supine position during the infusion. Blood pressure should be monitored every 5 minutes during the infusion. If hypotension requiring interruption of therapy occurs, patients should be placed in the Trendelenburg position and given an infusion of normal saline using a separate I.V. line.

It is recommended that antiemetic medication, including dexamethasone 20 mg I.V. and a serotonin 5-HT$_3$ receptor antagonist be administered prior to and in conjunction with amifostine.

Reports of clinically relevant hypocalcemia are rare, but serum calcium levels should be monitored in patients at risk of hypocalcemia, such as those with nephrotic syndrome
Adverse Reactions
>10%:
Cardiovascular: Flushing; hypotension (62%)
Central nervous system: Chills, dizziness, somnolence
Gastrointestinal: Nausea/vomiting (may be severe)
Respiratory: Sneezing
Miscellaneous: Feeling of warmth/coldness, hiccups
<1%: Mild rashes, hypocalcemia, rigors
Overdosage/Toxicology
Symptoms of overdose include increased nausea and vomiting, hypotension
Treatment includes infusion of normal saline and other supportive measures, as clinically indicated
Drug Interactions Increased toxicity: Special consideration should be given to patients receiving antihypertensive medications or other drugs that could potentiate hypotension
Stability
Store intact vials of lyophilized powder at room temperature (20°C to 25°C/68°F to 77°F)
Reconstitute with 9.7 mL of sterile 0.9% sodium chloride. The reconstituted solution (500 mg/10 mL) is chemically stable for up to 5 hours at room temperature (25°C) or up to 24 hours under refrigeration (2°C to 8°C).
Amifostine should be further diluted in 0.9% sodium chloride to a concentration of 5-40 mg/mL and is chemically stable for up to 5 hours at room temperature (25°C) or up to 24 hours under refrigeration (2°C to 8°C).
Mechanism of Action Prodrug that is dephosphorylated by alkaline phosphatase in tissues to a pharmacologically active free thiol metabolite that can reduce the toxic effects of cisplatin. The free thiol is available to bind to, and detoxify, reactive metabolites of cisplatin; and can also act as a scavenger of free radicals that may be generated in tissues exposed to cisplatin.
Pharmacodynamics/Kinetics
Absorption: Oral: Poor
Distribution: V$_d$: 3.5 L
Metabolism: Hepatic dephosphorylation to two metabolites (WR-33278 and WR-1065)
Half-life: 9 minutes
Elimination: Renal; plasma clearance: 2.17 L/minute
Usual Dosage Adults: I.V. (refer to individual protocols): 910 mg/m^2 administered once daily as a 15-minute I.V. infusion, starting 30 minutes prior to chemotherapy

Decrease in Systolic Blood Pressure

Baseline systolic blood pressure (mm Hg)	<100	100–119	120–139	140–179	≥180
Decrease in systolic blood pressure during infusion of amifostine (mm Hg)	20	25	30	40	50

Note: 15-minute infusion is better tolerated than more extended infusions. Further reductions in infusion times have not been systematically investigated. The infusion of amifostine should be interrupted if the systolic blood pressure decreases significantly from the baseline value. See table.

Mean onset of hypotension is 14 minutes into the 15-minute infusion and the mean duration was 6 minutes. Hypotension should be treated with fluid infusion and postural management of the patient (supine or Trendelenburg position). If the blood pressure returns to normal within 5 minutes and the patient is asymptomatic, the infusion may be restarted so that the full dose of amifostine may be administered. If the full dose of amifostine cannot be administered, the dose of amifostine for subsequent cycles should be 740 mg/m².

Administration I.V.: Administer over 15 minutes; administration as a longer infusion is associated with a higher incidence of side effects

Monitoring Parameters Blood pressure should be monitored every 5 minutes during the infusion

Dosage Forms Injection: 500 mg

Amikacin (am i KAY sin)

Related Information
    Antimicrobial Drugs of Choice *on page 1404*
    Community-Acquired Pneumonia in Adults *on page 1419*

U.S. Brand Names Amikin® Injection

Canadian Brand Names Amikin®

Synonyms Amikacin Sulfate

Therapeutic Category Antibiotic, Aminoglycoside

Use Treatment of serious infections due to organisms resistant to gentamicin and tobramycin including *Pseudomonas*, *Proteus*, *Serratia*, and other gram-positive bacilli (bone infections, respiratory tract infections, endocarditis, and septicemia); documented infection of mycobacterial organisms susceptible to amikacin

Pregnancy Risk Factor C

Contraindications Hypersensitivity to amikacin sulfate or any component; cross-sensitivity may exist with other aminoglycosides

Warnings/Precautions Dose and/or frequency of administration must be monitored and modified in patients with renal impairment; drug should be discontinued if signs of ototoxicity, nephrotoxicity, or hypersensitivity occur; ototoxicity is proportional to the amount of drug given and the duration of treatment; tinnitus or vertigo may be indications of vestibular injury and impending bilateral irreversible damage; renal damage is usually reversible

Adverse Reactions
    1% to 10%:
        Central nervous system: Neurotoxicity
        Otic: Ototoxicity (auditory), ototoxicity (vestibular)
        Renal: Nephrotoxicity
    <1%: Hypotension, headache, drowsiness, drug fever, rash, nausea, vomiting, eosinophilia, paresthesia, tremor, arthralgia, weakness, dyspnea

Overdosage/Toxicology
    Symptoms of overdose include ototoxicity, nephrotoxicity, and neuromuscular toxicity
    Treatment of choice following a single acute overdose appears to be the maintenance of good urine output of at least 3 mL/kg/hour. Dialysis is of questionable value in the enhancement of aminoglycoside elimination. If required, hemodialysis is preferred over peritoneal dialysis in patients with normal renal function.

Drug Interactions
    Decreased effect of aminoglycoside: High concentrations of penicillins and/or cephalosporins (*in vitro* data)
    Increased toxicity of aminoglycoside: Indomethacin I.V., amphotericin, loop diuretics, vancomycin, enflurane, methoxyflurane; increased toxicity of depolarizing and nondepolarizing neuromuscular blocking agents and polypeptide antibiotics with administration of aminoglycosides

Stability Stable for 24 hours at room temperature and 2 days at refrigeration when mixed in D_5W, $D_5^{1}/_4NS$, $D_5^{1}/_2NS$, NS, LR

Mechanism of Action Inhibits protein synthesis in susceptible bacteria by binding to 30S ribosomal subunits

Pharmacodynamics/Kinetics
    Absorption: I.M.: May be delayed in the bedridden patient
    Distribution: Crosses the placenta; primarily distributes into extracellular fluid (highly hydrophilic); penetrates the blood-brain barrier when meninges are inflamed
        Relative diffusion of antimicrobial agents from blood into cerebrospinal fluid (CSF): Good only with inflammation (exceeds usual MICs); ratio of CSF to blood level (%):
            Normal meninges: 10-20
            Inflamed meninges: 15-24
    Half-life (dependent on renal function):
        Infants: Low birthweight (1-3 days): 7-9 hours; Full term >7 days: 4-5 hours
        Children: 1.6-2.5 hours
        Adults: Normal renal function: 1.4-2.3 hours; Anuria: End-stage renal disease: 28-86 hours
    Time to peak serum concentration: I.M.: Within 45-120 minutes
    Elimination: 94% to 98% excreted unchanged in urine via glomerular filtration within 24 hours; clearance dependent on renal function and patient age
    (Continued)

Amikacin (Continued)

Usual Dosage Individualization is critical because of the low therapeutic index

Use of ideal body weight (IBW) for determining the mg/kg/dose appears to be more accurate than dosing on the basis of total body weight (TBW)

In morbid obesity, dosage requirement may best be estimated using a dosing weight of IBW + 0.4 (TBW - IBW)

Initial and periodic peak and trough plasma drug levels should be determined, particularly in critically ill patients with serious infections or in disease states known to significantly alter aminoglycoside pharmacokinetics (eg, cystic fibrosis, burns, or major surgery)

Infants, Children, and Adults: I.M., I.V.: 5-7.5 mg/kg/dose every 8 hours

Some clinicians suggest a daily dose of 15-20 mg/kg for all patients with normal renal function. This dose is at least as efficacious with similar, if not less, toxicity than conventional dosing.

Dosing interval in renal impairment: Some patients may require larger or more frequent doses if serum levels document the need (ie, cystic fibrosis or febrile granulocytopenic patients)

Cl_{cr} ≥60 mL/minute: Administer every 8 hours

Cl_{cr} 40-60 mL/minute: Administer every 12 hours

Cl_{cr} 20-40 mL/minute: Administer every 24 hours

Cl_{cr} <20 mL/minute: Loading dose, then monitor levels

Hemodialysis: Dialyzable (50% to 100%); administer dose postdialysis or administer $^2/_3$ normal dose as a supplemental dose postdialysis and follow levels

Peritoneal dialysis: Dose as Cl_{cr} <20 mL/minute: Follow levels

Continuous arteriovenous or venovenous hemodiafiltration (CAVH) effects: Dose as for Cl_{cr} 10-40 mL/minute and follow levels

Administration Administer I.M. injection in large muscle mass

Monitoring Parameters Urinalysis, BUN, serum creatinine, appropriately timed peak and trough concentrations, vital signs, temperature, weight, I & O, hearing parameters

Reference Range

Sample size: 0.5-2 mL blood (red top tube) or 0.1-1 mL serum (separated)

Therapeutic levels:

Peak:

Life-threatening infections: 25-30 µg/mL

Serious infections: 20-25 µg/mL

Urinary tract infections: 15-20 µg/mL

Trough:

Serious infections: 1-4 µg/mL

Life-threatening infections: 4-8 µg/mL

Toxic concentration: Peak: >35 µg/mL; Trough: >10 µg/mL

Timing of serum samples: Draw peak 30 minutes after completion of 30-minute infusion or at 1 hour following initiation of infusion or I.M. injection; draw trough within 30 minutes prior to next dose

Test Interactions Penicillin may decrease aminoglycoside serum concentrations *in vitro*

Patient Information Report loss of hearing, ringing or roaring in the ears, or feeling of fullness in head

Nursing Implications Aminoglycoside levels measured from blood taken from Silastic® central catheters can sometimes give falsely high readings (draw levels from alternate lumen or peripheral stick, if possible)

Additional Information Sodium content of 1 g: 29.9 mg (1.3 mEq)

Dosage Forms Injection, as sulfate: 50 mg/mL (2 mL, 4 mL); 250 mg/mL (2 mL, 4 mL)

♦ **Amikacin Sulfate** *see* Amikacin *on previous page*

♦ **Amikin®** *see* Amikacin *on previous page*

♦ **Amikin® Injection** *see* Amikacin *on previous page*

Amiloride (a MIL oh ride)

Related Information

Heart Failure: Management of Patients With Left-Ventricular Systolic Dysfunction *on page 1472*

U.S. Brand Names Midamor®

Synonyms Amiloride Hydrochloride

Therapeutic Category Diuretic, Potassium Sparing

Use Counteracts potassium loss induced by other diuretics in the treatment of hypertension or edematous conditions including CHF, hepatic cirrhosis, and hypoaldosteronism; usually used in conjunction with more potent diuretics such as thiazides or loop diuretics

Investigational: Cystic fibrosis

Pregnancy Risk Factor B

Contraindications Hyperkalemia, potassium supplementation and impaired renal function or potassium-sparing diuretics, hypersensitivity to amiloride or any component

Warnings/Precautions Use cautiously in patients with severe hepatic insufficiency; may cause hyperkalemia (serum levels >5.5 mEq/L) which, if uncorrected, is potentially fatal; medication should be discontinued if potassium level are >6.5 mEq/L

Adverse Reactions

1% to 10%:

Central nervous system: Headache, fatigue, dizziness

Endocrine & metabolic: Hyperkalemia, hyperchloremic metabolic acidosis, dehydration, hyponatremia, gynecomastia

Gastrointestinal: Nausea, diarrhea, vomiting, abdominal pain, gas pain, appetite changes, constipation

Genitourinary: Impotence

Neuromuscular & skeletal: Muscle cramps, weakness

Respiratory: Cough, dyspnea

<1%: Angina pectoris, orthostatic hypotension, arrhythmias, palpitations, chest pain, vertigo, nervousness, insomnia, depression, rash or dryness, pruritus, alopecia, decreased libido, GI bleeding, heartburn, flatulence, dyspepsia, polyuria, bladder spasms, dysuria, jaundice, arthralgia, tremor, neck/shoulder pain, back pain, increased intraocular pressure, shortness of breath, thirst

Overdosage/Toxicology
Clinical signs are consistent with dehydration and electrolyte disturbance; large amounts may result in life-threatening hyperkalemia (>6.5 mEq/L)

This can be treated with I.V. glucose (dextrose 25% in water), with rapid-acting insulin, with concurrent I.V. sodium bicarbonate and, if needed, Kayexalate® oral or rectal solutions in sorbitol; persistent hyperkalemia may require dialysis.

Drug Interactions
Decreased effect of amiloride: Nonsteroidal anti-inflammatory agents

Increased risk of amiloride-associated hyperkalemia: Avoid use or use with extreme caution with triamterene, spironolactone, angiotensin-converting enzyme (ACE) inhibitors, potassium preparations, indomethacin

Increased toxicity of amantadine and lithium by reduction of renal excretion

Mechanism of Action Interferes with potassium/sodium exchange (active transport) in the distal tubule, cortical collecting tubule and collecting duct by inhibiting sodium, potassium-ATPase; decreases calcium excretion; increases magnesium loss

Pharmacodynamics/Kinetics
Absorption: Oral: ~15% to 25%; Onset: 2 hours; Duration: 24 hours

Distribution: V_d: 350-380 L

Protein binding: 23%

Metabolism: No active metabolites

Half-life: Normal renal function: 6-9 hours; End-stage renal disease: 8-144 hours

Peak serum concentration: 6-10 hours

Elimination: Unchanged equally in the urine and the feces

Usual Dosage Oral:
Children: Although safety and efficacy have not been established by the FDA in children, a dosage of 0.625 mg/kg/day has been used in children weighing 6-20 kg

Adults: 5-10 mg/day (up to 20 mg)

Elderly: Initial: 5 mg once daily or every other day

Dosing adjustment in renal impairment:
Cl_{cr} 10-50 mL/minute: Administer at 50% of normal dose

Cl_{cr} <10 mL/minute: Avoid use

Monitoring Parameters I & O, daily weights, blood pressure, serum electrolytes, renal function

Test Interactions ↑ potassium (S)

Patient Information Take with food or milk; avoid salt substitutes; because of high potassium content, avoid bananas and oranges; report any muscle cramps, weakness, nausea, or dizziness; use caution operating machinery or performing other tasks requiring alertness

Nursing Implications Assess fluid status via daily weights, I & O ratios, standing and supine blood pressures; observe for hyperkalemia; if ordered once daily, dose should be given in the morning

Dosage Forms Tablet, as hydrochloride: 5 mg

Amiloride and Hydrochlorothiazide
(a MIL oh ride & hye droe klor oh THYE a zide)

U.S. Brand Names Moduretic®

Therapeutic Category Antihypertensive Agent, Combination

Dosage Forms Tablet: Amiloride hydrochloride 5 mg and hydrochlorothiazide 50 mg

♦ **Amiloride Hydrochloride** see Amiloride on previous page

♦ **2-Amino-6-Mercaptopurine** see Thioguanine on page 1133

♦ **2-Amino-6-Trifluoromethoxy-benzothiazole** see Riluzole on page 1027

♦ **Aminobenzylpenicillin** see Ampicillin on page 79

Aminocaproic Acid (a mee noe ka PROE ik AS id)

U.S. Brand Names Amicar®

Therapeutic Category Hemostatic Agent

Use Treatment of excessive bleeding from fibrinolysis

Pregnancy Risk Factor C

Contraindications Disseminated intravascular coagulation, hematuria of upper urinary tract

Warnings/Precautions Rapid I.V. administration of the undiluted drug is not recommended; aminocaproic acid may accumulate in patients with decreased renal function; do not use in hematuria of upper urinary tract origin unless possible benefits outweigh risks; use with caution in patients with cardiac, renal or hepatic disease; do not administer without a definite diagnosis of laboratory findings indicative of hyperfibrinolysis; should not be used in nursing women
(Continued)

Aminocaproic Acid (Continued)

Adverse Reactions
1% to 10%:
Cardiovascular: Hypotension, bradycardia, arrhythmia
Central nervous system: Dizziness, headache, malaise, fatigue
Dermatologic: Rash
Gastrointestinal: GI irritation, nausea, cramps, diarrhea
Hematologic: Decreased platelet function, elevated serum enzymes
Neuromuscular & skeletal: Myopathy, weakness
Otic: Tinnitus
Respiratory: Nasal congestion
<1%: Convulsions, ejaculation problems, rhabdomyolysis, renal failure

Overdosage/Toxicology Symptoms of overdose include nausea, diarrhea, delirium, hepatic necrosis, thromboembolism

Drug Interactions Increased toxic effect with oral contraceptives, estrogens

Mechanism of Action Competitively inhibits activation of plasminogen to plasmin, also, a lesser antiplasmin effect

Pharmacodynamics/Kinetics
Oral: Peak effect: Within 2 hours; Therapeutic effect: Within 1-72 hours after dose
Distribution: Widely distributes through intravascular and extravascular compartments
Metabolism: Minimal hepatic
Half-life: 1-2 hours
Elimination: 68% to 86% excreted as unchanged drug in urine within 12 hours

Usual Dosage In the management of acute bleeding syndromes, oral dosage regimens are the same as the I.V. dosage regimens in adults and children

Chronic bleeding: Oral, I.V.: 5-30 g/day in divided doses at 3- to 6-hour intervals
Acute bleeding syndrome:
Children: Oral, I.V.: 100 mg/kg or 3 g/m^2 during the first hour, followed by continuous infusion at the rate of 33.3 mg/kg/hour or 1 g/m^2/hour; total dosage should not exceed 18 g/m^2/24 hours
Traumatic hyphema: Oral: 100 mg/kg/dose every 6-8 hours
Adults:
Oral: For elevated fibrinolytic activity, administer 5 g during first hour, followed by 1-1.25 g/hour for approximately 8 hours or until bleeding stops
I.V.: 4-5 g in 250 mL of diluent during first hour followed by continuous infusion at the rate of 1-1.25 g/hour in 50 mL of diluent, continue for 8 hours or until bleeding stops
Maximum daily dose: Oral, I.V.: 30 g

Dosing adjustment in renal impairment: Oliguria or ESRD: Reduce dose by 15% to 25%

Administration Administration by infusion using appropriate I.V. solution (dextrose 5% or 0.9% sodium chloride); rapid I.V. injection (IVP) should be avoided since hypotension, bradycardia, and arrhythmia may result. Aminocaproic acid may accumulate in patients with decreased renal function.

Monitoring Parameters Fibrinogen, fibrin split products, creatine phosphokinase (with long-term therapy)

Reference Range Therapeutic concentration: >130 µg/mL (concentration necessary for inhibition of fibrinolysis)

Test Interactions ↑ potassium, creatine phosphokinase [CPK] (S)

Patient Information Report any signs of bleeding; change positions slowly to minimize dizziness

Dosage Forms
Injection: 250 mg/mL (20 mL, 96 mL, 100 mL)
Syrup: 1.25 g/5 mL (480 mL)
Tablet: 500 mg

♦ **Amino-Cerv™ Vaginal Cream** see Urea on page 1199

Aminoglutethimide (a mee noe gloo TETH i mide)

U.S. Brand Names Cytadren®

Therapeutic Category Adrenal Steroid Inhibitor; Antiadrenal Agent; Antineoplastic Agent, Miscellaneous

Use Suppression of adrenal function in selected patients with Cushing's syndrome; also used successfully in postmenopausal patients with advanced breast carcinoma and in patients with metastatic prostate carcinoma as salvage (third-line hormonal agent)

Pregnancy Risk Factor D

Pregnancy/Breast-Feeding Implications Suspected of causing virilization when given throughout pregnancy

Contraindications Hypersensitivity to aminoglutethimide or any component and glutethimide

Warnings/Precautions Monitor blood pressure in all patients at appropriate intervals; hypothyroidism may occur; **mineralocorticoid replacement therapy may be necessary in up to 50% of patients** (ie, fludrocortisone); if glucocorticoid replacement therapy is necessary, 20-30 mg of hydrocortisone daily in the morning will replace endogenous secretion (steroid replacement regimen is controversial - high-dose versus low-dose)

Adverse Reactions Most adverse effects will diminish in incidence and severity after the first 2-6 weeks

>10%:
Central nervous system: Headache, dizziness, drowsiness, and lethargy are frequent at the start of therapy, clumsiness
Dermatologic: Skin rash
Gastrointestinal: Nausea, vomiting, anorexia
Hepatic: Cholestatic jaundice
Neuromuscular & skeletal: Myalgia
Renal: Nephrotoxicity
Respiratory: Pulmonary alveolar damage
Miscellaneous: Systemic lupus erythematosus
1% to 10%:
Cardiovascular: Hypotension and tachycardia, orthostatic hypotension
Dermatologic: Hirsutism in females
Endocrine & metabolic: Adrenocortical insufficiency
Hematologic: Rare cases of neutropenia, leukopenia, thrombocytopenia, pancytopenia, and agranulocytosis have been reported
<1%: Adrenal suppression, lipid abnormalities (hypercholesterolemia), hyperkalemia, hypothyroidism, goiter

Overdosage/Toxicology
Symptoms of overdose include ataxia, somnolence, lethargy, dizziness, distress, fatigue, coma, hyperventilation, respiratory depression, hypovolemic shock
Treatment is supportive

Drug Interactions CYP 450 hepatic microsomal enzyme inducer
Decreased effect:
Dexamethasone: Reported to increase metabolism
Digitoxin: Increases clearance of digitoxin after 3-8 weeks of aminoglutethimide therapy
Theophylline: Aminoglutethimide increases metabolism of theophylline
Warfarin: Decreases anticoagulant response to warfarin
Increased toxicity: Propranolol: Case report of enhanced aminoglutethimide toxicity (rash and lethargy)

Mechanism of Action Blocks the enzymatic conversion of cholesterol to delta-5-pregnenolone, thereby reducing the synthesis of adrenal glucocorticoids, mineralocorticoids, estrogens, aldosterone, and androgens

Pharmacodynamics/Kinetics
Onset of action (adrenal suppression): 3-5 days
Absorption: Oral: Well absorbed (90%)
Distribution: Crosses the placenta
Protein binding: Minimally bound to plasma proteins (20% to 25%)
Metabolism: Major metabolite is N-acetylaminoglutethimide
Half-life: 7-15 hours; shorter following multiple administrations than following single doses (induces hepatic enzymes increasing its own metabolism)
Elimination: 34% to 50% excreted in urine as unchanged drug and 25% excreted as metabolite

Usual Dosage Adults: Oral:
250 mg every 6 hours may be increased at 1- to 2-week intervals to a total of 2 g/day; administer in divided doses, 2-3 times/day to reduce incidence of nausea and vomiting. Follow adrenal cortical response by careful monitoring of plasma cortisol until the desired level of suppression is achieved.
Mineralocorticoid (fludrocortisone) replacement therapy may be necessary in up to 50% of patients. If glucocorticoid replacement therapy is necessary, 20-30 mg hydrocortisone orally in the morning will replace endogenous secretion.
Dosing adjustment in renal impairment: Dose reduction may be necessary

Patient Information Masculinization can occur and is reversible after discontinuing treatment; may cause drowsiness or dizziness

Dosage Forms Tablet, scored: 250 mg

♦ **Amino-Opti-E® [OTC]** *see* Vitamin E *on page 1225*
♦ **Aminophyllin™** *see* Theophylline Salts *on page 1125*
♦ **Aminophylline** *see* Theophylline Salts *on page 1125*

Aminosalicylate Sodium (a MEE noe sa LIS i late SOW dee um)

U.S. Brand Names Sodium P.A.S.
Canadian Brand Names Tubasal®
Synonyms Para-Aminosalicylate Sodium; PAS
Therapeutic Category Anti-inflammatory Agent; Antitubercular Agent; Nonsteroidal Anti-inflammatory Drug (NSAID), Oral
Use Adjunctive treatment of tuberculosis used in combination with other antitubercular agents; has also been used in Crohn's disease
Pregnancy Risk Factor C
Contraindications Hypersensitivity to aminosalicylate sodium
Warnings/Precautions Use with caution in patients with hepatic or renal dysfunction, patients with gastric ulcer, patients with CHF, and patients who are sodium restricted
Adverse Reactions
1% to 10%: Gastrointestinal: Nausea, vomiting, diarrhea, abdominal pain
<1%: Vasculitis, fever, skin eruptions, goiter with or without myxedema, leukopenia, agranulocytosis, thrombocytopenia, hemolytic anemia, jaundice, hepatitis
Overdosage/Toxicology
Acute overdose results in crystalluria and renal failure, nausea, and vomiting
(Continued)

Aminosalicylate Sodium *(Continued)*

Alkalinization of the urine with sodium bicarbonate and forced diuresis can prevent crystalluria and nephrotoxicity

Drug Interactions Decreased levels of digoxin and vitamin B_{12}

Mechanism of Action Aminosalicylic acid (PAS) is a highly specific bacteriostatic agent active against *M. tuberculosis*. Structurally related to para-aminobenzoic acid (PABA) and its mechanism of action is thought to be similar to the sulfonamides, a competitive antagonism with PABA; disrupts plate biosynthesis in sensitive organisms.

Pharmacodynamics/Kinetics

Absorption: Readily absorbed >90%

Metabolism: >50% acetylated in liver

Elimination: >80% excreted through kidneys as parent drug and metabolites; elimination is reduced with renal dysfunction

Usual Dosage Oral:

Children: 150 mg/kg/day in 3-4 equally divided doses

Adults: 150 mg/kg/day in 2-3 equally divided doses (usually 12-14 g/day)

Dosing adjustment in renal impairment:

Cl_{cr} 10-50 mL/minute: Administer 50% to 75% of dose

Cl_{cr} <10 mL/minute: Administer 50% of dose

Administer after hemodialysis

Patient Information Notify physician if persistent sore throat, fever, unusual bleeding or bruising, persistent nausea, vomiting, or abdominal pain occurs; do not stop taking before consulting your physician; take with food or meals; do not use products that are brown or purple; store in a cool, dry place away from sunlight

Nursing Implications Do not administer if discolored

Dosage Forms Tablet: 500 mg

♦ **5-Aminosalicylic Acid** *see Mesalamine on page 734*

Amiodarone *(a MEE oh da rone)*

Related Information

Antiarrhythmic Drugs Comparison *on page 1297*

U.S. Brand Names Cordarone®; Pacerone®

Synonyms Amiodarone Hydrochloride

Therapeutic Category Antiarrhythmic Agent, Class III

Use

Oral: Management of life-threatening recurrent ventricular fibrillation (VF) or hemodynamically unstable ventricular tachycardia (VT)

I.V.: Initiation of treatment and prophylaxis of frequency recurring VF and unstable VT in patients refractory to other therapy. Also, for patients for whom oral amiodarone is indicated but who are unable to take oral medication.

Pregnancy Risk Factor D

Contraindications Hypersensitivity to amiodarone; severe sinus node dysfunction, second and third degree A-V block, marked sinus bradycardia except if pacemaker is placed, pregnancy and lactation; administration with ritonavir or sparfloxacin

Warnings/Precautions Not considered first-line antiarrhythmic due to high incidence of significant and potentially fatal toxicity (ie, hypersensitivity pneumonitis or interstitial/alveolar pneumonitis, hepatic failure, heart block, bradycardia or exacerbated arrhythmias), especially with large doses; reserve for use in arrhythmias refractory to other therapy; hospitalize patients while loading dose is administered; use cautiously in elderly due to predisposition to toxicity; use very cautiously and with close monitoring in patients with thyroid or liver disease. Due to an extensive tissue distribution and prolonged elimination period, the time at which a life-threatening arrhythmia will recur following discontinued therapy or an interaction with subsequent treatment may occur is unpredictable; patients must be observed carefully and extreme caution taken when other antiarrhythmic agents are substituted after discontinuation of amiodarone.

Adverse Reactions With large dosages (≥400 mg/day), adverse reactions occur in ~75% patients and require discontinuance in 5% to 20%

>10%:

Cardiovascular: Hypotension (especially with I.V. form)

Central nervous system: Ataxia, fatigue, malaise, dizziness, headache, insomnia, nightmares

Dermatologic: Photosensitivity

Gastrointestinal: Nausea, vomiting

Neuromuscular & skeletal: Tremor, paresthesias, muscle weakness

Respiratory: Pulmonary fibrosis (cough, fever, dyspnea, malaise), interstitial pneumonitis

Miscellaneous: Alveolitis

1% to 10%:

Cardiovascular: Congestive heart failure, cardiac arrhythmias (atropine-resistant bradycardia, heart block, sinus arrest, paroxysmal ventricular tachycardia), myocardial depression, flushing, edema

Central nervous system: Fever, sleep disturbances

Dermatologic: Solar dermatitis

Endocrine & metabolic: Hypothyroidism or hyperthyroidism (less common), decreased libido

Gastrointestinal: Constipation, anorexia, abdominal pain, abnormal salivation, abnormal taste (oral form)

Hematologic: Coagulation abnormalities
Hepatic: Abnormal LFTs
Local: Phlebitis with concentrations >3 mg/mL
Neuromuscular & skeletal: Paresthesia
Ocular: Visual disturbances
Miscellaneous: Abnormal smell (oral form)
<1%: Hypotension (with oral form), vasculitis, atrial fibrillation, increased Q-T interval, ventricular fibrillation, cardiogenic shock, pseudotumor cerebri, rash, alopecia, discoloration of skin (slate blue), Stevens-Johnson syndrome, hyperglycemia, hypertriglyceridemia, epididymitis, thrombocytopenia, cirrhosis, severe hepatotoxicity (potentially fatal hepatitis), increased ALT/AST, optic neuritis, corneal microdeposits, photophobia

Overdosage/Toxicology
Symptoms include extensions of pharmacologic effect, sinus bradycardia and/or heart block, hypotension and Q-T prolongation
Patients should be monitored for several days following ingestion. Intoxication with amiodarone necessitates EKG monitoring; bradycardia may be atropine resistant; injectable isoproterenol or a temporary pacemaker may be required.

Drug Interactions CYP3A3/4 enzyme substrate; CYP2C9, 2D6, and 3A3/4 enzyme inhibitor
Amiodarone appears to interfere with the hepatic metabolism of several drugs resulting in significantly increased plasma concentrations; see table.

Amiodarone Common Drug Interactions

Drug	Interaction
Anticoagulants, oral	The effects of the anticoagulant is increased due to inhibition of its metabolism.
β-adrenergic receptor antagonists	β-blocker effects are enhanced by amiodarone's inhibition of the β-blocker's hepatic metabolism.
Calcium channel antagonists	Additive effects of both drugs resulting in a reduction in cardiac sinus conduction, atrioventricular nodal conduction, and myocardial contractility.
Cholestyramine	Increased enterohepatic elimination of amiodarone may occur resulting in decreased serum levels and half-life.
Cimetidine	Increased amiodarone levels may result
Cyclosporine	Results in persistently elevated cyclosporine levels and elevated creatinine despite reduction in cyclosporine dosage.
Digoxin	Digoxin concentrations may be increased with resultant increases in activity and potential for toxicity.
Disopyramide	Q-T prolongation may occur in addition to arrhythmias.
Fentanyl	Concurrent use with amiodarone may result in hypotension, bradycardia, and decreased cardiac output.
Flecainide	Flecainide plasma concentrations are increased.
Methotrexate	Chronic use of amiodarone impairs MTX metabolism resulting in MTX toxicity.
Phenytoin	Phenytoin serum concentrations are increased due to reduction in phenytoin metabolism, with possible symptoms of phenytoin toxicity; amiodarone levels may be decreased.
Procainamide	Procainamide serum concentrations may be increased.
Quinidine	Quinidine serum concentrations may be increased and can potentially cause fatal cardiac dysrhythmias.
Ritonavir	Increased risk of amiodarone cardiotoxicity results.
Sparfloxacin	Risk of cardiotoxicity may be increased.
Theophylline	Increased theophylline levels and resultant toxicity may occur; effects may be delayed and may persist after amiodarone discontinuation

Stability I.V. infusions >2 hours must be administered in glass or polyolefin bottles; **incompatible** with aminophylline, cefamandole, cefazolin, heparin, mezlocillin, and sodium bicarbonate; store at room temperature; protect from light
Mechanism of Action Class III antiarrhythmic agent which inhibits adrenergic stimulation, prolongs the action potential and refractory period in myocardial tissue; decreases A-V conduction and sinus node function
Pharmacodynamics/Kinetics
Onset of effect: 3 days to 3 weeks after starting therapy
Peak effect: 1 week to 5 months
Duration of effect after discontinuation of therapy: 7-50 days
Note: Mean onset of effect and duration after discontinuation may be shorter in children versus adults
Distribution: V_d: 66 L/kg (range: 18-148 L/kg); crosses placenta; distributes into breast milk in concentrations higher than maternal plasma concentrations
Protein binding: 96%
Metabolism: In liver, major metabolite active
Bioavailability: ~50%
Half-life: Oral chronic therapy: 40-55 days (range: 26-107 days); shortened in children versus adults
(Continued)

Amiodarone *(Continued)*

Elimination: Via biliary excretion; possible enterohepatic recirculation; <1% excreted unchanged in urine

Usual Dosage

Oral:

Children (calculate doses for children <1 year on body surface area): Loading dose: 10-15 mg/kg/day or 600-800 mg/1.73 m²/day for 4-14 days or until adequate control of arrhythmia or prominent adverse effects occur (this loading dose may be given in 1-2 divided doses/day); dosage should then be reduced to 5 mg/kg/day or 200-400 mg/1.73 m²/day given once daily for several weeks; if arrhythmia does not recur, reduce to lowest effective dosage possible; usual daily minimal dose: 2.5 mg/kg/day; maintenance doses may be given for 5 of 7 days/week

Adults: Ventricular arrhythmias: 800-1600 mg/day in 1-2 doses for 1-3 weeks, then when adequate arrhythmia control is achieved decrease to 600-800 mg/day in 1-2 doses for 1 month; maintenance: 400 mg/day; lower doses are recommended for supraventricular arrhythmias

I.V.:

First 24 hours: 1000 mg according to following regimen

Step 1: 150 mg (10 mL) over first 10 minutes (mix 3 mL in 100 mL D₅W)

Step 2: 360 mg (200 mL) over next 6 hours (mix 18 mL in 500 mL D₅W)

Step 3: 540 mg (300 mL) over next 18 hours

After the first 24 hours: 0.5 mg/minute utilizing concentration of 1-6 mg/mL

Breakthrough VF or VT: 150 mg supplemental doses in 100 mL D₅W over 10 minutes

Note: When switching from I.V. to oral therapy, use the following as a guide:

<1-week I.V. infusion → 800-1600 mg/day

1- to 3-week I.V. infusion → 600-800 mg/day

>3-week I.V. infusion → 400 mg/day

Recommendations for conversion to intravenous amiodarone after oral administration: During long-term amiodarone therapy (ie, ≥4 months), the mean plasma-elimination half-life of the active metabolite of amiodarone is 61 days; replacement therapy may not be necessary in such patients if oral therapy is discontinued for a period <2 weeks, since any changes in serum amiodarone concentrations during this period may **not** be clinically significant

Dosing adjustment in hepatic impairment: Probably necessary in substantial hepatic impairment

Hemodialysis: Not dialyzable (0% to 5%); supplemental dose is not necessary

Peritoneal dialysis effects: Not dialyzable (0% to 5%); supplemental dose is not necessary

Administration Administer with food; if possible, gradually discontinue prior antiarrhythmic drugs when initiating therapy; if GI intolerance occurs with single-dose therapy, use twice daily dosing; give I.V. therapy through central venous catheter and with control of an infusion pump

Monitoring Parameters Monitor heart rate (EKG) and rhythm throughout therapy; assess patient for signs of thyroid dysfunction (thyroid function tests and liver enzymes), lethargy, edema of the hands, feet, weight loss, and pulmonary toxicity (baseline pulmonary function tests)

Reference Range Therapeutic: 0.5-2.5 mg/L (SI: 1-4 μmol/L) (parent); desethyl metabolite is active and is present in equal concentration to parent drug

Test Interactions Thyroid function tests: Amiodarone partially inhibits the peripheral conversion of thyroxine (T_4) to triiodothyronine (T_3); serum T_4 and reverse triiodothyronine (RT_3) concentrations may be increased and serum T_3 may be decreased; most patients remain clinically euthyroid, however, clinical hypothyroidism or hyperthyroidism may occur

Patient Information Take with food; use sunscreen or stay out of sun to prevent burns; skin discoloration is reversible; photophobia may make sunglasses necessary; do not discontinue abruptly; regular blood work for thyroid functions tests and ophthalmologic exams are necessary; notify physician if persistent dry cough or shortness of breath occurs

Nursing Implications Muscle weakness may present a great hazard for ambulation

Dosage Forms

Injection, as hydrochloride: 50 mg/mL with benzyl alcohol (3 mL)

Tablet, scored, as hydrochloride: 200 mg

Extemporaneous Preparations A 5 mg/mL oral suspension has been made from tablets and has an expected stability of 7 days under refrigeration; three 200 mg tablets are crushed in a mortar, 90 mL of methylcellulose 1%, and 10 mL of syrup (syrup NF (85% sucrose in water) or flavored syrup) are added in small amounts and triturated until uniform; purified water USP is used to make a quantity sufficient to 120 mL

Nahata MC and Hipple TF, *Pediatric Drug Formulations*, 2nd ed, Cincinnati, OH: Harvey Whitney Books Co, 1992.

♦ **Amiodarone Hydrochloride** *see* Amiodarone *on page 60*

♦ **Amitone® [OTC]** *see* Calcium Carbonate *on page 174*

Amitriptyline *(a mee TRIP ti leen)*

Related Information

Antidepressant Agents Comparison *on page 1301*

U.S. Brand Names Elavil®; Enovil®

Canadian Brand Names Apo®-Amitriptyline; Levate®; Novo-Tryptin

Synonyms Amitriptyline Hydrochloride

Therapeutic Category Antidepressant, Tricyclic; Antimigraine Agent

Use Treatment of various forms of depression, often in conjunction with psychotherapy; analgesic for certain chronic and neuropathic pain, prophylaxis against migraine headaches

Pregnancy Risk Factor D

Contraindications Hypersensitivity to amitriptyline (cross-sensitivity with other tricyclics may occur); patients receiving MAO inhibitors within past 14 days; narrow-angle glaucoma; avoid use during pregnancy and lactation

Warnings/Precautions

Amitriptyline should not be abruptly discontinued in patients receiving high doses for prolonged periods

Use with caution in patients with cardiac conduction disturbances; an EKG prior to initiation of therapy is advised; use with caution in patients with a history of hyperthyroidism, renal or hepatic impairment

The most anticholinergic and sedating of the antidepressants; pronounced effects on the cardiovascular system (hypotension), hence, many psychiatrists agree it is best to avoid in the elderly

Adverse Reactions Anticholinergic effects may be pronounced; moderate to marked sedation can occur (tolerance to these effects usually occurs)

>10%:

Central nervous system: Dizziness, drowsiness, headache

Gastrointestinal: Xerostomia, constipation, increased appetite, nausea, unpleasant taste, weight gain

Neuromuscular & skeletal: Weakness

1% to 10%:

Cardiovascular: Hypotension, postural hypotension, arrhythmias, tachycardia

Central nervous system: Nervousness, restlessness, parkinsonian syndrome, insomnia, sedation, fatigue, anxiety, impaired cognitive function, seizures have occurred occasionally, extrapyramidal symptoms are possible

Gastrointestinal: Diarrhea, heartburn

Genitourinary: Sexual dysfunction, urinary retention

Neuromuscular & skeletal: Tremor

Ocular: Eye pain, blurred vision

Miscellaneous: Diaphoresis (excessive)

<1%: Alopecia, photosensitivity, breast enlargement, galactorrhea, rarely SIADH, trouble with gums, decreased lower esophageal sphincter tone may cause GE reflux, testicular edema, leukopenia, eosinophilia, rarely agranulocytosis, cholestatic jaundice, increased liver enzymes, increased intraocular pressure, tinnitus, allergic reactions, sudden death

Overdosage/Toxicology

Symptoms of overdose include agitation, confusion, hallucinations, urinary retention, hypothermia, hypotension, ventricular tachycardia, seizures

Following initiation of essential overdose management, toxic symptoms should be treated. Sodium bicarbonate is indicated when QRS interval is >0.10 seconds or QT$_c$ >0.42 seconds. Ventricular arrhythmias often respond to phenytoin 15-20 mg/kg (adults) with concurrent systemic alkalinization (sodium bicarbonate 0.5-2 mEq/kg I.V.). Arrhythmias unresponsive to this therapy may respond to lidocaine 1 mg/kg I.V. followed by a titrated infusion. Physostigmine (1-2 mg I.V. slowly for adults or 0.5 mg I.V. slowly for children) may be indicated in reversing cardiac arrhythmias that are due to vagal blockade or for anticholinergic effects, but should only be used as a last measure in life-threatening situations. Seizures usually respond to diazepam I.V. boluses (5-10 mg for adults up to 30 mg or 0.25-0.4 mg/kg/dose for children up to 10 mg/dose). If seizures are unresponsive or recur, phenytoin or phenobarbital may be required.

Drug Interactions CYP1A2, 2C9, 2C18, 2C19, 2D6, and 3A3/4 enzyme substrate

Decreased effect: Phenobarbital may increase the metabolism of amitriptyline; amitriptyline blocks the uptake of guanethidine and thus prevents the hypotensive effect of guanethidine

Increased toxicity: Clonidine → hypertensive crisis; amitriptyline may be additive with or may potentiate the action of other CNS depressants such as sedatives or hypnotics; with MAO inhibitors, hyperpyrexia, hypertension, tachycardia, confusion, seizures, and **deaths have been reported**; amitriptyline may increase the prothrombin time in patients stabilized on warfarin; amitriptyline potentiates the pressor and cardiac effects of sympathomimetic agents such as isoproterenol, epinephrine, etc; cimetidine and methylphenidate may decrease the metabolism of amitriptyline; additive anticholinergic effects seen with other anticholinergic agents

Stability Protect injection and Elavil® 10 mg tablets from light

Mechanism of Action Increases the synaptic concentration of serotonin and/or norepinephrine in the central nervous system by inhibition of their reuptake by the presynaptic neuronal membrane

Pharmacodynamics/Kinetics

Onset of therapeutic effect: 7-21 days

Desired therapeutic effect (for depression) may take as long as 3-4 weeks, at that point dosage should be reduced to lowest effective level

When used for migraine headache prophylaxis, therapeutic effect may take as long as 6 weeks; a higher dosage may be required in a heavy smoker, because of increased metabolism

Distribution: Crosses placenta; enters breast milk

(Continued)

Amitriptyline (Continued)

Metabolism: In the liver to nortriptyline (active), hydroxy derivatives, and conjugated derivatives; metabolism may be impaired in the elderly

Half-life: Adults: 9-25 hours (15-hour average)

Time to peak serum concentration: Within 4 hours

Elimination: Renal excretion of 18% as unchanged drug; small amounts eliminated in feces by bile

Usual Dosage

Children: Pain management: Oral: Initial: 0.1 mg/kg at bedtime, may advance as tolerated over 2-3 weeks to 0.5-2 mg/day at bedtime

Adolescents: Oral: Initial: 25-50 mg/day; may administer in divided doses; increase gradually to 100 mg/day in divided doses

Adults:
Oral: 30-100 mg/day single dose at bedtime or in divided doses; dose may be gradually increased up to 300 mg/day; once symptoms are controlled, decrease gradually to lowest effective dose

I.M.: 20-30 mg 4 times/day

Dosing interval in hepatic impairment: Use with caution and monitor plasma levels and patient response

Hemodialysis: Nondialyzable

Dietary Considerations Alcohol: Additive CNS effects, avoid use

Monitoring Parameters Monitor blood pressure and pulse rate prior to and during initial therapy; evaluate mental status; monitor weight

Reference Range Therapeutic: Amitriptyline and nortriptyline 100-250 ng/mL (SI: 360-900 nmol/L); nortriptyline 50-150 ng/mL (SI: 190-570 nmol/L); Toxic: >0.5 µg/mL; plasma levels do not always correlate with clinical effectiveness

Test Interactions ↑ glucose

Patient Information Avoid alcohol ingestion; do not discontinue medication abruptly; may cause urine to turn blue-green; may cause drowsiness; full effect may not occur for 3-6 weeks; dry mouth may be helped by sips of water, sugarless gum, or hard candy

Nursing Implications May increase appetite and possibly a craving for sweets

Dosage Forms

Injection, as hydrochloride: 10 mg/mL (10 mL)

Tablet, as hydrochloride: 10 mg, 25 mg, 50 mg, 75 mg, 100 mg, 150 mg

Amitriptyline and Chlordiazepoxide

(a mee TRIP ti leen & klor dye az e POKS ide)

U.S. Brand Names Limbitrol® DS 10-25

Therapeutic Category Antidepressant, Tricyclic

Dosage Forms Tablet:

5-12.5: Amitriptyline hydrochloride 12.5 mg and chlordiazepoxide 5 mg

10-25: Amitriptyline hydrochloride 25 mg and chlordiazepoxide 10 mg

Amitriptyline and Perphenazine (a mee TRIP ti leen & per FEN a zeen)

U.S. Brand Names Etrafon®; Triavil®

Therapeutic Category Antidepressant/Phenothiazine

Dosage Forms Tablet:

2-10: Amitriptyline hydrochloride 10 mg and perphenazine 2 mg

4-10: Amitriptyline hydrochloride 10 mg and perphenazine 4 mg

2-25: Amitriptyline hydrochloride 25 mg and perphenazine 2 mg

4-25: Amitriptyline hydrochloride 25 mg and perphenazine 4 mg

4-50: Amitriptyline hydrochloride 50 mg and perphenazine 4 mg

♦ **Amitriptyline Hydrochloride** see Amitriptyline on page 62

Amlexanox (am LEKS an oks)

U.S. Brand Names Aphthasol™

Therapeutic Category Anti-inflammatory Agent, Locally Applied

Use Treatment of aphthous ulcers (ie, canker sores); has been investigated in many allergic disorders

Pregnancy Risk Factor B

Pregnancy/Breast-Feeding Implications Due to lack of data, avoid use in pregnancy or lactation, if possible

Contraindications Hypersensitivity to amlexanox or components

Warnings/Precautions Discontinue therapy if rash or contact mucositis develops

Adverse Reactions

1% to 2%:
Dermatologic: Allergic contact dermatitis
Gastrointestinal: Oral irritation

<1%: Contact mucositis

Mechanism of Action As a benzopyrano-bipyridine carboxylic acid derivative, amlexanox has anti-inflammatory and antiallergic properties; it inhibits chemical mediatory release of the slow-reacting substance of anaphylaxis (SRS-A) and may have antagonistic effect son interleukin-3

Pharmacodynamics/Kinetics

Absorption: Systemic absorption with swallowing of topical application of oral paste

Metabolism: Metabolized to hydroxylated and conjugated product

Half-life: 3.5 hours

Time to peak serum concentration: 2 hours
Elimination: 17% excreted unchanged
Usual Dosage Administer (0.5 cm - ¼") directly on ulcers 4 times/day following oral hygiene, after meals, and at bedtime
Patient Information Apply as soon as possible and continue 4 times/day (after meals and at bedtime); wash hands after use; contact physician if no reduction in pain occurs within 10 days
Dosage Forms Paste: 5% (5 g)

Amlodipine (am LOE di peen)
Related Information
  Calcium Channel Blockers Comparison *on page 1315*
U.S. Brand Names Norvasc®
Therapeutic Category Antihypertensive Agent; Calcium Channel Blocker
Use Treatment of hypertension and angina (chronic stable or Prinzmetal's) with or without other therapy
Pregnancy Risk Factor C
Pregnancy/Breast-Feeding Implications Teratogenic and embryotoxic effects have been demonstrated in small animals. No well controlled studies have been conducted in pregnant women. Use in pregnancy only when clearly needed and when the benefits outweigh the potential hazard to the fetus.

Clinical effects on the fetus: No data on crossing the placenta
Breast-feeding/lactation: No data on crossing into breast milk
Contraindications Hypersensitivity
Warnings/Precautions Use with caution and titrate dosages for patients with impaired renal or hepatic function; use caution when treating patients with congestive heart failure, sick-sinus syndrome, severe left ventricular dysfunction, hypertrophic cardiomyopathy (especially obstructive), concomitant therapy with beta-blockers or digoxin, edema, or increased intracranial pressure with cranial tumors; do not abruptly withdraw (may cause chest pain); elderly may experience hypotension and constipation more readily.
Adverse Reactions
  >10%: Cardiovascular: Peripheral edema (1.8%-14.6% dose-related)
  1% to 10%:
    Cardiovascular: Flushing, palpitations
    Central nervous system: Headache, fatigue, dizziness, somnolence (1% to 2%)
    Dermatologic: Dermatitis, rash (1% to 2%); pruritus, urticaria (1% to 2%)
    Endocrine & metabolic: Sexual dysfunction (1% to 2%)
    Gastrointestinal: Nausea, abdominal pain (1% to 2%)
    Respiratory: Shortness of breath (1% to 2%)
    Neuromuscular & skeletal: Muscle cramps (1% to 2%)
  <1%: Hypotension, bradycardia, arrhythmias, abnormal EKG, ventricular extrasystoles, syncope, tachycardia, nervousness, psychiatric disturbances, insomnia, malaise, alopecia, petechiae, weight gain, anorexia, diarrhea, constipation, vomiting, xerostomia, flatulence, micturition disorder, joint stiffness, weakness, paresthesia, tremor, tinnitus, nasal congestion, cough, epistaxis, diaphoresis
Overdosage/Toxicology The primary cardiac symptoms of calcium blocker overdose includes hypotension and bradycardia. The hypotension is caused by peripheral vasodilation, myocardial depression, and bradycardia. Bradycardia results from sinus bradycardia, second- or third-degree atrioventricular block, or sinus arrest with junctional rhythm. Intraventricular conduction is usually not affected so QRS duration is normal (verapamil does prolong the P-R interval and bepridil prolongs the Q-T and may cause ventricular arrhythmias, including torsade de pointes).

The noncardiac symptoms include confusion, stupor, nausea, vomiting, metabolic acidosis, and hyperglycemia. Following initial gastric decontamination, if possible, repeated calcium administration may promptly reverse the depressed cardiac contractility (but not sinus node depression or peripheral vasodilation); glucagon, epinephrine, and amrinone may treat refractory hypotension; glucagon and epinephrine also increase the heart rate (outside the U.S., 4-aminopyridine may be available as an antidote); dialysis and hemoperfusion are not effective in enhancing elimination although repeat-dose activated charcoal may serve as an adjunct with sustained-release preparations.

In a few reported cases, overdose with calcium channel blockers has been associated with hypotension and bradycardia, initially refractory to atropine but becoming more responsive to this agent when larger doses (approaching 1 gram per hour for more than 24 hours) of calcium chloride was administered.
Drug Interactions CYP3A3/4 enzyme substrate
  Increased effect:
    Amlodipine and benazepril may increase hypotensive effect
    Amlodipine and cyclosporine may increase cyclosporine levels
    Beta-blockers in combination with calcium antagonists may result in increased cardiac depression
    Severe hypotension or increased fluid volume requirements have occurred with fentanyl and calcium blockers
Mechanism of Action Inhibits calcium ion from entering the "slow channels" or select voltage-sensitive areas of vascular smooth muscle and myocardium during depolarization, producing a relaxation of coronary vascular smooth muscle and coronary vasodilation; increases myocardial oxygen delivery in patients with vasospastic angina
Pharmacodynamics/Kinetics
  Onset of action: 30-50 minutes
  (Continued)

Amlodipine *(Continued)*

Peak effect: 6-12 hours

Duration: 24 hours

Absorption: Oral: Well absorbed

Protein binding: 93%

Metabolism: Hepatic, >90% to inactive compound

Bioavailability: 64% to 90%

Half-life: 30-50 hours

Elimination: Metabolite and parent drug excreted renally

Usual Dosage Adults: Oral:

Hypertension: Initial dose: 2.5-5 mg once daily; usual dose: 5 mg once daily; maximum dose: 10 mg once daily; in general, titrate in 2.5 mg increments over 7-14 days

Angina: Usual dose: 10 mg; use lower doses for elderly or those with hepatic insufficiency (eg, 2.5-5 mg)

Dialysis: Hemodialysis and peritoneal dialysis does not enhance elimination; supplemental dose is not necessary

Dosage adjustment in hepatic impairment: 2.5 mg once daily

Patient Information Do not discontinue abruptly; report any dizziness, shortness of breath, palpitations, or edema

Additional Information Although there is some initial data which may show increased risk of myocardial infarction following treatment of hypertension with calcium antagonists, controlled trials (eg, ALL-HAT) are ongoing to examine the long-term effects of not only calcium antagonists but other antihypertensives in preventing heart disease. Until these studies are completed, patients taking calcium antagonists should be encouraged to continue with prescribed antihypertensive regimens, although a switch from high-dose, short-acting agents to sustained release products may be warranted.

Dosage Forms Tablet: 2.5 mg, 5 mg, 10 mg

Extemporaneous Preparations A 1 mg/mL suspension was stable for 91 days when refrigerated or 56 days when kept at room temperature when compounded as follows:

Triturate fifty 5 mg tablets in a mortar, reduce to a fine powder, then add a small amount of one of the following vehicles to make a paste; then add the remaining vehicle in small quantities while mixing:

Vehicle 1. Methylcellulose 1% (125 mL) and Simple Syrup N.F. (125 mL) mixed together in a graduate, **or**

Vehicle 2. Ora-Sweet® (125 mL) and Ora-Plus® (125 mL) mixed together in a graduate

Shake well before using and keep in refrigerator

Nahata MC, Morosco RS, and Hipple TF, *Stability of Amlodipine in Two Liquid Dosage Forms*, American Society of Health System Pharmacists Midyear Meeting, December 7-11, 1997.

Amlodipine and Benazepril *(am LOE di peen & ben AY ze pril)*

U.S. Brand Names Lotrel®

Therapeutic Category Angiotensin-Converting Enzyme (ACE) Inhibitor Combination; Antihypertensive Agent, Combination

Dosage Forms Capsule:

Amlodipine 2.5 mg and benazepril hydrochloride 10 mg

Amlodipine 5 mg and benazepril hydrochloride 10 mg

Amlodipine 5 mg and benazepril hydrochloride 20 mg

♦ **Ammonapse** *see* Sodium Phenylbutyrate *on page 1070*

Ammonium Chloride *(a MOE nee um KLOR ide)*

Therapeutic Category Diuretic, Miscellaneous; Metabolic Alkalosis Agent; Urinary Acidifying Agent

Use Diuretic or systemic and urinary acidifying agent; treatment of hypochloremic states

Pregnancy Risk Factor C

Contraindications Severe hepatic and renal dysfunction; patients with primary respiratory acidosis

Warnings/Precautions Safety and efficacy not established in children, use with caution in infants

Adverse Reactions Percentage unknown: Mental confusion, coma, headache (with large doses), rash, metabolic acidosis, hyperchloremia, hypokalemia (with large doses), gastric irritation, nausea, vomiting, pain at site of injection, hyperventilation (with large doses), may increase ammonia, may decrease potassium and sodium

Overdosage/Toxicology

Symptoms of overdose include acidosis, headache, drowsiness, confusion, hyperventilation, hypokalemia

Administer sodium bicarbonate or lactate to treat acidosis; supplemental potassium for hypokalemia

Mechanism of Action Increases acidity by increasing free hydrogen ion concentration

Pharmacodynamics/Kinetics

Absorption: Rapid from GI tract, complete within 3-6 hours

Metabolism: In the liver

Elimination: In urine

Usual Dosage Metabolic alkalosis: The following equations represent different methods of correction utilizing either the serum HCO_3^-, the serum chloride, or the base excess

Dosing of mEq NH₄Cl via the chloride-deficit method (hypochloremia):

Dose of mEq NH₄Cl = [0.2 L/kg x body weight (kg)] x [103 - observed serum chloride]; administer 100% of dose over 12 hours, then re-evaluate

Note: 0.2 L/kg is the estimated chloride space and 103 is the average normal serum chloride concentration

Dosing of mEq NH₄Cl via the bicarbonate-excess method (refractory hypochloremic metabolic alkalosis):

Dose of NH₄Cl = [0.5 L/kg x body weight (kg)] x (observed serum HCO₃⁻ - 24); administer 50% of dose over 12 hours, then re-evaluate

Note: 0.5 L/kg is the estimated bicarbonate space and 24 is the average normal serum bicarbonate concentration

Dosing of mEq NH₄Cl via the base-excess method:

Dose of NH₄Cl = [0.3 L/kg x body weight (kg)] x measured base excess (mEq/L); administer 50% of dose over 12 hours, then re-evaluate

Note: 0.3 L/kg is the estimated extracellular bicarbonate and base excess is measured by the chemistry lab and reported with arterial blood gases

These equations will yield different requirements of ammonium chloride

Equation #1 is inappropriate to use if the patient has severe metabolic alkalosis without hypochloremia or if the patient has uremia

Equation #3 is the most useful for the first estimation of ammonium chloride dosage

Children: Urinary acidifying agents: Oral, I.V.: 75 mg/kg/day in 4 divided doses; maximum daily dose: 6 g

Adults: Urinary acidifying agent/diuretic:

Oral: 1-2 g every 4-6 hours

I.V.: 1.5 g/dose every 6 hours

Administration Rapid I.V. injection may increase the likelihood of ammonia toxicity; rate should not exceed 1 mEq/kg/hour; 26.75% solution must be diluted prior to administration

Patient Information Take oral dose after meals

Dosage Forms

Injection: 26.75% [5 mEq/mL] (20 mL)

Tablet: 500 mg

Tablet, enteric coated: 486 mg

Amobarbital (am oh BAR bi tal)

U.S. Brand Names Amytal®

Canadian Brand Names Amobarbital; Novambarb®

Synonyms Amylobarbitone

Therapeutic Category Anticonvulsant; Barbiturate; Hypnotic; Sedative

Use

Oral: Hypnotic in short-term treatment of insomnia, to reduce anxiety and provide sedation preoperatively

I.M., I.V.: Control status epilepticus or acute seizure episodes; used in catatonic, negativistic, or manic reactions and in "Amytal® Interviewing" for narcoanalysis

Restrictions C-II

Pregnancy Risk Factor D

Contraindications Marked liver function impairment or latent porphyria; hypersensitivity to barbiturates; do not administer in presence of chronic or acute pain

Warnings/Precautions Safety has not been established in children <6 years of age; potential for drug dependency exists; avoid alcoholic beverages; use with caution in patients with CHF, hepatic or renal impairment, hypovolemic shock; when administered I.V., respiratory depression and hypotension are possible, have equipment and personnel available; this I.V. medication should be given only to hospitalized patients

Adverse Reactions

>10%:

Central nervous system: Dizziness, lightheadedness, "hangover" effect, drowsiness, CNS depression, fever

Local: Pain at injection site

1% to 10%:

Central nervous system: Confusion, mental depression, unusual excitement, nervousness, faint feeling, headache, insomnia, nightmares

Gastrointestinal: Nausea, vomiting, constipation

<1%: Hypotension, hallucinations, rash, exfoliative dermatitis, urticaria, Stevens-Johnson syndrome, agranulocytosis, megaloblastic anemia, thrombocytopenia, thrombophlebitis, respiratory depression, apnea, laryngospasm

Overdosage/Toxicology

Symptoms of overdose include unsteady gait, slurred speech, confusion, jaundice, hypothermia, fever, hypotension

If hypotension occurs, administer I.V. fluids and place the patient in the Trendelenburg position. If unresponsive, an I.V. vasopressor (eg, dopamine, epinephrine) may be required. Forced alkaline diuresis is of no value in the treatment of intoxications with short-acting barbiturates. Charcoal hemoperfusion or hemodialysis may be useful in the harder to treat intoxications, especially in the presence of very high serum barbiturate levels.

Drug Interactions

Decreased effect: Cimetidine's tricyclic antidepressants and doxycycline's efficacy may be reduced with amobarbital

Increased toxicity when combined with other CNS depressants or antidepressants, respiratory and CNS depression may be additive

(Continued)

Amobarbital *(Continued)*

Stability Hydrolyzes when exposed to air; use contents of vial within 30 minutes after constitution; use only clear solution

Mechanism of Action Interferes with transmission of impulses from the thalamus to the cortex of the brain resulting in an imbalance in central inhibitory and facilitatory mechanisms

Pharmacodynamics/Kinetics
Onset of action: Oral: Within 1 hour; I.V.: Within 5 minutes
Distribution: Readily crosses the placenta; small amounts appear in breast milk
Metabolism: Chiefly in the liver by microsomal enzymes
Half-life, biphasic: Initial: 40 minutes; Terminal: 20 hours

Usual Dosage
Children: Oral:
Sedation: 6 mg/kg/day divided every 6-8 hours
Insomnia: 2 mg/kg or 70 mg/m²/day in 4 equally divided doses
Hypnotic: 2-3 mg/kg
Adults:
Insomnia: Oral: 65-200 mg at bedtime
Sedation: Oral: 30-50 mg 2-3 times/day
Preanesthetic: Oral: 200 mg 1-2 hours before surgery
Hypnotic:
Oral: 65-200 mg at bedtime
I.M., I.V.: 65-500 mg, should not exceed 500 mg I.M. or 1000 mg I.V.

Dietary Considerations Alcohol: Avoid use

Administration I.M. injection should be deep to prevent against pain, sterile abscess, and sloughing

Monitoring Parameters Vital signs should be monitored during injection and for several hours after administration

Reference Range
Therapeutic: 1-5 µg/mL (SI: 4-22 µmol/L)
Toxic: >10 µg/mL (SI: >44 µmol/L)
Lethal: >50 µg/mL

Test Interactions ↑ ammonia (B); ↓ bilirubin (S)

Patient Information Avoid alcohol ingestion; physical dependency may result when used for an extended period of time (1-3 months); do not try to get out of bed without assistance, will cause drowsiness

Nursing Implications Raise bed rails at night

Dosage Forms
Capsule, as sodium: 65 mg, 200 mg
Injection, as sodium: 500 mg
Tablet: 30 mg, 50 mg, 100 mg

Amobarbital and Secobarbital *(am oh BAR bi tal & see koe BAR bi tal)*
U.S. Brand Names Tuinal®
Therapeutic Category Barbiturate
Dosage Forms Capsule:
100: Amobarbital sodium 50 mg and secobarbital sodium 50 mg
200: Amobarbital sodium 100 mg and secobarbital sodium 100 mg

♦ **AMO Vitrax®** *see* Sodium Hyaluronate *on page 1069*

Amoxapine *(a MOKS a peen)*
Related Information
Antidepressant Agents Comparison *on page 1301*
U.S. Brand Names Asendin®
Therapeutic Category Antidepressant, Tricyclic
Use Treatment of neurotic and endogenous depression and mixed symptoms of anxiety and depression

Pregnancy Risk Factor C

Contraindications Hypersensitivity to amoxapine; cross-sensitivity with other tricyclics may occur; narrow-angle glaucoma; patients receiving MAO inhibitors within past 14 days

Warnings/Precautions Use with caution in patients with seizures, cardiac conduction disturbances, cardiovascular diseases, urinary retention, hyperthyroidism, or those receiving thyroid replacement; do not discontinue abruptly in patients receiving high doses chronically; tolerance develops in 1-3 months in some patients, close medical follow-up is essential

Adverse Reactions
>10%:
Central nervous system: Drowsiness
Gastrointestinal: Xerostomia, constipation, nausea, unpleasant taste, weight gain
1% to 10%:
Central nervous system: Dizziness, headache, confusion, nervousness, restlessness, insomnia, ataxia, excitement
Dermatologic: Edema, skin rash
Endocrine: Elevated prolactin levels
Gastrointestinal: Increased appetite
Neuromuscular & skeletal: Tremor, weakness

Ocular: Blurred vision

Miscellaneous: Diaphoresis

<1%: Hypotension, tachycardia, pallor, anxiety, seizures, neuroleptic malignant syndrome, tardive dyskinesia, photosensitivity, breast enlargement, galactorrhea, SIADH, increased or decreased libido, impotence, menstrual irregularity, painful ejaculation, epigastric distress, vomiting, flatulence, abdominal pain, abnormal taste, diarrhea, testicular edema, urinary retention, agranulocytosis, leukopenia, elevated liver enzymes, paresthesia, increased intraocular pressure, mydriasis, lacrimation, tinnitus, allergic reactions

Overdosage/Toxicology

Symptoms of overdose include grand mal convulsions, acidosis, coma, renal failure

Following initiation of essential overdose management, toxic symptoms should be treated. Sodium bicarbonate is indicated when QRS interval is >0.10 seconds or QT$_c$ >0.42 seconds. Ventricular arrhythmias often respond to phenytoin 15-20 mg/kg (adults) with concurrent systemic alkalinization (sodium bicarbonate 0.5-2 mEq/kg I.V.). Arrhythmias unresponsive to this therapy may respond to lidocaine 1 mg/kg I.V. followed by a titrated infusion. Physostigmine (1-2 mg I.V. slowly for adults or 0.5 mg I.V. slowly for children) may be indicated in reversing cardiac arrhythmias that are due to vagal blockade or for anticholinergic effects, but should only be used as a last measure in life-threatening situations. Seizures usually respond to diazepam I.V. boluses (5-10 mg for adults up to 30 mg or 0.25-0.4 mg/kg/dose for children up to 10 mg/dose). If seizures are unresponsive or recur, phenytoin or phenobarbital may be required.

Drug Interactions

Decreased effect of clonidine, guanethidine

Increased effect of CNS depressants, adrenergic agents, anticholinergic agents

Increased toxicity of MAO inhibitors (hyperpyrexia, tachycardia, hypertension, seizures and death may occur); similar interactions as with other tricyclics may occur

Mechanism of Action Reduces the reuptake of serotonin and norepinephrine and blocks the response of dopamine receptors to dopamine

Pharmacodynamics/Kinetics

Onset of antidepressant effect: Usually occurs after 1-2 weeks

Absorption: Oral: Rapidly and well absorbed

Distribution: V$_d$: 0.9-1.2 L/kg; distributes into breast milk

Protein binding: 80%

Metabolism: Extensive in the liver

Half-life: Parent drug: 11-16 hours; Active metabolite (8-hydroxy): Adults: 30 hours

Time to peak serum concentration: Within 1-2 hours

Elimination: Excretion of metabolites and parent compound in urine

Usual Dosage Once symptoms are controlled, decrease gradually to lowest effective dose. Maintenance dose is usually given at bedtime to reduce daytime sedation. Oral:

Children: Not established in children <16 years of age

Adolescents: Initial: 25-50 mg/day; increase gradually to 100 mg/day; may administer as divided doses or as a single dose at bedtime

Adults: Initial: 25 mg 2-3 times/day, if tolerated, dosage may be increased to 100 mg 2-3 times/day; may be given in a single bedtime dose when dosage <300 mg/day

Elderly: Initial: 25 mg at bedtime increased by 25 mg weekly for outpatients and every 3 days for inpatients if tolerated; usual dose: 50-150 mg/day, but doses up to 300 mg may be necessary

Maximum daily dose:

Inpatient: 600 mg

Outpatient: 400 mg

Dietary Considerations Alcohol: Avoid use

Monitoring Parameters Monitor blood pressure and pulse rate prior to and during initial therapy evaluate mental status; monitor weight

Reference Range Therapeutic: Amoxapine: 20-100 ng/mL (SI: 64-319 nmol/L); 8-OH amoxapine: 150-400 ng/mL (SI: 478-1275 nmol/L); both: 200-500 ng/mL (SI: 637-1594 nmol/L)

Test Interactions ↑ glucose

Patient Information Dry mouth may be helped by sips of water, sugarless gum, or hard candy; avoid alcohol; very important to maintain established dosage regimen; photosensitivity to sunlight can occur, do not discontinue abruptly; full effect may not occur for 3-4 weeks; full dosage may be taken at bedtime to avoid daytime sedation

Nursing Implications May increase appetite and possibly a craving for sweets; recognize signs of neuroleptic malignant syndrome and tardive dyskinesia

Dosage Forms Tablet: 25 mg, 50 mg, 100 mg, 150 mg

Amoxicillin (a moks i SIL in)

Related Information

Animal and Human Bites Guidelines *on page 1399*

Antimicrobial Drugs of Choice *on page 1404*

Community-Acquired Pneumonia in Adults *on page 1419*

Helicobacter pylori Treatment *on page 1473*

Prevention of Bacterial Endocarditis *on page 1377*

Treatment of Sexually Transmitted Diseases *on page 1429*

U.S. Brand Names Amoxil®; Biomox®; Polymox®; Trimox®; Wymox®

Canadian Brand Names Apo®-Amoxi; Novamoxin®; Nu-Amoxi; Pro-Amox®

Synonyms Amoxicillin Trihydrate; Amoxycillin; p-Hydroxyampicillin

(Continued)

Amoxicillin *(Continued)*

Therapeutic Category Antibiotic, Penicillin

Use Treatment of otitis media, sinusitis, and infections caused by susceptible organisms involving the respiratory tract, skin, and urinary tract; prophylaxis of bacterial endocarditis in patients undergoing surgical or dental procedures; approved in combination for eradication of *H. pylori*

Pregnancy Risk Factor B

Contraindications Hypersensitivity to amoxicillin, penicillin, or any component

Warnings/Precautions In patients with renal impairment, doses and/or frequency of administration should be modified in response to the degree of renal impairment; a high percentage of patients with infectious mononucleosis have developed rash during therapy with amoxicillin; a low incidence of cross-allergy with other beta-lactams and cephalosporins exists

Adverse Reactions
1% to 10%:
Central nervous system: Fever
Dermatologic: Urticaria, rash
Miscellaneous: Allergic reactions (includes serum sickness, rash, angioedema, bronchospasm, hypotension, etc)
<1%: Seizures, anxiety, confusion, hallucinations, depression (with large doses or patients with renal dysfunction), nausea, vomiting, leukopenia, neutropenia, thrombocytopenia, jaundice, interstitial nephritis

Overdosage/Toxicology
Symptoms of penicillin overdose include neuromuscular hypersensitivity (agitation, hallucinations, asterixis, encephalopathy, confusion, and seizures) and electrolyte imbalance with potassium or sodium salts, especially in renal failure
Hemodialysis may be helpful to aid in the removal of the drug from the blood, otherwise most treatment is supportive or symptom directed

Drug Interactions
Decreased effect: Efficacy of oral contraceptives may be reduced
Increased effect: Disulfiram, probenecid may increase amoxicillin levels
Increased toxicity: Allopurinol theoretically has an additive potential for amoxicillin rash

Stability Oral suspension remains stable for 7 days at room temperature or 14 days if refrigerated; unit dose antibiotic oral syringes are stable for 48 hours

Mechanism of Action Inhibits bacterial cell wall synthesis by binding to one or more of the penicillin binding proteins (PBPs); which in turn inhibits the final transpeptidation step of peptidoglycan synthesis in bacterial cell walls, thus inhibiting cell wall biosynthesis. Bacteria eventually lyse due to ongoing activity of cell wall autolytic enzymes (autolysins and murein hydrolases) while cell wall assembly is arrested.

Pharmacodynamics/Kinetics
Absorption: Oral: Rapid and nearly complete; food does not interfere
Distribution: Widely distributed to most body fluids and bone; penetration into cells, eyes, and across normal meninges is poor
Protein binding: 17% to 20%
Ratio of CSF to blood: Normal meninges: <1%; Inflamed meninges: 8% to 90%
Metabolism: Partial
Half-life:
Neonates, full-term: 3.7 hours
Infants and Children: 1-2 hours
Adults with normal renal function: 0.7-1.4 hours
Patients with Cl_{cr} <10 mL/minute: 7-21 hours
Time to peak: 2 hours (capsule) and 1 hour (suspension)
Elimination: Renal excretion (80% as unchanged drug); lower in neonates

Usual Dosage Oral:
Children: 20-50 mg/kg/day in divided doses every 8 hours
Subacute bacterial endocarditis prophylaxis: 50 mg/kg 1 hour before procedure
Adults: 250-500 mg every 8 hours or 500-875 mg twice daily; maximum dose: 2-3 g/day
Endocarditis prophylaxis: 2 g 1 hour before procedure
Helicobacter pylori: 250-500 mg 3 times/day or 500-875 mg twice daily; clinically effective treatment regimens include triple therapy with amoxicillin or tetracycline, metronidazole, and bismuth subsalicylate; amoxicillin, metronidazole, and an H_2-receptor antagonist; amoxicillin, lansoprazole, and clarithromycin.
Dosing interval in renal impairment:
Cl_{cr} 10-50 mL/minute: Administer every 12 hours
Cl_{cr} <10 mL/minute: Administer every 24 hours
Dialysis: Moderately dialyzable (20% to 50%) by hemo- or peritoneal dialysis; approximately 50 mg of amoxicillin per liter of filtrate is removed by continuous arteriovenous or venovenous hemofiltration (CAVH); dose as per Cl_{cr} <10 mL/minute guidelines

Dietary Considerations Food: May be taken with food

Monitoring Parameters With prolonged therapy, monitor renal, hepatic, and hematologic function periodically; assess patient at beginning and throughout therapy for infection; monitor for signs of anaphylaxis during first dose

Test Interactions May interfere with urinary glucose tests using cupric sulfate (Benedict's solution, Clinitest®); may inactivate aminoglycosides *in vitro*

Patient Information Report diarrhea promptly; entire course of medication (10-14 days) should be taken to ensure eradication of organism; may interfere with oral contraceptives; females should report symptoms of vaginitis; pediatric drops may be placed on child's tongue or added to formula, milk, etc

Additional Information There is an increasing incidence of amoxicillin-resistant *H. influenzae* and *E. coli*; this should be taken into consideration when choosing treatment regimens

Dosage Forms

Capsule, as trihydrate: 250 mg, 500 mg

Powder for oral suspension, as trihydrate: 125 mg/5 mL (5 mL, 80 mL, 100 mL, 150 mL, 200 mL); 250 mg/5 mL (5 mL, 80 mL, 100 mL, 150 mL, 200 mL)

Powder for oral suspension, drops, as trihydrate: 50 mg/mL (15 mL, 30 mL)

Tablet, chewable, as trihydrate: 125 mg, 250 mg

Tablet, film coated: 500 mg, 875 mg

Amoxicillin and Clavulanate Potassium

(a moks i SIL in & klav yoo LAN ate poe TASS ee um)

Related Information

Animal and Human Bites Guidelines *on page 1399*

Antimicrobial Drugs of Choice *on page 1404*

Community-Acquired Pneumonia in Adults *on page 1419*

U.S. Brand Names Augmentin®

Canadian Brand Names Clavulin®

Synonyms Amoxicillin and Clavulanic Acid

Therapeutic Category Antibiotic, Penicillin; Antibiotic, Penicillin & Beta-lactamase Inhibitor

Use Treatment of otitis media, sinusitis, and infections caused by susceptible organisms involving the lower respiratory tract, skin and skin structure, and urinary tract; spectrum same as amoxicillin with additional coverage of beta-lactamase producing *B. catarrhalis*, *H. influenzae*, *N. gonorrhoeae*, and *S. aureus* (not MRSA).

Pregnancy Risk Factor B

Contraindications Known hypersensitivity to amoxicillin, clavulanic acid, or penicillin; concomitant use of disulfiram

Warnings/Precautions In patients with renal impairment, doses and/or frequency of administration should be modified in response to the degree of renal impairment; high percentage of patients with infectious mononucleosis have developed rash during therapy; a low incidence of cross-allergy with cephalosporins exists; incidence of diarrhea is higher than with amoxicillin alone. Hepatic dysfunction, although rare, is more common in elderly and/or males, and occurs more frequently with prolonged treatment.

Adverse Reactions

1% to 10%:

Dermatologic: Rash, urticaria

Gastrointestinal: Nausea, vomiting, diarrhea

Genitourinary: Vaginitis

<1%: Headache, abdominal discomfort, flatulence

Overdosage/Toxicology

Symptoms of penicillin overdose include neuromuscular hypersensitivity (agitation, hallucinations, asterixis, encephalopathy, confusion, and seizures) and electrolyte imbalance with potassium or sodium salts, especially in renal failure

Hemodialysis may be helpful to aid in the removal of the drug from the blood, otherwise most treatment is supportive or symptom directed

Drug Interactions

Decreased effect: Efficacy of oral contraceptives may be reduced

Increased effect: Disulfiram, probenecid may increase amoxicillin levels, increased effect of anticoagulants

Increased toxicity: Allopurinol theoretically has an additive potential for amoxicillin rash

Stability Discard unused suspension after 10 days; reconstituted oral suspension should be kept in refrigerator; unit dose antibiotic oral syringes are stable for 48 hours

Mechanism of Action Clavulanic acid binds and inhibits beta-lactamases that inactivate amoxicillin resulting in amoxicillin having an expanded spectrum of activity. Amoxicillin inhibits bacterial cell wall synthesis by binding to one or more of the penicillin binding proteins (PBPs); which in turn inhibits the final transpeptidation step of peptidoglycan synthesis in bacterial cell walls, thus inhibiting cell wall biosynthesis. Bacteria eventually lyse due to ongoing activity of cell wall autolytic enzymes (autolysins and murein hydrolases) while cell wall assembly is arrested.

Pharmacodynamics/Kinetics Amoxicillin pharmacokinetics are not affected by clavulanic acid

Absorption: Oral: Rapid and nearly complete; food does not interfere

Distribution: Both distribute into pleural fluids, lungs, and peritoneal fluid; high urine concentrations are attained; also into synovial fluid, liver, prostate, muscle, and gallbladder; penetrates into middle ear effusions, maxillary sinus secretions, tonsils, sputum, and bronchial secretions; crosses the placenta; low concentrations occur in breast milk

Protein binding: 17% to 20%

Metabolism: Partial (Clavulanic acid is hepatically metabolized)

Half-life:

Neonates, full-term: 3.7 hours

Infants and Children: 1-2 hours

Adults with normal renal function: ~1 hour for both agents

Patients with Cl_{cr} <10 mL/minute: 7-21 hours

Time to peak: 2 hours (capsule) and 1 hour (suspension)

Elimination: Amoxicillin excreted primarily (80%) unchanged and clavulanic acid is excreted 30% to 40% unchanged in the urine (lower in neonates)

(Continued)

Amoxicillin and Clavulanate Potassium *(Continued)*

Usual Dosage Oral:

Children ≤40 kg: 20-40 mg (amoxicillin)/kg/day in divided doses every 8 hours or 45 mg/kg in divided doses every 12 hours

Children >40 kg and Adults: 250-500 mg every 8 hours or 875 mg every 12 hours

Note: Augmentin® 200 suspension or chewable tablets 200 mg dosed every 12 hours is considered equivalent to Augmentin® "125" dosed every 8 hours; Augmentin® 400 suspension and chewable tablets may be similarly dosed every 12 hours and are equivalent to Augmentin® "250" every 8 hours

Dosing interval in renal impairment:

Cl$_{cr}$ 10-30 mL/minute: Administer every 12 hours

Cl$_{cr}$ <10 mL/minute: Administer every 24 hours

Hemodialysis: Moderately dialyzable (20% to 50%)

Amoxicillin/clavulanic acid: Administer dose after dialysis

Peritoneal dialysis: Moderately dialyzable (20% to 50%)

Amoxicillin: Administer 250 mg every 12 hours

Clavulanic acid: Dose for Cl$_{cr}$ <10 mL/minute

Continuous arteriovenous or venovenous hemofiltration (CAVH) effects:

Amoxicillin: ~50 mg of amoxicillin/L of filtrate is removed

Clavulanic acid: Dose for Cl$_{cr}$ <10 mL/minute

Monitoring Parameters Assess patient at beginning and throughout therapy for infection; with prolonged therapy, monitor renal, hepatic, and hematologic function periodically; monitor for signs of anaphylaxis during first dose

Test Interactions May interfere with urinary glucose tests using cupric sulfate (Benedict's solution, Clinitest®); may inactivate aminoglycosides *in vitro*

Patient Information Report diarrhea promptly; entire course of medication (10-14 days) should be taken to ensure eradication of organism; females should report onset of symptoms of candidal vaginitis; may interfere with the effects of oral contraceptives

Nursing Implications Two 250 mg tablets are not equivalent to a 500 mg tablet (both tablet sizes contain equivalent clavulanate); potassium content: 0.16 mEq of potassium per 31.25 mg of clavulanic acid

Dosage Forms

Suspension, oral:

125 (banana flavor): Amoxicillin trihydrate 125 mg and clavulanate potassium 31.25 mg per 5 mL (75 mL, 150 mL)

200: Amoxicillin 200 mg and clavulanate potassium 28.5 mg per 5 mL (50 mL, 75 mL, 100 mL)

250 (orange flavor): Amoxicillin trihydrate 250 mg and clavulanate potassium 62.5 mg per 5 mL (75 mL, 150 mL)

400: Amoxicillin 400 mg and clavulanate potassium 57 mg per 5 mL (50 mL, 75 mL, 100 mL)

Tablet:

250: Amoxicillin trihydrate 250 mg and clavulanate potassium 125 mg

500: Amoxicillin trihydrate 500 mg and clavulanate potassium 125 mg

875: Amoxicillin trihydrate 875 mg and clavulanate potassium 125 mg

Tablet, chewable:

125: Amoxicillin trihydrate 125 mg and clavulanate potassium 31.25 mg

200: Amoxicillin trihydrate 200 mg and clavulanate potassium 28.5 mg

250: Amoxicillin trihydrate 250 mg and clavulanate potassium 62.5 mg

400: Amoxicillin trihydrate 400 mg and clavulanate potassium 57 mg

- ◆ **Amoxicillin and Clavulanic Acid** *see* Amoxicillin and Clavulanate Potassium *on previous page*
- ◆ **Amoxicillin Trihydrate** *see* Amoxicillin *on page 69*
- ◆ **Amoxil®** *see* Amoxicillin *on page 69*
- ◆ **Amoxycillin** *see* Amoxicillin *on page 69*

Amphetamine *(am FET a meen)*

Related Information

Depression Disorders and Treatments *on page 1465*

Synonyms Amphetamine Sulfate; Racemic Amphetamine Sulfate

Therapeutic Category Amphetamine; Anorexiant; Central Nervous System Stimulant, Amphetamine

Use Treatment of narcolepsy; exogenous obesity; abnormal behavioral syndrome in children (minimal brain dysfunction); attention deficit/hyperactivity disorder (ADHD)

Restrictions C-II

Pregnancy Risk Factor C

Contraindications Patients with advanced arteriosclerosis, symptomatic cardiovascular disease, moderate to severe hypertension, hyperthyroidism, glaucoma, hypersensitivity, diabetes mellitus, agitated states, patients with a history of drug abuse, and during or within 14 days following MAO inhibitor therapy. Stimulant medications are contraindicated for use in children with attention deficit/hyperactivity disorders and concomitant Tourette's syndrome or tics.

Warnings/Precautions Cardiovascular disease, nephritis, angina pectoris, hypertension, glaucoma, patients with a history of drug abuse, known hypersensitivity to amphetamine

Adverse Reactions
>10%:
  Cardiovascular: Arrhythmia
  Central nervous system: False feeling of well being, nervousness, restlessness, insomnia
1% to 10%:
  Cardiovascular: Hypertension
  Central nervous system: Mood or mental changes, dizziness, lightheadedness, headache
  Endocrine & metabolic: Changes in libido
  Gastrointestinal: Diarrhea, nausea, vomiting, stomach cramps, constipation, anorexia, weight loss, xerostomia
  Ocular: Blurred vision
  Miscellaneous: Diaphoresis (increased)
<1%: Chest pain, CNS stimulation (severe), Tourette's syndrome, hyperthermia, seizures, paranoia, rash, urticaria, tolerance and withdrawal with prolonged use

Overdosage/Toxicology There is no specific antidote for amphetamine intoxication and the bulk of the treatment is supportive

Hyperactivity and agitation usually respond to reduced sensory input; however, with extreme agitation, haloperidol (2-5 mg I.M. for adults) may be required. Hyperthermia is best treated with external cooling measures, or when severe or unresponsive, muscle paralysis with pancuronium may be needed. Hypertension is usually transient and generally does not require treatment unless severe. For diastolic blood pressures >110 mm Hg, a nitroprusside infusion should be initiated. Seizures usually respond to diazepam IVP and/or phenytoin maintenance regimens.

Drug Interactions CYP2D6 enzyme substrate
Increased toxicity of MAO inhibitors (hyperpyrexia, hypertension, arrhythmias, seizures, cerebral hemorrhage, and death has occurred)

Mechanism of Action The amphetamines are noncatechol sympathomimetic amines with pharmacologic actions similar to ephedrine. They require breakdown by monoamine oxidase for inactivation; produce central nervous system and respiratory stimulation, a pressor response, mydriasis, bronchodilation, and contraction of the urinary sphincter; thought to have a direct effect on both alpha- and beta-receptor sites in the peripheral system, as well as release stores of norepinephrine in adrenergic nerve terminals. The central nervous system action is thought to occur in the cerebral cortex and reticular activating system. The anorexigenic effect is probably secondary to the CNS-stimulating effect; the site of action is probably the hypothalamic feeding center.

Usual Dosage Oral:
Narcolepsy:
  Children:
    6-12 years: 5 mg/day, increase by 5 mg at weekly intervals
    >12 years: 10 mg/day, increase by 10 mg at weekly intervals
  Adults: 5-60 mg/day in 2-3 divided doses
Attention deficit/hyperactivity disorder: Children:
    3-5 years: 2.5 mg/day, increase by 2.5 mg at weekly intervals
    >6 years: 5 mg/day, increase by 5 mg at weekly intervals not to exceed 40 mg/day
Short-term adjunct to exogenous obesity: Children >12 years and Adults: 10 mg or 15 mg long-acting capsule daily, up to 30 mg/day; or 5-30 mg/day in divided doses (immediate release tablets only)

Reference Range Therapeutic: 20-30 ng/mL; Toxic: >200 ng/mL
Patient Information Take during day to avoid insomnia; do not discontinue abruptly, may cause physical and psychological dependence with prolonged use
Nursing Implications Monitor CNS, dose should not be given in evening or at bedtime
Dosage Forms Tablet, as sulfate: 5 mg, 10 mg

◆ **Amphetamine Sulfate** see Amphetamine on previous page
◆ **Amphocin®** see Amphotericin B, Conventional on next page
◆ **Amphojel® [OTC]** see Aluminum Hydroxide on page 50
◆ **Amphotec®** see Amphotericin B Cholesteryl Sulfate Complex on this page

Amphotericin B Cholesteryl Sulfate Complex
(am foe TER i sin bee kole LES te ril SUL fate KOM plecks)
U.S. Brand Names Amphotec®
Synonyms ABCD; Amphotericin B Colloidal Dispersion
Therapeutic Category Antifungal Agent, Systemic
Use Treatment of invasive aspergillosis in patients who have failed amphotericin B deoxycholate treatment, or who have renal impairment or experience unacceptable toxicity which precludes treatment with amphotericin B deoxycholate in effective doses.
Pregnancy Risk Factor B
Pregnancy/Breast-Feeding Implications Breast-feeding/lactation: Due to limited data, consider discontinuing nursing during therapy
Contraindications Hypersensitivity to amphotericin B or its components
Warnings/Precautions Anaphylaxis has been reported with other amphotericin B-containing drugs. Facilities for cardiopulmonary resuscitation should be available during administration due to the possibility of anaphylactic reaction. If severe respiratory distress occurs, the infusion should be immediately discontinued. During the initial dosing, the drug should be administered under close clinical observation. Infusion reactions, sometimes, severe, usually subside with continued therapy - manage with decreased rate of infusion and pretreatment with antihistamines/corticosteroids;
(Continued)

Amphotericin B Cholesteryl Sulfate Complex *(Continued)*

pulmonary reactions may occur in neutropenic patients receiving leukocyte transfusions; separation of the infusions as much as possible is advised.

Adverse Reactions
>10%: Central nervous system: Chills, fever
1% to 10%:
    Cardiovascular: Hypotension, tachycardia
    Central nervous system: Headache
    Dermatologic: Rash
    Endocrine & metabolic: Hypokalemia, hypomagnesemia
    Gastrointestinal: Nausea, diarrhea, abdominal pain
    Hematologic: Thrombocytopenia
    Hepatic: LFT change
    Neuromuscular & skeletal: Rigors
    Renal: Elevated creatinine
    Respiratory: Dyspnea

Overdosage/Toxicology
Symptoms of overdose include renal dysfunction, anemia, thrombocytopenia, granulocytopenia, fever, nausea, vomiting
Treatment is supportive

Drug Interactions
Increased nephrotoxicity: Aminoglycosides, cyclosporine, other nephrotoxic drugs
Potentiation of hypokalemia: Corticosteroids, corticotropin
Increased digitalis and neuromuscular blocking agent toxicity due to hypokalemia
Decreased effect: Pharmacologic antagonism may occur with azole antifungal agents (eg, miconazole, ketoconazole)
Pulmonary toxicity has occurred with concomitant administration of amphotericin B and leukocyte transfusions

Stability
Store intact vials under refrigeration.
Reconstitute 50 mg and 100 mg vials with 10 mL and 20 mL of SWI, respectively. The reconstituted vials contain 5 mg/mL of amphotericin B. Shake the vial gently by hand until all solid particles have dissolved. After reconstitution, the solution should be refrigerated at 2°C to 8°C/36°F to 46°F and used within 24 hours.
Further dilute amphotericin B colloidal dispersion with dextrose 5% in water. Concentrations of 0.1-2 mg/mL in dextrose 5% in water are stable for 14 days at 4°C and 23°C if protected from light, however, due to the occasional formation of subvisual particles, solutions should be used within 48 hours.
Incompatible with sodium chloride solutions

Mechanism of Action Binds to ergosterol altering cell membrane permeability in susceptible fungi and causing leakage of cell components with subsequent cell death

Pharmacodynamics/Kinetics
Distribution: V_d: Total amphotericin B volume of distribution increases with increasing doses, reflects increasing uptake by tissues (with 4 mg/kg/day = 4 L/kg); predominantly distributed in the liver; concentrations in kidneys and other tissues are lower than observed with conventional amphotericin B
Half-life: 28-29 hours (increases with increasing doses)
Plasma concentration: Trough amphotericin B levels remain between 1-3 mcg/mL; little accumulation in plasma

Usual Dosage Children and Adults: I.V.:
Premedication: For patients who experience chills, fever, hypotension, nausea, or other nonanaphylactic infusion-related immediate reactions, premedicate with the following drugs, 30-60 minutes prior to drug administration: a nonsteroidal (eg, ibuprofen, choline magnesium trisalicylate, etc) with or without diphenhydramine; or acetaminophen with diphenhydramine; or hydrocortisone 50-100 mg. If the patient experiences rigors during the infusion, meperidine may be administered.
Range: 3-4 mg/kg/day (infusion of 1 mg/kg/hour); maximum: 7.5 mg/kg/day

Monitoring Parameters Liver function tests, electrolytes, BUN, Cr, temperature, CBC, I/O, signs of hypokalemia (muscle weakness, cramping, drowsiness, EKG changes)

Additional Information Controlled trials which compare the original formulation of amphotericin B to the newer liposomal formulations are lacking. Thus, comparative data discussing differences among the formulations should be interpreted cautiously.

Dosage Forms Suspension for injection: 50 mg (20 mL); 100 mg (50 mL)

♦ **Amphotericin B Colloidal Dispersion** *see* Amphotericin B Cholesteryl Sulfate Complex *on previous page*

Amphotericin B, Conventional *(am foe TER i sin bee)*

Related Information
Antifungal Agents Comparison *on page 1303*
Desensitization Protocols *on page 1347*
Guidelines for the Prevention of Opportunistic Infections in Persons with HIV *on page 1388*

U.S. Brand Names Amphocin®; Fungizone®

Synonyms Amphotericin B Desoxycholate

Therapeutic Category Antifungal Agent, Systemic; Antifungal Agent, Topical

Use Treatment of severe systemic and central nervous system infections caused by susceptible fungi such as *Candida* species, *Histoplasma capsulatum*, *Cryptococcus neoformans*, *Aspergillus* species, *Blastomyces dermatitidis*, *Torulopsis glabrata*, and

Coccidioides immitis; fungal peritonitis; irrigant for bladder fungal infections; and topically for cutaneous and mucocutaneous candidal infections; used in fungal infection in patients with bone marrow transplantation, amebic meningoencephalitis, ocular aspergillosis (intraocular injection), candidal cystitis (bladder irrigation), chemoprophylaxis (low-dose I.V.), immunocompromised patients at risk of aspergillosis (intranasal/nebulized), refractory meningitis (intrathecal), coccidioidal arthritis (intra-articular/I.M.)

Low-dose amphotericin B 0.1-0.25 mg/kg/day has been administered after bone marrow transplantation to reduce the risk of invasive fungal disease. Alternative routes of administration and extemporaneous preparations have been used when standard antifungal therapy is not available (eg, inhalation, intraocular injection, subconjunctival application, intracavitary administration into various joints and the pleural space).

Pregnancy Risk Factor B

Contraindications Hypersensitivity to amphotericin or any component

Warnings/Precautions Anaphylaxis has been reported with other amphotericin B-containing drugs. During the initial dosing, the drug should be administered under close clinical observation. Avoid additive toxicity with other nephrotoxic drugs; drug-induced renal toxicity usually improves with interrupting therapy, decreasing dosage, or increasing dosing interval. I.V. amphotericin is used primarily for the treatment of patients with progressive and potentially fatal fungal infections; topical preparations may stain clothing. Infusion reactions are most common 1-3 hours after starting the infusion and diminish with continued therapy. Use amphotericin B with caution in patients with decreased renal function. Pulmonary reactions may occur in neutropenic patients receiving leukocyte transfusions; separation of the infusions as much as possible is advised.

Adverse Reactions

>10%:

Central nervous system: Fever, chills, headache, malaise, generalized pain

Endocrine & metabolic: Hypokalemia, hypomagnesemia

Gastrointestinal: Anorexia

Hematologic: Anemia

Renal: Nephrotoxicity

1% to 10%:

Cardiovascular: Hypotension, hypertension, flushing

Central nervous system: Delirium, arachnoiditis, pain along lumbar nerves

Gastrointestinal: Nausea, vomiting

Genitourinary: Urinary retention

Hematologic: Leukocytosis

Local: Thrombophlebitis

Neuromuscular & skeletal: Paresthesia (especially with I.T. therapy)

Renal: Renal tubular acidosis, renal failure

<1%: Cardiac arrest, bone marrow suppression, convulsions, maculopapular rash, coagulation defects, thrombocytopenia, agranulocytosis, leukopenia, acute liver failure, vision changes, hearing loss, anuria, dyspnea

Overdosage/Toxicology

Symptoms of overdose include cardiac arrest, renal dysfunction, anemia, thrombocytopenia, granulocytopenia, fever, nausea, and vomiting

Treatment is supportive

Drug Interactions

Increased nephrotoxicity: Aminoglycosides, cyclosporine, other nephrotoxic drugs

Potentiation of hypokalemia: Corticosteroids, corticotropin

Increased digitalis and neuromuscular blocking agent toxicity due to hypokalemia

Decreased effect: Pharmacologic antagonism may occur with azole antifungal agents (eg, miconazole, ketoconazole)

Pulmonary toxicity has occurred with concomitant administration of amphotericin B and leukocyte transfusions

Stability

Reconstitute only with sterile water without preservatives, not bacteriostatic water. **Benzyl alcohol, sodium chloride, or other electrolyte solutions may cause precipitation.**

For I.V. infusion, an in-line filter (>1 micron mean pore diameter) may be used

Short-term exposure (<24 hours) to light during I.V. infusion does **not** appreciably affect potency

Reconstituted solutions with sterile water for injection and kept in the dark remain stable for 24 hours at room temperature and 1 week when refrigerated

Stability of parenteral admixture at room temperature (25°C): 24 hours; at refrigeration (4°C): 2 days

Standard diluent: Dose/250-500 mL D_5W

Mechanism of Action Binds to ergosterol altering cell membrane permeability in susceptible fungi and causing leakage of cell components with subsequent cell death

Pharmacodynamics/Kinetics

Distribution: Minimal amounts enter the aqueous humor, bile, CSF (inflamed or noninflamed meninges), amniotic fluid, pericardial fluid, pleural fluid, and synovial fluid

Protein binding, plasma: 90% infusion

Half-life, biphasic: Initial: 15-48 hours; Terminal: 15 days

Time to peak: Within 1 hour following a 4- to 6-hour dose

Elimination: 2% to 5% of dose eliminated in biologically active form in urine; approximately 40% eliminated over 7-day period and may be detected in urine for at least 7 weeks after discontinued use

(Continued)

Amphotericin B, Conventional *(Continued)*

Usual Dosage

I.V.: Premedication: For patients who experience chills, fever, hypotension, nausea, or other nonanaphylactic infusion-related immediate reactions, premedicate with the following drugs, 30-60 minutes prior to drug administration: a nonsteroidal (eg, ibuprofen, choline magnesium trisalicylate, etc) with or without diphenhydramine; or acetaminophen with diphenhydramine; or hydrocortisone 50-100 mg. If the patient experiences rigors during the infusion, meperidine may be administered.

Infants and Children:

Test dose: I.V.: 0.1 mg/kg/dose to a maximum of 1 mg; infuse over 30-60 minutes. Many clinicians believe a test dose is unnecessary.

Maintenance dose: 0.25-1 mg/kg/day given once daily; infuse over 2-6 hours. Once therapy has been established, amphotericin B can be administered on an every-other-day basis at 1-1.5 mg/kg/dose; cumulative dose: 1.5-2 g over 6-10 week

Adults:

Test dose: 1 mg infused over 20-30 minutes. Many clinicians believe a test dose is unnecessary.

Maintenance dose: Usual: 0.25-1.5 mg/kg/day; 1-1.5 mg/kg over 4-6 hours every other day may be given once therapy is established; aspergillosis, mucormycosis, rhinocerebral phycomycosis often require 1-1.5 mg/kg/day; do not exceed 1.5 mg/kg/day

Duration of therapy varies with nature of infection: Usual duration is 4-12 weeks or cumulative dose of 1-4 g

I.T.: Meningitis, coccidioidal or cryptococcal:

Children.: 25-100 mcg every 48-72 hours; increase to 500 mcg as tolerated

Adults: Initial: 25-300 mcg every 48-72 hours; increase to 500 mcg to 1 mg as tolerated; maximum total dose: 15 mg has been suggested

Oral: 1 mL (100 mg) 4 times/day

Topical: Apply to affected areas 2-4 times/day for 1-4 weeks of therapy depending on nature and severity of infection

Bladder irrigation: Candidal cystitis: Irrigate with 50 mcg/mL solution instilled periodically or continuously for 5-10 days or until cultures are clear

Dosing adjustment in renal impairment: If renal dysfunction is due to the drug, the daily total can be decreased by 50% or the dose can be given every other day; I.V. therapy may take several months

Dialysis: Poorly dialyzed; no supplemental dosage necessary when using hemo- or peritoneal dialysis or CAVH/CAVHD

Administration in dialysate: Children and Adults: 1-2 mg/L of peritoneal dialysis fluid either with or without low-dose I.V. amphotericin B (a total dose of 2-10 mg/kg given over 7-14 days). Precipitate may form in ionic dialysate solutions.

Monitoring Parameters Renal function (monitor frequently during therapy), electrolytes (especially potassium and magnesium), liver function tests, temperature, PT/PTT, CBC; monitor input and output; monitor for signs of hypokalemia (muscle weakness, cramping, drowsiness, EKG changes, etc)

Reference Range Therapeutic: 1-2 µg/mL (SI: 1-2.2 µmol/L)

Patient Information Amphotericin cream may slightly discolor skin and stain clothing; good personal hygiene may reduce the spread and recurrence of lesions; avoid covering topical applications with occlusive bandages; most skin lesions require 1-3 weeks of therapy; report any cramping, muscle weakness, or pain at or near injection site

Nursing Implications May be infused over 2-6 hours

Additional Information Renal toxicity may be minimized by sodium loading (500 mL NS with each dose), or pentoxifylline

Dosage Forms

Cream: 3% (20 g)

Lotion: 3% (30 mL)

Ointment, topical: 3% (20 g)

Powder for injection, lyophilized, as desoxycholate: 50 mg

Suspension, oral: 100 mg/mL (24 mL with dropper)

♦ **Amphotericin B Desoxycholate** *see* Amphotericin B, Conventional *on page 74*

Amphotericin B, Lipid Complex *(am foe TER i sin bee LIP id KOM pleks)*

U.S. Brand Names Abelcet™ Injection

Synonyms ABLC

Therapeutic Category Antifungal Agent, Systemic

Use Treatment of aspergillosis or any type of progressive fungal infection in patients who are refractory to or intolerant of conventional amphotericin B therapy

Orphan drug: Cryptococcal meningitis

Pregnancy Risk Factor B

Pregnancy/Breast-Feeding Implications Breast-feeding/lactation: Due to limited data, consider discontinuing nursing during therapy

Contraindications Hypersensitivity to amphotericin or any component in the formulation

Warnings/Precautions Anaphylaxis has been reported with other amphotericin B-containing drugs. Facilities for cardiopulmonary resuscitation should be available during administration due to the possibility of anaphylactic reaction. If severe respiratory distress occurs, the infusion should be immediately discontinued. During the initial dosing, the drug should be administered under close clinical observation. Acute reactions (including fever and chills) may occur 1-2 hours after starting an intravenous infusion. These reactions are usually more common with the first few doses and generally diminish with subsequent doses. Pulmonary reactions may occur in neutropenic patients receiving leukocyte transfusions; separation of the infusions as much as possible is advised.

Adverse Reactions Reduced nephrotoxicity as well as frequent infusion related side effects have been reported with this formulation

>10%:
  Central nervous system: Chills, fever
  Renal: Increased serum creatinine
1% to 10%:
  Cardiovascular: Hypotension, cardiac arrest
  Central nervous system: Headache, pain
  Dermatologic: Rash
  Endocrine & metabolic: Bilirubinemia, hypokalemia, acidosis
  Gastrointestinal: Nausea, vomiting, diarrhea, gastrointestinal hemorrhage, abdominal pain
  Renal: Renal failure
  Respiratory: Respiratory failure, dyspnea, pneumonia

Drug Interactions
  Increased nephrotoxicity: Aminoglycosides, cyclosporine, other nephrotoxic drugs
  Potentiation of hypokalemia: Corticosteroids, corticotropin
  Increased digitalis and neuromuscular blocking agent toxicity due to hypokalemia
  Decreased effect: Pharmacologic antagonism may occur with azole antifungal agents (eg, miconazole, ketoconazole)
  Pulmonary toxicity has occurred with concomitant administration of amphotericin B and leukocyte transfusions

Stability 100 mg vials in 20 mL of suspension in single-use vials (no preservative is present). Intact vials should be stored at 2°C to 8°C (35°F to 46°F) and protected from exposure to light; do not freeze intact vials. Shake the vial gently until there is no evidence of any yellow sediment at the bottom. Withdraw the appropriate dose and filter the contents (5 micron filter) prior to dilution. Dilute into D_5W to a final concentration of 1 mg/mL. For pediatric patients and patients with cardiovascular disease, the drug may be diluted with D_5W to a final concentration of 2 mg/mL.

Do not dilute with saline solutions or mix with other drugs or electrolytes - compatibility has not been established

Do not use an in-line filter <5 microns

Diluted solution is stable for up to 15 hours at 2°C to 8°C (38°F to 46°F) and an additional 6 hours at room temperature

Mechanism of Action Binds to ergosterol altering cell membrane permeability in susceptible fungi and causing leakage of cell components with subsequent cell death

Pharmacodynamics/Kinetics
  Distribution: V_d: Increases with increasing doses; reflects increased uptake by tissues (131 L/kg with 5 mg/kg/day)
  Half-life: ~24 hours
  Clearance: Increases with increasing doses [400 mL/hour/kg (with 5 mg/kg/day)]

Usual Dosage Children and Adults: I.V.:
  Premedication: For patients who experience chills, fever, hypotension, nausea, or other nonanaphylactic infusion-related immediate reactions, premedicate with the following drugs, 30-60 minutes prior to drug administration: a nonsteroidal (eg, ibuprofen, choline magnesium trisalicylate, etc) with or without diphenhydramine; or acetaminophen with diphenhydramine; or hydrocortisone 50-100 mg. If the patient experiences rigors during the infusion, meperidine may be administered.
  Range: 2.5-5 mg/kg/day as a single infusion
  Dosing adjustment in renal impairment: None necessary; effects of renal impairment are not currently known
  Hemodialysis: No supplemental dosage necessary
  Peritoneal dialysis: No supplemental dosage necessary
  Continuous arteriovenous or venovenous hemofiltration (CAVH/CAVHD): No supplemental dosage necessary

Monitoring Parameters Renal function (monitor frequently during therapy), electrolytes (especially potassium and magnesium), liver function tests, temperature, PT/PTT, CBC; monitor input and output; monitor for signs of hypokalemia (muscle weakness, cramping, drowsiness, EKG changes, etc)

Additional Information As a modification of dimyristoyl phosphatidylcholine:dimyristoyl phosphatidylglycerol 7:3 (DMPC:DMPG) liposome, amphotericin B lipid-complex has a higher drug to lipid ratio and the concentration of amphotericin B is 33 M; ABLC is a ribbon-like structure, not a liposome

Dosage Forms Injection: 5 mg/mL (20 mL)

Amphotericin B, Liposomal (am foe TER i sin bee lye po SO mal)

U.S. Brand Names AmBisome®
Synonyms L-AmB
Therapeutic Category Antifungal Agent, Systemic
Use Empirical therapy for presumed fungal infection in febrile, neutropenic patients. Treatment of patients with *Aspergillus* species, *Candida* species and/or *Cryptococcus* species infections refractory to amphotericin B desoxycholate, or in patients where renal impairment or unacceptable toxicity precludes the use of amphotericin B desoxycholate. Treatment of visceral leishmaniasis. In immunocompromised patients with visceral
(Continued)

Amphotericin B, Liposomal *(Continued)*

leishmaniasis treated with amphotericin B, liposomal, relapse rates were high following initial clearance of parasites.

Pregnancy Risk Factor B

Contraindications In those patients who have demonstrated or have known hypersensitivity to amphotericin B or any other constituents of the product unless, in the opinion of the treating physician, the benefit of therapy outweighs the risk

Warnings/Precautions Anaphylaxis has been reported with amphotericin B desoxycholate and other amphotericin B-containing drugs. Facilities for cardiopulmonary resuscitation should be available during administration due to the possibility of anaphylactic reaction. As with any amphotericin B-containing product the drug should be administered by medically trained personnel. During the initial dosing period, patients should be under close clinical observation. Amphotericin B, liposomal has been shown to be significantly less toxic than amphotericin B desoxycholate; however, adverse events may still occur. If severe respiratory distress occurs, the infusion should be immediately discontinued and the patient should not receive further infusions. Acute reactions (including fever and chills) may occur 1-2 hours after starting an intravenous infusion. These reactions are usually more common with the first few doses and generally diminish with subsequent doses.

Adverse Reactions

>10%:
  Central nervous system: Chills, fever
  Renal: Increased serum creatinine
  Miscellaneous: Multiple organ failure

1% to 10%:
  Cardiovascular: Hypotension, cardiac arrest
  Central nervous system: Headache, pain
  Dermatologic: Rash
  Endocrine & metabolic: Bilirubinemia, hypokalemia, acidosis
  Gastrointestinal: Nausea, vomiting, diarrhea, gastrointestinal hemorrhage, abdominal pain
  Renal: Renal failure
  Respiratory: Respiratory failure, dyspnea, pneumonia

Overdosage/Toxicology

The toxicity due to overdose has not been defined. Repeated daily doses up to 7.5 mg/kg have been administered in clinical trials with no reported dose-related toxicity.

If overdosage should occur, cease administration immediately. Symptomatic supportive measures should be instituted. Particular attention should be given to monitoring renal function.

Drug Interactions

Increased nephrotoxicity: Aminoglycosides, cyclosporine, other nephrotoxic drugs
Potentiation of hypokalemia: Corticosteroids, corticotropin
Increased digitalis and neuromuscular blocking agent toxicity due to hypokalemia
Decreased effect: Pharmacologic antagonism may occur with azole antifungal agents (eg, miconazole, ketoconazole)
Pulmonary toxicity has occurred with concomitant administration of amphotericin B and leukocyte transfusions

Stability Must be reconstituted using sterile water for injection, USP (without a bacteriostatic agent). Follow package insert instructions carefully for preparation. Do not reconstitute with saline or add saline to the reconstituted concentration, or mix with other drugs. The use of any solution other than those recommended, or the presence of a bacteriostatic agent in the solution, may cause precipitation.

Must be diluted with 5% dextrose injection to a final concentration of 1-2 mg/mL prior to administration. Lower concentrations (0.2-0.5 mg/mL) may be appropriate for infants and small children to provide sufficient volume for infusion.

Injection should commence within 6 hours of dilution with 5% dextrose injection.

An in-line membrane filter may be used for the intravenous infusion; provided, THE MEAN PORE DIAMETER OF THE FILTER SHOULD NOT BE LESS THAN 1 (one) MICRON.

Mechanism of Action Binds to ergosterol altering cell membrane permeability in susceptible fungi and causing leakage of cell components with subsequent cell death

Pharmacodynamics/Kinetics

Distribution: V_d: 131 L/kg
Half-life, terminal elimination: 174 hours
Poorly dialyzed

Usual Dosage Children and Adults: I.V.:

Premedication: For patients who experience chills, fever, hypotension, nausea, or other nonanaphylactic infusion-related immediate reactions, premedicate with the following drugs, 30-60 minutes prior to drug administration: a nonsteroidal (eg, ibuprofen, choline magnesium trisalicylate, etc) with or without diphenhydramine; or acetaminophen with diphenhydramine; or hydrocortisone 50-100 mg. If the patient experiences rigors during the infusion, meperidine may be administered.

Empiric therapy: Recommended initial dose: 3 mg/kg/day

Systemic fungal infections (*Aspergillus, Candida, Cryptococcus*): Recommended initial dose of 3-5 mg/kg/day

Treatment of visceral leishmaniasis: Amphotericin B liposomal achieved high rates of acute parasite clearance in immunocompetent patients when total doses of 12-30 mg/kg were administered. Most of these immunocompetent patients remained relapse-free during follow-up periods of 6 months or longer. While acute parasite clearance was achieved in most of the immunocompromised patients who received total doses of 30-40 mg/kg, the majority of these patients were observed to relapse in the 6 months following the completion of therapy.

Dosing adjustment in renal impairment: None necessary; effects of renal impairment are not currently known

Hemodialysis: No supplemental dosage necessary

Peritoneal dialysis effects: No supplemental dosage necessary

Continuous arteriovenous or venovenous hemofiltration (CAVH/CAVHD): No supplemental dosage necessary

Administration Should be administered by intravenous infusion, using a controlled infusion device, over a period of approximately 2 hours. Infusion time may be reduced to approximately 1 hour in patients in whom the treatment is well-tolerated. If the patient experiences discomfort during infusion, the duration of infusion may be increased. Administer at a rate of 2.5 mg/kg/hour; infusion bag or syringe should be shaken before start of infusion. If infusion time exceeds 2 hours, the contents of the infusion bag should be mixed every 2 hours by shaking.

Monitoring Parameters Renal function (monitor frequently during therapy), electrolytes (especially potassium and magnesium), liver function tests, temperature, PT/PTT, CBC; monitor input and output; monitor for signs of hypokalemia (muscle weakness, cramping, drowsiness, EKG changes, etc)

Additional Information Amphotericin B, liposomal is a true single bilayer liposomal drug delivery system. Liposomes are closed, spherical vesicles created by mixing specific proportions of amphophilic substances such as phospholipids and cholesterol so that they arrange themselves into multiple concentric bilayer membranes when hydrated in aqueous solutions. Single bilayer liposomes are then formed by microemulsification of multilamellar vesicles using a homogenizer. Amphotericin B, liposomal consists of these unilamellar bilayer liposomes with amphotericin B intercalated within the membrane. Due to the nature and quantity of amphophilic substances used, and the lipophilic moiety in the amphotericin B molecule, the drug is an integral part of the overall structure of the amphotericin B liposomes. Amphotericin B, liposomal contains true liposomes that are less than 100 nm in diameter.

Dosage Forms Injection: 50 mg

Ampicillin (am pi SIL in)

Related Information

Animal and Human Bites Guidelines *on page 1399*
Antibiotic Treatment of Adults With Infective Endocarditis *on page 1401*
Antimicrobial Drugs of Choice *on page 1404*
Desensitization Protocols *on page 1347*
Prevention of Bacterial Endocarditis *on page 1377*

U.S. Brand Names Marcillin®; Omnipen®; Omnipen®-N; Polycillin®; Polycillin-N®; Principen®; Totacillin®; Totacillin®-N

Canadian Brand Names Ampicin® Sodium; Apo®-Ampi Trihydrate; Jaa Amp® Trihydrate; Nu-Ampi Trihydrate; Pro-Ampi® Trihydrate; Taro-Ampicillin® Trihydrate

Synonyms Aminobenzylpenicillin; Ampicillin Sodium; Ampicillin Trihydrate

Therapeutic Category Antibiotic, Penicillin

Use Treatment of susceptible bacterial infections (nonbeta-lactamase-producing organisms); susceptible bacterial infections caused by streptococci, pneumococci, nonpenicillinase-producing staphylococci, *Listeria*, meningococci; some strains of *H. influenzae*, *Salmonella*, *Shigella*, *E. coli*, *Enterobacter*, and *Klebsiella*

Pregnancy Risk Factor B

Contraindications Known hypersensitivity to ampicillin or other penicillins

Warnings/Precautions Dosage adjustment may be necessary in patients with renal impairment; a low incidence of cross-allergy with other beta-lactams exists; high percentage of patients with infectious mononucleosis have developed rash during therapy with ampicillin. Appearance of a rash should be carefully evaluated to differentiate a nonallergic ampicillin rash from a hypersensitivity reaction. Ampicillin rash occurs in 5% to 10% of children receiving ampicillin and is a generalized dull red, maculopapular rash, generally appearing 3-14 days after the start of therapy. It normally begins on the trunk and spreads over most of the body. It may be most intense at pressure areas, elbows, and knees.

Adverse Reactions

>10%: Local: Pain at injection site

1% to 10%:

Dermatologic: Rash (appearance of a rash should be carefully evaluated to differentiate, if possible; nonallergic ampicillin rash from hypersensitivity reaction; incidence is higher in patients with viral infections, *Salmonella* infections, lymphocytic leukemia, or patients that have hyperuricemia)

Gastrointestinal: Diarrhea, vomiting, oral candidiasis, abdominal cramps

Miscellaneous: Allergic reaction (includes serum sickness, urticaria, angioedema, bronchospasm, hypotension, etc)

<1%: Penicillin encephalopathy, seizures (with large I.V. doses or patients with renal dysfunction), anemia, hemolytic anemia, thrombocytopenia, thrombocytopenic purpura, eosinophilia, leukopenia, granulocytopenia, decreased lymphocytes, interstitial nephritis (rare)

Overdosage/Toxicology

Symptoms of penicillin overdose include neuromuscular hypersensitivity (agitation, hallucinations, asterixis, encephalopathy, confusion, and seizures) and electrolyte imbalance with potassium or sodium salts, especially in renal failure

(Continued)

Ampicillin *(Continued)*

Hemodialysis may be helpful to aid in the removal of the drug from the blood, otherwise most treatment is supportive or symptom directed

Drug Interactions

Decreased effect: Efficacy of oral contraceptives may be reduced

Increased effect: Disulfiram, probenecid may increase penicillin levels, increased effect of anticoagulants

Increased toxicity: Allopurinol theoretically has an additive potential for amoxicillin (ampicillin) rash

Stability Oral suspension is stable for 7 days at room temperature or for 14 days under refrigeration; solutions for I.M. or direct I.V. should be used within 1 hour; solutions for I.V. infusion will be inactivated by dextrose at room temperature; if dextrose-containing solutions are to be used, the resultant solution will only be stable for 2 hours versus 8 hours in the 0.9% sodium chloride injection. D_5W has limited stability.

Minimum volume: Concentration should not exceed 30 mg/mL due to concentration-dependent stability restrictions. Manufacturer may supply as either the anhydrous or the trihydrate form.

Stability of parenteral admixture in NS at room temperature (25°C): 8 hours

Stability of parenteral admixture in NS at refrigeration temperature (4°C): 2 days

Standard diluent: 500 mg/50 mL NS; 1 g/50 mL NS; 2 g/100 mL NS

Mechanism of Action Inhibits bacterial cell wall synthesis by binding to one or more of the penicillin binding proteins (PBPs); which in turn inhibits the final transpeptidation step of peptidoglycan synthesis in bacterial cell walls, thus inhibiting cell wall biosynthesis. Bacteria eventually lyse due to ongoing activity of cell wall autolytic enzymes (autolysins and murein hydrolases) while cell wall assembly is arrested.

Pharmacodynamics/Kinetics

Absorption: Oral: 50%

Distribution: Distributes into bile; penetration into CSF occurs with inflamed meninges only, good only with inflammation (exceeds usual MICs)

Normal meninges: Nil

Inflamed meninges: 5-10

Protein binding: 15% to 25%

Half-life:

Neonates: 2-7 days: 4 hours; 8-14 days: 2.8 hours; 15-30 days: 1.7 hours

Children and Adults: 1-1.8 hours

Anuria/end-stage renal disease: 7-20 hours

Time to peak: Oral: Within 1-2 hours

Elimination: ~90% of the drug excreted unchanged in the urine within 24 hours

Usual Dosage

Neonates: I.M., I.V.:

Postnatal age ≤7 days:

≤2000 g: Meningitis: 50 mg/kg/dose every 12 hours; other infections: 25 mg/kg/dose every 12 hours

>2000 g: Meningitis: 50 mg/kg/dose every 8 hours; other infections: 25 mg/kg/dose every 8 hours

Postnatal age >7 days:

<1200 g: Meningitis: 50 mg/kg/dose every 12 hours; other infections: 25 mg/kg/dose every 12 hours

1200-2000 g: Meningitis: 50 mg/kg/dose every 8 hours; other infections: 25 mg/kg/dose every 8 hours

>2000 g: Meningitis: 50 mg/kg/dose every 6 hours; other infections: 25 mg/kg/dose every 6 hours

Infants and Children: I.M., I.V.: 100-400 mg/kg/day in doses divided every 4-6 hours

Meningitis: 200 mg/kg/day in doses divided every 4-6 hours; maximum dose: 12 g/day

Children: Oral: 50-100 mg/kg/day in doses divided every 6 hours; maximum dose: 2-3 g/day

Adults:

Oral: 250-500 mg every 6 hours

I.M.: 500 mg to 1.5 g every 4-6 hours

I.V.: 500 mg to 3 g every 4-6 hours; maximum dose: 12 g/day

Sepsis/meningitis: 150-250 mg/kg/24 hours divided every 3-4 hours

Dosing interval in renal impairment:

Cl_{cr} 30-50 mL/minute: Administer every 6-8 hours

Cl_{cr} 10-30 mL/minute: Administer every 8-12 hours

Cl_{cr} <10 mL/minute: Administer every 12 hours

Hemodialysis: Moderately dialyzable (20% to 50%); administer dose after dialysis

Peritoneal dialysis: Moderately dialyzable (20% to 50%)

Administer 250 mg every 12 hours

Continuous arteriovenous or venovenous hemofiltration (CAVH) effects: Dose as for Cl_{cr} 10-50 mL/minute; ~50 mg of ampicillin per liter of filtrate is removed

Dietary Considerations Food: Decreases drug absorption rate; decreases drug serum concentration. Take on an empty stomach 1 hour before or 2 hours after meals.

Administration Administer orally on an empty stomach (ie, 1 hour prior to, or 2 hours after meals) to increase total absorption

Monitoring Parameters With prolonged therapy monitor renal, hepatic, and hematologic function periodically; observe signs and symptoms of anaphylaxis during first dose

Test Interactions May interfere with urinary glucose tests using cupric sulfate (Benedict's solution, Clinitest®); may inactivate aminoglycosides *in vitro*

Patient Information Food decreases rate and extent of absorption; take oral on an empty stomach, if possible (ie, 1 hour prior to, or 2 hours after meals); report diarrhea promptly; entire course of medication should be taken to ensure eradication of organism; females should report onset of symptoms of candidal vaginitis; may interfere with the effects of oral contraceptives

Nursing Implications Ampicillin and gentamicin should not be mixed in the same I.V. tubing or administered concurrently

Additional Information

Sodium content of 5 mL suspension (250 mg/5 mL): 10 mg (0.4 mEq)

Sodium content of 1 g: 66.7 mg (3 mEq)

Dosage Forms

Capsule, as anhydrous: 250 mg, 500 mg

Capsule, as trihydrate: 250 mg, 500 mg

Powder for injection, as sodium: 125 mg, 250 mg, 500 mg, 1 g, 2 g, 10 g

Powder for oral suspension, as trihydrate: 125 mg/5 mL (5 mL unit dose, 80 mL, 100 mL, 150 mL, 200 mL); 250 mg/5 mL (5 mL unit dose, 80 mL, 100 mL, 150 mL, 200 mL); 500 mg/5 mL (5 mL unit dose, 100 mL)

Powder for oral suspension, drops, as trihydrate: 100 mg/mL (20 mL)

Ampicillin and Sulbactam (am pi SIL in & SUL bak tam)

Related Information

Animal and Human Bites Guidelines *on page 1399*

Antimicrobial Drugs of Choice *on page 1404*

U.S. Brand Names Unasyn®

Synonyms Sulbactam and Ampicillin

Therapeutic Category Antibiotic, Penicillin; Antibiotic, Penicillin & Beta-lactamase Inhibitor

Use Treatment of susceptible bacterial infections involved with skin and skin structure, intra-abdominal infections, gynecological infections; spectrum is that of ampicillin plus organisms producing beta-lactamases such as *S. aureus*, *H. influenzae*, *E. coli*, and anaerobes

Pregnancy Risk Factor B

Contraindications Hypersensitivity to ampicillin, sulbactam or any component, or penicillins

Warnings/Precautions Dosage adjustment may be necessary in patients with renal impairment; a low incidence of cross-allergy with other beta-lactams exists; high percentage of patients with infectious mononucleosis have developed rash during therapy with ampicillin. Appearance of a rash should be carefully evaluated to differentiate a nonallergic ampicillin rash from a hypersensitivity reaction. Ampicillin rash occurs in 5% to 10% of children receiving ampicillin and is a generalized dull red, maculopapular rash, generally appearing 3-14 days after the start of therapy. It normally begins on the trunk and spreads over most of the body. It may be most intense at pressure areas, elbows, and knees.

Adverse Reactions

>10%: Local: Pain at injection site (I.M.)

1% to 10%:

Dermatologic: Rash

Gastrointestinal: Diarrhea

Local: Pain at injection site (I.V.)

Miscellaneous: Allergic reaction (may include serum sickness, urticaria, bronchospasm, hypotension, etc)

<1%: Chest pain, fatigue, malaise, headache, chills, penicillin encephalopathy, seizures (with large I.V. doses or patients with renal dysfunction), itching, nausea, vomiting, enterocolitis, pseudomembranous colitis, hairy tongue, dysuria, vaginitis, leukopenia, neutropenia, thrombocytopenia, decreased hemoglobin and hematocrit, increased liver enzymes, thrombophlebitis, increased BUN/creatinine, interstitial nephritis (rare)

Overdosage/Toxicology

Symptoms of penicillin overdose include neuromuscular hypersensitivity (agitation, hallucinations, asterixis, encephalopathy, confusion, and seizures) and electrolyte imbalance with potassium or sodium salts, especially in renal failure

Hemodialysis may be helpful to aid in the removal of the drug from the blood, otherwise most treatment is supportive or symptom directed

Drug Interactions

Decreased effect: Efficacy of oral contraceptives may be reduced

Increased effect: Disulfiram, probenecid results in increased ampicillin levels

Increased toxicity: Allopurinol theoretically has an additive potential for ampicillin rash

Stability I.M. and direct I.V. administration: Use within 1 hour after preparation; reconstitute with sterile water for injection or 0.5% or 2% lidocaine hydrochloride injection (I.M.); sodium chloride 0.9% (NS) is the diluent of choice for I.V. piggyback use, solutions made in NS are stable up to 72 hours when refrigerated whereas dextrose solutions (same concentration) are stable for only 4 hours

Mechanism of Action The addition of sulbactam, a beta-lactamase inhibitor, to ampicillin extends the spectrum of ampicillin to include some beta-lactamase producing organisms; inhibits bacterial cell wall synthesis by binding to one or more of the penicillin binding proteins (PBPs); which in turn inhibits the final transpeptidation step of peptidoglycan synthesis in bacterial cell walls, thus inhibiting cell wall biosynthesis. Bacteria eventually lyse due to ongoing activity of cell wall autolytic enzymes (autolysins and murein hydrolases) while cell wall assembly is arrested.

(Continued)

Ampicillin and Sulbactam *(Continued)*

Pharmacodynamics/Kinetics

Distribution: Into bile, blister and tissue fluids; poor penetration into CSF with uninflamed meninges; higher concentrations attained with inflamed meninges

Protein binding: Ampicillin: 28%; Sulbactam: 38%

Half-life: Ampicillin and sulbactam are similar: 1-1.8 hours and 1-1.3 hours, respectively in patients with normal renal function

Elimination: ~75% to 85% of both drugs are excreted unchanged in the urine within 8 hours following administration

Usual Dosage Unasyn® (ampicillin/sulbactam) is a combination product. Each 3 g vial contains 2 g of ampicillin and 1 g of sulbactam. Sulbactam has very little antibacterial activity by itself, but effectively extends the spectrum of ampicillin to include beta-lactamase producing strains that are resistant to ampicillin alone. Therefore, dosage recommendations for Unasyn® are based on the ampicillin component.

I.M., I.V.:

Children (3 months to 12 years): 100-200 mg ampicillin/kg/day (150-300 mg Unasyn®) divided every 6 hours; maximum dose: 8 g ampicillin/day (12 g Unasyn®)

Adults: 1-2 g ampicillin (1.5-3 g Unasyn®) every 6-8 hours; maximum dose: 8 g ampicillin/day (12 g Unasyn®)

Dosing interval in renal impairment:

Cl$_{cr}$ 15-29 mL/minute: Administer every 12 hours

Cl$_{cr}$ 5-14 mL/minute: Administer every 24 hours

Monitoring Parameters With prolonged therapy, monitor hematologic, renal, and hepatic function; monitor for signs of anaphylaxis during first dose

Test Interactions May interfere with urinary glucose tests using cupric sulfate (Benedict's solution, Clinitest®); may inactivate aminoglycosides *in vitro*

Nursing Implications Ampicillin and gentamicin should not be mixed in the same I.V. tubing or administered concurrently

Additional Information Sodium content of 1.5 g injection: 115 mg (5 mEq)

Dosage Forms Powder for injection: 1.5 g [ampicillin sodium 1 g and sulbactam sodium 0.5 g]; 3 g [ampicillin sodium 2 g and sulbactam sodium 1 g]

♦ **Ampicillin Sodium** *see Ampicillin on page 79*

♦ **Ampicillin Trihydrate** *see Ampicillin on page 79*

♦ **Ampcin® Sodium** *see Ampicillin on page 79*

Amprenavir *(am PRE na veer)*

Related Information

Antiretroviral Agents *on page 1306*

Antiretroviral Therapy for HIV Infection *on page 1410*

Therapeutic Category Antiretroviral Agent, Protease Inhibitor; Protease Inhibitor

Use Treatment of HIV infections in combination with at least two other antiretroviral agents

Pregnancy Risk Factor Unknown

Contraindications Hypersensitivity to amprenavir or any component; concurrent therapy with rifampin, astemizole, bepridil, cisapride, dihydroergotamine, ergotamine, midazolam, and triazolam; severe previous allergic reaction to sulfonamides

Warnings/Precautions Because of hepatic metabolism and effect on cytochrome P-450 enzymes, amprenavir should be used with caution in combination with other agents metabolized by this system (see Contraindications and Drug Interactions). Use with caution in patients with diabetes mellitus, sulfonamide allergy, hepatic impairment, or hemophilia. Redistribution of fat may occur (eg, buffalo hump, peripheral wasting, cushingoid appearance). Additional vitamin E supplements should be avoided. Concurrent use of sildenafil should be avoided.

Adverse Reactions Protease inhibitors cause dyslipidemia which includes elevated cholesterol and triglycerides and a redistribution of body fat centrally to cause "protease paunch", buffalo hump, facial atrophy, and breast enlargement. These agents also cause hyperglycemia.

>10%:

Gastrointestinal: Nausea (38% to 73%), vomiting (20% to 29%), diarrhea (33% to 56%)

Dermatologic: Rash (28%)

Endocrine & metabolic: Hyperglycemia (37% to 41%), hypertriglyceridemia (38% to 27%)

Miscellaneous: Perioral tingling/numbness

1% to 10%:

Central nervous system: Depression (4% to 15%), headache, paresthesia, fatigue

Gastrointestinal: Taste disorders (1% to 10%)

Dermatologic: Stevens-Johnson syndrome (1% of total, 4% of patients who develop a rash)

Drug Interactions CYP3A4 inhibitor and substrate

Increased effect/toxicity: Abacavir, clarithromycin, indinavir, ketoconazole, and zidovudine increase the AUC of amprenavir. Nelfinavir had no effect on AUC, but increased the C$_{min}$ of amprenavir. Amprenavir increased the AUC of ketoconazole, rifabutin, and zidovudine during concurrent therapy. Amprenavir may enhance the toxicity of astemizole, bepridil, cisapride, dihydroergotamine, ergotamine, midazolam, and triazolam - concurrent therapy with these drugs and amprenavir is contraindicated. May increase serum concentration of HMGCoA reductase inhibitors, diltiazem, nicardipine, nifedipine, nimodipine, alprazolam, clorazepate, diazepam, flurazepam, itraconazole, dapsone, erythromycin, loratadine, sildenafil, carbamazepine, and pimozide. May also increase the toxic effect of amiodarone, lidocaine, quinidine, warfarin, and tricyclic antidepressants. Serum concentration monitoring of these drugs is necessary.

Mechanism of Action Binds to the protease activity site and inhibits the activity of the enzyme. HIV protease is required for the cleavage of viral polyprotein precursors into individual functional proteins found in infectious HIV. Inhibition prevents cleavage of these polyproteins, resulting in the formation of immature, noninfectious viral particles.

Pharmacodynamics/Kinetics
Absorption: 1-2 hours
Distribution: 430 L
Protein binding: 90%
Metabolism: Hepatic, via cytochrome P-450 isoenzymes (primarily CYP3A4)
Elimination: Biliary (75%) and urine (14%) as metabolites

Usual Dosage Oral:
Capsules:
Children 4-12 years and older (<50 kg): 20 mg/kg twice daily or 15 mg/kg 3 times daily; maximum: 2400 mg/day
Children >13 years (>50 kg) and Adults: 1200 mg twice daily
Solution: Children 4-12 years or older (up to 18 years weighing <50 kg): 22 mg/kg twice daily or 17 mg/kg 3 times daily; maximum: 2400/day
Dosage adjustment in hepatic impairment:
Child-Pugh score between 5-8: 450 mg twice daily
Child-Pugh score between 9-12: 300 mg twice daily

Patient Information Advise prescriber of any previous reactions to sulfonamides. Do not take this medication with antacids or high-fat meals. Do not take additional vitamin E supplements. Consult pharmacist or physician prior to taking any other medications, due to the potential for drug interactions. For women using oral contraceptives, an alternative method of contraception should be used.

Additional Information Capsules contain 109 Int. units of vitamin E per capsule; oral solution contains 46 Int. units of vitamin E per mL

Dosage Forms
Capsules: 50 mg, 150 mg
Solution: 15 mg/mL

♦ **AMPT** see Metyrosine on page 772

Amrinone (AM ri none)

Related Information
Adrenergic Agonists, Cardiovascular Comparison on page 1290
Adult ACLS Algorithm, Hypotension, Shock on page 1454

U.S. Brand Names Inocor®

Synonyms Amrinone Lactate®

Therapeutic Category Phosphodiesterase (Type 5) Enzyme Inhibitor

Use Congestive heart failure; adjunctive therapy of pulmonary hypertension; normally prescribed for patients who have not responded well to therapy with digitalis, diuretics, and vasodilators

Pregnancy Risk Factor C

Contraindications Hypersensitivity to amrinone lactate or sulfites (contains sodium metabisulfite)

Usual Dosage Dosage is based on clinical response (**Note:** Dose should not exceed 10 mg/kg/24 hours)

Children and Adults: 0.75 mg/kg I.V. bolus over 2-3 minutes followed by maintenance infusion of 5-10 mcg/kg/minute; I.V. bolus may need to be repeated in 30 minutes
Dosing adjustment in renal failure: Cl_{cr} <10 mL/minute: Administer 50% to 75% of dose

Additional Information Complete prescribing information for this medication should be consulted for additional detail

Dosage Forms Injection, as lactate: 5 mg/mL (20 mL)

♦ **Amrinone Lactate** see Amrinone on this page

♦ **Amvisc®** see Sodium Hyaluronate on page 1069

♦ **Amvisc® Plus** see Sodium Hyaluronate on page 1069

Amyl Nitrite (AM il NYE trite)

Synonyms Isoamyl Nitrite

Therapeutic Category Antidote, Cyanide; Vasodilator, Coronary

Use Coronary vasodilator in angina pectoris; adjunct in treatment of cyanide poisoning; used to produce changes in the intensity of heart murmurs

Pregnancy Risk Factor X

Contraindications Severe anemia; hypersensitivity to nitrates; pregnancy

Warnings/Precautions Use with caution in patients with increased intracranial pressure, low systolic blood pressure, and coronary artery disease

Adverse Reactions
1% to 10%:
Cardiovascular: Postural hypotension, cutaneous flushing of head, neck, and clavicular area
Central nervous system: Headache
<1%: Rash, hemolytic anemia
(Continued)

Amyl Nitrite (Continued)

Overdosage/Toxicology
Symptoms of overdose include hypotension

Treatment includes general supportive measures for transient hypotension; I.V. fluids; Trendelenburg position, vasopressors

Drug Interactions Increased toxicity: Alcohol

Stability Store in cool place; protect from light

Pharmacodynamics/Kinetics
Onset of action: Angina relieved within 30 seconds

Duration: 3-15 minutes

Usual Dosage Nasal inhalation:
Cyanide poisoning: Children and Adults: Inhale the vapor from a 0.3 mL crushed ampul every minute for 15-30 seconds until I.V. sodium nitrite infusion is available

Angina: Adults: 1-6 inhalations from 1 crushed ampul; may repeat in 3-5 minutes

Administration Administer nasally; patient should not be sitting; crush ampul in woven covering between fingers and then hold under patient's nostrils

Monitoring Parameters Monitor blood pressure during therapy

Patient Information Lie down during administration, crush ampul between fingers and then inhale through nostrils; may cause dizziness; call paramedics or have someone take you to the hospital immediately if pain is not relieved after 3 doses

Dosage Forms Inhalant, crushable glass perles: 0.18 mL, 0.3 mL

- ♦ **Amylobarbitone** see Amobarbital on page 67
- ♦ **Amytal®** see Amobarbital on page 67
- ♦ **Anabolin® Injection** see Nandrolone on page 816
- ♦ **Anacin® [OTC]** see Aspirin on page 102
- ♦ **Anadrol®** see Oxymetholone on page 876
- ♦ **Anafranil®** see Clomipramine on page 281

Anagrelide (an AG gre lide)

U.S. Brand Names Agrylin®

Synonyms Anagrelide Hydrochloride

Therapeutic Category Platelet Aggregation Inhibitor

Use Agent for essential thrombocythemia (ET); treatment of thrombocytopenia secondary to myeloproliferative disorders

Pregnancy Risk Factor C

Pregnancy/Breast-Feeding Implications Clinical effects on the fetus: The relative risks must be weighed carefully in relation to the potential benefits. Animal reproduction studies have shown an adverse effect on the fetus when anagrelide was administered during pregnancy. There are no adequate and well-controlled studies in humans; however, the potential benefits may warrant the use of this drug in pregnant women despite the potential risks.

Contraindications Hypersensitivity to anagrelide

Warnings/Precautions Anagrelide should be used with caution in patients with known or suspected heart disease, and only if the potential benefits of therapy outweigh the potential risks. Thrombocytopenia appears to be the main dose-limiting side effect of anagrelide; palpitations, orthostatic hypotension, and headache have also been reported. Caution is warranted when anagrelide is used in patients with reduced renal function or hepatic dysfunction.

Adverse Reactions
Cardiovascular: Palpitations (27.2%), chest pain (7.8%), tachycardia (7.3%), orthostatic hypotension, CHF, cardiomyopathy, myocardial infarction (rare), complete heart block, angina, and atrial fibrillation

Central nervous system: Headache (44%), dizziness (14.7%), bad dreams, impaired concentration ability

Hematologic: Anemia, thrombocytopenia, ecchymosis and lymphadenopathy have been reported rarely

Overdosage/Toxicology
Single oral doses of anagrelide at 2500, 1500, and 200 mg/kg in mice, rats, and monkeys, respectively, were not lethal. Symptoms of acute toxicity include decreased motor activity in mice and rats and softened stools and decreased appetite in monkeys. There are no reports of human overdosage with anagrelide. Platelet reduction from anagrelide therapy is dose-related; therefore, thrombocytopenia, which can potentially cause bleeding, is expected from overdosage.

Should overdosage occur, cardiac and central nervous system toxicity can also be expected. In the case of overdosage, close clinical supervision of the patient is required; this especially includes monitoring of the platelet count for thrombocytopenia. Dosage should be decreased or stopped, as appropriate, until the platelet count returns to within the normal range.

Drug Interactions There is a single case report that suggests sucralfate may interfere with anagrelide absorption

Mechanism of Action Anagrelide appears to inhibit cyclic nucleotide phosphodiesterase and the release of arachidonic acid from phospholipase, possibly by inhibiting phospholipase A2. It also causes a dose-related reduction in platelet production, which results from decreased megakaryocyte hypermaturation. The drug disrupts the postmitotic phase of maturation.

Pharmacodynamics/Kinetics
Metabolism: In the liver

Half-life, plasma: 1.3 hours

Peak serum concentrations: Oral: 1 hour

Elimination: <1% of dose appears unchanged in urine

Usual Dosage Adults: Oral: 0.5 mg 4 times/day or 1 mg twice daily

Maintain for ≥1 week, then adjust to the lowest effective dose to reduce and maintain platelet count <600,000 µL ideally to the normal range; the dose must not be increased by >0.5 mg/day in any 1 week; maximum dose: 10 mg/day or 2.5 mg/dose

Dietary Considerations Food: No clinically significant effect on absorption

Monitoring Parameters Anagrelide therapy requires close supervision of the patient. Because of the positive inotropic effects and side effects of anagrelide, a pretreatment cardiovascular examination is recommended along with careful monitoring during treatment; while the platelet count is being lowered (usually during the first 2 weeks of treatment), blood counts (hemoglobin, white blood cells), liver function test (AST, ALT) and renal function (serum creatinine, BUN) should be monitored.

Reference Range Thrombocythemia: 60-300 ng/mL

Patient Information Before using this drug, tell your physician your entire medical history, including any allergies (especially drug allergies), heart, kidney, or liver disease. Limit alcohol intake, as it may aggravate side effects. To avoid dizziness and lightheadedness when rising from a seated or lying position, get up slowly. This medication should be used only when clearly needed during pregnancy. Discuss the risks and benefits with your physician. It is not known whether this drug is excreted into breast milk. It is recommended to discontinue the drug or not to breast-feed, taking into account the risk to the infant. Tell your physician and pharmacist of all nonprescription and prescription medications you may use, especially sucralfate. Do not share this medication with others. Laboratory tests will be done to monitor the effectiveness and possible side effects of this drug.

Dosage Forms Capsule: 0.5 mg, 1 mg

♦ **Anagrelide Hydrochloride** see Anagrelide on previous page

♦ **Anandron®** see Nilutamide on page 840

♦ **Anapolon®** see Oxymetholone on page 876

♦ **Anaprox®** see Naproxen on page 818

♦ **Anaspaz®** see Hyoscyamine on page 590

Anastrozole (an AS troe zole)

U.S. Brand Names Arimidex®

Therapeutic Category Antineoplastic Agent, Hormone (Antiestrogen)

Use Treatment of advanced breast cancer in postmenopausal women with disease progression following tamoxifen therapy. Patients with ER-negative disease and patients who did not respond to tamoxifen therapy rarely responded to anastrozole.

Pregnancy Risk Factor C

Pregnancy/Breast-Feeding Implications Clinical effects on the fetus: Anastrozole can cause fetal harm when administered to a pregnant woman

Contraindications Hypersensitivity to any component

Warnings/Precautions Use with caution in patients with hyperlipidemias; mean serum total cholesterol and LDL cholesterol occurs in patients receiving anastrozole

Adverse Reactions

>5%:

Cardiovascular: Flushing

Gastrointestinal: Little to mild nausea (10%), vomiting

Neuromuscular & skeletal: Increased bone and tumor pain

2% to 5%:

Cardiovascular: Hypertension

Central nervous system: Somnolence, confusion, insomnia, anxiety, nervousness, fever, malaise, accidental injury

Dermatologic: Hair thinning, pruritus

Endocrine & metabolic: Breast pain

Gastrointestinal: Weight loss

Genitourinary: Urinary tract infection

Local: Thrombophlebitis

Neuromuscular & skeletal: Myalgia, arthralgia, pathological fracture, neck pain

Respiratory: Sinusitis, bronchitis, rhinitis

Miscellaneous: Flu-like syndrome, infection

Overdosage/Toxicology

Symptoms of overdose include severe irritation to the stomach (necrosis, gastritis, ulceration and hemorrhage)

There is no specific antidote; treatment must be symptomatic. Vomiting may be induced if the patient is alert. Dialysis may be helpful because anastrozole is not highly protein bound. General supportive care, including frequent monitoring of all vital signs and close observation.

Drug Interactions CYP3A3/4 enzyme substrate; CYP1A2, 2C8, 2C9, and 3A3/4 enzyme inhibitor

Anastrozole inhibited in vitro metabolic reactions catalyzed by cytochromes P-450 1A2, 2C8/9, and 3A4, but only at relatively high concentrations. It is unlikely that coadministration of anastrozole with other drugs will result in clinically significant inhibition of cytochrome P-450-mediated metabolism of other drugs.

Mechanism of Action Potent and selective nonsteroidal aromatase inhibitor. It significantly lowers serum estradiol concentrations and has no detectable effect on formation of adrenal corticosteroids or aldosterone. In postmenopausal women, the principal (Continued)

Anastrozole *(Continued)*

source of circulating estrogen is conversion of adrenally generated androstenedione to estrone by aromatase in peripheral tissues.

Pharmacodynamics/Kinetics

Absorption: Well absorbed from GI tract; food does not affect absorption

Protein binding, plasma: 40%

Metabolism: Extensively in the liver

Half-life: 50 hours

Elimination: Primarily via hepatic metabolism (85%) and to a lesser extent renal excretion (11%)

Usual Dosage Breast cancer: Adults: Oral (refer to individual protocols): 1 mg once daily

Dosage adjustment in renal impairment: Because only about 10% is excreted unchanged in the urine, dosage adjustment in patients with renal insufficiency is not necessary

Dosage adjustment in hepatic impairment: Plasma concentrations in subjects with hepatic cirrhosis were within the range concentrations in normal subjects across all clinical trials; therefore, no dosage adjustment is needed

Test Interactions Lab test abnormalities: GGT, AST, ALT, alkaline phosphatase, total cholesterol and LDL increased; threefold elevations of mean serum GGT levels have been observed among patients with liver metastases. These changes were likely related to the progression of liver metastases in these patients, although other contributing factors could not be ruled out. Mean serum total cholesterol levels increased by 0.5 mmol/L among patients.

Dosage Forms Tablet: 1 mg

♦ **Anbesol® [OTC]** *see* Benzocaine *on page 133*
♦ **Anbesol® Maximum Strength [OTC]** *see* Benzocaine *on page 133*
♦ **Ancef®** *see* Cefazolin *on page 206*
♦ **Ancobon®** *see* Flucytosine *on page 489*
♦ **Ancotil®** *see* Flucytosine *on page 489*
♦ **Androderm® Transdermal System** *see* Testosterone *on page 1117*
♦ **Andro/Fem® Injection** *see* Estradiol and Testosterone *on page 435*
♦ **Android®** *see* Methyltestosterone *on page 764*
♦ **Andro-L.A.® Injection** *see* Testosterone *on page 1117*
♦ **Androlone®-D Injection** *see* Nandrolone *on page 816*
♦ **Androlone® Injection** *see* Nandrolone *on page 816*
♦ **Andropository® Injection** *see* Testosterone *on page 1117*
♦ **Anectine® Chloride Injection** *see* Succinylcholine *on page 1087*
♦ **Anectine® Flo-Pack®** *see* Succinylcholine *on page 1087*
♦ **Anergan®** *see* Promethazine *on page 979*
♦ **Anestacon®** *see* Lidocaine *on page 679*
♦ **Aneurine Hydrochloride** *see* Thiamine *on page 1131*
♦ **Anexate®** *see* Flumazenil *on page 493*
♦ **Anexsia®** *see* Hydrocodone and Acetaminophen *on page 575*
♦ **Angiotensin Agents** *see page 1291*
♦ **Animal and Human Bites Guidelines** *see page 1399*

Anisotropine *(an iss oh TROE peen)*

U.S. Brand Names Valpin® 50

Canadian Brand Names Miradon®

Synonyms Anisotropine Methylbromide

Therapeutic Category Anticholinergic Agent

Use Adjunctive treatment of peptic ulcer

Pregnancy Risk Factor C

Contraindications Narrow-angle glaucoma, obstructive GI tract or uropathy, severe ulcerative colitis, myasthenia gravis, intestinal atony, hepatic disease, hypersensitivity

Warnings/Precautions Drug-induced heatstroke can develop in hot or humid climates

Adverse Reactions

>10%:

Cardiovascular: Palpitations

Dermatologic: Dry skin

Gastrointestinal: Constipation, dry throat, xerostomia

Respiratory: Dry nose

Miscellaneous: Diaphoresis (decreased)

1% to 10%:

Endocrine & metabolic: Decreased flow of breast milk

Gastrointestinal: Decreased salivary secretion

<1%: Orthostatic hypotension, confusion, drowsiness, headache, loss of memory, fatigue, rash, bloated feeling, nausea, vomiting, decreased urination, weakness, increased intraocular pain, blurred vision, increased sensitivity to light

Overdosage/Toxicology

Symptoms of overdose include blurred vision, dysphagia, urinary retention, tachycardia, hypertension

Anisotropine toxicity is caused by strong binding of the drug to cholinergic receptors. Anticholinesterase inhibitors reduce acetylcholinesterase, the enzyme that breaks down acetylcholine and thereby allows acetylcholine to accumulate and compete for receptor binding with this offending anticholinergic. For an overdose with severe life-threatening symptoms, physostigmine 1-2 mg (0.5 mg or 0.02 mg/kg for children) S.C. or I.V., slowly may be given to reverse these effects.

Mechanism of Action Blocks the action of acetylcholine at parasympathetic sites in smooth muscle, secretory glands, and the CNS; increases cardiac output, dries secretions, antagonizes histamine and serotonin

Pharmacodynamics/Kinetics
Absorption: Poor (~10%) from GI tract
Elimination: Principally in urine as unchanged drug and metabolites

Usual Dosage Adults: Oral: 50 mg 3 times/day

Administration Administer 30-60 minutes before meals

Monitoring Parameters Monitor patient's vital signs and I & O

Patient Information Dry mouth can be relieved by sugarless gum or hard candy; drink plenty of fluids

Dosage Forms Tablet, as methylbromide: 50 mg

♦ **Anisotropine Methylbromide** see Anisotropine on previous page

♦ **Anisoylated Plasminogen Streptokinase Activator Complex** see Anistreplase on this page

Anistreplase (a NISS tre plase)

U.S. Brand Names Eminase®

Synonyms Anisoylated Plasminogen Streptokinase Activator Complex; APSAC

Therapeutic Category Thrombolytic Agent

Use Management of acute myocardial infarction (AMI) in adults; lysis of thrombi obstructing coronary arteries, reduction of infarct size; and reduction of mortality associated with AMI

Pregnancy Risk Factor C

Contraindications Active internal bleeding, history of CVA, intracranial neoplasma, known hypersensitivity to anistreplase or other kinases (streptokinase); history of cerebrovascular accident; recent intracranial surgery or trauma; arteriovenous malformation or aneurysm; severe uncontrolled hypertension

Adverse Reactions
>10%:
Cardiovascular: Arrhythmias, hypotension, perfusion arrhythmias
Hematologic: Bleeding or oozing from cuts
1% to 10%: Miscellaneous: Anaphylactic reaction
<1%: Headache, chills, rash, nausea, vomiting, anemia, eye hemorrhage, bronchospasm, epistaxis, diaphoresis

Drug Interactions Increased efficacy and bleeding potential: Anticoagulants (heparin, warfarin), antiplatelet agents (aspirin)

Stability Store between 2°C and 8°C (36°F to 46°F); discard solution 30 minutes after reconstitution if not administered; do not shake solution

Mechanism of Action Activates the conversion of plasminogen to plasmin by forming a complex exposing plasminogen-activating site and cleavage of a peptide bond that converts plasminogen to plasmin; plasmin being capable of thrombolysis, by degrading fibrin, fibrinogen and other procoagulant proteins into soluble fragments, effective both outside and within the formed thrombus/embolus

Pharmacodynamics/Kinetics
Duration of action: Fibrinolytic effect persists for 4-6 hours following administration
Metabolism: Anistreplase is an acylated complex of streptokinase with lys-plasminogen; one of the purposes of this acylation is to extend the serum circulating time of anistreplase; because deacylation of the complex occurs more rapidly than dissociation, fibrinolytic activity is controlled by the rate of deacylation rather than of dissociation
Half-life: 70-120 minutes

Usual Dosage Adults: I.V.: 30 units injected over 2-5 minutes as soon as possible after onset of symptoms

Administration Can be given as a bolus; avoid I.M. injections and nonessential handling of patient after administration of drug

Nursing Implications Drug should not be used for any condition in which bleeding constitutes a significant hazard or would be particularly difficult to manage

Dosage Forms Powder for injection, lyophilized: 30 units

♦ **Anodynos-DHC**® see Hydrocodone and Acetaminophen on page 575
♦ **Anoquan**® see Butalbital Compound on page 165
♦ **Ansaid**® **Oral** see Flurbiprofen on page 507
♦ **Ansamycin** see Rifabutin on page 1022
♦ **Antabuse**® see Disulfiram on page 380
♦ **Antacid Drug Interactions** see page 1296
♦ **Antazone**® see Sulfinpyrazone on page 1096
♦ **Anthra-Derm**® see Anthralin on this page
♦ **Anthraforte**® see Anthralin on this page

Anthralin (AN thra lin)

U.S. Brand Names Anthra-Derm®; Drithocreme®; Drithocreme® HP 1%; Dritho-Scalp®; Micanol® Cream

Canadian Brand Names Anthraforte®; Anthranol®; Anthrascalp®

Therapeutic Category Antipsoriatic Agent, Topical; Keratolytic Agent
(Continued)

Anthralin *(Continued)*

Use Treatment of psoriasis (quiescent or chronic psoriasis)

Pregnancy Risk Factor C

Contraindications Hypersensitivity to anthralin or any component, acute psoriasis (acutely or actively inflamed psoriatic eruptions); use on the face

Warnings/Precautions If redness is observed, reduce frequency of dosage or discontinue application; avoid eye contact; should generally not be applied to intertriginous skin areas and high strengths should not be used on these sites; do not apply to face or genitalia; use caution in patients with renal disease and in those having extensive and prolonged applications; perform periodic urine tests for albuminuria.

Adverse Reactions

1% to 10%: Dermatologic: Transient primary irritation of uninvolved skin; temporary discoloration of hair and fingernails; may stain skin, hair, or fabrics

<1%: Rash, excessive irritation

Drug Interactions Increased toxicity: Long-term use of topical corticosteroids may destabilize psoriasis, and withdrawal may also give rise to a "rebound" phenomenon, allow an interval of at least 1 week between the discontinuance of topical corticosteroids and the commencement of therapy

Mechanism of Action Reduction of the mitotic rate and proliferation of epidermal cells in psoriasis by inhibiting synthesis of nucleic protein from inhibition of DNA synthesis to affected areas

Usual Dosage Adults: Topical: Generally, apply once a day or as directed. The irritant potential of anthralin is directly related to the strength being used and each patient's individual tolerance. Always commence treatment for at least one week using the lowest strength possible.

Skin application: Apply sparingly only to psoriatic lesions and rub gently and carefully into the skin until absorbed. Avoid applying an excessive quantity which may cause unnecessary soiling and staining of the clothing or bed linen.

Scalp application: Comb hair to remove scalar debris and, after suitably parting, rub cream well into the lesions, taking care to prevent the cream from spreading onto the forehead

Remove by washing or showering; optimal period of contact will vary according to the strength used and the patient's response to treatment. Continue treatment until the skin is entirely clear (ie, when there is nothing to feel with the fingers and the texture is normal)

Patient Information For external use only; may discolor skin, hair, or fabrics; avoid sunlight to treated areas

Nursing Implications Wear gloves; can discolor skin, hair, or clothes

Dosage Forms

Cream: 0.1% (50 g, 65 g); 0.2% (65 g); 0.25% (50 g); 0.4% (65 g); 0.5% (50 g); 1% (50 g, 65 g)

Ointment, topical: 0.1% (42.5 g); 0.25% (42.5 g); 0.4% (60 g); 0.5% (42.5 g); 1% (42.5 g)

◆ **Anthranol**® *see* Anthralin *on previous page*

◆ **Anthrascalp**® *see* Anthralin *on previous page*

◆ **Antiarrhythmic Drugs Comparison** *see page 1297*

◆ **AntibiOtic**® **Otic** *see* Neomycin, Polymyxin B, and Hydrocortisone *on page 827*

◆ **Antibiotic Treatment of Adults With Infective Endocarditis** *see page 1401*

◆ **Anti-CD20 Monoclonal Antibodies** *see* Rituximab *on page 1035*

◆ **Anticonvulsants by Seizure Type** *see page 1300*

◆ **Antidepressant Agents Comparison** *see page 1301*

◆ **Antidigoxin Fab Fragments** *see* Digoxin Immune Fab *on page 361*

◆ **Antidiuretic Hormone** *see* Vasopressin *on page 1211*

◆ **Antifungal Agents Comparison** *see page 1303*

Antihemophilic Factor (Human)

(an tee hee moe FIL ik FAK tor HYU man)

U.S. Brand Names Hemofil® M; Humate-P®; Koate®-HP; Koate®-HS; Kogenate®; Monoclate-P®; Profilate® OSD; Profilate® SD; Recombinate®

Synonyms AHF; Factor VIII

Therapeutic Category Antihemophilic Agent; Blood Product Derivative

Use Management of hemophilia A in patients whom a deficiency in factor VIII has been demonstrated. Can be of significant therapeutic value in patients with acquired factor VII inhibitors not exceeding 10 Bethesda units/mL.

Orphan drug status: von Willebrand disease and prevention of bleeding from surgery in hemophilia A

Pregnancy Risk Factor C

Contraindications Hypersensitivity to mouse protein (Monoclate-P®; Hemofil® M, Method M, Monoclonal Purified) and Antihemophilic Factor (Human); Method M, Monoclonal Purified contain trace amounts of mouse protein

Warnings/Precautions Risk of viral transmission is not totally eradicated. Risk of hepatitis: Because antihemophilic factor is prepared for pooled plasma, it may contain the causative agent of viral hepatitis. Antihemophilic factor contains trace amounts of blood groups A and B isohemagglutinins; when large or frequently repeated doses are given to individuals with blood groups A, B, and AB, the patient should be monitored for signs of progressive anemia and the possibility of intravascular hemolysis should be considered.

Adverse Reactions <1%: Flushing, tachycardia, headache, nausea, vomiting, paresthesia, allergic vasomotor reactions, tightness in neck or chest

Overdosage/Toxicology Intravascular hemolysis

Stability Dried concentrate should be refrigerated (2°C to 8°C/36°F to 46°F) but may be stored at room temperature for up to 6 months depending upon specific product; if refrigerated, the dried concentrate and diluent should be warmed to room temperature before reconstitution; gently agitate or rotate vial after adding diluent, do not shake vigorously; do **not** refrigerate after reconstitution, a precipitation may occur; Method M, monoclonal purified products should be administered within 1 hour after reconstitution

Stability of parenteral admixture at room temperature (25°C): 24 hours, but it is recommended to administer within 3 hours after reconstitution

Mechanism of Action Protein (factor VIII) in normal plasma which is necessary for clot formation and maintenance of hemostasis; activates factor X in conjunction with activated factor IX; activated factor X converts prothrombin to thrombin, which converts fibrinogen to fibrin and with factor XIII forms a stable clot

Pharmacodynamics/Kinetics

Distribution: Does not readily cross the placenta

Half-life, biphasic: 4-24 hours with a mean of 12 hours (biphasic: 12 hours is usually used for dosing interval estimates)

Usual Dosage I.V.: Individualize dosage based on coagulation studies performed prior to and during treatment at regular intervals; 1 AHF unit is the activity present in 1 mL of normal pooled human plasma; dosage should be adjusted to actual vial size currently stocked in the pharmacy.

Hospitalized patients: 20-50 units/kg/dose; may be higher for special circumstances; dose can be given every 12-24 hours and more frequently in special circumstances

Surgery patients: The factor VIII level should be raised to approximately 100% by giving a preoperative dose of 50 international units/kg, to maintain hemostatic levels, repeat infusions may be necessary every 6-12 hours initially and for a total of 10-14 days until healing is complete

Formula to approximate percentage increase in plasma antihemophilic factor:

Units required = desired level increase (desired level - actual level) x plasma volume (mL)

Total blood volume (mL blood/kg) = 70 mL/kg (adults); 80 mL/kg (children)

Plasma volume = total blood volume (mL) x [1 - Hct (in decimals)]

Example: For a 70 kg adult with a Hct = 40%: plasma volume = [70 kg x 70 mL/kg] x [1 - 0.4] = 2940 mL

To calculate number of units of factor VIII needed to increase level to desired range (highly individualized and dependent on patient's condition):

Number of units = desired level increase [desired level - actual level] x plasma volume (in mL)

Example: For a 100% level in the above patient who has an actual level of 20% the number of units needed = [1 (for a 100% level) - 0.2] x 2940 mL = 2352 units

Administration I.V. administration only; maximum rate of administration is product dependent: Monoclate-P® 2 mL/minute; Humate-P® 4 mL/minute; administration of other products should not exceed 10 mL/minute; use filter needle to draw product into syringe

Monitoring Parameters Heart rate (before and during I.V. administration); antihemophilic factor levels prior to and during treatment; in patients with circulating inhibitors, the inhibitor level should be monitored

Reference Range

Average normal antihemophilic factor plasma activity ranges 50% to 150%

Level to prevent spontaneous hemorrhage: 5%

Required peak postinfusion AHF activity in blood (as % of normal or units/dL plasma):

Early hemarthrosis or muscle bleed or oral bleed: 20% to 40%

More extensive hemarthrosis, muscle bleed, or hematoma: 30% to 60%

Life-threatening bleeds, such as head injury, throat bleed, severe abdominal pain

Minor surgery, including tooth extraction: 60% to 80%

Major surgery: 80% to 100% (pre- and postoperative)

Nursing Implications Reduce rate of administration or temporarily discontinue if patient becomes tachycardic

Dosage Forms Injection: 10 mL, 20 mL, 30 mL

Antihemophilic Factor (Porcine)

(an tee hee moe FIL ik FAK ter POR seen)

U.S. Brand Names Hyate:C®

Therapeutic Category Antihemophilic Agent; Blood Product Derivative

Use Treatment of congenital hemophiliacs with antibodies to human factor VIII:C and also for previously nonhemophiliac patients with spontaneously acquired inhibitors to human factor VIII:C; patients with inhibitors who are bleeding or who are to undergo surgery

Pregnancy Risk Factor C

Contraindications Should not be used to treat patients who have previously suffered acute allergic reaction to antihemophilic factor (porcine)

Warnings/Precautions Rarely administration has been associated with anaphylaxis; adrenaline, hydrocortisone, and facilities for cardiopulmonary resuscitation should be available in case such a reaction occurs; infusion may be followed by a rise in plasma levels of antibody to both human and porcine factor VIII:C; inhibitor levels should be monitored both during and after treatment

(Continued)

Antihemophilic Factor (Porcine) *(Continued)*

Adverse Reactions Reactions tend to lessen in frequency and severity as further infusions are given; hydrocortisone and/or antihistamines may help to prevent or alleviate side effects and may be prescribed as precautionary measures

1% to 10%:
Central nervous system: Fever, headache, chills
Dermatologic: Rashes
Gastrointestinal: Nausea, vomiting

Stability Store at temperature of -15°C to <20°C; use before expiration date; reconstituted Hyate:C® must not be stored, stable for 24 hours at room temperature

Mechanism of Action Factor VIII:C is the coagulation portion of the factor VIII complex in plasma. Factor VIII:C acts as a cofactor for factor IX to activate factor X in the intrinsic pathway of blood coagulation.

Usual Dosage Clinical response should be used to assess efficacy rather than relying upon a particular laboratory value for recovery of factor VIII:C.

Initial dose:
Antibody level to human factor VIII:C <50 Bethesda units/mL: 100-150 porcine units/kg (body weight) is recommended
Antibody level to human factor VIII:C >50 Bethesda units/mL: Activity of the antibody to porcine factor VIII:C should be determined; **an antiporcine antibody level** >20 Bethesda units/mL indicates that the patient is unlikely to benefit from treatment; for lower titers, a dose of 100-150 porcine units/kg is recommended
If a patient has previously been treated with Hyate:C®, this may provide a guide to his likely response and, therefore, assist in estimation of the preliminary dose
Subsequent doses: Following administration of the initial dose, if the recovery of factor VIII:C in the patient's plasma is not sufficient, a further higher dose should be administered; if recovery after the second dose is still insufficient, a third and higher dose may prove effective

Administration Administer by I.V. route only; infusion rate should be <10 mL/minute

Reference Range Treatment is not normally indicated in patients with an antibody titer <5 Bethesda units/mL (BU/mL) against human factor VIII:C and is likely to be ineffective in patients with an antibody titer >50 Bethesda units/mL against human factor VIII:C

If a patient has an antibody titer >50 Bethesda units/mL against human factor VIII:C, the activity of the antibody against porcine factor VIII should be determined
An antibody titer <15-20 Bethesda units/mL against porcine factor VIII:C indicates suitability for treatment with antihemophilic factor (Porcine) Hyate:C®
Factor VIII levels: 50% to 150%, draw 6-8 hours after dose administration

Additional Information Sodium ion concentration is not more than 200 mmol/L; the assayed amount of activity is stated on the label, but may vary depending on the type of assay and hemophilic substrate plasma used

Dosage Forms Powder for injection, lyophilized: 400-700 porcine units to be reconstituted with 20 mL sterile water

♦ **Antihist-1® [OTC]** *see* Clemastine *on page 274*

♦ **Antihist-D®** *see* Clemastine and Phenylpropanolamine *on page 275*

Anti-inhibitor Coagulant Complex

(an tee-in HI bi tor coe AG yoo lant KOM pleks)

U.S. Brand Names Autoplex® T; Feiba VH Immuno®

Synonyms Coagulant Complex Inhibitor

Therapeutic Category Antihemophilic Agent; Blood Product Derivative

Use Patients with factor VIII inhibitors who are to undergo surgery or those who are bleeding

Pregnancy Risk Factor C

Contraindications Disseminated intravascular coagulation; patients with normal coagulation mechanism

Warnings/Precautions Products are prepared from pooled human plasma; such plasma may contain the causative agents of viral diseases. Tests used to control efficacy such as APTT, WBCT, and TEG do not correlate with clinical efficacy. Dosing to normalize these values may result in DIC. Identification of the clotting deficiency as caused by factor VIII inhibitors is essential prior to starting therapy. Use with extreme caution in patients with impaired hepatic function.

Adverse Reactions <1%: Hypotension, flushing, fever, headache, chills, rash, urticaria, disseminated intravascular coagulation, anaphylaxis, indications of protein sensitivity

Overdosage/Toxicology Rapid infusion may cause hypotension, excessive administration can cause DIC

Stability Store at 2°C to 8°C (36°F to 46°F); use within 1-3 hours after reconstitution

Usual Dosage Dosage range: 25-100 factor VIII correctional units per kg depending on the severity of hemorrhage

Test Interactions ↑ ↓ PT, ↑ ↓ PTT, ↓ WBCT, ↓ fibrin, ↓ platelets, ↑ fibrin split products

Nursing Implications Monitor for hypotension, may reinitiate infusion at a slower rate; have epinephrine ready to treat hypersensitivity reactions

Dosage Forms Injection:
Autoplex® T, with heparin 2 units: Each bottle is labeled with correctional units of Factor VIII
Feiba VH Immuno®, heparin free: Each bottle is labeled with correctional units of Factor VIII

- **Antilirium**® *see* Physostigmine *on page 925*
- **Antimicrobial Drugs of Choice** *see page 1404*
- **Antimigraine Drugs: Pharmacokinetic Differences** *see page 1304*
- **Antiminth**® **[OTC]** *see* Pyrantel Pamoate *on page 995*
- **Antipsychotic Agents Comparison** *see page 1305*

Antipyrine and Benzocaine (an tee PYE reen & BEN zoe kane)

U.S. Brand Names Allergan® Ear Drops; Auralgan®; Auroto®; Otocalm® Ear
Therapeutic Category Otic Agent, Analgesic; Otic Agent, Cerumenolytic
Dosage Forms Solution, otic: Antipyrine 5.4% and benzocaine 1.4% (10 mL, 15 mL)

Antirabies Serum (Equine) (an tee RAY beez SEER um EE kwine)

Synonyms ARS
Therapeutic Category Serum
Use Rabies prophylaxis
Pregnancy Risk Factor C
Adverse Reactions 1% to 10%:
Central nervous system: Pain (local)
Dermatologic: Urticaria
Miscellaneous: Serum sickness
Mechanism of Action Affords passive immunity against rabies
Usual Dosage 1000 units/55 lb in a single dose, infiltrate up to 50% of dose around the wound
Nursing Implications Take careful history of asthma, angioneurotic edema, or other allergies
Additional Information Because of a significantly lower incidence of adverse reactions, Rabies Immune Globulin, Human is preferred over Antirabies Serum Equine
Dosage Forms Injection: 125 units/mL (8 mL)

- **Antiretroviral Agents** *see page 1306*
- **Antiretroviral Therapy for HIV Infection** *see page 1410*
- **Antispas**® **Injection** *see* Dicyclomine *on page 351*

Antithrombin III (an tee THROM bin three)

U.S. Brand Names ATnativ®; Thrombate III™
Synonyms ATIII; Heparin Cofactor I
Therapeutic Category Blood Product Derivative
Use Agent for hereditary antithrombin III deficiency
Unlabeled use: Has been used effectively for acquired antithrombin III deficiencies related to DIC, pre-eclampsia, liver disease, shock and surgery complicated by DIC
Pregnancy Risk Factor C
Contraindications Hypersensitivity to any component
Warnings/Precautions Test methods and treatment methods may not totally eradicate HBAg and HIV from pooled plasma used in processing of this product
Adverse Reactions <1%: Dizziness, lightheadedness, fever, chest tightness, chest pain, vasodilatory effects, edema, urticaria, fluid overload, nausea, foul taste in mouth, cramps, bowel fullness, hematoma formation, film over eye, diuretic effects, shortness of breath
Overdosage/Toxicology Levels of 150% to 200% have been documented in patients with no signs or symptoms of complications
Drug Interactions Increased toxicity: Anticoagulation effect of heparin is enhanced
Stability Reconstitute with 10 mL sterile water for injection, normal saline or D₅W; **do not shake**; stability of I.V. admixture: 24 hours at room temperature; do not refrigerate
Mechanism of Action Antithrombin III is the primary physiologic inhibitor of *in vivo* coagulation. It is an alpha₂-globulin. Its principal actions are the inactivation of thrombin, plasmin, and other active serine proteases of coagulation, including factors IXa, Xa, XIa, XIIa, and VIIa. The inactivation of proteases is a major step in the normal clotting process. The strong activation of clotting enzymes at the site of every bleeding injury facilitates fibrin formation and maintains normal hemostasis. Thrombosis in the circulation would be caused by active serine proteases if they were not inhibited by antithrombin III after the localized clotting process. Patients with congenital deficiency are in a prethrombotic state, even if asymptomatic, as evidenced by elevated plasma levels of prothrombin activation fragment, which are normalized following infusions of antithrombin III concentrate.
Usual Dosage After first dose of antithrombin III, level should increase to 120% of normal; thereafter maintain at levels >80%. Generally, achieved by administration of maintenance doses once every 24 hours; initially and until patient is stabilized, measure antithrombin III level at least twice daily, thereafter once daily and always immediately before next infusion. 1 unit = quantity of antithrombin III in 1 mL of normal pooled human plasma; administration of 1 unit/1 kg raises AT-III level by 1% to 2%; assume plasma volume of 40 mL/kg

Initial dosage (units) = [desired AT-III level % - baseline AT-III level %] x body weight (kg) divided by 1%/units/kg, eg, if a 70 kg adult patient had a baseline AT-III level of 57%, the initial dose would be (120% - 57%) x 70/1%/units/kg = 4,410 units
Measure antithrombin III preceding and 30 minutes after dose to calculate *in vivo* recovery rate; maintain level within normal range for 2-8 days depending on type of surgery or procedure
(Continued)

Antithrombin III *(Continued)*

Administration Infuse over 5-10 minutes; rate of infusion is 50 units/minute (1 mL/minute) not to exceed 100 units/minute (2 mL/minute)

Monitoring Parameters Monitor antithrombin III levels during treatment period

Reference Range Maintain antithrombin III level in plasma >80%

Dosage Forms Powder for injection: 500 units (50 mL)

♦ Antithymocyte Globulin (Equine) *see* Lymphocyte Immune Globulin *on page 702*

Antithymocyte Globulin (Rabbit)

(an te THY moe site GLOB yu lin (RAB bit)

U.S. Brand Names Thymoglobulin®

Synonyms Antithymocyte Immunoglobulin; ATG

Therapeutic Category Immunosuppressant Agent

Use Treatment of renal transplant acute rejection in conjunction with concomitant immunosuppression

Pregnancy Risk Factor C

Contraindications Patients with history of allergy or anaphylaxis to rabbit proteins, or who have an acute viral illness

Warnings/Precautions Infusion may produce fever and chills. To minimize, the first dose should be infused over a minimum of 6 hours into a high-flow vein. Also, premedication with corticosteroids, acetaminophen, and/or an antihistamine and/or slowing the infusion rate may reduce reaction incidence and intensity.

Prolonged use or overdosage of Thymoglobulin® in association with other immunosuppressive agents may cause over-immunosuppression resulting in severe infections and may increase the incidence of lymphoma or post-transplant lymphoproliferative disease (PTLD) or other malignancies. Appropriate antiviral, antibacterial, antiprotozoal, and/or antifungal prophylaxis is recommended.

Thymoglobulin® should only be used by physicians experienced in immunosuppressive therapy for the treatment of renal transplant patients. Medical surveillance is required during the infusion. In rare circumstances, anaphylaxis has been reported with use. In such cases, the infusion should be terminated immediately. Medical personnel should be available to treat patients who experience anaphylaxis. Emergency treatment such as 0.3-0.5 mL aqueous epinephrine (1:1000 dilution) subcutaneously and other resuscitative measures including oxygen, intravenous fluids, antihistamines, corticosteroids, pressor amines, and airway management, as clinically indicated, should be provided. Thymoglobulin® or other rabbit immunoglobulins should not be administered again for such patients. Thrombocytopenia or neutropenia may result from cross-reactive antibodies and is reversible following dose adjustments.

Adverse Reactions

>10%:
   Central nervous system: Fever, chills, headache
   Dermatologic: Rash
   Endocrine & metabolic: Hyperkalemia
   Gastrointestinal: Abdominal pain, diarrhea
   Hematologic: Leukopenia, thrombocytopenia
   Neuromuscular & skeletal: Weakness
   Respiratory: Dyspnea
   Miscellaneous: Systemic infection, pain

1% to 10%:
   Gastrointestinal: Gastritis
   Respiratory: Pneumonia
   Miscellaneous: Sensitivity reactions: Anaphylaxis may be indicated by hypotension, respiratory distress, serum sickness, viral infection

Stability

Store intact vials under refrigeration (2°C to 8°C/36°F to 46°F); protect from light and do not freeze

Allow Thymoglobulin® and diluent (sterile WFI) to reach room temperature before reconstituting the lyophilized product. Reconstitute Thymoglobulin® with the supplied diluent, sterile water for injection immediately before use. Thymoglobulin® should be used within 4 hours of reconstitution if kept at room temperature.

Reconstitute each vial of Thymoglobulin® lyophilized powder with 5 mL of sterile diluent to yield a concentration of 5 mg/mL of Thymoglobulin®.

The calculated dosage of Thymoglobulin® should be should be further diluted in 50-500 mL of 0.9% sodium chloride or 5% dextrose in water. Each vial of Thymoglobulin® should be further diluted to 50 mL of infusion solution.

Mechanism of Action May involve elimination of antigen-reactive T-lymphocytes (killer cells) in peripheral blood or alteration of T-cell function

Pharmacodynamics/Kinetics Half-life, plasma: 2-3 days

Usual Dosage I.V.: 1.5 mg/kg/day for 7-14 days

Administration For I.V. use only; administer via central line; use of high flow veins will minimize the occurrence of phlebitis and thrombosis; administer by slow I.V. infusion through an in-line filter with pore size of 0.2 micrometer over a minimum of 6 hours for the first infusion and over at least 4 hours on subsequent days of therapy.

Monitoring Parameters Lymphocyte profile, CBC with differential and platelet count, vital signs during administration

Nursing Implications For I.V. use only; mild itching and erythema can be treated with antihistamines; infuse first dose over at least 6 hours; any severe systemic reaction to the skin test such as generalized rash, tachycardia, dyspnea, hypotension, or anaphylaxis should preclude further therapy. **Epinephrine and resuscitation equipment should be nearby.** Patient may need to be pretreated with an antipyretic, antihistamine, and/or corticosteroid.

Dosage Forms Injection: 25 mg vials (with diluent)

- **Antithymocyte Immunoglobulin** *see* Antithymocyte Globulin (Rabbit) *on previous page*
- **Antithymocyte Immunoglobulin** *see* Lymphocyte Immune Globulin *on page 702*
- **Anti-Tuss® Expectorant [OTC]** *see* Guaifenesin *on page 549*
- **Antivert®** *see* Meclizine *on page 719*
- **Antizol®** *see* Fomepizole *on page 516*
- **Antrizine®** *see* Meclizine *on page 719*
- **Anturan®** *see* Sulfinpyrazone *on page 1096*
- **Anturane®** *see* Sulfinpyrazone *on page 1096*
- **Anucort-HC® Suppository** *see* Hydrocortisone *on page 579*
- **Anuprep HC® Suppository** *see* Hydrocortisone *on page 579*
- **Anusol® HC-1 [OTC]** *see* Hydrocortisone *on page 579*
- **Anusol® HC-2.5% [OTC]** *see* Hydrocortisone *on page 579*
- **Anusol-HC® Suppository** *see* Hydrocortisone *on page 579*
- **Anxanil®** *see* Hydroxyzine *on page 589*
- **Anzemet®** *see* Dolasetron *on page 385*
- **Apacet® [OTC]** *see* Acetaminophen *on page 19*
- **APAP** *see* Acetaminophen *on page 19*
- **Aphthasol™** *see* Amlexanox *on page 64*
- **A.P.L.®** *see* Chorionic Gonadotropin *on page 258*
- **Aplisol®** *see* Tuberculin Purified Protein Derivative *on page 1194*
- **Aplisol®** *see* Tuberculin Tests *on page 1194*
- **Aplitest®** *see* Tuberculin Purified Protein Derivative *on page 1194*
- **Aplitest®** *see* Tuberculin Tests *on page 1194*
- **Aplonidine** *see* Apraclonidine *on next page*
- **Apo®-Acetazolamide** *see* Acetazolamide *on page 22*
- **Apo®-Allopurinol** *see* Allopurinol *on page 44*
- **Apo®-Alpraz** *see* Alprazolam *on page 45*
- **Apo®-Amitriptyline** *see* Amitriptyline *on page 62*
- **Apo®-Amoxi** *see* Amoxicillin *on page 69*
- **Apo®-Ampi Trihydrate** *see* Ampicillin *on page 79*
- **Apo®-ASA** *see* Aspirin *on page 102*
- **Apo®-Atenol** *see* Atenolol *on page 106*
- **Apo® Bromocriptine** *see* Bromocriptine *on page 155*
- **Apo®-C** *see* Ascorbic Acid *on page 99*
- **Apo®-Cal** *see* Calcium Carbonate *on page 174*
- **Apo®-Capto** *see* Captopril *on page 185*
- **Apo®-Carbamazepine** *see* Carbamazepine *on page 188*
- **Apo®-Cefaclor** *see* Cefaclor *on page 202*
- **Apo®-Cephalex** *see* Cephalexin *on page 228*
- **Apo®-Chlordiazepoxide** *see* Chlordiazepoxide *on page 239*
- **Apo®-Chlorpromazine** *see* Chlorpromazine *on page 248*
- **Apo®-Chlorpropamide** *see* Chlorpropamide *on page 250*
- **Apo®-Chlorthalidone** *see* Chlorthalidone *on page 251*
- **Apo®-Cimetidine** *see* Cimetidine *on page 261*
- **Apo®-Clomipramine** *see* Clomipramine *on page 281*
- **Apo®-Clonidine** *see* Clonidine *on page 283*
- **Apo®-Clorazepate** *see* Clorazepate *on page 286*
- **Apo®-Cloxi** *see* Cloxacillin *on page 288*
- **Apo®-Diazepam** *see* Diazepam *on page 345*
- **Apo®-Diclo** *see* Diclofenac *on page 348*
- **Apo®-Diflunisal** *see* Diflunisal *on page 356*
- **Apo®-Diltiaz** *see* Diltiazem *on page 365*
- **Apo®-Dipyridamole FC** *see* Dipyridamole *on page 377*
- **Apo®-Dipyridamole SC** *see* Dipyridamole *on page 377*
- **Apo®-Doxepin** *see* Doxepin *on page 392*
- **Apo®-Doxy** *see* Doxycycline *on page 397*
- **Apo®-Doxy Tabs** *see* Doxycycline *on page 397*
- **Apo®-Enalapril** *see* Enalapril *on page 409*
- **Apo®-Erythro E-C** *see* Erythromycin *on page 427*
- **Apo®-Famotidine** *see* Famotidine *on page 469*
- **Apo®-Fenofibrate** *see* Fenofibrate *on page 472*
- **Apo-Ferrous® Gluconate** *see* Ferrous Gluconate *on page 479*
- **Apo-Ferrous® Sulfate** *see* Ferrous Sulfate *on page 480*
- **Apo®-Fluphenazine** *see* Fluphenazine *on page 504*
- **Apo®-Flurazepam** *see* Flurazepam *on page 506*

- **Apo®-Flurbiprofen** *see* Flurbiprofen *on page 507*
- **Apo®-Fluvoxamine** *see* Fluvoxamine *on page 511*
- **Apo®-Folic** *see* Folic Acid *on page 512*
- **Apo®-Furosemide** *see* Furosemide *on page 525*
- **Apo-Gain®** *see* Minoxidil *on page 783*
- **Apo®-Gemfibrozil** *see* Gemfibrozil *on page 532*
- **Apo®-Glyburide** *see* Glyburide *on page 540*
- **Apo®-Guanethidine** *see* Guanethidine *on page 552*
- **Apo®-Hydralazine** *see* Hydralazine *on page 572*
- **Apo®-Hydro** *see* Hydrochlorothiazide *on page 574*
- **Apo®-Hydroxyzine** *see* Hydroxyzine *on page 589*
- **Apo®-Ibuprofen** *see* Ibuprofen *on page 593*
- **Apo®-Imipramine** *see* Imipramine *on page 601*
- **Apo®-Indapadmide** *see* Indapamide *on page 607*
- **Apo®-Indomethacin** *see* Indomethacin *on page 609*
- **Apo®-ISDN** *see* Isosorbide Dinitrate *on page 637*
- **Apo®-Keto** *see* Ketoprofen *on page 650*
- **Apo®-Keto-E** *see* Ketoprofen *on page 650*
- **Apo®-Lisinopril** *see* Lisinopril *on page 686*
- **Apo®-Lorazepam** *see* Lorazepam *on page 694*
- **Apo®-Lovastatin** *see* Lovastatin *on page 699*
- **Apo®-Mefenamic** *see* Mefenamic Acid *on page 722*
- **Apo®-Meprobamate** *see* Meprobamate *on page 731*
- **Apo®-Methyldopa** *see* Methyldopa *on page 758*
- **Apo®-Metoclop** *see* Metoclopramide *on page 766*
- **Apo®-Metoprolol (Type L)** *see* Metoprolol *on page 768*
- **Apo®-Metronidazole** *see* Metronidazole *on page 770*
- **Apo®-Minocycline** *see* Minocycline *on page 782*
- **Apo®-Nadol** *see* Nadolol *on page 807*
- **Apo®-Naproxen** *see* Naproxen *on page 818*
- **Apo®-Nifed** *see* Nifedipine *on page 838*
- **Apo®-Nitrofurantoin** *see* Nitrofurantoin *on page 843*
- **Apo®-Nizatidine** *see* Nizatidine *on page 848*
- **Apo®-Nortriptyline** *see* Nortriptyline *on page 852*
- **Apo®-Oxazepam** *see* Oxazepam *on page 872*
- **Apo®-Pentoxifylline SR** *see* Pentoxifylline *on page 905*
- **Apo®-Pen VK** *see* Penicillin V Potassium *on page 898*
- **Apo®-Perphenazine** *see* Perphenazine *on page 909*
- **Apo®-Pindol** *see* Pindolol *on page 929*
- **Apo®-Piroxicam** *see* Piroxicam *on page 935*
- **Apo®-Prazo** *see* Prazosin *on page 959*
- **Apo®-Prednisone** *see* Prednisone *on page 963*
- **Apo®-Primidone** *see* Primidone *on page 966*
- **Apo®-Procainamide** *see* Procainamide *on page 968*
- **Apo®-Propranolol** *see* Propranolol *on page 986*
- **Apo®-Ranitidine** *see* Ranitidine Hydrochloride *on page 1011*
- **Apo®-Salvent** *see* Albuterol *on page 35*
- **Apo®-Selegiline** *see* Selegiline *on page 1053*
- **Apo®-Sulfamethoxazole** *see* Sulfamethoxazole *on page 1094*
- **Apo®-Sulfasalazine** *see* Sulfasalazine *on page 1095*
- **Apo®-Sulfatrim** *see* Co-Trimoxazole *on page 299*
- **Apo®-Sulfinpyrazone** *see* Sulfinpyrazone *on page 1096*
- **Apo®-Sulin** *see* Sulindac *on page 1099*
- **Apo®-Tamox** *see* Tamoxifen *on page 1106*
- **Apo®-Temazepam** *see* Temazepam *on page 1111*
- **Apo®-Tetra** *see* Tetracycline *on page 1122*
- **Apo®-Thioridazine** *see* Thioridazine *on page 1135*
- **Apo®-Timol** *see* Timolol *on page 1146*
- **Apo®-Timop** *see* Timolol *on page 1146*
- **Apo®-Tolbutamide** *see* Tolbutamide *on page 1155*
- **Apo®-Triazide** *see* Hydrochlorothiazide and Triamterene *on page 575*
- **Apo®-Triazo** *see* Triazolam *on page 1178*
- **Apo®-Trihex** *see* Trihexyphenidyl *on page 1182*
- **Apo®-Trimip** *see* Trimipramine *on page 1186*
- **Apo®-Verap** *see* Verapamil *on page 1214*
- **Apo®-Zidovudine** *see* Zidovudine *on page 1235*
- **APPG** *see* Penicillin G Procaine *on page 897*

Apraclonidine (a pra KLOE ni deen)
U.S. Brand Names Iopidine®
Synonyms Aplonidine; Apraclonidine Hydrochloride; p-Aminoclonidine

Therapeutic Category Alpha$_2$-Adrenergic Agonist Agent, Ophthalmic; Sympathomimetic Agent, Ophthalmic

Use Prevention and treatment of postsurgical intraocular pressure elevation

Pregnancy Risk Factor C

Contraindications Known hypersensitivity to apraclonidine or clonidine

Warnings/Precautions Closely monitor patients who develop exaggerated reductions in intraocular pressure; use with caution in patients with cardiovascular disease and in patients with a history of vasovagal reactions

Adverse Reactions
1% to 10%:
Central nervous system: Lethargy
Gastrointestinal: Xerostomia
Ocular: Upper lid elevation, conjunctival blanching, mydriasis, burning and itching eyes, discomfort, conjunctival microhemorrhage, blurred vision
Respiratory: Dry nose
<1%: Allergic response, some systemic effects have also been reported including GI, CNS, and cardiovascular symptoms (arrhythmias)

Drug Interactions Increased effect: Topical beta-blockers, pilocarpine → additive ↓ intraocular pressure

Stability Store in tight, light-resistant containers

Mechanism of Action Apraclonidine is a potent alpha-adrenergic agent similar to clonidine; relatively selective for alpha$_2$-receptors but does retain some binding to alpha$_1$-receptors; appears to result in reduction of aqueous humor formation; its penetration through the blood-brain barrier is more polar than clonidine which reduces its penetration through the blood-brain barrier and suggests that its pharmacological profile is characterized by peripheral rather than central effects.

Pharmacodynamics/Kinetics
Onset of action: 1 hour
Maximum IOP: 3-5 hours

Usual Dosage Adults: Ophthalmic:
0.5%: Instill 1-2 drops in the affected eye(s) 3 times/day; since apraclonidine 0.5% will be used with other ocular glaucoma therapies, use an approximate 5-minute interval between instillation of each medication to prevent washout of the previous dose
1%: Instill 1 drop in operative eye 1 hour prior to anterior segment laser surgery, second drop in eye immediately upon completion of procedure

Dosing adjustment in renal impairment: Although the topical use of apraclonidine has not been studied in renal failure patients, structurally related clonidine undergoes a significant increase in half-life in patients with severe renal impairment; close monitoring of cardiovascular parameters in patients with impaired renal function is advised if they are candidates for topical apraclonidine therapy

Dosing adjustment in hepatic impairment: Close monitoring of cardiovascular parameters in patients with impaired liver function is advised because the systemic dosage form of clonidine is partially metabolized in the liver

Monitoring Parameters Closely monitor patients who develop exaggerated reductions in intraocular pressure

Dosage Forms Solution, ophthalmic, as hydrochloride: 0.5% (5 mL); 1% (0.1 mL, 0.25 mL)

♦ **Apraclonidine Hydrochloride** *see Apraclonidine on previous page*

♦ **Apresazide®** *see Hydralazine and Hydrochlorothiazide on page 573*

♦ **Apresoline®** *see Hydralazine on page 572*

♦ **Aprodine® w/C** *see Triprolidine, Pseudoephedrine, and Codeine on page 1188*

Aprotinin (a proe TYE nin)

U.S. Brand Names Trasylol®

Therapeutic Category Blood Product Derivative; Hemostatic Agent

Use Reduction or prevention of blood loss in patients undergoing coronary artery bypass surgery when a high risk of excessive bleeding exists; this includes open heart reoperation, pre-existing coagulopathies, operations on the great vessels, and when a patient's beliefs prohibit blood transfusions

Pregnancy Risk Factor B

Contraindications Hypersensitivity to aprotinin or any component, patients with thromboembolic disease requiring anticoagulants or blood factor administration

Warnings/Precautions Patients with a previous exposure to aprotinin are at an increased risk of hypersensitivity reactions

Adverse Reactions
1% to 10%:
Cardiovascular: Atrial fibrillation, myocardial infarction, heart failure, atrial flutter, ventricular tachycardia, hypotension
Central nervous system: Fever, mental confusion
Local: Phlebitis
Renal: Increased potential for postoperative renal dysfunction
Respiratory: Dyspnea, bronchoconstriction
<1%: Cerebral embolism, cerebrovascular events, convulsions, hemolysis, liver damage, pulmonary edema, anaphylactic reactions have been reported in <0.5% of recipients, such reactions are more likely with repeated administration

Overdosage/Toxicology Maximum amount of aprotinin that can safely be given has not yet been determined. One case report of aprotinin overdose was associated with the development of hepatic and renal failure and eventually death. Autopsy demonstrated
(Continued)

Aprotinin *(Continued)*

severe hepatic necrosis and extensive renal tubular and glomerular necrosis. The relationship with these findings and aprotinin remains unclear.

Drug Interactions

Decreased effect: Blocks fibrinolytic effects of streptokinase or anistreplase; may decrease hypotensive effects of captopril (and other ACE inhibitors)

Increased effect: Heparin's whole blood clotting time may be prolonged; use with succinylcholine can produce prolonged or recurring apnea

Stability Vials should be stored between 2°C and 25°C and protected from freezing; it is **incompatible** with corticosteroids, heparin, tetracyclines, amino acid solutions, and fat emulsion

Mechanism of Action Serine protease inhibitor; inhibits plasmin, kallikrein, and platelet activation producing antifibrinolytic effects; a weak inhibitor of plasma pseudocholinesterase. It also inhibits the contact phase activation of coagulation and preserves adhesive platelet glycoproteins making them resistant to damage from increased circulating plasmin or mechanical injury occurring during bypass

Pharmacodynamics/Kinetics

Half-life: 150 minutes

Elimination: By the kidney

Usual Dosage

Test dose: **All** patients should receive a 1 mL I.V. test dose at least 10 minutes prior to the loading dose to assess the potential for allergic reactions

Regimen A (standard dose):

2 million units (280 mg) loading dose I.V. over 20-30 minutes

2 million units (280 mg) into pump prime volume

500,000 units/hour (70 mg/hour) I.V. during operation

Regimen B (low dose):

1 million units (140 mg) loading dose I.V. over 20-30 minutes

1 million units (140 mg) into pump prime volume

250,000 units/hour (35 mg/hour) I.V. during operation

Administration All intravenous doses should be administered through a central line

Monitoring Parameters Bleeding times, prothrombin time, activated clotting time, platelet count, red blood cell counts, hematocrit, hemoglobin and fibrinogen degradation products; for toxicity also include renal function tests and blood pressure

Reference Range Antiplasmin effects occur when plasma aprotinin concentrations are 125 KIU/mL and antikallikrein effects occur when plasma levels are 250-500 KIU/mL; it remains unknown if these plasma concentrations are required for clinical benefits to occur during cardiopulmonary bypass

Test Interactions Aprotinin prolongs whole blood clotting time of heparinized blood as determined by the Hemochrom® method or similar surface activation methods. Patients may require additional heparin even in the presence of activated clotting time levels that appear to represent adequate anticoagulation.

Dosage Forms Injection: 1.4 mg/mL [10,000 units/mL] (100 mL, 200 mL)

♦ **APSAC** *see* Anistreplase *on page 87*

♦ **Aquacare® Topical [OTC]** *see* Urea *on page 1199*

♦ **Aquachloral® Supprettes®** *see* Chloral Hydrate *on page 235*

♦ **AquaMEPHYTON® Injection** *see* Phytonadione *on page 926*

♦ **Aquaphyllin®** *see* Theophylline Salts *on page 1125*

♦ **Aquasol A®** *see* Vitamin A *on page 1223*

♦ **Aquasol E® [OTC]** *see* Vitamin E *on page 1225*

♦ **Aquatag®** *see* Benzthiazide *on page 135*

♦ **Aquatensen®** *see* Methyclothiazide *on page 757*

♦ **Aqueous Procaine Penicillin G** *see* Penicillin G Procaine *on page 897*

♦ **Aqueous Testosterone** *see* Testosterone *on page 1117*

♦ **Aquest®** *see* Estrone *on page 439*

♦ **Ara-A** *see* Vidarabine *on page 1217*

♦ **Arabinofuranosyladenine** *see* Vidarabine *on page 1217*

♦ **Arabinosylcytosine** *see* Cytarabine *on page 313*

♦ **Ara-C** *see* Cytarabine *on page 313*

♦ **Aralen® Phosphate** *see* Chloroquine Phosphate *on page 243*

♦ **Aralen® Phosphate With Primaquine Phosphate** *see* Chloroquine and Primaquine *on page 242*

♦ **Aramine®** *see* Metaraminol *on page 740*

♦ **Arava™** *see* Leflunomide *on page 661*

Ardeparin *(ar dee PA rin)*

Related Information

Heparins Comparison *on page 1324*

U.S. Brand Names Normiflo®

Synonyms Ardeparin Sodium

Therapeutic Category Low Molecular Weight Heparin

Use Prevention of deep vein thrombosis (DVT) which may lead to pulmonary embolism following knee replacement surgery

Pregnancy Risk Factor C

Contraindications Hypersensitivity to ardeparin, pork products, or other low-molecular weight heparins; cerebrovascular disease or other active hemorrhage; cerebral aneurysm; severe uncontrolled hypertension; thrombocytopenia associated with a positive *in vitro* test for antiplatelet antibodies in the presence of ardeparin

Warnings/Precautions Not intended for I.M. or I.V. use; use with extreme caution in patients with history of heparin-induced thrombocytopenia; may cause allergic-type reaction including anaphylactic symptoms and life-threatening or less severe asthmatic episodes in certain susceptible individuals; sulfite sensitivity more likely in asthmatics than nonasthmatics; use with extreme caution in patients with conditions having increased risk of hemorrhage (ie, bacterial endocarditis, congenital or acquired bleeding disorders, active ulcerative or angiodysplastic gastrointestinal disease, severe uncontrolled hypertension, hemorrhagic stroke, or shortly after brain, spinal, or ophthalmologic surgery) or in patients treated concomitantly with platelet inhibitors; use with caution in patients with hypersensitivity to methylparaben or propylparaben; use with caution in patients with bleeding diathesis, recent GI bleeding, thrombocytopenia or platelet defects, severe liver disease, hypertensive or diabetic retinopathy, or if undergoing invasive procedure especially if receiving other drugs known to interfere with hemostasis.

Patient should be observed closely for bleeding if ardeparin is administered during or immediately following diagnostic lumbar puncture, epidural anesthesia, or spinal anesthesia. If thromboembolism develops despite ardeparin prophylaxis, ardeparin should be discontinued and appropriate treatment should be initiated.

Carefully monitor patients receiving low molecular weight heparins or heparinoids. These drugs, when used concurrently with spinal or epidural anesthesia or spinal puncture, may cause bleeding or hematomas within the spinal column. Increased pressure on the spinal cord may result in permanent paralysis if not detected and treated immediately.

Adverse Reactions 1% to 10%:
Central nervous system: Fever (3%), confusion (<1%)
Dermatologic: Pruritus (2%), rash (2%), ecchymosis (2%)
Gastrointestinal: Nausea (3%), constipation (<1%), vomiting (1%)
Hematologic: Hemorrhage (5%), thrombocytopenia (2%), anemia (8%)

Overdosage/Toxicology
Main symptom of overdose is bleeding which may first be indicated with bleeding at the surgical site or at the venipuncture site; other symptoms include epistaxis, hematuria, or blood in stool; easy bruising or petechiae may precede frank bleeding.
Treatment includes discontinuing the drug and applying pressure to the site, if possible, and replacing volume and hemostatic blood elements (eg, fresh frozen plasma, platelets) as necessary. 1 mg protamine neutralizes approximately 100 anti-Xa units of ardeparin. Anti-IIa activity of I.V. ardeparin is completely neutralized within 10 minutes following I.V. infusion dose of equal weight protamine sulfate (about 1 mg protamine sulfate for each 100 anti-Xa units of ardeparin). The anti-Xa and Heptest® activities of ardeparin are reduced by ~75% within 10 minutes and are almost completely neutralized within 30 minutes after protamine sulfate administration. Protamine sulfate may cause anaphylactoid reactions that can be life-threatening; it should be given only when resuscitation techniques and treatment of anaphylactic shock are available (see Protamine Sulfate for additional information).

Drug Interactions Use with anticoagulants or platelet inhibitors, including aspirin and NSAIDs, may induce or augment bleeding

Stability Store at room temperature 15°C to 25°C (59°F to 77°F)

Mechanism of Action A low molecular weight heparin with antithrombotic properties; a partially depolymerized porcine mucosal heparin that has the same molecular subunits as heparin sodium, although its molecular weight is lower; acts at multiple sites in the normal coagulation system; binds to and accelerates the activity of antithrombin III, thereby inhibiting thrombosis by inactivating factor Xa and thrombin; inhibits thrombin by binding to heparin cofactor II

Pharmacodynamics/Kinetics
Absorption: S.C.: Well absorbed
Bioavailability: ~90%
Peak plasma levels: 2-3 hours (anti-Xa activity)
   Note: Peak anti-Xa plasma levels produced by ardeparin are about twice as high as those produced by heparin, and ardeparin anti-Xa half-life in plasma is longer than that for unfractionated heparin
Half-life: 3 hours
Elimination: Like other low-molecular-weight heparins, elimination of ardeparin appears to be via renal excretion as unchanged drug. Pharmacokinetic parameters for ardeparin suggest saturable elimination.

Usual Dosage Adults: S.C.: 50 anti-Xa units/kg every 12 hours for DVT prophylaxis
If the ardeparin formulation used contains 5000 anti-Xa units/0.5 mL (which is recommended for patients up to 100 kg or 220 lbs), the volume to be administered is calculated as follows:
Patient's weight (kg) x 0.005 mL/kg = volume (mL)
If the ardeparin formulation used contains 10,000 anti-Xa units/0.5 mL (which is recommended for patients >100 kg or 220 lbs), the volume to be administered is calculated as follows:
Patient's weight (kg) x 0.0025 mL/kg = volume (mL)
Dosage adjustment in renal impairment: No adjustment necessary
Not dialyzable

Administration Administer by deep S.C. injection; do not give I.M. Patient should be sitting or lying down. May be injected into abdomen (avoid the navel), the anterior aspect
(Continued)

Ardeparin *(Continued)*

of the thighs, or the outer aspect of the upper arms. Vary site with each injection. A skinfold held between the thumb and forefinger must be lifted. Entire length of the needle is inserted into the fold at a 45° to 90° angle. Before injecting, draw back on the plunger to ensure the needle is not in the intravascular space. Do not rub injection site after completing injection. Treatment should begin the evening of the day of surgery or the following morning and is continued for up to 14 days or until patient is fully ambulatory.

Monitoring Parameters Monitor CBC including platelet counts, urinalysis, and occult blood in stool. Patients should be observed closely for bleeding if administered during or immediately following diagnostic lumbar puncture, epidural anesthesia, or spinal anesthesia. If thromboembolism develops despite ardeparin prophylaxis, ardeparin should be discontinued and appropriate treatment should be initiated. It is recommended during therapy to monitor complete blood counts including platelet counts, urinalysis, and occult blood in stools. Monitoring of coagulation parameters (APTT) during thromboprophylaxis with ardeparin is not required nor recommended.

Test Interactions At recommended doses, ardeparin has no effect on PT; APTT may show no change or be prolonged; asymptomatic increases in AST and ALT levels >3 times the upper limit of normal have been reported in 20 of 16 and 4 of 16 normal subjects; because aminotransferase determinations are important in the differential diagnosis of myocardial infarction, liver disease, and pulmonary embolism, elevations should be interpreted with caution; ardeparin may increase activity of lipoprotein lipase; paradoxical elevations in serum triglyceride levels have been seen in clinical trials

Patient Information Tell your physician of any over-the-counter or prescription medication you may take including aspirin, warfarin, NSAID (eg, ibuprofen, naproxen). Because this drug can alter the effects of certain laboratory tests, be sure to remind your physician you are taking this medication when you are scheduled for any tests. This medication should not be mixed with, or added to, any other drug in the same syringe. Laboratory tests will be done periodically while taking this medication to monitor its effects and to prevent side effects. Use each dose at the scheduled time. If you miss a dose, use it as soon as remembered; do not use it if it is near the time for the next dose. Instead, skip the missed dose and resume your usual dosing schedule. Do not "double-up" the dose to catch up.

Nursing Implications See Administration

Dosage Forms Injection, as sodium: 5000 anti-Xa units (0.5 mL); 10,000 anti-Xa units (0.5 mL)

- ♦ **Ardeparin Sodium** *see Ardeparin on page 96*
- ♦ **Arduan®** *see Pipecuronium on page 930*
- ♦ **Aredia™** *see Pamidronate on page 882*
- ♦ **Argesic®-SA** *see Salsalate on page 1047*

Arginine *(AR ji neen)*

U.S. Brand Names R-Gene®

Therapeutic Category Diagnostic Agent, Pituitary Function; Metabolic Alkalosis Agent

Use Pituitary function test (growth hormone); management of severe, uncompensated, metabolic alkalosis (pH ≥7.55) **after** optimizing therapy with sodium and potassium supplements

Pregnancy Risk Factor C

Contraindications Known hypersensitivity to arginine; renal or hepatic failure

Usual Dosage I.V.:

Pituitary function test:
  Children: 500 mg kg/dose administered over 30 minutes
  Adults: 30 g (300 mL) administered over 30 minutes

Inborn errors of urea synthesis: Initial: 0.8 g/kg, then 0.2-0.8 g/kg/day as a continuous infusion

Metabolic alkalosis: Children and Adults: *Arginine hydrochloride is a fourth-line treatment for uncompensated metabolic alkalosis after sodium chloride, potassium chloride, and ammonium chloride supplementation has been optimized.*

  Arginine dose (G) = weight (kg) x 0.1 x (HCO$_3^-$ - 24) where HCO$_3^-$ = the patient's serum bicarbonate concentration in mEq/L

  Give ½ to ⅓ dose calculated then re-evaluate

  Note: Arginine hydrochloride should never be used as an alternative to chloride supplementation but used in the patient who is unresponsive to sodium chloride or potassium chloride supplementation

Hypochloremia: Children and Adults: Arginine dose (mL) = 0.4 x weight (kg) x (103-Cl$^-$) where Cl$^-$ = the patient's serum chloride concentration in mEq/L

  Give ½ to ⅓ dose calculated then re-evaluate

Additional Information Complete prescribing information for this medication should be consulted for additional detail

Dosage Forms Injection, as hydrochloride: 10% [100 mg/mL = 950 mOsm/L] (500 mL)

- ♦ **8-Arginine Vasopressin** *see Vasopressin on page 1211*
- ♦ **Aricept®** *see Donepezil on page 386*
- ♦ **Arimidex®** *see Anastrozole on page 85*
- ♦ **Aristocort®** *see Triamcinolone on page 1174*
- ♦ **Aristocort® A** *see Triamcinolone on page 1174*
- ♦ **Aristocort® Forte** *see Triamcinolone on page 1174*
- ♦ **Aristocort® Intralesional** *see Triamcinolone on page 1174*

- **Aristospan® Intra-Articular** *see* Triamcinolone *on page 1174*
- **Aristospan® Intralesional** *see* Triamcinolone *on page 1174*
- **Arm-a-Med® Isoetharine** *see* Isoetharine *on page 632*
- **Arm-a-Med® Isoproterenol** *see* Isoproterenol *on page 635*
- **Arm-a-Med® Metaproterenol** *see* Metaproterenol *on page 739*
- **Armour® Thyroid** *see* Thyroid *on page 1139*
- **Arrestin®** *see* Trimethobenzamide *on page 1183*
- **ARS** *see* Antirabies Serum (Equine) *on page 91*
- **Artane®** *see* Trihexyphenidyl *on page 1182*
- **Artha-G®** *see* Salsalate *on page 1047*
- **Arthritis Foundation® Pain Reliever [OTC]** *see* Aspirin *on page 102*
- **Arthritis Foundation® Pain Reliever, Aspirin Free [OTC]** *see* Acetaminophen *on page 19*
- **Arthropan® [OTC]** *see* Choline Salicylate *on page 256*
- **Arthrotec®** *see* Diclofenac and Misoprostol *on page 350*
- **Articulose-50® Injection** *see* Prednisolone *on page 961*
- **ASA®** *see* Aspirin *on page 102*
- **ASA** *see* Aspirin *on page 102*
- **A.S.A. [OTC]** *see* Aspirin *on page 102*
- **5-ASA** *see* Mesalamine *on page 734*
- **Asacol® Oral** *see* Mesalamine *on page 734*
- **Asaphen** *see* Aspirin *on page 102*
- **Ascorbic 500** *see* Ascorbic Acid *on this page*

Ascorbic Acid (a SKOR bik AS id)

U.S. Brand Names Ascorbicap® [OTC]; C-Crystals® [OTC]; Cebid® Timecelles® [OTC]; Cecon® [OTC]; Cevalin® [OTC]; Cevi-Bid® [OTC]; Ce-Vi-Sol® [OTC]; Dull-C® [OTC]; Flavorcee® [OTC]; N'ice® Vitamin C Drops [OTC]; Vita-C® [OTC]

Canadian Brand Names Apo®-C; Ascorbic 500; Redoxon®; Revitalose-C-1000®

Synonyms Vitamin C

Therapeutic Category Urinary Acidifying Agent; Vitamin, Water Soluble

Use Prevention and treatment of scurvy and to acidify the urine

Investigational: In large doses to decrease the severity of "colds"; dietary supplementation; a 20-year study was recently completed involving 730 individuals which indicates a possible decreased risk of death by stroke when ascorbic acid at doses ≥45 mg/day was administered

Pregnancy Risk Factor A (C if used in doses above RDA recommendation)

Contraindications Large doses during pregnancy

Warnings/Precautions Diabetics and patients prone to recurrent renal calculi (eg, dialysis patients) should not take excessive doses for extended periods of time

Adverse Reactions

1% to 10%: Renal: Hyperoxaluria with large doses

<1%: Flushing, faintness, dizziness, headache, fatigue, nausea, vomiting, heartburn, diarrhea, flank pain

Overdosage/Toxicology

Symptoms of overdose include renal calculi, nausea, gastritis, diarrhea

Diuresis with forced fluids may be useful following a massive ingestion

Drug Interactions

Decreased effect:

Aspirin (decreases ascorbate levels, increases aspirin)

Fluphenazine (decreases fluphenazine levels)

Warfarin (decreased effect)

Increased effect:

Iron (absorption enhanced)

Oral contraceptives (increased contraceptive effect)

Stability Injectable form should be stored under refrigeration (2°C to 8°C); protect oral dosage forms from light; is rapidly oxidized when in solution in air and alkaline media

Mechanism of Action Not fully understood; necessary for collagen formation and tissue repair; involved in some oxidation-reduction reactions as well as other metabolic pathways, such as synthesis of carnitine, steroids, and catecholamines and conversion of folic acid to folinic acid

Pharmacodynamics/Kinetics

Absorption: Oral: Readily absorbed; an active process and is thought to be dose-dependent

Distribution: Widely distributed

Metabolism: In the liver by oxidation and sulfation

Elimination: In urine; there is an individual specific renal threshold for ascorbic acid; when blood levels are high, ascorbic acid is excreted in the urine; whereas when the levels are subthreshold, very little if any ascorbic acid is cleared into the urine

Usual Dosage Oral, I.M., I.V., S.C.:

Recommended daily allowance (RDA):

<6 months: 30 mg

6 months to 1 year: 35 mg

1-3 years: 40 mg

4-10 years: 45 mg

11-14 years: 50 mg

(Continued)

Ascorbic Acid *(Continued)*

>14 years and Adults: 60 mg
Children:
Scurvy: 100-300 mg/day in divided doses for at least 2 weeks
Urinary acidification: 500 mg every 6-8 hours
Dietary supplement: 35-100 mg/day
Adults:
Scurvy: 100-250 mg 1-2 times/day for at least 2 weeks
Urinary acidification: 4-12 g/day in 3-4 divided doses
Prevention and treatment of colds: 1-3 g/day
Dietary supplement: 50-200 mg/day

Administration Avoid rapid I.V. injection

Monitoring Parameters Monitor pH of urine when using as an acidifying agent

Test Interactions False-positive urinary glucose with cupric sulfate reagent, false-negative urinary glucose with glucose oxidase method; false-negative stool occult blood 48-72 hours after ascorbic acid ingestion

Patient Information Do not take more than the recommended dose; take with plenty of water; report any pain on urination

Additional Information Sodium content of 1 g: ~5 mEq

Dosage Forms
Capsule, timed release: 500 mg
Crystals: 4 g/teaspoonful (100 g, 500 g); 5 g/teaspoonful (180 g)
Injection: 250 mg/mL (2 mL, 30 mL); 500 mg/mL (2 mL, 50 mL)
Liquid, oral: 35 mg/0.6 mL (50 mL)
Lozenges: 60 mg
Powder: 4 g/teaspoonful (100 g, 500 g)
Solution, oral: 100 mg/mL (50 mL)
Syrup: 500 mg/5 mL (5 mL, 10 mL, 120 mL, 480 mL)
Tablet: 25 mg, 50 mg, 100 mg, 250 mg, 500 mg, 1000 mg
Tablet:
Chewable: 100 mg, 250 mg, 500 mg
Timed release: 500 mg, 1000 mg, 1500 mg

- ◆ **Ascorbicap® [OTC]** *see* Ascorbic Acid *on previous page*
- ◆ **Ascriptin® [OTC]** *see* Aspirin *on page 102*
- ◆ **Asendin®** *see* Amoxapine *on page 68*
- ◆ **Asmalix®** *see* Theophylline Salts *on page 1125*

Asparaginase *(a SPIR a ji nase)*

Related Information
Cancer Chemotherapy Regimens *on page 1263*
Toxicities of Chemotherapeutic Agents *on page 1288*

U.S. Brand Names Elspar®

Synonyms L-asparaginase

Therapeutic Category Antineoplastic Agent, Protein Synthesis Inhibitor

Use Treatment of acute lymphocytic leukemia, lymphoma; used for induction therapy

Pregnancy Risk Factor C

Pregnancy/Breast-Feeding Implications Clinical effects on the fetus: Based on limited reports in humans, the use of asparaginase does not seem to pose a major risk to the fetus when used in the 2nd and 3rd trimesters, or when exposure occurs prior to conception in either females or males. Because of the teratogenicity observed in animals and the lack of human data after 1st trimester exposure, asparaginase should be used cautiously, if at all, during this period.

Contraindications Pancreatitis (active or any history of), hypersensitivity to asparaginase or any component; if a reaction occurs to Elspar®, obtain **Erwinia L-asparaginase** and use with caution

Warnings/Precautions The U.S. Food and Drug Administration (FDA) currently recommends that procedures for proper handling and disposal of antineoplastic agents be considered; monitor for severe allergic reactions; risk for hypersensitivity increases with successive doses

The following precautions should be taken when administering:
Only administer in hospital setting
Monitor blood pressure every 15 minutes for 1 hour
Administer a small test dose first; the intradermal skin test is commonly given prior to the initial injection, using a dose of 0.1 mL of 20 unit/mL dilute solution (~2 units); the skin test site should be observed for at least 1 hour for a wheal or erythema; note that a negative skin test does not preclude the possibility of an allergic reaction; desensitization should be performed in patients who have been found to be hypersensitive by the intradermal skin test or who have received previous courses of therapy with the drug
Have epinephrine, diphenhydramine, and hydrocortisone at the bedside
Have a running I.V. in place
A physician should be readily accessible
Avoid administering at night

Adverse Reactions
>10%:
Immediate effects: Fever, chills, nausea, and vomiting occur in 50% to 60% of patients

Gastrointestinal: Pancreatitis: Occurs in <15% of patients, but may progress to severe hemorrhagic pancreatitis

Emetic potential: Moderate (30% to 60%)

Renal: Prerenal azotemia

Miscellaneous: Hypersensitivity effects: Hypersensitivity and anaphylactic reactions occur in ~10% to 40% of patients and can be fatal; this reaction is more common in patients receiving asparaginase alone or by I.V. administration; hypersensitivity appears rarely with the first dose and more commonly after the second or third treatment; hypersensitivity may be treated with antihistamines and/or steroids; if an anaphylactic reaction occurs, a change in treatment to the *Erwinia* preparation may be made, since this preparation does not share antigenic cross-reactivity with the *E. coli* preparation; note that allergic reactions to the *Erwinia* preparation may also occur and ultimately develop in 5% to 20% of patients

1% to 10%:

Endocrine & metabolic: Hyperuricemia

Gastrointestinal: Mouth sores

<1%: Hypotension, leg vein thrombosis, chills, malaise, disorientation, drowsiness, seizures, and coma which may be due to elevated NH_4 levels; hyperthermia, drowsiness, fever, hallucinations, rash, pruritus, urticaria, transient diabetes mellitus, weight loss, inhibition of protein synthesis will cause a decrease in production of albumin, insulin (resulting in hyperglycemia), serum lipoprotein, antithrombin III, and clotting factors II, V, VII, VIII, IX, and X; the loss of the later two proteins may result in either thrombotic or hemorrhagic events; these protein losses occur in 100% of patients; increased serum bilirubin, AST/ALT, alkaline phosphatase, and possible decrease in mobilization of lipids, azotemia, laryngeal spasm, coughing

Myelosuppressive effects: Myelosuppression is uncommon

WBC: Mild

Platelets: Mild

Onset (days): 7

Nadir (days): 14

Recovery (days): 21

Overdosage/Toxicology Symptoms of overdose include nausea, diarrhea

Drug Interactions

Decreased effect: Methotrexate: Asparaginase terminates methotrexate action by inhibition of protein synthesis and prevention of cell entry into the S phase

Increased toxicity:

Vincristine and prednisone: An increase in toxicity has been noticed when asparaginase is administered with VCR and prednisone

Cyclophosphamide (decreases metabolism)

Mercaptopurine (increases hepatotoxicity)

Vincristine (increases neuropathy)

Prednisone (increases hyperglycemia)

Stability Intact vials of powder should be refrigerated (<8°C); lyophilized powder should be reconstituted with 1-5 mL sterile water for I.V. administration or NS for I.M. use, reconstituted solutions are stable 1 week at room temperature; shake well but not too vigorously; use of a 5 micron in-line filter is recommended to remove fiber-like particles in the solution (not 0.2 micron filter - has been associated with some loss of potency)

Standard I.M. dilution: 5000 international units/mL: 2 mL/syringe

Usually no >2 mL/injection site, however, contact RN first to clarify administration route.

Standard I.V. dilution: Dose/50-250 mL NS or D_5W

Stable for 8 hours at room temperature or refrigeration

Mechanism of Action Some malignant cells (ie, lymphoblastic leukemia cells and those of lymphocyte derivation) must acquire the amino acid asparagine from surrounding fluid such as blood, whereas normal cells can synthesize their own asparagine. Asparaginase is an enzyme that deaminates asparagine to aspartic acid and ammonia in the plasma and extracellular fluid and therefore deprives tumor cells of the amino acid for protein synthesis.

There are two purified preparations of the enzyme: one from *Escherichia coli* and one from *Erwinia carotovora*. These two preparations vary slightly in the gene sequencing and have slight differences in enzyme characteristics. Both are highly specific for asparagine and have less than 10% activity for the D-isomer. The preparation from *E. coli* has had the most use in clinical and research practice.

Pharmacodynamics/Kinetics

Absorption: Not absorbed from GI tract, therefore, requires parenteral administration; I.M. administration produces peak blood levels 50% lower than those from I.V. administration (I.M. may be less immunogenic)

Distribution: V_d: 4-5 L/kg; 70% to 80% of plasma volume; does not penetrate the CSF

Metabolism: Systemically degraded, only trace amounts are found in the urine

Half-life: 8-30 hours

Elimination: Clearance unaffected by age, renal function, or hepatic function

Usual Dosage Refer to individual protocols; dose must be individualized based upon clinical response and tolerance of the patient

I.M. administration is **preferred** over I.V. administration; I.M. administration may decrease the risk of anaphylaxis

Asparaginase is available from two different microbiological sources: One is from *Escherichia coli* and the other is from *Erwinia carotovora*; the *Erwinia* is restricted to patients who have sustained allergic reactions to the *E. coli* preparation

(Continued)

Asparaginase *(Continued)*

I.M., I.V.: 6000 units/m^2 every other day for 3-4 weeks or daily doses of 1000-20,000 units/m^2 for 10-20 days; other induction regimens have been utilized

Hemodialysis: Significant drug removal is unlikely based on physiochemical characteristics

Peritoneal dialysis: Significant drug removal is unlikely based on physiochemical characteristics

Desensitization should be performed before administering the first dose of asparaginase to patients who developed a positive reaction to the intradermal skin test or who are being retreated; one schedule begins with a total of 1 unit given I.V. and doubles the dose every 10 minutes until the total amount given in the planned dose for that day

Asparaginase Desensitization

Injection No.	Elspar Dose (IU)	Accumulated Total Dose
1	1	1
2	2	3
3	4	7
4	8	15
5	16	31
6	32	63
7	64	127
8	128	255
9	256	511
10	512	1023
11	1024	2047
12	2048	4095
13	4096	8191
14	8192	16,383
15	16,384	32,767
16	32,768	65,535
17	65,536	131,071
18	131,072	262,143

For example, if a patient was to receive a total dose of 4000 units, he/she would receive injections 1 through 12 during the desensitization

Administration Must only be given as a deep intramuscular injection into a large muscle; use two injection sites for I.M. doses >2 mL

May be administered I.V. infusion in 50 mL of D$_5$W or NS over more than 30 minutes; a small test dose (0.1 mL of a dilute 20 unit/mL solution) should be given first

Occasionally, gelatinous fiber-like particles may develop on standing; filtration through a 5 micron filter during administration will remove the particles with no loss of potency; some loss of potency has been observed with the use of a 0.2 micron filter

Monitoring Parameters Vital signs during administration, CBC, urinalysis, amylase, liver enzymes, prothrombin time, renal function tests, urine dipstick for glucose, blood glucose, uric acid

Test Interactions ↓ thyroxine and thyroxine-binding globulin

Patient Information Drowsiness may occur during therapy; nausea or vomiting may interrupt dosing schedule initially. Contraceptive measures are recommended during therapy.

Nursing Implications Appropriate agents for maintenance of an adequate airway and treatment of a hypersensitivity reaction (antihistamine, epinephrine, oxygen, I.V. corticosteroids) should be readily available. Be prepared to treat anaphylaxis at each administration; monitor for onset of abdominal pain and mental status changes.

Dosage Forms Injection:

10,000 units/10 mL

10,000 units/vial (*Erwinia*)

♦ **A-Spas® S/L** *see* Hyoscyamine *on page 590*

♦ **Aspergum® [OTC]** *see* Aspirin *on this page*

Aspirin (AS pir in)

U.S. Brand Names Anacin® [OTC]; Arthritis Foundation® Pain Reliever [OTC]; A.S.A. [OTC]; Ascriptin® [OTC]; Aspergum® [OTC]; Asprimox® [OTC]; Bayer® Aspirin [OTC]; Bayer® Buffered Aspirin [OTC]; Bayer® Low Adult Strength [OTC]; Bufferin® [OTC]; Buffex® [OTC]; Cama® Arthritis Pain Reliever [OTC]; Easprin®; Ecotrin® [OTC]; Ecotrin® Low Adult Strength [OTC]; Empirin® [OTC]; Extra Strength Adprin-B® [OTC]; Extra Strength Bayer® Enteric 500 Aspirin [OTC]; Extra Strength Bayer® Plus [OTC]; Halfprin® 81® [OTC]; Regular Strength Bayer® Enteric 500 Aspirin [OTC]; St Joseph® Adult Chewable Aspirin [OTC]; ZORprin®

Canadian Brand Names Apo®-ASA; ASA®; Asaphen; Entrophen®; MSD® Enteric Coated ASA; Novasen

Synonyms Acetylsalicylic Acid; ASA

Therapeutic Category Analgesic, Salicylate; Anti-inflammatory Agent; Antipyretic; Nonsteroidal Anti-inflammatory Drug (NSAID), Oral; Salicylate

Use Treatment of mild to moderate pain, inflammation, and fever; may be used as a prophylaxis of myocardial infarction and transient ischemic episodes; management of rheumatoid arthritis, rheumatic fever, osteoarthritis, and gout (high dose)

Pregnancy Risk Factor C (D if full-dose aspirin in 3rd trimester)

Contraindications Bleeding disorders (factor VII or IX deficiencies), hypersensitivity to salicylates or other NSAIDs, tartrazine dye and asthma

Warnings/Precautions Use with caution in patients with platelet and bleeding disorders, renal dysfunction, erosive gastritis, or peptic ulcer disease, previous nonreaction does not guarantee future safe taking of medication; do not use aspirin in children <16 years of age for chickenpox or flu symptoms due to the association with Reye's syndrome

Otic: Discontinue use if dizziness, tinnitus, or impaired hearing occurs; surgical patients: avoid ASA if possible, for 1 week prior to surgery because of the possibility of postoperative bleeding; use with caution in impaired hepatic function

Elderly are a high-risk population for adverse effects from nonsteroidal anti-inflammatory agents. As much as 60% of elderly with GI complications to NSAIDs can develop peptic ulceration and/or hemorrhage asymptomatically. Also, concomitant disease and drug use contribute to the risk for GI adverse effects. Use lowest effective dose for shortest period possible. Consider renal function decline with age. Use of NSAIDs can compromise existing renal function especially when Cl_{cr} is <30 mL/minute. Tinnitus may be a difficult and unreliable indication of toxicity due to age-related hearing loss or eighth cranial nerve damage. CNS adverse effects such as confusion, agitation, and hallucination are generally seen in overdose or high-dose situations, but elderly may demonstrate these adverse effects at lower doses than younger adults.

Adverse Reactions

>10%: Gastrointestinal: Nausea, vomiting, dyspepsia, epigastric discomfort, heartburn, stomach pains

1% to 10%:

Central nervous system: Fatigue

Dermatologic: Rash, urticaria

Gastrointestinal: Gastrointestinal ulceration

Hematologic: Hemolytic anemia

Neuromuscular & skeletal: Weakness

Respiratory: Dyspnea

Miscellaneous: Anaphylactic shock

<1%: Insomnia, nervousness, jitters, iron deficiency, occult bleeding, prolongation of bleeding time, leukopenia, thrombocytopenia, anemia, hepatotoxicity, impaired renal function, bronchospasm

Overdosage/Toxicology Refer to the nomogram in Toxicology Information *on page 1491* in the Appendix

Symptoms of overdose include tinnitus, headache, dizziness, confusion, metabolic acidosis, hyperpyrexia, hypoglycemia, coma

Treatment should also be based upon symptomatology.

Salicylates

Toxic Symptoms	Treatment
Overdose	Induce emesis with ipecac, and/or lavage with saline, followed with activated charcoal
Dehydration	I.V. fluids with KCl (no D_5W only)
Metabolic acidosis (must be treated)	Sodium bicarbonate
Hyperthermia	Cooling blankets or sponge baths
Coagulopathy/hemorrhage	Vitamin K I.V.
Hypoglycemia (with coma, seizures, or change in mental status)	Dextrose 25 g I.V.
Seizures	Diazepam 5-10 mg I.V.

Drug Interactions

Decreased effect: Possible decreased serum concentration of NSAIDs; aspirin may antagonize effects of probenecid

Increased toxicity: Aspirin may increase methotrexate serum levels and may displace valproic acid from binding sites which can result in toxicity; warfarin and aspirin may increase bleeding; NSAIDs and aspirin may increase GI adverse effects; buspirone increases free % *in vitro*; bleeding times may be additionally prolonged with verapamil

Stability Keep suppositories in refrigerator, do not freeze; hydrolysis of aspirin occurs upon exposure to water or moist air, resulting in salicylate and acetate, which possess a vinegar-like odor; do not use if a strong odor is present

Mechanism of Action Inhibits prostaglandin synthesis, acts on the hypothalamus heat-regulating center to reduce fever, blocks prostaglandin synthetase action which prevents formation of the platelet-aggregating substance thromboxane A_2

Pharmacodynamics/Kinetics

Absorption: From stomach and small intestine

Distribution: Readily distributes into most body fluids and tissues

Metabolism: Hydrolyzed to salicylate (active) by esterases in the GI mucosa, red blood cells, synovial fluid and blood; metabolism of salicylate occurs primarily by hepatic microsomal enzymes; metabolic pathways are saturable

(Continued)

Aspirin *(Continued)*

Half-life: Parent drug: 15-20 minutes; Salicylates (dose-dependent): From 3 hours at lower doses (300-600 mg), to 5-6 hours (after 1 g) to 10 hours with higher doses
Time to peak serum concentration: ~1-2 hours

Usual Dosage

Children:

Analgesic and antipyretic: Oral, rectal: 10-15 mg/kg/dose every 4-6 hours, up to a total of 60-80 mg/kg/24 hours

Anti-inflammatory: Oral: Initial: 60-90 mg/kg/day in divided doses; usual maintenance: 80-100 mg/kg/day divided every 6-8 hours, maximum dose: 3.6 g/day; monitor serum concentrations

Kawasaki disease: Oral: 80-100 mg/kg/day divided every 6 hours; after fever resolves: 8-10 mg/kg/day once daily; monitor serum concentrations

Antirheumatic: Oral: 60-100 mg/kg/day in divided doses every 4 hours

Adults:

Analgesic and antipyretic: Oral, rectal: 325-650 mg every 4-6 hours up to 4 g/day

Anti-inflammatory: Oral: Initial: 2.4-3.6 g/day in divided doses; usual maintenance: 3.6-5.4 g/day; monitor serum concentrations

TIA: Oral: 1.3 g/day in 2-4 divided doses

Myocardial infarction prophylaxis: 160-325 mg/day

Dosing adjustment in renal impairment: Cl_{cr} <10 mL/minute: Avoid use
Hemodialysis: Dialyzable (50% to 100%)

Dosing adjustment in hepatic disease: Avoid use in severe liver disease

Dietary Considerations

Alcohol: Combination causes GI irritation, possible bleeding; avoid or limit alcohol. Patients at increased risk include those prone to hypoprothrombinemia, vitamin K deficiency, thrombocytopenia, thrombotic thrombocytopenia purpura, severe hepatic impairment, and those receiving anticoagulants.

Food: May decrease the rate but not the extent of oral absorption. Drug may cause GI upset, bleeding, ulceration, perforation. Take with food or large volume of water or milk to minimize GI upset.

Folic acid: Hyperexcretion of folate; folic acid deficiency may result, leading to macrocytic anemia. Supplement with folic acid if necessary.

Iron: With chronic aspirin use and at doses of 3-4 g/day, iron deficiency anemia may result; supplement with iron if necessary

Sodium: Hypernatremia resulting from buffered aspirin solutions or sodium salicylate containing high sodium content. Avoid or use with caution in CHF or any condition where hypernatremia would be detrimental.

Curry powder, paprika, licorice, Benedictine liqueur, prunes, raisins, tea and gherkins: Potential salicylate accumulation. These foods contain 6 mg salicylate/100 g. An ordinarily American diet contains 10-200 mg/day of salicylate. Foods containing salicylates may contribute to aspirin hypersensitivity. Patients at greatest risk for aspirin hypersensitivity include those with asthma, nasal polyposis or chronic urticaria.

Fresh fruits containing vitamin C: Displaces drug from binding sites, resulting in increased urinary excretion of aspirin. Educate patients regarding the potential for a decreased analgesic effect of aspirin with consumption of foods high in vitamin C.

Administration Administer with food or a full glass of water to minimize GI distress

Reference Range Timing of serum samples: Peak levels usually occur 2 hours after ingestion. Salicylate serum concentrations correlate with the pharmacological actions and adverse effects observed. See table.

Serum Salicylate: Clinical Correlations

Serum Salicylate Concentration (mcg/mL)	Desired Effects	Adverse Effects/Intoxication
~100	Antiplatelet Antipyresis Analgesia	GI intolerance and bleeding, hypersensitivity, hemostatic defects
150-300	Anti-inflammatory	Mild salicylism
250-400	Treatment of rheumatic fever	Nausea/vomiting, hyperventilation, salicylism, flushing, sweating, thirst, headache, diarrhea, and tachycardia
>400-500		Respiratory alkalosis, hemorrhage, excitement, confusion, asterixis, pulmonary edema, convulsions, tetany, metabolic acidosis, fever, coma, cardiovascular collapse, renal and respiratory failure

Test Interactions False-negative results for glucose oxidase urinary glucose tests (Clinistix®); false-positives using the cupric sulfate method (Clinitest®); also, interferes with Gerhardt test, VMA determination; 5-HIAA, xylose tolerance test and T_3 and T_4

Patient Information Watch for bleeding gums or any signs of GI bleeding; take with food or milk to minimize GI distress, notify physician if ringing in ears or persistent GI pain occurs; avoid other concurrent aspirin or salicylate-containing products

Nursing Implications Do not crush sustained release or enteric coated tablet

Dosage Forms

Capsule: 356.4 mg and caffeine 30 mg

Suppository, rectal: 60 mg, 120 mg, 125 mg, 130 mg, 195 mg, 200 mg, 300 mg, 325 mg, 600 mg, 650 mg, 1.2 g
Tablet: 65 mg, 75 mg, 81 mg, 325 mg, 500 mg
Tablet: 400 mg and caffeine 32 mg
Tablet:
  Buffered: 325 mg and magnesium-aluminum hydroxide 150 mg; 325 mg, magnesium hydroxide 75 mg, aluminum hydroxide 75 mg, buffered with calcium carbonate; 325 mg and magnesium-aluminum hydroxide 75 mg
  Chewable: 81 mg
  Controlled release: 800 mg
  Delayed release: 81 mg
  Enteric coated: 81 mg, 325 mg, 500 mg, 650 mg, 975 mg
  Gum: 227.5 mg
  Timed release: 650 mg

Aspirin and Codeine (AS pir in & KOE deen)
Related Information
  Aspirin on page 102
  Codeine on page 291
U.S. Brand Names Empirin® With Codeine
Canadian Brand Names Coryphen® Codeine; 222® Tablets; 282® Tablets; 292® Tablets
Synonyms Codeine and Aspirin
Therapeutic Category Analgesic, Narcotic
Restrictions C-III
Dosage Forms Tablet:
  #2: Aspirin 325 mg and codeine phosphate 15 mg
  #3: Aspirin 325 mg and codeine phosphate 30 mg
  #4: Aspirin 325 mg and codeine phosphate 60 mg

Aspirin and Meprobamate (AS pir in & me proe BA mate)
U.S. Brand Names Equagesic®
Therapeutic Category Skeletal Muscle Relaxant
Dosage Forms Tablet: Aspirin 325 mg and meprobamate 200 mg

♦ **Aspirin Free Anacin® Maximum Strength [OTC]** see Acetaminophen on page 19
♦ **Asprimox® [OTC]** see Aspirin on page 102
♦ **Assessment of Liver Function** see page 1258
♦ **Assessment of Renal Function** see page 1259
♦ **Astelin® Nasal Spray** see Azelastine on page 117

Astemizole (a STEM mi zole)
U.S. Brand Names Hismanal®
Therapeutic Category Antihistamine, Nonsedating
Use Perennial and seasonal allergic rhinitis and other allergic symptoms including urticaria
Pregnancy Risk Factor C
Contraindications Hypersensitivity to astemizole or any component; concurrent use of erythromycin, quinine, ketoconazole, itraconazole, clarithromycin, troleandomycin, mibefradil dihydrochloride, or in patients with significant hepatic dysfunction
Warnings/Precautions Use with caution in patients receiving drugs which prolong QRS or rare cases of severe cardiovascular events (cardiac arrest, arrhythmias) have been reported. Safety and efficacy in children <12 years of age have not been established. Discontinue therapy immediately with signs of cardiotoxicity including syncope.

Concurrent use of fluoxetine, sertraline, fluvoxamine, nefazodone, paroxetine, ritonavir, indinavir, nelfinavir, saquinavir, zileuton, and other potent cytochrome P-450 3A4 inhibitors, including grapefruit juice is not recommended since these agents may inhibit astemizole clearance, thereby leading to increased astemizole serum concentrations and potential astemizole cardiotoxicity.

The recommended daily dose of astemizole should not be exceeded. Astemizole should not be used on an "as needed" (ie, prn) basis for immediate relief of symptoms. Patients should be advised that astemizole should not be taken with grapefruit juice because of the potential for grapefruit to influence the metabolism of astemizole.
Adverse Reactions
  1% to 10%:
    Central nervous system: Drowsiness, headache, fatigue, nervousness, dizziness
    Gastrointestinal: Appetite increase, weight gain, nausea, diarrhea, abdominal pain, xerostomia
    Neuromuscular & skeletal: Arthralgia
    Respiratory: Pharyngitis
  <1%: Palpitations, edema, depression, angioedema, photosensitivity, rash, hepatitis, myalgia, paresthesia, bronchospasm, epistaxis, thickening of mucous
Overdosage/Toxicology
  Symptoms of overdose include sedation, apnea, diminished mental alertness, ventricular tachycardia, torsade de pointes
  There is not a specific treatment for an antihistamine overdose, however most of its clinical toxicity is due to anticholinergic effects. Anticholinesterase inhibitors including physostigmine, neostigmine, pyridostigmine and edrophonium may be useful for the overdose with severe life-threatening symptoms. Physostigmine 1-2 mg (0.5 mg or 0.02 mg/kg for children) I.V., slowly may be given to reverse the anticholinergic effects.
(Continued)

Astemizole *(Continued)*

Cases of ventricular arrhythmias following dosages >200 mg have been reported, however, overdoses of up to 500 mg have been reported without ill effect. Patients should be carefully observed with EKG monitoring in cases of suspected overdose. Magnesium may be helpful for torsade de pointes or a lidocaine bolus followed by a titrated infusion.

Drug Interactions CYP3A3/4 enzyme substrate

Increased toxicity: CNS depressants (sedation), triazole antifungals, macrolide antibiotics, mibefradil, and quinine may inhibit the metabolism of astemizole resulting in potentially life-threatening arrhythmias (torsade de pointes, etc); see Warnings and Contraindications

Mechanism of Action Competes with histamine for H_1-receptor sites on effector cells in the gastrointestinal tract, blood vessels, and respiratory tract; binds to lung receptors significantly greater than it binds to cerebellar receptors, resulting in a reduced sedative potential

Pharmacodynamics/Kinetics Long-acting, with steady-state plasma levels seen within 4-8 weeks following initiation of chronic therapy

Distribution: Nonsedating action reportedly due to the drug's low lipid solubility and poor penetration through the blood-brain barrier

Protein binding: 97%

Metabolism: Undergoes exclusive first-pass metabolism

Half-life: 20 hours

Time to peak serum concentration: Oral: Long-acting, with steady-state plasma levels of parent compound and metabolites seen within 4-8 weeks following initiation of chronic therapy; peak plasma levels appear in 1-4 hours following administration

Elimination: By metabolism in the liver to active and inactive metabolites, which are thereby excreted in feces and to a lesser degree in urine

Usual Dosage Oral:

Children:

<6 years: 0.2 mg/kg/day

6-12 years: 5 mg/day (not to exceed 10 mg daily)

Children >12 years and Adults: 10-30 mg/day; administer 30 mg on first day, 20 mg on second day, then 10 mg/day in a single dose

Patient Information Take on an empty stomach at least 2 hours after a meal or 1 hour before a meal; may cause drowsiness; do not exceed recommended dose; notify physician or pharmacist if taking any heart medications. Because of its delayed onset, astemizole is useful for prophylaxis of allergic symptoms, rather than for acute relief.

Nursing Implications Raise bed rails at night; may need assistance with ambulation; administer on an empty stomach

Dosage Forms Tablet: 10 mg

♦ **Asthma, Guidelines for the Diagnosis and Management of** *see page 1456*

♦ **AsthmaHaler®** *see Epinephrine on page 415*

♦ **AsthmaNefrin® [OTC]** *see Epinephrine on page 415*

♦ **Astramorph™ PF Injection** *see Morphine Sulfate on page 797*

♦ **Atacand™** *see Candesartan on page 181*

♦ **Atamet®** *see Levodopa and Carbidopa on page 672*

♦ **Atarax®** *see Hydroxyzine on page 589*

♦ **Atasol®** *see Acetaminophen on page 19*

♦ **Atasol® 8, 15, 30 With Caffeine** *see Acetaminophen and Codeine on page 21*

Atenolol *(a TEN oh lole)*

Related Information

Beta-Blockers Comparison *on page 1311*

U.S. Brand Names Tenormin®

Canadian Brand Names Apo®-Atenol; Novo-Atenol; Nu-Atenol; Taro-Atenol®

Therapeutic Category Antianginal Agent; Antihypertensive Agent; Beta-Adrenergic Blocker

Use Treatment of hypertension, alone or in combination with other agents; management of angina pectoris, postmyocardial infarction patients

Unlabeled use: Acute alcohol withdrawal, supraventricular and ventricular arrhythmias, and migraine headache prophylaxis

Pregnancy Risk Factor C

Pregnancy/Breast-Feeding Implications

Clinical effects on the fetus: Crosses the placenta; persistent beta-blockade, bradycardia, IUGR; IUGR probably related to maternal hypertension. Available evidence suggest safe use during pregnancy and breast-feeding. Monitor breast-fed infant for symptoms of beta-blockade.

Breast-feeding/lactation: Crosses into breast milk. American Academy of Pediatrics considers **compatible** with breast-feeding.

Clinical effects on the infant: Symptoms have been reported of beta-blockade including cyanosis, hypothermia, bradycardia.

Contraindications Hypersensitivity to beta-blocking agents, pulmonary edema, cardiogenic shock, bradycardia, heart block without a pacemaker, uncompensated congestive heart failure, sinus node dysfunction, A-V conduction abnormalities

Warnings/Precautions Safety and efficacy in children have not been established; administer with caution to patients (especially the elderly) with bronchospastic disease,

CHF, renal dysfunction, severe peripheral vascular disease, myasthenia gravis, diabetes mellitus, hyperthyroidism. **Abrupt withdrawal of the drug should be avoided**, drug should be discontinued over 1-2 weeks; may potentiate hypoglycemia in a diabetic patient and mask signs and symptoms; modify dosage in patients with renal impairment.

Adverse Reactions

1% to 10%:

Cardiovascular: Persistent bradycardia (3%), hypotension (4%), second or third degree A-V block (0.7% to 1.7%), Raynaud's phenomenon (rare)

Central nervous system: Dizziness (4% to 13%), fatigue (3% to 6%), lethargy (1% to 3%), confusion (rare), mental impairment (rare)

Gastrointestinal: Diarrhea (2% to 3%), nausea (3% to 4%)

Genitourinary: Impotence (rare)

Respiratory: Dyspnea (especially with large doses), wheezing (0% to 3%)

Miscellaneous: Cold extremities (<10%)

<1%: Depression, headache, nightmares

Overdosage/Toxicology

Symptoms of intoxication include cardiac disturbances, CNS toxicity, bronchospasm, hypoglycemia and hyperkalemia. The most common cardiac symptoms include hypotension and bradycardia; atrioventricular block, intraventricular conduction disturbances, cardiogenic shock, and asystole may occur with severe overdose, especially with membrane-depressant drugs (eg, propranolol); CNS effects include convulsions, coma, and respiratory arrest (commonly seen with propranolol and other membrane-depressant and lipid-soluble drugs).

Treatment includes symptomatic treatment of seizures, hypotension, hyperkalemia, and hypoglycemia; bradycardia and hypotension resistant to atropine, isoproterenol, or pacing may respond to glucagon; wide QRS defects caused by the membrane-depressant poisoning may respond to hypertonic sodium bicarbonate; repeat-dose charcoal, hemoperfusion, or hemodialysis may be helpful in removal of only those beta-blockers with a small V_d, long half-life, or low intrinsic clearance (acebutolol, atenolol, nadolol, sotalol)

Drug Interactions

Decreased effect of some beta-blockers with aluminum salts, barbiturates, calcium salts, cholestyramine, colestipol, NSAIDs, penicillins (ampicillin), rifampin, salicylates, and sulfinpyrazone due to decreased bioavailability and plasma levels

Beta-blockers may decrease the effect of sulfonylureas

Increased effect/toxicity of beta-blockers with calcium blockers (diltiazem, felodipine, nicardipine), contraceptives, flecainide, hydralazine (metoprolol, propranolol), propafenone, quinidine (in extensive metabolizers), ciprofloxacin

Beta-blockers may increase the effect/toxicity of flecainide, hydralazine, clonidine (hypertensive crisis after or during withdrawal of either agent), epinephrine (initial hypertensive episode followed by bradycardia), nifedipine, verapamil, lidocaine, ergots, prazosin

Beta-blockers may affect the action or levels of ethanol, disopyramide, nondepolarizing muscle relaxants and theophylline although the effects are difficult to predict

Stability Protect from light

Mechanism of Action Competitively blocks response to beta-adrenergic stimulation, selectively blocks beta$_1$-receptors with little or no effect on beta$_2$-receptors except at high doses

Pharmacodynamics/Kinetics

Absorption: Incomplete from GI tract

Distribution: Low lipophilicity; does **not** cross the blood-brain barrier

Protein binding: Low at 3% to 15%

Metabolism: Partial hepatic

Half-life, beta:

Neonates: Mean: 16 hours, up to 35 hours

Children: 4.6 hours; children >10 years of age may have longer half-life (>5 hours) compared to children 5-10 years of age (<5 hours)

Adults:

Normal renal function: 6-9 hours, longer in those with renal impairment

End-stage renal disease: 15-35 hours

Time to peak: Oral: Within 2-4 hours

Elimination: 40% excreted as unchanged drug in urine, 50% in feces

Usual Dosage

Oral:

Children: 1-2 mg/kg/dose given daily

Adults:

Hypertension: 50 mg once daily, may increase to 100 mg/day; doses >100 mg are unlikely to produce any further benefit

Angina pectoris: 50 mg once daily, may increase to 100 mg/day; some patients may require 200 mg/day

Postmyocardial infarction: Follow I.V. dose with 100 mg/day or 50 mg twice daily for 6-9 days postmyocardial infarction

I.V.: Postmyocardial infarction: Early treatment: 5 mg slow I.V. over 5 minutes; may repeat in 10 minutes; if both doses are tolerated, may start oral atenolol 50 mg every 12 hours or 100 mg/day for 6-9 days postmyocardial infarction

Dosing interval for oral atenolol in renal impairment:

Cl_{cr} 15-35 mL/minute: Administer 50 mg/day maximum

Cl_{cr} <15 mL/minute: Administer 50 mg every other day maximum

(Continued)

Atenolol *(Continued)*

Hemodialysis: Moderately dialyzable (20% to 50%) via hemodialysis; administer dose postdialysis or administer 25-50 mg supplemental dose

Peritoneal dialysis: Elimination is not enhanced; supplemental dose is not necessary

Administration Administer I.V. at 1 mg/minute; intravenous administration requires a cardiac monitor and blood pressure monitor

Monitoring Parameters Monitor blood pressure, apical and radial pulses, fluid I & O, daily weight, respirations, and circulation in extremities before and during therapy

Test Interactions ↑ glucose; ↓ HDL

Patient Information Adhere to dosage regimen; watch for postural hypotension; **abrupt withdrawal of the drug should be avoided;** take at the same time each day; may mask diabetes symptoms; notify physician if any adverse effects occur; use with caution while driving or performing tasks requiring alertness; may be taken without regard to meals

Dosage Forms
Injection: 0.5 mg/mL (10 mL)
Tablet: 25 mg, 50 mg, 100 mg

Extemporaneous Preparations A 2 mg/mL atenolol oral liquid compounded from tablets and a commercially available oral diluent was found to be stable for up to 40 days when stored at 5°C or 25°C

Garner SS, Wiest DB, and Reynolds ER, "Stability of Atenolol in an Extemporaneously Compounded Oral Liquid," *Am J Hosp Pharm*, 1994, 51(4):508-11.

Atenolol and Chlorthalidone (a TEN oh lole & klor THAL i done)

U.S. Brand Names Tenoretic®
Therapeutic Category Antihypertensive Agent, Combination
Dosage Forms Tablet:
50: Atenolol 50 mg and chlorthalidone 25 mg
100: Atenolol 100 mg and chlorthalidone 25 mg

♦ **ATG** *see* Antithymocyte Globulin (Rabbit) *on page 92*
♦ **ATG** *see* Lymphocyte Immune Globulin *on page 702*
♦ **Atgam** *see* Lymphocyte Immune Globulin *on page 702*
♦ **ATIII** *see* Antithrombin III *on page 91*
♦ **Ativan®** *see* Lorazepam *on page 694*
♦ **ATnativ®** *see* Antithrombin III *on page 91*
♦ **Atolone®** *see* Triamcinolone *on page 1174*

Atorvastatin (a TORE va sta tin)

Related Information
Antacid Drug Interactions *on page 1296*
Lipid-Lowering Agents *on page 1327*

U.S. Brand Names Lipitor®
Therapeutic Category Antilipemic Agent; HMG-CoA Reductase Inhibitor
Use Adjunct to diet for the reduction of elevated total and LDL-cholesterol levels in patients with hypercholesterolemia (Type IIa, IIb, and IIc); used in hypercholesterolemic patients without clinically evident heart disease to reduce the risk of myocardial infarction, to reduce the risk for revascularization, and reduce the risk of death due to cardiovascular causes

Pregnancy Risk Factor X

Contraindications Hypersensitivity to atorvastatin or its components; patients with active liver disease; pregnancy or lactation

Warnings/Precautions Discontinue therapy if symptoms of myopathy or renal failure due to rhabdomyolysis develop. Use with caution in patients with history of liver disease or who consume excessive amounts of alcohol. It is recommended that liver function tests (LFTs) be performed prior to and at 12 weeks following both the initiation of therapy and any elevation in dose, and periodically (eg, semiannually) thereafter.

Adverse Reactions
>1%:
Central nervous system: Headache
Gastrointestinal: Diarrhea, flatulence, abdominal pain (2% to 3%)
Neuromuscular & skeletal: Myalgia (1% to 5%)
<1%: Giddiness, euphoria, mild confusion, impaired short-term memory, mild LFT increases, pharyngitis, rhinitis

Overdosage/Toxicology
Few symptoms of overdose anticipated
Treatment is supportive

Drug Interactions CYP3A3/4 enzyme substrate
Increased toxicity: Gemfibrozil (musculoskeletal effects such as myopathy, myalgia and/or muscle weakness accompanied by markedly elevated CK concentrations, rash and/or pruritus); clofibrate, niacin (myopathy), erythromycin, cyclosporine, oral anticoagulants (elevated PT)
Increased effect/toxicity of levothyroxine
Concurrent use of erythromycin and atorvastatin may result in rhabdomyolysis

Mechanism of Action Inhibitor of 3-hydroxy-3-methylglutaryl coenzyme A (HMG-CoA) reductase, the rate limiting enzyme in cholesterol synthesis (reduces the production of mevalonic acid from HMG-CoA); this then results in a compensatory increase in the expression of LDL receptors on hepatocyte membranes and a stimulation of LDL catabolism

Pharmacodynamics/Kinetics
  Absorption: Rapid
  Protein binding: 98%
  Metabolism: Undergoes enterohepatic recycling; not a prodrug; metabolized to active ortho- and parahydroxylated derivates and an inactive beta-oxidation product
  Half-life: 14 hours (parent)
  Time to peak serum concentration: 1-2 hours (maximal reduction in plasma cholesterol and triglycerides in 2 weeks)
  Elimination: 2% excreted as unchanged drug in the urine
Usual Dosage Adults: Oral: Initial: 10 mg once daily, titrate up to 80 mg/day if needed
  Dosing adjustment in renal impairment: No dosage adjustment necessary
  Dosing adjustment in hepatic impairment: Decrease dosage with severe disease (eg, chronic alcoholic liver disease)
Monitoring Parameters Lipid levels after 2-4 weeks; LFTs, CPK

It is recommended that liver function tests (LFTs) be performed prior to and at 12 weeks following both the initiation of therapy and any elevation in dose, and periodically (eg, semiannually) thereafter

Patient Information May take with food if desired; may take without regard to time of day
Dosage Forms Tablet: 10 mg, 20 mg, 40 mg

Atovaquone (a TOE va kwone)
U.S. Brand Names Mepron™
Therapeutic Category Antiprotozoal
Use Acute oral treatment of mild to moderate *Pneumocystis carinii* pneumonia (PCP) in patients who are intolerant to co-trimoxazole; prophylaxis of PCP in patients intolerant to co-trimoxazole; treatment/suppression of *Toxoplasma gondii* encephalitis, primary prophylaxis of HIV-infected persons at high risk for developing *Toxoplasma gondii* encephalitis
Pregnancy Risk Factor C
Contraindications Life-threatening allergic reaction to the drug or formulation
Warnings/Precautions Has only been indicated in mild to moderate PCP; use with caution in elderly patients due to potentially impaired renal, hepatic, and cardiac function
Adverse Reactions Note: Adverse reaction statistics have been compiled from studies including patients with advanced HIV disease; consequently, it is difficult to distinguish reactions attributed to atovaquone from those caused by the underlying disease or a combination, thereof.

  >10%:
    Central nervous system: Headache, fever, insomnia, anxiety
    Dermatologic: Rash
    Gastrointestinal: Nausea, diarrhea, vomiting
    Respiratory: Cough
  1% to 10%:
    Central nervous system: Dizziness
    Dermatologic: Pruritus
    Endocrine & metabolic: Hypoglycemia, hyponatremia
    Gastrointestinal: Abdominal pain, constipation, anorexia, dyspepsia, increased amylase
    Hematologic: Anemia, neutropenia, leukopenia
    Hepatic: Elevated liver enzymes
    Neuromuscular & skeletal: Weakness
    Renal: Elevated BUN/creatinine
    Miscellaneous: Oral moniliasis
Drug Interactions
  Decreased effect: Rifamycins used concurrently decrease the steady-state plasma concentrations of atovaquone
  Note: Possible increased toxicity with other highly protein bound drugs
Stability Do not freeze
Mechanism of Action Has not been fully elucidated; may inhibit electron transport in mitochondria inhibiting metabolic enzymes
Pharmacodynamics/Kinetics
  Absorption: Decreased significantly in single doses >750 mg; increased threefold when administered with a high-fat meal
  Distribution: Enterohepatically recirculated
  Protein binding: >99.9%
  Bioavailability: ~30%
  Half-life: 2.9 days
  Elimination: In feces
Usual Dosage Adults: Oral: 750 mg twice daily with food for 21 days
Patient Information Take only prescribed dose; take each dose with a meal, preferably one with high fat content
Dosage Forms
  Sachet: 750 mg/5 mL (42 sachets/box)
  Suspension, oral (citrus flavor): 750 mg/5 mL (210 mL)

♦ **Atozine®** *see* Hydroxyzine *on page 589*
♦ **ATRA** *see* Tretinoin, Oral *on page 1171*

Atracurium (a tra KYOO ree um)

Related Information
Neuromuscular Blocking Agents Comparison *on page 1331*

U.S. Brand Names Tracrium®

Synonyms Atracurium Besylate

Therapeutic Category Neuromuscular Blocker Agent, Nondepolarizing; Skeletal Muscle Relaxant

Use Drug of choice for neuromuscular blockade in patients with renal and/or hepatic failure; eases endotracheal intubation as an adjunct to general anesthesia and relaxes skeletal muscle during surgery or mechanical ventilation; does not relieve pain

Pregnancy Risk Factor C

Contraindications Hypersensitivity to atracurium besylate or any component

Warnings/Precautions Reduce initial dosage in patients in whom substantial histamine release would be potentially hazardous (eg, patients with clinically important cardiovascular disease); maintenance of an adequate airway and respiratory support is critical

Adverse Reactions Mild, rare, and generally suggestive of histamine release
1% to 10%: Cardiovascular: Flushing
<1%: Cardiovascular effects are minimal and transient, erythema, itching, urticaria, wheezing, bronchial secretions

Causes of prolonged neuromuscular blockade:
Excessive drug administration
Cumulative drug effect, decreased metabolism/excretion (hepatic and/or renal impairment)
Accumulation of active metabolites
Electrolyte imbalance (hypokalemia, hypocalcemia, hypermagnesemia, hypernatremia)
Hypothermia
Drug interactions
Increased sensitivity to muscle relaxants (eg, neuromuscular disorders such as myasthenia gravis or polymyositis)

Overdosage/Toxicology
Symptoms of overdose include respiratory depression, cardiovascular collapse
Neostigmine 1-3 mg slow I.V. push in adults (0.5 mg in children) antagonizes the neuromuscular blockade, and should be administered with or immediately after atropine 1-1.5 mg I.V. push (adults). This may be especially useful in the presence of bradycardia.

Drug Interactions Prolonged neuromuscular blockade:
Inhaled anesthetics:
Halothane has only a marginal effect, enflurane and isoflurane increases the potency and prolong duration of neuromuscular blockade induced by atracurium by 35% to 50%
Dosage should be reduced by 33% in patients receiving isoflurane or enflurane and by 20% in patients receiving halothane
Local anesthetics
Calcium channel blockers
Corticosteroids
Antiarrhythmics (eg, quinidine or procainamide)
Antibiotics (eg, aminoglycosides, tetracyclines, vancomycin, clindamycin)
Immunosuppressants (eg, cyclosporine)

Stability Refrigerate; unstable in alkaline solutions; **compatible** with D_5W, D_5NS, and NS; do not dilute in LR

Mechanism of Action Blocks neural transmission at the myoneural junction by binding with cholinergic receptor sites

Pharmacodynamics/Kinetics
Onset of action: I.V.: 2 minutes
Peak effect: Within 3-5 minutes
Duration: Recovery begins in 20-35 minutes when anesthesia is balanced
Metabolism: Some metabolites are active; undergoes rapid nonenzymatic degradation in the bloodstream, additional metabolism occurs via ester hydrolysis
Half-life, biphasic: Adults: Initial: 2 minutes; Terminal: 20 minutes

Usual Dosage I.V. (not to be used I.M.):
Children 1 month to 2 years: 0.3-0.4 mg/kg initially followed by maintenance doses of 0.3-0.4 mg/kg as needed to maintain neuromuscular blockade
Children >2 years to Adults: 0.4-0.5 mg/kg then 0.08-0.1 mg/kg 20-45 minutes after initial dose to maintain neuromuscular block
Infusions (require use of an infusion pump): 0.2 mg/mL or 0.5 mg/mL in D_5W or NS
Continuous infusion: Initial: 9-10 mcg/kg/minute followed by 5-9 mcg/kg/minute maintenance
Dosage adjustment for hepatic or renal impairment is not necessary

Administration Administer undiluted as a bolus injection; not for I.M. inject, too much tissue irritation; administration requires the use of an infusion pump

Monitoring Parameters Vital signs (heart rate, blood pressure, respiratory rate)

Patient Information May be difficult to talk because of head and neck muscle blockade

Dosage Forms
Injection, as besylate: 10 mg/mL (5 mL, 10 mL)
Injection, preservative-free, as besylate: 10 mg/mL (5 mL)

♦ **Atracurium Besylate** *see Atracurium on this page*

- **Atridox™** *see Doxycycline on page 397*
- **Atrohist® Plus** *see Chlorpheniramine, Phenylephrine, Phenylpropanolamine, and Belladonna Alkaloids on page 247*
- **Atromid-S®** *see Clofibrate on page 279*
- **Atropair® Ophthalmic** *see Atropine on this page*

Atropine (A troe peen)
Related Information
Adult ACLS Algorithm, Asystole *on page 1449*
Adult ACLS Algorithm, Bradycardia *on page 1452*
Adult ACLS Algorithm, Pulseless Electrical Activity *on page 1448*
Cycloplegic Mydriatics Comparison *on page 1321*
Pediatric ALS Algorithm, Bradycardia *on page 1444*
U.S. Brand Names Atropair® Ophthalmic; Atropine-Care® Ophthalmic; Atropisol® Ophthalmic; Isopto® Atropine Ophthalmic; I-Tropine® Ophthalmic; Ocu-Tropine® Ophthalmic
Synonyms Atropine Sulfate
Therapeutic Category Anticholinergic Agent; Anticholinergic Agent, Ophthalmic; Antidote, Organophosphate Poisoning; Antispasmodic Agent, Gastrointestinal; Bronchodilator; Ophthalmic Agent, Mydriatic
Use Preoperative medication to inhibit salivation and secretions; treatment of sinus bradycardia; management of peptic ulcer; treat exercise-induced bronchospasm; antidote for organophosphate pesticide poisoning; produce mydriasis and cycloplegia for examination of the retina and optic disc and accurate measurement of refractive errors; uveitis
Pregnancy Risk Factor C
Contraindications Hypersensitivity to atropine sulfate or any component; narrow-angle glaucoma; tachycardia; thyrotoxicosis; obstructive disease of the GI tract; obstructive uropathy
Warnings/Precautions Use with caution in children with spastic paralysis; use with caution in elderly patients. Low doses cause a paradoxical decrease in heart rates. Some commercial products contain sodium metabisulfite, which can cause allergic-type reactions. May accumulate with multiple inhalational administration, particularly in the elderly. Heat prostration may occur in hot weather. Use with caution in patients with autonomic neuropathy, prostatic hypertrophy, hyperthyroidism, congestive heart failure, cardiac arrhythmias, chronic lung disease, biliary tract disease; anticholinergic agents are generally not well tolerated in the elderly and their use should be avoided when possible; atropine is rarely used except as a preoperative agent or in the acute treatment of bradyarrhythmias.
Adverse Reactions
>10%:
Dermatologic: Dry, hot skin
Gastrointestinal: Impaired GI motility, constipation, dry throat, xerostomia
Local: Irritation at injection site
Respiratory: Dry nose
Miscellaneous: Diaphoresis (decreased)
1% to 10%:
Dermatologic: Increased sensitivity to light
Endocrine & metabolic: Decreased flow of breast milk
Gastrointestinal: Dysphagia
<1%: Orthostatic hypotension, tachycardia, palpitations, ventricular fibrillation, confusion, drowsiness, ataxia, fatigue, delirium, headache, loss of memory, restlessness; the elderly may be at increased risk for confusion and hallucinations, rash, bloated feeling, nausea, vomiting, dysuria, tremor, weakness, increased intraocular pain, blurred vision, mydriasis
Overdosage/Toxicology
Symptoms of overdose include dilated, unreactive pupils; blurred vision; hot, dry flushed skin; dryness of mucous membranes; difficulty in swallowing, foul breath, diminished or absent bowel sounds, urinary retention, tachycardia, hyperthermia, hypertension, increased respiratory rate
Anticholinergic toxicity is caused by strong binding of the drug to cholinergic receptors. Anticholinesterase inhibitors reduce acetylcholinesterase, the enzyme that breaks down acetylcholine and thereby allows acetylcholine to accumulate and compete for receptor binding with the offending anticholinergic. For anticholinergic overdose with severe life-threatening symptoms, physostigmine 1-2 mg (0.5 mg or 0.02 mg/kg for children) S.C. or I.V., slowly may be given to reverse these effects.
Drug Interactions
Decreased effect: Phenothiazines, levodopa, antihistamines with cholinergic mechanisms decrease anticholinergic effects of atropine
Increased toxicity: Amantadine increases anticholinergic effects, thiazides increase effect
Stability Store injection at <40°C, avoid freezing
Mechanism of Action Blocks the action of acetylcholine at parasympathetic sites in smooth muscle, secretory glands and the CNS; increases cardiac output, dries secretions, antagonizes histamine and serotonin
Pharmacodynamics/Kinetics
Absorption: Well absorbed from all dosage forms
Distribution: Widely distributes throughout the body; crosses the placenta; trace amounts appear in breast milk; crosses the blood-brain barrier
Metabolism: In the liver
(Continued)

Atropine *(Continued)*

Half-life: 2-3 hours

Elimination: Both metabolites and unchanged drug (30% to 50%) are excreted into urine

Usual Dosage Note: Doses <0.1 mg have been associated with paradoxical bradycardia

Neonates, Infants, and Children:

Preanesthetic: Oral, I.M., I.V., S.C.:

<5 kg: 0.02 mg/kg/dose 30-60 minutes preop then every 4-6 hours as needed; use of a minimum dosage of 0.1 mg in neonates <5 kg will result in dosages >0.02 mg/kg; there is no documented minimum dosage in this age group

>5 kg: 0.01-0.02 mg/kg/dose to a maximum 0.4 mg/dose 30-60 minutes preop; minimum dose: 0.1 mg

Bradycardia: I.V., intratracheal: 0.02 mg/kg, minimum dose 0.1 mg, maximum single dose: 0.5 mg in children and 1 mg in adolescents; may repeat in 5-minute intervals to a maximum total dose of 1 mg in children or 2 mg in adolescents. (**Note:** For intratracheal administration, the dosage must be diluted with normal saline to a total volume of 1-2 mL); when treating bradycardia in neonates, reserve use for those patients unresponsive to improved oxygenation and epinephrine.

Children:

Bronchospasm: Inhalation: 0.03-0.05 mg/kg/dose 3-4 times/day

Preprocedure: Ophthalmic: 0.5% solution: Instill 1-2 drops twice daily for 1-3 days before the procedure

Uveitis: Ophthalmic: 0.5% solution: Instill 1-2 drops up to 3 times/day

Adults (doses <0.5 mg have been associated with paradoxical bradycardia):

Asystole: I.V.: 1 mg; may repeat every 3-5 minutes as needed

Preanesthetic: I.M., I.V., S.C.: 0.4-0.6 mg 30-60 minutes preop and repeat every 4-6 hours as needed

Bradycardia: I.V.: 0.5-1 mg every 5 minutes, not to exceed a total of 2 mg or 0.04 mg/kg; may give intratracheal in 1 mg/10 mL dilution only, intratracheal dose should be 2-2.5 times the I.V. dose

Neuromuscular blockade reversal: I.V.: 25-30 mcg/kg 30 seconds before neostigmine or 10 mcg/kg 30 seconds before edrophonium

Organophosphate or carbamate poisoning: I.V.: 1-2 mg/dose every 10-20 minutes until atropine effect (dry flushed skin, tachycardia, mydriasis, fever) is observed, then every 1-4 hours for at least 24 hours; up to 50 mg in first 24 hours and 2 g over several days may be given in cases of severe intoxication

Bronchospasm: Inhalation: 0.025-0.05 mg/kg/dose every 4-6 hours as needed (maximum: 5 mg/dose)

Ophthalmic solution: 1%:

Preprocedure: Instill 1-2 drops 1 hour before the procedure

Uveitis: Instill 1-2 drops 4 times/day

Ophthalmic ointment: Apply a small amount in the conjunctival sac up to 3 times/day; compress the lacrimal sac by digital pressure for 1-3 minutes after instillation

Monitoring Parameters Heart rate, blood pressure, pulse, mental status; intravenous administration requires a cardiac monitor

Patient Information Maintain good oral hygiene habits because lack of saliva may increase chance of cavities. Observe caution while driving or performing other tasks requiring alertness, as drug may cause drowsiness, dizziness, or blurred vision. Notify physician if rash, flushing, or eye pain occurs, or if difficulty in urinating, constipation, or sensitivity to light becomes severe or persists. Do not allow dropper bottle or tube to touch eye during administration.

Nursing Implications Observe for tachycardia if patient has cardiac problems

Dosage Forms

Injection, as sulfate: 0.1 mg/mL (5 mL, 10 mL); 0.3 mg/mL (1 mL, 30 mL); 0.4 mg/mL (1 mL, 20 mL, 30 mL); 0.5 mg/mL (1 mL, 5 mL, 30 mL); 0.8 mg/mL (0.5 mL, 1 mL); 1 mg/mL (1 mL, 10 mL)

Ointment, ophthalmic, as sulfate: 0.5%, 1% (3.5 g)

Solution, ophthalmic, as sulfate: 0.5% (1 mL, 5 mL); 1% (1 mL, 2 mL, 5 mL, 15 mL); 2% (1 mL, 2 mL); 3% (5 mL)

Tablet, as sulfate: 0.4 mg

♦ **Atropine and Diphenoxylate** *see* Diphenoxylate and Atropine *on page 371*

♦ **Atropine-Care® Ophthalmic** *see* Atropine *on previous page*

♦ **Atropine Sulfate** *see* Atropine *on previous page*

♦ **Atropisol® Ophthalmic** *see* Atropine *on previous page*

♦ **Atrovent®** *see* Ipratropium *on page 625*

♦ **Attenuvax®** *see* Measles Virus Vaccine, Live, Attenuated *on page 715*

♦ **Augmentin®** *see* Amoxicillin and Clavulanate Potassium *on page 71*

♦ **Auralgan®** *see* Antipyrine and Benzocaine *on page 91*

Auranofin *(au RANE oh fin)*

U.S. Brand Names Ridaura®

Therapeutic Category Gold Compound

Use Management of active stage of classic or definite rheumatoid arthritis in patients that do not respond to or tolerate other agents; psoriatic arthritis; adjunctive or alternative therapy for pemphigus

Pregnancy Risk Factor C

Contraindications Renal disease, history of blood dyscrasias, congestive heart failure, exfoliative dermatitis, necrotizing enterocolitis, history of anaphylactic reactions

Warnings/Precautions NSAIDs and corticosteroids may be discontinued after starting gold therapy; therapy should be discontinued if platelet count falls to <100,000/mm^3; WBC <4000, granulocytes <1500/mm^3, explain possibility of adverse effects and their manifestations; use with caution in patients with renal or hepatic impairment

Adverse Reactions
>10%:
Dermatologic: Itching, rash
Gastrointestinal: Stomatitis
Ocular: Conjunctivitis
Renal: Proteinuria
1% to 10%:
Dermatologic: Urticaria, alopecia
Gastrointestinal: Glossitis
Hematologic: Eosinophilia, leukopenia, thrombocytopenia
Renal: Hematuria
<1%: Angioedema, ulcerative enterocolitis, GI hemorrhage, gingivitis, dysphagia, metallic taste, agranulocytosis, anemia, aplastic anemia, hepatotoxicity, peripheral neuropathy, interstitial pneumonitis

Overdosage/Toxicology
Symptoms of overdose include hematuria, proteinuria, fever, nausea, vomiting, diarrhea; signs of gold toxicity include decrease in hemoglobin, leukopenia, granulocytes and platelets, proteinuria, hematuria, pruritus, stomatitis or persistent diarrhea; advise patients to report any symptoms of toxicity; metallic taste may indicate stomatitis
Mild gold poisoning: Dimercaprol 2.5 mg/kg 4 times/day for 2 days or for more severe forms of gold intoxication, dimercaprol 3 mg/kg every 4 hours for 2 days, should be initiated; after 2 days the initial dose should be repeated twice daily on the third day and once daily thereafter for 10 days; other chelating agents have been used with some success

Drug Interactions Increased toxicity: Penicillamine, antimalarials, hydroxychloroquine, cytotoxic agents, immunosuppressants

Stability Store in tight, light-resistant containers at 15°C to 30°C

Mechanism of Action The exact mechanism of action of gold is unknown; gold is taken up by macrophages which results in inhibition of phagocytosis and lysosomal membrane stabilization; other actions observed are decreased serum rheumatoid factor and alterations in immunoglobulins. Additionally, complement activation is decreased, prostaglandin synthesis is inhibited, and lysosomal enzyme activity is decreased.

Pharmacodynamics/Kinetics
Therapeutic response may not be seen for 3-4 months after start of therapy
Absorption: Oral: ~20% gold in dose is absorbed
Protein binding: 60%
Half-life: 21-31 days (half-life dependent upon single or multiple dosing)
Time to peak serum concentration: Peak blood gold concentrations seen within 2 hours
Elimination: 60% of absorbed gold is eliminated in urine; remainder eliminated in feces

Usual Dosage Oral:
Children: Initial: 0.1 mg/kg/day divided daily; usual maintenance: 0.15 mg/kg/day in 1-2 divided doses; maximum: 0.2 mg/kg/day in 1-2 divided doses
Adults: 6 mg/day in 1-2 divided doses; after 3 months may be increased to 9 mg/day in 3 divided doses; if still no response after 3 months at 9 mg/day, discontinue drug
Dosing adjustment in renal impairment:
Cl$_{cr}$ 50-80 mL/minute: Reduce dose to 50%
Cl$_{cr}$ <50 mL/minute: Avoid use

Monitoring Parameters Monitor urine for protein; CBC and platelets; monitor for mouth ulcers and skin reactions; may monitor auranofin serum levels

Reference Range Gold: Normal: 0-0.1 µg/mL (SI: 0-0.0064 µmol/L); Therapeutic: 1-3 µg/mL (SI: 0.06-0.18 µmol/L); Urine: <0.1 µg/24 hours

Test Interactions May enhance the response to a tuberculin skin test

Patient Information Minimize exposure to sunlight; benefits from drug therapy may take as long as 3 months to appear; notify physician of pruritus, rash, sore mouth; metallic taste may occur; take shortly after a meal or light snack, can be given as bedtime dose if drowsiness occurs; optimum effect may take 2-4 weeks to be achieved; avoid alcohol; be aware of possible photosensitivity reaction; may cause painful erections; avoid sudden changes in position

Nursing Implications Discontinue therapy if platelet count falls <100,000/mm^3

Dosage Forms Capsule: 3 mg [29% gold]

♦ **Aureomycin®** see Chlortetracycline on page 251
♦ **Auro® Ear Drops [OTC]** see Carbamide Peroxide on page 190
♦ **Aurolate®** see Gold Sodium Thiomalate on page 543

Aurothioglucose (aur oh thye oh GLOO kose)

U.S. Brand Names Solganal®

Therapeutic Category Gold Compound

Use Adjunctive treatment in adult and juvenile active rheumatoid arthritis; alternative or adjunct in treatment of pemphigus; psoriatic patients who do not respond to NSAIDs

Pregnancy Risk Factor C

Contraindications Renal disease, history of blood dyscrasias, congestive heart failure, exfoliative dermatitis, hepatic disease, SLE, history of hypersensitivity

Warnings/Precautions Use with caution in patients with impaired renal or hepatic function; NSAIDs and corticosteroids may be discontinued over time after initiating gold

(Continued)

Aurothioglucose *(Continued)*

therapy; explain the possibility of adverse reactions before initiating therapy; pregnancy should be ruled out before therapy is started; therapy should be discontinued if platelet counts fall to <100,000/mm^3, WBC <4000/mm^3, granulocytes <1500/mm^3

Adverse Reactions
>10%:
Dermatologic: Itching, rash, exfoliative dermatitis, reddened skin
Gastrointestinal: Gingivitis, glossitis, metallic taste, stomatitis
1% to 10%: Renal: Proteinuria
<1%: Encephalitis, EEG abnormalities, fever, alopecia, ulcerative enterocolitis, vaginitis, agranulocytosis, aplastic anemia, eosinophilia, leukopenia, thrombocytopenia, hepato-toxicity, pharyngitis, bronchitis, pulmonary fibrosis, interstitial pneumonitis, peripheral neuropathy, conjunctivitis, corneal ulcers, iritis, glomerulitis, hematuria, nephrotic syndrome, anaphylactic shock, allergic reaction (severe)

Overdosage/Toxicology
Symptoms of overdose include hematuria, proteinuria, fever, nausea, vomiting, diarrhea; signs of gold toxicity include decrease in hemoglobin, leukopenia, granulocytes and platelets; proteinuria, hematuria, pruritus, stomatitis, persistent diarrhea, rash, or metallic taste; advise patients to report any symptoms of toxicity.

For mild gold poisoning, dimercaprol 2.5 mg/kg 4 times/day for 2 days or for more severe forms of gold intoxication, dimercaprol 3-5 mg/kg every 4 hours for 2 days, should be initiated; then after 2 days the initial dose should be repeated twice daily on the third day, and once daily thereafter for 10 days; other chelating agents have been used with some success

Drug Interactions Increased toxicity: Penicillamine, antimalarials, hydroxychloroquine, cytotoxic agents, immunosuppressants

Stability Protect from light and store at 15°C to 30°C

Mechanism of Action Unknown, may decrease prostaglandin synthesis or may alter cellular mechanisms by inhibiting sulfhydryl systems

Pharmacodynamics/Kinetics
Absorption: I.M.: Erratic and slow
Distribution: Crosses placenta; appears in breast milk
Protein binding: 95% to 99%
Half-life: 3-27 days (half-life dependent upon single or multiple dosing)
Time to peak serum concentration: Within 4-6 hours
Elimination: 70% renal excretion; 30% fecal

Usual Dosage I.M.: Doses should initially be given at weekly intervals
Children 6-12 years: Initial: 0.25 mg/kg/dose first week; increment at 0.25 mg/kg/dose increasing with each weekly dose; maintenance: 0.75-1 mg/kg/dose weekly not to exceed 25 mg/dose to a total of 20 doses, then every 2-4 weeks
Adults: 10 mg first week; 25 mg second and third week; then 50 mg/week until 800 mg to 1 g cumulative dose has been given; if improvement occurs without adverse reactions, administer 25-50 mg every 2-3 weeks, then every 3-4 weeks

Administration Administer by deep I.M. injection into the upper outer quadrant of the gluteal region

Monitoring Parameters CBC with differential, platelet count, urinalysis, baseline renal and liver function tests

Reference Range Gold: Normal: 0-0.1 µg/mL (SI: 0-0.0064 µmol/L); Therapeutic: 1-3 µg/mL (SI: 0.06-0.18 µmol/L); Urine: <0.1 µg/24 hours

Patient Information Minimize exposure to sunlight; benefits from drug therapy may take as long as 3 months to appear; notify physician of pruritus, rash, sore mouth; metallic taste may occur

Nursing Implications Therapy should be discontinued if platelet count falls <100,000/mm^3; vial should be thoroughly shaken before withdrawing a dose; explain the possibility of adverse reactions before initiating therapy; advise patients to report any symptoms of toxicity

Dosage Forms Injection, suspension: 50 mg/mL [gold 50%] (10 mL)

Azatadine (a ZA ta deen)
U.S. Brand Names Optimine®
Synonyms Azatadine Maleate
Therapeutic Category Antihistamine, H₁ Blocker
Use Treatment of perennial and seasonal allergic rhinitis and chronic urticaria
Pregnancy Risk Factor B
Contraindications Hypersensitivity to azatadine or to other related antihistamines including cyproheptadine; patients taking monoamine oxidase inhibitors should not use azatadine
Warnings/Precautions Sedation and somnolence are the most commonly reported adverse effects
Adverse Reactions
>10%:
  Central nervous system: Slight to moderate drowsiness
  Respiratory: Thickening of bronchial secretions
1% to 10%:
  Central nervous system: Headache, fatigue, nervousness, dizziness
  Gastrointestinal: Appetite increase, weight gain, nausea, diarrhea, abdominal pain, xerostomia
  Neuromuscular & skeletal: Arthralgia
  Respiratory: Pharyngitis
<1%: Palpitations, edema, depression, angioedema, photosensitivity, rash, hepatitis, myalgia, paresthesia, bronchospasm, epistaxis
Overdosage/Toxicology
Symptoms of overdose include CNS depression or stimulation, dry mouth, flushed skin, fixed and dilated pupils, apnea.
There is no specific treatment for an antihistamine overdose, however, most of its clinical toxicity is due to anticholinergic effects. Anticholinesterase inhibitors may be useful by reducing acetylcholinesterase; anticholinesterase inhibitors include physostigmine, neostigmine, pyridostigmine, and edrophonium. For anticholinergic overdose with severe life-threatening symptoms, physostigmine 1-2 mg (0.5 mg or 0.02 mg/kg for children) I.V., slowly may be given to reverse these effects.
Drug Interactions Increased effect/toxicity: Procarbazine, CNS depressants, tricyclic antidepressants, alcohol
Mechanism of Action Azatadine is a piperidine-derivative antihistamine; has both anti-cholinergic and antiserotonin activity; has been demonstrated to inhibit mediator release from human mast cells *in vitro*; mechanism of this action is suggested to prevent calcium entry into the mast cell through voltage-dependent calcium channels
Pharmacodynamics/Kinetics
  Absorption: Oral: Rapid and extensive
  Half-life, elimination: ~8.7 hours
  Elimination: ~20% of dose excreted unchanged in urine over 48 hours
Usual Dosage Children >12 years and Adults: Oral: 1-2 mg twice daily
Dietary Considerations Alcohol: Additive CNS effects, avoid use
Patient Information May cause drowsiness; avoid alcohol; can impair coordination and judgment
Nursing Implications Assist with ambulation
Dosage Forms Tablet, as maleate: 1 mg

Azatadine and Pseudoephedrine (a ZA ta deen & soo doe e FED rin)
U.S. Brand Names Trinalin®
Therapeutic Category Antihistamine/Decongestant Combination
Dosage Forms Tablet: Azatadine maleate 1 mg and pseudoephedrine sulfate 120 mg

♦ **Azatadine Maleate** *see* Azatadine *on this page*

Azathioprine (ay za THYE oh preen)
Related Information
  Toxicities of Chemotherapeutic Agents *on page 1288*
U.S. Brand Names Imuran®
Synonyms Azathioprine Sodium
Therapeutic Category Antineoplastic Agent, Miscellaneous; Immunosuppressant Agent
Use Adjunct with other agents in prevention of rejection of solid organ transplants; also used in severe active rheumatoid arthritis unresponsive to other agents; other autoimmune diseases (ITP, SLE, MS, Crohn's Disease); **azathioprine is an imidazolyl derivative of 6-mercaptopurine**
Pregnancy Risk Factor D
Contraindications Hypersensitivity to azathioprine or any component; pregnancy and lactation
Warnings/Precautions Chronic immunosuppression increases the risk of neoplasia; has mutagenic potential to both men and women and with possible hematologic toxicities; use with caution in patients with liver disease, renal impairment; monitor hematologic function closely
Adverse Reactions Dose reduction or temporary withdrawal allows reversal
>10%:
  Central nervous system: Fever, chills
  Gastrointestinal: Nausea, vomiting, anorexia, diarrhea
(Continued)

Azathioprine *(Continued)*

Hematologic: Thrombocytopenia, leukopenia, anemia
Miscellaneous: Secondary infection
1% to 10%:
Dermatologic: Rash
Hematologic: Pancytopenia
Hepatic: Hepatotoxicity
<1%: Hypotension, alopecia, maculopapular rash, aphthous stomatitis, arthralgias, which include myalgias, rigors, retinopathy, dyspnea, rare hypersensitivity reactions

Overdosage/Toxicology
Symptoms of overdose include nausea, vomiting, diarrhea, hematologic toxicity
Following initiation of essential overdose management, symptomatic and supportive treatment should be instituted. Dialysis has been reported to remove significant amounts of the drug and its metabolites, and should be considered as a treatment option in those patients who deteriorate despite established forms of therapy.

Drug Interactions Increased toxicity: Allopurinol (decreases azathioprine dose to $^1/_3$ to $^1/_4$ of normal dose)

Stability
Stability of parenteral admixture at room temperature (25°C): 24 hours
Stability of parenteral admixture at refrigeration temperature (4°C): 16 days
Stable in neutral or acid solutions, but is hydrolyzed to mercaptopurine in alkaline solutions

Mechanism of Action Antagonizes purine metabolism and may inhibit synthesis of DNA, RNA, and proteins; may also interfere with cellular metabolism and inhibit mitosis

Pharmacodynamics/Kinetics
Distribution: Crosses the placenta
Protein binding: ~30%
Metabolism: Extensively by hepatic xanthine oxidase to 6-mercaptopurine (active)
Half-life: Parent drug: 12 minutes; 6-mercaptopurine: 0.7-3 hours; End-stage renal disease: Slightly prolonged
Elimination: Small amounts eliminated as unchanged drug; metabolites eliminated eventually in urine

Usual Dosage I.V. dose is equivalent to oral dose (dosing should be based on ideal body weight):
Children and Adults: Solid organ transplantation: Oral, I.V.: 2-5 mg/kg/day to start, then 1-2 mg/kg/day maintenance
Adults: Rheumatoid arthritis: Oral: 1 mg/kg/day for 6-8 weeks; increase by 0.5 mg/kg every 4 weeks until response or up to 2.5 mg/kg/day

Dosing adjustment in renal impairment:
Cl_{cr} 10-50 mL/minute: Administer 75% of normal dose daily
Cl_{cr} <10 mL/minute: Administer 50% of normal dose daily
Hemodialysis: Slightly dialyzable (5% to 20%)
Administer dose posthemodialysis
CAPD effects: Unknown
CAVH effects: Unknown

Administration Azathioprine can be administered IVP over 5 minutes at a concentration not to exceed 10 mg/mL **or** azathioprine can be further diluted with normal saline or D_5W and administered by intermittent infusion over 15-60 minutes

Monitoring Parameters CBC, platelet counts, total bilirubin, alkaline phosphatase.

Patient Information Response in rheumatoid arthritis may not occur for up to 3 months; do not stop taking without the physician's approval, do not have any vaccinations before checking with your physician; check with your physician if you have a persistent sore throat, unusual bleeding or bruising, or fatigue. Contraceptive measures are recommended during therapy.

Dosage Forms
Injection, as sodium: 100 mg (20 mL)
Tablet (scored): 50 mg

Extemporaneous Preparations A 50 mg/mL suspension compounded from twenty 50 mg tablets, distilled water, Cologel® 5 mL, and then adding 2:1 simple syrup/cherry syrup mixture to a total volume of 20 mL, was stable for 8 weeks when stored in the refrigerator

Handbook on Extemporaneous Formulations, Bethesda, MD: American Society of Hospital Pharmacists, 1987.

♦ **Azathioprine Sodium** *see Azathioprine on previous page*
♦ **Azdone®** *see Hydrocodone and Aspirin on page 576*

Azelaic Acid *(a zeh LAY ik AS id)*

U.S. Brand Names Azelex®
Therapeutic Category Topical Skin Product, Acne
Use *Acne vulgaris*: Topical treatment of mild to moderate inflammatory acne vulgaris
Pregnancy Risk Factor B
Pregnancy/Breast-Feeding Implications Breast-feeding/lactation: Since <4% of a topically applied dose is systemically absorbed, the uptake of azelaic acid into breast milk is not expected to cause a significant change from baseline azelaic acid levels in the milk. However, exercise caution when administering to a nursing mother.
Contraindications Known hypersensitivity to any of components

Warnings/Precautions For external use only; not for ophthalmic use; there have been isolated reports of hypopigmentation after use. If sensitivity or severe irritation develops, discontinue treatment and institute appropriate therapy.

Adverse Reactions

1% to 10%:
Dermatologic: Pruritus, stinging
Local: Burning
Neuromuscular & skeletal: Paresthesia
<1%: Erythema, dryness, rash, peeling, dermatitis, contact dermatitis, irritation

Mechanism of Action Exact mechanism is not known; *in vitro*, azelaic acid possesses antimicrobial activity against *Propionibacterium acnes* and *Staphylococcus epidermidis*; may decrease microcomedo formation

Pharmacodynamics/Kinetics

Absorption: ~3% to 5% penetrates the stratum corneum; up to 10% is found in the epidermis and dermis; 4% is systemically absorbed
Half-life: Healthy subjects: 12 hours after topical dosing
Elimination: Mainly excreted unchanged in the urine

Usual Dosage Adults: Topical: After skin is thoroughly washed and patted dry, gently but thoroughly massage a thin film of azelaic acid cream into the affected areas twice daily, in the morning and evening. The duration of use can vary and depends on the severity of the acne. In the majority of patients with inflammatory lesions, improvement of the condition occurs within 4 weeks.

Patient Information Use for the full prescribed treatment period. Avoid the use of occlusive dressings or wrappings. Keep away from the mouth, eyes and other mucous membranes. If it does come in contact with the eyes, wash eyes with large amounts of water and consult a physician if eye irritation persists. If patients have dark complexions, they should report abnormal changes in skin color to their physician. Due in part to the low pH of azelaic acid, temporary skin irritation (pruritus, burning or stinging) may occur when azelaic acid is applied to broken or inflamed skin, usually at the start of treatment. However, this irritation commonly subsides if treatment is continued. If it continues, apply only once a day, or stop the treatment until these effects have subsided. If troublesome irritation persists, discontinue use and consult the physician.

Nursing Implications Wash hands following application

Dosage Forms Cream: 20% (30 g)

Azelastine (a ZEL as teen)

U.S. Brand Names Astelin® Nasal Spray

Synonyms Azelastine Hydrochloride

Therapeutic Category Antihistamine, Inhalation

Use Treatment of the symptoms of seasonal allergic rhinitis such as rhinorrhea, sneezing, and nasal pruritus in adults and children >12 years of age

Pregnancy Risk Factor C

Contraindications Hypersensitivity to azelastine or any component

Warnings/Precautions Use with caution in asthmatics; patients with hepatic or renal dysfunction may require lower doses

Adverse Reactions

>10%:
Central nervous system: Headache (14.8%), somnolence (11.5%)
Gastrointestinal: Bitter taste (19.7%)

2% to 10%:
Central nervous system: Dizziness (2%), fatigue (2.3%)
Gastrointestinal: Nausea (2.8%), weight increase (2%), dry mouth (2.8%)
Respiratory: Nasal burning (4.1%), pharyngitis (3.8%), paroxysmal sneezing (3.1%), rhinitis (2.3%), epistaxis (2%)

<2%:
Body as a whole: Allergic reactions, back pain, viral infections, malaise, extremity pain, abdominal pain
Cardiovascular: Flushing, hypertension, tachycardia
Central nervous system: Drowsiness, fatigue, vertigo, depression, nervousness, hypoesthesia
Dermatologic: Contact dermatitis, eczema, hair and follicle infection, furunculosis
Gastrointestinal: Constipation, gastroenteritis, glossitis, increased appetite, ulcerative stomatitis, vomiting, increased ALT, aphthous stomatitis
Genitourinary: Urinary frequency, hematuria, albuminuria, amenorrhea
Neuromuscular & skeletal: Myalgia, vertigo, temporomandibular dislocation, hypoesthesia, hyperkinesia
Ocular: Conjunctivitis, watery eyes, eye pain
Respiratory: Bronchospasm, coughing, throat burning, laryngitis
Psychological: Anxiety, depersonalization, sleep disorder, abnormal thinking

Drug Interactions May cause additive sedation when concomitantly administered with other CNS depressant medications; cimetidine can increase the AUC and C_{max} of azelastine by as much as 65%

Stability Stable 3 months after opening

Mechanism of Action Competes with histamine for H_1-receptor sites on effector cells in the blood vessels and respiratory tract; reduces hyper-reactivity of the airways; increases the motility of bronchial epithelial cilia, improving mucociliary transport

Pharmacodynamics/Kinetics

Peak effect: 3 hours
Duration of action: 12 hours
(Continued)

Azelastine *(Continued)*

Metabolism: Metabolized by cytochrome P-450 enzyme system; active metabolite desmethylazelastine

Bioavailability: After intranasal administration: 40%

Protein binding: 88%

Half-life, elimination: 22 hours

Time to peak serum concentration: 2-3 hours

Usual Dosage Children ≥12 years and Adults: 2 sprays (137 mcg/spray) each nostril twice daily. Before initial use, the delivery system should be primed with 4 sprays or until a fine mist appears. If 3 or more days have elapsed since last use, the delivery system should be reprimed.

Patient Information Causes drowsiness and may impair ability to perform hazardous activities requiring mental alertness or physical coordination; avoid spraying in eyes

Dosage Forms Solution, nasal: 1 mg/mL (137 mcg/spray) (17 mL)

♦ **Azelastine Hydrochloride** *see* Azelastine *on previous page*

♦ **Azelex®** *see* Azelaic Acid *on page 116*

♦ **Azidothymidine** *see* Zidovudine *on page 1235*

Azithromycin *(az ith roe MYE sin)*

Related Information

Antimicrobial Drugs of Choice *on page 1404*

Community-Acquired Pneumonia in Adults *on page 1419*

Guidelines for the Prevention of Opportunistic Infections in Persons with HIV *on page 1388*

Prevention of Bacterial Endocarditis *on page 1377*

Treatment of Sexually Transmitted Diseases *on page 1429*

U.S. Brand Names Zithromax™

Synonyms Azithromycin Dihydrate

Therapeutic Category Antibiotic, Macrolide

Use

Children: Treatment of acute otitis media due to *H. influenzae*, *M. catarrhalis*, or *S. pneumoniae*; pharyngitis/tonsillitis due to *S. pyogenes*

Adults:

Treatment of mild to moderate upper and lower respiratory tract infections, infections of the skin and skin structure, and sexually transmitted diseases due to susceptible strains of *C. trachomatis*, *M. catarrhalis*, *H. influenzae*, *S. aureus*, *S. pneumoniae*, *Mycoplasma pneumoniae*, and *C. psittaci*; community-acquired pneumonia, pelvic inflammatory disease (PID)

For preventing or delaying the onset of infection with *Mycobacterium avium* complex (MAC)

Prophylaxis of bacterial endocarditis in patients who are allergic to penicillin and undergoing surgical or dental procedures

Pregnancy Risk Factor B

Contraindications Hepatic impairment, known hypersensitivity to azithromycin, other macrolide antibiotics, or any azithromycin components; use with pimozide

Warnings/Precautions Use with caution in patients with hepatic dysfunction; hepatic impairment with or without jaundice has occurred chiefly in older children and adults; it may be accompanied by malaise, nausea, vomiting, abdominal colic, and fever; discontinue use if these occur; may mask or delay symptoms of incubating gonorrhea or syphilis, so appropriate culture and susceptibility tests should be performed prior to initiating azithromycin; pseudomembranous colitis has been reported with use of macrolide antibiotics; safety and efficacy have not been established in children <6 months of age with acute otitis media and in children <2 years of age with pharyngitis/tonsillitis

Adverse Reactions

1% to 10%: Gastrointestinal: Diarrhea, nausea, abdominal pain, cramping, vomiting (especially with high single-dose regimens)

<1%: Ventricular arrhythmias, fever, headache, dizziness, rash, angioedema, hypertrophic pyloric stenosis, vaginitis, eosinophilia, elevated LFTs, cholestatic jaundice, thrombophlebitis, ototoxicity, nephritis, allergic reactions

Overdosage/Toxicology

Symptoms of overdose include nausea, vomiting, diarrhea, prostration

Treatment is supportive and symptomatic

Drug Interactions May inhibit CYP3A3/4 enzyme (mild)

Decreased peak serum levels: Aluminum- and magnesium-containing antacids by 24% but not total absorption

Increased effect/toxicity: Azithromycin may increase levels of tacrolimus, phenytoin, ergot alkaloids, alfentanil, astemizole, terfenadine, bromocriptine, carbamazepine, cyclosporine, digoxin, disopyramide, and triazolam; azithromycin did not affect the response to warfarin or theophylline although caution is advised when administered together

Avoid use with pimozide due to significant risk of cardiotoxicity

Mechanism of Action Inhibits RNA-dependent protein synthesis at the chain elongation step; binds to the 50S ribosomal subunit resulting in blockage of transpeptidation

Pharmacodynamics/Kinetics

Absorption: Rapid from the GI tract

Distribution: Extensive tissue distribution; distributes well into skin, lungs, sputum, tonsils, and cervix; penetration into the CSF is poor

Protein binding: 7% to 50% (concentration-dependent)

Metabolism: In the liver

Bioavailability: 37%, decreased by food

Half-life, terminal: 68 hours

Peak serum concentration: 2.3-4 hours

Elimination: 4.5% to 12% of dose is excreted in urine; 50% of dose is excreted unchanged in bile

Usual Dosage

Oral:

Children ≥6 months: Otitis media and community-acquired pneumonia: 10 mg/kg on day 1 (maximum: 500 mg/day) followed by 5 mg/kg/day once daily on days 2-5 (maximum: 250 mg/day)

Children ≥2 years: Pharyngitis, tonsillitis: 12 mg/kg/day once daily for 5 days (maximum: 500 mg/day)

Children: *M. avium*-infected patients with acquired immunodeficiency syndrome: Not currently FDA approved for use; 10-20 mg/kg/day once daily (maximum: 40 mg/kg/day) has been used in clinical trials; prophylaxis for first episode of MAC: 5-12 mg/kg/day once daily (maximum: 500 mg/day)

Adolescents ≥16 years and Adults:

Respiratory tract, skin and soft tissue infections: 500 mg on day 1 followed by 250 mg/day on days 2-5 (maximum: 500 mg/day)

Uncomplicated chlamydial urethritis/cervicitis or chancroid: Single 1 g dose

Gonococcal urethritis/cervicitis: Single 2 g dose

Prophylaxis of disseminated *M. avium* complex disease in patient with advanced HIV infection: 1200 mg once weekly (may be combined with rifabutin)

Prophylaxis for bacterial endocarditis: 500 mg 1 hour prior to the procedure

I.V.: Adults:

Community-acquired pneumonia: 500 mg as a single dose for at least 2 days, follow I.V. therapy by the oral route with a single daily dose of 500 mg to complete a 7-10 day course of therapy

Pelvic inflammatory disease (PID): 500 mg as a single dose for 1-2 days, follow I.V. therapy by the oral route with a single daily dose of 250 mg to complete a 7 day course of therapy

Dietary Considerations Food: Rate and extent of GI absorption decreased; take on an empty stomach

Azithromycin suspension, not tablet form, has significantly increased absorption (46%) with food

Administration Do not administer the suspension with food; tablet may be taken without regard to food

Monitoring Parameters Liver function tests, CBC with differential

Patient Information Take suspension 1 hour prior to a meal or 2 hours after; do not take with aluminum- or magnesium-containing antacids; tablet form may be taken with food to decrease GI effects

Additional Information Capsules are no longer being produced in the United States

Dosage Forms

Capsule: 250 mg

Capsule (Z-Pak™): 6 caps/pkg

Powder for injection: 500 mg

Powder for oral suspension, as dihydrate: 100 mg/5 mL (15 mL); 200 mg/5 mL (15 mL, 22.5 mL); 1 g (single-dose packet)

Tablet, as dihydrate: 250 mg, 600 mg

♦ **Azithromycin Dihydrate** *see* Azithromycin *on previous page*

♦ **Azmacort™** *see* Triamcinolone *on page 1174*

♦ **Azopt™** *see* Brinzolamide *on page 154*

♦ **Azo-Standard® [OTC]** *see* Phenazopyridine *on page 910*

♦ **Azo-Sulfisoxazole** *see* Sulfisoxazole and Phenazopyridine *on page 1098*

♦ **AZT** *see* Zidovudine *on page 1235*

♦ **AZT + 3TC** *see* Zidovudine and Lamivudine *on page 1237*

♦ **Azthreonam** *see* Aztreonam *on this page*

Aztreonam (AZ tree oh nam)

Related Information

Antimicrobial Drugs of Choice *on page 1404*

Community-Acquired Pneumonia in Adults *on page 1419*

U.S. Brand Names Azactam®

Synonyms Azthreonam

Therapeutic Category Antibiotic, Miscellaneous

Use Treatment of patients with urinary tract infections, lower respiratory tract infections, septicemia, skin/skin structure infections, intra-abdominal infections, and gynecological infections caused by susceptible gram-negative bacilli; often useful in patients with allergies to penicillins or cephalosporins

Pregnancy Risk Factor B

Contraindications Hypersensitivity to aztreonam or any component

Warnings/Precautions Rare cross-allergenicity to penicillins and cephalosporins; requires dosing adjustment in renal impairment

(Continued)

Aztreonam *(Continued)*

Adverse Reactions

1% to 10%:

Dermatologic: Rash

Gastrointestinal: Diarrhea, nausea, vomiting

Local: Thrombophlebitis, pain at injection site

<1%: Hypotension, seizures, confusion, headache, vertigo, insomnia, dizziness, fever, breast tenderness, pseudomembranous colitis, aphthous ulcer, abnormal taste, halitosis, numb tongue, vaginitis, hepatitis, jaundice, elevated liver enzymes, thrombocytopenia, eosinophilia, leukopenia, neutropenia, myalgia, weakness, diplopia, tinnitus, sneezing, anaphylaxis

Overdosage/Toxicology

Symptoms of overdose include seizures

If necessary, dialysis can reduce the drug concentration in the blood

Stability Reconstituted solutions are colorless to light yellow straw and may turn pink upon standing without affecting potency; use reconstituted solutions and I.V. solutions (in NS and D_5W) within 48 hours if kept at room temperature or 7 days if kept in refrigerator

Stability of I.V. infusion solution: 48 hours at room temperature (25°C) and 7 days at refrigeration (4°C)

Mechanism of Action Inhibits bacterial cell wall synthesis by binding to one or more of the penicillin binding proteins (PBPs); which in turn inhibits the final transpeptidation step of peptidoglycan synthesis in bacterial cell walls, thus inhibiting cell wall biosynthesis. Bacteria eventually lyse due to ongoing activity of cell wall autolytic enzymes (autolysins and murein hydrolases) while cell wall assembly is arrested. Monobactam structure makes cross-allergenicity with beta-lactams unlikely.

Pharmacodynamics/Kinetics

Absorption: I.M.: Well absorbed; I.M. and I.V. doses produce comparable serum concentrations

Distribution: Relative diffusion of antimicrobial agents from blood into cerebrospinal fluid (CSF): Good only with inflammation (exceeds usual MICs); widely distributed to most body fluids and tissues including breast milk; crosses placenta

V_d: Neonates: 0.26-0.36 L/kg; Children: 0.2-0.29 L/kg; Adults: 0.2 L/kg

Ratio of CSF to blood level (%): Inflamed meninges: 8-40; Normal meninges: ~1

Protein binding: 56%

Metabolism: Partial

Half-life:

Neonates: <7 days, ≤2.5 kg: 5.5-9.9 hours; <7 days, >2.5 kg: 2.6 hours; 1 week to 1 month: 2.4 hours

Children 2 months to 12 years: 1.7 hours

Adults: Normal renal function: 1.7-2.9 hours

End-stage renal disease: 6-8 hours

Time to peak: Within 60 minutes (I.M., I.V. push) and 90 minutes (I.V. infusion)

Elimination: 60% to 70% excreted unchanged in urine and partially in feces

Usual Dosage

Neonates: I.M., I.V.:

Postnatal age ≤7 days:

<2000 g: 30 mg/kg/dose every 12 hours

>2000 g: 30 mg/kg/dose every 8 hours

Postnatal age >7 days:

<1200 g: 30 mg/kg/dose every 12 hours

1200-2000 g: 30 mg/kg/dose every 8 hours

>2000 g: 30 mg/kg/dose every 6 hours

Children >1 month: I.M., I.V.: 90-120 mg/kg/day divided every 6-8 hours

Cystic fibrosis: 50 mg/kg/dose every 6-8 hours (ie, up to 200 mg/kg/day); maximum: 6-8 g/day

Adults:

Urinary tract infection: I.M., I.V.: 500 mg to 1 g every 8-12 hours

Moderately severe systemic infections: 1 g I.V. or I.M. or 2 g I.V. every 8-12 hours

Severe systemic or life-threatening infections (especially caused by *Pseudomonas aeruginosa*): I.V.: 2 g every 6-8 hours; maximum: 8 g/day

Dosing adjustment in renal impairment: Adults:

Cl_{cr} >50 mL/minute: 500 mg to 1 g every 6-8 hours

Cl_{cr} 10-50 mL/minute: 50% to 75% of usual dose given at the usual interval

Cl_{cr} <10 mL/minute: 25% of usual dosage given at the usual interval

Hemodialysis: Moderately dialyzable (20% to 50%); administer dose postdialysis or supplemental dose of 500 mg after dialysis

Peritoneal dialysis: Administer as for Cl_{cr} <10 mL/minute

Continuous arteriovenous or venovenous hemofiltration (CAVH/CAVHD): Dose as for Cl_{cr} 10-50 mL/minute

Administration Administer by IVP over 3-5 minutes or by intermittent infusion over 20-60 minutes at a final concentration not to exceed 20 mg/mL

Monitoring Parameters Periodic liver function test; monitor for signs of anaphylaxis during first dose

Test Interactions May interfere with urine glucose tests containing cupric sulfate (Benedict's solution, Clinitest®)

Additional Information Although marketed as an agent similar to aminoglycosides, aztreonam is a monobactam antimicrobial with almost pure gram-negative aerobic activity; it cannot be used for gram-positive infections; aminoglycosides are often used for synergy in gram-positive infections

Dosage Forms Powder for injection: 500 mg (15 mL, 100 mL); 1 g (15 mL, 100 mL); 2 g (15 mL, 100 mL)

- **Azulfidine®** see Sulfasalazine on page 1095
- **Azulfidine® EN-tabs®** see Sulfasalazine on page 1095
- **Babee® Teething® [OTC]** see Benzocaine on page 133
- **B-A-C®** see Butalbital Compound on page 165

Bacampicillin (ba kam pi SIL in)

U.S. Brand Names Spectrobid®
Canadian Brand Names Penglobe®
Synonyms Bacampicillin Hydrochloride; Carampicillin Hydrochloride
Therapeutic Category Antibiotic, Penicillin
Use Treatment of susceptible bacterial infections involving the urinary tract, skin structure, upper and lower respiratory tract; activity is identical to that of ampicillin
Pregnancy Risk Factor B
Contraindications Hypersensitivity to bacampicillin or any component or penicillins
Warnings/Precautions Use with caution in patients allergic to cephalosporins; modify dosage in patients with renal impairment; high percentage of patients with infectious mononucleosis develop a rash during amoxicillin therapy
Adverse Reactions
  1% to 10%: Gastrointestinal: Gastric upset, diarrhea, nausea
  <1%: Rash, pseudomembranous colitis, agranulocytosis, mildly increased AST, hypersensitivity reactions
Overdosage/Toxicology
  Signs and symptoms: Neuromuscular sensitivity, many beta-lactam containing antibiotics have the potential to cause neuromuscular hyperirritability or convulsive seizures
  Treatment: Hemodialysis may be helpful to aid in the removal of the drug from the blood, otherwise most treatment is supportive or symptom directed
Drug Interactions
  Decreased effect of oral contraceptives
  Increased levels with probenecid; allopurinol theoretically has has an additive potential for amoxicillin/ampicillin rash
Stability Reconstituted suspension is stable for 10 days when stored in the refrigerator
Mechanism of Action Interferes with bacterial cell wall synthesis during active multiplication causing cell wall death and resultant bactericidal activity against susceptible bacteria
Pharmacodynamics/Kinetics
  Protein binding: 15% to 25%
  Metabolism: Hydrolyzed to ampicillin
  Bioavailability: 80% to 98%
  Half-life: 65 minutes, prolonged in patients with impaired renal function
  Time to peak serum concentration: Area under the serum concentration time curve is 40% higher for bacampicillin than after equivalent ampicillin doses
Usual Dosage Oral:
  Children <25 kg: 25-50 mg/kg/day in divided doses every 12 hours
  Children >25 kg and Adults: 400-800 mg every 12 hours
  Dosing interval in renal impairment:
    Cl_{cr} 10-30 mL/minute: Administer every 24 hours
    Cl_{cr} <10 mL/minute: Administer every 36 hours
Monitoring Parameters Renal, hepatic, and hematologic function tests
Test Interactions False-positive urine glucose with Clinitest®
Patient Information Take oral suspension 1 hour before or 2 hours after a meal; report diarrhea promptly; entire course of medication (10-14 days) should be taken to ensure eradication of organism; should be taken in equal intervals around-the-clock to maintain adequate blood levels; may interfere with oral contraceptives, females should report symptoms of vaginitis
Nursing Implications Assess patient at beginning and throughout therapy for infection; observe for signs and symptoms of anaphylaxis
Additional Information Each mg of bacampicillin is equivalent to ampicillin 700 mcg
Dosage Forms
  Powder for oral suspension, as hydrochloride: 125 mg/5 mL [chemically equivalent to ampicillin 87.5 mg per 5 mL] (70 mL)
  Tablet, as hydrochloride: 400 mg [chemically equivalent to ampicillin 280 mg]

- **Bacampicillin Hydrochloride** see Bacampicillin on this page
- **Bacid® [OTC]** see Lactobacillus acidophilus and Lactobacillus bulgaricus on page 655
- **Baciguent® Topical [OTC]** see Bacitracin on this page
- **Bacigvent** see Bacitracin on this page
- **Baci-IM® Injection** see Bacitracin on this page
- **Bacillus Calmette-Guérin (BCG) Live** see BCG Vaccine on page 126
- **Bacitin** see Bacitracin on this page

Bacitracin (bas i TRAY sin)

Related Information
  Antimicrobial Drugs of Choice on page 1404
  (Continued)

Bacitracin *(Continued)*

U.S. Brand Names AK-Tracin® Ophthalmic; Baciguent® Topical [OTC]; Baci-IM® Injection

Canadian Brand Names Bacigvent; Bacitin

Therapeutic Category Antibiotic, Ophthalmic; Antibiotic, Topical; Antibiotic, Miscellaneous

Use Treatment of susceptible bacterial infections mainly has activity against gram-positive bacilli; due to toxicity risks, systemic and irrigant uses of bacitracin should be limited to situations where less toxic alternatives would not be effective; oral administration has been successful in antibiotic-associated colitis and has been used for enteric eradication of vancomycin-resistant enterococci (VRE)

Pregnancy Risk Factor C

Contraindications Hypersensitivity to bacitracin or any component; I.M. use is contraindicated in patients with renal impairment

Warnings/Precautions Prolonged use may result in overgrowth of nonsusceptible organisms; I.M. use may cause renal failure due to tubular and glomerular necrosis; **do not administer intravenously** because severe thrombophlebitis occurs

Adverse Reactions 1% to 10%:
Cardiovascular: Hypotension, edema of the face/lips, tightness of chest
Central nervous system: Pain
Dermatologic: Rash, itching
Gastrointestinal: Anorexia, nausea, vomiting, diarrhea, rectal itching
Hematologic: Blood dyscrasias
Miscellaneous: Diaphoresis

Overdosage/Toxicology Symptoms of overdose include nephrotoxicity (parenteral), nausea, vomiting (oral)

Drug Interactions Increased toxicity: Nephrotoxic drugs, neuromuscular blocking agents, and anesthetics (↑ neuromuscular blockade)

Stability For I.M. use; bacitracin sterile powder should be dissolved in 0.9% sodium chloride injection containing 2% procaine hydrochloride; once reconstituted, bacitracin is stable for 1 week under refrigeration (2°C to 8°C); sterile powder should be stored in the refrigerator; do not use diluents containing parabens

Mechanism of Action Inhibits bacterial cell wall synthesis by preventing transfer of mucopeptides into the growing cell wall

Pharmacodynamics/Kinetics
Duration of action: 6-8 hours
Absorption: Poor from mucous membranes and intact or denuded skin; rapidly absorbed following I.M. administration; not absorbed by bladder irrigation, but absorption can occur from peritoneal or mediastinal lavage
Distribution: Relative diffusion of antimicrobial agents from blood into cerebrospinal fluid (CSF): Nil even with inflammation
Protein binding: Minimally bound to plasma proteins
Time to peak serum concentration: I.M.: Within 1-2 hours
Elimination: Slow elimination into urine with 10% to 40% of dose excreted within 24 hours

Usual Dosage Children and Adults (**do not administer I.V.**):
Infants: I.M.:
≤2.5 kg: 900 units/kg/day in 2-3 divided doses
>2.5 kg: 1000 units/kg/day in 2-3 divided doses
Children: I.M.: 800-1200 units/kg/day divided every 8 hours
Adults: Antibiotic-associated colitis: Oral: 25,000 units 4 times/day for 7-10 days
Topical: Apply 1-5 times/day
Ophthalmic, ointment: Instill ¼" to ½" ribbon every 3-4 hours into conjunctival sac for acute infections, or 2-3 times/day for mild to moderate infections for 7-10 days
Irrigation, solution: 50-100 units/mL in normal saline, lactated Ringer's, or sterile water for irrigation; soak sponges in solution for topical compresses 1-5 times/day or as needed during surgical procedures

Administration For I.M. administration, confirm any orders for parenteral use; pH of urine should be kept >6 by using sodium bicarbonate; bacitracin sterile powder should be dissolved in 0.9% sodium chloride injection containing 2% procaine hydrochloride; do not use diluents containing parabens

Monitoring Parameters I.M.: Urinalysis, renal function tests

Patient Information Ophthalmic ointment may cause blurred vision; do not share eye medications with others
Ophthalmic administration: Tilt head back, place medication in conjunctival sac and close eyes; apply light finger pressure on lacrimal sac for 1 minute following instillation
Topical bacitracin should not be used for longer than 1 week unless directed by a physician

Additional Information 1 unit is equivalent to 0.026 mg

Dosage Forms
Injection: 50,000 units
Ointment:
Ophthalmic: 500 units/g (1 g, 3.5 g, 3.75 g)
Topical: 500 units/g (1.5 g, 3.75 g, 15 g, 30 g, 120 g, 454 g)

Bacitracin and Polymyxin B (bas i TRAY sin & pol i MIKS in bee)

Related Information
Bacitracin *on previous page*

Polymyxin B *on page 943*
U.S. Brand Names AK-Poly-Bac® Ophthalmic; Betadine® First Aid Antibiotics + Moisturizer [OTC]; Polysporin® Ophthalmic; Polysporin® Topical
Canadian Brand Names Bioderm®; Polytopic
Therapeutic Category Antibiotic, Ophthalmic; Antibiotic, Topical
Dosage Forms
Ointment:
Ophthalmic: Bacitracin 500 units and polymyxin B sulfate 10,000 units per g (3.5 g)
Topical: Bacitracin 500 units and polymyxin B sulfate 10,000 units per g in white petrolatum (15 g, 30 g)
Powder: Bacitracin 500 units and polymyxin B sulfate 10,000 units per g (10 g)

Bacitracin, Neomycin, and Polymyxin B
(bas i TRAY sin, nee oh MYE sin & pol i MIKS in bee)
Related Information
Bacitracin *on page 121*
Neomycin *on page 824*
Polymyxin B *on page 943*
U.S. Brand Names AK-Spore® Ophthalmic Ointment; Medi-Quick® Topical Ointment [OTC]; Mycitracin® Topical [OTC]; Neomixin® Topical [OTC]; Neosporin® Ophthalmic Ointment; Neosporin® Topical Ointment [OTC]; Ocutricin® Topical Ointment; Septa® Topical Ointment [OTC]; Triple Antibiotic® Topical
Canadian Brand Names Neotopic
Therapeutic Category Antibiotic, Ophthalmic; Antibiotic, Topical
Dosage Forms Ointment:
Ophthalmic: Bacitracin 400 units, neomycin sulfate 3.5 mg, and polymyxin B sulfate 10,000 units and per g
Topical: Bacitracin 400 units, neomycin sulfate 3.5 mg, and polymyxin B sulfate 5000 units per g

Bacitracin, Neomycin, Polymyxin B, and Hydrocortisone
(bas i TRAY sin, nee oh MYE sin, pol i MIKS in bee & hye droe KOR ti sone)
Related Information
Bacitracin *on page 121*
Hydrocortisone *on page 579*
Neomycin *on page 824*
Polymyxin B *on page 943*
U.S. Brand Names AK-Spore H.C.® Ophthalmic Ointment; Cortisporin® Ophthalmic Ointment; Cortisporin® Topical Ointment; Neotricin HC® Ophthalmic Ointment
Therapeutic Category Antibiotic, Ophthalmic; Antibiotic, Otic; Antibiotic, Topical; Anti-inflammatory Agent; Corticosteroid, Ophthalmic; Corticosteroid, Otic; Corticosteroid, Topical (Low Potency)
Dosage Forms Ointment:
Ophthalmic: Bacitracin 400 units, neomycin sulfate 3.5 mg, polymyxin B sulfate 10,000 units, and hydrocortisone 10 mg per g (3.5 g)
Topical: Bacitracin 400 units, neomycin sulfate 3.5 mg, polymyxin B sulfate 10,000 units, and hydrocortisone 10 mg per g (15 g)

Baclofen (BAK loe fen)
U.S. Brand Names Lioresal®
Canadian Brand Names Alpha-Baclofen®; PMS-Baclofen
Therapeutic Category Skeletal Muscle Relaxant
Use Treatment of reversible spasticity associated with multiple sclerosis or spinal cord lesions
Unlabeled use: Intractable hiccups, intractable pain relief, and bladder spasticity
Pregnancy Risk Factor C
Contraindications Hypersensitivity to baclofen or any component
Warnings/Precautions Use with caution in patients with seizure disorder, impaired renal function; avoid abrupt withdrawal of the drug; elderly are more sensitive to the effects of baclofen and are more likely to experience adverse CNS effects at higher doses.
Adverse Reactions
>10%:
Central nervous system: Drowsiness, vertigo, psychiatric disturbances, insomnia, slurred speech, ataxia, hypotonia
Neuromuscular & skeletal: Weakness
1% to 10%:
Cardiovascular: Hypotension
Central nervous system: Fatigue, confusion, headache
Dermatologic: Rash
Gastrointestinal: Nausea, constipation
Genitourinary: Polyuria
<1%: Palpitations, chest pain, syncope, euphoria, excitement, depression, hallucinations, xerostomia, anorexia, abnormal taste, abdominal pain, vomiting, diarrhea, enuresis, urinary retention, dysuria, impotence, inability to ejaculate, nocturia, paresthesia, hematuria, dyspnea
Overdosage/Toxicology
Symptoms of overdose include vomiting, muscle hypotonia, salivation, drowsiness, coma, seizures, respiratory depression
(Continued)

Baclofen *(Continued)*

Atropine has been used to improve ventilation, heart rate, blood pressure, and core body temperature. Following initiation of essential overdose management, symptomatic and supportive treatment should be instituted.

Drug Interactions

Increased effect: Opiate analgesics, benzodiazepines, hypertensive agents

Increased toxicity: CNS depressants and alcohol (sedation), tricyclic antidepressants (short-term memory loss), clindamycin (neuromuscular blockade), guanabenz (sedation), MAO inhibitors (decrease blood pressure, CNS, and respiratory effects)

Mechanism of Action Inhibits the transmission of both monosynaptic and polysynaptic reflexes at the spinal cord level, possibly by hyperpolarization of primary afferent fiber terminals, with resultant relief of muscle spasticity

Pharmacodynamics/Kinetics

Onset of action: Muscle relaxation effect requires 3-4 days

Peak effect: Maximal clinical effect is not seen for 5-10 days

Absorption: Oral: Rapid; absorption from GI tract is thought to be dose dependent

Protein binding: 30%

Metabolism: Minimally in the liver

Half-life: 3.5 hours

Time to peak serum concentration: Oral: Within 2-3 hours

Elimination: 85% of oral dose excreted in urine and feces as unchanged drug

Usual Dosage

Oral (avoid abrupt withdrawal of drug):

Children:

2-7 years: Initial: 10-15 mg/24 hours divided every 8 hours; titrate dose every 3 days in increments of 5-15 mg/day to a maximum of 40 mg/day

≥8 years: Maximum: 60 mg/day in 3 divided doses

Adults: 5 mg 3 times/day, may increase 5 mg/dose every 3 days to a maximum of 80 mg/day

Hiccups: Adults: Usual effective dose: 10-20 mg 2-3 times/day

Intrathecal:

Test dose: 50-100 mcg, doses >50 mcg should be given in 25 mcg increments, separated by 24 hours

Maintenance: After positive response to test dose, a maintenance intrathecal infusion can be administered via an implanted intrathecal pump. Initial dose via pump: Infusion at a 24-hour rate dosed at twice the test dose.

Dosing adjustment in renal impairment: It is necessary to reduce dosage in renal impairment but there are no specific guidelines available

Hemodialysis: Poor water solubility allows for accumulation during chronic hemodialysis. Low-dose therapy is recommended. There have been several case reports of accumulation of baclofen resulting in toxicity symptoms (organic brain syndrome, myoclonia, deceleration and steep potentials in EEG) in patients with renal failure who have received normal doses of baclofen.

Test Interactions ↑ alkaline phosphatase, AST, glucose, ammonia (B); ↓ bilirubin (S)

Patient Information Take with food or milk; abrupt withdrawal after prolonged use may cause anxiety, hallucinations, tachycardia or spasticity; may cause drowsiness and impair coordination and judgment

Nursing Implications Epileptic patients should be closely monitored; supervise ambulation; avoid abrupt withdrawal of the drug

Dosage Forms

Injection, intrathecal, preservative free: 500 mcg/mL (20 mL); 2000 mcg/mL (5 mL)

Tablet: 10 mg, 20 mg

Extemporaneous Preparations Make a 5 mg/mL suspension by crushing fifteen 20 mg tablets; wet with glycerin, gradually add 45 mL simple syrup in 3 x 5 mL aliquots to make a total volume of 60 mL; refrigerate; stable 35 days

Johnson CE and Hart SM, "Stability of an Extemporaneously Compounded Baclofen Oral Liquid," *Am J Hosp Phar*, 1993, 50:2353-5.

◆ **Barbilixir®** *see* Phenobarbital *on page 912*

◆ **Barbita®** *see* Phenobarbital *on page 912*

◆ **Barc™ Liquid [OTC]** *see* Pyrethrins *on page 996*

◆ **Baridium® [OTC]** *see* Phenazopyridine *on page 910*

◆ **Barophen®** *see* Hyoscyamine, Atropine, Scopolamine, and Phenobarbital *on page 592*

Basiliximab (ba si LIKS i mab)

U.S. Brand Names Simulect®

Therapeutic Category Immunosuppressant Agent; Monoclonal Antibody

Use Prophylaxis of acute organ rejection in renal transplantation

Pregnancy Risk Factor B

Pregnancy/Breast-Feeding Implications IL-2 receptors play an important role in the development of the immune system. Use in pregnant women only when benefit exceeds potential risk to the fetus. Women of childbearing potential should use effective contraceptive measures before beginning treatment and for 2 months after completion of therapy with this agent.

It is not known whether basiliximab is excreted in human milk. Because many immunoglobulins are secreted in milk and the potential for serious adverse reactions exists, a decision should be made whether to discontinue nursing or discontinue the drug, taking into account the importance of the drug to the mother.

Contraindications Known hypersensitivity to murine proteins or any component of this product

Warnings/Precautions To be used as a component of immunosuppressive regimen which includes cyclosporine and corticosteroids. Only physicians experienced in transplantation and immunosuppression should prescribe, and patients should receive the drug in a facility with adequate equipment and staff capable of providing the laboratory and medical support required for transplantation.

The incidence of lymphoproliferative disorders and/or opportunistic infections may be increased by immunosuppressive therapy. Hypersensitivity reactions have not been observed in clinical trials. However, similar medications have been associated with reactions including urticaria, dyspnea, and hypotension. Discontinue the drug if a reaction occurs. Medications for the treatment of hypersensitivity reactions should be available for immediate use. Effects of readministration have not been evaluated in humans. Treatment may result in the development of human antimurine antibodies (HAMA); however, limited evidence suggesting the use of muromonab-CD3 or other murine products is not precluded.

Adverse Reactions Administration of basiliximab did not appear to increase the incidence or severity of adverse effects in clinical trials. Adverse events were reported in 99% of both the placebo and basiliximab groups.

>10%:
  Cardiovascular: Edema, peripheral edema, hypertension
  Central nervous system: Fever, headache, dizziness, insomnia
  Dermatologic: Wound complications, acne
  Endocrine and metabolic: Hypokalemia, hyperkalemia, hyperglycemia, hyperuricemia, hypophosphatemia, hypocalcemia, hypercholesterolemia, acidosis
  Gastrointestinal: Constipation, nausea, diarrhea, abdominal pain, vomiting, dyspepsia, moniliasis, weight gain
  Genitourinary: Dysuria, urinary tract infection
  Hematologic: Anemia
  Neuromuscular and skeletal: Leg pain, back pain, tremor
  Respiratory: Dyspnea, infection (upper respiratory), coughing, rhinitis, pharyngitis
  Miscellaneous: Viral infection, asthenia

3% to 10%:
  Cardiovascular: Chest pain, cardiac failure, hypotension, arrhythmia, tachycardia, vascular disorder, generalized edema
  Central nervous system: Hypoesthesia, neuropathy, agitation, anxiety, depression, malaise, fatigue, rigors
  Dermatologic: Cyst, herpes infection, hypertrichosis, pruritus, rash, skin disorder, skin ulceration
  Endocrine and metabolic: Dehydration, diabetes mellitus, fluid overload, hypercalcemia, hyperlipidemia, hypoglycemia, hypomagnesemia
  Gastrointestinal: Flatulence, gastroenteritis, GI hemorrhage, gingival hyperplasia, melena, esophagitis, stomatitis
  Genitourinary: Impotence, genital edema, albuminuria, bladder disorder, hematuria, urinary frequency, oliguria, abnormal renal function, renal tubular necrosis, ureteral disorder, urinary retention
  Hematologic: Hematoma, hemorrhage, purpura, thrombocytopenia, thrombosis, polycythemia
  Neuromuscular and skeletal: Arthralgia, arthropathy, cramps, fracture, hernia, myalgia, paresthesia
  Ocular: Cataract, conjunctivitis, abnormal vision
  Renal: Increased BUN
  Respiratory: Bronchitis, bronchospasm, pneumonia, pulmonary edema, sinusitis
  Miscellaneous: Accidental trauma, facial edema, sepsis, infection, increased glucocorticoids

Overdosage/Toxicology There have been no reports of overdose

(Continued)

Basiliximab (Continued)

Drug Interactions Basiliximab is an immunoglobulin; specific drug interactions have not been evaluated, but are not anticipated

Stability Store intact vials under refrigeration 2°C to 8°C (36°F to 46°F). Reconstitute 20 mg vials with 5 mL of sterile water for injection, USP. Shake the vial gently to dissolve. It is recommended that after reconstitution, the solution should be used immediately. If not used immediately, it can be stored at 2°C to 8°C for up to 24 hours or at room temperature for up to 4 hours. Discard the reconstituted solution within 24 hours. Further dilute reconstituted solution to a volume of 50 mL with 0.9% sodium chloride or dextrose 5% in water. When mixing the solution, gently invert the bag to avoid foaming. Do not shake.

Mechanism of Action Chimeric (murine/human) monoclonal antibody which blocks the alpha-chain of the interleukin-2 (IL-2) receptor complex; this receptor is expressed on activated T lymphocytes and is a critical pathway for activating cell-mediated allograft rejection

Pharmacodynamics/Kinetics
  Duration: Mean: 36 days (determined by IL-2R alpha saturation)
  Distribution, mean: V_c: Children: 1.7 L; V_d: Adults: 8.6 L
  Metabolism: Children: 20 mL/hour; Adults: Clearance (mean): 41 mL/hour
  Half-life: Children: 9.4 days; Adults: Mean: 7.2 days

Usual Dosage I.V.:
  Children 2-15 years of age: 12 mg/m² (maximum: 20 mg) within 2 hours prior to transplant surgery, followed by a second dose of 12 mg/m² (maximum: 20 mg/dose) 4 days after transplantation
  Adults: 20 mg within 2 hours prior to transplant surgery, followed by a second 20 mg dose 4 days after transplantation
  Dosing adjustment/comments in renal or hepatic impairment: No specific dosing adjustment recommended

Administration Intravenous infusion over 20-30 minutes via central or peripheral intravenous line

Monitoring Parameters Signs and symptoms of acute rejection

Dosage Forms Powder for injection: 20 mg

- Baycol™ see Cerivastatin on page 232
- Bayer® Aspirin [OTC] see Aspirin on page 102
- Bayer® Buffered Aspirin [OTC] see Aspirin on page 102
- Bayer® Low Adult Strength [OTC] see Aspirin on page 102
- BAY W6228 see Cerivastatin on page 232

BCG Vaccine (bee see jee vak SEEN)

U.S. Brand Names TheraCys®; TICE® BCG

Synonyms Bacillus Calmette-Guérin (BCG) Live

Therapeutic Category Biological Response Modulator; Vaccine, Live Bacteria

Use Immunization against tuberculosis and immunotherapy for cancer; treatment of bladder cancer
  BCG vaccine is not routinely recommended for use in the U.S. for prevention of tuberculosis
  BCG vaccine is strongly recommended for infants and children with negative tuberculin skin tests who:
      are at high risk of intimate and prolonged exposure to persistently untreated or ineffectively treated patients with infectious pulmonary tuberculosis, and
      cannot be removed from the source of exposure, and
      cannot be placed on long-term preventive therapy
      are continuously exposed with tuberculosis who have bacilli resistant to isoniazid and rifampin
  BCG is also recommended for tuberculin-negative infants and children in groups in which the rate of new infections exceeds 1% per year and for whom the usual surveillance and treatment programs have been attempted but are not operationally feasible

  BCG should be administered with caution to persons in groups at high risk for HIV infection or persons known to be severely immunocompromised. Although limited data suggest that the vaccine may be safe for use in asymptomatic children infected with HIV, BCG vaccination is not recommended for HIV infected adults or for persons with symptomatic disease. Until further research can clearly define the risks and benefits of BCG vaccination for this population, vaccination should be restricted to persons at exceptionally high risk for tuberculosis infection. HIV infected persons thought to be infected with Mycobacterium tuberculosis should be strongly recommended for tuberculosis preventive therapy.

Pregnancy Risk Factor C

Contraindications Tuberculin-positive individual, hypersensitivity to BCG vaccine or any component, immunocompromized, AIDS and burn patients

Warnings/Precautions Protection against tuberculosis is only relative, not permanent, nor entirely predictable; for live bacteria vaccine, proper aseptic technique and disposal of all equipment in contact with BCG vaccine as a biohazardous material is recommended; systemic reactions have been reported in patients treated as immunotherapy for bladder cancer

Adverse Reactions All serious adverse reactions must be reported to the U.S. Department of Health and Human Services (DHHS) Vaccine Adverse Event Reporting System (VAERS) 1-800-822-7967.

1% to 10%:
Genitourinary: Bladder infection, dysuria, polyuria, prostatitis
Miscellaneous: Flu-like syndrome

<1%: Skin ulceration, abscesses, hematuria, rarely anaphylactic shock in infants, lymphadenitis, tuberculosis in immunosuppressed patients

Drug Interactions Decreased effect: Antimicrobial or immunosuppressive drugs may impair response to BCG or increase risk of infection; antituberculosis drugs

Stability Refrigerate, protect from light, use within 2 (TICE® BCG) hours of mixing

Mechanism of Action BCG live is an attenuated strain of Bacillus Calmette-Guérin used as a biological response modifier; BCG live, when used intravesicular for treatment of bladder carcinoma *in situ*, is thought to cause a local, chronic inflammatory response involving macrophage and leukocyte infiltration of the bladder. By a mechanism not fully understood, this local inflammatory response leads to destruction of superficial tumor cells of the urothelium. Evidence of systemic immune response is also commonly seen, manifested by a positive PPD tuberculin skin test reaction, however, its relationship to clinical efficacy is not well-established. BCG is active immunotherapy which stimulates the host's immune mechanism to reject the tumor.

Usual Dosage Children >1 month and Adults:
Immunization against tuberculosis (Tice® BCG): 0.2-0.3 mL percutaneous; initial lesion usually appears after 10-14 days consisting of small red papule at injection site and reaches maximum diameter of 3 mm in 4-6 weeks; conduct postvaccinal tuberculin test (ie, 5 TU of PPD) in 2-3 months; if test is negative, repeat vaccination

Immunotherapy for bladder cancer:
Intravesical treatment: Instill into bladder for 2 hours
TheraCys®: One dose diluted in 50 mL NS (preservative free) instilled into bladder once weekly for 6 weeks followed by one treatment at 3, 6, 12, 18, and 24 months after initial treatment
Tice® BCG: One dose diluted in 50 mL NS (preservative free) instilled into the bladder once weekly for 6 weeks followed by one dose monthly for 6-12 months

Administration Should only be given intravesicularly or percutaneously; **do not administer I.V., S.C., or intradermally**; can be used for bladder irrigation

Test Interactions PPD intradermal test

Patient Information Notify physician of persistent pain on urination or blood in urine

Dosage Forms Freeze-dried suspension for reconstitution
Injection: 50 mg (2 mL)
Injection, intravesical: 27 mg (3 vials)

♦ **BCNU** see Carmustine on page 197
♦ **B Complex** see Vitamins, Multiple on page 1226
♦ **B Complex With C** see Vitamins, Multiple on page 1226

Becaplermin (be KAP ler min)

U.S. Brand Names Regranex®

Synonyms Recombinant Human Platelet-Derived Growth Factor B; rPDGF-BB

Therapeutic Category Growth Factor, Platelet-derived; Topical Skin Product

Use Debridement adjunct for the treatment of diabetic ulcers that occur on the lower limbs and feet

Pregnancy Risk Factor C

Contraindications Hypersensitivity to becaplermin or any component of its formulation; known neoplasm(s) at the site(s) of application; active infection at ulcer site

Warnings/Precautions Concurrent use of corticosteroids, cancer chemotherapy, or other immunosuppressive agents; ulcer wounds related to arterial or venous insufficiency. Thermal, electrical, or radiation burns at wound site. Malignancy (potential for tumor proliferation, although unproven; topical absorption is minimal). Should not be used in wounds that close by primary intention. For external use only.

Adverse Reactions <1%: Erythema with purulent discharge, ulcer infection, tunneling of ulcer, exuberant granulation tissue, local pain, skin ulceration

Stability Refrigerate at 2°C to 8°C (36°F to 46°F); do not freeze

Mechanism of Action Recombinant B-isoform homodimer of human platelet-derived growth factor (rPDGF-BB) which enhances formation of new granulation tissue, induces fibroblast proliferation, and differentiation to promote wound healing

Pharmacodynamics/Kinetics
Onset: Complete healing of diabetic ulcers in 15% of patients within 8 weeks and 25% of patients at 10 weeks
Absorption: Systemic absorption is minimal
Distribution: Binds to PGDF-beta receptors in normal skin and granulation tissue

Usual Dosage Adults: Topical:
Diabetic ulcers: Apply appropriate amount of gel once daily with a cotton swab or similar tool, as a coating over the ulcer
The amount of becaplermin to be applied will vary depending on the size of the ulcer area. To calculate the length of gel to apply to the ulcer, measure the greatest length

Formula to Calculate Length of Gel in Inches to be Applied Daily

Tube Size	Formula
15 or 7.5 g tube	length x width x 0.6
2 g tube	length x width x 1.3

(Continued)

Becaplermin (Continued)

of the ulcer by the greatest width of the ulcer in inches. Refer to following table to calculate the length of gel to administer.

Note: If the ulcer does not decrease in size by ~30% after 10 weeks of treatment or complete healing has not occurred in 20 weeks, continued treatment with becaplermin gel should be reassessed.

Monitoring Parameters Ulcer volume (pressure ulcers); wound area; evidence of closure; drainage (diabetic ulcers); signs/symptoms of toxicity (erythema, local infections)

Patient Information

Hands should be washed thoroughly before applying. The tip of the tube should not come into contact with the ulcer or any other surface; the tube should be recapped tightly after each use. A cotton swab, tongue depressor, or other application aid should be used to apply gel.

Step-by-step instructions for application:

Squeeze the calculated length of gel on to a clean, firm, nonabsorbable surface (wax paper)

With a clean cotton swab, tongue depressor, or similar application aid, spread the measured gel over the ulcer area to obtain an even layer

Cover with a saline-moistened gauze dressing. After ~12 hours, the ulcer should be gently rinsed with saline or water to remove residual gel and covered with a saline-moistened gauze dressing (**without** gel).

Dosage Forms Gel, topical: 0.01% (2 g, 7.5 g, 15 g)

◆ **Beclodisk®** see Beclomethasone on this page

◆ **Becloforte®** see Beclomethasone on this page

Beclomethasone (be kloe METH a sone)

Related Information

Asthma, Guidelines for the Diagnosis and Management of on page 1456

Estimated Clinical Comparability of Doses for Inhaled Corticosteroids on page 1463

U.S. Brand Names Beclovent® Oral Inhaler; Beconase AQ® Nasal Inhaler; Beconase® Nasal Inhaler; Vancenase® AQ Inhaler; Vancenase® Nasal Inhaler; Vanceril® Oral Inhaler

Canadian Brand Names Beclodisk®; Becloforte®; Propaderm®

Synonyms Beclomethasone Dipropionate

Therapeutic Category Anti-inflammatory Agent, Inhalant; Corticosteroid, Inhalant; Corticosteroid, Intranasal

Use

Oral inhalation: Treatment of bronchial asthma in patients who require chronic administration of corticosteroids

Nasal aerosol: Symptomatic treatment of seasonal or perennial rhinitis and nasal polyposis

Pregnancy Risk Factor C

Pregnancy/Breast-Feeding Implications Data does not support an association between drug and congenital defects in humans

Clinical effects on fetus: No data on crossing the placenta or effects on the fetus

Breast-feeding/lactation: No data on crossing into breast milk or effects on the infant

Contraindications Status asthmaticus; hypersensitivity to the drug or fluorocarbons, oleic acid in the formulation, systemic fungal infections

Warnings/Precautions Not to be used in status asthmaticus; safety and efficacy in children <6 years of age have not been established; avoid using higher than recommended dosages since suppression of hypothalamic, pituitary, or adrenal function may occur

Controlled clinical studies have shown that inhaled and intranasal corticosteroids may cause a reduction in growth velocity in pediatric patients. Growth velocity provides a means of comparing the rate of growth among children of the same age.

In studies involving inhaled corticosteroids, the average reduction in growth velocity was approximately 1 cm (about $1/3$ of an inch) per year. It appears that the reduction is related to dose and how long the child takes the drug.

FDA's Pulmonary and Allergy Drugs and Metabolic and Endocrine Drugs advisory committees discussed this issue at a July 1998 meeting. They recommended that the agency develop class-wide labeling to inform healthcare providers so they would understand this potential side effect and monitor growth routinely in pediatric patients who are treated with inhaled corticosteroids, intranasal corticosteroids or both.

Long-term effects of this reduction in growth velocity on final adult height are unknown. Likewise, it also has not yet been determined whether patients' growth will "catch up" if treatment in discontinued. Drug manufacturers will continue to monitor these drugs to learn more about long-term effects. Children are prescribed inhaled corticosteroids to treat asthma. Intranasal corticosteroids are generally used to prevent and treat allergy-related nasal symptoms.

Patients are advised not to stop using their inhaled or intranasal corticosteroids without first speaking to their healthcare providers about the benefits of these drugs compared to their risks.

Adverse Reactions

>10%:

Local: Growth of *Candida* in the mouth, irritation and burning of the nasal mucosa

Respiratory: Cough, hoarseness

1% to 10%:

Gastrointestinal: Xerostomia

Local: Nasal ulceration

Respiratory: Epistaxis

<1%: Headache, rash, dysphagia, bronchospasm, rhinorrhea, nasal congestion, sneezing, nasal septal perforations

Overdosage/Toxicology Symptoms of overdose include irritation and burning of the nasal mucosa, sneezing, intranasal and pharyngeal *Candida* infections, nasal ulceration, epistaxis, rhinorrhea, nasal stuffiness, headache. When consumed in excessive quantities, systemic hypercorticism and adrenal suppression may occur, in those cases discontinuation and withdrawal of the corticosteroid should be done judiciously.

Stability Do not store near heat or open flame

Mechanism of Action Controls the rate of protein synthesis, depresses the migration of polymorphonuclear leukocytes, fibroblasts, reverses capillary permeability, and lysosomal stabilization at the cellular level to prevent or control inflammation

Pharmacodynamics/Kinetics

Therapeutic effect: Within 1-4 weeks of use

Inhalation:

Absorption: Readily absorbed; quickly hydrolyzed by pulmonary esterases prior to absorption

Distribution: 10% to 25% of dose reaches respiratory tract

Oral:

Absorption: 90%

Distribution: Secreted into breast milk

Protein binding: 87%

Metabolism: Hepatic

Half-life:

Initial: 3 hours

Terminal: 15 hours

Elimination: Renal

Usual Dosage Nasal inhalation and oral inhalation dosage forms are not to be used interchangeably

Aqueous inhalation, nasal:

Vancenase® AQ, Beconase® AQ: Children ≥6 years and Adults: 1-2 inhalations each nostril twice daily

Vancenase® AQ 84 mcg: Children ≥6 years and Adults: 1-2 inhalations in each nostril once daily

Intranasal (Vancenase®, Beconase®):

Children 6-12 years: 1 inhalation in each nostril 3 times/day

Children ≥12 years and Adults: 1 inhalation in each nostril 2-4 times/day or 2 inhalations each nostril twice daily; usual maximum maintenance: 1 inhalation in each nostril 3 times/day

Oral inhalation (doses should be titrated to the lowest effective dose once asthma is controlled):

Beclovent®, Vanceril®:

Children 6-12 years: 1-2 inhalations 3-4 times/day (alternatively: 2-4 inhalations twice daily); maximum dose: 10 inhalations/day

Children ≥12 years and Adults: 2 inhalations 3-4 times/day (alternatively: 4 inhalations twice daily); maximum dose: 20 inhalations/day; patients with severe asthma: Initial: 12-16 inhalations/day (divided 3-4 times/day); dose should be adjusted downward according to patient's response

Vanceril® 84 mcg double strength:

Children 6-12 years: 2 inhalations twice daily; maximum dose: 5 inhalations/day

Children ≥12 years and Adults: 2 inhalations twice daily; maximum dose: 10 inhalations/day; patients with severe asthma: Initial: 6-8 inhalations/day (divided twice daily); dose should be adjusted downward according to patient's response

NIH Guidelines (NIH, 1997) (give in divided doses):

Children:

"Low" dose: 84-336 mcg/day (42 mcg/puff: 2-8 puffs/day or 84 mcg/puff: 1-4 puffs/day)

"Medium" dose: 336-672 mcg/day (42 mcg/puff: 8-16 puffs/day or 84 mcg/puff: 4-8 puffs/day)

"High" dose: >672 mcg/day (42 mcg/puff: >16 puffs/day or 84 mcg/puff >8 puffs/day)

Adults:

"Low" dose: 168-504 mcg/day (42 mcg/puff: 4-12 puffs/day or 84 mcg/puff: 2-6 puffs/day)

"Medium" dose: 504-840 mcg/day (42 mcg/puff: 12-20 puffs/day or 84 mcg/puff: 6-10 puffs/day)

"High" dose: >840 mcg/day (42 mcg/puff: >20 puffs/day or 84 mcg/puff: >10 puffs/day)

Patient Information Rinse mouth and throat after use to prevent *Candida* infection, report sore throat or mouth lesions to physician. Inhaled beclomethasone makes many asthmatics cough, to reduce chance, inhale drug slowly or use prescribed inhaled bronchodilator 5 minutes before beclomethasone is used; keep inhaler clean and unobstructed, wash in warm water and dry thoroughly; shake thoroughly before using.

(Continued)

Beclomethasone *(Continued)*

Nursing Implications Take drug history of patients with perennial rhinitis, may be drug related; check mucous membranes for signs of fungal infection

Dosage Forms

Nasal, as dipropionate:

Inhalation: (Beconase®, Vancenase®): 42 mcg/inhalation [200 metered doses] (16.8 g)

Spray, as dipropionate (Vancenase® AQ Nasal): 0.084% [120 actuations] (19 g)

Spray, aqueous, nasal, as dipropionate (Beconase® AQ, Vancenase® AQ): 42 mcg/ inhalation [≥200 metered doses] (25 g); 84 mcg/inhalation [≥200 metered doses] (25 g)

Oral: Inhalation, as dipropionate:

Beclovent®, Vanceril®: 42 mcg/inhalation [200 metered doses] (16.8 g)

Vanceril® Double Strength: 84 mcg/inhalation (5.4 g - 40 metered doses, 12.2 g - 120 metered doses)

- ♦ **Beclomethasone Dipropionate** *see Beclomethasone on page 128*
- ♦ **Beclovent® Oral Inhaler** *see Beclomethasone on page 128*
- ♦ **Beconase AQ® Nasal Inhaler** *see Beclomethasone on page 128*
- ♦ **Beconase® Nasal Inhaler** *see Beclomethasone on page 128*
- ♦ **Becotin® Pulvules®** *see Vitamins, Multiple on page 1226*
- ♦ **Beepen-VK®** *see Penicillin V Potassium on page 898*
- ♦ **Belix® Oral [OTC]** *see Diphenhydramine on page 369*

Belladonna and Opium *(bel a DON a & OH pee um)*

U.S. Brand Names B&O Supprettes®

Canadian Brand Names PMS-Opium & Beladonna

Synonyms Opium and Belladonna

Therapeutic Category Analgesic, Narcotic

Use Relief of moderate to severe pain associated with rectal or bladder tenesmus that may occur in postoperative states and neoplastic situations; pain associated with ureteral spasms not responsive to non-narcotic analgesics and to space intervals between injections of opiates

Restrictions C-II

Pregnancy Risk Factor C

Contraindications Glaucoma, severe renal or hepatic disease, bronchial asthma, respiratory depression, convulsive disorders, acute alcoholism, premature labor

Warnings/Precautions Usual precautions of opiate agonist therapy should be observed; infants <3 months of age are more susceptible to respiratory depression, use with caution and generally in reduced doses in this age group

Adverse Reactions

>10%:

Dermatologic: Dry skin

Gastrointestinal: Constipation, dry throat, xerostomia

Local: Irritation at injection site

Respiratory: Dry nose

Miscellaneous: Diaphoresis (decreased)

1% to 10%:

Dermatologic: Increased sensitivity to light

Endocrine & metabolic: Decreased flow of breast milk

Gastrointestinal: Dysphagia

<1%: Orthostatic hypotension, ventricular fibrillation, tachycardia, palpitations, confusion, drowsiness, headache, loss of memory, fatigue, ataxia, CNS depression, rash, antidiuretic hormone release, bloated feeling, nausea, vomiting, constipation, biliary tract spasm, dysuria, urinary retention, urinary tract spasm, increased intraocular pain, blurred vision, weakness, respiratory depression, histamine release, physical and psychological dependence, diaphoresis

Overdosage/Toxicology Primary attention should be directed to ensuring adequate respiratory exchange; opiate agonist-induced respiratory depression may be reversed with parenteral naloxone hydrochloride

Anticholinergic toxicity may be caused by strong binding of a belladonna alkaloid to cholinergic receptors

Anticholinesterase inhibitors reduce acetylcholinesterase, the enzyme that breaks down acetylcholine and thereby allows acetylcholine to accumulate and compete for receptor binding with the offending anticholinergic

For an overdose with severe life-threatening symptoms, physostigmine 1-2 mg (0.5 mg or 0.02 mg/kg for children) S.C. or I.V., slowly may be given to reverse these effects

Drug Interactions

Decreased effect: Phenothiazines

Increased effect/toxicity: CNS depressants, tricyclic antidepressants

Stability Store at 15°C to 30°C (avoid freezing)

Mechanism of Action Anticholinergic alkaloids act primarily by competitive inhibition of the muscarinic actions of acetylcholine on structures innervated by postganglionic cholinergic neurons and on smooth muscle; resulting effects include antisecretory activity on exocrine glands and intestinal mucosa and smooth muscle relaxation. Contains many narcotic alkaloids including morphine; its mechanism for gastric motility inhibition is primarily due to this morphine content; it results in a decrease in digestive secretions, an increase in GI muscle tone, and therefore a reduction in GI propulsion.

Pharmacodynamics/Kinetics
Onset of action: Belladonna: 1-2 hours; Opium: Within 30 minutes
Metabolism: Opium metabolized in the liver with formation of glucuronide metabolites
Elimination: Belladonna is excreted unchanged in urine

Usual Dosage Adults: Rectal: 1 suppository 1-2 times/day, up to 4 doses/day

Test Interactions ↑ aminotransferase [ALT (SGPT)/AST (SGOT)] (S)

Patient Information May cause drowsiness and blurred vision

Nursing Implications Prior to rectal insertion, the finger and suppository should be moistened; assist with ambulation, monitor for CNS depression

Dosage Forms Suppository:
#15 A: Belladonna extract 15 mg and opium 30 mg
#16 A: Belladonna extract 15 mg and opium 60 mg

Belladonna, Phenobarbital, and Ergotamine Tartrate
(bel a DON a, fee noe BAR bi tal, & er GOT a meen TAR trate)

U.S. Brand Names Bellergal-S®; Bel-Phen-Ergot-S®; Phenerbel-S®

Therapeutic Category Ergot Alkaloid and Derivative

Dosage Forms Tablet, sustained release: l-alkaloids of belladonna 0.2 mg, phenobarbital 40 mg, and ergotamine tartrate 0.6 mg

♦ **Bellergal-S®** see Belladonna, Phenobarbital, and Ergotamine Tartrate on this page

♦ **Bel-Phen-Ergot S®** see Belladonna, Phenobarbital, and Ergotamine Tartrate on this page

♦ **Benadryl® Injection** see Diphenhydramine on page 369

♦ **Benadryl® Oral [OTC]** see Diphenhydramine on page 369

♦ **Benadryl® Topical** see Diphenhydramine on page 369

♦ **Ben-Allergin-50® Injection** see Diphenhydramine on page 369

Benazepril (ben AY ze pril)
Related Information
Angiotensin Agents on page 1291
Drug-Drug Interactions With ACEIs on page 1295

U.S. Brand Names Lotensin®

Synonyms Benazepril Hydrochloride

Therapeutic Category Angiotensin-Converting Enzyme (ACE) Inhibitor; Antihypertensive Agent

Use Treatment of hypertension, either alone or in combination with other antihypertensive agents

Pregnancy Risk Factor C (1st trimester); D (2nd & 3rd trimester)

Pregnancy/Breast-Feeding Implications It is not known whether benazepril is excreted in human milk

Clinical effects on the fetus: No data available on crossing the placenta. Cranial defects, hypocalvaria/acalvaria, oligohydramnios, persistent anuria following delivery, hypotension, renal defects, renal dysgenesis/dysplasia, renal failure, pulmonary hypoplasia, limb contractures secondary to oligohydramnios and stillbirth reported. ACE inhibitors should be avoided during pregnancy.

Breast-feeding/lactation: Crosses into breast milk. American Academy of Pediatrics considers **compatible** with breast-feeding.

Contraindications Hypersensitivity to benazepril or any component or other ACE inhibitors

Warnings/Precautions Use with caution in patients with collagen vascular disease, hypovolemia, valvular stenosis, hyperkalemia, recent anesthesia; modify dosage in patients with renal impairment (especially renal artery stenosis), severe congestive heart failure, or with coadministered diuretic therapy; experience in children is limited; severe hypotension may occur in patients who are sodium and/or volume depleted; initiate lower doses and monitor closely when starting therapy in these patients

Adverse Reactions
1% to 10%:
Central nervous system: Headache, dizziness, fatigue
Gastrointestinal: Nausea (1% to 2%)
Respiratory: Transient cough
<1%: Hypotension, tachycardia, anxiety, insomnia, nervousness, rash, photosensitivity, angioedema, hyperkalemia, constipation, gastritis, vomiting, melena, impotence, urinary tract infection, hypertonia, paresthesia, arthralgia, arthritis, myalgia, weakness, asthma, bronchitis, dyspnea, sinusitis, diaphoresis

Overdosage/Toxicology
Mild hypotension has been the only toxic effect seen with acute overdose. Bradycardia may also occur; hyperkalemia occurs even with therapeutic doses, especially in patients with renal insufficiency and those taking NSAIDs.
Following initiation of essential overdose management, toxic symptom treatment and supportive treatment should be initiated. Hypotension usually responds to I.V. fluids or Trendelenburg positioning.

Drug Interactions See Drug-Drug Interactions With ACEIs on page 1295

Mechanism of Action Competitive inhibition of angiotensin I being converted to angiotensin II, a potent vasoconstrictor, through the angiotensin I-converting enzyme (ACE) activity, with resultant lower levels of angiotensin II which causes an increase in plasma renin activity and a reduction in aldosterone secretion
(Continued)

Benazepril *(Continued)*

Pharmacodynamics/Kinetics

Reduction in plasma angiotensin-converting enzyme activity: Oral:
Peak effect: 1-2 hours after administration of 2-20 mg dose
Duration of action: >90% inhibition for 24 hours has been observed after 5-20 mg dose
Reduction in blood pressure:
Peak effect after single oral dose: 2-6 hours
Maximum response With continuous therapy: 2 weeks
Absorption: Rapid (37% of each oral dose); food does not alter significantly; metabolite (benazeprilat) itself unsuitable for oral administration due to poor absorption
Distribution: V_d: ~8.7 L
Metabolism: Rapid and extensive in the liver to its active metabolite, benazeprilat, via enzymatic hydrolysis; undergoes significant first-pass metabolism and is completely eliminated from plasma in 4 hours
Half-life:
Parent drug: 0.6 hour
Metabolite elimination: 22 hours (from 24 hours after dosing onward)
Metabolite: 1.5-2 hours after fasting or 2-4 hours after a meal
Time to peak: 1-1.5 hours (unchanged parent drug)
Elimination: Nonrenal clearance (ie, biliary, metabolic) appears to contribute to the elimination of benazeprilat (11% to 12%), particularly in patients with severe renal impairment; hepatic clearance is the main elimination route of unchanged benazepril
Dialysis: ~6% of metabolite was removed by 4 hours of dialysis following 10 mg of benazepril administered 2 hours prior to procedure; parent compound was not found in the dialysate

Usual Dosage Adults: Oral: 20-40 mg/day as a single dose or 2 divided doses; base dosage adjustments on peak (2-6 hours after dosing) and trough responses

Dosing interval in renal impairment: Cl_{cr} <30 mL/minute: Administer 5 mg/day initially; maximum daily dose: 40 mg
Hemodialysis: Moderately dialyzable (20% to 50%); administer dose postdialysis or administer 25% to 35% supplemental dose
Peritoneal dialysis: Supplemental dose is not necessary

Administration Discontinue diuretics 2-3 days prior to benazepril initiation; if the diuretics cannot be discontinued, begin benazepril at 5 mg

Patient Information May be taken in disregard to meals; notify physician of persistent cough or other side effects; do not stop therapy except under prescriber advice; may cause dizziness, fainting, and lightheadedness, especially in first week of therapy; sit and stand up slowly; may cause changes in taste or rash; do not add a salt substitute (potassium) without advice of physician

Nursing Implications Watch for hypotensive effect within 1-3 hours of first dose or new higher dose; discontinue therapy immediately if angioedema of the face, extremities, lips, tongue, or glottis occurs

Dosage Forms Tablet, as hydrochloride: 5 mg, 10 mg, 20 mg, 40 mg

Benazepril and Hydrochlorothiazide

(ben AY ze pril & hye droe klor oh THYE a zide)

U.S. Brand Names Lotensin® HCT

Therapeutic Category Angiotensin-Converting Enzyme (ACE) Inhibitor Combination; Antihypertensive Agent, Combination

Dosage Forms Tablet:
Benazepril 5 mg and hydrochlorothiazide 6.25 mg
Benazepril 10 mg and hydrochlorothiazide 12.5 mg
Benazepril 20 mg and hydrochlorothiazide 12.5 mg
Benazepril 20 mg and hydrochlorothiazide 25 mg

♦ **Benazepril Hydrochloride** *see* Benazepril *on previous page*
♦ **BeneFix™** *see* Factor IX Complex (Human) *on page 464*
♦ **Benemid®** *see* Probenecid *on page 967*

Bentoquatam (ben to KWA tam)

U.S. Brand Names IvyBlock®

Synonyms Quaternium-18 Bentonite

Therapeutic Category Topical Skin Product

Use Skin protectant for the prevention of allergic contact dermatitis to poison oak, ivy, and sumac

Contraindications Hypersensitivity to bentoquatam

Warnings/Precautions Use with caution in patients with history of allergic-type responses to medications (especially topical formulations); open wounds, psoriatic lesions, or other cutaneous conditions. Use with caution in patients who are postexposure to poison oak, ivy, or sumac (lack of efficacy).

Adverse Reactions <1%: Erythema

Mechanism of Action An organoclay substance which is capable of absorbing or binding to urushiol, the active principle in poison oak, ivy, and sumac. Bentoquatam serves as a barrier, blocking urushiol skin contact/absorption.

Pharmacodynamics/Kinetics Absorption: Has not been studied

Usual Dosage Children >6 years and Adults: Topical: Apply to skin 15 minutes prior to potential exposure to poison ivy, poison oak, or poison sumac, and reapply every 4 hours

Monitoring Parameters Signs and symptoms of exposure to poison oak, ivy, or sumac (rash, swelling, blisters)

Patient Information Do not use this medication if you have had an allergic reaction to bentoquatam. Do not use this medication on children <6 years of age, unless ordered by your child's physician. Do not use this medication to treat a rash caused by poison ivy, oak, or sumac.

Use this medication on your skin only. Read and follow the instructions on the medicine label. The medication must be used at least 15 minutes **before** you are exposed to poison ivy, poison oak, or poison sumac. Shake the bottle well before each use. Rub a thin layer of the lotion on your skin to form a smooth wet layer. When the lotion dries, you will see a clay-like coating on the protected parts of your skin. You will need to apply more lotion on your skin at least every 4 hours or sooner if the medication rubs off. Do not use the medication in or near your eyes. If you do get the medication in your eyes, rinse them well with cool water for at least 20 minutes. Tell your physician if you have eye redness or eye pain that does not go away.

Dosage Forms Lotion: 5% (120 mL)

♦ **Bentyl® Hydrochloride Injection** *see Dicyclomine on page 351*

♦ **Bentyl® Hydrochloride Oral** *see Dicyclomine on page 351*

♦ **Bentylol®** *see Dicyclomine on page 351*

♦ **Benuryl™** *see Probenecid on page 967*

♦ **Benylin® Cough Syrup [OTC]** *see Diphenhydramine on page 369*

♦ **Benylin® Expectorant [OTC]** *see Guaifenesin and Dextromethorphan on page 550*

♦ **Benzamycin®** *see Erythromycin and Benzoyl Peroxide on page 429*

♦ **Benzathine Benzylpenicillin** *see Penicillin G Benzathine, Parenteral on page 895*

♦ **Benzathine Penicillin G** *see Penicillin G Benzathine, Parenteral on page 895*

♦ **Benzazoline Hydrochloride** *see Tolazoline on page 1155*

♦ **Benzene Hexachloride** *see Lindane on page 682*

♦ **Benzhexol Hydrochloride** *see Trihexyphenidyl on page 1182*

Benzocaine (BEN zoe kane)

U.S. Brand Names Americaine® [OTC]; Anbesol® [OTC]; Anbesol® Maximum Strength [OTC]; Babee® Teething® [OTC]; Benzocol® [OTC]; Benzodent® [OTC]; Chigger-Tox® [OTC]; Cylex® [OTC]; Dermoplast® [OTC]; Foille® [OTC]; Foille® Medicated First Aid [OTC]; Hurricaine®; Lanacane® [OTC]; Maximum Strength Anbesol® [OTC]; Maximum Strength Orajel® [OTC]; Mycinettes® [OTC]; Numzitdent® [OTC]; Numzit Teething® [OTC]; Orabase®-B [OTC]; Orabase®-O [OTC]; Orajel® Brace-Aid Oral Anesthetic [OTC]; Orajel® Maximum Strength [OTC]; Orajel® Mouth-Aid [OTC]; Orasept® [OTC]; Orasol® [OTC]; Oratect™ [OTC]; Rhulicaine® [OTC]; Rid-A-Pain® [OTC]; Slim-Mint® [OTC]; Solarcaine® [OTC]; Spec-T® [OTC]; Tanac® [OTC]; Trocaine® [OTC]; Unguentine® [OTC]; Vicks® Children's Chloraseptic® [OTC]; Vicks® Chloraseptic® Sore Throat [OTC]; Zilactin-B® Medicated [OTC]

Synonyms Ethyl Aminobenzoate

Therapeutic Category Local Anesthetic, Ester Derivative; Local Anesthetic, Oral; Local Anesthetic, Otic; Local Anesthetic, Topical

Use Temporary relief of pain associated with local anesthetic for pruritic dermatosis, pruritus, minor burns, acute congestive and serous otitis media, swimmer's ear, otitis externa, toothache, minor sore throat pain, canker sores, hemorrhoids, rectal fissures, anesthetic lubricant for passage of catheters and endoscopic tubes; nonprescription diet aide

Pregnancy Risk Factor C

Contraindications Children <1 year of age; secondary bacterial infection of area; ophthalmic use; known hypersensitivity to benzocaine or other ester type local anesthetics

Warnings/Precautions Not intended for use when infections are present

Adverse Reactions Dose-related and may result in high plasma levels

1% to 10%:
    Dermatologic: Angioedema, contact dermatitis
    Local: Burning, stinging
<1%: Edema, urticaria, urethritis, methemoglobinemia in infants, tenderness

Overdosage/Toxicology

Methemoglobinemia has been reported with benzocaine in oral overdose

Treatment is primarily symptomatic and supportive; termination of anesthesia by pneumatic tourniquet inflation should be attempted when the agent is administered by infiltration or regional injection. Seizures commonly respond to diazepam, while hypotension responds to I.V. fluids and Trendelenburg positioning. Bradyarrhythmias (when the heart rate is <60) can be treated with I.V., I.M., or S.C. atropine 15 mcg/kg. With the development of metabolic acidosis, I.V. sodium bicarbonate 0.5-2 mEq/kg and ventilatory assistance should be instituted.

Mechanism of Action Ester local anesthetic blocks both the initiation and conduction of nerve impulses by decreasing the neuronal membrane's permeability to sodium ions, which results in inhibition of depolarization with resultant blockade of conduction

Pharmacodynamics/Kinetics

Absorption: Topical: Poorly absorbed after administration to intact skin, but well absorbed from mucous membranes and traumatized skin

Metabolism: Hydrolyzed in the plasma and, to a lesser extent, the liver by cholinesterase

Elimination: Metabolites excreted in urine

(Continued)

Benzocaine *(Continued)*

Usual Dosage

Children and Adults:

Mucous membranes: Dosage varies depending on area to be anesthetized and vascularity of tissues

Oral mouth/throat preparations: Do not administer for >2 days or in children <2 years of age, unless directed by a physician; refer to specific package labeling

Topical: Apply to affected area as needed

Adults: Nonprescription diet aid: 6-15 mg just prior to food consumption, not to exceed 45 mg/day

Patient Information Do not eat for 1 hour after application to oral mucosa; chemical burns should be neutralized before application of benzocaine; avoid application to large areas of broken skin, especially in children

Dosage Forms

Mouth/throat preparations:

Cream: 5% (10 g)

Gel: 6.3% (7.5 g); 7.5% (7.2 g, 9.45 g, 14.1 g); 10% (6 g, 9.45 g, 10 g, 15 g); 15% (10.5 g); 20% (9.45 g, 14.1 g)

Liquid: (3.7 mL); 5% (8.8 mL); 6.3% (9 mL, 22 mL, 14.79 mL); 10% (13 mL); 20% (13.3 mL)

Lotion: 0.2% (15 mL); 2.5% (15 mL)

Lozenges: 5 mg, 6 mg, 10 mg, 15 mg

Ointment: 20% (30 g)

Paste: 20% (5 g, 15 g)

Nonprescription diet aid:

Candy: 6 mg

Gum: 6 mg

Topical for mucous membranes:

Gel: 6% (7.5 g); 20% (2.5 g, 3.75 g, 7.5 g, 30 g)

Liquid: 20% (3.75 mL, 9 mL, 13.3 mL, 30 mL)

Topical for skin disorders:

Aerosol, external use: 5% (92 mL, 105 g); 20% (82.5 mL, 90 mL, 92 mL, 150 mL)

Cream: (30 g, 60 g); 5% (30 g, 1 lb); 6% (28.4 g)

Lotion: (120 mL); 8% (90 mL)

Ointment: 5% (3.5 g, 28 g)

Spray: 5% (97.5 mL); 20% (20 g, 60 g, 120 g, 13.3 mL, 120 mL)

Benzocaine, Butyl Aminobenzoate, Tetracaine, and Benzalkonium Chloride

(BEN zoe kane, BYOO til a meen oh BENZ oh ate, TET ra kane, & benz al KOE nee um KLOR ide)

U.S. Brand Names Cetacaine®

Therapeutic Category Local Anesthetic

Dosage Forms Aerosol: Benzocaine 14%, butyl aminobenzoate 2%, tetracaine 2%, and benzalkonium chloride 0.5% (56 g)

- ♦ **Benzocol® [OTC]** *see Benzocaine on previous page*
- ♦ **Benzodent® [OTC]** *see Benzocaine on previous page*
- ♦ **Benzodiazepines Comparison** *see page 1310*

Benzonatate *(ben ZOE na tate)*

U.S. Brand Names Tessalon® Perles

Therapeutic Category Antitussive; Cough Preparation; Local Anesthetic, Oral

Use Symptomatic relief of nonproductive cough

Pregnancy Risk Factor C

Contraindications Known hypersensitivity to benzonatate or related compounds (such as tetracaine)

Adverse Reactions 1% to 10%:

Central nervous system: Sedation, headache, dizziness

Dermatologic: Rash

Gastrointestinal: GI upset

Neuromuscular & skeletal: Numbness in chest

Ocular: Burning sensation in eyes

Respiratory: Nasal congestion

Overdosage/Toxicology

Symptoms of overdose include restlessness, tremor, CNS stimulation. The drug's local anesthetic activity can reduce the patient's gag reflex and, therefore, may contradict the use of ipecac following ingestion, this is especially true when the capsules are chewed.

Gastric lavage may be indicated if initiated early on following an acute ingestion or in comatose patients. The remaining treatment is supportive and symptomatic.

Mechanism of Action Tetracaine congener with antitussive properties; suppresses cough by topical anesthetic action on the respiratory stretch receptors

Pharmacodynamics/Kinetics

Onset of action: Therapeutic: Within 15-20 minutes

Duration: 3-8 hours

Usual Dosage Children >10 years and Adults: Oral: 100 mg 3 times/day or every 4 hours up to 600 mg/day

Monitoring Parameters Monitor patient's chest sounds and respiratory pattern

Patient Information Swallow capsule whole (do not break or chew capsule); use of hard candy may increase saliva flow to aid in protecting pharyngeal mucosa

Nursing Implications Change patient position every 2 hours to prevent pooling of secretions in lung; capsules are not to be crushed

Dosage Forms Capsule: 100 mg

Benzoyl Peroxide and Hydrocortisone
(BEN zoe il peer OKS ide & hye droe KOR ti sone)

U.S. Brand Names Vanoxide-HC®

Therapeutic Category Acne Products

Dosage Forms Lotion: Benzoyl peroxide 5% and hydrocortisone alcohol 0.5% (25 mL)

Benzthiazide (benz THYE a zide)

Related Information

Sulfonamide Derivatives *on page 1337*

U.S. Brand Names Aquatag®; Exna®; Hydrex®; Marazide®; Proaqua®

Therapeutic Category Antihypertensive Agent; Diuretic, Thiazide

Use Management of mild to moderate hypertension; treatment of edema in congestive heart failure and hepatic cirrhosis, corticosteroid and estrogen therapy, and renal dysfunction

Unlabeled use: Calcium nephrolithiasis, osteoporosis, diabetes insipidus

Pregnancy Risk Factor C

Contraindications Anuria, renal decompensation, hypersensitivity to benzthiazide or any component, cross-sensitivity with other thiazides and sulfonamide derivatives

Warnings/Precautions Hypokalemia, renal disease, hepatic disease, gout, lupus erythematosus, diabetes mellitus; use with caution in severe renal diseases

Adverse Reactions

1% to 10%:

Cardiovascular: Orthostatic hypotension

Endocrine & metabolic: Hyponatremia, hypokalemia

Gastrointestinal: Anorexia, upset stomach, diarrhea

<1%: Drowsiness, hyperuricemia, nausea, vomiting, polyuria, aplastic anemia, hemolytic anemia, leukopenia, agranulocytosis, thrombocytopenia, hepatitis, hepatic function impairment, paresthesia, uremia, allergic reactions

Overdosage/Toxicology

Symptoms of overdose include hypermotility, diuresis, lethargy, confusion, muscle weakness

Following GI decontamination, therapy is supportive with I.V. fluids, electrolytes, and I.V. pressors if needed

Drug Interactions

Decreased effect of oral hypoglycemics; decreased absorption with cholestyramine and colestipol

Increased effect with furosemide and other loop diuretics

Increased toxicity/levels of lithium

Pharmacodynamics/Kinetics

Onset of action: Within 2 hours

Duration: 12 hours

Usual Dosage Adults: Oral:

Edema: 50-200 mg/day; maintenance: 50-150 mg/day; use divided doses after morning and evening meal if total dose exceeds 100 mg

Hypertension: 50-100 mg/day; maintenance: individualize dose (maximum effective dose: 200 mg/day)

Monitoring Parameters Assess weight, I & O reports daily to determine fluid loss; blood pressure, serum electrolytes, BUN, creatinine

Patient Information May be taken with food or milk; take early in day to avoid nocturia; take the last dose of multiple doses no later than 6 PM unless instructed otherwise. A few people who take this medication become more sensitive to sunlight and may experience skin rash, redness, itching, or severe sunburn, especially if sun block SPF ≥15 is not used on exposed skin areas.

Nursing Implications Take blood pressure with patient lying down and standing

Dosage Forms Tablet: 50 mg

Benztropine (BENZ troe peen)

Related Information

Parkinson's Disease, Dosing of Drugs Used for Treatment of *on page 1336*

U.S. Brand Names Cogentin®

Canadian Brand Names PMS-Benztropine

Synonyms Benztropine Mesylate

Therapeutic Category Anticholinergic Agent; Anti-Parkinson's Agent

Use Adjunctive treatment of Parkinson's disease; also used in treatment of drug-induced extrapyramidal effects (except tardive dyskinesia) and acute dystonic reactions

Pregnancy Risk Factor C

Contraindications Children <3 years of age, use with caution in older children (dosage not established); patients with narrow-angle glaucoma; hypersensitivity to any component; pyloric or duodenal obstruction, stenosing peptic ulcers; bladder neck obstructions; achalasia; myasthenia gravis

(Continued)

Benztropine *(Continued)*

Warnings/Precautions Use with caution in hot weather or during exercise. Elderly patients frequently develop increased sensitivity and require strict dosage regulation - side effects may be more severe in elderly patients with atherosclerotic changes. Use with caution in patients with tachycardia, cardiac arrhythmias, hypertension, hypotension, prostatic hypertrophy (especially in the elderly) or any tendency toward urinary retention, liver or kidney disorders and obstructive disease of the GI or GU tract. When given in large doses or to susceptible patients, may cause weakness and inability to move particular muscle groups.

Adverse Reactions

>10%:

Dermatologic: Dry skin

Gastrointestinal: Constipation, dry throat, xerostomia

Respiratory: Dry nose

Miscellaneous: Diaphoresis (decreased)

1% to 10%:

Dermatologic: Increased sensitivity to light

Endocrine & metabolic: Decreased flow of breast milk

Gastrointestinal: Dysphagia

<1%: Tachycardia, orthostatic hypotension, ventricular fibrillation, palpitations, coma, drowsiness, nervousness, hallucinations; the elderly may be at increased risk for confusion and hallucinations; headache, loss of memory, fatigue, ataxia, rash, nausea, vomiting, bloated feeling, dysuria, blurred vision, mydriasis, increased intraocular pain, weakness

Overdosage/Toxicology

Symptoms of overdose include CNS depression, confusion, nervousness, hallucinations, dizziness, blurred vision, nausea, vomiting, hyperthermia

For anticholinergic overdose with severe life-threatening symptoms, physostigmine 1-2 mg (0.5 mg or 0.02 mg/kg for children) S.C. or I.V., slowly may be given to reverse these effects. Anticholinergic toxicity is caused by strong binding of the drug to cholinergic receptors. Anticholinesterase inhibitors reduce acetylcholinesterase, the enzyme that breaks down acetylcholine and thereby allows acetylcholine to accumulate and compete for receptor binding with the offending anticholinergic.

Drug Interactions

Decreased effect: May increase gastric degradation of levodopa and decrease the amount of levodopa absorbed by delaying gastric emptying - the opposite may be true for digoxin

Increased toxicity: Central anticholinergic syndrome can occur when administered with narcotic analgesics, phenothiazines and other antipsychotics, tricyclic antidepressants, quinidine and some other antiarrhythmics, and antihistamines

Mechanism of Action Thought to partially block striatal cholinergic receptors to help balance cholinergic and dopaminergic activity

Pharmacodynamics/Kinetics

Onset of action: Oral: Within 1 hour; Parenteral: Within 15 minutes

Duration of action: 6-48 hours (wide range)

Usual Dosage Use in children <3 years of age should be reserved for life-threatening emergencies

Drug-induced extrapyramidal reaction: Oral, I.M., I.V.:

Children >3 years: 0.02-0.05 mg/kg/dose 1-2 times/day

Adults: 1-4 mg/dose 1-2 times/day

Acute dystonia: Adults: I.M., I.V.: 1-2 mg

Parkinsonism: Oral:

Adults: 0.5-6 mg/day in 1-2 divided doses; if one dose is greater, administer at bedtime; titrate dose in 0.5 mg increments at 5- to 6-day intervals

Elderly: Initial: 0.5 mg once or twice daily; increase by 0.5 mg as needed at 5-6 days; maximum: 6 mg/day

Dietary Considerations Alcohol: Additive CNS effects, avoid use

Patient Information Take after meals or with food if GI upset occurs; do not discontinue drug abruptly; notify physician if adverse GI effects, rapid or pounding heartbeat, confusion, eye pain, rash, fever, or heat intolerance occurs. Observe caution when performing hazardous tasks or those that require alertness such as driving, as may cause drowsiness. Avoid alcohol and other CNS depressants. May cause dry mouth - adequate fluid intake or hard sugar-free candy may relieve. Difficult urination or constipation may occur - notify physician if effects persist; may increase susceptibility to heat stroke.

Nursing Implications No significant difference in onset of I.M. or I.V. injection, therefore, there is usually no need to use the I.V. route. Improvement is sometimes noticeable a few minutes after injection.

Dosage Forms

Injection, as mesylate: 1 mg/mL (2 mL)

Tablet, as mesylate: 0.5 mg, 1 mg, 2 mg

♦ **Benztropine Mesylate** *see* Benztropine *on previous page*

♦ **Benzylpenicillin Benzathine** *see* Penicillin G Benzathine, Parenteral *on page 895*

♦ **Benzylpenicillin Potassium** *see* Penicillin G, Parenteral, Aqueous *on page 896*

♦ **Benzylpenicillin Sodium** *see* Penicillin G, Parenteral, Aqueous *on page 896*

Benzylpenicilloyl-polylysine (BEN zil pen i SIL oyl pol i LIE seen)

Related Information

Skin Tests *on page 1353*

U.S. Brand Names Pre-Pen®

Synonyms Penicilloyl-polylysine; PPL

Therapeutic Category Diagnostic Agent, Penicillin Allergy Skin Test

Use Adjunct in assessing the risk of administering penicillin (penicillin or benzylpenicillin) in adults with a history of clinical penicillin hypersensitivity

Pregnancy Risk Factor C

Contraindications Patients known to be extremely hypersensitive to penicillin

Warnings/Precautions PPL test alone does not identify those patients who react to a minor antigenic determinant and does not appear to predict reliably the occurrence of late reactions. A negative skin test is associated with an incidence of allergic reactions <5% after penicillin administration and a positive skin test is associated with a >20% incidence of allergic reaction after penicillin administration; have epinephrine 1:1000 available.

Adverse Reactions

1% to 10%: Local: Intense local inflammatory response at skin test site

<1%: Edema, pruritus, erythema, urticaria, wheal (locally), systemic allergic reactions occur rarely

Drug Interactions

Decreased effect: Corticosteroids and other immunosuppressive agents may inhibit the immune response to the skin test

Stability Refrigerate; discard if left at room temperature for longer than one day

Mechanism of Action Elicits IgE antibodies which produce type I accelerate urticarial reactions to penicillins

Usual Dosage PPL is administered by a scratch technique or by intradermal injection. For initial testing, PPL should always be applied via the scratch technique. **Do not administer intradermally to patients who have positive reactions to a scratch test.** PPL test alone does not identify those patients who react to a minor antigenic determinant and does not appear to predict reliably the occurrence of late reactions.

Scratch test: Use scratch technique with a 20-gauge needle to make 3-5 mm nonbleeding scratch on epidermis, apply a small drop of solution to scratch, rub in gently with applicator or toothpick. A positive reaction consists of a pale wheal surrounding the scratch site which develops within 10 minutes and ranges from 5-15 mm or more in diameter.

Intradermal test: Use intradermal test with a tuberculin syringe with a 26- to 30-gauge short bevel needle; a dose of 0.01-0.02 mL is injected intradermally. A control of 0.9% sodium chloride should be injected at least 1.5" from the PPL test site. Most skin responses to the intradermal test will develop within 5-15 minutes.

Interpretation:

(-) Negative: No reaction

(±) Ambiguous: Wheal only slightly larger than original bleb with or without erythematous flare and larger than control site

(+) Positive: Itching and marked increase in size of original bleb

Control site should be reactionless

Nursing Implications Always use scratch test for initial testing

Dosage Forms Solution: 0.25 mL

Bepridil (BE pri dil)

Related Information

Calcium Channel Blockers Comparison *on page 1315*

U.S. Brand Names Vascor®

Canadian Brand Names Bapadin®

Synonyms Bepridil Hydrochloride

Therapeutic Category Antianginal Agent; Calcium Channel Blocker

Use Treatment of chronic stable angina; due to side effect profile, reserve for patients who have been intolerant of other antianginal therapy; bepridil may be used alone or in combination with nitrates or beta-blockers

Pregnancy Risk Factor C

Contraindications History of serious ventricular or atrial arrhythmias (especially tachycardia or those associated with accessory conduction pathways), uncompensated cardiac insufficiency, congenital Q-T interval prolongation, patients taking other drugs that prolong the Q-T interval, history of hypersensitivity to bepridil or any component, calcium channel blockers, or adenosine; concurrent administration with ritonavir or sparfloxacin

Warnings/Precautions Use with great caution in patients with history of IHSS, second or third degree A-V block, cardiogenic shock; reserve for patients in whom other antianginals have failed. Carefully titrate dosages for patients with impaired renal or hepatic function; use caution when treating patients with congestive heart failure, significant hypotension, severe left ventricular dysfunction, hypertrophic cardiomyopathy (especially obstructive), concomitant therapy with beta-blockers or digoxin, edema, or increased intracranial pressure with cranial tumors; do not abruptly withdraw (may cause chest pain); elderly may experience hypotension and constipation more readily.

If dosage reduction does not maintain the Q-T within a safe range (not to exceed 0.52 seconds during therapy), discontinue the medication; has class I antiarrhythmic properties and can induce new arrhythmias, including VT/VF; it can also cause torsade de

(Continued)

Bepridil *(Continued)*

pointes type ventricular tachycardia due to its ability to prolong the Q-T interval; avoid use in patients in the immediate period postinfarction.

Adverse Reactions

>10%:

Central nervous system: Dizziness

Gastrointestinal: Nausea, dyspepsia

1% to 10%:

Cardiovascular: Bradycardia, edema, palpitations

Central nervous system: Nervousness, headache (7% to 13%), drowsiness, psychiatric disturbances (<2%), insomnia (2% to 3%)

Dermatologic: Rash (≤2%)

Endocrine & metabolic: Sexual dysfunction

Gastrointestinal: Diarrhea, anorexia, xerostomia, constipation, abdominal pain, dyspepsia, flatulence

Neuromuscular & skeletal: Weakness (6.5% to 14%), tremor (<9%), paresthesia (2.5%)

Ocular: Blurred vision

Otic: Tinnitus

Respiratory: Rhinitis, dyspnea (≤8.7%), cough (≤2%)

Miscellaneous (≤2%): Flu syndrome, diaphoresis

<1%: Ventricular premature contractions, hypertension, syncope, prolonged Q-T intervals, fever, altered behavior, akathisia, abnormal taste, arthritis, pharyngitis

Overdosage/Toxicology The primary cardiac symptoms of calcium blocker overdose include hypotension and bradycardia. The hypotension is caused by peripheral vasodilation, myocardial depression, and bradycardia. Bradycardia results from sinus bradycardia, second- or third-degree atrioventricular block, or sinus arrest with junctional rhythm. Intraventricular conduction is usually not affected so QRS duration is normal (verapamil does prolong the P-R interval and bepridil prolongs the Q-T and may cause ventricular arrhythmias, including torsade de pointes).

The noncardiac symptoms include confusion, stupor, nausea, vomiting, metabolic acidosis, and hyperglycemia. Following initial gastric decontamination, if possible, repeated calcium administration may promptly reverse the depressed cardiac contractility (but not sinus node depression or peripheral vasodilation); glucagon, epinephrine, and amrinone may treat refractory hypotension; glucagon and epinephrine also increase the heart rate (outside the U.S., 4-aminopyridine may be available as an antidote); dialysis and hemoperfusion are not effective in enhancing elimination although repeatdose activated charcoal may serve as an adjunct with sustained-release preparations.

In a few reported cases, overdose with calcium channel blockers has been associated with hypotension and bradycardia, initially refractory to atropine but becoming more responsive to this agent when larger doses (approaching 1 g/hour for more than 24 hours) of calcium chloride was administered.

Drug Interactions CYP3A3/4 enzyme substrate

Increased toxicity/effect/levels:

Bepridil and cyclosporine may increase cyclosporine levels (other calcium channel blockers have been shown to interact)

Bepridil and digitalis glycoside may increase digitalis glycoside levels

Use with ritonavir may increase risk of bepridil and sparfloxacin toxicity, especially its cardiotoxicity

Coadministration with beta-blocking agents may result in increased depressant effects on myocardial contractility or A-V conduction

Severe hypotension or increased fluid volume requirements may occur with concomitant fentanyl

Mechanism of Action Bepridil, a type 4 calcium antagonist, possesses characteristics of the traditional calcium antagonists, inhibiting calcium ion from entering the "slow channels" or select voltage-sensitive areas of vascular smooth muscle and myocardium during depolarization and producing a relaxation of coronary vascular smooth muscle and coronary vasodilation. However, bepridil may also inhibit fast sodium channels (inward), which may account for some of its side effects (eg, arrhythmias); a direct bradycardia effect of bepridil has been postulated via direct action on the S-A node.

Pharmacodynamics/Kinetics

Onset of action: 1 hour

Absorption: Oral: 100%

Distribution: Protein binding: >99%

Metabolism: Hepatic

Bioavailability: 60%

Half-life: 24 hours

Time to peak: 2-3 hours

Elimination: Metabolites renally excreted

Usual Dosage Adults: Oral: Initial: 200 mg/day, then adjust dose at 10-day intervals until optimal response is achieved; usual dose: 300 mg/day; maximum daily dose: 400 mg

Monitoring Parameters EKG and serum electrolytes, blood pressure, signs and symptoms of congestive heart failure; elderly may need very close monitoring due to underlying cardiac and organ system defects

Reference Range 1-2 ng/mL

Test Interactions ↑ aminotransferases, ↑ CPK, LDH

Patient Information May cause cardiac arrhythmias if potassium is low; can be taken with food or meals, maintain potassium supplementation as directed, routine EKGs will be necessary during start of therapy or dosage changes; notify physician if the following occur: irregular heartbeat, shortness of breath, pronounced dizziness, constipation, or hypotension

Nursing Implications EKG required; patient should be hospitalized during initiation or escalation of therapy

Additional Information Although there is some initial data which may show increased risk of myocardial infarction following treatment of hypertension with calcium antagonists, controlled trials (eg, ALL-HAT) are ongoing to examine the long-term effects of not only calcium antagonists but other antihypertensives in preventing heart disease. Until these studies are completed, patients taking calcium antagonists should be encouraged to continue with prescribed antihypertensive regimes, although a switch from high-dose, short-acting agents to sustained release products may be warranted.

Dosage Forms Tablet, as hydrochloride: 200 mg, 300 mg, 400 mg

♦ **Bepridil Hydrochloride** *see* Bepridil *on page 137*

Beractant (ber AKT ant)

U.S. Brand Names Survanta®
Synonyms Bovine Lung Surfactant; Natural Lung Surfactant
Therapeutic Category Lung Surfactant
Use Prevention and treatment of respiratory distress syndrome (RDS) in premature infants

Prophylactic therapy: Body weight <1250 g in infants at risk for developing or with evidence of surfactant deficiency

Rescue therapy: Treatment of infants with RDS confirmed by x-ray and requiring mechanical ventilation (administer as soon as possible - within 8 hours of age)

Warnings/Precautions Rapidly affects oxygenation and lung compliance and should be restricted to a highly supervised use in a clinical setting with immediate availability of clinicians experienced with intubation and ventilatory management of premature infants. If transient episodes of bradycardia and decreased oxygen saturation occur, discontinue the dosing procedure and initiate measures to alleviate the condition; produces rapid improvements in lung oxygenation and compliance that may require immediate reductions in ventilator settings and FiO_2.

Adverse Reactions During the dosing procedure:
>10%: Cardiovascular: Transient bradycardia
1% to 10%: Respiratory: Oxygen desaturation
<1%:
    Cardiovascular: Vasoconstriction, hypotension, hypertension, pallor
    Respiratory: Endotracheal tube blockage, hypocarbia, hypercarbia, apnea, pulmonary air leaks, pulmonary interstitial emphysema
    Miscellaneous: Increased probability of post-treatment nosocomial sepsis

Stability Refrigerate; protect from light, prior to administration warm by standing at room temperature for 20 minutes or held in hand for 8 minutes; **artificial warming methods should not be used**; unused, unopened vials warmed to room temperature may be returned to the refrigerator within 8 hours of warming only once

Mechanism of Action Replaces deficient or ineffective endogenous lung surfactant in neonates with respiratory distress syndrome (RDS) or in neonates at risk of developing RDS. Surfactant prevents the alveoli from collapsing during expiration by lowering surface tension between air and alveolar surfaces.

Pharmacodynamics/Kinetics Alveolar clearance is rapid

Usual Dosage
Prophylactic treatment: Administer 100 mg phospholipids (4 mL/kg) intratracheal as soon as possible; as many as 4 doses may be administered during the first 48 hours of life, no more frequently than 6 hours apart. The need for additional doses is determined by evidence of continuing respiratory distress; if the infant is still intubated and requiring at least 30% inspired oxygen to maintain a PaO_2 ≤80 torr.

Rescue treatment: Administer 100 mg phospholipids (4 mL/kg) as soon as the diagnosis of RDS is made; may repeat if needed, no more frequently than every 6 hours to a maximum of 4 doses

Administration
For intratracheal administration only
Suction infant prior to administration; inspect solution to verify complete mixing of the suspension

Administer intratracheally by instillation through a 5-French end-hole catheter inserted into the infant's endotracheal tube

Administer the dose in four 1 mL/kg aliquots. Each quarter-dose is instilled over 2-3 seconds; each quarter-dose is administered with the infant in a different position; slightly downward inclination with head turned to the right, then repeat with head turned to the left; then slightly upward inclination with head turned to the right, then repeat with head turned to the left.

Monitoring Parameters Continuous EKG and transcutaneous O_2 saturation should be monitored during administration; frequent arterial blood gases are necessary to prevent postdosing hyperoxia and hypocarbia

Nursing Implications Do not shake; if settling occurs during storage, swirl gently

Additional Information Each mL contains 25 mg phospholipids suspended in 0.9% sodium chloride solution. Contents of 1 mL: 0.5-1.75 mg triglycerides, 1.4-3.5 mg free fatty acids, and <1 mg protein.

Dosage Forms Suspension: 200 mg (8 mL)

♦ **Berocca®** *see* Vitamin B Complex With Vitamin C and Folic Acid *on page 1225*

♦ **Berubigen**® *see* Cyanocobalamin *on page 302*
♦ **Beta-2**® *see* Isoetharine *on page 632*
♦ **Beta-Blockers Comparison** *see page 1311*

Beta-Carotene (BAY tah KARE oh teen)
U.S. Brand Names Solatene®
Therapeutic Category Vitamin, Fat Soluble
Use Reduces severity of photosensitivity reactions in patients with erythropoietic protoporphyria (EPP)
>**Unlabeled use:** Prophylaxis and treatment of polymorphous light eruption and prophylaxis against photosensitivity reactions in erythropoietic protoporphyria
Pregnancy Risk Factor C
Contraindications Hypersensitivity to beta-carotene
Warnings/Precautions Use with caution in patients with renal or hepatic impairment; not proven effective as a sunscreen
Adverse Reactions
>10%: Dermatologic: Carotenodermia (yellowing of palms, hands, or soles of feet, and to a lesser extent the face)
<1%: Dizziness, bruising, diarrhea, arthralgia
Drug Interactions Fulfills vitamin A requirements, do not prescribe additional vitamin A
Mechanism of Action The exact mechanism of action in erythropoietic protoporphyria has not as yet been elucidated; although patient must become carotenemic before effects are observed, there appears to be more than a simple internal light screen responsible for the drug's action. A protective effect was achieved when beta-carotene was added to blood samples. The concentrations of solutions used were similar to those achieved in treated patients. Topically applied beta-carotene is considerably less effective than systemic therapy.
Pharmacodynamics/Kinetics
>Metabolism: Prior to absorption, converted to vitamin A in the wall of the small intestine and then further oxidized to retinoic acid and retinol in the presence of fat and bile acids; small amounts are then stored in the liver; retinol (active) is conjugated with glucuronic acid
Elimination: In urine and feces
Usual Dosage Oral:
>Children <14 years: 30-150 mg/day
Adults: 30-300 mg/day
Patient Information Take with meals; skin may appear slightly yellow-orange; not a proven sunscreen
Dosage Forms Capsule: 15 mg, 30 mg

♦ **Betachron E-R**® *see* Propranolol *on page 986*
♦ **Betadine**® [OTC] *see* Povidone-Iodine *on page 955*
♦ **Betadine**® **First Aid Antibiotics + Moisturizer** [OTC] *see* Bacitracin and Polymyxin B *on page 122*
♦ **9-Beta-D-ribofuranosyladenine** *see* Adenosine *on page 31*
♦ **Betagan**® [OTC] *see* Povidone-Iodine *on page 955*
♦ **Betagan**® **Liquifilm**® *see* Levobunolol *on page 670*

Betaine Anhydrous (BAY tayne an HY drus)
U.S. Brand Names Cystadane®
Therapeutic Category Homocystinuria Agent
Use Treatment of homocystinuria to decrease elevated homocysteine blood levels; included within the category of homocystinuria are deficiencies or defects in cystathionine beta-synthase (CBS), 5,10-methylenetetrahydrofolate reductase (MTHFR), and cobalamin cofactor metabolism (CBL).
Pregnancy Risk Factor C
Pregnancy/Breast-Feeding Implications Clinical effects on the fetus: Animal reproduction studies have not been conducted with betaine. It is also not known whether betaine can cause fetal harm when administered to a pregnant woman or can affect reproductive capacity. Betaine should be given to a pregnant woman only if needed.
Contraindications Hypersensitivity to betaine or its ingredients
Usual Dosage
>Children <3 years: Dosage may be started at 100 mg/kg/day and then increased weekly by 100 mg/kg increments
Children ≥3 years and Adults: Oral: 6 g/day administered in divided doses of 3 g twice daily. Dosages of up to 20 g/day have been necessary to control homocysteine levels in some patients.
Dosage in all patients can be gradually increased until plasma homocysteine is undetectable or present only in small amounts
Additional Information Betaine anhydrous is available through a specialty distribution system; please call 1-800- 900-4267 for ordering information. Complete prescribing information for this medication should be consulted for additional detail.
Dosage Forms Powder: 1 g/1.7 mL (180 g)

♦ **Betaloc**® *see* Metoprolol *on page 768*
♦ **Betaloc**® **Durules**® *see* Metoprolol *on page 768*

Betamethasone (bay ta METH a sone)

Related Information
Corticosteroids Comparison *on page 1319*

U.S. Brand Names Alphatrex®; Betatrex®; Beta-Val®; Celestone®; Celestone® Soluspan®; Cel-U-Jec®; Diprolene®; Diprolene® AF; Diprosone®; Luxiq™; Maxivate®; Psorion® Cream; Teladar®; Valisone®

Canadian Brand Names Betnesol® [Disodium Phosphate]; Diprolene® Glycol [Dipropionate]; Occlucort®; Rhoprolene; Rhoprosone; Taro-Sone; Topilene; Topisone

Synonyms Betamethasone Dipropionate; Betamethasone Dipropionate, Augmented; Betamethasone Sodium Phosphate; Betamethasone Valerate; Flubenisolone

Therapeutic Category Anti-inflammatory Agent; Corticosteroid; Corticosteroid, Systemic; Corticosteroid, Topical (Low Potency); Corticosteroid, Topical (Medium Potency); Corticosteroid, Topical (High Potency); Glucocorticoid

Use Inflammatory dermatoses such as seborrheic or atopic dermatitis, neurodermatitis, anogenital pruritus, psoriasis, inflammatory phase of xerosis

Pregnancy Risk Factor C

Pregnancy/Breast-Feeding Implications Clinical effects on the fetus: There are no reports linking the use of betamethasone with congenital defects in the literature; betamethasone is often used in patients with premature labor [26-34 weeks gestation] to stimulate fetal lung maturation

Contraindications Systemic fungal infections; hypersensitivity to betamethasone or any component

Warnings/Precautions Fatalities have occurred due to adrenal insufficiency in asthmatic patients during and after transfer from systemic corticosteroids to aerosol steroids; several months may be required for recovery of this syndrome; during this period, aerosol steroids do **not** provide the systemic steroid needed to treat patients having trauma, surgery, or infections; use with caution in patients with hypothyroidism, cirrhosis, ulcerative colitis; do not use occlusive dressings on weeping or exudative lesions and general caution with occlusive dressings should be observed; discontinue if skin irritation or contact dermatitis should occur; do not use in patients with decreased skin circulation

Adverse Reactions
>10%:
  Central nervous system: Insomnia
  Gastrointestinal: Increased appetite, indigestion
  Ocular: Temporary mild blurred vision
1% to 10%:
  Dermatologic: Erythema, itching
  Endocrine & metabolic: Diabetes mellitus
  Local: Dryness, irritation, papular rashes, burning
  Ocular: Cataracts
<1%: Hypertension, convulsions, vertigo, confusion, headache, thin fragile skin, hyperpigmentation or hypertrichosis, hypopigmentation, impaired wound healing, acneiform eruptions, perioral dermatitis, maceration of skin, skin atrophy, striae, miliaria, cushingoid state, sodium retention, peptic ulcer, sterile abscess, myalgia, osteoporosis, glaucoma, sudden blindness

Overdosage/Toxicology When consumed in excessive quantities for prolonged periods, systemic hypercorticism and adrenal suppression may occur; in those cases, discontinuation and withdrawal of the corticosteroid should be done judiciously

Drug Interactions CYP3A enzyme substrate
Decreased effect (corticosteroid) by barbiturates, phenytoin, rifampin

Mechanism of Action Controls the rate of protein synthesis, depresses the migration of polymorphonuclear leukocytes, fibroblasts, reverses capillary permeability, and lysosomal stabilization at the cellular level to prevent or control inflammation

Pharmacodynamics/Kinetics
Protein binding: 64%
Metabolism: Extensively in the liver
Half-life: 6.5 hours
Time to peak serum concentration: I.V.: Within 10-36 minutes
Elimination: <5% of dose excreted renally as unchanged drug

Usual Dosage
Base dosage on severity of disease and patient response
Children: Use lowest dose listed as initial dose for adrenocortical insufficiency (physiologic replacement)
  I.M.: 0.0175-0.125 mg base/kg/day divided every 6-12 hours **or** 0.5-7.5 mg base/m²/day divided every 6-12 hours
  Oral: 0.0175-0.25 mg/kg/day divided every 6-8 hours **or** 0.5-7.5 mg/m²/day divided every 6-8 hours
Adolescents and Adults:
  Oral: 2.4-4.8 mg/day in 2-4 doses; range: 0.6-7.2 mg/day
  I.M.: Betamethasone sodium phosphate and betamethasone acetate: 0.6-9 mg/day (generally, $\frac{1}{3}$ to $\frac{1}{2}$ of oral dose) divided every 12-24 hours
  Foam: Apply twice daily, once in the morning and once at night
Dosing adjustment in hepatic impairment: Adjustments may be necessary in patients with liver failure because betamethasone is extensively metabolized in the liver
Intrabursal, intra-articular, intradermal: 0.25-2 mL
Intralesional: Rheumatoid arthritis/osteoarthritis:
  Very large joints: 1-2 mL
  Large joints: 1 mL
  Medium joints: 0.5-1 mL
(Continued)

Betamethasone *(Continued)*

Small joints: 0.25-0.5 mL

Topical: Apply thin film 2-4 times/day

Patient Information Take oral with food or milk; apply topical sparingly to areas and gently rub in until it disappears, not for use on broken skin or in areas of infection; do not apply to face or inguinal areas

Nursing Implications Apply topical sparingly to areas; not for use on broken skin or in areas of infection; do not apply to wet skin unless directed; do not apply to face or inguinal area. Not for alternate day therapy; once daily doses should be given in the morning; do not administer injectable sodium phosphate/acetate suspension I.V.

Dosage Forms

Base (Celestone®), Oral:

Syrup: 0.6 mg/5 mL (118 mL)

Tablet: 0.6 mg

Dipropionate (Diprosone®)

Aerosol: 0.1% (85 g)

Cream: 0.05% (15 g, 45 g)

Lotion: 0.05% (20 mL, 30 mL, 60 mL)

Ointment: 0.05% (15 g, 45 g)

Dipropionate augmented (Diprolene®)

Cream: 0.05% (15 g, 45 g)

Gel: 0.05% (15 g, 45 g)

Lotion: 0.05% (30 mL, 60 mL)

Ointment, topical: 0.05% (15 g, 45 g)

Valerate (Betatrex®, Valisone®)

Cream: 0.01% (15 g, 60 g); 0.1% (15 g, 45 g, 110 g, 430 g)

Lotion: 0.1% (20 mL, 60 mL)

Ointment: 0.1% (15 g, 45 g)

Valerate (Beta-Val®)

Cream: 0.01% (15 g, 60 g); 0.1% (15 g, 45 g, 110 g, 430 g)

Lotion: 0.1% (20 mL, 60 mL)

Valerate (Luxiq™): Foam: 100 g aluminum can (box of 1)

Injection: Sodium phosphate (Celestone® Phosphate, Cel-U-Jec®): 4 mg betamethasone phosphate/mL (equivalent to 3 mg betamethasone/mL) (5 mL)

Injection, suspension: Sodium phosphate and acetate (Celestone® Soluspan®): 6 mg/mL (3 mg of betamethasone sodium phosphate and 3 mg of betamethasone acetate per mL) (5 mL)

Betamethasone and Clotrimazole

(bay ta METH a sone & kloe TRIM a zole)

U.S. Brand Names Lotrisone®

Therapeutic Category Antifungal/Corticosteroid

Dosage Forms Cream: Betamethasone dipropionate 0.05% and clotrimazole 1% (15 g, 45 g)

♦ **Betamethasone Dipropionate** *see* Betamethasone *on previous page*

♦ **Betamethasone Dipropionate, Augmented** *see* Betamethasone *on previous page*

♦ **Betamethasone Sodium Phosphate** *see* Betamethasone *on previous page*

♦ **Betamethasone Valerate** *see* Betamethasone *on previous page*

♦ **Betapace®** *see* Sotalol *on page 1074*

♦ **Betapen®-VK** *see* Penicillin V Potassium *on page 898*

♦ **Betasept® [OTC]** *see* Chlorhexidine Gluconate *on page 240*

♦ **Betaseron®** *see* Interferon Beta-1b *on page 621*

♦ **Betatrex®** *see* Betamethasone *on previous page*

♦ **Beta-Val®** *see* Betamethasone *on previous page*

♦ **Betaxin®** *see* Thiamine *on page 1131*

Betaxolol *(be TAKS oh lol)*

Related Information

Beta-Blockers Comparison *on page 1311*

Glaucoma Drug Therapy Comparison *on page 1322*

U.S. Brand Names Betoptic® Ophthalmic; Betoptic® S Ophthalmic; Kerlone® Oral

Synonyms Betaxolol Hydrochloride

Therapeutic Category Antihypertensive Agent; Beta-Adrenergic Blocker; Beta-Adrenergic Blocker, Ophthalmic

Use Treatment of chronic open-angle glaucoma and ocular hypertension; management of hypertension

Pregnancy Risk Factor C

Contraindications Bronchial asthma, sinus bradycardia, second and third degree A-V block, cardiac failure (unless a functioning pacemaker present), cardiogenic shock, hypersensitivity to betaxolol or any component

Warnings/Precautions Some products contain sulfites which can cause allergic reactions; diminished response occurs over time; use with caution in patients with decreased renal or hepatic function (dosage adjustment required); patients with a history of asthma, congestive heart failure, diabetes mellitus, or bradycardia appear to be at a higher risk for adverse effects

Adverse Reactions
1% to 10%:
Cardiovascular: Bradycardia, palpitations, edema, congestive heart failure
Central nervous system: Dizziness, fatigue, lethargy, headache
Dermatologic: Erythema, itching
Ocular: Mild ocular stinging and discomfort, tearing, photophobia, decreased corneal sensitivity, keratitis
Miscellaneous: Cold extremities
<1%: Chest pain, nervousness, depression, hallucinations, thrombocytopenia

Overdosage/Toxicology
Symptoms of intoxication include cardiac disturbances, CNS toxicity, bronchospasm, hypoglycemia and hyperkalemia. The most common cardiac symptoms include hypotension and bradycardia; atrioventricular block, intraventricular conduction disturbances, cardiogenic shock, and asystole may occur with severe overdose, especially with membrane-depressant drugs (eg, propranolol); CNS effects include convulsions, coma, and respiratory arrest (commonly seen with propranolol and other membrane-depressant and lipid-soluble drugs).

Treatment includes symptomatic treatment of seizures, hypotension, hyperkalemia, and hypoglycemia; bradycardia and hypotension resistant to atropine, isoproterenol, or pacing may respond to glucagon; wide QRS defects caused by the membrane-depressant poisoning may respond to hypertonic sodium bicarbonate; repeat-dose charcoal, hemoperfusion, or hemodialysis may be helpful in removal of only those beta-blockers with a small V_d, long half-life, or low intrinsic clearance (acebutolol, atenolol, nadolol, sotalol)

Drug Interactions CYP1A2 and 2D6 enzyme substrate
Decreased effect of some beta-blockers with aluminum salts, barbiturates, calcium salts, cholestyramine, colestipol, NSAIDs, penicillins (ampicillin), rifampin, salicylates and sulfinpyrazone due to decreased bioavailability and plasma levels

Beta-blockers may decrease the effect of sulfonylureas

Increased effect/toxicity of beta-blockers with calcium blockers (diltiazem, felodipine, nicardipine), contraceptives, flecainide, hydralazine (metoprolol, propranolol), propafenone, quinidine (in extensive metabolizers), ciprofloxacin

Beta-blockers may increase the effect/toxicity of flecainide, hydralazine, clonidine (hypertensive crisis after or during withdrawal of either agent), epinephrine (initial hypertensive episode followed by bradycardia), nifedipine, verapamil, lidocaine, ergots, prazosin

Beta-blockers may affect the action or levels of ethanol, disopyramide, nondepolarizing muscle relaxants and theophylline although the effects are difficult to predict

Stability Avoid freezing

Mechanism of Action Competitively blocks beta$_1$-receptors, with little or no effect on beta$_2$-receptors; ophthalmic reduces intraocular pressure by reducing the production of aqueous humor

Pharmacodynamics/Kinetics
Onset of action: 1-1.5 hours
Duration: ≥12 hours
Absorption: Systemically absorbed
Metabolism: Hepatic (multiple metabolites)
Half-life: 12-22 hours
Time to peak: Within 2 hours
Elimination: Renal

Usual Dosage Adults:
Ophthalmic: Instill 1 drop twice daily
Oral: 10 mg/day; may increase dose to 20 mg/day after 7-14 days if desired response is not achieved; initial dose in elderly patients: 5 mg/day

Monitoring Parameters Ophthalmic: Intraocular pressure. Systemic: Blood pressure, pulse

Patient Information Intended for twice daily dosing; keep eye open and do not blink for 30 seconds after instillation; wear sunglasses to avoid photophobic discomfort; apply gentle pressure to lacrimal sac during and immediately following instillation (1 minute)

Nursing Implications Monitor for systemic effect of beta-blockade

Dosage Forms
Solution, ophthalmic, as hydrochloride (Betoptic®): 0.5% (2.5 mL, 5 mL, 10 mL)
Suspension, ophthalmic, as hydrochloride (Betoptic® S): 0.25% (2.5 mL, 10 mL, 15 mL)
Tablet, as hydrochloride (Kerlone®): 10 mg, 20 mg

♦ **Betaxolol Hydrochloride** see Betaxolol on previous page

Bethanechol (be THAN e kole)
U.S. Brand Names Duvoid®; Myotonachol™; Urabeth®; Urecholine®
Canadian Brand Names PMS-Bethanechol Chloride
Synonyms Bethanechol Chloride
Therapeutic Category Cholinergic Agent
Use Nonobstructive urinary retention and retention due to neurogenic bladder; treatment and prevention of bladder dysfunction caused by phenothiazines; diagnosis of flaccid or atonic neurogenic bladder; gastroesophageal reflux
Pregnancy Risk Factor C
Contraindications Hypersensitivity to bethanechol; do not use in patients with mechanical obstruction of the GI or GU tract or when the strength or integrity of the GI or bladder wall is in question. It is also contraindicated in patients with hyperthyroidism, peptic ulcer
(Continued)

Bethanechol *(Continued)*

disease, epilepsy, obstructive pulmonary disease, bradycardia, vasomotor instability, atrioventricular conduction defects, hypotension, or parkinsonism; **contraindicated for I.M. or I.V. use due to a likely severe cholinergic reaction**

Warnings/Precautions Potential for reflux infection if the sphincter fails to relax as bethanechol contracts the bladder; use with caution when administering to nursing women, as it is unknown if the drug is excreted in breast milk; safety and efficacy in children <5 years of age have not been established; syringe containing atropine should be readily available for treatment of serious side effects; for S.C. injection only; do not administer I.M. or I.V.

Adverse Reactions

Oral: <1%: Hypotension, cardiac arrest, flushed skin, abdominal cramps, diarrhea, nausea, vomiting, salivation, bronchial constriction, diaphoresis, vasomotor response

Subcutaneous: 1% to 10%:

Cardiovascular: Hypotension, cardiac arrest, flushed skin

Gastrointestinal: Abdominal cramps, diarrhea, nausea, vomiting, salivation

Respiratory: Bronchial constriction

Miscellaneous: Diaphoresis, vasomotor response

Overdosage/Toxicology

Symptoms of overdose include nausea, vomiting, abdominal cramps, diarrhea, involuntary defecation, flushed skin, hypotension, bronchospasm

Atropine is the treatment of choice for intoxications manifesting with significant muscarinic symptoms; atropine I.V. 0.6 mg every 3-60 minutes (or 0.01 mg/kg I.V. every 2 hours if needed for children) should be repeated to control symptoms and then continued as needed for 1-2 days following the acute ingestion. Epinephrine 0.1-1 mg S.C. may be useful in reversing severe cardiovascular or pulmonary sequel.

Drug Interactions

Decreased effect: Procainamide, quinidine

Increased toxicity: Bethanechol and ganglionic blockers → critical fall in blood pressure; cholinergic drugs or anticholinesterase agents

Mechanism of Action Stimulates cholinergic receptors in the smooth muscle of the urinary bladder and gastrointestinal tract resulting in increased peristalsis, increased GI and pancreatic secretions, bladder muscle contraction, and increased ureteral peristaltic waves

Pharmacodynamics/Kinetics

Onset of action: Oral: 30-90 minutes; S.C.: 5-15 minutes

Duration of action: Oral: Up to 6 hours; S.C.: 2 hours

Absorption: Oral: Variable

Metabolism and elimination have not been determined

Usual Dosage

Children:

Oral:

Abdominal distention or urinary retention: 0.6 mg/kg/day divided 3-4 times/day

Gastroesophageal reflux: 0.1-0.2 mg/kg/dose given 30 minutes to 1 hour before each meal to a maximum of 4 times/day

S.C.: 0.15-0.2 mg/kg/day divided 3-4 times/day

Adults:

Oral: 10-50 mg 2-4 times/day

S.C.: 2.5-5 mg 3-4 times/day, up to 7.5-10 mg every 4 hours for neurogenic bladder

Administration Do **not** administer I.V. or I.M., a severe cholinergic reaction may occur

Monitoring Parameters Observe closely for side effects

Test Interactions ↑ lipase, AST, amylase (S), bilirubin, aminotransferase [ALT (SGPT)/ AST (SGOT)] (S)

Patient Information Oral should be taken 1 hour before meals or 2 hours after meals to avoid nausea or vomiting; may cause abdominal discomfort, salivation, diaphoresis, or flushing; notify physician if these symptoms become pronounced; rise slowly from sitting/ lying down

Nursing Implications Have bedpan readily available, if administered for urinary retention

Dosage Forms

Injection, as chloride: 5 mg/mL (1 mL)

Tablet, as chloride: 5 mg, 10 mg, 25 mg, 50 mg

Bicalutamide *(bye ka LOO ta mide)*

U.S. Brand Names Casodex®

Therapeutic Category Antiandrogen; Antineoplastic Agent, Miscellaneous

Use In combination therapy with LHRH agonist analogues in treatment of advanced prostatic carcinoma

Pregnancy Risk Factor X

Contraindications Known hypersensitivity to drug or any components of the product; pregnancy

Adverse Reactions

>10%: Endocrine & metabolic: Hot flashes (49%)

≥2% to <5%:

Cardiovascular: Angina pectoris, congestive heart failure, edema

Central nervous system: Anxiety, depression, confusion, somnolence, nervousness, fever, chills

Dermatologic: Dry skin, pruritus, alopecia

Endocrine & metabolic: Breast pain, diabetes mellitus, decreased libido, dehydration, gout

Gastrointestinal: Anorexia, dyspepsia, rectal hemorrhage, xerostomia, melena, weight gain

Genitourinary: Polyuria, urinary impairment, dysuria, urinary retention, urinary urgency

Hepatic: Alkaline phosphatase increased

Neuromuscular & skeletal: Myasthenia, arthritis, myalgia, leg cramps, pathological fracture, neck pain, hypertonia, neuropathy

Renal: Creatinine increased

Respiratory: Cough increased, pharyngitis, bronchitis, pneumonia, rhinitis, lung disorder

Miscellaneous: Sepsis, neoplasma

<1%: Diarrhea (0.5%)

Overdosage/Toxicology

Symptoms of overdose include hypoactivity, ataxia, anorexia, vomiting, slow respiration, lacrimation

Treatment is supportive, dialysis not of benefit; induce vomiting

Stability Store at room temperature

Mechanism of Action Pure nonsteroidal antiandrogen that binds to androgen receptors; specifically a competitive inhibitor for the binding of dihydrotestosterone and testosterone; prevents testosterone stimulation of cell growth in prostate cancer

Pharmacodynamics/Kinetics

Absorption: Rapid and complete

Protein binding: 96%

Metabolism: Extensive; stereospecific metabolism

Half-life: Up to 10 days; active enantiomer is 5.8 days

Elimination: Not yet studied

Usual Dosage Adults: Oral: 1 tablet once daily (morning or evening), with or without food. It is recommended that bicalutamide be taken at the same time each day; start treatment with bicalutamide at the same time as treatment with an LHRH analog.

Dosage adjustment in renal impairment: None necessary as renal impairment has no significant effect on elimination

Dosage adjustment in liver impairment: Limited data in subjects with severe hepatic impairment suggest that excretion of bicalutamide may be delayed and could lead to further accumulation. Use with caution in patients with moderate to severe hepatic impairment.

Administration Dose should be taken at the same time each day with or without food; start treatment at the same time as treatment with an LHRH analog

Monitoring Parameters Serum prostate-specific antigen, alkaline phosphatase, acid phosphatase, or prostatic acid phosphatase; prostate gland dimensions; skeletal survey; liver scans; chest x-rays; physical exam every 3 months; bone scan every 3-6 months; CBC, LFTs, EKG, echocardiograms, and serum testosterone and luteinizing hormone (periodically)

Patient Information Take at the same time as treatment with LHRH analog; advise of potential side effects; notify the physician if any visual disturbances or yellow discoloration of the skin or eyes

Dosage Forms Tablet: 50 mg

Bismuth (BIZ muth)

Related Information

(Continued)

Bismuth *(Continued)*

U.S. Brand Names Bismatrol® [OTC]; Devrom® [OTC]; Pepto-Bismol® [OTC]; Pink Bismuth® [OTC]

Synonyms Bismuth Subgallate; Bismuth Subsalicylate

Therapeutic Category Antidiarrheal

Use Symptomatic treatment of mild, nonspecific diarrhea; indigestion, nausea, control of traveler's diarrhea (enterotoxigenic *Escherichia coli*); an adjunct with other agents such as metronidazole, tetracycline, and an H_2-antagonist in the treatment of *Helicobacter pylori*-associated duodenal ulcer disease

Pregnancy Risk Factor C (D in 3rd trimester)

Contraindications Do not use subsalicylate in patients with influenza or chickenpox because of risk of Reye's syndrome; do not use in patients with known hypersensitivity to salicylates; history of severe GI bleeding; history of coagulopathy

Warnings/Precautions Subsalicylate should be used with caution if patient is taking aspirin; use with caution in children, especially those <3 years of age and those with viral illness; may be neurotoxic with very large doses

Adverse Reactions

>10%: Gastrointestinal: Discoloration of the tongue (darkening), grayish black stools

<1%: Anxiety, confusion, slurred speech, headache, mental depression, impaction may occur in infants and debilitated patients, muscle spasms, weakness, hearing loss, tinnitus

Overdosage/Toxicology

Symptoms of toxicity: **Subsalicylate**: Hyperpnea, nausea, vomiting, tinnitus, hyperpyrexia, metabolic acidoses/respiratory alkalosis, tachycardia, and confusion; seizures in severe overdose, pulmonary or cerebral edema, respiratory failure, cardiovascular collapse, coma, and death. **Note:** Each 262.4 mg tablet of bismuth subsalicylate contains an equivalent of 130 mg aspirin (150 mg/kg of aspirin is considered to be toxic; serious life-threatening toxicity occurs with >300mg/kg)

Treatment: Gastrointestinal decontamination (activated charcoal for immediate release formulations (10 x dose of ASA in g), whole bowel irrigation for enteric coated tablets or when serially increasing ASA plasma levels indicate the presence of an intestinal bezoar), supportive and symptomatic treatment with emphasis on correcting fluid, electrolyte, blood glucose and acid-base disturbances; elimination is enhanced with urinary alkalinization (sodium bicarbonate infusion with potassium), multiple dose activated charcoal, and hemodialysis.

Symptoms of toxicity: **Bismuth**: Rare with short-term administrations of bismuth salts; encephalopathy, methemoglobinemia, seizures

Treatment: Gastrointestinal decontamination; chelation with dimercaprol in doses of 3 mg/kg or penicillamine 100 mg/kg/day for 5 days can hasten recovery from bismuth-induced encephalopathy; methylene blue 1-2 mg/kg in a 1% sterile aqueous solution I.V. push over 4-6 minutes for methemoglobinemia. This may be repeated within 60 minutes if necessary, up to a total dose of 7 mg/kg. Seizures usually respond to I.V. diazepam.

Drug Interactions

Decreased effect: Tetracyclines and uricosurics

Increased toxicity: Aspirin, warfarin, hypoglycemics

Mechanism of Action Bismuth subsalicylate exhibits both antisecretory and antimicrobial action. This agent may provide some anti-inflammatory action as well. The salicylate moiety provides antisecretory effect and the bismuth exhibits antimicrobial directly against bacterial and viral gastrointestinal pathogens. Bismuth has some antacid properties.

Pharmacodynamics/Kinetics

Absorption: Minimally (<1%) absorbed across the GI tract while the salt (eg, salicylate) may be readily absorbed (80%); bismuth subsalicylate is rapidly cleaved to bismuth and salicylic acid in the stomach

Distribution: Salicylate: Volume of distribution: 170 mL/kg

Protein binding, plasma: Bismuth and salicylate: >90%

Metabolism: Bismuth salts undergo chemical dissociation after oral administration; salicylate is extensively metabolized in the liver

Half-life: Bismuth: Terminal: 21-72 days; Salicylate: Terminal: 2-5 hours

Elimination: Bismuth: Renal, biliary; clearance: 50 mL/minute; Salicylate: Only 10% excreted unchanged

Usual Dosage Oral:

Nonspecific diarrhea: Subsalicylate:

Children: Up to 8 doses/24 hours:

3-6 years: $1/3$ tablet or 5 mL every 30 minutes to 1 hour as needed

6-9 years: $2/3$ tablet or 10 mL every 30 minutes to 1 hour as needed

9-12 years: 1 tablet or 15 mL every 30 minutes to 1 hour as needed

Adults: 2 tablets or 30 mL every 30 minutes to 1 hour as needed up to 8 doses/24 hours

Prevention of traveler's diarrhea: 2.1 g/day or 2 tablets 4 times/day before meals and at bedtime

Subgallate: 1-2 tablets 3 times/day with meals

Helicobacter pylori: Chew 2 tablets 4 times/day with meals and at bedtime with other agents in selected regiment (eg, an H_2-antagonist, tetracycline and metronidazole) for 14 days

Dosing adjustment in renal impairment: Should probably be avoided in patients with renal failure

Test Interactions ↑ uric acid, ↑ AST; bismuth absorbs x-rays and may interfere with diagnostic procedures of GI tract

Patient Information Chew tablet well or shake suspension well before using; may darken stools; if diarrhea persists for more than 2 days, consult a physician; can turn tongue black; tinnitus may indicate toxicity and use should be discontinued

Nursing Implications Seek causes for diarrhea; monitor for tinnitus; may aggravate or cause gout attack; may enhance bleeding if used with anticoagulants

Dosage Forms
Liquid, as subsalicylate (Pepto-Bismol®, Bismatrol®): 262 mg/15 mL (120 mL, 240 mL, 360 mL, 480 mL); 524 mg/15 mL (120 mL, 240 mL, 360 mL)
Tablet:
Chewable, as subsalicylate (Pepto-Bismol®, Bismatrol®): 262 mg
Chewable, as subgallate (Devrom®): 200 mg

♦ **Bismuth Subgallate** *see* Bismuth *on page 145*
♦ **Bismuth Subsalicylate** *see* Bismuth *on page 145*

Bismuth Subsalicylate, Metronidazole, and Tetracycline
(BIZ muth sub sa LIS i late, me troe NI da zole, & tet ra SYE kleen)
Related Information
Bismuth *on page 145*
Metronidazole *on page 770*
Tetracycline *on page 1122*
U.S. Brand Names Helidac™
Therapeutic Category Antidiarrheal
Dosage Forms
Tablet:
Bismuth subsalicylate: Chewable: 262.4 mg
Metronidazole: 250 mg
Capsule: Tetracycline: 500 mg

Bisoprolol (bis OH proe lol)
Related Information
Beta-Blockers Comparison *on page 1311*
U.S. Brand Names Zebeta®
Synonyms Bisoprolol Fumarate
Therapeutic Category Antihypertensive Agent; Beta-Adrenergic Blocker
Use Treatment of hypertension, alone or in combination with other agents
Unlabeled use: Angina pectoris, supraventricular arrhythmias, PVCs
Pregnancy Risk Factor C
Contraindications Hypersensitivity to beta-blocking agents, uncompensated congestive heart failure; cardiogenic shock; bradycardia or heart block; sinus node dysfunction; A-V conduction abnormalities. Although bisoprolol primarily blocks beta₁-receptors, high doses can result in beta₂-receptor blockage. Therefore, use with caution in patients (especially elderly) with bronchospastic lung disease and renal dysfunction.
Warnings/Precautions Use with caution in patients with inadequate myocardial function, bronchospastic disease, hyperthyroidism, undergoing anesthesia; and in those with impaired hepatic function; acute withdrawal may exacerbate symptoms (gradually taper over a 2-week period)
Adverse Reactions
>10%: Central nervous system: Fatigue, lethargy
1% to 10%:
Cardiovascular: Hypotension, chest pain, heart failure, Raynaud's phenomenon, heart block, edema, bradycardia
Central nervous system: Headache, dizziness, insomnia, confusion, depression, abnormal dreams
Dermatologic: Rash
Gastrointestinal: Constipation, diarrhea, dyspepsia, nausea, flatulence, anorexia
Genitourinary: Polyuria, impotence, urinary retention
Hepatic: Increased LFTs
Neuromuscular & skeletal: Arthralgia, myalgia
Ocular: Abnormal vision
Respiratory: Dyspnea, rhinitis, cough
Overdosage/Toxicology
Symptoms of intoxication include cardiac disturbances, CNS toxicity, bronchospasm, hypoglycemia and hyperkalemia. The most common cardiac symptoms include hypotension and bradycardia; atrioventricular block, intraventricular conduction disturbances, cardiogenic shock, and asystole may occur with severe overdose, especially with membrane-depressant drugs (eg, propranolol); CNS effects include convulsions, coma, and respiratory arrest (commonly seen with propranolol and other membrane-depressant and lipid-soluble drugs).
Treatment includes symptomatic treatment of seizures, hypotension, hyperkalemia, and hypoglycemia; bradycardia and hypotension resistant to atropine, isoproterenol, or pacing may respond to glucagon; wide QRS defects caused by the membrane-depressant poisoning may respond to hypertonic sodium bicarbonate; repeat-dose charcoal, hemoperfusion, or hemodialysis may be helpful in removal of only those beta-blockers with a small V_d, long half-life, or low intrinsic clearance (acebutolol, atenolol, nadolol, sotalol)
Drug Interactions CYP2D6 enzyme substrate
(Continued)

Bisoprolol *(Continued)*

Decreased effect of some beta-blockers with aluminum salts, barbiturates, calcium salts, cholestyramine, colestipol, NSAIDs, penicillins (ampicillin), rifampin, salicylates, and sulfinpyrazone due to decreased bioavailability and plasma levels

Beta-blockers may decrease the effect of sulfonylureas

Increased effect/toxicity of beta-blockers with calcium blockers (diltiazem, felodipine, nicardipine), contraceptives, flecainide, hydralazine (metoprolol, propranolol), propafenone, quinidine (in extensive metabolizers), ciprofloxacin,

Beta-blockers may increase the effect/toxicity of flecainide, hydralazine, clonidine (hypertensive crisis after or during withdrawal of either agent), epinephrine (initial hypertensive episode followed by bradycardia), nifedipine, verapamil, lidocaine, ergots, prazosin

Beta-blockers may affect the action or levels of ethanol, disopyramide, nondepolarizing muscle relaxants and theophylline although the effects are difficult to predict

Mechanism of Action Selective inhibitor of beta$_1$-adrenergic receptors; competitively blocks beta$_1$-receptors, with little or no effect on beta$_2$-receptors at doses <10 mg

Pharmacodynamics/Kinetics

Absorption: Rapid and almost complete from GI tract

Distribution: Distributed widely to body tissues; highest concentrations in heart, liver, lungs, and saliva; crosses the blood-brain barrier; distributes into breast milk

Protein binding: 26% to 33%

Metabolism: Significant first-pass metabolism; extensively metabolized in the liver

Half-life: 9-12 hours

Time to peak: 1.7-3 hours

Elimination: In urine (3% to 10% as unchanged drug); <2% excreted in feces

Usual Dosage Oral:

Adults: 5 mg once daily, may be increased to 10 mg, and then up to 20 mg once daily, if necessary

Elderly: Initial dose: 2.5 mg/day; may be increased by 2.5-5 mg/day; maximum recommended dose: 20 mg/day

Dosing adjustment in renal/hepatic impairment: Cl$_{cr}$ <40 mL/minute: Initial: 2.5 mg/day; increase cautiously

Hemodialysis: Not dialyzable

Monitoring Parameters Blood pressure, EKG, neurologic status

Test Interactions ↑ thyroxine (S), cholesterol (S), glucose; ↑ triglycerides, uric acid; ↓ HDL

Patient Information Do not discontinue abruptly (angina may be precipitated); notify physician if CHF symptoms become worse or side effects occur; take at the same time each day; may mask diabetes symptoms; consult pharmacist or physician before taking with other adrenergic drugs (eg, cold medications); use with caution while driving or performing tasks requiring alertness; may be taken without regard to meals

Dosage Forms Tablet, as fumarate: 5 mg, 10 mg

Bisoprolol and Hydrochlorothiazide

(bis OH proe lol & hye droe klor oh THYE a zide)

U.S. Brand Names Ziac™

Therapeutic Category Antihypertensive Agent, Combination

Dosage Forms Tablet:

Bisoprolol fumarate 2.5 mg and hydrochlorothiazide 6.25 mg

Bisoprolol fumarate 5 mg and hydrochlorothiazide 6.25 mg

Bisoprolol fumarate 10 mg and hydrochlorothiazide 6.25 mg

- ♦ **Bisoprolol Fumarate** *see Bisoprolol on previous page*
- ♦ **Bistropamide** *see Tropicamide on page 1192*

Bitolterol *(bye TOLE ter ole)*

Related Information

Bronchodilators, Comparison of Inhaled and Sympathomimetic *on page 1314*

U.S. Brand Names Tornalate®

Synonyms Bitolterol Mesylate

Therapeutic Category Beta$_2$-Adrenergic Agonist Agent; Bronchodilator

Use Prevention and treatment of bronchial asthma and bronchospasm

Pregnancy Risk Factor C

Contraindications Known hypersensitivity to bitolterol

Warnings/Precautions Use with caution in patients with unstable vasomotor symptoms, diabetes, hyperthyroidism, prostatic hypertrophy or a history of seizures; also use caution in the elderly and those patients with cardiovascular disorders such as coronary artery disease, arrhythmias, and hypertension; excessive use may result in cardiac arrest and death; do not use concurrently with other sympathomimetic bronchodilators

Adverse Reactions

>10%: Neuromuscular & skeletal: Trembling

1% to 10%:

Cardiovascular: Flushing of face, hypertension, pounding heartbeat

Central nervous system: Dizziness, lightheadedness, nervousness

Gastrointestinal: Xerostomia, nausea, unpleasant taste

Respiratory: Bronchial irritation, coughing

<1%: Chest pain, arrhythmias, tachycardia, insomnia, paradoxical bronchospasm

Overdosage/Toxicology
Symptoms of overdose include tremor, dizziness, nervousness, headache, nausea, coughing

Treatment is symptomatic/supportive; in cases of severe overdose, supportive therapy should be instituted, and prudent use of a cardioselective beta-adrenergic blocker (eg, atenolol or metoprolol) should be considered, keeping in mind the potential for induction of bronchoconstriction in an asthmatic individual. Dialysis has not been shown to be of value in the treatment of an overdose with this agent.

Drug Interactions
Decreased effect: Beta-adrenergic blockers (eg, propranolol)

Increased effect: Inhaled ipratropium may increase duration of bronchodilation, nifedipine may increase FEV-1

Increased toxicity: MAO inhibitors, tricyclic antidepressants, sympathomimetic agents (eg, amphetamine, dopamine, dobutamine), inhaled anesthetics (eg, enflurane)

Mechanism of Action
Selectively stimulates beta$_2$-adrenergic receptors in the lungs producing bronchial smooth muscle relaxation; minor beta$_1$ activity

Pharmacodynamics/Kinetics
Duration of effect: 4-8 hours

Metabolism: Bitolterol, a prodrug, is hydrolyzed to colterol (active) following inhalation

Half-life: 3 hours

Time to peak serum concentration (colterol): Inhalation: Within 1 hour

Elimination: In urine and feces

Usual Dosage
Children >12 years and Adults:

Bronchospasm: 2 inhalations at an interval of at least 1-3 minutes, followed by a third inhalation if needed

Prevention of bronchospasm: 2 inhalations every 8 hours; do not exceed 3 inhalations every 6 hours or 2 inhalations every 4 hours

Administration
Administer around-the-clock rather than 3 times/day, to promote less variation in peak and trough serum levels

Monitoring Parameters
Assess lung sounds, pulse, and blood pressure before administration and during peak of medication; observe patient for wheezing after administration

Patient Information
Do not exceed recommended dosage, excessive use may lead to adverse effects or loss of effectiveness; shake canister well before use; administer pressurized inhalation during the second half of inspiration, as the airways are open, water and the aerosol distribution is more extensive. If more than one inhalation per dose is necessary, wait at least 1 full minute between inhalations - second inhalation is best delivered after 10 minutes. May cause nervousness, restlessness, and insomnia; if these effects continue after dosage reduction, notify physician. Also notify physician if palpitations, tachycardia, chest pain, muscle tremors, dizziness, headache, flushing, or if breathing difficulty persists.

Nursing Implications
Before using, the inhaler must be shaken well

Dosage Forms
Aerosol, oral, as mesylate: 0.8% [370 mcg/metered spray, 300 inhalations] (15 mL)

Solution, inhalation, as mesylate: 0.2% (10 mL, 30 mL, 60 mL)

♦ **Bitolterol Mesylate** see Bitolterol on previous page

♦ **Blenoxane®** see Bleomycin on this page

♦ **Bleo** see Bleomycin on this page

Bleomycin (blee oh MYE sin)
Related Information
Cancer Chemotherapy Regimens on page 1263
Toxicities of Chemotherapeutic Agents on page 1288

U.S. Brand Names Blenoxane®

Synonyms Bleo; Bleomycin Sulfate; BLM; NSC 125066

Therapeutic Category Antineoplastic Agent, Antibiotic

Use Treatment of squamous cell carcinomas, melanomas, sarcomas, testicular carcinoma, Hodgkin's lymphoma, and non-Hodgkin's lymphoma; may also be used as a sclerosing agent for malignant pleural effusion

Pregnancy Risk Factor D

Contraindications Hypersensitivity to bleomycin sulfate or any component, severe pulmonary disease

Warnings/Precautions The U.S. Food and Drug Administration (FDA) currently recommends that procedures for proper handling and disposal of antineoplastic agents be considered. Occurrence of pulmonary fibrosis is higher in elderly patients and in those receiving >400 units total and in smokers and patients with prior radiation therapy. A severe idiosyncratic reaction consisting of hypotension, mental confusion, fever, chills and wheezing (similar to anaphylaxis) has been reported in 1% of lymphoma patients treated with bleomycin. Since these reactions usually occur after the first or second dose, careful monitoring is essential after these doses. Check lungs prior to each treatment for fine rales (1st sign). Follow manufacturer recommendations for administering O_2 during surgery to patients who have received bleomycin.

Adverse Reactions
>10%:

Cardiovascular: Raynaud's phenomenon

Central nervous system: Mild febrile reaction, fever, chills, patients may become febrile after intracavitary administration

Dermatologic: Pruritic erythema

(Continued)

Bleomycin *(Continued)*

Integument: ~50% of patients will develop erythema, induration, and hyperkeratosis and peeling of the skin; hyperpigmentation, alopecia, nailbed changes may occur; this appears to be dose-related and is reversible after cessation of therapy

Irritant chemotherapy

Gastrointestinal: Mucocutaneous toxicity, stomatitis, nausea, vomiting, anorexia

Emetic potential: Moderately low (10% to 30%)

Local: Phlebitis, pain at tumor site

1% to 10%:

Dermatologic: Alopecia

Gastrointestinal: Weight loss

Respiratory: Toxicities (usually pneumonitis) occur in 10% of treated patients; 1% of patients progress to pulmonary fibrosis and death

Miscellaneous: Idiosyncratic: Similar to anaphylaxis and occurs in 1% of lymphoma patients; may include hypotension, confusion, fever, chills, and wheezing. May be immediate or delayed for several hours; symptomatic treatment includes volume expansion, pressor agents, antihistamines, and steroids

<1%: Myocardial infarction, cerebrovascular accident, skin thickening, hepatotoxicity, renal toxicity; respiratory effects are dose-related when total dose is >400 units or with single doses >30 units; pathogenesis is poorly understood, but may be related to damage of pulmonary, vascular, or connective tissue; manifested as an acute or chronic interstitial pneumonitis with interstitial fibrosis, hypoxia, and death; symptoms include cough, dyspnea, and bilateral pulmonary infiltrates noted on CXR; it is controversial whether steroids improve symptoms of bleomycin pulmonary toxicity; tachypnea, rales

Myelosuppressive:

WBC: Rare

Platelets: Rare

Onset (days): 7

Nadir (days): 14

Recovery (days): 21

Overdosage/Toxicology Symptoms of overdose include chills, fever, pulmonary fibrosis, hyperpigmentation

Drug Interactions

Decreased effect:

Digitalis glycosides: May decrease plasma levels and renal excretion of digoxin

Phenytoin: Results in decreased phenytoin levels, possibly due to decreased oral absorption

Increased toxicity: Cisplatin: Results in delayed bleomycin elimination due to decrease in creatinine clearance secondary to cisplatin

Stability

Refrigerate intact vials of powder; intact vials are stable for up to one month at 45°C

Reconstitute powder with 1-5 mL SWI or NS which is stable at room temperature for 28 days or in refrigerator for 14 days; may use bacteriostatic agent if prolonged storage is necessary

Incompatible with amino acid solutions, aminophylline, ascorbic acid, cefazolin, cisplatin, cytarabine, furosemide, diazepam, hydrocortisone sodium succinate, methotrexate, mitomycin, nafcillin, penicillin G

Compatible with amikacin, cyclophosphamide, dexamethasone, diphenhydramine, doxorubicin, fluorouracil, gentamicin, heparin, hydrocortisone mesna, phenytoin, sodium phosphate, streptomycin, tobramycin, vinblastine, vincristine

Standard I.V. dilution: Dose/50-1000 mL NS or D_5W

Stable for 96 hours at room temperature and 14 days under refrigeration

Mechanism of Action Inhibits synthesis of DNA; binds to DNA leading to single- and double-strand breaks; isolated from *Streptomyces verticillus*

Pharmacodynamics/Kinetics

Absorption: I.M. and intrapleural administration produces serum concentrations of 30% of I.V. administration; intraperitoneal and S.C. routes produce serum concentrations equal to those of I.V.

Distribution: V_d: 22 L/m^2; highest concentrations seen in skin, kidney, lung, heart tissues; low concentrations seen in testes and GI tract; does not cross blood-brain barrier

Protein binding: 1%

Metabolism: By several tissue types, including the liver, GI tract, skin, lungs, kidney, and serum

Half-life (biphasic): Dependent upon renal function:

Normal renal function:

Initial: 1.3 hours

Terminal: 9 hours

End-stage renal disease:

Initial: 2 hours

Terminal: 30 hours

Time to peak serum concentration: I.M.: Within 30 minutes

Elimination: 50% to 70% of dose excreted in urine as active drug; not removed by hemodialysis

Usual Dosage Refer to individual protocols; 1 unit = 1 mg

May be administered I.M., I.V., S.C., or intracavitary

Children and Adults:

Test dose for lymphoma patients: I.M., I.V., S.C.: Because of the possibility of an anaphylactoid reaction, ≤2 units of bleomycin for the first 2 doses; monitor vital signs every 15 minutes; wait a minimum of 1 hour before administering remainder of dose; if no acute reaction occurs, then the regular dosage schedule may be followed

Single-agent therapy:

I.M./I.V./S.C.: Squamous cell carcinoma, lymphoma, testicular carcinoma: 0.25-0.5 units/kg (10-20 units/m^2) 1-2 times/week

CIV: 15 units/m^2 over 24 hours daily for 4 days

Combination-agent therapy:

I.M./I.V.: 3-4 units/m^2

I.V.: ABVD: 10 units/m^2 on days 1 and 15

Maximum cumulative lifetime dose: 400 units

Dosing adjustment in renal impairment:

Cl$_{cr}$ 10-50 mL/minute: Administer 75% of normal dose

Cl$_{cr}$ <10 mL/minute: Administer 50% of normal dose

Hemodialysis: None

CAPD effects: None

CAVH effects: None

Adults: Intracavitary injection for malignant pleural effusion: 60 international units (range of 15-120 units; dose generally does not exceed 1 unit/kg) in 50-100 mL SWI

Administration I.V. doses should be administered slowly (≤1 unit/minute); I.M. or S.C. may cause pain at injection site

Monitoring Parameters Pulmonary function tests (total lung volume, forced vital capacity, carbon monoxide diffusion), renal function, chest x-ray, temperature initially, CBC with differential and platelet count

Patient Information Hair should reappear after discontinuance of medication; maintain excellent oral hygiene habits; report any coughing, shortness of breath, or wheezing; skin rashes, shaking, chills, or transient high fever may occur following administration. Contraceptive measures are recommended during therapy.

Nursing Implications Patients should be closely monitored for signs of pulmonary toxicity; check body weight at regular intervals

Dosage Forms Powder for injection, as sulfate: 15 units

- ◆ **Bleomycin Sulfate** see Bleomycin on page 149
- ◆ **Bleph®-10 Ophthalmic** see Sulfacetamide Sodium on page 1091
- ◆ **Blephamide® Ophthalmic** see Sulfacetamide Sodium and Prednisolone on page 1091
- ◆ **Blis-To-Sol® [OTC]** see Tolnaftate on page 1159
- ◆ **BLM** see Bleomycin on page 149
- ◆ **Blocadren® Oral** see Timolol on page 1146
- ◆ **Bonamine®** see Meclizine on page 719
- ◆ **Bonine® [OTC]** see Meclizine on page 719
- ◆ **B&O Supprettes®** see Belladonna and Opium on page 130
- ◆ **Botox®** see Botulinum Toxin Type A on this page

Botulinum Toxin Type A (BOT yoo lin num TOKS in type aye)

Replaces Oculinum®

U.S. Brand Names Botox®

Therapeutic Category Ophthalmic Agent, Toxin

Use Treatment of strabismus and blepharospasm associated with dystonia (including benign essential blepharospasm or VII nerve disorders in patients ≥12 years of age)

Unlabeled use: Treatment of hemifacial spasms, spasmodic torticollis (ie, cervical dystonia, clonic twisting of the head), oromandibular dystonia, spasmodic dysphonia (laryngeal dystonia) and other dystonias (ie, writer's cramp, focal task-specific dystonias)

Orphan drug: Treatment of dynamic muscle contracture in pediatric cerebral palsy patients

Pregnancy Risk Factor C

Contraindications Hypersensitivity to botulinum A toxin; relative contraindications to botulinum toxin therapy include diseases of neuromuscular transmission and coagulopathy, including anticoagulant therapy; injections into the central area of the upper eyelid (rapid diffusion of toxin into the levator can occur resulting in a marked ptosis).

Warnings/Precautions Use with caution in patients taking aminoglycosides or any other antibiotic or other drugs that interfere with neuromuscular transmission; do not exceed recommended dose

Adverse Reactions

>10%: Ocular: Dry eyes, lagophthalmos, ptosis, photophobia, vertical deviation

1% to 10%:

Dermatologic: Diffuse rash

Ocular: Eyelid edema, blepharospasm

<1%: Ectropion, keratitis, diplopia, entropion

Overdosage/Toxicology In the event of an overdosage or injection into the wrong muscle, additional information may be obtained by contacting Allergan Pharmaceuticals at (800)-347-5063 from 8 AM to 4 PM Pacific time, or at (714)-724-5954 at other times

Drug Interactions Increased effect: Botulinum toxin may be potentiated by aminoglycosides

(Continued)

Botulinum Toxin Type A *(Continued)*

Stability Keep in undiluted vials in freezer (at or below -5°C/23°F); administer within 4 hours after the vial is removed from the freezer and reconstituted; store reconstituted solution in refrigerator (2°C to 8°C/36°F to 46°F)

Mechanism of Action Botulinum A toxin is a neurotoxin produced by *Clostridium botulinum*, spore-forming anaerobic bacillus, which appears to affect only the presynaptic membrane of the neuromuscular junction in humans, where it prevents calcium-dependent release of acetylcholine and produces a state of denervation. Muscle inactivation persists until new fibrils grow from the nerve and form junction plates on new areas of the muscle-cell walls. The antagonist muscle shortens simultaneously ("contracture"), taking up the slack created by agonist paralysis; following several weeks of paralysis, alignment of the eye is measurably changed, despite return of innervation to the injected muscle.

Pharmacodynamics/Kinetics
Strabismus: Onset of action: 1-2 days after injection; Duration of paralysis: 2-6 weeks
Blepharospasm: Onset: 3 days after injection; Peak: 1-2 weeks; Duration of paralysis: 3 months

Usual Dosage
Strabismus: 1.25-5 units (0.05-0.15 mL) injected into any one muscle
Subsequent doses for residual/recurrent strabismus: Re-examine patients 7-14 days after each injection to assess the effect of that dose. Subsequent doses for patients experiencing incomplete paralysis of the target may be increased up to two fold the previously administered dose. Maximum recommended dose as a single injection for any one muscle is 25 units.
Blepharospasm: 1.25-2.5 units (0.05-0.10 mL) injected into the orbicularis oculi muscle
Subsequent doses: Each treatment lasts approximately 3 months. At repeat treatment sessions, the dose may be increased up to twofold if the response from the initial treatment is considered insufficient (usually defined as an effect that does not last >2 months). There appears to be little benefit obtainable from injecting >5 units per site. Some tolerance may be found if treatments are given any more frequently than every 3 months.
The cumulative dose should not exceed 200 units in a 30-day period

Administration Inject using a 27- to 30-gauge needle

Patient Information Patients with blepharospasm may have been extremely sedentary for a long time; caution these patients to resume activity slowly and carefully following administration

Nursing Implications To alleviate spatial disorientation or double vision in strabismic patients, cover the affected eye; have epinephrine ready for hypersensitivity reactions

Dosage Forms Injection: 100 units *Clostridium botulinum* toxin type A

Botulinum Toxoid, Pentavalent Vaccine (Against Types A, B, C, D, and E Strains of *C. botulinum*)
(BOT yoo lin num TOKS oyd pen ta VAY lent vak SEEN)

Therapeutic Category Toxoid

Additional Information For advice on vaccine administration and contraindications, contact the Division of Immunization, CDC, Atlanta, GA 30333 (404-639-3356).

♦ **Bovine Lung Surfactant** *see* Beractant *on page 139*
♦ **Breast-Feeding and Drugs** *see page 1506*
♦ **Breathe Free® [OTC]** *see* Sodium Chloride *on page 1067*
♦ **Breezee® Mist Antifungal [OTC]** *see* Miconazole *on page 775*
♦ **Breezee® Mist Antifungal [OTC]** *see* Tolnaftate *on page 1159*
♦ **Breonesin® [OTC]** *see* Guaifenesin *on page 549*
♦ **Brethaire® Inhalation Aerosol** *see* Terbutaline *on page 1115*
♦ **Brethine® Injection** *see* Terbutaline *on page 1115*
♦ **Brethine® Oral** *see* Terbutaline *on page 1115*
♦ **Bretylate®** *see* Bretylium *on this page*

Bretylium *(bre TIL ee um)*

Related Information
Adult ACLS Algorithm, Tachycardia *on page 1450*
Adult ACLS Algorithm, V. Fib and Pulseless V. Tach *on page 1447*
Antiarrhythmic Drugs Comparison *on page 1297*
Pediatric ALS Algorithm, Asystole and Pulseless Arrest *on page 1445*

Canadian Brand Names Bretylate®

Synonyms Bretylium Tosylate

Therapeutic Category Antiarrhythmic Agent, Class III

Use Prophylaxis and treatment of ventricular tachycardia and fibrillation; used in the treatment of other serious ventricular arrhythmias resistant to first-line agents (eg, lidocaine)

Pregnancy Risk Factor C

Contraindications Digitalis intoxication-induced arrhythmias, hypersensitivity to bretylium or any component, coadministration with sparfloxacin

Warnings/Precautions Hypotension occurs frequently; keep patients supine until tolerance develops; patients with fixed cardiac output (severe pulmonary hypertension or aortic stenosis) may experience severe hypotension due to decrease in peripheral resistance without ability to increase cardiac output; reduce dose in renal failure patients; may have prolonged half-life in the elderly; transient hypertension and increased frequency of arrhythmias may occur initially. Rapid I.V. injection may result in transient hypertension, nausea, and vomiting.

Adverse Reactions

>10%: Cardiovascular: Hypotension (both postural and supine)

1% to 10%: Gastrointestinal: Nausea, vomiting (especially after rapid I.V. administration)

<1%: Transient initial hypertension, increase in PVCs, bradycardia, angina, flushing, syncope, vertigo, confusion, hyperthermia, lightheadedness, rash, diarrhea, abdominal pain, muscle atrophy and necrosis with repeated I.M. injections at same site, conjunctivitis, renal impairment, respiratory depression, nasal congestion, hiccups

Overdosage/Toxicology

Symptoms of overdose include significant hypertension followed by severe hypotension due to inhibition of catecholamine release

After GI decontamination, supportive treatment is required. Note: Quinidine and other type Ia should not be used to treat cardiotoxicity caused by bretylium; continuously monitor vital signs and EKG for a minimum of 6 hours after exposure and admit the patient for 24 hours of intensive monitoring if there is evidence of toxicity. Dialysis and hemoperfusion unlikely to assist.

Drug Interactions

Increased toxicity: Other antiarrhythmic agents, pressor catecholamines, and digitalis

Risk of cardiotoxicity increased with concurrent sparfloxacin

Stability Standard diluent: 2 g/250 mL D_5W; the premix infusion should be stored at room temperature and protected from freezing

Mechanism of Action Class II antiarrhythmic; after an initial release of norepinephrine at the peripheral adrenergic nerve terminals, inhibits further release by postganglionic nerve endings in response to sympathetic nerve stimulation

Pharmacodynamics/Kinetics

Onset of antiarrhythmic effect: I.M.: May require 2 hours; I.V.: Within 6-20 minutes

Peak effect: 6-9 hours

Duration: 6-24 hours

Protein binding: 1% to 6%

Metabolism: Not metabolized

Half-life: 7-11 hours; average: 4-17 hours

End-stage renal disease: 16-32 hours

Elimination: 70% to 80% excreted over the first 24 hours; excreted unchanged in the urine

Usual Dosage Note: Patients should undergo defibrillation/cardioversion before and after bretylium doses as necessary

Children (**Note:** Not well established, although the following dosing has been suggested):

I.M.: 2-5 mg/kg as a single dose

I.V.: Acute ventricular fibrillation: Initial: 5 mg/kg, then attempt electrical defibrillation; repeat with 10 mg/kg if ventricular fibrillation persists at 15- to 30-minute intervals to maximum total of 30 mg/kg

Maintenance dose: I.M., I.V.: 5 mg/kg every 6 hours

Adults:

Immediate life-threatening ventricular arrhythmias (ventricular fibrillation, unstable ventricular tachycardia): Initial dose: I.V.: 5 mg/kg (undiluted) over 1 minute; if arrhythmia persists, administer 10 mg/kg (undiluted) over 1 minute and repeat as necessary (usually at 15- to 30-minute intervals) up to a total dose of 30-35 mg/kg

Other life-threatening ventricular arrhythmias:

Initial dose: I.M., I.V.: 5-10 mg/kg, may repeat every 1-2 hours if arrhythmia persists; administer I.V. dose (diluted) over 8-10 minutes

Maintenance dose: I.M.: 5-10 mg/kg every 6-8 hours; I.V. (diluted): 5-10 mg/kg every 6 hours; I.V. infusion (diluted): 1-2 mg/minute (little experience with doses >40 mg/kg/day)

Example dilution: 2 g/250 mL D_5W (infusion pump should be used for I.V. infusion administration)

Rate of I.V. infusion: 1-4 mg/minute

1 mg/minute = 7 mL/hour

2 mg/minute = 15 mL/hour

3 mg/minute = 22 mL/hour

4 mg/minute = 30 mL/hour

Dosing adjustment in renal impairment:

Cl_{cr} 10-50 mL/minute: Administer 25% to 50% of dose

Cl_{cr} <10 mL/minute: Administer 25% of dose

Dialysis: Not dialyzable (0% to 5%) via hemo- or peritoneal dialysis; supplemental doses are not needed

Administration I.M. injection in adults should not exceed 5 mL volume in any one site

Monitoring Parameters EKG, heart rate, blood pressure; requires a cardiac monitor

Patient Information Anticipate vomiting

Nursing Implications Monitor EKG and blood pressure throughout therapy; onset of action may be delayed 15-30 minutes; rapid infusion may result in nausea and vomiting

Dosage Forms

Injection, as tosylate: 50 mg/mL (10 mL, 20 mL)

Injection, as tosylate, premixed in D_5W: 1 mg/mL (500 mL); 2 mg/mL (250 mL); 4 mg/mL (250 mL, 500 mL)

♦ **Bretylium Tosylate** *see* Bretylium *on previous page*

- ◆ **Breviblloc® Injection** see Esmolol on page 430
- ◆ **Brevicon®** see Ethinyl Estradiol and Norethindrone on page 451
- ◆ **Brevital® Sodium** see Methohexital on page 750
- ◆ **Bricanyl® Injection** see Terbutaline on page 1115
- ◆ **Bricanyl® Oral** see Terbutaline on page 1115
- ◆ **Brietal® Sodium** see Methohexital on page 750

Brimonidine (bri MOE ni deen)

U.S. Brand Names Alphagan®
Synonyms Brimonidine Tartrate
Therapeutic Category Alpha$_2$-Adrenergic Agonist Agent, Ophthalmic; Sympathomimetic
Use Lowering of intraocular pressure in patients with open-angle glaucoma or ocular hypertension
Pregnancy Risk Factor B
Contraindications Known hypersensitivity to brimonidine tartrate or any component of this medication; patients receiving monoamine oxidase (MAO) inhibitor therapy
Warnings/Precautions Exercise caution in treating patients with severe cardiovascular disease. Use with caution in patients with depression, cerebral or coronary insufficiency, Raynaud's phenomenon, orthostatic hypotension or thromboangiitis obliterans

The preservative in brimonidine tartrate, benzalkonium chloride, may be absorbed by soft contact lenses; instruct patients wearing soft contact lenses to wait at least 15 minutes after instilling brimonidine tartrate to insert soft contact lenses

Use with caution in patients with hepatic or renal impairment

Loss of effect in some patients may occur. The IOP-lowering efficacy observed with brimonidine tartrate during the first of month of therapy may not always reflect the long term level of IOP reduction. Routinely monitor IOP.
Adverse Reactions
>10%:
Central nervous system: Headache, fatigue/drowsiness
Gastrointestinal: Xerostomia
Ocular: Ocular hyperemia, burning and stinging, blurring, foreign body sensation, conjunctival follicles, ocular allergic reactions and ocular pruritus
1% to 10%:
Central nervous system: Dizziness
Ocular: Corneal staining/erosion, photophobia, eyelid erythema, ocular ache/pain, ocular dryness, tearing, eyelid edema, conjunctival edema, blepharitis, ocular irritation, conjunctival blanching, abnormal vision, lid crusting, conjunctival hemorrhage, abnormal taste, conjunctival discharge
Respiratory: Upper respiratory symptoms
<1%: Allergic response, some systemic effects have also been reported including GI, CNS, and cardiovascular symptoms (arrhythmias)
Overdosage/Toxicology
Symptoms of overdose: No information is available on overdosage in humans
Treatment: Maintain a patent airway, supportive and symptomatic therapy
Drug Interactions
Increased effect:
CNS depressants (eg, alcohol, barbiturates, opiates, sedatives, anesthetics): Additive or potentiating effect
Topical beta-blockers, pilocarpine → additive decreased intraocular pressure, antihypertensives, cardiac glycosides
Decreased effect: Tricyclic antidepressants can affect the metabolism and uptake of circulating amines
Stability Store at or below 25°C (77°F)
Mechanism of Action Selective for alpha$_2$-receptors; appears to result in reduction of aqueous humor formation and increase uveoscleral outflow
Pharmacodynamics/Kinetics
Onset of action: 1-4 hours
Duration: 12 hours
Usual Dosage Adults: Ophthalmic: Instill 1 drop in affected eye(s) 3 times/day (approximately every 8 hours)
Monitoring Parameters Closely monitor patients who develop fatigue or drowsiness
Patient Information Instruct patients wearing soft contact lenses to wait at least 15 minutes after instilling brimonidine tartrate to insert soft contact lenses. As with other drugs in this class, brimonidine tartrate may cause fatigue or drowsiness in some patients. Caution patients who engage in hazardous activities of the potential for a decrease in mental alertness.
Dosage Forms Solution, ophthalmic, as tartrate: 0.2% (5 mL, 10 mL)

- ◆ **Brimonidine Tartrate** see Brimonidine on this page

Brinzolamide (brin ZOH la mide)

U.S. Brand Names Azopt™
Therapeutic Category Carbonic Anhydrase Inhibitor
Use Lowers intraocular pressure to treat glaucoma in patients with ocular hypertension or open-angle glaucoma
Pregnancy Risk Factor C

Contraindications Hypersensitivity to brinzolamide or any component

Warnings/Precautions Effects of prolonged use on corneal epithelial cells have not been evaluated; has not been studied in acute angle-closure glaucoma; renal impairment (parent and metabolite may accumulate). Patients with allergy to sulfonamides (brinzolamide is a sulfonamide); systemic absorption may cause serious hypersensitivity reactions to recur.

Adverse Reactions

1% to 10%:

Dermatologic: Dermatitis (1% to 5%)

Gastrointestinal: Taste disturbances (5% to 10%)

Ocular: Blurred vision (5% to 10%), blepharitis (1% to 5%), dry eye (1% to 5%), foreign body sensation (1% to 5%), eye discharge (1% to 5%), eye pain (1% to 5%), itching of eye (1% to 5%)

Respiratory: Rhinitis

<1%: Dizziness, headache, urticaria, alopecia, diarrhea, nausea, xerostomia, diplopia, eye fatigue, lid crusting, dyspnea, pharyngitis, allergic reactions

Overdosage/Toxicology

Theoretically, overdose could lead to electrolyte imbalance, acidosis and CNS effects; monitor serum electrolytes and blood pH

Treatment is supportive

Drug Interactions

Concurrent use of oral carbonic anhydrase inhibitors (CAIs) - additive effects and toxicity

High-dose salicylates may result in toxicity from CAIs

Stability Store at 4°C to 30°C (39°F to 86°F)

Mechanism of Action Inhibition of carbonic anhydrase decreases aqueous humor secretion. This results in a reduction of intraocular pressure.

Pharmacodynamics/Kinetics

Absorption: Topical: Into the systemic circulation

Distribution: Accumulates in red blood cells, binding to carbonic anhydrase (brinzolamide and metabolite)

Metabolism: To N-desmethyl brinzolamide

Elimination: Primarily in urine (unchanged drug and metabolites)

Usual Dosage Adults: Ophthalmic: Instill 1 drop in affected eye(s) 3 times/day

Administration May be used concomitantly with other topical ophthalmic drug products to lower intraocular pressure. If more than one topical ophthalmic drug is being used, administer drugs at least 10 minutes apart.

Monitoring Parameters Intraocular pressure

Dosage Forms Suspension, ophthalmic: 1% (2.5 mL, 5 mL, 10 mL, 15 mL)

♦ **British Anti-Lewisite** see Dimercaprol on page 367

♦ **Bromanate® DC** see Brompheniramine, Phenylpropanolamine, and Codeine on next page

♦ **Bromanyl® Cough Syrup** see Bromodiphenhydramine and Codeine on next page

Bromocriptine (broe moe KRIP teen)

Related Information

Parkinson's Disease, Dosing of Drugs Used for Treatment of on page 1336

U.S. Brand Names Parlodel®

Canadian Brand Names Apo® Bromocriptine

Synonyms Bromocriptine Mesylate

Therapeutic Category Anti-Parkinson's Agent; Ergot Alkaloid and Derivative

Use

Usually used with levodopa or levodopa/carbidopa to treat Parkinson's disease - treatment of parkinsonism in patients unresponsive or allergic to levodopa

Prolactin-secreting pituitary adenomas

Acromegaly

Amenorrhea/galactorrhea secondary to hyperprolactinemia in the absence of primary tumor

The indication for prevention of postpartum lactation has been withdrawn voluntarily by Sandoz Pharmaceuticals Corporation

Pregnancy Risk Factor C (See Contraindications)

Contraindications Hypersensitivity to bromocriptine or any component, severe ischemic heart disease or peripheral vascular disorders, pregnancy

Warnings/Precautions Use with caution in patients with impaired renal or hepatic function

Adverse Reactions Incidence of adverse effects is high, especially at beginning of treatment and with dosages >20 mg/day

1% to 10%:

Cardiovascular: Hypotension, Raynaud's phenomenon

Central nervous system: Mental depression, confusion, hallucinations

Gastrointestinal: Nausea, constipation, anorexia

Neuromuscular & skeletal: Leg cramps

Respiratory: Nasal congestion

<1%: Hypertension, myocardial infarction, syncope, dizziness, drowsiness, fatigue, insomnia, headache, seizures, vomiting, abdominal cramps

Overdosage/Toxicology

Symptoms of overdose include nausea, vomiting, hypotension

(Continued)

Bromocriptine *(Continued)*

Hypotension, when unresponsive to I.V. fluids or Trendelenburg positioning, often responds to norepinephrine infusions started at 0.1-0.2 mcg/kg/minute followed by a titrated infusion

Drug Interactions CYP3A3/4 enzyme substrate

Decreased effect: Amitriptyline, butyrophenones, imipramine, methyldopa, phenothiazines, reserpine, may decrease bromocriptine's efficacy at reducing prolactin

Increased toxicity: Ergot alkaloids (increased cardiovascular toxicity)

Mechanism of Action Semisynthetic ergot alkaloid derivative with dopaminergic properties; inhibits prolactin secretion and can improve symptoms of Parkinson's disease by directly stimulating dopamine receptors in the corpus stratum

Pharmacodynamics/Kinetics

Protein binding: 90% to 96%

Metabolism: Majority of drug metabolized in the liver

Half-life (biphasic): Initial: 6-8 hours; Terminal: 50 hours

Time to peak serum concentration: Oral: Within 1-2 hours

Elimination: In bile; only 2% to 6% excreted unchanged in urine

Usual Dosage Adults: Oral:

Parkinsonism: 1.25 mg 2 times/day, increased by 2.5 mg/day in 2- to 4-week intervals (usual dose range is 30-90 mg/day in 3 divided doses), though elderly patients can usually be managed on lower doses

Hyperprolactinemia: 2.5 mg 2-3 times/day

Acromegaly: Initial: 1.25-2.5 mg increasing as necessary every 3-7 days; usual dose: 20-30 mg/day

Dosing adjustment in hepatic impairment: No guidelines are available, however, may be necessary

Monitoring Parameters Monitor blood pressure closely as well as hepatic, hematopoietic, and cardiovascular function

Patient Information Take with food or milk; drowsiness commonly occurs upon initiation of therapy; limit use of alcohol; avoid exposure to cold; incidence of side effects is high (68%) with nausea the most common; hypotension occurs commonly with initiation of therapy, usually upon rising after prolonged sitting or lying

Discontinue immediately if pregnant; may restore fertility; women desiring not to become pregnant should use mechanical contraceptive means

Nursing Implications Raise bed rails and institute safety measures; aid patient with ambulation; may cause postural hypotension and drowsiness

Dosage Forms

Capsule, as mesylate: 5 mg

Tablet, as mesylate: 2.5 mg

- **Bromocriptine Mesylate** *see Bromocriptine on previous page*

Bromodiphenhydramine and Codeine

(brome oh dye fen HYE dra meen & KOE deen)

U.S. Brand Names Ambenyl® Cough Syrup; Amgenal® Cough Syrup; Bromanyl® Cough Syrup; Bromotuss® w/Codeine Cough Syrup

Therapeutic Category Antihistamine/Antitussive

Dosage Forms Liquid: Bromodiphenhydramine hydrochloride 12.5 mg and codeine phosphate 10 mg per 5 mL

- **Bromotuss® w/Codeine Cough Syrup** *see Bromodiphenhydramine and Codeine on this page*
- **Bromphen® DC w/Codeine** *see Brompheniramine, Phenylpropanolamine, and Codeine on this page*

Brompheniramine, Phenylpropanolamine, and Codeine

(brome fen IR a meen, fen il prop pa NOLE a meen, & KOE deen)

U.S. Brand Names Bromanate® DC; Bromphen® DC w/Codeine; Dimetane®-DC; Myphetane DC®; Poly-Histine CS®

Therapeutic Category Antihistamine/Decongestant/Antitussive

Dosage Forms Liquid: Brompheniramine maleate 2 mg, phenylpropanolamine hydrochloride 12.5 mg, and codeine phosphate 10 mg per 5 mL with alcohol 0.95% (480 mL)

- **Bronalide®** *see Flunisolide on page 494*
- **Bronchial®** *see Theophylline and Guaifenesin on page 1125*
- **Bronchodilators, Comparison of Inhaled and Sympathomimetic** *see page 1314*
- **Bronitin®** *see Epinephrine on page 415*
- **Bronkaid® Mist [OTC]** *see Epinephrine on page 415*
- **Bronkodyl®** *see Theophylline Salts on page 1125*
- **Bronkometer®** *see Isoetharine on page 632*
- **Bronkosol®** *see Isoetharine on page 632*
- **Brontex® Liquid** *see Guaifenesin and Codeine on page 550*
- **Brontex® Tablet** *see Guaifenesin and Codeine on page 550*
- **Bucladin®-S Softab®** *see Buclizine on this page*

Buclizine (BYOO kli zeen)

U.S. Brand Names Bucladin®-S Softab®; Vibazine®

Synonyms Buclizine Hydrochloride

Therapeutic Category Antiemetic; Antihistamine, H₁ Blocker

Use Prevention and treatment of motion sickness; symptomatic treatment of vertigo

Pregnancy Risk Factor C

Contraindications Known hypersensitivity to buclizine

Warnings/Precautions Product contains tartrazine; use with caution in patients with angle-closure glaucoma, peptic ulcer, urinary tract obstruction, hyperthyroidism; some preparations contain sodium bisulfite; syrup contains alcohol

Adverse Reactions

>10%: Central nervous system: Drowsiness

<1%: Hypotension, palpitations, sedation, dizziness, paradoxical excitement, fatigue, insomnia, nausea, vomiting, urinary retention, tremor, blurred vision

Overdosage/Toxicology

CNS stimulation or depression; overdose may result in death in infants and children

There is no specific treatment for an antihistamine overdose, however, most of its clinical toxicity is due to anticholinergic effects; anticholinesterase inhibitors including physostigmine, neostigmine, pyridostigmine, and edrophonium may be useful by reducing acetylcholinesterase; for anticholinergic overdose with severe life-threatening symptoms, physostigmine 1-2 mg (0.5 mg or 0.02 mg/kg for children) I.V., slowly may be given to reverse these effects

Drug Interactions Increased toxicity: CNS depressants, MAO inhibitors, tricyclic antidepressants

Mechanism of Action Buclizine acts centrally to suppress nausea and vomiting. It is a piperazine antihistamine closely related to cyclizine and meclizine. It also has CNS depressant, anticholinergic, antispasmodic, and local anesthetic effects, and suppresses labyrinthine activity and conduction in vestibular-cerebellar nerve pathways.

Usual Dosage Adults: Oral:

Motion sickness (prophylaxis): 50 mg 30 minutes prior to traveling; may repeat 50 mg after 4-6 hours

Vertigo: 50 mg twice daily, up to 150 mg/day

Patient Information May cause drowsiness

Nursing Implications Bucladin®-S Softab® may be chewed, swallowed whole, or allowed to dissolve in mouth

Dosage Forms Tablet, chewable, as hydrochloride: 50 mg

♦ **Buclizine Hydrochloride** see Buclizine on previous page

Budesonide (byoo DES oh nide)

Related Information

Asthma, Guidelines for the Diagnosis and Management of on page 1456
Estimated Clinical Comparability of Doses for Inhaled Corticosteroids on page 1463

U.S. Brand Names Pulmicort Turbuhaler®; Rhinocort®

Canadian Brand Names Entocort®; Pulmicort®

Therapeutic Category Corticosteroid, Inhalant; Corticosteroid, Intranasal; Corticosteroid, Topical (Medium Potency)

Use

Intranasal: Children and Adults: Management of symptoms of seasonal or perennial rhinitis

Oral inhalation: Maintenance and prophylactic treatment of asthma; includes patients who require corticosteroids and those who may benefit from systemic dose reduction/elimination

Pregnancy Risk Factor C

Warnings/Precautions Controlled clinical studies have shown that inhaled and intranasal corticosteroids may cause a reduction in growth velocity in pediatric patients. Growth velocity provides a means of comparing the rate of growth among children of the same age.

In studies involving inhaled corticosteroids, the average reduction in growth velocity was approximately 1 cm (about ⅓ of an inch) per year. It appears that the reduction is related to dose and how long the child takes the drug.

FDA's Pulmonary and Allergy Drugs and Metabolic and Endocrine Drugs advisory committees discussed this issue at a July 1998 meeting. They recommended that the agency develop class-wide labeling to inform healthcare providers so they would understand this potential side effect and monitor growth routinely in pediatric patients who are treated with inhaled corticosteroids, intranasal corticosteroids or both.

Long-term effects of this reduction in growth velocity on final adult height are unknown. Likewise, it also has not yet been determined whether patients' growth will "catch up" if treatment in discontinued. Drug manufacturers will continue to monitor these drugs to learn more about long-term effects. Children are prescribed inhaled corticosteroids to treat asthma. Intranasal corticosteroids are generally used to prevent and treat allergy-related nasal symptoms.

Patients are advised not to stop using their inhaled or intranasal corticosteroids without first speaking to their healthcare providers about the benefits of these drugs compared to their risks.

Adverse Reactions

>10%:

Cardiovascular: Pounding heartbeat

Central nervous system: Nervousness, headache, dizziness

Dermatologic: Itching, rash

(Continued)

Budesonide *(Continued)*

Gastrointestinal: GI irritation, bitter taste, oral candidiasis
Respiratory: Coughing, upper respiratory tract infection, bronchitis, hoarseness
Miscellaneous: Increased susceptibility to infections, diaphoresis

1% to 10%:
Central nervous system: Insomnia, psychic changes
Dermatologic: Acne, urticaria
Endocrine & metabolic: Menstrual problems
Gastrointestinal: Anorexia, increase in appetite, xerostomia, dry throat, loss of taste perception
Ocular: Cataracts
Respiratory: Epistaxis
Miscellaneous: Loss of smell

<1%: Abdominal fullness, bronchospasm, shortness of breath

Overdosage/Toxicology Symptoms of overdose include irritation and burning of the nasal mucosa, sneezing, intranasal and pharyngeal *Candida* infections, nasal ulceration, epistaxis, rhinorrhea, nasal stuffiness, headache. When consumed in excessive quantities, systemic hypercorticism and adrenal suppression may occur, in those cases discontinuation and withdrawal of the corticosteroid should be done judiciously.

Drug Interactions CYP3A3/4 enzyme substrate

Although there have been no reported drug interactions to date, one would expect budesonide could potentially interact with drugs known to interact with other corticosteroids

Mechanism of Action Controls the rate of protein synthesis, depresses the migration of polymorphonuclear leukocytes, fibroblasts, reverses capillary permeability, and lysosomal stabilization at the cellular level to prevent or control inflammation

Pharmacodynamics/Kinetics Oral inhalation:
Bioavailability: Systemic, 10%
Half-life, plasma: 2-3 hours

Usual Dosage
Children <6 years: Not recommended

Aerosol inhalation: Children ≥6 years and Adults: Nasal: Initial: 8 sprays (4 sprays/nostril) per day (256 mcg/day), given as either 2 sprays in each nostril in the morning and evening or as 4 sprays in each nostril in the morning; after symptoms decrease (usually by 3-7 days), reduce dose slowly every 2-4 weeks to the smallest amount needed to control symptoms

Oral inhalation:
Children ≥6 years:
Previous therapy of bronchodilators alone: 200 mcg twice initially which may be increased up to 400 mcg twice daily
Previous therapy of inhaled corticosteroids: 200 mcg twice initially which may be increased up to 400 mcg twice daily
Previous therapy of oral corticosteroids: The highest recommended dose in children is 400 mcg twice daily

Adults:
Previous therapy of bronchodilators alone: 200-400 mcg twice initially which may be increased up to 400 mcg twice daily
Previous therapy of inhaled corticosteroids: 200-400 mcg twice initially which may be increased up to 800 mcg twice daily
Previous therapy of oral corticosteroids: 400-800 mcg twice daily which may be increased up to 800 mcg twice daily

NIH Guidelines (NIH, 1997) (give in divided doses twice daily):
Children:
"Low" dose: 100-200 mcg/day
"Medium" dose: 200-400 mcg/day (1-2 inhalations/day)
"High" dose: >400 mcg/day (>2 inhalation/day)
Adults:
"Low" dose: 200-400 mcg/day (1-2 inhalations/day)
"Medium" dose: 400-600 mcg/day (2-3 inhalations/day)
"High" dose: >600 mcg/day (>3 inhalation/day)

Patient Information
Inhaler should be shaken well immediately prior to use; clear nasal passage by blowing nose prior to use; keep inhaler clean and unobstructed; wash in warm water and dry thoroughly; contact physician if symptoms are not improved by 3 weeks of treatment, if condition worsens, or if nasal irritation or burning persists

Medication is used for preventative therapy. Do **not** use to abort an acute asthmatic attack; use at regularly scheduled intervals as prescribed.

Dosage Forms
Aerosol: 50 mcg released per actuation to deliver ~32 mcg to patient via nasal adapter [200 metered doses] (7 g)
Turbuhaler: ~160 mcg delivered (200 mcg released) with each actuation (200 doses/inhaler)

♦ **Bufferin®** [OTC] *see* Aspirin *on page 102*
♦ **Buffex®** [OTC] *see* Aspirin *on page 102*

Bumetanide (byoo MET a nide)

Related Information

Heart Failure: Management of Patients With Left-Ventricular Systolic Dysfunction *on page 1472*

Sulfonamide Derivatives *on page 1337*

U.S. Brand Names Bumex®

Canadian Brand Names Burinex®

Therapeutic Category Antihypertensive Agent; Diuretic, Loop

Use Management of edema secondary to congestive heart failure or hepatic or renal disease including nephrotic syndrome; may be used alone or in combination with antihypertensives in the treatment of hypertension; can be used in furosemide-allergic patients; (1 mg = 40 mg furosemide)

Pregnancy Risk Factor D

Contraindications Hypersensitivity to bumetanide or any component; in anuria or increasing azotemia

Warnings/Precautions Profound diuresis with fluid and electrolyte loss is possible; close medical supervision and dose evaluation is required; use caution when dosing in patients with hepatic failure

Adverse Reactions

>10%:

Endocrine & metabolic: Hyperuricemia (18.4%), hypochloremia, hypokalemia

Renal: Azotemia

1% to 10%:

Central nervous system: Dizziness, encephalopathy, headache

Endocrine & metabolic: Hyponatremia

Neuromuscular & skeletal: Muscle cramps, weakness

<1%: Hypotension, rash, pruritus, hyperglycemia, cramps, nausea, vomiting, altered LFTs, hearing loss, increased serum creatinine

Overdosage/Toxicology

Symptoms of overdose include electrolyte depletion, volume depletion

Treatment is primarily symptomatic and supportive

Drug Interactions

Decreased effect: Indomethacin and other NSAIDs, probenecid

Increased effect: Other antihypertensive agents; lithium's excretion may be decreased

Stability I.V. infusion solutions should be used within 24 hours after preparation; light sensitive, discoloration may occur when exposed to light

Mechanism of Action Inhibits reabsorption of sodium and chloride in the ascending loop of Henle and proximal renal tubule, interfering with the chloride-binding cotransport system, thus causing increased excretion of water, sodium, chloride, magnesium, phosphate and calcium; it does not appear to act on the distal tubule

Pharmacodynamics/Kinetics

Onset of effect: Oral, I.M.: 0.5-1 hour; I.V.: 2-3 minutes

Duration of action: 6 hours

Distribution: V_d: 13-25 L/kg

Protein binding: 95%

Metabolism: Partial, occurs in the liver

Half-life: Infants <6 months: Possibly 2.5 hours; Children and Adults: 1-1.5 hours

Elimination: Majority of unchanged drug and metabolites excreted in urine

Usual Dosage

Children (not FDA-approved for use in children <18 years of age):

<6 months: Dose not established

>6 months:

Oral: Initial: 0.015 mg/kg/dose once daily or every other day; maximum dose: 0.1 mg/kg/day

I.M., I.V.: Dose not established

Adults:

Oral: 0.5-2 mg/dose 1-2 times/day; maximum: 10 mg/day

I.M., I.V.: 0.5-1 mg/dose; maximum: 10 mg/day

Continuous I.V. infusions of 0.9-1 mg/hour may be more effective than bolus dosing

Administration Administer I.V. slowly, over 1-2 minutes; an alternate-day schedule or a 3-4 daily dosing regimen with rest periods of 1-2 days in between may be the most tolerable and effective regimen for the continued control of edema; reserve I.V. administration for those unable to take oral medications

Monitoring Parameters Blood pressure, serum electrolytes, renal function

Patient Information May be taken with food or milk; rise slowly from a lying or sitting position to minimize dizziness, lightheadedness or fainting; also use extra care when exercising, standing for long periods of time, and during hot weather; take last dose of day early in the evening to prevent nocturia

Nursing Implications Be alert to complaints about hearing difficulty

Dosage Forms

Injection: 0.25 mg/mL (2 mL, 4 mL, 10 mL)

Tablet: 0.5 mg, 1 mg, 2 mg

♦ **Bumex®** *see Bumetanide on this page*

♦ **Buminate®** *see Albumin on page 34*

♦ **Buphenyl®** *see Sodium Phenylbutyrate on page 1070*

Bupivacaine (byoo PIV a kane)

U.S. Brand Names Marcaine®; Sensorcaine®; Sensorcaine®-MPF

Synonyms Bupivacaine Hydrochloride

Therapeutic Category Local Anesthetic, Injectable

Use Local anesthetic (injectable) for peripheral nerve block, infiltration, sympathetic block, caudal or epidural block, retrobulbar block

Pregnancy Risk Factor C

Contraindications Hypersensitivity to bupivacaine hydrochloride or any component, para-aminobenzoic acid or parabens

Warnings/Precautions Use with caution in patients with liver disease. Some commercially available formulations contain sodium metabisulfite, which may cause allergic-type reactions. Pending further data, should not be used in children <12 years of age and the solution for spinal anesthesia should not be used in children <18 years of age. **Do not use solutions containing preservatives for caudal or epidural block**; convulsions due to systemic toxicity leading to cardiac arrest have been reported, presumably following unintentional intravascular injection. 0.75% is **not** recommended for obstetrical anesthesia.

Adverse Reactions 1% to 10% (dose related):
Cardiovascular: Cardiac arrest, hypotension, bradycardia, palpitations
Central nervous system: Seizures, restlessness, anxiety, dizziness
Gastrointestinal: Nausea, vomiting
Neuromuscular & skeletal: Weakness
Ocular: Blurred vision
Otic: Tinnitus
Respiratory: Apnea

Overdosage/Toxicology Treatment is primarily symptomatic and supportive. Termination of anesthesia by pneumatic tourniquet inflation should be attempted when the agent is administered by infiltration or regional injection
Seizures commonly respond to diazepam, while hypotension responds to I.V. fluids and Trendelenburg positioning
Bradyarrhythmias (when the heart rate is <60) can be treated with I.V., or S.C. atropine 15 mcg/kg
With the development of metabolic acidosis, I.V. sodium bicarbonate 0.5-2 mEq/kg and ventilatory assistance should be instituted
Methemoglobinemia should be treated with methylene blue 1-2 mg/kg in a 1% sterile aqueous solution I.V. push over 4-6 minutes repeated up to a total dose of 7 mg/kg.

Drug Interactions
Increased effect: Hyaluronidase
Increased toxicity: Beta-blockers, ergot-type oxytocics, MAO inhibitors, TCAs, phenothiazines, vasopressors

Stability Solutions with epinephrine should be protected from light

Mechanism of Action Blocks both the initiation and conduction of nerve impulses by decreasing the neuronal membrane's permeability to sodium ions, which results in inhibition of depolarization with resultant blockade of conduction

Pharmacodynamics/Kinetics
Onset of anesthesia (dependent on route administered): Within 4-10 minutes generally
Duration of action: 1.5-8.5 hours
Metabolism: In the liver
Half-life (age dependent): Neonates: 8.1 hours; Adults: 1.5-5.5 hours
Elimination: Small amounts (~6%) excreted in urine

Usual Dosage Dose varies with procedure, depth of anesthesia, vascularity of tissues, duration of anesthesia and condition of patient. Metabisulfites (in epinephrine-containing injection); do not use solutions containing preservatives for caudal or epidural block.

Caudal block (with or without epinephrine):
Children: 1-3.7 mg/kg
Adults: 15-30 mL of 0.25% or 0.5%
Epidural block (other than caudal block):
Children: 1.25 mg/kg/dose
Adults: 10-20 mL of 0.25% or 0.5%
Peripheral nerve block: 5 mL dose of 0.25% or 0.5% (12.5-25 mg); maximum: 2.5 mg/kg (plain); 3 mg/kg (with epinephrine); up to a maximum of 400 mg/day
Sympathetic nerve block: 20-50 mL of 0.25% (no epinephrine) solution

Monitoring Parameters Monitor fetal heart rate during paracervical anesthesia

Patient Information Do not chew food in anesthetized region to prevent traumatizing tongue, lip, or buccal mucosa; single dose is usually sufficient in most applications

Dosage Forms
Injection, as hydrochloride: 0.25% (10 mL, 20 mL, 30 mL, 50 mL); 0.5% (10 mL, 20 mL, 30 mL, 50 mL); 0.75% (2 mL, 10 mL, 20 mL, 30 mL)
Injection, as hydrochloride, with epinephrine (1:200,000): 0.25% (10 mL, 30 mL, 50 mL); 0.5% (1.8 mL, 3 mL, 5 mL, 10 mL, 30 mL, 50 mL); 0.75% (30 mL)

♦ **Bupivacaine Hydrochloride** see Bupivacaine on this page
♦ **Buprenex®** see Buprenorphine on this page

Buprenorphine (byoo pre NOR feen)

Related Information
Narcotic Agonists Comparison on page 1328

U.S. Brand Names Buprenex®

Synonyms Buprenorphine Hydrochloride

Therapeutic Category Analgesic, Narcotic

Use Management of moderate to severe pain

Restrictions C-V

Pregnancy Risk Factor C

Contraindications Hypersensitivity to buprenorphine or any component

Warnings/Precautions Use with caution in patients with hepatic dysfunction or possible neurologic injury; may precipitate abstinence syndrome in narcotic-dependent patients; tolerance or drug dependence may result from extended use

Adverse Reactions
>10%: Central nervous system: Drowsiness
1% to 10%:
 Cardiovascular: Hypotension
 Central nervous system: Respiratory depression, dizziness, headache
 Gastrointestinal: Vomiting, nausea
<1%: Euphoria, slurred speech, malaise, allergic dermatitis, urinary retention, paresthesia, blurred vision

Overdosage/Toxicology
Symptoms of overdose include CNS depression, pinpoint pupils, hypotension, bradycardia

Treatment of an overdose includes support of the patient's airway, establishment of an I.V. line, and administration of naloxone 2 mg I.V. (0.01 mg/kg for children) with repeat administration as necessary up to a total of 10 mg

Drug Interactions Increased toxicity: Barbiturates, benzodiazepines (increase CNS and respiratory depression)

Stability Protect from excessive heat (>40°C/104°F) and light
 Compatible with 0.9% sodium chloride, lactated Ringer's solution, 5% dextrose in water, scopolamine, haloperidol, glycopyrrolate, droperidol, and hydroxyzine
 Incompatible with diazepam, lorazepam

Mechanism of Action Opiate agonist/antagonist that produces analgesia by binding to kappa and mu opiate receptors in the CNS

Pharmacodynamics/Kinetics
Onset of analgesia: Within 10-30 minutes
Absorption: I.M., S.C.: 30% to 40%
Distribution: V_d: 97-187 L/kg
Protein binding: High
Metabolism: Mainly in the liver; undergoes extensive first-pass metabolism
Half-life: 2.2-3 hours
Elimination: 70% excreted in feces via bile and 20% in urine as unchanged drug

Usual Dosage I.M., slow I.V.:
Children ≥13 years and Adults: 0.3-0.6 mg every 6 hours as needed
Elderly: 0.15 mg every 6 hours; elderly patients are more likely to suffer from confusion and drowsiness compared to younger patients
Long-term use is not recommended

Monitoring Parameters Pain relief, respiratory and mental status, CNS depression, blood pressure

Patient Information May cause drowsiness

Nursing Implications Gradual withdrawal of drug is necessary to avoid withdrawal symptoms

Additional Information 0.3 mg = 10 mg morphine or 75 mg meperidine, has longer duration of action than either agent

Dosage Forms Injection, as hydrochloride: 0.3 mg/mL (1 mL)

♦ **Buprenorphine Hydrochloride** see Buprenorphine on previous page

Bupropion (byoo PROE pee on)
Related Information
 Antidepressant Agents Comparison on page 1301

U.S. Brand Names Wellbutrin®; Wellbutrin® SR; Zyban™

Therapeutic Category Antidepressant, Miscellaneous

Use Treatment of depression; adjunct in smoking cessation

Pregnancy Risk Factor B

Contraindications Seizure disorder, prior diagnosis of bulimia or anorexia nervosa, known hypersensitivity to bupropion, concurrent use of a monoamine oxidase (MAO) inhibitor

Warnings/Precautions The estimated seizure potential is increased many fold in doses in the 450-600 mg/day range; giving a single dose <150 mg will lessen the seizure potential; use in patients with renal or hepatic impairment increases possible toxic effects

Adverse Reactions
>10%:
 Central nervous system: Agitation, insomnia, fever, headache, psychosis, confusion, anxiety, restlessness, dizziness, seizures, chills, akathisia
 Gastrointestinal: Nausea, vomiting, xerostomia, constipation, weight loss
 Genitourinary: Impotence
 Neuromuscular & skeletal: Tremor
1% to 10%:
 Central nervous system: Hallucinations, fatigue
 Dermatologic: Rash
 Ocular: Blurred vision
(Continued)

Bupropion *(Continued)*

<1%: Syncope, drowsiness

Overdosage/Toxicology

Symptoms of overdose include labored breathing, salivation, arched back, ataxia, convulsions, sedation, coma, and respiratory depression especially with coingestion of alcohol; bupropion may cause sinus tachycardia and seizures

Treatment is supportive following initial decontamination with activated charcoal (lavage with massive and recent doses). Treat seizures with I.V. benzodiazepines and supportive therapies; dialysis may be of limited value after drug absorption because of slow tissue to plasma diffusion.

Drug Interactions CYP2B6 and 2D6 enzyme substrate, CYP3A3/4 enzyme substrate (minor)

Decreased effects: Increased clearance: Carbamazepine, phenytoin, cimetidine, pheno-barbital

Increased effects: Levodopa, MAO inhibitors

Mechanism of Action Antidepressant structurally different from all other previously marketed antidepressants; like other antidepressants the mechanism of bupropion's activity is not fully understood; weak blocker of serotonin and norepinephrine re-uptake, inhibits neuronal dopamine re-uptake and is **not** a monoamine oxidase A or B inhibitor

Pharmacodynamics/Kinetics

Absorption: Rapidly absorbed from GI tract

Distribution: V_d: 19-21 L/kg

Protein binding: 82% to 88%

Metabolism: Extensively in the liver to multiple metabolites

Half-life: 14 hours

Time to peak serum concentration: Oral: Within 3 hours

Usual Dosage Oral:

Adults:

Depression: 100 mg 3 times/day; begin at 100 mg twice daily; may increase to a maximum dose of 450 mg/day

Smoking cessation: Initiate with 150 mg once daily for 3 days; increase to 150 mg twice daily; treatment should continue for 7-12 weeks

Elderly: Depression: 50-100 mg/day, increase by 50-100 mg every 3-4 days as tolerated; there is evidence that the elderly respond at 150 mg/day in divided doses, but some may require a higher dose

Dosing adjustment/comments in renal or hepatic impairment: Patients with renal or hepatic failure should receive a reduced dosage initially and be closely monitored

Dietary Considerations Alcohol: Additive CNS effects, avoid use

Monitoring Parameters Monitor body weight

Reference Range Therapeutic levels (trough, 12 hours after last dose): 50-100 ng/mL

Test Interactions Decreased prolactin levels

Patient Information Take in equally divided doses 3-4 times/day to minimize the risk of seizures; avoid alcohol; do not take more than recommended dose or more than 150 mg in a single dose; do not discontinue abruptly, may take 3-4 weeks for full effect; may impair driving or other motor or cognitive skills and judgment

Nursing Implications Be aware that drug may cause seizures; dose should not be increased by more than 50 mg/day once weekly

Dosage Forms

Tablet: 75 mg, 100 mg

Tablet, sustained release: 100 mg, 150 mg

Tablet, sustained release (Zyban™): 150 mg

- ◆ **Burinex**® *see* Bumetanide *on page 159*
- ◆ **BuSpar**® *see* Buspirone *on this page*

Buspirone *(byoo SPYE rone)*

U.S. Brand Names BuSpar®

Synonyms Buspirone Hydrochloride

Therapeutic Category Antianxiety Agent

Use Management of anxiety; has shown little potential for abuse

Pregnancy Risk Factor B

Contraindications Hypersensitivity to buspirone or any component

Warnings/Precautions Safety and efficacy not established in children <18 years of age; use in hepatic or renal impairment is not recommended; does not prevent or treat withdrawal from benzodiazepines

Adverse Reactions

>10%:

Central nervous system: Dizziness, lightheadedness, headache, restlessness

Gastrointestinal: Nausea

1% to 10%: Central nervous system: Drowsiness

<1%: Chest pain, tachycardia, confusion, insomnia, nightmares, sedation, disorientation, excitement, fever, ataxia, rash, urticaria, xerostomia, vomiting, diarrhea, flatulence, leukopenia, eosinophilia, muscle weakness, blurred vision, tinnitus

Overdosage/Toxicology

Symptoms of overdose include dizziness, drowsiness, pinpoint pupils, nausea, vomiting

There is no known antidote for buspirone, treatment is supportive

Drug Interactions CYP3A3/4 enzyme substrate

Increased effects/toxicity: MAO inhibitors, phenothiazines, CNS depressants; increased toxicity of digoxin and haloperidol; coadministration of buspirone with cimetidine was found to increase the maximal concentrations of buspirone, but to have no effects on the AUC

Mechanism of Action The mechanism of action of buspirone is unknown; it differs from typical benzodiazepine anxiolytics in that it does not exert anticonvulsant or muscle relaxant effects; it also lacks the prominent sedative effect that is associated with more typical anxiolytics; *in vitro* preclinical studies have shown that buspirone has a high affinity for serotonin (5-HT$_{1A}$) receptors; buspirone has no significant affinity for benzodiazepine receptors and does not affect GABA binding *in vitro* or *in vivo* when tested in preclinical models; buspirone has moderate affinity for brain D_2-dopamine receptors; some studies do suggest that buspirone may have indirect effects on other neurotransmitter systems

Pharmacodynamics/Kinetics

Protein binding: 86%

Metabolism: In the liver by oxidation and undergoes extensive first-pass metabolism

Half-life: 2-3 hours

Time to peak serum concentration: Oral: Within 40-60 minutes

Usual Dosage Adults: Oral: 15 mg/day (5 mg 3 times/day); may increase in increments of 5 mg/day every 2-4 days to a maximum of 60 mg/day

Note: The safety and efficacy profile of buspirone in elderly patients has been demonstrated to be similar to those in younger patients; there were no effects of age on its pharmacokinetics

Dosing adjustment in renal or hepatic impairment: Dosage should be decreased in patients with severe hepatic insufficiency; in anuric patients, doses should be reduced by 25% to 50% of usual dose

Monitoring Parameters Mental status, symptoms of anxiety; monitor for benzodiazepine withdrawal

Test Interactions ↑ AST, ALT, growth hormone(s), prolactin (S)

Patient Information Report any change in senses (ie, smelling, hearing, vision); cautious use with alcohol is recommended; cannot be substituted for benzodiazepines unless directed by a physician; takes 2-3 weeks to see the full effect of this medication; if you miss a dose, do **not** double your next dose

Dosage Forms Tablet, as hydrochloride: 5 mg, 10 mg, 15 mg

♦ **Buspirone Hydrochloride** *see* Buspirone *on previous page*

Busulfan (byoo SUL fan)

Related Information

Cancer Chemotherapy Regimens *on page 1263*

Toxicities of Chemotherapeutic Agents *on page 1288*

U.S. Brand Names Myleran®

Therapeutic Category Antineoplastic Agent, Alkylating Agent

Use

Oral: Chronic myelogenous leukemia and bone marrow disorders, such as polycythemia vera and myeloid metaplasia, conditioning regimens for bone marrow transplantation

I.V.: Combination therapy with cyclophosphamide as a conditioning regimen prior to allogeneic hematopoietic progenitor cell transplantation for chronic myelogenous leukemia

Pregnancy Risk Factor D

Contraindications Failure to respond to previous courses; should not be used in pregnancy or lactation; hypersensitivity to busulfan or any component

Warnings/Precautions The U.S. Food and Drug Administration (FDA) currently recommends that procedures for proper handling and disposal of antineoplastic agents be considered. May induce severe bone marrow hypoplasia; reduce or discontinue dosage at first sign, as reflected by an abnormal decrease in any of the formed elements of the blood; use with caution in patients recently given other myelosuppressive drugs or radiation treatment. If white blood count is high, hydration and allopurinol should be employed to prevent hyperuricemia.

Adverse Reactions

>10%:

Dermatologic: Urticaria, erythema, alopecia

Endocrine & metabolic: Ovarian suppression, amenorrhea, sterility

Genitourinary: Azospermia, testicular atrophy; malignant tumors have been reported in patients on busulfan therapy

Hematologic: Severe pancytopenia, leukopenia, thrombocytopenia, anemia, and bone marrow suppression are common and patients should be monitored closely while on therapy; since this is a delayed effect (busulfan affects the stem cells), the drug should be discontinued temporarily at the first sign of a large or rapid fall in any blood element; some patients may develop bone marrow fibrosis or chronic aplasia which is probably due to the busulfan toxicity; in large doses, busulfan is myeloablative and is used for this reason in BMT

Myelosuppressive:

WBC: Moderate

Platelets: Moderate

Onset (days): 7-10

Nadir (days): 14-21

Recovery (days): 28

(Continued)

Busulfan *(Continued)*

1% to 10%:
  Dermatologic: Skin hyperpigmentation (busulfan tan)
  Gastrointestinal: Nausea, vomiting, diarrhea; drug has little effect on the GI mucosal lining
    Emetic potential: Low (<10%)
  Hepatic: Elevated LFTs
  Neuromuscular & skeletal: Weakness
  Ocular: Cataracts
<1%: Generalized or myoclonic seizures and loss of consciousness have been associated with high-dose busulfan (4 mg/kg/day), endocardial fibrosis, adrenal suppression, gynecomastia, hyperuricemia, isolated cases of hemorrhagic cystitis have been reported, hepatic dysfunction, cataracts, blurred vision; after long-term or high-dose therapy, a syndrome known as busulfan lung may occur; this syndrome is manifested by a diffuse interstitial pulmonary fibrosis and persistent cough, fever, rales, and dyspnea. May be relieved by corticosteroids.

Overdosage/Toxicology
Symptoms of overdose include leukopenia, thrombocytopenia
Induction of vomiting or gastric lavage with charcoal is indicated for recent ingestions; the effects of dialysis are unknown

Drug Interactions CYP3A3/4 enzyme substrate

Stability Store unopened ampuls under refrigeration at 2°C to 8°C/36°F to 46°F
Dilute busulfan injection in 0.9% sodium chloride injection or dextrose 5% in water. The dilution volume should be ten times the volume of busulfan injection, ensuring that the final concentration of busulfan is ≥0.5 mg/mL. This solution is stable for up to 8 hours at room temperature (25°C) but the infusion must also be completed within that 8-hour time frame. Dilution of busulfan injection in 0.9% sodium chloride is stable for up to 12 hours at refrigeration (2°C to 8°C) but the infusion must also be completed within that 12-hour time frame.

Mechanism of Action Reacts with N-7 position of guanosine and interferes with DNA replication and transcription of RNA. Busulfan has a more marked effect on myeloid cells (and is, therefore, useful in the treatment of CML) than on lymphoid cells. The drug is also very toxic to hematopoietic stem cells (thus its usefulness in high doses in BMT preparative regimens). Busulfan exhibits little immunosuppressive activity. Interferes with the normal function of DNA by alkylation and cross-linking the strands of DNA.

Pharmacodynamics/Kinetics
Absorption: Rapidly and completely from the GI tract
Distribution: V_d: ~1 L/kg; distributed into the CSF and saliva with levels similar to plasma
Protein binding: ~14%
Metabolism: Extensive in the liver (may increase with multiple dosing)
Half-life: After first dose: 3.4 hours; After last dose: 2.3 hours
Time to peak serum concentration: Oral: Within 4 hours; I.V.: Within 5 minutes
Elimination: 10% to 50% excreted in the urine as metabolites within 24 hours; <2% seen as unchanged drug

Usual Dosage Busulfan should be based on adjusted ideal body weight because actual body weight, ideal body weight, or other factors can produce significant differences in busulfan clearance among lean, normal, and obese patients
Oral (refer to individual protocols):
  Children:
    For remission induction of CML: 0.06-0.12 mg/kg/day **OR** 1.8-4.6 mg/m²/day; titrate dosage to maintain leukocyte count above 40,000/mm³; reduce dosage by 50% if the leukocyte count reaches 30,000-40,000/mm³; discontinue drug if counts fall to ≤20,000/mm³
    BMT marrow-ablative conditioning regimen: 1 mg/kg/dose (ideal body weight) every 6 hours for 16 doses
  Adults:
    BMT marrow-ablative conditioning regimen: 1 mg/kg/dose (ideal body weight) every 6 hours for 16 doses
    Remission: Induction of CML: 4-8 mg/day (may be as high as 12 mg/day); Maintenance doses: Controversial, range from 1-4 mg/day to 2 mg/week; treatment is continued until WBC reaches 10,000-20,000 cells/mm³ at which time drug is discontinued; when WBC reaches 50,000/mm³, maintenance dose is resumed
  Unapproved uses:
    Polycythemia vera: 2-6 mg/day
    Thrombocytosis: 4-6 mg/day

I.V.: 0.8 mg/kg (ideal body weight or actual body weight, whichever is lower) every 6 hours for 4 days (a total of 16 doses)
  I.V. dosing in morbidly obese patients: Dosing should be based on adjusted ideal body weight (AIBW) which should be calculated as ideal body weight (IBW) + 0.25 times (actual weight minus ideal body weight)
    AIBW = IBW + 0.25 x (AW - IBW)
  Cyclophosphamide, in combination with busulfan, is given on each of two days as a 1-hour infusion at a dose of 160 mg/m² beginning on day 3, 6 hours following the 16th dose of busulfan

Administration Intravenous busulfan should be administered via a CENTRAL venous catheter as a 2-hour infusion - every 6 hours for 4 consecutive days for a total of 16 doses

Monitoring Parameters CBC with differential and platelet count, hemoglobin, liver function tests

Patient Information Contraceptive measures are recommended during therapy; watch for signs of bleeding; excellent oral hygiene is needed to minimize oral discomfort

Dosage Forms
Injection: 60 mg/10 mL ampuls
Tablet: 2 mg

Butabarbital Sodium (byoo ta BAR bi tal SOW dee um)

U.S. Brand Names Butalan®; Buticaps®; Butisol Sodium®

Therapeutic Category Barbiturate; Hypnotic; Sedative

Use Sedative, hypnotic

Restrictions C-III

Pregnancy Risk Factor D

Contraindications Hypersensitivity to butabarbital or any component, presence of acute or chronic pain, latent porphyria, marked liver impairment

Adverse Reactions
>10%: Central nervous system: Dizziness, lightheadedness, drowsiness, "hangover" effect

1% to 10%:
Central nervous system: Confusion, mental depression, unusual excitement, nervousness, faint feeling, headache, insomnia, nightmares
Gastrointestinal: Constipation, nausea, vomiting

<1%: Hypotension, hallucinations, rash, exfoliative dermatitis, Stevens-Johnson syndrome, angioedema, agranulocytosis, megaloblastic anemia, thrombocytopenia, thrombophlebitis, respiratory depression, dependence

Overdosage/Toxicology
Symptoms of overdose include slurred speech, confusion, nystagmus, tachycardia, hypotension
If hypotension occurs, administer I.V. fluids and place the patient in the Trendelenburg position; if unresponsive, an I.V. vasopressor (eg, dopamine, epinephrine) may be required. Forced alkaline diuresis is of no value in the treatment of intoxications with short-acting barbiturates. Charcoal hemoperfusion or hemodialysis may be useful in the harder to treat intoxications, especially in the presence of very high serum barbiturate levels.

Drug Interactions
Decreased effect: Phenothiazines, haloperidol, quinidine, cyclosporine, TCAs, corticosteroids, theophylline, ethosuximide, warfarin, oral contraceptives, chloramphenicol, griseofulvin, doxycycline, beta-blockers
Increased effect/toxicity: Propoxyphene, benzodiazepines, CNS depressants, valproic acid, methylphenidate, chloramphenicol

Mechanism of Action Interferes with transmission of impulses from the thalamus to the cortex of the brain resulting in an imbalance in central inhibitory and facilitatory mechanisms

Pharmacodynamics/Kinetics
Distribution: V_d: 0.8 L/kg
Protein binding: 26%
Metabolism: In the liver
Half-life: 40-140 hours
Time to peak serum concentration: Oral: Within 40-60 minutes
Elimination: In urine as metabolites

Usual Dosage Oral:
Children: Preop: 2-6 mg/kg/dose; maximum: 100 mg
Adults:
Sedative: 15-30 mg 3-4 times/day
Hypnotic: 50-100 mg
Preop: 50-100 mg 1-1½ hours before surgery

Dietary Considerations Alcohol: Additive CNS effects, avoid use

Reference Range Therapeutic: Not established; Toxic: 28-73 µg/mL

Test Interactions ↑ ammonia (B); ↓ bilirubin (S)

Patient Information May cause drowsiness, avoid alcohol or other CNS depressants, may impair judgment and coordination; may cause physical and psychological dependence with prolonged use; do not exceed recommended dose

Nursing Implications Raise bed rails; initiate safety measures; aid with ambulation; monitor for CNS depression

Dosage Forms
Capsule: 15 mg, 30 mg
Elixir, with alcohol 7%: 30 mg/5 mL (480 mL, 3780 mL); 33.3 mg/5 mL (480 mL, 3780 mL)
Tablet: 15 mg, 30 mg, 50 mg, 100 mg

◆ **Butace®** see Butalbital Compound on this page

◆ **Butalan®** see Butabarbital Sodium on this page

Butalbital Compound (byoo TAL bi tal KOM pound)

U.S. Brand Names Amaphen®; Anoquan®; Axotal®; B-A-C®; Bancap®; Butace®; Endolor®; Esgic®; Femcet®; Fiorgen PF®; Fioricet®; Fiorinal®; G-1®; Isollyl® Improved; Lanorinal®; Marnal®; Medigesic®; Phrenilin®; Phrenilin® Forte; Repan®; Sedapap-10®; Triapin®; Two-Dyne®
(Continued)

Butalbital Compound *(Continued)*

Canadian Brand Names Tecnal®

Therapeutic Category Barbiturate

Use Relief of symptomatic complex of tension or muscle contraction headache

Restrictions C-III (Fiorinal®)

Pregnancy Risk Factor D

Contraindications Patients with porphyria, known hypersensitivity to butalbital or any component

Warnings/Precautions Children and teenagers should not use for chickenpox or flu symptoms before a physician is consulted about Reye's syndrome (Fiorinal®)

Adverse Reactions

>10%:

Central nervous system: Dizziness, lightheadedness, drowsiness, "hangover" effect

Gastrointestinal: Nausea, heartburn, stomach pains, dyspepsia, epigastric discomfort

1% to 10%:

Central nervous system: Confusion, mental depression, unusual excitement, nervousness, faint feeling, headache, insomnia, nightmares, fatigue

Dermatologic: Rash

Gastrointestinal: Constipation, vomiting, gastrointestinal ulceration

Hematologic: Hemolytic anemia

Neuromuscular & skeletal: Weakness

Respiratory: Dyspnea

Miscellaneous: Anaphylactic shock

<1%: Hypotension, hallucinations, jitters, exfoliative dermatitis, Stevens-Johnson syndrome, agranulocytosis, megaloblastic anemia, occult bleeding, prolongation of bleeding time, leukopenia, thrombocytopenia, iron deficiency anemia, hepatotoxicity, thrombophlebitis, impaired renal function, respiratory depression, bronchospasm

Overdosage/Toxicology

Symptoms of overdose include slurred speech, confusion, nystagmus, tachycardia, hypotension, tinnitus, headache, dizziness, confusion, metabolic acidosis, hyperpyrexia, hypoglycemia, coma, hepatic necrosis, blood dyscrasias, respiratory depression

Forced alkaline diuresis is of no value in the treatment of intoxications with short-acting barbiturates. Charcoal hemoperfusion or hemodialysis may be useful in the harder to treat intoxications, especially in the presence of very high serum barbiturate levels; see also Acetaminophen for Fioricet® toxicology or Aspirin for Fiorinal® toxicology.

Drug Interactions

Decreased effect: Phenothiazines, haloperidol, quinidine, cyclosporine, TCAs, corticosteroids, theophylline, ethosuximide, warfarin, oral contraceptives, chloramphenicol, griseofulvin, doxycycline, beta-blockers

Increased effect/toxicity: Propoxyphene, benzodiazepines, CNS depressants, valproic acid, methylphenidate, chloramphenicol

Mechanism of Action Butalbital, like other barbiturates, has a generalized depressant effect on the central nervous system (CNS). Barbiturates have little effect on peripheral nerves or muscle at usual therapeutic doses. However, at toxic doses serious effects on the cardiovascular system and other peripheral systems may be observed. These effects may result in hypotension or skeletal muscle weakness. While all areas of the central nervous system are acted on by barbiturates, the mesencephalic reticular activating system is extremely sensitive to their effects. Barbiturates act at synapses where gamma-aminobenzoic acid is a neurotransmitter, but they may act in other areas as well.

Usual Dosage Adults: Oral: 1-2 tablets or capsules every 4 hours; not to exceed 6/day

Dosing interval in renal or hepatic impairment: Should be reduced

Dietary Considerations Alcohol: Additive CNS effects, avoid use

Patient Information Children and teenagers should not use this product; may cause drowsiness, avoid alcohol or other CNS depressants, may impair judgment and coordination; may cause physical and psychological dependence with prolonged use; do not exceed recommended dose

Nursing Implications Raise bed rails; initiate safety measures; aid with ambulation; monitor for CNS depression

Dosage Forms

Capsule, with acetaminophen:

Amaphen®, Anoquan®, Butace®, Endolor®, Esgic®, Femcet®, G-1®, Medigesic®, Repan®, Two-Dyne®: Butalbital 50 mg, caffeine 40 mg, and acetaminophen 325 mg

Bancap®, Triapin®: Butalbital 50 mg and acetaminophen 325 mg

Phrenilin® Forte: Butalbital 50 mg and acetaminophen 650 mg

Capsule, with aspirin: (Fiorgen PF®, Fiorinal®, Isollyl® Improved, Lanorinal®, Marnal®): Butalbital 50 mg, caffeine 40 mg, and aspirin 325 mg

Tablet, with acetaminophen:

Esgic®, Fioricet®, Repan®: Butalbital 50 mg, caffeine 40 mg, and acetaminophen 325 mg

Phrenilin®: Butalbital 50 mg and acetaminophen 325 mg

Sedapap-10®: Butalbital 50 mg and acetaminophen 650 mg

Tablet, with aspirin:

Axotal®: Butalbital 50 mg and aspirin 650 mg

B-A-C®: Butalbital 50 mg, caffeine 40 mg, and aspirin 650 mg

Fiorinal®, Isollyl® Improved, Lanorinal®, Marnal®: Butalbital 50 mg, caffeine 40 mg, and aspirin 325 mg

Butenafine (byoo TEN a fine)

U.S. Brand Names Mentax®

Synonyms Butenafine Hydrochloride

Therapeutic Category Antifungal Agent, Topical

Use Topical treatment of tinea pedis (athlete's foot) and tinea cruris (jock itch)

Pregnancy Risk Factor B

Contraindications Hypersensitivity to butenafine or components

Warnings/Precautions Only for topical use (not ophthalmic, vaginal, or internal routes); patients sensitive to other allylamine antifungals may cross-react with butenafine

Adverse Reactions
>1%: Dermatologic: Burning, stinging, irritation, erythema, pruritus (2%)
<1%: Contact dermatitis

Mechanism of Action Butenafine exerts antifungal activity by blocking squalene epoxidation, resulting in inhibition of ergosterol synthesis (antidermatophyte and *Sporothrix schenckii* activity). In higher concentrations, the drug disrupts fungal cell membranes (anticandidal activity).

Pharmacodynamics/Kinetics
Absorption: Minimal systemic absorption when topically applied
Metabolism: Hepatic; principle metabolite via hydroxylation
Half-life: 35 hours
Time to peak serum concentration: 6 hours (10 ng/mL)

Usual Dosage Children >12 years and Adults: Topical: Apply once daily for 4 weeks to the affected area and surrounding skin

Monitoring Parameters Culture and KOH exam, clinical signs of tinea pedis

Patient Information Report any signs of rash or allergy to your physician immediately; do not apply other topical medications on the same area as butenafine unless directed by your physician

Dosage Forms Cream, as hydrochloride: 1% (2 g, 15 g, 30 g)

♦ **Butenafine Hydrochloride** *see* Butenafine *on this page*
♦ **Buticaps®** *see* Butabarbital Sodium *on page 165*
♦ **Butisol Sodium®** *see* Butabarbital Sodium *on page 165*

Butoconazole (byoo toe KOE na zole)

Related Information
Treatment of Sexually Transmitted Diseases *on page 1429*

U.S. Brand Names Femstat®

Synonyms Butoconazole Nitrate

Therapeutic Category Antifungal Agent, Imidazole Derivative; Antifungal Agent, Vaginal

Use Local treatment of vulvovaginal candidiasis

Pregnancy Risk Factor C (For use only in 2nd or 3rd trimester)

Contraindications Known hypersensitivity to butoconazole

Warnings/Precautions In pregnancy, use only during 2nd or 3rd trimesters; if irritation or sensitization occurs, discontinue use

Adverse Reactions
1% to 10%: Genitourinary: Vulvar/vaginal burning
<1%: Vulvar itching, soreness, edema, or discharge; polyuria

Stability Do not store at temperatures >40°C/104°F; avoid freezing

Mechanism of Action Increases cell membrane permeability in susceptible fungi (*Candida*)

Pharmacodynamics/Kinetics
Absorption: Following intravaginal application small amounts of drug are absorbed systemically (25%) within 2-8 hours
Half-life: 21-24 hours
Elimination: Into urine and feces in approximate equal amounts

Usual Dosage Adults:
Nonpregnant: Insert 1 applicatorful (~5 g) intravaginally at bedtime as a single dose; therapy may extend for up to 6 days, if necessary, as directed by physician
Pregnant: **Use only during 2nd or 3rd trimester**

Patient Information May cause burning or stinging on application; if symptoms of vaginitis persist, contact physician

Dosage Forms Cream, vaginal, as nitrate: 2% with applicator (28 g)

♦ **Butoconazole Nitrate** *see* Butoconazole *on this page*

Butorphanol (byoo TOR fa nole)

Related Information
Narcotic Agonists Comparison *on page 1328*

U.S. Brand Names Stadol®; Stadol® NS

Synonyms Butorphanol Tartrate

Therapeutic Category Analgesic, Narcotic

Use Management of moderate to severe pain

Restrictions C-IV

Pregnancy Risk Factor B (D if used for prolonged periods or in high doses at term)

Contraindications Hypersensitivity to butorphanol or any component; avoid use in opiate-dependent patients who have not been detoxified, may precipitate opiate withdrawal

(Continued)

Butorphanol *(Continued)*

Warnings/Precautions Use with caution in patients with hepatic/renal dysfunction, may elevate CSF pressure, may increase cardiac workload; tolerance of drug dependence may result from extended use

Adverse Reactions

>10%: Central nervous system: Drowsiness

1% to 10%:

Cardiovascular: Flushing of the face, hypotension

Central nervous system: Dizziness, lightheadedness, headache

Gastrointestinal: Anorexia, nausea, vomiting

Genitourinary: Decreased urination

Miscellaneous: Diaphoresis (increased)

<1%: Bradycardia or tachycardia, hypertension, paradoxical CNS stimulation, confusion, hallucinations, mental depression, false sense of well being, malaise, restlessness, nightmares, CNS depression, rash, stomach cramps, constipation, xerostomia, painful urination, blurred vision, tinnitus, weakness, shortness of breath, dyspnea, respiratory depression, dependence with prolonged use

Overdosage/Toxicology

Symptoms of overdose include respiratory depression, cardiac and CNS depression

Treatment of an overdose includes support of the patient's airway, establishment of an I.V. line and administration of naloxone 2 mg I.V. (0.01 mg/kg for children) with repeat administration as necessary up to a total of 10 mg

Drug Interactions Increased toxicity: CNS depressants, phenothiazines, barbiturates, skeletal muscle relaxants, alfentanil, guanabenz, MAO inhibitors

Stability Store at room temperature, protect from freezing; **incompatible** when mixed in the same syringe with diazepam, dimenhydrinate, methohexital, pentobarbital, secobarbital, thiopental

Mechanism of Action Mixed narcotic agonist-antagonist with central analgesic actions; binds to opiate receptors in the CNS, causing inhibition of ascending pain pathways, altering the perception of and response to pain; produces generalized CNS depression

Pharmacodynamics/Kinetics

Peak effect: I.M.: Within 0.5-1 hour; I.V.: Within 4-5 minutes

Absorption: Rapidly and well absorbed

Protein binding: 80%

Metabolism: In the liver

Half-life: 2.5-4 hours

Elimination: Primarily in urine

Usual Dosage Adults:

I.M.: 1-4 mg every 3-4 hours as needed

I.V.: 0.5-2 mg every 3-4 hours as needed

Nasal spray: Headache: 1 spray in 1 nostril; if adequate pain relief is not achieved within 60-90 minutes, an additional 1 spray in 1 nostril may be given (each spray gives ~1 mg of butorphanol); may repeat in 3-4 hours after the last dose as needed

Dosing adjustment in renal impairment:

Cl_{cr} 10-50 mL/minute: Administer 75% of dose

Cl_{cr} <10 mL/minute: Administer 50% of dose

Dietary Considerations Alcohol: Additive CNS effects, avoid or limit use; watch for sedation

Monitoring Parameters Pain relief, respiratory and mental status, blood pressure

Reference Range 0.7-1.5 ng/mL

Patient Information May cause drowsiness; avoid alcohol

Nursing Implications Observe for excessive sedation or confusion, respiratory depression; raise bed rails; aid with ambulation

Dosage Forms

Injection, as tartrate: 1 mg/mL (1 mL); 2 mg/mL (1 mL, 2 mL, 10 mL)

Spray, nasal, as tartrate: 10 mg/mL [14-15 doses] (2.5 mL)

♦ **Butorphanol Tartrate** *see Butorphanol on previous page*

♦ **BW-430C** *see Lamotrigine on page 658*

♦ **Byclomine® Injection** *see Dicyclomine on page 351*

♦ **Bydramine® Cough Syrup [OTC]** *see Diphenhydramine on page 369*

♦ **C2B8 Monoclonal Antibody** *see Rituximab on page 1035*

♦ **C7E3** *see Abciximab on page 15*

Cabergoline *(ca BER go leen)*

Related Information

Parkinson's Disease, Dosing of Drugs Used for Treatment of *on page 1336*

U.S. Brand Names Dostinex®

Therapeutic Category Ergot Alkaloid and Derivative

Use Treatment of hyperprolactinemic disorders, either idiopathic or due to pituitary adenomas

Unlabeled use: Adjunct for the treatment of Parkinson's disease

Pregnancy Risk Factor B

Contraindications Patients with uncontrolled hypertension or hypersensitivity to ergot derivatives

Warnings/Precautions Initial doses >1 mg may cause orthostatic hypotension. Use caution when patients are receiving other medications which may reduce blood pressure. Not indicated for the inhibition or suppression of physiologic lactation since it has been associated with cases of hypertension, stroke, and seizures. Because cabergoline is extensively metabolized by the liver, careful monitoring in patients with hepatic impairment is warranted. Female patients should instruct the physician if they are pregnant, become pregnant, or intend to become pregnant. Should not be used in patients with pregnancy-induced hypertension unless benefit outweighs potential risk. Do not give to postpartum women who are breast-feeding or planning to breast-feed. In all patients, prolactin concentrations should be monitored monthly until normalized.

Adverse Reactions

>10%:
Central nervous system: Headache (26%), dizziness (17%)
Gastrointestinal: Nausea (29%)

1% to 10%:
Body as whole: Asthenia (6%), fatigue (5%), syncope (1%), influenza-like symptoms (1%), malaise (1%), periorbital edema (1%), peripheral edema (1%)
Cardiovascular: Hot flashes (3%), hypotension (1%), dependent edema (1%), palpitations (1%)
Central nervous system: Vertigo (4%), depression (3%), somnolence (2%), anxiety (1%), insomnia (1%), impaired concentration (1%), nervousness (1%)
Dermatologic: Acne (1%), pruritus (1%)
Endocrine: Breast pain (2%), dysmenorrhea (1%)
Gastrointestinal: Constipation (7%), abdominal pain (5%), dyspepsia (5%), vomiting (4%), xerostomia (2%), diarrhea (2%), flatulence (2%), throat irritation (1%), toothache (1%), anorexia (1%)
Neuromuscular & skeletal: Pain (2%), arthralgia (1%), paresthesias (2%)
Ocular: Abnormal vision (1%)
Respiratory: Rhinitis (1%)

Overdosage/Toxicology

An overdose may produce nasal congestion, syncope, hallucinations, or hypotension
Measures to support blood pressure should be taken if necessary

Drug Interactions

Additive hypotensive effects may occur when cabergoline is administered with antihypertensive medications; dosage adjustment of the antihypertensive medication may be required
Decreased effect: Dopamine antagonists (eg, phenothiazines, butyrophenones, thioxanthenes, or metoclopramide) may reduce the therapeutic effects of cabergoline and should not be used concomitantly

Mechanism of Action Cabergoline is a long-acting dopamine receptor agonist with a high affinity for D_2 receptors; prolactin secretion by the anterior pituitary is predominantly under hypothalamic inhibitory control exerted through the release of dopamine

Pharmacodynamics/Kinetics

Distribution: Extensive tissue distribution, particularly to the pituitary
Metabolism: Extensively metabolized by the liver; minimal cytochrome P-450 metabolism
Bioavailability: The absolute bioavailability of cabergoline is unknown
Protein binding: 40% to 42%
Half-life: 63-69 hours
Time to peak: 2-3 hours

Usual Dosage Initial dose: Oral: 0.25 mg twice weekly; the dose may be increased by 0.25 mg twice weekly up to a maximum of 1 mg twice weekly according to the patient's serum prolactin level. Dosage increases should not occur more rapidly than every 4 weeks. Once a normal serum prolactin level is maintained for 6 months, the dose may be discontinued and prolactin levels monitored to determine if cabergoline is still required. The durability of efficacy beyond 24 months of therapy has not been established.

Patient Information Patient should be instructed to notify physician if she suspects she is pregnant, becomes pregnant, or intends to become pregnant during therapy with cabergoline. A pregnancy test should be done if there is any suspicion of pregnancy and continuation of treatment should be discussed with physician.

Additional Information Bromocriptine and cabergoline are the only drugs indicated for the treatment of hyperprolactinemia. In the largest comparative clinical trial, prolactin levels normalized in 77% of patients treated with cabergoline compared to 59% of patients treated with bromocriptine. In that trial, 3% of patients discontinued treatment due to adverse effects in the cabergoline group versus 12% of patients in the bromocriptine group. In addition to the improved safety and efficacy profile, cabergoline (administered twice weekly) is more convenient than bromocriptine (administered 1-3 times/day) for patients to take.

If the drug is used to prevent lactation, a single 1 mg dose is recommended on the first day after delivery. The drug is not approved for the inhibition of established lactation and should only be used to prevent lactation when there are medical reasons whereby which the potential benefits of therapy outweigh the risks, since it has been associated with cases of hypertension, stroke, and seizures.

Dosage Forms Tablet: 0.5 mg

♦ **Cafatine®** *see Ergotamine on page 426*
♦ **Cafatine-PB®** *see Ergotamine on page 426*
♦ **Cafergot®** *see Ergotamine on page 426*
♦ **Cafetrate®** *see Ergotamine on page 426*

Caffeine and Sodium Benzoate (KAF een & SOW dee um BEN zoe ate)

Therapeutic Category Diuretic, Miscellaneous
Dosage Forms Injection: Caffeine 125 mg and sodium benzoate 125 mg per mL (2 mL)

- **Calan®** *see* Verapamil *on page 1214*
- **Calan® SR** *see* Verapamil *on page 1214*
- **Cal Carb-HD®** [OTC] *see* Calcium Carbonate *on page 174*
- **Calci-Chew™** [OTC] *see* Calcium Carbonate *on page 174*
- **Calciday-667®** [OTC] *see* Calcium Carbonate *on page 174*

Calcifediol (kal si fe DYE ole)
U.S. Brand Names Calderol®
Synonyms 25-HCC; 25-Hydroxycholecalciferol; 25-Hydroxyvitamin D_3
Therapeutic Category Vitamin, Fat Soluble
Use Treatment and management of metabolic bone disease associated with chronic renal failure or hypocalcemia in patients on chronic renal dialysis
Pregnancy Risk Factor C
Contraindications Hypercalcemia; known hypersensitivity to calcifediol; malabsorption syndrome; hypervitaminosis D; significantly decreased renal function
Warnings/Precautions Adequate (supplemental) dietary calcium is necessary for clinical response to vitamin D; calcium-phosphate product (serum calcium times phosphorus) must not exceed 70; avoid hypercalcemia
Adverse Reactions Percentage unknown:
  Cardiovascular: Hypotension, cardiac arrhythmias, hypertension
  Central nervous system: Irritability, headache, somnolence, seizures (rare)
  Dermatologic: Pruritus
  Endocrine & metabolic: Hypercalcemia, polydipsia, hypermagnesemia
  Gastrointestinal: Nausea, vomiting, constipation, anorexia, pancreatitis, metallic taste, xerostomia
  Genitourinary: Polyuria
  Hepatic: Elevated LFTs
  Neuromuscular & skeletal: Myalgia, bone pain
  Ocular: Conjunctivitis, photophobia
Overdosage/Toxicology
  Rarely toxicity occurs from acute overdose. Symptoms of chronic overdose include hypercalcemia, hypercalciuria with weakness, altered mental status, GI upset, renal tubular injury, and occasionally cardiac arrhythmias.
  Following withdrawal of the drug, treatment consists of bed rest, liberal intake of fluids, reduced calcium intake, and cathartic administration. Severe hypercalcemia requires I.V. hydration and forced diuresis. I.V. saline may increase excretion of calcium. Calcitonin, cholestyramine, prednisone, sodium EDTA, biphosphonates, and mithramycin have all been used successfully to treat the more resistant cases of vitamin D-induced hypercalcemia.
Drug Interactions
  Decreased effect: Cholestyramine, colestipol
  Increased effect: Thiazide diuretics
  Additive effect: Antacids (magnesium)
Mechanism of Action Vitamin D analog that (along with calcitonin and parathyroid hormone) regulates serum calcium homeostasis by promoting absorption of calcium and phosphorus in the small intestine; promotes renal tubule resorption of phosphate; increases rate of accretion and resorption in bone minerals
Pharmacodynamics/Kinetics
  Absorption: Rapid from the small intestines
  Distribution: Activated in the kidneys; stored in liver and fat depots
  Half-life: 12-22 days
  Time to peak: Within 4 hours (oral)
  Elimination: In bile and feces
Usual Dosage Oral: Hepatic osteodystrophy:
  Infants: 5-7 mcg/kg/day
  Children and Adults: Usual dose: 20-100 mcg/day or 20-200 mcg every other day; titrate to obtain normal serum calcium/phosphate levels; increase dose at 4-week intervals; initial dose: 300-350 mcg/week, administered daily or on alternate days
Test Interactions ↑ calcium (S), cholesterol (S), magnesium, BUN, AST, ALT; ↓ alk phos
Patient Information Compliance with dose, diet, and calcium supplementation is essential; avoid taking magnesium supplements or magnesium-containing antacids; notify physician if weakness, lethargy, headache, and decreased appetite occur
Dosage Forms Capsule: 20 mcg, 50 mcg

- **Calciferol™ Injection** *see* Ergocalciferol *on page 424*
- **Calciferol™ Oral** *see* Ergocalciferol *on page 424*
- **Calcijex™** *see* Calcitriol *on page 172*
- **Calcilean®** *see* Heparin *on page 560*
- **Calcimar® Injection** *see* Calcitonin *on next page*
- **Calci-Mix™** [OTC] *see* Calcium Carbonate *on page 174*

Calcipotriene (kal si POE try een)
U.S. Brand Names Dovonex®
Therapeutic Category Topical Skin Product; Vitamin, Fat Soluble
Use Treatment of moderate plaque psoriasis
Pregnancy Risk Factor C
Contraindications Hypersensitivity to any components of the preparation; patients with demonstrated hypercalcemia or evidence of vitamin D toxicity; use on the face

Warnings/Precautions Use may cause irritations of lesions and surrounding uninvolved skin. If irritation develops, discontinue use. Transient, rapidly reversible elevation of serum calcium has occurred during use. If elevation in serum calcium occurs above the normal range, discontinue treatment until calcium levels are normal. For external use only; not for ophthalmic, oral or intravaginal use.

Adverse Reactions
>10%: Dermatologic: Burning, itching, skin irritation, erythema, dry skin, peeling, rash, worsening of psoriasis
1% to 10%: Dermatologic: Dermatitis
<1%: Skin atrophy, hyperpigmentation, folliculitis, hypercalcemia

Mechanism of Action Synthetic vitamin D_3 analog which regulates skin cell production and proliferation

Usual Dosage Adults: Topical: Apply in a thin film to the affected skin twice daily and rub in gently and completely

Patient Information For external use only; avoid contact with the face or eyes; wash hands after application

Nursing Implications Wear gloves

Dosage Forms
Cream: 0.005% (30 g, 60 g, 100 g)
Ointment, topical: 0.005% (30 g, 60 g, 100 g)
Solution, topical: 0.005%

♦ **Calcite-500** see Calcium Carbonate on page 174

Calcitonin (kal si TOE nin)

U.S. Brand Names Calcimar® Injection; Cibacalcin® Injection; Miacalcin® Injection; Miacalcin® Nasal Spray; Osteocalcin® Injection; Salmonine® Injection

Canadian Brand Names Caltine®

Synonyms Calcitonin (Human); Calcitonin (Salmon)

Therapeutic Category Antidote, Hypercalcemia

Use
Calcitonin (salmon): Treatment of Paget's disease of bone and as adjunctive therapy for hypercalcemia; also used in postmenopausal osteoporosis and osteogenesis imperfecta
Calcitonin (human): Treatment of Paget's disease of bone

Pregnancy Risk Factor C

Contraindications Hypersensitivity to salmon protein or gelatin diluent

Warnings/Precautions A skin test should be performed prior to initiating therapy of calcitonin salmon; have epinephrine immediately available for a possible hypersensitivity reaction

Adverse Reactions
>10%:
Cardiovascular: Facial flushing
Gastrointestinal: Nausea, diarrhea, anorexia
Local: Edema at injection site
1% to 10%: Genitourinary: Polyuria
<1%: Edema, chills, headache, dizziness, rash, urticaria, paresthesia, weakness, shortness of breath, nasal congestion

Overdosage/Toxicology Symptoms of overdose include nausea, vomiting, hypocalcemia, hypocalcemic tetany

Stability
Salmon calcitonin: Injection: Store under refrigeration at 2°C to 6°C/36°F to 43°F; stable for up to 2 weeks at room temperature; NS has been recommended for the dilution to prepare a skin test
Salmon calcitonin: Nasal: Store unopened bottle under refrigeration at 2°C to 8°C; Once the pump has been activated, store at room temperature
Human calcitonin: Store at <25°C/77°F and protect from light

Mechanism of Action Structurally similar to human calcitonin; it directly inhibits osteoclastic bone resorption; promotes the renal excretion of calcium, phosphate, sodium, magnesium and potassium by decreasing tubular reabsorption; increases the jejunal secretion of water, sodium, potassium, and chloride

Pharmacodynamics/Kinetics
Hypercalcemia: Onset of reduction in calcium: 2 hours; Duration of effect: 6-8 hours
Distribution: Does not cross into the placenta
Metabolism: Rapidly by the kidneys
Half-life: S.C.: 1.2 hours
Elimination: As inactive metabolites in urine

Usual Dosage
Children: Dosage not established
Adults:
Paget's disease:
Salmon calcitonin: I.M., S.C.: 100 units/day to start, 50 units/day or 50-100 units every 1-3 days maintenance dose
Human calcitonin: S.C.: Initial: 0.5 mg/day (maximum: 0.5 mg twice daily); maintenance: 0.5 mg 2-3 times/week or 0.25 mg/day
Hypercalcemia: Salmon calcitonin: I.M., S.C.: 4 units/kg every 12 hours; may increase up to 8 units/kg every 12 hours to a maximum of every 6 hours
Osteogenesis imperfecta: Salmon calcitonin: I.M., S.C.: 2 units/kg 3 times/week
(Continued)

171

Calcitonin *(Continued)*

Postmenopausal osteoporosis: Salmon calcitonin:
I.M., S.C.: 100 units/day
Intranasal: 200 units (1 spray)/day

Monitoring Parameters Serum electrolytes and calcium; alkaline phosphatase and 24-hour urine collection for hydroxyproline excretion (Paget's disease); serum calcium

Reference Range Therapeutic: <19 pg/mL (SI: 19 ng/L) basal, depending on the assay

Patient Information Nasal spray: Notify physician if you develop significant nasal irritation. To activate the pump, hold the bottle upright and depress the two white side arms toward the bottle six times until a faint spray is emitted. The pump is activated once this first faint spray has been emitted; at this point, firmly place the nozzle into the bottle. It is not necessary to reactivate the pump before each daily use. Alternate nostrils with the spray formulation.

Nursing Implications Skin test should be performed prior to administration of salmon calcitonin; refrigerate; I.M. administration is preferred if the volume to injection exceeds 2 mL

Dosage Forms

Injection:
Human (Cibacalcin®): 0.5 mg/vial
Salmon: 200 units/mL (2 mL)
Spray, nasal: **Salmon** (Miacalcin®): 200 units/activation (0.09 mL/dose) (2 mL glass bottle with pump)

♦ **Calcitonin (Human)** *see* Calcitonin *on previous page*
♦ **Calcitonin (Salmon)** *see* Calcitonin *on previous page*

Calcitriol *(kal si TRYE ole)*

Related Information
Antacid Drug Interactions *on page 1296*

U.S. Brand Names Calcijex™; Rocaltrol®

Synonyms 1,25 Dihydroxycholecalciferol

Therapeutic Category Vitamin, Fat Soluble

Use Management of hypocalcemia in patients on chronic renal dialysis; reduce elevated parathyroid hormone levels

Unlabeled use: Decrease severity of psoriatic lesions in psoriatic vulgaris; vitamin D resistant rickets

Pregnancy Risk Factor C

Contraindications Hypercalcemia; vitamin D toxicity; abnormal sensitivity to the effects of vitamin D; malabsorption syndrome

Warnings/Precautions Adequate dietary (supplemental) calcium is necessary for clinical response to vitamin D; maintain adequate fluid intake; calcium-phosphate product (serum calcium times phosphorus) must not exceed 70; avoid hypercalcemia or use with renal function impairment and secondary hyperparathyroidism

Adverse Reactions

Percentage unknown:
Cardiovascular: Hypotension, cardiac arrhythmias, hypertension
Central nervous system: Irritability, headache, somnolence, seizures (rare)
Dermatologic: Pruritus
Endocrine & metabolic: Polydipsia, hypermagnesemia
Gastrointestinal: Nausea, vomiting, constipation, anorexia, pancreatitis, metallic taste, xerostomia
Genitourinary: Polyuria
Hepatic: Elevated LFTs
Neuromuscular & skeletal: Myalgia, bone pain
Ocular: Conjunctivitis, photophobia
>10%: Endocrine & metabolic: Hypercalcemia (33%)

Overdosage/Toxicology

Rarely toxicity occurs from acute overdose. Symptoms of chronic overdose include hypercalcemia, hypercalciuria with weakness, altered mental status, GI upset, renal tubular injury, and occasionally cardiac arrhythmias.

Following withdrawal of the drug, treatment consists of bed rest, liberal intake of fluids, reduced calcium intake, and cathartic administration. Severe hypercalcemia requires I.V. hydration and forced diuresis. I.V. saline may increase excretion of calcium. Calcitonin, cholestyramine, prednisone, sodium EDTA, biphosphonates, and mithramycin have all been used successfully to treat the more resistant cases of vitamin D-induced hypercalcemia.

Drug Interactions

Decreased effect/absorption: Cholestyramine, colestipol
Increased effect: Thiazide diuretics
Additive effect: Magnesium-containing antacids

Stability Store in tight, light-resistant container; calcitriol degrades upon prolonged exposure to light

Mechanism of Action Promotes absorption of calcium in the intestines and retention at the kidneys thereby increasing calcium levels in the serum; decreases excessive serum phosphatase levels, parathyroid hormone levels, and decreases bone resorption; increases renal tubule phosphate resorption

Pharmacodynamics/Kinetics

Onset of action: ~2-6 hours

Duration: 3-5 days

Absorption: Oral: Rapid

Metabolism: Primarily to 1,24,25-trihydroxycholecalciferol and 1,24,25-trihydroxy ergocalciferol

Half-life: 3-8 hours

Elimination: Principally in bile and feces with 4% to 6% excreted in urine

Usual Dosage Individualize dosage to maintain calcium levels of 9-10 mg/dL

Renal failure:

Children:

Oral: 0.25-2 mcg/day have been used (with hemodialysis); 0.014-0.041 mcg/kg/day (not receiving hemodialysis); increases should be made at 4- to 8-week intervals

I.V.: 0.01-0.05 mcg/kg 3 times/week if undergoing hemodialysis

Adults:

Oral: 0.25 mcg/day or every other day (may require 0.5-1 mcg/day); increases should be made at 4- to 8-week intervals

I.V.: 0.5 mcg/day 3 times/week (may require from 0.5-3 mcg/day given 3 times/week) if undergoing hemodialysis

Hypoparathyroidism/pseudohypoparathyroidism: Oral (evaluate dosage at 2- to 4-week intervals):

Children:

<1 year: 0.04-0.08 mcg/kg once daily

1-5 years: 0.25-0.75 mcg once daily

Children >6 years and Adults: 0.5-2 mcg once daily

Vitamin D-dependent rickets: Children and Adults: Oral: 1 mcg once daily

Vitamin D-resistant rickets (familial hypophosphatemia): Children and Adults: Oral: Initial: 0.015-0.02 mcg/kg once daily; maintenance: 0.03-0.06 mcg/kg once daily; maximum dose: 2 mcg once daily

Hypocalcemia in premature infants: Oral: 1 mcg once daily for 5 days

Hypocalcemic tetany in premature infants: I.V.: 0.05 mcg/kg once daily for 5-12 days

Monitoring Parameters Monitor symptoms of hypercalcemia (weakness, fatigue, somnolence, headache, anorexia, dry mouth, metallic taste, nausea, vomiting, cramps, diarrhea, muscle pain, bone pain and irritability)

Reference Range Calcium (serum) 9-10 mg/dL (4.5-5 mEq/L) but do not include the I.V. dosages; phosphate: 2.5-5 mg/dL

Test Interactions ↑ calcium, cholesterol, magnesium, BUN, AST, ALT, calcium (S), cholesterol (S); ↓ alkaline phosphatase

Patient Information Compliance with dose, diet, and calcium supplementation is essential; notify physician if weakness, lethargy, headache, and decreased appetite occur; avoid taking magnesium supplements or magnesium-containing antacids

Dosage Forms

Capsule: 0.25 mcg, 0.5 mcg

Injection: 1 mcg/mL (1 mL); 2 mcg/mL (1 mL)

Solution, oral: 1 mcg/mL

Calcium Acetate (KAL see um AS e tate)

U.S. Brand Names Calphron®; Phos-Ex® 125; PhosLo®

Therapeutic Category Antidote, Hyperphosphatemia; Calcium Salt; Electrolyte Supplement, Oral; Electrolyte Supplement, Parenteral

Use

Oral: Control of hyperphosphatemia in end-stage renal failure; calcium acetate binds to phosphorus in the GI tract better than other calcium salts due to its lower solubility and subsequent reduced absorption and increased formation of calcium phosphate; calcium acetate does not promote aluminum absorption

I.V.: Calcium supplementation in parenteral nutrition therapy

Pregnancy Risk Factor C

Contraindications Hypercalcemia, renal calculi, hypophosphatemia

Warnings/Precautions Calcium absorption is impaired in achlorhydria (common in elderly - try alternate salt, administer with food); administration is followed by increased gastric acid secretion within 2 hours of administration; while hypercalcemia and hypercalciuria may result when therapeutic replacement amounts are given for prolonged periods, they are most likely to occur in hypoparathyroid patients receiving high doses of vitamin D

Adverse Reactions

Mild hypercalcemia (calcium: >10.5 mg/dL) may be asymptomatic or manifest itself as constipation, anorexia, nausea, and vomiting

More severe hypercalcemia (calcium: >12 mg/dL) is associated with confusion, delirium, stupor, and coma

<1%: Headache, hypophosphatemia, hypercalcemia, nausea, anorexia, vomiting, abdominal pain, constipation, thirst

Overdosage/Toxicology

Acute single ingestions of calcium salts may produce mild gastrointestinal distress, but hypercalcemia or other toxic manifestations are extremely unlikely

Treatment is supportive

Drug Interactions

Decreased effect:

Calcium acetate may significantly decrease the bioavailability of tetracyclines

Large intakes of dietary fiber may decrease calcium absorption due to a decreased GI transit time and the formation of fiber-calcium complexes

(Continued)

Calcium Acetate *(Continued)*

Increased effect: Calcium acetate may increase the effects of quinidine

Mechanism of Action Combines with dietary phosphate to form insoluble calcium phosphate which is excreted in feces

Pharmacodynamics/Kinetics

Absorption: From the GI tract requires vitamin D; minimal absorption unless chronic, high doses are given; calcium is absorbed in soluble, ionized form; solubility of calcium is increased in an acid environment

Distribution: Crosses the placenta; appears in breast milk

Elimination: Mainly in feces as unabsorbed calcium with 20% eliminated by the kidneys

Usual Dosage

Oral: Adults, on dialysis: Initial: 2 tablets with each meal, can be increased gradually to 3-4 tablets with each meal to bring the serum phosphate value <6 mg/dL as long as hypercalcemia does not develop

I.V.: Dose is dependent on the requirements of the individual patient; in central venous total parental nutrition (TPN), calcium is administered at a concentration of 5 mEq (10 mL)/L of TPN solution; the additive maintenance dose in neonatal TPN is 0.5 mEq calcium/kg/day (1.0 mL/kg/day)

Neonates: 70-200 mg/kg/day

Infants and Children: 70-150 mg/kg/day

Adolescents: 18-35 mg/kg/day

Reference Range

Serum calcium: 8.4-10.2 mg/dL

Due to a poor correlation between the serum ionized calcium (free) and total serum calcium, particularly in states of low albumin or acid/base imbalances, direct measurement of ionized calcium is recommended

In low albumin states, the corrected **total** serum calcium may be estimated by this equation (assuming a normal albumin of 4 g/dL)

Corrected total calcium = total serum calcium + 0.8 (4.0 - measured serum albumin)

or

Corrected calcium = measured calcium - measured albumin + 4.0

Test Interactions ↑ calcium (S); ↓ magnesium

Patient Information Can take with food; do not take calcium supplements within 1-2 hours of taking other medicine by mouth or eating large amounts of fiber-rich foods; do not use nonprescription antacids or drink large amounts of alcohol, caffeine-containing beverages, or use tobacco

Additional Information 12.7 mEq/g; 250 mg/g elemental calcium (25% elemental calcium)

Dosage Forms Elemental calcium listed in brackets

Capsule: Phos-Ex® 125: 500 mg (125 mg)

Injection, 0.5 mEq calcium/mL (39.55 mg calcium acetate/mL) 10 mL vial

Tablet:

Calphron®: 667 mg [169 mg]

PhosLo®: 667 mg [169 mg]

Calcium Carbonate *(KAL see um KAR bun ate)*

U.S. Brand Names Alka-Mints® [OTC]; Amitone® [OTC]; Cal Carb-HD® [OTC]; Calci-Chew™ [OTC]; Calciday-667® [OTC]; Calci-Mix™ [OTC]; Cal-Plus® [OTC]; Caltrate® 600 [OTC]; Caltrate, Jr.® [OTC]; Chooz® [OTC]; Dicarbosil® [OTC]; Equilet® [OTC]; Florical® [OTC]; Gencalc® 600 [OTC]; Mallamint® [OTC]; Nephro-Calci® [OTC]; Os-Cal® 500 [OTC]; Oyst-Cal 500 [OTC]; Oystercal® 500; Rolaids® Calcium Rich [OTC]; Tums® [OTC]; Tums® E-X Extra Strength Tablet [OTC]; Tums® Extra Strength Liquid [OTC]

Canadian Brand Names Apo®-Cal; Calcite-500; Calsan®; Pharmacal®

Therapeutic Category Antacid; Antidote; Hyperphosphatemia; Calcium Salt; Electrolyte Supplement, Oral

Use As an antacid, and treatment and prevention of calcium deficiency or hyperphosphatemia (eg, osteoporosis, osteomalacia, mild/moderate renal insufficiency, hypoparathyroidism, postmenopausal osteoporosis, rickets); has been used to bind phosphate

Pregnancy Risk Factor C

Pregnancy/Breast-Feeding Implications

Clinical effects on the fetus: No data available; available evidence suggests safe use during pregnancy and breast-feeding

Breast-feeding/lactation: No data available

Contraindications Hypercalcemia, renal calculi, hypophosphatemia

Warnings/Precautions Calcium carbonate absorption is impaired in achlorhydria (common in elderly - use alternate salt, administer with food); administration is followed by increased gastric acid secretion within 2 hours of administration; while hypercalcemia and hypercalciuria may result when therapeutic replacement amounts are given for prolonged periods, they are most likely to occur in hypoparathyroid patients receiving high doses of vitamin D

Adverse Reactions Well tolerated; 1% to 10%:

Central nervous system: Headache

Endocrine & metabolic: Hypophosphatemia, hypercalcemia

Gastrointestinal: Constipation, laxative effect, acid rebound, nausea, vomiting, anorexia, abdominal pain, xerostomia, flatulence

Miscellaneous: Milk alkali syndrome with very high, chronic dosing and/or renal failure (headache, nausea, irritability, and weakness or alkalosis, hypercalcemia, renal impairment)

Overdosage/Toxicology
Acute single ingestions of calcium salts may produce mild gastrointestinal distress, but hypercalcemia or other toxic manifestations are extremely unlikely
Treatment is supportive

Drug Interactions Decreased effect:
May significantly decrease the bioavailability of tetracyclines and fluoroquinolones, iron salts, and salicylates
Large intakes of dietary fiber may decrease calcium absorption due to a decreased GI transit time and the formation of fiber-calcium complexes

Mechanism of Action As dietary supplements to prevent or treat negative calcium balance (eg, osteoporosis), the calcium in calcium salts moderates nerve and muscle performance and allows normal cardiac function; also used to treat hyperphosphatemia in patients with advanced renal insufficiency by combining with dietary phosphate to form insoluble calcium phosphate, which is excreted in feces; calcium salts as antacids neutralize gastric acidity resulting in increased gastric an duodenal bulb pH; they additionally inhibit proteolytic activity of peptic if the pH is increased >4 and increase lower esophageal sphincter tone.

Pharmacodynamics/Kinetics
Absorption: From the GI tract requires vitamin D; minimal absorption unless chronic, high doses are given; calcium is absorbed in soluble, ionized form; solubility of calcium is increased in an acid environment
Distribution: Crosses the placenta; appears in breast milk
Elimination: Mainly in feces as unabsorbed calcium with 20% eliminated by the kidneys

Usual Dosage Oral (dosage is in terms of elemental calcium):
Adequate intakes:
0-6 months: 210 mg/day
7-12 months: 270 mg/day
1-3 years: 500 mg/day
4-8 years: 800 mg/day
Adults, male/female:
9-18 years: 1300 mg/day
19-50 years: 1000 mg/day
>51 years: 1200 mg/day
Female: Pregnancy:
≤18 years: 1300 mg/day
>19 years: 1000 mg/day
Female: Lactating:
≤18 years: 1300 mg/day
>19 years: 1000 mg/day
Hypocalcemia (dose depends on clinical condition and serum calcium level): Dose expressed in mg of **elemental calcium**
Neonates: 50-150 mg/kg/day in 4-6 divided doses; not to exceed 1 g/day
Children: 45-65 mg/kg/day in 4 divided doses
Adults: 1-2 g or more/day in 3-4 divided doses
Adults:
Dietary supplementation: 500 mg to 2 g divided 2-4 times/day
Antacid: 2 tablets or 10 mL every 2 hours, up to 12 times/day
Adults >51 years of age: Osteoporosis: 1200 mg/day
Dosing adjustment in renal impairment: Cl_{cr} <25 mL/minute: Dosage adjustments may be necessary depending on the serum calcium levels

Reference Range
Serum calcium: 8.4-10.2 mg/dL: Monitor plasma calcium levels if using calcium salts as electrolyte supplements for deficiency
Due to a poor correlation between the serum ionized calcium (free) and total serum calcium, particularly in states of low albumin or acid/base imbalances, direct measurement of ionized calcium is recommended
In low albumin states, the corrected **total** serum calcium may be estimated by: Corrected total calcium = total serum calcium + 0.8 (4.0 - measured serum albumin)

Test Interactions ↑ calcium (S); ↓ magnesium

Patient Information Shake suspension well; chew tablets thoroughly; take with large quantities of water or juice; do not take calcium supplements within 1-2 hours of taking other medicine by mouth or eating large amounts of fiber-rich foods; do not take other antacids or calcium supplements or drink large amounts of alcohol or caffeine-containing beverages; if the maximum dosage of antacids is required for >2 weeks, consult your physician

Additional Information 20 mEq calcium/g; 400 mg calcium/g calcium carbonate (40% elemental calcium)

Dosage Forms Elemental calcium listed in brackets
Capsule: 1500 mg [600 mg]
Calci-Mix™: 1250 mg [500 mg]
Florical®: 364 mg [145.6 mg] with sodium fluoride 8.3 mg
Liquid (Tums® Extra Strength): 1000 mg/5 mL (360 mL)
Lozenge (Mylanta® Soothing Antacids): 600 mg [240 mg]
Powder (Cal Carb-HD®): 6.5 g/packet [2.6 g]
Suspension, oral: 1250 mg/5 mL [500 mg]
Tablet: 650 mg [260 mg], 1500 mg [600 mg]
Calciday-667®: 667 mg [267 mg]
Os-Cal® 500, Oyst-Cal 500, Oystercal® 500: 1250 mg [500 mg]
Cal-Plus®, Caltrate® 600, Gencalc® 600, Nephro-Calci®: 1500 mg [600 mg]
(Continued)

Calcium Carbonate *(Continued)*

Chewable:
Alka-Mints®: 850 mg [340 mg]
Amitone®: 350 mg [140 mg]
Caltrate, Jr.®: 750 mg [300 mg]
Calci-Chew™, Os-Cal®: 750 mg [300 mg]
Chooz®, Dicarbosil®, Equilet®, Tums®: 500 mg [200 mg]
Mallamint®: 420 mg [168 mg]
Rolaids® Calcium Rich: 550 mg [220 mg]
Tums® E-X Extra Strength: 750 mg [300 mg]
Tums® Ultra®: 1000 mg [400 mg]
Florical®: 364 mg [145.6 mg] with sodium fluoride 8.3 mg

Calcium Carbonate and Magnesium Carbonate

(KAL see um KAR bun ate & mag NEE zhum KAR bun ate)
U.S. Brand Names Mylanta® Gelcaps®
Therapeutic Category Antacid
Dosage Forms Capsule: Calcium carbonate 311 mg and magnesium carbonate 232 mg

♦ **Calcium Channel Blockers Comparison** *see page 1315*

Calcium Chloride (KAL see um KLOR ide)

Related Information
Extravasation Treatment of Other Drugs *on page 1287*
Therapeutic Category Calcium Salt; Electrolyte Supplement, Parenteral
Use Cardiac resuscitation when epinephrine fails to improve myocardial contractions, cardiac disturbances of hyperkalemia, hypocalcemia, or calcium channel blocking agent toxicity; emergent treatment of hypocalcemic tetany, treatment of hypermagnesemia
Pregnancy Risk Factor C
Contraindications In ventricular fibrillation during cardiac resuscitation, hypercalcemia, and in patients with risk of digitalis toxicity, renal or cardiac disease
Warnings/Precautions Avoid too rapid I.V. administration (<1 mL/minute) and extravasation; use with caution in digitalized patients, respiratory failure, or acidosis; hypercalcemia may occur in patients with renal failure, and frequent determination of serum calcium is necessary; avoid metabolic acidosis (ie, administer only 2-3 days then change to another calcium salt)
Adverse Reactions <1%: Vasodilation, hypotension, bradycardia, cardiac arrhythmias, ventricular fibrillation, syncope, lethargy, coma, mania, erythema, decreased serum magnesium, hypercalcemia, elevated serum amylase, tissue necrosis, muscle weakness, hypercalciuria
Overdosage/Toxicology
Symptoms of overdose include lethargy, nausea, vomiting, coma
Following withdrawal of the drug, treatment consists of bed rest, liberal intake of fluids, reduced calcium intake, and cathartic administration. Severe hypercalcemia requires I.V. hydration and forced diuresis. Urine output should be monitored and maintained at >3 mL/kg/hour. I.V. saline and natriuretic agents (eg, furosemide) can quickly and significantly increase excretion of calcium.
Drug Interactions
Decreased effect: Calcium may antagonize the effects of calcium channel blockers, atenolol, and sodium polystyrene sulfonate
Increased toxicity: Administer cautiously to a digitalized patient, may precipitate arrhythmias; hypercalcemia induced by thiazides may be increased with calcium administration
Stability
Do not refrigerate solutions; IVPB solutions/I.V. infusion solutions are stable for 24 hours at room temperature
Maximum concentration in parenteral nutrition solutions: 15 mEq/L of calcium and 30 mmol/L of phosphate
Incompatible with sodium bicarbonate, carbonates, phosphates, sulfates, and tartrates
Mechanism of Action Moderates nerve and muscle performance via action potential excitation threshold regulation
Pharmacodynamics/Kinetics
Absorption: I.V. calcium salts are absorbed directly into the bloodstream
Distribution: Crosses the placenta; appears in breast milk
Elimination: Mainly in feces as unabsorbed calcium with 20% eliminated by the kidneys
Usual Dosage Note: Calcium chloride is 3 times as potent as calcium gluconate
Cardiac arrest in the presence of hyperkalemia or hypocalcemia, magnesium toxicity, or calcium antagonist toxicity: I.V.:
Infants and Children: 20 mg/kg; may repeat in 10 minutes if necessary
Adults: 2-4 mg/kg (10% solution), repeated every 10 minutes if necessary
Hypocalcemia: I.V.:
Infants and Children: 10-20 mg/kg/dose (infants <1 mEq; children 1-7 mEq), repeat every 4-6 hours if needed
Adults: 500 mg to 1 g (7-14 mEq)/dose repeated every 4-6 hours if needed
Hypocalcemic tetany: I.V.:
Infants and Children: 10 mg/kg (0.5-0.7 mEq/kg) over 5-10 minutes; may repeat after 6-8 hours or follow with an infusion with a maximum dose of 200 mg/kg/day
Adults: 1 g over 10-30 minutes; may repeat after 6 hours

Hypocalcemia secondary to citrated blood transfusion: I.V.:
Neonates: Give 0.45 mEq **elemental** calcium for each 100 mL citrated blood infused
Adults: 1.35 mEq calcium with each 100 mL of citrated blood infused
Dosing adjustment in renal impairment: Cl_{cr} <25 mL/minute: Dosage adjustments may be necessary depending on the serum calcium levels

Reference Range
Serum calcium: 8.4-10.2 mg/dL
Due to a poor correlation between the serum ionized calcium (free) and total serum calcium, particularly in states of low albumin or acid/base imbalances, direct measurement of ionized calcium is recommended
In low albumin states, the corrected **total** serum calcium may be estimated by this equation (assuming a normal albumin of 4 g/dL)
Corrected total calcium = total serum calcium + 0.8 (4.0 - measured serum albumin)
or
Corrected calcium = measured calcium - measured albumin + 4.0
Serum/plasma chloride: 95-108 mEq/L

Test Interactions ↑ calcium (S); ↓ magnesium

Nursing Implications Do not inject calcium chloride I.M. or administer S.C. or use scalp, small hand or foot veins for I.V. administration since severe necrosis and sloughing may occur. Monitor EKG if calcium is infused faster than 2.5 mEq/minute; usual: 0.7-1.5 mEq/minute (0.5-1 mL/minute); **stop the infusion if the patient complains of pain or discomfort.** Warm to body temperature; administer slowly, do not exceed 1 mL/minute (inject into ventricular cavity - not myocardium); **do not infuse calcium chloride in the same I.V. line as phosphate-containing solutions.**

Extravasation treatment (example):
Hyaluronidase: Add 1 mL NS to 150 unit vial to make 150 units/mL of concentration; mix 0.1 mL of above with 0.9 mL NS in 1 mL syringe to make final concentration = 15 units/mL

Additional Information 14 mEq/g/10 mL; 270 mg elemental calcium/g (27% elemental calcium)

Dosage Forms Elemental calcium listed in brackets
Injection: 10% = 100 mg/mL [27.2 mg/mL, 1.36 mEq/mL] (10 mL)

♦ **Calcium Disodium Edetate** see Edetate Calcium Disodium on page 404
♦ **Calcium Disodium Versenate®** see Edetate Calcium Disodium on page 404
♦ **Calcium EDTA** see Edetate Calcium Disodium on page 404

Calcium Glubionate (KAL see um gloo BYE oh nate)

U.S. Brand Names Neo-Calglucon® [OTC]
Therapeutic Category Calcium Salt
Use Adjunct in treatment and prevention of postmenopausal osteoporosis; treatment and prevention of calcium depletion or hyperphosphatemia (eg, osteoporosis, osteomalacia, mild/moderate renal insufficiency, hypoparathyroidism, rickets)
Pregnancy Risk Factor C
Contraindications Hypercalcemia, renal calculi, ventricular fibrillation
Warnings/Precautions Calcium absorption is impaired in achlorhydria (common in elderly - try alternate salt, administer with food); administration is followed by increased gastric acid secretion within 2 hours of administration; while hypercalcemia and hypercalciuria may result when therapeutic replacement amounts are given for prolonged periods, they are most likely to occur in hypoparathyroid patients receiving high doses of vitamin D
Adverse Reactions
Mild hypercalcemia (calcium: >10.5 mg/dL) may be asymptomatic or manifest itself as constipation, anorexia, nausea, and vomiting
More severe hypercalcemia (calcium: >12 mg/dL) is associated with confusion, delirium, stupor, and coma

<1%: Headache, hypophosphatemia, hypercalcemia, nausea, anorexia, vomiting, abdominal pain, constipation, thirst
Overdosage/Toxicology
Acute single ingestions of calcium salts may produce mild gastrointestinal distress, but hypercalcemia or other toxic manifestations are extremely unlikely
Treatment is supportive
Drug Interactions
Decreased effect:
Calcium glubionate may significantly decrease the bioavailability of tetracyclines
Large intakes of dietary fiber may decrease calcium absorption due to a decreased GI transit time and the formation of fiber-calcium complexes
Increased effect: Calcium glubionate may increase the effects of quinidine
Mechanism of Action As dietary supplements, to prevent or treat negative calcium balance (eg, osteoporosis), the calcium in calcium salts moderates nerve and muscle performance and allows normal cardiac function
Pharmacodynamics/Kinetics
Absorption: From the GI tract requires vitamin D; minimal absorption unless chronic, high doses are given; calcium is absorbed in soluble, ionized form; solubility of calcium is increased in an acid environment
Distribution: Crosses the placenta; appears in breast milk
Elimination: Mainly in feces as unabsorbed calcium with 20% eliminated by the kidneys
Usual Dosage Dosage is in terms of **elemental** calcium
(Continued)

Calcium Glubionate *(Continued)*

Adequate intakes:
0-6 months: 210 mg/day
7-12 months: 270 mg/day
1-3 years: 500 mg/day
4-8 years: 800 mg/day
Adults, male/female:
9-18 years: 1300 mg/day
19-50 years: 1000 mg/day
>51 years: 1200 mg/day
Female: Pregnancy:
≤18 years: 1300 mg/day
>19 years: 1000 mg/day
Female: Lactating:
≤18 years: 1300 mg/day
>19 years: 1000 mg/day

Syrup is a hyperosmolar solution; dosage is in terms of calcium glubionate, elemental calcium is in parentheses

Neonatal hypocalcemia: 1200 mg (77 mg Ca^{++})/kg/day in 4-6 divided doses

Maintenance: Infants and Children: 600-2000 mg (38-128 mg Ca^{++})/kg/day in 4 divided doses up to a maximum of 9 g (575 mg Ca^{++})/day

Adults: 6-18 g (~0.5-1 g Ca^{++})/day in divided doses

Dosing adjustment in renal impairment: Cl_{cr} <25 mL/minute: Dosage adjustments may be necessary depending on the serum calcium levels

Reference Range
Serum calcium: 8.4-10.2 mg/dL: Monitor plasma calcium levels if using calcium salts as electrolyte supplements for deficiency

Due to a poor correlation between the serum ionized calcium (free) and total serum calcium, particularly in states of low albumin or acid/base imbalances, direct measurement of ionized calcium is recommended

In low albumin states, the corrected **total** serum calcium may be estimated by: Corrected total calcium = total serum calcium + 0.8 (4.0 - measured serum albumin)

Test Interactions ↑ calcium (S); ↓ magnesium

Patient Information Do not take calcium supplements within 1-2 hours of taking other medicine by mouth or eating large amounts of fiber-rich foods; do not take other calcium-containing products or antacids, drink large amounts of alcohol or caffeine-containing beverages

Additional Information 3.3 mEq/g; 64 mg elemental calcium/g (6% elemental calcium)

Dosage Forms Elemental calcium listed in brackets
Syrup: 1.8 g/5 mL [115 mg/5 mL] (480 mL)

Calcium Gluceptate *(KAL see um gloo SEP tate)*

Therapeutic Category Calcium Salt; Electrolyte Supplement, Parenteral

Use Treatment of cardiac disturbances of hyperkalemia, hypocalcemia, or calcium channel blocker toxicity; cardiac resuscitation when epinephrine fails to improve myocardial contractions; treatment of hypermagnesemia and hypocalcemia

Pregnancy Risk Factor C

Contraindications In ventricular fibrillation during cardiac resuscitation; patients with risk of digitalis toxicity, renal or cardiac disease; hypercalcemia

Warnings/Precautions Avoid too rapid I.V. administration; avoid extravasation; use with caution in digitalized patients, respiratory failure or acidosis; metabolic acidosis (administer for only 2-3 days then change to another calcium salt)

Adverse Reactions <1%: Vasodilation, hypotension, bradycardia, cardiac arrhythmias, ventricular fibrillation, syncope, lethargy, mania, coma, erythema, hypomagnesemia, hypercalcemia, elevated serum amylase, tissue necrosis, muscle weakness, hypercalciuria

Overdosage/Toxicology
Symptoms of overdose include lethargy, nausea, vomiting, coma

Following withdrawal of the drug, treatment consists of bed rest, liberal intake of fluids, reduced calcium intake, and cathartic administration. Severe hypercalcemia requires I.V. hydration and forced diuresis. Urine output should be monitored and maintained at >3 mL/kg/hour. I.V. saline and natriuretic agents (eg, furosemide) can quickly and significantly increase excretion of calcium.

Drug Interactions
Decreased effect: Calcium may antagonize the effects of calcium channel blockers, atenolol, and sodium polystyrene sulfonate

Increased toxicity: Administer cautiously to a digitalized patient, may precipitate arrhythmias; hypercalcemia induced by thiazides may be increased with calcium administration

Stability Admixture **incompatibilities** include carbonates, phosphates, sulfates, tartrates

Mechanism of Action Moderates nerve and muscle performance via action potential excitation threshold regulation

Pharmacodynamics/Kinetics
Absorption: I.M. and I.V. calcium salts are absorbed directly into the bloodstream
Distribution: Crosses the placenta; appears in breast milk
Elimination: Mainly in feces as unabsorbed calcium with 20% eliminated by the kidneys

Usual Dosage Dose expressed in mg of calcium gluceptate (elemental calcium is in parentheses)

Cardiac resuscitation in the presence of hypocalcemia, hyperkalemia, magnesium toxicity, or calcium channel blocker toxicity: I.V.:
Children: 110 mg (9 mg Ca++)/kg/dose
Adults: 1.1-1.5 g (90-123 mg Ca++)
Hypocalcemia:
I.M.:
Children: 200-500 mg (16.4-41 mg Ca++)/kg/day divided every 6 hours
Adults: 500 mg to 1.1 g/dose as needed
I.V.: Adults: 1.1-4.4 g (90-360 mg Ca++) administered slowly as needed (≤2 mL/minute)
After citrated blood administration: Children and Adults: I.V.: 0.45 mEq Ca++/100 mL blood infused
Dosing adjustment in renal impairment: Cl$_{cr}$ <25 mL/minute: Dosage adjustments may be necessary depending on the serum calcium levels

Reference Range
Serum calcium: 8.4-10.2 mg/dL
Due to a poor correlation between the serum ionized calcium (free) and total serum calcium, particularly in states of low albumin or acid/base imbalances, direct measurement of ionized calcium is recommended
In low albumin states, the corrected **total** serum calcium may be estimated by this equation (assuming a normal albumin of 4 g/dL)
Corrected total calcium = total serum calcium + 0.8 (4.0 - measured serum albumin)
or
Corrected calcium = measured calcium - measured albumin + 4.0

Test Interactions ↑ calcium (S); ↓ magnesium

Nursing Implications Warm to body temperature; administer slowly, do not exceed 2 mL/minute

Additional Information 4.1 mEq/g; 82 mg elemental calcium/g (8% elemental calcium)

Dosage Forms Elemental calcium listed in brackets
Injection: 220 mg/mL [18 mg/mL, 0.9 mEq/mL] (5 mL, 50 mL)

Calcium Gluconate (KAL see um GLOO koe nate)

U.S. Brand Names Kalcinate®

Therapeutic Category Calcium Salt; Electrolyte Supplement, Oral; Electrolyte Supplement, Parenteral

Use Treatment and prevention of hypocalcemia; treatment of tetany, cardiac disturbances of hyperkalemia, cardiac resuscitation when epinephrine fails to improve myocardial contractions, hypocalcemia, or calcium channel blocker toxicity; calcium supplementation

Pregnancy Risk Factor C

Contraindications In ventricular fibrillation during cardiac resuscitation; patients with risk of digitalis toxicity, renal or cardiac disease, hypercalcemia, renal calculi, hypophosphatemia

Warnings/Precautions Avoid too rapid I.V. administration (1.5-3.3 mL/minute); use with caution in digitalized patients, severe hyperphosphatemia, respiratory failure or acidosis; avoid extravasation; may produce cardiac arrest; hypercalcemia may occur in patients with renal failure and frequent determination of serum calcium is necessary; the serum calcium level should be monitored twice weekly during the early dose adjustment period

Adverse Reactions <1%: Vasodilation, hypotension, bradycardia, cardiac arrhythmias, ventricular fibrillation, syncope, lethargy, mania, coma, erythema, decrease serum magnesium, hypercalcemia, elevated serum amylase, constipation, nausea, vomiting, abdominal pain, tissue necrosis, muscle weakness, hypercalciuria

Overdosage/Toxicology
Acute single oral ingestions of calcium salts may produce mild gastrointestinal distress, but hypercalcemia or other toxic manifestations are extremely unlikely. Symptoms of hypercalcemia include lethargy, nausea, vomiting, and coma.
Treatment is supportive. Severe hypercalcemia following parenteral overdose requires I.V. hydration. Urine output should be monitored and maintained at >3 mL/kg/hour. I.V. saline and natriuretic agents (eg, furosemide) can quickly and significantly increase excretion of calcium into urine.

Drug Interactions
Decreased effect:
Calcium may decrease the bioavailability of tetracyclines, fluoroquinolones, iron salts and salicylates, atenolol, and sodium polystyrene sulfonate
I.V. calcium may antagonize the effects of verapamil; large intakes of dietary fiber may decrease calcium absorption due to a decreased GI transit time and the formation of fiber-calcium complexes
Increased effect: I.V. calcium may increase the effects of quinidine and digitalis

Stability
Do not refrigerate solutions; IVPB solutions/I.V. infusion solutions are stable for 24 hours at room temperature
Standard diluent: 1 g/100 mL D$_5$W or NS; 2 g/100 mL D$_5$W or NS
Maximum concentration in parenteral nutrition solutions is 15 mEq/L of calcium and 30 mmol/L of phosphate
Incompatible with sodium bicarbonate, carbonates, phosphates, sulfates, and tartrates

Mechanism of Action When used to prevent or treat negative calcium balance (eg, osteoporosis), the calcium in calcium salts moderates nerve and muscle performance and allows normal cardiac function
(Continued)

Calcium Gluconate *(Continued)*

Pharmacodynamics/Kinetics

Absorption: From the GI tract requires vitamin D; minimal absorption unless chronic, high doses are given; calcium is absorbed in soluble, ionized form; solubility of calcium is increased in an acid environment

Distribution: Crosses the placenta; appears in breast milk

Elimination: Mainly in feces as unabsorbed calcium with 20% eliminated by the kidneys

Usual Dosage Dosage is in terms of **elemental** calcium

Adequate intakes:

0-6 months: 210 mg/day

7-12 months: 270 mg/day

1-3 years: 500 mg/day

4-8 years: 800 mg/day

Adults, male/female:

9-18 years: 1300 mg/day

19-50 years: 1000 mg/day

>51 years: 1200 mg/day

Female: Pregnancy:

≤18 years: 1300 mg/day

>19 years: 1000 mg/day

Female: Lactating:

≤18 years: 1300 mg/day

>19 years: 1000 mg/day

Dosage expressed in terms of **calcium gluconate**

Hypocalcemia: I.V.:

Neonates: 200-800 mg/kg/day as a continuous infusion or in 4 divided doses

Infants and Children: 200-500 mg/kg/day as a continuous infusion or in 4 divided doses

Adults: 2-15 g/24 hours as a continuous infusion or in divided doses

Hypocalcemia: Oral:

Children: 200-500 mg/kg/day divided every 6 hours

Adults: 500 mg to 2 g 2-4 times/day

Osteoporosis/bone loss: Oral: 1000-1500 mg in divided doses/day

Hypocalcemia secondary to citrated blood infusion: I.V.: Give 0.45 mEq **elemental** calcium for each 100 mL citrated blood infused

Hypocalcemic tetany: I.V.:

Neonates: 100-200 mg/kg/dose, may follow with 500 mg/kg/day in 3-4 divided doses or as an infusion

Infants and Children: 100-200 mg/kg/dose (0.5-0.7 mEq/kg/dose) over 5-10 minutes; may repeat every 6-8 hours or follow with an infusion of 500 mg/kg/day

Adults: 1-3 g (4.5-16 mEq) may be administered until therapeutic response occurs

Calcium antagonist toxicity, magnesium intoxication or cardiac arrest in the presence of hyperkalemia or hypocalcemia: Calcium chloride is recommended calcium salt: I.V.:

Infants and Children: 100 mg/kg/dose (maximum: 3 g/dose)

Adults: 500-800 mg; maximum: 3 g/dose

Maintenance electrolyte requirements for total parenteral nutrition: I.V.: Daily requirements: Adults: 8-16 mEq/1000 kcal/24 hours

Dosing adjustment in renal impairment: Cl_{cr} <25 mL/minute: Dosage adjustments may be necessary depending on the serum calcium levels

Administration
I.M. injections should be administered in the gluteal region in adults, usually in volumes <2 mL; avoid I.M. injections in children and adults with muscle mass wasting; do not use scalp veins or small hand or foot veins for I.V. administration; generally, I.V. infusion rates should not exceed 0.7-1.5 mEq/minute (1.5-3.3 mL/minute); **stop the infusion if the patient complains of pain or discomfort.** Warm to body temperature; do not inject into the myocardium when using calcium during advanced cardiac life support.

Reference Range

Serum calcium: 8.4-10.2 mg/dL: Monitor plasma calcium levels if using calcium salts as electrolyte supplements for deficiency

Due to a poor correlation between the serum ionized calcium (free) and total serum calcium, particularly in states of low albumin or acid/base imbalances, direct measurement of ionized calcium is recommended

In low albumin states, the corrected **total** serum calcium may be estimated by: Corrected total calcium = total serum calcium + 0.8 (4.0 - measured serum albumin)

Test Interactions ↑ calcium (S); ↓ magnesium

Patient Information
Do not take calcium supplements within 1-2 hours of taking other medicine by mouth or eating large amounts of fiber-rich foods; do not drink large amounts of alcohol or caffeine-containing beverages; take with food

Nursing Implications

Extravasation treatment (example):

Hyaluronidase: Add 1 mL NS to 150 unit vial to make 150 units/mL of concentration; mix 0.1 mL of above with 0.9 mL NS in 1 mL syringe to make final concentration = 15 units/mL

Do not infuse calcium gluconate solutions in the same I.V. line as phosphate-containing solutions (eg, TPN)

Additional Information 4.5 mEq/g; 90 mg elemental calcium/g (9% elemental calcium)

Dosage Forms Elemental calcium listed in brackets

Injection: 10% = 100 mg/mL [9 mg/mL] (10 mL, 50 mL, 100 mL, 200 mL)

Tablet: 500 mg [45 mg], 650 mg [58.5 mg], 975 mg [87.75 mg], 1 g [90 mg]

♦ **Calcium Leucovorin** see Leucovorin on page 666
♦ **CaldeCORT®** see Hydrocortisone on page 579
♦ **CaldeCORT® Anti-Itch Spray** see Hydrocortisone on page 579
♦ **Calderol®** see Calcifediol on page 170

Calfactant (cal FAC tant)
U.S. Brand Names Infasurf®
Therapeutic Category Lung Surfactant
Use Prevention of respiratory distress syndrome (RDS) in premature infants at high risk for RDS and for the treatment ("rescue") of premature infants who develop RDS

Prophylaxis: Therapy at birth with calfactant is indicated for premature infants <29 weeks of gestational age at significant risk for RDS. Should be administered as soon as possible, preferably within 30 minutes after birth.

Treatment: For infants ≤72 hours of age with RDS (confirmed by clinical and radiologic findings) and requiring endotracheal intubation.

Warnings/Precautions For intratracheal administration only; the administration of exogenous surfactants often rapidly improves oxygenation and lung compliance. Transient episodes of cyanosis, bradycardia, reflux of surfactant into the endotracheal tube, and airway obstruction were observed more frequently among infants treated with calfactant in clinical trials.

Adverse Reactions
Cardiovascular: Bradycardia (34%), cyanosis (65%)
Respiratory: Airway obstruction (39%), reflux (21%), requirement for manual ventilation (16%), reintubation (1% to 10%)

Overdosage/Toxicology There have been no known reports of overdosage. While there are no known adverse effects of excess lung surfactant, overdoses would result in overloading the lungs with an isotonic solution. Ventilation should be supported until clearance of the liquid is accomplished.

Stability Gently swirling or agitation of the vial of suspension is often necessary for redispersion. **Do not shake.** Visible flecks of the suspension and foaming at the surface are normal. Calfactant should be stored at refrigeration (2°C to 8°C/36°F to 46°F). Warming before administration is not necessary. Unopened and unused vials of calfactant that have been warmed to room temperature can be returned to the refrigeration storage within 24 hours for future use. Repeated warming to room temperature should be avoided. Each single-use vial should be entered only once and the vial with any unused material should be discarded after the initial entry.

Mechanism of Action Endogenous lung surfactant is essential for effective ventilation because it modifies alveolar surface tension, thereby stabilizing the alveoli. Lung surfactant deficiency is the cause of respiratory distress syndrome (RDS) in premature infants and lung surfactant restores surface activity to the lungs of these infants.

Pharmacodynamics/Kinetics No human studies of absorption, biotransformation, or excretion of calfactant have been performed

Usual Dosage Intratracheal administration **only:** Each dose is 3 mL/kg body weight at birth; should be administered every 12 hours for a total of up to 3 doses

Administration Should be administered intratracheally through an endotracheal tube. Dose is drawn into a syringe from the single-use vial using a 20-gauge or larger needle with care taken to avoid excessive foaming. Should be administered in 2 aliquots of 1.5 mL/kg each. After each aliquot is instilled, the infant should be positioned with either the right or the left side dependent. Administration is made while ventilation is continued over 20-30 breaths for each aliquot, with small bursts timed only during the inspiratory cycles. A pause followed by evaluation of the respiratory status and repositioning should separate the two aliquots.

Monitoring Parameters Following administration, patients should be carefully monitored so that oxygen therapy and ventilatory support can be modified in response to changes in respiratory status

Dosage Forms Suspension, intratracheal: 6 mL

♦ **Calmylin Expectorant** see Guaifenesin on page 549
♦ **Calphron®** see Calcium Acetate on page 173
♦ **Cal-Plus® [OTC]** see Calcium Carbonate on page 174
♦ **Calsan®** see Calcium Carbonate on page 174
♦ **Caltine®** see Calcitonin on page 171
♦ **Caltrate® 600 [OTC]** see Calcium Carbonate on page 174
♦ **Caltrate, Jr.® [OTC]** see Calcium Carbonate on page 174
♦ **Cama® Arthritis Pain Reliever [OTC]** see Aspirin on page 102
♦ **Camphorated Tincture of Opium** see Paregoric on page 886
♦ **Camptosar®** see Irinotecan on page 627
♦ **Camptothecin-11** see Irinotecan on page 627
♦ **Cancer Chemotherapy Regimens** see page 1263
♦ **Cancer Pain Management** see page 1284

Candesartan (kan de SAR tan)
Related Information
Angiotensin Agents on page 1291
U.S. Brand Names Atacand™
Synonyms Candesartan Cilexetil
(Continued)

Candesartan *(Continued)*

Therapeutic Category Angiotensin II Antagonist; Antihypertensive Agent

Use Alone or in combination with other antihypertensive agents in treating essential hypertension; may have an advantage over losartan due to minimal metabolism requirements and consequent use in mild to moderate hepatic impairment

Pregnancy Risk Factor C (1st trimester); D (2nd and 3rd trimester)

Pregnancy/Breast-Feeding Implications Avoid use in the nursing mother, if possible, since candesartan may be excreted in breast milk. The drug should be discontinued as soon as possible when pregnancy is detected. Drugs which act directly on renin-angiotensin can cause fetal and neonatal morbidity and death.

Contraindications Hypersensitivity to candesartan or any component; sensitivity to other A-II receptor antagonists; pregnancy; hyperaldosteronism (primary); renal artery stenosis (bilateral)

Warnings/Precautions Avoid use or use smaller dose in volume-depleted patients. Drugs which alter renin-angiotensin system have been associated with deterioration in renal function, including oliguria, acute renal failure and progressive azotemia. Use with caution in patients with renal artery stenosis (unilateral or bilateral) to avoid decrease in renal function; use caution in patients with pre-existing renal insufficiency (may decrease renal perfusion).

Adverse Reactions

1% to 10%:
  Cardiovascular: Flushing, chest pain, peripheral edema
  Central nervous system: Dizziness, lightheadedness, drowsiness, fatigue, headache
  Gastrointestinal: Nausea, diarrhea, vomiting
  Neuromuscular & skeletal: Back pain, arthralgia
  Respiratory: Upper respiratory tract infection, pharyngitis, rhinitis, bronchitis, cough, sinusitis

<1%: Tachycardia, palpitations, angina, myocardial infarction, vertigo, anxiety, depression, somnolence, fever, angioedema, rash (>0.5%), hyperglycemia, hypertriglyceridemia, hyperuricemia, dyspepsia, gastroenteritis, paresthesias, increased CPK, myalgia, weakness, hematuria, epistaxis, dyspnea, diaphoresis (increased)

Overdosage/Toxicology

Signs and symptoms of overdose: Hypotension and tachycardia

Treatment is supportive

Drug Interactions Potassium salts/supplements; candesartan is not metabolized by cytochrome P-450

Mechanism of Action Candesartan is an angiotensin receptor antagonist. Angiotensin II acts as a vasoconstrictor. In addition to causing direct vasoconstriction, angiotensin II also stimulates the release of aldosterone. Once aldosterone is released, sodium as well as water are reabsorbed. The end result is an elevation in blood pressure. Candesartan binds to the AT1 angiotensin II receptor. This binding prevents angiotensin II from binding to the receptor thereby blocking the vasoconstriction and the aldosterone secreting effects of angiotensin II.

Pharmacodynamics/Kinetics

Onset of action: 2-3 hours

Peak effect: 6-8 hours

Duration: >24 hours

Distribution: V_d: 0.13 L/kg

Protein binding: 99%

Metabolism: Candesartan cilexetil is metabolized to candesartan by the intestinal wall cells

Bioavailability: 15%

Half-life (dose dependent): 5-9 hours

Time to peak: 3-4 hours

Elimination: Total body clearance: 0.37 mL/kg/minute; renal clearance: 0.19 mL/kg/minute; 26% renal excretion

High concentrations occur in elderly compared to younger subjects; AUC may be doubled in patients with renal impairment

Usual Dosage Adults: Oral: Usual dose is 4-32 mg once daily; dosage must be individualized; blood pressure response is dose-related over the range of 2-32 mg; the usual recommended starting dose of 16 mg once daily when it is used as monotherapy in patients who are not volume depleted; it can be administered once or twice daily with total daily doses ranging from 8-32 mg; larger doses do not appear to have a greater effect and there is relatively little experience with such doses

No initial dosage adjustment is necessary for elderly patients (although higher concentrations (C_{max}) and AUC were observed in these populations), for patients with mildly impaired renal function, or for patients with mildly impaired hepatic function.

Dietary Considerations Food reduces the time to maximal concentration and increases the C_{max}

Monitoring Parameters Supine blood pressure, electrolytes, serum creatinine, BUN, urinalysis, symptomatic hypotension, and tachycardia

Patient Information Patients of childbearing age should be informed about the consequences of 2nd- and 3rd-trimester exposure to drugs that act on the renin-angiotensin system, and that these consequences do not appear to have resulted from intrauterine drug exposure that has been limited to the 1st trimester. Patients should report pregnancy to their physician as soon as possible.

Dosage Forms Tablet, as cilexetil: 4 mg, 8 mg, 16 mg, 32 mg

♦ **Candesartan Cilexetil** *see Candesartan on page 181*
♦ **Capastat® Sulfate** *see Capreomycin on page 185*

Capecitabine (ka pe SITE a been)

U.S. Brand Names Xeloda™

Therapeutic Category Antineoplastic Agent, Antimetabolite

Use Treatment of patients with metastatic breast cancer resistant to both paclitaxel and an anthracycline-containing chemotherapy regimen or resistant to paclitaxel and for whom further anthracycline therapy is not indicated (eg, patients who have received cumulative doses of 400 mg/m^2 of doxorubicin or doxorubicin equivalents). Resistance is defined as progressive disease while on treatment, with or without an initial response, or relapse within 6 months of completing treatment with an anthracycline-containing adjuvant regimen.

Pregnancy Risk Factor D

Pregnancy/Breast-Feeding Implications It is not known if the drug is excreted in breast milk. Because of the potential for serious adverse reactions in nursing infants, it is recommended that nursing be discontinued when receiving capecitabine therapy.

Contraindications Hypersensitivity to capecitabine, fluorouracil, or any component

Warnings/Precautions The U.S. Food and Drug Administration (FDA) currently recommends that procedures for proper handling and disposal of antineoplastic agents be considered. Use with caution in patients with bone marrow suppression, poor nutritional status, or renal or hepatic dysfunction. The drug should be discontinued if intractable diarrhea, stomatitis, bone marrow suppression, or myocardial ischemia develop. Use with caution in patients who have received extensive pelvic radiation or alkylating therapy.

Capecitabine can cause severe diarrhea; median time to first occurrence is 31 days; subsequent doses should be reduced after grade 3 or 4 diarrhea

Hand-and-foot syndrome (palmar-plantar erythrodysesthesia or chemotherapy-induced acral erythema) is characterized by numbness, dysesthesia/paresthesia, tingling, painless or painful swelling, erythema, desquamation, blistering, and severe pain. If grade 2 or 3 hand-and-foot syndrome occurs, interrupt administration of capecitabine until the event resolves or decreases in intensity to grade 1. Following grade 3 hand-and-foot syndrome, decrease subsequent doses of capecitabine.

There has been cardiotoxicity associated with fluorinated pyrimidine therapy, including myocardial infarction, angina, dysrhythmias, cardiogenic shock, sudden death, and EKG changes. These adverse events may be more common in patients with a history of coronary artery disease.

Adverse Reactions
>10%:
  Central nervous system: Fatigue (41%), fever (12%)
  Gastrointestinal: Diarrhea (57%), may be dose limiting; mild to moderate nausea (53%), vomiting (37%), stomatitis (24%), anorexia (23%), abdominal pain (20%), constipation (15%)
  Dermatologic: Palmar-plantar erythrodysesthesia (hand-and-foot syndrome) (57%), may be dose limiting; dermatitis (37%)
  Hematologic: Lymphopenia (94%), anemia (72%), neutropenia (26%), thrombocytopenia (24%)
  Hepatic: Increased bilirubin (22%)
  Neuromuscular & skeletal: Paresthesia (21%)
  Ocular: Eye irritation (15%)
1% to 10%:
  Central nervous system: Headache (9%), dizziness (8%), insomnia (8%)
  Dermatologic: Nail disorders (7%)
  Gastrointestinal: Intestinal obstruction (1.1%)
  Endocrine & metabolic: Dehydration (7%)
  Neuromuscular & skeletal: Myalgia (9%)
<1%: Chest pain, cardiomyopathy, hypotension, cerebral vascular accident, ataxia, encephalopathy, change in consciousness, confusion, photosensitization, radiation recall, alopecia, hypertriglyceridemia, necrotizing enterocolitis, gastritis, colitis, duodenitis, hematemesis, GI hemorrhage, esophagitis, cachexia, oral candidiasis, nocturia, thrombocytopenic purpura, pancytopenia, cholestasis, hepatitis, hepatic fibrosis, thrombophlebitis, deep vein thrombosis, bone pain, joint stiffness, dyspnea, epistaxis, bronchospasm, respiratory distress, pulmonary embolism, increased diaphoresis, infections, hypersensitivity, lymphedema

Overdosage/Toxicology Symptoms of overdose include myelosuppression, nausea, vomiting, diarrhea, and alopecia. No specific antidote exists. Monitor hematologically for at least 4 weeks.

Treatment is supportive

Drug Interactions
  Increased effect: Taking capecitabine immediately before an aluminum hydroxide/magnesium hydroxide antacid, or a meal, increases the absorption of capecitabine
  Increased toxicity: The concentration of 5-fluorouracil is increased and its toxicity may be enhanced by leucovorin. Deaths from severe enterocolitis, diarrhea, and dehydration have been reported in elderly patients receiving weekly leucovorin and fluorouracil. Warfarin: Altered coagulation parameters have been noted in cancer patients receiving coumarin derivatives concomitantly with capecitabine.

Stability Tablets are stored at room temperature

(Continued)

Capecitabine *(Continued)*

Mechanism of Action Capecitabine is a prodrug of fluorouracil. It undergoes hydrolysis in the liver and tissues to form fluorouracil which is the active moiety. Fluorouracil is a fluorinated pyrimidine antimetabolite that inhibits thymidylate synthetase, blocking the methylation of deoxyuridylic acid to thymidylic acid, interfering with DNA, and to a lesser degree, RNA synthesis. Fluorouracil appears to be phase specific for the G_1 and S phases of the cell cycle.

Pharmacodynamics/Kinetics

Absorption: Rapid and extensive

Protein binding: <60% (35% to albumin)

Metabolism: Hepatic: Inactive metabolites: 5′-deoxy-5-fluorocytidine, 5′-deoxy-5-fluorouridine; Tissues: Active metabolite: 5-fluorouracil

Half-life: Elimination: 0.5-1 hour

Elimination: Renal: 70%, 50% as α-fluoro-β-alanine

Usual Dosage Oral:

Adults: 2500 mg/m^2/day in 2 divided doses (~12 hours apart) at the end of a meal for 2 weeks followed by a 1-week rest period given as 3-week cycles

Capecitabine Dose Calculation According to BSA Table

Dose Level 2500 mg/m^2/day		# of tablets per dose (morning and evening)	
Surface Area (m^2)	Total Daily Dose (mg)	150 mg	500 mg
≤1.24	3000	0	3
1.25-1.36	3300	1	3
1.37-1.51	3600	2	3
1.52-1.64	4000	0	4
1.65-1.76	4300	1	4
1.77-1.91	4600	2	4
1.92-2.04	5000	0	5
2.05-2.17	5300	1	5
≥2.18	5600	2	5

Recommended Dose Modifications

Toxicity NCI Grades	During a Course of Therapy	Dose Adjustment for Next Cycle (% of starting dose)
Grade 1	Maintain dose level	Maintain dose level
Grade 2		
1st appearance	Interrupt until resolved to grade 0-1	100%
2nd appearance	Interrupt until resolved to grade 0-1	75%
3rd appearance	Interrupt until resolved to grade 0-1	50%
4th appearance	Discontinue treatment permanently	
Grade 3		
1st appearance	Interrupt until resolved to grade 0-1	75%
2nd appearance	Interrupt until resolved to grade 0-1	50%
3rd appearance	Discontinue treatment permanently	
Grade 4	Discontinue permanently	50%
	OR	
1st appearance	If physician deems it to be in the patient's best interest to continue, interrupt until resolved to grade 0-1	

Dosing adjustment in renal impairment: There is little experience in patients with renal impairment; use with caution. There is insufficient data to provide a dosage recommendation.

Dosing adjustment in hepatic impairment:

Mild to moderate impairment: No starting dose adjustment is necessary; however, carefully monitor patients

Severe hepatic impairment: Patients have not been studied

Dosing adjustment in elderly patients: The elderly may be pharmacodynamically more sensitive to the toxic effects of 5-fluorouracil. Use with caution in monitoring the effects of capecitabine. Insufficient data are available to provide dosage modifications.

Dosage modification guidelines: Carefully monitor patients for toxicity. Toxicity caused by capecitabine administration may be managed by symptomatic treatment, dose interruptions, and adjustment of dose. Once the dose has been reduced, it should not be increased at a later time.

Dietary Considerations Food reduced the rate and extent of absorption of capecitabine. Because current safety and efficacy data are based upon administration with food, it is recommended that capecitabine be administered with food. In all clinical trials, patients were instructed to administer capecitabine within 30 minutes after a meal.

Administration Capecitabine is administered orally, usually in two divided doses taken 12 hours apart. Doses should be taken after meals with water.

Monitoring Parameters CBC with differential, hepatic function, renal function

Patient Information Report any diarrhea, soreness in the mouth or throat, fever, chills, bruising or prolonged bleeding, chest pain, or shortness of breath. The drug may cause hair loss; nausea and vomiting are usually mild.

Dosage Forms Tablet: 150 mg, 500 mg

♦ **Capital® and Codeine** see Acetaminophen and Codeine on page 21

♦ **Capoten®** see Captopril on this page

♦ **Capozide®** see Captopril and Hydrochlorothiazide on page 187

Capreomycin (kap ree oh MYE sin)

Related Information
Antimicrobial Drugs of Choice on page 1404
Tuberculosis Treatment Guidelines on page 1432

U.S. Brand Names Capastat® Sulfate

Synonyms Capreomycin Sulfate

Therapeutic Category Antibiotic, Miscellaneous; Antitubercular Agent

Use Treatment of tuberculosis in conjunction with at least one other antituberculosis agent

Pregnancy Risk Factor C

Contraindications Known hypersensitivity to capreomycin sulfate

Warnings/Precautions Use in patients with renal insufficiency or pre-existing auditory impairment must be undertaken with great caution, and the risk of additional eighth nerve impairment or renal injury should be weighed against the benefits to be derived from therapy. Since other parenteral antituberculous agents (eg, streptomycin) also have similar and sometimes irreversible toxic effects, particularly on eighth cranial nerve and renal function, simultaneous administration of these agents with capreomycin is not recommended. Use with nonantituberculous drugs (ie, aminoglycoside antibiotics) having ototoxic or nephrotoxic potential should be undertaken only with great caution.

Adverse Reactions
>10%:
  Otic: Ototoxicity [subclinical hearing loss (11%), clinical loss (3%)], tinnitus
  Renal: Nephrotoxicity (36%, increased BUN)
1% to 10%: Hematologic: Eosinophilia (dose-related, mild)
<1%: Vertigo, hypokalemia, leukocytosis, thrombocytopenia (rare); pain, induration, and bleeding at injection site; hypersensitivity (urticaria, rash, fever)

Overdosage/Toxicology
Symptoms of overdose include renal failure, ototoxicity, thrombocytopenia
Treatment is supportive

Drug Interactions
Increased effect/duration of nondepolarizing neuromuscular blocking agents
Additive toxicity (nephro- and ototoxicity, respiratory paralysis): Aminoglycosides (eg, streptomycin)

Mechanism of Action Capreomycin is a cyclic polypeptide antimicrobial. It is administered as a mixture of capreomycin IA and capreomycin IB. The mechanism of action of capreomycin is not well understood. Mycobacterial species that have become resistant to other agents are usually still sensitive to the action of capreomycin. However, significant cross-resistance with viomycin, kanamycin, and neomycin occurs.

Pharmacodynamics/Kinetics
Absorption: Oral: Poor absorption necessitates parenteral administration
Half-life: Dependent upon renal function and varies with creatinine clearance; 4-6 hours
Time to peak serum concentration: I.M.: Within 1 hour
Elimination: Essentially excreted unchanged in the urine; no significant accumulation after ≥30 day of 1 g/day dosing in patients with normal renal function

Usual Dosage I.M.:
Infants and Children: 15 mg/kg/day, up to 1 g/day maximum
Adults: 15-20 mg/kg/day up to 1 g/day for 60-120 days, followed by 1 g 2-3 times/week
  Dosing interval in renal impairment: Adults:
    Cl_{cr} >100 mL/minute: Administer 13-15 mg/kg every 24 hours
    Cl_{cr} 80-100 mL/minute: Administer 10-13 mg/kg every 24 hours
    Cl_{cr} 60-80 mL/minute: Administer 7-10 mg/kg every 24 hours
    Cl_{cr} 40-60 mL/minute: Administer 11-14 mg/kg every 48 hours
    Cl_{cr} 20-40 mL/minute: Administer 10-14 mg/kg every 72 hours
    Cl_{cr} <20 mL/minute: Administer 4-7 mg/kg every 72 hours

Reference Range 10 µg/mL

Patient Information Report any hearing loss to physician immediately; do not discontinue without notifying physician

Nursing Implications The solution for injection may acquire a pale straw color and darken with time; this is not associated with a loss of potency or development of toxicity

Dosage Forms Injection, as sulfate: 100 mg/mL (10 mL)

♦ **Capreomycin Sulfate** see Capreomycin on this page

Captopril (KAP toe pril)

Related Information
Angiotensin Agents on page 1291
Antacid Drug Interactions on page 1296
Drug-Drug Interactions With ACEIs on page 1295
(Continued)

Captopril *(Continued)*

Heart Failure: Management of Patients With Left-Ventricular Systolic Dysfunction *on page 1472*
Hypertension Therapy *on page 1479*

U.S. Brand Names Capoten®

Canadian Brand Names Apo®-Capto; Novo-Captopril; Nu-Capto; Syn-Captopril

Synonyms ACE

Therapeutic Category Angiotensin-Converting Enzyme (ACE) Inhibitor; Antihypertensive Agent

Use Management of hypertension and treatment of congestive heart failure; left ventricular dysfunction after myocardial infarction (MI), diabetic nephropathy

Unlabeled use: Hypertensive crisis, rheumatoid arthritis, diagnosis of anatomic renal artery stenosis, hypertension secondary to scleroderma renal crisis, diagnosis of aldosteronism, idiopathic edema, Bartter's syndrome, increase circulation in Raynaud's phenomenon

Pregnancy Risk Factor C (1st trimester); D (2nd and 3rd trimesters)

Pregnancy/Breast-Feeding Implications

Clinical effects on the fetus: No data available on crossing the placenta. Cranial defects, hypocalvaria/acalvaria, oligohydramnios, persistent anuria following delivery, hypotension, renal defects, renal dysgenesis/dysplasia, renal failure, pulmonary hypoplasia, limb contractures secondary to oligohydramnios and stillbirth reported. ACE inhibitors should be avoided during pregnancy.

Breast-feeding/lactation: Crosses into breast milk. American Academy of Pediatrics considers **compatible** with breast-feeding.

Contraindications Hypersensitivity to captopril, other ACE inhibitors, or any component

Warnings/Precautions Use with caution and decrease dosage in patients with renal impairment (especially renal artery stenosis), severe congestive heart failure, or with coadministered diuretic therapy; experience in children is limited. Severe hypotension may occur in patients who are sodium and/or volume depleted, initiate lower doses and monitor closely when starting therapy in these patients; ACE inhibitors may be preferred agents in elderly patients with congestive heart failure and diabetes mellitus (diabetic proteinuria is reduced, minimal CNS effects, and enhanced insulin sensitivity); however due to decreased renal function, tolerance must be carefully monitored.

Adverse Reactions

>1%:

Cardiovascular: Tachycardia, chest pain, palpitations

Central nervous system: Insomnia, headache, dizziness, fatigue, malaise

Dermatologic: Rash (4% to 7%), pruritus, alopecia

Gastrointestinal: Abdominal pain, vomiting, nausea, diarrhea, anorexia, constipation, abnormal taste (2% to 4%), xerostomia

Neuromuscular & skeletal: Paresthesias

Renal: Oliguria

Respiratory: Transient cough (0.5% to 2%)

<1%: Hypotension, angioedema, hyperkalemia, neutropenia, agranulocytosis, proteinuria, increased BUN/serum creatinine

Overdosage/Toxicology

Mild hypotension has been the only toxic effect seen with acute overdose. Bradycardia may also occur; hyperkalemia occurs even with therapeutic doses, especially in patients with renal insufficiency and those taking NSAIDs.

Following initiation of essential overdose management, toxic symptom treatment and supportive treatment should be initiated. Hypotension usually responds to I.V. fluids or Trendelenburg positioning.

Drug Interactions CYP2D6 enzyme substrate

Increased toxicity: See Drug-Drug Interactions With ACEIs table *on page 1295*

Stability Unstable in aqueous solutions; to prepare solution for oral administration, mix prior to administration and use within 10 minutes

Mechanism of Action Competitive inhibitor of angiotensin-converting enzyme (ACE); prevents conversion of angiotensin I to angiotensin II, a potent vasoconstrictor; results in lower levels of angiotensin II which causes an increase in plasma renin activity and a reduction in aldosterone secretion

Pharmacodynamics/Kinetics

Onset of effect: Maximal decrease in blood pressure 1-1.5 hours after dose

Duration: Dose related, may require several weeks of therapy before full hypotensive effect is seen

Absorption: Oral: 60% to 75%; food decreases absorption of captopril 30% to 40%

Protein binding: 25% to 30%

Metabolism: 50%

Half-life (dependent upon renal and cardiac function):

Adults, normal: 1.9 hours

Congestive heart failure: 2.06 hours

Anuria: 20-40 hours

Time to peak: Within 1-2 hours

Elimination: 95% excreted in urine in 24 hours

Usual Dosage Note: Dosage must be titrated according to patient's response; use lowest effective dose. Oral:

Infants: Initial: 0.15-0.3 mg/kg/dose; titrate dose upward to maximum of 6 mg/kg/day in 1-4 divided doses; usual required dose: 2.5-6 mg/kg/day

Children: Initial: 0.5 mg/kg/dose; titrate upward to maximum of 6 mg/kg/day in 2-4 divided doses

Older Children: Initial: 6.25-12.5 mg/dose every 12-24 hours; titrate upward to maximum of 6 mg/kg/day

Adolescents: Initial: 12.5-25 mg/dose given every 8-12 hours; increase by 25 mg/dose to maximum of 450 mg/day

Adults:

Hypertension:

Initial dose: 12.5-25 mg 2-3 times/day; may increase by 12.5-25 mg/dose at 1- to 2-week intervals up to 50 mg 3 times/day; add diuretic before further dosage increases

Maximum dose: 150 mg 3 times/day

Congestive heart failure:

Initial dose: 6.25-12.5 mg 3 times/day in conjunction with cardiac glycoside and diuretic therapy; initial dose depends upon patient's fluid/electrolyte status

Target dose: 50 mg 3 times/day

Maximum dose: 150 mg 3 times/day

LVD after MI: Initial dose: 6.25 mg followed by 12.5 mg 3 times/day; then increase to 25 mg 3 times/day during next several days and then over next several weeks to target dose of 50 mg 3 times/day

Diabetic nephropathy: 25 mg 3 times/day; other antihypertensives often given concurrently

Dosing adjustment in renal impairment:

Cl_{cr} 10-50 mL/minute: Administer at 75% of normal dose

Cl_{cr} <10 mL/minute: Administer at 50% of normal dose

Note: Smaller dosages given every 8-12 hours are indicated in patients with renal dysfunction; renal function and leukocyte count should be carefully monitored during therapy

Hemodialysis: Moderately dialyzable (20% to 50%); administer dose postdialysis or administer 25% to 35% supplemental dose

Peritoneal dialysis: Supplemental dose is not necessary

Monitoring Parameters BUN, serum creatinine, urine dipstick for protein, complete leukocyte count, and blood pressure

Test Interactions ↑ BUN, creatinine, potassium, positive Coombs' [direct]; ↓ cholesterol (S); may cause false-positive results in urine acetone determinations using sodium nitroprusside reagent

Patient Information Take 1 hour before meals; do not stop therapy except under prescriber advice; notify physician if you develop sore throat, fever, swelling, rash, difficult breathing, irregular heartbeats, chest pains, or cough. May cause dizziness, fainting, and lightheadedness, especially in first week of therapy; sit and stand up slowly; do not add a salt substitute (potassium) without advice of physician.

Nursing Implications Watch for hypotensive effect within 1-3 hours of first dose or new higher dose

Additional Information A dosage ratio of 5:1 (captopril:lisinopril) was established and a regimen of 3 times/day vs 1 time/day (captopril vs lisinopril) was tolerated without an increased in adverse drug reactions

Dosage Forms Tablet: 12.5 mg, 25 mg, 50 mg, 100 mg

Extemporaneous Preparations Captopril has limited stability in aqueous preparations. The addition of an antioxidant (sodium ascorbate) has been shown to increase the stability of captopril in solution; captopril (1 mg/mL) in syrup with methylcellulose is stable for 7 days stored either at 4°C or 22°C; captopril (1 mg/mL) in distilled water (no additives) is stable for 14 days if stored at 4°C and 7 days if stored at 22°C; captopril (1 mg/mL) with sodium ascorbate (5 mg/mL) in distilled water is stable for 56 days at 4°C and 14 days at 22°C. Captopril 0.75 mg/mL was found stable for up to 60 days at 5°C and 25°C in a 1:1 mixture of Ora-Sweet® and Ora-Plus®, in Ora-Sweet® SF and Ora-Plus®, and in cherry syrup.

Powder papers can also be made; powder papers are stable for 12 weeks when stored at room temperature

Allen LV and Erickson III MA, "Stability of Baclofen, Captopril, Diltiazem Hydrochloride, Dipyridamole, and Flecainide Acetate in Extemporaneously Compounded Oral Liquids," *Am J Health Syst Pharm*, 1996, 53:2179-84.

Nahata MC, Morosco RS, and Hipple TF, "Stability of Captopril in Three Liquid Dosage Forms," *Am J Hosp Pharm*, 1994, 51(1):95-96.

Taketomo CK, Chu SA, Cheng MH, et al, "Stability of Captopril in Powder Papers Under Three Storage Conditions," *Am J Hosp Pharm*, 1990;47(8):1799-1801.

Captopril and Hydrochlorothiazide

(KAP toe pril & hye droe klor oh THYE a zide)

U.S. Brand Names Capozide®

Therapeutic Category Angiotensin-Converting Enzyme (ACE) Inhibitor Combination; Antihypertensive Agent, Combination

Dosage Forms Tablet:

25/15: Captopril 25 mg and hydrochlorothiazide 15 mg

25/25: Captopril 25 mg and hydrochlorothiazide 25 mg

50/15: Captopril 50 mg and hydrochlorothiazide 15 mg

50/25: Captopril 50 mg and hydrochlorothiazide 25 mg

♦ **Carafate®** *see* Sucralfate *on page 1088*

~aramiphen and Phenylpropanolamine
(kar AM i fen & fen il proe pa NOLE a meen)

U.S. Brand Names Ordrine AT® Extended Release Capsule; Rescaps-D® S.R. Capsule; Tuss-Allergine® Modified T.D. Capsule; Tussogest® Extended Release Capsule

Therapeutic Category Antihistamine/Decongestant Combination

Dosage Forms
Capsule, timed release: Caramiphen edisylate 40 mg and phenylpropanolamine hydrochloride 75 mg
Liquid: Caramiphen edisylate 6.7 mg and phenylpropanolamine hydrochloride 12.5 mg per 5 mL

♦ **Carampicillin Hydrochloride** see Bacampicillin on page 121

Carbachol (KAR ba kole)

Related Information
Glaucoma Drug Therapy Comparison on page 1322

U.S. Brand Names Carbastat® Ophthalmic; Carboptic® Ophthalmic; Isopto® Carbachol Ophthalmic; Miostat® Intraocular

Synonyms Carbacholine; Carbamylcholine Chloride

Therapeutic Category Cholinergic Agent, Ophthalmic; Ophthalmic Agent, Miotic

Use Lowers intraocular pressure in the treatment of glaucoma; cause miosis during surgery

Pregnancy Risk Factor C

Contraindications Acute iritis, acute inflammatory disease of the anterior chamber, hypersensitivity to carbachol or any component

Warnings/Precautions Use with caution in patients undergoing general anesthesia and in presence of corneal abrasion

Adverse Reactions
1% to 10%: Ocular: Blurred vision, eye pain
<1%: Transient fall in blood pressure, headache, stomach cramps, diarrhea, ciliary spasm with temporary decrease of visual acuity, corneal clouding, persistent bullous keratopathy, postoperative keratitis, retinal detachment, transient ciliary and conjunctival injection, asthma, increased peristalsis

Overdosage/Toxicology
Symptoms of overdose include miosis, flushing, vomiting, bradycardia, bronchospasm, involuntary urination
Atropine is the treatment of choice for intoxications manifesting with significant muscarinic symptoms. Atropine I.V. 2-4 mg every 3-60 minutes (or 0.04-0.08 mg I.V. every 5-60 minutes if needed for children) should be repeated to control symptoms and then continued as needed for 1-2 days following the acute ingestion. Epinephrine 0.1-1 mg S.C. may be useful in reversing severe cardiovascular or pulmonary sequelae.

Stability
Intraocular: Store at room temperature of 15°C to 30°C/59°F to 86°F
Topical: Store at 8°C to 27°C/46°F to 80°F

Mechanism of Action Synthetic direct-acting cholinergic agent that causes miosis by stimulating muscarinic receptors in the eye

Pharmacodynamics/Kinetics
Ophthalmic instillation: Onset of miosis: 10-20 minutes; Duration of reduction in intraocular pressure: 4-8 hours
Intraocular administration: Onset of miosis: Within 2-5 minutes; Duration: 24 hours

Usual Dosage Adults:
Ophthalmic: Instill 1-2 drops up to 3 times/day
Intraocular: 0.5 mL instilled into anterior chamber before or after securing sutures

Patient Information May sting on instillation; may cause headache, altered distance vision, and decreased night vision

Nursing Implications Finger pressure should be applied on the lacrimal sac for 1-2 minutes following topical instillation; remove excess around the eye with a tissue. Instillation for miosis prior to eye surgery should be gentle and parallel to the iris face and tangential to the pupil border; discard unused portion.

Dosage Forms Solution:
Intraocular (Carbastat®, Miostat®): 0.01% (1.5 mL)
Topical, ophthalmic:
Carboptic®: 3% (15 mL)
Isopto® Carbachol: 0.75% (15 mL, 30 mL); 1.5% (15 mL, 30 mL); 2.25% (15 mL); 3% (15 mL, 30 mL)

♦ **Carbacholine** see Carbachol on this page

Carbamazepine (kar ba MAZ e peen)

Related Information
Anticonvulsants by Seizure Type on page 1300
Depression Disorders and Treatments on page 1465
Epilepsy Treatment on page 1468

U.S. Brand Names Carbatrol®; Epitol®; Tegretol®; Tegretol®-XR

Canadian Brand Names Apo®-Carbamazepine; Mazepine®; Novo-Carbamaz; Nu-Carbamazepine; PMS-Carbamazepine

Therapeutic Category Anticonvulsant

Use Prophylaxis of generalized tonic-clonic, partial (especially complex partial), and mixed partial or generalized seizure disorder; pain relief of trigeminal neuralgia

Unlabeled use: Treat bipolar disorders and other affective disorders; resistant schizophrenia, alcohol withdrawal, restless leg syndrome, and psychotic behavior associated with dementia

Pregnancy Risk Factor D

Pregnancy/Breast-Feeding Implications

Clinical effects on the fetus: Crosses the placenta. Dysmorphic facial features, cranial defects, cardiac defects, spina bifida, IUGR, and multiple other malformations reported. Epilepsy itself, number of medications, genetic factors, or a combination of these probably influence the teratogenicity of anticonvulsant therapy. Benefit:risk ratio usually favors continued use during pregnancy and breast-feeding.

Breast-feeding/lactation: Crosses into breast milk. American Academy of Pediatrics considers **compatible** with breast-feeding.

Contraindications Hypersensitivity to carbamazepine or any component; **may have cross-sensitivity with tricyclic antidepressants**; should not be used in any patient with bone marrow suppression, MAO inhibitor use; the oral suspension should not be administered simultaneously with other liquid medicinal agents or diluents

Warnings/Precautions MAO inhibitors should be discontinued for a minimum of 14 days before carbamazepine is begun; administer with caution to patients with history of cardiac damage or hepatic disease; potentially fatal blood cell abnormalities have been reported following treatment; early detection of hematologic change is important; advise patients of early signs and symptoms including fever, sore throat, mouth ulcers, infections, easy bruising, petechial or purpuric hemorrhage; carbamazepine is not effective in absence, myoclonic or akinetic seizures; exacerbation of certain seizure types have been seen after initiation of carbamazepine therapy in children with mixed seizure disorders. Elderly may have increased risk of SIADH-like syndrome.

Adverse Reactions

Dermatologic: Rash; but does not necessarily mean the drug should not be stopped

>10%:

Central nervous system: Sedation, dizziness, fatigue, ataxia, confusion

Gastrointestinal: Nausea, vomiting

Ocular: Blurred vision, nystagmus

1% to 10%:

Dermatologic: Stevens-Johnson syndrome, toxic epidermal necrolysis

Endocrine & metabolic: Hyponatremia, SIADH

Gastrointestinal: Diarrhea

Miscellaneous: Diaphoresis

<1%: Edema, congestive heart failure, syncope, bradycardia, hypertension or hypotension, A-V block, arrhythmias, slurred speech, mental depression, hypocalcemia, hyponatremia, urinary retention, sexual problems in males, neutropenia (can be transient), aplastic anemia, agranulocytosis, eosinophilia, leukopenia, pancytopenia, thrombocytopenia, bone marrow suppression, hepatitis, peripheral neuritis, diplopia, swollen glands, hypersensitivity

Overdosage/Toxicology

Symptoms of overdose include dizziness ataxia, drowsiness, nausea, vomiting, tremor, agitation, nystagmus, urinary retention, dysrhythmias, coma, seizures, twitches, respiratory depression, neuromuscular disturbances

Provide general supportive care. Activated charcoal is effective at binding certain chemicals and this is especially true for carbamazepine; other treatment is supportive/symptomatic. Treatment consists of inducing emesis or gastric lavage. EKG should also be monitored to detect cardiac dysfunction. Monitor blood pressure, body temperature, pupillary reflexes, bladder function for several days following ingestion.

Drug Interactions CYP2C8 and CYP3A3/4 enzyme substrate; CYP1A2, 2C, 2C9, 2C18, 2C19, 2D6, and 3A3/4 inducer

Decreased effect: Carbamazepine may induce the metabolism of warfarin, cyclosporine, doxycycline, oral contraceptives, phenytoin, theophylline, benzodiazepines, ethosuximide, valproic acid, corticosteroids, and thyroid hormones

Increased toxicity: Erythromycin, isoniazid, propoxyphene, verapamil, danazol, diltiazem, and cimetidine may inhibit hepatic metabolism of carbamazepine with resultant increase of carbamazepine serum concentrations and toxicity

Carbamazepine suspension is **incompatible** with chlorpromazine solution and thioridazine liquid; a number of patients have found rubbery orange mass to indicate a decreased bioavailability. Schedule carbamazepine suspension at least 1-2 hours apart from other liquid medicinals.

Mechanism of Action In addition to anticonvulsant effects, carbamazepine has anticholinergic, antineuralgic, antidiuretic, muscle relaxant and antiarrhythmic properties; may depress activity in the nucleus ventralis of the thalamus or decrease synaptic transmission or decrease summation of temporal stimulation leading to neural discharge by limiting influx of sodium ions across cell membrane or other unknown mechanisms; stimulates the release of ADH and potentiates its action in promoting reabsorption of water; chemically related to tricyclic antidepressants

Pharmacodynamics/Kinetics

Absorption: Slowly absorbed from GI tract

Distribution: V_d: Neonates: 1.5 L/kg; Children: 1.9 L/kg; Adults: 0.59-2 L/kg

Protein binding: 75% to 90%; may be decreased in newborns

Metabolism: In the liver to active epoxide metabolite; induces liver enzymes to increase metabolism and shorten half-life over time

Bioavailability, oral: 85%

Half-life: Initial: 18-55 hours; Multiple dosing: Children: 8-14 hours; Adults: 12-17 hours

Time to peak serum concentration: Unpredictable, within 4-8 hours

(Continued)

Carbamazepine *(Continued)*

Elimination: 1% to 3% excreted unchanged in urine

Usual Dosage Oral (adjust dose according to patient's response and serum concentrations):

Children:

<6 years: Initial: 5 mg/kg/day; dosage may be increased every 5-7 days to 10 mg/kg/day; then up to 20 mg/kg/day if necessary; administer in 2-4 divided doses/day

6-12 years: Initial: 100 mg twice daily or 10 mg/kg/day in 2 divided doses; increase by 100 mg/day at weekly intervals depending upon response; usual maintenance: 20-30 mg/kg/day in 2-4 divided doses; maximum dose: 1000 mg/day

Children >12 years and Adults: 200 mg twice daily to start, increase by 200 mg/day at weekly intervals until therapeutic levels achieved; usual dose: 800-1200 mg/day in 3-4 divided doses; some patients have required up to 1.6-2.4 g/day

Trigeminal or glossopharyngeal neuralgia: Initial: 100 mg twice daily with food, gradually increasing in increments of 100 mg twice daily as needed; usual maintenance: 400-800 mg daily in 2 divided doses

Dosing adjustment in renal impairment: Cl$_{cr}$ <10 mL/minute: Administer 75% of dose

Dietary Considerations

Food: Drug may cause GI upset, take with large amount of water or food to decrease GI upset. May need to split doses to avoid GI upset.

Sodium: SIADH and water intoxication; monitor fluid status; may need to restrict fluid

Reference Range

Timing of serum samples: Absorption is slow, peak levels occur 6-8 hours after ingestion of the first dose; the half-life ranges from 8-60 hours, therefore, steady-state is achieved in 2-5 days

Therapeutic levels: 6-12 µg/mL (SI: 25-51 µmol/L)

Toxic concentration: >15 µg/mL; patients who require higher levels of 8-12 µg/mL (SI: 34-51 µmol/L) should be watched closely. Side effects including CNS effects occur commonly at higher dosage levels. If other anticonvulsants are given therapeutic range is 4-8 µg/mL.

Test Interactions ↑ BUN, AST, ALT, bilirubin, alkaline phosphatase (S); ↓ calcium, T$_3$, T$_4$, sodium (S)

Patient Information Take with food, may cause drowsiness, periodic blood test monitoring required; notify physician if you observe bleeding, bruising, jaundice, abdominal pain, pale stools, mental disturbances, fever, chills, sore throat, or mouth ulcers

Nursing Implications Observe patient for excessive sedation; suspension dosage form must be given on a 3-4 times/day schedule versus tablets which can be given 2-4 times/day

Dosage Forms

Suspension, oral (citrus-vanilla flavor): 100 mg/5 mL (450 mL)

Tablet: 200 mg

Tablet, chewable: 100 mg

Tablet, extended release: 100 mg, 200 mg, 400 mg

♦ **Carbamide** *see* Urea *on page 1199*

Carbamide Peroxide *(KAR ba mide per OKS ide)*

U.S. Brand Names Auro® Ear Drops [OTC]; Debrox® Otic [OTC]; E•R•O Ear [OTC]; Gly-Oxide® Oral [OTC]; Mollifene® Ear Wax Removing Formula [OTC]; Murine® Ear Drops [OTC]; Orajel® Perioseptic [OTC]; Proxigel® Oral [OTC]

Canadian Brand Names Clamurid®

Synonyms Urea Peroxide

Therapeutic Category Anti-infective Agent, Oral; Otic Agent, Cerumenolytic

Use Relief of minor inflammation of gums, oral mucosal surfaces and lips including canker sores and dental irritation; emulsify and disperse ear wax

Pregnancy Risk Factor C

Contraindications Otic preparation should not be used in patients with a perforated tympanic membrane; ear drainage, ear pain or rash in the ear; do not use in the eye; do not use otic preparation longer than 4 days; oral preparation should not be used in children <3 years

Warnings/Precautions

Oral: With prolonged use of oral carbamide peroxide, there is a potential for overgrowth of opportunistic organisms; damage to periodontal tissues; delayed wound healing; should not be used for longer than 7 days

Otic: Do not use if ear drainage or discharge, ear pain, irritation, or rash in ear; should not be used for longer than 4 days

Adverse Reactions 1% to 10%:

Dermatologic: Rash

Local: Irritation, redness

Miscellaneous: Superinfections

Stability Store in tight, light-resistant containers; oral gel should be stored under refrigeration

Mechanism of Action Carbamide peroxide releases hydrogen peroxide which serves as a source of nascent oxygen upon contact with catalase; deodorant action is probably due to inhibition of odor-causing bacteria; softens impacted cerumen due to its foaming action

Pharmacodynamics/Kinetics Onset of effect: Slight disintegration of hard ear wax in 24 hours

Usual Dosage Children and Adults:

Gel: Gently massage on affected area 4 times/day; do not drink or rinse mouth for 5 minutes after use

Oral solution (should not be used for >7 days): Oral preparation should not be used in children <3 years of age; apply several drops undiluted on affected area 4 times/day after meals and at bedtime; expectorate after 2-3 minutes **or** place 10 drops onto tongue, mix with saliva, swish for several minutes, expectorate

Otic:

Children <12 years: Tilt head sideways and individualize the dose according to patient size; 3 drops (range: 1-5 drops) twice daily for up to 4 days, tip of applicator should not enter ear canal; keep drops in ear for several minutes by keeping head tilted and placing cotton in ear

Children ≥12 years and Adults: Tilt head sideways and instill 5-10 drops twice daily up to 4 days, tip of applicator should not enter ear canal; keep drops in ear for several minutes by keeping head tilted and placing cotton in ear

Patient Information Contact physician if dizziness or otic redness, rash, irritation, tenderness, pain, drainage, or discharge develop; do not drink or rinse mouth for 5 minutes after oral use of gel

Nursing Implications Patient may complain of foaming

Additional Information Otic preparation should not be used for >4 days; oral preparation should not be used for longer than 7 days

Dosage Forms

Gel, oral (Proxigel®): 10% (34 g)

Solution:

Oral:

Gly-Oxide®: 10% in glycerin (15 mL, 60 mL)

Orajel® Perioseptic: 15% in glycerin (13.3 mL)

Otic (Auro® Ear Drops, Debrox®, Mollifene® Ear Wax Removing, Murine® Ear Drops): 6.5% in glycerin (15 mL, 30 mL)

- ♦ **Carbamylcholine Chloride** *see* Carbachol *on page 188*
- ♦ **Carbastat® Ophthalmic** *see* Carbachol *on page 188*
- ♦ **Carbatrol®** *see* Carbamazepine *on page 188*

Carbenicillin (kar ben i SIL in)

U.S. Brand Names Geocillin®

Canadian Brand Names Geopen®

Synonyms Carindacillin; Indanyl Sodium

Therapeutic Category Antibiotic, Penicillin

Use Treatment of serious urinary tract infections and prostatitis caused by susceptible gram-negative aerobic bacilli

Pregnancy Risk Factor B

Contraindications Hypersensitivity to carbenicillin or any component or penicillins

Warnings/Precautions Do not use in patients with severe renal impairment (Cl_{cr} <10 mL/minute); dosage modification required in patients with impaired renal and/or hepatic function; oral carbenicillin should be limited to treatment of urinary tract infections. Use with caution in patients with history of hypersensitivity to cephalosporins.

Adverse Reactions

>10%: Gastrointestinal: Diarrhea

1% to 10%: Gastrointestinal: Nausea, bad taste, vomiting, flatulence, glossitis

<1%: Headache, skin rash, urticaria, anemia, thrombocytopenia, leukopenia, neutropenia, eosinophilia, hyperthermia, itchy eyes, vaginitis, hypokalemia, hematuria, thrombophlebitis

Overdosage/Toxicology

Symptoms of overdose include neuromuscular hypersensitivity, convulsions; many beta-lactam containing antibiotics have the potential to cause neuromuscular hyperirritability or convulsive seizures

Hemodialysis may be helpful to aid in the removal of the drug from the blood, otherwise most treatment is supportive or symptom directed

Drug Interactions

Decreased effect with administration of aminoglycosides within 1 hour; may inactivate both drugs

Increased duration of half-life with probenecid

Mechanism of Action Inhibits bacterial cell wall synthesis by binding to one or more of the penicillin binding proteins (PBPs); which in turn inhibits the final transpeptidation step of peptidoglycan synthesis in bacterial cell walls, thus inhibiting cell wall biosynthesis. Bacteria eventually lyse due to ongoing activity of cell wall autolytic enzymes (autolysins and murein hydrolases) while cell wall assembly is arrested.

Pharmacodynamics/Kinetics

Absorption: Oral: 30% to 40%

Distribution: Crosses the placenta; small amounts appear in breast milk; distributes into bile, low concentrations attained in CSF

Half-life: Children: 0.8-1.8 hours; Adults: 1-1.5 hours, prolonged to 10-20 hours with renal insufficiency

Time to peak serum concentration: Within 0.5-2 hours in patients with normal renal function; serum concentrations following oral absorption are inadequate for treatment of systemic infections

Elimination: ~80% to 99% excreted unchanged in urine

(Continued)

Carbenicillin *(Continued)*

Usual Dosage Oral:

Children: 30-50 mg/kg/day divided every 6 hours; maximum dose: 2-3 g/day

Adults: 1-2 tablets every 6 hours for urinary tract infections or 2 tablets every 6 hours for prostatitis

Dosing interval in renal impairment: Adults:

Cl_{cr} 10-50 mL/minute: Administer 382-764 mg every 12-24 hours

Cl_{cr} <10 mL/minute: Administer 382-764 mg every 24-48 hours

Moderately dialyzable (20% to 50%)

Monitoring Parameters Renal, hepatic, and hematologic function tests

Reference Range Therapeutic: Not established; Toxic: >250 µg/mL (SI: >660 µmol/L)

Test Interactions May interfere with urinary glucose tests using cupric sulfate (Benedict's solution, Clinitest®); may inactivate aminoglycosides *in vitro*; false-positive urine or serum proteins

Patient Information Tablets have a bitter taste; take with a full glass of water; take all medication for 7-14 days, do not skip doses; may interfere with oral contraceptives

Additional Information Sodium content of 382 mg tablet: 23 mg (1 mEq)

Dosage Forms Tablet, film coated: 382 mg

Carbidopa *(kar bi DOE pa)*

U.S. Brand Names Lodosyn®

Therapeutic Category Anti-Parkinson's Agent

Use Given with levodopa in the treatment of parkinsonism to enable a lower dosage of levodopa to be used and a more rapid response to be obtained and to decrease side-effects; for details of administration and dosage, see Levodopa; has no effect without levodopa

Pregnancy Risk Factor C

Contraindications Hypersensitivity to carbidopa or levodopa

Adverse Reactions Adverse reactions are associated with concomitant administration with levodopa

>10%: Central nervous system: Anxiety, confusion, nervousness, mental depression

1% to 10%:

Cardiovascular: Orthostatic hypotension, palpitations, cardiac arrhythmias

Central nervous system: Memory loss, nervousness, insomnia, fatigue, hallucinations, ataxia, dystonic movements

Gastrointestinal: Nausea, vomiting, GI bleeding

Ocular: Blurred vision

<1%: Hypertension, duodenal ulcer, hemolytic anemia

Drug Interactions Increased toxicity: Tricyclic antidepressant → hypertensive reactions and dyskinesia

Mechanism of Action Carbidopa is a peripheral decarboxylase inhibitor with little or no pharmacological activity when given alone in usual doses. It inhibits the peripheral decarboxylation of levodopa to dopamine; and as it does not cross the blood-brain barrier, unlike levodopa, effective brain concentrations of dopamine are produced with lower doses of levodopa. At the same time, reduced peripheral formation of dopamine reduces peripheral side-effects, notably nausea and vomiting, and cardiac arrhythmias, although the dyskinesias and adverse mental effects associated with levodopa therapy tend to develop earlier.

Pharmacodynamics/Kinetics

Absorption: Rapid but incomplete from GI tract

Distribution: Does not cross the blood-brain barrier; in rats, it has been reported to cross the placenta and to be excreted in milk

Elimination: Rapidly excreted in urine both unchanged and in the form of metabolites

Usual Dosage Adults: Oral: 70-100 mg/day; maximum daily dose: 200 mg

Administration Administer with meals to decrease GI upset

Patient Information Can take with food to prevent GI upset, do not stop taking this drug even if you do not think it is working; dizziness, lightheadedness, fainting may occur when getting up from a sitting or lying position

Dosage Forms Tablet: 25 mg

♦ **Carbidopa and Levodopa** *see* Levodopa and Carbidopa *on page 672*

Carbinoxamine and Pseudoephedrine

(kar bi NOKS a meen & soo doe e FED rin)

Related Information

Pseudoephedrine *on page 993*

U.S. Brand Names Biohist-LA®; Carbiset® Tablet; Carbiset-TR® Tablet; Carbodec® Syrup; Carbodec® Tablet; Carbodec® TR Tablet; Cardec-S® Syrup; Rondec® Drops; Rondec® Filmtab®; Rondec® Syrup; Rondec-TR®

Therapeutic Category Adrenergic Agonist Agent; Antihistamine, H_1 Blocker; Decongestant

Use Temporary relief of nasal congestion, running nose, sneezing, itching of nose or throat, and itchy, watery eyes due to the common cold, hay fever, or other respiratory allergies

Pregnancy Risk Factor C

Contraindications Hypersensitivity to carbinoxamine or pseudoephedrine or any component; severe hypertension or coronary artery disease, MAO inhibitor therapy, GI or GU obstruction, narrow-angle glaucoma; avoid use in premature or term infants due to a possible association with SIDS

Warnings/Precautions Narrow-angle glaucoma, bladder neck obstruction, symptomatic prostatic hypertrophy, asthmatic attack, and stenosing peptic ulcer

Adverse Reactions

>10%:
  Central nervous system: Slight to moderate drowsiness
  Respiratory: Thickening of bronchial secretions

1% to 10%:
  Central nervous system: Headache, fatigue, nervousness, dizziness
  Gastrointestinal: Appetite increase, weight gain, nausea, diarrhea, abdominal pain, xerostomia
  Neuromuscular & skeletal: Arthralgia
  Respiratory: Pharyngitis

<1%: Edema, palpitations, depression, angioedema, photosensitivity, rash, hepatitis, myalgia, paresthesia, bronchospasm, epistaxis

Overdosage/Toxicology

Symptoms of overdose include dry mouth, flushed skin, dilated pupils, CNS depression There is no specific treatment for an antihistamine overdose, however, most of its clinical toxicity is due to anticholinergic effects. Anticholinesterase inhibitors including physostigmine, neostigmine, pyridostigmine, and edrophonium may be useful by reducing acetylcholinesterase; for anticholinergic overdose with severe life-threatening symptoms, physostigmine 1-2 mg (0.5 mg or 0.02 mg/kg for children) I.V., slowly may be given to reverse these effects.

Drug Interactions Increased toxicity: Barbiturates, TCAs, MAO inhibitors, ethanolamine antihistamines

Mechanism of Action Carbinoxamine competes with histamine for H_1-receptor sites on effector cells in the gastrointestinal tract, blood vessels, and respiratory tract

Usual Dosage Oral:
  Children:
    Drops: 1-18 months: 0.25-1 mL 4 times/day
    Syrup:
      18 months to 6 years: 2.5 mL 3-4 times/day
      >6 years: 5 mL 2-4 times/day
  Adults:
    Liquid: 5 mL 4 times/day
    Tablets: 1 tablet 4 times/day

Patient Information May cause drowsiness, impaired coordination, or judgment; may cause blurred vision; may also cause CNS excitation and difficulty sleeping

Nursing Implications Raise bed rails; institute safety measures; assist with ambulation

Dosage Forms

Drops: Carbinoxamine maleate 2 mg and pseudoephedrine hydrochloride 25 mg per mL (30 mL with dropper)

Syrup: Carbinoxamine maleate 4 mg and pseudoephedrine hydrochloride 60 mg per 5 mL (120 mL, 480 mL)

Tablet:
  Film-coated: Carbinoxamine maleate 4 mg and pseudoephedrine hydrochloride 60 mg
  Sustained release: Carbinoxamine maleate 8 mg and pseudoephedrine hydrochloride 120 mg

Carbinoxamine, Pseudoephedrine, and Dextromethorphan

(kar bi NOKS a meen, soo doe e FED rin, & deks troe meth OR fan)

U.S. Brand Names Carbodec DM®; Cardec DM®; Pseudo-Car® DM; Rondamine-DM® Drops; Rondec®-DM; Tussafed® Drops

Therapeutic Category Antihistamine/Decongestant/Antitussive

Dosage Forms

Drops: Carbinoxamine maleate 2 mg, pseudoephedrine hydrochloride 25 mg, and dextromethorphan hydrobromide 4 mg per mL (30 mL)

Syrup: Carbinoxamine maleate 4 mg, pseudoephedrine hydrochloride 60 mg, and dextromethorphan hydrobromide 15 mg per 5 mL (120 mL, 480 mL, 4000 mL)

- **Carbiset® Tablet** *see Carbinoxamine and Pseudoephedrine on previous page*
- **Carbiset-TR® Tablet** *see Carbinoxamine and Pseudoephedrine on previous page*
- **Carbocaine®** *see Mepivacaine on page 730*
- **Carbodec DM®** *see Carbinoxamine, Pseudoephedrine, and Dextromethorphan on this page*
- **Carbodec® Syrup** *see Carbinoxamine and Pseudoephedrine on previous page*
- **Carbodec® Tablet** *see Carbinoxamine and Pseudoephedrine on previous page*
- **Carbodec® TR Tablet** *see Carbinoxamine and Pseudoephedrine on previous page*

Carboplatin (KAR boe pla tin)

Related Information
Cancer Chemotherapy Regimens on page 1263
Toxicities of Chemotherapeutic Agents on page 1288

U.S. Brand Names Paraplatin®

Synonyms CBDCA

Therapeutic Category Antineoplastic Agent, Alkylating Agent; Antineoplastic Agent, Irritant

(Continued)

Carboplatin *(Continued)*

Use Ovarian carcinoma, cervical, small cell lung carcinoma, esophageal, testicular, bladder cancer, mesothelioma, pediatric brain tumors, sarcoma, neuroblastoma, osteosarcoma

Pregnancy Risk Factor D

Contraindications Hypersensitivity to carboplatin or any component (anaphylactic-like reactions may occur), severe bone marrow suppression, or excessive bleeding

Warnings/Precautions The U.S. Food and Drug Administration (FDA) currently recommends that procedures for proper handling and disposal of antineoplastic agents be considered. High doses have resulted in severe abnormalities of liver function tests. Bone marrow suppression, which may be severe, and vomiting are dose related; reduce dosage in patients with bone marrow suppression and impaired renal function.

Adverse Reactions

>10%:
Endocrine & metabolic: Electrolyte abnormalities such as hypocalcemia and hypomagnesemia, hyponatremia, hypokalemia
Gastrointestinal: Nausea, vomiting, stomatitis
Emetic potential: Moderate
Time course for nausea and vomiting: Onset: 2-6 hours; Duration: 1-48 hours
Hematologic: Neutropenia, leukopenia, thrombocytopenia, anemia
Myelosuppressive: Dose-limiting toxicity
WBC: Severe (dose-dependent)
Platelets: Severe
Nadir: 21-24 days
Recovery: 28-35 days
Hepatic: Abnormal LFTs
Local: Pain at injection site
Neuromuscular & skeletal: Asthenia

1% to 10%:
Dermatologic: Alopecia
Gastrointestinal: Diarrhea, anorexia
Hematologic: Hemorrhagic complications
Neuromuscular & skeletal: Peripheral neuropathy
Otic: Ototoxicity in 1% of patients

<1%: Neurotoxicity has only been noted in patients previously treated with cisplatin, urticaria, rash, blurred vision, nephrotoxicity (uncommon)

Overdosage/Toxicology Symptoms of overdose include bone marrow suppression, hepatic toxicity

Drug Interactions Increased toxicity: Nephrotoxic drugs; aminoglycosides increase risk of ototoxicity

Stability
Store intact vials at room temperature (15°C to 30°C/59°F to 86°F) and protect from light
Reconstitute powder to yield a final concentration of 10 mg/mL which is stable for 5 days at room temperature (25°C)
Aluminum needles should not be used for administration due to binding with the platinum ion
Compatible with etoposide
Standard I.V. dilution: Dose/250-1000 mL D_5W
Further dilution to a concentration as low as 0.5 mg/mL is stable at room temperature (25°C) or under refrigeration for 8 days in D_5W

Mechanism of Action Analogue of cisplatin which covalently binds to DNA; possible cross-linking and interference with the function of DNA

Pharmacodynamics/Kinetics Possible cross-linking and interference with the function of DNA
Distribution: V_d: 16 L/kg; distributes into liver, kidney, skin, and tumor tissue
Metabolism: To aquated and hydroxylated compounds
Protein binding: 0%; however, platinum is 30% irreversibly bound
Half-life: Terminal: 22-40 hours; 2.5-5.9 hours in patients with Cl_{cr} >60 mL/minute
Elimination: ~60% to 90% is excreted renally in the first 24 hours

Usual Dosage IVPB, I.V. infusion, intraperitoneal (refer to individual protocols):
Children:
Solid tumor: 300-600 mg/m² once every 4 weeks
Brain tumor: 175 mg/m² once weekly for 4 weeks with a 2-week recovery period between courses; dose is then adjusted on platelet count and neutrophil count values
Adults:
Ovarian cancer: Usual doses range from 360 mg/m² I.V. every 3 weeks single agent therapy to 300 mg/m² every 4 weeks as combination therapy

Carboplatin Dosage Adjustment Based on Pretreatment Platelet Counts

Platelets (cells/mm³)	Neutrophils (cells/mm³)	Adjusted Dose (from prior course)
>100,000	>2000	125%
50-100,000	500-2000	No adjustment
<50,000	<500	75%

In general, however, single intermittent courses of carboplatin should not be repeated until the neutrophil count is at least 2000 and the platelet count is at least 100,000 The dose adjustments in the table are modified from a controlled trial in previously treated patients with ovarian carcinoma. Blood counts were done weekly, and the recommendations are based on the lowest post-treatment platelet or neutrophil value.

Carboplatin dosage adjustment based on the Egorin formula (based on platelet counts):

Previously untreated patients:

$$\text{dosage (mg/m}^2) = \frac{(0.091)\ (Cl_{cr})}{(BSA)} \left(\frac{\text{Pretreat Plt count - Plt nadir count desired x 100}}{\text{(Pretreatment Plt count)}}\right) + 86$$

Previously treated patients with heavily myelosuppressive agents:

$$\text{dosage (mg/m}^2) = \frac{(0.091)\ (Cl_{cr})}{(BSA)} \left[\frac{\text{(Pretreat Plt count - Plt nadir count desired x 100) - 17}}{\text{(Pretreatment Plt count)}}\right] + 86$$

Autologous BMT: I.V.: 1600 mg/m^2 (total dose) divided over 4 days **requires BMT (ie, FATAL without BMT)**

Dosing adjustment in hepatic impairment: There are no published studies available on the dosing of carboplatin in patients with impaired liver function. Human data regarding the biliary elimination of carboplatin are not available; however, pharmacokinetic studies in rabbits and rats reflect a biliary excretion of 0.4% to 0.7% of the dose (ie, 0.05 mL/minute/kg biliary clearance).

Dosing adjustment in renal impairment: These dosing recommendations apply to the initial course of treatment. Subsequent dosages should be adjusted according to the patient's tolerance based on the degree of bone marrow suppression.

Cl_{cr} <60 mL/minute: Increased risk of severe bone marrow suppression. In renally impaired patients who received single agent carboplatin therapy, the incidence of severe leukopenia, neutropenia, or thrombocytopenia has been about 25% when the following dosage modifications have been used:

Cl_{cr} 41-59 mL/minute: Recommended dose on day 1 is 250 mg/m^2

Cl_{cr} 16-40 mL/minute: Recommended dose on day 1 is 200 mg/m^2

Cl_{cr} <15 mL/minute: The data available for patients with severely impaired kidney function are too limited to permit a recommendation for treatment

or

Dosing adjustment in renal impairment: CALVERT FORMULA

Total dose (mg) = Target AUC (mg/mL/minute) x (GFR [mL/minute] + 25)

Note: The dose of carboplatin calculated is TOTAL mg DOSE not mg/m^2. AUC is the area under the concentration versus time curve.

Target AUC value will vary depending upon:

Number of agents in the regimen

Treatment status (ie, previously untreated or treated)

Single Agent Carboplatin/No Prior Chemotherapy	Total dose (mg): 6-8 (GFR + 25)
Single Agent Carboplatin/Prior Chemotherapy	Total dose (mg): 4-6 (GFR + 25)
Combination Chemotherapy/No Prior Chemotherapy	Total dose (mg): 4.5-6 (GFR + 25)
Combination Chemotherapy/Prior Chemotherapy	A reasonable approach for these patients would be to use a target AUC value <5 for the initial cycle

Note: The Jelliffe formula (below) substantially underestimates the creatinine clearance in patients with a serum creatinine <1.5 mg/dL. However, the Jelliffe formula is more accurate in estimating creatinine clearance in patients with significant renal impairment than the Cockroft and Gault formula.

Cl_{cr} (mL/minute/1.73 m^2) for males = 98 - [(0.8) (Age - 20)]/S_{cr}

Cl_{cr} (mL/minute/1.73 m^2) for females = 98 - [(0.8) (Age - 20)]/S_{cr} multiplied by 90%

Intraperitoneal: 200-650 mg/m^2 in 2 L of dialysis fluid have been administered into the peritoneum of ovarian cancer patients

Administration

Do not use needles or I.V. administration sets containing aluminum parts that may come in contact with carboplatin (aluminum can react causing precipitate formation and loss of potency)

Administer as IVPB over 15 minutes up to a CIV over 24 hours; may also be administered intraperitoneally

Monitoring Parameters CBC (with differential and platelet count), serum electrolytes, urinalysis, creatinine clearance, liver function tests

Patient Information Contraceptive measures are recommended during therapy; report any loss of hearing, numbness, or tingling in the extremities to the physician

Dosage Forms Powder for injection, lyophilized: 50 mg, 150 mg, 450 mg

Carboprost Tromethamine (KAR boe prost tro METH a meen)

Replaces Prostin/15M®

U.S. Brand Names Hemabate™

(Continued)

Carboprost Tromethamine (Continued)

Therapeutic Category Abortifacient; Prostaglandin
Use Termination of pregnancy and refractory postpartum uterine bleeding
  Investigational: Hemorrhagic cystitis
Pregnancy Risk Factor X
Contraindications Hypersensitivity to carboprost tromethamine or any component; acute pelvic inflammatory disease; pregnancy
Warnings/Precautions Use with caution in patients with history of asthma, hypotension or hypertension, cardiovascular, adrenal, renal or hepatic disease, anemia, jaundice, diabetes, epilepsy or compromised uteri
Adverse Reactions
  >10%: Gastrointestinal: Nausea (33%)
  1% to 10%: Cardiovascular: Flushing (7%)
  <1%: Hypertension, hypotension, drowsiness, vertigo, nervousness, fever, headache, dystonia, vasovagal syndrome, breast tenderness, xerostomia, vomiting, diarrhea, hematemesis, abnormal taste, bladder spasms, myalgia, blurred vision, coughing, asthma, respiratory distress, septic shock, hiccups
Drug Interactions Increased toxicity: Oxytocic agents
Stability Refrigerate ampuls
  Bladder irrigation: Dilute immediately prior to administration in NS; stability unknown
Mechanism of Action Carboprost tromethamine is a prostaglandin similar to prostaglandin F_2 alpha (dinoprost) except for the addition of a methyl group at the C-15 position. This substitution produces longer duration of activity than dinoprost; carboprost stimulates uterine contractility which usually results in expulsion of the products of conception and is used to induce abortion between 13-20 weeks of pregnancy. Hemostasis at the placentation site is achieved through the myometrial contractions produced by carboprost.
Usual Dosage Adults: I.M.:
  Abortion: Initial: 250 mcg, then 250 mcg at $1^1/_2$-hour to $3^1/_2$-hour intervals depending on uterine response; a 500 mcg dose may be given if uterine response is not adequate after several 250 mcg doses; do not exceed 12 mg total dose or continuous administration for >2 days
  Refractory postpartum uterine bleeding: Initial: 250 mcg; may repeat at 15- to 90-minute intervals to a total dose of 2 mg
  Bladder irrigation for hemorrhagic cystitis (refer to individual protocols): [0.4-1.0 mg/dL as solution] 50 mL instilled into bladder 4 times/day for 1 hour
Administration Do not inject I.V.; may result in bronchospasm, hypertension, vomiting, and anaphylaxis
Dosage Forms Injection: Carboprost 250 mcg and tromethamine 83 mcg per mL (1 mL)

Carisoprodol (kar i soe PROE dole)

U.S. Brand Names Rela®; Sodol®; Soma®; Soprodol®; Soridol®
Synonyms Carisoprodate; Isobamate
Therapeutic Category Skeletal Muscle Relaxant
Use Skeletal muscle relaxant
Pregnancy Risk Factor C
Contraindications Acute intermittent porphyria, hypersensitivity to carisoprodol, meprobamate or any component
Warnings/Precautions Use with caution in renal and hepatic dysfunction
Adverse Reactions
  >10%: Central nervous system: Drowsiness
  1% to 10%:
    Cardiovascular: Tachycardia, tightness in chest, flushing of face, syncope
    Central nervous system: Mental depression, allergic fever, dizziness, lightheadedness, headache, paradoxical CNS stimulation
    Dermatologic: Angioedema
    Gastrointestinal: Nausea, vomiting, stomach cramps
    Neuromuscular & skeletal: Trembling
    Ocular: Burning eyes
    Respiratory: Shortness of breath
    Miscellaneous: Hiccups

<1%: Ataxia, rash, urticaria, erythema multiforme, aplastic anemia, leukopenia, eosino-philia, blurred vision

Overdosage/Toxicology
Symptoms of overdose include CNS depression, stupor, coma, shock, respiratory depression
Treatment is supportive following attempts to enhance drug elimination. Hypotension should be treated with I.V. fluids and/or Trendelenburg positioning.

Drug Interactions CYP2C19 enzyme substrate
Increased toxicity: Alcohol, CNS depressants, phenothiazines

Mechanism of Action Precise mechanism is not yet clear, but many effects have been ascribed to its central depressant actions

Pharmacodynamics/Kinetics
Onset of action: Within 30 minutes
Duration: 4-6 hours
Distribution: Crosses the placenta; appears in high concentrations in breast milk
Metabolism: By the liver
Half-life: 8 hours
Elimination: By the kidneys

Usual Dosage Adults: Oral: 350 mg 3-4 times/day; take last dose at bedtime; compound: 1-2 tablets 4 times/day

Dietary Considerations Alcohol: Additive CNS effects, avoid use

Monitoring Parameters Look for relief of pain and/or muscle spasm and avoid excessive drowsiness

Patient Information May cause drowsiness or dizziness; avoid alcohol and other CNS depressants

Nursing Implications Raise bed rails; institute safety measures; assist with ambulation

Dosage Forms Tablet: 350 mg

Extemporaneous Preparations A suspension can be prepared by triturating 60 carisoprodol 350 mg tablets, a small amount of water or glycerin, then mixing with a sufficient quantity of cherry syrup to bring the final volume to 60 mL; when refrigerated, the suspension is stable for 14 days; shake well before administration

Carisoprodol and Aspirin (kar i soe PROE dole & AS pir in)
U.S. Brand Names Soma® Compound
Therapeutic Category Skeletal Muscle Relaxant
Dosage Forms Tablet: Carisoprodol 200 mg and aspirin 325 mg

Carisoprodol, Aspirin, and Codeine
(kar i soe PROE dole, AS pir in, and KOE deen)
U.S. Brand Names Soma® Compound w/Codeine
Therapeutic Category Skeletal Muscle Relaxant
Dosage Forms Tablet: Carisoprodol 200 mg, aspirin 325 mg, and codeine phosphate 16 mg

♦ Carmol-HC® Topical see Urea and Hydrocortisone on page 1199
♦ Carmol® Topical [OTC] see Urea on page 1199

Carmustine (kar MUS teen)
Related Information
Cancer Chemotherapy Regimens on page 1263
Toxicities of Chemotherapeutic Agents on page 1288

U.S. Brand Names BiCNU®

Synonyms BCNU

Therapeutic Category Antineoplastic Agent, Alkylating Agent (Nitrosourea); Antineo-plastic Agent, Vesicant; Vesicant

Use Treatment of brain tumors (glioblastoma, brainstem glioma, medulloblastoma, astro-cytoma, ependymoma, and metastatic brain tumors), multiple myeloma, Hodgkin's disease (secondary therapy in combination with other approved drugs in patients who relapse while being treated with primary therapy or who fail to respond to primary therapy) and non-Hodgkin's lymphomas (secondary therapy in combination with other approved drugs in patients who relapse while being treated with primary therapy or who fail to respond to primary therapy), melanoma, lung cancer, colon cancer

Pregnancy Risk Factor D

Contraindications Hypersensitivity to carmustine or any component, myelosuppression from previous chemotherapy or other causes

Warnings/Precautions The U.S. Food and Drug Administration (FDA) currently recommends that procedures for proper handling and disposal of antineoplastic agents be considered. Administer with caution to patients with depressed platelet, leukocyte or erythrocyte counts, renal or hepatic impairment. Bone marrow depression, notably thrombocytopenia and leukopenia, may lead to bleeding and overwhelming infections in an already compromised patient; will last for at least 6 weeks after a dose, **do not give courses more frequently than every 6 weeks because the toxicity is cumulative.**

Baseline pulmonary function tests are recommended. Delayed onset pulmonary fibrosis occurring up to 17 years after treatment has been reported in children (1-16 years) who received carmustine in cumulative doses ranging from 770-1800 mg/m^2 combined with cranial radiotherapy for intracranial tumors.
(Continued)

Carmustine *(Continued)*

Adverse Reactions

>10%:

Cardiovascular: Hypotension is associated with HIGH-DOSE administration secondary to the high alcohol content of the diluent

Central nervous system: Dizziness and ataxia

Dermatologic: Hyperpigmentation of skin

Gastrointestinal: Nausea and vomiting occur within 2-4 hours after drug injection; dose-related

Emetic potential:

<200 mg: Moderately high (60% to 90%)

≥200 mg: High (>90%)

Time course of nausea/vomiting: Onset: 2-6 hours; Duration: 4-6 hours

Hematologic: Myelosuppressive: Delayed, occurs 4-6 weeks after administration and is dose-related; usually persists for 1-2 weeks; thrombocytopenia is usually more severe than leukopenia. Myelofibrosis and preleukemic syndromes have been reported.

WBC: Moderate

Platelets: Severe

Onset (days): 14

Nadir (days): 21-35

Recovery (days): 42-50

Local: Burning at injection site

Irritant chemotherapy: Pain at injection site

Ocular: Ocular toxicity, and retinal hemorrhages

1% to 10%:

Dermatologic: Facial flushing is probably due to the ethanol used in reconstitution, alopecia

Gastrointestinal: Stomatitis, diarrhea, anorexia

Hematologic: Anemia

<1%: Hyperpigmentation, dermatitis, reversible toxicity, increased LFTs in 20%, fibrosis occurs mostly in patients treated with prolonged total doses >1400 mg/m^2 or with bone marrow transplantation doses; risk factors include a history of lung disease, concomitant bleomycin, or radiation therapy; PFTs should be conducted prior to therapy and monitored; patients with predicted FVC or DL$_{co}$ <70% are at a higher risk; azotemia, decrease in kidney size

Overdosage/Toxicology

Symptoms of overdose include nausea, vomiting, thrombocytopenia, leukopenia

There are no known antidotes and treatment is primarily symptomatic and supportive

Drug Interactions Increased toxicity:

Cimetidine: Reported to cause bone marrow suppression

Etoposide: Reported to cause severe hepatic dysfunction with hyperbilirubinemia, ascites, and thrombocytopenia

Stability

Store intact vials under refrigeration; vials are stable for 36 days at room temperature

Initially dilute with 3 mL of absolute alcohol diluent. Further dilute with 27 mL SWI to result in a concentration of 3.3 mg/mL with 10% ethanol. Initial solutions are stable for 8 hours at room temperature (25°C) and 24 hours at refrigeration (2°C to 8°C) and protected from light.

Further dilution in D$_5$W or NS is stable for 8 hours at room temperature (25°C) and 48 hours at refrigeration (4°C) in glass or Excel® protected from light

Incompatible with sodium bicarbonate; **compatible** with cisplatin

Standard I.V. dilution: Dose/150-500 mL D$_5$W or NS

Must use glass or Excel® containers for administration

Protect from light

Stable for 8 hours at room temperature (25°C) and 48 hours under refrigeration (4°C)

Mechanism of Action Interferes with the normal function of DNA by alkylation and cross-linking the strands of DNA, and by possible protein modification

Pharmacodynamics/Kinetics

Absorption: Highly lipid soluble

Distribution: Readily crosses the blood-brain barrier producing CSF levels equal to 15% to 70% of blood plasma levels; distributes into breast milk

Metabolism: Rapid

Half-life (biphasic): Initial: 1.4 minutes; Secondary: 20 minutes (active metabolites may persist for days and have a plasma half-life of 67 hours)

Elimination: ~60% to 70% excreted in the urine within 96 hours and 6% to 10% excreted as CO$_2$ by the lungs

Suggested Carmustine Dose Following Initial Dose

Nadir After Prior Dose		% of Prior Dose to Be Given
Leukocytes/mm^3	Platelets/mm^3	
>4000	>100,000	100
3000-3999	75,000-99,999	100
2000-2999	25,000-74,999	70
<2000	<25,000	50

Usual Dosage I.V. (refer to individual protocols):

Children: 200-250 mg/m² every 4-6 weeks as a single dose

Adults: 150-200 mg/m² every 6 weeks as a single dose or divided into daily injections on 2 successive days; next dose is to be determined based on hematologic response to the previous dose. See table.

Primary brain cancer: 150-200 mg/m² every 6-8 weeks

Autologous BMT: ALL OF THE FOLLOWING DOSES ARE FATAL WITHOUT BMT

Combination therapy: Up to 300-900 mg/m²

Single agent therapy: Up to 1200 mg/m² (fatal necrosis is associated with doses >2 g/m²)

Hemodialysis: Supplemental dosing is not required

Dosing adjustment in hepatic impairment: Dosage adjustment may be necessary; however, no specific guidelines are available

Administration

Significant absorption to PVC containers - should be administered in either glass or Excel® container

Infuse I.V. infusion over ≥15-45 minutes is recommended to minimize severe burning/vein irritation; longer infusion times (1-2 hours) can alleviate venous pain/irritation

High-dose carmustine: Maximum rate of infusion of ≤3 mg/m²/minute to avoid excessive flushing, agitation, and hypotension; infusions should run over at least 2 hours; some investigational protocols dictate shorter infusions.

Monitoring Parameters CBC with differential and platelet count, pulmonary function, liver function, and renal function tests; monitor blood pressure during administration

Patient Information Contraceptive measures are recommended during therapy

Dosage Forms Powder for injection: 100 mg/vial packaged with 3 mL of absolute alcohol for use as a sterile diluent

Carteolol (KAR tee oh lole)

Related Information

Beta-Blockers Comparison *on page 1311*

Glaucoma Drug Therapy Comparison *on page 1322*

U.S. Brand Names Cartrol® Oral; Ocupress® Ophthalmic

Synonyms Carteolol Hydrochloride

Therapeutic Category Antihypertensive Agent; Beta-Adrenergic Blocker; Beta-Adrenergic Blocker, Ophthalmic

Use Management of hypertension; treatment of chronic open-angle glaucoma and intraocular hypertension

Pregnancy Risk Factor C

Contraindications Bronchial asthma, sinus bradycardia, second and third degree A-V block, cardiac failure (unless a functioning pacemaker present), cardiogenic shock, hypersensitivity to betaxolol or any component

Warnings/Precautions Some products contain sulfites which can cause allergic reactions; diminished response over time; may increase muscle weaknesses; use with a miotic in angle-closure glaucoma; use with caution in patients with decreased renal or hepatic function (dosage adjustment required) or patients with a history of asthma, congestive heart failure, or bradycardia; severe CNS, cardiovascular, and respiratory adverse effects have been seen following ophthalmic use

Adverse Reactions

1% to 10%:

Cardiovascular: Congestive heart failure, arrhythmia

Central nervous system: Mental depression, headache, dizziness

Neuromuscular & skeletal: Back pain, arthralgia

<1%: Bradycardia, chest pain, mesenteric arterial thrombosis, A-V block, persistent bradycardia, hypotension, edema, Raynaud's phenomenon, fatigue, insomnia, lethargy, nightmares, confusion, purpura, hyperglycemia, ischemic colitis, constipation, nausea, diarrhea, impotence, thrombocytopenia, bronchospasm, cold extremities

Overdosage/Toxicology

Symptoms of intoxication include cardiac disturbances, CNS toxicity, bronchospasm, hypoglycemia, and hyperkalemia. The most common cardiac symptoms include hypotension and bradycardia; atrioventricular block, intraventricular conduction disturbances, cardiogenic shock, and asystole may occur with severe overdose, especially with membrane-depressant drugs (eg, propranolol); CNS effects include convulsions, coma, and respiratory arrest (commonly seen with propranolol and other membrane-depressant and lipid-soluble drugs)

Treatment includes symptomatic treatment of seizures, hypotension, hyperkalemia, and hypoglycemia; bradycardia and hypotension resistant to atropine, isoproterenol, or pacing may respond to glucagon; wide QRS defects caused by the membrane-depressant poisoning may respond to hypertonic sodium bicarbonate; repeat-dose charcoal, hemoperfusion, or hemodialysis may be helpful in removal of only those beta-blockers with a small V_d, long half-life, or low intrinsic clearance (acebutolol, atenolol, nadolol, sotalol).

Drug Interactions

Decreased effect of beta-blockers with aluminum salts, barbiturates, calcium salts, cholestyramine, colestipol, NSAIDs, penicillins (ampicillin), rifampin, salicylates, and sulfinpyrazone due to decreased bioavailability and plasma levels

Beta-blockers may decrease the effect of sulfonylureas

Increased effect/toxicity of beta-blockers with calcium blockers (diltiazem, felodipine, nicardipine), contraceptives, flecainide, haloperidol (propranolol, hypotensive effects), (Continued)

Carteolol *(Continued)*

H₂-antagonists (metoprolol, propranolol only by cimetidine, possibly ranitidine), hydralazine (metoprolol, propranolol), loop diuretics (propranolol, not atenolol), MAO inhibitors (metoprolol, nadolol, bradycardia), phenothiazines (propranolol), propafenone (metoprolol, propranolol), quinidine (in extensive metabolizers), ciprofloxacin, thyroid hormones (metoprolol, propranolol, when hypothyroid patient is converted to euthyroid state)

Beta-blockers may increase the effect/toxicity of flecainide, haloperidol (hypotensive effects), hydralazine, phenothiazines, acetaminophen, anticoagulants (propranolol, warfarin), benzodiazepines (not atenolol), clonidine (hypertensive crisis after or during withdrawal of either agent), epinephrine (initial hypertensive episode followed by bradycardia), nifedipine and verapamil lidocaine, ergots (peripheral ischemia), prazosin (postural hypotension)

Beta-blockers may affect the action or levels of ethanol, disopyramide, nondepolarizing muscle relaxants and theophylline although the effects are difficult to predict

Mechanism of Action Blocks both beta₁- and beta₂-receptors and has mild intrinsic sympathomimetic activity; has negative inotropic and chronotropic effects and can significantly slow A-V nodal conduction

Pharmacodynamics/Kinetics
Onset of effect: Oral: 1-1.5 hours
Peak effect: 2 hours
Duration: 12 hours
Absorption: Oral: 80%
Protein binding: 23% to 30%
Metabolism: 30% to 50%
Half-life: 6 hours
Elimination: Renally excreted metabolites

Usual Dosage Adults:
Oral: 2.5 mg as a single daily dose, with a maintenance dose normally 2.5-5 mg once daily; doses >10 mg do not increase response and may in fact decrease effect
Ophthalmic: Instill 1 drop in affected eye(s) twice daily
Dosing interval in renal impairment:
Cl$_{cr}$ >60 mL/minute/1.73 m²: Administer every 24 hours
Cl$_{cr}$ 20-60 mL/minute/1.73 m²: Administer every 48 hours
Cl$_{cr}$ <20 mL/minute/1.73 m²: Administer every 72 hours

Monitoring Parameters Ophthalmic: Intraocular pressure; Systemic: Blood pressure, pulse, CNS status

Patient Information Intended for twice daily dosing; keep eye open and do not blink for 30 seconds after instillation; wear sunglasses to avoid photophobic discomfort; apply gentle pressure to lacrimal sac during and immediately following instillation (1 minute); do not discontinue medication abruptly, sudden stopping of medication may precipitate or cause angina; consult pharmacist or physician before taking with other adrenergic drugs (eg, cold medications); notify physician if any systemic side effects occur; use with caution while driving or performing tasks requiring alertness; may mask signs of hypoglycemia in diabetics; may be taken without regard to meals

Nursing Implications Advise against abrupt withdrawal; monitor orthostatic blood pressures, apical and peripheral pulse, and mental status changes (ie, confusion, depression)

Dosage Forms
Solution, ophthalmic, as hydrochloride (Ocupress®): 1% (5 mL, 10 mL)
Tablet, as hydrochloride (Cartrol®): 2.5 mg, 5 mg

♦ **Carteolol Hydrochloride** see Carteolol *on previous page*
♦ **Cartrol® Oral** see Carteolol *on previous page*

Carvedilol *(KAR ve dil ole)*

Related Information
Beta-Blockers Comparison *on page 1311*
U.S. Brand Names Coreg®
Therapeutic Category Antihypertensive Agent; Beta-Adrenergic Blocker
Use Management of hypertension; can be used alone or in combination with other agents, especially thiazide-type diuretics; treatment of mild or moderate congestive heart failure of ischemia or cardiomyopathic origin in conjunction with digitalis, diuretics, and ACE inhibitors to reduce the progression of disease as evidenced by cardiovascular death, cardiovascular hospitalizations, or the need to adjust other heart failure medications
Unlabeled use: Appears to be effective in the treatment of angina and idiopathic cardiomyopathy

Pregnancy Risk Factor C
Pregnancy/Breast-Feeding Implications
Clinical effects on the fetus: Use during pregnancy only if the potential benefit justifies the risk
Breast-feeding/lactation: Possible excretion in breast milk; avoid administration in lactating women, if possible

Contraindications Uncompensated congestive heart failure (NYHA Class IV), asthma or bronchospastic disease (status asthmaticus may result), cardiogenic shock, severe bradycardia or second or third degree heart block, and symptomatic hepatic disease; hypersensitivity to any component

Warnings/Precautions Use with caution in patients with congestive heart failure treated with digitalis, diuretic, or ACE inhibitor since A-V conduction may be slowed; discontinue therapy if any evidence of liver injury occurs; use caution in patients with peripheral vascular disease, those undergoing anesthesia, in hyperthyroidism and diabetes mellitus. If no other antihypertensive is tolerated, very small doses may be cautiously used in patients with bronchospastic disease. Abrupt withdrawal of the drug should be avoided, drug should be discontinued over 1-2 weeks; do not use in pregnant or nursing women; may potentiate hypoglycemia in a diabetic patient and mask signs and symptoms; safety and efficacy in children have not been established.

Adverse Reactions
>1%:
Cardiovascular: Bradycardia, postural hypotension, edema
Central nervous system: Dizziness, somnolence, insomnia, fatigue
Gastrointestinal: Diarrhea, abdominal pain
Neuromuscular & skeletal: Back pain
Respiratory: Rhinitis, pharyngitis, dyspnea
<1%: A-V block, extrasystoles, hypertension, hypotension, palpitations, peripheral ischemia, syncope, ataxia, vertigo, depression, nervousness, malaise, pruritus, rash, decreased male libido, hypercholesterolemia, hyperglycemia, hyperuricemia, constipation, flatulence, xerostomia, impotence, anemia, leukopenia, hyperbilirubinemia, increased LFTs, paresthesia, myalgia, weakness, abnormal vision, tinnitus, asthma, cough, diaphoresis (increased)

Overdosage/Toxicology
Symptoms of intoxication include cardiac disturbances, CNS toxicity, bronchospasm, hypoglycemia, and hyperkalemia. The most common cardiac symptoms include hypotension and bradycardia; atrioventricular block, intraventricular conduction disturbances, cardiogenic shock, and asystole may occur with severe overdose, especially with membrane-depressant drugs (eg, propranolol); CNS effects include convulsions, coma, and respiratory arrest which are commonly seen with propranolol and other membrane-depressant and lipid-soluble drugs.

Treatment includes symptomatic treatment of seizures, hypotension, hyperkalemia, and hypoglycemia; bradycardia and hypotension resistant to atropine, isoproterenol, or pacing may respond to glucagon; wide QRS defects caused by the membrane-depressant poisoning may respond to hypertonic sodium bicarbonate; repeat-dose charcoal, hemoperfusion, or hemodialysis may be helpful in removal of only those beta-blockers with a small V_d, long half-life, or low intrinsic clearance (acebutolol, atenolol, nadolol, sotalol)

Drug Interactions CYP2C, 2C9, and 2D6 enzyme substrate
Decreased effect: Rifampin may reduce the plasma concentration of carvedilol by up to 70%; decreased effect of other beta-blockers has also occurred with aluminum salts, barbiturates, calcium salts, cholestyramine, colestipol, NSAIDs, penicillins (ampicillin), salicylates, and sulfinpyrazone due to decreased bioavailability and plasma levels; beta-blockers may decrease the effect of sulfonylureas

Increased effect: Carvedilol may enhance the action of antidiabetic agents, calcium channel blockers, digoxin; clonidine and carvedilol may result in augmented blood pressure and heart rate lowering effects; cimetidine increases the effect and AUC of carvedilol. Other drugs likely to increase carvedilol's levels and effects include quinidine, fluoxetine, paroxetine, and propafenone since these drugs inhibit CYP2D6.

Increased effect/toxicity of other beta-blockers occurs with contraceptives, flecainide, epinephrine (initial hypertensive episode followed by bradycardia), lidocaine, ergots (peripheral ischemia), and prazosin (postural hypotension)

Mechanism of Action
As a racemic mixture, carvedilol has nonselective beta-adrenoreceptor and alpha-adrenergic blocking activity at equal potency. No intrinsic sympathomimetic activity has been documented. Associated effects include reduction of cardiac output, exercise- or beta agonist-induced tachycardia, reduction of reflex orthostatic tachycardia, vasodilation, decreased peripheral vascular resistance (especially in standing position), decreased renal vascular resistance, reduced plasma renin activity, and increased levels of atrial natriuretic peptide.

Pharmacodynamics/Kinetics
Absorption: Rapid; food decreases the rate but not the extent of absorption; administration with food minimizes risks of orthostatic hypotension
Metabolism: First-pass metabolism; extensively metabolized primarily by aromatic ring oxidation and glucuronidation (2% excreted unchanged); three active metabolites (4-hydroxphenyl metabolite is 13 times more potent than parent drug); plasma concentrations in the elderly and those with cirrhotic liver disease are 50% and 4-7 times higher, respectively
Bioavailability: 25% to 35%
Half-life: 7-10 hours
Elimination: Primarily via bile into feces

Usual Dosage Adults: Oral:
Hypertension: 6.25 mg twice daily; if tolerated, dose should be maintained for 1-2 weeks, then increased to 12.5 mg twice daily; dosage may be increased to a maximum of 25 mg twice daily after 1-2 weeks; reduce dosage if heart rate drops to <55 beats/minute
Congestive heart failure: 3.125 mg twice daily for 2 weeks; if this dose is tolerated, may increase to 6.25 mg twice daily. Double the dose every 2 weeks to the highest dose tolerated by patient. (Prior to initiating therapy, other heart failure medications should be stabilized.)
Maximum recommended dose:
<85 kg: 25 mg twice daily
>85 kg: 50 mg twice daily
Angina pectoris (unlabeled use): 25-50 mg twice daily
Idiopathic cardiomyopathy (unlabeled use): 6.25-25 mg twice daily
(Continued)

Carvedilol *(Continued)*

Dosing adjustment in renal impairment: None necessary

Dosing adjustment in hepatic impairment: Use is contraindicated in liver dysfunction

Monitoring Parameters Heart rate, blood pressure (base need for dosage increase on trough blood pressure measurements and for tolerance on standing systolic pressure 1 hour after dosing)

Patient Information Take with food to minimize the risk of hypotension; do not interrupt or discontinue using carvedilol without a physician's advice; use care to avoid standing abruptly or standing still for long periods; lie down if dizziness or faintness occurs and consult a physician for a reduced dosage; contact lens wearers may experience dry eyes

Nursing Implications Minimize risk of bradycardia with initiation of treatment with a low dose, slow upward titration, and administration with food; decrease dose if pulse rate drops <55 beats per minute

Dosage Forms Tablet: 3.125 mg, 6.25 mg, 12.5 mg, 25 mg

Cascara Sagrada *(kas KAR a sah GRAH dah)*

Related Information

Laxatives, Classification and Properties *on page 1326*

Therapeutic Category Laxative, Stimulant

Use Temporary relief of constipation; sometimes used with milk of magnesia ("black and white" mixture)

Pregnancy Risk Factor C

Contraindications Nausea, vomiting, abdominal pain, fecal impaction, intestinal obstruction, GI bleeding, appendicitis, congestive heart failure

Warnings/Precautions Excessive use can lead to electrolyte imbalance, fluid imbalance, vitamin deficiency, steatorrhea, osteomalacia, cathartic colon, and dependence; should be avoided during nursing because it may have a laxative effect on the infant

Adverse Reactions 1% to 10%:

Central nervous system: Faintness

Endocrine & metabolic: Electrolyte and fluid imbalance

Gastrointestinal: Abdominal cramps, nausea, diarrhea

Genitourinary: Discoloration of urine (reddish pink or brown)

Drug Interactions Decreased effect of oral anticoagulants

Stability Protect from light and heat

Mechanism of Action Direct chemical irritation of the intestinal mucosa resulting in an increased rate of colonic motility and change in fluid and electrolyte secretion

Pharmacodynamics/Kinetics

Onset of action: 6-10 hours

Absorption: Oral: Small amount absorbed from small intestine

Metabolism: In the liver

Usual Dosage Note: Cascara sagrada fluid extract is 5 times more potent than cascara sagrada aromatic fluid extract

Oral (aromatic fluid extract):

Infants: 1.25 mL/day (range: 0.5-1.5 mL) as needed

Children 2-11 years: 2.5 mL/day (range: 1-3 mL) as needed

Children ≥12 years and Adults: 5 mL/day (range: 2-6 mL) as needed at bedtime (1 tablet as needed at bedtime)

Test Interactions ↓ calcium (S), ↓ potassium (S)

Patient Information Should not be used regularly for more than 1 week

Dosage Forms

Aromatic fluid extract: 120 mL, 473 mL

Tablet: 325 mg

- ♦ **Casodex®** *see* Bicalutamide *on page 144*
- ♦ **Cataflam® Oral** *see* Diclofenac *on page 348*
- ♦ **Catapres® Oral** *see* Clonidine *on page 283*
- ♦ **Catapres-TTS® Transdermal** *see* Clonidine *on page 283*
- ♦ **Caverject® Injection** *see* Alprostadil *on page 46*
- ♦ **CBDCA** *see* Carboplatin *on page 193*
- ♦ **CCNU** *see* Lomustine *on page 691*
- ♦ **C-Crystals® [OTC]** *see* Ascorbic Acid *on page 99*
- ♦ **2-CdA** *see* Cladribine *on page 271*
- ♦ **CDDP** *see* Cisplatin *on page 267*
- ♦ **Cebid® Timecelles® [OTC]** *see* Ascorbic Acid *on page 99*
- ♦ **Ceclor®** *see* Cefaclor *on this page*
- ♦ **Ceclor® CD** *see* Cefaclor *on this page*
- ♦ **Cecon® [OTC]** *see* Ascorbic Acid *on page 99*
- ♦ **Cedax®** *see* Ceftibuten *on page 221*
- ♦ **Cedocard®-SR** *see* Isosorbide Dinitrate *on page 637*
- ♦ **CeeNU®** *see* Lomustine *on page 691*

Cefaclor *(SEF a klor)*

Related Information

Antimicrobial Drugs of Choice *on page 1404*

Cephalosporins by Generation *on page 1373*

U.S. Brand Names Ceclor®; Ceclor® CD

Canadian Brand Names Apo®-Cefaclor

Therapeutic Category Antibiotic, Cephalosporin (Second Generation)

Use Infections caused by susceptible organisms including *Staphylococcus aureus* and *H. influenzae*; treatment of otitis media, sinusitis, and infections involving the respiratory tract, skin and skin structure, bone and joint, and urinary tract

Pregnancy Risk Factor B

Contraindications Hypersensitivity to cefaclor, any component, or cephalosporins

Warnings/Precautions Modify dosage in patients with severe renal impairment; prolonged use may result in superinfection; a low incidence of cross-hypersensitivity to penicillins exists

Adverse Reactions

1% to 10%:

Gastrointestinal: Diarrhea (1.5%)

Hematologic: Eosinophilia (2%)

Hepatic: Elevated transaminases (2.5%)

Dermatologic: Rash (maculopapular, erythematous, or morbilliform) (1% to 1.5%)

<1%: Anaphylaxis, urticaria, pruritus, angioedema, serum-sickness, arthralgia, hepatitis, cholestatic jaundice, Stevens-Johnson syndrome, nausea, vomiting, pseudomembranous colitis, vaginitis, hemolytic anemia, neutropenia, interstitial nephritis, CNS irritability, hyperactivity, agitation, nervousness, insomnia, confusion, dizziness, hallucinations, somnolence, seizures, prolonged PT

Reactions reported with other cephalosporins include fever, abdominal pain, superinfection, renal dysfunction, toxic nephropathy, hemorrhage, cholestasis

Overdosage/Toxicology

After acute overdose, most agents cause only nausea, vomiting, and diarrhea, although neuromuscular hypersensitivity and seizures are possible, especially in patients with renal insufficiency; many beta-lactam antibiotics have the potential to cause neuromuscular hyperirritability or seizures

Hemodialysis may be helpful to aid in the removal of the drug from the blood but not usually indicated, otherwise most treatment is supportive or symptom directed following GI decontamination

Drug Interactions

Increased effect: Probenecid may decrease cephalosporin elimination

Increased toxicity: Furosemide, aminoglycosides may be a possible additive to nephrotoxicity

Stability Refrigerate suspension after reconstitution; discard after 14 days; do not freeze

Mechanism of Action Inhibits bacterial cell wall synthesis by binding to one or more of the penicillin-binding proteins (PBPs) which in turn inhibits the final transpeptidation step of peptidoglycan synthesis in bacterial cell walls, thus inhibiting cell wall biosynthesis. Bacteria eventually lyse due to ongoing activity of cell wall autolytic enzymes (autolysins and murein hydrolases) while cell wall assembly is arrested.

Pharmacodynamics/Kinetics

Absorption: Oral: Well absorbed, acid stable

Distribution: Widely distributed throughout the body and reaches therapeutic concentration in most tissues and body fluids, including synovial, pericardial, pleural, and peritoneal fluids; also bile, sputum, and urine; also bone, myocardium, gallbladder, skin and soft tissue; crosses the placenta and appears in breast milk

Protein binding: 25%

Metabolism: Partially

Half-life: 0.5-1 hour, prolonged with renal impairment

Time to peak: Capsule: 60 minutes; Suspension: 45 minutes

Elimination: 80% excreted unchanged in urine

Usual Dosage Oral:

Children >1 month: 20-40 mg/kg/day divided every 8-12 hours; maximum dose: 2 g/day (total daily dose may be divided into two doses for treatment of otitis media or pharyngitis)

Adults: 250-500 mg every 8 hours

Extended release tablets: 500 mg every 12 hours for 7 days for acute bacterial exacerbations of or secondary infections with chronic bronchitis or 375 mg every 12 hour for 10 days for pharyngitis or tonsillitis or for uncomplicated skin and skin structure infections

Dosing adjustment in renal impairment: Cl_{cr} <50 mL/minute: Administer 50% of dose

Hemodialysis: Moderately dializable (20% to 50%)

Monitoring Parameters Assess patient at beginning and throughout therapy for infection; monitor for signs of anaphylaxis during first dose

Test Interactions Positive direct Coombs', false-positive urinary glucose test using cupric sulfate (Benedict's solution, Clinitest®, Fehling's solution), false-positive serum or urine creatinine with Jaffé reaction

Patient Information Chilling of the oral suspension improves flavor (do not freeze); report persistent diarrhea; entire course of medication (10-14 days) should be taken to ensure eradication of organism; may interfere with oral contraceptives; females should report symptoms of vaginitis

Dosage Forms

Capsule: 250 mg, 500 mg

Powder for oral suspension (strawberry flavor): 125 mg/5 mL (75 mL, 150 mL); 187 mg/5 mL (50 mL, 100 mL); 250 mg/5 mL (75 mL, 150 mL); 375 mg/5 mL (50 mL, 100 mL)

Tablet, extended release: 375 mg, 500 mg

Cefadroxil (sef a DROKS il)

Related Information
Cephalosporins by Generation *on page 1373*
Prevention of Bacterial Endocarditis *on page 1377*

U.S. Brand Names Duricef®; Ultracef®

Synonyms Cefadroxil Monohydrate

Therapeutic Category Antibiotic, Cephalosporin (First Generation)

Use Treatment of susceptible gram-positive bacilli and cocci (not enterococcus); some gram-negative bacilli including *E. coli*, *Proteus*, and *Klebsiella* may be susceptible

Pregnancy Risk Factor B

Contraindications Hypersensitivity to cefadroxil or other cephalosporins

Warnings/Precautions Modify dosage in patients with severe renal impairment; prolonged use may result in superinfection; use with caution in patients with a history of penicillin allergy especially IgE-mediated reactions (eg, anaphylaxis, urticaria); may cause antibiotic-associated colitis or colitis secondary to *C. difficile*

Adverse Reactions
1% to 10%: Gastrointestinal: Diarrhea

<1%: Anaphylaxis, rash (maculopapular and erythematous), erythema multiforme, Stevens-Johnson syndrome, serum sickness, arthralgia, urticaria, pruritus, angioedema, pseudomembranous colitis, abdominal pain, dyspepsia, nausea, vomiting, elevated transaminases, cholestasis, vaginitis, neutropenia, agranulocytosis, thrombocytopenia, fever

Reactions reported with other cephalosporins include toxic epidermal necrolysis, abdominal pain, superinfection. renal dysfunction, toxic nephropathy, aplastic anemia, hemolytic anemia, hemorrhage, prolonged prothrombin time, increased BUN, increased creatinine, eosinophilia, pancytopenia, seizures

Overdosage/Toxicology
After acute overdose, most agents cause only nausea, vomiting, and diarrhea, although neuromuscular hypersensitivity and seizures are possible, especially in patients with renal insufficiency; many beta-lactam antibiotics have the potential to cause neuromuscular hyperirritability or seizures

Hemodialysis may be helpful to aid in the removal of the drug from the blood but not usually indicated, otherwise most treatment is supportive or symptom directed following GI decontamination

Drug Interactions
Increased effect: Probenecid may decrease cephalosporin elimination
Increased toxicity: Furosemide, aminoglycosides may be a possible additive to nephrotoxicity

Stability Refrigerate suspension after reconstitution; discard after 14 days

Mechanism of Action Inhibits bacterial cell wall synthesis by binding to one or more of the penicillin-binding proteins (PBPs) which in turn inhibits the final transpeptidation step of peptidoglycan synthesis in bacterial cell walls, thus inhibiting cell wall biosynthesis. Bacteria eventually lyse due to ongoing activity of cell wall autolytic enzymes (autolysins and murein hydrolases) while cell wall assembly is arrested.

Pharmacodynamics/Kinetics
Absorption: Oral: Rapid and well absorbed from GI tract
Distribution: Widely distributed throughout the body and reaches therapeutic concentrations in most tissues and body fluids, including synovial, pericardial, pleural, and peritoneal fluids; also bile, sputum, and urine; also bone, the myocardium, gallbladder, skin and soft tissue; crosses the placenta and appears in breast milk
Protein binding: 20%
Half-life: 1-2 hours; 20-24 hours in renal failure
Time to peak serum concentration: Within 70-90 minutes
Elimination: >90% of dose excreted unchanged in urine within 8 hours

Usual Dosage Oral:
Children: 30 mg/kg/day divided twice daily up to a maximum of 2 g/day
Adults: 1-2 g/day in 2 divided doses
Prophylaxis against bacterial endocarditis: 2 g 1 hour prior to the procedure
Dosing interval in renal impairment:
Cl$_{cr}$ 10-25 mL/minute: Administer every 24 hours
Cl$_{cr}$ <10 mL/minute: Administer every 36 hours

Monitoring Parameters Observe for signs and symptoms of anaphylaxis during first dose

Test Interactions Positive direct Coombs', false-positive urinary glucose test using cupric sulfate (Benedict's solution, Clinitest®, Fehling's solution), false-positive serum or urine creatinine with Jaffé reaction

Patient Information Report persistent diarrhea; entire course of medication (10-14 days) should be taken to ensure eradication of organism; may interfere with oral contraceptives; females should report symptoms of vaginitis

Dosage Forms
Capsule, as monohydrate: 500 mg
Suspension, oral, as monohydrate: 125 mg/5 mL, 250 mg/5 mL, 500 mg/5 mL (50 mL, 100 mL)
Tablet, as monohydrate: 1 g

♦ **Cefadroxil Monohydrate** *see* Cefadroxil *on this page*
♦ **Cefadyl®** *see* Cephapirin *on page 230*

Cefamandole (sef a MAN dole)

Related Information
Cephalosporins by Generation *on page 1373*

U.S. Brand Names Mandol®

Synonyms Cefamandole Nafate

Therapeutic Category Antibiotic, Cephalosporin (Second Generation)

Use Treatment of susceptible bacterial infection; mainly respiratory tract, skin and skin structure, bone and joint, urinary tract and gynecologic, septicemia; surgical prophylaxis. Active against methicillin-sensitive staphylococci, many streptococci, and various gram-negative bacilli including *E. coli*, some *Klebsiella, P. mirabilis, H. influenzae,* and *Moraxella.*

Pregnancy Risk Factor B

Contraindications Hypersensitivity to cefamandole nafate, any component, or cephalosporins

Warnings/Precautions Modify dosage in patients with severe renal impairment; prolonged use may result in superinfection; although rare, cefamandole may interfere with hemostasis via destruction of vitamin K producing intestinal bacteria, prevention of activation of prothrombin by the attachment of a methyltetrazolethiol side chain, and by an immune-mediated thrombocytopenia. Use with caution in patients with a history of penicillin allergy especially IgE-mediated reactions (eg, anaphylaxis, urticaria); may cause antibiotic-associated colitis or colitis secondary to *C. difficile.*

Adverse Reactions Contains MTT side chain which may lead to increased risk of hypoprothrombinemia and bleeding.

1% to 10%:
  Gastrointestinal: Diarrhea
  Local: Thrombophlebitis

<1%: Anaphylaxis, rash (maculopapular and erythematous), urticaria, pseudomembranous colitis, nausea, vomiting, elevated transaminases, cholestasis, eosinophilia, neutropenia, thrombocytopenia, increased BUN, increased creatinine, fever, prolonged PT

Reactions reported with other cephalosporins include toxic epidermal necrolysis, Stevens-Johnson syndrome, abdominal pain, superinfection, renal dysfunction, toxic nephropathy, aplastic anemia, hemolytic anemia, hemorrhage, pancytopenia, vaginitis, seizures

Overdosage/Toxicology
Symptoms of overdose include neuromuscular hypersensitivity, convulsions, especially in patients with renal insufficiency; many beta-lactam antibiotics have the potential to cause neuromuscular hyperirritability or seizures

Hemodialysis may be helpful to aid in the removal of the drug from the blood, otherwise most treatment is supportive or symptom directed

Drug Interactions
Disulfiram-like reaction has been reported when taken within 72 hours of alcohol consumption

Increased cefamandole plasma levels: Probenecid

Increased nephrotoxicity: Aminoglycosides, furosemide

Hypoprothrombinemic effect increased: Warfarin and heparin

Stability After reconstitution, CO_2 gas is liberated which allows solution to be withdrawn without injecting air; solution is stable for 24 hours at room temperature and 96 hours when refrigerated; for I.V., infusion in NS and D_5W is stable for 24 hours at room temperature, 1 week when refrigerated, or 26 weeks when frozen

Mechanism of Action Inhibits bacterial cell wall synthesis by binding to one or more of the penicillin-binding proteins (PBPs) which in turn inhibits the final transpeptidation step of peptidoglycan synthesis in bacterial cell walls, thus inhibiting cell wall biosynthesis. Bacteria eventually lyse due to ongoing activity of cell wall autolytic enzymes (autolysins and murein hydrolases) while cell wall assembly is arrested.

Pharmacodynamics/Kinetics
Distribution: Well throughout the body, except CSF; poor penetration even with inflamed meninges

Protein binding: 56% to 78%

Half-life: 30-60 minutes

Time to peak serum concentration: I.M.: Within 1-2 hours

Elimination: Extensive enterohepatic circulation; high concentrations in bile; majority of drug excreted unchanged in urine

Usual Dosage I.M., I.V.:
Children: 50-150 mg/kg/day in divided doses every 4-8 hours
Adults: Usual dose: 500-1000 mg every 4-8 hours; in life-threatening infections: 2 g every 4 hours may be needed

Dosing interval in renal impairment:
Cl_{cr} 25-50 mL/minute: 1-2 g every 8 hours
Cl_{cr} 10-25 mL/minute: 1 g every 8 hours
Cl_{cr} <10 mL/minute: 1 g every 12 hours
Hemodialysis: Moderately dialyzable (20% to 50%)

Monitoring Parameters Monitor for signs of bruising or bleeding; observe for signs and symptoms of anaphylaxis during first dose

Test Interactions Positive direct Coombs', false-positive urinary glucose test using cupric sulfate (Benedict's solution, Clinitest®, Fehling's solution), false-positive serum or urine creatinine with Jaffé reaction
(Continued)

Cefamandole *(Continued)*

Nursing Implications Do not admix with aminoglycosides in same bottle/bag; observe for signs and symptoms of anaphylaxis during first dose

Additional Information Sodium content of 1 g: 76 mg (3.3 mEq); contains the n-methylthiotetrazole side chain

Dosage Forms Powder for injection, as nafate: 500 mg (10 mL); 1 g (10 mL, 100 mL); 2 g (20 mL, 100 mL); 10 g (100 mL)

♦ **Cefamandole Nafate** *see Cefamandole on previous page*

Cefazolin (sef A zoe lin)

Related Information

Animal and Human Bites Guidelines *on page 1399*
Antibiotic Treatment of Adults With Infective Endocarditis *on page 1401*
Cephalosporins by Generation *on page 1373*
Community-Acquired Pneumonia in Adults *on page 1419*
Prevention of Bacterial Endocarditis *on page 1377*
Prevention of Wound Infection & Sepsis in Surgical Patients *on page 1381*

U.S. Brand Names Ancef®; Kefzol®; Zolicef®

Synonyms Cefazolin Sodium

Therapeutic Category Antibiotic, Cephalosporin (First Generation)

Use Treatment of gram-positive bacilli and cocci (except enterococcus); some gram-negative bacilli including *E. coli*, *Proteus*, and *Klebsiella* may be susceptible

Pregnancy Risk Factor B

Contraindications Hypersensitivity to cefazolin sodium, any component, or cephalosporins

Warnings/Precautions Modify dosage in patients with severe renal impairment; prolonged use may result in superinfection; use with caution in patients with a history of penicillin allergy especially IgE-mediated reactions (eg, anaphylaxis, urticaria); may cause antibiotic-associated colitis or colitis secondary to *C. difficile*

Adverse Reactions

1% to 10%:
Gastrointestinal: Diarrhea
Local: Pain at injection site

<1%: Anaphylaxis, rash, pruritus, Stevens-Johnson syndrome, oral candidiasis, nausea, vomiting, abdominal cramps, anorexia, pseudomembranous colitis, eosinophilia, neutropenia, leukopenia, thrombocytopenia, thrombocytosis, elevated transaminases, phlebitis, vaginitis, fever, seizures

Other reactions with cephalosporins include toxic epidermal necrolysis, abdominal pain, cholestasis, superinfection, renal dysfunction, toxic nephropathy, aplastic anemia, hemolytic anemia, hemorrhage, prolonged prothrombin time, pancytopenia

Overdosage/Toxicology

Symptoms of overdose include neuromuscular hypersensitivity, convulsions especially with renal insufficiency; many beta-lactam antibiotics have the potential to cause neuromuscular hyperirritability or seizures

Hemodialysis may be helpful to aid in the removal of the drug from the blood, otherwise most treatment is supportive or symptom directed

Drug Interactions

Increased effect: High-dose probenecid decreases clearance
Increased toxicity: Aminoglycosides increase nephrotoxic potential

Stability

Store intact vials at room temperature and protect from temperatures exceeding 40°C
Reconstituted solutions of cefazolin are light yellow to yellow
Protection from light is recommended for the powder and for the reconstituted solutions
Reconstituted solutions are stable for 24 hours at room temperature and 10 days under refrigeration
Stability of parenteral admixture at room temperature (25°C): 48 hours
Stability of parenteral admixture at refrigeration temperature (4°C): 14 days
Standard diluent: 1 g/50 mL D_5W; 2 g/50 mL D_5W

Mechanism of Action Inhibits bacterial cell wall synthesis by binding to one or more of the penicillin-binding proteins (PBPs) which in turn inhibits the final transpeptidation step of peptidoglycan synthesis in bacterial cell walls, thus inhibiting cell wall biosynthesis. Bacteria eventually lyse due to ongoing activity of cell wall autolytic enzymes (autolysins and murein hydrolases) while cell wall assembly is arrested.

Pharmacodynamics/Kinetics

Distribution: Widely distributed into most body tissues and fluids including gallbladder, liver, kidneys, bone, sputum, bile, pleural and synovial fluids; CSF penetration is poor; crosses the placenta and small amounts appear in breast milk
Protein binding: 74% to 86%
Metabolism: Hepatic is minimal
Half-life: 90-150 minutes (prolonged with renal impairment)
Time to peak serum concentration: I.M.: Within 0.5-2 hours
Elimination: 80% to 100% is excreted unchanged in urine

Usual Dosage I.M., I.V.:

Children >1 month: 25-100 mg/kg/day divided every 6-8 hours; maximum: 6 g/day
Adults: 250 mg to 2 g every 6-12 (usually 8) hours, depending on severity of infection; maximum dose: 12 g/day

Dosing adjustment in renal impairment:
Cl$_{cr}$ 10-30 mL/minute: Administer every 12 hours
Cl$_{cr}$ <10 mL/minute: Administer every 24 hours
Hemodialysis: Moderately dialyzable (20% to 50%); administer dose postdialysis or administer supplemental dose of 0.5-1 g after dialysis
Peritoneal dialysis: Administer 0.5 g every 12 hours
Continuous arteriovenous or venovenous hemofiltration (CAVH/CAVHD): Dose as for Cl$_{cr}$ 10-30 mL/minute; removes 30 mg of cefazolin per liter of filtrate per day

Monitoring Parameters Renal function periodically when used in combination with other nephrotoxic drugs, hepatic function tests, CBC; monitor for signs of anaphylaxis during first dose

Test Interactions Positive direct Coombs', false-positive urinary glucose test using cupric sulfate (Benedict's solution, Clinitest®, Fehling's solution), false-positive serum or urine creatinine with Jaffé reaction

Nursing Implications Do not admix with aminoglycosides in same bottle/bag; observe for signs and symptoms of anaphylaxis during first dose

Additional Information Sodium content of 1 g: 47 mg (2 mEq)

Dosage Forms
Infusion, premixed, as sodium, in D$_5$W (frozen) (Ancef®): 500 mg (50 mL); 1 g (50 mL)
Injection, as sodium (Kefzol®): 500 mg, 1 g
Powder for injection, as sodium (Ancef®, Zolicef®): 250 mg, 500 mg, 1 g, 5 g, 10 g, 20 g

• **Cefazolin Sodium** *see* Cefazolin *on previous page*

Cefdinir (SEF di ner)

Related Information
Cephalosporins by Generation *on page 1373*

U.S. Brand Names Omnicef®

Synonyms CFDN

Therapeutic Category Antibiotic, Cephalosporin (Third Generation)

Use Treatment of community-acquired pneumonia, acute exacerbations of chronic bronchitis, acute bacterial otitis media, acute maxillary sinusitis, pharyngitis/tonsillitis, and uncomplicated skin and skin structure infections.

Pregnancy Risk Factor B

Contraindications Hypersensitivity to cephalosporins or related antibiotics

Warnings/Precautions Administer cautiously to penicillin-sensitive patients. There is evidence of partial cross-allergenicity and cephalosporins cannot be assumed to be an absolutely safe alternative to penicillin in the penicillin-allergic patient. Serum sickness-like reactions have been reported. Signs and symptoms occur after a few days of therapy and resolve a few days after drug discontinuation with no serious sequelae. Pseudo-membranous colitis occurs; consider its diagnosis in patients who develop diarrhea with antibiotic use.

Adverse Reactions
>1%: Gastrointestinal: Diarrhea
<1%: Seizures (with high doses and renal dysfunction), headache, nervousness, rash, urticaria, pruritus, Stevens-Johnson syndrome, nausea, vomiting, pseudomembranous colitis, eosinophilia, hemolytic anemia, neutropenia, positive Coombs' test, thrombocytopenia, cholestatic jaundice, slightly increased AST/ALT, arthralgia, nephrotoxicity with transient elevations of BUN/creatinine, interstitial nephritis, serum sickness, candidiasis

Overdosage/Toxicology
After acute overdose, most agents cause only nausea, vomiting, and diarrhea, although neuromuscular hypersensitivity and seizures are possible, especially in patients with renal insufficiency
Hemodialysis may be helpful to aid in the removal of the drug from the blood but not usually indicated, otherwise most treatment is supportive or symptom directed following GI decontamination

Drug Interactions
Decreased effect: Coadministration with iron or antacids reduces the rate and extent of cefdinir absorption
Increased effect: Probenecid increases the effects of cephalosporins by decreasing the renal elimination in those which are secreted by tubular secretion
Increased toxicity: Anticoagulant effects may be increased when administered with cephalosporins

Stability Oral suspension should be mixed with 39 mL water for the 60 mL bottle and 65 mL of water for the 120 mL bottle. After mixing, the suspension can be stored at room temperature (25°C/77°F). The suspension may be used for 10 days. The suspension should be shaken well before each administration.

Mechanism of Action Inhibits bacterial cell wall synthesis by binding to one or more of the penicillin-binding proteins (PBPs) which in turn inhibits the final transpeptidation step of peptidoglycan synthesis in bacterial cell walls, thus inhibiting cell wall biosynthesis. Bacteria eventually lyse due to ongoing activity of cell wall autolytic enzymes (autolysins and murein hydrolases) while cell wall assembly is arrested.

Usual Dosage Oral:
Children: 7 mg/kg/dose twice daily or 14 mg/kg/dose once daily for 10 days (maximum: 600 mg/day)
Adolescents and Adults: 300 mg twice daily or 600 mg once daily for 10 days
Dosing adjustment in renal impairment: Cl$_{cr}$ <30 mL/minute: 300 mg once daily
(Continued)

Cefdinir *(Continued)*

Hemodialysis removes cefdinir; recommended initial dose: 300 mg (or 7 mg/kg/dose) every other day. At the conclusion of each hemodialysis session, 300 mg (or 7 mg/kg/dose) should be given. Subsequent doses (300 mg or 7 mg/kg/dose) should be administered every other day.

Monitoring Parameters Observe for signs and symptoms of anaphylaxis during first dose

Dosage Forms
Capsule: 300 mg
Suspension, oral: 125 mg/5 mL (60 mL, 100 mL)

Cefepime (SEF e pim)

Related Information
Antimicrobial Drugs of Choice *on page 1404*
Cephalosporins by Generation *on page 1373*
Community-Acquired Pneumonia in Adults *on page 1419*

U.S. Brand Names Maxipime®

Synonyms Cefepime Hydrochloride

Therapeutic Category Antibiotic, Cephalosporin (Fourth Generation)

Use Treatment of uncomplicated and complicated urinary tract infections, including pyelonephritis caused by typical urinary tract pathogens; monotherapy for febrile neutropenia; uncomplicated skin and skin structure infections caused by *Streptococcus pyogenes*; moderate to severe pneumonia caused by pneumococcus, *Pseudomonas aeruginosa*, and other gram-negative organisms; complicated intra-abdominal infections (in combination with metronidazole). Also active against methicillin-susceptible staphylococci, *Enterobacter* sp, and many other gram-negative bacilli.

Pediatrics (2 months to 16 years of age): Empiric therapy of febrile neutropenia patients, uncomplicated skin/soft tissue infections, pneumonia, and uncomplicated/complicated urinary tract infections.

Pregnancy Risk Factor B

Contraindications Hypersensitivity to cefepime or its components, or other cephalosporins

Warnings/Precautions Modify dosage in patients with severe renal impairment; prolonged use may result in superinfection; use with caution in patients with a history of penicillin or cephalosporin allergy, especially IgE-mediated reactions (eg, anaphylaxis, urticaria); may cause antibiotic-associated colitis or colitis secondary to *C. difficile*

Adverse Reactions
>10%: Hematologic: Positive Coombs' test without hemolysis
1% to 10%:
Dermatologic: Rash, pruritus
Gastrointestinal: : Diarrhea, nausea, vomiting
Central nervous system: Fever (1%), headache (1%)
Local: Pain, erythema at injection site
<1%: Leukopenia, neutropenia, agranulocytosis, thrombocytopenia, myoclonus, seizures, encephalopathy, neuromuscular excitability

Other reactions with cephalosporins include toxic epidermal necrolysis, Stevens-Johnson syndrome, erythema multiforme, renal dysfunction, toxic nephropathy, aplastic anemia, hemolytic anemia, hemorrhage, prolonged PT, pancytopenia, vaginitis, superinfection

Overdosage/Toxicology
Symptoms of overdose include neuromuscular hypersensitivity, convulsions; many beta-lactam antibiotics have the potential to cause neuromuscular hyperirritability or seizures
Hemodialysis may be helpful to aid in the removal of the drug from the blood; however, most often treatment is supportive and symptom directed

Drug Interactions
Increased effect: High-dose probenecid decreases clearance
Increased toxicity: Aminoglycosides increase nephrotoxic potential

Stability Cefepime is **compatible** and stable with normal saline, D_5W, and a variety of other solutions for 24 hours at room temperature and 7 days refrigerated

Mechanism of Action Inhibits bacterial cell wall synthesis by binding to one or more of the penicillin-binding proteins (PBPs) which in turn inhibits the final transpeptidation step of peptidoglycan synthesis in bacterial cell walls, thus inhibiting cell wall biosynthesis. Bacteria eventually lyse due to ongoing activity of cell wall autolytic enzymes (autolysis and murein hydrolases) while cell wall assembly is arrested.

Pharmacodynamics/Kinetics
Absorption: I.M.: Rapid and complete; T_{max}: 0.5-1.5 hours
Distribution: V_d: Adults: 14-20 L; penetrates into inflammatory fluid at concentrations ~80% of serum levels and into bronchial mucosa at levels ~60% of those reached in the plasma, crosses blood-brain barrier
Protein binding, plasma: 16% to 19%
Metabolism: Very little
Half-life: 2 hours
Elimination: 85% eliminated as unchanged drug in urine

Usual Dosage I.V.:
Children:
Febrile neutropenia: 50 mg/kg every 8 hours for 7-10 days

Uncomplicated skin/soft tissue infections, pneumonia, and complicated/uncomplicated UTI: 50 mg/kg twice daily

Adults:

Most infections: 1-2 g every 12 hours for 5-10 days; higher doses or more frequent administration may be required in pseudomonal infections

Urinary tract infections, uncomplicated: 500 mg every 12 hours

Monotherapy for febrile neutropenic patients: 2 g every 8 hours for 7 days or until the neutropenia resolves

Dosing adjustment in renal impairment:

Cefepime Hydrochloride

Creatinine Clearance (mL/minute)	Recommended Maintenance Schedule		
>60 Normal recommended dosing schedule	500 mg every 12 hours	1 g every 12 hours	2 g every 12 hours
30-60	500 mg every 24 hours	1 g every 24 hours	1 g every 24 hours
11-29	500 mg every 24 hours	500 mg every 24 hours	1 g every 24 hours
<10	250 mg every 24 hours	250 mg every 24 hours	500 mg every 24 hours

Hemodialysis: Removed by dialysis; administer supplemental dose of 250 mg after each dialysis session

Peritoneal dialysis: Removed to a lesser extent than hemodialysis; administer 250 mg every 48 hours

Continuous arteriovenous or venovenous hemofiltration (CAVH/CAVHD): Dose as normal Cl$_{cr}$ (eg, >30 mL/minute)

Administration May be administered either I.M. or I.V.

Monitoring Parameters Obtain specimen for culture and sensitivity prior to the first dose; monitor for signs of anaphylaxis during first dose

Test Interactions Positive direct Coombs', false-positive urinary glucose test using cupric sulfate (Benedict's solution, Clinitest®, Fehling's solution), false-positive serum or urine creatinine with Jaffé reaction, false-positive urinary proteins and steroids

Patient Information Report side effects such as diarrhea, dyspepsia, headache, blurred vision, and lightheadedness to your physician

Nursing Implications Do not admix with aminoglycosides in the same bottle/bag; observe for signs and symptoms of bacterial infection, including defervescence; observe for anaphylaxis during first dose

Dosage Forms

Infusion, piggy-back: 1 g (100 mL); 2 g (100 mL)

Infusion (ADD-Vantage®): 1 g

Injection: 500 mg, 1 g, 2 g

♦ **Cefepime Hydrochloride** see Cefepime on previous page

Cefixime (sef IKS eem)

Related Information

Antimicrobial Drugs of Choice on page 1404

Cephalosporins by Generation on page 1373

Treatment of Sexually Transmitted Diseases on page 1429

U.S. Brand Names Suprax®

Therapeutic Category Antibiotic, Cephalosporin (Third Generation)

Use Treatment of urinary tract infections, otitis media, respiratory infections due to susceptible organisms including *S. pneumoniae* and *S. pyogenes*, *H. influenzae* and many Enterobacteriaceae; documented poor compliance with other oral antimicrobials; outpatient therapy of serious soft tissue or skeletal infections due to susceptible organisms; single-dose oral treatment of uncomplicated cervical/urethral gonorrhea due to *N. gonorrhoeae*

Pregnancy Risk Factor B

Contraindications Hypersensitivity to cefixime or cephalosporins

Warnings/Precautions Prolonged use may result in superinfection; modify dosage in patients with renal impairment; use with caution in patients with a history of penicillin allergy especially IgE-mediated reactions (eg, anaphylaxis, urticaria); may cause antibiotic-associated colitis or colitis secondary to *C. difficile*

Adverse Reactions

>10%: Gastrointestinal: Diarrhea (16%)

1% to 10%: Gastrointestinal: Abdominal pain, nausea, dyspepsia, flatulence

<1%: Rash, urticaria, pruritus, erythema multiforme, Stevens-Johnson syndrome, serum sickness -like reaction, fever, vomiting, pseudomembranous colitis, transaminase elevations, increased BUN, increased creatinine, headache, dizziness, thrombocytopenia, leukopenia, eosinophilia, prolonged PT, vaginitis, candidiasis

Other reactions with cephalosporins include anaphylaxis, seizures, toxic epidermal necrolysis, renal dysfunction, toxic nephropathy, interstitial nephritis, cholestasis, aplastic anemia, hemolytic anemia, hemorrhage, pancytopenia, neutropenia, agranulocytosis, colitis, superinfection

(Continued)

Cefixime *(Continued)*

Overdosage/Toxicology

After acute overdose, most agents cause only nausea, vomiting, and diarrhea, although neuromuscular hypersensitivity and seizures are possible, especially in patients with renal insufficiency; many beta-lactam antibiotics have the potential to cause neuromuscular hyperirritability or seizures

Hemodialysis may be helpful to aid in the removal of the drug from the blood but not usually indicated, otherwise most treatment is supportive or symptom directed following GI decontamination

Drug Interactions

Increased effect: Probenecid may decrease cephalosporin elimination

Increased toxicity: Furosemide, aminoglycosides may be a possible additive to nephrotoxicity

Stability After reconstitution, suspension may be stored for 14 days at room temperature

Mechanism of Action Inhibits bacterial cell wall synthesis by binding to one or more of the penicillin binding proteins (PBPs); which in turn inhibits the final transpeptidation step of peptidoglycan synthesis in bacterial cell walls, thus inhibiting cell wall biosynthesis. Bacteria eventually lyse due to ongoing activity of cell wall autolytic enzymes (autolysins and murein hydrolases) while cell wall assembly is arrested.

Pharmacodynamics/Kinetics

Absorption: Oral: 40% to 50%

Distribution: Widely distributed throughout the body and reaches therapeutic concentration in most tissues and body fluids, including synovial, pericardial, pleural, and peritoneal fluids; also bile, sputum, and urine; also bone, myocardium, gallbladder, and skin and soft tissue

Protein binding: 65%

Half-life: Normal renal function: 3-4 hours; Renal failure: Up to 11.5 hours

Time to peak serum concentrations: Within 2-6 hours; peak serum concentrations are 15% to 50% higher for the oral suspension versus tablets; presence of food delays the time to reach peak concentrations

Elimination: 50% of absorbed dose excreted as active drug in urine and 10% in bile

Usual Dosage Oral:

Children: 8 mg/kg/day divided every 12-24 hours

Adolescents and Adults: 400 mg/day divided every 12-24 hours

Uncomplicated cervical/urethral gonorrhea due to *N. gonorrhoeae*: 400 mg as a single dose

For *S. pyogenes* infections, treat for 10 days; use suspension for otitis media due to increased peak serum levels as compared to tablet form

Dosing adjustment in renal impairment:

Cl$_{cr}$ 21-60 mL/minute or with renal hemodialysis: Administer 75% of the standard dose

Cl$_{cr}$ <20 mL/minute or with CAPD: Administer 50% of the standard dose

Moderately dialyzable (10%)

Administration Oral: May be administered with or without food; administer with food to decrease GI distress

Monitoring Parameters With prolonged therapy, monitor renal and hepatic function periodically; observe for signs and symptoms of anaphylaxis during first dose

Test Interactions Positive direct Coombs', false-positive urinary glucose test using cupric sulfate (Benedict's solution, Clinitest®, Fehling's solution), false-positive serum or urine creatinine with Jaffé reaction

Patient Information Report diarrhea promptly; entire course of medication (10-14 days) should be taken to ensure eradication of organism; may interfere with oral contraceptives, females should report symptoms of vaginitis

Additional Information Otitis media should be treated with the suspension since it results in higher peak blood levels than the tablet

Dosage Forms

Powder for oral suspension (strawberry flavor): 100 mg/5 mL (50 mL, 100 mL)

Tablet, film coated: 200 mg, 400 mg

♦ **Cefizox®** *see* Ceftizoxime *on page 222*

Cefmetazole *(sef MET a zole)*

Related Information

Antimicrobial Drugs of Choice *on page 1404*

Cephalosporins by Generation *on page 1373*

U.S. Brand Names Zefazone®

Synonyms Cefmetazole Sodium

Therapeutic Category Antibiotic, Cephalosporin (Second Generation)

Use Second generation cephalosporin, useful for susceptible aerobic and anaerobic gram-positive and gram-negative bacteria; surgical prophylaxis, specifically colorectal and OB-GYN

Pregnancy Risk Factor B

Contraindications Hypersensitivity to cefmetazole or any component or cephalosporins

Warnings/Precautions Modify dosage in patients with severe renal impairment; prolonged use may result in superinfection; use with caution in patients with a history of penicillin allergy especially IgE-mediated reactions (eg, anaphylaxis, urticaria); may cause antibiotic-associated colitis or colitis secondary to *C. difficile*

Adverse Reactions Contains MTT side chain which may lead to increased risk of hypoprothrombinemia and bleeding.

1% to 10%:
Dermatologic: Rash
Gastrointestinal: Diarrhea

<1%: Pain at injection site, phlebitis, pseudomembranous colitis, epigastric pain, candidiasis, bleeding, shock, hypotension, headache, hot flashes, dyspnea, epistaxis, respiratory distress, fever, vaginitis

Other reactions with cephalosporins include anaphylaxis, seizures, toxic epidermal necrolysis, erythema multiforme, Stevens-Johnson syndrome, renal dysfunction, interstitial nephritis, toxic nephropathy, cholestasis, aplastic anemia, hemolytic anemia, hemorrhage, pancytopenia, neutropenia, agranulocytosis, colitis, superinfection

Overdosage/Toxicology
Symptoms of overdose include neuromuscular hypersensitivity, convulsions especially with renal insufficiency; many beta-lactam antibiotics have the potential to cause neuromuscular hyperirritability or seizures

Hemodialysis may be helpful to aid in the removal of the drug from the blood, otherwise most treatment is supportive or symptom directed.

Drug Interactions
Increased effect: Probenecid may decrease cephalosporin elimination
Increased toxicity: Furosemide, aminoglycosides may be a possible additive to nephrotoxicity

Stability Reconstituted solution and I.V. infusion in NS or D_5W solution are stable for 24 hours at room temperature, 7 days when refrigerated, or 6 weeks when frozen; after freezing, thawed solution is stable for 24 hours at room temperature or 7 days when refrigerated

Mechanism of Action Inhibits bacterial cell wall synthesis by binding to one or more of the penicillin-binding proteins (PBPs) which in turn inhibits the final transpeptidation step of peptidoglycan synthesis in bacterial cell walls, thus inhibiting cell wall biosynthesis. Bacteria eventually lyse due to ongoing activity of cell wall autolytic enzymes (autolysins and murein hydrolases) while cell wall assembly is arrested.

Pharmacodynamics/Kinetics
Absorption: I.M.: Well absorbed
Distribution: Widely distributed
Protein binding: 65%
Metabolism: <15%
Half-life: 72 minutes
Elimination: Renal

Usual Dosage Adults: I.V.:
Infections: 2 g every 6-12 hours for 5-14 days
Prophylaxis: 2 g 30-90 minutes before surgery **or** 1 g 30-90 minutes before surgery; repeat 8 and 16 hours later

Dosing interval in renal impairment:
Cl_{cr} 50-90 mL/minute: Administer every 12 hours
Cl_{cr} 10-50 mL/minute: Administer every 16-24 hours
Cl_{cr} <10 mL/minute: Administer every 48 hours

Monitoring Parameters Monitor prothrombin times; observe for signs and symptoms of anaphylaxis during first dose

Test Interactions Positive direct Coombs', false-positive urinary glucose test using cupric sulfate (Benedict's solution, Clinitest®, Fehling's solution), false-positive serum or urine creatinine with Jaffé reaction

Patient Information Do not drink alcohol for at least 24 hours after receiving dose; report persistent diarrhea; may interfere with oral contraceptives, females should report symptoms of vaginitis

Nursing Implications Do not admix with aminoglycosides in same bottle/bag

Additional Information Sodium content of 1 g: 47 mg (2 mEq)

Dosage Forms Powder for injection, as sodium: 1 g, 2 g

♦ **Cefmetazole Sodium** see Cefmetazole on previous page
♦ **Cefobid®** see Cefoperazone on next page
♦ **Cefol® Filmtab®** see Vitamins, Multiple on page 1226

Cefonicid (se FON i sid)
Related Information
Cephalosporins by Generation on page 1373
U.S. Brand Names Monocid®
Synonyms Cefonicid Sodium
Therapeutic Category Antibiotic, Cephalosporin (Second Generation)
Use Treatment of susceptible bacterial infection; mainly respiratory tract, skin and skin structure, bone and joint, urinary tract and gynecologic, septicemia; active against methicillin-sensitive staphylococci, many streptococci, and various gram-negative bacilli including E. coli, some Klebsiella, P. mirabilis, H. influenzae, and Moraxella.
Pregnancy Risk Factor B
Contraindications Hypersensitivity to cefonicid sodium, any component, or cephalosporins
Warnings/Precautions Modify dosage in patients with severe renal impairment; prolonged use may result in superinfection; use with caution in patients with a history of penicillin allergy especially IgE-mediated reactions (eg, anaphylaxis, urticaria); may cause antibiotic-associated colitis or colitis secondary to C. difficile
(Continued)

Cefonicid *(Continued)*

Adverse Reactions
1% to 10%:

Hematologic: Increased eosinophils (2.9%), increased platelets (1.7%)

Hepatic: Altered liver function tests (increased transaminases, LDH, alkaline phosphatase) (1.6%)

Local: Pain, burning at injection site (5.7%)

<1%: Fever, rash, pruritus, erythema, anaphylactoid reactions, diarrhea, pseudomembranous colitis, abdominal pain, increased transaminases, increased BUN, increased creatinine, interstitial nephritis, neutropenia, decreased WBC, thrombocytopenia

Other reactions with cephalosporins include anaphylaxis, seizures, Stevens-Johnson syndrome, toxic epidermal necrolysis, renal dysfunction, toxic nephropathy, cholestasis, aplastic anemia, hemolytic anemia, hemorrhage, pancytopenia, agranulocytosis, colitis, superinfection

Overdosage/Toxicology
Symptoms of overdose include neuromuscular hypersensitivity, convulsions especially with renal insufficiency; many beta-lactam antibiotics have the potential to cause neuromuscular hyperirritability or seizures

Hemodialysis may be helpful to aid in the removal of the drug from the blood, otherwise most treatment is supportive or symptom directed

Drug Interactions
Increased effect: Probenecid may decrease cephalosporin elimination

Increased toxicity: Furosemide, aminoglycosides may be a possible additive to nephrotoxicity

Stability Reconstituted solution and I.V. infusion in NS or D_5W solution are stable for 24 hours at room temperature or 72 hours if refrigerated

Mechanism of Action Inhibits bacterial cell wall synthesis by binding to one or more of the penicillin-binding proteins (PBPs) which in turn inhibits the final transpeptidation step of peptidoglycan synthesis in bacterial cell walls, thus inhibiting cell wall biosynthesis. Bacteria eventually lyse due to ongoing activity of cell wall autolytic enzymes (autolysins and murein hydrolases) while cell wall assembly is arrested.

Pharmacodynamics/Kinetics
Absorption: I.M.: Well absorbed

Distribution: Widely distributed into most body tissues with low concentrations in CSF and eye

Protein binding: 98%

Metabolism: None

Half-life: 3.5-5.8 hours

Elimination: Unchanged in urine

Usual Dosage Adults: I.M., I.V.: 0.5-2 g every 24 hours

Prophylaxis: Preop: 1 g/hour

Dosing interval in renal impairment: See table.

Cefonicid Sodium

Cl_{cr} (mL/min/1.73 m²)	Dose (mg/kg) for Each Dosing Interval
60-79	10-24 q24h
40-59	8-20 q24h
20-39	4-15 q24h
10-19	4-15 q48h
5-9	4-15 q3-5d
<5	3-4 q3-5d

Monitoring Parameters Observe for signs and symptoms of anaphylaxis during first dose

Test Interactions Positive direct Coombs', false-positive urinary glucose test using cupric sulfate (Benedict's solution, Clinitest®, Fehling's solution), false-positive serum or urine creatinine with Jaffé reaction

Additional Information Sodium content of 1 g: 85.1 mg (3.7 mEq)

Dosage Forms Powder for injection, as sodium: 500 mg, 1 g, 10 g

♦ Cefonicid Sodium *see* Cefonicid *on previous page*

Cefoperazone *(sef oh PER a zone)*

Related Information
Cephalosporins by Generation *on page 1373*

U.S. Brand Names Cefobid®

Synonyms Cefoperazone Sodium

Therapeutic Category Antibiotic, Cephalosporin (Third Generation)

Use Treatment of susceptible bacterial infection; mainly respiratory tract, skin and skin structure, bone and joint, urinary tract and gynecologic as well as septicemia. Active against a variety of gram-negative bacilli, some gram-positive cocci, and has some activity against *Pseudomonas aeruginosa*.

Pregnancy Risk Factor B

Contraindications Hypersensitivity to cefoperazone or any component or cephalosporins

Warnings/Precautions Modify dosage in patients with severe renal or hepatic impairment; prolonged use may result in superinfection; although rare, cefoperazone may interfere with hemostasis via destruction of vitamin K-producing intestinal bacteria, prevention of activation of prothrombin by the attachment of a methyltetrazolethiol side chain, and by an immune-mediated thrombocytopenia; use with caution in patients with a history of penicillin allergy especially IgE-mediated reactions (eg, anaphylaxis, urticaria); may cause antibiotic-associated colitis or colitis secondary to *C. difficile*

Adverse Reactions Contains MTT side chain which may lead to increased risk of hypoprothrombinemia and bleeding.

1% to 10%:
    Dermatologic: Rash (maculopapular or erythematous) (2%)
    Gastrointestinal: Diarrhea (3%)
    Hematologic: Decreased neutrophils (2%), decreased hemoglobin or hematocrit (5%), eosinophilia (10%)
    Hepatic: Increased transaminases (5% to 10%)
<1%: Hypoprothrombinemia, bleeding, pseudomembranous colitis, nausea, vomiting, elevated BUN, elevated creatinine, pain at injection site, induration at injection site, phlebitis, drug fever

Other reactions with cephalosporins include anaphylaxis, seizures, Stevens-Johnson syndrome, toxic epidermal necrolysis, renal dysfunction, toxic nephropathy, cholestasis, aplastic anemia, hemolytic anemia, pancytopenia, agranulocytosis, colitis, superinfection

Overdosage/Toxicology
Symptoms of overdose include neuromuscular hypersensitivity, convulsions especially with renal insufficiency; many beta-lactam antibiotics have the potential to cause neuromuscular hyperirritability or seizures
Hemodialysis may be helpful to aid in the removal of the drug from the blood, otherwise most treatment is supportive or symptom directed

Drug Interactions
Disulfiram-like reaction has been reported when taken within 72 hours of alcohol consumption
Increased nephrotoxicity: Aminoglycosides, furosemide

Stability Reconstituted solution and I.V. infusion in NS or D_5W solution are stable for 24 hours at room temperature, 5 days when refrigerated or 3 weeks, when frozen; after freezing, thawed solution is stable for 48 hours at room temperature or 10 days when refrigerated

Mechanism of Action Inhibits bacterial cell wall synthesis by binding to one or more of the penicillin-binding proteins (PBPs) which in turn inhibits the final transpeptidation step of peptidoglycan synthesis in bacterial cell walls, thus inhibiting cell wall biosynthesis. Bacteria eventually lyse due to ongoing activity of cell wall autolytic enzymes (autolysins and murein hydrolases) while cell wall assembly is arrested.

Pharmacodynamics/Kinetics
Distribution: Widely distributed in most body tissues and fluids; highest concentrations in bile; low penetration in CSF; variable when meninges are inflamed; crosses placenta; small amounts into breast milk
Half-life: 2 hours, higher with hepatic disease or biliary obstruction
Time to peak serum concentration: I.M.: Within 1-2 hours
Elimination: Principally in bile (70% to 75%); 20% to 30% recovered unchanged in urine within 6-12 hours

Usual Dosage I.M., I.V.:
Children (not approved): 100-150 mg/kg/day divided every 8-12 hours; up to 12 g/day
Adults: 2-4 g/day in divided doses every 12 hours; up to 12 g/day
Dosing adjustment in hepatic impairment: Reduce dose 50% in patients with advanced liver cirrhosis; maximum daily dose: 4 g

Monitoring Parameters Monitor for coagulation abnormalities and diarrhea; observe for signs and symptoms of anaphylaxis during first dose

Test Interactions Positive direct Coombs', false-positive urinary glucose test using cupric sulfate (Benedict's solution, Clinitest®, Fehling's solution), false-positive serum or urine creatinine with Jaffé reaction

Nursing Implications Do not admix with aminoglycosides in same bottle/bag

Additional Information Sodium content of 1 g: 34.5 mg (1.5 mEq); contains the n-methylthiotetrazole side chain

Dosage Forms
Injection, as sodium, premixed (frozen): 1 g (50 mL); 2 g (50 mL)
Powder for injection, as sodium: 1 g, 2 g

♦ **Cefoperazone Sodium** *see Cefoperazone on previous page*

♦ **Cefotan®** *see Cefotetan on page 215*

Cefotaxime (sef oh TAKS eem)

Related Information
Antibiotic Treatment of Adults With Infective Endocarditis *on page 1401*
Antimicrobial Drugs of Choice *on page 1404*
Cephalosporins by Generation *on page 1373*
Community-Acquired Pneumonia in Adults *on page 1419*
Treatment of Sexually Transmitted Diseases *on page 1429*
U.S. Brand Names Claforan®
Synonyms Cefotaxime Sodium

(Continued)

Cefotaxime *(Continued)*

Therapeutic Category Antibiotic, Cephalosporin (Third Generation)

Use Treatment of susceptible infection in respiratory tract, skin and skin structure, bone and joint, urinary tract, gynecologic as well as septicemia, and documented or suspected meningitis. Active against most gram-negative bacilli (not *Pseudomonas*) and gram-positive cocci (not enterococcus). Active against many penicillin-resistant pneumococci.

Pregnancy Risk Factor B

Contraindications Hypersensitivity to cefotaxime, any component, or cephalosporins

Warnings/Precautions Modify dosage in patients with severe renal impairment; prolonged use may result in superinfection; a potentially life-threatening arrhythmia has been reported in patients who received a rapid bolus injection via central line. Use caution in patients with colitis; minimize tissue inflammation by changing infusion sites when needed. Use with caution in patients with a history of penicillin allergy especially IgE-mediated reactions (eg, anaphylaxis, urticaria); may cause antibiotic-associated colitis or colitis secondary to *C. difficile*.

Adverse Reactions

1% to 10%:
  Dermatologic: Rash, pruritus
  Gastrointestinal: Diarrhea, nausea, vomiting, colitis
  Local: Pain at injection site

<1%: Anaphylaxis, urticaria, arrhythmias (after rapid IV injection via central catheter), pseudomembranous colitis, neutropenia, thrombocytopenia, eosinophilia, headache, fever, transaminase elevations, interstitial nephritis, increased BUN, increased creatinine, increased transaminases, phlebitis, candidiasis, vaginitis

Other reactions with cephalosporins include seizures, Stevens-Johnson syndrome, toxic epidermal necrolysis, renal dysfunction, toxic nephropathy, cholestasis, aplastic anemia, hemolytic anemia, hemorrhage, pancytopenia, agranulocytosis, colitis, super-infection

Overdosage/Toxicology

Usually well tolerated even in overdose, convulsions possible; many beta-lactam antibiotics have the potential to cause neuromuscular hyperirritability or seizures

Hemodialysis may be helpful to aid in the removal of the drug from the blood, otherwise most treatment is supportive or symptom directed

Drug Interactions

Increased effect: Probenecid may decrease cephalosporin elimination

Increased toxicity: Furosemide, aminoglycosides may be a possible additive to nephrotoxicity

Stability Reconstituted solution is stable for 12-24 hours at room temperature and 7-10 days when refrigerate and for 13 weeks when frozen; for I.V. infusion in NS or D_5W, solution is stable for 24 hours at room temperature, 5 days when refrigerated, or 13 weeks when frozen in Viaflex® plastic containers; thawed solutions previously of frozen premixed bags are stable for 24 hours at room temperature or 10 days when refrigerated

Mechanism of Action Inhibits bacterial cell wall synthesis by binding to one or more of the penicillin-binding proteins (PBPs) which in turn inhibits the final transpeptidation step of peptidoglycan synthesis in bacterial cell walls, thus inhibiting cell wall biosynthesis. Bacteria eventually lyse due to ongoing activity of cell wall autolytic enzymes (autolysins and murein hydrolases) while cell wall assembly is arrested.

Pharmacodynamics/Kinetics

Distribution: Widely distributed to body tissues and fluids including aqueous humor, ascitic and prostatic fluids, and bone; penetrates CSF best when meninges are inflamed; crosses the placenta and appears in breast milk

Metabolism: Partially in the liver to active metabolite, desacetylcefotaxime

Half-life:
  Cefotaxime: Premature neonates <1 week: 5-6 hours; Full-term neonates <1 week: 2-3.4 hours; Adults: 1-1.5 hours (prolonged with renal and/or hepatic impairment)
  Desacetylcefotaxime: 1.5-1.9 hours (prolonged with renal impairment)

Time to peak serum concentration: I.M.: Within 30 minutes

Elimination: Renal excretion of parent drug and metabolites

Usual Dosage

Neonates: I.V.:
  0-1 week: 50 mg/kg every 12 hours
  1-4 weeks: 50 mg/kg every 8 hours

Infants and Children 1 month to 12 years: I.M., I.V.: <50 kg: 50-180 mg/kg/day in divided doses every 4-6 hours
  Meningitis: 200 mg/kg/day in divided doses every 6 hours

Children >12 years and Adults:
  Gonorrhea: I.M.: 1 g as a single dose
  Uncomplicated infections: I.M., I.V.: 1 g every 12 hours
  Moderate/severe infections: I.M., I.V.: 1-2 g every 8 hours
  Infections commonly needing higher doses (eg, septicemia): I.V.: 2 g every 6-8 hours
  Life-threatening infections: I.V.: 2 g every 4 hours
  Preop: I.M., I.V.: 1 g 30-90 minutes before surgery
  C-section: 1 g as soon as the umbilical cord is clamped, then 1 g I.M., I.V. at 6- and 12-hours intervals

Dosing interval in renal impairment:
  Cl_{cr} 10-50 mL/minute: Administer every 8-12 hours
  Cl_{cr} <10 mL/minute: Administer every 24 hours

Hemodialysis: Moderately dialyzable

Dosing adjustment in hepatic impairment: Moderate dosage reduction is recommended in severe liver disease

Continuous arteriovenous or venovenous hemodiafiltration (CAVH) effects: Administer 1 g every 12 hour

Administration Can be administered IVP over 3-5 minutes or I.V. retrograde or I.V. intermittent infusion over 15-30 minutes

Monitoring Parameters Observe for signs and symptoms of anaphylaxis during first dose; CBC with differential (especially with long courses)

Test Interactions Positive direct Coombs', false-positive urinary glucose test using cupric sulfate (Benedict's solution, Clinitest®, Fehling's solution), false-positive serum or urine creatinine with Jaffé reaction

Nursing Implications Cefotaxime can be administered IVP over 3-5 minutes or I.V. retrograde or I.V. intermittent infusion over 15-30 minutes; do not admix with aminoglycosides in same bottle/bag; observe for signs and symptoms of anaphylaxis during first dose

Additional Information Sodium content of 1 g: 50.6 mg (2.2 mEq)

Dosage Forms
Infusion, as sodium, premixed, in D_5W (frozen): 1 g (50 mL); 2 g (50 mL)
Powder for injection, as sodium: 500 mg, 1 g, 2 g, 10 g

♦ **Cefotaxime Sodium** *see* Cefotaxime *on page 213*

Cefotetan (SEF oh tee tan)

Related Information
Animal and Human Bites Guidelines *on page 1399*
Antimicrobial Drugs of Choice *on page 1404*
Cephalosporins by Generation *on page 1373*
Prevention of Wound Infection & Sepsis in Surgical Patients *on page 1381*
Treatment of Sexually Transmitted Diseases *on page 1429*

U.S. Brand Names Cefotan®

Synonyms Cefotetan Disodium

Therapeutic Category Antibiotic, Cephalosporin (Second Generation)

Use Less active against staphylococci and streptococci than first generation cephalosporins, but active against anaerobes including *Bacteroides fragilis*; active against gram-negative enteric bacilli including *E. coli*, *Klebsiella*, and *Proteus*; used predominantly for respiratory tract, skin and skin structure, bone and joint, urinary tract and gynecologic as well as septicemia; surgical prophylaxis; intra-abdominal infections and other mixed infections

Pregnancy Risk Factor B

Contraindications Hypersensitivity to cefotetan, any component, or cephalosporins

Warnings/Precautions Modify dosage in patients with severe renal impairment; prolonged use may result in superinfection; although cefotetan contains the methyltetrazolethial side chain, bleeding has not been a significant problem; use with caution in patients with a history of penicillin allergy especially IgE-mediated reactions (eg, anaphylaxis, urticaria); may cause antibiotic-associated colitis or colitis secondary to *C. difficile*

Adverse Reactions Contains MTT side chain which may lead to increased risk of hypoprothrombinemia and bleeding.

1% to 10%:
Gastrointestinal: Diarrhea (1.3%)
Hepatic: Increased transaminases (1.2%)
Miscellaneous: Hypersensitivity reactions (1.2%)

<1%: Anaphylaxis, urticaria, rash, pruritus, pseudomembranous colitis, nausea, vomiting, eosinophilia, thrombocytosis, agranulocytosis, hemolytic anemia, leukopenia, thrombocytopenia, prolonged PT, bleeding, elevated BUN, elevated creatinine, nephrotoxicity, phlebitis, fever

Other reactions with cephalosporins include: Seizures, Stevens-Johnson syndrome, toxic epidermal necrolysis, renal dysfunction, toxic nephropathy, cholestasis, aplastic anemia, hemolytic anemia, hemorrhage, pancytopenia, agranulocytosis, colitis, superinfection

Overdosage/Toxicology
Symptoms of overdose include neuromuscular hypersensitivity, convulsions especially with renal insufficiency; many beta-lactam antibiotics have the potential to cause neuromuscular hyperirritability or seizures

Hemodialysis may be helpful to aid in the removal of the drug from the blood, otherwise most treatment is supportive or symptom directed

Drug Interactions
Disulfiram-like reaction has been reported when taken within 72 hours of alcohol consumption

Increased cefamandole plasma levels: Probenecid

Increased nephrotoxicity: Aminoglycosides, furosemide

Stability Reconstituted solution is stable for 24 hours at room temperature and 96 hours when refrigerated; for I.V. infusion in NS or D_5W solution and after freezing, thawed solution is stable for 24 hours at room temperature or 96 hours when refrigerated; frozen solution is stable for 12 weeks

Mechanism of Action Inhibits bacterial cell wall synthesis by binding to one or more of the penicillin-binding proteins (PBPs) which in turn inhibits the final transpeptidation step of peptidoglycan synthesis in bacterial cell walls, thus inhibiting cell wall biosynthesis. (Continued)

Cefotetan *(Continued)*

Bacteria eventually lyse due to ongoing activity of cell wall autolytic enzymes (autolysins and murein hydrolases) while cell wall assembly is arrested.

Pharmacodynamics/Kinetics

Distribution: Widely distributed to body tissues and fluids including bile, sputum, prostatic and peritoneal fluids; low concentrations enter CSF; crosses the placenta and appears in breast milk

Protein binding: 76% to 90%

Half-life: 3-5 hours

Time to peak serum concentration: I.M.: Within 1.5-3 hours

Elimination: Primarily excreted unchanged in urine with 20% excreted in bile

Usual Dosage I.M., I.V.:

Children: 20-40 mg/kg/dose every 12 hours

Adults: 1-6 g/day in divided doses every 12 hours; usual dose: 1-2 g every 12 hours for 5-10 days; 1-2 g may be given every 24 hours for urinary tract infection

Dosing interval in renal impairment:

Cl_{cr} 10-30 mL/minute: Administer every 24 hours

Cl_{cr} <10 mL/minute: Administer every 48 hours

Hemodialysis: Slightly dialyzable (5% to 20%)

Continuous arteriovenous or venovenous hemodiafiltration (CAVH) effects: Administer 750 mg every 12 hours

Monitoring Parameters Observe for signs and symptoms of anaphylaxis during first dose

Test Interactions Positive direct Coombs', false-positive urinary glucose test using cupric sulfate (Benedict's solution, Clinitest®, Fehling's solution), false-positive serum or urine creatinine with Jaffé reaction

Nursing Implications Do not admix with aminoglycosides in same bottle/bag

Additional Information Sodium content of 1 g: 34.5 mg (1.5 mEq); contains the n-methylthiotetrazole side chain

Dosage Forms Powder for injection, as disodium: 1 g (10 mL, 100 mL); 2 g (20 mL, 100 mL); 10 g (100 mL)

♦ **Cefotetan Disodium** *see Cefotetan on previous page*

Cefoxitin (se FOKS i tin)

Related Information

Antimicrobial Drugs of Choice *on page 1404*

Cephalosporins by Generation *on page 1373*

Prevention of Wound Infection & Sepsis in Surgical Patients *on page 1381*

Treatment of Sexually Transmitted Diseases *on page 1429*

U.S. Brand Names Mefoxin®

Synonyms Cefoxitin Sodium

Therapeutic Category Antibiotic, Cephalosporin (Second Generation)

Use Less active against staphylococci and streptococci than first generation cephalosporins, but active against anaerobes including *Bacteroides fragilis*; active against gram-negative enteric bacilli including *E. coli*, *Klebsiella*, and *Proteus*; used predominantly for respiratory tract, skin and skin structure, bone and joint, urinary tract and gynecologic as well as septicemia; surgical prophylaxis; intra-abdominal infections and other mixed infections

Pregnancy Risk Factor B

Contraindications Hypersensitivity to cefoxitin, any component, or cephalosporins

Warnings/Precautions Use with caution in patients with history of colitis; cefoxitin may increase resistance of organisms by inducing beta-lactamase; modify dosage in patients with severe renal impairment; prolonged use may result in superinfection; use with caution in patients with a history of penicillin allergy especially IgE-mediated reactions (eg, anaphylaxis, urticaria); may cause antibiotic-associated colitis or colitis secondary to *C. difficile*

Adverse Reactions

1% to 10%: Gastrointestinal: Diarrhea

<1%: Anaphylaxis, dyspnea, fever, rash, exfoliative dermatitis, toxic epidermal necrolysis, pruritus, angioedema, nausea, hypotension, vomiting, dyspnea, pseudomembranous colitis, phlebitis, interstitial nephritis, increased BUN, increased creatinine, leukopenia, thrombocytopenia, hemolytic anemia, bone marrow suppression, eosinophilia, increased transaminases, jaundice, thrombophlebitis, increased nephrotoxicity (with aminoglycosides), exacerbation of myasthenia gravis, prolonged PT

Other reactions with cephalosporins include: Seizures, Stevens-Johnson syndrome, toxic epidermal necrolysis, erythema multiforme, urticaria, serum-sickness reactions, renal dysfunction, toxic nephropathy, cholestasis, aplastic anemia, hemolytic anemia, hemorrhage, pancytopenia, agranulocytosis, colitis, vaginitis, superinfection

Overdosage/Toxicology

Symptoms of overdose include neuromuscular hypersensitivity, convulsions especially with renal insufficiency; many beta-lactam antibiotics have the potential to cause neuromuscular hyperirritability or seizures

Hemodialysis may be helpful to aid in the removal of the drug from the blood, otherwise most treatment is supportive or symptom directed

Drug Interactions

Increased effect: Probenecid may decrease cephalosporin elimination

Increased toxicity: Furosemide, aminoglycosides may be a possible additive to nephro-toxicity

Stability Reconstituted solution is stable for 24 hours at room temperature and 48 hours when refrigerated; I.V. infusion in NS or D_5W solution is stable for 24 hours at room temperature, 1 week when refrigerated, or 26 weeks when frozen; after freezing, thawed solution is stable for 24 hours at room temperature or 5 days when refrigerated

Mechanism of Action Inhibits bacterial cell wall synthesis by binding to one or more of the penicillin-binding proteins (PBPs) which in turn inhibits the final transpeptidation step of peptidoglycan synthesis in bacterial cell walls, thus inhibiting cell wall biosynthesis. Bacteria eventually lyse due to ongoing activity of cell wall autolytic enzymes (autolysins and murein hydrolases) while cell wall assembly is arrested.

Pharmacodynamics/Kinetics

Distribution: Widely distributed to body tissues and fluids including pleural, synovial, ascitic fluid, and bile; poorly penetrates into CSF even with inflammation of the meninges; crosses the placenta and small amounts appear in breast milk

Protein binding: 65% to 79%

Half-life: 45-60 minutes, increases significantly with renal insufficiency

Time to peak serum concentration: I.M.: Within 20-30 minutes

Elimination: Rapidly excreted as unchanged drug (85%) in urine

Usual Dosage I.M., I.V.:

Infants >3 months and Children:

Mild to moderate infection: 80-100 mg/kg/day in divided doses every 4-6 hours

Severe infection: 100-160 mg/kg/day in divided doses every 4-6 hours

Maximum dose: 12 g/day

Adults: 1-2 g every 6-8 hours (I.M. injection is painful); up to 12 g/day

Dosing interval in renal impairment:

Cl_{cr} 30-50 mL/minute: Administer every 8-12 hours

Cl_{cr} 10-30 mL/minute: Administer every 12-24 hours

Cl_{cr} <10 mL/minute: Administer every 24-48 hours

Hemodialysis: Moderately dialyzable (20% to 50%)

Continuous arteriovenous or venovenous hemodiafiltration (CAVH) effects: Dose as for Cl_{cr} 10-50 mL/minute

Monitoring Parameters Monitor renal function periodically when used in combination with other nephrotoxic drugs; observe for signs and symptoms of anaphylaxis during first dose

Test Interactions Positive direct Coombs', false-positive urinary glucose test using cupric sulfate (Benedict's solution, Clinitest®, Fehling's solution), false-positive serum or urine creatinine with Jaffé reaction

Additional Information Sodium content of 1 g: 53 mg (2.3 mEq)

Dosage Forms

Infusion, as sodium, premixed, in D_5W (frozen): 1 g (50 mL); 2 g (50 mL)

Powder for injection, as sodium: 1 g, 2 g, 10 g

♦ **Cefoxitin Sodium** see Cefoxitin on previous page

Cefpodoxime (sef pode OKS eem)

Related Information

Antimicrobial Drugs of Choice on page 1404
Cephalosporins by Generation on page 1373
Community-Acquired Pneumonia in Adults on page 1419
Treatment of Sexually Transmitted Diseases on page 1429

U.S. Brand Names Vantin®

Synonyms Cefpodoxime Proxetil

Therapeutic Category Antibiotic, Cephalosporin (Second Generation)

Use Treatment of susceptible acute, community-acquired pneumonia caused by *S. pneumoniae* or nonbeta-lactamase producing *H. influenzae*; acute uncomplicated gonorrhea caused by *N. gonorrhoeae*; uncomplicated skin and skin structure infections caused by *S. aureus* or *S. pyogenes*; acute otitis media caused by *S. pneumoniae, H. influenzae*, or *M. catarrhalis*; pharyngitis or tonsillitis; and uncomplicated urinary tract infections caused by *E. coli, Klebsiella*, and *Proteus*

Pregnancy Risk Factor B

Contraindications Hypersensitivity to cefpodoxime or cephalosporins

Warnings/Precautions Modify dosage in patients with severe renal impairment; prolonged use may result in superinfection; a low incidence of cross-hypersensitivity to penicillins exists

Adverse Reactions

>10%:

Dermatologic: Diaper rash (12.1%)

Gastrointestinal: Diarrhea in infants and toddlers (15.4%)

1% to 10%:

Central nervous system: Headache (1.1%)

Dermatologic: Rash (1.4%)

Gastrointestinal: Diarrhea (7.2%), nausea (3.8%), abdominal pain (1.6%), vomiting (1.1% to 2.1%)

Genitourinary: Vaginal infections (3.1%)

<1%: Anaphylaxis, chest pain, hypotension, fungal skin infection, pseudomembranous colitis, vaginal candidiasis, pruritus, flatulence, decreased salivation, malaise, fever, decreased appetite, cough, epistaxis, dizziness, fatigue, anxiety, insomnia, flushing, weakness, nightmares, taste alteration, eye itching, tinnitus, purpuric nephritis

(Continued)

Cefpodoxime *(Continued)*

Other reactions with cephalosporins include seizures, Stevens-Johnson syndrome, toxic epidermal necrolysis, erythema multiforme, urticaria, serum-sickness reactions, renal dysfunction, interstitial nephritis toxic nephropathy, cholestasis, aplastic anemia, hemolytic anemia, hemorrhage, pancytopenia, agranulocytosis, colitis, vaginitis, superinfection

Overdosage/Toxicology

After acute overdose, most agents cause only nausea, vomiting, and diarrhea, although neuromuscular hypersensitivity and seizures are possible, especially in patients with renal insufficiency; many beta-lactam antibiotics have the potential to cause neuro-muscular hyperirritability or seizures

Hemodialysis may be helpful to aid in the removal of the drug from the blood but not usually indicated, otherwise most treatment is supportive or symptom directed following GI decontamination

Drug Interactions

Decreased effect: Antacids and H_2-receptor antagonists (reduce absorption and serum concentration of cefpodoxime)

Increased effect: Probenecid may decrease cephalosporin elimination

Increased toxicity: Furosemide, aminoglycosides may be a possible additive to nephro-toxicity

Stability After mixing, keep suspension in refrigerator, shake well before using; discard unused portion after 14 days

Mechanism of Action Inhibits bacterial cell wall synthesis by binding to one or more of the penicillin-binding proteins (PBPs) which in turn inhibits the final transpeptidation step of peptidoglycan synthesis in bacterial cell walls, thus inhibiting cell wall biosynthesis. Bacteria eventually lyse due to ongoing activity of cell wall autolytic enzymes (autolysins and murein hydrolases) while cell wall assembly is arrested.

Pharmacodynamics/Kinetics

Absorption: Oral: Rapidly and well absorbed (50%), acid stable; enhanced in the presence of food or low gastric pH

Distribution: Good tissue penetration, including lung and tonsils; penetrates into pleural fluid

Protein binding: 18% to 23%

Metabolism: Oral: De-esterified in the GI tract to the active metabolite, cefpodoxime

Half-life: 2.2 hours (prolonged with renal impairment)

Time to peak: Within 1 hour (oral)

Elimination: Primarily eliminated by the kidney with 80% of dose excreted unchanged in urine in 24 hours

Usual Dosage Oral:

Children >5 months to 12 years:

Acute otitis media: 10 mg/kg/day as a single dose or divided every 12 hours (400 mg/day)

Pharyngitis/tonsillitis: 10 mg/kg/day in 2 divided doses (maximum: 200 mg/day)

Children ≥13 years and Adults:

Acute community-acquired pneumonia and bacterial exacerbations of chronic bronchitis: 200 mg every 12 hours for 14 days and 10 days, respectively

Skin and skin structure: 400 mg every 12 hours for 7-14 days

Uncomplicated gonorrhea (male and female) and rectal gonococcal infections (female): 200 mg as a single dose

Pharyngitis/tonsillitis: 100 mg every 12 hours for 10 days

Uncomplicated urinary tract infection: 100 mg every 12 hours for 7 days

Dosing adjustment in renal impairment: Cl_{cr} <30 mL/minute: Administer every 24 hours

Monitoring Parameters Observe for signs and symptoms of anaphylaxis during first dose

Test Interactions Positive direct Coombs', false-positive urinary glucose test using cupric sulfate (Benedict's solution, Clinitest®, Fehling's solution), false-positive serum or urine creatinine with Jaffé reaction

Patient Information Take with food; chilling improves flavor (do not freeze); report persistent diarrhea; entire course of medication (10-14 days) should be taken to ensure eradication of organism; may interfere with oral contraceptives; females should report symptoms of vaginitis

Dosage Forms

Granules for oral suspension, as proxetil (lemon creme flavor): 50 mg/5 mL (100 mL); 100 mg/5 mL (100 mL)

Tablet, film coated, as proxetil: 100 mg, 200 mg

♦ **Cefpodoxime Proxetil** *see Cefpodoxime on previous page*

Cefprozil *(sef PROE zil)*

Related Information

Cephalosporins by Generation *on page 1373*
Community-Acquired Pneumonia in Adults *on page 1419*

U.S. Brand Names Cefzil®

Therapeutic Category Antibiotic, Cephalosporin (Second Generation)

Use Treatment of otitis media and infections involving the respiratory tract and skin and skin structure; Active against methicillin-sensitive staphylococci, many streptococci, and various gram-negative bacilli including *E. coli*, some *Klebsiella*, *P. mirabilis*, *H. influenzae*, and *Moraxella*.

Pregnancy Risk Factor B

Contraindications Hypersensitivity to cefprozil or any component or cephalosporins

Warnings/Precautions Modify dosage in patients with severe renal impairment; prolonged use may result in superinfection; use with caution in patients with a history of penicillin allergy especially IgE-mediated reactions (eg, anaphylaxis, urticaria); may cause antibiotic-associated colitis or colitis secondary to *C. difficile*

Adverse Reactions

1% to 10%:

Central nervous system: Dizziness (1%)

Dermatologic: Diaper rash (1.5%)

Gastrointestinal: Diarrhea (2.9%), nausea (3.5%), vomiting (1%), abdominal pain (1%)

Genitourinary: Vaginitis, genital pruritus (1.6%)

Hepatic: Increased transaminases (2%)

Miscellaneous: Superinfection

<1%: Anaphylaxis, angioedema, pseudomembranous colitis, rash, urticaria, erythema multiforme, serum sickness, Stevens-Johnson syndrome, hyperactivity, headache, insomnia, confusion, somnolence, leukopenia, eosinophilia, thrombocytopenia, elevated BUN, elevated creatinine, arthralgia, cholestatic jaundice, fever

Other reactions with cephalosporins include: Seizures, toxic epidermal necrolysis, renal dysfunction, interstitial nephritis, toxic nephropathy, aplastic anemia, hemolytic anemia, hemorrhage, pancytopenia, agranulocytosis, colitis, vaginitis, superinfection

Overdosage/Toxicology

After acute overdose, most agents cause only nausea, vomiting, and diarrhea, although neuromuscular hypersensitivity and seizures are possible, especially in patients with renal insufficiency; many beta-lactam antibiotics have the potential to cause neuromuscular hyperirritability or seizures

Hemodialysis may be helpful to aid in the removal of the drug from the blood but not usually indicated, otherwise most treatment is supportive or symptom directed following GI decontamination

Drug Interactions

Increased effect: Probenecid may decrease cephalosporin elimination

Increased toxicity: Furosemide, aminoglycosides may be a possible additive to nephrotoxicity

Mechanism of Action Inhibits bacterial cell wall synthesis by binding to one or more of the penicillin-binding proteins (PBPs) which in turn inhibits the final transpeptidation step of peptidoglycan synthesis in bacterial cell walls, thus inhibiting cell wall biosynthesis. Bacteria eventually lyse due to ongoing activity of cell wall autolytic enzymes (autolysins and murein hydrolases) while cell wall assembly is arrested.

Pharmacodynamics/Kinetics

Absorption: Oral: Well absorbed (94%)

Distribution: Low distribution into breast milk

Protein binding: 35% to 45%

Half-life, elimination: 1.3 hours (normal renal function)

Peak serum levels: 1.5 hours (fasting state)

Elimination: 61% excreted unchanged in urine

Usual Dosage Oral:

Infants and Children >6 months to 12 years: Otitis media: 15 mg/kg every 12 hours for 10 days

Pharyngitis/tonsillitis:

Children 2-12 years: 7.5 -15 mg/kg/day divided every 12 hours for 10 days (administer for >10 days if due to *S. pyogenes*); maximum: 1 g/day

Children >13 years and Adults: 500 mg every 24 hours for 10 days

Uncomplicated skin and skin structure infections:

Children 2-12 years: 20 mg/kg every 24 hours for 10 days; maximum: 1 g/day

Children >13 years and Adults: 250 mg every 12 hours, or 500 mg every 12-24 hours for 10 days

Secondary bacterial infection of acute bronchitis or acute bacterial exacerbation of chronic bronchitis: 500 mg every 12 hours for 10 days

Dosing adjustment in renal impairment: Cl_{cr} <30 mL/minute: Reduce dose by 50%

Hemodialysis: Reduced by hemodialysis; administer dose after the completion of hemodialysis

Monitoring Parameters Assess patient at beginning and throughout therapy for infection; monitor for signs of anaphylaxis during first dose

Test Interactions Positive direct Coombs', false-positive urinary glucose test using cupric sulfate (Benedict's solution, Clinitest®, Fehling's solution), false-positive serum or urine creatinine with Jaffé reaction

Patient Information Chilling improves flavor (do not freeze); report persistent diarrhea; entire course of medication (10-14 days) should be taken to ensure eradication of organism; may interfere with oral contraceptives; females should report symptoms of vaginitis

Dosage Forms

Powder for oral suspension, as anhydrous: 125 mg/5 mL (50 mL, 75 mL, 100 mL); 250 mg/5 mL (50 mL, 75 mL, 100 mL)

Tablet, as anhydrous: 250 mg, 500 mg

Ceftazidime (SEF tay zi deem)

Related Information

Antimicrobial Drugs of Choice *on page 1404*
Cephalosporins by Generation *on page 1373*

(Continued)

Ceftazidime *(Continued)*

U.S. Brand Names Ceptaz™; Fortaz®; Tazicef®; Tazidime®

Canadian Brand Names Ceptaz™

Therapeutic Category Antibiotic, Cephalosporin (Third Generation)

Use Treatment of documented susceptible *Pseudomonas aeruginosa* infection and infections due to other susceptible aerobic gram-negative organisms; empiric therapy of a febrile, granulocytopenic patient

Pregnancy Risk Factor B

Contraindications Hypersensitivity to ceftazidime, any component, or cephalosporins

Warnings/Precautions Modify dosage in patients with severe renal impairment; prolonged use may result in superinfection; use with caution in patients with a history of penicillin allergy especially IgE-mediated reactions (eg, anaphylaxis, urticaria); may cause antibiotic-associated colitis or colitis secondary to *C. difficile*

Adverse Reactions

1% to 10%:
   Gastrointestinal: Diarrhea (1.3%)
   Local: Pain at injection site (1.4%)
   Miscellaneous: Hypersensitivity reactions (2%)

<1%: Anaphylaxis, fever, headache, dizziness, paresthesia, pruritus, rash, Stevens-Johnson syndrome, toxic epidermal necrolysis, erythema multiforme, angioedema, nausea, vomiting, pseudomembranous colitis, eosinophilia, thrombocytosis, leukopenia, hemolytic anemia, elevated transaminases, increased BUN, increased creatinine, phlebitis, candidiasis, vaginitis, encephalopathy, asterixis, neuromuscular excitability

Other reactions with cephalosporins include seizures, urticaria, serum-sickness reactions, renal dysfunction, interstitial nephritis, toxic nephropathy, elevated BUN, elevated creatinine, cholestasis, aplastic anemia, hemolytic anemia, pancytopenia, agranulocytosis, colitis, prolonged PT, hemorrhage, superinfection

Overdosage/Toxicology

Symptoms of overdose include neuromuscular hypersensitivity, convulsions especially with renal insufficiency; many beta-lactam antibiotics have the potential to cause neuromuscular hyperirritability or seizures

Hemodialysis may be helpful to aid in the removal of the drug from the blood, otherwise most treatment is supportive or symptom directed

Drug Interactions

Increased effect: Probenecid may decrease cephalosporin elimination; aminoglycosides: *in vitro* studies indicate additive or synergistic effect against some strains of Enterobacteriaceae and *Pseudomonas aeruginosa*

Increased toxicity: Furosemide, aminoglycosides may be a possible additive to nephrotoxicity

Stability Reconstituted solution and I.V. infusion in NS or D_5W solution are stable for 24 hours at room temperature, 10 days when refrigerated, or 12 weeks when frozen; after freezing, thawed solution is stable for 24 hours at room temperature or 4 days when refrigerated; 96 hours under refrigeration, after mixing

Mechanism of Action Inhibits bacterial cell wall synthesis by binding to one or more of the penicillin-binding proteins (PBPs) which in turn inhibits the final transpeptidation step of peptidoglycan synthesis in bacterial cell walls, thus inhibiting cell wall biosynthesis. Bacteria eventually lyse due to ongoing activity of cell wall autolytic enzymes (autolysins and murein hydrolases) while cell wall assembly is arrested.

Pharmacodynamics/Kinetics

Distribution: Widely distributes throughout the body including bone, bile, skin, CSF (diffuses into CSF with higher concentrations when the meninges are inflamed), endometrium, heart, pleural and lymphatic fluids

Protein binding: 17%

Half-life: 1-2 hours (prolonged with renal impairment); Neonates <23 days: 2.2-4.7 hours

Time to peak serum concentration: I.M.: Within 1 hour

Elimination: By glomerular filtration with 80% to 90% of the dose excreted as unchanged drug within 24 hours

Usual Dosage

Neonates 0-4 weeks: I.V.: 30 mg/kg every 12 hours

Infants and Children 1 month to 12 years: I.V.: 30-50 mg/kg/dose every 8 hours; maximum dose: 6 g/day

Adults: I.M., I.V.: 500 mg to 2 g every 8-12 hours
   Urinary tract infections: 250-500 mg every 12 hours

Dosing interval in renal impairment:
   Cl_{cr} 30-50 mL/minute: Administer every 12 hours
   Cl_{cr} 10-30 mL/minute: Administer every 24 hours
   Cl_{cr} <10 mL/minute: Administer every 48-72 hours
   Hemodialysis: Dialyzable (50% to 100%)
   Continuous arteriovenous or venovenous hemodiafiltration (CAVH) effects: Dose as for Cl_{cr} 30-50 mL/minute

Administration Any carbon dioxide bubbles that may be present in the withdrawn solution should be expelled prior to injection; administer around-the-clock to promote less variation in peak and trough serum levels; ceftazidime can be administered IVP over 3-5 minutes, or I.V. retrograde or I.V. intermittent infusion over 15-30 minutes; do not admix with aminoglycosides in same bottle/bag; final concentration for I.V. administration should not exceed 100 mg/mL

Monitoring Parameters Observe for signs and symptoms of anaphylaxis during first dose

Test Interactions Positive direct Coombs', false-positive urinary glucose test using cupric sulfate (Benedict's solution, Clinitest®, Fehling's solution), false-positive serum or urine creatinine with Jaffé reaction

Additional Information Sodium content of 1 g: 2.3 mEq

Dosage Forms

Infusion, premixed (frozen) (Fortaz®): 1 g (50 mL); 2 g (50 mL)

Powder for injection: 500 mg, 1 g, 2 g, 6 g

Ceftibuten (sef TYE byoo ten)

U.S. Brand Names Cedax®

Therapeutic Category Antibiotic, Cephalosporin (Third Generation)

Use Oral cephalosporin for bronchitis, otitis media, and pharyngitis/tonsillitis due to *H. influenzae* and *M. catarrhalis*, both beta-lactamase-producing and nonproducing strains, as well as *S. pneumoniae* (weak) and *S. pyogenes*

Pregnancy Risk Factor B

Contraindications In patients with known allergy to the cephalosporin group of antibiotics

Warnings/Precautions Modify dosage in patients with severe renal impairment, prolonged use may result in superinfection; use with caution in patients with a history of penicillin allergy, especially IgE-mediated reactions (eg, anaphylaxis, urticaria); may cause antibiotic-associated colitis or colitis secondary to *C. difficile*

Adverse Reactions

1% to 10%:

Central nervous system: Headache (3%), dizziness (1%)

Gastrointestinal: Nausea (4%), diarrhea (3%), dyspepsia (2%), vomiting (1%), abdominal pain (1%)

Hematologic: Increased eosinophils (3%), decreased hemoglobin (2%), thrombocytosis

Hepatic: Increased ALT (1%), increased bilirubin (1%)

Renal: Increased BUN (4%)

<1%: Anorexia, agitation, constipation, diaper rash, dry mouth, dyspnea, dysuria, fatigue, candidiasis, rash, urticaria, irritability, paresthesia, nasal congestion, insomnia, rigors, increased transaminases, increased creatinine, leukopenia

Other reactions with cephalosporins include anaphylaxis, fever, paresthesia, pruritus, Stevens-Johnson syndrome, toxic epidermal necrolysis, erythema multiforme, angioedema, pseudomembranous colitis, hemolytic anemia, candidiasis, vaginitis, encephalopathy, asterixis, neuromuscular excitability, seizures, serum-sickness reactions, renal dysfunction, interstitial nephritis, toxic nephropathy, cholestasis, aplastic anemia, hemolytic anemia, pancytopenia, agranulocytosis, colitis, prolonged PT, hemorrhage, superinfection

Overdosage/Toxicology

After acute overdose, most agents cause only nausea, vomiting, and diarrhea, although neuromuscular hypersensitivity and seizures are possible, especially in patients with renal insufficiency; many beta-lactam antibiotics have the potential to cause neuromuscular hyperirritability or seizures

Hemodialysis may be helpful to aid in the removal of the drug from the blood but not usually indicated, otherwise most treatment is supportive or symptom directed following GI decontamination

Drug Interactions

Increased effect: High-dose probenecid decreases clearance

Increased toxicity: Aminoglycosides increase nephrotoxic potential

Stability Reconstituted suspension is stable for 14 days in the refrigerator

Mechanism of Action Inhibits bacterial cell wall synthesis by binding to one or more of the penicillin-binding proteins (PBPs) which in turn inhibits the final transpeptidation step of peptidoglycan synthesis in bacterial cell walls, thus inhibiting cell wall biosynthesis. Bacteria eventually lyse due to ongoing activity of cell wall autolytic enzymes (autolysins and murein hydrolases) while cell wall assembly is arrested.

Pharmacodynamics/Kinetics

Absorption: Rapid (T_{max}: 2-3 hours); food decreases peak concentrations, delays T_{max} and lowers the AUC (total amount of drug absorbed)

Distribution: V_d: Children: 0.5 L/kg; Adults: 0.21 L/kg

Half-life: 2 hours

Elimination: In urine

Usual Dosage Oral:

Children <12 years: 9 mg/kg/day for 10 days; maximum daily dose: 400 mg

Children ≥12 years and Adults: 400 mg once daily for 10 days; maximum: 400 mg

Dosage adjustment in renal impairment:

Cl_{cr} 30-49 mL//minute: Administer 4.5 mg/kg or 200 mg every 24 hours

Cl_{cr} <29 mL/minute: Administer 2.25 mg/kg or 100 mg every 24 hours

Monitoring Parameters Observe for signs and symptoms of anaphylaxis during first dose; with prolonged therapy, monitor renal, hepatic, and hematologic function periodically

Test Interactions Positive direct Coombs', false-positive urinary glucose test using cupric sulfate (Benedict's solution, Clinitest®, Fehling's solution), false-positive serum or urine creatinine with Jaffé reaction

(Continued)

Ceftibuten *(Continued)*

Patient Information Must be administered at least 2 hours before meals or 1 hour after a meal; shake suspension well before use; suspension may be kept for 14 days if stored in refrigerator; discard any unused portion after 14 days; report prolonged diarrhea; entire course of medication should be taken to ensure eradication of organism; take at the same time each day to maintain adequate blood levels; may interfere with oral contraceptive; females should report symptoms of vaginitis

Additional Information Oral suspension contains 1 g of sucrose per 5 mL

Dosage Forms

Capsule: 400 mg

Powder for oral suspension (cherry flavor): 90 mg/5 mL (30 mL, 60 mL, 120 mL); 180 mg/5 mL (30 mL, 60 mL, 120 mL)

♦ **Ceftin® Oral** *see* Cefuroxime *on page 224*

Ceftizoxime *(sef ti ZOKS eem)*

Related Information

Antimicrobial Drugs of Choice *on page 1404*

Cephalosporins by Generation *on page 1373*

Treatment of Sexually Transmitted Diseases *on page 1429*

U.S. Brand Names Cefizox®

Synonyms Ceftizoxime Sodium

Therapeutic Category Antibiotic, Cephalosporin (Third Generation)

Use Treatment of susceptible bacterial infection, mainly respiratory tract, skin and skin structure, bone and joint, urinary tract and gynecologic, as well as septicemia; active against many gram-negative bacilli (not *Pseudomonas*), some gram-positive cocci (not *Enterococcus*), and some anaerobes

Pregnancy Risk Factor B

Contraindications Hypersensitivity to ceftizoxime, any component, or cephalosporins

Warnings/Precautions Modify dosage in patients with severe renal impairment, prolonged use may result in superinfection; use with caution in patients with a history of penicillin allergy, especially IgE-mediated reactions (eg, anaphylaxis, urticaria); may cause antibiotic-associated colitis or colitis secondary to *C. difficile*

Adverse Reactions

1% to 10%:

Central nervous system: Fever

Dermatologic: Rash, pruritus

Hematologic: Eosinophilia, thrombocytosis

Hepatic: Elevated transaminases, alkaline phosphatase

Local: Pain, burning at injection site

<1%: Anaphylaxis, diarrhea, nausea, vomiting, injection site reactions, phlebitis, paresthesia, numbness, increased bilirubin, increased BUN, increased creatinine, anemia, leukopenia, neutropenia, thrombocytopenia, vaginitis

Other reactions reported with cephalosporins include Stevens-Johnson syndrome, toxic epidermal necrolysis, erythema multiforme, pseudomembranous colitis, angioedema, hemolytic anemia, candidiasis, encephalopathy, asterixis, neuromuscular excitability, seizures, serum-sickness reactions, renal dysfunction, interstitial nephritis, toxic nephropathy, cholestasis, aplastic anemia, hemolytic anemia, pancytopenia, agranulocytosis, colitis, prolonged PT, hemorrhage, superinfection

Overdosage/Toxicology

Symptoms of overdose include neuromuscular hypersensitivity, convulsions especially with renal insufficiency; many beta-lactam antibiotics have the potential to cause neuromuscular hyperirritability or seizures

Hemodialysis may be helpful to aid in the removal of the drug from the blood, otherwise most treatment is supportive or symptom directed

Drug Interactions

Increased effect: Probenecid may decrease cephalosporin elimination

Increased toxicity: Furosemide, aminoglycosides may be a possible additive to nephrotoxicity

Stability Reconstituted solution is stable for 24 hours at room temperature and 96 hours when refrigerated; for I.V. infusion in NS or D₅W solution is stable for 24 hours at room temperature, 96 hours when refrigerated or 12 weeks when frozen; after freezing, thawed solution is stable for 24 hours at room temperature or 10 days when refrigerated

Mechanism of Action Inhibits bacterial cell wall synthesis by binding to one or more of the penicillin-binding proteins (PBPs) which in turn inhibits the final transpeptidation step of peptidoglycan synthesis in bacterial cell walls, thus inhibiting cell wall biosynthesis. Bacteria eventually lyse due to ongoing activity of cell wall autolytic enzymes (autolysins and murein hydrolases) while cell wall assembly is arrested.

Pharmacodynamics/Kinetics

Distribution: V_d: 0.35-0.5 L/kg; widely distributed into most body tissues and fluids including gallbladder, liver, kidneys, bone, sputum, bile, and pleural and synovial fluids; has good CSF penetration; crosses placenta; small amounts excreted in breast milk

Protein binding: 30%

Half-life: 1.6 hours, increases to 25 hours when Cl_{cr} falls to <10 mL/minute

Time to peak serum concentration: I.M.: Within 0.5-1 hour

Elimination: Excreted unchanged in urine

Usual Dosage I.M., I.V.:

Children ≥6 months: 150-200 mg/kg/day divided every 6-8 hours (maximum of 12 g/24 hours)

Adults: 1-2 g every 8-12 hours, up to 2 g every 4 hours or 4 g every 8 hours for life-threatening infections

Dosing adjustment in renal impairment: Adults:

Cl_{cr} 10-30 mL/minute: Administer 1 g every 12 hours

Cl_{cr} <10 mL/minute: Administer 1 g every 24 hours

Moderately dialyzable (20% to 50%)

Continuous arteriovenous or venovenous hemodiafiltration (CAVH) effects: Dose as for Cl_{cr} 10-50 mL/minute

Monitoring Parameters Observe for signs and symptoms of anaphylaxis during first dose

Test Interactions Positive direct Coombs', false-positive urinary glucose test using cupric sulfate (Benedict's solution, Clinitest®, Fehling's solution), false-positive serum or urine creatinine with Jaffé reaction

Nursing Implications Do not admix with aminoglycosides in same bottle/bag

Additional Information Sodium content of 1 g: 60 mg (2.6 mEq)

Dosage Forms

Injection, as sodium, in D_5W (frozen): 1 g (50 mL); 2 g (50 mL)

Powder for injection, as sodium: 500 mg, 1 g, 2 g, 10 g

♦ **Ceftizoxime Sodium** see Ceftizoxime on previous page

Ceftriaxone (sef trye AKS one)

Related Information

Animal and Human Bites Guidelines on page 1399

Antibiotic Treatment of Adults With Infective Endocarditis on page 1401

Antimicrobial Drugs of Choice on page 1404

Cephalosporins by Generation on page 1373

Community-Acquired Pneumonia in Adults on page 1419

Treatment of Sexually Transmitted Diseases on page 1429

U.S. Brand Names Rocephin®

Synonyms Ceftriaxone Sodium

Therapeutic Category Antibiotic, Cephalosporin (Third Generation)

Use Treatment of lower respiratory tract infections, skin and skin structure infections, bone and joint infections, intra-abdominal and urinary tract infections, sepsis and meningitis due to susceptible organisms; documented or suspected infection due to susceptible organisms in home care patients and patients without I.V. line access; treatment of documented or suspected gonococcal infection or chancroid; emergency room management of patients at high risk for bacteremia, periorbital or buccal cellulitis, salmonellosis or shigellosis, and pneumonia of unestablished etiology (<5 years of age); treatment of Lyme disease, depends on the stage of the disease (used in Stage II and Stage III, but not stage I; doxycycline is the drug of choice for Stage I)

Pregnancy Risk Factor B

Contraindications Hypersensitivity to ceftriaxone sodium, any component, or cephalosporins; do not use in hyperbilirubinemic neonates, particularly those who are premature since ceftriaxone is reported to displace bilirubin from albumin binding sites

Warnings/Precautions Modify dosage in patients with severe renal impairment, prolonged use may result in superinfection; use with caution in patients with a history of penicillin allergy, especially IgE-mediated reactions (eg, anaphylaxis, urticaria); may cause antibiotic-associated colitis or colitis secondary to C. difficile

Adverse Reactions

1% to 10%:

Dermatologic: Rash (1.7%)

Gastrointestinal: Diarrhea (2.7%)

Hematologic: Eosinophilia (6%), thrombocytosis (5.1%), leukopenia (2.1%)

Hepatic: Elevated transaminases (3.1% to 3.3%)

Local: Pain, induration at injection site (1%)

Renal: Increased BUN (1.2%)

<1%: Phlebitis, pruritus, fever, chills, anemia, hemolytic anemia, neutropenia, lymphopenia, thrombocytopenia, prolonged PT, nausea, vomiting, dysgeusia, increased alkaline phosphatase, increased bilirubin, increased creatinine, urinary casts, headache, dizziness, candidiasis, vaginitis, diaphoresis, flushing

Other reactions with cephalosporins include anaphylaxis, paresthesia, Stevens-Johnson syndrome, toxic epidermal necrolysis, erythema multiforme, angioedema, pseudomembranous colitis, hemolytic anemia, encephalopathy, asterixis, neuromuscular excitability, seizures, serum-sickness reactions, renal dysfunction, interstitial nephritis, toxic nephropathy, cholestasis, aplastic anemia, hemolytic anemia, pancytopenia, agranulocytosis, colitis, hemorrhage, superinfection

Overdosage/Toxicology

Symptoms of overdose include neuromuscular hypersensitivity, convulsions especially with renal insufficiency; many beta-lactam antibiotics have the potential to cause neuromuscular hyperirritability or seizures

Hemodialysis may be helpful to aid in the removal of the drug from the blood, otherwise most treatment is supportive or symptom directed

(Continued)

Ceftriaxone *(Continued)*

Drug Interactions

Increased effect:

Aminoglycosides may result in synergistic antibacterial activity

High-dose probenecid decreases clearance

Increased toxicity: Aminoglycosides increase nephrotoxic potential

Stability Reconstituted solution (100 mg/mL) is stable for 3 days at room temperature and 3 days when refrigerated; for I.V. infusion in NS or D_5W solution is stable for 3 days at room temperature, 10 days when refrigerated, or 26 weeks when frozen; after freezing, thawed solution is stable for 3 days at room temperature or 10 days when refrigerated

Mechanism of Action Inhibits bacterial cell wall synthesis by binding to one or more of the penicillin-binding proteins (PBPs) which in turn inhibits the final transpeptidation step of peptidoglycan synthesis in bacterial cell walls, thus inhibiting cell wall biosynthesis. Bacteria eventually lyse due to ongoing activity of cell wall autolytic enzymes (autolysins and murein hydrolases) while cell wall assembly is arrested.

Pharmacodynamics/Kinetics

Absorption: I.M.: Well absorbed

Distribution: Widely distributed throughout the body including gallbladder, lungs, bone, bile, CSF (diffuses into the CSF at higher concentrations when the meninges are inflamed); crosses placenta, reaches amniotic fluid and milk

Protein binding: 85% to 95%

Half-life: Normal renal and hepatic function: 5-9 hours

Neonates: Postnatal: 1-4 days: 16 hours; 9-30 days: 9 hours

Time to peak serum concentration: I.M.: Within 1-2 hours

Elimination: Excreted unchanged in urine (33% to 65%) by glomerular filtration and in feces

Usual Dosage I.M., I.V.:

Neonates:

Postnatal age ≤7 days: 50 mg/kg/day given every 24 hours

Postnatal age >7 days:

≤2000 g: 50 mg/kg/day given every 24 hours

>2000 g: 50-75 mg/kg/day given every 24 hours

Gonococcal prophylaxis: 25-50 mg/kg as a single dose (dose not to exceed 125 mg)

Gonococcal infection: 25-50 mg/kg/day (maximum dose: 125 mg) given every 24 hours for 10-14 days

Infants and Children: 50-75 mg/kg/day in 1-2 divided doses every 12-24 hours; maximum: 2 g/24 hours

Meningitis: 100 mg/kg/day divided every 12-24 hours, up to a maximum of 4 g/24 hours; loading dose of 75 mg/kg/dose may be given at start of therapy

Otitis media: Single I.M. injection

Uncomplicated gonococcal infections, sexual assault, and STD prophylaxis: I.M.: 125 mg as a single dose plus doxycycline

Complicated gonococcal infections:

Infants: I.M., I.V.: 25-50 mg/kg/day in a single dose (maximum: 125 mg/dose); treat for 7 days for disseminated infection and 7-14 days for documented meningitis

<45 kg: 50 mg/kg/day once daily; maximum: 1 g/day; for ophthalmia, peritonitis, arthritis, or bacteremia: 50-100 mg/kg/day divided every 12-24 hours; maximum: 2 g/day for meningitis or endocarditis

>45 kg: 1 g/day once daily for disseminated gonococcal infections; 1-2 g dose every 12 hours for meningitis or endocarditis

Acute epididymitis: I.M.: 250 mg in a single dose

Adults: 1-2 g every 12-24 hours (depending on the type and severity of infection); maximum dose: 2 g every 12 hours for treatment of meningitis

Uncomplicated gonorrhea: I.M.: 250 mg as a single dose

Surgical prophylaxis: 1 g 30 minutes to 2 hours before surgery

Dosing adjustment in renal or hepatic impairment: No change necessary

Hemodialysis: Not dialyzable (0% to 5%); administer dose postdialysis

Peritoneal dialysis: Administer 750 mg every 12 hours

Continuous arteriovenous or venovenous hemofiltration (CAVH/CAVHD): Removes 10 mg of ceftriaxone per liter of filtrate per day

Monitoring Parameters Observe for signs and symptoms of anaphylaxis

Test Interactions Positive direct Coombs', false-positive urinary glucose test using cupric sulfate (Benedict's solution, Clinitest®, Fehling's solution), false-positive serum or urine creatinine with Jaffé reaction

Nursing Implications For I.M. injection, the maximum concentration is 250 mg/mL; ceftriaxone can be diluted with 1:1 water and 1% lidocaine for I.M. administration. Do not admix with aminoglycosides in same bottle/bag.

Additional Information Sodium content of 1 g: 60 mg (2.6 mEq)

Dosage Forms

Infusion, as sodium, premixed (frozen): 1 g in $D_{3.8}W$ (50 mL); 2 g in $D_{2.4}W$ (50 mL)

Powder for injection, as sodium: 250 mg, 500 mg, 1 g, 2 g, 10 g

♦ **Ceftriaxone Sodium** *see Ceftriaxone on previous page*

Cefuroxime *(se fyoor OKS eem)*

Related Information

Antimicrobial Drugs of Choice *on page 1404*
Cephalosporins by Generation *on page 1373*
Community-Acquired Pneumonia in Adults *on page 1419*

Prevention of Wound Infection & Sepsis in Surgical Patients on page 1381

U.S. Brand Names Ceftin® Oral; Kefurox® Injection; Zinacef® Injection

Synonyms Cefuroxime Axetil; Cefuroxime Sodium

Therapeutic Category Antibiotic, Cephalosporin (Second Generation)

Use Treatment of infections caused by staphylococci, group B streptococci, *H. influenzae* (type A and B), *E. coli*, *Enterobacter*, *Salmonella*, and *Klebsiella*; treatment of susceptible infections of the lower respiratory tract, otitis media, urinary tract, skin and soft tissue, bone and joint, sepsis and gonorrhea

Pregnancy Risk Factor B

Contraindications Hypersensitivity to cefuroxime, any component, or cephalosporins

Warnings/Precautions Modify dosage in patients with severe renal impairment, prolonged use may result in superinfection; use with caution in patients with a history of penicillin allergy, especially IgE-mediated reactions (eg, anaphylaxis, urticaria); may cause antibiotic-associated colitis or colitis secondary to *C. difficile*

Adverse Reactions

1% to 10%:

Hematologic: Eosinophilia (7%), decreased hemoglobin and hematocrit (10%)

Hepatic: Increased transaminases (4%), increased alkaline phosphatase (2%)

Local: Thrombophlebitis (1.7%)

<1%: Anaphylaxis, erythema multiforme, toxic epidermal necrolysis, Stevens-Johnson syndrome, interstitial nephritis, dizziness, fever, headache, rash, nausea, vomiting, diarrhea, stomach cramps, GI bleeding, colitis, neutropenia, leukopenia, increased creatinine, increased BUN, pain at injection site, vaginitis, seizures, angioedema, pseudomembranous colitis

Other reactions with cephalosporins include toxic nephropathy, cholestasis, agranulocytosis, colitis, pancytopenia, aplastic anemia, hemolytic anemia, hemorrhage, prolonged PT, encephalopathy, asterixis, neuromuscular excitability, serum-sickness reactions, superinfection

Overdosage/Toxicology

After acute overdose, most agents cause only nausea, vomiting, and diarrhea, although neuromuscular hypersensitivity and seizures are possible, especially in patients with renal insufficiency; many beta-lactam antibiotics have the potential to cause neuromuscular hyperirritability or seizures

Hemodialysis may be helpful to aid in the removal of the drug from the blood but not usually indicated, otherwise most treatment is supportive or symptom directed following GI decontamination

Drug Interactions

Increased effect: High-dose probenecid decreases clearance

Increased toxicity: Aminoglycosides increase nephrotoxic potential

Stability Reconstituted solution is stable for 24 hours at room temperature and 48 hours when refrigerated; I.V. infusion in NS or D₅W solution is stable for 24 hours at room temperature, 7 days when refrigerated, or 26 weeks when frozen; after freezing, thawed solution is stable for 24 hours at room temperature or 21 days when refrigerated

Mechanism of Action Inhibits bacterial cell wall synthesis by binding to one or more of the penicillin-binding proteins (PBPs) which in turn inhibits the final transpeptidation step of peptidoglycan synthesis in bacterial cell walls, thus inhibiting cell wall biosynthesis. Bacteria eventually lyse due to ongoing activity of cell wall autolytic enzymes (autolysins and murein hydrolases) while cell wall assembly is arrested.

Pharmacodynamics/Kinetics

Absorption: Oral (cefuroxime axetil): Increased when given with or shortly after food or infant formula (37% to 52%)

Distribution: Widely distributed to body tissues and fluids; crosses blood-brain barrier; therapeutic concentrations achieved in CSF even when meninges are not inflamed; crosses placenta and reaches breast milk

Protein binding: 33% to 50%

Bioavailability, axetil: Oral: 37% to 52%

Half-life:

Neonates: ≤3 days: 5.1-5.8 hours; 6-14 days: 2-4.2 hours; 3-4 weeks: 1-1.5 hours

Adults: 1-2 hours (prolonged in renal impairment)

Time to peak serum concentration: I.M.: Within 15-60 minutes

Elimination: Primarily excreted 66% to 100% as unchanged drug in urine by both glomerular filtration and tubular secretion

Usual Dosage

Children:

Pharyngitis, tonsillitis: Oral:

Suspension: 20 mg/kg/day (maximum: 500 mg/day) in 2 divided doses

Tablet: 125 mg every 12 hours

Acute otitis media, impetigo: Oral:

Suspension: 30 mg/kg/day (maximum: 1 g/day) in 2 divided doses

Tablet: 250 mg every 12 hours

I.M., I.V.: 75-150 mg/kg/day divided every 8 hours; maximum dose: 6 g/day

Meningitis: Not recommended (doses of 200-240 mg/kg/day divided every 6-8 hours have been used); maximum dose: 9 g/day

Adults:

Oral: 250-500 mg twice daily; uncomplicated urinary tract infection: 125-250 mg every 12 hours

I.M., I.V.: 750 mg to 1.5 g/dose every 8 hours or 100-150 mg/kg/day in divided doses every 6-8 hours; maximum: 6 g/24 hours

(Continued)

Cefuroxime *(Continued)*

Dosing adjustment in renal impairment:
Cl$_{cr}$ 10-20 mL/minute: Administer every 12 hours
Cl$_{cr}$ <10 mL/minute: Administer every 24 hours
Hemodialysis: Dialyzable (25%)
Note: Cefuroxime axetil film-coated tablets and oral suspension are not bioequivalent and are not substitutable on a mg/mg basis
Continuous arteriovenous or venovenous hemodiafiltration (CAVH) effects: Dose as for Cl$_{cr}$ 10-20 mL/minute

Monitoring Parameters Observe for signs and symptoms of anaphylaxis during first dose; with prolonged therapy, monitor renal, hepatic, and hematologic function periodically

Test Interactions Positive direct Coombs', false-positive urinary glucose test using cupric sulfate (Benedict's solution, Clinitest®, Fehling's solution), false-positive serum or urine creatinine with Jaffé reaction

Patient Information Report prolonged diarrhea; entire course of medication (10-14 days) should be taken to ensure eradication of organism; may interfere with oral contraceptives; females should report symptoms of vaginitis

Nursing Implications Do not admix with aminoglycosides in same bottle/bag; obtain specimens for culture and sensitivity prior to the first dose

Additional Information Sodium content of 1 g: 54.2 mg (2.4 mEq)

Dosage Forms
Infusion, as sodium, premixed (frozen) (Zinacef®): 750 mg (50 mL); 1.5 g (50 mL)
Powder for injection, as sodium: 750 mg, 1.5 g, 7.5 g
Powder for injection, as sodium (Kefurox®, Zinacef®): 750 mg, 1.5 g, 7.5 g
Powder for oral suspension, as axetil (tutti-frutti flavor) (Ceftin®): 125 mg/5 mL (50 mL, 100 mL, 200 mL)
Tablet, as axetil (Ceftin®): 125 mg, 250 mg, 500 mg

♦ **Cefuroxime Axetil** *see Cefuroxime on page 224*
♦ **Cefuroxime Sodium** *see Cefuroxime on page 224*
♦ **Cefzil®** *see Cefprozil on page 218*
♦ **Celebrex®** *see Celecoxib on this page*

Celecoxib *(ce le COX ib)*

U.S. Brand Names Celebrex®

Therapeutic Category Selective Cyclooxygenase-2 Inhibitor

Use Relief of the signs and symptoms of osteoarthritis; relief of the signs and symptoms of rheumatoid arthritis in adults

Pregnancy Risk Factor C (D after 34 weeks gestation or close to delivery)

Pregnancy/Breast-Feeding Implications In late pregnancy may cause premature closure of the ductus arteriosus. In animal studies, celecoxib has been found to be excreted in milk; it is not known whether celecoxib is excreted in human milk. Because many drugs are excreted in milk, and the potential for serious adverse reactions exists, a decision should be made whether to discontinue nursing or discontinue the drug, taking into account the importance of the drug to the mother.

Contraindications Hypersensitivity to celecoxib or any component, sulfonamides, aspirin, or other nonsteroidal anti-inflammatory drugs (NSAIDs)

Warnings/Precautions Gastrointestinal irritation, ulceration, bleeding, and perforation may occur with NSAIDs (it is unclear whether celecoxib is associated with rates of these events which are similar to nonselective NSAIDs). Use with caution in patients with a history of GI disease (bleeding or ulcers), decreased renal function, hepatic disease, congestive heart failure, hypertension, or asthma. Anaphylactoid reactions may occur, even with no prior exposure to celecoxib. Use caution in patients with known or suspected deficiency of cytochrome P-450 isoenzyme 2C9.

Adverse Reactions
>10%: Central nervous system: Headache (15.8%)
2% to 10%:
Cardiovascular: Peripheral edema (2.1%)
Central nervous system: Insomnia (2.3%), dizziness (2%)
Dermatologic: Skin rash (2.2%)
Gastrointestinal: Dyspepsia (8.8%), diarrhea (5.6%), abdominal pain (4.1%), nausea (3.5%), flatulence (2.2%)
Neuromuscular & skeletal: Back pain (2.8%)
Respiratory: Upper respiratory tract infection (8.1%), sinusitis (5%), pharyngitis (2.3%), rhinitis (2%)
Miscellaneous: Accidental injury (2.9%)
0.1% to 2%:
Cardiovascular: Hypertension (aggravated), chest pain, myocardial infarction, palpitation, tachycardia, facial edema, peripheral edema
Central nervous system: Migraine, vertigo, hypoesthesia, fatigue, fever, pain, hypotonia, anxiety, depression, nervousness, somnolence
Dermatologic: Alopecia, dermatitis, photosensitivity, pruritus, rash (maculopapular), rash (erythematous), dry skin, urticaria
Endocrine & metabolic: Hot flashes, diabetes mellitus, hyperglycemia, hypercholesterolemia, breast pain, dysmenorrhea, menstrual disturbances, hypokalemia
Gastrointestinal: Constipation, tenesmus, diverticulitis, eructation, esophagitis, gastroenteritis, vomiting, gastroesophageal reflux, hemorrhoids, hiatal hernia, melena,

stomatitis, anorexia, increased appetite, taste disturbance, dry mouth, tooth disorder, weight gain

Genitourinary: Prostate disorder, vaginal bleeding, vaginitis, monilial vaginitis, dysuria, cystitis, urinary frequency, incontinence, urinary tract infection,

Hepatic: Elevated transaminases, increased alkaline phosphatase

Hematologic: Anemia, thrombocytopenia, ecchymosis

Neuromuscular & skeletal: Leg cramps, increased CPK, neck stiffness, arthralgia, myalgia, bone disorder, fracture, synovitis, tendonitis, neuralgia, paresthesia, neuropathy, weakness

Ocular: Glaucoma, blurred vision, cataract, conjunctivitis, eye pain

Otic: Deafness, tinnitus, earache, otitis media

Renal: Increased BUN, increased creatinine, albuminuria, hematuria, renal calculi

Respiratory: Bronchitis, bronchospasm, cough, dyspnea, laryngitis, pneumonia, epistaxis

Miscellaneous: Allergic reactions, flu-like syndrome, breast cancer, herpes infection, bacterial infection, moniliasis, viral infection, increased diaphoresis

<0.1% (limited to severe): Congestive heart failure, ventricular fibrillation, pulmonary embolism, syncope, cerebrovascular accident, gangrene, thrombophlebitis, thrombocytopenia, ataxia, acute renal failure, intestinal obstruction, pancreatitis, intestinal perforation, gastrointestinal bleeding, colitis, esophageal perforation, sepsis, sudden death

Overdosage/Toxicology

Symptoms may include epigastric pain, drowsiness, lethargy, nausea, and vomiting; gastrointestinal bleeding may occur. Rare manifestations include hypertension, respiratory depression, coma, and acute renal failure.

Treatment is symptomatic and supportive; forced diuresis, hemodialysis and/or urinary alkalinization may not be useful

Drug Interactions Celecoxib may be a cytochrome oxidase P-450 isoenzyme 2C9 substrate and an inhibitor of isoenzyme 2D6

Decreased effect: Efficacy of thiazide diuretics, loop diuretics (furosemide), or ACE-inhibitors may be diminished by celecoxib; aluminum and magnesium-containing antacids may decrease AUC and C_{max} of celecoxib 10% and 37% respectively

Increased effect: Inhibitors of isoenzyme 2C9 may result in significant increases in celecoxib concentrations. Coadministration of drugs by 2D6 may result in increased serum concentrations of these agents. Fluconazole increases celecoxib concentrations two-fold. Lithium concentrations may be increased by celecoxib. Celecoxib may be used with low-dose aspirin, however rates of gastrointestinal bleeding may be increased with coadministration. Celecoxib has not been shown to alter warfarin effects, although bleeding complications may be increased.

Mechanism of Action Inhibits prostaglandin synthesis by decreasing the activity of the enzyme, cyclo-oxygenase-2 (COX-2), which results in decreased formation of prostaglandin precursors. Celecoxib does not inhibit cyclo-oxygenase-1 (COX-1) at therapeutic concentrations.

Pharmacodynamics/Kinetics

Distribution: V_d (apparent): 400 L

Protein binding: 97% (albumin)

Metabolism: Metabolized by cytochrome P-450 isoenzyme 2C9 (CYP 2C9)

Bioavailability, absolute: Has not been determined

Half-life: 11 hours

Time to peak: 3 hours

Elimination: In urine as metabolites (<3% unchanged drug)

Usual Dosage Adults: Oral:

Osteoarthritis: 200 mg/day as a single dose or in divided dose twice daily

Rheumatoid arthritis: 100-200 mg twice daily

Dosing adjustment in renal impairment: No specific dosage adjustment is recommended

Dosing adjustment in hepatic impairment: Reduced dosage is recommended (AUC may be increased by 40% to 180%)

Dosing adjustment for elderly: No specific adjustment is recommended. However, the AUC in elderly patients may be increased by 50% as compared to younger subjects. Use the lowest recommended dose in patients weighing <50 kg.

Dietary Considerations Peak concentrations are delayed and AUC is increased by 10% to 20% when taken with a high-fat meal; celecoxib may be taken without regard to meals

Monitoring Parameters Periodic LFTs

Patient Information Patients should be informed of the signs and symptoms of gastrointestinal bleeding. Gastrointestinal bleeding may occur as well as ulceration and perforation; pain may or may not be present. If gastric upset occurs, take with food, milk, or antacid; if gastric upset persists, contact physician.

Dosage Forms Capsule: 100 mg, 200 mg

♦ Cenolate® see Sodium Ascorbate on page 1065

Cephalexin (sef a LEKS in)
Related Information
Animal and Human Bites Guidelines on page 1399
Cephalosporins by Generation on page 1373
Prevention of Bacterial Endocarditis on page 1377

U.S. Brand Names Biocef; Keflex®; Keftab®

Canadian Brand Names Apo®-Cephalex; Novo-Lexin; Nu-Cephalex

Synonyms Cephalexin Hydrochloride; Cephalexin Monohydrate

Therapeutic Category Antibiotic, Cephalosporin (First Generation)

Use Treatment of susceptible bacterial infections, including those caused by group A beta-hemolytic *Streptococcus*, *Staphylococcus*, *Klebsiella pneumoniae*, *E. coli*, *Proteus mira-bilis*, and *Shigella*; predominantly used for lower respiratory tract, urinary tract, skin and soft tissue, and bone and joint; prophylaxis against bacterial endocarditis in high-risk patients undergoing surgical or dental procedures who are allergic to penicillin

Pregnancy Risk Factor B

Contraindications Hypersensitivity to cephalexin, any component, or cephalosporins

Warnings/Precautions Modify dosage in patients with severe renal impairment, prolonged use may result in superinfection; use with caution in patients with a history of penicillin allergy, especially IgE-mediated reactions (eg, anaphylaxis, urticaria); may cause antibiotic-associated colitis or colitis secondary to *C. difficile*

Adverse Reactions
1% to 10%: Gastrointestinal: Diarrhea

<1%: Dizziness, fatigue, headache, rash, urticaria, angioedema, anaphylaxis, erythema multiforme, toxic epidermal necrolysis, Stevens-Johnson syndrome, serum-sickness reaction, nausea, vomiting, dyspepsia, gastritis, abdominal pain, pseudomembranous colitis, interstitial nephritis, agitation, hallucinations, confusion, arthralgia, eosinophilia, neutropenia, thrombocytopenia, anemia, increased transaminases, hepatitis, cholestasis

Other reactions with cephalosporins include anaphylaxis, vomiting, agranulocytosis, colitis, pancytopenia, aplastic anemia, hemolytic anemia, hemorrhage, prolonged PT, encephalopathy, asterixis, neuromuscular excitability, seizures, superinfection

Overdosage/Toxicology
After acute overdose, most agents cause only nausea, vomiting, and diarrhea, although neuromuscular hypersensitivity and seizures are possible, especially in patients with renal insufficiency; many beta-lactam antibiotics have the potential to cause neuromuscular hyperirritability or seizures

Hemodialysis may be helpful to aid in the removal of the drug from the blood but not usually indicated, otherwise most treatment is supportive or symptom directed following GI decontamination

Drug Interactions
Increased effect: High-dose probenecid decreases clearance
Increased toxicity: Aminoglycosides increase nephrotoxic potential

Stability Refrigerate suspension after reconstitution; discard after 14 days

Mechanism of Action Inhibits bacterial cell wall synthesis by binding to one or more of the penicillin-binding proteins (PBPs) which in turn inhibits the final transpeptidation step of peptidoglycan synthesis in bacterial cell walls, thus inhibiting cell wall biosynthesis. Bacteria eventually lyse due to ongoing activity of cell wall autolytic enzymes (autolysins and murein hydrolases) while cell wall assembly is arrested.

Pharmacodynamics/Kinetics
Absorption: Delayed in young children; may be decreased up to 50% in neonates

Distribution: Widely distributed into most body tissues and fluids, including gallbladder, liver, kidneys, bone, sputum, bile, and pleural and synovial fluids; CSF penetration is poor; crosses placenta; appears in breast milk

Protein binding: 6% to 15%

Half-life: Neonates: 5 hours; Children 3-12 months: 2.5 hours; Adults: 0.5-1.2 hours (prolonged with renal impairment)

Time to peak serum concentration: Oral: Within 1 hour

Elimination: 80% to 100% of dose excreted as unchanged drug in urine within 8 hours

Usual Dosage Oral:
Children: 25-50 mg/kg/day every 6 hours; severe infections: 50-100 mg/kg/day in divided doses every 6 hours; maximum: 3 g/24 hours

Adults: 250-1000 mg every 6 hours; maximum: 4 g/day
Prophylaxis of bacterial endocarditis: 2 g 1 hour prior to the procedure

Dosing adjustment in renal impairment: Adults:
Cl_{cr} 10-40 mL/minute: 250-500 mg every 8-12 hours
Cl_{cr} <10 mL/minute: 250 mg every 12-24 hours

Hemodialysis: Moderately dialyzable (20% to 50%)

Dietary Considerations Food: Peak antibiotic serum concentration is lowered and delayed, but total drug absorbed is not affected; take on an empty stomach. If GI distress, take with food.

Administration Administer on an empty stomach (ie, 1 hour prior to, or 2 hours after meals) to increase total absorption

Monitoring Parameters With prolonged therapy monitor renal, hepatic, and hematologic function periodically; monitor for signs of anaphylaxis during first dose

Test Interactions Positive direct Coombs', false-positive urinary glucose test using cupric sulfate (Benedict's solution, Clinitest®, Fehling's solution), false-positive serum or urine creatinine with Jaffé reaction, false-positive urinary proteins and steroids

Patient Information Report prolonged diarrhea; entire course of medication (10-14 days) should be taken to ensure eradication of organism; may interfere with oral contraceptives; females should report symptoms of vaginitis

Dosage Forms

Capsule, as monohydrate: 250 mg, 500 mg

Powder for oral suspension, as monohydrate: 125 mg/5 mL (5 mL unit dose, 60 mL, 100 mL, 200 mL); 250 mg/5 mL (5 mL unit dose, 100 mL, 200 mL)

Suspension, oral, as monohydrate, pediatric: 100 mg/mL [5 mg/drop] (10 mL)

Tablet, as monohydrate: 250 mg, 500 mg, 1 g

Tablet, as hydrochloride: 500 mg

♦ **Cephalexin Hydrochloride** *see Cephalexin on previous page*

♦ **Cephalexin Monohydrate** *see Cephalexin on previous page*

♦ **Cephalosporins by Generation** *see page 1373*

Cephalothin (sef A loe thin)

Related Information

Cephalosporins by Generation *on page 1373*

Canadian Brand Names Ceporacin®

Synonyms Cephalothin Sodium

Therapeutic Category Antibiotic, Cephalosporin (First Generation)

Use Treatment of infections when caused by susceptible strains in respiratory, genitourinary, gastrointestinal, skin and soft tissue, bone and joint infections; septicemia; treatment of susceptible gram-positive bacilli and cocci (never enterococcus); some gram-negative bacilli including *E. coli*, *Proteus*, and *Klebsiella* may be susceptible

Pregnancy Risk Factor B

Contraindications Hypersensitivity to cephalothin or cephalosporins

Warnings/Precautions Modify dosage in patients with severe renal impairment, prolonged use may result in superinfection; use with caution in patients with a history of penicillin allergy, especially IgE-mediated reactions (eg, anaphylaxis, urticaria); may cause antibiotic-associated colitis or colitis secondary to *C. difficile*

Adverse Reactions

1% to 10%: Gastrointestinal: Diarrhea, nausea, vomiting

<1%: Maculopapular and erythematous rash, dyspepsia, pseudomembranous colitis, bleeding, pain and induration at injection site

Other reactions with cephalosporins include anaphylaxis, erythema multiforme, toxic epidermal necrolysis, Stevens-Johnson syndrome, dizziness, fever, headache, CNS irritability, seizures, decreased hemoglobin, neutropenia, leukopenia, agranulocytosis, pancytopenia, aplastic anemia, hemolytic anemia, interstitial nephritis, toxic nephropathy, vaginitis, angioedema, cholestasis, hemorrhage, prolonged PT, serum-sickness reactions, superinfection

Overdosage/Toxicology

Symptoms of overdose include neuromuscular hypersensitivity, convulsions especially with renal insufficiency; many beta-lactam antibiotics have the potential to cause neuromuscular hyperirritability or seizures

Hemodialysis may be helpful to aid in the removal of the drug from the blood, otherwise most treatment is supportive or symptom directed

Stability Reconstituted solution is stable for 12-24 hours at room temperature and 96 hours when refrigerated; for I.V. infusion in NS or D_5W solution is stable for 24 hours at room temperature, 96 hours when refrigerated or 12 weeks when frozen; after freezing, thawed solution is stable for 24 hours at room temperature or 96 hours when refrigerated

Mechanism of Action Inhibits bacterial cell wall synthesis by binding to one or more of the penicillin-binding proteins (PBPs) which in turn inhibits the final transpeptidation step of peptidoglycan synthesis in bacterial cell walls, thus inhibiting cell wall biosynthesis. Bacteria eventually lyse due to ongoing activity of cell wall autolytic enzymes (autolysins and murein hydrolases) while cell wall assembly is arrested.

Pharmacodynamics/Kinetics

Distribution: Does not penetrate the CSF unless the meninges are inflamed; crosses the placenta; small amounts appear in breast milk

Protein binding: 65% to 80%

Metabolism: Partially deacetylated in the liver and kidney

Half-life: 30-60 minutes

Time to peak serum concentration: I.M.: Within 30 minutes

Elimination: 50% to 75% of a dose appearing as unchanged drug in urine

Usual Dosage I.M., I.V.:

Neonates:

Postnatal age <7 days:

<2000 g: 20 mg every 12 hours

>2000 g: 20 mg every 8 hours

Postnatal age >7 days:

<2000 g: 20 mg every 8 hours

>2000 g: 20 mg every 6 hours

Children: 75-125 mg/kg/day divided every 4-6 hours; maximum dose: 10 g in a 24-hour period

Adults: 500 mg to 2 g every 4-6 hours

(Continued)

Cephalothin *(Continued)*

Dosing interval in renal impairment:
Cl$_{cr}$ 10-50 mL/minute: Administer every 6-8 hours
Cl$_{cr}$ <10 mL/minute: Administer every 12 hours
Continuous arteriovenous or venovenous hemodiafiltration (CAVH) effects: Administer 1 g every 8 hours

Monitoring Parameters Observe for signs and symptoms of anaphylaxis during first dose

Test Interactions Positive direct Coombs', false-positive urinary glucose test using cupric sulfate (Benedict's solution, Clinitest®, Fehling's solution), false-positive serum or urine creatinine with Jaffé reaction, false-positive urinary proteins and steroids

Nursing Implications Do not admix with aminoglycosides in same bottle/bag

Additional Information Sodium content of 1 g: 64.4 mg (2.8 mEq)

Dosage Forms Powder for injection, as sodium: 1 g, 2 g (50 mL)

♦ **Cephalothin Sodium** *see Cephalothin on previous page*

Cephapirin *(sef a PYE rin)*

Related Information
Cephalosporins by Generation *on page 1373*

U.S. Brand Names Cefadyl®

Synonyms Cephapirin Sodium

Therapeutic Category Antibiotic, Cephalosporin (First Generation)

Use Treatment of infections when caused by susceptible strains in respiratory, genitourinary, gastrointestinal, skin and soft tissue, bone and joint infections, septicemia; treatment of susceptible gram-positive bacilli and cocci (never enterococcus); some gram-negative bacilli including *E. coli*, *Proteus*, and *Klebsiella* may be susceptible

Pregnancy Risk Factor B

Contraindications Hypersensitivity to cephapirin sodium, any component, or cephalosporins

Warnings/Precautions Modify dosage in patients with severe renal impairment, prolonged use may result in superinfection; use with caution in patients with a history of penicillin allergy, especially IgE-mediated reactions (eg, anaphylaxis, urticaria); may cause antibiotic-associated colitis or colitis secondary to *C. difficile*

Adverse Reactions
1% to 10%: Gastrointestinal: Diarrhea
<1%: CNS irritation, seizures, fever, rash, urticaria, leukopenia, thrombocytopenia, increased transaminases

Other reactions with cephalosporins include anaphylaxis, erythema multiforme, toxic epidermal necrolysis, Stevens-Johnson syndrome, dizziness, fever, headache, encephalopathy, asterixis, neuromuscular excitability, seizures, nausea, vomiting, pseudomembranous colitis, decreased hemoglobin, agranulocytosis, pancytopenia, aplastic anemia, hemolytic anemia, interstitial nephritis, toxic nephropathy, pain at injection site, vaginitis, angioedema, cholestasis, hemorrhage, prolonged PT, serum-sickness reactions, superinfection

Overdosage/Toxicology
Symptoms of overdose include neuromuscular hypersensitivity, convulsions especially with renal insufficiency; many beta-lactam antibiotics have the potential to cause neuromuscular hyperirritability or seizures
Hemodialysis may be helpful to aid in the removal of the drug from the blood, otherwise most treatment is supportive or symptom directed

Drug Interactions
Increased effect: High-dose probenecid decreases clearance
Increased toxicity: Aminoglycosides increase nephrotoxic potential

Stability Reconstituted solution is stable for 24 hours at room temperature and 10 days when refrigerated; for I.V. infusion in NS or D$_5$W solution is stable for 24 hours at room temperature, 10 days when refrigerated or 14 days when frozen; after freezing, thawed solution is stable for 12 hours at room temperature or 10 days when refrigerated

Mechanism of Action Inhibits bacterial cell wall synthesis by binding to one or more of the penicillin-binding proteins (PBPs) which in turn inhibits the final transpeptidation step of peptidoglycan synthesis in bacterial cell walls, thus inhibiting cell wall biosynthesis. Bacteria eventually lyse due to ongoing activity of cell wall autolytic enzymes (autolysins and murein hydrolases) while cell wall assembly is arrested.

Pharmacodynamics/Kinetics
Distribution: Widely distributed into most body tissues and fluids including gallbladder, liver, kidneys, bone, sputum, bile, and pleural and synovial fluids; CSF penetration is poor; crosses the placenta and small amounts appear in breast milk
Protein binding: 22% to 25%
Metabolism: Partially in the liver, kidney, and plasma to metabolites (50% active)
Half-life: 36-60 minutes
Time to peak serum concentration: I.M.: Within 30 minutes
Elimination: 60% to 85% excreted as unchanged drug in urine

Usual Dosage I.M., I.V.:
Children: 10-20 mg/kg/dose every 6 hours up to 4 g/24 hours
Adults: 500 mg to 1 g every 6 hours up to 12 g/day
Perioperative prophylaxis: 1-2 g 30 minutes to 1 hour prior to surgery and every 6 hours as needed for 24 hours following

Dosing interval in renal impairment:
Cl_{cr} 10-50 mL/minute: Administer every 6-8 hours
Cl_{cr} <10 mL/minute: Administer every 12 hours
Continuous arteriovenous or venovenous hemodiafiltration (CAVH) effects: Administer 1 g every 8 hours

Monitoring Parameters Observe for signs and symptoms of anaphylaxis during first dose

Test Interactions Positive direct Coombs', false-positive urinary glucose test using cupric sulfate (Benedict's solution, Clinitest®, Fehling's solution), false-positive serum or urine creatinine with Jaffé reaction, false-positive urinary proteins and steroids

Nursing Implications Do not admix with aminoglycosides in same bottle/bag; obtain specimens for culture and sensitivity prior to administration of first dose

Additional Information Sodium content of 1 g: 55.2 mg (2.4 mEq)

Dosage Forms Powder for injection, as sodium: 500 mg, 1 g, 2 g, 4 g, 20 g

♦ **Cephapirin Sodium** see Cephapirin on previous page

Cephradine (SEF ra deen)

Related Information
Cephalosporins by Generation on page 1373

U.S. Brand Names Velosef®

Therapeutic Category Antibiotic, Cephalosporin (First Generation)

Use Treatment of infections when caused by susceptible strains in respiratory, genitourinary, gastrointestinal, skin and soft tissue, bone and joint infections; treatment of susceptible gram-positive bacilli and cocci (never enterococcus); some gram-negative bacilli including E. coli, Proteus, and Klebsiella may be susceptible

Pregnancy Risk Factor B

Contraindications Hypersensitivity to cephradine, any component, or cephalosporins

Warnings/Precautions Modify dosage in patients with severe renal impairment, prolonged use may result in superinfection; use with caution in patients with a history of penicillin allergy, especially IgE-mediated reactions (eg, anaphylaxis, urticaria); may cause antibiotic-associated colitis or colitis secondary to C. difficile

Adverse Reactions
1% to 10%: Gastrointestinal: Diarrhea
<1%: Rash, nausea, vomiting, pseudomembranous colitis, increased BUN, increased creatinine

Other reactions with cephalosporins include anaphylaxis, erythema multiforme, toxic epidermal necrolysis, Stevens-Johnson syndrome, dizziness, fever, headache, encephalopathy, asterixis, neuromuscular excitability, seizures, neutropenia, leukopenia, agranulocytosis, pancytopenia, aplastic anemia, hemolytic anemia, interstitial nephritis, toxic nephropathy, vaginitis, angioedema, cholestasis, hemorrhage, prolonged PT, serum-sickness reactions, superinfection

Overdosage/Toxicology
Symptoms of overdose include neuromuscular hypersensitivity, convulsions especially with renal insufficiency; many beta-lactam antibiotics have the potential to cause neuromuscular hyperirritability or seizures
Hemodialysis may be helpful to aid in the removal of the drug from the blood, otherwise most treatment is supportive or symptom directed.

Drug Interactions
Increased effect: High-dose probenecid decreases clearance
Increased toxicity: Aminoglycosides increase nephrotoxic potential

Mechanism of Action Inhibits bacterial cell wall synthesis by binding to one or more of the penicillin-binding proteins (PBPs) which in turn inhibits the final transpeptidation step of peptidoglycan synthesis in bacterial cell walls, thus inhibiting cell wall biosynthesis. Bacteria eventually lyse due to ongoing activity of cell wall autolytic enzymes (autolysins and murein hydrolases) while cell wall assembly is arrested.

Pharmacodynamics/Kinetics
Absorption: Well absorbed
Distribution: Widely distributed into most body tissues and fluids including gallbladder, liver, kidneys, bone, sputum, bile, and pleural and synovial fluids; CSF penetration is poor; crosses the placenta and appears in breast milk
Protein binding: 18% to 20%
Half-life: 1-2 hours
Time to peak serum concentration: Oral: Within 1-2 hours
Elimination: ~80% to 90% unchanged drug is recovered in urine within 6 hours

Usual Dosage Oral:
Children ≥9 months: 25-50 mg/kg/day in divided doses every 6 hours
Adults: 250-500 mg every 6-12 hours
Dosing adjustment in renal impairment: Adults:
Cl_{cr} 10-50 mL/minute: 250 mg every 6 hours
Cl_{cr} <10 mL/minute: 125 mg every 6 hours

Monitoring Parameters Observe for signs and symptoms of anaphylaxis during first dose

Test Interactions Positive direct Coombs', false-positive urinary glucose test using cupric sulfate (Benedict's solution, Clinitest®, Fehling's solution), false-positive serum or urine creatinine with Jaffé reaction, false-positive urinary proteins and steroids

Patient Information Take until gone, do not miss doses; report diarrhea promptly; entire course of medication (10-14 days) should be taken to ensure eradication of organism; may interfere with oral contraceptives; females should report symptoms of vaginitis
(Continued)

Cephradine *(Continued)*

Dosage Forms
Capsule: 250 mg, 500 mg
Powder for injection: 250 mg, 500 mg, 1 g, 2 g, (in ready-to-use infusion bottles)
Powder for oral suspension: 125 mg/5 mL (5 mL, 100 mL, 200 mL); 250 mg/5 mL (5 mL, 100 mL, 200 mL)

♦ **Cephulac®** *see* Lactulose *on page 656*
♦ **Ceporacin®** *see* Cephalothin *on page 229*
♦ **Ceptaz™** *see* Ceftazidime *on page 219*
♦ **Ceptaz™** *see* Ceftazidime *on page 219*
♦ **Cerebyx®** *see* Fosphenytoin *on page 523*
♦ **Ceredase®** *see* Alglucerase *on page 42*
♦ **Cerezyme®** *see* Alglucerase *on page 42*

Cerivastatin *(se ree va STAT in)*
U.S. Brand Names Baycol™
Synonyms BAY W6228; Cerivastatin Sodium; Rivastatin
Therapeutic Category Antilipemic Agent; HMG-CoA Reductase Inhibitor
Use Adjunct to dietary therapy to for the reduction of elevated total and LDL cholesterol levels in patients with primary hypercholesterolemia and mixed dyslipidemia when the response to dietary restriction of saturated fat and cholesterol and other nonpharmacological measures alone has been inadequate
Pregnancy Risk Factor X
Pregnancy/Breast-Feeding Implications Breast-feeding/lactation: Breast-feeding is not recommended by manufacturer
Contraindications Hypersensitivity or severe adverse reactions to cerivastatin or other statins; active hepatic disease, pregnancy
Warnings/Precautions Use with caution in patients with history of liver disease, those who are breast-feeding, and those predisposed to renal failure
Adverse Reactions
1% to 10%:
Cardiovascular: Chest pain, peripheral edema (2%)
Central nervous system: Headache, dizziness, insomnia, asthenia (2%)
Gastrointestinal: Pain (3%), diarrhea (4%), dyspepsia (6%), nausea (3%), constipation (2%)
Neuromuscular & skeletal: Myalgia (3%), arthralgia (7%), leg pain (2%)
<1%: Increased LFTs, myopathy, possible rhabdomyolysis with renal failure, sinusitis, rhinitis, cough
Drug Interactions CYP3A3/4 enzyme substrate
Concurrent therapy with cyclosporine, fibric acid derivative, erythromycin, azole antifungals, and niacin may increase risk of myopathy/rhabdomyolysis with renal failure
Decreased effect of cerivastatin with cholestyramine
Increased cerivastatin with erythromycin
Mechanism of Action As an HMG-CoA reductase inhibitor, cerivastatin competitively inhibits 3-hydroxyl-3-methylglutaryl coenzyme A (HMG-CoA) reductase, the enzyme that catalyzes the rate-limiting step in cholesterol biosynthesis
Pharmacodynamics/Kinetics
Distribution: V_d: 0.3 L/kg
Protein binding: >99%
Metabolism: Hepatic; active metabolite, demethylation and hydroxylation
Bioavailability: 60%, no effect with food
Half-life: 2-3 hours
Elimination: 26% renally, as metabolites; 70% in feces
Usual Dosage Adults: Oral: 0.3 mg once daily in the evening; may be taken with or without food

Dosing adjustment with renal impairment: Moderate to severe impairment (<60 mL/minute): Starting dose: 0.2 mg
Dosing adjustment in hepatic impairment: Avoidance suggested; no guidelines for dosage reduction available
Monitoring Parameters Serum total cholesterol, LDL, HDL, triglycerides, apolipoprotein B, diet, weight, LFTs
Patient Information Call physician if you experience unexplained fever, rash, muscle pain, GI upset, or headache
Dosage Forms Tablet, as sodium: 0.2 mg, 0.3 mg

♦ **Cerivastatin Sodium** *see* Cerivastatin *on this page*
♦ **Certiva™** *see* Diphtheria, Tetanus Toxoids, and Acellular Pertussis Vaccine *on page 373*
♦ **Cerubidine®** *see* Daunorubicin Hydrochloride *on page 327*
♦ **Cerumenex® Otic** *see* Triethanolamine Polypeptide Oleate-Condensate *on page 1180*
♦ **Cervidil® Vaginal Insert** *see* Dinoprostone *on page 368*
♦ **C.E.S.™** *see* Estrogens, Conjugated *on page 436*
♦ **C.E.S.** *see* Estrogens, Conjugated *on page 436*
♦ **Cetacaine®** *see* Benzocaine, Butyl Aminobenzoate, Tetracaine, and Benzalkonium Chloride *on page 134*
♦ **Cetacort®** *see* Hydrocortisone *on page 579*
♦ **Cetamide® Ophthalmic** *see* Sulfacetamide Sodium *on page 1091*

♦ **Cetapred® Ophthalmic** *see* Sulfacetamide Sodium and Prednisolone *on page 1091*

Cetirizine (se TI ra zeen)
U.S. Brand Names Zyrtec®
Canadian Brand Names Reactine™
Synonyms Cetirizine Hydrochloride; P-071; UCB-P071
Therapeutic Category Antihistamine, Nonsedating
Use Perennial and seasonal allergic rhinitis and other allergic symptoms including urticaria
Pregnancy Risk Factor B
Contraindications Hypersensitivity to cetirizine, hydroxyzine, or any component
Warnings/Precautions Cetirizine should be used cautiously in patients with hepatic or renal dysfunction, the elderly and in nursing mothers. Doses >10 mg/day may cause significant drowsiness
Adverse Reactions
>10%: Central nervous system: Headache has been reported to occur in 10% to 12% of patients, drowsiness has been reported in as much as 26% of patients on high doses
1% to 10%:
Central nervous system: Somnolence, fatigue, dizziness
Gastrointestinal: Xerostomia
<1%: Depression
Overdosage/Toxicology
Symptoms of overdose include seizures, sedation, hypotension. There is no specific treatment for an antihistamine overdose, however, most of its clinical toxicity is due to anticholinergic effects
Anticholinesterase inhibitors may be useful by reducing acetylcholinesterase. For anticholinergic overdose with severe life-threatening symptoms, physostigmine 1-2 mg (0.5 mg or 0.02 mg/kg for children) I.V., slowly may be given to reverse these effects.
Drug Interactions Increased toxicity: CNS depressants, anticholinergics
Mechanism of Action Competes with histamine for H_1-receptor sites on effector cells in the gastrointestinal tract, blood vessels, and respiratory tract
Pharmacodynamics/Kinetics
Onset of effect: Within 15-30 minutes
Absorption: Oral: Rapid
Metabolism: Exact fate is unknown, limited hepatic metabolism
Half-life: 8-11 hours
Time to peak serum concentration: Within 30-60 minutes
Usual Dosage Children ≥6 years and Adults: Oral: 5-10 mg once daily, depending upon symptom severity

Dosing interval in renal/hepatic impairment: Cl_{cr} ≤31 mL/minute: Administer 5 mg once daily
Monitoring Parameters Relief of symptoms, sedation and anticholinergic effects
Dosage Forms
Syrup, as hydrochloride: 5 mg/5 mL (120 mL)
Tablet, as hydrochloride: 5 mg, 10 mg

♦ **Cetirizine Hydrochloride** *see* Cetirizine *on this page*
♦ **Cevalin® [OTC]** *see* Ascorbic Acid *on page 99*
♦ **Cevi-Bid® [OTC]** *see* Ascorbic Acid *on page 99*
♦ **Ce-Vi-Sol® [OTC]** *see* Ascorbic Acid *on page 99*
♦ **CFDN** *see* Cefdinir *on page 207*
♦ **CG** *see* Chorionic Gonadotropin *on page 258*
♦ **Charcoaid® [OTC]** *see* Charcoal *on this page*

Charcoal (CHAR kole)
U.S. Brand Names Actidose-Aqua® [OTC]; Actidose® With Sorbitol [OTC]; Charcoaid® [OTC]; Charcocaps® [OTC]; Insta-Char® [OTC]; Liqui-Char® [OTC]
Canadian Brand Names Charcodole®; Charcodole® AQ; Charcodole® TFS
Synonyms Activated Carbon; Activated Charcoal; Adsorbent Charcoal; Liquid Antidote; Medicinal Carbon; Medicinal Charcoal
Therapeutic Category Antidiarrheal; Antidote, Adsorbent; Antiflatulent
Use Emergency treatment in poisoning by drugs and chemicals; repetitive doses in gastric dialysis in uremia to adsorb various waste products, and repetitive doses have proven useful to enhance the elimination of certain drugs (eg, theophylline, phenobarbital, and aspirin)
Pregnancy Risk Factor C
Contraindications Not effective for cyanide, mineral acids, caustic alkalis, organic solvents, iron, ethanol, methanol poisoning, lithium; do not use charcoal with sorbitol in patients with fructose intolerance; charcoal with sorbitol is not recommended in children <1 year.
Warnings/Precautions When using ipecac with charcoal, induce vomiting with ipecac before administering activated charcoal since charcoal adsorbs ipecac syrup; charcoal may cause vomiting which is hazardous in petroleum distillate and caustic ingestions; if charcoal in sorbitol is administered, doses should be limited to prevent excessive fluid and electrolyte losses; do not mix charcoal with milk, ice cream, or sherbet
Adverse Reactions
>10%:
Gastrointestinal: Vomiting, diarrhea with sorbitol, constipation
Miscellaneous: Stools will turn black
(Continued)

Charcoal *(Continued)*

<1%: Swelling of abdomen

Drug Interactions Do not administer concomitantly with syrup of ipecac; do not mix with milk, ice cream, or sherbet

Stability Adsorbs gases from air, store in closed container

Mechanism of Action Adsorbs toxic substances or irritants, thus inhibiting GI absorption; adsorbs intestinal gas; the addition of sorbitol results in hyperosmotic laxative action causing catharsis

Pharmacodynamics/Kinetics

Absorption: Not absorbed from GI tract

Metabolism: Not metabolized

Elimination: As charcoal in feces

Usual Dosage Oral:

Acute poisoning:

Charcoal with sorbitol: Single-dose:

Children 1-12 years: 1-2 g/kg/dose or 15-30 g or approximately 5-10 times the weight of the ingested poison; 1 g adsorbs 100-1000 mg of poison; the use of repeat oral charcoal with sorbitol doses is not recommended. In young children, sorbitol should be repeated no more than 1-2 times/day.

Adults: 30-100 g

Charcoal in water:

Single-dose:

Infants <1 year: 1 g/kg

Children 1-12 years: 15-30 g or 1-2 g/kg

Adults: 30-100 g or 1-2 g/kg

Multiple-dose:

Infants <1 year: 0.5 g/kg every 4-6 hours

Children 1-12 years: 20-60 g or 0.5-1 g/kg every 2-6 hours until clinical observations, serum drug concentration have returned to a subtherapeutic range, or charcoal stool apparent

Adults: 20-60 g or 0.5-1 g/kg every 2-6 hours

Gastric dialysis: Adults: 20-50 g every 6 hours for 1-2 days

Intestinal gas, diarrhea, GI distress: Adults: 520-975 mg after meals or at first sign of discomfort; repeat as needed to a maximum dose of 4.16 g/day

Administration Flavoring agents (eg, chocolate) and sorbitol can enhance charcoal's palatability; marmalade, milk, ice cream, and sherbet should be avoided since they can reduce charcoal's effectiveness

Patient Information Charcoal causes the stools to turn black; should not be used prior to calling a poison control center or a physician

Nursing Implications Too concentrated of slurries may clog airway; often given with a laxative or cathartic; check for presence of bowel sounds before administration

Dosage Forms

Capsule (Charcocaps®): 260 mg

Liquid, activated:

Actidose-Aqua®: 12.5 g (60 mL); 25 g (120 mL)

Liqui-Char®: 12.5 g (60 mL); 15 g (75 mL); 25 g (120 mL); 30 g (120 mL); 50 g (240 mL)

SuperChar®: 30 g (240 mL)

Liquid, activated, with propylene glycol: 12.5 g (60 mL); 25 g (120 mL)

Liquid, activated, with sorbitol:

Actidose® With Sorbitol: 25 g (120 mL); 50 g (240 mL)

Charcoaid®: 30 g (150 mL)

SuperChar®: 30 g (240 mL)

Powder for suspension, activated:

15 g, 30 g, 40 g, 120 g, 240 g

SuperChar®: 30 g

- ◆ **Charcocaps® [OTC]** *see Charcoal on previous page*
- ◆ **Charcodole®** *see Charcoal on previous page*
- ◆ **Charcodole® AQ** *see Charcoal on previous page*
- ◆ **Charcodole® TFS** *see Charcoal on previous page*
- ◆ **Chealamide®** *see Edetate Disodium on page 405*
- ◆ **Chelated Manganese® [OTC]** *see Manganese on page 710*
- ◆ **Chemet®** *see Succimer on page 1086*
- ◆ **Chenix®** *see Chenodiol on this page*
- ◆ **Chenodeoxycholic Acid** *see Chenodiol on this page*

Chenodiol *(kee noe DYE ole)*

U.S. Brand Names Chenix®

Synonyms Chenodeoxycholic Acid

Therapeutic Category Bile Acid; Gallstone Dissolution Agent

Use Oral dissolution of cholesterol gallstones in selected patients

Pregnancy Risk Factor X

Contraindications Presence of known hepatocyte dysfunction or bile ductal abnormalities; a gallbladder confirmed as nonvisualizing after two consecutive single doses of dye; radiopaque stones; gallstone complications or compelling reasons for gallbladder surgery; inflammatory bowel disease or active gastric or duodenal ulcer; pregnancy

Warnings/Precautions Chenodiol is hepatotoxic in animal models including subhuman Primates; chenodiol should be discontinued if aminotransferases exceed 3 times the upper normal limit; chenodiol may contribute to colon cancer in otherwise susceptible individuals

Adverse Reactions
>10%:
Gastrointestinal: Diarrhea (mild), biliary pain
Miscellaneous: Aminotransferase increases
1% to 10%:
Endocrine & metabolic: Increases in cholesterol and LDL cholesterol
Gastrointestinal: Dyspepsia
<1%: Diarrhea (severe), cramps, nausea, vomiting, flatulence, constipation, leukopenia, intrahepatic cholestasis, higher cholecystectomy rates

Overdosage/Toxicology
Symptoms of overdose may include diarrhea; a rise in liver function tests has been observed
No specific antidote, institute supportive therapy

Drug Interactions Decreased effect: Antacids, cholestyramine, colestipol, oral contraceptives

Mechanism of Action Chenodiol is a primary acid excreted into bile, normally constituting one-third of the total biliary bile acids. Synthesis of chenodiol is regulated by the relative composition and flux of cholesterol and bile acids through the hepatocyte by a negative feedback effect on the rate-limiting enzymes for synthesis of cholesterol (HMG CoA reductase) and bile acids (cholesterol 7 alpha-hydroxyl).

Usual Dosage Adults: Oral: 13-16 mg/kg/day in 2 divided doses, starting with 250 mg twice daily the first 2 weeks and increasing by 250 mg/day each week thereafter until the recommended or maximum tolerated dose is achieved

Dosing comments in hepatic impairment: Contraindicated for use in presence of known hepatocyte dysfunction or bile ductal abnormalities

Monitoring Parameters Oral cholecystograms and/or ultrasonograms should be used to monitor response; dissolutions of stones should be confirmed 1-3 months later

Test Interactions ↑ aminotransferases, ↑ cholesterol, ↑ LDL cholesterol, ↓ triglycerides, ↑ bilirubin (I)

Patient Information Periodic liver function tests and oral cholecystograms are required to monitor therapy; contact the physician immediately if nonspecific abdominal pain, right upper quadrant pain, nausea, and vomiting are severe

Dosage Forms Tablet, film coated: 250 mg

Chloral Hydrate (KLOR al HYE drate)

Related Information
Depression Disorders and Treatments on page 1465
U.S. Brand Names Aquachloral® Supprettes®
Canadian Brand Names Novo-Chlorhydrate; PMS-Chloral Hydrate
Synonyms Chloral; Hydrated Chloral; Trichloroacetaldehyde Monohydrate
Therapeutic Category Hypnotic; Sedative
Use Short-term sedative and hypnotic (<2 weeks), sedative/hypnotic for dental and diagnostic procedures; sedative prior to EEG evaluations
Restrictions C-IV
Pregnancy Risk Factor C
Contraindications Hypersensitivity to chloral hydrate or any component; hepatic or renal impairment; gastritis or ulcers; severe cardiac disease
Warnings/Precautions Use with caution in patients with porphyria; use with caution in neonates, drug may accumulate with repeated use, prolonged use in neonates associated with hyperbilirubinemia; tolerance to hypnotic effect develops, therefore, not recommended for use >2 weeks; taper dosage to avoid withdrawal with prolonged use; trichloroethanol (TCE), a metabolite of chloral hydrate, is a carcinogen in mice; there is no data in humans. Chloral hydrate is considered a second line hypnotic agent in the elderly. Recent interpretive guidelines from the Health Care Financing Administration (HCFA) discourage the use of chloral hydrate in residents of long-term care facilities.
Adverse Reactions
>10%: Gastrointestinal: Gastric irritation, nausea, vomiting, diarrhea
1% to 10%:
Central nervous system: Ataxia, hallucinations, drowsiness, "hangover" effect
Dermatologic: Rash, urticaria
(Continued)

Chloral Hydrate *(Continued)*

<1%: Disorientation, sedation, ataxia, excitement (paradoxical), dizziness, fever, headache, confusion, flatulence, leukopenia, eosinophilia, physical and psychological dependence may occur with prolonged use of large doses

Overdosage/Toxicology

Symptoms of overdose include hypotension, respiratory depression, coma, hypothermia, cardiac arrhythmias

Treatment is supportive and symptomatic; lidocaine or propranolol may be used for ventricular dysrhythmias, while isoproterenol or atropine may be required for torsade de pointes; activated charcoal may prevent drug absorption

Drug Interactions Increased toxicity: May potentiate effects of warfarin, central nervous system depressants, alcohol; vasodilation reaction (flushing, tachycardia, etc) may occur with concurrent use of alcohol; concomitant use of furosemide (I.V.) may result in flushing, diaphoresis, and blood pressure changes

Stability Sensitive to light; exposure to air causes volatilization; store in light-resistant, airtight container

Mechanism of Action Central nervous system depressant effects are due to its active metabolite trichloroethanol, mechanism unknown

Pharmacodynamics/Kinetics

Peak effect: Within 0.5-1 hour

Duration: 4-8 hours

Absorption: Oral, rectal: Well absorbed

Distribution: Crosses the placenta; negligible amounts appear in breast milk

Metabolism: Rapidly to trichloroethanol (active metabolite); variable amounts metabolized in liver and kidney to trichloroacetic acid (inactive)

Half-life: Active metabolite: 8-11 hours

Elimination: Metabolites excreted in urine, small amounts excreted in feces via bile

Usual Dosage

Children:

Sedation, anxiety: Oral, rectal: 5-15 mg/kg/dose every 8 hours, maximum: 500 mg/dose

Prior to EEG: Oral, rectal: 20-25 mg/kg/dose, 30-60 minutes prior to EEG; may repeat in 30 minutes to maximum of 100 mg/kg or 2 g total

Hypnotic: Oral, rectal: 20-40 mg/kg/dose up to a maximum of 50 mg/kg/24 hours or 1 g/dose or 2 g/24 hours

Sedation, nonpainful procedure: Oral: 50-75 mg/kg/dose 30-60 minutes prior to procedure; may repeat 30 minutes after initial dose if needed, to a total maximum dose of 120 mg/kg or 1 g total

Adults: Oral, rectal:

Sedation, anxiety: 250 mg 3 times/day

Hypnotic: 500-1000 mg at bedtime or 30 minutes prior to procedure, not to exceed 2 g/24 hours

Dosing adjustment/comments in renal impairment: Cl$_{cr}$ <50 mL/minute: Avoid use
Hemodialysis: Dialyzable (50% to 100%); supplemental dose is not necessary

Dosing adjustment/comments in hepatic impairment: Avoid use in patients with severe hepatic impairment

Dietary Considerations Alcohol: Additive CNS effects, avoid use

Administration Do not crush capsule, contains drug in liquid form

Monitoring Parameters Vital signs, O$_2$ saturation and blood pressure with doses used for conscious sedation

Test Interactions False-positive urine glucose using Clinitest® method; may interfere with fluorometric urine catecholamine and urinary 17-hydroxycorticosteroid tests

Patient Information Take a capsule with a full glass of water or fruit juice; swallow capsules whole, do not chew; avoid alcohol and other CNS depressants; avoid activities needing good psychomotor coordination until CNS effects are known; drug may cause physical or psychological dependence; avoid abrupt discontinuation after prolonged use; if taking at home prior to a diagnostic procedure, have someone else transport

Nursing Implications Gastric irritation may be minimized by diluting dose in water or other oral liquid

Dosage Forms

Suppository, rectal: 324 mg, 500 mg, 648 mg

Syrup: 250 mg/5 mL (10 mL); 500 mg/5 mL (5 mL, 10 mL, 480 mL)

Chlorambucil *(klor AM byoo sil)*

Related Information

Cancer Chemotherapy Regimens *on page 1263*
Toxicities of Chemotherapeutic Agents *on page 1288*

U.S. Brand Names Leukeran®

Therapeutic Category Antineoplastic Agent, Alkylating Agent

Use Management of chronic lymphocytic leukemia, Hodgkin's and non-Hodgkin's lymphoma; breast and ovarian carcinoma; Waldenström's macroglobulinemia, testicular carcinoma, thrombocythemia, choriocarcinoma

Pregnancy Risk Factor D

Pregnancy/Breast-Feeding Implications Clinical effects on the fetus: Carcinogenic and mutagenic in humans

Contraindications Previous resistance; hypersensitivity to chlorambucil or any component or other alkylating agents

Warnings/Precautions The U.S. Food and Drug Administration (FDA) currently recommends that procedures for proper handling and disposal of antineoplastic agents be considered. Use with caution in patients with seizure disorder and bone marrow suppression; reduce initial dosage if patient has received radiation therapy, myelosuppressive drugs or has a depressed baseline leukocyte or platelet count within the previous 4 weeks. Can severely suppress bone marrow function; affects human fertility; carcinogenic in humans and probably mutagenic and teratogenic as well; chromosomal damage has been documented; secondary AML may be associated with chronic therapy.

Adverse Reactions
>10%:
Hematologic: Myelosuppressive: Use with caution when receiving radiation; bone marrow suppression frequently occurs and occasionally bone marrow failure has occurred; blood counts should be monitored closely while undergoing treatment; leukopenia, thrombocytopenia, anemia
WBC: Moderate
Platelets: Moderate
Onset (days): 7
Nadir (days): 10-14
Recovery (days): 28
1% to 10%:
Dermatologic: Skin rashes
Endocrine & metabolic: Hyperuricemia, menstrual changes
Gastrointestinal: Nausea, vomiting, diarrhea, oral ulceration are all infrequent
Emetic potential: Low (<10%)
<1%: Confusion, agitation, drug fever, ataxia, hallucination; rarely generalized or focal seizures, rash, fertility impairment: Has caused chromosomal damage in men, both reversible and permanent sterility have occurred in both sexes; can produce amenorrhea in females, oral ulceration, oligospermia, hepatotoxicity, hepatic necrosis, weakness, tremors, muscular twitching, peripheral neuropathy, pulmonary fibrosis, secondary malignancies; Increased incidence of AML; skin hypersensitivity

Overdosage/Toxicology
Symptoms of overdose include vomiting, ataxia, coma, seizures, pancytopenia
There are no known antidotes for chlorambucil intoxication, and treatment is mainly supportive, directed at decontaminating the GI tract and controlling symptoms; blood products may be used to treat the hematologic toxicity

Stability Store at room temperature

Mechanism of Action Interferes with DNA replication and RNA transcription by alkylation and cross-linking the strands of DNA

Pharmacodynamics/Kinetics
Absorption/bioavailability: 70% to 80%; **food will interfere with absorption** resulting in a 10% to 20% decrease in bioavailability
Distribution: V_d: 0.14-0.24 L/kg, thought to cross the placenta
Protein binding: ~99% bound to albumin; extensive binding to tissues and plasma proteins
Metabolism: In the liver to an active metabolite
Half-life: 90 minutes to 2 hours
Elimination: 60% excreted in urine within 24 hours, principally as metabolites; probably not dialyzable

Usual Dosage Oral (refer to individual protocols):
Children:
General short courses: 0.1-0.2 mg/kg/day OR 4.5 mg/m^2/day for 3-6 weeks for remission induction (usual: 4-10 mg/day); maintenance therapy: 0.03-0.1 mg/kg/day (usual: 2-4 mg/day)
Nephrotic syndrome: 0.1-0.2 mg/kg/day every day for 5-15 weeks with low-dose prednisone
Chronic lymphocytic leukemia (CLL):
Biweekly regimen: Initial: 0.4 mg/kg/dose every 2 weeks; increase dose by 0.1 mg/kg every 2 weeks until a response occurs and/or myelosuppression occurs
Monthly regimen: Initial: 0.4 mg/kg, increase dose by 0.2 mg/kg every 4 weeks until a response occurs and/or myelosuppression occurs
Malignant lymphomas:
Non-Hodgkin's lymphoma: 0.1 mg/kg/day
Hodgkin's lymphoma: 0.2 mg/kg/day
Adults: 0.1-0.2 mg/kg/day OR 3-6 mg/m^2/day for 3-6 weeks, then adjust dose on basis of blood counts. Pulse dosing has been used in CLL as intermittent, biweekly, or monthly doses of 0.4 mg/kg and increased by 0.1 mg/kg until the disease is under control or toxicity ensues. An alternate regimen is 14 mg/m^2/day for 5 days, repeated every 21-28 days.
Hemodialysis: Supplemental dosing is not necessary
Peritoneal dialysis: Supplemental dosing is not necessary

Monitoring Parameters Liver function tests, CBC, leukocyte counts, platelets, serum uric acid

Patient Information Notify physician immediately if sore throat or bleeding occurs, contraceptive measures are recommended during therapy

Dosage Forms Tablet, sugar coated: 2 mg

Extemporaneous Preparations A 2 mg/mL suspension was stable for 7 days when refrigerated and compounded as follows: Pulverize sixty 2 mg tablets; levigate with a small amount of glycerin; add 20 mL Cologel® and levigate until a uniform mixture is obtained; add a 2:1 simple syrup/cherry syrup mixture to make a total volume of 60 mL
(Continued)

Chlorambucil *(Continued)*

Handbook in Extemporaneous Formulations, Bethesda, MD: American Society of Hospital Pharmacists, 1987.

Chloramphenicol *(klor am FEN i kole)*

Related Information
Antimicrobial Drugs of Choice *on page 1404*
Community-Acquired Pneumonia in Adults *on page 1419*

U.S. Brand Names AK-Chlor® Ophthalmic; Chloromycetin®; Chloroptic® Ophthalmic

Canadian Brand Names Diochloram; Pentamycetin®; Sopamycetin

Therapeutic Category Antibiotic, Ophthalmic; Antibiotic, Otic; Antibiotic, Miscellaneous

Use Treatment of serious infections due to organisms resistant to other less toxic antibiotics or when its penetrability into the site of infection is clinically superior to other antibiotics to which the organism is sensitive; useful in infections caused by *Bacteroides*, *H. influenzae*, *Neisseria meningitidis*, *Salmonella*, and *Rickettsia*; active against many vancomycin-resistant enterococci

Pregnancy Risk Factor C

Contraindications Hypersensitivity to chloramphenicol or any component

Warnings/Precautions Use with caution in patients with impaired renal or hepatic function and in neonates; reduce dose with impaired liver function; use with care in patients with glucose 6-phosphate dehydrogenase deficiency. Serious and fatal blood dyscrasias have occurred after both short-term and prolonged therapy; should not be used when less potentially toxic agents are effective; prolonged use may result in superinfection.

Adverse Reactions <1%: Nightmares, headache, rash, diarrhea, stomatitis, enterocolitis, nausea, vomiting, bone marrow suppression, aplastic anemia, peripheral neuropathy, optic neuritis, gray syndrome

Three (3) major toxicities associated with chloramphenicol include:
  Aplastic anemia, an idiosyncratic reaction which can occur with any route of administration; usually occurs 3 weeks to 12 months after initial exposure to chloramphenicol
  Bone marrow suppression is thought to be dose-related with serum concentrations >25 μg/mL and reversible once chloramphenicol is discontinued; anemia and neutropenia may occur during the first week of therapy
  Gray syndrome is characterized by circulatory collapse, cyanosis, acidosis, abdominal distention, myocardial depression, coma, and death; reaction appears to be associated with serum levels ≥50 μg/mL; may result from drug accumulation in patients with impaired hepatic or renal function

Overdosage/Toxicology
Symptoms of overdose include anemia, metabolic acidosis, hypotension, hypothermia
Treatment is supportive following GI decontamination

Drug Interactions CYP2C9 enzyme inhibitor
Decreased effect: Phenobarbital and rifampin may decrease concentration of chloramphenicol
Increased toxicity: Chloramphenicol inhibits the metabolism of chlorpropamide, phenytoin, oral anticoagulants

Stability Refrigerate ophthalmic solution; constituted solutions remain stable for 30 days; use only clear solutions; frozen solutions remain stable for 6 months

Mechanism of Action Reversibly binds to 50S ribosomal subunits of susceptible organisms preventing amino acids from being transferred to growing peptide chains thus inhibiting protein synthesis

Pharmacodynamics/Kinetics
Distribution: Readily crosses placenta; appears in breast milk; distributes to most tissues and body fluids
  Ratio of CSF to blood level (%): Normal meninges: 66; Inflamed meninges: 66+
Protein binding: 60%
Metabolism: Extensive in the liver (90%) to inactive metabolites, principally by glucuronidation, chloramphenicol palmitate is hydrolyzed by lipases in the GI tract to the active base; chloramphenicol sodium succinate is hydrolyzed by esterases to active base
Half-life: (Prolonged with markedly reduced liver function or combined liver/kidney dysfunction):
  Normal renal function: 1.6-3.3 hours
  End-stage renal disease: 3-7 hours
  Cirrhosis: 10-12 hours
  Neonates: Postnatal: 1-2 days: 24 hours; 10-16 days: 10 hours
Elimination: 5% to 15% excreted as unchanged drug in the urine, 4% excreted in bile; in neonates, 6% to 80% may be excreted unchanged in urine

Usual Dosage
Meningitis: I.V.: Infants >30 days and Children: 50-100 mg/kg/day divided every 6 hours
Other infections: I.V.:
  Infants >30 days and Children: 50-75 mg/kg/day divided every 6 hours; maximum daily dose: 4 g/day
  Adults: 50-100 mg/kg/day in divided doses every 6 hours; maximum daily dose: 4 g/day
Ophthalmic: Children and Adults: Instill 1-2 drops or 1.25 cm (½" of ointment every 3-4 hours); increase interval between applications after 48 hours to 2-3 times/day
Otic solution: Instill 2-3 drops into ear 3 times/day

Topical: Gently rub into the affected area 1-4 times/day

Dosing adjustment/comments in hepatic impairment: Avoid use in severe liver impairment as increased toxicity may occur

Hemodialysis: Slightly dialyzable (5% to 20%) via hemo- and peritoneal dialysis; no supplemental doses needed in dialysis or continuous arteriovenous or veno-venous hemofiltration (CAVH/CAVHD)

Dietary Considerations Folic acid, iron salts, vitamin B_{12}: May decrease intestinal absorption of vitamin B_{12}; may have increased dietary need for riboflavin, pyridoxine, and vitamin B_{12}; monitor hematological status

Administration Do not administer I.M.

Monitoring Parameters CBC with reticulocyte and platelet counts, periodic liver and renal function tests, serum drug concentration

Reference Range

Therapeutic levels: 15-20 µg/mL; Toxic concentration: >40 µg/mL; Trough: 5-10 µg/mL

Timing of serum samples: Draw levels 1.5 hours and 3 hours after completion of I.V. or oral dose; trough levels may be preferred; should be drawn ≤1 hour prior to dose

Additional Information Sodium content of 1 g (injection): 51.8 mg (2.25 mEq)

Dosage Forms

Capsule: 250 mg

Ointment, ophthalmic: 1% [10 mg/g] (3.5 g)

AK-Chlor®, Chloromycetin®, Chloroptic® S.O.P.: 1% [10 mg/g] (3.5 g)

Powder for injection, as sodium succinate: 1 g

Powder for ophthalmic solution (Chloromycetin®): 25 mg/vial (15 mL)

Solution: 0.5% [5 mg/mL] (7.5 mL, 15 mL)

Ophthalmic (AK-Chlor®, Chloroptic®): 0.5% [5 mg/mL] (2.5 mL, 7.5 mL, 15 mL)

Otic (Chloromycetin®): 0.5% (15 mL)

Chloramphenicol and Prednisolone

(klor am FEN i kole & pred NIS oh lone)

U.S. Brand Names Chloroptic-P® Ophthalmic

Therapeutic Category Antibiotic/Corticosteroid, Ophthalmic

Dosage Forms Ointment, ophthalmic: Chloramphenicol 1% and prednisolone 0.5% (3.5 g)

Chloramphenicol, Polymyxin B, and Hydrocortisone

(klor am FEN i kole, pol i MIKS in bee, & hye droe KOR ti sone)

Therapeutic Category Antibiotic/Corticosteroid, Ophthalmic

Dosage Forms Solution, ophthalmic: Chloramphenicol 1%, polymyxin B sulfate 10,000 units, and hydrocortisone acetate 0.5% per g (3.75 g)

Chlordiazepoxide (klor dye az e POKS ide)

Related Information

Benzodiazepines Comparison *on page 1310*

U.S. Brand Names Libritabs®; Librium®; Mitran® Oral; Reposans-10® Oral

Canadian Brand Names Apo®-Chlordiazepoxide; Corax®; Medilium®; Novo-Poxide; Solium®

Synonyms Methaminodiazepoxide Hydrochloride

Therapeutic Category Benzodiazepine; Hypnotic; Sedative

Use Approved for anxiety, may be useful for acute alcohol withdrawal symptoms

Restrictions C-IV

Pregnancy Risk Factor D

Contraindications Hypersensitivity to chlordiazepoxide or any component, pre-existing CNS depression, severe uncontrolled pain

Warnings/Precautions Use with caution in patients with respiratory depression, CNS impairment, liver dysfunction, or a history of drug dependence

Adverse Reactions

>10%:

Cardiovascular: Chest pain

Central nervous system: Drowsiness, fatigue, lightheadedness, memory impairment, insomnia, anxiety, depression, headache

Dermatologic: Skin eruptions, rash

Endocrine & metabolic: Decreased libido

Gastrointestinal: Nausea, constipation, vomiting, diarrhea, xerostomia, increased or decreased appetite, decreased salivation

Neuromuscular & skeletal: Dysarthria

Ocular: Blurred vision

Miscellaneous: Diaphoresis

1% to 10%:

Cardiovascular: Hypotension, tachycardia, edema, syncope

Central nervous system: Ataxia (more commonly in the elderly), confusion, mental impairment, nervousness, dizziness, akathisia

Dermatologic: Dermatitis

Gastrointestinal: Weight gain or loss, increased salivation

Neuromuscular & skeletal: Rigidity, tremor, muscle cramps

Otic: Tinnitus

Respiratory: Nasal congestion, hyperventilation

<1%: Menstrual irregularities, blood dyscrasias, depressed reflexes, drug dependence

(Continued)

Chlordiazepoxide *(Continued)*

Overdosage/Toxicology

Symptoms of overdose include hypotension, respiratory depression, coma, hypothermia, cardiac arrhythmias

Treatment for benzodiazepine overdose is supportive; rarely is mechanical ventilation required; flumazenil has been shown to selectively block the binding of benzodiazepines to CNS receptors, resulting in a reversal of benzodiazepine-induced CNS depression. Respiratory depression may not be reversed.

Drug Interactions Increased toxicity (CNS depression): Oral anticoagulants, alcohol, tricyclic antidepressants, sedative-hypnotics, MAO inhibitors

Stability Refrigerate injection; protect from light; **incompatible** when mixed with Ringer's solution, normal saline, ascorbic acid, benzquinamide, heparin, phenytoin, promethazine, secobarbital

Pharmacodynamics/Kinetics

Distribution: V_d: 3.3 L/kg; crosses the placenta; appears in breast milk

Protein binding: 90% to 98%

Metabolism: Extensive in the liver to desmethyldiazepam (active and long-acting)

Half-life: 6.6-25 hours; End-stage renal disease: 5-30 hours; Cirrhosis: 30-63 hours

Time to peak serum concentration: Oral: Within 2 hours; I.M.: Results in lower peak plasma levels than oral

Elimination: Very little excretion in urine as unchanged drug

Usual Dosage

Children:

<6 years: Not recommended

>6 years: Anxiety: Oral, I.M.: 0.5 mg/kg/24 hours divided every 6-8 hours

Adults:

Anxiety:

Oral: 15-100 mg divided 3-4 times/day

I.M., I.V.: Initial: 50-100 mg followed by 25-50 mg 3-4 times/day as needed

Preoperative anxiety: I.M.: 50-100 mg prior to surgery

Alcohol withdrawal symptoms: Oral, I.V.: 50-100 mg to start, dose may be repeated in 2-4 hours as necessary to a maximum of 300 mg/24 hours

Dosing adjustment in renal impairment: Cl_{cr} <10 mL/minute: Administer 50% of dose

Hemodialysis: Not dialyzable (0% to 5%)

Dosing adjustment/comments in hepatic impairment: Avoid use

Dietary Considerations Alcohol: Additive CNS effects, avoid use

Administration Up to 300 mg may be given I.M. or I.V. during a 6-hour period, but not more than this in any 24-hour period; do not use diluent provided with parenteral form for I.V. administration; dissolve with normal saline instead; I.V. form is a powder and should be reconstituted with 5 mL of sterile water or saline prior to administration

Monitoring Parameters Respiratory and cardiovascular status, mental status, check for orthostasis

Reference Range Therapeutic: 0.1-3 µg/mL (SI: 0-10 µmol/L); Toxic: >23 µg/mL (SI: >77 µmol/L)

Test Interactions ↓ HDL, ↑ triglycerides (S)

Patient Information Avoid alcohol and other CNS depressants; avoid activities needing good psychomotor coordination until CNS effects are known; drug may cause physical or psychological dependence; avoid abrupt discontinuation after prolonged use, may cause drowsiness, poor balance

Nursing Implications Raise bed rails; initiate safety measures; aid with ambulation

Dosage Forms

Capsule, as hydrochloride: 5 mg, 10 mg, 25 mg

Powder for injection, as hydrochloride: 100 mg

Tablet: 10 mg, 25 mg

Chlorhexidine Gluconate *(klor HEKS i deen GLOO koe nate)*

U.S. Brand Names BactoShield® Topical [OTC]; Betasept® [OTC]; Dyna-Hex® Topical [OTC]; Exidine® Scrub [OTC]; Hibiclens® Topical [OTC]; Hibistat® Topical [OTC]; Peridex® Oral Rinse; PerioChip®; PerioGard®

Therapeutic Category Antibacterial, Oral Rinse; Mouthwash

Use Skin cleanser for surgical scrub, cleanser for skin wounds, germicidal hand rinse, and as antibacterial dental rinse. Chlorhexidine is active against gram-positive and gramnegative organisms, facultative anaerobes, aerobes, and yeast.

Pregnancy Risk Factor B

Contraindications Known hypersensitivity to chlorhexidine gluconate

Warnings/Precautions Staining of oral surfaces, tooth restorations, and dorsum of tongue may occur; keep out of eyes and ears; for topical use only; there have been case reports of anaphylaxis following chlorhexidine disinfection

Adverse Reactions

>10%: Oral: Increase of tartar on teeth, changes in taste. Staining of oral surfaces (mucosa, teeth, dorsum of tongue) may be visible as soon as 1 week after therapy begins and is more pronounced when there is a heavy accumulation of unremoved plaque and when teeth fillings have rough surfaces. Stain does not have a clinically adverse effect but because removal may not be possible, patient with frontal restoration should be advised of the potential permanency of the stain.

1% to 10%: Gastrointestinal: Tongue irritation, oral irritation

<1%: Facial edema, nasal congestion, shortness of breath

Overdosage/Toxicology Symptoms of oral overdose include gastric distress, nausea, or signs of alcohol intoxication

Mechanism of Action The bactericidal effect of chlorhexidine is a result of the binding of this cationic molecule to negatively charged bacterial cell walls and extramicrobial complexes. At low concentrations, this causes an alteration of bacterial cell osmotic equilibrium and leakage of potassium and phosphorous resulting in a bacteriostatic effect. At high concentrations of chlorhexidine, the cytoplasmic contents of the bacterial cell precipitate and result in cell death.

Pharmacodynamics/Kinetics

Absorption: ~30% of chlorhexidine is retained in the oral cavity following rinsing and is slowly released into the oral fluids; chlorhexidine is poorly absorbed from the GI tract

Serum concentrations: Detectable levels are not present in the plasma 12 hours after administration

Elimination: Primarily through the feces (approximately 90%); <1% excreted in the urine

Usual Dosage Adults:

Oral rinse (Peridex®):

Precede use of solution by flossing and brushing teeth; completely rinse toothpaste from mouth. Swish 15 mL undiluted oral rinse around in mouth for 30 seconds, then expectorate. Caution patient not to swallow the medicine. Avoid eating for 2-3 hours after treatment. (The cap on bottle of oral rinse is a measure for 15 mL.)

When used as a treatment of gingivitis, the regimen begins with oral prophylaxis. Patient treats mouth with 15 mL chlorhexidine, swishes for 30 seconds, then expectorates. This is repeated twice daily (morning and evening). Patient should have a re-evaluation followed by a dental prophylaxis every 6 months.

Cleanser:

Surgical scrub: Scrub 3 minutes and rinse thoroughly, wash for an additional 3 minutes

Hand wash: Wash for 15 seconds and rinse

Hand rinse: Rub 15 seconds and rinse

Periodontal chip: Adults: One chip is inserted into a periodontal pocket with a probing pocket depth ≥5 mm. Up to 8 chips may be inserted in a single visit. Treatment is recommended every 3 months in pockets with a remaining depth ≥5 mm. If dislodgment occurs 7 days or more after placement, the subject is considered to have had the full course of treatment. If dislodgment occurs within 48 hours, a new chip should be inserted.

Insertion of periodontal chip: Pocket should be isolated and surrounding area dried prior to chip insertion. The chip should be grasped using forceps with the rounded edges away from the forceps. The chip should be inserted into the periodontal pocket to its maximum depth. It may be maneuvered into position using the tips of the forceps or a flat instrument. The chip biodegrades completely and does not need to be removed. Patients should avoid dental floss at the site of PerioChip® insertion for 10 days after placement because flossing might dislodge the chip.

Patient Information

Oral rinse: Do not swallow, do not rinse after use; may cause reduced taste perception which is reversible; may cause discoloration of teeth

Topical administration is for external use only

Dosage Forms

Chip, for periodontal pocket insertion (PerioChip®): 2.5 mg

Foam, topical, with isopropyl alcohol 4% (BactoShield®): 4% (180 mL)

Liquid, topical, with isopropyl alcohol 4%:

Dyna-Hex® Skin Cleanser: 2% (120 mL, 240 mL, 480 mL, 960 mL, 4000 mL); 4% (120 mL, 240 mL, 480 mL, 4000 mL)

BactoShield® 2: 2% (960 mL)

BactoShield®, Betasept®, Exidine® Skin Cleanser, Hibiclens® Skin Cleanser: 4% (15 mL, 120 mL, 240 mL, 480 mL, 960 mL, 4000 mL)

Rinse:

Oral (mint flavor) (Peridex®, PerioGard®): 0.12% with alcohol 11.6% (480 mL)

Topical (Hibistat® Hand Rinse): 0.5% with isopropyl alcohol 70% (120 mL, 240 mL)

Sponge/Brush (Hibiclens®): 4% with isopropyl alcohol 4% (22 mL)

Wipes (Hibistat®): 0.5% (50s)

♦ **2-Chlorodeoxyadenosine** see Cladribine on page 271

♦ **Chloromycetin®** see Chloramphenicol on page 238

Chloroprocaine (klor oh PROE kane)

U.S. Brand Names Nesacaine®; Nesacaine®-MPF

Synonyms Chloroprocaine Hydrochloride

Therapeutic Category Local Anesthetic, Injectable

Use Infiltration anesthesia and peripheral and epidural anesthesia

Pregnancy Risk Factor C

Contraindications Known hypersensitivity to chloroprocaine, or other ester type anesthetics; myasthenia gravis; concurrent use of bupivacaine; do not use for subarachnoid administration

Warnings/Precautions Use with caution in patients with cardiac disease, renal disease, and hyperthyroidism; convulsions and cardiac arrest have been reported presumably due to intravascular injection

Adverse Reactions <1%: Myocardial depression, hypotension, bradycardia, cardiovascular collapse, edema, anxiety, restlessness, disorientation, confusion, seizures, drowsiness, unconsciousness, chills, urticaria, nausea, vomiting, transient stinging or burning

(Continued)

Chloroprocaine *(Continued)*

at injection site, tremor, blurred vision, tinnitus, respiratory arrest, anaphylactoid reactions, shivering

Overdosage/Toxicology Treatment is primarily symptomatic and supportive. Termination of anesthesia by pneumatic tourniquet inflation should be attempted when the agent is administered by infiltration or regional injection. Hypotension responds to I.V. fluids and Trendelenburg positioning. Other symptoms (seizures, bradyarrhythmias, metabolic acidosis, methemoglobinemia) respond to conventional treatments.

Mechanism of Action Chloroprocaine HCl is benzoic acid, 4-amino-2-chloro-2-(diethylamino) ethyl ester monohydrochloride. Chloroprocaine is an ester-type local anesthetic, which stabilizes the neuronal membranes and prevents initiation and transmission of nerve impulses thereby affecting local anesthetic actions. Local anesthetics including chloroprocaine, reversibly prevent generation and conduction of electrical impulses in neurons by decreasing the transient increase in permeability to sodium. The differential sensitivity generally depends on the size of the fiber; small fibers are more sensitive than larger fibers and require a longer period for recovery. Sensory pain fibers are usually blocked first, followed by fibers that transmit sensations of temperature, touch, and deep pressure. High concentrations block sympathetic somatic sensory and somatic motor fibers. The spread of anesthesia depends upon the distribution of the solution. This is primarily dependent on the volume of drug injected.

Usual Dosage Dosage varies with anesthetic procedure, the area to be anesthetized, the vascularity of the tissues, depth of anesthesia required, degree of muscle relaxation required, and duration of anesthesia; range: 1.5-25 mL of 2% to 3% solution; single adult dose should not exceed 800 mg

Infiltration and peripheral nerve block: 1% to 2%

Infiltration, peripheral and central nerve block, including caudal and epidural block: 2% to 3%, without preservatives

Administration Before injecting, withdraw syringe plunger to ensure injection is not into vein or artery

Nursing Implications Must have resuscitative equipment available

Dosage Forms Injection, as hydrochloride:

Preservative free (Nesacaine®-MPF): 2% (30 mL); 3% (30 mL)

With preservative (Nesacaine®): 1% (30 mL); 2% (30 mL)

♦ **Chloroprocaine Hydrochloride** *see Chloroprocaine on previous page*

♦ **Chloroptic® Ophthalmic** *see Chloramphenicol on page 238*

♦ **Chloroptic-P® Ophthalmic** *see Chloramphenicol and Prednisolone on page 239*

Chloroquine and Primaquine (KLOR oh kwin & PRIM a kween)

U.S. Brand Names Aralen® Phosphate With Primaquine Phosphate

Synonyms Primaquine and Chloroquine

Therapeutic Category Antimalarial Agent

Use Prophylaxis of malaria, regardless of species, in all areas where the disease is endemic

Pregnancy Risk Factor C

Contraindications Retinal or visual field changes, known hypersensitivity to chloroquine or primaquine

Warnings/Precautions Use with caution in patients with psoriasis, porphyria, hepatic dysfunction, G-6-PD deficiency

Adverse Reactions

1% to 10%: Gastrointestinal: Diarrhea, nausea

<1%: Hypotension, EKG changes, fatigue, personality changes, headache, pruritus, hair bleaching, anorexia, vomiting, stomatitis, blood dyscrasias, retinopathy, blurred vision

Overdosage/Toxicology

Symptoms of overdose include headache, visual changes, cardiovascular collapse, seizures, abdominal cramps, vomiting, cyanosis, methemoglobinemia, leukopenia, respiratory and cardiac arrest

Following initial measures (immediate GI decontamination), treatment is supportive and symptomatic

Drug Interactions

Decreased absorption if administered concomitantly with kaolin and magnesium trisilicate

Increased toxicity/levels with cimetidine

Mechanism of Action Chloroquine concentrates within parasite acid vesicles and raises internal pH resulting in inhibition of parasite growth; may involve aggregates of ferriprotoporphyrin IX acting as chloroquine receptors causing membrane damage; may also interfere with nucleoprotein synthesis. Primaquine eliminates the primary tissue exoerythrocytic forms of *P. falciparum*; disrupts mitochondria and binds to DNA.

Pharmacodynamics/Kinetics

Absorption: Oral: Both drugs are readily absorbed

Distribution: Concentrated in liver, spleen, kidney, heart, and brain

Protein binding: ~55%; binds strongly to melanin

Metabolism: 25% of chloroquine is metabolized

Elimination: Drug may remain in tissue for 3-5 days; up to 70% excreted unchanged

Usual Dosage Oral: Start at least 1 day before entering the endemic area; continue for 8 weeks after leaving the endemic area

Children: For suggested weekly dosage (based on body weight), see table:

Weight		Chloroquine Base (mg)	Primaquine Base (mg)	Dose* (mL)
lb	kg			
10-15	4.5-6.8	20	3	2.5
16-25	7.3-11.4	40	6	5
26-35	11.8-15.9	60	9	7.5
36-45	16.4-20.5	80	12	10
46-55	20.9-25	100	15	12.5
56-100	25.4-45.4	150	22.5	½ tablet
100+	>45.4	300	45	1 tablet

*Dose based on liquid containing approximately 40 mg of chloroquine base and 6 mg primaquine base per 5 mL, prepared from chloroquine phosphate with primaquine phosphate tablets.

Adults: 1 tablet/week on the same day each week

Monitoring Parameters Periodic CBC, examination for muscular weakness, and ophthalmologic examination in patients receiving prolonged therapy

Patient Information Take with meals; report any visual disturbances or difficulty in hearing or ringing in the ears; tablets are bitter tasting; may cause diarrhea, loss of appetite, nausea, stomach pain; notify physician if these become severe

Dosage Forms Tablet: Chloroquine phosphate 500 mg [base 300 mg] and primaquine phosphate 79 mg [base 45 mg]

Chloroquine Phosphate (KLOR oh kwin FOS fate)

Related Information

Malaria Treatment on page 1425
Prevention of Malaria on page 1372

U.S. Brand Names Aralen® Phosphate

Therapeutic Category Amebicide; Antimalarial Agent

Use Suppression or chemoprophylaxis of malaria; treatment of uncomplicated or mild to moderate malaria; extraintestinal amebiasis

Unlabeled use: Rheumatoid arthritis; discoid lupus erythematosus, scleroderma, pemphigus

Pregnancy Risk Factor C

Contraindications Retinal or visual field changes; patients with psoriasis; known hypersensitivity to chloroquine

Warnings/Precautions Use with caution in patients with liver disease, G-6-PD deficiency, alcoholism or in conjunction with hepatotoxic drugs, psoriasis, porphyria may be exacerbated; retinopathy (irreversible) has occurred with long or high-dose therapy; discontinue drug if any abnormality in the visual field or if muscular weakness develops during treatment

Adverse Reactions

>1%: Gastrointestinal: Nausea, diarrhea

<1%: Hypotension, EKG changes, fatigue, personality changes, headache, pruritus, hair bleaching, anorexia, vomiting, stomatitis, blood dyscrasias, retinopathy, blurred vision

Overdosage/Toxicology

Symptoms of overdose include headache, visual changes, cardiovascular collapse, seizures, abdominal cramps, vomiting, cyanosis, methemoglobinemia, leukopenia, respiratory and cardiac arrest

Following initial measures (immediate GI decontamination), treatment is supportive and symptomatic

Drug Interactions

Chloroquine and other 4-aminoquinolones may be decreased due to GI binding with kaolin or magnesium trisilicate

Increased effect: Cimetidine increases levels of chloroquine and probably other 4-aminoquinolones

Mechanism of Action Binds to and inhibits DNA and RNA polymerase; interferes with metabolism and hemoglobin utilization by parasites; inhibits prostaglandin effects; chloroquine concentrates within parasite acid vesicles and raises internal pH resulting in inhibition of parasite growth; may involve aggregates of ferriprotoporphyrin IX acting as chloroquine receptors causing membrane damage; may also interfere with nucleoprotein synthesis

Pharmacodynamics/Kinetics

Absorption: Oral: Rapid (~89%)

Distribution: Widely distributed in body tissues such as eyes, heart, kidneys, liver, and lungs where retention is prolonged; crosses the placenta; appears in breast milk

Metabolism: Partial hepatic metabolism occurs

Half-life: 3-5 days

Time to peak serum concentration: Within 1-2 hours

Elimination: ~70% excreted unchanged in urine; acidification of the urine increases elimination of drug; small amounts of drug may be present in urine months following discontinuation of therapy

Usual Dosage Oral (dosage expressed in terms of mg of base):

Suppression or prophylaxis of malaria:

Children: Administer 5 mg base/kg/week on the same day each week (not to exceed 300 mg base/dose); begin 1-2 weeks prior to exposure; continue for 4-6 weeks after leaving endemic area; if suppressive therapy is not begun prior to exposure, double

(Continued)

Chloroquine Phosphate *(Continued)*

the initial loading dose to 10 mg base/kg and administer in 2 divided doses 6 hours apart, followed by the usual dosage regimen

Adults: 300 mg/week (base) on the same day each week; begin 1-2 weeks prior to exposure; continue for 4-6 weeks after leaving endemic area; if suppressive therapy is not begun prior to exposure, double the initial loading dose to 600 mg base and administer in 2 divided doses 6 hours apart, followed by the usual dosage regimen

Acute attack:

Oral:

Children: 10 mg/kg on day 1, followed by 5 mg/kg 6 hours later and 5 mg/kg on days 2 and 3

Adults: 600 mg on day 1, followed by 300 mg 6 hours later, followed by 300 mg on days 2 and 3

I.M. (as hydrochloride):

Children: 5 mg/kg, repeat in 6 hours

Adults: Initial: 160-200 mg, repeat in 6 hours if needed; maximum: 800 mg first 24 hours; begin oral dosage as soon as possible and continue for 3 days until 1.5 g has been given

Extraintestinal amebiasis:

Children: Oral: 10 mg/kg once daily for 2-3 weeks (up to 300 mg base/day)

Adults:

Oral: 600 mg base/day for 2 days followed by 300 mg base/day for at least 2-3 weeks

I.M., as hydrochloride: 160-200 mg/day for 10 days; resume oral therapy as soon as possible

Dosing adjustment in renal impairment: Cl_{cr} <10 mL/minute: Administer 50% of dose
Hemodialysis: Minimally removed by hemodialysis

Monitoring Parameters Periodic CBC, examination for muscular weakness, and ophthalmologic examination in patients receiving prolonged therapy

Patient Information Take with meals; report any visual disturbances or difficulty in hearing or ringing in the ears; tablets are bitter tasting; may cause diarrhea, loss of appetite, nausea, stomach pain; notify physician if these become severe

Dosage Forms

Injection: 50 mg [40 mg base]/mL (5 mL)

Tablet: 250 mg [150 mg base]; 500 mg [300 mg base]

Extemporaneous Preparations A 10 mg chloroquine base/mL suspension is made by pulverizing two Aralen® 500 mg phosphate = 300 mg base/tablet, levigating with sterile water, and adding by geometric proportion, a significant amount of the cherry syrup and levigating until a uniform mixture is obtained; qs ad to 60 mL with cherry syrup, stable for up to 4 weeks when stored in the refrigerator or at a temperature of 29°C

Mirochnick M, Barnett E, Clarke DF, et al, "Stability of Chloroquine in an Extemporaneously Prepared Suspension Stored at Three Temperatures," *Pediatr Infect Dis J,* 1994, 13(9):827-8.

Chlorothiazide (klor oh THYE a zide)

Related Information

Sulfonamide Derivatives *on page 1337*

U.S. Brand Names Diurigen®; Diuril®

Therapeutic Category Antihypertensive Agent; Diuretic, Thiazide

Use Management of mild to moderate hypertension, or edema associated with congestive heart failure, pregnancy, or nephrotic syndrome in patients unable to take oral hydrochlorothiazide, when a thiazide is the diuretic of choice

Pregnancy Risk Factor B

Pregnancy/Breast-Feeding Implications

Clinical effects on the fetus: Crosses the placenta. Hypoglycemia, thrombocytopenia, hemolytic anemia, electrolyte disturbances reported. May exhibit a tocolytic effect. Generally, use of diuretics during pregnancy is avoided due to risk of decreased placental perfusion.

Breast-feeding/lactation: Crosses into breast milk; may suppress lactation with high doses. American Academy of Pediatrics considers **compatible** with breast-feeding.

Contraindications Hypersensitivity to chlorothiazide or any component; cross-sensitivity with other thiazides or sulfonamides; do not use in anuric patients.

Warnings/Precautions Injection must not be administered S.C. or I.M.; may cause hyperbilirubinemia, hypokalemia, alkalosis, hyperglycemia, hyperuricemia; chlorothiazide is minimally effective in patients with a Cl_{cr} <40 mL/minute; this may limit the usefulness of chlorothiazide in the elderly; use the I.V. form only when oral therapy is prohibitive or in an emergency, do not use in children if possible; avoid coadministration with blood

Adverse Reactions

1% to 10%: Endocrine & metabolic: Hypokalemia, hyponatremia

<1%: Arrhythmia, weak pulse, orthostatic hypotension, dizziness, vertigo, headache, fever, rash, photosensitivity, hypochloremic alkalosis, hyperglycemia, hyperlipidemia, hyperuricemia, rarely blood dyscrasias, leukopenia, agranulocytosis, aplastic anemia, paresthesias, prerenal azotemia

Overdosage/Toxicology

Symptoms of overdose include hypermotility, diuresis, lethargy, confusion, muscle weakness, coma

Following GI decontamination, therapy is supportive with I.V. fluids, electrolytes, and I.V. pressors if needed

Drug Interactions
Decreased effect:
Thiazides may decrease the effect of anticoagulants, antigout agents, sulfonylureas
Bile acid sequestrants, methenamine, and NSAIDs may decrease the effect of the thiazides
Increased effect: Thiazides may increase the toxicity of allopurinol, anesthetics, antineoplastics, calcium salts, diazoxide, digitalis, lithium, loop diuretics, methyldopa, nondepolarizing muscle relaxants, vitamin D; amphotericin B and anticholinergics may increase the toxicity of thiazides

Stability Reconstituted solution is stable for 24 hours at room temperature; precipitation will occur in <24 hours in pH <7.4

Mechanism of Action Inhibits sodium reabsorption in the distal tubules causing increased excretion of sodium and water as well as potassium and hydrogen ions, magnesium, phosphate, calcium

Pharmacodynamics/Kinetics
Absorption: Oral: Poor
Onset of diuresis: Oral: 2 hours
Duration of diuretic action: Oral: 6-12 hours; I.V.: ~2 hours
Half-life: 1-2 hours
Time to peak serum concentration: Within 4 hours

Usual Dosage
Infants <6 months:
Oral: 20-40 mg/kg/day in 2 divided doses
I.V.: 2-8 mg/kg/day in 2 divided doses
Infants >6 months and Children:
Oral: 20 mg/kg/day in 2 divided doses
I.V.: 4 mg/kg/day
Adults:
Oral: 500 mg to 2 g/day divided in 1-2 doses
I.V.: 100-500 mg/day (for edema only)
Elderly: Oral: 500 mg once daily **or** 1 g 3 times/week

Administration Injection must **not** be administered S.C. or I.M.; intermittent schedules for edema are often safer and more effective

Monitoring Parameters Serum electrolytes, renal function, blood pressure; assess weight, I & O reports daily to determine fluid loss

Test Interactions ↑ creatine phosphokinase [CPK] (S), ammonia (B), amylase (S), calcium (S), chloride (S), cholesterol (S), glucose, ↑ acid (S), ↓ chloride (S), magnesium, potassium (S), sodium (S)

Patient Information Shake well; may be taken with food or milk; take early in day to avoid nocturia; take the last dose of multiple doses no later than 6 PM unless instructed otherwise; to avoid photosensitivity, use sun block SPF ≥15 on exposed skin areas

Nursing Implications Take blood pressure with patient lying down and standing; avoid extravasation of parenteral solution since it is extremely irritating to tissues

Additional Information Sodium content of injection, 500 mg: 57.5 mg (2 mEq)

Dosage Forms
Powder for injection, lyophilized, as sodium: 500 mg
Suspension, oral: 250 mg/5 mL (237 mL)
Tablet: 250 mg, 500 mg

Chlorothiazide and Methyldopa (klor oh THYE a zide & meth il DOE pa)
U.S. Brand Names Aldoclor®
Therapeutic Category Antihypertensive Agent, Combination
Dosage Forms Tablet:
150: Chlorothiazide 150 mg and methyldopa 250 mg
250: Chlorothiazide 250 mg and methyldopa 250 mg

Chlorothiazide and Reserpine (klor oh THYE a zide & re SER peen)
Therapeutic Category Antihypertensive Agent, Combination
Dosage Forms Tablet:
250: Chlorothiazide 250 mg and reserpine 0.125 mg
500: Chlorothiazide 500 mg and reserpine 0.125 mg

Chlorotrianisene (klor oh trye AN i seen)
U.S. Brand Names TACE®
Therapeutic Category Estrogen Derivative, Oral
Use Treat inoperable prostatic cancer; management of atrophic vaginitis, female hypogonadism, vasomotor symptoms of menopause
Pregnancy Risk Factor X
Contraindications Thrombophlebitis, breast cancer, undiagnosed abnormal vaginal bleeding, known or suspected pregnancy
Warnings/Precautions Estrogens have been reported to increase the risk of endometrial carcinoma; do not use estrogens during pregnancy
Adverse Reactions
>10%:
Cardiovascular: Peripheral edema
Endocrine & metabolic: Enlargement of breasts (female and male), breast tenderness
(Continued)

Chlorotrianisene *(Continued)*

Gastrointestinal: Nausea, anorexia, bloating

1% to 10%:

Central nervous system: Headache

Endocrine & metabolic: Increased libido (female), decreased libido (male)

Gastrointestinal: Vomiting, diarrhea

<1%: Hypertension, thromboembolism, myocardial infarction, edema, depression, dizziness, anxiety, stroke, chloasma, melasma, rash, amenorrhea, alterations in frequency and flow of menses, decreased glucose tolerance, increased triglycerides and LDL, nausea, GI distress, cholestatic jaundice, intolerance to contact lenses, increased susceptibility to *Candida* infection, breast tumors

Overdosage/Toxicology Serious adverse effects have not been reported following ingestion of large doses of estrogen-containing oral contraceptives; overdosage of estrogen may cause nausea; withdrawal bleeding may occur in females

Mechanism of Action Diethylstilbestrol derivative with similar estrogenic actions

Pharmacodynamics/Kinetics

Onset of therapeutic effect: Commonly occurs within 14 days of therapy

Distribution: Stored in fat tissues and slowly released

Metabolism: In the liver to a more potent estrogen compound

Usual Dosage Adults: Oral:

Atrophic vaginitis: 12-25 mg/day in 28-day cycles (21 days on and 7 days off)

Female hypogonadism: 12-25 mg cyclically for 21 days. May be followed by I.M. progesterone 100 mg or 5 days of oral progestin; next course may begin on day 5 of induced uterine bleeding.

Postpartum breast engorgement: 12 mg 4 times/day for 7 days or 50 mg every 6 hours for 6 doses; administer first dose within 8 hours after delivery

Vasomotor symptoms associated with menopause: 12-25 mg cyclically for 30 days; one or more courses may be prescribed

Prostatic cancer (inoperable/progressing): 12-25 mg/day

Patient Information Patients should inform their physicians if signs or symptoms of thromboembolic or thrombotic disorders including sudden severe headache or vomiting, disturbance of vision or speech, loss of vision, numbness or weakness in an extremity, sharp or crushing chest pain, calf pain, shortness of breath, severe abdominal pain or mass, mental depression or unusual bleeding.

Dosage Forms Capsule: 12 mg, 25 mg

Chlorpheniramine and Phenylephrine

(klor fen IR a meen & fen il EF rin)

U.S. Brand Names Dallergy-D® Syrup; Ed A-Hist® Liquid; Histatab® Plus Tablet [OTC]; Histor-D® Syrup; Rolatuss® Plain Liquid; Ru-Tuss® Liquid

Therapeutic Category Antihistamine/Decongestant Combination

Dosage Forms

Capsule, sustained release: Chlorpheniramine maleate 8 mg and phenylephrine hydrochloride 20 mg

Liquid:

Dallergy-D®, Histor-D®, Rolatuss® Plain, Ru-Tuss®: Chlorpheniramine maleate 2 mg and phenylephrine hydrochloride 5 mg per 5 mL

Ed A-Hist® Liquid: Chlorpheniramine maleate 4 mg and phenylephrine hydrochloride 10 mg per 5 mL

Tablet (Histatab® Plus): Chlorpheniramine maleate 2 mg and phenylephrine hydrochloride 5 mg

Chlorpheniramine, Ephedrine, Phenylephrine, and Carbetapentane

(klor fen IR a meen, e FED rin, fen il EF rin, & kar bay ta PEN tane)

U.S. Brand Names Rentamine®; Rynatuss® Pediatric Suspension; Tri-Tannate Plus®

Therapeutic Category Antihistamine/Decongestant/Antitussive

Dosage Forms Liquid: Carbetapentane tannate 30 mg, ephedrine tannate 5 mg, phenylephrine tannate 5 mg, and chlorpheniramine tannate 4 mg per 5 mL

Chlorpheniramine, Phenindamine, and Phenylpropanolamine

(klor fen IR a meen, fen IN dah meen, & fen il proe pa NOLE a meen)

U.S. Brand Names Nolamine®

Therapeutic Category Antihistamine/Decongestant Combination

Dosage Forms Tablet, timed release: Chlorpheniramine maleate 4 mg, phenindamine tartrate 24 mg, and phenylpropanolamine hydrochloride 50 mg

Chlorpheniramine, Phenylephrine, and Codeine

(klor fen IR a meen, fen il EF rin, & KOE deen)

U.S. Brand Names Pediacof®; Pedituss®

Therapeutic Category Antihistamine/Decongestant/Antitussive

Dosage Forms Liquid: Chlorpheniramine maleate 0.75 mg, phenylephrine hydrochloride 2.5 mg, and codeine phosphate 5 mg with potassium iodide 75 mg per 5 mL

Chlorpheniramine, Phenylephrine, and Methscopolamine
(klor fen IR a meen, fen il EF rin, & meth skoe POL a meen)

U.S. Brand Names D.A.II® Tablet; Dallergy®; Dura-Vent/DA®; Extendryl® SR; Histor-D® Timecelles®

Therapeutic Category Antihistamine/Decongestant/Anticholinergic

Dosage Forms

Caplet, sustained release: Chlorpheniramine maleate 8 mg, phenylephrine hydrochloride 20 mg, and methscopolamine nitrate 2.5 mg

Capsule, sustained release: Chlorpheniramine maleate 8 mg, phenylephrine hydrochloride 10 mg, and methscopolamine nitrate 2.5 mg

Syrup: Chlorpheniramine maleate 2 mg, phenylephrine hydrochloride 10 mg, and methscopolamine nitrate 0.625 mg per 5 mL

Tablet: Chlorpheniramine maleate 4 mg, phenylephrine hydrochloride 10 mg, and methscopolamine nitrate 1.25 mg

Chlorpheniramine, Phenylephrine, and Phenylpropanolamine
(klor fen IR a meen, fen il EF rin, & fen il proe pa NOLE a meen)

U.S. Brand Names Hista-Vadrin® Tablet

Therapeutic Category Antihistamine/Decongestant Combination

Dosage Forms Tablet: Chlorpheniramine maleate 6 mg, phenylephrine hydrochloride 5 mg, and phenylpropanolamine hydrochloride 40 mg

Chlorpheniramine, Phenylephrine, and Phenyltoloxamine
(klor fen IR a meen, fen il EF rin, & fen il tole LOKS a meen)

U.S. Brand Names Comhist®; Comhist® LA

Therapeutic Category Antihistamine/Decongestant Combination

Dosage Forms

Capsule, sustained release (Comhist® LA): Chlorpheniramine maleate 4 mg, phenylephrine hydrochloride 20 mg, and phenyltoloxamine citrate 50 mg

Tablet (Comhist®): Chlorpheniramine maleate 2 mg, phenylephrine hydrochloride 10 mg, and phenyltoloxamine citrate 25 mg

Chlorpheniramine, Phenylephrine, Phenylpropanolamine, and Belladonna Alkaloids
(klor fen IR a meen, fen il EF rin, fen il proe pa NOLE a meen, & bel a DON a AL ka loydz)

U.S. Brand Names Atrohist® Plus; Phenahist-TR®; Phenchlor® S.H.A.; Ru-Tuss®; Stahist®

Therapeutic Category Cold Preparation

Dosage Forms Tablet, sustained release: Chlorpheniramine 8 mg, phenylephrine 25 mg, phenylpropanolamine 50 mg, hyoscyamine 0.19 mg, atropine 0.04 mg, and scopolamine 0.01 mg

Chlorpheniramine, Phenyltoloxamine, Phenylpropanolamine, and Phenylephrine
(klor fen IR a meen, fen il tole LOKS a meen, fen il proe pa NOLE a meen & fen il EF rin)

U.S. Brand Names Naldecon®; Naldelate®; Nalgest®; Nalspan®; New Decongestant®; Par Decon®; Tri-Phen-Chlor®; Uni-Decon®

Therapeutic Category Antihistamine/Decongestant Combination

Dosage Forms

Drops, pediatric: Chlorpheniramine maleate 0.5 mg, phenyltoloxamine citrate 2 mg, phenylpropanolamine hydrochloride 5 mg, and phenylephrine hydrochloride 1.25 mg per mL

Syrup: Chlorpheniramine maleate 2.5 mg, phenyltoloxamine citrate 7.5 mg, phenylpropanolamine hydrochloride 20 mg, and phenylephrine hydrochloride 5 mg per 5 mL

Syrup, pediatric: Chlorpheniramine maleate 0.5 mg, phenyltoloxamine citrate 2 mg, phenylpropanolamine hydrochloride 5 mg, and phenylephrine hydrochloride 1.25 mg per 5 mL

Tablet, sustained release: Chlorpheniramine maleate 5 mg, phenyltoloxamine citrate 15 mg, phenylpropanolamine hydrochloride 40 mg, and phenylephrine hydrochloride 10 mg

Chlorpheniramine, Pseudoephedrine, and Codeine
(klor fen IR a meen, soo doe e FED rin, & KOE deen)

U.S. Brand Names Codehist® DH; Decohistine® DH; Dihistine® DH; Ryna-C® Liquid

Therapeutic Category Antihistamine/Decongestant/Antitussive

Dosage Forms Liquid: Chlorpheniramine maleate 2 mg, pseudoephedrine hydrochloride 30 mg, and codeine phosphate 10 mg (120 mL, 480 mL)

Chlorpheniramine, Pyrilamine, and Phenylephrine
(klor fen IR a meen, pye RIL a meen, & fen il EF rin)

U.S. Brand Names Rhinatate® Tablet; R-Tannamine® Tablet; R-Tannate® Tablet; Rynatan® Pediatric Suspension; Rynatan® Tablet; Tanoral® Tablet; Triotann® Tablet; Tri-Tannate® Tablet

Therapeutic Category Antihistamine/Decongestant Combination

(Continued)

Chlorpheniramine, Pyrilamine, and Phenylephrine
(Continued)

Dosage Forms
Liquid: Chlorpheniramine tannate 2 mg, pyrilamine tannate 12.5 mg, and phenylephrine tannate 5 mg per 5 mL
Tablet: Chlorpheniramine tannate 8 mg, pyrilamine maleate 12.5 mg, and phenylephrine tannate 25 mg

Chlorpheniramine, Pyrilamine, Phenylephrine, and Phenylpropanolamine
(klor fen IR a meen, pye RIL a meen, fen il EF rin, & fen il proe pa NOLE a meen)
U.S. Brand Names Histalet Forte® Tablet
Therapeutic Category Antihistamine/Decongestant Combination
Dosage Forms Tablet: Chlorpheniramine maleate 4 mg, pyrilamine maleate 25 mg, phenylephrine hydrochloride 10 mg, and phenylpropanolamine hydrochloride 50 mg

♦ **Chlorprom®** *see* Chlorpromazine *on this page*
♦ **Chlorpromanyl®** *see* Chlorpromazine *on this page*

Chlorpromazine (klor PROE ma zeen)
Related Information
Antipsychotic Agents Comparison *on page 1305*
U.S. Brand Names Ormazine; Thorazine®
Canadian Brand Names Apo®-Chlorpromazine; Chlorprom®; Chlorpromanyl®; Largactil®; Novo-Chlorpromazine
Synonyms Chlorpromazine Hydrochloride
Therapeutic Category Antiemetic; Antipsychotic Agent; Phenothiazine Derivative
Use Treatment of nausea and vomiting; psychoses; Tourette's syndrome; mania; intractable hiccups (adults); behavioral problems (children)
Pregnancy Risk Factor C
Contraindications Hypersensitivity to chlorpromazine hydrochloride or any component; cross-sensitivity with other phenothiazines may exist; avoid use in patients with narrow-angle glaucoma
Warnings/Precautions Safety in children <6 months of age has not been established; use with caution in patients with seizures, bone marrow suppression, or severe liver disease
Significant hypotension may occur, especially when the drug is administered parenterally; injection contains benzyl alcohol; injection also contains sulfites which may cause allergic reaction
Tardive dyskinesia: Prevalence rate may be 40% in elderly; development of the syndrome and the irreversible nature are proportional to duration and total cumulative dose over time. May be reversible if diagnosed early in therapy.
Extrapyramidal reactions are more common in elderly with up to 50% developing these reactions after 60 years of age. Drug-induced **Parkinson's syndrome** occurs often. **Akathisia** is the most common extrapyramidal reaction in elderly.
Increased confusion, memory loss, psychotic behavior, and agitation frequently occur as a consequence of anticholinergic effects
Orthostatic hypotension is due to alpha-receptor blockade, the elderly are at greater risk for orthostatic hypotension
Antipsychotic associated sedation in nonpsychotic patients is extremely unpleasant due to feelings of depersonalization, derealization, and dysphoria
Life-threatening arrhythmias have occurred at therapeutic doses of antipsychotics
Adverse Reactions
>10%:
Cardiovascular: Hypotension (especially with I.V. use), tachycardia, arrhythmias, orthostatic hypotension
Central nervous system: Pseudoparkinsonism, akathisia, dystonias, tardive dyskinesia (persistent), dizziness
Gastrointestinal: Constipation
Ocular: Pigmentary retinopathy
Respiratory: Nasal congestion
Miscellaneous: Diaphoresis (decreased)
1% to 10%:
Dermatologic: Pruritus, rash, increased sensitivity to sun
Endocrine & metabolic: Amenorrhea, galactorrhea, gynecomastia, changes in libido, pain in breasts
Gastrointestinal: GI upset, nausea, vomiting, stomach pain, weight gain, xerostomia
Genitourinary: Dysuria, ejaculatory disturbances, urinary retention
Neuromuscular & skeletal: Trembling of fingers
Ocular: Blurred vision
<1%: Sedation, drowsiness, restlessness, anxiety, extrapyramidal reactions, seizures, altered central temperature regulation, lowering of seizures threshold, neuroleptic malignant syndrome (NMS), discoloration of skin (blue-gray), photosensitivity, galactorrhea, priapism, agranulocytosis (more often in women between 4th and 10th weeks of therapy), leukopenia (usually in patients with large doses for prolonged periods), cholestatic jaundice, hepatotoxicity, cornea and lens changes, anaphylactoid reactions

Overdosage/Toxicology

Symptoms of overdose include deep sleep, coma, extrapyramidal symptoms, abnormal involuntary muscle movements, hypotension

Following initiation of essential overdose management, toxic symptom treatment and supportive treatment should be initiated. Hypotension usually responds to I.V. fluids or Trendelenburg positioning. If unresponsive to these measures, the use of a parenteral inotrope may be required. Seizures commonly respond to diazepam (I.V. 5-10 mg bolus in adults every 15 minutes if needed up to a total of 30 mg; I.V. 0.25-0.4 mg/kg/dose up to a total of 10 mg in children) or to phenytoin or phenobarbital; critical cardiac arrhythmias often respond to I.V. phenytoin (15 mg/kg up to 1 g), while other antiarrhythmics can be used. Neuroleptics often cause extrapyramidal symptoms (eg, dystonic reactions) requiring management with benztropine mesylate I.V. 1-2 mg (adults) may be effective. These agents are generally effective within 2-5 minutes.

Drug Interactions CYP1A2, 2D6, and 3A3/4 enzyme substrate; CYP2D6 enzyme inhibitor

Increased toxicity: Additive effects with other CNS-depressants; epinephrine (hypotension); may increase valproic acid serum concentrations

Stability Protect from light; a slightly yellowed solution does not indicate potency loss, but a markedly discolored solution should be discarded; diluted injection (1 mg/mL) with NS and stored in 5 mL vials remains stable for 30 days

Mechanism of Action Blocks postsynaptic mesolimbic dopaminergic receptors in the brain; exhibits a strong alpha-adrenergic blocking effect and depresses the release of hypothalamic and hypophyseal hormones; believed to depress the reticular activating system, thus affecting basal metabolism, body temperature, wakefulness, vasomotor tone, and emesis

Pharmacodynamics/Kinetics

Distribution: Crosses the placenta; appears in breast milk

Metabolism: Extensively in the liver to active and inactive metabolites

Half-life, biphasic: Initial: 2 hours; Terminal: 30 hours

Elimination: <1% excreted in urine as unchanged drug within 24 hours

Usual Dosage

Children >6 months:

Psychosis:

Oral: 0.5-1 mg/kg/dose every 4-6 hours; older children may require 200 mg/day or higher

I.M., I.V.: 0.5-1 mg/kg/dose every 6-8 hours; maximum dose for <5 years (22.7 kg): 40 mg/day; maximum for 5-12 years (22.7-45.5 kg): 75 mg/day

Nausea and vomiting:

Oral: 0.5-1 mg/kg/dose every 4-6 hours as needed

I.M., I.V.: 0.5-1 mg/kg/dose every 6-8 hours; maximum dose for <5 years (22.7 kg): 40 mg/day; maximum for 5-12 years (22.7-45.5 kg): 75 mg/day

Rectal: 1 mg/kg/dose every 6-8 hours as needed

Adults:

Psychosis:

Oral: Range: 30-800 mg/day in 1-4 divided doses, initiate at lower doses and titrate as needed; usual dose: 200 mg/day; some patients may require 1-2 g/day

I.M., I.V.: Initial: 25 mg, may repeat (25-50 mg) in 1-4 hours, gradually increase to a maximum of 400 mg/dose every 4-6 hours until patient is controlled; usual dose: 300-800 mg/day

Intractable hiccups: Oral, I.M.: 25-50 mg 3-4 times/day

Nausea and vomiting:

Oral: 10-25 mg every 4-6 hours

I.M., I.V.: 25-50 mg every 4-6 hours

Rectal: 50-100 mg every 6-8 hours

Elderly (nonpsychotic patient; dementia behavior): Initial: 10-25 mg 1-2 times/day; increase at 4- to 7-day intervals by 10-25 mg/day. Increase dose intervals (bid, tid, etc) as necessary to control behavior response or side effects; maximum daily dose: 800 mg; gradual increases (titration) may prevent some side effects or decrease their severity.

Hemodialysis: Not dialyzable (0% to 5%)

Dosing adjustment/comments in hepatic impairment: Avoid use in severe hepatic dysfunction

Dietary Considerations Alcohol: Additive CNS effects, avoid use

Administration Dilute oral concentrate solution in juice before administration

Monitoring Parameters Orthostatic blood pressures; tremors, gait changes, abnormal movement in trunk, neck, buccal area, or extremities; monitor target behaviors for which the agent is given; watch for hypotension when administering I.M. or I.V.

Reference Range

Therapeutic: 50-300 ng/mL (SI: 157-942 nmol/L)

Toxic: >750 ng/mL (SI: >2355 nmol/L); serum concentrations poorly correlate with expected response

Test Interactions False-positives for phenylketonuria, amylase, uroporphyrins, urobilinogen; may cause photosensitivity; avoid excessive sunlight; do not stop taking without consulting physician

Patient Information Do not stop taking unless informed by your physician; oral concentrate must be diluted in 2-4 oz of liquid (water, fruit juice, carbonated drinks, milk, or pudding); do not take antacid within 1 hour of taking drug; avoid alcohol; avoid excess sun exposure (use sun block); may cause drowsiness, rise slowly from recumbent position; use of supportive stockings may help prevent orthostatic hypotension

(Continued)

Chlorpromazine *(Continued)*

Nursing Implications Avoid contact of oral solution or injection with skin (contact dermatitis)

Dosage Forms

Capsule, as hydrochloride, sustained action: 30 mg, 75 mg, 150 mg, 200 mg, 300 mg

Concentrate, oral, as hydrochloride: 30 mg/mL (120 mL); 100 mg/mL (60 mL, 240 mL)

Injection, as hydrochloride: 25 mg/mL (1 mL, 2 mL, 10 mL)

Suppository, rectal, as base: 25 mg, 100 mg

Syrup, as hydrochloride: 10 mg/5 mL (120 mL)

Tablet, as hydrochloride: 10 mg, 25 mg, 50 mg, 100 mg, 200 mg

♦ Chlorpromazine Hydrochloride *see* Chlorpromazine *on page 248*

Chlorpropamide *(klor PROE pa mide)*

Related Information

Hypoglycemic Drugs, Comparison of Oral Agents *on page 1325*

Sulfonamide Derivatives *on page 1337*

U.S. Brand Names Diabinese®

Canadian Brand Names Apo®-Chlorpropamide; Novo-Propamide

Therapeutic Category Antidiabetic Agent, Oral; Hypoglycemic Agent, Oral; Sulfonylurea Agent

Use Control blood sugar in adult onset, noninsulin-dependent diabetes (type II)

Unlabeled use: Neurogenic diabetes insipidus

Pregnancy Risk Factor D

Pregnancy/Breast-Feeding Implications

Clinical effects on the fetus: Crosses the placenta. Hypoglycemia; ear defects reported; other malformations reported but may have been secondary to poor maternal glucose control/diabetes. Insulin is the drug of choice for the control of diabetes mellitus during pregnancy.

Breast-feeding/lactation: Crosses into breast milk

Contraindications Cross-sensitivity may exist with other hypoglycemics or sulfonamides; do not use with type I diabetes or with severe renal, hepatic, thyroid, or other endocrine disease

Warnings/Precautions

Patients should be properly instructed in the early detection and treatment of hypoglycemia; long half-life may complicate recovery from excess effects

Because of chlorpropamide's long half-life, duration of action, and the increased risk for hypoglycemia, it is not considered a hypoglycemic agent of choice in the elderly; see Pharmacodynamics/Kinetics

Adverse Reactions

>10%:

Central nervous system: Headache, dizziness

Gastrointestinal: Anorexia, constipation, heartburn, epigastric fullness, nausea, vomiting, diarrhea

1% to 10%: Dermatologic: Skin rash, urticaria, photosensitivity

<1%: Edema, hypoglycemia, hyponatremia, SIADH, blood dyscrasias, aplastic anemia, hemolytic anemia, bone marrow suppression, thrombocytopenia, agranulocytosis, cholestatic jaundice

Overdosage/Toxicology

Symptoms of overdose include low blood glucose levels, tingling of lips and tongue, tachycardia, convulsions, stupor, coma

Antidote is glucose; intoxications with sulfonylureas can cause hypoglycemia and are best managed with glucose administration (oral for milder hypoglycemia or by injection in more severe forms); prolonged effects lasting up to 1 week may occur with this agent

Drug Interactions

Decreased effect: Thiazides and hydantoins (eg, phenytoin) decrease chlorpropamide effectiveness may increase blood glucose

Increased toxicity:

Increases alcohol-associated disulfiram reactions

Increases oral anticoagulant effects

Salicylates may increase chlorpropamide effects may decrease blood glucose

Sulfonamides may decrease sulfonylureas clearance

Mechanism of Action Stimulates insulin release from the pancreatic beta cells; reduces glucose output from the liver; insulin sensitivity is increased at peripheral target sites

Pharmacodynamics/Kinetics

Peak effect: Oral: Within 6-8 hours

Distribution: V_d: 0.13-0.23 L/kg; appears in breast milk

Protein binding: 60% to 90%

Metabolism: Extensive (~80%) in the liver

Half-life: 30-42 hours; prolonged in the elderly or with renal disease

End-stage renal disease: 50-200 hours

Time to peak serum concentration: Within 3-4 hours

Elimination: 10% to 30% excreted in the urine as unchanged drug

Usual Dosage Oral: The dosage of chlorpropamide is variable and should be individualized based upon the patient's response

Initial dose:

Adults: 250 mg/day in mild to moderate diabetes in middle-aged, stable diabetic

Elderly: 100-125 mg/day in older patients

Subsequent dosages may be increased or decreased by 50-125 mg/day at 3- to 5-day intervals

Maintenance dose: 100-250 mg/day; severe diabetics may require 500 mg/day; avoid doses >750 mg/day

Dosing adjustment/comments in renal impairment: Cl$_{cr}$ <50 mL/minute: Avoid use

Hemodialysis: Removed with hemoperfusion

Peritoneal dialysis: Supplemental dose is not necessary

Dosing adjustment in hepatic impairment: Dosage reduction is recommended. Conservative initial and maintenance doses are recommended in patients with liver impairment because chlorpropamide undergoes extensive hepatic metabolism.

Dietary Considerations

Alcohol: A disulfiram-like reaction characterized by flushing, headache, nausea, vomiting, sweating or tachycardia; avoid use. Inform patient of chlorpropamide-alcohol flush (facial reddening and an increase in facial temperature).

Food: Chlorpropamide may cause GI upset; take with food. Take at the same time each day; eat regularly and do not skip meals.

Glucose: Decreases blood glucose concentration; hypoglycemia may occur. Educate patients how to detect and treat hypoglycemia. Monitor for signs and symptoms of hypoglycemia. Administer glucose if necessary. Evaluate patient's diet and exercise regimen. May need to decrease or discontinue dose of sulfonylurea.

Sodium: Reports of hyponatremia and SIADH. Those at increased risk include patients on medications or who have medical conditions that predispose them to hyponatremia. Monitor sodium serum concentration and fluid status. May need to restrict water intake.

Monitoring Parameters Fasting blood glucose, normal Hgb A$_{1c}$ or fructosamine levels; monitor for signs and symptoms of hypoglycemia, (fatigue, sweating, numbness of extremities); monitor urine for glucose and ketones

Reference Range Target range: Adults:

Fasting blood glucose: <120 mg/dL

Glycosylated hemoglobin: <7%

Patient Information Avoid alcohol; take at the same time each day; avoid hypoglycemia, eat regularly, do not skip meals; carry a quick source of sugar

Dosage Forms Tablet: 100 mg, 250 mg

Chlortetracycline (klor tet ra SYE kleen)

U.S. Brand Names Aureomycin®

Synonyms Chlortetracycline Hydrochloride

Therapeutic Category Antibiotic, Ophthalmic; Antibiotic, Tetracycline Derivative; Antibiotic, Topical

Use

Ophthalmic: Treatment of superficial ocular infections involving the conjunctiva or cornea due to strains of susceptible microorganisms

Topical: Treatment of superficial infections of the skin due to susceptible organisms, also infection prophylaxis in minor skin abrasions

Pregnancy Risk Factor D

Contraindications Hypersensitivity to tetracycline or any component; do not use topical formulation in eyes

Warnings/Precautions Prolonged use may cause superinfection; ophthalmic ointments may retard corneal epithelial healing

Adverse Reactions

1% to 10%: Dermatologic: Faint yellowing of skin

<1%: Edema, reddening of skin, photosensitivity, irritation

Mechanism of Action Inhibits bacterial protein synthesis by binding with the 30S and possibly the 50S ribosomal subunit(s) of susceptible bacteria; may also cause alterations in the cytoplasmic membrane; usually bacteriostatic, may be bactericidal

Usual Dosage

Ophthalmic:

Acute infections: Instill ½" (1.25 cm) every 3-4 hours until improvement

Mild to moderate infections: Instill ½" (1.25 cm) 2-3 times/day

Topical: Apply 1-4 times/day, cover with sterile bandage if needed

Patient Information

For ophthalmic use, tilt head back, place medication in conjunctival sac and close eye, apply light finger pressure on lacrimal sac following instillation

Topical is for external use only, contact physician if rash or irritation develops, may stain clothing

Nursing Implications Cleanse affected area of skin prior to application unless otherwise directed

Dosage Forms Ointment, as hydrochloride:

Ophthalmic: 1% [10 mg/g] (3.5 g)

Topical: 3% (14.2 g, 30 g)

♦ Chlortetracycline Hydrochloride see Chlortetracycline on this page

Chlorthalidone (klor THAL i done)

Related Information

Heart Failure: Management of Patients With Left-Ventricular Systolic Dysfunction on page 1472

Sulfonamide Derivatives on page 1337

(Continued)

Chlorthalidone *(Continued)*

U.S. Brand Names Hygroton®; Thalitone®

Canadian Brand Names Apo®-Chlorthalidone; Novo-Thalidone; Uridon®

Therapeutic Category Antihypertensive Agent; Diuretic, Miscellaneous

Use Management of mild to moderate hypertension, used alone or in combination with other agents; treatment of edema associated with congestive heart failure, nephrotic syndrome, or pregnancy. Recent studies have found chlorthalidone effective in the treatment of isolated systolic hypertension in the elderly.

Pregnancy Risk Factor B

Contraindications Hypersensitivity to chlorthalidone or any component, cross-sensitivity with other thiazides or sulfonamides; do not use in anuric patients

Warnings/Precautions Use with caution in patients with hypokalemia, renal disease, hepatic disease, gout, lupus erythematosus, diabetes mellitus; use with caution in severe renal diseases

Adverse Reactions

1% to 10%: Endocrine & metabolic: Hypokalemia

<1%: Hypotension, photosensitivity, fluid and electrolyte imbalances (hypocalcemia, hypomagnesemia, hyponatremia), hyperglycemia, rarely blood dyscrasias, prerenal azotemia

Overdosage/Toxicology

Symptoms of overdose include hypermotility, diuresis, lethargy, confusion, muscle weakness, coma

Following GI decontamination, therapy is supportive with I.V. fluids, electrolytes, and I.V. pressors if needed

Drug Interactions

Decreased effect: NSAIDs + chlorthalidone → decreased antihypertensive effect; decreased absorption of thiazides with cholestyramine resins; chlorthalidone causes a decreased effect of oral hypoglycemics

Increased toxicity: Digitalis glycosides, lithium (decreased clearance), probenecid

Increased effect: Furosemide and other loop diuretics

Mechanism of Action Sulfonamide-derived diuretic that inhibits sodium and chloride reabsorption in the cortical-diluting segment of the ascending loop of Henle

Pharmacodynamics/Kinetics

Peak effect: 2-6 hours

Absorption: Oral: 65%

Distribution: Crosses placenta; appears in breast milk

Metabolism: In the liver

Half-life: 35-55 hours; may be prolonged with renal impairment, with anuria: 81 hours

Elimination: ~50% to 65% excreted unchanged in urine

Usual Dosage Oral:

Children (nonapproved): 2 mg/kg/dose 3 times/week or 1-2 mg/kg/day

Adults:

Edema: 50-100 mg/day or 100 mg every other day; may increase to 200 mg but greater doses do not usually result in increased response

Hypertension: Initial: 25 mg/day, increase slowly to 100 mg/day or add additional antihypertensives

Elderly: Initial: 12.5-25 mg/day or every other day; there is little advantage to using doses >25 mg/day

Note: Thalidone 30 mg = chlorthalidone 25 mg

Dosing interval in renal impairment: Cl_{cr} <10 mL/minute: Administer every 48 hours

Monitoring Parameters Assess weight, I & O records daily to determine fluid loss; blood pressure, serum electrolytes, renal function

Test Interactions ↑ creatine phosphokinase [CPK] (S), ammonia (B), amylase (S), calcium (S), chloride (S), cholesterol (S), glucose (S), ↑ acid (S), ↓ chloride (S), magnesium, potassium (S), sodium (S)

Patient Information May be taken with food or milk; take early in day to avoid nocturia; take the last dose of multiple doses no later than 6 PM unless instructed otherwise; to avoid photosensitivity, use sun block SPF ≥15 on exposed skin areas

Nursing Implications Take blood pressure with patient lying down and standing

Dosage Forms

Tablet: 25 mg, 50 mg, 100 mg

Hygroton®: 25 mg, 50 mg, 100 mg

Thalitone®: 15 mg, 25 mg

Chlorzoxazone *(klor ZOKS a zone)*

U.S. Brand Names Flexaphen®; Paraflex®; Parafon Forte™ DSC

Synonyms Chlorzoxazone with Acetaminophen

Therapeutic Category Centrally Acting Muscle Relaxant; Skeletal Muscle Relaxant

Use Symptomatic treatment of muscle spasm and pain associated with acute musculoskeletal conditions

Pregnancy Risk Factor C

Contraindications Known hypersensitivity to chlorzoxazone; impaired liver function

Adverse Reactions

>10%: Central nervous system: Drowsiness

1% to 10%:

Cardiovascular: Tachycardia, tightness in chest, flushing of face, syncope

Central nervous system: Mental depression, allergic fever, dizziness, lightheadedness, headache, paradoxical stimulation

Dermatologic: Angioedema
Gastrointestinal: Nausea, vomiting, stomach cramps
Neuromuscular & skeletal: Trembling
Ocular: Burning of eyes
Respiratory: Shortness of breath
Miscellaneous: Hiccups
<1%: Ataxia, rash, urticaria, erythema multiforme, aplastic anemia, leukopenia, eosinophilia, blurred vision

Overdosage/Toxicology
Symptoms of overdose include nausea, vomiting, diarrhea, drowsiness, dizziness, headache, absent tendon reflexes, hypotension
Treatment is supportive following attempts to enhance drug elimination. Hypotension should be treated with I.V. fluids and/or Trendelenburg positioning. Dialysis and hemoperfusion and osmotic diuresis have all been useful in reducing serum drug concentrations; patient should be observed for possible relapses due to incomplete gastric emptying.

Drug Interactions CYP2E1 enzyme substrate
Increased effect/toxicity: Alcohol, CNS depressants

Mechanism of Action Acts on the spinal cord and subcortical levels by depressing polysynaptic reflexes

Pharmacodynamics/Kinetics
Onset of action: Within 1 hour
Absorption: Oral: Readily absorbed
Metabolism: Extensively in the liver by glucuronidation
Elimination: Excretion in urine as conjugates

Usual Dosage Oral:
Children: 20 mg/kg/day or 600 mg/m^2/day in 3-4 divided doses
Adults: 250-500 mg 3-4 times/day up to 750 mg 3-4 times/day

Dietary Considerations Alcohol: Additive CNS effects, avoid use

Monitoring Parameters Periodic liver functions tests

Patient Information May cause drowsiness or dizziness; avoid alcohol and other CNS depressants

Nursing Implications Raise bed rails; institute safety measures; assist with ambulation

Dosage Forms
Caplet (Parafon Forte™ DSC): 500 mg
Capsule (Flexaphen®, Mus-Lax®): 250 mg with acetaminophen 300 mg
Tablet (Paraflex®): 250 mg

♦ **Chlorzoxazone with Acetaminophen** see Chlorzoxazone on previous page
♦ **Cholac®** see Lactulose on page 656
♦ **Choledyl®** see Theophylline Salts on page 1125

Cholera Vaccine (KOL er a vak SEEN)

Therapeutic Category Vaccine, Inactivated Bacteria

Use The World Health Organization no longer recommends cholera vaccination for travel to or from cholera-endemic areas. Some countries may still require evidence of a complete primary series or a booster dose given within 6 months of arrival. Vaccination should not be considered as an alternative to continued careful selection of foods and water. Ideally, cholera and yellow fever vaccines should be administered at least 3 weeks apart.

Pregnancy Risk Factor C

Contraindications Presence of any acute illness, history of severe systemic reaction, or allergic response following a prior dose of cholera vaccine

Warnings/Precautions There is no data on the safety of cholera vaccination during pregnancy. Use in pregnancy should reflect actual increased risk. Persons who have had severe local or systemic reactions to a previous dose should not be revaccinated. Have epinephrine (1:1000) available for immediate use.

Adverse Reactions All serious adverse reactions must be reported to the U.S. Department of Health and Human Services (DHHS) Vaccine Adverse Event Reporting System (VAERS) 1-800-822-7967.
>10%:
Central nervous system: Malaise, fever, headache
Local: Pain, edema, tenderness, erythema, and induration at injection site

Drug Interactions Decreased effect with yellow fever vaccine; data suggests that giving both vaccines within 3 weeks of each other may decrease the response to both

Stability Refrigerate, avoid freezing

Mechanism of Action Inactivated vaccine producing active immunization

Usual Dosage
Children:
6 months to 4 years: Two 0.2 mL doses I.M./S.C. 1 week to 1 month apart; booster doses (0.2 mL I.M./S.C.) every 6 months
5-10 years: Two 0.3 mL doses I.M./S.C. or two 0.2 mL intradermal doses 1 week to 1 month apart; booster doses (0.3 mL I.M./S.C. or 0.2 mL I.D.) every 6 months
Children ≥10 years and Adults: Two 0.5 mL doses given I.M./S.C. or two 0.2 mL doses I.D. 1 week to 1 month apart; booster doses (0.5 mL I.M. or S.C. or 0.2 mL I.D.) every 6 months

Administration Do not administer I.V.

Patient Information Local reactions can occur up to 7 days after injection
(Continued)

Cholera Vaccine *(Continued)*

Nursing Implications Defer immunization in individuals with moderate or severe febrile illness

Additional Information Inactivated bacteria vaccine

Dosage Forms Injection: Suspension of killed *Vibrio cholerae* (Inaba and Ogawa types) 8 units of each serotype per mL (1.5 mL, 20 mL)

Cholestyramine Resin *(koe LES tir a meen REZ in)*

Related Information

Lipid-Lowering Agents *on page 1327*

U.S. Brand Names LoCHOLEST®; LoCHOLEST® Light; Prevalite®; Questran®; Questran® Light

Canadian Brand Names PMS-Cholestyramine

Therapeutic Category Antilipemic Agent

Use Adjunct in the management of primary hypercholesterolemia; pruritus associated with elevated levels of bile acids; diarrhea associated with excess fecal bile acids; binding toxicologic agents; pseudomembranous colitis

Pregnancy Risk Factor C

Contraindications Avoid using in complete biliary obstruction; hypersensitivity to cholestyramine or any component; hypolipoproteinemia types III, IV, V

Warnings/Precautions Use with caution in patients with constipation (GI dysfunction); caution patients with phenylketonuria (Questran® Light contains aspartame); overdose may result in GI obstruction

Adverse Reactions

1% to 10%: Gastrointestinal: Constipation

<1%: Rash, irritation of perianal area or skin, hyperchloremic acidosis, nausea, vomiting, abdominal distention and pain, malabsorption of fat-soluble vitamins, intestinal obstruction, steatorrhea, tongue irritation, hypoprothrombinemia (secondary to vitamin K deficiency), increased urinary calcium excretion

Overdosage/Toxicology

Symptoms of overdose include GI obstruction

Treatment is supportive

Drug Interactions Decreased effect: Decreased absorption (oral) of digitalis glycosides, warfarin, thyroid hormones, valproic acid, thiazide diuretics, propranolol, phenobarbital, amiodarone, methotrexate, NSAIDs, fat-soluble vitamins, aspirin, clofibrate, furosemide, glipizide, hydrocortisone, imipramine, methyldopa, niacin, penicillin G, phenytoin, phosphate, tetracyclines, tolbutamide, and other drugs by binding to the drug in the intestine

Mechanism of Action Forms a nonabsorbable complex with bile acids in the intestine, releasing chloride ions in the process; inhibits enterohepatic reuptake of intestinal bile salts and thereby increases the fecal loss of bile salt-bound low density lipoprotein cholesterol

Pharmacodynamics/Kinetics

Peak effect: 21 days

Absorption: Not absorbed from the GI tract

Elimination: In feces as an insoluble complex with bile acids

Usual Dosage Oral (dosages are expressed in terms of anhydrous resin):

Powder:

Children: 240 mg/kg/day in 3 divided doses; need to titrate dose depending on indication

Adults: 4 g 1-2 times/day to a maximum of 24 g/day and 6 doses/day

Tablet: Adults: Initial: 4 g once or twice daily; maintenance: 8-16 g/day in 2 divided doses

Dialysis: Not removed by hemo- or peritoneal dialysis; supplemental doses not necessary with dialysis or continuous arteriovenous or venovenous hemofiltration effects

Test Interactions ↑ prothrombin time; ↓ cholesterol (S), iron (B)

Patient Information Do not administer the powder in its dry form, mix with fluid or with applesauce; chew bars thoroughly; drink plenty of fluids; take other medications 1 hour before or 4-6 hours after binding resin; GI adverse reactions may decrease over time with continued use; adhere to prescribed diet

Nursing Implications Administer warfarin and other drugs at least 1-2 hours prior to, or 6 hours after cholestyramine because cholestyramine may bind to them, decreasing their total absorption. (**Note:** Cholestyramine itself may cause hypoprothrombinemia in patients with impaired enterohepatic circulation.)

Dosage Forms

Powder: 4 g of resin/9 g of powder (9 g, 378 g)

Powder, for oral suspension, with aspartame: 4 g of resin/5 g of powder (5 g, 210 g)

Powder, for oral suspension, with phenylalanine: 4 g of resin/5.5 g of powder (60s)

Choline Magnesium Trisalicylate

(KOE leen mag NEE zhum trye sa LIS i late)

U.S. Brand Names Tricosal®; Trilisate®

Therapeutic Category Analgesic, Salicylate; Anti-inflammatory Agent; Nonsteroidal Anti-inflammatory Drug (NSAID), Oral; Salicylate

Use Management of osteoarthritis, rheumatoid arthritis, and other arthritis; salicylate salts may not inhibit platelet aggregation and, therefore, should not be substituted for aspirin in the prophylaxis of thrombosis

Pregnancy Risk Factor C

Contraindications Bleeding disorders; hypersensitivity to salicylates or other nonacetylated salicylates or other NSAIDs; tartrazine dye hypersensitivity, asthma

Warnings/Precautions Use with caution in patients with impaired renal function, erosive gastritis, or peptic ulcer; avoid use in patients with suspected varicella or influenza (salicylates have been associated with Reye's syndrome in children <16 years of age when used to treat symptoms of chickenpox or the flu). Tinnitus or impaired hearing may indicate toxicity; discontinue use 1 week prior to surgical procedures.

Elderly are a high-risk population for adverse effects from nonsteroidal anti-inflammatory agents. As much as 60% of elderly can develop peptic ulceration and/or hemorrhage asymptomatically. Use lowest effective dose for shortest period possible. Tinnitus may be a difficult and unreliable indication of toxicity due to age-related hearing loss or eighth cranial nerve damage. CNS adverse effects may be observed in the elderly at lower doses than younger adults.

Adverse Reactions

>10%: Gastrointestinal: Nausea, heartburn, stomach pains, dyspepsia, epigastric discomfort

1% to 10%:
Central nervous system: Fatigue
Dermatologic: Rash
Gastrointestinal: Gastrointestinal ulceration
Hematologic: Hemolytic anemia
Neuromuscular & skeletal: Weakness
Respiratory: Dyspnea
Miscellaneous: Anaphylactic shock

<1%: Insomnia, nervousness, jitters, occult bleeding, prolongation of bleeding time, leukopenia, thrombocytopenia, iron deficiency anemia, hepatotoxicity, impaired renal function, bronchospasm, increased uric acid

Overdosage/Toxicology

Symptoms of overdose include tinnitus, vomiting, acute renal failure, hyperthermia, irritability, seizures, coma, metabolic acidosis

For acute ingestions, determine serum salicylate levels 6 hours after ingestion; the "Done" nomogram may be helpful for estimating the severity of aspirin poisoning and directing treatment using serum salicylate levels. Treatment can also be based upon symptomatology.

Salicylates

Toxic Symptoms	Treatment
Overdose	Induce emesis with ipecac, and/or lavage with saline, followed with activated charcoal
Dehydration	I.V. fluids with KCl (no D_5W only)
Metabolic acidosis (must be treated)	Sodium bicarbonate
Hyperthermia	Cooling blankets or sponge baths
Coagulopathy/hemorrhage	Vitamin K I.V.
Hypoglycemia (with coma, seizures, or change in mental status)	Dextrose 25 g I.V.
Seizures	Diazepam 5-10 mg I.V.

Drug Interactions

Decreased effect: Antacids + Trilisate® may decrease salicylate concentration
Increased toxicity: Warfarin + Trilisate® may possibly increase hypoprothrombinemic effect

Mechanism of Action Inhibits prostaglandin synthesis; acts on the hypothalamus heat-regulating center to reduce fever; blocks the generation of pain impulses

Pharmacodynamics/Kinetics

Absorption: Absorbed from the stomach and small intestine
Distribution: Readily distributes into most body fluids and tissues; crosses the placenta; appears in breast milk
Half-life: Dose-dependent ranging from 2-3 hours at low doses to 30 hours at high doses
Time to peak serum concentration: ~2 hours

Usual Dosage Oral (based on total salicylate content):
Children <37 kg: 50 mg/kg/day given in 2 divided doses
Adults: 500 mg to 1.5 g 2-3 times/day; usual maintenance dose: 1-4.5 g/day
Dosing adjustment/comments in renal impairment: Avoid use in severe renal impairment

Dietary Considerations

Alcohol: Combination causes GI irritation, possible bleeding; avoid or limit alcohol. Patients at increased risk include those prone to hypoprothrombinemia, vitamin K deficiency, thrombocytopenia, thrombotic thrombocytopenia purpura, severe hepatic impairment, and those receiving anticoagulants.

Food: May decrease the rate but not the extent of oral absorption. Drug may cause GI upset, bleeding, ulceration, perforation. Take with food or or large volume of water or milk to minimize GI upset.

Folic acid: Hyperexcretion of folate; folic acid deficiency may result, leading to macrocytic anemia. Supplement with folic acid if necessary.

Iron: With chronic use and at doses of 3-4 g/day, iron deficiency anemia may result; supplement with iron if necessary

Magnesium: Hypermagnesemia resulting from magnesium salicylate; avoid or use with caution in renal insufficiency

(Continued)

Choline Magnesium Trisalicylate *(Continued)*

Sodium: Hypernatremia resulting from buffered aspirin solutions or sodium salicylate containing high sodium content. Avoid or use with caution in CHF or any condition where hypernatremia would be detrimental.

Curry powder, paprika, licorice, Benedictine liqueur, prunes, raisins, tea and gherkins: Potential salicylate accumulation. These foods contain 6 mg salicylate/100 g. An ordinary American diet contains 10-200 mg/day of salicylate. Foods containing salicylates may contribute to aspirin hypersensitivity. Patients at greatest risk for aspirin hypersensitivity include those with asthma, nasal polyposis, or chronic urticaria.

Monitoring Parameters Serum magnesium with high dose therapy or in patients with impaired renal function; serum salicylate levels, renal function, hearing changes or tinnitus, abnormal bruising, weight gain and response (ie, pain)

Reference Range Salicylate blood levels for anti-inflammatory effect: 150-300 µg/mL; analgesia and antipyretic effect: 30-50 µg/mL

Test Interactions False-negative results for glucose oxidase urinary glucose tests (Clinistix®); false-positives using the cupric sulfate method (Clinitest®); also, interferes with Gerhardt test (urinary ketone analysis), VMA determination; 5-HIAA, xylose tolerance test, and T_3 and T_4; increased PBI

Patient Information Take with food; do not take with antacids; watch for bleeding gums or any signs of GI bleeding; take with food or milk to minimize GI distress, notify physician if ringing in ears or persistent GI pain occurs

Nursing Implications Liquid may be mixed with fruit juice just before drinking; do not administer with antacids

Dosage Forms See table.

Brand Name	Dosage Form	Total Salicylate	Choline Salicylate	Magnesium Salicylate
Trilisate®	Liquid	500 mg/5 mL	293 mg/5 mL	362 mg/5 mL
Trilisate 500®	Tablet	500 mg	293 mg	362 mg
Trilisate 750®	Tablet	750 mg	440 mg	544 mg
Trilisate 1000®	Tablet	1000 mg	587 mg	725 mg

Choline Salicylate *(KOE leen sa LIS i late)*

U.S. Brand Names Arthropan® [OTC]

Canadian Brand Names Teejel®

Therapeutic Category Analgesic, Salicylate; Anti-inflammatory Agent; Nonsteroidal Anti-inflammatory Drug (NSAID), Oral; Salicylate

Use Temporary relief of pain of rheumatoid arthritis, rheumatic fever, osteoarthritis, and other conditions for which oral salicylates are recommended; useful in patients in which there is difficulty in administering doses in a tablet or capsule dosage form, because of the liquid dosage form

Pregnancy Risk Factor C

Contraindications Hypersensitivity to salicylates or any component or other nonacetylated salicylates

Warnings/Precautions Use with caution in patients with impaired renal function, erosive gastritis, or peptic ulcer; avoid use in patients with suspected varicella or influenza (salicylates have been associated with Reye's syndrome in children <16 years of age when used to treat symptoms of chickenpox or the flu)

Adverse Reactions

>10%: Gastrointestinal: Nausea, heartburn, stomach pains, dyspepsia, epigastric discomfort

1% to 10%:

Central nervous system: Fatigue

Dermatologic: Rash

Gastrointestinal: Gastrointestinal ulceration

Hematologic: Hemolytic anemia

Neuromuscular & skeletal: Weakness

Respiratory: Dyspnea

Miscellaneous: Anaphylactic shock

<1%: Insomnia, nervousness, jitters, occult bleeding, prolongation of bleeding time, leukopenia, thrombocytopenia, iron deficiency anemia, hepatotoxicity, impaired renal function, bronchospasm

Salicylates

Toxic Symptoms	Treatment
Overdose	Induce emesis with ipecac, and/or lavage with saline, followed with activated charcoal
Dehydration	I.V. fluids with KCl (no D_5W only)
Metabolic acidosis (must be treated)	Sodium bicarbonate
Hyperthermia	Cooling blankets or sponge baths
Coagulopathy/hemorrhage	Vitamin K I.V.
Hypoglycemia (with coma, seizures, or change in mental status)	Dextrose 25 g I.V.
Seizures	Diazepam 5-10 mg I.V.

Overdosage/Toxicology

Symptoms of overdose include tinnitus, vomiting, acute renal failure, hyperthermia, irritability, seizures, coma, metabolic acidosis

For acute ingestions, determine serum salicylate levels 6 hours after ingestion; the "Done" nomogram may be helpful for estimating the severity of aspirin poisoning and directing treatment using serum salicylate levels. Treatment can also be based upon symptomatology.

Drug Interactions

Decreased effect with antacids

Increased effect of warfarin

Mechanism of Action Inhibits prostaglandin synthesis; acts on the hypothalamus heat-regulating center to reduce fever; blocks the generation of pain impulses

Pharmacodynamics/Kinetics

Absorption: From the stomach and small intestine within ~2 hours

Distribution: Readily distributes into most body fluids and tissues; crosses the placenta; appears in breast milk

Protein binding: 75% to 90%

Metabolism: Hydrolyzed to salicylate in the liver

Half-life: Dose-dependent ranging from 2-3 hours at low doses to 30 hours at high doses

Time to peak serum concentration: 1-2 hours

Elimination: In urine

Usual Dosage

Children >12 years and Adults: Oral: 5 mL (870 mg) every 3-4 hours, if necessary, but not more than 6 doses in 24 hours

Rheumatoid arthritis: 870-1740 mg (5-10 mL) up to 4 times/day

Dosing adjustment/comments in renal impairment: Avoid use in severe renal impairment

Test Interactions False-negative results for Clinistix® urine test; false-positive results with Clinitest®

Patient Information Take with food; do not take with antacids; watch for bleeding gums or any signs of GI bleeding; take with food or milk to minimize GI distress, notify physician if ringing in ears or persistent GI pain occurs

Nursing Implications Liquid may be mixed with fruit juice just before drinking; do not administer with antacids

Dosage Forms Liquid (mint flavor): 870 mg/5 mL (240 mL, 480 mL)

- **Choline Theophyllinate** see Theophylline Salts on page 1125
- **Choloxin®** see Dextrothyroxine on page 344

Chondroitin Sulfate-Sodium Hyaluronate

(kon DROY tin SUL fate-SOW de um hye al yoor ON ate)

U.S. Brand Names Duovisc® With Kit; Viscoat®

Synonyms Sodium Hyaluronate-Chrondroitin Sulfate

Therapeutic Category Ophthalmic Agent, Viscoelastic

Use Surgical aid in anterior segment procedures, protects corneal endothelium and coats intraocular lens thus protecting it

Pregnancy Risk Factor C

Contraindications Hypersensitivity to hyaluronate

Warnings/Precautions Product is extracted from avian tissues and contains minute amounts of protein, potential risks of hypersensitivity may exist. Intraocular pressure may be elevated as a result of pre-existing glaucoma, compromised outflow and by operative procedures and sequelae, including coma, compromised outflow and by operative procedures and sequelae, including enzymatic zonulysis, absence of an iridectomy, trauma to filtration structures and by blood and lenticular remnants in the anterior chamber. Monitor IOP, especially during the immediate postoperative period.

Adverse Reactions 1% to 10%: Ocular: Increased intraocular pressure

Stability Store at 2°C to 8°C/36°F to 46°F; do not freeze

Mechanism of Action Functions as a tissue lubricant and is thought to play an important role in modulating the interactions between adjacent tissues

Pharmacodynamics/Kinetics

Absorption: Following intravitreous injection, diffusion occurs slowly

Elimination: By way of the Canal of Schlemm

Usual Dosage Carefully introduce (using a 27-gauge needle or cannula) into anterior chamber after thoroughly cleaning the chamber with a balanced salt solution

Administration May inject prior to or following delivery of the crystalline lens. Installation prior to lens delivery provides additional protection to corneal endothelium, protecting it from possible damage arising from surgical instrumentation. May also be used to coat intraocular lens and tips of surgical instruments prior to implantation surgery. May inject additional solution during anterior segment surgery to fully maintain the solution lost during surgery. At the end of surgery, remove solution by thoroughly irrigating with a balanced salt solution.

Test Interactions False-negative results for Clinistix® urine test; false-positive results with Clinitest®

Dosage Forms Solution: Sodium chondroitin 40 mg and sodium hyaluronate 30 mg (0.25 mL, 0.5 mL)

♦ **Chooz®** [OTC] *see* Calcium Carbonate *on page 174*

♦ **Chorex®** *see* Chorionic Gonadotropin *on this page*

Chorionic Gonadotropin (kor ee ON ik goe NAD oh troe pin)

U.S. Brand Names A.P.L.®; Chorex®; Choron®; Follutein®; Glukor®; Gonic®; Pregnyl®; Profasi® HP

Synonyms CG; hCG

Therapeutic Category Ovulation Stimulator

Use Induces ovulation and pregnancy in anovulatory, infertile females; treatment of hypo-gonadotropic hypogonadism, prepubertal cryptorchidism

Pregnancy Risk Factor C

Contraindications Hypersensitivity to chorionic gonadotropin or any component; precocious puberty, prostatic carcinoma or similar neoplasms

Warnings/Precautions Use with caution in asthma, seizure disorders, migraine, cardiac or renal disease; **not** effective in the treatment of obesity

Adverse Reactions
1% to 10%:
Central nervous system: Mental depression, fatigue
Endocrine & metabolic: Pelvic pain, ovarian cysts, enlargement of breasts, precocious puberty
Local: Pain at the injection site
Neuromuscular & skeletal: Premature closure of epiphyses
<1%: Peripheral edema, irritability, restlessness, headache, ovarian hyperstimulation syndrome, gynecomastia

Stability Following reconstitution with the provided diluent, solutions are stable for 30-90 days, depending on the specific preparation, when stored at 2°C to 15°C

Mechanism of Action Stimulates production of gonadal steroid hormones by causing production of androgen by the testis; as a substitute for luteinizing hormone (LH) to stimulate ovulation

Pharmacodynamics/Kinetics
Half-life, biphasic: Initial: 11 hours; Terminal: 23 hours
Elimination: Excreted unchanged in urine within 3-4 days

Usual Dosage I.M.:
Children:
Prepubertal cryptorchidism: 1000-2000 units/m²/dose 3 times/week for 3 weeks **OR** 4000 units 3 times/week for 3 weeks **OR** 5000 units every second day for 4 injections **OR** 500 units 3 times/week for 4-6 weeks
Hypogonadotropic hypogonadism: 500-1000 units 3 times/week for 3 weeks, followed by the same dose twice weekly for 3 weeks **OR** 1000-2000 units 3 times/week for 3 weeks **OR** 4000 units 3 times/week for 6-9 months; reduce dosage to 2000 units 3 times/week for additional 3 months
Adults: Induction of ovulation: 5000-10,000 units one day following last dose of menotropins

Administration I.M. administration only

Reference Range Depends on application and methodology; <3 mIU/mL (SI: <3 units/L) usually normal (nonpregnant)

Patient Information Discontinue immediately if possibility of pregnancy

Dosage Forms Powder for injection (human origin): 200 units/mL (10 mL, 25 mL); 500 units/mL (10 mL); 1000 units/mL (10 mL); 2000 units/mL (10 mL)

♦ **Choron®** *see* Chorionic Gonadotropin *on this page*

♦ **Chromagen® OB** [OTC] *see* Vitamins, Multiple *on page 1226*

♦ **Chronulac®** *see* Lactulose *on page 656*

♦ **Cibacalcin® Injection** *see* Calcitonin *on page 171*

Ciclopirox (sye kloe PEER oks)

U.S. Brand Names Loprox®

Synonyms Ciclopirox Olamine

Therapeutic Category Antifungal Agent, Topical

Use Treatment of tinea pedis (athlete's foot), tinea cruris (jock itch), tinea corporis (ringworm), cutaneous candidiasis, and tinea versicolor (pityriasis)

Pregnancy Risk Factor B

Contraindications Known hypersensitivity to ciclopirox or any of its components; avoid occlusive wrappings or dressings

Warnings/Precautions For external use only; avoid contact with eyes

Adverse Reactions 1% to 10%:
Dermatologic: Pruritus
Local: Irritation, redness, burning, or pain

Mechanism of Action Inhibiting transport of essential elements in the fungal cell causing problems in synthesis of DNA, RNA, and protein

Pharmacodynamics/Kinetics
Absorption: <2% absorbed through intact skin
Distribution: To epidermis, corium (dermis), including hair, hair follicles, and sebaceous glands
Protein binding: 94% to 98%
Half-life: 1.7 hours
Elimination: Of the small amounts of systemically absorbed drug, majority excreted by the kidney with small amounts excreted in feces

Usual Dosage Children >10 years and Adults: Apply twice daily, gently massage into affected areas; if no improvement after 4 weeks of treatment, re-evaluate the diagnosis

Patient Information Avoid contact with eyes; if sensitivity or irritation occurs, discontinue use

Dosage Forms

Cream, topical, as olamine: 1% (15 g, 30 g, 90 g)

Lotion, as olamine: 1% (30 mL, 60 mL)

♦ **Ciclopirox Olamine** see Ciclopirox on previous page

Cidofovir (si DOF o veer)

U.S. Brand Names Vistide®

Therapeutic Category Antiviral Agent, Parenteral

Use Treatment of cytomegalovirus (CMV) retinitis in patients with acquired immunodeficiency syndrome (AIDS). **Note:** Should be administered with probenecid.

Pregnancy Risk Factor C

Pregnancy/Breast-Feeding Implications

Clinical effect on the fetus: Although studies are inconclusive, adenocarcinomas have occurred in animal studies with cidofovir; use during pregnancy only if the potential benefit justifies the potential risk to the fetus

Breast-feeding/lactation: Excretion of cidofovir into breast milk is unknown

Contraindications Patients with hypersensitivity to cidofovir and in patients with a history of clinically severe hypersensitivity to probenecid or other sulfa-containing medications

Warnings/Precautions Dose-dependent nephrotoxicity requires dose adjustment or discontinuation if changes in renal function occur during therapy (eg, proteinuria, glycosuria, decreased serum phosphate, uric acid or bicarbonate, and elevated creatinine); avoid use in patients with creatinine >1.5 mg/dL; Cl_{cr} <55 mL/minute; use great caution with elderly patients; neutropenia and ocular hypotony have also occurred; safety and efficacy have not been established in children; administration must be accompanied by oral probenecid and intravenous saline prehydration; prepare admixtures in a class two laminar flow hood, wearing protective gear; dispose of cidofovir as directed

Adverse Reactions

>10%:

Central nervous system: Infection, chills, fever, headache, amnesia, anxiety, confusion, seizures, insomnia

Dermatologic: Alopecia, rash, acne, skin discoloration

Gastrointestinal: Nausea, vomiting, diarrhea, anorexia, abdominal pain, constipation, dyspepsia, gastritis

Hematologic: Thrombocytopenia, neutropenia, anemia

Neuromuscular & skeletal: Weakness, paresthesia

Ocular: Amblyopia, conjunctivitis, ocular hypotony

Renal: Tubular damage, proteinuria, elevated creatinine

Respiratory: Asthma, bronchitis, coughing, dyspnea, pharyngitis

1% to 10%:

Cardiovascular: Hypotension, pallor, syncope, tachycardia

Central nervous system: Dizziness, hallucinations, depression, somnolence, malaise

Dermatologic: Pruritus, urticaria

Endocrine & metabolic: Hyperglycemia, hyperlipidemia, hypocalcemia, hypokalemia, dehydration

Gastrointestinal: Abnormal taste, stomatitis

Genitourinary: Glycosuria, urinary incontinence, urinary tract infections

Neuromuscular & skeletal: Skeletal pain

Ocular: Retinal detachment, iritis, uveitis, abnormal vision

Renal: Hematuria

Respiratory: Pneumonia, rhinitis, sinusitis

Miscellaneous: Diaphoresis, allergic reactions

Overdosage/Toxicology No reports of acute toxicity have been reported, however, hemodialysis and hydration may reduce drug plasma concentrations; probenecid may assist in decreasing active tubular secretion

Drug Interactions Increased effect/toxicity: Drugs with nephrotoxic potential (eg, amphotericin B, aminoglycosides, foscarnet, and I.V. pentamidine) should be avoided during cidofovir therapy

Stability Store admixtures under refrigeration for ≤24 hours

Mechanism of Action Cidofovir is converted to cidofovir diphosphate which is the active intracellular metabolite; cidofovir diphosphate suppresses CMV replication by selective inhibition of viral DNA synthesis. Incorporation of cidofovir into growing viral DNA chain results in reductions in the rate of viral DNA synthesis.

Pharmacodynamics/Kinetics The following pharmacokinetic data is based on a combination of cidofovir administered with probenecid:

Distribution: V_d: 0.54 L/kg; does not cross significantly into the CSF

Protein binding: <6%

Metabolism: Minimal; phosphorylation occurs intracellularly

Half-life, plasma: ~2.6 hours

Elimination: Renal tubular secretion and glomerular filtration

Usual Dosage

Induction: 5 mg/kg I.V. over 1 hour once weekly for 2 consecutive weeks

Maintenance: 5 mg/kg over 1 hour once every other week

Administer with probenecid - 2 g orally 3 hours prior to each cidofovir dose and 1 g at 2 and 8 hours after completion of the infusion (total: 4 g)

(Continued)

Cidofovir (Continued)

Hydrate with 1 L of 0.9% NS I.V. prior to cidofovir infusion; a second liter may be administered over a 1- to 3-hour period immediately following infusion, if tolerated

Dosing adjustment in renal impairment:
Cl_{cr} 41-55 mL/minute: 2 mg/kg
Cl_{cr} 30-40 mL/minute: 1.5 mg/kg
Cl_{cr} 20-29 mL/minute: 1 mg/kg
Cl_{cr} <19 mL/minute: 0.5 mg/kg

If the creatinine increases by 0.3-0.4 mg/dL, reduce the cidofovir dose to 3 mg/kg; discontinue therapy for increases ≥0.5 mg/dL or development of ≥3+ proteinuria

Monitoring Parameters Renal function (Cr, BUN, UAs), LFTs, WBCs, intraocular pressure and visual acuity

Patient Information Cidofovir is not a cure for CMV retinitis; regular follow-up ophthalmologic exams and careful monitoring of renal function are necessary; probenecid must be administered concurrently with cidofovir; report rash immediately to your physician; avoid use during pregnancy; use contraception during and for 3 months following treatment

Nursing Implications Administration of probenecid with a meal may decrease associated nausea; acetaminophen and antihistamines may ameliorate hypersensitivity reactions; dilute in 100 mL 0.9% saline; administer probenecid and I.V. saline before each infusion; allow the admixture to come to room temperature before administration

Dosage Forms Injection: 75 mg/mL (5 mL)

Cilostazol (sil OH sta zol)

U.S. Brand Names Pletal®

Synonyms OPC13013

Therapeutic Category Platelet Aggregation Inhibitor

Use Symptomatic management of peripheral vascular disease, primarily intermittent claudication; currently being investigated for the treatment of acute coronary syndromes

Pregnancy Risk Factor C

Pregnancy/Breast-Feeding Implications In animal studies, abnormalities of the skeletal, renal and cardiovascular system were increased. In addition, the incidence of stillbirth and decreased birth weights were increased. It is not known whether cilostazol is excreted in human milk. Because of the potential risk to nursing infants, a decision to discontinue the drug or discontinue nursing should be made.

Contraindications Hypersensitivity to cilostazol or any component of the formulation; heart failure (of any severity)

Warnings/Precautions Use with caution in patients receiving platelet aggregation inhibitors (effects are unknown), hepatic impairment (not studied). Use with caution in patients receiving inhibitors of CYP3A4 (such as ketoconazole or erythromycin) or inhibitors of CYP2C19 (such as omeprazole); use with caution in severe underlying heart disease; use is not recommended in nursing mothers

Adverse Reactions
>10%:
Central nervous system: Headache (27% to 34%)
Gastrointestinal: Abnormal stools (12% to 15%), diarrhea (12% to 19%)
Miscellaneous: Infection (10% to 14%)
2% to 10%:
Cardiovascular: Peripheral edema (7% to 9%), palpitation (5% to 10%), tachycardia (4%)
Central nervous system: Dizziness (9% to 10%)
Gastrointestinal: Dyspepsia (6%), nausea (6% to 7%), abdominal pain (4% to 5%), flatulence (2% to 3%)
Neuromuscular & skeletal: Back pain (6% to 7%), myalgia (2% to 3%)
Respiratory: Rhinitis (7% to 12%), pharyngitis (7% to 10%), cough (3% to 4%)
<2%: Chills, facial edema, fever, edema, malaise, nuchal rigidity, pelvic pain, retroperitoneal hemorrhage, cerebral infarction/ischemia, congestive heart failure, cardiac arrest, hemorrhage, hypotension, myocardial infarction/ischemia, postural hypotension, ventricular arrhythmia, supraventricular arrhythmia, syncope, anorexia, cholelithiasis, colitis, duodenitis, peptic ulcer, duodenal ulcer, esophagitis, esophageal hemorrhage, gastritis, hematemesis, melena, tongue edema, diabetes mellitus, anemia, ecchymosis, polycythemia, purpura, increased creatinine, gout, hyperlipidemia, hyperuricemia, arthralgia, bone pain, bursitis, anxiety, insomnia, neuralgia, dry skin, urticaria, amblyopia, blindness, conjunctivitis, diplopia, retinal hemorrhage, cystitis, albuminuria, vaginitis, vaginal hemorrhage, urinary frequency

Overdosage/Toxicology Experience with overdosage in humans is limited. Headache, diarrhea, hypotension, tachycardia and/or cardiac arrhythmias may occur. Treatment is symptomatic and supportive. Hemodialysis is unlikely to be of value. In some animal models, high-dose or long-term administration was associated with a variety of cardiovascular lesions, including endocardial hemorrhage, hemosiderin deposition and left ventricular fibrosis, coronary arteritis, and periarteritis.

Drug Interactions CYP3A4 and CYP2C19 cytochrome enzyme substrate
Increased effect/toxicity: Increased concentrations of cilostazol have been observed during concurrent therapy with omeprazole, an inhibitor of CYP2C19 and during concurrent therapy with inhibitors of CYP3A4 such as clarithromycin, erythromycin, itraconazole, fluconazole, miconazole, fluvoxamine, fluoxetine, nefazodone, sertraline,

and diltiazem. Platelet aggregation with aspirin is further inhibited when coadministered with cilostazol, it remains unclear whether concurrent oral anticoagulants or other antiplatelet drugs can increase cilostazol toxicity.

Mechanism of Action Cilostazol and its metabolites are inhibitors of phosphodiesterase III. As a result cyclic AMP is increased leading to inhibition of platelet aggregation and vasodilation. Other effects of phosphodiesterase III inhibition include increased cardiac contractility, accelerated AV nodal conduction, increased ventricular automaticity, heart rate, and coronary blood flow.

Pharmacodynamics/Kinetics

Onset: 2-4 weeks; treatment for up to 12 weeks may be required before benefit is experienced

Protein binding: 97% to 98%

Metabolism: Hepatic, via CYP3A4 and CYP2C19; at least one metabolite has significant activity

Half-life: 11-13 hours

Elimination: In urine (74%) and feces (20%), as metabolites

Usual Dosage Adults: Oral: 100 mg twice daily taken at least one-half hour before or 2 hours after breakfast and dinner; dosage should be reduced to 50 mg twice daily during concurrent therapy with inhibitors of CYP3A4 or CYP2C19 (see Drug Interactions)

Dietary Considerations Avoid concurrent ingestion of grapefruit juice due to the potential to inhibit CYP3A4. Avoid administration with meals. Taking cilostazol with a high-fat meal increases the AUC by 25% and the peak concentration may be increased by 90%; it is best to take cilostazol 30 minutes before or 2 hours after meals.

Dosage Forms Tablet: 50 mg, 100 mg

♦ **Ciloxan™ Ophthalmic** see Ciprofloxacin on page 263

Cimetidine (sye MET i deen)

Related Information

Antacid Drug Interactions on page 1296

Depression Disorders and Treatments on page 1465

U.S. Brand Names Tagamet®; Tagamet® HB [OTC]

Canadian Brand Names Apo®-Cimetidine; Novo-Cimetine; Nu-Cimet; Peptol®

Therapeutic Category Antihistamine, H₂ Blocker; Histamine H₂ Antagonist

Use Short-term treatment of active duodenal ulcers and benign gastric ulcers; long-term prophylaxis of duodenal ulcer; gastric hypersecretory states; gastroesophageal reflux; prevention of upper GI bleeding in critically ill patients.

Pregnancy Risk Factor B

Contraindications Hypersensitivity to cimetidine, other component, or other H₂-antagonists

Warnings/Precautions Adjust dosages in renal/hepatic impairment or patients receiving drugs metabolized through the P-450 system

Adverse Reactions

1% to 10%:

Central nervous system: Dizziness, agitation, headache, drowsiness

Gastrointestinal: Diarrhea, nausea, vomiting

<1%: Bradycardia, hypotension, tachycardia, confusion, fever, rash, gynecomastia, edema of the breasts, decreased sexual ability, neutropenia, agranulocytosis, thrombocytopenia, increased AST/ALT, myalgia, elevated creatinine

Overdosage/Toxicology Treatment is primarily symptomatic and supportive. No experience with intentional overdose; reported ingestions of 20 g have had transient side effects seen with recommended doses; animal data have shown respiratory failure, tachycardia, muscle tremors, vomiting, restlessness, hypotension, salivation, emesis, and diarrhea.

Drug Interactions CYP3A3/4 enzyme substrate; CYP1A2, 2C9, 2C18, 2C19, 2D6, and 3A3/4 enzyme inhibitor

Increased toxicity: Decreased elimination of lidocaine, theophylline, phenytoin, metronidazole, triamterene, procainamide, quinidine, and propranolol

Inhibition of warfarin metabolism, tricyclic antidepressant metabolism, diazepam elimination and cyclosporine elimination

Stability

Intact vials of cimetidine should be stored at room temperature and protected from light; cimetidine may precipitate from solution upon exposure to cold but can be redissolved by warming without degradation

Stability at room temperature:

Prepared bags: 7 days

Premixed bags: Manufacturer expiration dating and out of overwrap stability: 15 days

Stable in parenteral nutrition solutions for up to 7 days when protected from light

Physically incompatible with barbiturates, amphotericin B, and cephalosporins

Mechanism of Action Competitive inhibition of histamine at H₂-receptors of the gastric parietal cells resulting in reduced gastric acid secretion, gastric volume and hydrogen ion concentration reduced

Pharmacodynamics/Kinetics

Distribution: Crosses the placenta; appears in breast milk

Protein binding: 20%

Bioavailability: 60% to 70%

Half-life: Neonates: 3.6 hours; Children: 1.4 hours; Adults (with normal renal function): 2 hours

Time to peak serum concentration: Oral: Within 1-2 hours

(Continued)

Cimetidine *(Continued)*

Elimination: Principally as unchanged drug by the kidney; some excretion in bile and feces

Usual Dosage

Children: Oral, I.M., I.V.: 20-40 mg/kg/day in divided doses every 4 hours

Adults: Short-term treatment of active ulcers:

Oral: 300 mg 4 times/day or 800 mg at bedtime or 400 mg twice daily for up to 8 weeks

I.M., I.V.: 300 mg every 6 hours or 37.5 mg/hour by continuous infusion; I.V. dosage should be adjusted to maintain an intragastric pH ≥5

Patients with an active bleed: Administer cimetidine as a continuous infusion (see above)

Duodenal ulcer prophylaxis: Oral: 400-800 mg at bedtime

Gastric hypersecretory conditions: Oral, I.M., I.V.: 300-600 mg every 6 hours; dosage not to exceed 2.4 g/day

Dosing adjustment/interval in renal impairment: Children and Adults:

Cl_{cr} 20-40 mL/minute: Administer every 8 hours or 75% of normal dose

Cl_{cr} 0-20 mL/minute: Administer every 12 hours or 50% of normal dose

Hemodialysis: Slightly dialyzable (5% to 20%)

Dosing adjustment/comments in hepatic impairment: Usual dose is safe in mild liver disease but use with caution and in reduced dosage in severe liver disease; increased risk of CNS toxicity in cirrhosis suggested by enhanced penetration of CNS

Dietary Considerations Alcohol: Additive CNS effects, avoid or limit use

Administration Administer with meals so that the drug's peak effect occurs at the proper time (peak inhibition of gastric acid secretion occurs at 1 and 3 hours after dosing in fasting subjects and approximately 2 hours in nonfasting subjects; this correlates well with the time food is no longer in the stomach offering a buffering effect)

Monitoring Parameters Blood pressure with I.V. push administration, CBC, gastric pH, signs and symptoms of peptic ulcer disease, occult blood with GI bleeding, monitor renal function to correct dose; monitor for side effects

Test Interactions ↑ creatinine, AST, ALT, creatinine (S)

Patient Information Take with or immediately after meals; take 1 hour before or 2 hours after antacids; may cause drowsiness, impaired judgment, or coordination; avoid excessive alcohol

Dosage Forms

Infusion, as hydrochloride, in NS: 300 mg (50 mL)

Injection, as hydrochloride: 150 mg/mL (2 mL, 8 mL)

Liquid, oral, as hydrochloride (mint-peach flavor): 300 mg/5 mL with alcohol 2.8% (5 mL, 240 mL)

Tablet: 200 mg, 300 mg, 400 mg, 800 mg

♦ **Cinobac® Pulvules®** *see Cinoxacin on this page*

Cinoxacin *(sin OKS a sin)*

U.S. Brand Names Cinobac® Pulvules®

Therapeutic Category Antibiotic, Quinolone

Use Treatment of urinary tract infections

Pregnancy Risk Factor B

Contraindications History of convulsive disorders, hypersensitivity to cinoxacin or any component or other quinolones

Warnings/Precautions CNS stimulation may occur (tremor, restlessness, confusion, and very rarely hallucinations or seizures). Use with caution in patients with known or suspected CNS disorders or renal impairment. Not recommended in children <18 years of age, ciprofloxacin (a related compound), has caused a transient arthropathy in children; prolonged use may result in superinfection; modify dosage in patients with renal impairment.

Adverse Reactions Generally well tolerated

1% to 10%:

Central nervous system: Headache, dizziness

Gastrointestinal: Heartburn, abdominal pain, GI bleeding, belching, flatulence, anorexia, nausea

<1%: Insomnia, confusion, seizures (rare), diarrhea, thrombocytopenia, photophobia, tinnitus

Overdosage/Toxicology

Symptoms of overdose include acute renal failure, seizures

GI decontamination and supportive care; not removed by peritoneal or hemodialysis

Drug Interactions

Decreased effect: Decreased urine levels with probenecid; decreased absorption with aluminum-, magnesium-, calcium-containing antacids

Increased serum levels: Probenecid

Mechanism of Action Inhibits microbial synthesis of DNA with resultant inhibition of protein synthesis

Pharmacodynamics/Kinetics

Absorption: Oral: Rapid and complete; food decreases peak levels by 30% but not total amount absorbed

Distribution: Crosses the placenta; concentrates in prostate tissue

Protein binding: 60% to 80%

Half-life: 1.5 hours, prolonged in renal impairment

Time to peak serum concentration: Oral: Within 2-3 hours

Elimination: ~60% excreted as unchanged drug in urine

Usual Dosage Children >12 years and Adults: Oral: 1 g/day in 2-4 doses for 7-14 days

Dosing interval in renal impairment:
Cl_{cr} 20-50 mL/minute: 250 mg twice daily
Cl_{cr} <20 mL/minute: 250 mg/day

Patient Information May be taken with food to minimize upset stomach; avoid antacid use; drink fluid liberally; may cause dizziness; use caution when driving or performing other tasks requiring alertness

Nursing Implications Hold antacids for 3-4 hours after giving

Dosage Forms Capsule: 250 mg, 500 mg

♦ Cipro™ see Ciprofloxacin *on this page*

Ciprofloxacin (sip roe FLOKS a sin)

Related Information
Antimicrobial Drugs of Choice *on page 1404*
Desensitization Protocols *on page 1347*
Guidelines for the Prevention of Opportunistic Infections in Persons with HIV *on page 1388*
Treatment of Sexually Transmitted Diseases *on page 1429*
Tuberculosis Treatment Guidelines *on page 1432*

U.S. Brand Names Ciloxan™ Ophthalmic; Cipro™; Cipro™ I.V.

Synonyms Ciprofloxacin Hydrochloride

Therapeutic Category Antibiotic, Ophthalmic; Antibiotic, Quinolone

Use Treatment of documented or suspected infections of the lower respiratory tract, sinuses, skin and skin structure, bone/joints, and urinary tract including prostatitis, due to susceptible bacterial strains; especially indicated for *Pseudomonal* infections and those due to multidrug resistant gram-negative organisms, chronic bacterial prostatitis, infectious diarrhea, complicated gram-negative and anaerobic intra-abdominal infections (with metronidazole) due to *E. coli* (enteropathic strains), *B. fragilis, P. mirabilis, K. pneumoniae, P. aeruginosa, Campylobacter jejuni* or *Shigella*; approved for acute sinusitis caused by *H. influenzae* or *M. catarrhalis*; also used to treat typhoid fever due to *Salmonella typhi* (although eradication of the chronic typhoid carrier state has not been proven), osteomyelitis when parenteral therapy is not feasible, and sexually transmitted diseases such as uncomplicated cervical and urethral gonorrhea due to *Neisseria gonorrhoeae*; used ophthalmologically for superficial ocular infections (corneal ulcers, conjunctivitis) due to susceptible strains

Pregnancy Risk Factor C

Contraindications Hypersensitivity to ciprofloxacin, any component or other quinolones

Warnings/Precautions Not recommended in children <18 years of age; has caused transient arthropathy in children; CNS stimulation may occur (tremor, restlessness, confusion, and very rarely hallucinations or seizures); use with caution in patients with known or suspected CNS disorder; green discoloration of teeth in newborns has been reported; prolonged use may result in superinfection; may rarely cause inflamed or ruptured tendons (discontinue use immediately with signs of inflammation or tendon pain)

Adverse Reactions
1% to 10%:
Central nervous system: Headache, restlessness
Gastrointestinal: Nausea, diarrhea, vomiting, abdominal pain
Dermatologic: Rash
<1%: Dizziness, confusion, seizures, anemia, increased liver enzymes, tremor, arthralgia, ruptured tendons, acute renal failure

Overdosage/Toxicology
Symptoms of overdose include acute renal failure, seizures
GI decontamination and supportive care; not removed by peritoneal or hemodialysis

Drug Interactions CYP1A2 enzyme inhibitor
Decreased effect:
Enteral feedings may decrease plasma concentrations of ciprofloxacin probably by >30% inhibition of absorption. Ciprofloxacin should not be administered with enteral feedings. The feeding would need to be discontinued for 1-2 hours prior to and after ciprofloxacin administration. Nasogastric administration produces a greater loss of ciprofloxacin bioavailability than does nasoduodenal administration.
Aluminum/magnesium products, didanosine, and sucralfate may decrease absorption of ciprofloxacin by ≥90% if administered concurrently
RECOMMENDATION: Administer ciprofloxacin 2 hours before dose OR administer ciprofloxacin at least 4 hours and preferably 6 hours after the dose of these agents OR change to an H_2-antagonist or omeprazole
Calcium, iron, zinc, and multivitamins with minerals products may decrease absorption of ciprofloxacin significantly if administered concurrently
RECOMMENDATION: Administer ciprofloxacin 2 hours before dose OR administer ciprofloxacin at least 2 hours after the dose of these agents
Increased toxicity:
Caffeine and theophylline → CNS stimulation when concurrent with ciprofloxacin
Cyclosporine may increase serum creatinine levels

Stability Refrigeration and room temperature: Prepared bags: 14 days; Premixed bags: Manufacturer expiration dating

Mechanism of Action Inhibits DNA-gyrase in susceptible organisms; inhibits relaxation of supercoiled DNA and promotes breakage of double-stranded DNA

Pharmacodynamics/Kinetics
Absorption: Oral: Rapid from GI tract (~50% to 85%)
(Continued)

Ciprofloxacin *(Continued)*

Distribution: Crosses the placenta; appears in breast milk; distributes widely throughout body; tissue concentrations often exceed serum concentrations especially in the kidneys, gallbladder, liver, lungs, gynecological tissue, and prostatic tissue; CSF concentrations reach 10% with noninflamed meninges and 14% to 37% with inflamed meninges

Protein binding: 16% to 43%

Metabolism: Partially metabolized in the liver

Half-life: Children: 2.5 hours; Adults with normal renal function: 3-5 hours

Time to peak: Oral: T_{max}: 0.5-2 hours

Elimination: 30% to 50% excreted as unchanged drug in urine; 20% to 40% of dose excreted in feces primarily from biliary excretion

Usual Dosage

Children (see Warnings/Precautions):

Oral: 20-30 mg/kg/day in 2 divided doses; maximum: 1.5 g/day

Cystic fibrosis: 20-40 mg/kg/day divided every 12 hours

I.V.: 15-20 mg/kg/day divided every 12 hours

Cystic fibrosis: 15-30 mg/kg/day divided every 8-12 hours

Adults: Oral:

Urinary tract infection: 250-500 mg every 12 hours for 7-10 days, depending on severity of infection and susceptibility; (3 investigations (n=975) indicate the minimum effective dose for women with acute, uncomplicated urinary tract infection may be 100 mg twice daily for 3 days)

Lower respiratory tract, skin/skin structure infections: 500-750 mg twice daily for 7-14 days depending on severity and susceptibility

Bone/joint infections: 500-750 mg twice daily for 4-6 weeks, depending on severity and susceptibility

Infectious diarrhea: 500 mg every 12 hours for 5-7 days

Typhoid fever: 500 mg every 12 hours for 10 days

Urethral/cervical gonococcal infections: 250-500 mg as a single dose (CDC recommends concomitant doxycycline or azithromycin due to developing resistance; avoid use in Asian or Western Pacific travelers)

Disseminated gonococcal infection: 500 mg twice daily to complete 7 days of therapy (initial treatment with ceftriaxone 1 g I.M./I.V. daily for 24-48 hours after improvement begins)

Chancroid: 500 mg twice daily for 3 days

Mild to moderate sinusitis: 500 mg every 12 hours for 10 days

Adults: I.V.

Urinary tract infection: 200-400 mg every 12 hours for 7-10 days

Lower respiratory tract, skin/skin structure infection (mild to moderate): 400 mg every 12 hours for 7-14 days

Ophthalmic: Instill 1-2 drops in eye(s) every 2 hours while awake for 2 days and 1-2 drops every 4 hours while awake for the next 5 days

Dosing adjustment in renal impairment:

Cl_{cr} >30 mL/minute:

250 mg every 12 hours or

500 mg every 12 hours or

750 mg every 12 hours

Cl_{cr} <30 mL/minute:

500 mg every 24 hours or

750 mg every 24 hours

Dialysis: Only small amounts of ciprofloxacin are removed by hemo- or peritoneal dialysis (<10%); usual dose: 250-500 mg every 24 hours following dialysis

Continuous arteriovenous or venovenous hemodiafiltration (CAVH) effects: Administer 200-400 mg I.V. every 12 hours

Dietary Considerations

Food: Decreases rate, but not extent, of absorption. Drug may cause GI upset; take without regard to meals (manufacturer prefers that drug is taken 2 hours after meals)

Dairy products, oral multivitamins, and mineral supplements: Absorption decreased by divalent and trivalent cations. These cations bind to and form insoluble complexes with quinolones. Avoid taking these substrates with ciprofloxacin. The manufacturer states that the usual dietary intake of calcium has not been shown to interfere with ciprofloxacin absorption.

Caffeine: Possible exaggerated or prolonged effects of caffeine. Ciprofloxacin reduces total body clearance of caffeine. Patients consuming regular large quantities of caffeinated beverages may need to restrict caffeine intake if excessive cardiac or CNS stimulation occurs.

Administration

Oral: May administer with food to minimize GI upset; avoid antacid use; drink plenty of fluids to maintain proper hydration and urine output

Parenteral: Administer by slow I.V. infusion over 60 minutes to reduce the risk of venous irritation (burning, pain, erythema, and swelling); final concentration for administration should not exceed 2 mg/mL

Monitoring Parameters Patients receiving concurrent ciprofloxacin, theophylline, or cyclosporine should have serum levels monitored

Reference Range Therapeutic: 2.6-3 μg/mL; Toxic: >5 μg/mL

Patient Information May be taken with food to minimize upset stomach; avoid antacids containing magnesium or aluminum, or products containing zinc or iron within 4 hours before or 2 hours after dosing; may cause dizziness or drowsiness; drink fluid liberally; consult your physician immediately if inflammation or tendon pain develop

Nursing Implications Hold antacids for 2 hours after giving

Dosage Forms

Infusion, as hydrochloride, in D$_5$W: 400 mg (200 mL)

Infusion, as hydrochloride, in NS or D$_5$W: 200 mg (100 mL)

Injection, as hydrochloride: 200 mg (20 mL); 400 mg (40 mL)

Solution, ophthalmic, as hydrochloride: 3.5 mg/mL (2.5 mL, 5 mL)

Suspension, oral, as hydrochloride: 250 mg/5 mL x 100 mL, 500 mg/5 mL x 100 mL

Tablet, as hydrochloride: 100 mg, 250 mg, 500 mg, 750 mg

Ciprofloxacin and Hydrocortisone

(sip roe FLOKS a sin & hye droe KOR ti sone)

U.S. Brand Names Cipro® HC Otic

Therapeutic Category Antibiotic/Corticosteroid, Otic

Dosage Forms Suspension, otic: Ciprofloxacin hydrochloride 0.2% and hydrocortisone 1%

♦ **Ciprofloxacin Hydrochloride** *see Ciprofloxacin on page 263*

♦ **Cipro® HC Otic** *see Ciprofloxacin and Hydrocortisone on this page*

♦ **Cipro™ I.V.** *see Ciprofloxacin on page 263*

Cisapride (SIS a pride)

U.S. Brand Names Propulsid®

Canadian Brand Names Prepulsid®

Therapeutic Category Cholinergic Agent; Gastroprokinetic Agent

Use Treatment of nocturnal symptoms of gastroesophageal reflux disease (GERD), also demonstrated effectiveness for gastroparesis, refractory constipation, and nonulcer dyspepsia

Pregnancy Risk Factor C

Contraindications

Hypersensitivity to cisapride or any of its components; GI hemorrhage, mechanical obstruction, GI perforation, or other situations when GI motility stimulation is dangerous

Serious cardiac arrhythmias including ventricular tachycardia, ventricular fibrillation, torsade de pointes, and Q-T prolongation have been reported in patients taking cisapride with other drugs that inhibit CYP3A4. Some of these events have been fatal. Concomitant oral or intravenous administration of the following drugs with cisapride may lead to elevated cisapride blood levels and is contraindicated:

Antibiotics: Oral or I.V. erythromycin, clarithromycin, troleandomycin

Antidepressants: Nefazodone

Antifungals: Oral or I.V. fluconazole, itraconazole, miconazole, oral ketoconazole

Protease inhibitors: Indinavir, ritonavir

Cisapride is also contraindicated for patients with history of prolonged electrocardiographic Q-T intervals, renal failure, history of ventricular arrhythmias, ischemic heart disease, and congestive heart failure; uncorrected electrolyte disorders (hypokalemia, hypomagnesemia); respiratory failure; and concomitant medications known to prolong the Q-T interval and increase the risk of arrhythmia, such as certain antiarrhythmics, certain antipsychotics, certain antidepressants, astemizole, bepridil, sparfloxacin, and terodiline. The preceding lists of drugs are not comprehensive. Cisapride should not be used in patients with uncorrected hypokalemia or hypomagnesemia or who might experience rapid reduction of plasma potassium such as those administered potassium-wasting diuretics and/or insulin in acute settings.

Warnings/Precautions Serious cardiac arrhythmias including ventricular tachycardia, ventricular fibrillation, torsade de pointes, and QT prolongation have been reported in patients taking this drug. Many of these patients also took drugs expected to increase cisapride blood levels by inhibiting the cytochrome P-450 3A4 enzymes that metabolize cisapride. These drugs include clarithromycin, erythromycin, troleandomycin, nefazodone, fluconazole, itraconazole, ketoconazole, indinavir and ritonavir. Some of these events have been fatal. Cisapride is contraindicated in patients taking any of these drugs. **QT prolongation, torsade de pointes (sometimes with syncope), cardiac arrest and sudden death have been reported in patients taking cisapride without the above-mentioned contraindicated drugs.** Most patients had disorders that may have predisposed them to arrhythmias with cisapride. Cisapride is contraindicated for those patients with: history of prolonged electrocardiographic Q-T intervals; renal failure; history of ventricular arrhythmias; ischemic heart disease, and congestive heart failure; uncorrected electrolyte disorders (hypokalemia, hypomagnesemia); respiratory failure; and concomitant medications known to prolong the Q-T interval and increase the risk of arrhythmia, such as certain antiarrhythmics, including those of Class 1A (such as quinidine and procainamide) and Class III (such as sotalol); tricyclic antidepressants (such as amitriptyline); certain tetracyclic antidepressants (such as maprotiline); certain antipsychotic medications (such as certain phenothiazines and sertindole); astemizole, bepridil, sparfloxacin and terodiline. (The preceding lists of drugs are not comprehensive.) Recommended doses of cisapride should not be exceeded.

Potential benefits should be weighed against risks prior administration of cisapride to patients who have or may develop prolongation of cardiac conduction intervals, particularly QT$_c$. These include patients with conditions that could predispose them to the development of serious arrhythmias, such as multiple organ failure, COPD, apnea and advanced cancer. Cisapride should not be used in patients with uncorrected

(Continued)

Cisapride *(Continued)*

hypokalemia or hypomagnesemia, such as those with severe dehydration, vomiting or malnutrition, or those taking potassium-wasting diuretics. Cisapride should not be used in patients who might experience rapid reduction of plasma potassium, such as those administered potassium-wasting diuretics and/or insulin in acute settings.

Adverse Reactions

>5%:

Central nervous system: Headache

Dermatologic: Rash

Gastrointestinal: Diarrhea, GI cramping, dyspepsia, flatulence, nausea, xerostomia

Respiratory: Rhinitis

<5%:

Cardiovascular: Tachycardia

Central nervous system: Extrapyramidal effects, somnolence, fatigue, seizures, insomnia, anxiety

Hematologic: Thrombocytopenia, increased LFTs, pancytopenia, leukopenia, granulocytopenia, aplastic anemia

Respiratory: Sinusitis, coughing, upper respiratory tract infection, increased incidence of viral infection

Drug Interactions CYP3A3/4 enzyme substrate

Decreased effect: Atropine, digoxin

Increased toxicity: Warfarin, diazepam increased levels, cimetidine, and ranitidine, CNS depressants; diltiazem, erythromycin and other macrolides and the azole-derivative antifungal agents such as ketoconazole, miconazole, itraconazole, and fluconazole have increased cisapride levels, which has been associated with prolonged Q-T intervals and the potential for torsade de pointes

Mechanism of Action Enhances the release of acetylcholine at the myenteric plexus. *In vitro* studies have shown cisapride to have serotonin-4 receptor agonistic properties which may increase gastrointestinal motility and cardiac rate; increases lower esophageal sphincter pressure and lower esophageal peristalsis; accelerates gastric emptying of both liquids and solids.

Pharmacodynamics/Kinetics

Onset of effect: 0.5-1 hour

Bioavailability: 35% to 40%

Protein binding: 97.5% to 98%

Metabolism: Extensively to norcisapride, which is eliminated in urine and feces

Half-life: 6-12 hours

Elimination: <10% of dose excreted into feces and urine

Usual Dosage Oral:

Children: 0.15-0.3 mg/kg/dose 3-4 times/day; maximum: 10 mg/dose

Adults: Initial: 10 mg 4 times/day at least 15 minutes before meals and at bedtime; in some patients the dosage will need to be increased to 20 mg to obtain a satisfactory result

Additional Information Safety and effectiveness in children have not been established

Dosage Forms

Suspension, oral (cherry cream flavor): 1 mg/mL (450 mL)

Tablet, scored: 10 mg, 20 mg

Cisatracurium *(sis a tra KYOO ree um)*

Related Information

Neuromuscular Blocking Agents Comparison *on page 1331*

U.S. Brand Names Nimbex®

Synonyms Cisatracurium Besylate

Therapeutic Category Neuromuscular Blocker Agent, Nondepolarizing; Skeletal Muscle Relaxant

Use Drug for neuromuscular blockade in patients with renal and/or hepatic failure; eases endotracheal intubation as an adjunct to general anesthesia and relaxes skeletal muscle during surgery or mechanical ventilation; does not relieve pain

Pregnancy Risk Factor C

Contraindications Hypersensitivity to cisatracurium besylate or any component

Warnings/Precautions Not recommended for rapid sequence intubation; may produce profound effects in patients with neuromuscular disorders (myasthenia gravis); patients with severe burns may develop resistance; maintenance of an adequate airway and respiratory support is critical

Adverse Reactions <1%: Effects are minimal and transient, bradycardia and hypotension, flushing, rash, bronchospasm

Overdosage/Toxicology

Symptoms of overdose include respiratory depression, cardiovascular collapse

Neostigmine 1-3 mg slow I.V. push in adults (0.5 mg in children) antagonizes the neuromuscular blockade, and should be administered with or immediately after atropine 1-1.5 mg I.V. push (adults). This may be especially useful in the presence of bradycardia.

Drug Interactions

Prolonged neuromuscular blockade:

Inhaled anesthetics:

Halothane has only a marginal effect, enflurane and isoflurane increase the potency and prolong duration of neuromuscular blockade induced by cisatracurium

Dosage should be reduced by 30% to 40% in patients receiving isoflurane or enflurane

Local anesthetics

Lithium

Magnesium salts

Antiarrhythmics (eg, quinidine or procainamide)

Antibiotics (eg, aminoglycosides, tetracyclines, vancomycin, clindamycin)

Resistance to neuromuscular blockade: Chronic phenytoin or carbamazepine

Stability Refrigerate intact vials at 2°C to 8°C/36°F to 46°F; use vials within 21 days upon removal from the refrigerator to room temperature (25°C to 77°F). Dilutions of 0.1-0.2 mg/mL in 0.9% sodium chloride or dextrose 5% in water are stable for up to 24 hours at room temperature. **Incompatible** with sodium bicarbonate, ketorolac, propofol; **compatible** with alfentanil, droperidol, fentanyl, midazolam, and sufentanil.

Mechanism of Action Blocks neural transmission at the myoneural junction by binding with cholinergic receptor sites

Pharmacodynamics/Kinetics

Onset of action: I.V.: 2-3 minutes

Peak effect: Within 3-5 minutes

Duration: Recovery begins in 20-35 minutes when anesthesia is balanced; recovery is attained in 90% of patients in 25-93 minutes

Metabolism: Some metabolites are active; undergoes rapid nonenzymatic degradation in the bloodstream, additional metabolism occurs via ester hydrolysis

Half-life: 22 minutes

Usual Dosage I.V. (not to be used I.M.):

Operating room administration:

Children 2-12 years: Intubating doses: 0.1 mg over 5-15 seconds during either halothane or opioid anesthesia. (**Note:** When given during stable opioid nitrous oxide/oxygen anesthesia, 0.1 mg/kg produces maximum neuromuscular block in an average of 2.8 minutes and clinically effective block for 28 minutes.)

Adults: Intubating doses: 0.15-0.2 mg/kg as components of propofol/nitrous oxide/oxygen induction-intubation technique. (**Note:** May produce generally good or excellent conditions for tracheal intubation in 1.5-2 minutes with clinically effective duration of action during propofol anesthesia of 55-61 minutes.)

Children ≥2 years and Adults: Continuous infusion: After an initial bolus, a diluted solution can be given by continuous infusion for maintenance of neuromuscular blockade during extended surgery; adjust the rate of administration according to the patient's response as determined by peripheral nerve stimulation. An initial infusion rate of 3 mcg/kg/minute may be required to rapidly counteract the spontaneous recovery of neuromuscular function; thereafter, a rate of 1-2 mcg/kg/minute should be adequate to maintain continuous neuromuscular block in the 89% to 99% range in most pediatric and adult patients. Consider reduction of the infusion rate by 30% to 40% when administering during stable isoflurane or enflurane anesthesia. Spontaneous recovery from neuromuscular blockade following discontinuation of infusion of cisatracurium may be expected to proceed at a rate comparable to that following single bolus administration.

Intensive care unit administration: Follow the principles for infusion in the operating rooms. An infusion rate of ~3 mcg/kg/minute should provide adequate neuromuscular blockade in adult patients. Following recovery from neuromuscular block, readministration of a bolus dose may be necessary to quickly re-establish neuromuscular block prior to reinstituting the infusion; dosage ranges of 0.5-10 mcg/kg/minute have been reported.

Dosing adjustment in renal impairment: Because slower times to onset of complete neuromuscular block were observed in renal dysfunction patients, extending the interval between the administration of cisatracurium and intubation attempt may be required to achieve adequate intubation conditions

Administration Administer I.V. only; the use of a peripheral nerve stimulator will permit the most advantageous use of cisatracurium, minimize the possibility of overdosage or underdosage and assist in the evaluation of recovery

Monitoring Parameters Vital signs (heart rate, blood pressure, respiratory rate)

Patient Information May be difficult to talk because of head and neck muscle blockade

Additional Information Neuromuscular blocking potency is 3 times that of atracurium; maximum block is up to 2 minutes longer than for equipotent doses of atracurium

Dosage Forms Injection, as besylate: 2 mg/mL (5 mL, 10 mL); 10 mg/mL (20 mL)

♦ **Cisatracurium Besylate** see Cisatracurium on previous page

Cisplatin (SIS pla tin)

Related Information

Cancer Chemotherapy Regimens on page 1263
Toxicities of Chemotherapeutic Agents on page 1288

U.S. Brand Names Platinol®; Platinol®-AQ

Synonyms CDDP

Therapeutic Category Antineoplastic Agent, Alkylating Agent; Antineoplastic Agent, Vesicant; Vesicant

Use Treatment of head and neck, breast, testicular, and ovarian cancer; Hodgkin's and non-Hodgkin's lymphoma; neuroblastoma; sarcomas; bladder, gastric, lung, esophageal, cervical, and prostate cancer; myeloma, melanoma, mesothelioma, small cell lung cancer, and osteosarcoma

Pregnancy Risk Factor D

(Continued)

Cisplatin *(Continued)*

Contraindications Hypersensitivity to cisplatin or any other platinum-containing compounds or any component, anaphylactic-like reactions have been reported; pre-existing renal insufficiency, myelosuppression, hearing impairment

Warnings/Precautions The U.S. Food and Drug Administration (FDA) currently recommends that procedures for proper handling and disposal of antineoplastic agents be considered. All patients should receive adequate hydration prior to and for 24 hours after cisplatin administration, with or without mannitol and/or furosemide, to ensure good urine output and decrease the chance of nephrotoxicity; reduce dosage in renal impairment. Cumulative renal toxicity may be severe; dose-related toxicities include myelosuppression, nausea, and vomiting; cumulative ototoxicity, especially pronounced in children, is manifested by tinnitus or loss of high frequency hearing and occasionally, deafness. **Serum magnesium, as well as other electrolytes, should be monitored both before and within 48 hours after cisplatin therapy.** Patients who are magnesium depleted should receive replacement therapy before the cisplatin is administered.

Adverse Reactions

>10%:

Endocrine & metabolic: Hyperuricemia

Gastrointestinal: Cisplatin is one of the most emetogenic agents used in cancer chemotherapy; nausea and vomiting occur in 76% to 100% of patients and is dose related. **Prophylactic antiemetics should always be prescribed**; nausea and vomiting may last up to 1 week after therapy. Antiemetics should be included in discharge medications.

Emetic potential:

<50 mg/m^2: Moderately high (60% to 90%)

≥50 mg/m^2: High (>90%)

Time course of nausea/vomiting: Onset: 1-4 hours; Duration: 12-96 hours

Hematologic: Myelosuppressive: Mild with moderate doses, mild to moderate with high-dose therapy

WBC: Mild

Platelets: Mild

Onset (days): 10

Nadir (days): 14-23

Recovery (days): 21-39

Anemia: Can be chronic, when high dose cisplatin is given for multiple cycles which is responsive to epoetin alfa. Cisplatin has also been associated with Coombs' positive hemolytic anemia.

Neuromuscular & skeletal: Neurotoxicity: Peripheral neuropathy is dose- and duration-dependent. The mechanism is through axonal degeneration with subsequent damage to the long sensory nerves. Toxicity can first be noted at doses of 200 mg/m^2, with measurable toxicity at doses >350 mg/m^2. This process is irreversible and progressive with continued use. Ototoxicity occurs in 10% to 30%, and is manifested as high frequency hearing loss. Baseline audiography should be performed.

Otic: Ototoxicity (especially pronounced in children)

Renal: Nephrotoxicity: Related to elimination, protein binding, and uptake of cisplatin; two types of nephrotoxicity: acute renal failure and chronic renal insufficiency

Acute renal failure and azotemia is a dose-dependent process and can be minimized with proper administration and prophylaxis. Damage to the proximal tubules by the aquation products of cisplatin is suspected to cause the toxicity. Proper preplatinum hydration with a chloride containing intravenous fluid is believed to minimize the production of the more nephrotoxic aqua products. It is manifested as increased BUN and creatinine, oliguria, protein wasting, and potassium, calcium, and magnesium wasting.

Chronic renal dysfunction can develop in patients receiving multiple courses of cisplatin. This occurs with slow release of the platinum ion from tissues, which then accumulates in the distal tubules. Manifestations of this toxicity are varied, and can include sodium and water wasting, nephropathy, decreased Cl_{cr}, and magnesium wasting.

Recommendations for minimizing nephrotoxicity include:

Prepare cisplatin in saline-containing vehicles

Vigorous hydration with saline-containing intravenous fluids (125-150 mL/hour) before, during, and after cisplatin administration

Simultaneous administration of either mannitol or furosemide

Infuse dose over 24 hours

Pretreatment with amifostine

Avoid other nephrotoxic agents (aminoglycosides, amphotericin, etc)

Miscellaneous: Anaphylactic reaction occurs within minutes after administration and can be controlled with epinephrine, antihistamines, and steroids

1% to 10%:

Extravasation: May cause thrombophlebitis and tissue damage if infiltrated; may use sodium thiosulfate as antidote, but consult UCH extravasation policy for guidelines

Irritant chemotherapy

<1%: Bradycardia, arrhythmias, mild alopecia, SIADH, hypomagnesemia, hypocalcemia, hypokalemia, hypophosphatemia, mouth sores, elevated liver enzymes, phlebitis, optic neuritis, blurred vision, papilledema

Overdosage/Toxicology

Symptoms of overdose include severe myelosuppression, intractable nausea and vomiting, kidney and liver failure, deafness, ocular toxicity, and neuritis

No known antidote; hemodialysis appears to have little effect; treatment is supportive therapy

Drug Interactions

Decreased toxicity: Sodium thiosulfate theoretically inactivates drug systemically; has been used clinically to reduce systemic toxicity with intraperitoneal administration of cisplatin

Increased toxicity:

Ethacrynic acid has resulted in severe ototoxicity in animals

Delayed bleomycin elimination with decreased glomerular filtration rate

Stability

Store intact vials at room temperature (15°C to 25°C/59°F to 77°F); protect from light

Do not refrigerate solution - a precipitate may form. If inadvertently refrigerated, the precipitate will slowly dissolve within hours to days, when placed at room temperature. The precipitate may be dissolved without loss of potency by warming solution to 37°C/98.6°F.

Multidose (preservative-free) vials: After initial entry into the vial, solution is stable for 28 days protected from light or for at least 7 days under fluorescent room light at room temperature

Further dilution **stability is dependent on the chloride ion concentration** and should be mixed in solutions of NS (at least 0.3% NaCl). Further dilution in NS, D_5/0.45% NaCl or D_5/NS to a concentration of 0.05-2 mg/mL are stable for 72 hours at 4°C to 25°C in combination with mannitol; may administer 12.5-50 g mannitol/L

Do **NOT** administer with D_5W or other chloride-lacking solutions because nephrotoxicity increases in solutions which do not contain a chloride ion.

Aluminum-containing I.V. infusion sets and needles should NOT be used due to binding with the platinum

Incompatible with sodium bicarbonate

Standard I.V. dilution: Dose/250-1000 mL NS, D_5/NS or D_5/0.45% NaCl

Stable for 72 hours at 4°C to 25°C (in combination with mannitol)

Mechanism of Action

Inhibits DNA synthesis by the formation of DNA cross-links; denatures the double helix; covalently binds to DNA bases and disrupts DNA function; may also bind to proteins; the *cis*-isomer is 14 times more cytotoxic than the *trans*-isomer; both forms cross-link DNA but cis-platinum is less easily recognized by cell enzymes and, therefore, not repaired. Cisplatin can also bind two adjacent guanines on the same strand of DNA producing intrastrand cross-linking and breakage.

Pharmacodynamics/Kinetics

Distribution: I.V.: Rapidly distributes into tissue; found in high concentrations in the kidneys, liver, ovaries, uterus, and lungs

Protein binding: >90%

Half-life: Initial: 20-30 minutes; Beta: 60 minutes; Terminal: ~24 hours; Secondary half-life: 44-73 hours

Metabolism: Undergoes nonenzymatic metabolism; the drug is inactivated (in both the cell and the bloodstream) by sulfhydryl groups; cisplatin covalently binds to glutathione and to thiosulfate

Elimination: >90% excreted in the urine and 10% in bile

Usual Dosage

I.V. (refer to individual protocols):

An estimated Cl_{cr} should be on all cisplatin chemotherapy orders along with other patient parameters (ie, patient's height, weight, and body surface area). Pharmacy and nursing staff should check the Cl_{cr} on the order and determine the appropriateness of cisplatin dosing.

The manufacturer recommends that subsequent cycles should only be given when serum creatinine <1.5 mg%, WBC ≥4,000/mm^3, platelets ≥ 100,000/mm^3, and BUN <25.

It is recommended that a 24-hour urine creatinine clearance be checked prior to a patient's first dose of cisplatin and periodically thereafter (ie, after every 2-3 cycles of cisplatin)

Pretreatment hydration with 1-2 L of chloride-containing fluid is recommended prior to cisplatin administration; adequate hydration and urinary output (>100 mL/hour) should be maintained for 24 hours after administration

If the dose prescribed is a reduced dose, then this should be indicated on the chemotherapy order

Children: Various dosage schedules range from 30-100 mg/m^2 once every 2-3 weeks; may also dose similar to adult dosing

Recurrent brain tumors: 60 mg/m^2 once daily for 2 consecutive days every 3-4 weeks

Adults:

Advanced bladder cancer: 50-70 mg/m^2 every 3-4 weeks

Head and neck cancer: 100-120 mg/m^2 every 3-4 weeks

Testicular cancer: 10-20 mg/m^2/day for 5 days repeated every 3-4 weeks

Metastatic ovarian cancer: 75-100 mg/m^2 every 3 weeks

Intraperitoneal: cisplatin has been administered intraperitoneal with systemic sodium thiosulfate for ovarian cancer; doses up to 90-270 mg/m^2 have been administered and retained for 4 hours before draining

Dosing adjustment in renal impairment:

Cl_{cr} 10-50 mL/minute: Administer 50% of normal dose

Cl_{cr} <10 mL/minute: Do not administer

Hemodialysis: Partially cleared by hemodialysis; administer dose posthemodialysis

CAPD effects: Unknown

CAVH effects: Unknown

(Continued)

Cisplatin *(Continued)*

Administration

I.V.: Rate of administration has varied from a 15- to 120-minute infusion, 1 mg/minute infusion, 6- to 8-hour infusion, 24-hour infusion, or per protocol

Maximum rate of infusion of 1 mg/minute in patients with CHF

Pretreatment hydration with 1-2 Liters of fluid is recommended prior to cisplatin administration; adequate hydration and urinary output (>100 mL/hour) should be maintained for 24 hours after administration

Needles, syringes, catheters, or I.V. administration sets that contain aluminum parts should not be used for administration of drug

Monitoring Parameters Renal function tests (serum creatinine, BUN, Cl$_{cr}$), electrolytes (particularly magnesium, calcium, potassium); hearing test, neurologic exam (with high dose), liver function tests periodically, CBC with differential and platelet count; urine output, urinalysis

Patient Information Contraceptive measures are recommended during therapy. Drink plenty of fluids to maintain urine output, be prepared for severe nausea and vomiting following drug administration which can be delayed up to 48 hours; notify physician of numbness or tingling in extremities or hearing loss

Nursing Implications Perform pretreatment hydration (see Usual Dosage); monitor for possible anaphylactoid reaction; monitor renal, hematologic, otic, and neurologic function frequently

Management of extravasation:

Large extravasations (>20 mL) of concentrated solutions (>0.5 mg/mL) produce tissue necrosis. **Treatment is not recommended unless a large amount of highly concentrated solution is extravasated.**

Mix 4 mL of 10% sodium thiosulfate with 6 mL sterile water for injection: Inject 1-4 mL through existing I.V. line cannula. Administer 1 mL for each mL extravasated; inject S.C. if needle is removed.

Additional Information

Sodium content: 9 mg/mL (equivalent to 0.9% sodium chloride solution)

Osmolality of Platinol®-AQ = 285-286 mOsm

Dosage Forms

Injection, aqueous: 1 mg/mL (50 mL, 100 mL)

Powder for injection: 10 mg, 50 mg

♦ **13-*cis*-Retinoic Acid** *see* Isotretinoin *on page 640*

Citalopram *(sye TAL oh pram)*

Related Information

Antidepressant Agents Comparison *on page 1301*

U.S. Brand Names Celexa®

Synonyms Nitalapram

Therapeutic Category Antidepressant, Miscellaneous

Use Treatment of depression; currently being evaluated for use in the treatment of dementia, smoking cessation, alcohol abuse, obsessive-compulsive disorder, and diabetic neuropathy

Pregnancy Risk Factor C

Pregnancy/Breast-Feeding Implications Animal reproductive studies have revealed adverse effects on fetal and postnatal development (at doses higher than human therapeutic doses). Should be used in pregnancy only if potential benefit justifies potential risk. Citalopram is excreted in human milk; a decision should be made whether to continue or discontinue nursing or discontinue the drug.

Contraindications Known hypersensitivity to citalopram; hypersensitivity or other adverse sequelae during therapy with other SSRIs; concomitant use with MAO inhibitors or within 2 weeks of discontinuing MAO inhibitors. Potential for severe reaction when used with MAO inhibitors - serotonin syndrome (hyperthermia, muscular rigidity, mental status changes/agitation, autonomic instability) may occur, possibly resulting in death. Do not use citalopram and MAO inhibitors within 14 days of each other.

Warnings/Precautions As with all antidepressants, use with caution in patients with a history of mania (may activate hypomania/mania). Use with caution in patients with a history of seizures and patients at high risk of suicide. Has potential to impair cognitive/motor performance - should use caution operating hazardous machinery. Elderly and patients with hepatic insufficiency should receive lower dosages. Use with caution in renal insufficiency and other concomitant illness (due to limited drug experience). May cause hyponatremia/SIADH.

Adverse Reactions

>10%:

Central nervous system: Somnolence (18%), insomnia (15%)

Gastrointestinal: Nausea (21%), dry mouth (20%)

Miscellaneous: Increased diaphoresis (11%)

1% to 10%:

Central nervous system: Fatigue (5%), anxiety (4%), agitation (3%), yawning (2%), fever (2%)

Endocrine/metabolic: Dysmenorrhea (3%), decreased libido (males 3.8%, females 1.3%), anorgasmia (females 1.1%)

Gastrointestinal: Diarrhea (8%), dyspepsia (5%), vomiting (4%), anorexia (4%), abdominal pain (3%)

Genitourinary: Ejaculation disorder (6%), impotence (3%)

Neuromuscular/skeletal: Tremor (8%), arthralgia (2%), myalgia (2%)
Respiratory: Upper respiratory tract infection (5%), rhinitis (5%), sinusitis (3%)

The following events had an incidence >2% in clinical trials but the incidence on placebo was greater than or equal to the incidence on citalopram: Headache, asthenia, dizziness, constipation, palpitation, abnormal vision, sleep disorder, nervousness, pharyngitis, micturition disorder, back pain

The following treatment emergent effects were also noted at a frequency ≥1% in premarketing trials: Migraine, impaired concentration, confusion, hypotension, postural hypotension, tachycardia, suicide attempt, rash, pruritus, weight gain or loss, abnormal taste, increased appetite, amenorrhea, paresthesia, abnormal accommodation, cough

Several cases of hyponatremia and SIADH have been reported with citalopram. As with other antidepressants, hypomania/mania may be activated in a small proportion of patients with major affective disorders.

Overdosage/Toxicology Signs of overdose include: Dizziness, nausea, vomiting, sweating, tremor, somnolence, sinus tachycardia. Rare symptoms have included amnesia, confusion, coma, seizures, hyperventilation, EKG changes (including QT_c prolongation, ventricular arrhythmia, and torsade de pointes); management is supportive.

Drug Interactions Extensive metabolism via CYP450 isoenzymes 3A4 and 2C19. Decreases in citalopram clearance are possible when used with inhibitors of these isoenzymes (including ketoconazole, itraconazole, fluconazole, and erythromycin). Citalopram is also a weak inhibitor of CYP450 isoenzymes 1A2, 2D6, and 2C19.

Caution when use with other CNS active agents. See Contraindications and Warnings regarding the use of MAO inhibitors. Cimetidine increases AUC by 43%, lithium may enhance serotonergic effects, and carbamazepine may increase clearance of citalopram via enzyme induction. Citalopram may increase the serum concentration of metoprolol. Serum concentrations of imipramine metabolite (desipramine) may be increased.

Stability Store below 25°C

Mechanism of Action Inhibits CNS neuronal reuptake of serotonin, which enhances serotonergic activity. Activity as an antidepressant has been presumed to be associated with this effect. Has limited or no affinity for histamine, dopamine, acetylcholine (muscarinic), GABA, benzodiazepine, and adrenergic (alpha- and beta-) receptors. Antagonism of these receptors is believed to be associated with sedative, anticholinergic and cardiovascular adverse effects of tricyclic antidepressants.

Pharmacodynamics/Kinetics
Distribution: V_d: 12 L/kg
Protein binding, plasma: ~80%
Metabolism: Extensive hepatic metabolism, including cytochrome P-450 oxidase system, to N-demethylated, N-oxide, and deaminated metabolites
Bioavailability: 80%
Half-life: 24-48 hours; average 35 hours (doubled in patients with hepatic impairment)
Time to peak serum concentration: 1-6 hours, average within 4 hours
Elimination: 10% recovered unchanged in urine; systemic clearance: 330 mL/minute (20% renal)

Clearance was decreased, while AUC and half-life were significantly increased in elderly patients and in patients with hepatic impairment. Mild to moderate renal impairment may reduce clearance of citalopram (17% reduction noted in trials). No pharmacokinetic information is available concerning patients with severe renal impairment.

Usual Dosage Oral: 20 mg once daily, in the morning or evening. Dose is generally increased to 40 mg once daily. Doses should be increased by 20 mg at intervals of not less than 1 week. Doses >40 mg/day are not generally recommended, although some patients may respond to doses up to 60 mg/day.

Elderly or hepatically impaired patients: Initial dose of 20 mg is recommended; increase dose to 40 mg/day only in nonresponders
Maintenance: Generally, patients are maintained on the dose required for acute stabilization. If side effects are bothersome, dose reduction by 20 mg/day may be considered.

Dosing adjustment in renal impairment: None necessary in mild to moderate renal impairment; best avoided in severely impaired renal function (Cl_{cr} <20 mL/minute)

Monitoring Parameters Monitor patient periodically for symptom resolution, heart rate, blood pressure, liver function tests, and CBC with continued therapy

Patient Information Citalopram does not impair psychomotor performance, nevertheless, patients receiving treatment may have an impaired ability to drive or operate machinery; they should be warned of this possibility and advised to avoid these tasks if so affected

Dosage Forms Tablet, as hydrobromide: 20 mg, 40 mg, 60 mg

♦ **Citrate of Magnesia** see Magnesium Citrate on page 704
♦ **Citrovorum Factor** see Leucovorin on page 666
♦ **CI-719** see Gemfibrozil on page 532
♦ **Cla** see Clarithromycin on page 273

Cladribine (KLA dri been)

Related Information
Cancer Chemotherapy Regimens on page 1263
Toxicities of Chemotherapeutic Agents on page 1288
U.S. Brand Names Leustatin™
Synonyms 2-CdA; 2-Chlorodeoxyadenosine
Therapeutic Category Antineoplastic Agent, Antimetabolite (Purine)
(Continued)

Cladribine *(Continued)*

Use Treatment of hairy cell leukemia (HCL) and chronic lymphocytic leukemias

Pregnancy Risk Factor D

Contraindications Patients with a prior history of hypersensitivity to cladribine

Warnings/Precautions The U.S. Food and Drug Administration (FDA) currently recommends that procedures for proper handling and disposal of antineoplastic agents be considered. Because of its myelosuppressive properties, cladribine should be used with caution in patients with pre-existing hematologic or immunologic abnormalities; prophylactic administration of allopurinol should be considered in patients receiving cladribine because of the potential for hyperuricemia secondary to tumor lysis; appropriate antibiotic therapy should be administered promptly in patients exhibiting signs and symptoms of neutropenia and infection.

Adverse Reactions

>10%:

Bone marrow suppression: Commonly observed in patients treated with cladribine, especially at high doses; at the initiation of treatment, however, most patients in clinical studies had hematologic impairment as a result of HCL. During the first 2 weeks after treatment initiation, mean platelet counts decline and subsequently increased with normalization of mean counts by day 12. Absolute neutrophil counts and hemoglobin declined and subsequently increased with normalization of mean counts by week 5 and week 6. CD4 counts nadir at approximately 270, 4-6 months after treatments. Mean CD4 counts after 15 months were <500/mm^3. Patients should be considered immunosuppressed for up to one year after cladribine therapy.

Central nervous system: Fatigue, headache

Fever: Temperature ≥101°F has been associated with the use of cladribine in approximately 66% of patients in the first month of therapy. Although 69% of patients developed fevers, <33% of febrile events were associated with documented infection.

Dermatologic: Rash

Gastrointestinal: Nausea and vomiting are not severe with cladribine at any dose level. Most cases of nausea were mild, not accompanied by vomiting and did not require treatment with antiemetics. In patients requiring antiemetics, nausea was easily controlled most often by chlorpromazine.

Local: Injection site reactions

1% to 10%:

Cardiovascular: Edema, tachycardia

Central nervous system: Dizziness, insomnia, pain, chills, malaise

Dermatologic: Pruritus, erythema

Gastrointestinal: Constipation, abdominal pain

Neuromuscular & skeletal: Myalgia, arthralgia, weakness

Miscellaneous: Diaphoresis, trunk pain

Stability

Store intact vials under refrigeration (2°C to 8°C); stable for 7 days at room temperature Further dilution in 100-1000 mL NS is stable for 72 hours. Stable in PVC containers for 24 hours at room temperature and 7 days in Pharmacia Deltec® medication cassettes at room temperature. For 7-day infusion, dilute with bacteriostatic NS and filter through 0.22 μ filter prior to addition into infusion reservoir.

Incompatible with D$_5$W

Standard I.V. 24-hour infusion dilution:

24-hour dose/500 mL NS

24-hour infusion solution is stable for 24 hours at room temperature

Standard I.V. 7-day infusion dilution:

7-day dose/q.s. to 100 mL with bacteriostatic NS

7-day infusion solution is stable for 7 days at room temperature

Mechanism of Action A purine nucleoside analogue; prodrug which is activated via phosphorylation by deoxycytidine kinase to a 5'-triphosphate derivative. This active form incorporates into susceptible cells and into DNA to result in the breakage of DNA strand and shutdown of DNA synthesis. This also results in a depletion of nicotinamide adenine dinucleotide and adenosine triphosphate (ATP). The induction of strand breaks results in a drop in the cofactor nicotinamide adenine dinucleotide and disruption of cell metabolism. ATP is depleted to deprive cells of an important source of energy. Cladribine effectively kills resting as well as dividing cells.

Pharmacodynamics/Kinetics

Distribution: V$_d$: 4.52±2.82 L/kg

Protein binding: 20% to plasma proteins

Half-life: Biphasic: Alpha: 25 minutes; Beta: 6.7 hours; Terminal, mean (normal renal function): 5.4 hours

Elimination: Mean: 978±422 mL/hour/kg; estimated systemic clearance: 640 mL/hour/kg

Usual Dosage I.V.:

Children:

Acute leukemia: The safety and effectiveness of cladribine in children have not been established; in a phase I study involving patients 1-21 years of age with relapsed acute leukemia, cladribine was administered by CIV at doses ranging from 3-10.7 mg/m^2/day for 5 days (0.5-2 times the dose recommended in HCL). Investigators reported beneficial responses in this study; the dose-limiting toxicity was severe myelosuppression with profound neutropenia and thrombocytopenia.

CIV: 15-18 mg/m^2/day for 5 days

Adults:
Hairy cell leukemia:
CIV: 0.09-0.1 mg/kg/day continuous infusion for 7 consecutive days
CIV: 4 mg/m^2/day for 7 days
Non-Hodgkin's lymphoma: CIV: 0.1 mg/kg/day for 7 days
Administration Single daily infusion: Administer diluted in an infusion bag containing 500 mL of 0.9% sodium chloride and repeated for a total of 7 consecutive days

7-day infusion: Prepare with bacteriostatic 0.9% sodium chloride. Both cladribine and diluent should be passed through a sterile 0.22 micron hydrophilic filter as it is being introduced into the infusion reservoir. The calculated dose of cladribine (7 days x 0.09 mg/kg) should first be added to the infusion reservoir then the bacteriostatic 0.9% sodium chloride should be added to the reservoir to obtain a total volume of 100 mL.

Dosage Forms Injection, preservative free: 1 mg/mL (10 mL)

♦ **Claforan**® *see Cefotaxime on page 213*
♦ **Clamurid**® *see Carbamide Peroxide on page 190*
♦ **Claripex**® *see Clofibrate on page 279*

Clarithromycin (kla RITH roe mye sin)
Related Information
Antimicrobial Drugs of Choice *on page 1404*
Community-Acquired Pneumonia in Adults *on page 1419*
Guidelines for the Prevention of Opportunistic Infections in Persons with HIV *on page 1388*
Helicobacter pylori Treatment *on page 1473*
Prevention of Bacterial Endocarditis *on page 1377*
U.S. Brand Names Biaxin™
Synonyms Cla
Therapeutic Category Antibiotic, Macrolide
Use In adults, for treatment of pharyngitis/tonsillitis, acute maxillary sinusitis, acute exacerbation of chronic bronchitis, pneumonia, uncomplicated skin/skin structure infections due to susceptible *S. pyogenes, S. pneumoniae, S. agalactiae,* viridans *Streptococcus, M. catarrhalis, C. trachomatis, Legionella* sp, *Mycoplasma pneumoniae,S. aureus, H. influenzae*; has activity against *M. avium* and *M. intracellulare* infection and is indicated for treatment of and prevention of disseminated mycobacterial infections due to *M. avium* complex disease (eg, patients with advanced HIV infection); indicated for the treatment of duodenal ulcer disease due to *H. pylori* in regimens with other drugs including amoxicillin and lansoprazole or omeprazole, ranitidine, bismuth citrate, bismuth subsalicylate, tetracycline and/or an H$_2$-antagonist (see index); also indicated for prophylaxis of bacterial endocarditis in patients who are allergic to penicillin and undergoing surgical or dental procedures

In children, for treatment of pharyngitis/tonsillitis, acute maxillary sinusitis, acute otitis media, uncomplicated skin/skin structure infections due to the above organisms; treatment of and prevention of disseminated mycobacterial infections due to *M. avium* complex disease (eg, patients with advanced HIV infection)

Exhibits the same spectrum of *in vitro* activity as erythromycin, but with significantly increased potency against those organisms
Pregnancy Risk Factor C
Contraindications Hypersensitivity to clarithromycin, erythromycin, or any macrolide antibiotic; use with pimozide, astemizole, cisapride, terfenadine
Warnings/Precautions In presence of severe renal impairment with or without coexisting hepatic impairment, decreased dosage or prolonged dosing interval may be appropriate; antibiotic-associated colitis has been reported with use of clarithromycin; elderly patients have experienced increased incidents of adverse effects due to known age-related decreases in renal function
Adverse Reactions
1% to 10%:
Central nervous system: Headache
Gastrointestinal: Diarrhea, nausea, abnormal taste, dyspepsia, abdominal pain
<1%: Ventricular tachycardia, manic behavior, tremor, hypoglycemia, torsade de pointes, neutropenia, leukopenia, prolonged PT, increased AST, alkaline phosphatase, and bilirubin; elevated BUN/serum creatinine
Overdosage/Toxicology
Symptoms of overdose include nausea, vomiting, diarrhea, prostration, reversible pancreatitis, hearing loss with or without tinnitus or vertigo
Treatment includes symptomatic and supportive care
Drug Interactions CYP3A3/4 enzyme substrate; CYP1A2 and 3A3/4 enzyme inhibitor
Increased levels:
Clarithromycin increases serum theophylline levels by as much as 20%
Increased concentration of HMG CoA-reductase inhibitors (lovastatin and simvastatin)
Significantly increases carbamazepine levels and those of cyclosporine, digoxin, ergot alkaloid, tacrolimus, omeprazole and triazolam
Peak levels (but not AUC) of zidovudine are often increased; terfenadine and astemizole should be avoided with use of clarithromycin since plasma levels may be increased by >3 times; serious arrhythmias have occurred with cisapride and other drugs which inhibit cytochrome P-450 3A4 (eg, clarithromycin)
(Continued)

Clarithromycin *(Continued)*

Fluconazole increases clarithromycin levels and AUC by ~25%; death has been reported with administration of pimozide and clarithromycin

Note: While other drug interactions (bromocriptine, disopyramide, lovastatin, phenytoin, and valproate) known to occur with erythromycin have not been reported in clinical trials with clarithromycin, concurrent use of these drugs should be monitored closely

Mechanism of Action Exerts its antibacterial action by binding to 50S ribosomal subunit resulting in inhibition of protein synthesis. The 14-OH metabolite of clarithromycin is twice as active as the parent compound against certain organisms.

Pharmacodynamics/Kinetics

Absorption: Highly stable in the presence of gastric acid (unlike erythromycin)

Distribution: Widely distributes into most body tissues with the exception of the CNS

Metabolism: Partially converted to the microbiologically active metabolite, 14-OH clarithromycin

Bioavailability: 50%; food delays but does not affect extent of bioavailability; T_{max}: 2-4 hours

Half-life: 5-7 hours

Elimination: Primarily renal excretion; clearance approximates normal GFR

Usual Dosage Safe use in children has not been established

Children ≥6 months: 15 mg/kg/day divided every 12 hours; dosages of 7.5 mg/kg twice daily up to 500 mg twice daily children with AIDS and disseminated MAC infection

Adults: Oral: Usual dose: 250-500 mg every 12 hours for 7-14 days

Upper respiratory tract: 250-500 mg every 12 hours for 10-14 days

Pharyngitis/tonsillitis: 250 mg every 12 hours for 10 days

Acute maxillary sinusitis: 500 mg every 12 hours for 14 days

Lower respiratory tract: 250-500 mg every 12 hours for 7-14 days

Acute exacerbation of chronic bronchitis due to:

M. catarrhalis and *S. pneumoniae*: 250 mg every 12 hours for 7-14 days

H. influenzae: 500 mg every 12 hours for 7-14 days

Pneumonia due to *M. pneumoniae* and *S. pneumoniae*: 250 mg every 12 hours for 7-14 days

Mycobacterial infection (prevention and treatment): 500 mg twice daily (use with other antimycobacterial drugs, eg, ethambutol, clofazimine, or rifampin)

Prophylaxis of bacterial endocarditis: 500 mg 1 hour prior to procedure

Uncomplicated skin and skin structure: 250 mg every 12 hours for 7-14 days

Helicobacter pylori: In combination regimen with bismuth subsalicylate, tetracycline, and an H_2-receptor antagonist; or in combination with omeprazole (and possibly metronidazole or amoxicillin) or ranitidine bismuth citrate (Tritec®) (and possibly tetracycline or amoxicillin or lansoprazole and amoxicillin): 250 mg twice daily to 500 mg 3 times/day (for first 2 weeks only of regimen with Tritec® or omeprazole)

Dosing adjustment in renal impairment: Adults: Oral:

Cl_{cr} <30 mL/minute: 500 mg loading dose, then 250 mg once or twice daily

Dosing adjustment in severe renal impairment: Decreased doses or prolonged dosing intervals are recommended

Patient Information May be taken with meals; finish all medication; do not skip doses; do not refrigerate oral suspension, more palatable when taken at room temperature

Dosage Forms

Granules for oral suspension: 125 mg/5 mL (50 mL, 100 mL); 250 mg/5 mL (50 mL, 100 mL)

Tablet, film coated: 250 mg, 500 mg

- **Claritin®** *see* Loratadine *on page 694*
- **Claritin-D®** *see* Loratadine and Pseudoephedrine *on page 694*
- **Claritin-D® 24-Hour** *see* Loratadine and Pseudoephedrine *on page 694*
- **Clavulin®** *see* Amoxicillin and Clavulanate Potassium *on page 71*
- **Clear Eyes® [OTC]** *see* Naphazoline *on page 817*
- **Clear Tussin® 30** *see* Guaifenesin and Dextromethorphan *on page 550*

Clemastine *(KLEM as teen)*

U.S. Brand Names Antihist-1® [OTC]; Tavist®; Tavist®-1 [OTC]

Synonyms Clemastine Fumarate

Therapeutic Category Antihistamine, H_1 Blocker

Use Perennial and seasonal allergic rhinitis and other allergic symptoms including urticaria

Pregnancy Risk Factor C

Contraindications Narrow-angle glaucoma, hypersensitivity to clemastine or any component

Warnings/Precautions Safety and efficacy have not been established in children <6 years of age; bladder neck obstruction, symptomatic prostate hypertrophy, asthmatic attacks, and stenosing peptic ulcer

Adverse Reactions

>10%:

Central nervous system: Slight to moderate drowsiness

Respiratory: Thickening of bronchial secretions

1% to 10%:

Central nervous system: Headache, fatigue, nervousness, increased dizziness

Gastrointestinal: Appetite increase, weight gain, nausea, diarrhea, abdominal pain, xerostomia

Neuromuscular & skeletal: Arthralgia

Respiratory: Pharyngitis

<1%: Edema, palpitations, depression, angioedema, photosensitivity, rash, hepatitis, myalgia, paresthesia, bronchospasm, epistaxis

Overdosage/Toxicology

Symptoms of overdose include anemia, metabolic acidosis, hypotension, hypothermia

There is no specific treatment for an antihistamine overdose, however, most of its clinical toxicity is due to anticholinergic effects. For anticholinergic overdose with severe life-threatening symptoms, physostigmine 1-2 mg (0.5 mg or 0.02 mg/kg for children) I.V., slowly may be given to reverse these effects.

Drug Interactions Increased toxicity (CNS depression): CNS depressants, MAO inhibitors, tricyclic antidepressants, phenothiazines

Mechanism of Action Competes with histamine for H_1-receptor sites on effector cells in the gastrointestinal tract, blood vessels, and respiratory tract

Pharmacodynamics/Kinetics

Peak therapeutic effect: Within 5-7 hours

Absorption: Almost 100% from GI tract

Metabolism: In the liver

Elimination: In urine

Usual Dosage Oral:

Children: <12 years: 0.4-1 mg twice daily

Children >12 years and Adults: 1.34 mg twice daily to 2.68 mg 3 times/day; do not exceed 8.04 mg/day; lower doses should be considered in patients >60 years

Dietary Considerations Alcohol: Additive CNS effects, avoid use

Monitoring Parameters Look for a reduction of rhinitis, urticaria, eczema, pruritus, or other allergic symptoms

Patient Information Avoid alcohol; may cause drowsiness, may impair coordination or judgment

Nursing Implications Raise bed rails, institute safety measures, assist with ambulation

Dosage Forms

Syrup, as fumarate (citrus flavor): 0.67 mg/5 mL with alcohol 5.5% (120 mL)

Tablet, as fumarate: 1.34 mg, 2.68 mg

Clemastine and Phenylpropanolamine

(KLEM as teen & fen il proe pa NOLE a meen)

U.S. Brand Names Antihist-D®; Tavist-D®

Therapeutic Category Antihistamine/Decongestant Combination

Dosage Forms Tablet: Clemastine fumarate 1.34 mg and phenylpropanolamine hydrochloride 75 mg

♦ **Clemastine Fumarate** see Clemastine on previous page

♦ **Cleocin HCl®** see Clindamycin on this page

♦ **Cleocin Pediatric®** see Clindamycin on this page

♦ **Cleocin Phosphate®** see Clindamycin on this page

♦ **Cleocin T®** see Clindamycin on this page

Clidinium and Chlordiazepoxide

(kli DI nee um & klor dye az e POKS ide)

U.S. Brand Names Clindex®; Librax®

Therapeutic Category Anticholinergic Agent

Dosage Forms Capsule: Clidinium bromide 2.5 mg and chlordiazepoxide hydrochloride 5 mg

♦ **Climara® Transdermal** see Estradiol on page 433

♦ **Clinda-Derm® Topical Solution** see Clindamycin on this page

Clindamycin (klin da MYE sin)

Related Information

Animal and Human Bites Guidelines on page 1399

Antimicrobial Drugs of Choice on page 1404

Community-Acquired Pneumonia in Adults on page 1419

Guidelines for the Prevention of Opportunistic Infections in Persons with HIV on page 1388

Prevention of Bacterial Endocarditis on page 1377

Prevention of Wound Infection & Sepsis in Surgical Patients on page 1381

Treatment of Sexually Transmitted Diseases on page 1429

U.S. Brand Names Cleocin HCl®; Cleocin Pediatric®; Cleocin Phosphate®; Cleocin T®; Clinda-Derm® Topical Solution; C/T/S® Topical Solution

Canadian Brand Names Dalacin® C [Hydrochloride]

Synonyms Clindamycin Hydrochloride; Clindamycin Phosphate

Therapeutic Category Acne Products; Antibiotic, Anaerobic; Antibiotic, Topical

Use Treatment against aerobic and anaerobic streptococci (except enterococci), most staphylococci, *Bacteroides* sp and *Actinomyces*; used topically in treatment of severe acne, vaginally for *Gardnerella vaginalis*, alternate treatment for toxoplasmosis; prophylaxis in the prevention of bacterial endocarditis in high-risk patients undergoing surgical or dental procedures in patients allergic to penicillin; may be useful in PCP

Pregnancy Risk Factor B

Contraindications Hypersensitivity to clindamycin or any component; previous pseudomembranous colitis, hepatic impairment

(Continued)

Clindamycin *(Continued)*

Warnings/Precautions Dosage adjustment may be necessary in patients with severe hepatic dysfunction; can cause severe and possibly fatal colitis; use with caution in patients with a history of pseudomembranous colitis; discontinue drug if significant diarrhea, abdominal cramps, or passage of blood and mucus occurs

Adverse Reactions

>10%: Gastrointestinal: Diarrhea

1% to 10%:

Dermatologic: Rashes

Gastrointestinal: Pseudomembranous colitis (more common with oral form), nausea, vomiting

<1%: Hypotension, urticaria, Stevens-Johnson syndrome, eosinophilia, neutropenia, granulocytopenia, thrombocytopenia, elevated liver enzymes, thrombophlebitis, sterile abscess at I.M. injection site, polyarthritis, rare renal dysfunction

Overdosage/Toxicology

Symptoms of overdose include diarrhea, nausea, vomiting; following GI decontamination Treatment is supportive

Drug Interactions CYP3A3/4 enzyme substrate

Increased duration of neuromuscular blockade from tubocurarine, pancuronium

Stability Do **not** refrigerate reconstituted oral solution because it will thicken; oral solution is stable for 2 weeks at room temperature following reconstitution; I.V. infusion solution in NS or D_5W solution is stable for 16 days at room temperature

Mechanism of Action Reversibly binds to 50S ribosomal subunits preventing peptide bond formation thus inhibiting bacterial protein synthesis; bacteriostatic or bactericidal depending on drug concentration, infection site, and organism

Pharmacodynamics/Kinetics

Absorption: ~10% of topically applied drug is absorbed systemically; 90% absorbed rapidly from GI tract following oral administration

Distribution: No significant levels are seen in CSF, even with inflamed meninges; crosses the placenta; distributes into breast milk; high concentrations in bone and urine

Metabolism: Hepatic

Half-life: Neonates: Premature: 8.7 hours; Full-term: 3.6 hours; Adults: 1.6-5.3 hours, average: 2-3 hours

Time to peak serum concentration: Oral: Within 60 minutes; I.M.: Within 1-3 hours

Elimination: Most of drug eliminated by hepatic metabolism

Usual Dosage Avoid in neonates (contains benzyl alcohol)

Infants and Children:

Oral: 8-20 mg/kg/day as hydrochloride; 8-25 mg/kg/day as palmitate in 3-4 divided doses; minimum dose of palmitate: 37.5 mg 3 times/day

I.M., I.V.:

<1 month: 15-20 mg/kg/day

>1 month: 20-40 mg/kg/day in 3-4 divided doses

Children and Adults: Topical: Apply a thin film twice daily

Adults:

Oral: 150-450 mg/dose every 6-8 hours; maximum dose: 1.8 g/day

I.M., I.V.: 1.2-1.8 g/day in 2-4 divided doses; maximum dose: 4.8 g/day

Bacterial endocarditis prophylaxis: 600 mg 1 hour prior to the procedure

Pelvic inflammatory disease: I.V.: 900 mg every 8 hours with gentamicin 2 mg/kg, then 1.5 mg/kg every 8 hours; continue after discharge with doxycycline 100 mg twice daily or oral clindamycin 450 mg 5 times/day for 10-14 days

Pneumocystis carinii pneumonia:

Oral: 300-450 mg 4 times/day with primaquine

I.M., I.V.: 1200-2400 mg/day with pyrimethamine

I.V.: 600 mg 4 times/day with primaquine

Vaginal: One full applicator (100 mg) inserted intravaginally once daily before bedtime for 3 or 7 consecutive days

Dosing adjustment in hepatic impairment: Adjustment recommended in patients with severe hepatic disease

Administration Administer oral dosage form with a full glass of water to minimize esophageal ulceration

Monitoring Parameters Observe for changes in bowel frequency, monitor for colitis and resolution of symptoms; during prolonged therapy monitor CBC, liver and renal function tests periodically

Patient Information Report any severe diarrhea immediately and do not take antidiarrheal medication; take each oral dose with a full glass of water; finish all medication; do not skip doses; should not engage in sexual intercourse during treatment with vaginal product; avoid contact of topical gel/solution with eyes, abraded skin, or mucous membranes

Dosage Forms

Capsule, as hydrochloride: 75 mg, 150 mg, 300 mg

Cream, vaginal: 2% (40 g)

Gel, topical, as phosphate: 1% [10 mg/g] (7.5 g, 30 g)

Granules for oral solution, as palmitate: 75 mg/5 mL (100 mL)

Infusion, as phosphate, in D_5W: 300 mg (50 mL); 600 mg (50 mL)

Injection, as phosphate: 150 mg/mL (2 mL, 4 mL, 6 mL, 50 mL, 60 mL)

Lotion: 1% [10 mg/mL] (60 mL)

Pledgets: 1%

Solution, topical, as phosphate: 1% [10 mg/mL] (30 mL, 60 mL, 480 mL)

- **Clindamycin Hydrochloride** *see* Clindamycin *on page 275*
- **Clindamycin Phosphate** *see* Clindamycin *on page 275*
- **Clindex®** *see* Clidinium and Chlordiazepoxide *on page 275*
- **Clinical Syndromes Associated With Food-Borne Diseases** *see page 1418*
- **Clinoril®** *see* Sulindac *on page 1099*

Clioquinol (klye oh KWIN ole)

U.S. Brand Names Vioform® [OTC]
Canadian Brand Names Clioquinol®
Synonyms Iodochlorhydroxyquin
Therapeutic Category Antifungal Agent, Topical
Use Topically in the treatment of tinea pedis, tinea cruris, and skin infections caused by dermatophytic fungi (ringworm)
Pregnancy Risk Factor C
Contraindications Not effective in the treatment of scalp or nail fungal infections; children <2 years of age, hypersensitivity to any component
Warnings/Precautions May irritate sensitized skin; topical application poses a potential risk of toxicity to infants and children; known to cause serious and irreversible optic atrophy and peripheral neuropathy with muscular weakness, sensory loss, spastic paraparesis, and blindness; use with caution in patients with iodine intolerance
Adverse Reactions 1% to 10%:
Dermatologic: Skin irritation, rash
Neuromuscular & skeletal: Peripheral neuropathy
Ocular: Optic atrophy
Mechanism of Action Chelates bacterial surface and trace metals needed for bacterial growth
Pharmacodynamics/Kinetics
Absorption: With an occlusive dressing, up to 40% of dose can be absorbed systemically during a 12-hour period; absorption is enhanced when applied under diapers
Half-life: 11-14 hours
Elimination: Conjugated and excreted in urine
Usual Dosage Children and Adults: Topical: Apply 2-3 times/day; do not use for longer than 7 days
Test Interactions Thyroid function tests (decreased ^{131}I uptake); false-positive ferric chloride test for phenylketonuria
Patient Information Cleanse affected area before application; can stain skin and fabrics; for external use only; avoid contact with eyes and mucous membranes
Nursing Implications Watch affected area for increased irritation
Dosage Forms
Cream: 3% (30 g)
Ointment, topical: 3% (30 g)

- **Clioquinol®** *see* Clioquinol *on this page*

Clioquinol and Hydrocortisone

(klye oh KWIN ole & hye droe KOR ti sone)
U.S. Brand Names Corque® Topical; Pedi-Cort V® Creme
Therapeutic Category Antifungal/Corticosteroid
Dosage Forms Cream: Clioquinol 3% and hydrocortisone 1% (20 g)

Clobetasol (kloe BAY ta sol)

Related Information
Corticosteroids Comparison *on page 1319*
U.S. Brand Names Temovate® Topical
Canadian Brand Names Dermasone; Dermovate®; Gen-Clobetasol; Novo-Clobetasol
Synonyms Clobetasol Propionate
Therapeutic Category Anti-inflammatory Agent; Corticosteroid, Topical (Low Potency); Corticosteroid, Topical (Very High Potency)
Use Short-term relief of inflammation of moderate to severe corticosteroid-responsive dermatosis (very high potency topical corticosteroid)
Pregnancy Risk Factor C
Contraindications Known hypersensitivity to clobetasol; viral, fungal, or tubercular skin lesions
Warnings/Precautions Adrenal suppression can occur if used for >14 days
Adverse Reactions
1% to 10%:
Dermatologic: Itching, erythema
Local: Burning, dryness, irritation, papular rashes
<1%: Hypertrichosis, acneiform eruptions, maceration of skin, skin atrophy, striae, hypopigmentation, perioral dermatitis, miliaria
Mechanism of Action Stimulates the synthesis of enzymes needed to decrease inflammation, suppress mitotic activity, and cause vasoconstriction
Pharmacodynamics/Kinetics
Absorption: Percutaneous absorption variable and dependent upon many factors including vehicle used, integrity of epidermis, dose, and use of occlusive dressings
Metabolism: Remains to be defined
Elimination: In urine and bile
(Continued)

Clobetasol *(Continued)*

Usual Dosage Adults: Topical: Apply twice daily for up to 2 weeks with no more than 50 g/week

Patient Information A thin film of cream or ointment is effective; do not overuse; do not use tight-fitting diapers or plastic pants on children being treated in the diaper area; use only as prescribed and for no longer than the period prescribed; apply sparingly in light film; rub in lightly; avoid contact with eyes; notify physician if condition being treated persists or worsens

Nursing Implications For external use only; do not use on open wounds; apply sparingly to occlusive dressings; should not be used in the presence of open or weeping lesions

Dosage Forms
Cream, as propionate: 0.05% (15 g, 30 g, 45 g)
Cream, as propionate, in emollient base: 0.05% (15 g, 30 g, 60 g)
Gel, as propionate: 0.05% (15 g, 30 g, 45 g)
Ointment, topical, as propionate: 0.05% (15 g, 30 g, 45 g)
Scalp application, as propionate: 0.05% (25 mL, 50 mL)

♦ **Clobetasol Propionate** *see* Clobetasol *on previous page*

♦ **Clocort® Maximum Strength** *see* Hydrocortisone *on page 579*

Clocortolone (kloe KOR toe lone)

Related Information
Corticosteroids Comparison *on page 1319*

U.S. Brand Names Cloderm® Topical

Synonyms Clocortolone Pivalate

Therapeutic Category Corticosteroid, Topical (Medium Potency)

Use Inflammation of corticosteroid-responsive dermatoses (medium potency topical corticosteroid)

Pregnancy Risk Factor C

Contraindications Known hypersensitivity to clocortolone; viral, fungal, or tubercular skin lesions

Warnings/Precautions Adrenal suppression can occur if used for >14 days

Adverse Reactions
1% to 10%:
Dermatologic: Itching, erythema
Local: Burning, dryness, irritation, papular rashes
<1%: Hypertrichosis, acneiform eruptions, maceration of skin, skin atrophy, striae, hypopigmentation, perioral dermatitis, miliaria

Mechanism of Action Stimulates the synthesis of enzymes needed to decrease inflammation, suppress mitotic activity, and cause vasoconstriction

Pharmacodynamics/Kinetics
Absorption: Percutaneous absorption is variable and dependent upon many factors including vehicle used, integrity of epidermis, dose, and use of occlusive dressings;
Distribution: Small amounts enter systemic circulation mostly throughout skin
Metabolism: Remains to be defined (largely in liver)
Elimination: In urine and bile

Usual Dosage Adults: Apply sparingly and gently; rub into affected area from 1-4 times/day

Patient Information A thin film of cream or ointment is effective; do not overuse; do not use tight-fitting diapers or plastic pants on children being treated in the diaper area; use only as prescribed, and for no longer than the period prescribed; apply sparingly in light film; rub in lightly; avoid contact with eyes; notify physician if condition being treated persists or worsens

Nursing Implications For external use only; do not use on open wounds; apply sparingly to occlusive dressings; should not be used in the presence of open or weeping lesions

Dosage Forms Cream, as pivalate: 0.1% (15 g, 45 g)

♦ **Clocortolone Pivalate** *see* Clocortolone *on this page*

♦ **Cloderm® Topical** *see* Clocortolone *on this page*

Clofazimine (kloe FA zi meen)

Related Information
Antimicrobial Drugs of Choice *on page 1404*
Tuberculosis Treatment Guidelines *on page 1432*

U.S. Brand Names Lamprene®

Synonyms Clofazimine Palmitate

Therapeutic Category Antibiotic, Miscellaneous; Leprostatic Agent

Use Orphan drug: Treatment of dapsone-resistant leprosy; multibacillary dapsone-sensitive leprosy; erythema nodosum leprosum; *Mycobacterium avium-intracellulare* (MAI) infections

Pregnancy Risk Factor C

Contraindications Hypersensitivity to clofazimine or any component

Warnings/Precautions Use with caution in patients with GI problems; dosages >100 mg/day should be used for as short a duration as possible; skin discoloration may lead to depression

Adverse Reactions
>10%:
  Dermatologic: Dry skin
  Gastrointestinal: Abdominal pain, nausea, vomiting, diarrhea
  Miscellaneous: Pink to brownish-black discoloration of the skin and conjunctiva
1% to 10%:
  Dermatologic: Rash, pruritus
  Endocrine & metabolic: Elevated blood sugar
  Gastrointestinal: Fecal discoloration
  Genitourinary: Discoloration of urine
  Ocular: Irritation of the eyes
  Miscellaneous: Discoloration of sputum, sweat
<1%: Edema, vascular pain, dizziness, drowsiness, fatigue, headache, giddiness, taste disorder, fever, erythroderma, acneiform eruptions, monilial cheilosis, phototoxicity, hypokalemia, bowel obstruction, GI bleeding, anorexia, constipation, weight loss, eosinophilic enteritis, cystitis, eosinophilia, anemia, hepatitis, jaundice, enlarged liver; increased albumin, serum bilirubin, and AST; bone pain, neuralgia, diminished vision, lymphadenopathy

Overdosage/Toxicology Following GI decontamination, treatment is supportive
Drug Interactions Decreased effect with dapsone (unconfirmed)
Mechanism of Action Binds preferentially to mycobacterial DNA to inhibit mycobacterial growth; also has some anti-inflammatory activity through an unknown mechanism
Pharmacodynamics/Kinetics
Absorption: Oral: 45% to 70% absorbed slowly
Distribution: Remains in tissues for prolonged periods; appears in breast milk; highly lipophilic; deposited primarily in fatty tissue and cells of the reticuloendothelial system; taken up by macrophages throughout the body; also distributed to breast milk, mesenteric lymph nodes, adrenal glands, subcutaneous fat, liver, bile, gallbladder, spleen, small intestine, muscles, bones, and skin; does not appear to cross blood-brain barrier
Metabolism: Partially in the liver to two metabolites
Half-life: Terminal: 8 days; Tissue: 70 days
Time to peak serum concentration: 1-6 hours with chronic therapy
Elimination: Mainly in feces; negligible amounts excreted unchanged in urine; small amounts excreted in sputum, saliva, and sweat

Usual Dosage Oral:
Children: Leprosy: 1 mg/kg/day every 24 hours in combination with dapsone and rifampin
Adults:
  Dapsone-resistant leprosy: 100 mg/day in combination with one or more antileprosy drugs for 3 years; then alone 100 mg/day
  Dapsone-sensitive multibacillary leprosy: 100 mg/day in combination with two or more antileprosy drugs for at least 2 years and continue until negative skin smears are obtained, then institute single drug therapy with appropriate agent
  Erythema nodosum leprosum: 100-200 mg/day for up to 3 months or longer then taper dose to 100 mg/day when possible
  Pyoderma gangrenosum: 300-400 mg/day for up to 12 months
Dosing adjustment in hepatic impairment: Should be considered in severe hepatic dysfunction
Patient Information Drug may cause a pink to brownish-black discoloration of the skin, conjunctiva, tears, sweat, urine, feces, and nasal secretions; although reversible, may take months to years to disappear after therapy is complete; take with meals
Dosage Forms Capsule, as palmitate: 50 mg

♦ **Clofazimine Palmitate** *see* Clofazimine *on previous page*

Clofibrate (kloe FYE brate)
Related Information
  Lipid-Lowering Agents *on page 1327*
U.S. Brand Names Atromid-S®
Canadian Brand Names Abitrate®; Claripex®; Novo-Fibrate
Therapeutic Category Antilipemic Agent
Use Adjunct to dietary therapy in the management of hyperlipidemias associated with high triglyceride levels (types III, IV, V); primarily lowers triglycerides and very low density lipoprotein
Pregnancy Risk Factor C
Contraindications Hypersensitivity to clofibrate or any component, severe hepatic or renal impairment, primary biliary cirrhosis
Warnings/Precautions Clofibrate has been shown to be tumorigenic in animal studies; increased risk of cholelithiasis, cholecystitis; discontinue if lipid response is not obtained; no evidence substantiates a beneficial effect on cardiovascular mortality
Adverse Reactions Percentage unknown:
  Cardiovascular: Angina, cardiac arrhythmias
  Central nervous system: Headache, dizziness, fatigue
  Dermatologic: Rash, urticaria, pruritus, alopecia
  Gastrointestinal: Nausea, diarrhea, vomiting, dyspepsia, flatulence, abdominal distress, gallstones
  Genitourinary: Impotence
  Hematologic: Leukopenia, anemia, eosinophilia, agranulocytosis
  Hepatic: Increased LFTs
(Continued)

Clofibrate *(Continued)*

Neuromuscular & skeletal: Muscle cramping, aching, weakness, myalgia
Renal: Renal toxicity, rhabdomyolysis-induced renal failure
Miscellaneous: Dry, brittle hair

Overdosage/Toxicology
Symptoms of overdose include nausea, vomiting, diarrhea, GI distress
Following GI decontamination, treatment is supportive

Drug Interactions
Decreased effect: Oral contraceptives may increase elimination of clofibrate
Increased effect: Effects of warfarin, insulin, dantrolene, furosemide, and sulfonylureas may be increased
Increased toxicity/levels: Clofibrate's levels may be increased with probenecid

Mechanism of Action Mechanism is unclear but thought to reduce cholesterol synthesis and triglyceride hepatic-vascular transference

Pharmacodynamics/Kinetics
Absorption: Occurs completely; intestinal transformation is required to activate the drug
Distribution: V_d: 5.5 L/kg; crosses the placenta
Protein binding: 95%
Metabolism: In the liver to an inactive glucuronide ester
Half-life: 6-24 hours, increases significantly with reduced renal function; with anuria: 110 hours
Time to peak serum concentration: Within 3-6 hours
Elimination: 40% to 70% excreted in urine

Usual Dosage Adults: Oral: 500 mg 4 times/day; some patients may respond to lower doses
Dosing interval in renal impairment:
Cl_{cr} >50 mL/minute: Administer every 6-12 hours
Cl_{cr} 10-50 mL/minute: Administer every 12-18 hours
Cl_{cr} <10 mL/minute: Avoid use
Hemodialysis: Elimination is not enhanced via hemodialysis; supplemental dose is not necessary

Monitoring Parameters Serum lipids, cholesterol and triglycerides, LFTs, CBC

Test Interactions ↑ creatine phosphokinase [CPK] (S); ↓ alkaline phosphatase (S), cholesterol (S), glucose, uric acid (S)

Patient Information If GI upset occurs, may be taken with food; notify physician of chest pain, shortness of breath, irregular heartbeat, severe stomach pain with nausea and vomiting, persistent fever, sore throat, or unusual bleeding or bruising; adhere to prescribed diet

Dosage Forms Capsule: 500 mg

♦ **Clomid**® *see* Clomiphene *on this page*

Clomiphene *(KLOE mi feen)*

U.S. Brand Names Clomid®; Milophene®; Serophene®
Synonyms Clomiphene Citrate
Therapeutic Category Ovulation Stimulator
Use Treatment of ovulatory failure in patients desiring pregnancy
Unlabeled use: Male infertility
Pregnancy Risk Factor X
Contraindications Hypersensitivity or allergy to clomiphene citrate or any of its components; liver disease, abnormal uterine bleeding, suspected pregnancy, enlargement or development of ovarian cyst, uncontrolled thyroid or adrenal dysfunction in the presence of an organic intracranial lesion such as pituitary tumor
Warnings/Precautions Patients unusually sensitive to pituitary gonadotropins (eg, polycystic ovary disease); multiple pregnancies, blurring or other visual symptoms can occur, ovarian hyperstimulation syndrome, and abdominal pain

Adverse Reactions
>10%: Endocrine & metabolic: Hot flashes, ovarian enlargement
1% to 10%:
Cardiovascular: Thromboembolism
Central nervous system: Mental depression, headache
Endocrine & metabolic: Breast enlargement (males), breast discomfort (females), abnormal menstrual flow
Gastrointestinal: Distention, bloating, nausea, vomiting, hepatotoxicity
Ocular: Blurring of vision, diplopia, floaters, after-images, phosphenes, photophobia
<1%: Insomnia, fatigue, alopecia (reversible), weight gain, polyuria

Stability Protect from light
Mechanism of Action Induces ovulation by stimulating the release of pituitary gonadotropins

Pharmacodynamics/Kinetics
Half-life: 5-7 days
Elimination: Enterohepatically circulated; excreted primarily in feces with small amounts appearing in urine

Usual Dosage Adults: Oral:
Male (infertility): 25 mg/day for 25 days with 5 days rest, or 100 mg every Monday, Wednesday, Friday
Female (ovulatory failure): 50 mg/day for 5 days (first course); start the regimen on or about the fifth day of cycle. The dose should be increased only in those patients who

do not ovulate in response to cyclic 50 mg Clomid®. A low dosage or duration of treatment course is particularly recommended if unusual sensitivity to pituitary gonadotropin is suspected, such as in patients with polycystic ovary syndrome.

If ovulation does not appear to occur after the first course of therapy, a second course of 100 mg/day (two 50 mg tablets given as a single daily dose) for 5 days should be given. This course may be started as early as 30 days after the previous one after precautions are taken to exclude the presence of pregnancy. Increasing the dosage or duration of therapy beyond 100 mg/day for 5 days is not recommended. The majority of patients who are going to ovulate will do so after the first course of therapy. If ovulation does not occur after 3 courses of therapy, further treatment is not recommended and the patient should be re-evaluated. If 3 ovulatory responses occur, but pregnancy has not been achieved, further treatment is not recommended. If menses does not occur after an ovulatory response, the patient should be re-evaluated. Long-term cyclic therapy is not recommended beyond a total of about 6 cycles.

Reference Range FSH and LH are expected to peak 5-9 days after completing clomiphene; ovulation assessed by basal body temperature or serum progesterone 2 weeks after last clomiphene dose

Test Interactions Clomiphene may increase levels of serum thyroxine and thyroxine-binding globulin (TBG)

Patient Information May cause visual disturbances, dizziness, lightheadedness; if possibility of pregnancy, stop the drug and consult your physician

Dosage Forms Tablet, as citrate: 50 mg

♦ **Clomiphene Citrate** see Clomiphene on previous page

Clomipramine (kloe MI pra meen)

Related Information

Antidepressant Agents Comparison on page 1301

U.S. Brand Names Anafranil®

Canadian Brand Names Apo®-Clomipramine

Synonyms Clomipramine Hydrochloride

Therapeutic Category Antidepressant, Tricyclic

Use Treatment of obsessive-compulsive disorder (OCD); may also relieve depression, panic attacks, and chronic pain

Pregnancy Risk Factor C

Contraindications Patients in acute recovery stage of recent myocardial infarction; not to be used within 14 days of MAO inhibitors

Warnings/Precautions Seizures are likely and are dose-related; can be additive when coadministered with other drugs that can lower the seizure threshold; use with caution in patients with asthma, bladder outlet destruction, narrow-angle glaucoma

Adverse Reactions

>10%:

Central nervous system: Dizziness, drowsiness, headache

Gastrointestinal: Xerostomia, constipation, increased appetite, nausea, unpleasant taste, weight gain

Neuromuscular & skeletal: Weakness

1% to 10%:

Cardiovascular: Arrhythmias, hypotension

Central nervous system: Confusion, delirium, hallucinations, nervousness, restlessness, parkinsonian syndrome, insomnia

Gastrointestinal: Diarrhea, heartburn

Genitourinary: Dysuria, sexual dysfunction

Neuromuscular & skeletal: Fine muscle tremors

Ocular: Blurred vision, eye pain

Miscellaneous: Diaphoresis (excessive)

<1%: Anxiety, seizures, alopecia, photosensitivity, breast enlargement, galactorrhea, SIADH, trouble with gums, decreased lower esophageal sphincter tone may cause GE reflux, testicular edema, agranulocytosis, leukopenia, eosinophilia, cholestatic jaundice, increased liver enzymes, increased intraocular pressure, tinnitus, allergic reactions

Overdosage/Toxicology

Symptoms of overdose include agitation, confusion, hallucinations, urinary retention, hypothermia, hypotension, tachycardia, ventricular tachycardia, seizures, coma

Following initiation of essential overdose management, toxic symptoms should be treated. Sodium bicarbonate is indicated when QRS interval is >0.10 seconds or QT_c >0.42 seconds. Ventricular arrhythmias and EKG abnormalities (eg, QRS widening) often respond to systemic alkalinization (sodium bicarbonate 0.5-2 mEq/kg I.V.) and/or phenytoin 15-20 mg/kg (adults). Arrhythmias unresponsive to this therapy may respond to lidocaine 1 mg/kg I.V. followed by a titrated infusion. Physostigmine (1-2 mg I.V. slowly for adults or 0.5 mg I.V. slowly for children) may be indicated in reversing cardiac arrhythmias that are life-threatening. Seizures usually respond to diazepam I.V. boluses (5-10 mg for adults up to 30 mg or 0.25-0.4 mg/kg/dose for children up to 10 mg/dose). If seizures are unresponsive or recur, phenytoin or phenobarbital may be required.

Drug Interactions CYP1A2, 2C9, 2C18, 2C19, 2D6, and 3A3/4 enzyme substrate; CYP2D6 enzyme inhibitor

Decreased effect with barbiturates, carbamazepine, phenytoin

Increased effect of alcohol, CNS depressants, anticholinergics, sympathomimetics

Increased toxicity: MAO inhibitors (increase temperature, seizures, coma, and death)

(Continued)

Clomipramine *(Continued)*

Mechanism of Action Clomipramine appears to affect serotonin uptake while its active metabolite, desmethylclomipramine, affects norepinephrine uptake

Pharmacodynamics/Kinetics
Absorption: Oral: Rapid
Metabolism: Extensive first-pass metabolism; metabolized to desmethylclomipramine (active) in the liver
Half-life: 20-30 hours

Usual Dosage Oral: Initial:
Children >10 years of age: 25 mg/day and gradually increase, as tolerated, to a maximum of 3 mg/kg/day or 200 mg/day, whichever is smaller
The safety and efficacy of clomipramine in pediatric patients <10 years of age have not been established and, therefore, dosing recommendations cannot be made
Adults: 25 mg/day and gradually increase, as tolerated, to 100 mg/day the first 2 weeks, may then be increased to a total of 250 mg/day maximum

Test Interactions ↑ glucose

Patient Information May cause seizures; caution should be used in activities that require alertness like driving, operating machinery, or swimming; effect of drug may take several weeks to appear

Dosage Forms Capsule, as hydrochloride: 25 mg, 50 mg, 75 mg

♦ **Clomipramine Hydrochloride** *see Clomipramine on previous page*

Clonazepam *(kloe NA ze pam)*

Related Information
Anticonvulsants by Seizure Type *on page 1300*
Benzodiazepines Comparison *on page 1310*
Epilepsy Treatment *on page 1468*
U.S. Brand Names Klonopin™
Canadian Brand Names PMS-Clonazepam; Rivotril®
Therapeutic Category Anticonvulsant
Use Prophylaxis of petit mal, petit mal variant (Lennox-Gastaut), akinetic, and myoclonic seizures
Unlabeled use: Restless legs syndrome, neuralgia, multifocal tic disorder, parkinsonian dysarthria, acute manic episodes, and adjunct therapy for schizophrenia

Restrictions C-IV
Pregnancy Risk Factor C
Pregnancy/Breast-Feeding Implications
Clinical effects on the fetus: Two reports of cardiac defects; respiratory depression, lethargy, hypotonia may be observed in newborns exposed near time of delivery. Epilepsy itself, number of medications, genetic factors, or a combination of these probably influence the teratogenicity of anticonvulsant therapy. Benefit:risk ratio usually favors continued use during pregnancy and breast-feeding.
Breast-feeding/lactation: Crosses into breast milk
Clinical effects on the infant: CNS depression, respiratory depression reported. No recommendation from the American Academy of Pediatrics.

Contraindications Hypersensitivity to clonazepam, any component, or other benzodiazepines; severe liver disease, acute narrow-angle glaucoma

Warnings/Precautions Use with caution in patients with chronic respiratory disease or impaired renal function; abrupt discontinuance may precipitate withdrawal symptoms, status epilepticus or seizures, in patients with a history of substance abuse; clonazepam-induced behavioral disturbances may be more frequent in mentally handicapped patients

Adverse Reactions
>10%:
Cardiovascular: Tachycardia, chest pain
Central nervous system: Drowsiness, fatigue, ataxia, lightheadedness, memory impairment, insomnia, anxiety, depression, headache
Dermatologic: Rash
Endocrine & metabolic: Decreased libido
Gastrointestinal: Xerostomia, constipation, diarrhea, nausea, increased or decreased appetite, vomiting, decreased salivation
Neuromuscular & skeletal: Dysarthria
Ocular: Blurred vision
Miscellaneous: Diaphoresis
1% to 10%:
Cardiovascular: Syncope, hypotension
Central nervous system: Confusion, nervousness, dizziness, akathisia
Dermatologic: Dermatitis
Gastrointestinal: Weight gain or loss, increased salivation
Neuromuscular & skeletal: Rigidity, tremor, muscle cramps
Otic: Tinnitus
Respiratory: Nasal congestion, hyperventilation
<1%: Menstrual irregularities, blood dyscrasias, reflex slowing, drug dependence

Overdosage/Toxicology
May produce somnolence, confusion, ataxia, diminished reflexes, or coma
Treatment for benzodiazepine overdose is supportive. Rarely is mechanical ventilation required. Flumazenil has been shown to selectively block the binding of benzodiazepines to CNS receptors, resulting in a reversal of benzodiazepine-induced CNS depression, but not respiratory depression.

Drug Interactions CYP3A3/4 enzyme substrate

Decreased effect: Phenytoin, barbiturates may increase clonazepam clearance

Increased toxicity: CNS depressants may increase sedation

Mechanism of Action Suppresses the spike-and-wave discharge in absence seizures by depressing nerve transmission in the motor cortex

Pharmacodynamics/Kinetics

Onset of effect: 20-60 minutes

Duration: Up to 6-8 hours in infants and young children, up to 12 hours in adults

Absorption: Oral: Well absorbed

Distribution: Adults: V_d: 1.5-4.4 L/kg

Protein binding: 85%

Metabolism: Extensive; glucuronide and sulfate conjugation

Half-life: Children: 22-33 hours; Adults: 19-50 hours

Time to peak serum concentration: Oral: 1-3 hours; Steady-state: 5-7 days

Elimination: <2% excreted unchanged in urine; metabolites excreted as glucuronide or sulfate conjugates

Usual Dosage Oral:

Children <10 years or 30 kg:

Initial daily dose: 0.01-0.03 mg/kg/day (maximum: 0.05 mg/kg/day) given in 2-3 divided doses; increase by no more than 0.5 mg every third day until seizures are controlled or adverse effects seen

Usual maintenance dose: 0.1-0.2 mg/kg/day divided 3 times/day; not to exceed 0.2 mg/kg/day

Adults:

Initial daily dose not to exceed 1.5 mg given in 3 divided doses; may increase by 0.5-1 mg every third day until seizures are controlled or adverse effects seen

Usual maintenance dose: 0.05-0.2 mg/kg; do not exceed 20 mg/day

Hemodialysis: Supplemental dose is not necessary

Dietary Considerations Alcohol: Additive CNS depression has been reported with benzodiazepines; avoid or limit alcohol

Reference Range Relationship between serum concentration and seizure control is not well established

Timing of serum samples: Peak serum levels occur 1-3 hours after oral ingestion; the half-life is 20-40 hours; therefore, steady-state occurs in 5-7 days

Therapeutic levels: 20-80 ng/mL; Toxic concentration: >80 ng/mL

Patient Information Avoid alcohol and other CNS depressants; avoid activities needing good psychomotor coordination until CNS effects are known; drug may cause physical or psychological dependence; avoid abrupt discontinuation after prolonged use

Nursing Implications Observe patient for excess sedation, respiratory depression; raise bed rails, initiate safety measures, assist with ambulation

Dosage Forms Tablet: 0.5 mg, 1 mg, 2 mg

Extemporaneous Preparations A 0.1 mg/mL oral suspension has been made using five 2 mg tablets, purified water USP (10 mL) and methylcellulose 1% (qs ad 100 mL); the expected stability of this preparation is 2 weeks if stored under refrigeration; shake well before use

Nahata MC and Hipple TF, *Pediatric Drug Formulations*, 2nd ed, Cincinnati, OH: Harvey Whitney Books Co, 1992.

Clonidine (KLOE ni deen)

Related Information

Depression Disorders and Treatments *on page 1465*

Hypertension Therapy *on page 1479*

U.S. Brand Names Catapres® Oral; Catapres-TTS® Transdermal; Duraclon® Injection

Canadian Brand Names Apo®-Clonidine; Dixarit®; Novo-Clonidine; Nu-Clonidine

Synonyms Clonidine Hydrochloride

Therapeutic Category Alpha$_2$-Adrenergic Agonist Agent; Antihypertensive Agent; Antimigraine Agent

Use Management of mild to moderate hypertension; either used alone or in combination with other antihypertensives; not recommended for first-line therapy for hypertension; as a second-line agent for decreasing heroin or nicotine withdrawal symptoms in patients with severe symptoms; indicated by the epidural route, in combination with opiates, for treatment of severe pain in refractory cancer patients (most effective in patients with neuropathic pain); other uses may include prophylaxis of migraines, glaucoma, and diabetes-associated diarrhea

Pregnancy Risk Factor C

Pregnancy/Breast-Feeding Implications

Clinical effects on the fetus: Crosses the placenta. Caution should be used with this drug due to the potential of rebound hypertension with abrupt discontinuation.

Breast-feeding/lactation: Crosses into breast milk. American Academy of Pediatrics has NO RECOMMENDATION.

Contraindications Hypersensitivity to clonidine hydrochloride or any component

Warnings/Precautions Use with caution in cerebrovascular disease, coronary insufficiency, renal impairment, sinus node dysfunction; do not abruptly discontinue as rapid increase in blood pressure and symptoms of sympathetic overactivity (ie, increased heart rate, tremor, agitation, anxiety, insomnia, sweating, palpitations) may occur; **if need to discontinue, taper dose gradually over 1 week or more (2-4 days with epidural product)**; adjust dosage in patients with renal dysfunction (especially the elderly); not recommended for obstetrical, postpartum or perioperative pain management or in those (Continued)

Clonidine *(Continued)*

with severe hemodynamic instability due to unacceptable risk of hypotension and brady-cardia; clonidine injection should be administered via a continuous epidural infusion device

Adverse Reactions

>10%:

Cardiovascular: Orthostatic hypotension (especially with epidural route), rebound hypertension, bradycardia

Central nervous system: Drowsiness, dizziness, confusion, anxiety

Gastrointestinal: Xerostomia, constipation, nausea

1% to 10%:

Central nervous system: Mental depression, headache, fatigue, hyperaesthesia, pain

Dermatologic: Rash, skin ulcer

Respiratory: Dyspnea, hypoventilation

Cardiovascular: Chest pain

Endocrine & metabolic: Decreased sexual activity, loss of libido

Gastrointestinal: vomiting, constipation

Genitourinary: Nocturia, impotence

Hepatic: Abnormal LFTs

Neuromuscular & skeletal: Weakness

Otic: Tinnitus

<1%: Palpitations, tachycardia, Raynaud's phenomenon, congestive heart failure, insomnia, vivid dreams, delirium, fever, pruritus, urticaria, alopecia, gynecomastia, weight gain, urinary retention, dysuria, infection possible, burning eyes, blurred vision

Overdosage/Toxicology

Symptoms of overdose include bradycardia, CNS depression, hypothermia, diarrhea, respiratory depression, apnea

Treatment is primarily supportive and symptomatic. Hypotension usually responds to I.V. fluids or Trendelenburg positioning. Naloxone may be utilized in treating CNS depression and/or apnea and should be given I.V. 0.4-2 mg, with repeated doses as needed or as an infusion.

Drug Interactions

Decreased effect: Tricyclic antidepressants antagonize hypotensive effects of clonidine

Increased toxicity: Beta-blockers may potentiate bradycardia in patients receiving cloni-dine and may increase the rebound hypertension of withdrawal; discontinue beta-blocker several days before clonidine is tapered; tricyclic antidepressants may enhance the hypertensive response associated with abrupt clonidine withdrawal; narcotic analgesics may potentiate hypotensive effects of clonidine; alcohol and barbi-turates may increase the CNS depression; epidural clonidine may prolong the sensory and motor blockade of local anesthetics

Mechanism of Action Stimulates alpha$_2$-adrenoceptors in the brain stem, thus activating an inhibitory neuron, resulting in reduced sympathetic outflow, producing a decrease in vasomotor tone and heart rate; epidural clonidine may produce pain relief at spinal presynaptic and postjunctional alpha$_2$-adrenoceptors by preventing pain signal transmis-sion; pain relief occurs only for the body regions innervated by the spinal segments where analgesic concentrations of clonidine exist

Pharmacodynamics/Kinetics

Onset of effect: Oral: 0.5-1 hour; T_{max}: 2-4 hours

Duration: 6-10 hours

Distribution: V_d: 2.1 L/kg (adults); highly lipid soluble; distributes readily into extravas-cular sites; protein binding: 20% to 40%

Metabolism: Hepatic (enterohepatic recirculation); extensively metabolized to inactive metabolites

Bioavailability: 75% to 95%

Half-life: Adults: Normal renal function: 6-20 hours; Renal impairment: 18-41 hours

Elimination: 65% excreted in urine, 32% unchanged, and 22% excreted in feces; not removed significantly by hemodialysis

Usual Dosage

Oral:

Children: Initial: 5-10 mcg/kg/day in divided doses every 8-12 hours; increase gradu-ally at 5- to 7-day intervals to 25 mcg/kg/day in divided doses every 6 hours; maximum: 0.9 mg/day

Clonidine tolerance test (test of growth hormone release from pituitary): 0.15 mg/m^2 or 4 mcg/kg as single dose

Adults: Initial dose: 0.1 mg twice daily, usual maintenance dose: 0.2-1.2 mg/day in 2-4 divided doses; maximum recommended dose: 2.4 mg/day

Nicotine withdrawal symptoms: 0.1 mg twice daily to maximum of 0.4 mg/day for 3-4 weeks

Elderly: Initial: 0.1 mg once daily at bedtime, increase gradually as needed

Transdermal: Apply once every 7 days; for initial therapy start with 0.1 mg and increase by 0.1 mg at 1- to 2-week intervals; dosages >0.6 mg do not improve efficacy

Epidural infusion: Starting dose: 30 mcg/hour; titrate as required for relief of pain or presence of side effects; minimal experience with doses >40 mcg/hour; should be considered an adjunct to intraspinal opiate therapy

Dosing adjustment in renal impairment: Cl_{cr} <10 mL/minute: Administer 50% to 75% of normal dose initially

Dialysis: Not dialyzable (0% to 5%) via hemo- or peritoneal dialysis; supplemental dose not necessary

Monitoring Parameters Blood pressure, standing and sitting/supine, respiratory rate and depth, pain relief, mental status, heart rate (bradycardia may be treated with atropine)

Reference Range Therapeutic: 1-2 ng/mL (SI: 4.4-8.7 nmol/L)

Test Interactions ↑ sodium (S); ↓ catecholamines (U)

Patient Information Do not discontinue drug except on instruction of physician; check daily to be sure patch is present; may cause drowsiness, impaired coordination, and judgment; use extreme caution while driving or operating machines

Nursing Implications Patches should be applied weekly at bedtime to a clean, hairless area of the upper outer arm or chest; rotate patch sites weekly; redness under patch may be reduced if a topical corticosteroid spray is applied to the area before placement of the patch; if needed, gradually reduce dose over 2-4 days to avoid rebound hypertension; during epidural administration, monitor cardiovascular and respiratory status carefully

Dosage Forms

Injection, preservative free, as hydrochloride: 100 mcg/mL (10 mL)

Patch, transdermal, as hydrochloride: 1, 2, and 3 (0.1, 0.2, 0.3 mg/day, 7-day duration)

Tablet, as hydrochloride: 0.1 mg, 0.2 mg, 0.3 mg

Clonidine and Chlorthalidone (KLOE ni deen & klor THAL i done)

U.S. Brand Names Combipres®

Therapeutic Category Antihypertensive Agent, Combination

Dosage Forms Tablet:

0.1: Clonidine 0.1 mg and chlorthalidone 15 mg

0.2: Clonidine 0.2 mg and chlorthalidone 15 mg

0.3: Clonidine 0.3 mg and chlorthalidone 15 mg

♦ **Clonidine Hydrochloride** see Clonidine on page 283

Clopidogrel (kloh PID oh grel)

U.S. Brand Names Plavix®

Synonyms Clopidogrel Bisulfate

Therapeutic Category Antiplatelet Agent

Use The reduction of atherosclerotic events (myocardial infarction, stroke, vascular deaths) in patients with atherosclerosis documented by recent myocardial infarctions, recent stroke or established peripheral arterial disease

Pregnancy Risk Factor B

Contraindications In patients with active bleeding (eg, peptic ulcer disease, intracranial hemorrhage), patients with coagulation disorders, or patients who have demonstrated hypersensitivity to the drug or any components of the drug product

Warnings/Precautions Patients receiving anticoagulants or other antiplatelet drugs concurrently, liver disease, patients having a previous hypersensitivity or other untoward effects related to ticlopidine, hypertension, renal impairment, history of bleeding or hemostatic disorders or drug-related hematologic disorders, and consider discontinuing in patients scheduled for major surgery, 7 days prior to that surgery

Adverse Reactions

>10%: Gastrointestinal: Indigestion, nausea, vomiting (15%)

1% to 10%:

Dermatologic: Rash (4.2%), pruritus (3.3%)

Gastrointestinal: Diarrhea (4.5%), GI hemorrhage (2%)

Hepatic: Hepatotoxicity (≤3%)

<1%: Neutropenia (0.1%), prolonged bleeding time, intracranial bleeding (0.35%)

Overdosage/Toxicology

Symptoms of acute toxicity include vomiting, prostration, difficulty breathing, and gastrointestinal hemorrhage. Only one case of overdose with clopidogrel has been reported to date, no symptoms were reported with this case and no specific treatments were required.

Based on its pharmacology, platelet transfusions may be an appropriate treatment when attempting to reverse the effects of clopidogrel. After decontamination, treatment is symptomatic and supportive.

Drug Interactions Increased effect/toxicity: When used with other drugs that can increase bleeding risk such as heparins, warfarins, NSAIDs and other antiplatelet drugs

Mechanism of Action Blocks the ADP receptors, which prevent fibrinogen binding at that site and thereby reduce the possibility of platelet adhesion and aggregation

Pharmacodynamics/Kinetics

Onset:

Maximal effect on bleeding time: 5-6 days

Maximal effect on platelet function: 3-7 days

Metabolism: Hydrolysis in the liver; biotransformation of clopidogrel is needed to produce inhibition of platelet aggregation, but an active metabolite responsible for the activity of the drug has not yet been isolated

Half-life, elimination: ~8 hours

Time to peak serum concentration: Oral: ~1 hour

Elimination: Excretion via the kidneys

Usual Dosage Adults: Oral: 75 mg once daily

Dosing adjustment in renal impairment and elderly: None necessary

Dietary Considerations Food: May be taken without regard to meals

Monitoring Parameters Signs of bleeding

(Continued)

Clopidogrel *(Continued)*

Patient Information Report any unusual or prolonged bleeding or fever; inform your physician before starting any new medications, changing your diet, or undergoing any procedures that may be associated with a risk of bleeding

Dosage Forms Tablet, as bisulfate: 75 mg

♦ **Clopidogrel Bisulfate** *see Clopidogrel on previous page*

♦ **Clopra®** *see Metoclopramide on page 766*

Clorazepate (klor AZ e pate)

Related Information
Benzodiazepines Comparison *on page 1310*
Epilepsy Treatment *on page 1468*

U.S. Brand Names Gen-XENE®; Tranxene®

Canadian Brand Names Apo®-Clorazepate; Novo-Clopate

Synonyms Clorazepate Dipotassium

Therapeutic Category Anticonvulsant; Benzodiazepine; Sedative

Use Treatment of generalized anxiety and panic disorders; management of alcohol withdrawal; adjunct anticonvulsant in management of partial seizures

Restrictions C-IV

Pregnancy Risk Factor D

Contraindications Hypersensitivity to clorazepate dipotassium or any component; cross-sensitivity with other benzodiazepines may exist; avoid using in patients with pre-existing CNS depression, severe uncontrolled pain, or narrow-angle glaucoma

Warnings/Precautions Use with caution in patients with hepatic or renal disease; abrupt discontinuation may cause withdrawal symptoms or seizures

Adverse Reactions
>10%:
Cardiovascular: Tachycardia, chest pain
Central nervous system: Drowsiness, fatigue, ataxia, lightheadedness, memory impairment, insomnia, anxiety, headache, depression
Dermatologic: Rash
Endocrine & metabolic: Decreased libido
Gastrointestinal: Xerostomia, constipation, diarrhea, decreased salivation, nausea, vomiting, increased or decreased appetite
Neuromuscular & skeletal: Dysarthria
Ocular: Blurred vision
Miscellaneous: Diaphoresis
1% to 10%:
Cardiovascular: Syncope, hypotension
Central nervous system: Confusion, nervousness, dizziness, akathisia
Dermatologic: Dermatitis
Gastrointestinal: Nausea, increased salivation, weight gain or loss
Neuromuscular & skeletal: Rigidity, tremor, muscle cramps
Otic: Tinnitus
Respiratory: Nasal congestion, hyperventilation
<1%: Menstrual irregularities, blood dyscrasias, reflex slowing, drug dependence, long-term use may also be associated with renal or hepatic injury and reduced hematocrit

Overdosage/Toxicology
May produce somnolence, confusion, ataxia, diminished reflexes, coma
Treatment for benzodiazepine overdose is supportive; rarely is mechanical ventilation required; flumazenil has been shown to selectively block the binding of benzodiazepines to CNS receptors, resulting in a reversal of benzodiazepine-induced CNS depression, but not respiratory depression.

Drug Interactions Increased effect: Cimetidine, CNS depressants, alcohol

Stability Unstable in water

Mechanism of Action Facilitates gamma aminobutyric acid (GABA)-mediated transmission inhibitory neurotransmitter action, depresses subcortical levels of CNS

Pharmacodynamics/Kinetics
Distribution: Crosses the placenta; appears in urine
Metabolism: Rapidly decarboxylated to desmethyldiazepam (active) in acidic stomach prior to absorption; metabolized in the liver to oxazepam (active)
Half-life: Adults: Desmethyldiazepam: 48-96 hours; Oxazepam: 6-8 hours
Time to peak serum concentration: Oral: Within 1 hour
Elimination: Primarily in urine

Usual Dosage Oral:
Children 9-12 years: Anticonvulsant: Initial: 3.75-7.5 mg/dose twice daily; increase dose by 3.75 mg at weekly intervals, not to exceed 60 mg/day in 2-3 divided doses
Children >12 years and Adults: Anticonvulsant: Initial: Up to 7.5 mg/dose 2-3 times/day; increase dose by 7.5 mg at weekly intervals; not to exceed 90 mg/day
Adults:
Anxiety: 7.5-15 mg 2-4 times/day, or given as single dose of 11.25 or 22.5 mg at bedtime
Alcohol withdrawal: Initial: 30 mg, then 15 mg 2-4 times/day on first day; maximum daily dose: 90 mg; gradually decrease dose over subsequent days

Dietary Considerations Alcohol: Additive CNS effects, avoid use

Monitoring Parameters Respiratory and cardiovascular status, excess CNS depression

Reference Range Therapeutic: 0.12-1 µg/mL (SI: 0.36-3.01 µmol/L)

Test Interactions ↓ hematocrit, abnormal liver and renal function tests

Patient Information Avoid alcohol and other CNS depressants; avoid activities needing good psychomotor coordination until CNS effects are known; drug may cause physical or psychological dependence; avoid abrupt discontinuation after prolonged use

Nursing Implications Observe patient for excess sedation, respiratory depression; raise bed rails, initiate safety measures, assist with ambulation

Dosage Forms
Capsule, as dipotassium: 3.75 mg, 7.5 mg, 15 mg
Tablet, as dipotassium: 3.75 mg, 7.5 mg, 15 mg
Tablet, as dipotassium, single dose: 11.25 mg, 22.5 mg

♦ **Clorazepate Dipotassium** *see Clorazepate on previous page*

Clotrimazole (kloe TRIM a zole)

Related Information
Guidelines for the Prevention of Opportunistic Infections in Persons with HIV *on page 1388*
Treatment of Sexually Transmitted Diseases *on page 1429*

U.S. Brand Names Femizole-7® [OTC]; Fungoid® Solution; Gyne-Lotrimin® [OTC]; Gynix®; Lotrimin®; Lotrimin® AF Cream [OTC]; Lotrimin® AF Lotion [OTC]; Lotrimin® AF Solution [OTC]; Mycelex®; Mycelex®-7; Mycelex®-G

Therapeutic Category Antifungal Agent, Oral Nonabsorbed; Antifungal Agent, Topical; Antifungal Agent, Vaginal

Use Treatment of susceptible fungal infections, including oropharyngeal, candidiasis, dermatophytoses, superficial mycoses, and cutaneous candidiasis, as well as vulvovaginal candidiasis; limited data suggest that clotrimazole troches may be effective for prophylaxis against oropharyngeal candidiasis in neutropenic patients

Pregnancy Risk Factor B; C (oral)

Contraindications Hypersensitivity to clotrimazole or any component

Warnings/Precautions Clotrimazole should not be used for treatment of systemic fungal infection; safety and effectiveness of clotrimazole lozenges (troches) in children <3 years of age have not been established

Adverse Reactions
>10%: Hepatic: Abnormal LFTs, causal relationship between troches and elevated LFTs not clearly established
1% to 10%:
Gastrointestinal: Nausea and vomiting may occur in patients on clotrimazole troches
Local: Mild burning, irritation, stinging to skin or vaginal area

Drug Interactions CYP3A3/4 and 3A5-7 enzyme inhibitor

Mechanism of Action Binds to phospholipids in the fungal cell membrane altering cell wall permeability resulting in loss of essential intracellular elements

Pharmacodynamics/Kinetics
Absorption: Topical: Negligible through intact skin
Time to peak serum concentration:
Oral topical administration: Salivary levels occur within 3 hours following 30 minutes of dissolution time in the mouth
Vaginal cream: High vaginal levels occur within 8-24 hours
Vaginal tablet: High vaginal levels occur within 1-2 days
Elimination: As metabolites via bile

Usual Dosage
Children >3 years and Adults:
Oral:
Prophylaxis: 10 mg troche dissolved 3 times/day for the duration of chemotherapy or until steroids are reduced to maintenance levels
Treatment: 10 mg troche dissolved slowly 5 times/day for 14 consecutive days
Topical: Apply twice daily; if no improvement occurs after 4 weeks of therapy, re-evaluate diagnosis
Children >12 years and Adults:
Vaginal:
Cream: Insert 1 applicatorful of 1% vaginal cream daily (preferably at bedtime) for 7 consecutive days
Tablet: Insert 100 mg/day for 7 days or 500 mg single dose
Topical: Apply to affected area twice daily (morning and evening) for 7 consecutive days

Monitoring Parameters Periodic liver function tests during oral therapy with clotrimazole lozenges

Patient Information May cause irritation to the skin; avoid contact with eyes; lozenge (troche) must be dissolved slowly in the mouth

Dosage Forms
Combination pack (Mycelex®-7): Vaginal tablet 100 mg (7's) and vaginal cream 1% (7 g)
Cream:
Topical (Lotrimin®, Lotrimin® AF, Mycelex®, Mycelex® OTC) : 1% (15 g, 30 g, 45 g, 90 g)
Vaginal (Femizole-7®, Gyne-Lotrimin®, Mycelex®-G): 1% (45 g, 90 g)
Lotion (Lotrimin®): 1% (30 mL)
Solution, topical (Fungoid®, Lotrimin®, Lotrimin® AF, Mycelex®, Mycelex® OTC): 1% (10 mL, 30 mL)
Tablet, vaginal (Gyne-Lotrimin®, Gynix®, Mycelex®-G): 100 mg (7s); 500 mg (1s)
Troche (Mycelex®): 10 mg
(Continued)

Clotrimazole *(Continued)*

Twin pack (Mycelex®): Vaginal tablet 500 mg (1's) and vaginal cream 1% (7 g)

Cloxacillin (kloks a SIL in)

U.S. Brand Names Cloxapen®; Tegopen®
Canadian Brand Names Apo®-Cloxi; Novo-Cloxin; Nu-Cloxi; Orbenin®; Taro-Cloxacillin®
Synonyms Cloxacillin Sodium
Therapeutic Category Antibiotic, Penicillin
Use Treatment of susceptible bacterial infections, notably penicillinase-producing staphylococci causing respiratory tract, skin and skin structure, bone and joint, urinary tract infections
Pregnancy Risk Factor B
Contraindications Hypersensitivity to cloxacillin or any component, or penicillins
Warnings/Precautions Monitor PT if patient concurrently on warfarin, elimination of drug is slow in renally impaired; use with caution in patients allergic to cephalosporins due to a low incidence of cross-hypersensitivity
Adverse Reactions
1% to 10%: Gastrointestinal: Nausea, diarrhea, abdominal pain
<1%: Fever, seizures with extremely high doses and/or renal failure, rash (maculopapular to exfoliative), vomiting, pseudomembranous colitis, vaginitis, eosinophilia, leukopenia, neutropenia, thrombocytopenia, agranulocytosis, anemia, hemolytic anemia, prolonged PT, hepatotoxicity, transient elevated LFTs, hematuria, interstitial nephritis, increased BUN/creatinine, serum sickness-like reactions, hypersensitivity
Overdosage/Toxicology
Symptoms of penicillin overdose include neuromuscular hypersensitivity (agitation, hallucinations, asterixis, encephalopathy, confusion, and seizures) and electrolyte imbalance with potassium or sodium salts, especially in renal failure
Hemodialysis may be helpful to aid in the removal of the drug from the blood, otherwise most treatment is supportive or symptom directed
Drug Interactions
Decreased effect: Efficacy of oral contraceptives may be reduced
Increased effect: Disulfiram, probenecid may increase penicillin levels, increased effect of anticoagulants
Stability Refrigerate oral solution after reconstitution; discard after 14 days; stable for 3 days at room temperature
Mechanism of Action Inhibits bacterial cell wall synthesis by binding to one or more of the penicillin-binding proteins (PBPs) which in turn inhibits the final transpeptidation step of peptidoglycan synthesis in bacterial cell walls, thus inhibiting cell wall biosynthesis. Bacteria eventually lyse due to ongoing activity of cell wall autolytic enzymes (autolysins and murein hydrolases) while cell wall assembly is arrested.
Pharmacodynamics/Kinetics
Absorption: Oral: ~50%
Distribution: Crosses the placenta; appears in breast milk; distributed widely to most body fluids and bone; penetration into cells, into the eye, and across normal meninges is poor; inflammation increased amount that crosses the blood-brain barrier
Protein binding: 90% to 98%
Metabolism: Significant in the liver to active and inactive metabolites
Half-life: 0.5-1.5 hours (prolonged with renal impairment and in neonates)
Time to peak serum concentration: Oral: Within 0.5-2 hours
Elimination: In urine and through bile
Usual Dosage Oral:
Children >1 month (<20 kg): 50-100 mg/kg/day in divided doses every 6 hours; up to a maximum of 4 g/day
Children (>20 kg) and Adults: 250-500 mg every 6 hours
Hemodialysis: Not dialyzable (0% to 5%)
Monitoring Parameters Observe for signs and symptoms of anaphylaxis during first dose
Test Interactions May interfere with urinary glucose tests using cupric sulfate (Benedict's solution, Clinitest®); may inactivate aminoglycosides *in vitro*; false-positive urine and serum proteins; false-positive in uric acid, urinary steroids
Patient Information Take 1 hour before or 2 hours after meals; finish all medication; do not skip doses
Additional Information Sodium content of 250 mg capsule: 13.8 mg (0.6 mEq); 5 mL of 125 mg/5 mL: 11 mg (0.48 mEq)
Dosage Forms
Capsule, as sodium: 250 mg, 500 mg
Powder for oral suspension, as sodium: 125 mg/5 mL (100 mL, 200 mL)

♦ **Cloxacillin Sodium** *see Cloxacillin on this page*
♦ **Cloxapen®** *see Cloxacillin on this page*

Clozapine (KLOE za peen)

Related Information
Antipsychotic Agents Comparison *on page 1305*
U.S. Brand Names Clozaril®
Therapeutic Category Antipsychotic Agent
Use Management of schizophrenic patients

Pregnancy Risk Factor B

Contraindications In patients with WBC ≤3500 cells/mm³ before therapy; if WBC falls to <3000 cells/mm³ during therapy the drug should be withheld until signs and symptoms of infection disappear and WBC rises to >3000 cells/mm³

Warnings/Precautions Medication should not be stopped abruptly; taper off over 1-2 weeks. WBC testing should occur weekly for the first 6 months of therapy; thereafter, if acceptable WBC counts are maintained (WBC ≥3000/mm³, ANC ≥1500/mm³) then WBC counts can be monitored every other week. WBCs must be monitored weekly for the first 4 weeks after therapy discontinuation. Significant risk of agranulocytosis, potentially life-threatening. Use with caution in patients receiving other marrow suppressive agents.

Adverse Reactions

>10%:
    Cardiovascular: Tachycardia, hypotension, orthostatic hypotension
    Central nervous system: Fever, headache, drowsiness
    Gastrointestinal: Constipation, nausea, vomiting, unusual weight gain

1% to 10%:
    Cardiovascular: EKG changes, hypertension
    Central nervous system: Agitation, akathisia
    Gastrointestinal: Abdominal discomfort, heartburn, xerostomia
    Ocular: Blurred vision
    Miscellaneous: Diaphoresis (increased)

<1%: Insomnia, seizures, tardive dyskinesia, neuroleptic malignant syndrome, dysuria, impotence, agranulocytosis, eosinophilia, granulocytopenia, leukopenia, thrombocytopenia, rigidity, tremor

Overdosage/Toxicology

Symptoms of overdose include altered states of consciousness, tachycardia, hypotension, hypersalivation, respiratory depression

Following initiation of essential overdose management, toxic symptom treatment and supportive treatment should be initiated. Hypotension usually responds to I.V. fluids or Trendelenburg positioning. If unresponsive to these measures, the use of a parenteral inotrope may be required. Seizures commonly respond to diazepam (I.V. 5-10 mg bolus in adults every 15 minutes if needed up to a total of 30 mg; I.V. 0.25-0.4 mg/kg/dose up to a total of 10 mg in children) or to phenytoin or phenobarbital; critical cardiac arrhythmias often respond to I.V. phenytoin (15 mg/kg up to 1 g), while other antiarrhythmics can be used. Neuroleptics often cause extrapyramidal symptoms (eg, dystonic reactions) requiring management with benztropine mesylate I.V. 1-2 mg (adults) may be effective. These agents are generally effective within 2-5 minutes.

Drug Interactions CYP1A2, 2C, 2E1, 3A3/4 enzyme substrate, CYP2D6 enzyme substrate (minor)

Decreased effect of epinephrine; decreased effect with phenytoin
Increased effect of CNS depressants, guanabenz, anticholinergics
Increased toxicity with cimetidine, MAO inhibitors, neuroleptics, TCAs

Mechanism of Action Clozapine is a weak dopamine₁ and dopamine₂ receptor blocker; in addition, it blocks the serotonin₂, alpha-adrenergic, and histamine H₁ central nervous system receptors

Pharmacodynamics/Kinetics

Metabolism: Undergoes extensive metabolism primarily to unconjugated forms
Elimination: In urine

Usual Dosage Adults: Oral: 25 mg once or twice daily initially and increased, as tolerated to a target dose of 300-450 mg/day after 2 weeks, but may require doses as high as 600-900 mg/day

Patient Information Report any lethargy, fever, sore throat, flu-like symptoms, or any other signs or symptoms of infection; may cause drowsiness; frequent blood samples must be taken; do not stop taking even if you think it is not working

Nursing Implications Benign, self-limiting temperature elevations sometimes occur during the first 3 weeks of treatment, weekly CBC mandatory

Additional Information Clozapine is available only through the Clozaril® Patient Management System, a program that combines WBC testing, pharmacy services, patient monitoring services, and safety monitoring. No more than a one-week supply should be dispensed at a time.

Dosage Forms Tablet: 25 mg, 100 mg

♦ **Clozaril®** *see Clozapine on previous page*

♦ **CMV-IGIV** *see Cytomegalovirus Immune Globulin (Intravenous-Human) on page 315*

♦ **Coagulant Complex Inhibitor** *see Anti-inhibitor Coagulant Complex on page 90*

♦ **Coagulation Factor VIIa** *see Factor VIIa, Recombinant on page 467*

♦ **Cobex®** *see Cyanocobalamin on page 302*

Cocaine (koe KANE)

Synonyms Cocaine Hydrochloride

Therapeutic Category Local Anesthetic, Ester Derivative; Local Anesthetic, Topical

Use Topical anesthesia (ester derivative) for mucous membranes

Restrictions C-II

Pregnancy Risk Factor C (X if nonmedicinal use)

Contraindications Systemic use, hypersensitivity to cocaine or any component; pregnancy if nonmedicinal use

Warnings/Precautions Use with caution in patients with hypertension, severe cardiovascular disease, or thyrotoxicosis; use with caution in patients with severely traumatized mucosa and sepsis in the region of intended application. Repeated topical application
(Continued)

Cocaine *(Continued)*

can result in psychic dependence and tolerance. May cause cornea to become clouded or pitted, therefore, normal saline should be used to irrigate and protect cornea during surgery; not for injection.

Adverse Reactions
>10%:
Central nervous system: CNS stimulation
Gastrointestinal: Loss of taste perception
Respiratory: Chronic rhinitis, nasal congestion
Miscellaneous: Loss of smell
1% to 10%:
Cardiovascular: Decreased heart rate with low doses, increased heart rate with moderate doses, hypertension, tachycardia, cardiac arrhythmias
Central nervous system: Nervousness, restlessness, euphoria, excitement, hallucination, seizures
Gastrointestinal: Vomiting
Neuromuscular & skeletal: Tremors and clonic-tonic reactions
Ocular: Sloughing of the corneal epithelium, ulceration of the cornea
Respiratory: Tachypnea, respiratory failure

Overdosage/Toxicology
Symptoms of overdose include anxiety, excitement, confusion, nausea, vomiting, headache, rapid pulse, irregular respiration, delirium, fever, seizures, respiratory arrest, hallucinations, dilated pupils, muscle spasms, sensory aberrations, cardiac arrhythmias
Fatal dose: Oral: 500 mg to 1.2 g; severe toxic effects have occurred with doses as low as 20 mg
Since no specific antidote for cocaine exists, serious toxic effects are treated symptomatically. Maintain airway and respiration. Attempt delay of absorption (if ingested) with activated charcoal, gastric lavage or emesis. Seizures are treated with diazepam while propranolol or labetalol may be useful for life-threatening arrhythmias, agitation, and/or hypertension.

Drug Interactions CYP3A3/4 enzyme substrate
Increased toxicity: MAO inhibitors

Stability Store in well closed, light-resistant containers

Mechanism of Action Ester local anesthetic blocks both the initiation and conduction of nerve impulses by decreasing the neuronal membrane's permeability to sodium ions, which results in inhibition of depolarization with resultant blockade of conduction; interferes with the uptake of norepinephrine by adrenergic nerve terminals producing vasoconstriction

Pharmacodynamics/Kinetics Following topical administration to mucosa:
Onset of action: Within 1 minute
Peak action: Within 5 minutes
Duration: ≥30 minutes, depending on dosage administered
Absorption: Well absorbed through mucous membranes; limited by drug-induced vasoconstriction; enhanced by inflammation
Distribution: Appears in breast milk
Metabolism: In the liver; major metabolites are ecgonine methyl ester and benzoyl ecgonine
Half-life: 75 minutes
Elimination: Primarily in urine as metabolites and unchanged drug (<10%); cocaine metabolites may appear in the urine of neonates for up to 5 days after birth due to maternal cocaine use shortly before birth

Usual Dosage Dosage depends on the area to be anesthetized, tissue vascularity, technique of anesthesia, and individual patient tolerance; use the lowest dose necessary to produce adequate anesthesia should be used, not to exceed 1 mg/kg. Use reduced dosages for children, elderly, or debilitated patients.

Topical application (ear, nose, throat, bronchoscopy): Concentrations of 1% to 4% are used; concentrations >4% are not recommended because of potential for increased incidence and severity of systemic toxic reactions

Monitoring Parameters Vital signs

Reference Range Therapeutic: 100-500 ng/mL (SI: 330 nmol/L); Toxic: >1000 ng/mL (SI: >3300 nmol/L)

Nursing Implications Use only on mucous membranes of the oral, laryngeal, and nasal cavities, do not use on extensive areas of broken skin

Dosage Forms
Powder, as hydrochloride: 5 g, 25 g
Solution, topical:
As hydrochloride: 4% [40 mg/mL] (2 mL, 4 mL, 10 mL); 10% [100 mg/mL] (4 mL, 10 mL)
Viscous, as hydrochloride: 4% [40 mg/mL] (4 mL, 10 mL); 10% [100 mg/mL] (4 mL, 10 mL)
Tablet, soluble, for topical solution, as hydrochloride: 135 mg

- ♦ **Cocaine Hydrochloride** *see* Cocaine *on previous page*
- ♦ **Codafed® Expectorant** *see* Guaifenesin, Pseudoephedrine, and Codeine *on page 551*
- ♦ **Codamine®** *see* Hydrocodone and Phenylpropanolamine *on page 579*
- ♦ **Codamine® Pediatric** *see* Hydrocodone and Phenylpropanolamine *on page 579*
- ♦ **Codehist® DH** *see* Chlorpheniramine, Pseudoephedrine, and Codeine *on page 247*

Codeine (KOE deen)

Related Information
Narcotic Agonists Comparison *on page 1328*

Canadian Brand Names Codeine Contin®; Linctus Codeine Blac; Linctus With Codeine Phosphate; Paveral Stanley Syrup With Codeine Phosphate

Synonyms Codeine Phosphate; Codeine Sulfate; Methylmorphine

Therapeutic Category Analgesic, Narcotic; Antitussive

Use Treatment of mild to moderate pain; antitussive in lower doses; dextromethorphan has equivalent antitussive activity but has much lower toxicity in accidental overdose

Restrictions C-II

Pregnancy Risk Factor C (D if used for prolonged periods or in high doses at term)

Contraindications Hypersensitivity to codeine or any component

Warnings/Precautions Use with caution in patients with hypersensitivity reactions to other phenanthrene derivative opioid agonists (morphine, hydrocodone, hydromorphone, levorphanol, oxycodone, oxymorphone); respiratory diseases including asthma, emphysema, COPD, or severe liver or renal insufficiency; some preparations contain sulfites which may cause allergic reactions; tolerance or drug dependence may result from extended use

Not recommended for use for cough control in patients with a productive cough; not recommended as an antitussive for children <2 years of age; the elderly may be particularly susceptible to the CNS depressant and confusion as well as constipating effects of narcotics

Adverse Reactions
Percentage unknown: Increased AST, ALT
>10%:
Central nervous system: Drowsiness
Gastrointestinal: Constipation
1% to 10%:
Cardiovascular: Tachycardia or bradycardia, hypotension
Central nervous system: Dizziness, lightheadedness, false feeling of well being, malaise, headache, restlessness, paradoxical CNS stimulation, confusion
Dermatologic: Rash, urticaria
Gastrointestinal: Xerostomia, anorexia, nausea, vomiting,
Genitourinary: Decreased urination, ureteral spasm
Hepatic: Increased LFTs
Local: Burning at injection site
Ocular: Blurred vision
Neuromuscular & skeletal: Weakness
Respiratory: Shortness of breath, dyspnea
Miscellaneous: Histamine release
<1%: Convulsions, hallucinations, mental depression, nightmares, insomnia, paralytic ileus, biliary spasm, stomach cramps, muscle rigidity, trembling

Overdosage/Toxicology
Symptoms of overdose include CNS and respiratory depression, gastrointestinal cramping, constipation
Naloxone 2 mg I.V. (0.01 mg/kg for children) with repeat administration as necessary up to a total of 10 mg

Drug Interactions CYP2D6 and 3A3/4 enzyme substrate; CYP2D6 enzyme inhibitor
Decreased effect with cigarette smoking
Increased toxicity: CNS depressants, phenothiazines, TCAs, other narcotic analgesics, guanabenz, MAO inhibitors, neuromuscular blockers

Stability Store injection between 15°C to 30°C, avoid freezing; do not use if injection is discolored or contains a precipitate; protect injection from light

Mechanism of Action Binds to opiate receptors in the CNS, causing inhibition of ascending pain pathways, altering the perception of and response to pain; causes cough supression by direct central action in the medulla; produces generalized CNS depression

Pharmacodynamics/Kinetics
Onset of action: Oral: 0.5-1 hour; I.M.: 10-30 minutes
Peak action: Oral: 1-1.5 hours; I.M.: 0.5-1 hour
Duration of action: 4-6 hours
Absorption: Oral: Adequate
Distribution: Crosses the placenta; appears in breast milk
Protein binding: 7%
Metabolism: Hepatic to morphine (active)
Half-life: 2.5-3.5 hours
Elimination: 3% to 16% excreted in urine as unchanged drug, norcodeine, and free and conjugated morphine

Usual Dosage Doses should be titrated to appropriate analgesic effect; when changing routes of administration, note that oral dose is ²/₃ as effective as parenteral dose

Analgesic:
Children: Oral, I.M., S.C.: 0.5-1 mg/kg/dose every 4-6 hours as needed; maximum: 60 mg/dose
Adults: Oral, I.M., I.V., S.C.: 30 mg/dose; range: 15-60 mg every 4-6 hours as needed; maximum: 360 mg/24 hours
Antitussive: Oral (for nonproductive cough):
Children: 1-1.5 mg/kg/day in divided doses every 4-6 hours as needed: Alternative dose according to age:
2-6 years: 2.5-5 mg every 4-6 hours as needed; maximum: 30 mg/day

(Continued)

Codeine *(Continued)*

      6-12 years: 5-10 mg every 4-6 hours as needed; maximum: 60 mg/day

      Adults: 10-20 mg/dose every 4-6 hours as needed; maximum: 120 mg/day

    Dosing adjustment in renal impairment:

      Cl$_{cr}$ 10-50 mL/minute: Administer 75% of dose

      Cl$_{cr}$ <10 mL/minute: Administer 50% of dose

    Dosing adjustment in hepatic impairment: Probably necessary in hepatic insufficiency

Dietary Considerations

    Alcohol: Additive CNS effects, avoid or limit alcohol; watch for sedation

    Food: Glucose may cause hyperglycemia; monitor blood glucose concentrations

Monitoring Parameters Pain relief, respiratory and mental status, blood pressure, heart rate

Reference Range Therapeutic: Not established; Toxic: >1.1 µg/mL

Patient Information Avoid alcohol, may cause drowsiness, impaired judgment, or coordination; may cause physical and psychological dependence with prolonged use

Nursing Implications Observe patient for excessive sedation, respiratory depression, implement safety measures, assist with ambulation

Dosage Forms

    Injection, as phosphate: 30 mg (1 mL, 2 mL); 60 mg (1 mL, 2 mL)

    Solution, oral: 15 mg/5 mL

    Tablet, as sulfate: 15 mg, 30 mg, 60 mg

    Tablet, as phosphate, soluble: 30 mg, 60 mg

    Tablet, as sulfate, soluble: 15 mg, 30 mg, 60 mg

- ◆ **Codeine and Acetaminophen** *see Acetaminophen and Codeine on page 21*
- ◆ **Codeine and Aspirin** *see Aspirin and Codeine on page 105*
- ◆ **Codeine and Guaifenesin** *see Guaifenesin and Codeine on page 550*
- ◆ **Codeine Contin®** *see Codeine on previous page*
- ◆ **Codeine Phosphate** *see Codeine on previous page*
- ◆ **Codeine Sulfate** *see Codeine on previous page*
- ◆ **Codiclear® DH** *see Hydrocodone and Guaifenesin on page 577*
- ◆ **Codoxy®** *see Oxycodone and Aspirin on page 876*
- ◆ **Codroxomin®** *see Hydroxocobalamin on page 585*
- ◆ **Cogentin®** *see Benztropine on page 135*
- ◆ **Co-Gesic®** *see Hydrocodone and Acetaminophen on page 575*
- ◆ **Cognex®** *see Tacrine on page 1102*
- ◆ **Colace® [OTC]** *see Docusate on page 384*
- ◆ **Colax-C®** *see Docusate on page 384*

Colchicine *(KOL chi seen)*

Therapeutic Category Anti-inflammatory Agent; Uricosuric Agent

Use Treat acute gouty arthritis attacks and prevent recurrences of such attacks, management of familial Mediterranean fever

Pregnancy Risk Factor C (oral)/D (parenteral)

Contraindications Hypersensitivity to colchicine or any component; serious renal, gastrointestinal, hepatic, or cardiac disorders; blood dyscrasias

Warnings/Precautions Severe local irritation can occur following S.C. or I.M. administration; use with caution in debilitated patients or elderly patients or patients with severe GI, renal, or liver disease

Adverse Reactions

    >10%: Gastrointestinal: Nausea, vomiting, diarrhea, abdominal pain

    1% to 10%:

      Dermatologic: Alopecia

      Gastrointestinal: Anorexia

    <1%: Rash, azoospermia, agranulocytosis, aplastic anemia, bone marrow suppression, hepatotoxicity, myopathy, peripheral neuritis

Overdosage/Toxicology

    Symptoms of overdose include nausea, vomiting, abdominal pain, shock, kidney damage, muscle weakness, burning in throat, watery to bloody diarrhea, hypotension, anuria, cardiovascular collapse, delirium, convulsions

    Treatment includes gastric lavage and measures to prevent shock, hemodialysis or peritoneal dialysis; atropine and morphine may relieve abdominal pain

Drug Interactions

    Decreased effect: Vitamin B$_{12}$ absorption may be decreased

    Increased toxicity:

      Sympathomimetic agents

      CNS depressant effects are enhanced

Stability Protect tablets from light; I.V. colchicine is **incompatible** with I.V. solutions with preservatives; **incompatible** with dextrose

Mechanism of Action Decreases leukocyte motility, decreases phagocytosis in joints and lactic acid production, thereby reducing the deposition of urate crystals that perpetuates the inflammatory response

Pharmacodynamics/Kinetics

    Onset of effect: Oral: Pain relief begins within 12 hours if adequately dosed

    Distribution: Concentrates in leukocytes, kidney, spleen, and liver; does not distribute in heart, skeletal muscle, and brain

    Protein binding: 10% to 31%

Metabolism: Partially deacetylated in the liver
Half-life: 12-30 minutes
End-stage renal disease: 45 minutes
Time to peak serum concentration: Oral: Within 0.5-2 hours declining for the next 2 hours before increasing again due to enterohepatic recycling
Elimination: Primarily in the feces via bile; 10% to 20% excreted in the urine

Usual Dosage
Prophylaxis of familial Mediterranean fever: Oral:
Children:
≤5 years: 0.5 mg/day
>5 years: 1-1.5 mg/day in 2-3 divided doses
Adults: 1-2 mg/day in 2-3 divided doses
Gouty arthritis, acute attacks: Adults:
Oral: Initial: 0.5-1.2 mg, then 0.5-0.6 mg every 1-2 hours or 1-1.2 mg every 2 hours until relief or GI side effects (nausea, vomiting, or diarrhea) occur to a maximum total dose of 8 mg; wait 3 days before initiating another course of therapy
I.V.: Initial: 1-3 mg, then 0.5 mg every 6 hours until response, not to exceed 4 mg/day; if pain recurs, it may be necessary to administer a daily dose of 1-2 mg for several days, however, do not administer more colchicine by any route for at least 7 days after a full course of I.V. therapy (4 mg), transfer to oral colchicine in a dose similar to that being given I.V.
Gouty arthritis, prophylaxis of recurrent attacks: Adults: Oral: 0.5-0.6 mg/day or every other day
Dosing adjustment in renal impairment:
Cl_{cr} <50 mL/minute: Avoid chronic use or administration
Cl_{cr} <10 mL/minute: Decrease dose by 50% for treatment of acute attacks
Hemodialysis: Not dialyzable (0% to 5%); supplemental dose is not necessary
Peritoneal dialysis: Supplemental dose is not necessary

Dietary Considerations
Alcohol: Avoid use
Food: Cyanocobalamin (Vitamin B_{12}): Malabsorption of the substrate. May result in macrocytic anemia or neurologic dysfunction. May need to supplement with Vitamin B_{12}.

Administration Injection should be made over 2-5 minutes into tubing of free-flowing I.V. with compatible fluid; do not administer I.M. or S.C.

Monitoring Parameters CBC and renal function test

Test Interactions May cause false-positive results in urine tests for erythrocytes or hemoglobin

Patient Information Avoid alcohol; discontinue if nausea or vomiting occurs; if taking for acute attack, discontinue as soon as pain resolves or if nausea, vomiting, or diarrhea occurs

Dosage Forms
Injection: 0.5 mg/mL (2 mL)
Tablet: 0.5 mg, 0.6 mg

Colchicine and Probenecid (KOL chi seen & proe BEN e sid)
Therapeutic Category Antigout Agent
Dosage Forms Tablet: Colchicine 0.5 mg and probenecid 0.5 g

♦ Colestid® see Colestipol on this page

Colestipol (koe LES ti pole)
Related Information
Lipid-Lowering Agents on page 1327
U.S. Brand Names Colestid®
Synonyms Colestipol Hydrochloride
Therapeutic Category Antilipemic Agent
Use Adjunct in management of primary hypercholesterolemia; regression of arteriolosclerosis; relief of pruritus associated with elevated levels of bile acids; possibly used to decrease plasma half-life of digoxin in toxicity
Pregnancy Risk Factor C
Contraindications Hypersensitivity to colestipol or any component; avoid using in complete biliary obstruction
Warnings/Precautions Avoid in patients with high triglycerides, GI dysfunction (constipation); may be associated with increased bleeding tendency as a result of hypothrombinemia secondary to vitamin K deficiency; may cause depletion of vitamins A, D, E
Adverse Reactions
>10%: Gastrointestinal: Constipation
1% to 10%: Gastrointestinal: Abdominal pain and distention, belching, flatulence, nausea, vomiting, diarrhea
<1%: Headache, dizziness, anxiety, vertigo, drowsiness, fatigue, dermatitis, urticaria, peptic ulceration, GI irritation and bleeding, anorexia, cholelithiasis, cholecystitis, arthralgia, arthritis, weakness, shortness of breath, increased serum phosphorous and chloride with decrease of sodium and potassium
Overdosage/Toxicology
Symptoms of overdose include GI obstruction, nausea, GI distress
Treatment is supportive
Drug Interactions Decreased absorption of tetracycline, penicillin G, vitamins A, D, E and K, digitalis glycosides, warfarin, thyroid hormones, thiazide diuretics, propranolol, (Continued)

Colestipol (Continued)

phenobarbital, amiodarone, methotrexate, NSAIDs, gemfibrozil, ursodiol, aspirin, clinda-mycin, clofibrate, furosemide, glipizide, hydrocortisone, imipramine, methyldopa, niacin, phenytoin, phosphate, tolbutamide, and other drugs by binding to the drug in the intestine

Mechanism of Action Binds with bile acids to form an insoluble complex that is eliminated in feces; it thereby increases the fecal loss of bile acid-bound low density lipoprotein cholesterol

Pharmacodynamics/Kinetics Absorption: Oral: Not absorbed

Usual Dosage Adults: Oral:

Granules: 5-30 g/day given once or in divided doses 2-4 times/day; initial dose: 5 g 1-2 times/day; increase by 5 g at 1- to 2-month intervals

Tablets: 2-16 g/day; initial dose: 2 g 1-2 times/day; increase by 2 g at 1- to 2-month intervals

Administration Dry powder should be added to at least 90 mL of liquid and stirred until completely mixed; other drugs should be administered at least 1 hour before or 4 hours after colestipol

Test Interactions ↑ prothrombin time; ↓ cholesterol (S)

Patient Information Take granules in water or fruit juice (~90 mL) or sprinkled on food, swallow tablets whole with plenty of fluids; other drugs should not be taken at least 1 hour before or 4 hours after colestipol; rinse glass with small amount of liquid to ensure full dose is taken

Dosage Forms

Granules, as hydrochloride: 5 g packet, 300 g, 500 g

Tablet, as hydrochloride: 1 g

♦ **Colestipol Hydrochloride** see Colestipol on previous page

Colfosceril Palmitate (kole FOS er il PALM i tate)

U.S. Brand Names Exosurf® Neonatal

Synonyms Dipalmitoylphosphatidylcholine; DPPC; Synthetic Lung Surfactant

Therapeutic Category Lung Surfactant

Use Neonatal respiratory distress syndrome:

Prophylactic therapy: Body weight <1350 g in infants at risk for developing RDS; body weight >1350 g in infants with evidence of pulmonary immaturity

Rescue therapy: Treatment of infants with RDS based on respiratory distress not attributable to any other causes and chest radiographic findings consistent with RDS

Warnings/Precautions Pulmonary hemorrhaging may occur especially in infants <700 g. Mucous plugs may have formed in the endotracheal tube in those infants whose ventilation was markedly impaired during or shortly after dosing. If chest expansion improves substantially, the ventilator PIP setting should be reduced immediately. Hyperoxia and hypocarbia (hypocarbia can decrease blood flow to the brain) may occur requiring appropriate ventilator adjustments.

Adverse Reactions 1% to 10%: Respiratory: Pulmonary hemorrhage, apnea, mucous plugging, decrease in transcutaneous O_2 of >20%

Stability Reconstituted suspension should be used immediately and unused portion discarded; store at room temperature of 15°C to 30°C (59°F to 86°F); do not refrigerate

Mechanism of Action Replaces deficient or ineffective endogenous lung surfactant in neonates with respiratory distress syndrome (RDS) or in neonates at risk of developing RDS; reduces surface tension and stabilizes the alveoli from collapsing

Pharmacodynamics/Kinetics

Absorption: Intratracheal: Absorbed from the alveolus

Metabolism: Catabolized and reutilized for further synthesis and secretion in lung tissue

Usual Dosage For intratracheal use only. Neonates:

Prophylactic treatment: Administer 5 mL/kg (as two 2.5 mL/kg half-doses) as soon as possible; the second and third doses should be administered at 12 and 24 hours later to those infants remaining on ventilators

Rescue treatment: Administer 5 mL/kg (as two 2.5 mL/kg half-doses) as soon as the diagnosis of RDS is made; the second 5 mL/kg (as two 2.5 mL/kg half-doses) dose should be administered 12 hours later

Administration For intratracheal administration only. Suction infant prior to administration; inspect solution to verify complete mixing of the suspension. Administer via sideport on the special ETT adapter without interrupting mechanical ventilation. Administer the dose in two 2.5 mL/kg aliquots. Each half-dose is instilled slowly over 1-2 minutes in small bursts with each inspiration. After the first 2.5 mL/kg dose, turn the infant's head and torso 45° to the right for 30 seconds, then return to the midline position and administer the second dose as above. Following the second dose, turn the infant's head and torso 45° to the left for 30 seconds and return the infant to the midline position.

Monitoring Parameters Continuous EKG and transcutaneous O_2 saturation should be monitored during administration; frequent ABG sampling is necessary to prevent postdosing hyperoxia and hypocarbia

Dosage Forms Powder for injection, lyophilized: 108 mg (10 mL)

Colistimethate (koe lis ti METH ate)

U.S. Brand Names Coly-Mycin® M Parenteral

Therapeutic Category Antibiotic, Miscellaneous

Use Treatment of infections due to sensitive strains of certain gram-negative bacilli which are resistant to other antibacterials or in patients allergic to other antibacterials

Not FDA approved: Used as inhalation in the prevention of *Pseudomonas aeruginosa* respiratory tract infections in immunocompromised patients, and used as inhalation adjunct agent for the treatment of *P. aeruginosa* infections in patients with cystic fibrosis and other seriously ill or chronically ill patients

Pregnancy Risk Factor B

Contraindications Hypersensitivity to colistimethate or any component

Warnings/Precautions Use with caution in patients with pre-existing renal disease

Adverse Reactions 1% to 10%: Respiratory arrest, nephrotoxicity, GI upset, vertigo, slurring of speech, urticaria

Drug Interactions Other nephrotoxic drugs, neuromuscular blocking agents

Stability Freshly prepare any infusion and use for no longer than 24 hours

Mechanism of Action Hydrolyzed to colistin, which acts as a cationic detergent which damages the bacterial cytoplasmic membrane causing leaking of intracellular substances and cell death

Pharmacodynamics/Kinetics
  Distribution: Widely distributed, except for CNS, synovial, pleural, and pericardial fluids
  Half-life: 1.5-8 hours; may be as high as 2-3 days in anuric patients
  Elimination: Excreted primarily unchanged in urine
  Peak: About 2 hours

Usual Dosage Children and Adults:
  I.M., I.V.: 2.5-5 mg/kg/day in 2-4 divided doses
  Inhalation: 75 mg in 3 mL NS (4 mL total) via nebulizer twice daily
  Dosing interval in renal impairment: Adults:
    S_{cr} 0.7-1.2 mg/dL: 100-125 mg 2-4 times/day
    S_{cr} 1.3-1.5 mg/dL: 75-115 mg twice daily
    S_{cr} 1.6-2.5 mg/dL: 66-150 mg once or twice daily
    S_{cr} 2.6-4 mg/dL: 100-150 mg every 36 hours

Dosage Forms Powder for injection, lyophilized: 150 mg

Colistin (koe LIS tin)

U.S. Brand Names Coly-Mycin® S Oral

Synonyms Polymyxin E

Therapeutic Category Antibiotic, Miscellaneous; Antidiarrheal

Use Treatment of diarrhea in infants and children caused by susceptible organisms, especially *E. coli* and *Shigella*, however, other agents are preferred; treatment of superficial infections of external ear canal and of mastoidectomy and fenestration cavities

Pregnancy Risk Factor C

Contraindications Known hypersensitivity to colistin

Warnings/Precautions Use with caution in patients with impaired renal function; some systemic absorption may occur; potential for renal toxicity exists; prolonged use may lead to superinfection

Adverse Reactions <1%: Neuromuscular blockade, nephrotoxicity, respiratory arrest, nausea, vomiting, hypersensitivity reactions, superinfections

Stability Stable for 2 weeks when refrigerated, shake well; discard after 14 days

Mechanism of Action Polypeptide antibiotic that binds to and damages the bacterial cell membrane

Pharmacodynamics/Kinetics
  Absorption: Oral: Slightly absorbed from GI tract (adults); unpredictable absorption occurs in infants, can lead to significant serum levels
  Half-life: 2.8-4.8 hours, prolonged in renal insufficiency; with anuria: 48-72 hours
  Elimination: ~65% to 75% excreted unchanged in urine

Usual Dosage Diarrhea: Children: Oral: 5-15 mg/kg/day in 3 divided doses given every 8 hours

Dosage Forms Powder for oral suspension: 25 mg/5 mL (60 mL)

Colistin, Neomycin, and Hydrocortisone
(koe LIS tin, nee oh MYE sin & hye droe KOR ti sone)

U.S. Brand Names Coly-Mycin® S Otic Drops; Cortisporin-TC® Otic *New Brand*

Therapeutic Category Antibiotic/Corticosteroid, Otic

Dosage Forms Suspension, otic:
  Coly-Mycin® S Otic Drops: Colistin sulfate 0.3%, neomycin sulfate 0.47%, and hydrocortisone acetate 1% (5 mL, 10 mL)
  Cortisporin-TC®: Colistin sulfate 0.3%, neomycin sulfate 0.33%, and hydrocortisone acetate 1% (5 mL, 10 mL)

◆ **Collagen** *see* Microfibrillar Collagen Hemostat *on page 776*

Collagenase (KOL la je nase)

U.S. Brand Names Biozyme-C®; Santyl®

Therapeutic Category Enzyme, Topical Debridement

Use Promotes debridement of necrotic tissue in dermal ulcers and severe burns

Pregnancy Risk Factor C

Contraindications Known hypersensitivity to collagenase

Warnings/Precautions For external use only; avoid contact with eyes; monitor debilitated patients for systemic bacterial infections because debriding enzymes may increase the risk of bacteremia

Adverse Reactions
  1% to 10%: Local: Irritation
  (Continued)

Collagenase *(Continued)*

<1%: Pain and burning may occur at site of application

Overdosage/Toxicology Action of enzyme may be stopped by applying Burow's solution

Drug Interactions Decreased effect: Enzymatic activity is inhibited by detergents, benzalkonium chloride, hexachlorophene, nitrofurazone, tincture of iodine, and heavy metal ions (silver and mercury)

Mechanism of Action Collagenase is an enzyme derived from the fermentation of *Clostridium histolyticum* and differs from other proteolytic enzymes in that its enzymatic action has a high specificity for native and denatured collagen. Collagenase will not attack collagen in healthy tissue or newly formed granulation tissue. In addition, it does not act on fat, fibrin, keratin, or muscle.

Usual Dosage Topical: Apply once daily (or more frequently if the dressing becomes soiled)

Nursing Implications Do not introduce into major body cavities; monitor debilitated patients for systemic bacterial infections

Dosage Forms Ointment, topical: 250 units/g (15 g, 30 g)

- **Colovage**® see Polyethylene Glycol-Electrolyte Solution *on page 942*
- **Coly-Mycin**® **M Parenteral** see Colistimethate *on page 294*
- **Coly-Mycin**® **S Oral** see Colistin *on previous page*
- **Coly-Mycin**® **S Otic Drops** see Colistin, Neomycin, and Hydrocortisone *on previous page*
- **Colyte**® see Polyethylene Glycol-Electrolyte Solution *on page 942*
- **Combipres**® see Clonidine and Chlorthalidone *on page 285*
- **Combivent**® see Ipratropium and Albuterol *on page 626*
- **Combivir**® see Zidovudine and Lamivudine *on page 1237*
- **Comfort**® [OTC] see Naphazoline *on page 817*
- **Comhist**® see Chlorpheniramine, Phenylephrine, and Phenyltoloxamine *on page 247*
- **Comhist**® **LA** see Chlorpheniramine, Phenylephrine, and Phenyltoloxamine *on page 247*
- **Community-Acquired Pneumonia in Adults** see page 1419
- **Compazine**® see Prochlorperazine *on page 973*
- **Compound E** see Cortisone Acetate *on next page*
- **Compound F** see Hydrocortisone *on page 579*
- **Compound S** see Zidovudine *on page 1235*
- **Compoz**® **Gel Caps [OTC]** see Diphenhydramine *on page 369*
- **Compoz**® **Nighttime Sleep Aid [OTC]** see Diphenhydramine *on page 369*
- **Comvax**™ see Haemophilus b Conjugate and Hepatitis b Vaccine *on page 553*
- **Congest** see Estrogens, Conjugated *on page 436*
- **Constant-T**® see Theophylline Salts *on page 1125*
- **Constilac**® see Lactulose *on page 656*
- **Constulose**® see Lactulose *on page 656*
- **Contac**® **Cough Formula Liquid [OTC]** see Guaifenesin and Dextromethorphan *on page 550*
- **Contrast Media Reactions, Premedication for Prophylaxis** see page 1464
- **Control**® [OTC] see Phenylpropanolamine *on page 919*
- **Convulsive Status Epilepticus** see page 1470
- **Copaxone**® see Glatiramer Acetate *on page 537*
- **Cophene XP**® see Hydrocodone, Pseudoephedrine, and Guaifenesin *on page 579*
- **Copolymer-1** see Glatiramer Acetate *on page 537*
- **Coptin**® see Sulfadiazine *on page 1092*
- **Coradur**® see Isosorbide Dinitrate *on page 637*
- **Corax**® see Chlordiazepoxide *on page 239*
- **Cordarone**® see Amiodarone *on page 60*
- **Cordran**® see Flurandrenolide *on page 506*
- **Cordran**® **SP** see Flurandrenolide *on page 506*
- **Coreg**® see Carvedilol *on page 200*
- **Corgard**® see Nadolol *on page 807*
- **Corlopam**® see Fenoldopam *on page 472*
- **Corque**® **Topical** see Clioquinol and Hydrocortisone *on page 277*
- **CortaGel**® [OTC] see Hydrocortisone *on page 579*
- **Cortaid**® **Maximum Strength [OTC]** see Hydrocortisone *on page 579*
- **Cortaid**® **With Aloe [OTC]** see Hydrocortisone *on page 579*
- **Cortatrigen**® **Otic** see Neomycin, Polymyxin B, and Hydrocortisone *on page 827*
- **Cort-Dome**® see Hydrocortisone *on page 579*
- **Cortef**® see Hydrocortisone *on page 579*
- **Cortef**® **Feminine Itch** see Hydrocortisone *on page 579*
- **Cortenema**® see Hydrocortisone *on page 579*
- **Corticaine**® **Topical** see Dibucaine and Hydrocortisone *on page 348*
- **Corticosteroids Comparison** see page 1319
- **Cortifoam**® see Hydrocortisone *on page 579*
- **Cortisol** see Hydrocortisone *on page 579*

Cortisone Acetate (KOR ti sone AS e tate)

Related Information
Corticosteroids Comparison *on page 1319*

U.S. Brand Names Cortone® Acetate

Synonyms Compound E

Therapeutic Category Anti-inflammatory Agent; Corticosteroid; Corticosteroid, Adrenal; Corticosteroid, Systemic; Diagnostic Agent, Adrenocortical Insufficiency; Glucocorticoid; Mineralocorticoid

Use Management of adrenocortical insufficiency

Pregnancy Risk Factor D

Contraindications Serious infections, except septic shock or tuberculous meningitis; administration of live virus vaccines

Warnings/Precautions Use with caution in patients with hypothyroidism, cirrhosis, hypertension, congestive heart failure, ulcerative colitis, thromboembolic disorders, osteoporosis, convulsive disorders, peptic ulcer, diabetes mellitus, myasthenia gravis; prolonged therapy (>5 days) of pharmacologic doses of corticosteroids may lead to hypothalamic-pituitary-adrenal suppression, the degree of adrenal suppression varies with the degree and duration of glucocorticoid therapy; this must be taken into consideration when taking patients off steroids

Adverse Reactions
>10%:
Central nervous system: Insomnia, nervousness
Gastrointestinal: Increased appetite, indigestion
1% to 10%:
Dermatologic: Hirsutism
Endocrine & metabolic: Diabetes mellitus
Neuromuscular & skeletal: Arthralgia
Ocular: Cataracts, glaucoma
Respiratory: Epistaxis
<1%: Edema, hypertension, vertigo, seizures, headache, psychoses, pseudotumor cerebri, mood swings, delirium, hallucinations, euphoria, acne, skin atrophy, bruising, hyperpigmentation, Cushing's syndrome, pituitary-adrenal axis suppression, growth suppression, glucose intolerance, hypokalemia, alkalosis, amenorrhea, sodium and water retention, hyperglycemia, peptic ulcer, nausea, vomiting, abdominal distention, ulcerative esophagitis, pancreatitis, myalgia, osteoporosis, fractures, muscle wasting, hypersensitivity reactions

Overdosage/Toxicology When consumed in excessive quantities for prolonged periods, systemic hypercorticism and adrenal suppression may occur; in those cases, discontinuation and withdrawal of the corticosteroid should be done judiciously. Cushingoid changes from continued administration of large doses results in moon face, central obesity, striae, hirsutism, acne, ecchymoses, hypertension, osteoporosis, myopathy, sexual dysfunction, diabetes, hyperlipidemia, peptic ulcer, increased susceptibility to infection, and electrolyte and fluid imbalance.

Drug Interactions CYP3A3/4 enzyme substrate
Decreased effect:
Barbiturates, phenytoin, rifampin may decrease cortisone effects
Live virus vaccines
Anticholinesterase agents may decrease effect
Cortisone may decrease warfarin effects
Cortisone may decrease effects of salicylates
Increased effect: Estrogens (increase cortisone effects)
Increased toxicity:
Cortisone + NSAIDs may increase ulcerogenic potential
Cortisone may increase potassium deletion due to diuretics

Mechanism of Action Decreases inflammation by suppression of migration of polymorphonuclear leukocytes and reversal of increased capillary permeability

Pharmacodynamics/Kinetics
Peak effect: Oral: Within 2 hours
Duration of action: 30-36 hours
Absorption: Slow rate of absorption
Distribution: Crosses the placenta; appears in breast milk; distributes to muscles, liver, skin, intestines, and kidneys
Metabolism: In the liver to inactive metabolites
Half-life: 30 minutes to 2 hours
End-stage renal disease: 3.5 hours
Elimination: In bile and urine
Note: Insoluble in water; supplemental doses may be warranted during times of stress in the course of withdrawing therapy

Usual Dosage If possible, administer glucocorticoids before 9 AM to minimize adrenocortical suppression; dosing depends upon the condition being treated and the response of the patient; supplemental doses may be warranted during times of stress in the course of withdrawing therapy

Children:
Anti-inflammatory or immunosuppressive: Oral: 2.5-10 mg/kg/day **or** 20-300 mg/m²/day in divided doses every 6-8 hours
Physiologic replacement: Oral: 0.5-0.75 mg/kg/day **or** 20-25 mg/m²/day in divided doses every 8 hours
Adults: Oral: 25-300 mg/day in divided doses every 12-24 hours
(Continued)

Cortisone Acetate *(Continued)*

Hemodialysis: Supplemental dose is not necessary

Peritoneal dialysis: Supplemental dose is not necessary

Patient Information Take with meals or take with food or milk; do not discontinue drug without notifying physician

Nursing Implications Withdraw gradually following long-term therapy

Dosage Forms Tablet: 5 mg, 10 mg, 25 mg

- ◆ **Cortisporin® Ophthalmic Ointment** *see* Bacitracin, Neomycin, Polymyxin B, and Hydrocortisone *on page 123*
- ◆ **Cortisporin® Ophthalmic Suspension** *see* Neomycin, Polymyxin B, and Hydrocortisone *on page 827*
- ◆ **Cortisporin® Otic** *see* Neomycin, Polymyxin B, and Hydrocortisone *on page 827*
- ◆ **Cortisporin-TC® Otic** *New Brand see* Colistin, Neomycin, and Hydrocortisone *on page 295*
- ◆ **Cortisporin® Topical Cream** *see* Neomycin, Polymyxin B, and Hydrocortisone *on page 827*
- ◆ **Cortisporin® Topical Ointment** *see* Bacitracin, Neomycin, Polymyxin B, and Hydrocortisone *on page 123*
- ◆ **Cortizone®-5 [OTC]** *see* Hydrocortisone *on page 579*
- ◆ **Cortizone®-10 [OTC]** *see* Hydrocortisone *on page 579*
- ◆ **Cortone® Acetate** *see* Cortisone Acetate *on previous page*
- ◆ **Cortrosyn®** *see* Cosyntropin *on this page*
- ◆ **Corvert®** *see* Ibutilide *on page 595*
- ◆ **Coryphen® Codeine** *see* Aspirin and Codeine *on page 105*
- ◆ **Cosmegen®** *see* Dactinomycin *on page 318*

Cosyntropin (koe sin TROE pin)

U.S. Brand Names Cortrosyn®

Synonyms Synacthen; Tetracosactide

Therapeutic Category Diagnostic Agent, Adrenocortical Insufficiency

Use Diagnostic test to differentiate primary adrenal from secondary (pituitary) adrenocortical insufficiency

Pregnancy Risk Factor C

Contraindications Known hypersensitivity to cosyntropin

Warnings/Precautions Use with caution in patients with pre-existing allergic disease or a history of allergic reactions to corticotropin

Adverse Reactions

1% to 10%:

Cardiovascular: Flushing

Central nervous system: Mild fever

Dermatologic: Pruritus

Gastrointestinal: Chronic pancreatitis

<1%: Hypersensitivity reactions

Stability Reconstitute with NS

Stability of parenteral admixture at room temperature (25°C): 24 hours

Stability of parenteral admixture at refrigeration temperature (4°C): 21 days

I.V. infusion in NS or D_5W is stable 12 hours at room temperature

Mechanism of Action Stimulates the adrenal cortex to secrete adrenal steroids (including hydrocortisone, cortisone), androgenic substances, and a small amount of aldosterone

Pharmacodynamics/Kinetics

Distribution: Crosses the placenta

Metabolism: Unknown

Time to peak serum concentration: Within 1 hour (plasma cortisol levels rise in healthy individuals within 5 minutes of administration I.M. or I.V. push)

Usual Dosage

Adrenocortical insufficiency: I.M., I.V. (over 2 minutes): Peak plasma cortisol concentrations usually occur 45-60 minutes after cosyntropin administration

Neonates: 0.015 mg/kg/dose

Children <2 years: 0.125 mg

Children >2 years and Adults: 0.25-0.75 mg

When greater cortisol stimulation is needed, an I.V. infusion may be used:

Children >2 years and Adults: 0.25 mg administered at 0.04 mg/hour over 6 hours

Congenital adrenal hyperplasia evaluation: 1 mg/m²/dose up to a maximum of 1 mg

Reference Range Normal baseline cortisol; increase in serum cortisol after cosyntropin injection of >7 µg/dL or peak response >18 µg/dL; plasma cortisol concentrations should be measured immediately before and exactly 30 minutes after a dose

Test Interactions Decreased effect: Spironolactone, hydrocortisone, cortisone

Nursing Implications Patient should not receive corticosteroids or spironolactone the day prior and the day of the test

Additional Information Each 0.25 mg of cosyntropin is equivalent to 25 units of corticotropin

Dosage Forms Powder for injection: 0.25 mg

- ◆ **Cotazym®** *see* Pancrelipase *on page 883*
- ◆ **Cotazym-S®** *see* Pancrelipase *on page 883*
- ◆ **Cotrim®** *see* Co-Trimoxazole *on next page*

♦ **Cotrim® DS** *see* Co-Trimoxazole *on this page*

Co-Trimoxazole (koe trye MOKS a zole)

Related Information

Animal and Human Bites Guidelines *on page 1399*
Antimicrobial Drugs of Choice *on page 1404*
Community-Acquired Pneumonia in Adults *on page 1419*
Desensitization Protocols *on page 1347*
Guidelines for the Prevention of Opportunistic Infections in Persons with HIV *on page 1388*

U.S. Brand Names Bactrim™; Bactrim™ DS; Cotrim®; Cotrim® DS; Septra®; Septra® DS; Sulfatrim®

Canadian Brand Names Apo®-Sulfatrim; Novo-Trimel; Nu-Cotrimox; Pro-Trin®; Roubac®; Trisulfa®; Trisulfa-S®

Synonyms SMX-TMP; SMZ-TMP; Sulfamethoxazole and Trimethoprim; TMP-SMX; TMP-SMZ; Trimethoprim and Sulfamethoxazole

Therapeutic Category Antibiotic, Sulfonamide Derivative

Use

Oral treatment of urinary tract infections due to *E. coli*, *Klebsiella* and *Enterobacter* sp, *M. morganii*, *P. mirabilis* and *P. vulgaris*; acute otitis media in children and acute exacerbations of chronic bronchitis in adults due to susceptible strains of *H. influenzae* or *S. pneumoniae*; prophylaxis of *Pneumocystis carinii* pneumonitis (PCP), traveler's diarrhea due to enterotoxigenic *E. coli* or *Cyclospora*

I.V. treatment or severe or complicated infections when oral therapy is not feasible, for documented PCP, empiric treatment of PCP in immune compromised patients; treatment of documented or suspected shigellosis, typhoid fever, *Nocardia asteroides* infection, or other infections caused by susceptible bacteria

Unlabeled use: Cholera and salmonella-type infections and nocardiosis; chronic prostatitis; as prophylaxis in neutropenic patients with *P. carinii* infections, in leukemics, and in patients following renal transplantation, to decrease incidence of gram-negative rod infections

Pregnancy Risk Factor C

Pregnancy/Breast-Feeding Implications Do not use at term to avoid kernicterus in the newborn and use during pregnancy only if risks outweigh the benefits since folic acid metabolism may be affected

Contraindications Hypersensitivity to any sulfa drug or any component; porphyria; megaloblastic anemia due to folate deficiency; infants <2 months of age; marked hepatic damage

Warnings/Precautions Use with caution in patients with G-6-PD deficiency, impaired renal or hepatic function; maintain adequate hydration to prevent crystalluria; adjust dosage in patients with renal impairment. Injection vehicle contains benzyl alcohol and sodium metabisulfite. Fatalities associated with severe reactions including Stevens-Johnson syndrome, toxic epidermal necrolysis, hepatic necrosis, agranulocytosis, aplastic anemia and other blood dyscrasias; discontinue use at first sign of rash. Elderly patients appear at greater risk for more severe adverse reactions. May cause hypoglycemia, particularly in malnourished, or patients with renal or hepatic impairment. Use with caution in patients with porphyria or thyroid dysfunction. Slow acetylators may be more prone to adverse reactions.

Adverse Reactions

>10%:
Dermatologic: Allergic skin reactions including rashes and urticaria, photosensitivity
Gastrointestinal: Nausea, vomiting, anorexia

1% to 10%:
Dermatologic: Stevens-Johnson syndrome, toxic epidermal necrolysis (rare)
Hematologic: Blood dyscrasias
Hepatic: Hepatitis

<1%: Confusion, depression, hallucinations, seizures, fever, ataxia, kernicterus in neonates, erythema multiforme, stomatitis, diarrhea, pseudomembranous colitis, pancytopenia, pancreatitis, rhabdomyolysis, thrombocytopenia, megaloblastic anemia, granulocytopenia, aplastic anemia, hemolysis (with G-6-PD deficiency), cholestatic jaundice, interstitial nephritis, serum sickness

Overdosage/Toxicology

Symptoms of acute overdose include nausea, vomiting, GI distress, hematuria, crystalluria

Following GI decontamination, treatment is supportive; adequate fluid intake is essential; peritoneal dialysis is not effective and hemodialysis only moderately effective in removing co-trimoxazole

Drug Interactions CYP2C9 enzyme inhibitor

Decreased effect: Cyclosporines

Increased effect/toxicity: Phenytoin, cyclosporines (nephrotoxicity), methotrexate (displaced from binding sites), dapsone, sulfonylureas, and oral anticoagulants; may compete for renal secretion of methotrexate; digoxin concentrations increased

Stability Do not refrigerate injection; is less soluble in more alkaline pH; protect from light; do not use NS as a diluent; injection vehicle contains benzyl alcohol and sodium metabisulfite

Stability of parenteral admixture at room temperature (25°C):
5 mL/125 mL D_5W = 6 hours
5 mL/100 mL D_5W = 4 hours
5 mL/75 mL D_5W = 2 hours
(Continued)

Co-Trimoxazole *(Continued)*

Mechanism of Action Sulfamethoxazole interferes with bacterial folic acid synthesis and growth via inhibition of dihydrofolic acid formation from para-aminobenzoic acid; trimethoprim inhibits dihydrofolic acid reduction to tetrahydrofolate resulting in sequential inhibition of enzymes of the folic acid pathway

Pharmacodynamics/Kinetics

Absorption: Oral: 90% to 100%

Distribution: Crosses the placenta; distributes widely into body tissues, breast milk, and fluids including middle ear fluid, prostatic fluid, bile, aqueous humor, and CSF

Protein binding: SMX: 68%; TMP: 68%

Metabolism: SMX is N-acetylated and glucuronidated; TMP is metabolized to oxide and hydroxylated metabolites

Half-life: SMX: 9 hours; TMP: 6-17 hours, both are prolonged in renal failure

Time to peak serum concentration: Within 1-4 hours

Elimination: In urine as metabolites and unchanged drug

Usual Dosage Dosage recommendations are based on the trimethoprim component

Children >2 months:

Mild to moderate infections: Oral, I.V.: 8 mg TMP/kg/day in divided doses every 12 hours

Serious infection/*Pneumocystis*: I.V.: 20 mg TMP/kg/day in divided doses every 6 hours

Urinary tract infection prophylaxis: Oral: 2 mg TMP/kg/dose daily

Prophylaxis of *Pneumocystis*: Oral, I.V.: 10 mg TMP/kg/day or 150 mg TMP/m^2/day in divided doses every 12 hours for 3 days/week; dose should not exceed 320 mg trimethoprim and 1600 mg sulfamethoxazole 3 days/week

Adults:

Urinary tract infection/chronic bronchitis: Oral: 1 double strength tablet every 12 hours for 10-14 days

Sepsis: I.V.: 20 TMP/kg/day divided every 6 hours

Pneumocystis carinii:

Prophylaxis: Oral: 1 double strength tablet daily or 3 times/week

Treatment: Oral, I.V.: 15-20 mg TMP/kg/day in 3-4 divided doses

Dosing adjustment in renal impairment: Adults:

I.V.:

Cl_{cr} 15-30 mL/minute: Administer 2.5-5 mg/kg every 12 hours

Cl_{cr} <15 mL/minute: Administer 2.5-5 mg/kg every 24 hours

Oral:

Cl_{cr} 15-30 mL/minute: Administer 1 double strength tablet every 24 hours or 1 single strength tablet every 12 hours

Cl_{cr} <15 mL/minute: Not recommended

Administration Infuse over 60-90 minutes, must dilute well before giving; may be given less diluted in a central line; not for I.M. injection; maintain adequate fluid intake to prevent crystalluria

Test Interactions ↑ creatinine (Jaffé alkaline picrate reaction); increased serum methotrexate by dihydrofolate reductase method

Patient Information Take oral medication with 8 oz of water on an empty stomach (1 hour before or 2 hours after meals) for best absorption; report any skin rashes immediately; finish all medication, do not skip doses

Dosage Forms The 5:1 ratio (SMX to TMP) remains constant in all dosage forms:

Injection: Sulfamethoxazole 80 mg and trimethoprim 16 mg per mL (5 mL, 10 mL, 20 mL, 30 mL, 50 mL)

Suspension, oral: Sulfamethoxazole 200 mg and trimethoprim 40 mg per 5 mL (20 mL, 100 mL, 150 mL, 200 mL, 480 mL)

Tablet: Sulfamethoxazole 400 mg and trimethoprim 80 mg

Tablet, double strength: Sulfamethoxazole 800 mg and trimethoprim 160 mg

- **Coumadin®** *see* Warfarin *on page 1228*
- **Covera-HS®** *see* Verapamil *on page 1214*
- **Cozaar®** *see* Losartan *on page 696*
- **CP-99,219-27** *see* Trovafloxacin *on page 1192*
- **CPM** *see* Cyclophosphamide *on page 305*
- **CPT-11** *see* Irinotecan *on page 627*
- **Creon 10®** *see* Pancrelipase *on page 883*
- **Creon 20®** *see* Pancrelipase *on page 883*
- **Crinone™ Vaginal Gel** *see* Progesterone *on page 976*
- **Crixivan®** *see* Indinavir *on page 607*
- **Crolom® Ophthalmic Solution** *see* Cromolyn Sodium *on this page*
- **Cromoglycic Acid** *see* Cromolyn Sodium *on this page*

Cromolyn Sodium *(KROE moe lin SOW dee um)*

Related Information

Asthma, Guidelines for the Diagnosis and Management of *on page 1456*

U.S. Brand Names Crolom® Ophthalmic Solution; Gastrocrom® Oral; Intal® Nebulizer Solution; Intal® Oral Inhaler; Nasalcrom® Nasal Solution

Canadian Brand Names Novo-Cromolyn; Opticrom®; PMS-Sodium Cromoglycate; Rynacrom®

Synonyms Cromoglycic Acid; Disodium Cromoglycate; DSCG

Therapeutic Category Antiallergic, Inhalation; Antiallergic, Ophthalmic

Use Adjunct in the prophylaxis of allergic disorders, including rhinitis, giant papillary conjunctivitis, and asthma; inhalation product may be used for prevention of exercise-induced bronchospasm; systemic mastocytosis, food allergy, and treatment of inflammatory bowel disease; **cromolyn is a prophylactic drug with no benefit for acute situations**

Pregnancy Risk Factor B

Pregnancy/Breast-Feeding Implications

Clinical effects on the fetus: No data on whether cromolyn crosses the placenta or clinical effects on the fetus. Available evidence suggests safe use during pregnancy.

Breast-feeding/lactation: No data on whether cromolyn crosses into breast milk or clinical effects on the infant

Contraindications Hypersensitivity to cromolyn or any component; acute asthma attacks

Warnings/Precautions Severe anaphylactic reactions may occur rarely; cromolyn is a prophylactic drug with no benefit for acute situations; do not use in patients with severe renal or hepatic impairment; caution should be used when withdrawing the drug or tapering the dose as symptoms may reoccur; use with caution in patients with a history of cardiac arrhythmias

Adverse Reactions

>10%:

Gastrointestinal: Unpleasant taste (inhalation aerosol)

Respiratory: Hoarseness, coughing

1% to 10%:

Dermatologic: Angioedema

Gastrointestinal: Xerostomia

Genitourinary: Dysuria

Respiratory: Sneezing, nasal congestion

<1%: Dizziness, headache, rash, urticaria, nausea, vomiting, diarrhea, arthralgia, ocular stinging, lacrimation, wheezing, throat irritation, eosinophilic pneumonia, pulmonary infiltrates, nasal burning, anaphylactic reactions

Overdosage/Toxicology Symptoms of overdose include bronchospasm, laryngeal edema, dysuria

Stability Nebulizer solution is **compatible** with metaproterenol sulfate, isoproterenol hydrochloride, 0.25% isoetharine hydrochloride, epinephrine hydrochloride, terbutaline sulfate, and 20% acetylcysteine solution for at least 1 hour after their admixture; store nebulizer solution protected from direct light

Mechanism of Action Prevents the mast cell release of histamine, leukotrienes and slow-reacting substance of anaphylaxis by inhibiting degranulation after contact with antigens

Pharmacodynamics/Kinetics

Absorption:

Inhalation: ~8% of dose reaches the lungs upon inhalation of the powder and is well absorbed

Oral: Only 0.5% to 2% of dose absorbed

Half-life: 80-90 minutes

Time to peak serum concentration: Inhalation: Within 15 minutes

Elimination: Absorbed cromolyn is equally excreted unchanged in the urine and the feces (via bile); small amounts are exhaled

Usual Dosage

Oral:

Systemic mastocytosis:

Neonates and preterm Infants: Not recommended

Infants and Children <2 years: 20 mg/kg/day in 4 divided doses; may increase in patients 6 months to 2 years of age if benefits not seen after 2-3 weeks; do not exceed 30 mg/kg/day

Children 2-12 years: 100 mg 4 times/day; not to exceed 40 mg/kg/day

Children >12 years and Adults: 200 mg 4 times/day

Food allergy and inflammatory bowel disease:

Children <2 years: Not recommended

Children 2-12 years: Initial dose: 100 mg 4 times/day; may double the dose if effect is not satisfactory within 2-3 weeks; not to exceed 40 mg/kg/day

Children >12 years and Adults: Initial dose: 200 mg 4 times/day; may double the dose if effect is not satisfactory within 2-3 weeks; up to 400 mg 4 times/day

Once desired effect is achieved, dose may be tapered to lowest effective dose

Inhalation:

For chronic control of asthma, taper frequency to the lowest effective dose (ie, 4 times/day to 3 times/day to twice daily):

Nebulization solution: Children >2 years and Adults: Initial: 20 mg 4 times/day; usual dose: 20 mg 3-4 times/day

Metered spray:

Children 5-12 years: Initial: 2 inhalations 4 times/day; usual dose: 1-2 inhalations 3-4 times/day

Children ≥12 years and Adults: Initial: 2 inhalations 4 times/day; usual dose: 2-4 inhalations 3-4 times/day

Prevention of allergen- or exercise-induced bronchospasm: Administer 10-15 minutes prior to exercise or allergen exposure but no longer than 1 hour before:

Nebulization solution: Children >2 years and Adults: Single dose of 20 mg

Metered spray: Children >5 years and Adults: Single dose of 2 inhalations

Monitoring Parameters Periodic pulmonary function tests

(Continued)

Cromolyn Sodium *(Continued)*

Patient Information Do not discontinue abruptly; not effective for acute relief of symptoms; must be taken on a regularly scheduled basis; do not mix oral capsule with fruit juice, milk, or foods

Nursing Implications Advise patient to clear as much mucus as possible before inhalation treatments

Dosage Forms
Inhalation, oral (Intal®): 800 mcg/spray (8.1 g)
Solution, for nebulization:
10 mg/mL (2 mL)
Intal®: 10 mg/mL (2 mL)
Solution, as sodium (Gastrocrom®): 100 mg/5 mL
Solution, nasal (Nasalcrom®): 40 mg/mL (13 mL)
Solution, ophthalmic (Crolom®): 4% (2.5 mL, 10 mL)

Crotamiton *(kroe TAM i tonn)*

U.S. Brand Names Eurax® Topical

Therapeutic Category Scabicidal Agent

Use Treatment of scabies (*Sarcoptes scabiei*) and symptomatic treatment of pruritus

Pregnancy Risk Factor C

Contraindications Hypersensitivity to crotamiton or other components; patients who manifest a primary irritation response to topical medications

Warnings/Precautions Avoid contact with face, eyes, mucous membranes, and urethral meatus; do not apply to acutely inflamed or raw skin; for external use only

Adverse Reactions <1%: Local irritation, pruritus, contact dermatitis, warm sensation

Overdosage/Toxicology
Symptoms of ingestion include burning sensation in mouth, irritation of the buccal, esophageal and gastric mucosa, nausea, vomiting and abdominal pain
There is no specific antidote; general measures to eliminate the drug and reduce its absorption, combined with symptomatic treatment, are recommended

Mechanism of Action Crotamiton has scabicidal activity against *Sarcoptes scabiei*; mechanism of action unknown

Usual Dosage Topical:
Scabicide: Children and Adults: Wash thoroughly and scrub away loose scales, then towel dry; apply a thin layer and massage drug onto skin of the entire body from the neck to the toes (with special attention to skin folds, creases, and interdigital spaces). Repeat application in 24 hours. Take a cleansing bath 48 hours after the final application. Treatment may be repeated after 7-10 days if live mites are still present.
Pruritus: Massage into affected areas until medication is completely absorbed; repeat as necessary

Patient Information For topical use only; all contaminated clothing and bed linen should be washed to avoid reinfestation

Nursing Implications Lotion: Shake well before using; avoid contact with face, eyes, mucous membranes, and urethral meatus

Dosage Forms
Cream: 10% (60 g)
Lotion: 10% (60 mL, 454 mL)

- **Crystalline Penicillin** *see* Penicillin G, Parenteral, Aqueous *on page 896*
- **Crystal Violet** *see* Gentian Violet *on page 536*
- **Crystamine®** *see* Cyanocobalamin *on this page*
- **Crysti 1000®** *see* Cyanocobalamin *on this page*
- **Crysticillin® A.S.** *see* Penicillin G Procaine *on page 897*
- **Crystodigin®** *see* Digitoxin *on page 357*
- **CsA** *see* Cyclosporine *on page 308*
- **C/T/S® Topical Solution** *see* Clindamycin *on page 275*
- **CTX** *see* Cyclophosphamide *on page 305*
- **Cuprid®** *see* Trientine *on page 1179*
- **Cuprimine®** *see* Penicillamine *on page 893*
- **Curretab®** *see* Medroxyprogesterone Acetate *on page 721*
- **Cutivate™** *see* Fluticasone *on page 509*
- **CyA** *see* Cyclosporine *on page 308*

Cyanocobalamin *(sye an oh koe BAL a min)*

U.S. Brand Names Berubigen®; Cobex®; Crystamine®; Crysti 1000®; Cyanoject®; Cyomin®; Ener-B® [OTC]; Kaybovite-1000®; Nascobal®; Redisol®; Rubramin-PC®; Sytobex®

Canadian Brand Names Rubramin®

Synonyms Vitamin B_{12}

Therapeutic Category Vitamin, Water Soluble

Use Treatment of pernicious anemia; vitamin B_{12} deficiency; increased B_{12} requirements due to pregnancy, thyrotoxicosis, hemorrhage, malignancy, liver or kidney disease

Pregnancy Risk Factor A (C if dose exceeds RDA recommendation)

Contraindications Hypersensitivity to cyanocobalamin or any component, cobalt; patients with hereditary optic nerve atrophy

Warnings/Precautions I.M. route used to treat pernicious anemia; vitamin B_{12} deficiency for >3 months results in irreversible degenerative CNS lesions; treatment of vitamin B_{12} megaloblastic anemia may result in severe hypokalemia, sometimes, fatal, when anemia corrects due to cellular potassium requirements. B_{12} deficiency masks signs of polycythemia vera; vegetarian diets may result in B_{12} deficiency; pernicious anemia occurs more often in gastric carcinoma than in general population.

Adverse Reactions
1% to 10%:
Dermatologic: Itching
Gastrointestinal: Diarrhea
<1%: Peripheral vascular thrombosis, urticaria, anaphylaxis

Stability Clear pink to red solutions are stable at room temperature; protect from light; **incompatible** with chlorpromazine, phytonadione, prochlorperazine, warfarin, ascorbic acid, dextrose, heavy metals, oxidizing or reducing agents

Mechanism of Action Coenzyme for various metabolic functions, including fat and carbohydrate metabolism and protein synthesis, used in cell replication and hematopoiesis

Pharmacodynamics/Kinetics
Absorption: Absorbed from the terminal ileum in the presence of calcium; for absorption to occur gastric "intrinsic factor" must be present to transfer the compound across the intestinal mucosa
Distribution: Principally stored in the liver, also stored in the kidneys and adrenals
Protein binding: Bound to transcobalamin II
Metabolism: Converted in the tissues to active coenzymes methylcobalamin and deoxyadenosylcobalamin

Usual Dosage
Recommended daily allowance (RDA):
Children: 0.3-2 mcg
Adults: 2 mcg
Nutritional deficiency: Oral: 25-250 mcg/day
Anemias: I.M. or deep S.C. (oral is not generally recommended due to poor absorption and I.V. is not recommended due to more rapid elimination):
Pernicious anemia, congenital (if evidence of neurologic involvement): 1000 mcg/day for at least 2 weeks; maintenance: 50-100 mcg/month or 100 mcg for 6-7 days; if there is clinical improvement, give 100 mcg every other day for 7 doses, then every 3-4 days for 2-3 weeks; follow with 100 mcg/month for life. Administer with folic acid if needed.
Children: 30-50 mcg/day for 2 or more weeks (to a total dose of 1000-5000 mcg), then follow with 100 mcg/month as maintenance dosage
Adults: 100 mcg/day for 6-7 days; if improvement, administer same dose on alternate days for 7 doses; then every 3-4 days for 2-3 weeks; once hematologic values have returned to normal, maintenance dosage: 100 mcg/month. **Note:** Use only parenteral therapy as oral therapy is not dependable.
Vitamin B_{12} deficiency:
Children:
Neurologic signs: 100 mcg/day for 10-15 days (total dose of 1-1.5 mg), then once or twice weekly for several months; may taper to 60 mcg every month
Hematologic signs: 10-50 mcg/day for 5-10 days, followed by 100-250 mcg/dose every 2-4 weeks
Adults: Initial: 30 mcg/day for 5-10 days; maintenance: 100-200 mcg/month
Schilling test: I.M.: 1000 mcg

Administration I.M. or deep S.C. are preferred routes of administration

Monitoring Parameters Serum potassium, erythrocyte and reticulocyte count, hemoglobin, hematocrit

Reference Range Normal range of serum B_{12} is 150-750 pg/mL; this represents 0.1% of total body content. Metabolic requirements are 2-5 µg/day; years of deficiency required before hematologic and neurologic signs and symptoms are seen. Occasional patients with significant neuropsychiatric abnormalities may have no hematologic abnormalities and normal serum cobalamin levels, 200 pg/mL (SI: >150 pmol/L), or more commonly between 100-200 pg/mL (SI: 75-150 pmol/L). There exists evidence that people, particularly elderly whose serum cobalamin concentrations <300 pg/mL, should receive replacement parenteral therapy; this recommendation is based upon neuropsychiatric disorders and cardiovascular disorders associated with lower sodium cobalamin concentrations.

Test Interactions Methotrexate, pyrimethamine, and most antibiotics invalidate folic acid and vitamin B_{12} diagnostic microbiological blood assays

Patient Information Pernicious anemia will require monthly injections for life

Nursing Implications Oral therapy is markedly inferior to parenteral therapy; monitor potassium concentrations during early therapy

Dosage Forms
Gel, nasal:
Ener-B®: 400 mcg/0.1 mL
Nascobal™: 500 mcg/0.1 mL (5 mL)
Injection: 30 mcg/mL (30 mL); 100 mcg/mL (1 mL, 10 mL, 30 mL); 1000 mcg/mL (1 mL, 10 mL, 30 mL)
Tablet [OTC]: 25 mcg, 50 mcg, 100 mcg, 250 mcg, 500 mcg, 1000 mcg

♦ **Cyanoject®** see Cyanocobalamin *on previous page*
♦ **Cyclen®** see Ethinyl Estradiol and Norgestimate *on page 453*

Cyclobenzaprine (sye kloe BEN za preen)

U.S. Brand Names Flexeril®

Canadian Brand Names Novo-Cycloprine

Synonyms Cyclobenzaprine Hydrochloride

Therapeutic Category Skeletal Muscle Relaxant

Use Treatment of muscle spasm associated with acute painful musculoskeletal conditions; supportive therapy in tetanus

Pregnancy Risk Factor B

Contraindications Hypersensitivity to cyclobenzaprine or any component; do not use concomitantly or within 14 days of MAO inhibitors; hyperthyroidism, congestive heart failure, arrhythmias

Warnings/Precautions Cyclobenzaprine shares the toxic potentials of the tricyclic antidepressants and the usual precautions of tricyclic antidepressant therapy should be observed; use with caution in patients with urinary hesitancy or angle-closure glaucoma

Adverse Reactions

>10%:

Central nervous system: Drowsiness, dizziness, lightheadedness

Gastrointestinal: Xerostomia

1% to 10%:

Cardiovascular: Edema of the face/lips, syncope

Gastrointestinal: Bloated feeling

Genitourinary: Problems in urinating, polyuria

Hepatic: Hepatitis

Neuromuscular & skeletal: Problems in speaking, muscle weakness

Ocular: Blurred vision

Otic: Tinnitus

<1%: Tachycardia, hypotension, arrhythmia, headache, fatigue, nervousness, confusion, ataxia, rash, dermatitis, dyspepsia, nausea, constipation, stomach cramps, unpleasant taste

Overdosage/Toxicology

Symptoms of overdose include troubled breathing, drowsiness, syncope, seizures, tachycardia, hallucinations, vomiting

Following initiation of essential overdose management, toxic symptoms should be treated. Ventricular arrhythmias often respond to systemic alkalinization (sodium bicarbonate 0.5-2 mEq/kg I.V.) and/or phenytoin 15-20 mg/kg (adults). Arrhythmias unresponsive to this therapy may respond to lidocaine 1 mg/kg I.V. followed by a titrated infusion. Physostigmine (1-2 mg I.V. slowly for adults or 0.5 mg I.V. slowly for children) may be indicated in reversing cardiac arrhythmias that are life-threatening. Seizures usually respond to diazepam I.V. boluses (5-10 mg for adults up to 30 mg or 0.25-0.4 mg/kg/dose for children up to 10 mg/dose). If seizures are unresponsive or recur, phenytoin or phenobarbital may be required.

Drug Interactions CYP1A2, 2D6 and 3A3/4 enzyme substrate

Increased toxicity:

Do not use concomitantly or within 14 days after MAO inhibitors

Because of similarities to the tricyclic antidepressants, may have additive toxicities

Anticholinergics: Because of cyclobenzaprine's anticholinergic action, use with caution in patients receiving these agents

Alcohol, barbiturates, and other CNS depressants: Effects may be enhanced by cyclobenzaprine

Mechanism of Action Centrally acting skeletal muscle relaxant pharmacologically related to tricyclic antidepressants; reduces tonic somatic motor activity influencing both alpha and gamma motor neurons

Pharmacodynamics/Kinetics

Onset of action: Commonly occurs within 1 hour

Absorption: Oral: Completely

Metabolism: Hepatic; may undergo enterohepatic recycling

Time to peak serum concentration: Within 3-8 hours

Elimination: Renally as inactive metabolites and in feces (via bile) as unchanged drug

Usual Dosage Oral: **Note:** Do not use longer than 2-3 weeks

Children: Dosage has not been established

Adults: 20-40 mg/day in 2-4 divided doses; maximum dose: 60 mg/day

Patient Information Drug may impair ability to perform hazardous activities requiring mental alertness or physical coordination, such as operating machinery or driving a motor vehicle

Nursing Implications Raise bed rails, institute safety measures, assist with ambulation

Dosage Forms Tablet, as hydrochloride: 10 mg

♦ **Cyclobenzaprine Hydrochloride** see Cyclobenzaprine on this page

♦ **Cyclocort®** see Amcinonide on page 53

♦ **Cyclogyl®** see Cyclopentolate on this page

♦ **Cyclomen®** see Danazol on page 322

♦ **Cyclomydril® Ophthalmic** see Cyclopentolate and Phenylephrine on next page

Cyclopentolate (sye kloe PEN toe late)

Related Information

Cycloplegic Mydriatics Comparison on page 1321

U.S. Brand Names AK-Pentolate®; Cyclogyl®; I-Pentolate®

Synonyms Cyclopentolate Hydrochloride

Therapeutic Category Anticholinergic Agent, Ophthalmic; Ophthalmic Agent, Mydriatic

Use Diagnostic procedures requiring mydriasis and cycloplegia

Pregnancy Risk Factor C

Contraindications Narrow-angle glaucoma, known hypersensitivity to drug

Warnings/Precautions 2% solution may result in psychotic reactions and behavioral disturbances in children, usually occurring approximately 30-45 minutes after instillation; use with caution in elderly patients and other patients who may be predisposed to increased intraocular pressure

Adverse Reactions 1% to 10%:
Cardiovascular: Tachycardia
Central nervous system: Restlessness, hallucinations, psychosis, hyperactivity, seizures, incoherent speech, ataxia
Dermatologic: Burning sensation
Ocular: Increase in intraocular pressure, loss of visual accommodation
Miscellaneous: Allergic reaction

Overdosage/Toxicology Antidote, if needed, is pilocarpine

Drug Interactions Decreased effect of carbachol, cholinesterase inhibitors

Stability Store in tight containers

Mechanism of Action Prevents the muscle of the ciliary body and the sphincter muscle of the iris from responding to cholinergic stimulation, causing mydriasis and cycloplegia

Pharmacodynamics/Kinetics
Peak effect: Cycloplegia: 25-75 minutes; Mydriasis: 30-60 minutes
Duration: Recovery takes up to 24 hours

Usual Dosage
Infants: Instill 1 drop of 0.5% into each eye 5-10 minutes before examination
Children: Instill 1 drop of 0.5%, 1%, or 2% in eye followed by 1 drop of 0.5% or 1% in 5 minutes, if necessary
Adults: Instill 1 drop of 1% followed by another drop in 5 minutes; 2% solution in heavily pigmented iris

Patient Information May cause blurred vision and increased sensitivity to light

Nursing Implications Finger pressure should be applied to lacrimal sac for 1-2 minutes after instillation to decrease risk of absorption and systemic reactions

Dosage Forms Solution, ophthalmic, as hydrochloride: 0.5% (2 mL, 5 mL, 15 mL); 1% (2 mL, 5 mL, 15 mL); 2% (2 mL, 5 mL, 15 mL)

Cyclopentolate and Phenylephrine
(sye kloe PEN toe late & fen il EF rin)

U.S. Brand Names Cyclomydril® Ophthalmic

Therapeutic Category Anticholinergic/Adrenergic Agonist

Dosage Forms Solution, ophthalmic: Cyclopentolate hydrochloride 0.2% and phenylephrine hydrochloride 1% (2 mL, 5 mL)

♦ **Cyclopentolate Hydrochloride** see Cyclopentolate on previous page

Cyclophosphamide (sye kloe FOS fa mide)

Related Information
Cancer Chemotherapy Regimens on page 1263
Toxicities of Chemotherapeutic Agents on page 1288

U.S. Brand Names Cytoxan® Injection; Cytoxan® Oral; Neosar® Injection

Canadian Brand Names Procytox®

Synonyms CPM; CTX; CYT

Therapeutic Category Antineoplastic Agent, Alkylating Agent

Use Treatment of Hodgkin's and non-Hodgkin's lymphoma, Burkitt's lymphoma, chronic lymphocytic leukemia, chronic granulocytic leukemia, AML, ALL, mycosis fungoides, breast cancer, multiple myeloma, neuroblastoma, retinoblastoma, rhabdomyosarcoma, Ewing's sarcoma; testicular, endometrium and ovarian, and lung cancer, and as a conditioning regimen for BMT; prophylaxis of rejection for kidney, heart, liver, and BMT transplants, severe rheumatoid disorders, nephrotic syndrome, Wegener's granulomatosis, idiopathic pulmonary hemosideroses, myasthenia gravis, multiple sclerosis, systemic lupus erythematosus, lupus nephritis, autoimmune hemolytic anemia, idiopathic thrombocytic purpura, macroglobulinemia, and antibody-induced pure red cell aplasia

Pregnancy Risk Factor D

Contraindications Hypersensitivity to cyclophosphamide or any component

Warnings/Precautions The U.S. Food and Drug Administration (FDA) currently recommends that procedures for proper handling and disposal of antineoplastic agents be considered. Possible dosage adjustment needed for renal or hepatic failure; use with caution in patients with bone marrow suppression.

Adverse Reactions
>10%:
Dermatologic: Alopecia is frequent, but hair will regrow although it may be of a different color or texture; alopecia usually occurs 3 weeks after therapy
Endocrine & metabolic: Fertility: May cause sterility; interferes with oogenesis and spermatogenesis; may be irreversible in some patients; gonadal suppression (amenorrhea)
Gastrointestinal: Nausea and vomiting occur more frequently with larger doses, usually beginning 6-10 hours after administration; also seen are anorexia, diarrhea, stomatitis; mucositis

(Continued)

Cyclophosphamide *(Continued)*

Emetic potential:
Oral: Low (<10%)
<1 g: Moderate (30% to 60%)
≥1 g: High (>90%)
Time course of nausea/vomiting: Onset: 6-8 hours; Duration: 8-24 hours
Hepatic: Jaundice seen occasionally

1% to 10%:
Central nervous system: Headache
Dermatologic: Skin rash, facial flushing
Hematologic: Myelosuppressive: Thrombocytopenia occurs less frequently than with mechlorethamine, anemia
WBC: Moderate
Platelets: Moderate
Onset (days): 7
Nadir (days): 10-14
Recovery (days): 21

<1%: High-dose therapy may cause cardiac dysfunction manifested as congestive heart failure; cardiac necrosis or hemorrhagic myocarditis has occurred rarely, but is fatal. Cyclophosphamide may also potentiate the cardiac toxicity of anthracyclines.

Dizziness, darkening of skin/fingernails, hyperglycemia, hypokalemia, distortion, hyperuricemia, SIADH has occurred with I.V. doses >50 mg/kg, stomatitis, acute hemorrhagic cystitis is believed to be a result of chemical irritation of the bladder by acrolein, a cyclophosphamide metabolite. Acute hemorrhagic cystitis occurs in 7% to 12% of patients, and has been reported in up to 40% of patients. Hemorrhagic cystitis can be severe and even fatal. Patients should be encouraged to drink plenty of fluids (3-4 L/day) during therapy, void frequently, and avoid taking the drug at nighttime. If large I.V. doses are being administered, I.V. hydration should be given during therapy. The administration of mesna or continuous bladder irrigation may also be warranted.

Hepatic toxicity, renal tubular necrosis has occurred, but usually resolves after the discontinuation of therapy, nasal congestion occurs when given in large I.V. doses via 30-60 minute infusion; patients experience runny eyes, nasal burning, rhinorrhea, sinus congestion, and sneezing during or immediately after the infusion; interstitial pulmonary fibrosis with prolonged high dosage has occurred; secondary malignancy has developed with cyclophosphamide alone or in combination with other antineoplastics; both bladder carcinoma and acute leukemia are well documented; rare instances of anaphylaxis have been reported

Overdosage/Toxicology

Symptoms of overdose include myelosuppression, alopecia, nausea, vomiting
Treatment is supportive; cyclophosphamide is moderately dialyzable (20% to 50%)

Drug Interactions CYP2B6, 2D6, and 3A3/4 enzyme substrate

Decreased effect: Digoxin: Cyclophosphamide may decrease digoxin serum levels
Increased toxicity:
Allopurinol may cause increase in bone marrow depression and may result in significant elevations of cyclophosphamide cytotoxic metabolites
Anesthetic agents: Cyclophosphamide reduces serum pseudocholinesterase concentrations and may prolong the neuromuscular blocking activity of succinylcholine; use with caution with halothane, nitrous oxide, and succinylcholine
Chloramphenicol results in prolonged cyclophosphamide half-life to increase toxicity
Cimetidine inhibits hepatic metabolism of drugs and may decrease or increase the activation of cyclophosphamide
Doxorubicin: Cyclophosphamide may enhance cardiac toxicity of anthracyclines
Phenobarbital and phenytoin induce hepatic enzymes and cause a more rapid production of cyclophosphamide metabolites with a concurrent decrease in the serum half-life of the parent compound
Tetrahydrocannabinol results in enhanced immunosuppression in animal studies
Thiazide diuretics: Leukopenia may be prolonged

Stability

Store intact vials of powder at room temperature (25°C to 35°C)
Reconstitute vials with SWI to a concentration of 20 mg/mL as follows below; reconstituted solutions are stable for 24 hours at room temperature (25°C) and 6 days at refrigeration (5°C)
100 mg vial = 5 mL
200 mg vial = 10 mL
500 mg vial = 25 mL
1 g vial = 50 mL
2 g vial = 100 mL
Further dilutions in D_5W or NS are stable for 48 hours at room temperature (25°C) and 28 days at refrigeration (5°C)

Maximum concentration of cyclophosphamide is **limited** to 20 mg/mL due to solubility of cyclophosphamide

Standard I.V. push dilution: Dose up to 500 mg/30 mL syringe
Maximum syringe size for IVP is a 30 mL syringe syringe should be ≤75% full
Standard IVPB dilution:
May further dilute in D_5W or NS after initial reconstitution with SWI
Doses up to 2 g/250 mL volume
Doses up to 4 g/500 mL volume

Mechanism of Action Interferes with the normal function of DNA by alkylation and cross-linking the strands of DNA, and by possible protein modification; cyclophosphamide also possesses potent immunosuppressive activity; note that cyclophosphamide must be metabolized to its active form in the liver

Pharmacodynamics/Kinetics

Absorption: Completely from the GI tract (>75%)

Distribution: V_d: 0.48-0.71 L/kg; well distributed; crosses the placenta; appears in breast milk; does cross into the CSF, but not in concentrations high enough to treat meningeal leukemia

Protein binding: 10% to 56%

Metabolism: In the liver into its active components, one of which is 4-HC

Bioavailability: >75%

Half-life: 4-6.5 hours

Time to peak serum concentration: Oral: Within 1 hour

Elimination: In the urine as unchanged drug (<10%) and as metabolites (85% to 90%); most of which are inactive

Usual Dosage Refer to individual protocols

Patients with compromised bone marrow function may require a 33% to 50% reduction in initial loading dose

Children:

SLE: I.V.: 500-750 mg/m^2 every month; maximum dose: 1 g/m^2

JRA/vasculitis: I.V.: 10 mg/kg every 2 weeks

Children and Adults:

Oral: 50-100 mg/m^2/day as continuous therapy or 400-1000 mg/m^2 in divided doses over 4-5 days as intermittent therapy

I.V.:

Single Doses: 400-1800 mg/m^2 (30-50 mg/kg) per treatment course (1-5 days) which can be repeated at 2-4 week intervals

MAXIMUM SINGLE DOSE WITHOUT BMT is 7 g/m^2 (190 mg/kg) SINGLE AGENT THERAPY

Continuous daily doses: 60-120 mg/m^2 (1-2.5 mg/kg) per day

Autologous BMT: IVPB: 50 mg/kg/dose x 4 days or 60 mg/kg/dose for 2 days; total dose is usually divided over 2-4 days

Nephrotic syndrome: Oral: 2-3 mg/kg/day every day for up to 12 weeks when corticosteroids are unsuccessful

Dosing adjustment in renal impairment: A large fraction of cyclophosphamide is eliminated by hepatic metabolism

Some authors recommend no dose adjustment unless severe renal insufficiency (Cl_{cr} <20 mL/minute)

Cl_{cr} >10 mL/minute: Administer 100% of normal dose

Cl_{cr} <10 mL/minute: Administer 75% of normal dose

Hemodialysis: Moderately dialyzable (20% to 50%); administer dose posthemodialysis or administer supplemental 50% dose

CAPD effects: Unknown

CAVH effects: Unknown

Dosing adjustment in hepatic impairment: Some authors recommend dosage reductions (of up to 30%); however, the pharmacokinetics of cyclophosphamide are not significantly altered in the presence of hepatic insufficiency. Cyclophosphamide undergoes hepatic transformation in the liver to its 4-hydroxycyclophosphamide, which breaks down to its active form, phosphoramide mustard.

Administration

May be administered I.M., I.P., intrapleurally, IVPB, or continuous I.V. infusion

I.V. infusions may be administered over 1-2 hours

Doses >500 mg to approximately 1 g may be administered over 20-30 minutes

May also be administered slow IVP in lower doses

Force fluids up to 2 L/day to minimize bladder toxicity; high-dose regimens should be accompanied by vigorous hydration ± MESNA therapy

Monitoring Parameters CBC with differential and platelet count, BUN, UA, serum electrolytes, serum creatinine

Patient Information Drink plenty of fluids before and after doses; report any blood in the urine. Contraceptive measures are recommended during therapy.

Nursing Implications Encourage adequate hydration and frequent voiding to help prevent hemorrhagic cystitis

Dosage Forms

Powder for injection: 100 mg, 200 mg, 500 mg, 1 g, 2 g

Powder for injection, lyophilized: 100 mg, 200 mg, 500 mg, 1 g, 2 g

Tablet: 25 mg, 50 mg

Extemporaneous Preparations A 2 mg/mL oral elixir was stable for 14 days when refrigerated when made as follows:

Withdraw the liquid injection (50 mg) from the vial and qs to 100 mL with Aromatic Elixir U.S.P.

Keep in refrigerator (Store in amber glass)

Brook D, Davis RE, and Bequette RJ, "Chemical Stability of Cyclophosphamide in Aromatic Elixir U.S.P.," *Am J Health Syst Pharm*, 1973, 30:618-20.

♦ **Cycloplegic Mydriatics Comparison** *see page 1321*

Cycloserine (sye kloe SER een)

Related Information
Antimicrobial Drugs of Choice *on page 1404*
Depression Disorders and Treatments *on page 1465*
Tuberculosis Treatment Guidelines *on page 1432*

U.S. Brand Names Seromycin® Pulvules®

Therapeutic Category Antibiotic, Miscellaneous; Antitubercular Agent

Use Adjunctive treatment in pulmonary or extrapulmonary tuberculosis; has been studied for use in Gaucher's disease

Pregnancy Risk Factor C

Contraindications Known hypersensitivity to cycloserine

Warnings/Precautions Epilepsy, depression, severe anxiety, psychosis, severe renal insufficiency, chronic alcoholism

Adverse Reactions Percentage unknown: Cardiac arrhythmias, drowsiness, headache, dizziness, vertigo, seizures, confusion, psychosis, paresis, coma, rash, folate deficiency, elevated liver enzymes, tremor, vitamin B_{12} deficiency

Overdosage/Toxicology
Symptoms of overdose include confusion, agitation, CNS depression, psychosis, coma, seizures

Decontaminate with activated charcoal; can be hemodialyzed; management is supportive; administer 100-300 mg/day of pyridoxine to reduce neurotoxic effects; acute toxicity can occur with ingestions >1 g; chronic toxicity: >500 mg/day

Drug Interactions Increased toxicity: Alcohol, isoniazid, ethionamide increase toxicity of cycloserine; cycloserine inhibits the hepatic metabolism of phenytoin

Mechanism of Action Inhibits bacterial cell wall synthesis by competing with amino acid (D-alanine) for incorporation into the bacterial cell wall; bacteriostatic or bactericidal

Pharmacodynamics/Kinetics
Absorption: Oral: ~70% to 90% from the GI tract

Distribution: Crosses the placenta; appears in breast milk; distributed widely to most body fluids and tissues including CSF, breast milk, bile, sputum, lymph tissue, lungs, and ascitic, pleural, and synovial fluids

Half-life: 10 hours in patients with normal renal function

Metabolism: Extensive in liver

Time to peak serum concentration: Oral: Within 3-4 hours

Elimination: 60% to 70% of oral dose excreted unchanged in urine by glomerular filtration within 72 hours, small amounts excreted in feces, remainder is metabolized

Usual Dosage Some of the neurotoxic effects may be relieved or prevented by the concomitant administration of pyridoxine

Tuberculosis: Oral:
Children: 10-20 mg/kg/day in 2 divided doses up to 1000 mg/day for 18-24 months
Adults: Initial: 250 mg every 12 hours for 14 days, then administer 500 mg to 1 g/day in 2 divided doses for 18-24 months (maximum daily dose: 1 g)

Dosing interval in renal impairment:
Cl_{cr} 10-50 mL/minute: Administer every 24 hours
Cl_{cr} <10 mL/minute: Administer every 36-48 hours

Monitoring Parameters Periodic renal, hepatic, hematological tests, and plasma cycloserine concentrations

Reference Range Toxicity is greatly increased at levels >30 µg/mL

Patient Information May cause drowsiness; notify physician if skin rash, mental confusion, dizziness, headache, or tremors occur; do not skip doses; do not drink excessive amounts of alcoholic beverages

Dosage Forms Capsule: 250 mg

♦ Cyclosporin A *see* Cyclosporine *on this page*

Cyclosporine (SYE kloe spor een)

U.S. Brand Names Neoral® Oral; Sandimmune® Injection; Sandimmune® Oral; Sang® CyA

Synonyms CsA; CyA; Cyclosporin A

Therapeutic Category Immunosuppressant Agent

Use Immunosuppressant which may be used with azathioprine and/or corticosteroids to prolong organ and patient survival in kidney, liver, heart, and bone marrow transplants; severe psoriasis; also used in some cases of severe autoimmune disease that are resistant to corticosteroids and other therapy.

Pregnancy Risk Factor C

Pregnancy/Breast-Feeding Implications Clinical effects on the fetus: Based on small numbers of patients, the use of cyclosporine during pregnancy apparently does not pose a major risk to the fetus

Contraindications
Hypersensitivity to cyclosporine, Cremaphor EL® (I.V. solution), or any other I.V. component (ie, polyoxyl 35 castor oil is an ingredient of the parenteral formulation and polyoxyl 40 hydrogenated castor oil is an ingredient of the cyclosporine capsules and solution for microemulsion)

Use in severe psoriasis therapy: Concomitant treatment of cyclosporine with other psoriasis treatments such as psoralens + ultraviolet A (UVA) light PUVA, UVB therapy, other radiation therapy or other immunosuppressive agents may result in excessive immunosuppression and increased risk of malignancies. Concomitant treatment of cyclosporine with methotrexate or coal tar. The risk of skin malignancies is increased in patients who have previously been treated with these other psoriasis therapies prior to cyclosporine therapy.

Warnings/Precautions Infection and possible development of lymphoma may result. Make dose adjustments to avoid toxicity or possible organ rejection using cyclosporine blood levels because absorption is erratic and elimination is highly variable. Adjustment of dose should only be made under the direct supervision of an experienced physician; reserve the use of I.V. for use only in patients who cannot take oral; adequate airway and other supportive measures and agents for treating anaphylaxis should be present when I.V. drug is given. Nephrotoxic, if possible avoid concomitant use of other potentially nephrotoxic drugs (eg, acyclovir, aminoglycoside antibiotics, amphotericin B, ciprofloxacin). Can cause systemic hypertension or nephrotoxicity when used with other psoriasis therapies.

Adverse Reactions
>10%:
Cardiovascular: Hypertension
Dermatologic: Hirsutism
Endocrine & metabolic: Hypomagnesemia, hypokalemia
Gastrointestinal: Gingival hypertrophy
Neuromuscular & skeletal: Tremor
Renal: Nephrotoxicity

1% to 10%:
Central nervous system: Seizure, headache
Dermatologic: Acne
Gastrointestinal: Abdominal discomfort, nausea, vomiting
Neuromuscular & skeletal: Leg cramps

<1%: Hypotension, tachycardia, warmth, flushing, hyperkalemia, hypomagnesemia, hyperuricemia, pancreatitis, hepatotoxicity, myositis, paresthesias, respiratory distress, sinusitis, anaphylaxis, increased susceptibility to infection, and sensitivity to temperature extremes

Overdosage/Toxicology Symptoms of overdose include hepatotoxicity, nephrotoxicity, nausea, vomiting, tremor. CNS secondary to direct action of the drug may not be reflected in serum concentrations, may be more predictable by renal magnesium loss.

Drug Interactions CYP3A3/4 enzyme substrate

Decreased effect: Drugs that decrease cyclosporine concentrations: Carbamazepine, phenobarbital, phenytoin, rifampin, isoniazid

Increased toxicity:
Drugs that increase cyclosporine concentrations: Azithromycin, clarithromycin, diltiazem, erythromycin, fluconazole, itraconazole, ketoconazole, nicardipine, verapamil, grapefruit juice
Drugs that enhance nephrotoxicity of cyclosporine: Aminoglycosides, amphotericin B, acyclovir
Lovastatin - myositis, myalgias, rhabdomyolysis, acute renal failure
Nifedipine - increases risk of gingival hyperplasia

Stability
Cyclosporine injection is a clear, faintly brown-yellow solution which should be stored at <30°C and protected from light

Cyclosporine concentrate for injection should be further diluted [1 mL (50 mg) of concentrate in 20-100 mL of D_5W or or NS] for administration by intravenous infusion. Light protection is not required for intravenous admixtures of cyclosporine.

Stability of injection of parenteral admixture at room temperature (25°C): 6 hours in PVC; 24 hours in Excel, PAB containers, or glass

Polyoxyethylated castor oil (Cremophor EL®) surfactant in cyclosporin injection may leach phthalate from PVC containers such as bags and tubing. The actual amount of diethylhexyl phthalate (DEHP) plasticizer leached from PVC containers and administration sets may vary in clinical situations, depending on surfactant concentration, bag size, and contact time.

Doses <250 mg should be prepared in 100 mL of D_5W or NS
Doses >250 mg should be prepared in 250 mL of D_5W or NS
Minimum volume: 100 mL D_5W or NS
Do not refrigerate oral or I.V. solution

Oral solution: Use the contents of the oral solution within two months after opening; should be mixed in glass containers

Mechanism of Action Inhibition of production and release of interleukin II and inhibits interleukin II-induced activation of resting T-lymphocytes

Pharmacodynamics/Kinetics
Absorption: Oral:
Solution or soft gelatin capsule (Sandimmune®): Erratically and incompletely absorbed; dependent on the presence of food, bile acids, and GI motility; larger oral doses of cyclosporine are needed in pediatric patients versus adults due to a shorter bowel length resulting in limited intestinal absorption
Solution in microemulsion or soft gelatin capsule in a microemulsion are bioequivalent (Neoral®): Erratically and incompletely absorbed; increased absorption, up to 30% when compared to Sandimmune®; absorption is less dependent on food intake, bile, or GI motility when compared to Sandimmune®

Distribution: Widely distributed in tissues and body fluids including the liver, pancreas, and lungs; crosses the placenta; excreted into breast milk
V_{dss}: 4-6 L/kg in renal, liver, and marrow transplant recipients (slightly lower values in cardiac transplant patients; children <10 years of age have higher values)

Protein binding: 90% to 98% of cyclosporine in the blood is bound to lipoproteins
(Continued)

Cyclosporine *(Continued)*

Metabolism: Undergoes extensive first-pass metabolism following oral administration; extensively metabolized by the cytochrome P-450 system in the liver

Bioavailability:

Solution or soft gelatin capsule (Sandimmune®): Dependent on patient population and transplant type (<10% in adult liver transplant patients and as high as 89% in renal patients)

Children: 28% (range: 17% to 42%); with gut dysfunction commonly seen in BMT patients, oral bioavailability is further reduced

Solution or soft gelatin capsule in a microemulsion (Neoral®):

Children: 43% (range: 30% to 68%)

Adults: 23% greater than with Sandimmune® in renal transplant patients. 50% greater in liver transplant patients

Half-life:

Solution or soft gelatin capsule (Sandimmune®): Biphasic, alpha phase: 1.4 hours and terminal phase 6-24 hours (prolonged in patients with hepatic dysfunction)

Solution or soft gelatin capsule in a microemulsion (Neoral®): 8.4 hours, lower in pediatric patients versus adults due to the higher metabolism rate

Time to peak serum concentration:

Oral solution or capsule (Sandimmune®): 2-6 hours; some patients have a second peak at 5-6 hours

Oral solution or capsule in a microemulsion (Neoral®): 1.5-2 hours (in renal transplant patients)

Elimination: Primarily in the bile; clearance is more rapid in pediatric patients than in adults; clearance is decreased in patients with liver disease; 6% of dose excreted in the urine as unchanged drug (0.1%) and metabolites

Usual Dosage Children and Adults (oral dosage is ~3 times the I.V. dosage); dosage should be based on ideal body weight:

I.V.:

Initial: 5-6 mg/kg/day beginning 4-12 hours prior to organ transplantation; patients should be switched to oral cyclosporine as soon as possible; dose should be infused over 2-24 hours

Maintenance: 2-10 mg/kg/day in divided doses every 8-12 hours; dose should be adjusted to maintain whole blood FPIA trough concentrations in the reference range

Oral: Solution or soft gelatin capsule (Sandimmune®):

Initial: 14-18 mg/kg/day, beginning 4-12 hours prior to organ transplantation

Maintenance: 5-15 mg/kg/day divided every 12-24 hours; maintenance dose is usually tapered to 3-10 mg/kg/day

Focal segmental glomerulosclerosis: Initial: 3 mg/kg/day divided every 12 hours

Autoimmune diseases: 1-3 mg/kg/day

Dosing considerations of cyclosporine, see table.

Cyclosporine

Condition	Cyclosporine
Switch from I.V. to oral therapy	Threefold increase in dose
T-tube clamping	Decrease dose; increase availability of bile facilitates absorption of CsA
Pediatric patients	About 2-3 times higher dose compared to adults
Liver dysfunction	Decrease I.V. dose; increase oral dose
Renal dysfunction	Decrease dose to decrease levels if renal dysfunction is related to the drug
Dialysis	Not removed
Inhibitors of hepatic metabolism	Decrease dose
Inducers of hepatic metabolism	Monitor drug level; may need to increase dose

Oral: **Solution or soft gelatin capsule in a microemulsion (Neoral®):** Based on the organ transplant population:

Initial: Same as the initial dose for solution or soft gelatin capsule (listed above) **or**

Renal: 9 mg/kg/day (range: 6-12 mg/kg/day)

Liver: 8 mg/kg/day (range: 4-12 mg/kg/day)

Heart: 7 mg/kg/day (range: 4-10 mg/kg/day)

Note: A 1:1 ratio conversion from Sandimmune® to Neoral® has been recommended initially; however, lower doses of Neoral® may be required after conversion to prevent overdose. Total daily doses should be adjusted based on the cyclosporine trough blood concentration and clinical assessment of organ rejection. CsA blood trough levels should be determined prior to conversion. After conversion to Neoral®, CsA trough levels should be monitored every 4-7 days. **Neoral® and Sandimmune® are not bioequivalent and cannot be used interchangeably.**

Hemodialysis: Supplemental dose is not necessary

Peritoneal dialysis: Supplemental dose is not necessary

Dosing adjustment in hepatic impairment: Probably necessary, monitor levels closely

Dosing adjustment recommendations for renal impairment during cyclosporine therapy for severe psoriasis:

Serum creatinine levels ≥25% above pretreatment levels: Take another sample within 2 weeks. If the level remains ≥25% above pretreatment levels, decrease dosage of cyclosporine microemulsion by 25% to 50%. If 2 dosage adjustments do

not reverse the increase in serum creatinine levels, treatment should be discontinued.

Serum creatinine ≥50% above pretreatment levels: Decrease cyclosporine dosage by 25% to 50%. If 2 dosage adjustments do not reverse the increase in serum creatinine levels, treatment should be discontinued.

Note: Increase the frequency of blood pressure monitoring after each alteration in dosage of cyclosporine. Cyclosporine dosage should be decreased by 25% to 50% in patients with no history of hypertension who develop sustained hypertension during therapy and, if hypertension persists, treatment with cyclosporine should be discontinued.

Monitoring Parameters
Cyclosporine trough levels, serum electrolytes, renal function, hepatic function, blood pressure, serum cholesterol

Psoriasis therapy: Biweekly monitoring of blood pressure, complete blood count, and levels of BUN, uric acid, potassium, lipids and magnesium during the first three months of treatment for psoriasis. Monthly monitoring is recommended after this initial period.

Reference Range Reference ranges are method dependent and specimen dependent; use the same analytical method consistently; trough levels should be obtained immediately prior to next dose

Method-dependent and specimen-dependent
Trough levels should be obtained:
Oral: 12-18 hours after dose (chronic usage)
I.V.: 12 hours after dose **or** immediately prior to next dose

Therapeutic range: Not absolutely defined, dependent on organ transplanted, time after transplant, organ function and CsA toxicity
General range of 100-400 ng/mL
Toxic level: Not well defined, nephrotoxicity may occur at any level

Test Interactions Cyclosporine adsorbs to silicone; specific whole blood assay for cyclosporine may be falsely elevated if sample is drawn from the same line through which dose was administered (even if flush has been administered and/or dose was given hours before)

Patient Information Use glass droppers or glass to hold dose; rinse container to get full dose; mix with milk, chocolate milk, or orange juice preferably at room temperature, improves palatability; stir well and drink at once. Take dose at same time each day. The patient should be instructed not to change brands unless directed to do so by their physician.

Nursing Implications Do not administer liquid from plastic or styrofoam cup; mixing with milk, chocolate milk, or orange juice preferably at room temperature, improves palatability; stir well; do not allow to stand before drinking; rinse with more diluent to ensure that the total dose is taken; after use, dry outside of pipette; do not rinse with water or other cleaning agents; may cause inflamed gums

Dosage Forms
Capsule, microemulsion (Neoral®): 25 mg; 100 mg
Capsule, soft gelatin (Sandimmune®): 25 mg; 50 mg; 100 mg
Injection: 50 mg/mL (5 mL)
Solution, oral (Sandimmune®): 100 mg/mL (50 mL)
Solution, oral, microemulsion (Neoral®): 100 mg/mL (50 mL)

♦ **Cycofed® Pediatric** see Guaifenesin, Pseudoephedrine, and Codeine on page 551
♦ **Cycrin®** see Medroxyprogesterone Acetate on page 721
♦ **Cyklokapron®** see Tranexamic Acid on page 1167
♦ **Cylert®** see Pemoline on page 892
♦ **Cylex® [OTC]** see Benzocaine on page 133
♦ **Cyomin®** see Cyanocobalamin on page 302

Cyproheptadine (si proe HEP ta deen)

U.S. Brand Names Periactin®
Canadian Brand Names PMS-Cyproheptadine
Synonyms Cyproheptadine Hydrochloride
Therapeutic Category Antihistamine, H₁ Blocker
Use Perennial and seasonal allergic rhinitis and other allergic symptoms including urticaria

Unlabeled use: Appetite stimulation, blepharospasm, cluster headaches, migraine headaches, Nelson's syndrome, pruritus, schizophrenia, spinal cord damage associated spasticity, and tardive dyskinesia

Pregnancy Risk Factor B

Contraindications Hypersensitivity to cyproheptadine or any component; narrow-angle glaucoma, bladder neck obstruction, acute asthmatic attack, stenosing peptic ulcer, GI tract obstruction, those on MAO inhibitors; avoid use in premature and term newborns due to potential association with SIDS

Warnings/Precautions Do not use in neonates, safety and efficacy have not been established in children <2 years of age; symptomatic prostate hypertrophy; antihistamines are more likely to cause dizziness, excessive sedation, syncope, toxic confusion states, and hypotension in the elderly. In case reports, cyproheptadine has promoted weight gain in anorexic adults, though it has not been specifically studied in the elderly. All cases of weight loss or decreased appetite should be adequately assessed.

Adverse Reactions
>10%:
Central nervous system: Slight to moderate drowsiness
Respiratory: Thickening of bronchial secretions
(Continued)

Cyproheptadine *(Continued)*

1% to 10%:
Central nervous system: Headache, fatigue, nervousness, dizziness
Gastrointestinal: Appetite stimulation, nausea, diarrhea, abdominal pain, xerostomia
Neuromuscular & skeletal: Arthralgia
Respiratory: Pharyngitis
<1%: Tachycardia, palpitations, edema, sedation, CNS stimulation, seizures, depression, photosensitivity, rash, angioedema, hemolytic anemia, leukopenia, thrombocytopenia, hepatitis, myalgia, paresthesia, bronchospasm, epistaxis, allergic reactions

Overdosage/Toxicology
Symptoms of overdose include CNS depression or stimulation, dry mouth, flushed skin, fixed and dilated pupils, apnea

There is no specific treatment for an antihistamine overdose, however, most of its clinical toxicity is due to anticholinergic effects. Anticholinesterase inhibitors may be useful by reducing acetylcholinesterase. Anticholinesterase inhibitors include physostigmine, neostigmine, pyridostigmine, and edrophonium. For anticholinergic overdose with severe life-threatening symptoms, physostigmine 1-2 mg (0.5 mg or 0.02 mg/kg for children) I.V., slowly may be given to reverse these effects.

Drug Interactions Increased toxicity: MAO inhibitors → hallucinations

Mechanism of Action A potent antihistamine and serotonin antagonist, competes with histamine for H_1-receptor sites on effector cells in the gastrointestinal tract, blood vessels, and respiratory tract

Pharmacodynamics/Kinetics
Metabolism: Almost completely
Elimination: >50% excreted in urine (primarily as metabolites); ~25% excreted in feces

Usual Dosage Oral:
Children: 0.25 mg/kg/day in 2-3 divided doses or 8 mg/m²/day in 2-3 divided doses
2-6 years: 2 mg every 8-12 hours (not to exceed 12 mg/day)
7-14 years: 4 mg every 8-12 hours (not to exceed 16 mg/day)
Adults: 4-20 mg/day divided every 8 hours (not to exceed 0.5 mg/kg/day)
Dosing adjustment in hepatic impairment: Dosage should be reduced in patients with significant hepatic dysfunction

Dietary Considerations Alcohol: Additive CNS effects, avoid use

Test Interactions Diagnostic antigen skin tests, ↑ amylases (S), ↓ fasting glucose (S)

Patient Information May cause drowsiness; may stimulate appetite; avoid alcohol and other CNS depressants; may impair judgment and coordination

Nursing Implications Raise bed rails, institute safety measures, assist with ambulation

Dosage Forms
Syrup, as hydrochloride: 2 mg/5 mL with alcohol 5% (473 mL)
Tablet, as hydrochloride: 4 mg

♦ **Cyproheptadine Hydrochloride** *see Cyproheptadine on previous page*
♦ **Cystadane®** *see Betaine Anhydrous on page 140*
♦ **Cystagon®** *see Cysteamine on this page*

Cysteamine *(sis TEE a meen)*

U.S. Brand Names Cystagon®
Synonyms Cysteamine Bitartrate
Therapeutic Category Anticystine Agent; Urinary Tract Product
Use Orphan drug: Management of nephropathic cystinosis
Pregnancy Risk Factor C
Pregnancy/Breast-Feeding Implications
Clinical effects on the fetus: Use only when the potential benefits outweigh the potential hazards to the fetus; in animal studies, cysteamine reduced the fertility of rats and offspring survival at very large doses
Breast-feeding/lactation: It is unknown whether cysteamine is excreted in breast milk; discontinue nursing or discontinue drug during lactation

Contraindications Hypersensitivity to cysteamine or penicillamine

Warnings/Precautions Withhold cysteamine if a mild rash develops; restart at a lower dose and titrate to therapeutic dose; adjust cysteamine dose if CNS symptoms due to the drug develop, rather than the disease; adjust cysteamine dose downward if severe GI symptoms develop (most common during initiation of therapy)

Adverse Reactions
>5%:
Central nervous system: Fever, lethargy (11%)
Dermatologic: Rash (7%)
Gastrointestinal: Vomiting (35%), anorexia (31%), diarrhea (16%)
<5%:
Cardiovascular: Hypertension
Central nervous system: Somnolence, encephalopathy, headache, seizures, ataxia, confusion, dizziness, jitteriness, nervousness, impaired cognition, emotional changes, hallucinations, nightmares
Dermatologic: Urticaria
Endocrine & metabolic: Dehydration
Gastrointestinal: Bad breath, abdominal pain, dyspepsia, constipation, gastroenteritis, duodenitis, duodenal ulceration
Hematologic: Anemia, leukopenia
Hepatic: Abnormal LFTs

Neuromuscular & skeletal: Tremor, hyperkinesia
Otic: Decreased hearing

Overdosage/Toxicology
Symptoms may include vomiting, reduction of motor activity, GI or renal hemorrhage
Treatment is generally supportive; hemodialysis may be appropriate

Mechanism of Action Reacts with cystine in the lysosome to convert it to cysteine and to a cysteine-cysteamine mixed disulfide, both of which can then exit the lysosome in patients with cystinosis, an inherited defect of lysosomal transport

Usual Dosage Initiate therapy with $1/4$ to $1/8$ of maintenance dose; titrate slowly upward over 4-6 weeks

Children <12 years: Oral: Maintenance: 1.3 g/m^2/day divided into 4 doses

Children >12 years and Adults (>110 lbs): 2 g/day in 4 divided doses; dosage may be increased to 1.95 g/m^2/day if cystine levels are <1 nmol/$1/2$ cystine/mg protein, although intolerance and incidence of adverse events may be increased

Administration Sprinkle capsule contents over food for children <6 years of age

Monitoring Parameters Blood counts and LFTs during therapy; monitor leukocyte cystine measurements every 3 months to determine adequate dosage and compliance (measure 5-6 hours after administration); monitor more frequently when switching salt forms

Reference Range Leukocyte cystine: <1 nmol/$1/2$ cystine/mg protein

Patient Information Following initiation of therapy, do not engage in hazardous tasks until the effects of the drug on mental performance are known

Dosage Forms Capsule, as bitartrate: 50 mg, 150 mg

- **Cysteamine Bitartrate** see Cysteamine on previous page
- **Cystospaz®** see Hyoscyamine on page 590
- **Cystospaz-M®** see Hyoscyamine on page 590
- **CYT** see Cyclophosphamide on page 305
- **Cytadren®** see Aminoglutethimide on page 58

Cytarabine (sye TARE a been)

Related Information
Cancer Chemotherapy Regimens on page 1263
Toxicities of Chemotherapeutic Agents on page 1288

U.S. Brand Names Cytosar-U®

Synonyms Arabinosylcytosine; Ara-C; Cytarabine Hydrochloride; Cytosine Arabinosine Hydrochloride

Therapeutic Category Antineoplastic Agent, Antimetabolite (Purine)

Use Ara-C is one of the most active agents in leukemia; also active against lymphoma, meningeal leukemia, and meningeal lymphoma; has little use in the treatment of solid tumors

Pregnancy Risk Factor D

Contraindications Hypersensitivity to cytarabine or any component

Warnings/Precautions The U.S. Food and Drug Administration (FDA) currently recommends that procedures for proper handling and disposal of antineoplastic agents be considered. Use with caution in pregnant women or women of childbearing age and in infants; must monitor drug tolerance, protect and maintain a patient compromised by drug toxicity that includes bone marrow suppression with leukopenia, thrombocytopenia and anemia along with nausea, vomiting, diarrhea, abdominal pain, oral ulceration and hepatic impairment; marked bone marrow suppression necessitates dosage reduction by a decrease in the number of days of administration.

Adverse Reactions
>10%:

High-dose therapy toxicities: Cerebellar toxicity, conjunctivitis (make sure the patient is on steroid eye drops during therapy), corneal keratitis, hyperbilirubinemia, pulmonary edema, pericarditis, and tamponade

Central nervous system: Has produced seizures when given I.T.; cerebellar syndrome (or cerebellar toxicity), manifested as ataxia, dysarthria, and dysdiadochokinesia, has been reported to be dose-related. This may or may not be reversible.

Dermatologic: Oral/anal ulceration, rash

Gastrointestinal: Nausea, vomiting, diarrhea, and mucositis which subside quickly after discontinuing the drug; GI effects may be more pronounced with divided I.V. bolus doses than with continuous infusion

Emetic potential:
<500 mg: Moderately low (10% to 30%)
500 mg to 1500 mg: Moderately high (60% to 90%)
>1-1.5 g: High (>90%)

Time course of nausea/vomiting: Onset: 1-3 hours; Duration: 3-8 hours

Hematologic: Bleeding

Myelosuppressive: Occurs within the first week of treatment and lasts for 10-14 days; primarily manifested as granulocytopenia, but anemia can also occur
WBC: Severe
Platelets: Severe
Onset (days): 4-7
Nadir (days): 14-18
Recovery (days): 21-28

Hepatic: Hepatic dysfunction, mild jaundice and acute increase in transaminases can be produced

(Continued)

Cytarabine *(Continued)*

Local: Thrombophlebitis

1% to 10%:

Cardiovascular: Cardiomegaly

Central nervous system: Dizziness, headache, somnolence, confusion, neuritis, malaise

Dermatologic: Skin freckling, itching, alopecia, cellulitis at injection site

Genitourinary: Urinary retention

Neuromuscular & skeletal: Myalgia, bone pain, peripheral neuropathy

Respiratory: Syndrome of sudden respiratory distress progressing to pulmonary edema, pneumonia

Miscellaneous: Sepsis

Overdosage/Toxicology Symptoms of overdose include myelosuppression, megaloblastosis, nausea, vomiting, respiratory distress, pulmonary edema. A syndrome of sudden respiratory distress progressing to pulmonary edema and cardiomegaly has been reported following high doses.

Drug Interactions

Decreased effect of gentamicin, flucytosine; decreases digoxin oral tablet absorption

Increased toxicity: Alkylating agents and radiation; purine analogs; methotrexate

Stability Store intact vials of powder at room temperature 15°C to 30°C (59°F to 86°F)

WARNING: Bacteriostatic diluent should not be used for the preparation of either high-doses or intrathecal doses of cytarabine

Reconstitute with SWI, D_5W or NS; dilute to a concentration of 100 mg/mL as follows; reconstituted solutions are stable for 48 hours at 15°C to 30°C

100 mg vial = 1 mL

500 mg vial = 5 mL

1 g vial = 10 mL

2 g vial = 20 mL

Further dilution in D_5W or NS is stable for 8 days at room temperature (25°C)

Standard I.V. dilution:

I.V. push: Dose/syringe (concentration: 100 mg/mL)

Maximum syringe size for IVP is 30 mL syringe and syringe should be ≤75% full

IVPB: Dose/100 mL D_5W or NS

CIV: Dose/250-1000 mL D_5W or NS

Compatible with calcium, idarubicin, magnesium, potassium chloride, and vincristine

Incompatible with 5-FU, gentamicin, heparin, insulin, methylprednisolone, nafcillin, oxacillin, penicillin G sodium

Intrathecal solutions in 3-20 mL lactated Ringer's are stable for 7 days at room temperature (30°C); however, should be used within 24 hours due to sterility concerns

Standard intrathecal dilutions: Dose/3-5 mL lactated Ringer's ± methotrexate (12 mg) ± hydrocortisone (15-50 mg)

Compatible with methotrexate and hydrocortisone in lactated Ringer's or NS for 24 hours at room temperature (25°C)

Mechanism of Action Inhibition of DNA synthesis; cell cycle-specific for the S phase of cell division; cytosine gains entry into cells by a carrier process, and then must be converted to its active compound; cytosine acts as an analog and is incorporated into DNA; however, the primary action is inhibition of DNA polymerase resulting in decreased DNA synthesis and repair; degree of its cytotoxicity correlates linearly with its incorporation into DNA; therefore, incorporation into the DNA is responsible for drug activity and toxicity

Pharmacodynamics/Kinetics

Absorption: Because high concentrations of cytidine deaminase are in the GI mucosa and liver, 3-10 fold higher doses than I.V. would need to be given orally; therefore, the oral route is not used

Distribution: V_d = total body water. Widely and rapidly distributed since it enters the cells readily; crosses the blood-brain barrier, and CSF levels of 40% to 50% of the plasma level are reached

Metabolism: Primarily in the liver; Ara-C must be metabolized to Ara-CTP to be active

Half-life: Initial: 7-20 minutes; Terminal: 0.5-2.6 hours

Elimination: ~80% of dose excreted in the urine as metabolites within 36 hours

Usual Dosage I.V. bolus, IVPB, and CIV doses of cytarabine are very different. Bolus doses are relatively well tolerated since the drug is rapidly metabolized; bolus doses are associated with greater gastrointestinal and neurotoxicity; continuous infusion uniformly results in myelosuppression. Refer to individual protocols.

Children and Adults:

Induction remission:

I.V.: 200 mg/m²/day for 5 days at 2-week intervals

100-200 mg/m²/day for 5- to 10-day therapy course or every day until remission

I.T.: 5-75 mg/m² every 4 days until CNS findings normalize

or

<1 year: 20 mg

1-2 years: 30 mg

2-3 years: 50 mg

>3 years: 70 mg

Maintenance remission:

I.V.: 70-200 mg/m²/day for 2-5 days at monthly intervals

I.M., S.C.: 1-1.5 mg/kg single dose for maintenance at 1- to 4-week intervals

High-dose therapies:
 Doses as high as 1-3 g/m^2 have been used for refractory or secondary leukemias or refractory non-Hodgkin's lymphoma
 Doses of 3 g/m^2 every 12 hours for up to 12 doses have been used
Bone marrow transplant: 1.5 g/m^2 continuous infusion over 48 hours
Dosage adjustment of high-dose therapy in patients with renal insufficiency: In one study, 76% of patients with a Cl$_{cr}$ <60 mL/minute experienced neurotoxicity; dosage adjustment should be considered in these patients
Hemodialysis: Supplemental dose is not necessary
Peritoneal dialysis: Supplemental dose is not necessary
Dose may need to be adjusted in patients with liver failure since cytarabine is partially detoxified in the liver

Administration
 Can be administered I.M., IVP, I.V. infusion, I.T., or S.C. at a concentration not to exceed 100 mg/mL
 I.V. may be administered either as a bolus, IVPB (high-doses of >500 mg/m^2) or continuous intravenous infusion (doses of 100-200 mg/m^2)
 I.V. doses of >200 mg/m^2 may produce conjunctivitis which can be ameliorated with prophylactic use of corticosteroid (0.1% dexamethasone) eye drops. Dexamethasone eye drops should be administered at 1-2 drops every 6 hours for 2-7 days after cytarabine is done.

Monitoring Parameters Liver function tests, CBC with differential and platelet count, serum creatinine, BUN, serum uric acid

Patient Information Notify physician of any fever, sore throat, bleeding, or bruising; contraceptive measures are recommended during therapy

Additional Information
 Supplied with diluent containing benzyl alcohol, which should not be used when preparing either high-dose or I.T. doses
 Latex-free products: 100 mg, 500 mg, 1 g, 2 g vials (Cytosar-U®) by Pharmacia-Upjohn

Dosage Forms
 Powder for injection, as hydrochloride: 100 mg, 500 mg, 1 g, 2 g
 Powder for injection, as hydrochloride (Cytosar-U®): 100 mg, 500 mg, 1 g, 2 g

- ♦ **Cytarabine Hydrochloride** see Cytarabine on page 313
- ♦ **Cytochrome P-450 and Drug Interactions** see page 1338
- ♦ **CytoGam™** see Cytomegalovirus Immune Globulin (Intravenous-Human) on this page

Cytomegalovirus Immune Globulin (Intravenous-Human)
(sye toe meg a low VYE rus i MYUN GLOB yoo lin in tra VEE nus HYU man)

U.S. Brand Names CytoGam™

Synonyms CMV-IGIV

Therapeutic Category Immune Globulin

Use Attenuation of primary CMV disease associated with immunosuppressed recipients of kidney transplantation; especially indicated for CMV-negative recipients of CMV-positive donor; has been used as adjunct therapy in the treatment of CMV disease in immuno-compromised patients

Pregnancy Risk Factor C

Contraindications Hypersensitivity to any component, patients with selective immuno-globulin A deficiency (↑ potential for anaphylaxis); persons with IgA deficiency

Warnings/Precautions Studies indicate that product carries little or no risk for transmission of HIV; give with caution to patients with prior allergic reactions to human immuno-globulin preparations; do not perform skin testing

Adverse Reactions
 1% to 10%:
  Cardiovascular: Flushing of face
  Gastrointestinal: Nausea, vomiting
  Neuromuscular & skeletal: Muscle cramps, back pain
  Respiratory: Wheezing
  Miscellaneous: Diaphoresis
 <1%: Tightness in the chest, dizziness, fever, headache, chills, aseptic meningitis syndrome, hypersensitivity reactions

Drug Interactions May inactivate live virus vaccines (eg, measles, mumps, rubella); if IGIV administration within 3 months of vaccination with live virus products, revaccinate

Stability Use reconstituted product within 6 hours; do not admix with other medications

Mechanism of Action CMV-IGIV is a preparation of immunoglobulin G derived from pooled healthy blood donors with a high titer of CMV antibodies; administration provides a passive source of antibodies against cytomegalovirus

Usual Dosage I.V.:
 Dosing schedule:
  Initial dose (within 72 hours after transplant): 150 mg/kg/dose
  2, 4, 6, 8 weeks after transplant: 100 mg/kg/dose
  12 and 16 weeks after transplant: 50 mg/kg/dose
  Severe CMV pneumonia: Regimens of 400 mg/kg on days 1, 2, 7 or 8, followed by 200 mg/kg have been used

 Administration rate: Administer at 15 mg/kg/hour initially, then increase to 30 mg/kg/hour after 30 minutes if no untoward reactions, then increase to 60 mg/kg/hour after another 30 minutes; volume not to exceed 75 mL/hour
(Continued)

Cytomegalovirus Immune Globulin (Intravenous-Human)
(Continued)

Administration I.V. use only; administer as separate infusion; infuse beginning at 15 mg/kg/hour; may titrate up to 60 mg/kg/hour; do not administer faster than 75 mL/hour

Dosage Forms Powder for injection, lyophilized, detergent treated: 2500 mg ± 250 mg (50 mL)

- ◆ **Cytomel® Oral** *see* Liothyronine *on page 683*
- ◆ **Cytosar-U®** *see* Cytarabine *on page 313*
- ◆ **Cytosine Arabinosine Hydrochloride** *see* Cytarabine *on page 313*
- ◆ **Cytotec®** *see* Misoprostol *on page 785*
- ◆ **Cytovene®** *see* Ganciclovir *on page 529*
- ◆ **Cytoxan® Injection** *see* Cyclophosphamide *on page 305*
- ◆ **Cytoxan® Oral** *see* Cyclophosphamide *on page 305*
- ◆ **D-3-Mercaptovaline** *see* Penicillamine *on page 893*
- ◆ **d4T** *see* Stavudine *on page 1080*

Dacarbazine (da KAR ba zeen)
Related Information
Cancer Chemotherapy Regimens *on page 1263*
U.S. Brand Names DTIC-Dome®
Synonyms DIC; Dimethyl Triazeno Imidazol Carboxamide; Imidazole Carboxamide
Therapeutic Category Antineoplastic Agent, Vesicant; Antineoplastic Agent, Miscellaneous; Vesicant
Use Treatment of malignant melanoma, Hodgkin's disease, soft-tissue sarcomas, fibrosarcomas, rhabdomyosarcoma, islet cell carcinoma, medullary carcinoma of the thyroid, and neuroblastoma
Pregnancy Risk Factor C
Contraindications Hypersensitivity to dacarbazine or any component
Warnings/Precautions The U.S. Food and Drug Administration (FDA) currently recommends that procedures for proper handling and disposal of antineoplastic agents be considered. Use with caution in patients with bone marrow suppression; in patients with renal and/or hepatic impairment since dosage reduction may be necessary; avoid extravasation of the drug.
Adverse Reactions
>10%:
    Extravasation: Dacarbazine is an irritant; may cause tissue necrosis after extravasation; apply ice and consult extravasation policy if this occurs
    Irritant chemotherapy: Pain and burning at infusion site
    Gastrointestinal: Moderate to severe nausea and vomiting in 90% of patients and lasting up to 12 hours after administration; nausea and vomiting are dose-related and occur more frequently when given as a one-time dose, as opposed to a less intensive 5-day course; diarrhea may also occur
    Emetic potential:
        <500 mg: Moderately high (60% to 90%)
        ≥500 mg: High (>90%)
    Time course of nausea/vomiting: Onset: 1-2 hours; Duration: 2-4 hours
1% to 10%:
    Cardiovascular: Facial flushing
    Dermatologic: Alopecia, rash
    Flu-like effects: Fever, malaise, headache, myalgia, and sinus congestion may last up to several days after administration
    Gastrointestinal: Anorexia, metallic taste
    Hematologic: Myelosuppressive: Mild to moderate is common and dose-related; leukopenia and thrombocytopenia may be delayed 2-3 weeks and may be the dose-limiting toxicity
    WBC: Mild (primarily leukocytes)
    Platelets: Mild
    Onset (days): 7
    Nadir (days): 21-25
    Recovery (days): 21-28
    Neuromuscular & skeletal: Paresthesias
    Respiratory: Sinus congestion
    Miscellaneous: Anaphylactic reactions, hypocalcemia with high-dose Dtic®
<1%: Orthostatic hypotension, polyneuropathy, headache, and seizures have been reported, photosensitivity reactions, stomatitis, diarrhea, elevated LFTs, hepatic vein thrombosis and hepatocellular necrosis, weakness, blurred vision, anaphylaxis
Overdosage/Toxicology
Symptoms of overdose include myelosuppression, diarrhea
There are no known antidotes and treatment is primarily symptomatic and supportive
Stability
Store intact vials under refrigeration (2°C to 8°C) and protect from light; vials are stable for 4 weeks at room temperature
Reconstitute with a minimum of 2 mL (100 mg vial) or 4 mL (200 mg vial) of SWI, D₅W, or NS; dilute to a concentration of 10 mg/mL as follows; reconstituted solution is stable for 24 hours at room temperature (20°C) and 96 hours under refrigeration (4°C)
    100 mg vial = 9.9 mL

200 mg vial = 19.7 mL
500 mg vial = 49.5 mL
Further dilution in 200-500 mL of D_5W or NS is stable for 24 hours at room temperature and protected from light
Decomposed drug turns pink

Standard I.V. dilution:
Dose/250-500 mL D_5W or NS
Stable for 24 hours at room temperature and refrigeration (4°C) when protected from light

Mechanism of Action Alkylating agent which forms methylcarbonium ions that attack nucleophilic groups in DNA; cross-links strands of DNA resulting in the inhibition of DNA, RNA, and protein synthesis, but the exact mechanism of action is still unclear; originally developed as a purine antimetabolite, but it does not interfere with purine synthesis; metabolism by the host is necessary for activation of dacarbazine, then the methylated species acts by alkylation of nucleic acids; dacarbazine is active in all phases of the cell cycle

Pharmacodynamics/Kinetics
Onset of action: I.V.: 18-24 days
Absorption: Oral administration demonstrates slow and variable absorption; preferable to administer by I.V. route
Distribution: V_d: 0.6 L/kg, exceeding total body water and suggesting binding to some tissue (probably the liver)
Protein binding: Minimal (5%)
Metabolism: Extensive in the liver, and hepatobiliary excretion is probably of some importance; metabolites may also have an antineoplastic effect
Half-life (biphasic): Initial: 20-40 minutes; Terminal: 5 hours
Elimination: Hepatobiliary; ~30% to 50% of dose excreted unchanged in the urine by tubular secretion

Usual Dosage I.V. (refer to individual protocols):
Children:
Pediatric solid tumors: 200-470 mg/m²/day over 5 days every 21-28 days
Pediatric neuroblastoma: 800-900 mg/m² as a single dose on day 1 of therapy every 3-4 weeks in combination therapy
Hodgkin's disease: 375 mg/m² on days 1 and 15 of treatment course, repeat every 28 days
Adults:
Malignant melanoma: 2-4.5 mg/kg/day for 10 days, repeat in 4 weeks **OR** may use 250 mg/m²/day for 5 days, repeat in 3 weeks
Hodgkin's disease: 150 mg/m²/day for 5 days, repeat every 4 weeks **OR** 375 mg/m² on day 1, repeat in 15 days of each 28-day cycle in combination with other agents **OR** 375 mg/m² repeated in 15 days of each 28-day cycle

Dosing adjustment in renal impairment: Adjustment is warranted

Dosing adjustment/comments in hepatic impairment: Monitor closely for signs of toxicity

Monitoring Parameters CBC (with differential, erythrocyte, and platelet count), liver function tests

Patient Information Report any persistent fever, sore throat, malaise, or fatigue; contraceptive measures are recommended during therapy

Nursing Implications
Extravasation management: Local pain, burning sensation, and irritation at the injection site may be relieved by local application of hot packs; if extravasation occurs, apply cold packs; protect exposed tissue from light following extravasation

Dosage Forms Injection: 100 mg (10 mL, 20 mL); 200 mg (20 mL, 30 mL); 500 mg (50 mL)

Dacliximab (da KLIK si mab)

U.S. Brand Names Zenapax®

Therapeutic Category Immunosuppressant Agent

Use Prophylaxis of acute organ rejection in patients receiving renal transplants; used as part of an immunosuppressive regimen that includes cyclosporine and corticosteroids

Pregnancy Risk Factor C

Contraindications Hypersensitivity to any component of the product

Warnings/Precautions Only physicians experienced in immunosuppressive therapy and management of organ transplant patients should prescribe dacliximab. Manage patients receiving the drug in facilities equipped and staffed with adequate laboratory and supportive medical resources. Readmission of dacliximab after an initial course of therapy has not been studied in humans. The potential risks of such readmistration, specifically those associated with immunosuppression or the occurrence of anaphylaxis/anaphylactoid reactions, are not known.

Adverse Reactions
>10%: Endocrine & metabolic: Hyperglycemia (32%)
1% to 10%:
Cardiovascular: Peripheral edema, hypertension, hypotension, aggravated hypertension, tachycardia, thrombosis, bleeding, chest pain
Central nervous system: Headache, dizziness, prickly sensation, depression, anxiety, fever, fatigue, insomnia, shivering, generalized weakness
Dermatologic: Impaired wound healing without infection, acne, pruritus, hirsutism, rash
Endocrine & metabolic: Fluid overload, diabetes mellitus, dehydration, edema
(Continued)

Dacliximab *(Continued)*

Gastrointestinal: Constipation, nausea, diarrhea, vomiting, abdominal pain, pyrosis, dyspepsia, abdominal distention, epigastric pain (not food-related), flatulence, gastritis, hemorrhoids

Genitourinary: Dysuria, urinary tract disorder, urinary retention

Hematologic: Urinary tract bleeding

Local: Injection site pain

Neuromuscular & skeletal: Tremor, musculoskeletal pain, back pain, arthralgia, leg cramps, myalgia, pain

Ocular: Blurred vision

Renal: Oliguria, renal tubular necrosis, renal damage, hydronephrosis, renal insufficiency

Respiratory: Dyspnea, pulmonary edema, coughing, atelectasis, congestion, rhinitis, pharyngitis, hypoxia, rales, abnormal breath sounds, pleural effusion

Miscellaneous: Increased diaphoresis, night sweats, post-traumatic pain

Overdosage/Toxicology Overdose has not been reported; a maximum tolerated dose has not been determined in patients. A dose of 1.5 mg/kg has been administered to bone marrow transplant recipients without any associated adverse events.

Stability Refrigerate vials at 2°C to 8°C/36°F to 46°F. Do not shake or freeze; protect undiluted solution against direct sunlight. Dose should be further diluted in 50 mL 0.9% sodium chloride solution. Diluted solution is stable for 24 hours at 4°C or for 4 hours at room temperature.

Mechanism of Action Inhibits the binding of IL-2 to the high affinity IL-2 receptor, thus suppressing T cell activity against allografts. Its active ingredient, dacliximab, a humanized monoclonal antibody, binds to the alpha subunit of the high affinity interleukin-2 receptor (IL-2R) which is expressed on activated T cells.

Pharmacodynamics/Kinetics

Volume of central compartment: 2.5 L

Volume of peripheral compartment: 3.4 L

Estimated half-life (terminal elimination): 20 days (480 hours)

Usual Dosage Children and Adults: IVPB: 1 mg/kg, used as part of an immunosuppressive regimen that includes cyclosporine and corticosteroids for a total of 5 doses; give the first dose ≤24 hours before transplantation. The 4 remaining doses should be administered at intervals of 14 days.

Dosing adjustment in renal impairment: None necessary

Administration Administer I.V. via a peripheral or central line over 15 minutes

Dosage Forms Injection: 5 mg/mL (5 mL)

Dactinomycin *(dak ti noe MYE sin)*

Related Information

Cancer Chemotherapy Regimens *on page 1263*

Toxicities of Chemotherapeutic Agents *on page 1288*

U.S. Brand Names Cosmegen®

Synonyms ACT; Actinomycin D

Therapeutic Category Antineoplastic Agent, Antibiotic; Antineoplastic Agent, Vesicant; Vesicant

Use Treatment of testicular tumors, melanoma, choriocarcinoma, Wilms' tumor, neuroblastoma, retinoblastoma, rhabdomyosarcoma, uterine sarcomas, Ewing's sarcoma, Kaposi's sarcoma, and soft tissue sarcoma

Pregnancy Risk Factor C

Contraindications Hypersensitivity to dactinomycin or any component; patients with chickenpox or herpes zoster; avoid in infants <6 months of age

Warnings/Precautions The U.S. Food and Drug Administration (FDA) currently recommends that procedures for proper handling and disposal of antineoplastic agents be considered. Drug is extremely irritating to tissues and must be administered I.V.; if extravasation occurs during I.V. use, severe damage to soft tissues will occur; use with caution in patients who have received radiation therapy or in the presence of hepatobiliary dysfunction; reduce dosage in patients who are receiving radiation therapy simultaneously.

Adverse Reactions

>10%:

Central nervous system: Unusual fatigue, malaise, fever

Dermatologic: Alopecia (reversible), skin eruptions, acne, increased pigmentation of previously irradiated skin

Extravasation: An irritant and should be administered through a rapidly running I.V. line; extravasation can lead to tissue necrosis, pain, and ulceration

Vesicant chemotherapy

Endocrine & metabolic: Hypocalcemia

Gastrointestinal: **Highly emetogenic**

Severe nausea and vomiting occurs in most patients and persists for up to 24 hours; stomatitis, anorexia, abdominal pain, esophagitis, diarrhea

Time course of nausea/vomiting: Onset: 2-5 hours; Duration: 4-24 hours

Hematologic: Myelosuppressive: Dose-limiting toxicity; anemia, aplastic anemia, agranulocytosis, pancytopenia

WBC: Moderate

Platelets: Moderate

Onset (days): 7

Nadir (days): 14-21

Recovery (days): 21-28

1% to 10%: Gastrointestinal: Diarrhea, mucositis

<1%: Hyperuricemia, hepatitis, LFT abnormalities, anaphylactoid reaction

Overdosage/Toxicology

Symptoms of overdose include myelosuppression, nausea, vomiting, glossitis, oral ulceration

There are no known antidotes and treatment is primarily symptomatic and supportive

Drug Interactions

Increased toxicity: Dactinomycin potentiates the effects of radiation therapy: Radiation may cause skin erythema which may become severe and is also associated with ↑ incidence of GI toxicity

Stability

Store intact vials at room temperature (30°C) and protect from light; storage at high temperatures (up to 50°C) for up to 2 weeks is permissible

Dilute with 1.1 mL of preservative-free SWI to yield a final concentration of 500 mcg/mL; do not use preservative diluent as precipitation may occur. Solution is chemically stable for 24 hours at room temperature (25°C). Significant binding of the drug occurs with micrometer nitrocellulose filter materials.

Compatible with D_5W or NS

Standard I.V. dilution:

I.V. push: Dose/syringe (500 mcg/mL)

IVPB: Dose/50 mL D_5W or NS

Stable for 24 hours at room temperature

Mechanism of Action Binds to the guanine portion of DNA intercalated between guanine and cytosine base pairs inhibiting DNA and RNA synthesis and protein synthesis; product of *Streptomyces parvullus* (a yeast species)

Pharmacodynamics/Kinetics

Distribution: Poor penetration into CSF; crosses placenta; high concentrations found in bone marrow and tumor cells, submaxillary gland, liver, and kidney

Metabolism: Minimal

Half-life: 36 hours

Time to peak serum concentration: I.V.: Within 2-5 minutes

Elimination: ~10% of dose excreted as unchanged drug in the urine, 14% excreted in feces, while 50% appears in the bile

Usual Dosage Refer to individual protocols

Calculation of the dosage for obese or edematous patients should be on the basis of surface area in an effort to relate dosage to lean body mass

Children >6 months and Adults: I.V.:

15 mcg/kg/day **or** 400-600 mcg/m²/day (maximum: 500 mcg) for 5 days, may repeat every 3-6 weeks **or**

2.5 mg/m² given in divided doses over 1-week period and repeated at 2-week intervals **or**

0.75-2 mg/m² as a single dose given at intervals of 1-4 weeks have been used

Dosing in renal impairment: No adjustment necessary

Administration

Administer slow I.V. push over 10-15 minutes

An in-line cellulose membrane filter should not be used during administration of dactinomycin solutions; do not administer I.M. or S.C.

Avoid extravasation: Extremely damaging to soft tissue and will cause a severe local reaction if extravasation occurs

Monitoring Parameters CBC with differential and platelet count, liver function tests, and renal function tests

Patient Information Notify physician if fever, persistent sore throat, bleeding, bruising, fatigue, or malaise occurs; contraceptive measures are recommended during therapy

Nursing Implications Care should be taken to avoid extravasation of the drug; an in-line cellulose membrane filter should not be used during administration of dactinomycin solutions; do not administer I.M. or S.C.

Management of extravasation: Apply ice immediately for 30-60 minutes; then alternate off/on every 15 minutes for one day. Data is not currently available regarding potential antidotes for dactinomycin.

Dosage Forms Powder for injection, lyophilized: 0.5 mg

♦ **D.A.II®** Tablet *see* Chlorpheniramine, Phenylephrine, and Methscopolamine *on page 247*

♦ **Dakin's Solution** *see* Sodium Hypochlorite Solution *on page 1070*

♦ **Dalacin® C [Hydrochloride]** *see* Clindamycin *on page 275*

♦ **Dalalone D.P.®** *see* Dexamethasone *on page 337*

♦ **Dalalone L.A.®** *see* Dexamethasone *on page 337*

♦ **Dalgan®** *see* Dezocine *on page 344*

♦ **Dallergy®** *see* Chlorpheniramine, Phenylephrine, and Methscopolamine *on page 247*

♦ **Dallergy-D® Syrup** *see* Chlorpheniramine and Phenylephrine *on page 246*

♦ **Dalmane®** *see* Flurazepam *on page 506*

♦ **d-Alpha Tocopherol** *see* Vitamin E *on page 1225*

Dalteparin (dal TE pa rin)

Related Information

Heparins Comparison *on page 1324*

U.S. Brand Names Fragmin®

(Continued)

Dalteparin *(Continued)*

Therapeutic Category Low Molecular Weight Heparin

Use Prevention of deep vein thrombosis which may lead to pulmonary embolism, in patients requiring hip arthroplasty or abdominal surgery who are at risk for thromboembolism complications (ie, patients >40 years of age, obese, patients with malignancy, history of deep vein thrombosis or pulmonary embolism, and surgical procedures requiring general anesthesia and lasting longer than 30 minutes)

Pregnancy Risk Factor B

Contraindications Hypersensitivity to dalteparin or other low-molecular weight heparins; cerebrovascular disease or other active hemorrhage; cerebral aneurysm; severe uncontrolled hypertension

Warnings/Precautions Use with caution in patients with pre-existing thrombocytopenia, recent childbirth, subacute bacterial endocarditis, peptic ulcer disease, pericarditis or pericardial effusion, liver or renal function impairment, recent lumbar puncture, vasculitis, concurrent use of aspirin (increased bleeding risk), previous hypersensitivity to heparin, heparin-associated thrombocytopenia. Patients should be observed closely for bleeding if dalteparin is administered during or immediately following diagnostic lumbar puncture, epidural anesthesia, or spinal anesthesia. If thromboembolism develops despite dalteparin prophylaxis, dalteparin should be discontinued and appropriate treatment should be initiated.

Adverse Reactions 1% to 10%:

Central nervous system: Allergic fever

Dermatologic: Pruritus, rash, bullous eruption, skin necrosis

Hematologic: Bleeding, thrombocytopenia, wound hematoma

Local: Pain at injection site, injection site hematoma, injection site reactions

Miscellaneous: Anaphylactoid reactions, allergic reactions

Drug Interactions Increased toxicity: Caution should be used when using aspirin, other platelet inhibitors, and oral anticoagulants in combination with dalteparin due to an increased risk of bleeding

Stability Store at temperatures ≤25°C

Mechanism of Action Low molecular weight heparin analog with a molecular weight of 4000-6000 daltons; the commercial product contains 3% to 15% heparin with a molecular weight <3000 daltons, 65% to 78% with a molecular weight of 3000-8000 daltons and 14% to 26% with a molecular weight >8000 daltons; while dalteparin has been shown to inhibit both factor Xa and factor IIa (thrombin), the antithrombotic effect of dalteparin is characterized by a higher ratio of antifactor Xa to antifactor IIa activity (ratio = 4)

Usual Dosage Adults: S.C.:

Low-moderate risk patients undergoing abdominal surgery: 2500 units 1-2 hours prior to surgery, then once daily for 5-10 days postoperatively

High risk patients undergoing abdominal surgery: 5000 units 1-2 hours prior to surgery and then once daily for 5-10 days postoperatively

Patients undergoing total hip surgery: 2500 units 1-2 hours prior to surgery, then 2500 units 6 hours after surgery (evening of the day of surgery), followed by 5000 units once daily for 7-10 days

Monitoring Parameters Periodic CBC including platelet count; stool occult blood tests; monitoring of PT and PTT is not necessary

Dosage Forms Injection:

Prefilled syringe: Antifactor Xa 2500 units per 0.2 mL; antifactor Xa 5000 units per 0.2 mL

Multidose vial: 95,000 international units

♦ **Damason-P®** *see* Hydrocodone and Aspirin *on page 576*

Danaparoid *(da NAP a roid)*

Related Information

Heparins Comparison *on page 1324*

U.S. Brand Names Orgaran®

Synonyms Danaparoid Sodium

Therapeutic Category Heparinoid

Use Prevention of postoperative deep vein thrombosis following elective hip replacement surgery

Unlabeled use: System anticoagulation for patients with heparin-induced thrombocytopenia: Factor Xa inhibition is used to monitor degree of anticoagulation if necessary

Pregnancy Risk Factor B

Contraindications Patients with severe hemorrhagic diathesis including active major bleeding, hemorrhagic stroke in the acute phase, hemophilia and idiopathic thrombocytopenic purpura; type II thrombocytopenia associated with a positive *in vitro* test for antiplatelet antibody in the presence of danaparoid, hypersensitivity to danaparoid or known hypersensitivity to pork products

Warnings/Precautions Do not administer intramuscularly; use with extreme caution in patients with a history of bacterial endocarditis, hemorrhagic stroke, recent CNS or ophthalmological surgery, bleeding diathesis, uncontrolled arterial hypertension, or a history of recent gastrointestinal ulceration and hemorrhage. Danaparoid shows a low cross-sensitivity with antiplatelet antibodies in individuals with type II heparin-induced thrombocytopenia. This product contains sodium sulfite which may cause allergic-type reactions, including anaphylactic symptoms and life-threatening asthmatic episodes in susceptible people; this is seen more frequently in asthmatics.

Carefully monitor patients receiving low molecular weight heparins or heparinoids. These drugs, when used concurrently with spinal or epidural anesthesia or spinal puncture, may cause bleeding or hematomas within the spinal column. Increased pressure on the spinal cord may result in permanent paralysis if not detected and treated immediately.

Note: Danaparoid is **not** effectively antagonized by protamine sulfate. No other antidote is available, so extreme caution is needed in monitoring dose given and resulting Xa inhibition effect.

Adverse Reactions 1% to 10%:
Cardiovascular: Peripheral edema, generalized edema
Central nervous system: Fever, insomnia, headache, dizziness
Dermatologic: Rash, pruritus
Gastrointestinal: Nausea, constipation, vomiting
Genitourinary: Urinary tract infections, urinary retention
Hematologic: Anemia, hemorrhage, hematoma
Local: Injection site pain
Neuromuscular & skeletal: Joint disorder, weakness

Overdosage/Toxicology
Symptoms of overdose include hemorrhage
Protamine zinc has been used to reverse effects

Drug Interactions Increased toxicity with oral anticoagulants, platelet inhibitors

Stability Store intact vials or ampuls under refrigeration

Pharmacodynamics/Kinetics
Onset of effect: Maximum antifactor Xa and antithrombin (antifactor IIa) activities occur 2-5 hours after S.C. administration
Half-life, plasma: Mean terminal half-life: ~24 hours
Elimination: Primarily by the kidneys

Usual Dosage S.C.:
Children: Safety and effectiveness have not been established
Adults: 750 anti-Xa units twice daily; beginning 1-4 hours before surgery and then not sooner than 2 hours after surgery and every 12 hours until the risk of DVT has diminished, the average duration of therapy is 7-10 days
Treatment: See table.

Adult Danaparoid Treatment Dosing Regimens

	Body Weight (kg)	I.V. Bolus aFXaU	Long–Term Infusion aFXaU	Level of aFXaU/mL	Monitoring
Deep Vein Thrombosis OR Acute Pulmonary Embolism	<55	1250	400 units/h over 4 h then		Days 1-3 daily, then every alternate day
	55-90	2500	300 units/h over 4 h, then	0.5-0.8	
	>90	3750	150-200 units/h maintenance dose		
Deep Vein Thrombosis OR Pulmonary Embolism >5 d old	<90	1250	S.C.: 3 x 750/d	<0.5	Not necessary
	>90	1250	S.C.: 3 x 1250/d		
Embolectomy	<90	2500 preoperatively	S.C.: 2 x 1250/d postoperatively	<0.4	Not necessary
	>90 and high risk	2500 preoperatively	750 units/20 mL NaCl perioperatively, arterial irrigation if necessary	0.5-0.8	Days 1-3 daily, then every alternate day
Peripheral Arterial Bypass		2500 preoperatively	150-200 units/h	0.5-0.8	Days 1-3 daily, then every alternate day
Cardiac Catheter	<90	2500 preoperatively			
	>90	3750 preoperatively			
Surgery (excluding vascular)			S.C.: 750, 1-4 h preoperatively S.C.: 750, 2-5 h postoperatively, then 2 x 750/d	<0.35	Not necessary

Dosing adjustment in elderly and severe renal impairment: Adjustment may be necessary; patients with serum creatinine levels ≥2.0 mg/dL should be carefully monitored
Hemodialysis: See table on following page.

Monitoring Parameters Platelets, occult blood, and anti-Xa activity, if available; the monitoring of PT and/or PTT is not necessary

Additional Information A 750 anti-Xa unit dose of danaparoid is approximately equivalent to 55 mg of danaparoid

Dosage Forms Injection, as sodium: 750 anti-Xa units/0.6 mL
(Continued)

Danazol *(Continued)*

Haemodialysis With Danaparoid Sodium

Dialysis on alternate days	Dosage prior to dialysis in aFXaU (dosage for body wt <55 kg)	
First dialysis	3750 (2500)	
Second dialysis	3750 (2000)	
Further dialysis:		
aFXa level before dialysis (eg, day 5)	Bolus before next dialysis, aFXaU (eg, day 7)	aFXa level during dialysis
<0.3	3000 (<55 kg 2000)	0.5-0.8
0.3-0.35	2500 (2000)	
0.35-0.4	2000 (1500)	
>0.4	0	
	if fibrin strands occur, 1500 aFXaU I.V.	
Monitoring: 30 minutes before dialysis and after 4 hours of dialysis		
Daily Dialysis		
First dialysis	3750 (2500)	
Second dialysis	2500 (2000)	
Further dialyses	See above	

As with "dialysis on alternate days", always take the aFXa activity preceding the previous dialysis as a basis for the current dosage.

Danazol (DA na zole)
U.S. Brand Names Danocrine®
Canadian Brand Names Cyclomen®
Therapeutic Category Androgen; Antigonadotropic Agent
Use Treatment of endometriosis, fibrocystic breast disease, and hereditary angioedema
Pregnancy Risk Factor X
Contraindications Undiagnosed genital bleeding, hypersensitivity to danazol or any component; pregnancy
Warnings/Precautions Use with caution in patients with seizure disorders, migraine, or conditions influenced by edema; impaired hepatic, renal, or cardiac disease, pregnancy, lactation
Adverse Reactions
>10%:
Cardiovascular: Edema
Dermatologic: Oily skin, acne, hirsutism
Endocrine & metabolic: Fluid retention, breakthrough bleeding, irregular menstrual periods, decreased breast size
Gastrointestinal: Weight gain
Hepatic: Hepatic impairment
Miscellaneous: Voice deepening
1% to 10%:
Endocrine & metabolic: Virilization, androgenic effects, amenorrhea, hypoestrogenism
Neuromuscular & skeletal: Weakness
<1%: Benign intracranial hypertension, dizziness, headache, skin rashes, photosensitivity, pancreatitis, bleeding gums, monilial vaginitis, testicular atrophy, enlarged clitoris, cholestatic jaundice, carpal tunnel syndrome
Drug Interactions CYP3A3/4 enzyme inhibitor
Increased toxicity: Decreased insulin requirements; warfarin may increase anticoagulant effects
Mechanism of Action Suppresses pituitary output of follicle-stimulating hormone and luteinizing hormone that causes regression and atrophy of normal and ectopic endometrial tissue; decreases rate of growth of abnormal breast tissue; reduces attacks associated with hereditary angioedema by increasing levels of C4 component of complement
Pharmacodynamics/Kinetics
Onset of therapeutic effect: Within 4 weeks following daily doses
Metabolism: Extensive hepatic metabolism, primarily to 2-hydroxymethylethisterone
Half-life: 4.5 hours (variable)
Time to peak serum concentration: Within 2 hours
Elimination: In urine
Usual Dosage Adults: Oral:
Female: Endometriosis: Initial: 200-400 mg/day in 2 divided doses for mild disease; individualize dosage. Usual maintenance dose: 800 mg/day in 2 divided doses to achieve amenorrhea and rapid response to painful symptoms. Continue therapy uninterrupted for 3-6 months (up to 9 months).
Female: Fibrocystic breast disease: Range: 10-400 mg/day in 2 divided doses
Male/Female: Hereditary angioedema: Initial: 200 mg 2-3 times/day; after favorable response, decrease the dosage by 50% or less at intervals of 1-3 months or longer if

the frequency of attacks dictates. If an attack occurs, increase the dosage by up to 200 mg/day.

Patient Information Notify physician if masculinity effects occur; virilization may occur in female patients; report menstrual irregularities; male patients report persistent penile erections; all patients should report persistent GI distress, diarrhea, or jaundice

Dosage Forms Capsule: 50 mg, 100 mg, 200 mg

♦ Danocrine® *see Danazol on page 322*
♦ Dantrium® *see Dantrolene on this page*

Dantrolene (DAN troe leen)

U.S. Brand Names Dantrium®

Synonyms Dantrolene Sodium

Therapeutic Category Antidote, Malignant Hyperthermia; Hyperthermia, Treatment; Skeletal Muscle Relaxant

Use Treatment of spasticity associated with spinal cord injury, stroke, cerebral palsy, or multiple sclerosis; also used as treatment of malignant hyperthermia

Pregnancy Risk Factor C

Contraindications Active hepatic disease; should not be used where spasticity is used to maintain posture or balance

Warnings/Precautions Use with caution in patients with impaired cardiac function or impaired pulmonary function; has potential for hepatotoxicity; overt hepatitis has been most frequently observed between the third and twelfth month of therapy; hepatic injury appears to be greater in females and in patients >35 years of age

Adverse Reactions

>10%:
   Central nervous system: Drowsiness, dizziness, lightheadedness, fatigue
   Dermatologic: Rash
   Gastrointestinal: Diarrhea (mild), nausea, vomiting
   Neuromuscular & skeletal: Muscle weakness

1% to 10%:
   Cardiovascular: Pleural effusion with pericarditis
   Central nervous system: Chills, fever, headache, insomnia, nervousness, mental depression
   Gastrointestinal: Diarrhea (severe), constipation, anorexia, stomach cramps
   Ocular: Blurred vision
   Respiratory: Respiratory depression

<1%: Seizures, confusion, hepatitis

Overdosage/Toxicology

Symptoms of overdose include CNS depression, hypotension, nausea, vomiting

For decontamination, lavage/activated charcoal with cathartic; do not use ipecac; hypotension can be treated with isotonic I.V. fluids with the patient placed in the Trendelenburg position; dopamine or norepinephrine can be given if hypotension is refractory to above therapy

Drug Interactions Increased toxicity: Estrogens (hepatotoxicity), CNS depressants (sedation), MAO inhibitors, phenothiazines, clindamycin (increased neuromuscular blockade), verapamil (hyperkalemia and cardiac depression), warfarin, clofibrate and tolbutamide

Stability Reconstitute vial by adding 60 mL of sterile water for injection USP (**not bacteriostatic water for injection**); protect from light; use within 6 hours; avoid glass bottles for I.V. infusion

Mechanism of Action Acts directly on skeletal muscle by interfering with release of calcium ion from the sarcoplasmic reticulum; prevents or reduces the increase in myoplasmic calcium ion concentration that activates the acute catabolic processes associated with malignant hyperthermia

Pharmacodynamics/Kinetics

Absorption: Slow and incomplete from GI tract
Metabolism: Slowly in liver
Half-life: 8.7 hours
Elimination: 25% excreted in urine as metabolites and unchanged drug, 45% to 50% excreted in feces via bile

Usual Dosage

Spasticity: Oral:
   Children: Initial: 0.5 mg/kg/dose twice daily, increase frequency to 3-4 times/day at 4- to 7-day intervals, then increase dose by 0.5 mg/kg to a maximum of 3 mg/kg/dose 2-4 times/day up to 400 mg/day
   Adults: 25 mg/day to start, increase frequency to 2-4 times/day, then increase dose by 25 mg every 4-7 days to a maximum of 100 mg 2-4 times/day or 400 mg/day

Malignant hyperthermia: Children and Adults:
   Oral: 4-8 mg/kg/day in 4 divided doses
      Preoperative prophylaxis: Begin 1-2 days prior to surgery with last dose 3-4 hours prior to surgery
   I.V.: 1 mg/kg; may repeat dose up to cumulative dose of 10 mg/kg (mean effective dose is 2.5 mg/kg), then switch to oral dosage
      Preoperative: 2.5 mg/kg ~1¼ hours prior to anesthesia and infused over 1 hour with additional doses as needed and individualized

Dietary Considerations Alcohol: Additive CNS effects, avoid use

Monitoring Parameters Motor performance should be monitored for therapeutic outcomes; nausea, vomiting, and liver function tests should be monitored for potential (Continued)

Dantrolene *(Continued)*

hepatotoxicity; intravenous administration requires cardiac monitor and blood pressure monitor

Test Interactions ↑ serum AST (SGOT), ALT (SGPT), alkaline phosphatase, LDH, BUN, and total serum bilirubin

Patient Information Avoid unnecessary exposure to sunlight (or use sunscreen, protective clothing); avoid alcohol and other CNS depressants; patients should use caution while driving or performing other tasks requiring alertness

Nursing Implications 36 vials needed for adequate hyperthermia therapy; exercise caution at meals on the day of administration because difficulty swallowing and choking has been reported; avoid extravasation as is a tissue irritant

Dosage Forms

Capsule, as sodium: 25 mg, 50 mg, 100 mg

Powder for injection, as sodium: 20 mg

Extemporaneous Preparations A 5 mg/mL suspension may be made by adding five 100 mg capsules to a citric acid solution (150 mg citric acid powder in 10 mL water) and then adding syrup to a total volume of 100 mL; stable 2 days in refrigerator

Nahata MC and Hipple TF, *Pediatric Drug Formulations*, 1st ed, Cincinnati, OH: Harvey Whitney Books Co, 1990.

♦ **Dantrolene Sodium** see Dantrolene *on previous page*

Dapiprazole *(DA pi pray zole)*

U.S. Brand Names Rēv-Eyes™

Synonyms Dapiprazole Hydrochloride

Therapeutic Category Alpha-Adrenergic Blocking Agent, Ophthalmic

Use Reverse dilation due to drugs (adrenergic or parasympathomimetic) after eye exams

Pregnancy Risk Factor B

Contraindications Contraindicated in the presence of conditions where miosis is unacceptable, such as acute iritis and in patients with a history of hypersensitivity to any component of the formulation

Warnings/Precautions For ophthalmic use only

Adverse Reactions

>10%:

Central nervous system: Headache

Ocular: Conjunctival injection, burning and itching eyes, lid edema, ptosis, lid erythema, chemosis, punctate keratitis, corneal edema, photophobia

1% to 10%: Ocular: Dry eyes, blurring of vision, tearing of eye

Stability After reconstitution, drops are stable at room temperature for 21 days. Store at room temperature (15°C to 30°C/59°F to 86°F)

Mechanism of Action Dapiprazole is a selective alpha-adrenergic blocking agent, exerting effects primarily on alpha$_1$-adrenoceptors. It induces miosis via relaxation of the smooth dilator (radial) muscle of the iris, which causes pupillary constriction. It is devoid of cholinergic effects. Dapiprazole also partially reverses the cycloplegia induced with parasympatholytic agents such as tropicamide. Although the drug has no significant effect on the ciliary muscle *per se*, it may increase accommodative amplitude, therefore relieving the symptoms of paralysis of accommodation.

Usual Dosage Adults: Administer 2 drops followed 5 minutes later by an additional 2 drops applied to the conjunctiva of each eye; should not be used more frequently than once a week in the same patient

Administration Shake container for several minutes to ensure mixing. Instill 2 drops into the conjunctiva of each eye followed 5 minutes later by an additional 2 drops. Administer after the ophthalmic examination to reverse the diagnostic mydriasis.

Patient Information May still be sensitive to sunlight and sensitivity may return in 2 or more hours; exercise caution when driving at night or performing other activities in poor illumination. To avoid contamination, do not touch tip of container to any surface.

Nursing Implications Finger pressure should be applied to lacrimal sac for 1-2 minutes after instillation to decrease risk of absorption and systemic reactions

Dosage Forms Powder, lyophilized, as hydrochloride: 25 mg [0.5% solution when mixed with supplied diluent]

♦ **Dapiprazole Hydrochloride** see Dapiprazole *on this page*

Dapsone *(DAP sone)*

Related Information

Antimicrobial Drugs of Choice *on page 1404*

Guidelines for the Prevention of Opportunistic Infections in Persons with HIV *on page 1388*

U.S. Brand Names Avlosulfon®

Synonyms Diaminodiphenylsulfone

Therapeutic Category Antibiotic, Sulfone; Leprostatic Agent

Use Treatment of leprosy and dermatitis herpetiformis (infections caused by *Mycobacterium leprae*)

Prophylaxis of toxoplasmosis in severely immunocompromised patients; alternative agent for *Pneumocystis carinii* pneumonia prophylaxis (given alone) and treatment (given with trimethoprim)

May be useful in relapsing polychondritis, prophylaxis of malaria, inflammatory bowel disorders, *Leishmaniasis*, rheumatic/connective tissue disorders, brown recluse spider bites

Pregnancy Risk Factor C

Contraindications Hypersensitivity to dapsone or any component

Warnings/Precautions Use with caution in patients with severe anemia, G-6-PD, methemoglobin reductase or hemoglobin M deficiency; hypersensitivity to other sulfonamides; aplastic anemia, agranulocytosis and other severe blood dyscrasias have resulted in death; monitor carefully; treat severe anemia prior to therapy; serious dermatologic reactions (including toxic epidermal necrolysis) are rare but potential occurrences; sulfone reactions may also occur as potentially fatal hypersensitivity reactions; these, but not leprosy reactional states, require drug discontinuation; dapsone is carcinogenic in small animals

Adverse Reactions

1% to 10%: Hematologic: Hemolysis, methemoglobinemia

<1%: Reactional states (ie, abrupt changes in clinical activity occurring during any leprosy treatment; classified as reversal of erythema nodosum leprosum reactions); insomnia, headache, exfoliative dermatitis, photosensitivity, nausea, vomiting, anemia, leukopenia, agranulocytosis, hepatitis, cholestatic jaundice, peripheral neuropathy (usually in nonleprosy patients), blurred vision, tinnitus, SLE

Overdosage/Toxicology

Symptoms of overdose include nausea, vomiting, confusion, hyperexcitability, seizures, cyanosis, hemolysis, methemoglobinemia, sulfhemoglobinemia, metabolic acidosis, hallucinations, hepatitis

Following decontamination, methylene blue 1-2 mg/kg I.V. is treatment of choice if MHb level is >15%; may repeat every 6-8 hours for 2-3 days if needed; if hemolysis is present, give I.V. fluids and alkalinize urine to prevent acute tubular necrosis

Drug Interactions CYP2C9, 2E1, and 3A3/4 enzyme substrate

Decreased effect/levels: Para-aminobenzoic acid, didanosine, and rifampin decrease dapsone effects

Increased toxicity: Folic acid antagonists may increase the risk of hematologic reactions of dapsone; probenecid decreases dapsone excretion; trimethoprim with dapsone may increase toxic effects of both drugs

Stability Protect from light

Mechanism of Action Competitive antagonist of para-aminobenzoic acid (PABA) and prevents normal bacterial utilization of PABA for the synthesis of folic acid

Pharmacodynamics/Kinetics

Absorption: Oral: Well absorbed

Distribution: V_d: 1.5 L/kg; throughout total body water and present in all tissues, especially liver and kidney

Metabolism: In the liver

Half-life, elimination: 30 hours (range: 10-50 hours)

Elimination: In urine

Usual Dosage Oral:

Leprosy:

Children: 1-2 mg/kg/24 hours, up to a maximum of 100 mg/day

Adults: 50-100 mg/day for 3-10 years

Dermatitis herpetiformis: Adults: Start at 50 mg/day, increase to 300 mg/day, or higher to achieve full control, reduce dosage to minimum level as soon as possible

Prophylaxis of *Pneumocystis carinii* pneumonia:

Children >1 month: 1 mg/kg/day; maximum: 100 mg

Adults: 100 mg/day

Treatment of *Pneumocystis carinii* pneumonia: Adults: 100 mg/day in combination with trimethoprim (15-20 mg/kg/day) for 21 days

Dosing in renal impairment: No specific guidelines are available

Monitoring Parameters Monitor patient for signs of jaundice and hemolysis; CBC weekly for first month, monthly for 6 months, and semiannually thereafter

Patient Information Frequent blood tests are required during early therapy; discontinue if rash develops and contact physician if persistent sore throat, fever, malaise, or fatigue occurs; may cause photosensitivity

Dosage Forms Tablet: 25 mg, 100 mg

Extemporaneous Preparations One report indicated that dapsone may not be well absorbed when administered to children as suspensions made from pulverized tablets

Mirochnick M, Clarke D, Brenn A, et al, "Low Serum Dapsone Concentrations in Children Receiving an Extemporaneously Prepared Oral Formulation," [Abstract Th B 365], APS-SPR, Baltimore, MD: 1992.

Jacobus Pharmaceutical Company (609) 921-7447 makes a 2 mg/mL proprietary liquid formulation available under an IND for the prophylaxis of *Pneumocystis carinii* pneumonia

Daunorubicin Citrate (Liposomal)

(daw noe ROO bi sin SI trate lip po SOE mal)

Related Information

Daunorubicin Hydrochloride *on next page*

U.S. Brand Names DaunoXome®

Therapeutic Category Antineoplastic Agent, Anthracycline; Antineoplastic Agent, Antibiotic

Use Advanced HIV-associated Kaposi's sarcoma; first-line cytotoxic therapy for advanced HIV-associated Kaposi's sarcoma

Pregnancy Risk Factor D

Contraindications Hypersensitivity to previous doses or any constituents of the product

Warnings/Precautions The U.S. Food and Drug Administration (FDA) currently recommends that procedures for proper handling and disposal of antineoplastic agents be considered.

The primary toxicity is myelosuppression, especially off the granulocytic series, which may be severe, with much less marked effects on platelets and erythroid series. Potential cardiac toxicity, particularly in patients who have received prior anthracyclines or who have pre-existing cardiac disease, may occur. Refer to Daunorubicin monograph.

Although grade 3-4 injection site inflammation has been reported in patients treated with the liposomal daunorubicin, no instances of local tissue necrosis were observed with extravasation. However, refer to daunorubicin monograph and avoid extravasation.

Reduce dosage in patients with impaired hepatic function. Hyperuricemia can be induced secondary to rapid lysis of leukemic cells. As a precaution, administer allopurinol prior to initiating antileukemic therapy.

Adverse Reactions

>10%:

Central nervous system: Fatigue, headache

Gastrointestinal: Abdominal pain, anorexia, diarrhea, nausea, vomiting

Hematologic: Neutropenia

Neuromuscular & skeletal: Neuropathy

Respiratory: Cough, dyspnea, rhinitis

Miscellaneous: Infection

5% to 10%:

Cardiovascular: Hypertension, palpitations, syncope, tachycardia, chest pain, edema

Central nervous system: Depression, dizziness, insomnia, malaise

Dermatologic: Alopecia, pruritus

Endocrine & metabolic: Hot flashes

Gastrointestinal: Constipation, stomatitis, tenesmus

Neuromuscular & skeletal: Arthralgia, myalgia

Ocular: Abnormal vision

Respiratory: Sinusitis

Overdosage/Toxicology

Symptoms of acute overdose are increased severities of the observed dose-limiting toxicities of therapeutic doses, myelosuppression (especially granulocytopenia), fatigue, nausea, vomiting

Treatment is symptomatic

Stability Store intact vials under refrigeration (2°C to 8°C/36°F to 46°F). Reconstitute liposomal daunorubicin 1:1 with 5% dextrose injection before administration. Store reconstituted solution for a maximum of 6 hours. Do not freeze and protect from light. Do not use an in-line filter for intravenous infusion.

Mechanism of Action Liposomal daunorubicin contains an aqueous solution of the citrate salt of daunorubicin encapsulated with lipid vesicles (liposomes) composed of a lipid bilayer of distearoylphosphatidylcholine and cholesterol (2:1 molar ratio). This liposomal daunorubicin is formulated to maximum the selectivity of daunorubicin for solid tumors *in situ*; refer to Daunorubicin monograph.

Pharmacodynamics/Kinetics

Distribution: V_d: 6.4 L

Half-life: 4.4 hours

Elimination: Plasma clearance: 17.3 mL/minute

Usual Dosage Adults: I.V.: 40 mg/m^2 over 1 hour; repeat every 2 weeks; continue treatment until there is evidence of progressive disease

Dosing adjustment in renal/hepatic impairment:

Serum Bilirubin	Serum Creatinine	Recommended Dose
1.2-3 mg/dL		$^3/_4$ normal dose
>3 mg/dL	>3 mg/dL	$^1/_2$ normal dose

Administration Administer intravenously over 1 hour; avoid extravasation; refer to Daunorubicin monograph

Monitoring Parameters Observe patient closely and monitor chemical and laboratory tests extensively. Evaluate cardiac, renal, and hepatic function prior to each course of treatment. Repeat blood counts prior to each dose and withhold if the absolute granulocyte count is <750 cells/mm^3. Monitor serum uric acid levels.

Dosage Forms Injection: 2 mg/mL (equivalent to 50 mg daunorubicin base) (1 mL, 4 mL, 10 mL unit packs)

Daunorubicin Hydrochloride (daw noe ROO bi sin hye droe KLOR ide)
Related Information
Cancer Chemotherapy Regimens *on page 1263*
Extravasation Management of Chemotherapeutic Agents *on page 1285*
U.S. Brand Names Cerubidine®
Synonyms Daunomycin; DNR; Rubidomycin Hydrochloride
Therapeutic Category Antineoplastic Agent, Anthracycline; Antineoplastic Agent, Antibiotic; Antineoplastic Agent, Vesicant; Vesicant
Use Treatment of ANLL and myeloblastic leukemia; lymphoma
Pregnancy Risk Factor D
Contraindications Congestive heart failure, cardiopathy or arrhythmias; hypersensitivity to daunorubicin or any component
Warnings/Precautions The U.S. Food and Drug Administration (FDA) currently recommends that procedures for proper handling and disposal of antineoplastic agents be considered. I.V. use only, severe local tissue necrosis will result if extravasation occurs; reduce dose in patients with impaired hepatic, renal, or biliary function; severe myelosuppression is possible when used in therapeutic doses. Total cumulative dose should take into account previous or concomitant treatment with cardiotoxic agents or irradiation of chest.

Irreversible myocardial toxicity may occur as total dosage approaches:
$550 \ mg/m^2$ in adults
$400 \ mg/m^2$ in patients receiving chest radiation
$300 \ mg/m^2$ in children >2 years of age or
$10 \ mg/kg$ in children <2 years; this may occur during therapy or several months after therapy

Adverse Reactions
>10%:
Dermatologic: Alopecia (reversible)
Gastrointestinal: Mild nausea or vomiting occurs in 50% of patients within the first 24 hours; stomatitis may occur 3-7 days after administration, but is not as severe as that caused by doxorubicin
Time course for nausea/vomiting: Onset: 1-3 hours; Duration 4-24 hours
Genitourinary: Discoloration of urine (red)
1% to 10%:
Cardiovascular: Congestive heart failure; maximum lifetime dose: Refer to Warnings/Precautions
Extravasation: Daunorubicin is a vesicant; infiltration can cause severe inflammation, tissue necrosis, and ulceration; if the drug is infiltrated, consult institutional policy, apply ice to the area, and elevate the limb
Vesicant chemotherapy
Endocrine & metabolic: Hyperuricemia
Gastrointestinal: GI ulceration, diarrhea
Hematologic: Myelosuppressive: Dose-limiting toxicity; occurs in all patients; leukopenia is more significant than thrombocytopenia
WBC: Severe
Platelets: Severe
Onset (days): 7
Nadir (days): 14
Recovery (days): 21-28
<1%: Pericarditis; myocarditis; chills; skin rash; pigmentation of nail beds; urticaria; elevated serum bilirubin, AST, and alkaline phosphatase; fertility impairment

Overdosage/Toxicology
Symptoms of overdose include myelosuppression, nausea, vomiting, stomatitis
There are no known antidotes; treatment is primarily symptomatic and supportive

Stability
Store intact vials at room temperature and protect from light
Dilute vials with 4 mL SWI for a final concentration of 5 mg/mL; reconstituted solution is stable for 4 days at 15°C to 25°C
Protect from fluorescent light to decrease photo-inactivation after storage in solution for several days; protect from direct sunlight
Decomposed drug turns purple
For I.V. push administration, desired dose is withdrawn into a syringe containing 10-15 mL NS
Further dilution in D_5W, LR, or NS is stable for 24 hours at room temperature (25°C) and up to 4 weeks if protected from light
Incompatible with dexamethasone, heparin, sodium bicarbonate, 5-FU

Standard I.V. dilution:
I.V. push: Dose/syringe (initial concentration is 5 mg/mL; however, qs to 10-15 mL with NS)
Maximum syringe size for IVP is a 30 mL syringe and syringe should be <75% full
IVPB: Dose/50-100 mL NS or D_5W
Stable for 24 hours at room temperature (25°C)
Mechanism of Action Inhibition of DNA and RNA synthesis, by intercalating between DNA base pairs and by steric obstruction; is not cell cycle-specific for the S phase of cell division; daunomycin is preferred over doxorubicin for the treatment of ANLL because of its dose-limiting toxicity (myelosuppression) is not of concern in the therapy of this disease; has less mucositis associated with its use
(Continued)

Daunorubicin Hydrochloride *(Continued)*

Pharmacodynamics/Kinetics

Distribution: V_d: 40 L/kg; crosses the placenta; distributed to many body tissues, particularly the liver, kidneys, lung, spleen, and heart; does not distribute into the CNS

Metabolism: Primarily in the liver to daunorubicinol (active), which circulates

Half-life: Distribution: 2 minutes; Elimination: 14-20 hours; Terminal: 18.5 hours; Daunorubicinol plasma half-life: 24-48 hours

Elimination: 40% of dose excreted in the bile; ~25% is excreted in the urine as metabolite and unchanged drug; can turn the urine red during first 24-48 hours after treatment

Usual Dosage I.V. (refer to individual protocols):

Children:

ALL combination therapy: Remission induction: 25-45 mg/m² on day 1 every week for 4 cycles **or** 30-45 mg/m²/day for 3 days

AML combination therapy: Induction: I.V. continuous infusion: 30-60 mg/m²/day on days 1-3 of cycle

Note: In children <2 years or <0.5 m², daunorubicin should be based on weight - mg/kg: 1 mg/kg per protocol with frequency dependent on regimen employed

Cumulative dose should not exceed 300 mg/m² in children >2 years or 10 mg/kg in children <2 years

Adults:

30-60 mg/m²/day for 3-5 days, repeat dose in 3-4 weeks

AML: Single agent induction: 60 mg/m²/day for 3 days; repeat every 3-4 weeks

AML: Combination therapy induction: 45 mg/m²/day for 3 days of the first course of induction therapy; subsequent courses: Every day for 2 days

ALL combination therapy: 45 mg/m²/day for 3 days

Cumulative dose should not exceed 400-600 mg/m²

Dosing adjustment in renal impairment:

Cl_{cr} <10 mL/minute: Administer 75% of normal dose

S_{cr} >3 mg/dL: Administer 50% of normal dose

Dosing adjustment in hepatic impairment:

Serum bilirubin 1.2-3 mg/dL or AST 60-180 int. units: Reduce dose to 75%

Serum bilirubin 3.1-5 mg/dL or AST >180 int. units: Reduce dose to 50%

Serum bilirubin >5 mg/dL: Omit use

Administration

Administer IVP over 1-5 minutes into the tubing of a rapidly infusing I.V. solution of D_5W or NS; daunorubicin has also been diluted in 100 mL of D_5W or NS and infused over 15-30 minutes

Avoid extravasation, can cause severe tissue damage; flush with 5-10 mL of I.V. solution before and after drug administration

Monitoring Parameters CBC with differential and platelet count, liver function test, EKG, ventricular ejection fraction, renal function test

Patient Information Discoloration of urine (red) may occur transiently; immediately report any change in sensation (eg, stinging) at injection site during infusion (may be an early sign of infiltration); contraceptive measures are recommended during therapy

Nursing Implications Daunorubicin is a vesicant and should never be administered I.M. or S.C.

Extravasation management:

Apply ice immediately for 30-60 minutes; then alternate off/on every 15 minutes for one day

Topical cooling may be achieved using ice packs or cooling pad with circulating ice water; cooling of site for 24 hours as tolerated by the patient. Elevate and rest extremity 24-48 hours, then resume normal activity as tolerated. Application of cold inhibits vesicant's cytotoxicity.

Application of heat or sodium bicarbonate can be harmful and is contraindicated

If pain, erythema, and/or swelling persist beyond 48 hours, refer patient immediately to plastic surgeon for consultation and possible debridement

Dosage Forms Powder for injection, lyophilized: 20 mg

- ◆ **Decohistine® DH** *see* Chlorpheniramine, Pseudoephedrine, and Codeine *on page 247*
- ◆ **Decohistine® Expectorant** *see* Guaifenesin, Pseudoephedrine, and Codeine *on page 551*
- ◆ **Deconsal® Sprinkle®** *see* Guaifenesin and Phenylephrine *on page 551*

Deferoxamine (de fer OKS a meen)

U.S. Brand Names Desferal® Mesylate
Synonyms Deferoxamine Mesylate
Therapeutic Category Antidote, Aluminum Toxicity; Antidote, Iron Toxicity
Use Acute iron intoxication when serum iron is >450-500 mcg/dL or when clinical signs of significant iron toxicity exist; chronic iron overload secondary to multiple transfusions; diagnostic test for iron overload; iron overload secondary to congenital anemias; hemochromatosis; removal of corneal rust rings following surgical removal of foreign bodies
Investigational: Treatment of aluminum accumulation in renal failure
Pregnancy Risk Factor C
Contraindications Patients with anuria, primary hemochromatosis
Warnings/Precautions Use with caution in patients with severe renal disease, pyelonephritis; may increase susceptibility to *Yersinia enterocolitica*
Adverse Reactions
1% to 10%: Local: Pain and induration at injection site
<1%: Flushing, hypotension (especially with rapid injection), tachycardia, shock, edema, fever, erythema, urticaria, pruritus, rash, cutaneous wheal formation, abdominal discomfort, diarrhea, leg cramps, blurred vision, cataracts, hearing loss, anaphylaxis
Overdosage/Toxicology
Symptoms of overdose include hypotension, blurring of vision, diarrhea, leg cramps, tachycardia
Treatment is symptomatic and supportive
Stability Protect from light; reconstituted solutions (sterile water) may be stored at room temperature for 7 days
Mechanism of Action Complexes with trivalent ions (ferric ions) to form ferrioxamine, which are removed by the kidneys
Pharmacodynamics/Kinetics
Absorption: Oral: <15%
Metabolism: In the liver to ferrioxamine
Half-life: Parent drug: 6.1 hours; Ferrioxamine: 5.8 hours
Elimination: Renal excretion of the metabolite and unchanged drug
Usual Dosage
Children and Adults:
Acute iron toxicity: I.V. route is preferred in all cases: 15 mg/kg/hour (although rates up to 40-50 mg/kg/hour have been given in patients with massive iron intoxication); maximum recommended dose: 6 g/day
End points: Loss of vin rosé-colored urine and serum iron level <350 μ/dL and resolution of clinical signs of intoxication
Note: Test dose I.M. injection is not recommended due to risk of sterile abscess formation and hypotension, however, usual dose is 50 mg/kg; observe for vin rosé-colored urine
Children:
Chronic iron overload: S.C.: 20-40 mg/kg/day over 8-12 hours (via a portable, controlled infusion device)
Aluminum-induced bone disease: 20-40 mg/kg every hemodialysis treatment, frequency dependent on clinical status of the patient
Adults: Chronic iron overload:
I.V.: 2 g after each unit of blood infusion at 15 mg/kg/hour
S.C.: 1-2 g every day over 8-24 hours
Dosing adjustment in renal impairment: Cl_{cr} <10 mL/minute: Administer 50% of dose
Has been used investigationally as a single 40 mg/kg I.V. dose over 2 hours, to promote mobilization of aluminum from tissue stores as an aid in the diagnosis of aluminum-associated osteodystrophy
Administration I.M. is preferred route; maximum I.V. rate is 15 mg/kg/hour. Urticaria, hypotension, and shock have occurred following rapid I.V. administration; administer I.M., slow S.C., or I.V. infusion. Add 2 mL sterile water to 500 mg vial; for I.M. or S.C. administration, no further dilution is required; for I.V. infusion, dilute in dextrose, normal saline, or lactated Ringer's; 10 mg/mL (maximum: 25 mg/mL); maximum rate of infusion: 15 mg/kg/hour.
Monitoring Parameters Serum iron, total iron binding capacity; ophthalmologic exam and audiometry with chronic therapy
Patient Information May turn urine pink; blood and urine tests are necessary to follow therapy
Nursing Implications Iron chelate colors urine salmon pink
Dosage Forms Powder for injection, as mesylate: 500 mg

- ◆ **Deferoxamine Mesylate** *see* Deferoxamine *on this page*
- ◆ **Degest® 2 [OTC]** *see* Naphazoline *on page 817*
- ◆ **Dehydral™** *see* Methenamine *on page 747*
- ◆ **Dekasol-L.A.®** *see* Dexamethasone *on page 337*
- ◆ **Deladumone® Injection** *see* Estradiol and Testosterone *on page 435*
- ◆ **Delatest® Injection** *see* Testosterone *on page 1117*
- ◆ **Delatestryl® Injection** *see* Testosterone *on page 1117*

Delavirdine (de la VIR deen)

Related Information
Antiretroviral Agents *on page 1306*
Antiretroviral Therapy for HIV Infection *on page 1410*

U.S. Brand Names Rescriptor®

Synonyms U-90152S

Therapeutic Category Antiretroviral Agent, Reverse Transcriptase Inhibitor; Reverse Transcriptase Inhibitor

Use Treatment of HIV-1 infection in combination with at least two additional antiretroviral agents

Pregnancy Risk Factor C

Pregnancy/Breast-Feeding Implications
Clinical effects on the fetus: Administer during pregnancy only if benefits to mother outweigh risks to the fetus
Breast-feeding/lactation: HIV-infected mothers are discouraged from breast-feeding to decrease potential transmission of HIV

Contraindications Known hypersensitivity to delavirdine or any components

Warnings/Precautions Avoid use with terfenadine, astemizole, benzodiazepines, clarithromycin, dapsone, cisapride, rifabutin, rifampin; use with caution in patients with hepatic or renal dysfunction; due to rapid emergence of resistance, delavirdine should not be used as monotherapy; cross-resistance may be conferred to other non-nucleoside reverse transcriptase inhibitors, although potential for cross-resistance with protease inhibitors is low. Long-term effects of delavirdine are not known. Safety and efficacy have not been established in children. Rash, which occurs frequently, may require discontinuation of therapy; usually occurs within 1-3 weeks and lasts <2 weeks. Most patients may resume therapy following a treatment interruption.

Adverse Reactions >2%:
Central nervous system: Headache, fatigue
Dermatologic: Rash, pruritus
Gastrointestinal: Nausea, diarrhea, vomiting
Metabolic: Increased ALT/AST

Overdosage/Toxicology
Human reports of overdose with delavirdine are not available
GI decontamination and supportive measures are recommended, dialysis unlikely to be of benefit in removing drug since it is extensively metabolized by the liver and is highly protein bound

Drug Interactions CYP2D6 and 3A3/4 enzyme substrate; CYP2D6 and 3A3/4 enzyme inhibitor
Increased plasma concentrations of delavirdine: Clarithromycin, ketoconazole, fluoxetine
Decreased plasma concentrations of delavirdine: Carbamazepine, phenobarbital, phenytoin, rifabutin, rifampin, didanosine, saquinavir
Decreased absorption of delavirdine: Antacids, histamine-2 receptor antagonists, didanosine
Delavirdine increases plasma concentrations of: Indinavir, saquinavir, terfenadine, astemizole, clarithromycin, dapsone, rifabutin, ergot derivatives, alprazolam, midazolam, triazolam, dihydropyridines, cisapride, quinidine, warfarin
Delavirdine decreases plasma concentrations of: Didanosine

Mechanism of Action Delavirdine binds directly to reverse transcriptase, blocking RNA-dependent and DNA-dependent DNA polymerase activities

Pharmacodynamics/Kinetics
Absorption: Rapid; peak plasma concentrations at 1 hour
Distribution: Not reported
Metabolism: Hepatic; extensively metabolized by the cytochrome P-450 3A or possibly 2D6
Bioavailability: 85%; AUC may be higher in female patients
Protein binding: ~98%, primarily albumin
Half-life: 2-11 hours
Elimination: 44% in feces, 51% in urine, and <5% unchanged in urine; nonlinear kinetics exhibited. (Note: May reduce CYP3A activity and inhibit its own metabolism.)

Usual Dosage Adults: Oral: 400 mg 3 times/day

Dietary Considerations Delavirdine may be taken without regard to food

Administration Patients with achlorhydria should take the drug with an acidic beverage; antacids and delavirdine should be separated by 1 hour

Monitoring Parameters Liver function tests if administered with saquinavir

Patient Information Delavirdine is not a cure for HIV-1 nor has it been shown to reduce the risk of transmission; illnesses associated with HIV-1 infection may continue to be acquired at the same frequency. Stay under the care of a physician when using delavirdine; notify your physician if a rash occurs or symptoms of rash with fever, blistering, oral lesions, conjunctivitis, swelling, or muscle/joint pain

Additional Information Potential compliance problems, frequency of administration and adverse effects should be discussed with patients before initiating therapy to help prevent the emergence of resistance.

Dosage Forms Tablet: 100 mg

Extemporaneous Preparations A dispersion of delavirdine may be prepared by adding 4 tablets to at least 3 oz of water; allow to stand for a few minutes and stir until uniform dispersion; drink immediately; rinse glass and mouth following ingestion to ensure total dose administered

♦ **Delaxin®** *see* Methocarbamol *on page 749*

- **Delcort®** *see* Hydrocortisone *on page 579*
- **Delestrogen® Injection** *see* Estradiol *on page 433*
- **Delta-Cortef® Oral** *see* Prednisolone *on page 961*
- **Deltacortisone** *see* Prednisone *on page 963*
- **Deltadehydrocortisone** *see* Prednisone *on page 963*
- **Deltahydrocortisone** *see* Prednisolone *on page 961*
- **Deltasone®** *see* Prednisone *on page 963*
- **Delta-Tritex®** *see* Triamcinolone *on page 1174*
- **Del-Vi-A®** *see* Vitamin A *on page 1223*
- **Demadex®** *see* Torsemide *on page 1164*

Demecarium (dem e KARE ee um)

Related Information
Glaucoma Drug Therapy Comparison *on page 1322*
U.S. Brand Names Humorsol® Ophthalmic
Synonyms Demecarium Bromide
Therapeutic Category Cholinergic Agent, Ophthalmic; Ophthalmic Agent, Miotic
Use Management of chronic simple glaucoma; chronic and acute angle-closure glaucoma; strabismus
Pregnancy Risk Factor C
Pregnancy/Breast-Feeding Implications Although there are no reports of use in pregnancy, demecarium is an ophthalmic medication and transplacental passage in significant amounts would not be expected
Contraindications Hypersensitivity to demecarium or any component, acute inflammatory disease of anterior chamber; pregnancy
Adverse Reactions
1% to 10%: Ocular: Stinging, burning eyes, myopia, visual blurring
<1%: Bradycardia, hypotension, flushing, nausea, vomiting, diarrhea, muscle weakness, retinal detachment, miosis, twitching eyelids, watering eyes, dyspnea, diaphoresis
Overdosage/Toxicology Antidote: Atropine sulfate: Adults: 0.4-0.6 mg (1/150-1/100 grain) or more parenterally
Stability Do not freeze; protect from heat
Mechanism of Action Cholinesterase inhibitor (anticholinesterase) which causes acetylcholine to accumulate at cholinergic receptor sites and produces effects equivalent to excessive stimulation of cholinergic receptors. Demecarium mainly acts by inhibiting true (erythrocyte) cholinesterase and causes a reduction in intraocular pressure due to facilitation of outflow of aqueous humor; the reduction is likely to be particularly marked in eyes in which the pressure is elevated.
Usual Dosage Children/Adults: Ophthalmic:
Glaucoma: Instill 1 drop into eyes twice weekly to a maximum dosage of 1 or 2 drops twice daily for up to 4 months
Strabismus:
Diagnosis: Instill 1 drop daily for 2 weeks, then 1 drop every 2 days for 2-3 weeks. If eyes become straighter, an accommodative factor is demonstrated.
Therapy: Instill not more than 1 drop at a time in both eyes every day for 2-3 weeks. Then reduce dosage to 1 drop every other day for 3-4 weeks and re-evaluate. Continue at 1 drop every 2 days to 1 drop twice a week and evaluate the patient's condition every 4-12 weeks. If improvement continues, reduce dose to 1 drop once a week and eventually off of medication. Discontinue therapy after 4 months if control of the condition still requires 1 drop every 2 days.
Patient Information For the eye; do not touch dropper to eye; transient burning or stinging may occur; do not use more often than directed
Nursing Implications Finger pressure should be applied to lacrimal sac for 1-2 minutes after instillation to decrease risk of absorption and systemic reactions; patient must be under supervision and tonometric examinations performed every 3-4 hours following initiation of therapy
Dosage Forms Solution, ophthalmic, as bromide: 0.125% (5 mL); 0.25% (5 mL)

- **Demecarium Bromide** *see* Demecarium *on this page*

Demeclocycline (dem e kloe SYE kleen)

U.S. Brand Names Declomycin®
Synonyms Demeclocycline Hydrochloride; Demethylchlortetracycline
Therapeutic Category Antibiotic, Tetracycline Derivative
Use Treatment of susceptible bacterial infections (acne, gonorrhea, pertussis and urinary tract infections) caused by both gram-negative and gram-positive organisms; used when penicillin is contraindicated (other agents are preferred); treatment of chronic syndrome of inappropriate secretion of antidiuretic hormone (SIADH)
Pregnancy Risk Factor D
Contraindications Hypersensitivity to demeclocycline, tetracyclines, or any component
Warnings/Precautions Do not administer to children <9 years of age; photosensitivity reactions occur frequently with this drug, avoid prolonged exposure to sunlight, do not use tanning equipment
Adverse Reactions
1% to 10%:
Dermatologic: Photosensitivity
Gastrointestinal: Nausea, diarrhea
(Continued)

Demeclocycline (Continued)

<1%: Pericarditis, increased intracranial pressure, bulging fontanels in infants, dermatologic effects, pruritus, exfoliative dermatitis, diabetes insipidus syndrome, vomiting, esophagitis, anorexia, abdominal cramps, paresthesia, acute renal failure, azotemia, superinfections, anaphylaxis, pigmentation of nails

Overdosage/Toxicology
Symptoms of overdose include diabetes insipidus, nausea, anorexia, diarrhea
Following GI decontamination, treatment is supportive

Drug Interactions
Decreased effect with antacids (aluminum, calcium, zinc, or magnesium), bismuth salts, sodium bicarbonate, barbiturates, carbamazepine, hydantoins
Decreased effect of oral contraceptives
Increased effect of warfarin

Mechanism of Action Inhibits protein synthesis by binding with the 30S and possibly the 50S ribosomal subunit(s) of susceptible bacteria; may also cause alterations in the cytoplasmic membrane; inhibits the action of ADH in patients with chronic SIADH

Pharmacodynamics/Kinetics
Onset of action for diuresis in SIADH: Several days
Absorption: ~50% to 80% from GI tract; food and dairy products reduce absorption
Protein binding: 41% to 50%
Metabolism: Small amounts metabolized in the liver to inactive metabolites; enterohepatically recycled
Half-life: Reduced renal function: 10-17 hours
Time to peak serum concentration: Oral: Within 3-6 hours
Elimination: As unchanged drug (42% to 50%) in urine

Usual Dosage Oral:
Children ≥8 years: 8-12 mg/kg/day divided every 6-12 hours
Adults: 150 mg 4 times/day or 300 mg twice daily
Uncomplicated gonorrhea (penicillin sensitive): 600 mg stat, 300 mg every 12 hours for 4 days (3 g total)
SIADH: 900-1200 mg/day or 13-15 mg/kg/day divided every 6-8 hours initially, then decrease to 600-900 mg/day
Dosing adjustment/comments in renal/hepatic impairment: Should be avoided in patients with renal/hepatic dysfunction

Administration Administer 1 hour before or 2 hours after food or milk with plenty of fluid

Monitoring Parameters CBC, renal and hepatic function

Test Interactions May interfere with tests for urinary glucose (false-negative urine glucose using Clinistix®, Tes-Tape®)

Patient Information Avoid prolonged exposure to sunlight or sunlamps; avoid taking antacids before tetracyclines

Dosage Forms
Capsule, as hydrochloride: 150 mg
Tablet, as hydrochloride: 150 mg, 300 mg

- ◆ **Demeclocycline Hydrochloride** see Demeclocycline on previous page
- ◆ **Demerol®** see Meperidine on page 728
- ◆ **4-Demethoxydaunorubicin** see Idarubicin on page 596
- ◆ **Demethylchlortetracycline** see Demeclocycline on previous page
- ◆ **Demser®** see Metyrosine on page 772
- ◆ **Demulen®** see Ethinyl Estradiol and Ethynodiol Diacetate on page 447
- ◆ **Denavir™** see Penciclovir on page 892
- ◆ **Deodorized Opium Tincture** see Opium Tincture on page 864
- ◆ **Deoxycoformycin** see Pentostatin on page 904
- ◆ **2'-deoxycoformycin** see Pentostatin on page 904
- ◆ **Depacon®** see Valproic Acid and Derivatives on page 1203
- ◆ **Depakene®** see Valproic Acid and Derivatives on page 1203
- ◆ **Depakote®** see Valproic Acid and Derivatives on page 1203
- ◆ **depAndrogyn® Injection** see Estradiol and Testosterone on page 435
- ◆ **depAndro® Injection** see Testosterone on page 1117
- ◆ **Depen®** see Penicillamine on page 893
- ◆ **depGynogen® Injection** see Estradiol on page 433
- ◆ **depMedalone® Injection** see Methylprednisolone on page 762
- ◆ **Depo®-Estradiol Injection** see Estradiol on page 433
- ◆ **Depogen® Injection** see Estradiol on page 433
- ◆ **Depoject® Injection** see Methylprednisolone on page 762
- ◆ **Depo-Medrol® Injection** see Methylprednisolone on page 762
- ◆ **Deponit® Patch** see Nitroglycerin on page 845
- ◆ **Depopred® Injection** see Methylprednisolone on page 762
- ◆ **Depo-Provera® Injection** see Medroxyprogesterone Acetate on page 721
- ◆ **Depo-Testadiol® Injection** see Estradiol and Testosterone on page 435
- ◆ **Depotest® Injection** see Testosterone on page 1117
- ◆ **Depotestogen® Injection** see Estradiol and Testosterone on page 435
- ◆ **Depo®-Testosterone Injection** see Testosterone on page 1117
- ◆ **Deprenyl** see Selegiline on page 1053
- ◆ **Depression Disorders and Treatments** see page 1465

Desipramine (des IP ra meen)

Related Information
Antidepressant Agents Comparison on page 1301

U.S. Brand Names Norpramin®

Canadian Brand Names PMS-Desipramine

Synonyms Desipramine Hydrochloride; Desmethylimipramine Hydrochloride

Therapeutic Category Antidepressant, Tricyclic

Use Treatment of various forms of depression, often in conjunction with psychotherapy; analgesic adjunct in chronic pain

Unlabeled use: Peripheral neuropathies

Pregnancy Risk Factor C

Contraindications Hypersensitivity to desipramine (cross-sensitivity with other tricyclic antidepressants may occur); patients receiving MAO inhibitors within past 14 days; narrow-angle glaucoma; use immediately postmyocardial infarction

Warnings/Precautions Use with caution in patients with cardiovascular disease, conduction disturbances, urinary retention, seizure disorders, hyperthyroidism or those receiving thyroid replacement; do not discontinue abruptly in patients receiving long-term high-dose therapy

Adverse Reactions
>10%:

Central nervous system: Dizziness, drowsiness, headache

Gastrointestinal: Xerostomia, constipation, increased appetite, nausea, unpleasant taste, weight gain

Neuromuscular & skeletal: Weakness

1% to 10%:

Cardiovascular: Arrhythmias, hypotension

Central nervous system: Confusion, delirium, hallucinations, nervousness, restlessness, parkinsonian syndrome, insomnia

Gastrointestinal: Diarrhea, heartburn

Genitourinary: Dysuria, sexual dysfunction

Neuromuscular & skeletal: Fine muscle tremors

Ocular: Blurred vision, eye pain

Miscellaneous: Diaphoresis (excessive)

<1%: Anxiety, seizures, alopecia, photosensitivity, breast enlargement, galactorrhea, SIADH, trouble with gums, decreased lower esophageal sphincter tone may cause GE reflux, testicular edema, agranulocytosis, leukopenia, eosinophilia, cholestatic jaundice, increased liver enzymes, increased intraocular pressure, tinnitus, allergic reactions

Overdosage/Toxicology
Symptoms of overdose include severe hypotension, agitation, confusion, hyperthermia, urinary retention, CNS depression (including coma), cyanosis, dry mucous membranes, cardiac arrhythmias, seizures, changes in EKG (particularly in QRS axis and width), transient visual hallucinations, stupor, muscle rigidity

Following GI decontamination, treatment is supportive. Sodium bicarbonate is indicated when QRS interval is ≥0.10 seconds or QT_c >0.42 seconds. Ventricular arrhythmias and EKG changes (eg, QRS widening) often respond with concurrent systemic alkalinization (sodium bicarbonate 0.5-2 mEq/kg I.V.). Arrhythmias unresponsive to phenytoin 15-20 mg/kg (adults) may respond to lidocaine 1 mg/kg I.V. followed by a titrated infusion. Physostigmine (1-2 mg I.V. slowly for adults or 0.5 mg I.V. slowly for children) may be indicated in reversing cardiac arrhythmias that are life-threatening. Seizures usually respond to diazepam I.V. boluses (5-10 mg for adults up to 30 mg or 0.25-0.4 mg/kg/dose for children up to 10 mg/dose). If seizures are unresponsive or recur, phenytoin or phenobarbital may be required.

Drug Interactions CYP1A2 and 2D6 enzyme substrate; CYP2D6 inhibitor

Decreased effects of guanethidine, clonidine; decreased effect of desipramine with barbiturates, carbamazepine, phenytoin

Increased effects: Sympathomimetics, benzodiazepines

(Continued)

Desipramine *(Continued)*

Increased toxicity: Anticholinergics; increased toxicity with MAO inhibitors (hyperpyrexia, tachycardia, hypertension, seizures, and death may occur), alcohol, CNS depressants, cimetidine

Mechanism of Action Traditionally believed to increase the synaptic concentration of norepinephrine in the central nervous system by inhibition of its reuptake by the presynaptic neuronal membrane. However, additional receptor effects have been found including desensitization of adenyl cyclase, down regulation of beta-adrenergic receptors, and down regulation of serotonin receptors.

Pharmacodynamics/Kinetics

Onset of action: 1-3 weeks (maximum antidepressant effects: after >2 weeks)

Absorption: Well absorbed from GI tract

Metabolism: In the liver

Half-life: Adults: 7-60 hours

Peak plasma levels occur within 4-6 hours

Elimination: 70% excreted in urine

Usual Dosage Oral:

Children 6-12 years: 10-30 mg/day or 1-5 mg/kg/day in divided doses; do not exceed 5 mg/kg/day

Adolescents: Initial: 25-50 mg/day; gradually increase to 100 mg/day in single or divided doses; maximum: 150 mg/day

Adults: Initial: 75 mg/day in divided doses; increase gradually to 150-200 mg/day in divided or single dose; maximum: 300 mg/day

Elderly: Initial dose: 10-25 mg/day; increase by 10-25 mg every 3 days for inpatients and every week for outpatients if tolerated; usual maintenance dose: 75-100 mg/day, but doses up to 150 mg/day may be necessary

Hemodialysis/peritoneal dialysis: Supplemental dose is not necessary

Dietary Considerations Alcohol: Additive CNS effects, avoid use

Monitoring Parameters Monitor blood pressure and pulse rate prior to and during initial therapy; evaluate mental status; monitor weight

Reference Range

Plasma levels do not always correlate with clinical effectiveness

Timing of serum samples: Draw trough just before next dose

Therapeutic: 50-300 ng/mL

In elderly patients the response rate is greatest with steady-state plasma concentrations >115 ng/mL

Possible toxicity: >300 ng/mL

Toxic: >1000 ng/mL

Patient Information Avoid alcohol ingestion; do not discontinue medication abruptly; may cause urine to turn blue-green; may cause drowsiness; avoid unnecessary exposure to sunlight; sugarless hard candy or gum can help with dry mouth; full effect may not occur for 3-4 weeks

Dosage Forms Tablet, as hydrochloride: 10 mg, 25 mg, 50 mg, 75 mg, 100 mg, 150 mg

♦ **Desipramine Hydrochloride** *see Desipramine on previous page*

♦ **Desmethylimipramine Hydrochloride** *see Desipramine on previous page*

Desmopressin Acetate (des moe PRES in AS e tate)

U.S. Brand Names DDAVP® Nasal Spray; Stimate® Nasal

Canadian Brand Names Octostim®

Synonyms 1-Deamino-8-D-Arginine Vasopressin

Therapeutic Category Antihemophilic Agent; Hemostatic Agent; Vasopressin Analog, Synthetic

Use Treatment of diabetes insipidus and controlling bleeding in mild hemophilia, von Willebrand disease, and thrombocytopenia (eg, uremia), nocturnal enuresis

Pregnancy Risk Factor B

Contraindications Hypersensitivity to desmopressin or any component; avoid using in patients with type IIB or platelet-type von Willebrand disease, patients with <5% factor VIII activity level

Warnings/Precautions Avoid overhydration especially when drug is used for its hemostatic effect

Adverse Reactions

1% to 10%:

Cardiovascular: Facial flushing

Central nervous system: Headache, dizziness

Gastrointestinal: Nausea, abdominal cramps

Genitourinary: Vulval pain

Local: Pain at the injection site

Respiratory: Nasal congestion

<1%: Increase in blood pressure, hyponatremia, water intoxication

Overdosage/Toxicology Symptoms of overdose include drowsiness, headache, confusion, anuria, water intoxication

Drug Interactions

Decreased effect: Demeclocycline, lithium may decrease ADH effects

Increased effect: Chlorpropamide, fludrocortisone may increase ADH response

Stability Keep in refrigerator, avoid freezing; discard discolored solutions; nasal solution stable for 3 weeks at room temperature; injection stable for 2 weeks at room temperature

Mechanism of Action Enhances reabsorption of water in the kidneys by increasing cellular permeability of the collecting ducts; possibly causes smooth muscle constriction with resultant vasoconstriction; raises plasma levels of von Willebrand factor and factor VIII

Pharmacodynamics/Kinetics

Intranasal administration: Onset of ADH effects: Within 1 hour; Peak effect: Within 1-5 hours; Duration: 5-21 hours

I.V. infusion: Onset of increased factor VIII activity: Within 15-30 minutes; Peak effect: 90 minutes to 3 hours

Absorption: Nasal: Slow; 10% to 20%

Metabolism: Unknown

Half-life: Elimination (terminal): 75 minutes

Usual Dosage

Children:

Diabetes insipidus: 3 months to 12 years: Intranasal (using 100 mcg/mL nasal solution): Initial: 5 mcg/day (0.05 mL/day) divided 1-2 times/day; range: 5-30 mcg/day (0.05-0.3 mL/day) divided 1-2 times/day; adjust morning and evening doses separately for an adequate diurnal rhythm of water turnover

Hemophilia: >3 months: I.V. 0.3 mcg/kg; may repeat dose if needed; begin 30 minutes before procedure; dilute I.V. dose in 50 mL 0.9% sodium chloride and infuse over 15-30 minutes

Nocturnal enuresis: ≥6 years: Intranasal (using 100 mcg/mL nasal solution): Initial: 20 mcg (0.2 mL) at bedtime; range: 10-40 mcg; it is recommended that $^1/_2$ of the dose be given in each nostril

Children 12 years and Adults:

Diabetes insipidus:

I.V., S.C.: 2-4 mcg/day in 2 divided doses or $^1/_{10}$ of the maintenance intranasal dose; dilute I.V. dose in 50 mL 0.9% sodium chloride and infuse over 15-30 minutes

Intranasal (using 100 mcg/mL nasal solution): 5-40 mcg/day (0.05-0.4 mL) divided 1-3 times/day; adjust morning and evening doses separately for an adequate diurnal rhythm of water turnover. **Note:** The nasal spray pump can only deliver doses of 10 mcg (0.1 mL) or multiples of 10 mcg (0.1 mL), if doses other than this are needed, the rhinal tube delivery system is preferred.

Hemophilia/uremic bleeding:

I.V.: 0.3 mcg/kg by slow infusion, begin 30 minutes before procedure; dilute I.V. dose in 50 mL 0.9% sodium chloride and infuse over 15-30 minutes

Nasal spray: Using high concentration spray: <50 kg: 150 mcg (1 spray); >50 kg: 300 mcg (1 spray each nostril); repeat use is determined by the patient's clinical condition and laboratory work; if using preoperatively, administer 2 hours before surgery

Oral: Begin therapy 12 hours after the last intranasal dose for patients previously on intranasal therapy

Children: Initial: 0.05 mg; fluid restrictions are required in children to prevent hyponatremia and water intoxication

Adults: 0.05 mg twice daily; adjust individually to optimal therapeutic dose. Total daily dose should be increased or decreased (range: 0.1-1.2 mg divided 2-3 times/day) as needed to obtain adequate antidiuresis.

Administration For I.V. administration, dilute in 10-50 mL 0.9% sodium chloride and infuse over 15-30 minutes

Monitoring Parameters Blood pressure and pulse should be monitored during I.V. infusion

Diabetes insipidus: Fluid intake, urine volume, specific gravity, plasma and urine osmolality, serum electrolytes

Hemophilia: Factor VIII antigen levels, APTT, bleeding time (for von Willebrand disease and thrombocytopathies)

Patient Information Avoid overhydration; notify physician if headache, shortness of breath, heartburn, nausea, abdominal cramps, or vulval pain occur

Dosage Forms

Injection (DDAVP®): 4 mcg/mL (1 mL)

Solution, nasal:

DDAVP®: 100 mcg/mL (2.5 mL, 5 mL)

Stimate™: 1.5 mg/mL (2.5 mL)

Tablet (DDAVP®): 0.1 mg, 0.2 mg

♦ **Desocort®** see Desonide on this page

♦ **Desogen®** see Ethinyl Estradiol and Desogestrel on page 447

Desonide (DES oh nide)

Related Information

Corticosteroids Comparison on page 1319

U.S. Brand Names DesOwen® Topical; Tridesilon® Topical

Canadian Brand Names Desocort®

Therapeutic Category Anti-inflammatory Agent; Corticosteroid, Topical (Low Potency); Corticosteroid, Topical (Medium Potency)

Use Adjunctive therapy for inflammation in acute and chronic corticosteroid responsive dermatosis (low potency corticosteroid)

Pregnancy Risk Factor C

Contraindications Known hypersensitivity to desonide, fungal infections, tuberculosis of skin, herpes simplex

(Continued)

Desonide (Continued)

Warnings/Precautions Use with caution in patients with impaired circulation, skin infections

Adverse Reactions <1%: Itching, dry skin, folliculitis, hypertrichosis, acneiform eruptions, hypopigmentation, perioral dermatitis, allergic contact dermatitis, skin maceration, skin atrophy, striae; local burning, irritation, miliaria; secondary infection

Overdosage/Toxicology Symptoms of overdose include moon face, central obesity, hypertension, diabetes, hyperlipidemia, peptic ulcer, increased susceptibility to infection, electrolyte and fluid imbalance, psychosis, hallucinations. When consumed in excessive quantities, systemic hypercorticism and adrenal suppression may occur; in those cases discontinuation and withdrawal of the corticosteroid should be done judiciously.

Mechanism of Action Stimulates the synthesis of enzymes needed to decrease inflammation, suppress mitotic activity, and cause vasoconstriction

Pharmacodynamics/Kinetics

Onset of effect: Commonly noted within 7 days of continued therapy

Absorption: Topical absorption extensive from the scalp, face, axilla and scrotum; adequate through epidermis on appendages; absorption can be increased with occlusion or the addition of penetrants (eg, urea, DMSO)

Metabolism: By the liver

Elimination: Primarily in urine

Usual Dosage Children and Adults: Topical: Apply 2-4 times/day sparingly

Patient Information A thin film of cream or ointment is effective, do not overuse; rub in lightly; do not use tight-fitting diapers or plastic pants on children being treated in the diaper area; use only as prescribed and for no longer than the period prescribed; avoid contact with eyes; notify physician if condition being treated persists or worsens

Nursing Implications For external use only; do not use on open wounds; apply sparingly to occlusive dressings; should not be used in the presence of open or weeping lesions

Dosage Forms

Cream, topical: 0.05% (15 g, 60 g)

Lotion: 0.05% (60 mL, 120 mL)

Ointment, topical: 0.05% (15 g, 60 g)

♦ **DesOwen® Topical** see Desonide on previous page

Desoximetasone (des oks i MET a sone)

Related Information

Corticosteroids Comparison on page 1319

U.S. Brand Names Topicort®; Topicort®-LP

Therapeutic Category Corticosteroid, Topical (Medium Potency); Corticosteroid, Topical (High Potency)

Use Relieves inflammation and pruritic symptoms of corticosteroid-responsive dermatosis [medium to high potency topical corticosteroid]

Pregnancy Risk Factor C

Contraindications Known hypersensitivity to desoximetasone, topical fungal infections, tuberculosis of skin herpes simplex

Warnings/Precautions Use with caution in patients with impaired circulation; skin infections

Adverse Reactions <1%: Itching, dry skin, folliculitis, hypertrichosis, acneiform eruptions, allergic contact dermatitis, skin maceration, skin atrophy, striae, perioral dermatitis, hypopigmentation; local burning, irritation, miliaria; secondary infection

Overdosage/Toxicology Symptoms of overdose include moon face, central obesity, hypertension, diabetes, hyperlipidemia, peptic ulcer, increased susceptibility to infection, electrolyte and fluid imbalance, psychosis, hallucinations. When consumed in excessive quantities, systemic hypercorticism and adrenal suppression may occur; in those cases discontinuation and withdrawal of the corticosteroid should be done judiciously.

Mechanism of Action Stimulates the synthesis of enzymes needed to decrease inflammation, suppress mitotic activity, and cause vasoconstriction; high potency, fluorinated topical corticosteroid

Pharmacodynamics/Kinetics Topical:

Absorption: Extensive from the scalp, face, axilla, and scrotum and adequate through epidermis on appendages; absorption can be increased with occlusion or the addition of penetrants

Distribution: Only small amounts reach the systemic circulation or dermal layers

Usual Dosage Desoximetasone is a potent fluorinated topical corticosteroid. All of the preparations are considered high potency.

Children: Apply sparingly in a very thin film to affected area 1-2 times/day

Adults: Apply sparingly in a thin film twice daily

Patient Information A thin film of cream or ointment is effective, do not overuse; rub in lightly; do not use tight-fitting diapers or plastic pants on children being treated in the diaper area; use only as prescribed and for no longer than the period prescribed; avoid contact with eyes; notify physician if condition being treated persists or worsens

Nursing Implications For external use only; apply sparingly to occlusive dressings; should not be used in the presence of open or weeping lesions

Dosage Forms Topical:

Cream:

Topicort®: 0.25% (15 g, 60 g, 120 g)

Topicort®-LP: 0.05% (15 g, 60 g)

Gel, topical: 0.05% (15 g, 60 g)
Ointment (Topicort®): 0.25% (15 g, 60 g)

- ♦ **Desoxyephedrine Hydrochloride** see Methamphetamine *on page 745*
- ♦ **Desoxyn®** see Methamphetamine *on page 745*
- ♦ **Desoxyn Gradumet®** see Methamphetamine *on page 745*
- ♦ **Desoxyphenobarbital** see Primidone *on page 966*
- ♦ **Desyrel®** see Trazodone *on page 1170*
- ♦ **Detensol®** see Propranolol *on page 986*
- ♦ **Detrol™** see Tolterodine *on page 1160*
- ♦ **Detussin® Expectorant** see Hydrocodone, Pseudoephedrine, and Guaifenesin *on page 579*
- ♦ **Detussin® Liquid** see Hydrocodone and Pseudoephedrine *on page 579*
- ♦ **Devrom® [OTC]** see Bismuth *on page 145*
- ♦ **Dexacidin®** see Neomycin, Polymyxin B, and Dexamethasone *on page 826*
- ♦ **Dexair®** see Dexamethasone *on this page*

Dexamethasone (deks a METH a sone)

Related Information
Cancer Chemotherapy Regimens *on page 1263*
Corticosteroids Comparison *on page 1319*

U.S. Brand Names Aeroseb-Dex®; AK-Dex®; Alba-Dex®; Baldex®; Dalalone D.P.®; Dalalone L.A.®; Decaderm®; Decadron®; Decadron®-LA; Decadron® Turbinaire®; Decaject-L.A.®; Decaspray®; Dekasol-L.A.®; Dexair®; Dexasone L.A.®; Dexone®; Dexone L.A.®; Dezone®; Hexadrol®; I-Methasone®; Maxidex®; Ocu-Dex®; Solurex L.A.®

Synonyms Dexamethasone Acetate; Dexamethasone Sodium Phosphate

Therapeutic Category Antiemetic; Anti-inflammatory Agent; Anti-inflammatory Agent, Inhalant; Anti-inflammatory Agent, Ophthalmic; Corticosteroid, Inhalant; Corticosteroid, Ophthalmic; Corticosteroid, Systemic; Corticosteroid, Topical (Low Potency); Glucocorticoid

Use Systemically and locally for chronic inflammation, allergic, hematologic, neoplastic, and autoimmune diseases; may be used in management of cerebral edema, septic shock, as a diagnostic agent, antiemetic

Pregnancy Risk Factor C

Pregnancy/Breast-Feeding Implications Dexamethasone has been used in patients with premature labor (26-34 weeks gestation) to stimulate fetal lung maturation

Clinical effects on the fetus: Crosses the placenta; transient leukocytosis reported. Available evidence suggests safe use during pregnancy

Breast-feeding/lactation: No data on crossing into breast milk or effects on the infant

Contraindications Active untreated infections; use in ophthalmic viral, fungal, or tuberculosis diseases of the eye

Warnings/Precautions Fatalities have occurred due to adrenal insufficiency in asthmatic patients during and after transfer from systemic corticosteroids to aerosol steroids; aerosol steroids do **not** provide the systemic steroid needed to treat patients having trauma, surgery, or infections; use with caution in patients with hypothyroidism, cirrhosis, hypertension, congestive heart failure, ulcerative colitis, thromboembolic disorders. Because of the risk of adverse effects, systemic corticosteroids should be used cautiously in the elderly in the smallest possible dose and for the shortest possible time.

Controlled clinical studies have shown that inhaled and intranasal corticosteroids may cause a reduction in growth velocity in pediatric patients. Growth velocity provides a means of comparing the rate of growth among children of the same age.

In studies involving inhaled corticosteroids, the average reduction in growth velocity was approximately 1 cm (about 1/3 of an inch) per year. It appears that the reduction is related to dose and how long the child takes the drug.

FDA's Pulmonary and Allergy Drugs and Metabolic and Endocrine Drugs advisory committees discussed this issue at a July 1998 meeting. They recommended that the agency develop class-wide labeling to inform health care providers so they would understand this potential side effect and monitor growth routinely in pediatric patients who are treated with inhaled corticosteroids, intranasal corticosteroids or both.

Long-term effects of this reduction in growth velocity on final adult height are unknown. Likewise, it also has not yet been determined whether patients' growth will "catch up" if treatment in discontinued. Drug manufacturers will continue to monitor these drugs to learn more about long-term effects. Children are prescribed inhaled corticosteroids to treat asthma. Intranasal corticosteroids are generally used to prevent and treat allergy-related nasal symptoms.

Patients are advised not to stop using their inhaled or intranasal corticosteroids without first speaking to their health care providers about the benefits of these drugs compared to their risks.

Adverse Reactions
Systemic:
>10%:
Central nervous system: Insomnia, nervousness
Gastrointestinal: Increased appetite, indigestion
1% to 10%:
Dermatologic: Hirsutism
Endocrine & metabolic: Diabetes mellitus
(Continued)

Dexamethasone *(Continued)*

Neuromuscular & skeletal: Arthralgia

Ocular: Cataracts

Respiratory: Epistaxis

<1%: Seizures, mood swings, headache, delirium, hallucinations, euphoria, skin atrophy, bruising, hyperpigmentation, acne, amenorrhea, sodium and water retention, Cushing's syndrome, hyperglycemia, bone growth suppression, abdominal distention, ulcerative esophagitis, pancreatitis, muscle wasting, hypersensitivity reactions

Topical: <1%: Itching, dryness, folliculitis, hypertrichosis, acneiform eruptions, hypopigmentation, perioral dermatitis, allergic contact dermatitis, skin maceration, skin atrophy, striae; miliaria, local burning, irritation; secondary infection

Overdosage/Toxicology Symptoms of overdose include moon face, central obesity, hypertension, psychosis, hallucinations, diabetes, hyperlipidemia, peptic ulcer, increased susceptibility to infection, electrolyte and fluid imbalance. When consumed in excessive quantities, systemic hypercorticism and adrenal suppression may occur; in those cases, discontinuation and withdrawal of the corticosteroid should be done judiciously.

Drug Interactions CYP3A3/4 enzyme substrate; CYP3A3/4 enzyme inducer; CYP3A3/4 enzyme inhibitor

Decreased effect: Barbiturates, phenytoin, rifampin may decrease dexamethasone effects; dexamethasone decreases effect of salicylates, vaccines, toxoids

Stability

Dexamethasone 4 mg/mL injection solution is clear and colorless and dexamethasone 24 mg/mL injection solution is clear and colorless to light yellow. Injection solution should be protected from light and freezing.

Stability of injection of parenteral admixture at room temperature (25°C): 24 hours

Stability of injection of parenteral admixture at refrigeration temperature (4°C): 2 days; protect from light and freezing

Standard diluent: 4 mg/50 mL D_5W; 10 mg/50 mL D_5W

Minimum volume: 50 mL D_5W

Mechanism of Action Decreases inflammation by suppression of migration of polymorphonuclear leukocytes and reversal of increased capillary permeability; suppresses normal immune response

Pharmacodynamics/Kinetics

Duration of metabolic effect: Can last for 72 hours; acetate is a long-acting repository preparation with a prompt onset of action

Metabolism: In the liver

Half-life: Normal renal function: 1.8-3.5 hours; Biological half-life: 36-54 hours

Time to peak serum concentration: Oral: Within 1-2 hours; I.M.: Within 8 hours

Elimination: In the urine and bile

Usual Dosage

Neonates:

Airway edema or extubation: I.V.: Usual: 0.25 mg/kg/dose given 4 hours prior to scheduled extubation and then every 8 hours for 3 doses total; range: 0.25-1 mg/kg/dose for 1-3 doses; maximum dose: 1 mg/kg/day. **Note:** A longer duration of therapy may be needed with more severe cases.

Bronchopulmonary dysplasia (to facilitate ventilator weaning): Oral;, I.V.: Numerous dosing schedules have been proposed; range: 0.5-0.6 mg/kg/day given in divided doses every 12 hours for 3-7 days, then taper over 1-6 weeks

Children:

Antiemetic (prior to chemotherapy): I.V. (should be given as sodium phosphate): 10 mg/m²/dose (maximum: 20 mg) for first dose then 5 mg/m²/dose every 6 hours as needed

Anti-inflammatory immunosuppressant: Oral, I.M., I.V. (injections should be given as sodium phosphate): 0.08-0.3 mg/kg/day or 2.5-10 mg/m²/day in divided doses every 6-12 hours

Extubation or airway edema: Oral, I.M., I.V. (injections should be given as sodium phosphate): 0.5-2 mg/kg/day in divided doses every 6 hours beginning 24 hours prior to extubation and continuing for 4-6 doses afterwards

Cerebral edema: I.V. (should be given as sodium phosphate): Loading dose: 1-2 mg/kg/dose as a single dose; maintenance: 1-1.5 mg/kg/day (maximum: 16 mg/day) in divided doses every 4-6 hours for 5 days then taper for 5 days, then discontinue

Bacterial meningitis in infants and children >2 months: I.V. (should be given as sodium phosphate): 0.6 mg/kg/day in 4 divided doses every 6 hours for the first 4 days of antibiotic treatment; start dexamethasone at the time of the first dose of antibiotic

Physiologic replacement: Oral, I.M., I.V.: 0.03-0.15 mg/kg/day or 0.6-0.75 mg/m²/day in divided doses every 6-12 hours

Adults:

Acute nonlymphoblastic leukemia (ANLL) protocol: I.V.: 2 mg/m²/dose every 8 hours for 12 doses

Antiemetic (prior to chemotherapy): Oral/I.V. (should be given as sodium phosphate): 10 mg/m²/dose (usually 20 mg) for first dose then 5 mg/m²/dose every 6 hours as needed

Anti-inflammatory:

Oral, I.M., I.V. (injections should be given as sodium phosphate): 0.75-9 mg/day in divided doses every 6-12 hours

I.M. (as acetate): 8-16 mg; may repeat in 1-3 weeks

Intralesional (as acetate): 0.8-1.6 mg

Intra-articular/soft tissue (as acetate): 4-16 mg; may repeat in 1-3 weeks

Intra-articular, intralesional, or soft tissue (as sodium phosphate): 0.4-6 mg/day

Cerebral edema: I.V. 10 mg stat, 4 mg I.M./I.V. (should be given as sodium phosphate) every 6 hours until response is maximized, then switch to oral regimen, then taper off if appropriate; dosage may be reduced after 24 days and gradually discontinued over 5-7 days

Diagnosis for Cushing's syndrome: Oral: 1 mg at 11 PM, draw blood at 8 AM the following day for plasma cortisol determination

Physiological replacement: Oral, I.M., I.V. (should be given as sodium phosphate): 0.03-0.15 mg/kg/day OR 0.6-0.75 mg/m²/day in divided doses every 6-12 hours

Shock therapy:

Addisonian crisis/shock (ie, adrenal insufficiency/responsive to steroid therapy): I.V. (given as sodium phosphate): 4-10 mg as a single dose, which may be repeated if necessary

Unresponsive shock (ie, unresponsive to steroid therapy): I.V. (given as sodium phosphate): 1-6 mg/kg as a single I.V. dose or up to 40 mg initially followed by repeat doses every 2-6 hours while shock persists

Hemodialysis: Supplemental dose is not necessary

Peritoneal dialysis: Supplemental dose is not necessary

Ophthalmic:

Ointment: Apply thin coating into conjunctival sac 3-4 times/day; gradually taper dose to discontinue

Suspension: Instill 2 drops into conjunctival sac every hour during the day and every other hour during the night; gradually reduce dose to every 3-4 hours, then to 3-4 times/day

Topical: Apply 1-4 times/day

Administration Administer oral formulation with meals to decrease GI upset

Monitoring Parameters Hemoglobin, occult blood loss, serum potassium, and glucose

Reference Range Dexamethasone suppression test, overnight: 8 AM cortisol <6 µg/100 mL (dexamethasone 1 mg); plasma cortisol determination should be made on the day after giving dose

Patient Information Notify physician of any signs of infection or injuries during therapy; inform physician or dentist before surgery if you are taking a corticosteroid; may cause GI upset, take with food; do not overuse; use only as prescribed and for no longer than the period prescribed; notify physician if condition being treated persists or worsens

Topical: Thin film of cream or ointment is effective, do not overuse; do not use tight-fitting diapers or plastic pants on children being treated in the diaper area; use only as prescribed, and for no longer than the period prescribed; rub in lightly; avoid contact with eyes; notify physician if condition being treated persists or worsens

Nursing Implications Topical formation is for external use, do not use on open wounds; apply sparingly to occlusive dressings; should not be used in the presence of open or weeping lesions; **acetate injection is not for I.V. use**

Dosage Forms

Aerosol:

Oral, as sodium phosphate: 84 mcg dexamethasone per activation (12.6 g)

Nasal, as sodium phosphate: 84 mcg dexamethasone/spray (12.6 g)

Topical: 0.01% (58 g); 0.04% (25 g)

Cream, as sodium phosphate: 0.1% (15 g, 30 g)

Elixir: 0.5 mg/5 mL (5 mL, 20 mL, 100 mL, 120 mL, 237 mL, 240 mL, 500 mL)

Injection, as acetate suspension: 8 mg/mL (1 mL, 5 mL); 16 mg/mL (1 mL, 5 mL)

Injection, as sodium phosphate: 4 mg/mL (1 mL, 5 mL, 10 mL, 25 mL, 30 mL); 10 mg/mL (1 mL, 10 mL); 20 mg/mL (5 mL); 24 mg/mL (5 mL, 10 mL)

Ointment, ophthalmic, as sodium phosphate: 0.05% (3.5 g)

Solution, oral:

Concentrate: 0.5 mg/0.5 mL (30 mL) (30% alcohol)

Oral: 0.5 mg/5 mL (5 mL, 20 mL, 500 mL)

Suspension, ophthalmic, as sodium phosphate: 0.1% with methylcellulose 0.5% (5 mL, 15 mL)

Tablet: 0.25 mg, 0.5 mg, 0.75 mg, 1 mg, 1.5 mg, 2 mg, 4 mg, 6 mg

Tablet, therapeutic pack: 6 x 1.5 mg; 8 x 0.75 mg

- ◆ **Dexamethasone Acetate** see Dexamethasone on page 337
- ◆ **Dexamethasone and Tobramycin** see Tobramycin and Dexamethasone on page 1152
- ◆ **Dexamethasone Sodium Phosphate** see Dexamethasone on page 337
- ◆ **Dexasone L.A.®** see Dexamethasone on page 337
- ◆ **Dexasporin®** see Neomycin, Polymyxin B, and Dexamethasone on page 826
- ◆ **Dexatrim® Pre-Meal [OTC]** see Phenylpropanolamine on page 919
- ◆ **Dexchlor®** see Dexchlorpheniramine on this page

Dexchlorpheniramine (deks klor fen EER a meen)

U.S. Brand Names Dexchlor®; Poladex®; Polaramine®

Synonyms Dexchlorpheniramine Maleate

Therapeutic Category Antihistamine, H₁ Blocker

Use Perennial and seasonal allergic rhinitis and other allergic symptoms including urticaria

Pregnancy Risk Factor B

Contraindications Narrow-angle glaucoma, hypersensitivity to dexchlorpheniramine or any component

(Continued)

Dexchlorpheniramine *(Continued)*

Usual Dosage Oral:

Children:

2-5 years: 0.5 mg every 4-6 hours (do not use timed release)

6-11 years: 1 mg every 4-6 hours or 4 mg timed release at bedtime

Adults: 2 mg every 4-6 hours or 4-6 mg timed release at bedtime or every 8-10 hours

Additional Information Complete prescribing information for this medication should be consulted for additional detail

Dosage Forms

Syrup, as maleate (orange flavor): 2 mg/5 mL with alcohol 6% (480 mL)

Tablet, as maleate: 2 mg

Tablet, as maleate, sustained action: 4 mg, 6 mg

- **Dexchlorpheniramine Maleate** *see Dexchlorpheniramine on previous page*
- **Dexedrine®** *see Dextroamphetamine on page 342*
- **Dexferrum®** *see Iron Dextran Complex on page 630*
- **Dexone®** *see Dexamethasone on page 337*
- **Dexone L.A.®** *see Dexamethasone on page 337*

Dexpanthenol *(deks PAN the nole)*

U.S. Brand Names Ilopan®; Ilopan-Choline®; Panthoderm® [OTC]

Synonyms Pantothenyl Alcohol

Therapeutic Category Gastrointestinal Agent, Stimulant

Use Prophylactic use to minimize paralytic ileus, treatment of postoperative distention

Pregnancy Risk Factor C

Contraindications Hemophilia; mechanical obstruction of ileus

Usual Dosage

Children and Adults: Relief of itching and aid in skin healing: Topical: Apply to affected area 1-2 times/day

Adults:

Relief of gas retention: Oral: 2-3 tablets 3 times/day

Prevention of postoperative ileus: I.M.: 250-500 mg stat, repeat in 2 hours, followed by doses every 6 hours until danger passes

Paralyzed ileus: I.M.: 500 mg stat, repeat in 2 hours, followed by doses every 6 hours, if needed

Additional Information Complete prescribing information for this medication should be consulted for additional detail

Dosage Forms

Cream: 2% (30 g, 60 g)

Injection (Ilopan®): 250 mg/mL (2 mL, 10 mL, 30 mL)

Tablet (Ilopan-Choline®): 50 mg with choline bitartrate 25 mg

Dexrazoxane *(deks ray ZOKS ane)*

U.S. Brand Names Zinecard®

Therapeutic Category Cardioprotective Agent

Use Reduction of the incidence and severity of cardiomyopathy associated with doxorubicin administration in women with metastatic breast cancer who have received a cumulative doxorubicin dose of 300 mg/m^2 and who would benefit from continuing therapy with doxorubicin. It is not recommended for use with the initiation of doxorubicin therapy.

Pregnancy Risk Factor C

Pregnancy/Breast-Feeding Implications

Clinical effects on the fetus: Avoid use in pregnant women unless the potential benefit justifies the potential risk to the fetus

Breast-feeding/lactation: Discontinue nursing during dexrazoxane therapy

Contraindications Do not use with chemotherapy regimens that do not contain an anthracycline

Warnings/Precautions Dexrazoxane may add to the myelosuppression caused by chemotherapeutic agents. There is some evidence that the use of dexrazoxane concurrently with the initiation of fluorouracil, doxorubicin, and cyclophosphamide (FAC) therapy interferes with the antitumor efficacy of the regimen, and this use is not recommended. Dexrazoxane should only be used in those patients who have received a cumulative doxorubicin dose of 300 mg/m^2 and are continuing with doxorubicin therapy. Dexrazoxane does not eliminate the potential for anthracycline-induced cardiac toxicity. Carefully monitor cardiac function.

Adverse Reactions The adverse experiences are likely attributable to the FAC regimen, with the exception of pain on injection that was observed mainly with dexrazoxane. Patients receiving FAC with dexrazoxane experienced more severe leukopenia, granulocytopenia, and thrombocytopenia at nadir than patients receiving FAC without dexrazoxane; but recovery counts were similar for the two groups.

1% to 2%: Dermatologic: Urticaria, recall skin reaction, extravasation

Overdosage/Toxicology Management includes good supportive care until resolution of myelosuppression, and related conditions, is complete. Management of overdose should include treatment of infections, fluid regulation, and management of nutritional requirements. Retention of a significant dose fraction of the unchanged drug in the plasma pool, minimal tissue partitioning or binding and availability of >90% of the systemic drug levels in the unbound form suggest that dexrazoxane could be removed using conventional peritoneal or hemodialysis.

Drug Interactions Decreased effect: There is some evidence that the use of dexrazoxane concurrently with the initiation of FAC therapy interferes with the antitumor efficacy of the regimen, and this use is not recommended

Stability

Store intact vials at controlled room temperature, (15°C to 30°C/59°F to 86°F). Reconstituted and diluted solutions are stable for 6 hours at controlled room temperature or under refrigeration (2°C to 8°C/36°F to 46°F).

Must be reconstituted with 0.167 Molar (M/6) sodium lactate injection to a concentration of 10 mg dexrazoxane/mL sodium lactate. Reconstituted dexrazoxane solution may be diluted with either 0.9% sodium chloride injection or 5% dextrose injection to a concentration of 1.3-5 mg/mL in intravenous infusion bags.

Caution should be exercised in the handling and preparation of the reconstituted solution; the use of gloves is recommended. If dexrazoxane powder or solutions contact the skin or mucosae, immediately wash with soap and water.

Mechanism of Action Derivative of EDTA and potent intracellular chelating agent. The mechanism of cardioprotectant activity is not fully understood. Appears to be converted intracellularly to a ring-opened chelating agent that interferes with iron-mediated free radical generation thought to be responsible, in part, for anthracycline-induced cardiomyopathy.

Pharmacodynamics/Kinetics

Distribution: V_d: 22-22.4 L/m^2; not bound to plasma proteins

Half-life: 2.1-2.5 hours

Elimination: 42% of dose excreted in the urine; renal clearance: 3.35 L/hour/m^2; plasma clearance: 6.25-7.88 L/hour/m^2

Usual Dosage Adults: I.V.: The recommended dosage ratio of dexrazoxane:doxorubicin is 10:1 (eg, 500 mg/m^2 dexrazoxane:50 mg/m^2 doxorubicin). Administer the reconstituted solution by slow I.V. push or rapid I.V. infusion from a bag. After completing the infusion, and prior to a total elapsed time of 30 minutes (from the beginning of the dexrazoxane infusion), administer the I.V. injection of doxorubicin.

Administration Doxorubicin should not be given prior to the I.V. injection of dexrazoxane. Administer dexrazoxane by slow I.V. push or rapid drip I.V. infusion from a bag. Administer doxorubicin within 30 minutes after beginning the infusion with dexrazoxane.

Monitoring Parameters Since dexrazoxane will always be used with cytotoxic drugs, and since it may add to the myelosuppressive effects of cytotoxic drugs, frequent complete blood counts are recommended

Nursing Implications Observe for signs and symptoms of cardiac toxicity, infection, and anemia

Additional Information Reimbursement Guarantee Program: 1-800-808-9111

Dosage Forms Powder for injection, lyophilized: 250 mg, 500 mg (10 mg/mL when reconstituted)

Dextran (DEKS tran)

U.S. Brand Names Gentran®; LMD®; Macrodex®; Rheomacrodex®

Synonyms Dextran 40; Dextran 70; Dextran, High Molecular Weight; Dextran, Low Molecular Weight

Therapeutic Category Plasma Volume Expander, Colloid

Use Blood volume expander used in treatment of shock or impending shock when blood or blood products are not available

Pregnancy Risk Factor C

Contraindications Hypersensitivity to dextrans or components (see Dextran 1)

Warnings/Precautions Use caution in patients with CHF, renal insufficiency, thrombocytopenia, or active hemorrhage; **observe patients closely during the first minute of infusion and have other means of maintaining circulation and epinephrine and diphenhydramine available should dextran therapy result in an anaphylactoid reaction;** patients should be well hydrated at the start of therapy; discontinue dextran if urine specific gravity is low and/or if oliguria or anuria occurs or if there is a precipitous rise in central venous pressure and signs of circulatory overload

Adverse Reactions <1%: Mild hypotension, tightness of chest, fever, urticaria, nausea, vomiting, arthralgia, nasal congestion, wheezing, anaphylaxis

Overdosage/Toxicology

Symptoms include fluid overload, pulmonary edema, increased bleeding time, decreased platelet function

Treatment is supportive, blood products containing clotting factors may be necessary

Stability Store at room temperature; discard partially used containers

Mechanism of Action Produces plasma volume expansion by virtue of its highly colloidal starch structure, similar to albumin

Pharmacodynamics/Kinetics

Onset of action: I.V.: Within minutes to 1 hour (depending upon the molecular weight polysaccharide administered), infusion volume expansion occurs

Elimination: ~75% excreted in urine within 24 hours

Usual Dosage I.V.: (requires an infusion pump):

Children: Total dose should not be >20 mL/kg during first 24 hours

Adults: 500-1000 mL at rate of 20-40 mL/minute; if therapy continues beyond 24 hours, total daily dosage should not exceed 10 mL/kg and therapy should not continue beyond 5 days

Dosing in renal and/or hepatic impairment: Use with extreme caution

Administration I.V. infusion only (use an infusion pump)

(Continued)

Dextran *(Continued)*

Monitoring Parameters Observe patient for signs of circulatory overload and/or monitor central venous pressure; observe patients closely during the first minute of infusion and have other means of maintaining circulation should dextran therapy result in an anaphylactoid reaction

Nursing Implications Patients should be well hydrated at the start of therapy; discontinue dextran if urine specific gravity is low, and/or if oliguria or anuria occurs, or if there is a precipitous rise in central venous pressure or sign of circulatory overloading

Dosage Forms Injection:

High molecular weight:

6% dextran 75 in dextrose 5% (500 mL)

Gentran®: 6% dextran 75 in sodium chloride 0.9% (500 mL)

Gentran®, Macrodex®: 6% dextran 70 in sodium chloride 0.9% (500 mL)

Macrodex®: 6% dextran 70 in dextrose 5% (500 mL)

Low molecular weight: Gentran®, LMD®, Rheomacrodex®:

10% dextran 40 in dextrose 5% (500 mL)

10% dextran 40 in sodium chloride 0.9% (500 mL)

Dextran 1 (DEKS tran won)

U.S. Brand Names Promit®

Therapeutic Category Dextran Adjunct; Plasma Volume Expander, Colloid

Use Prophylaxis of serious anaphylactic reactions to I.V. infusion of dextran

Pregnancy Risk Factor C

Contraindications Known hypersensitivity to dextrans or any component

Warnings/Precautions If immune adverse reactions occur, do not administer large volumes of dextran solutions for clinical use

Adverse Reactions <1%: Mild hypotension, tightness of chest, fever, urticaria, nausea, vomiting, cutaneous reactions, arthralgia, nasal congestion, wheezing

Stability Protect from freezing

Mechanism of Action Binds to dextran-reactive immunoglobulin without bridge formation and no formation of large immune complexes

Usual Dosage I.V. (time between dextran 1 and dextran solution should not exceed 15 minutes):

Children: 0.3 mL/kg 1-2 minutes before I.V. infusion of dextran

Adults: 20 mL 1-2 minutes before I.V. infusion of dextran

Nursing Implications Do not dilute or admix with dextrans

Dosage Forms Injection: 150 mg/mL (20 mL)

♦ **Dextran 40** *see Dextran on previous page*

♦ **Dextran 70** *see Dextran on previous page*

♦ **Dextran, High Molecular Weight** *see Dextran on previous page*

♦ **Dextran, Low Molecular Weight** *see Dextran on previous page*

Dextranomer (deks TRAN oh mer)

U.S. Brand Names Debrisan® [OTC]

Therapeutic Category Topical Skin Product

Use Clean exudative ulcers and wounds such as venous stasis ulcers, decubitus ulcers, and infected traumatic and surgical wounds; no controlled studies have found dextranomer to be more effective than conventional therapy

Pregnancy Risk Factor C

Contraindications Deep fistulas, sinus tracts, hypersensitivity to any component

Warnings/Precautions Do not use in deep fistulas or any area where complete removal is not assured; do not use on dry wounds (ineffective); avoid contact with eyes

Adverse Reactions 1% to 10%:

Local: Transitory pain, blistering

Dermatologic: Maceration may occur, erythema

Hematologic: Bleeding

Mechanism of Action Dextranomer is a network of dextran-sucrose beads possessing a great many exposed hydroxy groups; when this network is applied to an exudative wound surface, the exudate is drawn by capillary forces generated by the swelling of the beads, with vacuum forces producing an upward flow of exudate into the network

Usual Dosage Debride and clean wound prior to application; apply to affected area once or twice daily in a 1/4" layer; apply a dressing and seal on all four sides; removal should be done by irrigation

Patient Information For external use only; avoid contact with eyes; contact physician if condition worsens or persists beyond 14-21 days

Nursing Implications Sprinkle beads into ulcer (or apply paste) to 1/4" thickness; change dressings 1-4 times/day depending on drainage; change dressing before it is completely dry to facilitate removal

Dosage Forms

Beads: 4 g, 25 g, 60 g, 120 g

Paste: 10 g foil packets

Dextroamphetamine (deks troe am FET a meen)

U.S. Brand Names Dexedrine®; Oxydess® II; Spancap® No. 1

Synonyms Dextroamphetamine Sulfate

Therapeutic Category Amphetamine; Anorexiant; Central Nervous System Stimulant, Amphetamine

Use Narcolepsy, exogenous obesity, abnormal behavioral syndrome in children (minimal brain dysfunction), attention deficit/hyperactivity disorder (ADHD)

Restrictions C-II

Pregnancy Risk Factor C

Contraindications Hypersensitivity to dextroamphetamine or any component; advanced arteriosclerosis, hypertension, hyperthyroidism, glaucoma, MAO inhibitors

Warnings/Precautions Use with caution in patients with psychopathic personalities, cardiovascular disease, HTN, angina, and glaucoma; has high potential for abuse; use in weight reduction programs only when alternative therapy has been ineffective; prolonged administration may lead to drug dependence

Adverse Reactions

>10%:

Cardiovascular: Arrhythmia

Central nervous system: False feeling of well being, nervousness, restlessness, insomnia

1% to 10%:

Cardiovascular: Hypertension

Central nervous system: Mood or mental changes, dizziness, lightheadedness, headache

Endocrine & metabolic: Changes in libido

Gastrointestinal: Diarrhea, nausea, vomiting, stomach cramps, constipation, anorexia, weight loss, xerostomia

Ocular: Blurred vision

Miscellaneous: Diaphoresis (increased)

<1%: Chest pain, CNS stimulation (severe), Tourette's syndrome, hyperthermia, seizures, paranoia, rash, urticaria, tolerance and withdrawal with prolonged use

Overdosage/Toxicology

Symptoms of overdose include restlessness, tremor, confusion, hallucinations, panic, dysrhythmias, nausea, vomiting

There is no specific antidote for dextroamphetamine intoxication and the bulk of the treatment is supportive. Hyperactivity and agitation usually respond to reduced sensory input; however, with extreme agitation, haloperidol (2-5 mg I.M. for adults) may be required.

Hyperthermia is best treated with external cooling measures, or when severe or unresponsive, muscle paralysis with pancuronium may be needed

Hypertension is usually transient and generally does not require treatment unless severe. For diastolic blood pressures >110 mm Hg, a nitroprusside infusion should be initiated.

Seizures usually respond to diazepam I.V. and/or phenytoin maintenance regimens

Drug Interactions

Decreased effect: Methyldopa decreased antihypertensive efficacy; ethosuximide; decreased effect with acidifiers, psychotropics

Increased toxicity: May precipitate hypertensive crisis in patients receiving MAO inhibitors and arrhythmias in patients receiving general anesthetics

Increased effect/toxicity of TCAs, phenytoin, phenobarbital, propoxyphene, norepinephrine and meperidine

Stability Protect from light

Mechanism of Action Blocks reuptake of dopamine and norepinephrine from the synapse, thus increases the amount of circulating dopamine and norepinephrine in cerebral cortex to reticular activating system; inhibits the action of monoamine oxidase and causes catecholamines to be released

Pharmacodynamics/Kinetics

Onset of action: 1-1.5 hours

Metabolism: In the liver

Half-life: Adults: 34 hours (pH dependent)

Time to peak serum concentration: Oral: Within 3 hours

Elimination: In urine as unchanged drug and inactive metabolites after oral dose

Usual Dosage Oral:

Children:

Narcolepsy: 6-12 years: Initial: 5 mg/day, may increase at 5 mg increments in weekly intervals until side effects appear; maximum dose: 60 mg/day

Attention deficit/hyperactivity disorder:

3-5 years: Initial: 2.5 mg/day given every morning; increase by 2.5 mg/day in weekly intervals until optimal response is obtained, usual range: 0.1-0.5 mg/kg/dose every morning with maximum of 40 mg/day

≥6 years: 5 mg once or twice daily; increase in increments of 5 mg/day at weekly intervals until optimal response is reached, usual range: 0.1-0.5 mg/kg/dose every morning (5-20 mg/day) with maximum of 40 mg/day

Children >12 years and Adults:

Narcolepsy: Initial: 10 mg/day, may increase at 10 mg increments in weekly intervals until side effects appear; maximum: 60 mg/day

Exogenous obesity: 5-30 mg/day in divided doses of 5-10 mg 30-60 minutes before meals

Administration Administer as single dose in morning or as divided doses with breakfast and lunch

Monitoring Parameters Growth in children and CNS activity in all

(Continued)

Dextroamphetamine *(Continued)*

Patient Information Take during day to avoid insomnia; do not discontinue abruptly, may cause physical and psychological dependence with prolonged use

Nursing Implications Last daily dose should be given 6 hours before retiring; do not crush sustained release drug product

Dosage Forms
Capsule, as sulfate, sustained release: 5 mg, 10 mg, 15 mg
Elixir, as sulfate: 5 mg/5 mL (480 mL)
Tablet, as sulfate: 5 mg, 10 mg (5 mg tablets contain tartrazine)

Dextroamphetamine and Amphetamine
(deks troe am FET a meen & am FET a meen)

U.S. Brand Names Adderall®

Therapeutic Category Amphetamine

Dosage Forms Tablet:
10 mg [dextroamphetamine sulfate 2.5 mg, dextroamphetamine saccharate 2.5 mg and amphetamine aspartate 2.5 mg, amphetamine sulfate 2.5 mg]
30 mg [dextroamphetamine sulfate 7.5 mg, dextroamphetamine saccharate 7.5 mg and amphetamine aspartate 7.55 mg, amphetamine sulfate 7.5 mg]

+ **Dextroamphetamine Sulfate** *see* Dextroamphetamine *on page 342*
+ **Dextromethorphan and Guaifenesin** *see* Guaifenesin and Dextromethorphan *on page 550*
+ **Dextropropoxyphene** *see* Propoxyphene *on page 985*

Dextrothyroxine (deks troe thye ROKS een)

U.S. Brand Names Choloxin®

Synonyms Dextrothyroxine Sodium

Therapeutic Category Antilipemic Agent

Use Reduction of elevated serum cholesterol

Pregnancy Risk Factor C

Contraindications Organic heart disease, congestive heart failure, advanced renal or hepatic disease

Usual Dosage Oral:
Children: 0.05 mg/kg/day, increase at 1-month intervals by 0.05 mg/kg/day to a maximum of 0.4 mg/kg/day or 4 mg/day
Adults: 1-2 mg/day, increase at 1-2 mg at intervals of 4 weeks, up to a maximum of 8 mg/day

Additional Information Complete prescribing information for this medication should be consulted for additional detail

Dosage Forms Tablet, as sodium: 2 mg, 4 mg, 6 mg

+ **Dextrothyroxine Sodium** *see* Dextrothyroxine *on this page*
+ **Dey-Dose® Isoproterenol** *see* Isoproterenol *on page 635*
+ **Dey-Dose® Metaproterenol** *see* Metaproterenol *on page 739*
+ **Dey-Drop® Ophthalmic Solution** *see* Silver Nitrate *on page 1061*
+ **Dey-Lute® Isoetharine** *see* Isoetharine *on page 632*

Dezocine (DEZ oh seen)

Related Information
Narcotic Agonists Comparison *on page 1328*

U.S. Brand Names Dalgan®

Therapeutic Category Analgesic, Narcotic

Use Relief of moderate to severe postoperative, acute renal and ureteral colic, and cancer pain

Pregnancy Risk Factor C

Contraindications Patients experiencing immediate type hypersensitivity reactions (anaphylaxis) to dezocine or structurally related compounds should not receive this drug. Use of other central nervous system depressants concurrently to dezocine is contraindicated.

Warnings/Precautions Use with caution in patients with head injuries or increased intracranial pressure, respiratory depression, asthma, emphysema, COPD, renal or hepatic disease, labor and delivery, biliary surgery, or in patients with a history of drug abuse; abuse potential is apparent; may be better tolerated than other opioid agonist-antagonist; does not affect cardiac performance; contains bisulfites, avoid use in those sensitive to bisulfites

Adverse Reactions
1% to 10%:
Central nervous system: Sedation, dizziness, vertigo
Gastrointestinal: Nausea, vomiting
Local: Injection site reactions
<1%: Hypotension, palpitations, bradycardia, peripheral vasodilation, increased intracranial pressure, CNS depression, drowsiness, antidiuretic hormone release, constipation, biliary tract spasm, urinary tract spasm, miosis, respiratory depression, histamine release, physical and psychological dependence with prolonged use

Overdosage/Toxicology
Symptoms of overdose include CNS and respiratory depression, gastrointestinal cramping, constipation

Naloxone 2 mg I.V. (0.01 mg/kg for children) with repeat administration as necessary up to a total of 10 mg

Drug Interactions Increased effect with CNS depressants

Stability Store at room temperature; protect from light

Mechanism of Action Binds to opiate receptors in the CNS, causing inhibition of ascending pain pathways, altering the perception of and response to pain; produces generalized CNS depression; it is a mixed agonist-antagonist that appears to bind selectively to CNS μ and Δ opiate receptors

Pharmacodynamics/Kinetics
Onset of analgesia: Within 15-30 minutes
Peak effect: 1 hour
Duration of analgesia: 4-6 hours
Half-life: 2.6-2.8 hours
Metabolism: Glucuronidated in liver
Elimination: Excretion of inactive metabolites and unchanged drug in the urine

Usual Dosage Adults (not recommended for patients <18 years):
I.M.: Initial: 5-20 mg; may be repeated every 3-6 hours as needed; maximum: 120 mg/day and 20 mg/dose
I.V.: Initial: 2.5-10 mg; may be repeated every 2-4 hours as needed
Dosing adjustment in renal impairment: Should be used cautiously at reduced doses

Monitoring Parameters Monitor blood pressure and heart rate during adjustment of dose

Patient Information Avoid driving or operating machinery until the effect of drug wears off; may cause physical and psychological dependence with prolonged use

Nursing Implications Watch closely for respiratory depression; induced respiratory depression is greater than that seen with morphine during the first hour after administration

Dosage Forms Injection, single-dose vial: 5 mg/mL (2 mL); 10 mg/mL (2 mL); 15 mg/mL (2 mL)

Diazepam (dye AZ e pam)

Related Information
Adult ACLS Algorithm, Electrical Conversion on page 1453
Anticonvulsants by Seizure Type on page 1300
Benzodiazepines Comparison on page 1310
Convulsive Status Epilepticus on page 1470
Febrile Seizures on page 1469

U.S. Brand Names Diastat® Rectal Delivery System; Diazemuls® Injection; Diazepam Intensol®; Dizac® Injectable Emulsion; Valium® Injection; Valium® Oral

Canadian Brand Names Apo®-Diazepam; Diazemuls®; E Pam®; Meval®; Novo-Dipam; PMS-Diazepam; Vivol®

Therapeutic Category Antianxiety Agent; Anticonvulsant; Benzodiazepine; Sedative

Use Management of general anxiety disorders, panic disorders, and provide preoperative sedation, light anesthesia, and amnesia; treatment of status epilepticus, alcohol withdrawal symptoms; used as a skeletal muscle relaxant

Restrictions C-IV

Pregnancy Risk Factor D

Pregnancy/Breast-Feeding Implications
Clinical effects on the fetus: Crosses the placenta. Oral clefts reported, however, more recent data does not support an association between drug and oral clefts; inguinal hernia, cardiac defects, spina bifida, dysmorphic facial features, skeletal defects, (Continued)

Diazepam *(Continued)*

multiple other malformations reported; hypotonia and withdrawal symptoms reported following use near time of delivery

Breast-feeding/lactation: Crosses into breast milk

Clinical effects on the infant: Sedation; American Academy of Pediatrics reports that USE MAY BE OF CONCERN.

Contraindications Hypersensitivity to diazepam or any component; there may be a cross-sensitivity with other benzodiazepines; do not use in a comatose patient, in those with pre-existing CNS depression, respiratory depression, narrow-angle glaucoma, or severe uncontrolled pain; do not use in pregnant women

Warnings/Precautions Use with caution in patients receiving other CNS depressants, patients with low albumin, hepatic dysfunction, and in the elderly and young infants. Due to its long-acting metabolite, diazepam is not considered a drug of choice in the elderly; long-acting benzodiazepines have been associated with falls in the elderly.

Adverse Reactions

>10%:

Cardiovascular: Cardiac arrest, bradycardia, cardiovascular collapse, tachycardia, chest pain

Central nervous system: Drowsiness, ataxia, amnesia, slurred speech, paradoxical excitement or rage, fatigue, lightheadedness, insomnia, memory impairment, headache, anxiety, depression

Dermatologic: Rash

Endocrine & metabolic: Decreased libido

Gastrointestinal: Xerostomia, changes in salivation, constipation, nausea, vomiting, diarrhea, increased or decreased appetite

Local: Phlebitis, pain with injection

Neuromuscular & skeletal: Dysarthria

Ocular: Blurred vision, diplopia

Respiratory: Decrease in respiratory rate, apnea, laryngospasm

Miscellaneous: Diaphoresis

1% to 10%:

Cardiovascular: Syncope, hypotension

Central nervous system: Confusion, nervousness, dizziness, akathisia

Dermatologic: Dermatitis

Gastrointestinal: Weight gain or loss

Neuromuscular & skeletal: Rigidity, tremor, muscle cramps

Otic: Tinnitus

Respiratory: Nasal congestion, hyperventilation

Miscellaneous: Hiccups

<1%: Menstrual irregularities, blood dyscrasias, reflex slowing, physical and psychological dependence with prolonged use

Overdosage/Toxicology

Symptoms of overdose include somnolence, confusion, coma, hypoactive reflexes, dyspnea, hypotension, slurred speech, impaired coordination

Treatment for benzodiazepine overdose is supportive. Rarely is mechanical ventilation required. Flumazenil has been shown to selectively block the binding of benzodiazepines to CNS receptors, resulting in a reversal of benzodiazepine-induced CNS depression, but not respiratory depression.

Drug Interactions CYP1A2, 2C8, and 2C9 enzyme substrate, CYP3A3/4 enzyme substrate (minor), and diazepam and desmethyldiazepam are CYP2C19 enzyme substrates

Decreased effect: Enzyme inducers may increase the metabolism of diazepam

Increased toxicity: CNS depressants (alcohol, barbiturates, opioids) may enhance sedation and respiratory depression; cimetidine may decrease the metabolism of diazepam; cisapride can significantly increase diazepam levels; valproic acid may displace diazepam from binding sites which may result in an increase in sedative effects; selective serotonin reuptake inhibitors (eg, fluoxetine, sertraline, paroxetine) have greatly increased diazepam levels by altering its clearance

Stability Protect parenteral dosage form from light; potency is retained for up to 3 months when kept at room temperature; most stable at pH 4-8, hydrolysis occurs at pH <3; do not mix I.V. product with other medications

Mechanism of Action Depresses all levels of the CNS, including the limbic and reticular formation, probably through the increased action of gamma-aminobutyric acid (GABA), which is a major inhibitory neurotransmitter in the brain

Pharmacodynamics/Kinetics

I.V. for status epilepticus: Onset of action: Almost immediate; Duration: Short, 20-30 minutes

Absorption: Oral: 85% to 100%, more reliable than I.M.

Protein binding: 98%

Metabolism: In the liver

Half-life:

Parent drug: Adults: 20-50 hours, increased half-life in neonates, elderly, and those with severe hepatic disorders

Active major metabolite (desmethyldiazepam): 50-100 hours, can be prolonged in neonates

Usual Dosage Oral absorption is more reliable than I.M.

Children:

Conscious sedation for procedures: Oral: 0.2-0.3 mg/kg (maximum: 10 mg) 45-60 minutes prior to procedure

Sedation or muscle relaxation or anxiety:

Oral: 0.12-0.8 mg/kg/day in divided doses every 6-8 hours

I.M., I.V.: 0.04-0.3 mg/kg/dose every 2-4 hours to a maximum of 0.6 mg/kg within an 8-hour period if needed

Status epilepticus:

Infants 30 days to 5 years: I.V.: 0.05-0.3 mg/kg/dose given over 2-3 minutes, every 15-30 minutes to a maximum total dose of 5 mg; repeat in 2-4 hours as needed **or** 0.2-0.5 mg/dose every 2-5 minutes to a maximum total dose of 5 mg

>5 years: I.V.: 0.05-0.3 mg/kg/dose given over 2-3 minutes every 15-30 minutes to a maximum total dose of 10 mg; repeat in 2-4 hours as needed **or** 1 mg/dose given over 2-3 minutes, every 2-5 minutes to a maximum total dose of 10 mg

Rectal: 0.5 mg/kg, then 0.25 mg/kg in 10 minutes if needed

Adolescents: Conscious sedation for procedures:

Oral: 10 mg

I.V.: 5 mg, may repeat with ½ dose if needed

Adults:

Anxiety/sedation/skeletal muscle relaxation:

Oral: 2-10 mg 2-4 times/day

I.M., I.V.: 2-10 mg, may repeat in 3-4 hours if needed

Status epilepticus: I.V.: 5-10 mg every 10-20 minutes, up to 30 mg in an 8-hour period; may repeat in 2-4 hours if necessary

Elderly: Oral: Initial:

Anxiety: 1-2 mg 1-2 times/day; increase gradually as needed, rarely need to use >10 mg/day

Skeletal muscle relaxant: 2-5 mg 2-4 times/day

Hemodialysis: Not dialyzable (0% to 5%); supplemental dose is not necessary

Dosing adjustment in hepatic impairment: Reduce dose by 50% in cirrhosis and avoid in severe/acute liver disease

Dietary Considerations Alcohol: Additive CNS depression has been reported with benzodiazepines; avoid or limit alcohol

Administration In children, do not exceed 1-2 mg/minute IVP; adults 5 mg/minute

Monitoring Parameters Respiratory rate, heart rate, blood pressure with I.V. use

Reference Range Therapeutic: Diazepam: 0.2-1.5 µg/mL (SI: 0.7-5.3 µmol/L); N-desmethyldiazepam (nordiazepam): 0.1-0.5 µg/mL (SI: 0.35-1.8 µmol/L)

Test Interactions False-negative urinary glucose determinations when using Clinistix® or Diastix®

Patient Information Avoid alcohol and other CNS depressants; avoid activities needing good psychomotor coordination until CNS effects are known; drug may cause physical or psychological dependence; avoid abrupt discontinuation after prolonged use

Nursing Implications Provide safety measures (ie, side rails, night light, and call button); supervise ambulation

Dosage Forms

Gel, rectal delivery system (Diastat®):

Pediatric rectal tip (4.4 cm): 5 mg/mL (2.5 mg, 5 mg, 10 mg) [twin packs]

Adult rectal tip (6 cm): 5 mg/mL (10 mg, 15 mg, 20 mg) [twin packs]

Injection: 5 mg/mL (1 mL, 2 mL, 5 mL, 10 mL)

Injection, emulsified:

Dizac®: 5 mg/mL (3 mL)

Diazemuls®: 5 mg/mL (2 mL)

Solution, oral (wintergreen-spice flavor): 5 mg/5 mL (5 mL, 10 mL, 500 mL)

Solution, oral concentrate (Diazepam Intensol®): 5 mg/mL (30 mL)

Tablet: 2 mg, 5 mg, 10 mg

♦ **Diazepam Intensol®** see Diazepam on page 345

Diazoxide (dye az OKS ide)

Related Information

Hypertension Therapy on page 1479

U.S. Brand Names Hyperstat® I.V.; Proglycem® Oral

Therapeutic Category Hyperglycemic Agent; Hypoglycemic Agent, Oral

Use

Oral: Hypoglycemia related to islet cell adenoma, carcinoma, hyperplasia, or adenomatosis, nesidioblastosis, leucine sensitivity, or extrapancreatic malignancy

I.V.: Severe hypertension

Pregnancy Risk Factor C

Contraindications Hypersensitivity to diazoxide, thiazides, or other sulfonamide derivatives; hypertension associated with aortic coarctation, arteriovenous shunts, pheochromocytoma, dissecting aortic aneurysm

Warnings/Precautions Diabetes mellitus, renal or liver disease, coronary artery disease, or cerebral vascular insufficiency; patients may require a diuretic with repeated I.V. doses; use caution when reducing severely elevated blood pressure (use 150 mg minibolus only)

Adverse Reactions

1% to 10%:

Cardiovascular: Hypotension

(Continued)

Diazoxide *(Continued)*

Central nervous system: Dizziness
Gastrointestinal: Nausea, vomiting
Neuromuscular & skeletal: Weakness

<1%: Tachycardia, flushing, angina, myocardial infarction, seizures, headache, extrapyramidal symptoms and development of abnormal facies with chronic oral use, cerebral infarction, rash, hirsutism, cellulitis, hyperglycemia, ketoacidosis, sodium and water retention, hyperuricemia, inhibition of labor, anorexia, constipation, leukopenia, thrombocytopenia, pain, burning, phlebitis upon extravasation

Overdosage/Toxicology

Symptoms of overdose include hyperglycemia, ketoacidosis, hypotension
Treatment: Insulin, fluid, and electrolyte restoration; I.V. pressors may be needed to support blood pressure

Drug Interactions

Decreased effect: Diazoxide may increase phenytoin metabolism or free fraction
Increased toxicity:
Diuretics and hypotensive agents may potentiate diazoxide adverse effects
Diazoxide may decrease warfarin protein binding

Stability Protect from light, heat, and freezing; avoid using darkened solutions

Mechanism of Action Inhibits insulin release from the pancreas; produces direct smooth muscle relaxation of the peripheral arterioles which results in decrease in blood pressure and reflex increase in heart rate and cardiac output

Pharmacodynamics/Kinetics

Hyperglycemic effect: Oral: Onset of action: Within 1 hour; Duration (normal renal function): 8 hours
Hypotensive effect: I.V.: Peak: Within 5 minutes; Duration: Usually 3-12 hours
Protein binding: 90%
Half-life: Children: 9-24 hours; Adults: 20-36 hours; End-stage renal disease: >30 hours
Elimination: 50% excreted unchanged in urine

Usual Dosage

Hypertension: Children and Adults: I.V.: 1-3 mg/kg up to a maximum of 150 mg in a single injection; repeat dose in 5-15 minutes until blood pressure adequately reduced; repeat administration at intervals of 4-24 hours; monitor the blood pressure closely; do not use longer than 10 days
Hyperinsulinemic hypoglycemia: Oral: **Note:** Use lower dose listed as initial dose
Newborns and Infants: 8-15 mg/kg/day in divided doses every 8-12 hours
Children and Adults: 3-8 mg/kg/day in divided doses every 8-12 hours
Dosing adjustment in renal impairment: None
Dialysis: Elimination is not enhanced via hemo- or peritoneal dialysis; supplemental dose is not necessary

Administration I.V. diazoxide is given undiluted by rapid I.V. injection over a period of 30 seconds or less but may also be given by continuous infusion

Monitoring Parameters Blood pressure, blood glucose, serum uric acid; intravenous administration requires cardiac monitor and blood pressure monitor

Test Interactions False-negative insulin response to glucagon

Patient Information Check blood glucose carefully, monitor urine glucose/ketones; shake suspension well before using

Nursing Implications Extravasation can be treated with warm compresses; monitor blood glucose daily in patients receiving I.V. therapy

Dosage Forms

Capsule (Proglycem®): 50 mg
Injection (Hyperstat®): 15 mg/mL (1 mL, 20 mL)
Suspension, oral (chocolate-mint flavor) (Proglycem®): 50 mg/mL (30 mL)

♦ **Dibent® Injection** *see* Dicyclomine *on page 351*
♦ **Dibenzyline®** *see* Phenoxybenzamine *on page 915*

Dibucaine and Hydrocortisone *(DYE byoo kane & hye droe KOR ti sone)*

U.S. Brand Names Corticaine® Topical
Therapeutic Category Anesthetic/Corticosteroid
Dosage Forms Cream: Dibucaine 5% and hydrocortisone 5%

♦ **DIC** *see* Dacarbazine *on page 316*
♦ **Dicarbosil® [OTC]** *see* Calcium Carbonate *on page 174*

Dichlorodifluoromethane and Trichloromonofluoromethane *(dye klor oh dye flor oh METH ane & tri klor oh mon oh flor oh METH ane)*

U.S. Brand Names Fluori-Methane® Topical Spray
Therapeutic Category Analgesic, Topical
Dosage Forms Spray, topical: Dichlorodifluoromethane 15% and trichloromonofluoromethane 85%

♦ **Dichysterol** *see* Dihydrotachysterol *on page 364*

Diclofenac *(dye KLOE fen ak)*

Related Information

Nonsteroidal Anti-Inflammatory Agents Comparison *on page 1335*

U.S. Brand Names Cataflam® Oral; Voltaren® Ophthalmic; Voltaren® Oral; Voltaren-XR® Oral

Canadian Brand Names Apo®-Diclo; Novo-Difenac®; Novo-Difenac®-SR; Nu-Diclo; Voltaren Rapide®

Synonyms Diclofenac Potassium; Diclofenac Sodium

Therapeutic Category Analgesic, Nonsteroidal Anti-inflammatory Drug; Anti-inflammatory Agent; Anti-inflammatory Agent, Ophthalmic; Nonsteroidal Anti-inflammatory Drug (NSAID), Ophthalmic; Nonsteroidal Anti-inflammatory Drug (NSAID), Oral

Use Acute treatment of mild to moderate pain; acute and chronic treatment of rheumatoid arthritis, ankylosing spondylitis, and osteoarthritis; used for juvenile rheumatoid arthritis, gout, dysmenorrhea; ophthalmic solution for postoperative inflammation after cataract extraction

Pregnancy Risk Factor B

Contraindications Known hypersensitivity to diclofenac, any component, aspirin or other nonsteroidal anti-inflammatory drugs (NSAIDs); porphyria

Warnings/Precautions Use with caution in patients with congestive heart failure, hypertension, decreased renal or hepatic function, history of GI disease, or those receiving anticoagulants

Adverse Reactions

>10%:
  Dermatologic: Rash
  Gastrointestinal: Abdominal cramps, heartburn, indigestion, nausea

1% to 10%:
  Cardiovascular: Angina pectoris, arrhythmias
  Central nervous system: Dizziness, nervousness
  Dermatologic: Itching
  Gastrointestinal: GI ulceration, vomiting
  Genitourinary: Vaginal bleeding
  Otic: Tinnitus

<1%: Chest pain, congestive heart failure, hypertension, tachycardia, convulsions, forgetfulness, mental depression, drowsiness, insomnia, urticaria, exfoliative dermatitis, erythema multiforme, Stevens-Johnson syndrome, angioedema, stomatitis, cystitis, agranulocytosis, anemia, pancytopenia, leukopenia, thrombocytopenia, hepatitis, peripheral neuropathy, trembling, weakness, blurred vision, change in vision, decreased hearing, interstitial nephritis, nephrotic syndrome, renal impairment, wheezing, laryngeal edema, shortness of breath, epistaxis, anaphylaxis, diaphoresis (increased)

Overdosage/Toxicology

Symptoms of overdose include acute renal failure, vomiting, drowsiness, leukocytosis

Management of a nonsteroidal anti-inflammatory drug (NSAID) intoxication is primarily supportive and symptomatic. Fluid therapy is commonly effective in managing the hypotension that may occur following an acute NSAID overdose, except when this is due to an acute blood loss.

Drug Interactions CYP2C8 and 2C9 enzyme substrate; CYP2C9 enzyme inhibitor

Decreased effect with aspirin; decreased effect of thiazides, furosemide

Increased toxicity of digoxin, methotrexate, cyclosporine, lithium, insulin, sulfonylureas, potassium-sparing diuretics, aspirin, warfarin

Mechanism of Action Inhibits prostaglandin synthesis by decreasing the activity of the enzyme, cyclo-oxygenase, which results in decreased formation of prostaglandin precursors

Pharmacodynamics/Kinetics

Onset of action: Cataflam® has a more rapid onset of action than does the sodium salt (Voltaren®), because it is absorbed in the stomach instead of the duodenum

Protein binding: 99%

Metabolism: In the liver to inactive metabolites

Half-life: 2 hours

Time to peak serum concentration: Cataflam®: Within 1 hour; Voltaren®: Within 2 hours

Elimination: Primarily in urine

Usual Dosage Adults:

Oral:

Analgesia: Starting dose: 50 mg 3 times/day

Rheumatoid arthritis: 150-200 mg/day in 2-4 divided doses (100 mg/day of sustained release product)

Osteoarthritis: 100-150 mg/day in 2-3 divided doses (100-200 mg/day of sustained release product)

Ankylosing spondylitis: 100-125 mg/day in 4-5 divided doses

Ophthalmic: Instill 1 drop into affected eye 4 times/day beginning 24 hours after cataract surgery and continuing for 2 weeks

Monitoring Parameters Monitor CBC, liver enzymes; monitor urine output and BUN/serum creatinine in patients receiving diuretics; occult blood loss

Patient Information Do not crush tablets; take with food, milk, or water; report any signs of blood in stool

Nursing Implications Do not crush tablets

Additional Information

Diclofenac potassium = Cataflam®; potassium content: 5.8 mg (0.15 mEq) per 50 mg tablet

Diclofenac sodium = Voltaren®

Diclofenac sodium = Voltaren®-XR

Dosage Forms

Solution, ophthalmic, as sodium (Voltaren®): 0.1% (2.5 mL, 5 mL)

Tablet, enteric coated, as sodium: 25 mg, 50 mg, 75 mg

(Continued)

Diclofenac *(Continued)*

Voltaren®: 25 mg, 50 mg, 75 mg
Tablet, extended release, as sodium (Voltaren®-XR): 100 mg
Tablet, as potassium (Cataflam®): 50 mg

Diclofenac and Misoprostol *(dye KLOE fen ak & mye soe PROST ole)*

U.S. Brand Names Arthrotec®

Therapeutic Category Analgesic, Nonsteroidal Anti-inflammatory Drug; Prostaglandin

Dosage Forms Tablet: Diclofenac 50 mg and misoprostol 200 mcg; diclofenac 75 mg and misoprostol 200 mcg

♦ **Diclofenac Potassium** *see* Diclofenac *on page 348*
♦ **Diclofenac Sodium** *see* Diclofenac *on page 348*

Dicloxacillin *(dye kloks a SIL in)*

Related Information
Animal and Human Bites Guidelines *on page 1399*

U.S. Brand Names Dycill®; Dynapen®; Pathocil®

Synonyms Dicloxacillin Sodium

Therapeutic Category Antibiotic, Penicillin

Use Treatment of systemic infections such as pneumonia, skin and soft tissue infections, and osteomyelitis caused by penicillinase-producing staphylococci

Pregnancy Risk Factor B

Contraindications Known hypersensitivity to dicloxacillin, penicillin, or any components

Warnings/Precautions Monitor PT if patient concurrently on warfarin; elimination of drug is slow in neonates; use with caution in patients allergic to cephalosporins; bad taste of suspension may make compliance difficult

Adverse Reactions
1% to 10%: Gastrointestinal: Nausea, diarrhea, abdominal pain
<1%: Fever, seizures with extremely high doses and/or renal failure, rash (maculopapular to exfoliative), vomiting, pseudomembranous colitis, vaginitis, eosinophilia, leukopenia, neutropenia, thrombocytopenia, agranulocytosis, anemia, hemolytic anemia, prolonged PT, hepatotoxicity, transient elevated LFTs, hematuria, interstitial nephritis, increased BUN/creatinine, serum sickness-like reactions, hypersensitivity

Overdosage/Toxicology
Symptoms of penicillin overdose include neuromuscular hypersensitivity (agitation, hallucinations, asterixis, encephalopathy, confusion, and seizures) and electrolyte imbalance with potassium or sodium salts, especially in renal failure
Hemodialysis may be helpful to aid in the removal of the drug from the blood, otherwise most treatment is supportive or symptom directed

Drug Interactions
Decreased effect: Efficacy of oral contraceptives may be reduced; decreased effect of warfarin
Increased effect: Disulfiram, probenecid may increase penicillin levels

Stability Refrigerate suspension after reconstitution; discard after 14 days if refrigerated or 7 days if kept at room temperature; unit dose antibiotic oral syringes are stable for 48 hours

Mechanism of Action Inhibits bacterial cell wall synthesis by binding to one or more of the penicillin binding proteins (PBPs); which in turn inhibits the final transpeptidation step of peptidoglycan synthesis in bacterial cell walls, thus inhibiting cell wall biosynthesis. Bacteria eventually lyse due to ongoing activity of cell wall autolytic enzymes (autolysins and murein hydrolases) while cell wall assembly is arrested.

Pharmacodynamics/Kinetics
Absorption: 35% to 76% from GI tract; food decreases rate and extent of absorption
Distribution: Crosses the placenta; distributes into breast milk; distributed throughout body with highest concentrations in kidney and liver; CSF penetration is low
Protein binding: 96%
Half-life: 0.6-0.8 hours, slightly prolonged in patients with renal impairment
Time to peak serum concentration: Within 0.5-2 hours
Elimination: Prolonged in neonates; partially eliminated by the liver and excreted in bile, 56% to 70% is eliminated in urine as unchanged drug

Usual Dosage Oral:
Use in newborns not recommended
Children <40 kg: 12.5-25 mg/kg/day divided every 6 hours; doses of 50-100 mg/kg/day in divided doses every 6 hours have been used for therapy of osteomyelitis
Children >40 kg and Adults: 125-250 mg every 6 hours
Dosage adjustment in renal impairment: Not necessary
Hemodialysis: Not dialyzable (0% to 5%); supplemental dosage not necessary
Peritoneal dialysis: Supplemental dosage not necessary
Continuous arteriovenous or venovenous hemofiltration (CAVH/CAVHD): Supplemental dosage not necessary

Dietary Considerations Food: Decreases drug absorption rate; decreases drug serum concentration. Administer on an empty stomach 1 hour before or 2 hours after meals.

Monitoring Parameters Monitor prothrombin time if patient concurrently on warfarin; monitor for signs of anaphylaxis during first dose

Test Interactions False-positive urine and serum proteins; false-positive in uric acid, urinary steroids; may interfere with urinary glucose tests using cupric sulfate (Benedict's solution, Clinitest®); may inactivate aminoglycosides *in vitro*

Patient Information Take until all medication used; take 1 hour before or 2 hours after meals, do not skip doses

Additional Information
    Sodium content of 250 mg capsule: 13 mg (0.6 mEq)
    Sodium content of suspension 65 mg/5 mL: 27 mg (1.2 mEq)

Dosage Forms
    Capsule, as sodium: 125 mg, 250 mg, 500 mg
    Powder for oral suspension, as sodium: 62.5 mg/5 mL (80 mL, 100 mL, 200 mL)

♦ **Dicloxacillin Sodium** *see* Dicloxacillin *on previous page*

Dicyclomine (dye SYE kloe meen)

U.S. Brand Names Antispas® Injection; Bentyl® Hydrochloride Injection; Bentyl® Hydrochloride Oral; Byclomine® Injection; Dibent® Injection; Dilomine® Injection; Di-Spaz® Injection; Di-Spaz® Oral; Or-Tyl® Injection

Canadian Brand Names Bentylol®; Formulex®

Synonyms Dicyclomine Hydrochloride; Dicycloverine Hydrochloride

Therapeutic Category Antispasmodic Agent, Gastrointestinal

Use Treatment of functional disturbances of GI motility such as irritable bowel syndrome
    Unlabeled use: Urinary incontinence

Pregnancy Risk Factor B

Contraindications Hypersensitivity to any anticholinergic drug; narrow-angle glaucoma, myasthenia gravis; should not be used in infants <6 months of age; nursing mothers

Warnings/Precautions Use with caution in patients with hepatic or renal disease, ulcerative colitis, hyperthyroidism, cardiovascular disease, hypertension, tachycardia, GI obstruction, obstruction of the urinary tract. The elderly are at increased risk for anticholinergic effects, confusion and hallucinations.

Adverse Reactions Adverse reactions are included here that have been reported for pharmacologically similar drugs with anticholinergic/antispasmodic action

    Cardiovascular: Syncope, tachycardia, palpitations
    Central nervous system: Dizziness, lightheadedness, tingling, headache, drowsiness, nervousness, numbness, mental confusion and/or excitement, dyskinesia, lethargy, speech disturbance, insomnia
    Dermatologic: Rash, urticaria, itching, and other dermal manifestations; severe allergic reaction or drug idiosyncrasies including anaphylaxis
    Endocrine & metabolic: Suppression of lactation
    Gastrointestinal: Xerostomia, nausea, vomiting, constipation, bloated feeling, abdominal pain, taste loss, anorexia
    Genitourinary: Urinary hesitancy, urinary retention, impotence
    Neuromuscular & skeletal: Weakness
    Ocular: Blurred vision, diplopia, mydriasis, cycloplegia, increased ocular tension
    Respiratory: Dyspnea, apnea, asphyxia, nasal stuffiness or congestion, sneezing, throat congestion
    Miscellaneous: Decreased diaphoresis

Overdosage/Toxicology
    Symptoms of overdose include CNS stimulation followed by depression, confusion, delusions, nonreactive pupils, tachycardia, hypertension
    Anticholinergic toxicity is caused by strong binding of the drug to cholinergic receptors. For anticholinergic overdose with severe life-threatening symptoms, physostigmine 1-2 mg (0.5 mg or 0.02 mg/kg for children) S.C. or I.V., slowly may be given to reverse these effects.

Drug Interactions
    Decreased effect: Phenothiazines, anti-Parkinson's drugs, haloperidol, sustained release dosage forms; decreased effect with antacids
    Increased toxicity: Anticholinergics, amantadine, narcotic analgesics, type I antiarrhythmics, antihistamines, phenothiazines, TCAs

Mechanism of Action Blocks the action of acetylcholine at parasympathetic sites in smooth muscle, secretory glands and the CNS

Pharmacodynamics/Kinetics
    Onset of effect: 1-2 hours
    Duration: Up to 4 hours
    Absorption: Oral: Well absorbed
    Metabolism: Extensive
    Half-life: Initial phase: 1.8 hours; Terminal phase: 9-10 hours
    Elimination: In urine with only a small amount excreted as unchanged drug

Usual Dosage
    Oral:
        Infants >6 months: 5 mg/dose 3-4 times/day
        Children: 10 mg/dose 3-4 times/day
        Adults: Begin with 80 mg/day in 4 equally divided doses, then increase up to 160 mg/day
    I.M. **(should not be used I.V.):** Adults: 80 mg/day in 4 divided doses (20 mg/dose)

Dietary Considerations Alcohol: Additive CNS effects, avoid use

Administration Do not administer I.V.

Monitoring Parameters Pulse, anticholinergic effect, urinary output, GI symptoms

Patient Information May cause drowsiness; avoid alcohol; may impair coordination and judgment; may cause blurred vision or dizziness; take 30-60 minutes before a meal; may cause dry mouth, difficult urination, or constipation

Nursing Implications Raise bed rails, institute safety measures
(Continued)

Dicyclomine *(Continued)*

Dosage Forms

Capsule, as hydrochloride: 10 mg, 20 mg

Injection, as hydrochloride: 10 mg/mL (2 mL, 10 mL)

Syrup, as hydrochloride: 10 mg/5 mL (118 mL, 473 mL, 946 mL)

Tablet, as hydrochloride: 20 mg

♦ **Dicyclomine Hydrochloride** *see Dicyclomine on previous page*

♦ **Dicycloverine Hydrochloride** *see Dicyclomine on previous page*

Didanosine *(dye DAN oh seen)*

Related Information

Antiretroviral Agents *on page 1306*

Antiretroviral Therapy for HIV Infection *on page 1410*

U.S. Brand Names Videx®

Synonyms ddl

Therapeutic Category Antiretroviral Agent, Reverse Transcriptase Inhibitor; Antiviral Agent, Oral; Reverse Transcriptase Inhibitor

Use Treatment of HIV infection; always to be used in combination with at least two other antiretroviral agents

Pregnancy Risk Factor B

Pregnancy/Breast-Feeding Implications

Clinical effects on the fetus: Administer during pregnancy only if benefits to mother outweigh risks to the fetus

Breast-feeding/lactation: HIV-infected mothers are discouraged from breast-feeding to decrease potential transmission of HIV

Contraindications Hypersensitivity to any component

Warnings/Precautions Peripheral neuropathy occurs in ~35% of patients receiving the drug; pancreatitis (sometimes fatal) occurs in ~9%; risk factors for developing pancreatitis include a previous history of the condition, concurrent cytomegalovirus or *Mycobacterium avium-intracellulare* infection, and concomitant use of pentamidine or cotrimoxazole; discontinue didanosine if clinical signs of pancreatitis occur. Didanosine may cause retinal depigmentation in children receiving doses >300 mg/m²/day. Patients should undergo retinal examination every 6-12 months. Use with caution in patients with decreased renal or hepatic function, phenylketonuria, sodium-restricted diets, or with edema, congestive heart failure or hyperuricemia; in high concentrations, didanosine is mutagenic. Lactic acidosis and severe hepatomegaly have occurred with antiretroviral nucleoside analogues.

Adverse Reactions

>10%:

Central nervous system: Anxiety, headache, irritability, insomnia, restlessness

Gastrointestinal: Abdominal pain, nausea, diarrhea

Neuromuscular & skeletal: Peripheral neuropathy

1% to 10%:

Central nervous system: Depression

Dermatologic: Rash, pruritus

Gastrointestinal: Pancreatitis (2% to 3%)

<1%: Seizures, anemia, granulocytopenia, leukopenia, thrombocytopenia, hepatitis, lactic acidosis/hepatomegaly, alopecia, anaphylactoid reaction, diabetes mellitus, optic neuritis, retinal depigmentation, renal impairment, hypersensitivity

Overdosage/Toxicology

Chronic overdose may cause pancreatitis, peripheral neuropathy, diarrhea, hyperuricemia, and hepatic impairment

There is no known antidote for didanosine overdose; treatment is asymptomatic

Drug Interactions Drugs whose absorption depends on the level of acidity in the stomach such as ketoconazole, itraconazole, and dapsone should be administered at least 2 hours prior to didanosine

Decreased effect: Didanosine may decrease absorption of quinolones or tetracyclines, didanosine should be held during PCP treatment with pentamidine; didanosine may decrease levels of indinavir

Increased toxicity: Concomitant administration of other drugs which have the potential to cause peripheral neuropathy or pancreatitis may increase the risk of these toxicities

Stability Tablets should be stored in tightly closed bottles at 15°C to 30°C; undergoes rapid degradation when exposed to an acidic environment; tablets dispersed in water are stable for 1 hour at room temperature; reconstituted buffered solution is stable for 4 hours at room temperature; reconstituted pediatric solution is stable for 30 days if refrigerated; unbuffered powder for oral solution must be reconstituted and mixed with an equal volume of antacid at time of preparation

Mechanism of Action Didanosine, a purine nucleoside analogue and the deamination product of dideoxyadenosine (ddA), inhibits HIV replication *in vitro* in both T cells and monocytes. Didanosine is converted within the cell to the mono-, di-, and triphosphates of ddA. These ddA triphosphates act as substrate and inhibitor of HIV reverse transcriptase substrate and inhibitor of HIV reverse transcriptase thereby blocking viral DNA synthesis and suppressing HIV replication.

Pharmacodynamics/Kinetics

Absorption: Subject to degradation by the acidic pH of the stomach; buffered to resist the acidic pH; as much as 50% reduction in the peak plasma concentration is observed in the presence of food

Distribution: V_d: 1.08 L/kg; children: 35.6 L/m²

Protein binding: <5%

Metabolism: Has not been evaluated in man; studies conducted in dogs, shows didanosine extensively metabolized with allantoin, hypoxanthine, xanthine, and uric acid
being the major metabolites found in the urine

Bioavailability: 42%

Half-life:

Children and Adolescents: 0.8 hour

Adults:

Normal renal function: 1.5 hours; however, its active metabolite ddATP has an
intracellular half-life >12 hours *in vitro*; this permits the drug to be dosed at 12-hour
intervals; total body clearance averages 800 mL/minute

Impaired renal function: Half-life is increased, with values ranging from 2.5-5 hours

Elimination: ~55% of drug is eliminated unchanged in urine

Usual Dosage Oral (administer on an empty stomach):

Children: 180 mg/m²/day divided every 12 hours **or** dosing is based on body surface
area (m²): See table.

Didanosine — Pediatric Dosing

Body Surface Area (m²)	Dosing (Tablets) (mg bid)
≤0.4	25
0.5-0.7	50
0.8-1	75
1.1-1.4	100

Adults: Dosing is based on patient weight: See table.

Didanosine — Adult Dosing

Patient Weight (kg)	Dosing (Tablets) (mg bid)
35-49	125
50-74	200
≥75	300

Note: Children >1 year and Adults should receive 2 tablets per dose and children <1
year should receive 1 tablet per dose for adequate buffering and absorption; tablets
should be chewed; didanosine has also been used as 300 mg once daily

Dosing adjustment in renal impairment:

Recommended Dose (mg) of Didanosine by Body Weight

Creatinine Clearance (mL/min)	≥60 kg		<60 kg		Interval (hours)
	Tablet[a]	Solution[b]	Tablet[a]	Solution[b]	
≥60	200	250	125	167	12
30-59	100	100	75	100	12
10-29	150	167	100	100	24
<10	100	100	75	100	24

[a] Chewable/dispersible buffered tablet; 2 tablets must be taken with each dose; different strengths
of tablets may be combined to yield the recommended dose.

[b] Buffered powder for oral solution

Hemodialysis: Removed by hemodialysis (40% to 60%)

Dosing adjustment in hepatic impairment: Should be considered

Monitoring Parameters Serum potassium, uric acid, creatinine; hemoglobin, CBC with
neutrophil and platelet count, CD4 cells; viral load; liver function tests; amylase; weight
gain; perform dilated retinal exam every 6 months

Patient Information Thoroughly chew tablets or manually crush or disperse 2 tablets in 1
oz of water prior to taking; for powder, open packet and pour contents into 4 oz of liquid;
do not mix with fruit juice or other acid-containing liquid; stir until dissolved, drink immediately; do not take with meals

Nursing Implications Administer liquified powder immediately after dissolving; avoid
creating dust if powder spilled, use wet mop or damp sponge

Additional Information Sodium content of buffered tablets: 264.5 mg (11.5 mEq)

Dosage Forms

Powder for oral solution:

Buffered (single dose packet): 100 mg, 167 mg, 250 mg, 375 mg

Pediatric: 2 g, 4 g

Tablet, buffered, chewable (mint flavor): 25 mg, 50 mg, 100 mg, 150 mg

♦ **Dideoxycytidine** see Zalcitabine on page 1233

♦ **Didronel®** see Etidronate Disodium on page 457

Dienestrol (dye en ES trole)

U.S. Brand Names DV® Vaginal Cream; Ortho® Dienestrol Vaginal

Therapeutic Category Estrogen Derivative, Vaginal

(Continued)

Dienestrol *(Continued)*

Use Symptomatic management of atrophic vaginitis or kraurosis vulvae in postmenopausal women

Pregnancy Risk Factor X

Contraindications Pregnancy; should not be used during lactation or undiagnosed vaginal bleeding

Warnings/Precautions Use with caution in patients with a history of thromboembolism, stroke, myocardial infarction (especially age >40 who smoke), liver tumor, hypertension, cardiac, renal or hepatic insufficiency

Adverse Reactions

1% to 10%:

Cardiovascular: Peripheral edema

Gastrointestinal: Anorexia, abdominal cramping

<1%: Hypertension, thromboembolism, myocardial infarction, stroke, migraine, dizziness, anxiety, depression, headache, chloasma, melasma, rash, decreased glucose tolerance, alterations in frequency and flow of menses, breast tenderness or enlargement, increased triglycerides and LDL, nausea, GI distress, cholestatic jaundice, increased susceptibility to *Candida* infection

Mechanism of Action Increases the synthesis of DNA, RNA, and various proteins in target tissues; reduces the release of gonadotropin-releasing hormone from the hypothalamus; reduces FSH and LH release from the pituitary

Pharmacodynamics/Kinetics

Time to peak serum concentration: Topical: Within 3-4 hours

Metabolism: In the liver

Usual Dosage Adults: Vaginal: Insert 1 applicatorful once or twice daily for 1-2 weeks and then $1/2$ of that dose for 1-2 weeks; maintenance dose: 1 applicatorful 1-3 times/week for 3-6 months

Patient Information Insert applicator high into vagina. Patients should inform their physician if signs or symptoms of any of the following occur: Thromboembolic or thrombotic disorders including sudden severe headache or vomiting, disturbance of vision or speech, loss of vision, numbness or weakness in an extremity, sharp or crushing chest pain, calf pain, shortness of breath, severe abdominal pain or mass, mental depression, or unusual bleeding. Patients should discontinue taking the medication if they suspect they are pregnant or become pregnant.

Dosage Forms Cream, vaginal: 0.01% (30 g with applicator; 78 g with applicator)

Diethylpropion *(dye eth il PROE pee on)*

U.S. Brand Names Tenuate®; Tenuate® Dospan®

Canadian Brand Names Nobesine®

Synonyms Amfepramone; Diethylpropion Hydrochloride

Therapeutic Category Anorexiant

Use Short-term adjunct in exogenous obesity

Restrictions C-IV

Pregnancy Risk Factor B

Contraindications Known hypersensitivity to diethylpropion; during or within 14 days following administration of MAO inhibitors (hypertensive crises may result)

Warnings/Precautions Prolonged administration may lead to dependence; use with caution in patients with mental illness or diabetes mellitus, advanced arteriosclerosis, cardiovascular disease, nephritis, angina pectoris, hypertension, glaucoma, and patients with a history of drug abuse

Adverse Reactions

>10%:

Cardiovascular: Hypertension

Central nervous system: Euphoria, nervousness, insomnia

1% to 10%:

Central nervous system: Confusion, mental depression

Endocrine & metabolic: Changes in libido

Gastrointestinal: Nausea, vomiting, restlessness, constipation

Hematologic: Blood dyscrasias

Neuromuscular & skeletal: Tremor

Ocular: Blurred vision

<1%: Tachycardia, arrhythmias, depression, headache, alopecia, diarrhea, abdominal cramps, dysuria, polyuria, myalgia, dyspnea, diaphoresis (increased)

Overdosage/Toxicology There is no specific antidote for amphetamine intoxication and the bulk of the treatment is supportive. Hyperactivity and agitation usually respond to reduced sensory input; however, with extreme agitation, haloperidol (2-5 mg I.M. for adults) may be required. Hyperthermia is best treated with external cooling measures, or when severe or unresponsive, muscle paralysis with pancuronium may be needed. Hypertension is usually transient and generally does not require treatment unless severe. For diastolic blood pressures >110 mm Hg, a nitroprusside infusion should be initiated. Seizures usually respond to diazepam I.V. and/or phenytoin maintenance regimens.

Drug Interactions

Decreased effect of guanethidine; decreased effect with phenothiazines

Increased effect/toxicity with MAO inhibitors (hypertensive crisis), CNS depressants, general anesthetics (arrhythmias), sympathomimetics

Mechanism of Action Diethylpropion is used as an anorexiant agent possessing pharmacological and chemical properties similar to those of amphetamines. The mechanism of action of diethylpropion in reducing appetite appears to be secondary to CNS effects, specifically stimulation of the hypothalamus to release catecholamines into the central nervous system; anorexiant effects are mediated via norepinephrine and dopamine metabolism. An increase in physical activity and metabolic effects (inhibition of lipogenesis and enhancement of lipolysis) may also contribute to weight loss.

Usual Dosage Adults: Oral:
Tablet: 25 mg 3 times/day before meals or food
Tablet, controlled release: 75 mg at midmorning

Dietary Considerations Alcohol: Avoid use

Monitoring Parameters Monitor CNS

Patient Information Avoid alcoholic beverages; take during day to avoid insomnia; do not discontinue abruptly, may cause physical and psychological dependence with prolonged use

Nursing Implications Do not crush 75 mg controlled release tablets; dose should not be given in evening or at bedtime

Dosage Forms
Tablet, as hydrochloride: 25 mg
Tablet, as hydrochloride, controlled release: 75 mg

♦ **Diethylpropion Hydrochloride** see Diethylpropion on previous page

Diethylstilbestrol (dye eth il stil BES trole)

U.S. Brand Names Stilphostrol®

Canadian Brand Names Honvol®

Synonyms DES; Diethylstilbestrol Diphosphate Sodium; Stilbestrol

Therapeutic Category Estrogen Derivative; Estrogen Derivative, Oral; Estrogen Derivative, Parenteral

Use Palliative treatment of inoperable metastatic prostatic carcinoma and postmenopausal inoperable, progressing breast cancer

Pregnancy Risk Factor X

Contraindications Undiagnosed vaginal bleeding, during pregnancy; breast cancer except in select patients with metastatic disease

Warnings/Precautions Use with caution in patients with a history of thromboembolism, stroke, myocardial infarction (especially >40 years of age who smoke), liver tumor, hypertension, cardiac, renal or hepatic insufficiency; estrogens have been reported to increase the risk of endometrial carcinoma; do not use estrogens during pregnancy

Adverse Reactions
>10%:
Cardiovascular: Peripheral edema
Endocrine & metabolic: Enlargement of breasts (female and male), breast tenderness
Gastrointestinal: Anorexia, bloating
1% to 10%:
Central nervous system: Headache
Endocrine & metabolic: Increased libido (female), decreased libido (male)
Gastrointestinal: Vomiting, diarrhea
<1%: Hypertension, thromboembolism, myocardial infarction, edema, stroke, depression, dizziness, anxiety, chloasma, melasma, rash, amenorrhea, alterations in frequency and flow of menses, increased triglycerides, nausea, GI distress, increased LDL, cholestatic jaundice, intolerance to contact lenses, decreased glucose tolerance, increased susceptibility to *Candida* infection, breast tumors

Overdosage/Toxicology Symptoms of overdose include nausea

Stability Intravenous solution should be stored at room temperature and away from direct light; solution is stable for 3 days as long as cloudiness or precipitation has not occurred

Mechanism of Action Competes with estrogenic and androgenic compounds for binding onto tumor cells and thereby inhibits their effects on tumor growth

Pharmacodynamics/Kinetics
Metabolism: In the liver
Elimination: In urine and feces

Usual Dosage Adults:
Male:
Prostate carcinoma (inoperable, progressing): Oral: 1-3 mg/day
Diphosphate: (inoperable, progressing): Oral: 50 mg 3 times/day; increase up to 200 mg or more 3 times/day; maximum daily dose: 1 g
I.V.: Administer 0.5 g, dissolved in 250 mL of saline or D_5W, administer slowly the first 10-15 minutes then adjust rate so that the entire amount is given in 1 hour; repeat for ≥5 days depending on patient response, then repeat 0.25-0.5 g 1-2 times for one week or change to oral therapy
Female: Postmenopausal (inoperable, progressing) breast carcinoma: Oral: 15 mg/day

Test Interactions
Increased prothrombin and factors VII, VIII, IX, X
Decreased antithrombin III
Increased platelet aggregability
Increased thyroid binding globulin
Increased total thyroid hormone (T_4)
Decreased serum folate concentration
Increased serum triglycerides/phospholipids

Patient Information Patients should inform their physicians if signs or symptoms of thromboembolic or thrombotic disorders including sudden severe headache or vomiting, disturbance of vision or speech, loss of vision, numbness or weakness in an extremity, (Continued)

Diethylstilbestrol *(Continued)*

sharp or crushing chest pain, calf pain, shortness of breath, severe abdominal pain or mass, mental depression or unusual bleeding.

Dosage Forms
Injection, as diphosphate sodium (Stilphostrol®): 0.25 g (5 mL)
Tablet: 1 mg, 2.5 mg, 5 mg
Tablet (Stilphostrol®): 50 mg

♦ **Diethylstilbestrol Diphosphate Sodium** *see Diethylstilbestrol on previous page*

Difenoxin and Atropine (dye fen OKS in & A troe peen)
U.S. Brand Names Motofen®
Therapeutic Category Antidiarrheal
Dosage Forms Tablet: Difenoxin hydrochloride 1 mg and atropine sulfate 0.025 mg

♦ **Differin®** *see Adapalene on page 30*

Diflorasone (dye FLOR a sone)
Related Information
Corticosteroids Comparison *on page 1319*
U.S. Brand Names Florone®; Florone E®; Maxiflor®; Psorcon™
Synonyms Diflorasone Diacetate
Therapeutic Category Corticosteroid, Topical (High Potency); Corticosteroid, Topical (Very High Potency)
Use Relieves inflammation and pruritic symptoms of corticosteroid-responsive dermatosis (high to very high potency topical corticosteroid)

Maxiflor®: High potency topical corticosteroid
Psorcon™: Very high potency topical corticosteroid
Pregnancy Risk Factor C
Contraindications Known hypersensitivity to diflorasone
Warnings/Precautions Use with caution in patients with impaired circulation; skin infections
Adverse Reactions <1%: Itching, folliculitis, maceration, burning, dryness, muscle atrophy, arthralgia, secondary infection
Overdosage/Toxicology Symptoms of overdose include moon face, central obesity, hypertension, diabetes, hyperlipidemia, peptic ulcer, increased susceptibility to infection, electrolyte and fluid imbalance, psychosis, hallucinations. When consumed in excessive quantities, systemic hypercorticism and adrenal suppression may occur; in those cases discontinuation and withdrawal of the corticosteroid should be done judiciously.
Mechanism of Action Decreases inflammation by suppression of migration of polymorphonuclear leukocytes and reversal of increased capillary permeability
Pharmacodynamics/Kinetics
Absorption: Topical: Negligible, around 1% reaches dermal layers or systemic circulation; occlusive dressings increase absorption percutaneously
Metabolism: Primarily in the liver
Usual Dosage Topical: Apply ointment sparingly 1-3 times/day; apply cream sparingly 2-4 times/day
Patient Information A thin film of cream or ointment is effective; do not overuse; do not use tight-fitting diapers or plastic pants on children being treated in the diaper area; use only as prescribed, and for no longer than the period prescribed; apply sparingly in light film; rub in lightly; avoid contact with eyes; notify physician if condition being treated persists or worsens
Nursing Implications For external use only; do not use on open wounds; apply sparingly to occlusive dressings; should not be used in the presence of open or weeping lesions
Dosage Forms
Cream, as diacetate: 0.05% (15 g, 30 g, 60 g)
Ointment, topical, as diacetate: 0.05% (15 g, 30 g, 60 g)

♦ **Diflorasone Diacetate** *see Diflorasone on this page*
♦ **Diflucan®** *see Fluconazole on page 488*

Diflunisal (dye FLOO ni sal)
U.S. Brand Names Dolobid®
Canadian Brand Names Apo®-Diflunisal; Novo-Diflunisal; Nu-Diflunisal
Therapeutic Category Analgesic, Nonsteroidal Anti-inflammatory Drug; Anti-inflammatory Agent; Nonsteroidal Anti-inflammatory Drug (NSAID), Oral
Use Management of inflammatory disorders usually including rheumatoid arthritis and osteoarthritis; can be used as an analgesic for treatment of mild to moderate pain
Pregnancy Risk Factor C (D if used in the 3rd trimester)
Contraindications Hypersensitivity to diflunisal or any component, may be a cross-sensitivity with other nonsteroidal anti-inflammatory agents including aspirin; should not be used in patients with active GI bleeding
Warnings/Precautions Peptic ulceration and GI bleeding have been reported; platelet function and bleeding time are inhibited; ophthalmologic effects; impaired renal function, use lower dosage; peripheral edema; possibility of Reye's syndrome; elevation in liver tests

Adverse Reactions

>10%:

Central nervous system: Headache

Endocrine & metabolic: Fluid retention

1% to 10%:

Cardiovascular: Angina pectoris, arrhythmias

Central nervous system: Dizziness

Dermatologic: Rash

Gastrointestinal: GI ulceration

Genitourinary: Vaginal bleeding

Otic: Tinnitus

<1%: Chest pain, vasculitis, tachycardia, convulsions, hallucinations, mental depression, drowsiness, nervousness, insomnia, toxic epidermal necrolysis, urticaria, exfoliative dermatitis, itching, erythema multiforme, Stevens-Johnson syndrome, angioedema, stomatitis, esophagitis or gastritis, cystitis, hemolytic anemia, agranulocytosis, thrombocytopenia, hepatitis, peripheral neuropathy, trembling, weakness, blurred vision, change in vision, decreased hearing, interstitial nephritis, nephrotic syndrome, renal impairment, wheezing, shortness of breath, anaphylaxis, diaphoresis (increased)

Overdosage/Toxicology

Symptoms of overdose include drowsiness, nausea, vomiting, hyperventilation, tachycardia, tinnitus, stupor, coma, renal failure, leukocytosis

Management of a nonsteroidal anti-inflammatory drug (NSAID) intoxication is primarily supportive and symptomatic. Fluid therapy is commonly effective in managing the hypotension that may occur following an acute NSAID overdose, except when this is due to an acute blood loss.

Drug Interactions

Decreased effect with antacids

Increased effect/toxicity of digoxin, methotrexate, anticoagulants, phenytoin, sulfonylureas, sulfonamides, lithium, indomethacin, hydrochlorothiazide, acetaminophen (levels)

Mechanism of Action Inhibits prostaglandin synthesis by decreasing the activity of the enzyme, cyclo-oxygenase, which results in decreased formation of prostaglandin precursors

Pharmacodynamics/Kinetics

Onset of analgesia: Within 1 hour

Duration of action: 8-12 hours

Absorption: Well absorbed from GI tract

Distribution: Appears in breast milk

Metabolism: Extensively in the liver

Half-life: 8-12 hours, prolonged with renal impairment

Time to peak serum concentration: Oral: Within 2-3 hours

Elimination: In urine within 72-96 hours, ~3% as unchanged drug and 90% as glucuronide conjugates

Usual Dosage Adults: Oral:

Pain: Initial: 500-1000 mg followed by 250-500 mg every 8-12 hours; maximum daily dose: 1.5 g

Inflammatory condition: 500-1000 mg/day in 2 divided doses; maximum daily dose: 1.5 g

Dosing adjustment in renal impairment: Cl_{cr} <50 mL/minute: Administer 50% of normal dose

Test Interactions Decrease in uric acid (S), increase in salicylate levels (S), increase in bleeding time

Patient Information May cause GI upset, take with water, milk, or meals; do not take aspirin with diflunisal, swallow tablets whole, do not crush or chew

Dosage Forms Tablet: 250 mg, 500 mg

♦ **Digibind**® see Digoxin Immune Fab on page 361
♦ **Digitaline**® see Digoxin on this page

Digitoxin (di ji TOKS in)

U.S. Brand Names Crystodigin®

Canadian Brand Names Digitaline®

Therapeutic Category Antiarrhythmic Agent, Miscellaneous; Cardiac Glycoside

Use Treatment of congestive heart failure, atrial fibrillation, atrial flutter, paroxysmal atrial tachycardia, and cardiogenic shock

Pregnancy Risk Factor C

Contraindications Hypersensitivity to digitoxin or any component (rare); digitalis toxicity, beriberi heart disease, A-V block, idiopathic hypertrophic subaortic stenosis, constrictive pericarditis, ventricular fibrillation, or tachycardia

Warnings/Precautions Use with caution in patients with hypoxia, hypothyroidism, acute myocarditis,; do not use to treat obesity; patients with incomplete A-V block (Stokes-Adams attack) may progress to complete block with digitalis drug administration; use with caution in patients with acute myocardial infarction, severe pulmonary disease, advanced heart failure, idiopathic hypertrophic subaortic stenosis, Wolff-Parkinson-White syndrome, sick-sinus syndrome (bradyarrhythmias), amyloid heart disease, and constrictive cardiomyopathies; adjust dose with renal or hepatic impairment and aged patients; elderly may develop exaggerated serum/tissue concentrations due to decreased lean body mass, total body water, and age-related reduction in renal/hepatic function; exercise will reduce serum concentrations of digoxin due to increased skeletal muscle uptake

(Continued)

Digitoxin *(Continued)*

Adverse Reactions

1% to 10%: Gastrointestinal: Anorexia, nausea, vomiting

<1%: Sinus bradycardia, A-V block, S-A block, atrial or nodal ectopic beats, ventricular arrhythmias, bigeminy, trigeminy, atrial tachycardia with A-V block, drowsiness, headache, fatigue, lethargy, vertigo, disorientation, hyperkalemia with acute toxicity, feeding intolerance, abdominal pain, diarrhea, neuralgia, blurred vision, halos, yellow or green vision, diplopia, photophobia, flashing lights

Overdosage/Toxicology

Symptoms of acute overdose: Vomiting, hyperkalemia, sinus bradycardia, S-A arrest and A-V block are common, ventricular tachycardia, and fibrillation may occur

Chronic intoxication: Visual disturbances, weakness, sinus bradycardia, atrial fibrillation with slowed ventricular response, and ventricular arrhythmias

After GI decontamination, treat hyperkalemia if >5.5 mEq/L with sodium bicarbonate and glucose with insulin or Kayexalate®. Treat bradycardia or heart block with atropine or pacemaker and other arrhythmias with conventional antiarrhythmics. Use Digibind® for severe hyperkalemia, symptomatic arrhythmias unresponsive to other drugs, and for prophylactic treatment in massive overdose.

Drug Interactions CYP3A3/4 enzyme substrate

Decreased effect/levels of digoxin: Antacids (magnesium, aluminum)•, penicillamine••, dietary bran fiber•, radiotherapy+, antineoplastic drugs+, sucralfate+, sulfasalazine+, thiazide and loop diuretics+, aminosalicylic acid+, neomycin••, phenytoin••, cholestyramine/colestipol/kaolin-pectin••, aminoglutethimide••

Decreased effect/levels of digitoxin: Antacids (magnesium, aluminum)•, phenylbutazone••, phenobarbital••, phenytoin••, cholestyramine••, aminoglutethimide••, rifampin++

Increased effect/toxicity/levels of digoxin: Diltiazem•, spironolactone/triamterene•, ibuprofen•, cimetidine•, omeprazole•, flecainide+, acetylsalicylic acid+, indomethacin+, benzodiazepines+, bepridil•, reserpine••, amphotericin B••, erythromycin••, quinine sulfate••, tetracycline••, cyclosporin••, amiodarone++, propafenone++, quinidine++, verapamil++, calcium preparations++, itraconazole++

Increased effect/toxicity/levels of digitoxin: Diltiazem•, spironolactone•, amphotericin B••, quinidine++, calcium preparations++

Note:

- • = improbable clinical importance
- + = uncertain clinical significance
- •• = interaction proven needing monitoring for possible dosage adjustments
- ++ important interaction needing monitoring, dosage adjustments are likely

Mechanism of Action

Digitalis binds to and inhibits magnesium and adenosine triphosphate dependent sodium and potassium adenosine ATPase thereby increasing the influx of calcium ions, from extracellular to intracellular cytoplasm due to the inhibition of sodium and potassium ion movement across the myocardial membranes; this increase in calcium ions results in a potentiation of the activity of the contractile heart muscle fibers and an increase in the force of myocardial contraction (positive inotropic effect); digitalis may also increase intracellular entry of calcium via slow calcium channel influx; stimulates release and blocks re-uptake of norepinephrine; decreases conduction through the S-A and A-V nodes

Pharmacodynamics/Kinetics

Absorption: 90% to 100%

Distribution: V_d: 7 L/kg

Protein binding: 90% to 97%

Metabolism: Hepatic, 50% to 70%

Time to peak: 8-12 hours

Half-life: 7-8 days

Elimination: 30% to 50% excreted unchanged in urine/feces

Usual Dosage Oral:

Children: Doses are very individualized; **when recommended**, digitalizing dose is as follows:

<1 year: 0.045 mg/kg

1-2 years: 0.04 mg/kg

>2 years: 0.03 mg/kg which is equivalent to 0.75 mg/m²

Maintenance: Approximately 1/10 of the digitalizing dose

Adults: Oral:

Rapid loading dose: Initial: 0.6 mg followed by 0.4 mg and then 0.2 mg at intervals of 4-6 hours

Slow loading dose: 0.2 mg twice daily for a period of 4 days followed by a maintenance dose

Maintenance: 0.05-0.3 mg/day

Most common dose: 0.15 mg/day

Dosing adjustment in renal impairment: Cl_{cr} <10 mL/minute: Administer 50% to 75% of normal dose

Hemodialysis: Not dialyzable (0% to 5%)

Dosing adjustment in hepatic impairment: Dosage reduction is necessary in severe liver disease

Reference Range

Therapeutic: 20-35 ng/mL; Toxic: >45 ng/mL

Patient Information

Do not discontinue medication without physician's advice; instruct patients to notify physician if they suffer loss of appetite, visual changes, nausea, vomiting, weakness, drowsiness, headache, confusion, or depression

Nursing Implications Observe patients for noncardiac signs of toxicity: anorexia, vision changes (blurred), confusion, and depression

Dosage Forms Tablet: 0.1 mg, 0.2 mg

Digoxin (di JOKS in)

Related Information

Adult ACLS Algorithm, Hypotension, Shock *on page 1454*
Adult ACLS Algorithm, Tachycardia *on page 1450*
Antacid Drug Interactions *on page 1296*
Antiarrhythmic Drugs Comparison *on page 1297*
Heart Failure: Management of Patients With Left-Ventricular Systolic Dysfunction *on page 1472*

U.S. Brand Names Lanoxicaps®; Lanoxin®

Canadian Brand Names Novo-Digoxin

Therapeutic Category Antiarrhythmic Agent, Miscellaneous; Cardiac Glycoside

Use Treatment of congestive heart failure and to slow the ventricular rate in tachyarrhythmias such as atrial fibrillation, atrial flutter, and supraventricular tachycardia (paroxysmal atrial tachycardia); cardiogenic shock; may not slow progression of heart failure or affect survival but proven to relieve signs and symptoms of heart failure.

Pregnancy Risk Factor C

Contraindications Hypersensitivity to digoxin or any component; A-V block, idiopathic hypertrophic subaortic stenosis, or constrictive pericarditis

Warnings/Precautions Use with caution in patients with hypoxia, myxedema, hypothyroidism, acute myocarditis; patients with incomplete A-V block (Stokes-Adams attack) may progress to complete block with digitalis drug administration; use with caution in patients with acute myocardial infarction, severe pulmonary disease, advanced heart failure, idiopathic hypertrophic subaortic stenosis, Wolff-Parkinson-White syndrome, sick-sinus syndrome (bradyarrhythmias), amyloid heart disease, and constrictive cardiomyopathies; adjust dose with renal impairment; elderly and neonates may develop exaggerated serum/tissue concentrations due to age-related alterations in clearance and pharmacodynamic differences; exercise will reduce serum concentrations of digoxin due to increased skeletal muscle uptake; recent studies indicate photopsia, chromatopsia and decreased visual acuity may occur even with therapeutic serum drug levels

Adverse Reactions

1% to 10%: Gastrointestinal: Anorexia, nausea, vomiting

<1%: Sinus bradycardia, A-V block, S-A block, atrial or nodal ectopic beats, ventricular arrhythmias, bigeminy, trigeminy, atrial tachycardia with A-V block, drowsiness, headache, fatigue, lethargy, vertigo, disorientation, hyperkalemia with acute toxicity, feeding intolerance, abdominal pain, diarrhea, neuralgia, blurred vision, halos, yellow or green vision, diplopia, photophobia, flashing lights

Overdosage/Toxicology

Symptoms of acute overdose: Vomiting, hyperkalemia, sinus bradycardia, S-A arrest and A-V block are common, ventricular tachycardia, and fibrillation may occur

Chronic intoxication: Visual disturbances, weakness, sinus bradycardia, atrial fibrillation with slowed ventricular response, and ventricular arrhythmias

After GI decontamination, treat hyperkalemia if >5.5 mEq/L with sodium bicarbonate and glucose with insulin or Kayexalate®. Treat bradycardia or heart block with atropine or pacemaker and other arrhythmias with conventional antiarrhythmics. Use Digibind® for severe hyperkalemia, symptomatic arrhythmias unresponsive to other drugs, and for prophylactic treatment in massive overdose.

Drug Interactions

Decreased effect/levels of digoxin: Antacids (magnesium, aluminum)•, penicillamine•, dietary bran fiber•, radiotherapy⁺, antineoplastic drugs⁺, sucralfate⁺, sulfasalazine⁺, thiazide and loop diuretics⁺, aminosalicylic acid⁺, neomycin••, phenytoin••, cholestyramine/colestipol/kaolin-pectin••, aminoglutethimide••

Decreased effect/levels of digitoxin: Antacids (magnesium, aluminum)•, phenylbutazone••, phenobarbital••, phenytoin••, cholestyramine••, aminoglutethimide••, rifampin⁺⁺

Increased effect/toxicity/levels of digoxin: Diltiazem•, spironolactone/triamterene•, ibuprofen•, cimetidine•, omeprazole•, flecainide⁺, acetylsalicylic acid⁺, indomethacin⁺, benzodiazepines⁺, bepridil••, reserpine••, amphotericin B••, erythromycin••, clarithromycin, quinine sulfate••, tetracycline••, nefazodone, cyclosporin••, amiodarone⁺⁺, propafenone⁺⁺, quinidine⁺⁺, verapamil⁺⁺, calcium preparations⁺⁺, itraconazole⁺⁺

Increased effect/toxicity/levels of digitoxin: diltiazem•, spironolactone•, amphotericin B••, quinidine⁺⁺, calcium preparations⁺⁺

Note:

• = improbable clinical importance

⁺ = uncertain clinical significance

•• = interaction proven needing monitoring for possible dosage adjustments

⁺⁺ = important interaction needing monitoring, dosage adjustments are likely

Stability Protect elixir and injection from light; solution **compatibility**: D₅W, D₁₀W, NS, sterile water for injection (when diluted fourfold or greater)

Mechanism of Action

Congestive heart failure: Inhibition of the sodium/potassium ATPase pump which acts to increase the intracellular sodium-calcium exchange to increase intracellular calcium leading to increased contractility

Supraventricular arrhythmias: Direct suppression of the A-V node conduction to increase effective refractory period and decrease conduction velocity - positive inotropic effect, enhanced vagal tone, and decreased ventricular rate to fast atrial arrhythmias. Atrial
(Continued)

Digoxin *(Continued)*

fibrillation may decrease sensitivity and increase tolerance to higher serum digoxin concentrations.

Pharmacodynamics/Kinetics

Onset of action: Oral: 1-2 hours; I.V.: 5-30 minutes

Peak effect: Oral: 2-8 hours; I.V.: 1-4 hours

Duration: Adults: 3-4 days both forms

Absorption: By passive nonsaturable diffusion in the upper small intestine; food may delay, but does not affect extent of digoxin absorption

Distribution:

Normal renal function: 6-7 L/kg

V_d: Extensive to peripheral tissues, with a distinct distribution phase which lasts 6-8 hours; concentrates in heart, liver, kidney, skeletal muscle and intestines. Heart/serum concentration is 70:1. Pharmacologic effects are delayed and do not correlate well with serum concentrations during distribution phase.

Hyperthyroidism: Increased V_d

Hyperkalemia, hyponatremia: Decreased digoxin distribution to heart and muscle

Hypokalemia: Increased digoxin distribution to heart and muscles

Concomitant quinidine therapy: Decreased V_d

Chronic renal failure: 4-6 L/kg

Decreased sodium/potassium ATPase activity - decreased tissue binding

Neonates, full term: 7.5-10 L/kg

Children: 16 L/kg

Adults: 7 L/kg, decreased with renal disease

Protein binding: 30% (in uremic patients, digoxin is displaced from plasma protein binding sites)

Metabolism: By sequential sugar hydrolysis in the stomach or by reduction of lactone ring by intestinal bacteria (in ~10% of population, gut bacteria may metabolize up to 40% of digoxin dose); metabolites may contribute to therapeutic and toxic effects of digoxin; metabolism is reduced in patients with CHF

Bioavailability: Oral (dependent upon formulation): Elixir: 75% to 85%; Tablets: 70% to 80%

Half-life: Dependent upon age, renal and cardiac function:

Neonates: Premature: 61-170 hours; Full-term: 35-45 hours

Infants: 18-25 hours

Children: 35 hours

Adults: 38-48 hours

Adults, anephric: 4-6 days

Half-life: Parent drug: 38 hours; Metabolites: Digoxigenin: 4 hours; Monodigitoxoside: 3-12 hours

Time to peak serum concentration: Oral: Within 1 hour

Elimination: 50% to 70% excreted unchanged in urine

Usual Dosage When changing from oral (tablets or liquid) or I.M. to I.V. therapy, dosage should be reduced by 20% to 25%. See table.

Dosage Recommendations for Digoxin

Age	Total Digitalizing Dose† (mcg/kg*)		Daily Maintenance Dose‡ (mcg/kg*)	
	P.O.	I.V. or I.M.	P.O.	I.V. or I.M.
Preterm infant*	20-30	15-25	5-7.5	4-6
Full-term infant*	25-35	20-30	6-10	5-8
1 mo - 2 y*	35-60	30-50	10-15	7.5-12
2-5 y*	30-40	25-35	7.5-10	6-9
5-10 y*	20-35	15-30	5-10	4-8
>10 y*	10-15	8-12	2.5-5	2-3
Adults	0.75-1.5 mg	0.5-1 mg	0.125-0.5 mg	0.1-0.4 mg

*Based on lean body weight and normal renal function for age. Decrease dose in patients with ↓ renal function; digitalizing dose often not recommended in infants and children.

†Give one-half of the total digitalizing dose (TDD) in the initial dose, then give one-quarter of the TDD in each of two subsequent doses at 8- to 12-hour intervals. Obtain EKG 6 hours after each dose to assess potential toxicity.

‡Divided every 12 hours in infants and children <10 years of age. Given once daily to children >10 years of age and adults.

Dosing adjustment/interval in renal impairment:

Cl_{cr} 10-50 mL/minute: Administer 25% to 75% of dose or every 36 hours

Cl_{cr} <10 mL/minute: Administer 10% to 25% of dose or every 48 hours

Reduce loading dose by 50% in ESRD

Hemodialysis: Not dialyzable (0% to 5%)

Monitoring Parameters

When to draw serum digoxin concentrations: Digoxin serum concentrations are monitored because digoxin possesses a narrow therapeutic serum range; the therapeutic endpoint is difficult to quantify and digoxin toxicity may be life-threatening. Digoxin serum levels should be drawn **at least 4 hours after an intravenous dose** and at **least 6 hours after an oral dose (optimally 12-24 hours after a dose).**

Initiation of therapy:

If a loading dose is given: Digoxin serum concentration may be drawn within 12-24 hours after the initial loading dose administration. Levels drawn this early may confirm the relationship of digoxin plasma levels and response but are of little value in determining maintenance doses.

If a loading dose is not given: Digoxin serum concentration should be obtained after 3-5 days of therapy

Maintenance therapy:

Trough concentrations should be followed just prior to the next dose or at a minimum of 4 hours after an I.V. dose and at least 6 hours after an oral dose

Digoxin serum concentrations should be obtained within 5-7 days (approximate time to steady-state) after any dosage changes. Continue to obtain digoxin serum concentrations 7-14 days after any change in maintenance dose. **Note:** In patients with end-stage renal disease, it may take 15-20 days to reach steady-state.

Additionally, patients who are receiving potassium-depleting medications such as diuretics, should be monitored for potassium, magnesium, and calcium levels

Digoxin serum concentrations should be obtained whenever any of the following conditions occur:

Questionable patient compliance or to evaluate clinical deterioration following an initial good response

Changing renal function

Suspected digoxin toxicity

Initiation or discontinuation of therapy with drugs (amiodarone, quinidine, verapamil) which potentially interact with digoxin; if quinidine therapy is started; digoxin levels should be drawn within the first 24 hours after starting quinidine therapy, then 7-14 days later or empirically skip one day's digoxin dose and decrease the daily dose by 50%

Any disease changes (hypothyroidism)

Heart rate and rhythm should be monitored along with periodic EKGs to assess both desired effects and signs of toxicity

Follow closely (especially in patients receiving diuretics or amphotericin) for decreased serum potassium and magnesium or increased calcium, all of which predispose to digoxin toxicity

Assess renal function

Be aware of drug interactions

Reference Range

Digoxin therapeutic serum concentrations:
Congestive heart failure: 0.8-2 ng/mL
Arrhythmias: 1.5-2.5 ng/mL

Adults: <0.5 ng/mL; probably indicates underdigitalization unless there are special circumstances

Toxic: >2.5 ng/mL; tachyarrhythmias commonly require levels >2 ng/mL

Digoxin-like immunoreactive substance (DLIS) may cross-react with digoxin immunoassay. DLIS has been found in patients with renal and liver disease, congestive heart failure, neonates, and pregnant women (3rd trimester).

Patient Information Do not discontinue medication without checking with physician; notify physician if loss of appetite or visual changes occur

Nursing Implications Observe patients for noncardiac signs of toxicity, ie, anorexia, vision changes (blurred), confusion, and depression

Dosage Forms

Capsule: 50 mcg, 100 mcg, 200 mcg
Elixir, pediatric (lime flavor): 50 mcg/mL with alcohol 10% (60 mL)
Injection: 250 mcg/mL (1 mL, 2 mL)
Injection, pediatric: 100 mcg/mL (1 mL)
Tablet: 125 mcg, 250 mcg, 500 mcg

Digoxin Immune Fab (di JOKS in i MYUN fab)

U.S. Brand Names Digibind®

Synonyms Antidigoxin Fab Fragments

Therapeutic Category Antidote, Digoxin

Use Digoxin immune Fab are specific antibodies for the treatment of digitalis intoxication in carefully selected patients; use in life-threatening ventricular arrhythmias secondary to digoxin, acute digoxin ingestion (ie, >10 mg in adults or >4 mg in children), hyperkalemia (serum potassium >5 mEq/L) in the setting of digoxin toxicity

Pregnancy Risk Factor C

Contraindications Hypersensitivity to sheep products

Warnings/Precautions Use with caution in renal or cardiac failure; allergic reactions possible (sheep product)-skin testing not routinely recommended; epinephrine should be immediately available, Fab fragments may be eliminated more slowly in patients with renal failure, heart failure may be exacerbated as digoxin level is reduced; total serum digoxin concentration may rise precipitously following administration of Digibind®, but this will be almost entirely bound to the Fab fragment and not able to react with receptors in the body; Digibind® will interfere with digitalis immunoassay measurements - this will result in clinically misleading serum digoxin concentrations until the Fab fragment is eliminated from the body (several days to >1 week after Digibind® administration). Hypokalemia has been reported to occur following reversal of digitalis intoxication as has exacerbation of underlying heart failure. Serum digoxin levels drawn prior to therapy may be difficult to evaluate if 6-8 hours have not elapsed after the last dose of digoxin (time to equilibration between serum and tissue); redigitalization should not be initiated until Fab (Continued)

Digoxin Immune Fab (Continued)

fragments have been eliminated from the body, which may occur over several days or greater than a week in patients with impaired renal function.

Adverse Reactions <1%: Worsening of low cardiac output or congestive heart failure, rapid ventricular response in patients with atrial fibrillation as digoxin is withdrawn, facial edema and redness, hypokalemia, urticarial rash, allergic reactions

Overdosage/Toxicology

Symptoms of overdose include delayed serum sickness

Treatment of serum sickness includes acetaminophen, histamine$_1$ and possibly histamine$_2$ blockers and corticosteroids

Stability Should be refrigerated (2°C to 8°C); reconstituted solutions should be used within 4 hours if refrigerated

Mechanism of Action Binds with molecules of digoxin or digitoxin and then is excreted by the kidneys and removed from the body

Pharmacodynamics/Kinetics

Onset of action: I.V.: Improvement in signs and symptoms occur within 2-30 minutes

Half-life: 15-20 hours; prolonged in patients with renal impairment

Elimination: Renally with levels declining to undetectable amounts within 5-7 days

Usual Dosage Each vial of Digibind® 40 mg will bind ~0.6 mg of digoxin or digitoxin

Estimation of the dose is based on the body burden of digitalis. This may be calculated if the amount ingested is known or the postdistribution serum drug level is known.

Tablets Ingested (0.25 mg)	Fab Dose (mg)	(vials)
5	68	1.7
10	136	3.4
25	340	8.5
50	680	17
75	1000	25
100	1360	34
150	2000	50

Fab dose based on serum drug level postdistribution:

Digoxin:

No. of vials = level (ng/mL) x body weight (kg) divided by 100

Digitoxin:

No. of vials = digitoxin (ng/mL) x body weight (kg) divided by 1000

If neither amount ingested nor drug level are known, dose empirically with 10 and 5 vials for acute and chronic toxicity, respectively

Administration Continuous I.V. infusion over 15-30 minutes is preferred; digoxin immune Fab is reconstituted by adding 4 mL sterile water, resulting in 10 mg/mL for I.V. infusion, the reconstituted solution may be further diluted with NS to a convenient volume (eg, 1 mg/mL)

Monitoring Parameters Serum potassium, serum digoxin concentration prior to first dose of digoxin immune Fab; **digoxin levels will greatly increase with Digibind® use and are not an accurate determination of body stores**

Dosage Forms Powder for injection, lyophilized: 38 mg

- ◆ **Dihistine® DH** see Chlorpheniramine, Pseudoephedrine, and Codeine on page 247
- ◆ **Dihistine® Expectorant** see Guaifenesin, Pseudoephedrine, and Codeine on page 551
- ◆ **Dihydrex® Injection** see Diphenhydramine on page 369

Dihydrocodeine Compound (dye hye droe KOE deen KOM pound)

U.S. Brand Names DHC Plus®; Synalgos®-DC

Therapeutic Category Analgesic, Narcotic

Use Management of mild to moderate pain that requires relaxation

Restrictions C-III

Pregnancy Risk Factor B (D if used for prolonged periods or in high doses at term)

Contraindications Hypersensitivity to dihydrocodeine or any component

Warnings/Precautions Use with caution in patients with hypersensitivity reactions to other phenanthrene derivative opioid agonists (morphine, hydrocodone, hydromorphone, levorphanol, oxycodone, oxymorphone); respiratory diseases including asthma, emphysema, COPD, or severe liver or renal insufficiency; some preparations contain sulfites which may cause allergic reactions; dextromethorphan has equivalent antitussive activity but has much lower toxicity in accidental overdose; tolerance of drug dependence may result from extended use

Adverse Reactions

>10%:

Central nervous system: Lightheadedness, dizziness, drowsiness, sedation

Dermatologic: Pruritus, skin reactions

Gastrointestinal: Nausea, vomiting, constipation

1% to 10%:

Cardiovascular: Hypotension, palpitations, bradycardia, peripheral vasodilation

Central nervous system: Increased intracranial pressure

Endocrine & metabolic: Antidiuretic hormone release

Gastrointestinal: Biliary tract spasm

Genitourinary: Urinary tract spasm

Ocular: Miosis

Respiratory: Respiratory depression

Miscellaneous: Histamine release, physical and psychological dependence with prolonged use

Overdosage/Toxicology Naloxone 2 mg I.V. (0.01 mg/kg for children) with repeat administration as necessary up to a total of 10 mg

Drug Interactions CYP2D6 enzyme substrate

Increased toxicity: MAO inhibitors may increase adverse symptoms

Mechanism of Action Binds to opiate receptors in the CNS, causing inhibition of ascending pain pathways, altering the perception of and response to pain; causes cough suppression by direct central action in the medulla; produces generalized CNS depression

Usual Dosage Adults: Oral: 1-2 capsules every 4-6 hours as needed for pain

Dietary Considerations Alcohol: Additive CNS effects, avoid use

Patient Information Avoid alcohol, may cause drowsiness, impaired judgment or coordination; may cause physical and psychological dependence with prolonged use

Nursing Implications Observe patient for excessive sedation, respiratory depression; implement safety measures, assist with ambulation

Dosage Forms Capsule:

DHC Plus®: Dihydrocodeine bitartrate 16 mg, acetaminophen 356.4 mg, and caffeine 30 mg

Synalgos®-DC: Dihydrocodeine bitartrate 16 mg, aspirin 356.4 mg, and caffeine 30 mg

Dihydroergotamine (dye hye droe er GOT a meen)

U.S. Brand Names D.H.E. 45® Injection; Migranal® Nasal Spray

Synonyms Dihydroergotamine Mesylate

Therapeutic Category Ergot Alkaloid and Derivative

Use Aborts or prevents vascular headaches; also as an adjunct for DVT prophylaxis for hip surgery, for orthostatic hypotension, xerostomia secondary to antidepressant use, and pelvic congestion with pain

Pregnancy Risk Factor X

Contraindications High-dose aspirin therapy, hypersensitivity to dihydroergotamine or any component. DHE should not be used within 24 hours of sumatriptan, zolmitriptan, other serotonin agonists or ergot-like agents. DHE should be avoided during or within 2 weeks of discontinuing MAO inhibitors. Pregnancy is contraindicated.

Warnings/Precautions Use with caution in hypertension, angina, peripheral vascular disease, impaired renal or hepatic function; avoid pregnancy

Adverse Reactions

>10%:

Cardiovascular: Localized edema, peripheral vascular effects (numbness and tingling of fingers and toes)

Central nervous system: Drowsiness, dizziness

Gastrointestinal: Xerostomia, diarrhea, nausea, vomiting

1% to 10%:

Cardiovascular: Precordial distress and pain, transient tachycardia or bradycardia

Neuromuscular & skeletal: Muscle pain in the extremities, weakness in the legs

Overdosage/Toxicology

Symptoms of overdose include peripheral ischemia, paresthesia, headache, nausea, vomiting

Activated charcoal is effective at binding certain chemicals; this is especially true for ergot alkaloids

Drug Interactions

Increased effect of heparin

Increased toxicity with erythromycin, clarithromycin, nitroglycerin, propranolol, troleandomycin

Stability Store in refrigerator

Mechanism of Action Ergot alkaloid alpha-adrenergic blocker directly stimulates vascular smooth muscle to vasoconstrict peripheral and cerebral vessels; also has effects on serotonin receptors

Pharmacodynamics/Kinetics

Onset of action: Within 15-30 minutes

Duration: 3-4 hours

Distribution: V_d: 14.5 L/kg

Protein binding: 90%

Metabolism: Extensively in the liver

Half-life: 1.3-3.9 hours

Time to peak serum concentration: I.M.: Within 15-30 minutes

Elimination: Predominately into bile and feces and 10% excreted in urine, mostly as metabolites

Usual Dosage Adults:

I.M.: 1 mg at first sign of headache; repeat hourly to a maximum dose of 3 mg total

I.V.: Up to 2 mg maximum dose for faster effects; maximum dose: 6 mg/week

Intranasal: 1 spray (0.5 mg) of nasal spray should be administered into each nostril; repeat as needed within 15 minutes, up to a total of 6 sprays in any 24-hour period and no more than 8 sprays in a week

Dosing adjustment in hepatic impairment: Dosage reductions are probably necessary but specific guidelines are not available

(Continued)

Dihydroergotamine *(Continued)*

Reference Range Minimum concentration for vasoconstriction is reportedly 0.06 ng/mL

Patient Information Rare feelings of numbness or tingling of fingers, toes, or face may occur; avoid using this medication if you are pregnant, have heart disease, hypertension, liver disease, infection, itching

Additional Information Nasal spray contains caffeine

Dosage Forms
Injection, as mesylate: 1 mg/mL (1 mL)
Spray, nasal: 4 mg/mL [0.5 mg/spray] (1 mL)

♦ **Dihydroergotamine Mesylate** *see Dihydroergotamine on previous page*

♦ **Dihydroergotoxine** *see Ergoloid Mesylates on page 425*

♦ **Dihydrogenated Ergot Alkaloids** *see Ergoloid Mesylates on page 425*

♦ **Dihydrohydroxycodeinone** *see Oxycodone on page 874*

♦ **Dihydromorphinone** *see Hydromorphone on page 583*

Dihydrotachysterol *(dye hye droe tak IS ter ole)*

U.S. Brand Names DHT™; Hytakerol®

Synonyms Dichysterol

Therapeutic Category Vitamin, Fat Soluble

Use Treatment of hypocalcemia associated with hypoparathyroidism; prophylaxis of hypocalcemic tetany following thyroid surgery

Pregnancy Risk Factor A (D if used in doses above the recommended daily allowance)

Contraindications Hypercalcemia, known hypersensitivity to dihydrotachysterol

Warnings/Precautions Calcium-phosphate product (serum calcium and phosphorus) must not exceed 70; avoid hypercalcemia; use with caution in coronary artery disease, decreased renal function (especially with secondary hyperparathyroidism), renal stones, and elderly

Adverse Reactions
>10%:
Endocrine & metabolic: Hypercalcemia
Renal: Elevated serum creatinine, hypercalciuria
<1%: Convulsions, polydipsia, nausea, vomiting, anorexia, weight loss, polyuria, anemia, weakness, metastatic calcification, renal damage

Overdosage/Toxicology
Symptoms of overdose include hypercalcemia, anorexia, nausea, weakness, constipation, diarrhea, vague aches, mental confusion, tinnitus, ataxia, depression, hallucinations, syncope, coma; polyuria, polydypsia, nocturia, hypercalciuria, irreversible renal insufficiency or proteinuria, azotemia; will spread tissue calcifications, hypertension
Following withdrawal of the drug, treatment consists of bed rest, reduced calcium intake, and cathartic administration. Severe hypercalcemia requires I.V. hydration and forced diuresis. Urine output should be monitored and maintained at >3 mL/kg/hour. I.V. saline can quickly and significantly increase excretion of calcium into the urine. Calcitonin, cholestyramine, prednisone, sodium EDTA and mithramycin have all been used successfully to treat the more resistant cases of vitamin D-induced hypercalcemia.

Drug Interactions
Decreased effect/levels of vitamin D: Cholestyramine, colestipol, mineral oil; phenytoin and phenobarbital may inhibit activation may decrease effectiveness
Increased toxicity: Thiazide diuretics increase calcium

Stability Protect from light

Mechanism of Action Synthetic analogue of vitamin D with a faster onset of action; stimulates calcium and phosphate absorption from the small intestine, promotes secretion of calcium from bone to blood; promotes renal tubule resorption of phosphate

Pharmacodynamics/Kinetics
Peak hypercalcemic effect: Within 2-4 weeks
Duration: Can be as long as 9 weeks
Absorption: Well absorbed from the GI tract
Elimination: In bile and feces; stored in liver, fat, skin, muscle, and bone

Usual Dosage Oral:
Hypoparathyroidism:
Infants and young Children: Initial: 1-5 mg/day for 4 days, then 0.1-0.5 mg/day
Older Children and Adults: Initial: 0.8-2.4 mg/day for several days followed by maintenance doses of 0.2-1 mg/day
Nutritional rickets: 0.5 mg as a single dose or 13-50 mcg/day until healing occurs
Renal osteodystrophy: Maintenance: 0.25-0.6 mg/24 hours adjusted as necessary to achieve normal serum calcium levels and promote bone healing

Monitoring Parameters Monitor renal function, serum calcium, and phosphate concentrations; if hypercalcemia is encountered, discontinue agent until serum calcium returns to normal

Reference Range Calcium (serum): 9-10 mg/dL (4.5-5 mEq/L)

Patient Information Do not take more than the recommended amount. While taking this medication, your physician may want you to follow a special diet or take a calcium supplement; follow this diet closely. Avoid taking magnesium supplements or magnesium-containing antacids. Early symptoms of hypercalcemia include weakness, fatigue, headache, metallic taste, stomach upset, muscle or bone pain, and irritability.

Nursing Implications Monitor symptoms of hypercalcemia (weakness, fatigue, somnolence, headache, anorexia, dry mouth, metallic taste, nausea, vomiting, cramps, diarrhea, muscle pain, bone pain, and irritability)

Dosage Forms
Capsule (Hytakerol®): 0.125 mg
Solution:
Oral Concentrate (DHT™): 0.2 mg/mL (30 mL)
Oral, in oil (Hytakerol®): 0.25 mg/mL (15 mL)
Tablet (DHT™): 0.125 mg, 0.2 mg, 0.4 mg

♦ **1,25 Dihydrocholecalciferol** see Calcitriol on page 172
♦ **Diiodohydroxyquin** see Iodoquinol on page 623
♦ **Diisopropyl Fluorophosphate** see Isoflurophate on page 633
♦ **Dilacor™ XR** see Diltiazem on this page
♦ **Dilantin®** see Phenytoin on page 921
♦ **Dilatrate®-SR** see Isosorbide Dinitrate on page 637
♦ **Dilaudid®** see Hydromorphone on page 583
♦ **Dilaudid-5®** see Hydromorphone on page 583
♦ **Dilaudid-HP®** see Hydromorphone on page 583
♦ **Dilocaine®** see Lidocaine on page 679
♦ **Dilomine® Injection** see Dicyclomine on page 351

Diloxanide Furoate (dye LOKS ah nide FYOOR oh ate)
U.S. Brand Names Furamide®
Therapeutic Category Amebicide
Use Treatment of amebiasis (asymptomatic cyst passers)
Additional Information Available from:
The Centers for Disease Control Drug and Immunobiologic Service
1600 Clifton Road
Building 1
Room 1259
Atlanta, GA 30333
Monday-Friday 8 AM to 4:30 PM
(404) 639-3670
Nonbusiness hours (emergencies only): (404) 639-3670

Diltiazem (dil TYE a zem)
Related Information
Adult ACLS Algorithm, Tachycardia on page 1450
Antiarrhythmic Drugs Comparison on page 1297
Calcium Channel Blockers Comparison on page 1315
Hypertension Therapy on page 1479
U.S. Brand Names Cardizem® CD; Cardizem® Injectable; Cardizem® SR; Cardizem® Tablet; Dilacor™ XR; Tiamate®; Tiazac™
Canadian Brand Names Apo®-Diltiaz; Novo-Diltazem; Nu-Diltiaz; Syn-Diltiazem
Synonyms Diltiazem Hydrochloride
Therapeutic Category Antianginal Agent; Antihypertensive Agent; Calcium Channel Blocker
Use
Capsule: Essential hypertension (alone or in combination) - sustained release only; chronic stable angina or angina from coronary artery spasm
Injection: Atrial fibrillation or atrial flutter; paroxysmal supraventricular tachycardia (PSVT)
Unlabeled use: Prevention of reinfarction of non-Q-wave myocardial infarction, dyskinesia, and Raynaud's syndrome
Pregnancy Risk Factor C
Pregnancy/Breast-Feeding Implications
Clinical effects on the fetus: Teratogenic and embryotoxic effects have been demonstrated in small animals given doses 5-10 times the adult dose (mg/kg)
Breast-feeding/lactation: Freely diffuses into breast milk; however, the American Academy of Pediatrics considers diltiazem to be **compatible** with breast-feeding. Available evidence suggest safe use during breast-feeding.
Contraindications Severe hypotension (<90 mm Hg systolic) or second and third degree heart block except with a functioning pacemaker; hypersensitivity to diltiazem; sick sinus syndrome, acute myocardial infarction, and pulmonary congestion
Warnings/Precautions Use with caution and titrate dosages for patients with hypotension or patients taking antihypertensives, impaired renal or hepatic function, or when treating patients with congestive heart failure. Use caution with concomitant therapy with beta-blockers or digoxin. Monitor LFTs during therapy since these enzymes may rarely be increased and symptoms of hepatic injury may occur; usually reverses with drug discontinuation; avoid abrupt withdrawal of calcium blockers since rebound angina is theoretically possible.
Adverse Reactions
1% to 10% (generally well tolerated):
Cardiovascular: Bradycardia, A-V block (0.6% to 7.6%), EKG abnormality, peripheral edema, flushing
Central nervous system: Dizziness, headache
Gastrointestinal: Nausea
(Continued)

Diltiazem *(Continued)*

Neuromuscular & skeletal: Weakness

<1%: Congestive heart failure, tachycardia, angina, hypotension, palpitations, sleep disturbances, psychiatric disturbances, insomnia, nervousness, somnolence, urticaria, photosensitivity, alopecia, rash, petechiae, ecchymosis, anorexia, constipation, diarrhea, abnormal taste, dyspepsia, vomiting, abdominal cramps, xerostomia, micturition disorder, sexual difficulties, leukopenia, paresthesia, tremor, joint stiffness, amblyopia, retinopathy, tinnitus, nasal or chest congestion, shortness of breath

Overdosage/Toxicology The primary cardiac symptoms of calcium blocker overdose includes hypotension and bradycardia. The hypotension is caused by peripheral vasodilation, myocardial depression, and bradycardia. Bradycardia results from sinus bradycardia, second- or third-degree atrioventricular block, or sinus arrest with junctional rhythm. Intraventricular conduction is usually not affected so QRS duration is normal (verapamil does prolong the P-R interval and bepridil prolongs the Q-T and may cause ventricular arrhythmias, including torsade de pointes).

The noncardiac symptoms include confusion, stupor, nausea, vomiting, metabolic acidosis and hyperglycemia. Following initial gastric decontamination, if possible, repeated calcium administration may promptly reverse the depressed cardiac contractility (but not sinus node depression or peripheral vasodilation); glucagon, epinephrine, and amrinone may treat refractory hypotension; glucagon and epinephrine also increase the heart rate (outside the U.S., 4-aminopyridine may be available as an antidote); dialysis and hemoperfusion are not effective in enhancing elimination although repeat-dose activated charcoal may serve as an adjunct with sustained-release preparations.

In a few reported cases, overdose with calcium channel blockers has been associated with hypotension and bradycardia, initially refractory to atropine but becoming more responsive to this agent when larger doses (approaching 1 gram per hour for more than 24 hours) of calcium chloride was administered.

Drug Interactions CYP3A3/4 enzyme substrate; CYP1A2, 2D6, and 3A3/4 enzyme inhibitor

Decreased effect: Moricizine has decreased diltiazem concentrations and decreased its half-life

Increased toxicity:

Diltiazem has increased peak plasma moricizine levels and decreased oral clearance; side effect frequency increases

Diltiazem and amiodarone may cause increased bradycardia and decreased cardiac output

Diltiazem and cimetidine may cause increased bioavailability of diltiazem

Severe hypotension possible with concurrent administration with fentanyl

Both increased and decreased lithium levels have occurred with diltiazem; use caution with coadministration

Diltiazem and cyclosporine may cause increased cyclosporine levels and subsequent renal toxicity

Diltiazem and digoxin may cause increased digoxin levels and additive effects

Diltiazem and beta-blockers may result in increased cardiac depression

Cisapride toxicity (Q-T prolongation) may be increased with diltiazem

Theophylline effects possibly enhanced with diltiazem

Diltiazem with carbamazepine may result in increased carbamazepine levels and possible toxic effects

Mechanism of Action Inhibits calcium ion from entering the "slow channels" or select voltage-sensitive areas of vascular smooth muscle and myocardium during depolarization, producing a relaxation of coronary vascular smooth muscle and coronary vasodilation; increases myocardial oxygen delivery in patients with vasospastic angina

Pharmacodynamics/Kinetics

Onset of action: Oral: 30-60 minutes (including sustained release)

Absorption: 80% to 90%

Time to peak serum concentration: Short-acting tablets: Within 2-3 hours; Sustained release: 6-11 hours

Distribution: V_d: 3-13 L/kg; appears in breast milk

Protein binding: 77% to 85%

Metabolism: Extensive first-pass metabolism; metabolized in the liver; following single I.V. injection, plasma concentrations of N-monodesmethyldiltiazem and desacetyldiltiazem are typically undetectable; however, these metabolites accumulate to detectable concentrations following 24-hour constant rate infusion. N-monodesmethyldiltiazem appears to have 20% of the potency of diltiazem; desacetyldiltiazem is about 50% as potent as the parent compound.

Bioavailability: ~40% to 60% due to significant first-pass effect

Half-life: 4-6 hours, may increase with renal impairment; 5-7 hours with sustained release

Elimination: In urine and bile mostly as metabolites

Usual Dosage Adults:

Angina: Oral: Usual starting dose: 30 mg 4 times/day; sustained release: 120-180 mg once daily; dosage should be increased gradually at 1- to 2-day intervals until optimum response is obtained. Doses up to 360 mg/day have been effectively used. Hypertension is controllable with single daily doses of sustained release products, or divided daily doses of regular release products, in the range of 240-360 mg/day

Sustained-release capsules:

Cardizem® SR: Initial: 60-120 mg twice daily; adjust to maximum antihypertensive effect (usually within 14 days); usual range: 240-360 mg/day

Cardizem® CD, Tiazac™: Hypertension: Total daily dose of short-acting administered once daily or initially 180 or 240 mg once daily; adjust to maximum effect (usually within 14 days); maximum: 480 mg/day; usual range: 240-360 mg/day

Cardizem® CD: Angina: Initial: 120-180 mg once daily; maximum: 480 mg once/day

Dilacor™ XR:

Hypertension: 180-240 mg once daily; maximum: 540 mg/day; usual range: 180-480 mg/day; use lower dose in elderly

Angina: Initial: 120 mg/day; titrate slowly over 7-14 days up to 480 mg/day, as needed

I.V. (requires an infusion pump): See table.

Diltiazem — I.V. Dosage and Administration

Initial Bolus Dose	0.25 mg/kg actual body weight over 2 min (average adult dose: 20 mg)
Repeat Bolus Dose May be administered after 15 min if the response is inadequate.	0.35 mg/kg actual body weight over 2 min (average adult dose: 25 mg)
Continuous Infusion Infusions >24 h or infusion rates >15 mg/h are not recommended.	Initial infusion rate of 10 mg/h; rate may be increased in 5 mg/h increments up to 15 mg/h as needed; some patients may respond to an initial rate of 5 mg/h.

If Cardizem® injectable is administered by continuous infusion for >24 hours, the possibility of decreased diltiazem clearance, prolonged elimination half-life, and increased diltiazem and/or diltiazem metabolite plasma concentrations should be considered

Conversion from I.V. diltiazem to oral diltiazem: Start oral approximately 3 hours after bolus dose

Oral dose (mg/day) is approximately equal to [rate (mg/hour) x 3 + 3] x 10

3 mg/hour = 120 mg/day
5 mg/hour = 180 mg/day
7 mg/hour = 240 mg/day
11 mg/hour = 360 mg/day

Dosing comments in renal/hepatic impairment: Use with caution as extensively metabolized by the liver and excreted in the kidneys and bile

Dialysis: Not removed by hemo- or peritoneal dialysis; supplemental dose is not necessary

Dietary Considerations Alcohol: Avoid use

Monitoring Parameters Liver function tests, blood pressure, EKG

Patient Information Sustained release products should be taken in the morning; do not crush or chew; limit caffeine intake; notify physician if angina pain is not reduced when taking this drug, irregular heartbeat, shortness of breath, swelling, dizziness, constipation, nausea, or hypotension occurs; do not stop therapy without advice of physician

Nursing Implications Do not crush sustained release capsules

Additional Information Although there is some initial epidemiology data which may show increased risk of myocardial infarction with the treatment of hypertension with some short-acting calcium antagonists, controlled trials (eg, ALL-HAT) are ongoing to examine the long-term effects of not only these agents but other antihypertensives in preventing heart disease. Until these studies are completed, patients taking calcium antagonists should be encouraged to continue with the prescribed antihypertensive regimens although a switch from high-dose short-acting products to sustained release agents may be warranted.

An investigation (n=121) found diltiazem superior to nitroglycerin infusion in decreasing cardiac ischemia events at 48 hours

Dosage Forms

Capsule, sustained release, as hydrochloride:
Cardizem® CD: 120 mg, 180 mg, 240 mg, 300 mg
Cardizem® SR: 60 mg, 90 mg, 120 mg
Dilacor™ XR: 180 mg, 240 mg
Tiazac™: 120 mg, 180 mg, 240 mg, 300 mg, 360 mg
Injection, as hydrochloride: 5 mg/mL (5 mL, 10 mL)
Cardizem®: 5 mg/mL (5 mL, 10 mL)
Tablet, as hydrochloride (Cardizem®): 30 mg, 60 mg, 90 mg, 120 mg
Tablet, extended release, as hydrochloride (Tiamate®): 120 mg, 180 mg, 240 mg

Extemporaneous Preparations Diltiazem 12 mg/mL was found to be stable for up to 60 days at 5°C and 25°C in a 1:1 mixture of Ora-Sweet® and Ora-Plus®, a 1:1 mixture of Ora-Sweet® SF and Ora-Plus® and of cherry syrup

Allen LV and Erickson III MA, "Stability of Baclofen, Captopril, Diltiazem, hydrochloride, Dipyridamole, and Flecainide Acetate in Extemporaneously Compounded Oral Liquids," *Am J Health Syst Pharm*, 1996, 53:2179-84.

♦ **Diltiazem Hydrochloride** see Diltiazem on page 365

Dimercaprol (dye mer KAP role)

U.S. Brand Names BAL in Oil®

Synonyms BAL; British Anti-Lewisite; Dithioglycerol

Therapeutic Category Antidote, Arsenic Toxicity; Antidote, Gold Toxicity; Antidote, Lead Toxicity; Antidote, Mercury Toxicity

(Continued)

Dimercaprol *(Continued)*

Use Antidote to gold, arsenic (except arsine), and mercury poisoning (except nonalkyl mercury); adjunct to edetate calcium disodium in lead poisoning; possibly effective for antimony, bismuth, chromium, copper, nickel, tungsten, or zinc

Pregnancy Risk Factor C

Contraindications Hepatic insufficiency (unless due to arsenic poisoning); do not use on iron, cadmium, or selenium poisoning

Warnings/Precautions Potentially a nephrotoxic drug, use with caution in patients with oliguria or glucose 6-phosphate dehydrogenase deficiency; keep urine alkaline to protect kidneys; administer all injections deep I.M. at different sites

Adverse Reactions
>10%:
  Cardiovascular: Hypertension, tachycardia (dose-related)
  Central nervous system: Headache
1% to 10%: Gastrointestinal: Nausea, vomiting
<1%: Nervousness, fever, convulsions, salivation, transient neutropenia, thrombocytopenia, increased PT, pain at the injection site, abscess formation, myalgia, paresthesia, blepharospasm, burning eyes, nephrotoxicity, dysuria, burning sensation of the lips, mouth, throat, and penis

Drug Interactions Toxic complexes with iron, cadmium, selenium, or uranium

Mechanism of Action Sulfhydryl group combines with ions of various heavy metals to form relatively stable, nontoxic, soluble chelates which are excreted in urine

Pharmacodynamics/Kinetics
Distribution: Distributes to all tissues including the brain
Metabolism: Rapidly to inactive products
Time to peak serum concentration: 0.5-1 hour
Elimination: In urine

Usual Dosage Children and Adults: Deep I.M.:
  Arsenic, mercury, and gold poisoning: 3 mg/kg every 4-6 hours for 2 days, then every 12 hours for 7-10 days or until recovery (initial dose may be up to 5 mg if severe poisoning)
  Lead poisoning (in conjunction with calcium EDTA): For symptomatic acute encephalopathy or blood level >100 mcg/dL: 4-5 mg/kg every 4 hours for 3-5 days

Administration Administer deep I.M. only; keep urine alkaline to protect renal function

Test Interactions Iodine ^{131}I thyroidal uptake values may be decreased

Patient Information Frequent blood and urine tests may be required

Nursing Implications Urine should be kept alkaline because chelate dissociates in acid media

Dosage Forms Injection: 100 mg/mL (3 mL)

♦ **Dimetane®-DC** *see* Brompheniramine, Phenylpropanolamine, and Codeine *on page 156*

♦ **Dimethoxyphenyl Penicillin Sodium** *see* Methicillin *on page 748*

♦ **β,β-Dimethylcysteine** *see* Penicillamine *on page 893*

♦ **Dimethyl Triazeno Imidazol Carboxamide** *see* Dacarbazine *on page 316*

Dinoprostone *(dye noe PROST one)*

U.S. Brand Names Cervidil® Vaginal Insert; Prepidil® Vaginal Gel; Prostin E₂® Vaginal Suppository

Synonyms PGE₂; Prostaglandin E₂

Therapeutic Category Abortifacient; Prostaglandin

Use
Gel: Promote cervical ripening prior to labor induction; usage for gel include any patient undergoing induction of labor with an unripe cervix, most commonly for pre-eclampsia, eclampsia, postdates, diabetes, intrauterine growth retardation, and chronic hypertension
Suppositories: Terminate pregnancy from 12th through 28th week of gestation; evacuate uterus in cases of missed abortion or intrauterine fetal death; manage benign hydatidiform mole

Pregnancy Risk Factor X

Contraindications
Gel: Hypersensitivity to prostaglandins or any constituents of the cervical gel, history of asthma, contracted pelvis, malpresentation of the fetus
Gel: The following are "relative" contraindications and should only be considered by the physician under these circumstances: Patients in whom vaginal delivery is not indicated (ie, herpes genitalia with a lesion at the time of delivery), prior uterine surgery, breech presentation, multiple gestation, polyhydramnios, premature rupture of membranes
Suppository: Known hypersensitivity to dinoprostone, acute pelvic inflammatory disease, uterine fibroids, cervical stenosis

Warnings/Precautions Dinoprostone should be used only by medically trained personnel in a hospital; caution in patients with cervicitis, infected endocervical lesions, acute vaginitis, compromised (scarred) uterus or history of asthma, hypertension or hypotension, epilepsy, diabetes mellitus, anemia, jaundice, or cardiovascular, renal, or hepatic disease. Oxytocin should not be used simultaneously with Prepidil® (>6 hours of the last dose of Prepidil®).

Adverse Reactions
>10%:
  Central nervous system: Headache

Gastrointestinal: Vomiting, diarrhea, nausea

1% to 10%:

Cardiovascular: Bradycardia

Central nervous system: Fever

Neuromuscular & skeletal: Back pain

<1%: Hypotension, cardiac arrhythmias, syncope, flushing, tightness of the chest, vaso-motor and vasovagal reactions, dizziness, chills, pain, hot flashes, wheezing, dyspnea, coughing, bronchospasm, shivering

Overdosage/Toxicology

Symptoms of overdose include vomiting, bronchospasm, hypotension, chest pain, abdominal cramps, uterine contractions

Treatment is symptomatic

Drug Interactions Increased effect of oxytocics

Stability Suppositories must be kept frozen, store in freezer not above -20°F (-4°C); bring to room temperature just prior to use; cervical gel should be stored under refrigeration 2°C to 8°C (36°F to 46°F)

Mechanism of Action A synthetic prostaglandin E_2 abortifacient that stimulates uterine contractions similar to those seen during natural labor

Pharmacodynamics/Kinetics

Onset of effect (uterine contractions): Within 10 minutes

Duration: Up to 2-3 hours

Absorption: Vaginal: Slow following administration

Metabolism: In many tissues including the kidney, lungs, and spleen

Elimination: Primarily in urine with small amounts excreted in feces

Usual Dosage

Abortifacient: Insert 1 suppository high in vagina, repeat at 3- to 5-hour intervals until abortion occurs up to 240 mg (maximum dose); continued administration for longer than 2 days is not advisable

Cervical ripening:

Gel:

Intracervical: 0.25-1 mg

Intravaginal: 2.5 mg

Suppositories: Intracervical: 2-3 mg

Administration Intracervically: For cervical ripening, patient should be supine in the dorsal position

Nursing Implications Bring suppository to room temperature just prior to use; patient should remain supine for 10 minutes following insertion; commercially available suppositories should not be used for extemporaneous preparation of any other dosage form of drug

Dosage Forms

Insert, vaginal (Cervidil®): 10 mg

Gel, endocervical: 0.5 mg in 3 g syringes [each package contains a 10-mm and 20-mm shielded catheter]

Suppository, vaginal: 20 mg

♦ **Diocaine** see Proparacaine on page 982

♦ **Diochloram** see Chloramphenicol on page 238

♦ **Diocto®** [OTC] see Docusate on page 384

♦ **Diocto-K®** [OTC] see Docusate on page 384

♦ **Dioctyl Calcium Sulfosuccinate** see Docusate on page 384

♦ **Dioctyl Potassium Sulfosuccinate** see Docusate on page 384

♦ **Dioctyl Sodium Sulfosuccinate** see Docusate on page 384

♦ **Diodoquin®** see Iodoquinol on page 623

♦ **Dioeze®** [OTC] see Docusate on page 384

♦ **Diomycin** see Erythromycin on page 427

♦ **Dionephrine** see Phenylephrine on page 918

♦ **Dioval® Injection** see Estradiol on page 433

♦ **Diovan™** see Valsartan on page 1205

♦ **Diovan™ HCT** see Valsartan and Hydrochlorothiazide on page 1206

♦ **Dipalmitoylphosphatidylcholine** see Colfosceril Palmitate on page 294

♦ **Dipentum®** see Olsalazine on page 861

♦ **Diphenacen-50® Injection** see Diphenhydramine on this page

♦ **Diphen® Cough [OTC]** see Diphenhydramine on this page

♦ **Diphenhist [OTC]** see Diphenhydramine on this page

Diphenhydramine (dye fen HYE dra meen)

Related Information

Contrast Media Reactions, Premedication for Prophylaxis on page 1464

U.S. Brand Names AllerMax® Oral [OTC]; Banophen® Oral [OTC]; Belix® Oral [OTC]; Benadryl® Injection; Benadryl® Oral [OTC]; Benadryl® Topical; Ben-Allergin-50® Injection; Benylin® Cough Syrup [OTC]; Bydramine® Cough Syrup [OTC]; Compoz® Gel Caps [OTC]; Compoz® Nighttime Sleep Aid [OTC]; Dihydrex® Injection; Diphenacen-50® Injection; Diphen® Cough [OTC]; Diphenhist [OTC]; Dormarex® 2 Oral [OTC]; Dormin® Oral [OTC]; Genahist® Oral; Hydramyn® Syrup [OTC]; Hyrexin-50® Injection; Maximum Strength Nytol® [OTC]; Miles Nervine® Caplets [OTC]; Nordryl® Injection; Nordryl® Oral; Nytol® Oral [OTC]; Phendry® Oral [OTC]; Siladryl® Oral [OTC]; Silphen® Cough [OTC]; (Continued)

Diphenhydramine *(Continued)*

Sleep-eze 3® Oral [OTC]; Sleepinal® [OTC]; Sleepwell 2-nite® [OTC]; Sominex® Oral [OTC]; Tusstat® Syrup; Twilite® Oral [OTC]; Uni-Bent® Cough Syrup; 40 Winks® [OTC]

Canadian Brand Names Allerdryl®; Allernix®; Nytol® Extra Strength

Synonyms Diphenhydramine Hydrochloride

Therapeutic Category Antidote, Hypersensitivity Reactions; Antihistamine, H₁ Blocker; Sedative

Use Symptomatic relief of allergic symptoms caused by histamine release which include nasal allergies and allergic dermatosis; can be used for mild nighttime sedation; prevention of motion sickness and as an antitussive; has antinauseant and topical anesthetic properties; treatment of phenothiazine-induced dystonic reactions

Pregnancy Risk Factor C

Contraindications Hypersensitivity to diphenhydramine or any component; should not be used in acute attacks of asthma

Warnings/Precautions Use with caution in patients with angle-closure glaucoma, peptic ulcer, urinary tract obstruction, hyperthyroidism; some preparations contain sodium bisulfite; syrup contains alcohol; diphenhydramine has high sedative and anticholinergic properties, so it may not be considered the antihistamine of choice for prolonged use in the elderly

Adverse Reactions

>10%:

Central nervous system: Slight to moderate drowsiness

Respiratory: Thickening of bronchial secretions

1% to 10%:

Central nervous system: Headache, fatigue, nervousness

Gastrointestinal: Nausea, vomiting, diarrhea, abdominal pain, xerostomia, appetite increase, weight gain, dry mucous membranes

Neuromuscular & skeletal: Arthralgia

Respiratory: Pharyngitis

<1%: Hypotension, palpitations, edema, sedation, dizziness, paradoxical excitement, insomnia, depression, photosensitivity, rash, angioedema, urinary retention, hepatitis, myalgia, paresthesia, tremor, blurred vision, bronchospasm, epistaxis

Overdosage/Toxicology

Symptoms of overdose include CNS stimulation or depression; overdose may result in death in infants and children

There is no specific treatment for an antihistamine overdose, however, most of its clinical toxicity is due to anticholinergic effects. Anticholinesterase inhibitors (eg, physostigmine, neostigmine, pyridostigmine, or edrophonium) may be useful by reducing acetylcholinesterase. For anticholinergic overdose with severe life-threatening symptoms, physostigmine 1-2 mg (0.5 mg or 0.02 mg/kg for children) I.V., slowly may be given to reverse these effects.

Drug Interactions CYP2D6 enzyme substrate

Increased toxicity: CNS depressants worsens CNS and respiratory depression, monoamine oxidase inhibitors may increase anticholinergic effects; syrup should not be given to patients taking drugs that can cause disulfiram reactions (ie, metronidazole, chlorpropamide) due to high alcohol content

Stability Protect from light; the following drugs are **incompatible** with diphenhydramine when mixed in the same syringe: Amobarbital, amphotericin B, cephalothin, diatrizoate, foscarnet, heparin, hydrocortisone, hydroxyzine, pentobarbital, phenobarbital, phenytoin, prochlorperazine, promazine, promethazine, tetracycline, thiopental

Mechanism of Action Competes with histamine for H₁-receptor sites on effector cells in the gastrointestinal tract, blood vessels, and respiratory tract

Pharmacodynamics/Kinetics

Maximum sedative effect: 1-3 hours

Duration of action: 4-7 hours

Absorption: Oral: 40% to 60% reaches systemic circulation due to first-pass metabolism

Metabolism: Extensive in the liver and, to smaller degrees, in the lung and kidney

Half-life: 2-8 hours; elderly: 13.5 hours

Protein binding: 78%

Time to peak serum concentration: 2-4 hours

Usual Dosage

Children:

Oral: (>10 kg): 12.5-25 mg 3-4 times/day; maximum daily dose: 300 mg

I.M., I.V.: 5 mg/kg/day or 150 mg/m²/day in divided doses every 6-8 hours, not to exceed 300 mg/day

Adults:

Oral: 25-50 mg every 6-8 hours

Nighttime sleep aid: 50 mg at bedtime

I.M., I.V.: 10-50 mg in a single dose every 2-4 hours, not to exceed 400 mg/day

Topical: For external application, not longer than 7 days

Dietary Considerations Alcohol: Additive CNS effects, avoid use

Reference Range

Antihistamine effects at levels >25 ng/mL

Drowsiness at levels 30-40 ng/mL

Mental impairment at levels >60 ng/mL

Therapeutic: Not established

Toxic: >0.1 µg/mL

Test Interactions May suppress the wheal and flare reactions to skin test antigens

Patient Information May cause drowsiness; swallow whole, do not crush or chew sustained release product; avoid alcohol, may impair coordination and judgment

Nursing Implications Raise bed rails, institute safety measures, assist with ambulation

Dosage Forms
Capsule, as hydrochloride: 25 mg, 50 mg
Cream, as hydrochloride: 1%, 2%
Elixir, as hydrochloride: 12.5 mg/5 mL (5 mL, 10 mL, 20 mL, 120 mL, 480 mL, 3780 mL)
Injection, as hydrochloride: 10 mg/mL (10 mL, 30 mL); 50 mg/mL (1 mL, 10 mL)
Lotion, as hydrochloride: 1% (75 mL)
Solution, topical spray, as hydrochloride: 1% (60 mL)
Syrup, as hydrochloride: 12.5 mg/5 mL (5 mL, 120 mL, 240 mL, 480 mL, 3780 mL)
Tablet, as hydrochloride: 25 mg, 50 mg

♦ **Diphenhydramine Hydrochloride** *see* Diphenhydramine *on page 369*

Diphenoxylate and Atropine (dye fen OKS i late & A troe peen)

U.S. Brand Names Lofene®; Logen®; Lomanate®; Lomodix®; Lomotil®; Lonox®; Low-Quel®

Synonyms Atropine and Diphenoxylate

Therapeutic Category Antidiarrheal

Use Treatment of diarrhea

Restrictions C-V

Pregnancy Risk Factor C

Contraindications Hypersensitivity to diphenoxylate, atropine or any component; severe liver disease, jaundice, dehydrated patient, and narrow-angle glaucoma; it should not be used for children <2 years of age

Warnings/Precautions High doses may cause physical and psychological dependence with prolonged use; use with caution in patients with ulcerative colitis, dehydration, and hepatic dysfunction; reduction of intestinal motility may be deleterious in diarrhea resulting from *Shigella*, *Salmonella*, toxigenic strains of *E. coli*, and from pseudomembranous enterocolitis associated with broad spectrum antibiotics; children may develop signs of atropinism (dryness of skin and mucous membranes, thirst, hyperthermia, tachycardia, urinary retention, flushing) even at the recommended dosages; if there is no response with 48 hours, the drug is unlikely to be effective and should be discontinued; if chronic diarrhea is not improved symptomatically within 10 days at maximum dosage of 20 mg/day, control is unlikely with further use.

Adverse Reactions
1% to 10%:
Central nervous system: Nervousness, restlessness, dizziness, drowsiness, headache, mental depression
Gastrointestinal: Paralytic ileus, xerostomia
Genitourinary: Urinary retention and dysuria
Ocular: Blurred vision
Respiratory: Respiratory depression
<1%: Tachycardia, sedation, euphoria, hyperthermia, pruritus, urticaria, nausea, vomiting, abdominal discomfort, pancreatitis, stomach cramps, muscle cramps, weakness, diaphoresis (increased)

Overdosage/Toxicology
Symptoms of overdose include drowsiness, hypotension, blurred vision, flushing, dry mouth, miosis
Administration of activated charcoal will reduce bioavailability of diphenoxylate; naloxone 2 mg I.V. (0.01 mg/kg for children) with repeat administration as necessary up to a total of 10 mg; for anticholinergic overdose with severe life-threatening symptoms, physostigmine 1-2 mg (0.5 mg or 0.02 mg/kg for children) S.C. or I.V., slowly may be given to reverse these effects

Drug Interactions Increased toxicity: MAO inhibitors (hypertensive crisis), CNS depressants, antimuscarinics (paralytic ileus); may prolong half-life of drugs metabolized in liver

Stability Protect from light

Mechanism of Action Diphenoxylate inhibits excessive GI motility and GI propulsion; commercial preparations contain a subtherapeutic amount of atropine to discourage abuse

Pharmacodynamics/Kinetics
Onset of action: Within 45-60 minutes
Peak effect: Within 2 hours
Duration: 3-4 hours
Absorption: Oral: Well absorbed
Metabolism: Extensively in the liver to diphenoxylic acid (active)
Half-life: Diphenoxylate: 2.5 hours
Time to peak serum concentration: 2 hours
Elimination: Primarily in feces (via bile); ~14% excreted in urine; <1% excreted unchanged in urine

Usual Dosage Oral:
Children (use with caution in young children due to variable responses): Liquid: 0.3-0.4 mg of diphenoxylate/kg/day in 2-4 divided doses **or**
<2 years: Not recommended
2-5 years: 2 mg of diphenoxylate 3 times/day
5-8 years: 2 mg of diphenoxylate 4 times/day
8-12 years: 2 mg of diphenoxylate 5 times/day
(Continued)

Diphenoxylate and Atropine *(Continued)*

Adults: 15-20 mg/day of diphenoxylate in 3-4 divided doses; maintenance: 5-15 mg/day in 2-3 divided doses

Dietary Considerations Alcohol: Additive CNS effects, avoid use

Monitoring Parameters Watch for signs of atropinism (dryness of skin and mucous membranes, tachycardia, thirst, flushing); monitor number and consistency of stools; observe for signs of toxicity, fluid and electrolyte loss, hypotension, and respiratory depression

Patient Information Drowsiness, dizziness, dry mouth; use caution while driving or performing hazardous tasks; avoid alcohol or other CNS depressants; do not exceed prescribed dose; report persistent diarrhea, fever, or palpitations to physician

Nursing Implications Raise bed rails, institute safety measures

Dosage Forms

Solution, oral: Diphenoxylate hydrochloride 2.5 mg and atropine sulfate 0.025 mg per 5 mL (4 mL, 10 mL, 60 mL)

Tablet: Diphenoxylate hydrochloride 2.5 mg and atropine sulfate 0.025 mg

♦ **Diphenylan Sodium®** *see* Phenytoin *on page 921*

♦ **Diphenylhydantoin** *see* Phenytoin *on page 921*

Diphtheria and Tetanus Toxoid (dif THEER ee a & TET a nus TOKS oyd)

Related Information

Adverse Events and Vaccination *on page 1369*

Immunization Recommendations *on page 1358*

Recommendations of the Advisory Committee on Immunization Practices (ACIP) *on page 1360*

Skin Tests *on page 1353*

Synonyms DT; Td; Tetanus and Diphtheria Toxoid

Therapeutic Category Toxoid

Use Active immunity against diphtheria and tetanus when pertussis vaccine is contraindicated; tetanus prophylaxis in wound management

DT: Infants and children through 6 years of age

Td: Children and adults ≥7 years of age

Pregnancy Risk Factor C

Pregnancy/Breast-Feeding Implications Clinical effects on the fetus: Td and T vaccines are not known to cause special problems for pregnant women or their unborn babies. While physicians do not usually recommend giving any drugs or vaccines to pregnant women, a pregnant women who needs Td vaccine should get it; wait until 2nd trimester if possible.

Contraindications Patients receiving immunosuppressive agents, prior anaphylactic, allergic, or systemic reactions; hypersensitivity to diphtheria and tetanus toxoid or any component; acute respiratory infection or other active infection

Warnings/Precautions History of a neurologic reaction or immediate hypersensitivity reaction following a previous dose. History of severe local reaction (Arthus-type) following previous dose (such individuals should not be given further routine or emergency doses of tetanus and diphtheria toxoids for 10 years). Do not confuse pediatric DT with adult diphtheria and tetanus toxoid (Td), absorbed (Td) is used in patients >7 years of age; primary immunization should be postponed until the second year of life due to possibility of CNS damage or convulsion; have epinephrine 1:1000 available.

Adverse Reactions Severe adverse reactions must be reported to the FDA

>10%: Central nervous system: Fretfulness, drowsiness

1% to 10%:

Central nervous system: Persistent crying

Gastrointestinal: Anorexia, vomiting

<1%: Tachycardia, hypotension, edema, convulsions (rarely), pain, redness, urticaria, pruritus, tenderness, Arthus-type hypersensitivity reactions, transient fever

Drug Interactions Decreased effect with immunosuppressive agents, immunoglobulins if given within 1 month (eg, concomitant administration with tetanus immune globulin decreased the immune response to Td)

Stability Refrigerate

Tetanus Prophylaxis in Wound Management

Number of Prior Tetanus Toxoid Doses	Clean, Minor Wounds		All Other Wounds	
	Td*	TIG†	Td*	TIG†
Unknown or <3	Yes	No	Yes	Yes
≥3‡	No#	No	No¶	No

*Adult tetanus and diphtheria toxoids; use pediatric preparations (DT or DTP) if the patient is <7 years old.

†Tetanus immune globulin.

‡If only three doses of fluid tetanus toxoid have been received, a fourth dose of toxoid, preferably an adsorbed toxoid, should be given.

#Yes, if >10 years since last dose.

¶Yes, if >5 years since last dose.

Adapted from Report of the Committee on Infectious Diseases, American Academy of Pediatrics, Elk Grove Village, IL: American Academy of Pediatrics, 1986.

Usual Dosage I.M.:

Infants and Children (DT):

6 weeks to 1 year: Three 0.5 mL doses at least 4 weeks apart; administer a reinforcing dose 6-12 months after the third injection

1-6 years: Two 0.5 mL doses at least 4 weeks apart; reinforcing dose 6-12 months after second injection; if final dose is given after seventh birthday, use adult preparation

4-6 years (booster immunization): 0.5 mL; not necessary if all 4 doses were given after fourth birthday - routinely administer booster doses at 10-year intervals with the adult preparation

Children >7 years and Adults: Should receive Td; 2 primary doses of 0.5 mL each, given at an interval of 4-6 weeks; third (reinforcing) dose of 0.5 mL 6-12 months later; boosters every 10 years

Administration Administer only I.M.; do not inject the same site more than once

Patient Information DT, Td and T vaccines cause few problems (mild fever or soreness, swelling, and redness/knot at the injection site); these problems usually last 1-2 days, but this does not happen nearly as often as with DTP vaccine

Nursing Implications Shake well before giving

Additional Information Pediatric dosage form should only be used in patients ≤6 years of age. Federal law requires that the date of administration, the vaccine manufacturer, lot number of vaccine, and the administering person's name, title, and address be entered into the patient's permanent medical record.

Since protective tetanus and diphtheria antibodies decline with age, only 28% of persons >70 years of age in the U.S. are believed to be immune to tetanus, and most of the tetanus-induced deaths occur in people >60 years of age, it is advisable to offer Td especially to the elderly concurrent with their influenza and other immunization programs if history of vaccination is unclear; boosters should be given at 10-year intervals; earlier for wounds

Dosage Forms Injection:

Pediatric use:

Diphtheria 6.6 Lf units and tetanus 5 Lf units per 0.5 mL (5 mL)

Diphtheria 10 Lf units and tetanus 5 Lf units per 0.5 mL (0.5 mL, 5 mL)

Diphtheria 12.5 Lf units and tetanus 5 Lf units per 0.5 mL (5 mL)

Diphtheria 15 Lf units and tetanus 10 Lf units per 0.5 mL (5 mL)

Adult use:

Diphtheria 1.5 Lf units and tetanus 5 Lf units per 0.5 mL (0.5 mL, 5 mL)

Diphtheria 2 Lf units and tetanus 5 Lf units per 0.5 mL (5 mL)

Diphtheria 2 Lf units and tetanus 10 Lf units per 0.5 mL (5 mL)

♦ **Diphtheria CRM$_{197}$ Protein Conjugate** see Haemophilus b Conjugate Vaccine on page 554

Diphtheria, Tetanus Toxoids, and Acellular Pertussis Vaccine

(dif THEER ee a, TET a nus TOKS oyds & ay CEL yoo lar per TUS sis vak SEEN)

Related Information

Adverse Events and Vaccination on page 1369

Guidelines for the Prevention of Opportunistic Infections in Persons with HIV on page 1388

Immunization Recommendations on page 1358

Prophylaxis for Patients Exposed to Common Communicable Diseases on page 1384

Recommendations of the Advisory Committee on Immunization Practices (ACIP) on page 1360

Recommended Childhood Immunization Schedule - US - January-December, 1999 on page 1359

Recommended Immunization Schedule for HIV-Infected Children on page 1363

U.S. Brand Names Acel-Imune®; Certiva™; Infanrix™; TriHIBit®; Tripedia®

Synonyms DTaP

Therapeutic Category Toxoid; Vaccine

Use As fourth and fifth dose in primary immunization series against diphtheria, tetanus, and pertussis from age 15 months (Tripedia®) or 17 months (Acel-Imune®) through 7th birthday (recipients must have previously received 3 doses of whole-cell DTP (DTwP))

Pregnancy Risk Factor C

Pregnancy/Breast-Feeding Implications Clinical effects on the fetus: Animal reproduction studies have not been conducted. It is not known whether the vaccine can cause fetal harm when administered to a pregnant woman or can affect reproductive capacity. Tripedia® vaccine is NOT recommended for use in a pregnant woman.

Contraindications Patients >7 years of age, patients with cancer, immunodeficiencies, an acute respiratory infection, or any other active infection; children with a history of neurologic disorders should not receive the pertussis or any component; history of any of the following effects from previous administration of pertussis vaccine precludes further use: >103°F fever (39.4°C), convulsions, focal neurologic signs, screaming episodes, shock, collapse, sleepiness or encephalopathy; known hypersensitivity to diphtheria and tetanus toxoids or pertussis vaccine; do not use for treatment of actual tetanus, diphtheria, or whooping cough infections

Warnings/Precautions DTaP should not be used in children <15 months of age and should not be used in children who have received fewer than 3 doses of DTP

(Continued)

Diphtheria, Tetanus Toxoids, and Acellular Pertussis Vaccine *(Continued)*

Adverse Reactions All serious adverse reactions must be reported to the U.S. Department of Health and Human Services (DDHS) Vaccine Adverse Event Reporting System (VAERS) 1-800-822-7967.

<1%: Edema, convulsions, screaming episodes, malaise, sleepiness, focal neurological signs, shock, collapse, fever, chills, erythema, induration, rash, urticaria, tenderness, arthralgias

Drug Interactions Decreased effect with immunosuppressive agents, corticosteroids within 1 month

Stability Refrigerate at 2°C to 8°C (35°F to 46°F); do not freeze

Mechanism of Action Promotes active immunity to diphtheria, tetanus, and pertussis by inducing production of specific antibodies and antitoxins.

Usual Dosage Before administration, ensure that at least 3 doses of whole-cell DTP vaccine have been given. Give the fourth dose of DTaP at ~18 months of age, at least 6 months after the third DTwP. Give a fifth 0.5 mL dose at 4-6 years of age. Tetanus and diphtheria toxoids for adult use (Td) is the preferred agent for adults and older children.

Administration Administer only I.M. in anterolateral aspect of thigh or deltoid muscle of upper arm

Patient Information A nodule may be palpable at the injection site for a few weeks

Nursing Implications Acetaminophen 10-15 mg/kg before and every 4 hours to 12-24 hours may reduce or prevent fever; shake well before administering; the child's medical record should document that the small risk of postvaccination seizure and the benefits of the pertussis vaccination were discussed with the patient

Additional Information This preparation contains less endotoxin relative to DTP and, although immunogenic, it apparently is less reactogenic than DTP. Federal law requires that the date of administration, the vaccine manufacturer, lot number of vaccine, and the administering person's name, title, and address be entered into the patient's permanent medical record.

Dosage Forms Injection:

Acel-Imune®: Diphtheria 7.5 Lf units, tetanus 5 Lf units, and acellular pertussis vaccine 40 mcg per 0.5 mL (7.5 mL)

Tripedia®: Diphtheria 6.7 Lf units, tetanus 5 Lf units, and acellular pertussis vaccine 46.8 mcg per 0.5 mL (7.5 mL)

Infanrix™: Diphtheria 25 Lf units, tetanus 10 Lf units, and acellular pertussis vaccine 25 mcg per 0.5 mL (0.5 mL)

TriHIBit® vaccine [Tripedia® vaccine used to reconstitute ActHIB®]: 0.5 mL

Certiva™: Diphtheria 15 Lf units, tetanus 6 Lf, and acellular pertussis vaccine 40 mcg per 0.5 mL (7.5 mL)

Diphtheria, Tetanus Toxoids, and Whole-Cell Pertussis Vaccine, Adsorbed

(dif THEER ee a & TET a nus TOKS oyds & hole-sel per TUS sis vak SEEN)

Related Information

Recommended Immunization Schedule for HIV-Infected Children *on page 1363*

U.S. Brand Names Tri-Immunol®

Synonyms DTP

Therapeutic Category Toxoid and Vaccine

Use Active immunization of infants and children through 6 years of age (between 2 months and the seventh birthday) against diphtheria, tetanus, and pertussis; recommended for primary immunization; start immunization if whooping cough or diphtheria is present in the community

For children who are severely immunocompromised or who are infected with HIV, DTP vaccine is indicated in the same schedule and dose as for immunocompetent children, including the use of acellular pertussis-containing vaccines (DTaP) as a booster. Although no specific studies with pertussis vaccine are available, if immunosuppressive therapy is to be discontinued shortly, it would be reasonable to defer immunization until at least 3 months after the patient last received therapy; otherwise, the patient should be vaccinated while still receiving therapy.

Pregnancy Risk Factor C

Contraindications

Known hypersensitivity to diphtheria and tetanus toxoids or pertussis vaccine, known hypersensitivity to thimerosal, thrombocytopenia

Patients >7 years of age history of any of the following effects from previous administration of pertussis vaccine precludes further use

Temperature of 105°F or higher **within 2 days** after getting DTP

Shock-collapse (becoming blue or pale, limp, and not responsive) **within 2 days** after getting DTP

Convulsion **within 3 days** after getting DTP

Crying that cannot be stopped which lasts for more than 3 hours at a time **within 2 days** after getting DTP

Warnings/Precautions Do not use DTP for treatment of actual tetanus, diphtheria, or whooping cough infections. The child's medical record should document that the small risk of past vaccination seizure and the benefits of the pertussis vaccination were discussed with the patient. If adverse reactions occurred with previous doses, immunization should be completed with diphtheria and tetanus toxoid absorbed (pediatric); have epinephrine 1:1000 available.

Adverse Reactions All serious adverse reactions must be reported to the U.S. Department of Health and Human Services (DHHS) Vaccine Adverse Event Reporting System (VAERS). Reporting forms and information about reporting requirements or completion of the form can be obtained from VAERS through a toll-free number 1-800-822-7967.

<1%: Convulsions, screaming episodes, malaise, sleepiness, focal neurological signs, shock, collapse, mild to moderate fever, chills, erythema, swelling induration, rash, urticaria, local tenderness, arthralgia

Drug Interactions Decreased effect: Immunosuppressive agents may result in aberrant responses to active immunization

Stability Refrigerate

Mechanism of Action Promotes active immunity to diphtheria, tetanus, and pertussis by inducing production of specific antibodies and antitoxins.

Usual Dosage For pediatric use only. Do not give to patients >7 years of age; primary immunization for children 2-6 years of age, ideally beginning at the age of 2-3 months

Primary immunization: Administer 0.5 mL I.M. on three occasions at 8-week intervals with a re-enforcing dose administered at 15-18 months of age

The booster doses are given when children are 4-6 years of age, 0.5 mL I.M.

For booster doses thereafter, use the recommended dose of diphtheria and tetanus toxoids, adsorbed (adults) every 10 years; for patients not receiving immunization at usual times, consult authoritative source

Patient Information Most children have little or no problem from the DTP shot; many children will have fever or soreness, swelling, and redness where the shot was given. Usually these problems are mild and last 1-2 days. Some children will be cranky, drowsy, or not want to eat during this time.

Nursing Implications Acetaminophen 10-15 mg/kg before and every 4 hours to 12-24 hours may reduce fever; give vaccine only I.M.

The child's medical record should document that the small risk of past vaccination seizure and the benefits of the pertussis vaccination were discussed with the patient

Additional Information

Inactivated/killed bacterial vaccine

Federal law requires that the date of administration, the vaccine manufacturer, lot number of vaccine and the administering person's name, title and address be entered into the patient's permanent medical record

Dosage Forms Injection: 0.5 mL

Diphtheria, Tetanus Toxoids, Whole-Cell Pertussis, and *Haemophilus influenzae* Type b Conjugate Vaccines

(dif THEER ee a, TET a nus TOKS oyds, hole-sel per TUS sis, & hem OF fil us in floo EN za)

U.S. Brand Names Tetramune®; Tripedia/ActHIB®

Synonyms DTwP-HIB

Therapeutic Category Toxoid

Use Active immunization of infants and children through 5 years of age (between 2 months and the sixth birthday) against diphtheria, tetanus, and pertussis and *Haemophilus* b disease when indications for immunization with DTP vaccine and HIB vaccine coincide

Pregnancy Risk Factor C

Contraindications Children with any febrile illness or active infection, known hypersensitivity to *Haemophilus* b polysaccharide vaccine (thimerosal), children who are immunosuppressed or receiving immunosuppressive therapy; patients >7 years of age, patients with cancer, immunodeficiencies, an acute respiratory infection, or any other active infection; children with a history of neurologic disorders should not receive the pertussis any component; history of any of the following effects from previous administration of pertussis vaccine precludes further use: fever >103°F (39.4°C), convulsions, focal neurologic signs, screaming episodes, shock, collapse, sleepiness or encephalopathy; known hypersensitivity to diphtheria and tetanus toxoids or pertussis vaccine; do not use DTP for treatment of actual tetanus, diphtheria or whooping cough infections

Warnings/Precautions If adverse reactions occurred with previous doses, immunization should be completed with diphtheria and tetanus toxoid absorbed (pediatric); any febrile illness or active infection is reason for delaying use of *Haemophilus* b conjugate vaccine

Adverse Reactions

>10%:

Central nervous system: Fever, chills, irritability, restlessness, drowsiness

Local: Erythema, edema, induration, pain and warmth at injection site

1% to 10%:

Dermatologic: Rash

Gastrointestinal: Vomiting, diarrhea, loss of appetite

<1%: Convulsions, screaming episodes, malaise, sleepiness, focal neurological signs, shock, collapse, chills, urticaria, local tenderness, arthralgia, increased risk of *Haemophilus* b infections in the week after vaccination, rarely allergic or anaphylactic reactions

Drug Interactions Decreased effect: Immunosuppressive agents; may interfere with antigen detection tests

Stability Keep in refrigerator, may be frozen (not diluent) without affecting potency; unopened vials are stable for up to 24 hours at <70°C

Mechanism of Action Promotes active immunity to diphtheria, tetanus, pertussis, and *H. influenzae* by inducing production of specific antibodies and antitoxins.

(Continued)

Diphtheria, Tetanus Toxoids, Whole-Cell Pertussis, and *Haemophilus influenzae* Type b Conjugate Vaccines (Continued)

Usual Dosage The primary immunization for children 2 months to 5 years of age, ideally beginning at the age of 2-3 months or at 6-week check-up. Administer 0.5 mL I.M. on 3 occasions at ~2-month intervals, followed by a fourth 0.5 mL dose at ~15 months of age.

Administration Administer I.M. only

Patient Information A nodule may be palpable at the injection site for a few weeks

Nursing Implications

Acetaminophen 10-15 mg/kg before and every 4 hours to 12-24 hours may reduce or prevent fever

Shake well before administering

The child's medical record should document that the small risk of past vaccination seizure and the benefits of the pertussis vaccination were discussed with the patient

Additional Information Inactivated bacterial vaccine; Federal law requires that the date of administration, the vaccine manufacturer, lot number of vaccine and the administering person's name, title, and address be entered into the patient's permanent medical record. (**Note:** Diphtheria and Tetanus Toxoids, and Acellular Pertussis and *Haemophilus influenzae* Type B Conjugate Vaccine is Tripedia/ActHIB®)

Dosage Forms Injection: Diphtheria toxoid 12.5 Lf units, tetanus toxoid 5 Lf units, and whole-cell pertussis vaccine 4 units, and *Haemophilus influenzae* type b oligosaccharide 10 mcg per 0.5 mL (5 mL)

- ♦ **Diphtheria Toxoid Conjugate** *see Haemophilus* b Conjugate Vaccine *on page 554*
- ♦ **Dipivalyl Epinephrine** *see Dipivefrin on this page*

Dipivefrin (dye PI ve frin)

Related Information

Glaucoma Drug Therapy Comparison *on page 1322*

U.S. Brand Names AKPro® Ophthalmic; Propine® Ophthalmic

Canadian Brand Names DPE™; Ophtho-Dipivefrin™

Synonyms Dipivalyl Epinephrine; Dipivefrin Hydrochloride; DPE

Therapeutic Category Adrenergic Agonist Agent, Ophthalmic; Ophthalmic Agent, Vasoconstrictor

Use Reduces elevated intraocular pressure in chronic open-angle glaucoma; also used to treat ocular hypertension, low tension, and secondary glaucomas

Pregnancy Risk Factor B

Contraindications Hypersensitivity to dipivefrin, ingredients in the formulation, or epinephrine; contraindicated in patients with angle-closure glaucoma

Warnings/Precautions Use with caution in patients with vascular hypertension or cardiac disorders and in aphakic patients; contains sodium metabisulfite

Adverse Reactions

1% to 10%:

Central nervous system: Headache

Local: Burning, stinging

Ocular: Ocular congestion, photophobia, mydriasis, blurred vision, ocular pain, bulbar conjunctival follicles, blepharoconjunctivitis, cystoid macular edema

<1%: Arrhythmias, hypertension

Drug Interactions Increased or synergistic effect when used with other agents to lower intraocular pressure

Stability Avoid exposure to light and air; discolored or darkened solutions indicate loss of potency

Mechanism of Action Dipivefrin is a prodrug of epinephrine which is the active agent that stimulates alpha- and/or beta-adrenergic receptors increasing aqueous humor outflow

Pharmacodynamics/Kinetics

Ocular pressure effect: Onset of action: Within 30 minutes; Duration: ≥12 hours

Mydriasis: Onset of action: May occur within 30 minutes; Duration: Several hours

Absorption: Rapid into the aqueous humor

Metabolism: Converted to epinephrine

Usual Dosage Adults: Ophthalmic: Instill 1 drop every 12 hours into the eyes

Patient Information Discolored solutions should be discarded; may cause transient burning or stinging

Nursing Implications Finger pressure should be applied to lacrimal sac for 1-2 minutes after instillation to decrease risk of absorption and systemic reactions

Dosage Forms Solution, ophthalmic, as hydrochloride: 0.1% (5 mL, 10 mL, 15 mL)

- ♦ **Dipivefrin Hydrochloride** *see Dipivefrin on this page*
- ♦ **Diprivan®** *see Propofol on page 983*
- ♦ **Diprolene®** *see Betamethasone on page 141*
- ♦ **Diprolene® AF** *see Betamethasone on page 141*
- ♦ **Diprolene® Glycol [Dipropionate]** *see Betamethasone on page 141*
- ♦ **Dipropylacetic Acid** *see Valproic Acid and Derivatives on page 1203*
- ♦ **Diprosone®** *see Betamethasone on page 141*

Dipyridamole (dye peer ID a mole)

U.S. Brand Names Persantine®

Canadian Brand Names Apo®-Dipyridamole FC; Apo®-Dipyridamole SC; Novo-Dipiradol

Therapeutic Category Antiplatelet Agent; Vasodilator, Coronary

Use Maintains patency after surgical grafting procedures including coronary artery bypass; used with warfarin to decrease thrombosis in patients after artificial heart valve replacement; used with aspirin to prevent coronary artery thrombosis; in combination with aspirin or warfarin to prevent other thromboembolic disorders. Dipyridamole may also be given 2 days prior to open heart surgery to prevent platelet activation by extracorporeal bypass pump and as a diagnostic agent in CAD; also approved as an alternative to exercise during Thallium myocardial perfusion imaging for the evaluation of coronary artery disease in patients who cannot exercise adequately

Pregnancy Risk Factor B

Contraindications Hypersensitivity to dipyridamole or any component

Warnings/Precautions Safety and effectiveness in children <12 years of age have not been established; may further decrease blood pressure in patients with hypotension due to peripheral vasodilation; use with caution in patients taking other drugs which affect platelet function or coagulation and in patients with hemostatic defects. Since evidence suggests that clinically used doses are ineffective for prevention of platelet aggregation, consideration for low-dose aspirin (81-325 mg/day) alone may be necessary; this will decrease cost as well as inconvenience.

Adverse Reactions

>10%:
  Cardiovascular: Exacerbation of angina pectoris (I.V.), headache (I.V.)
  Central nervous system: Dizziness

1% to 10%:
  Cardiovascular: Hypotension, hypertension, tachycardia
  Central nervous system: Headache
  Dermatologic: Rash
  Gastrointestinal: Abdominal distress
  Respiratory: Dyspnea

<1%: Vasodilatation, flushing, syncope, edema, angina, migraine, diarrhea, vomiting, hepatic dysfunction, weakness, hypertonia, rhinitis, hyperventilation, allergic reaction, pleural pain

Overdosage/Toxicology

Symptoms of overdose include hypotension, peripheral vasodilation; dialysis is not effective

Treatment includes fluids and vasopressors although hypotension is often transient

Drug Interactions

Increased toxicity: Heparin may increase anticoagulation

Decreased hypotensive effect (I.V.): Theophylline

Stability Do not freeze, protect I.V. preparation from light

Mechanism of Action Inhibits the activity of adenosine deaminase and phosphodiesterase, which causes an accumulation of adenosine, adenine nucleotides, and cyclic AMP; these mediators then inhibit platelet aggregation and may cause vasodilation; may also stimulate release of prostacyclin or PGD_2; causes coronary vasodilation

Pharmacodynamics/Kinetics

Absorption: Readily absorbed from GI tract but variable

Distribution: V_d: 2-3 L/kg in adults

Protein binding: 91% to 99%

Metabolism: Concentrated and metabolized in the liver

Half-life, terminal: 10-12 hours

Time to peak serum concentration: 2-2.5 hours

Elimination: In feces via bile as glucuronide conjugates and unchanged drug

Usual Dosage

Children: Oral: 3-6 mg/kg/day in 3 divided doses
  Doses of 4-10 mg/kg/day have been used investigationally to treat proteinuria in pediatric renal disease
  Mechanical prosthetic heart valves: Oral: 2-5 mg/kg/day (used in combination with an oral anticoagulant in children who have systemic embolism despite adequate oral anticoagulant therapy, and used in combination with low-dose oral anticoagulation (INR 2-3) plus aspirin in children in whom full-dose oral anticoagulation is contraindicated)

Adults:
  Oral: 75-400 mg/day in 3-4 divided doses
  Evaluation of coronary artery disease: I.V.: 0.14 mg/kg/minute for 4 minutes; maximum dose: 60 mg

Hemodialysis: Significant drug removal is unlikely based on physiochemical characteristics

Patient Information Notify physician or pharmacist if taking other medications that affect bleeding, such as NSAIDs or warfarin

Dosage Forms

Injection: 10 mg/2 mL

Tablet: 25 mg, 50 mg, 75 mg

Extemporaneous Preparations A 10 mg/mL oral suspension has been made using four 25 mg tablets and purified water USP qs ad to 10 mL; expected stability is 3 days.

(Continued)

Dipyridamole *(Continued)*

Dipyridamole 10 mg/mL was stable for up to 60 days at 5°C and 25°C in 1:1 mixtures of Ora-Sweet® and Ora-Plus®, Ora-Sweet® SF and Ora-Plus® and in cherry syrup

Allen LV and Erickson III MA, "Stability of Baclofen, Captopril, Diltiazem, Hydrochloride, Dipyridamole, and Flecainide Acetate in Extemporaneously Compounded Oral Liquids," *Am J Health Syst Pharm*, 1996, 53:2179-84.

Nahata MC and Hipple TF, *Pediatric Drug Formulations*, 2nd ed, Cincinnati, OH: Harvey Whitney Books Co, 1992.

Dirithromycin *(dye RITH roe mye sin)*

U.S. Brand Names Dynabac®

Therapeutic Category Antibiotic, Macrolide

Use Treatment of mild to moderate upper and lower respiratory tract infections due to *Moraxella catarrhalis*, *Streptococcus pneumoniae*, *Legionella pneumophila*, *H. influenzae*, or *S. pyogenes* ie, acute exacerbation of chronic bronchitis, secondary bacterial infection of acute bronchitis, community-acquired pneumonia, pharyngitis/tonsillitis, and uncomplicated infections of the skin and skin structure due to *Staphylococcus aureus*

Pregnancy Risk Factor C

Pregnancy/Breast-Feeding Implications

Clinical effects on the fetus: Animal studies indicate the use of dirithromycin during pregnancy should be avoided if possible

Breast-feeding/lactation: Use caution when administering to nursing women

Contraindications Hypersensitivity to any macrolide or component of dirithromycin; use with pimozide

Warnings/Precautions Contrary to potential serious consequences with other macrolides (eg, cardiac arrhythmias), the combination of terfenadine and dirithromycin has not shown alteration of terfenadine metabolism; however, caution should be taken during coadministration of dirithromycin and terfenadine; pseudomembranous colitis has been reported and should be considered in patients presenting with diarrhea subsequent to therapy with dirithromycin

Adverse Reactions

1% to 10%:

Central nervous system: Headache, dizziness, vertigo, insomnia

Dermatologic: Rash, pruritus, urticaria

Endocrine & metabolic: Hyperkalemia

Gastrointestinal: Abdominal pain, nausea, diarrhea, vomiting, dyspepsia, flatulence

Hematologic: Thrombocytosis, eosinophilia, segmented neutrophils

Neuromuscular & skeletal: Weakness, pain, increased CPK

Respiratory: Increased cough, dyspnea

<1%: Palpitations, vasodilation, syncope, edema, anxiety, depression, somnolence, fever, malaise, dysmenorrhea, hypochloremia, hypophosphatemia, increased uric acid, dehydration, abnormal stools, anorexia, gastritis, constipation, abnormal taste, xerostomia, abdominal pain, mouth ulceration, polyuria, vaginitis, neutropenia, thrombocytopenia, decreased hemoglobin/hematocrit; increased alkaline phosphatase, bands, basophils; leukocytosis, monocytosis, Increased ALT/AST, GGT; hyperbilirubinemia, paresthesia, tremor, myalgia, amblyopia, tinnitus, increased creatinine, phosphorus, epistaxis, hemoptysis, hyperventilation, hypoalbuminemia, flu-like syndrome, diaphoresis, thirst

Overdosage/Toxicology

Symptoms of overdose include nausea, vomiting, abdominal pain, diarrhea

Treatment is supportive; dialysis has not been found effective

Drug Interactions CYP3A3/4 enzyme inhibitor

Increased effect: Absorption of dirithromycin is slightly enhanced with concomitant antacids and H_2-antagonists; dirithromycin may, like erythromycin, increase the effect of alfentanil, anticoagulants, bromocriptine, carbamazepine, cyclosporine, digoxin, disopyramide, ergots, methylprednisolone, cisapride, astemizole

Increased toxicity: Avoid use with pimozide (due to risk of significant cardiotoxicity) and triazolam

Note: Interactions with nonsedating antihistamines (eg, terfenadine, astemizole), cisapride, and theophylline are not known to occur, however, caution is advised with coadministration.

Mechanism of Action After being converted during intestinal absorption to its active form, erythromycylamine, dirithromycin inhibits protein synthesis by binding to the 50S ribosomal subunits of susceptible microorganisms

Pharmacodynamics/Kinetics

Absorption: Rapidly absorbed and nonenzymatically hydrolyzed to erythromycylamine; T_{max}: 4 hours

Distribution: V_d: 800 L; rapidly and widely distributed (higher levels in tissues than plasma)

Protein binding: 14% to 30%

Metabolism: Hydrolyzed to erythromycylamine

Bioavailability: 10%

Half-life: 8 hours (range: 2-36 hours)

Elimination: Via bile (81% to 97% of dose)

Usual Dosage Adults: Oral: 500 mg once daily for 5-14 days (14 days required for treatment of community-acquired pneumonia due to *Legionella*, *Mycoplasma*, or *S. pneumoniae*; 10 days is recommended for treatment of *S. pyogenes* pharyngitis/tonsillitis)

Dosing adjustment in renal impairment: None necessary

Dosing adjustment in hepatic impairment: None needed in mild dysfunction; not studied in moderate to severe dysfunction

Administration Administer with food or within an hour following a meal

Monitoring Parameters Temperature, CBC

Patient Information Take with food or within an hour following a meal; do not cut, chew, or crush tablets; entire course of medication should be taken to ensure eradication of organism

Nursing Implications Do not crush tablets

Dosage Forms Tablet, enteric coated: 250 mg

♦ **Disalcid®** see Salsalate on page 1047

♦ **Disalicylic Acid** see Salsalate on page 1047

♦ **Disipal™** see Orphenadrine on page 867

♦ **Disodium Cromoglycate** see Cromolyn Sodium on page 300

♦ **d-Isoephedrine Hydrochloride** see Pseudoephedrine on page 993

♦ **Disonate®** [OTC] see Docusate on page 384

Disopyramide (dye soe PEER a mide)

Related Information
Antiarrhythmic Drugs Comparison on page 1297

U.S. Brand Names Norpace®

Synonyms Disopyramide Phosphate

Therapeutic Category Antiarrhythmic Agent, Class I-A

Use Suppression and prevention of unifocal and multifocal premature, ventricular premature complexes, coupled ventricular tachycardia; effective in the conversion of atrial fibrillation, atrial flutter, and paroxysmal atrial tachycardia to normal sinus rhythm and prevention of the reoccurrence of these arrhythmias after conversion by other methods

Pregnancy Risk Factor C

Contraindications Pre-existing second or third degree A-V block, cardiogenic shock, or known hypersensitivity to the drug; coadministration with sparfloxacin

Warnings/Precautions Pre-existing urinary retention, family history, or existing angle-closure glaucoma, myasthenia gravis, hypotension during initiation of therapy, congestive heart failure unless caused by an arrhythmias, widening of QRS complex during therapy or Q-T interval (>25% to 50% of baseline QRS complex or Q-T interval), sick-sinus syndrome or WPW, renal or hepatic impairment require decrease in dosage; disopyramide ineffective in hypokalemia and potentially toxic with hyperkalemia. Due to changes in total clearance (decreased) in elderly, monitor closely; the anticholinergic action may be intolerable and require discontinuation.

Adverse Reactions
>10%: Genitourinary: Urinary retention/hesitancy
1% to 10%:
  Cardiovascular: Chest pains, congestive heart failure, hypotension
  Endocrine & metabolic: Hypokalemia
  Gastrointestinal: Stomach pain, bloating, xerostomia
  Neuromuscular & skeletal: Muscle weakness
  Ocular: Blurred vision
<1%: Syncope and conduction disturbances including A-V block, widening QRS complex and lengthening of Q-T interval, fatigue, malaise, nervousness, acute psychosis, depression, dizziness, headache, pain, generalized rashes, hypoglycemia, may initiate contractions of pregnant uterus, hyperkalemia may enhance toxicities, increased cholesterol and triglycerides, constipation, nausea, vomiting, diarrhea, flatulence, anorexia, weight gain, dry throat, hepatic cholestasis, elevated liver enzymes, dry eyes, dyspnea, dry nose

Overdosage/Toxicology
Has a low toxic therapeutic ratio and may easily produce fatal intoxication (acute toxic dose: 1 g in adults); symptoms of overdose include sinus bradycardia, sinus node arrest or asystole, P-R, QRS or Q-T interval prolongation, torsade de pointes (polymorphous ventricular tachycardia) and depressed myocardial contractility, which along with alpha-adrenergic or ganglionic blockade, may result in hypotension and pulmonary edema; other effects are anticholinergic (dry mouth, dilated pupils, and delirium) as well as seizures, coma and respiratory arrest.
Treatment is primarily symptomatic and effects usually respond to conventional therapies (fluids, positioning, vasopressors, anticonvulsants, antiarrhythmics). **Note:** Do not use other type Ia or Ic antiarrhythmic agents to treat ventricular tachycardia; sodium bicarbonate may treat wide QRS intervals or hypotension; markedly impaired conduction or high degree A-V block, unresponsive to bicarbonate, indicates consideration of a pacemaker.

Drug Interactions CYP3A3/4 enzyme substrate
Decreased effect with hepatic microsomal enzyme-inducing agents (ie, phenytoin, phenobarbital, rifampin)
Increased effect/levels/toxicity with sparfloxacin; increased levels of digoxin
Increased effect/levels/toxicity with erythromycin; disopyramide levels when administered with erythromycin resulting in excessive QRS complex widening and/or prolongation of the Q-T interval

Mechanism of Action Class IA antiarrhythmic: Decreases myocardial excitability and conduction velocity; reduces disparity in refractory between normal and infarcted myocardium; possesses anticholinergic, peripheral vasoconstrictive, and negative inotropic effects

(Continued)

Disopyramide *(Continued)*

Pharmacodynamics/Kinetics
Onset of action: 0.5-3.5 hours
Duration of effect: 1.5-8.5 hours
Absorption: 60% to 83%
Protein binding: Concentration dependent, ranges from 20% to 60%
Metabolism: In the liver to inactive metabolites
Half-life: Adults: 4-10 hours, increased half-life with hepatic or renal disease
Elimination: 40% to 60% excreted unchanged in urine and 10% to 15% in feces

Usual Dosage Oral:
Children:
<1 year: 10-30 mg/kg/24 hours in 4 divided doses
1-4 years: 10-20 mg/kg/24 hours in 4 divided doses
4-12 years: 10-15 mg/kg/24 hours in 4 divided doses
12-18 years: 6-15 mg/kg/24 hours in 4 divided doses
Adults:
<50 kg: 100 mg every 6 hours or 200 mg every 12 hours (controlled release)
>50 kg: 150 mg every 6 hours or 300 mg every 12 hours (controlled release); if no response, may increase to 200 mg every 6 hours; maximum dose required for patients with severe refractory ventricular tachycardia is 400 mg every 6 hours
Dosing adjustment in renal impairment: 100 mg (nonsustained release) given at the following intervals: See table.

Disopyramide Phosphate

Creatinine Clearance (mL/min)	Dosage Interval
30-40	q8h
15-30	q12h
<15	q24h

or alter the dose as follows:
Cl_{cr} 30-<40 mL/minute: Reduce dose 50%
Cl_{cr} 15-30 mL/minute: Reduce dose 75%
Dialysis: Not dialyzable (0% to 5%) by hemo- or peritoneal methods; supplemental dose not necessary
Dosing interval in hepatic impairment: 100 mg every 6 hours or 200 mg every 12 hours (controlled release)
Administration Administer around-the-clock rather than 4 times/day (ie, 12-6-12-6, not 9-1-5-9) to promote less variation in peak and trough serum levels
Monitoring Parameters EKG, blood pressure, disopyramide drug level, urinary retention, CNS anticholinergic effects (confusion, agitation, hallucinations, etc)
Reference Range
Therapeutic concentration:
Atrial arrhythmias: 2.8-3.2 µg/mL
Ventricular arrhythmias 3.3-7.5 µg/mL
Toxic concentration: >7 µg/mL
Patient Information Notify physician if urinary retention or worsening CHF; do not break or chew sustained release capsules
Nursing Implications Do not crush controlled release capsules
Dosage Forms
Capsule, as phosphate: 100 mg, 150 mg
Capsule, sustained action, as phosphate: 100 mg, 150 mg
Extemporaneous Preparations Extemporaneous suspensions in cherry syrup (1 mg/mL and 10 mg/mL) are stable for 4 weeks in amber glass bottles stored at 5°C, 30°C, or at room temperature; shake well before use; do not use extended release capsules for this suspension

Mathur LK, Lai PK, and Shively CD, "Stability of Disopyramide Phosphate in Cherry Syrup," *J Hosp Pharm*, 1982, 39(2):309-10.

♦ **Disopyramide Phosphate** *see* Disopyramide *on previous page*
♦ **Disotate®** *see* Edetate Disodium *on page 405*
♦ **Di-Spaz® Injection** *see* Dicyclomine *on page 351*
♦ **Di-Spaz® Oral** *see* Dicyclomine *on page 351*
♦ **Dispos-a-Med® Isoproterenol** *see* Isoproterenol *on page 635*

Disulfiram *(dye SUL fi ram)*
Related Information
Depression Disorders and Treatments *on page 1465*
U.S. Brand Names Antabuse®
Therapeutic Category Aldehyde Dehydrogenase Inhibitor Agent; Antialcoholic Agent
Use Management of chronic alcoholism
Pregnancy Risk Factor C
Contraindications Severe myocardial disease and coronary occlusion, hypersensitivity to disulfiram or any component, patient receiving alcohol, paraldehyde, alcohol-containing preparations like cough syrup or tonics

Warnings/Precautions Use with caution in patients with diabetes, hypothyroidism, seizure disorders, hepatic cirrhosis, or insufficiency; should never be administered to a patient when he/she is in a state of alcohol intoxication, or without his/her knowledge

Adverse Reactions

>10%: Central nervous system: Drowsiness

1% to 10%:

Central nervous system: Headache, fatigue, mood changes, neurotoxicity

Dermatologic: Rash

Gastrointestinal: Metallic or garlic-like aftertaste

Genitourinary: Impotence

<1%: Encephalopathy, hepatitis

Disulfiram reaction with alcohol: Flushing, diaphoresis, cardiovascular collapse, myocardial infarction, vertigo, seizures, headache, nausea, vomiting, dyspnea, chest pain, death

Overdosage/Toxicology Management of disulfiram reaction: Institute support measures to restore blood pressure (pressors and fluids); monitor for hypokalemia

Drug Interactions CYP2C9 and 2E1 enzyme inhibitor, both disulfiram and diethyldithio-carbamate (disulfiram metabolite) are CYP3A/4 enzyme inhibitors

Increased effect: Diazepam, chlordiazepoxide

Increased toxicity:

Alcohol and disulfiram: Antabuse® reaction

Tricyclic antidepressants, metronidazole, isoniazid: Encephalopathy

Phenytoin may increase serum levels and toxicity

Warfarin may increase prothrombin time

Mechanism of Action Disulfiram is a thiuram derivative which interferes with aldehyde dehydrogenase. When taken concomitantly with alcohol, there is an increase in serum acetaldehyde levels. High acetaldehyde causes uncomfortable symptoms including flushing, nausea, thirst, palpitations, chest pain, vertigo, and hypotension. This reaction is the basis for disulfiram use in postwithdrawal long-term care of alcoholism.

Pharmacodynamics/Kinetics

Absorption: Rapid from GI tract

Full effect: 12 hours

Metabolism: To diethylthiocarbamate

Duration: May persist for 1-2 weeks after last dose

Usual Dosage Adults: Oral: Do not administer until the patient has abstained from alcohol for at least 12 hours

Initial: 500 mg/day as a single dose for 1-2 weeks; maximum daily dose is 500 mg

Average maintenance dose: 250 mg/day; range: 125-500 mg; duration of therapy is to continue until the patient is fully recovered socially and a basis for permanent self control has been established; maintenance therapy may be required for months or even years

Dietary Considerations Alcohol: Avoid use, including alcohol-containing products

Patient Information Do not drink any alcohol, including products containing alcohol (cough and cold syrups), or use alcohol-containing skin products for at least 3 days and preferably 14 days after stopping this medication or while taking this medication; not for treatment of alcohol intoxication; may cause drowsiness; tablets can be crushed or mixed with water

Nursing Implications Administration of any medications containing alcohol including topicals is contraindicated

Dosage Forms Tablet: 250 mg, 500 mg

♦ **Dithioglycerol** see Dimercaprol on page 367

♦ **Ditropan®** see Oxybutynin on page 873

♦ **Ditropan XL®** see Oxybutynin on page 873

♦ **Diucardin®** see Hydroflumethiazide on page 582

♦ **Diuchlor®** see Hydrochlorothiazide on page 574

♦ **Diurigen®** see Chlorothiazide on page 244

♦ **Diuril®** see Chlorothiazide on page 244

♦ **Divalproex Sodium** see Valproic Acid and Derivatives on page 1203

♦ **Dixarit®** see Clonidine on page 283

♦ **Dizac® Injectable Emulsion** see Diazepam on page 345

♦ **Dizmiss® [OTC]** see Meclizine on page 719

♦ **dl-Alpha Tocopherol** see Vitamin E on page 1225

♦ **dl-Norephedrine Hydrochloride** see Phenylpropanolamine on page 919

♦ **D-Mannitol** see Mannitol on page 711

♦ **4-DMDR** see Idarubicin on page 596

♦ **D-Med® Injection** see Methylprednisolone on page 762

♦ **DNase** see Dornase Alfa on page 388

♦ **DNR** see Daunorubicin Hydrochloride on page 327

Dobutamine (doe BYOO ta meen)

Related Information

Adrenergic Agonists, Cardiovascular Comparison on page 1290

Adult ACLS Algorithm, Hypotension, Shock on page 1454

Extravasation Treatment of Other Drugs on page 1287

U.S. Brand Names Dobutrex® Injection

Synonyms Dobutamine Hydrochloride

(Continued)

Dobutamine *(Continued)*

Therapeutic Category Adrenergic Agonist Agent; Sympathomimetic

Use Short-term management of patients with cardiac decompensation

Pregnancy Risk Factor C

Contraindications Hypersensitivity to sulfites (commercial preparation contains sodium bisulfite); patients with idiopathic hypertrophic subaortic stenosis, atrial fibrillation or atrial flutter

Warnings/Precautions Hypovolemia should be corrected prior to use; infiltration causes local inflammatory changes, extravasation may cause dermal necrosis; use with extreme caution following myocardial infarction; potent drug, must be diluted prior to use

Adverse Reactions

>10%: Cardiovascular: Ectopic heartbeats, increased heart rate, chest pain, angina, palpitations, elevated blood pressure; in higher doses ventricular tachycardia or arrhythmias may be seen; patients with atrial fibrillation or flutter are at risk of developing a rapid ventricular response

1% to 10%:

Cardiovascular: Premature ventricular beats

Central nervous system: Headache

Gastrointestinal: Nausea, vomiting

Neuromuscular & skeletal: Mild leg cramps, paresthesia

Respiratory: Dyspnea, shortness of breath

Overdosage/Toxicology

Symptoms of overdose include fatigue, nervousness, tachycardia, hypertension, arrhythmias

Reduce rate of administration or discontinue infusion until condition stabilizes

Drug Interactions

Decreased effect: Beta-adrenergic blockers (increased peripheral resistance)

Increased toxicity: General anesthetics (ie, halothane or cyclopropane) and usual doses of dobutamine have resulted in ventricular arrhythmias in animals

Stability Remix solution every 24 hours; store reconstituted solution under refrigeration for 48 hours or 6 hours at room temperature; pink discoloration of solution indicates slight oxidation but **no** significant loss of potency.

Stability of parenteral admixture at room temperature (25°C): 48 hours; at refrigeration (4°C): 7 days

Standard adult diluent: 250 mg/500 mL D_5W; 500 mg/500 mL D_5W

Incompatible with heparin, cefazolin, penicillin, and sodium bicarbonate; **incompatible** in alkaline solutions (sodium bicarbonate)

Compatible with dopamine, epinephrine, isoproterenol, lidocaine

Mechanism of Action Stimulates $beta_1$-adrenergic receptors, causing increased contractility and heart rate, with little effect on $beta_2$- or alpha-receptors

Pharmacodynamics/Kinetics

Onset of action: I.V.: 1-10 minutes

Peak effect: Within 10-20 minutes

Metabolism: In tissues and the liver to inactive metabolites

Half-life: 2 minutes

Elimination: Metabolites are excreted in urine

Usual Dosage Administration requires the use of an infusion pump; I.V. infusion: See table.

Infusion Rates of Various Dilutions of Dobutamine

Desired Delivery Rate (mcg/kg/min)	Infusion Rate (mL/kg/min)	
	250 mg/500 mL diluent (500 mcg/mL)	500 mg/500 mL diluent (1 mg/mL)
2.5	0.005	0.0025
5	0.01	0.005
7.5	0.015	0.0075
10	0.02	0.01
12.5	0.025	0.0125
15	0.03	0.015
20	0.04	0.02

Neonates: 2-15 mcg/kg/minute, titrate to desired response

Children and Adults: 2.5-20 mcg/kg/minute; maximum: 40 mcg/kg/minute, titrate to desired response

Administration Use infusion device to control rate of flow; administer into large vein

To prepare for infusion:

$$\frac{6 \times weight\ (kg) \times desired\ dose\ (mcg/kg/min)}{I.V.\ infusion\ rate\ (mL/h)} = \begin{array}{l} mg\ of\ drug\ to\ be\ added\ to \\ 100\ mL\ of\ I.V.\ fluid \end{array}$$

Do not administer through same I.V. line as heparin, hydrocortisone sodium succinate, cefazolin, or penicillin

Monitoring Parameters Blood pressure, EKG, heart rate, CVP, RAP, MAP, urine output; if pulmonary artery catheter is in place, monitor CI, PCWP, and SVR; also monitor serum potassium

Patient Information May affect serum assay of chloramphenicol

Nursing Implications Management of extravasation: Phentolamine: Mix 5 mg with 9 mL of NS; inject a small amount of this dilution into extravasation area; blanching should reverse immediately. Monitor site; if blanching should recur, additional injections of phentolamine may be needed.

Dosage Forms Infusion, as hydrochloride: 12.5 mg/mL (20 mL)

♦ **Dobutamine Hydrochloride** see Dobutamine on page 381

♦ **Dobutrex® Injection** see Dobutamine on page 381

Docetaxel (doe se TAKS el)

Related Information
Toxicities of Chemotherapeutic Agents on page 1288

U.S. Brand Names Taxotere®

Therapeutic Category Antineoplastic Agent, Antimicrotubular

Use Treatment of patients with locally advanced or metastatic breast cancer who have progressed during anthracycline-based therapy or have relapsed during anthracycline-based adjuvant therapy

Investigational: Treatment of nonsmall cell lung cancer, gastric, pancreatic, head and neck, ovarian, soft tissue sarcoma, and melanoma

Pregnancy Risk Factor D

Contraindications History of hypersensitivity to any component

Warnings/Precautions Early studies reported severe hypersensitivity reactions characterized by hypotension, bronchospasms, or minor reactions characterized by generalized rash/erythema. The overall incidence was 25% in patients who did not receive premedication.

Fluid retention syndrome characterized by pleural effusions, ascites, edema, and weight gain (2-15 kg) has also been reported. It has not been associated with cardiac, pulmonary, renal, hepatic, or endocrine dysfunction. The incidence and severity of the syndrome increase sharply at cumulative doses ≥400 mg/m².

Premedication to reduce fluid retention and hypersensitivity reactions: Oral dexamethasone 8 mg twice daily for 5 days starting one day prior to docetaxel exposure. There is also data to support that a 3-day corticosteroid regimen (oral dexamethasone 8 mg twice daily for 3 days starting one day prior to docetaxel exposure) was as effective as the standard 5-day regimen in reducing the incidence and severity of fluid retention. In addition, the 3-day regimen had a more favorable safety profile.

Neutropenia was the dose-limiting toxicity; however this rarely resulted in treatment delays and prophylactic colony stimulating factors have not been routinely used. Patients with increased liver function tests experienced more episodes of neutropenia with a greater number of severe infections. Patients with an absolute neutrophil count <1500 cells/mm³ should not receive docetaxel.

Adverse Reactions
Irritant chemotherapy
>10%:
    Central nervous system: Fever
    Dermatologic: Alopecia
    Gastrointestinal: Nausea, vomiting, diarrhea, stomatitis
    Hematologic: Neutropenia, leukopenia, thrombocytopenia, anemia
    Neuromuscular & skeletal: Myalgia
1% to 10%: Cardiovascular: Severe fluid retention: poorly tolerated peripheral edema, generalized edema, pleural effusion requiring urgent drainage, dyspnea at rest, cardiac tamponade or pronounced abdominal distention (due to ascites)
<1%: Hypersensitivity reactions, myocardial infarction, gastrointestinal perforation, neutropenic enterocolitis

Drug Interactions CYP3A3/4 enzyme substrate
Increased toxicity: Possibility of an inhibition of metabolism in patients treated with ketoconazole, erythromycin, terfenadine, and cyclosporine

Stability Docetaxel is available in 20 mg and 80 mg vials prepackaged with a special diluent and formulated in polysorbate 80. Docetaxel is diluted with 13% (w/w) ethanol in water giving a final concentration of 10 mg/mL. Docetaxel is slightly more water soluble than paclitaxel. Intact vials should stored under refrigeration (2°C to 8°C/36°F to 46°F) and protected from light. Vials should be stored at room temperature for approximately 5 minutes before using.

Docetaxel is **compatible** with 0.9% sodium chloride or 5% dextrose in water and should be diluted to a final concentration of 0.3-0.9 mg/mL. Diluted solutions are stable for 8 hours at either room temperature (15°C to 25°C/59°F to 77°F) or refrigeration (2°C to 8°C/36°F to 46°F). Solutions must be prepared in a glass bottle, polypropylene, or polyolefin plastic bag to prevent leaching of plasticizers. Nonpolyvinyl chloride tubing should be used.

Mechanism of Action Semisynthetic agent prepared from a noncytotoxic precursor which is extracted from the needles of the European Yew *Taxus baccata*. Docetaxel differs structurally from the prototype taxoid, paclitaxel, by substitutions at the C-10 and C-5 positions. It is an antimicrotubule agent, but exhibits a unique mechanism of action. Unlike other antimicrotubule agents that induce microtubule disassembly (eg, vinca alkaloids and colchicine), docetaxel promotes the assembly of microtubules from tubulin dimers, and inhibits the depolymerization of tubulin which leads to bundles of microtubules in the cell.

(Continued)

Docetaxel (Continued)

Pharmacodynamics/Kinetics Administered by I.V. infusion and exhibits linear pharmacokinetics at the recommended dosage range

Distribution: Exhibits a triphasic decline in plasma concentrations. Initial rapid decline represents distribution to the peripheral compartment and the terminal phase reflects a relatively slow efflux of docetaxel from the peripheral compartment. mean steady state: 36.6-95.6 L/m², indicating extensive extravascular distribution and/or tissue binding. Mean steady state volume of distribution is 113 Liters.

Protein binding: 94% mainly to alpha₁-acid glycoprotein, albumin, and lipoproteins

Metabolism: Oxidative metabolism by the liver. Isoenzymes of cytochrome P-450 (CYA3A) are involved in the metabolism

Half-lifes: α, β, and γ phases are 4 minutes, 36 minutes, and 11.1 hours, respectively

Elimination: Following oxidative metabolism, docetaxel is eliminated in both urine (6%) and feces (75%) with approximately 80% eliminated in the first 48 hours

Mean values for total body clearance 21 L/hour/m²

Usual Dosage Corticosteroids (oral dexamethasone 8 mg twice daily for 3 days or 5 days starting 1 day prior to docetaxel administration) are necessary to reduce the potential for hypersensitivity and severe fluid retention

Adults: I.V. infusion: Refer to individual protocols:

Locally advanced or metastatic carcinoma of the breast: 60-100 mg/m² over 1 hour every 3 weeks

Dosage adjustment in patients who are initially started at 100 mg/m² (>1 week), cumulative cutaneous reactions, or severe peripheral neuropathy: 75 mg/m²

Note: If the patient continues to experience these adverse reactions, the dosage should be reduced to 55 mg/m² or therapy should be discontinued

Dosing adjustment in hepatic impairment:

Total bilirubin ≥ the upper limit of normal (ULN), or AST/ALT >1.5 times the ULN concomitant with alkaline phosphatase >2.5 times the ULN: Docetaxel **should not be administered** secondary to increased incidence of treatment-related mortality

Administration

Anaphylactoid-like reactions have been reported: Premedication with dexamethasone (8 mg orally twice daily for 5 days starting one day prior to administration of docetaxel)

Administer I.V. infusion over 1-hour

Monitoring Parameters Monitor for hypersensitivity reactions and fluid retention

Patient Information Alopecia occurs in almost all patients; contraceptive measures are recommended during therapy

Dosage Forms Injection: 40 mg/mL (0.5 mL, 2 mL)

Docusate (DOK yoo sate)

Related Information

Laxatives, Classification and Properties on page 1326

U.S. Brand Names Colace® [OTC]; DC 240® Softgels® [OTC]; Dialose® [OTC]; Diocto® [OTC]; Diocto-K® [OTC]; Dioeze® [OTC]; Disonate® [OTC]; DOK® [OTC]; DOS® Softgel® [OTC]; D-S-S® [OTC]; Kasof® [OTC]; Modane® Soft [OTC]; Pro-Cal-Sof® [OTC]; Regulax SS® [OTC]; Sulfalax® [OTC]; Surfak® [OTC]

Canadian Brand Names Albert® Docusate; Colax-C®; PMS-Docusate Calcium; Regulex®; Selax®; SoFlax™

Synonyms Dioctyl Calcium Sulfosuccinate; Dioctyl Potassium Sulfosuccinate; Dioctyl Sodium Sulfosuccinate; Docusate Calcium; Docusate Potassium; Docusate Sodium; DOSS; DSS

Therapeutic Category Laxative, Surfactant; Stool Softener

Use Stool softener in patients who should avoid straining during defecation and constipation associated with hard, dry stools; prophylaxis for straining (Valsalva) following myocardial infarction. A safe agent to be used in elderly; some evidence that doses <200 mg are ineffective; stool softeners are unnecessary if stool is well hydrated or "mushy" and soft; shown to be ineffective used long-term.

Pregnancy Risk Factor C

Contraindications Concomitant use of mineral oil; intestinal obstruction, acute abdominal pain, nausea, vomiting; hypersensitivity to docusate or any component

Warnings/Precautions Prolonged, frequent or excessive use may result in dependence or electrolyte imbalance

Adverse Reactions 1% to 10%:

Gastrointestinal: Intestinal obstruction, diarrhea, abdominal cramping

Miscellaneous: Throat irritation

Overdosage/Toxicology

Symptoms of overdose include abdominal cramps, diarrhea, fluid loss, hypokalemia Treatment is symptomatic

Drug Interactions

Decreased effect of Coumadin® with high doses of docusate

Increased toxicity with mineral oil, phenolphthalein

Mechanism of Action Reduces surface tension of the oil-water interface of the stool resulting in enhanced incorporation of water and fat allowing for stool softening

Pharmacodynamics/Kinetics Onset of action: 12-72 hours

Usual Dosage Docusate salts are interchangeable; the amount of sodium, calcium, or potassium per dosage unit is clinically insignificant

Infants and Children <3 years: Oral: 10-40 mg/day in 1-4 divided doses

Children: Oral:
   3-6 years: 20-60 mg/day in 1-4 divided doses
   6-12 years: 40-150 mg/day in 1-4 divided doses
Adolescents and Adults: Oral: 50-500 mg/day in 1-4 divided doses
Older Children and Adults: Rectal: Add 50-100 mg of docusate liquid to enema fluid (saline or water); administer as retention or flushing enema

Test Interactions ↓ potassium (S), ↓ chloride (S)

Patient Information Adults: Docusate should be taken with a full glass of water; do not use if abdominal pain, nausea, or vomiting are present; laxative use should be used for a short period of time (<1 week); prolonged use may result in abuse, dependence, as well as fluid and electrolyte loss; notify physician if bleeding occurs or if constipation is not relieved

Nursing Implications Docusate liquid should be given with milk, fruit juice, or infant formula to mask the bitter taste

Dosage Forms
Capsule, as calcium:
   DC 240® Softgels®, Pro-Cal-Sof®, Sulfalax®: 240 mg
   Surfak®: 50 mg, 240 mg
Capsule, as potassium:
   Diocto-K®: 100 mg
   Kasof®: 240 mg
Capsule, as sodium:
   Colace®: 50 mg, 100 mg
   Dioeze®: 250 mg
   Disonate®: 100 mg, 240 mg
   DOK®: 100 mg, 250 mg
   DOS® Softgel®: 100 mg, 250 mg
   D-S-S®: 100 mg
   Modane® Soft: 100 mg
   Regulax SS®: 100 mg, 250 mg
Liquid, as sodium (Diocto®, Colace®, Disonate®, DOK®): 150 mg/15 mL (30 mL, 60 mL, 480 mL)
Solution, oral, as sodium (Doxinate®): 50 mg/mL with alcohol 5% (60 mL, 3780 mL)
Syrup, as sodium:
   50 mg/15 mL (15 mL, 30 mL)
   Colace®, Diocto®, Disonate®, DOK®: 60 mg/15 mL (240 mL, 480 mL, 3780 mL)
Tablet, as sodium (Dialose®): 100 mg

♦ **Docusate Calcium** see Docusate on previous page
♦ **Docusate Potassium** see Docusate on previous page
♦ **Docusate Sodium** see Docusate on previous page
♦ **DOK® [OTC]** see Docusate on previous page
♦ **Doktors® Nasal Solution [OTC]** see Phenylephrine on page 918
♦ **Dolacet®** see Hydrocodone and Acetaminophen on page 575

Dolasetron (dol A se tron)

U.S. Brand Names Anzemet®

Synonyms Dolasetron Mesylate

Therapeutic Category Antiemetic, Serotonin Antagonist; 5-HT₃ Receptor Antagonist; Serotonin Antagonist

Use Prevention of nausea and vomiting associated with emetogenic cancer chemotherapy, including initial and repeat courses; prevention of postoperative nausea and vomiting and treatment of postoperative nausea and vomiting (injectable form only)

Pregnancy Risk Factor B

Contraindications Patients known to have hypersensitivity to the drug

Warnings/Precautions Dolasetron should be administered with caution in patients who have or may develop prolongation of cardiac conduction intervals, particularly QT$_c$ intervals. These include patients with hypokalemia or hypomagnesemia, patients taking diuretics with potential for inducing electrolyte abnormalities, patients with congenital Q-T syndrome, patients taking antiarrhythmic drugs or other drugs which lead to Q-T prolongation, and cumulative high-dose anthracycline therapy.

Adverse Reactions Dolasetron can cause electrocardiographic interval changes, which are related in frequency and magnitude to blood levels of the metabolite, hydrodolasetron

>2%:
   Cardiovascular: Hypertension
   Central nervous system: Headache, fatigue, dizziness, fever, chills and shivering
   Gastrointestinal: Diarrhea, abdominal pain
   Genitourinary: Urinary retention
   Hepatic: Transient increases in liver enzymes

Overdosage/Toxicology
In animal toxicity studies, doses 6.3-12.6 times the recommended human dose based upon surface area were lethal and symptoms of acute poisoning included tremors, depression, and convulsions
There is no known specific antidote for dolasetron and patients with suspected overdose should be managed with supportive therapy

Drug Interactions CYP2D6 and 3A3/4 enzyme substrate

(Continued)

Dolasetron *(Continued)*

Blood levels of the active metabolite are increased when dolasetron is coadministered with cimetidine, decreased with rifampin. Clearance of hydrodolasetron decreases when dolasetron is given with atenolol.

Stability After dilution, I.V. dolasetron is stable under normal lighting conditions at room temperature for 24 hours or under refrigeration for 48 hours with the following **compatible** intravenous fluids: 0.9% sodium chloride injection, 5% dextrose injection, 5% dextrose and 0.45% sodium chloride injection, 5% dextrose and lactated Ringer's injection, lactated Ringer's injection, and 10% mannitol injection

Mechanism of Action Dolasetron is a pseudopelletierine-derived serotonin antagonist. Serotonin antagonists block the serotonin receptors in the chemoreceptor trigger zone and in the gastrointestinal tract. Once the receptor site is blocked, antagonism of vomiting occurs.

Usual Dosage

Children <2 years: Not recommended for use

Nausea and vomiting associated with chemotherapy (including initial and repeat courses):

Children 2-16 years:

Oral: 1.8 mg/kg within 1 hour before chemotherapy; maximum: 100 mg/dose

I.V.: 1.8 mg/kg ~30 minutes before chemotherapy; maximum: 100 mg/dose

Adults:

Oral: 100 mg within 1 hour before chemotherapy

I.V.: 1.8 mg/kg ~30 minutes before chemotherapy or may give 100 mg

Prevention of postoperative nausea and vomiting:

Children 2-16 years:

Oral: 1.2 mg within 2 hours before surgery; maximum: 100 mg/dose

I.V.: 0.35 mg/kg (maximum: 12.5 mg) ~15 minutes before stopping anesthesia

Adults:

Oral: 100 mg within 2 hours before surgery

I.V.: 12.5 mg ~15 minutes before stopping anesthesia

Treatment of postoperative nausea and vomiting: I.V. only:

Children 2-16 years: 0.35 mg/kg as soon as needed

Adults: 12.5 mg as soon as needed

Dosing adjustment for elderly, renal/hepatic impairment: No dosage adjustment is recommended

Administration I.V. injection may be given either undiluted IVP over 30 seconds or diluted to 50 mL and infused as an IVPB over 15 minutes. Dolasetron injection may be diluted in apple or apple-grape juice and taken orally (Note: Timing and doses are different with oral and I.V. routes of administration)

Monitoring Parameters Liver function tests, blood pressure and pulse, and EKG in patients with cardiovascular disease

Nursing Implications Dolasetron injection may be diluted in apple or apple-grape juice and taken orally

Additional Information A single I.V. dose of dolasetron mesylate (1.8 or 2.4 mg/kg) has comparable safety and efficacy to a single 32 mg I.V. dose of ondansetron in patients receiving cisplatin chemotherapy

Dosage Forms

Injection, as mesylate: 20 mg/mL (0.625 mL, 5 mL)

Tablet, as mesylate: 50 mg, 100 mg

♦ **Dolasetron Mesylate** *see Dolasetron on previous page*

♦ **Dolene®** *see Propoxyphene on page 985*

♦ **Dolobid®** *see Diflunisal on page 356*

♦ **Dolophine®** *see Methadone on page 744*

♦ **Dome Paste Bandage** *see Zinc Gelatin on page 1238*

Donepezil *(don EH pa zil)*

U.S. Brand Names Aricept®

Synonyms E2020

Therapeutic Category Cholinergic Agent

Use Treatment of mild to moderate dementia of the Alzheimer's type

Pregnancy Risk Factor C

Contraindications Patients who are hypersensitive to donepezil or piperidine derivatives

Warnings/Precautions Use with caution in patients with sick sinus syndrome or other supraventricular cardiac conduction abnormalities, in patients with seizures or asthma; avoid use in nursing mothers

Adverse Reactions

>10%:

Central nervous system: Headache

Gastrointestinal: Nausea, diarrhea

1% to 10%:

Cardiovascular: Syncope, chest pain

Central nervous system: Fatigue, insomnia, dizziness, depression, abnormal dreams, somnolence

Dermatologic: Bruising

Gastrointestinal: Anorexia, vomiting, weight loss

Genitourinary: Polyuria

Neuromuscular & skeletal: Muscle cramps, arthritis, body pain

Overdosage/Toxicology

General supportive measures; can cause a cholinergic crisis characterized by severe nausea, vomiting, salivation, sweating, bradycardia, hypotension, collapse, and convulsions; increased muscle weakness is a possibility and may result in death if respiratory muscles are involved

Tertiary anticholinergics, such as atropine, may be used as an antidote for overdosage. I.V. atropine sulfate titrated to effect is recommended; initial dose of 1-2 mg I.V. with subsequent doses based upon clinical response. Atypical increases in blood pressure and heart rate have been reported with other cholinomimetics when coadministered with quaternary anticholinergics such as glycopyrrolate.

Drug Interactions CYP2D6 and 3A3/4 enzyme substrate

Increased effects of succinylcholine, cholinesterase inhibitors, or cholinergic agonists (bethanechol). Concomitant NSAIDs may increase the risk of gastrointestinal bleeding.

Mechanism of Action Alzheimer's disease is characterized by cholinergic deficiency in the cortex and basal forebrain, which contributes to cognitive deficits. Donepezil reversibly and noncompetitively inhibits centrally-active acetylcholinesterase, the enzyme responsible for hydrolysis of acetylcholine. This appears to result in increased concentrations of acetylcholine available for synaptic transmission in the central nervous system.

Usual Dosage Adults: Initial: 5 mg/day at bedtime; may increase to 10 mg/day at bedtime after 4-6 weeks

Dosage Forms Tablet: 5 mg, 10 mg

Dopamine (DOE pa meen)

Related Information

Adrenergic Agonists, Cardiovascular Comparison on page 1290
Adult ACLS Algorithm, Bradycardia on page 1452
Adult ACLS Algorithm, Hypotension, Shock on page 1454
Extravasation Treatment of Other Drugs on page 1287

U.S. Brand Names Intropin® Injection

Synonyms Dopamine Hydrochloride

Therapeutic Category Adrenergic Agonist Agent; Sympathomimetic; Vesicant

Use Adjunct in the treatment of shock which persists after adequate fluid volume replacement

Pregnancy Risk Factor C

Contraindications Hypersensitivity to sulfites (commercial preparation contains sodium bisulfite); pheochromocytoma or ventricular fibrillation

Warnings/Precautions Safety in children has not been established; hypovolemia should be corrected by appropriate plasma volume expanders before administration; extravasation may cause tissue necrosis; potent drug, must be diluted prior to use; patient's hemodynamic status should be monitored; use with caution in patients with cardiovascular disease or cardiac arrhythmias or patients with occlusive vascular disease

Adverse Reactions

>10%:

Cardiovascular: Ectopic heartbeats, tachycardia, vasoconstriction, hypotension, cardiac conduction abnormalities, widened QRS complex, ventricular arrhythmias

Central nervous system: Headache

Gastrointestinal: Nausea, vomiting

Respiratory: Dyspnea

1% to 10%: Cardiovascular: Bradycardia, hypertension, gangrene of the extremities

<1%: Vasoconstriction, anxiety, piloerection, azotemia, decreased urine output

Overdosage/Toxicology

Symptoms of overdose include severe hypertension, cardiac arrhythmias, acute renal failure

Important: Antidote for peripheral ischemia: To prevent sloughing and necrosis in ischemic areas, the area should be infiltrated as soon as possible with 10-15 mL of saline solution containing from 5-10 mg of Regitine® (brand of phentolamine), an adrenergic blocking agent. A syringe with a fine hypodermic needle should be used, and the solution liberally infiltrated throughout the ischemic area. Sympathetic blockade with phentolamine causes immediate and conspicuous local hyperemic changes if the area is infiltrated within 12 hours. Therefore, phentolamine should be given as soon as possible after the extravasation is noted.

Drug Interactions Increased effect: Dopamine's effects are prolonged and intensified by MAO inhibitors, alpha- and beta-adrenergic blockers, general anesthetics, phenytoin

Stability Protect from light; solutions that are darker than slightly yellow should not be used; **incompatible** with alkaline solutions or iron salts; **compatible** when coadministered with dobutamine, epinephrine, isoproterenol, and lidocaine

Mechanism of Action Stimulates both adrenergic and dopaminergic receptors, lower doses are mainly dopaminergic stimulating and produce renal and mesenteric vasodilation, higher doses also are both dopaminergic and beta$_1$-adrenergic stimulating and produce cardiac stimulation and renal vasodilation; large doses stimulate alpha-adrenergic receptors

(Continued)

Dopamine *(Continued)*

Pharmacodynamics/Kinetics

Children: With medication changes, may not achieve steady-state for ~1 hour rather than 20 minutes

Adults: Onset of action: 5 minutes; Duration: <10 minutes

Metabolism: In the plasma, kidneys, and liver 75% to inactive metabolites by monoamine oxidase and 25% to norepinephrine (active)

Half-life: 2 minutes

Elimination: Metabolites are excreted in urine; neonatal clearance varies and appears to be age related; clearance is more prolonged with combined hepatic and renal dysfunction

Dopamine has exhibited nonlinear kinetics in children

Usual Dosage I.V. infusion (administration requires the use of an infusion pump):

Neonates: 1-20 mcg/kg/minute continuous infusion, titrate to desired response

Children: 1-20 mcg/kg/minute, maximum: 50 mcg/kg/minute continuous infusion, titrate to desired response

Adults: 1-5 mcg/kg/minute up to 50 mcg/kg/minute, titrate to desired response; infusion may be increased by 1-4 mcg/kg/minute at 10- to 30-minute intervals until optimal response is obtained

If dosages >20-30 mcg/kg/minute are needed, a more direct-acting pressor may be more beneficial (ie, epinephrine, norepinephrine)

The hemodynamic effects of dopamine are dose-dependent:

Low-dose: 1-3 mcg/kg/minute, increased renal blood flow and urine output

Intermediate-dose: 3-10 mcg/kg/minute, increased renal blood flow, heart rate, cardiac contractility, and cardiac output

High-dose: >10 mcg/kg/minute, alpha-adrenergic effects begin to predominate, vasoconstriction, increased blood pressure

Administration

Administer into large vein to prevent the possibility of extravasation; monitor continuously for free flow; use infusion device to control rate of flow; administration into an umbilical arterial catheter is not recommended; central line administration

To prepare for infusion:

$$\frac{6 \times \text{weight (kg)} \times \text{desired dose (mcg/kg/min)}}{\text{I.V. infusion rate (mL/h)}} = \frac{\text{mg of drug to be added to}}{\text{100 mL of I.V. fluid}}$$

Monitoring Parameters Blood pressure, EKG, heart rate, CVP, RAP, MAP, urine output; if pulmonary artery catheter is in place, monitor CI, PCWP, SVR, and PVR

Nursing Implications Extravasation: Due to short half-life, withdrawal of drug is often only necessary treatment. Use phentolamine as antidote; mix 5 mg with 9 mL of NS; inject a small amount of this dilution into extravasated area; blanching should reverse immediately. Monitor site; if blanching should recur, additional injections of phentolamine may be needed.

Dosage Forms

Infusion, as hydrochloride, in D₅W: 0.8 mg/mL (250 mL, 500 mL); 1.6 mg/mL (250 mL, 500 mL); 3.2 mg/mL (250 mL, 500 mL)

Injection, as hydrochloride: 40 mg/mL (5 mL, 10 mL, 20 mL); 80 mg/mL (5 mL, 20 mL); 160 mg/mL (5 mL)

- ◆ **Dopamine Hydrochloride** *see Dopamine on previous page*
- ◆ **Dopar®** *see Levodopa on page 671*
- ◆ **Dopram® Injection** *see Doxapram on page 391*
- ◆ **Doral®** *see Quazepam on page 1000*
- ◆ **Dormarex® 2 Oral [OTC]** *see Diphenhydramine on page 369*
- ◆ **Dormin® Oral [OTC]** *see Diphenhydramine on page 369*

Dornase Alfa *(DOOR nase AL fa)*

U.S. Brand Names Pulmozyme®

Synonyms DNase; Recombinant Human Deoxyribonuclease

Therapeutic Category Enzyme

Use Management of cystic fibrosis patients to reduce the frequency of respiratory infections that require parenteral antibiotics, and to improve pulmonary function; has also demonstrated value in the treatment of chronic bronchitis

Pregnancy Risk Factor B

Contraindications Contraindicated in patients with known hypersensitivity to dornase alfa, Chinese hamster ovary cell products (eg, epoetin alfa), or any component

Warnings/Precautions No clinical trials have been conducted to demonstrate safety and effectiveness of dornase in children <5 years of age, in patients with pulmonary function <40% of normal, or in patients for longer treatment periods >12 months; no data exists regarding safety during lactation

Adverse Reactions

>10%:

Respiratory: Pharyngitis

Miscellaneous: Voice alteration

1% to 10%:

Cardiovascular: Chest pain

Dermatologic: Rash

Ocular: Conjunctivitis

Respiratory: Laryngitis, cough, dyspnea, hemoptysis, rhinitis, hoarse throat, wheezing

Stability Must be stored in the refrigerator at 2°C to 8°C (36°F to 46°F) and protected from strong light; should not be exposed to room temperature for a total of 24 hours

Mechanism of Action The hallmark of cystic fibrosis lung disease is the presence of abundant, purulent airway secretions composed primarily of highly polymerized DNA. The principal source of this DNA is the nuclei of degenerating neutrophils, which is present in large concentrations in infected lung secretions. The presence of this DNA produces a viscous mucous that may contribute to the decreased mucociliary transport and persistent infections that are commonly seen in this population. Dornase alfa is a deoxyribonuclease (DNA) enzyme produced by recombinant gene technology. Dornase selectively cleaves DNA, thus reducing mucous viscosity and as a result, airflow in the lung is improved and the risk of bacterial infection may be decreased.

Pharmacodynamics/Kinetics Following nebulization, enzyme levels are measurable in the sputum within 15 minutes and decline rapidly thereafter

Usual Dosage Children >5 years and Adults: Inhalation: 2.5 mg once daily through selected nebulizers in conjunction with a Pulmo-Aide® or a Pari-Proneb® compressor

Nursing Implications Should not be diluted or mixed with any other drugs in the nebulizer, this may inactivate the drug

Dosage Forms Solution, inhalation: 1 mg/mL (2.5 mL)

♦ **Doryx®** see Doxycycline on page 397

Dorzolamide (dor ZOLE a mide)

Related Information

Glaucoma Drug Therapy Comparison on page 1322

U.S. Brand Names Trusopt®

Synonyms Dorzolamide Hydrochloride

Therapeutic Category Carbonic Anhydrase Inhibitor

Use Lowers intraocular pressure to treat glaucoma in patients with ocular hypertension or open-angle glaucoma

Pregnancy Risk Factor C

Contraindications Hypersensitivity to any component of the product; contains benzalkonium chloride as a preservative

Warnings/Precautions

Although administered topically, systemic absorption occurs. Same types of adverse reactions attributed to sulfonamides may occur with topical administration.

Because dorzolamide and its metabolite are excreted predominantly by the kidney, it is not recommended for use in patients with severe renal impairment (Cl_{cr} <30 mL/minute); use with caution in patients with hepatic impairment

Local ocular adverse effects (conjunctivitis and lid reactions) were reported with chronic administration. Many resolved with discontinuation of drug therapy. If such reactions occur, discontinue dorzolamide.

There is a potential for an additive effect in patients receiving an oral carbonic anhydrase inhibitor and dorzolamide. The concomitant administration of dorzolamide and oral carbonic anhydrase inhibitors is not recommended.

Benzalkonium chloride is the preservative in dorzolamide which may be absorbed by soft contact lenses. Dorzolamide should not be administered while wearing soft contact lenses.

Adverse Reactions

>10%:

Gastrointestinal: Bitter taste following administration (25%)

Ocular: Burning, stinging or discomfort immediately following administration (33%); superficial punctate keratitis (10% to 15%); signs and symptoms of ocular allergic reaction (10%)

5% to 10% Ocular: Blurred vision, tearing, dryness, photophobia

<1%: Headache, fatigue, rashes, nausea, urolithiasis, weakness, iridocyclitis

Overdosage/Toxicology

Symptoms of overdose include electrolyte imbalance, development of an acidotic state and possible CNS effects

Treatment is symptomatic

Drug Interactions Increased toxicity: Salicylates use may result in carbonic anhydrase inhibitor accumulation and toxicity including CNS depression and metabolic acidosis

Stability Store at room temperature (25°C)

Mechanism of Action Reversible inhibition of the enzyme carbonic anhydrase resulting in reduction of hydrogen ion secretion at renal tubule and an increased renal excretion of sodium, potassium, bicarbonate, and water to decrease production of aqueous humor; also inhibits carbonic anhydrase in central nervous system to retard abnormal and excessive discharge from CNS neurons

Pharmacodynamics/Kinetics

Peak effect: 2 hours

Duration: 8-12 hours

Absorption: Topical: Reaches the systemic circulation where it accumulates in RBCs during chronic dosing as a result of binding to CA-11

Distribution: Accumulates in RBCs during chronic administration

Protein binding: 33%

Half-life: Terminal RBC half-life of 147 days

Metabolism: Metabolized to N-desethyl metabolite that also inhibits carbonic anhydrase less potently than the parent drug

(Continued)

Dorzolamide *(Continued)*

Elimination: Dorzolamide and its metabolite (N-desethyl) are excreted in the urine. After dosing is stopped, dorzolamide washes out of RBCs nonlinearly, resulting in a rapid decline of drug concentration initially, followed by a slower elimination phase with a half-life of about 4 months.

Usual Dosage Adults: Glaucoma: Instill 1 drop in the affected eye(s) 3 times/day

Administration If more than one topical ophthalmic drug is being used, administer the drugs at least 10 minutes apart. Instruct patients to avoid allowing the tip of the dispensing container to contact the eye or surrounding structures. Ocular solutions can become contaminated by common bacteria known to cause ocular infections. Serious damage to the eye and subsequent loss of vision may occur from using contaminated solutions.

Monitoring Parameters Monitor serum electrolyte levels (potassium) and blood pH levels; Ophthalmic exams and IOP periodically

Patient Information

If serious or unusual reactions or signs of hypersensitivity occur, discontinue use of the product

If any ocular reactions, particularly conjunctivitis and lid reactions, discontinue use and seek physician's advice. If an intercurrent ocular condition (eg, trauma, ocular surgery, infection) occur, immediately seek your physician's advice concerning the continued use of the present multidose container.

Avoid allowing the tip of the dispensing container to contact the eye or surround structures

Dosage Forms Solution, ophthalmic, as hydrochloride: 2%

♦ **Dorzolamide Hydrochloride** *see* Dorzolamide *on previous page*

♦ **DOSS** *see* Docusate *on page 384*

♦ **DOS® Softgel® [OTC]** *see* Docusate *on page 384*

♦ **Dostinex®** *see* Cabergoline *on page 168*

♦ **Dovonex®** *see* Calcipotriene *on page 170*

Doxacurium *(doks a KYOO ri um)*

Related Information

Neuromuscular Blocking Agents Comparison *on page 1331*

U.S. Brand Names Nuromax® Injection

Synonyms Doxacurium Chloride

Therapeutic Category Neuromuscular Blocker Agent, Nondepolarizing; Skeletal Muscle Relaxant

Use Adjunct to general anesthesia; provides skeletal muscle relaxation during surgery. Doxacurium is a long-acting nondepolarizing neuromuscular blocker with virtually no cardiovascular side effects. The characteristics of this agent make it especially useful in procedures requiring careful maintenance of hemodynamic stability for prolonged periods.

Pregnancy Risk Factor C

Contraindications Hypersensitivity to doxacurium or any component

Warnings/Precautions Use with caution in the elderly, effects and duration are more variable; product contains benzoyl alcohol; use with caution in newborns; use with caution in patients with neuromuscular diseases such as myasthenia gravis; resistance may develop in burn patients; ensure proper electrolyte balance prior to use; use with caution in patients with renal or hepatic impairment

Adverse Reactions <1%: Hypotension, fever, urticaria, skeletal muscle weakness, diplopia, respiratory insufficiency and apnea, wheezing, produces little, if any, histamine release

Overdosage/Toxicology

Overdosage is manifested by prolonged neuromuscular blockage

Treatment is supportive; reverse blockade with neostigmine, pyridostigmine, or edrophonium

Drug Interactions

Decreased effect: Phenytoin, carbamazepine (decreases neuromuscular blockade)

Increased effect: Magnesium, lithium

Prolonged neuromuscular blockade:

Corticosteroids

Inhaled anesthetics

Local anesthetics

Calcium channel blockers

Antiarrhythmics (eg, quinidine or procainamide)

Antibiotics (eg, aminoglycosides, tetracyclines, vancomycin, clindamycin)

Immunosuppressants (eg, cyclosporine)

Mechanism of Action Doxacurium is a long-acting nondepolarizing skeletal muscle relaxant. The drug is a bis-quaternary benzylisoquinolinium diester, with a chemical structure similar to that of atracurium. Similar to other nondepolarizing neuromuscular blocking agents, doxacurium produces muscle relaxation by competing with acetylcholine for cholinergic receptor sites on the postjunctional membrane; significant presynaptic depressant activity is also observed.

Pharmacodynamics/Kinetics

Onset of effect: 5-11 minutes

Duration: 30 minutes (range: 12-54 minutes)

Protein binding: 30%

Elimination: Primarily as unchanged drug via the kidneys and biliary tract
Recovery time is longer in elderly patients

Usual Dosage I.V. (in obese patients, use ideal body weight to calculate dose):

Children >2 years: Initial: 0.03-0.05 mg/kg followed by maintenance doses of 0.005-0.01 mg/kg after 30-45 minutes

Adults: Surgery: 0.05 mg/kg with thiopental/narcotic or 0.025 mg/kg with succinylcholine; maintenance doses of 0.005-0.01 mg/kg after 60-100 minutes

Dosing adjustment in renal or hepatic impairment: Reduce initial dose and titrate carefully as duration may be prolonged

Monitoring Parameters Blockade is monitored with a peripheral nerve stimulator, should also evaluate EKG, blood pressure, and heart rate

Dosage Forms Injection, as chloride: 1 mg/mL (5 mL)

♦ **Doxacurium Chloride** see Doxacurium on previous page

Doxapram (DOKS a pram)

U.S. Brand Names Dopram® Injection

Synonyms Doxapram Hydrochloride

Therapeutic Category Central Nervous System Stimulant, Nonamphetamine; Respiratory Stimulant

Use Respiratory and CNS stimulant; stimulates respiration in patients with drug-induced CNS depression or postanesthesia respiratory depression; in hospitalized patients with COPD associated with acute hypercapnia

Pregnancy Risk Factor B

Contraindications Hypersensitivity to doxapram or any component; epilepsy, cerebral edema, head injury, severe pulmonary disease, pheochromocytoma, cardiovascular disease, hypertension, hyperthyroidism

Usual Dosage Not for use in newborns since doxapram contains a significant amount of benzyl alcohol (0.9%)

Neonatal apnea (apnea of prematurity): I.V.:
Initial: 1-1.5 mg/kg/hour
Maintenance: 0.5-2.5 mg/kg/hour, titrated to the lowest rate at which apnea is controlled

Adults: Respiratory depression following anesthesia: I.V.:
Initial: 0.5-1 mg/kg; may repeat at 5-minute intervals; maximum total dose: 2 mg/kg
I.V. infusion: Initial: 5 mg/minute until adequate response or adverse effects seen; decrease to 1-3 mg/minute; usual total dose: 0.5-4 mg/kg; maximum: 300 mg
Hemodialysis: Not dialyzable

Additional Information Complete prescribing information for this medication should be consulted for additional detail

Dosage Forms Injection, as hydrochloride: 20 mg/mL (20 mL)

♦ **Doxapram Hydrochloride** see Doxapram on this page

Doxazosin (doks AYE zoe sin)

U.S. Brand Names Cardura®

Therapeutic Category Alpha-Adrenergic Blocking Agent, Oral; Antihypertensive Agent

Use Treatment of hypertension alone or in conjunction with diuretics, cardiac glycosides, ACE inhibitors or calcium antagonists (particularly appropriate for those with hypertension and other cardiovascular risk factors such as hypercholesterolemia and diabetes mellitus); treatment of urinary outflow obstruction and/or obstructive and irritative symptoms associated with benign prostatic hyperplasia (particularly useful in patients with troublesome symptoms who are unable or unwilling to undergo invasive procedures, but who require rapid symptomatic relief)

Pregnancy Risk Factor B

Contraindications Hypersensitivity to doxazosin or any component

Warnings/Precautions Use with caution in patients with renal impairment. Can cause marked hypotension and syncope with sudden loss of consciousness with the first dose. Anticipate a similar effect if therapy is interrupted for a few days, if dosage is increased rapidly, or if another antihypertensive drug is introduced.

Adverse Reactions

>10%: Central nervous system: Dizziness

1% to 10%:
Cardiovascular: Palpitations, arrhythmia
Central nervous system: Vertigo, nervousness, somnolence, anxiety
Endocrine & metabolic: Decreased libido
Gastrointestinal: Nausea, vomiting, xerostomia, diarrhea, constipation
Neuromuscular & skeletal: Shoulder, neck, back pain
Ocular: Abnormal vision
Respiratory: Rhinitis

<1%: Hypotension, tachycardia, depression, abdominal discomfort, flatulence, incontinence, polyuria, conjunctivitis, tinnitus, dyspnea, sinusitis, epistaxis

Overdosage/Toxicology

Symptoms of overdose include severe hypotension, drowsiness, tachycardia
Hypotension usually responds to I.V. fluids, Trendelenburg positioning, or parenteral vasoconstrictor; treatment is primarily supportive and symptomatic.

Drug Interactions

Decreased effect with NSAIDs
(Continued)

Doxazosin *(Continued)*

Increased effect with diuretics and antihypertensive medications (especially beta-blockers)

Mechanism of Action Competitively inhibits postsynaptic alpha-adrenergic receptors which results in vasodilation of veins and arterioles and a decrease in total peripheral resistance and blood pressure; approximately 50% as potent on a weight by weight basis as prazosin

Usual Dosage Oral:

Adults: 1 mg once daily in morning or evening; may be increased to 2 mg once daily; thereafter titrate upwards, if needed, over several weeks, balancing therapeutic benefit with doxazosin-induced postural hypotension; maximum dose for hypertension: 16 mg/day, for BPH: 8 mg/day

Elderly: Initial: 0.5 mg once daily

Monitoring Parameters Blood pressure, standing and sitting/supine

Test Interactions Increased urinary VMA 17%, norepinephrine metabolite 42%

Patient Information Rise from sitting/lying position carefully; may cause dizziness; report to physician if painful persistent erection occurs; take the first dose at bedtime

Nursing Implications Syncope may occur usually within 90 minutes of the initial dose

Dosage Forms Tablet: 1 mg, 2 mg, 4 mg, 8 mg

Doxepin *(DOKS e pin)*

Related Information

Antidepressant Agents Comparison *on page 1301*

U.S. Brand Names Adapin® Oral; Sinequan® Oral; Zonalon® Topical Cream

Canadian Brand Names Apo®-Doxepin; Novo-Doxepin; Triadapin®

Synonyms Doxepin Hydrochloride

Therapeutic Category Antianxiety Agent; Antidepressant, Tricyclic

Use

Oral: Treatment of various forms of depression, usually in conjunction with psychotherapy; treatment of anxiety disorders

Unlabeled use: Analgesic for certain chronic and neuropathic pain

Topical: Short-term (<8 days) management of moderate pruritus in adults with atopic dermatitis or lichen simplex chronicus

Pregnancy Risk Factor C

Contraindications Hypersensitivity to doxepin or any component (cross-sensitivity with other tricyclic antidepressants may occur); narrow-angle glaucoma

Warnings/Precautions Use with caution in patients with cardiovascular disease, conduction disturbances, seizure disorders, urinary retention, hyperthyroidism, or those receiving thyroid replacement; avoid use during lactation; use with caution in pregnancy; do not discontinue abruptly in patients receiving chronic high-dose therapy

Adverse Reactions

>10%:

Central nervous system: Sedation, drowsiness, dizziness, headache

Gastrointestinal: Xerostomia, constipation, increased appetite, nausea, unpleasant taste, weight gain

Neuromuscular & skeletal: Weakness

1% to 10%:

Cardiovascular: Hypotension, arrhythmias

Central nervous system: Confusion, delirium, hallucinations, nervousness, restlessness, parkinsonian syndrome, insomnia

Gastrointestinal: Diarrhea, heartburn

Genitourinary: Sexual dysfunction, dysuria

Neuromuscular & skeletal: Fine muscle tremors

Ocular: Blurred vision, eye pain

Miscellaneous: Diaphoresis (excessive)

<1%: Anxiety, seizures, alopecia, photosensitivity, breast enlargement, galactorrhea, SIADH, trouble with gums, decreased lower esophageal sphincter tone may cause GE reflux, urinary retention, testicular edema, agranulocytosis, leukopenia, eosinophilia, hepatitis, cholestatic jaundice and increased liver enzymes, increased intraocular pressure, tinnitus, allergic reactions

Overdosage/Toxicology

Symptoms of overdose include confusion, hallucinations, seizures, urinary retention, hypothermia, hypotension, tachycardia, cyanosis

Following initiation of essential overdose management, toxic symptoms should be treated. Sodium bicarbonate is indicated when QRS interval is >0.10 seconds or QT_c >0.42 seconds. Ventricular arrhythmias often respond to systemic alkalinization with or without phenytoin 15-20 mg/kg (adults) (sodium bicarbonate 0.5-2 mEq/kg I.V.). Arrhythmias unresponsive to this therapy may respond to lidocaine 1 mg/kg I.V. followed by a titrated infusion. Physostigmine (1-2 mg I.V. slowly for adults or 0.5 mg I.V. slowly for children) may be indicated in reversing cardiac arrhythmias that are life-threatening. Seizures usually respond to diazepam I.V. boluses (5-10 mg for adults up to 30 mg or 0.25-0.4 mg/kg/dose for children up to 10 mg/dose). If seizures are unresponsive or recur, phenytoin or phenobarbital may be required.

Drug Interactions CYP2D6 enzyme substrate

Decreased effect of bretylium, guanethidine, clonidine, levodopa; decreased effect with ascorbic acid, cholestyramine

Increased effect/toxicity of carbamazepine, amphetamines, thyroid preparations, sympathomimetics

Increased toxicity with fluoxetine (seizures), thyroid preparations, MAO inhibitors, albuterol, CNS depressants (ie, benzodiazepines, opiate analgesics, phenothiazines, alcohol), anticholinergics, cimetidine

Stability Protect from light

Mechanism of Action Increases the synaptic concentration of serotonin and/or norepinephrine in the central nervous system by inhibition of their reuptake by the presynaptic neuronal membrane

Pharmacodynamics/Kinetics

Peak effect (antidepressant): Usually more than 2 weeks; anxiolytic effects may occur sooner

Distribution: Crosses the placenta; appears in breast milk

Protein binding: 80% to 85%

Metabolism: Hepatic; metabolites include desmethyldoxepin (active)

Half-life: Adults: 6-8 hours

Elimination: Renal

Usual Dosage

Oral (entire daily dose may be given at bedtime):

Adolescents: Initial: 25-50 mg/day in single or divided doses; gradually increase to 100 mg/day

Adults: Initial: 30-150 mg/day at bedtime or in 2-3 divided doses; may gradually increase up to 300 mg/day; single dose should not exceed 150 mg; select patients may respond to 25-50 mg/day

Dosing adjustment in hepatic impairment: Use a lower dose and adjust gradually

Topical: Adults: Apply a thin film 4 times/day with at least 3- to 4-hour interval between applications

Dietary Considerations Alcohol: Additive CNS effect, avoid use

Monitoring Parameters Monitor blood pressure and pulse rate prior to and during initial therapy; monitor mental status, weight

Reference Range Therapeutic: 30-150 ng/mL; Toxic: >500 ng/mL; utility of serum level monitoring is controversial

Test Interactions ↑ glucose

Patient Information Avoid unnecessary exposure to sunlight; avoid alcohol ingestion; do not discontinue medication abruptly; may cause urine to turn blue-green; may cause drowsiness; can use sugarless gum or hard candy for dry mouth; full effect may not occur for 4-6 weeks

Nursing Implications May increase appetite; may cause drowsiness, raise bed rails, institute safety precautions

Dosage Forms

Capsule, as hydrochloride: 10 mg, 25 mg, 50 mg, 75 mg, 100 mg, 150 mg

Concentrate, oral, as hydrochloride: 10 mg/mL (120 mL)

Cream: 5% (30 g)

♦ **Doxepin Hydrochloride** see Doxepin on previous page

♦ **Doxil®** see Doxorubicin (Liposomal) on page 396

Doxorubicin (doks oh ROO bi sin)

Related Information

Cancer Chemotherapy Regimens on page 1263

Extravasation Management of Chemotherapeutic Agents on page 1285

Toxicities of Chemotherapeutic Agents on page 1288

U.S. Brand Names Adriamycin® PFS; Adriamycin® RDF; Rubex®

Synonyms ADR; Doxorubicin Hydrochloride; Hydroxydaunomycin Hydrochloride

Therapeutic Category Antineoplastic Agent, Anthracycline; Antineoplastic Agent, Antibiotic; Vesicant

Use Treatment of leukemias, lymphomas, multiple myeloma, osseous and nonosseous sarcomas, mesotheliomas, germ cell tumors of the ovary or testis, and carcinomas of the head and neck, thyroid, lung, Wilms' tumor, breast, stomach, pancreas, liver, ovary, bladder, prostate, and uterus, neuroblastoma

Pregnancy Risk Factor D

Contraindications Hypersensitivity to doxorubicin or any component, severe congestive heart failure, cardiomyopathy, pre-existing myelosuppression, patients with impaired cardiac function, patients who received previous treatment with complete cumulative doses of doxorubicin, idarubicin, and/or daunorubicin

Warnings/Precautions The U.S. Food and Drug Administration (FDA) currently recommends that procedures for proper handling and disposal of antineoplastic agents be considered. Total dose should not exceed 550 mg/m^2 or 400 mg/m^2 in patients with previous or concomitant treatment (with daunorubicin, cyclophosphamide, or irradiation of the cardiac region); irreversible myocardial toxicity may occur as total dosage approaches 550 mg/m^2. A baseline cardiac evaluation (EKG, LVEF, +/- ECHO) is recommended, especially in patients with risk factors for increased cardiac toxicity. I.V. use only, severe local tissue necrosis will result if extravasation occurs; reduce dose in patients with impaired hepatic function; severe myelosuppression is also possible.

Adverse Reactions

>10%:

Dermatologic: Alopecia

Extravasation: Doxorubicin is one of the most notorious vesicants. Infiltration can cause severe inflammation, tissue necrosis, and ulceration. If the drug is infiltrated, consult institutional policy, apply ice to the area, and elevate the limb. Can have

(Continued)

Doxorubicin *(Continued)*

ongoing tissue destruction secondary to propagation of free radicals; may require debridement.

Vesicant chemotherapy

Gastrointestinal: Acute nausea and vomiting may be seen in 21% to 55% of patients; mucositis, ulceration, and necrosis of the colon, anorexia, and diarrhea, stomatitis, esophagitis

Emetic potential:

≤20 mg: Moderately low (10% to 30%)

>20 mg or < 60 mg: Moderate (30% to 60%)

≥60 mg: Moderately high (60% to 90%)

Time course for nausea/vomiting: Onset: 1-3 hours; Duration 4-24 hours

Genitourinary: Discoloration of urine (red)

Hematologic: Myelosuppressive: 60% to 80% of patients will have leukopenia; dose-limiting toxicity

WBC: Moderate

Platelets: Moderate

Onset (days): 7

Nadir (days): 10-14

Recovery (days): 21-28

1% to 10%:

Cardiac toxicity: Dose-limiting and related to cumulative dose; usually a maximum total lifetime dose of 450-550 mg/m^2 is administered; although, it has been demonstrated that if given by continuous infusion in breast cancer patients, higher doses may be tolerated. Patients may present with acute toxicity (arrhythmias, heart block, pericarditis-myocarditis) which may be fatal. More commonly, chronic toxicity is seen, in which patients present with signs of congestive heart failure. Treatment includes aggressive management of CHF with digoxin, diuretics and peripheral vasodilators. Several methods of monitoring cardiac toxicity have been utilized, including myocardial biopsy (expensive and hazardous procedure).

Cardiovascular: Facial flushing

Dermatologic: Hyperpigmentation of nail beds, erythematous streaking along the vein if administered too rapidly

Endocrine & metabolic: Hyperuricemia

<1%: Fever, chills, urticaria, conjunctivitis, allergic reaction, anaphylaxis; radiation recall noticed in patients who have had prior irradiation; reactions include redness, warmth, erythema, and dermatitis in the radiation port. Can progress to severe desquamation and ulceration. Occurs 5-7 days after doxorubicin administration; local therapy with topical corticosteroids and cooling have given the best relief.

Overdosage/Toxicology Symptoms of overdose include myelosuppression, nausea, vomiting, myocardial toxicity

Drug Interactions CYP3A3/4 enzyme substrate; CYP2D6 enzyme inhibitor

Decreased effect:

Doxorubicin may decrease digoxin plasma levels and renal excretion

Phenobarbital increases elimination of doxorubicin

Phenytoin levels decreased by doxorubicin

Increased toxicity:

Cyclosporine may induce coma or seizures. The addition of cyclosporine to doxorubicin may result in increases in AUC for both doxorubicin and doxorubicinol possibly due to a decrease in clearance of parent drug and a decrease in metabolism of the doxorubicinol. Literature reports suggest that adding cyclosporine to doxorubicin results in more profound and prolonged hematologic toxicity than doxorubicin alone.

Cyclophosphamide enhances the cardiac toxicity of doxorubicin by producing additional myocardial cell damage

Mercaptopurine increases toxicities

Paclitaxel: Two published studies report that initial administration of paclitaxel infused over 24 hours followed by doxorubicin administered over 48 hours resulted in a significant decrease in doxorubicin clearance with more profound neutropenic and stomatitis episodes than the reverse sequence administration

Progesterone: Enhanced doxorubicin-induced neutropenia and thrombocytopenia were observed with progesterone given intravenously to patients with advanced malignancies at high doses concomitantly with a fixed doxorubicin dose (60 mg/m^2) via bolus.

Streptozocin greatly enhances leukopenia and thrombocytopenia by inhibiting doxorubicin metabolism

Verapamil alters the cellular distribution of doxorubicin; may result in increased cell toxicity by inhibition of the P-glycoprotein pump

Stability

Store intact vials of solution under refrigeration (2°C to 8°C) and protect from light; store intact vials of lyophilized powder at room temperature (15°C to 30°C). Gensia formulation of generic doxorubicin is stable for up to 30 days at room temperature.

Reconstitute lyophilized powder with SWI or NS to a final concentration of 2 mg/mL as follows. Reconstituted solution is stable for 7 days at room temperature (25°C) and 15 days under refrigeration (5°C) when protected from light.

10 mg vial = 5 mL

20 mg vial = 10 mL

50 mg vial = 25 mL

Further dilution in D$_5$W or NS is stable for 48 hours at room temperature (25°C) when protected from light

Unstable in solutions with a pH <3 or >7; avoid aluminum needles and bacteriostatic diluents as precipitation occurs; decomposing drug turns purple; protect from direct sunlight

Incompatible with aminophylline, cephalothin, dexamethasone, diazepam, fluorouracil, furosemide, heparin, hydrocortisone, sodium bicarbonate

Y-site compatible with bleomycin, cyclophosphamide, dacarbazine, vinblastine, vincristine

Standard I.V. dilution:

I.V. push: Dose/syringe (concentration: 2 mg/mL)

Maximum syringe size for IVP is a 30 mL syringe and syringe should be ≤75% full

Syringes are stable for 7 days at room temperature (25°C) and 15 days under refrigeration (5°C) when protected from light

IVPB: Dose/50-100 mL D_5W or NS

IVPB solutions are stable for 48 hours at room temperature (25°C) when protected from light

Mechanism of Action Doxorubicin works through inhibition of topoisomerase-II at the point of DNA cleavage. A second mechanism of action is the production of free radicals (the hydroxy radical OH) by doxorubicin, which in turn can destroy DNA and cancerous cells. Doxorubicin is also a very powerful iron chelator, equal to deferoxamine. The iron-doxorubicin complex can bind DNA and cell membranes rapidly and produce free radicals that immediately cleave the DNA and cell membranes. Inhibits DNA and RNA synthesis by intercalating between DNA base pairs and by steric obstruction; active throughout entire cell cycle.

Pharmacodynamics/Kinetics

Absorption: Oral: Poor, <50%

Distribution: V_d: 25 L/kg; rapidly distributed into the liver, spleen, kidney, lung and heart, also distributes into breast milk

Protein binding: 70% bound to plasma proteins

Metabolism: In both the liver and in plasma to both active and inactive metabolites

Half-life, triphasic: Primary: 30 minutes; Secondary: 3-3.5 hours for metabolites; Terminal: 17-30 hours for doxorubicin and its metabolites

Elimination: Triphasic; 80% eventually excreted in bile and feces; clearance has been shown to be significantly reduced in obese women with weight >130% of IBW

Usual Dosage Refer to individual protocols

I.V. (patient's ideal weight should be used to calculate body surface area):

Children: 35-75 mg/m² as a single dose, repeat every 21 days; **or** 20-30 mg/m² once weekly; **or** 60-90 mg/m² given as a continuous infusion over 96 hours every 3-4 weeks

Adults: 60-75 mg/m² as a single dose, repeat every 21 days **or** other dosage regimens like 20-30 mg/m²/day for 2-3 days, repeat in 4 weeks **or** 20 mg/m² once weekly

The lower dose regimen should be given to patients with decreased bone marrow reserve, prior therapy or marrow infiltration with malignant cells

Currently the maximum cumulative dose is 550 mg/m² or 450 mg/m² in patients who have received RT to the mediastinal areas; a baseline MUGA should be performed prior to initiating treatment. If the LVEF is <30% to 40%, therapy should not be instituted; LVEF should be monitored during therapy.

Doxorubicin has also been administered intraperitoneal (phase I in refractory ovarian cancer patients) and intra-arterially.

Dosing adjustment in renal impairment: Adjustments not required in mild to moderate renal failure

Cl_{cr} <10 mL/minute: Reduce dose to 75% of normal dose in severe renal failure

Hemodialysis: Supplemental dose is not necessary

Dosing adjustment in hepatic impairment:

Bilirubin 1.2-3 mg/dL: Administer 50% of dose

Bilirubin 3.1-5 mg/dL: Administer 25% of dose

Bilirubin >5 mg/dL: Avoid use

Administration

Administer I.V. push over 1-2 minutes or IVPB; may be further diluted in either NS of D_5W for I.V. administration. Continuous infusions must be administered via central line.

Avoid extravasation, associated with severe ulceration and soft tissue necrosis; flush with 5-10 mL of I.V. solution before and after drug administration

Monitoring Parameters CBC with differential and platelet count, echocardiogram, liver function tests

Patient Information Discolors urine red/orange; immediately report any change in sensation (eg, stinging) at injection site during infusion (may be an early sign of infiltration); contraceptive measures are recommended during therapy

Nursing Implications

Local erythematous streaking along the vein and/or facial flushing may indicate too rapid a rate of administration

Extravasation management:

Apply ice immediately for 30-60 minutes; then alternate off/on every 15 minutes for one day

Topical cooling may be achieved using ice packs or cooling pad with circulating ice water. Cooling of site for 24 hours as tolerated by the patient. Elevate and rest extremity 24-48 hours, then resume normal activity as tolerated. Application of cold inhibits vesicant's cytotoxicity.

Application of heat or sodium bicarbonate can be harmful and is contraindicated

If pain, erythema, and/or swelling persist beyond 48 hours, refer patient immediately to plastic surgeon for consultation and possible debridement

(Continued)

Doxorubicin *(Continued)*

Dosage Forms
Injection, as hydrochloride:
Aqueous, with NS: 2 mg/mL (5 mL, 10 mL, 25 mL)
Preservative free: 2 mg/mL (5 mL, 10 mL, 25 mL, 100 mL)
Powder for injection, as hydrochloride, lyophilized: 10 mg, 20 mg, 50 mg, 100 mg
Powder for injection, as hydrochloride, lyophilized, rapid dissolution formula: 10 mg, 20 mg, 50 mg, 150 mg

♦ **Doxorubicin Hydrochloride** *see* Doxorubicin *on page 393*
♦ **Doxorubicin Hydrochloride (Liposomal)** *see* Doxorubicin (Liposomal) *on this page*

Doxorubicin (Liposomal) (doks oh ROO bi sin lip pah SOW mal)
U.S. Brand Names Doxil®
Synonyms Doxorubicin Hydrochloride (Liposomal)
Therapeutic Category Antineoplastic Agent, Anthracycline; Antineoplastic Agent, Antibiotic
Use Treatment of AIDS-related Kaposi's sarcoma in patients with disease that has progressed on prior combination chemotherapy or in patients who are intolerant to such therapy
Unlabeled use: Breast cancer, ovarian cancer, and solid tumors
Pregnancy Risk Factor D
Contraindications Hypersensitivity to doxorubicin or the components of Doxil®
Warnings/Precautions The U.S. Food and Drug Administration (FDA) currently recommends that procedures for proper handling and disposal of antineoplastic agents be considered. Total dose should not exceed 550 mg/m^2 or 400 mg/m^2 in patients with previous or concomitant treatment (with daunorubicin, cyclophosphamide, or irradiation of the cardiac region); irreversible myocardial toxicity may occur as total dosage approaches 550 mg/m^2. I.V. use only, severe local tissue necrosis will result if extravasation occurs; reduce dose in patients with impaired hepatic function; severe myelosuppression is also possible.
Adverse Reactions Information on adverse events is based on the experience reported in 753 patients with AIDS-related Kaposi's sarcoma enrolled in four studies

>10%:
Extravasation: Doxorubicin is one of the most notorious vesicants. Infiltration can cause severe inflammation, tissue necrosis, and ulceration. If the drug is infiltrated, consult institutional policy, apply ice to the area, and elevate the limb. Can have ongoing tissue destruction secondary to propagation of free radicals; may require debridement.
Irritant chemotherapy
Gastrointestinal: Nausea; emetic potential:
≤20 mg: Moderately low (10% to 30%)
>20 mg or <75 mg: Moderate (30% to 60%)
≥75 mg: Moderately high (49%)
Hematologic: Myelosuppressive: 60% to 80% of patients will have leukopenia; dose-limiting toxicity
WBC: Moderate
Platelets: Moderate
Onset (days): 7
Nadir (days): 10-14
Recovery (days): 21-28
1% to 10%:
Cardiovascular: Cardiac toxicity (9.7%): Cardiomyopathy, congestive heart failure, arrhythmia, pericardial effusion, tachycardia, facial flushing
Dermatologic: Hyperpigmentation of nail beds, erythematous streaking along the vein if administered too rapidly
Endocrine & metabolic: Hyperuricemia
<1%: Allergic reaction, anaphylaxis, fever, chills, urticaria, conjunctivitis
Overdosage/Toxicology
Symptoms of overdose include increases in mucositis, leukopenia, and thrombocytopenia
Treatment of acute overdosage consists of treatment of the severely myelosuppressed patient with hospitalization, antibiotics, platelet and granulocyte transfusions and symptomatic treatment of mucositis
Drug Interactions
No formal drug interaction studies have been conducted with doxorubicin hydrochloride liposome injection, however, may interact with drugs known to interact with the conventional formulation of doxorubicin hydrochloride
Decreased effect: Doxorubicin may decrease digoxin plasma levels and renal excretion
Increased effect: Allopurinol may enhance the antitumor activity of doxorubicin (animal data only)
Increased toxicity:
Cyclophosphamide enhances the cardiac toxicity of doxorubicin by producing additional myocardial cell damage
Mercaptopurine enhances toxicities
Streptozocin greatly enhances leukopenia and thrombocytopenia
Verapamil alters the cellular distribution of doxorubicin; may result in increased cell toxicity by inhibition of the P-glycoprotein pump

Stability Store intact vials of solution under refrigeration (2°C to 8°C) and avoid freezing. Prolonged freezing may adversely affect liposomal drug products, however, short-term freezing (<1 month) does not appear to have a deleterious effect.

The appropriate dose (up to a maximum of 90 mg) must be diluted in 250 mL of dextrose 5% in water prior to administration. Diluted doxorubicin hydrochloride liposome injection should be refrigerated at 2°C to 8°C and administered within 24 hours. **Do not use with in-line filters.**

Mechanism of Action Doxil® is doxorubicin hydrochloride encapsulated in long-circulating STEALTH® liposomes. Liposomes are microscopic vesicles composed of a phospholipid bilayer that are capable of encapsulating active drugs. Doxorubicin works through inhibition of topoisomerase-II at the point of DNA cleavage. A second mechanism of action is the production of free radicals (the hydroxy radical OH) by doxorubicin, which in turn can destroy DNA and cancerous cells. Doxorubicin is also a very powerful iron chelator, equal to deferoxamine. The iron-doxorubicin complex can bind DNA and cell membranes rapidly and produce free radicals that immediately cleave the DNA and cell membranes. Inhibits DNA and RNA synthesis by intercalating between DNA base pairs and by steric obstruction; active throughout entire cell cycle.

Pharmacodynamics/Kinetics
Distribution: V_d: Steady state volume of distribution is confined mostly to the vascular fluid volume
Protein binding (doxorubicin): 70% bound to plasma proteins
Metabolism: In both the liver and in plasma to both active and inactive metabolites
Elimination: Mean clearance value of 0.041 L/hour/m²

Usual Dosage Refer to individual protocols
I.V. (patient's ideal weight should be used to calculate body surface area): 20 mg/m² over 30 minutes, once every 3 weeks, for as long as patients respond satisfactorily and tolerate treatment.
Breast cancer: I.V.: 20-80 mg/m²/dose has been studied in a limited number of phase I/II trials
Ovarian cancer: I.V.: 50 mg/m²/dose repeated every 3 weeks has been studied in a limited number of phase I/II trials
Solid tumors: I.V.: 50-60 mg/m²/dose repeated every 3-4 weeks has been studied in a limited number of phase I/II trials
Dosing adjustment in hepatic impairment:
Bilirubin 1.2-3 mg/dL or AST 60-180 units/L: Administer 50% of dose
Bilirubin >3 mg/dL: Administer 25% of dose

Administration
Administer IVPB over 30 minutes; further dilute in D₅W; do not administer as a bolus injection or undiluted solution
Do not administer intramuscular or subcutaneous
Avoid extravasation, associated with severe ulceration and soft tissue necrosis; flush with 5-10 mL of D₅W solution before and after drug administration

Monitoring Parameters CBC with differential and platelet count, echocardiogram, liver function tests

Patient Information Discolors urine red/orange; immediately report any change in sensation (eg, stinging) at injection site during infusion (may be an early sign of infiltration)

Nursing Implications
Local erythematous streaking along the vein and/or facial flushing may indicate too rapid a rate of administration
Extravasation management:
Apply ice immediately for 30-60 minutes; then alternate off/on every 15 minutes for one day
Topical cooling may be achieved using ice packs or cooling pad with circulating ice water. Cooling of site for 24 hours as tolerated by the patient. Elevate and rest extremity 24-48 hours, then resume normal activity as tolerated. Application of cold inhibits vesicant's cytotoxicity.
Application of heat or sodium bicarbonate can be harmful and is contraindicated
If pain, erythema, and/or swelling persist beyond 48 hours, refer patient immediately to plastic surgeon for consultation and possible debridement

Dosage Forms Injection, as hydrochloride: 2 mg/mL (10 mL)

♦ **Doxy®** *see* Doxycycline *on this page*
♦ **Doxychel®** *see* Doxycycline *on this page*
♦ **Doxycin** *see* Doxycycline *on this page*

Doxycycline (doks i SYE kleen)
Related Information
Animal and Human Bites Guidelines *on page 1399*
Antimicrobial Drugs of Choice *on page 1404*
Community-Acquired Pneumonia in Adults *on page 1419*
Prevention of Malaria *on page 1372*
Prevention of Wound Infection & Sepsis in Surgical Patients *on page 1381*
Treatment of Sexually Transmitted Diseases *on page 1429*
U.S. Brand Names Atridox™; Bio-Tab® Oral; Doryx®; Doxy®; Doxychel®; Periostat™; Vibramycin®; Vibramycin® IV; Vibra-Tabs®
Canadian Brand Names Apo®-Doxy; Apo®-Doxy Tabs; Doxycin; Doxytec; Novo-Doxylin; Nu-Doxycycline
Synonyms Doxycycline Hyclate; Doxycycline Monohydrate
(Continued)

Doxycycline *(Continued)*

Therapeutic Category Antibiotic, Tetracycline Derivative

Use Principally in the treatment of infections caused by susceptible *Rickettsia*, *Chlamydia*, and *Mycoplasma* along with uncommon susceptible gram-negative and gram-positive organisms; alternative to mefloquine for malaria prophylaxis; treatment for syphilis in penicillin-allergic patients; often active against vancomycin-resistant enterococci; used for community-acquired pneumonia and other common infections due to susceptible organisms; sclerosing agent for pleural effusions

Pregnancy Risk Factor D

Contraindications Hypersensitivity to doxycycline, tetracycline or any component; children <8 years of age; severe hepatic dysfunction

Warnings/Precautions Use of tetracyclines during tooth development may cause permanent discoloration of the teeth and enamel hypoplasia; prolonged use may result in superinfection; photosensitivity reaction may occur with this drug; avoid prolonged exposure to sunlight or tanning equipment. Do not administer to children ≤8 years of age.

Adverse Reactions
>10%: Miscellaneous: Discoloration of teeth in children
1% to 10%: Gastrointestinal: Esophagitis
<1%: Increased intracranial pressure, bulging fontanels in infants, rash, photosensitivity, nausea, diarrhea, neutropenia, eosinophilia, hepatotoxicity, phlebitis

Overdosage/Toxicology
Symptoms of overdose include nausea, anorexia, diarrhea
Following GI decontamination, supportive care only; fluid support may be required for hypotension

Drug Interactions CYP3A3/4 enzyme substrate
Decreased effect with antacids containing aluminum, calcium, or magnesium
Iron and bismuth subsalicylate may decrease doxycycline bioavailability
Barbiturates, phenytoin, and carbamazepine decrease doxycycline's half-life
Increased effect of warfarin

Stability Tetracyclines form toxic products when outdated or when exposed to light, heat, or humidity; reconstituted solution is stable for 72 hours (refrigerated); for I.V. infusion in NS or D_5W solution, complete infusion should be completed within 12 hours; discard remaining solution

Mechanism of Action Inhibits protein synthesis by binding with the 30S and possibly the 50S ribosomal subunit(s) of susceptible bacteria; may also cause alterations in the cytoplasmic membrane

Pharmacodynamics/Kinetics
Absorption: Almost completely from the GI tract; absorption can be reduced by food or milk by 20%
Distribution: Widely distributed into body tissues and fluids including synovial, pleural, prostatic, seminal fluids, and bronchial secretions; saliva, aqueous humor, and CSF penetration is poor; readily crosses placenta and appears in breast milk
Protein binding: 90%
Metabolism: Not metabolized in the liver, instead is partially inactivated in the GI tract by chelate formation
Half-life: 12-15 hours (usually increases to 22-24 hours with multiple dosing)
End-stage renal disease: 18-25 hours
Time to peak serum concentration: Within 1.5-4 hours
Elimination: In urine (23%) and feces (30%)

Usual Dosage Oral, I.V.:
Children ≥8 years (<45 kg): 2-5 mg/kg/day in 1-2 divided doses, not to exceed 200 mg/day
Children >8 years (>45 kg) and Adults: 100-200 mg/day in 1-2 divided doses
Acute gonococcal infection: 200 mg immediately, then 100 mg at bedtime on the first day followed by 100 mg twice daily for 3 days **OR** 300 mg immediately followed by 300 mg in 1 hour
Primary and secondary syphilis: 300 mg/day in divided doses for ≥10 days
Uncomplicated chlamydial infections: 100 mg twice daily for ≥7 days
Endometritis, salpingitis, parametritis, or peritonitis: 100 mg I.V. twice daily with cefoxitin 2 g every 6 hours for 4 days and for ≥48 hours after patient improves; then continue with oral therapy 100 mg twice daily to complete a 10- to 14-day course of therapy
Sclerosing agent for pleural effusion injection: 500 mg as a single dose in 30-50 mL of NS or SWI

Dosing adjustment in renal impairment: Cl_{cr} <10 mL/minute: 100 mg every 24 hours
Dialysis: Not dialyzable; 0% to 5% by hemo- and peritoneal methods or by continuous arteriovenous or venovenous hemofiltration (CAVH/CAVHD); no supplemental dosage necessary

Administration Infuse I.V. doxycycline over 1 hour; may administer with meals to decrease GI upset

Test Interactions False-negative urine glucose using Clinistix®, Tes-Tape®

Patient Information Avoid unnecessary exposure to sunlight; finish all medication; do not skip doses

Nursing Implications Avoid extravasation

Dosage Forms
Capsule, as hyclate:
Doxychel®, Vibramycin®: 50 mg
Doxy®, Doxychel®, Vibramycin®: 100 mg

Periostat™: 20 mg
Capsule, as monohydrate (Monodox®): 50 mg, 100 mg
Capsule, coated pellets, as hyclate (Doryx®): 100 mg
Gel, for subgingival application: Atridox™: 50 mg in each 500 mg of blended formulation; 2-syringe system contains doxycycline syringe (50 mg) and delivery system syringe (450 mg) along with a blunt cannula
Powder for injection, as hyclate (Doxy®, Doxychel®, Vibramycin® IV): 100 mg, 200 mg
Powder for oral suspension, as monohydrate (raspberry flavor) (Vibramycin®): 25 mg/5 mL (60 mL)
Syrup, as calcium (raspberry-apple flavor) (Vibramycin®): 50 mg/5 mL (30 mL, 473 mL)
Tablet, as hyclate
  Doxychel®: 50 mg
  Bio-Tab®, Doxychel®, Vibra-Tabs®: 100 mg

- **Doxycycline Hyclate** *see* Doxycycline *on page 397*
- **Doxycycline Monohydrate** *see* Doxycycline *on page 397*
- **Doxytec** *see* Doxycycline *on page 397*
- **DPA** *see* Valproic Acid and Derivatives *on page 1203*
- **DPE™** *see* Dipivefrin *on page 376*
- **DPE** *see* Dipivefrin *on page 376*
- **D-Penicillamine** *see* Penicillamine *on page 893*
- **DPH** *see* Phenytoin *on page 921*
- **DPPC** *see* Colfosceril Palmitate *on page 294*
- **Dramamine® II [OTC]** *see* Meclizine *on page 719*
- **Drenison®** *see* Flurandrenolide *on page 506*
- **Drisdol® Oral** *see* Ergocalciferol *on page 424*
- **Dristan® Saline Spray [OTC]** *see* Sodium Chloride *on page 1067*
- **Drithocreme®** *see* Anthralin *on page 87*
- **Drithocreme® HP 1%** *see* Anthralin *on page 87*
- **Dritho-Scalp®** *see* Anthralin *on page 87*
- **Drixoral® Non-Drowsy [OTC]** *see* Pseudoephedrine *on page 993*

Dronabinol (droe NAB i nol)

U.S. Brand Names Marinol®
Synonyms Tetrahydrocannabinol; THC
Therapeutic Category Antiemetic
Use When conventional antiemetics fail to relieve the nausea and vomiting associated with cancer chemotherapy, AIDS-related anorexia
Restrictions C-II
Pregnancy Risk Factor B
Contraindications Use only for cancer chemotherapy-induced nausea; should not be used in patients with a history of schizophrenia or in patients with known hypersensitivity to dronabinol or any component
Warnings/Precautions Use with caution in patients with heart disease, hepatic disease, or seizure disorders; reduce dosage in patients with severe hepatic impairment
Adverse Reactions
  >10%: Central nervous system: Drowsiness, dizziness, detachment, anxiety, difficulty concentrating, mood change
  1% to 10%:
    Cardiovascular: Orthostatic hypotension, tachycardia
    Central nervous system: Ataxia, depression, headache, vertigo, hallucinations, memory lapse
    Gastrointestinal: Xerostomia
    Neuromuscular & skeletal: Paresthesia, weakness
  <1%: Syncope, nightmares, speech difficulties, diarrhea, myalgia, tinnitus, diaphoresis
Overdosage/Toxicology Symptoms of overdose include tachycardia, hypertension, and hypotension
Drug Interactions CYP2C18 and 3A3/4 enzyme substrate
  Increased toxicity (drowsiness) with alcohol, barbiturates, benzodiazepines
Stability Store in a cool place
Mechanism of Action Not well defined, probably inhibits the vomiting center in the medulla oblongata
Pharmacodynamics/Kinetics
  Absorption: Oral: Erratic
  Protein binding: 97% to 99%
  Metabolism: Extensive first-pass metabolism; metabolized in the liver to several metabolites, some of which are active
  Half-life: 19-24 hours
  Time to peak serum concentration: Within 2-3 hours
  Elimination: In feces and urine
Usual Dosage Oral:
  Children: NCI protocol recommends 5 mg/m^2 starting 6-8 hours before chemotherapy and every 4-6 hours after to be continued for 12 hours after chemotherapy is discontinued
  Adults: 5 mg/m^2 1-3 hours before chemotherapy, then administer 5 mg/m^2/dose every 2-4 hours after chemotherapy for a total of 4-6 doses/day; dose may be increased up to
(Continued)

Dronabinol *(Continued)*

a maximum of 15 mg/m²/dose if needed (dosage may be increased by 2.5 mg/m² increments)

Appetite stimulant (AIDS-related): Initial: 2.5 mg twice daily (before lunch and dinner); titrate up to a maximum of 20 mg/day

Dietary Considerations Alcohol: Additive CNS effect, avoid use

Monitoring Parameters CNS effects, heart rate, blood pressure

Reference Range Antinauseant effects: 5-10 ng/mL

Test Interactions ↓ FSH, ↓ LH, ↓ growth hormone, ↓ testosterone

Patient Information Avoid activities such as driving which require motor coordination, avoid alcohol and other CNS depressants; may impair coordination and judgment

Nursing Implications Raise bed rails, institute safety measures, assist with ambulation

Dosage Forms Capsule: 2.5 mg, 5 mg, 10 mg

Droperidol (droe PER i dole)

U.S. Brand Names Inapsine®

Therapeutic Category Antiemetic; Antipsychotic Agent

Use Tranquilizer and antiemetic in surgical and diagnostic procedures; antiemetic for cancer chemotherapy; preoperative medication; has good antiemetic effect as well as sedative and antianxiety effects

Pregnancy Risk Factor C

Pregnancy/Breast-Feeding Implications

Clinical effects on the fetus: Crosses the placenta

Breast-feeding/lactation: No data available

Contraindications Hypersensitivity to droperidol or any component

Warnings/Precautions Safety in children <6 months of age has not been established; use with caution in patients with seizures, bone marrow suppression, or severe liver disease

Significant hypotension may occur, especially when the drug is administered parenterally; injection contains benzyl alcohol; injection also contains sulfites which may cause allergic reaction

Tardive dyskinesia: Prevalence rate may be 40% in elderly; development of the syndrome and the irreversible nature are proportional to duration and total cumulative dose over time. May be reversible if diagnosed early in therapy.

Extrapyramidal reactions are more common in elderly with up to 50% developing these reactions after 60 years of age. Drug-induced **Parkinson's syndrome** occurs often. **Akathisia** is the most common extrapyramidal reaction in elderly.

Increased confusion, memory loss, psychotic behavior, and agitation frequently occur as a consequence of anticholinergic effects

Orthostatic hypotension is due to alpha-receptor blockade, the elderly are at greater risk for orthostatic hypotension

Antipsychotic associated sedation in nonpsychotic patients is extremely unpleasant due to feelings of depersonalization, derealization, and dysphoria

Life-threatening arrhythmias have occurred at therapeutic doses of antipsychotics

Adverse Reactions

>10%:

Cardiovascular: Mild to moderate hypotension, tachycardia

Central nervous system: Postoperative drowsiness

1% to 10%:

Cardiovascular: Hypertension

Central nervous system: Extrapyramidal reactions

Respiratory: Respiratory depression

<1%: Dizziness, chills, postoperative hallucinations, laryngospasm, bronchospasm, shivering

Overdosage/Toxicology

Symptoms of overdose include hypotension, tachycardia, hallucinations, extrapyramidal symptoms

Following initiation of essential overdose management, toxic symptom treatment and supportive treatment should be initiated. Hypotension usually responds to I.V. fluids or Trendelenburg positioning. If unresponsive to these measures, the use of a parenteral inotrope may be required (eg, norepinephrine 0.1-0.2 mcg/kg/minute titrated to response). Seizures commonly respond to diazepam (I.V. 5-10 mg bolus in adults every 15 minutes if needed up to a total of 30 mg; I.V. 0.25-0.4 mg/kg/dose up to a total of 10 mg in children) or to phenytoin or phenobarbital. Critical cardiac arrhythmias often respond to I.V. phenytoin (15 mg/kg up to 1 g), while other antiarrhythmics can be used. Neuroleptics often cause extrapyramidal symptoms (eg, dystonic reactions) requiring management with diphenhydramine 1-2 mg/kg (adults) up to a maximum of 50 mg I.M. or I.V. slow push followed by a maintenance dose for 48-72 hours. When these reactions are unresponsive to diphenhydramine, benztropine mesylate I.V. 1-2 mg (adults) may be effective. These agents are generally effective within 2-5 minutes.

Drug Interactions Increased toxicity: CNS depressants, fentanyl and other analgesics increased blood pressure; conduction anesthesia decreased blood pressure; epinephrine decreased blood pressure; atropine, lithium

Stability

Droperidol ampuls/vials should be stored at room temperature and protected from light

Stability of parenteral admixture at room temperature (25°C): 7 days

Standard diluent: 2.5 mg/50 mL D₅W

Incompatible with barbiturates

Mechanism of Action Alters the action of dopamine in the CNS, at subcortical levels, to produce sedation; reduces emesis by blocking dopamine stimulation of the chemotrigger zone

Pharmacodynamics/Kinetics

Following parenteral administration: Peak effect: Within 30 minutes; Duration: 2-4 hours, may extend to 12 hours

Metabolism: In the liver

Half-life: Adults: 2.3 hours

Elimination: In urine (75%) and feces (22%)

Usual Dosage Titrate carefully to desired effect

Children 2-12 years:

Premedication: I.M.: 0.1-0.15 mg/kg; smaller doses may be sufficient for control of nausea or vomiting

Adjunct to general anesthesia: I.V. induction: 0.088-0.165 mg/kg

Nausea and vomiting: I.M., I.V.: 0.05-0.06 mg/kg/dose every 4-6 hours as needed

Adults:

Premedication: I.M.: 2.5-10 mg 30 minutes to 1 hour preoperatively

Adjunct to general anesthesia: I.V. induction: 0.22-0.275 mg/kg; maintenance: 1.25-2.5 mg/dose

Alone in diagnostic procedures: I.M.: Initial: 2.5-10 mg 30 minutes to 1 hour before; then 1.25-2.5 mg if needed

Nausea and vomiting: I.M., I.V.: 2.5-5 mg/dose every 3-4 hours as needed

Administration Administer I.M. or I.V.; I.V. should be administered slow IVP (over 2-5 minutes) or IVPB

Monitoring Parameters Blood pressure, heart rate, respiratory rate; observe for dystonias, extrapyramidal side effects, and temperature changes

Dosage Forms Injection: 2.5 mg/mL (1 mL, 2 mL, 5 mL, 10 mL)

Droperidol and Fentanyl (droe PER i dole & FEN ta nil)

U.S. Brand Names Innovar®

Therapeutic Category Analgesic, Narcotic

Dosage Forms Injection: Droperidol 2.5 mg and fentanyl 50 mcg per mL (2 mL, 5 mL)

- **Dura-Vent/DA**® *see* Chlorpheniramine, Phenylephrine, and Methscopolamine *on page 247*
- **Duricef**® *see* Cefadroxil *on page 204*
- **Durrax**® *see* Hydroxyzine *on page 589*
- **Duvoid**® *see* Bethanechol *on page 143*
- **DV**® **Vaginal Cream** *see* Dienestrol *on page 353*
- **Dyazide**® *see* Hydrochlorothiazide and Triamterene *on page 575*
- **Dycill**® *see* Dicloxacillin *on page 350*
- **Dyclone**® *see* Dyclonine *on this page*

Dyclonine (DYE kloe neen)

U.S. Brand Names Dyclone®; Sucrets® [OTC]
Synonyms Dyclonine Hydrochloride
Therapeutic Category Local Anesthetic, Mucous Membrane; Local Anesthetic, Oral
Use Local anesthetic prior to laryngoscopy, bronchoscopy, or endotracheal intubation; use topically for temporary relief of pain associated with oral mucosa or anogenital lesions
Pregnancy Risk Factor C
Contraindications Contraindicated in patients allergic to chlorobutanol (preservative used in dyclonine) or dyclonine
Warnings/Precautions Use with caution in patients with sepsis or traumatized mucosa in the area of application to avoid rapid systemic absorption; may impair swallowing and enhance the danger of aspiration; use with caution in patients with shock or heart block; resuscitative equipment, oxygen, and resuscitative drugs should be immediately available when dyclonine topical solution is administered to mucous membranes; **not for injection or ophthalmic use**
Adverse Reactions <1%: Hypotension, bradycardia, respiratory arrest, cardiac arrest, excitation, drowsiness, nervousness, dizziness, seizures, slight irritation and stinging may occur when applied, blurred vision, allergic reactions
Overdosage/Toxicology
  Symptoms of overdose are primarily CNS (seizures, excitation) and cardiovascular (hypotension, myocardial depression)
  Treatment is supportive with fluids and pressors (particularly those that stimulate the myocardium); diazepam 0.1 mg/kg can be used to control seizures
Stability Store in tight, light-resistant containers
Mechanism of Action Blocks impulses at peripheral nerve endings in skin and mucous membranes by altering cell membrane permeability to ionic transfer
Pharmacodynamics/Kinetics
  Onset of local anesthesia: 2-10 minutes
  Duration: 30-60 minutes
Usual Dosage Use the lowest dose needed to provide effective anesthesia
  Children and Adults: Topical solution:
    Mouth sores: 5-10 mL of 0.5% or 1% to oral mucosa (swab or swish and then spit) 3-4 times/day as needed; maximum single dose: 200 mg (40 mL of 0.5% solution or 20 mL of 1% solution)
    Bronchoscopy: Use 2 mL of the 1% solution or 4 mL of the 0.5% solution sprayed onto the larynx and trachea every 5 minutes until the reflex has been abolished
Patient Information Food should not be ingested for 60 minutes following application in the mouth or throat area; numbness of the tongue and buccal mucosa may result in increased risk of biting trauma; may impair swallowing; not for use in small infants or children
Dosage Forms
  Lozenges, as hydrochloride: 1.2 mg, 3 mg
  Solution, topical, as hydrochloride: 0.5% (30 mL); 1% (30 mL)

- **Dyclonine Hydrochloride** *see* Dyclonine *on this page*
- **Dyflos** *see* Isoflurophate *on page 633*
- **Dymelor**® *see* Acetohexamide *on page 25*
- **Dynabac**® *see* Dirithromycin *on page 378*
- **Dynacin**® **Oral** *see* Minocycline *on page 782*
- **DynaCirc**® *see* Isradipine *on page 641*
- **Dyna-Hex**® **Topical [OTC]** *see* Chlorhexidine Gluconate *on page 240*
- **Dynapen**® *see* Dicloxacillin *on page 350*
- **Dyrenium**® *see* Triamterene *on page 1177*
- **7E3** *see* Abciximab *on page 15*
- **E2020** *see* Donepezil *on page 386*
- **Ear-Eze**® **Otic** *see* Neomycin, Polymyxin B, and Hydrocortisone *on page 827*
- **Easprin**® *see* Aspirin *on page 102*
- **E-Base**® *see* Erythromycin *on page 427*

Echothiophate Iodide (ek oh THYE oh fate EYE oh dide)

Related Information
  Glaucoma Drug Therapy Comparison *on page 1322*
U.S. Brand Names Phospholine Iodide® Ophthalmic
Synonyms Ecostigmine Iodide
Therapeutic Category Ophthalmic Agent, Miotic

Use Reverse toxic CNS effects caused by anticholinergic drugs; used as miotic in treatment of open-angle glaucoma; may be useful in specific case of narrow-angle glaucoma; accommodative esotropia

Pregnancy Risk Factor C

Contraindications Hypersensitivity to echothiophate or any component; most cases of angle-closure glaucoma; active uveal inflammation or any inflammatory disease of the iris or ciliary body, glaucoma associated with iridocyclitis

Warnings/Precautions Tolerance may develop after prolonged use; a rest period restores response to the drug

Adverse Reactions

1% to 10%: Ocular: Stinging, burning eyes, myopia, visual blurring

<1%: Bradycardia, hypotension, flushing, nausea, vomiting, diarrhea, muscle weakness, retinal detachment, diaphoresis, browache, miosis, twitching eyelids, watering eyes, dyspnea

Overdosage/Toxicology

Symptoms of overdose include excessive salivation, urinary incontinence, dyspnea, diarrhea, profuse sweating

If systemic effects occur, administer parenteral atropine; for severe muscle weakness, pralidoxime may be used in addition to atropine

Drug Interactions Increased toxicity: Carbamate or organophosphate insecticides and pesticides; succinylcholine; systemic acetylcholinesterases may increase neuromuscular effects

Stability Store undiluted vials at room temperature (15°C to 30°C/59°F to 86°F); reconstituted solutions remain stable for 30 days at room temperature or 6 months when refrigerated

Mechanism of Action Produces miosis and changes in accommodation by inhibiting cholinesterase, thereby preventing the breakdown of acetylcholine; acetylcholine is, therefore, allowed to continuously stimulate the iris and ciliary muscles of the eye

Pharmacodynamics/Kinetics

Onset of action: Miosis: 10-30 minutes; Intraocular pressure decrease: 4-8 hours

Peak intraocular pressure decrease: 24 hours

Duration: Up to 1-4 weeks

Usual Dosage Adults:

Ophthalmic: Glaucoma: Instill 1 drop twice daily into eyes with 1 dose just prior to bedtime; some patients have been treated with 1 dose daily or every other day

Accommodative esotropia:

Diagnosis: Instill 1 drop of 0.125% once daily into both eyes at bedtime for 2-3 weeks

Treatment: Use lowest concentration and frequency which gives satisfactory response, with a maximum dose of 0.125% once daily, although more intensive therapy may be used for short periods of time

Patient Information Be sure of solution expiration date; local irritation and headache may occur; notify physician if abdominal cramps, diarrhea, or salivation occurs; use caution if driving at night or performing hazardous tasks; do not touch dropper to eye; report any change in vision to physician

Nursing Implications Keep refrigerated; do not touch dropper to eye

Dosage Forms Powder for reconstitution, ophthalmic: 1.5 mg [0.03%] (5 mL); 3 mg [0.06%] (5 mL); 6.25 mg [0.125%] (5 mL); 12.5 mg [0.25%] (5 mL)

♦ **E-Complex-600® [OTC]** see Vitamin E on page 1225

Econazole (e KONE a zole)

U.S. Brand Names Spectazole™ Topical

Canadian Brand Names Ecostatin®

Synonyms Econazole Nitrate

Therapeutic Category Antifungal Agent, Topical

Use Topical treatment of tinea pedis (athlete's foot), tinea cruris (jock itch), tinea corporis (ringworm), tinea versicolor, and cutaneous candidiasis

Pregnancy Risk Factor C

Pregnancy/Breast-Feeding Implications Clinical effect on the fetus: Do not use during the 1st trimester of pregnancy, unless essential to a patient's welfare; use during the second and third trimesters only if clearly needed

Contraindications Known hypersensitivity to econazole or any component

Warnings/Precautions Discontinue drug if sensitivity or chemical irritation occurs; not for ophthalmic or intravaginal use

Adverse Reactions 1% to 10%:

Dermatologic: Pruritus, erythema

Local: Burning, stinging

Mechanism of Action Alters fungal cell wall membrane permeability; may interfere with RNA and protein synthesis, and lipid metabolism

Pharmacodynamics/Kinetics

Absorption: Topical: <10%

Metabolism: In the liver to >20 metabolites

Elimination: <1% of applied dose recovered in urine or feces

Usual Dosage Children and Adults: Topical:

Tinea pedis, tinea cruris, tinea corporis, tinea versicolor: Apply sufficient amount to cover affected areas once daily

Cutaneous candidiasis: Apply sufficient quantity twice daily (morning and evening)

(Continued)

Econazole *(Continued)*

Duration of treatment: Candidal infections and tinea cruris, versicolor, and corporis should be treated for 2 weeks and tinea pedis for 1 month; occasionally, longer treatment periods may be required

Patient Information For external use only; avoid eye contact; if condition worsens or persists, or irritation occurs, notify physician

Dosage Forms Cream, as nitrate: 1% (15 g, 30 g, 85 g)

- ◆ **Econazole Nitrate** *see Econazole on previous page*
- ◆ **Econopred® Ophthalmic** *see Prednisolone on page 961*
- ◆ **Econopred® Plus Ophthalmic** *see Prednisolone on page 961*
- ◆ **Ecostatin®** *see Econazole on previous page*
- ◆ **Ecostigmine Iodide** *see Echothiophate Iodide on page 402*
- ◆ **Ecotrin® [OTC]** *see Aspirin on page 102*
- ◆ **Ecotrin® Low Adult Strength [OTC]** *see Aspirin on page 102*
- ◆ **Ed A-Hist® Liquid** *see Chlorpheniramine and Phenylephrine on page 246*
- ◆ **Edathamil Disodium** *see Edetate Disodium on next page*
- ◆ **Edecrin®** *see Ethacrynic Acid on page 443*

Edetate Calcium Disodium *(ED e tate KAL see um dye SOW dee um)*

U.S. Brand Names Calcium Disodium Versenate®

Synonyms Calcium Disodium Edetate; Calcium EDTA

Therapeutic Category Antidote, Lead Toxicity

Use Treatment of symptomatic acute and chronic lead poisoning or for symptomatic patients with high blood lead levels; used as an aid in the diagnosis of lead poisoning; possibly useful in poisoning by zinc, manganese, and certain heavy radioisotopes

Pregnancy Risk Factor C

Contraindications Severe renal disease, anuria

Warnings/Precautions Potentially nephrotoxic; renal tubular acidosis and fatal nephrosis may occur, especially with high doses; EKG changes may occur during therapy; do not exceed recommended daily dose; avoid rapid I.V. infusion in the management of lead encephalopathy, may increase intracranial pressure to lethal levels. If anuria, increasing proteinuria, or hematuria occurs during therapy, discontinue calcium EDTA. Minimize nephrotoxicity by adequate hydration, establishment of good urine output, avoidance of excessive doses, and limitation of continuous administration to ≤5 days.

Adverse Reactions

1% to 10%: Renal: Renal tubular necrosis

<1%: Hypotension, arrhythmias, fever, headache, chills, skin lesions, hypercalcemia, nausea, vomiting, transient marrow suppression, pain at injection site following I.M. injection, thrombophlebitis following I.V. infusion (when concentration >0.5%), numbness, paresthesia, lacrimation, proteinuria, microscopic hematuria, sneezing, nasal congestion

Drug Interactions Decreased effect: Do not use simultaneously with zinc insulin preparations; do not mix in the same syringe with dimercaprol

Stability Dilute with 0.9% sodium chloride or D_5W; physically **incompatible** with $D_{10}W$, LR, Ringer's

Mechanism of Action Calcium is displaced by divalent and trivalent heavy metals, forming a nonionizing soluble complex that is excreted in urine

Pharmacodynamics/Kinetics

Absorption: I.M., S.C.: Well absorbed

Distribution: Into extracellular fluid; minimal CSF penetration

Half-life, plasma: I.M.: 1.5 hours; I.V.: 20 minutes

Elimination: Rapidly excreted in urine as metal chelates or unchanged drug, decreased GFR decreases elimination; when administered I.V., urinary excretion of chelated lead begins in 1 hour and peak excretion of chelated lead occurs within 24-48 hours

Usual Dosage Children and Adults:

Lead poisoning with encephalopathy or blood levels >100 mcg/dL: 1500 mg/m²/day (~30 mg/kg) in 2-3 divided doses deep I.M. or as a slow I.V. infusion (diluted to 2-4 mg/mL in D_5W or NS). Usual duration of therapy is 5 days. Some clinicians advocate initiation with single dose of dimercaprol (BAL) followed 4 hours later by concomitant BAL and calcium EDTA.

Symptomatic lead poisoning without encephalopathy and blood lead levels 50-100 mcg/dL: 1000-1500 mg/m²/day (20-30 mg/kg) in 2-3 divided doses deep I.M. or as a continuous infusion (diluted to 2-4 mg/mL) for 3-5 days

Note: An additional course may be considered based on post-treatment lead levels and the persistence or recurrence of symptoms; separate courses by ≥2 days and an interval of ≥2 weeks may be indicated to assess the extent of post-treatment rebound in lead levels.

Single dose EDTA chelation lead mobilization tests to assess the need for a full course in patients with moderately elevated levels are very controversial

Dosing adjustment/comments in renal impairment: Calcium disodium EDTA is almost exclusively eliminated in urine and should not be administered during periods of anuria

Administration For intermittent I.V. infusion, administer the dose I.V. over at least 1 hour in asymptomatic patients, 2 hours in symptomatic patients; for I.V. continuous infusion, dilute to 2-4 mg/mL in D_5W or NS and infuse over at least 8 hours, usually over 12-24

hours; for I.M. injection, 1 mL of 1% procaine hydrochloride may be added to each mL of EDTA calcium to minimize pain at injection site

Monitoring Parameters BUN, creatinine, urinalysis, I & O, and EKG during therapy; intravenous administration requires a cardiac monitor

Test Interactions If calcium EDTA is given as a continuous I.V. infusion, stop the infusion for at least 1 hour before blood is drawn for lead concentration to avoid a falsely elevated value

Dosage Forms Injection: 200 mg/mL (5 mL)

Edetate Disodium (ED e tate dye SOW dee um)

U.S. Brand Names Chealamide®; Disotate®; Endrate®

Synonyms Edathamil Disodium; EDTA; Sodium Edetate

Therapeutic Category Antidote, Hypercalcemia; Chelating Agent, Parenteral

Use Emergency treatment of hypercalcemia; control digitalis-induced cardiac dysrhythmias (ventricular arrhythmias)

Pregnancy Risk Factor C

Contraindications Severe renal failure or anuria

Warnings/Precautions Use of this drug is recommended only when the severity of the clinical condition justifies the aggressive measures associated with this type of therapy; use with caution in patients with renal dysfunction, intracranial lesions, seizure disorders, coronary or peripheral vascular disease

Adverse Reactions

Rapid I.V. administration or excessive doses may cause a sudden drop in serum calcium concentration which may lead to hypocalcemic tetany, seizures, arrhythmias, and death from respiratory arrest. Do **not** exceed recommended dosage and rate of administration.

1% to 10%: Gastrointestinal: Nausea, vomiting, abdominal cramps, diarrhea

<1%: Arrhythmias, transient hypotension, acute tubular necrosis, seizures, fever, headache, tetany, chills, eruptions, dermatologic lesions, hypomagnesemia, hypokalemia, anemia, thrombophlebitis, pain at the site of injection, paresthesia may occur, back pain, muscle cramps, nephrotoxicity, death from respiratory arrest

Overdosage/Toxicology

Symptoms of overdose include hypotension, dysrhythmias, tetany, seizures

Treatment includes immediate I.V. calcium salts for hypocalcemia related adverse reactions; replace calcium cautiously in patients on digitalis

Drug Interactions Increased effect of insulin (edetate disodium may decrease blood glucose concentrations and reduce insulin requirements in diabetic patients treated with insulin)

Mechanism of Action Chelates with divalent or trivalent metals to form a soluble complex that is then eliminated in urine

Pharmacodynamics/Kinetics

Metabolism: Not metabolized

Half-life: 20-60 minutes

Elimination: Following chelation, 95% excreted in urine as chelates within 24-48 hours

Usual Dosage Hypercalcemia: I.V.:

Children: 40-70 mg/kg/day slow infusion over 3-4 hours or more to a maximum of 3 g/24 hours; administer for 5 days and allow 5 days between courses of therapy

Adults: 50 mg/kg/day over 3 or more hours to a maximum of 3 g/24 hours; a suggested regimen of 5 days followed by 2 days without drug and repeated courses up to 15 total doses

Administration Must be diluted before use in 500 mL D_5W or NS to <30 mg/mL

Monitoring Parameters Cardiac function (EKG monitoring); blood pressure during infusion; renal function should be assessed before and during therapy; monitor calcium, magnesium, and potassium levels; cardiac monitor required

Nursing Implications Avoid extravasation; patient should remain supine for a short period after infusion; infuse over 3-4 hours

Additional Information Sodium content of 1 g: 5.4 mEq

Dosage Forms Injection: 150 mg/mL (20 mL)

♦ Edex™ Injection see Alprostadil on page 46

Edrophonium (ed roe FOE nee um)

U.S. Brand Names Enlon® Injection; Reversol® Injection; Tensilon® Injection

Synonyms Edrophonium Chloride

Therapeutic Category Antidote, Neuromuscular Blocking Agent; Cholinergic Agent; Diagnostic Agent, Myasthenia Gravis

Use Diagnosis of myasthenia gravis; differentiation of cholinergic crises from myasthenia crises; reversal of nondepolarizing neuromuscular blockers; treatment of paroxysmal atrial tachycardia

Pregnancy Risk Factor C

Contraindications Hypersensitivity to edrophonium or any component, GI or GU obstruction, hypersensitivity to sulfite agents

Warnings/Precautions Use with caution in patients with bronchial asthma and those receiving a cardiac glycoside; atropine sulfate should always be readily available as an antagonist. Overdosage can cause cholinergic crisis which may be fatal. I.V. atropine should be readily available for treatment of cholinergic reactions.

(Continued)

Edrophonium *(Continued)*

Adverse Reactions

>10%:
Gastrointestinal: Nausea, vomiting, diarrhea, excessive salivation, stomach cramps
Miscellaneous: Diaphoresis (increased)

1% to 10%:
Genitourinary: Polyuria
Ocular: Small pupils, lacrimation
Respiratory: Increased bronchial secretions

<1%: Bradycardia, A-V block, seizures, headache, drowsiness, dysphoria, weakness, muscle cramps, muscle spasms, thrombophlebitis, diplopia, miosis, laryngospasm, bronchospasm, respiratory paralysis, hypersensitivity, hyper-reactive cholinergic responses

Overdosage/Toxicology

Symptoms of overdose include muscle weakness, nausea, vomiting, miosis, bronchospasm, respiratory paralysis

Maintain adequate airway; antidote is atropine for muscarinic symptoms; pralidoxime (2-PAM) may also be needed to reverse severe muscle weakness or paralysis; skeletal muscle effects of edrophonium not alleviated by atropine.

Drug Interactions

Decreased effect: Atropine, nondepolarizing muscle relaxants, procainamide, quinidine
Increased effect: Succinylcholine, digoxin, I.V. acetazolamide, neostigmine, physostigmine

Mechanism of Action Inhibits destruction of acetylcholine by acetylcholinesterase. This facilitates transmission of impulses across myoneural junction and results in increased cholinergic responses such as miosis, increased tonus of intestinal and skeletal muscles, bronchial and ureteral constriction, bradycardia, and increased salivary and sweat gland secretions.

Pharmacodynamics/Kinetics

I.M.: Onset of effect: Within 2-10 minutes; Duration: 5-30 minutes
I.V.: Onset of effect: Within 30-60 seconds; Duration: 10 minutes
Distribution: V_d: 1.1 L/kg
Half-life: 1.8 hours

Usual Dosage Usually administered I.V., however, if not possible, I.M. or S.C. may be used:

Infants:
I.M.: 0.5-1 mg
I.V.: Initial: 0.1 mg, followed by 0.4 mg if no response; total dose = 0.5 mg

Children:
Diagnosis: Initial: 0.04 mg/kg over 1 minute followed by 0.16 mg/kg if no response, to a maximum total dose of 5 mg for children <34 kg, or 10 mg for children >34 kg
I.M.:
<34 kg: 1 mg
>34 kg: 5 mg
Titration of oral anticholinesterase therapy: 0.04 mg/kg once given 1 hour after oral intake of the drug being used in treatment; if strength improves, an increase in neostigmine or pyridostigmine dose is indicated

Adults:
Diagnosis:
I.V.: 2 mg test dose administered over 15-30 seconds; 8 mg given 45 seconds later if no response is seen; test dose may be repeated after 30 minutes
I.M.: Initial: 10 mg; if no cholinergic reaction occurs, administer 2 mg 30 minutes later to rule out false-negative reaction
Titration of oral anticholinesterase therapy: 1-2 mg given 1 hour after oral dose of anticholinesterase; if strength improves, an increase in neostigmine or pyridostigmine dose is indicated
Reversal of nondepolarizing neuromuscular blocking agents (neostigmine with atropine usually preferred): I.V.: 10 mg over 30-45 seconds; may repeat every 5-10 minutes up to 40 mg
Termination of paroxysmal atrial tachycardia: I.V. rapid injection: 5-10 mg
Differentiation of cholinergic from myasthenic crisis: I.V.: 1 mg; may repeat after 1 minute. **Note:** Intubation and controlled ventilation may be required if patient has cholinergic crisis

Dosing adjustment in renal impairment: Dose may need to be reduced in patients with chronic renal failure

Test Interactions ↑ aminotransferase [ALT (SGPT)/AST (SGOT)] (S), amylase (S)
Dosage Forms Injection, as chloride: 10 mg/mL (1 mL, 10 mL, 15 mL)

♦ **Edrophonium Chloride** *see* Edrophonium *on previous page*

♦ **ED-SPAZ®** *see* Hyoscyamine *on page 590*

♦ **EDTA** *see* Edetate Disodium *on previous page*

♦ **E.E.S.®** *see* Erythromycin *on page 427*

Efavirenz *(e FAV e renz)*

Related Information

Antiretroviral Agents *on page 1306*
Antiretroviral Therapy for HIV Infection *on page 1410*

U.S. Brand Names Sustiva™
Therapeutic Category Non-nucleoside Reverse Transcriptase Inhibitor (NNRTI)

Use Treatment of HIV-1 infections in combination with at least two other antiretroviral agents. Also has some activity against hepatitis B virus and herpes viruses.

Pregnancy Risk Factor C

Pregnancy/Breast-Feeding Implications Teratogenic effects have been observed in Primates receiving efavirenz. Pregnancy should be avoided. Women of childbearing potential should undergo pregnancy testing prior to initiation of efavirenz. Barrier contraception should be used in combination with other (hormonal) methods of contraception.

Contraindications Clinically significant hypersensitivity to any component of the formulation

Warnings/Precautions Do not use as single-agent therapy; avoid pregnancy; women of childbearing potential should undergo pregnancy testing prior to initiation of therapy; do not administer with other agents metabolized by cytochrome P-450 isoenzyme 3A4 including astemizole, cisapride, midazolam, triazolam or ergot alkaloids (potential for life-threatening adverse effects); history of mental illness/drug abuse (predisposition to psychological reactions); may cause depression and/or other psychiatric symptoms including impaired concentration, dizziness or drowsiness (avoid potentially hazardous tasks such as driving or operating machinery if these effects are noted); discontinue if severe rash (involving blistering, desquamation, mucosal involvement or fever) develops. Caution in patients with known or suspected hepatitis B or C infection (monitoring of liver function is recommended); hepatic impairment. Persistent elevations of serum transaminases >5 times the upper limit of normal should prompt evaluation - benefit of continued therapy should be weighed against possible risk of hepatotoxicity. Children are more susceptible to development of rash - prophylactic antihistamines may be used.

Adverse Reactions

2% to 10%:
Central nervous system: Dizziness (2% to 10%), inability to concentrate (0% to 9%), insomnia (0% to 7%), headache (5% to 6%) abnormal dreams (0% to 4%), somnolence (0% to 3%), depression (0% to 2%), anorexia (0% to 5%), nervousness (0% to 2%), fatigue (2% to 7%), hypoesthesia (1% to 2%)
Dermatologic: Rash (5% to 20%), pruritus (0% to 2%)
Gastrointestinal: Nausea (0% to 12%), vomiting (0% to 7%), diarrhea (2% to 12%), dyspepsia (0% to 4%), elevated transaminases (2% to 3%), abdominal pain (0% to 3%)
Miscellaneous: Increased sweating (0% to 2%)

<2%: Edema (peripheral), syncope, flushing, palpitations, tachycardia, fever, pain, malaise, ataxia, depression, seizures, hallucinations, psychosis, depersonalization, amnesia, anxiety, apathy, emotional lability, agitation, confusion, euphoria, impaired coordination, migraine, speech disorder, vertigo, alopecia, eczema, folliculitis, skin exfoliation, urticaria, increased cholesterol and triglycerides, hot flashes, pancreatitis, dry mouth, taste disturbance, flatulence, renal calculus, hematuria, hepatitis, thrombophlebitis, asthenia, neuralgia, paresthesia, peripheral neuropathy, tremor, arthralgia, myalgia, abnormal vision, diplopia, tinnitus, asthma, alcohol intolerance, allergic reaction, parosmia

Pediatric patients: Rash (40%), diarrhea (39%), fever (26%), cough (25%), nausea/vomiting (16%), central nervous system reactions (9%)

Overdosage/Toxicology

Increased central nervous system symptoms and involuntary muscle contractions have been reported in accidental overdose

Treatment is supportive, activated charcoal may enhance elimination; dialysis is unlikely to remove drug

Drug Interactions

Increased effect: CYP3A4, 2C9, 2C19 inhibitor; CYP3A4 inducer; coadministration with medications metabolized by these enzymes may lead to increased concentration-related effects. Astemizole, cisapride, midazolam, triazolam and ergot alkaloids may result in life-threatening toxicities. The AUC of nelfinavir is increased (20%); AUC of both ritonavir and efavirenz are increased by 20% during concurrent therapy. The AUC of ethinyl estradiol is increased 37% by efavirenz (clinical significance unknown). May increase effect of warfarin.

Decreased effect: Other inducers of this enzyme (including phenobarbital, rifampin and rifabutin) may decrease serum concentrations of efavirenz. Concentrations of indinavir may be reduced; dosage increase to 1000 mg 3 times/day is recommended. Concentrations of saquinavir may be decreased (use as sole protease inhibitor is not recommended). Plasma concentrations of clarithromycin are decreased (clinical significance unknown). May decrease effect of warfarin.

Stability Store below 25°C (77°F)

Mechanism of Action As a non-nucleoside reverse transcriptase inhibitor, efavirenz has activity against HIV-1 by binding to reverse transcriptase. It consequently blocks the RNA-dependent and DNA-dependent DNA polymerase activities including HIV-1 replication. It does not require intracellular phosphorylation for antiviral activity.

Pharmacodynamics/Kinetics

Absorption: Increased 50% by fatty meals

Distribution: Highly protein bound (>99%) primarily to albumin; CSF concentrations exceed free fraction in serum

Metabolism: Hepatic

Half-life: Single dose: 52-76 hours; after multiple doses: 40-55 hours

Time to peak concentration: 3-8 hours

Elimination: 14% to 34% in urine (as metabolites) and 16% to 41% in feces (primarily as efavirenz)

(Continued)

Efavirenz *(Continued)*

Usual Dosage Oral: Dosing at bedtime is recommended to limit central nervous system effects; should not be used as single-agent therapy

Children: Dosage is based on body weight
   10 kg to <15 kg: 200 mg once daily
   15 kg to <20 kg: 250 mg once daily
   20 kg to <25 kg: 300 mg once daily
   25 kg to <32.5 kg: 350 mg once daily
   32.5 kg to <40 kg: 400 mg once daily
   ≥40 kg: 600 mg once daily
Adults: 600 mg once daily

Dosing adjustment in renal impairment: None recommended

Dosing comments in hepatic impairment: Limited clinical experience, use with caution

Dietary Considerations May be taken with or without food. Avoid high-fat meals when taking this medication. High-fat meals increase the absorption of efavirenz.

Monitoring Parameters Serum transaminases (discontinuation of treatment should be considered for persistent elevations greater than five times the upper limit of normal), cholesterol, triglycerides, signs and symptoms of infection

Test Interactions False positive test for cannabinoids have been reported when the CEDIA DAU Multilevel THC assay is used. False positive results with other assays for cannabinoids have not been observed

Patient Information Take efavirenz exactly as prescribed; report all side effects to your physician; do not alter dose or discontinue without consulting physician; may cause dizziness, drowsiness, impaired concentration, delusions or depression; taking at bedtime may minimize these effects; caution in performing potentially hazardous tasks such as operating machinery or driving; do not get pregnant; avoid high-fat meals

Dosage Forms Capsule: 50 mg, 100 mg, 200 mg

- **Effer-K™** *see* Potassium Bicarbonate and Potassium Citrate, Effervescent *on page 948*
- **Effer-Syllium® [OTC]** *see* Psyllium *on page 994*
- **Effexor®** *see* Venlafaxine *on page 1213*
- **Effexor® XR** *see* Venlafaxine *on page 1213*
- **Efidac/24® [OTC]** *see* Pseudoephedrine *on page 993*

Eflornithine *(ee FLOR ni theen)*

U.S. Brand Names Ornidyl®

Synonyms DFMO; Eflornithine Hydrochloride

Therapeutic Category Antiprotozoal

Use Treatment of meningoencephalitic stage of *Trypanosoma brucei gambiense* infection (sleeping sickness)

Pregnancy Risk Factor C

Contraindications Hypersensitivity to eflornithine or any component

Warnings/Precautions Must be diluted before use; frequent monitoring for myelosuppression should be done; use with caution in patients with a history of seizures and in patients with renal impairment; serial audiograms should be obtained; due to the potential for relapse, patients should be followed up for at least 24 months

Adverse Reactions

>10%: Hematologic (reversible): Anemia (55%), leukopenia (37%), thrombocytopenia (14%)

1% to 10%:
   Central nervous system: Seizures (may be due to the disease) (8%), dizziness
   Dermatologic: Alopecia
   Gastrointestinal: Vomiting, diarrhea
   Hematologic: Eosinophilia
   Otic: Hearing impairment

<1%: Facial edema, headache, abdominal pain, anorexia, weakness

Overdosage/Toxicology No known antidote; treatment is supportive; in mice and rats, CNS depression, seizures, death have occurred

Stability Must be diluted before use and used within 24 hours of preparation

Mechanism of Action Eflornithine exerts antitumor and antiprotozoal effects through specific, irreversible ("suicide") inhibition of the enzyme ornithine decarboxylase (ODC). ODC is the rate-limiting enzyme in the biosynthesis of putrescine, spermine, and spermidine, the major polyamines in nucleated cells. Polyamines are necessary for the synthesis of DNA, RNA, and proteins and are, therefore, necessary for cell growth and differentiation. Although many microorganisms and higher plants are able to produce polyamines from alternate biochemical pathways, all mammalian cells depend on ornithine decarboxylase to produce polyamines. Eflornithine inhibits ODC and rapidly depletes animal cells of putrescine and spermidine; the concentration of spermine remains the same or may even increase. Rapidly dividing cells appear to most susceptible to the effects of eflornithine.

Pharmacodynamics/Kinetics

Absorption: Well absorbed from GI tract
Bioavailability: 54% to 58%
Half-life: 3-3.5 hours
Elimination: Mainly excreted unchanged in urine via glomerular filtration

Usual Dosage Adults: I.V. infusion: 100 mg/kg/dose given every 6 hours (over at least 45 minutes) for 14 days

Dosing adjustment in renal impairment: Dose should be adjusted although no specific guidelines are available

Monitoring Parameters CBC with platelet counts

Patient Information Report any persistent or unusual fever, sore throat, fatigue, bleeding, or bruising; frequent blood tests are needed during therapy

Dosage Forms Injection, as hydrochloride: 200 mg/mL (100 mL)

- **Eflornithine Hydrochloride** see Eflornithine on previous page
- **Efodine® [OTC]** see Povidone-Iodine on page 955
- **Efudex® Topical** see Fluorouracil on page 500
- **EHDP** see Etidronate Disodium on page 457
- **E-IPV** see Polio Vaccines on page 940
- **Elase-Chloromycetin® Topical** see Fibrinolysin and Desoxyribonuclease on page 482
- **Elase® Topical** see Fibrinolysin and Desoxyribonuclease on page 482
- **Elavil®** see Amitriptyline on page 62
- **Eldecort®** see Hydrocortisone on page 579
- **Eldepryl®** see Selegiline on page 1053
- **Eldercaps® [OTC]** see Vitamins, Multiple on page 1226
- **Eldopaque® [OTC]** see Hydroquinone on page 584
- **Eldopaque Forte®** see Hydroquinone on page 584
- **Eldoquin® [OTC]** see Hydroquinone on page 584
- **Eldoquin® Forte®** see Hydroquinone on page 584
- **Electrolyte Lavage Solution** see Polyethylene Glycol-Electrolyte Solution on page 942
- **Elimite™ Cream** see Permethrin on page 908
- **Elixophyllin®** see Theophylline Salts on page 1125
- **Elixophyllin® SR** see Theophylline Salts on page 1125
- **Elmiron®** see Pentosan Polysulfate Sodium on page 904
- **Elocom** see Mometasone Furoate on page 794
- **Elocon® Topical** see Mometasone Furoate on page 794
- **Elspar®** see Asparaginase on page 100
- **Eltor®** see Pseudoephedrine on page 993
- **Eltroxin®** see Levothyroxine on page 677
- **Emcyt®** see Estramustine on page 435
- **Eminase®** see Anistreplase on page 87
- **EMLA®** see Lidocaine and Prilocaine on page 681
- **Empirin® [OTC]** see Aspirin on page 102
- **Empirin® With Codeine** see Aspirin and Codeine on page 105
- **Empracet® 30, 60** see Acetaminophen and Codeine on page 21
- **Emtec-30®** see Acetaminophen and Codeine on page 21
- **E-Mycin®** see Erythromycin on page 427

Enalapril (e NAL a pril)

Related Information

Angiotensin Agents on page 1291

Drug-Drug Interactions With ACEIs on page 1295

Heart Failure: Management of Patients With Left-Ventricular Systolic Dysfunction on page 1472

U.S. Brand Names Vasotec®; Vasotec® I.V.

Canadian Brand Names Apo®-Enalapril

Synonyms Enalaprilat; Enalapril Maleate

Therapeutic Category Angiotensin-Converting Enzyme (ACE) Inhibitor; Antihypertensive Agent

Use Management of mild to severe hypertension and congestive heart failure; believed to prolong survival in heart failure

Unlabeled use: Hypertensive crisis, diabetic nephropathy, rheumatoid arthritis, diagnosis of anatomic renal artery stenosis, hypertension secondary to scleroderma renal crisis, diagnosis of aldosteronism, idiopathic edema, Bartter's syndrome, postmyocardial infarction for prevention of ventricular failure

Pregnancy Risk Factor C (1st trimester); D (2nd and 3rd trimester)

Pregnancy/Breast-Feeding Implications

Clinical effects on the fetus: No data available on crossing the placenta. Cranial defects, hypocalvaria/acalvaria, oligohydramnios, persistent anuria following delivery, hypotension, renal defects, renal dysgenesis/dysplasia, renal failure, pulmonary hypoplasia, limb contractures secondary to oligohydramnios and stillbirth reported. ACE inhibitors should be avoided during pregnancy.

Breast-feeding/lactation: Crosses into breast milk. Detectable levels but appears clinically insignificant. American Academy of Pediatrics considers **compatible** with breast-feeding.

Contraindications Hypersensitivity to enalapril, enalaprilat, other ACE inhibitors, or any component

Warnings/Precautions Use with caution and modify dosage in patients with renal impairment (especially renal artery stenosis), severe congestive heart failure, or with coadministered diuretic therapy, valvular stenosis, hyperkalemia (>5.7 mEq/L); experience in children is limited. Severe hypotension may occur in patients who are sodium (Continued)

409

Enalapril (Continued)

and/or volume depleted; initiate lower doses and monitor closely when starting therapy in these patients.

Adverse Reactions

1% to 10%:

Cardiovascular: Chest pain (2%), syncope (2%), hypotension (6.7%)

Central nervous system: Headache (2% to 5%), dizziness (4% to 8%), fatigue (2% to 3%)

Dermatologic: Rash (1.5%)

Gastrointestinal: Abnormal taste, abdominal pain, vomiting, nausea, diarrhea, anorexia, constipation

Neuromuscular & skeletal: Weakness

Respiratory (1% to 2%): Bronchitis, cough, dyspnea

<1%: Angina pectoris, pulmonary edema, palpitations, arrest, CVA, myocardial infarction, orthostatic hypotension, rhythm, insomnia, ataxia, drowsiness, confusion, depression, nervousness, vertigo, alopecia, erythema multiforme, pruritus, Stevens-Johnson syndrome, urticaria, angioedema, pemphigus, hypoglycemia, hyperkalemia, gynecomastia, stomatitis, xerostomia, dyspepsia, glossitis, pancreatitis, ileus, urinary tract infection. impotence, agranulocytosis, neutropenia, anemia, hemolysis with G-6-PD, jaundice, hepatitis, paresthesia, blurred vision, conjunctivitis, tinnitus, oliguria, renal dysfunction, asthma, bronchospasm, URI, diaphoresis

Overdosage/Toxicology

Mild hypotension has been the only toxic effect seen with acute overdose. Bradycardia may also occur; hyperkalemia occurs even with therapeutic doses, especially in patients with renal insufficiency and those taking NSAIDs

Following initiation of essential overdose management, toxic symptom treatment and supportive treatment should be initiated. Hypotension usually responds to I.V. fluids or Trendelenburg positioning.

Drug Interactions CYP3A3/4 enzyme substrate

See Drug-Drug Interactions With ACEIs on page 1295

Stability Enalapril: Clear, colorless solution which should be stored at <30°C; I.V. is 24 hours at room temperature in D_5W or NS

Mechanism of Action Competitive inhibitor of angiotensin-converting enzyme (ACE); prevents conversion of angiotensin I to angiotensin II, a potent vasoconstrictor; results in lower levels of angiotensin II which causes an increase in plasma renin activity and a reduction in aldosterone secretion

Pharmacodynamics/Kinetics

Oral: Onset of action: ~1 hour; Duration: 12-24 hours

Absorption: Oral: 55% to 75%

Protein binding: 50% to 60%

Metabolism: Enalapril is a prodrug and undergoes biotransformation to enalaprilat in the liver

Half-life:

Enalaprilat: Adults:

Healthy: 2 hours

With congestive heart failure: 3.4-5.8 hours

Enalaprilat:

Infants 6 weeks to 8 months: 6-10 hours

Adults: 35-38 hours

Time to peak serum concentration: Oral:

Enalapril: Within 0.5-1.5 hours

Enalaprilat (active): Within 3-4.5 hours

Elimination: Principally in urine (60% to 80%) with some fecal excretion

Usual Dosage Use lower listed initial dose in patients with hyponatremia, hypovolemia, severe congestive heart failure, decreased renal function, or in those receiving diuretics

Infants and Children:

Investigational initial oral doses of **enalapril**: 0.1 mg/kg/day increasing as needed over 2 weeks to 0.5 mg/kg/day have been used to treat severe congestive heart failure in infants

Investigational I.V. doses of **enalaprilat**: 5-10 mcg/kg/dose administered every 8-24 hours have been used for the treatment of neonatal hypertension; monitor patients carefully; select patients may require higher doses

Adults:

Oral: **Enalapril**

Hypertension: 2.5-5 mg/day then increase as required, usual therapeutic dose for hypertension: 10-40 mg/day in 1-2 divided doses. **Note:** Initiate with 2.5 mg if patient taking diuretic which cannot be discontinued; may add a diuretic if blood pressure cannot be controlled with enalapril alone

Heart failure: As adjunct with diuretics and digitalis, initiate with 2.5 mg once or twice daily (usual range: 5-20 mg/day in 2 divided doses; maximum: 40 mg)

Asymptomatic left ventricular dysfunction: 2.5 mg twice daily, titrated as tolerated to 20 mg/day

I.V.: **Enalaprilat**

Hypertension: 1.25 mg/dose, given over 5 minutes every 6 hours; doses as high as 5 mg/dose every 6 hours have been tolerated for up to 36 hours. **Note:** If patients are concomitantly receiving diuretic therapy, begin with 0.625 mg I.V. over 5 minutes; if the effect is not adequate after 1 hour, repeat the dose and administer

1.25 mg at 6-hour intervals thereafter; if adequate, administer 0.625 mg I.V. every 6 hours

Conversion from I.V. to oral therapy if not concurrently on diuretics: 5 mg once daily; subsequent titration as needed; if concurrently receiving diuretics and responding to 0.625 mg I.V. every 6 hours, initiate with 2.5 mg/day

Dosing adjustment in renal impairment:

Oral: Enalapril:

Cl_{cr} 30-80 mL/minute: Administer 5 mg/day titrated upwards to maximum of 40 mg

Cl_{cr} <30 mL/minute: Administer 2.5 mg day; titrated upward until blood pressure is controlled

For heart failure patients with sodium <130 mEq/L or serum creatinine >1.6 mg/dL, initiate dosage with 2.5 mg/day, increasing to twice daily as needed; increase further in increments of 2.5 mg/dose at >4-day intervals to a maximum daily dose of 40 mg

I.V.: Enalaprilat:

Cl_{cr} >30 mL/minute: Initiate with 1.25 mg every 6 hours and increase dose based on response

Cl_{cr} <30 mL/minute: Initiate with 0.625 mg every 6 hours and increase dose based on response

Hemodialysis: Moderately dialyzable (20% to 50%); administer dose postdialysis (eg, 0.625 mg I.V. every 6 hours) or administer 20% to 25% supplemental dose following dialysis; Clearance: 62 mL/minute

Peritoneal dialysis: Supplemental dose is not necessary, although some removal of drug occurs

Dosing adjustment in hepatic impairment: Hydrolysis of enalapril to enalaprilat may be delayed and/or impaired in patients with severe hepatic impairment, but the pharmacodynamic effects of the drug do not appear to be significantly altered; no dosage adjustment

Administration Administer direct IVP over at least 5 minutes or dilute up to 50 mL and infuse; discontinue diuretic, if possible, for 2-3 days before beginning enalapril therapy

Monitoring Parameters Blood pressure, renal function, WBC, serum potassium; blood pressure monitor required during intravenous administration

Test Interactions Positive Coombs' [direct]; may cause false-positive results in urine acetone determinations using sodium nitroprusside reagent

Patient Information Notify physician if vomiting, diarrhea, excessive perspiration, or dehydration should occur; also if swelling of face, lips, tongue, or difficulty in breathing occurs or if persistent cough develops

Nursing Implications May cause depression in some patients; discontinue if angioedema of the face, extremities, lips, tongue, or glottis occurs; watch for hypotensive effects within 1-3 hours of first dose or new higher dose

Dosage Forms

Injection, as enalaprilat: 1.25 mg/mL (1 mL, 2 mL)

Tablet, as maleate: 2.5 mg, 5 mg, 10 mg, 20 mg

Extemporaneous Preparations An enalapril oral suspension (0.2 mg/mL) has been made using one 2.5 mg tablet and 12.5 mL sterile water; stability unknown; suspension should be used immediately and the remaining amount discarded

Young TE and Mangum OB, "Neofax®, '95: A Manual of Drugs Used in Neonatal Care," 8th ed, Columbus, OH: Ross Products Division, Abbott Laboratories, 1995, 85.

Enalapril and Diltiazem (e NAL a pril & dil TYE a zem)

U.S. Brand Names Teczem®

Therapeutic Category Angiotensin-Converting Enzyme (ACE) Inhibitor Combination; Antihypertensive Agent, Combination

Dosage Forms Tablet, extended release: Enalapril maleate 5 mg and diltiazem maleate 180 mg

Enalapril and Felodipine (e NAL a pril & fe LOE di peen)

U.S. Brand Names Lexxel™

Therapeutic Category Angiotensin-Converting Enzyme (ACE) Inhibitor Combination; Antihypertensive Agent, Combination

Dosage Forms Tablet, extended release: Enalapril maleate 5 mg and felodipine 5 mg

Enalapril and Hydrochlorothiazide

(e NAL a pril & hye droe klor oh THYE a zide)

U.S. Brand Names Vaseretic® 10-25

Therapeutic Category Angiotensin-Converting Enzyme (ACE) Inhibitor Combination; Antihypertensive Agent, Combination

Dosage Forms Tablet:

Enalapril maleate 5 mg and hydrochlorothiazide 12.5 mg

Enalapril maleate 10 mg and hydrochlorothiazide 25 mg

- ◆ **Endodan**® see Oxycodone and Aspirin on page 876
- ◆ **Endolor**® see Butalbital Compound on page 165
- ◆ **Endrate**® see Edetate Disodium on page 405
- ◆ **Enduron**® see Methyclothiazide on page 757
- ◆ **Enduronyl**® see Methyclothiazide and Deserpidine on page 757
- ◆ **Enduronyl**® **Forte** see Methyclothiazide and Deserpidine on page 757
- ◆ **Ener-B**® [OTC] see Cyanocobalamin on page 302
- ◆ **Engerix-B**® see Hepatitis B Vaccine on page 565
- ◆ **Enhanced-potency Inactivated Poliovirus Vaccine** see Polio Vaccines on page 940
- ◆ **Enlon**® **Injection** see Edrophonium on page 405
- ◆ **Enovil**® see Amitriptyline on page 62

Enoxacin (en OKS a sin)

U.S. Brand Names Penetrex™

Therapeutic Category Antibiotic, Quinolone

Use Treatment of complicated and uncomplicated urinary tract infections caused by susceptible gram-negative and gram-positive bacteria and uncomplicated urethral or cervical gonorrhea due to *N. gonorrhoeae*

Pregnancy Risk Factor C

Contraindications Hypersensitivity to enoxacin, any component, or other quinolones

Warnings/Precautions Use with caution in patients with a history of convulsions or epilepsy, renal dysfunction, psychosis, elevated intracranial pressure, prepubertal children, and pregnancy; nalidixic acid and ciprofloxacin (related compounds) have been associated with erosions of the cartilage in weight-bearing joints and other signs of arthropathy in immature animals and children; similar precautions are advised for enoxacin although no data is available; has rarely caused ruptured tendons (discontinue immediately with signs of inflammation or tendon pain)

Adverse Reactions

1% to 10%:

Central nervous system: Dizziness (<3%), headache (<2%), vertigo (3%)

Gastrointestinal: Nausea (2.9%), vomiting (6% to 9%), abdominal pain (1% to 2%), diarrhea (1% to 2%)

<1%: Palpitations, syncope, edema, restlessness, confusion, seizures, fatigue, drowsiness, depression, insomnia, confusion, chills, fever, rash, photosensitivity, pruritus, exfoliative dermatitis, hypo/hyperkalemia, GI bleeding, dyspepsia, xerostomia, constipation, flatulence, anorexia, vaginitis, anemia, leukopenia, eosinophilia, leukocytosis, increased liver enzymes, tremor, arthralgia, ruptured tendons, paresthesias, visual disturbances, increased serum creatinine/BUN, acute renal failure, proteinuria

Overdosage/Toxicology

Symptoms of overdose include acute renal failure, seizures

GI decontamination and supportive care; diazepam for seizures; not removed by peritoneal or hemodialysis

Drug Interactions CYP1A2 enzyme inhibitor

Decreased effect of enoxacin with antacids (magnesium, aluminum), iron and zinc salts, sucralfate, bismuth salts, antineoplastics

Increased toxicity/levels of warfarin, cyclosporine, digoxin, caffeine, and theophylline with enoxacin

Increased levels of enoxacin with cimetidine, probenecid

Mechanism of Action Inhibits DNA-gyrase in susceptible organisms; inhibits relaxation of supercoiled DNA and promotes breakage of double-stranded DNA

Pharmacodynamics/Kinetics

Absorption: 98%

Distribution: Penetrates well into tissues and body secretions

Half-life: 3-6 hours (average)

Elimination: Primarily in urine, however, significant drug concentrations are achieved in feces

Usual Dosage Adults: Oral:

Complicated urinary tract infection: 400 mg twice daily for 14 days

Cystitis: 200 mg twice daily for 7 days

Uncomplicated gonorrhea: 400 mg as single dose

Dosing adjustment in renal impairment: Cl_{cr} <50 mL/minute: Administer 50% of dose

Patient Information May be taken with food to minimize upset stomach; avoid antacid use; drink fluid liberally

Dosage Forms Tablet: 200 mg, 400 mg

Enoxaparin (ee noks a PA rin)

Related Information

Heparins Comparison on page 1324

U.S. Brand Names Lovenox® Injection

Synonyms Enoxaparin Sodium

Therapeutic Category Low Molecular Weight Heparin

Use

Prophylaxis of thromboembolic disorders (deep vein thrombosis) which may lead to pulmonary embolism following hip replacement therapy or total knee replacement

Prophylaxis of thromboembolic disorders (deep vein thrombosis) which may lead to pulmonary embolism in high-risk patients who are undergoing abdominal surgery. High-risk patients include those with one or more of the following risk factors: >40 years of age, obese, general anesthesia lasting >30 minutes, malignancy, history of deep vein thrombosis or pulmonary embolism.

Prevention of ischemic complications of unstable angina and non-Q-wave myocardial infarction when concurrently administered with aspirin

Treatment of thromboembolic disorders (deep vein thrombosis with or without pulmonary embolism)

Pregnancy Risk Factor B

Contraindications Patients with active major bleeding, thrombocytopenia associated with a positive *in vitro* test for antiplatelet antibody or enoxaparin-induced platelet aggregation; hypersensitivity to enoxaparin; known hypersensitivity to heparin or pork products

Warnings/Precautions Do not administer intramuscularly; use with extreme caution in patients with a history of heparin-induced thrombocytopenia; bacterial endocarditis, hemorrhagic stroke, recent CNS or ophthalmological surgery, bleeding diathesis, uncontrolled arterial hypertension, or a history of recent gastrointestinal ulceration and hemorrhage. Elderly and patients with renal insufficiency may show delayed elimination of enoxaparin; avoid use in lactation. Patients should be observed closely for bleeding if enoxaparin is administered during or immediately following diagnostic lumbar puncture, epidural anesthesia, or spinal anesthesia. If thromboembolism develops despite enoxaparin prophylaxis, enoxaparin should be discontinued and appropriate treatment should be initiated.

Carefully monitor patients receiving low molecular weight heparins or heparinoids. These drugs, when used concurrently with spinal or epidural anesthesia or spinal puncture, may cause bleeding or hematomas within the spinal column. Increased pressure on the spinal cord may result in permanent paralysis if not detected and treated immediately.

Adverse Reactions 1% to 10%:
Central nervous system: Fever, confusion, pain
Dermatologic: Erythema, bruising
Gastrointestinal: Nausea
Hematologic: Hemorrhage, thrombocytopenia, hypochromic anemia, hematoma
Local: Irritation
At the recommended doses, single injections of enoxaparin do not significantly influence platelet aggregation or affect global clotting time (ie, PT or APTT)

Overdosage/Toxicology
Symptoms of overdose include hemorrhage
Protamine sulfate has been used to reverse effects

Drug Interactions Increased toxicity with oral anticoagulants, platelet inhibitors

Mechanism of Action Standard heparin consists of components with molecular weights ranging from 4000-30,000 daltons with a mean of 16,000 daltons. Heparin acts as an anticoagulant by enhancing the inhibition rate of clotting proteases by antithrombin III impairing normal hemostasis and inhibition of factor Xa. Low molecular weight heparins have a small effect on the activated partial thromboplastin time and strongly inhibit factor Xa. Enoxaparin is derived from porcine heparin that undergoes benzylation followed by alkaline depolymerization. The average molecular weight of enoxaparin is 4500 daltons which is distributed as (≤20%) 2000 daltons, (≥68%) 2000-8000 daltons, and (≤15%) >8000 daltons. Enoxaparin has a higher ratio of antifactor Xa to antifactor IIa activity than unfractionated heparin.

Pharmacodynamics/Kinetics
Onset of effect: Maximum antifactor Xa and antithrombin (antifactor IIa) activities occur 3-5 hours after S.C. administration
Duration: Following a 40 mg dose, significant antifactor Xa activity persists in plasma for ~12 hours
Protein binding: Low molecular weight heparins do not bind to heparin binding proteins
Half-life, plasma: Low molecular weight heparin is 2-4 times longer than standard heparin independent of the dose

Usual Dosage S.C.:
Prophylaxis of DVT following abdominal, hip replacement or knee replacement surgery:
Children: Safety and effectiveness have not been established
Adults:
DVT prophylaxis in hip replacement:
30 mg twice daily: First dose within 12-24 hours after surgery and every 12 hours until risk of deep vein thrombosis has diminished or the patient is adequately anticoagulated on warfarin. Average duration of therapy: 7-10 days
40 mg once daily: First dose within 9-15 hours before surgery and daily until risk of deep vein thrombosis has diminished or the patient is adequately anticoagulated on warfarin. Average duration of therapy: 7-10 days unless warfarin is not given concurrently, then 40 mg S.C. once daily should be continued for 3 more weeks (4 weeks total)
DVT prophylaxis in knee replacement:
30 mg twice daily: First dose within 12-24 hours after surgery and every 12 hours until risk of deep vein thrombosis has diminished. Average duration of therapy: 7-10 days; maximum course: 14 days
Patients who weigh <100 lbs or are >65 years of age: Some clinicians recommend 0.5 mg/kg/dose every 12 hours to reduce the risk of bleeding
DVT prophylaxis in high-risk patients undergoing abdominal surgery: 40 mg once daily, with initial dose given 2 hours prior to surgery; usual duration: 7-10 days and up to 12 days has been tolerated in clinical trials
Treatment of acute proximal DVT: Start warfarin within 72 hours and continue enoxaparin until INR is between 2.0 and 3.0 (usually 7 days)
(Continued)

413

Enoxaparin *(Continued)*

Inpatient treatment of DVT with or without pulmonary embolism: Adults: S.C. 1 mg/kg/dose every 12 hours or 1.5 mg/kg once daily

Outpatient treatment of DCT without pulmonary embolism: Adults: S.C.: 1 mg/kg/dose every 12 hours

Prevention of ischemic complications with unstable angina or non-Q-wave myocardial infarction: S.C.: 1 mg/kg twice daily in conjunction with oral aspirin therapy (100-325 mg once daily); treatment should be continued for a minimum of 2 days and continued until clinical stabilization (usually 2-8 days)

Dosing adjustment in renal impairment: Total clearance is lower and elimination is delayed in patients with renal failure; adjustment may be necessary in elderly and patients with severe renal impairment

Hemodialysis: Supplemental dose is not necessary

Peritoneal dialysis: Significant drug removal is unlikely based on physiochemical characteristics

Monitoring Parameters Platelets, occult blood, and anti-Xa activity, if available; the monitoring of PT and/or PTT is not necessary

Dosage Forms Injection, as sodium, preservative free:
Prefilled syringes: 30 mg/0.3 mL, 40 mg/0.4 mL
Graduated prefilled syringe: 60 mg/0.6 mL, 80 mg/0.8 mL, 100 mg/1.0 mL
Ampul: 30 mg/0.3 mL

♦ **Enoxaparin Sodium** *see* Enoxaparin *on page 412*

♦ **Entocort®** *see* Budesonide *on page 157*

♦ **Entrophen®** *see* Aspirin *on page 102*

♦ **Entuss-D® Liquid** *see* Hydrocodone and Pseudoephedrine *on page 579*

♦ **Enulose®** *see* Lactulose *on page 656*

♦ **Enzone®** *see* Pramoxine and Hydrocortisone *on page 958*

♦ **E Pam®** *see* Diazepam *on page 345*

Ephedrine *(e FED rin)*

Related Information
Contrast Media Reactions, Premedication for Prophylaxis *on page 1464*

U.S. Brand Names Kondon's Nasal® [OTC]; Pretz-D® [OTC]

Synonyms Ephedrine Sulfate

Therapeutic Category Adrenergic Agonist Agent; Bronchodilator; Sympathomimetic

Use Treatment of bronchial asthma, nasal congestion, acute bronchospasm, idiopathic orthostatic hypotension

Pregnancy Risk Factor C

Contraindications Hypersensitivity to ephedrine or any component, cardiac arrhythmias, angle-closure glaucoma, patients on other sympathomimetic agents

Warnings/Precautions Blood volume depletion should be corrected before ephedrine therapy is instituted; use caution in patients with unstable vasomotor symptoms, diabetes, hyperthyroidism, prostatic hypertrophy, or a history of seizures; also use caution in the elderly and those patients with cardiovascular disorders such as coronary artery disease, arrhythmias, and hypertension. Ephedrine may cause hypertension resulting in intracranial hemorrhage. Long-term use may cause anxiety and symptoms of paranoid schizophrenia. Avoid as a bronchodilator; generally not used as a bronchodilator since new beta$_2$ agents are less toxic. Use with caution in the elderly, since it crosses the blood-brain barrier and may cause confusion.

Adverse Reactions
>10%: Central nervous system: CNS stimulating effects, nervousness, anxiety, apprehension, fear, tension, agitation, excitation, restlessness, irritability, insomnia, hyperactivity

1% to 10%:
Cardiovascular: Hypertension, tachycardia, palpitations, elevation or depression of blood pressure, unusual pallor
Central nervous system: Dizziness, headache
Gastrointestinal: Xerostomia, nausea, anorexia, GI upset, vomiting
Genitourinary: Painful urination
Neuromuscular & skeletal: Trembling, tremor (more common in the elderly), weakness
Miscellaneous: Diaphoresis (increased)

<1%: Chest pain, arrhythmias, dyspnea

Overdosage/Toxicology
Symptoms of overdose include dysrhythmias, CNS excitation, respiratory depression, vomiting, convulsions

There is no specific antidote for ephedrine intoxication and the bulk of the treatment is supportive. Hyperactivity and agitation usually respond to reduced sensory input; however, with extreme agitation, haloperidol (2-5 mg I.M. for adults) may be required. Hyperthermia is best treated with external cooling measures; or when severe or unresponsive, muscle paralysis with pancuronium may be needed. Hypertension is usually transient and generally does not require treatment unless severe. For diastolic blood pressures >110 mm Hg, a nitroprusside infusion should be initiated. Seizures usually respond to diazepam I.V. and/or phenytoin maintenance regimens.

Drug Interactions
Decreased effect: Alpha- and beta-adrenergic blocking agents decrease ephedrine vasopressor effects

Increased toxicity: Additive cardiostimulation with other sympathomimetic agents; theophylline → cardiostimulation; MAO inhibitors or atropine may increase blood pressure; cardiac glycosides or general anesthetics may increase cardiac stimulation

Stability Protect all dosage forms from light

Mechanism of Action Releases tissue stores of epinephrine and thereby produces an alpha- and beta-adrenergic stimulation; longer-acting and less potent than epinephrine

Pharmacodynamics/Kinetics

Onset of bronchodilation: Within 0.25-1 hour; Duration of action: 3-6 hours

Distribution: Crosses the placenta; appears in breast milk

Metabolism: Little hepatic metabolism

Half-life: 2.5-3.6 hours

Elimination: 60% to 77% of dose excreted as unchanged drug in urine within 24 hours

Usual Dosage

Children:

Oral, S.C.: 3 mg/kg/day or 25-100 mg/m²/day in 4-6 divided doses every 4-6 hours

I.M., slow I.V. push: 0.2-0.3 mg/kg/dose every 4-6 hours

Adults:

Oral: 25-50 mg every 3-4 hours as needed

I.M., S.C.: 25-50 mg, parenteral adult dose should not exceed 150 mg in 24 hours

I.V.: 5-25 mg/dose slow I.V. push repeated after 5-10 minutes as needed, then every 3-4 hours not to exceed 150 mg/24 hours

Monitoring Parameters Blood pressure, pulse, urinary output, mental status; cardiac monitor and blood pressure monitor required

Test Interactions Can cause a false-positive amphetamine EMIT assay

Patient Information May cause wakefulness or nervousness; take last dose 4-6 hours before bedtime

Nursing Implications Do not administer unless solution is clear

Dosage Forms

Capsule, as sulfate: 25 mg, 50 mg

Injection, as sulfate: 25 mg/mL (1 mL); 50 mg/mL (1 mL, 10 mL)

Jelly, as sulfate (Kondon's Nasal®): 1% (20 g)

Spray, as sulfate (Pretz-D®): 0.25% (15 mL)

♦ **Ephedrine Sulfate** see Ephedrine on previous page

♦ **Epi E-Z Pen™** see Epinephrine on this page

♦ **Epi E-Z Pen™ Jr** see Epinephrine on this page

♦ **Epifrin®** see Epinephrine on this page

♦ **Epilepsy Treatment** see page 1468

♦ **E-Pilo-x® Ophthalmic** see Pilocarpine and Epinephrine on page 928

♦ **Epimorph®** see Morphine Sulfate on page 797

♦ **Epinal®** see Epinephrine on this page

Epinephrine (ep i NEF rin)

Related Information

Adrenergic Agonists, Cardiovascular Comparison on page 1290

Adult ACLS Algorithm, Asystole on page 1449

Adult ACLS Algorithm, Bradycardia on page 1452

Adult ACLS Algorithm, Pulseless Electrical Activity on page 1448

Adult ACLS Algorithm, V. Fib and Pulseless V. Tach on page 1447

Bronchodilators, Comparison of Inhaled and Sympathomimetic on page 1314

Extravasation Treatment of Other Drugs on page 1322

Glaucoma Drug Therapy Comparison on page 1287

Pediatric ALS Algorithm, Asystole and Pulseless Arrest on page 1445

Pediatric ALS Algorithm, Bradycardia on page 1444

U.S. Brand Names Adrenalin®; AsthmaHaler®; AsthmaNefrin® [OTC]; Bronitin®; Bronkaid® Mist [OTC]; Epifrin®; Epinal®; EpiPen® Auto-Injector; EpiPen® Jr Auto-Injector; Glaucon®; microNefrin®; Primatene® Mist [OTC]; Sus-Phrine®; Vaponefrin®

Canadian Brand Names Epi E-Z Pen™; Epi E-Z Pen™ Jr

Synonyms Adrenaline; Epinephrine Bitartrate; Epinephrine Hydrochloride; Racemic Epinephrine

Therapeutic Category Adrenergic Agonist Agent; Antidote, Hypersensitivity Reactions; Bronchodilator; Sympathomimetic

Use Treatment of bronchospasms, anaphylactic reactions, cardiac arrest, management of open-angle (chronic simple) glaucoma

Pregnancy Risk Factor C

Pregnancy/Breast-Feeding Implications

Clinical effects on the fetus: Crosses the placenta. Reported association with malformations in 1 study; may be secondary to severe maternal disease.

Breast-feeding/lactation: No data on crossing into breast milk or clinical effects on the infant

Contraindications Hypersensitivity to epinephrine or any component; cardiac arrhythmias, angle-closure glaucoma

Warnings/Precautions Use with caution in elderly patients, patients with diabetes mellitus, cardiovascular diseases (angina, tachycardia, myocardial infarction), thyroid disease, or cerebral arteriosclerosis, Parkinson's; some products contain sulfites as preservatives. Rapid I.V. infusion may cause death from cerebrovascular hemorrhage or cardiac arrhythmias. Oral inhalation of epinephrine is **not** the preferred route of administration.

(Continued)

Epinephrine *(Continued)*

Adverse Reactions

>10%:
Cardiovascular: Tachycardia (parenteral), pounding heartbeat
Central nervous system: Nervousness, restlessness

1% to 10%:
Cardiovascular: Flushing, hypertension
Central nervous system: Headache, dizziness, lightheadedness, insomnia
Gastrointestinal: Nausea, vomiting
Neuromuscular & skeletal: Weakness, trembling
Miscellaneous: Diaphoresis (increased)

<1%: Pallor, tachycardia, chest pain, increased myocardial oxygen consumption, cardiac arrhythmias, sudden death, anxiety, xerostomia, dry throat, decreased renal and splanchnic blood flow, acute urinary retention in patients with bladder outflow obstruction, precipitation of or exacerbation of narrow-angle glaucoma, wheezing

Overdosage/Toxicology

Hypertension which may result in subarachnoid hemorrhage and hemiplegia; symptoms of overdose include arrhythmias, unusually large pupils, pulmonary edema, renal failure, metabolic acidosis

There is no specific antidote for epinephrine intoxication and the bulk of the treatment is supportive. Hyperactivity and agitation usually respond to reduced sensory input; however, with extreme agitation, haloperidol (2-5 mg I.M. for adults) may be required. Hyperthermia is best treated with external cooling measures; or when severe or unresponsive, muscle paralysis with pancuronium may be needed. Hypertension is usually transient and generally does not require treatment unless severe. For diastolic blood pressures >110 mm Hg, a nitroprusside infusion should be initiated. Seizures usually respond to diazepam I.V. and/or phenytoin maintenance regimens.

Drug Interactions Increased toxicity: Increased cardiac irritability if administered concurrently with halogenated inhalational anesthetics, beta-blocking agents, alpha-blocking agents

Stability

Epinephrine is sensitive to light and air; protection from light is recommended

Oxidation turns drug pink, then a brown color; **solutions should not be used if they are discolored or contain a precipitate**

Stability of injection of parenteral admixture at room temperature (25°C) or refrigeration (4°C): 24 hours

Standard diluent: 1 mg/250 mL NS

Compatible with dopamine, dobutamine, diltiazem

Incompatible with aminophylline, sodium bicarbonate or other alkaline solutions

Mechanism of Action Stimulates alpha-, beta$_1$-, and beta$_2$-adrenergic receptors resulting in relaxation of smooth muscle of the bronchial tree, cardiac stimulation, and dilation of skeletal muscle vasculature; small doses can cause vasodilation via beta$_2$-vascular receptors; large doses may produce constriction of skeletal and vascular smooth muscle; decreases production of aqueous humor and increases aqueous outflow; dilates the pupil by contracting the dilator muscle

Pharmacodynamics/Kinetics

Onset of bronchodilation: Subcutaneous: Within 5-10 minutes; Inhalation: Within 1 minute

Conjunctival instillation: Onset of effect: Intraocular pressures fall within 1 hour; Peak effect: Within 4-8 hours

Duration of ocular effect: 12-24 hours

Absorption: Orally ingested doses are rapidly metabolized in the GI tract and liver; pharmacologically active concentrations are not achieved

Distribution: Crosses the placenta; appears in breast milk

Metabolism: Following administration, drug is taken up into the adrenergic neuron and metabolized by monoamine oxidase and catechol-o-methyltransferase; circulating drug is metabolized in the liver

Elimination: Inactive metabolites (metanephrine and the sulfate and hydroxy derivatives of mandelic acid) and a small amount of unchanged drug is excreted in urine

Usual Dosage

Neonates: Cardiac arrest: I.V.: Intratracheal: 0.01-0.03 mg/kg (0.1-0.3 mL/kg of **1:10,000** solution) every 3-5 minutes as needed; dilute intratracheal doses to 1-2 mL with normal saline

Infants and Children:
Bronchodilator: S.C.: 10 mcg/kg (0.01 mL/kg of 1:1000) (single doses not to exceed 0.5 mg) **or** suspension (1:200): 0.005 mL/kg/dose (0.025 mg/kg/dose) to a maximum of 0.15 mL (0.75 mg for single dose) every 8-12 hours

Bradycardia:
I.V.: 0.01 mg/kg (0.1 mL/kg of **1:10,000** solution) every 3-5 minutes as needed (maximum: 1 mg/10 mL)
Intratracheal: 0.1 mg/kg (0.1 mL/kg of **1:1000** solution every 3-5 minutes); doses as high as 0.2 mg/kg may be effective

Asystole or pulseless arrest:
I.V. or intraosseous: **First dose:** 0.01 mg/kg (0.1 mL/kg of a **1:10,000** solution); **subsequent doses:** 0.1 mg/kg (0.1 mL/kg of a **1:1000** solution); doses as high as 0.2 mg/kg may be effective; repeat every 3-5 minutes
Intratracheal: 0.1 mg/kg (0.1 mL/kg of a **1:1000** solution); doses as high as 0.2 mg/kg may be effective

Hypersensitivity reaction: S.C.: 0.01 mg/kg every 15 minutes for 2 doses then every 4 hours as needed (single doses not to exceed 0.5 mg)

Refractory hypotension (refractory to dopamine/dobutamine): Continuous I.V. infusions of 0.1-1 mcg/kg/minute; titrate dosage to desired effect

Nebulization: 0.25-0.5 mL of 2.25% **racemic epinephrine** solution diluted in 3 mL normal saline, or L-epinephrine at an equivalent dose; racemic epinephrine 10 mg = 5 mg L-epinephrine; use lower end of dosing range for younger infants

Intranasal: Children ≥6 years and Adults: Apply locally as drops or spray or with sterile swab

Adults:

Asystole:

I.V.: 1 mg every 3-5 minutes; if this approach fails, alternative regimens include:
Intermediate: 2-5 mg every 3-5 minutes
Escalating: 1 mg, 3 mg, 5 mg at 3-minute intervals
High: 0.1 mg/kg every 3-5 minutes
Intratracheal: 1 mg (although optimal dose is unknown, doses of 2-2.5 times the I.V. dose may be needed)

Bronchodilator: I.M., S.C. (**1:1000**): 0.1-0.5 mg every 10-15 minutes to 4 hours

Hypersensitivity reaction: I.M., S.C.: 0.2-0.5 mg every 20 minutes to 4 hours (single dose maximum: 1 mg)

Refractory hypotension (refractory to dopamine/dobutamine): Continuous I.V. infusion 1 mg/minute (range: 1-10 mcg/minute); titrate dosage to desired effect; severe cardiac dysfunction may require doses >10 mcg/minute (up to 0.1 mcg/kg/minute)

Nebulization: Instill 8-15 drops into nebulizer reservoirs; administer 1-3 inhalations 4-6 times/day

Ophthalmic: Instill 1-2 drops in eye(s) once or twice daily; when treating open-angle glaucoma, the concentration and dosage must be adjusted to the response of the patient

Administration Central line administration only; intravenous infusions require an infusion pump

Endotracheal: Doses (2-2.5 times the I.V. dose) should be diluted to 10 mL with NS or distilled water prior to administration

Epinephrine can be administered S.C., I.M., I.V., or intracardiac injection

I.M. administration into the buttocks should be avoided

Desired pediatric intravenous infusion solution preparation:

To prepare for infusion:

$$\frac{6 \times \text{weight (kg)} \times \text{desired dose (mcg/kg/min)}}{\text{I.V. infusion rate (mL/h)}} = \text{mg of drug to be added to 100 mL of I.V. fluid}$$

Preparation of adult I.V. infusion: Dilute 1 mg in 250 mL of D$_5$W or NS (4 mcg/mL); administer at an initial rate of 1 mcg/minute and increase to desired effects; at 20 mcg/minute pure alpha effects occur
1 mcg/minute: 15 mL/hour
2 mcg/minute: 30 mL/hour
3 mcg/minute: 45 mL/hour, etc

Monitoring Parameters Pulmonary function, heart rate, blood pressure, site of infusion for blanching, extravasation; cardiac monitor and blood pressure monitor required

Reference Range Therapeutic: 31-95 pg/mL (SI: 170-520 pmol/L)

Test Interactions ↑ bilirubin (S), catecholamines (U), glucose, uric acid (S)

Nursing Implications Patients should be cautioned to avoid the use of over-the-counter epinephrine inhalation products; beta$_2$-adrenergic agents for inhalation are preferred

Management of extravasation: Use phentolamine as antidote; mix 5 mg with 9 mL of NS; inject a small amount of this dilution into extravasated area; blanching should reverse immediately. Monitor site; if blanching should recur, additional injections of phentolamine may be needed.

Additional Information

Epinephrine: Primatene® Mist, Bronkaid® Mist, Sus-Phrine®

Epinephrine bitartrate: AsthmaHaler®, Bronitin®, Epitrate®, Medihaler-Epi®; Primatene® Mist

Epinephrine hydrochloride: Adrenalin®, Epifrin®, EpiPen®, EpiPen® Jr

Racemic epinephrine: AsthmaHaler®, Breatheasy®, microNefrin®, Vaponefrin®

Epinephryl borate: Epinal®

Dosage Forms

Aerosol, oral:

Bitartrate (AsthmaHaler®, Bronitin®, Medihaler-Epi®, Primatene® Suspension): 0.3 mg/spray [epinephrine base 0.16 mg/spray] (10 mL, 15 mL, 22.5 mL)

Bronkaid®: 0.5% (10 mL, 15 mL, 22.5 mL)

Primatene®: 0.2 mg/spray (15 mL, 22.5 mL)

Auto-injector:

EpiPen®: Delivers 0.3 mg I.M. of epinephrine 1:1000 (2 mL)

EpiPen® Jr.: Delivers 0.15 mg I.M. of epinephrine 1:2000 (2 mL)

Solution:

Inhalation:

Adrenalin®: 1% [10 mg/mL, 1:100] (7.5 mL)

AsthmaNefrin®, microNefrin®, Nephron®, S-2®: Racepinephrine 2% [epinephrine base 1.125%] (7.5 mL, 15 mL, 30 mL)

Vaponefrin®: Racepinephrine 2% [epinephrine base 1%] (15 mL, 30 mL)

(Continued)

417

Epinephrine *(Continued)*

Injection:
Adrenalin®: 0.01 mg/mL [1:100,000] (5 mL); 0.1 mg/mL [1:10,000] (3 mL, 10 mL); 1 mg/mL [1:1000] (1 mL, 2 mL, 30 mL)
Suspension (Sus-Phrine®): 5 mg/mL [1:200] (0.3 mL, 5 mL)
Nasal (Adrenalin®): 0.1% [1 mg/mL] (30 mL)
Ophthalmic, as borate (Epinal®): 0.5% (7.5 mL); 1% (7.5 mL)
Ophthalmic, as hydrochloride (Epifrin®, Glaucon®): 0.1% (1 mL, 30 mL); 0.5% (15 mL); 1% (1 mL, 10 mL, 15 mL); 2% (10 mL, 15 mL)
Topical (Adrenalin®): 0.1% [1 mg/mL, 1:1000] (10 mL, 30 mL)

+ **Epinephrine Bitartrate** *see* Epinephrine *on page 415*
+ **Epinephrine Hydrochloride** *see* Epinephrine *on page 415*
+ **EpiPen® Auto-Injector** *see* Epinephrine *on page 415*
+ **EpiPen® Jr Auto-Injector** *see* Epinephrine *on page 415*
+ **Epipodophyllotoxin** *see* Etoposide *on page 459*
+ **Epitol®** *see* Carbamazepine *on page 188*
+ **Epivir®** *see* Lamivudine *on page 657*
+ **Epivir® HBV** *see* Lamivudine *on page 657*

Epoetin Alfa (e POE e tin AL fa)

U.S. Brand Names Epogen®; Procrit®
Synonyms EPO; Erythropoietin; rHuEPO-α
Therapeutic Category Colony Stimulating Factor; Growth Factor; Recombinant Human Erythropoietin
Use

Treatment of anemia associated with chronic renal failure, including patients on dialysis (end-stage renal disease) and patients not on dialysis

Treatment of anemia related to zidovudine therapy in HIV-infected patients; in patients when the endogenous erythropoietin level is ≤500 mIU/mL and the dose of zidovudine is ≤4200 mg/week

Treatment of anemia in cancer patients on chemotherapy; in patients with nonmyeloid malignancies where anemia is caused by the effect of the concomitantly administered chemotherapy; to decrease the need for transfusions in patients who will be receiving chemotherapy for a minimum of 2 months

Reduction of allogeneic block transfusion in surgery patients scheduled to undergo elective, noncardiac, nonvascular surgery

Pregnancy Risk Factor C

Pregnancy/Breast-Feeding Implications Clinical effect on the fetus: Epoetin alfa has been shown to have adverse effects in rats when given in doses 5X the human dose. There are no adequate and well-controlled studies in pregnant women. Epoetin alfa should be used only if potential benefit justifies the potential risk to the fetus.

Contraindications Known hypersensitivity to albumin (human) or mammalian cell-derived products; uncontrolled hypertension

Warnings/Precautions Use with caution in patients with porphyria, hypertension, or a history of seizures; prior to and during therapy, iron stores must be evaluated. It is recommended that the epoetin dose be decreased if the hematocrit increase exceeds 4 points in any 2-week period.

Pretherapy parameters:
Serum ferritin >100 ng/dL
Transferrin saturation (serum iron/iron binding capacity x 100) of 20% to 30%
Iron supplementation (usual oral dosing of 325 mg 2-3 times/day) should be given during therapy to provide for increased requirements during expansion of the red cell mass secondary to marrow stimulation by EPO unless iron stores are already in excess
For patients with endogenous serum EPO levels which are inappropriately low for hemoglobin level, documentation of the serum EPO level will help indicate which patients may benefit from EPO therapy. Serum EPO levels can be ordered routinely from Clinical Chemistry (red-top serum separator tube). Refer to "Reference Range" for information on interpretation of EPO levels.

See table:

Factors Limiting Response to Epoetin Alfa

Factor	Mechanism
Iron deficiency	Limits hemoglobin synthesis
Blood loss/hemolysis	Counteracts epoetin alfa-stimulated erythropoiesis
Infection/inflammation	Inhibits iron transfer from storage to bone marrow
	Suppresses erythropoiesis through activated macrophages
Aluminum overload	Inhibits iron incorporation into heme protein
Bone marrow replacement Hyperparathyroidsm Metastatic, neoplastic	Limits bone marrow volume
Folic acid/vitamin B_{12} deficiency	Limits hemoglobin synthesis
Patient compliance	Self-administered epoetin alfa or iron therapy

Increased mortality has occurred when aggressive dosing is used in CHF or anginal patients undergoing hemodialysis. An Amgen-funded study determined that when patients were targeted for a hematocrit of 42% versus a less aggressive 30%, mortality was higher (35% versus 29%).

Adverse Reactions

>10%:
Cardiovascular: Hypertension
Central nervous system: Fatigue, headache, fever
1% to 10%:
Cardiovascular: Edema, chest pain
Gastrointestinal: Nausea, vomiting, diarrhea
Hematologic: Clotted access
Neuromuscular & skeletal: Arthralgias, asthenia
<1%: Myocardial infarction, CVA/TIA, rash, hypersensitivity reactions

Overdosage/Toxicology

Symptoms of overdose include erythrocytosis
Adequate airway and other supportive measures and agents for treating anaphylaxis should be present when I.V. drug is given

Stability

Vials should be stored at 2°C to 8°C (36°F to 46°F); **do not freeze or shake**; single-use vials are stable 2 weeks at room temperature and multidose vials are stable for 1 week at room temperature
Single-dose 1 mL vial contains no preservative: Use one dose per vial; do not re-enter vial; discard unused portions
Multidose 2 mL vial contains preservative; store at 2°C to 8°C after initial entry and between doses; discard 21 days after initial entry
For minimal dilution: Mix with bacteriostatic 0.9% sodium chloride, containing 20 mL of 0.9% sodium chloride and benzyl alcohol as the bacteriostatic agent; dilutions of 1:10 and 1:20 (1 part to epoetin:19 parts sodium chloride) are stable for 18 hours at room temperature; results showed no loss of epoetin alfa after a 1:20 dilution; 250 mcg/mL albumin remaining after a 1:10 dilution of formulated epoetin alfa should be sufficient to prevent it from binding to commonly encountered containers

Mechanism of Action Induces erythropoiesis by stimulating the division and differentiation of committed erythroid progenitor cells; induces the release of reticulocytes from the bone marrow into the bloodstream, where they mature to erythrocytes. There is a dose response relationship with this effect. This results in an increase in reticulocyte counts followed by a rise in hematocrit and hemoglobin levels.

Pharmacodynamics/Kinetics

Onset of action: Several days
Peak effect: 2-3 weeks
Distribution: V_d: 9 L; rapid in the plasma compartment; majority of drug is taken up by the liver, kidneys, and bone marrow
Metabolism: Some metabolic degradation does occur
Bioavailability: S.C.: ~21% to 31%; intraperitoneal epoetin in a few patients demonstrated a bioavailability of only 3%
Half-life: Circulating: 4-13 hours in patients with chronic renal failure; 20% shorter in patients with normal renal function
Time to peak serum concentrations: S.C.: 2-8 hours
Elimination: Small amounts recovered in the urine; majority hepatically eliminated; 10% excreted unchanged in the urine of normal volunteers

Usual Dosage

Chronic renal failure patients: I.V., S.C.:
Initial dose: 50-100 units/kg 3 times/week
Reduce dose by 25 units/kg when
  1) hematocrit approaches 36% **or**
  2) when hematocrit increases >4 points in any 2-week period
Increase dose if hematocrit does not increase by 5-6 points after 8 weeks of therapy and hematocrit is below suggested target range
Suggested target hematocrit range: 30% to 36%
Maintenance dose: Individualize to target range
  Dialysis patients: Median dose: 75 units/kg 3 times/week
  Nondialysis patients: Doses of 75-150 units/kg
Zidovudine-treated, HIV-infected patients: Patients with erythropoietin levels >500 mIU/mL are **unlikely** to respond
Initial dose: I.V., S.C.: 100 units/kg 3 times/week for 8 weeks
Increase dose by 50-100 units/kg 3 times/week if response is not satisfactory in terms of reducing transfusion requirements or increasing hematocrit after 8 weeks of therapy
Evaluate response every 4-8 weeks thereafter and adjust the dose accordingly by 50-100 units/kg increments 3 times/week
If patients have not responded satisfactorily to a 300 unit/kg dose 3 times/week, it is unlikely that they will respond to higher doses
Stop dose if hematocrit exceeds 40% and resume treatment at a 25% dose reduction when hematocrit drops to 36%
Cancer patients on chemotherapy: Treatment of patients with erythropoietin levels >200 mU/mL is **not recommended**
(Continued)

Epoetin Alfa *(Continued)*

Initial dose: S.C.: 150 units/kg 3 times/week

Dose adjustment: If response is not satisfactory in terms of reducing transfusion requirement or increasing hematocrit after 8 weeks of therapy, the dose may be increased up to 300 units/kg 3 times/week. If patients do not respond, it is unlikely that they will respond to higher doses.

If hematocrit exceeds 40%, hold the dose until it falls to 36% and reduce the dose by 25% when treatment is resumed

Surgery patients: Prior to initiating treatment, obtain a hemoglobin to establish that is is >10 mg/dL or ≤13 mg/dL

Initial dose: S.C.: 300 units/kg/day for 10 days before surgery, on the day of surgery, and for 4 days after surgery

Alternative dose: S.C.: 600 units/kg in once-weekly doses (21, 14, and 7 days before surgery) plus a fourth dose on the day of surgery

Monitoring Parameters

Careful monitoring of blood pressure is indicated; problems with hypertension have been noted especially in renal failure patients treated with rHuEPO. Other patients are less likely to develop this complication.

See table.

Test	Initial Phase Frequency	Maintenance Phase Frequency
Hematocrit/hemoglobin	2 x/week	2-4 x/month
Blood pressure	3 x/week	3 x/week
Serum ferritin	Monthly	Quarterly
Transferrin saturation	Monthly	Quarterly
Serum chemistries including CBC with differential, creatinine, blood urea nitrogen, potassium, phosphorous	Regularly per routine	Regularly per routine

Hematocrit should be determined twice weekly until stabilization within the target range (30% to 36%), and twice weekly for at least 2 to 6 weeks after a dose increase

Reference Range Guidelines should be based on the following figure or published literature

Guidelines for estimating appropriateness of endogenous EPO levels for varying levels of anemia via the EIA assay method: See figure. The reference range for erythropoietin in serum, for subjects with normal hemoglobin and hematocrit, is 4.1-22.2 mIU/mL by the EIA method. Erythropoietin levels are typically inversely related to hemoglobin (and hematocrit) levels in anemias not attributed to impaired erythropoietin production.

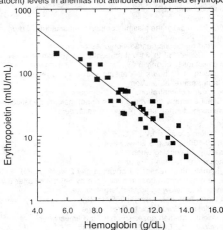

Zidovudine-treated HIV patients: Available evidence indicates patients with endogenous serum erythropoietin levels >500 mIU/mL are unlikely to respond

Cancer chemotherapy patients: Treatment of patients with endogenous serum erythropoietin levels >200 mIU/mL is not recommended

Patient Information

If necessary, the patient should be instructed as to the proper dosage and self-administration of epoetin alpha

Frequent blood tests are needed to determine the correct dose; notify physician if any severe headache develops

Additional Information

Reimbursement Hotline (Epogen®): 1-800-272-9376

Professional Services [Amgen]: 1-800-77-AMGEN

Reimbursement Hotline (Procrit®): 1-800-553-3851

Professional services [Ortho Biotech]: 1-800-325-7504

Dosage Forms

1 mL single-dose vials: Preservative-free solution
- 2000 units/mL
- 3000 units/mL
- 4000 units/mL
- 10,000 units/mL

2 mL multidose vials: Preserved solution: 10,000 units/mL

♦ **Epogen®** *see* Epoetin Alfa *on page 418*

Epoprostenol (e poe PROST en ole)

U.S. Brand Names Flolan® Injection

Synonyms Epoprostenol Sodium; PGI_2; PGX; Prostacyclin

Therapeutic Category Prostaglandin

Use Treatment of primary pulmonary hypertension in NYHA Class III and IV patients

Off-label uses: Other potential uses include pulmonary hypertension associated with ARDS, SLE, or CHF, neonatal pulmonary hypertension, cardiopulmonary bypass surgery, hemodialysis, atherosclerosis, peripheral vascular disorders, and neonatal purpura fulminans

Pregnancy Risk Factor B

Contraindications Chronic use in patients with CHF due to severe left ventricular systolic dysfunction; hypersensitivity to epoprostenol or to structurally-related compounds

Warnings/Precautions Abrupt interruptions or large sudden reductions in dosage may result in rebound pulmonary hypertension; some patients with primary pulmonary hypertension have developed pulmonary edema during dose ranging, which may be associated with pulmonary veno-occlusive disease; during chronic use, unless contraindicated, anticoagulants should be coadministered to reduce the risk of thromboembolism

Adverse Reactions

>10%:
- Cardiovascular: Flushing, tachycardia, shock, syncope, heart failure
- Central nervous system: Fever, chills, anxiety, nervousness, dizziness, headache, hyperesthesia, pain
- Gastrointestinal: Diarrhea, nausea, vomiting
- Neuromuscular & skeletal: Jaw pain, myalgia, tremor, paresthesia
- Respiratory: Hypoxia
- Miscellaneous: Sepsis, flu-like symptoms

1% to 10%:
- Cardiovascular: Bradycardia, hypotension, angina pectoris, edema, arrhythmias, pallor, cyanosis, palpitations, cerebrovascular accident, myocardial ischemia, chest pain
- Central nervous system: Seizures, confusion, depression, insomnia
- Dermatologic: Pruritus, rash
- Endocrine & metabolic: Hypokalemia, weight change
- Gastrointestinal: Abdominal pain, anorexia, constipation
- Hematologic: Hemorrhage
- Hepatic: Ascites
- Neuromuscular & skeletal: Arthralgias, bone pain, weakness
- Hematologic: Disseminated intravascular coagulation
- Ocular: Amblyopia
- Respiratory: Cough increase, dyspnea, epistaxis, pleural effusion
- Miscellaneous: Diaphoresis

Overdosage/Toxicology

Symptoms of overdose include headache, hypotension, tachycardia, nausea, vomiting, diarrhea, and flushing

If any of these symptoms occur, the infusion rate should be reduced until the symptoms subside; if symptoms do not subside should then consider drug discontinuation; no fatal events have been reported following overdosage with epoprostenol

Drug Interactions Increased toxicity: The hypotensive effects of epoprostenol may be exacerbated by other vasodilators, diuretics, or by using acetate in dialysis fluids. Patients treated with anticoagulants and epoprostenol should be monitored for increased bleeding risk because of shared effects on platelet aggregation.

Stability Refrigerate ampuls; protect from freezing; prepare fresh solutions every 24 hours;

Stable only when reconstituted with the diluent solution packaged with the medication

Mechanism of Action Epoprostenol is also known as prostacyclin and PGI_2. It is a strong vasodilator of all vascular beds. In addition, it is a potent endogenous inhibitor of platelet aggregation. The reduction in platelet aggregation results from epoprostenol's activation of intracellular adenylate cyclase and the resultant increase in cyclic adenosine monophosphate concentrations within the platelets. Additionally, it is capable of decreasing thrombogenesis and platelet clumping in the lungs by inhibiting platelet aggregation.

Pharmacodynamics/Kinetics

Steady state levels are reached in about 15 minutes with continuous infusions

Metabolism: Rapidly hydrolyzed at neutral pH in blood and is subject to some enzymatic degradation to one active metabolite, and 13 inactive metabolites

Half-life: 2.7-6 minutes

Elimination: 12% excreted unchanged in urine

(Continued)

Epoprostenol *(Continued)*

Usual Dosage I.V.: The drug is administered by continuous intravenous infusion via a central venous catheter using an ambulatory infusion pump; during dose ranging it may be administered peripherally

Acute dose ranging: The initial infusion rate should be 2 ng/kg/minute by continuous I.V. and increased in increments of 2 ng/kg/minute every 15 minutes or longer until dose-limiting effects are elicited (such as chest pain, anxiety, dizziness, changes in heart rate, dyspnea, nausea, vomiting, headache, hypotension and/or flushing)

Continuous chronic infusion: Initial: 4 ng/kg/minute **less** than the maximum-tolerated infusion rate determined during acute dose ranging

If maximum-tolerated infusion rate is <5 ng/kg/minute, the chronic infusion rate should be 1/2 the maximum-tolerated acute infusion rate

Dosage adjustments: Dose adjustments in the chronic infusion rate should be based on persistence, recurrence, or worsening of patient symptoms of pulmonary hypertension

If symptoms persist or recur after improving, the infusion rate should be increased by 1-2 ng/kg/minute increments, every 15 minutes or greater; following establishment of a new chronic infusion rate, the patient should be observed and vital signs monitored.

Preparation of Infusion

To make 100 mL of solution with concentration:	Directions
3000 ng/mL	Dissolve one 0.5 mg vial with 5 mL supplied diluent, withdraw 3 mL, and add to sufficient diluent to make a total of 100 mL.
5000 ng/mL	Dissolve one 0.5 mg vial with 5 mL supplied diluent, withdraw entire vial contents, and add a sufficient volume of diluent to make a total of 100 mL.
10,000 ng/mL	Dissolve two 0.5 mg vials each with 5 mL supplied diluent, withdraw entire vial contents, and add a sufficient volume of diluent to make a total of 100 mL.
15,000 ng/mL	Dissolve one 1.5 mg vial with 5 mL supplied diluent, withdraw entire vial contents, and add a sufficient volume of diluent to make a total of 100 mL.

Monitoring Parameters Monitor for improvements in pulmonary function, decreased exertional dyspnea, fatigue, syncope and chest pain, pulmonary vascular resistance, pulmonary arterial pressure and quality of life. In addition, the pump device and catheters should be monitored frequently to avoid "system" related failure.

Patient Information Therapy with epoprostenol requires commitment to drug reconstitution, administration, and care of the permanent central venous catheter. The decision to receive epoprostenol should be based upon the understanding that there is a high likelihood that therapy will be needed for prolonged periods, possibly for life, and that the care of the catheter and infusion pump will be required and should be carefully considered. Promptly report any adverse drug reactions with epoprostenol, this may require dosage adjustments.

Nursing Implications Monitor arterial pressure; assess all vital functions; hypoxia, flushing, and tachycardia may indicate overdose. Epoprostenol must be reconstituted with manufacturer-supplied sterile diluent only and when given on an ongoing basis, it must be infused through a permanent indwelling central venous catheter via a portable infusion pump. Instruct patient to report ADRs since dosage adjustments may be necessary.

Additional Information All orders for epoprostenol are distributed only by Olsten Health Services; to order the drug or to request reimbursement assistance, call 1-800-935-6526

Dosage Forms Injection, as sodium: 0.5 mg/vial and 1.5 mg/vial, each supplied with 50 mL of sterile diluent

♦ **Epoprostenol Sodium** *see* Epoprostenol *on previous page*
♦ **Epsom Salts** *see* Magnesium Sulfate *on page 708*
♦ **EPT** *see* Teniposide *on page 1112*

Eptifibatide *(ep TIF i ba tide)*

Related Information
Glycoprotein Antagonists *on page 1323*

U.S. Brand Names Integrilin™

Synonyms Intrifiban

Therapeutic Category Antiplatelet Agent; Glycoprotein IIb/IIIa Inhibitor, Reversible; Platelet Aggregation Inhibitor

Use Treatment of patients with acute coronary syndrome (UA/NQMI), including patients who are to be managed medically and those undergoing percutaneous coronary intervention (PCI)

Pregnancy Risk Factor B

Contraindications History of hypersensitivity to eptifibatide or related compounds, tirofiban, lamifiban; history of bleeding diathesis or abnormal bleeding (within 30 days); severe hypertension, major surgery within preceding 6 weeks, history of stroke (within 30 days) or any hemorrhagic stroke, platelet count <100,000/mm^3; dependence on renal dialysis; renal impairment - serum creatinine >2.0 (180 mcg/kg bolus), >4.0 (135 mcg/kg bolus); concomitant or anticipated other parenteral glycoprotein IIb/IIIa inhibitors

Warnings/Precautions Bleeding is the most common complication encountered during eptifibatide therapy. Most major bleeding has been at the arterial access site for cardiac catheterization or from the gastrointestinal or genitourinary tract. To minimize bleeding complications, care must be taken in sheath insertion/removal. Sheath hemostasis should be achieved at least 4 hours before hospital discharge. Use with caution when administered with other anticoagulants; minimize vascular trauma and other trauma. Avoid obtaining intravenous access via noncompressible sites (eg, subclavian or jugular vein) or I.M. injections.

Adverse Reactions Bleeding is the major drug-related adverse effect. Major bleeding was reported in 4.4% to 10.5%, minor bleeding was reported in 10.5% to 14.2%, requirement for transfusion was reported in 5.5% to 12.8%.

Incidence unknown:
Cardiovascular: Hypotension
Local: Injection site reaction
Neuromuscular & skeletal: Back pain

1% to 10%: Hematologic: Thrombocytopenia (2.8% to 3.2%)
<1%:
Central nervous system: Intracranial hemorrhage (0.5% to 0.7%)
Miscellaneous: Anaphylaxis (0.4% to 0.6%)

Overdosage/Toxicology Two cases of human overdosage have been reported; neither case was eventful and these were not associated with major bleeding. Symptoms of overdose in animal studies include loss of righting reflex, dyspnea, ptosis, decreased muscle tone, and petechial hemorrhages.

Drug Interactions Drugs which affect hemostasis: Thrombolytics, oral anticoagulants, nonsteroidal anti-inflammatory agents, dipyridamole, ticlopidine, clopidogrel; avoid concomitant use of other IIb/IIIa inhibitors

Stability Vials should be stored refrigerated at 2°C to 8°C (36°F to 46°F). Protect from light until administration. Do not use beyond the expiration date. Discard any unused portion left in the vial.

Mechanism of Action Eptifibatide is a cyclic heptapeptide which blocks the platelet glycoprotein IIb/IIIa receptor, the binding site for fibrinogen, von Willebrand factor, and other ligands. Inhibition of binding at this final common receptor reversibly blocks platelet aggregation and prevents thrombosis.

Pharmacodynamics/Kinetics
Onset of action: Within 1 hour
Half-life: 2.5 hours
Metabolism: Total body clearance: 55-58 mL/kg/hour; renal clearance is ~50% of total in healthy subjects
Protein binding: ~25%
Elimination: Renal excretion of eptifibatide and metabolites accounts for majority of drug elimination; significant renal impairment is expected to alter the disposition of this compound
Reversibility: Platelet function is restored in about 4 hours following discontinuation

Usual Dosage Adults: I.V.:
Acute coronary syndrome: Bolus of 180 mcg/kg over 1-2 minutes, begun as soon as possible following diagnosis, followed by a continuous infusion of 2 mcg/kg/minute (maximum: 15 mg/hour) until hospital discharge or initiation of CABG surgery, up to 72 hours. If a patient is to undergo a percutaneous coronary intervention (PCI) while receiving eptifibatide, consideration can be given to decreasing the infusion rate to 0.5 mcg/kg/minute at the time of the procedure. Infusion should be continued for an additional 20-24 hours after the procedure, allowing for up to 96 hours of therapy.
Percutaneous coronary intervention (PCI) in patients not presenting with an acute coronary syndrome: Bolus of 135 mcg/kg administered immediately before the initiation of PCI followed by a continuous infusion of 0.5 mcg/kg/minute for 20-24 hours.

Administration
Visually inspect for discoloration or particulate matter prior to administration
The bolus dose should be withdrawn from the 10 mL vial into a syringe and administered by I.V. push over 1-2 minutes
Begin continuous infusion immediately following bolus administration, administered directly from the 100 mL vial
The 100 mL vial should be spiked with a vented infusion set

Monitoring Parameters Coagulation parameters, signs/symptoms of excessive bleeding. Laboratory tests at baseline and monitoring during therapy: hematocrit and hemoglobin, platelet count, serum creatinine, PT/APTT, and ACT with PCI (maintain ACT between 300-350 seconds).

Nursing Implications Do not shake the vial; maintain bleeding precautions, avoid unnecessary arterial and venous punctures, use saline or heparin lock for blood drawing, assess sheath insertion site and distal pulses of affected leg every 15 minutes for the first hour and then every 1 hour for the next 6 hours. Arterial access site care is important to prevent bleeding. Care should be taken when attempting vascular access that only the anterior wall of the femoral artery is punctured, avoiding a Seldinger (through and through) technique for obtaining sheath access. Femoral vein sheath placement should be avoided unless needed. While the vascular sheath is in place, patients should be maintained on complete bed rest with the head of the bed at a 30° angle and the affected limb restrained in a straight position.
(Continued)

Eptifibatide *(Continued)*

Observe patient for mental status changes, hemorrhage, assess nose and mouth mucous membranes, puncture sites for oozing, ecchymosis and hematoma formation, and examine urine, stool and emesis for presence of occult or frank blood; gentle care should be provided when removing dressings.

Dosage Forms Injection: 0.75 mg/mL (100 mL); 2 mg/mL (10 mL)

* **Equagesic®** *see* Aspirin and Meprobamate *on page 105*
* **Equanil®** *see* Meprobamate *on page 731*
* **Equilet® [OTC]** *see* Calcium Carbonate *on page 174*
* **Eramycin®** *see* Erythromycin *on page 427*
* **Ercaf®** *see* Ergotamine *on page 426*
* **Ergamisol®** *see* Levamisole *on page 669*

Ergocalciferol *(er goe kal SIF e role)*

U.S. Brand Names Calciferol™ Injection; Calciferol™ Oral; Drisdol® Oral
Canadian Brand Names Ostoforte®; Radiostol®
Synonyms Activated Ergosterol; Viosterol; Vitamin D_2
Therapeutic Category Vitamin, Fat Soluble
Use Treatment of refractory rickets, hypophosphatemia, hypoparathyroidism
Pregnancy Risk Factor A (C if dose exceeds RDA recommendation)
Contraindications Hypercalcemia, hypersensitivity to ergocalciferol or any component; malabsorption syndrome; evidence of vitamin D toxicity
Warnings/Precautions Administer with extreme caution in patients with impaired renal function, heart disease, renal stones, or arteriosclerosis; must administer concomitant calcium supplementation; maintain adequate fluid intake; avoid hypercalcemia; renal function impairment with secondary hyperparathyroidism
Adverse Reactions Generally well tolerated; percentage unknown:
Cardiovascular: Cardiac arrhythmias, hypertension (late)
Central nervous system: Irritability, headache, psychosis (rare), somnolence, hyperthermia (late)
Dermatologic: Pruritus
Endocrine & metabolic: Decreased libido (late), hypercholesterolemia, mild acidosis (late), polydipsia (late)
Gastrointestinal: Nausea, vomiting, anorexia, pancreatitis, metallic taste, weight loss (rare), xerostomia, constipation
Genitourinary: Polyuria (late), increased BUN (late)
Hepatic: Increased LFTs (late)
Neuromuscular & skeletal: Bone pain, myalgia, weakness
Ocular: Conjunctivitis, photophobia (late)
Miscellaneous: Vascular/nephrocalcinosis (rare)
Overdosage/Toxicology
Symptoms of chronic overdose include hypercalcemia, weakness, fatigue, lethargy, anorexia
Following withdrawal of the drug and oral decontamination, treatment consists of bedrest, liberal intake of fluids, reduced calcium intake, and cathartic administration. Severe hypercalcemia requires I.V. hydration and forced diuresis with I.V. furosemide. Urine output should be monitored and maintained at >3 mL/kg/hour. I.V. saline can quickly and significantly increase excretion of calcium into urine. Calcitonin, mithramycin, and biphosphonates have all been used successfully to treat the more resistant cases of vitamin D-induced hypercalcemia.
Drug Interactions
Decreased effect: Cholestyramine, colestipol, mineral oil may decrease oral absorption
Increased effect: Thiazide diuretics may increase vitamin D effects
Increased toxicity: Cardiac glycosides may increase toxicity
Stability Protect from light
Mechanism of Action Stimulates calcium and phosphate absorption from the small intestine, promotes secretion of calcium from bone to blood; promotes renal tubule phosphate resorption
Pharmacodynamics/Kinetics
Peak effect: In ~1 month following daily doses
Absorption: Readily absorbed from GI tract; absorption requires intestinal presence of bile
Metabolism: Inactive until hydroxylated in the liver and the kidney to calcifediol and then to calcitriol (most active form)
Usual Dosage Oral dosing is preferred; I.M. therapy required with GI, liver, or biliary disease associated with malabsorption
Dietary supplementation (each mcg = 40 USP units):
Premature infants: 10-20 mcg/day (400-800 units), up to 750 mcg/day (30,000 units)
Infants and healthy Children: 10 mcg/day (400 units)
Adults: 10 mcg/day (400 units)
Renal failure:
Children: 100-1000 mcg/day (4000-40,000 units)
Adults: 500 mcg/day (20,000 units)
Hypoparathyroidism:
Children: 1.25-5 mg/day (50,000-200,000 units) and calcium supplements
Adults: 625 mcg to 5 mg/day (25,000-200,000 units) and calcium supplements

Vitamin D-dependent rickets:
    Children: 75-125 mcg/day (3000-5000 units); maximum: 1500 mcg/day
    Adults: 250 mcg to 1.5 mg/day (10,000-60,000 units)
Nutritional rickets and osteomalacia:
    Children and Adults (with normal absorption): 25-125 mcg/day (1000-5000 units)
    Children with malabsorption: 250-625 mcg/day (10,000-25,000 units)
    Adults with malabsorption: 250-7500 mcg (10,000-300,000 units)
Vitamin D-resistant rickets:
    Children: Initial: 1000-2000 mcg/day (40,000-80,000 units) with phosphate supple-
        ments; daily dosage is increased at 3- to 4-month intervals in 250-500 mcg (10,000-
        20,000 units) increments
    Adults: 250-1500 mcg/day (10,000-60,000 units) with phosphate supplements
Familial hypophosphatemia: 10,000-80,000 units daily plus 1-2 g/day elemental phos-
    phorus
Osteoporosis prophylaxis: Adults:
    51-70 years of age: 400 units/day
    >70 years of age: 600 units/day
    Maximum daily dose: 2000 units/day

Administration Parenteral injection for I.M. use only

Monitoring Parameters Measure serum calcium, BUN, and phosphorus every 1-2 weeks; x-ray bones monthly until stabilized

Reference Range Serum calcium times phosphorus should not exceed 70 mg/dL to avoid ectopic calcification; ergocalciferol levels: 10-60 ng/mL; serum calcium: 9-10 mg/dL, phosphorus: 2.5-5 mg/dL

Patient Information Early symptoms of hypercalcemia include weakness, fatigue, somnolence, headache, anorexia, dry mouth, metallic taste, nausea, vomiting, cramps, diarrhea, muscle pain, bone pain, and irritability. Your physician may place you on a special diet or have you take a calcium supplement. Follow this diet closely; do not take magnesium supplements or magnesium-containing antacids.

Nursing Implications Monitor serum calcium, phosphorus, and BUN every 2 weeks

Additional Information 1.25 mg ergocalciferol provides 50,000 units of vitamin D activity

Dosage Forms
    Capsule (Drisdol®): 50,000 units [1.25 mg]
    Injection (Calciferol™): 500,000 units/mL [12.5 mg/mL] (1 mL)
    Liquid (Calciferol™, Drisdol®): 8000 units/mL [200 mcg/mL] (60 mL)
    Tablet (Calciferol™): 50,000 units [1.25 mg]

Ergoloid Mesylates (ER goe loid MES i lates)

U.S. Brand Names Germinal®; Hydergine®; Hydergine® LC
Synonyms Dihydroergotoxine; Dihydrogenated Ergot Alkaloids
Therapeutic Category Ergot Alkaloid and Derivative
Use Treatment of cerebrovascular insufficiency in primary progressive dementia, Alzheimer's dementia, and senile onset
Pregnancy Risk Factor C
Contraindications Acute or chronic psychosis, hypersensitivity to ergot or any compo-
nent
Usual Dosage Adults: Oral: 1 mg 3 times/day up to 4.5-12 mg/day; up to 6 months of therapy may be necessary
Additional Information Complete prescribing information for this medication should be consulted for additional detail
Dosage Forms
    Capsule, liquid (Hydergine® LC): 1 mg
    Liquid (Hydergine®): 1 mg/mL (100 mL)
    Tablet: Oral: 0.5 mg
        Gerimal®, Hydergine®: 1 mg
        Sublingual: Gerimal®, Hydergine®: 0.5 mg, 1 mg

♦ **Ergomar®** see Ergotamine on next page
♦ **Ergometrine Maleate** see Ergonovine on this page

Ergonovine (er goe NOE veen)

U.S. Brand Names Ergotrate® Maleate
Synonyms Ergometrine Maleate; Ergonovine Maleate
Therapeutic Category Ergot Alkaloid and Derivative
Use Prevention and treatment of postpartum and postabortion hemorrhage caused by uterine atony or subinvolution
    Unlabeled use: Migraine headaches, diagnostically to identify Prinzmetal's angina
Pregnancy Risk Factor X
Contraindications Induction of labor, threatened spontaneous abortion, hypersensitivity to ergonovine or any component
Warnings/Precautions Use with caution in patients with sepsis, heart disease, hyper-
tension, or with hepatic or renal impairment; restore uterine responsiveness in calcium-
deficient patients who do not respond to ergonovine by I.V. calcium administration; avoid
prolonged use; discontinue if ergotism develops
Adverse Reactions
    1% to 10%: Gastrointestinal: Nausea, vomiting
(Continued)

Ergonovine (Continued)

<1%: Palpitations, bradycardia, transient chest pain, hypertension (sometimes extreme - treat with I.V. chlorpromazine), cerebrovascular accidents, shock, myocardial infarction, ergotism, seizures, dizziness, headache, thrombophlebitis, tinnitus, dyspnea, diaphoresis

Overdosage/Toxicology

Symptoms of overdose include gangrene (chronic), seizures (acute), chest pain, numbness in extremities, weak pulse, confusion, excitement, delirium, hallucinations

Treatment is supportive following GI decontamination (for oral overdose). I.V. or intra-arterial nitroprusside for arterial venospasm; nitroglycerin for coronary vasospasm.

Stability Refrigerate injection, protect from light; store intact ampuls in refrigerator, stable for 60-90 days; do not use if discoloration occurs

Mechanism of Action Ergot alkaloid alpha-adrenergic agonist directly stimulates vascular smooth muscle to vasoconstrict peripheral and cerebral vessels; may also have antagonist effects on serotonin

Pharmacodynamics/Kinetics

Onset of effect: I.M.: Within 2-5 minutes

Duration: Uterine effects persist for 3 hours, except when given I.V., then effects persist for ~45 minutes

Usual Dosage Adults: I.M., I.V. (I.V. should be reserved for emergency use only): 0.2 mg, repeat dose in 2-4 hours as needed

Administration I.V. doses should be administered over a period of not <1 minute; dilute in NS to 5 mL for I.V. administration

Patient Information May cause nausea, vomiting, dizziness, increased blood pressure, headache, ringing in the ears, chest pain, or shortness of breath

Nursing Implications I.V. use should be limited to patients with severe uterine bleeding or other life-threatening emergency situations

Dosage Forms Injection, as maleate: 0.2 mg/mL (1 mL)

♦ **Ergonovine Maleate** see Ergonovine on previous page

Ergotamine (er GOT a meen)

U.S. Brand Names Cafatine®; Cafatine-PB®; Cafergot®; Cafetrate®; Ercaf®; Ergomar®; Wigraine®

Canadian Brand Names Gynergen®

Synonyms Ergotamine Tartrate; Ergotamine Tartrate and Caffeine

Therapeutic Category Adrenergic Blocking Agent; Antimigraine Agent; Ergot Alkaloid and Derivative

Use Abort or prevent vascular headaches, such as migraine or cluster

Pregnancy Risk Factor X

Contraindications Hypersensitivity to ergotamine, caffeine, or any component; peripheral vascular disease, hepatic or renal disease, hypertension, peptic ulcer disease, sepsis; avoid during pregnancy

Warnings/Precautions Avoid prolonged administration or excessive dosage because of the danger of ergotism and gangrene; patients who take ergotamine for extended periods of time may become dependent on it. May be harmful due to reduction in cerebral blood flow; may precipitate angina, myocardial infarction, or aggravate intermittent claudication; therefore, not considered a drug of choice in the elderly.

Adverse Reactions

>10%:

Cardiovascular: Tachycardia, bradycardia, arterial spasm, claudication and vasoconstriction; rebound headache may occur with sudden withdrawal of the drug in patients on prolonged therapy; localized edema, peripheral vascular effects (numbness and tingling of fingers and toes)

Central nervous system: Drowsiness, dizziness

Gastrointestinal: Nausea, vomiting, diarrhea, xerostomia

1% to 10%:

Cardiovascular: Transient tachycardia or bradycardia, precordial distress and pain

Neuromuscular & skeletal: Weakness in the legs, abdominal or muscle pain, muscle pains in the extremities, paresthesia

Overdosage/Toxicology

Symptoms include vasospastic effects, nausea, vomiting, lassitude, impaired mental function, hypotension, hypertension, unconsciousness, seizures, shock, and death

Treatment includes general supportive therapy, gastric lavage, or induction of emesis, activated charcoal, saline cathartic; keep extremities warm. Activated charcoal is effective at binding certain chemicals, and this is especially true for ergot alkaloids; treatment is symptomatic with heparin, vasodilators (nitroprusside); vasodilators should be used with caution to avoid exaggerating any pre-existing hypotension.

Drug Interactions Increased toxicity:

Propranolol: One case of severe vasoconstriction with pain and cyanosis has been reported

Erythromycin, troleandomycin and other macrolide antibiotics: Monitor for signs of ergot toxicity

Mechanism of Action Has partial agonist and/or antagonist activity against tryptaminergic, dopaminergic and alpha-adrenergic receptors depending upon their site; is a highly active uterine stimulant; it causes constriction of peripheral and cranial blood vessels and produces depression of central vasomotor centers

Pharmacodynamics/Kinetics

Absorption: Oral, rectal: Erratic; enhanced by caffeine coadministration

Metabolism: Extensively in the liver

Bioavailability: Poor overall (<5%)

Time to peak serum concentration: Within 0.5-3 hours following coadministration with caffeine

Elimination: In bile as metabolites (90%)

Usual Dosage Adults:

Oral:

Cafergot®: 2 tablets at onset of attack; then 1 tablet every 30 minutes as needed; maximum: 6 tablets per attack; do not exceed 10 tablets/week

Ergostat®: 1 tablet under tongue at first sign, then 1 tablet every 30 minutes, 3 tablets/ 24 hours, 5 tablets/week

Rectal (Cafergot® suppositories, Wigraine® suppositories, Cafatine® suppositories): 1 at first sign of an attack; follow with second dose after 1 hour, if needed; maximum dose: 2 per attack; do not exceed 5/week

Patient Information Any symptoms such as nausea, vomiting, numbness or tingling, and chest, muscle, or abdominal pain should be reported to the physician. Initiate therapy at first sign of attack. Do **not** exceed recommended dosage.

Nursing Implications Do not crush sublingual drug product

Additional Information

Ergotamine tartrate: Ergostat®

Ergotamine tartrate and caffeine: Cafergot®

Dosage Forms

Suppository, rectal (Cafatine®, Cafergot®, Cafetrate®, Wigraine®): Ergotamine tartrate 2 mg and caffeine 100 mg (12s)

Tablet (Ercaf®, Wigraine®): Ergotamine tartrate 1 mg and caffeine 100 mg

Tablet, sublingual (Ergomar®): Ergotamine tartrate 2 mg

♦ **Ergotamine Tartrate** see Ergotamine on previous page

♦ **Ergotamine Tartrate and Caffeine** see Ergotamine on previous page

♦ **Ergotrate® Maleate** see Ergonovine on page 425

♦ **E•R•O Ear [OTC]** see Carbamide Peroxide on page 190

♦ **Erybid™** see Erythromycin on this page

♦ **Eryc®** see Erythromycin on this page

♦ **EryPed®** see Erythromycin on this page

♦ **Ery-Tab®** see Erythromycin on this page

♦ **Erythro-Base®** see Erythromycin on this page

♦ **Erythrocin®** see Erythromycin on this page

Erythromycin (er ith roe MYE sin)

Related Information

Animal and Human Bites Guidelines on page 1399

Antimicrobial Drugs of Choice on page 1404

Community-Acquired Pneumonia in Adults on page 1419

Prevention of Wound Infection & Sepsis in Surgical Patients on page 1381

Treatment of Sexually Transmitted Diseases on page 1429

U.S. Brand Names E-Base®; E.E.S.®; E-Mycin®; Eramycin®; Eryc®; EryPed®; Ery-Tab®; Erythrocin®; Ilosone®; PCE®

Canadian Brand Names Apo®-Erythro E-C; Diomycin; Erybid™; Erythro-Base®; Novo-Rythro Encap; PMS-Erythromycin

Synonyms Erythromycin Base; Erythromycin Estolate; Erythromycin Ethylsuccinate; Erythromycin Gluceptate; Erythromycin Lactobionate; Erythromycin Stearate

Therapeutic Category Antibiotic, Macrolide; Antibiotic, Ophthalmic

Use Treatment of susceptible bacterial infections including *S. pyogenes*, some *S. pneumoniae*, some *S. aureus*, *M. pneumoniae*, *Legionella pneumophila*, diphtheria, pertussis, chancroid, *Chlamydia*, erythrasma, *N. gonorrhoeae*, *E. histolytica*, syphilis and nongonococcal urethritis, and *Campylobacter* gastroenteritis; used in conjunction with neomycin for decontaminating the bowel; treatment of gastroparesis

Pregnancy Risk Factor B

Contraindications Hepatic impairment, known hypersensitivity to erythromycin or its components; pre-existing liver disease (erythromycin estolate); concomitant use with pimozide, terfenadine, astemizole, or cisapride

Warnings/Precautions Hepatic impairment with or without jaundice has occurred, it may be accompanied by malaise, nausea, vomiting, abdominal colic, and fever; discontinue use if these occur; avoid using erythromycin lactobionate in neonates since formulations may contain benzyl alcohol which is associated with toxicity in neonates; observe for superinfections

Adverse Reactions

>10%: Gastrointestinal: Abdominal pain, cramping, nausea, vomiting

1% to 10%:

Gastrointestinal: Oral candidiasis

Hepatic: Cholestatic jaundice

Local: Phlebitis at the injection site

Miscellaneous: Hypersensitivity reactions

<1%: Ventricular arrhythmias, fever, rash, hypertrophic pyloric stenosis, diarrhea, pseudomembranous colitis, eosinophilia, cholestatic jaundice (most common with estolate), thrombophlebitis, allergic reactions

(Continued)

Erythromycin *(Continued)*

Overdosage/Toxicology

Symptoms of overdose include nausea, vomiting, and diarrhea

General and supportive care only

Drug Interactions CYP3A3/4 enzyme substrate; CYP1A2 and 3A3/4 enzyme inhibitor

Increased toxicity:

Erythromycin decreases clearance of carbamazepine, cyclosporine, and triazolam, alfentanil, bromocriptine, digoxin (~10% of patients), disopyramide, ergot alkaloids, methylprednisolone; may decrease clearance of protease inhibitors

Erythromycin may decrease theophylline clearance and increase theophylline's half-life by up to 60% (patients on high-dose theophylline and erythromycin or who have received erythromycin for >5 days may be at higher risk)

Decreases metabolism of terfenadine, cisapride, and astemizole resulting in an increase in Q-T interval and potential heart failure

Inhibits felodipine (and other dihydropyridine calcium antagonist) metabolism in the liver resulting in a twofold increase in levels and consequent toxicity

Death has been reported by potentiation of pimozide's cardiotoxicity when given concurrently with erythromycin

May potentiate anticoagulant effect of warfarin and decrease metabolism of vinblastine

Concurrent use of erythromycin and lovastatin and simvastatin may result in significantly increased levels and rhabdomyolysis

Stability

Erythromycin lactobionate should be reconstituted with sterile water for injection without preservatives to avoid gel formation; the reconstituted solution is stable for 2 weeks when refrigerated for 24 hours at room temperature

Erythromycin I.V. infusion solution is stable at pH 6-8. Stability of lactobionate is pH dependent; I.V. form has the longest stability in 0.9% sodium chloride (NS) and should be prepared in this base solution whenever possible. Do not use D_5W as a diluent unless sodium bicarbonate is added to solution. If I.V. must be prepared in D_5W, 0.5 mL of the 8.4% sodium bicarbonate solution should be added per each 100 mL of D_5W.

Stability of parenteral admixture at room temperature (25°C) and at refrigeration temperature (4°C): 24 hours

Standard diluent: 500 mg/250 mL D_5W/NS; 750 mg/250 mL D_5W/NS; 1 g/250 mL D_5W/NS

Refrigerate oral suspension

Mechanism of Action Inhibits RNA-dependent protein synthesis at the chain elongation step; binds to the 50S ribosomal subunit resulting in blockage of transpeptidation

Pharmacodynamics/Kinetics

Absorption: Variable but better with salt forms than with base form; 18% to 45% absorbed orally, ethylsuccinate may be better absorbed with food

Distribution: Crosses the placenta; appears in breast milk

Relative diffusion of antimicrobial agents from blood into cerebrospinal fluid (CSF): Minimal even with inflammation

Ratio of CSF to blood level (%): Normal meninges: 1-12; Inflamed meninges: 7-25

Protein binding: 75% to 90%

Metabolism: In the liver by demethylation

Half-life: 1.5-2 hours (peak)

End-stage renal disease: 5-6 hours

Time to peak serum concentration: 4 hours for the base, 30 minutes to 2.5 hours for the ethylsuccinate; delayed in the presence of food; due to differences in absorption

Elimination: 2% to 15% excreted as unchanged drug in urine and major excretion in feces (via bile)

Usual Dosage

Infants and Children (Note: 400 mg ethylsuccinate = 250 mg base, stearate, or estolate salts):

Oral: 30-50 mg/kg/day divided every 6-8 hours; may double doses in severe infections

Preop bowel preparation: 20 mg/kg erythromycin base at 1, 2, and 11 PM on the day before surgery combined with mechanical cleansing of the large intestine and oral neomycin

I.V.: Lactobionate: 20-40 mg/kg/day divided every 6 hours

Adults:

Oral:

Base: 250-500 mg every 6-12 hours

Ethylsuccinate: 400-800 mg every 6-12 hours

Preop bowel preparation: Oral: 1 g erythromycin base at 1, 2, and 11 PM on the day before surgery combined with mechanical cleansing of the large intestine and oral neomycin

I.V.: Lactobionate: 15-20 mg/kg/day divided every 6 hours or 500 mg to 1 g every 6 hours, or given as a continuous infusion over 24 hours (maximum: 4 g/24 hours)

Children and Adults: Ophthalmic: Instill ½" (1.25 cm) 2-8 times/day depending on the severity of the infection

Dialysis: Slightly dialyzable (5% to 20%); no supplemental dosage necessary in hemo or peritoneal dialysis or in continuous arteriovenous or venovenous hemofiltration (CAVH/CAVHD)

Erythromycin has been used as a prokinetic agent to improve gastric emptying time and intestinal motility. In adults, 200 mg was infused I.V. initially followed by 250 mg orally 3 times/day 30 minutes before meals. In children, erythromycin 3 mg/kg I.V. has been infused over 60 minutes initially followed by 20 mg/kg/day orally in 3-4 divided doses before meals or before meals and at bedtime

Dietary Considerations Food: Increased drug absorption with meals. Drug may cause GI upset; may take with food.

Administration Can administer with food to decrease GI upset

Test Interactions False-positive urinary catecholamines

Patient Information Refrigerate after reconstitution, take until gone, do not skip doses; chewable tablets should not be swallowed whole; report to physician if persistent diarrhea occurs; discard any unused portion after 10 days; absorption of estolate, ethylsuccinate, and base in a delayed release form are unaffected by food; take stearate salt and nondelayed release base preparations 2 hours before or after meals

Nursing Implications Some formulations may contain benzyl alcohol as a preservative; use with extreme care in neonates; do not crush enteric coated drug product; GI upset, including diarrhea, is common; I.V. infusion may be very irritating to the vein; if phlebitis/pain occurs with used dilution, consider diluting further (eg, 1:5) and administer over ≥20-60 minutes, if fluid status of the patient will tolerate, or consider administering in larger available vein

Additional Information Due to differences in absorption, 400 mg erythromycin ethylsuccinate produces the same serum levels as 250 mg erythromycin base, stearate, or estolate. Do not use D_5W as a diluent unless sodium bicarbonate is added to solution; infuse over 30 minutes.

Sodium content of oral suspension (ethylsuccinate) 200 mg/5 mL: 29 mg (1.3 mEq)

Sodium content of base Filmtab® 250 mg: 70 mg (3 mEq)

Dosage Forms

Erythromycin base:
Capsule, delayed release: 250 mg
Capsule, delayed release, enteric coated pellets (Eryc®): 250 mg
Ointment, ophthalmic: 0.55 mg (3.5 g)
Tablet, delayed release: 333 mg
Tablet, enteric coated (E-Mycin®, Ery-Tab®, E-Base®): 250 mg, 333 mg, 500 mg
Tablet, film coated: 250 mg, 500 mg
Tablet, polymer coated particles (PCE®): 333 mg, 500 mg

Erythromycin estolate:
Capsule (Ilosone® Pulvules®): 250 mg
Suspension, oral (Ilosone®): 125 mg/5 mL (480 mL); 250 mg/5 mL (480 mL)
Tablet (Ilosone®): 500 mg

Erythromycin ethylsuccinate:
Granules for oral suspension (EryPed®): 400 mg/5 mL (60 mL, 100 mL, 200 mL)
Powder for oral suspension (E.E.S.®): 200 mg/5 mL (100 mL, 200 mL)
Suspension, oral (E.E.S.®, EryPed®): 200 mg/5 mL (5 mL, 100 mL, 200 mL, 480 mL); 400 mg/5 mL (5 mL, 60 mL, 100 mL, 200 mL, 480 mL)
Suspension, oral [drops] (EryPed®): 100 mg/2.5 mL (50 mL)
Tablet (E.E.S.®): 400 mg
Tablet, chewable (EryPed®): 200 mg

Erythromycin gluceptate: Injection: 1000 mg (30 mL)

Erythromycin lactobionate: Powder for injection: 500 mg, 1000 mg

Erythromycin stearate: Tablet, film coated (Eramycin®, Erythrocin®): 250 mg, 500 mg

Erythromycin and Benzoyl Peroxide
(er ith roe MYE sin & BEN zoe il per OKS ide)

U.S. Brand Names Benzamycin®

Therapeutic Category Acne Products

Dosage Forms Gel: Erythromycin 30 mg and benzoyl peroxide 50 mg per g

Erythromycin and Sulfisoxazole (er ith roe MYE sin & sul fi SOKS a zole)

U.S. Brand Names Eryzole®; Pediazole®

Synonyms Sulfisoxazole and Erythromycin

Therapeutic Category Antibiotic, Macrolide; Antibiotic, Sulfonamide Derivative

Use Treatment of susceptible bacterial infections of the upper and lower respiratory tract, otitis media in children caused by susceptible strains of *Haemophilus influenzae*, and many other infections in patients allergic to penicillin

Pregnancy Risk Factor C

Contraindications Hepatic dysfunction, known hypersensitivity to erythromycin or sulfonamides; infants <2 months of age (sulfas compete with bilirubin for binding sites); patients with porphyria; concurrent use with pimozide, terfenadine, astemizole, or cisapride

Warnings/Precautions Use with caution in patients with impaired renal or hepatic function, G-6-PD deficiency (hemolysis may occur)

Adverse Reactions
>10%: Gastrointestinal: Abdominal pain, cramping, nausea, vomiting
1% to 10%:
Gastrointestinal: Oral candidiasis
Local: Phlebitis at the injection site
Miscellaneous: Hypersensitivity reactions
<1%: Ventricular arrhythmias, fever, headache, rash, Stevens-Johnson syndrome, toxic epidermal necrolysis, hypertrophic pyloric stenosis, diarrhea, pseudomembranous colitis, crystalluria, eosinophilia, agranulocytosis, aplastic anemia, hepatic necrosis, cholestatic jaundice, thrombophlebitis, toxic nephrosis

(Continued)

Erythromycin and Sulfisoxazole (Continued)

Overdosage/Toxicology
Symptoms of overdose include nausea, vomiting, diarrhea, prostration, reversible pancreatitis, hearing loss with or without tinnitus or vertigo

General and supportive care only; keep patient well hydrated

Drug Interactions
Increased effect/toxicity/levels with erythromycin/sulfisoxazole on alfentanil, astemizole, terfenadine (resulting in potentially life-threatening prolonged Q-T interval), bromocriptine, carbamazepine, cyclosporine, digoxin, disopyramide, theophylline, triazolam, lovastatin/simvastatin, ergots, methylprednisolone, cisapride, pimozide, felodipine, phenytoin, barbiturate anesthetics, methotrexate, sulfonylureas, uricosuric agents, and warfarin; may inhibit metabolism of protease inhibitors

Increased toxicity of sulfonamides occurs with concurrent diuretics, indomethacin, methenamine, probenecid, and salicylates

Stability Reconstituted suspension is stable for 14 days when refrigerated

Mechanism of Action Erythromycin inhibits bacterial protein synthesis; sulfisoxazole competitively inhibits bacterial synthesis of folic acid from para-aminobenzoic acid

Pharmacodynamics/Kinetics
Erythromycin ethylsuccinate:
Absorption: Well absorbed from GI tract
Distribution: Crosses the placenta; appears in breast milk
Protein binding: 75% to 90%
Metabolism: In the liver
Half-life: 1-1.5 hours
Elimination: Unchanged drug is excreted and concentrated in bile
Sulfisoxazole acetyl: Hydrolyzed in the GI tract to sulfisoxazole which has the following characteristics:
Absorption: Readily absorbed
Distribution: Crosses the placenta; appears in breast milk
Protein binding: 85%
Half-life: 6 hours, prolonged in renal impairment
Elimination: 50% excreted in urine as unchanged drug

Usual Dosage Oral (dosage recommendation is based on the product's erythromycin content):

Children ≥2 months: 50 mg/kg/day erythromycin and 150 mg/kg/day sulfisoxazole in divided doses every 6 hours; not to exceed 2 g erythromycin/day or 6 g sulfisoxazole/day for 10 days

Adults >45 kg: 400 mg erythromycin and 1200 mg sulfisoxazole every 6 hours

Dosing adjustment in renal impairment (sulfisoxazole must be adjusted in renal impairment):
Cl_{cr} 10-50 mL/minute: Administer every 8-12 hours
Cl_{cr} <10 mL/minute: Administer every 12-24 hours

Monitoring Parameters CBC and periodic liver function test

Test Interactions False-positive urinary protein

Patient Information Maintain adequate fluid intake; avoid prolonged exposure to sunlight; discontinue if rash appears; take until gone, do not skip doses

Dosage Forms Suspension, oral: Erythromycin ethylsuccinate 200 mg and sulfisoxazole acetyl 600 mg per 5 mL (100 mL, 150 mL, 200 mL, 250 mL)

- **Erythromycin Base** see Erythromycin on page 427
- **Erythromycin Estolate** see Erythromycin on page 427
- **Erythromycin Ethylsuccinate** see Erythromycin on page 427
- **Erythromycin Gluceptate** see Erythromycin on page 427
- **Erythromycin Lactobionate** see Erythromycin on page 427
- **Erythromycin Stearate** see Erythromycin on page 427
- **Erythropoietin** see Epoetin Alfa on page 418
- **Eryzole®** see Erythromycin and Sulfisoxazole on previous page
- **Esclim® Transdermal** see Estradiol on page 433
- **Eserine Salicylate** see Physostigmine on page 925
- **Esgic®** see Butalbital Compound on page 165
- **Esidrix®** see Hydrochlorothiazide on page 574
- **Eskalith®** see Lithium on page 688
- **Eskalith CR®** see Lithium on page 688

Esmolol (ES moe lol)

Related Information
Antiarrhythmic Drugs Comparison on page 1297
Beta-Blockers Comparison on page 1311
Extravasation Treatment of Other Drugs on page 1287
Hypertension Therapy on page 1479

U.S. Brand Names Brevibloc® Injection

Synonyms Esmolol Hydrochloride

Therapeutic Category Antiarrhythmic Agent, Class II; Antihypertensive Agent; Beta-Adrenergic Blocker

Use Treatment of supraventricular tachycardia, atrial fibrillation/flutter (primarily to control ventricular rate), and hypertension (especially perioperatively)

Pregnancy Risk Factor C

Contraindications Sinus bradycardia or heart block; uncompensated congestive heart failure; cardiogenic shock; hypersensitivity to esmolol, any component, or other beta-blockers

Warnings/Precautions Must be diluted for continuous I.V. infusion; use with extreme caution in patients with hyper-reactive airway disease; use lowest dose possible and discontinue infusion if bronchospasm occurs; use with caution in diabetes mellitus, hypoglycemia, renal failure; avoid extravasation; caution should be exercised when discontinuing esmolol infusions to avoid withdrawal effects; esmolol shares the toxic potentials of beta-adrenergic blocking agents and the usual precautions of these agents should be observed

Adverse Reactions
>10%:
Cardiovascular: Asymptomatic and symptomatic hypotension (12%)
Miscellaneous: Diaphoresis (12%)
1% to 10%:
Cardiovascular: Peripheral ischemia
Central nervous system: Dizziness (3%), somnolence (3%), confusion (2%), headache (2%), agitation (2%), fatigue (1%)
Gastrointestinal: Nausea (7%), vomiting (1%)
<1%: Pallor, flushing, bradycardia, chest pain, syncope, heart block, edema, depression, abnormal thinking, anxiety, fever, lightheadedness, seizures, erythema, skin discoloration, anorexia, dyspepsia, constipation, xerostomia, abdominal discomfort, urinary retention, thrombophlebitis, infusion site reactions, paresthesia, rigors, midcapsular pain, weakness, abnormal vision, bronchospasm, wheezing, dyspnea, nasal congestion, pulmonary edema

Overdosage/Toxicology
Symptoms of intoxication include cardiac disturbances, CNS toxicity, bronchospasm, hypoglycemia and hyperkalemia. The most common cardiac symptoms include hypotension and bradycardia; atrioventricular block, intraventricular conduction disturbances, cardiogenic shock, and asystole may occur with severe overdose, especially with membrane-depressant drugs (eg, propranolol); CNS effects include convulsions, coma, and respiratory arrest is commonly seen with propranolol and other membrane-depressant and lipid-soluble drugs.
Treatment includes symptomatic treatment of seizures, hypotension, hyperkalemia, and hypoglycemia; bradycardia and hypotension resistant to atropine, isoproterenol, or pacing may respond to glucagon; wide QRS defects caused by the membrane-depressant poisoning may respond to hypertonic sodium bicarbonate; repeat-dose charcoal, hemoperfusion, or hemodialysis may be helpful in removal of only those beta-blockers with a small V_d, long half-life, or low intrinsic clearance (acebutolol, atenolol, nadolol, sotalol)

Drug Interactions
Decreased effect of beta-blockers with aluminum salts, barbiturates, calcium salts, cholestyramine, colestipol, NSAIDs, penicillins (ampicillin), rifampin, salicylates and sulfinpyrazone due to decreased bioavailability and plasma levels
Beta-blockers may decrease the effect of sulfonylureas
Increased effect/toxicity of beta-blockers with calcium blockers (diltiazem, felodipine, nicardipine), contraceptives, flecainide, quinidine (in extensive metabolizers), ciprofloxacin
Beta-blockers may increase the effect/toxicity of flecainide, acetaminophen, benzodiazepines (not atenolol), clonidine (hypertensive crisis after or during withdrawal of either agent), epinephrine (initial hypertensive episode followed by bradycardia), nifedipine and verapamil lidocaine, ergots (peripheral ischemia), prazosin (postural hypotension)
Beta-blockers may affect the action or levels of ethanol, disopyramide, nondepolarizing muscle relaxants and theophylline although the effects are difficult to predict

Stability Clear, colorless to light yellow solution which should be stored at room temperature and protected from temperatures >40°C
Stability of parenteral admixture at room temperature (25°C) and at refrigeration temperature (4°C): 24 hours
Standard diluent: 5 g/500 mL NS

Mechanism of Action Class II antiarrhythmic: Competitively blocks response to beta$_1$-adrenergic stimulation with little or no effect of beta$_2$-receptors except at high doses, no intrinsic sympathomimetic activity, no membrane stabilizing activity

Pharmacodynamics/Kinetics
Onset of beta-blockade: I.V.: Within 2-10 minutes (onset of effect is quickest when loading doses are administered)
Duration of activity: Short, 10-30 minutes; prolonged following higher cumulative doses, extended duration of use
Protein binding: 55%
Metabolism: In blood by esterases
Half-life: Adults: 9 minutes
Elimination: ~69% of dose excreted in urine as metabolites and 2% as unchanged drug

Usual Dosage I.V. administration requires an infusion pump (must be adjusted to individual response and tolerance):

Children: An extremely limited amount of information regarding esmolol use in pediatric patients is currently available
Some centers have utilized doses of 100-500 mcg/kg given over 1 minute for control of supraventricular tachycardias
(Continued)

Esmolol *(Continued)*

Loading doses of 500 mcg/kg/minute over 1 minute with maximal doses of 50-250 mcg/kg/minute (mean 173) have been used in addition to nitroprusside to treat postoperative hypertension after coarctation of aorta repair

Adults: Loading dose: 500 mcg/kg over 1 minute; follow with a 50 mcg/kg/minute infusion for 4 minutes; if response is inadequate, rebolus with another 500 mcg/kg loading dose over 1 minute, and increase the maintenance infusion to 100 mcg/kg/minute. Repeat this process until a therapeutic effect has been achieved or to a maximum recommended maintenance dose of 200 mcg/kg/minute. Usual dosage range: 50-200 mcg/kg/minute with average dose of 100 mcg/kg/minute.

Esmolol: Hemodynamic effects of beta-blockade return to baseline within 20-30 minutes after discontinuing esmolol infusions

Guidelines for withdrawal of therapy:

Transfer to alternative antiarrhythmic drug (propranolol, digoxin, verapamil)

Infusion should be reduced by 50% 30 minutes following the first dose of the alternative agent

Following the second dose of the alternative drug, patient's response should be monitored and if control is adequate for the first hours, esmolol may be discontinued

Dialysis: Not removed by hemo- or peritoneal dialysis; supplemental dose is not necessary

Administration The 250 mg/mL ampul is **not** for direct I.V. injection, but rather must first be diluted to a final concentration of 10 mg/mL (ie, 2.5 g in 250 mL or 5 g in 500 mL); decrease or discontinue infusion if hypotension, congenital heart failure occur

Monitoring Parameters Blood pressure, heart rate, MAP, EKG, respiratory rate, I.V. site; cardiac monitor and blood pressure monitor required

Test Interactions Increases cholesterol (S), glucose

Dosage Forms Injection, as hydrochloride: 10 mg/mL (10 mL); 250 mg/mL (10 mL)

♦ **Esmolol Hydrochloride** *see Esmolol on page 430*

♦ **Esoterica® Facial [OTC]** *see Hydroquinone on page 584*

♦ **Esoterica® Regular [OTC]** *see Hydroquinone on page 584*

♦ **Esoterica® Sensitive Skin Formula [OTC]** *see Hydroquinone on page 584*

♦ **Esoterica® Sunscreen [OTC]** *see Hydroquinone on page 584*

Estazolam *(es TA zoe lam)*

Related Information

Benzodiazepines Comparison *on page 1310*

U.S. Brand Names ProSom™

Therapeutic Category Benzodiazepine; Hypnotic; Sedative

Use Short-term management of insomnia; there has been little experience with this drug in the elderly, but because of its lack of active metabolites, it is a reasonable choice when a benzodiazepine hypnotic is indicated

Restrictions C-IV

Pregnancy Risk Factor X

Contraindications Pregnancy; hypersensitivity to estazolam, cross-sensitivity with other benzodiazepines may occur, pre-existing CNS depression, sleep apnea, narrow-angle glaucoma

Warnings/Precautions Abrupt discontinuance may precipitate withdrawal or rebound insomnia; use with caution in patients receiving other CNS depressants, patients with low albumin, hepatic dysfunction, and in the elderly; do not use in pregnant women; may cause drug dependency; safety and efficacy have not been established in children <15 years of age, not recommended in nursing mothers

Adverse Reactions

>10%:

Cardiovascular: Tachycardia, chest pain

Central nervous system: Drowsiness, fatigue, ataxia, lightheadedness, memory impairment, insomnia, anxiety, depression, headache

Dermatologic: Rash

Endocrine & metabolic: Decreased libido

Gastrointestinal: Xerostomia, constipation, decreased salivation, nausea, vomiting, diarrhea, increased or decreased appetite

Neuromuscular & skeletal: Dysarthria

Ocular: Blurred vision

Miscellaneous: Diaphoresis

1% to 10%:

Cardiovascular: Syncope, hypotension

Central nervous system: Confusion, nervousness, dizziness, akathisia

Dermatologic: Dermatitis

Gastrointestinal: Weight gain or loss, increased salivation

Neuromuscular & skeletal: Rigidity, tremor, muscle cramps

Otic: Tinnitus

Respiratory: Nasal congestion, hyperventilation

<1%: Menstrual irregularities, blood dyscrasias, reflex slowing, drug dependence

Overdosage/Toxicology

Symptoms of overdose include respiratory depression, hypoactive reflexes, unsteady gait, hypotension

Treatment for benzodiazepine overdose is supportive; rarely is mechanical ventilation required; flumazenil has been shown to selectively block the binding of benzodiazepines to CNS receptors, resulting in a reversal of benzodiazepine-induced CNS depression.

Drug Interactions
Decreased effect: Enzyme inducers may increase the metabolism of estazolam
Increased toxicity: CNS depressants may increase CNS adverse effects; cimetidine may decrease metabolism of estazolam

Mechanism of Action Benzodiazepines may exert their pharmacologic effect through potentiation of the inhibitory activity of GABA. Benzodiazepines do not alter the synthesis, release, reuptake, or enzymatic degradation of GABA.

Usual Dosage Adults: Oral: 1 mg at bedtime, some patients may require 2 mg; start at doses of 0.5 mg in debilitated or small elderly patients

Dosing adjustment in hepatic impairment: May be necessary

Dietary Considerations Alcohol: Additive CNS effect, avoid use

Monitoring Parameters Respiratory and cardiovascular status

Patient Information May cause daytime drowsiness, avoid alcohol and drugs with CNS depressant effects; avoid activities needing good psychomotor coordination until CNS effects are known; drug may cause physical or psychological dependence; avoid abrupt discontinuation after prolonged use

Nursing Implications Provide safety measures (ie, side rails, night light, and call button); remove smoking materials from area; supervise ambulation; avoid abrupt discontinuance in patients with prolonged therapy or seizure disorders

Dosage Forms Tablet: 1 mg, 2 mg

- ◆ **Estimated Clinical Comparability of Doses for Inhaled Corticosteroids** see page 1463
- ◆ **Estinyl®** see Ethinyl Estradiol on page 446
- ◆ **Estivin® II [OTC]** see Naphazoline on page 817
- ◆ **Estrace® Oral** see Estradiol on this page
- ◆ **Estraderm® Transdermal** see Estradiol on this page
- ◆ **Estra-D® Injection** see Estradiol on this page

Estradiol (es tra DYE ole)

U.S. Brand Names Alora® Transdermal; Climara® Transdermal; Delestrogen® Injection; depGynogen® Injection; Depo®-Estradiol Injection; Depogen® Injection; Dioval® Injection; Dura-Estrin® Injection; Duragen® Injection; Esclim® Transdermal; Estrace® Oral; Estraderm® Transdermal; Estra-D® Injection; Estra-L® Injection; Estring®; Estro-Cyp® Injection; Estroject-L.A.® Injection; FemPatch® Transdermal; Gynogen L.A.® Injection; Valergen® Injection; Vivelle® Transdermal

Synonyms Estradiol Cypionate; Estradiol Transdermal; Estradiol Valerate

Therapeutic Category Estrogen Derivative, Intramuscular; Estrogen Derivative, Oral; Estrogen Derivative, Topical; Estrogen Derivative, Vaginal

Use Treatment of atrophic vaginitis, atrophic dystrophy of vulva, menopausal symptoms, female hypogonadism, ovariectomy, primary ovarian failure, inoperable breast cancer, inoperable prostatic cancer, mild to severe vasomotor symptoms associated with menopause

Pregnancy Risk Factor X

Contraindications Known or suspected pregnancy, undiagnosed genital bleeding, carcinoma of the breast (except in patients treated for metastatic disease), estrogen-dependent tumors, history of thrombophlebitis, thrombosis, or thromboembolic disorders associated with estrogen use

Warnings/Precautions Use with caution in patients with renal or hepatic insufficiency; estrogens may cause premature closure of epiphyses in young individuals; in patients with a history of thromboembolism, stroke, myocardial infarction (especially >40 years of age who smoke), liver tumor, hypertension.

Estrogens have been reported to increase the risk of endometrial carcinoma; do not use estrogens during pregnancy. Before prescribing estrogen therapy to postmenopausal women, the risks and benefits must be weighed for each patient. Women should be informed of these risks and benefits, as well as possible side effects and the return of menstrual bleeding (when cycled with a progestin), and be involved in the decision to prescribe. Oral therapy may be more convenient for vaginal atrophy and stress incontinence.

Adverse Reactions
>10%:
Cardiovascular: Peripheral edema
Endocrine & metabolic: Enlargement of breasts (female and male), breast tenderness
Gastrointestinal: Nausea, anorexia, bloating
1% to 10%:
Central nervous system: Headache
Endocrine & metabolic: Increased libido (female), decreased libido (male)
Gastrointestinal: Vomiting, diarrhea
<1%: Increase in blood pressure, edema, thromboembolic disorders, myocardial infarction, depression, dizziness, anxiety, stroke, chloasma, melasma, rash, hypercalcemia, folate deficiency, change in menstrual flow, breast tumors, amenorrhea, decreased glucose tolerance, increased triglycerides and LDL, GI distress, cholestatic jaundice, pain at injection site, intolerance to contact lenses, increased susceptibility to *Candida* infection
(Continued)

Estradiol *(Continued)*

Overdosage/Toxicology

Symptoms of overdose include fluid retention, jaundice, thrombophlebitis, nausea, vomiting

Toxicity is unlikely following single exposures of excessive doses, any treatment following emesis and charcoal administration should be supportive and symptomatic

Drug Interactions CYP1A2 and 3A3/4 enzyme substrate

Decreased effect: Rifampin decreases estrogen serum concentrations

Increased toxicity: Hydrocortisone increases corticosteroid toxic potential; increased potential for thromboembolic events with anticoagulants

Mechanism of Action Increases the synthesis of DNA, RNA, and various proteins in target tissues; reduces the release of gonadotropin-releasing hormone from the hypothalamus; reduces FSH and LH release from the pituitary

Pharmacodynamics/Kinetics

Absorption: Readily absorbed through skin and GI tract; reabsorbed from bile in GI tract and enterohepatically recycled

Distribution: Crosses the placenta; appears in breast milk

Metabolism: Principally degraded in the liver

Protein binding: 80%

Half-life: 50-60 minutes

Elimination: In urine as conjugates; small amounts excreted in feces via bile, reabsorbed from the GI tract and enterohepatically recycled

Usual Dosage Adults (all dosage needs to be adjusted based upon the patient's response):

Male:

Prostate cancer: Valerate: I.M.: ≥30 mg or more every 1-2 weeks

Prostate cancer (androgen-dependent, inoperable, progressing): Oral: 10 mg 3 times/day for at least 3 months

Female:

Breast cancer (inoperable, progressing): Oral: 10 mg 3 times/day for at least 3 months

Osteoporosis prevention: Oral: 0.5 mg/day in a cyclic regimen (3 weeks on and 1 week off of drug)

Hypogonadism, moderate to severe vasomotor symptoms:

Oral: 1-2 mg/day in a cyclic regimen for 3 weeks on drug, then 1 week off drug

I.M.: Valerate: 10-20 mg every 4 weeks given cyclically

Moderate to severe vasomotor symptoms:

Oral: 1-2 mg/day; adjust to control presenting symptoms and titrate to the minimal effective dose for maintenance therapy. Use the lowest dose and regimen that will control symptoms and discontinue medication as soon as possible. Attempt to discontinue or taper medication at 3- to 6-month intervals.

I.M.: Cypionate: 1-5 mg every 3-4 weeks; attempt to discontinue or taper medication at 3- to 6-month intervals

I.M.: Valerate: 10-20 mg every 4 weeks

Postpartum breast engorgement: I.M.: Valerate: 10-25 mg at end of first stage of labor

Transdermal: Apply 0.05 mg patch initially (titrate dosage to response) applied twice weekly (once weekly for Climara® Transdermal) in a cyclic regimen, for 3 weeks on drug and 1 week off drug in patients with an intact uterus and continuously in patients without a uterus

Atrophic vaginitis, kraurosis vulvae: Vaginal: Insert 2-4 g/day for 2 weeks then gradually reduce to $1/2$ the initial dose for 2 weeks followed by a maintenance dose of 1 g 1-3 times/week

Dosing adjustment in hepatic impairment:

Mild to moderate liver impairment: Dosage reduction of estrogens is recommended

Severe liver impairment: **Not recommended**

Administration Injection for intramuscular use only

Reference Range

Children: <10 pg/mL (SI: <37 pmol/L)

Male: 10-50 pg/mL (SI: 37-184 pmol/L)

Female:

Premenopausal: 30-400 pg/mL (SI: 110-1468 pmol/L)

Postmenopausal: 0-30 pg/mL (SI: 0-110 pmol/L)

Test Interactions

Decreased antithrombin III

Decreased serum folate concentration

Increased prothrombin and factors VII, VIII, IX, X

Increased platelet aggregability

Increased thyroid binding globulin

Increased total thyroid hormone (T_4)

Increased serum triglycerides/phospholipids

Patient Information Patients should inform their physicians if signs or symptoms of any of the following occur: Thromboembolic or thrombotic disorders including sudden severe headache or vomiting, disturbance of vision or speech, loss of vision, numbness or weakness in an extremity, sharp or crushing chest pain, calf pain, shortness of breath, severe abdominal pain or mass, mental depression, or unusual bleeding.

Patients should discontinue taking the medication if they suspect they are pregnant or become pregnant. Notify physician if area under dermal patch becomes irritated or a rash develops. Patient package insert is available with product; insert vaginal product high into the vagina.

Nursing Implications Aerosol topical corticosteroids applied under the patch may reduce allergic reactions; do not apply transdermal system to breasts, but place on trunk of body (preferably abdomen); rotate application sites

Additional Information
Estradiol: Estraderm®, Estrace®
Estradiol cypionate: Depo®-Estradiol, depGynogen®, Depogen®, Dura-Estrin®, Estra-D®, Estro-Cyp®, Estroject-L.A.®
Estradiol valerate: Delestrogen®, Dioval®, Duragen®, Estra-L®Gynogen®, Valergen®

Dosage Forms
Cream, vaginal (Estrace®): 0.1 mg/g (42.5 g)
Injection, as cypionate (depGynogen®, Depo®-Estradiol, Depogen®, Dura-Estrin®, Estra-D®, Estro-Cyp®, Estroject-L.A.®): 5 mg/mL (5 mL, 10 mL)
Injection, as valerate:
  Delestrogen®, Valergen®: 10 mg/mL (5 mL, 10 mL); 20 mg/mL (1 mL, 5 mL, 10 mL); 40 mg/mL (5 mL, 10 mL)
  Dioval®, Duragen®, Estra-L®, Gynogen L.A.®: 20 mg/mL (10 mL); 40 mg/mL (10 mL)
Tablet, micronized (Estrace®): 1 mg, 2 mg
Transdermal system
  Alora®:
    0.05 mg/24 hours [18 cm^2], total estradiol 1.5 mg
    0.075 mg/24 hours [27 cm^2], total estradiol 2.3 mg
    0.1 mg/24 hours [36 cm^2], total estradiol 3 mg
  Climara®:
    0.05 mg/24 hours [12.5 cm^2], total estradiol 3.9 mg
    0.1 mg/24 hours [25 cm^2], total estradiol 7.8 mg
  Estraderm®:
    0.05 mg/24 hours [10 cm^2], total estradiol 4 mg
    0.1 mg/24 hours [20 cm^2], total estradiol 8 mg
  Vivelle™:
    0.0375 mg/day
    0.05 mg/day
    0.075 mg/day
Vaginal ring (Estring®): 2 mg gradually released over 90 days

Estradiol and Testosterone (es tra DYE ole & tes TOS ter one)

U.S. Brand Names Andro/Fem® Injection; Deladumone® Injection; depAndrogyn® Injection; Depo-Testadiol® Injection; Depotestogen® Injection; Duo-Cyp® Injection; Duratestrin® Injection; Valertest No.1® Injection

Therapeutic Category Estrogen and Androgen Combination

Dosage Forms Injection:
Andro/Fem®, depAndrogyn®, Depo-Testadiol®, Depotestogen®, Duo-Cyp®, Duratestrin®: Estradiol cypionate 2 mg and testosterone cypionate 50 mg per mL in cottonseed oil (1 mL, 10 mL)
Androgyn L.A.®, Deladumone®, Estra-Testrin®, Valertest No.1®: Estradiol valerate 4 mg and testosterone enanthate 90 mg per mL in sesame oil (5 mL, 10 mL)

♦ **Estradiol Cypionate** see Estradiol on page 433
♦ **Estradiol Transdermal** see Estradiol on page 433
♦ **Estradiol Valerate** see Estradiol on page 433
♦ **Estra-L® Injection** see Estradiol on page 433

Estramustine (es tra MUS teen)

U.S. Brand Names Emcyt®

Synonyms Estramustine Phosphate Sodium

Therapeutic Category Antineoplastic Agent, Alkylating Agent; Antineoplastic Agent, Hormone; Antineoplastic Agent, Nitrogen Mustard

Use Palliative treatment of prostatic carcinoma (progressive or metastatic)

Pregnancy Risk Factor C

Contraindications Active thrombophlebitis or thromboembolic disorders, hypersensitivity to estramustine or any component, estradiol or nitrogen mustard

Warnings/Precautions The U.S. Food and Drug Administration (FDA) currently recommends that procedures for proper handling and disposal of antineoplastic agents be considered. Glucose tolerance may be decreased; elevated blood pressure may occur; exacerbation of peripheral edema or congestive heart disease may occur; use with caution in patients with impaired liver function, renal insufficiency, or metabolic bone diseases.

Adverse Reactions
>10%:
  Cardiovascular: Edema
  Gastrointestinal: Diarrhea, nausea, mild increases in AST (SGOT) or LDH
  Endocrine & metabolic: Decreased libido, breast tenderness, breast enlargement
  Respiratory: Dyspnea
1% to 10%:
  Cardiovascular: Myocardial infarction
  Central nervous system: Insomnia, lethargy
  Gastrointestinal: Anorexia, flatulence
  Hematologic: Leukopenia
  Local: Thrombophlebitis
  Neuromuscular & skeletal: Leg cramps
(Continued)

Estramustine *(Continued)*

Respiratory: Pulmonary embolism

<1%: Cardiac arrest, depression, pigment changes, hypercalcemia, hot flashes, tinnitus, night sweats

Overdosage/Toxicology

Symptoms of overdose include nausea, vomiting, myelosuppression

There are no known antidotes, treatment is primarily symptomatic and supportive

Drug Interactions Decreased effect: Milk products and calcium-rich foods/drugs may impair the oral absorption of estramustine phosphate sodium

Stability Refrigerate at 2°C to 8°C (36°F to 46°F); capsules may be stored outside of refrigerator for up to 24-48 hours without affecting potency

Mechanism of Action Mechanism is not completely clear, thought to act as an alkylating agent and as estrogen

Pharmacodynamics/Kinetics

Absorption: Oral: Well absorbed (75%)

Metabolism: Dephosphorylated in the intestines and eventually oxidized and hydrolyzed to estramustine, estrone, estradiol, and nitrogen mustard

Half-life: 20 hours

Time to peak serum concentration: Within 2-3 hours

Elimination: In feces via bile

Usual Dosage Adults: Oral: 14 mg/kg/day (range: 10-16 mg/kg/day) in 3-4 divided doses for 30-90 days; some patients have been maintained for >3 years on therapy

Patient Information Take on an empty stomach, particularly avoid taking with milk

Dosage Forms Capsule, as phosphate sodium: 140 mg

- ◆ **Estramustine Phosphate Sodium** *see* Estramustine *on previous page*
- ◆ **Estratab®** *see* Estrogens, Esterified *on page 438*
- ◆ **Estratest®** *see* Estrogens and Methyltestosterone *on this page*
- ◆ **Estratest® H.S.** *see* Estrogens and Methyltestosterone *on this page*
- ◆ **Estring®** *see* Estradiol *on page 433*
- ◆ **Estro-Cyp® Injection** *see* Estradiol *on page 433*
- ◆ **Estrogenic Substance Aqueous** *see* Estrone *on page 439*
- ◆ **Estrogenic Substances, Conjugated** *see* Estrogens, Conjugated *on this page*

Estrogens and Medroxyprogesterone

(ES troe jenz & me DROKS ee proe JES te rone)

U.S. Brand Names Premphase™; Prempro™

Therapeutic Category Estrogen and Progestin Combination

Dosage Forms

Premphase™: Two separate tablets in therapy pack: Conjugated estrogens 0.625 mg [Premarin®] (28s) taken orally for 28 days and medroxyprogesterone acetate [Cycrin®] 5 mg (14s) which are taken orally with a Premarin® tablet on days 15 through 28

Prempro™: Conjugated estrogens 0.625 mg and medroxyprogesterone acetate 2.5 mg (14s)

Estrogens and Methyltestosterone

(ES troe jenz & meth il tes TOS te rone)

U.S. Brand Names Estratest®; Estratest® H.S.; Premarin® With Methyltestosterone

Therapeutic Category Estrogen and Androgen Combination

Dosage Forms Tablet:

Estratest®, Menogen®: Esterified estrogen 1.25 mg and methyltestosterone 2.5 mg

Estratest® H.S., Menogen H.S.®: Esterified estrogen 0.625 mg and methyltestosterone 1.25 mg

Premarin® With Methyltestosterone: Conjugated estrogen 0.625 mg and methyltestosterone 5 mg; conjugated estrogen 1.25 mg and methyltestosterone 10 mg

Estrogens, Conjugated (ES troe jenz KON joo gate ed)

Related Information

Depression Disorders and Treatments *on page 1465*

U.S. Brand Names Premarin®

Canadian Brand Names C.E.S.™; Congest

Synonyms C.E.S.; Estrogenic Substances, Conjugated

Therapeutic Category Estrogen Derivative; Estrogen Derivative, Intramuscular; Estrogen Derivative, Oral; Estrogen Derivative, Parenteral; Estrogen Derivative, Vaginal

Use Atrophic vaginitis; hypogonadism; primary ovarian failure; vasomotor symptoms of menopause; prostatic carcinoma; osteoporosis prophylactic

Pregnancy Risk Factor X

Contraindications Undiagnosed vaginal bleeding; hypersensitivity to estrogens or any component; thrombophlebitis, liver disease, known or suspected pregnancy, carcinoma of the breast, estrogen dependent tumor

Warnings/Precautions Use with caution in patients with asthma, epilepsy, migraine, diabetes, cardiac or renal dysfunction; estrogens may cause premature closure of the epiphyses in young individuals; safety and efficacy in children have not been established; estrogens have been reported to increase the risk of endometrial carcinoma; do not use estrogens during pregnancy

Adverse Reactions

>10%:

Cardiovascular: Peripheral edema

Endocrine & metabolic: Breast tenderness, hypercalcemia, enlargement of breasts

Gastrointestinal: Nausea, anorexia, bloating

1% to 10%:

Central nervous system: Headache

Endocrine & metabolic: Increased libido

Gastrointestinal: Vomiting, diarrhea

Local: Pain at injection site

<1%: Increase in blood pressure, edema, thromboembolic disorder, myocardial infarction, hypertension, depression, dizziness, anxiety, stroke, chloasma, melasma, rash, breast tumors, amenorrhea, alterations in frequency and flow of menses, decreased glucose tolerance, increased triglycerides and LDL, GI distress, cholestatic jaundice, intolerance to contact lenses, increased susceptibility to *Candida* infection

Overdosage/Toxicology

Symptoms of overdose include fluid retention, jaundice, thrombophlebitis

Toxicity is unlikely following single exposures of excessive doses, any treatment following emesis and charcoal administration should be supportive and symptomatic

Drug Interactions CYP1A2 enzyme inducer

Decreased effect: Rifampin decreases estrogen serum concentrations

Increased toxicity:

Hydrocortisone increases corticosteroid toxic potential

Increased potential for thromboembolic events with anticoagulants

Stability

Refrigerate injection; at room temperature, the injection is stable for 24 months

Reconstituted solution is stable for 60 days at refrigeration

Compatible with normal saline, dextrose, and inert sugar solution

Incompatible with proteins, ascorbic acid, or solutions with acidic pH

Mechanism of Action Increases the synthesis of DNA, RNA, and various proteins in target tissues; reduces the release of gonadotropin-releasing hormone from the hypothalamus; reduces FSH and LH release from the pituitary

Pharmacodynamics/Kinetics

Absorption: Readily absorbed from GI tract

Metabolism: To inactive compounds in the liver

Elimination: In bile and urine

Usual Dosage Adolescents and Adults:

Male: Prostate cancer: Oral: 1.25-2.5 mg 3 times/day

Female:

Osteoporosis in postmenopausal women: Oral: 0.625 mg/day, cyclically (3 weeks on, 1 week off)

Dysfunctional uterine bleeding:

Stable hematocrit: Oral: 1.25 mg twice daily for 21 days; if bleeding persists after 48 hours, increase to 2.5 mg twice daily; if bleeding persists after 48 more hours, increase to 2.5 mg 4 times/day; some recommend starting at 2.5 mg 4 times/day. **(Note:** Medroxyprogesterone acetate 10 mg/day is also given on days 17-21.)

Unstable hematocrit: I.V.: 5 mg 2-4 times/day; if bleeding is profuse, 20-40 mg every 4 hours up to 24 hours may be used. **Note:** A progestational-weighted contraception pill should also be given (eg, Ovral® 2 tablets stat and 1 tablet 4 times/day or medroxyprogesterone acetate 5-10 mg 4 times/day)

Alternatively: I.V.: 25 mg every 6-12 hours until bleeding stops

Hypogonadism: Oral: 2.5-7.5 mg/day for 20 days, off 10 days and repeat until menses occur. If bleeding does not occur by the end of this period, repeat dosage schedule. If bleeding occurs before the end of the 10-day period, begin a 20-day estrogen-progestin cyclic regimen with 2.5-7.5 mg estrogen daily in divided doses for 1-20 days. During the last 5 days of estrogen therapy, give an oral progestin. If bleeding occurs before this regimen is concluded, discontinue therapy and resume on day 5 of bleeding.

Moderate to severe vasomotor symptoms: Oral: 1.25 mg/day if patient has not menstruated in ≥2 months, start cyclic administration arbitrarily. If patient is menstruating, begin administration on day 5 of bleeding.

Postpartum breast engorgement: Oral: 3.75 mg every 4 hours for 5 doses, then 1.25 mg every 4 hours for 5 days

Atrophic vaginitis, kraurosis vulvae:

Oral: 0.3-1.25 mg or more daily depending on tissue response of the patient; administer cyclically (3 weeks of daily estrogen and 1 week off)

Vaginal: 2-4 g instilled/day 3 weeks on and 1 week off

Female castration and primary ovarian failure: Oral: 1.25 mg/day cyclically (3 weeks on, 1 week off). Adjust according to severity of symptoms and patient response. For maintenance, adjust to the lowest effective dose.

Male/Female: Uremic bleeding: I.V.: 0.6 mg/kg/dose daily for 5 days

Dosing adjustment in hepatic impairment:

Mild to moderate liver impairment: Dosage reduction of estrogens is recommended

Severe liver impairment: **Not recommended**

Administration May also be administered intramuscularly; when administered I.V., drug should be administered slowly to avoid the occurrence of a flushing reaction

Reference Range

Children: <10 µg/24 hours (SI: <35 µmol/day) (values at Mayo Medical Laboratories)

(Continued)

Estrogens, Conjugated *(Continued)*

Adults:
  Male: 15-40 µg/24 hours (SI: 52-139 µmol/day)
  Female:
    Menstruating: 15-80 µg/24 hours (SI: 52-277 µmol/day)
    Postmenopausal: <20 µg/24 hours (SI: <69 µmol/day)

Test Interactions
  Decreased antithrombin III
  Decreased serum folate concentration
  Increased prothrombin and factors VII, VIII, IX, X
  Increased platelet aggregability
  Increased thyroid binding globulin
  Increased total thyroid hormone (T_4)
  Increased serum triglycerides/phospholipids

Patient Information Insert vaginal product high into vagina
  Patient package insert available with product
  Women should inform their physicians if signs or symptoms of any of the following occur: Thromboembolic or thrombotic disorders including sudden severe headache or vomiting, disturbance of vision or speech, loss of vision, numbness or weakness in an extremity, sharp or crushing chest pain, calf pain, shortness of breath, severe abdominal pain or mass, mental depression or unusual bleeding
  Women should discontinue taking the medication if they suspect they are pregnant or become pregnant

Nursing Implications May also be administered intramuscularly; administer at bedtime to minimize occurrence of adverse effects; when administered I.V., drug should be administered slowly to avoid the occurrence of a flushing reaction

Additional Information Contains 50% to 65% sodium estrone sulfate and 20% to 35% sodium equilin sulfate

Dosage Forms
  Cream, vaginal: 0.625 mg/g (42.5 g)
  Injection: 25 mg (5 mL)
  Tablet: 0.3 mg, 0.625 mg, 0.9 mg, 1.25 mg, 2.5 mg

Estrogens, Esterified *(ES troe jenz, es TER i fied)*

U.S. Brand Names Estratab®; Menest®

Canadian Brand Names Neo-Estrone®

Therapeutic Category Estrogen Derivative; Estrogen Derivative, Oral

Use Atrophic vaginitis; hypogonadism; primary ovarian failure; vasomotor symptoms of menopause; prostatic carcinoma; osteoporosis prophylactic

Pregnancy Risk Factor X

Contraindications Known or suspected cancer of the breast, except in appropriately selected patients being treated for metastatic disease; known or suspected estrogen-dependent neoplasia; known or suspected pregnancy; undiagnosed abnormal genital bleeding; active thrombophlebitis or thromboembolic disorders; past history of thrombophlebitis, thrombosis, or thromboembolic disorders associated with previous estrogen use except when used in the treatment of breast or prostatic malignancy

Warnings/Precautions Use with caution in patients with asthma, epilepsy, migraine, diabetes, cardiac or renal dysfunction; estrogens may cause premature closure of the epiphyses in young individuals; safety and efficacy in children have not been established; estrogens have been reported to increase the risk of endometrial carcinoma, do not use estrogens during pregnancy

Adverse Reactions
  >10%:
    Cardiovascular: Peripheral edema
    Endocrine & metabolic: Enlargement of breasts, breast tenderness
    Gastrointestinal: Nausea, anorexia, bloating
  1% to 10%:
    Central nervous system: Headache
    Endocrine & metabolic: Increased libido
    Gastrointestinal: Vomiting, diarrhea
  <1%: Hypertension, thromboembolism, myocardial infarction, edema, stroke, depression, dizziness, anxiety, chloasma, melasma, rash, amenorrhea, alterations in frequency and flow of menses, decreased glucose tolerance, increased triglycerides and LDL, GI distress, cholestatic jaundice, intolerance to contact lenses, increased susceptibility to *Candida* infection, breast tumors

Overdosage/Toxicology
  Symptoms of overdose include fluid retention, jaundice, thrombophlebitis
  Toxicity is unlikely following single exposures of excessive doses, any treatment following emesis and charcoal administration should be supportive and symptomatic

Drug Interactions
  Decreased effect: Rifampin decreases estrogen serum concentrations
  Increased toxicity:
    Hydrocortisone increases corticosteroid toxic potential
    Anticoagulants: Increases potential for thromboembolic events with anticoagulants
    Carbamazepine, tricyclic antidepressants, and corticosteroids; increased thromboembolic potential with oral anticoagulants

Mechanism of Action Primary effects on the interphase DNA-protein complex (chromatin) by binding to a receptor (usually located in the cytoplasm of a target cell) and initiating translocation of the hormone-receptor complex to the nucleus

Pharmacodynamics/Kinetics

Absorption: Readily absorbed from GI tract

Metabolism: Rapidly in the liver to less active metabolites

Elimination: In urine as unchanged compound and metabolites

Usual Dosage Adults: Oral:

Male: Prostate cancer (inoperable, progressing): 1.25-2.5 mg 3 times/day

Female:

Hypogonadism: 2.5-7.5 mg of estrogen daily for 20 days followed by a 10-day rest period. Administer cyclically (3 weeks on and 1 week off). If bleeding does not occur by the end of the 10-day period, begin an estrogen-progestin cyclic regimen of 2.5-7.5 mg/day in divided doses for 20 days. During the last days of estrogen therapy, give an oral progestin. If bleeding occurs before this regimen is concluded, discontinue therapy and resume on the fifth day of bleeding.

Moderate to severe vasomotor symptoms: 1.25 mg/day administered cyclically (3 weeks on and 1 week off). If patient has not menstruated within the last 2 months or more, cyclic administration is started arbitrary. If the patient is menstruating, cyclical administration is started on day 5 of the bleeding. For short-term use only and should be discontinued as soon as possible. Re-evaluate at 3- to 6-month intervals for tapering or discontinuation of therapy.

Atopic vaginitis and kraurosis vulvae: 0.3 to ≥1.25 mg/day, depending on the tissue response of the individual patient. Administer cyclically. For short-term use only and should be discontinued as soon as possible. Re-evaluate at 3- to 6-month intervals for tapering or discontinuation of therapy.

Breast cancer (inoperable, progressing): 10 mg 3 times/day for at least 3 months

Osteoporosis, in postmenopausal women: Initial: 0.3 mg/day and increase to a maximum daily dose of 1.25 mg/day; initiate therapy as soon as possible after menopause; cyclical therapy is recommended

Female castration and primary ovarian failure: 1.25 mg/day, cyclically. Adjust dosage up- or downward according to the severity of symptoms and patient response. For maintenance, adjust dosage to lowest level that will provide effective control.

Dosing adjustment in hepatic impairment:

Mild to moderate liver impairment: Dosage reduction of estrogens is recommended

Severe liver impairment: **Not recommended**

Test Interactions Endocrine function test may be altered

Decreased antithrombin III

Decreased serum folate concentration

Increased prothrombin and factors VII, VIII, IX, X

Increased platelet aggregability

Increased thyroid binding globulin

Increased total thyroid hormone (T_4)

Increased serum triglycerides/phospholipids

Patient Information Patients should inform their physicians if signs or symptoms of thromboembolic or thrombotic disorders occur including sudden severe headache or vomiting, disturbance of vision or speech, loss of vision, numbness or weakness in an extremity, sharp or crushing chest pain, calf pain, shortness of breath, severe abdominal pain or mass, mental depression or unusual bleeding; patients should discontinue taking the medication if they suspect they are pregnant or become pregnant.

Additional Information Esterified estrogens are a combination of the sodium salts of the sulfate esters of estrogenic substances; the principal component is estrone, with preparations containing 75% to 85% sodium estrone sulfate and 6% to 15% sodium equilin sulfate such that the total is not <90%

Dosage Forms Tablet: 0.3 mg, 0.625 mg, 1.25 mg, 2.5 mg

♦ **Estroject-L.A.®** Injection *see* Estradiol *on page 433*

Estrone (ES trone)

U.S. Brand Names Aquest®; Kestrone®

Canadian Brand Names Femogen®; Neo-Estrone®; Oestrilin®

Synonyms Estrogenic Substance Aqueous

Therapeutic Category Estrogen Derivative; Estrogen Derivative, Intramuscular

Use Hypogonadism; primary ovarian failure; vasomotor symptoms of menopause; prostatic carcinoma; inoperable breast cancer, kraurosis vulvae, abnormal uterine bleeding due to hormone imbalance

Pregnancy Risk Factor X

Contraindications Thrombophlebitis, undiagnosed vaginal bleeding, hypersensitivity to estrogens or any component, pregnancy

Warnings/Precautions Use with caution in patients with asthma, epilepsy, migraine, diabetes, cardiac or renal dysfunction; estrogens may cause premature closure of the epiphyses in young individuals; safety and efficacy in children have not been established; estrogens have been reported to increase the risk of endometrial carcinoma, do not use estrogens during pregnancy

Adverse Reactions

>10%:

Cardiovascular: Peripheral edema

Endocrine & metabolic: Enlargement of breasts, breast tenderness

Gastrointestinal: Nausea, anorexia, bloating

(Continued)

439

Estrone *(Continued)*

1% to 10%:
Central nervous system: Headache
Endocrine & metabolic: Increased libido
Gastrointestinal: Vomiting, diarrhea

<1%: Hypertension, thromboembolism, myocardial infarction, edema, stroke, depression, dizziness, anxiety, chloasma, melasma, rash, amenorrhea, alterations in frequency and flow of menses, decreased glucose tolerance, increased triglycerides and LDL, GI distress, cholestatic jaundice, intolerance to contact lenses, increased susceptibility to *Candida* infection, breast tumors

Overdosage/Toxicology
Symptoms of overdose include fluid retention, jaundice, thrombophlebitis
Toxicity is unlikely following single exposures of excessive doses, any treatment should be supportive and symptomatic

Drug Interactions
Decreased effect: Rifampin decreases estrogen serum concentrations
Increased toxicity:
Hydrocortisone increases corticosteroid toxic potential
Anticoagulants: Increases potential for thromboembolic events with anticoagulants
Carbamazepine, tricyclic antidepressants, and corticosteroids; increased thromboembolic potential with oral anticoagulants

Mechanism of Action Estrone is a natural ovarian estrogenic hormone that is available as an aqueous mixture of water insoluble estrone and water soluble estrone potassium sulfate; all estrogens, including estrone, act in a similar manner; there is no evidence that there are biological differences among various estrogen preparations other than their ability to bind to cellular receptors inside the target cells

Usual Dosage Adults: I.M.:
Male: Prostatic carcinoma: 2-4 mg 2-3 times/week
Female:
Senile vaginitis and kraurosis vulvae: 0.1-0.5 mg 2-3 times/week; cyclical (3 weeks on and 1 week off)
Breast cancer (inoperable, progressing): 5 mg 3 or more times/week
Primary ovarian failure, hypogonadism: 0.1-1 mg/week, up to 2 mg/week in single or divided doses; cyclical (3 weeks on and 1 week off)
Abnormal uterine bleeding: Brief courses of intensive therapy: 2-5 mg/day for several days

Dosing adjustment in hepatic impairment:
Mild to moderate liver impairment: Dosage reduction of estrogens is recommended
Severe liver impairment: **Not recommended**

Administration Intramuscular injection only

Test Interactions
Decreased antithrombin III
Decreased serum folate concentration
Increased prothrombin and factors VII, VIII, IX, X
Increased platelet aggregability
Increased thyroid binding globulin
Increased total thyroid hormone (T_4)
Increased serum triglycerides/phospholipids

Patient Information Patients should inform their physicians if signs or symptoms of any of the following occur: Thromboembolic or thrombotic disorders including sudden severe headache or vomiting, disturbance of vision or speech, loss of vision, numbness or weakness in an extremity, sharp or crushing chest pain, calf pain, shortness of breath, severe abdominal pain or mass, mental depression or unusual bleeding; patients should discontinue taking the medication if they suspect they are pregnant or become pregnant

Dosage Forms Injection: 2 mg/mL (10 mL, 30 mL); 5 mg/mL (10 mL)

Estropipate *(ES troe pih pate)*

U.S. Brand Names Ogen® Oral; Ogen® Vaginal; Ortho-Est® Oral
Canadian Brand Names Estrouis®
Synonyms Piperazine Estrone Sulfate
Therapeutic Category Estrogen Derivative; Estrogen Derivative, Oral; Estrogen Derivative, Vaginal
Use Atrophic vaginitis; hypogonadism; primary ovarian failure; vasomotor symptoms of menopause; osteoporosis prophylactic
Pregnancy Risk Factor X
Contraindications Thrombophlebitis, undiagnosed vaginal bleeding, hypersensitivity to estrogens or any component; pregnancy
Warnings/Precautions Use with caution in patients with asthma, epilepsy, migraine, diabetes, cardiac or renal dysfunction; estrogens may cause premature closure of the epiphyses in young individuals; safety and efficacy in children have not been established; estrogens have been reported to increase the risk of endometrial carcinoma, do not use estrogens during pregnancy
Adverse Reactions
>10%:
Cardiovascular: Peripheral edema
Endocrine & metabolic: Enlargement of breasts, breast tenderness
Gastrointestinal: Nausea, anorexia, bloating

1% to 10%:
Central nervous system: Headache
Endocrine & metabolic: Increased libido
Gastrointestinal: Vomiting, diarrhea

<1%: Hypertension, thromboembolism, myocardial infarction, edema, stroke, depression, dizziness, anxiety, chloasma, melasma, rash, amenorrhea, alterations in frequency and flow of menses, decreased glucose tolerance, increased triglycerides and LDL, GI distress, cholestatic jaundice, intolerance to contact lenses, increased susceptibility to *Candida* infection, breast tumors

Overdosage/Toxicology
Symptoms of overdose include fluid retention, jaundice, thrombophlebitis
Toxicity is unlikely following single exposures of excessive doses, any treatment following emesis and charcoal administration should be supportive and symptomatic

Drug Interactions
Decreased effect: Rifampin decreases estrogen serum concentrations
Increased toxicity:
Hydrocortisone increases corticosteroid toxic potential
Anticoagulants: Increases potential for thromboembolic events with anticoagulants
Carbamazepine, tricyclic antidepressants, and corticosteroids; increased thromboembolic potential with oral anticoagulants

Mechanism of Action Crystalline estrone that has been solubilized as the sulfate and stabilized with piperazine. Primary effects on the interphase DNA-protein complex (chromatin) by binding to a receptor (usually located in the cytoplasm of a target cell) and initiating translocation of the hormone receptor complex to the nucleus.

Usual Dosage Adults: Female:
Moderate to severe vasomotor symptoms: Oral: Usual dosage range: 0.75-6 mg estropipate daily. Use the lowest dose and regimen that will control symptoms, and discontinue as soon as possible. Attempt to discontinue or taper medication at 3- to 6-month intervals. If a patient with vasomotor symptoms has not menstruated within the last ≥2 months, start cyclic administration arbitrarily. If the patient has menstruated, start cyclic administration on day 5 of bleeding.

Hypogonadism or primary ovarian failure: Oral: 1.5-9 mg/day for the first 3 weeks, followed by a rest period of 8-10 days. Repeat if bleeding does not occur by the end of the rest period. The duration of therapy necessary to product the withdrawal bleeding will vary according to the responsiveness of the endometrium. If satisfactory withdrawal bleeding does not occur, give an oral progestin in addition to estrogen during the third week of the cycle.

Osteoporosis prevention: Oral: 0.625 mg/day for 25 days of a 31-day cycle

Atrophic vaginitis or kraurosis vulvae: Vaginal: Instill 2-4 g/day 3 weeks on and 1 week off

Dosing adjustment in hepatic impairment:
Mild to moderate liver impairment: Dosage reduction of estrogens is recommended
Severe liver impairment: **Not recommended**

Test Interactions
Decreased antithrombin III
Decreased serum folate concentration
Increased prothrombin and factors VII, VIII, IX, X
Increased platelet aggregability
Increased thyroid binding globulin
Increased total thyroid hormone (T_4)
Increased serum triglycerides/phospholipids

Patient Information Patients should inform their physicians if signs or symptoms of any of the following occur: Thromboembolic or thrombotic disorders including sudden severe headache or vomiting, disturbance of vision or speech, loss of vision, numbness or weakness in an extremity, sharp or crushing chest pain, calf pain, shortness of breath, severe abdominal pain or mass, mental depression or unusual bleeding; patients should discontinue taking the medication if they suspect they are pregnant or become pregnant. Patient package insert is available; insert product high into the vagina.

Dosage Forms
Cream, vaginal: 0.15% [estropipate 1.5 mg/g] (42.5 g tube)
Tablet: 0.625 mg [estropipate 0.75 mg]; 1.25 mg [estropipate 1.5 mg]; 2.5 mg [estropipate 3 mg]; 5 mg [estropipate 6 mg]

♦ **Estrostep® 21** *see* Ethinyl Estradiol and Norethindrone *on page 451*

♦ **Estrostep® Fe** *see* Ethinyl Estradiol and Norethindrone *on page 451*

♦ **Estrouis®** *see* Estropipate *on previous page*

Etanercept (et a NER cept)

U.S. Brand Names Enbrel®

Therapeutic Category Antirheumatic, Disease Modifying

Use Reduction in signs and symptoms of moderately to severely active rheumatoid arthritis in patients who have had an inadequate response to one or more disease-modifying antirheumatic drugs (DMARDs).

Pregnancy Risk Factor B

Pregnancy/Breast-Feeding Implications Developmental toxicity studies performed in animals have revealed no evidence of harm to the fetus. There are no studies in pregnant women; this drug should be used during pregnancy only if clearly needed.

It is not known whether etanercept is excreted in human milk or absorbed systemically after ingestion. Because many immunoglobulins are excreted in human milk, and (Continued)

Etanercept (Continued)

because of the potential for serious adverse reactions in nursing infants from etanercept, a decision should be made whether to discontinue nursing or to discontinue the drug.

Contraindications Etanercept should not be administered to patients with sepsis (mortality may be increased). Do not administer to patients with known hypersensitivity to etanercept or any of its components.

Warnings/Precautions Etanercept may affect defenses against infections and malignancies. Safety and efficacy in patients with immunosuppression or chronic infections have not been evaluated. Discontinue administration if patient develops a serious infection. Do not start drug administration in patients with an active infection.

Impact on the development and course of malignancies is not fully defined. Treatment may result in the formation of autoimmune antibodies; cases of autoimmune disease have not been described. Non-neutralizing antibodies to etanercept may also be formed. No correlation of antibody development to clinical response or adverse events has been observed. The long-term immunogenicity, carcinogenic potential, or effect on fertility are unknown. No evidence of mutagenic activity has been observed *in vitro* or *in vivo*. The safety of etanercept has not been studied in children <4 years of age.

Allergic reactions may occur (<0.5%), but anaphylaxis has not been observed. If an anaphylactic reaction or other serious allergic reaction occurs, administration of etanercept should be discontinued immediately and appropriate therapy initiated.

Patients should be brought up to date with all immunizations before initiating therapy. No data are available concerning the effects of etanercept on vaccination. Live vaccines should not be given concurrently. No data are available concerning secondary transmission of live vaccines in patients receiving etanercept. Patients with a significant exposure to varicella virus should temporarily discontinue etanercept. Treatment with varicella zoster immune globulin should be considered.

Adverse Reactions Events reported include those >3% with incidence higher than placebo

>10%:
    Central nervous system: Headache (17%)
    Local: Injection site reaction (37%)
    Respiratory: Respiratory tract infection (38%), upper respiratory tract infection (29%), rhinitis (12%)
    Miscellaneous: Infection (35%), positive ANA (11%), positive anti-double stranded DNA antibodies (15% by RIA, 3% by *Crithidia lucilae* assay)

>3% to 10%:
    Central nervous system: Dizziness (7%)
    Dermatologic: Rash (5%)
    Gastrointestinal: Abdominal pain (5%), dyspepsia (4%)
    Neuromuscular and skeletal: Weakness (5%)
    Respiratory: Pharyngitis (7%), respiratory disorder (5%), sinusitis (3%)

<3%: Malignancies, serious infection, heart failure, myocardial infarction, myocardial ischemia, cerebral ischemia, hypertension, hypotension, cholecystitis, pancreatitis, gastrointestinal hemorrhage, bursitis, depression, dyspnea

Pediatric patients (JRA): The percentages of patients reporting abdominal pain (17%) and vomiting (14.5%) was higher than in adult RA. Two patients developed varicella infection associated with aseptic meningitis which resolved without complications (see Warnings/Precautions).

Overdosage/Toxicology No dose-limiting toxicities have been observed during clinical trials. Single I.V. doses up to 60 mg/m^2 have been administered to healthy volunteers in an endotoxemia study without evidence of dose-limiting toxicities.

Drug Interactions Specific drug interaction studies have not been conducted with etanercept

Stability The dose tray containing etanercept (sterile powder) must be refrigerated at 2°C to 8°C (36°F to 46°F). Do not freeze. Reconstituted solutions of etanercept should be administered as soon as possible after reconstitution. If not administered immediately after reconstitution, etanercept may be stored in the vial at 2°C to 8°C (36°F to 46°F) for up to 6 hours.

Mechanism of Action Etanercept is a recombinant DNA-derived protein composed of tumor necrosis factor receptor (TNFR) linked to the Fc portion of human IgG1. Etanercept binds tumor necrosis factor (TNF) and blocks its interaction with cell surface receptors. TNF plays an important role in the inflammatory processes of rheumatoid arthritis (RA) and the resulting joint pathology.

Pharmacodynamics/Kinetics

Metabolism: Children: Clearance: 45.9 mL/hour/m^2; Adults: Clearance: 89 mL/hour (52 mL/hour/m^2)

Half-life: 115 hours (98-300 hours)

Time to peak: 72 hours (48-96 hours)

Usual Dosage S.C.:

Children: 0.4 mg/kg (maximum: 25 mg dose)

Adult: 25 mg given twice weekly; if the physician determines that it is appropriate, patients may self-inject after proper training in injection technique

Elderly: Although greater sensitivity of some elderly patients cannot be ruled out, no overall differences in safety or effectiveness were observed

Administration Follow package instructions carefully for reconstitution. **Note:** The needle cover of the diluent syringe contains dry natural rubber (latex) which should not be handled by persons sensitive to this substance. Injection sites should be rotated. New injections should be given at least 1" from an old site and never into areas where the skin is tender, bruised, red, or hard.

Patient Information If a patient is to self-administer etanercept, they should be instructed in injection techniques to ensure the safe self-administration of etanercept. The first injection should be performed under the supervision of a qualified healthcare professional. The ability of that patient to self-inject subcutaneously should be assessed. A puncture-resistant container for disposal of needles and syringes should be used. Patients should be instructed in the technique and told the importance of proper syringe and needle disposal, and be cautioned against reuse of these items. Sites for self-injection include thigh, abdomen, or upper arm. Injection sites should be rotated. New injections should be given at least one inch from an old site and never into areas where the skin is tender, bruised, red, or hard.

Dosage Forms Powder for injection: 25 mg

♦ **Etacrynate Sodium** see Ethacrynic Acid on this page

Ethacrynic Acid (eth a KRIN ik AS id)

Related Information

Heart Failure: Management of Patients With Left-Ventricular Systolic Dysfunction on page 1472

U.S. Brand Names Edecrin®

Synonyms Ethacrynate Sodium

Therapeutic Category Diuretic, Loop

Use Management of edema associated with congestive heart failure; hepatic cirrhosis or renal disease; short-term management of ascites due to malignancy, idiopathic edema, and lymphedema

Pregnancy Risk Factor B

Pregnancy/Breast-Feeding Implications

Clinical effects on the fetus: No data available. Generally, use of diuretics during pregnancy is avoided due to risk of decreased placental perfusion.

Breast-feeding/lactation: No data available

Contraindications Hypersensitivity to ethacrynic acid or any component; anuria, hypotension, dehydration with low serum sodium concentrations; metabolic alkalosis with hypokalemia, or history of severe, watery diarrhea from ethacrynic acid

Warnings/Precautions Use with caution in patients with advanced hepatic cirrhosis, diabetes mellitus, hypotension, dehydration, history of watery diarrhea from ethacrynic acid, hearing impairment; ototoxicity occurs more frequently than with other loop diuretics; safety and efficacy in infants have not been established

Adverse Reactions

>10%: Gastrointestinal: Diarrhea

1% to 10%:

Cardiovascular: Orthostatic hypotension

Central nervous system: Headache

Endocrine & metabolic: Hyponatremia, hypochloremic alkalosis, hypokalemia

Gastrointestinal: Loss of appetite, nausea, vomiting

Ocular: Blurred vision

<1%: Nervousness, confusion, fatigue, malaise, fever, chills, rash, hyperuricemia, gout, GI bleeding, pancreatitis, stomach cramps, dysphagia, hepatic dysfunction, abnormal LFTs, jaundice, leukopenia, agranulocytosis, thrombocytopenia, irritation, ototoxicity (irreversible), renal injury, hematuria

Overdosage/Toxicology

Symptoms of overdose include electrolyte depletion, volume depletion, dehydration, circulatory collapse

Following GI decontamination, treatment is supportive; hypotension responds to fluids and Trendelenburg position

Drug Interactions

Increased toxicity:

Thiazide diuretics may synergistically result in profound diuresis and serious electrolyte disturbances

Hypotensive agents → additive decreased blood pressure

Drugs affected by or causing potassium depletion → additive decreased potassium

Increased ototoxicity potential with aminoglycosides, cisplatin

Ethacrynic acid increases digoxin's cardiotoxic potential → arrhythmias

Increased warfarin anticoagulant effects; increased lithium levels

Decreased effect:

Probenecid, NSAIDs, salicylates decrease diuretic effects

Decreased effectiveness of antidiabetic agents

Mechanism of Action Inhibits reabsorption of sodium and chloride in the ascending loop of Henle and distal renal tubule, interfering with the chloride-binding cotransport system, thus causing increased excretion of water, sodium, chloride, magnesium, and calcium

Pharmacodynamics/Kinetics

Onset of diuretic effect: Oral: Within 30 minutes; I.V.: 5 minutes

Peak effect: Oral: 2 hours; I.V.: 30 minutes

Duration of action: Oral: 12 hours; I.V.: 2 hours

Absorption: Oral: Rapid

Metabolism: In the liver to active cysteine conjugate (35% to 40%)

Protein binding: >90%

Half-life: Normal renal function: 2-4 hours

Elimination: 30% to 60% excreted unchanged in bile and urine

(Continued)

Ethacrynic Acid *(Continued)*

Usual Dosage I.V. formulation should be diluted in D_5W or NS (1 mg/mL) and infused over several minutes

Children: Oral: 1 mg/kg/dose once daily; increase at intervals of 2-3 days as needed, to a maximum of 3 mg/kg/day

Adults:

Oral: 50-200 mg/day in 1-2 divided doses; may increase in increments of 25-50 mg at intervals of several days; doses up to 200 mg twice daily may be required with severe, refractory edema

I.V.: 0.5-1 mg/kg/dose (maximum: 100 mg/dose); repeat doses not routinely recommended; however, if indicated, repeat doses every 8-12 hours

Dosing adjustment/comments in renal impairment: Cl_{cr} <10 mL/minute: Avoid use

Dialysis: Not removed by hemo- or peritoneal dialysis; supplemental dose is not necessary

Administration Injection should **not** be given S.C. or I.M. due to local pain and irritation; single I.V. doses should not exceed 100 mg; if a second dose is needed, use a new injection site to avoid possible thrombophlebitis

Monitoring Parameters Blood pressure, renal function, serum electrolytes, and fluid status closely, including weight and I & O daily; hearing

Patient Information May be taken with food or milk; get up slowly from a lying or sitting position to minimize dizziness, lightheadedness, or fainting; also use extra care when exercising, standing for long periods of time, and during hot weather. Take in morning, take last dose of multiple doses before 6 PM unless instructed otherwise.

Dosage Forms

Powder for injection, as ethacrynate sodium: 50 mg (50 mL)

Tablet: 25 mg, 50 mg

Extemporaneous Preparations To make a 1 mg/mL suspension: Dissolve 120 mg ethacrynic acid powder in a small amount of 10% alcohol. Add a small amount of 50% sorbitol solution and stir. Adjust pH to 7 with 0.1N sodium hydroxide solution. Add sufficient 50% sorbitol solution to make a final volume of 120 mL. (Methylparaben 6 mg and propylparaben 2.4 mg are added as preservatives.) Stable 220 days at room temperature.

Handbook on Extemporaneous Formulations, Bethesda, MD: American Society of Hospital Pharmacists, 1987.

Ethambutol (e THAM byoo tole)

Related Information

Antimicrobial Drugs of Choice *on page 1404*

Depression Disorders and Treatments *on page 1465*

Desensitization Protocols *on page 1347*

Tuberculosis Prophylaxis *on page 1386*

Tuberculosis Treatment Guidelines *on page 1432*

U.S. Brand Names Myambutol®

Canadian Brand Names Etibi®

Synonyms Ethambutol Hydrochloride

Therapeutic Category Antitubercular Agent

Use Treatment of tuberculosis and other mycobacterial diseases in conjunction with other antituberculosis agents

Pregnancy Risk Factor B

Contraindications Hypersensitivity to ethambutol or any component; optic neuritis

Warnings/Precautions Use only in children whose visual acuity can accurately be determined and monitored (not recommended for use in children <13 years of age); dosage modification required in patients with renal insufficiency

Adverse Reactions

1% to 10%:

Central nervous system: Headache, confusion, disorientation

Endocrine & metabolic: Acute gout or hyperuricemia

Gastrointestinal: Abdominal pain, anorexia, nausea, vomiting

<1%: Malaise, mental confusion, fever, rash, pruritus, abnormal LFTs, peripheral neuritis, optic neuritis, anaphylaxis

Overdosage/Toxicology

Symptoms of overdose include decrease in visual acuity, anorexia, joint pain, numbness of the extremities

Following GI decontamination, treatment is supportive

Drug Interactions Decreased absorption with aluminum salts

Mechanism of Action Suppresses mycobacteria multiplication by interfering with RNA synthesis

Pharmacodynamics/Kinetics

Absorption: Oral: ~80%

Distribution: Well distributed throughout the body with high concentrations in kidneys, lungs, saliva, and red blood cells

Relative diffusion of antimicrobial agents from blood into CSF: Adequate with or without inflammation (exceeds usual MICs)

Ratio of CSF to blood level (%): Normal meninges: 0; Inflamed meninges: 25

Protein binding: 20% to 30%

Metabolism: 20% metabolized by the liver to inactive metabolite

Half-life: 2.5-3.6 hours

End-stage renal disease: 7-15 hours
Time to peak serum concentration: 2-4 hours
Elimination: ~50% excreted in the urine and 20% excreted in the feces as unchanged drug

Usual Dosage Oral:

Ethambutol is generally not recommended in children whose visual acuity cannot be monitored (<6 years of age). However, ethambutol should be considered for all children with organisms resistant to other drugs, when susceptibility to ethambutol has been demonstrated, or susceptibility is likely.

Note: A four-drug regimen (isoniazid, rifampin, pyrazinamide, and either streptomycin or ethambutol) is preferred for the initial, empiric treatment of TB. When the drug susceptibility results are available, the regimen should be altered as appropriate.

Children (>6 years) and Adults:
Daily therapy: 15-25 mg/kg/day (maximum: 2.5 g/day)
Directly observed therapy (DOT): Twice weekly: 50 mg/kg (maximum: 2.5 g)
DOT: 3 times/week: 25-30 mg/kg (maximum: 2.5 g)

Dosing interval in renal impairment:
Cl_{cr} 10-50 mL/minute: Administer every 24-36 hours
Cl_{cr} <10 mL/minute: Administer every 48 hours
Hemodialysis: Slightly dialyzable (5% to 20%); Administer dose postdialysis
Peritoneal dialysis: Dose for Cl_{cr} <10 mL/minute
Continuous arteriovenous or venovenous hemofiltration: Administer every 24-36 hours

Monitoring Parameters Periodic visual testing in patients receiving more than 15 mg/kg/day; periodic renal, hepatic, and hematopoietic tests

Patient Information Report any visual changes or rash to physician; may cause stomach upset, take with food; do not take within 2 hours of aluminum-containing antacids

Dosage Forms Tablet, as hydrochloride: 100 mg, 400 mg

♦ **Ethambutol Hydrochloride** see Ethambutol on previous page
♦ **Ethamolin®** see Ethanolamine Oleate on this page
♦ **Ethanoic Acid** see Acetic Acid on page 24

Ethanolamine Oleate (ETH a nol a meen OH lee ate)

U.S. Brand Names Ethamolin®
Therapeutic Category Sclerosing Agent
Use Mild sclerosing agent used for bleeding esophageal varices
Pregnancy Risk Factor C
Contraindications Hypersensitivity to agent or oleic acid
Warnings/Precautions Fatal anaphylactic shock has been reported following administration; use with caution and decrease doses in patients with significant liver dysfunction (child class C), with concomitant cardiorespiratory disease, or in the elderly or critically ill
Adverse Reactions

1% to 10%:
Central nervous system: Pyrexia (1.8%)
Gastrointestinal: Esophageal ulcer (2%), esophageal stricture (1.3%)
Respiratory: Pleural effusion (2%), pneumonia (1.2%)
Miscellaneous: Retrosternal pain (1.6%)
<1%: Esophagitis, perforation, injection necrosis, acute renal failure, anaphylaxis

Overdosage/Toxicology
Anaphylaxis after administration of larger than normal volumes, severe intramural necrosis
Treatment is supportive with epinephrine, corticosteroids, fluids, and pressors

Mechanism of Action Derived from oleic acid and similar in physical properties to sodium morrhuate; however, the exact mechanism of the hemostatic effect used in endoscopic injection sclerotherapy is not known. Intravenously injected ethanolamine oleate produces a sterile inflammatory response resulting in fibrosis and occlusion of the vein; a dose-related extravascular inflammatory reaction occurs when the drug diffuses through the venous wall. Autopsy results indicate that variceal obliteration occurs secondary to mural necrosis and fibrosis. Thrombosis appears to be a transient reaction.

Usual Dosage Adults: 1.5-5 mL per varix, up to 20 mL total or 0.4 mL/kg for a 50 kg patient; doses should be decreased in patients with severe hepatic dysfunction and should receive less than recommended maximum dose

Administration Use care to use acceptable technique to avoid necrosis
Nursing Implications Have epinephrine and resuscitative equipment nearby
Dosage Forms Injection: 5% [50 mg/mL] (2 mL)

Ethchlorvynol (eth klor VI nole)

U.S. Brand Names Placidyl®
Therapeutic Category Hypnotic; Sedative
Use Short-term management of insomnia
Restrictions C-IV
Pregnancy Risk Factor C
Contraindications Porphyria, hypersensitivity to ethchlorvynol or any component
Warnings/Precautions Administer with caution to depressed or suicidal patients or to patients with a history of drug abuse; intoxication symptoms may appear with prolonged daily doses of as little as 1 g; withdrawal symptoms may be seen upon abrupt discontinuation; use with caution in the elderly and in patients with hepatic or renal dysfunction; use with caution in patients who have a history of paradoxical restlessness to barbiturates or alcohol; some products may contain tartrazine
(Continued)

Ethchlorvynol *(Continued)*

Adverse Reactions
>10%:
Central nervous system: Dizziness
Gastrointestinal: Indigestion, nausea, stomach pain, unpleasant aftertaste
Neuromuscular & skeletal: Weakness
Ocular: Blurred vision
1% to 10%:
Central nervous system: Nervousness, excitement, ataxia, confusion, drowsiness (daytime)
Dermatologic: Rash
<1%: Bradycardia, hyperthermia, slurred speech, cholestatic jaundice, trembling, weakness (severe), shortness of breath

Overdosage/Toxicology
Symptoms of overdose include prolonged deep coma, respiratory depression, hypothermia, bradycardia, hypotension, nystagmus
Treatment is supportive in nature; hemoperfusion may be helpful in enhancing elimination

Drug Interactions
Decreased effect of oral anticoagulants
Increased toxicity (CNS depression) with alcohol, CNS depressants, MAO inhibitors, TCAs (delirium)

Stability Capsules should not be crushed and should not be refrigerated
Mechanism of Action Causes nonspecific depression of the reticular activating system

Pharmacodynamics/Kinetics
Onset of action: 15-60 minutes
Duration: 5 hours
Absorption: Rapid from GI tract
Metabolism: In the liver
Half-life: 10-20 hours
Time to peak serum concentration: 2 hours

Usual Dosage Adults: Oral: 500-1000 mg at bedtime
Dosing adjustment in renal impairment: Cl_{cr} <50 mL/minute: Avoid use
Dietary Considerations Alcohol: Additive CNS effect, avoid use
Monitoring Parameters Cardiac and respiratory function and abuse potential
Reference Range Therapeutic: 2-9 µg/mL; Toxic: >20 µg/mL
Patient Information May cause drowsiness, can impair judgment and coordination; avoid alcohol and other CNS depressants; ataxia can be reduced if taken with food, do not crush or refrigerate capsules
Nursing Implications Raise bed rails, institute safety measures, assist with ambulation
Dosage Forms Capsule: 200 mg, 500 mg, 750 mg

Ethinyl Estradiol *(ETH in il es tra DYE ole)*

U.S. Brand Names Estinyl®
Therapeutic Category Estrogen Derivative; Estrogen Derivative, Oral
Use Hypogonadism; primary ovarian failure; vasomotor symptoms of menopause; prostatic carcinoma; breast cancer
Pregnancy Risk Factor X
Contraindications Thrombophlebitis, undiagnosed vaginal bleeding, hypersensitivity to ethinyl estradiol or any component, pregnancy, estrogen-dependent neoplasia
Warnings/Precautions Use with caution in patients with asthma, seizure disorders, migraine, cardiac, renal or hepatic impairment, cerebrovascular disorders or history of breast cancer, past or present thromboembolic disease, smokers >35 years of age

Adverse Reactions
>10%:
Cardiovascular: Peripheral edema
Endocrine & metabolic: Enlargement of breasts, breast tenderness, bloating
Gastrointestinal: Nausea, anorexia
1% to 10%:
Central nervous system: Headache
Endocrine & metabolic: Increased libido
Gastrointestinal: Vomiting, diarrhea
<1%: Hypertension, thromboembolism, myocardial infarction, edema, stroke, depression, dizziness, anxiety, chloasma, melasma, rash, breast tumors, amenorrhea, alterations in frequency and flow of menses, decreased glucose tolerance, increased triglycerides and LDL, GI distress, cholestatic jaundice, intolerance to contact lenses, increased susceptibility to *Candida* infection

Overdosage/Toxicology
Symptoms of overdose include fluid retention, jaundice, thrombophlebitis, nausea
Toxicity is unlikely following single exposures of excessive doses, any treatment following emesis and charcoal administration should be supportive and symptomatic

Drug Interactions CYP3A3/4 and 3A5-7 enzyme substrate; CYP1A2 enzyme inhibitor
Increased toxicity:
Carbamazepine, tricyclic antidepressants, and corticosteroids
Increased thromboembolic potential with oral anticoagulants
Mechanism of Action Increases the synthesis of DNA, RNA, and various proteins in target tissues; reduces the release of gonadotropin-releasing hormone from the hypothalamus; reduces FSH and LH release from the pituitary

Pharmacodynamics/Kinetics
  Absorption: Absorbed well from GI tract
  Protein binding: 50% to 80%
  Metabolism: Inactivated by liver
  Elimination: By the kidneys
Usual Dosage Adults: Oral:
  Male: Prostatic cancer (inoperable, progressing): 0.15-2 mg/day for palliation
  Female:
    Hypogonadism: 0.05 mg 1-3 times/day during the first 2 weeks of a theoretical menstrual cycle. Follow with a progesterone during the last half of the arbitrary cycle. Continue for 3-6 months. The patient should not be treated for the following 2 months.
    Vasomotor symptoms: Usual dosage range: 0.02-0.05 mg/day; give cyclically for short-term use only and use the lowest dose that will control symptoms. Discontinue as soon as possible and administer cyclically (3 weeks on and 1 week off). Attempt to discontinue or taper medication at 3- to 6-month intervals.
    Breast cancer (inoperable, progressing): 1 mg 3 times/day for palliation
  Dosing adjustment in hepatic impairment:
    Mild to moderate liver impairment: Dosage reduction of estrogens is recommended
    Severe liver impairment: **Not recommended**
Test Interactions
  Decreased antithrombin III
  Decreased serum folate concentration
  Increased prothrombin and factors VII, VIII, IX, X
  Increased platelet aggregability
  Increased thyroid binding globulin
  Increased total thyroid hormone (T_4)
  Increased serum triglycerides/phospholipids
Patient Information Photosensitivity may occur
  Women should inform their physicians if signs or symptoms of any of the following occur: Thromboembolic or thrombotic disorders including sudden severe headache or vomiting, disturbance of vision or speech, loss of vision, numbness or weakness in an extremity, sharp or crushing chest pain, calf pain, shortness of breath, severe abdominal pain or mass, mental depression or unusual bleeding
  Women should discontinue taking the medication if they suspect they are pregnant or become pregnant
Nursing Implications Administer at bedtime to minimize occurrence of adverse effects
Dosage Forms Tablet: 0.02 mg, 0.05 mg, 0.5 mg

Ethinyl Estradiol and Desogestrel

(ETH in il es tra DYE ole & des oh JES trel)
U.S. Brand Names Desogen®; Ortho-Cept®
Therapeutic Category Contraceptive, Oral
Dosage Forms Tablet: Ethinyl estradiol 0.03 mg and desogestrel 0.15 mg (21s, 28s)

Ethinyl Estradiol and Ethynodiol Diacetate

(ETH in il es tra DYE ole & e thye noe DYE ole dye AS e tate)
U.S. Brand Names Demulen®; Zovia®
Synonyms Ethynodiol Diacetate and Ethinyl Estradiol
Therapeutic Category Contraceptive, Oral (Intermediate Potency Estrogen, Intermediate Potency Progestin); Contraceptive, Oral (Low Potency Estrogen, Intermediate Potency Progestin); Contraceptive, Oral (Monophasic); Estrogen Derivative, Oral; Progestin
Use Prevention of pregnancy; treatment of hypermenorrhea, endometriosis, female hypogonadism
Pregnancy Risk Factor X
Contraindications Known or suspected pregnancy, undiagnosed genital bleeding, carcinoma of the breast, estrogen-dependent tumor
Warnings/Precautions In patients with a history of thromboembolism, stroke, myocardial infarction (especially >40 years of age who smoke), liver tumor, hypertension, cardiac, renal or hepatic insufficiency; use of any progestin during the first 4 months of pregnancy is not recommended; risk of cardiovascular side effects increases in those women who smoke cigarettes and in women >35 years of age
Adverse Reactions
  >10%:
    Cardiovascular: Peripheral edema
    Endocrine & metabolic: Enlargement of breasts, breast tenderness
    Gastrointestinal: Nausea, anorexia, bloating
  1% to 10%:
    Central nervous system: Headache
    Endocrine & metabolic: Increased libido
    Gastrointestinal: Vomiting, diarrhea
  <1%: Hypertension, thromboembolism, stroke, myocardial infarction, edema, depression, dizziness, anxiety, chloasma, melasma, rash, decreased glucose tolerance, amenorrhea, alterations in frequency and flow of menses, increased triglycerides and LDL, GI distress, cholestatic jaundice, intolerance to contact lenses, increased susceptibility to *Candida* infection, breast tumors
  See tables.
  (Continued)

Ethinyl Estradiol and Ethynodiol Diacetate *(Continued)*

Achieving Proper Hormonal Balance in an Oral Contraceptive

Estrogen		Progestin	
Excess	Deficiency	Excess	Deficiency
Nausea, bloating	Early or midcycle	Increased appetite	Late breakthrough
Cervical mucorrhea,	breakthrough	Weight gain	bleeding
polyposis	bleeding	Tiredness, fatigue	Amenorrhea
Melasma	Increased spotting	Hypomenorrhea	Hypermenorrhea
Migraine headache	Hypomenorrhea	Acne, oily scalp*	
Breast fullness or		Hair loss, hirsutism*	
tenderness		Depression	
Edema		Monilial vaginitis	
Hypertension		Breast regression	

*Result of androgenic activity of progestins.

Pharmacological Effects of Progestins Used in Oral Contraceptives

	Progestin	Estrogen	Antiestrogen	Androgen
Norgestrel/levonorgestrel	+++	0	++	+++
Ethynodiol diacetate	++	+*	+*	+
Norethindrone acetate	+	+	+++	+
Norethindrone	+	+*	+*	+
Norethynodrel	+	+++	0	0

*Has estrogenic effect at low doses; may have antiestrogenic effect at higher doses.

+++ = pronounced effect

++ = moderate effect

+ = slight effect

0 = no effect

Overdosage/Toxicology

Toxicity is unlikely following single exposures of excessive doses

Any treatment following emesis and charcoal administration should be supportive and symptomatic

Drug Interactions Ethinyl estradiol is a CYP3A3/4 and 3A5-7 enzyme substrate; CYP1A2 enzyme inhibitor

Decreased effect of oral contraceptives with barbiturates, hydantoins - phenytoin, rifampin, antibiotics - penicillins, tetracyclines, griseofulvin

Increased toxicity of acetaminophen, anticoagulants, benzodiazepines, caffeine, corticosteroids, metoprolol, theophylline, tricyclic antidepressants

Mechanism of Action Combination oral contraceptives inhibit ovulation via a negative feedback mechanism on the hypothalamus, which alters the normal pattern of gonadotropin secretion of a follicle-stimulating hormone (FSH) and luteinizing hormone by the anterior pituitary. The follicular phase FSH and midcycle surge of gonadotropins are inhibited. In addition, oral contraceptives produce alterations in the genital tract, including changes in the cervical mucus, rendering it unfavorable for sperm penetration even if ovulation occurs. Changes in the endometrium may also occur, producing an unfavorable environment for nidation. Oral contraceptive drugs may alter the tubal transport of the ova through the fallopian tubes. Progestational agents may also alter sperm fertility.

Pharmacodynamics/Kinetics

Ethinyl estradiol:

Absorption: Absorbed well from GI tract

Protein binding: 50% to 80%

Metabolism: Inactivated by liver

Elimination: By the kidneys

Ethynodiol diacetate:

Converted to norethindrone

Metabolism: By conjugation in the liver

Half-life, terminal: 5-14 hours

Usual Dosage Adults: Female: Oral:

For 21-tablet cycle packs, with 21 active tablets (28-day packs have 21 active tablets and 7 inert tablets): Take 1 tablet daily starting on the fifth day of menstrual cycle, with day 1 being the first day of menstruation; begin taking a new cycle pack on the eighth day after taking the last tablet from the previous pack

With 28-tablet packages, dosage is 1 tablet daily without interruption; extra tablets are placebos or contain iron. If next menstrual period does not begin on schedule, rule out pregnancy before starting new dosing cycle. If menstrual period begins, start new dosing cycle 7 days after last tablet was taken. If all doses have been taken on schedule and one menstrual period is missed, continue dosing cycle. If two consecutive menstrual periods are missed, pregnancy test is required before new dosing cycle is started.

One dose missed: Take as soon as remembered or take 2 tablets next day

Two doses missed: Take 2 tablets as soon as remembered or 2 tablets next 2 days

Three doses missed: Begin new compact of tablets starting on day 1 of next cycle

Test Interactions
Decreased antithrombin III
Decreased serum folate concentration
Increased prothrombin and factors VII, VIII, IX, X
Increased platelet aggregability
Increased thyroid binding globulin
Increased total thyroid hormone (T_4)
Increased serum triglycerides/phospholipids

Patient Information Photosensitivity may occur
Inform your physician if signs or symptoms of any of the following occur: Thromboembolic or thrombotic disorders including sudden severe headache or vomiting, disturbance of vision or speech, loss of vision, numbness or weakness in an extremity, sharp or crushing chest pain, calf pain, shortness of breath, severe abdominal pain or mass, mental depression or unusual bleeding.
If any doses are missed, alternative contraceptive methods should be used for the next 2 days or until 2 days into the new cycle
Discontinue taking the medication if you suspect you are pregnant or become pregnant

Additional Information Monophasic oral contraceptive

Dosage Forms Tablet:
1/35: Ethinyl estradiol 0.035 mg and ethynodiol diacetate 1 mg (21s, 28s)
1/50: Ethinyl estradiol 0.05 mg and ethynodiol diacetate 1 mg (21s, 28s)

Ethinyl Estradiol and Levonorgestrel

(ETH in il es tra DYE ole & LEE voe nor jes trel)

U.S. Brand Names Alesse™; Levlen®; Levlite®; Levora®; Nordette®; Tri-Levlen®; Triphasil®

Synonyms Levonorgestrel and Ethinyl Estradiol

Therapeutic Category Contraceptive, Oral (Low Potency Estrogen, Intermediate Potency Progestin); Contraceptive, Oral (Low Potency Estrogen, Low Potency Progestin); Contraceptive, Oral (Monophasic); Contraceptive, Oral (Triphasic); Estrogen Derivative, Oral; Progestin

Use Prevention of pregnancy; treatment of hypermenorrhea, endometriosis, female hypogonadism

Pregnancy Risk Factor X

Contraindications Thrombophlebitis, undiagnosed vaginal bleeding, hypersensitivity to ethinyl estradiol or any component, known or suspected pregnancy, carcinoma of the breast, estrogen-dependent tumor

Warnings/Precautions Use of any progestin during the first 4 months of pregnancy is not recommended; use with caution in patients with asthma, seizure disorders, migraine, cardiac, renal or hepatic impairment, cerebrovascular disorders or history of breast cancer, past and present thromboembolic disease, smokers >35 years of age

Adverse Reactions

Achieving Proper Hormonal Balance in an Oral Contraceptive

Estrogen		Progestin	
Excess	Deficiency	Excess	Deficiency
Nausea, bloating	Early or midcycle breakthrough bleeding	Increased appetite*	Late breakthrough bleeding
Cervical mucorrhea, polyposis		Weight gain	
Melasma	Increased spotting	Tiredness, fatigue	Amenorrhea
Migraine headache	Hypomenorrhea	Hypomenorrhea	Hypermenorrhea
Breast fullness or tenderness		Acne, oily scalp*	
		Hair loss, hirsutism*	
Edema		Depression	
Hypertension		Monilial vaginitis	
		Breast regression	

*Result of androgenic activity of progestins.

Pharmacological Effects of Progestins Used in Oral Contraceptives

	Progestin	Estrogen	Antiestrogen	Androgen
Norgestrel/levonorgestrel	+++	0	++	+++
Ethynodiol diacetate	++	+*	+*	+
Norethindrone acetate	+	+	+++	+
Norethindrone	+	+*	+*	+
Norethynodrel	+	+++	0	0

*Has estrogenic effect at low doses; may have antiestrogenic effect at higher doses.

+++ = pronounced effect

++ = moderate effect

+ = slight effect

0 = no effect

>10%:
Cardiovascular: Peripheral edema
Endocrine & metabolic: Enlargement of breasts, breast tenderness
Gastrointestinal: Nausea, anorexia, bloating

(Continued)

Ethinyl Estradiol and Levonorgestrel *(Continued)*

1% to 10%:
Central nervous system: Headache
Endocrine & metabolic: Increased libido
Gastrointestinal: Vomiting, diarrhea

<1%: Hypertension, thromboembolism, stroke, myocardial infarction, edema, depression, dizziness, anxiety, chloasma, melasma, rash, decreased glucose tolerance, amenorrhea, alterations in frequency and flow of menses, increased triglycerides and LDL, GI distress, cholestatic jaundice, intolerance to contact lenses, increased susceptibility to *Candida* infection, breast tumors

See tables.

Overdosage/Toxicology
Toxicity is unlikely following single exposures of excessive doses
Any treatment following emesis and charcoal administration should be supportive and symptomatic

Drug Interactions
Ethinyl estradiol is a CYP3A3/4 and 3A5-7 enzyme substrate; CYP1A2 enzyme inhibitor

Decreased effect of oral contraceptives with barbiturates, hydantoins - phenytoin, rifampin, antibiotics - penicillins, tetracyclines, griseofulvin

Increased toxicity of acetaminophen, anticoagulants, benzodiazepines, caffeine, corticosteroids, metoprolol, theophylline, tricyclic antidepressants

Mechanism of Action
Combination oral contraceptives inhibit ovulation via a negative feedback mechanism on the hypothalamus, which alters the normal pattern of gonadotropin secretion of a follicle-stimulating hormone (FSH) and luteinizing hormone by the anterior pituitary. The follicular phase FSH and midcycle surge of gonadotropins are inhibited. In addition, oral contraceptives produce alterations in the genital tract, including changes in the cervical mucus, rendering it unfavorable for sperm penetration even if ovulation occurs. Changes in the endometrium may also occur, producing an unfavorable environment for nidation. Oral contraceptive drugs may alter the tubal transport of the ova through the fallopian tubes. Progestational agents may also alter sperm fertility.

Pharmacodynamics/Kinetics
Ethinyl estradiol:
Absorption: Absorbed well from GI tract
Protein binding: 98%
Metabolism: Inactivated by liver
Half-life: 6-20 hours
Elimination: Bile and urine, enterohepatic recycling

Levonorgestrel:
Metabolism: Does not undergo first-pass effect; chiefly metabolized by reduction and conjugation
Bioavailability: Completely
Half-life, terminal: 11-45 hours
Time to peak: 0.5-2 hours

Usual Dosage
Adults: Female: Oral:
Contraception: 1 tablet daily, beginning on day 5 of menstrual cycle (first day of menstrual flow is day 1). With 20-tablet and 21-tablet packages, new dosing cycle begins 7 days after last tablet taken. With 28-tablet packages, dosage is 1 tablet daily without interruption; extra tablets are placebos or contain iron. If next menstrual period does not begin on schedule, rule out pregnancy before starting new dosing cycle. If menstrual period begins, start new dosing cycle 7 days after last tablet was taken. If all doses have been taken on schedule and one menstrual period is missed, continue dosing cycle. If two consecutive menstrual periods are missed, pregnancy test is required before new dosing cycle is started.

One dose missed: Take as soon as remembered or take 2 tablets next day
Two doses missed: Take 2 tablets as soon as remembered or 2 tablets next 2 days
Three doses missed: Begin new compact of tablets starting on day 1 of next cycle

Triphasic oral contraceptive (Tri-Levlen®, Triphasil®): 1 tablet/day in the sequence specified by the manufacturer

Test Interactions
Decreased antithrombin III
Decreased serum folate concentration
Increased prothrombin and factors VII, VIII, IX, X
Increased platelet aggregability
Increased thyroid binding globulin
Increased total thyroid hormone (T_4)
Increased serum triglycerides/phospholipids

Patient Information
Inform your physician if signs or symptoms of any of the following occur: Thromboembolic or thrombotic disorders including sudden severe headache or vomiting, disturbance of vision or speech, loss of vision, numbness or weakness in an extremity, sharp or crushing chest pain, calf pain, shortness of breath, severe abdominal pain or mass, mental depression or unusual bleeding

If any doses are missed, alternative contraceptive methods should be used for the next 2 days or until 2 days into the new cycle

Discontinue taking the medication if you suspect you are pregnant or become pregnant

Additional Information
Monophasic oral contraceptives: Levlen®, Levora®, Nordette®
Triphasic oral contraceptives: Tri-Levlen® and Triphasil®

Dosage Forms Tablet:

Alesse™: Ethinyl estradiol 0.02 mg and levonorgestrel 0.1 mg (21s, 28s)

Levlen®, Levora®, Nordette®: Ethinyl estradiol 0.03 mg and levonorgestrel 0.15 mg (21s, 28s)

Tri-Levlen®, Triphasil®: Phase 1 (6 brown tablets): Ethinyl estradiol 0.03 mg and levonorgestrel 0.05 mg; Phase 2 (5 white tablets): Ethinyl estradiol 0.04 mg and levonorgestrel 0.075 mg; Phase 3 (10 yellow tablets): Ethinyl estradiol 0.03 mg and levonorgestrel 0.125 mg (21s, 28s)

Ethinyl Estradiol and Norethindrone

(ETH in il es tra DYE ole & nor eth IN drone)

U.S. Brand Names Brevicon®; Estrostep® 21; Estrostep® Fe; Genora® 0.5/35; Genora® 1/35; Jenest-28™; Loestrin®; Modicon™; N.E.E.® 1/35; Nelova™ 0.5/35E; Nelova™ 10/11; Norethin™ 1/35E; Norinyl™ 1+35; Ortho-Novum® 1/35; Ortho-Novum® 7/7/7; Ortho-Novum® 10/11; Ovcon® 35; Ovcon® 50; Tri-Norinyl®

Canadian Brand Names Ortho®0.5/35; Synphasic®

Synonyms Norethindrone Acetate and Ethinyl Estradiol

Therapeutic Category Contraceptive, Oral (Biphasic); Contraceptive, Oral (Intermediate Potency Estrogen, Intermediate Potency Progestin); Contraceptive, Oral (Intermediate Potency Estrogen, Low Potency Progestin); Contraceptive, Oral (Low Potency Estrogen, Low Potency Progestin); Contraceptive, Oral (Monophasic); Contraceptive, Oral (Triphasic); Estrogen Derivative, Oral; Progestin

Use Prevention of pregnancy; treatment of hypermenorrhea, endometriosis, female hypogonadism

Pregnancy Risk Factor X

Contraindications Thrombophlebitis, cerebral vascular disease, coronary artery disease, known or suspected breast carcinoma, undiagnosed abnormal genital bleeding, hypersensitivity to any component; pregnancy

Warnings/Precautions Use of any progestin during the first 4 months of pregnancy is not recommended; in patients with a history of thromboembolism, stroke, myocardial infarction (especially >40 years of age who smoke), liver tumor, hypertension, cardiac, renal or hepatic insufficiency; risk of cardiovascular side effects increases in those women who smoke cigarettes and in women >35 years of age

Adverse Reactions

>10%:

Cardiovascular: Peripheral edema

Endocrine & metabolic: Enlargement of breasts, breast tenderness

Gastrointestinal: Nausea, anorexia, bloating

1% to 10%:

Central nervous system: Headache

Endocrine & metabolic: Increased libido

Gastrointestinal: Vomiting, diarrhea

<1%: Hypertension, thromboembolism, stroke, myocardial infarction, edema, depression, dizziness, anxiety, chloasma, melasma, rash, decreased glucose tolerance, breast tumors, amenorrhea, alterations in frequency and flow of menses, increased triglycerides and LDL, GI distress, cholestatic jaundice, intolerance to contact lenses, increased susceptibility to *Candida* infection

Achieving Proper Hormonal Balance in an Oral Contraceptive

Estrogen		Progestin	
Excess	**Deficiency**	**Excess**	**Deficiency**
Nausea, bloating	Early or midcycle	Increased appetite	Late breakthrough
Cervical mucorrhea,	breakthrough	Weight gain	bleeding
polyposis	bleeding	Tiredness, fatigue	Amenorrhea
Melasma	Increased spotting	Hypomenorrhea	Hypermenorrhea
Migraine headache	Hypomenorrhea	Acne, oily scalp*	
Breast fullness or		Hair loss, hirsutism*	
tenderness		Depression	
Edema		Monilial vaginitis	
Hypertension		Breast regression	

*Result of androgenic activity of progestins.

Pharmacological Effects of Progestins Used in Oral Contraceptives

	Progestin	Estrogen	Antiestrogen	Androgen
Norgestrel/levonorgestrel	+++	0	++	+++
Ethynodiol diacetate	++	+*	+*	+
Norethindrone acetate	+	+	+++	+
Norethindrone	+	+*	+*	+
Norethynodrel	+	+++	0	0

*Has estrogenic effect at low doses; may have antiestrogenic effect at higher doses.

+++ = pronounced effect

++ = moderate effect

+ = slight effect

0 = no effect

(Continued)

Ethinyl Estradiol and Norethindrone *(Continued)*

Minimize these effects by adjusting the estrogen/progestin balance or dosage. The table categorizes products by both their estrogenic and progestational potencies; because overall activity is influenced by the interaction of components, it is difficult to precisely classify products; placement in the table is only approximate. Differences between products within a group are probably not clinically significant. See tables.

Overdosage/Toxicology

Toxicity is unlikely following single exposures of excessive doses

Any treatment following emesis and charcoal administration should be supportive and symptomatic

Drug Interactions Ethinyl estradiol is a CYP3A3/4 and 3A5-7 enzyme substrate; CYP1A2 enzyme inhibitor

Decreased effect:

Potential contraceptive failure with barbiturates, hydantoins, and rifampin

Concomitant penicillins or tetracyclines may lead to contraceptive failure

Increased toxicity:

Increased toxicity of carbamazepine, tricyclic antidepressants, and corticosteroids

Increased thromboembolic potential with oral anticoagulants

Mechanism of Action Combination oral contraceptives inhibit ovulation via a negative feedback mechanism on the hypothalamus, which alters the normal pattern of gonadotropin secretion of a follicle-stimulating hormone (FSH) and luteinizing hormone by the anterior pituitary. The follicular phase FSH and midcycle surge of gonadotropins are inhibited. In addition, oral contraceptives produce alterations in the genital tract, including changes in the cervical mucus, rendering it unfavorable for sperm penetration even if ovulation occurs. Changes in the endometrium may also occur, producing an unfavorable environment for nidation. Oral contraceptive drugs may alter the tubal transport of the ova through the fallopian tubes. Progestational agents may also alter sperm fertility.

Pharmacodynamics/Kinetics

Ethinyl estradiol:

Absorption: Absorbed well from GI tract

Protein binding: 98%

Metabolism: Inactivated by liver

Half-life: 6-20 hours

Elimination: Bile and urine, enterohepatic recycling

Norethindrone:

Bioavailability: Overall 65% with first-pass metabolism

Half-life, terminal: 5-14 hours

Time to peak: Oral: 0.5-4 hours

Usual Dosage Adults: Female: Oral:

For 21-tablet cycle packs, with 21 active tablets (28-day packs have 21 active tablets and 7 inert tablets): Take 1 tablet daily starting on the fifth day of menstrual cycle, with day 1 being the first day of menstruation; begin taking a new cycle pack on the eighth day after taking the last tablet from the previous pack

With 28-tablet packages, dosage is 1 tablet daily without interruption; extra tablets are placebos or contain iron. If next menstrual period does not begin on schedule, rule out pregnancy before starting new dosing cycle. If menstrual period begins, start new dosing cycle 7 days after last tablet was taken. If all doses have been taken on schedule and one menstrual period is missed, continue dosing cycle. If two consecutive menstrual periods are missed, pregnancy test is required before new dosing cycle is started.

One dose missed: Take as soon as remembered or take 2 tablets next day

Two doses missed: Take 2 tablets as soon as remembered or 2 tablets next 2 days

Three doses missed: Begin new compact of tablets starting on day 1 of next cycle

Biphasic oral contraceptive (Jenest™-28, Ortho-Novum™ 10/11, Nelova™ 10/11): 1 color tablet/day for 10 days, then next color tablet for 11 days

Triphasic oral contraceptive (Ortho-Novum™ 7/7/7, Tri-Norinyl®, Triphasil®): 1 tablet/day in the sequence specified by the manufacturer

Test Interactions

Decreased antithrombin III

Decreased serum folate concentration

Increased prothrombin and factors VII, VIII, IX, X

Increased platelet aggregability

Increased thyroid binding globulin

Increased total thyroid hormone (T_4)

Increased serum triglycerides/phospholipids

Patient Information Take exactly as directed; use additional method of birth control during first week of administration of first cycle; photosensitivity may occur. Women should inform their physicians if signs or symptoms of any of the following occur thromboembolic or thrombotic disorders including sudden severe headache or vomiting, disturbance of vision or speech, loss of vision, numbness or weakness in an extremity, sharp or crushing chest pain, calf pain, shortness of breath, severe abdominal pain or mass, mental depression, or unusual bleeding.

When any doses are missed, alternative contraceptive methods should be used for the next 2 days or until 2 days into the new cycle

Women should discontinue taking the medication if they suspect they are pregnant or become pregnant

Nursing Implications Administer at bedtime to minimize occurrence of adverse effects
Additional Information
   Monophasic oral contraceptives: Ovcon®, Genora®, Loestrin®, N.E.E.®, Nelova®, Norethin®, Norinyl®, Ortho-Novum®
   Biphasic oral contraceptives: Jenest®, Nelova™ 10/11, Ortho-Novum™ 10/11
   Triphasic oral contraceptives: Tri-Norinyl®, Ortho-Novum™ 7/7/7
Dosage Forms Tablet:
   Brevicon®, Genora® 0.5/35, Modicon™, Nelova™ 0.5/35E: Ethinyl estradiol 0.035 mg and norethindrone 0.5 mg (21s, 28s)
   Estrostep®:
      Triangular tablet (white): Ethinyl estradiol 0.02 mg and norethindrone acetate 1 mg
      Square tablet (white): Ethinyl estradiol 0.03 mg and norethindrone acetate 1 mg
      Round tablet (white): Ethinyl estradiol 0.035 mg and norethindrone acetate 1 mg
   Estrostep® Fe:
      Triangular tablet (white): Ethinyl estradiol 0.02 mg and norethindrone acetate 1 mg
      Square tablet (white): Ethinyl estradiol 0.03 mg and norethindrone acetate 1 mg
      Round tablet (white): Ethinyl estradiol 0.035 mg and norethindrone acetate 1 mg
      Brown tablet: Ferrous fumarate 75 mg
   Loestrin® 1.5/30: Ethinyl estradiol 0.03 mg and norethindrone acetate 1.5 mg (21s)
   Loestrin® Fe 1.5/30: Ethinyl estradiol 0.03 mg and norethindrone acetate 1.5 mg with ferrous fumarate 75 mg in 7 inert tablets (28s)
   Loestrin® 1/20: Ethinyl estradiol 0.02 mg and norethindrone acetate 1 mg (21s)
   Loestrin® Fe 1/20: Ethinyl estradiol 0.02 mg and norethindrone acetate 1 mg with ferrous fumarate 75 mg in 7 inert tablets (28s)
   Genora® 1/35, N.E.E.® 1/35, Nelova® 1/35E, Norethin™ 1/35E, Norinyl® 1+35, Ortho-Novum® 1/35: Ethinyl estradiol 0.035 mg and norethindrone 1 mg (21s, 28s)
   Jenest-28™: Phase 1 (7 white tablets): Ethinyl estradiol 0.035 mg and norethindrone 0.5 mg; Phase 2 (14 peach tablets): Ethinyl estradiol 0.035 mg and norethindrone 1 mg and 7 green inert tablets (28s)
   Ortho-Novum® 7/7/7: Phase 1 (7 white tablets): Ethinyl estradiol 0.035 mg and norethindrone 0.5 mg; Phase 2 (7 light peach tablets): Ethinyl estradiol 0.035 mg and norethindrone 0.75 mg; Phase 3 (7 peach tablets): Ethinyl estradiol 0.035 mg and norethindrone 1 mg (21s, 28s)
   Ortho-Novum® 10/11: Phase 1 (10 white tablets): Ethinyl estradiol 0.035 mg and norethindrone 0.5 mg; Phase 2 (11 dark yellow tablets): Ethinyl estradiol 0.035 mg and norethindrone 1 mg (21s, 28s)
   Ovcon® 35: Ethinyl estradiol 0.035 mg and norethindrone 0.4 mg (21s, 28s)
   Ovcon® 50: Ethinyl estradiol 0.050 mg and norethindrone 1 mg (21s, 28s)
   Tri-Norinyl®: Phase 1 (7 blue tablets): Ethinyl estradiol 0.035 mg and norethindrone 0.5 mg; Phase 2 (9 green tablets): Ethinyl estradiol 0.035 mg and norethindrone 1 mg; Phase 3 (5 blue tablets): Ethinyl estradiol 0.035 mg and norethindrone 0.5 mg (21s, 28s)

Ethinyl Estradiol and Norgestimate
   (ETH in il es tra DYE ole & nor JES ti mate)
Canadian Brand Names Cyclen®; Tri-Cyclen®
Synonyms Norgestimate and Ethinyl Estradiol
Therapeutic Category Contraceptive, Oral
Use Prevention of pregnancy
Pregnancy Risk Factor X
Contraindications Thrombophlebitis, undiagnosed vaginal bleeding, hypersensitivity to ethinyl estradiol or any component, known or suspected pregnancy, carcinoma of the breast, estrogen-dependent tumor
Warnings/Precautions Use of any progestin during the first 4 months of pregnancy is not recommended; use with caution in patients with asthma, seizure disorders, migraine, cardiac, renal or hepatic impairment, cerebrovascular disorders or history of breast cancer, past and present thromboembolic disease, smokers >35 years of age
Overdosage/Toxicology
   Signs and symptoms: Toxicity is unlikely following single exposures of excessive doses
   Treatment: Any treatment following emesis and charcoal administration should be supportive and symptomatic
Drug Interactions Ethinyl estradiol is a CYP3A3/4 and 3A5-7 enzyme substrate; CYP1A2 enzyme inhibitor
   Anticonvulsants, rifampin, tetracyclines → ↓ efficacy of BCPs
Mechanism of Action Combination oral contraceptives inhibit ovulation via a negative feedback mechanism on the hypothalamus, which alters the normal pattern of gonadotropin secretion of a follicle-stimulating hormone (FSH) and luteinizing hormone by the anterior pituitary. The follicular phase FSH and midcycle surge of gonadotropins are inhibited. In addition, oral contraceptives produce alterations in the genital tract, including changes in the cervical mucus, rendering it unfavorable for sperm penetration even if ovulation occurs. Changes in the endometrium may also occur, producing an unfavorable environment for nidation. Oral contraceptive drugs may alter the tubal transport of the ova through the fallopian tubes. Progestational agents may also alter sperm fertility.
Pharmacodynamics/Kinetics Ethinyl estradiol:
   Absorption: Absorbed well from GI tract
   Protein binding: 98%
   Metabolism: Inactivated by liver
   Half-life: 6-20 hours
   Elimination: Bile and urine, enterohepatic recycling
   (Continued)

Ethinyl Estradiol and Norgestimate *(Continued)*

Usual Dosage

Contraception: Oral: 1 tablet daily, beginning on day 5 of menstrual cycle (first day of menstrual flow is day 1). With 21-tablet packages, new dosing cycle begins 7 days after last tablet taken. With 28-tablet packages, dosage is 1 tablet daily without interruption; extra tablets are placebos or contain iron. If next menstrual period does not begin on schedule, rule out pregnancy before starting new dosing cycle. If menstrual period begins, start new dosing cycle 7 days after last tablet was taken. If all doses have been taken on schedule and one menstrual period is missed, continue dosing cycle. If two consecutive menstrual periods are missed, pregnancy test is required before new dosing cycle is started.

One dose missed: Take as soon as remembered or take 2 tablets next day

Two doses missed: Take 2 tablets as soon as remembered or 2 tablets next 2 days

Three doses missed: Begin new compact of tablets starting on day 1 of next cycle

Triphasic oral contraceptive: 1 tablet/day in the sequence specified by the manufacturer

Test Interactions ↑ amylase (S), cholesterol (S), iron (B), sodium (S), thyroxine (S); ↓ calcium (S), protein, prothrombin time

Patient Information Women should inform their physicians if signs or symptoms of any of the following occur: thromboembolic or thrombotic disorders including sudden severe headache or vomiting, disturbance of vision or speech, loss of vision, numbness or weakness in an extremity, sharp or crushing chest pain, calf pain, shortness of breath, severe abdominal pain or mass, mental depression or unusual bleeding. Women should be advised that when any doses are missed, alternative contraceptive methods should be used for the next 2 days or until 2 days into the new cycle; women should discontinue taking the medication if they suspect they are pregnant or become pregnant.

Dosage Forms Tablet:

Ortho-Cyclen®: Ethinyl estradiol 0.035 mg and norgestimate 0.25 mg (21s, 28s)

Ortho Tri-Cyclen®: Phase 1 (7 white tablets): Ethinyl estradiol 0.035 mg and norgestimate 0.18 mg; Phase 2 (5 light blue tablets): Ethinyl estradiol 0.035 mg and norgestimate 0.215 mg; Phase 3 (10 blue tablets): Ethinyl estradiol 0.035 mg and norgestimate 0.25 mg (21s, 28s)

Ethinyl Estradiol and Norgestrel *(ETH in il es tra DYE ole & nor JES trel)*

U.S. Brand Names Lo/Ovral®; Ovral®

Synonyms Morning After Pill; Norgestrel and Ethinyl Estradiol

Therapeutic Category Contraceptive, Oral (Intermediate Potency Estrogen, High Potency Progestin); Contraceptive, Oral (Low Potency Estrogen, Intermediate Potency Progestin); Contraceptive, Oral (Monophasic); Estrogen Derivative, Oral; Progestin

Use Prevention of pregnancy; oral: postcoital contraceptive or "morning after" pill; treatment of hypermenorrhea, endometriosis, female hypogonadism

Pregnancy Risk Factor X

Contraindications Thromboembolic disorders, cerebrovascular or coronary artery disease; known or suspected breast cancer; undiagnosed abnormal vaginal bleeding; women smokers >35 years of age; all women >40 years of age, hypersensitivity to drug or components; pregnancy

Warnings/Precautions Use of any progestin during the first 4 months of pregnancy is not recommended; in patients with a history of thromboembolism, stroke, myocardial infarction (especially >40 years of age who smoke), liver tumor, hypertension, cardiac, renal or hepatic insufficiency; risk of cardiovascular side effects increases in those women who smoke cigarettes and in women >35 years of age

Adverse Reactions Effects can be minimized by adjusting the estrogen/progestin balance or dosage. See tables in Ethinyl Estradiol and Norethindrone monograph.

>10%:

Cardiovascular: Peripheral edema

Endocrine & metabolic: Enlargement of breasts, breast tenderness

Gastrointestinal: Nausea, anorexia, bloating

1% to 10%:

Central nervous system: Headache

Endocrine & metabolic: Increased libido

Gastrointestinal: Vomiting, diarrhea

<1%: Hypertension, thromboembolism, myocardial infarction, edema, depression, dizziness, anxiety, stroke, chloasma, melasma, rash, decreased glucose tolerance, breast tumors, amenorrhea, alterations in frequency and flow of menses, increased triglycerides and LDL, GI distress, cholestatic jaundice, intolerance to contact lenses, increased susceptibility to *Candida* infection

Overdosage/Toxicology

Toxicity is unlikely following single exposures of excessive doses

Any treatment following emesis and charcoal administration should be supportive and symptomatic

Drug Interactions Ethinyl estradiol is a CYP3A3/4 and 3A5-7 enzyme substrate; CYP1A2 enzyme inhibitor

Decreased effect:

Potential contraceptive failure with barbiturates, hydantoins, and rifampin

Concomitant penicillins or tetracyclines may lead to contraceptive failure

Increased toxicity:

Increased toxicity of carbamazepine, tricyclic antidepressants, and corticosteroids

Increased thromboembolic potential with oral anticoagulants

Mechanism of Action Combination oral contraceptives inhibit ovulation via a negative feedback mechanism on the hypothalamus, which alters the normal pattern of gonadotropin secretion of a follicle-stimulating hormone (FSH) and luteinizing hormone by the anterior pituitary. The follicular phase FSH and midcycle surge of gonadotropins are inhibited. In addition, oral contraceptives produce alterations in the genital tract, including changes in the cervical mucus, rendering it unfavorable for sperm penetration even if ovulation occurs. Changes in the endometrium may also occur, producing an unfavorable environment for nidation. Oral contraceptive drugs may alter the tubal transport of the ova through the fallopian tubes. Progestational agents may also alter sperm fertility.

Pharmacodynamics/Kinetics
    Ethinyl estradiol:
        Absorption: Absorbed well from GI tract
        Protein binding: 98%
        Metabolism: Inactivated by liver
        Half-life: 6-20 hours
        Elimination: Bile and urine, enterohepatic recycling
    Norgestrel:
        Metabolism: Reduction and conjugation
        Bioavailability: Complete with no first-pass effect
        Half-life, terminal: 11-45 hours
        Time to peak: 0.5-2 hours

Usual Dosage Female: Oral: Contraceptive: 1 tablet daily, beginning on day 5 of menstrual cycle (first day of menstrual flow is day 1). With 20-tablet and 21-tablet packages, new dosing cycle begins 7 days after last tablet taken; with 28-tablet packages, dosage is 1 tablet daily without interruption; extra tablets are placebos or contain iron. If next menstrual period does not begin on schedule, rule out pregnancy before starting new dosing cycle; if menstrual period begins, start new dosing cycle 7 days after last tablet was taken; if all doses have been taken on schedule and one menstrual period is missed, continue dosing cycle; if two consecutive menstrual periods are missed, pregnancy test is required before new dosing cycle is started.
    One dose missed: Take as soon as remembered or take 2 tablets next day
    Two doses missed: Take 2 tablets as soon as remembered or 2 tablets next 2 days
    Three doses missed: Begin new compact of tablets starting on day 1 of next cycle
    Postcoital contraception or "morning after" pill: Oral (50 mcg ethinyl estradiol and 0.5 mg norgestrel): 2 tablets at initial visit and 2 tablets 12 hours later

Test Interactions
    Decreased antithrombin III
    Decreased serum folate concentration
    Increased prothrombin and factors VII, VIII, IX, X
    Increased platelet aggregability
    Increased thyroid binding globulin
    Increased total thyroid hormone (T_4)
    Increased serum triglycerides/phospholipids

Patient Information Take exactly as directed; use additional method of birth control during first week of administration of first cycle; photosensitivity may occur. Women should inform their physicians if signs or symptoms of any of the following occur: Thromboembolic or thrombotic disorders including sudden severe headache or vomiting, disturbance of vision or speech, loss of vision, numbness or weakness in an extremity, sharp or crushing chest pain, calf pain, shortness of breath, severe abdominal pain or mass, mental depression or unusual bleeding.

Women should be advised that when any doses are missed, alternative contraceptive methods should be used for the next 2 days or until 2 days into the new cycle

Women should discontinue taking the medication if they suspect they are pregnant or become pregnant

Nursing Implications Administer at bedtime to minimize occurrence of adverse effects

Additional Information Monophasic oral contraceptives

Dosage Forms Tablet:
    Lo/Ovral®: Ethinyl estradiol 0.03 mg and norgestrel 0.3 mg (21s and 28s)
    Ovral®: Ethinyl estradiol 0.05 mg and norgestrel 0.5 mg (21s and 28s)

 ◆ **Ethiofos** see Amifostine on page 54

Ethionamide (e thye on AM ide)
Related Information
    Antimicrobial Drugs of Choice on page 1404
    Tuberculosis Prophylaxis on page 1386
    Tuberculosis Treatment Guidelines on page 1432

U.S. Brand Names Trecator®-SC

Therapeutic Category Antitubercular Agent

Use Treatment of tuberculosis and other mycobacterial diseases, in conjunction with other antituberculosis agents, when first-line agents have failed or resistance has been demonstrated

Pregnancy Risk Factor C

Contraindications Contraindicated in patients with severe hepatic impairment or in patients who are sensitive to the drug

Warnings/Precautions Use with caution in patients receiving cycloserine or isoniazid, in diabetics

Adverse Reactions
    >10%: Gastrointestinal: Anorexia, nausea, vomiting
    (Continued)

Ethionamide (Continued)

1% to 10%:
Cardiovascular: Postural hypotension
Central nervous system: Psychiatric disturbances, drowsiness
Gastrointestinal: Metallic taste, diarrhea
Hepatic: Hepatitis (5%), jaundice
Neuromuscular & skeletal: Weakness
<1%: Dizziness, seizures, headache, peripheral neuritis, rash, alopecia, hypothyroidism or goiter, hypoglycemia, gynecomastia, stomatitis, abdominal pain, thrombocytopenia, optic neuritis, blurred vision, olfactory disturbances

Overdosage/Toxicology
Symptoms of overdose include peripheral neuropathy, anorexia, joint pain
Following GI decontamination, treatment is supportive; pyridoxine may be given to prevent peripheral neuropathy

Mechanism of Action Inhibits peptide synthesis

Pharmacodynamics/Kinetics
Absorption: Rapid from GI tract (~80%)
Distribution: Crosses the placenta
Protein binding: 10%
Bioavailability: 80%
Half-life: 2-3 hours
Time to peak serum concentration: Oral: Within 3 hours
Elimination: As metabolites (active and inactive) and parent drug in urine

Usual Dosage Oral:
Children: 15-20 mg/kg/day in 2 divided doses, not to exceed 1 g/day
Adults: 500-1000 mg/day in 1-3 divided doses
Dosing adjustment in renal impairment: Cl_{cr} <50 mL/minute: Administer 50% of dose

Monitoring Parameters Initial and periodic serum ALT and AST

Patient Information Take with meals; notify physician of persistent or severe stomach upset, loss of appetite, or metallic taste; frequent blood tests are needed for monitoring; increase dietary intake of pyridoxine

Additional Information Neurotoxic effects may be relieved by the administration of pyridoxine

Dosage Forms Tablet, sugar coated: 250 mg

♦ **Ethmozine®** see Moricizine on page 796

Ethosuximide (eth oh SUKS i mide)

Related Information
Anticonvulsants by Seizure Type on page 1300
Epilepsy Treatment on page 1468

U.S. Brand Names Zarontin®

Therapeutic Category Anticonvulsant

Use Management of absence (petit mal) seizures, myoclonic seizures, and akinetic epilepsy; considered to be drug of choice for simple absence seizures

Pregnancy Risk Factor C

Contraindications Known hypersensitivity to ethosuximide

Drug Interactions CYP3A3/4 enzyme substrate; CYP3A3/4 enzyme inducer

Usual Dosage Oral:
Children 3-6 years: Initial: 250 mg/day (or 15 mg/kg/day) in 2 divided doses; increase every 4-7 days; usual maintenance dose: 15-40 mg/kg/day in 2 divided doses
Children >6 years and Adults: Initial: 250 mg twice daily; increase by 250 mg as needed every 4-7 days up to 1.5 g/day in 2 divided doses; usual maintenance dose: 20-40 mg/kg/day in 2 divided doses

Additional Information Complete prescribing information for this medication should be consulted for additional detail

Dosage Forms
Capsule: 250 mg
Syrup (raspberry flavor): 250 mg/5 mL (473 mL)

♦ **Ethoxynaphthamido Penicillin Sodium** see Nafcillin on page 810
♦ **Ethyl Aminobenzoate** see Benzocaine on page 133

Ethyl Chloride and Dichlorotetrafluoroethane

(ETH il KLOR ide & dye klor oh te tra floo or oh ETH ane)

U.S. Brand Names Fluro-Ethyl® Aerosol

Therapeutic Category Local Anesthetic

Dosage Forms Aerosol: Ethyl chloride 25% and dichlorotetrafluoroethane 75% (225 g)

♦ **Ethylenediamine** see Theophylline Salts on page 1125
♦ **Ethynodiol Diacetate and Ethinyl Estradiol** see Ethinyl Estradiol and Ethynodiol Diacetate on page 447
♦ **Ethyol®** see Amifostine on page 54
♦ **Etibi®** see Ethambutol on page 444

Etidocaine (e TI doe kane)

U.S. Brand Names Duranest®

Synonyms Etidocaine Hydrochloride

Therapeutic Category Local Anesthetic, Injectable

Use Infiltration anesthesia; peripheral nerve blocks; central neural blocks

Pregnancy Risk Factor B

Contraindications Heart block, severe hemorrhage, severe hypotension, known hypersensitivity to etidocaine or other amide local anesthetics

Warnings/Precautions Use with caution in patients with cardiac disease and hyperthyroidism; fetal bradycardia may occur up to 20% of the time; use with caution in areas of inflammation or sepsis, in debilitated or elderly patients, and those with severe cardiovascular disease or hepatic dysfunction; some products may contain sulfites

Adverse Reactions <1%: Myocardial depression, hypotension, bradycardia, cardiovascular collapse, anxiety, restlessness, disorientation, confusion, seizures, drowsiness, unconsciousness, chills, urticaria, nausea, vomiting, transient stinging or burning at injection site, tremor, blurred vision, tinnitus, respiratory arrest, anaphylactoid reactions, shivering

Overdosage/Toxicology

Symptoms of overdose include seizures, hypoventilation, apnea, hypotension, cardiac depression, arrhythmias, cardiac arrest

Treatment is supportive; seizures may be treated with diazepam; hypotension, circulatory collapse respond best to fluids and Trendelenburg position

Mechanism of Action Blocks nervous conduction through the stabilization of neuronal membranes. By preventing the transient increase in membrane permeability to sodium, the ionic fluxes necessary for initiation and transmission of electrical impulses are inhibited and local anesthesia is induced.

Pharmacodynamics/Kinetics

Onset of anesthesia: Within 2-5 minutes

Duration: ~4-10 hours

Absorption: Rapid

Distribution: Wide V_d allows wide distribution into neuronal tissues

Protein binding: High

Metabolism: Extensively in the liver

Elimination: Small amounts excreted in urine

Usual Dosage Varies with procedure; use 1% for peripheral nerve block, central nerve block, lumbar peridural caudal; use 1.5% for maxillary infiltration or inferior alveolar nerve block; use 1% or 1.5% for intra-abdominal or pelvic surgery, lower limb surgery, or caesarean section

Reference Range Toxic concentration: >0.1 μg/mL

Nursing Implications Before injecting withdraw syringe plunger to ensure injection is not into vein or artery; have resuscitative equipment nearby

Dosage Forms

Injection, as hydrochloride: 1% [10 mg/mL] (30 mL)

Injection, as hydrochloride, with epinephrine 1:200,000: 1% [10 mg/mL] (30 mL); 1.5% [15 mg/mL] (20 mL)

♦ **Etidocaine Hydrochloride** see Etidocaine on previous page

Etidronate Disodium (e ti DROE nate dye SOW dee um)

U.S. Brand Names Didronel®

Synonyms EHDP; Sodium Etidronate

Therapeutic Category Antidote, Hypercalcemia; Bisphosphonate Derivative

Use Symptomatic treatment of Paget's disease and heterotopic ossification due to spinal cord injury or after total hip replacement, hypercalcemia associated with malignancy

Pregnancy Risk Factor B (oral)/C (parenteral)

Contraindications Patients with serum creatinine >5 mg/dL; hypersensitivity to biphosphonates

Warnings/Precautions Use with caution in patients with restricted calcium and vitamin D intake; dosage modification required in renal impairment; I.V. form may be nephrotoxic and should be used with caution, if at all, in patients with impaired renal function (serum creatinine: 2.5-4.9 mg/dL)

Adverse Reactions

1% to 10%:

Central nervous system: Fever, convulsions

Endocrine & metabolic: Hypophosphatemia, hypomagnesemia, fluid overload

Neuromuscular & skeletal: Bone pain

Respiratory: Dyspnea

<1%: Pain, angioedema, rash, abnormal taste, occult blood in stools, increased risk of fractures, nephrotoxicity, hypersensitivity reactions

Overdosage/Toxicology

Symptoms of overdose include diarrhea, nausea, vomiting, paresthesias, tetany, coma

Antidote is calcium

Stability Store ampuls at room temperature and avoid excess heat (>40°C/104°F); intravenous solution diluted in ≥250 mL normal saline is stable for 48 hours at room temperature or refrigerated

Mechanism of Action Decreases bone resorption by inhibiting osteocystic osteolysis; decreases mineral release and matrix or collagen breakdown in bone

Pharmacodynamics/Kinetics

Onset of therapeutic effect: Within 1-3 months of therapy

Duration: Can persist for 12 months without continuous therapy

Absorption: Dependent upon dose administered

Metabolism: Not metabolized

(Continued)

Etidronate Disodium (Continued)

Elimination: As unchanged drug primarily in urine with unabsorbed drug being eliminated in feces

Usual Dosage Adults: Oral formulation should be taken on an empty stomach 2 hours before any meal.

Paget's disease: Oral

Initial: 5-10 mg/kg/day (not to exceed 6 months) or 11-20 mg/kg/day (not to exceed 3 months). Doses >10 mg/kg/day are **not** recommended.

Retreatment: Initiate only after etidronate-free period ≥90 days. Monitor patients every 3-6 months. Retreatment regimens are the same as for initial treatment.

Heterotopic ossification: Oral:

Caused by spinal cord injury: 20 mg/kg/day for 2 weeks, then 10 mg/kg/day for 10 weeks; total treatment period: 12 weeks

Complicating total hip replacement: 20 mg/kg/day for 1 month preoperatively then 20 mg/kg/day for 3 months postoperatively; total treatment period is 4 months

Hypercalcemia associated with malignancy:

I.V. (dilute dose in at least 250 mL NS): 7.5 mg/kg/day for 3 days; there should be at least 7 days between courses of treatment

Oral: Start 20 mg/kg/day on the last day of infusion and continue for 30-90 days

Dosing adjustment in renal impairment:

S_{cr} 2.5-5 mg/dL: Use with caution

S_{cr} >5 mg/dL: **Not recommended**

Administration Administer intravenous dose over at least 2 hours; I.V. doses should be diluted in at least 250 mL 0.9% sodium chloride

Monitoring Parameters Serum calcium and phosphorous; serum creatinine and BUN

Reference Range Calcium (total): Adults: 9.0-11.0 mg/dL

Patient Information Maintain adequate intake of calcium and vitamin D; take medicine on an empty stomach 2 hours before meals

Nursing Implications Ensure adequate hydration

Dosage Forms

Injection: 50 mg/mL (6 mL)

Tablet: 200 mg, 400 mg

Etodolac (ee toe DOE lak)

Related Information

Nonsteroidal Anti-Inflammatory Agents Comparison on page 1335

U.S. Brand Names Lodine®; Lodine® XL

Canadian Brand Names Utradol™

Synonyms Etodolic Acid

Therapeutic Category Analgesic, Nonsteroidal Anti-inflammatory Drug; Anti-inflammatory Agent; Nonsteroidal Anti-inflammatory Drug (NSAID), Oral

Use Acute and long-term use in the management of signs and symptoms of osteoarthritis and management of pain

Unapproved use: Rheumatoid arthritis

Pregnancy Risk Factor C

Contraindications Hypersensitivity to etodolac, aspirin, or other NSAIDs

Warnings/Precautions Use with caution in patients with congestive heart failure, hypertension, decreased renal or hepatic function, history of GI disease, or those receiving anticoagulants

Adverse Reactions

>10%:

Central nervous system: Dizziness

Dermatologic: Rash

Gastrointestinal: Abdominal cramps, heartburn, indigestion, nausea

1% to 10%:

Central nervous system: Headache, nervousness

Dermatologic: Itching

Endocrine & metabolic: Fluid retention

Gastrointestinal: Vomiting

Otic: Tinnitus

<1%: Congestive heart failure, hypertension, arrhythmia, tachycardia, confusion, hallucinations, aseptic meningitis, mental depression, drowsiness, insomnia, urticaria, erythema multiforme, toxic epidermal necrolysis, Stevens-Johnson syndrome, angioedema, polydipsia, hot flashes, gastritis, GI ulceration, cystitis, polyuria, agranulocytosis, anemia, hemolytic anemia, bone marrow suppression, leukopenia, thrombocytopenia, hepatitis, peripheral neuropathy, toxic amblyopia, blurred vision, conjunctivitis, dry eyes, decreased hearing, acute renal failure, allergic rhinitis, shortness of breath, epistaxis

Overdosage/Toxicology

Symptoms of overdose include acute renal failure, vomiting, drowsiness, leukocytes

Management of a nonsteroidal anti-inflammatory drug (NSAID) intoxication is primarily supportive and symptomatic. Fluid therapy is commonly effective in managing the hypotension that may occur following an acute NSAID overdose, except when this is due to an acute blood loss.

Drug Interactions

Decreased effect with aspirin

Increased effect/toxicity with aspirin (GI irritation), probenecid; increased effect/toxicity of lithium, methotrexate, digoxin, cyclosporin (nephrotoxicity), warfarin (bleeding)

Stability Protect from moisture

Mechanism of Action Inhibits prostaglandin synthesis by decreasing the activity of the enzyme, cyclo-oxygenase, which results in decreased formation of prostaglandin precursors

Pharmacodynamics/Kinetics
Absorption: Oral: Well absorbed
Distribution: V_d: 0.4 L/kg
Protein binding: High
Half-life: 7 hours
Time to peak serum concentration: 1 hour

Usual Dosage Single dose of 76-100 mg is comparable to the analgesic effect of aspirin 650 mg; in patients ≥65 years, no substantial differences in the pharmacokinetics or side-effects profile were seen compared with the general population

Adults: Oral:
Acute pain: 200-400 mg every 6-8 hours, as needed, not to exceed total daily doses of 1200 mg; for patients weighing <60 kg, total daily dose should not exceed 20 mg/kg/day
Osteoarthritis: Initial: 800-1200 mg/day given in divided doses: 400 mg 2 or 3 times/day; 300 mg 2, 3 or 4 times/day; 200 mg 3 or 4 times/day; total daily dose should not exceed 1200 mg; for patients weighing <60 kg, total daily dose should not exceed 20 mg/kg/day

Monitoring Parameters Monitor CBC, liver enzymes; in patients receiving diuretics, monitor urine output and BUN/serum creatinine

Test Interactions False-positive for urinary bilirubin and ketone ↑ bleeding time

Patient Information Do not crush tablets; take with food, milk, or water; report any signs of blood in stool

Dosage Forms
Capsule (Lodine®): 200 mg, 300 mg
Tablet (Lodine®): 400 mg, 500 mg
Tablet, extended release (Lodine® XL): 400 mg, 500 mg, 600 mg

♦ **Etodolic Acid** see Etodolac on previous page

Etomidate (e TOM i date)
Related Information
Adult ACLS Algorithm, Electrical Conversion on page 1453
U.S. Brand Names Amidate®
Therapeutic Category General Anesthetic
Use Induction of general anesthesia
Pregnancy Risk Factor C
Contraindications Known hypersensitivity to etomidate
Warnings/Precautions Consider exogenous corticosteroid replacement in patients undergoing severe stress
Adverse Reactions
>10%:
Gastrointestinal: Nausea, vomiting
Local: Pain at injection site
Neuromuscular & skeletal: Transient skeletal movements
Ocular: Uncontrolled eye movements
1% to 10%: Hiccups
<1%: Hypertension, hypotension, tachycardia, bradycardia, arrhythmias, hyperventilation, hypoventilation, apnea, laryngospasm
Overdosage/Toxicology
Symptoms of overdose include respiratory arrest, coma
Supportive treatment
Stability Store in at room temperature
Mechanism of Action Ultrashort-acting nonbarbiturate hypnotic used for the induction of anesthesia; chemically, it is a carboxylated imidazole and has been shown to produce a rapid induction of anesthesia with minimal cardiovascular and respiratory effects
Pharmacodynamics/Kinetics
Distribution: V_d: 3.6 to 4.5 L/kg; rapid into body tissues; penetrates the central nervous system rapidly
Protein binding: 76%
Metabolism: Rapid in both liver and blood
Half-life: Terminal: 2.6 hours
Usual Dosage Children >10 years and Adults: I.V.: 0.2-0.6 mg/kg over a period of 30-60 seconds for induction of anesthesia
Dosage Forms Injection: 2 mg/mL (10 mL, 20 mL)

♦ **Etopophos®** see Etoposide Phosphate on page 462
♦ **Etopophos® Injection** see Etoposide on this page

Etoposide (e toe POE side)
Related Information
Cancer Chemotherapy Regimens on page 1263
Extravasation Management of Chemotherapeutic Agents on page 1285
Toxicities of Chemotherapeutic Agents on page 1288
U.S. Brand Names Etopophos® Injection; Toposar® Injection; VePesid® Injection; VePesid® Oral
(Continued)

Etoposide *(Continued)*

Synonyms Epipodophyllotoxin; VP-16; VP-16-213

Therapeutic Category Antineoplastic Agent, Irritant; Antineoplastic Agent, Podophyllotoxin Derivative; Vesicant

Use Treatment of lymphomas, ANLL, lung, testicular, bladder, and prostate carcinoma, hepatoma, rhabdomyosarcoma, uterine carcinoma, neuroblastoma, mycosis fungoides, Kaposi's sarcoma, histiocytosis, gestational trophoblastic disease, Ewing's sarcoma, Wilms' tumor, and brain tumors

Pregnancy Risk Factor D

Contraindications Hypersensitivity to etoposide or any component; **I.T. administration is contraindicated**

Warnings/Precautions The U.S. Food and Drug Administration (FDA) currently recommends that procedures for proper handling and disposal of antineoplastic agents be considered. Severe myelosuppression with resulting infection or bleeding may occur.

Dosage should be adjusted in patients with hepatic or renal impairment

Adverse Reactions

>10%:

Dermatologic: Alopecia (reversible)

Gastrointestinal: Occasional diarrhea and infrequent nausea and vomiting at standard doses; severe mucositis occurs with high (BMT) doses, anorexia

Emetic potential: Moderately low (10% to 30%)

Hematologic: Myelosuppressive: Principal dose-limiting toxicity of VP-16. White blood cell count nadir is 5-15 days after administration and is more frequent than thrombocytopenia. Recovery is usually within 24-28 days and cumulative toxicity has not been noted with VP-16 as a single agent. No difference in toxicity is seen when VP-16 is administered over a 24-hour period or over 2 hours on 5 consecutive days.

WBC: Mild to severe

Platelets: Mild

Onset (days): 10

Nadir (days): granulocytes 7-14 days; platelets 9-16 days

Recovery (days): 21-28

1% to 10%:

Cardiovascular: Hypotension: Related to drug infusion time; may be related to vehicle used in the I.V. preparation (polysorbate 80 plus polyethylene glycol); best to administer the drug over 1 hour

Central nervous system: Unusual fatigue

Gastrointestinal: Stomatitis, diarrhea, abdominal pain, hepatitic dysfunction

<1%: Irritant chemotherapy, tachycardia, unusual tiredness, thrombophlebitis has been reported, toxic hepatitis (with high-dose therapy), reports of flushing or bronchospasm, which did not reoccur in one report if patients were pretreated with corticosteroids and antihistamine, peripheral neuropathy

Overdosage/Toxicology Symptoms of overdose include bone marrow depression, leukopenia, thrombocytopenia, nausea, vomiting

Drug Interactions CYP3A3/4 enzyme substrate

Increased toxicity:

Warfarin may elevate prothrombin time with concurrent use

Methotrexate: Alteration of MTX transport has been found as a slow efflux of MTX and its polyglutamated form out of the cell, leading to intercellular accumulation of MTX

Calcium antagonists: Increases the rate of VP-16-induced DNA damage and cytotoxicity *in vitro*

Carmustine: Reports of frequent hepatic dysfunction with hyperbilirubinemia, ascites, and thrombocytopenia

Cyclosporine: Additive cytotoxic effects on tumor cells

Stability

Store intact vials of injection at room temperature and protected from light; injection solution contains polyethylene glycol vehicle with absolute alcohol; store oral capsules under refrigeration

VP-16 should be further diluted in D_5W or NS for administration; diluted solutions have CONCENTRATION-DEPENDENT stability: More concentrated solutions have shorter stability times

At room temperature in D_5W or NS in polyvinyl chloride, the concentration is stable as follows:

0.2 mg/mL: 96 hours

0.4 mg/mL: 48 hours

0.6 mg/mL: 8 hours

1 mg/mL: 2 hours

2 mg/mL: 1 hour

20 mg/mL (undiluted): 24 hours

Y-site compatible with carboplatin, cytarabine, daunorubicin, mesna

Standard I.V. dilution:

Lower dose regimens (<1 g/dose):

Doses may be diluted in 100-1000 mL of D_5W or NS

If the concentration is less than or equal to 0.6 mg/mL, the bag should be mixed with the appropriate expiration dating

If the concentration is >0.6 mg/mL, the concentration is highly unstable and a syringe of UNDILUTED etoposide accompanied with the appropriate volume of diluent will be sent to the nursing unit to be mixed by the nursing staff just prior to administration

High dose regimens (>1g/dose):

Total dose should be drawn into an empty viaflex container and the appropriate amount of diluent (for a final concentration of 1 mg/mL) will be sent

Use the **2-Channel Pump Method:** Instill all of the etoposide dose into one viaflex container (concentration = 20 mg/mL). Infuse this into one channel (Baxter Flow-Guard 6300 Dual Channel Volumetric Infusion Pump - or any 2-channel infusion pump that does not require a "hard" plastic cassette). Infuse the indicated diluent (ie, D_5W or NS) at a rate of at least 20 times the infusion rate of the etoposide to simulate a 1 mg/mL concentration in the line. The etoposide should be Y-sited into the port most proximal to the patient. A 0.22 micron filter should be attached to the line after the Y-site and before entry into the patient.

Mechanism of Action Inhibits mitotic activity; inhibits cells from entering prophase; inhibits DNA synthesis. Initially thought to be mitotic inhibitors similar to podophyllotoxin, but actually have no effect on microtubule assembly. However, later shown to induce DNA strand breakage and inhibition of topoisomerase II (an enzyme which breaks and repairs DNA); etoposide acts in late S or early G2 phases.

Pharmacodynamics/Kinetics

Absorption: Oral: 32% to 57%

Distribution: Poor penetration across blood-brain barrier, with concentrations in the CSF being <10% that of plasma; Average V_d: 3-36 L/m^2

Protein binding: 94% to 97%

Metabolism: In the liver (with a biphasic decay)

Half-life: Terminal: 4-15 hours; Children: 6-8 hours with normal renal and hepatic function

Time to peak serum concentration: Oral: 1-1.5 hours

Elimination: Both unchanged drug and metabolites are excreted in the urine and a small amount (2% to 16%) excreted in feces; up to 55% of an I.V. dose is excreted unchanged in urine in children

Usual Dosage Refer to individual protocols:

Oral: Twice the I.V. dose rounded to the nearest 50 mg given once daily if total dose ≤400 mg or in divided doses if >400 mg

Children: I.V.: 60-120 mg/m^2/day for 3-5 days every 3-6 weeks

AML:

Remission induction: 150 mg/m^2/day for 2-3 days for 2-3 cycles

Intensification or consolidation: 250 mg/m^2/day for 3 days, courses 2-5

Brain tumor: 150 mg/m^2/day on days 2 and 3 of treatment course

Neuroblastoma: 100 mg/m^2/day over 1 hour on days 1-5 of cycle; repeat cycle every 4 weeks

BMT conditioning regimen used in patients with rhabdomyosarcoma or neuroblastoma: I.V. continuous infusion: 160 mg/m^2/day for 4 days

Conditioning regimen for allogenic BMT: 60 mg/kg/dose as a single dose

Adults:

Small cell lung cancer:

Oral: Twice the I.V. dose rounded to the nearest 50 mg given once daily if tolerated

I.V.: 35 mg/m^2/day for 4 days or 50 mg/m^2/day for 5 days every 3-4 weeks total dose ≤400 mg/day or in divided doses if >400 mg/day

IVPB: 60-100 mg/m^2/day for 3 days (with cisplatin)

CIV: 500 mg/m^2 over 24 hours every 3 weeks

Testicular cancer:

IVPB: 50-100 mg/m^2/day for 5 days repeated every 3-4 weeks

I.V.: 100 mg/m^2 every other day for 3 doses repeated every 3-4 weeks

BMT/relapsed leukemia: I.V.: 2.4-3.5 g/m^2 or 25-70 mg/kg administered over 4-36 hours

Dosing adjustment in renal impairment:

Cl_{cr} 10-50 mL/minute: Administer 75% of normal dose

Cl_{cr} <10 mL minute: Administer 50% of normal dose

Hemodialysis: Supplemental dose is not necessary

Peritoneal dialysis: Supplemental dose is not necessary

CAPD effects: Unknown

CAVH effects: Unknown

Dosing adjustment in hepatic impairment:

Bilirubin 1.5-3 mg/dL or AST 60-180 units: Reduce dose by 50%

Bilirubin 3-5 mg/dL or AST >180 units: Reduce by 75%

Bilirubin >5 mg/dL: Do not administer

Administration

Administer lower doses IVPB over at least 30 minutes to minimize the risk of hypotensive reactions

Administer high-doses (>1 g/dose) via the 2-channel pump method.

An in-line 0.22 micron filter should be attached to ALL etoposide infusions due to the high potential for precipitation

If necessary, the injection may be used for oral administration; mix with orange juice, apple juice, or lemonade to a concentration of 0.4 mg/mL or less, and use within a 3-hour period

Monitoring Parameters CBC with differential, platelet count, and hemoglobin, vital signs (blood pressure), bilirubin, and renal function tests

Patient Information Any signs of infection, easy bruising or bleeding, shortness of breath, or painful or burning urination should be brought to physician's attention. Nausea, vomiting, or hair loss sometimes occurs. The drug may cause permanent sterility and may cause birth defects. Contraceptive measures are recommended during therapy. The (Continued)

Etoposide (Continued)

drug may be excreted in breast milk, therefore, an alternative form of feeding your baby should be used.

Nursing Implications

Extravasation treatment:

Inject 150-900 units of hyaluronidase S.C. clockwise into the infiltrated area using a 25-gauge needle; change the needle with each injection; apply heat immediately for 1 hour, repeat 4 times/day for 3-5 days

Application of cold or hydrocortisone is contraindicated.

If necessary, the injection may be used for oral administration; mix with orange juice, apple juice, or lemonade to a concentration of 0.4 mg/mL or less, and use within a 3-hour period

Dosage Forms

Capsule: 50 mg

Injection: 20 mg/mL (5 mL, 10 mL, 25 mL)

Etoposide Phosphate (e toe POE side FOS fate)

Related Information

Etoposide on page 459

U.S. Brand Names Etopophos®

Therapeutic Category Antineoplastic Agent, Irritant; Antineoplastic Agent, Podophyllotoxin Derivative; Vesicant

Use Treatment of refractory testicular tumors and small cell lung cancer

Pregnancy Risk Factor D

Contraindications Hypersensitivity to etoposide, etoposide phosphate, or any component; **I.T. administration is contraindicated**

Warnings/Precautions The U.S. Food and Drug Administration (FDA) currently recommends that procedures for proper handling and disposal of antineoplastic agents be considered. Severe myelosuppression with resulting infection or bleeding may occur.

Dosage should be adjusted in patients with hepatic or renal impairment

Adverse Reactions Refer to Etoposide on page 459 monograph for details

Overdosage/Toxicology Refer to Etoposide on page 459 monograph for details

Drug Interactions Refer to Etoposide on page 459 monograph for details

Stability

Store intact vials of injection under refrigeration 2°C to 8°C (36°F to 46°F); protect from light

Reconstituted vials with 5 mL or 10 mL SWI, D₅W, NS, bacteriostatic SWI, or bacteriostatic NS to a concentration of 20 mg/mL or 10 mg/mL etoposide (22.7 mg/mL or 11.4 mg/mL etoposide phosphate), respectively. These solutions may be administered without further dilution or may be further diluted to a concentration as low as 0.1 mg/mL etoposide with either D₅W or NS. Solutions are stable in glass or plastic containers for at least 7 days at room temperature 20°C to 25°C (68°F to 77°F) or at least 31 days under refrigeration 2°C to 8°C (36°F to 47°F) for up to 24 hours.

Y-site **incompatible** with: Amphotericin B, cefepime hydrochloride, chlorpromazine hydrochloride, imipenem-cilastin sodium, methylprednisolone sodium phosphate, mitomycin, prochlorperazine edisylate

Y-site **compatible** with: Bleomycin, carboplatin, carmustine, cisplatin, cyclophosphamide, cytarabine, dacarbazine, dactinomycin, daunorubicin, doxorubicin, floxuridine, fludarabine, fluorouracil, idarubicin, ifosfamide, methotrexate, mitoxantrone, paclitaxel, plicamycin, streptozocin, teniposide, thiotepa, vinblastine, vincristine, acyclovir, amikacin, ampicillin, ampicillin sodium-sulbactam sodium, aztreonam, cefazolin, cefoperazone, cefonicid, cefotaxime, cefotetan, cefoxitin, ceftazidime, ceftizoxime, ceftriaxone, cefuroxime, ciprofloxacin, clindamycin, doxycycline, fluconazole, ganciclovir, gentamicin, metronidazole, mezlocillin, minocycline, netilmicin, ofloxacin, piperacillin, piperacillin sodium-tazobactam, ticarcillin, ticarcillin disodium-clavulanate potassium, tobramycin, trimethoprim-sulfamethoxazole, vancomycin, zidovudine, aminophylline, bumetanide, buprenorphine, butorphanol, calcium gluconate, cimetidine, dexamethasone, diphenhydramine, dobutamine, dopamine, droperidol, enalaprilat, famotidine, furosemide, gallium nitrate, granisetron, haloperidol, heparin, hydrocortisone sodium phosphate, hydrocortisone sodium succinate, hydroxyzine, leucovorin, lorazepam, magnesium sulfate, mannitol, meperidine, mesna, metoclopramide, morphine, nalbuphine, ondansetron, potassium chloride, promethazine, ranitidine, sodium bicarbonate

Mechanism of Action Etoposide phosphate is converted in vivo to the active moiety, etoposide, by dephosphorylation. Etoposide inhibits mitotic activity; inhibits cells from entering prophase; inhibits DNA synthesis. Initially thought to be mitotic inhibitors similar to podophyllotoxin, but actually have no effect on microtubule assembly. However, later shown to induce DNA strand breakage and inhibition of topoisomerase II (an enzyme which breaks and repairs DNA); etoposide acts in late S or early G2 phases.

Pharmacodynamics/Kinetics

Distribution: Average V d: 3-36 L/m²; poor penetration across blood-brain barrier, with concentrations in the CSF being <10% that of plasma

Protein binding: 94% to 97%

Metabolism: In the liver (with a biphasic decay)

Half-life: Terminal: 4-15 hours; Children: 6-8 hours with normal renal and hepatic function

Elimination: Both unchanged drug and metabolites are excreted in the urine and a small amount (2% to 16%) excreted in feces; up to 55% of an I.V. dose is excreted unchanged in urine in children

Usual Dosage Refer to individual protocols. Adults:

Small cell lung cancer: I.V. (in combination with other approved chemotherapeutic drugs): **Equivalent doses of etoposide phosphate to an etoposide dosage** range of 35 mg/m^2/day for 4 days to 50 mg/m^2/day for 5 days. Courses are repeated at 3- to 4-week intervals after adequate recovery from any toxicity.

Testicular cancer: I.V. (in combination with other approved chemotherapeutic agents): **Equivalent dose of etoposide phosphate to etoposide dosage** range of 50-100 mg/m^2/day on days 1-5 to 100 mg/m^2/day on days 1, 3, and 5. Courses are repeated at 3- to 4-week intervals after adequate recovery from any toxicity.

Dosage adjustment in renal impairment:

Cl$_{cr}$ 15-50 mL/minute: Administer 75% of normal dose

Cl$_{cr}$ <15 mL minute: Data are not available and further dose reduction should be considered in these patients.

Hemodialysis: Supplemental dose is not necessary

Peritoneal dialysis: Supplemental dose is not necessary

CAPD effects: Unknown

CAVH effects: Unknown

Dosage adjustment in hepatic impairment:

Bilirubin 1.5-3 mg/dL or AST 60-180 units: Reduce dose by 50%

Bilirubin 3-5 mg/dL or AST >180 units: Reduce by 75%

Bilirubin >5 mg/dL: Do not administer

Administration Etoposide phosphate solutions may be administered at infusion rates from 5-210 minutes

Monitoring Parameters CBC with differential, platelet count, and hemoglobin, vital signs (blood pressure), bilirubin, and renal function tests

Patient Information Any signs of infection, easy bruising or bleeding, shortness of breath, or painful or burning urination should be brought to physician's attention. Nausea, vomiting, or hair loss sometimes occur. The drug may cause permanent sterility and may cause birth defects. The drug may be excreted in breast milk, therefore, an alternative form of feeding your baby should be used.

Dosage Forms Powder for injection, lyophilized: 119.3 mg (100 mg base)

♦ **Etrafon**® see Amitriptyline and Perphenazine on page 64

Etretinate (e TRET i nate)

U.S. Brand Names Tegison®

Therapeutic Category Antipsoriatic Agent, Systemic

Use Treatment of severe recalcitrant psoriasis in patients intolerant of or unresponsive to standard therapies

Pregnancy Risk Factor X

Contraindications Pregnancy, known hypersensitivity to etretinate; because of the high likelihood of long lasting teratogenic effects, do not prescribe etretinate for women who are or who are likely to become pregnant while or after using the drug

Warnings/Precautions Not to be used in severe obesity or women of childbearing potential unless woman is capable of complying with effective contraceptive measures; therapy is normally begun on the second or third day of next normal menstrual period; effective contraception must be used for at least 1 month before beginning therapy, during therapy, and for 1 month after discontinuation of therapy; pregnancy test must be performed prior to starting therapy

Adverse Reactions

>10%:

Central nervous system: Fatigue, headache, fever

Dermatologic: Chapped lips, alopecia

Endocrine & metabolic: Hypercholesterolemia, hypertriglyceridemia

Gastrointestinal: Nausea, appetite change, xerostomia, sore tongue

Neuromuscular & skeletal: Hyperostosis, bone pain, arthralgia

Ocular: Eye irritation

Respiratory: Epistaxis

1% to 10%:

Cardiovascular: Edema

Central nervous system: Dizziness, lethargy

Hepatic: Hepatitis

Neuromuscular & skeletal: Myalgia

Ocular: Blurred vision

Otic: Otitis externa

Respiratory: Dyspnea

<1%: Syncope, amnesia, confusion, pseudotumor cerebri, depression, urticaria, mouth ulcers, diarrhea, constipation, flatulence, weight loss, gingival bleeding, gout, dysuria, polyuria, phlebitis, hyperkinesia, hypertonia, photophobia, ear infection, kidney stones, rhinorrhea

Drug Interactions

Increased effect: Milk increases absorption of etretinate

Increased toxicity: Additive toxicity with vitamin A

Mechanism of Action Unknown; related to retinoic acid and retinol (vitamin A)

Pharmacodynamics/Kinetics

Absorption: Oral: Absorbed from small intestine; absorption enhanced when coadministered with whole milk or a high lipid meal (highly lipophilic)

Protein binding: 99%

Metabolism: Undergoes significant first-pass metabolism to form acitretin (active)

Half-life: 4-8 days (with multiple doses)

(Continued)

Etretinate *(Continued)*

Elimination: By metabolism and by excretion in feces of unchanged drug and metabolites

Usual Dosage Adults: Oral: Individualized; Initial: 0.75-1 mg/kg/day in divided doses, increase by 0.25 mg/kg/day at weekly intervals up to 1.5 mg/kg/day; maintenance dose established after 8-10 weeks of therapy 0.5-0.75 mg/kg/day

Patient Information Do not become pregnant while taking this drug, use effective contraceptive measures; if severe persistent nausea, abdominal pain, or vomiting recur stop taking the drug; if persistent or severe headache or visual disturbance occur, stop taking the drug; take with food, do not take vitamin A supplements while taking this drug, may have decreased tolerance to contact lenses before and after therapy

Dosage Forms Capsule: 10 mg, 25 mg

♦ **Euglucon®** *see* Glyburide *on page 540*
♦ **Eulexin®** *see* Flutamide *on page 508*
♦ **Eurax® Topical** *see* Crotamiton *on page 302*
♦ **Eutron®** *see* Methyclothiazide and Pargyline *on page 757*
♦ **Evac-Q-Mag® [OTC]** *see* Magnesium Citrate *on page 704*
♦ **Evalose®** *see* Lactulose *on page 656*
♦ **Everone® Injection** *see* Testosterone *on page 1117*
♦ **Evista®** *see* Raloxifene *on page 1008*
♦ **E-Vitamin® [OTC]** *see* Vitamin E *on page 1225*
♦ **Excedrin® IB [OTC]** *see* Ibuprofen *on page 593*
♦ **Exelderm®** *see* Sulconazole *on page 1090*
♦ **Exidine® Scrub [OTC]** *see* Chlorhexidine Gluconate *on page 240*
♦ **Exna®** *see* Benzthiazide *on page 135*
♦ **Exosurf® Neonatal** *see* Colfosceril Palmitate *on page 294*
♦ **Exsel®** *see* Selenium Sulfide *on page 1055*
♦ **Extendryl® SR** *see* Chlorpheniramine, Phenylephrine, and Methscopolamine *on page 247*
♦ **Extra Action Cough Syrup [OTC]** *see* Guaifenesin and Dextromethorphan *on page 550*
♦ **Extra Strength Adprin-B® [OTC]** *see* Aspirin *on page 102*
♦ **Extra Strength Bayer® Enteric 500 Aspirin [OTC]** *see* Aspirin *on page 102*
♦ **Extra Strength Bayer® Plus [OTC]** *see* Aspirin *on page 102*
♦ **Extravasation Management of Chemotherapeutic Agents** *see page 1285*
♦ **Extravasation Treatment of Other Drugs** *see page 1287*
♦ **Eye-Sed® [OTC]** *see* Zinc Supplements *on page 1239*
♦ **Ezide®** *see* Hydrochlorothiazide *on page 574*
♦ **F₃T** *see* Trifluridine *on page 1182*

Factor IX Complex (Human) (FAK ter nyne KOM pleks HYU man)

U.S. Brand Names AlphaNine® SD; BeneFix™; Hemonyne®; Konÿne® 80; Profilnine® SD; Proplex® T

Synonyms Prothrombin Concentrate

Therapeutic Category Antihemophilic Agent

Use

Control bleeding in patients with factor IX deficiency (hemophilia B or Christmas disease)
NOTE: Factor IX concentrate containing ONLY factor IX is also available and preferable for this indication.
Prevention/control of bleeding in hemophilia A patients with inhibitors to factor VIII
Prevention/control of bleeding in patients with factor VII deficiency
Emergency correction of the coagulopathy of warfarin excess in critical situations.

Pregnancy Risk Factor C

Contraindications Liver disease with signs of intravascular coagulation or fibrinolysis, not for use in factor VII deficiencies, patients undergoing elective surgery

Warnings/Precautions Use with caution in patients with liver dysfunction; prepared from pooled human plasma - the risk of viral transmission is not totally eradicated; monitor patients who receive repeated doses twice daily with PTT and prothrombin time and level of factor being replaced (eg, usually VII or IX); if PT is <10 seconds, this may indicate risk of hypercoagulable complication

Adverse Reactions

1% to 10%:
Central nervous system: Fever, headache, chills
Neuromuscular & skeletal: Tingling
Miscellaneous: Following rapid administration: Transient fever

<1%: Flushing, DIC, thrombosis following high dosages because of presence of activated clotting factors, tightness in chest, somnolence, urticaria, nausea, vomiting, tightness in neck

Overdosage/Toxicology Symptoms of overdose include disseminated intravascular coagulation (DIC)

Drug Interactions Increased toxicity: Do not coadminister with aminocaproic acid may increase risk for thrombosis

Stability When stored at refrigerator temperature, 2°C to 8°C (36°F to 46°F), Coagulation Factor IX is stable for the period indicated by the expiration date on its label. Avoid freezing which may damage container for the diluent.
Stability of parenteral admixture at room temperature (25°C): 24 hours

Standard diluent: Dose in units/bag

Minimum volume: Use complete vial(s) for entire dose

Comments: Infusion rate should be 2 mL/minute

Mechanism of Action Replaces deficient clotting factor including factor X; hemophilia B, or Christmas disease, is an X-linked recessively inherited disorder of blood coagulation characterized by insufficient or abnormal synthesis of the clotting protein factor IX. Factor IX is a vitamin K-dependent coagulation factor which is synthesized in the liver. Factor IX is activated by factor XIa in the intrinsic coagulation pathway. Activated factor IX (IXa), in combination with factor VII:C activates factor X to Xa, resulting ultimately in the conversion of prothrombin to thrombin and the formation of a fibrin clot. The infusion of exogenous factor IX to replace the deficiency present in hemophilia B temporarily restores hemostasis.

Pharmacodynamics/Kinetics Half-life:

VII component: Cleared rapidly from the serum in two phases; initial: 4-6 hours; terminal: 22.5 hours

IX component: 24 hours

Usual Dosage Children and Adults: Dosage is expressed in units of factor IX activity and must be individualized. I.V. only:

Formula for units required to raise blood level %:

Total blood volume (mL blood/kg) = 70 mL/kg (adults), 80 mL/kg (children)

Plasma volume = total blood volume (mL) x [1 - Hct (in decimals)]

For example, for a 70 kg adult with a Hct = 40%: Plasma volume = [70 kg x 70 mL/kg] x [1 - 0.4] = 2940 mL

To calculate number of units needed to increase level to desired range (highly individualized and dependent on patient's condition): Number of units = desired level increase [desired level - actual level] x plasma volume (in mL)

For example, for a 100% level in the above patient who has an actual level of 20%: Number of units needed = [1 (for a 100% level) - 0.2] x 2940 mL = 2352 units

As a general rule, the level of factor IX required for treatment of different conditions is shown in the table.

Level of Factor IX Required for Treatment

	Minor Spontaneous Hemorrhage, Prophylaxis	Major Trauma or Surgery
Desired levels of factor IX for hemostasis	15%-25%	25%-50%
Initial loading dose to achieve desired level	<20-30 units/kg	<75 units/kg
Frequency of dosing	Once; repeated in 24 h if necessary	q18-30h, depending on half-life and measured factor IX levels
Duration of treatment	Once; repeated if necessary	Up to 10 days, depending upon nature of insult

Factor VIII inhibitor patients: 75 units/kg/dose; may be given every 6-12 hours

Anticoagulant overdosage: I.V.: 15 units/kg

Administration Solution should be infused at room temperature

I.V. administration only: Should be infused slowly: Start infusion at a rate of 2-3 mL/minute. If headache, flushing, changes in pulse rate or blood pressure appear, the infusion rate should be decreased. Initially, stop the infusion until the symptoms disappear, then resume the infusion at a slower rate. **Infuse at a rate not exceeding 3 mL/minute.**

Monitoring Parameters Levels of factors being replaced (eg, VII or IX), PT, PTT

Reference Range Average normal factor VII and factor IX levels are 50% to 150%; patients with severe hemophilia will have levels <1%, often undetectable. Moderate forms of the disease have levels of 1% to 10% while some mild cases may have 11% to 49% of normal factor IX.

Maintain factor IX plasma level at least 20% until hemostasis achieved after acute joint or muscle bleeding

In preparation for and following surgery:

Level to prevent spontaneous hemorrhage: 5%

Minimum level for hemostasis following trauma and surgery: 30% to 50%

Severe hemorrhage: >60%

Major surgery: >60% prior to procedure, 30% to 50% for several days after surgery, and >20% for 7-10 days thereafter

Patient Information Early signs of hypersensitivity reactions including hives, generalized urticaria, tightness of the chest, wheezing, hypotension, and anaphylaxis indicate discontinuation of use of the concentrate and physician should be contacted if these symptoms occur

Dosage Forms Injection:

AlphaNine® SD: Single dose vial

BeneFix™: 250 units, 500 units, 1000 units

Konÿne® 80: 20 mL, 40 mL

Hemonyne®: 20 mL, 40 mL

Profilnine® SD: Single dose vial

Proplex® T: 30 mL vial

♦ **Factor IX Purified** see Factor IX, Purified (Human) *on next page*

Factor IX, Purified (Human) (FAK ter nyne, PURE eh fide HYU man)

U.S. Brand Names Mononine®

Synonyms Factor IX Purified; Monoclonal Antibody Purified

Therapeutic Category Antihemophilic Agent

Use

Control bleeding in patients with factor IX deficiency (hemophilia B or Christmas disease)

Mononine® contains **nondetectable levels of factors II, VII, and X** (<0.0025 units per factor IX unit using standard coagulation assays) and is, therefore, **NOT INDICATED** for replacement therapy of any of these clotting factors

Mononine® is also **NOT INDICATED** in the treatment or reversal of coumarin-induced anticoagulation or in a hemorrhagic state caused by hepatitis-induced lack of production of liver dependent coagulation factors.

Pregnancy Risk Factor C

Contraindications Known hypersensitivity to mouse protein

Warnings/Precautions Use with caution in patients with liver dysfunction; prepared from pooled human plasma - the risk of viral transmission is not totally eradicated; monitor patients who receive repeated doses twice daily with PTT and level of factor being replaced (eg, IX). Observe closely for signs or symptoms of intravascular coagulation or thrombosis. Caution should be exercised when administering to patients with liver disease, postoperatively, neonates, or patients at risk of thromboembolic phenomena or disseminated intravascular coagulation because of the potential risk of thromboembolic complications.

Adverse Reactions

1% to 10%:

Central nervous system: Fever, headache, chills

Neuromuscular & skeletal: Tingling

Miscellaneous: Following rapid administration: Transient fever

<1%: Flushing, DIC, thrombosis following high dosages because of presence of activated clotting factors, tightness in chest, somnolence, urticaria, nausea, vomiting, tightness in neck

Overdosage/Toxicology Symptoms of overdose include disseminated intravascular coagulation (DIC)

Drug Interactions Increased toxicity: Do not coadminister with aminocaproic acid may increase the risk for thrombosis

Stability When stored at refrigerator temperature, 2°C to 8°C (36°F to 46°F), coagulation factor IX is stable for the period indicated by the expiration date on its label. Avoid freezing which may damage container for the diluent.

Stability of parenteral admixture at room temperature (25°C): 24 hours

Standard diluent: Dose in units/bag

Minimum volume: Use complete vial(s) for entire dose

Comments: Infusion rate should be up to 225 units/minute (2 mL/minute)

Mechanism of Action Replaces deficient clotting factor IX; concentrate of factor IX; hemophilia B, or Christmas disease, is an X-linked inherited disorder of blood coagulation characterized by insufficient or abnormal synthesis of the clotting protein factor IX. Factor IX is a vitamin K-dependent coagulation factor which is synthesized in the liver. Factor IX is activated by factor XIa in the intrinsic coagulation pathway. Activated factor IX (IXa), in combination with factor VII:C activates factor X to Xa, resulting ultimately in the conversion of prothrombin to thrombin and the formation of a fibrin clot. The infusion of exogenous factor IX to replace the deficiency present in hemophilia B temporarily restores hemostasis. Depending upon the patient's level of biologically active factor IX, clinical symptoms range from moderate skin bruising or excessive hemorrhage after trauma or surgery to spontaneous hemorrhage into joints, muscles, or internal organs including the brain. Severe or recurring hemorrhages can produce death, organ dysfunction, or orthopedic deformity.

Pharmacodynamics/Kinetics Half-life for IX component: 23-31 hours

Usual Dosage Children and Adults: Dosage is expressed in units of factor IX activity and must be individualized. I.V. only:

Formula for units required to raise blood level %:

Number of Factor IX Units Required = body weight (in kg) x desired Factor IX level increase (% normal) x 1 unit/kg

For example, for a 100% level a patient who has an actual level of 20%: Number of Factor IX Units needed = 70 kg x 80% x 1 Unit/kg = 5,600 Units

As a general rule, the level of factor IX required for treatment of different conditions is shown in the table.

Level of Factor IX Required for Treatment

	Minor Spontaneous Hemorrhage, Prophylaxis	Major Trauma or Surgery
Desired levels of factor IX for hemostasis	15%-25%	25%-50%
Initial loading dose to achieve desired level	<20-30 units/kg	<75 units/kg
Frequency of dosing	Once; repeated in 24 h if necessary	q18-30h, depending on half-life and measured factor IX levels
Duration of treatment	Once; repeated if necessary	Up to 10 days, depending upon nature of insult

Administration
Solution should be infused at room temperature

I.V. administration only:

Should be infused **slowly**: The rate of administration should be determined by the response and comfort of the patient; intravenous dosage administration rates of up to 225 units/minute (~2 mL/minute) have been regularly tolerated without incident.

Infuse at a rate not exceeding 2 mL/minute

Monitoring Parameters Levels of factors being replaced (eg, IX), PTT

Reference Range Average normal factor IX levels are 50% to 150%; patients with severe hemophilia will have levels <1%, often undetectable. Moderate forms of the disease have levels of 1% to 10% while some mild cases may have 11% to 49% of normal factor IX.

Maintain factor IX plasma level at least 20% until hemostasis achieved after acute joint or muscle bleeding

In preparation for and following surgery:

Level to prevent spontaneous hemorrhage: 5%

Minimum level for hemostasis following trauma and surgery: 30% to 50%

Severe hemorrhage: >60%

Major surgery: ≥50% prior to procedure, 30% to 50% for several days after surgery, and >20% for 10-14 days thereafter

Patient Information Early signs of hypersensitivity reactions including hives, generalized urticaria, tightness of the chest, wheezing, hypotension, and anaphylaxis indicate discontinuation of use of the concentrate and physician should be contacted if these symptoms occur

Dosage Forms Factor IX units listed per vial and per lot to lot variation of factor IX

Injection: 250 units, 500 units, 1000 units

Factor VIIa, Recombinant (FAK ter SE ven two aye ree KOM be nant)

U.S. Brand Names Novo-Seven®

Synonyms Coagulation Factor VIIa; rFVIIa

Therapeutic Category Antihemophilic Agent; Blood Product Derivative

Use Treatment of bleeding episodes in patients with hemophilia A or B when inhibitors to Factor VIII or Factor IX are present

Pregnancy Risk Factor C

Contraindications Known hypersensitivity to Factor VII or any component of the product, or known hypersensitivity to mouse, hamster, or bovine proteins

Warnings/Precautions Patients should be monitored for signs and symptoms of activation of the coagulation system or thrombosis. Thrombotic events may be increased in patients with disseminated intravascular coagulation (DIC), advanced atherosclerotic disease, sepsis or crush injury. Decreased dosage or discontinuation is warranted in confirmed DIC. Efficacy with prolonged infusions and data evaluating this agent's long-term adverse effects are limited.

Adverse Reactions
1% to 10%:

Cardiovascular: Hypertension

Hematologic: Hemorrhage, decreased plasma fibrinogen

Musculoskeletal: Hemarthrosis

<1%: Allergic reactions, pruritus, purpura, rash, injection-site reactions, vomiting, headache, hypotension, bradycardia, edema, arthrosis, coagulation disorder, increased fibrinolysis, disseminate intravascular coagulation (DIC), decreased prothrombin, pneumonia, abnormal renal function.

Overdosage/Toxicology Experience with overdose in humans is limited; an increased risk of thrombotic events may occur in overdosage; treatment is symptomatic and supportive

Stability Store under refrigeration (2°C to 8°C/36°F to 46°F); reconstituted solutions may be stored at room temperature or under refrigeration, but must be infused within 3 hours of reconstitution

Mechanism of Action Recombinant Factor VIIa, a vitamin K-dependent glycoprotein, promotes hemostasis by activating the extrinsic pathway of the coagulation cascade. It replaces deficient activated coagulation Factor VII, which complexes with tissue factor and may activate coagulation Factor X to Xa and Factor IX to IXa. When complexed with other factors, coagulation Factor Xa converts prothrombin to thrombin, a key step in the formation of a fibrin-platelet hemostatic plug

Pharmacodynamics/Kinetics
Distribution: V_d: 103 mL/kg (78-139)

Half-life: 2.3 hours (1.7-2.7)

Clearance: 33 mL/kg/hour (27-49)

Usual Dosage Children and Adults: I.V. administration only: 90 mcg/kg every 2 hours until hemostasis is achieved or until the treatment is judged ineffective. The dose and interval may be adjusted based upon the severity of bleeding and the degree of hemostasis achieved. The duration of therapy following hemostasis has not been fully established; for patients experiencing severe bleeds, dosing should be continued at 3-6 hour intervals after hemostasis has been achieved and the duration of dosing should be minimized.

In clinical trials, dosages have ranged from 35-120 mcg/kg and a decision on the final therapeutic dosages was reached within 8 hours in the majority of patients

Administration I.V. administration only; reconstitute only with the specified volume of sterile water for injection, USP; administer within 3 hours after reconstitution

(Continued)

Factor VIIa, Recombinant *(Continued)*

Monitoring Parameters Monitor for evidence of hemostasis; although the prothrombin time, aPTT, and factor VII clotting activity have no correlation with achieving hemostasis, these parameters may be useful as adjunct tests to evaluate efficacy and guide dose or interval adjustments

Dosage Forms Powder for injection: 1.2 mg, 2.4 mg, 4.8 mg

♦ **Factor VIII** *see* Antihemophilic Factor (Human) *on page 88*

♦ **Factrel®** *see* Gonadorelin *on page 544*

Famciclovir *(fam SYE kloe veer)*

U.S. Brand Names Famvir™

Therapeutic Category Antiviral Agent, Oral

Use Management of acute herpes zoster (shingles) and recurrent episodes of genital herpes; treatment of recurrent herpes simplex in immunocompetent patients

Pregnancy Risk Factor B

Pregnancy/Breast-Feeding Implications

Clinical effects on the fetus: Use only if the benefit to the patient clearly exceeds the potential risk to the fetus

Breast-feeding/lactation: Due to potential for excretion of famciclovir in breast milk and for its associated tumorigenicity, discontinue nursing or discontinue the drug during lactation

Contraindications Hypersensitivity to famciclovir

Warnings/Precautions Has not been studied in immunocompromised patients or patients with ophthalmic or disseminated zoster; dosage adjustment is required in patients with renal insufficiency (Cl_{cr} <60 mL/minute) and in patients with noncompensated hepatic disease; safety and efficacy have not been established in children <18 years of age; animal studies indicated increases in incidence of carcinomas, mutagenic changes, and decreases in fertility with extremely large doses

Adverse Reactions

1% to 10%:

Central nervous system: Fatigue (4% to 6%), fever (1% to 3%), dizziness (3% to 5%), somnolence (1% to 2%), headache

Dermatologic: Pruritus (1% to 4%)

Gastrointestinal: Diarrhea (4% to 8%), vomiting (1% to 5%), constipation (1% to 5%), anorexia (1% to 3%), abdominal pain (1% to 4%), nausea

Neuromuscular & skeletal: Paresthesia (1% to 3%)

Respiratory: Sinusitis/pharyngitis (2%)

<1%: Rigors, arthralgia, upper respiratory infection

Overdosage/Toxicology Supportive and symptomatic care is recommended; hemodialysis may enhance elimination

Drug Interactions Increased effect/toxicity:

Cimetidine: Penciclovir AUC may increase due to impaired metabolism

Digoxin: C_{max} of digoxin increases by ~19%

Probenecid: Penciclovir serum levels significantly increase

Theophylline: Penciclovir AUC/C_{max} may increase and renal clearance decrease, although not clinically significant

Mechanism of Action After undergoing rapid biotransformation to the active compound, penciclovir, famciclovir is phosphorylated by viral thymidine kinase in HSV-1, HSV-2, and VZV-infected cells to a monophosphate form; this is then converted to penciclovir triphosphate and competes with deoxyguanosine triphosphate to inhibit HSV-2 polymerase (ie, herpes viral DNA synthesis/replication is selectively inhibited)

Pharmacodynamics/Kinetics

Absorption: Food decreases the maximum peak concentration and delays the time to peak; AUC remains the same

Distribution: V_{dss}: 0.98-1.08 L/kg

Protein binding: 20%

Metabolism: Rapidly deacetylated and oxidized to penciclovir (not by cytochrome P-450)

Bioavailability: 77%; T_{max}: 0.9 hours

Half-life: Penciclovir: 2-3 hours (10, 20, and 7 hours in HSV-1, HSV-2, and VZV-infected cells); linearly decreased with reductions in renal failure

Elimination: >90% of penciclovir is eliminated unchanged in urine; C_{max} and T_{max} are decreased and prolonged, respectively in patients with noncompensated hepatic impairment

Usual Dosage Adults: Oral:

Acute herpes zoster: 500 mg every 8 hours for 7 days

Recurrent herpes simplex in immunocompetent patients: 125 mg twice daily for 5 days

Genital herpes:

Recurrent episodes: 125 mg twice daily for 5 days

Prophylaxis: 250 mg twice daily

Dosing interval in renal impairment:

Cl_{cr} 40-59 mL/minute: Administer 500 mg every 12 hours

Cl_{cr} 20-39 mL/minute: Administer 500 mg every 24 hours

Cl_{cr} <20 mL/minute: Unknown

Patient Information Initiate therapy as soon as herpes zoster is diagnosed; may take medication with food or on an empty stomach

Additional Information Most effective if therapy is initiated within 72 hours of initial lesion

Dosage Forms Tablet: 125 mg, 250 mg, 500 mg

Famotidine (fa MOE ti deen)

U.S. Brand Names Pepcid®; Pepcid® AC Acid Controller [OTC]

Canadian Brand Names Apo®-Famotidine; Novo-Famotidine; Nu-Famotidine

Therapeutic Category Antihistamine, H_2 Blocker; Histamine H_2 Antagonist

Use

Pepcid®: Therapy and treatment of duodenal ulcer, gastric ulcer, control gastric pH in critically ill patients, symptomatic relief in gastritis, gastroesophageal reflux, active benign ulcer, and pathological hypersecretory conditions

Pepcid® AC Acid Controller: Relieves heartburn, acid indigestion and sour stomach

Pregnancy Risk Factor B

Pregnancy/Breast-Feeding Implications

Clinical effects on the fetus: Crosses the placenta. No data on effects on the fetus (insufficient data).

Breast-feeding/lactation: Crosses into breast milk. American Academy of Pediatrics has NO RECOMMENDATIONS.

Contraindications Hypersensitivity to famotidine or other H_2-antagonists

Warnings/Precautions Modify dose in patients with renal impairment

Adverse Reactions

1% to 10%:

Central nervous system: Dizziness, headache

Gastrointestinal: Constipation, diarrhea

<1%: Bradycardia, tachycardia, palpitations, hypertension, fever, fatigue, seizures, insomnia, drowsiness, acne, pruritus, urticaria, dry skin, abdominal discomfort, flatulence, belching, anorexia, agranulocytosis, neutropenia, thrombocytopenia, increased AST/ALT, paresthesia, weakness, increased BUN/creatinine, proteinuria, bronchospasm, allergic reaction

Overdosage/Toxicology

Symptoms of overdose include hypotension, tachycardia, vomiting, drowsiness

Treatment is primarily symptomatic and supportive

Drug Interactions Decreased effect of ketoconazole, itraconazole

Stability Reconstituted I.V. solution is stable for 48 hours at room temperature; I.V. infusion in NS or D_5W solution is stable for 48 hours at room temperature; reconstituted oral solution is stable for 30 days at room temperature

Mechanism of Action Competitive inhibition of histamine at H_2 receptors of the gastric parietal cells, which inhibits gastric acid secretion

Pharmacodynamics/Kinetics

Onset of GI effect: Oral: Within 1 hour

Duration: 10-12 hours

Protein binding: 15% to 20%

Bioavailability: Oral: 40% to 50%

Half-life: 2.5-3.5 hours; increases with renal impairment, oliguric patients: 20 hours

Time to peak serum concentration: Oral: Within 1-3 hours

Elimination: In urine as unchanged drug

Usual Dosage

Children: Oral, I.V.: Doses of 1-2 mg/kg/day have been used; maximum dose: 40 mg

Adults:

Oral:

Duodenal ulcer, gastric ulcer: 40 mg/day at bedtime for 4-8 weeks

Hypersecretory conditions: Initial: 20 mg every 6 hours, may increase up to 160 mg every 6 hours

GERD: 20 mg twice daily for 6 weeks

I.V.: 20 mg every 12 hours

Dosing adjustment in renal impairment:

Cl_{cr} <10 mL/minute: Administer every 24 hours or 50% of dose

Administration Administer over 15-30 minutes; may be given undiluted I.V. push

Dosage Forms

Infusion, premixed in NS: 20 mg (50 mL)

Injection: 10 mg/mL (2 mL, 4 mL)

Powder for oral suspension (cherry-banana-mint flavor): 40 mg/5 mL (50 mL)

Tablet, film coated: 20 mg, 40 mg

Tablet, disintegrating: 20 mg, 40 mg

Pepcid® AC Acid Controller: 10 mg

◆ **Famvir™** see Famciclovir on previous page

◆ **Fareston®** see Toremifene on page 1163

◆ **Fastin®** see Phentermine on page 915

Fat Emulsion (fat e MUL shun)

U.S. Brand Names Intralipid®; Liposyn®; Nutrilipid®; Soyacal®

Synonyms Intravenous Fat Emulsion

Therapeutic Category Caloric Agent

Use Source of calories and essential fatty acids for patients requiring parenteral nutrition of extended duration

Pregnancy Risk Factor B/C

Contraindications Pathologic hyperlipidemia, lipoid nephrosis, known hypersensitivity to fat emulsion and severe egg or legume (soybean) allergies, pancreatitis with hyperlipemia

(Continued)

Fat Emulsion *(Continued)*

Warnings/Precautions Use caution in patients with severe liver damage, pulmonary disease, anemia, or blood coagulation disorder; use with caution in jaundiced, premature, and low birth weight children

Adverse Reactions
>10%: Local: Thrombophlebitis
1% to 10%: Endocrine & metabolic: Hyperlipemia
<1%: Cyanosis, flushing, chest pain, nausea, vomiting, diarrhea, hepatomegaly, dyspnea, sepsis

Overdosage/Toxicology
Too rapid administration results in fluid or fat overloading to cause dilution of serum electrolytes, overhydration, pulmonary edema, impaired pulmonary diffusion capacity, metabolic acidosis
Treatment is supportive

Stability May be stored at room temperature; do not store partly used bottles for later use; do not use if emulsion appears to be oiling out

Mechanism of Action Essential for normal structure and function of cell membranes

Pharmacodynamics/Kinetics
Metabolism: Undergoes lipolysis to free fatty acids, which are utilized by reticuloendothelial cells
Half-life: 0.5-1 hour

Usual Dosage Fat emulsion should not exceed 60% of the total daily calories
Premature Infants: Initial dose: 0.25-0.5 g/kg/day, increase by 0.25-0.5 g/kg/day to a maximum of 3 g/kg/day depending on needs/nutritional goals; limit to 1 g/kg/day if on phototherapy; maximum rate of infusion: 0.15 g/kg/hour (0.75 mL/kg/hour of 20% solution)
Infants and Children: Initial dose: 0.5-1 g/kg/day, increase by 0.5 g/kg/day to a maximum of 3 g/kg/day depending on needs/nutritional goals; maximum rate of infusion: 0.25 g/kg/hour (1.25 mL/kg/hour of 20% solution)
Adolescents and Adults: Initial dose: 1 g/kg/day, increase by 0.5-1 g/kg/day to a maximum of 2.5 g/kg/day of 10% and 3 g/kg/day of 20% depending on needs/nutritional goals; maximum rate of infusion: 0.25 g/kg/hour (1.25 mL/kg/hour of 20% solution); do not exceed 50 mL/hour (20%) or 100 mL/hour (10%)
Prevention of essential fatty acid deficiency (8% to 10% of total caloric intake): 0.5-1 g/kg/24 hours
Children: 5-10 mL/kg/day at 0.1 mL/minute then up to 100 mL/hour
Adults: 500 mL (10%) twice weekly at rate of 1 mL/minute for 30 minutes, then increase to 42 mL/hour (500 mL over 12 hours)
Note: At the onset of therapy, the patient should be observed for any immediate allergic reactions such as dyspnea, cyanosis, and fever; slower initial rates of infusion may be used for the first 10-15 minutes of the infusion (eg, 0.1 mL/minute of 10% or 0.05 mL/minute of 20% solution)

Administration May be simultaneously infused with amino acid dextrose mixtures by means of Y-connector located near infusion site. The 10% isotonic solution which has 1.1 cal/mL (10%) and may be administered peripherally; the 20% (2 cal/mL) is not recommended for use in low birth weight infants.

Monitoring Parameters Serum triglycerides; before initiation of therapy and at least weekly during therapy

Dosage Forms Injection: 10% [100 mg/mL] (100 mL, 250 mL, 500 mL); 20% [200 mg/mL] (100 mL, 250 mL, 500 mL)

♦ **5-FC** *see* Flucytosine *on page 489*

♦ **Febrile Seizures** *see page 1469*

♦ **Feiba VH Immuno®** *see* Anti-inhibitor Coagulant Complex *on page 90*

♦ **Feldene®** *see* Piroxicam *on page 935*

Felodipine *(fe LOE di peen)*

Related Information
Calcium Channel Blockers Comparison *on page 1315*

U.S. Brand Names Plendil®

Canadian Brand Names Renedil®

Therapeutic Category Antihypertensive Agent; Calcium Channel Blocker

Use Treatment of hypertension, congestive heart failure

Pregnancy Risk Factor C

Contraindications Hypersensitivity to felodipine or any component or other calcium channel blocker; severe hypotension or second and third degree heart block

Warnings/Precautions Use with caution and titrate dosages for patients with impaired renal or hepatic function; use caution when treating patients with congestive heart failure, sick-sinus syndrome, severe left ventricular dysfunction, hypertrophic cardiomyopathy (especially obstructive), concomitant therapy with beta-blockers or digoxin, edema, or increased intracranial pressure with cranial tumors; do not abruptly withdraw (may cause chest pain); elderly may experience hypotension and constipation more readily.

Adverse Reactions
>10%:
Cardiovascular: Peripheral edema (22%)
Central nervous system: Headache (18%)
1% to 10%:
Cardiovascular: Chest pain, palpitations (2%), flushing (6%)

Central nervous system: Dizziness/lightheadedness (6%)

Dermatologic: Rash (1% to 2%)

Gastrointestinal: Constipation/diarrhea (1% to 2%), nausea (2%), abdominal pain (1% to 2%)

Neuromuscular & skeletal: Weakness (5%), paresthesia (2.5%)

Respiratory: Cough (3%), upper respiratory infection (5.5%)

<1%: Hypotension, arrhythmia, tachycardia, syncope, A-V block, myocardial infarction, angina, mental depression, nervousness, somnolence, insomnia, pruritus, sexual disorder, gingival hyperplasia, xerostomia, vomiting, flatulence, micturition disorder, anemia, marked elevations in LFTs, blurred vision, shortness of breath, rhinitis, epistaxis

Overdosage/Toxicology The primary cardiac symptoms of calcium blocker overdose include hypotension and bradycardia. The hypotension is caused by peripheral vasodilation, myocardial depression, and bradycardia. Bradycardia results from sinus bradycardia, second- or third-degree atrioventricular block, or sinus arrest with junctional rhythm. Intraventricular conduction is usually not affected so QRS duration is normal (verapamil does prolong the P-R interval and bepridil prolongs the Q-T and may cause ventricular arrhythmias, including torsade de pointes).

The noncardiac symptoms include confusion, stupor, nausea, vomiting, metabolic acidosis and hyperglycemia. Following initial gastric decontamination, if possible, repeated calcium administration may promptly reverse the depressed cardiac contractility (but not sinus node depression or peripheral vasodilation); glucagon, epinephrine, and amrinone may treat refractory hypotension; glucagon and epinephrine also increase the heart rate (outside the U.S., 4-aminopyridine may be available as an antidote); dialysis and hemoperfusion are not effective in enhancing elimination although repeat-dose activated charcoal may serve as an adjunct with sustained-release preparations.

In a few reported cases, overdose with calcium channel blockers has been associated with hypotension and bradycardia, initially refractory to atropine but becoming more responsive to this agent when larger doses (approaching 1 g/hour for more than 24 hours) of calcium chloride was administered.

Drug Interactions CYP3A3/4 enzyme substrate

Decreased effect:

Felodipine and carbamazepine may decrease felodipine effect

Felodipine and theophylline may decrease pharmacologic actions of theophylline

Increased toxicity/effect/levels:

Felodipine and metoprolol may increase cardiac depressant effects on A-V conduction

Felodipine and erythromycin inhibits felodipine (and other dihydropyridine calcium antagonist) metabolism resulting in a twofold increase in levels and consequent toxicity

Mechanism of Action Inhibits calcium ions from entering the "slow channels" or select voltage-sensitive areas of vascular smooth muscle and myocardium during depolarization, producing a relaxation of coronary vascular smooth muscle and coronary vasodilation; increases myocardial oxygen delivery in patients with vasospastic angina

Pharmacodynamics/Kinetics

Onset of effect: 2-5 hours

Duration: 16-24 hours

Absorption: 100%; absolute: 20% due to first-pass effect

Protein binding: >99%

Metabolism: >99% in liver

Half-life: 11-16 hours

Elimination: In urine as metabolites

Usual Dosage

Adults: Oral: 2.5-10 mg once daily; usual initial dose: 5 mg; increase by 5 mg at 2-week intervals, as needed; maximum: 10 mg

Elderly: Begin with 2.5 mg/day

Dosing adjustment/comments in hepatic impairment: Begin with 2.5 mg/day; do not use doses >10 mg/day

Dietary Considerations Should be taken without food; the bioavailability of felodipine is influenced by the presence of food and has been shown to increase more than twofold when taken with concentrated grapefruit juice

Patient Information Do not crush or chew tablets; do not discontinue abruptly; report any dizziness, shortness of breath, palpitations or edema occurs

Additional Information Although there is some initial data which may show increased risk of myocardial infarction following treatment of hypertension with calcium antagonists, controlled trials (eg, ALL-HAT) are ongoing to examine the long-term effects of not only calcium antagonists but other antihypertensives in preventing heart disease. Until these studies are completed, patients taking calcium antagonists should be encouraged to continue with prescribed antihypertensive regimes, although a switch from high-dose, short-acting agents to sustained release products may be warranted.

Dosage Forms Tablet, extended release: 2.5 mg, 5 mg, 10 mg

Fenofibrate (fen oh FYE brate)

U.S. Brand Names TriCor™

Canadian Brand Names Apo®-Fenofibrate

Synonyms Procetofene; Proctofene

Therapeutic Category Antilipemic Agent

Use Adjunct to dietary therapy for the treatment of adults with very high elevations of serum triglyceride levels (types IV and V hyperlipidemia) who are at risk of pancreatitis and who do not respond adequately to a determined dietary effort; its efficacy can be enhanced by combination with other hypolipidemic agents that have a different mechanism of action; safety and efficacy may be greater than that of clofibrate

Pregnancy Risk Factor C

Pregnancy/Breast-Feeding Implications Although teratogenicity and mutagenicity tests in animals have been negative, significant risk has been identified with clofibrate, an agent similar in action to fenofibrate. Use should be avoided, if possible, in pregnant women since the neonatal glucuronide conjugation pathways are immature.

Warnings/Precautions The hypoprothrombinemic effect of anticoagulants is significantly increased with concomitant fenofibrate administration; use with caution in patients with severe renal dysfunction

Adverse Reactions

>10%: Gastrointestinal: Nausea, gastric discomfort

1% to 10%:

Dermatologic: Skin reactions

Gastrointestinal: Constipation, diarrhea

<1%: Dizziness, headache, fatigue, insomnia, transient increases in LFTs, arthralgia, myalgia

Overdosage/Toxicology Symptoms of overdose include nausea, vomiting, diarrhea, and GI distress; treatment is supportive

Drug Interactions Increased effect/toxicity: Increased hypolipidemic effect when used with cholestyramine or colestipol; increased hypoprothrombinemic effect when used with warfarin

Mechanism of Action Fenofibric acid is believed to increase VLDL catabolism by enhancing the synthesis of lipoprotein lipase; as a result of a decrease in VLDL levels, total plasma triglycerides are reduced by 30% to 60%; modest increase in HDL occurs in some hypertriglyceridemic patients

Pharmacodynamics/Kinetics

Absorption: 60% to 90% when given with meals

Distribution: Distributes well to most tissues except brain or eye; concentrates in liver, kidneys, and gut

Protein binding: >99%

Metabolism: Metabolized to its active form, fenofibric acid, by tissue and plasma esterases; then undergoes inactivation by glucuronidation in the liver or kidneys

Half-life, elimination: 21 hours (30 hours in elderly, 44-54 hours in hepatic impairment)

Time to peak: 4-6 hours

Elimination: 60% to 93% excreted in metabolized form; 5% to 25% excreted fecally; hemodialysis has no effect on removal of fenofibric acid from the plasma

Usual Dosage Adults: Oral: Initial: 67 mg/day, up to 3 capsules (201 mg); requires 6-8 weeks of therapy to determine efficacy

Dosing adjustment/comments in renal impairment: Decrease dose or increase dosing interval for patients with renal failure

Monitoring Parameters Total serum cholesterol and triglyceride concentration and CLDL, LDL, and HDL levels should be measured periodically; if only marginal changes are noted in 6-8 weeks, the drug should be discontinued; serum transaminases should be measured every 3 months; if ALT values increase >100 units/L, therapy should be discontinued. Monitor LFTs prior to initiation, at 6 and 12 weeks after initiation of first dose, then periodically thereafter.

Patient Information Take with food. Do not change dosage without consulting prescriber. Maintain diet and exercise program as prescribed. You may experience mild GI disturbances (eg, gas, diarrhea, constipation, nausea); inform prescriber if these are severe. Report skin rash or irritation, insomnia, unusual muscle pain or tremors, or persistent dizziness. Inform prescriber if you are or intend to be pregnant; consult prescriber if breast-feeding.

Dosage Forms Capsule: 67 mg

Fenoldopam (fe NOL doe pam)

U.S. Brand Names Corlopam®

Synonyms Fenoldopam Mesylate; SKF 82526

Therapeutic Category Antihypertensive Agent

Use Treatment of severe hypertension particularly I.V. and in patients with renal compromise; potential use for congestive heart failure

Pregnancy Risk Factor B

Contraindications Previous hypersensitive reaction to fenoldopam

Warnings/Precautions Use with caution in patients with cirrhosis, portal hypertension (due to possible increases in portal venous pressure), unstable angina, or glaucoma

Adverse Reactions Percentage unknown: Hypotension, edema, tachycardia, facial flushing, asymptomatic T-wave flattening, flutter (atrial), fibrillation (atrial), chest pain, angina in patients with history of unstable angina, headache, dizziness, nausea, vomiting, diarrhea, xerostomia, intraocular pressure (increased), blurred vision, increases in portal pressure in cirrhotic patients

Drug Interactions

Increased effect: Concurrent acetaminophen may increase fenoldopam levels (30% to 70%)

Decreased effect: Administration with food may result in a decreased peak level and time to peak may be delayed; overall, extent of absorption is unaffected

Stability Store ampuls at room temperature; diluted solution is stable for ≤24 hours; discard any diluted solution that is not used after 24 hours

Mechanism of Action A selective postsynaptic dopamine agonist (D_1-receptors) which exerts hypotensive effects by decreasing peripheral vasculature resistance with increased renal blood flow, diuresis, and natriuresis; 6 times as potent as dopamine in producing renal vasodilitation; has minimal adrenergic effects

Pharmacodynamics/Kinetics

Onset of action: I.V.: 10 minutes

Duration: Oral: 2-4 hours; I.V.: 1 hour

Absorption: Oral: Good, however, undergoes extensive first-pass metabolism; peak serum levels at 1 hour after oral doses

Distribution: V_d: 0.6 L/kg

Half-life: I.V.: 9.8 minutes

Metabolism: Hepatic to multiple metabolites; the 8-sulfate metabolite may have some activity

Elimination: Renal (80%), fecal (20%)

Usual Dosage I.V.: Severe hypertension: Initial: 0.1 mcg/kg/minute; may be increased in increments of 0.05-0.2 mcg/kg/minute until target blood pressure is achieved; average rate: 0.25-0.5 mcg/kg/minute; usual length of treatment is 1-6 hours with tapering of 12% every 15-30 minutes

Dosing adjustment in renal impairment: None required

Dosing adjustment in hepatic impairment: None published

Monitoring Parameters Blood pressure, heart rate, EKG, renal/hepatic function tests

Reference Range Mean plasma fenoldopam levels after a 2 hour infusion (at 0.5 µg/kg/minute) and a 100 mg dose is approximately 13 ng/mL and 50 ng/mL

Additional Information Since the drug has the ability to induce natriuresis, diuresis, and increased creatinine clearance, it may have an advantage over nitroprusside, especially in patients with severe renal insufficiency and in volume overloaded patients (ie, CHF)

Dosage Forms Injection: 10 mg/mL (5 mL)

♦ **Fenoldopam Mesylate** see Fenoldopam on previous page

Fenoprofen (fen oh PROE fen)

Related Information

Nonsteroidal Anti-Inflammatory Agents Comparison on page 1335

U.S. Brand Names Nalfon®

Synonyms Fenoprofen Calcium

Therapeutic Category Analgesic, Nonsteroidal Anti-inflammatory Drug; Anti-inflammatory Agent; Nonsteroidal Anti-inflammatory Drug (NSAID), Oral

Use Symptomatic treatment of acute and chronic rheumatoid arthritis and osteoarthritis; relief of mild to moderate pain

Pregnancy Risk Factor B (D if used in the 3rd trimester or near delivery)

Contraindications Known hypersensitivity to fenoprofen or other NSAIDs

Warnings/Precautions Use with caution in patients with congestive heart failure, hypertension, decreased renal or hepatic function, history of GI disease, or those receiving anticoagulants

Adverse Reactions

>10%:

Central nervous system: Dizziness

Dermatologic: Rash

Gastrointestinal: Abdominal cramps, heartburn, indigestion, nausea

1% to 10%:

Central nervous system: Headache, nervousness

Dermatologic: Itching

Endocrine & metabolic: Fluid retention

Gastrointestinal: Vomiting

Otic: Tinnitus

<1%: Congestive heart failure, hypertension, arrhythmias, tachycardia, confusion, hallucinations, aseptic meningitis, mental depression, drowsiness, insomnia, urticaria, erythema multiforme, toxic epidermal necrolysis, Stevens-Johnson syndrome, angioedema, polydipsia, hot flashes, gastritis, GI ulceration, cystitis, polyuria, agranulocytosis, anemia, hemolytic anemia, bone marrow suppression, leukopenia, thrombocytopenia, hepatitis, peripheral neuropathy, toxic amblyopia, blurred vision, conjunctivitis, dry eyes, decreased hearing, acute renal failure, allergic rhinitis, shortness of breath, epistaxis

Overdosage/Toxicology

Symptoms of overdose include acute renal failure, vomiting, drowsiness, leukocytosis
(Continued)

Fenoprofen (Continued)

Management of a nonsteroidal anti-inflammatory drug (NSAID) intoxication is primarily supportive and symptomatic. Fluid therapy is commonly effective in managing the hypotension that may occur following an acute NSAID overdose, except when this is due to an acute blood loss.

Drug Interactions
Decreased effect with phenobarbital
Increased effect/toxicity of phenytoin, sulfonamides, sulfonylureas
Increased toxicity with salicylates, oral anticoagulants

Mechanism of Action Inhibits prostaglandin synthesis by decreasing the activity of the enzyme, cyclo-oxygenase, which results in decreased formation of prostaglandin precursors

Pharmacodynamics/Kinetics
Absorption: Rapid (to 80%) from upper GI tract
Distribution: Does not cross the placenta
Protein binding: 99%
Metabolism: Extensively in the liver
Half-life: 2.5-3 hours
Time to peak serum concentration: Within 2 hours
Elimination: In urine 2% to 5% as unchanged drug; small amounts appear in feces

Usual Dosage Adults: Oral:
Rheumatoid arthritis: 300-600 mg 3-4 times/day up to 3.2 g/day
Mild to moderate pain: 200 mg every 4-6 hours as needed

Monitoring Parameters Monitor CBC, liver enzymes; monitor urine output and BUN/serum creatinine in patients receiving diuretics

Reference Range Therapeutic: 20-65 µg/mL (SI: 82-268 µmol/L)

Test Interactions ↑ chloride (S), ↑ sodium (S)

Patient Information Do not crush tablets; take with food, milk, or water; report any signs of blood in stool

Dosage Forms
Capsule, as calcium: 200 mg, 300 mg
Tablet, as calcium: 600 mg

♦ **Fenoprofen Calcium** see Fenoprofen on previous page

Fentanyl (FEN ta nil)

Related Information
Adult ACLS Algorithm, Electrical Conversion on page 1453
Narcotic Agonists Comparison on page 1328

U.S. Brand Names Duragesic® Transdermal; Fentanyl Oralet®; Sublimaze® Injection

Synonyms Fentanyl Citrate

Therapeutic Category Analgesic, Narcotic

Use Sedation, relief of pain, preoperative medication, adjunct to general or regional anesthesia, management of chronic pain (transdermal product)

Restrictions C-II

Pregnancy Risk Factor B (D if used for prolonged periods or in high doses at term)

Contraindications Hypersensitivity to fentanyl or any component; increased intracranial pressure; severe respiratory depression; severe liver or renal insufficiency

Transmucosal is contraindicated in unmonitored settings where a risk of unrecognized hypoventilation exists or in treating acute or chronic pain

Warnings/Precautions Fentanyl shares the toxic potentials of opiate agonists, and precautions of opiate agonist therapy should be observed; use with caution in patients with bradycardia; rapid I.V. infusion may result in skeletal muscle and chest wall rigidity → impaired ventilation → respiratory distress → apnea, bronchoconstriction, laryngospasm; inject slowly over 3-5 minutes; nondepolarizing skeletal muscle relaxant may be required. Tolerance of drug dependence may result from extended use.

Transmucosal fentanyl: Fentanyl Oralet® is not indicated for use in unmonitored settings where there is a risk of unrecognized hypoventilation or in treating acute or chronic pain. Patients should be monitored by direct visual observation and by some means of measuring respiratory function such as pulse oximetry until they are recovered. Facilities for the administration of fluids, opioid antagonists, oxygen and resuscitation equipment (including facilities for endotracheal intubation) should be readily available.

Topical patches: Serum fentanyl concentrations may increase approximately one-third for patients with a body temperature of 40°C secondary to a temperature-dependent increase in fentanyl release from the system and increased skin permeability. Patients who experience adverse reactions should be monitored for at least 12 hours after removal of the patch.

The elderly may be particularly susceptible to the CNS depressant and constipating effects of narcotics

Adverse Reactions
>10%:
Cardiovascular: Hypotension, bradycardia
Central nervous system: CNS depression, drowsiness, sedation
Gastrointestinal: Nausea, vomiting, constipation
Respiratory: Respiratory depression
1% to 10%:
Cardiovascular: Cardiac arrhythmias, orthostatic hypotension

Central nervous system: Confusion
Gastrointestinal: Biliary tract spasm
Ocular: Miosis
<1%: Circulatory depression, convulsions, dysesthesia, paradoxical CNS excitation or delirium; cold, clammy skin; dizziness, erythema, pruritus, rash, urticaria, itching, ADH release, urinary tract spasm, bronchospasm, laryngospasm, physical and psychological dependence with prolonged use

Overdosage/Toxicology
Symptoms of overdose include CNS depression, respiratory depression, miosis
Treatment of an overdose includes support of the patient's airway, establishment of an I.V. line, and administration of naloxone 2 mg I.V. (0.01 mg/kg for children) with repeat administration as necessary up to a total of 10 mg

Drug Interactions CYP3A3/4 enzyme substrate
Increased toxicity: CNS depressants, phenothiazines, tricyclic antidepressants may potentiate fentanyl's adverse effects

Stability Protect from light; **incompatible** when mixed in the same syringe with pentobarbital
Transmucosal: Store at controlled room temperature of 15°C to 30°C (59°F to 86°F)

Mechanism of Action Binds with stereospecific receptors at many sites within the CNS, increases pain threshold, alters pain reception, inhibits ascending pain pathways

Pharmacodynamics/Kinetics Respiratory depressant effect may last longer than analgesic effect
I.M.: Onset of analgesia: 7-15 minutes; Duration: 1-2 hours
I.V.: Onset of analgesia: Almost immediate; Duration: 0.5-1 hour
Transmucosal:
    Onset of effect: 5-15 minutes with a maximum reduction in activity/apprehension
    Peak analgesia: Within 20-30 minutes
    Duration: Related to blood level of the drug
Absorption: Transmucosal: Rapid, ~25% from the buccal mucosa; 75% swallowed with saliva and slowly absorbed from gastrointestinal tract
Distribution: Highly lipophilic, redistributes into muscle and fat
Metabolism: In the liver
Bioavailability: Transmucosal: ~50% (range: 36% to 71%)
Half-life: 2-4 hours
    Transmucosal: 6.6 hours (range: 5-15 hours)
Elimination: In urine primarily as metabolites and 10% as unchanged drug

Usual Dosage Doses should be titrated to appropriate effects; wide range of doses, dependent upon desired degree of analgesia/anesthesia

Children 1-12 years:
    Sedation for minor procedures/analgesia:
        I.M., I.V.: 1-2 mcg/kg/dose; may repeat at 30- to 60-minute intervals. **Note:** Children 18-36 months of age may require 2-3 mcg/kg/dose
        Transmucosal (dosage strength is based on patient weight): 5 mcg/kg if child is not fearful; fearful children and some younger children may require doses of 5-15 mcg/kg (which also carries an increased risk of hypoventilation); drug effect begins within 10 minutes, with sedation beginning shortly thereafter
    Continuous sedation/analgesia: Initial I.V. bolus: 1-2 mcg/kg then 1 mcg/kg/hour; titrate upward; usual: 1-3 mcg/kg/hour
    Pain control: Transdermal: Not recommended
Children >12 years and Adults:
    Sedation for minor procedures/analgesia:
        I.M., I.V.: 0.5-1 mcg/kg/dose; higher doses are used for major procedures
        Transmucosal: 5 mcg/kg, suck on lozenge vigorously approximately 20-40 minutes before the start of procedure, drug effect begins within 10 minutes, with sedation beginning shortly thereafter; see table.

Dosage Recommendations for Transmucosal Fentanyl (Oralet®)

Patient Age/Weight	5-10 mcg/kg/dose	10-15 mcg/kg/dose
Children <2 years of age OR <15 kg	NOT RECOMMENDED	NOT RECOMMENDED
<15 kg	NOT AVAILABLE	200 mcg
20 kg	200 mcg	200-300 mcg
25 kg	200 mcg	300 mcg
30 kg	300 mcg	300-400 mcg
35 kg	300 mcg	400 mcg
>40 kg	400 mcg	400 mcg
Adults	400 mcg	400 mcg

Preoperative sedation, adjunct to regional anesthesia, postoperative pain: I.M., I.V.: 50-100 mcg/dose
Adjunct to general anesthesia: I.M., I.V.: 2-50 mcg/kg
General anesthesia without additional anesthetic agents: I.V. 50-100 mcg/kg with O$_2$ and skeletal muscle relaxant
Pain control: Transdermal: Initial: 25 mcg/hour system; if currently receiving opiates, convert to fentanyl equivalent and administer equianalgesic dosage titrated to minimize the adverse effects and provide analgesia. To convert patients from oral or
(Continued)

Fentanyl *(Continued)*

parenteral opioids to Duragesic®, the previous 24-hour analgesic requirement should be calculated. This analgesic requirement should be converted to the equianalgesic oral morphine dose. See tables.

Equianalgesic Doses of Opioid Agonists

Drug	Equianalgesic Dose (mg)	
	I.M.	P.O.
Codeine	130	200
Hydromorphone	1.5	7.5
Levorphanol	2	4
Meperidine	75	—
Methadone	10	20
Morphine	10	60
Oxycodone	15	30
Oxymorphone	1	10 (PR)

From *N Engl J Med*, 1985, 313:84-95.

Corresponding Doses of Oral/Intramuscular Morphine and Duragesic™

P.O. 24-Hour Morphine (mg/d)	I.M. 24-Hour Morphine (mg/d)	Duragesic™ Dose (mcg/h)
45-134	8-22	25
135-224	28-37	50
225-314	38-52	75
315-404	53-67	100
405-494	68-82	125
495-584	83-97	150
585-674	98-112	175
675-764	113-127	200
765-854	128-142	225
855-944	143-157	250
945-1034	158-172	275
1035-1124	173-187	300

Product information, Duragesic™ — Janssen Pharmaceutica, January, 1991.

The dosage should not be titrated more frequently than every 3 days after the initial dose or every 6 days thereafter. The majority of patients are controlled on every 72-hour administration, however, a small number of patients require every 48-hour administration.

Elderly >65 years: Transmucosal: Dose should be reduced to 2.5-5 mcg/kg; elderly have been found to be twice as sensitive as younger patients to the effects of fentanyl

Dosing adjustment in renal impairment:
Cl_{cr} 10-50 mL/minute: Administer at 75% of normal dose
Cl_{cr} <10 mL/minute: Administer at 50% of normal dose

Dietary Considerations
Alcohol: Additive CNS effects, avoid or limit alcohol; watch for sedation
Food: Glucose may cause hyperglycemia; monitor blood glucose concentrations

Administration Transmucosal product should begin 20-40 minutes prior to the anticipated start of surgery, diagnostic, or therapeutic procedure; foil overwrap should be removed just prior to administration; once removed, patient should place the unit in mouth and suck (not chew) it; unit should be removed after it is consumed or if patient has achieved an adequate sedation and anxiolytic level, and/or shows signs of respiratory depression

Monitoring Parameters Respiratory and cardiovascular status, blood pressure, heart rate

Nursing Implications
May cause rebound respiratory depression postoperatively
Patients with increased temperature may have increased fentanyl absorption transdermally, observe for adverse effects, dosage adjustment may be needed
Pharmacologic and adverse effects can be seen after discontinuation of transdermal system, observe patients for at least 12 hours after transdermal product removed; keep transdermal product (both used and unused) out of the reach of children
Do **not** use soap, alcohol, or other solvents to remove transdermal gel if it accidentally touches skin as they may increase transdermal absorption, use copious amounts of water For patients who have received transmucosal product within 6-12 hours, it is recommended that if other narcotics are required, they should be used at starting doses 1/4 to 1/3 those usually recommended.

Dosage Forms
Injection, as citrate: 0.05 mg/mL (2 mL, 5 mL, 10 mL, 20 mL, 50 mL)

Lozenge, oral transmucosal (raspberry flavored): 200 mcg, 300 mcg, 400 mcg, 600 mcg, 800 mcg, 1200 mcg, 1600 mcg

Transdermal system: 25 mcg/hour [10 cm^2]; 50 mcg/hour [20 cm^2]; 75 mcg/hour [30 cm^2]; 100 mcg/hour [40 cm^2] (all available in 5s)

- ♦ **Fentanyl Citrate** *see* Fentanyl *on page 474*
- ♦ **Fentanyl Oralet**® *see* Fentanyl *on page 474*
- ♦ **Feosol**® [OTC] *see* Ferrous Sulfate *on page 480*
- ♦ **Feostat**® [OTC] *see* Ferrous Fumarate *on next page*
- ♦ **Feratab**® [OTC] *see* Ferrous Sulfate *on page 480*
- ♦ **Fergon**® [OTC] *see* Ferrous Gluconate *on page 479*
- ♦ **Fer-Iron**® [OTC] *see* Ferrous Sulfate *on page 480*
- ♦ **Fermalac**® *see* Lactobacillus acidophilus *and* Lactobacillus bulgaricus *on page 655*
- ♦ **Ferodan**® *see* Ferrous Sulfate *on page 480*
- ♦ **Fero-Gradumet**® [OTC] *see* Ferrous Sulfate *on page 480*
- ♦ **Ferospace**® [OTC] *see* Ferrous Sulfate *on page 480*
- ♦ **Ferralet**® [OTC] *see* Ferrous Gluconate *on page 479*
- ♦ **Ferralyn**® **Lanacaps**® [OTC] *see* Ferrous Sulfate *on page 480*
- ♦ **Ferra-TD**® [OTC] *see* Ferrous Sulfate *on page 480*

Ferric Gluconate (FER ik GLOO koe nate)

U.S. Brand Names Ferrlecit®

Synonyms Sodium Ferric Gluconate

Therapeutic Category Iron Salt

Use Repletion of total body iron content in patients with iron deficiency anemia who are undergoing hemodialysis in conjunction with erythropoietin therapy

Pregnancy Risk Factor B

Pregnancy/Breast-Feeding Implications There are no well-controlled studies available. Should be used in pregnancy only when the potential benefit to the mother clearly outweighs the potential risk to the fetus. It is not known if ferrous gluconate is excreted in human milk. Use caution if the drug is administered to women who are breast-feeding.

Contraindications Hypersensitivity to ferric gluconate, benzyl alcohol, or any component of the formulation; use in any anemia not caused by iron deficiency, heart failure (of any severity)

Warnings/Precautions Potentially serious hypersensitivity reactions may occur. Fatal immediate hypersensitivity reactions have occurred with other iron carbohydrate complexes. Avoid rapid administration - flushing and hypotension may occur. Administration rate should not exceed 2.1 mg/minute. Do not administer to patients with iron overload. Use with caution in elderly patients.

Adverse Reactions Major adverse reactions which are likely to be related ferrous gluconate include hypotension and hypersensitivity reactions. Hypersensitivity reactions have included pruritus, chest pain, hypotension, nausea, abdominal pain, flank pain, fatigue and rash. Fatal hypersensitivity reactions have occurred with other iron polysaccharide complexes. A test dose is recommended.

1% to 10%:

Cardiovascular: Hypotension (serious hypotension in 1.3%), chest pain, hypertension, syncope, tachycardia, angina, myocardial infarction, pulmonary edema, hypovolemia, peripheral edema

Central nervous system: Headache, fatigue, fever, malaise, dizziness, paresthesia, insomnia, agitation, somnolence

Dermatologic: Pruritus, rash

Endocrine & metabolic: Hyperkalemia, hypoglycemia, hypokalemia

Gastrointestinal: Abdominal pain, nausea, vomiting, diarrhea, rectal disorder, dyspepsia, flatulence, melena

Genitourinary: Urinary tract infection

Hematologic: Anemia, abnormal erythrocytes, lymphadenopathy

Local: Injection site reactions, pain

Neuromuscular & skeletal: Weakness, back pain, leg cramps, myalgia, arthralgia, paresthesia

Ocular: Blurred vision, conjunctivitis

Respiratory: Dyspnea, cough, rhinitis, upper respiratory infection, pneumonia

Miscellaneous: Hypersensitivity reactions (3%), infection, rigors, chills, flu-like syndrome, sepsis, carcinoma, increased sweating, diaphoresis (increased)

<1% Epigastric pain, groin pain

Overdosage/Toxicology Symptoms of iron overdose include CNS toxicity, acidosis, hepatic and renal impairment, hematemesis, and lethargy. A serum iron level ≥300 μg/mL requires treatment due to severe toxicity. Treatment is generally symptomatic and supportive, but severe overdoses may be treated with deferoxamine. Deferoxamine may be administered I.V. (80 mg/kg over 24 hours) or I.M. (40-90 mg/kg every 8 hours). Usual toxic dose of elemental iron: ≥35 mg/kg.

Mechanism of Action Supplies a source to elemental iron necessary to the function of hemoglobin, myoglobin and specific enzyme systems; allows transport of oxygen via hemoglobin

Pharmacodynamics/Kinetics Pharmacokinetic studies have not been conducted; the total body iron content normally ranges from 2-4 g of elemental iron

Usual Dosage Adults:

Test dose (recommended): 2 mL diluted in 50 mL 0.9% sodium chloride over 60 minutes

(Continued)

477

Ferric Gluconate *(Continued)*

Repletion of iron in hemodialysis patients: I.V.: 125 mg (10 mL) in 100 mL 0.9% sodium chloride over 1 hour during hemodialysis. Most patients will require a cumulative dose of 1 g elemental iron over approximately 8 sequential dialysis treatments to achieve a favorable response.

Administration Dilute prior to administration; avoid rapid administration. Infusion rate should not exceed 2.1 mg/minute. Monitor patient for hypotension or hypersensitivity reactions during infusion.

Monitoring Parameters Hemoglobin and hematocrit, serum ferritin, iron saturation

Additional Information Contains benzyl alcohol 9 mg/mL

Dosage Forms Injection: 12.5 mg/mL (5 mL ampuls)

♦ **Ferrlecit®** see Ferric Gluconate *on previous page*

♦ **Ferro-Sequels® [OTC]** see Ferrous Fumarate *on this page*

Ferrous Fumarate *(FER us FYOO ma rate)*

U.S. Brand Names Femiron® [OTC]; Feostat® [OTC]; Ferro-Sequels® [OTC]; Fumasorb® [OTC]; Fumerin® [OTC]; Hemocyte® [OTC]; Ircon® [OTC]; Nephro-Fer™ [OTC]; Span-FF® [OTC]

Canadian Brand Names Palafer®

Therapeutic Category Iron Salt

Use Prevention and treatment of iron deficiency anemias

Pregnancy Risk Factor A

Contraindications Hemochromatosis, hemolytic anemia, known hypersensitivity to iron salts

Warnings/Precautions Avoid in patients with peptic ulcer, enteritis, or ulcerative colitis. Administration of iron for >6 months should be avoided except in patients with continuous bleeding or menorrhagia. Anemia in the elderly is often caused by "anemia of chronic disease" or associated with inflammation rather than blood loss. Iron stores are usually normal or increased, with a serum ferritin >50 ng/mL and a decreased total iron binding capacity. Hence, the "anemia of chronic disease" is not secondary to iron deficiency but the inability of the reticuloendothelial system to reclaim available iron stores.

Adverse Reactions

>10%: Gastrointestinal: Stomach cramping, constipation, nausea, vomiting, dark stools

1% to 10%:

Gastrointestinal: Heartburn, diarrhea, staining of teeth

Genitourinary: Discoloration of urine

<1%: Contact irritation

Overdosage/Toxicology

Symptoms of overdose include acute GI irritation, erosion of GI mucosa, hepatic and renal impairment, coma, hematemesis, lethargy, acidosis, serum Fe level >300 mcg/mL requires treatment of overdose due to severe toxicity

Following treatment for fluid losses, metabolic acidosis, and shock, a severe iron overdose may be treated with deferoxamine. Deferoxamine may be administered I.V. (80 mg/kg over 24 hours) or I.M. (40-90 mg/kg every 8 hours). Usual toxic dose of elemental iron: ≥35 mg/kg.

Drug Interactions

Decreased effect: Absorption of oral preparation of iron and tetracyclines are decreased when both of these drugs are given together; concurrent administration of antacids may decrease iron absorption; iron may decrease absorption of penicillamine when given at the same time; response to iron therapy may be delayed in patients receiving chloramphenicol

Milk may decrease absorption of iron

Increased effect: Current administration ≥200 mg vitamin C per 30 mg elemental iron increases absorption of oral iron

Mechanism of Action Replaces iron found in hemoglobin, myoglobin, and enzymes; allows the transportation of oxygen via hemoglobin

Pharmacodynamics/Kinetics

Onset of hematologic response (essentially the same to either oral or parenteral iron salts): Red blood cell form and color changes within 3-10 days

Peak reticulocytosis: Within 5-10 days; hemoglobin values increase within 2-4 weeks

Absorption: Iron is absorbed in the duodenum and upper jejunum; in persons with normal iron stores 10% of an oral dose is absorbed, this is increased to 20% to 30% in persons with inadequate iron stores; food and achlorhydria will decrease absorption

Elimination: Iron is largely bound to serum transferrin and excreted in the urine, sweat, sloughing of intestinal mucosa, and by menses

Usual Dosage Oral **(dose expressed in terms of elemental iron):**

Children:

Severe iron deficiency anemia: 4-6 mg Fe/kg/day in 3 divided doses

Mild to moderate iron deficiency anemia: 3 mg Fe/kg/day in 1-2 divided doses

Prophylaxis: 1-2 mg Fe/kg/day

Adults:

Iron deficiency: 60-100 mg twice daily up to 60 mg 2 times/day

Prophylaxis: 60-100 mg/day

To avoid GI upset, start with a single daily dose and increase by 1 tablet/day each week or as tolerated until desired daily dose is achieved

Elderly: 200 mg 3-4 times/day

Reference Range

Serum iron:

Male: 75-175 µg/dL (SI: 13.4-31.3 µmol/L)

Female: 65-165 µg/dL (SI: 11.6-29.5 µmol/L)

Total iron binding capacity: 230-430 µg/dL

Transferrin: 204-360 mg/dL

Percent transferrin saturation: 20% to 50%

Iron levels >300 µg/dL can be considered toxic, should be treated as an overdose

Patient Information May color stool black, take between meals for maximum absorption; may take with food if GI upset occurs, do not take with milk or antacids; keep out of reach of children

Additional Information Elemental iron content of ferrous fumarate: 33%

Dosage Forms Amount of elemental iron is listed in brackets

Capsule, controlled release (Span-FF®): 325 mg [106 mg]

Drops (Feostat®): 45 mg/0.6 mL [15 mg/0.6 mL] (60 mL)

Suspension, oral (Feostat®): 100 mg/5 mL [33 mg/5 mL] (240 mL)

Tablet:

325 mg [106 mg]

Chewable (chocolate flavor) (Feostat®): 100 mg [33 mg]

Femiron®: 63 mg [20 mg]

Fumerin®: 195 mg [64 mg]

Fumasorb®, Ircon®: 200 mg [66 mg]

Hemocyte®: 324 mg [106 mg]

Nephro-Fer™: 350 mg [115 mg]

Timed release (Ferro-Sequels®): Ferrous fumarate 150 mg [50 mg] and docusate sodium 100 mg

Ferrous Gluconate (FER us GLOO koe nate)

U.S. Brand Names Fergon® [OTC]; Ferralet® [OTC]; Simron® [OTC]

Canadian Brand Names Apo-Ferrous® Gluconate

Therapeutic Category Iron Salt

Use Prevention and treatment of iron deficiency anemias

Pregnancy Risk Factor A

Contraindications Hemochromatosis, hemolytic anemia; known hypersensitivity to iron salts

Warnings/Precautions Administration of iron for >6 months should be avoided except in patients with continued bleeding, menorrhagia, or repeated pregnancies; avoid in patients with peptic ulcer, enteritis, or ulcerative colitis. Anemia in the elderly is often caused by "anemia of chronic disease" or associated with inflammation rather than blood loss. Iron stores are usually normal or increased, with a serum ferritin >50 ng/mL and a decreased total iron binding capacity. Hence, the "anemia of chronic disease" is not secondary to iron deficiency but the inability of the reticuloendothelial system to reclaim available iron stores.

Adverse Reactions

>10%: Gastrointestinal: Stomach cramping, constipation, nausea, vomiting, dark stools

1% to 10%:

Gastrointestinal: Heartburn, diarrhea, staining of teeth

Genitourinary: Discoloration of urine

<1%: Contact irritation

Overdosage/Toxicology

Symptoms of overdose include acute GI irritation; erosion of GI mucosa, hepatic and renal impairment, coma, hematemesis, lethargy, acidosis

Following treatment for fluid losses, metabolic acidosis, and shock, a severe iron overdose may be treated with deferoxamine. Deferoxamine may be administered I.V. (80 mg/kg over 24 hours) or I.M. (40-90 mg/kg every 8 hours). Usual toxic dose of elemental iron: ≥35 mg/kg.

Drug Interactions Absorption of oral preparation of iron and tetracyclines is decreased when both of these drugs are given together; concurrent administration of antacids may decrease iron absorption; iron may decrease absorption of penicillamine when given at the same time. Response to iron therapy may be delayed in patients receiving chloramphenicol. Concurrent administration ≥200 mg vitamin C/30 mg elemental iron increases absorption of oral iron; milk may decrease absorption of iron.

Mechanism of Action Replaces iron found in hemoglobin, myoglobin, and enzymes; allows the transportation of oxygen via hemoglobin

Pharmacodynamics/Kinetics Onset of hematologic response (essentially the same to either oral or parenteral iron salts): Red blood cells form and color changes within 3-10 days, peak reticulocytosis occurs in 5-10 days, and hemoglobin values increase within 2-4 weeks

Usual Dosage Oral (dose expressed in terms of elemental iron):

Children:

Severe iron deficiency anemia: 4-6 mg Fe/kg/day in 3 divided doses

Mild to moderate iron deficiency anemia: 3 mg Fe/kg/day in 1-2 divided doses

Prophylaxis: 1-2 mg Fe/kg/day

Adults:

Iron deficiency: 60 mg twice daily up to 60 mg 4 times/day

Prophylaxis: 60 mg/day

Reference Range Therapeutic: Male: 75-175 µg/dL (SI: 13.4-31.3 µmol/L); Female: 65-165 µg/dL (SI: 11.6-29.5 µmol/L); serum iron level >300 µg/dL usually requires treatment of overdose due to severe toxicity

(Continued)

Ferrous Gluconate *(Continued)*

Test Interactions False-positive for blood in stool by the guaiac test

Patient Information May color stool black, take between meals for maximum absorption; may take with food if GI upset occurs, do not take with milk or antacids; keep out of reach of children

Additional Information Elemental iron content of gluconate: 12%

Dosage Forms Amount of elemental iron is listed in brackets

Capsule, soft gelatin (Simron®): 86 mg [10 mg]

Elixir (Fergon®): 300 mg/5 mL [34 mg/5 mL] with alcohol 7% (480 mL)

Tablet: 300 mg [34 mg]; 325 mg [38 mg]

    Fergon®, Ferralet®: 320 mg [37 mg]

    Sustained release (Ferralet® Slow Release): 320 mg [37 mg]

Ferrous Sulfate *(FER us SUL fate)*

U.S. Brand Names Feosol® [OTC]; Feratab® [OTC]; Fer-Iron® [OTC]; Fero-Gradumet® [OTC]; Ferospace® [OTC]; Ferralyn® Lanacaps® [OTC]; Ferra-TD® [OTC]; Mol-Iron® [OTC]; Slow FE® [OTC]

Canadian Brand Names Apo-Ferrous® Sulfate; Ferodan®

Synonyms FeSO₄

Therapeutic Category Iron Salt

Use Prevention and treatment of iron deficiency anemias

Pregnancy Risk Factor A

Contraindications Hemochromatosis, hemolytic anemia; known hypersensitivity to iron salts

Warnings/Precautions Administration of iron for >6 months should be avoided except in patients with continued bleeding, menorrhagia, or repeated pregnancies; avoid in patients with peptic ulcer, enteritis, or ulcerative colitis. Anemia in the elderly is often caused by "anemia of chronic disease" or associated with inflammation rather than blood loss. Iron stores are usually normal or increased, with a serum ferritin >50 ng/mL and a decreased total iron binding capacity. Hence, the "anemia of chronic disease" is not secondary to iron deficiency but the inability of the reticuloendothelial system to reclaim available iron stores.

Adverse Reactions

>10%: Gastrointestinal: GI irritation, epigastric pain, nausea, dark stool, vomiting, stomach cramping, constipation

1% to 10%:

    Gastrointestinal: Heartburn, diarrhea

    Genitourinary: Discoloration of urine

    Miscellaneous: Liquid preparations may temporarily stain the teeth

<1%: Contact irritation

Overdosage/Toxicology

Symptoms of overdose include acute GI irritation; erosion of GI mucosa, hepatic and renal impairment, coma, hematemesis, lethargy, acidosis

Following treatment for fluid losses, metabolic acidosis, and shock, a severe iron overdose may be treated with deferoxamine. Deferoxamine may be administered I.V. (80 mg/kg over 24 hours) or I.M. (40-90 mg/kg every 8 hours). Usual toxic dose of elemental iron: ≥35 mg/kg.

Drug Interactions

Decreased effect: Absorption of oral preparation of iron and tetracyclines are decreased when both of these drugs are given together; concurrent administration of antacids may decrease iron absorption; iron may decrease absorption of penicillamine when given at the same time; response to iron therapy may be delayed in patients receiving chloramphenicol; milk may decrease absorption of iron

Increased effect: Concurrent administration ≥200 mg vitamin C per 30 mg elemental Fe increases absorption of oral iron

Mechanism of Action Replaces iron, found in hemoglobin, myoglobin, and other enzymes; allows the transportation of oxygen via hemoglobin

Pharmacodynamics/Kinetics

Onset of hematologic response (essentially the same to either oral or parenteral iron salts): Red blood cell form and color changes within 3-10 days

Peak reticulocytosis: Occurs in 5-10 days, and hemoglobin values increase within 2-4 weeks

Absorption: Iron is absorbed in the duodenum and upper jejunum; in persons with normal serum iron stores, 10% of an oral dose is absorbed; this is increased to 20% to 30% in persons with inadequate iron stores. Food and achlorhydria will decrease absorption

Elimination: Iron is largely bound to serum transferrin and excreted in the urine, sweat, sloughing of the intestinal mucosa, and by menstrual bleeding

Usual Dosage Oral:

Children **(dose expressed in terms of elemental iron):**

    Severe iron deficiency anemia: 4-6 mg Fe/kg/day in 3 divided doses

    Mild to moderate iron deficiency anemia: 3 mg Fe/kg/day in 1-2 divided doses

    Prophylaxis: 1-2 mg Fe/kg/day up to a maximum of 15 mg/day

Adults **(dose expressed in terms of ferrous sulfate):**

    Iron deficiency: 300 mg twice daily up to 300 mg 4 times/day or 250 mg (extended release) 1-2 times/day

    Prophylaxis: 300 mg/day

Administration Administer ferrous sulfate 2 hours prior to, or 4 hours after antacids

Reference Range
Serum iron:
Male: 75-175 µg/dL (SI: 13.4-31.3 µmol/L)
Female: 65-165 µg/dL (SI: 11.6-29.5 µmol/L)
Total iron binding capacity: 230-430 µg/dL
Transferrin: 204-360 mg/dL
Percent transferrin saturation: 20% to 50%

Test Interactions False-positive for blood in stool by the guaiac test

Patient Information May color stool black, take between meals for maximum absorption; may take with food if GI upset occurs, do not take with milk or antacids; keep out of reach of children

Additional Information Elemental iron content of iron salts in ferrous sulfate is 20% (ie, 300 mg ferrous sulfate is equivalent to 60 mg ferrous iron)

Dosage Forms Amount of elemental iron is listed in brackets
Capsule:
Exsiccated, timed release (Feosol®): 159 mg [50 mg]
Exsiccated, timed release (Ferralyn® Lanacaps®, Ferra-TD®): 250 mg [50 mg]
Ferospace®: 250 mg [50 mg]
Drops, oral:
Fer-In-Sol®: 75 mg/0.6 mL [15 mg/0.6 mL] (50 mL)
Fer-Iron®: 125 mg/mL [25 mg/mL] (50 mL)
Elixir (Feosol®): 220 mg/5 mL [44 mg/5 mL] with alcohol 5% (473 mL, 4000 mL)
Syrup (Fer-In-Sol®): 90 mg/5 mL [18 mg/5 mL] with alcohol 5% (480 mL)
Tablet: 324 mg [65 mg]
Exsiccated (Feosol®) 200 mg [65 mg]
Exsiccated, timed release (Slow FE®): 160 mg [50 mg]
Feratab®: 300 mg [60 mg]
Mol-Iron®: 195 mg [39 mg]
Timed release (Fero-Gradumet®): 525 mg [105 mg]

Ferrous Sulfate, Ascorbic Acid, Vitamin B-Complex, and Folic Acid

(FER us SUL fate, a SKOR bik AS id, VYE ta min bee KOM pleks, & FOE lik AS id)
U.S. Brand Names Iberet-Folic-500®
Therapeutic Category Vitamin
Dosage Forms Tablet, controlled release:
Ferrous sulfate: 105 mg
Ascorbic acid: 500 mg
B_1: 6 mg
B_2: 6 mg
B_3: 30 mg
B_5: 10 mg
B_6: 5 mg
B_{12}: 25 mcg
Folic acid: 800 mcg

♦ **Fertinex™** see Follitropins on page 513
♦ **FeSO₄** see Ferrous Sulfate on previous page
♦ **Feverall™ [OTC]** see Acetaminophen on page 19
♦ **Feverall™ Sprinkle Caps [OTC]** see Acetaminophen on page 19

Fexofenadine (feks oh FEN a deen)
U.S. Brand Names Allegra®
Synonyms Fexofenadine Hydrochloride
Therapeutic Category Antihistamine, Nonsedating
Use Nonsedating antihistamine indicated for the relief of seasonal allergic rhinitis
Pregnancy Risk Factor C
Contraindications Individuals demonstrating hypersensitivity to fexofenadine or any components of its formulation
Warnings/Precautions Safety and effectiveness in pediatric patients <12 years of age has not been established. Fexofenadine is classified in FDA pregnancy category C and no data is yet available evaluating its use in breast-feeding women.
Adverse Reactions 1% to 10%:
Central nervous system: Drowsiness (1.3%), fatigue (1.3%)
Endocrine & metabolic: Dysmenorrhea (1.5%)
Gastrointestinal: Nausea (1.5%), dyspepsia (1.3%)
Miscellaneous: Viral infection (2.5%)
Drug Interactions CYP3A3/4 enzyme substrate

Fexofenadine levels have increased when administered with erythromycin (82% higher) and with ketoconazole (135% higher); this has not been associated with any increased incidence of side effects

In two separate studies, fexofenadine 120 mg twice daily (high doses) was coadministered with standard doses of erythromycin or ketoconazole to healthy volunteers and although fexofenadine peak plasma concentrations increased, no differences in adverse events or QT_c intervals were observed. **It remains unknown if a similar interaction occurs with other azole antifungal agents (eg, itraconazole) or other macrolide antibiotics (eg, clarithromycin).**
(Continued)

Fexofenadine *(Continued)*

Stability Capsules should be stored at controlled room temperature 20°C to 25°C and protected from excessive moisture

Mechanism of Action Fexofenadine is an active metabolite of terfenadine and like terfenadine it competes with histamine for H_1-receptor sites on effector cells in the gastrointestinal tract, blood vessels and respiratory tract; it appears that fexofenadine does not cross the blood brain barrier to any appreciable degree, resulting in a reduced potential for sedation

Pharmacodynamics/Kinetics
Onset of action: 60 minutes
Duration of antihistaminic effect: At least 12 hours
Metabolism: ~5% metabolized mostly by gut flora; only 0.5% to 1.5% metabolized by cytochrome P-450 enzymes
Half-life: 14.4 hours
Time to peak serum concentration: ~2.6 hours after oral administration
Elimination: Primarily in feces (~80%) and in urine (~11%) as unchanged drug

Usual Dosage Oral:
Children <12 years: Not recommended
Children ≥12 years and Adults: 1 capsule (60 mg) twice daily
Dosing adjustment in renal impairment: Recommended initial doses of 60 mg once daily

Monitoring Parameters Relief of symptoms

Patient Information Although relatively uncommon (1.3%), fexofenadine may cause drowsiness; contact your physician or pharmacist if you experience drowsiness, upset stomach, increased pain or cramping during menstruation while taking this medication

Dosage Forms Capsule, as hydrochloride: 60 mg

Fexofenadine and Pseudoephedrine

(feks oh FEN a deen & soo doe e FED rin)

U.S. Brand Names Allegra-D™

Therapeutic Category Antihistamine/Decongestant Combination

Dosage Forms Tablet, extended release: Fexofenadine hydrochloride 60 mg and pseudoephedrine hydrochloride 120 mg

- ♦ **Fexofenadine Hydrochloride** *see Fexofenadine on previous page*
- ♦ **Fiberall® Powder [OTC]** *see Psyllium on page 994*
- ♦ **Fiberall® Wafer [OTC]** *see Psyllium on page 994*
- ♦ **Fibrepur®** *see Psyllium on page 994*

Fibrinolysin and Desoxyribonuclease

(fye brin oh LYE sin & des oks i rye boe NOO klee ase)

U.S. Brand Names Elase-Chloromycetin® Topical; Elase® Topical

Therapeutic Category Enzyme

Dosage Forms
Ointment, topical:
Elase®: Fibrinolysin 1 unit and desoxyribonuclease 666.6 units per g (10 g, 30 g)
Elase-Chloromycetin®: Fibrinolysin 1 unit and desoxyribonuclease 666.6 units per g with chloramphenicol 10 mg per g (10 g, 30 g)
Powder, dry: Fibrinolysin 25 units and desoxyribonuclease 15,000 units per 30 g

Filgrastim *(fil GRA stim)*

Related Information
Cancer Chemotherapy Regimens *on page 1263*
Sargramostim *on page 1049*

U.S. Brand Names Neupogen® Injection

Synonyms G-CSF; Granulocyte Colony Stimulating Factor

Therapeutic Category Colony Stimulating Factor

Use
Patients with nonmyeloid malignancies receiving myelosuppressive anticancer drugs associated with a significant incidence of neutropenia (FDA-approved indication)
Cancer patients receiving bone marrow transplant (BMT) (FDA-approved indication)
Patients undergoing peripheral blood progenitor cell (PBPC) collection
Patients with severe chronic neutropenia (SCN) (FDA-approved indication)
Chronic administration in symptomatic patients with congenital neutropenia, cyclic neutropenia, or idiopathic neutropenic; filgrastim should not be started until the diagnosis of SCN is confirmed, as it may interfere with diagnostic efforts
Safety and efficacy of G-CSF given simultaneously with cytotoxic chemotherapy have not been established; concurrent treatment may increase myelosuppression; G-CSF should be avoided in patients receiving concomitant chemotherapy and radiation therapy

Pregnancy Risk Factor C

Contraindications Patients with known hypersensitivity to *E. coli*-derived proteins or G-CSF

Warnings/Precautions Complete blood count and platelet count should be obtained prior to chemotherapy. Do not use G-CSF in the period 12-24 hours before to 24 hours after administration of cytotoxic chemotherapy because of the potential sensitivity of rapidly dividing myeloid cells to cytotoxic chemotherapy. Precaution should be exercised in the usage of G-CSF in any malignancy with myeloid characteristics. G-CSF can potentially act as a growth factor for any tumor type, particularly myeloid malignancies. Tumors of nonhematopoietic origin may have surface receptors for G-CSF.

Allergic-type reactions have occurred in patients receiving G-CSF with first or later doses. Reactions tended to occur more frequently with intravenous administration and within 30 minutes of infusion. Most cases resolved rapidly with antihistamines, steroids, bronchodilators, and/or epinephrine. Symptoms recurred in >50% of patients on rechallenge.

Adverse Reactions Effects are generally mild and dose related

>10%:
  Central nervous system: Neutropenic fever, fever
  Dermatologic: Alopecia
  Gastrointestinal: Nausea, vomiting, diarrhea, mucositis,
    Splenomegaly: This occurs more commonly in patients with cyclic neutropenia/congenital agranulocytosis who received S.C. injections for a prolonged (>14 days) period of time; ~33% of these patients experience subclinical splenomegaly (detected by MRI or CT scan); ~3% of these patients experience clinical splenomegaly
  Neuromuscular & skeletal: Medullary bone pain (24% incidence): This occurs most commonly in lower back pain, posterior iliac crest, and sternum and is controlled with non-narcotic analgesics

1% to 10%:
  Cardiovascular: Chest pain, fluid retention
  Central nervous system: Headache
  Dermatologic: Skin rash
  Gastrointestinal: Anorexia, stomatitis, constipation
  Hematologic: Leukocytosis
  Local: Pain at injection site
  Neuromuscular & skeletal: Weakness
  Respiratory: Dyspnea, cough, sore throat

<1%: Transient supraventricular arrhythmia, pericarditis, thrombophlebitis, anaphylactic reaction

Overdosage/Toxicology
No clinical adverse effects seen with high dose producing ANC >10,000/mm^3; leukocytosis which was not associated with any clinical adverse effects
After discontinuing in patients receiving myelosuppressive chemotherapy, there is a 50% decrease in circulating levels of neutrophils within 1-2 days, return to pretreatment levels within 1-7 days

Drug Interactions Drugs which may potentiate the release of neutrophils (eg, lithium) should be used with caution

Stability
Filgrastim is a clear, colorless solution and should be stored under refrigeration at 2°C to 8°C (36°F to 46°F) and protected from direct sunlight. Filgrastim should be protected from freezing and temperatures >30°C to avoid aggregation. Filgrastim unopened vials are stable at controlled room temperatures (9°C to 30°C/47°F to 86°F) for up to 7 days.
The solution should not be shaken since bubbles and/or foam may form. If foaming occurs, the solution should be left undisturbed for a few minutes until bubbles dissipate.
Filgrastim is stable for 7 days at 9°C to 30°C, however, the manufacturer recommends discarding after 6 hours because of microbiological concerns. The product is packaged as single-use vial without a preservative.
Undiluted filgrastim is stable for 7 days at 15°C to 30°C and 14 days at 2°C to 8°C in tuberculin syringes. However, refrigeration and use within 24 hours are recommended because of concern for bacterial contamination.
Filgrastim may be diluted in dextrose 5% in water to a concentration of ≥15 mcg/mL for I.V. infusion administration
  Minimum concentration is 15 mcg/mL; concentrations of 5-15 mcg/mL require the addition of albumin (1 mL of 5%) to the bag to prevent absorption to plastics/PVC. Concentrations of <5 mcg/mL **should not** be used.
  This diluted solution is stable for 7 days under refrigeration or at room temperature
Standard diluent: ≥375 mcg/25 mL D$_5$W; filgrastim is **incompatible** with 0.9% sodium chloride (normal saline)

Mechanism of Action Stimulates the production, maturation, and activation of neutrophils, G-CSF activates neutrophils to increase both their migration and cytotoxicity

Pharmacodynamics/Kinetics
Onset of action: Rapid elevation in neutrophil counts within the first 24 hours, reaching a plateau in 3-5 days
Duration: ANC decreases by 50% within 2 days after discontinuing G-CSF; white counts return to the normal range in 4-7 days
Absorption: S.C.: 100% absorbed; peak plasma levels can be maintained for up to 12 hours
Distribution: V$_d$: 150 mL/kg; no evidence of drug accumulation over a 11- to 20-day period
Metabolism: Systemically metabolized
Bioavailability: Oral: Not bioavailable
Half-life: 1.8-3.5 hours
Time to peak serum concentration: S.C.: Within 2-6 hours

Usual Dosage Children and Adults:
Dosage should be based on actual body weight (even in morbidly obese patients)
(Continued)

Filgrastim *(Continued)*

Existing clinical data suggest that starting G-CSF between 24 and 72 hours subsequent to chemotherapy may provide optimal neutrophil recover; continue therapy until the occurrence of an absolute neutrophil count of 10,000 µL after the neutrophil nadir

The available data suggest that rounding the dose to the nearest vial size may enhance patient convenience and reduce costs without clinical detriment

Neonates: 5-10 mcg/kg/day once daily for 3-5 days has been administered to neutropenic neonates with sepsis; there was a rapid and significant increase in peripheral neutrophil counts and the neutrophil storage pool

Children and Adults:

Myelosuppressive chemotherapy S.C. or I.V. infusion: 5 mcg/kg/day

Doses may be increased in increments of 5 mcg/kg for each chemotherapy cycle, according to the duration and severity of the absolute neutrophil count (ANC) nadir

Bone marrow transplant patients: 5-10 mcg/kg/day as an I.V. infusion of 4 or 24 hours or as continuous 24-hour S.C. infusion; administer first dose at least 24 hours after cytotoxic chemotherapy and at least 24 hours after bone marrow infusion; if ANC decreases <1000/mm^3 during the 5 mcg/kg/day dose, increase filgrastim to 10 mcg/kg/day and follow the steps in the table

Filgrastim Dose Based on Neutrophil Response

Absolute Neutrophil Count	Filgrastim Dose Adjustment
When ANC >1000/mm^3 for 3 consecutive days	Reduce to 5 mcg/kg/day
If ANC remains >1000/mm^3 for 3 more consecutive days	Discontinue filgrastim
If ANC decreases to <1000/mm^3	Resume at 5 mcg/kg/day

If ANC decreases <1000/mm^3 during the 5 mcg/kg/day dose, increase filgrastim to 10 mcg/kg/day and follow the above steps in the table.

Peripheral blood progenitor cell (PBPC) collection: 10 mcg/kg/day either S.C. or a bolus or continuous I.V. infusion. It is recommended that G-CSF be given for at least 4 days before the first leukapheresis procedure and continued until the last leukapheresis; although the optimal duration of administration and leukapheresis schedule have not been established, administration of G-CSF for 6-7 days with leukaphereses on days 5,6 and 7 was found to be safe and effective; neutrophil counts should be monitored after 4 days of G-CSF, and G-CSF dose-modification should be considered for those patients who develop a white blood cell count >100,000/mm^3

Severe chronic neutropenia: S.C.:

Congenital neutropenia: 6 mcg/kg/dose twice daily

Idiopathic/cyclic neutropenia: 5 mcg/kg single dose daily

Chronic daily administration is required to maintain clinical benefit; adjust dose based on the patients' clinical course as well as ANC; in phase III studies, the target ANC was 1500-10,000/mm^3. Reduce the dose if the ANC is persistently >10,000/mm^3

Premature discontinuation of G-CSF therapy prior to the time of recovery from the expected neutrophil is generally not recommended; a transient increase in neutrophil counts is typically seen 1-2 days after initiation of therapy

Hemodialysis: Supplemental dose is not necessary

Peritoneal dialysis: Supplemental dose is not necessary

Administration May be administered undiluted by S.C. or by I.V. infusion over 15-60 minutes in D$_5$W; **incompatible** with sodium chloride solutions

Monitoring Parameters Complete blood cell count and platelet count should be obtained twice weekly after chemotherapy or three times weekly after transplant. Leukocytosis (white blood cell counts of ≥100,000/mm^3) has been observed in ~2% of patients receiving G-CSF at doses above 5 mcg/kg/day. Monitor platelets and hematocrit regularly. Monitor patients with pre-existing cardiac conditions closely as cardiac events (myocardial infarctions, arrhythmias) have been reported in premarketing clinical studies.

Reference Range No clinical benefit seen with ANC >10,000/mm^3

Patient Information Possible bone pain

Nursing Implications Do not mix with sodium chloride solutions

Additional Information

Reimbursement Hotline: 1-800-272-9376

Professional Services [AMGEN]: 1-800-77-AMGEN

Dosage Forms Injection, preservative free: 300 mcg/mL (1 mL, 1.6 mL)

♦ **Filibon®** [OTC] *see* Vitamins, Multiple *on page 1226*

Finasteride *(fi NAS teer ide)*

U.S. Brand Names Propecia®; Proscar®

Therapeutic Category Antiandrogen; Antineoplastic Agent, Miscellaneous

Use Early data indicate that finasteride is useful in the treatment of symptomatic benign prostatic hyperplasia (BPH); male pattern baldness

Unlabeled use: Adjuvant monotherapy after radical prostatectomy in the treatment of prostatic cancer

Pregnancy Risk Factor X

Contraindications History of hypersensitivity to drug, pregnancy, lactation, children

Warnings/Precautions A minimum of 6 months of treatment may be necessary to determine whether an individual will respond to finasteride. Use with caution in those patients with liver function abnormalities. Carefully monitor patients with a large residual urinary volume or severely diminished urinary flow for obstructive uropathy. These patients may not be candidates for finasteride therapy.

Adverse Reactions 1% to 10%:

Endocrine & metabolic: Decreased libido

Genitourinary: <4% incidence of impotence, decreased volume of ejaculate

Drug Interactions CYP3A3/4 enzyme substrate

Mechanism of Action Finasteride is a 4-azo analog of testosterone and is a competitive inhibitor of both tissue and hepatic 5-alpha reductase. This results in inhibition of the conversion of testosterone to dihydrotestosterone and markedly suppresses serum dihydrotestosterone levels; depending on dose and duration, serum testosterone concentrations may or may not increase. Testosterone-dependent processes such as fertility, muscle strength, potency, and libido are not affected by finasteride.

Pharmacodynamics/Kinetics

Onset of clinical effect: Within 12 weeks to 6 months of ongoing therapy

Duration of action:

After a single oral dose as small as 0.5 mg: 65% depression of plasma dihydrotestosterone levels persists 5-7 days

After 6 months of treatment with 5 mg/day: Circulating dihydrotestosterone levels are reduced to castrate levels without significant effects on circulating testosterone; levels return to normal within 14 days of discontinuation of treatment

Absorption: Oral: Extent may be reduced if administered with food

Metabolism: Unchanged finasteride is major circulating component; two active metabolites have been identified

Protein binding: 90%

Bioavailability: Mean: 63%

Half-life, serum: Parent drug: ~5-17 hours (mean: 1.9 fasting, 4.2 with breakfast)

Half-life: Elderly: 8 hours; Adults: 6 hours (3-16)

Time to peak serum concentration: Oral: 2-6 hours

Elimination: As metabolites in urine (39%) and feces (57%); elimination rate is decreased in the elderly, but no dosage adjustment is needed

Usual Dosage Adults: Male:

Benign prostatic hyperplasia: Oral: 5 mg/day as a single dose; clinical responses occur within 12 weeks to 6 months of initiation of therapy; long-term administration is recommended for maximal response

Male pattern baldness: Oral: 1 mg daily

Dosing adjustment in renal impairment: No dosage adjustment is necessary

Dosing adjustment in hepatic impairment: Use with caution in patients with liver function abnormalities because finasteride is metabolized extensively in the liver

Dietary Considerations Food: Administration with food may delay the rate and reduce the extent of oral absorption

Monitoring Parameters Objective and subjective signs of relief of benign prostatic hyperplasia, including improvement in urinary flow, reduction in symptoms of urgency, and relief of difficulty in micturition

Dosage Forms Tablet, film coated: 1 mg, 5 mg

♦ **Fiorgen PF®** see Butalbital Compound on page 165

♦ **Fioricet®** see Butalbital Compound on page 165

♦ **Fiorinal®** see Butalbital Compound on page 165

♦ **Fisalamine** see Mesalamine on page 734

♦ **FK506** see Tacrolimus on page 1103

♦ **Flagyl ER® Oral** see Metronidazole on page 770

♦ **Flagyl® Oral** see Metronidazole on page 770

♦ **Flamazine®** see Silver Sulfadiazine on page 1062

♦ **Flarex®** see Fluorometholone on page 499

♦ **Flavorcee® [OTC]** see Ascorbic Acid on page 99

Flavoxate (fla VOKS ate)

U.S. Brand Names Urispas®

Synonyms Flavoxate Hydrochloride

Therapeutic Category Antispasmodic Agent, Urinary

Use Antispasmodic to provide symptomatic relief of dysuria, nocturia, suprapubic pain, urgency, and incontinence due to detrusor instability and hyper-reflexia in elderly with cystitis, urethritis, urethrocystitis, and urethrotrigonitis, and prostatitis

Pregnancy Risk Factor B

Contraindications Pyloric or duodenal obstruction, GI hemorrhage, GI obstruction; ileus; achalasia; obstructive uropathies of lower urinary tract (BPH)

Warnings/Precautions May cause drowsiness, vertigo, and ocular disturbances; administer cautiously in patients with suspected glaucoma

Adverse Reactions

>10%:

Central nervous system: Drowsiness

Gastrointestinal: Xerostomia, dry throat

1% to 10%:

Cardiovascular: Tachycardia, palpitations

Central nervous system: Nervousness, fatigue, vertigo, headache, hyperpyrexia

Gastrointestinal: Constipation, nausea, vomiting

<1%: Confusion (especially in the elderly), rash, leukopenia, increased intraocular pressure

(Continued)

Flavoxate *(Continued)*

Overdosage/Toxicology
Symptoms of overdose include clumsiness, dizziness, drowsiness, flushing, hallucinations, irritability
Supportive care only

Mechanism of Action
Synthetic antispasmotic with similar actions to that of propantheline; it exerts a direct relaxant effect on smooth muscles via phosphodiesterase inhibition, providing relief to a variety of smooth muscle spasms; it is especially useful for the treatment of bladder spasticity, whereby it produces an increase in urinary capacity

Pharmacodynamics/Kinetics
Onset of action: 55-60 minutes
Metabolism: To methyl; flavone carboxylic acid active
Elimination: 10% to 30% of dose excreted in urine within 6 hours

Usual Dosage
Children >12 years and Adults: Oral: 100-200 mg 3-4 times/day; reduce the dose when symptoms improve

Monitoring Parameters
Monitor I & O closely

Patient Information
May cause drowsiness, dizziness, or visual disturbances; use with caution if performing tasks requiring coordination or mental alertness; avoid other substances that may cause similar effects (eg, alcohol); may cause dry mouth

Dosage Forms
Tablet, film coated, as hydrochloride: 100 mg

♦ **Flavoxate Hydrochloride** *see Flavoxate on previous page*

Flecainide *(fle KAY nide)*

Related Information
Antacid Drug Interactions *on page 1296*
Antiarrhythmic Drugs Comparison *on page 1297*

U.S. Brand Names
Tambocor™

Synonyms
Flecainide Acetate

Therapeutic Category
Antiarrhythmic Agent, Class I-C

Use
Prevention and suppression of documented life-threatening ventricular arrhythmias (ie, sustained ventricular tachycardia); controlling symptomatic, disabling supraventricular tachycardias in patients without structural heart disease in whom other agents fail

Pregnancy Risk Factor
C

Contraindications
Pre-existing second or third degree A-V block; right bundle-branch block associated with left hemiblock (bifascicular block) or trifascicular block; cardiogenic shock, myocardial depression; known hypersensitivity to the drug; concurrent use of ritonavir

Warnings/Precautions
Pre-existing sinus node dysfunction, sick-sinus syndrome, history of congestive heart failure or myocardial dysfunction; increases in P-R interval ≥300 MS, QRS ≥180 MS, QT_c interval increases, and/or new bundle-branch block; patients with pacemakers, renal impairment, and/or hepatic impairment.

The manufacturer and FDA recommend that this drug be reserved for life-threatening ventricular arrhythmias unresponsive to conventional therapy. Its use for symptomatic nonsustained ventricular tachycardia, frequent premature ventricular complexes (PVCs), uniform and multiform PVCs and/or coupled PVCs is no longer recommended. Flecainide can worsen or cause arrhythmias with an associated risk of death. Proarrhythmic effects range from an increased number of PVCs to more severe ventricular tachycardias (eg, tachycardias that are more sustained or more resistant to conversion to sinus rhythm).

Adverse Reactions
>10%:
Central nervous system: Dizziness (19%)
Ocular: Visual disturbances (16%)
Respiratory: Dyspnea (~10%)

1% to 10%:
Cardiovascular: Palpitations (6%), chest pain (5%), edema (3.5%), tachycardia (1% to 3%)
Central nervous system: Headache (4%), fatigue (8%), fever (1% to 3%), malaise (1% to 3%)
Dermatologic: Rash (1% to 3%)
Gastrointestinal: Nausea (9%), constipation, abdominal pain (3%), anorexia (1% to 3%)
Neuromuscular & skeletal: Tremor (5%), weakness (5%)
Ocular: Diplopia (1% to 3%)

<1%: Bradycardia, heart block, increased P-R, QRS duration, worsening ventricular arrhythmias, congestive heart failure, flushing, A-V block, angina, hyper/hypotension, nervousness, hypoesthesia, ataxia, vertigo, somnolence, alopecia, flatulence, xerostomia, blood dyscrasias, possible hepatic dysfunction, paresthesia, eye pain, photophobia, tinnitus

Overdosage/Toxicology
Has a narrow therapeutic index and severe toxicity may occur slightly above the therapeutic range, especially if combined with other antiarrhythmic drugs. (Acute single ingestion of twice the daily therapeutic dose is life-threatening.) Symptoms of overdose include increases in P-R, QRS, Q-T intervals and amplitude of the T wave, A-V block, bradycardia, hypotension, ventricular arrhythmias (monomorphic or polymorphic ventricular tachycardia), and asystole; other symptoms include dizziness, blurred vision, headache, and GI upset.

Treatment is supportive, using conventional treatment (fluids, positioning, anticonvulsants, antiarrhythmics). **Note:** Type Ia antiarrhythmic agents should not be used to treat cardiotoxicity caused by type Ic drugs; sodium bicarbonate may reverse QRS prolongation, bradycardia and hypotension; ventricular pacing may be needed; hemodialysis only of possible benefit for tocainide or flecainide overdose in patients with renal failure.

Drug Interactions CYP2D6 enzyme substrate

Increased toxicity:

Flecainide increases the bioavailability/toxicity of propranolol

Digoxin, amiodarone increase plasma concentrations of flecainide and may increase toxicity

Beta-adrenergic blockers, disopyramide, verapamil (possible additive negative inotropic effects)

Alkalinizing agents (high dose antacids, cimetidine, carbonic anhydrase inhibitors or sodium bicarbonate) may decrease flecainide clearance

Avoid use with ritonavir due to increased risk of flecainide toxicity, especially cardiotoxicity

Decreased toxicity: Smoking and acid urine (increases flecainide clearance)

Mechanism of Action Class Ic antiarrhythmic; slows conduction in cardiac tissue by altering transport of ions across cell membranes; causes slight prolongation of refractory periods; decreases the rate of rise of the action potential without affecting its duration; increases electrical stimulation threshold of ventricle, HIS-Purkinje system; possesses local anesthetic and moderate negative inotropic effects

Pharmacodynamics/Kinetics

Absorption: Oral: Rapid

Distribution: Adults: V_d: 5-13.4 L/kg

Protein binding: 40% to 50% (alpha$_1$ glycoprotein)

Bioavailability: 85% to 90%

Metabolism: In the liver

Half-life: Infants: 11-12 hours; Children: 8 hours; Adults: 7-22 hours, increased with congestive heart failure or renal dysfunction; End-stage renal disease: 19-26 hours

Time to peak serum concentration: Within 1.5-3 hours

Elimination: 80% to 90% excreted in urine as unchanged drug and metabolites (10% to 50%)

Usual Dosage Oral:

Children:

Initial: 3 mg/kg/day or 50-100 mg/m^2/day in 3 divided doses

Usual: 3-6 mg/kg/day or 100-150 mg/m^2/day in 3 divided doses; up to 11 mg/kg/day or 200 mg/m^2/day for uncontrolled patients with subtherapeutic levels

Adults:

Life-threatening ventricular arrhythmias:

Initial: 100 mg every 12 hours

Increase by 50-100 mg/day (given in 2 doses/day) every 4 days; maximum: 400 mg/day

Use of higher initial doses and more rapid dosage adjustments have resulted in an increased incidence of proarrhythmic events and congestive heart failure, particularly during the first few days. Do not use a loading dose. Use very cautiously in patients with history of congestive heart failure or myocardial infarction.

Prevention of paroxysmal supraventricular arrhythmias in patients with disabling symptoms but no structural heart disease:

Initial: 50 mg every 12 hours

Increase by 50 mg twice daily at 4-day intervals; maximum: 300 mg/day

Dosing adjustment in severe renal impairment: Cl$_{cr}$ <35 mL/minute: Decrease initial dose to 50 mg every 12 hours; increase doses at intervals >4 days monitoring plasma levels closely

Dialysis: Not dialyzable (0% to 5%) via hemo- or peritoneal dialysis; no supplemental dose necessary

Dosing adjustment/comments in hepatic impairment: Monitoring of plasma levels is recommended because of significantly increased half-life

When transferring from another antiarrhythmic agent, allow for 2-4 half-lives of the agent to pass before initiating flecainide therapy

Administration Administer around-the-clock to promote less variation in peak and trough serum levels

Monitoring Parameters EKG, blood pressure, pulse, periodic serum concentrations, especially in patients with renal or hepatic impairment

Reference Range Therapeutic: 0.2-1 µg/mL; pediatric patients may respond at the lower end of the recommended therapeutic range

Patient Information Notify physician if chest pain, faintness, or palpitations occurs; take only as prescribed

Dosage Forms Tablet, as acetate: 50 mg, 100 mg, 150 mg

Extemporaneous Preparations A 5 mg/mL suspension compounded from tablets and an oral flavored commercially available diluent (Roxane®) was stable for up to 45 days when stored at 5°C or 25°C in amber glass bottles. Flecainide 20 mg/mL was found stable for up to 60 days at 5°C and 25°C in a 1:1 preparation of Ora-Sweet® and Ora-Plus®, in Ora-Sweet® SF and Ora-Plus® and in cherry syrup

Allen LV and Erickson III MA, "Stability of Baclofen, Captopril, Diltiazem, Hydrochloride, Dipyridamole, and Flecainide Acetate in Extemporaneously Compounded Oral Liquids," *Am J Health Syst Pharm*, 53:2179-84.

(Continued)

Flecainide *(Continued)*

Wiest DB, Garner SS, and Pagacz LR, "Stability of Flecainide Acetate in an Extemporaneously Compounded Oral Suspension," *Am J Hosp Pharm*, 1992, 49(6):1467-70.

- ◆ **Flecainide Acetate** *see* Flecainide *on page 486*
- ◆ **Flexaphen®** *see* Chlorzoxazone *on page 252*
- ◆ **Flexeril®** *see* Cyclobenzaprine *on page 304*
- ◆ **Flodine®** *see* Folic Acid *on page 512*
- ◆ **Flolan® Injection** *see* Epoprostenol *on page 421*
- ◆ **Flomax®** *see* Tamsulosin *on page 1107*
- ◆ **Flonase®** *see* Fluticasone *on page 509*
- ◆ **Florical® [OTC]** *see* Calcium Carbonate *on page 174*
- ◆ **Florinef® Acetate** *see* Fludrocortisone Acetate *on page 492*
- ◆ **Florone®** *see* Diflorasone *on page 356*
- ◆ **Florone E®** *see* Diflorasone *on page 356*
- ◆ **Floropryl® Ophthalmic** *see* Isoflurophate *on page 633*
- ◆ **Florvite®** *see* Vitamins, Multiple *on page 1226*
- ◆ **Flovent®** *see* Fluticasone *on page 509*
- ◆ **Floxin®** *see* Ofloxacin *on page 859*
- ◆ **Flubenisolone** *see* Betamethasone *on page 141*

Fluconazole *(floo KOE na zole)*

Related Information

Antifungal Agents Comparison *on page 1303*

Guidelines for the Prevention of Opportunistic Infections in Persons with HIV *on page 1388*

Treatment of Sexually Transmitted Diseases *on page 1429*

U.S. Brand Names Diflucan®

Therapeutic Category Antifungal Agent, Systemic

Use Indications for use in adult patients: Oral or vaginal candidiasis unresponsive to nystatin or clotrimazole; nonlife-threatening *Candida* infections (eg, cystitis, esophagitis); treatment of hepatosplenic candidiasis and other *Candida* infections in persons unable to tolerate amphotericin B; treatment of cryptococcal infections; secondary prophylaxis for cryptococcal meningitis in persons with AIDS; antifungal prophylaxis in allogeneic bone marrow transplant recipients

Oral fluconazole should be used in persons able to tolerate oral medications; parenteral fluconazole should be reserved for patients who are both unable to take oral medications and are unable to tolerate amphotericin B (eg, due to hypersensitivity or renal insufficiency)

Pregnancy Risk Factor C

Contraindications Known hypersensitivity to fluconazole or other azoles; concomitant administration with terfenadine

Warnings/Precautions Should be used with caution in patients with renal and hepatic dysfunction or previous hepatotoxicity from other azole derivatives. Patients who develop abnormal liver function tests during fluconazole therapy should be monitored closely and discontinued if symptoms consistent with liver disease develop. **Should be used with caution in patients receiving cisapride or astemizole.**

Adverse Reactions

1% to 10%:

Central nervous system: Headache

Dermatologic: Rash

Gastrointestinal: Nausea, vomiting, abdominal pain, diarrhea

<1%: Pallor, dizziness, hypokalemia, increased AST/ALT, or alkaline phosphatase

Overdosage/Toxicology

Symptoms of overdose include decreased lacrimation, salivation, respiration and motility, urinary incontinence, cyanosis

Treatment includes supportive measures, a 3-hour hemodialysis will remove 50%

Drug Interactions CYP2C9 enzyme inducer; CYP2C9, 2C18, and 2C19 enzyme inhibitor and CYP3A3/4 enzyme inhibitor (weak)

Decreased effect: Rifampin and cimetidine decrease concentrations of fluconazole; fluconazole may decrease the effect of oral contraceptives

Increased effect/toxicity:

Coadministration with terfenadine or cisapride is contraindicated; use with caution with astemizole due to increased risk of significant cardiotoxicity

Hydrochlorothiazide may decrease fluconazole clearance

Fluconazole may also inhibit warfarin, phenytoin, cyclosporine, and theophylline, zidovudine, sulfonylureas, rifabutin, and warfarin clearance

Nephrotoxicity of tacrolimus may be increased

Stability Parenteral admixture at room temperature (25°C): Manufacturer expiration dating; do not refrigerate

Standard diluent: 200 mg/100 mL NS (premixed); 400 mg/200 mL NS (premixed)

Mechanism of Action Interferes with cytochrome P-450 activity, decreasing ergosterol synthesis (principal sterol in fungal cell membrane) and inhibiting cell membrane formation

Pharmacodynamics/Kinetics

Distribution: Widely distributed throughout body with good penetration into CSF, eye, peritoneal fluid, sputum, skin, and urine; relative diffusion of antimicrobial agents from blood into CSF: Adequate with or without inflammation (exceeds usual MICs)

Ratio of CSF to blood level (%): Normal meninges: 70-80; Inflamed meninges: >70-80

Protein binding, plasma: 11% to 12%

Bioavailability: Oral: >90%

Half-life: 25-30 hours with normal renal function

Time to peak serum concentration: Oral: Within 2-4 hours

Elimination: 80% of a dose excreted unchanged in the urine

Usual Dosage The daily dose of fluconazole is the same for oral and I.V. administration

Neonates: First 2 weeks of life, especially premature neonates: Same dose as older children every 72 hours

Children: See table for once daily dosing

Fluconazole — Once-Daily Dosing (Children)

Indication	Day 1	Daily Therapy	Minimum Duration of Therapy
Oropharyngeal candidiasis	6 mg/kg	3 mg/kg	14 d
Esophageal candidiasis	6 mg/kg	3-12 mg/kg	21 d and for at least 2 wks following resolution of symptoms
Systemic candidiasis	—	6-12 mg/kg	28 d
Cryptococcal meningitis	12 mg/kg	6-12 mg/kg	10-12 wk after CSF culture becomes negative
relapse	6 mg/kg	6 mg/kg	

Adults: Oral, I.V.: See table for once daily dosing.

Fluconazole — Once-Daily Dosing (Adults)

Indication	Day 1	Daily Therapy	Minimum Duration of Therapy
Oropharyngeal candidiasis	200 mg	100 mg	14 d
Esophageal candidiasis	200 mg	100 mg	21 d and for at least 14 d following resolution of symptoms
Prevention of candidiasis in bone marrow transplant	400 mg	400 mg	3 d before neutropenia, 7 d after neutrophils >1000 cells/mm³
Candidiasis UTIs, peritonitis	Twice daily dose	50-200 mg	
Systemic candidiasis	400 mg	200 mg	28 d
Cryptococcal meningitis			10-12 wk after CSF culture becomes negative
acute	400 mg	200 mg	
relapse	200 mg	200 mg	
Vaginal candidiasis	150 mg	Single dose	

Dosing adjustment/interval in renal impairment:

No adjustment for vaginal candidiasis single-dose therapy

For multiple dosing, administer usual load then adjust daily doses

Cl_{cr} 11-50 mL/minute: Administer 50% of recommended dose or administer every 48 hours

Hemodialysis: One dose after each dialysis

Continuous arteriovenous or venovenous hemodiafiltration (CAVH) effects: Dose as for Cl_{cr} 10-50 mL/minute

Administration Parenteral fluconazole must be administered by I.V. infusion over approximately 1-2 hours; do not exceed 200 mg/hour when giving I.V. infusion; maximum rate of infusion: 200 mg/hour

Monitoring Parameters Periodic liver function tests (AST, ALT, alkaline phosphatase) and renal function tests, potassium

Patient Information May take with food; complete full course of therapy; contact physician or pharmacist if side effects develop; consider using an alternative method of contraception if taking concurrently with birth control pills

Dosage Forms

Injection: 2 mg/mL (100 mL, 200 mL)

Powder for oral suspension: 10 mg/mL (35 mL); 40 mg/mL (35 mL)

Tablet: 50 mg, 100 mg, 150 mg, 200 mg

Flucytosine (floo SYE toe seen)

Related Information

Antifungal Agents Comparison *on page 1303*

U.S. Brand Names Ancobon®

Canadian Brand Names Ancotil®

Synonyms 5-FC; 5-Flurocytosine

Therapeutic Category Antifungal Agent, Systemic

(Continued)

Flucytosine *(Continued)*

Use Adjunctive treatment of susceptible fungal infections (usually *Candida* or *Crypto-coccus*); synergy with amphotericin B for certain fungal infections (*Cryptococcus* spp., *Candida* spp.)

Pregnancy Risk Factor C

Contraindications Hypersensitivity to flucytosine or any component

Warnings/Precautions Use with extreme caution in patients with renal impairment, bone marrow suppression, or in patients with AIDS; dosage modification required in patients with impaired renal function

Adverse Reactions

1% to 10%:

  Dermatologic: Rash

  Gastrointestinal: Abdominal pain, diarrhea, loss of appetite, nausea, vomiting

  Hematologic: Anemia, leukopenia, thrombocytopenia

  Hepatic: Hepatitis, jaundice

<1%: Cardiac arrest, confusion, hallucinations, dizziness, drowsiness, headache, parkinsonism, psychosis, ataxia, photosensitivity, temporary growth failure, hypoglycemia, hypokalemia, bone marrow suppression, elevated liver enzymes, paresthesia, hearing loss, respiratory arrest, anaphylaxis

Overdosage/Toxicology

Symptoms of overdose include nausea, vomiting, diarrhea, bone marrow suppression

Treatment is supportive

Drug Interactions Increased effect/toxicity with concurrent amphotericin administration; cytosine may inactivate flucytosine activity

Stability Protect from light

Mechanism of Action Penetrates fungal cells and is converted to fluorouracil which competes with uracil interfering with fungal RNA and protein synthesis

Pharmacodynamics/Kinetics

Absorption: Oral: 75% to 90%

Distribution: Into CSF, aqueous humor, joints, peritoneal fluid, and bronchial secretions

Metabolism: Minimal

Protein binding: 2% to 4%

Half-life: 3-8 hours

  Anuria: May be as long as 200 hours

  End-stage renal disease: 75-200 hours

Time to peak serum concentration: Within 2-6 hours

Elimination: 75% to 90% excreted unchanged in the urine by glomerular filtration

Usual Dosage Children and Adults: Oral: 50-150 mg/kg/day in divided doses every 6 hours

Dosing interval in renal impairment: Use lower initial dose:

  Cl_{cr} >50 mL/minute: Administer every 12 hours

  Cl_{cr} 10-50 mL/minute: Administer every 16 hours

  Cl_{cr} <10 mL/minute: Administer every 24 hours

Hemodialysis: Dialyzable (50% to 100%); administer dose posthemodialysis

Peritoneal dialysis: Adults: Administer 0.5-1 g every 24 hours

Continuous arteriovenous or venovenous hemodiafiltration (CAVH) effects: Dose as for Cl_{cr} 10-50 mL/minute

Monitoring Parameters Serum creatinine, BUN, alkaline phosphatase, AST, ALT, CBC; serum flucytosine concentrations

Reference Range

Therapeutic: 25-100 µg/mL (SI: 195-775 µmol/L); levels should not exceed 100-120 µg/mL to avoid toxic bone marrow depressive effects

Trough: Draw just prior to dose administration

Peak: Draw 2 hours after an oral dose administration

Test Interactions Flucytosine causes markedly false elevations in serum creatinine values when the Ektachem® analyzer is used

Patient Information Take capsules a few at a time with food over a 15-minute period to avoid nausea

Dosage Forms Capsule: 250 mg, 500 mg

Extemporaneous Preparations Flucytosine oral liquid has been prepared by using the contents of ten 500 mg capsules triturated in a mortar and pestle with a small amount of distilled water; the mixture was transferred to a 500 mL volumetric flask; the mortar was rinsed several times with a small amount of distilled water and the fluid added to the flask; sufficient distilled water was added to make a total volume of 500 mL of a 10 mg/mL liquid; oral liquid was stable for 70 days when stored in glass or plastic prescription bottles at 4°C or for up to 14 days at room temperature.

Wintermeyer SM and Nahata MC, "Stability of Flucytosine in an Extemporaneously Compounded Oral Liquid," *Am J Health Syst Pharm*, 1996, 53:407-9.

◆ **Fludara**® *see Fludarabine on this page*

Fludarabine *(floo DARE a been)*

Related Information

Cancer Chemotherapy Regimens *on page 1263*
Toxicities of Chemotherapeutic Agents *on page 1288*

U.S. Brand Names Fludara®

Synonyms Fludarabine Phosphate

Therapeutic Category Antineoplastic Agent, Antimetabolite (Purine)

Use Treatment of chronic lymphocytic leukemia (B-cell) in patients who have not responded to other alkylating agent regimen

Pregnancy Risk Factor D

Contraindications Hypersensitivity of fludarabine; patients with severe infections

Warnings/Precautions The U.S. Food and Drug Administration (FDA) currently recommends that procedures for proper handling and disposal of antineoplastic agents be considered. Use with caution in renal insufficiency, patients with a fever, documented infection, or pre-existing hematological disorders (particularly granulocytopenia) or in patients with pre-existing central nervous system disorder (epilepsy), spasticity, or peripheral neuropathy. Use with caution in patients with pre-existing renal insufficiency. Life-threatening and sometimes fatal autoimmune hemolytic anemia have occurred.

Adverse Reactions
>10%:
  Cardiovascular: Edema
  Central nervous system: Fever, chills, fatigue, pain
  Dermatologic: Rash
  Gastrointestinal: Mild nausea, vomiting, diarrhea, stomatitis, GI bleeding
  Genitourinary: Urinary infection
  Hematologic: Myelosuppression: Dose-limiting toxicity; myelosuppression may not be related to cumulative dose
    Granulocyte nadir: 13 days (3-25)
    Platelet nadir: 16 days (2-32)
    WBC nadir: 8 days
    Recovery: 5-7 weeks
  Neuromuscular & skeletal: Paresthesia, myalgia, weakness
  Respiratory: Manifested as dyspnea and a nonproductive cough; lung biopsy has shown pneumonitis in some patients, pneumonia
  Miscellaneous: Infection
1% to 10%:
  Cardiovascular: Congestive heart failure
  Central nervous system: Malaise, headache
  Dermatologic: Alopecia
  Endocrine & metabolic: Hyperglycemia
  Gastrointestinal: Anorexia
  Otic: Hearing loss
<1%: Reported with higher dose levels; most patients shown to have CNS demyelination; somnolence, blindness, coma, and death also occurred; severe neurotoxicity; skin rash, metabolic acidosis, metallic taste, life-threatening and sometimes fatal autoimmune hemolytic anemia; often recurs on rechallenge; steroid treatment may or may not be beneficial; reversible hepatotoxicity, renal failure, hematuria, increased serum creatinine, interstitial pneumonitis, tumor lysis syndrome

Overdosage/Toxicology There are clear dose-dependent toxic neurologic effects associated with fludarabine. Doses of 96 mg/m²/day for 5-7 days are associated with a syndrome characterized by delayed blindness, coma, and death. Symptoms appeared from 21-60 days following the last dose. The central nervous system toxicity has distinctive features of delayed onset and progressive encephalopathy resulting in fatal outcomes. It is reported at an incidence rate of 36% at high doses (≥96 mg/m²/day for 5-7 days) and <0.2% for low doses (≤125 mg/m²/course).

Drug Interactions Increased toxicity: Cytarabine when administered with or prior to a fludarabine dose competes for deoxycytidine kinase decreasing the metabolism of F-ara-A to the active F-ara-ATP (inhibits the antineoplastic effect of fludarabine); however, administering fludarabine prior to cytarabine may stimulate activation of cytarabine

Stability
Store intact vials under refrigeration (2°C to 8°C); stable for 48 hours at room temperature
  Reconstitute vials with 2 mL SWI to result in a concentration of 25 mg/mL; solution is stable for 16 days at room temperature (22°C to 25°C) and under refrigeration (2°C to 8°C)
  Further dilution in 100 mL D₅W or NS is stable for 48 hours at room temperature or refrigeration

Standard I.V. dilution:
  Dose/100 mL D₅W or NS
  Stable for 48 hours at 4°C to 25°C

Mechanism of Action Fludarabine is analogous to that of Ara-C and Ara-A. Following systemic administration, FAMP is rapidly dephosphorylated to 2-fluoro-Ara-A. 2-Fluoro-Ara-A enters the cell by a carrier-mediated transport process, then is phosphorylated intracellularly by deoxycytidine kinase to form the active metabolite 2-fluoro-Ara-ATP. 2-Fluoro-Ara-ATP inhibits DNA synthesis by inhibition of DNA polymerase and ribonucleotide reductase.

Pharmacodynamics/Kinetics
Absorption: Oral preparation is under study
Bioavailability: 75%
Distribution: V_d: 38-96 L/m²; widely distributed with extensive tissue binding
Metabolism: I.V.: Fludarabine phosphate is rapidly dephosphorylated to 2-fluoro-vidarabine, which subsequently enters tumor cells and is phosphorylated to the active triphosphate derivative; rapidly dephosphorylated in the serum
Half-life, elimination: 2-fluoro-vidarabine: 9 hours
Elimination: 23% of a dose of fludarabine is recovered in urine as 2-fluoro-vidarabine
(Continued)

Fludarabine *(Continued)*

Usual Dosage I.V.:

Children:

Acute leukemia: 10 mg/m^2 bolus over 15 minutes followed by continuous infusion of 30.5 mg/m^2/day over 5 days **or**

10.5 mg/m^2 bolus over 15 minutes followed by 30.5 mg/m^2/day over 48 hours followed by cytarabine has been used in clinical trials

Solid tumors: 9 mg/m^2 bolus followed by 27 mg/m^2/day continuous infusion over 5 days

Adults:

Chronic lymphocytic leukemia: 25 mg/m^2/day over a 30-minute period for 5 days; 5-day courses are repeated every 28 days days

Non-Hodgkin's lymphoma: Loading dose: 20 mg/m^2 followed by 30 mg/m^2/day for 48 hours

Dosing in renal impairment: Cl$_{cr}$ <50 mL/minute: Monitor closely for toxicity; dose reduction is indicated in patients with renal failure. However, no specific guidelines are available

Administration Administer I.V. over 15-30 minutes or continuous infusion

Monitoring Parameters CBC with differential, platelet count, AST, ALT, creatinine, serum albumin, uric acid

Reference Range Peak plasma levels: 0.3-0.9 µg/mL following a short infusion of 25 mg/m^2

Dosage Forms Powder for injection, as phosphate, lyophilized: 50 mg (6 mL)

♦ **Fludarabine Phosphate** *see* Fludarabine *on page 490*

Fludrocortisone Acetate (floo droe KOR ti sone AS e tate)

Related Information

Corticosteroids Comparison *on page 1319*

U.S. Brand Names Florinef® Acetate

Synonyms Fluohydrisone Acetate; Fluohydrocortisone Acetate; 9α-Fluorohydrocortisone Acetate

Therapeutic Category Mineralocorticoid

Use Partial replacement therapy for primary and secondary adrenocortical insufficiency in Addison's disease; treatment of salt-losing adrenogenital syndrome

Pregnancy Risk Factor C

Contraindications Known hypersensitivity to fludrocortisone; systemic fungal infections

Warnings/Precautions Taper dose gradually when therapy is discontinued; use with caution with Addison's disease, sodium retention and potassium loss

Adverse Reactions 1% to 10%:

Cardiovascular: Hypertension, edema, congestive heart failure

Central nervous system: Convulsions, headache, dizziness

Dermatologic: Acne, rash, bruising

Endocrine & metabolic: Hypokalemic alkalosis, suppression of growth, hyperglycemia, HPA suppression

Gastrointestinal: Peptic ulcer

Neuromuscular & skeletal: Muscle weakness

Ocular: Cataracts

Miscellaneous: Diaphoresis

Overdosage/Toxicology Symptoms of overdose include hypertension, edema, hypokalemia, excessive weight gain. When consumed in excessive quantities, systemic hypercorticism and adrenal suppression may occur; in those cases, discontinuation and withdrawal of the corticosteroid should be done judiciously.

Drug Interactions Decreased effect:

Anticholinesterases effects are antagonized

Decreased corticosteroid effects by rifampin, barbiturates, and hydantoins

Decreased salicylate levels

Mechanism of Action Promotes increased reabsorption of sodium and loss of potassium from renal distal tubules

Pharmacodynamics/Kinetics

Absorption: Rapid and complete from GI tract, partially absorbed through skin

Protein binding: 42%

Metabolism: In the liver

Half-life: Plasma: 30-35 minutes; Biological: 18-36 hours

Time to peak serum concentration: Within 1.7 hours

Usual Dosage Oral:

Infants and Children: 0.05-0.1 mg/day

Adults: 0.1-0.2 mg/day with ranges of 0.1 mg 3 times/week to 0.2 mg/day

Addison's disease: Initial: 0.1 mg/day; if transient hypertension develops, reduce the dose to 0.05 mg/day. Preferred administration with cortisone (10-37.5 mg/day) or hydrocortisone (10-30 mg/day).

Salt-losing adrenogenital syndrome: 0.1-0.2 mg/day

Administration Administration in conjunction with a glucocorticoid is preferable

Monitoring Parameters Monitor blood pressure and signs of edema when patient is on chronic therapy; very potent mineralocorticoid with high glucocorticoid activity; monitor serum electrolytes, serum renin activity, and blood pressure; monitor for evidence of infection

Patient Information Notify physician if dizziness, severe or continuing headaches, swelling of feet or lower legs or unusual weight gain occur

Dosage Forms Tablet: 0.1 mg

♦ **Flumadine**® *see* Rimantadine *on page 1028*

Flumazenil (FLO may ze nil)

Replaces Mazicon™

U.S. Brand Names Romazicon™ Injection

Canadian Brand Names Anexate®

Therapeutic Category Antidote, Benzodiazepine

Use Benzodiazepine antagonist - reverses sedative effects of benzodiazepines used in general anesthesia; for management of benzodiazepine overdose; flumazenil does **not** antagonize the CNS effects of other GABA agonists (such as ethanol, barbiturates, or general anesthetics), **does not** reverse narcotics

Pregnancy Risk Factor C

Contraindications Known hypersensitivity to flumazenil or benzodiazepines; patients given benzodiazepines for control of potentially life-threatening conditions (eg, control of intracranial pressure or status epilepticus); patients who are showing signs of serious cyclic-antidepressant overdosage

Warnings/Precautions

Risk of seizures = high-risk patients:

Patients on benzodiazepines for long-term sedation

Tricyclic antidepressant overdose patients

Concurrent major sedative-hypnotic drug withdrawal

Recent therapy with repeated doses of parenteral benzodiazepines

Myoclonic jerking or seizure activity prior to flumazenil administration

Hypoventilation: Does not reverse respiratory depression/hypoventilation or cardiac depression

Resedation: Occurs more frequently in patients where a large single dose or cumulative dose of a benzodiazepine is administered along with a neuromuscular blocking agent and multiple anesthetic agents

Flumazenil should be used with caution in the intensive care unit because of increased risk of unrecognized benzodiazepine dependence in such settings.

Flumazenil

Pediatric Dosage	
Further studies are needed	
Pediatric dosage for **reversal of conscious sedation:** Intravenously through a freely running intravenous infusion into a large vein to minimize pain at the injection site	
Initial dose	0.01 mg/kg over 15 seconds (maximum dose of 0.2 mg)
Repeat doses	0.005-0.01 mg/kg (maximum dose of 0.2 mg) repeated at 1-minute intervals
Maximum total cumulative dose	1 mg
Pediatric dosage for **management of benzodiazepine overdose:** Intravenously through a freely running intravenous infusion into a large vein to minimize pain at the injection site	
Initial dose	0.01 mg/kg (maximum dose: 0.2 mg)
Repeat doses	0.01 mg/kg (maximum dose of 0.2 mg) repeated at 1-minute intervals
Maximum total cumulative dose	1 mg
In place of repeat bolus doses, follow-up continuous infusions of 0.005-0.01 mg/kg/hour have been used; further studies are needed.	
Adult Dosage	
Adult dosage for **reversal of conscious sedation:** Intravenously through a freely running intravenous infusion into a large vein to minimize pain at the injection site	
Initial dose	0.2 mg intravenously over 15 seconds
Repeat doses	If desired level of consciousness is not obtained, 0.2 mg may be repeated at 1-minute intervals.
Maximum total cumulative dose	1 mg (usual dose 0.6-1 mg) **In the event of resedation:** Repeat doses may be given at 20-minute intervals with maximum of 1 mg/dose and 3 mg/hour
Adult dosage for **suspected benzodiazepine overdose:** Intravenously through a freely running intravenous infusion into a large vein to minimize pain at the injection site	
Initial dose	0.2 mg intravenously over 30 seconds
Repeat doses	0.5 mg over 30 seconds repeated at 1-minute intervals
Maximum total cumulative dose	3 mg (usual dose 1-3 mg) Patients with a partial response at 3 mg may require additional titration up to a total dose of 5 mg. If a patient has not responded 5 minutes after cumulative dose of 5 mg, the major cause of sedation is not likely due to benzodiazepines. **In the event of resedation:** May repeat doses at 20-minute intervals with maximum of 1 mg/dose and 3 mg/hour

(Continued)

Flumazenil *(Continued)*

Adverse Reactions

>10%:
  Central nervous system: Dizziness
  Gastrointestinal: Vomiting, nausea

1% to 10%:
  Central nervous system: Headache, asthenia, malaise, anxiety, nervousness, insomnia, abnormal crying, euphoria, depression
  Endocrine & metabolic: Hot flashes
  Gastrointestinal: Xerostomia
  Local: Pain at injection site
  Neuromuscular & skeletal: Tremor
  Ocular: Abnormal vision
  Respiratory: Dyspnea, hyperventilation
  Miscellaneous: Increased sweating disorders

<1%: Bradycardia, tachycardia, chest pain, hypertension, ventricular extrasystoles, altered blood pressure (increases and decreases), anxiety and sensation of coldness, generalized convulsions, somnolence, thick tongue, abnormal hearing, hiccups

Drug Interactions Increased toxicity: Use with caution in overdosage involving mixed drug overdose; toxic effects may emerge (especially with cyclic antidepressants) with the reversal of the benzodiazepine effect by flumazenil

Stability For I.V. use only; **compatible** with D₅W, lactated Ringer's, or normal saline; once drawn up in the syringe or mixed with solution use within 24 hours; discard any unused solution after 24 hours

Mechanism of Action Antagonizes the effect of benzodiazepines on the GABA/benzodiazepine receptor complex. Flumazenil is benzodiazepine specific and does not antagonize other nonbenzodiazepine GABA agonists (including ethanol, barbiturates, general anesthetics); flumazenil does not reverse the effects of opiates

Pharmacodynamics/Kinetics

Onset of action: 1-3 minutes; 80% response within 3 minutes

Peak effect: 6-10 minutes

Duration: Resedation occurs usually within 1 hour; duration is related to dose given and benzodiazepine plasma concentrations; reversal effects of flumazenil may wear off before effects of benzodiazepine

Distribution: 0.63-1.06 L/kg; Initial V_d: 0.5 L/kg; V_{dss} 0.77-1.6 L/kg

Protein binding: 40% to 50%

Half-life, adults: Alpha: 7-15 minutes; Terminal: 41-79 minutes

Elimination: Clearance dependent upon hepatic blood flow; hepatically eliminated, 0.2% unchanged in urine

Usual Dosage See table.

Resedation: Repeated doses may be given at 20-minute intervals as needed; repeat treatment doses of 1 mg (at a rate of 0.5 mg/minute) should be given at any time and no more than 3 mg should be given in any hour. After intoxication with high doses of benzodiazepines, the duration of a single dose of flumazenil is not expected to exceed 1 hour; if desired, the period of wakefulness may be prolonged with repeated low intravenous doses of flumazenil, or by an infusion of 0.1-0.4 mg/hour. Most patients with benzodiazepine overdose will respond to a cumulative dose of 1-3 mg and doses >3 mg do not reliably produce additional effects. Rarely, patients with a partial response at 3 mg may require additional titration up to a total dose of 5 mg. **If a patient has not responded 5 minutes after receiving a cumulative dose of 5 mg, the major cause of sedation is not likely to be due to benzodiazepines.**

Dosing in renal impairment: Not significantly affected by renal failure (Cl$_{cr}$ <10 mL/minute) or hemodialysis beginning 1 hour after drug administration

Dosing in hepatic impairment: Initial dose of flumazenil used for initial reversal of benzodiazepine effects is not changed; however, subsequent doses in liver disease patients should be reduced in size or frequency

Monitoring Parameters Monitor patients for return of sedation or respiratory depression

Patient Information Flumazenil does not consistently reverse amnesia; do not engage in activities requiring alertness for 18-24 hours after discharge; resedation may occur in patients on long-acting benzodiazepines (such as diazepam)

Dosage Forms Injection: 0.1 mg/mL (5 mL, 10 mL)

Flunisolide *(floo NIS oh lide)*

Related Information

Asthma, Guidelines for the Diagnosis and Management of *on page 1456*
Estimated Clinical Comparability of Doses for Inhaled Corticosteroids *on page 1463*

U.S. Brand Names AeroBid®-M Oral Aerosol Inhaler; AeroBid® Oral Aerosol Inhaler; Nasalide® Nasal Aerosol; Nasarel™

Canadian Brand Names Bronalide®; Rhinalar®; Rhinaris®-F; Syn-Flunisolide

Therapeutic Category Anti-inflammatory Agent, Inhalant; Corticosteroid, Inhalant; Corticosteroid, Intranasal

Use Steroid-dependent asthma; nasal solution is used for seasonal or perennial rhinitis

Pregnancy Risk Factor C

Pregnancy/Breast-Feeding Implications

Clinical effects on the fetus: No data on crossing the placenta or effects on the fetus
Breast-feeding/lactation: No data on crossing into breast milk or effects on the infant

Contraindications Known hypersensitivity to flunisolide, acute status asthmaticus; viral, tuberculosis, fungal or bacterial respiratory infections, or infections of nasal mucosa

Warnings/Precautions Use with caution in patients with hypothyroidism, cirrhosis, hypertension, congestive heart failure, ulcerative colitis, thromboembolic disorders; do not stop medication abruptly if on prolonged therapy; fatalities have occurred due to adrenal insufficiency in asthmatic patients during and after transfer from systemic corticosteroids to aerosol steroids; several months may be required for recovery of this syndrome; during this period, aerosol steroids do **not** provide the systemic steroid needed to treat patients having trauma, surgery or infections. When consumed in excessive quantities, systemic hypercorticism and adrenal suppression may occur; withdrawal and discontinuation of the corticosteroid should be done carefully. Controlled clinical studies have shown that inhaled and intranasal corticosteroids may cause a reduction in growth velocity in pediatric patients. Growth velocity provides a means of comparing the rate of growth among children of the same age.

In studies involving inhaled corticosteroids, the average reduction in growth velocity was approximately 1 cm (about 1/3 of an inch) per year. It appears that the reduction is related to dose and how long the child takes the drug.

FDA's Pulmonary and Allergy Drugs and Metabolic and Endocrine Drugs advisory committees discussed this issue at a July 1998 meeting. They recommended that the agency develop class-wide labeling to inform healthcare providers so they would understand this potential side effect and monitor growth routinely in pediatric patients who are treated with inhaled corticosteroids, intranasal corticosteroids or both.

Long-term effects of this reduction in growth velocity on final adult height are unknown. Likewise, it also has not yet been determined whether patients' growth will "catch up" if treatment in discontinued. Drug manufacturers will continue to monitor these drugs to learn more about long-term effects. Children are prescribed inhaled corticosteroids to treat asthma. Intranasal corticosteroids are generally used to prevent and treat allergy-related nasal symptoms.

Patients are advised not to stop using their inhaled or intranasal corticosteroids without first speaking to their healthcare providers about the benefits of these drugs compared to their risks.

Adverse Reactions
>10%:
    Cardiovascular: Pounding heartbeat
    Central nervous system: Dizziness, headache, nervousness
    Dermatologic: Itching, rash
    Endocrine & metabolic: Adrenal suppression, menstrual problems
    Gastrointestinal: GI irritation, anorexia, sore throat, bitter taste
    Local: Nasal burning, *Candida* infections of the nose or pharynx, atrophic rhinitis
    Respiratory: Sneezing, coughing, upper respiratory tract infection, bronchitis, nasal congestion, nasal dryness
    Miscellaneous: Increased susceptibility to infections
1% to 10%:
    Central nervous system: Insomnia, psychic changes
    Dermatologic: Acne, urticaria
    Gastrointestinal: Increase in appetite, xerostomia, dry throat, loss of taste perception
    Ocular: Cataracts
    Respiratory: Epistaxis
    Miscellaneous: Diaphoresis, loss of smell
<1%: Abdominal fullness, bronchospasm, shortness of breath

Overdosage/Toxicology When consumed in excessive quantities, systemic hypercorticism and adrenal suppression may occur; in those cases; discontinuation and withdrawal of the corticosteroid should be done judiciously

Drug Interactions Expected interactions similar to other corticosteroids

Mechanism of Action Decreases inflammation by suppression of migration of polymorphonuclear leukocytes and reversal of increased capillary permeability; does not depress hypothalamus

Pharmacodynamics/Kinetics
    Absorption: Nasal inhalation: ~50%
    Metabolism: Rapidly in the liver to active metabolites
    Half-life: 1.8 hours
    Elimination: Equally in urine and feces

Usual Dosage
    Children >6 years:
        Oral inhalation: 2 inhalations twice daily (morning and evening) up to 4 inhalations/day
        Nasal: 1 spray each nostril twice daily (morning and evening), not to exceed 4 sprays/day each nostril
    Adults:
        Oral inhalation: 2 inhalations twice daily (morning and evening) up to 8 inhalations/day maximum
        Nasal: 2 sprays each nostril twice daily (morning and evening); maximum dose: 8 sprays/day in each nostril

Patient Information Inhaler should be shaken well immediately prior to use; while activating inhaler, deep breathe for 3-5 seconds, hold breath for ~10 seconds and allow ≥1 minute between inhalations

Nursing Implications Shake well before giving; do not use Nasalide® orally; throw out product after it has been opened for 3 months

Additional Information Does not contain fluorocarbons; contains polyethylene glycol vehicle

(Continued)

Flunisolide *(Continued)*

Dosage Forms

Inhalant:

Nasal (Nasalide®, Nasarel™): 25 mcg/actuation [200 sprays] (25 mL)

Oral:

AeroBid®: 250 mcg/actuation [100 metered doses] (7 g)

AeroBid-M® (menthol flavor): 250 mcg/actuation [100 metered doses] (7 g)

Solution, spray: 0.025% [200 actuations] (25 mL)

Fluocinolone (floo oh SIN oh lone)

Related Information

Corticosteroids Comparison *on page 1319*

U.S. Brand Names Derma-Smoothe/FS®; Fluonid®; Flurosyn®; FS Shampoo®; Synalar®; Synalar-HP®; Synemol®

Canadian Brand Names Lidemol®

Synonyms Fluocinolone Acetonide

Therapeutic Category Anti-inflammatory Agent; Corticosteroid, Shampoo; Corticosteroid, Topical (Low Potency); Corticosteroid, Topical (Medium Potency); Corticosteroid, Topical (High Potency)

Use Relief of susceptible inflammatory dermatosis [low, medium, high potency topical corticosteroid]

Pregnancy Risk Factor C

Contraindications Fungal infection, hypersensitivity to fluocinolone or any component, TB of skin, herpes (including varicella)

Warnings/Precautions Adverse systemic effects may occur when used on large areas of the body, denuded areas, for prolonged periods of time, with an occlusive dressing, and/or in infants or small children. Infants and small children may be more susceptible to adrenal axis suppression from topical corticosteroid therapy.

Adverse Reactions <1%: Acne, hypopigmentation, allergic dermatitis, maceration of the skin, skin atrophy, folliculitis, hypertrichosis, dry skin, itching, HPA suppression, Cushing's syndrome, growth retardation, burning, irritation, secondary infection

Overdosage/Toxicology When consumed in excessive quantities, systemic hypercorticism and adrenal suppression may occur; in those cases, discontinuation and withdrawal of the corticosteroid should be done judiciously

Mechanism of Action A synthetic corticosteroid which differs structurally from triamcinolone acetonide in the presence of an additional fluorine atom in the 6-alpha position on the steroid nucleus. The mechanism of action for all topical corticosteroids is not well defined, however, is believed to be a combination of three important properties: anti-inflammatory activity, immunosuppressive properties, and antiproliferative actions.

Pharmacodynamics/Kinetics

Absorption: Dependent on strength of preparation, amount applied, and nature of skin at application site; ranges from ~1% in thick stratum corneum areas (palms, soles, elbows, etc) to 36% in areas of thinnest stratum corneum (face, eyelids, etc); increased absorption in areas of skin damage, inflammation, or occlusion

Distribution: Throughout the local skin; absorbed drug is distributed rapidly into muscle, liver, skin, intestines, and kidneys

Metabolism: Primarily in the skin; small amount absorbed into systemic circulation is metabolized primarily in the liver to inactive compounds

Elimination: By the kidneys primarily as glucuronides and sulfate, but also as unconjugated products; small amounts of metabolites are excreted in feces

Usual Dosage Children and Adults: Topical: Apply a thin layer to affected area 2-4 times/day

Patient Information A thin film of cream or ointment is effective; do not overuse; do not use tight-fitting diapers or plastic pants on children being treated in the diaper area; use only as prescribed, and for no longer than the period prescribed; apply sparingly in light film; rub in lightly; avoid contact with eyes; notify physician if condition being treated persists or worsens

Dosage Forms

Cream, as acetonide: 0.01% (15 g, 60 g); 0.025% (15 g, 60 g)

Flurosyn®, Synalar®: 0.01% (15 g, 30 g, 60 g, 425 g)

Flurosyn®, Synalar®, Synemol®: 0.025% (15 g, 60 g, 425 g)

Synalar-HP®: 0.2% (12 g)

Ointment, topical, as acetonide: 0.025% (15 g, 60 g)

Flurosyn®, Synalar®: 0.025% (15 g, 30 g, 60 g, 425 g)

Oil, as acetonide (Derma-Smoothe/FS®): 0.01% (120 mL)

Shampoo, as acetonide (FS Shampoo®): 0.01% (180 mL)

Solution, topical, as acetonide: 0.01% (20 mL, 60 mL)

Fluonid®, Synalar®: 0.01% (20 mL, 60 mL)

♦ **Fluocinolone Acetonide** *see Fluocinolone on this page*

Fluocinonide (floo oh SIN oh nide)

Related Information

Corticosteroids Comparison *on page 1319*

U.S. Brand Names Fluonex®; Lidex®; Lidex-E®

Canadian Brand Names Lyderm; Lydonide; Tiamol®; Topactin®; Topsyn®

Therapeutic Category Corticosteroid, Topical (High Potency)

Use Anti-inflammatory, antipruritic, relief of inflammatory and pruritic manifestations [high potency topical corticosteroid]

Pregnancy Risk Factor C

Contraindications Viral, fungal, or tubercular skin lesions, herpes simplex, known hypersensitivity to fluocinonide

Warnings/Precautions Adverse systemic effects may occur when used on large areas of the body, denuded areas, for prolonged periods of time, with an occlusive dressing, and/or in infants or small children

Adverse Reactions <1%: Intracranial hypertension, acne, hypopigmentation, allergic dermatitis, maceration of the skin, skin atrophy, dry skin, itching, folliculitis, hypertrichosis, HPA suppression, Cushing's syndrome, growth retardation, burning, irritation, secondary infection

Mechanism of Action Fluorinated topical corticosteroid considered to be of high potency. The mechanism of action for all topical corticosteroids is not well defined, however, is felt to be a combination of three important properties: anti-inflammatory activity, immunosuppressive properties, and antiproliferative actions.

Pharmacodynamics/Kinetics

Absorption: Dependent on amount applied and nature of skin at application site; ranges from ~1% in areas of thick stratum corneum (palms, soles, elbows, etc) to 36% in areas of thin stratum corneum (face, eyelids, etc); absorption is increased in areas of skin damage, inflammation, or occlusion

Distribution: Distributed throughout local skin; any absorbed drug is removed rapidly from the blood and distributed into muscle, liver, skin, intestines, and kidneys

Metabolism: Primarily in the skin; small amount absorbed into systemic circulation is metabolized primarily in the liver to inactive compounds

Elimination: By the kidneys primarily as glucuronides and sulfates, but also as unconjugated products; small amounts of metabolites are excreted in feces

Usual Dosage Children and Adults: Topical: Apply thin layer to affected area 2-4 times/day depending on the severity of the condition

Patient Information Do not use tight-fitting diapers or plastic pants on children being treated in the diaper area; use only as prescribed, and for no longer than the period prescribed; apply sparingly in a light film; rub in lightly; notify physician if condition being treated persists or worsens; avoid contact with eyes

Dosage Forms

Cream: 0.05% (15 g, 30 g, 60 g, 120 g)

  Anhydrous, emollient (Lidex®): 0.05% (15 g, 30 g, 60 g, 120 g)

  Aqueous, emollient (Lidex-E®): 0.05% (15 g, 30 g, 60 g, 120 g)

Gel, topical: 0.05% (15 g, 60 g)

  Lidex®: 0.05% (15 g, 30 g, 60 g, 120 g)

Ointment, topical: 0.05% (15 g, 30 g, 60 g)

  Lidex®: 0.05% (15 g, 30 g, 60 g, 120 g)

Solution, topical: 0.05% (20 mL, 60 mL)

  Lidex®: 0.05% (20 mL, 60 mL)

♦ **Fluogen®** *see* Influenza Virus Vaccine *on page 611*

♦ **Fluohydrisone Acetate** *see* Fludrocortisone Acetate *on page 492*

♦ **Fluohydrocortisone Acetate** *see* Fludrocortisone Acetate *on page 492*

♦ **Fluonex®** *see* Fluocinonide *on previous page*

♦ **Fluonid®** *see* Fluocinolone *on previous page*

♦ **Fluoracaine® Ophthalmic** *see* Proparacaine and Fluorescein *on page 983*

Fluorescein Sodium (FLURE e seen SOW dee um)

U.S. Brand Names AK-Fluor; Fluorescite®; Fluorets®; Fluor-I-Strip®; Fluor-I-Strip-AT®; Fluress®; Ful-Glo®; Funduscein®; Ophthifluor®

Synonyms Soluble Fluorescein

Therapeutic Category Diagnostic Agent, Ophthalmic Dye

Use Demonstrates defects of corneal epithelium; diagnostic aid in ophthalmic angiography

Pregnancy Risk Factor C (topical); X (parenteral)

Contraindications Hypersensitivity to fluorescein or any other component of the product; do not use with soft contact lenses, as this will cause them to discolor; pregnancy with parenteral product

Warnings/Precautions Use with caution in patients with history of hypersensitivity, allergies, or asthma; avoid extravasation; should not be used in patients with soft contact lenses, will cause them to discolor

Adverse Reactions

1% to 10%:

  Dermatologic: Burning sensation

  Local: Temporary stinging

<1%: Syncope, hypotension, cardiac arrest, basilar artery ischemia, severe shock, headache, nausea, GI distress, vomiting, thrombophlebitis

Mechanism of Action Yellow, water soluble, dibasic acid xanthine dye which penetrates any break in epithelial barrier to permit rapid penetration

Usual Dosage

Ophthalmic:

  Solution: Instill 1-2 drops of 2% solution and allow a few seconds for staining; wash out excess with sterile water or irrigating solution

  Strips: Moisten strip with sterile water. Place moistened strip at the fornix into the lower cul-de-sac close to the punctum. For best results, patient should close lid tightly over

(Continued)

Fluorescein Sodium *(Continued)*

strip until desired amount of staining is obtained. Patient should blink several times after application.

Removal of foreign bodies, sutures or tonometry (Fluress®): Instill 1 or 2 drops (single instillations) into each eye before operating

Deep ophthalmic anesthesia (Fluress®): Instill 2 drops into each eye every 90 seconds up to 3 doses

Injection: Prior to use, perform intradermal skin test; have epinephrine 1:1000, an antihistamine, and oxygen available

Children: 3.5 mg/lb (7.5 mg/kg) injected rapidly into antecubital vein

Adults: 500-750 mg injected rapidly into antecubital vein

Patient Information Do not replace soft contact lenses for at least 1 hour, flush eye before replacing; skin discoloration may last 6-12 hours, urine 24-36 hours if given systemically

Nursing Implications Avoid extravasation, results in severe local tissue damage; have epinephrine 1:1000, an antihistamine, and oxygen available

Dosage Forms

Injection (AK-Fluor, Fluorescite®, Funduscein®, Ophthifluor®): 10% [100 mg/mL] (5 mL); 25% [250 mg/mL] (2 mL, 3 mL)

Ophthalmic:

Solution: 2% [20 mg/mL] (1 mL, 2 mL, 15 mL)

Fluress®: 0.25% [2.5 mg/mL] with benoxinate 0.4% (5 mL)

Strip:

Ful-Glo®: 0.6 mg

Fluorets®, Fluor-I-Strip-AT®: 1 mg

Fluor-I-Strip®: 9 mg

♦ **Fluorescite**® *see* Fluorescein Sodium *on previous page*

♦ **Fluorets**® *see* Fluorescein Sodium *on previous page*

Fluoride *(FLOR ide)*

U.S. Brand Names ACT® [OTC]; Fluorigard® [OTC]; Fluorinse®; Fluoritab®; Flura®; Flura-Drops®; Flura-Loz®; Gel Kam®; Gel-Tin® [OTC]; Karidium®; Karigel®; Karigel®-N; Listermint® with Fluoride [OTC]; Luride®; Luride® Lozi-Tab®; Luride®-SF Lozi-Tab®; Minute-Gel®; Pediaflor®; Pharmaflur®; Phos-Flur®; Point-Two®; PreviDent®; Stop® [OTC]; Thera-Flur®; Thera-Flur-N®

Synonyms Acidulated Phosphate Fluoride; Sodium Fluoride; Stannous Fluoride

Therapeutic Category Mineral, Oral; Mineral, Oral Topical

Use Prevention of dental caries

Pregnancy Risk Factor C

Contraindications Hypersensitivity to fluoride, tartrazine, or any component; when fluoride content of drinking water exceeds 0.7 ppm; low sodium or sodium-free diets; do not use 1 mg tablets in children <3 years of age or when drinking water fluoride content is ≥0.3 ppm; do not use 1 mg/5 mL rinse (as supplement) in children <6 years of age

Warnings/Precautions Prolonged ingestion with excessive doses may result in dental fluorosis and osseous changes; do **not** exceed recommended dosage; some products contain tartrazine

Adverse Reactions <1%: Rash, nausea, vomiting, products containing stannous fluoride may stain the teeth

Overdosage/Toxicology

Symptoms of overdose include hypersalivation, salty or soapy taste, epigastric pain, nausea, vomiting, diarrhea, rash muscle weakness, tremor, seizures, cardiac failure, respiratory arrest, shock, death

Fatal dose not known. Children: 500 mg; Adults: 7-140 mg/kg

Treatment of overdose: Gastric lavage with $CaCl_2$ or $Ca(OH)_2$ solution; administer large quantity of milk at frequent intervals; $Al(OH)_3$ may also bind the fluoride ion

Drug Interactions Decreased effect/absorption with magnesium-, aluminum-, and calcium-containing products

Fluoride Ion

Fluoride Content of Drinking Water	Daily Dose, Oral (mg)
<0.3 ppm	
Birth - 6 mo	0
6 mo - 3 y	0.25
3-6 y	0.5
6-16 y	1
0.3-0.6 ppm	
Birth - 3 y	0
3-6 y	0.25
6-16 y	0.5
>0.6 ppm	
All ages	0

Adapted from *AAP News*, 1995, 11(2):18.

Stability Store in tight plastic containers (not glass)

Mechanism of Action Promotes remineralization of decalcified enamel; inhibits the cariogenic microbial process in dental plaque; increases tooth resistance to acid dissolution

Pharmacodynamics/Kinetics

Absorption: Absorbed in GI tract, lungs, and skin; calcium, iron, or magnesium may delay absorption

Distribution: 50% of fluoride is deposited in teeth and bone after ingestion; topical application works superficially on enamel and plaque; crosses placenta; appears in breast milk

Elimination: In urine and feces

Usual Dosage Oral:

Recommended daily fluoride supplement (2.2 mg of sodium fluoride is equivalent to 1 mg of fluoride ion): See table.

Dental rinse or gel:

Children 6-12 years: 5-10 mL rinse or apply to teeth and spit daily after brushing

Adults: 10 mL rinse or apply to teeth and spit daily after brushing

Patient Information Take with food (but not milk) to eliminate GI upset; with dental rinse or dental gel do **not** swallow, do **not** eat or drink for 30 minutes after use

Nursing Implications Avoid giving with milk or dairy products

Dosage Forms Fluoride ion content listed in brackets

Drops, oral, as sodium:

Fluoritab®, Flura-Drops®: 0.55 mg/drop [0.25 mg/drop] (22.8 mL, 24 mL)

Karidium®, Luride®: 0.275 mg/drop [0.125 mg/drop] (30 mL, 60 mL)

Pediaflor®: 1.1 mg/mL [0.5 mg/mL] (50 mL)

Gel, topical:

Acidulated phosphate fluoride (Minute-Gel®): 1.23% (480 mL)

Sodium fluoride (Karigel®, Karigel®-N, PreviDent®): 1.1% [0.5%] (24 g, 30 g, 60 g, 120 g, 130 g, 250 g)

Stannous fluoride (Gel Kam®, Gel-Tin®, Stop®): 0.4% [0.1%] (60 g, 65 g, 105 g, 120 g)

Lozenge, as sodium (Flura-Loz®) (raspberry flavor): 2.2 mg [1 mg]

Rinse, topical, as sodium:

ACT®, Fluorigard®: 0.05% [0.02%] (90 mL, 180 mL, 300 mL, 360 mL, 480 mL)

Fluorinse®, Point-Two®: 0.2% [0.09%] (240 mL, 480 mL, 3780 mL)

Listermint® with Fluoride: 0.02% [0.01%] (180 mL, 300 mL, 360 mL, 480 mL, 540 mL, 720 mL, 960 mL, 1740 mL)

Solution, oral, as sodium (Phos-Flur®): 0.44 mg/mL [0.2 mg/mL] (250 mL, 500 mL, 3780 mL)

Tablet, as sodium:

Chewable:

Fluoritab®, Luride® Lozi-Tab®, Pharmaflur®: 1.1 mg [0.5 mg]

Fluoritab®, Karidium®, Luride® Lozi-Tab®, Luride®-SF Lozi-Tab®, Pharmaflur®: 2.2 mg [1 mg]

Oral: Flura®, Karidium®: 2.2 mg [1 mg]

♦ **Fluorigard®** [OTC] see Fluoride on previous page

♦ **Fluori-Methane® Topical Spray** see Dichlorodifluoromethane and Trichloromonofluoromethane on page 348

♦ **Fluorinse®** see Fluoride on previous page

♦ **Fluor-I-Strip®** see Fluorescein Sodium on page 497

♦ **Fluor-I-Strip-AT®** see Fluorescein Sodium on page 497

♦ **Fluoritab®** see Fluoride on previous page

♦ **9α-Fluorohydrocortisone Acetate** see Fludrocortisone Acetate on page 492

Fluorometholone (flure oh METH oh lone)

U.S. Brand Names Flarex®; Fluor-Op®; FML®; FML® Forte

Therapeutic Category Anti-inflammatory Agent; Corticosteroid, Ophthalmic; Corticosteroid, Topical (Low Potency)

Use Inflammatory conditions of the eye, including keratitis, iritis, cyclitis, and conjunctivitis

Pregnancy Risk Factor C

Contraindications Herpes simplex, keratitis, fungal diseases of ocular structures, most viral diseases, hypersensitivity to any component

Warnings/Precautions Not recommended in children <2 years of age, prolonged use may result in glaucoma, elevated intraocular pressure, or other ocular damage; some products contain sulfites

Adverse Reactions

1% to 10%: Ocular: Blurred vision

<1%: Stinging, burning eyes, increased intraocular pressure, open-angle glaucoma, defect in visual acuity and field of vision, cataracts

Overdosage/Toxicology When consumed in excessive quantities, systemic hypercorticism and adrenal suppression may occur; in those cases, discontinuation and withdrawal of the corticosteroid should be done judiciously

Mechanism of Action Decreases inflammation by suppression of migration of polymorphonuclear leukocytes and reversal of increased capillary permeability

Pharmacodynamics/Kinetics Absorption: Into aqueous humor with slight systemic absorption

Usual Dosage Children >2 years and Adults: Ophthalmic:

Ointment: May be applied every 4 hours in severe cases; 1-3 times/day in mild to moderate cases

(Continued)

Fluorometholone *(Continued)*

Solution: Instill 1-2 drops into conjunctival sac every hour during day, every 2 hours at night until favorable response is obtained, then use 1 drop every 4 hours; for mild to moderate inflammation, instill 1-2 drops into conjunctival sac 2-4 times/day

Patient Information Do not discontinue use without consulting a physician; photosensitivity may occur; notify physician if improvement does not occur after 7-8 days

Nursing Implications Use a separate individual container for each patient

Dosage Forms Ophthalmic:

Ointment (FML®): 0.1% (3.5 g)

Suspension:

Flarex®, Fluor-Op®, FML®: 0.1% (2.5 mL, 5 mL, 10 mL)

FML® Forte: 0.25% (2 mL, 5 mL, 10 mL, 15 mL)

♦ **Fluor-Op®** *see Fluorometholone on previous page*

♦ **Fluoroplex® Topical** *see Fluorouracil on this page*

Fluorouracil (flure oh YOOR a sil)

Related Information

Cancer Chemotherapy Regimens *on page 1263*
Toxicities of Chemotherapeutic Agents *on page 1288*

U.S. Brand Names Adrucil® Injection; Efudex® Topical; Fluoroplex® Topical

Synonyms 5-Fluorouracil; 5-FU

Therapeutic Category Antineoplastic Agent, Antimetabolite (Pyrimidine)

Use Treatment of carcinoma of stomach, colon, rectum, breast, and pancreas; also used topically for management of multiple actinic keratoses and superficial basal cell carcinomas

Pregnancy Risk Factor D (injection); X (topical)

Contraindications Hypersensitivity to fluorouracil or any component, poor nutritional status, bone marrow depression, or potentially serious infections; pregnancy with topical product

Warnings/Precautions The U.S. Food and Drug Administration (FDA) currently recommends that procedures for proper handling and disposal of antineoplastic agents be considered. Use with caution in patients with impaired kidney or liver function. The drug should be discontinued if intractable vomiting or diarrhea, precipitous falls in leukocyte or platelet counts, stomatitis, hemorrhage, or myocardial ischemia occurs. Use with caution in patients who have had high-dose pelvic radiation or previous use of alkylating agents. Patient should be hospitalized during initial course of therapy.

Adverse Reactions Toxicity depends on route and duration of infusion

>10%:

Dermatologic: Dermatitis, pruritic maculopapular rash, alopecia

Irritant chemotherapy

Gastrointestinal (route and schedule dependent): Heartburn, nausea, vomiting, anorexia, stomatitis, esophagitis, anorexia, stomatitis, and diarrhea; bolus dosing produces milder GI problems, while continuous infusion tends to produce severe mucositis and diarrhea; vomiting is moderate, occurring in 30% to 60% of patients, and responds well to phenothiazines and dexamethasone

Emetic potential:

<1000 mg: Moderately low (10% to 30%)

≥1000 mg: Moderate (30% to 60%)

Hematologic: Myelosuppressive: Granulocytopenia occurs around 9-14 days after 5-FU and thrombocytopenia around 7-17 days. The marrow recovers after 22 days. Myelosuppression tends to be more pronounced in patients receiving bolus dosing of 5-FU.

WBC: Moderate

Platelets: Mild to moderate

Onset (days): 7-10

Nadir (days): 14

Recovery (days): 21

1% to 10%:

Dermatologic: Dry skin

Gastrointestinal: GI ulceration

<1%: Hypotension, chest pain, EKG changes similar to ischemic changes, and possibly cardiac enzyme abnormalities. Usually occurs within the first two days of therapy, and may resolve with nitroglycerin and calcium channel blockers. May be due to coronary vessel vasospasm induced by 5-FU.

Cerebellar ataxia, headache, somnolence, ataxia are seen primarily in intracarotid arterial infusions for head and neck tumors. This is believed to be caused by fluorocitrate, a neurotoxic metabolite of the parent compound.

Pruritic maculopapular rash, alopecia, hyperpigmentation of nailbeds, face, hands, and veins used in infusion; photosensitization with UV light; palmar-plantar syndrome (hand-foot syndrome); coagulopathy, hepatotoxicity, conjunctivitis, tear duct stenosis, excessive lacrimation, visual disturbances, shortness of breath

Overdosage/Toxicology

Symptoms of overdose include myelosuppression, nausea, vomiting, diarrhea, alopecia

No specific antidote exists; monitor hematologically for at least 4 weeks; supportive therapy

Drug Interactions

Methotrexate: This interaction is schedule dependent; **5-FU should be given following MTX, not prior to**

If MTX is given first: The cells exposed to MTX before 5-FU have a depleted reduced folate pool which inhibits the binding of the 5dUMP to TS. However, it does not interfere with FUTP incorporation into RNA. Polyglutamines, which accumulate in the presence of MTX may be substituted for the folates and allow binding of FdUMP to TS. MTX given prior to 5-FU may actually activate 5-FU due to MTX inhibition of purine synthesis.

If 5-FU is given first: 5-FU inhibits the TS binding and thus the reduced folate pool is not depleted, thereby negating the effect of MTX

Increased effect: Leucovorin: ↑ the folate pool and in certain tumors, may promote TS inhibition and ↑ 5-FU activity. Must be given before or with the 5-FU to prime the cells; it is not used as a rescue agent in this case.

Increased toxicity:
Allopurinol: Inhibits thymidine phosphorylase (an enzyme that activates 5-FU). The antitumor effect of 5-FU appears to be unaltered, but decreases toxicity

Cimetidine: Results in increased plasma levels of 5-FU due to drug metabolism inhibition and reduction of liver blood flow induced by cimetidine

Stability

Store intact vials at room temperature and protect from light; slight discoloration does not usually denote decomposition

Further dilution in D_5W or NS at concentrations of 0.5-10 mg/mL are stable for 72 hours at 4°C to 25°C

Incompatible with cytarabine, diazepam, doxorubicin, methotrexate; concentrations of >25 mg/mL of fluorouracil and >2 mg/mL of leucovorin are incompatible (precipitation occurs)

Compatible with vincristine, methotrexate, potassium chloride, magnesium sulfate

Standard I.V. dilution: I.V. push: Dose/syringe (concentration: 50 mg/mL)

Maximum syringe size for IVP is a 30 mL syringe and syringe should be <75% full

CIV/IVPB: Dose/50-1000 mL D_5W or NS

Syringe and solution are stable for 72 hours at 4°C to 25°C

Mechanism of Action A pyrimidine antimetabolite that interferes with DNA synthesis by blocking the methylation of deoxyuridylic acid; 5-FU rapidly enters the cell and is activated to the nucleotide level; there it inhibits thymidylate synthetase (TS), or is incorporated into RNA (most evident during the GI phase of the cell cycle). The reduced folate cofactor is required for tight binding to occur between the 5-FdUMP and TS.

Pharmacodynamics/Kinetics

Absorption: Oral: Erratic and rarely used

Distribution: V_d: ~22% of total body water; penetrates the extracellular fluid, CSF, and third space fluids (such as pleural effusions and ascitic fluid)

Metabolism: 5-FU must be metabolized to be active. 90% metabolized; accomplished by a dehydrogenase enzyme primarily found in the liver; dose may need to be omitted in patients with liver failure (bilirubin >5 mg/dL)

Bioavailability: <75%, erratic and unpredendable

Half-life (biphasic): Initial: 6-20 minutes; doses of 400-600 mg/m² produce drug concentrations above the threshold for cytotoxicity for normal tissue and remain there for 6 hours; 2 metabolites, FdUMP and FUTP, have prolonged half-lives depending on the type of tissue; the clinical effect of these metabolites has not been determined

Elimination: 5% of dose excreted as unchanged drug in the urine in 6 hours, and a large amount excreted as CO_2 from the lung

Usual Dosage Refer to individual protocols

All dosages are based on the patient's actual weight. However, the estimated lean body mass (dry weight) is used if the patient is obese or if there has been a spurious weight gain due to edema, ascites or other forms of abnormal fluid retention.

Children and Adults:
I.V.: Initial: 400-500 mg/m²/day (12 mg/kg/day; maximum: 800 mg/day) for 4-5 days either as a single daily I.V. push or 4-day CIV

I.V.: Maintenance dose regimens:
200-250 mg/m² (6 mg/kg) every other day for 4 days repeated in 4 weeks
500-600 mg/m² (15 mg/kg) weekly as a CIV or I.V. push

I.V.: Concomitant with leucovorin:
370 mg/m²/day x 5 days
500-1000 mg/m² every 2 weeks
600 mg/m² weekly for 6 weeks

Although the manufacturer recommends no daily dose >800 mg, higher doses of up to 2 g/day are routinely administered by CIV; higher daily doses have been successfully used

Hemodialysis: Administer dose posthemodialysis

Dosing adjustment/comments in hepatic impairment: Bilirubin >5 mg/dL: Omit use

Topical:
Actinic or solar keratosis: Apply twice daily for 2-6 weeks
Superficial basal cell carcinomas: Apply 5% twice daily for at least 3-6 weeks and up to 10-12 weeks

Administration Direct I.V. push injection (50 mg/mL solution needs no further dilution) or by I.V. infusion; myelotoxicity may be reduced by giving the drug as a constant infusion. Bolus doses may be administered by slow IVP or IVPB; continuous infusions may be administered in D_5W or NS. Solution should be protected from direct sunlight; 5-FU may also be administered intra-arterially or intrahepatically (refer to specific protocols); may be given orally mixed in water, grape juice, or carbonated beverage.

(Continued)

Fluorouracil *(Continued)*

Monitoring Parameters CBC with differential and platelet count, renal function tests, liver function tests

Test Interactions Fecal discoloration

Patient Information Avoid unnecessary exposure to sunlight; any signs of infection, easy bruising or bleeding, shortness of breath, or painful or burning urination should be brought to physician's attention. Nausea, vomiting, or hair loss sometimes occurs. The drug may cause permanent sterility and may cause birth defects. Contraceptive measures are recommended during therapy. The drug may be excreted in breast milk, therefore, an alternative form of feeding your baby should be used.

Nursing Implications Cool to body temperature before using; after vial has been entered, any unused portion should be discarded within 1 hour; wash hands immediately after topical application of the 5% cream; I.V. formulation may be given orally mixed in water, grape juice, or carbonated beverage

Dosage Forms

Cream, topical:
Efudex®: 5% (25 g)
Fluoroplex®: 1% (30 g)
Injection (Adrucil®): 50 mg/mL (10 mL, 20 mL, 50 mL, 100 mL)
Solution, topical:
Efudex®: 2% (10 mL); 5% (10 mL)
Fluoroplex®: 1% (30 mL)

- **5-Fluorouracil** *see Fluorouracil on page 500*
- **Fluostigmin** *see Isoflurophate on page 633*

Fluoxetine *(floo OKS e teen)*

Related Information

Antidepressant Agents Comparison *on page 1301*

U.S. Brand Names Prozac®

Synonyms Fluoxetine Hydrochloride

Therapeutic Category Antidepressant, Serotonin Reuptake Inhibitor

Use Treatment of major depression; treatment of binge-eating and vomiting in patients with moderate-to-severe bulimia nervosa; obsessive-compulsive disorder

Pregnancy Risk Factor B

Contraindications Hypersensitivity to fluoxetine; patients receiving MAO inhibitors currently or in past 2 weeks

Warnings/Precautions Use with caution in patients with hepatic impairment, history of seizures; MAO inhibitors should be discontinued at least 14 days before initiating fluoxetine therapy; add or initiate other antidepressants with caution for up to 5 weeks after stopping fluoxetine

Adverse Reactions Predominant adverse effects are CNS and GI

>10%:
Central nervous system: Headache, nervousness, insomnia, drowsiness
Gastrointestinal: Nausea, diarrhea, xerostomia

1% to 10%:
Central nervous system: Anxiety, dizziness, fatigue, sedation
Dermatologic: Rash, pruritus
Endocrine & metabolic: SIADH, hypoglycemia, hyponatremia (elderly or volume-depleted patients)
Gastrointestinal: Anorexia, dyspepsia, constipation
Neuromuscular & skeletal: Tremor
Miscellaneous: Diaphoresis (excessive)

<1%: Extrapyramidal reactions (rare), visual disturbances, anaphylactoid reactions, allergies, suicidal ideation

Overdosage/Toxicology Symptoms of overdose include ataxia, sedation, and coma; respiratory depression may occur, especially with coingestion of alcohol or other drugs; seizures very rarely occur

Drug Interactions CYP2D6 enzyme substrate (minor), CYP2C enzyme substrate (minor), CYP3A3/4 enzyme substrate; CYP2C9 enxyme inducer; CYP1A2, 2C9, 2C18, 2C19, 2D6, and 3A3/4 enzyme inhibitor

Increased effect with tricyclics (2 times increased plasma level)
Increased/decreased effect of lithium (both increased and decreased level has been reported)
Increased toxicity of diazepam, trazodone via decreased clearance; increased toxicity with MAO inhibitors (hyperpyrexia, tremors, seizures, delirium, coma)
May displace highly protein bound drugs (warfarin)

Mechanism of Action Inhibits CNS neuron serotonin uptake; minimal or no effect on reuptake of norepinephrine or dopamine; does not significantly bind to alpha-adrenergic, histamine or cholinergic receptors; may therefore be useful in patients at risk from sedation, hypotension, and anticholinergic effects of tricyclic antidepressants

Pharmacodynamics/Kinetics

Peak antidepressant effect: After >4 weeks
Absorption: Oral: Well absorbed
Metabolism: To norfluoxetine (active)
Half-life: Adults: 2-3 days; due to long half-life, resolution of adverse reactions after discontinuation may be slow
Time to peak serum concentration: Within 4-8 hours

Elimination: In urine as fluoxetine (2.5% to 5%) and norfluoxetine (10%)

Usual Dosage Oral:

Children <18 years: Dose and safety not established; preliminary experience in children 6-14 years using initial doses of 20 mg/day have been reported

Adults: 20 mg/day in the morning; may increase after several weeks by 20 mg/day increments; maximum: 80 mg/day; doses >20 mg should be divided into morning and noon doses

Usual dosage range:

20-80 mg/day for depression and OCD

20-60 mg/day for obesity

60-80 mg/day for bulimia nervosa

Note: Lower doses of 5 mg/day have been used for initial treatment

Elderly: Some patients may require an initial dose of 10 mg/day with dosage increases of 10 and 20 mg every several weeks as tolerated; should not be taken at night unless patient experiences sedation

Dosing adjustment in renal impairment:

Single dose studies: Pharmacokinetics of fluoxetine and norfluoxetine were similar among subjects with all levels of impaired renal function, including anephric patients on chronic hemodialysis

Chronic administration: Additional accumulation of fluoxetine or norfluoxetine may occur in patients with severely impaired renal function

Hemodialysis: Not removed by hemodialysis

Dosing adjustment in hepatic impairment: Elimination half-life of fluoxetine is prolonged in patients with hepatic impairment; a lower or less frequent dose of fluoxetine should be used in these patients

Cirrhosis patients: Administer a lower dose or less frequent dosing interval

Compensated cirrhosis without ascites: Administer 50% of normal dose

Dietary Considerations Alcohol: Avoid use

Reference Range Therapeutic levels have not been well established

Therapeutic: Fluoxetine: 100-800 ng/mL (SI: 289-2314 nmol/L); Norfluoxetine: 100-600 ng/mL (SI: 289-1735 nmol/L)

Toxic: Fluoxetine plus norfluoxetine: >2000 ng/mL

Test Interactions ↑ albumin in urine

Patient Information Avoid alcoholic beverages, take in morning to avoid insomnia; fluoxetine's potential stimulating and anorexic effects may be bothersome to some patients. Use sugarless hard candy for dry mouth; avoid alcoholic beverages, may cause drowsiness, improvement may take several weeks; rise slowly to prevent dizziness.

Nursing Implications Offer patient sugarless hard candy for dry mouth

Dosage Forms

Capsule, as hydrochloride: 10 mg, 20 mg

Liquid, as hydrochloride (mint flavor): 20 mg/5 mL (120 mL)

Extemporaneous Preparations A 20 mg capsule may be mixed with 4 oz of water, apple juice, or Gatorade® to provide a solution that is stable for 14 days under refrigeration

♦ **Fluoxetine Hydrochloride** see Fluoxetine *on previous page*

Fluoxymesterone (floo oks i MES te rone)

Related Information

Cancer Chemotherapy Regimens *on page 1263*

U.S. Brand Names Halotestin®

Therapeutic Category Androgen

Use Replacement of endogenous testicular hormone; in females, used as palliative treatment of breast cancer; stimulation of erythropoiesis, angioneurotic edema, postpartum breast engorgement

Restrictions C-III

Pregnancy Risk Factor X

Contraindications Serious cardiac disease, liver or kidney disease, hypersensitivity to fluoxymesterone or any component; pregnancy

Warnings/Precautions May accelerate bone maturation without producing compensatory gain in linear growth in children; in prepubertal children perform radiographic examination of the hand and wrist every 6 months to determine the rate of bone maturation and to assess the effect of treatment on the epiphyseal centers

Adverse Reactions

>10%:

Males: Priapism

Females: Menstrual problems (amenorrhea), virilism, breast soreness

Cardiovascular: Edema

Dermatologic: Acne

1% to 10%:

Males: Prostatic carcinoma, hirsutism (increase in pubic hair growth), impotence, testicular atrophy

Cardiovascular: Edema

Gastrointestinal: GI irritation, nausea, vomiting

Genitourinary: Prostatic hypertrophy

Hepatic: Hepatic dysfunction

<1%:

Males: Gynecomastia

Females: Amenorrhea

(Continued)

Fluoxymesterone *(Continued)*

Hypercalcemia, leukopenia, polycythemia, hepatic necrosis, cholestatic hepatitis, hypersensitivity reactions

Overdosage/Toxicology Symptoms of overdose include abnormal liver function tests, water retention

Drug Interactions
Decreased effect:
Fluphenazine effectiveness with anticholinergics
Barbiturate levels and decreased fluphenazine effectiveness when given together
Increased toxicity:
Anticoagulants: Fluoxymesterone may suppress clotting factors II, V, VII, and X; therefore, bleeding may occur in patients on anticoagulant therapy
Cyclosporine: May elevate cyclosporine serum levels
Insulin: May enhance hypoglycemic effect of insulin therapy
May decrease blood glucose concentrations and insulin requirements in patients with diabetes
With ethanol, effects of both drugs may increase
EPSEs and other CNS effects may increase when coadministered with lithium
May potentiate the effects of narcotics including respiratory depression

Stability Protect from light

Mechanism of Action Synthetic androgenic anabolic hormone responsible for the normal growth and development of male sex hormones and development of male sex organs and maintenance of secondary sex characteristics; synthetic testosterone derivative with significant androgen activity; stimulates RNA polymerase activity resulting in an increase in protein production; increases bone development

Pharmacodynamics/Kinetics
Absorption: Oral: Rapid
Protein binding: 98%
Metabolism: In the liver
Half-life: 10-100 minutes
Elimination: Enterohepatic circulation and urinary excretion (90%)
Halogenated derivative of testosterone with up to 5 times the activity of methyltestosterone

Usual Dosage Adults: Oral:
Male:
Hypogonadism: 5-20 mg/day
Delayed puberty: 2.5-20 mg/day for 4-6 months
Female:
Inoperable breast carcinoma: 10-40 mg/day in divided doses for 1-3 months
Breast engorgement: 2.5 mg after delivery, 5-10 mg/day in divided doses for 4-5 days

Monitoring Parameters In prepubertal children, perform radiographic examination of the head and wrist every 6 months

Test Interactions Decreased levels of thyroxine-binding globulin; decreased total T_4 serum levels; increased resin uptake of T_3 and T_4

Patient Information Men should report overly frequent or persistent penile erections; women should report menstrual irregularities; all patients should report persistent GI distress, diarrhea, or jaundice

Dosage Forms Tablet: 2 mg, 5 mg, 10 mg

Fluphenazine *(floo FEN a zeen)*

Related Information
Antipsychotic Agents Comparison *on page 1305*

U.S. Brand Names Permitil® Oral; Prolixin Decanoate® Injection; Prolixin Enanthate® Injection; Prolixin® Injection; Prolixin® Oral

Canadian Brand Names Apo®-Fluphenazine; Modecate®; Modecate® Enanthate; Moditen® Hydrochloride; PMS-Fluphenazine

Synonyms Fluphenazine Decanoate; Fluphenazine Enanthate; Fluphenazine Hydrochloride

Therapeutic Category Antipsychotic Agent; Phenothiazine Derivative

Use Management of manifestations of psychotic disorders

Pregnancy Risk Factor C

Contraindications Hypersensitivity to fluphenazine or any component, cross-sensitivity with other phenothiazines may exist; avoid use in patients with narrow-angle glaucoma

Warnings/Precautions Safety in children <6 months of age has not been established; use with caution in patients with cardiovascular disease or seizures; benefits of therapy must be weighed against risks of therapy; adverse effects may be of longer duration with Depot® form; watch for hypotension when administering I.M. or I.V.; use with caution in patients with severe liver or renal disease

Adverse Reactions
>10%:
Cardiovascular: Orthostatic hypotension, hypotension, tachycardia, arrhythmias
Central nervous system: Parkinsonian symptoms, akathisia, dystonias, tardive dyskinesia (persistent), dizziness
Gastrointestinal: Constipation
Ocular: Pigmentary retinopathy
Respiratory: Nasal congestion
Miscellaneous: Diaphoresis (decreased)

1% to 10%:
  Dermatologic: Increased sensitivity to sun, rash
  Endocrine & metabolic: Changes in menstrual cycle, breast pain, amenorrhea, galactorrhea, gynecomastia, changes in libido
  Gastrointestinal: Weight gain, nausea, vomiting, stomach pain
  Genitourinary: Dysuria, ejaculatory disturbances
  Neuromuscular & skeletal: Trembling of fingers
<1%: Sedation, drowsiness, restlessness, anxiety, extrapyramidal reactions, pseudoparkinsonian signs and symptoms, seizures, altered central temperature regulation, photosensitivity, hyperpigmentation, pruritus, rash, discoloration of skin (bluegray), galactorrhea, xerostomia, priapism, urinary retention, agranulocytosis (more often in women between 4th and 10th weeks of therapy), leukopenia (usually in patients with large doses for prolonged periods), cholestatic jaundice, hepatotoxicity, cornea and lens changes, blurred vision

Overdosage/Toxicology
  Symptoms of overdose include deep sleep, hypotension, hypertension, dystonia, seizures, extrapyramidal symptoms, respiratory failure
  Following initiation of essential overdose management, toxic symptom treatment and supportive treatment should be initiated. Hypotension usually responds to I.V. fluids or Trendelenburg positioning. If unresponsive to these measures, the use of a parenteral inotrope may be required. Seizures commonly respond to diazepam (I.V. 5-10 mg bolus in adults every 15 minutes if needed up to a total of 30 mg; I.V. 0.25-0.4 mg/kg/dose up to a total of 10 mg in children) or to phenytoin or phenobarbital. Cardiac arrhythmias often respond to I.V. lidocaine while other antiarrhythmics can be used. Neuroleptics often cause extrapyramidal symptoms (eg, dystonic reactions) requiring management; benztropine mesylate I.V. 1-2 mg (adults) may be effective. These agents are generally effective within 2-5 minutes.

Drug Interactions CYP2D6 enzyme substrate; CYP2D6 enzyme inhibitor
  Decreased effect: Barbiturate levels and decreased fluphenazine effectiveness when given together
  Increased toxicity: With ethanol, effects of both drugs may be increased; EPSEs and other CNS effects may be increased when coadministered with lithium; may potentiate the effects of narcotics including respiratory depression

Mechanism of Action Blocks postsynaptic mesolimbic dopaminergic D_1 and D_2 receptors in the brain; exhibits a strong alpha-adrenergic blocking and anticholinergic effect, depresses the release of hypothalamic and hypophyseal hormones; believed to depress the reticular activating system thus affecting basal metabolism, body temperature, wakefulness, vasomotor tone, and emesis

Pharmacodynamics/Kinetics
  Following I.M. or S.C. administration (derivative dependent):
    Decanoate (lasts the longest and requires more time for onset):
      Onset of action: 24-72 hours
      Peak neuroleptic effect: Within 48-96 hours
    Hydrochloride salt (acts quickly and persists briefly):
      Onset of activity: Within 1 hour
      Duration: 6-8 hours
  Distribution: Crosses the placenta; appears in breast milk
  Metabolism: In the liver
  Half-life: Derivative dependent:
    Enanthate: 84-96 hours
    Hydrochloride: 33 hours
    Decanoate: 163-232 hours

Usual Dosage Adults:
  Oral: 0.5-10 mg/day in divided doses at 6- to 8-hour intervals; some patients may require up to 40 mg/day
  I.M.: 2.5-10 mg/day in divided doses at 6- to 8-hour intervals (parenteral dose is $^1/_3$ to $^1/_2$ the oral dose for the hydrochloride salts)
  I.M., S.C. (decanoate): 12.5 mg every 3 weeks
    Conversion from hydrochloride to decanoate I.M. 0.5 mL (12.5 mg) decanoate every 3 weeks is approximately equivalent to 10 mg hydrochloride/day
  I.M., S.C. (enanthate): 12.5-25 mg every 3 weeks
  Hemodialysis: Not dialyzable (0% to 5%)

Dietary Considerations Alcohol: Additive CNS effect, avoid use

Reference Range Therapeutic: 5-20 ng/mL; correlation of serum concentrations and efficacy is controversial; most often dosed to best response

Test Interactions $\uparrow$ cholesterol (S), $\uparrow$ glucose; $\downarrow$ uric acid (S)

Patient Information Avoid alcoholic beverages, may cause drowsiness, do not discontinue without consulting physician

Nursing Implications Avoid contact of oral solution or injection with skin (contact dermatitis); watch for hypotension when administering I.M. or I.V.; oral liquid to be diluted in the following only: water, saline, 7-UP®, homogenized milk, carbonated orange beverages, pineapple, apricot, prune, orange, V8® juice, tomato, and grapefruit juices

Dosage Forms
  Concentrate, as hydrochloride:
    Permitil®: 5 mg/mL with alcohol 1% (118 mL)
    Prolixin®: 5 mg/mL with alcohol 14% (120 mL)
  Elixir, as hydrochloride (Prolixin®): 2.5 mg/5 mL with alcohol 14% (60 mL, 473 mL)
  Injection, as decanoate (Prolixin Decanoate®): 25 mg/mL (1 mL, 5 mL)
  Injection, as enanthate (Prolixin Enanthate®): 25 mg/mL (5 mL)
  (Continued)

Fluphenazine *(Continued)*

Injection, as hydrochloride (Prolixin®): 2.5 mg/mL (10 mL)
Tablet, as hydrochloride
    Permitil®: 2.5 mg, 5 mg, 10 mg
    Prolixin®: 1 mg, 2.5 mg, 5 mg, 10 mg

♦ **Fluphenazine Decanoate** *see* Fluphenazine *on page 504*
♦ **Fluphenazine Enanthate** *see* Fluphenazine *on page 504*
♦ **Fluphenazine Hydrochloride** *see* Fluphenazine *on page 504*
♦ **Flura**® *see* Fluoride *on page 498*
♦ **Flura-Drops**® *see* Fluoride *on page 498*
♦ **Flura-Loz**® *see* Fluoride *on page 498*

Flurandrenolide *(flure an DREN oh lide)*

Related Information
Corticosteroids Comparison *on page 1319*
U.S. Brand Names Cordran®; Cordran® SP
Canadian Brand Names Drenison®
Synonyms Flurandrenolone
Therapeutic Category Anti-inflammatory Agent; Corticosteroid, Topical (Low Potency); Corticosteroid, Topical (Medium Potency)
Use Inflammation of corticosteroid-responsive dermatoses [medium potency topical corticosteroid]
Pregnancy Risk Factor C
Contraindications Viral, fungal, or tubercular skin lesions, known hypersensitivity to flurandrenolide
Warnings/Precautions Adverse systemic effects may occur when used on large areas of the body, denuded areas, for prolonged periods of time, with an occlusive dressing, and/or in infants or small children
Adverse Reactions <1%: Itching, dry skin, folliculitis, hypertrichosis, acneiform eruptions, hypopigmentation, perioral dermatitis, allergic contact dermatitis, skin atrophy, striae, miliaria, intracranial hypertension, acne, maceration of the skin; HPA suppression, Cushing's syndrome, growth retardation, burning, irritation, secondary infection
Overdosage/Toxicology When consumed in excessive quantities, systemic hypercorticism and adrenal suppression may occur; in those cases, discontinuation and withdrawal of the corticosteroid should be done judiciously
Mechanism of Action Decreases inflammation by suppression of migration of polymorphonuclear leukocytes and reversal of increased capillary permeability
Pharmacodynamics/Kinetics
Absorption: Adequate with intact skin
Metabolism: In the liver
Elimination: By the kidney with small amounts appearing in bile
Repeated applications lead to depot effects on skin, potentially resulting in enhanced percutaneous absorption
Usual Dosage Topical:
Children:
    Ointment, cream: Apply sparingly 1-2 times/day
    Tape: Apply once daily
Adults: Cream, lotion, ointment: Apply sparingly 2-3 times/day
Patient Information A thin film of cream or ointment is effective; do not overuse; do not use tight-fitting diapers or plastic pants on children being treated in the diaper area; use only as prescribed, and for no longer than the period prescribed; apply sparingly in light film; rub in lightly; avoid contact with eyes; notify physician if condition being treated persists or worsens
Dosage Forms
Cream, emulsified base (Cordran® SP): 0.025% (30 g, 60 g); 0.05% (15 g, 30 g, 60 g)
Lotion (Cordran®): 0.05% (15 mL, 60 mL)
Ointment, topical (Cordran®): 0.025% (30 g, 60 g); 0.05% (15 g, 30 g, 60 g)
Tape, topical (Cordran®): 4 mcg/cm^2 (7.5 cm x 60 cm, 7.5 cm x 200 cm rolls)

♦ **Flurandrenolone** *see* Flurandrenolide *on this page*

Flurazepam *(flure AZ e pam)*

Related Information
Benzodiazepines Comparison *on page 1310*
U.S. Brand Names Dalmane®
Canadian Brand Names Apo®-Flurazepam; Novo-Flupam; PMS-Flupam; Somnol®; Som Pam®
Synonyms Flurazepam Hydrochloride
Therapeutic Category Benzodiazepine; Hypnotic; Sedative
Use Short-term treatment of insomnia
Restrictions C-IV
Pregnancy Risk Factor X
Contraindications Hypersensitivity to flurazepam or any component (there may be cross-sensitivity with other benzodiazepines); pregnancy, pre-existing CNS depression, respiratory depression, narrow-angle glaucoma
Warnings/Precautions Use with caution in patients receiving other CNS depressants, patients with low albumin, hepatic dysfunction, and in the elderly; do not use in pregnant

women; may cause drug dependency; safety and efficacy have not been established in children <15 years of age

Adverse Reactions

>10%:

Cardiovascular: Tachycardia, chest pain

Central nervous system: Drowsiness, fatigue, ataxia, lightheadedness, memory impairment, insomnia, anxiety, depression, headache

Dermatologic: Rash

Endocrine & metabolic: Decreased libido

Gastrointestinal: Xerostomia, constipation, decreased salivation, nausea, vomiting, diarrhea, increased or decreased appetite

Neuromuscular & skeletal: Dysarthria

Ocular: Blurred vision

Miscellaneous: Diaphoresis

1% to 10%:

Cardiovascular: Syncope, hypotension

Central nervous system: Confusion, nervousness, dizziness, akathisia

Dermatologic: Dermatitis

Gastrointestinal: Weight gain or loss, increased salivation

Neuromuscular & skeletal: Rigidity, tremor, muscle cramps

Otic: Tinnitus

Respiratory: Hyperventilation, nasal congestion

<1%: Menstrual irregularities, blood dyscrasias, reflex slowing, drug dependence

Overdosage/Toxicology

Symptoms of overdose include respiratory depression, hypoactive reflexes, unsteady gait, hypotension

Treatment for benzodiazepine overdose is supportive. Rarely is mechanical ventilation required. Flumazenil has been shown to selectively block the binding of benzodiazepines to CNS receptors, resulting in a reversal of benzodiazepine-induced CNS depression.

Drug Interactions

Decreased effect with enzyme inducers

Increased toxicity with other CNS depressants and cimetidine

Stability Store in light-resistant containers

Mechanism of Action Depresses all levels of the CNS, including the limbic and reticular formation, probably through the increased action of gamma-aminobutyric acid (GABA), which is a major inhibitory neurotransmitter in the brain

Pharmacodynamics/Kinetics

Onset of hypnotic effect: 15-20 minutes

Peak: 3-6 hours

Duration of action: 7-8 hours

Metabolism: In the liver to N-desalkylflurazepam (active)

Half-life: Adults: 40-114 hours

Usual Dosage Oral:

Children:

<15 years: Dose not established

>15 years: 15 mg at bedtime

Adults: 15-30 mg at bedtime

Dietary Considerations Alcohol: Additive CNS effect, avoid use

Monitoring Parameters Respiratory and cardiovascular status

Reference Range Therapeutic: 0-4 ng/mL (SI: 0-9 nmol/L); Metabolite N-desalkylflurazepam: 20-110 ng/mL (SI: 43-240 nmol/L); Toxic: >0.12 µg/mL

Patient Information Avoid alcohol and other CNS depressants; avoid activities needing good psychomotor coordination until CNS effects are known; drug may cause physical or psychological dependence; avoid abrupt discontinuation after prolonged use

Nursing Implications Provide safety measures (ie, side rails, night light, and call button); remove smoking materials from area; supervise ambulation; avoid abrupt discontinuation in patients with prolonged therapy or seizure disorders

Dosage Forms Capsule, as hydrochloride: 15 mg, 30 mg

♦ **Flurazepam Hydrochloride** see Flurazepam on previous page

Flurbiprofen (flure BI proe fen)

Related Information

Nonsteroidal Anti-Inflammatory Agents Comparison on page 1335

U.S. Brand Names Ansaid® Oral; Ocufen® Ophthalmic

Canadian Brand Names Apo®-Flurbiprofen; Froben®; Froben-SR®; Novo-Flurprofen; Nu-Flurprofen

Synonyms Flurbiprofen Sodium

Therapeutic Category Analgesic, Nonsteroidal Anti-inflammatory Drug; Anti-inflammatory Agent; Nonsteroidal Anti-inflammatory Drug (NSAID), Ophthalmic; Nonsteroidal Anti-inflammatory Drug (NSAID), Oral

Use Inhibition of intraoperative miosis; acute or long-term treatment of signs and symptoms of rheumatoid arthritis and osteoarthritis; prevention and management of postoperative ocular inflammation and postoperative cystoid macular edema remains to be determined

Pregnancy Risk Factor C

Contraindications Dendritic keratitis, hypersensitivity to flurbiprofen or any component

(Continued)

Flurbiprofen (Continued)

Warnings/Precautions Should be used with caution in patients with a history of herpes simplex, keratitis, and patients who might be affected by inhibition of platelet aggregation; slowing of corneal wound healing patients in whom asthma, rhinitis, or urticaria is precipitated by aspirin or other NSAIDs.

Adverse Reactions

Ophthalmic:
>10%: Ocular: Slowing of corneal wound healing, mild ocular stinging, itching and burning eyes, ocular irritation
1% to 10%: Ocular: Eye redness

Oral:
>10%:
Central nervous system: Dizziness
Dermatologic: Rash
Gastrointestinal: Abdominal cramps, heartburn, indigestion, nausea
1% to 10%:
Central nervous system: Headache, nervousness
Dermatologic: Itching
Endocrine & metabolic: Fluid retention
Gastrointestinal: Vomiting
Otic: Tinnitus
<1%: Congestive heart failure, hypertension, arrhythmias, tachycardia, confusion, hallucinations, aseptic meningitis, mental depression, drowsiness, insomnia, urticaria, erythema multiforme, toxic epidermal necrolysis, Stevens-Johnson syndrome, angioedema, polydipsia, hot flashes, gastritis, GI ulceration, cystitis, polyuria, agranulocytosis, anemia, hemolytic anemia, bone marrow suppression, leukopenia, thrombocytopenia, hepatitis, peripheral neuropathy, toxic amblyopia, blurred vision, conjunctivitis, dry eyes, decreased hearing, acute renal failure, shortness of breath, allergic rhinitis, epistaxis

Overdosage/Toxicology

Symptoms include apnea, metabolic acidosis, coma, and nystagmus; leukocytosis, renal failure

Management of a nonsteroidal anti-inflammatory drug (NSAID) intoxication is primarily supportive and symptomatic. Fluid therapy is commonly effective in managing the hypotension that may occur following an acute NSAIDs overdose, except when this is due to an acute blood loss. Seizures tend to be very short-lived and often do not require drug treatment; although, recurrent seizures should be treated with I.V. diazepam. Since many of the NSAID undergo enterohepatic cycling, multiple doses of charcoal may be needed to reduce the potential for delayed toxicities.

Drug Interactions CYP2C9 enzyme substrate; CYP2C9 enzyme inhibitor
Decreased effect: When used concurrently with flurbiprofen, reports acetylcholine chloride and carbachol being ineffective

Mechanism of Action Inhibits prostaglandin synthesis by decreasing the activity of the enzyme, cyclo-oxygenase, which results in decreased formation of prostaglandin precursors

Pharmacodynamics/Kinetics Onset of effect: Within 1-2 hours

Usual Dosage
Oral: Rheumatoid arthritis and osteoarthritis: 200-300 mg/day in 2, 3, or 4 divided doses
Ophthalmic: Instill 1 drop every 30 minutes, 2 hours prior to surgery (total of 4 drops to each affected eye)

Patient Information Take the oral formulation with food to decrease any abdominal complaints. Eye drops may cause mild burning or stinging, notify physician if this becomes severe or persistent; do not touch dropper to eye, visual acuity may be decreased after administration.

Nursing Implications Care should be taken to avoid contamination of the solution container tip

Dosage Forms
Solution, ophthalmic, as sodium (Ocufen®): 0.03% (2.5 mL, 5 mL, 10 mL)
Tablet, as sodium (Ansaid®): 50 mg, 100 mg

- ◆ **Flurbiprofen Sodium** see Flurbiprofen on previous page
- ◆ **Fluress®** see Fluorescein Sodium on page 497
- ◆ **5-Flurocytosine** see Flucytosine on page 489
- ◆ **Fluro-Ethyl® Aerosol** see Ethyl Chloride and Dichlorotetrafluoroethane on page 456
- ◆ **Flurosyn®** see Fluocinolone on page 496
- ◆ **Flushield®** see Influenza Virus Vaccine on page 611

Flutamide (FLOO ta mide)

Related Information
Cancer Chemotherapy Regimens on page 1263
U.S. Brand Names Eulexin®
Canadian Brand Names Novo-Flutamide
Therapeutic Category Antiandrogen; Antineoplastic Agent, Miscellaneous
Use In combination therapy with LHRH agonist analogues in treatment of metastatic prostatic carcinoma. A study has shown that the addition of flutamide to leuprolide therapy in patients with advanced prostatic cancer increased median actuarial survival time to 34.9 months versus 27.9 months with leuprolide alone. To achieve benefit to combination therapy, both drugs need to be started simultaneously.

Pregnancy Risk Factor D

Contraindications Known hypersensitivity to flutamide

Warnings/Precautions The U.S. Food and Drug Administration (FDA) currently recommends that procedures for proper handling and disposal of antineoplastic agents be considered. Animal data (based on using doses higher than recommended for humans) produced testicular interstitial cell adenoma. Do not discontinue therapy without physician's advice.

Adverse Reactions
>10%:
Gastrointestinal: Nausea, vomiting, diarrhea
Genitourinary: Impotence
Endocrine & metabolic: Loss of libido, hot flashes
1% to 10%:
Endocrine & metabolic: Gynecomastia
Gastrointestinal: Anorexia
Neuromuscular & skeletal: Numbness in extremities
<1%: Hypertension, edema, drowsiness, nervousness, confusion, hepatitis

Overdosage/Toxicology
Symptoms of overdose include hypoactivity, ataxia, anorexia, vomiting, slow respiration, lacrimation
Management is supportive, dialysis not of benefit; induce vomiting

Drug Interactions CYP3A3/4 enzyme substrate

Stability Store at room temperature

Mechanism of Action Nonsteroidal antiandrogen that inhibits androgen uptake or inhibits binding of androgen in target tissues

Pharmacodynamics/Kinetics
Absorption: Rapid and complete
Metabolism: Extensively to more than 10 metabolites
Half-life: 5-6 hours
Elimination: All metabolites excreted primarily in urine

Usual Dosage Adults: Oral: 2 capsules every 8 hours for a total daily dose of 750 mg

Administration Contents of capsule may be opened and mixed with applesauce, pudding, or other soft foods; mixing with a beverage is not recommended

Monitoring Parameters LFTs, tumor reduction, testosterone/estrogen, and phosphatase serum levels

Patient Information Flutamide and the drug used for medical castration should be administered concomitantly; do not interrupt or stop taking medication; frequent blood tests may be needed to monitor therapy

Dosage Forms Capsule: 125 mg

♦ **Flutex®** see Triamcinolone on page 1174

Fluticasone (floo TIK a sone)

Related Information
Asthma, Guidelines for the Diagnosis and Management of on page 1456
Corticosteroids Comparison on page 1319
Estimated Clinical Comparability of Doses for Inhaled Corticosteroids on page 1463

U.S. Brand Names Cutivate™; Flonase®; Flovent®

Synonyms Fluticasone Propionate

Therapeutic Category Corticosteroid, Inhalant; Corticosteroid, Topical (Medium Potency)

Use
Inhalation: Maintenance treatment of asthma as prophylactic therapy. It is also indicated for patients requiring oral corticosteroid therapy for asthma to assist in total discontinuation or reduction of total oral dose. NOT indicated for the relief of acute bronchospasm.
Intranasal: Management of seasonal and perennial allergic rhinitis in patients ≥12 years of age
Topical: Relief of inflammation and pruritus associated with corticosteroid-responsive dermatoses [medium potency topical corticosteroid]

Pregnancy Risk Factor C

Contraindications Hypersensitivity to any component, bacterial infections, ophthalmic use

Warnings/Precautions Adverse systemic effects may occur when used on large areas of the body, denuded areas, for prolonged periods of time, with an occlusive dressing, and/or in infants or small children Controlled clinical studies have shown that inhaled and intranasal corticosteroids may cause a reduction in growth velocity in pediatric patients. Growth velocity provides a means of comparing the rate of growth among children of the same age.

In studies involving inhaled corticosteroids, the average reduction in growth velocity was approximately 1 cm (about 1/3 of an inch) per year. It appears that the reduction is related to dose and how long the child takes the drug.

FDA's Pulmonary and Allergy Drugs and Metabolic and Endocrine Drugs advisory committees discussed this issue at a July 1998 meeting. They recommended that the agency develop class-wide labeling to inform healthcare providers so they would understand this potential side effect and monitor growth routinely in pediatric patients who are treated with inhaled corticosteroids, intranasal corticosteroids or both.
(Continued)

Fluticasone *(Continued)*

Long-term effects of this reduction in growth velocity on final adult height are unknown. Likewise, it also has not yet been determined whether patients' growth will "catch up" if treatment is discontinued. Drug manufacturers will continue to monitor these drugs to learn more about long-term effects. Children are prescribed inhaled corticosteroids to treat asthma. Intranasal corticosteroids are generally used to prevent and treat allergy-related nasal symptoms.

Patients are advised not to stop using their inhaled or intranasal corticosteroids without first speaking to their healthcare providers about the benefits of these drugs compared to their risks.

Adverse Reactions
>10%: Oral inhalation:
Central nervous system: Headache
Respiratory: Respiratory infection, pharyngitis, nasal congestion
1% to 10%: Oral Inhalation:
Central nervous system: Dysphonia
Gastrointestinal: Oral candidiasis
Respiratory: Sinusitis
<1%: Acne, hypopigmentation, allergic dermatitis, maceration of the skin, skin atrophy, folliculitis, hypertrichosis, itching, dry skin, HPA suppression, Cushing's syndrome, growth retardation, burning, irritation, secondary infection

Overdosage/Toxicology When consumed in excessive quantities, systemic hypercorticism and adrenal suppression may occur; in those cases, discontinuation and withdrawal of the corticosteroid should be done judiciously

Mechanism of Action Fluticasone belongs to a new group of corticosteroids which utilizes a fluorocarbothioate ester linkage at the 17 carbon position; extremely potent vasoconstrictive and anti-inflammatory activity; has a weak hypothalamic -pituitary- adrenocortical axis (HPA) inhibitory potency when applied topically, which gives the drug a high therapeutic index. The mechanism of action for all topical corticosteroids is believed to be a combination of three important properties: anti-inflammatory activity, immunosuppressive properties, and antiproliferative actions.

Usual Dosage Flovent® Rotadisk can now be used in children ≥4 years; Flovent® is still indicated for use ≥12 years of age
Adolescents:
Topical: Apply sparingly in a thin film twice daily
Intranasal: Initially 1 spray (50 mcg/spray) per nostril once daily. Patients not adequately responding or patients with more severe symptoms may use 2 sprays (200 mcg) per nostril. Depending on response, dosage may be reduced to 100 mcg daily. Total daily dosage should not exceed 4 sprays (200 mcg)/day.
Adults:
Topical: Apply sparingly in a thin film twice daily
Inhalation, Oral:

Recommended Oral Inhalation Doses

Previous Therapy	Recommended Starting Dose	Recommended Highest Dose
Bronchodilator alone	88 mcg twice daily	440 mcg twice daily
Inhaled corticosteroids	88–220 mcg twice daily	440 mcg twice daily
Oral corticosteroids	880 mcg twice daily	880 mcg twice daily

Intranasal: Initial: 2 sprays (50 mcg/spray) per nostril once daily; after the first few days, dosage may be reduced to 1 spray per nostril once daily for maintenance therapy; maximum total daily dose should not exceed 4 sprays (200 mcg)/day

Patient Information A thin film of cream or ointment is effective; do not overuse; do not use tight-fitting diapers or plastic pants on children being treated in the diaper area; use only as prescribed, and for no longer than the period prescribed; apply sparingly in light film; rub in lightly; avoid contact with eyes; notify physician if condition being treated persists or worsens

Dosage Forms
Spray, aerosol, oral inhalation (Flovent®): 44 mcg/actuation (7.9 g = 60 actuations or 13 g = 120 actuations), 110 mcg/actuation (13 g = 120 actuations); 220 mcg/actuation (13 g = 120 actuations)
Spray, intranasal (Flonase®): 50 mcg/actuation (16 g = 120 actuations)
Topical (Cutivate™):
Cream: 0.05% (15 g, 30 g, 60 g)
Ointment: 0.005% (15 g, 60 g)

♦ **Fluticasone Propionate** *see* Fluticasone *on previous page*

Fluvastatin *(FLOO va sta tin)*
Related Information
Lipid-Lowering Agents *on page 1327*
U.S. Brand Names Lescol®
Therapeutic Category Antilipemic Agent; HMG-CoA Reductase Inhibitor
Use Adjunct to dietary therapy to decrease elevated serum total and LDL cholesterol concentrations in primary hypercholesterolemia
Pregnancy Risk Factor X

Pregnancy/Breast-Feeding Implications
Clinical effects on the fetus: Skeletal malformations have occurred in animals following agents with similar structure; avoid use in women of childbearing age; discontinue if pregnancy occurs
Breast-feeding/lactation: Avoid use in nursing mothers

Contraindications Pregnancy; myopathy or marked elevations of CPK

Warnings/Precautions Avoid combination of clofibrate and fluvastatin due to possible myopathy; consider temporarily withholding therapy in patients with risk of developing renal failure; avoid prolonged exposure to the sun or other ultraviolet light

Adverse Reactions
>10%: Respiratory: Upper respiratory infection (16%)
1% to 10%:
Central nervous system: Headache (9%), dizziness (2%), insomnia (2% to 3%), fatigue (2% to 3%)
Dermatologic: Rash (2% to 3%)
Gastrointestinal: Dyspepsia (8%), diarrhea (5%), nausea/vomiting (3%), constipation (2% to 3%), flatulence (2% to 3%), abdominal pain (5%)
Neuromuscular & skeletal: Back pain/myalgia (5% to 6%), arthropathy (2% to 4%)
Miscellaneous: Cold/flu symptoms (2% to 5%)

Overdosage/Toxicology No symptomatology has been reported in cases of significant overdosage, however, supportive measure should be instituted, as required; dialyzability is not known

Drug Interactions CYP2C9 enzyme substrate; CYP2C9, 2C18, and 2C19 enzyme inhibitor
Anticoagulant effect of warfarin, digoxin may be increased
Concurrent use of erythromycin, cyclosporine, niacin, gemfibrozil, and HMG-CoA reductase inhibitors may result in rhabdomyolysis
Increased effect/toxicity of fluvastatin with alcohol, itraconazole
Decreased effect of fluvastatin or other HMG-CoA reductase inhibitors with bile acid sequestrants, nicotinic acid, propranolol, rifampin, and digoxin

Mechanism of Action Acts by competitively inhibiting 3-hydroxyl-3-methylglutaryl-coenzyme A (HMG-CoA) reductase, the enzyme that catalyzes the reduction of HMG-CoA to mevalonate; this is an early rate-limiting step in cholesterol biosynthesis. HDL is increased while total, LDL and VLDL cholesterols, apolipoprotein B, and plasma triglycerides are decreased.

Pharmacodynamics/Kinetics
Protein binding: >98%
Metabolism: Undergoes extensive first pass hepatic extraction; metabolized to inactive and active metabolites although the active forms do not circulate systemically
Bioavailability: Absolute (24%); T_{max}: ≤1 hour
Half-life: 1.2 hours
Elimination: Urine (5%), feces (90%)

Usual Dosage Adults: Oral:
Initial dose: 20-40 mg at bedtime
Usual dose: 20-80 mg at bedtime
Note: Splitting the 80 mg dose into a twice daily regimen may provide a modest improvement in LDL response; maximum response occurs within 4-6 weeks; decrease dose and monitor effects carefully in patients with hepatic insufficiency

Administration Place patient on a standard cholesterol-lowering diet before and during treatment; fluvastatin may be taken without regard to meals; adjust dosage as needed in response to periodic lipid determinations during the first 4 weeks after a dosage change; lipid-lowering effects are additive when fluvastatin is combined with a bile-acid binding resin or niacin, however, it must be administered at least 2 hours following these drugs.

Test Interactions Increased serum transaminases, CPK, alkaline phosphatase, and bilirubin and thyroid function tests

Patient Information Avoid prolonged exposure to the sun and other ultraviolet light; report unexplained muscle pain or weakness, especially if accompanied by fever or malaise

Dosage Forms Capsule: 20 mg, 40 mg

♦ **Fluviral®** see Influenza Virus Vaccine on page 611
♦ **Fluviron®** see Influenza Virus Vaccine on page 611

Fluvoxamine (floo VOKS ah meen)

Related Information
Antidepressant Agents Comparison on page 1301
U.S. Brand Names Luvox®
Canadian Brand Names Apo®-Fluvoxamine
Therapeutic Category Antidepressant, Serotonin Reuptake Inhibitor
Use Treatment of obsessive-compulsive disorder (OCD); effective in the treatment of major depression; may be useful for the treatment of panic disorder
Pregnancy Risk Factor C
Contraindications Concomitant terfenadine or astemizole; during or within 14 days of MAO inhibitors; hypersensitivity to fluvoxamine or any congeners (eg, fluoxetine)
Warnings/Precautions Use with caution in patients with liver dysfunction, suicidal tendencies, history of seizures, mania, or drug abuse, ECT, cardiovascular disease, and the elderly

Adverse Reactions
>10%: Gastrointestinal: Nausea
(Continued)

Fluvoxamine (Continued)

1% to 10%:
Cardiovascular: Palpitations
Central nervous system: Somnolence, headache, insomnia, dizziness, nervousness, mania, hypomania, vertigo, abnormal thinking, agitation, anxiety, malaise, amnesia
Endocrine & metabolic: Decreased libido
Gastrointestinal: Xerostomia, abdominal pain, vomiting, dyspepsia, constipation, diarrhea, abnormal taste, anorexia
Neuromuscular & skeletal: Tremors, weakness
Miscellaneous: Diaphoresis
<1%: Seizures, toxic epidermal necrolysis, thrombocytopenia, hepatic dysfunction, increases in serum creatinine, extrapyramidal reactions

Overdosage/Toxicology
Symptoms of overdose include drowsiness, nausea, vomiting, abdominal pain, tremors, sinus bradycardia, and seizures
Specific antidote does not exist; treatment is supportive. Although vomiting has not been extensive in overdose to date, patients should be monitored for fluid and electrolyte loss, and appropriate replacement therapy instituted when necessary.

Drug Interactions CYP1A2 enzyme substrate; CYP1A2, 2C9, 2C19, 2D6, and 3A3/4 enzyme inhibitor

Increased toxicity: Terfenadine, astemizole, and cisapride are metabolized by the CYP3A4 isozyme, increased levels of these drugs have been associated with prolongation of the Q-T interval and potentially fatal, torsade de pointes ventricular arrhythmias. Since fluvoxamine inhibits the enzyme responsible for their clearance, the concomitant use of these agents is contraindicated.

Potentiates triazolam and alprazolam (dose should be reduced by at least 50%), hypertensive crisis with MAO inhibitors, theophylline (doses should be reduced by $\frac{1}{3}$ and plasma levels monitored), warfarin (reduce its dose and monitor PT/INR), carbamazepine (monitor levels), tricyclic antidepressants (monitor effects and reduce doses accordingly), methadone, beta-blockers (reduce dose of propranolol or metoprolol), diltiazem. Caution with other benzodiazepines, phenytoin, lithium, clozapine, alcohol, other CNS drugs, quinidine, ketoconazole.

Mechanism of Action Inhibits CNS neuron serotonin uptake; minimal or no effect on reuptake of norepinephrine or dopamine; does not significantly bind to alpha-adrenergic, histamine or cholinergic receptors

Usual Dosage
Adults: Initial: 50 mg at bedtime; adjust in 50 mg increments at 4- to 7-day intervals; usual dose range: 100-300 mg/day; divide total daily dose into 2 doses; administer larger portion at bedtime
Elderly or hepatic impairment: Reduce dose, titrate slowly

Dietary Considerations Alcohol: Additive CNS effect, avoid use

Monitoring Parameters Signs and symptoms of depression, anxiety, weight gain or loss, nutritional intake, sleep

Patient Information Its favorable side effect profile makes it a useful alternative to the traditional agents; use sugarless hard candy for dry mouth; avoid alcoholic beverages, may cause drowsiness; improvement may take several weeks; rise slowly to prevent dizziness. As with all psychoactive drugs, fluvoxamine may impair judgment, thinking, or motor skills, so use caution when operating hazardous machinery, including automobiles, especially early on into therapy. Inform your physician of any concurrent medications you may be taking.

Dosage Forms Tablet: 50 mg, 100 mg

♦ **Fluzone®** see Influenza Virus Vaccine on page 611
♦ **FML®** see Fluorometholone on page 499
♦ **FML® Forte** see Fluorometholone on page 499
♦ **FML-S® Ophthalmic Suspension** see Sulfacetamide Sodium and Fluorometholone on page 1091
♦ **Foille® [OTC]** see Benzocaine on page 133
♦ **Foille® Medicated First Aid [OTC]** see Benzocaine on page 133
♦ **Folacin** see Folic Acid on this page
♦ **Folate** see Folic Acid on this page
♦ **Folex® PFS** see Methotrexate on page 751

Folic Acid (FOE lik AS id)

U.S. Brand Names Folvite®
Canadian Brand Names Apo®-Folic; Flodine®; Novo-Folacid
Synonyms Folacin; Folate; Pteroylglutamic Acid
Therapeutic Category Vitamin, Water Soluble
Use Treatment of megaloblastic and macrocytic anemias due to folate deficiency; dietary supplement to prevent neural tube defects
Pregnancy Risk Factor A (C if dose exceeds RDA recommendation)
Contraindications Pernicious, aplastic, or normocytic anemias
Warnings/Precautions Doses >0.1 mg/day may obscure pernicious anemia with continuing irreversible nerve damage progression. Resistance to treatment may occur with depressed hematopoiesis, alcoholism, deficiencies of other vitamins. Injection contains benzyl alcohol (1.5%) as preservative (use care in administration to neonates).

Adverse Reactions <1%: Slight flushing, general malaise, pruritus, rash, bronchospasm, allergic reaction

Drug Interactions Decreased effect: In folate-deficient patients, folic acid therapy may increase phenytoin metabolism. Phenytoin, primidone, para-aminosalicylic acid, and sulfasalazine may decrease serum folate concentrations and cause deficiency. Oral contraceptives may also impair folate metabolism producing depletion, but the effect is unlikely to cause anemia or megaloblastic changes. Concurrent administration of chloramphenicol and folic acid may result in antagonism of the hematopoietic response to folic acid; dihydrofolate reductase inhibitors (eg, methotrexate, trimethoprim) may interfere with folic acid utilization.

Stability Incompatible with oxidizing and reducing agents and heavy metal ions

Mechanism of Action Folic acid is necessary for formation of a number of coenzymes in many metabolic systems, particularly for purine and pyrimidine synthesis; required for nucleoprotein synthesis and maintenance in erythropoiesis; stimulates WBC and platelet production in folate deficiency anemia

Pharmacodynamics/Kinetics
Peak effect: Oral: Within 0.5-1 hour
Absorption: In the proximal part of the small intestine

Usual Dosage
Infants: 0.1 mg/day
Children <4 years: Up to 0.3 mg/day
Children >4 years and Adults: 0.4 mg/day
Pregnant and lactating women: 0.8 mg/day
RDA:
Adult male: 0.15-0.2 mg/day
Adult female: 0.15-0.18 mg/day

Administration Oral preferred, but may also be administered by deep I.M., S.C., or I.V. injection; a diluted solution for oral or for parenteral administration may be prepared by diluting 1 mL of folic acid injection (5 mg/mL), with 49 mL sterile water for injection; resulting solution is 0.1 mg folic acid per 1 mL

Reference Range Therapeutic: 0.005-0.015 µg/mL

Test Interactions Falsely low serum concentrations may occur with the *Lactobacillus casei* assay method in patients on anti-infectives (eg, tetracycline)

Patient Information Take folic acid replacement only under recommendation of physician

Dosage Forms
Injection, as sodium folate: 5 mg/mL (10 mL); 10 mg/mL (10 mL)
Folvite®: 5 mg/mL (10 mL)
Tablet: 0.1 mg, 0.4 mg, 0.8 mg, 1 mg
Folvite®: 1 mg

Extemporaneous Preparations A 1 mg/mL folic acid solution may be prepared by crushing fifty 1 mg tablets. Dissolve in a small amount of distilled water, then add sufficient distilled water to make a final volume of 50 mL. Adjust the pH to 8 with sodium hydroxide. It is stable for 42 days at room temperature.

Nahata MC and Hipple TF, *Pediatric Drug Formulations*, Harvey Whitney Books Company, 1992.

♦ **Folinic Acid** see Leucovorin on page 666
♦ **Follistim™** see Follitropins on this page
♦ **Follitropin Alpha** see Follitropins on this page
♦ **Follitropin Beta** see Follitropins on this page

Follitropins (foe li TRO pins)

U.S. Brand Names Fertinex™; Follistim™; Gonal-F®
Synonyms Follitropin Alpha; Follitropin Beta; Recombinant Human Follicle Stimulating Hormone; rFSH-alpha; rFSH-beta; rhFSH-alpha; rhFSH-beta; Urofollitropin
Therapeutic Category Ovulation Stimulator
Use

Urofollitropin (Fertinex™):
Polycystic ovary syndrome: Give sequentially with hCG for the stimulation of follicular recruitment and development and the induction of ovulation in patients with polycystic ovary syndrome and infertility, who have failed to respond or conceive following adequate clomiphene citrate therapy
Follicle stimulation: Stimulate the development of multiple follicles in ovulatory patients undergoing Assisted Reproductive Technologies such as *in vitro* fertilization

Follitropin alpha (Gonal-F™)/follitropin beta (Follistim™):
Ovulation induction: For the induction of ovulation and pregnancy in anovulatory infertile patients in whom the cause of infertility is functional and not caused by primary ovarian failure
Follicle stimulation: To stimulate the development of multiple follicles in ovulatory patients undergoing Assisted Reproductive Technologies such as *in vitro* fertilization

Pregnancy Risk Factor X

Contraindications High levels of FSH indicating primary ovarian failure; uncontrolled thyroid or adrenal dysfunction; the presence of any cause of infertility other than anovulation; tumor of the ovary, breast, uterus, hypothalamus, or pituitary gland; abnormal vaginal bleeding of undetermined origin; ovarian cysts or enlargement not due to polycystic ovary syndrome; hypersensitivity to the product or any of its components; pregnancy
(Continued)

Follitropins *(Continued)*

Warnings/Precautions These medications should only be used by physicians who are thoroughly familiar with infertility problems and their management. To minimize risks, use only at the lowest effective dose. Monitor ovarian response with serum estradiol and vaginal ultrasound on a regular basis.

Ovarian enlargement which may be accompanied by abdominal distention or abdominal pain, occurs in ~20% of those treated with urofollitropin and hCG, and generally regresses without treatment within 2-3 weeks. Ovarian hyperstimulation syndrome, characterized by severe ovarian enlargement, abdominal pain/distention, nausea, vomiting, diarrhea, dyspnea, and oliguria, and may be accompanied by ascites, pleural effusion, hypovolemia, electrolyte imbalance, hemoperitoneum, and thromboembolic events is reported in about 6% of patients. If hyperstimulation occurs, stop treatment and hospitalize patient. This syndrome develops rapidly within 24 hours to several days and generally occurs during the 7-10 days immediately following treatment. Hemoconcentration associated with fluid loss into the abdominal cavity has occurred and should be assessed by fluid intake & output, weight, hematocrit, serum & urinary electrolytes, urine specific gravity, BUN and creatinine, and abdominal girth. Determinations should be performed daily or more often if the need arises. Treatment is primarily symptomatic and consists of bed rest, fluid and electrolyte replacement and analgesics. The ascitic, pleural and pericardial fluids should never be removed because of the potential danger of injury.

Serious pulmonary conditions (atelectasis, acute respiratory distress syndrome and exacerbation of asthma) have been reported. Thromboembolic events, both in association with and separate from ovarian hyperstimulation syndrome, have been reported.

Multiple pregnancies have been associated with these medications, including triplet and quintuplet gestations. Advise patient of the potential risk of multiple births before starting the treatment.

Adverse Reactions 1% to 10%:

Dermatologic: Dry skin, body rash, hair loss, hives

Endocrine & metabolic: Ovarian hyperstimulation syndrome, adnexal torsion, mild to moderate ovarian enlargement, abdominal pain, ovarian cysts, breast tenderness

Gastrointestinal: Nausea, vomiting, diarrhea, abdominal cramps, bloating

Local: Pain, rash, swelling, or irritation at the site of injection

Respiratory: Atelectasis, acute respiratory distress syndrome, exacerbation of asthma

Miscellaneous: Febrile reactions accompanied by chills, musculoskeletal, joint pains, malaise, headache, and fatigue

Overdosage/Toxicology

Symptoms of overdose: Aside from possible ovarian hyperstimulation and multiple gestations, little is known concerning the consequences of an acute overdose

Treatment is symptomatic

Stability

Urofollitropin (Fertinex™): Lyophilized powder may be stored in the refrigerator or at room temperature (3°C to 25°C/37°F to 77°F). Protect from light; use immediately after reconstitution.

Urofollitropin (Fertinex™): Dissolve the contents of one or more ampuls of urofollitropin in 0.5-1 mL of sterile saline (concentration should not exceed 225 international units/0.5 mL)

Follitropin alpha (Gonal-F®)/follitropin beta (Follistim™): Store powder refrigerated or at room temperature (2°C to 25°C/36°F to 77°F). Protect from light; use immediately after reconstitution.

Follitropin alpha (Gonal-F®): Dissolve the contents of one or more ampuls in 0.5-1 mL of sterile water for injection (concentration should not exceed 225 international units/0.5 mL)

Follitropin beta (Follistim™): Inject 1 mL of 0.45% sodium chloride injection into vial of follitropin beta. **Do not shake,** but gently swirl until solution is clear; generally the follitropin beta dissolves immediately

Mechanism of Action Urofollitropin is a preparation of highly purified follicle-stimulating hormone (FSH) extracted from the urine of postmenopausal women. Follitropin alpha and follitropin beta are human FSH preparations of recombinant DNA origin. Follitropins stimulate ovarian follicular growth in women who do not have primary ovarian failure. FSH is required for normal follicular growth, maturation, and gonadal steroid production.

Pharmacodynamics/Kinetics

Absorption: Absorption-rate limited pharmacokinetics; absorption rate following I.M. or S.C. administration is slower than the elimination rate

Mean T_{max}:

Follitropin alpha: 16 hours after subcutaneous administration; 25 hours after intramuscular administration

Follitropin beta: 27 hours after intramuscular administration

Urofollitropin: 15 hours after subcutaneous administration; 10 hours after intramuscular administration

Distribution: Mean V_d: Follitropin alpha: 10 L; Follitropin beta: 8 L

Bioavailability: Ranges from ~66% to 78% depending on the agent

Metabolism: Total clearance of follitropin alpha was 0.6 Liters/hour following IV administration

Half-life:

Mean elimination:

Follitropin alpha: 24-32 hours after subcutaneous administration

Follitropin beta: ~30 hours after intramuscular administration

Mean terminal: Follitropin alpha (intramuscular) & follitropin beta (subcutaneous): ~30 hours with multiple dosing

Usual Dosage

Urofollitropin (Fertinex™): Adults: S.C.:

Polycystic ovary syndrome: Initial recommended dose of the first cycle: 75 international units/day; consider dose adjustment after 5-7 days; additional dose adjustments may be considered based on individual patient response. The dose should not be increased more than twice in any cycle or by more than 75 international units per adjustment. To complete follicular development and affect ovulation in the absence of an endogenous LH surge, give 5000 to 10,000 units hCG, 1 day after the last dose of urofollitropin. Withhold hCG if serum estradiol is >2000 pg/mL.

Individualize the initial dose administered in subsequent cycles for each patient based on her response in the preceding cycle. Doses of >300 international units of FSH/day are not routinely recommended. As in the initial cycle, 5000 to 10,000 units of hCG must be given 1 day after the last dose of urofollitropin to complete follicular development and induce ovulation.

Give the lowest dose consistent with the expectation of good results. Over the course of treatment, doses may range between 75 to 300 international units/day depending on individual patient response. Administer urofollitropin until adequate follicular development as indicated by serum estradiol and vaginal ultrasonography. A response is generally evident after 5-7 days.

Encourage the couple to have intercourse daily, beginning on the day prior to the administration of hCG until ovulation becomes apparent from the indices employed for determination of progestational activity. Take care to ensure insemination.

Follicle stimulation: For Assisted Reproductive Technologies, initiate therapy with urofollitropin in the early follicular phase (cycle day 2 or 3) at a dose of 150 international units/day, until sufficient follicular development is attained. In most cases, therapy should not exceed 10 days.

Follitropin alpha (Gonal-F®): Adults: S.C.:

Ovulation induction: Initial recommended dose of the first cycle: 75 international units/day. Consider dose adjustment after 5-7 days; additional dose adjustments of up to 37.5 international units may be considered after 14 days. Further dose increases of the same magnitude can be made, if necessary, every 7 days. To complete follicular development and affect ovulation in the absence of an endogenous LH surge, give 5000 to 10,000 units hCG, 1 day after the last dose of follitropin alpha. Withhold hCG if serum estradiol is >2000 pg/mL.

Individualize the initial dose administered in subsequent cycles for each patient based on her response in the preceding cycle. Doses of >300 international units of FSH/day are not routinely recommended. As in the initial cycle, 5000 to 10,000 units of hCG must be given 1 day after the last dose of urofollitropin to complete follicular development and induce ovulation.

Give the lowest dose consistent with the expectation of good results. Over the course of treatment, doses may range between 75 to 300 international units/day depending on individual patient response. Administer urofollitropin until adequate follicular development as indicated by serum estradiol and vaginal ultrasonography. A response is generally evident after 5-7 days.

Encourage the couple to have intercourse daily, beginning on the day prior to the administration of hCG until ovulation becomes apparent from the indices employed for determination of progestational activity. Take care to ensure insemination.

Follicle stimulation: Initiate therapy with follitropin alpha in the early follicular phase (cycle day 2 or 3) at a dose of 150 international units/day, until sufficient follicular development is attained. In most cases, therapy should not exceed 10 days.

In patients undergoing Assisted Reproductive Technologies, whose endogenous gonadotropin levels are suppressed, initiate follitropin alpha at a dose of 225 international units/day. Continue treatment until adequate follicular development is indicated as determined by ultrasound in combination with measurement of serum estradiol levels. Consider adjustments to dose after 5 days based on the patient's response; adjust subsequent dosage every 3-5 days by ≤75-150 international units additionally at each adjustment. Doses >450 international units/day are not recommended. Once adequate follicular development is evident, administer hCG (5000-10,000 units) to induce final follicular maturation in preparation for oocyte.

Follitropin beta (Follistim™): Adults: S.C. or I.M.:

Ovulation induction: Stepwise approach: Initiate therapy with 75 international units/day for up to 14 days. Increase by 37.5 international units at weekly intervals until follicular growth or serum estradiol levels indicate an adequate response. The maximum, individualized, daily dose that has been safely used for ovulation induction in patients during clinical trials is 300 international units. Treat the patient until ultrasonic visualizations or serum estradiol determinations indicate preovulatory conditions greater than or equal to normal values followed by 5000 to 10,000 units hCG.

During treatment and during a 2-week post-treatment period, examine patients at least every other day for signs of excessive ovarian stimulation. Discontinue follitropin beta administration if the ovaries become abnormally enlarged or abdominal pain occurs.

Encourage the couple to have intercourse daily, beginning on the day prior to the administration of hCG until ovulation becomes apparent from the indices employed for determination of progestational activity. Take care to ensure insemination.

(Continued)

Follitropins (Continued)

Follicle stimulation: A starting dose of 150-225 international units of follitropin beta is recommended for at least the first 4 days of treatment. The dose may be adjusted for the individual patient based upon their ovarian response. Daily maintenance doses ranging from 75-300 international units for 6-12 days are usually sufficient, although longer treatment may be necessary. However, maintenance doses of up to 375-600 international units may be necessary according to individual response. The maximum daily dose used in clinical studies is 600 international units. When a sufficient number of follicles of adequate size are present, the final maturation of the follicles is induced by administering hCG at a dose of 5000-10,000 international units. Oocyte retrieval is performed 34-36 hours later. Withhold hCG in cases where the ovaries are abnormally enlarged on the last day of follitropin beta therapy.

Administration
Urofollitropin (Fertinex™)/follitropin alpha (Gonal-F®): Administer S.C.
Follitropin beta (Follistim™): Administer S.C. or I.M. The most convenient sites for S.C. injection are either in the abdomen around the navel or in the upper thigh. The best site for I.M. injection is the upper outer quadrant of the buttock muscle.

Monitoring Parameters Monitor sufficient follicular maturation. This may be directly estimated by sonographic visualization of the ovaries and endometrial lining or measuring serum estradiol levels. The combination of both ultrasonography and measurement of estradiol levels is useful for monitoring for the growth and development of follicles and timing hCG administration.

The clinical evaluation of estrogenic activity (changes in vaginal cytology and changes in appearance and volume of cervical mucus) provides an indirect estimate of the estrogenic effect upon the target organs and, therefore, it should only be used adjunctively with more direct estimates of follicular development (ultrasonography and serum estradiol determinations).

The clinical confirmation of ovulation is obtained by direct and indirect indices of progesterone production. The indices most generally used are: rise in basal body temperature, increase in serum progesterone, and menstruation following the shift in basal body temperature.

Patient Information Discontinue immediately if possibility of pregnancy. Prior to therapy, inform patients of the following: Duration of treatment and monitoring required; possible adverse reactions; risk of multiple births.

Dosage Forms
Urofollitropin (Fertinex®): Powder for injection: 75 international units (1, 10, 100 mL ampuls with diluent), 150 international units (1 mL ampuls with diluent)
Follitropin alpha (Gonal-F®): Powder for injection: 75 international units (1, 10, 100 mL ampuls with diluent), 150 international units (1 mL ampuls with diluent)
Follitropin beta (Follistim®): Powder for injection:: 75 international units (1, 5 mL vials with diluent)

♦ **Follutein®** see Chorionic Gonadotropin on page 258
♦ **Folvite®** see Folic Acid on page 512

Fomepizole (foe ME pi zole)

U.S. Brand Names Antizol®
Synonyms 4-Methylpyrazole; 4-MP
Therapeutic Category Antidote, Antifreeze Toxicity
Use Ethylene glycol and methanol toxicity; may be useful in propylene glycol; unclear whether it is useful in disulfiram-ethanol reactions
Pregnancy Risk Factor C
Pregnancy/Breast-Feeding Implications Clinical effects on the fetus: Animal reproduction studies have not been conducted and it is not known whether fomepizole can cause fetal harm when administered to pregnant women; should only be used in pregnant women if the benefits clearly outweigh the risks
Contraindications Fomepizole should not be administered to patients with a documented serious hypersensitivity reaction to fomepizole or other pyrazoles
Warnings/Precautions Should not be given undiluted or by bolus injection. It is not known whether this drug is excreted in human milk, therefore, caution should be exercised when given to a nursing woman; safety and effectiveness in pediatric patients have not been established. This drug is known to be substantially excreted by the kidney, and the risk of toxic reactions to this drug may be greater in patients with impaired renal function and because elderly patients are more likely to have decreased renal function, care should be taken in geriatric dose selection. Hemodialysis can accumulate the drug and as a result dosage adjustments may be required and patients with liver disease may accumulate fomepizole.
Adverse Reactions Unless noted, all adverse reactions have a reported incidence of ≤6%:
Cardiovascular: Bradycardia, tachycardia, hypotension
Central nervous system: Dizziness (7%), seizures, headache (12%), vertigo, lightheadedness, feeling of drunkenness, strange feelings, slurred speech, decreased environmental awareness, somnolence, hangover
Dermatologic: Rash
Gastrointestinal: Vomiting, nausea (11%), diarrhea, anorexia, heartburn, abdominal pain, bad metallic taste
Hematologic: Lymphangitis, eosinophilia, anemia
Local: Injection site reactions

Ocular: Nystagmus, blurred vision, visual problems
Respiratory: Pharyngitis, abnormal smell
Miscellaneous: Phlebosclerosis, hiccups

Overdosage/Toxicology

Nausea, dizziness, and vertigo were noted in healthy volunteers receiving 3-6 times the recommended dose. This dose-dependent CNS effect was short-lived in most subjects and lasted up to 30 hours in one subject.

Because fomepizole is dialyzable, dialysis may be useful in treating cases of overdosage

Drug Interactions Inhibitory effects on alcohol dehydrogenase are increased in presence of ethanol; ethanol also decreases metabolism of 4-MP; 4-MPO induces cytochrome P-450 mixed function oxidases *in vitro*; 4-MP may worsen the ethanol-chlorohydrate central nervous system interaction

Stability

Fomepizole diluted in 0.9% sodium chloride injection or dextrose 5% injection is stable for at least 48 hours when stored refrigerated or at room temperature; although, it is chemically and physically stable when diluted as recommended, sterile precautions should be observed because diluents generally do not contain preservatives.

After dilution, do not use beyond 24 hours. Fomepizole solidifies at temperatures <25°C (77°F). If the fomepizole solution has become solid in the vial, the solution should carefully be warmed by running the vial under warm water or by holding in the hand. Solidification does not affect the efficacy, safety, or stability of the drug.

Mechanism of Action Complexes and inactivates alcohol dehydrogenase thus preventing formation of the toxic metabolites of the alcohols

Pharmacodynamics/Kinetics

Maximum effect: 1.5-2 hours

Absorption: Oral: Readily absorbed

Distribution: V_d: 0.6-1.02 L/kg; rapidly distributes into total body water

Protein binding: Negligible

Elimination: Nonlinear elimination; at suggested therapeutic doses of 10-20 mg/kg, the apparent elimination rate is 4-5 µmol/L/hour

Usual Dosage A loading dose of 15 mg/kg should be administered, followed by doses of 10 mg/kg every 12 hours for 4 doses, then 15 mg/kg every 12 hours thereafter until ethylene glycol levels have been reduced <20 mg/dL

Dialysis should be considered in addition to fomepizole in the case of renal failure, significant or worsening metabolic acidosis, or a measured ethylene glycol level of >50 mg/dL. Patients should be dialyzed to correct metabolic abnormalities and to lower the ethylene glycol level <50 mg/dL

Fomepizole is dialyzable and the frequency of dosing should be increased to every 4 hours during hemodialysis

Dosage with hemodialysis: See table.

DOSE AT THE BEGINNING OF HEMODIALYSIS:	
If <6 hours since last fomepizole dose	If ≥6 hours since last fomepizole dose
Do not administer dose	Administer next scheduled dose
DOSING DURING HEMODIALYSIS:	
Dose every 4 hours	
DOSING AT THE TIME HEMODIALYSIS IS COMPLETE:	
Time Between Last Dose and the End of Hemodialysis	
<1 hour	Do not administer dose at the end of hemodialysis
1-3 hours	Administer 1/2 of next scheduled dose
>3 hours	Administer next scheduled dose
MAINTENANCE DOSE WHEN OFF HEMODIALYSIS:	
Give next scheduled dose 12 hours from last dose administered	

Administration The appropriate dose of fomepizole should be drawn from the vial with a syringe and injected into at least 100 mL of sterile 0.9% sodium chloride injection or dextrose 5% injection. All doses should be administered as a slow intravenous infusion (IVPB) over 30 minutes.

Monitoring Parameters Fomepizole plasma levels should be monitored as well as the response of ethylene glycol intoxication to fomepizole; monitor plasma/urinary ethylene glycol, urinary oxalate, plasma/urinary osmolality, renal/hepatic function, serum electrolytes, arterial blood gases; look for continued signs of severe metabolic acidosis, elevated anion and osmolar gaps, significant creatinine increases and resolution of clinical signs and symptoms of ethylene glycol intoxication (eg, arrhythmias, seizures, coma)

Reference Range Concentrations >10 µmol/L should result in enzyme inhibition

Nursing Implications This agent is intended as an antidote for ethylene glycol poisoning, the main ingredient in antifreeze and coolants, which can cause severe CNS depression, severe metabolic acidosis, renal failure, coma, and possibly death. The most common reactions to be aware of with the use of this agent are minor allergic reactions, headache, nausea, and dizziness.

Dosage Forms Injection: 1 g/mL (1.5 mL)

Fomivirsen (foe MI vir sen)

U.S. Brand Names Vitravene™

Synonyms Fomivirsen Sodium

Therapeutic Category Antiviral Agent, Ophthalmic

Use Local treatment of cytomegalovirus (CMV) retinitis in patients with acquired immuno-deficiency syndrome who are intolerant or insufficiently responsive to other treatments for CMV retinitis or when other treatments for CMV retinitis are contraindicated

Pregnancy Risk Factor C

Pregnancy/Breast-Feeding Implications Studies have not been conducted in pregnant women. Should be used in pregnancy only when potential benefit to the mother outweighs the potential risk to the fetus. Excretion in human milk is unknown. Use during breast-feeding is contraindicated - a decision to discontinue nursing or discontinue the drug is should be made.

Contraindications Hypersensitivity to fomivirsen or any component

Warnings/Precautions For ophthalmic use via intravitreal injection only. Uveitis occurs frequently, particularly during induction dosing. Do not use in patients who have received intravenous or intravitreal cidofovir within 2-4 weeks (risk of exaggerated inflammation is increased). Patients should be monitored for CMV disease in the contralateral eye and/or extraocular disease. Commonly increases intraocular pressure - monitoring is recommended.

Adverse Reactions

5% to 10%:

Central nervous system: Fever, headache

Gastrointestinal: Abdominal pain, diarrhea, nausea, vomiting

Hematologic: Anemia

Neuromuscular & skeletal: Asthenia

Ocular: Uveitis, abnormal vision, anterior chamber inflammation, blurred vision, cataract, conjunctival hemorrhage, decreased visual acuity, loss of color vision, eye pain, increased intraocular pressure, photophobia, retinal detachment, retinal edema, retinal hemorrhage, retinal pigment changes, vitreitis

Respiratory: Pneumonia, sinusitis

Miscellaneous: Systemic CMV, sepsis, infection

2% to 5%:

Cardiovascular: Chest pain

Central nervous system: Confusion, depression, dizziness, neuropathy, pain

Endocrine and metabolic: Dehydration

Gastrointestinal: Abnormal LFTs, pancreatitis, anorexia, weight loss

Hematologic: Thrombocytopenia, lymphoma

Neuromuscular & skeletal: Back pain, cachexia

Ocular: Application site reaction, conjunctival hyperemia, conjunctivitis, corneal edema, decreased peripheral vision, eye irritation, keratic precipitates, optic neuritis, photopsia, retinal vascular disease, visual field defect, vitreous hemorrhage, vitreous opacity

Renal: Kidney failure

Respiratory: Bronchitis, dyspnea, cough

Miscellaneous: Allergic reaction, flu-like syndrome, diaphoresis (increased)

Drug Interactions Drug interactions between fomivirsen and other medications have not been conducted.

Stability Store between 2°C to 25°C (35°F to 77°F); protect from excessive heat or light

Mechanism of Action Inhibits synthesis of viral protein by binding to mRNA which blocks replication of cytomegalovirus through an antisense mechanism

Pharmacodynamics/Kinetics Pharmacokinetic studies have not been conducted in humans. In animal models, the drug is cleared from the eye after 7-10 days. It is metabolized by sequential nucleotide removal, with a small amount of the radioactivity from a dose appearing in the urine.

Usual Dosage Adults: Intravitreal injection: Induction: 330 mcg (0.05 mL) every other week for 2 doses, followed by maintenance dose of 330 mcg (0.05 mL) every 4 weeks If progression occurs during maintenance, a repeat of the induction regimen may be attempted to establish resumed control. Unacceptable inflammation during therapy may be managed by temporary interruption, provided response has been established. Topical corticosteroids have been used to reduce inflammation.

Administration Administered by intravitreal injection following application of standard topical and/or local anesthetics and antibiotics.

Monitoring Parameters Immediately after injection, light perception and optic nerve head perfusion should be monitored. Anterior chamber paracentesis may be necessary if perfusion is not complete within 7-10 minutes after injection. Subsequent patient evaluation should include monitoring for contralateral CMV infection or extraocular CMV disease, and intraocular pressure prior to each injection.

Additional Information Because the mechanism of action of fomivirsen is different than other antiviral agents active against CMV, fomivirsen may be active against isolates resistant to ganciclovir, foscarnet, or cidofovir. The converse may also be true.

Dosage Forms Solution, for ocular injection: 6.6 mg/mL (0.25 mL)

◆ **Fortovase**® *see* Saquinavir *on page 1048*
◆ **Fosamax**® *see* Alendronate *on page 40*

Foscarnet (fos KAR net)

Related Information
Guidelines for the Prevention of Opportunistic Infections in Persons with HIV *on page 1388*

U.S. Brand Names Foscavir® Injection

Synonyms PFA; Phosphonoformate; Phosphonoformic Acid

Therapeutic Category Antiviral Agent, Parenteral

Use
Herpesvirus infections suspected to be caused by acyclovir - (HSV, VZV) or ganciclovir - (CMV) resistant strains (this occurs almost exclusively in immunocompromised persons, eg, with advanced AIDS), who have received prolonged treatment for a herpesvirus infection

CMV retinitis in persons with AIDS

Other CMV infections in persons unable to tolerate ganciclovir; may be given in combination with ganciclovir in patients who relapse after monotherapy with either drug

Pregnancy Risk Factor C

Contraindications Hypersensitivity to foscarnet, Cl_{cr} <0.4 mL/minute/kg during therapy

Warnings/Precautions Renal impairment occurs to some degree in the majority of patients treated with foscarnet; renal impairment may occur at any time and is usually reversible within 1 week following dose adjustment or discontinuation of therapy, however, several patients have died with renal failure within 4 weeks of stopping foscarnet; therefore, renal function should be closely monitored. Foscarnet is deposited in teeth and bone of young, growing animals; it has adversely affected tooth enamel development in rats; safety and effectiveness in children has not been studied. Imbalance of serum electrolytes or minerals occurs in 6% to 18% of patients (hypocalcemia, low ionized calcium, hypo- or hyperphosphatemia, hypomagnesemia or hypokalemia).

Patients with a low ionized calcium may experience perioral tingling, numbness, paresthesias, tetany, and seizures. Seizures have been experienced by up to 10% of AIDS patients. Risk factors for seizures include a low baseline absolute neutrophil count (ANC), impaired baseline renal function and low total serum calcium. Some patients who have experienced seizures have died, while others have been able to continue or resume foscarnet treatment after their mineral or electrolyte abnormality has been corrected, their underlying disease state treated, or their dose decreased. Foscarnet has been shown to be mutagenic *in vitro* and in mice at very high doses. Information on the use of foscarnet is lacking in the elderly; dose adjustments and proper monitoring must be performed because of the decreased renal function common in older patients.

Adverse Reactions
>10%:
Central nervous system: Fever (65%), headache (26%), seizures (10%)
Gastrointestinal: Nausea (47%), diarrhea (30%), vomiting
Hematologic: Anemia (33%)
Renal: Abnormal renal function/decreased creatinine clearance (27%)
1% to 10%:
Central nervous system: Fatigue, malaise, dizziness, hypoesthesia, depression/confusion/anxiety (≥5%)
Dermatologic: Rash
Endocrine & metabolic: Electrolyte imbalance (especially potassium, calcium, magnesium, and phosphorus)
Gastrointestinal: Anorexia
Hematologic: Granulocytopenia, leukopenia (≥5%), thrombocytopenia, thrombosis
Local: Injection site pain
Neuromuscular & skeletal: Paresthesia, involuntary muscle contractions, rigors, neuropathy (peripheral), weakness
Ocular: Vision abnormalities
Respiratory: Coughing, dyspnea (≥5%)
Miscellaneous: Sepsis, diaphoresis (increased)
<1%: Cardiac failure, bradycardia, arrhythmias, cerebral edema, leg edema, peripheral edema, syncope, substernal chest pain, hypothermia, abnormal crying, malignant hyperpyrexia, vertigo, coma, speech disorders, gynecomastia, decreased gonadotropins, cholecystitis, cholelithiasis, hepatitis, hepatosplenomegaly, ascites, abnormal gait, dyskinesia, hypertonia, nystagmus, vocal cord paralysis

Overdosage/Toxicology
Symptoms of overdose include seizures, renal dysfunction, perioral or limb paresthesias, hypocalcemia
Treatment is supportive; I.V. calcium salts for hypocalcemia

Drug Interactions Increased toxicity: Pentamidine increases hypocalcemia; concurrent use with ciprofloxacin increases seizure potential; acute renal failure (reversible) has been reported with cyclosporin due most likely to toxic synergistic effect; other nephrotoxic drugs (amphotericin B, I.V. pentamidine, aminoglycosides, etc) should be avoided, if possible, to minimize additive renal risk with foscarnet

Stability
Foscarnet injection is a clear, colorless solution; it should be stored at room temperature and protected from temperatures >40°C and from freezing
Foscarnet should be diluted in D_5W or NS and transferred to PVC containers; stable for 24 hours at room temperature or refrigeration
(Continued)

Foscarnet *(Continued)*

For peripheral line administration, foscarnet **must** be diluted to 12 mg/mL with D₅W or NS

For central line administration, foscarnet may be administered undiluted

Incompatible with dextrose 30%, I.V. solutions containing calcium, magnesium, vancomycin, TPN

Mechanism of Action Pyrophosphate analogue which acts as a noncompetitive inhibitor of many viral RNA and DNA polymerases as well as HIV reverse transcriptase. Similar to ganciclovir, foscarnet is a virostatic agent. Foscarnet does not require activation by thymidine kinase.

Pharmacodynamics/Kinetics

Absorption: Oral: Poorly absorbed; I.V. therapy is needed for the treatment of viral infections in AIDS patients

Distribution: Up to 28% of cumulative I.V. dose may be deposited in bone

Metabolism: Biotransformation does not occur

Half-life: ~3 hours

Elimination: Up to 28% excreted unchanged in urine

Usual Dosage Adolescents and Adults: I.V.:

CMV retinitis:

Induction treatment: 60 mg/kg/dose every 8 hours **or** 100 mg/kg every 12 hours for 14-21 days

Maintenance therapy: 90-120 mg/kg/day as a single infusion

Acyclovir-resistant HSV induction treatment: 40 mg/kg/dose every 8-12 hours for 14-21 days

Dosage adjustment in renal impairment: Refer to tables

Induction Dosing of Foscarnet in Patients with Abnormal Renal Function

Cl$_{cr}$ (mL/min/kg)	HSV Equivalent to 40 mg/kg q12h	HSV Equivalent to 40 mg/kg q8h	CMV Equivalent to 60 mg/kg q8h
<0.4	not recommended	not recommended	not recommended
≥0.4-0.5	20 mg/kg every 24 hours	35 mg/kg every 24 hours	50 mg/kg every 24 hours
≥0.5-0.6	25 mg/kg every 24 hours	40 mg/kg every 24 hours	60 mg/kg every 24 hours
≥0.6-0.8	35 mg/kg every 24 hours	25 mg/kg every 12 hours	40 mg/kg every 12 hours
≥0.8-1.0	20 mg/kg every 12 hours	35 mg/kg every 12 hours	50 mg/kg every 12 hours
≥1.0-1.4	30 mg/kg every 12 hours	30 mg/kg every 8 hours	45 mg/kg every 8 hours
1.4	40 mg/kg every 12 hours	40 mg/kg every 8 hours	60 mg/kg every 8 hours

Maintenance Dosing of Foscarnet in Patients with Abnormal Renal Function

Cl$_{cr}$ (mL/min/kg)	CMV Equivalent to 90 mg/kg q24h	CMV Equivalent to 120 mg/kg q24h
<0.4	not recommended	not recommended
≥0.4-0.5	50 mg/kg every 48 hours	65 mg/kg every 48 hours
≥0.5-0.6	60 mg/kg every 48 hours	80 mg/kg every 48 hours
≥0.6-0.8	80 mg/kg every 48 hours	105 mg/kg every 48 hours
≥0.8-1.0	50 mg/kg every 24 hours	65 mg/kg every 24 hours
≥1-1.4	70 mg/kg every 24 hours	90 mg/kg every 24 hours
≥1.4	90 mg/kg every 24 hours	120 mg/kg every 24 hours

Hemodialysis:

Foscarnet is highly removed by hemodialysis (30% in 4 hours HD)

Doses of 50 mg/kg/dose posthemodialysis have been found to produce similar serum concentrations as doses of 90 mg/kg twice daily in patients with normal renal function

Doses of 60-90 mg/kg/dose loading dose (posthemodialysis) followed by 45 mg/kg/dose posthemodialysis (3 times/week) with the monitoring of weekly plasma concentrations to maintain peak plasma concentrations in the range of 400-800 μMolar has been recommended by some clinicians

Continuous arteriovenous or venovenous hemodiafiltration (CAVH) effects: Dose as for Cl$_{cr}$ 10-50 mL/minute

Administration

Foscarnet is administered by intravenous infusion, using an infusion pump, at a rate not exceeding 1 mg/kg/minute

Undiluted (24 mg/mL) solution can be administered without further dilution when using a central venous catheter for infusion

For peripheral vein administration, the solution **must** be diluted to a final concentration **not to exceed** 12 mg/mL

The recommended dosage, frequency, and rate of infusion should not be exceeded

Patient Information Close monitoring is important and any symptom of electrolyte abnormalities should be reported immediately; maintain adequate fluid intake and hydration; regular ophthalmic examinations are necessary. Foscarnet is not a cure; disease progression may occur during or following treatment. Report any numbness in the extremities, paresthesias, or perioral tingling.

Nursing Implications Do not administer by rapid or bolus injection; follow administration guidelines carefully

Additional Information Sodium loading with 500 mL of 0.9% sodium chloride solution before and after foscarnet infusion helps to minimize the risk of nephrotoxicity

Dosage Forms Injection: 24 mg/mL (250 mL, 500 mL)

♦ **Foscavir® Injection** see Foscarnet on page 519

Fosfomycin (fos foe MYE sin)

Related Information
Antimicrobial Drugs of Choice on page 1404

U.S. Brand Names Monurol™

Synonyms Fosfomycin Tromethamine

Therapeutic Category Antibiotic, Miscellaneous

Use A single oral dose in the treatment of uncomplicated urinary tract infections in women due to susceptible strains of E. coli and Enterococcus; multiple doses have been investigated for complicated urinary tract infections in men; may have an advantage over other agents since it maintains high concentration in the urine for up to 48 hours

Pregnancy Risk Factor B

Pregnancy/Breast-Feeding Implications Breast-feeding/lactation: Milk concentration approximates 10% of plasma

Adverse Reactions
>1%:
  Central nervous system: Headache
  Dermatologic: Rash
  Gastrointestinal: Diarrhea (2% to 8%), nausea, vomiting, epigastric discomfort, anorexia
<1%: Dizziness, drowsiness, fatigue, pruritus

Overdosage/Toxicology Symptomatic and supportive treatment is recommended in the event of an overdose.

Drug Interactions
Decreased effect: Antacids or calcium salts may cause precipitate formation and decrease fosfomycin absorption
Metoclopramide: Increased gastrointestinal motility may lower fosfomycin tromethamine serum concentrations and urinary excretion. This drug interaction possibly could be extrapolated to other medications which increase gastrointestinal motility.

Mechanism of Action As a phosphonic acid derivative, fosfomycin inhibits bacterial wall synthesis (bactericidal) by inactivating the enzyme, pyruvyl transferase, which is critical in the synthesis of cell walls by bacteria; the tromethamine salt is preferable to the calcium salt due to its superior absorption

Pharmacodynamics/Kinetics
Absorption: Well absorbed
Distribution: V_d: 2 L/kg; high concentrations in urine; distributed well into other tissues, crosses maximally into CSF with inflamed meninges
Protein binding: Minimal (<3%)
Metabolism: None
Bioavailability: 34% to 58%
Half-life: 4-8 hours; prolonged in renal failure (50 hours with Cl_{cr} <10 mL/minute)
Time to peak serum concentration: 2 hours
Elimination: High urinary levels persist for >48 hours (100 mcg/mL); excreted unchanged

Usual Dosage Adults: Urinary tract infections: Oral:
Female: Single dose of 3 g in 4 oz of water
Male: 3 g once daily for 2-3 days for complicated urinary tract infections
  Dosing adjustment in renal impairment: Decrease dose; 80% removed by dialysis, repeat dose after dialysis
  Dosing adjustment in hepatic impairment: No dosage decrease needed

Administration Always mix with water before ingesting; do not administer in its dry form; pour contents of envelope into 90-120 mL of water (not hot), stir to dissolve and take immediately

Monitoring Parameters Signs and symptoms of urinary tract infection

Patient Information May be taken with or without food; avoid use of antacids or calcium salts within 4 hours before or 2 hours after taking fosfomycin; contact your physician if signs of allergy develop; if symptoms do not improve after 2-3 days, contact your healthcare provider

Additional Information Many gram-positive and gram-negative organisms such as staphylococci, pneumococci, E. coli, Salmonella, Shigella, H. influenzae, Neisseria spp, and some strains of P. aeruginosa, indole-negative Proteus, and Providencia are inhibited; B. fragilis, and anaerobic gram-negative cocci are resistant

Dosage Forms Powder, as tromethamine: 3 g, to be mixed in 4 oz of water

♦ **Fosfomycin Tromethamine** see Fosfomycin on this page

Fosinopril (foe SIN oh pril)

Related Information

Angiotensin Agents *on page 1291*
Drug-Drug Interactions With ACEIs *on page 1295*
Heart Failure: Management of Patients With Left-Ventricular Systolic Dysfunction *on page 1472*

U.S. Brand Names Monopril®

Therapeutic Category Angiotensin-Converting Enzyme (ACE) Inhibitor; Antihypertensive Agent

Use Treatment of hypertension, either alone or in combination with other antihypertensive agents; congestive heart failure; believed to prolong survival in heart failure

Pregnancy Risk Factor C (1st trimester); D (2nd and 3rd trimester)

Contraindications Renal impairment, collagen vascular disease, hypersensitivity to fosinopril, any component, or other angiotensin-converting enzyme inhibitors

Warnings/Precautions Use with caution and modify dosage in patients with renal impairment (decrease dosage) (especially renal artery stenosis), severe congestive heart failure or with coadministered diuretic therapy; experience in children is limited. Severe hypotension may occur in patients who are sodium and/or volume depleted; initiate lower doses and monitor closely when starting therapy in these patients.

Adverse Reactions

1% to 10%:
 Cardiovascular: Orthostatic hypotension (especially after initial dose)
 Central nervous system: Headache (3%), dizziness (1% to 2%), fatigue (1% to 2%)
 Gastrointestinal: Diarrhea/nausea/vomiting (1% to 2%)
 Respiratory: Cough (2%)
<1%: Syncope, hypotension, hypertensive crisis, claudication, edema, vertigo, insomnia, memory disturbance, drowsiness, angioedema, rash, hypoglycemia, hyperkalemia, abnormal taste, dysphagia, abdominal distention, dyspepsia, impotence, neutropenia, agranulocytosis, anemia, muscle cramps, tremor, deterioration in renal function, cold/flu symptoms

Overdosage/Toxicology

Mild hypotension has been the only toxic effect seen with acute overdose. Bradycardia may also occur; hyperkalemia occurs even with therapeutic doses, especially in patients with renal insufficiency and those taking NSAIDs

Following initiation of essential overdose management, toxic symptom treatment and supportive treatment should be initiated. Hypotension usually responds to I.V. fluids or Trendelenburg positioning.

Drug Interactions Increased toxicity: See Drug-Drug Interactions With ACEIs *on page 1295*

Mechanism of Action Competitive inhibitor of angiotensin-converting enzyme (ACE); prevents conversion of angiotensin I to angiotensin II, a potent vasoconstrictor; results in lower levels of angiotensin II which causes an increase in plasma renin activity and a reduction in aldosterone secretion; a CNS mechanism may also be involved in hypotensive effect as angiotensin II increases adrenergic outflow from CNS; vasoactive kallikreins may be decreased in conversion to active hormones by ACE inhibitors, thus reducing blood pressure

Pharmacodynamics/Kinetics

Absorption: 36%
Metabolism: Fosinopril is a prodrug and is hydrolyzed to its active metabolite fosinoprilat by intestinal wall and hepatic esterases
Half-life, serum (fosinoprilat): 12 hours
Time to peak serum concentration: ~3 hours
Elimination: In the urine and bile as fosinoprilat and it conjugates in roughly equal proportions (45% to 50%)

Usual Dosage Adults: Oral:

Hypertension: Initial: 10 mg/day; most patients are maintained on 20-40 mg/day; may need to divide the dose into two if trough effect is inadequate; discontinue the diuretic, if possible 2-3 days before initiation of therapy; resume diuretic therapy carefully, if needed.

Heart failure: Initial: 10 mg/day (5 mg if renal dysfunction present) and increase, as needed, to a maximum of 40 mg once daily over several weeks; usual dose: 20-40 mg/day; if hypotension, orthostasis, or azotemia occur during titration, consider decreasing concomitant diuretic dose, if any

Dosing adjustment/comments in renal impairment: None needed since hepatobiliary elimination compensates adequately diminished renal elimination

Hemodialysis: Moderately dialyzable (20% to 50%)

Monitoring Parameters Blood pressure (supervise for at least 2 hours after the initial dose or any increase for significant orthostasis); serum potassium, calcium, creatinine, BUN, WBC

Test Interactions Positive Coombs' [direct]; may cause false-positive results in urine acetone determinations using sodium nitroprusside reagent

Patient Information Notify physician if vomiting, diarrhea, excessive perspiration, or dehydration should occur; also if swelling of face, lips, tongue, or difficulty in breathing occurs or if persistent cough develops; may be taken with meals; do not stop therapy or add a potassium salt replacement without physician's advice

Nursing Implications May cause depression in some patients; discontinue if angioedema of the face, extremities, lips, tongue, or glottis occurs; watch for hypotensive effects within 1-3 hours of first dose or new higher dose

Dosage Forms Tablet: 10 mg, 20 mg

Fosphenytoin (FOS fen i toyn)

Related Information

Fosphenytoin and Phenytoin, Parenteral Comparison on page 1321

U.S. Brand Names Cerebyx®

Synonyms Fosphenytoin Sodium; 3-Phosphoryloxymethyl Phenytoin Disodium

Therapeutic Category Anticonvulsant

Use Indicated for short-term parenteral administration when other means of phenytoin administration are unavailable, inappropriate or deemed less advantageous; the safety and effectiveness of fosphenytoin in this use has not been systematically evaluated for more than 5 days; may be used for the control of generalized convulsive status epilepticus and prevention and treatment of seizures occurring during neurosurgery

Pregnancy Risk Factor D

Pregnancy/Breast-Feeding Implications

Clinical effects on the fetus: Crosses placenta with fetal serum concentrations equal to those of mother; eye, cardiac, cleft palate, and skeletal malformations have been noted; fetal hydantoin syndrome associated with maternal ingestion of 100-800 mg/kg during 1st trimester

Breast-feeding/lactation: Distributes into breast milk

Contraindications Hypersensitivity to phenytoin or fosphenytoin; occurrence of any rash while on treatment; the drug should not be resumed if rash is exfoliative, purpuric, or bullous; not recommended for use in children <4 years of age

Warnings/Precautions Use with caution in patients with severe cardiovascular, hepatic, renal disease or diabetes mellitus; avoid abrupt discontinuation; dosing should be slowly reduced to avoid precipitation of seizures; increased toxicity with nephrotic syndrome patient; may increase frequency of petit mal seizures; use with caution in patients with porphyria, fever, or hypothyroidism

Adverse Reactions

Percentage unknown:

Local: Pain on injection

Neuromuscular & skeletal: Sensory paresthesia (long-term treatment)

Renal: Nephrotic syndrome

>10%:

Central nervous system: Dizziness (31%), somnolence (21%), ataxia (11%)

Dermatologic: Pruritus (48.9%)

Ocular: Nystagmus (44%)

1% to 10%:

Cardiovascular: Hypotension (7.7%), vasodilation (>1%), tachycardia (2.2%)

Central nervous system: Stupor (7.7%), incooridnation (4.4%), paresthesia (4.4%), choreathetosis (4.4%), tremor (3.3%), agitation (3.3%)

Gastrointestinal: Nausea (>5%), vomiting (2%)

Ocular: Blurred vision (2%), diplopia (3.3%)

<1%: Rash, exfoliative dermatitis, erythema multiforme, acne, diabetes insipidis, lymphadenopathy, neutropenia, thrombocytopenia, anemia (megaloblastic)

Overdosage/Toxicology

Signs and symptoms of toxicity include unsteady gait, tremors, hyperglycemia, chorea (extrapyramidal), gingival hyperplasia, gynecomastia, myoglobinuria, nephrotic syndrome, slurred speech, mydriasis, myoclonus, confusion, encephalopathy, hyperthermia, drowsiness, nausea, hypothermia, fever, hypotension, respiratory depression, leukopenia; neutropenia; agranulocytosis; granulocytopenia; hyper-reflexia, coma, systemic lupus erythematosus (SLE), ophthalmoplegia

Treatment is supportive for hypotension; treat with I.V. fluids and place patient in Trendelenburg position; seizures may be controlled with lorazepam or diazepam 5-10 mg (0.25-0.4 mg/kg in children); intravenous albumin (25 g every 6 hours has been used to increase bound fraction of drug). Multiple dosing of activated charcoal may be effective; peritoneal dialysis, diuresis, hemodialysis, hemoperfusion, and plasmapheresis is of little value

Drug Interactions No drug interaction noted with diazepam

Stability Refrigerated vials are stable for 2 years; at room temperature, stable for 3 months; I.V. solutions are stable for one day when refrigerated

Compatible with all diluents and does not require propylene glycol or ethanol for solubility

Mechanism of Action Diphosphate ester salt of phenytoin which acts as a water soluble prodrug of phenytoin; after administration, plasma esterases convert fosphenytoin to phosphate, formaldehyde and phenytoin as the active moiety; phenytoin works by stabilizing neuronal membranes and decreasing seizure activity by increasing efflux or decreasing influx of sodium ions across cell membranes in the motor cortex during generation of nerve impulses

Usual Dosage The dose, concentration in solutions, and infusion rates for fosphenytoin are expressed as phenytoin sodium equivalents; fosphenytoin should always be prescribed and dispensed in phenytoin sodium equivalents

Status epilepticus: I.V.: Adults: Loading dose: Phenytoin equivalent: 15-20 mg/kg I.V. administered at 100-150 mg/minute

Nonemergent loading and maintenance dosing: I.V. or I.M.: Adults:

Loading dose: Phenytoin equivalent: 10-20 mg/kg I.V. or I.M. (maximum I.V. rate: 150 mg/minute)

Initial daily maintenance dose: Phenytoin equivalent: 4-6 mg/kg/day I.V. or I.M.

(Continued)

Fosphenytoin *(Continued)*

I.M. or I.V. substitution for oral phenytoin therapy: May be substituted for oral phenytoin sodium at the same total daily dose, however, Dilantin® capsules are ~90% bioavailable by the oral route; phenytoin, supplied as fosphenytoin, is 100% bioavailable by both the I.M. and I.V. routes; for this reason, plasma phenytoin concentrations may increase when I.M. or I.V. fosphenytoin is substituted for oral phenytoin sodium therapy; in clinical trials I.M. fosphenytoin was administered as a single daily dose utilizing either 1 or 2 injection sites; some patients may require more frequent dosing

Dosing adjustments in renal/hepatic impairment: Phenytoin clearance may be substantially reduced in cirrhosis and plasma level monitoring with dose adjustment advisable; free phenytoin levels should be monitored closely in patients with renal or hepatic disease or in those with hypoalbuminemia; furthermore, fosphenytoin clearance to phenytoin may be increased without a similar increase in phenytoin in these patients leading to increase frequency and severity of adverse events

Administration Since there is no precipitation problem with fosphenytoin, no I.V. filter is required

Monitoring Parameters Blood pressure, vital signs (with I.V. use), plasma level monitoring, CBC, liver function tests

Reference Range

Therapeutic: 10-20 µg/mL (SI: 40-79 µmol/L); toxicity is measured clinically, and some patients require levels outside the suggested therapeutic range

Toxic: 30-50 µg/mL (SI: 120-200 µmol/L)

Lethal: >100 µg/mL (SI: >400 µmol/L)

Manifestations of toxicity:

Nystagmus: 20 µg/mL (SI: 79 µmol/L)

Ataxia: 30 µg/mL (SI: 118.9 µmol/L)

Decreased mental status: 40 µg/mL (SI: 159 µmol/L)

Coma: 50 µg/mL (SI: 200 µmol/L)

Peak serum phenytoin level after a 375 mg I.M. fosphenytoin dose in healthy males: 5.7 µg/mL

Peak serum fosphenytoin levels and phenytoin levels after a 1.2 g infusion (I.V.) in healthy subjects over 30 minutes were 129 µg/mL and 17.2 µg/mL respectively

Test Interactions Increases glucose, alkaline phosphatase (S); decreases thyroxine (S), calcium (S); serum sodium increases in overdose setting

Nursing Implications I.V. injections should be followed by normal saline flushes through the same needle or I.V. catheter to avoid local irritation of the vein; must be diluted to concentrations <6 mg/mL, in normal saline, for I.V. infusion

Additional Information 1.5 mg fosphenytoin is approximately equivalent to 1 mg phenytoin; equimolar fosphenytoin dose is 375 mg (75 mg/mL solution) to phenytoin 250 mg (50 mg/mL)

Water solubility: 142 mg/mL at pH of 9

Antiarrhythmic effects may be similar to phenytoin; parenteral product contains no propylene sterol; this should allow for rapid intravenous bolus dosing without cardiovascular complications; formaldehyde production is not expected to be clinically consequential (about 200 mg) if used for one week

Dosage Forms Injection, as sodium: 150 mg [equivalent to phenytoin sodium 100 mg] in 2 mL vials; 750 mg [equivalent to phenytoin sodium 500 mg] in 10 mL vials

+ **Fosphenytoin and Phenytoin, Parenteral Comparison** *see page 1321*
+ **Fosphenytoin Sodium** *see Fosphenytoin on previous page*
+ **Fragmin®** *see Dalteparin on page 319*
+ **Froben®** *see Flurbiprofen on page 507*
+ **Froben-SR®** *see Flurbiprofen on page 507*
+ **Frusemide** *see Furosemide on next page*
+ **FS Shampoo®** *see Fluocinolone on page 496*
+ **5-FU** *see Fluorouracil on page 500*
+ **Ful-Glo®** *see Fluorescein Sodium on page 497*
+ **Fulvicin® P/G** *see Griseofulvin on page 548*
+ **Fulvicin-U/F®** *see Griseofulvin on page 548*
+ **Fumasorb® [OTC]** *see Ferrous Fumarate on page 478*
+ **Fumerin® [OTC]** *see Ferrous Fumarate on page 478*
+ **Funduscein®** *see Fluorescein Sodium on page 497*
+ **Fungizone®** *see Amphotericin B, Conventional on page 74*
+ **Fungoid® Creme** *see Miconazole on page 775*
+ **Fungoid® Solution** *see Clotrimazole on page 287*
+ **Fungoid® Tincture** *see Miconazole on page 775*
+ **Furacin® Topical** *see Nitrofurazone on page 844*
+ **Furadantin®** *see Nitrofurantoin on page 843*
+ **Furalan®** *see Nitrofurantoin on page 843*
+ **Furamide®** *see Diloxanide Furoate on page 365*
+ **Furan®** *see Nitrofurantoin on page 843*
+ **Furanite®** *see Nitrofurantoin on page 843*

Furazolidone *(fyoor a ZOE li done)*

Related Information

Tyramine Content of Foods *on page 1525*

U.S. Brand Names Furoxone®

Therapeutic Category Antibiotic, Miscellaneous; Antidiarrheal; Antiprotozoal

Use Treatment of bacterial or protozoal diarrhea and enteritis caused by susceptible organisms *Giardia lamblia* and *Vibrio cholerae*

Pregnancy Risk Factor C

Contraindications Known hypersensitivity to furazolidone; concurrent use of alcohol; patients <1 month of age because of the possibility of producing hemolytic anemia

Warnings/Precautions Use caution in patients with G-6-PD deficiency when administering large doses for prolonged periods; furazolidone inhibits monoamine oxidase

Adverse Reactions
>10%: Genitourinary: Discoloration of urine (dark yellow to brown)
1% to 10%:
    Central nervous system: Headache
    Gastrointestinal: Abdominal pain, diarrhea, nausea, vomiting
<1%: Orthostatic hypotension, fever, dizziness, drowsiness, malaise, rash, hypoglycemia, disulfiram-like reaction after alcohol ingestion, leukopenia, agranulocytosis, hemolysis in patients with G-6-PD deficiency, arthralgia

Overdosage/Toxicology
Symptoms of overdose include nausea, vomiting, serotonin crisis
Treatment is supportive care only; serotonin crisis may require dantrolene/bromocriptine

Drug Interactions
Increases toxicity of sympathomimetic amines, tricyclic antidepressants, MAO inhibitors, meperidine, anorexiants, dextromethorphan, fluoxetine, paroxetine, sertraline, trazodone
Increased effect/toxicity of levodopa
Disulfiram-like reaction with alcohol

Mechanism of Action Inhibits several vital enzymatic reactions causing antibacterial and antiprotozoal action

Pharmacodynamics/Kinetics
Absorption: Oral: Poor
Elimination: Oral: $1/3$ of dose is excreted in urine as active drug and metabolites

Usual Dosage Oral:
Children >1 month: 5-8 mg/kg/day in 4 divided doses for 7 days, not to exceed 400 mg/day or 8.8 mg/kg/day
Adults: 100 mg 4 times/day for 7 days

Dietary Considerations
Alcohol: Avoid use
Food: Marked elevation of blood pressure, hypertensive crisis, or hemorrhagic stroke may occur with foods high in amine content

Monitoring Parameters CBC

Test Interactions False-positive results for urine glucose with Clinitest®

Patient Information May discolor urine to a brown tint; avoid drinking alcohol during or for 4 days after therapy or eating tyramine-containing foods; consult with physician or pharmacist for a list of these foods. Do not take any prescription or nonprescription drugs without consulting the physician or pharmacist; if result not achieved at the end of treatment contact physician.

Dosage Forms
Liquid: 50 mg/15 mL (60 mL, 473 mL)
Tablet: 100 mg

♦ **Furazosin** *see* Prazosin *on page 959*

Furosemide (fyoor OH se mide)

Related Information
Adrenergic Agonists, Cardiovascular Comparison *on page 1290*
Adult ACLS Algorithm, Hypotension, Shock *on page 1454*
Heart Failure: Management of Patients With Left-Ventricular Systolic Dysfunction *on page 1472*
Sulfonamide Derivatives *on page 1337*

U.S. Brand Names Lasix®

Canadian Brand Names Apo®-Furosemide; Furoside®; Novo-Semide; Uritol®

Synonyms Frusemide

Therapeutic Category Antihypertensive Agent; Diuretic, Loop

Use Management of edema associated with congestive heart failure and hepatic or renal disease; used alone or in combination with antihypertensives in treatment of hypertension

Pregnancy Risk Factor C

Pregnancy/Breast-Feeding Implications
Clinical effects on the fetus: Crosses the placenta. Increased fetal urine production, electrolyte disturbances reported. Generally, use of diuretics during pregnancy is avoided due to risk of decreased placental perfusion.
Breast-feeding/lactation: Crosses into breast milk; may suppress lactation. American Academy of Pediatrics has NO RECOMMENDATION.

Contraindications Hypersensitivity to furosemide, any component, or other sulfonamides; use with sparfloxacin; anuric patients

Warnings/Precautions Loop diuretics are potent diuretics; close medical supervision and dose evaluation is required to prevent fluid and electrolyte imbalance; use caution with other nephrotoxic or ototoxic drugs

(Continued)

Furosemide (Continued)

Adverse Reactions
>10%:
- Cardiovascular: Orthostatic hypotension
- Central nervous system: Dizziness

1% to 10%:
- Central nervous system: Headache
- Dermatologic: Photosensitivity
- Endocrine & metabolic: Electrolyte imbalance (hypokalemia, hyponatremia, hypochloremia, hypercalciuria, hyperuricemia), alkalosis, dehydration
- Gastrointestinal: Diarrhea, loss of appetite, stomach cramps or pain
- Ocular: Blurred vision

<1%: Rash, pancreatitis, nausea, hepatic dysfunction, agranulocytosis, leukopenia, anemia, thrombocytopenia, redness at injection site, gout, xanthopsia, ototoxicity, nephrocalcinosis, interstitial nephritis, prerenal azotemia

Overdosage/Toxicology
Symptoms of overdose include electrolyte imbalance, volume depletion, hypotension, dehydration, hypokalemia and hypochloremic alkalosis

Following GI decontamination, treatment is supportive; hypotension responds to fluids and Trendelenburg position

Drug Interactions
Decreased effect:
- Furosemide interferes with hypoglycemic effect of antidiabetic agents; decreased furosemide concentrations with metformin have been observed
- Furosemide may antagonize the skeletal muscle relaxing effect of tubocurarine and decrease the responsiveness of norepinephrine (although not to a major extent)
- Indomethacin may reduce natriuretic and hypotensive effects of furosemide
- Furosemide effects may be significantly decreased when given within 2 hours of sucralfate

Increased effect: Effects of antihypertensive agents may be enhanced

Increased toxicity:
- High-dose salicylates with furosemide may predispose patients to salicylate toxicity due to competitive renal excretory sites
- Lithium → renal clearance decreased; furosemide may increase toxicity of metformin (eg, ethacrynic acid)
- Concomitant use of furosemide with aminoglycoside antibiotics or other ototoxic drugs should be avoided, especially with renal dysfunction
- Avoid use with sparfloxacin due to increased risk of cardiotoxicity
- Succinylcholine's action may be potentiated by furosemide as is ganglionic or peripheral adrenergic-blocking drugs
- Aspirin and furosemide in combination may reduce temporarily Cl$_{cr}$ in patients with chronic renal insufficiency; other NSAIDs may result in increased BUN, creatinine, potassium, and weight gain when used in conjunction with furosemide

Stability
Furosemide injection should be stored at controlled room temperature and protected from light

Exposure to light may cause discoloration; do not use furosemide solutions if they have a yellow color

Refrigeration may result in precipitation or crystallization, however, resolubilization at room temperature or warming may be performed without affecting the drugs stability

Furosemide solutions are unstable in acidic media but very stable in basic media

I.V. infusion solution mixed in NS or D$_5$W solution is stable for 24 hours at room temperature

Mechanism of Action Inhibits reabsorption of sodium and chloride in the ascending loop of Henle and distal renal tubule, interfering with the chloride-binding cotransport system, thus causing increased excretion of water, sodium, chloride, magnesium, and calcium

Pharmacodynamics/Kinetics
Onset of diuresis: Oral: Within 30-60 minutes; I.M.: 30 minutes; I.V.: Within 5 minutes

Peak effect: Oral: Within 1-2 hours

Duration: Oral: 6-8 hours; I.V.: 2 hours

Absorption: Oral: 60% to 67%

Protein binding: >98%

Half-life: Normal renal function: 0.5-1.1 hours; End-stage renal disease: 9 hours

Elimination: 50% of an oral or 80% of an I.V. dose is excreted in the urine within 24 hours; the remainder is eliminated by other nonrenal pathways, including liver metabolism and excretion of unchanged drug in the feces

Usual Dosage
Infants and Children:
- Oral: 1-2 mg/kg/dose increased in increments of 1 mg/kg/dose with each succeeding dose until a satisfactory effect is achieved to a maximum of 6 mg/kg/dose no more frequently than 6 hours
- I.M., I.V.: 1 mg/kg/dose, increasing by each succeeding dose at 1 mg/kg/dose at intervals of 6-12 hours until a satisfactory response up to 6 mg/kg/dose

Adults:
- Oral: 20-80 mg/dose initially increased in increments of 20-40 mg/dose at intervals of 6-8 hours; usual maintenance dose interval is twice daily or every day; may be titrated up to 600 mg/day with severe edematous states
- I.M., I.V.: 20-40 mg/dose, may be repeated in 1-2 hours as needed and increased by 20 mg/dose until the desired effect has been obtained; usual dosing interval: 6-12

hours; for acute pulmonary edema, the usual dose is 40 mg I.V. over 1-2 minutes; if not adequate, may increase dose to 80 mg

Continuous I.V. infusion: Initial I.V. bolus dose of 0.1 mg/kg followed by continuous I.V. infusion doses of 0.1 mg/kg/hour doubled every 2 hours to a maximum of 0.4 mg/kg/hour if urine output is <1 mL/kg/hour have been found to be effective and result in a lower daily requirement of furosemide than with intermittent dosing. Other studies have used a rate of ≤4 mg/minute as a continuous I.V. infusion.

Elderly: Oral, I.M., I.V.: Initial: 20 mg/day; increase slowly to desired response

Refractory heart failure: Oral, I.V.: Doses up to 8 g/day have been used

Dosing adjustment/comments in renal impairment: Acute renal failure: High doses (up to 1-3 g/day - oral/I.V.) have been used to initiate desired response; avoid use in oliguric states

Dialysis: Not removed by hemo- or peritoneal dialysis; supplemental dose is not necessary

Dosing adjustment/comments in hepatic disease: Diminished natriuretic effect with increased sensitivity to hypokalemia and volume depletion in cirrhosis; monitor effects, particularly with high doses

Administration I.V. injections should be given slowly over 1-2 minutes; maximum rate of administration for IVPB or infusion: 4 mg/minute; replace parenteral therapy with oral therapy as soon as possible

Monitoring Parameters Monitor weight and I & O daily; blood pressure, serum electrolytes, renal function; in high doses, monitor hearing

Patient Information May be taken with food or milk; rise slowly from a lying or sitting position to minimize dizziness, lightheadedness, or fainting; also use extra care when exercising, standing for long periods of time, and during hot weather; take last dose of day early in the evening to prevent nocturia

Additional Information Sodium content of 1 mL (injection): 0.162 mEq

Dosage Forms
Injection: 10 mg/mL (2 mL, 4 mL, 5 mL, 6 mL, 8 mL, 10 mL, 12 mL)
Solution, oral: 10 mg/mL (60 mL, 120 mL); 40 mg/5 mL (5 mL, 10 mL, 500 mL)
Tablet: 20 mg, 40 mg, 80 mg

- ◆ **Furoside®** see Furosemide on page 525
- ◆ **Furoxone®** see Furazolidone on page 524
- ◆ **G-1®** see Butalbital Compound on page 165

Gabapentin (GA ba pen tin)

Related Information
Anticonvulsants by Seizure Type on page 1300
Epilepsy Treatment on page 1468

U.S. Brand Names Neurontin®

Therapeutic Category Anticonvulsant

Use Adjunct for treatment of drug-refractory partial and secondarily generalized seizures in adults with epilepsy; not effective for absence seizures

Pregnancy Risk Factor C

Pregnancy/Breast-Feeding Implications
Clinical effects on the fetus: No data on crossing the placenta; 4 reports of normal pregnancy outcomes; 1 report of infant with respiratory distress, pyloric stenosis, inguinal hernia following 1st trimester exposure to gabapentin plus carbamazepine; epilepsy itself, number of medications, genetic factors, or a combination of these probably influence the teratogenicity of anticonvulsant therapy
Breast-feeding/lactation: No data available

Contraindications Hypersensitivity to the drug or its ingredients

Warnings/Precautions Avoid abrupt withdrawal, may precipitate seizures; may be associated with a slight incidence (0.6%) of status epilepticus and sudden deaths (0.0038 deaths/patient year); use cautiously in patients with severe renal dysfunction; rat studies demonstrated an association with pancreatic adenocarcinoma in male rats; clinical implication unknown

Adverse Reactions
>10%: Central nervous system: Somnolence, dizziness, ataxia, fatigue
1% to 10%:
Cardiovascular: Peripheral edema
Central nervous system: Nervousness, amnesia, depression, anxiety, abnormal coordination
Dermatologic: Pruritus
Gastrointestinal: Dyspepsia, dry throat, xerostomia, nausea, constipation, appetite stimulation (weight gain)
Genitourinary: Impotence
Hematologic: Leukopenia
Neuromuscular & skeletal: Back pain, myalgia, dysarthria, tremor
Ocular: Diplopia, blurred vision, nystagmus
Respiratory: Rhinitis, bronchospasm
Miscellaneous: Hiccups

Overdosage/Toxicology
Decontaminate using lavage/activated charcoal with cathartic
Multiple dosing of activated charcoal may be useful; hemodialysis will be useful

Drug Interactions
Gabapentin does not modify plasma concentrations of standard anticonvulsant medications (ie, valproic acid, carbamazepine, phenytoin, or phenobarbital)

(Continued)

Gabapentin *(Continued)*

Decreased effect: Antacids reduce the bioavailability of gabapentin by 20%

Increased toxicity: Cimetidine may decrease clearance of gabapentin; gabapentin may increase levels of norethindrone by 13%

Mechanism of Action Exact mechanism of action is not known, but does have properties in common with other anticonvulsants; although structurally related to GABA, it does not interact with GABA receptors

Pharmacodynamics/Kinetics

Absorption: Oral: 50% to 60%

Distribution: V_d: 0.6-0.8 L/kg

Protein binding: 0%

Half-life: 5-6 hours

Elimination: Renal, 56% to 80%

Usual Dosage If gabapentin is discontinued or if another anticonvulsant is added to therapy, it should be done slowly over a minimum of 1 week

Children >12 years and Adults: Oral:

Initial: 300 mg on day 1 (at bedtime to minimize sedation), then 300 mg twice daily on day 2, and then 300 mg 3 times/day on day 3

Total daily dosage range: 900-1800 mg/day administered in 3 divided doses at 8-hour intervals

Pain: 300-1800 mg/day given in 3 divided doses has been the most common dosage range

Dosing adjustment in renal impairment:

Cl_{cr} >60 mL/minute: Administer 1200 mg/day

Cl_{cr} 30-60 mL/minute: Administer 600 mg/day

Cl_{cr} 15-30 mL/minute: Administer 300 mg/day

Cl_{cr} <15 mL/minute: Administer 150 mg/day

Hemodialysis: 200-300 mg after each 4-hour dialysis following a loading dose of 300-400 mg

Dietary Considerations

Food: Does not change rate or extent of absorption; take without regard to meals

Serum lipids: May see increases in total cholesterol, HDL cholesterol and triglycerides. Hyperlipidemia and hypercholesterolemia have been reported with gabapentin.

Administration Administer first dose on first day at bedtime to avoid somnolence and dizziness

Monitoring Parameters Monitor serum levels of concomitant anticonvulsant therapy; routine monitoring of gabapentin levels is not mandatory

Reference Range Minimum effective serum concentration may be 2 µg/mL; **routine monitoring of drug levels is not required**

Patient Information Take only as prescribed; may cause dizziness, somnolence, and other symptoms and signs of CNS depression; do not operate machinery or drive a car until you have experience with the drug; may be administered without regard to meals

Nursing Implications Dosage must be adjusted for renal function and elderly often have reduced renal function

Dosage Forms Capsule: 100 mg, 300 mg, 400 mg, 600 mg, 800 mg

Extemporaneous Preparations A 100 mg/mL suspension was stable for 91 days when refrigerated or 56 days when kept at room temperature when compounded as follows:

Triturate sixty-seven 300 mg tablets in a mortar, reduce to a fine powder, then add a small amount of one of the following vehicles to make a paste; then add the remaining vehicle in small quantities while mixing:

Vehicle 1. Methylcellulose 1% (100 mL) and Simple Syrup N.F. (100 mL) mixed together in a graduate, **or**

Vehicle 2. Ora-Sweet® (100 mL) and Ora-Plus® (100 mL) mixed together in a graduate

Shake well before using and keep in refrigerator

Nahata MC, Morosco RS, and Hipple TF, *Stability of Gabapentin in Extemporaneously Prepared Suspensions at Two Temperatures*, American Society of Health System Pharmacists Midyear Meeting, December 7-11, 1997.

♦ **Gabitril®** *see* Tiagabine *on page 1141*

Gallium Nitrate *(GAL ee um NYE trate)*

U.S. Brand Names Ganite™

Therapeutic Category Antidote, Hypercalcemia

Use Treatment of clearly symptomatic cancer-related hypercalcemia that has not responded to adequate hydration

Pregnancy Risk Factor C

Contraindications Should not be used in patients with a serum creatinine >2.5 mg/dL, hypersensitivity to any component

Warnings/Precautions Safety and efficacy in children have not been established. Concurrent use of gallium nitrate with other potentially nephrotoxic drugs may increase the risk for developing severe renal insufficiency in patients with cancer-related hypercalcemia; use with caution in patients with impaired renal function or dehydration

Adverse Reactions

>10%:

Endocrine & metabolic: Hypophosphatemia

Gastrointestinal: Nausea, vomiting, diarrhea, metallic taste

Renal: Renal toxicity

1% to 10%: Endocrine & metabolic: Hypocalcemia

<1%: Anemia, optic neuritis, hearing impairment

Overdosage/Toxicology
Symptoms of overdose include nausea, vomiting, renal failure, hypocalcemia, tetany
Supportive measures ensure adequate hydration, calcium salts

Drug Interactions Increased toxicity: Nephrotoxic drugs (eg, aminoglycosides, amphotericin B)

Stability Store at room temperature (15°C to 30°C/59°F to 86°F); when diluted in NS or D_5W, stable for 48 hours at room temperature or 7 days at refrigeration (2°C to 8°C/36°F to 46°F)

Mechanism of Action Primarily via inhibition of bone resorption with associated reduction in urinary calcium excretion. Gallium has increased the calcium content of newly mineralized bone following short-term treatment *in vitro*, and this effect combined with its ability to inhibit bone resorption has suggested the use of gallium for other disorders associated with increased bone loss.

Pharmacodynamics/Kinetics
Metabolism: Not metabolized by liver or kidneys
Half-life, elimination: Terminal: 25-111 hours
Elimination: Up to 70% of dose excreted by the kidneys

Usual Dosage Adults:
I.V. infusion (over 24 hours): 200 mg/m² for 5 consecutive days in 1 L of NS or D_5W
Mild hypercalcemia/few symptoms: 100 mg/m²/day for 5 days in 1 L of NS or D_5W
Dosing adjustment/comments in renal impairment: Cl_{cr} <30 mL/minute: Avoid use

Monitoring Parameters Serum creatinine, BUN, and calcium

Reference Range Steady-state gallium serum levels: Generally obtained within 2 days following initiation of continuous I.V. infusions of gallium nitrate

Nursing Implications Patients should have adequate I.V. hydration, serum creatinine levels should be monitored during gallium nitrate therapy

Dosage Forms Injection: 25 mg/mL (20 mL)

♦ **Gamimune® N** see Immune Globulin, Intravenous *on page 604*
♦ **Gamma Benzene Hexachloride** see Lindane *on page 682*
♦ **Gammabulin Immuno** see Immune Globulin, Intramuscular *on page 603*
♦ **Gammagard® S/D** see Immune Globulin, Intravenous *on page 604*
♦ **Gamma Globulin** see Immune Globulin, Intramuscular *on page 603*
♦ **Gammaphos** see Amifostine *on page 54*
♦ **Gammar®-P I.V.** see Immune Globulin, Intravenous *on page 604*
♦ **Gamulin® Rh** see Rh₀(D) Immune Globulin (Intramuscular) *on page 1019*

Ganciclovir (gan SYE kloe veer)

Related Information
Guidelines for the Prevention of Opportunistic Infections in Persons with HIV *on page 1388*

U.S. Brand Names Cytovene®; Vitrasert®

Synonyms DHPG Sodium; GCV Sodium; Nordeoxyguanosine

Therapeutic Category Antiviral Agent, Parenteral

Use
Parenteral: Treatment of CMV retinitis in immunocompromised individuals, including patients with acquired immunodeficiency syndrome; prophylaxis of CMV infection in transplant patients; may be given in combination with foscarnet in patients who relapse after monotherapy with either drug
Oral: Alternative to the I.V. formulation for maintenance treatment of CMV retinitis in immunocompromised patients, including patients with AIDS, in whom retinitis is stable following appropriate induction therapy and for whom the risk of more rapid progression is balanced by the benefit associated with avoiding daily I.V. infusions
Implant: Treatment of CMV retinitis

Pregnancy Risk Factor C

Contraindications Absolute neutrophil count <500/mm³; platelet count <25,000/mm³; known hypersensitivity to ganciclovir or acyclovir

Warnings/Precautions Dosage adjustment or interruption of ganciclovir therapy may be necessary in patients with neutropenia and/or thrombocytopenia and patients with impaired renal function. Use with extreme caution in children since long-term safety has not been determined and due to ganciclovir's potential for long-term carcinogenic and adverse reproductive effects; ganciclovir may adversely affect spermatogenesis and fertility; due to its mutagenic potential, contraceptive precautions for female and male patients need to be followed during and for at least 90 days after therapy with the drug; take care to administer only into veins with good blood flow.

Adverse Reactions
>10%:
Central nervous system: Fever (38% to 48%)
Dermatologic: Rash (15% - oral, 10% - I.V.)
Gastrointestinal: Abdominal pain (17% to 19%), diarrhea (40%), nausea (25%), anorexia (15%), vomiting (13%)
Hematologic: Anemia (20% to 25%), leukopenia (30% to 40%)
1% to 10%:
Central nervous system: Confusion, neuropathy (8% to 9%), headache (4%)
Dermatologic: Pruritus (5%)
Hematologic: Thrombocytopenia (6%), neutropenia with ANC <500/mm³ (5% - oral, 14% - I.V.)
(Continued)

Ganciclovir *(Continued)*

Neuromuscular & skeletal: Paresthesia (6% to 10%), weakness (6%)

Miscellaneous: Sepsis (4% - oral, 15% - I.V.)

<1%: Arrhythmia, hypertension, hypotension, edema, ataxia, dizziness, nervousness, psychosis, malaise, coma, seizures, alopecia, urticaria, eosinophilia, hemorrhage, increased LFTs, increased serum creatinine, azotemia, inflammation or pain at injection site, tremor, retinal detachment, visual loss, hyphema, uveitis (intravitreal implant), creatinine increased 2.5%, dyspnea

Overdosage/Toxicology

Symptoms of overdose include neutropenia, vomiting, hypersalivation, bloody diarrhea, cytopenia, testicular atrophy

Treatment is supportive; hemodialysis removes 50% of drug; hydration may be of some benefit

Drug Interactions

Decreased effect: Didanosine: A decrease in steady-state ganciclovir AUC may occur

Increased toxicity:

Immunosuppressive agents may increase cytotoxicity of ganciclovir

Imipenem/cilastatin may increase seizure potential

Zidovudine: Oral ganciclovir increased the AUC of zidovudine, although zidovudine decreases steady state levels of ganciclovir. Since both drugs have the potential to cause neutropenia and anemia, some patients may not tolerate concomitant therapy with these drugs at full dosage.

Probenecid: The renal clearance of ganciclovir is decreased in the presence of probenecid

Didanosine levels are increased with concurrent ganciclovir

Other nephrotoxic drugs (eg, amphotericin and cyclosporine) may have additive nephrotoxicity with ganciclovir

Stability

Preparation should take place in a vertical laminar flow hood with the same precautions as antineoplastic agents

Intact vials should be stored at room temperature and protected from temperatures >40°C

Reconstitute powder with sterile water **not** bacteriostatic water because parabens may cause precipitation

Reconstituted solution is stable for 12 hours at room temperature, however, conflicting data indicates that reconstituted solution is stable for 60 days under refrigeration (4°C)

Drug product should be reconstituted immediately before use and any unused portion should be discarded

Stability of parenteral admixture at room temperature (25°C) and at refrigeration temperature (4°C): 5 days

An in-line filter of 0.22-5 micron is recommended during the infusion of all ganciclovir solutions

Mechanism of Action

Ganciclovir is phosphorylated to a substrate which competitively inhibits the binding of deoxyguanosine triphosphate to DNA polymerase resulting in inhibition of viral DNA synthesis

Pharmacodynamics/Kinetics

Absorption: Oral: Absolute bioavailability under fasting conditions: 5% and following food: 6% to 9%; following fatty meal: 28% to 31%

Distribution: V_d: 15.26 L/1.73 m^2; widely distributed to all tissues including CSF and ocular tissue

Protein binding: 1% to 2%

Half-life: 1.7-5.8 hours; increases with impaired renal function

End-stage renal disease: 5-28 hours

Elimination: Majority (80% to 99%) excreted as unchanged drug in the urine

Usual Dosage

CMV retinitis: Slow I.V. infusion (dosing is based on total body weight):

Children >3 months and Adults:

Induction therapy: 5 mg/kg/dose every 12 hours for 14-21 days followed by maintenance therapy

Maintenance therapy: 5 mg/kg/day as a single daily dose for 7 days/week or 6 mg/kg/day for 5 days/week

CMV retinitis: Oral: 1000 mg 3 times/day with food **or** 500 mg 6 times/day with food

Prevention of CMV disease in patients with advanced HIV infection and normal renal function: Oral: 1000 mg 3 times/day with food

Prevention of CMV disease in transplant patients: Same initial and maintenance dose as CMV retinitis except duration of initial course is 7-14 days, duration of maintenance therapy is dependent on clinical condition and degree of immunosuppression

Intravitreal implant: One implant for 5- to 8-month period; following depletion of ganciclovir, as evidenced by progression of retinitis, implant may be removed and replaced

Dosing adjustment in renal impairment:

I.V. (Induction):

Cl_{cr} 50-69 mL/minute: Administer 2.5 mg/kg/dose every 12 hours

Cl_{cr} 25-49 mL/minute: Administer 2.5 mg/kg/dose every 24 hours

Cl_{cr} 10-24 mL/minute: Administer 12.5 mg/kg/dose every 24 hours

Cl_{cr} <10 mL/minute: Administer 1.25 mg/kg/dose 3 times/week following hemodialysis

I.V. (Maintenance):

Cl_{cr} 50-69 mL/minute: Administer 2.5 mg/kg/dose every 24 hours

Cl_{cr} 25-49 mL/minute: Administer 1.25 mg/kg/dose every 24 hours

Cl$_{cr}$ 10-24 mL/minute: Administer 0.625 mg/kg/dose every 24 hours
Cl$_{cr}$ <10 mL/minute: Administer 0.625 mg/kg/dose 3 times/week following hemodialysis

Oral:
Cl$_{cr}$ 50-69 mL/minute: Administer 1500 mg/day or 500 mg 3 times/day
Cl$_{cr}$ 25-49 mL/minute: Administer 1000 mg/day or 500 mg twice daily
Cl$_{cr}$ 10-24 mL/minute: Administer 500 mg/day
Cl$_{cr}$ <10 mL/minute: Administer 500 mg 3 times/week following hemodialysis

Hemodialysis effects: Dialyzable (50%) following hemodialysis; administer dose postdialysis. During peritoneal dialysis, dose as for Cl$_{cr}$ <10 mL/minute. During continuous arteriovenous or venovenous hemofiltration (CAVH/CAVHD), administer 2.5 mg/kg/dose every 24 hours.

Administration The same precautions utilized with antineoplastic agents should be followed with ganciclovir administration. Ganciclovir should not be administered by I.M., S.C., or rapid IVP administration; administer by slow I.V. infusion over at least 1 hour at a final concentration for administration not to exceed 10 mg/mL. **An IN-LINE filter of 0.22-5 micron is recommended during the infusion of all ganciclovir solutions.** Oral ganciclovir should be administered with food.

Monitoring Parameters CBC with differential and platelet count, serum creatinine, ophthalmologic exams

Patient Information Ganciclovir is not a cure for CMV retinitis; regular ophthalmologic examinations should be done; close monitoring of blood counts should be done while on therapy and dosage adjustments may need to be made; take with food to increase absorption

Nursing Implications Must be prepared in vertical flow hood; use chemotherapy precautions during administration; discard appropriately

Additional Information Sodium content of 500 mg vial: 46 mg

Dosage Forms
Capsule: 250 mg
Implant, intravitreal: 4.5 mg released gradually over 5-8 months
Powder for injection, lyophilized: 500 mg (10 mL)

♦ **Ganite™** see Gallium Nitrate on page 528
♦ **Gantanol®** see Sulfamethoxazole on page 1094
♦ **Garamycin®** see Gentamicin on page 533
♦ **Gastrocrom® Oral** see Cromolyn Sodium on page 300
♦ **Gastrosed™** see Hyoscyamine on page 590
♦ **G-CSF** see Filgrastim on page 482
♦ **GCV Sodium** see Ganciclovir on page 529
♦ **Gee Gee® [OTC]** see Guaifenesin on page 549
♦ **Gel Kam®** see Fluoride on page 498
♦ **Gel-Tin® [OTC]** see Fluoride on page 498
♦ **Gelucast®** see Zinc Gelatin on page 1238

Gemcitabine (jem SIT a been)

Related Information
Toxicities of Chemotherapeutic Agents on page 1288

U.S. Brand Names Gemzar®

Synonyms Gemcitabine Hydrochloride

Therapeutic Category Antineoplastic Agent, Antimetabolite

Use Adenocarcinoma of the pancreas; first-line therapy for patients with locally advanced (nonresectable stage II of stage III) or metastatic (stage IV) adenocarcinoma of the pancreas (indicated for patients previously treated with 5-FU); combination with cisplatin for the first-line treatment of patients with inoperable, locally advanced (stage IIIA or IIIB) or metastatic (stage IV) non-small cell lung cancer

Pregnancy Risk Factor D

Contraindications Known hypersensitivity to gemcitabine

Warnings/Precautions The U.S. Food & Drug Administration (FDA) recommends that procedures for proper handling and disposal of antineoplastic agents be considered. Prolongation of the infusion time >60 minutes and more frequent than weekly dosing have been shown to increase toxicity. Gemcitabine can suppress bone marrow function manifested by leukopenia, thrombocytopenia and anemia, and myelosuppression is usually the dose-limiting ototoxicity. The incidence of fever is 41% and gemcitabine may cause fever in the absence of clinical infection. Rash has been reported in 30% of patients - typically a macular or finely granular maculopapular pruritic eruption of mild to moderate severity involving the trunk and extremities. Gemcitabine should be used with caution in patients with pre-existing renal impairment (mild proteinuria and hematuria were commonly reported; hemolytic uremic syndrome has been reported) and hepatic impairment (associated with transient elevations of serum transaminases in ²/₃ of patients - but no evidence of increasing hepatic toxicity).

Adverse Reactions >10%:
Cardiovascular: Peripheral edema
Central nervous system: Fever
Dermatologic: Rash, alopecia
Gastrointestinal: Nausea, vomiting, constipation, diarrhea, stomatitis
Hematologic: Anemia, leukopenia, neutropenia, thrombocytopenia
Hepatic: Elevated liver enzymes (ALT/AST, alkaline phosphatase) and bilirubin
Neuromuscular & skeletal: Pain
(Continued)

Gemcitabine *(Continued)*

Renal: Proteinuria, hematuria, increased BUN
Respiratory: Dyspnea
Miscellaneous: Infection

Overdosage/Toxicology
Symptoms of overdose include myelosuppression, paresthesia, and severe rash - the principle toxicities seen when a single dose as high as 5,700 mg/m^2 was administered by I.V. infusion over 30 minutes every 2 weeks
Treatment: Monitor blood counts and administer supportive therapy as needed

Stability
Store intact vials at room temperature (20°C to 25°C/68°F to 77°F). Reconstitute gemcitabine with 0.9% sodium chloride (preservative-free). Dilute as follows:
200 mg vial - 5 mL
1 g vial - 25 mL
These dilutions yield a concentration of 40 mg/mL - maximum concentration for reconstitution is 40 mg/mL. Store at room temperature (20°C to 25°C/68°F to 77°F) for up to 24 hours. The appropriate dose should be further diluted with 0.9% sodium chloride injection to concentrations as low as 0.1 mg/mL. Store at room temperature for up to 24 hours. Do not refrigerate.

Mechanism of Action Nucleoside analogue that primarily kills cells undergoing DNA synthesis (S-phase) and blocks the progression of cells through the G1/S-phase boundary

Pharmacodynamics/Kinetics
Distribution: V_d: 50 mL/m^2 (short infusions); 370 L/m^2 (long infusions)
Metabolism: To inactive metabolite (dFdU)
Half-life: 42-94 minutes
Elimination: In urine

Usual Dosage Adults: I.V. (refer to individual protocols): 1000 mg/m^2 once weekly for up to 7 weeks (or until toxicity necessitates reducing or holding a dose), followed by a week of rest from treatment; subsequent cycles should consist of infusions once weekly for 3 consecutive weeks out of every 4 weeks

Dosing reductions based on hematologic function: Patients who complete an entire 7-week initial cycle of gemcitabine therapy or a subsequent 3-week cycle at a dose of 1000 mg/m^2 may have the dose for subsequent cycles increased by 25% (1250 mg/m^2), provided that the absolute granulocyte count and platelet nadirs exceed 1500 x 10^6/L and 100,000 x 10^6/L, respectively, and if nonhematologic toxicity has not been more than World Health Organization Grade 1

For patients who tolerate the subsequent course, at a dose of 1250 mg/m^2, the dose for the next cycle can be increased to 1500 mg/m^2, provided again that the AGC and platelet nadirs exceed 1500 x 10^6/L and 100,000 x 10^6/L, respectively, and again, if nonhematologic toxicity is not greater than WHO Grade 1

Dosing adjustment in renal/hepatic impairment: Use with caution; gemcitabine has not been studied in patients with significant renal or hepatic dysfunction

Administration I.V. over 30 minutes

Monitoring Parameters Patients should be monitored prior to each dose with a complete blood count (CBC), including differential and platelet count; suspension or modification of therapy should be considered when marrow suppression is detected
Hepatic and renal function should be performed prior to initiation of therapy and periodically, thereafter

Dosage Forms Powder for injection, as hydrochloride, lyophilized: 20 mg/mL (10 mL, 50 mL)

♦ **Gemcitabine Hydrochloride** *see Gemcitabine on previous page*
♦ **Gemcor®** *see Gemfibrozil on this page*

Gemfibrozil *(jem FI broe zil)*

Related Information
Lipid-Lowering Agents *on page 1327*

U.S. Brand Names Gemcor®; Lopid®

Canadian Brand Names Apo®-Gemfibrozil; Nu-Gemfibrozil

Synonyms CI-719

Therapeutic Category Antilipemic Agent

Use Treatment of hypertriglyceridemia in types IV and V hyperlipidemia for patients who are at greater risk for pancreatitis and who have not responded to dietary intervention; reduction of coronary heart disease in type IIB patients who have low HDL cholesterol, increased LDL cholesterol, and increased triglycerides

Pregnancy Risk Factor B

Contraindications Renal or hepatic dysfunction, gallbladder disease, hypersensitivity to gemfibrozil or any component

Warnings/Precautions Abnormal elevation of AST, ALT, LDH, bilirubin, and alkaline phosphatase has occurred; if no appreciable triglyceride or cholesterol lowering effect occurs after 3 months, the drug should be discontinued; not useful for type I hyperlipidemia; myositis may be more common in patients with poor renal function

Adverse Reactions
>10%:
Gastrointestinal: Dyspepsia (20%), abdominal pain (10%)
Hepatic: Cholelithiasis

1% to 10%:
  Central nervous system: Fatigue (4%), vertigo (1.5%), headache (1.2%)
  Dermatologic: Eczema/rash (1% to 2%)
  Gastrointestinal: Diarrhea (7%), nausea/vomiting (2.5%), constipation (1.4%), acute appendicitis (1.2%)
  <1%: Atrial fibrillation, hyperesthesia, dizziness, drowsiness, somnolence, mental depression, paresthesia, blurred vision

Overdosage/Toxicology
  Symptoms of overdose include abdominal pain, diarrhea, nausea, vomiting
  Following GI decontamination, treatment is supportive

Drug Interactions Increased toxicity:
  May potentiate the effects of warfarin
  Manufacturer warns against the use of gemfibrozil with concomitant lovastatin therapy

Mechanism of Action The exact mechanism of action of gemfibrozil is unknown, however, several theories exist regarding the VLDL effect; it can inhibit lipolysis and decrease subsequent hepatic fatty acid uptake as well as inhibit hepatic secretion of VLDL; together these actions decrease serum VLDL levels; increases HDL cholesterol; the mechanism behind HDL elevation is currently unknown

Pharmacodynamics/Kinetics
  Absorption: Well absorbed
  Protein binding: 99%
  Metabolism: In the liver by oxidation to two inactive metabolites
  Half-life: 1.4 hours
  Time to peak serum concentration: Within 1-2 hours
  Elimination: A portion of the drug undergoes enterohepatic recycling; excreted in urine, primarily as unchanged drug (70%)

Usual Dosage Adults: Oral: 1200 mg/day in 2 divided doses, 30 minutes before breakfast and dinner
  Hemodialysis: Not removed by hemodialysis; supplemental dose is not necessary

Monitoring Parameters Serum cholesterol, LFTs

Patient Information May cause dizziness or blurred vision, abdominal or epigastric pain, diarrhea, nausea, or vomiting; notify physician if these become pronounced

Dosage Forms
  Capsule: 300 mg
  Tablet, film coated: 600 mg

Gentamicin (jen ta MYE sin)

Related Information
  Antibiotic Treatment of Adults With Infective Endocarditis *on page 1401*
  Antimicrobial Drugs of Choice *on page 1404*
  Community-Acquired Pneumonia in Adults *on page 1419*
  Prevention of Bacterial Endocarditis *on page 1377*
  Prevention of Wound Infection & Sepsis in Surgical Patients *on page 1381*
  Treatment of Sexually Transmitted Diseases *on page 1429*

U.S. Brand Names Garamycin®; Genoptic® Ophthalmic; Genoptic® S.O.P. Ophthalmic; Gentacidin® Ophthalmic; Gentafair®; Gentak® Ophthalmic; Gentrasul®; G-myticin® Topical; I-Gent®; Jenamicin® Injection; Ocumycin®

Synonyms Gentamicin Sulfate
(Continued)

Gentamicin *(Continued)*

Therapeutic Category Antibiotic, Aminoglycoside; Antibiotic, Ophthalmic; Antibiotic, Topical

Use Treatment of susceptible bacterial infections, normally gram-negative organisms including *Pseudomonas*, *Proteus*, *Serratia*, and gram-positive *Staphylococcus*; treatment of bone infections, respiratory tract infections, skin and soft tissue infections, as well as abdominal and urinary tract infections, endocarditis, and septicemia; used topically to treat superficial infections of the skin or ophthalmic infections caused by susceptible bacteria; prevention of bacterial endocarditis prior to dental or surgical procedures

Pregnancy Risk Factor C

Contraindications Hypersensitivity to gentamicin or other aminoglycosides

Warnings/Precautions Not intended for long-term therapy due to toxic hazards associated with extended administration; pre-existing renal insufficiency, vestibular or cochlear impairment, myasthenia gravis, hypocalcemia, conditions which depress neuromuscular transmission

Parenteral aminoglycosides have been associated with significant nephrotoxicity or ototoxicity; the ototoxicity may be directly proportional to the amount of drug given and the duration of treatment; tinnitus or vertigo are indications of vestibular injury and impending hearing loss; renal damage is usually reversible

Adverse Reactions
>10%:
  Central nervous system: Neurotoxicity (vertigo, ataxia)
  Neuromuscular & skeletal: Gait instability
  Otic: Ototoxicity (auditory), ototoxicity (vestibular)
  Renal: Nephrotoxicity, decreased creatinine clearance
1% to 10%:
  Cardiovascular: Edema
  Dermatologic: Skin itching, reddening of skin, rash
<1%: Drowsiness, headache, pseudomotor cerebri, photosensitivity, erythema, anorexia, nausea, vomiting, weight loss, increased salivation, enterocolitis, granulocytopenia, agranulocytosis, thrombocytopenia, elevated LFTs, burning, stinging, tremors, muscle cramps, weakness, dyspnea

Overdosage/Toxicology
Symptoms of overdose include ototoxicity, nephrotoxicity, and neuromuscular toxicity; serum level monitoring is recommended

The treatment of choice, following a single acute overdose, appears to be the maintenance of good urine output of at least 3 mL/kg/hour. Dialysis is of questionable value in the enhancement of aminoglycoside elimination. If required, hemodialysis is preferred over peritoneal dialysis in patients with normal renal function. Careful hydration may be all that is required to promote diuresis and therefore the enhancement of the drug's elimination. Chelation with penicillins is experimental.

Drug Interactions Increased toxicity:
Penicillins, cephalosporins, amphotericin B, loop diuretics may increase nephrotoxic potential
Neuromuscular blocking agents may increase neuromuscular blockade

Stability
Gentamicin is a colorless to slightly yellow solution which should be stored between 2°C to 30°C, but refrigeration is not recommended
I.V. infusion solutions mixed in NS or D_5W solution are stable for 24 hours at room temperature and refrigeration
Premixed bag: Manufacturer expiration date
Out of overwrap stability: 30 days

Mechanism of Action Interferes with bacterial protein synthesis by binding to 30S and 50S ribosomal subunits resulting in a defective bacterial cell membrane

Aminoglycoside Penetration Into Various Tissues

Site	Extent of Distribution
Eye	Poor
CNS	Poor (<25%)
Pleural	Excellent
Bronchial secretions	Poor
Sputum	Fair (10%-50%)
Pulmonary tissue	Excellent
Ascitic fluid	Variable (43%-132%)
Peritoneal fluid	Poor
Bile	Variable (25%-90%)
Bile with obstruction	Poor
Synovial fluid	Excellent
Bone	Poor
Prostate	Poor
Urine	Excellent
Renal tissue	Excellent

Pharmacodynamics/Kinetics

Absorption: Oral: Not absorbed

Distribution: Crosses the placenta

V_d: Increased by edema, ascites, fluid overload; decreased in patients with dehydration. See table.

Neonates: 0.4-0.6 L/kg

Children: 0.3-0.35 L/kg

Adults: 0.2-0.3 L/kg

Relative diffusion of antimicrobial agents from blood into cerebrospinal fluid (CSF): Minimal even with inflammation

Ratio of CSF to blood level (%): Normal meninges: Nil; Inflamed meninges: 10-30

Protein binding: <30%

Half-life:

Infants: <1 week: 3-11.5 hours; 1 week to 6 months: 3-3.5 hours

Adults: 1.5-3 hours; end-stage renal disease: 36-70 hours

Time to peak serum concentration: I.M.: Within 30-90 minutes; I.V.: 30 minutes after a 30-minute infusion

Elimination: Clearance is directly related to renal function, eliminated almost completely by glomerular filtration of unchanged drug with excretion into the urine

Usual Dosage

Individualization is critical because of the low therapeutic index

Use of ideal body weight (IBW) for determining the mg/kg/dose appears to be more accurate than dosing on the basis of total body weight (TBW).

In morbid obesity, dosage requirement may best be estimated using a dosing weight of IBW + 0.4 (TBW - IBW)

Initial and periodic peak and trough plasma drug levels should be determined, particularly in critically ill patients with serious infections or in disease states known to significantly alter aminoglycoside pharmacokinetics (eg, cystic fibrosis, burns, or major surgery)

Newborns: Intrathecal: 1 mg every day

Infants >3 months: Intrathecal: 1-2 mg/day

Infants and Children <5 years: I.M., I.V.: 2.5 mg/kg/dose every 8 hours*

Cystic fibrosis: 2.5 mg/kg/dose every 6 hours

Children >5 years: I.M., I.V.: 1.5-2.5 mg/kg/dose every 8 hours*

Prevention of bacterial endocarditis: Dental, oral, upper respiratory procedures, GI/GU procedures: 2 mg/kg with ampicillin (50 mg/kg) 30 minutes prior to procedure

*Some patients may require larger or more frequent doses (eg, every 6 hours) if serum levels document the need (ie, cystic fibrosis or febrile granulocytopenic patients)

Adults: I.M., I.V.:

Severe life-threatening infections: 2-2.5 mg/kg/dose

Urinary tract infections: 1.5 mg/kg/dose

Synergy (for gram-positive infections): 1 mg/kg/dose

Prevention of bacterial endocarditis:

Dental, oral, or upper respiratory procedures: 1.5 mg/kg not to exceed 80 mg with ampicillin (1-2 g) 30 minutes prior to procedure

GI/GU surgery: 1.5 mg/kg not to exceed 80 mg with ampicillin 2 g 30 minutes prior to procedure

Children and Adults:

Intrathecal: 4-8 mg/day

Ophthalmic:

Ointment: Instill ½" (1.25 cm) 2-3 times/day to every 3-4 hours

Solution: Instill 1-2 drops every 2-4 hours, up to 2 drops every hour for severe infections

Topical: Apply 3-4 times/day to affected area

Some clinicians suggest a daily dose of 4-7 mg/kg for all patients with normal renal function. This dose is at least as efficacious with similar, if not less, toxicity than conventional dosing.

Dosing interval in renal impairment:

Cl_{cr} ≥60 mL/minute: Administer every 8 hours

Cl_{cr} 40-60 mL/minute: Administer every 12 hours

Cl_{cr} 20-40 mL/minute: Administer every 24 hours

Cl_{cr} <20 mL/minute: Loading dose, then monitor levels

Hemodialysis: Dialyzable; removal by hemodialysis: 30% removal of aminoglycosides occurs during 4 hours of HD; administer dose after dialysis and follow levels

Removal by continuous ambulatory peritoneal dialysis (CAPD):

Administration via CAPD fluid:

Gram-negative infection: 4-8 mg/L (4-8 mcg/mL) of CAPD fluid

Gram-positive infection (ie, synergy): 3-4 mg/L (3-4 mcg/mL) of CAPD fluid

Administration via I.V., I.M. route during CAPD: Dose as for Cl_{cr} <10 mL/minute and follow levels

Removal via continuous arteriovenous or venovenous hemofiltration (CAVH/CAVHD): Dose as for Cl_{cr} 10-40 mL/minute and follow levels

Dosing adjustment/comments in hepatic disease: Monitor plasma concentrations

Dietary Considerations Calcium, magnesium, potassium: Renal wasting may cause hypocalcemia, hypomagnesemia, and/or hypokalemia

Monitoring Parameters Urinalysis, urine output, BUN, serum creatinine; hearing should be tested before, during, and after treatment; particularly in those at risk for ototoxicity or who will be receiving prolonged therapy (>2 weeks)

Reference Range

Timing of serum samples: Draw peak 30 minutes after 30-minute infusion has been completed or 1 hour after I.M. injection; draw trough immediately before next dose

(Continued)

Gentamicin *(Continued)*

Sample size: 0.5-2 mL blood (red top tube) or 0.1-1 mL serum (separated)

Therapeutic levels:

Peak:

Serious infections: 6-8 µg/mL (12-17 µmol/L)

Life-threatening infections: 8-10 µg/mL (17-21 µmol/L)

Urinary tract infections: 4-6 µg/mL

Synergy against gram-positive organisms: 3-5 µg/mL

Trough:

Serious infections: 0.5-1 µg/mL

Life-threatening infections: 1-2 µg/mL

Obtain drug levels after the third dose unless renal dysfunction/toxicity suspected

Test Interactions Penicillin may decrease aminoglycoside serum concentrations *in vitro*

Patient Information Report any dizziness or sensations of ringing or fullness in ears; do not touch ophthalmics to eye; use no other eye drops within 5-10 minutes of instilling ophthalmic

Nursing Implications Slower absorption and lower peak concentrations probably due to poor circulation in the atrophic muscle, may occur following I.M. injection in paralyzed patients (suggest I.V. route); aminoglycoside levels measured in blood taken from Silastic® central catheters can sometimes give falsely high readings (draw via separate lumen or peripheral site if possible, otherwise flush very well). Monitor serum creatinine and urine output; obtain drug levels after the third dose unless otherwise directed (eg, suspected toxicity or renal dysfunction). Peak levels are drawn 30 minutes after the end of a 30-minute infusion or 60 minutes following I.M. injection; trough levels are drawn within 30 minutes before the next dose; administer other antibiotic drugs at least 1 hour before or after gentamicin. Hearing should be tested before, during, and after treatment in patients at risk for ototoxicity.

Dosage Forms

Cream, topical, as sulfate (Garamycin®, G-myticin®): 0.1% (15 g)

Infusion, in D₅W, as sulfate: 60 mg, 80 mg, 100 mg

Infusion, in NS, as sulfate: 40 mg, 60 mg, 80 mg, 90 mg, 100 mg, 120 mg

Injection, as sulfate: 40 mg/mL (1 mL, 1.5 mL, 2 mL)

Pediatric, as sulfate: 10 mg/mL (2 mL)

Intrathecal, preservative free, as sulfate (Garamycin®): 2 mg/mL (2 mL)

Ointment, as sulfate:

Ophthalmic: 0.3% [3 mg/g] (3.5 g)

Garamycin®, Genoptic® S.O.P., Gentacidin®, Gentak®: 0.3% [3 mg/g] (3.5 g)

Topical, as sulfate (Garamycin®, G-myticin®): 0.1% (15 g)

Solution, ophthalmic, as sulfate: 0.3% (5 mL, 15 mL)

Garamycin®, Genoptic®, Gentacidin®, Gentak®: 0.3% (1 mL, 5 mL, 15 mL)

♦ **Gentamicin Sulfate** *see Gentamicin on page 533*

Gentian Violet *(JEN shun VYE oh let)*

U.S. Brand Names Genapax®

Synonyms Crystal Violet; Methylrosaniline Chloride

Therapeutic Category Antibacterial, Topical; Antifungal Agent, Topical

Use Treatment of cutaneous or mucocutaneous infections caused by *Candida albicans* and other superficial skin infections

Pregnancy Risk Factor C

Contraindications Known hypersensitivity to gentian violet; ulcerated areas; patients with porphyria

Warnings/Precautions Infants should be turned face down after application to minimize amount of drug swallowed; may result in tattooing of the skin when applied to granulation tissue; solution is for external use only; avoid contact with eyes

Adverse Reactions 1% to 10%: Esophagitis, burning, irritation, vesicle formation, sensitivity reactions, ulceration of mucous membranes, laryngitis, tracheitis, laryngeal obstruction

Overdosage/Toxicology Signs and symptoms: Laryngeal obstruction

Mechanism of Action Topical antiseptic/germicide effective against some vegetative gram-positive bacteria, particularly *Staphylococcus* sp, and some yeast; it is much less effective against gram-negative bacteria and is ineffective against acid-fast bacteria

Usual Dosage

Children and Adults: Topical: Apply 0.5% to 2% locally with cotton to lesion 2-3 times/day for 3 days, do not swallow and avoid contact with eyes

Adults: Intravaginal: Insert one tampon for 3-4 hours once or twice daily for 12 days

Patient Information Drug stains skin and clothing purple; do not apply to an ulcerative lesion; may result in "tattooing" of the skin; when used for the treatment of vaginal candidiasis, coitus should be avoided; insert vaginal product high into vagina. Use condoms or refrain from sexual intercourse to avoid reinfection.

Dosage Forms

Solution, topical: 1% (30 mL); 2% (30 mL)

Tampons: 5 mg (12s)

♦ **Gen-Timolol** *see Timolol on page 1146*

♦ **Gentran®** *see Dextran on page 341*

♦ **Gentrasul®** *see Gentamicin on page 533*

♦ **Gen-Triazolam** *see Triazolam on page 1178*

♦ **Gen-XENE®** *see Clorazepate on page 286*

Glatiramer Acetate (gla TIR a mer AS e tate)

U.S. Brand Names Copaxone®

Synonyms Copolymer-1

Therapeutic Category Biological, Miscellaneous

Use Relapsing-remitting type multiple sclerosis; studies indicate that it reduces the frequency of attacks and the severity of disability; appears to be most effective for patients with minimal disability

Pregnancy Risk Factor B

Contraindications Previous hypersensitivity to any component of the copolymer formulation

Adverse Reactions
>10%:
    Cardiovascular: Chest pain (26%)
    Local: Pain
1% to 10%:
    Cardiovascular: Chest tightness, flushing, tachycardia, vasodilitation
    Central nervous system: Anxiety, depression, dizziness
    Dermatologic: Erythema (4%), urticaria
    Hematologic: Transient eosinophilia
    Local: Injection site reactions (6.5%)
    Neuromuscular & skeletal: Tremor
    Respiratory: Dyspnea
    Miscellaneous: Diaphoresis, unintended pregnancy

Overdosage/Toxicology Well tolerated; no serious toxicities can be anticipated

Stability Reconstituted product contains no preservative, use immediately; store unreconstituted product in refrigerator at 2°C to 8°C (36°F to 46°F); diluent may be stored at room temperature

Mechanism of Action Glatiramer is a mixture of random polymers of four amino acids; L-alanine, L-glutamic acid, L-lysine and L-tyrosine, the resulting mixture is antigenically similar to myelin basic protein, which is an important component of the myelin sheath of nerves; glatiramer is thought to suppress T-lymphocytes specific for a myelin antigen, it is also proposed that glatiramer interferes with the antigen-presenting function of certain immune cells opposing pathogenic T-cell function

Usual Dosage Adults: S.C.: 20 mg daily

Patient Information It is essential to provide the patient with proper handling and reconstitution instruction, since they will most likely have to self-administer the drug for an extended period

Dosage Forms Injection: Single-use vials containing 20 mg of glatiramer and 40 mg mannitol; packaged in 2 mL vials along with 1 mL vial of diluent (sterile water for injection)

Glimepiride (GLYE me pye ride)

Related Information
Hypoglycemic Drugs, Comparison of Oral Agents *on page 1325*

U.S. Brand Names Amaryl®

Therapeutic Category Antidiabetic Agent, Oral; Hypoglycemic Agent, Oral; Sulfonylurea Agent

Use
Management of noninsulin-dependent diabetes mellitus (type II) as an adjunct to diet and exercise to lower blood glucose
Use in combination with insulin to lower blood glucose in patients whose hyperglycemia cannot be controlled by diet and exercise in conjunction with an oral hypoglycemic agent

Pregnancy Risk Factor C

Contraindications Hypersensitivity to glimepiride or any component, other sulfonamides; diabetic ketoacidosis (with or without coma)

Warnings/Precautions
The administration of oral hypoglycemic drugs (ie, tolbutamide) has been reported to be associated with increased cardiovascular mortality as compared to treatment with diet alone or diet plus insulin
All sulfonylurea drugs are capable of producing severe hypoglycemia. Hypoglycemia is more likely to occur when caloric intake is deficient, after severe or prolonged exercise, when alcohol is ingested, or when more than one glucose-lowering drug is used.
(Continued)

Glimepiride (Continued)

Adverse Reactions
1% to 10%: Central nervous system: Headache

<1%: Edema, rash, urticaria, photosensitivity, hypoglycemia, hyponatremia, anorexia, nausea, vomiting, diarrhea, epigastric fullness, constipation, heartburn, blood dyscrasias, aplastic anemia, hemolytic anemia, bone marrow suppression, thrombocytopenia, agranulocytosis, cholestatic jaundice, diuretic effect

Overdosage/Toxicology
Symptoms of overdose include low blood sugar, tingling of lips and tongue, nausea, yawning, confusion, agitation, tachycardia, sweating, convulsions, stupor, and coma

Intoxications with sulfonylureas can cause hypoglycemia and are best managed with glucose administration (oral for milder hypoglycemia or by injection in more severe forms). Patients should be monitored for a minimum of 24-48 hours after ingestion.

Drug Interactions CYP2C9 enzyme substrate
Decreased effects: Cholestyramine, hydantoins, rifampin, thiazide diuretics, urinary alkalines, charcoal

Increased effects: H_2-antagonists, anticoagulants, androgens, beta-blockers, fluconazole, salicylates, gemfibrozil, sulfonamides, tricyclic antidepressants, probenecid, MAO inhibitors, methyldopa, NSAIDs, salicylates, sulfonamides, chloramphenicol, coumarins, probenecid, MAO inhibitors, digitalis glycosides, urinary acidifiers

Increased toxicity: Cimetidine may increase hypoglycemic effects; certain drugs tend to produce hyperglycemia and may lead to loss of control. These drugs include the thiazides and other diuretics, corticosteroids, phenothiazines, thyroid products, estrogens, oral contraceptives, phenytoin, nicotinic acid, sympathomimetics, and isoniazid.

Mechanism of Action
Stimulates insulin release from the pancreatic beta cells; reduces glucose output from the liver; insulin sensitivity is increased at peripheral target sites

Pharmacodynamics/Kinetics
Duration of action: 24 hours

Peak blood glucose reductions: Within 2-3 hours

Protein binding: >99.5%

Absorption: 100% absorbed; delayed when given with food

Metabolism: Completely in the liver

Half-life: 5-9 hours

Elimination: Metabolites excreted in urine and feces

Usual Dosage Oral (allow several days between dose titrations):
Adults: Initial: 1-2 mg once daily, administered with breakfast or the first main meal; usual maintenance dose: 1-4 mg once daily; after a dose of 2 mg once daily, increase in increments of 2 mg at 1- to 2-week intervals based upon the patient's blood glucose response to a maximum of 8 mg once daily

Elderly: Initial: 1 mg/day

Combination with insulin therapy (fasting glucose level for instituting combination therapy is in the range of >150 mg/dL in plasma or serum depending on the patient): 8 mg once daily with the first main meal

After starting with low-dose insulin, upward adjustments of insulin can be done approximately weekly as guided by frequent measurements of fasting blood glucose. Once stable, combination-therapy patients should monitor their capillary blood glucose on an ongoing basis, preferably daily.

Dosing adjustment/comments in renal impairment: Cl_{cr} <22 mL/minute: Initial starting dose should be 1 mg and dosage increments should be based on fasting blood glucose levels

Dosing adjustment in hepatic impairment: No data available

Administration May be taken with a meal/food

Monitoring Parameters
Urine for glucose and ketones; monitor for signs and symptoms of hypoglycemia (fatigue, excessive hunger, profuse sweating, numbness of extremities), fasting blood glucose, hemoglobin A_{1c}, fructosamine

Reference Range Target range: Adults:
Fasting blood glucose: <120 mg/dL

Glycosylated hemoglobin: <7%

Patient Information
Patients must be counseled by someone experienced in diabetes education, signs and symptoms of hyper- and hypoglycemia, exercise and diet, blood glucose monitoring, and other related topics; eat regularly, do not skip meals; carry quick source of sugar; medical alert bracelet

Nursing Implications
Patients who are NPO may need to have their dose held to avoid hypoglycemia

Dosage Forms Tablet: 1 mg, 2 mg, 4 mg

Glipizide (GLIP i zide)

Related Information
Hypoglycemic Drugs, Comparison of Oral Agents on page 1325

Sulfonamide Derivatives on page 1337

U.S. Brand Names Glucotrol®; Glucotrol® XL

Synonyms Glydiazinamide

Therapeutic Category Antidiabetic Agent, Oral; Hypoglycemic Agent, Oral; Sulfonylurea Agent

Use Management of noninsulin-dependent diabetes mellitus (type II)

Pregnancy Risk Factor C

Pregnancy/Breast-Feeding Implications
Clinical effects on the fetus: Crosses the placenta. Insulin is the drug of choice for the control of diabetes mellitus during pregnancy.
Breast-feeding/lactation: No data available

Contraindications Hypersensitivity to glipizide or any component, other sulfonamides, type I diabetes mellitus

Warnings/Precautions Use with caution in patients with severe hepatic disease; a useful agent since few drug to drug interactions and not dependent upon renal elimination of active drug

Adverse Reactions
>10%:
Central nervous system: Headache
Gastrointestinal: Anorexia, nausea, vomiting, diarrhea, epigastric fullness, constipation, heartburn
1% to 10%: Dermatologic: Rash, urticaria, photosensitivity
<1%: Edema, hypoglycemia, hyponatremia, blood dyscrasias, aplastic anemia, hemolytic anemia, bone marrow suppression, thrombocytopenia, agranulocytosis, cholestatic jaundice, diuretic effect

Overdosage/Toxicology
Symptoms of overdose include low blood sugar, tingling of lips and tongue, nausea, yawning, confusion, agitation, tachycardia, sweating, convulsions, stupor, and coma
Intoxications with sulfonylureas can cause hypoglycemia and are best managed with glucose administration (oral for milder hypoglycemia or by injection in more severe forms)

Drug Interactions
Decreased effects: Beta-blockers, cholestyramine, hydantoins, rifampin, thiazide diuretics, urinary alkalines, charcoal
Increased effects: H_2-antagonists, anticoagulants, androgens, fluconazole, salicylates, gemfibrozil, sulfonamides, tricyclic antidepressants, probenecid, MAO inhibitors, methyldopa, digitalis glycosides, urinary acidifiers
Increased toxicity: Cimetidine may increase hypoglycemic effects

Mechanism of Action Stimulates insulin release from the pancreatic beta cells; reduces glucose output from the liver; insulin sensitivity is increased at peripheral target sites

Pharmacodynamics/Kinetics
Duration of action: 12-24 hours
Peak blood glucose reductions: Within 1.5-2 hours
Protein binding: 92% to 99%
Absorption: Delayed when given with food
Metabolism: In the liver with metabolites (91% to 97%)
Half-life: 2-4 hours
Elimination: Metabolites (91% to 97%) excreted in urine (60% to 80%) and feces (11%)

Usual Dosage Oral (allow several days between dose titrations): Give ~30 minutes before a meal to obtain the greatest reduction in postprandial hyperglycemia
Adults: Initial: 5 mg/day; adjust dosage at 2.5-5 mg daily increments as determined by blood glucose response at intervals of several days. Maximum recommended once-daily dose: 15 mg; maximum recommended total daily dose: 40 mg.
Elderly: Initial: 2.5 mg/day; increase by 2.5-5 mg/day at 1- to 2-week intervals
Dosing adjustment/comments in renal impairment: Cl_{cr} <10 mL/minute: Some investigators recommend not using
Dosing adjustment in hepatic impairment: Initial dosage should be 2.5 mg/day

Dietary Considerations
Alcohol: A disulfiram-like reaction characterized by flushing, headache, nausea, vomiting, sweating, or tachycardia; avoid use
Food: Food delays absorption by 40%; take glipizide before meals
Glucose: Decreases blood glucose concentration. Hypoglycemia may occur. Educate patients how to detect and treat hypoglycemia. Monitor for signs and symptoms of hypoglycemia. Administer glucose if necessary. Evaluate patient's diet and exercise regimen. May need to decrease or discontinue dose of sulfonylurea.
Sodium: Reports of hyponatremia and SIADH. Those at increased risk include patients on medications or who have medical conditions that predispose them to hyponatremia. Monitor sodium serum concentration and fluid status. May need to restrict water intake.

Administration Administer 30 minutes before a meal to achieve greatest reduction in postprandial hyperglycemia

Monitoring Parameters Urine for glucose and ketones; monitor for signs and symptoms of hypoglycemia (fatigue, excessive hunger, profuse sweating, numbness of extremities), fasting blood glucose, hemoglobin A_{1c}, fructosamine

Reference Range Target range: Adults:
Fasting blood glucose: <120 mg/dL
Glycosylated hemoglobin: <7%

Patient Information Patients must be counseled by someone experienced in diabetes education, signs and symptoms of hyper- and hypoglycemia, exercise and diet, blood glucose monitoring, and other related topics; eat regularly, do not skip meals; carry quick source of sugar; medical alert bracelet

Nursing Implications Patients who are NPO may need to have their dose held to avoid hypoglycemia

Dosage Forms
Tablet: 5 mg, 10 mg
Tablet, extended release: 5 mg, 10 mg

Glucagon (GLOO ka gon)

Therapeutic Category Antidote, Hypoglycemia; Diagnostic Agent, Gastrointestinal

Use Management of hypoglycemia; diagnostic aid in the radiologic examination of GI tract when a hypnotic state is needed; used with some success as a cardiac stimulant in management of severe cases of beta-adrenergic blocking agent overdosage

Pregnancy Risk Factor B

Contraindications Hypersensitivity to glucagon or any component

Warnings/Precautions Use with caution in patients with a history of insulinoma and/or pheochromocytoma

Adverse Reactions 1% to 10%:
Cardiovascular: Hypotension
Dermatologic: Urticaria
Gastrointestinal: Nausea, vomiting
Respiratory: Respiratory distress

Overdosage/Toxicology Symptoms of overdose include hypokalemia, nausea, vomiting

Drug Interactions Increased toxicity: Oral anticoagulant - hypoprothrombinemic effects may be increased possibly with bleeding

Stability After reconstitution, use immediately; may be kept at 5°C for up to 48 hours if necessary

Mechanism of Action Stimulates adenylate cyclase to produce increased cyclic AMP, which promotes hepatic glycogenolysis and gluconeogenesis, causing a raise in blood glucose levels

Pharmacodynamics/Kinetics
Peak effect on blood glucose levels: Parenteral: Within 5-20 minutes
Duration of action: 60-90 minutes
Metabolism: In the liver with some inactivation occurring in the kidneys and plasma
Half-life, plasma: 3-10 minutes

Usual Dosage
Hypoglycemia or insulin shock therapy: I.M., I.V., S.C.:
Children: 0.025-0.1 mg/kg/dose, not to exceed 1 mg/dose, repeated in 20 minutes as needed
Adults: 0.5-1 mg, may repeat in 20 minutes as needed
If patient fails to respond to glucagon, I.V. dextrose must be given
Diagnostic aid: Adults: I.M., I.V.: 0.25-2 mg 10 minutes prior to procedure

Administration Reconstitute powder for injection by adding 1 or 10 mL of sterile diluent to a vial containing 1 or 10 units of the drug, respectively, to provide solutions containing 1 mg of glucagon/mL; if dose to be administered is <2 mg of the drug → use only the diluent provided by the manufacturer; if >2 mg → use sterile water for injection; use immediately after reconstitution

Monitoring Parameters Blood pressure, blood glucose

Patient Information Instruct a close associate on how to prepare and administer as a treatment for insulin shock

Additional Information 1 unit = 1 mg

Dosage Forms Powder for injection, lyophilized: 1 mg [1 unit]; 10 mg [10 units]

- ♦ **Glucocerebrosidase** see Alglucerase on page 42
- ♦ **Glucophage®** see Metformin on page 741
- ♦ **Glucotrol®** see Glipizide on page 538
- ♦ **Glucotrol® XL** see Glipizide on page 538
- ♦ **Glukor®** see Chorionic Gonadotropin on page 258
- ♦ **Glyate® [OTC]** see Guaifenesin on page 549
- ♦ **Glybenclamide** see Glyburide on this page
- ♦ **Glybenzcyclamide** see Glyburide on this page

Glyburide (GLYE byoor ide)

Related Information
Hypoglycemic Drugs, Comparison of Oral Agents on page 1325
Sulfonamide Derivatives on page 1337

U.S. Brand Names DiaβΕta®; Glynase™ PresTab™; Micronase®

Canadian Brand Names Albert® Glyburide; Apo®-Glyburide; Euglucon®; Gen-Glybe; Novo-Glyburide; Nu-Glyburide

Synonyms Glibenclamide; Glybenclamide; Glybenzcyclamide

Therapeutic Category Antidiabetic Agent, Oral; Hypoglycemic Agent, Oral; Sulfonylurea Agent

Use Management of noninsulin-dependent diabetes mellitus (type II)

Pregnancy Risk Factor C

Pregnancy/Breast-Feeding Implications
Clinical effects on the fetus: Crosses the placenta. Hypoglycemia; ear defects reported; other malformations reported but may have been secondary to poor maternal glucose control/diabetes. Insulin is the drug of choice for the control of diabetes mellitus during pregnancy.
Breast-feeding/lactation: No data available

Contraindications Hypersensitivity to glyburide or any component, or other sulfonamides; type I diabetes mellitus, diabetic ketoacidosis with or without coma

Warnings/Precautions Use with caution in patients with hepatic impairment. Elderly: Rapid and prolonged hypoglycemia (>12 hours) despite hypertonic glucose injections have been reported; age and hepatic and renal impairment are independent risk factors for hypoglycemia; dosage titration should be made at weekly intervals. Use with caution in patients with renal and hepatic impairment, malnourished or debilitated conditions, or adrenal or pituitary insufficiency. The administration of oral hypoglycemic drugs (ie, tolbutamide) has been reported to be associated with increased cardiovascular mortality as compared to treatment with diet alone or diet plus insulin.

Adverse Reactions
>10%:
 Central nervous system: Headache, dizziness
 Gastrointestinal: Nausea, epigastric fullness, heartburn, constipation, diarrhea, anorexia
 Ocular: Blurred vision
1% to 10%: Dermatologic: Pruritus, rash, urticaria, photosensitivity reaction
<1%: Hypoglycemia, nocturia, leukopenia, thrombocytopenia, hemolytic anemia, aplastic anemia, bone marrow suppression, agranulocytosis, cholestatic jaundice, arthralgia, paresthesia, diuretic effect

Overdosage/Toxicology
Symptoms of overdose include severe hypoglycemia, seizures, cerebral damage, tingling of lips and tongue, nausea, yawning, confusion, agitation, tachycardia, sweating, convulsions, stupor, and coma
Intoxications with sulfonylureas can cause hypoglycemia and are best managed with glucose administration (oral for milder hypoglycemia or by injection in more severe forms)

Drug Interactions CYP3A3/4 enzyme substrate
Decreased effect: Thiazides may decrease effectiveness of glyburide
Increased effect: Possible interaction between glyburide and fluoroquinolone antibiotics has been reported resulting in a potentiation of hypoglycemic action of glyburide
Increased toxicity:
 Since this agent is highly protein bound, the toxic potential is increased when given concomitantly with other highly protein bound drugs (ie, phenylbutazone, oral anticoagulants, hydantoins, salicylates, NSAIDs, beta-blockers, sulfonamides) - increase hypoglycemic effect
 Alcohol increases disulfiram reactions
 Phenylbutazone can increase hypoglycemic effects
 Certain drugs tend to produce hyperglycemia and may lead to loss of control (ie, thiazides and other diuretics, corticosteroids, phenothiazines, thyroid products, estrogens, oral contraceptives, phenytoin, nicotinic acid, sympathomimetics, calcium channel blocking drugs, and isoniazid)
Possible interactions between glyburide and coumarin derivatives have been reported that may either potentiate or weaken the effects of coumarin derivatives

Mechanism of Action Stimulates insulin release from the pancreatic beta cells; reduces glucose output from the liver; insulin sensitivity is increased at peripheral target sites

Pharmacodynamics/Kinetics
Onset of action: Oral: Insulin levels in the serum begin to increase within 15-60 minutes after a single dose
Duration: Up to 24 hours
Metabolism: To one moderately active and several inactive metabolites
Plasma protein binding: High (>99%)
Half-life: 5-16 hours; may be prolonged with renal insufficiency or hepatic insufficiency
Time to peak serum concentration: Adults: Within 2-4 hours

Usual Dosage Oral:
Adults:
 Initial: 2.5-5 mg/day, administered with breakfast or the first main meal of the day. In patients who are more sensitive to hypoglycemic drugs, start at 1.25 mg/day.
 Increase in increments of no more than 2.5 mg/day at weekly intervals based on the patient's blood glucose response
 Maintenance: 1.25-20 mg/day given as single or divided doses; maximum: 20 mg/day
Elderly: Initial: 1.25-2.5 mg/day, increase by 1.25-2.5 mg/day every 1-3 weeks
Micronized tablets (Glynase PresTab™): Adults:
 Initial: 1.5-3 mg/day, administered with breakfast or the first main meal of the day in patients who are more sensitive to hypoglycemic drugs, start at 0.75 mg/day.
 Increase in increments of no more than 1.5 mg/day in weekly intervals based on the patient's blood glucose response.
 Maintenance: 0.75-12 mg/day given as a single dose or in divided doses. Some patients (especially those receiving >6 mg/day) may have a more satisfactory response with twice-daily dosing.

Dosing adjustment/comments in renal impairment: Cl$_{cr}$ <50 mL/minute: **Not recommended**

Dosing adjustment in hepatic impairment: Use conservative initial and maintenance doses and avoid use in severe disease

Dietary Considerations
Alcohol: A disulfiram-like reaction characterized by flushing, headache, nausea, vomiting, sweating, or tachycardia; avoid use
Food: Food does not affect absorption; glyburide may be taken with food
Glucose: Decreases blood glucose concentration. Hypoglycemia may occur. Educate patients how to detect and treat hypoglycemia. Monitor for signs and symptoms of hypoglycemia. Administer glucose if necessary. Evaluate patient's diet and exercise regimen. May need to decrease or discontinue dose of sulfonylurea.

(Continued)

Glyburide *(Continued)*

Sodium: Reports of hyponatremia and SIADH. Those at increased risk include patients on medications or who have medical conditions that predispose them to hyponatremia. Monitor sodium serum concentration and fluid status. May need to restrict water intake.

Monitoring Parameters Signs and symptoms of hypoglycemia, fasting blood glucose, hemoglobin A_{1c}, fructosamine

Reference Range Target range: Adults:
Fasting blood glucose: <120 mg/dL
Glycosylated hemoglobin: <7%

Patient Information Patients must be counseled by someone experienced in diabetes education, signs and symptoms of hyper- and hypoglycemia, exercise and diet, blood glucose monitoring, and other related topics; eat regularly, do not skip meals; carry quick source of sugar; medical alert bracelet

Nursing Implications Patients who are anorexic or NPO, may need to have their dose held to avoid hypoglycemia

Dosage Forms
Tablet (Diaβeta®, Micronase®): 1.25 mg, 2.5 mg, 5 mg
Tablet, micronized (Glynase™ PresTab™): 1.5 mg, 3 mg, 6 mg

- ♦ **Glycerol Guaiacolate** see Guaifenesin on page 549
- ♦ **Glycerol-T®** see Theophylline and Guaifenesin on page 1125
- ♦ **Glyceryl Trinitrate** see Nitroglycerin on page 845
- ♦ **Glycoprotein Antagonists** see page 1323

Glycopyrrolate *(glye koe PYE roe late)*

U.S. Brand Names Robinul®; Robinul® Forte

Synonyms Glycopyrronium Bromide

Therapeutic Category Anticholinergic Agent; Antispasmodic Agent, Gastrointestinal

Use Adjunct in treatment of peptic ulcer disease; inhibit salivation and excessive secretions of the respiratory tract preoperatively; reversal of neuromuscular blockade; control of upper airway secretions

Pregnancy Risk Factor B

Contraindications Narrow-angle glaucoma, acute hemorrhage, tachycardia, hypersensitivity to glycopyrrolate or any component; ulcerative colitis, obstructive uropathy, paralytic ileus, obstructive disease of GI tract

Warnings/Precautions Not recommended in children <12 years of age for the management of peptic ulcer; infants, patients with Down syndrome, and children with spastic paralysis or brain damage may be hypersensitive to antimuscarine effects. Use caution in elderly, patients with autonomic neuropathy, hepatic or renal disease, ulcerative colitis may predispose megacolon, hyperthyroidism, CAD, CHF, arrhythmias, tachycardia, BPH, hiatal hernia, with reflux.

Adverse Reactions
>10%:
Dermatologic: Dry skin
Gastrointestinal: Constipation, dry throat, xerostomia
Local: Irritation at injection site
Respiratory: Dry nose
Miscellaneous: Diaphoresis (decreased)
1% to 10%:
Dermatologic: Increased sensitivity to light
Endocrine & metabolic: Decreased flow of breast milk
Gastrointestinal: Dysphagia
<1%: Orthostatic hypotension, ventricular fibrillation, tachycardia, palpitations, confusion, drowsiness, headache, loss of memory, fatigue, ataxia, rash, bloated feeling, nausea, vomiting, dysuria, weakness, increased intraocular pain, blurred vision

Overdosage/Toxicology
Symptoms of overdose include blurred vision, urinary retention, tachycardia, absent bowel sounds
Anticholinergic toxicity is caused by strong binding of the drug to cholinergic receptors. For anticholinergic overdose with severe life-threatening symptoms, physostigmine 1-2 mg (0.5 mg or 0.02 mg/kg for children) S.C. or I.V., slowly may be given to reverse these effects.

Drug Interactions
Decreased effect of levodopa
Increased toxicity with amantadine, cyclopropane

Stability Unstable at pH >6; **incompatible** with secobarbital (immediate precipitation), sodium bicarbonate (gas evolves), thiopental (immediate precipitation)

Mechanism of Action Blocks the action of acetylcholine at parasympathetic sites in smooth muscle, secretory glands, and the CNS

Pharmacodynamics/Kinetics
Oral: Onset of action: Within 50 minutes; Peak effect: Within 1 hour
I.M.: Onset of action: 20-40 minutes
I.V.: Onset of action: 10-15 minutes
Absorption: Oral: Poor and erratic
Bioavailability: ~10%

Usual Dosage

Children:

Control of secretions:

Oral: 40-100 mcg/kg/dose 3-4 times/day

I.M., I.V.: 4-10 mcg/kg/dose every 3-4 hours; maximum: 0.2 mg/dose or 0.8 mg/24 hours

Intraoperative: I.V.: 4 mcg/kg not to exceed 0.1 mg; repeat at 2- to 3-minute intervals as needed

Preoperative: I.M.:

<2 years: 4.4-8.8 mcg/kg 30-60 minutes before procedure

>2 years: 4.4 mcg/kg 30-60 minutes before procedure

Children and Adults: Reverse neuromuscular blockade: I.V.: 0.2 mg for each 1 mg of neostigmine or 5 mg of pyridostigmine administered

Adults:

Intraoperative: I.V.: 0.1 mg repeated as needed at 2- to 3-minute intervals

Preoperative: I.M.: 4.4 mcg/kg 30-60 minutes before procedure

Peptic ulcer:

Oral: 1-2 mg 2-3 times/day

I.M., I.V.: 0.1-0.2 mg 3-4 times/day

Administration For I.V. administration, glycopyrrolate may also be administered via the tubing of a running I.V. infusion of a compatible solution

Patient Information Maintain good oral hygiene habits, because lack of saliva may increase chance of cavities. Observe caution when driving or performing other tasks requiring alertness, as may cause drowsiness, dizziness, or blurred vision. Notify physician if skin rash, flushing or eye pain occurs; or if difficulty in urinating, constipation, or sensitivity to light becomes severe or persists.

Dosage Forms

Injection, as bromide: 0.2 mg/mL (1 mL, 2 mL, 5 mL, 20 mL)

Robinul®: 0.2 mg/mL (1 mL, 2 mL, 5 mL, 20 mL)

Tablet, as bromide:

Robinul®: 1 mg

Robinul® Forte: 2 mg

♦ **Glycopyrronium Bromide** see Glycopyrrolate on previous page

♦ **Glycotuss®** [OTC] see Guaifenesin on page 549

♦ **Glycotuss-DM®** [OTC] see Guaifenesin and Dextromethorphan on page 550

♦ **Glydiazinamide** see Glipizide on page 538

♦ **Glynase™ PresTab™** see Glyburide on page 540

♦ **Gly-Oxide® Oral** [OTC] see Carbamide Peroxide on page 190

♦ **Glyset®** see Miglitol on page 780

♦ **Glytuss®** [OTC] see Guaifenesin on page 549

♦ **GM-CSF** see Sargramostim on page 1049

♦ **G-myticin® Topical** see Gentamicin on page 533

♦ **GnRH** see Gonadorelin on next page

Gold Sodium Thiomalate (gold SOW dee um thye oh MAL ate)

U.S. Brand Names Aurolate®

Therapeutic Category Gold Compound

Use Treatment of progressive rheumatoid arthritis

Pregnancy Risk Factor C

Contraindications Hypersensitivity to gold compounds or any component; systemic lupus erythematosus; history of blood dyscrasias; congestive heart failure, exfoliative dermatitis, colitis

Warnings/Precautions Frequent monitoring of patients for signs and symptoms of toxicity will prevent serious adverse reactions; nonsteroidal anti-inflammatory drugs (NSAIDs) and corticosteroids may be discontinued after initiating gold therapy; must not be injected I.V.

Explain the possibility of adverse reactions before initiating therapy; signs of gold toxicity include decrease in hemoglobin, leukopenia, granulocytes and platelets; proteinuria, hematuria, pigmentation, pruritus, stomatitis or persistent diarrhea, rash, metallic taste; advise patient to report any symptoms of toxicity; use with caution in patients with liver or renal disease

Adverse Reactions

>10%:

Dermatologic: Itching, rash

Gastrointestinal: Stomatitis, gingivitis, glossitis

Ocular: Conjunctivitis

1% to 10%:

Dermatologic: Urticaria, alopecia

Hematologic: Eosinophilia, leukopenia, thrombocytopenia

Renal: Proteinuria, hematuria

<1%: Angioedema, ulcerative enterocolitis, GI hemorrhage, dysphagia, metallic taste, agranulocytosis, anemia, aplastic anemia, hepatotoxicity, peripheral neuropathy, interstitial pneumonitis

Overdosage/Toxicology

Symptoms of overdose include hematuria, proteinuria, fever, nausea, vomiting, diarrhea

For mild gold poisoning, dimercaprol 2.5 mg/kg 4 times/day for 2 days or for more severe forms of gold intoxication, dimercaprol 3-5 mg/kg every 4 hours for 2 days should be

(Continued)

Gold Sodium Thiomalate *(Continued)*

initiated; then after 2 days, the initial dose should be repeated twice daily on the third day, and once daily thereafter for 10 days. Other chelating agents have been used with some success.

Drug Interactions Decreased effect with penicillamine, acetylcysteine

Stability Should not be used if solution is darker than pale yellow

Mechanism of Action Unknown, may decrease prostaglandin synthesis or may alter cellular mechanisms by inhibiting sulfhydryl systems

Pharmacodynamics/Kinetics

Half-life: 5 days; may lengthen with multiple doses

Time to peak serum concentration: Within 4-6 hours

Elimination: Majority (60% to 90%) excreted in urine with smaller amounts (10% to 40%) excreted in feces (via bile)

Usual Dosage I.M.:

Children: Initial: Test dose of 10 mg is recommended, followed by 1 mg/kg/week for 20 weeks; maintenance: 1 mg/kg/dose at 2- to 4-week intervals thereafter for as long as therapy is clinically beneficial and toxicity does not develop. Administration for 2-4 months is usually required before clinical improvement is observed.

Adults: 10 mg first week; 25 mg second week; then 25-50 mg/week until 1 g cumulative dose has been given; if improvement occurs without adverse reactions, administer 25-50 mg every 2-3 weeks for 2-20 weeks, then every 3-4 weeks indefinitely

Dosing adjustment in renal impairment:

Cl_{cr} 50-80 mL/minute: Administer 50% of normal dose

Cl_{cr} <50 mL/minute: Avoid use

Administration Deep I.M. injection into the upper outer quadrant of the gluteal region addition of 0.1 mL of 1% lidocaine to each injection may reduce the discomfort associated with I.M. administration

Monitoring Parameters Signs and symptoms of gold toxicity, CBC with differential and platelet count, urinalysis

Reference Range Gold: Normal: 0-0.1 µg/mL (SI: 0-0.0064 µmol/L); Therapeutic: 1-3 µg/mL (SI: 0.06-0.18 µmol/L); Urine: <0.1 µg/24 hour

Patient Information Minimize exposure to sunlight; benefits from drug therapy may take as long as 3 months to appear; notify physician of pruritus, rash, sore mouth; metallic taste may occur

Nursing Implications Explain the possibility of adverse reactions before initiating therapy

Additional Information Approximately 50% gold

Dosage Forms Injection: 25 mg/mL (1 mL); 50 mg/mL (1 mL, 2 mL, 10 mL)

♦ GoLYTELY® *see* Polyethylene Glycol-Electrolyte Solution *on page 942*

Gonadorelin (goe nad oh REL in)

U.S. Brand Names Factrel®; Lutrepulse®

Synonyms GnRH; Gonadorelin Acetate; Gonadorelin Hydrochloride; Gonadotropin Releasing Hormone; LHRH; LRH; Luteinizing Hormone Releasing Hormone

Therapeutic Category Diagnostic Agent, Gonadotrophic Hormone; Gonadotropin

Use Evaluation of the functional capacity and response of gonadotrophic hormones; evaluate abnormal gonadotropin regulation as in precocious puberty and delayed puberty. Lutrepulse®: Induction of ovulation in females with hypothalamic amenorrhea.

Pregnancy Risk Factor B

Contraindications Known hypersensitivity to gonadorelin, women with any condition that could be exacerbated by pregnancy; patients who have ovarian cysts or causes of anovulation other than those of hypothalamic origin; any condition that may worsened by reproductive hormones

Warnings/Precautions Hypersensitivity and anaphylactic reactions have occurred following multiple-dose administration; multiple pregnancy is a possibility; use with caution in women in whom pregnancy could worsen pre-existing conditions (eg, pituitary prolactinemia). Multiple pregnancy is a possibility with Lutrepulse®.

Adverse Reactions

1% to 10%: Local: Pain at injection site

<1%: Flushing, lightheadedness, headache, rash, nausea, abdominal discomfort

Overdosage/Toxicology

Symptoms of overdose include abdominal discomfort, nausea, headache, flushing Treatment is symptomatic

Drug Interactions

Decreased levels/effect: Oral contraceptives, digoxin, phenothiazines, dopamine antagonists

Increased levels/effect: Androgens, estrogens, progestins, glucocorticoids, spironolactone, levodopa

Stability

Factrel®: Prepare immediately prior to use; after reconstitution, store at room temperature and use within 1 day; discard unused portion

Lutrepulse®: Store at room temperature; reconstitute with diluent immediately prior to use and transfer to plastic reservoir. The solution will supply 90 minute pulsatile doses for 7 consecutive days (Lutrepulse® pump).

Mechanism of Action Stimulates the release of luteinizing hormone (LH) from the anterior pituitary gland

Pharmacodynamics/Kinetics
Peak effect: Maximal LH release occurs within 20 minutes
Duration of action: 3-5 hours
Half-life: 4 minutes

Usual Dosage
Diagnostic test: Children >12 years and Adults (female): I.V., S.C. hydrochloride salt: 100 mcg administered in women during early phase of menstrual cycle (day 1-7)

Primary hypothalamic amenorrhea: Female adults: Acetate: I.V.: 5 mcg every 90 minutes via Lutrepulse® pump kit at treatment intervals of 21 days (pump will pulsate every 90 minutes for 7 days)

Administration
Factrel®: Dilute in 3 mL of normal saline; administer I.V. push over 30 seconds

Lutrepulse®: A presterilized reservoir bag with the infusion catheter set supplied with the kit should be filled with the reconstituted solution and administered I.V. using the Lutrepulse® pump. Set the pump to deliver 25-50 mL of solution, based upon the dose, over a pulse period of 1 minute and at a pulse frequency of 90 minutes.

Monitoring Parameters LH, FSH

Dosage Forms
Injection, as acetate (Lutrepulse®): 0.8 mg, 3.2 mg
Injection, as hydrochloride (Factrel®): 100 mcg, 500 mcg

♦ **Gonadorelin Acetate** *see Gonadorelin on previous page*
♦ **Gonadorelin Hydrochloride** *see Gonadorelin on previous page*
♦ **Gonadotropin Releasing Hormone** *see Gonadorelin on previous page*
♦ **Gonal-F®** *see Follitropins on page 513*
♦ **Gonic®** *see Chorionic Gonadotropin on page 258*
♦ **Gormel® Creme [OTC]** *see Urea on page 1199*

Goserelin (GOE se rel in)

Related Information
Cancer Chemotherapy Regimens *on page 1263*

U.S. Brand Names Zoladex® Implant

Synonyms Goserelin Acetate

Therapeutic Category Antineoplastic Agent, Miscellaneous; Gonadotropin Releasing Hormone Analog; Luteinizing Hormone-Releasing Hormone Analog

Use
Prostate carcinoma: Palliative treatment of advanced carcinoma of the prostate. An alternative treatment of prostatic cancer when orchiectomy or estrogen administration are either not indicated or unacceptable to the patient. Combination with flutamide for the management of locally confined stage T2b-T4 (stage B2-C) carcinoma of the prostate.

3.6 mg implant only:
Endometriosis: Management of endometriosis, including pain relief and reduction of endometriotic lesions for the duration of therapy

Advanced breast cancer: Palliative treatment of advanced breast cancer in pre- and perimenopausal women. Estrogen and progesterone receptor values may help to predict whether goserelin therapy is likely to be beneficial.

Note: The 10.8 mg implant is not indicated in women as the data are insufficient to support reliable suppression of serum estradiol

Pregnancy Risk Factor X

Contraindications In women who are or may become pregnant, patients who are hypersensitive to the drug

Warnings/Precautions Initially, goserelin, transiently increases serum levels of testosterone. Transient worsening of signs and symptoms, usually manifested by an increase in cancer-related pain which was managed symptomatically, may develop during the first few weeks of treatment. Isolated cases of ureteral obstruction and spinal cord compression have been reported; patient's symptoms may initially worsen temporarily during first few weeks of therapy, cancer-related pain can usually be controlled by analgesics

Adverse Reactions
General: Worsening of signs and symptoms may occur during the first few weeks of therapy and are usually manifested by an increase in bone pain, increased difficulty in urinating, hot flashes, injection site irritation, and weakness; this will subside, but patients should be aware

>10%:
Endocrine & metabolic: Gynecomastia, postmenopausal symptoms, sexual dysfunction, loss of libido, hot flashes
Genitourinary: Impotence, decreased erection

1% to 10%:
Cardiovascular: Edema
Central nervous system: Headache, spinal cord compression (possible result of tumor flare), lethargy, dizziness, insomnia
Dermatologic: Rash
Gastrointestinal: Nausea and vomiting, anorexia, diarrhea, weight gain
Genitourinary: Vaginal spotting and breakthrough bleeding, breast tenderness/enlargement
Local: Pain on injection
Neuromuscular & skeletal: Bone loss, increased bone pain
Miscellaneous: Diaphoresis

(Continued)

Goserelin *(Continued)*

Overdosage/Toxicology Symptomatic management

Stability Zoladex® should be stored at room temperature not to exceed 25°C or 77°F; must be dispensed in an amber bag

Mechanism of Action LHRH synthetic analog of luteinizing hormone-releasing hormone also known as gonadotropin-releasing hormone (GnRH) incorporated into a biodegradable depot material which allows for continuous slow release over 28 days; mechanism of action is similar to leuprolide

Pharmacodynamics/Kinetics

Absorption: Oral: Inactive when administered orally; S.C.: Rapid and can be detected in the serum in 10 minutes

Distribution: V_d: 13.7 L

Time to peak serum concentration: S.C.: 12-15 days

Half-life: Following a bolus S.C. dose: 5 hours

Elimination: By the kidney; elimination time: 4.2 hours (prolonged in impaired renal function - 12 hours)

Usual Dosage

Adults: S.C.:

Monthly implant: 3.6 mg injected into upper abdomen every 28 days; do not try to aspirate with the goserelin syringe; if the needle is in a large vessel, blood will immediately appear in syringe chamber. While a delay of a few days is permissible, attempt to adhere to the 28-day schedule.

3-month implant: 10.8 mg injected into the upper abdominal wall every 12 weeks; do not try to aspirate with the goserelin syringe; if the needle is in a large vessel, blood will immediately appear in syringe chamber. While a delay of a few days is permissible, attempt to adhere to the 12-week schedule.

Prostate carcinoma: Intended for long-term administration

Endometriosis: Recommended duration: 6 months; retreatment is not recommended since safety data is not available. If symptoms recur after a course of therapy, and further treatment is contemplated, consider monitoring bone mineral density. Currently, there are no clinical data on the effect of treatment of benign gynecological conditions with goserelin for periods >6 months.

Dosing adjustment in renal/hepatic impairment: No adjustment is necessary

Administration

Do not remove the sterile syringe until immediately before use.

After cleaning with an alcohol swab, a local anesthetic may be used on an area of skin on the upper abdominal wall.

Stretch the patient's skin with one hand, and grip the needle with fingers around the barrel of the syringe. Insert the hypodermic needle into the SC fat. Do not aspirate. If the hypodermic needle penetrates a large vessel, blood will be seen instantly in the syringe chamber.

Change the direction of the needle so it parallels the abdominal wall. Push the needle in until the barrel hub touches the patient's skin. Withdraw the needle 1 cm to create a space to discharge the drug; fully depress the plunger to discharge.

Withdraw needle and bandage the site. Confirm discharge by ensuring tip of the plunger is visible within the tip of the needle.

Test Interactions Serum alkaline phosphatase, serum acid phosphatase, serum testosterone, serum LH and FSH, serum estradiol

Patient Information Females must use reliable contraception during therapy; symptoms may worsen temporarily during first weeks of therapy

Dosage Forms Injection, implant: 3.6 mg single dose disposable syringe with 16-gauge hypodermic needle; 10.8 mg single dose disposable syringe with 14-gauge hypodermic needle

♦ **Goserelin Acetate** *see Goserelin on previous page*
♦ **GR1222311X** *see Ranitidine Bismuth Citrate on page 1010*

Granisetron *(gra NI se tron)*

U.S. Brand Names Kytril™

Therapeutic Category Antiemetic, Serotonin Antagonist; 5-HT₃ Receptor Antagonist; Serotonin Antagonist

Use Prophylaxis and treatment of chemotherapy-related emesis; may be prescribed for patients who are refractory to or have severe adverse reactions to standard antiemetic therapy. Granisetron may be prescribed for young patients (ie, <45 years of age who are more likely to develop extrapyramidal reactions to high-dose metoclopramide) who are to receive highly emetogenic chemotherapeutic agents as listed:

Agents with high emetogenic potential (>90%) (dose/m²):

Amifostine

Azacitidine

Carmustine ≥200 mg/m²

Cisplatin ≥50 mg/m²

Cyclophosphamide ≥1 g/m²

Cytarabine ≥1500 mg/m²

Dacarbazine ≥500 mg/m²

Dactinomycin

Doxorubicin ≥60 mg/m²

Lomustine ≥60 mg/m²

Mechlorethamine

Melphalan ≥100 mg/m²

Streptozocin
Thiotepa ≥100 mg/m^2

or two agents classified as having high or moderately high emetogenic potential as listed:

Agents with moderately high emetogenic potential (60% to 90%) (dose/m^2):
Carboplatin 200-400 mg/m^2
Carmustine <200 mg/m^2
Cisplatin <50 mg/m^2
Cyclophosphamide 600-999 mg/m^2
Dacarbazine <500 mg/m^2
Doxorubicin 21-59 mg/m^2
Hexamethyl melamine
Ifosfamide ≥5000 mg/m^2
Lomustine <60 mg/m^2
Methotrexate ≥250 mg/m^2
Pentostatin
Procarbazine

Granisetron should not be prescribed for chemotherapeutic agents with a low emetogenic potential (eg, bleomycin, busulfan, cyclophosphamide <1000 mg, etoposide, 5-fluorouracil, vinblastine, vincristine)

Pregnancy Risk Factor B

Contraindications Previous hypersensitivity to granisetron

Warnings/Precautions Use with caution in patients with liver disease or in pregnant patients

Adverse Reactions
>10%: Central nervous system: Headache
1% to 10%:
Cardiovascular: Hyper/hypotension
Central nervous system: Dizziness, insomnia, anxiety
Gastrointestinal: Constipation, abdominal pain, diarrhea
Neuromuscular & skeletal: Weakness
<1%: Arrhythmias, somnolence, agitation, hot flashes, liver enzyme elevations

Drug Interactions CYP3A3/4 enzyme substrate

Stability I.V.: Stable when mixed in NS or D$_5$W for 24 hours at room temperature; protect from light; do not freeze vials

Mechanism of Action Selective 5-HT$_3$-receptor antagonist, blocking serotonin, both peripherally on vagal nerve terminals and centrally in the chemoreceptor trigger zone

Pharmacodynamics/Kinetics
Onset of action: Commonly controls emesis within 1-3 minutes of administration
Duration: Effects generally last no more than 24 hours maximum
Distribution: V$_d$: 2-3 L/kg; widely distributed throughout the body
Half-life: Cancer patients: 10-12 hours; Healthy volunteers: 3-4 hours
Elimination: Primarily nonrenal, 8% to 15% of a dose is excreted unchanged in urine

Usual Dosage
I.V.: Children and Adults: 10 mcg/kg for 1-3 doses. Doses should be administered as a single IVPB over 5 minutes to 1 hour or by undiluted IV push over 30 seconds, given just prior to chemotherapy (15-60 minutes before); as intervention therapy for breakthrough nausea and vomiting, during the first 24 hours following chemotherapy, 2 or 3 repeat infusions (same dose) have been administered, separated by at least 10 minutes
Oral: Adults: 1 mg twice daily; the first 1 mg dose should be given up to 1 hour before chemotherapy, and the second tablet, 12 hours after the first; alternatively may give a single dose of 2 mg, up to 1 hour before chemotherapy
Note: Granisetron should only be given on the day(s) of chemotherapy
Dosing interval in renal impairment: Creatinine clearance values have no relationship to granisetron clearance
Dosing interval in hepatic impairment: Kinetic studies in patients with hepatic impairment showed that total clearance was approximately halved, however, standard doses were very well tolerated

Nursing Implications Doses should be given at least 15 minutes prior to initiation of chemotherapy

Dosage Forms
Injection: 1 mg/mL
Tablet: 1 mg (2s), (20s)

Extemporaneous Preparations A 0.2 mg/mL oral suspension may be prepared by crushing twelve (12) 1 mg tablets and mixing with 30 mL water and enough cherry syrup to provide a final volume of 60 mL; this preparation is stable for 14 days at room temperature or when refrigerated

♦ **Granulex** see Trypsin, Balsam Peru, and Castor Oil on page 1193
♦ **Granulocyte Colony Stimulating Factor** see Filgrastim on page 482
♦ **Granulocyte-Macrophage Colony Stimulating Factor** see Sargramostim on page 1049

Grepafloxacin (grep a FLOX a sin)
Related Information
Antimicrobial Drugs of Choice on page 1404
Community-Acquired Pneumonia in Adults on page 1419
U.S. Brand Names Raxar®
(Continued)

Grepafloxacin *(Continued)*

Synonyms OPC-17116

Therapeutic Category Antibiotic, Quinolone

Use Treatment of acute bacterial exacerbations of chronic bronchitis caused by *Haemophilus influenzae*, *Streptococcus pneumoniae*, or *Moraxella catarrhalis*; community-acquired pneumonia caused by *Mycoplasma pneumoniae* or the organisms previously mentioned; uncomplicated gonorrhea caused by *Neisseria gonorrhoeae*, and nongonococcal cervicitis and urethritis caused by *Chlamydia trachomatis*

In vitro studies suggest similar or lesser activity against *Enterobacteriaceae* and *P. aeruginosa* but greater activity against gram-positive cocci, especially *S. pneumoniae*, and some anaerobes and *Chlamydia* spp.

Pregnancy Risk Factor C

Contraindications Previous hypersensitivity to grepafloxacin and other quinolone derivatives; in patients with hepatic failure; given concomitantly with class I and III antiarrhythmics or bepridil due to the potential risk of cardiac arrhythmias (including torsade de pointes); patients with QT_c prolongation and use with drugs which prolong QT_c interval

Warnings/Precautions Use caution in patients with cerebral arteriosclerosis or epilepsy, and in patients with GI disorders or hepatic or renal dysfunction; there is no data to support safety and efficacy in children <18 years of age

Adverse Reactions Percentage unknown: Syncope, headache, dizziness, fatigue, nausea, emesis due to medicinal taste, hepatotoxicity (ie, elevated serum transaminases), abdominal pain, diarrhea, hypersensitivity

Drug Interactions CYP1A2 enzyme substrate

Antacids decrease grepafloxacin levels by 60%; grepafloxacin decreases theophylline clearance by 50%; may inhibit the metabolism of other drugs metabolized by cytochrome P-450 enzymes; may have additive effect of $Q-T_c$ prolongation when administered with other agent that may prolong $Q-T_c$ interval

Mechanism of Action Inhibits DNA-gyrase in susceptible organisms; inhibits relaxation of supercoiled DNA and promotes breakage of double-stranded DNA

Pharmacodynamics/Kinetics

Absorption: Peak plasma levels at 2-3 hours

Distribution: High concentrations have been achieved in bile, gynecologic tissue, hair, blister fluid, lung and other tissue; V_d: 5 L/kg

Metabolism: Liver, unknown activity of metabolites

Bioavailability: 70%

Half-life: 15.7 hours

Elimination: Eliminated unchanged in urine (10%); the rest in bile, feces, and metabolites

Usual Dosage Oral:

Bronchitis: 400-600 mg/day for 10 days

Community-acquired pneumonia: 600 mg/day for 10 days

Nongonococcal urethritis or cervicitis: 400 mg/day for 7 days

Uncomplicated gonorrhea: 400 mg as a single dose

Monitoring Parameters CBC, signs/symptoms of infection, liver/renal function tests

Patient Information Call physician immediately if hallucinations, confusion, seizures, rash, itching, facial swelling, or shortness of breath develops

Dosage Forms Tablet, as hydrochloride: 200 mg, 400 mg, 600 mg

- ♦ **Grifulvin® V** *see Griseofulvin on this page*
- ♦ **Grisactin-500®** *see Griseofulvin on this page*
- ♦ **Grisactin® Ultra** *see Griseofulvin on this page*

Griseofulvin *(gri see oh FUL vin)*

Related Information

Antifungal Agents Comparison *on page 1303*

U.S. Brand Names Fulvicin® P/G; Fulvicin-U/F®; Grifulvin® V; Grisactin-500®; Grisactin® Ultra; Gris-PEG®

Canadian Brand Names Grisovin®-FP

Synonyms Griseofulvin Microsize; Griseofulvin Ultramicrosize

Therapeutic Category Antifungal Agent, Systemic

Use Treatment of susceptible tinea infections of the skin, hair, and nails

Pregnancy Risk Factor C

Contraindications Hypersensitivity to griseofulvin or any component; severe liver disease, porphyria (interferes with porphyrin metabolism)

Warnings/Precautions Safe use in children <2 years of age has not been established; during long-term therapy, periodic assessment of hepatic, renal, and hematopoietic functions should be performed; may cause fetal harm when administered to pregnant women; avoid exposure to intense sunlight to prevent photosensitivity reactions; hypersensitivity cross reaction between penicillins and griseofulvin is possible

Adverse Reactions

>10%: Dermatologic: Rash, urticaria

1% to 10%:

Central nervous system: Headache, fatigue, dizziness, insomnia, mental confusion

Dermatologic: Photosensitivity

Gastrointestinal: Nausea, vomiting, epigastric distress, diarrhea

Miscellaneous: Oral thrush

<1%: Angioneurotic edema, menstrual toxicity, GI bleeding, leukopenia, hepatotoxicity, proteinuria, nephrosis

Overdosage/Toxicology
Symptoms of overdose include lethargy, vertigo, blurred vision, nausea, vomiting, diarrhea
Following GI decontamination, treatment is supportive

Drug Interactions
Decreased effect:
Barbiturates may decrease levels of griseofulvin
Decreased warfarin, cyclosporine, and salicylate activity with griseofulvin
Griseofulvin decreases oral contraceptive effectiveness
Increased toxicity: With alcohol → tachycardia and flushing

Mechanism of Action Inhibits fungal cell mitosis at metaphase; binds to human keratin making it resistant to fungal invasion

Pharmacodynamics/Kinetics
Absorption: Ultramicrosize griseofulvin absorption is almost complete; absorption of microsize griseofulvin is variable (25% to 70% of an oral dose); absorption is enhanced by ingestion of a fatty meal (GI absorption of ultramicrosize is ~1.5 times that of microsize)
Distribution: Crosses the placenta
Metabolism: Extensive in the liver
Half-life: 9-22 hours
Elimination: <1% excreted unchanged in urine; also excreted in feces and perspiration

Usual Dosage Oral:
Children:
Microsize: 10-20 mg/kg/day in single or 2 divided doses
Ultramicrosize: >2 years: 5-10 mg/kg/day in single or 2 divided doses
Adults:
Microsize: 500-1000 mg/day in single or divided doses
Ultramicrosize: 330-375 mg/day in single or divided doses; doses up to 750 mg/day have been used for infections more difficult to eradicate such as tinea unguium
Duration of therapy depends on the site of infection:
Tinea corporis: 2-4 weeks
Tinea capitis: 4-6 weeks or longer
Tinea pedis: 4-8 weeks
Tinea unguium: 3-6 months or longer

Monitoring Parameters Periodic renal, hepatic, and hematopoietic function tests

Test Interactions False-positive urinary VMA levels

Patient Information Avoid exposure to sunlight, take with fatty meal; if patient gets headache, it usually goes away with continued therapy; may cause dizziness, drowsiness, and impair judgment; do not take if pregnant; if you become pregnant, discontinue immediately

Dosage Forms
Microsize:
Capsule: 125 mg, 250 mg
Suspension, oral (Grifulvin® V): 125 mg/5 mL with alcohol 0.2% (120 mL)
Tablet:
Fulvicin-U/F®, Grifulvin® V: 250 mg
Fulvicin-U/F®, Grifulvin® V, Grisactin-500®: 500 mg
Ultramicrosize:
Tablet:
Fulvicin® P/G: 165 mg, 330 mg
Fulvicin® P/G, Grisactin Ultra, Gris-PEG®: 125 mg, 250 mg
Grisactin® Ultra: 330 mg

♦ **Griseofulvin Microsize** see Griseofulvin on previous page
♦ **Griseofulvin Ultramicrosize** see Griseofulvin on previous page
♦ **Grisovin®-FP** see Griseofulvin on previous page
♦ **Gris-PEG®** see Griseofulvin on previous page
♦ **Growth Hormone** see Human Growth Hormone on page 569

Guaifenesin (gwye FEN e sin)

U.S. Brand Names Anti-Tuss® Expectorant [OTC]; Breonesin® [OTC]; Diabetic Tussin EX® [OTC]; Durafuss-G®; Fenesin™; Gee Gee® [OTC]; Genatuss® [OTC]; GG-Cen® [OTC]; Glyate® [OTC]; Glycotuss® [OTC]; Glytuss® [OTC]; Guaifenex LA®; GuiaCough® Expectorant [OTC]; Guiatuss® [OTC]; Halotussin® [OTC]; Humibid® L.A.; Humibid® Sprinkle; Hytuss® [OTC]; Hytuss-2X® [OTC]; Liquibid®; Malotuss® [OTC]; Medi-Tuss® [OTC]; Monafed®; Muco-Fen-LA®; Mytussin® [OTC]; Naldecon® Senior EX [OTC]; Organidin® NR; Pneumomist®; Respa-GF®; Robitussin® [OTC]; Scot-Tussin® [OTC]; Siltussin® [OTC]; Sinumist®-SR Capsulets®; Touro Ex®; Tusibron® [OTC]; Uni-Tussin® [OTC]

Canadian Brand Names Balminil® Expectorant; Calmylin Expectorant

Synonyms GG; Glycerol Guaiacolate

Therapeutic Category Cough Preparation; Expectorant

Use Temporary control of cough due to minor throat and bronchial irritation

Pregnancy Risk Factor C

Contraindications Hypersensitivity to guaifenesin or any component

Warnings/Precautions Not for persistent cough such as occurs with smoking, asthma, or emphysema or cough accompanied by excessive secretions

Adverse Reactions 1% to 10%:
Central nervous system: Drowsiness, headache
(Continued)

Guaifenesin *(Continued)*

Dermatologic: Rash
Gastrointestinal: Nausea, vomiting, stomach pain

Overdosage/Toxicology
Symptoms of overdose include vomiting, lethargy, coma, respiratory depression
Treatment is supportive

Stability Protect from light

Mechanism of Action Thought to act as an expectorant by irritating the gastric mucosa and stimulating respiratory tract secretions, thereby increasing respiratory fluid volumes and decreasing phlegm viscosity

Pharmacodynamics/Kinetics
Absorption: Well absorbed from GI tract
Metabolism: Hepatic, 60%
Half-life: ~1 hour
Elimination: Renal excretion of changed and unchanged drug

Usual Dosage Oral:
Children:
<2 years: 12 mg/kg/day in 6 divided doses
2-5 years: 50-100 mg every 4 hours, not to exceed 600 mg/day
6-11 years: 100-200 mg every 4 hours, not to exceed 1.2 g/day
Children >12 years and Adults: 200-400 mg every 4 hours to a maximum of 2.4 g/day

Test Interactions Possible color interference with determination of 5-HIAA and VMA

Patient Information Take with a large quantity of fluid to ensure proper action; if cough persists for more than 1 week or is accompanied by fever, rash, or persistent headache, physician should be consulted

Additional Information Syrup contains 3.5% alcohol

Dosage Forms
Caplet, sustained release (Touro Ex®): 600 mg
Capsule (Breonesin®, GG-Cen®, Hytuss-2X®): 200 mg
Capsule, sustained release (Humibid® Sprinkle): 300 mg
Liquid:
Diabetic Tussin EX®, Organidin® NR, Tusibron®: 100 mg/5 mL (118 mL)
Naldecon® Senior EX: 200 mg/5 mL (118 mL, 480 mL)
Syrup (Anti-Tuss® Expectorant, Genatuss®, Glyate®, GuiaCough® Expectorant, Guiatuss®, Halotussin®, Malotuss®, Medi-Tuss®, Mytussin®, Robitussin®, Scot-Tussin®, Siltussin®, Tusibron®, Uni-Tussin®): 100 mg/5 mL with alcohol 3.5% (30 mL, 120 mL, 240 mL, 473 mL, 946 mL)
Tablet:
Duratuss-G®: 1200 mg
Gee Gee®, Glytuss®, Organidin® NR: 200 mg
Glycotuss®, Hytuss®: 100 mg
Sustained release:
Fenesin™, Guaifenex LA®, Humibid® L.A., Liquibid®, Monafed®, Muco-Fen-LA®, Pneumomist®, Respa-GF®, Sinumist®-SR Capsulets®: 600 mg

Guaifenesin and Codeine *(gwye FEN e sin & KOE deen)*

Related Information
Codeine *on page 291*
Guaifenesin *on previous page*

U.S. Brand Names Brontex® Liquid; Brontex® Tablet; Cheracol®; Guaituss AC®; Guiatussin® With Codeine; Mytussin® AC; Robafen® AC; Robitussin® A-C; Tussi-Organidin® NR

Synonyms Codeine and Guaifenesin

Therapeutic Category Antitussive; Cough Preparation; Expectorant

Restrictions C-V

Dosage Forms
Liquid (Brontex®): Guaifenesin 75 mg and codeine phosphate 2.5 mg per 5 mL
Syrup (Cheracol®, Guaituss AC®, Guiatussin® with Codeine, Mytussin® AC, Robafen® AC, Tussi-Organidin® A-C, Tussi-Organidin® NR): Guaifenesin 100 mg and codeine phosphate 10 mg per 5 mL (60 mL, 120 mL, 480 mL)
Tablet (Brontex®): Guaifenesin 300 mg and codeine phosphate 10 mg

Guaifenesin and Dextromethorphan

(gwye FEN e sin & deks troe meth OR fan)

U.S. Brand Names Benylin® Expectorant [OTC]; Cheracol® D [OTC]; Clear Tussin® 30; Contac® Cough Formula Liquid [OTC]; Diabetic Tussin DM® [OTC]; Extra Action Cough Syrup [OTC]; Fenesin™ DM; Genatuss DM® [OTC]; Glycotuss-DM® [OTC]; Guaifenex DM®; GuiaCough® [OTC]; Guiatuss-DM® [OTC]; Halotussin®-DM [OTC]; Humibid® DM [OTC]; Iobid DM®; Kolephrin® GG/DM [OTC]; Monafed® DM; Muco-Fen-DM®; Mytussin® DM [OTC]; Naldecon® Senior DX [OTC]; Phanatuss® Cough Syrup [OTC]; Phenadex® Senior [OTC]; Queltuss®; Respa-DM®; Rhinosyn-DMX® [OTC]; Robafen DM® [OTC]; Robitussin®-DM [OTC]; Safe Tussin® 30 [OTC]; Scot-Tussin® Senior Clear [OTC]; Siltussin DM® [OTC]; Synacol® CF [OTC]; Syracol-CF® [OTC]; Tolu-Sed® DM [OTC]; Tusibron-DM® [OTC]; Tuss-DM® [OTC]; Tussi-Organidin® DM NR; Uni-tussin® DM [OTC]; Vicks® 44E [OTC]; Vicks® Pediatric Formula 44E [OTC]

Synonyms Dextromethorphan and Guaifenesin

Therapeutic Category Antitussive; Cough Preparation; Expectorant

Use Temporary control of cough due to minor throat and bronchial irritation

Pregnancy Risk Factor C

Contraindications Hypersensitivity to guaifenesin, dextromethorphan or any component

Warnings/Precautions Should not be used for persistent or chronic cough such as that occurring with smoking, asthma, chronic bronchitis, or emphysema or for cough associated with excessive phlegm

Adverse Reactions 1% to 10%:

Central nervous system: Drowsiness, headache

Dermatologic: Rash

Gastrointestinal: Nausea, vomiting

Pharmacodynamics/Kinetics Refer to Dextromethorphan and Guaifenesin monographs

Onset of action: Exerts its antitussive effect in 15-30 minutes after oral administration

Usual Dosage Oral:

Children: Dextromethorphan: 1-2 mg/kg/24 hours divided 3-4 times/day

Children >12 years and Adults: 5 mL every 4 hours or 10 mL every 6-8 hours not to exceed 40 mL/24 hours

Patient Information Take with a large quantity of fluid to ensure proper action; if cough persists for more than one week, is recumbent, or is accompanied by fever, rash or persistent headache, physician should be consulted

Dosage Forms

Syrup:

Benylin® Expectorant: Guaifenesin 100 mg and dextromethorphan hydrobromide 5 mg per 5 mL (118 mL, 236 mL)

Cheracol® D, Clear Tussin® 30, Genatuss® DM, Mytussin® DM, Robitussin®-DM, Siltussin DM®, Tolu-Sed® DM, Tussi-Organidin® DM NR: Guaifenesin 100 mg and dextromethorphan hydrobromide 10 mg per 5 mL (5 mL, 10 mL, 120 mL, 240 mL, 360 mL, 480 mL, 3780 mL)

Contac® Cough Formula Liquid: Guaifenesin 67 mg and dextromethorphan hydrobromide 10 mg per 5 mL (120 mL)

Extra Action Cough Syrup, GuiaCough®, Guiatuss DM®, Halotussin® DM, Rhinosyn-DMX®, Tusibron-DM®, Uni Tussin® DM: Guaifenesin 100 mg and dextromethorphan hydrobromide 15 mg per 5 mL (120 mL, 240 mL, 480 mL)

Kolephrin® GG/DM: Guaifenesin 150 mg and dextromethorphan hydrobromide 10 mg per 5 mL (120 mL)

Naldecon® Senior DX: Guaifenesin 200 mg and dextromethorphan hydrobromide 15 mg per 5 mL (118 mL, 480 mL)

Phanatuss®: Guaifenesin 85 mg and dextromethorphan hydrobromide 10 mg per 5 mL

Vicks® 44E: Guaifenesin 66.7 mg and dextromethorphan hydrobromide 6.7 mg per 5 mL

Tablet:

Extended release

Guaifenex DM®, Iobid DM®, Fenesin™ DM, Humibid® DM, Monafed® DM, Respa-DM®: Guaifenesin 600 mg and dextromethorphan hydrobromide 30 mg

Glycotuss-dM®: Guaifenesin 100 mg and dextromethorphan hydrobromide 10 mg

Queltuss®: Guaifenesin 100 mg and dextromethorphan hydrobromide 15 mg

Syracol-CF®: Guaifenesin 200 mg and dextromethorphan hydrobromide 15 mg

Tuss-DM®: Guaifenesin 200 mg and dextromethorphan hydrobromide 10 mg

Guaifenesin and Phenylephrine (gwye FEN e sin & fen il EF rin)

U.S. Brand Names Deconsal® Sprinkle®; Endal®; Sinupan®

Therapeutic Category Cold Preparation

Dosage Forms

Capsule, sustained release:

Deconsal® Sprinkle®: Guaifenesin 300 mg and phenylephrine hydrochloride 10 mg

Sinupan®: Guaifenesin 200 mg and phenylephrine hydrochloride 40 mg

Tablet, timed release (Endal®): Guaifenesin 300 mg and phenylephrine hydrochloride 20 mg

Guaifenesin, Pseudoephedrine, and Codeine

(gwye FEN e sin, soo doe e FED rin, & KOE deen)

U.S. Brand Names Codafed® Expectorant; Cycofed® Pediatric; Decohistine® Expectorant; Deproist® Expectorant With Codeine; Dihistine® Expectorant; Guiatuss DAC®; Guiatussin® DAC; Halotussin® DAC; Isoclor® Expectorant; Mytussin® DAC; Nucofed®; Nucofed® Pediatric Expectorant; Nucotuss®; Phenhist® Expectorant; Robitussin®-DAC; Ryna-CX®; Tussar® SF Syrup

Therapeutic Category Antitussive/Decongestant/Expectorant

Dosage Forms

Liquid:

C-III: Nucofed®, Nucotuss®: Guaifenesin 200 mg, pseudoephedrine hydrochloride 60 mg, and codeine phosphate 20 mg per 5 mL (480 mL)

C-V: Codafed® Expectorant, Decohistine® Expectorant, Deproist® Expectorant with Codeine, Dihistine® Expectorant, Guiatuss DAC®, Guiatussin® DAC, Halotussin® DAC, Isoclor® Expectorant, Mytussin® DAC, Nucofed® Pediatric Expectorant, Phenhist® Expectorant, Robitussin®-DAC, Ryna-CX®, Tussar® SF: Guaifenesin 100 mg, pseudoephedrine hydrochloride 30 mg, and codeine phosphate 10 mg per 5 mL (120 mL, 480 mL, 4000 mL)

♦ **Guaifenex DM®** see Guaifenesin and Dextromethorphan *on previous page*

♦ **Guaifenex LA®** see Guaifenesin *on page 549*

♦ **Guaituss AC**® *see Guaifenesin and Codeine on page 550*

Guanabenz (GWAHN a benz)
U.S. Brand Names Wytensin®
Synonyms Guanabenz Acetate
Therapeutic Category Alpha₂-Adrenergic Agonist Agent; Antihypertensive Agent
Use Management of hypertension
Pregnancy Risk Factor C
Contraindications Hypersensitivity to guanabenz or any component
Usual Dosage Adults: Oral: Initial: 4 mg twice daily, increase in increments of 4-8 mg/day every 1-2 weeks to a maximum of 32 mg twice daily
    Dosing adjustment in hepatic impairment: Probably necessary
Additional Information Complete prescribing information for this medication should be consulted for additional detail
Dosage Forms Tablet, as acetate: 4 mg, 8 mg

♦ **Guanabenz Acetate** *see Guanabenz on this page*

Guanadrel (GWAHN a drel)
U.S. Brand Names Hylorel®
Synonyms Guanadrel Sulfate
Therapeutic Category Adrenergic Blocking Agent, Peripherally Acting; Antihypertensive Agent
Use Considered a second line agent in the treatment of hypertension, usually with a diuretic
Pregnancy Risk Factor B
Contraindications Known hypersensitivity to guanadrel, pheochromocytoma, patients taking MAO inhibitors
Usual Dosage Oral:
    Adults: Initial: 10 mg/day (5 mg twice daily); adjust dosage weekly or monthly until blood pressure is controlled, usual dosage: 20-75 mg/day, given twice daily; for larger dosage, 3-4 times/day dosing may be needed
    Elderly: Initial: 5 mg once daily
    Dosing interval in renal impairment:
      Cl_{cr} 10-50 mL/minute: Administer every 12-24 hours
      Cl_{cr} <10 mL/minute: Administer every 24-48 hours
Additional Information Complete prescribing information for this medication should be consulted for additional detail
Dosage Forms Tablet, as sulfate: 10 mg, 25 mg

♦ **Guanadrel Sulfate** *see Guanadrel on this page*

Guanethidine (gwahn ETH i deen)
Related Information
    Depression Disorders and Treatments *on page 1465*
U.S. Brand Names Ismelin®
Canadian Brand Names Apo®-Guanethidine
Synonyms Guanethidine Monosulfate
Therapeutic Category Alpha₂-Adrenergic Agonist Agent; Antihypertensive Agent
Use Treatment of moderate to severe hypertension
Pregnancy Risk Factor C
Contraindications Pheochromocytoma, patients taking MAO inhibitors, hypersensitivity to guanethidine or any component
Usual Dosage Oral:
    Children: Initial: 0.2 mg/kg/day, increase by 0.2 mg/kg/day at 7- to 10-day intervals to a maximum of 3 mg/kg/day
    Adults:
      Ambulatory patients: Initial: 10 mg/day, increase at 5- to 7-day intervals to an average of 25-50 mg/day
      Hospitalized patients: Initial: 25-50 mg/day, increase by 25-50 mg/day or every other day to desired therapeutic response
    Elderly: Initial: 5 mg once daily
    Dosing interval in renal impairment: Cl_{cr} <10 mL/minute: Administer every 24-36 hours
Additional Information Complete prescribing information for this medication should be consulted for additional detail
Dosage Forms Tablet, as monosulfate: 10 mg, 25 mg

♦ **Guanethidine Monosulfate** *see Guanethidine on this page*

Guanfacine (GWAHN fa seen)
U.S. Brand Names Tenex®
Therapeutic Category Alpha₂-Adrenergic Agonist Agent; Antihypertensive Agent
Use Management of hypertension
Pregnancy Risk Factor B
Contraindications Hypersensitivity to guanfacine or any component
Usual Dosage Adults: Oral: 1 mg usually at bedtime, may increase if needed at 3- to 4-week intervals; 1 mg/day is most common dose

Additional Information Complete prescribing information for this medication should be consulted for additional detail

Dosage Forms Tablet, as hydrochloride: 1 mg, 2 mg

Haemophilus b Conjugate and Hepatitis b Vaccine

(he MOF i lus bee KON joo gate & hep a TYE tis bee vak SEEN)

U.S. Brand Names Comvax™

Synonyms *Haemophilus* b (meningococcal protein conjugate) Conjugate Vaccine; Hib

Therapeutic Category Vaccine

Use

Immunization against invasive disease caused by *H. influenzae* type b and against infection caused by all known subtypes of hepatitis B virus in infants 8 weeks to 15 months of age born of HB_sAg-negative mothers

Infants born of HB_sAg-positive mothers or mothers of unknown HB_sAg status should receive hepatitis B immune globulin and hepatitis B vaccine (Recombinant) at birth and should complete the hepatitis B vaccination series given according to a particular schedule

Pregnancy Risk Factor C

Contraindications Hypersensitivity to any component of the vaccine

Warnings/Precautions If used in persons with malignancies or those receiving immuno-suppressive therapy or who are otherwise immunocompromised, the expected immune response may not be obtained.

Patients who develop symptoms suggestive of hypersensitivity after an injection should not receive further injections of the vaccine.

The decision to administer or delay vaccination because of current or recent febrile illness depends on the severity of symptoms and the etiology of the disease. Immunization should be delayed during the course of an acute febrile illness.

Adverse Reactions When administered during the same visit that DTP, OPV, IPV, Varicella Virus Vaccine, and M-M-R II vaccines are given, the rates of systemic reactions do not differ from those observed only when any of the vaccines are administered **All serious adverse reactions must be reported to the U.S. Department of Health and Human Services (DHHS) Vaccine Adverse Event Reporting System (VAERS) 1-800-822-7967.**

>10%: Central nervous system: Acute febrile reactions

1% to 10%:
    Central nervous system: Fever (up to 102.2°F), irritability, lethargy
    Gastrointestinal: Anorexia, diarrhea
    Local: Irritation at injection site

<1%: Convulsions, fever (>102.2°F), vomiting, allergic or anaphylactic reactions (difficulty in breathing, hives, itching, swelling of eyes, face, unusual tiredness or weakness)

Stability Store at 2°C to 8°C/36°F to 48°F

Mechanism of Action Hib conjugate vaccines use covalent binding of capsular polysaccharide of *Haemophilus influenzae* type b to OMPC carrier to produce an antigen which is postulated to convert a T-independent antigen into a T-dependent antigen to result in enhanced antibody response and on immunologic memory. Recombinant hepatitis B vaccine is a noninfectious subunit viral vaccine. The vaccine is derived from hepatitis B surface antigen (HB_sAg) produced through recombinant DNA techniques from yeast cells. The portion of the hepatitis B gene which codes for HB_sAg is cloned into yeast which is then cultured to produce hepatitis B vaccine.

Pharmacodynamics/Kinetics

The seroconversion following one dose of Hib vaccine for children 18 months or 24 months of age or older is 75% to 90% respectively

Onset of Hib serum antibody responses: 1-2 weeks after vaccination

Duration: Hib Immunity appears to last 1.5 years

Duration of action: Following all 3 doses of hepatitis B vaccine, immunity will last ~5-7 years

(Continued)

Haemophilus b Conjugate and Hepatitis b Vaccine
(Continued)

Usual Dosage Infants (>8 weeks of age): I.M.: 0.5 mL at 2, 4, and 12-15 months of age (total of 3 doses)

If the recommended schedule cannot be followed, the interval between the first two doses should be at least 2 months and the interval between the second and third dose should be as close as possible to 8-11 months.

Modified Schedule: Children who receive one dose of hepatitis B vaccine at or shortly after birth may receive Comvax™ on a schedule of 2,4, and 12-15 months of age

Administration Administer 0.5 mL I.M. into anterolateral thigh [data suggests that injections given in the buttocks frequently are given into fatty tissue instead of into muscle to result in lower seroconversion rates]; **do not administer intravenously, intradermally, or subcutaneously**

Patient Information May use acetaminophen for postdose fever

Nursing Implications Defer immunization if infection or febrile illness present

Additional Information

Inactivated bacterial vaccine and inactivated viral vaccine

Federal law requires that the date of administration, the vaccine manufacturer, lot number of vaccine and the administering person's name, title and address be entered into the patient's permanent medical record

Dosage Forms Injection: 7.5 mcg *Haemophilus* b PRP and 5 mcg $HB_sAg/0.5$ mL

Haemophilus b Conjugate Vaccine
(hem OF fi lus bee KON joo gate vak SEEN)

Related Information

Guidelines for the Prevention of Opportunistic Infections in Persons with HIV *on page 1388*

Haemophilus influenzae Vaccination *on page 1367*

Immunization Recommendations *on page 1358*

Recommendations of the Advisory Committee on Immunization Practices (ACIP) *on page 1360*

Recommended Immunization Schedule for HIV-Infected Children *on page 1363*

U.S. Brand Names ActHIB®; HibTITER®; OmniHIB™; PedvaxHIB™; ProHIBiT®; TriHIBIT®

Synonyms Diphtheria CRM$_{197}$ Protein Conjugate; Diphtheria Toxoid Conjugate; *Haemophilus* b Oligosaccharide Conjugate Vaccine; *Haemophilus* b Polysaccharide Vaccine; HbCV; Hib Polysaccharide Conjugate; PRP-D

Therapeutic Category Vaccine, Inactivated Bacteria

Use Routine immunization of children 2 months to 5 years of age against invasive disease caused by *H. influenzae*

Unimmunized children ≥5 years of age with a chronic illness known to be associated with increased risk of *Haemophilus influenzae* type b disease, specifically, persons with anatomic or functional asplenia or sickle cell anemia or those who have undergone splenectomy, should receive Hib vaccine.

Haemophilus b conjugate vaccines are not indicated for prevention of bronchitis or other infections due to *H. influenzae* in adults; adults with specific dysfunction or certain complement deficiencies who are at especially high risk of *H. influenzae* type b infection (HIV-infected adults); patients with Hodgkin's disease (vaccinated at least 2 weeks before the initiation of chemotherapy or 3 months after the end of chemotherapy)

Pregnancy Risk Factor C

Contraindications Children with any febrile illness or active infection, known hypersensitivity to *Haemophilus* b polysaccharide vaccine (thimerosal), children who are immunosuppressed or receiving immunosuppressive therapy

Warnings/Precautions Have epinephrine 1:1000 available; children in whom DTP or DT vaccination is deferred: The carrier proteins used in HbOC (but not PRP-OMP) are chemically and immunologically related to toxoids contained in DTP vaccine. Earlier or simultaneous vaccination with diphtheria or tetanus toxoids may be required to elicit an optimal anti-PRP antibody response to HbOC. In contrast, the immunogenicity of PRP-OMP is not affected by vaccination with DTP. In infants in whom DTP or DT vaccination is deferred, PRP-OMP may be advantageous for *Haemophilus influenzae* type b vaccination.

Children with immunologic impairment: Children with chronic illness associated with increased risk of *Haemophilus influenzae* type b disease may have impaired anti-PRP antibody responses to conjugate vaccination. Examples include those with HIV infection, immunoglobulin deficiency, anatomic or functional asplenia, and sickle cell disease, as well as recipients of bone marrow transplants and recipients of chemotherapy for malignancy. Some children with immunologic impairment may benefit from more doses of conjugate vaccine than normally indicated.

Adverse Reactions When administered during the same visit that DTP vaccine is given, the rates of systemic reactions do not differ from those observed only when DTP vaccine is administered. **All serious adverse reactions must be reported to the U.S. Department of Health and Human Services (DHHS) Vaccine Adverse Event Reporting System (VAERS) 1-800-822-7967.**

25%:

Cardiovascular: Edema

Dermatologic: Local erythema

♦ **Halfprin**® **81**® **[OTC]** *see* Aspirin *on page 102*

Halobetasol (hal oh BAY ta sol)

Related Information
  Corticosteroids Comparison *on page 1319*
U.S. Brand Names Ultravate™ Topical
Synonyms Halobetasol Propionate
Therapeutic Category Corticosteroid, Topical (Very High Potency)
Use Relief of inflammatory and pruritic manifestations of corticosteroid-response dermatoses [very high potency topical corticosteroid]
Pregnancy Risk Factor C
Contraindications Hypersensitivity to halobetasol or any component; viral, fungal, or tubercular skin lesions
Warnings/Precautions Not for ophthalmic use; may cause adrenal suppression or insufficiency; application to abraded or inflamed areas or too large of areas of the body may increase the risk of systemic absorption and the risk of adrenal suppression, as may prolonged use or the use of >50 g/week. Topical halobetasol should not be used for the treatment of rosacea or perioral dermatitis.
Adverse Reactions <1%: Itching, dry skin, folliculitis, hypertrichosis, acneiform eruptions, hypopigmentation, perioral dermatitis, allergic contact dermatitis, skin maceration, skin atrophy, striae; local burning, irritation, miliaria; secondary infection
Overdosage/Toxicology When consumed in excessive quantities, systemic hypercorticism and adrenal suppression may occur; in those cases, discontinuation and withdrawal of the corticosteroid should be done judiciously
Mechanism of Action Corticosteroids inhibit the initial manifestations of the inflammatory process (ie, capillary dilation and edema, fibrin deposition, and migration and diapedesis of leukocytes into the inflamed site) as well as later sequelae (angiogenesis, fibroblast proliferation)
Pharmacodynamics/Kinetics
  Absorption: Percutaneous absorption varies by location of topical application and the use of occlusive dressings; ~3% of a topically applied dose of ointment enters the circulation within 96 hours
  Metabolism: Primarily in the liver
  Elimination: By the kidneys
Usual Dosage Children and Adults: Topical: Apply sparingly to skin twice daily, rub in gently and completely; treatment should not exceed 2 consecutive weeks and total dosage should not exceed 50 g/week
Patient Information A thin film of cream or ointment is effective; do not overuse; do not use tight-fitting diapers or plastic pants on children being treated in the diaper area; use only as prescribed, and for no longer than the period prescribed; apply sparingly in light film; rub in lightly; avoid contact with eyes; notify physician if condition being treated persists or worsens
Dosage Forms
  Cream, as propionate: 0.05% (15 g, 45 g)
  Ointment, topical, as propionate: 0.05% (15 g, 45 g)

♦ **Halobetasol Propionate** *see* Halobetasol *on this page*

Halofantrine (ha loe FAN trin)

U.S. Brand Names Halfan®
Synonyms Halofantrine Hydrochloride
Therapeutic Category Antimalarial Agent
Use Treatment of mild to moderate acute malaria caused by susceptible strains of *Plasmodium falciparum* and *Plasmodium vivax*
Pregnancy Risk Factor C
Contraindications Family history of congenital Q-T$_c$ prolongation; hypersensitivity to halofantrine
Warnings/Precautions Monitor closely for decreased hematocrit and hemoglobin, patients with chronic liver disease
Adverse Reactions
  >10%: Dermatologic: Pruritus
  1% to 10%:
    Cardiovascular: Edema
    Central nervous system: Malaise, headache
    Gastrointestinal: Nausea, vomiting
    Hematologic: Leukocytosis
    Hepatic: Elevated LFTs
    Local: Tenderness
    Neuromuscular & skeletal: Myalgia
    Respiratory: Cough
    Miscellaneous: Lymphadenopathy
  <1%: Tachycardia, hypotension, urticaria, hypoglycemia, sterile abscesses, asthma, anaphylactic shock
Drug Interactions CYP2D6 and 3A3/4 enzyme substrate
  Increased toxicity (Q-T$_c$ interval prolongation) with other agents that cause Q-T$_c$ interval prolongation, especially mefloquine
Mechanism of Action Similar to mefloquine; destruction of asexual blood forms, possible inhibition of proton pump
  (Continued)

Halofantrine *(Continued)*

Pharmacodynamics/Kinetics
Mean time to parasite clearance: 40-84 hours

Absorption: Erratic and variable; serum levels are proportional to dose up to 1000 mg; doses greater than this should be divided; may be increased 60% with high fat meals

Distribution: V_d: 570 L/kg; widely distributed in most tissues

Metabolism: To active metabolite in liver

Half-life: 23 hours; metabolite: 82 hours; may be increased in active disease

Elimination: Essentially unchanged in urine

Usual Dosage Oral:
Children <40 kg: 8 mg/kg every 6 hours for 3 doses; repeat in 1 week

Adults: 500 mg every 6 hours for 3 doses; repeat in 1 week

Monitoring Parameters CBC, LFTs, parasite counts

Test Interactions Increased serum transaminases, bilirubin

Patient Information Take on an empty stomach; avoid high fat meals; notify physician of persistent nausea, vomiting, abdominal pain, light stools, dark urine

Nursing Implications Monitor closely for jaundice, other signs of hepatotoxicity

Dosage Forms Tablet, as hydrochloride: 250 mg

- ◆ **Halofantrine Hydrochloride** *see Halofantrine on previous page*
- ◆ **Halog®** *see Halcinonide on page 556*
- ◆ **Halog®-E** *see Halcinonide on page 556*

Haloperidol *(ha loe PER i dole)*

Related Information
Antipsychotic Agents Comparison *on page 1305*

Depression Disorders and Treatments *on page 1465*

U.S. Brand Names Haldol®; Haldol® Decanoate

Canadian Brand Names Haldol® LA; Peridol

Synonyms Haloperidol Decanoate; Haloperidol Lactate

Therapeutic Category Antipsychotic Agent; Sedative

Use Treatment of psychoses, Tourette's disorder, and severe behavioral problems in children; may be used for the emergency sedation of severely agitated or delirious patients; may be effective for infantile autism and has been commonly used to reduce disabling choreiform movements associated with Huntington's disease

Pregnancy Risk Factor C

Contraindications Hypersensitivity to haloperidol or any component; narrow-angle glaucoma, bone marrow suppression, CNS depression, severe liver or cardiac disease, subcortical brain damage; circulatory collapse; severe hypotension or hypertension

Warnings/Precautions Safety and efficacy have not been established in children <3 years of age; watch for hypotension when administering I.M. or I.V.; use with caution in patients with cardiovascular disease or seizures; benefits of therapy must be weighed against risks of therapy; decanoate form should never be given I.V.; some tablets contain tartrazine which may cause allergic reactions; use caution with CNS depression and severe liver or cardiac disease

Adverse Reactions EKG changes, retinal pigmentation are more common than with chlorpromazine

>10%:
Central nervous system: Restlessness, anxiety, extrapyramidal reactions, dystonic reactions, pseudoparkinsonian signs and symptoms, tardive dyskinesia, neuroleptic malignant syndrome (NMS), seizures, altered central temperature regulation, akathisia

Endocrine & metabolic: Edema of the breasts

Gastrointestinal: Weight gain, constipation

1% to 10%:
Cardiovascular: Hypotension (especially orthostatic), tachycardia, arrhythmias, abnormal T waves with prolonged ventricular repolarization

Central nervous system: Hallucinations, sedation, drowsiness, persistent tardive dyskinesia

Genitourinary: Dysuria

<1%: Tardive dystonia, hyperpigmentation, pruritus, rash, contact dermatitis, alopecia, photosensitivity (rare), amenorrhea, galactorrhea, gynecomastia, sexual dysfunction, adynamic ileus, nausea, vomiting, xerostomia (problem for denture user), urinary retention, overflow incontinence, priapism, agranulocytosis, leukopenia (usually inpatients with large doses for prolonged periods), cholestatic jaundice, obstructive jaundice, blurred vision, retinal pigmentation, decreased visual acuity (may be irreversible), laryngospasm, respiratory depression, heat stroke

Overdosage/Toxicology
Symptoms of overdose include deep sleep, dystonia, agitation, dysrhythmias, extrapyramidal symptoms

Following initiation of essential overdose management, toxic symptom treatment and supportive treatment should be initiated. Critical cardiac arrhythmias often respond to I.V. lidocaine, while other antiarrhythmics can be used. Neuroleptics often cause extrapyramidal symptoms (eg, dystonic reactions) requiring management with benztropine mesylate I.V. 1-2 mg (adult) may be effective. These agents are generally effective within 2-5 minutes.

Drug Interactions CYP1A2 enzyme substrate, CYP2D6 enzyme substrate (minor); CYP2D6 enzyme inhibitor

Decreased effect: Carbamazepine and phenobarbital may increase metabolism and decreased effectiveness of haloperidol

Increased toxicity: CNS depressants may increase adverse effects; epinephrine may cause hypotension; haloperidol and anticholinergic agents may increase intraocular pressure; concurrent use with lithium has occasionally caused acute encephalopathy-like syndrome

Stability

Protect oral dosage forms from light

Haloperidol lactate injection should be stored at controlled room temperature and protected from light, freezing and temperatures >40°C; exposure to light may cause discoloration and the development of a grayish-red precipitate over several weeks

Haloperidol lactate may be administered IVPB or I.V. infusion in D_5W solutions; NS solutions should not be used due to reports of decreased stability and incompatibility

Standardized dose: 0.5-100 mg/50-100 mL D_5W

Stability of standardized solutions is 38 days at room temperature (24°C)

Mechanism of Action Blocks postsynaptic mesolimbic dopaminergic D_1 and D_2 receptors in the brain; exhibits a strong alpha-adrenergic blocking and anticholinergic effect, depresses the release of hypothalamic and hypophyseal hormones; believed to depress the reticular activating system thus affecting basal metabolism, body temperature, wakefulness, vasomotor tone, and emesis

Pharmacodynamics/Kinetics

Onset of sedation: I.V.: Within 1 hour

Duration of action: ~3 weeks for decanoate form

Distribution: Crosses the placenta; appears in breast milk

Protein binding: 90%

Metabolism: In the liver to inactive compounds

Bioavailability: Oral: 60%

Half-life: 20 hours

Time to peak serum concentration: 20 minutes

Elimination: 33% to 40% excreted in urine within 5 days; an additional 15% excreted in feces

Usual Dosage

Children: 3-12 years (15-40 kg): Oral:

Initial: 0.05 mg/kg/day or 0.25-0.5 mg/day given in 2-3 divided doses; increase by 0.25-0.5 mg every 5-7 days; maximum: 0.15 mg/kg/day

Usual maintenance:

Agitation or hyperkinesia: 0.01-0.03 mg/kg/day once daily

Nonpsychotic disorders: 0.05-0.075 mg/kg/day in 2-3 divided doses

Psychotic disorders: 0.05-0.15 mg/kg/day in 2-3 divided doses

Children 6-12 years: I.M. (as lactate): 1-3 mg/dose every 4-8 hours to a maximum of 0.15 mg/kg/day; change over to oral therapy as soon as able

Adults:

Oral: 0.5-5 mg 2-3 times/day; usual maximum: 30 mg/day; some patients may require up to 100 mg/day

I.M. (as lactate): 2-5 mg every 4-8 hours as needed

I.M. (as decanoate): Initial: 10-15 times the daily oral dose administered at 3- to 4-week intervals

Sedation in the Intensive Care Unit:

I.M./IVP/IVPB: May repeat bolus doses after 30 minutes until calm achieved then administer 50% of the maximum dose every 6 hours

Mild agitation: 0.5-2 mg

Moderate agitation: 2-5 mg

Severe agitation: 10-20 mg

Continuous intravenous infusion (100 mg/100 mL D_5W): Rates of 1-40 mg/hour have been used

Elderly (nonpsychotic patients, dementia behavior):

Initial: Oral: 0.25-0.5 mg 1-2 times/day; increase dose at 4- to 7-day intervals by 0.25-0.5 mg/day; increase dosing intervals (twice daily, 3 times/day, etc) as necessary to control response or side effects

Maximum daily dose: 50 mg; gradual increases (titration) may prevent side effects or decrease their severity

Hemodialysis/peritoneal dialysis: Supplemental dose is not necessary

Dietary Considerations Alcohol: Additive CNS effect, avoid use

Administration The decanoate injectable formulation should be administered I.M. only, **do not administer decanoate I.V.** Dilute the oral concentrate with water or juice before administration

Monitoring Parameters Monitor orthostatic blood pressures 3-5 days after initiation of therapy or a dose increase; observe for tremor and abnormal movement or posturing (extrapyramidal symptoms)

Reference Range

Therapeutic: 5-15 ng/mL (SI: 10-30 nmol/L) (psychotic disorders - less for Tourette's and mania)

Toxic: >42 ng/mL (SI: >84 nmol/L)

Test Interactions ↓ cholesterol (S)

Patient Information May cause drowsiness, restlessness, avoid alcohol and other CNS depressants, rise slowly from recumbent position; use of supportive stockings may help prevent orthostatic hypotension; do not alter dosage or discontinue without consulting physician; oral concentrate must be diluted in 2-4 oz of liquid (water, fruit juice, carbonated drinks, milk, or pudding)

(Continued)

Haloperidol *(Continued)*

Nursing Implications Avoid skin contact with oral suspension or solution; may cause contact dermatitis

Dosage Forms
Concentrate, oral, as lactate: 2 mg/mL (5 mL, 10 mL, 15 mL, 120 mL, 240 mL)
Injection, as decanoate: 50 mg/mL (1 mL, 5 mL); 100 mg/mL (1 mL, 5 mL)
Injection, as lactate: 5 mg/mL (1 mL, 2 mL, 2.5 mL, 10 mL)
Tablet: 0.5 mg, 1 mg, 2 mg, 5 mg, 10 mg, 20 mg

- **Haloperidol Decanoate** *see Haloperidol on page 558*
- **Haloperidol Lactate** *see Haloperidol on page 558*

Haloprogin *(ha loe PROE jin)*

U.S. Brand Names Halotex®

Therapeutic Category Antifungal Agent, Topical

Use Topical treatment of tinea pedis (athlete's foot), tinea cruris (jock itch), tinea corporis (ringworm), tinea manuum caused by *Trichophyton rubrum*, *Trichophyton tonsurans*, *Trichophyton mentagrophytes*, *Microsporum canis*, or *Epidermophyton floccosum*; topical treatment of *Malassezia furfur*

Pregnancy Risk Factor B

Contraindications Hypersensitivity to haloprogin or any component

Warnings/Precautions Safety and efficacy have not been established in children

Adverse Reactions <1%: Pruritus, folliculitis, vesicle formation, erythema, irritation, burning sensation

Mechanism of Action Interferes with fungal DNA replication to inhibit yeast cell respiration and disrupt its cell membrane

Pharmacodynamics/Kinetics
Absorption: Poorly through the skin (~11%)
Metabolism: To trichlorophenol
Elimination: In urine, 75% as unchanged drug

Usual Dosage Topical: Children and Adults: Apply liberally twice daily for 2-3 weeks; intertriginous areas may require up to 4 weeks of treatment

Patient Information Avoid contact with eyes; for external use only; improvement should occur within 4 weeks; discontinue use if sensitization or irritation occur

Dosage Forms
Cream: 1% (15 g, 30 g)
Solution, topical: 1% with alcohol 75% (10 mL, 30 mL)

- **Halotestin®** *see Fluoxymesterone on page 503*
- **Halotex®** *see Haloprogin on this page*
- **Halotussin® [OTC]** *see Guaifenesin on page 549*
- **Halotussin® DAC** *see Guaifenesin, Pseudoephedrine, and Codeine on page 551*
- **Halotussin®-DM [OTC]** *see Guaifenesin and Dextromethorphan on page 550*
- **Haltran® [OTC]** *see Ibuprofen on page 593*
- **Havrix®** *see Hepatitis A Vaccine on page 563*
- **HbCV** *see Haemophilus b Conjugate Vaccine on page 554*
- **HBIG** *see Hepatitis B Immune Globulin on page 564*
- **H-BIG®** *see Hepatitis B Immune Globulin on page 564*
- **25-HCC** *see Calcifediol on page 170*
- **hCG** *see Chorionic Gonadotropin on page 258*
- **HCTZ** *see Hydrochlorothiazide on page 574*
- **HDCV** *see Rabies Virus Vaccine on page 1007*
- **Head & Shoulders® Intensive Treatment [OTC]** *see Selenium Sulfide on page 1055*
- **Healon®** *see Sodium Hyaluronate on page 1069*
- **Healon® GV** *see Sodium Hyaluronate on page 1069*
- **Heart Failure: Management of Patients With Left-Ventricular Systolic Dysfunction** *see page 1472*
- *Helicobacter pylori* **Treatment** *see page 1473*
- **Helidac™** *see Bismuth Subsalicylate, Metronidazole, and Tetracycline on page 147*
- **Helistat®** *see Microfibrillar Collagen Hemostat on page 776*
- **Hemabate™** *see Carboprost Tromethamine on page 195*
- **Hemocyte® [OTC]** *see Ferrous Fumarate on page 478*
- **Hemofil® M** *see Antihemophilic Factor (Human) on page 88*
- **Hemonyne®** *see Factor IX Complex (Human) on page 464*
- **Hemotene®** *see Microfibrillar Collagen Hemostat on page 776*
- **Hemril-HC® Uniserts®** *see Hydrocortisone on page 579*
- **HepaLean®** *see Heparin on this page*
- **HepaLean® LCO** *see Heparin on this page*
- **HepaLean®-LOK** *see Heparin on this page*

Heparin *(HEP a rin)*

Related Information
Heparins Comparison *on page 1324*

U.S. Brand Names Hep-Lock®; Liquaemin®

Canadian Brand Names Calcilean®; HepaLean®; HepaLean® LCO; HepaLean®-LOK

Synonyms Heparin Calcium; Heparin Lock Flush; Heparin Sodium

Therapeutic Category Anticoagulant

Use Prophylaxis and treatment of thromboembolic disorders

Pregnancy Risk Factor C

Contraindications Hypersensitivity to heparin or any component; severe thrombocytopenia, subacute bacterial endocarditis, suspected intracranial hemorrhage, uncontrollable bleeding (unless secondary to disseminated intravascular coagulation)

Warnings/Precautions

Use with caution as hemorrhaging may occur; risk factors for hemorrhage include I.M. injections, peptic ulcer disease, increased capillary permeability, menstruation; severe renal, hepatic or biliary disease; use with caution in patients with shock, severe hypotension

Some preparations contain benzyl alcohol as a preservative. In neonates, large amounts of benzyl alcohol (>100 mg/kg/day) have been associated with fatal toxicity (gasping syndrome). The use of preservative-free heparin is, therefore, recommended in neonates. Some preparations contain sulfite which may cause allergic reactions.

Heparin does not possess fibrinolytic activity and, therefore, cannot lyse established thrombi; discontinue heparin if hemorrhage occurs; severe hemorrhage or overdosage may require protamine

Use caution with white clot syndrome (new thrombus associated with thrombocytopenia) and heparin resistance

Adverse Reactions

>10%:

Dermatologic: Unexplained bruising

Gastrointestinal: Constipation, vomiting of blood

Hematologic: Hemorrhage, blood in urine, bleeding from gums

1% to 10%:

Cardiovascular: Chest pain

Genitourinary: Frequent or persistent erection

Neuromuscular & skeletal: Peripheral neuropathy

Miscellaneous: Allergic reactions

<1%: Fever, headache, chills, urticaria, nausea, vomiting; thrombocytopenia (heparin-associated thrombocytopenia occurs in <1% of patients, immune thrombocytopenia occurs with progressive fall in platelet counts and, in some cases, thromboembolic complications; daily platelet counts for 5-7 days at initiation of therapy may help detect the onset of this complication); elevated liver enzymes, irritation, ulceration, cutaneous necrosis have been rarely reported with deep S.C. injections, osteoporosis (chronic therapy effect)

Overdosage/Toxicology

The primary symptom of overdose is bleeding

Antidote is protamine; dose 1 mg per 1 mg (100 units) of heparin. Discontinue all heparin if evidence of progressive immune thrombocytopenia occurs.

Drug Interactions

Decreased effect with digoxin, tetracycline, nicotine, antihistamine, I.V. NTG

Increased toxicity with NSAIDs, ASA, dipyridamole, dextran, hydroxychloroquine

Stability

Heparin solutions are colorless to slightly yellow; minor color variations do not affect therapeutic efficacy

Heparin should be stored at controlled room temperature and protected from freezing and temperatures >40°C

Stability at room temperature and refrigeration:

Prepared bag: 24 hours

Premixed bag: After seal is broken 4 days

Out of overwrap stability: 30 days

Standard diluent: 25,000 units/500 mL D_5W (premixed)

Minimum volume: 250 mL D_5W

Mechanism of Action Potentiates the action of antithrombin III and thereby inactivates thrombin (as well as activated coagulation factors IX, X, XI, XII, and plasmin) and prevents the conversion of fibrinogen to fibrin; heparin also stimulates release of lipoprotein lipase (lipoprotein lipase hydrolyzes triglycerides to glycerol and free fatty acids)

Pharmacodynamics/Kinetics

Onset of anticoagulation: I.V.: Immediate with use; S.C.: Within 20-30 minutes

Absorption: Oral, rectal, I.M.: Erratic at best from all these routes of administration; S.C. absorption is also erratic, but considered acceptable for prophylactic use

Distribution: Does not cross placenta; does not appear in breast milk

Metabolism: Hepatic; believed to be partially metabolized in the reticuloendothelial system

Half-life: Mean: 1.5 hours; Range: 1-2 hours; affected by obesity, renal function, hepatic function, malignancy, presence of pulmonary embolism, and infections

Elimination: Renal, small amount excreted unchanged in urine

Usual Dosage

Line flushing: When using daily flushes of heparin to maintain patency of single and double lumen central catheters, 10 units/mL is commonly used for younger infants (eg, <10 kg) while 100 units/mL is used for older infants, children, and adults. Capped PVC catheters and peripheral heparin locks require flushing more frequently (eg, every 6-8 hours). Volume of heparin flush is usually similar to volume of catheter (or slightly greater). Additional flushes should be given when stagnant blood is observed in catheter, after catheter is used for drug or blood administration, and after blood withdrawal from catheter.

(Continued)

Heparin (Continued)

Addition of heparin (0.5-1 unit/mL) to peripheral and central TPN has been shown to increase duration of line patency. The final concentration of heparin used for TPN solutions may need to be decreased to 0.5 units/mL in small infants receiving larger amounts of volume in order to avoid approaching therapeutic amounts. Arterial lines are heparinized with a final concentration of 1 unit/mL.

Children:

Intermittent I.V.: Initial: 50-100 units/kg, then 50-100 units/kg every 4 hours

I.V. infusion: Initial: 50 units/kg, then 15-25 units/kg/hour; increase dose by 2-4 units/kg/hour every 6-8 hours as required

Adults:

Prophylaxis (low-dose heparin): S.C.: 5000 units every 8-12 hours

Intermittent I.V.: Initial: 10,000 units, then 50-70 units/kg (5000-10,000 units) every 4-6 hours

I.V. infusion: 50 units/kg to start, then 15-25 units/kg/hour as continuous infusion; increase dose by 5 units/kg/hour every 4 hours as required according to PTT results, usual range: 10-30 units/hour

Weight-based protocol: 80 units/kg I.V. push followed by continuous infusion of 18 units/kg/hour; see table.

Standard Heparin Solution
(25,000 units/500 mL D$_5$W)

To Administer a Dose of	Set Infusion Rate at
400 units/h	8 mL/h
500 units/h	10 mL/h
600 units/h	12 mL/h
700 units/h	14 mL/h
800 units/h	16 mL/h
900 units/h	18 mL/h
1000 units/h	20 mL/h
1100 units/h	22 mL/h
1200 units/h	24 mL/h
1300 units/h	26 mL/h
1400 units/h	28 mL/h
1500 units/h	30 mL/h
1600 units/h	32 mL/h
1700 units/h	34 mL/h
1800 units/h	36 mL/h
1900 units/h	38 mL/h
2000 units/h	40 mL/h

Administration Do not administer I.M. due to pain, irritation, and hematoma formation; central venous catheters must be flushed with heparin solution when newly inserted, daily (at the time of tubing change), after blood withdrawal or transfusion, and after an intermittent infusion through an injectable cap. A volume of at least 10 mL of blood should be removed and discarded from a heparinized line before blood samples are sent for coagulation testing.

Monitoring Parameters Platelet counts, PTT, hemoglobin, hematocrit, signs of bleeding

For intermittent I.V. injections, PTT is measured 3.5-4 hours after I.V. injection

Note: Continuous I.V. infusion is preferred vs I.V. intermittent injections. For full-dose heparin (ie, nonlow-dose), the dose should be titrated according to PTT results. For anticoagulation, an APTT 1.5-2.5 times normal is usually desired. APTT is usually measured prior to heparin therapy, 6-8 hours after initiation of a continuous infusion (following a loading dose), and 6-8 hours after changes in the infusion rate; increase or decrease infusion by 2-4 units/kg/hour dependent on PTT. See table.

Heparin Infusion Dose Adjustment

APTT	Adjustment
>3x control	↓ Infusion rate 50%
2-3x control	↓ Infusion rate 25%
1.5-2x control	No change
<1.5x control	↑ Rate of infusion 25%; max 2500 units/h

Reference Range Heparin: 0.3-0.5 unit/mL; APTT: 1.5-2.5 times **the patient's baseline**
Test Interactions ↑ thyroxine (S) (competitive protein binding methods); ↑ PT, ↑ PTT, ↑ bleeding time
Dosage Forms

Heparin sodium:

Lock flush injection:

Beef lung source: 10 units/mL (1 mL, 2 mL, 2.5 mL, 3 mL, 5 mL, 10 mL, 30 mL); 100 units/mL (1 mL, 2 mL, 2.5 mL, 3 mL, 5 mL, 10 mL, 30 mL)

Porcine intestinal mucosa source: 10 units/mL (1 mL, 2 mL, 10 mL, 30 mL); 100 units/mL (1 mL, 2 mL, 10 mL, 30 mL)

Porcine intestinal mucosa source, preservative free: 10 units/mL (1 mL); 100 units/mL (1 mL)

Multiple-dose vial injection:

Beef lung source, with preservative: 1000 units/mL (5 mL, 10 mL, 30 mL); 5000 units/mL (10 mL); 10,000 units/mL (4 mL, 5 mL, 10 mL); 20,000 units/mL (2 mL, 5 mL, 10 mL); 40,000 units/mL (5 mL)

Porcine intestinal mucosa source, with preservative: 1000 units/mL (10 mL, 30 mL); 5000 units/mL (10 mL); 10,000 units/mL (4 mL); 20,000 units/mL (2 mL, 5 mL)

Single-dose vial injection:

Beef lung source: 1000 units/mL (1 mL); 5000 units/mL (1 mL); 10,000 units/mL (1 mL); 20,000 units/mL (1 mL); 40,000 units/mL (1 mL)

Porcine intestinal mucosa: 1000 units/mL (1 mL); 5000 units/mL (1 mL); 10,000 units/mL (1 mL); 20,000 units/mL (1 mL); 40,000 units/mL (1 mL)

Unit dose injection:

Porcine intestinal mucosa source, with preservative: 1000 units/dose (1 mL, 2 mL); 2500 units/dose (1 mL); 5000 units/dose (0.5 mL, 1 mL); 7500 units/dose (1 mL); 10,000 units/dose (1 mL); 15,000 units/dose (1 mL); 20,000 units/dose (1 mL)

Heparin sodium infusion, porcine intestinal mucosa source:

D_5W: 40 units/mL (500 mL); 50 units/mL (250 mL, 500 mL); 100 units/mL (100 mL, 250 mL)

NaCl 0.45%: 2 units/mL (500 mL, 1000 mL); 50 units/mL (250 mL); 100 units/mL (250 mL)

NaCl 0.9%: 2 units/mL (500 mL, 1000 mL); 5 units/mL (1000 mL); 50 units/mL (250 mL, 500 mL, 1000 mL)

Heparin calcium:

Unit dose injection, porcine intestinal mucosa, preservative free (Calciparine®): 5000 units/dose (0.2 mL); 12,500 units/dose (0.5 mL); 20,000 units/dose (0.8 mL)

♦ **Heparin Calcium** *see* Heparin *on page 560*
♦ **Heparin Cofactor I** *see* Antithrombin III *on page 91*
♦ **Heparin Lock Flush** *see* Heparin *on page 560*
♦ **Heparins Comparison** *see page 1324*
♦ **Heparin Sodium** *see* Heparin *on page 560*

Hepatitis A Vaccine (hep a TYE tis aye vak SEEN)

Related Information

Immunization Recommendations *on page 1358*
Prevention of Hepatitis A Through Active or Passive Immunization *on page 1370*
Prophylaxis for Patients Exposed to Common Communicable Diseases *on page 1384*

U.S. Brand Names Havrix®; VAQTA®

Therapeutic Category Vaccine, Inactivated Virus

Use For populations desiring protection against hepatitis A or for populations at high risk of exposure to hepatitis A virus (travelers to developing countries, household and sexual contacts of persons infected with hepatitis A), child day care employees, patients with chronic liver disease, illicit drug users, male homosexuals, institutional workers (eg, institutions for the mentally and physically handicapped persons, prisons, etc), and healthcare workers who may be exposed to hepatitis A virus (eg, laboratory employees); protection lasts for approximately 15 years

Pregnancy Risk Factor C

Contraindications Hypersensitivity to any component of hepatitis A vaccine

Warnings/Precautions Use caution in patients with serious active infection, cardiovascular disease, or pulmonary disorders; treatment for anaphylactic reactions should be immediately available

Adverse Reactions All serious adverse reactions must be reported to the U.S. Department of Health and Human Services (DHHS) Vaccine Adverse Event Reporting System (VAERS) 1-800-822-7967.

Percentage unknown: Fatigue, fever (rare), transient LFT abnormalities

>10%:

Central nervous system: Headache

Local: Pain, tenderness, and warmth

1% to 10%:

Endocrine & metabolic: Pharyngitis (1.2%)

Gastrointestinal: Abdominal pain (1.2%)

Local: Cutaneous reactions at the injection site (soreness, edema, and redness)

Drug Interactions No interference of immunogenicity was reported when mixed with hepatitis B vaccine

Mechanism of Action As an inactivated virus vaccine, hepatitis A vaccine offers active immunization against hepatitis A virus infection at an effective immune response rate in up to 99% of subjects

Pharmacodynamics/Kinetics

Onset of action (protection): 3 weeks after a single dose

Duration: Neutralizing antibodies have persisted for >3 years; unconfirmed evidence indicates that antibody levels may persist for 5-10 years

(Continued)

Hepatitis A Vaccine *(Continued)*

Usual Dosage I.M.:
> Havrix®:
>> Children 2-18 years: 720 ELISA units (administered as 2 injections of 360 ELISA units [0.5 mL]) 15-30 days prior to travel with a booster 6-12 months following primary immunization; the deltoid muscle should be used for I.M. injection
>> Adults: 1440 ELISA units(1 mL) 15-30 days prior to travel with a booster 6-12 months following primary immunization; injection should be in the deltoid
> VAQTA®:
>> Children 2-17 years: 25 units (0.5 mL) with 25 units (0.5 mL) booster to be given 6-18 months after primary immunization
>> Adults: 50 units (1 mL) with 50 units (1 mL) booster to be given 6 months after primary immunization

Administration Inject I.M. into the deltoid muscle, if possible

Monitoring Parameters Liver function tests

Reference Range Seroconversion for Havrix®: Antibody >20 milli-international units/mL

Additional Information Some investigators suggest simultaneous or sequential administration of inactivated hepatitis A vaccine and immune globulin for postexposure protection, especially for travelers requiring rapid immunization, although a slight decrease in vaccine immunogenicity may be observed with this technique

Dosage Forms
> Injection: 360 ELISA units/0.5 mL (0.5 mL); 1440 ELISA units/mL (1 mL)
> Injection, pediatric: 720 ELISA units/0.5 mL (0.5 mL)
> Injection (VAQTA®): 50 units/mL (1 mL)

Hepatitis B Immune Globulin (hep a TYE tis bee i MYUN GLOB yoo lin)

Related Information
> Immunization Recommendations *on page 1358*
> Postexposure Prophylaxis for Hepatitis B *on page 1383*

U.S. Brand Names H-BIG®; Hep-B Gammagee®; HyperHep®

Synonyms HBIG

Therapeutic Category Immune Globulin

Use Provide prophylactic passive immunity to hepatitis B infection to those individuals exposed; newborns of mothers known to be hepatitis B surface antigen positive; hepatitis B immune globulin is not indicated for treatment of active hepatitis B infections and is ineffective in the treatment of chronic active hepatitis B infection

Pregnancy Risk Factor C

Contraindications Hypersensitivity to hepatitis B immune globulin or any component; allergies to gamma globulin or anti-immunoglobulin antibodies; allergies to thimerosal; IgA deficiency; I.M. injections in patients with thrombocytopenia or coagulation disorders

Adverse Reactions
> 1% to 10%:
>> Central nervous system: Dizziness, malaise
>> Dermatologic: Urticaria, angioedema, rash, erythema
>> Local: Pain and tenderness at injection site
>> Neuromuscular & skeletal: Arthralgia
> <1%: Anaphylaxis

Drug Interactions Interferes with immune response of live virus vaccines

Stability Refrigerate at 2°C to 8°C (36°F to 46°F); do not freeze

Mechanism of Action Hepatitis B immune globulin (HBIG) is a nonpyrogenic sterile solution containing 10% to 18% protein of which at least 80% is monomeric immunoglobulin G (IgG). HBIG differs from immune globulin in the amount of anti-HB$_s$. Immune globulin is prepared from plasma that is not preselected for anti-HB$_s$ content. HBIG is prepared from plasma preselected for high titer anti-HB$_s$. In the U.S., HBIG has an anti-HB$_s$ high titer >1:100,000 by IRA. There is no evidence that the causative agent of AIDS (HTLV-III/LAV) is transmitted by HBIG.

Pharmacodynamics/Kinetics
> Absorption: Slow
> Time to peak serum concentration: 1-6 days

Usual Dosage I.M.:
> Newborns: Hepatitis B: 0.5 mL as soon after birth as possible (within 12 hours); may repeat at 3 months in order for a higher rate of prevention of the carrier state to be achieved; at this time an active vaccination program with the vaccine may begin
> Adults: Postexposure prophylaxis: 0.06 mL/kg as soon as possible after exposure (ie, within 24 hours of needlestick, ocular, or mucosal exposure or within 14 days of sexual exposure); usual dose: 3-5 mL; repeat at 28-30 days after exposure
> Note: HBIG may be administered at the same time (but at a different site) or up to 1 month preceding hepatitis B vaccination without impairing the active immune response

Administration I.M. injection only in gluteal or deltoid region; to prevent injury from injection, care should be taken when giving to patients with thrombocytopenia or bleeding disorders; has been administered intravenously in hepatitis B-positive liver transplant patients

Additional Information Has been administered intravenously in hepatitis B-positive liver transplant patients

Dosage Forms Injection:
> H-BIG®: 4 mL, 5 mL
> HyperHep®: 0.5 mL, 1 mL, 5 mL

♦ **Hepatitis B Inactivated Virus Vaccine (plasma derived)** *see* Hepatitis B Vaccine *on this page*

♦ **Hepatitis B Inactivated Virus Vaccine (recombinant DNA)** *see* Hepatitis B Vaccine *on this page*

Hepatitis B Vaccine (hep a TYE tis bee vak SEEN)

Related Information

Adverse Events and Vaccination *on page 1369*
Guidelines for the Prevention of Opportunistic Infections in Persons with HIV *on page 1388*
Immunization Recommendations *on page 1358*
Postexposure Prophylaxis for Hepatitis B *on page 1383*
Prophylaxis for Patients Exposed to Common Communicable Diseases *on page 1384*
Recommendations of the Advisory Committee on Immunization Practices (ACIP) *on page 1360*
Recommended Childhood Immunization Schedule - US - January-December, 1999 *on page 1359*
Recommended Immunization Schedule for HIV-Infected Children *on page 1363*

U.S. Brand Names Engerix-B®; Recombivax HB®

Synonyms Hepatitis B Inactivated Virus Vaccine (plasma derived); Hepatitis B Inactivated Virus Vaccine (recombinant DNA)

Therapeutic Category Vaccine, Inactivated Virus

Use Immunization against infection caused by all known subtypes of hepatitis B virus, in individuals considered at high risk of potential exposure to hepatitis B virus or HB_sAg-positive materials; see chart.

Pre-exposure Prophylaxis for Hepatitis B
Health care workers*
Special patient groups (eg, adolescents, infants born to HB_sAg–positive mothers, military personnel, etc)
Hemodialysis patients†
Recipients of certain blood products‡
Lifestyle factors
Homosexual and bisexual men
Intravenous drug abusers
Heterosexually active persons with multiple sexual partners or recently acquired sexually transmitted diseases
Environmental factors
Household and sexual contacts of HBV carriers
Prison inmates
Clients and staff of institutions for the mentally handicapped
Residents, immigrants and refugees from areas with endemic HBV infection
International travelers at increased risk of acquiring HBV infection

*The risk of hepatitis B virus (HBV) infection for health care workers varies both between hospitals and within hospitals. Hepatitis B vaccination is recommended for all health care workers with blood exposure.

†Hemodialysis patients often respond poorly to hepatitis B vaccination; higher vaccine doses or increased number of doses are required. A special formulation of one vaccine is now available for such persons (Recombivax HB®, 40 mcg/mL). The anti-HB$_s$ (antibody to hepatitis B surface antigen) response of such persons should be tested after they are vaccinated, and those who have not responded should be revaccinated with 1-3 additional doses

Patients with chronic renal disease should be vaccinated as early as possible, ideally before they require hemodialysis. In addition, their anti-HB$_s$ levels should be monitored at 6-12 month intervals to assess the need for revaccination.

‡Patients with hemophilia should be immunized subcutaneously, not intramuscularly.

Pregnancy Risk Factor C

Contraindications Hypersensitivity to yeast, hypersensitivity to hepatitis B vaccine or any component

Adverse Reactions All serious adverse reactions must be reported to the U.S. Department of Health and Human Services (DHHS) Vaccine Adverse Event Reporting System (VAERS) 1-800-822-7967.
>10%:
    Central nervous system: Fever, malaise, fatigue (14%), headache
    Local: Mild local tenderness (22%), local inflammatory reaction
1% to 10%:
    Gastrointestinal: Nausea, vomiting
    Respiratory: Pharyngitis
<1%: Tachycardia, hypotension, sensation of warmth, flushing, lightheadedness, chills, somnolence, insomnia, irritability, agitation, pruritus, rash, erythema, urticaria, GI disturbances, constipation, abdominal cramps, dyspepsia, anorexia, dysuria, arthralgia, myalgia, stiffness in back/neck/arm or shoulder, earache, rhinitis, cough, epistaxis, diaphoresis

Drug Interactions Decreased effect: Immunosuppressive agents

Stability Refrigerate, do not freeze

Mechanism of Action Recombinant hepatitis B vaccine is a noninfectious subunit viral vaccine. The vaccine is derived from hepatitis B surface antigen (HB_sAg) produced through recombinant DNA techniques from yeast cells. The portion of the hepatitis B
(Continued)

565

Hepatitis B Vaccine *(Continued)*

gene which codes for HB$_s$Ag is cloned into yeast which is then cultured to produce hepatitis B vaccine.

Pharmacodynamics/Kinetics Duration of action: Following all 3 doses of hepatitis B vaccine, immunity will last approximately 5-7 years

Usual Dosage See tables.

Routine Immunization Regimen of Three I.M. Hepatitis B Vaccine Doses

Age	Initial		1 mo		6 mo	
	Recom-bivax HB® (mL)	Engerix-B® (mL)	Recom-bivax HB® (mL)	Engerix-B® (mL)	Recom-bivax HB® (mL)	Engerix-B® (mL)
Birth* - 10 y	0.25**	0.5	0.25**	0.5	0.25**	0.5
11-19 y	0.5	1	0.5	1	0.5	1
≥20 y	1	1	1	1	1	1
Dialysis or immunocom-promised patients		2†		2†		2†

*Infants born of HB$_s$ Ag **negative** mothers.

**0.5 mL of the 5 mcg/0.5 mL (adolescent/high-risk infant) product or 0.5 mL of the 25 mcg/0.5 mL pediatric formulation

†Two 1 mL doses given at different sites.

Postexposure Prophylaxis Recommended Dosage for Infants Born to HB$_s$Ag-Positive Mothers

Treatment	Birth	Within 7 d	1 mo	6 mo
Engerix-B® (pediatric product dose 10 mcg/0.5 mL)	*	0.5 mL*	0.5 mL	0.5 mL
Recombivax HB® (high-risk infant product dose 5 mcg/0.5 mL)	*	0.25 mL*†	0.25 mL†	0.25 mL†
Hepatitis B immune globulin	0.5 mL	—	—	—

Note: An alternate regimen is administration of the vaccine at birth, within 7 days of birth, and 1, 2, and 12 months later.

*The first dose may be given at birth at the same time as HBIG, but give in the opposite anterolateral thigh. This may better ensure vaccine absorption.

†Or 0.5 mL of the pediatric product (0.25 mcg/0.5 mL)

Dialysis regimen: Use Recombivax HB® formulation (40 mcg/mL); initial: 40 mcg/mL, then at 1 and 6 months; revaccination: if anti-HB$_s$ <10 mIU/mL ≥1-2 months after 3rd dose

Administration I.M. injection only; in adults, the deltoid muscle is the preferred site; the anterolateral thigh is the recommended site in infants and young children

Patient Information Must complete full course of injections for adequate immunization

Nursing Implications Rare chance of anaphylactoid reaction; have epinephrine available

Additional Information Inactivated virus vaccine; federal law requires that the date of administration, the vaccine manufacturer, lot number of vaccine, and the administering person's name, title and address be entered into the patient's permanent medical record

Dosage Forms Injection:

Recombinant DNA (Engerix-B®)

Pediatric formulation: Hepatitis B surface antigen 10 mcg/0.5 mL (0.5 mL)

Adult formulation: Hepatitis B surface antigen 20 mcg/mL (1 mL)

Recombinant DNA (Recombivax HB®):

Pediatric formulation: Hepatitis B surface antigen 2.5 mg/0.5 mL (0.5 mL/3 mL)

Adolescent/high-risk infant formulation: Hepatitis B surface antigen 5 mcg/0.5 mL (0.5 mL)

Adult formulation: Hepatitis B surface antigen 10 mcg/mL (1 mL, 3 mL)

Dialysis formulation, recombinant DNA: Hepatitis B surface antigen 40 mcg/mL (1 mL)

♦ **Hep-B Gammagee®** *see* Hepatitis B Immune Globulin *on page 564*

♦ **Hep-Lock®** *see* Heparin *on page 560*

♦ **Heptalac®** *see* Lactulose *on page 656*

♦ **Herceptin®** *see* Trastuzumab *on page 1169*

♦ **HES** *see* Hetastarch *on this page*

♦ **Hespan®** *see* Hetastarch *on this page*

Hetastarch *(HET a starch)*

U.S. Brand Names Hespan®

Synonyms HES; Hydroxyethyl Starch

Therapeutic Category Plasma Volume Expander, Colloid

Use Blood volume expander used in treatment of shock or impending shock when blood or blood products are not available; does not have oxygen-carrying capacity and is not a substitute for blood or plasma

Pregnancy Risk Factor C

Contraindications Severe bleeding disorders, renal failure with oliguria or anuria, or severe congestive heart failure

Warnings/Precautions Anaphylactoid reactions have occurred; use with caution in patients with thrombocytopenia (may interfere with platelet function); large volume may cause drops in hemoglobin concentrations; use with caution in patients at risk from overexpansion of blood volume, including the very young or aged patients, those with congestive heart failure or pulmonary edema; large volumes may interfere with platelet function and prolong PT and PTT times

Adverse Reactions <1%: Peripheral edema, heart failure, circulatory overload, fever, chills, headaches, itching, pruritus, vomiting, bleeding, prolongation of PT, PTT, clotting time, and bleeding time, myalgia, hypersensitivity

Overdosage/Toxicology
Symptoms of overdose include heart failure, nausea, vomiting, circulatory overload, bleeding
Treatment is supportive

Stability Do not use if crystalline precipitate forms or is turbid deep brown

Mechanism of Action Produces plasma volume expansion by virtue of its highly colloidal starch structure, similar to albumin

Pharmacodynamics/Kinetics
Onset of volume expansion: I.V.: Within 30 minutes
Duration: 24-36 hours
Metabolism: Molecules >50,000 daltons require enzymatic degradation by the reticuloen-dothelial system or amylases in the blood prior to urinary and fecal excretion
Elimination: Smaller molecular weight molecules are readily excreted in urine

Usual Dosage I.V. infusion (requires an infusion pump):
Children: Safety and efficacy have not been established
Adults: 500-1000 mL (up to 1500 mL/day) or 20 mL/kg/day (up to 1500 mL/day); larger volumes (15,000 mL/24 hours) have been used safely in small numbers of patients
Dosing adjustment in renal impairment: Cl_{cr} <10 mL/minute: Initial dose is the same but subsequent doses should be reduced by 20% to 50% of normal

Administration I.V. only; may administer up to 1.2 g/kg/hour (20 mL/kg/hour)

Nursing Implications Anaphylactoid reactions can occur, have epinephrine and resuscitative equipment available

Dosage Forms Infusion, in sodium chloride 0.9%: 6% (500 mL)

♦ **Hexachlorocyclohexane** see Lindane on page 682

Hexachlorophene (heks a KLOR oh feen)

U.S. Brand Names pHisoHex®; Septisol®

Therapeutic Category Antibacterial, Topical; Soap

Use Surgical scrub and as a bacteriostatic skin cleanser; control an outbreak of gram-positive infection when other procedures have been unsuccessful

Pregnancy Risk Factor C

Contraindications Known hypersensitivity to halogenated phenol derivatives or hexachlorophene; use in premature infants; use on burned or denuded skin; occlusive dressing; application to mucous membranes

Warnings/Precautions Discontinue use if signs of cerebral irritability occur; exposure of preterm infants or patients with extensive burns has been associated with apnea, convulsions, agitation and coma; do not use for bathing infants, premature infants are particularly susceptible to hexachlorophene topical absorption

Adverse Reactions <1%: CNS injury, seizures, irritability, photosensitivity, dermatitis, redness, dry skin

Overdosage/Toxicology
Symptoms of overdose include anorexia, vomiting, abdominal cramps, diarrhea, dehydration, seizures, hypotension, shock
Treatment is supportive

Stability Store in nonmetallic container (**incompatible** with many metals); prolonged direct exposure to strong light may cause brownish surface discoloration, but this does not affect its action

Mechanism of Action Bacteriostatic polychlorinated biphenyl which inhibits membrane-bound enzymes and disrupts the cell membrane

Pharmacodynamics/Kinetics
Absorption: Percutaneously through inflamed, excoriated, and intact skin
Distribution: Crosses the placenta
Half-life: Infants: 6.1-44.2 hours

Usual Dosage Children and Adults: Topical: Apply 5 mL cleanser and water to area to be cleansed; lather and rinse thoroughly under running water

Patient Information Do not leave on skin for prolonged contact; for external use only; discontinue product if condition persists or worsens and call physician; if suds enter eye, rinse out thoroughly with water

Dosage Forms
Foam (Septisol®): 0.23% with alcohol 56% (180 mL, 600 mL)
Liquid, topical (pHisoHex®): 3% (8 mL, 150 mL, 500 mL, 3840 mL)

♦ **Hexadrol®** see Dexamethasone on page 337
♦ **Hexalen®** see Altretamine on page 50
♦ **Hexamethylenetetramine** see Methenamine on page 747
♦ **Hexamethylmelamine** see Altretamine on page 50
♦ **Hexavitamin** see Vitamins, Multiple on page 1226
♦ **Hexit®** see Lindane on page 682
♦ **Hib** see Haemophilus b Conjugate and Hepatitis b Vaccine on page 553

- **Hibiclens®** Topical [OTC] *see* Chlorhexidine Gluconate *on page 240*
- **Hibistat®** Topical [OTC] *see* Chlorhexidine Gluconate *on page 240*
- **Hib Polysaccharide Conjugate** *see* Haemophilus b Conjugate Vaccine *on page 554*
- **HibTITER®** *see* Haemophilus b Conjugate Vaccine *on page 554*
- **Hi-Cor-1.0®** *see* Hydrocortisone *on page 579*
- **Hi-Cor-2.5®** *see* Hydrocortisone *on page 579*
- **Hip-Rex™** *see* Methenamine *on page 747*
- **Hiprex®** *see* Methenamine *on page 747*
- **Hismanal®** *see* Astemizole *on page 105*
- **Histalet Forte® Tablet** *see* Chlorpheniramine, Pyrilamine, Phenylephrine, and Phenylpropanolamine *on page 248*
- **Histatab® Plus Tablet [OTC]** *see* Chlorpheniramine and Phenylephrine *on page 246*
- **Hista-Vadrin® Tablet** *see* Chlorpheniramine, Phenylephrine, and Phenylpropanolamine *on page 247*
- **Histerone® Injection** *see* Testosterone *on page 1117*
- **Histor-D® Syrup** *see* Chlorpheniramine and Phenylephrine *on page 246*
- **Histor-D® Timecelles®** *see* Chlorpheniramine, Phenylephrine, and Methscopolamine *on page 247*

Histrelin (his TREL in)

U.S. Brand Names Supprelin™ Injection

Therapeutic Category Gonadotropin Releasing Hormone Analog; Luteinizing Hormone-Releasing Hormone Analog

Use Treatment of central idiopathic precocious puberty; treatment of estrogen-associated gynecological disorders such as acute intermittent porphyria, endometriosis, leiomyomata uteri, and premenstrual syndrome

Pregnancy Risk Factor X

Contraindications Hypersensitivity to histrelin, pregnancy, breast-feeding

Warnings/Precautions The site of injection should be varied daily; the dose should be administered at the same time each day. In precocious puberty, changing the dosage schedule or noncompliance may result in inadequate control of the pubertal process.

Adverse Reactions

>10%:
  Cardiovascular: Vasodilation
  Central nervous system: Headache
  Gastrointestinal: Abdominal pain
  Genitourinary: Vaginal bleeding, vaginal dryness
  Local: Skin reaction at injection site

1% to 10%:
  Central nervous system: Mood swings, headache, pain
  Dermatologic: Rashes, urticaria
  Endocrine & metabolic: Breast tenderness, hot flashes
  Gastrointestinal: Nausea, vomiting
  Genitourinary: Increased urinary calcium excretion
  Neuromuscular & skeletal: Joint stiffness

Stability Refrigerate at 2°C to 8°C (36°F to 46°F) and protect from light; allow vial to reach room temperature before injecting contents

Mechanism of Action Histrelin is a synthetic long-acting gonadotropin-releasing hormone analog; with daily administration, it desensitizes the pituitary to endogenous gonadotropin-releasing hormone (ie, suppresses gonadotropin release by causing down regulation of the pituitary); this results in a decrease in gonadal sex steroid production which stops the secondary sexual development

Pharmacodynamics/Kinetics

Precocious puberty: Onset of hormonal responses: Within 3 months of initiation of therapy

Acute intermittent porphyria associated with menses: Amelioration of symptoms: After 1-2 months of therapy

Treatment of endometriosis or leiomyomata uteri: Onset of responses: After 3-6 months of treatment

Usual Dosage

Central idiopathic precocious puberty: S.C.: Usual dose is 10 mcg/kg/day given as a single daily dose at the same time each day

Acute intermittent porphyria in women: S.C.: 5 mcg/day

Endometriosis: S.C.: 100 mcg/day

Leiomyomata uteri: S.C.: 20-50 mcg/day or 4 mcg/kg/day

Administration Injection site should be varied daily; dose should be administered at the same time each day

Monitoring Parameters Precocious puberty: Prior to initiating therapy: Height and weight, hand and wrist x-rays, total sex steroid levels, beta-hCG level, adrenal steroid level, gonadotropin-releasing hormone stimulation test, pelvic/adrenal/testicular ultrasound/head CT; during therapy monitor 3 months after initiation and then every 6-12 months; serial levels of sex steroids and gonadotropin-releasing hormone testing; physical exam; secondary sexual development; histrelin may be discontinued when the patient reaches the appropriate age for puberty

Dosage Forms Injection: 7-day kits of single use: 120 mcg/0.6 mL; 300 mcg/0.6 mL; 600 mcg/0.6 mL

- **Histussin D® Liquid** *see* Hydrocodone and Pseudoephedrine *on page 579*

♦ **Hivid**® *see* Zalcitabine *on page 1233*
♦ **HMS Liquifilm**® *see* Medrysone *on page 722*
♦ **HN₂** *see* Mechlorethamine *on page 717*

Homatropine (hoe MA troe peen)

Related Information
Cycloplegic Mydriatics Comparison *on page 1321*

U.S. Brand Names AK-Homatropine® Ophthalmic; Isopto® Homatropine Ophthalmic

Synonyms Homatropine Hydrobromide

Therapeutic Category Anticholinergic Agent, Ophthalmic; Ophthalmic Agent, Mydriatic

Use Producing cycloplegia and mydriasis for refraction; treatment of acute inflammatory conditions of the uveal tract

Pregnancy Risk Factor C

Contraindications Narrow-angle glaucoma, acute hemorrhage or hypersensitivity to the drug or any component in the formulation

Warnings/Precautions Use with caution in patients with hypertension, cardiac disease, or increased intraocular pressure; safety and efficacy not established in infants and young children, therefore, use with extreme caution due to susceptibility of systemic effects; use with caution in obstructive uropathy, paralytic ileus, ulcerative colitis, unstable cardiovascular status in acute hemorrhage

Adverse Reactions
>10%: Ocular: Blurred vision, photophobia
1% to 10%:
  Local: Stinging, local irritation
  Ocular: Increased intraocular pressure
  Respiratory: Congestion
<1%: Vascular congestion, edema, drowsiness, exudate, eczematoid dermatitis, follicular conjunctivitis

Overdosage/Toxicology
Symptoms of overdose include blurred vision, urinary retention, tachycardia
Anticholinergic toxicity is caused by strong binding of the drug to cholinergic receptors. For anticholinergic overdose with severe life-threatening symptoms, physostigmine 1-2 mg (0.5 mg or 0.02 mg/kg for children) S.C. or I.V., slowly may be given to reverse these effects.

Stability Protect from light

Mechanism of Action Blocks response of iris sphincter muscle and the accommodative muscle of the ciliary body to cholinergic stimulation resulting in dilation and loss of accommodation

Pharmacodynamics/Kinetics
Onset of accommodation and pupil effect: Ophthalmic:
  Maximum mydriatic effect: Within 10-30 minutes
  Maximum cycloplegic effect: Within 30-90 minutes
Duration:
  Mydriasis: 6 hours to 4 days
  Cycloplegia: 10-48 hours

Usual Dosage
Children:
  Mydriasis and cycloplegia for refraction: Instill 1 drop of 2% solution immediately before the procedure; repeat at 10-minute intervals as needed
  Uveitis: Instill 1 drop of 2% solution 2-3 times/day
Adults:
  Mydriasis and cycloplegia for refraction: Instill 1-2 drops of 2% solution or 1 drop of 5% solution before the procedure; repeat at 5- to 10-minute intervals as needed; maximum of 3 doses for refraction
  Uveitis: Instill 1-2 drops of 2% or 5% 2-3 times/day up to every 3-4 hours as needed

Patient Information May cause blurred vision; if irritation persists or increases, discontinue use

Nursing Implications Finger pressure should be applied to lacrimal sac for 1-2 minutes after instillation to decrease risk of absorption and systemic reactions

Dosage Forms Solution, ophthalmic, as hydrobromide:
2% (1 mL, 5 mL); 5% (1 mL, 2 mL, 5 mL)
AK-Homatropine®: 5% (15 mL)
Isopto® Homatropine 2% (5 mL, 15 mL); 5% (5 mL, 15 mL)

♦ **Homatropine and Hydrocodone** *see* Hydrocodone and Homatropine *on page 577*
♦ **Homatropine Hydrobromide** *see* Homatropine *on this page*
♦ **Honvol**® *see* Diethylstilbestrol *on page 355*
♦ **Horse Antihuman Thymocyte Gamma Globulin** *see* Lymphocyte Immune Globulin *on page 702*
♦ **Humalog**® *see* Insulin Preparations *on page 613*
♦ **Human Diploid Cell Cultures Rabies Vaccine** *see* Rabies Virus Vaccine *on page 1007*
♦ **Human Diploid Cell Cultures Rabies Vaccine (Intradermal use)** *see* Rabies Virus Vaccine *on page 1007*

Human Growth Hormone (HYU man grothe HOR mone)

U.S. Brand Names Genotropin® Injection; Humatrope® Injection; Norditropin® Injection; Nutropin® AQ Injection; Nutropin® Injection; Protropin® Injection; Saizen® Injection; Serostim® Injection
(Continued)

Human Growth Hormone *(Continued)*

Synonyms Growth Hormone; Somatrem; Somatropin

Therapeutic Category Growth Hormone

Use

Long-term treatment of growth failure from lack of adequate endogenous growth hormone secretion

Nutropin®: Treatment of children who have growth failure associated with chronic renal insufficiency up until the time of renal transplantation

Pregnancy Risk Factor C

Contraindications Closed epiphyses, known hypersensitivity to drug, benzyl alcohol (somatrem), or m-Cresol or glycerin (somatropin); progression of any underlying intracranial lesion or actively growing intracranial tumor

Warnings/Precautions Use with caution in patients with diabetes; when administering to newborns, reconstitute with sterile water for injection

Adverse Reactions S.C. administration can cause local lipoatrophy or lipodystrophy and may enhance the development of neutralizing antibodies

1% to 10%: Endocrine & metabolic: Hypothyroidism

<1%: Rash, itching, hypoglycemia, pain at injection site, small risk for developing leukemia, pain in hip/knee

Overdosage/Toxicology Symptoms include hypoglycemia, hyperglycemia, acromegaly

Drug Interactions Decreased effect: Glucocorticoid therapy may inhibit growth-promoting effects.

Stability

Somatrem (Protropin®): Store vials at 2°C to 8°C/36°F to 46°F; reconstitute each 5 mg vial with 1-5 mL of bacteriostatic water for injection; use reconstituted vials within 7 days; avoid freezing

Somatropin (Humatrope®/Nutropin®): Store vials at 2°C to 8°C/36°F to 46°F; avoid freezing; reconstitute each 5 mg vial with 1-5 mL of bacteriostatic water for injection; use reconstituted vials within 14 days; avoid freezing

Mechanism of Action Somatropin and somatrem are purified polypeptide hormones of recombinant DNA origin; somatropin contains the identical sequence of amino acids found in human growth hormone while somatrem's amino acid sequence is identical plus an additional amino acid, methionine; human growth hormone stimulates growth of linear bone, skeletal muscle, and organs; stimulates erythropoietin which increases red blood cell mass; exerts both insulin-like and diabetogenic effects

Pharmacodynamics/Kinetics Somatrem and somatropin have equivalent pharmacokinetic properties

Duration of action: Maintains supraphysiologic levels for 18-20 hours

Absorption: I.M.: Well absorbed

Metabolism: ~90% in the liver

Half-life: 15-50 minutes

Elimination: 0.1% excreted in urine unchanged

Usual Dosage Children (individualize dose):

Somatrem (Protropin®): I.M., S.C.: Up to 0.1 mg (0.26 units)/kg/dose 3 times/week

Somatropin (Genotropin®): S.C.: Weekly dosage of 0.16-0.24 mg/kg divided into 6-7 doses

Somatropin (Humatrope®): I.M., S.C.: Up to 0.06 mg (0.16 units)/kg/dose 3 times/week

Somatropin (Nutropin®): S.C.:

Growth hormone inadequacy: Weekly dosage of 0.3 mg/kg (0.78 units/kg) administered daily

Chronic renal insufficiency: Weekly dosage of 0.35 mg/kg (0.91 units/kg) administered daily

Therapy should be discontinued when patient has reached satisfactory adult height, when epiphyses have fused, or when the patient ceases to respond

Growth of 5 cm/year or more is expected, if growth rate does not exceed 2.5 cm in a 6-month period, double the dose for the next 6 months, if there is still no satisfactory response, discontinue therapy

Administration Do not shake; administer S.C. or I.M.; refer to product labeling; when administering to newborns, reconstitute with sterile water for injection

Monitoring Parameters Growth curve, periodic thyroid function tests, bone age (annually), periodical urine testing for glucose, somatomedin C levels

Nursing Implications Watch for glucose intolerance

Dosage Forms Powder for injection (lyophilized):

Somatropin:

Genotropin®: 1.5 mg ~4.5 units (5 mL); 5.8 mg ~17.4 units (5 mL)

Humatrope®: 5 mg ~15 units

Norditropin®: 4 mg ~12 units; 8 mg ~24 units

Nutropin®: 5 mg ~15 units (10 mL); 10 mg ~30 units (10 mL)

Nutropin® AQ: 10 mg ~30 units (2 mL)

Saizen® (rDNA origin): 5 mg ~15 units

Serostim®: 5 mg ~15 units (5 mL); 6 mg ~18 units (5 mL)

Somatrem, Protropin®: 5 mg ~15 units (10 mL); 10 mg ~30 units (10 mL)

- ◆ **Human Thyroid Stimulating Hormone** *see* Thyrotropin Alpha *on page 1140*
- ◆ **Humate-P®** *see* Antihemophilic Factor (Human) *on page 88*
- ◆ **Humatin®** *see* Paromomycin *on page 888*
- ◆ **Humatrope® Injection** *see* Human Growth Hormone *on previous page*
- ◆ **Humegon™** *see* Menotropins *on page 727*

Hyaluronidase (hye al yoor ON i dase)

Related Information
Extravasation Treatment of Other Drugs *on page 1287*
U.S. Brand Names Wydase® Injection
Therapeutic Category Antidote, Extravasation
Use Increases the dispersion and absorption of other drugs; increases rate of absorption of parenteral fluids given by hypodermoclysis; enhances diffusion of locally irritating or toxic drugs in the management of I.V. extravasation
Pregnancy Risk Factor C
Contraindications Hypersensitivity to hyaluronidase or any component; do not inject in or around infected, inflamed, or cancerous areas
Warnings/Precautions Drug infiltrates in which hyaluronidase is contraindicated: Dopamine, alpha-adrenergic agonists; an intradermal skin test for sensitivity should be performed before actual administration using 0.02 mL of a 150 units/mL of hyaluronidase solution
Adverse Reactions <1%: Tachycardia, hypotension, dizziness, chills, urticaria, erythema, nausea, vomiting
Overdosage/Toxicology Symptoms of overdose include local edema, urticaria, erythema, chills, nausea, vomiting, hypotension
Drug Interactions Decreased effect: Salicylates, cortisone, ACTH, estrogens, antihistamines
Stability Reconstituted hyaluronidase solution remains stable for only 24 hours when stored in the refrigerator; do not use discolored solutions
Mechanism of Action Modifies the permeability of connective tissue through hydrolysis of hyaluronic acid, one of the chief ingredients of tissue cement which offers resistance to diffusion of liquids through tissues
Pharmacodynamics/Kinetics
Onset of action: Immediate by the subcutaneous or intradermal routes for the treatment of extravasation
Duration: 24-48 hours
Usual Dosage
Infants and Children:
Management of I.V. extravasation: Reconstitute the 150 unit vial of lyophilized powder with 1 mL normal saline; take 0.1 mL of this solution and dilute with 0.9 mL normal saline to yield 15 units/mL; using a 25- or 26-gauge needle, five 0.2 mL injections are made subcutaneously or intradermally into the extravasation site at the leading edge, changing the needle after each injection
Hypodermoclysis:
S.C.: 1 mL (150 units) is added to 1000 mL of infusion fluid and 0.5 mL (75 units) in injected into each clysis site at the initiation of the infusion
I.V.: 15 units is added to each 100 mL of I.V. fluid to be administered
Children <3 years: Limit volume of single clysis to 200 mL
Premature Infants: Do not exceed 25 mL/kg/day and not >2 mL/minute
Adults: Absorption and dispersion of drugs: 150 units are added to the vehicle containing the drug
Administration Administer hyaluronidase within the first few minutes to 1 hour after the extravasation of a necrotizing agent is recognized; do not administer I.V.
Nursing Implications Appropriate drugs for the management of an acute hypersensitivity (epinephrine, corticosteroids, and antihistamines) should be readily available
Additional Information The USP hyaluronidase unit is equivalent to the turbidity-reducing (TR) unit and the International Unit; each unit is defined as being the activity contained in 100 mcg of the International Standard Preparation
Dosage Forms
Injection, stabilized solution: 150 units/mL (1 mL, 10 mL)
Powder for injection, lyophilized: 150 units, 1500 units

- **Hycodan®** *see* Hydrocodone and Homatropine *on page 577*
- **Hycomine®** *see* Hydrocodone and Phenylpropanolamine *on page 579*
- **Hycomine® Compound** *see* Hydrocodone, Chlorpheniramine, Phenylephrine, Acetaminophen and Caffeine *on page 579*
- **Hycomine® Pediatric** *see* Hydrocodone and Phenylpropanolamine *on page 579*
- **Hycort®** *see* Hydrocortisone *on page 579*
- **Hycotuss® Expectorant Liquid** *see* Hydrocodone and Guaifenesin *on page 577*
- **Hydergine®** *see* Ergoloid Mesylates *on page 425*
- **Hydergine® LC** *see* Ergoloid Mesylates *on page 425*

Hydralazine (hye DRAL a zeen)

Related Information
Depression Disorders and Treatments *on page 1465*
Heart Failure: Management of Patients With Left-Ventricular Systolic Dysfunction *on page 1472*
Hypertension Therapy *on page 1479*

U.S. Brand Names Apresoline®
Canadian Brand Names Apo®-Hydralazine; Novo-Hylazin; Nu-Hydral
Synonyms Hydralazine Hydrochloride
Therapeutic Category Antihypertensive Agent; Vasodilator
Use Management of moderate to severe hypertension, congestive heart failure, hypertension secondary to pre-eclampsia/eclampsia; also used to treat primary pulmonary hypertension

Pregnancy Risk Factor C
Pregnancy/Breast-Feeding Implications
Clinical effects on the fetus: Crosses the placenta. One report of fetal arrhythmia; transient neonatal thrombocytopenia and fetal distress reported following late 3rd trimester use. A large amount of clinical experience with the use of these drugs for management of hypertension during pregnancy is available. Available evidence suggests safe use during pregnancy and breast-feeding.
Breast-feeding/lactation: Crosses into breast milk in extremely small amounts. American Academy of Pediatrics considers **compatible** with breast-feeding.

Contraindications Hypersensitivity to hydralazine or any component, dissecting aortic aneurysm, mitral valve rheumatic heart disease

Warnings/Precautions Discontinue hydralazine in patients who develop SLE-like syndrome or positive ANA. Use with caution in patients with severe renal disease or cerebral vascular accidents or with known or suspected coronary artery disease; monitor blood pressure closely with I.V. use; some formulations may contain tartrazines or sulfites. Slow acetylators, patients with decreased renal function, and patients receiving >200 mg/day (chronically) are at higher risk for SLE. Titrate dosage to patient's response. Usually administered with diuretic and a beta-blocker to counteract side effects of sodium and water retention and reflex tachycardia.

Adverse Reactions
>10%:
Cardiovascular: Palpitations, flushing, tachycardia, angina pectoris
Central nervous system: Headache
Gastrointestinal: Nausea, vomiting, diarrhea, anorexia
1% to 10%:
Cardiovascular: Hypotension, redness or flushing of face
Gastrointestinal: Constipation
Ocular: Lacrimation
Respiratory: Dyspnea, nasal congestion
<1%: Malaise, fever, dizziness, rash, edema, arthralgias, weakness, peripheral neuritis, positive ANA, positive LE cells
Note: Because of blunted beta-receptor response, the elderly are less likely to experience reflex tachycardia; this puts them at greater risk for orthostatic hypotension

Overdosage/Toxicology
Symptoms of overdose include hypotension, tachycardia, shock
Hypotension usually responds to I.V. fluid, Trendelenburg positioning or vasoconstrictors; treatment is primarily supportive and symptomatic

Drug Interactions Increased toxicity: MAO inhibitors → significant decrease in blood pressure indomethacin may decrease hypotensive effects; hydralazine serum levels may be increased by beta-blockers (metoprolol, propranolol) while hydralazine increases serum levels/toxic risk of beta-blockers

Stability
Intact ampuls/vials of hydralazine should not be stored under refrigeration because of possible precipitation or crystallization
Hydralazine should be diluted in NS for IVPB administration due to decreased stability in D_5W
Stability of IVPB solution in NS: 4 days at room temperature

Mechanism of Action Direct vasodilation of arterioles (with little effect on veins) with decreased systemic resistance

Pharmacodynamics/Kinetics
Onset of action: Oral: 20-30 minutes; I.V.: 5-20 minutes
Duration: Oral: 2-4 hours; I.V.: 2-6 hours
Distribution: Crosses placenta; appears in breast milk
Metabolism: Large first-pass effect orally, acetylated in liver
Protein binding: 85% to 90%

Bioavailability: 30% to 50%; enhanced by concurrent administration with food
Half-life: Normal renal function: 2-8 hours; End-stage renal disease: 7-16 hours
Elimination: 14% excreted unchanged in urine

Usual Dosage
Children:
Oral: Initial: 0.75-1 mg/kg/day in 2-4 divided doses; increase over 3-4 weeks to maximum of 7.5 mg/kg/day in 2-4 divided doses; maximum daily dose: 200 mg/day
I.M., I.V.: 0.1-0.2 mg/kg/dose (not to exceed 20 mg) every 4-6 hours as needed, up to 1.7-3.5 mg/kg/day in 4-6 divided doses
Adults:
Oral: Hypertension:
Initial dose: 10 mg 4 times/day for first 2-4 days; increase to 25 mg 4 times/day for the balance of the first week
Increase by 10-25 mg/dose gradually to 50 mg 4 times/day; 300 mg/day may be required for some patients
Oral: Congestive heart failure:
Initial dose: 10-25 mg 3 times/day
Target dose: 75 mg 3 times/day
Maximum dose: 100 mg 3 times/day
I.M., I.V.:
Hypertension: Initial: 10-20 mg/dose every 4-6 hours as needed, may increase to 40 mg/dose; change to oral therapy as soon as possible
Pre-eclampsia/eclampsia: 5 mg/dose then 5-10 mg every 20-30 minutes as needed
Elderly: Oral: Initial: 10 mg 2-3 times/day; increase by 10-25 mg/day every 2-5 days

Dosing interval in renal impairment:
Cl$_{cr}$ 10-50 mL/minute: Administer every 8 hours
Cl$_{cr}$ <10 mL/minute: Administer every 8-16 hours in fast acetylators and every 12-24 hours in slow acetylators
Hemodialysis: Supplemental dose is not necessary
Peritoneal dialysis: Supplemental dose is not necessary

Dietary Considerations Food enhances bioavailability of hydralazine

Monitoring Parameters Blood pressure (monitor closely with I.V. use), standing and sitting/supine, heart rate, ANA titer

Patient Information Report flu-like symptoms, rise slowly from sitting/lying position; take with meals

Nursing Implications Aid with ambulation, rising may cause orthostasis

Dosage Forms
Injection, as hydrochloride: 20 mg/mL (1 mL)
Tablet, as hydrochloride: 10 mg, 25 mg, 50 mg, 100 mg

Extemporaneous Preparations An oral solution (20 mg/5 mL) has been made from 20 mL of the hydralazine injection (20 mg/mL), 8 mL of propylene glycol and purified water USP qs ad 50 mL; expected stability: 30 days if refrigerated

A flavored syrup (1.25 mg/mL) has been made using seventy-five hydralazine hydrochloride 50 mg tablets, dissolved in 250 mL of distilled water with 2250 g of Lycasin® (75% w/w maltitol syrup vehicle); edetate disodium 3 g and sodium saccharin 3 g dissolved in 50 mL distilled water was added; solution was preserved with 30 mL of a solution containing methylparaben 10% (w/v) and propylparaben 2% (w/v) in propylene glycol; flavored with 3 mL orange flavoring; qs ad to 3 L with distilled water and then pH adjusted to pH of 3.7 using glacial acetic acid; measured stability was 5 days at room temperature (25°C); less than 2% loss of hydralazine occurred at 2 weeks when syrup was stored at 5°C

Alexander KS, Pudipeddi M, and Parker GA, "Stability of Hydralazine Hydrochloride Syrup Compounded From Tablets," *Am J Hosp Pharm*, 1993, 50(4):683-6.

Nahata MC and Hipple TF, *Pediatric Drug Formulations*, 2nd ed, Cincinnati, OH: Harvey Whitney Books Co, 1992.

Hydralazine and Hydrochlorothiazide
(hye DRAL a zeen & hye droe klor oh THYE a zide)
U.S. Brand Names Apresazide®
Therapeutic Category Antihypertensive Agent, Combination
Dosage Forms Capsule:
25/25: Hydralazine hydrochloride 25 mg and hydrochlorothiazide 25 mg
50/50: Hydralazine hydrochloride 50 mg and hydrochlorothiazide 50 mg
100/50: Hydralazine hydrochloride 100 mg and hydrochlorothiazide 50 mg

♦ **Hydralazine Hydrochloride** *see Hydralazine on previous page*

Hydralazine, Hydrochlorothiazide, and Reserpine
(hye DRAL a zeen, hye droe klor oh THYE a zide, & re SER peen)
U.S. Brand Names Hydrap-ES®; Marpres®; Ser-Ap-Es®
Therapeutic Category Antihypertensive Agent, Combination
Dosage Forms Tablet: Hydralazine 25 mg, hydrochlorothiazide 15 mg, and reserpine 0.1 mg

♦ **Hydramyn® Syrup [OTC]** *see Diphenhydramine on page 369*
♦ **Hydrap-ES®** *see Hydralazine, Hydrochlorothiazide, and Reserpine on this page*
♦ **Hydrated Chloral** *see Chloral Hydrate on page 235*
♦ **Hydrea®** *see Hydroxyurea on page 587*
♦ **Hydrex®** *see Benzthiazide on page 135*

♦ **Hydrocet®** *see Hydrocodone and Acetaminophen on next page*

Hydrochlorothiazide (hye droe klor oh THYE a zide)

Related Information
Heart Failure: Management of Patients With Left-Ventricular Systolic Dysfunction *on page 1472*

Sulfonamide Derivatives *on page 1337*

U.S. Brand Names Esidrix®; Ezide®; HydroDIURIL®; Hydro-Par®; Microzide™; Oretic®

Canadian Brand Names Apo®-Hydro; Diuchlor®; Neo-Codema®; Novo-Hydrazide; Urozide®

Synonyms HCTZ

Therapeutic Category Antihypertensive Agent; Diuretic, Thiazide

Use Management of mild to moderate hypertension; treatment of edema in congestive heart failure and nephrotic syndrome

Pregnancy Risk Factor B

Contraindications Anuria, renal decompensation, hypersensitivity to hydrochlorothiazide or any component, cross-sensitivity with other thiazides and sulfonamide derivatives

Warnings/Precautions Use with caution in renal disease, hepatic disease, gout, lupus erythematosus, diabetes mellitus; some products may contain tartrazine. Hydrochlorothiazide is not effective in patients with a Cl_{cr} 25-50 mL/minute, therefore, it may not be a useful agent in many elderly patients.

Adverse Reactions
1% to 10%: Endocrine & metabolic: Hypokalemia

<1%: Hypotension, photosensitivity, fluid and electrolyte imbalances, hyperglycemia, rarely blood dyscrasias, prerenal azotemia

Overdosage/Toxicology
Symptoms of overdose include hypermotility, diuresis, lethargy, confusion, muscle weakness

Following GI decontamination, therapy is supportive with I.V. fluids, electrolytes, and I.V. pressors if needed

Drug Interactions
Decreased effect:

Thiazides may decrease the effect of anticoagulants, antigout agents, sulfonylureas Bile acid sequestrants, methenamine, and NSAIDs may decrease the effect of the thiazides

Increased effect: Thiazides may increase the toxicity of allopurinol, anesthetics, antineoplastics, calcium salts, diazoxide, digitalis, lithium, loop diuretics, methyldopa, nondepolarizing muscle relaxants, vitamin D; amphotericin B and anticholinergics may increase the toxicity of thiazides

Mechanism of Action Inhibits sodium reabsorption in the distal tubules causing increased excretion of sodium and water as well as potassium and hydrogen ions

Pharmacodynamics/Kinetics
Onset of diuretic action: Oral: Within 2 hours

Peak effect: 4 hours

Duration: 6-12 hours

Absorption: Oral: ~60% to 80%

Half-life: 5.6-14.8 hours

Elimination: Excreted unchanged in urine

Usual Dosage Oral (effect of drug may be decreased when used every day):
Children (In pediatric patients, chlorothiazide may be preferred over hydrochlorothiazide as there are more dosage formulations (eg, suspension) available):
<6 months: 2-3 mg/kg/day in 2 divided doses
>6 months: 2 mg/kg/day in 2 divided doses
Adults: 25-100 mg/day in 1-2 doses
Maximum: 200 mg/day
Elderly: 12.5-25 mg once daily
Minimal increase in response and more electrolyte disturbances are seen with doses >50 mg/day

Dosing adjustment/comments in renal impairment: Cl_{cr} 25-50 mL/minute: Not effective

Monitoring Parameters Assess weight, I & O reports daily to determine fluid loss; blood pressure, serum electrolytes, BUN, creatinine

Test Interactions ↑ creatine phosphokinase [CPK] (S), ammonia (B), amylase (S), calcium (S), chloride (S), cholesterol (S), glucose, ↑ acid (S), ↓ chloride (S), magnesium, potassium, sodium (S); Tyramine and phentolamine tests, histamine tests for pheochromocytoma

Patient Information May be taken with food or milk; take early in day to avoid nocturia; take the last dose of multiple doses no later than 6 PM unless instructed otherwise. A few people who take this medication become more sensitive to sunlight and may experience skin rash, redness, itching, or severe sunburn, especially if sun block SPF ≥15 is not used on exposed skin areas. May increase blood glucose levels in diabetics.

Nursing Implications Take blood pressure with patient lying down and standing

Dosage Forms
Capsule: 12.5 mg
Solution, oral (mint flavor): 50 mg/5 mL (50 mL)
Tablet: 25 mg, 50 mg, 100 mg

♦ **Hydrochlorothiazide and Irbesartan** *see Irbesartan and Hydrochlorothiazide on page 627*

Hydrochlorothiazide and Reserpine
(hye droe klor oh THYE a zide & re SER peen)
U.S. Brand Names Hydropres®; Hydro-Serp®; Hydroserpine®
Therapeutic Category Antihypertensive Agent, Combination
Dosage Forms Tablet:
25: Hydrochlorothiazide 25 mg and reserpine 0.125 mg
50: Hydrochlorothiazide 50 mg and reserpine 0.125 mg

Hydrochlorothiazide and Spironolactone
(hye droe klor oh THYE a zide & speer on oh LAK tone)
U.S. Brand Names Aldactazide®
Therapeutic Category Antihypertensive Agent, Combination
Dosage Forms Tablet:
25/25: Hydrochlorothiazide 25 mg and spironolactone 25 mg
50/50: Hydrochlorothiazide 50 mg and spironolactone 50 mg

Hydrochlorothiazide and Triamterene
(hye droe klor oh THYE a zide & trye AM ter een)
Related Information
Hydrochlorothiazide *on previous page*
Triamterene *on page 1177*
U.S. Brand Names Dyazide®; Maxzide®
Canadian Brand Names Apo®-Triazide; Novo-Triamzide; Nu-Triazide
Therapeutic Category Antihypertensive Agent; Diuretic, Potassium Sparing; Diuretic, Thiazide
Dosage Forms
Capsule (Dyazide®): Hydrochlorothiazide 25 mg and triamterene 37.5 mg
Tablet:
Maxzide®-25: Hydrochlorothiazide 25 mg and triamterene 37.5 mg
Maxzide®: Hydrochlorothiazide 50 mg and triamterene 75 mg

♦ **Hydrocil® [OTC]** *see* Psyllium *on page 994*
♦ **Hydro-Cobex®** *see* Hydroxocobalamin *on page 585*

Hydrocodone and Acetaminophen
(hye droe KOE done & a seet a MIN oh fen)
Related Information
Narcotic Agonists Comparison *on page 1328*
U.S. Brand Names Anexsia®; Anodynos-DHC®; Bancap HC®; Co-Gesic®; Dolacet®; DuoCet™; Duradyne DHC®; Hydrocet®; Hydrogesic®; Hy-Phen™; Lorcet®-HD; Lorcet® Plus; Lortab®; Margesic® H; Medipain 5®; Norcet®; Stagesic®; T-Gesic®; Vicodin®; Vicodin® ES; Vicodin® HP; Zydone®
Canadian Brand Names Vapocet®
Synonyms Acetaminophen and Hydrocodone
Therapeutic Category Analgesic, Narcotic
Use Relief of moderate to severe pain; antitussive (hydrocodone)
Restrictions C-III
Pregnancy Risk Factor C
Contraindications CNS depression, hypersensitivity to hydrocodone, acetaminophen or any component; severe respiratory depression
Warnings/Precautions Use with caution in patients with hypersensitivity reactions to other phenanthrene derivative opioid agonists (morphine, hydrocodone, hydromorphone, levorphanol, oxycodone, oxymorphone); tablets contain metabisulfite which may cause allergic reactions; tolerance or drug dependence may result from extended use
Adverse Reactions
>10%:
Cardiovascular: Hypotension
Central nervous system: Lightheadedness, dizziness, sedation, drowsiness, fatigue
Neuromuscular & skeletal: Weakness
1% to 10%:
Cardiovascular: Bradycardia
Central nervous system: Confusion
Gastrointestinal: Nausea, vomiting
Genitourinary: Decreased urination
Respiratory: Shortness of breath, dyspnea
<1%: Hypertension, hallucinations, xerostomia, anorexia, biliary tract spasm, urinary tract spasm, diplopia, miosis, histamine release, physical and psychological dependence with prolonged use
Overdosage/Toxicology
Symptoms of overdose include hepatic necrosis, blood dyscrasias, respiratory depression
Acetylcysteine 140 mg/kg orally (loading) followed by 70 mg/kg every 4 hours for 17 doses. Therapy should be initiated based upon laboratory analysis suggesting high probability of hepatotoxic potential. Naloxone (2 mg I.V.) can also be used to reverse the toxic effects of the opiate. Activated charcoal is effective at binding certain chemicals, and this is especially true for acetaminophen.
Drug Interactions
Decreased effect with phenothiazines
(Continued)

Hydrocodone and Acetaminophen *(Continued)*

Increased effect with dextroamphetamine
Increased toxicity with CNS depressants, TCAs; effect of warfarin may be enhanced

Mechanism of Action See individual agents

Pharmacodynamics/Kinetics

Onset of narcotic analgesia: Within 10-20 minutes

Duration: 3-6 hours

Distribution: Crosses the placenta

Metabolism: In the liver

Half-life: 3.8 hours

Elimination: In urine

Usual Dosage Oral (doses should be titrated to appropriate analgesic effect):

Children:

Antitussive (hydrocodone): 0.6 mg/kg/day in 3-4 divided doses

A single dose should not exceed 10 mg in children >12 years, 5 mg in children 2-12 years, and 1.25 mg in children <2 years of age

Analgesic (acetaminophen): Refer to Acetaminophen monograph

Adults: Analgesic: 1-2 tablets or capsules every 4-6 hours or 5-10 mL solution every 4-6 hours as needed for pain

Monitoring Parameters Pain relief, respiratory and mental status, blood pressure

Patient Information May cause drowsiness; do not exceed recommended dose; do not take for more than 10 days without physician's advice

Nursing Implications Observe patient for excessive sedation, respiratory depression

Dosage Forms

Capsule:

Bancap HC®, Dolacet®, Hydrocet®, Hydrogesic®, Lorcet®-HD, Margesic® H, Medipain 5®, Norcet®, Stagesic®, T-Gesic®, Zydone®: Hydrocodone bitartrate 5 mg and acetaminophen 500 mg

Elixir (tropical fruit punch flavor) (Lortab®): Hydrocodone bitartrate 2.5 mg and acetaminophen 167 mg per 5 mL with alcohol 7% (480 mL)

Solution, oral (tropical fruit punch flavor) (Lortab®): Hydrocodone bitartrate 2.5 mg and acetaminophen 167 mg per 5 mL with alcohol 7% (480 mL)

Tablet: Hydrocodone bitartrate 5 mg and acetaminophen 400 mg; hydrocodone bitartrate 7.5 mg and acetaminophen 400 mg; hydrocodone bitartrate 10 mg and acetaminophen 400 mg; hydrocodone bitartrate 5 mg and acetaminophen 500 mg; hydrocodone bitartrate 7.5 mg and acetaminophen 750 mg; hydrocodone bitartrate 7.5 mg and acetaminophen 500 mg; hydrocodone bitartrate 7.5 mg and acetaminophen 650 mg; hydrocodone bitartrate 10 mg and acetaminophen 650 mg

Lortab® 2.5/500: Hydrocodone bitartrate 2.5 mg and acetaminophen 500 mg

Anexsia® 5/500, Anodynos-DHC®, Co-Gesic®, DuoCet™, DHC®; Hy-Phen®, Lorcet®, Lortab®® 5/500, Vicodin®: Hydrocodone bitartrate 5 mg and acetaminophen 500 mg

Lortab® 7.5/500: Hydrocodone bitartrate 7.5 mg and acetaminophen 500 mg

Anexsia® 7.5/650, Lorcet® Plus: Hydrocodone bitartrate 7.5 mg and acetaminophen 650 mg

Vicodin® ES: Hydrocodone bitartrate 7.5 mg and acetaminophen 750 mg

Norco®: Hydrocodone bitartrate 10 mg and acetaminophen 325 mg

Lortab® 10/500: Hydrocodone bitartrate 10 mg and acetaminophen 500 mg

Lorcet® 10/650: Hydrocodone bitartrate 10 mg and acetaminophen 650 mg

Vicodin® HP: Hydrocodone bitartrate 10 mg and acetaminophen 660 mg

Zydone®: Hydrocodone bitartrate 5 mg and acetaminophen 400 mg; hydrocodone bitartrate 7.5 mg and acetaminophen 400 mg; Hydrocodone bitartrate 10 mg and acetaminophen 400 mg

Hydrocodone and Aspirin *(hye droe KOE done & AS pir in)*

Related Information

Narcotic Agonists Comparison *on page 1328*

U.S. Brand Names Alor® 5/500; Azdone®; Damason-P®; Lortab® ASA; Panasal® 5/500

Therapeutic Category Analgesic, Narcotic

Use Relief of moderate to moderately severe pain

Restrictions C-III

Pregnancy Risk Factor D

Warnings/Precautions Use with caution in patients with impaired renal function, erosive gastritis, or peptic ulcer disease; children and teenagers should not use for chickenpox or flu symptoms before a physician is consulted about Reye's syndrome; tolerance or drug dependence may result from extended use

Adverse Reactions

>10%:

Cardiovascular: Hypotension

Central nervous system: Lightheadedness, dizziness, sedation, drowsiness, fatigue

Gastrointestinal: Nausea, heartburn, stomach pains, dyspepsia, epigastric discomfort

Neuromuscular & skeletal: Weakness

1% to 10%:

Cardiovascular: Bradycardia

Central nervous system: Confusion

Dermatologic: Rash

Gastrointestinal: Vomiting, gastrointestinal ulceration

Genitourinary: Decreased urination

Hematologic: Hemolytic anemia

Respiratory: Shortness of breath, dyspnea
Miscellaneous: Anaphylactic shock
<1%: Hypertension, hallucinations, insomnia, nervousness, jitters, xerostomia, anorexia, biliary tract spasm, urinary tract spasm, occult bleeding, prolonged bleeding time, leukopenia, thrombocytopenia, iron deficiency anemia, hepatotoxicity, diplopia, miosis, impaired renal function, bronchospasm, histamine release, physical and psychological dependence with prolonged use

Overdosage/Toxicology Antidote is naloxone for codeine. Naloxone 2 mg I.V. (0.01 mg/kg for children) with repeat administration as necessary up to a total of 10 mg. The "Done" nomogram is very helpful for estimating the severity of aspirin poisoning and directing treatment using serum salicylate levels. Treatment can also be based upon symptomatology; see Aspirin.

Drug Interactions Increased toxicity with CNS depressants, warfarin (bleeding)
Mechanism of Action Refer to individual agents
Usual Dosage Adults: Oral: 1-2 tablets every 4-6 hours as needed for pain
Dietary Considerations Alcohol: Additive CNS effect, avoid use
Administration Administer with food or a full glass of water to minimize GI distress
Monitoring Parameters Observe patient for excessive sedation, respiratory depression
Test Interactions Urine glucose, urinary 5-HIAA, serum uric acid
Patient Information May cause drowsiness; avoid alcohol; watch for bleeding gums or any signs of GI bleeding; take with food or milk to minimize GI distress, notify physician if ringing in ears or persistent GI pain occurs
Dosage Forms Tablet: Hydrocodone bitartrate 5 mg and aspirin 500 mg

Hydrocodone and Chlorpheniramine
(hye droe KOE done & klor fen IR a meen)
U.S. Brand Names Tussionex®
Therapeutic Category Antihistamine/Antitussive
Dosage Forms Syrup, alcohol free: Hydrocodone polistirex 10 mg and chlorpheniramine polistirex 8 mg per 5 mL (480 mL, 900 mL)

Hydrocodone and Guaifenesin (hye droe KOE done & gwye FEN e sin)
U.S. Brand Names Codiclear® DH; HycoClear Tuss®; Hycotuss® Expectorant Liquid; Kwelcof®
Therapeutic Category Antitussive/Expectorant
Dosage Forms Liquid: Hydrocodone bitartrate 5 mg and guaifenesin 100 mg per 5 mL (120 mL, 480 mL)

Hydrocodone and Homatropine
(hye droe KOE done & hoe MA troe peen)
Related Information
Narcotic Agonists Comparison on page 1328
U.S. Brand Names Hycodan®; Hydromet®; Hydropane®; Hydrotropine®; Oncet®; Tussigon®
Synonyms Homatropine and Hydrocodone
Therapeutic Category Antitussive; Cough Preparation
Use Symptomatic relief of cough
Restrictions C-III
Pregnancy Risk Factor C
Contraindications Increased intracranial pressure, narrow-angle glaucoma, depressed ventilation, hypersensitivity to hydrocodone, homatropine, or any component
Warnings/Precautions Use with caution in patients with hypersensitivity to other phenanthrene derivatives; use with caution in patients with respiratory diseases, or severe liver or renal failure; use with caution in children with spastic paralysis, in the elderly, and in patients with prostatic hypertrophy
Adverse Reactions
>10%:
Cardiovascular: Hypotension
Central nervous system: Lightheadedness, dizziness, sedation, drowsiness, fatigue
Neuromuscular & skeletal: Weakness
1% to 10%:
Cardiovascular: Bradycardia, tachycardia
Central nervous system: Confusion
Gastrointestinal: Nausea, vomiting
Genitourinary: Decreased urination
Respiratory: Shortness of breath, dyspnea
<1%: Hallucinations, hypertension, dry hot skin, xerostomia, anorexia, impaired GI motility, biliary tract spasm, urinary tract spasm, diplopia, miosis, mydriasis, blurred vision, histamine release, physical and psychological dependence with prolonged use
Overdosage/Toxicology
Symptoms of overdose include CNS and respiratory depression; gastrointestinal cramping; dilated, unreactive pupils; blurred vision; hot, dry flushed skin; dryness of mucous membranes; difficulty in swallowing, foul breath, diminished or absent bowel sounds, urinary retention, tachycardia, hyperthermia, hypertension, increased respiratory rate
CNS depression is an extension of pharmacologic effect; treatment is supportive; naloxone 0.4 mg I.V. (0.01 mg/kg for children) with repeat administrations as necessary; anticholinergic toxicity is caused by strong binding of the drug to cholinergic
(Continued)

Hydrocodone and Homatropine *(Continued)*

receptors. For anticholinergic overdose with severe life-threatening symptoms, physostigmine 1-2 mg (0.5 or 0.02 mg/kg for children) S.C. or I.V., slowly may be given to reverse these effects.

Usual Dosage Oral (based on hydrocodone component):

Children: 0.6 mg/kg/day in 3-4 divided doses; do not administer more frequently than every 4 hours

A single dose should not exceed 1.25 mg in children <2 years of age, 5 mg in children 2-12 years, and 10 mg in children >12 years

Adults: 5-10 mg every 4-6 hours, a single dose should not exceed 15 mg; do not administer more frequently than every 4 hours

Dietary Considerations Alcohol: Additive CNS effect, avoid use

Test Interactions ↑ ALT, AST (S)

Patient Information Avoid alcohol; may cause drowsiness and impair judgment or coordination; may cause physical and psychological dependence with prolonged use; lack of saliva may enhance cavities; maintain good oral hygiene; use caution while driving; may cause blurred vision; notify physician if difficulty in urinating or constipation becomes severe

Nursing Implications Dispense in light-resistant container; observe patient for excessive sedation, respiratory depression, implement safety measures, assist with ambulation

Dosage Forms

Syrup (Hycodan®, Hydromet®): Hydrocodone bitartrate 5 mg and homatropine methylbromide 1.5 mg per 5 mL (120 mL, 480 mL, 4000 mL)

Tablet (Hycodan®, Oncet®, Tussigon®): Hydrocodone bitartrate 5 mg and homatropine methylbromide 1.5 mg

Hydrocodone and Ibuprofen *(hye droe KOE done & eye byoo PROE fen)*

Related Information

Narcotic Agonists Comparison *on page 1328*

U.S. Brand Names Vicoprofen®

Therapeutic Category Analgesic, Narcotic

Use Short-term (generally <10 days) management of moderate to severe acute pain; is not indicated for treatment of such conditions as osteoarthritis or rheumatoid arthritis

Restrictions C-III

Pregnancy Risk Factor C

Pregnancy/Breast-Feeding Implications Clinical effects on the fetus: As with other NSAID-containing products, this agent should be avoided in late pregnancy because it may cause premature closure of the ductus arteriosus

Contraindications Hypersensitivity to any of the ingredients, aspirin allergy, and 3rd trimester pregnancy

Warnings/Precautions As with any opioid analgesic agent, this agent should be used with caution in elderly or debilitated patients, and those with severe impairment of hepatic or renal function, hypothyroidism, Addison's disease, prostatic hypertrophy, or urethral stricture. The usual precautions should be observed and the possibility of respiratory depression should be kept in mind. Patients with head injury, increased intracranial pressure, acute abdomen, active peptic ulcer disease, history of upper GI disease, impaired thyroid function, asthma, hypertension, edema, heart failure, and any bleeding disorder should use this agent cautiously. Hydrocodone suppresses the cough reflex; as with opioids, caution should be exercised when this agent is used postoperatively and in patients with pulmonary disease.

Adverse Reactions

>10%:

Cardiovascular: Hypotension

Central nervous system: Lightheadedness, dizziness, sedation, drowsiness, fatigue

Dermatologic: Rash, urticaria

Gastrointestinal: Abdominal cramps, heartburn, indigestion, nausea

Neuromuscular & skeletal: Weakness

1% to 10%:

Cardiovascular: Bradycardia

Central nervous system: Headache, nervousness, confusion

Dermatologic: Itching

Endocrine & metabolic: Fluid retention

Gastrointestinal: Dyspepsia, vomiting, abdominal pain, GI ulceration

Genitourinary: Decreased urination

Otic: Tinnitus

Respiratory: Shortness of breath, dyspnea

<1%: Edema, congestive heart failure, arrhythmias, tachycardia, hypertension, confusion, hallucinations, mental depression, insomnia, aseptic meningitis, urticaria, erythema multiforme, toxic epidermal necrolysis, Stevens-Johnson syndrome, polydipsia, hot flashes, gastritis, xerostomia, anorexia, biliary tract spasm, cystitis, urinary tract spasm, neutropenia, anemia, agranulocytosis, inhibition of platelet aggregation, hemolytic anemia, bone marrow suppression, leukopenia, thrombocytopenia, hepatitis, peripheral neuropathy, vision changes, blurred vision, conjunctivitis, dry eyes, toxic amblyopia, diplopia, miosis, decreased hearing, acute renal failure, polyuria, allergic rhinitis, shortness of breath, epistaxis, histamine release, physical and psychological dependence with prolonged use

Overdosage/Toxicology Treat according to separate ingredient (hydrocodone and ibuprofen) toxicology

Drug Interactions
Decreased effect: May decrease efficacy of ACE inhibitors and diuretics
Increased toxicity potential: Aspirin, other CNS depressants, alcohol, MAO inhibitors, ACE inhibitors, tricyclic antidepressants, lithium, anticoagulants, anticholinergics, methotrexate

Mechanism of Action Refer to individual agents

Usual Dosage Adults: Oral: 1-2 tablets every 4-6 hours as needed for pain; maximum: 5 tablets/day

Patient Information Hydrocodone and ibuprofen, like other opioid-containing analgesics, may impair mental and/or physical abilities required for the performance of potentially hazardous tasks such as driving a car or operating machinery; patients should be cautioned accordingly. Alcohol and other CNS depressants may produce an additive CNS depression, when taken with this combination product, and should be avoided. This agent may be habit-forming. Patients should take the drug only for as long as it is prescribed, in the amounts prescribed, and no more frequently than prescribed.

Additional Information The antipyretic and anti-inflammatory activity of ibuprofen may reduce fever and inflammation, thus diminishing their utility as diagnostic signs in detecting complications of presumed noninfectious, noninflammatory painful conditions.

Dosage Forms Tablet: Hydrocodone bitartrate 7.5 mg and ibuprofen 200 mg

Hydrocodone and Phenylpropanolamine
(hye droe KOE done & fen il proe pa NOLE a meen)
U.S. Brand Names Codamine®; Codamine® Pediatric; Hycomine®; Hycomine® Pediatric; Hydrocodone PA® Syrup
Therapeutic Category Antitussive/Decongestant
Dosage Forms Syrup:
Codamine®, Hycomine®: Hydrocodone bitartrate 5 mg and phenylpropanolamine hydrochloride 25 mg per 5 mL (480 mL)
Codamine® Pediatric, Hycomine® Pediatric: Hydrocodone bitartrate 2.5 mg and phenylpropanolamine hydrochloride 12.5 mg per 5 mL (480 mL)

Hydrocodone and Pseudoephedrine
(hye droe KOE done & soo doe e FED rin)
U.S. Brand Names Detussin® Liquid; Entuss-D® Liquid; Histussin D® Liquid; Tyrodone® Liquid
Therapeutic Category Cough and Cold Combination
Dosage Forms Liquid:
Entuss-D®: Hydrocodone bitartrate 5 mg and pseudoephedrine hydrochloride 30 mg per 5 mL
Detussin®, Histussin D®, Tyrodone®: Hydrocodone bitartrate 5 mg and pseudoephedrine hydrochloride 60 mg per 5 mL

Hydrocodone, Chlorpheniramine, Phenylephrine, Acetaminophen and Caffeine
(hye droe KOE done, klor fen IR a meen, fen il EF rin, a seet a MIN oh fen, & KAF een)
U.S. Brand Names Hycomine® Compound
Therapeutic Category Antitussive
Dosage Forms Tablet: Hydrocodone bitartrate 5 mg, chlorpheniramine maleate 2 mg, phenylephrine hydrochloride 10 mg, acetaminophen 250 mg, and caffeine 30 mg

♦ **Hydrocodone PA® Syrup** see Hydrocodone and Phenylpropanolamine *on this page*

Hydrocodone, Phenylephrine, Pyrilamine, Phenindamine, Chlorpheniramine, and Ammonium Chloride
(hye droe KOE done, fen il EF rin, peer IL a meen, fen IN da meen, klor fen IR a meen, & a MOE nee um KLOR ide)
U.S. Brand Names P-V-Tussin®
Therapeutic Category Antihistamine/Decongestant/Antitussive
Dosage Forms Syrup: Hydrocodone bitartrate 2.5 mg, phenylephrine hydrochloride 5 mg, pyrilamine maleate 6 mg, phenindamine tartrate 5 mg, chlorpheniramine maleate 2 mg, and ammonium chloride 50 mg per 5 mL with alcohol 5% (480 mL, 3780 mL)

Hydrocodone, Pseudoephedrine, and Guaifenesin
(hye droe KOE done, soo doe e FED rin & gwye FEN e sin)
U.S. Brand Names Cophene XP®; Detussin® Expectorant; SRC® Expectorant; Tussafin® Expectorant
Therapeutic Category Antitussive/Decongestant/Expectorant
Dosage Forms Liquid: Hydrocodone bitartrate 5 mg, pseudoephedrine hydrochloride 60 mg, and guaifenesin 200 mg per 5 mL with alcohol 12.5% (480 mL)

♦ **Hydrocort®** see Hydrocortisone *on this page*

Hydrocortisone (hye droe KOR ti sone)
Related Information
Corticosteroids Comparison *on page 1319*
(Continued)

Hydrocortisone (Continued)

U.S. Brand Names Acticort 100®; Aeroseb-HC®; A-hydroCort®; Ala-Cort®; Ala-Scalp®; Anucort-HC® Suppository; Anuprep HC® Suppository; Anusol® HC-1 [OTC]; Anusol® HC-2.5% [OTC]; Anusol-HC® Suppository; CaldeCORT®; CaldeCORT® Anti-Itch Spray; Cetacort®; Clocort® Maximum Strength; CortaGel® [OTC]; Cortaid® Maximum Strength [OTC]; Cortaid® With Aloe [OTC]; Cort-Dome®; Cortef®; Cortef® Feminine Itch; Cortenema®; Cortifoam®; Cortizone®-5 [OTC]; Cortizone®-10 [OTC]; Delcort®; Dermacort®; Dermarest Dricort®; DermiCort®; Dermolate® [OTC]; Dermtex® HC With Aloe; Eldecort®; Gynecort® [OTC]; Hemril-HC® Uniserts®; Hi-Cor-1.0®; Hi-Cor-2.5®; Hycort®; Hydrocort®; Hydrocortone® Acetate; Hydrocortone® Phosphate; HydroSKIN®; Hydro-Tex® [OTC]; Hytone®; LactiCare-HC®; Lanacort® [OTC]; Locoid®; Nutracort®; Orabase® HCA; Pandel®; Penecort®; Procort® [OTC]; Proctocort™; Scalpicin®; Solu-Cortef®; S-T Cort®; Synacort®; Tegrin®-HC U-Cort™; Westcort®

Synonyms Compound F; Cortisol; Hydrocortisone Acetate; Hydrocortisone Buteprate; Hydrocortisone Butyrate; Hydrocortisone Cypionate; Hydrocortisone Sodium Phosphate; Hydrocortisone Sodium Succinate; Hydrocortisone Valerate

Therapeutic Category Anti-inflammatory Agent; Anti-inflammatory Agent, Rectal; Corticosteroid; Corticosteroid, Rectal; Corticosteroid, Systemic; Corticosteroid, Topical (Low Potency); Corticosteroid, Topical (Medium Potency); Glucocorticoid; Mineralocorticoid

Use Management of adrenocortical insufficiency; relief of inflammation of corticosteroid-responsive dermatoses (low and medium potency topical corticosteroid); adjunctive treatment of ulcerative colitis

Pregnancy Risk Factor C

Contraindications Serious infections, except septic shock or tuberculous meningitis; known hypersensitivity to hydrocortisone; viral, fungal, or tubercular skin lesions

Warnings/Precautions

Use with caution in patients with hyperthyroidism, cirrhosis, nonspecific ulcerative colitis, hypertension, osteoporosis, thromboembolic tendencies, CHF, convulsive disorders, myasthenia gravis, thrombophlebitis, peptic ulcer, diabetes

Acute adrenal insufficiency may occur with abrupt withdrawal after long-term therapy or with stress; young pediatric patients may be more susceptible to adrenal axis suppression from topical therapy

Because of the risk of adverse effects, systemic corticosteroids should be used cautiously in the elderly, in the smallest possible dose, and for the shortest possible time

Adverse Reactions

>10%:

Central nervous system: Insomnia, nervousness

Gastrointestinal: Increased appetite, indigestion

1% to 10%:

Dermatologic: Hirsutism

Endocrine & metabolic: Diabetes mellitus

Neuromuscular & skeletal: Arthralgia

Ocular: Cataracts

Respiratory: Epistaxis

<1%: Hypertension, edema, euphoria, headache, delirium, hallucinations, seizures, mood swings, acne, dermatitis, skin atrophy, bruising, hyperpigmentation, hypokalemia, hyperglycemia, Cushing's syndrome, sodium and water retention, bone growth suppression, amenorrhea, peptic ulcer, abdominal distention, ulcerative esophagitis, pancreatitis, muscle wasting, hypersensitivity reactions, immunosuppression

Overdosage/Toxicology Symptoms of overdose include cushingoid appearance (systemic), muscle weakness (systemic), osteoporosis (systemic) all with long-term use only. When consumed in excessive quantities for prolonged periods, systemic hypercorticism and adrenal suppression may occur. In those cases, discontinuation and withdrawal of the corticosteroid should be done judiciously.

Drug Interactions CYP2D6 and 3A3/4 enzyme substrate

Decreased effect:

Insulin decreases hypoglycemic effect

Phenytoin, phenobarbital, ephedrine, and rifampin increase metabolism of hydrocortisone and decrease steroid blood level

Increased toxicity:

Oral anticoagulants change prothrombin time; potassium-depleting diuretics increase risk of hypokalemia

Cardiac glucosides increase risk of arrhythmias or digitalis toxicity secondary to hypokalemia

Stability

Hydrocortisone sodium phosphate and hydrocortisone sodium succinate are clear, light yellow solutions which are heat labile

After initial reconstitution, hydrocortisone sodium succinate solutions are stable for 3 days at room temperature and refrigeration if protected from light

Stability of parenteral admixture (Solu-Cortef®) at room temperature (25°C) and at refrigeration temperature (4°C) is concentration dependent

Minimum volume: Concentration should not exceed 1 mg/mL

Stability of concentration ≤1 mg/mL: 24 hours

Stability of concentration >1 mg/mL to <25 mg/mL: Unpredictable, 4-6 hours

Stability of concentration ≥25 mg/mL: 3 days

Standard diluent (Solu-Cortef®): 50 mg/50 mL D_5W; 100 mg/100 mL D_5W

Comments: Should be administered in a 0.1-1 mg/mL concentration due to stability problems

Mechanism of Action Decreases inflammation by suppression of migration of polymorphonuclear leukocytes and reversal of increased capillary permeability

Pharmacodynamics/Kinetics

Absorption: Rapid by all routes, except rectally

Metabolism: In the liver

Half-life, biologic: 8-12 hours

Elimination: Renally, mainly as 17-hydroxysteroids and 17-ketosteroids

Hydrocortisone acetate salt has a slow onset but long duration of action when compared with more soluble preparations

Hydrocortisone sodium phosphate salt is a water soluble salt with a rapid onset but short duration of action

Hydrocortisone sodium succinate salt is a water soluble salt with is rapidly active

Usual Dosage Dose should be based on severity of disease and patient response

Acute adrenal insufficiency: I.M., I.V.:

Infants and young Children: Succinate: 1-2 mg/kg/dose bolus, then 25-150 mg/day in divided doses every 6-8 hours

Older Children: Succinate: 1-2 mg/kg bolus then 150-250 mg/day in divided doses every 6-8 hours

Adults: Succinate: 100 mg I.V. bolus, then 300 mg/day in divided doses every 8 hours or as a continuous infusion for 48 hours; once patient is stable change to oral, 50 mg every 8 hours for 6 doses, then taper to 30-50 mg/day in divided doses

Chronic adrenal corticoid insufficiency: Adults: Oral: 20-30 mg/day

Anti-inflammatory or immunosuppressive:

Infants and Children:

Oral: 2.5-10 mg/kg/day **or** 75-300 mg/m^2/day every 6-8 hours

I.M., I.V.: Succinate: 1-5 mg/kg/day **or** 30-150 mg/m^2/day divided every 12-24 hours

Adolescents and Adults: Oral, I.M., I.V.: Succinate: 15-240 mg every 12 hours

Congenital adrenal hyperplasia: Oral: Initial: 30-36 mg/m^2/day with $^1/_3$ of dose every morning and $^2/_3$ every evening or $^1/_4$ every morning and mid-day and $^1/_2$ every evening; maintenance: 20-25 mg/m^2/day in divided doses

Physiologic replacement: Children:

Oral: 0.5-0.75 mg/kg/day **or** 20-25 mg/m^2/day every 8 hours

I.M.: Succinate: 0.25-0.35 mg/kg/day **or** 12-15 mg/m^2/day once daily

Shock: I.M., I.V.: Succinate:

Children: Initial: 50 mg/kg, then repeated in 4 hours and/or every 24 hours as needed

Adolescents and Adults: 500 mg to 2 g every 2-6 hours

Status asthmaticus: Children and Adults: I.V.: Succinate: 1-2 mg/kg/dose every 6 hours for 24 hours, then maintenance of 0.5-1 mg/kg every 6 hours

Rheumatic diseases:

Adults: Intralesional, intra-articular, soft tissue injection: Acetate:

Large joints: 25 mg (up to 37.5 mg)

Small joints: 10-25 mg

Tendon sheaths: 5-12.5 mg

Soft tissue infiltration: 25-50 mg (up to 75 mg)

Bursae: 25-37.5 mg

Ganglia: 12.5-25 mg

Dermatosis: Children >2 years and Adults: Topical: Apply to affected area 3-4 times/day (Buteprate: Apply once or twice daily)

Ulcerative colitis: Adults: Rectal: 10-100 mg 1-2 times/day for 2-3 weeks

Administration

Oral: Administer with food or milk to decrease GI upset

Parenteral: Hydrocortisone sodium succinate may be administered by I.M. or I.V. routes

I.V. bolus: Dilute to 50 mg/mL and administer over 30 seconds to several minutes (depending on the dose)

I.V. intermittent infusion: Dilute to 1 mg/mL and administer over 20-30 minutes

Topical: Apply a thin film to clean, dry skin and rub in gently

Monitoring Parameters Blood pressure, weight, serum glucose, and electrolytes

Reference Range Therapeutic: AM: 5-25 µg/dL (SI: 138-690 nmol/L), PM: 2-9 µg/dL (SI: 55-248 nmol/L) depending on test, assay

Patient Information Notify surgeon or dentist before surgical repair; oral formulation may cause GI upset, take with food; notify physician if any sign of infection occurs; avoid abrupt withdrawal when on long-term therapy. Before applying, gently wash area to reduce risk of infection; apply a thin film to cleansed area and rub in gently and thoroughly until medication vanishes; avoid exposure to sunlight, severe sunburn may occur.

Additional Information

Sodium content of 1 g (sodium succinate injection): 47.5 mg (2.07 mEq)

Hydrocortisone base topical cream, lotion, and ointments in concentrations of 0.25%, 0.5%, and 1% may be OTC or prescription depending on the product labeling

Dosage Forms

Hydrocortisone acetate:

Aerosol, rectal: 10% (20 g)

Cream, topical: 0.5% (15 g, 22.5 g, 30 g); 1% (15 g, 30 g, 120 g)

Ointment, topical: 0.5% (15 g, 30 g); 1% (15 g, 21 g, 30 g)

Injection, suspension: 25 mg/mL (5 mL, 10 mL); 50 mg/mL (5 mL, 10 mL)

Suppositories, rectal: 10 mg, 25 mg

Hydrocortisone base:

Aerosol, topical: 0.5% (45 g, 58 g); 1% (45 mL)

(Continued)

Hydrocortisone *(Continued)*

Cream, rectal: 1% (30 g); 2.5% (30 g)
Cream, topical: 0.5% (15 g, 30 g, 60 g, 120 g, 454 g); 1% (15 g, 20 g, 30 g, 60 g, 90 g, 120 g, 240 g, 454 g); 2.5% (15 g, 20 g, 30 g, 60 g, 120 g, 240 g, 454 g)
Gel, topical: 0.5% (15 g, 30 g); 1% (15 g, 30 g)
Lotion, topical: 0.25% (120 mL); 0.5% (30 mL, 60 mL, 120 mL); 1% (60 mL, 118 mL, 120 mL) ; 2% (30 mL) ; 2.5% (60 mL, 120 mL)
Ointment, rectal: 1% (30 g)
Ointment, topical: 0.5% (30 g) ; 1% (15 g, 20 g, 28 g, 30 g, 60 g, 120 g, 240 g, 454 g); 2.5% (20 g, 30 g)
Paste: 0.5% (5 g)
Solution, topical: 1% (45 mL, 75 mL, 120 mL)
Suspension, rectal: 100 mg/60 mL (7s)
Tablet, oral: 5 mg, 10 mg, 20 mg
Hydrocortisone buteprate: Cream: 1% (15 g, 45 g)
Hydrocortisone butyrate:
Cream: 0.1% (15 g, 45 g)
Ointment, topical: 0.1% (15 g, 45 g)
Solution, topical: 0.1% (20 mL, 50 mL)
Hydrocortisone cypionate:
Suspension, oral: 10 mg/5 mL (120 mL)
Hydrocortisone sodium phosphate:
Injection, I.M./I.V./S.C.: 50 mg/mL (2 mL, 10 mL)
Hydrocortisone sodium succinate:
Injection, IM/I.V.: 100 mg, 250 mg, 500 mg, 1000 mg
Hydrocortisone valerate:
Cream, topical: 0.2% (15 g, 45 g, 60 g)
Ointment, topical: 0.2% (15 g, 45 g, 60 g, 120 g)

♦ **Hydrocortisone Acetate** *see* Hydrocortisone *on page 579*
♦ **Hydrocortisone Buteprate** *see* Hydrocortisone *on page 579*
♦ **Hydrocortisone Butyrate** *see* Hydrocortisone *on page 579*
♦ **Hydrocortisone Cypionate** *see* Hydrocortisone *on page 579*
♦ **Hydrocortisone Sodium Phosphate** *see* Hydrocortisone *on page 579*
♦ **Hydrocortisone Sodium Succinate** *see* Hydrocortisone *on page 579*
♦ **Hydrocortisone Valerate** *see* Hydrocortisone *on page 579*
♦ **Hydrocortone® Acetate** *see* Hydrocortisone *on page 579*
♦ **Hydrocortone® Phosphate** *see* Hydrocortisone *on page 579*
♦ **Hydro-Crysti-12®** *see* Hydroxocobalamin *on page 585*
♦ **HydroDIURIL®** *see* Hydrochlorothiazide *on page 574*

Hydroflumethiazide *(hye droe floo meth EYE a zide)*

Related Information
Sulfonamide Derivatives *on page 1337*

U.S. Brand Names Diucardin®; Saluron®

Therapeutic Category Antihypertensive Agent; Diuretic, Thiazide

Use Management of mild to moderate hypertension; treatment of edema in congestive heart failure and nephrotic syndrome

Pregnancy Risk Factor C

Contraindications Anuria, renal decompensation, hypersensitivity to hydrochlorothiazide or any component, cross-sensitivity with other thiazides and sulfonamide derivatives

Warnings/Precautions Use with caution in renal disease, hepatic disease, gout, lupus erythematosus, diabetes mellitus; some products may contain tartrazine

Adverse Reactions
1% to 10%: Endocrine & metabolic: Hypokalemia
<1%: Hypotension, drowsiness, photosensitivity, rash, fluid and electrolyte imbalances (hypocalcemia, hypomagnesemia, hyponatremia), hyperglycemia, anorexia, polyuria, aplastic anemia, hemolytic anemia, leukopenia, agranulocytosis, thrombocytopenia, rarely blood dyscrasias, hepatitis, paresthesia, prerenal azotemia, uremia

Overdosage/Toxicology
Symptoms of overdose include hypermotility, diuresis, lethargy
Following GI decontamination, therapy is supportive with I.V. fluids, electrolytes, and I.V. pressors if needed

Drug Interactions
Decreased effect:
Thiazides may decrease the effect of anticoagulants, antigout agents, sulfonylureas
Bile acid sequestrants, methenamine, and NSAIDs may decrease the effect of the thiazides
Increased effect: Thiazides may increase the toxicity of allopurinol, anesthetics, antineoplastics, calcium salts, diazoxide, digitalis, lithium, loop diuretics, methyldopa, nondepolarizing muscle relaxants, vitamin D; amphotericin B and anticholinergics may increase the toxicity of thiazides

Mechanism of Action The diuretic mechanism of action is primarily inhibition of sodium, chloride, and water reabsorption in the renal distal tubules, thereby producing diuresis with a resultant reduction in plasma volume

Pharmacodynamics/Kinetics
Onset of diuretic effect: Within ~2 hours
Peak effect: Within ~4 hours

Duration of action: 12-24 hours
Usual Dosage Oral:
Children (not approved): 1 mg/kg/24 hours
Adults:
Edema:
Initial: 50 mg 1-2 times/day
Maintenance: 25-200 mg/day (use divided doses when >100 mg/day)
Hypertension:
Initial: 50 mg twice daily
Maintenance: 50-100 mg/day; maximum: 200 mg/day
Monitoring Parameters Assess weight, I & O reports daily to determine fluid loss; blood pressure, serum electrolytes, BUN, creatinine
Test Interactions ↑ ammonia (B), ↑ amylase (S), ↑ calcium (S), ↑ chloride (S), ↑ glucose, ↑ uric acid (S); ↓ chloride (S), ↓ magnesium, ↓ potassium (S), ↓ sodium (S)
Patient Information May be taken with food or milk; take early in day to avoid nocturia; take the last dose of multiple doses no later than 6 PM unless instructed otherwise. A few people who take this medication become more sensitive to sunlight and may experience skin rash, redness, itching or severe sunburn, especially if sun block SPF ≥15 is not used on exposed skin areas.
Nursing Implications Take blood pressure with patient lying down and standing
Dosage Forms Tablet: 50 mg

Hydroflumethiazide and Reserpine
(hye droe floo meth EYE a zide & re SER peen)
U.S. Brand Names Hydro-Fluserpine®; Salutensin®; Salutensin®-Demi
Therapeutic Category Antihypertensive Agent, Combination
Dosage Forms
Tablet (Salutensin®): Hydroflumethiazide 50 mg and reserpine 0.125 mg
Tablet (Hydro-Fluserpine®, Salutensin-Demi®): Hydroflumethiazide 25 mg and reserpine 0.125 mg

◆ **Hydro-Fluserpine®** see Hydroflumethiazide and Reserpine on this page
◆ **Hydrogesic®** see Hydrocodone and Acetaminophen on page 575
◆ **Hydromet®** see Hydrocodone and Homatropine on page 577
◆ **Hydromorph Contin®** see Hydromorphone on this page

Hydromorphone (hye droe MOR fone)
Related Information
Narcotic Agonists Comparison on page 1328
U.S. Brand Names Dilaudid®; Dilaudid-5®; Dilaudid-HP®; HydroStat IR®
Canadian Brand Names Hydromorph Contin®; PMS-Hydromorphone
Synonyms Dihydromorphinone; Hydromorphone Hydrochloride
Therapeutic Category Analgesic, Narcotic; Antitussive
Use Management of moderate to severe pain; antitussive at lower doses
Restrictions C-II
Pregnancy Risk Factor B (D if used for prolonged periods or in high doses at term)
Contraindications Hypersensitivity to hydromorphone or any component or other phenanthrene derivative
Warnings/Precautions Tablet and cough syrup contain tartrazine which may cause allergic reactions; hydromorphone shares toxic potential of opiate agonists, and precaution of opiate agonist therapy should be observed; extreme caution should be taken to avoid confusing the highly concentrated injection with the less concentrated injectable product, injection contains benzyl alcohol; use with caution in patients with hypersensitivity to other phenanthrene opiates, in patients with respiratory disease, or severe liver or renal failure; tolerance or drug dependence may result from extended use
Adverse Reactions
Percentage unknown: Antidiuretic hormone release, biliary tract spasm, urinary tract spasm, miosis, histamine release, physical and psychological dependence, increased AST, ALT
>10%:
Cardiovascular: Palpitations, hypotension, peripheral vasodilation
Central nervous system: Dizziness, lightheadedness, drowsiness
Gastrointestinal: Anorexia
1% to 10%:
Cardiovascular: Tachycardia, bradycardia, flushing of face
Central nervous system: CNS depression, increased intracranial pressure, fatigue, headache, nervousness, restlessness
Gastrointestinal: Nausea, vomiting, constipation, stomach cramps, xerostomia
Genitourinary: Decreased urination, ureteral spasm
Hepatic: Increased LFTs
Neuromuscular & skeletal: Trembling, weakness
Respiratory: Respiratory depression, dyspnea, shortness of breath
<1%: Hallucinations, mental depression, pruritus, rash, urticaria, paralytic ileus
Overdosage/Toxicology
Symptoms of overdose include CNS depression, respiratory depression, miosis, apnea, pulmonary edema, convulsions
Maintain airway, establish I.V. line; naloxone 2 mg I.V. (0.01 mg/kg for children) with repeat administration as necessary up to a total of 10 mg.
(Continued)

Hydromorphone *(Continued)*

Drug Interactions Increased toxicity: CNS depressants, phenothiazines, tricyclic antidepressants may potentiate the adverse effects of hydromorphone

Stability Protect tablets from light; do not store intact ampuls in refrigerator; a slightly yellowish discoloration has not been associated with a loss of potency; I.V. is **incompatible** when mixed with minocycline, prochlorperazine, sodium bicarbonate, tetracycline, thiopental

Mechanism of Action Binds to opiate receptors in the CNS, causing inhibition of ascending pain pathways, altering the perception of and response to pain; causes cough supression by direct central action in the medulla; produces generalized CNS depression

Pharmacodynamics/Kinetics
  Onset of analgesic effect: Within 15-30 minutes
  Peak effect: Within 0.5-1.5 hours
  Duration: 4-5 hours
  Metabolism: Primarily in the liver
  Bioavailability: 62%
  Half-life: 1-3 hours
  Elimination: In urine, principally as glucuronide conjugates

Usual Dosage
  Doses should be titrated to appropriate analgesic effects; when changing routes of administration, note that oral doses are less than half as effective as parenteral doses (may be only one-fifth as effective)
  Pain: Older Children and Adults:
    Oral, I.M., I.V., S.C.: 1-4 mg/dose every 4-6 hours as needed; usual adult dose: 2 mg/dose
    Rectal: 3 mg every 6-8 hours
  Antitussive: Oral:
    Children 6-12 years: 0.5 mg every 3-4 hours as needed
    Children >12 years and Adults: 1 mg every 3-4 hours as needed
  Dosing adjustment in hepatic impairment: Should be considered

Dietary Considerations
  Alcohol: Additive CNS effects, avoid or limit alcohol; watch for sedation
  Food: Glucose may cause hyperglycemia; monitor blood glucose concentrations

Monitoring Parameters Pain relief, respiratory and mental status, blood pressure

Patient Information May cause drowsiness; avoid alcohol; take with food or milk to minimize GI distress

Nursing Implications Observe patient for oversedation, respiratory depression, implement safety measures

Additional Information Equianalgesic doses: Morphine 10 mg I.M. = hydromorphone 1.5 mg I.M.

Dosage Forms
  Injection, as hydrochloride:
    Dilaudid®: 1 mg/mL (1 mL); 2 mg/mL (1 mL, 20 mL); 3 mg/mL (1 mL); 4 mg/mL (1 mL)
    Dilaudid-HP®: 10 mg/mL (1 mL, 2 mL, 5 mL)
  Liquid, as hydrochloride: 5 mg/5 mL (480 mL)
  Powder for injection, as hydrochloride: (Dilaudid-HP®): 250 mg
  Suppository, rectal, as hydrochloride: 3 mg (6s)
  Tablet, as hydrochloride: 1 mg, 2 mg, 3 mg, 4 mg, 8 mg

• **Hydromorphone Hydrochloride** *see* Hydromorphone *on previous page*
• **Hydromox®** *see* Quinethazone *on page 1003*
• **Hydropane®** *see* Hydrocodone and Homatropine *on page 577*
• **Hydro-Par®** *see* Hydrochlorothiazide *on page 574*
• **Hydrophed®** *see* Theophylline, Ephedrine, and Hydroxyzine *on page 1125*
• **Hydropres®** *see* Hydrochlorothiazide and Reserpine *on page 575*
• **Hydroquinol** *see* Hydroquinone *on this page*

Hydroquinone *(HYE droe kwin one)*

U.S. Brand Names Ambi® Skin Tone [OTC]; Eldopaque® [OTC]; Eldopaque Forte®; Eldoquin® [OTC]; Eldoquin® Forte®; Esoterica® Facial [OTC]; Esoterica® Regular [OTC]; Esoterica® Sensitive Skin Formula [OTC]; Esoterica® Sunscreen [OTC]; Melanex®; Melpaque HP®; Melquin HP®; Nuquin HP®; Porcelana® [OTC]; Porcelana® Sunscreen [OTC]; Solaquin® [OTC]; Solaquin Forte®

Canadian Brand Names Neostrata™ HQ; Ultraquin™

Synonyms Hydroquinol; Quinol

Therapeutic Category Depigmenting Agent

Use Gradual bleaching of hyperpigmented skin conditions

Pregnancy Risk Factor C

Contraindications Sunburn, depilatory usage, known hypersensitivity to hydroquinone

Warnings/Precautions Limit application to area no larger than face and neck or hands and arms

Adverse Reactions 1% to 10%:
  Dermatologic: Dermatitis, dryness, erythema, stinging, inflammatory reaction, sensitization
  Local: Irritation

Mechanism of Action Produces reversible depigmentation of the skin by suppression of melanocyte metabolic processes, in particular the inhibition of the enzymatic oxidation of tyrosine to DOPA (3,4-dihydroxyphenylalanine); sun exposure reverses this effect and will cause repigmentation.

Pharmacodynamics/Kinetics Onset and duration of depigmentation produced by hydroquinone varies among individuals

Usual Dosage Children >12 years and Adults: Topical: Apply thin layer and rub in twice daily

Patient Information Use sunscreens or clothing; do not use on irritated or denuded skin; stop using if rash or irritation develops; for external use only, avoid eye contact

Dosage Forms
Cream, topical:
Esoterica® Sensitive Skin Formula: 1.5% (85 g)
Eldopaque®, Eldoquin®, Esoterica® Facial, Esoterica® Regular, Porcelana®: 2% (14.2 g, 28.4 g, 60 g, 85 g, 120 g)
Eldopaque Forte®, Eldoquin® Forte®, Melquin HP®: 4% (14.2 g, 28.4 g)
Cream, topical, with sunscreen:
Esoterica® Sunscreen, Porcelana®, Solaquin®: 2% (28.4 g, 120 g)
Melpaque HP®, Nuquin HP®, Solaquin Forte®: 4% (14.2 g, 28.4 g)
Gel, topical, with sunscreen (Solaquin Forte®): 4% (14.2 g, 28.4 g)
Solution, topical (Melanex®): 3% (30 mL)

♦ **Hydro-Serp®** see Hydrochlorothiazide and Reserpine on page 575
♦ **Hydroserpine®** see Hydrochlorothiazide and Reserpine on page 575
♦ **HydroSKIN®** see Hydrocortisone on page 579
♦ **HydroStat IR®** see Hydromorphone on page 583
♦ **Hydro-Tex® [OTC]** see Hydrocortisone on page 579
♦ **Hydrotropine®** see Hydrocodone and Homatropine on page 577

Hydroxocobalamin (hye droks oh koe BAL a min)

U.S. Brand Names Alphamin®; Codroxomin®; Hybalamin®; Hydro-Cobex®; Hydro-Crysti-12®; LA-12®
Canadian Brand Names Acti-B$_{12}$®
Synonyms Vitamin B$_{12}$
Therapeutic Category Vitamin, Water Soluble
Use Treatment of pernicious anemia, vitamin B$_{12}$ deficiency, increased B$_{12}$ requirements due to pregnancy, thyrotoxicosis, hemorrhage, malignancy, liver or kidney disease
Pregnancy Risk Factor C
Contraindications Hypersensitivity to cyanocobalamin or any component, cobalt; patients with hereditary optic nerve atrophy
Warnings/Precautions Some products contain benzoyl alcohol; avoid use in premature infants; an intradermal test dose should be performed for hypersensitivity; use only if oral supplementation not possible or when treating pernicious anemia
Adverse Reactions
1% to 10%:
Dermatologic: Itching
Gastrointestinal: Diarrhea
<1%: Peripheral vascular thrombosis, urticaria, anaphylaxis
Mechanism of Action Coenzyme for various metabolic functions, including fat and carbohydrate metabolism and protein synthesis, used in cell replication and hematopoiesis
Usual Dosage Vitamin B$_{12}$ deficiency: I.M.:
Children: 1-5 mg given in single doses of 100 mcg over 2 or more weeks, followed by 30-50 mcg/month
Adults: 30 mcg/day for 5-10 days, followed by 100-200 mcg/month
Administration Administer I.M. only; may require coadministration of folic acid
Patient Information Therapy is required throughout life; do not take folic acid instead of B$_{12}$ to prevent anemia
Dosage Forms Injection: 1000 mcg/mL (10 mL, 30 mL)

Hydroxyamphetamine and Tropicamide
(hye droks ee am FET a meen & troe PIK a mide)
U.S. Brand Names Paremyd® Ophthalmic
Therapeutic Category Adrenergic Agonist Agent
Dosage Forms Solution, ophthalmic: Hydroxyamphetamine hydrobromide 1% and tropicamide 0.25% (5 mL, 15 mL)

♦ **Hydroxycarbamide** see Hydroxyurea on page 587

Hydroxychloroquine (hye droks ee KLOR oh kwin)

U.S. Brand Names Plaquenil®
Synonyms Hydroxychloroquine Sulfate
Therapeutic Category Antimalarial Agent
Use Suppresses and treats acute attacks of malaria; treatment of systemic lupus erythematosus and rheumatoid arthritis
Pregnancy Risk Factor C
Contraindications Retinal or visual field changes attributable to 4-aminoquinolines; hypersensitivity to hydroxychloroquine, 4-aminoquinoline derivatives, or any component
Warnings/Precautions Use with caution in patients with hepatic disease, G-6-PD deficiency, psoriasis, and porphyria; long-term use in children is not recommended; perform
(Continued)

Hydroxychloroquine *(Continued)*

baseline and periodic (6 months) ophthalmologic examinations; test periodically for muscle weakness

Adverse Reactions

>10%:

Central nervous system: Headache

Dermatologic: Itching

Gastrointestinal: Diarrhea, loss of appetite, nausea, stomach cramps, vomiting

Ocular: Ciliary muscle dysfunction

1% to 10%:

Central nervous system: Dizziness, lightheadedness, nervousness, restlessness

Dermatologic: Bleaching of hair, rash, discoloration of skin (black-blue)

Ocular: Ocular toxicity, keratopathy, retinopathy

<1%: Emotional changes, seizures, agranulocytosis, aplastic anemia, neutropenia, thrombocytopenia, neuromyopathy, ototoxicity

Overdosage/Toxicology

Symptoms of overdose include headache, drowsiness, visual changes, cardiovascular collapse, and seizures followed by respiratory and cardiac arrest

Treatment is symptomatic; activated charcoal will bind the drug following GI decontamination; urinary alkalinization will enhance renal elimination

Drug Interactions

Chloroquine and other 4-aminoquinolones may be decreased due to GI binding with kaolin or magnesium trisilicate

Increased effect: Cimetidine increases levels of chloroquine and probably other 4-aminoquinolones

Mechanism of Action Interferes with digestive vacuole function within sensitive malarial parasites by increasing the pH and interfering with lysosomal degradation of hemoglobin; inhibits locomotion of neutrophils and chemotaxis of eosinophils; impairs complement-dependent antigen-antibody reactions

Pharmacodynamics/Kinetics

Absorption: Oral: Complete

Protein binding: 55%

Metabolism: In the liver

Half-life: 32-50 days

Elimination: Metabolites and unchanged drug slowly excreted in urine, may be enhanced by urinary acidification

Usual Dosage Note: Hydroxychloroquine sulfate 200 mg is equivalent to 155 mg hydroxychloroquine base and 250 mg chloroquine phosphate. Oral:

Children:

Chemoprophylaxis of malaria: 5 mg/kg (base) once weekly; should not exceed the recommended adult dose; begin 2 weeks before exposure; continue for 4-6 weeks after leaving endemic area; if suppressive therapy is not begun prior to the exposure, double the initial dose and give in 2 doses, 6 hours apart

Acute attack: 10 mg/kg (base) initial dose; followed by 5 mg/kg at 6, 24, and 48 hours

JRA or SLE: 3-5 mg/kg/day divided 1-2 times/day; avoid exceeding 7 mg/kg/day

Adults:

Chemoprophylaxis of malaria: 310 mg base weekly on same day each week; begin 2 weeks before exposure; continue for 4-6 weeks after leaving endemic area; if suppressive therapy is not begun prior to the exposure, double the initial dose and give in 2 doses, 6 hours apart

Acute attack: 620 mg first dose day 1; 310 mg in 6 hours day 1; 310 mg in 1 dose day 2; and 310 mg in 1 dose on day 3

Rheumatoid arthritis: 310-465 mg/day to start taken with food or milk; increase dose until optimum response level is reached; usually after 4-12 weeks dose should be reduced by ½ and a maintenance dose of 155-310 mg/day given

Lupus erythematosus: 310 mg every day or twice daily for several weeks depending on response; 155-310 mg/day for prolonged maintenance therapy

Administration Administer with food or milk

Monitoring Parameters Ophthalmologic exam, CBC

Patient Information Take with food or milk; complete full course of therapy; wear sunglasses in bright sunlight; notify physician if blurring or other vision changes, ringing in the ears, or hearing loss occurs

Nursing Implications Periodic blood counts and eye examinations are recommended when patient is on chronic therapy

Dosage Forms Tablet, as sulfate: 200 mg [base 155 mg]

Extemporaneous Preparations A 25 mg/mL hydroxychloroquine sulfate suspension is made by removing the coating off of fifteen 200 mg hydroxychloroquine sulfate tablets with a towel moistened with alcohol; tablets are ground to a fine powder and levigated to a paste with 15 mL of Ora-Plus® suspending agent; add an additional 45 mL of suspending agent and levigate until a uniform mixture is obtained; qs ad to 120 mL with sterile water for irrigation; a 30 day expiration date is recommended, although stability testing has not been performed

Pesko LJ, "Compounding: Hydroxychloroquine," *Am Druggist*, 1993, 207:57.

♦ **Hydroxychloroquine Sulfate** *see* Hydroxychloroquine *on previous page*

♦ **25-Hydroxycholecalciferol** *see* Calcifediol *on page 170*

♦ **Hydroxydaunomycin Hydrochloride** *see* Doxorubicin *on page 393*

♦ **Hydroxyethyl Starch** *see* Hetastarch *on page 566*

Hydroxyprogesterone Caproate
(hye droks ee proe JES te rone KAP roe ate)

U.S. Brand Names Hylutin® Injection; Hyprogest® 250 Injection

Therapeutic Category Progestin

Use Treatment of amenorrhea, abnormal uterine bleeding, endometriosis, uterine carcinoma

Pregnancy Risk Factor D

Contraindications Thrombophlebitis, thromboembolic disorders, cerebral hemorrhage, liver impairment, carcinoma of the breast, hypersensitivity to hydroxyprogesterone or any component, undiagnosed vaginal bleeding

Warnings/Precautions Use with caution in patients with asthma, seizure disorders, migraine, cardiac or renal impairment, history of mental depression; use of any progestin during the first 4 months of pregnancy is not recommended; observe patients closely for signs and symptoms of thrombotic disorders

Adverse Reactions
>10%:
  Cardiovascular: Edema
  Endocrine & metabolic: Breakthrough bleeding, spotting, changes in menstrual flow, amenorrhea
  Gastrointestinal: Anorexia
  Local: Pain at injection site
  Neuromuscular & skeletal: Weakness
1% to 10%:
  Central nervous system: Mental depression, insomnia, fever
  Dermatologic: Melasma or chloasma, allergic rash with or without pruritus
  Gastrointestinal: Weight gain or loss
  Genitourinary: Changes in cervical erosion and secretions, increased breast tenderness
  Hepatic: Cholestatic jaundice

Overdosage/Toxicology Toxicity is unlikely following single exposures of excessive doses; supportive treatment is adequate in most cases

Drug Interactions Decreased effect: Rifampin may increase clearance of hydroxyprogesterone

Stability Store at <40°C (15°C to 30°C); avoid freezing

Mechanism of Action Natural steroid hormone that induces secretory changes in the endometrium, promotes mammary gland development, relaxes uterine smooth muscle, blocks follicular maturation and ovulation and maintains pregnancy

Pharmacodynamics/Kinetics
Metabolism: Hepatic
Peak serum concentration: I.M.: 3-7 days; concentrations are measurable for 3-4 weeks after injection
Elimination: Renal

Usual Dosage Adults: Female: I.M.: *Long-acting progestin*
Amenorrhea: 375 mg; if no bleeding, begin cyclic treatment with estradiol valerate
Production of secretory endometrium and desquamation: (Medical D and C): 125-250 mg administered on day 10 of cycle; repeat every 7 days until suppression is no longer desired.
Uterine carcinoma: 1 g one or more times/day (1-7 g/week) for up to 12 weeks

Administration Administer deep I.M. only

Test Interactions Thyroid function tests and liver function tests and endocrine function tests

Patient Information Take this medicine only as directed; do not exceed recommended dosage nor take it for a longer period of time; if you suspect you may have become pregnant, stop taking this medicine; take with food; patient package insert is available upon request; notify physician of pain in calves along with swelling and warmth, severe headache, visual disturbance

Nursing Implications Patients should receive a copy of the patient labeling for the drug

Dosage Forms Injection:
125 mg/mL (10 mL)
Hylutin®, Hyprogest®: 250 mg/mL (5 mL)

Hydroxyurea (hye droks ee yoor EE a)

Related Information
Cancer Chemotherapy Regimens *on page 1263*
Toxicities of Chemotherapeutic Agents *on page 1288*

U.S. Brand Names Droxia™; Hydrea®

Synonyms Hydroxycarbamide

Therapeutic Category Antineoplastic Agent, Antimetabolite (Ribonucleotide Reductase Inhibitor)

Use CML in chronic phase; radiosensitizing agent in the treatment of primary brain tumors, head and neck tumors, uterine cervix and nonsmall cell lung cancer, psoriasis, sickle cell anemia and other hemoglobinopathies; treatment of hematologic conditions such as essential thrombocythemia, polycythemia vera, hypereosinophilia, and hyperleukocytosis due to acute leukemia. Has shown activity against renal cell cancer, melanoma, ovarian cancer, head and neck cancer, and prostate cancer. Management of sickle cell anemia - to reduce the frequency of painful crises and to reduce the need for blood transfusions in adult patients with sickle cell anemia with recurrent moderate to severe
(Continued)

Hydroxyurea *(Continued)*

painful crises (generally at least 3 during the preceding 12 months). Has been used in combination with didanosine and other antiretrovirals in the treatment of HIV.

Pregnancy Risk Factor D

Contraindications Severe anemia, severe bone marrow suppression; WBC <2500/mm^3 or platelet count <100,000/mm^3; hypersensitivity to hydroxyurea

Warnings/Precautions The U.S. Food and Drug Administration (FDA) currently recommends that procedures for proper handling and disposal of antineoplastic agents be considered. Use with caution in patients with renal impairment, in patients who have received prior irradiation therapy, and in the elderly.

Adverse Reactions
>10%:
  Central nervous system: Drowsiness
  Gastrointestinal: Mild to moderate nausea and vomiting may occur, as well as diarrhea, constipation, mucositis, ulceration of the GI tract, anorexia, and stomatitis
  Hematologic: Myelosuppression: Dose-limiting toxicity, causes a rapid drop in leukocyte count (seen in 4-5 days in nonhematologic malignancy and more rapidly in leukemia); thrombocytopenia and anemia occur less often; reversal of WBC count occurs rapidly, but the platelet count may take 7-10 days to recover
    WBC: Moderate
    Platelets: Moderate
    Onset (days): 7
    Nadir (days): 10
    Recovery (days): 21
1% to 10%:
  Dermatologic: Dermatologic changes (hyperpigmentation, erythema of the hands and face, maculopapular rash, or dry skin), alopecia
  Hepatic: Abnormal LFTs and hepatitis
  Renal: Increased creatinine and BUN due to impairment of renal tubular function
  Miscellaneous: Carcinogenic potential
<1%: Neurotoxicity, dizziness, disorientation, hallucination, seizures, headache, fever, facial erythema, hyperuricemia, dysuria, elevated hepatic enzymes, rarely, acute diffuse pulmonary infiltrates; dyspnea

Overdosage/Toxicology
Symptoms of overdose: Myelosuppression, facial swelling, hallucinations, disorientation
Treatment is supportive

Drug Interactions
Increased effect: Zidovudine, zalcitabine, didanosine: Synergy
Increased toxicity:
  Fluorouracil: The potential for neurotoxicity may increase with concomitant administration
  Cytarabine: Modulation of its metabolism and cytotoxicity → reduction of cytarabine dose is recommended

Stability Store capsules at room temperature; capsules may be opened and emptied into water (will not dissolve completely)

Mechanism of Action Thought to interfere (unsubstantiated hypothesis) with synthesis of DNA, during the S phase of cell division, without interfering with RNA synthesis; inhibits ribonucleoside diphosphate reductase, preventing conversion of ribonucleotides to deoxyribonucleotides; cell-cycle specific for the S phase and may hold other cells in the G$_1$ phase of the cell cycle.

Pharmacodynamics/Kinetics
Absorption: Readily from the GI tract (≥80%)
Distribution: Readily crosses the blood-brain barrier; well distributed into intestine, brain, lung, kidney tissues, effusions and ascites; appears in breast milk
Metabolism: In the liver; 50% degradation by enzymes of intestinal bacteria
Half-life: 3-4 hours
Time to peak serum concentration: Within 2 hours
Elimination: Renal excretion of urea (metabolite) and respiratory excretion of CO$_2$ (metabolic end product); 50% of the drug is excreted unchanged in urine

Usual Dosage Oral (refer to individual protocols): All dosage should be based on ideal or actual body weight, whichever is less:

Children:
  No FDA-approved dosage regimens have been established; dosages of 1500-3000 mg/m^2 as a single dose in combination with other agents every 4-6 weeks have been used in the treatment of pediatric astrocytoma, medulloblastoma, and primitive neuroectodermal tumors
  CML: Initial: 10-20 mg/kg/day once daily; adjust dose according to hematologic response
Adults: Dose should always be titrated to patient response and WBC counts; usual oral doses range from 10-30 mg/kg/day or 500-3000 mg/day; if WBC count falls to <2500 cells/mm^3, or the platelet count to <100,000/mm^3, therapy should be stopped for at least 3 days and resumed when values rise toward normal
  Solid tumors:
    Intermittent therapy: 80 mg/kg as a single dose every third day
    Continuous therapy: 20-30 mg/kg/day given as a single dose/day
  Concomitant therapy with irradiation: 80 mg/kg as a single dose every third day starting at least 7 days before initiation of irradiation
  Resistant chronic myelocytic leukemia: 20-30 mg/kg/day divided daily

HIV: 1000-1500 mg daily in a single dose or divided doses

Sickle cell anemia (moderate/severe disease): Initial: 15 mg/kg/day, increased by 5 mg/kg every 12 weeks if blood counts are in an acceptable range until the maximum tolerated dose of 35 mg/kg/day is achieved or the dose that does not produce toxic effects

Acceptable range:

Neutrophils ≥2500 cells/mm³

Platelets ≥95,000/mm³

Hemoglobin >5.3 g/dL, and

Reticulocytes ≥95,000/mm³ if the hemoglobin concentration is <9 g/dL

Toxic range:

Neutrophils <2000 cells/mm³

Platelets <80,000/mm³

Hemoglobin <4.5 g/dL

Reticulocytes <80,000/mm³ if the hemoglobin concentration is <9 g/dL

Monitor for toxicity every 2 weeks; if toxicity occurs, stop treatment until the bone marrow recovers; restart at 2.5 mg/kg/day less than the dose at which toxicity occurs; if no toxicity occurs over the next 12 weeks, then the subsequent dose should be increased by 2.5 mg/kg/day; reduced dosage of hydroxyurea alternating with erythropoietin may decrease myelotoxicity and increase levels of fetal hemoglobin in patients who have not been helped by hydroxyurea alone

Dosing adjustment in renal impairment:

Cl_{cr} 10-50 mL/minute: Administer 50% of normal dose

Cl_{cr} <10 mL/minute: Administer 20% of normal dose

Hemodialysis: Supplemental dose is not necessary. Hydroxyurea is a low molecular weight compound with high aqueous solubility that may be freely dialyzable, however, clinical studies confirming this hypothesis have not been performed; peak serum concentrations are reached within 2 hours after oral administration and by 24 hours, the concentration in the serum is zero

CAPD effects: Unknown

CAVH effects: Unknown

Monitoring Parameters CBC with differential, platelets, hemoglobin, renal function and liver function tests, serum uric acid

Patient Information Contents of capsule may be emptied into a glass of water if taken immediately; inform the physician if you develop fever, sore throat, bruising, or bleeding; may cause drowsiness, constipation, and loss of hair. Contraceptive measures are recommended during therapy.

Dosage Forms

Capsule (Droxia™): 200 mg, 300 mg, 400 mg

Capsule: 500 mg

♦ **25-Hydroxyvitamin D₃** see Calcifediol on page 170

Hydroxyzine (hye DROKS i zeen)

U.S. Brand Names Anxanil®; Atarax®; Atozine®; Durrax®; Hy-Pam®; Hyzine-50®; Neucalm®; Quiess®; QYS®; Rezine®; Vamate®; Vistacon-50®; Vistaject-25®; Vistaject-50®; Vistaquel®; Vistaril®; Vistazine®

Canadian Brand Names Apo®-Hydroxyzine; Multipax®; Novo-Hydroxyzin; PMS-Hydroxyzine

Synonyms Hydroxyzine Hydrochloride; Hydroxyzine Pamoate

Therapeutic Category Antianxiety Agent; Antiemetic; Antihistamine, H₁ Blocker; Sedative

Use Treatment of anxiety, as a preoperative sedative, an antipruritic, an antiemetic, and in alcohol withdrawal symptoms

Pregnancy Risk Factor C

Contraindications Hypersensitivity to hydroxyzine or any component

Warnings/Precautions S.C., intra-arterial and I.V. administration **not** recommended since thrombosis and digital gangrene can occur; extravasation can result in sterile abscess and marked tissue induration; should be used with caution in patients with narrow-angle glaucoma, prostatic hypertrophy, and bladder neck obstruction; should also be used with caution in patients with asthma or COPD

Anticholinergic effects are not well tolerated in the elderly. Hydroxyzine may be useful as a short-term antipruritic, but it is not recommended for use as a sedative or anxiolytic in the elderly.

Adverse Reactions

>10%:

Central nervous system: Slight to moderate drowsiness

Respiratory: Thickening of bronchial secretions

1% to 10%:

Central nervous system: Headache, fatigue, nervousness, dizziness

Gastrointestinal: Appetite increase, weight gain, nausea, diarrhea, abdominal pain, xerostomia

Neuromuscular & skeletal: Arthralgia

Respiratory: Pharyngitis

<1%: Palpitations, hypotension, edema, depression, sedation, paradoxical excitement, insomnia, angioedema, photosensitivity, rash, urinary retention, hepatitis, myalgia, tremor, paresthesia, blurred vision, bronchospasm, epistaxis

(Continued)

Hydroxyzine *(Continued)*

Overdosage/Toxicology

Symptoms of overdose include seizures, sedation, hypotension

There is no specific treatment for an antihistamine overdose, however, most of its clinical toxicity is due to anticholinergic effects. Anticholinesterase inhibitors may be useful by reducing acetylcholinesterase. For anticholinergic overdose with severe life-threatening symptoms, physostigmine 1-2 mg (0.5 mg or 0.02 mg/kg for children) I.V., slowly may be given to reverse these effects.

Drug Interactions

Decreased effect: Epinephrine decreased vasopressor effect

Increased toxicity: CNS depressants, anticholinergics

Stability Protect from light; store at 15°C to 30°C and protected from freezing; I.V. is **incompatible** when mixed with aminophylline, amobarbital, chloramphenicol, dimenhydrinate, heparin, penicillin G, pentobarbital, phenobarbital, phenytoin, ranitidine, sulfisoxazole, vitamin B complex with C

Mechanism of Action Competes with histamine for H_1-receptor sites on effector cells in the gastrointestinal tract, blood vessels, and respiratory tract

Pharmacodynamics/Kinetics

Onset of effect: Within 15-30 minutes

Duration: 4-6 hours

Absorption: Oral: Rapid

Metabolism: Exact fate is unknown

Half-life: 3-7 hours

Time to peak serum concentration: Within 2 hours

Usual Dosage

Children:

Oral: 0.6 mg/kg/dose every 6 hours

I.M.: 0.5-1 mg/kg/dose every 4-6 hours as needed

Adults:

Antiemetic: I.M.: 25-100 mg/dose every 4-6 hours as needed

Anxiety: Oral: 25-100 mg 4 times/day; maximum dose: 600 mg/day

Preoperative sedation:

Oral: 50-100 mg

I.M.: 25-100 mg

Management of pruritus: Oral: 25 mg 3-4 times/day

Dosing interval in hepatic impairment: Change dosing interval to every 24 hours in patients with primary biliary cirrhosis

Dietary Considerations Alcohol: Additive CNS effect, avoid use

Administration For I.M. administration in children, injections should be made into the midlateral muscles of the thigh; S.C., intra-arterial, and I.V. administration **not** recommended since thrombosis and digital gangrene can occur

Monitoring Parameters Relief of symptoms, mental status, blood pressure

Patient Information Will cause drowsiness, avoid alcohol and other CNS depressants, avoid driving and other hazardous tasks until the CNS effects are known

Nursing Implications Extravasation can result in sterile abscess and marked tissue induration; provide safety measures (ie, side rails, night light, and call button); remove smoking materials from area; supervise ambulation

Additional Information

Hydroxyzine hydrochloride: Anxanil®, Atarax®, Hydroxacen®, Quiess®, Vistaril® injection, Vistazine®

Hydroxyzine pamoate: Hy-Pam®, Vistaril® capsule and suspension

Dosage Forms

Hydroxyzine hydrochloride:

Injection: 25 mg/mL (1 mL, 2 mL, 10 mL); 50 mg/mL (1 mL, 2 mL, 10 mL)

Syrup: 10 mg/5 mL (120 mL, 480 mL, 4000 mL)

Tablet: 10 mg, 25 mg, 50 mg, 100 mg

Hydroxyzine pamoate:

Capsule: 25 mg, 50 mg, 100 mg

Suspension, oral: 25 mg/5 mL (120 mL, 480 mL)

- **Hydroxyzine Hydrochloride** *see Hydroxyzine on previous page*
- **Hydroxyzine Pamoate** *see Hydroxyzine on previous page*
- **Hygroton®** *see Chlorthalidone on page 251*
- **Hylorel®** *see Guanadrel on page 552*
- **Hylutin® Injection** *see Hydroxyprogesterone Caproate on page 587*
- **Hyoscine** *see Scopolamine on page 1051*

Hyoscyamine *(hye oh SYE a meen)*

U.S. Brand Names Anaspaz®; A-Spas® S/L; Cystospaz®; Cystospaz-M®; Donnamar®; ED-SPAZ®; Gastrosed™; Levbid®; Levsin®; Levsinex®; Levsin/SL®

Synonyms Hyoscyamine Sulfate; *l*-Hyoscyamine Sulfate

Therapeutic Category Anticholinergic Agent; Antispasmodic Agent, Gastrointestinal

Use Treatment of GI tract disorders caused by spasm, adjunctive therapy for peptic ulcers

Pregnancy Risk Factor C

Contraindications Narrow-angle glaucoma, obstructive uropathy, obstructive GI tract disease, myasthenia gravis, known hypersensitivity to belladonna alkaloids

Warnings/Precautions Use with caution in children with spastic paralysis; use with caution in elderly patients. Low doses cause a paradoxical decrease in heart rates.

Some commercial products contain sodium metabisulfite, which can cause allergic-type reactions. May accumulate with multiple inhalational administration, particularly in the elderly. Heat prostration may occur in hot weather. Use with caution in patients with autonomic neuropathy, prostatic hypertrophy, hyperthyroidism, congestive heart failure, cardiac arrhythmias, chronic lung disease, biliary tract disease.

Adverse Reactions

>10%:
Dermatologic: Dry skin
Gastrointestinal: Dry throat, xerostomia
Local: Irritation at injection site
Respiratory: Dry nose
Miscellaneous: Diaphoresis (decreased)

1% to 10%:
Dermatologic: Photosensitivity
Gastrointestinal: Constipation, dysphagia
Ocular: Blurred vision, mydriasis

<1%: Palpitations, orthostatic hypotension, headache, lightheadedness, memory loss, fatigue, delirium, restlessness, ataxia, rash, dysuria, tremor, increased intraocular pressure

Overdosage/Toxicology

Symptoms of overdose include dilated, unreactive pupils; blurred vision; hot, dry flushed skin; dryness of mucous membranes; difficulty in swallowing, foul breath, diminished or absent bowel sounds, urinary retention, tachycardia, hyperthermia, hypertension, increased respiratory rate

Anticholinergic toxicity is caused by strong binding of the drug to cholinergic receptors. Anticholinesterase inhibitors reduce acetylcholinesterase, the enzyme that breaks down acetylcholine and thereby allows acetylcholine to accumulate and compete for receptor binding with the offending anticholinergic. For anticholinergic overdose with severe life-threatening symptoms, physostigmine 1-2 mg (0.5 mg or 0.02 mg/kg for children) S.C. or I.V., slowly may be given to reverse these effects.

Drug Interactions

Decreased effect with antacids
Increased toxicity with amantadine, antimuscarinics, haloperidol, phenothiazines, TCAs, MAO inhibitors

Mechanism of Action Blocks the action of acetylcholine at parasympathetic sites in smooth muscle, secretory glands and the CNS; increases cardiac output, dries secretions, antagonizes histamine and serotonin

Pharmacodynamics/Kinetics

Onset of effect: 2-3 minutes
Duration: 4-6 hours
Absorption: Oral: Absorbed well
Distribution: Crosses the placenta; small amounts appear in breast milk
Protein binding: 50%
Metabolism: In the liver
Half-life: 13% to 38%
Elimination: In urine

Usual Dosage

Children: Oral, S.L.: Dose as per table repeated every 4 hours as needed

Hyoscyamine

Weight (kg)	Dose (mcg)	Maximum 24-Hour Dose (mcg)
Children <2 y		
2.3	12.5	75
3.4	16.7	100
5	20.8	125
7	25	150
10	31.3-33.3	200
15	45.8	275
Children 2-10 y		
10	31.3-33.3	
20	62.5	Do not exceed
40	93.8	0.75 mg
50	125	

Adults:
Oral or S.L.: 0.125-0.25 mg 3-4 times/day before meals or food and at bedtime
Oral: 0.375-0.75 mg (timed release) every 12 hours
I.M., I.V., S.C.: 0.25-0.5 mg every 6 hours

Patient Information Maintain good oral hygiene habits, because lack of saliva may increase chance of cavities. Observe caution while driving or performing other tasks requiring alertness, as may cause drowsiness, dizziness, or blurred vision. Notify physician if skin rash, flushing or eye pain occurs; or if difficulty in urinating, constipation or sensitivity to light becomes severe or persists.

Nursing Implications Observe for tachycardia if patient has cardiac problems.
(Continued)

Hyoscyamine *(Continued)*

Dosage Forms

Capsule, as sulfate, timed release (Cystospaz-M®, Levsinex®): 0.375 mg

Elixir, as sulfate (Levsin®): 0.125 mg/5 mL with alcohol 20% (480 mL)

Injection, as sulfate (Levsin®): 0.5 mg/mL (1 mL, 10 mL)

Solution, oral (Gastrosed™, Levsin®): 0.125 mg/mL (15 mL)

Tablet, as sulfate:

Anaspaz®, Gastrosed™, Levsin®, Neoquess®: 0.125 mg

Cystospaz®: 0.15 mg

Extended release (Levbid®): 0.375 mg

Hyoscyamine, Atropine, Scopolamine, and Phenobarbital

(hye oh SYE a meen, A troe peen, skoe POL a meen & fee noe BAR bi tal)

U.S. Brand Names Barbidonna®; Barophen®; Donnapine®; Donna-Sed®; Donnatal®; Hyosophen®; Kinesed®; Malatal®; Relaxadon®; Spaslin®; Spasmolin®; Spasmophen®; Spasquid®; Susano®

Therapeutic Category Anticholinergic Agent; Antispasmodic Agent, Gastrointestinal

Use Adjunct in treatment of peptic ulcer disease, irritable bowel, spastic colitis, spastic bladder, and renal colic

Pregnancy Risk Factor C

Contraindications Hypersensitivity to hyoscyamine, atropine, scopolamine, phenobarbital, or any component; narrow-angle glaucoma, tachycardia, GI and GU obstruction, myasthenia gravis

Warnings/Precautions Use with caution in patients with hepatic or renal disease, hyperthyroidism, cardiovascular disease, hypertension, prostatic hypertrophy, autonomic neuropathy in the elderly; abrupt withdrawal may precipitate status epilepticus. Because of the anticholinergic effects of this product, it is not recommended for use in the elderly.

Adverse Reactions

>10%:

Dermatologic: Dry skin

Gastrointestinal: Constipation, dry throat, xerostomia

Local: Irritation at injection site

Respiratory: Dry nose

Miscellaneous: Diaphoresis (decreased)

1% to 10%:

Dermatologic: Increased sensitivity to light

Endocrine & metabolic: Decreased flow of breast milk

Gastrointestinal: Dysphagia

<1%: Orthostatic hypotension, ventricular fibrillation, tachycardia, palpitations, confusion, drowsiness, headache, loss of memory, fatigue, ataxia, rash, bloated feeling, nausea, vomiting, dysuria, increased intraocular pain, blurred vision

Overdosage/Toxicology

Symptoms of overdose include unsteady gait, slurred speech, confusion, hypotension, respiratory collapse, dilated unreactive pupils, hot or flushed skin, diminished bowel sounds, urinary retention

Anticholinergic toxicity is caused by strong binding of the drug to cholinergic receptors. Anticholinesterase inhibitors reduce acetylcholinesterase, the enzyme that breaks down acetylcholine and thereby allows acetylcholine to accumulate and compete for receptor binding with the offending anticholinergic. For anticholinergic overdose with severe life-threatening symptoms, physostigmine 1-2 mg (0.5 mg or 0.02 mg/kg for children) S.C. or I.V., slowly may be given to reverse these effects.

Drug Interactions Increased toxicity: CNS depressants, coumarin anticoagulants, amantadine, antihistamine, phenothiazines, antidiarrheal suspensions, corticosteroids, digitalis, griseofulvin, tetracyclines, anticonvulsants, MAO inhibitors, tricyclic antidepressants

Mechanism of Action Refer to individual agents

Pharmacodynamics/Kinetics Absorption: Well absorbed from GI tract

Usual Dosage Oral:

Children 2-12 years: Kinesed® dose: 1/2 to 1 tablet 3-4 times/day

Children: Donnatal® elixir: 0.1 mL/kg/dose every 4 hours; maximum dose: 5 mL **or** see table for alternative.

Hyoscyamine, Atropine, Scopolamine, and Phenobarbital

Weight	Dose (mL)	
(kg)	q4h	q6h
4.5	0.5	0.75
10	1	1.5
14	1.5	2
23	2.5	3.8
34	3.8	5
≥45	5	7.5

Adults: 1-2 capsules or tablets 3-4 times/day; or 1 Donnatal® Extentab® in sustained release form every 12 hours; or 5-10 mL elixir 3-4 times/day or every 8 hours

Patient Information Maintain good oral hygiene habits, because lack of saliva may increase chance of cavities. Observe caution while driving or performing other tasks requiring alertness, as may cause drowsiness, dizziness, or blurred vision. Notify physician if skin rash, flushing or eye pain occurs; or if difficulty in urinating, constipation, or sensitivity to light becomes severe or persists. Do not attempt tasks requiring mental alertness or physical coordination until you know the effects of the drug. Swallow extended release tablet whole, do not crush or chew.

Dosage Forms
Capsule (Donnatal®, Spasmolin®): Hyoscyamine sulfate 0.1037 mg, atropine sulfate 0.0194 mg, scopolamine hydrobromide 0.0065 mg, and phenobarbital 16.2 mg

Elixir (Donnatal®, Hyosophen®, Spasmophen®): Hyoscyamine sulfate 0.1037 mg, atropine sulfate 0.0194 mg, scopolamine hydrobromide 0.0065 mg, and phenobarbital 16.2 mg per 5 mL (120 mL, 480 mL, 4000 mL)

Tablet:
Barbidonna®: Hyoscyamine hydrobromide 0.1286 mg, atropine sulfate 0.025 mg, scopolamine hydrobromide 0.0074 mg, and phenobarbital 16 mg

Barbidonna® No. 2: Hyoscyamine hydrobromide 0.1286 mg, atropine sulfate 0.025 mg, scopolamine hydrobromide 0.0074 mg, and phenobarbital 32 mg

Donnatal®, Hyosophen®: Hyoscyamine sulfate 0.1037 mg, atropine sulfate 0.0194 mg, scopolamine hydrobromide 0.0065 mg, and phenobarbital 16.2 mg

Long-acting (Donnatal®): Hyoscyamine sulfate 0.3111 mg, atropine sulfate 0.0582 mg, scopolamine hydrobromide 0.0195 mg, and phenobarbital 48.6 mg

Spasmophen®: Hyoscyamine sulfate 0.1037 mg, atropine sulfate 0.0194 mg, scopolamine hydrobromide 0.0065 mg, and phenobarbital 15 mg

Hyoscyamine, Atropine, Scopolamine, Kaolin, Pectin, and Opium

(hye oh SYE a meen, A troe peen, skoe POL a meen, KAY oh lin, PEK tin, & OH pee um)

U.S. Brand Names Donnapectolin-PG®; Kapectolin PG®
Therapeutic Category Anticholinergic Agent
Dosage Forms Suspension, oral: Hyoscyamine sulfate 0.1037 mg, atropine sulfate 0.0194 mg, scopolamine hydrobromide 0.0065 mg, kaolin 6 g, pectin 142.8 mg, and powdered opium 24 mg per 30 mL with alcohol 5%

Ibuprofen (eye byoo PROE fen)

Related Information
Nonsteroidal Anti-Inflammatory Agents Comparison on page 1335
U.S. Brand Names Aches-N-Pain® [OTC]; Advil® [OTC]; Children's Advil® Oral Suspension [OTC]; Children's Motrin® Oral Suspension [OTC]; Excedrin® IB [OTC]; Genpril® [OTC]; Haltran® [OTC]; Ibuprin® [OTC]; Ibuprohm® [OTC]; Ibu-Tab®; Junior Strength Motrin® [OTC]; Medipren® [OTC]; Menadol® [OTC]; Midol® 200 [OTC]; Motrin®; Motrin® IB [OTC]; Nuprin® [OTC]; Pamprin IB® [OTC]; PediaProfen™; Saleto-200® [OTC]; Saleto-400®; Trendar® [OTC]; Uni-Pro® [OTC]
Canadian Brand Names Actiprofen®; Apo®-Ibuprofen; Novo-Profen®; Nu-Ibuprofen
Synonyms p-Isobutylhydratropic Acid
(Continued)

Ibuprofen *(Continued)*

Therapeutic Category Analgesic, Nonsteroidal Anti-inflammatory Drug; Anti-inflammatory Agent; Antimigraine Agent; Antipyretic; Nonsteroidal Anti-inflammatory Drug (NSAID), Oral

Use Inflammatory diseases and rheumatoid disorders including juvenile rheumatoid arthritis, mild to moderate pain, fever, dysmenorrhea, gout, ankylosing spondylitis, acute migraine headache

Pregnancy Risk Factor B (D if used in the 3rd trimester)

Contraindications Hypersensitivity to ibuprofen, any component, aspirin, or other nonsteroidal anti-inflammatory drugs (NSAIDs)

Warnings/Precautions Do not exceed 3200 mg/day; use with caution in patients with congestive heart failure, hypertension, decreased renal or hepatic function, history of GI disease (bleeding or ulcers), or those receiving anticoagulants; safety and efficacy in children <6 months of age have not yet been established; elderly are a high-risk population for adverse effects from nonsteroidal anti-inflammatory agents. As much as 60% of elderly can develop peptic ulceration and/or hemorrhage asymptomatically.

Use lowest effective dose for shortest period possible. Use of NSAIDs can compromise existing renal function especially when Cl_{cr} is <30 mL/minute. CNS adverse effects such as confusion, agitation, and hallucination are generally seen in overdose or high dose situations; but elderly may demonstrate these adverse effects at lower doses than younger adults.

Adverse Reactions

>10%:
    Central nervous system: Dizziness, fatigue
    Dermatologic: Rash, urticaria
    Gastrointestinal: Abdominal cramps, heartburn, indigestion, nausea

1% to 10%:
    Central nervous system: Headache, nervousness
    Dermatologic: Itching
    Endocrine & metabolic: Fluid retention
    Gastrointestinal: Dyspepsia, vomiting, abdominal pain, peptic ulcer, GI bleed, GI perforation
    Otic: Tinnitus

<1%: Edema, congestive heart failure, arrhythmias, tachycardia, hypertension, confusion, hallucinations, mental depression, drowsiness, insomnia, aseptic meningitis, erythema multiforme, toxic epidermal necrolysis, Stevens-Johnson syndrome, polydipsia, hot flashes, gastritis, GI ulceration, cystitis, polyuria, neutropenia, anemia, agranulocytosis, inhibition of platelet aggregation, hemolytic anemia, bone marrow suppression, leukopenia, thrombocytopenia, hepatitis, peripheral neuropathy, vision changes, blurred vision, conjunctivitis, dry eyes, toxic amblyopia, decreased hearing, acute renal failure, allergic rhinitis, shortness of breath, epistaxis

Overdosage/Toxicology

Symptoms include apnea, metabolic acidosis, coma, and nystagmus; leukocytosis, renal failure

Management of a nonsteroidal anti-inflammatory drug (NSAID) intoxication is primarily supportive and symptomatic. Fluid therapy is commonly effective in managing the hypotension that may occur following an acute NSAID overdose, except when this is due to an acute blood loss. Seizures tend to be very short-lived and often do not require drug treatment; although, recurrent seizures should be treated with I.V. diazepam. Since many of the NSAIDs undergo enterohepatic cycling, multiple doses of charcoal may be needed to reduce the potential for delayed toxicities.

Drug Interactions CYP2C8 and 2C9 enzyme substrate

Decreased effect: Aspirin may decrease ibuprofen serum concentrations

Increased toxicity: May increase digoxin, methotrexate, and lithium serum concentrations; other nonsteroidal anti-inflammatories may increase adverse gastrointestinal effects

Mechanism of Action Inhibits prostaglandin synthesis by decreasing the activity of the enzyme, cyclo-oxygenase, which results in decreased formation of prostaglandin precursors

Pharmacodynamics/Kinetics

Onset of analgesia: 30-60 minutes
Duration: 4-6 hours
Onset of anti-inflammatory effect: Up to 7 days
Peak action: 1-2 weeks
Absorption: Oral: Rapid (85%)
Time to peak serum concentration: Within 1-2 hours
Protein binding: 90% to 99%
Metabolism: In the liver by oxidation
Half-life: 2-4 hours
End-stage renal disease: Unchanged
Elimination: In urine (1% as free drug); some biliary excretion occurs

Usual Dosage Oral:

Children:
    Antipyretic: 6 months to 12 years: Temperature <102.5°F (39°C): 5 mg/kg/dose; temperature >102.5°F: 10 mg/kg/dose given every 6-8 hours; maximum daily dose: 40 mg/kg/day
    Juvenile rheumatoid arthritis: 30-70 mg/kg/24 hours divided every 6-8 hours
        <20 kg: Maximum: 400 mg/day

20-30 kg: Maximum: 600 mg/day

30-40 kg: Maximum: 800 mg/day

>40 kg: Adult dosage

Start at lower end of dosing range and titrate upward; maximum: 2.4 g/day

Analgesic: 4-10 mg/kg/dose every 6-8 hours

Adults:

Inflammatory disease: 400-800 mg/dose 3-4 times/day; maximum dose: 3.2 g/day

Analgesia/pain/fever/dysmenorrhea: 200-400 mg/dose every 4-6 hours; maximum daily dose: 1.2 g (unless directed by physician)

Dosing adjustment/comments in severe hepatic impairment: Avoid use

Dietary Considerations Food: May decrease the rate but not the extent of oral absorption; drug may cause GI upset, bleeding, ulceration, perforation; take with food or milk to minimize GI upset

Administration Administer with food

Monitoring Parameters CBC; occult blood loss and periodic liver function tests; monitor response (pain, range of motion, grip strength, mobility, ADL function), inflammation; observe for weight gain, edema; monitor renal function (urine output, serum BUN and creatinine); observe for bleeding, bruising; evaluate gastrointestinal effects (abdominal pain, bleeding, dyspepsia); mental confusion, disorientation; with long-term therapy, periodic ophthalmic exams

Reference Range Plasma concentrations >200 µg/mL may be associated with severe toxicity

Patient Information Serious gastrointestinal bleeding can occur as well as ulceration and perforation. Pain may or may not be present. Avoid aspirin and aspirin-containing products while taking this medication. If gastric upset occurs, take with food, milk, or antacid. If gastric adverse effects persist, contact physician. May cause drowsiness, dizziness, blurred vision, and confusion. Use caution when performing tasks that require alertness (eg, driving). Do not take for more than 3 days for fever or 10 days for pain without physician's advice.

Nursing Implications Do not crush tablet

Additional Information Sucrose content of 5 mL (suspension): 2.5 g

Dosage Forms

Caplet: 100 mg

Drops, oral (berry flavor): 40 mg/mL (15 mL)

Suspension, oral: 100 mg/5 mL [OTC] (60 mL, 120 mL, 480 mL)

Suspension, oral, drops: 40 mg/mL [OTC]

Tablet: 100 mg [OTC], 200 mg [OTC], 300 mg, 400 mg, 600 mg, 800 mg

Tablet, chewable: 50 mg, 100 mg

♦ **Ibuprohm® [OTC]** *see* Ibuprofen *on page 593*

♦ **Ibu-Tab®** *see* Ibuprofen *on page 593*

Ibutilide (i BYOO ti lide)

Related Information

Antiarrhythmic Drugs Comparison *on page 1297*

U.S. Brand Names Corvert®

Synonyms Ibutilide Fumarate

Therapeutic Category Antiarrhythmic Agent, Class III

Use Acute termination of atrial fibrillation or flutter of recent onset; the effectiveness of ibutilide has not been determined in patients with arrhythmias of >90 days in duration

Pregnancy Risk Factor C

Pregnancy/Breast-Feeding Implications

Clinical effects on the fetus: Teratogenic and embryocidal in rats; avoid use in pregnancy

Breast-feeding/lactation: Avoid breast-feeding during therapy

Contraindications Hypersensitivity to the drug or any component

Warnings/Precautions Potentially fatal arrhythmias (eg, polymorphic ventricular tachycardia) can occur with ibutilide, **usually** in association with torsade de pointes (Q-T prolongation). Studies indicate a 1.7% incidence of arrhythmias in treated patients. The drug should be given in a setting of continuous EKG monitoring and by personnel trained in treating arrhythmias particularly polymorphic ventricular tachycardia. Patients with chronic atrial fibrillation may not be the best candidates for ibutilide since they often revert after conversion and the risks of treatment may not be justified when compared to alternative management. Dosing adjustments in patients with renal or hepatic dysfunction since a maximum of only two 10-minute infusions are indicated and drug distribution is one of the primary mechanisms responsible for termination of the pharmacologic effect; safety and efficacy in children have not been established.

Adverse Reactions

1% to 10%:

Cardiovascular: Sustained polymorphic ventricular tachycardia (ie, torsade de pointes) (1.7%), often requiring cardioversion, nonsustained polymorphic ventricular tachycardia (2.7%), nonsustained monomorphic ventricular extrasystoles (5.1%), nonsustained monomorphic VT (4.9%), tachycardia/supraventricular tachycardia, hypotension (2%), bundle branch block (1.9%), A-V block (1.5%), bradycardia, Q-T segment prolongation, hypertension (1.2%), palpitations (1%)

Central nervous system: Headache (3.6%)

Gastrointestinal: Nausea (>1%)

<1%: Supraventricular extrasystoles (0.9%), nodal arrhythmia (0.7%), congestive heart failure (0.5%), syncope, idioventricular rhythm, sustained monomorphic VT (0.2%), renal failure (0.3%)

(Continued)

Ibutilide *(Continued)*

Overdosage/Toxicology
Symptoms include CNS depression, rapid gasping breathing, and convulsions; arrhythmias occur

Treatment is supportive and includes measures appropriate for the condition; antiarrhythmics are generally avoided; pharmacologic therapies may include magnesium sulfate, correction of other electrolyte abnormalities, overdrive cardiac pacing, electrical cardioversion, or defibrillation

Drug Interactions Increased toxicity: Class Ia antiarrhythmic drugs (disopyramide, quinidine, and procainamide) and other class III drugs such as amiodarone and sotalol, should not be given concomitantly with ibutilide due to their potential to prolong refractoriness; the potential for prolongation of the Q-T interval may occur if ibutilide is given concurrently with phenothiazines, tricyclic and tetracyclic antidepressants, and the nonsedating antihistamines (terfenadine and astemizole); signs of digoxin toxicity may be masked when coadministered with ibutilide

Stability Admixtures are chemically and physically stable for 24 hours at room temperature and for 48 hours at refrigerated temperatures

Mechanism of Action Exact mechanism of action is unknown; prolongs the action potential in cardiac tissue

Pharmacodynamics/Kinetics
Absorption: Onset: Within 90 minutes after start of infusion ($\frac{1}{2}$ of conversions to sinus rhythm occur during infusion)

Metabolism: Extensively metabolized in the liver

Half-life: 2-12 hours (average: 6 hours)

Elimination: Parent and metabolite excreted predominantly in the urine

Usual Dosage I.V.: Initial:
<60 kg: 0.01 mg/kg over 10 minutes
≥60 kg: 1 mg over 10 minutes
If the arrhythmia does not terminate within 10 minutes after the end of the initial infusion, a second infusion of equal strength may be infused over a 10-minute period

Administration May be administered undiluted or diluted in 50 mL diluent (0.9% NS or D_5W)

Monitoring Parameters Observe patient with continuous EKG monitoring for at least 4 hours following infusion or until QT_c has returned to baseline; skilled personnel and proper equipment should be available during administration of ibutilide and subsequent monitoring of the patient

Nursing Implications See Monitoring Parameters; EKG, electrolytes

Dosage Forms Injection, as fumarate: 0.1 mg/mL (10 mL)

♦ **Ibutilide Fumarate** *see Ibutilide on previous page*

♦ **Idamycin®** *see Idarubicin on this page*

Idarubicin *(eye da ROO bi sin)*

Related Information
Cancer Chemotherapy Regimens *on page 1263*
Extravasation Management of Chemotherapeutic Agents *on page 1285*
Toxicities of Chemotherapeutic Agents *on page 1288*

U.S. Brand Names Idamycin®

Synonyms 4-Demethoxydaunorubicin; 4-DMDR; Idarubicin Hydrochloride

Therapeutic Category Antineoplastic Agent, Anthracycline; Antineoplastic Agent, Antibiotic; Vesicant

Use In combination treatment of acute myeloid leukemia (AML), this includes classifications M1 through M7 of the French-American-British (FAB) classification system; also used for the treatment of acute lymphocytic leukemia (ALL) in children

Pregnancy Risk Factor D

Contraindications Hypersensitivity to idarubicin, daunorubicin, or any component

Warnings/Precautions The U.S. Food and Drug Administration (FDA) currently recommends that procedures for proper handling and disposal of antineoplastic agents be considered. Administer I.V. slowly into a freely flowing I.V. infusion; do not administer I.M. or S.C., severe necrosis can result if extravasation occurs; can cause myocardial toxicity and is more common in patients who have previously received anthracyclines or have pre-existing cardiac disease; reduce dose in patients with impaired hepatic function; irreversible myocardial toxicity may occur as total dosage approaches 137.5 mg/m^2; severe myelosuppression is also possible.

Adverse Reactions
>10%:
Central nervous system: Headache, fever
Dermatologic: Alopecia, rash, urticaria
Gastrointestinal: Mucositis, nausea, vomiting, diarrhea, stomatitis
Genitourinary: Reddish urine
Hematologic: Hemorrhage, anemia
Leukopenia (nadir: 8-29 days)
Thrombocytopenia (nadir: 10-15 days)
Local: Tissue necrosis upon extravasation, erythematous streaking
Vesicant chemotherapy
Miscellaneous: Infection
1% to 10%:
Central nervous system: Seizures

Neuromuscular & skeletal: Peripheral neuropathy

Miscellaneous: Pulmonary allergy

<1%: Arrhythmias, EKG changes, cardiomyopathy, congestive heart failure, myocardial toxicity, acute life-threatening arrhythmias, hyperuricemia, elevated liver enzymes or bilirubin

Overdosage/Toxicology

Symptoms of overdose include severe myelosuppression and increased GI toxicity

Treatment is supportive; it is unlikely that therapeutic efficacy or toxicity would be altered by conventional peritoneal or hemodialysis

Stability

Store intact vials of lyophilized powder at room temperature and protect from light

Dilute powder with sterile water for injection to a concentration of 1 mg/mL as follows:

Solution is stable for 72 hours at room temperature and 7 days under refrigeration. Bacteriostatic diluents are **not** recommended.

5 mg = 5 mL

10 mg = 10 mL

Further dilution in D_5W or NS is stable for 4 weeks at room temperature and protected from light

Incompatible with dexamethasone, etoposide, fluorouracil, heparin, hydrocortisone, methotrexate, vincristine

Standard I.V. dilution:

I.V. push: Dose/syringe (concentration: 1 mg/mL)

Maximum syringe size for IVP: 30 mL syringe and syringe should be ≤75% full

IVPB: Dose/100 mL D_5W or NS

Syringe and IVPB solutions are stable for 72 hours at room temperature and 7 days under refrigeration

Mechanism of Action Derivative of daunorubicin; the only structural difference between idarubicin and the parent compound, daunorubicin, is lack of the methoxyl group at the C4 position of the aglycone. Similar to daunorubicin, idarubicin exhibits inhibitory effects on DNA and RNA polymerase *in vitro*. Idarubicin has an affinity for DNA similar to the parent compound and somewhat higher efficacy than daunorubicin in stabilizing the DNA double helix against heat denaturation.

Pharmacodynamics/Kinetics

Absorption: Oral: Rapid but erratic (20% to 30%) from the GI tract

Distribution: Large V_d due to extensive tissue binding and distributes into CSF

Protein binding: 94% to 97%

Metabolism: In the liver to idarubicinol, which is pharmacologically active

Half-life, elimination: Oral: 14-35 hours; I.V.: 12-27 hours

Time to peak serum concentration: Within 2-4 hours and varies considerably

Elimination: ~15% of an I.V. dose has been recovered in urine as idarubicin and idarubicinol; urinary recovery of idarubicin and idarubicinol is lower following oral doses; similar amounts are excreted via the bile

Usual Dosage I.V.:

Children:

Leukemia: 10-12 mg/m² once daily for 3 days and repeat every 3 weeks

Solid tumors: 5 mg/m² once daily for 3 days and repeat every 3 weeks

Adults: 12 mg/m²/day for 3 days by slow (10-15 minutes) intravenous injection in combination with Ara-C

The Ara-C may be given as 100 mg/m²/day by continuous infusion for 7 days or as Ara-C 25 mg/m² bolus followed by Ara-C 200 mg/m²/day for 5 days continuous infusion

Dosing adjustment in renal impairment: Dose reduction is recommended

Serum creatinine ≥2 mg/dL: Reduce dose by 25%

Hemodialysis: Significant drug removal is unlikely based on physiochemical characteristics

Peritoneal dialysis: Significant drug removal is unlikely based on physiochemical characteristics

Dosing adjustment/comments in hepatic impairment:

Bilirubin 1.5-5.0 mg/dL or AST 60-180 units/L: Reduce dose 50%

Bilirubin >5 mg/dL or AST >180 units/L: Do not administer

Administration

Administer by intermittent infusion over 10-15 minutes into a free flowing I.V. solution of NS or D_5W

Avoid extravasation - potent vesicant

Monitoring Parameters CBC with differential, platelet count, ECHO, EKG, serum electrolytes, creatinine, uric acid, ALT, AST, bilirubin, signs of extravasation

Patient Information May cause hair loss; notify physician if pain, burning, or stinging around injection site occur. Contraceptive measures are recommended during therapy.

Nursing Implications

Local erythematous streaking along the vein may indicate too rapid a rate of administration

Unless specific data available, do not mix with other drugs

Extravasation management:

Apply ice immediately for 30-60 minutes; then alternate off/on every 15 minutes for one day

Topical cooling may be achieved using ice packs or cooling pad with circulating ice water. Cooling of site for 24 hours as tolerated by the patient. Elevate and rest extremity 24-48 hours, then resume normal activity as tolerated. Application of cold inhibits vesicant's cytotoxicity.

(Continued)

Idarubicin (Continued)

Application of heat or sodium bicarbonate can be harmful and is contraindicated
If pain, erythema, and/or swelling persist beyond 48 hours, refer patient immediately to plastic surgeon for consultation and possible debridement

Dosage Forms Powder for injection, lyophilized, as hydrochloride: 5 mg, 10 mg

- **Idarubicin Hydrochloride** see Idarubicin on page 596
- **Ifex® Injection** see Ifosfamide on this page
- **IFLrA** see Interferon Alfa-2a on page 616
- **IFN** see Interferon Alfa-2a on page 616

Ifosfamide (eye FOSS fa mide)

Related Information
Cancer Chemotherapy Regimens on page 1263
Toxicities of Chemotherapeutic Agents on page 1288

U.S. Brand Names Ifex® Injection

Therapeutic Category Antineoplastic Agent, Alkylating Agent; Antineoplastic Agent, Nitrogen Mustard

Use In combination with certain other antineoplastics in treatment of lung cancer, Hodgkin's and non-Hodgkin's lymphoma, breast cancer, acute and chronic lymphocytic leukemia, ovarian cancer, testicular cancer, and sarcomas, pancreatic and gastric carcinoma, osteosarcoma

Pregnancy Risk Factor D

Contraindications Patients who have demonstrated a previous hypersensitivity to ifosfamide; patients with severely depressed bone marrow function

Warnings/Precautions The U.S. Food and Drug Administration (FDA) currently recommends that procedures for proper handling and disposal of antineoplastic agents be considered. May require therapy cessation if confusion or coma occurs; be aware of hemorrhagic cystitis and severe myelosuppression. Use with caution in patients with impaired renal function or those with compromised bone marrow reserve.

Adverse Reactions

>10%:

Central nervous system: Somnolence, confusion, hallucinations in 12% and coma (rare) have occurred and are usually reversible; usually occur with higher doses or in patients with reduced renal function; depressive psychoses, polyneuropathy

Dermatologic: Alopecia occurs in 50% to 83% of patients 2-4 weeks after initiation of therapy; may be as high as 100% in combination therapy

Gastrointestinal: Nausea and vomiting in 58% of patients is dose and schedule related (more common with higher doses and after bolus regimens); nausea and vomiting can persist up to 3 days after therapy; also anorexia, diarrhea, constipation, transient increase in LFTs and stomatitis noted.

Emetic potential: Moderate (58%)

Time course of nausea/vomiting: Onset: 2-3 hours; Duration: 12-72 hours

Genitourinary: Hemorrhagic cystitis has been frequently associated with the use of ifosfamide. A urinalysis prior to each dose should be obtained. **Ifosfamide should never be administered without a uroprotective agent (MESNA).** Hematuria has been reported in 6% to 92% of patients. Renal toxicity occurs in 6% of patients and is manifested as an increase in BUN or serum creatinine and is most likely related to tubular damage. Renal toxicity, including ARF, may occur more frequently with high-dose ifosfamide. Metabolic acidosis may occur in up to 31% of patients.

1% to 10%:

Dermatologic: Phlebitis, dermatitis, nail ridging, skin hyperpigmentation, impaired wound healing

Endocrine & metabolic: SIADH

Hematologic: Myelosuppression: Less of a problem than with cyclophosphamide if used alone. Leukopenia is mild to moderate, thrombocytopenia and anemia are rare. However, myelosuppression can be severe when used with other chemotherapeutic agents or with high-dose therapy. Be cautious with patients with compromised bone marrow reserve.

WBC: Moderate

Platelets: Mild

Onset (days): 7

Nadir (days): 10-14

Hepatic: Elevated liver enzymes

Respiratory: Nasal congestion, pulmonary fibrosis

Miscellaneous: Immunosuppression, sterility, possible secondary malignancy, allergic reactions

<1%: Cardiotoxicity, pulmonary toxicity

Overdosage/Toxicology
Symptoms of overdose include myelosuppression, nausea, vomiting, diarrhea, alopecia; direct extension of the drug's pharmacologic effect
Treatment is supportive

Drug Interactions CYP2B6 and 3A3/4 enzyme substrate
Because ifosfamide undergoes hepatic activation by microsomal enzymes, induction of these enzymes is potentially possible by pretreatment with various enzyme-inducers such as phenobarbital, phenytoin, and chloral hydrate

Stability
Store intact vials at room temperature or under refrigeration

Dilute powder with SWI or NS to a concentration of 50 mg/mL as follows. **Do not use bacteriostatic SWI or NS** - incompatible; solution is stable for 7 days at room temperature and 6 weeks under refrigeration

1 g vial = 20 mL

3 g vial = 60 mL

Further dilution in NS, D_5W or LR is stable for 7 days at room temperature and 6 weeks under refrigeration

Compatible with mesna in NS for up to 9 days at room temperature

Standard I.V. dilution:

I.V. push: Dose/syringe (concentration = 50 mg/mL)

Maximum syringe size for IVP is a 30 mL syringe and syringe should be ≤75% full

IVPB: Dose/100-1000 mL D_5W or NS

Syringe and IVPB are stable for 7 days at room temperature and 6 weeks under refrigeration

Mechanism of Action Causes cross-linking of strands of DNA by binding with nucleic acids and other intracellular structures; inhibits protein synthesis and DNA synthesis; an analogue of cyclophosphamide; like cyclophosphamide, it undergoes activation by microsomal enzymes in the liver. Ifosfamide is metabolized to active compounds, ifosfamide mustard, and acrolein

Pharmacodynamics/Kinetics Pharmacokinetics are dose-dependent

Absorption: Oral: Peak plasma levels occur within 1 hour

Bioavailability: Estimated at 100%

Distribution: V_d: Has been calculated to be 5.7-49 L; does penetrate CNS, but not in therapeutic levels

Protein binding: Not appreciably protein bound

Metabolism: In the liver to active species; requires biotransformation in the liver before it can act as an alkylating agent; the metabolite acrolein is the toxic agent implicated in the development of hemorrhagic cystitis

Half-life: Beta phase: 11-15 hours with high-dose (3800-5000 mg/m²) or 4-7 hours with lower doses (1800 mg/m²)

Elimination: 15% to 50% excreted unchanged in urine

Usual Dosage I.V. (refer to individual protocols):

Children: 1200-1800 mg/m²/day for 3-5 days every 21-28 days

Adults:

Doses may be given as 50 mg/kg/day **or** 700-2000 mg/m²/day for 5 days

Alternatives include 2400 mg/m²/day for 3 days **or** 5000 mg/m² as a single dose

Doses of 700-900 mg/m²/day for 5 days may be given IVP; courses may be repeated every 3-4 weeks

To prevent bladder toxicity, ifosfamide should be given with extensive hydration consisting of at least 2 L of oral or I.V. fluid per day. A protector, such as mesna, should also be used to prevent hemorrhagic cystitis. The dose-limiting toxicity is hemorrhagic cystitis and ifosfamide should be used in conjunction with a uroprotective agent.

Dosing adjustment in renal impairment:

S_{cr} >3.0 mg/dL: Withhold drug

S_{cr} 2.1-3.0 mg/dL: Reduce dose by 25% to 50%

Dosing adjustment in hepatic impairment: Although no specific guidelines are available, it is possible that higher doses are indicated in hepatic disease. One author [Falkson G, et al, "An extended phase II trial of ifosfamide plus mesna in malignant mesothelioma," *Invest New Drugs*: 1992;10:337-343.] recommended the following dosage adjustments:

AST >300 or bilirubin >3.0 mg/dL: Decrease ifosfamide dose by 75%

Administration

Administer slow I.V. push, IVPB over 30 minutes or continuous I.V. over 5 days

Adequate hydration (at least 2 L/day) of the patient before and for 72 hours after therapy is recommended to minimize the risk of hemorrhagic cystitis

MESNA should be administered concomitantly (20% of the ifosfamide dose 15 minutes before, 4 hours after and 8 hours after ifosfamide administration)

Monitoring Parameters CBC with differential, hemoglobin, and platelet count, urine output, urinalysis, liver function, and renal function tests

Patient Information Drink plenty of fluids after dose; notify physician if persistent sore throat, fever, sores on mucous membranes, fatigue, or unusual bleeding or bruising occur

Nursing Implications Mesna to be used concomitantly for prophylaxis against hemorrhagic cystitis

Dosage Forms Powder for injection: 1 g, 3 g

♦ **Imidazole Carboxamide** *see* Dacarbazine *on page 316*
♦ **Imipemide** *see* Imipenem and Cilastatin *on this page*

Imipenem and Cilastatin (i mi PEN em & sye la STAT in)

Related Information
Animal and Human Bites Guidelines *on page 1399*
Antimicrobial Drugs of Choice *on page 1404*

U.S. Brand Names Primaxin®

Synonyms Imipemide

Therapeutic Category Antibiotic, Anaerobic; Antibiotic, Carbapenem

Use Treatment of respiratory tract, urinary tract, intra-abdominal, gynecologic, bone and joint, skin structure, and polymicrobic infections as well as bacterial septicemia and endocarditis. Antibacterial activity includes resistant gram-negative bacilli (*Pseudomonas aeruginosa* and *Enterobacter* sp), gram-positive bacteria (methicillin-sensitive *Staphylococcus aureus* and *Streptococcus* sp) and anaerobes.

Pregnancy Risk Factor C

Contraindications Hypersensitivity to imipenem/cilastatin or any component

Warnings/Precautions Dosage adjustment required in patients with impaired renal function; safety and efficacy in children <12 years of age have not yet been established; prolonged use may result in superinfection; use with caution in patients with a history of seizures or hypersensitivity to beta-lactams; elderly patients often require lower doses

Adverse Reactions
1% to 10%:
  Gastrointestinal: Nausea/diarrhea/vomiting (1% to 2%)
  Local: Phlebitis (3%)
<1%: Hypotension, palpitations, seizures, rash, pseudomembranous colitis, neutropenia (including agranulocytosis), eosinophilia, anemia, (+) Coombs' test, thrombocytopenia, increased PT, increased LFTs, pain at injection site, increased BUN/creatine, abnormal urinalysis, emergence of resistant strains of *P. aeruginosa*

Overdosage/Toxicology
Symptoms of overdose include neuromuscular hypersensitivity, seizures
Hemodialysis may be helpful to aid in the removal of the drug from the blood; otherwise most treatment is supportive or symptom directed

Drug Interactions Increased toxicity: Beta-lactam antibiotics, probenecid may increase toxic potential

Stability
Imipenem/cilastatin powder for injection should be stored at <30°C
Reconstituted solutions are stable 10 hours at room temperature and 48 hours at refrigeration (4°C) with NS
If reconstituted with 5% or 10% dextrose injection, 5% dextrose and sodium bicarbonate, 5% dextrose and 0.9% sodium chloride, is stable for 4 hours at room temperature and 24 hours when refrigerated
Imipenem/cilastatin is most stable at a pH of 6.5-7.5; imipenem is inactivated at acidic or alkaline pH
Standard diluent: 500 mg/100 mL NS; 1 g/250 mL NS
Comments: All IVPB should be prepared fresh; do not use dextrose as a diluent due to limited stability

Mechanism of Action Inhibits bacterial cell wall synthesis by binding to one or more of the penicillin binding proteins (PBPs); which in turn inhibits the final transpeptidation step of peptidoglycan synthesis in bacterial cell walls, thus inhibiting cell wall biosynthesis. Bacteria eventually lyse due to ongoing activity of cell wall autolytic enzymes (autolysins and murein hydrolases) while cell wall assembly is arrested. Cilastatin prevents renal metabolism of imipenem by competitive inhibition of dehydropeptidase along the brush border of the renal tubules.

Pharmacodynamics/Kinetics
Absorption: I.M.: Imipenem: 60% to 75%; cilastatin: 95% to 100%
Distribution: Imipenem appears in breast milk; crosses the placenta; distributed rapidly and widely to most tissues and fluids including sputum, pleural fluid, peritoneal fluid, interstitial fluid, bile, aqueous humor, reproductive organs, and bone; highest concentrations in pleural fluid, interstitial fluid, peritoneal fluid, and reproductive organs; low concentrations in cerebrospinal fluid
Metabolism: Imipenem is metabolized in the kidney by dehydropeptidase, this activity is blocked by cilastatin; cilastatin is partially metabolized in the kidneys
Half-life: Both: 60 minutes, extended with renal insufficiency
Elimination: Both: ~70% excreted unchanged in urine

Usual Dosage Dosing based on imipenem component:
Children: I.V.:
  3 months to 3 years: 25 mg/kg every 6 hours; maximum: 2 g/day
  ≥3 years: 15 mg/kg/every 6 hours
Adults: I.V.:
  Mild to moderate infection: 250-500 mg every 6-8 hours
  Severe infections with only **moderately susceptible** organisms: 1 g every 6-8 hours
  Mild to moderate infection **only**: I.M.: 500-750 mg every 12 hours (**Note:** 750 mg is recommended for intra-abdominal and more severe respiratory, dermatologic, or gynecologic infections; total daily I.M. dosages >1500 mg are not recommended; deep I.M. injection should be carefully made into a large muscle mass only)
Dosing adjustment in renal impairment: See table.
Hemodialysis: Imipenem (**not cilastatin**) is moderately dialyzable (20% to 50%); administer dose postdialysis

Imipenem/Cilastatin

Creatinine Clearance (mL/min/1.73 m²)	Frequency	Dose (mg)
30-70	q8h	500
20-30	q12h	500
5-20	q12h	250

Peritoneal dialysis: Dose as for Cl_{cr} <10 mL/minute

Continuous arteriovenous or venovenous hemofiltration (CAVH/CAVHD): Dose as for Cl_{cr} 20-30 mL/minute; monitor for seizure activity; imipenem is well removed by CAVH but cilastatin is not; removes 20 mg of imipenem per liter of filtrate per day

Administration Not for direct infusion; vial contents must be transferred to 100 mL of infusion solution; final concentration should not exceed 5 mg/mL; infuse each 250-500 mg dose over 20-30 minutes; infuse each 1 g dose over 40-60 minutes; watch for convulsions. If nausea and/or vomiting occur during administration, decrease the rate of I.V. infusion; do not mix with or physically add to other antibiotics; however, may administer concomitantly

Monitoring Parameters Periodic renal, hepatic, and hematologic function tests; monitor for signs of anaphylaxis during first dose

Test Interactions Interferes with urinary glucose determination using Clinitest®

Additional Information Sodium content of 1 g injection:
I.M.: 64.4 mg (2.8 mEq)
I.V.: 73.6 mg (3.2 mEq)

Dosage Forms Powder for injection:
I.M.:
Imipenem 500 mg and cilastatin 500 mg
Imipenem 750 mg and cilastatin 750 mg
I.V.:
Imipenem 250 mg and cilastatin 250 mg
Imipenem 500 mg and cilastatin 500 mg

Imipramine (im IP ra meen)

Related Information
Antidepressant Agents Comparison *on page 1301*

U.S. Brand Names Janimine®; Tofranil®; Tofranil-PM®

Canadian Brand Names Apo®-Imipramine; Novo-Pramine; PMS-Imipramine

Synonyms Imipramine Hydrochloride; Imipramine Pamoate

Therapeutic Category Antidepressant, Tricyclic

Use Treatment of various forms of depression, often in conjunction with psychotherapy; enuresis in children; certain types of chronic and neuropathic pain

Pregnancy Risk Factor D

Contraindications Hypersensitivity to imipramine (cross-sensitivity with other tricyclics may occur); patients receiving MAO inhibitors or fluoxetine within past 14 days; narrow-angle glaucoma

Warnings/Precautions Use with caution in patients with cardiovascular disease, conduction disturbances, seizure disorders, urinary retention, hyperthyroidism or those receiving thyroid replacement; do not discontinue abruptly in patients receiving long-term, high-dose therapy; some oral preparations contain tartrazine and injection contains sulfites, both of which can cause allergic reactions

Orthostatic hypotension is a concern with this agent, especially in patients taking other medications that may affect blood pressure; may precipitate arrhythmias in predisposed patients; may aggravate seizures; a less anticholinergic antidepressant may be a better choice

Adverse Reactions Less sedation and anticholinergic effects than amitriptyline
>10%:
Central nervous system: Dizziness, drowsiness, headache
Gastrointestinal: Increased appetite, nausea, unpleasant taste, weight gain, xerostomia, constipation
Genitourinary: Urinary retention
Neuromuscular & skeletal: Weakness
1% to 10%:
Cardiovascular: Postural hypotension, arrhythmias, tachycardia
Central nervous system: Confusion, delirium, hallucinations, nervousness, restlessness, parkinsonian syndrome, insomnia
Endocrine & metabolic: Sexual dysfunction
Gastrointestinal: Diarrhea, heartburn
Genitourinary: Dysuria
Neuromuscular & skeletal: Fine muscle tremors
Ocular: Blurred vision, eye pain
Miscellaneous: Diaphoresis (excessive)
<1%: Anxiety, seizures, alopecia, photosensitivity, breast enlargement, galactorrhea, SIADH, trouble with gums, decreased lower esophageal sphincter tone may cause GE reflux, testicular edema, leukopenia, eosinophilia, rarely agranulocytosis, increased liver enzymes, cholestatic jaundice, increased intraocular pressure, tinnitus, allergic reactions, has been associated with falls, sudden death
(Continued)

Imipramine *(Continued)*

Overdosage/Toxicology

Symptoms of overdose include confusion, hallucinations, constipation, cyanosis, tachycardia, urinary retention, ventricular tachycardia, seizures

Following initiation of essential overdose management, toxic symptoms should be treated. Sodium bicarbonate is indicated when QRS interval is >0.10 seconds or QT_c >0.42 seconds. Ventricular arrhythmias often respond to concurrent systemic alkalinization (sodium bicarbonate 0.5-2 mEq/kg I.V.). Arrhythmias unresponsive to this therapy may respond to lidocaine 1 mg/kg I.V. followed by a titrated infusion. Physostigmine (1-2 mg I.V. slowly for adults or 0.5 mg I.V. slowly for children) may be indicated in reversing cardiac arrhythmias that are life-threatening. Seizures usually respond to diazepam I.V. boluses (5-10 mg for adults up to 30 mg or 0.25-0.4 mg/kg/dose for children up to 10 mg/dose). If seizures are unresponsive or recur, phenytoin or phenobarbital may be required.

Drug Interactions CYP1A2, 2C9, 2C18, 2C19, 2D6, and 3A3/4 enzyme substrate

Decreased effect: Imipramine inhibits the antihypertensive effects of clonidine

Increased toxicity: MAO inhibitors: Hyperpyrexia, hypertension, tachycardia, confusion, seizures, and death; may increase the prothrombin time in patients stabilized on warfarin; may potentiate the action of other CNS depressants; potentiates the pressor and cardiac effects of sympathomimetic agents such as isoproterenol, epinephrine, etc; additive anticholinergic effects seen with other anticholinergic agents; cimetidine reduces the hepatic metabolism of imipramine; tricyclic antidepressants like imipramine may enhance the hypertensive response associated with abrupt clonidine withdrawal

Stability Solutions stable at a pH of 4-5; turns yellowish or reddish on exposure to light. Slight discoloration does not affect potency; marked discoloration is associated with loss of potency. Capsules stable for 3 years following date of manufacture.

Mechanism of Action Traditionally believed to increase the synaptic concentration of serotonin and/or norepinephrine in the central nervous system by inhibition of their reuptake by the presynaptic neuronal membrane. However, additional receptor effects have been found including desensitization of adenyl cyclase, down regulation of beta-adrenergic receptors, and down regulation of serotonin receptors.

Pharmacodynamics/Kinetics

Peak antidepressant effect: Usually after ≥2 weeks

Absorption: Oral: Well absorbed

Distribution: Crosses the placenta

Metabolism: In the liver by microsomal enzymes to desipramine (active) and other metabolites; significant first-pass metabolism

Half-life: 6-18 hours

Elimination: Almost all compounds following metabolism are excreted in urine

Usual Dosage Maximum antidepressant effect may not be seen for 2 or more weeks after initiation of therapy.

Children: Oral:

Depression: 1.5 mg/kg/day with dosage increments of 1 mg/kg every 3-4 days to a maximum dose of 5 mg/kg/day in 1-4 divided doses; monitor carefully especially with doses ≥3.5 mg/kg/day

Enuresis: ≥6 years: Initial: 10-25 mg at bedtime, if inadequate response still seen after 1 week of therapy, increase by 25 mg/day; dose should not exceed 2.5 mg/kg/day or 50 mg at bedtime if 6-12 years of age or 75 mg at bedtime if ≥12 years of age

Adjunct in the treatment of cancer pain: Initial: 0.2-0.4 mg/kg at bedtime; dose may be increased by 50% every 2-3 days up to 1-3 mg/kg/dose at bedtime

Adolescents: Oral: Initial: 25-50 mg/day; increase gradually; maximum: 100 mg/day in single or divided doses

Adults:

Oral: Initial: 25 mg 3-4 times/day, increase dose gradually, total dose may be given at bedtime; maximum: 300 mg/day

I.M.: Initial: Up to 100 mg/day in divided doses; change to oral as soon as possible

Elderly: Initial: 10-25 mg at bedtime; increase by 10-25 mg every 3 days for inpatients and weekly for outpatients if tolerated; average daily dose to achieve a therapeutic concentration: 100 mg/day; range: 50-150 mg/day

Dietary Considerations Alcohol: Additive CNS effect, avoid use

Monitoring Parameters Monitor blood pressure and pulse rate prior to and during initial therapy; EKG, CBC; evaluate mental status

Reference Range Therapeutic: Imipramine and desipramine: 150-250 ng/mL (SI: 530-890 nmol/L); desipramine: 150-300 ng/mL (SI: 560-1125 nmol/L); Toxic: >500 ng/mL (SI: 446-893 nmol/L); utility of serum level monitoring controversial

Test Interactions ↑ glucose

Patient Information May require 2-4 weeks to achieve desired effect; avoid alcohol ingestion; do not discontinue medication abruptly; may cause urine to turn blue-green; may cause drowsiness, avoid alcohol and other CNS depressants; dry mouth may be helped by sips of water, sugarless gum, or hard candy; rise slowly to avoid dizziness

Nursing Implications Raise bed rails, institute safety measures

Additional Information

Imipramine hydrochloride: Tofranil®, Janimine®

Imipramine pamoate: Tofranil-PM®

Dosage Forms

Capsule, as pamoate (Tofranil-PM®): 75 mg, 100 mg, 125 mg, 150 mg

Injection, as hydrochloride (Tofranil®): 12.5 mg/mL (2 mL)
Tablet, as hydrochloride (Janimine®, Tofranil®): 10 mg, 25 mg, 50 mg

◆ **Imipramine Hydrochloride** *see Imipramine on page 601*

◆ **Imipramine Pamoate** *see Imipramine on page 601*

Imiquimod (i mi KWI mod)

U.S. Brand Names Aldara™

Therapeutic Category Skin and Mucous Membrane Agent; Topical Skin Product

Use Treatment of external genital and perianal warts/condyloma acuminata in adults

Pregnancy Risk Factor B

Contraindications Hypersensitivity to imiquimod

Warnings/Precautions Imiquimod has not been evaluated for the treatment of urethral, intravaginal, cervical, rectal, or intra-anal human papilloma viral disease and is not recommended for these conditions. Topical imiquimod is not intended for ophthalmic use. Topical imiquimod administration is not recommended until genital/perianal tissue is healed from any previous drug or surgical treatment. Imiquimod has the potential to exacerbate inflammatory conditions of the skin.

Adverse Reactions

>10%: Local, mild/moderate: Erythema, itching, erosion, burning, excoriation/flaking, edema

1% to 10%:

Local, severe: Erythema, erosion, edema

Local, mild/moderate: Pain, induration, ulceration, scabbing, vesicles, soreness

Overdosage/Toxicology

Overdosage is unlikely because of minimal percutaneous absorption. Persistent topical overdosing of imiquimod could result in severe local skin reactions. The most clinically serious adverse event reported following multiple oral imiquimod doses of ≥200 mg was hypotension that resolved following oral or I.V. fluid administration.
Treat symptomatically

Stability Do not store at ≥30°C (86°F); avoid freezing

Mechanism of Action Mechanism of action is unknown; however, induces cytokines, including interferon-alpha and others

Pharmacodynamics/Kinetics

Absorption: Minimal

Elimination: Less than 0.9% of dose is excreted in urine and feces following topical administration

Usual Dosage

Adults: Topical: Apply 3 times/week prior to normal sleeping hours and leave on the skin for 6-10 hours. Following treatment period, remove cream by washing the treated area with mild soap and water. Examples of 3 times/week application schedules are: Monday, Wednesday, Friday; or Tuesday, Thursday, Saturday. Continue imiquimod treatment until there is total clearance of the genital/perianal warts for ≤16 weeks. A rest period of several days may be taken if required by the patient's discomfort or severity of the local skin reaction. Treatment may resume once the reaction subsides. Nonocclusive dressings such as cotton gauze or cotton underwear may be used in the management of skin reactions. Handwashing before and after cream application is recommended. Imiquimod is packaged in single-use packets that contain sufficient cream to cover a wart area of up to 20 cm²; avoid use of excessive amounts of cream. Instruct patients to apply imiquimod to external or perianal warts. Apply a thin layer to the wart area and rub in until the cream is no longer visible. Do not occlude the application site.

Monitoring Parameters Reduction in wart size is indicative of a therapeutic response; patients should be monitored for signs and symptoms of hypersensitivity to imiquimod

Patient Information Imiquimod may weaken condoms and vaginal diaphragms; therefore, concurrent use is not recommended. This medication is for external use only; avoid contact with eyes. Do not occlude the treatment area with bandages or other covers or wraps. Avoid sexual (genital, anal, oral) contact while the cream is on the skin. Wash the treatment area with mild soap and water 6-10 hours following application of imiquimod.

Patients commonly experience local skin reactions such as erythema, erosion, excoriation/flaking, and edema at the site of application or surrounding areas. Most skin reactions are mild to moderate. Severe skin reactions can occur; promptly report severe reactions to physician. Uncircumcised males treating warts under the foreskin should retract the foreskin and clean the area daily.

Imiquimod is not a cure; new warts may develop during therapy.

Dosage Forms Cream, topical: 5% (250 mg single dose packets in boxes of 12)

◆ **Imitrex®** *see Sumatriptan Succinate on page 1100*

Immune Globulin, Intramuscular

(i MYUN GLOB yoo lin, IN tra MUS kyoo ler)

Related Information

Immunization Recommendations *on page 1358*

Prevention of Hepatitis A Through Active or Passive Immunization *on page 1370*

Prophylaxis for Patients Exposed to Common Communicable Diseases *on page 1384*

Canadian Brand Names Gammabulin Immuno; Iveegam®

Synonyms Gamma Globulin; IG; IGIM; Immune Serum Globulin; ISG

Therapeutic Category Immune Globulin

(Continued)

Immune Globulin, Intramuscular *(Continued)*

Use Household and sexual contacts of persons with hepatitis A, measles, varicella, and possibly rubella; travelers to high-risk areas outside tourist routes; staff, attendees, and parents of diapered attendees in day-care center outbreaks

For travelers, IG is not an alternative to careful selection of foods and water; immune globulin can interfere with the antibody response to parenterally administered live virus vaccines. Frequent travelers should be tested for hepatitis A antibody, immune hemolytic anemia, and neutropenia (with ITP, I.V. route is usually used).

Pregnancy Risk Factor C

Contraindications Thrombocytopenia, hypersensitivity to immune globulin, thimerosal, IgA deficiency

Warnings/Precautions Skin testing should not be performed as local irritation can occur and be misinterpreted as a positive reaction; do not administer I.V.; IG should **not** be used to control outbreaks of measles; epidemiologic and laboratory data indicate current IMIG products do not have a discernible risk of transmitting HIV

Adverse Reactions
>10%: Local: Pain, tenderness, muscle stiffness at I.M. site
1% to 10%:
  Cardiovascular: Flushing
  Central nervous system: Chills
  Gastrointestinal: Nausea
<1%: Lethargy, fever, urticaria, angioedema, erythema, vomiting, myalgia, hypersensitivity reactions

Drug Interactions Increased toxicity: Live virus, vaccines (measles, mumps, rubella); do not administer within 3 months after administration of these vaccines

Stability Keep in refrigerator; do not freeze

Mechanism of Action Provides passive immunity by increasing the antibody titer and antigen-antibody reaction potential

Pharmacodynamics/Kinetics
Duration of immune effect: Usually 3-4 weeks
Half-life: 23 days
Time to peak serum concentration: I.M.: Within 24-48 hours

Usual Dosage I.M.:
Hepatitis A:
  Pre-exposure prophylaxis upon travel into endemic areas (hepatitis A vaccine preferred):
    0.02 mL/kg for anticipated risk 1-3 months
    0.06 mL/kg for anticipated risk >3 months
    Repeat approximate dose every 4-6 months if exposure continues
  Postexposure prophylaxis: 0.02 mL/kg given within 2 weeks of exposure
Measles:
  Prophylaxis: 0.25 mL/kg/dose (maximum dose: 15 mL) given within 6 days of exposure followed by live attenuated measles vaccine in 3 months or at 15 months of age (whichever is later)
  For patients with leukemia, lymphoma, immunodeficiency disorders, generalized malignancy, or receiving immunosuppressive therapy: 0.5 mL/kg (maximum dose: 15 mL)
Poliomyelitis: Prophylaxis: 0.3 mL/kg/dose as a single dose
Rubella: Prophylaxis: 0.55 mL/kg/dose within 72 hours of exposure
Varicella:: Prophylaxis: 0.6-1.2 mL/kg (varicella zoster immune globulin preferred) within 72 hours of exposure
IgG deficiency: 1.3 mL/kg, then 0.66 mL/kg in 3-4 weeks
Hepatitis B: Prophylaxis: 0.06 mL/kg/dose (HBIG preferred)

Administration Intramuscular injection only

Test Interactions Skin tests should **not** be done

Nursing Implications Do not mix with other medications; skin testing should not be performed as local irritation can occur and be misinterpreted as a positive reaction

Dosage Forms Injection: I.M.: 165±15 mg (of protein)/mL (2 mL, 10 mL)

Immune Globulin, Intravenous (i MYUN GLOB yoo lin, IN tra VEE nus)

Related Information
  Immunization Recommendations *on page 1358*

U.S. Brand Names Gamimune® N; Gammagard® S/D; Gammar®-P I.V.; Polygam®; Polygam® S/D; Sandoglobulin®; Venoglobulin®-I; Venoglobulin®-S

Synonyms IVIG

Therapeutic Category Immune Globulin

Use Treatment of immunodeficiency sufficiency (hypogammaglobulinemia, agammaglobulinemia, IgG subclass deficiencies, severe combined immunodeficiency syndromes (SCIDS), Wiskott-Aldrich syndrome), idiopathic thrombocytopenic purpura; used in conjunction with appropriate anti-infective therapy *to prevent or modify acute bacterial or viral infections* in patients with iatrogenically-induced or disease-associated immunodepression; *chronic lymphocytic leukemia (CLL) - chronic prophylaxis autoimmune neutropenia, bone marrow transplantation patients, autoimmune hemolytic anemia or neutropenia, refractory dermatomyositis/polymyositis, autoimmune diseases* (myasthenia gravis, SLE, bullous pemphigoid, severe rheumatoid arthritis), Guillain-Barré syndrome; pediatric HIV infection to decrease frequency of serious bacterial infections

Pregnancy Risk Factor C

Contraindications Hypersensitivity to immune globulin or any component, IgA deficiency (except with the use of Gammagard®, Polygam®)

Warnings/Precautions Anaphylactic hypersensitivity reactions can occur, especially in IgA-deficient patients; studies indicate that the currently available products have no discernible risk of transmitting HIV or hepatitis B; aseptic meningitis may occur with high doses (≥2 g/kg)

Intravenous Immune Globulin Product Comparison

	Gamimune® N	Gammagard® SD	Gammar®-IV	Polygam®	Sandoglobulin®	Venoglobulin®-I
FDA indication	Primary immunodeficiency, ITP	Primary immunodeficiency, ITP, CLL prophylaxis	Primary immunodeficiency	Primary immunodeficiency, ITP, CLL	Primary immunodeficiency, ITP	Primary immunodeficiency, ITP
Contraindication	IgA deficiency	None (caution with IgA deficiency)	IgA deficiency	None (caution with IgA deficiency)	IgA deficiency	IgA deficiency
IgA content	270 mcg/mL	0.92-1.6 mcg/mL	<20 mcg/mL	0.74±0.33 mcg/mL	720 mcg/mL	20-24 mcg/mL
Adverse reactions (%)	5.2	6	15	6	2.5-6.6	6
Plasma source	>2000 paid donors	4000-5000 paid donors	>8000 paid donors	50,000 voluntary donors	8000-15,000 voluntary donors	6000-9000 paid donors
Half-life	21 d	24 d	21-24 d	21-25 d	21-23 d	29 d
IgG subclass (%)						
IgG$_1$ (60-70)	60	67 (66.8)[1]	69	67	60.5 (55.3)[1]	62.3[2]
IgG$_2$ (19-31)	29.4	25 (25.4)	23	25	30.2 (35.7)	32.8
IgG$_3$ (5-8.4)	6.5	5 (7.4)	6	5	6.6 (6.3)	2.9
IgG$_4$ (0.7-4)	4.1	3 (0.3)	2	3	2.6 (2.6)	2
Monomers (%)	>95	>95	>98	>95	>92	>98
Gammaglobulin (%)	>98	>90	>98	>90	>96	>98
Storage	Refrigerate	Room temp	Room temp	Room temp	Room temp	Room temp
Recommendations for initial infusion rate	0.01-0.02 mL/kg/min	0.5 mL/kg/h	0.01-0.02 mL/kg/min	0.5 mL/kg/h	0.01-0.03 mL/kg/min	0.01-0.02 mL/kg/min
Maximum infusion rate	0.08 mL/kg/min	4 mL/kg/h	0.06 mL/kg/min	4 mL/kg/h	2.5 mL/min	0.04 mL/kg/min
Maximum concentration for infusion (%)	10	5	5	10	12	10

[1]Skvaril F and Gardi A, "Differences Among Available Immunoglobulin Preparations for Intravenous Use," *Pediatr Infect Dis J*, 1988, 7:543-48.
[2]Roomer J, Morgenthaler JJ, Scherz R, et al, "Characterization of Various Immunoglobulin Preparations for Intravenous Application," *Vox Sang*, 1982, 42:62-73.

Adverse Reactions

1% to 10%:

Cardiovascular: Flushing of the face, tachycardia

Central nervous system: Chills

(Continued)

Immune Globulin, Intravenous (Continued)

Gastrointestinal: Nausea

Respiratory: Dyspnea

<1%: Hypotension, tightness in the chest, dizziness, fever, headache, diaphoresis, hypersensitivity reactions

Drug Interactions Increased toxicity: Live virus, vaccines (measles, mumps, rubella); do not administer within 3 months after administration of these vaccines

Stability Stability and dilution is dependent upon the manufacturer and brand; do not mix with other drugs

Mechanism of Action Replacement therapy for primary and secondary immunodeficiencies; interference with F_c receptors on the cells of the reticuloendothelial system for autoimmune cytopenias and ITP; possible role of contained antiviral-type antibodies

Pharmacodynamics/Kinetics I.V. provides immediate antibody levels

Duration of immune effects: 3-4 weeks

Half-life: 21-24 days

Usual Dosage Children and Adults: I.V.:

Dosages should be based on ideal body weight and not actual body weight in morbidly obese patients; approved doses and regimens may vary between brands; check manufacturer guidelines

Primary immunodeficiency disorders: 200-400 mg/kg every 4 weeks or as per monitored serum IgG concentrations

Chronic lymphocytic leukemia (CLL): 400 mg/kg/dose every 3 weeks

Idiopathic thrombocytopenic purpura (ITP): Maintenance dose:

400 mg/kg/day for 2-5 consecutive days; or 1000 mg/kg every other day for 3 doses, if needed or

1000 mg/kg/day for 2 consecutive days; or up to 2000 mg/kg/day over 2-7 consecutive days

Chronic ITP: 400-2000 mg/kg/dose as needed to maintain appropriate platelet counts

Kawasaki disease:

400 mg/kg/day for 4 days within 10 days of onset of fever

800 mg/kg/day for 1-2 days within 10 days of onset of fever

2 g/kg for one dose only

Acquired immunodeficiency syndrome (patients must be symptomatic):

200-250 mg/kg/dose every 2 weeks

400-500 mg/kg/dose every month or every 4 weeks

Pediatric HIV: 400 mg/kg every 28 days

Autoimmune hemolytic anemia and neutropenia: 1000 mg/kg/dose for 2-3 days

Autoimmune diseases: 400 mg/kg/day for 4 days

Bone marrow transplant: 500 mg/kg beginning on days 7 and 2 pretransplant, then 500 mg/kg/week for 90 days post-transplant

Adjuvant to severe cytomegalovirus infections: 500 mg/kg/dose every other day for 7 doses

Severe systemic viral and bacterial infections: Children: 500-1000 mg/kg/week

Prevention of gastroenteritis: Infants and Children: Oral: 50 mg/kg/day divided every 6 hours

Guillain-Barré syndrome:

400 mg/kg/day for 4 days

1000 mg/kg/day for 2 days

2000 mg/kg/day for one day

Refractory dermatomyositis: 2 g/kg/dose every month x 3-4 doses

Refractory polymyositis: 1 g/kg/day x 2 days every month x 4 doses

Chronic inflammatory demyelinating polyneuropathy:

400 mg/kg/day for 5 doses once each month

800 mg/kg/day for 3 doses once each month

1000 mg/kg/day for 2 days once each month

Dosing adjustment/comments in renal impairment: Cl_{cr} <10 mL/minute: Avoid use

Administration I.V. use only; for initial treatment, a lower concentration and/or a slower rate of infusion should be used

Dosage Forms

Injection: Gamimune® N: 5% [50 mg/mL] (10 mL, 50 mL, 100 mL, 250 mL); 10% [100 mg/mL] (10 mL, 50 mL, 100 mL, 200 mL)

Powder for injection, lyophilized:

Gammar®-P I.V. (5% IgG and 3% albumin): 1 g, 2.5 g, 5 g, 10 g

Polygam®: 0.5 g, 2.5 g, 5 g, 10 g

Sandoglobulin®: 1 g, 3 g, 6 g, 12 g

Venoglobulin®-I: 0.5 g, 2.5 g, 5 g, 10 g

Detergent treated:

Gammagard® S/D: 2.5 g, 5 g, 10 g

Polygam® S/D: 2.5 g, 5 g, 10 g

Venoglobulin®-S: 5% [50 mg/mL] (50 mL, 100 mL, 200 mL); 10% [100 mg/mL] (50 mL, 100 mL, 200 mL)

+ **Immune Serum Globulin** see Immune Globulin, Intramuscular on page 603

+ **Immunization Recommendations** see page 1358

+ **Imodium®** see Loperamide on page 692

+ **Imodium® A-D [OTC]** see Loperamide on page 692

+ **Imogam®** see Rabies Immune Globulin (Human) on page 1006

+ **Imovax® Rabies I.D. Vaccine** see Rabies Virus Vaccine on page 1007

- **Imovax® Rabies Vaccine** *see Rabies Virus Vaccine on page 1007*
- **Imuran®** *see Azathioprine on page 115*
- **I-Naphline®** *see Naphazoline on page 817*
- **Inapsine®** *see Droperidol on page 400*
- **Indanyl Sodium** *see Carbenicillin on page 191*

Indapamide (in DAP a mide)
Related Information
Depression Disorders and Treatments *on page 1465*
Sulfonamide Derivatives *on page 1337*
U.S. Brand Names Lozol®
Canadian Brand Names Apo®-Indapadmide; Lozide®
Therapeutic Category Antihypertensive Agent; Diuretic, Miscellaneous
Use Management of mild to moderate hypertension; treatment of edema in congestive heart failure and nephrotic syndrome
Pregnancy Risk Factor D
Contraindications Anuria, hypersensitivity to indapamide or any component, cross-sensitivity with other thiazides and sulfonamide derivatives
Warnings/Precautions Use with caution in patients with renal or hepatic disease, gout, lupus erythematosus, or diabetes mellitus
Adverse Reactions
1% to 10%: Endocrine & metabolic: Hypokalemia
<1%: Arrhythmia, weak pulse, hypotension, mood changes, photosensitivity, fluid and electrolyte imbalances (hypocalcemia, hypomagnesemia, hyponatremia), hyperglycemia, xerostomia, rarely blood dyscrasias, numbness or paresthesia in hands, feet or lips, muscle cramps or pain, unusual weakness, prerenal azotemia, shortness of breath, increased thirst
Overdosage/Toxicology
Symptoms of overdose include lethargy, diuresis, hypermotility, confusion, muscle weakness
Following GI decontamination, therapy is supportive with I.V. fluids, electrolytes, and I.V. pressors if needed
Drug Interactions
Decreased effect:
Thiazides may decrease the effect of anticoagulants, antigout agents, sulfonylureas
Bile acid sequestrants, methenamine, and NSAIDs may decrease the effect of the thiazides
Increased effect: Thiazides may increase the toxicity of allopurinol, anesthetics, antineoplastics, calcium salts, diazoxide, digitalis, lithium, loop diuretics, methyldopa, nondepolarizing muscle relaxants, vitamin D; amphotericin B and anticholinergics may increase the toxicity of thiazides
Mechanism of Action Diuretic effect is localized at the proximal segment of the distal tubule of the nephron; it does not appear to have significant effect on glomerular filtration rate nor renal blood flow; like other diuretics, it enhances sodium, chloride, and water excretion by interfering with the transport of sodium ions across the renal tubular epithelium
Pharmacodynamics/Kinetics
Absorption: Completely from GI tract
Plasma protein binding: 71% to 79%
Metabolism: Extensively in the liver
Half-life: 14-18 hours
Time to peak serum concentration: 2-2.5 hours
Elimination: ~60% of dose excreted in urine within 48 hours, ~16% to 23% excreted via bile in feces
Usual Dosage Adults: Oral:
Edema: 2.5-5 mg/day. **Note:** There is little therapeutic benefit to increasing the dose >5 mg/day; there is, however, an increased risk of electrolyte disturbances
Hypertension: 1.25 mg in the morning, may increase to 5 mg/day by increments of 1.25-2.5 mg; consider adding another antihypertensive and decreasing the dose if response is not adequate
Monitoring Parameters Blood pressure (both standing and sitting/supine), serum electrolytes, renal function, assess weight, I & O reports daily to determine fluid loss
Patient Information May be taken with food or milk; take early in day to avoid nocturia; take the last dose of multiple doses no later than 6 PM unless instructed otherwise. A few people who take this medication become more sensitive to sunlight and may experience skin rash, redness, itching, or severe sunburn, especially if sun block SPF ≥15 is not used on exposed skin areas.
Nursing Implications Take blood pressure with patient lying down and standing; may increase serum glucose in diabetic patients
Dosage Forms Tablet: 1.25 mg, 2.5 mg

- **Inderal®** *see Propranolol on page 986*
- **Inderal® LA** *see Propranolol on page 986*
- **Inderide®** *see Propranolol and Hydrochlorothiazide on page 989*

Indinavir (in DIN a veer)
Related Information
Antiretroviral Agents *on page 1306*
(Continued)

Indinavir *(Continued)*

Antiretroviral Therapy for HIV Infection *on page 1410*
Management of Healthcare Worker Exposures to HIV *on page 1374*

U.S. Brand Names Crixivan®

Therapeutic Category Antiretroviral Agent, Protease Inhibitor; Protease Inhibitor

Use Treatment of HIV infection; should always be used as part of a multidrug regimen (at least three antiretroviral agents)

Pregnancy Risk Factor C

Pregnancy/Breast-Feeding Implications

Clinical effects on the fetus: Administer during pregnancy only if benefits to mother outweigh risks to the fetus; hyperbilirubinemia may be exacerbated in neonates

Breast-feeding/lactation: HIV-infected mothers are discouraged from breast-feeding to decrease potential transmission of HIV

Contraindications Hypersensitivity to the drug or its components

Warnings/Precautions Because indinavir may cause nephrolithiasis the drug should be discontinued if signs and symptoms occur. Indinavir should not be administered concurrently with terfenadine, astemizole, cisapride, triazolam, and midazolam because of competition for metabolism of these drugs through the CYP3A4 system, and potential serious or life-threatening events. Patients with hepatic insufficiency due to cirrhosis should have dose reduction.

Adverse Reactions Protease inhibitors cause dyslipidemia which includes elevated cholesterol and triglycerides and a redistribution of body fat centrally to cause "protease paunch", buffalo hump, facial atrophy, and breast enlargement. These agents also cause hyperglycemia.

1% to 10%:

Central nervous system: Headache (5.6%), insomnia (3.1%)

Gastrointestinal: Mild elevation of indirect bilirubin (10%), abdominal pain (8.7%), nausea (11.7%), diarrhea/vomiting (4% to 5%), taste perversion (2.6%)

Neuromuscular & skeletal: Weakness (3.6%), flank pain (2.6%)

Renal: Kidney stones (2% to 3%)

<1%: Malaise, dizziness, somnolence, anorexia, xerostomia, decreased hemoglobin

Drug Interactions CYP3A3/4 enzyme substrate; CYP3A3/4 enzyme inhibitor

Decreased effect: Concurrent use of rifampin and rifabutin may decrease the effectiveness of indinavir (dosage increase of indinavir is recommended), dosage decreases of rifampin/rifabutin is recommended; the efficacy of protease inhibitors may be decreased when given with nevirapine

Increased toxicity: Gastric pH is lowered and absorption may be decreased when didanosine and indinavir are taken <1 hour apart; a reduction of dose is often required when coadministered with ketoconazole; terfenadine, astemizole, cisapride should be avoided with indinavir due to life-threatening cardiotoxicity; benzodiazepines with indinavir may result in prolonged sedation and respiratory depression

Stability Capsules are sensitive to moisture; medication should be stored and used in the original container and the desiccant should remain in the bottle

Mechanism of Action Indinavir is a human immunodeficiency virus protease inhibitor, binding to the protease activity site and inhibiting the activity of this enzyme. HIV protease is an enzyme required for the cleavage of viral polyprotein precursors into individual functional proteins found in infectious HIV. Inhibition prevents cleavage of these polyproteins resulting in the formation of immature noninfectious viral particles.

Pharmacodynamics/Kinetics

Absorption: Administration of indinavir with a high fat, high calorie diet resulted in a reduction in AUC and in maximum serum concentration (77% and 84% respectively). Administration with a lighter meal resulted in little or no change in these parameters.

Protein binding: 60% in the plasma

Metabolism: Highly metabolized by the cytochrome P-450 3A4 enzymes; seven metabolites of indinavir have been identified

Bioavailability: Oral: Good; T_{max}: 0.8 ± 0.3 hour

Half-life: 1.8 ± 0.4 hour

Elimination: In feces and urine

Usual Dosage Adults: Oral: 800 mg every 8 hours

Dosage adjustment in hepatic impairment: 600 mg every 8 hours with mild/medium impairment due to cirrhosis or with ketoconazole coadministration

Dietary Considerations Meals high in calories, fat, and protein result in a significant decrease in drug levels; grapefruit juice may decrease indinavir's AUC

Monitoring Parameters Monitor viral load, CD4 count, triglycerides, cholesterol, glucose

Patient Information Take with a full glass of water; any symptoms of kidney stones, including flank pain, dysuria, etc, indicates the drug should be discontinued and physician or pharmacist should be contacted. Drug should be administered on an empty stomach 1 hour before or 2 hours after a large meal. May take with a small, light meal. Indinavir should be stored and used in the original container.

Nursing Implications Administer around-the-clock to avoid significant fluctuation in serum levels; administer with plenty of water

Dosage Forms Capsule: 200 mg, 333 mg, 400 mg

♦ **Indochron E-R®** *see* Indomethacin *on next page*
♦ **Indocid®** *see* Indomethacin *on next page*
♦ **Indocid® SR** *see* Indomethacin *on next page*
♦ **Indocin®** *see* Indomethacin *on next page*
♦ **Indocin® I.V.** *see* Indomethacin *on next page*

♦ **Indocin® SR** see Indomethacin on this page
♦ **Indometacin** see Indomethacin on this page

Indomethacin (in doe METH a sin)

Related Information
Antacid Drug Interactions on page 1296
Depression Disorders and Treatments on page 1465
Nonsteroidal Anti-Inflammatory Agents Comparison on page 1335

U.S. Brand Names Indochron E-R®; Indocin®; Indocin® I.V.; Indocin® SR

Canadian Brand Names Apo®-Indomethacin; Indocid®; Indocid® SR; Novo-Methacin; Nu-Indo; Pro-Indo®

Synonyms Indometacin; Indomethacin Sodium Trihydrate

Therapeutic Category Analgesic, Nonsteroidal Anti-inflammatory Drug; Anti-inflammatory Agent; Antipyretic; Nonsteroidal Anti-inflammatory Drug (NSAID), Oral; Nonsteroidal Anti-inflammatory Drug (NSAID), Parenteral

Use Management of inflammatory diseases and rheumatoid disorders; moderate pain; acute gouty arthritis; I.V. form used as alternative to surgery for closure of patent ductus arteriosus in neonates

Pregnancy Risk Factor B (D if used longer than 48 hours or after 34-week gestation)

Contraindications Hypersensitivity to indomethacin, any component, aspirin, or other nonsteroidal anti-inflammatory drugs (NSAIDs); active GI bleeding, ulcer disease; premature neonates with necrotizing enterocolitis, impaired renal function, active bleeding, thrombocytopenia

Warnings/Precautions Use with caution in patients with cardiac dysfunction, hypertension, renal or hepatic impairment, epilepsy, history of GI bleeding, patients receiving anticoagulants, and for treatment of JRA in children (fatal hepatitis has been reported); may have adverse effects on fetus; may affect platelet and renal function in neonates; elderly are a high-risk population for adverse effects from nonsteroidal anti-inflammatory agents. As much as 60% of elderly can develop peptic ulceration and/or hemorrhage asymptomatically.

Use lowest effective dose for shortest period possible. Use of NSAIDs can compromise existing renal function especially when Cl_{cr} is <30 mL/minute.

CNS adverse effects such as confusion, agitation, and hallucination are generally seen in overdose or high-dose situations; but elderly may demonstrate these adverse effects at lower doses than younger adults.

Adverse Reactions
>10%:
Central nervous system: Dizziness
Dermatologic: Rash
Gastrointestinal: Nausea, epigastric pain, abdominal pain, anorexia, GI bleeding, ulcers, perforation, abdominal cramps, heartburn, indigestion
1% to 10%:
Central nervous system: Headache, nervousness
Dermatologic: Itching
Endocrine & metabolic: Fluid retention
Gastrointestinal: Vomiting
Otic: Tinnitus
<1%: Hypertension, congestive heart failure, arrhythmias, tachycardia, somnolence, fatigue, depression, confusion, drowsiness, hallucinations, aseptic meningitis, urticaria, erythema multiforme, toxic epidermal necrolysis, Stevens-Johnson syndrome, angioedema, hyperkalemia, dilutional hyponatremia (I.V.), hypoglycemia (I.V.), polydipsia, hot flashes, gastritis, GI ulceration, cystitis, polyuria, hemolytic anemia, bone marrow suppression, agranulocytosis, thrombocytopenia, inhibition of platelet aggregation, anemia, leukopenia, hepatitis, peripheral neuropathy, corneal opacities, blurred vision, conjunctivitis, dry eyes, toxic amblyopia, decreased hearing, oliguria, renal failure, shortness of breath, allergic rhinitis, epistaxis, hypersensitivity reactions

Overdosage/Toxicology
Symptoms of overdose include drowsiness, lethargy, nausea, vomiting, seizures, paresthesia, headache, dizziness, GI bleeding, cerebral edema, tinnitus, leukocytosis, renal failure

Management of a nonsteroidal anti-inflammatory drug (NSAID) intoxication is primarily supportive and symptomatic. Fluid therapy is commonly effective in managing the hypotension that may occur following an acute NSAID overdose, except when this is due to an acute blood loss. Seizures tend to be very short-lived and often do not require drug treatment. Although, recurrent seizures should be treated with I.V. diazepam.

Drug Interactions CYP2C9 enzyme substrate
Decreased effect: May decrease antihypertensive effects of beta-blockers, hydralazine and captopril; indomethacin may decrease antihypertensive and diuretic effects of furosemide and thiazides
Increased toxicity: May increase serum potassium with potassium-sparing diuretics; probenecid may increase indomethacin serum concentrations; other NSAIDs may increase GI adverse effects; may increase nephrotoxicity of cyclosporin
Indomethacin may increase serum concentrations of digoxin, methotrexate, lithium, and aminoglycosides (reported with I.V. use in neonates)

Stability I.V.: Protect from light; not stable in alkaline solution; reconstitute just prior to administration; discard any unused portion; do not use preservative-containing diluents for reconstitution; suppositories do not require refrigeration

(Continued)

Indomethacin *(Continued)*

Mechanism of Action Inhibits prostaglandin synthesis by decreasing the activity of the enzyme, cyclo-oxygenase, which results in decreased formation of prostaglandin precursors

Pharmacodynamics/Kinetics

Onset of action: Within 30 minutes

Duration: 4-6 hours

Absorption: Prompt and extensive

Distribution: V_d: 0.34-1.57 L/kg; crosses the placenta; appears in breast milk

Protein binding: 90%

Metabolism: In the liver with significant enterohepatic cycling

Half-life: 4.5 hours, longer in neonates

Time to peak serum concentration: Oral: Within 3-4 hours

Elimination: Significant enterohepatic recycling; excreted in urine principally as glucuronide conjugates

Usual Dosage

Patent ductus arteriosus: Neonates: I.V.: Initial: 0.2 mg/kg; followed with: 2 doses of 0.1 mg/kg at 12- to 24-hour intervals if age <48 hours at time of first dose; 0.2 mg/kg 2 times if 2-7 days old at time of first dose; or 0.25 mg/kg 2 times if over 7 days at time of first dose; discontinue if significant adverse effects occur. Dose should be withheld if patient has anuria or oliguria.

Analgesia:

Children: Oral: Initial: 1-2 mg/kg/day in 2-4 divided doses; maximum: 4 mg/kg/day; not to exceed 150-200 mg/day

Adults: Oral, rectal: 25-50 mg/dose 2-3 times/day; maximum dose: 200 mg/day; extended release capsule should be given on a 1-2 times/day schedule

Dietary Considerations

Food: May decrease the rate but not the extent of oral absorption. Drug may cause GI upset, bleeding, ulceration, perforation; take with food or milk to minimize GI upset.

Potassium: Hyperkalemia has been reported. The elderly and those with renal insufficiency are at greatest risk. Monitor potassium serum concentration in those at greatest risk. Avoid salt substitutes.

Sodium: Hyponatremia from sodium retention. Suspect secondary to suppression of renal prostaglandin. Monitor serum concentration and fluid status. May need to restrict fluid.

Administration Administer orally with food, milk, or antacids to decrease GI adverse effects

I.V.: Administer over 20-30 minutes at a concentration of 0.5-1 mg/mL in preservative-free sterile water for injection or normal saline. Reconstitute I.V. formulation just prior to administration; discard any unused portion; avoid I.V. bolus administration or infusion via an umbilical catheter into vessels near the superior mesenteric artery as these may cause vasoconstriction and can compromise blood flow to the intestines. Do not administer intra-arterially.

Monitoring Parameters Monitor response (pain, range of motion, grip strength, mobility, ADL function), inflammation; observe for weight gain, edema; monitor renal function (serum creatinine, BUN); observe for bleeding, bruising; evaluate gastrointestinal effects (abdominal pain, bleeding, dyspepsia); mental confusion, disorientation, CBC, liver function tests

Test Interactions Positive direct Coombs'; increased sodium, chloride, prolonged bleeding time

Patient Information Take with food, milk, or with antacids; sustained release capsules must be swallowed whole/intact, can cause dizziness or drowsiness

Nursing Implications Extended release capsules must be swallowed intact

Dosage Forms

Capsule: 25 mg, 50 mg

Indocin®: 25 mg, 50 mg

Capsule, sustained release (Indocin® SR): 75 mg

Powder for injection, as sodium trihydrate (Indocin® I.V.): 1 mg

Suppository, rectal (Indocin®): 50 mg

Suspension, oral (Indocin®): 25 mg/5 mL (5 mL, 10 mL, 237 mL, 500 mL)

♦ **Indomethacin Sodium Trihydrate** *see* Indomethacin *on previous page*

♦ **INF** *see* Interferon Alfa-2b *on page 617*

♦ **INF-alpha 2** *see* Interferon Alfa-2b *on page 617*

♦ **Infanrix™** *see* Diphtheria, Tetanus Toxoids, and Acellular Pertussis Vaccine *on page 373*

♦ **Infants Feverall™ [OTC]** *see* Acetaminophen *on page 19*

♦ **Infants' Silapap® [OTC]** *see* Acetaminophen *on page 19*

♦ **Infasurf®** *see* Calfactant *on page 181*

♦ **InFed™ Injection** *see* Iron Dextran Complex *on page 630*

♦ **Inflamase® Forte Ophthalmic** *see* Prednisolone *on page 961*

♦ **Inflamase® Mild Ophthalmic** *see* Prednisolone *on page 961*

Infliximab *(in FLIKS e mab)*

U.S. Brand Names Remicade™

Therapeutic Category Gastrointestinal Agent, Miscellaneous; Monoclonal Antibody

Use Treatment of moderately to severely active Crohn's disease for the reduction of the signs and symptoms in patients who have an inadequate response to conventional therapy or for the treatment of patients with fistulizing Crohn's disease for the reduction in the number of draining enterocutaneous fistula(s)

Pregnancy Risk Factor C

Pregnancy/Breast-Feeding Implications It is not known whether infliximab is secreted in human milk. Because many immunoglobulins are secreted in milk, and the potential for serious adverse reactions exists, a decision should be made whether to discontinue nursing or discontinue the drug, taking into account the importance of the drug to the mother.

Contraindications Known hypersensitivity to murine proteins or any component

Warnings/Precautions Hypersensitivity reactions, including urticaria, dyspnea, and hypotension have occurred; discontinue the drug if a reaction occurs. Medications for the treatment of hypersensitivity reactions should be available for immediate use. Autoimmune antibodies and a lupus-like syndrome have been reported; if antibodies to double-stranded DNA are confirmed in a patient with lupus-like symptoms, treatment should be discontinued. May affect normal immune responses; effects on development of lymphoma and infection in Crohn's patients are unknown. Treatment may result in the development of human antichimeric antibodies (HACA); presence of these antibodies may predispose patients to infusion reactions.

Adverse Reactions

>10%:

Central nervous system: Headache (22.6%), fatigue (10.6%), fever (10.1%)
Gastrointestinal: Nausea (16.6%), abdominal pain (12.1%)
Local: Infusion reactions (16%)
Respiratory: Upper respiratory tract infection (16.1%)
Miscellaneous: Infections (21%)

1% to 10%:

Cardiovascular: Chest pain (5.5%)
Central nervous system: Pain (8.5%), dizziness (8%)
Dermatologic: Rash (6%), pruritus (5%)
Gastrointestinal: Vomiting (8.5%)
Neuromuscular & skeletal: Myalgia (5%), back pain (5%)
Respiratory: Pharyngitis (8.5%), bronchitis (7%), rhinitis (6%), cough (5%), sinusitis (5%)
Miscellaneous: Development of antibodies to double-stranded DNA (9%), candidiasis (5%), serious infection (3%)

<1%: Lupus-like syndrome (2 patients); a proportion of patients (12%) with fistulizing disease developed new abscess 8-16 weeks after the last infusion of infliximab

Drug Interactions Specific drug interaction studies have not been conducted

Stability Store vials at 2°C to 8°C (36°F to 46°F); do not freeze; does not contain preservative

Pharmacodynamics/Kinetics

Distribution: V_d: 3.0 L (volume may be increased 17% in patients receiving corticosteroids)
Half-life: 9.5 days

Usual Dosage

Moderately to severely active Crohn's disease: Adults: I.V.: 5 mg/kg as a single infusion over a minimum of 2 hours
Fistulizing Crohn's disease: 5 mg/kg as an infusion over a minimum of 2 hours, dose repeated at 2 and 6 weeks after the initial infusion
Dosing adjustment in renal impairment: No specific adjustment recommended
Dosing adjustment in hepatic impairment: No specific adjustment recommended

Administration Reconstitute vials with 10 mL sterile water for injection; total dose of reconstituted product should be further diluted to 250 mL of 0.9% sodium chloride injection and infused over at least 2 hours (use in-line filter). Do not infuse with other agents.

Nursing Implications Do not shake reconstituted vials

Dosage Forms Powder for injection: 100 mg

Influenza Virus Vaccine (in floo EN za VYE rus vak SEEN)

Related Information

Guidelines for the Prevention of Opportunistic Infections in Persons with HIV on page 1388
Immunization Recommendations on page 1358
Recommended Immunization Schedule for HIV-Infected Children on page 1363

U.S. Brand Names Fluogen®; Flushield®; Fluviron®; Fluzone®

Canadian Brand Names Fluviral®

Synonyms Influenza Virus Vaccine (inactivated whole-virus); Influenza Virus Vaccine (split-virus) Influenza Virus Vaccine (purified surface antigen)

Therapeutic Category Vaccine, Inactivated Virus

Use Provide active immunity to influenza virus strains contained in the vaccine; for high-risk persons, previous year vaccines should not be to prevent present year influenza

Groups at Increased Risk for Influenza Related Complications:
• Persons ≥65 years of age
• Residents of nursing homes and other chronic-care facilities that house persons of any age with chronic medical conditions

(Continued)

Influenza Virus Vaccine *(Continued)*

- Adults and children with chronic disorders of the pulmonary or cardiovascular systems, including children with asthma
- Adults and children who have required regular medical follow-up or hospitalization during the preceding year because of chronic metabolic diseases (including diabetes mellitus), renal dysfunction, hemoglobinopathies, or immunosuppression (including immunosuppression caused by medications)

Children and teenagers (6 months to 18 years of age) who are receiving long-term aspirin therapy and therefore, may be at risk for developing Reye's syndrome after influenza

Pregnancy Risk Factor C

Contraindications Persons with allergy history to eggs or egg products, chicken, chicken feathers or chicken dander, hypersensitivity to thimerosal, influenza virus vaccine or any component, presence of acute respiratory disease or other active infections or illnesses, delay immunization in a patient with an active neurological disorder

Warnings/Precautions Although there is no evidence of maternal or fetal risk when vaccine is given in pregnancy, waiting until the 2nd or 3rd trimester to vaccinate the pregnant woman with a high-risk condition may be reasonable. Antigenic response may not be as great as expected in patients requiring immunosuppressive drug; hypersensitivity reactions may occur; because of potential for febrile reactions, risks and benefits must carefully be considered in patients with history of febrile convulsions; influenza vaccines from previous seasons must not be used; patients with sulfite sensitivity may be affected by this product.

Adverse Reactions All serious adverse reactions must be reported to the U.S. Department of Health and Human Services (DHHS) Vaccine Adverse Event Reporting System (VAERS) 1-800-822-7967.

1% to 10%:

Central nervous system: Fever, malaise

Local: Tenderness, redness, or induration at the site of injection (<33%)

<1%: Guillain-Barré syndrome, fever, urticaria, angioedema, myalgia, asthma, anaphylactoid reactions (most likely to residual egg protein), allergic reactions

Drug Interactions

Decreased effect with immunosuppressive agents; some manufacturers and clinicians recommend that the flu vaccine not be administered with the DTP for the potential for increased febrile reactions (specifically whole-cell pertussis), and that one should wait at least 3 days. ACIP recommends that children at high risk for influenza may get the vaccine concomitantly with DTP.

Increased effect/toxicity of theophylline and warfarin possible

Stability Refrigerate

Mechanism of Action Promotes immunity to influenza virus by inducing specific antibody production. Each year the formulation is standardized according to the U.S. Public Health Service. Preparations from previous seasons must not be used.

Usual Dosage I.M.:

Children:

6-35 months: 1-2 doses of 0.25 mL with ≥4 weeks between doses and the last dose administered before December

3-8 years: 1-2 doses of 0.5 mL (in anterolateral aspect of thigh) with ≥4 weeks between doses and the last dose administered before December

Children ≥9 years and Adults: 0.5 mL each year of appropriate vaccine for the year, one dose is all that is necessary; administer in late fall to allow maximum titers to develop by peak epidemic periods usually occurring in early December

Note: The split virus or purified surface antigen is recommended for children ≤12 years of age; if the child has received at least one dose of the 1978-79 or later vaccine, one dose is sufficient

Administration Inspect for particulate matter and discoloration prior to administration; for I.M. administration only

Additional Information Pharmacies will stock the formulations(s) standardized according to the USPHS requirements for the season. Influenza vaccines from previous seasons must not be used. Federal law requires that the date of administration, the vaccine manufacturer, lot number of vaccine, and the administering person's name, title and address be entered into the patient's permanent medical record.

Dosage Forms Injection:

Purified surface antigen (Flu-Imune®): 5 mL

Split-virus (Fluogen®, Fluzone®): 0.5 mL, 5 mL

Whole-virus (Fluzone®): 5 mL

Insulin Preparations (IN su lin prep a RAY shuns)

Related Information
Desensitization Protocols *on page 1347*
Diabetes Mellitus Treatment *on page 1467*

U.S. Brand Names Humalog®; Humulin® 50/50; Humulin® 70/30; Humulin® L; Humulin® N; Humulin® R; Humulin® U; Lente® Iletin® I; Lente® Iletin® II; Lente® Insulin; Lente® L; Novolin® 70/30; Novolin® L; Novolin® N; Novolin® R; NPH Iletin® I; NPH Insulin; NPH-N; Pork NPH Iletin® II; Pork Regular Iletin® II; Regular (Concentrated) Iletin® II U-500; Regular Iletin® I; Regular Insulin; Regular Purified Pork Insulin; Velosulin® Human

Therapeutic Category Antidiabetic Agent, Parenteral; Antidote, Hyperglycemia

Use Treatment of insulin-dependent diabetes mellitus, also noninsulin-dependent diabetes mellitus unresponsive to treatment with diet and/or oral hypoglycemics; to assure proper utilization of glucose and reduce glucosuria in nondiabetic patients receiving parenteral nutrition whose glucosuria cannot be adequately controlled with infusion rate adjustments or those who require assistance in achieving optimal caloric intakes; hyperkalemia (use with glucose to shift potassium into cells to lower serum potassium levels)

Pregnancy Risk Factor B

Pregnancy/Breast-Feeding Implications
Clinical effects on the fetus: Does not cross the placenta. Insulin is the drug of choice for the control of diabetes mellitus during pregnancy.

Breast-feeding/lactation: The gastrointestinal tract destroys insulin when administered orally and therefore would not be expected to be absorbed intact by the breast-feeding infant.

Warnings/Precautions Any change of insulin should be made cautiously; changing manufacturers, type and/or method of manufacture, may result in the need for a change of dosage; human insulin differs from animal-source insulin; regular insulin is the only insulin to be used I.V.; hypoglycemia may result from increased work or exercise without eating

Adverse Reactions 1% to 10%:
Cardiovascular: Palpitation, tachycardia, pallor

Central nervous system: Fatigue, mental confusion, loss of consciousness, headache, hypothermia

Dermatologic: Urticaria, redness

Endocrine & metabolic: Hypoglycemia

Gastrointestinal: Hunger, nausea, numbness of mouth

Local: Itching, edema, stinging, or warmth at injection site, atrophy or hypertrophy of S.C. fat tissue

Neuromuscular & skeletal: Muscle weakness, paresthesia, tremors

Ocular: Transient presbyopia or blurred vision, blurred vision

Miscellaneous: Diaphoresis, anaphylaxis

Overdosage/Toxicology
Symptoms of overdose include tachycardia, anxiety, hunger, tremors, pallor, headache, motor dysfunction, speech disturbances, sweating, palpitations, coma, death

Antidote is glucose and glucagon, if necessary

Drug Interactions See table.

Drug Interactions With Insulin Injection

Decrease Hypoglycemic Effect of Insulin	Increase Hypoglycemic Effect of Insulin
Contraceptives, oral	Alcohol
Corticosteroids	Alpha-blockers
Dextrothyroxine	Anabolic steroids
Diltiazem	Beta-blockers*
Dobutamine	Clofibrate
Epinephrine	Fenfluramine
Niacin	Guanethidine
Smoking	MAO inhibitors
Thiazide diuretics	Pentamidine
Thyroid hormone	Phenylbutazone
	Salicylates
	Sulfinpyrazone
	Tetracyclines

*Nonselective beta-blockers may delay recovery from hypoglycemic episodes and mask signs/symptoms of hypoglycemia. Cardioselective agents may be alternatives.

Insulin Preparations	Compatible Mixed With
Rapid-Acting	
Insulin injection (regular)	All
Lispro (Humalog®)	Ultralente / NPH
Intermediate-Acting	
Isophane insulin suspension (NPH)	Regular
Long-Acting	
Protamine zinc insulin suspension* (PZI)	Regular

(Continued)

Insulin Preparations *(Continued)*

Stability

Newer neutral formulation of insulin is stable at room temperature up to one month (studies indicate up to 24-30 months)

Freezing causes more damage to insulin than room temperatures up to 100°F

Avoid direct sunlight; for compatibility, see table.

When mixing with NPH insulin in any proportion, the excess protamine may combine with regular insulin and may reduce or delay activity of regular insulin (does not appear to be clinically significant); phosphate-buffered regular insulins bind with Lente® insulins forming short-acting insulin; excess protamine in PZI combines with regular insulin and prolongs its action, therefore, should not be mixed; administer as a separate injection

Stability of parenteral admixture of regular insulin at room temperature (25°C) and at refrigeration temperature (4°C): 24 hours

Standard diluent: 100 units/100 mL NS

Comments: All bags should be prepared fresh; tubing should be flushed 30 minutes prior to administration to allow adsorption as time permits

Mechanism of Action The principal hormone required for proper glucose utilization in normal metabolic processes; it is obtained from beef or pork pancreas or a biosynthetic process converting pork insulin to human insulin; insulins are categorized into 3 groups related to promptness, duration, and intensity of action

Pharmacodynamics/Kinetics

Onset and duration of hypoglycemic effects depend upon preparation administered. See table.

Pharmacokinetics/Pharmacodynamics: Onset and Duration of Hypoglycemic Effects Depend Upon Preparation Administered

	Onset (h)	Peak (h)	Duration (h)
Lispro (Humalog®)	0.25	0.5-1.5	6-8
Insulin, regular (Novolin® R)	0.5-1	2-3	8-12
Isophane insulin suspension (NPH) (Novolin® N)	1-1.5	4-12	24
Insulin zinc suspension (Lente®)	1-2.5	8-12	18-24
Isophane insulin suspension and regular insulin injection (Novolin® 70/30)	0.5 (0.5)	4-8 (2-12)	24 (24)
Prompt zinc insulin suspension (PZI)	4-8	14-24	36
Extended insulin zinc suspension (Ultralente®)	4-8	16-18	>36

Onset and duration: Biosynthetic NPH human insulin shows a more rapid onset and shorter duration of action than corresponding porcine insulins; human insulin and purified porcine regular insulin are similarly efficacious following S.C. administration. The duration of action of highly purified porcine insulins is shorter than that of conventional insulin equivalents. Duration depends on type of preparation and route of administration as well as patient related variables. In general, the larger the dose of insulin, the longer the duration of activity.

Absorption: Biosynthetic regular human insulin is absorbed from the S.C. injection site more rapidly than insulins of animal origin (60-90 minutes peak vs 120-150 minutes peak respectively) and lowers the initial blood glucose much faster. Human Ultralente® insulin is absorbed about twice as quickly as its bovine equivalent, and bioavailability is also improved. Human Lente® insulin preparations are also absorbed more quickly than their animal equivalents.

Bioavailability: Medium-acting S.C. Lente®-type human insulins did not differ from the corresponding porcine insulins

Usual Dosage Dose requires continuous medical supervision; may administer I.V. (regular), I.M., S.C.

Diabetes mellitus: The number and size of daily doses, time of administration, and diet and exercise require continuous medical supervision. Lispro should be given within 15 minutes of a meal and human regular insulin should be given within 30-60 minutes before a meal. Maintenance doses should be administered subcutaneously and sites should be rotated to prevent lipodystrophy.

Children and Adults: 0.5-1 unit/kg/day in divided doses

Adolescents (growth spurts): 0.8-1.2 units/kg/day in divided doses

Adjust dose to maintain premeal and bedtime blood glucose of 80-140 mg/dL (children <5 years: 100-200 mg/dL)

Hyperkalemia: Administer calcium gluconate and $NaHCO_3$ first then 50% dextrose at 0.5-1 mL/kg and insulin 1 unit for every 4-5 g dextrose given

Diabetic ketoacidosis: Children and Adults: Regular Insulin: I.V. loading dose: 0.1 unit/kg, then maintenance continuous infusion: 0.1 unit/kg/hour (range: 0.05-0.2 units/kg/hour depending upon the rate of decrease of serum glucose - too rapid decrease of serum glucose may lead to cerebral edema).

Optimum rate of decrease (serum glucose): 80-100 mg/dL/hour

Note: Newly diagnosed patients with IDDM presenting in DKA and patients with blood sugars <800 mg/dL may be relatively "sensitive" to insulin and should receive loading and initial maintenance doses approximately $\frac{1}{2}$ of those indicated above.

Dosing adjustment in renal impairment (regular): Insulin requirements are reduced due to changes in insulin clearance or metabolism

Cl_{cr} 10-50 mL/minute: Administer at 75% of normal dose

Cl_{cr} <10 mL/minute: Administer at 25% to 50% of normal dose and monitor glucose closely

Hemodialysis: Because of a large molecular weight (6000 daltons), insulin is not significantly removed by either peritoneal or hemodialysis

Supplemental dose is not necessary

Peritoneal dialysis: Supplemental dose is not necessary

Continuous arteriovenous or venovenous hemofiltration effects: Supplemental dose is not necessary

Dietary Considerations

Alcohol: Increase in hypoglycemic effect of insulin; monitor blood glucose concentration; avoid or limit use

Food:

Potassium: Shifts potassium from extracellular to intracellular space. Decreases potassium serum concentration; monitor potassium serum concentration.

Sodium: SIADH; water retention and dilutional hyponatremia may occur. Patients at greatest risk are those with CHF or hepatic cirrhosis. Monitor sodium serum concentration and fluid status.

Administration

Regular insulin may be administered by S.C., I.M., or I.V. routes

S.C. administration is usually made into the thighs, arms, buttocks, or abdomen, with sites rotated

When mixing regular insulin with other preparations of insulin, regular insulin should be drawn into syringe first

I.V. administration (requires use of an infusion pump): **Only regular insulin** may be administered I.V.

I.V. infusions: To minimize adsorption problems to I.V. solution bag:

If new tubing is **not** needed: Wait a minimum of 30 minutes between the preparation of the solution and the initiation of the infusion

If new tubing is needed: After receiving the insulin drip solution, the administration set should be attached to the I.V. container and the line should be flushed with the insulin solution. The nurse should then wait 30 minutes, then flush the line again with the insulin solution prior to initiating the infusion

If insulin is required prior to the availability of the insulin drip, regular insulin should be administered by I.V. push injection

Because of adsorption, the actual amount of insulin being administered could be substantially less than the apparent amount. Therefore, adjustment of the insulin drip rate should be based on effect and not solely on the apparent insulin dose. Furthermore, the apparent dose should not be used as the basis for determining the subsequent insulin dose upon discontinuing the insulin drip. Dose requires continuous medical supervision.

To be ordered as units/hour

Example: Standard diluent of regular insulin only: 100 units/100 mL NS (can be given as a more diluted solution, ie, 100 units/250 mL NS)

Insulin rate of infusion (100 units regular/100 mL NS)

1 unit/hour: 1 mL/hour

2 units/hour: 2 mL/hour

3 units/hour: 3 mL/hour

4 units/hour: 4 mL/hour

5 units/hour: 5 mL/hour, etc

Monitoring Parameters Urine sugar and acetone, serum glucose, electrolytes

Reference Range

Therapeutic, serum insulin (fasting): 5-20 µIU/mL (SI: 35-145 pmol/L)

Glucose, fasting:

Newborns: 60-110 mg/dL

Adults: 60-110 mg/dL

Elderly: 100-180 mg/dL

Patient Information Do not change insulins without physician's approval; titrate vials to mix, do not shake; store in a cool place; when mixing insulins, draw up regular insulin into syringe first and use as soon as possible after mixing. Patients must be counseled by someone experienced in diabetes education, signs and symptoms of hyper- and hypoglycemia, exercise and diet, blood glucose monitoring, and other related topics.

Nursing Implications Patients using human insulin may be less likely to recognize hypoglycemia than if they use pork insulin, patients on pork insulin that have low blood sugar exhibit hunger and sweating; regular insulin is the only form for I.V. use. Patients who are unable to accurately draw up their dose will need assistance such as prefilled syringes.

Additional Information The term "purified" refers to insulin preparations containing no more than 10 ppm proinsulin (purified and human insulins are less immunogenic)

Dosage Forms All insulins are 100 units/mL (10 mL) except where indicated:

RAPID ACTING:

Insulin lispro rDNA origin: Humalog® [Lilly] (1.5 mL, 10 mL)

Insulin Injection (Regular Insulin)

Beef and pork: Regular Iletin® I [Lilly]

(Continued)

Insulin Preparations *(Continued)*

Human:
 rDNA: Humulin® R [*Lilly*], Novolin® R [*Novo Nordisk*]
 Semisynthetic: Velosulin® Human [*Novo Nordisk*]
Pork: Regular Insulin [*Novo Nordisk*]
Purified pork:
 Pork Regular Iletin® II [*Lilly*], Regular Purified Pork Insulin [*Novo Nordisk*]
 Regular (Concentrated) Iletin® II U-500 (*Lilly*): 500 units/mL

INTERMEDIATE-ACTING:
Insulin Zinc Suspension (Lente)
 Beef and pork: Lente® Iletin® I [*Lilly*]
 Human, rDNA: Humulin® L [*Lilly*], Novolin® L [*Novo Nordisk*]
 Purified pork: Lente® Iletin® II [*Lilly*], Lente® L [*Novo Nordisk*]

Isophane Insulin Suspension (NPH)
 Beef and pork: NPH Iletin® I [*Lilly*]
 Human, rDNA: Humulin® N [*Lilly*], Novolin® N [*Novo Nordisk*]
 Purified pork: Pork NPH Iletin® II [*Lilly*], NPH-N [*Novo Nordisk*]

LONG-ACTING:
Insulin zinc suspension, extended (Ultralente®)
 Human, rDNA: Humulin® U [Lilly]

COMBINATIONS:
Isophane Insulin Suspension and Insulin Injection
 Isophane insulin suspension (50%) and insulin injection (50%) human (rDNA): Humulin® 50/50 [*Lilly*]
 Isophane insulin suspension (70%) and insulin injection (30%) human (rDNA): Humulin® 70/30 [*Lilly*], Novolin® 70/30 [*Novo Nordisk*]

- **Intal® Nebulizer Solution** *see* Cromolyn Sodium *on page 300*
- **Intal® Oral Inhaler** *see* Cromolyn Sodium *on page 300*
- **Integrilin™** *see* Eptifibatide *on page 422*
- **α-2-interferon** *see* Interferon Alfa-2b *on next page*

Interferon Alfa-2a (in ter FEER on AL fa too aye)
Related Information
 Toxicities of Chemotherapeutic Agents *on page 1288*
U.S. Brand Names Roferon-A®
Synonyms IFLrA; IFN; rIFN-A
Therapeutic Category Biological Response Modulator; Interferon
Use Patients >18 years of age: Hairy cell leukemia, AIDS-related Kaposi's sarcoma, chronic myelogenous leukemia (CML), chronic hepatitis C, adjuvant treatment to surgery for primary or recurrent malignant melanoma; multiple unlabeled uses; indications and dosage regimens are specific for a particular brand of interferon
Pregnancy Risk Factor C
Contraindications Hypersensitivity to alfa-2a interferon or any component of the product
Warnings/Precautions Use with caution in patients with seizure disorders, brain metastases, compromised CNS, multiple sclerosis, and patients with pre-existing cardiac disease, severe renal or hepatic impairment, or myelosuppression; safety and efficacy in children <18 years of age have not been established. Higher doses in the elderly or in malignancies other than hairy cell leukemia may result in severe obtundation.
Adverse Reactions
>10%:
 Central nervous system: Dizziness, fatigue, malaise, fever (usually within 4-6 hours), chills
 Dermatologic: Rash
 Gastrointestinal: Xerostomia, nausea, vomiting, diarrhea, abdominal cramps, weight loss, metallic taste
 Hematologic: Mildly myelosuppressive and well tolerated if used without adjunct antineoplastic agents; thrombocytosis has been reported, leukopenia (mainly neutropenia), anemia, thrombocytopenia, decreased hemoglobin, hematocrit, platelets
 Myelosuppressive:
  WBC: Mild
  Platelets: Mild
  Onset (days): 7-10
  Nadir (days): 14
  Recovery (days): 21
 Neuromuscular & skeletal: Rigors, arthralgia
 Miscellaneous: Flu-like syndrome, diaphoresis
1% to 10%:
 Central nervous system: Headache, delirium, somnolence, neurotoxicity
 Dermatologic: Alopecia, dry skin
 Gastrointestinal: Anorexia, stomatitis
 Hepatic: Hepatotoxicity
 Neuromuscular & skeletal: Peripheral neuropathy, leg cramps
 Ocular: Blurred vision
 Miscellaneous: Diaphoresis

<1%: Tachycardia, arrhythmias, chest pain, hypotension, SVT, edema, confusion, sensory neuropathy, psychiatric effects, EEG abnormalities, depression, hypothyroidism, increased uric acid level, change in taste, increased hepatic transaminase, myalgia, visual disturbances, proteinuria, increased BUN/creatinine, coughing, dyspnea, nasal congestion, neutralizing antibodies, local sensitivity to injection; usually patient can build up a tolerance to side effects

Overdosage/Toxicology
Symptoms of overdose include CNS depression, obtundation, flu-like symptoms, myelosuppression
Treatment is supportive

Drug Interactions
Increased effect:
Cimetidine: May augment the antitumor effects of interferon in melanoma
Theophylline: Clearance has been reported to be decreased in hepatitis patients receiving interferon
Increased toxicity: Vinblastine: Enhances interferon toxicity in several patients; increased incidence of paresthesia has also been noted

Stability Refrigerate (2°C to 8°C/36°F to 46°F); do not freeze; do not shake; after reconstitution, the solution is stable for 24 hours at room temperature and for 1 month when refrigerated

Mechanism of Action Alpha interferons are a family of proteins, produced by nucleated cells, that have antiviral, antiproliferative, and immune-regulating activity. There are 16 known subtypes of alpha interferons. Interferons interact with cells through high affinity cell surface receptors. Following activation, multiple effects can be detected including induction of gene transcription. Inhibits cellular growth, alters the state of cellular differentiation, interferes with oncogene expression, alters cell surface antigen expression, increases phagocytic activity of macrophages, and augments cytotoxicity of lymphocytes for target cells

Pharmacodynamics/Kinetics
Absorption: Filtered and absorbed at the renal tubule
Distribution: The V_d of interferon is 31 L; but has been noted to be much greater (370-720 L) in leukemia patients receiving continuous infusion IFN; IFN does not penetrate the CSF
Metabolism: Majority of dose thought to be metabolized in the kidney
Bioavailability: I.M.: 83%; S.C.: 90%
Half-life: Elimination: I.M., I.V.: 2 hours after administration; S.C.: 3 hours
Time to peak serum concentration: I.M., S.C.: ~6-8 hours

Usual Dosage Refer to individual protocols
Infants and Children: Hemangiomas of infancy, pulmonary hemangiomatosis: S.C.: 1-3 million units/m²/day once daily
Adults >18 years: I.M., S.C.:
Hairy cell leukemia:
Induction: 3 million units/day for 16-24 weeks.
Maintenance: 3 million units 3 times/week (may be treated for up to 20 consecutive weeks)
AIDS-related Kaposi's sarcoma:
Induction: 36 million units/day for 10-12 weeks
Maintenance: 36 million units 3 times/week (may begin with dose escalation from 3-9-18 million units each day over 3 consecutive days followed by 36 million units/day for the remainder of the 10-12 weeks of induction)
If severe adverse reactions occur, modify dosage (50% reduction) or temporarily discontinue therapy until adverse reactions abate

Administration S.C. administration is suggested for those who are at risk for bleeding or are thrombocytopenic; rotate S.C. injection site; patient should be well hydrated

Monitoring Parameters Baseline chest x-ray, EKG, CBC with differential, liver function tests, electrolytes, platelets, weight; patients with pre-existing cardiac abnormalities, or in advanced stages of cancer should have EKGs taken before and during treatment

Patient Information Do not change brands as changes in dosage may result; possible mental status changes may occur while on therapy; report to physician any persistent or severe sore throat, fever, fatigue, unusual bleeding, or bruising; do not operate heavy machinery while on therapy since changes in mental status may occur

Nursing Implications Do not freeze or shake solution; a flu-like syndrome (fever, chills) occurs in the majority of patients 2-6 hours after a dose; pretreatment with nonsteroidal anti-inflammatory drug (NSAID) or acetaminophen can decrease fever and its severity and alleviate headache

Dosage Forms
Injection: 3 million units/mL (1 mL); 6 million units/mL (3 mL); 9 million units/mL (0.9 mL, 3 mL); 36 million units/mL (1 mL)
Powder for injection: 6 million units/mL when reconstituted

Interferon Alfa-2b (in ter FEER on AL fa too bee)

Related Information
Cancer Chemotherapy Regimens on page 1263
Toxicities of Chemotherapeutic Agents on page 1288

U.S. Brand Names Intron® A

Synonyms INF; INF-alpha 2; α-2-interferon; rLFN-α2

Therapeutic Category Biological Response Modulator; Interferon

Use Hairy-cell leukemia in patients >18 years, condylomata acuminata, AIDS-related Kaposi's sarcoma in patients >18 years, chronic non-A/non-B/C hepatitis in patients >18
(Continued)

Interferon Alfa-2b *(Continued)*

years, chronic hepatitis B in patients >18 years (indications and dosage are specific for a particular brand of interferon)

Pregnancy Risk Factor C

Contraindications Known hypersensitivity to interferon alfa-2b or any components, patients with pre-existing thyroid disease uncontrolled by medication, coagulation disorders, diabetics prone to DKA, pulmonary disease

Warnings/Precautions Use with caution in patients with seizure disorders, brain metastases, compromised CNS, multiple sclerosis, and patients with pre-existing cardiac disease, severe renal or hepatic impairment, or myelosuppression; safety and efficacy in children <18 years has not been established. Higher doses in the elderly or in malignancies other than hairy cell leukemia may result in severe obtundation. A baseline ocular exam is recommended in patients with diabetes or hypertension.

Adverse Reactions

>10%:

Central nervous system: Dizziness, fatigue, malaise, fever (usually within 4-6 hours), chills

Dermatologic: Skin rash

Gastrointestinal: Xerostomia, nausea, vomiting, diarrhea, dizziness, abdominal cramps, weight loss, metallic taste, anorexia

Hematologic: Mildly myelosuppressive and well tolerated if used without adjunct antineoplastic agents; thrombocytosis has been reported, leukopenia (mainly neutropenia), anemia, thrombocytopenia, decreased hemoglobin, hematocrit, platelets

Myelosuppressive:

WBC: Mild

Platelets: Mild

Onset (days): 7-10

Nadir (days): 14

Recovery (days): 21

Neuromuscular & skeletal: Rigors, arthralgia

Miscellaneous: Flu-like syndrome, diaphoresis

1% to 10%:

Central nervous system: Neurotoxicity

Dermatologic: Dry skin, alopecia

Gastrointestinal: Stomatitis

Hepatic: Hepatotoxicity

Neuromuscular & skeletal: Peripheral neuropathy, leg cramps

Ocular: Blurred vision

Miscellaneous: Diaphoresis

<1%: Cardiotoxicity, tachycardia, arrhythmias, hypotension, SVT, arrhythmias, chest pain, edema, EEG abnormalities, confusion, sensory neuropathy, headache, psychiatric effects, delirium, somnolence, partial alopecia, increased uric acid level, hypothyroidism, change in taste, increased hepatic transaminase, increased ALT/AST, sensitivity to injection, myalgia, rigors, visual disturbances, proteinuria, increased creatinine, increased BUN, coughing, dyspnea, nasal congestion, neutralizing antibodies; usually patient can build up a tolerance to side effects

Overdosage/Toxicology

Symptoms of overdose include CNS depression, obtundation, flu-like symptoms, myelosuppression

Treatment is supportive

Drug Interactions

Increased effect: Cimetidine: May augment the antitumor effects of interferon in melanoma

Increased toxicity:

Theophylline: Clearance has been reported to be decreased in hepatitis patients receiving interferon

Vinblastine: Enhances interferon toxicity in several patients; increased incidence of paresthesia has also been noted

Zidovudine: Increased myelosuppression

Stability

Store intact vials at refrigeration (2°C to 8°C); powder and premixed solutions are stable at 95°F to 113°F for 7 days

Reconstitute vials with diluent; solution is stable for 30 days under refrigeration (2°C to 8°C)

Standard I.M./S.C. dilution: Dose/syringe or dispense vial to floor

Solution is stable for 7 days at room temperature and 30 days under refrigeration (2°C to 8°C)

Mechanism of Action Alpha interferons are a family of proteins, produced by nucleated cells, that have antiviral, antiproliferative, and immune-regulating activity. There are 16 known subtypes of alpha interferons. Interferons interact with cells through high affinity cell surface receptors. Following activation, multiple effects can be detected including induction of gene transcription. Inhibits cellular growth, alters the state of cellular differentiation, interferes with oncogene expression, alters cell surface antigen expression, increases phagocytic activity of macrophages, and augments cytotoxicity of lymphocytes for target cells

Pharmacodynamics/Kinetics

Absorption: Filtered and absorbed at the renal tubule

Distribution: The V_d of interferon is 31 L; but has been noted to be much greater (370-720 L) in leukemia patients receiving continuous infusion IFN; IFN does not penetrate the CSF

Metabolism: Majority of dose thought to be metabolized in the kidney

Bioavailability: I.M.: 83%; S.C.: 90%

Half-life: Elimination: I.M., I.V.: 2 hours; S.C.: 3 hours

Time to peak serum concentration: I.M., S.C.: ~6-8 hours

Usual Dosage Adults (refer to individual protocols):

Hairy cell leukemia: I.M., S.C.: 2 million units/m^2 3 times/week for 2 to ≥6 months of therapy

AIDS-related Kaposi's sarcoma: I.M., S.C. (use 50 million international unit vial): 30 million units/m^2 3 times/week

Condylomata acuminata: Intralesionally (use 10 million international unit vial): 1 million units/lesion 3 times/week for 4-8 weeks; not to exceed 5 million units per treatment (maximum: 5 lesions at one time)

Chronic hepatitis C (non-A/non-B): I.M., S.C.: 3 million units 3 times/week for approximately a 6-month course

Chronic hepatitis B: I.M., S.C.: 5 million international units/day or 10 million international units 3 times/week for 16 weeks; if severe adverse reactions occur, reduce dosage 50% or temporarily discontinue therapy until adverse reactions abate; when platelet/granulocyte count returns to normal, reinstitute therapy

Hemodialysis: Supplemental dose is not necessary

Peritoneal dialysis: Supplemental dose is not necessary

Monitoring Parameters Baseline chest x-ray, EKG, CBC with differential, liver function tests, electrolytes, thyroid function tests, platelets, weight; patients with pre-existing cardiac abnormalities, or in advanced stages of cancer should have EKGs taken before and during treatment

Patient Information Do not change brands of interferon as changes in dosage may result; do not operate heavy machinery while on therapy since changes in mental status may occur; report to physician any persistent or severe sore throat, fever, fatigue, unusual bleeding, or bruising

Nursing Implications Use acetaminophen to prevent or partially alleviate headache and fever; do not use 3, 5, 18, and 25 million unit strengths intralesionally, solutions are hypertonic; 50 million unit strength is not for use in condylomata, hairy cell leukemia, or chronic hepatitis.

Dosage Forms

Injection, albumin free: 3 million units (0.5 mL); 5 million units (0.5 mL); 10 million units (1 mL); 25 million units

Powder for injection, lyophilized: 18 million units, 50 million units

Interferon Alfa-2b and Ribavirin Combination Pack

(in ter FEER on AL fa too bee & rye ba VYE rin com bi NAY shun pak)

U.S. Brand Names Rebetron™

Therapeutic Category Antiviral Agent; Biological Response Modulator

Use The combination therapy of oral ribavirin with interferon alfa-2b, recombinant (Intron® A) injection is indicated for the treatment of chronic hepatitis C in patients with compensated liver disease who have relapsed after alpha interferon therapy.

Usual Dosage The recommended dosage of combination therapy is 3 million int. units of Intron® A injected subcutaneously 3 times/week and 1000-1200 mg of Rebetol® capsules administered orally in a divided daily (morning and evening) dose for 24 weeks; patients weighing 75 kg (165 pounds) or less should receive 1000 mg of Rebetol® daily (2 x 200 mg capsules in the morning and 3 x 200 mg capsules in the evening); while patients weighing more than 75 kg should receive 1200 mg of Rebetol® daily (3 x 200 mg capsules in the morning and 3 x 200 mg capsules in the evening)

Dosage Forms Combination package:

For patients ≤75 kg:

Each Rebetron™ combination package consists of:

A box containing 6 vials of Intron® A (3 million int. units in 0.5 mL per vial) and 6 syringes and alcohol swabs; two boxes containing 35 Rebetol® 200 mg capsules each for a total of 70 capsules (5 capsules per blister card)

One 18 million int. units multidose vial of Intron® A injection (22.8 million int. units per 3.8 mL; 3 million int. units/0.5 mL) and 6 syringes and alcohol swabs; two boxes containing 35 Rebetol® 200 mg capsules each for a total of 70 capsules (5 capsules per blister card)

One 18 million int. units Intron® A injection multidose pen (22.5 million int. units per 1.5 mL; 3 million int. units/0.2 mL) and 6 disposable needles and alcohol swabs; two boxes containing 35 Rebetol® 200 mg capsules each for a total of 70 capsules (5 capsules per blister card)

For patients >75 kg:

A box containing 6 vials of Intron® A injection (3 million int. units in 0.5 mL per vial) and 6 syringes and alcohol swabs; two boxes containing 42 Rebetol® 200 mg capsules each for a total of 84 capsules (6 capsules per blister card)

One 18 million int. units multidose vial of Intron® A injection (22.5 million int. units per 3.8 mL; 3 million int. units/0.5 mL) and 6 syringes and alcohol swabs; two boxes containing 42 Rebetol® 200 mg capsules each for a total of 84 capsules (6 capsules per blister card)

One 18 million int. units Intron® A injection multidose pen (22.5 million int. units per 1.5 mL; 3 million int. units/0.2 mL) and 6 disposable needles and alcohol swabs; two

(Continued)

Interferon Alfa-2b and Ribavirin Combination Pack
(Continued)

boxes containing 42 Rebetol® 200 mg capsules each for a total of 84 capsules (6 capsules per blister card)

For Rebetol® dose reduction:

A box containing 6 vials of Intron® A injection (3 million int. units in 0.5 mL per vial) and 6 syringes and alcohol swabs; one box containing 42 Rebetol® 200 mg capsules (6 capsules per blister card)

One 18 million int. units multidose vial of Intron® A injection (22.8 million int. units per 3.8 mL; 3 million int. units/0.5 mL) and 6 syringes and alcohol swabs; one box containing 42 Rebetol® 200 mg capsules (6 capsules per blister card)

One 18 million int. units Introl® A injection multidose pen (22.5 million int. units per 1.5 mL; 3 million int. units/0.2 mL) and 6 disposable needles and alcohol swabs; one box containing 42 Rebetol® 200 mg capsules (6 capsules per blister card)

Interferon Alfa-n3 (in ter FEER on AL fa en three)
Related Information
Toxicities of Chemotherapeutic Agents *on page 1288*
U.S. Brand Names Alferon® N
Therapeutic Category Interferon
Use Patients ≥18 years of age: Condylomata acuminata, intralesional treatment of refractory or recurring genital or venereal warts; useful in patients who do not respond or are not candidates for usual treatments; indications and dosage regimens are specific for a particular brand of interferon
Pregnancy Risk Factor C
Contraindications Patients with known hypersensitivity to alpha interferon, mouse immunoglobulin, or any component of the product
Warnings/Precautions Use with caution in patients with seizure disorders, brain metastases, compromised CNS function, cardiac disease, severe renal or hepatic impairment, multiple sclerosis; safety and efficacy in children <18 years have not been established.
Adverse Reactions
>10%:
Central nervous system: Fatigue, malaise, fever (usually within 4-6 hours), chills, dizziness
Dermatologic: Rash
Gastrointestinal: Xerostomia, nausea, vomiting, diarrhea, abdominal cramps, weight loss, metallic taste, anorexia
Hematologic: Mildly myelosuppressive and well tolerated if used without adjunct antineoplastic agents; thrombocytosis has been reported, leukopenia (mainly neutropenia), anemia, thrombocytopenia, decreased hemoglobin, hematocrit, platelets
Myelosuppressive:
WBC: Mild
Platelets: Mild
Onset (days): 7-10
Nadir (days): 14
Recovery (days): 21
Neuromuscular & skeletal: Arthralgia, rigors
Miscellaneous: Flu-like syndrome, diaphoresis
1% to 10%:
Central nervous system: Headache, delirium, somnolence, neurotoxicity
Dermatologic: Alopecia, dry skin
Gastrointestinal: Stomatitis
Hepatic: Hepatotoxicity
Neuromuscular & skeletal: Peripheral neuropathy, leg cramps
Ocular: Blurred vision
Miscellaneous: Diaphoresis
<1%: Tachycardia, arrhythmias, chest pain, hypotension, SVT, edema, EEG abnormalities, confusion, sensory neuropathy, confusion, psychiatric effects, depression, hypothyroidism, increased uric acid level, change in taste, increased hepatic transaminase, increased ALT/AST, sensitivity to injection, myalgia, visual disturbances, proteinuria, increased BUN/creatinine, coughing, dyspnea, cough, nasal congestion, neutralizing antibodies, usually patient can build up a tolerance to side effects
Overdosage/Toxicology
Symptoms of overdose include CNS depression, obtundation, flu-like symptoms, myelosuppression
Treatment is supportive
Drug Interactions
Increased effect: Cimetidine: May augment the antitumor effects of interferon in melanoma
Increased toxicity:
Vinblastine: Enhances interferon toxicity in several patients; increased incidence of paresthesia has also been noted
Theophylline: Clearance has been reported to be decreased in hepatitis patients receiving interferon
Stability Store solution at 2°C to 8°C (36°F to 46°F); do not freeze or shake solution
Mechanism of Action Interferons interact with cells through high affinity cell surface receptors. Following activation, multiple effects can be detected including induction of gene transcription. Inhibits cellular growth, alters the state of cellular differentiation,

interferes with oncogene expression, alters cell surface antigen expression, increases phagocytic activity of macrophages, and augments cytotoxicity of lymphocytes for target cells

Usual Dosage Adults: Inject 250,000 units (0.05 mL) in each wart twice weekly for a maximum of 8 weeks; therapy should not be repeated for at least 3 months after the initial 8-week course of therapy

Administration Inject into base of wart with a small 30-gauge needle

Patient Information Warts are highly contagious until they completely disappear, abstain from sexual activity or use barrier protection; inform nurse or physician if allergy exists to eggs, neomycin, mouse immunoglobulin, or to human interferon alpha; acetaminophen can be used to treat flu-like symptoms

Dosage Forms Injection: 5 million units (1 mL)

Interferon Beta-1a (in ter FEER on BAY ta won aye)

U.S. Brand Names Avonex™

Synonyms rIFN-b

Therapeutic Category Interferon

Use Treatment of relapsing forms of multiple sclerosis (MS); to slow the accumulation of physical disability and decrease the frequency of clinical exacerbations

Pregnancy Risk Factor C

Contraindications History of hypersensitivity to natural or recombinant interferon beta, human albumin, or any other component of the formulation

Warnings/Precautions Interferon beta-1a should be used with caution in patients with a history of depression, seizures, or cardiac disease; because its use has not been evaluated during lactation, its use in breast-feeding mothers may not be safe and should be warned against

Adverse Reactions 1% to 10%:

Cardiovascular: CHF (rare), tachycardia, syncope

Central nervous system: Headache, lethargy, depression, emotional lability, anxiety, suicidal ideations, somnolence, agitation, confusion

Dermatologic: Alopecia (rare)

Endocrine & metabolic: Hypocalcemia

Gastrointestinal: Nausea, anorexia, vomiting, diarrhea, chronic weight loss

Hematologic: Leukopenia, thrombocytopenia, anemia (frequent, dose-related, but not usually severe)

Hepatic: Elevated liver enzymes (mild, transient)

Local: Pain/redness at injection site (80%)

Neuromuscular & skeletal: Weakness

Ocular: Retinal toxicity/visual changes

Renal: Elevated BUN and S_{cr}

Miscellaneous: Flu-like syndrome (fever, nausea, malaise, myalgia) occurs in most patients, but is usually controlled by acetaminophen or NSAIDs; dose related abortifacient activity was reported in Rhesus monkeys

Overdosage/Toxicology

Symptoms of overdose include CNS depression, obtundation, flu-like symptoms, myelosuppression

Treatment is supportive

Drug Interactions Decreases clearance of zidovudine thus increasing zidovudine toxicity

Stability The reconstituted product contains no preservative and is for single use only; discard unused portion; store unreconstituted vial or reconstituted vial at 2°C to 8°C (36°F to 46°F); use the reconstituted product within 6 hours

Mechanism of Action Interferon beta differs from naturally occurring human protein by a single amino acid substitution and the lack of carbohydrate side chains; alters the expression and response to surface antigens and can enhance immune cell activities. Properties of interferon beta that modify biologic responses are mediated by cell surface receptor interactions; mechanism in the treatment of MS is unknown.

Pharmacodynamics/Kinetics Limited data due to small doses used

Half-life: 10 hours

Time to peak serum concentration: 3-15 hours

Usual Dosage Adults >18 years: I.M.: 30 mcg once weekly

Administration Reconstitute with 1.1 mL of diluent and swirl gently to dissolve

Monitoring Parameters Hemoglobin, liver function, and blood chemistries

Patient Information Flu-like symptoms are not uncommon following initiation of therapy. Acetaminophen may reduce these symptoms. Do not change the dosage or schedule of administration without medical consultation. Report depression or suicide ideation to physicians. Avoid prolonged exposure to sunlight or sunlamps.

Nursing Implications Patient should be informed of possible side effects, especially depression, suicidal ideations, and the risk of abortion; flu-like symptoms such as chills, fever, malaise, diaphoresis, and myalgia are common

Dosage Forms Powder for injection, lyophilized: 33 mcg [6.6 million units]

Interferon Beta-1b (in ter FEER on BAY ta won bee)

Related Information

Toxicities of Chemotherapeutic Agents *on page 1288*

U.S. Brand Names Betaseron®

Synonyms rIFN-b

Therapeutic Category Interferon

(Continued)

Interferon Beta-1b *(Continued)*

Use Reduces the frequency of clinical exacerbations in ambulatory patients with relapsing-remitting multiple sclerosis (MS)

Pregnancy Risk Factor C

Contraindications Hypersensitivity to *E. coli* derived products, natural or recombinant interferon beta, albumin human or any other component of the formulation

Warnings/Precautions The safety and efficacy of interferon beta-1b in chronic progressive MS have not been evaluated; use with caution in women who are breast-feeding; flu-like symptoms complex (ie, myalgia, fever, chills, malaise, sweating) is reported in 53% of patients who receive interferon beta-1b

Adverse Reactions Due to the pivotal position of interferon in the immune system, toxicities can affect nearly every organ system: Injection site reactions, injection site necrosis, flu-like symptoms, menstrual disorders, depression (with suicidal ideations), somnolence, palpitations, peripheral vascular disorders, hypertension, blood dyscrasias, dyspnea, laryngitis, cystitis, gastrointestinal complaints, seizures, headache, and liver enzyme elevations

Overdosage/Toxicology

Symptoms of overdose include CNS depression, obtundation, flu-like symptoms, myelo-suppression

Treatment is supportive

Stability Store solution at 2°C to 8°C (36°F to 46°F); do not freeze or shake solution; use product within 3 hours of reconstitution

Mechanism of Action Interferon beta-1b differs from naturally occurring human protein by a single amino acid substitution and the lack of carbohydrate side chains; alters the expression and response to surface antigens and can enhance immune cell activities. Properties of interferon beta-1b that modify biologic responses are mediated by cell surface receptor interactions; mechanism in the treatment of MS is unknown.

Usual Dosage S.C.:

Children <18 years: Not recommended

Adults >18 years: 0.25 mg (8 million units) every other day

Administration Withdraw 1 mL of reconstituted solution from the vial into a sterile syringe fitted with a 27-gauge needle and inject the solution subcutaneously; sites for self-injection include arms, abdomen, hips, and thighs

Monitoring Parameters Hemoglobin, liver function, and blood chemistries

Patient Information Instruct patients on self-injection technique and procedures. If possible, perform first injection under the supervision of an appropriately qualified health-care professional. Injection site reactions may occur during therapy. They are usually transient and do not require discontinuation of therapy, but careful assessment of the nature and severity of all reported reactions. Flu-like symptoms are not uncommon following initiation of therapy. Acetaminophen may reduce these symptoms. Do not change the dosage or schedule of administration without medical consultation. Report depression or suicide ideation to physicians. Avoid prolonged exposure to sunlight or sunlamps.

Nursing Implications Patient should be informed of possible side effects, especially depression, suicidal ideations, and the risk of abortion; flu-like symptoms such as chills, fever, malaise, sweating, and myalgia are common

Additional Information May be available only in small supplies; for information on availability and distribution, call the patient information line at 800-580-3837

Dosage Forms Powder for injection, lyophilized: 0.3 mg [9.6 million units]

Iodinated Glycerol *(EYE oh di nay ted GLI ser ole)*

U.S. Brand Names Iophen®; Organidin®; Par Glycerol®; R-Gen®

Therapeutic Category Expectorant

Use Mucolytic expectorant in adjunctive treatment of bronchitis, bronchial asthma, pulmonary emphysema, cystic fibrosis, or chronic sinusitis

Pregnancy Risk Factor X

Contraindications Hypersensitivity to inorganic iodides, iodinated glycerol, or any component; pregnancy, newborns

Warnings/Precautions Use with caution in patients with thyroid disease or renal impairment

Adverse Reactions

1% to 10%: Gastrointestinal: Diarrhea, nausea, vomiting

<1%: Headache, acne, dermatitis, acute parotitis, thyroid gland enlargement, GI irritation, eyelid edema, pulmonary edema, hypersensitivity

Overdosage/Toxicology Symptoms include metallic taste, swollen eyelids, sneezing, nausea, vomiting, diarrhea

Drug Interactions Increased toxicity: Disulfiram, metronidazole, procarbazine, MAO inhibitors, CNS depressants, lithium

Mechanism of Action Increases respiratory tract secretions by decreasing surface tension and thereby decreases the viscosity of mucus, which aids in removal of the mucus

Pharmacodynamics/Kinetics
  Absorption: From GI tract
  Distribution: Accumulates in the thyroid gland
  Elimination: In urine

Usual Dosage Oral:
  Children: Up to 30 mg 4 times/day
  Adults: 60 mg 4 times/day

Test Interactions Thyroid function tests may be altered

Patient Information Take with a full glass of water; not for use in coughs lasting longer than 1 week or associated with a fever

Nursing Implications Administer with plenty of fluids; elixir contains 21.75% alcohol; watch for sedation; avoid elixir in children due to high alcohol content

Dosage Forms Organically bound iodine in brackets
  Elixir: 60 mg/5 mL [30 mg/5 mL] (120 mL, 480 mL)
  Solution: 50 mg/mL [25 mg/mL] (30 mL)
  Tablet: 30 mg [15 mg]

♦ **Iodochlorhydroxyquin** see Clioquinol on page 277

Iodoquinol (eye oh doe KWIN ole)

U.S. Brand Names Yodoxin®
Canadian Brand Names Diodoquin®
Synonyms Diiodohydroxyquin
Therapeutic Category Amebicide
Use Treatment of acute and chronic intestinal amebiasis; asymptomatic cyst passers; *Blastocystis hominis* infections; ineffective for amebic hepatitis or hepatic abscess
Pregnancy Risk Factor C
Contraindications Known hypersensitivity to iodine or iodoquinol; hepatic damage; pre-existing optic neuropathy
Warnings/Precautions Optic neuritis, optic atrophy, and peripheral neuropathy have occurred following prolonged use; avoid long-term therapy
Adverse Reactions
  >10%: Gastrointestinal: Diarrhea, nausea, vomiting, stomach pain
  1% to 10%:
    Central nervous system: Fever, chills, agitation, retrograde amnesia, headache
    Dermatologic: Rash, urticaria
    Endocrine & metabolic: Thyroid gland enlargement
    Neuromuscular & skeletal: Peripheral neuropathy, weakness
    Ocular: Optic neuritis, optic atrophy, visual impairment
    Miscellaneous: Itching of rectal area
Overdosage/Toxicology
  Chronic overdose can result in vomiting, diarrhea, abdominal pain, metallic taste, paresthesias, paraplegia, and loss of vision; can lead to destruction of the long fibers of the spinal cord and optic nerve
  Acute overdose: Delirium, stupor, coma, amnesia
  Following GI decontamination, treatment is symptomatic
Mechanism of Action Contact amebicide that works in the lumen of the intestine by an unknown mechanism
Pharmacodynamics/Kinetics
  Absorption: Oral: Poor and irregular
  Metabolism: In the liver
  Elimination: High percentage of the dose excreted in feces
Usual Dosage Oral:
  Children: 30-40 mg/kg/day (maximum: 650 mg/dose) in 3 divided doses for 20 days; not to exceed 1.95 g/day
  Adults: 650 mg 3 times/day after meals for 20 days; not to exceed 1.95 g/day
Monitoring Parameters Ophthalmologic exam
Test Interactions May increase protein-bound serum iodine concentrations reflecting a decrease in ^{131}I uptake; false-positive ferric chloride test for phenylketonuria
Patient Information May take with food or milk to reduce stomach upset; complete full course of therapy
Nursing Implications Tablets may be crushed and mixed with applesauce or chocolate syrup
Dosage Forms
  Powder: 25 g
  Tablet: 210 mg, 650 mg

Iodoquinol and Hydrocortisone

  (eye oh doe KWIN ole & hye droe KOR ti sone)
U.S. Brand Names Vytone® Topical
Therapeutic Category Antifungal/Corticosteroid
Dosage Forms Cream: Iodoquinol 1% and hydrocortisone 1% (30 g)

Ioxilan (eye OKS ee lan)

U.S. Brand Names Oxilan®

Therapeutic Category Radiopaque Agents

Use
Intra-arterial: Ioxilan 300 mgI/mL is indicated for cerebral arteriography. Ioxilan 350 mgI/ mL is indicated for coronary arteriography and left ventriculography, visceral angiography, aortography, and peripheral arteriography
Intravenous: Both products are indicated for excretory urography and contrast enhanced computed tomographic (CECT) imaging of the head and body

Pregnancy Risk Factor B

Contraindications Ioxilan injection is not indicated for intrathecal use

Warnings/Precautions Clotting has been reported when blood remains in contact with syringes containing ioxilan; use of plastic syringes in place of glass syringes has been reported to decrease, but not eliminate, the likelihood of *in vitro* clotting. Serious, rarely fatal, thromboembolic events causing myocardial infarction and stroke have been reported during angiographic procedures with both ionic and nonionic contrast media. Therefore, meticulous intravascular administration technique is necessary; caution must be exercised in patients with severely impaired renal function, combined renal and hepatic disease, combined renal and cardiac disease, severe thyrotoxicosis, myelomatosis, or anuria, particularly when large doses are administered.

Intravascularly administered ioxilan is potentially hazardous in patients with multiple myeloma or other paraproteinacious diseases, who are prone to disease-induced renal insufficiency and/or failure. Partial dehydration in the preparation of these patients prior to injection is not recommended since this may predispose the patient to precipitation of the myeloma protein. Reports of thyroid storm following the intravascular use of iodinated radiopaque agents in patients with hyperthyroidism, or with an autonomously functioning thyroid nodule, suggest that this additional risk be evaluated in such patients before use of any contrast agent. Administration of radiopaque materials to patients with known or suspected pheochromocytoma should be performed with extreme caution. Contrast agents may promote sickling in individuals who are homozygous for sickle cell disease when administered intravascularly.

Adverse Reactions
1% to 10%:
Cardiovascular: Angina (1.3%), hypertension (1.1%)
Central nervous system: Headache (3.6%), fever (1.7%)
Gastrointestinal: Nausea (1.5%)
<1%: Bradycardia (0.8%), hypotension (0.9%), dizziness (0.8%), chills (0.6%), urticaria (0.8%), rash (0.6%), vomiting (0.9%), diarrhea (0.9%), injection site hematomas (0.8%)

Drug Interactions Increased toxicity: Renal toxicity has been reported in a few patients with liver dysfunction who were given an oral cholecystographic agent followed by intravascular contrast agents such as ioxilan

Mechanism of Action Ioxilan is a nonionic, water soluble, tri-iodinated x-ray contrast agent for intravascular injection. Intravascular injection of a radiopaque diagnostic agent opacifies those vessels in the path of flow of the contrast medium, permitting radiographic visualization of the internal structures of the human body until significant hemodilution occurs.

Usual Dosage
Intra-arterial: Coronary arteriography and left ventriculography: For visualization of coronary arteries and left ventricle, ioxilan injection with a concentration of 350 mg iodine/ mL is recommended
Usual injection volumes:
Left and right coronary: 2-10 mL (0.7-3.5 g iodine)
Left ventricle: 25-50 mL (8.75-17.5 g iodine)
Total doses should not exceed 250 mL; the injection rate of ioxilan should approximate the flow rate in the vessel injected
Cerebral arteriography: For evaluation of arterial lesions of the brain, a concentration of 300 mg iodine/mL is indicated
Recommended doses: 8-12 mL (2.4-3.6 g iodine)
Total dose should not exceed 150 mL

Administration Patients should be adequately hydrated prior to and following intravascular administration of ioxilan. If during administration a reaction occurs, the injection should be immediately stopped.

Monitoring Parameters Prior to and 24-48 hours after intravascular administration: Thyroid function tests, renal function tests, blood counts, serum electrolytes, and urinalysis should be monitored for and blood pressure, heart rate, electrocardiogram, and temperature should be monitored throughout the procedure

Test Interactions The results of protein-bound iodine and radioactive iodine uptake studies, which depend on iodine estimations, will not accurately reflect thyroid function for at least 16 days following administration of iodinated contrast media. However, thyroid function tests that do not depend on iodine estimations (eg, T_3 resin uptake and total or free thyroxine (T_4) assays), are not affected.

Patient Information Patients receiving iodinated intravascular contrast agents should be instructed to:

Inform physician if pregnant

Inform physician if diabetic or have multiple myeloma, pheochromocytoma, homozygous sickle cell disease, or known thyroid disorder

Inform physician if allergic to any drugs or food, or have immune, autoimmune, or immune deficiency disorders; also inform physician if previous reactions to injections of dyes used for x-ray procedures

Inform physician about all medications currently being taken, including nonprescription (over-the-counter) drugs, before having this procedure

Nursing Implications Patients receiving contrast agents, and especially those who are medically unstable, must be closely supervised. Diagnostic procedures that involve the use of iodinated intravascular contrast agents should be carried out under the direction of personnel skilled and experienced in the particular procedure to be performed. A fully equipped emergency cart, or equivalent supplies and equipment, and personnel competent in recognizing and treating adverse reactions of all types should always be available. Since severe delayed reactions have been known to occur, emergency facilities and competent personnel should be available for at least 30-60 minutes after administration.

Dosage Forms Solution for injection: 300 mgI/mL (Oxilan® 300), 350 mgI/mL (Oxilan® 350)

♦ **I-Paracaine®** *see* Proparacaine *on page 982*

Ipecac Syrup (IP e kak SIR up)

Therapeutic Category Antidote, Emetic

Use Treatment of acute oral drug overdosage and in certain poisonings

Pregnancy Risk Factor C

Contraindications Do not use in unconscious patients when time elapsed since exposure is >1 hour, patients with no gag reflex; following ingestion of strong bases or acids, volatile oils; when seizures are likely

Warnings/Precautions Do not confuse ipecac syrup with ipecac fluid extract, which is 14 times more potent; use with caution in patients with cardiovascular disease and bulimics; may not be effective in antiemetic overdose

Adverse Reactions 1% to 10%:

Cardiovascular: Cardiotoxicity

Central nervous system: Lethargy

Gastrointestinal: Protracted vomiting, diarrhea

Neuromuscular & skeletal: Myopathy

Overdosage/Toxicology

Contains cardiotoxin; symptoms of overdose include tachycardia, CHF, atrial fibrillation, depressed myocardial contractility, myocarditis, diarrhea, persistent vomiting, hypotension

Treatment is activated charcoal, gastric lavage

Drug Interactions

Decreased effect: Activated charcoal, milk, carbonated beverages

Increased toxicity: Phenothiazines (chlorpromazine has been associated with serious dystonic reactions)

Mechanism of Action Irritates the gastric mucosa and stimulates the medullary chemoreceptor trigger zone to induce vomiting

Pharmacodynamics/Kinetics

Onset of action: Within 15-30 minutes

Duration: 20-25 minutes; can last longer, 60 minutes in some cases

Absorption: Significant amounts, mainly when it does not produce emesis

Elimination: Emetine (alkaloid component) may be detected in urine 60 days after excess dose or chronic use

Usual Dosage Oral:

Children:

6-12 months: 5-10 mL followed by 10-20 mL/kg of water; repeat dose one time if vomiting does not occur within 20 minutes

1-12 years: 15 mL followed by 10-20 mL/kg of water; repeat dose one time if vomiting does not occur within 20 minutes

If emesis does not occur within 30 minutes after second dose, ipecac must be removed from stomach by gastric lavage

Adults: 15-30 mL followed by 200-300 mL of water; repeat dose one time if vomiting does not occur within 20 minutes

Patient Information Call Poison Center before administering. Patients should be kept active and moving following administration of ipecac; follow dose with 8 oz of water following initial episode; if vomiting, no food or liquids should be ingested for 1 hour

Nursing Implications Do **not** administer to unconscious patients; patients should be kept active and moving following administration of ipecac; if vomiting does not occur after second dose, gastric lavage may be considered to remove ingested substance

Dosage Forms Syrup: 70 mg/mL (15 mL, 30 mL, 473 mL, 4000 mL)

♦ **I-Pentolate®** *see* Cyclopentolate *on page 304*

♦ **I-Phrine® Ophthalmic Solution** *see* Phenylephrine *on page 918*

♦ **IPOL™** *see* Polio Vaccines *on page 940*

Ipratropium (i pra TROE pee um)

U.S. Brand Names Atrovent®

Synonyms Ipratropium Bromide

(Continued)

Ipratropium *(Continued)*

Therapeutic Category Anticholinergic Agent; Bronchodilator

Use Anticholinergic bronchodilator in bronchospasm associated with COPD, bronchitis, and emphysema

Pregnancy Risk Factor B

Contraindications Hypersensitivity to atropine or its derivatives

Warnings/Precautions Not indicated for the initial treatment of acute episodes of bronchospasm; use with caution in patients with narrow-angle glaucoma, prostatic hypertrophy, or bladder neck obstruction; ipratropium has not been specifically studied in the elderly, but it is poorly absorbed from the airways and appears to be safe in this population.

Adverse Reactions Note: Ipratropium is poorly absorbed from the lung, so systemic effects are rare

>10%:
Central nervous system: Nervousness, dizziness, fatigue, headache
Gastrointestinal: Nausea, xerostomia, stomach upset
Respiratory: Cough

1% to 10%:
Cardiovascular: Palpitations, hypotension
Central nervous system: Insomnia
Genitourinary: Urinary retention
Neuromuscular & skeletal: Trembling
Ocular: Blurred vision
Respiratory: Nasal congestion

<1%: Rash, urticaria, stomatitis

Overdosage/Toxicology

Symptoms of overdose include dry mouth, drying of respiratory secretions, cough, nausea, GI distress, blurred vision or impaired visual accommodation, headache, nervousness

Acute overdosage with ipratropium by inhalation is unlikely since it is so poorly absorbed. However, if poisoning occurs, it can be treated like any other anticholinergic toxicity. An anticholinergic overdose with severe life-threatening symptoms may be treated with physostigmine 1-2 mg (0.5 mg or 0.02 mg/kg for children) S.C. or I.V., slowly.

Drug Interactions

Increased effect with albuterol

Increased toxicity with anticholinergics or drugs with anticholinergic properties, dronabinol

Mechanism of Action Blocks the action of acetylcholine at parasympathetic sites in bronchial smooth muscle causing bronchodilation

Pharmacodynamics/Kinetics

Onset of bronchodilation: 1-3 minutes after administration
Peak effect: Within 1.5-2 hours
Duration: Up to 4-6 hours
Absorption: Not readily absorbed into the systemic circulation from the surface of the lung or from the GI tract
Distribution: Inhalation: 15% of dose reaches the lower airways

Usual Dosage

Children:
<2 years: Nebulization: 250 mcg 3 times/day
3-14 years: Metered dose inhaler: 1-2 inhalations 3 times/day, up to 6 inhalations/24 hours
Children >12 years and Adults: Nebulization: 500 mcg (1 unit-dose vial) administered 3-4 times/day by oral nebulization, with doses 6-8 hours apart
Children >14 years and Adults: Metered dose inhaler: 2 inhalations 4 times/day every 4-6 hours up to 12 inhalations in 24 hours

Patient Information

Inhaler directions: Effects are enhanced by breath-holding 10 seconds after inhalation; temporary blurred vision may occur if sprayed into eyes; shake canister well before each use of the inhaler; follow instructions for use accompanying the product; close eyes when administering ipratropium; wait at least one full minute between inhalations

Nebulizer directions: Twist open the top of one unit dose vial and squeeze the contents into the nebulizer reservoir. Connect the nebulizer reservoir to the mouthpiece or face mask. Connect the nebulizer to the compressor. Sit in a comfortable, upright position; place the mouthpiece in your mouth or put on the face mask and turn on the compressor. If a face mask is used, care should be taken to avoid leakage around the mask as temporary blurring of vision, precipitation or worsening of narrow-angle glaucoma, or eye pain may occur if the solution comes into direct contact with the eyes. Breathe as calmly, deeply, and evenly as possible until no more mist is formed in the nebulizer chamber (about 5-15 minutes). At this point, the treatment is finished. Clean the nebulizer.

Dosage Forms Solution, as bromide:

Inhalation: 18 mcg/actuation (14 g)
Nasal spray: 0.03% (30 mL); 0.06% (15 mL)
Nebulizing: 0.02% (2.5 mL)

Ipratropium and Albuterol *(i pra TROE pee um & al BYOO ter ole)*

U.S. Brand Names Combivent®

Therapeutic Category Bronchodilator

Dosage Forms Aerosol: Ipratropium bromide 18 mcg and albuterol sulfate 103 mcg per actuation [200 doses] (14.7 g)

♦ **Ipratropium Bromide** see Ipratropium on page 625
♦ **Iproveratril Hydrochloride** see Verapamil on page 1214

Irbesartan (ir be SAR tan)

Related Information
Angiotensin Agents on page 1291
U.S. Brand Names Avapro®
Therapeutic Category Angiotensin II Antagonist; Antihypertensive Agent
Use Treatment of hypertension alone or in combination with other antihypertensives
Pregnancy Risk Factor C (1st trimester); D (2nd and 3rd trimesters)
Contraindications Hypersensitivity to any component
Warnings/Precautions Avoid use or use a much smaller dose in patients who are intravascularly volume-depleted; use caution in patients with unilateral or bilateral renal artery stenosis to avoid a decrease in renal function; AUCs of irbesartan (not the active metabolite) are about 50% greater in patients with Cl_{cr} <30 mL/minute and are doubled in hemodialysis patients
Adverse Reactions 1% to 10%:
Cardiovascular: Edema, chest pain, tachycardia
Central nervous system: Dizziness, headache, fatigue, anxiety, nervousness
Dermatologic: Rash
Gastrointestinal: Diarrhea, dyspepsia/heartburn, nausea, vomiting, abdominal pain
Genitourinary: Urinary tract infection
Neuromuscular & skeletal: Pain, trauma
Respiratory: Upper respiratory infection, cough, sinus disorder, pharyngitis, rhinitis, influenza
Overdosage/Toxicology
Most likely manifestation of an overdosage would be hypotension and tachycardia; bradycardia could occur from parasympathetic (vagal) stimulation
If symptomatic hypotension should occur, institute supportive treatment
Drug Interactions CYP2C9 enzyme substrate
Mechanism of Action Irbesartan is an angiotensin receptor antagonist. Angiotensin II acts as a vasoconstrictor. In addition to causing direct vasoconstriction, angiotensin II also stimulates the release of aldosterone. Once aldosterone is released, sodium as well as water are reabsorbed. The end result is an elevation in blood pressure. Irbesartan binds to the AT1 angiotensin II receptor. This binding prevents angiotensin II from binding to the receptor thereby blocking the vasoconstriction and the aldosterone secreting effects of angiotensin II.
Pharmacodynamics/Kinetics
Distribution: V_d: 53-93 L
Protein binding, plasma: 90%
Metabolism: Hepatic
Bioavailability: 60% to 80%
Half-life: Terminal: 11-15 hours
Time to peak serum concentration: 1.5-2 hours
Elimination: Urine (20%), feces (80%)
Usual Dosage Adults: Oral: 150 mg once daily with or without food; patients may be titrated to 300 mg once daily
Patient Information Patients of childbearing age should be informed about the consequences of 2nd- and 3rd-trimester exposure to drugs that act on the renin-angiotensin system, and that these consequences do not appear to have resulted from intrauterine drug exposure that has been limited to the 1st trimester. Patients should report pregnancy to their physician as soon as possible.
Dosage Forms Tablet: 75 mg, 150 mg, 300 mg

Irbesartan and Hydrochlorothiazide
(ir be SAR tan & hye droe klor oh THYE a zide)
U.S. Brand Names Avapro® HCT
Synonyms Hydrochlorothiazide and Irbesartan
Therapeutic Category Angiotensin II Antagonist Combination; Antihypertensive Agent, Combination
Dosage Forms Tablet: Irbesartan 150 mg and hydrochlorothiazide 12.5 mg; irbesartan 300 mg and hydrochlorothiazide 12.5 mg

♦ **Ircon® [OTC]** see Ferrous Fumarate on page 478

Irinotecan (eye rye no TEE kan)

Related Information
Toxicities of Chemotherapeutic Agents on page 1288
U.S. Brand Names Camptosar®
Synonyms Camptothecin-11; CPT-11
Therapeutic Category Antineoplastic Agent, Miscellaneous
Use Treatment of metastatic carcinoma of the colon or rectum which has recurred or progressed following fluorouracil-based therapy
Unlabeled use: Clinical trials are assessing efficacy in the treatment of lung cancer (small cell and nonsmall cell), cervical cancer, ovarian cancer, gastric cancer, leukemia, lymphoma
(Continued)

Irinotecan *(Continued)*

Pregnancy Risk Factor D

Contraindications Hypersensitivity to irinotecan or any component

Warnings/Precautions The U.S. Food and Drug Administration (FDA) currently recommends that procedures for proper handling and disposal of antineoplastic agents be considered

Irinotecan can induce both early and late forms of diarrhea that appear to be mediated by different mechanisms. Early diarrhea (during or within 24 hours of administration) is cholinergic in nature. It can be preceded by complaints of diaphoresis and abdominal cramping and may be ameliorated by the administration of atropine. The elderly (≥65 years of age) are at particular risk for diarrhea. Late diarrhea (occurring >24 hours after administration) can be prolonged and may lead to dehydration and electrolyte imbalance, and can be life-threatening. Late diarrhea should be treated promptly with loperamide. If grade 3 diarrhea (7-9 stools daily, incontinence, or severe cramping) or grade 4 diarrhea (≥10 stools daily, grossly bloody stool, or need for parenteral support), the administration of irinotecan should be delayed until the patient recovers and subsequent doses should be decreased.

> Early diarrhea treatment: 0.25-1 mg of intravenous atropine should be considered (unless clinically contraindicated) in patients experiencing diaphoresis, abdominal cramping, or early diarrhea
>
> Late diarrhea treatment: High-dose loperamide: Oral: 4 mg at the first onset of late diarrhea and then 2 mg every 2 hours until the patient is diarrhea-free for at least 12 hours. During the night, the patient may take 4 mg of loperamide every 4 hours. **Premedication with loperamide is not recommended.**

Deaths due to sepsis following severe myelosuppression have been reported. Therapy should be discontinued if neutropenic fever occurs or if the absolute neutrophil count is <500/mm^3. The dose of irinotecan should be reduced if there is a clinically significant decrease in the total WBC (<200/mm^3), neutrophil count (<1000/mm^3), hemoglobin (<8 g/dL), or platelet count (<100,000/mm^3). Routine administration of a colony-stimulating factor is generally not necessary. Avoid extravasation.

Patients with even modest elevations in total serum bilirubin levels (1.0-2.0 mg/dL) have a significantly greater likelihood of experiencing first-course grade 3 or 4 neutropenia than those with bilirubin levels that were <1.0 mg/dL. Patients with abnormal glucuronidation of bilirubin, such as those with Gilbert's syndrome, may also be at greater risk of myelosuppression when receiving therapy with irinotecan.

Adverse Reactions

>10%:

> Cardiovascular: Vasodilation
>
> Central nervous system: Insomnia, dizziness, fever (45.4%)
>
> Dermatologic: Alopecia (60.5%), rash
>
> Gastrointestinal: Irinotecan therapy may induce two different forms of diarrhea. Onset, symptoms, proposed mechanisms and treatment are different. Overall, 56.9% of patients treated experience abdominal pain and/or cramping during therapy. Anorexia, constipation, flatulence, stomatitis, and dyspepsia have also been reported.
>
> Diarrhea: Dose-limiting toxicity with weekly dosing regimen
>
> Early diarrhea (50.7% incidence) usually occurs during or within 24 hours of administration. May be accompanied by symptoms of cramping, vomiting, flushing, and diaphoresis. It is thought to be mediated by cholinergic effects which can be successfully managed with atropine (refer to Warnings/Precautions).
>
> Late diarrhea (87.8% incidence) usually occurs >24 hours after treatment. National Cancer Institute (NCI) grade 3 or 4 diarrhea occurs in 30.6% of patients. Late diarrhea generally occurs with a median of 11 days after therapy and lasts approximately 3 days. Patients experiencing grade 3 or 4 diarrhea were noted to have symptoms a total of 7 days. Correlated with irinotecan or SN-38 levels in plasma and bile. Due to the duration, dehydration and electrolyte imbalances are significant clinical concerns. Loperamide therapy is recommended. The incidence of grade 3 or 4 late diarrhea is significantly higher in patients ≥65 years of age; close monitoring and prompt initiation of high-dose loperamide therapy is prudent (refer to Warnings/Precautions).
>
> Emetic potential: Moderately high (86.2% incidence, however, only 12.5% grade 3 or 4 vomiting)
>
> Hematologic: Myelosuppressive: Dose-limiting toxicity with 3 week dosing regimen
>
> Grade 1-4 neutropenia occurred in 53.9% of patients. Patients who had previously received pelvic or abdominal radiation therapy were noted to have a significantly increased incidence of grade 3 or 4 neutropenia. White blood cell count nadir is 15 days after administration and is more frequent than thrombocytopenia. Recovery is usually within 24-28 days and cumulative toxicity has not been observed.
>
> WBC: Mild to severe
>
> Platelets: Mild
>
> Onset (days): 10
>
> Nadir (days): 14-16
>
> Recovery (days): 21-28
>
> Neuromuscular & skeletal: Weakness (75.7%)
>
> Respiratory: Dyspnea (22%), coughing, rhinitis
>
> Miscellaneous: Diaphoresis

1% to 10%: **Irritant chemotherapy**; thrombophlebitis has been reported

Overdosage/Toxicology

Symptoms of overdose include bone marrow suppression, leukopenia, thrombocytopenia, nausea, vomiting

Treatment is supportive

Drug Interactions Increased toxicity: Prochlorperazine: Increased incidence of akathisia

Stability

Store intact vials of injection at room temperature and protected from light

Doses should be diluted in D_5W or NS to a final concentration of 0.12-1.1 mg/mL. Due to the relatively acidic pH, irinotecan appears to be more stable in D_5W than NS. D_5W (500 mL) is the preferred diluent for most doses

Standardized dose: Dose/500 mL D_5W

Stability at room temperature (15°C to 30°C/59°F to 86°F): 24 hours

Stability at refrigeration (2°C to 8°C/36°F to 46°F): 48 hours

Standardized dose: Dose/500 mL NS

Stability at room temperature (15°C to 30°C/59°F to 86°F): 24 hours

Stability at refrigeration (2°C to 8°C/36°F to 46°F): NOT RECOMMENDED DUE TO THE OCCURRENCE OF VISIBLE PARTICULATES

Mechanism of Action Irinotecan and its active metabolite (SN-38) bind reversibly to topoisomerase I and stabilize the cleavable complex so that religation of the cleaved DNA strand cannot occur. This results in the accumulation of cleavable complexes and single-strand DNA breaks. This interaction results in double-stranded DNA breaks and cell death consistent with S-phase cell cycle specificity.

Pharmacodynamics/Kinetics

Distribution: Average V_d: 263 L/m^2

Protein binding: 30% to 68%; SN-38 is highly protein bound (95%) predominately to albumin

Metabolism: Irinotecan is a water-soluble prodrug of SN-38, which is approximately 1,000 times the potency of the potency of irinotecan. In the liver, irinotecan undergoes metabolic conversion to the active metabolite SN-38; high interpatient variability.

Half-life: Terminal: Irinotecan = 10 hours; SN-38 = 10 hours

Elimination: Irinotecan is eliminated via biliary excretion, urinary excretion, and conversion to SN-38. SN-38 is eliminated via glucuronidation and biliary excretion.

Usual Dosage Refer to individual protocols:

Adults: I.V.: Metastatic colon or rectal carcinoma:

Initial: 125 mg/m^2 I.V. over 90 minutes

Recommended Irinotecan Dosage Modifications

Toxicity NCI Grade (Value)	During a Course of Therapy*	At the Start of the Next Courses of Therapy* (After Adequate Recovery), Compared to the Starting Dose in the Previous Courses
No toxicity	Maintain dose level	↑ 25 mg/m^2 up to a maximum dose of 150 mg/m^2
Neutropenia		
1 (1500-1900/mm^3)	Maintain dose level	Maintain dose level
2 (1000-1400/mm^3)	↓ 25 mg/m^2	Maintain dose level
3 (500-900/mm^3)	Omit dose, then ↓ 25 mg/m^2 when resolved to ≤ grade 2	↓ 25 mg/m^2
4 (<500/mm^3)	Omit dose, then ↓ 50 mg/m^2 when resolved to ≤ grade 2	↓ 50 mg/m^2
Neutropenic Fever (grade 4 neutropenia and ≥ grade 2 fever)	Omit dose then ↓ 50 mg/m^2 when resolved	↓ 50 mg/m^2
Other hematologic toxicities	Dose modifications for leukopenia, thrombocytopenia, and anemia during a course of therapy and at the start of subsequent courses of therapy are also based on NCI toxicity criteria and are the same as recommended for neutropenia above.	
Diarrhea		
1 (2-3 stools/day > pretreatment)	Maintain dose level	Maintain dose level
2 (4-6 stools/day > pretreatment)	↓ 25 mg/m^2	Maintain, if only grade 2 toxicity
3 (7-9 stools/day > pretreatment)	Omit dose, then ↓ 25 mg/m^2 when resolved to ≤ grade 2	↓ 25 mg/m^2, if only grade 3 toxicity
4 (≥10 stools/day > pretreatment)	Omit dose then ↓ 50 mg/m^2, when resolved to ≤ grade 2	↓ 50 mg/m^2
Other Nonhematologic Toxicities		
1	Maintain dose level	Maintain dose level
2	↓ 25 mg/m^2	↓ 25 mg/m^2
3	Omit dose, then ↓ 25 mg/m^2 when resolved to ≤ grade 2	↓ 50 mg/m^2
4	Omit dose, then ↓ 50 mg/m^2 when resolved to ≤ grade 2	↓ 50 mg/m^2

*All dose modifications should be based on the worst preceding toxicity.

(Continued)

Irinotecan *(Continued)*

The recommended treatment regimen (ie, one treatment course) is once weekly treatment for 4 weeks, followed by a 2-week rest period. The first treatment course is shown in the following table. Thereafter, additional courses of treatment may be repeated every 6 weeks (4 weeks on therapy, followed by 2 weeks rest). Provided intolerable toxicity does not develop, treatment and additional courses may be continued indefinitely in patients who attain a response or in patients whose disease remains stable. Patients should be carefully monitored for toxicity.

First 6-Week Dosing Schedule for Irinotecan for a Patient Experiencing No Toxicity Requiring Dosing Delays

Week	1	2	3	4	5	6 (the second 6-week course of treatment may begin week 7 - day 43)
(day)	1	8	15	22	29	36
Treatment (given on first day of weeks 1-4)	One 90-minute I.V. infusion	One 90-minute I.V. infusion	One 90-minute I.V. infusion	One 90-minute I.V. infusion	Rest	Rest

Dosing adjustment in hepatic impairment: In patients with a combined history of prior pelvic/abdominal irradiation and modestly elevated total serum bilirubin levels (1.0-2.0 mg/dL) prior to treatment with irinotecan, there may be substantially increased likelihood of grade 3 or 4 neutropenia. Consideration may be given to starting irinotecan at a lower dose (eg, 100 mg/m^2) in such patients. Definite recommendations regarding the most appropriate starting dose in patients who have pretreatment total serum bilirubin elevations >2.0 mg/dL are not available, but it is likely that lower starting doses will need to be considered in such patients.

Note: It is recommended that new courses begin only after the granulocyte count recovers to ≥1500/mm^3, the platelet counts recovers to ≥100,000/mm^3, and treatment-related diarrhea has fully resolved. Depending on the patient's ability to tolerate therapy, doses should be adjusted in increments of 25-50 mg/m^2. Irinotecan doses may range 50-150 mg/m^2. Treatment should be delayed 1-2 weeks to allow for recovery from treatment-related toxicities. If the patient has not recovered after a 2-week delay, consideration should be given to discontinuing irinotecan.

Dosing adjustment for toxicities: See table.

Dosing adjustment in renal impairment: Effects have not been evaluated

Dosing adjustment in hepatic impairment:

AUC of irinotecan and SN-38 have been reported to be higher in patients with known hepatic tumor involvement. The manufacturer recommends that no change in dosage or administration be made for patients with liver metastases and normal hepatic function.

Use caution when treating patients with known hepatic dysfunction or hyperbilirubinemia

Administration Administer I.V. infusion over 90 minutes

Monitoring Parameters CBC with differential, platelet count, and hemoglobin with each dose

Patient Information

Patients and patients' caregivers should be informed of the expected toxic effects of irinotecan, particularly of its gastrointestinal manifestations, such as nausea, vomiting, and diarrhea

Each patient should be instructed to have loperamide readily available and to begin treatment for late diarrhea (occurring >24 hours after administration of irinotecan) at the first episode of poorly formed or loose stools or the earliest onset of bowel movements more frequent than normally expected for the patient. Refer to Warnings/Precautions.

The patient should also be instructed to notify the physician if diarrhea occurs. Premedication with loperamide is not recommended. The use of drugs with laxative properties should be avoided because of the potential for exacerbation of diarrhea. Patients should be advised to contact their physician to discuss any laxative use.

Patients should consult their physician if vomiting occurs, fever or evidence of infection develops, or if symptoms of dehydration, such as fainting, lightheadedness, or dizziness, are noted following therapy

Nursing Implications Monitor infusion site for signs of inflammation and avoid extravasation

Extravasation treatment: Flush the site with sterile water and apply ice

Dosage Forms Injection: 20 mg/mL (5 mL)

Iron Dextran Complex *(EYE ern DEKS tran KOM pleks)*

Related Information

Antacid Drug Interactions *on page 1296*

U.S. Brand Names Dexferrum®; InFed™ Injection

Canadian Brand Names Infufer®

Therapeutic Category Iron Salt

Use Treatment of microcytic hypochromic anemia resulting from iron deficiency in whom oral administration is infeasible or ineffective

Pregnancy Risk Factor C

Contraindications Hypersensitivity to iron dextran, all anemias that are not involved with iron deficiency, hemochromatosis, hemolytic anemia

Warnings/Precautions Use with caution in patients with history of asthma, hepatic impairment, rheumatoid arthritis; not recommended in children <4 months of age; deaths associated with parenteral administration following anaphylactic-type reactions have been reported; use only in patients where the iron deficient state is not amenable to oral iron therapy. A test dose of 0.5 mL I.V. or I.M. should be given to observe for adverse reactions. Anemia in the elderly is often caused by "anemia of chronic disease" or associated with inflammation rather than blood loss. Iron stores are usually normal or increased, with a serum ferritin >50 ng/mL and a decreased total iron binding capacity. I.V. administration of iron dextran is often preferred over I.M. in the elderly secondary to a decreased muscle mass and the need for daily injections.

Adverse Reactions

>10%:
    Cardiovascular: Flushing
    Central nervous system: Dizziness, fever, headache, pain
    Gastrointestinal: Nausea, vomiting, metallic taste
    Local: Staining of skin at the site of I.M. injection
    Miscellaneous: Diaphoresis

1% to 10%:
    Cardiovascular: Hypotension (1% to 2%)
    Dermatologic: Urticaria (1% to 2%), phlebitis (1% to 2%)
    Gastrointestinal: Diarrhea
    Genitourinary: Discoloration of urine

<1%: Cardiovascular collapse, leukocytosis, chills, arthralgia, respiratory difficulty, lymphadenopathy

Note: Diaphoresis, urticaria, arthralgia, fever, chills, dizziness, headache, and nausea may be delayed 24-48 hours after I.V. administration or 3-4 days after I.M. administration

Anaphylactoid reactions: Respiratory difficulties and cardiovascular collapse have been reported and occur most frequently within the first several minutes of administration

Overdosage/Toxicology
    Symptoms of overdose include erosion of GI mucosa, pulmonary edema, hyperthermia, convulsions, tachycardia, hepatic and renal impairment, coma, hematemesis, lethargy, tachycardia, acidosis, serum Fe level >300 mcg/mL requires treatment of overdose due to severe toxicity
    Although rare, if a severe iron overdose (when the serum iron concentration exceeds the total iron-binding capacity) occurs, it may be treated with deferoxamine. Deferoxamine may be administered I.V. (80 mg/kg over 24 hours) or I.M. (40-90 mg/kg every 8 hours).

Drug Interactions Decreased effect with chloramphenicol

Stability Store at room temperature
    Stability of parenteral admixture at room temperature (25°C): 3 months
    Standard diluent: Dose/250-1000 mL NS
    Minimum volume: 250 mL NS

Mechanism of Action The released iron, from the plasma, eventually replenishes the depleted iron stores in the bone marrow where it is incorporated into hemoglobin

Pharmacodynamics/Kinetics
    Absorption:
        I.M.: 50% to 90% is promptly absorbed, the balance is slowly absorbed over month
        I.V.: Uptake of iron by the reticuloendothelial system appears to be constant at about 10-20 mg/hour
    Elimination: By the reticuloendothelial system and excreted in the urine and feces (via bile)

Usual Dosage I.M. (Z-track method should be used for I.M. injection), I.V.:
    A 0.5 mL test dose (0.25 mL in infants) should be given prior to starting iron dextran therapy; total dose should be divided into a daily schedule for I.M., total dose may be given as a single continuous infusion
    Iron deficiency anemia: Dose (mL) = 0.0476 x wt (kg) x (normal hemoglobin - observed hemoglobin) + (1 mL/5 kg) to maximum of 14 mL for iron stores
    Iron replacement therapy for blood loss: Replacement iron (mg) = blood loss (mL) x hematocrit
    Maximum daily dose (can administer total dose at one time I.V.):
        Infants <5 kg: 25 mg iron (0.5 mL)
        Children:
            5-10 kg: 50 mg iron (1 mL)
            10-50 kg: 100 mg iron (2 mL)
        Adults >50 kg: 100 mg iron (2 mL)

Administration Use Z-track technique for I.M. administration (deep into the upper outer quadrant of buttock); may be administered I.V. bolus at rate ≤50 mg/minute or diluted in 250-1000 mL NS and infused over 1-6 hours; infuse initial 25 mL slowly, observe for allergic reactions; have epinephrine nearby

Monitoring Parameters Hemoglobin, hematocrit, reticulocyte count, serum ferritin

Reference Range
    Hemoglobin 14.8 mg % (for weight >15 kg), hemoglobin 12.0 mg % (for weight <15 kg)
(Continued)

Iron Dextran Complex *(Continued)*

Serum iron: 40-160 µg/dL
Total iron binding capacity: 230-430 µg/dL
Transferrin: 204-360 mg/dL
Percent transferrin saturation: 20% to 50%
Test Interactions May cause falsely elevated values of serum bilirubin and falsely decreased values of serum calcium
Dosage Forms Injection: 50 mg/mL (2 mL, 10 mL)

♦ **ISD** *see* Isosorbide Dinitrate *on page 637*
♦ **ISDN** *see* Isosorbide Dinitrate *on page 637*
♦ **ISG** *see* Immune Globulin, Intramuscular *on page 603*
♦ **Ismelin**® *see* Guanethidine *on page 552*
♦ **ISMN** *see* Isosorbide Mononitrate *on page 639*
♦ **Ismo**® *see* Isosorbide Mononitrate *on page 639*
♦ **Ismotic**® *see* Isosorbide *on page 637*
♦ **Isoamyl Nitrite** *see* Amyl Nitrite *on page 83*
♦ **Isobamate** *see* Carisoprodol *on page 196*
♦ **Isocaine**® **HCl** *see* Mepivacaine *on page 730*
♦ **Isoclor**® **Expectorant** *see* Guaifenesin, Pseudoephedrine, and Codeine *on page 551*
♦ **Isocom**® *see* Acetaminophen, Isometheptene, and Dichloralphenazone *on page 22*
♦ **Isodine**® **[OTC]** *see* Povidone-Iodine *on page 955*

Isoetharine *(eye soe ETH a reen)*

Related Information
Bronchodilators, Comparison of Inhaled and Sympathomimetic *on page 1314*
U.S. Brand Names Arm-a-Med® Isoetharine; Beta-2®; Bronkometer®; Bronkosol®; Dey-Lute® Isoetharine
Synonyms Isoetharine Hydrochloride; Isoetharine Mesylate
Therapeutic Category Adrenergic Agonist Agent; Bronchodilator; Sympathomimetic
Use Bronchodilator in bronchial asthma and for reversible bronchospasm occurring with bronchitis and emphysema
Pregnancy Risk Factor C
Contraindications Known hypersensitivity to isoetharine
Warnings/Precautions Excessive or prolonged use may result in decreased effectiveness
Adverse Reactions
1% to 10%:
Cardiovascular: Tachycardia, hypertension, pounding heartbeat
Central nervous system: Dizziness, lightheadedness, headache, nervousness, insomnia
Gastrointestinal: Xerostomia, nausea, vomiting
Neuromuscular & skeletal: Trembling, weakness
<1%: Paradoxical bronchospasm
Overdosage/Toxicology
Symptoms of overdose include nausea, vomiting, hypertension, tremors; beta-adrenergic stimulation can cause increased heart rate, decreased blood pressure, and CNS excitation
Heart rate can be treated with beta-blockers, decreased blood pressure can be treated with pure alpha-adrenergic agents, diazepam 0.07 mg/kg can be used for excitation, seizures
Drug Interactions
Decreased effect with beta-blockers
Increased toxicity with other sympathomimetics (eg, epinephrine)
Stability Do not use if solution is discolored or a precipitation is present; **compatible** with sterile water, 0.45% sodium chloride, and 0.9% sodium chloride; protect from light
Mechanism of Action Relaxes bronchial smooth muscle by action on beta$_2$-receptors with very little effect on heart rate
Pharmacodynamics/Kinetics
Peak effect: Inhaler: Within 5-15 minutes
Duration: 1-4 hours
Metabolism: In many tissues including the liver and lungs
Elimination: Renal, primarily (90%) as metabolites
Usual Dosage Treatments are not usually repeated more than every 4 hours, except in severe cases

Nebulizer: Children: 0.01 mL/kg; minimum dose 0.1 mL; maximum dose: 0.5 mL diluted in 2-3 mL normal saline
Inhalation: Oral: Adults: 1-2 inhalations every 4 hours as needed
Administration Administer around-the-clock to promote less variation in peak and trough serum levels
Monitoring Parameters Heart rate, blood pressure, respiratory rate
Test Interactions ↓ potassium (S)
Patient Information Do not exceed recommended dosage - excessive use may lead to adverse effects or loss of effectiveness. Shake canister well before use. Administer pressurized inhalation during the second half of inspiration, as the airways are open wider and the aerosol distribution is more extensive. If more than one inhalation per dose

is necessary, wait at least 1 full minute between inhalations - second inhalation is best delivered after 10 minutes. May cause nervousness, restlessness, insomnia; if these effects continue after dosage reduction, notify physician. Also notify physician if palpitations, tachycardia, chest pain, muscle tremors, dizziness, headache, flushing, or if breathing difficulty persists.

Additional Information
Isoetharine hydrochloride: Arm-a-Med® isoetharine, Beta-2®, Bronkosol®, Dey-Lute® isoetharine
Isoetharine mesylate: Bronkometer®

Dosage Forms
Aerosol, oral, as mesylate: 340 mcg/metered spray
Solution, inhalation, as hydrochloride: 0.062% (4 mL); 0.08% (3.5 mL); 0.1% (2.5 mL, 5 mL); 0.125% (4 mL); 0.167% (3 mL); 0.17% (3 mL); 0.2% (2.5 mL); 0.25% (2 mL, 3.5 mL); 0.5% (0.5 mL); 1% (0.5 mL, 0.25 mL, 10 mL, 14 mL, 30 mL)

♦ **Isoetharine Hydrochloride** see Isoetharine on previous page

♦ **Isoetharine Mesylate** see Isoetharine on previous page

Isoflurophate (eye soe FLURE oh fate)

Related Information
Glaucoma Drug Therapy Comparison on page 1322

U.S. Brand Names Floropryl® Ophthalmic

Synonyms DFP; Diisopropyl Fluorophosphate; Dyflos; Fluostigmin

Therapeutic Category Cholinergic Agent, Ophthalmic; Ophthalmic Agent, Miotic

Use Treat primary open-angle glaucoma and conditions that obstruct aqueous outflow and to treat accommodative convergent strabismus

Pregnancy Risk Factor X

Contraindications Active uveal inflammation, angle-closure (narrow-angle) glaucoma, known hypersensitivity to isoflurophate, pregnancy

Warnings/Precautions May retard corneal healing; because of the tendency to produce more severe adverse effects, use the lowest dose possible; keep frequency of use to a minimum to avoid cyst formation; some products may contain sulfites

Adverse Reactions
1% to 10%: Ocular: Stinging, burning eyes, myopia, visual blurring
<1%: Bradycardia, hypotension, flushing, nausea, vomiting, diarrhea, muscle weakness, retinal detachment, browache, miosis, twitching eyelids, watering eyes, dyspnea, diaphoresis

Overdosage/Toxicology
Symptoms of overdose include excessive salivation, urinary incontinence, dyspnea, diarrhea, profuse sweating
If systemic effects occur, administer parenteral atropine; for severe muscle weakness; pralidoxime may be used in addition to atropine

Drug Interactions Increased toxicity: Succinylcholine, systemic anticholinesterases, carbamate or organic phosphate insecticides, may decrease cholinesterase levels

Stability Protect from moisture, freezing, excessive heat

Mechanism of Action Cholinesterase inhibitor that causes contraction of the iris and ciliary muscles producing miosis, reduced intraocular pressure, and increased aqueous humor outflow

Pharmacodynamics/Kinetics
Peak IOP reduction: 24 hours; Duration: 1 week
Onset of miosis: Within 5-10 minutes; Duration: Up to 4 weeks

Usual Dosage Adults: Ophthalmic:
Glaucoma: Instill 0.25" strip in eye every 8-72 hours
Strabismus: Instill 0.25" strip to each eye every night for 2 weeks then reduce to 0.25" every other night to once weekly for 2 months

Patient Information Notify physician if abdominal cramps, diarrhea, or salivation occur

Nursing Implications Keep tube tightly closed to prevent absorption of moisture and loss of potency

Dosage Forms Ointment, ophthalmic: 0.025% in polyethylene mineral oil gel (3.5 g)

♦ **Isollyl® Improved** see Butalbital Compound on page 165

Isoniazid (eye soe NYE a zid)

Related Information
Antacid Drug Interactions on page 1296
Guidelines for the Prevention of Opportunistic Infections in Persons with HIV on page 1388
Tuberculosis Prophylaxis on page 1386
Tuberculosis Treatment Guidelines on page 1432
Tyramine Content of Foods on page 1525

U.S. Brand Names Laniazid®; Nydrazid®

Canadian Brand Names PMS-Isoniazid

Synonyms INH; Isonicotinic Acid Hydrazide

Therapeutic Category Antitubercular Agent

Use Treatment of susceptible tuberculosis infections and prophylactically to those individuals exposed to tuberculosis

Pregnancy Risk Factor C

Contraindications Acute liver disease; hypersensitivity to isoniazid or any component; previous history of hepatic damage during isoniazid therapy
(Continued)

Isoniazid *(Continued)*

Warnings/Precautions Use with caution in patients with renal impairment and chronic liver disease. Severe and sometimes fatal hepatitis may occur or develop even after many months of treatment; patients must report any prodromal symptoms of hepatitis, such as fatigue, weakness, malaise, anorexia, nausea, or vomiting. Children with low milk and low meat intake should receive concomitant pyridoxine therapy. Periodic ophthalmic examinations are recommended even when usual symptoms do not occur; pyridoxine (10-50 mg/day) is recommended in individuals likely to develop peripheral neuropathies.

Adverse Reactions

>10%:
Gastrointestinal: Loss of appetite, nausea, vomiting, stomach pain
Hepatic: Mild increased LFTs (10% to 20%)
Neuromuscular & skeletal: Weakness, peripheral neuropathy (dose-related incidence, 10% to 20% incidence with 10 mg/kg/day)

1% to 10%:
Central nervous system: Dizziness, slurred speech, lethargy
Hepatic: Progressive liver damage (increases with age; 2.3% in patients >50 years of age)
Neuromuscular & skeletal: Hyper-reflexia

<1%: Fever, seizures, mental depression, psychosis, rash, blood dyscrasias, arthralgia, blurred vision, loss of vision

Overdosage/Toxicology

Symptoms of overdose include nausea, vomiting, slurred speech, dizziness, blurred vision, hallucinations, stupor, coma, intractable seizures, onset of metabolic acidosis is 30 minutes to 3 hours. Because of the severe morbidity and high mortality rates with isoniazid overdose, patients who are asymptomatic after an overdose, should be monitored for 4-6 hours.

Pyridoxine has been shown to be effective in the treatment of intoxication, especially when seizures occur. Pyridoxine I.V. is administered on a milligram to milligram dose. If the amount of isoniazid ingested is unknown, 5 g of pyridoxine should be given over 3-5 minutes and may be followed by an additional 5 g in 30 minutes. Treatment is supportive; may require airway protection, ventilation; diazepam for seizures, sodium bicarbonate for acidosis; forced diuresis and hemodialysis can result in more rapid removal.

Drug Interactions CYP2E1 enzyme substrate; CYP2E1 enzyme inducer; and CYP1A2, 2C, 2C9, 2C18, 2C19, and 3A3/4 enzyme inhibitor
Decreased effect of ketoconazole with isoniazid
Decreased effect/levels of isoniazid with aluminum salts
Increased toxicity/levels of oral anticoagulants, carbamazepine, cycloserine, meperidine, hydantoins, hepatically metabolized benzodiazepines with isoniazid; reaction with disulfiram occurs; enflurane with isoniazid may result in renal failure especially in rapid acetylators
Increased hepatic toxicity with alcohol or with rifampin and isoniazid

Stability Protect oral dosage forms from light

Mechanism of Action Unknown, but may include the inhibition of myocolic acid synthesis resulting in disruption of the bacterial cell wall

Pharmacodynamics/Kinetics

Absorption: Rapid and complete; rate can be slowed when orally administered with food
Distribution: Crosses the placenta; appears in breast milk; distributes into all body tissues and fluids including the CSF
Protein binding: 10% to 15%
Metabolism: By the liver with decay rate determined genetically by acetylation phenotype
Half-life: Fast acetylators: 30-100 minutes; Slow acetylators: 2-5 hours; half-life may be prolonged in patients with impaired hepatic function or severe renal impairment
Time to peak serum concentration: Within 1-2 hours
Elimination: In urine (75% to 95%), feces, and saliva

Usual Dosage Recommendations often change due to resistant strains and newly developed information; consult *MMWR* for current CDC recommendations: **Oral** (intramuscular is available in patients who are unable to either take or absorb oral therapy):
Note: A four-drug regimen (isoniazid, rifampin, pyrazinamide, and either streptomycin or ethambutol) is preferred for the initial, empiric treatment of TB. When the drug susceptibility results are available, the regimen should be altered as appropriate.

Infants and Children:
Prophylaxis: 10 mg/kg/day in 1-2 divided doses (maximum: 300 mg/day) 6 months in patients who do not have HIV infection and 12 months in patients who have HIV infection
Treatment:
Daily therapy: 10-20 mg/kg/day in 1-2 divided doses (maximum: 300 mg/day)
Directly observed therapy (DOT): Twice weekly therapy: 20-40 mg/kg (maximum: 900 mg/day); 3 times/week therapy: 20-40 mg/kg (maximum: 900 mg)

Adults:
Prophylaxis: 300 mg/day for 6 months in patients who do not have HIV infection and 12 months in patients who have HIV infection
Treatment:
Daily therapy: 5 mg/kg/day given daily (usual dose: 300 mg/day); 10 mg/kg/day in 1-2 divided doses in patients with disseminated disease
Directly observed therapy (DOT): Twice weekly therapy: 15 mg/kg (maximum: 900 mg); 3 times/week therapy: 15 mg/kg (maximum: 900 mg)

Note: Concomitant administration of 6-50 mg/day pyridoxine is recommended in malnourished patients or those prone to neuropathy (eg, alcoholics, diabetics)

Hemodialysis: Dialyzable (50% to 100%)
Administer dose postdialysis

Peritoneal dialysis effects: Dose for Cl_{cr} <10 mL/minute

Continuous arteriovenous or venovenous hemofiltration (CAVH/CAVHD): Dose for Cl_{cr} <10 mL/minute

Dosing adjustment in hepatic impairment: Dose should be reduced in severe hepatic disease

Monitoring Parameters Periodic liver function tests; monitoring for prodromal signs of hepatitis

Reference Range Therapeutic: 1-7 µg/mL (SI: 7-51 µmol/L); Toxic: 20-710 µg/mL (SI: 146-5176 µmol/L)

Test Interactions False-positive urinary glucose with Clinitest®

Patient Information Report any prodromal symptoms of hepatitis (fatigue, weakness, nausea, vomiting, dark urine, or yellowing of eyes) or any burning, tingling, or numbness in the extremities

Dosage Forms
Injection: 100 mg/mL (10 mL)
Syrup (orange flavor): 50 mg/5 mL (473 mL)
Tablet: 50 mg, 100 mg, 300 mg

Extemporaneous Preparations A 10 mg/mL oral suspension was stable for 21 days when refrigerated when compounded as follows:
Triturate ten 10 mg tablets in a mortar, reduce to a fine powder, then add 10 mL of purified water U.S.P. to make a paste; then transfer to a graduate and qs to 100 mL with sorbitol (do not use sugar-based solutions)
Shake well before using and keep in refrigerator

Nahata MC and Hipple TF, *Pediatric Drug Formulations*, 3rd ed, Cincinnati, OH: Harvey Whitney Books Co, 1997.

- ♦ **Isonicotinic Acid Hydrazide** see Isoniazid *on page 633*
- ♦ **Isonipecaine Hydrochloride** see Meperidine *on page 728*
- ♦ **Isopap®** see Acetaminophen, Isometheptene, and Dichloralphenazone *on page 22*
- ♦ **Isoprenaline Hydrochloride** see Isoproterenol *on this page*
- ♦ **Isopro®** see Isoproterenol *on this page*

Isoproterenol (eye soe proe TER e nole)

Related Information
Adrenergic Agonists, Cardiovascular Comparison *on page 1290*
Adult ACLS Algorithm, Bradycardia *on page 1452*
Bronchodilators, Comparison of Inhaled and Sympathomimetic *on page 1314*

U.S. Brand Names Aerolone®; Arm-a-Med® Isoproterenol; Dey-Dose® Isoproterenol; Dispos-a-Med® Isoproterenol; Isopro®; Isuprel®; Medihaler-Iso®; Norisodrine®; Vapo-Iso®

Synonyms Isoprenaline Hydrochloride; Isoproterenol Hydrochloride; Isoproterenol Sulfate

Therapeutic Category Adrenergic Agonist Agent; Bronchodilator; Sympathomimetic

Use Treatment of reversible airway obstruction as in asthma or COPD; used parenterally in ventricular arrhythmias due to A-V nodal block; hemodynamically compromised brady-arrhythmias or atropine-resistant bradyarrhythmias; temporary use in third degree A-V block until pacemaker insertion; low cardiac output; vasoconstrictive shock states

Pregnancy Risk Factor C

Contraindications Angina, pre-existing cardiac arrhythmias (ventricular); tachycardia or A-V block caused by cardiac glycoside intoxication; allergy to sulfites or isoproterenol or other sympathomimetic amines

Warnings/Precautions Elderly patients, diabetics, renal or cardiovascular disease, hyperthyroidism; excessive or prolonged use may result in decreased effectiveness

Adverse Reactions
>10%:
Central nervous system: Insomnia, restlessness
Gastrointestinal: Dry throat, xerostomia, discoloration of saliva (pinkish-red)
1% to 10%:
Cardiovascular: Flushing of the face or skin, ventricular arrhythmias, tachycardias, profound hypotension, hypertension
Central nervous system: Nervousness, anxiety, dizziness, headache, lightheadedness
Gastrointestinal: Vomiting, nausea
Neuromuscular & skeletal: Trembling, tremor, weakness
Miscellaneous: Diaphoresis
<1%: Arrhythmias, chest pain, paradoxical bronchospasm

Overdosage/Toxicology
Symptoms of overdose include tremors, nausea, vomiting, hypotension; beta-adrenergic stimulation can cause increased heart rate, decreased blood pressure, and CNS excitation
Heart rate can be treated with beta-blockers, decreased blood pressure can be treated with pure alpha-adrenergic agents, diazepam 0.07 mg/kg can be used for excitation, seizures

Drug Interactions Increased toxicity: Sympathomimetic agents may cause headaches and elevate blood pressure; general anesthetics may cause arrhythmias
(Continued)

Isoproterenol *(Continued)*

Stability

Isoproterenol solution should be stored at room temperature; it should not be used if a color or precipitate is present

Exposure to air, light, or increased temperature may cause a pink to brownish pink color to develop

Stability of parenteral admixture at room temperature (25°C) or at refrigeration (4°C): 24 hours

Standard diluent: 2 mg/500 mL D_5W; 4 mg/500 mL D_5W

Minimum volume: 1 mg/100 mL D_5W

Incompatible with alkaline solutions, aminophylline and furosemide

Mechanism of Action Stimulates beta$_1$- and beta$_2$-receptors resulting in relaxation of bronchial, GI, and uterine smooth muscle, increased heart rate and contractility, vasodilation of peripheral vasculature

Pharmacodynamics/Kinetics

Onset of bronchodilation: Oral inhalation: Immediately

Time to peak serum concentration: Oral: Within 1-2 hours

Duration: Oral inhalation: 1 hour; S.C.: Up to 2 hours

Metabolism: By conjugation in many tissues including the liver and lungs

Half-life: 2.5-5 minutes

Elimination: In urine principally as sulfate conjugates

Usual Dosage

Children:

Bronchodilation: Inhalation: Metered dose inhaler: 1-2 metered doses up to 5 times/day

Bronchodilation (using 1:200 inhalation solution) 0.01 mL/kg/dose every 4 hours as needed (maximum: 0.05 mL/dose) diluted with NS to 2 mL

Sublingual: 5-10 mg every 3-4 hours, not to exceed 30 mg/day

Cardiac arrhythmias: I.V.: Start 0.1 mcg/kg/minute (usual effective dose 0.2-2 mcg/kg/minute)

Adults:

Bronchodilation: Inhalation: Metered dose inhaler: 1-2 metered doses 4-6 times/day

Bronchodilation: 1-2 inhalations of a 0.25% solution, no more than 2 inhalations at any one time (1-5 minutes between inhalations); no more than 6 inhalations in any hour during a 24-hour period; maintenance therapy: 1-2 inhalations 4-6 times/day. Alternatively: 0.5% solution via hand bulb nebulizer is 5-15 deep inhalations repeated once in 5-10 minutes if necessary; treatments may be repeated up to 5 times/day.

Sublingual: 10-20 mg every 3-4 hours; not to exceed 60 mg/day

Cardiac arrhythmias: I.V.: 5 mcg/minute initially, titrate to patient response (2-20 mcg/minute)

Shock: I.V.: 0.5-5 mcg/minute; adjust according to response

Administration Administer around-the-clock to promote less variation in peak and trough serum levels; I.V. infusion administration requires the use of an infusion pump

To prepare for infusion:

$$\frac{6 \times weight~(kg) \times desired~dose~(mcg/kg/min)}{I.V.~infusion~rate~(mL/h)} = \frac{mg~of~drug~to~be~added~to}{100~mL~of~I.V.~fluid}$$

Monitoring Parameters EKG, heart rate, respiratory rate, arterial blood gas, arterial blood pressure, CVP

Patient Information Do not exceed recommended dosage; excessive use may lead to adverse effects or loss of effectiveness. Shake canister well before use. Administer pressurized inhalation during the second half of inspiration, as the airways are open wider and the aerosol distribution is more extensive. If more than one inhalation per dose is necessary, wait at least 1 full minute between inhalations - second inhalation is best delivered after 10 minutes. May cause nervousness, restlessness, insomnia; if these effects continue after dosage reduction, notify physician. Notify physician if palpitations, tachycardia, chest pain, muscle tremors, dizziness, headache, flushing or if breathing difficulty persists. Do not chew or swallow sublingual tablet.

Nursing Implications Elderly may find it useful to utilize a spacer device when using a metered dose inhaler

Additional Information

Isoproterenol hydrochloride: Aerolone®, Dey-Dose® isoproterenol, Dispos-a-Med® isoproterenol, Isopro®, Isuprel®, Norisodrine®, Vapo-Iso®

Isoproterenol sulfate: Medihaler-Iso®

Dosage Forms

Inhalation:

Aerosol: 0.2% (1:500) (15 mL, 22.5 mL); 0.25% (1:400) (15 mL)

Solution for nebulization: 0.031% (4 mL); 0.062% (4 mL); 0.25% (0.5 mL, 30 mL); 0.5% (0.5 mL, 1 mL, 60 mL); 1% (10 mL)

Injection: 0.2 mg/mL (1:5000) (1 mL, 5 mL, 10 mL)

Tablet, sublingual: 10 mg, 15 mg

Isoproterenol and Phenylephrine

(eye soe proe TER e nole & fen il EF rin)

U.S. Brand Names Duo-Medihaler® Aerosol

Therapeutic Category Adrenergic Agonist Agent

Dosage Forms Aerosol: Each actuation releases isoproterenol hydrochloride 0.16 mg and phenylephrine bitartrate 0.24 mg (15 mL, 22.5 mL)

♦ **Isoproterenol Hydrochloride** *see Isoproterenol on page 635*

♦ **Isoproterenol Sulfate** *see Isoproterenol on page 635*

♦ **Isoptin®** *see Verapamil on page 1214*

♦ **Isoptin® SR** *see Verapamil on page 1214*

♦ **Isopto® Atropine Ophthalmic** *see Atropine on page 111*

♦ **Isopto® Carbachol Ophthalmic** *see Carbachol on page 188*

♦ **Isopto® Carpine Ophthalmic** *see Pilocarpine on page 927*

♦ **Isopto® Cetamide® Ophthalmic** *see Sulfacetamide Sodium on page 1091*

♦ **Isopto® Cetapred® Ophthalmic** *see Sulfacetamide Sodium and Prednisolone on page 1091*

♦ **Isopto® Eserine** *see Physostigmine on page 925*

♦ **Isopto® Frin Ophthalmic Solution** *see Phenylephrine on page 918*

♦ **Isopto® Homatropine Ophthalmic** *see Homatropine on page 569*

♦ **Isopto® Hyoscine Ophthalmic** *see Scopolamine on page 1051*

♦ **Isordil®** *see Isosorbide Dinitrate on this page*

Isosorbide (eye soe SOR bide)

U.S. Brand Names Ismotic®

Therapeutic Category Diuretic, Osmotic; Ophthalmic Agent, Osmotic

Use Short-term emergency treatment of acute angle-closure glaucoma and short-term reduction of intraocular pressure prior to and following intraocular surgery; may be used to interrupt an acute glaucoma attack; preferred agent when need to avoid nausea and vomiting

Pregnancy Risk Factor B

Contraindications Severe renal disease, anuria, severe dehydration, acute pulmonary edema, severe cardiac decompensation, known hypersensitivity to isosorbide

Warnings/Precautions Use with caution in patients with impending pulmonary edema and in the elderly due to the elderly's predisposition to dehydration and the fact that they frequently have concomitant diseases which may be aggravated by the use of isosorbide; hypernatremia and dehydration may begin to occur after 72 hours of continuous administration. Maintain fluid/electrolyte balance with multiple doses; monitor urinary output; if urinary output declines, need to review clinical status.

Adverse Reactions
1% to 10%:
 Central nervous system: Headache, confusion, disorientation
 Gastrointestinal: Vomiting
<1%: Syncope, lethargy, vertigo, dizziness, lightheadedness, irritability, rash, hypernatremia, hyperosmolarity, nausea, abdominal/gastric discomfort (infrequently), anorexia, hiccups, thirst

Overdosage/Toxicology
Symptoms of overdose include dehydration, hypotension, hyponatremia
General supportive care, fluid administration, electrolyte balance, discontinue agent

Mechanism of Action Elevates osmolarity of glomerular filtrate to hinder the tubular resorption of water and increase excretion of sodium and chloride to result in diuresis; creates an osmotic gradient between plasma and ocular fluids

Pharmacodynamics/Kinetics
Onset of action: Within 10-30 minutes
Peak action: 1-1.5 hours
Duration: 5-6 hours
Distribution: In total body water
Metabolism: Not metabolized
Half-life: 5-9.5 hours
Elimination: By glomerular filtration; see Mechanism of Action

Usual Dosage Adults: Oral: Initial: 1.5 g/kg with a usual range of 1-3 g/kg 2-4 times/day as needed

Monitoring Parameters Monitor for signs of dehydration, blood pressure, renal output, intraocular pressure reduction

Nursing Implications Palatability may be improved if poured over ice and sipped

Additional Information Each 220 mL contains isosorbide 100 g, sodium 4.6 mEq, and potassium 0.9 mEq

Dosage Forms Solution: 45% [450 mg/mL] (220 mL)

Isosorbide Dinitrate (eye soe SOR bide dye NYE trate)

Related Information
Heart Failure: Management of Patients With Left-Ventricular Systolic Dysfunction *on page 1472*
Nitrates Comparison *on page 1334*

U.S. Brand Names Dilatrate®-SR; Isordil®; Sorbitrate®

Canadian Brand Names Apo®-ISDN; Cedocard®-SR; Coradur®

Synonyms ISD; ISDN

Therapeutic Category Antianginal Agent; Nitrate; Vasodilator, Coronary

Use Prevention and treatment of angina pectoris; for congestive heart failure; to relieve pain, dysphagia, and spasm in esophageal spasm with GE reflux

Pregnancy Risk Factor C
(Continued)

Isosorbide Dinitrate *(Continued)*

Contraindications Severe anemia, closed-angle glaucoma, postural hypotension, cerebral hemorrhage, head trauma, hypersensitivity to isosorbide dinitrate or any component

Warnings/Precautions Use with caution in patients with increased intracranial pressure, hypotension, hypovolemia, glaucoma; sustained release products may be absorbed erratically in patients with GI hypermotility or malabsorption syndrome; do not crush or chew sublingual dosage form; abrupt withdrawal may result in angina; tolerance may develop (adjust dose or change agent)

Adverse Reactions
>10%:
　　Cardiovascular: Flushing, postural hypotension
　　Central nervous system: Headache, lightheadedness, dizziness
　　Neuromuscular & skeletal: Weakness
1% to 10%: Dermatologic: Drug rash, exfoliative dermatitis
<1%: Nausea, vomiting, methemoglobinemia (overdose)

Overdosage/Toxicology
Symptoms of overdose which are most common include hypotension, throbbing headache, tachycardia, and flushing. Methemoglobinemia may occur with massive doses; hypotension may aggravate symptoms of cardiac ischemia or cerebrovascular disease and may even cause seizures (rare).

Treatment consists of placing patient in recumbent position and administering fluids; alpha-adrenergic vasopressors may be required; treat methemoglobinemia with oxygen and methylene blue at a dose of 1-2 mg/kg I.V. slowly.

Mechanism of Action Stimulation of intracellular cyclic-GMP results in vascular smooth muscle relaxation of both arterial and venous vasculature. Increased venous pooling decreases left ventricular pressure (preload) and arterial dilatation decreases arterial resistance (afterload). Therefore, this reduces cardiac oxygen demand by decreasing left ventricular pressure and systemic vascular resistance by dilating arteries. Additionally, coronary artery dilation improves collateral flow to ischemic regions; esophageal smooth muscle is relaxed via the same mechanism.

Pharmacodynamics/Kinetics See table.

Dosage Form	Onset of Action	Duration
Sublingual tablet	2-10 min	1-2 h
Chewable tablet	3 min	0.5-2 h
Oral tablet	45-60 min	4-6 h
Sustained release tablet	30 min	6-12 h

Metabolism: Extensive in the liver to conjugated metabolites, including isosorbide 5-mononitrate (active) and 2-mononitrate (active)
Half-life: Parent drug: 1-4 hours; Metabolite (5-mononitrate): 4 hours
Elimination: In urine and feces

Usual Dosage Adults (elderly should be given lowest recommended daily doses initially and titrate upward): Oral:
Angina: 5-40 mg 4 times/day or 40 mg every 8-12 hours in sustained-release dosage form
Congestive heart failure:
　　Initial dose: 10 mg 3 times/day
　　Target dose: 40 mg 3 times/day
　　Maximum dose: 80 mg 3 times/day
　　Sublingual: 2.5-10 mg every 4-6 hours
　　Chew: 5-10 mg every 2-3 hours
Tolerance to nitrate effects develops with chronic exposure
Dose escalation does not overcome this effect. Tolerance can only be overcome by short periods of nitrate absence from the body. Short periods (14 hours) or nitrate withdrawal help minimize tolerance.
Hemodialysis: During hemodialysis, administer dose postdialysis or administer supplemental 10-20 mg dose
Peritoneal dialysis: Supplemental dose is not necessary
See Administration

Administration Do not administer around-the-clock; the first dose of nitrates should be administered in a physician's office to observe for maximal cardiovascular dynamic effects and adverse effects (orthostatic blood pressure drop, headache); when immediate release products are prescribed twice daily - recommend 7 AM and noon; for 3 times/day dosing - recommend 7 AM, noon, and 5 PM; when sustained-release products are indicated, suggest once a day in morning or via twice daily dosing at 8 AM and 2 PM

Monitoring Parameters Monitor for orthostasis

Test Interactions ↓ cholesterol (S)

Patient Information Do not chew or crush sublingual or sustained release dosage form; do not change brands without consulting your pharmacist or physician; keep tablets or capsules in original container and keep container tightly closed; if no relief from sublingual tablets after 15 minutes, report to nearest emergency room or seek emergency help

Nursing Implications 8- to 12-hour nitrate-free interval is needed each day to prevent tolerance

Dosage Forms
Capsule, sustained release: 40 mg

Tablet:
    Chewable: 5 mg, 10 mg
    Oral: 5 mg, 10 mg, 20 mg, 30 mg, 40 mg
    Sublingual: 2.5 mg, 5 mg, 10 mg
    Sustained release: 40 mg

Isosorbide Mononitrate (eye soe SOR bide mon oh NYE trate)

Related Information
  Nitrates Comparison *on page 1334*

U.S. Brand Names Imdur™; Ismo®; Monoket®

Synonyms ISMN

Therapeutic Category Antianginal Agent; Nitrate; Vasodilator, Coronary

Use Long-acting metabolite of the vasodilator isosorbide dinitrate used for the prophylactic treatment of angina pectoris

Pregnancy Risk Factor B

Contraindications Contraindicated due to potential increases in intracranial pressure in patients with head trauma or cerebral hemorrhage; hypersensitivity or idiosyncrasy to nitrates

Warnings/Precautions Postural hypotension, transient episodes of weakness, dizziness, or syncope may occur even with small doses; alcohol accentuates these effects; tolerance and cross-tolerance to nitrate antianginal and hemodynamic effects may occur during prolonged isosorbide mononitrate therapy; (minimized by using the smallest effective dose, by alternating coronary vasodilators or offering drug-free intervals of as little as 12 hours). Excessive doses may result in severe headache, blurred vision, or dry mouth; increased anginal symptoms may be a result of dosage increases.

Adverse Reactions
  >10%: Central nervous system: Headache
  1% to 10%: Gastrointestinal: Dizziness, nausea, vomiting
  <1%: Angina pectoris, arrhythmias, atrial fibrillation, hypotension, palpitations, postural hypotension, premature ventricular contractions, supraventricular tachycardia, syncope, edema, malaise, agitation, anxiety, confusion, hypoesthesia, insomnia, nervousness, nightmares, pruritus, rash, abdominal pain, diarrhea, dyspepsia, tenesmus, increased appetite, tooth disorder, impotence, polyuria, dysuria, methemoglobinemia (rarely with very high doses), neck stiffness, rigors, arthralgia, dyscoordination, weakness, blurred vision, diplopia, bronchitis, pneumonia, upper respiratory tract infection, cold sweat

Overdosage/Toxicology
  Symptoms of overdose which are most common include hypotension, throbbing headache, tachycardia, and flushing. Methemoglobinemia may occur with massive doses; hypotension may aggravate symptoms of cardiac ischemia or cerebrovascular disease and may even cause seizures (rare).
  Treatment consists of placing patient in recumbent position and administering fluids; alpha-adrenergic vasopressors may be required; treat methemoglobinemia with oxygen and methylene blue at a dose of 1-2 mg/kg I.V. slowly.

Stability Tablets should be stored in a tight container at room temperature of 15°C to 30°C (59°F to 86°F)

Mechanism of Action Prevailing mechanism of action for nitroglycerin (and other nitrates) is systemic venodilation, decreasing preload as measured by pulmonary capillary wedge pressure and left ventricular end diastolic volume and pressure; the average reduction in left ventricular end diastolic volume is 25% at rest, with a corresponding increase in ejection fractions of 50% to 60%. This effect improves congestive symptoms in heart failure and improves the myocardial perfusion gradient in patients with coronary artery disease.

Pharmacodynamics/Kinetics
  Absorption: Oral: Nearly complete and low intersubject variability in its pharmacokinetic parameters and plasma concentrations
  Metabolism: Metabolite of isosorbide dinitrate
  Half-life: Mononitrate: ~4 hours (8 times that of dinitrate)

Usual Dosage Adults: Oral:
  Regular tablet: 20 mg twice daily separated by 7 hours; may initiate with 5-10 mg
  Extended release tablet (Imdur™): Initial: 30-60 mg once daily; after several days the dosage may be increased to 120 mg/day (given as two 60 mg tablets); daily dose should be taken in the morning upon arising; rarely, 240 mg may be needed
  Asymmetrical dosing regimen of 7 AM and 3 PM or 9 AM and 5 PM to allow for a nitrate-free dosing interval to minimize nitrate tolerance
  Dosing adjustment in renal impairment: Not necessary for elderly or patients with altered renal or hepatic function

Dietary Considerations Alcohol: Has been found to exhibit additive effects of this variety

Administration Do not administer around-the-clock; Monoket® and Ismo® should be scheduled twice daily with doses 7 hours apart (8 AM and 3 PM); Imdur™ may be given once daily

Monitoring Parameters Monitor for orthostasis

Patient Information Dispense drug in easy-to-open container; do not change brands without consulting pharmacist or physician; keep tablets or capsules tightly closed in original container; extended release tablets should not be chewed or crushed and should be swallowed together with a half-glassful of fluid; the antianginal efficacy of tablets can be maintained by carefully following the prescribed schedule of dosing (2 doses taken 7 hours apart); headaches are sometimes a marker of the activity of the drug
(Continued)

Isosorbide Mononitrate *(Continued)*

Nursing Implications Do not crush; 8- to 12-hour nitrate-free interval is needed each day to prevent tolerance

Dosage Forms
Tablet (Ismo®, Monoket®): 10 mg, 20 mg
Tablet, extended release (Imdur™): 30 mg, 60 mg, 120 mg

Isotretinoin *(eye soe TRET i noyn)*

U.S. Brand Names Accutane®

Canadian Brand Names Isotrex®

Synonyms 13-*cis*-Retinoic Acid

Therapeutic Category Acne Products; Retinoic Acid Derivative; Vitamin A Derivative; Vitamin, Fat Soluble

Use Treatment of severe recalcitrant cystic and/or conglobate acne unresponsive to conventional therapy

Investigational: Treatment of children with metastatic neuroblastoma or leukemia that does not respond to conventional therapy

Pregnancy Risk Factor X

Contraindications Sensitivity to parabens, vitamin A, or other retinoids; patients who are pregnant or intend to become pregnant during treatment

Warnings/Precautions Use with caution in patients with diabetes mellitus, hypertriglyceridemia; **not to be used in women of childbearing potential** unless woman is capable of complying with effective contraceptive measures; therapy is normally begun on the second or third day of next normal menstrual period; effective contraception must be used for at least 1 month before beginning therapy, during therapy, and for 1 month after discontinuation of therapy. Because of the high likelihood of teratogenic effects (~20%), do not prescribe isotretinoin for women who are or who are likely to become pregnant while using the drug. Isolated reports of depression, psychosis and rarely suicidal thoughts and actions have been reported during isotretinoin usage.

Adverse Reactions
>10%:
Dermatologic: Redness, cheilitis, inflammation of lips, dry skin, pruritus, photosensitivity
Endocrine & metabolic: Increased serum concentration of triglycerides
Gastrointestinal: Xerostomia
Local: Burning
Neuromuscular & skeletal: Bone pain, arthralgia, myalgia
Ocular: Itching eyes
Respiratory: Epistaxis, dry nose
1% to 10%:
Cardiovascular: Facial edema, pallor
Central nervous system: Fatigue, headache, mental depression, hypothermia
Dermatologic: Skin peeling on hands or soles of feet, rash, cellulitis
Endocrine & metabolic: Fluid imbalance, acidosis
Gastrointestinal: Stomach upset
Hepatic: Ascites
Neuromuscular & skeletal: Flank pain
Ocular: Dry eyes, photophobia
Miscellaneous: Lymph disorders
<1%: Mood change, pseudomotor cerebri, alopecia, pruritus, hyperuricemia, xerostomia, anorexia, nausea, vomiting, inflammatory bowel syndrome, bleeding of gums, increase in erythrocyte sedimentation rate, decrease in hemoglobin and hematocrit, hepatitis, conjunctivitis, corneal opacities, optic neuritis, cataracts

Overdosage/Toxicology Symptoms of overdose include headache, vomiting, flushing, abdominal pain, ataxia; all signs and symptoms have been transient

Drug Interactions
Decreased effect: Increased clearance of carbamazepine
Increased toxicity: Avoid other vitamin A products; may interfere with medications used to treat hypertriglyceridemia

Stability Store at room temperature and protect from light

Mechanism of Action Reduces sebaceous gland size and reduces sebum production; regulates cell proliferation and differentiation

Pharmacodynamics/Kinetics
Absorption: Oral: Demonstrates biphasic absorption
Distribution: Crosses the placenta; appears in breast milk
Protein binding: 99% to 100%
Metabolism: In the liver; major metabolite: 4-oxo-isotretinoin (active)
Half-life, terminal: Parent drug: 10-20 hours; Metabolite: 11-50 hours
Time to peak serum concentration: Within 3 hours
Elimination: Equally in urine and feces

Usual Dosage Oral:
Children: Maintenance therapy for neuroblastoma: 100-250 mg/m^2/day in 2 divided doses has been used investigationally
Children and Adults: 0.5-2 mg/kg/day in 2 divided doses (dosages as low as 0.05 mg/kg/day have been reported to be beneficial) for 15-20 weeks or until the total cyst count decreases by 70%, whichever is sooner
Dosing adjustment in hepatic impairment: Dose reductions empirically are recommended in hepatitis disease

Monitoring Parameters CBC with differential and platelet count, baseline sedimentation rate, serum triglycerides, liver enzymes

Patient Information Avoid pregnancy during therapy; effective contraceptive measures must be used since this drug may harm the fetus; there is information from manufacturers about this product that you should receive. Discontinue therapy if visual difficulties, abdominal pain, rectal bleeding, diarrhea; exacerbation of acne may occur during first weeks of therapy. Avoid use of other vitamin A products. Decreased tolerance to contact lenses may occur. Do not donate blood for at least 1 month following stopping of the drug. Loss of night vision may occur, avoid prolonged exposure to sunlight. Do not double next dose if dose is skipped. Isolated reports of depression, psychosis, and rarely suicidal thoughts and actions have been reported during isotretinoin usage.

Nursing Implications Capsules can be swallowed, or chewed and swallowed. The capsule may be opened with a large needle and the contents placed on applesauce or ice cream for patients unable to swallow the capsule.

Dosage Forms Capsule: 10 mg, 20 mg, 40 mg

♦ **Isotrex**® *see Isotretinoin on previous page*

Isoxsuprine (eye SOKS syoo preen)

U.S. Brand Names Vasodilan®; Voxsuprine®

Therapeutic Category Vasodilator

Use Treatment of peripheral vascular diseases, such as arteriosclerosis obliterans and Raynaud's disease

Pregnancy Risk Factor C

Contraindications Presence of arterial bleeding; do not administer immediately postpartum

Usual Dosage Adults: 10-20 mg 3-4 times/day; start with lower dose in elderly due to potential hypotension

Additional Information Complete prescribing information for this medication should be consulted for additional detail

Dosage Forms Tablet, as hydrochloride: 10 mg, 20 mg

Isradipine (iz RA di peen)

Related Information

Calcium Channel Blockers Comparison *on page 1315*

U.S. Brand Names DynaCirc®

Therapeutic Category Antihypertensive Agent; Antimigraine Agent; Calcium Channel Blocker

Use Treatment of hypertension, congestive heart failure, migraine prophylaxis

Pregnancy Risk Factor C

Pregnancy/Breast-Feeding Implications

Clinical effects on the fetus: No data on crossing the placenta

Breast-feeding/lactation: No data on crossing into breast milk. Not recommended due to potential harm to infant.

Contraindications Sinus bradycardia; advanced heart block; ventricular tachycardia; cardiogenic shock, hypotension, congestive heart failure; hypersensitivity to isradipine or any component, hypersensitivity to calcium channel blockers and adenosine; atrial fibrillation or flutter associated with accessory conduction pathways; not to be given within a few hours of I.V. beta-blocking agents

Warnings/Precautions Avoid use in hypotension, congestive heart failure, cardiac conduction defects, PVCs, idiopathic hypertrophic subaortic stenosis; may cause platelet inhibition; do not abruptly withdraw (chest pain); may cause hepatic dysfunction or increased angina; increased intracranial pressure with cranial tumors; elderly may have greater hypotensive effect

Adverse Reactions

>10%: Central nervous system: Headache (14%)

1% to 10%:

Cardiovascular: Edema (7%), palpitations (4%), flushing (2.6%), angina (2.4%), tachycardia (1.5%), hypotension

Central nervous system: Dizziness (7%), fatigue (4%)

Dermatologic: Rash (1.5%)

Gastrointestinal: Nausea (1.8%), abdominal discomfort (1.7%), vomiting/diarrhea (1%)

Neuromuscular & skeletal: Weakness (1% to 2%)

Respiratory: Dyspnea (1.8%)

<1%: Heart failure, atrial and ventricular fibrillation, TIAs, A-V block, myocardial infarction, abnormal EKG, disturbed sleep, pruritus, urticaria, xerostomia, nocturia, leukopenia, foot cramps, paresthesia, numbness, visual disturbance, cough

Overdosage/Toxicology The primary cardiac symptoms of calcium blocker overdose include hypotension and bradycardia. The hypotension is caused by peripheral vasodilation, myocardial depression, and bradycardia. Bradycardia results from sinus bradycardia, second- or third-degree atrioventricular block, or sinus arrest with junctional rhythm. Intraventricular conduction is usually not affected so QRS duration is normal (verapamil does prolong the P-R interval and bepridil prolongs the Q-T and may cause ventricular arrhythmias, including torsade de pointes).

The noncardiac symptoms include confusion, stupor, nausea, vomiting, metabolic acidosis and hyperglycemia. Following initial gastric decontamination, if possible, repeated calcium administration may promptly reverse the depressed cardiac contractility (but not sinus node depression or peripheral vasodilation); glucagon, epinephrine, and amrinone may treat refractory hypotension; glucagon and epinephrine also increase (Continued)

Isradipine *(Continued)*

the heart rate (outside the U.S., 4-aminopyridine may be available as an antidote); dialysis and hemoperfusion are not effective in enhancing elimination although repeat-dose activated charcoal may serve as an adjunct with sustained-release preparations.

In a few reported cases, overdose with calcium channel blockers has been associated with hypotension and bradycardia, initially refractory to atropine but becoming more responsive to this agent when larger doses (approaching 1 g/hour for more than 24 hours) of calcium chloride was administered.

Drug Interactions CYP3A3/4 enzyme substrate

Decreased effect:

Isradipine and NSAIDs (diclofenac) may decrease antihypertensive response

Isradipine and lovastatin causes decrease lovastatin effect

Increased toxicity/effect/levels:

Isradipine and beta-blockers may increase cardiovascular adverse effects; with fentanyl, isradipine therapy may cause severe hypotension

Isradipine and cyclosporine may minimally increase cyclosporine levels

Mechanism of Action Inhibits calcium ion from entering the "slow channels" or select voltage-sensitive areas of vascular smooth muscle and myocardium during depolarization, producing a relaxation of coronary vascular smooth muscle and coronary vasodilation; increases myocardial oxygen delivery in patients with vasospastic angina

Pharmacodynamics/Kinetics

Absorption: Oral: 90% to 95%

Protein binding: 95%

Metabolism: In the liver

Bioavailability: Absolute due to first-pass elimination 15% to 24%

Half-life: 8 hours

Time to peak: Serum concentration: 1-1.5 hours

Elimination: Renal excretion by metabolites (cyclic lactone and monoacids)

Usual Dosage Adults: 2.5 mg twice daily; antihypertensive response occurs in 2-3 hours; maximal response in 2-4 weeks; increase dose at 2- to 4-week intervals at 2.5-5 mg increments; usual dose range: 5-20 mg/day. **Note:** Most patients show no improvement with doses >10 mg/day except adverse reaction rate increases

Patient Information Do not discontinue abruptly; report any dizziness, shortness of breath, palpitations, or edema

Additional Information Although there is some initial data which may show increased risk of myocardial infarction following treatment of hypertension with calcium antagonists, controlled trials (eg, ALL-HAT) are ongoing to examine the long-term effects of not only calcium antagonists but other antihypertensives in preventing heart disease. Until these studies are completed, patients taking calcium antagonists should be encouraged to continue with prescribed antihypertensive regimes, although a switch from high-dose, short-acting agents to sustained release products may be warranted.

Dosage Forms Capsule: 2.5 mg, 5 mg

Extemporaneous Preparations A 1 mg/mL oral liquid was stable for 35 days when refrigerated when compounded as follows:

Dissolve the contents of ten 5 mg capsules in simple syrup, qs ad 50 mL

Shake well before using and keep in refrigerator

MacDonald JL, Johnson CE, and Jacobson P, "Stability of Isradipine in Extemporaneously Compounded Oral Liquids," *Am J Hosp Pharm*, 1994, 51(19):2409-11.

♦ **Isuprel®** *see* Isoproterenol *on page 635*

Itraconazole *(i tra KOE na zole)*

Related Information

Antifungal Agents Comparison *on page 1303*

Guidelines for the Prevention of Opportunistic Infections in Persons with HIV *on page 1388*

U.S. Brand Names Sporanox®

Therapeutic Category Antifungal Agent, Imidazole Derivative; Antifungal Agent, Systemic

Use Treatment of susceptible fungal infections in immunocompromised and immunocompetent patients including blastomycosis and histoplasmosis; indicated for aspergillosis, and onychomycosis of the toenail; treatment of onychomycosis of the fingernail without concomitant toenail infection via a pulse-type dosing regimen; has activity against *Aspergillus, Candida, Coccidioides, Cryptococcus, Sporothrix,* tinea unguium

Oral solution (not capsules) is marketed for oral and esophageal candidiasis

Useful in superficial mycoses including dermatophytes (eg, tinea capitis), pityriasis versicolor, sebopsoriasis, vaginal and chronic mucocutaneous candidiases; systemic mycoses including candidiasis, meningeal and disseminated cryptococcal infections, paracoccidioidomycosis, coccidioidomycoses; miscellaneous mycoses such as sporotrichosis, chromomycosis, leishmaniasis, fungal keratitis, alternariosis, zygomycosis

Intravenous solution is indicated in the treatment of blastomycosis, histoplasmosis (nonmeningeal), and aspergillosis (in patients intolerant or refractory to amphotericin B therapy)

Pregnancy Risk Factor C

Contraindications Known hypersensitivity to other azoles; concurrent administration with astemizole, cisapride, lovastatin, midazolam, simvastatin, or triazolam

Warnings/Precautions Rare cases of serious cardiovascular adverse event, including death, ventricular tachycardia and torsade de pointes have been observed due to increased terfenadine and cisapride concentrations induced by itraconazole; patients who develop abnormal liver function tests during itraconazole therapy should be monitored and therapy discontinued if symptoms of liver disease develop

Adverse Reactions Listed incidences are for higher doses appropriate for systemic fungal infections

>10%: Gastrointestinal: Nausea (10.6%)

1% to 10%:

Cardiovascular: Edema (3.5%), hypertension (3.2%)

Central nervous system: Headache (4%), fatigue (2% to 3%), malaise (1.2%), fever (2.5%)

Dermatologic: Rash (8.6%)

Endocrine & metabolic: Decreased libido (1.2%), hypertriglyceridemia

Gastrointestinal: Abdominal pain (1.5%), vomiting (5%), diarrhea (3%)

Hepatic: Abnormal LFTs (2.7%), hepatitis

<1%: Fatigue, dizziness, somnolence, pruritus, hypokalemia, anorexia, impotence, adrenal suppression, gynecomastia, albuminuria

Overdosage/Toxicology

Overdoses are well tolerated

Following decontamination, if possible, supportive measures only are required; dialysis is not effective

Drug Interactions CYP3A3/4 enzyme substrate; CYP3A3/4 enzyme inhibitor

Decreased effect:

Decreased serum levels with carbamazepine, didanosine, isoniazid, phenobarbital, phenytoin, rifabutin, and rifampin; may cause a decreased effect of oral contraceptives; alternative birth control is recommended

Decreased/undetectable serum levels with rifampin - **should not be administered concomitantly with rifampin**

Absorption requires gastric acidity; therefore, antacids, H_2-antagonists (cimetidine and ranitidine), omeprazole, and sucralfate significantly reduce bioavailability resulting in treatment failures and should not be administered concomitantly; amphotericin B or fluconazole should be used instead

Increased toxicity:

May increase cyclosporine or tacrolimus levels (by 50%) when high doses are used

Itraconazole increases serum levels of lovastatin (possibly 20-fold) and other HMG-CoA inhibitors due to inhibition of CYP3A4

May increase phenytoin serum concentration

May inhibit warfarins metabolism

May increase digoxin serum levels

May increase astemizole, busulfan, cisapride, terfenadine, and vinca alkaloid levels - **concomitant administration is not recommended** due to increased risk of cardiotoxicity

Itraconazole may increase astemizole levels resulting in prolonged Q-T intervals - concomitant administration is contraindicated

Itraconazole may increase levels of cisapride - concomitant administration is contraindicated due to increased risk of cardiotoxicity

May increase amlodipine, benzodiazepine, buspirone, corticosteroids, and oral hypoglycemic levels; use with caution in patients prescribed medications eliminated by CYP3A4 metabolism

Stability Dilute with 0.9% sodium chloride only; do not dilute in dextrose or lactated Ringer's; may be stored refrigerated or at room temperature for 48 hours; use dedicated infusion line; do not mix with any other medication

Mechanism of Action Interferes with cytochrome P-450 activity, decreasing ergosterol synthesis (principal sterol in fungal cell membrane) and inhibiting cell membrane formation

Pharmacodynamics/Kinetics

Absorption: Requires gastric acidity; capsule better absorbed with food, solution better absorbed on empty stomach

Distribution: Apparent volume averaged 796±185 L or 10 L/kg; highly lipophilic and tissue concentrations are higher than plasma concentrations. The highest itraconazole concentrations are achieved in adipose, omentum, endometrium, cervical and vaginal mucus, and skin/nails. Aqueous fluids, such as cerebrospinal fluid and urine, contain negligible amounts of itraconazole; steady-state concentrations are achieved in 13 days with multiple administration of itraconazole 100-400 mg/day.

Protein binding: 99.9% bound to plasma proteins; metabolite hydroxy-itraconazole is 99.5% bound to plasma proteins

Metabolism: Extensive by the liver into >30 metabolites including hydroxy-itraconazole which is the major metabolite and appears to have in vitro antifungal activity. The main metabolic pathway is oxidation; may undergo saturation metabolism with multiple dosing

Bioavailability: Increased from 40% fasting to 100% postprandial; absolute oral bioavailability: 55%; hypochlorhydria has been reported in HIV-infected patients; therefore, oral absorption in these patients may be decreased

Half-life: Oral: After single 200 mg dose: 21±5 hours; 64 hours at steady-state; I.V.: steady-state: 35 hours

Elimination: ~3% to 18% excreted in feces; ~0.03% of parent drug excreted renally and 40% of dose excreted as inactive metabolites in urine

(Continued)

Itraconazole *(Continued)*

Usual Dosage Oral: Capsule: Absorption is best if taken with food, therefore, it is best to administer itraconazole after meals; Solution: Should be taken on an empty stomach. Absorption of both products is significantly increased when taken with a cola beverage.

Children: Efficacy and safety have not been established; a small number of patients 3-16 years of age have been treated with 100 mg/day for systemic fungal infections with no serious adverse effects reported

Adults:

Oral:

Blastomycosis/histoplasmosis: 200 mg once daily, if no obvious improvement or there is evidence of progressive fungal disease, increase the dose in 100 mg increments to a maximum of 400 mg/day; doses >200 mg/day are given in 2 divided doses; length of therapy varies from 1 day to >6 months depending on the condition and mycological response

Aspergillosis: 200-400 mg/day

Onychomycosis: 200 mg once daily for 12 consecutive weeks

Life-threatening infections: Loading dose: 200 mg 3 times/day (600 mg/day) should be given for the first 3 days of therapy

Oropharyngeal and esophageal candidiasis: Oral solution: 100-200 mg once daily

I.V.: 200 mg twice daily for 4 doses, followed by 200 mg daily

Dosing adjustment in renal impairment: Not necessary; itraconazole injection is not recommended in patients with Cl_{cr} <30 mL/minute

Hemodialysis: Not dialyzable

Dosing adjustment in hepatic impairment: May be necessary, but specific guidelines are not available

Dietary Considerations Food increases absorption of capsule and decreases absorption of the solution

Administration

Oral: Doses >200 mg/day are given in 2 divided doses; do not administer with antacids.

I.V.: Infuse over 1 hour

Patient Information Take capsule with food; take solution on an empty stomach; report any signs and symptoms that may suggest liver dysfunction so that the appropriate laboratory testing can be done; signs and symptoms may include unusual fatigue, anorexia, nausea and/or vomiting, jaundice, dark urine, or pale stool

Dosage Forms

Capsule: 100 mg

Injection kit: 10 mg/mL - 25 mL ampul, one 50 mL (100 mL capacity) bag 0.9% sodium chloride, one filtered infusion set

Solution, oral: 100 mg/10 mL (150 mL)

♦ **I-Tropine® Ophthalmic** *see* Atropine *on page 111*

♦ **Iveegam®** *see* Immune Globulin, Intramuscular *on page 603*

Ivermectin *(eye ver MEK tin)*

U.S. Brand Names Mectizan®; Stromectol®

Therapeutic Category Antibiotic, Miscellaneous

Use Treatment of the following infections: Strongyloidiasis of the intestinal tract due the nematode parasite *Strongyloides stercoralis*. Onchocerciasis due to the nematode parasite *Onchocerca volvulus*. Ivermectin is only active against the immature form of *Onchocerca volvulus*, and the intestinal forms of *Strongyloides stercoralis*. Ivermectin has been used for other parasitic infections including *Ascaris lumbricoides*, bancroftian filariasis, *Brugia malayi*, scabies, *Enterobius vermicularis*, *Mansonella ozzardi*, *Trichuris trichiura*.

Pregnancy Risk Factor C

Contraindications Hypersensitivity to ivermectin or any component

Warnings/Precautions Data have shown that antihelmintic drugs like ivermectin may cause cutaneous and/or systemic reactions (Mazzoti reaction) of varying severity including ophthalmological reactions in patients with onchocerciasis. These reactions are probably due to allergic and inflammatory responses to the death of microfilariae. Patients with hyper-reactive onchodermatitis may be more likely than others to experience severe adverse reactions, especially edema and aggravation of the onchodermatitis. Repeated treatment may be required in immunocompromised patients (eg, HIV); control of extraintestinal strongyloidiasis may necessitate suppressive (once monthly) therapy

Adverse Reactions

Percentage unknown: Transient tachycardia, peripheral and facial edema, hypotension, mild EKG changes, dizziness, headache, somnolence, vertigo, insomnia, hyperthermia, pruritus, rash, urticaria, diarrhea, nausea, abdominal pain, vomiting, leukopenia, eosinophilia, increased ALT/AST, weakness, myalgia, tremor, limbitis, punctate opacity, mild conjunctivitis, blurred vision

Mazzotti reaction (with onchocerciasis): Pruritus, edema, rash, fever, lymphadenopathy, ocular damage

Overdosage/Toxicology

Accidental intoxication with, or significant exposure to unknown quantities of veterinary formulations of ivermectin in humans, either by ingestion, inhalation, injection, or exposure to body surfaces, has resulted in the following adverse effects: rash, edema, headache, dizziness, asthenia, nausea, vomiting, and diarrhea; other adverse effects that have been reported include seizure and ataxia

Treatment is supportive; usual methods for decontamination are recommended

Mechanism of Action Ivermectin is a semisynthetic antihelminthic agent; it binds selectively and with strong affinity to glutamate-gated chloride ion channels which occur in invertebrate nerve and muscle cells. This leads to increased permeability of cell membranes to chloride ions then hyperpolarization of the nerve or muscle cell, and death of the parasite.

Pharmacodynamics/Kinetics
Peak response: 3-6 months
Absorption: Well absorbed
Distribution: Does not cross the blood-brain barrier
Half-life: 16-35 hours
Metabolism: Hepatic, >97%
Elimination: <1% excreted in urine, the remainder in feces

Usual Dosage Oral:
Children ≥5 years: 150 mcg/kg as a single dose; treatment for onchocerciasis may need to be repeated every 3-12 months until the adult worms die
Adults:
Strongyloidiasis: 200 mcg/kg as a single dose; follow-up stool examinations
Onchocerciasis: 150 mcg/kg as a single dose; retreatment may be required every 3-12 months until the adult worms die

Monitoring Parameters Skin and eye microfilarial counts, periodic ophthalmologic exams

Patient Information If infected with strongyloidiasis, repeated stool examinations are required to document clearance of the organisms; repeated follow-up and retreatment is usually required in the treatment of onchocerciasis

Nursing Implications Ensure that patients take ivermectin with water

Additional Information Available from:
The Centers for Disease Control Drug and Immunobiologic Service
1600 Clifton Road
Building 1
Room 1259
Atlanta, GA 30333
Monday-Friday 8 AM to 4:30 PM
(404) 639-3670
Nonbusiness hours (emergencies only): (404) 639-2888

Dosage Forms Tablet: 6 mg

♦ **IVIG** see Immune Globulin, Intravenous on page 604
♦ **IvyBlock®** see Bentoquatam on page 132
♦ **Jaa Amp® Trihydrate** see Ampicillin on page 79
♦ **Jaa-Prednisone®** see Prednisone on page 963
♦ **Janimine®** see Imipramine on page 601

Japanese Encephalitis Virus Vaccine, Inactivated
(jap a NEESE en sef a LYE tis VYE rus vak SEEN, in ak ti VAY ted)

U.S. Brand Names JE-VAX®

Therapeutic Category Vaccine, Live Virus

Use Active immunization against Japanese encephalitis for persons 1 year of age and older who plan to spend 1 month or more in endemic areas in Asia, especially persons traveling during the transmission season or visiting rural areas; consider vaccination for shorter trips to epidemic areas or extensive outdoor activities in rural endemic areas; elderly (>55 years of age) individuals should be considered for vaccination, since they have increased risk of developing symptomatic illness after infection; those planning travel to or residence in endemic areas should consult the Travel Advisory Service (Central Campus) for specific advice

Pregnancy Risk Factor C

Contraindications Serious adverse reaction (generalized urticaria or angioedema) to a prior dose of this vaccine; proven or suspected hypersensitivity to proteins or rodent or neural origin; hypersensitivity to thimerosal (used as a preservative). *CDC recommends that the following should not generally receive the vaccine, unless benefit to the individual clearly outweighs the risk:*
* those acutely ill or with active infections
* persons with heart, kidney, or liver disorders
* persons with generalized malignancies such as leukemia or lymphoma
* persons with a history of multiple allergies or hypersensitivity to components of the vaccine
* pregnant women, unless there is a very high risk of Japanese encephalitis during the woman's stay in Asia

Warnings/Precautions Severe adverse reactions manifesting as generalized urticaria or angioedema may occur within minutes following vaccination, or up to 17 days later; most reactions occur within 10 days, with the majority within 48 hours; observe vaccinees for 30 minutes after vaccination; warn them of the possibility of delayed generalized urticaria and to remain where medical care is readily available for 10 days following any dose of the vaccine; because of the potential for severe adverse reactions, Japanese encephalitis vaccine is **not** recommended for all persons traveling to or residing in Asia; safety and efficacy in infants <1 year of age have not been established; therefore, immunization of infants should be deferred whenever possible; it is not known whether the vaccine is excreted in breast milk

Adverse Reactions Report allergic or unusual adverse reactions to the Vaccine Adverse Event Reporting System (VAERS) 1-800-822-7967.
(Continued)

Japanese Encephalitis Virus Vaccine, Inactivated
(Continued)

Percentage unknown: Commonly tenderness, redness, and swelling at injection site; systemic side effects include fever, headache, malaise, rash, chills, dizziness, myalgia, nausea, vomiting, abdominal pain, urticaria, itching with or without accompanying rash, and hypotension; rarely, anaphylactic reaction, encephalitis, encephalopathy, seizure, peripheral neuropathy, erythema multiforme, erythema nodosum, angioedema, dyspnea, and joint swelling

Drug Interactions Simultaneous administration of DTP vaccine and Japanese encephalitis vaccine does not compromise the immunogenicity of either vaccine; data on administration with other vaccines, chloroquine, or mefloquine are lacking

Stability Refrigerate, discard 8 hours after reconstitution

Usual Dosage U.S. recommended primary immunization schedule:

Children >3 years and Adults: S.C.: Three 1 mL doses given on days 0, 7, and 30. Give third dose on day 14 when time does not permit waiting; 2 doses a week apart produce immunity in about 80% of vaccines; the longest regimen yields highest titers after 6 months.

Children 1-3 years: S.C.: Three 0.5 mL doses given on days 0, 7, and 30; abbreviated schedules should be used only when necessary due to time constraints

Booster dose: Give after 2 years, or according to current recommendation

Note: Travel should not commence for at least 10 days after the last dose of vaccine, to allow adequate antibody formation and recognition of any delayed adverse reaction

Advise concurrent use of other means to reduce the risk of mosquito exposure when possible, including bed nets, insect repellents, protective clothing, avoidance of travel in endemic areas, and avoidance of outdoor activity during twilight and evening periods

Patient Information Adverse reactions may occur shortly after vaccination or up to 17 days (usually within 10 days) after vaccination

Additional Information Japanese encephalitis vaccine is currently available only from the Centers for Disease Control. Contact Centers for Disease Control at (404) 639-6370 (Mon-Fri) or (404) 639-2888 (nights, weekends, or holidays).

Dosage Forms Powder for injection, lyophilized: 1 mL, 10 mL

- ◆ **Jenamicin®** Injection *see* Gentamicin *on page 533*
- ◆ **Jenest-28**™ *see* Ethinyl Estradiol and Norethindrone *on page 451*
- ◆ **JE-VAX®** *see* Japanese Encephalitis Virus Vaccine, Inactivated *on previous page*
- ◆ **Junior Strength Motrin®** [OTC] *see* Ibuprofen *on page 593*
- ◆ **Junior Strength Panadol®** [OTC] *see* Acetaminophen *on page 19*
- ◆ **K+ 10®** *see* Potassium Chloride *on page 949*
- ◆ **Kabikinase®** *see* Streptokinase *on page 1081*
- ◆ **Kadian**™ *see* Morphine Sulfate *on page 797*
- ◆ **Kalcinate®** *see* Calcium Gluconate *on page 179*

Kanamycin (kan a MYE sin)
Related Information

Antimicrobial Drugs of Choice *on page 1404*
Tuberculosis Prophylaxis *on page 1386*
Tuberculosis Treatment Guidelines *on page 1432*

U.S. Brand Names Kantrex®

Synonyms Kanamycin Sulfate

Therapeutic Category Antibiotic, Aminoglycoside

Use

Oral: Preoperative bowel preparation in the prophylaxis of infections and adjunctive treatment of hepatic coma (oral kanamycin is not indicated in the treatment of systemic infections); treatment of susceptible bacterial infection including gram-negative aerobes, gram-positive *Bacillus* as well as some mycobacteria

Parenteral: Rarely used in antibiotic irrigations during surgery

Pregnancy Risk Factor D

Contraindications Hypersensitivity to kanamycin or any component or other aminoglycosides

Warnings/Precautions Use with caution in patients with pre-existing renal insufficiency, vestibular or cochlear impairment, myasthenia gravis, conditions which depress neuromuscular transmission

Parenteral aminoglycosides are associated with nephrotoxicity or ototoxicity; the ototoxicity may be proportional to the amount of drug given and the duration of treatment; tinnitus or vertigo are indications of vestibular injury and impending hearing loss; renal damage is usually reversible

Adverse Reactions Percentage unknown: Edema, neurotoxicity, drowsiness, headache, pseudomotor cerebri, skin itching, redness, rash, photosensitivity, erythema, nausea, vomiting, diarrhea (most common with oral form), malabsorption syndrome with prolonged and high-dose therapy of hepatic coma; anorexia, weight loss, increased salivation, enterocolitis, granulocytopenia, agranulocytosis, thrombocytopenia, burning, stinging, weakness, tremors, muscle cramps, ototoxicity (auditory), ototoxicity (vestibular), nephrotoxicity, dyspnea

Overdosage/Toxicology

Symptoms of overdose include ototoxicity, nephrotoxicity, and neuromuscular toxicity

The treatment of choice following a single acute overdose appears to be the maintenance of good urine output of at least 3 mL/kg/hour. Dialysis is of questionable value in the enhancement of aminoglycoside elimination. If required, hemodialysis is preferred over peritoneal dialysis in patients with normal renal function. Careful hydration may be all that is required to promote diuresis and, therefore, the enhancement of the drug's elimination.

Drug Interactions
Increased toxicity:
Penicillins, cephalosporins, amphotericin B, diuretics may increase nephrotoxicity; polypeptide antibiotics may increase risk of respiratory paralysis and renal dysfunction

Neuromuscular blocking agents with oral kanamycin may increase neuromuscular blockade; a small increase in warfarin's effect may occur due to decreased absorption of vitamin K

Decreased toxicity: Methotrexate with kanamycin (oral) may be less well absorbed as may digoxin (minor) and vitamin A

Stability Darkening of vials does not indicate loss of potency

Mechanism of Action Interferes with protein synthesis in bacterial cell by binding to ribosomal subunit

Pharmacodynamics/Kinetics
Absorption: Oral: Not absorbed following administration
Relative diffusion of antimicrobial agents from blood into cerebrospinal fluid (CSF): Good only with inflammation (exceeds usual MICs)
Ratio of CSF to blood level (%): Normal meninges: Nil; Inflamed meninges: 43
Half-life: 2-4 hours, increases in anuria to 80 hours
End-stage renal disease: 40-96 hours
Time to peak serum concentration: I.M.: 1-2 hours
Elimination: Entirely in the kidney, principally by glomerular filtration

Usual Dosage
Children: Infections: I.M., I.V.: 15 mg/kg/day in divided doses every 8-12 hours
Adults:
Infections: I.M., I.V.: 5-7.5 mg/kg/dose in divided doses every 8-12 hours (<15 mg/kg/day)
Preoperative intestinal antisepsis: Oral: 1 g every 4-6 hours for 36-72 hours
Hepatic coma: Oral: 8-12 g/day in divided doses
Intraperitoneal: After contamination in surgery: 500 mg diluted in 20 mL distilled water; other irrigations: 0.25% solutions
Aerosol: 250 mg 2-4 times/day (250 mg diluted with 3 mL of NS and nebulized)
Dosing adjustment/interval in renal impairment:
Cl_{cr} 50-80 mL/minute: Administer 60% to 90% of dose or administer every 8-12 hours
Cl_{cr} 10-50 mL/minute: Administer 30% to 70% of dose or administer every 12 hours
Cl_{cr} <10 mL/minute: Administer 20% to 30% of dose or administer every 24-48 hours
Hemodialysis: Dialyzable (50% to 100%)

Administration Adults: Dilute to 100-200 mL and infuse over 30 minutes; give I.M. deeply in gluteal muscle

Monitoring Parameters Serum creatinine and BUN every 2-3 days; peak and trough concentrations; hearing

Reference Range Therapeutic: Peak: 25-35 µg/mL; Trough: 4-8 µg/mL; Toxic: Peak: >35 µg/mL; Trough: >10 µg/mL

Patient Information Report any dizziness or sensations of ringing or fullness in ears

Dosage Forms
Capsule, as sulfate: 500 mg
Injection, as sulfate:
Pediatric: 75 mg (2 mL)
Adults: 500 mg (2 mL); 1 g (3 mL)

♦ **Kanamycin Sulfate** see Kanamycin on previous page

♦ **Kantrex®** see Kanamycin on previous page

♦ **Kaochlor®** see Potassium Chloride on page 949

♦ **Kaochlor-Eff®** see Potassium Bicarbonate, Potassium Chloride, and Potassium Citrate on page 949

♦ **Kaochlor® SF** see Potassium Chloride on page 949

Kaolin and Pectin With Opium (KAY oh lin & PEK tin with OH pee um)
U.S. Brand Names Parepectolin®
Therapeutic Category Antidiarrheal
Dosage Forms Suspension, oral: Kaolin 5.5 g, pectin 162 mg, and opium 15 mg per 30 mL [3.7 mL paregoric] (240 mL)

♦ **Kaon®** see Potassium Gluconate on page 951

♦ **Kaon-Cl®** see Potassium Chloride on page 949

♦ **Kaon Cl-10®** see Potassium Chloride on page 949

♦ **Kaopectate® II [OTC]** see Loperamide on page 692

♦ **Kapectolin PG®** see Hyoscyamine, Atropine, Scopolamine, Kaolin, Pectin, and Opium on page 593

♦ **Karidium®** see Fluoride on page 498

♦ **Karigel®** see Fluoride on page 498

♦ **Karigel®-N** see Fluoride on page 498

♦ **Kasof® [OTC]** see Docusate on page 384

Ketamine (KEET a meen)

Related Information

Adult ACLS Algorithm, Electrical Conversion *on page 1453*

U.S. Brand Names Ketalar®

Synonyms Ketamine Hydrochloride

Therapeutic Category General Anesthetic

Use Induction of anesthesia; short surgical procedures; dressing changes

Pregnancy Risk Factor D

Contraindications Elevated intracranial pressure; patients with hypertension, aneurysms, thyrotoxicosis, congestive heart failure, angina, psychotic disorders; hypersensitivity to ketamine or any component

Warnings/Precautions Should be used by or under the direct supervision of physicians experienced in administering general anesthetics and in maintenance of an airway, and in the control of respiration. Resuscitative equipment should be available for use.

Postanesthetic emergence reactions which can manifest as vivid dreams, hallucinations and/or frank delirium occur in 12% of patients; these reactions are less common in patients >65 and when given I.M.; emergence reactions, confusion, or irrational behavior may occur up to 24 hours postoperatively and may be reduced by minimization of verbal, tactile, and visual patient stimulation during recovery or by pretreatment with a benzodiazepine. Avoid postsurgery stimulation which may cause agitation and hallucinations in patients.

Adverse Reactions

>10%:

Cardiovascular: Hypertension, tachycardia, increased cardiac output, paradoxical direct myocardial depression

Central nervous system: Increased intracranial pressure, vivid dreams, visual hallucinations

Neuromuscular & skeletal: Tonic-clonic movements, tremors

Miscellaneous: Emergence reactions, vocalization

1% to 10%:

Cardiovascular: Bradycardia, hypotension

Dermatologic: Pain at injection site, skin rash

Gastrointestinal: Vomiting, anorexia, nausea

Ocular: Nystagmus, diplopia

Respiratory: Respiratory depression

<1%: Cardiac arrhythmias, myocardial depression, increased intracranial pressure, increases in cerebral blood, increased metabolic rate, increased intraocular pressure, hypersalivation, increased skeletal muscle tone, fasciculations, increased intraocular pressure, increased airway resistance, cough reflex may be depressed, decreased bronchospasm, apnea with large doses or rapid infusions, laryngospasm

Overdosage/Toxicology

Symptoms of overdose include respiratory depression with excessive dosing or too rapid administration

Supportive care is the treatment of choice; mechanical support of respiration is preferred

Drug Interactions CYP3A enzyme substrate

Increased effect: Barbiturates, narcotics, hydroxyzine increase prolonged recovery; nondepolarizing may increase effects

Increased toxicity: Muscle relaxants, thyroid hormones may increase blood pressure and heart rate; halothane may decrease BP

Stability Do not mix with barbiturates or diazepam → precipitation may occur

Mechanism of Action Produces dissociative anesthesia by direct action on the cortex and limbic system

Pharmacodynamics/Kinetics Duration of action (following a single dose):
Anesthesia: I.M.: 12-25 minutes; I.V.: 5-10 minutes
Analgesia: I.M.: 15-30 minutes
Amnesia: May persist for 1-2 hours
Recovery: I.M.: 3-4 hours; I.V.: 1-2 hours

Usual Dosage Used in combination with anticholinergic agents to decrease hypersalivation
Children:
Oral: 6-10 mg/kg for 1 dose (mixed in 0.2-0.3 mL/kg of cola or other beverage) given 30 minutes before the procedure
I.M.: 3-7 mg/kg
I.V.: Range: 0.5-2 mg/kg, use smaller doses (0.5-1 mg/kg) for sedation for minor procedures; usual induction dosage: 1-2 mg/kg
Continuous I.V. infusion: Sedation: 5-20 mcg/kg/minute
Adults:
I.M.: 3-8 mg/kg
I.V.: Range: 1-4.5 mg/kg; usual induction dosage: 1-2 mg/kg
Children and Adults: Maintenance: Supplemental doses of 1/3 to 1/2 of initial dose

Administration
Oral: Use 100 mg/mL I.V. solution and mix the appropriate dose in 0.2-0.3 mL/kg of cola or other beverage
Parenteral: I.V.: Do not exceed 0.5 mg/kg/minute or administer faster than 60 seconds; do not exceed final concentration of 2 mg/mL

Monitoring Parameters Cardiovascular effects, heart rate, blood pressure, respiratory rate, transcutaneous O_2 saturation

Dosage Forms Injection, as hydrochloride: 10 mg/mL (20 mL, 25 mL, 50 mL); 50 mg/mL (10 mL); 100 mg/mL (5 mL)

♦ **Ketamine Hydrochloride** see Ketamine on previous page

Ketoconazole (kee toe KOE na zole)

Related Information
Antacid Drug Interactions on page 1296
Antifungal Agents Comparison on page 1303
Guidelines for the Prevention of Opportunistic Infections in Persons with HIV on page 1388

U.S. Brand Names Nizoral®

Therapeutic Category Antifungal Agent, Imidazole Derivative; Antifungal Agent, Systemic; Antifungal Agent, Topical

Use Treatment of susceptible fungal infections, including candidiasis, oral thrush, blastomycosis, histoplasmosis, paracoccidioidomycosis, coccidioidomycosis, chromomycosis, candiduria, chronic mucocutaneous candidiasis, as well as, certain recalcitrant cutaneous dermatophytoses; used topically for treatment of tinea corporis, tinea cruris, tinea versicolor, and cutaneous candidiasis, seborrheic dermatitis

Pregnancy Risk Factor C

Contraindications Hypersensitivity to ketoconazole or any component; CNS fungal infections (due to poor CNS penetration); coadministration with terfenadine, astemizole, or cisapride is contraindicated due to risk of potentially fatal cardiac arrhythmias

Warnings/Precautions Rare cases of serious cardiovascular adverse event, including death, ventricular tachycardia and torsade de pointes have been observed due to increased terfenadine concentrations induced by ketoconazole. Use with caution in patients with impaired hepatic function; has been associated with hepatotoxicity, including some fatalities; perform periodic liver function tests; high doses of ketoconazole may depress adrenocortical function.

Adverse Reactions
Oral:
1% to 10%:
Dermatologic: Pruritus (1.5%)
Gastrointestinal: Nausea/vomiting (3% to 10%), abdominal pain (1.2%)
<1%: Headache, dizziness, somnolence, fever, chills, bulging fontanelles, depression, gynecomastia, diarrhea, impotence, thrombocytopenia, leukopenia, hemolytic anemia, hepatotoxicity, photophobia
Cream: Severe irritation, pruritus, stinging (~5%)
Shampoo: Increases in normal hair loss, irritation (<1%), abnormal hair texture, scalp pustules, mild dryness of skin, itching, oiliness/dryness of hair

Overdosage/Toxicology
Symptoms of overdose include dizziness, headache, nausea, vomiting, diarrhea; overdoses are well tolerated
Treatment includes supportive measures and gastric decontamination

Drug Interactions CYP3A3/4 enzyme substrate; CYP1A2, 2C, 2C9, 2C18, 2C19, 3A3/4, and 3A5-7 enzyme inhibitor
(Continued)

Ketoconazole (Continued)

Decreased effect:

Decreased ketoconazole serum levels with isoniazid and phenytoin; decreased/undetectable serum levels with rifampin - **should not be administered concomitantly with rifampin**; theophylline and oral hypoglycemic serum levels may be decreased

Absorption requires gastric acidity; therefore, antacids, H₂-antagonists (cimetidine and ranitidine), omeprazole, and sucralfate significantly reduce bioavailability resulting in treatment failures; should not be administered concomitantly

Increased toxicity:

May increase cyclosporine levels (by 50%) when high doses are used

Inhibits warfarin metabolism resulting in increased anticoagulant effect

Increases corticosteroid bioavailability and decreases steroid clearance

Increases phenytoin, digoxin, terfenadine, astemizole, and cisapride concentrations; **concomitant administration with astemizole or cisapride is contraindicated**; may significantly increase levels and toxicity of lovastatin and simvastatin due to CYP3A4 inhibition; a disulfiram-type reaction may occur with concomitant ethanol

Mechanism of Action Alters the permeability of the cell wall by blocking fungal cytochrome P-450; inhibits biosynthesis of triglycerides and phospholipids by fungi; inhibits several fungal enzymes that results in a build-up of toxic concentrations of hydrogen peroxide

Pharmacodynamics/Kinetics

Absorption: Oral: Rapid (~75%); no detectable absorption following use of the shampoo

Distribution: Well distributed to inflamed joint fluid, saliva, bile, urine, breast milk, sebum, cerumen, feces, tendons, skin and soft tissues, and testes; crosses blood-brain barrier poorly; only negligible amounts reach CSF

Protein binding: 93% to 96%

Metabolism: Partially in the liver by enzymes to inactive compounds

Bioavailability: Decreases as pH of the gastric contents increases

Half-life, biphasic: Initial: 2 hours; Terminal: 8 hours

Time to peak serum concentration: 1-2 hours

Elimination: Primarily in feces (57%) with smaller amounts excreted in urine (13%)

Usual Dosage

Oral:

Children ≥2 years: 3.3-6.6 mg/kg/day as a single dose for 1-2 weeks for candidiasis, for at least 4 weeks in recalcitrant dermatophyte infections, and for up to 6 months for other systemic mycoses

Adults: 200-400 mg/day as a single daily dose for durations as stated above

Shampoo: Apply twice weekly for 4 weeks with at least 3 days between each shampoo

Topical: Rub gently into the affected area once daily to twice daily

Dosing adjustment in hepatic impairment: Dose reductions should be considered in patients with severe liver disease

Hemodialysis: Not dialyzable (0% to 5%)

Monitoring Parameters Liver function tests

Patient Information Cream is for topical application to the skin only; avoid contact with the eye; avoid taking antacids at the same time as ketoconazole; may take with food; may cause drowsiness, impair judgment or coordination. Notify physician of unusual fatigue, anorexia, vomiting, dark urine, or pale stools.

Nursing Implications Administer 2 hours prior to antacids to prevent decreased absorption due to the high pH of gastric contents

Dosage Forms

Cream: 2% (15 g, 30 g, 60 g)

Shampoo: 2% (120 mL)

Tablet: 200 mg

Extemporaneous Preparations A 20 mg/mL suspension may be made by pulverizing twelve 200 mg ketoconazole tablets to a fine powder; add 40 mL Ora-Plus® in small portions with thorough mixing; incorporate Ora-Sweet® to make a final volume of 120 mL and mix thoroughly; refrigerate (no stability information is available)

Allen LV, "Ketoconazole Oral Suspension," *US Pharm*, 1993, 18(2):98-9, 101.

Ketoprofen (kee toe PROE fen)

Related Information

Nonsteroidal Anti-Inflammatory Agents Comparison *on page 1335*

U.S. Brand Names Actron® [OTC]; Orudis®; Orudis® KT [OTC]; Oruvail®

Canadian Brand Names Apo®-Keto; Apo®-Keto-E; Novo-Keto-EC; Nu-Ketoprofen; Nu-Ketoprofen-E; Orafen; PMS-Ketoprofen; Rhodis™; Rhodis-EC™

Therapeutic Category Analgesic, Nonsteroidal Anti-inflammatory Drug; Anti-inflammatory Agent; Nonsteroidal Anti-inflammatory Drug (NSAID), Oral

Use Acute or long-term treatment of rheumatoid arthritis and osteoarthritis; primary dysmenorrhea; mild to moderate pain

Pregnancy Risk Factor B

Contraindications Known hypersensitivity to ketoprofen or other NSAIDs/aspirin

Warnings/Precautions Use with caution in patients with congestive heart failure, hypertension, decreased renal or hepatic function, history of GI disease (bleeding or ulcers), or those receiving anticoagulants; safety and efficacy in children <6 months of age have not yet been established

Adverse Reactions

>10%:

Central nervous system: Dizziness

Dermatologic: Rash
Gastrointestinal: Abdominal cramps, heartburn, indigestion, nausea
1% to 10%:
Central nervous system: Headache, nervousness
Dermatologic: Itching
Endocrine & metabolic: Fluid retention
Gastrointestinal: Vomiting
Otic: Tinnitus
<1%: Congestive heart failure, hypertension, arrhythmias, tachycardia, confusion, hallucinations, mental depression, drowsiness, insomnia, aseptic meningitis, urticaria, erythema multiforme, toxic epidermal necrolysis, Stevens-Johnson syndrome, angiodema, polydipsia, hot flashes, gastritis, GI ulceration, cystitis, polyuria, agranulocytosis, anemia, hemolytic anemia, bone marrow suppression, leukopenia, thrombocytopenia, hepatitis, peripheral neuropathy, toxic amblyopia, blurred vision, conjunctivitis, dry eyes, decreased hearing, acute renal failure, allergic rhinitis, shortness of breath, epistaxis

Overdosage/Toxicology
Symptoms of overdose include apnea, metabolic acidosis, coma, and nystagmus; leukocytosis, renal failure
Management of a nonsteroidal anti-inflammatory drug (NSAID) intoxication is primarily supportive and symptomatic. Fluid therapy is commonly effective in managing the hypotension that may occur following an acute NSAID overdose, except when this is due to an acute blood loss. Seizures tend to be very short-lived and often do not require drug treatment. Although, recurrent seizures should be treated with I.V. diazepam. Since many of the NSAIDs undergo enterohepatic cycling, multiple doses of charcoal may be needed to reduce the potential for delayed toxicities.

Drug Interactions CYP2C and 2C9 enzyme inhibitor
Decreased effect of diuretics
Increased effect/toxicity with probenecid, lithium, anticoagulants
Increased toxicity of methotrexate

Mechanism of Action Inhibits prostaglandin synthesis by decreasing the activity of the enzyme, cyclo-oxygenase, which results in decreased formation of prostaglandin precursors

Pharmacodynamics/Kinetics
Absorption: Almost completely
Metabolism: In the liver
Half-life: 1-4 hours
Time to peak serum concentration: 0.5-2 hours
Elimination: Renal excretion (60% to 75%), primarily as glucuronide conjugates

Usual Dosage Oral:
Children 3 months to 14 years: Fever: 0.5-1 mg/kg every 6-8 hours
Children >12 years and Adults:
Rheumatoid arthritis or osteoarthritis: 50-75 mg 3-4 times/day up to a maximum of 300 mg/day
Mild to moderate pain: 25-50 mg every 6-8 hours up to a maximum of 300 mg/day

Test Interactions ↑ chloride (S), ↑ sodium (S), ↑ bleeding time

Patient Information Take with food; may cause dizziness or drowsiness

Dosage Forms
Capsule (Orudis®): 25 mg, 50 mg, 75 mg
Actron®, Orudis® KT [OTC]: 12.5 mg
Capsule, extended release (Oruvail®): 100 mg, 200 mg

Ketorolac Tromethamine (KEE toe role ak troe METH a meen)

Related Information
Nonsteroidal Anti-Inflammatory Agents Comparison *on page 1335*

U.S. Brand Names Acular® Ophthalmic; Toradol® Injection; Toradol® Oral

Therapeutic Category Analgesic, Nonsteroidal Anti-inflammatory Drug; Anti-inflammatory Agent; Nonsteroidal Anti-inflammatory Drug (NSAID), Oral; Nonsteroidal Anti-inflammatory Drug (NSAID), Parenteral

Use Short-term (<5 days) management of pain; first parenteral NSAID for analgesia; 30 mg provides the analgesia comparable to 12 mg of morphine or 100 mg of meperidine

Pregnancy Risk Factor B (D if used in the 3rd trimester)

Contraindications In patients who have developed nasal polyps, angioedema, or bronchospastic reactions to other NSAIDs, active peptic ulcer disease, recent GI bleeding or perforation, patients with advanced renal disease or risk of renal failure, labor and delivery, nursing mothers, patients with hypersensitivity to ketorolac, aspirin, or other NSAIDs, **prophylaxis before major surgery**, suspected or confirmed cerebrovascular bleeding, hemorrhagic diathesis, concurrent ASA or other NSAIDs, epidural or intrathecal administration, concomitant probenecid

Warnings/Precautions Use extra caution and reduce dosages in the elderly because it is cleared renally somewhat slower, and the elderly are also more sensitive to the renal effects of NSAIDs; use with caution in patients with congestive heart failure, hypertension, decreased renal or hepatic function, history of GI disease (bleeding or ulcers), or those receiving anticoagulants

Adverse Reactions
Percentage unknown: Renal impairment, wound bleeding (with I.M.), postoperative hematomas
(Continued)

651

Ketorolac Tromethamine *(Continued)*

1% to 10%:
Cardiovascular: Edema
Central nervous system: Drowsiness, dizziness, headache, pain
Gastrointestinal: Nausea, dyspepsia, diarrhea, gastric ulcers, indigestion
Local: Pain at injection site
Miscellaneous: Diaphoresis (increased)
<1%: Mental depression, purpura, aphthous stomatitis, rectal bleeding, peptic ulceration, change in vision, oliguria, dyspnea

Overdosage/Toxicology

Symptoms of overdose include diarrhea, pallor, vomiting, labored breathing, apnea, metabolic acidosis, leukocytosis, renal failure

Management of a nonsteroidal anti-inflammatory drug (NSAID) intoxication is primarily supportive and symptomatic. Fluid therapy is commonly effective in managing the hypotension that may occur following an acute NSAID overdose, except when this is due to an acute blood loss. Seizures tend to be very short-lived and often do not require drug treatment; although, recurrent seizures should be treated with I.V. diazepam. Since many of the NSAIDs undergo enterohepatic cycling, multiple doses of charcoal may be needed to reduce the potential for delayed toxicities; NSAIDs are highly bound to plasma proteins; therefore, hemodialysis and peritoneal dialysis are not useful.

Drug Interactions

Decreased effect of diuretics
Increased toxicity: Lithium, methotrexate increased drug level; increased effect/toxicity with salicylates, probenecid, anticoagulants

Stability

Ketorolac tromethamine injection should be stored at controlled room temperature and protected from light; injection is clear and has a slight yellow color; precipitation may occur at relatively low pH values

Compatible with NS, D_5W, D_5NS, LR

Incompatible with meperidine, morphine, promethazine, and hydroxyzine

Mechanism of Action Inhibits prostaglandin synthesis by decreasing the activity of the enzyme, cyclo-oxygenase, which results in decreased formation of prostaglandin precursors

Pharmacodynamics/Kinetics

Analgesic effect: Onset of action: I.M.: Within 10 minutes; Peak effect: Within 75-150 minutes; Duration of action: 6-8 hours
Absorption: Oral: Well absorbed
Time to peak serum concentration: I.M.: 30-60 minutes
Distribution: Crosses placenta; crosses into breast milk; poor penetration into CSF
Protein binding: 99%
Metabolism: In the liver
Half-life: 2-8 hours; increased 30% to 50% in elderly
Elimination: Renal excretion, 61% appearing in the urine as unchanged drug

Usual Dosage Note: The use of ketorolac in children <16 years of age is outside of product labeling

Children 2-16 years: Dosing guidelines are not established; **do not exceed adult doses**
Single-dose treatment:
I.M., I.V.: 0.4-1 mg/kg as a single dose; **Note:** Limited information exists. Single I.V. doses of 0.5 mg/kg, 0.75 mg/kg, 0.9 mg/kg and 1 mg/kg have been studied in children 2-16 years of age for postoperative analgesia. One study (Maunuksela, 1992) used a titrating dose starting with 0.2 mg/kg up to a total of 0.5 mg/kg (median dose required: 0.4 mg/kg).
Oral: One study used 1 mg/kg as a single dose for analgesia in 30 children (mean ± SD age: 3 ± 2.5 years) undergoing bilateral myringotomy
Multiple-dose treatment: I.M., I.V., Oral: No pediatric studies exist; one report (Buck, 1994) of the clinical experience with ketorolac in 112 children, 6 months to 19 years of age (mean: 9 years), described usual I.V. maintenance doses of 0.5 mg/kg every 6 hours (mean dose: 0.52 mg/kg; range: 0.17-1 mg/kg)
Adults (pain relief usually begins within 10 minutes with parenteral forms):
Oral: 10 mg every 4-6 hours as needed for a maximum of 40 mg/day; on day of transition from I.M. to oral: maximum oral dose: 40 mg (or 120 mg combined oral and I.M.); maximum 5 days administration
I.M.: Initial: 30-60 mg, then 15-30 mg every 6 hours as needed for up to 5 days maximum; maximum dose in the first 24 hours: 150 mg with 120 mg/24 hours for up to 5 days total
I.V.: Initial: 30 mg, then 15-30 mg every 6 hours as needed for up to 5 days **maximum**; maximum daily dose: 120 mg for up to 5 days total
Ophthalmic: Instill 1 drop in eye(s) 4 times/day for up to 7 days
Elderly >65 years: Renal insufficiency or weight <50 kg:
I.M.: 30 mg, then 15 mg every 6 hours
I.V.: 15 mg every 6 hours as needed for up to 5 days total; maximum daily dose: 60 mg

Dietary Considerations

Potassium: Hyperkalemia has been reported. The elderly and those with renal insufficiency are at greatest risk. Monitor potassium serum concentration in those at greatest risk. Avoid salt substitutes.

Sodium: Hyponatremia from sodium retention. Suspect secondary to suppression of renal prostaglandin. Monitor serum concentration and fluid status. May need to restrict fluid.

Monitoring Parameters Monitor response (pain, range of motion, grip strength, mobility, ADL function), inflammation; observe for weight gain, edema; monitor renal function (serum creatinine, BUN, urine output); observe for bleeding, bruising; evaluate gastrointestinal effects (abdominal pain, bleeding, dyspepsia); mental confusion, disorientation, CBC, liver function tests

Reference Range Serum concentration: Therapeutic: 0.3-5 µg/mL; Toxic: >5 µg/mL

Test Interactions ↑ chloride (S), ↑ sodium (S), ↑ bleeding time

Patient Information Serious gastrointestinal bleeding can occur as well as ulceration and perforation. Pain may or may not be present. Avoid aspirin and aspirin-containing products while taking this medication. If gastric adverse effects persist, contact physician. May cause drowsiness, dizziness, blurred vision, and confusion. Use caution when performing tasks which require alertness (eg, driving).

Nursing Implications Monitor for signs of pain relief, such as an increased appetite and activity

Dosage Forms
Injection: 15 mg/mL (1 mL); 30 mg/mL (1 mL, 2 mL)
Solution, ophthalmic: 0.5% (5 mL)
Tablet: 10 mg

- **Key-Pred® Injection** see Prednisolone on page 961
- **Key-Pred-SP® Injection** see Prednisolone on page 961
- **K-G®** see Potassium Gluconate on page 951
- **KI** see Potassium Iodide on page 952
- **K-Ide®** see Potassium Bicarbonate and Potassium Citrate, Effervescent on page 948
- **Kinesed®** see Hyoscyamine, Atropine, Scopolamine, and Phenobarbital on page 592
- **Klaron® Lotion** see Sulfacetamide Sodium on page 1091
- **Klean-Prep®** see Polyethylene Glycol-Electrolyte Solution on page 942
- **K-Lease®** see Potassium Chloride on page 949
- **Klonopin™** see Clonazepam on page 282
- **K-Lor™** see Potassium Chloride on page 949
- **Klor-Con®** see Potassium Chloride on page 949
- **Klor-Con® 8** see Potassium Chloride on page 949
- **Klor-Con® 10** see Potassium Chloride on page 949
- **Klor-Con/25®** see Potassium Chloride on page 949
- **Klor-Con®/EF** see Potassium Bicarbonate and Potassium Citrate, Effervescent on page 948
- **Klorvess®** see Potassium Chloride on page 949
- **Klorvess® Effervescent** see Potassium Bicarbonate and Potassium Chloride, Effervescent on page 948
- **Klotrix®** see Potassium Chloride on page 949
- **K-Lyte®** see Potassium Bicarbonate and Potassium Citrate, Effervescent on page 948
- **K/Lyte/CL®** see Potassium Bicarbonate and Potassium Chloride, Effervescent on page 948
- **K-Lyte/Cl®** see Potassium Chloride on page 949
- **K-Norm®** see Potassium Chloride on page 949
- **Koate®-HP** see Antihemophilic Factor (Human) on page 88
- **Koate®-HS** see Antihemophilic Factor (Human) on page 88
- **Kogenate®** see Antihemophilic Factor (Human) on page 88
- **Kolephrin® GG/DM [OTC]** see Guaifenesin and Dextromethorphan on page 550
- **Kolyum®** see Potassium Chloride and Potassium Gluconate on page 951
- **Konakion® Injection** see Phytonadione on page 926
- **Kondon's Nasal® [OTC]** see Ephedrine on page 414
- **Konsyl® [OTC]** see Psyllium on page 994
- **Konsyl-D® [OTC]** see Psyllium on page 994
- **Konÿne® 80** see Factor IX Complex (Human) on page 464
- **K-Phos® Neutral** see Potassium Phosphate and Sodium Phosphate on page 955
- **K-Phos® Original** see Potassium Acid Phosphate on page 947
- **K-Tab®** see Potassium Chloride on page 949
- **Ku-Zyme® HP** see Pancrelipase on page 883
- **K-Vescent®** see Potassium Bicarbonate and Potassium Citrate, Effervescent on page 948
- **Kwelcof®** see Hydrocodone and Guaifenesin on page 577
- **Kwell®** see Lindane on page 682
- **Kwellada™** see Lindane on page 682
- **Kytril™** see Granisetron on page 546
- **L-3-Hydroxytyrosine** see Levodopa on page 671
- **LA-12®** see Hydroxocobalamin on page 585

Labetalol (la BET a lole)

Related Information
Beta-Blockers Comparison on page 1311
Hypertension Therapy on page 1479
(Continued)

Labetalol *(Continued)*

U.S. Brand Names Normodyne®; Trandate®

Synonyms Ibidomide Hydrochloride; Labetalol Hydrochloride

Therapeutic Category Antihypertensive Agent; Beta-Adrenergic Blocker

Use Treatment of mild to severe hypertension with or without other agents; I.V. for hypertensive emergencies

Unlabeled use: Pheochromocytoma, clonidine withdrawal hypertension

Pregnancy Risk Factor C

Pregnancy/Breast-Feeding Implications

Clinical effects on the fetus: Crosses the placenta. Bradycardia, hypotension, hypoglycemia, intrauterine growth rate (IUGR). IUGR probably related to maternal hypertension. Available evidence suggests safe use during pregnancy and breast-feeding. Monitor breast-fed infant for symptoms of beta-blockade.

Breast-feeding/lactation: Crosses into breast milk. American Academy of Pediatrics considers **compatible** with breast-feeding.

Contraindications Cardiogenic shock, uncompensated congestive heart failure, bradycardia, pulmonary edema, or heart block

Warnings/Precautions Paradoxical increase in blood pressure has been reported with treatment of pheochromocytoma or clonidine withdrawal syndrome; use with caution in patients with hyper-reactive airway disease, congestive heart failure, diabetes mellitus, hepatic dysfunction; orthostatic hypotension may occur with I.V. administration; patient should remain supine during and for up to 3 hours after I.V. administration; use with caution in impaired hepatic function (discontinue if signs of liver dysfunction occur); may mask the signs and symptoms of hypoglycemia; a lower hemodynamic response rate and higher incidence of toxicity may be observed with administration to elderly patients.

Adverse Reactions

1% to 10%:

Cardiovascular: Orthostatic hypotension (dose-related, usual 1% to 5%), edema (1%)

Central nervous system: Dizziness (11%), fatigue (2% to 5%), vertigo (2%), headache (2%)

Endocrine & metabolic: Decreased sexual ability (1% to 2%)

Gastrointestinal: Nausea (1% to 4%), stomach discomfort (3%), abnormal taste (1%)

Neuromuscular & skeletal: Paresthesia (1% to 2%)

Respiratory: Dyspnea (2%), nasal congestion (1% to 3%)

<1%: Drowsiness, rash (1%), diarrhea, vomiting, vision abnormality

Overdosage/Toxicology

Symptoms of intoxication include cardiac disturbances, CNS toxicity, bronchospasm, hypoglycemia and hyperkalemia. The most common cardiac symptoms include hypotension and bradycardia; atrioventricular block, intraventricular conduction disturbances, cardiogenic shock, and asystole may occur with severe overdose, especially with membrane-depressant drugs (eg, propranolol); CNS effects include convulsions, coma, and respiratory arrest is commonly seen with propranolol and other membrane-depressant and lipid-soluble drugs.

Treatment includes symptomatic treatment of seizures, hypotension, hyperkalemia and hypoglycemia; bradycardia and hypotension resistant to atropine, isoproterenol or pacing may respond to glucagon; wide QRS defects caused by the membrane-depressant poisoning may respond to hypertonic sodium bicarbonate; repeat-dose charcoal, hemoperfusion, or hemodialysis may be helpful in removal of only those beta-blockers with a small V_d, long half-life or low intrinsic clearance (acebutolol, atenolol, nadolol, sotalol)

Drug Interactions CYP2D6 enzyme substrate; CYP2D6 enzyme inhibitor

Decreased effect of beta-blockers with aluminum salts, barbiturates, calcium salts, cholestyramine, colestipol, NSAIDs, penicillins (ampicillin), rifampin, salicylates and sulfinpyrazone due to decreased bioavailability and plasma levels

Beta-blockers may decrease the effect of sulfonylureas and bronchodilators

Increased effect/toxicity of beta-blockers with calcium blockers (diltiazem, felodipine, nicardipine), contraceptives, flecainide, H_2-antagonists (cimetidine), quinidine (in extensive metabolizers), ciprofloxacin, nitroglycerin, and halothane

Beta-blockers may increase the effect/toxicity of flecainide, haloperidol (hypotensive effects), hydralazine, phenothiazines, acetaminophen, benzodiazepines (not atenolol), clonidine (hypertensive crisis after or during withdrawal of either agent), epinephrine (initial hypertensive episode followed by bradycardia), nifedipine and verapamil, lidocaine, ergots, prazosin

Beta-blockers may affect the action or levels of ethanol, disopyramide, nondepolarizing muscle relaxants and theophylline although the effects are difficult to predict

Stability

Labetalol should be stored at room temperature or under refrigeration and should be protected from light and freezing; the solution is clear to slightly yellow

Stability of parenteral admixture at room temperature (25°C) and refrigeration temperature (4°C): 3 days

Standard diluent: 500 mg/250 mL D_5W

Minimum volume: 250 mL D_5W

Incompatible with sodium bicarbonate, most stable at pH of 2-4; **incompatible** with alkaline solutions

Mechanism of Action Blocks alpha-, beta$_1$-, and beta$_2$-adrenergic receptor sites; elevated renins are reduced

Pharmacodynamics/Kinetics

Onset of action: Oral: 20 minutes to 2 hours; I.V.: 2-5 minutes

Peak effect: Oral: 1-4 hours; I.V.: 5-15 minutes

Duration: Oral: 8-24 hours (dose-dependent); I.V.: 2-4 hours

Distribution: Crosses placenta; small amounts in breast milk; moderately lipid soluble, therefore, can enter CNS

V_d: Adults: 3-16 L/kg; mean: <9.4 L/kg

Protein binding: 50%

Metabolism: Extensive first-pass effect; metabolized in liver primarily via glucuronide conjugation

Bioavailability: Oral: 25%; increased with liver disease, elderly, and concurrent cimetidine

Half-life, normal renal function: 2.5-8 hours

Elimination: <5% excreted in urine unchanged; possible decreased clearance in neonates/infants

Usual Dosage Due to limited documentation of its use, labetalol should be initiated cautiously in pediatric patients with careful dosage adjustment and blood pressure monitoring

Children:

Oral: Limited information regarding labetalol use in pediatric patients is currently available in literature. Some centers recommend initial oral doses of 4 mg/kg/day in 2 divided doses. Reported oral doses have started at 3 mg/kg/day and 20 mg/kg/day and have increased up to 40 mg/kg/day.

I.V., intermittent bolus doses of 0.3-1 mg/kg/dose have been reported

For treatment of pediatric hypertensive emergencies, initial continuous infusions of 0.4-1 mg/kg/hour with a maximum of 3 mg/kg/hour have been used; administration requires the use of an infusion pump

Adults:

Oral: Initial: 100 mg twice daily, may increase as needed every 2-3 days by 100 mg until desired response is obtained; usual dose: 200-400 mg twice daily; may require up to 2.4 g/day

I.V.: 20 mg (0.25 mg/kg for an 80 kg patient) IVP over 2 minutes, may administer 40-80 mg at 10-minute intervals, up to 300 mg total dose

I.V. infusion: Initial: 2 mg/minute; titrate to response up to 300 mg total dose, if needed; administration requires the use of an infusion pump

I.V. infusion (500 mg/250 mL D_5W) rates:

1 mg/minute: 30 mL/hour
2 mg/minute: 60 mL/hour
3 mg/minute: 90 mL/hour
4 mg/minute: 120 mL/hour
5 mg/minute: 150 mL/hour
6 mg/minute: 180 mL/hour

Dialysis: Not removed by hemo- or peritoneal dialysis; supplemental dose is not necessary

Dosage adjustment in hepatic impairment: Dosage reduction may be necessary

Monitoring Parameters Blood pressure, standing and sitting/supine, pulse, cardiac monitor and blood pressure monitor required for I.V. administration

Test Interactions False-positive urine catecholamines, VMA if measured by fluorometric or photometric methods; use HPLC or specific catecholamine radioenzymatic technique

Patient Information Do not stop medication without aid of physician; may mask signs and symptoms of diabetes

Dosage Forms

Injection, as hydrochloride: 5 mg/mL (20 mL, 40 mL, 60 mL)

Tablet, as hydrochloride: 100 mg, 200 mg, 300 mg

Extemporaneous Preparations A mixture of labetalol 40 mg/mL plus hydrochlorothiazide 5 mg/mL was found stable for 60 days in the refrigerator when prepared in a 1:1 mixture of Ora-Sweet® and Ora-Plus®, or Ora-Sweet® SF and Ora-Plus®, and of cherry syrup

Allen LV and Erickson III MA, "Stability of Labetalol Hydrochloride, Metoprolol Tartrate, Verapamil Hydrochloride, and Spironolactone With Hydrochlorothiazide in Extemporaneously Compounded Oral Liquids," *Am J Health Syst Pharm*, 1996, 53:2304-9.

♦ **Labetalol Hydrochloride** *see* Labetalol *on page 653*

♦ **LaBID®** *see* Theophylline Salts *on page 1125*

♦ **LactiCare-HC®** *see* Hydrocortisone *on page 579*

♦ **Lactinex® [OTC]** *see Lactobacillus acidophilus* and *Lactobacillus bulgaricus on this page*

Lactobacillus acidophilus and *Lactobacillus bulgaricus*

(lak toe ba SIL us as i DOF fil us & lak toe ba SIL us bul GAR i cus)

U.S. Brand Names Bacid® [OTC]; Lactinex® [OTC]; More-Dophilus® [OTC]

Canadian Brand Names Fermalac®

Therapeutic Category Antidiarrheal

Use Treatment of uncomplicated diarrhea particularly that caused by antibiotic therapy; reestablish normal physiologic and bacterial flora of the intestinal tract

Contraindications Allergy to milk or lactose

Warnings/Precautions Discontinue if high fever present; do not use in children <3 years of age

Adverse Reactions 1% to 10%: Gastrointestinal: Intestinal flatus

Stability Store in the refrigerator

(Continued)

Lactobacillus acidophilus and *Lactobacillus bulgaricus* (Continued)

Mechanism of Action Creates an environment unfavorable to potentially pathogenic fungi or bacteria through the production of lactic acid, and favors establishment of an aciduric flora, thereby suppressing the growth of pathogenic microorganisms; helps re-establish normal intestinal flora

Pharmacodynamics/Kinetics

Absorption: Oral: Not absorbed

Distribution: Locally, primarily in the colon

Elimination: In feces

Usual Dosage Children >3 years and Adults: Oral:

Capsules: 2 capsules 2-4 times/day

Granules: 1 packet added to or taken with cereal, food, milk, fruit juice, or water, 3-4 times/day

Powder: 1 teaspoonful daily with liquid

Tablet, chewable: 4 tablets 3-4 times/day; may follow each dose with a small amount of milk, fruit juice, or water

Administration Granules may be added to or given with cereal, food, milk, fruit juice, or water

Patient Information Refrigerate; granules may be added to or taken with cereal, food, milk, fruit juice, or water

Dosage Forms

Capsule: 50s, 100s

Granules: 1 g/packet (12 packets/box)

Powder: 12 oz

Tablet, chewable: 50s

♦ **Lactoflavin** *see Riboflavin on page 1022*

Lactulose (LAK tyoo lose)

Related Information

Laxatives, Classification and Properties *on page 1326*

U.S. Brand Names Cephulac®; Cholac®; Chronulac®; Constilac®; Constulose®; Duphalac®; Enulose®; Evalose®; Heptalac®; Lactulose PSE®

Therapeutic Category Ammonium Detoxicant; Laxative, Miscellaneous

Use Adjunct in the prevention and treatment of portal-systemic encephalopathy (PSE); treatment of chronic constipation

Pregnancy Risk Factor B

Contraindications Patients with galactosemia and require a low galactose diet, hypersensitivity to any component

Warnings/Precautions Use with caution in patients with diabetes mellitus; monitor periodically for electrolyte imbalance when lactulose is used >6 months or in patients predisposed to electrolyte abnormalities (eg, elderly); patients receiving lactulose and an oral anti-infective agent should be monitored for possible inadequate response to lactulose

Adverse Reactions

>10%: Gastrointestinal: Flatulence, diarrhea (excessive dose)

1% to 10%: Gastrointestinal: Abdominal discomfort, nausea, vomiting

Overdosage/Toxicology

Symptoms of overdose include diarrhea, abdominal pain, hypochloremic alkalosis, dehydration, hypotension, hypokalemia

Treatment includes supportive care

Drug Interactions Decreased effect: Oral neomycin, laxatives, antacids

Stability Keep solution at room temperature to reduce viscosity; discard solution if cloudy or very dark

Mechanism of Action The bacterial degradation of lactulose resulting in an acidic pH inhibits the diffusion of NH_3 into the blood by causing the conversion of NH_3 to NH_4+; also enhances the diffusion of NH_3 from the blood into the gut where conversion to NH_4+ occurs; produces an osmotic effect in the colon with resultant distention promoting peristalsis

Pharmacodynamics/Kinetics

Absorption: Oral: Not absorbed appreciably following administration; this is desirable since the intended site of action is within the colon

Metabolism: By colonic flora to lactic acid and acetic acid, requires colonic flora for primary drug activation

Elimination: Primarily in feces and urine (~3%)

Usual Dosage Diarrhea may indicate overdosage and responds to dose reduction

Prevention of portal systemic encephalopathy (PSE): Oral:

Infants: 2.5-10 mL/day divided 3-4 times/day; adjust dosage to produce 2-3 stools/day

Older Children: Daily dose of 40-90 mL divided 3-4 times/day; if initial dose causes diarrhea, then reduce it immediately; adjust dosage to produce 2-3 stools/day

Constipation:

Children: 5 g/day (7.5 mL) after breakfast

Adults:

Acute PSE:

Oral: 20-30 g (30-45 mL) every 1-2 hours to induce rapid laxation; adjust dosage daily to produce 2-3 soft stools; doses of 30-45 mL may be given hourly to cause rapid laxation, then reduce to recommended dose; usual daily dose: 60-100 g (90-150 mL) daily

Rectal administration: 200 g (300 mL) diluted with 700 mL of H_2O or NS; administer rectally via rectal balloon catheter and retain 30-60 minutes every 4-6 hours

Constipation: Oral: 15-30 mL/day increased to 60 mL/day if necessary

Monitoring Parameters Blood pressure, standing/supine; serum potassium, bowel movement patterns, fluid status, serum ammonia

Patient Information Lactulose can be taken "as is" or diluted with water, fruit juice or milk, or taken in a food; laxative results may not occur for 24-48 hours

Nursing Implications Dilute lactulose in water, usually 60-120 mL, prior to administering through a gastric or feeding tube

Dosage Forms Syrup: 10 g/15 mL (15 mL, 30 mL, 237 mL, 473 mL, 946 mL, 1890 mL)

♦ **Lactulose PSE**® *see Lactulose on previous page*

♦ **L-AmB** *see Amphotericin B, Liposomal on page 77*

♦ **Lamictal**® *see Lamotrigine on next page*

♦ **Lamisil**® *see Terbinafine on page 1114*

Lamivudine (la MI vyoo deen)

Related Information

Antiretroviral Agents *on page 1306*

Antiretroviral Therapy for HIV Infection *on page 1410*

Management of Healthcare Worker Exposures to HIV *on page 1374*

U.S. Brand Names Epivir®; Epivir® HBV

Synonyms 3TC

Therapeutic Category Antiretroviral Agent, Reverse Transcriptase Inhibitor; Reverse Transcriptase Inhibitor

Use Treatment of HIV infection when antiretroviral therapy is warranted; should always be used as part of a multidrug regimen (at least three antiretroviral agents); indicated for the treatment of chronic hepatitis B associated with evidence of hepatitis B viral replication and active liver inflammation

Pregnancy Risk Factor C

Pregnancy/Breast-Feeding Implications

Clinical effects on the fetus: Use only if the potential benefits outweigh the risks. Combination therapy with zidovudine and lamivudine is currently being investigated to decrease the maternal/fetal transmission of HIV.

Breast-feeding/lactation: HIV-infected mothers are discouraged from breast-feeding to decrease postnatal transmission of HIV

Contraindications Hypersensitivity to lamivudine or any component

Warnings/Precautions A decreased dosage is recommended in patients with renal dysfunction since AUC, C_{max}, and half-life increased with diminishing renal function; use with extreme caution in children with history of pancreatitis or risk factors for development of pancreatitis. Do not use as monotherapy in treatment of HIV.

Adverse Reactions

>10%:

Central nervous system: Headache, insomnia, malaise, fatigue, pain

Gastrointestinal: Nausea, diarrhea, vomiting

Neuromuscular & skeletal: Peripheral neuropathy, paresthesia

Respiratory: Nasal signs and symptoms, cough

1% to 10%:

Central nervous system: Dizziness, depression, fever, chills

Dermatologic: Rashes

Gastrointestinal: Anorexia, abdominal pain, dyspepsia, increased amylase

Hematologic: Neutropenia, anemia

Hepatic: Elevated AST/ALT

Neuromuscular & skeletal: Myalgia, arthralgia

<1%: Pancreatitis, thrombocytopenia, hyperbilirubinemia

Overdosage/Toxicology

Very limited information is available although there have been no clinical signs or symptoms noted and hematologic tests remained normal in overdose

No antidote is available; unknown dialyzability

Drug Interactions Increased effect: Zidovudine concentrations increase (~39%) with coadministration with lamivudine; trimethoprim/sulfamethoxazole increases lamivudine's AUC and decreases its renal clearance by 44% and 29%, respectively; although the AUC was not significantly affected, absorption of lamivudine was slowed and C_{max} was 40% lower when administered to patients in the fed versus the fasted state

Stability Store solution at 2°C to 25°C tightly closed

Mechanism of Action After lamivudine is triphosphorylated, the principle mode of action is inhibition of HIV reverse transcription via viral DNA chain termination; inhibits RNA- and DNA-dependent DNA polymerase activities of reverse transcriptase. The monophosphate form of lamivudine is incorporated into the viral DNA by hepatitis B virus polymerase, resulting in DNA chain termination.

Pharmacodynamics/Kinetics

Absorption: Oral: Rapid

Distribution: V_d: 1.3 L/kg

Protein binding, plasma: <36%

Metabolism: 5.6% metabolized to trans-sulfoxide metabolite

Bioavailability: Absolute; Cp_{max} decreased with food although AUC not significantly affected

(Continued)

Lamivudine *(Continued)*

Children: 66%
Adults: 87%
Half-life: Children: 2 hours; Adults: 5-7 hours
Elimination: Most eliminated unchanged in urine

Usual Dosage Oral: Use with at least two other antiretroviral agents when treating HIV
Children 3 months to 12 years: 4 mg/kg twice daily (maximum: 150 mg twice daily)
Adolescents 12-16 years and Adults: 150 mg twice daily
Prevention of HIV following needlesticks: 150 mg twice daily (with zidovudine and a protease inhibitor)
Adults <50 kg: 2 mg/kg twice daily
Treatment of hepatitis B: 100 mg/day
Dosing interval in renal impairment in patients >16 years for HIV:
Cl_{cr} 30-49 mL/minute: Administer 150 mg once daily
Cl_{cr} 15-29 mL/minute: Administer 150 mg first dose, then 100 mg once daily
Cl_{cr} 5-14 mL/minute: Administer 150 mg first dose, then 50 mg once daily
Cl_{cr} <5 mL/minute: Administer 50 mg first dose, then 25 mg once daily
Dosing interval in renal impairment in patients with hepatitis B:
Cl_{cr} 30-49: Administer 100 mg first dose then 50 mg once daily
Cl_{cr} 15-29: Administer 100 mg first dose then 25 mg once daily
Cl_{cr} 5-14: Administer 35 mg first dose then 15 mg once daily
Cl_{cr} <5: Administer 35 mg first dose then 10 mg once daily
Dialysis: No data available

Monitoring Parameters Amylase, bilirubin, liver enzymes, hematologic parameters, viral load, and CD4 count; signs and symptoms of pancreatitis

Patient Information Patients may still experience illnesses associated with HIV infection; lamivudine is not a cure for HIV infection nor has it been shown to reduce the risk of transmission to others; long-term effects are unknown; take exactly as prescribed; children should be monitored for symptoms of pancreatitis

Additional Information Lamivudine has been well studied in the treatment of chronic hepatitis B infection. Potential compliance problems, frequency of administration and adverse effects should be discussed with patients before initiating therapy to help prevent the emergence of resistance.

Dosage Forms
Solution, oral: 5 mg/mL (240 mL); 10 mg/mL (240 mL)
Tablet: 100 mg, 150 mg

Lamotrigine *(la MOE tri jeen)*

Related Information
Anticonvulsants by Seizure Type *on page 1300*
Epilepsy Treatment *on page 1468*
U.S. Brand Names Lamictal®
Synonyms BW-430C; LTG
Therapeutic Category Anticonvulsant
Use Partial/secondary generalized seizures in adults; childhood epilepsy, including Lennox-Gastaut disorder **(not approved for use in children <2 years of age)**
Pregnancy Risk Factor C
Contraindications History of hypersensitivity to lamotrigine or any component
Warnings/Precautions Lactation, impaired renal, hepatic, or cardiac function; avoid abrupt cessation, taper over at least 2 weeks if possible. Severe and potentially life-threatening skin rashes have been reported; this appears to occur most frequently in pediatric patients.
Adverse Reactions 1% to 10%:
Central nervous system: Dizziness, sedation, ataxia
Dermatologic: Hypersensitivity rash, Stevens-Johnson syndrome, angioedema
Ocular: Nystagmus, diplopia
Renal: Hematuria
Overdosage/Toxicology
Decontaminate using lavage/activated charcoal with cathartic
Multiple dosing of activated charcoal may be useful
Drug Interactions
Decreased effect: Acetaminophen (increased renal clearance); carbamazepine, phenobarbital, and phenytoin (increased metabolic clearance)
Increased effect: Valproic acid increases half-life of lamotrigine (decreased metabolic clearance)
Mechanism of Action A triazine derivative which inhibits release of glutamate (an excitatory amino acid) and inhibits voltage-sensitive sodium channels, which stabilizes neuronal membranes
Pharmacodynamics/Kinetics
Distribution: V_d: 1.1 L/kg
Protein binding: 55%
Metabolism: Hepatic and renal
Half-life: 24 hours; increases to 59 hours with concomitant valproic acid therapy; decreases with concomitant phenytoin or carbamazepine therapy to 15 hours
Peak levels: Within 1-4 hours
Elimination: In urine as the glucuronide conjugate

Usual Dosage Oral:

Children 2-12 years:

With concomitant AEDs including valproic acid therapy: Initial: 0.15 mg/kg/day in 1-2 divided doses for 2 weeks; may increase by 0.3 mg/kg/day in 1-2 divided doses for 2 weeks; may increase by 0.3 mg/kg/day at 1- to 2-week intervals in 1-2 divided doses; see table

With concomitant AEDs without valproic acid therapy: Initial: 0.6 mg/kg/day in 2 divided doses for 2 weeks, then 1-2 mg/kg/day in 2 divided doses for 2 weeks; may increase by 1.2 mg/kg/day (round down to nearest 5 mg) at 1- to 2-week intervals; usual maintenance dose: 5-15 mg/kg/day; maximum: 400 mg/day in 2 divided doses

Lamictal Added to an AED Regimen Containing VPA in Patients 2-12 Years of Age

Weeks 1 and 2	0.15 mg/kg/day in 1 or 2 divided doses, rounded down to the nearest 5 mg; if the initial calculated dose is 2.5-5 mg, then 5 mg should be taken on alternate days for the first 2 weeks
Weeks 3 and 4	0.3 mg/kg/day in 1 or 2 divided doses, rounded down to the nearest 5 mg

Usual maintenance dose: 1-5 mg/kg/day (maximum: 200 mg/day in 1-2 divided doses). To achieve usual maintenance dose, subsequent doses should be increased every 1-2 weeks as follows: Calculate 0.3 mg/kg/day, round this amount down to the neares 5 mg, and add this amount to the previously administered daily dose

Adults: Initial: 50-100 mg/day then titrate to daily maintenance dose of 100-400 mg/day in 1-2 divided daily doses

With concomitant valproic acid therapy: Start initial dose at 25 mg/day then titrate to maintenance dose of 50-200 mg/day in 1-2 divided daily doses

Dietary Considerations Food: Has no effect on absorption, take without regard to meals; drug may cause GI upset

Monitoring Parameters Seizure (frequency and duration); serum levels of concurrent anticonvulsants; hypersensitivity reactions (especially rash)

Reference Range Therapeutic range: 2-4 µg/mL

Additional Information Low water solubility

Dosage Forms

Tablet: 25 mg, 100 mg, 150 mg, 200 mg

Tablet, dispersable, chewable: 5 mg, 25 mg

Extemporaneous Preparations A 1 mg/mL oral suspension was stable for 28 days stored at room temperature when compounded as follows:

Triturate five 25 mg tablets in a mortar, reduce to a fine powder, then make a paste with a small amount of syrup, add the remaining syrup to almost desired volume, then transfer to a graduate and qs to 125 mL

Shake well before using and keep in refrigerator

Stability information from Glaxo Wellcome Co.

- **Lamprene®** see Clofazimine on page 278
- **Lanacane® [OTC]** see Benzocaine on page 133
- **Lanacort® [OTC]** see Hydrocortisone on page 579
- **Lanaphilic® Topical [OTC]** see Urea on page 1199
- **Laniazid®** see Isoniazid on page 633
- **Lanorinal®** see Butalbital Compound on page 165
- **Lanoxicaps®** see Digoxin on page 359
- **Lanoxin®** see Digoxin on page 359

Lansoprazole (lan SOE pra zole)

Related Information

Helicobacter pylori Treatment on page 1473

U.S. Brand Names Prevacid®

Therapeutic Category Gastric Acid Secretion Inhibitor; Proton Pump Inhibitor

Use Short-term treatment (up to 4 weeks) for healing and symptom relief of active duodenal ulcers (should not be used for maintenance therapy of duodenal ulcers); as part of a multiple drug regimen for *H. pylori* eradication; short-term treatment of symptomatic GERD; up to 8 weeks of treatment for all grades of erosive esophagitis (8 additional weeks can be given for incompletely healed esophageal erosions or for recurrence); and long-term treatment of pathological hypersecretory conditions, including Zollinger-Ellison syndrome

Pregnancy Risk Factor B

Contraindications Should not be taken by anyone with a known hypersensitivity to lansoprazole or any of the formulation's components

Warnings/Precautions Liver disease may require dosage reductions

Adverse Reactions

1% to 10%:

Central nervous system: Fatigue, dizziness, headache

Gastrointestinal: Abdominal pain, diarrhea, nausea, increased appetite, hypergastrinoma

<1%: Rash, tinnitus, proteinuria

(Continued)

Lansoprazole *(Continued)*

Overdosage/Toxicology
Symptoms of overdose include hypothermia, sedation, convulsions, decreased respiratory rate demonstrated in animals only

Treatment is supportive; not dialyzable

Drug Interactions CYP2C19 enzyme substrate, CYP3A3/4 enzyme substrate (minor)

Decreased effect: Ketoconazole, itraconazole, and other drugs dependent upon acid for absorption; theophylline clearance increased slightly; sucralfate delays and reduces lansoprazole absorption by 30%

Stability Lansoprazole is unstable in acidic media (eg, stomach contents) and is, therefore, administered as enteric coated granules in capsule form; the capsule contents (granules) may be given via nasogastric tube when mixed (not crushed) with apple juice

Pharmacodynamics/Kinetics
Absorption: Food affected

Bioavailability: 80% (50% if given 30 minutes after food)

Peak plasma levels: 1.7 hours

Protein binding: 97%

Metabolism: Hepatic and in parietal cells

Half-life: 2 hours (2.9 hours in elderly, 7 hours with hepatic impairment)

Excretion: 33% in urine; 67% in feces

Usual Dosage
Duodenal ulcer: 15 mg once daily for 4 weeks; maintenance therapy: 15 mg once daily

Gastric ulcer: 30 mg once daily for up to 8 weeks

GERD: 15 mg once daily for up to 8 weeks

Erosive esophagitis: 30 mg once daily for up to 8 weeks, continued treatment for an additional 8 weeks may be considered for recurrence or for patients that do not heal after the first 8 weeks of therapy. Maintenance therapy: 15 mg once daily.

Hypersecretory conditions: Initial: 60 mg once daily; adjust dose based upon patient response and to reduce acid secretion to <10 mEq/hour (5 mEq/hour in patients with prior gastric surgery); doses of 90 mg twice daily have been used; administer doses >120 mg/day in divided doses.

Helicobacter pylori-associated antral gastritis: 30 mg/day for 2 weeks (in combination with 1 g amoxicillin and 500 mg clarithromycin given twice daily for 14 days). Alternatively, in patients allergic to or intolerant of clarithromycin or in whom resistance to clarithromycin is known or suspected, lansoprazole 30 mg every 8 hours and amoxicillin 1 g every 8 hours may be given for 2 weeks

Dosing adjustment in hepatic impairment: Dose reduction is necessary for severe hepatic impairment

Administration For nasogastric tube administration, the capsules can be opened, the granules mixed (not crushed) with 40 mL of apple juice and then injected through the NG tube into the stomach, then flush tube with additional apple juice

Monitoring Parameters Patients with Zollinger-Ellison syndrome should be monitored for gastric acid output, which should be maintained at 10 mEq/hour or less during the last hour before the next lansoprazole dose; lab monitoring should include CBC, liver function, renal function, and serum gastrin levels

Patient Information Take before eating; do not crush or chew capsules

Dosage Forms Capsule, delayed release: 15 mg, 30 mg

- ◆ **Largactil**® *see* Chlorpromazine *on page 248*
- ◆ **Lariam**® *see* Mefloquine *on page 723*
- ◆ **Larodopa**® *see* Levodopa *on page 671*
- ◆ **Lasix**® *see* Furosemide *on page 525*
- ◆ **L-asparaginase** *see* Asparaginase *on page 100*

Latanoprost *(la TAN oh prost)*

Related Information
Glaucoma Drug Therapy Comparison *on page 1322*

U.S. Brand Names Xalatan®

Therapeutic Category Prostaglandin, Ophthalmic

Use Reduction of elevated intraocular pressure in patients with open-angle glaucoma and ocular hypertension who are intolerant of the other IOP lowering medications or insufficiently responsive (failed to achieve target IOP determined after multiple measurements over time) to another IOP lowering medication

Pregnancy Risk Factor C

Contraindications Hypersensitivity to any component of product

Warnings/Precautions Latanoprost may gradually change eye color, increasing the amount of brown pigment in the iris by increasing the number of melanosome in melanocytes. The long-term effects on the melanocytes and the consequences of potential injury to the melanocytes or deposition of pigment granules to other areas of the eye is currently unknown. Patients should be examined regularly, and depending on the clinical situation, treatment may be stopped if increased pigmentation ensues.

There have been reports of bacterial keratitis associated with the use of multiple-dose containers of topical ophthalmic products. Do not administer while wearing contact lenses.

Adverse Reactions
>10%: Ocular: Blurred vision, burning and stinging, conjunctival hyperemia, foreign body sensation, itching, increased pigmentation of the iris, and punctate epithelial keratopathy

1% to 10%:
Cardiovascular: Chest pain, angina pectoris
Dermatologic: Rash, allergic skin reaction
Neuromuscular & skeletal: Myalgia, arthralgia, back pain
Ocular: Dry eye, excessive tearing, eye pain, lid crusting, lid edema, lid erythema, lid discomfort/pain, photophobia
Respiratory: Upper respiratory tract infection, cold, flu
<1%: Conjunctivitis, diplopia, discharge from the eye, retinal artery embolus, retinal detachment, vitreous hemorrhage from diabetic retinopathy

Overdosage/Toxicology
Symptoms include ocular irritation and conjunctival or episcleral hyperemia
Treatment should be symptomatic

Drug Interactions Decreased effect: *In vitro* studies have shown that precipitation occurs when eye drops containing thimerosal are mixed with latanoprost. If such drugs are used, administer with an interval of at least 5 minutes between applications

Stability Protect from light; store intact bottles under refrigeration (2°C to 8°C/36°F to 46°F). Once opened, the container may be stored at room temperature up to 25°C (77°F) for 6 weeks.

Mechanism of Action Latanoprost is a prostaglandin F_2-alpha analog believed to reduce intraocular pressure by increasing the outflow of the aqueous humor

Pharmacodynamics/Kinetics
Onset of effect: 3-4 hours
Maximum effect: 8-12 hours
Absorption: Through the cornea where the isopropyl ester prodrug is hydrolyzed by esterases to the biologically active acid. Peak concentration is reached in 2 hours after topical administration in the aqueous humor.
Distribution: V_d: 0.16 L/kg
Half-life: 17 minutes
Metabolism: Primarily metabolized by the liver via fatty acid beta-oxidation
Elimination: After hepatic metabolism, the metabolites are mainly eliminated via the kidneys

Usual Dosage Adults: Ophthalmic: 1 drop (1.5 mcg) in the affected eye(s) once daily in the evening; do not exceed the once daily dosage because it has been shown that more frequent administration may decrease the IOP lowering effect

Administration If more than one topical ophthalmic drug is being used, administer the drugs at least 5 minutes apart

Patient Information Inform patients about the possibility of iris color change because of an increase of the brown pigment and resultant cosmetically different eye coloration that may occur. Iris pigmentation changes may be more noticeable in patients with green-brown, blue/gray-brown, or yellow-brown irides.

Advise patients to avoid allowing the tip of the dispensing container to contact the eye or surrounding structures because this could cause the tip to become contaminated by common bacteria known to cause ocular infections. Serious damage to the eye and subsequent loss of vision may result from using contaminated solutions.

Advise patients that if they develop any ocular reactions, particularly conjunctivitis and lid reactions, they should immediately seek their physician's advice.

Latanoprost contains benzalkonium chloride, which may be absorbed by contact lenses. Remove contact lenses prior to administration of the solution. Lenses may be reinserted 15 minutes following latanoprost administration.

If more than one topical ophthalmic drug is being used, administer the drugs at least 5 minutes apart.

Dosage Forms Solution, ophthalmic: 0.005% (2.5 mL)

♦ **Laxatives, Classification and Properties** *see page 1326*
♦ **LazerSporin-C® Otic** *see Neomycin, Polymyxin B, and Hydrocortisone on page 827*
♦ **l-Bunolol Hydrochloride** *see Levobunolol on page 670*
♦ **LCR** *see Vincristine on page 1219*
♦ **L-Deprenyl** *see Selegiline on page 1053*
♦ **L-Dopa** *see Levodopa on page 671*

Leflunomide (le FLU no mide)

U.S. Brand Names Arava™
Therapeutic Category Antimetabolite
Use Treatment of active rheumatoid arthritis to reduce signs and symptoms and to retard structural damage as evidenced by x-ray erosions and joint space narrowing
Pregnancy Risk Factor X
Pregnancy/Breast-Feeding Implications Has been associated with teratogenic and embryolethal effects in animal models at low doses. Leflunomide is contraindicated in pregnant women or women of childbearing potential who are not using reliable contraception. Pregnancy must be excluded prior to initiating treatment. Following treatment, pregnancy should be avoided until the drug elimination procedure is completed (see Additional Information).

Breast-feeding is contraindicated. It is not known whether leflunomide is secreted in human milk; however, there is a potential for serious adverse reactions in nursing infants. A decision should be made whether to discontinue nursing or discontinue the drug, taking into account the importance of the drug to the mother.
(Continued)

Leflunomide *(Continued)*

Contraindications Pregnancy/breast-feeding; known hypersensitivity to leflunomide or any component

Warnings/Precautions Hepatic disease (including seropositive hepatitis B or C patients) may increase risk of hepatotoxicity; immunosuppression may increase the risk of lymphoproliferative disorders or other malignancies; women of childbearing potential should not receive leflunomide until pregnancy has been excluded, patients have been counseled concerning fetal risk and reliable contraceptive measures have been confirmed. Caution in renal impairment, immune deficiency, bone marrow dysplasia or severe, uncontrolled infection. Use of live vaccines is not recommended; will increase uric acid excretion.

Adverse Reactions

>10%:
  Gastrointestinal: Diarrhea (17%)
  Respiratory: Respiratory tract infection (15%)

1% to 10%:
  Cardiovascular: Hypertension (10%), chest pain (2%), palpitation, tachycardia, vasculitis, vasodilation, varicose vein, edema (peripheral)
  Central nervous system: Headache (7%), dizziness (4%), pain (2%), fever, malaise, migraine, anxiety, depression, insomnia, sleep disorder
  Dermatologic: Alopecia (10%), rash (10%), pruritus (4%), dry skin (2%), eczema (2%), acne, dermatitis, hair discoloration, hematoma, herpes infection, nail disorder, subcutaneous nodule, skin disorder/discoloration, skin ulcer, bruising
  Endocrine & metabolic: Hypokalemia (1%), diabetes mellitus, hyperglycemia, hyperlipidemia, hyperthyroidism, menstrual disorder
  Gastrointestinal: Nausea (9%), abdominal pain (5%), dyspepsia (5%), weight loss (4%), anorexia (3%), gastroenteritis (3%), stomatitis (3%), vomiting (3%), cholelithiasis, colitis, constipation, esophagitis, flatulence, gastritis, gingivitis, melena, candidiasis (oral), enlarged salivary gland, tooth disorder, xerostomia, taste disturbance
  Genitourinary: Urinary tract infection (5%), albuminuria, cystitis, dysuria, hematuria, vaginal candidiasis, prostate disorder, urinary frequency
  Hematologic: Anemia
  Hepatic: Abnormal LFTs (5%)
  Neuromuscular & skeletal: Back pain (5%), joint disorder (4%), weakness (3%), tenosynovitis (3%), synovitis (2%), arthralgia (1%), paresthesia (2%), muscle cramps (1%), neck pain, pelvic pain, increased CPK, arthrosis, bursitis, myalgia, bone necrosis, bone pain, tendon rupture, neuralgia, neuritis
  Ocular: Blurred vision, cataract, conjunctivitis, eye disorder
  Respiratory: Bronchitis (7%), cough (3%), pharyngitis (3%), pneumonia (2%), rhinitis (2%), sinusitis (2%), asthma, dyspnea, epistaxis, lung disorder
  Miscellaneous: Infection (4%), accidental injury (5%), allergic reactions (2%), diaphoresis

<1%: Anaphylaxis, urticaria, eosinophilia, thrombocytopenia, leukopenia

Overdosage/Toxicology There is no human experience with overdosage. Leflunomide is not dialyzable. Cholestyramine and/or activated charcoal enhance elimination of leflunomide's active metabolite (MI). In cases of significant overdose or toxicity, cholestyramine 8 g every 8 hours for 1-3 days may be administered to enhance elimination. Plasma levels are reduced by approximately 40% in 24 hours and 49% to 65% after 48 hours of cholestyramine dosing.

Drug Interactions Cytochrome P-450 2C9 enzyme inhibitor
  Increased effect: Theoretically, the concomitant use of drugs metabolized by this enzyme, which includes many NSAIDs, may result in increased serum concentrations. Coadministration with methotrexate increases the risk of hepatotoxicity. Leflunomide may also enhance the hepatotoxicity of other drugs. Tolbutamide free fraction may be increased. Rifampin may increase the serum concentrations of the active metabolite of leflunomide. Leflunomide has uricosuric activity and may enhance activity of other uricosuric agents.
  Decreased effect: Administration of cholestyramine and activated charcoal enhance the elimination of leflunomide's active metabolite

Stability Protect from light; store at 25°C (77°F)

Mechanism of Action Inhibits pyrimidine synthesis, resulting in antiproliferative and anti-inflammatory effects

Pharmacodynamics/Kinetics
  Distribution: V_d: 0.13 L/kg
  Metabolism: Hepatic, to A77 1726 (MI) which accounts for nearly all pharmacologic activity; further metabolism to multiple inactive metabolites
  Bioavailability: 80%
  Half-life: Mean 14-15 days; enterohepatic recycling appears to contribute to the long half-life of this agent, since activated charcoal and cholestyramine substantially reduce plasma half-life
  Time to peak: 6-12 hours
  Elimination: Urine 43%; Feces 48%

Usual Dosage
  Adults: Oral: Initial: 100 mg/day for 3 days, followed by 20 mg/day; dosage may be decreased to 10 mg/day in patients who have difficulty tolerating the 20 mg dose. Due to the long half-life of the active metabolite, plasma levels may require a prolonged period to decline after dosage reduction.
  Dosing adjustment in renal impairment: No specific dosage adjustment is recommended. There is no clinical experience in the use of leflunomide in patients with renal

impairment. The free fraction of MI is doubled in dialysis patients. Patients should be monitored closely for adverse effects requiring dosage adjustment.

Dosing adjustment in hepatic impairment: No specific dosage adjustment is recommended. Since the liver is involved in metabolic activation and subsequent metabolism/elimination of leflunomide, patients with hepatic impairment should be monitored closely for adverse effects requiring dosage adjustment.

Guidelines for dosage adjustment or discontinuation based on the severity and persistence of ALT elevation secondary to leflunomide have been developed. For ALT elevations >2 times the upper limit of normal, dosage reduction to 10 mg/day may allow continued administration. Cholestyramine 8 g 3 times/day for 1-3 days may be administered to decrease plasma levels. If elevations >2 times but ≤3 times the upper limit of normal persist, liver biopsy is recommended. If elevations >3 times the upper limit of normal persist despite cholestyramine administration and dosage reduction, leflunomide should be discontinued and drug elimination should be enhanced with additional cholestyramine as indicated.

Elderly: Although hepatic function may decline with age, no specific dosage adjustment is recommended. Patients should be monitored closely for adverse effects which may require dosage adjustment.

Dietary Considerations No interactions with food have been noted

Monitoring Parameters Serum transaminase determinations at baseline and monthly during the initial phase of treatment; if stable, monitoring frequency may be decreased to intervals determined by the individual clinical situation

Patient Information Do not take leflunomide if pregnant

Additional Information To enhance elimination, a drug elimination procedure has been developed. Without this procedure, it may take up to 2 years to reach plasma concentrations <0.02 mg/L (a concentration expected to have minimal risk of teratogenicity based on animal models). The procedure consists of the following steps: Administer cholestyramine 8 g 3 times/day for 11 days (the 11 days do not need to be consecutive). Plasma levels <0.02 mg/L should be verified by two separate tests performed at least 14 days apart. If plasma levels are >0.02 mg/L, additional cholestyramine treatment should be considered.

Dosage Forms Tablet: 10 mg, 20 mg, 100 mg

♦ **Lenoltec No 1, 2, 3, 4** see Acetaminophen and Codeine on page 21

♦ **Lente® Iletin® I** see Insulin Preparations on page 613

♦ **Lente® Iletin® II** see Insulin Preparations on page 613

♦ **Lente® Insulin** see Insulin Preparations on page 613

♦ **Lente® L** see Insulin Preparations on page 613

Lepirudin (leh puh ROO din)

U.S. Brand Names Refludan™

Therapeutic Category Anticoagulant

Use Anticoagulation in patients with heparin-induced thrombocytopenia (HIT) and associated thromboembolic disease in order to prevent further thromboembolic complications

Pregnancy Risk Factor B

Pregnancy/Breast-Feeding Implications Lepirudin crosses the placenta in pregnant rats; however, it is not known if lepirudin crosses the placenta in humans. It is not known if lepirudin is excreted in human milk.

Contraindications Patients with known hypersensitivity to hirudins

Warnings/Precautions

Hemorrhagic events: Intracranial bleeding following concomitant thrombolytic therapy with rt-PA or streptokinase may be life threatening. For patients with an increased risk of bleeding, a careful assessment weighing the risk of lepirudin administration versus its anticipated benefit has to be made by the treating physician. In particular, this includes the following conditions:

Recent puncture of large vessels or organ biopsy

Anomaly of vessels or organs

Recent cerebrovascular accident, stroke, intracerebral surgery, or other neuroaxial procedures

Severe uncontrolled hypertension

Bacterial endocarditis

Advanced renal impairment

Hemorrhagic diathesis

Recent major surgery

Recent major bleeding (eg, intracranial, gastrointestinal, intraocular, or pulmonary bleeding)

With renal impairment, relative overdose might occur even with standard dosage regimen. The bolus dose and rate of infusion must be reduced in patients with known or suspected renal insufficiency.

Formation of antihirudin antibodies was observed in ~40% of HIT patients treated with lepirudin. This may increase the anticoagulant effect of lepirudin possibly due to delayed renal elimination of active lepirudin-antihirudin complexes. Therefore, strict monitoring of APTT is necessary also during prolonged therapy. No evidence of neutralization of lepirudin or of allergic reactions associated with positive antibody test results was found.

Serious liver injury (eg, liver cirrhosis) may enhance the anticoagulant effect of lepirudin due to coagulation defects secondary to reduced generation of vitamin K-dependent clotting factors

(Continued)

Lepirudin *(Continued)*

Clinical trials have provided limited information to support any recommendations for re-exposure to lepirudin

Adverse Reactions

>10%: Bleeding was the most frequent adverse event observed in patients treated with lepirudin

Hematologic: Bleeding from puncture sites and wounds, anemia or isolated drop in hemoglobin, other hematoma and unclassified bleeding

1% to 10%:

Central nervous system: Fever

Dermatologic: Allergic skin reactions

Gastrointestinal: Gastrointestinal and rectal bleeding

Genitourinary: Hematuria, vaginal bleeding

Hepatic: Abnormal LFTs

Respiratory: Hemothorax

Miscellaneous: Epistaxis

Overdosage/Toxicology

Symptoms of overdosage: In case of overdose (eg, suggested by excessively high APTT values), the risk of bleeding is increased

Treatment: No specific antidote for lepirudin is available; if life-threatening bleeding occurs and excessive plasma levels of lepirudin are suspected, the following steps should be followed:

Immediately STOP LEPIRUDIN administration

Determine APTT and other coagulation levels as appropriate

Determine hemoglobin and prepare for blood transfusion

Follow current guidelines for treating patients with shock

Individual clinical case reports and *in vitro* data suggest that either hemofiltration or hemodialysis (using high-flux dialysis membranes with a cutoff point of 50,000 daltons, eg, AN/69) may be useful in this situation

Drug Interactions

Increased toxicity:

Concomitant treatment with thrombolytics (eg, rt-PA or streptokinase) may: ↑ the risk of bleeding complications and considerably enhance the effect of lepirudin on APTT prolongation

Concomitant treatment with coumarin derivatives (vitamin K antagonists) and drugs that affect platelet function may also increase the risk of bleeding

Stability

Intact vials should be stored at 2°C to 25°C (36°F to 77°F)

Intravenous bolus: Use a solution with a concentration of 5 mg/mL

Preparation of a lepirudin solution with a concentration of 5 mg/mL: Reconstitute one vial (50 mg) of lepirudin with 1 mL of sterile water for injection or 0.9% sodium chloride injection; the final concentration of 5 mg/mL is obtained by transferring the contents of the vial into a sterile, single-use syringe (of at least 10 mL capacity) and diluting the solution to a total volume of 10 mL using sterile water for injection, 0.9% sodium chloride, or 5% dextrose in water

Intravenous infusion: For continuous intravenous infusion, solutions with concentrations of 0.2 or 0.4 mg/mL may be used

Preparation of a lepirudin solution with a concentration of 0.2 mg/mL or 0.4 mg/mL: Reconstitute 2 vials (50 mg each) of lepirudin with 1 mL each using either sterile water for injection or 0.9% sodium chloride injection; the final concentration of 0.2 mg/mL or 0.4 mg/mL is obtained by transferring the contents of both vials into an infusion bag containing 500 mL or 250 mL of 0.9% sodium chloride injection or 5% dextrose injection

Reconstituted solutions of lepirudin are stable for 24 hours at room temperature

Mechanism of Action

Lepirudin is a highly specific direct inhibitor of thrombin; lepirudin is a recombinant hirudin derived from yeast cells

Pharmacodynamics/Kinetics

Distribution: Lepirudin follows a two-compartment model. Distribution is essential confined to extracellular fluids.

Metabolism: Metabolized by release of amino acids via catabolic hydrolysis of the parent drug. ~ 48% of the administered dose is excreted in the urine which consists of unchanged drug (35%) and other fragments of the parent drug.

Half-life:

Initial: ~10 minutes

Terminal: 1.3 hours in health volunteers; however, systemic clearance is proportional to glomerular filtration rate or creatinine clearance. Terminal half-life in patients with marked renal insufficiency (creatinine clearance <15 mL/minute) and on hemodialysis is prolonged up to 2 days.

Elimination: Renal

Usual Dosage

Adults:

I.V. bolus: 0.4 mg/kg body weight (up to 110 kg) slowly (eg, over 15-20 seconds)

Followed by a continuous I.V. infusion of 0.15 mg/kg body weight (up to 110 kg)/hour for 2-10 days or longer if clinically indicated.

Note: Normally the initial dose depends on the patient's body weight. This is valid up to a body weight of 110 kg. In patients with a body weight exceeding 110 kg, the initial dose should not be increased beyond the 110 kg body weight dose (maximum initial dose of 44 mg, maximum initial infusion dose of 16.5 mg/hour).

Monitoring and adjusting therapy: Standard recommendations:
Monitoring:
In general, the dosage (infusion rate) should be adjusted according to the APTT ratio (patient APTT at a given time over an APTT reference value, usually median of the laboratory normal range for aPTT)

The target range for the APTT ratio during treatment (therapeutic window) should be 1.5-2.5; data from clinical trials in HIT patients suggest that with APTT ratios higher than this target range, the risk of bleeding increases, while there is no incremental increase in clinical efficacy

Lepirudin should not be started in patients presenting with a baseline APTT ratio of 2.5 or more, in order to avoid initial overdosing

The first APTT determination for monitoring treatment should be done 4 hours after start of the lepirudin infusion

Follow-up APTT determinations are recommended at least once daily, as long as treatment with lepirudin is ongoing

More frequent APTT monitoring is highly recommended in patients with renal impairment or serious liver injury

Dose modifications:
Any APTT ratio out of the target range is to be confirmed at once before drawing conclusions with respect to dose modifications, unless there is a clinical need to react immediately

If the confirmed APTT ratio is above the target range, the infusion should be stopped for 2 hours; at restart, the infusion rate should be decreased by 50% (no additional intravenous bolus should be administered); the APTT ratio should be determined again 4 hours later

If the confirmed APTT ratio is below the target range, the infusion rate should be increased in steps of 20%; the APTT ratio should be determined again 4 hours later

In general, an infusion rate of 0.21 mg/kg/hour should not be exceeded without checking for coagulation abnormalities which might be preventive of an appropriate APTT response

Dosing adjustment in renal impairment: All patients with a creatinine clearance of <60 mL/minute or a serum creatinine of >1.5 mg should receive a reduction in lepirudin dosage; there is only limited information on the therapeutic use of lepirudin in HIT patients with significant renal impairment; the following dosage recommendations are mainly based on single-dose studies in a small number of patients with renal impairment

Bolus dose: Reduce to 0.4 mg/kg body weight

Infusion dose reductions: In hemodialysis patients or in case of acute renal failure (creatinine clearance below 15 mL/minutes or serum creatinine >6.0 mg/dL), infusion of lepirudin is to be avoided or stopped; additional intravenous bolus doses of 0.1 mg/kg body weight should be considered every other day only if the APTT ratio falls below the lower therapeutic limit of 1.5; see table.

Lepirudin Infusion Rates in Patients With Renal Impairment

Creatinine Clearance (mL/minute)	Serum Creatinine (mg/dL)	Adjusted Infusion Rate	
		% of Standard Initial Infusion Rate	mg/kg/hour
45-60	1.6-2.0	50%	0.075
30-44	2.1-3.0	30%	0.045
15-29	3.1-6.0	15%	0.0225
<15*	>6.0*	Avoid or STOP infusion*	

Concomitant use with thrombolytic therapy:
I.V. bolus: 0.2 mg/kg body weight
I.V. infusion: 0.1 mg/kg body weight/hour

Use in patients scheduled for a switch to oral anticoagulation: If a patient is scheduled to receive coumarin derivatives for oral anticoagulation after lepirudin therapy, the dose of lepirudin should first be gradually reduced in order to reach an a APTT ratio just above 1.5 before initiating oral anticoagulation; as soon as an INR of 2.0 is reached, lepirudin should be stopped

Administration Administer only intravenously; administer I.V. bolus over 15-20 seconds
Monitoring Parameters APTT levels
Reference Range APTT 1.5 to 2.5 times the control value
Dosage Forms Injection: 50 mg vials

♦ **Lescol®** see Fluvastatin on page 510

Letrozole (LET roe zole)

U.S. Brand Names Femara™
Therapeutic Category Antineoplastic Agent, Hormone Antagonist; Antineoplastic Agent, Hormone (Antiestrogen); Aromatase Inhibitor
Use Treatment of advanced breast cancer in postmenopausal women with disease progression following antiestrogen therapy
Pregnancy Risk Factor D
(Continued)

Letrozole *(Continued)*

Pregnancy/Breast-Feeding Implications

Clinical effects on the fetus: Letrozole may cause fetal harm when administered to pregnant women. Letrozole is embryotoxic and fetotoxic when administered to rats. There are no studies in pregnant women and letrozole is indicated for postmenopausal women.

Breast-feeding/lactation: It is not known if letrozole is excreted in breast milk; exercise caution when letrozole is administered to nursing women

Contraindications Hypersensitivity to letrozole or any of its excipients

Warnings/Precautions Letrozole was not mutagenic in *in vitro* tests but was observed to be a potential clastogen in *in vitro* assays. Repeated dosing caused sexual inactivity in females and atrophy in the reproductive tract in males and females at doses of 0.6 mg/kg, 0.1 mg/kg, and 0.03 mg/kg in mice, rats, and dogs, respectively (~1 mg/kg, 0.4 mg/kg, and 0.4 mg/kg the maximum recommended human doses, respectively).

Moderate decreases in lymphocyte counts, of uncertain clinical significance, were observed in some patients receiving letrozole 2.5 mg. This depression was transient in ~50% of those affected. Two patients on letrozole developed thrombocytopenia; relationship to the drug was unclear.

Increases in AST, ALT, and GGT ≥5 times the upper limit of normal (ULN) and of bilirubin ≥1.5 times the ULN were most often associated with metastatic disease in the liver.

Adverse Reactions

>10%: Gastrointestinal: Nausea

1% to 10%:

Central nervous system: Headache, somnolence, dizziness

Dermatologic: Hot flashes, rash, pruritus

Gastrointestinal: Vomiting, constipation, diarrhea, abdominal pain, anorexia, dyspepsia

Neuromuscular: Arthralgia

Respiratory: Dyspnea, coughing

<1%: Thromboembolic events, vaginal bleeding

Overdosage/Toxicology

No experience with letrozole overdose has been reported. In single-dose studies, the highest dose used was 30 mg, which was well tolerated. Lethality was observed in mice and rats following single oral doses that were ≥2000 mg/kg (~4000 to 8000 times the maximum daily doses recommended in humans); death was associated with reduced motor activity, ataxia, and dyspnea. Lethality was observed in cats following single I.V. doses that were ≥10 mg/kg (~50 times the maximum daily dose recommended in humans): death was preceded by depressed blood pressure and arrhythmias.

Firm recommendations for treatment are not possible; emesis could be induced if the patient is alert. In general, supportive care and frequent monitoring of vital signs are appropriate.

Drug Interactions CYP3A3/4 and 2A6 enzyme substrate; CYP2A6 and 2C19 enzyme inhibitor

Mechanism of Action Nonsteroidal, competitive inhibitor of the aromatase enzyme system which binds to the heme group of aromatase, a cytochrome P-450 enzyme which catalyzes conversion of androgens to estrogens (specifically, androstenedione to estrone and testosterone to estradiol). This leads to inhibition of the enzyme and a significant reduction in plasma estrogen levels. Approximately 30% of breast cancers are sensitive to this estrogen deprivation.

Pharmacodynamics/Kinetics

Absorption: Well absorbed from GI tract; not affected by food

Distribution: V_d: ~1.9 L/kg

Protein binding, plasma: Weakly bound

Metabolism: In the liver to a pharmacologically inactive carbinol metabolite

Half-life: Terminal elimination: ~2 days

Time to steady state plasma concentrations: 2-6 weeks

Elimination: Renally of the glucuronide conjugate of the metabolite; ~90% of letrozole is recovered in urine

Usual Dosage Oral (refer to individual protocols):

Adults: 2.5 mg once daily without regard to meals; continue treatment until tumor progression is evident. Patients treated with letrozole do not require glucocorticoid or mineralocorticoid replacement therapy.

Dosage adjustment in renal impairment: No dosage adjustment is required in patients with renal impairment if Cl_{cr} ≥10 mL/minute

Dosage adjustment in hepatic impairment: No dosage adjustment is recommended for patients with mild-to-moderate hepatic impairment. Patients with severe impairment of liver function have not been studied; dose patients with severe impairment of liver function with caution.

Monitoring Parameters Clinical/radiologic evidence of tumor regression in advanced breast cancer patients. Until the toxicity has been defined in larger patient populations, monitor the following laboratory tests periodically during therapy: complete blood counts, thyroid function tests, serum electrolytes, serum transaminases, and serum creatinine.

Dosage Forms Tablet: 2.5 mg

Leucovorin (loo koe VOR in)

Related Information

Cancer Chemotherapy Regimens *on page 1263*

Guidelines for the Prevention of Opportunistic Infections in Persons with HIV on page 1388

U.S. Brand Names Wellcovorin®

Synonyms Calcium Leucovorin; Citrovorum Factor; Folinic Acid; 5-Formyl Tetrahydrofolate; Leucovorin Calcium

Therapeutic Category Antidote, Folic Acid Antagonist; Antidote, Methotrexate; Folic Acid Derivative; Vitamin, Water Soluble

Use Antidote for folic acid antagonists (methotrexate [>100 mg/m²], trimethoprim, pyrimethamine); treatment of megaloblastic anemias when folate is deficient as in infancy, sprue, pregnancy, and nutritional deficiency when oral folate therapy is not possible; in combination with fluorouracil in the treatment of malignancy

Pregnancy Risk Factor C

Contraindications Pernicious anemia or vitamin B_{12} deficient megaloblastic anemias; should **NOT** be administered Intrathecally/Intraventricularly

Warnings/Precautions Use with caution in patients with a history of hypersensitivity

Adverse Reactions <1%: Rash, pruritus, erythema, urticaria, thrombocytosis, wheezing, anaphylactoid reactions

Stability

Leucovorin injection should be stored at room temperature and protected from light

Reconstituted solution is stated to be chemically stable for 7 days; reconstitutions with bacteriostatic water for injection, U.S.P., must be used within 7 days. Doses >10 mg/m² must be prepared using leucovorin reconstituted with sterile water for injection, U.S.P., and used immediately.

Stability of parenteral admixture at room temperature (25°C): 24 hours

Stability of parenteral admixture at refrigeration temperature (4°C): 4 days

Standard diluent: 50-100 mg/50 mL D_5W

Minimum volume: 50 mL D_5W

Concentrations of >2 mg/mL of leucovorin and >25 mg/mL of fluorouracil are **incompatible** (precipitation occurs)

Mechanism of Action A reduced form of folic acid, but does not require a reduction reaction by an enzyme for activation, allows for purine and thymidine synthesis, a necessity for normal erythropoiesis; leucovorin supplies the necessary cofactor blocked by MTX, enters the cells via the same active transport system as MTX

Pharmacodynamics/Kinetics

Onset of activity: Oral: Within 30 minutes; rapid, well absorbed but decreases at doses >25 mg; I.V.: Within 5 minutes

Absorption: Oral, I.M.: Rapid

Metabolism: Rapidly converted to (5MTHF) 5-methyl-tetrahydrofolate (active) in the intestinal mucosa and by the liver

Half-life: Leucovorin: 15 minutes; 5MTHF: 33-35 minutes

Elimination: Primarily in urine (80% to 90%) with small losses appearing in feces (5% to 8%)

Usual Dosage Children and Adults:

Treatment of folic acid antagonist overdosage (eg, pyrimethamine or trimethoprim): Oral: 2-15 mg/day for 3 days or until blood counts are normal or 5 mg every 3 days; doses of 6 mg/day are needed for patients with platelet counts <100,000/mm³

Folate-deficient megaloblastic anemia: I.M.: 1 mg/day

Megaloblastic anemia secondary to congenital deficiency of dihydrofolate reductase: I.M.: 3-6 mg/day

Rescue dose (rescue therapy should start within 24 hours of MTX therapy): I.V.: 10 mg/m² to start, then 10 mg/m² every 6 hours orally for 72 hours until serum MTX concentration is <10⁻⁸ molar; if serum creatinine 24 hours after methotrexate is elevated 50% or more above the pre-MTX serum creatinine **or** the serum MTX concentration is >5 x 10⁻⁶ molar (see graph), increase dose to 100 mg/m²/dose (preservative-free) every 3 hours until serum methotrexate level is <1 x 10⁻⁸ molar

Investigational: Post I.T. methotrexate: Oral, I.V.: 12 mg/m² as a single dose; post high-dose methotrexate: 100-1000 mg/m²/dose until the serum methotrexate level is less than 1 x 10⁻⁷ molar

The drug should be given parenterally instead of orally in patients with GI toxicity, nausea, vomiting, and when individual doses are >25 mg

Administration Leucovorin calcium should be administered I.M. or I.V.; rate of I.V. infusion should not exceed 160 mg/minute

Monitoring Parameters Plasma MTX concentration as a therapeutic guide to high-dose MTX therapy with leucovorin factor rescue

Leucovorin is continued until the plasma MTX level is <1 x 10⁻⁷ molar

Each dose of leucovorin is increased if the plasma MTX concentration is excessively high (see graph)

With 4- to 6-hour high-dose MTX infusions, plasma drug values in excess of 5 x 10⁻⁵ and 10⁻⁶ molar at 24 and 48 hours after starting the infusion, respectively, are often predictive of delayed MTX clearance; see graph.

Patient Information Patients should be informed to:

Contact their physician immediately, if they have an allergic reaction after taking leucovorin calcium (trouble breathing, wheezing, fainting, skin rash, or hives)

Let their physician know if they are pregnant or are trying to get pregnant before taking leucovorin calcium

Leucovorin calcium can be taken with or without food

Take exactly as directed; take at evenly spaced times day and night

(Continued)

Leucovorin *(Continued)*

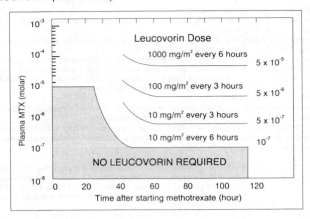

Dosage Forms
Injection, as calcium: 3 mg/mL (1 mL)
Powder for injection, as calcium: 25 mg, 50 mg, 100 mg, 350 mg
Powder for oral solution, as calcium: 1 mg/mL (60 mL)
Tablet, as calcium: 5 mg, 10 mg, 15 mg, 25 mg

- ◆ **Leucovorin Calcium** *see* Leucovorin *on page 666*
- ◆ **Leukeran®** *see* Chlorambucil *on page 236*
- ◆ **Leukine™** *see* Sargramostim *on page 1049*

Leuprolide Acetate (loo PROE lide AS e tate)
Related Information
Cancer Chemotherapy Regimens *on page 1263*
U.S. Brand Names Lupron®; Lupron Depot®; Lupron Depot®-3 Month; Lupron Depot®-4 Month; Lupron Depot-Ped®
Synonyms Leuprorelin Acetate
Therapeutic Category Gonadotropin Releasing Hormone Analog
Use Palliative treatment of advanced prostate carcinoma (alternative when orchiectomy or estrogen administration are not indicated or are unacceptable to the patient); combination therapy with flutamide for treating metastatic prostatic carcinoma; endometriosis (3.75 mg depot only); central precocious puberty (may be used an agent to treat precocious puberty because of its effect in lowering levels of LH and FSH, testosterone, and estrogen).
Unlabeled use: Treatment of breast, ovarian, and endometrial cancer; leiomyoma uteri; infertility; prostatic hypertrophy
Pregnancy Risk Factor X
Contraindications Hypersensitivity to leuprolide; spinal cord compression (orchiectomy suggested); undiagnosed abnormal vaginal bleeding; women who are or may be pregnant should not receive Lupron® Depot®
Warnings/Precautions Use with caution in patients hypersensitive to benzyl alcohol; after 6 months use of Depot® leuprolide, vertebral bone density decreased (average 13.5%); long-term safety of leuprolide in children has not been established; urinary tract obstruction may occur upon initiation of therapy. Closely observe patients for weakness, paresthesias, and urinary tract obstruction in first few weeks of therapy. Tumor flare and bone pain may occur at initiation of therapy; transient weakness and paresthesia of lower limbs, hematuria, and urinary tract obstruction in first week of therapy; animal studies have shown dose-related benign pituitary hyperplasia and benign pituitary adenomas after 2 years of use.
Adverse Reactions
>10%:
Central nervous system: Depression, pain
Endocrine & metabolic: Hot flashes
Gastrointestinal: Weight gain, nausea, vomiting
1% to 10%:
Cardiovascular: Cardiac arrhythmias, edema
Central nervous system: Dizziness, lethargy, insomnia, headache
Dermatologic: Rash
Endocrine: Estrogenic effects (gynecomastia, breast tenderness)
Gastrointestinal: Nausea, vomiting, diarrhea, GI bleed
Hematologic: Decreased hemoglobin and hematocrit
Neuromuscular & skeletal: Paresthesia, myalgia
Ocular: Blurred vision
<1%: Myocardial infarction, thrombophlebitis, pulmonary embolism
Overdosage/Toxicology General supportive care

Stability

Store unopened vials of injection in refrigerator, vial in use can be kept at room temperature (≤30°C/86°F) for several months with minimal loss of potency. Protect from light and store vial in carton until use. Do not freeze.

Depot® may be stored at room temperature. Upon reconstitution, the suspension is stable for 24 hours; does not contain a preservative.

Mechanism of Action Continuous daily administration results in suppression of ovarian and testicular steroidogenesis due to decreased levels of LH and FSH with subsequent decrease in testosterone (male) and estrogen (female) levels

Pharmacodynamics/Kinetics

Onset of action: Serum testosterone levels first increase within 3 days of therapy

Duration: Levels decrease after 2-4 weeks with continued therapy

Metabolism: Destroyed within the GI tract

Bioavailability: Orally not bioavailable; S.C. and I.V. doses are comparable

Half-life: 3-4.25 hours

Elimination: Not well defined

Usual Dosage Requires parenteral administration

Children: Precocious puberty:

S.C.: 20-45 mcg/kg/day

I.M. (Depot®) formulation: 0.3 mg/kg/dose given every 28 days

≤25 kg: 7.5 mg

>25-37.5 kg: 11.25 mg

>37.5 kg: 15 mg

Adults:

Male: Advanced prostatic carcinoma:

S.C.: 1 mg/day **or**

I.M., Depot® (suspension): 7.5 mg/dose given monthly (every 28-33 days)

Female: Endometriosis: I.M., Depot® (suspension): 3.75 mg monthly for up to 6 months

Administration When administering the Depot® form, do not use needles smaller than 22-gauge; reconstitute only with diluent provided

Monitoring Parameters Precocious puberty: GnRH testing (blood LH and FSH levels), testosterone in males and estradiol in females; closely monitor patients with prostatic carcinoma for weakness, paresthesias, and urinary tract obstruction in first few weeks of therapy

Test Interactions Interferes with pituitary gonadotropic and gonadal function tests during and up to 4-8 weeks after therapy

Patient Information Do not discontinue medication without physician's advice

Nursing Implications Patient must be taught aseptic technique and S.C. injection technique. Rotate S.C. injection sites frequently. Disease flare (increased bone pain, urinary retention) can briefly occur with initiation of therapy.

Dosage Forms

Injection: 5 mg/mL (2.8 mL)

Powder for injection (depot):

Depot®: 3.75 mg, 7.5 mg

Depot-3® Month: 11.25 mg, 22.5 mg

Depot-4® Month: 30 mg

Depot-Ped™: 7.5 mg, 11.25 mg, 15 mg

♦ **Leuprorelin Acetate** see Leuprolide Acetate on previous page

♦ **Leurocristine** see Vincristine on page 1219

♦ **Leustatin™** see Cladribine on page 271

Levamisole (lee VAM i sole)

Related Information

Cancer Chemotherapy Regimens on page 1263

U.S. Brand Names Ergamisol®

Synonyms Levamisole Hydrochloride

Therapeutic Category Immune Modulator

Use Adjuvant treatment with fluorouracil in Dukes stage C colon cancer

Pregnancy Risk Factor C

Contraindications Previous hypersensitivity to the drug

Warnings/Precautions Agranulocytosis can occur asymptomatically and flu-like symptoms can occur without hematologic adverse effects; frequent hematologic monitoring is necessary

Adverse Reactions

>10%: Gastrointestinal: Nausea, diarrhea

1% to 10%:

Cardiovascular: Edema

Central nervous system: Fatigue, fever, dizziness, headache, somnolence, depression, nervousness, insomnia

Dermatologic: Dermatitis, alopecia

Gastrointestinal: Stomatitis, vomiting, anorexia, abdominal pain, constipation, taste perversion

Hematologic: Leukopenia

Neuromuscular & skeletal: Rigors, arthralgia, myalgia, paresthesia

Miscellaneous: Infection

(Continued)

Levamisole *(Continued)*

<1%: Chest pain, anxiety, pruritus, urticaria, flatulence, dyspepsia, thrombocytopenia, anemia, granulocytopenia, abnormal tearing, blurred vision, conjunctivitis, epistaxis, altered sense of smell

Overdosage/Toxicology Treatment following decontamination is symptomatic and supportive

Drug Interactions
Increased toxicity/serum levels of phenytoin
Disulfiram-like reaction with alcohol

Mechanism of Action Clinically, combined therapy with levamisole and 5-fluorouracil has been effective in treating colon cancer patients, whereas demonstrable activity has been demonstrated. Due to the broad range of pharmacologic activities of levamisole, it has been suggested that the drug may act as a biochemical modulator (of fluorouracil, for example, in colon cancer), an effect entirely independent of immune modulation. Further studies are needed to evaluate the mechanisms of action of the drug in cancer patients.

Pharmacodynamics/Kinetics
Absorption: Well absorbed
Metabolism: In the liver, >70%
Half-life, elimination: 2-6 hours
Time to peak serum concentration: 1-2 hours
Elimination: In urine and feces; elimination is virtually complete within 48 hours after an oral dose

Usual Dosage Adults: Oral: Initial: 50 mg every 8 hours for 3 days, then 50 mg every 8 hours for 3 days every 2 weeks (fluorouracil is always given concomitantly)

Dosing adjustment in hepatic impairment: May be necessary in patients with liver disease, but no specific guidelines are available

Monitoring Parameters CBC with platelet count prior to therapy and weekly prior to treatment; LFTs every 3 months

Patient Information Notify physician immediately if flu-like symptoms appear; may cause dizziness, drowsiness, impair judgment or coordination

Dosage Forms Tablet, as base: 50 mg

◆ **Levamisole Hydrochloride** *see* Levamisole *on previous page*
◆ **Levaquin™** *see* Levofloxacin *on page 674*
◆ **Levarterenol Bitartrate** *see* Norepinephrine *on page 849*
◆ **Levate®** *see* Amitriptyline *on page 62*
◆ **Levbid®** *see* Hyoscyamine *on page 590*
◆ **Levlen®** *see* Ethinyl Estradiol and Levonorgestrel *on page 449*
◆ **Levlite®** *see* Ethinyl Estradiol and Levonorgestrel *on page 449*

Levobunolol *(lee voe BYOO noe lole)*

Related Information
Glaucoma Drug Therapy Comparison *on page 1322*

U.S. Brand Names AKBeta®; Betagan® Liquifilm®
Synonyms *l*-Bunolol Hydrochloride; Levobunolol Hydrochloride
Therapeutic Category Beta-Adrenergic Blocker, Ophthalmic
Use To lower intraocular pressure in chronic open-angle glaucoma or ocular hypertension
Pregnancy Risk Factor C

Contraindications Known hypersensitivity to levobunolol; bronchial asthma, severe COPD, sinus bradycardia, second or third degree A-V block, cardiac failure, cardiogenic shock

Warnings/Precautions Use with caution in patients with congestive heart failure, diabetes mellitus, hyperthyroidism; contains metabisulfite. Because systemic absorption does occur with ophthalmic administration, the elderly with other disease states or syndromes that may be affected by a beta-blocker (CHF, COPD, etc) should be monitored closely.

Adverse Reactions
>10%: Ocular: Stinging/burning eyes
1% to 10%:
Cardiovascular: Bradycardia, arrhythmia, hypotension
Central nervous system: Dizziness, headache
Dermatologic: Alopecia, erythema
Local: Stinging, burning
Ocular: Blepharoconjunctivitis, conjunctivitis
Respiratory: Bronchospasm
<1%: Rash, itching, visual disturbances, keratitis, decreased visual acuity

Overdosage/Toxicology
Symptoms of intoxication include cardiac disturbances, CNS toxicity, bronchospasm, hypoglycemia and hyperkalemia. The most common cardiac symptoms include hypotension and bradycardia; atrioventricular block, intraventricular conduction disturbances, cardiogenic shock, and asystole may occur with severe overdose, especially with membrane-depressant drugs (eg, propranolol); CNS effects include convulsions, coma, and respiratory arrest is commonly seen with propranolol and other membrane-depressant and lipid-soluble drugs
Treatment includes symptomatic treatment of seizures, hypotension, hyperkalemia and hypoglycemia; bradycardia and hypotension resistant to atropine, isoproterenol or

pacing may respond to glucagon; wide QRS defects caused by the membrane-depressant poisoning may respond to hypertonic sodium bicarbonate; repeat-dose charcoal, hemoperfusion, or hemodialysis may be helpful in removal of only those beta-blockers with a small V_d, long half-life or low intrinsic clearance (acebutolol, atenolol, nadolol, sotalol).

Drug Interactions Increased toxicity:
Systemic beta-adrenergic blocking agents
Ophthalmic epinephrine (increased blood pressure/loss of IOP effect)
Quinidine (sinus bradycardia)
Verapamil (bradycardia and asystole have been reported)

Mechanism of Action A nonselective beta-adrenergic blocking agent that lowers intraocular pressure by reducing aqueous humor production and possibly increases the outflow of aqueous humor

Pharmacodynamics/Kinetics
Onset of action: Decreases in intraocular pressure (IOP) can be noted within 1 hour
Peak effect: 2-6 hours
Duration: 1-7 days
Elimination: Not well defined

Usual Dosage Adults: Instill 1 drop in the affected eye(s) 1-2 times/day

Monitoring Parameters Intraocular pressure, heart rate, funduscopic exam, visual field testing

Patient Information May sting on instillation, do not touch dropper to eye; visual acuity may be decreased after administration; night vision may be decreased; distance vision may be altered; apply finger pressure between the bridge of the nose and corner of the eye to decrease systemic absorption; assess patient's or caregiver's ability to administer

Nursing Implications Apply finger pressure over nasolacrimal duct to decrease systemic absorption

Dosage Forms Solution, ophthalmic, as hydrochloride: 0.25% (5 mL, 10 mL, 15 mL); 0.5% (2 mL, 5 mL, 10 mL, 15 mL)

♦ **Levobunolol Hydrochloride** see Levobunolol on previous page

Levocabastine (LEE voe kab as teen)

U.S. Brand Names Livostin®

Synonyms Levocabastine Hydrochloride

Therapeutic Category Antiallergic, Ophthalmic; Antihistamine, H_1 Blocker; Antihistamine, H_1 Blocker, Ophthalmic

Use Treatment of allergic conjunctivitis

Pregnancy Risk Factor B

Contraindications Hypersensitivity to any component of product; while soft contact lenses are being worn

Warnings/Precautions Safety and efficacy in children <12 years of age have not been established; not for injection; not for use in patients wearing soft contact lenses during treatment

Adverse Reactions
>10%: Local: Transient burning, stinging, discomfort
1% to 10%:
Central nervous system: Headache, somnolence, fatigue
Dermatologic: Rash
Gastrointestinal: Xerostomia
Ocular: Blurred vision, eye pain, somnolence, red eyes, eyelid edema
Respiratory: Dyspnea

Mechanism of Action Potent, selective histamine H_1-receptor antagonist for topical ophthalmic use

Pharmacodynamics/Kinetics Absorption: Topical: Systemically absorbed

Usual Dosage Children >12 years and Adults: Instill 1 drop in affected eye(s) 4 times/day for up to 2 weeks

Dosage Forms Suspension, ophthalmic, as hydrochloride: 0.05% (2.5 mL, 5 mL, 10 mL)

♦ **Levocabastine Hydrochloride** see Levocabastine on this page

Levodopa (lee voe DOE pa)

Related Information
Antacid Drug Interactions on page 1296
Depression Disorders and Treatments on page 1465

U.S. Brand Names Dopar®; Larodopa®

Synonyms L-3-Hydroxytyrosine; L-Dopa

Therapeutic Category Anti-Parkinson's Agent

Use Treatment of Parkinson's disease; used as a diagnostic agent for growth hormone deficiency

Pregnancy Risk Factor C

Contraindications Hypersensitivity to levodopa or any component; narrow-angle glaucoma, MAO inhibitor therapy, melanomas or any undiagnosed skin lesions

Warnings/Precautions Use with caution in patients with history of myocardial infarction, arrhythmias, asthma, wide-angle glaucoma, peptic ulcer disease; sudden discontinuation of levodopa may cause a worsening of Parkinson's disease; some products may contain tartrazine. Elderly may be more sensitive to CNS effects of levodopa.
(Continued)

Levodopa *(Continued)*

Adverse Reactions
>10%:
Cardiovascular: Orthostatic hypotension, arrhythmias
Central nervous system: Dizziness, anxiety, confusion, nightmares
Gastrointestinal: Anorexia, nausea, vomiting, constipation
Genitourinary: Dysuria
Neuromuscular & skeletal: Choreiform and involuntary movements
Ocular: Blepharospasm
1% to 10%:
Central nervous system: Headache
Gastrointestinal: Diarrhea, xerostomia
Genitourinary: Discoloration of urine
Neuromuscular & skeletal: Muscle twitching
Ocular: Eyelid spasms
Miscellaneous: Discoloration of sweat
<1%: Hypertension, duodenal ulcer, GI bleeding, hemolytic anemia, blurred vision

Overdosage/Toxicology
Symptoms of overdose include palpitations, dysrhythmias, spasms, hypertension
Use fluids judiciously to maintain pressures; may precipitate a variety of arrhythmias

Drug Interactions
Decreased effect:
Hydantoins may decrease effectiveness
Phenothiazines and hypotensive agents may decrease effect of levodopa
Pyridoxine may increase peripheral conversion, may decrease levodopa effectiveness
Increased toxicity with antacids
Monoamine oxidase inhibitors → hypertensive reactions

Mechanism of Action
Increases dopamine levels in the brain, then stimulates dopaminergic receptors in the basal ganglia to improve the balance between cholinergic and dopaminergic activity

Pharmacodynamics/Kinetics
Time to peak serum concentration: Oral: 1-2 hours
Metabolism: Majority of drug is peripherally decarboxylated to dopamine; small amounts of levodopa reach the brain where it is also decarboxylated to active dopamine
Half-life: 1.2-2.3 hours
Elimination: Primarily in urine (80%) as dopamine, norepinephrine, and homovanillic acid

Usual Dosage
Oral:
Children (administer as a single dose to evaluate growth hormone deficiency):
0.5 g/m^2 **or**
<30 lbs: 125 mg
30-70 lbs: 250 mg
>70 lbs: 500 mg
Adults: 500-1000 mg/day in divided doses every 6-12 hours; increase by 100-750 mg/day every 3-7 days until response or total dose of 8,000 mg is reached
A significant therapeutic response may not be obtained for 6 months

Administration
Administer with meals to decrease GI upset

Monitoring Parameters
Serum growth hormone concentration

Test Interactions
False-positive reaction for urinary glucose with Clinitest®; false-negative reaction using Clinistix®; false-positive urine ketones with Acetest®, Ketostix®, Labstix®

Patient Information
Avoid vitamins with B$_6$ (pyridoxine); can take with food to prevent GI upset; do not stop taking this drug even if you do not think it is working; dizziness, lightheadedness, fainting may occur when you get up from a sitting or lying position.

Nursing Implications
Sustained release product should not be crushed

Dosage Forms
Capsule: 100 mg, 250 mg, 500 mg
Tablet: 100 mg, 250 mg, 500 mg

Levodopa and Carbidopa *(lee voe DOE pa & kar bi DOE pa)*

Related Information
Carbidopa *on page 192*
Parkinson's Disease, Dosing of Drugs Used for Treatment of *on page 1336*

U.S. Brand Names
Atamet®; Sinemet®; Sinemet® CR

Synonyms
Carbidopa and Levodopa

Therapeutic Category
Anti-Parkinson's Agent

Use
Treatment of parkinsonian syndrome; 50-100 mg/day of carbidopa is needed to block the peripheral conversion of levodopa to dopamine. "On-off" can be managed by giving smaller, more frequent doses of Sinemet® or adding a dopamine agonist or selegiline; when adding a new agent, doses of Sinemet® should usually be decreased.

Pregnancy Risk Factor
C

Contraindications
Narrow-angle glaucoma, MAO inhibitors, hypersensitivity to levodopa, carbidopa, or any component; do not use in patients with malignant melanoma or undiagnosed skin lesions

Warnings/Precautions
Use with caution in patients with history of myocardial infarction, arrhythmias, asthma, wide angle glaucoma, peptic ulcer disease; sudden discontinuation of levodopa may cause a worsening of Parkinson's disease; some tablets may contain tartrazine. The elderly may be more sensitive to the CNS effects of levodopa. Protein in

the diet should be distributed throughout the day to avoid fluctuations in levodopa absorption.

Adverse Reactions
>10%:
  Cardiovascular: Orthostatic hypotension, palpitations, cardiac arrhythmias
  Central nervous system: Confusion, nightmares, dizziness, anxiety
  Gastrointestinal: Nausea, vomiting, anorexia, constipation
  Neuromuscular & skeletal: Dystonic movements, "on-off", choreiform and involuntary movements
  Ocular: Blepharospasm
  Renal: Dysuria
1% to 10%:
  Central nervous system: Headache
  Gastrointestinal: Diarrhea, xerostomia
  Genitourinary: Discoloration of urine
  Neuromuscular & skeletal: Muscle twitching
  Ocular: Eyelid spasms
  Miscellaneous: Discoloration of sweat
<1%: Hypertension, memory loss, nervousness, insomnia, fatigue, hallucinations, ataxia, duodenal ulcer, GI bleeding, hemolytic anemia, blurred vision

Overdosage/Toxicology
Symptoms of overdose include palpitations, arrhythmias, spasms, hypotension; may cause hypertension or hypotension
Treatment is supportive; initiate gastric lavage, administer I.V. fluids judiciously and monitor EKG; use fluids judiciously to maintain pressures; may precipitate a variety of arrhythmias

Drug Interactions
Decreased effect:
  Hydantoins, pyridoxine
  Phenothiazines and hypotensive agents may decrease effects of levodopa
Increased toxicity with antacids
Monoamine oxidase inhibitors → hypertensive reactions

Mechanism of Action Parkinson's symptoms are due to a lack of striatal dopamine; levodopa circulates in the plasma to the blood-brain-barrier (BBB), where it crosses, to be converted by striatal enzymes to dopamine; carbidopa inhibits the peripheral plasma breakdown of levodopa by inhibiting its decarboxylation, and thereby increases available levodopa at the BBB

Pharmacodynamics/Kinetics
Carbidopa:
  Absorption: Oral: 40% to 70%
  Protein binding: 36%
  Half-life: 1-2 hours
  Elimination: Excreted unchanged
Levodopa:
  Absorption: May be decreased if given with a high protein meal
  Half-life: 1.2-2.3 hours
  Elimination: Primarily in urine (80%) as dopamine, norepinephrine, and homovanillic acid

Usual Dosage Oral:
Adults: Initial: 25/100 2-4 times/day, increase as necessary to a maximum of 200/2000 mg/day
Elderly: Initial: 25/100 twice daily, increase as necessary
Conversion from Sinemet® to Sinemet® CR (50/200): (Sinemet® [total daily dose of levodopa] / Sinemet® CR)
  300-400 mg / 1 tablet twice daily
  500-600 mg / 1½ tablets twice daily or one 3 times/day
  700-800 mg / 4 tablets in 3 or more divided doses
  900-1000 mg / 5 tablets in 3 or more divided doses
Intervals between doses of Sinemet® CR should be 4-8 hours while awake

Administration Administer with meals to decrease GI upset

Monitoring Parameters Blood pressure, standing and sitting/supine; symptoms of parkinsonism, dyskinesias, mental status

Test Interactions False-positive reaction for urinary glucose with Clinitest®; false-negative reaction using Clinistix®; false-positive urine ketones with Acetest®, Ketostix®, Labstix®

Patient Information Do not stop taking this drug even if you do not think it is working; take on an empty stomach if possible; if GI distress occurs, take with meals; rise carefully from lying or sitting position as dizziness, lightheadedness, or fainting may occur; do not crush or chew sustained release product

Nursing Implications Space doses evenly over the waking hours; sustained release product should not be crushed

Dosage Forms Tablet:
  10/100: Carbidopa 10 mg and levodopa 100 mg
  25/100: Carbidopa 25 mg and levodopa 100 mg
  25/250: Carbidopa 25 mg and levodopa 250 mg
  Sustained release: Carbidopa 25 mg and levodopa 100 mg; carbidopa 50 mg and levodopa 200 mg

♦ Levo-Dromoran® see Levorphanol on page 676

Levofloxacin (lee voe FLOKS a sin)

Related Information
Antimicrobial Drugs of Choice *on page 1404*
Community-Acquired Pneumonia in Adults *on page 1419*

U.S. Brand Names Levaquin™

Therapeutic Category Antibiotic, Quinolone

Use Acute maxillary sinusitis due to *S. pneumoniae*, *H. influenzae*, or *M. catarrhalis*; uncomplicated urinary tract infection due to *E. coli*, *K. pneumoniae*, or *S. saprophyticus*; also for acute bacterial exacerbation of chronic bronchitis and community-acquired pneumonia due to *S. aureus*, *S. pneumoniae*, *H. influenzae*, *H. parainfluenza*, or *M. catarrhalis*, *C. pneumoniae*, *L. pneumophila*, or *M. pneumoniae*; may be used for uncomplicated skin and skin structure infection (due to *S. aureus* or *S. pyogenes*) and complicated urinary tract infection due to gram-negative *Enterobacter* sp, including acute pyelonephritis (caused by *E. coli*)

Pregnancy Risk Factor C

Pregnancy/Breast-Feeding Implications
Clinical effects on the fetus: Avoid use in pregnant women unless the benefit justifies the potential risk to the fetus
Breast-feeding/lactation: Quinolones are known to distribute well into breast milk; consequently, use during lactation should be avoided, if possible

Contraindications Hypersensitivity to levofloxacin, any component, or other quinolones; pregnancy; lactation

Warnings/Precautions Not recommended in children <18 years of age; other quinolones have caused transient arthropathy in children; CNS stimulation may occur (tremor, restlessness, confusion, and very rarely hallucinations or seizures); use with caution in patients with known or suspected CNS disorders or renal dysfunction; prolonged use may result in superinfection; if an allergic reaction (itching, urticaria, dyspnea, pharyngeal or facial edema, loss of consciousness, tingling, cardiovascular collapse) occurs, discontinue the drug immediately; use caution to avoid possible photosensitivity reactions during and for several days following fluoroquinolone therapy; pseudomembranous colitis may occur and should be considered in patients who present with diarrhea

Adverse Reactions >1%:
Central nervous system: Dizziness, headache, insomnia
Dermatologic: Rash
Gastrointestinal: Nausea, vomiting, increased transaminases
Hematologic: Leukopenia, thrombocytopenia
Neuromuscular & skeletal: Tremor, arthralgia

Overdosage/Toxicology
Symptoms of overdose include acute renal failure, seizures
Treatment should include GI decontamination and supportive care; not removed by peritoneal or hemodialysis

Drug Interactions CYP1A2 enzyme inhibitor (minor)
Decreased effect: Decreased absorption with antacids containing aluminum, magnesium, and/or calcium (by up to 98% if given at the same time); phenytoin serum levels may be reduced by quinolones; antineoplastic agents may also decrease serum levels of fluoroquinolones
Increased toxicity/serum levels: Quinolones may cause increased levels of digoxin, caffeine, warfarin, cyclosporine. Cimetidine and probenecid increase quinolone levels; an increased incidence of seizures may occur with foscarnet.

Stability Stable for 72 hours when diluted to 5 mg/mL in a compatible I.V. fluid and stored at room temperature; stable for 14 days when stored at room temperature; stable for 6 months when frozen, do not refreeze; do not thaw in microwave or by bath immersion; **incompatible** with mannitol and sodium bicarbonate

Mechanism of Action As the S (-) enantiomer of the fluoroquinolone, ofloxacin, levofloxacin, inhibits DNA-gyrase in susceptible organisms thereby inhibits relaxation of supercoiled DNA and promotes breakage of DNA strands. DNA gyrase (topoisomerase II), is an essential bacterial enzyme that maintains the superhelical structure of DNA and is required for DNA replication and transcription, DNA repair, recombination, and transposition.

Pharmacodynamics/Kinetics
Absorption: Well absorbed
Distribution: V_d: 1.25 L/kg; CSF concentrations ~15% of serum levels; high concentrations are achieved in prostate and gynecological tissues, sinus, breast milk, and saliva
Protein binding: 50%
Metabolism: Hepatic, minimal
Half-life: 6 hours
Bioavailability: 100%
Time to peak serum concentration: 1 hour
Elimination: Most excreted unchanged in urine

Usual Dosage Adults: Oral, I.V. (infuse I.V. solution over 60 minutes):
Acute bacterial exacerbation of chronic bronchitis: 500 mg every 24 hours for at least 7 days
Community acquired pneumonia: 500 mg every 24 hours for 7-14 days
Acute maxillary sinusitis: 500 mg every 24 hours for 10-14 days
Uncomplicated skin infections: 500 mg every 24 hours for 7-10 days
Uncomplicated urinary tract infections: 250 mg once daily for 3 days
Complicated urinary tract infections include acute pyelonephritis: 250 mg every 24 hours for 10 days

Dosing adjustment in renal impairment:
Cl$_{cr}$ 20-49 mL/minute: Administer 250 mg every 24 hours (initial: 500 mg)
Cl$_{cr}$ 10-19 mL/minute: Administer 250 mg every 48 hours (initial: 500 mg for most infections; 250 mg for renal infections)
Hemodialysis/CAPD: 250 mg every 48 hours (initial: 500 mg)

Monitoring Parameters Evaluation of organ system functions (renal, hepatic, ophthalmologic, and hematopoietic) is recommended periodically during therapy; the possibility of crystalluria should be assessed; WBC and signs of infection

Patient Information May be taken with or without food; drink plenty of fluids; avoid exposure to direct sunlight during therapy and for several days following; do not take antacids within 4 hours before or 2 hours after dosing; contact your physician immediately if signs of allergy occur; do not discontinue therapy until your course has been completed; take a missed dose as soon as possible, unless it is almost time for your next dose.

Nursing Implications Infuse I.V. solutions over 60 minutes

Dosage Forms
Infusion, in D$_5$W: 5 mg/mL (50 mL, 100 mL)
Injection: 25 mg/mL (20 mL)
Tablet: 250 mg, 500 mg

Levomethadyl Acetate Hydrochloride
(lee voe METH a dil AS e tate hye droe KLOR ide)

U.S. Brand Names ORLAAM®

Therapeutic Category Analgesic, Narcotic

Use Management of opiate dependence

Restrictions C-II; must be dispensed in a designated clinic setting only

Warnings/Precautions Not recommended for use outside of the treatment of opiate addiction; shall be dispensed only by treatment programs approved by FDA, DEA, and the designated state authority. Approved treatment programs shall dispense and use levomethadyl in oral form only and according to the treatment requirements stipulated in federal regulations. Failure to abide by these requirements may result in injunction precluding operation of the program, seizure of the drug supply, revocation of the program approval, and possible criminal prosecution.

Adverse Reactions
>10%:
Cardiovascular: Bradycardia, hypotension
Central nervous system: Drowsiness
Gastrointestinal: Nausea, vomiting
Respiratory: Respiratory depression
1% to 10%:
Cardiovascular: Peripheral vasodilation, orthostatic hypotension, increased intracranial pressure
Central nervous system: Dizziness/vertigo, CNS depression, confusion, sedation
Endocrine & metabolic: Antidiuretic hormone release
Gastrointestinal: Constipation, biliary tract spasm
Genitourinary: Urinary tract spasm
Ocular: Miosis, blurred vision

Drug Interactions Decreased effect/levels with phenobarbital

Usual Dosage Adults: Oral: 20-40 mg 3 times/week, with ranges of 10 mg to as high as 140 mg 3 times/week; always dilute before administration and mix with diluent prior to dispensing

Monitoring Parameters Patient adherence with regimen and avoidance of illicit substances; random drug testing is recommended

Nursing Implications Drug administration and dispensing is to take place in an authorized clinic setting only; can potentially cause Q-T prolongation on EKG (not dose related)

Dosage Forms Solution, oral: 10 mg/mL (474 mL)

Levonorgestrel (LEE voe nor jes trel)

U.S. Brand Names Norplant® Implant

Therapeutic Category Contraceptive, Implant (Progestin); Contraceptive, Oral (Progestin); Progestin

Use Prevention of pregnancy. The net cumulative 5-year pregnancy rate for levonorgestrel implant use has been reported to be from 1.5-3.9 pregnancies/100 users. Norplant® is a very efficient, yet reversible, method of contraception. The long duration of action may be particularly advantageous in women who desire an extended period of contraceptive protection without sacrificing the possibility of future fertility.

Pregnancy Risk Factor X

Contraindications Women with undiagnosed abnormal uterine bleeding, hemorrhagic diathesis, known or suspected pregnancy, active hepatic disease, active thrombophlebitis, thromboembolic disorders, or known or suspected carcinoma of the breast

Warnings/Precautions Patients presenting with lower abdominal pain should be evaluated for follicular atresia and ectopic pregnancy

Adverse Reactions
>10%: Hormonal: Prolonged menstrual flow, spotting
1% to 10%:
Central nervous system: Headache, nervousness, dizziness
Dermatologic: Dermatitis, acne
(Continued)

Levonorgestrel *(Continued)*

Endocrine & metabolic: Amenorrhea, irregular menstrual cycles, scanty bleeding, breast discharge

Gastrointestinal: Nausea, change in appetite, weight gain

Genitourinary: Vaginitis, leukorrhea

Local: Pain or itching at implant site

Neuromuscular & skeletal: Myalgia

<1%: Infection at implant site

Overdosage/Toxicology

Can result if >6 capsules are *in situ*; symptoms include uterine bleeding irregularities and fluid retention

Treatment includes removal of all implanted capsules

Drug Interactions Decreased effect: Carbamazepine/phenytoin

Mechanism of Action First, ovulation is inhibited in about 50% to 60% of implant users from a negative feedback mechanism on the hypothalamus, leading to reduced secretion of follicle stimulating hormone (FSH) and luteinizing hormone (LH). An insufficient luteal phase has also been demonstrated with levonorgestrel administration and may result from defective gonadotropin stimulation of the ovary or from a direct effect of the drug on progesterone synthesis by the corpora lutea.

Pharmacodynamics/Kinetics

Protein binding: Following release from the implant, levonorgestrel enters the bloodstream highly bound to sex hormone binding globulin (SHBG), albumin, and alpha$_1$ glycoprotein

Metabolism: In the liver

Half-life, terminal: 11-45 hours

Elimination: In urine primarily as conjugates of sulfate and glucuronide

Usual Dosage Total administration doses (implanted): 216 mg in 6 capsules which should be implanted during the first 7 days of onset of menses subdermally in the upper arm; each Norplant® silastic capsule releases 80 mcg of drug/day for 6-18 months, following which a rate of release of 25-30 mcg/day is maintained for ≤5 years; capsules should be removed by end of 5th year

Patient Information Notify physician if unusual or persistent nausea, vomiting, abdominal pain, dark urine, or pale stools; may cause changes in vision or contact lens tolerability

Dosage Forms Capsule, subdermal implantation: 36 mg (6s)

♦ **Levonorgestrel and Ethinyl Estradiol** *see* Ethinyl Estradiol and Levonorgestrel *on page 449*

♦ **Levophed® Injection** *see* Norepinephrine *on page 849*

♦ **Levora®** *see* Ethinyl Estradiol and Levonorgestrel *on page 449*

Levorphanol *(lee VOR fa nole)*

Related Information

Narcotic Agonists Comparison *on page 1328*

U.S. Brand Names Levo-Dromoran®

Synonyms Levorphanol Tartrate; Levorphan Tartrate

Therapeutic Category Analgesic, Narcotic

Use Relief of moderate to severe pain; also used parenterally for preoperative sedation and an adjunct to nitrous oxide/oxygen anesthesia; 2 mg levorphanol produces analgesia comparable to that produced by 10 mg of morphine

Restrictions C-II

Pregnancy Risk Factor B (D if used for prolonged periods or in high doses at term)

Contraindications Hypersensitivity to levorphanol or any component

Warnings/Precautions Use with caution in patients with hypersensitivity reactions to other phenanthrene derivative opioid agonists (morphine, hydrocodone, hydromorphone, levorphanol, oxycodone, oxymorphone); respiratory diseases including asthma, emphysema, COPD or severe liver or renal insufficiency; some preparations contain sulfites which may cause allergic reactions; tolerance or dependence may result from extended use; dextromethorphan has equivalent antitussive activity but has much lower toxicity in accidental overdose. Elderly may be particularly susceptible to the CNS depressant and constipating effects of narcotics.

Adverse Reactions

>10%:

Cardiovascular: Palpitations, hypotension, bradycardia, peripheral vasodilation

Central nervous system: CNS depression, fatigue, drowsiness, dizziness

Dermatologic: Pruritus

Gastrointestinal: Nausea, vomiting

Neuromuscular & skeletal: Weakness

1% to 10%:

Central nervous system: Nervousness, headache, restlessness, anorexia, malaise, confusion

Gastrointestinal: Stomach cramps, xerostomia, constipation

Endocrine & metabolic: Antidiuretic hormone release

Gastrointestinal: Biliary tract spasm

Genitourinary: Decreased urination, urinary tract spasm

Local: Pain at injection site

Ocular: Miosis

Respiratory: Respiratory depression

<1%: Paralytic ileus, mental depression, hallucinations, paradoxical CNS stimulation, increased intracranial pressure, rash, urticaria, histamine release, physical and psychological dependence, histamine release

Overdosage/Toxicology
Symptoms of overdose include CNS depression, respiratory depression, miosis, apnea, pulmonary edema, convulsions
Naloxone 2 mg I.V. (0.01 mg/kg for children) with repeat administration as necessary up to a total of 10 mg

Drug Interactions Increased toxicity: CNS depressants increase CNS depression

Stability Store at room temperature, protect from freezing; I.V. is **incompatible** when mixed with aminophylline, barbiturates, heparin, methicillin, phenytoin, sodium bicarbonate

Mechanism of Action Levorphanol tartrate is a synthetic opioid agonist that is classified as a morphinan derivative. Opioids interact with stereospecific opioid receptors in various parts of the central nervous system and other tissues. Analgesic potency parallels the affinity for these binding sites. These drugs do not alter the threshold or responsiveness to pain, but the perception of pain.

Usual Dosage Adults:
Oral: 2 mg every 6-24 hours as needed
S.C.: 2 mg, up to 3 mg if necessary, every 6-8 hours
Dosing adjustment in hepatic disease: Reduction is necessary in patients with liver disease

Dietary Considerations
Alcohol: Additive CNS effects, avoid or limit alcohol; watch for sedation
Food: Glucose may cause hyperglycemia; monitor blood glucose concentrations

Monitoring Parameters Pain relief, respiratory and mental status, blood pressure

Patient Information Avoid alcohol, may cause drowsiness, impaired judgment or coordination; may cause physical and psychological dependence with prolonged use

Nursing Implications Observe patient for excessive sedation, respiratory depression; implement safety measures, assist with ambulation

Dosage Forms
Injection, as tartrate: 2 mg/mL (1 mL, 10 mL)
Tablet, as tartrate: 2 mg

♦ **Levorphanol Tartrate** see Levorphanol on previous page

♦ **Levorphan Tartrate** see Levorphanol on previous page

♦ **Levo-T™** see Levothyroxine on this page

♦ **Levothroid®** see Levothyroxine on this page

Levothyroxine (lee voe thye ROKS een)

U.S. Brand Names Eltroxin®; Levo-T™; Levothroid®; Levoxyl®; Synthroid®
Canadian Brand Names PMS-Levothyroxine Sodium
Synonyms Levothyroxine Sodium; L-Thyroxine Sodium; T_4
Therapeutic Category Thyroid Product
Use Replacement or supplemental therapy in hypothyroidism; some clinicians suggest levothyroxine is the drug of choice for replacement therapy
Pregnancy Risk Factor A
Contraindications Recent myocardial infarction or thyrotoxicosis, uncorrected adrenal insufficiency, hypersensitivity to levothyroxine sodium or any component
Warnings/Precautions Ineffective for weight reduction; high doses may produce serious or even life-threatening toxic effects particularly when used with some anorectic drugs. Use with caution and reduce dosage in patients with angina pectoris or other cardiovascular disease; levothyroxine tablets contain tartrazine dye which may cause allergic reactions in susceptible individuals; use cautiously in elderly since they may be more likely to have compromised cardiovascular functions. Patients with adrenal insufficiency, myxedema, diabetes mellitus and insipidus may have symptoms exaggerated or aggravated; thyroid replacement requires periodic assessment of thyroid status. Chronic hypothyroidism predisposes patients to coronary artery disease.
Adverse Reactions <1%: Palpitations, cardiac arrhythmias, tachycardia, chest pain, nervousness, headache, insomnia, fever, ataxia, alopecia, changes in menstrual cycle, weight loss, increased appetite, diarrhea, abdominal cramps, constipation, myalgia, hand tremors, tremor, shortness of breath, diaphoresis
Overdosage/Toxicology
Chronic overdose is treated by withdrawal of the drug; massive overdose may require beta-blockers for increased sympathomimetic activity. Chronic overdose may cause hyperthyroidism, weight loss, nervousness, sweating, tachycardia, insomnia, heat intolerance, menstrual irregularities, palpitations, psychosis, fever; acute overdose may cause fever, hypoglycemia, CHF, unrecognized adrenal insufficiency
Reduce dose or temporarily discontinue therapy; normal hypothalamic-pituitary-thyroid axis will return to normal in 6-8 weeks; serum T_4 levels do not correlate well with toxicity; in massive acute ingestion, reduce GI absorption, administer general supportive care; treat congestive heart failure with digitalis glycosides; excessive adrenergic activity (tachycardia) require propranolol 1-3 mg I.V. over 10 minutes or 80-160 mg orally/day; fever may be treated with acetaminophen.
Drug Interactions
Decreased effect:
Phenytoin may decrease levothyroxine levels
Cholestyramine may decrease absorption of levothyroxine
Increased oral hypoglycemic requirements
(Continued)

677

Levothyroxine *(Continued)*

Increased effect: Increased effects of oral anticoagulants

Increased toxicity: Tricyclic antidepressants may increase toxic potential of both drugs

Stability Protect tablets from light; do not mix I.V. solution with other I.V. infusion solutions; reconstituted solutions should be used immediately and any unused portions discarded

Mechanism of Action Exact mechanism of action is unknown; however, it is believed the thyroid hormone exerts its many metabolic effects through control of DNA transcription and protein synthesis; involved in normal metabolism, growth, and development; promotes gluconeogenesis, increases utilization and mobilization of glycogen stores, and stimulates protein synthesis, increases basal metabolic rate

Pharmacodynamics/Kinetics

Onset of therapeutic effect: Oral: 3-5 days; I.V. Within 6-8 hours

Peak effect: I.V.: Within 24 hours

Absorption: Oral: Erratic

Metabolism: In the liver to triiodothyronine (active)

Time to peak serum concentration: 2-4 hours

Half-life: Euthyroid: 6-7 days; Hypothyroid: 9-10 days; Hyperthyroid: 3-4 days

Elimination: In feces and urine

Usual Dosage

Children: Congenital hypothyroidism:

Oral:

0-6 months: 8-10 mcg/kg/day **or** 25-50 mcg/day

6-12 months: 6-8 mcg/kg/day **or** 50-75 mcg/day

1-5 years: 5-6 mcg/kg/day **or** 75-100 mcg/day

6-12 years: 4-5 mcg/kg/day **or** 100-150 mcg/day

>12 years: 2-3 mcg/kg/day **or** ≥150 mcg/day

I.M., I.V.: 50% to 75% of the oral dose

Adults:

Oral: Initial: 0.05 mg/day, then increase by increments of 25 mcg/day at intervals of 2-3 weeks; average adult dose: 100-200 mcg/day; maximum dose: 200 mcg/day

I.M., I.V.: 50% of the oral dose

Myxedema coma or stupor: I.V.: 200-500 mcg one time, then 100-300 mcg the next day if necessary

Thyroid suppression therapy: Oral: 2-6 mcg/kg/day for 7-10 days

Administration

Oral: Administer on an empty stomach

Parenteral: Dilute vial with 5 mL normal saline; use immediately after reconstitution; administer by direct I.V. infusion over 2- to 3-minute period. I.V. form must be prepared immediately prior to administration; should not be admixed with other solutions

Monitoring Parameters Thyroid function test (serum thyroxine, thyrotropin concentrations), resin triiodothyronine uptake (RT$_3$U), free thyroxine index (FTI), T$_4$, TSH, heart rate, blood pressure, clinical signs of hypo- and hyperthyroidism; TSH is the most reliable guide for evaluating adequacy of thyroid replacement dosage. TSH may be elevated during the first few months of thyroid replacement despite patients being clinically euthyroid. In cases where T$_4$ remains low and TSH is within normal limits, an evaluation of "free" (unbound) T$_4$ is needed to evaluate further increase in dosage

Reference Range Pediatrics: Cord T$_4$ and values in the first few weeks are much higher, falling over the first months and years. ≥10 years: ~5.8-11 μg/dL (SI: 75-142 nmol/L). Borderline low: ≤4.5-5.7 μg/dL (SI: 58-73 nmol/L); low: ≤4.4 μg/dL (SI: 57 nmol/L); results <2.5 μg/dL (SI: <32 nmol/L) are strong evidence for hypothyroidism.

Approximate adult normal range: 4-12 μg/dL (SI: 51-154 nmol/L). Borderline high: 11.1-13 μg/dL (SI: 143-167 nmol/L); high: ≥13.1 μg/dL (SI: 169 nmol/L). Normal range is increased in women on birth control pills (5.5-12 μg/dL); normal range in pregnancy: ~5.5-16 μg/dL (SI: ~71-206 nmol/L). TSH: 0.4-10 (for those ≥80 years) mIU/L; T$_4$: 4-12 μg/dL (SI: 51-154 nmol/L); T$_3$ (RIA) (total T$_3$): 80-230 ng/dL (SI: 1.2-3.5 nmol/L); T$_4$ free (free T$_4$): 0.7-1.8 ng/dL (SI: 9-23 pmol/L).

Test Interactions Many drugs may have effects on thyroid function tests; para-aminosalicylic acid, aminoglutethimide, amiodarone, barbiturates, carbamazepine, chloral hydrate, clofibrate, colestipol, corticosteroids, danazol, diazepam, estrogens, ethionamide, fluorouracil, I.V. heparin, insulin, lithium, methadone, methimazole, mitotane, nitroprusside, oxyphenbutazone, phenylbutazone, PTU, perphenazine, phenytoin, propranolol, salicylates, sulfonylureas, and thiazides

Patient Information Do not change brands without physician's knowledge; report immediately to physician any chest pain, increased pulse, palpitations, heat intolerances, excessive sweating; do not discontinue without notifying your physician

Nursing Implications I.V. form must be prepared immediately prior to administration; should not be admixed with other solutions

Additional Information Levothroid® tablets contain lactose and tartrazine dye

Equivalent doses: Thyroid USP 60 mg ~ levothyroxine 0.05-0.06 mg ~ liothyronine 0.015-0.0375 mg

50-60 mg thyroid ~ 50-60 mcg levothyroxine and 12.5-15 mcg liothyronine Liotrix®

Dosage Forms

Powder for injection, as sodium, lyophilized: 200 mcg/vial (6 mL, 10 mL); 500 mcg/vial (6 mL, 10 mL)

Tablet, as sodium: 25 mcg, 50 mcg, 75 mcg, 88 mcg, 100 mcg, 112 mcg, 125 mcg, 150 mcg, 175 mcg, 200 mcg, 300 mcg

♦ **Levothyroxine Sodium** *see* Levothyroxine *on previous page*

Lidocaine (LYE doe kane)

Related Information

Adult ACLS Algorithm, Tachycardia *on page 1450*
Adult ACLS Algorithm, V. Fib and Pulseless V. Tach *on page 1447*
Antiarrhythmic Drugs Comparison *on page 1297*
Pediatric ALS Algorithm, Asystole and Pulseless Arrest *on page 1445*

U.S. Brand Names Anestacon®; Dermaflex® Gel; Dilocaine®; Dr Scholl's® Cracked Heel Relief Cream [OTC]; Duo-Trach®; LidoPen® Auto-Injector; Nervocaine®; Octocaine®; Solarcaine® Aloe Extra Burn Relief [OTC]; Xylocaine®; Zilactin-L® [OTC]

Canadian Brand Names PMS-Lidocaine Viscous; Xylocard®

Synonyms Lidocaine Hydrochloride; Lignocaine Hydrochloride

Therapeutic Category Antiarrhythmic Agent, Class I-B; Local Anesthetic, Injectable; Local Anesthetic, Topical

Use Local anesthetic and acute treatment of ventricular arrhythmias from myocardial infarction, cardiac manipulation, digitalis intoxication; topical local anesthetic; drug of choice for ventricular ectopy, ventricular tachycardia, ventricular fibrillation; for pulseless VT or VF preferably administer **after** defibrillation and epinephrine; control of premature ventricular contractions, wide-complex PSVT

Pregnancy Risk Factor B

Contraindications Known hypersensitivity to amide-type local anesthetics; patients with Adams-Stokes syndrome or with severe degree of S-A, A-V, or intraventricular heart block (without a pacemaker)

Warnings/Precautions Avoid use of preparations containing preservatives for spinal or epidural (including caudal) anesthesia. Use extreme caution in patients with hepatic disease, heart failure, marked hypoxia, severe respiratory depression, hypovolemia or shock, incomplete heart block or bradycardia, and atrial fibrillation.

Due to decreases in phase I metabolism and possibly decrease in splanchnic perfusion with age, there may be a decreased clearance or increased half-life in elderly and increased risk for CNS side effects and cardiac effects

Adverse Reactions

1% to 10%:
Cardiovascular: Hypotension
Central nervous system: Positional headache
Miscellaneous: Shivering
<1%: Heart block, arrhythmias, cardiovascular collapse, lethargy, coma, agitation, slurred speech, seizures, anxiety, euphoria, hallucinations, itching, rash, edema of the skin, nausea, vomiting, paresthesias, blurred vision, diplopia, dyspnea, respiratory depression or arrest

Overdosage/Toxicology

Has a narrow therapeutic index and severe toxicity may occur slightly above the therapeutic range, especially with other antiarrhythmic drugs; symptoms of overdose include sedation, confusion, coma, seizures, respiratory arrest and cardiac toxicity (sinus arrest, A-V block, asystole, and hypotension); the QRS and Q-T intervals are usually normal, although they may be prolonged after massive overdose; other effects include dizziness, paresthesias, tremor, ataxia, and GI disturbance.

Treatment is supportive, using conventional therapies (fluids, positioning, vasopressors, antiarrhythmics, anticonvulsants); sodium bicarbonate may reverse QRS prolongation, bradyarrhythmias and hypotension; enhanced elimination with dialysis, hemoperfusion or repeat charcoal is not effective.

Drug Interactions CYP3A3/4 enzyme substrate

Increased toxicity:
Concomitant cimetidine or beta-blockers may result in increased serum concentrations of lidocaine with resultant toxicity; procainamide and tocainide may result in additive cardiodepressant action
Effect of succinylcholine may be enhanced

Stability

Lidocaine injection is stable at room temperature
Stability of parenteral admixture at room temperature (25°C): Expiration date on premixed bag; out of overwrap stability: 30 days
Standard diluent: 2 g/250 mL D_5W
(Continued)

Lidocaine *(Continued)*

Mechanism of Action Class IB antiarrhythmic; suppresses automaticity of conduction tissue, by increasing electrical stimulation threshold of ventricle, HIS-Purkinje system, and spontaneous depolarization of the ventricles during diastole by a direct action on the tissues; blocks both the initiation and conduction of nerve impulses by decreasing the neuronal membrane's permeability to sodium ions, which results in inhibition of depolarization with resultant blockade of conduction

Pharmacodynamics/Kinetics

Onset of action (single bolus dose): 45-90 seconds

Duration: 10-20 minutes

Distribution: V_d: Alterable by many patient factors; decreased in CHF and liver disease

Protein binding: 60% to 80%; binds to alpha$_1$ acid glycoprotein

Metabolism: 90% metabolized in liver; active metabolites monoethylglycinexylidide (MEGX) and glycinexylidide (GX) can accumulate and may cause CNS toxicity

Half-life (biphasic): Increased with CHF, liver disease, shock, severe renal disease

Initial: 7-30 minutes

Terminal: Infants, premature: 3.2 hours; Adults: 1.5-2 hours

Usual Dosage

Topical: Apply to affected area as needed; maximum: 3 mg/kg/dose; do not repeat within 2 hours

Injectable local anesthetic: Varies with procedure, degree of anesthesia needed, vascularity of tissue, duration of anesthesia required, and physical condition of patient; maximum: 4.5 mg/kg/dose; do not repeat within 2 hours

I.M.: Adults: 300 mg (best in deltoid muscle; only 10% solution)

Children: Endotracheal, I.O., I.V.: Loading dose: 1 mg/kg; may repeat in 10-15 minutes x 2 doses; after loading dose, start I.V. continuous infusion 20-50 mcg/kg/minute (300 mcg/kg/minute per American Heart Association)

Use 20 mcg/kg/minute in patients with shock, hepatic disease, mild congestive heart failure (CHF)

Moderate to severe CHF may require ½ loading dose and lower infusion rates to avoid toxicity

Adults: Antiarrhythmic:

I.V.: 1-1.5 mg/kg bolus over 2-3 minutes; may repeat doses of 0.5-0.75 mg/kg in 5-10 minutes up to a total of 3 mg/kg; continuous infusion: 1-4 mg/minute

I.V. (2 g/250 mL D$_5$W) infusion rates (infusion pump should be used for I.V. infusion administration):

1 mg/minute: 7 mL/hour

2 mg/minute: 15 mL/hour

3 mg/minute: 21 mL/hour

4 mg/minute: 30 mL/hour

Ventricular fibrillation (after defibrillation and epinephrine): Initial dose: 1.5 mg/kg, may repeat boluses as above; follow with continuous infusion after return of perfusion

Prevention of ventricular fibrillation: I.V.: Initial bolus: 0.5 mg/kg; repeat every 5-10 minutes to a total dose of 2 mg/kg

Refractory ventricular fibrillation: Repeat 1.5 mg/kg bolus may be given 3-5 minutes after initial dose

Endotracheal: 2-2.5 times the I.V. dose

Decrease dose in patients with CHF, shock, or hepatic disease

Dosing adjustment/comments in hepatic disease: Reduce dose in acute hepatitis and decompensated cirrhosis by 50%

Dialysis: Not dialyzable (0% to 5%) by hemo- or peritoneal dialysis; supplemental dose not necessary; supplemental dose is not necessary

Reference Range

Therapeutic: 1.5-5.0 µg/mL (SI: 6-21 µmol/L)

Potentially toxic: >6 µg/mL (SI: >26 µmol/L)

Toxic: >9 µg/mL (SI: >38 µmol/L)

Nursing Implications Local thrombophlebitis may occur in patients receiving prolonged I.V. infusions

Dosage Forms

Cream, as hydrochloride: 2% (56 g)

Injection, as hydrochloride: 0.5% [5 mg/mL] (50 mL); 1% [10 mg/mL] (2 mL, 5 mL, 10 mL, 20 mL, 30 mL, 50 mL); 1.5% [15 mg/mL] (20 mL); 2% [20 mg/mL] (2 mL, 5 mL, 10 mL, 20 mL, 30 mL, 50 mL); 4% [40 mg/mL] (5 mL); 10% [100 mg/mL] (10 mL); 20% [200 mg/mL] (10 mL, 20 mL)

Injection, as hydrochloride:

I.M. use: 10% [100 mg/mL] (3 mL, 5 mL)

Direct I.V.: 1% [10 mg/mL] (5 mL, 10 mL); 20 mg/mL (5 mL)

I.V. admixture, preservative free: 4% [40 mg/mL] (25 mL, 30 mL); 10% [100 mg/mL] (10 mL); 20% [200 mg/mL] (5 mL, 10 mL)

I.V. infusion, in D$_5$W: 0.2% [2 mg/mL] (500 mL); 0.4% [4 mg/mL] (250 mL, 500 mL, 1000 mL); 0.8% [8 mg/mL] (250 mL, 500 mL)

Gel, , as hydrochloride, topical: 2% (30 mL); 2.5% (15 mL)

Liquid, as hydrochloride, topical: 2.5% (7.5 mL)

Liquid, as hydrochloride, viscous: 2% (20 mL, 100 mL)

Ointment, as hydrochloride, topical: 2.5% [OTC]; 5% (35 g)

Solution, as hydrochloride, topical: 2% (15 mL, 240 mL); 4% (50 mL)

Lidocaine and Epinephrine (LYE doe kane & ep i NEF rin)

U.S. Brand Names Octocaine® With Epinephrine; Xylocaine® With Epinephrine

Therapeutic Category Local Anesthetic, Injectable

Use Local infiltration anesthesia; AVS for nerve block

Pregnancy Risk Factor B

Contraindications Hypersensitivity to local anesthetics of the amide type, myasthenia gravis, shock, or cardiac conduction disease

Warnings/Precautions Do not use solutions in distal portions of the body (digits, nose, ears, penis); use with caution in endocrine, heart, hepatic, or thyroid disease

Adverse Reactions Refer to Lidocaine monograph

Overdosage/Toxicology Refer to Lidocaine monograph

Stability Solutions with epinephrine should be protected from light

Mechanism of Action Lidocaine blocks both the initiation and conduction of nerve impulses via decreased permeability of sodium ions; epinephrine increases the duration of action of lidocaine by causing vasoconstriction (via alpha effects) which slows the vascular absorption of lidocaine

Pharmacodynamics/Kinetics
Peak effect: Within 5 minutes
Duration: ~2 hours, dependent on dose and anesthetic procedure

Usual Dosage
Children: Use lidocaine concentrations of 0.5% to 1% (or even more diluted) to decrease possibility of toxicity; lidocaine dose should not exceed 7 mg/kg/dose; do not repeat within 2 hours
Adults: Dosage varies with the anesthetic procedure, degree of anesthesia needed, vascularity of tissue, duration of anesthesia required, and physical condition of patient

Nursing Implications Before injecting, withdraw syringe plunger to ensure injection is not into vein or artery

Additional Information Contains metabisulfites

Dosage Forms Injection with epinephrine:
1:200,000: Lidocaine hydrochloride 0.5% [5 mg/mL] (50 mL); 1% [10 mg/mL] (30 mL); 1.5% [15 mg/mL] (5 mL, 10 mL, 30 mL); 2% [20 mg/mL] (20 mL)
1:100,000: Lidocaine hydrochloride 1% [10 mg/mL] (20 mL, 50 mL); 2% [20 mg/mL] (1.8 mL, 20 mL, 50 mL)
1:50,000: Lidocaine hydrochloride 2% [20 mg/mL] (1.8 mL)

Lidocaine and Hydrocortisone (LYE doe kane & hye droe KOR ti sone)

U.S. Brand Names Lida-Mantle HC® Topical

Therapeutic Category Anesthetic/Corticosteroid

Dosage Forms Cream: Lidocaine 3% and hydrocortisone 0.5% (15 g, 30 g)

Lidocaine and Prilocaine (LYE doe kane & PRIL oh kane)

U.S. Brand Names EMLA®

Therapeutic Category Analgesic, Topical; Anesthetic, Topical; Local Anesthetic, Topical

Use Topical anesthetic for use on normal intact skin to provide local analgesia for minor procedures such as I.V. cannulation or venipuncture; has also been used for painful procedures such as lumbar puncture and skin graft harvesting

Pregnancy Risk Factor B

Contraindications
Children <1 month of age
Administration on mucous membranes
Administration on broken or inflamed skin
Children with congenital or idiopathic methemoglobinemia, or in children who are receiving medications associated with drug-induced methemoglobinemia [ie, acetaminophen (overdosage), benzocaine, chloroquine, dapsone, nitrofurantoin, nitroglycerin, nitroprusside, phenazopyridine, phenelzine, phenobarbital, phenytoin, quinine, sulfonamides]
Patients with a documented hypersensitivity to amide type anesthetic agents [ie, lidocaine, prilocaine, dibucaine, mepivacaine, bupivacaine, etidocaine]
Patients with a documented hypersensitivity to any components of EMLA® cream or Tegaderm®

Adverse Reactions
1% to 10%:
Dermatologic: Angioedema, contact dermatitis
Local: Burning, stinging
<1%: Bradycardia, hypotension, shock, edema, nervousness, euphoria, confusion, dizziness, drowsiness, convulsions, CNS excitation, erythema, itching, rash, urticaria, methemoglobinemia in infants, blanching, alteration in temperature sensation, tenderness, tremors, blurred vision, tinnitus, respiratory depression, bronchospasm

Drug Interactions Increased toxicity:
Class I antiarrhythmic drugs (tocainide, mexiletine): Effects are additive and potentially synergistic
Drugs known to induce methemoglobinemia

Stability Store at room temperature

Mechanism of Action Local anesthetic action occurs by stabilization of neuronal membranes and inhibiting the ionic fluxes required for the initiation and conduction of impulses

(Continued)

Lidocaine and Prilocaine *(Continued)*

Pharmacodynamics/Kinetics

Onset of action: 1 hour for sufficient dermal analgesia

Peak effect: 2-3 hours

Duration: 1-2 hours after removal of the cream

Absorption: Related to the duration of application and to the area over which it is applied

3-hour application: 3.6% lidocaine and 6.1% prilocaine were absorbed

24-hour application: 16.2% lidocaine and 33.5% prilocaine were absorbed

Distribution: Both cross the blood-brain barrier

V_d:

Lidocaine: 1.1-2.1 L/kg

Prilocaine: 0.7-4.4 L/kg

Protein binding:

Lidocaine: 70%

Prilocaine: 55%

Metabolism:

Lidocaine: Metabolized by the liver to inactive and active metabolites

Prilocaine: Metabolized in both the liver and kidneys

Half-life:

Lidocaine: 65-150 minutes, prolonged with cardiac or hepatic dysfunction

Prilocaine: 10-150 minutes, prolonged in hepatic or renal dysfunction

Usual Dosage Children and Adults:

EMLA® cream should not be used in infants under the age of 1 month or in infants, under the age of 12 months, who are receiving treatment with methemogloblin-inducing agents

Choose 2 application sites available for intravenous access

Apply a thick layer (2.5 g/site ~½ of a 5 g tube) of cream to each designated site of intact skin

Cover each site with the occlusive dressing (Tegaderm®)

Mark the time on the dressing

Allow at least 1 hour for optimum therapeutic effect. Remove the dressing and wipe off excess EMLA® cream (gloves should be worn).

EMLA® Cream Maximum Recommended Application Area* for Infants and Children Based on Application to Intact Skin

Body Weight (kg)	Maximum Application Area (cm²)†
<10	100
10-20	600
>20	2000

*These are broad guidelines for avoiding systemic toxicity in applying EMLA® to patients with normal intact skin and with normal renal and hepatic function.

†For more individualized calculation of how much lidocaine and prilocaine may be absorbed, use the following estimates of lidocaine and prilocaine absorption for children and adults:

Estimated mean (±SD) absorption of lidocaine: 0.045 (±0.016) mg/cm²/h.

Estimated mean (±SD) absorption of prilocaine: 0.077 (±0.036) mg/cm²/h.

Debilitated patients, small children or patients with impaired elimination (ie, hepatic or renal dysfunction): Smaller areas of treatment are recommended

Patient Information Not for ophthalmic use; for external use only. EMLA® may block sensation in the treated skin.

Nursing Implications In small infants and children, an occlusive bandage should be placed over the EMLA® cream to prevent the child from placing the cream in his mouth

Dosage Forms Cream: Lidocaine 2.5% and prilocaine 2.5% [2 Tegaderm® dressings] (5 g, 30 g)

♦ **Lidocaine Hydrochloride** *see Lidocaine on page 679*

♦ **LidoPen® Auto-Injector** *see Lidocaine on page 679*

♦ **Lignocaine Hydrochloride** *see Lidocaine on page 679*

♦ **Limbitrol® DS 10-25** *see Amitriptyline and Chlordiazepoxide on page 64*

♦ **Linctus Codeine Blac** *see Codeine on page 291*

♦ **Linctus With Codeine Phosphate** *see Codeine on page 291*

Lindane *(LIN dane)*

U.S. Brand Names G-well®; Kwell®; Scabene®

Canadian Brand Names Hexit®; Kwellada™; PMS-Lindane

Synonyms Benzene Hexachloride; Gamma Benzene Hexachloride; Hexachlorocyclohexane

Therapeutic Category Antiparasitic Agent, Topical; Pediculocide; Scabicidal Agent; Shampoos

Use Treatment of scabies (*Sarcoptes scabiei*), *Pediculus capitis* (head lice), and *Pediculus pubis* (crab lice); FDA recommends reserving lindane as a second-line agent or with inadequate response to other therapies

Pregnancy Risk Factor B

Pregnancy/Breast-Feeding Implications Clinical effects on the fetus: There are no well controlled studies in pregnant women; treat no more than twice during a pregnancy

Contraindications Hypersensitivity to lindane or any component; premature neonates; acutely inflamed skin or raw, weeping surfaces

Warnings/Precautions Not considered a drug of first choice; use with caution in infants and small children, and patients with a history of seizures; avoid contact with face, eyes, mucous membranes, and urethral meatus. Because of the potential for systemic absorption and CNS side effects, lindane should be used with caution; consider permethrin or crotamiton agent first.

Adverse Reactions <1%: Cardiac arrhythmia, dizziness, restlessness, seizures, headache, ataxia, eczematous eruptions, contact dermatitis, skin and adipose tissue may act as repositories, nausea, vomiting, aplastic anemia, hepatitis, burning and stinging, hematuria, pulmonary edema

Overdosage/Toxicology

Symptoms of overdose include vomiting, restlessness, ataxia, seizures, arrhythmias, pulmonary edema, hematuria, hepatitis. Absorbed through skin and mucous membranes and GI tract, has occasionally caused serious CNS, hepatic and renal toxicity when used excessively for prolonged periods, or when accidental ingestion has occurred

If ingested, perform gastric lavage and general supportive measures; diazepam 0.01 mg/kg can be used to control seizures.

Drug Interactions Increased toxicity: Oil-based hair dressing may increase toxic potential

Mechanism of Action Directly absorbed by parasites and ova through the exoskeleton; stimulates the nervous system resulting in seizures and death of parasitic arthropods

Pharmacodynamics/Kinetics

Absorption: Systemic absorption of up to 13% may occur

Distribution: Stored in body fat and accumulates in brain; skin and adipose tissue may act as repositories

Metabolism: By the liver

Half-life: Children: 17-22 hours

Time to peak serum concentration: Topical: Children: 6 hours

Elimination: In urine and feces

Usual Dosage Children and Adults: Topical:

Scabies: Apply a thin layer of lotion or cream and massage it on skin from the neck to the toes (head to toe in infants). For adults, bathe and remove the drug after 8-12 hours; for children, wash off 6-8 hours after application (for infants, wash off 6 hours after application); repeat treatment in 7 days if lice or nits are still present

Pediculosis, capitis and pubis: 15-30 mL of shampoo is applied and lathered for 4-5 minutes; rinse hair thoroughly and comb with a fine tooth comb to remove nits; repeat treatment in 7 days if lice or nits are still present

Administration Drug should not be administered orally, for topical use only; apply to dry, cool skin

Patient Information Topical use only, do not apply to face, avoid getting in eyes; do **not** apply lotion immediately after a hot, soapy bath. Clothing and bedding should be washed in hot water or by dry cleaning to kill the scabies mite. Combs and brushes may be washed with lindane shampoo then thoroughly rinsed with water. Notify physician if condition worsens; treat sexual contact simultaneously.

Dosage Forms

Cream: 1% (60 g, 454 g)

Lotion: 1% (60 mL, 473 mL, 4000 mL)

Shampoo: 1% (60 mL, 473 mL, 4000 mL)

♦ **Lioresal®** see Baclofen on page 123

Liothyronine (lye oh THYE roe neen)

U.S. Brand Names Cytomel® Oral; Triostat™ Injection

Synonyms Liothyronine Sodium; Sodium L-Triiodothyronine; T_3 Sodium

Therapeutic Category Thyroid Product

Use Replacement or supplemental therapy in hypothyroidism, management of nontoxic goiter, chronic lymphocytic thyroiditis, as an adjunct in thyrotoxicosis and as a diagnostic aid; **levothyroxine is recommended for chronic therapy**; although previously thought to benefit cardiac patients with severely reduced fractions, liothyronine injection is no longer considered beneficial

Pregnancy Risk Factor A

Contraindications Recent myocardial infarction or thyrotoxicosis, hypersensitivity to liothyronine sodium or any component, undocumented or uncorrected adrenal insufficiency

Warnings/Precautions Ineffective for weight reduction; high doses may produce serious or even life-threatening toxic effects particularly when used with some anorectic drugs. Use with extreme caution in patients with angina pectoris or other cardiovascular disease (including hypertension) or coronary artery disease; use with caution in elderly patients since they may be more likely to have compromised cardiovascular function. Patients with adrenal insufficiency, myxedema, diabetes mellitus and insipidus may have symptoms exaggerated or aggravated; thyroid replacement requires periodic assessment of thyroid status. Chronic hypothyroidism predisposes patients to coronary artery disease.

Adverse Reactions <1%: Palpitations, tachycardia, cardiac arrhythmias, chest pain, nervousness, insomnia, fever, headache, ataxia, alopecia, changes in menstrual cycle, weight loss, increased appetite, diarrhea, abdominal cramps, constipation, myalgia, hand tremors, tremor, shortness of breath, diaphoresis

(Continued)

Liothyronine *(Continued)*

Overdosage/Toxicology

Chronic overdose may cause hyperthyroidism, weight loss, nervousness, sweating, tachycardia, insomnia, heat intolerance, menstrual irregularities, palpitations, psychosis, fever; acute overdose may cause fever, hypoglycemia, CHF, unrecognized adrenal insufficiency.

Reduce dose or temporarily discontinue therapy; normal hypothalamic-pituitary-thyroid axis will return to normal in 6-8 weeks; serum T_4 levels do not correlate well with toxicity

In massive acute ingestion, reduce GI absorption, administer general supportive care; treat congestive heart failure with digitalis glycosides; excessive adrenergic activity (tachycardia) requires propranolol 1-3 mg I.V. over 10 minutes or 80-160 mg orally/day; fever may be treated with acetaminophen.

Drug Interactions

Decreased effect:
Cholestyramine resin may decrease absorption
Antidiabetic drug requirements are increased
Estrogens may increase thyroid requirements
Increased effect: Increased oral anticoagulant effects

Stability
Vials must be stored under refrigeration at 2°C to 8°C (36°F to 46°F)

Mechanism of Action
Primary active compound is T_3 (triiodothyronine), which may be converted from T_4 (thyroxine) and then circulates throughout the body to influence growth and maturation of various tissues; exact mechanism of action is unknown; however, it is believed the thyroid hormone exerts its many metabolic effects through control of DNA transcription and protein synthesis; involved in normal metabolism, growth, and development; promotes gluconeogenesis, increases utilization and mobilization of glycogen stores, and stimulates protein synthesis, increases basal metabolic rate

Pharmacodynamics/Kinetics

Onset of effect: Within 24-72 hours
Duration: Up to 72 hours
Absorption: Oral: Well absorbed (~85% to 90%)
Metabolism: In the liver to inactive compounds
Half-life: 16-49 hours
Elimination: In urine

Usual Dosage

Congenital hypothyroidism: Children: Oral: 5 mcg/day increase by 5 mcg every 3-4 days until the desired response is achieved. Usual maintenance dose: 20 mcg/day for infants, 50 mcg/day for children 1-3 years of age, and adult dose for children >3 years.

Hypothyroidism: Oral:
Adults: 25 mcg/day increase by increments of 12.5-25 mcg/day every 1-2 weeks to a maximum of 100 mcg/day; usual maintenance dose: 25-75 mcg/day
Elderly: Initial: 5 mcg/day, increase by 5 mcg/day every 1-2 weeks; usual maintenance dose: 25-75 mcg/day

T_3 suppression test: Oral: 75-100 mcg/day for 7 days; use lowest dose for elderly

Myxedema: Oral: Initial: 5 mcg/day; increase in increments of 5-10 mcg/day every 1-2 weeks. When 25 mcg/day is reached, dosage may be increased at intervals of 12.5-25 mcg/day every 1-2 weeks. Usual maintenance dose: 50-100 mcg/day.

Myxedema coma: I.V.: 25-50 mcg
Patients with known or suspected cardiovascular disease: 10-20 mcg
Note: Normally, at least 4 hours should be allowed between doses to adequately assess therapeutic response and no more than 12 hours should elapse between doses to avoid fluctuations in hormone levels. Oral therapy should be resumed as soon as the clinical situation has been stabilized and the patient is able to take oral medication. If levothyroxine rather than liothyronine sodium is used in initiating oral therapy, the physician should bear in mind that there is a delay of several days in the onset of levothyroxine activity and that I.V. therapy should be discontinued gradually.

Administration
For I.V. use only - **do not administer I.M. or S.C.**

Administer doses at least 4 hours, and no more than 12 hours, apart
Resume oral therapy as soon as the clinical situation has been stabilized and the patient is able to take oral medication
When switching to tablets, discontinue the injectable, initiate oral therapy at a low dosage and increase gradually according to response
If levothyroxine is used for oral therapy, there is a delay of several days in the onset of activity; therefore, discontinue I.V. therapy gradually

Monitoring Parameters
T_4, TSH, heart rate, blood pressure, clinical signs of hypo- and hyperthyroidism; TSH is the most reliable guide for evaluating adequacy of thyroid replacement dosage. TSH may be elevated during the first few months of thyroid replacement despite patients being clinically euthyroid. In cases where T_4 remains low and TSH is within normal limits, an evaluation of "free" (unbound) T_4 is needed to evaluate further increase in dosage.

Reference Range
Free T_3, serum: 250-390 pg/dL; TSH: 0.4 and up to 10 (≥80 years of age) mIU/L; remains normal in pregnancy

Test Interactions
Many drugs may have effects on thyroid function tests; para-aminosalicylic acid, aminoglutethimide, amiodarone, barbiturates, carbamazepine, chloral hydrate, clofibrate, colestipol, corticosteroids, danazol, diazepam, estrogens, ethionamide, fluorouracil, I.V. heparin, insulin, lithium, methadone, methimazole, mitotane, nitroprusside, oxyphenbutazone, phenylbutazone, PTU, perphenazine, phenytoin, propranolol, salicylates, sulfonylureas, and thiazides

Patient Information Do not change brands without physician's knowledge; report immediately to physician any chest pain, increased pulse, palpitations, heat intolerances, excessive sweating; do not discontinue without notifying physician

Additional Information
Equivalent doses: Thyroid USP 60 mg ~ levothyroxine 0.05-0.06 mg ~ liothyronine 0.015-0.0375 mg
50-60 mg thyroid ~ 50-60 mcg levothyroxine and 12.5-15 mcg liothyronine Liotrix®

Dosage Forms
Injection, as sodium: 10 mcg/mL (1 mL)
Tablet, as sodium: 5 mcg, 25 mcg, 50 mcg

♦ **Liothyronine Sodium** see Liothyronine on page 683

Liotrix (LYE oh triks)

U.S. Brand Names Thyrolar®

Synonyms T_3/T_4 Liotrix

Therapeutic Category Thyroid Product

Use Replacement or supplemental therapy in hypothyroidism (uniform mixture of T_4:T_3 in 4:1 ratio by weight); little advantage to this product exists and cost is not justified

Pregnancy Risk Factor A

Contraindications Hypersensitivity to liotrix or any component; recent myocardial infarction or thyrotoxicosis, uncomplicated by hypothyroidism; uncorrected adrenal insufficiency, hypersensitivity to active or extraneous constituents

Warnings/Precautions Ineffective for weight reduction; high doses may produce serious or even life-threatening toxic effects particularly when used with some anorectic drugs; use cautiously in patients with pre-existing cardiovascular disease (angina, CHD), elderly since they may be more likely to have compromised cardiovascular function

Adverse Reactions <1%: Palpitations, tachycardia, cardiac arrhythmias, chest pain, nervousness, headache, insomnia, fever, ataxia, alopecia, excessive bone loss with overtreatment (excess thyroid replacement), heat intolerance, changes in menstrual cycle, weight loss, increased appetite, diarrhea, abdominal cramps, vomiting, constipation, tremor, myalgia, hand tremors, shortness of breath, diaphoresis

Overdosage/Toxicology
Chronic overdose may cause weight loss, nervousness, sweating, tachycardia, insomnia, heat intolerance, menstrual irregularities, palpitations, psychosis, fever; acute overdose may cause fever, hypoglycemia, CHF, unrecognized adrenal insufficiency
Reduce dose or temporarily discontinue therapy; normal hypothalamic-pituitary-thyroid axis will return to normal in 6-8 weeks; serum T_4 levels do not correlate well with toxicity
In massive acute ingestion, reduce GI absorption, administer general supportive care; treat congestive heart failure with digitalis glycosides; excessive adrenergic activity (tachycardia) require propranolol 1-3 mg I.V. over 10 minutes or 80-160 mg orally/day; fever may be treated with acetaminophen

Drug Interactions
Decreased effect:
Thyroid hormones increase hypoglycemic drug requirements
Phenytoin → clinical lymphothyroidism
Cholestyramine may decrease drug absorption
Increased effect: Increased oral anticoagulant effect
Increased toxicity: Tricyclic antidepressants may increase potential of both drugs

Mechanism of Action The primary active compound is T_3 (triiodothyronine), which may be converted from T_4 (thyroxine) and then circulates throughout the body to influence growth and maturation of various tissues. Liotrix is uniform mixture of synthetic T_4 and T_3 in 4:1 ratio; exact mechanism of action is unknown; however, it is believed the thyroid hormone exerts its many metabolic effects through control of DNA transcription and protein synthesis; involved in normal metabolism, growth, and development; promotes gluconeogenesis, increases utilization and mobilization of glycogen stores and stimulates protein synthesis, increases basal metabolic rate

Pharmacodynamics/Kinetics
Absorption: 50% to 95% from GI tract
Time to peak serum concentration: 12-48 hours
Metabolism: Partially in the liver, kidneys, and intestines
Half-life: 6-7 days
Elimination: Partially in feces and bile as conjugated metabolites

Usual Dosage Oral:
Congenital hypothyroidism:
Children (dose of T_4 or levothyroxine/day):
0-6 months: 8-10 mcg/kg or 25-50 mcg/day
6-12 months: 6-8 mcg/kg or 50-75 mcg/day
1-5 years: 5-6 mcg/kg or 75-100 mcg/day
6-12 years: 4-5 mcg/kg or 100-150 mcg/day
>12 years: 2-3 mcg/kg or >150 mcg/day
Hypothyroidism (dose of thyroid equivalent):
Adults: 30 mg/day (15 mg/day if cardiovascular impairment), increasing by increments of 15 mg/day at 2- to 3-week intervals to a maximum of 180 mg/day (usual maintenance dose: 60-120 mg/day)
Elderly: Initial: 15 mg, adjust dose at 2- to 4-week intervals by increments of 15 mg
(Continued)

Liotrix *(Continued)*

Monitoring Parameters T₄, TSH, heart rate, blood pressure, clinical signs of hypo- and hyperthyroidism; TSH is the most reliable guide for evaluating adequacy of thyroid replacement dosage. TSH may be elevated during the first few months of thyroid replacement despite patients being clinically euthyroid. In cases where T₄ remains low and TSH is within normal limits, an evaluation of "free" (unbound) T₄ is needed to evaluate further increase in dosage.

Reference Range

TSH: 0.4-10 (for those ≥80 years) mIU/L

T₄: 4-12 µg/dL (SI: 51-154 nmol/L)

T₃ (RIA) (total T₃): 80-230 ng/dL (SI: 1.2-3.5 nmol/L)

T₄ free (Free T₄): 0.7-1.8 ng/dL (SI: 9-23 pmol/L)

Test Interactions Many drugs may have effects on thyroid function tests; para-aminosalicylic acid, aminoglutethimide, amiodarone, barbiturates, carbamazepine, chloral hydrate, clofibrate, colestipol, corticosteroids, danazol, diazepam, estrogens, ethionamide, fluorouracil, I.V. heparin, insulin, lithium, methadone, methimazole, mitotane, nitroprusside, oxyphenbutazone, phenylbutazone, PTU, perphenazine, phenytoin, propranolol, salicylates, sulfonylureas, and thiazides

Patient Information Do not change brands without physician's knowledge; report immediately to physician any chest pain, increased pulse, palpitations, heat intolerances, excessive sweating; do not discontinue without notifying your physician; replacement therapy will be for life; take as a single dose before breakfast

Additional Information

Equivalent doses: Thyroid USP 60 mg ~ levothyroxine 0.05-0.06 mg ~ liothyronine 0.015-0.0375 mg

50-60 mg thyroid ~50-60 mcg levothyroxine and 12.5-15 mcg liothyronine Liotrix®. Since T₃ is produced by monodeiodination of T₄ in peripheral tissues (80%) and since elderly have decreased T₃ (25% to 40%), little advantage to this product exists and cost is not justified; no advantage over synthetic levothyroxine sodium.

Comparison of Liotrix Products

Product	T₄ Content (mcg)	T₃ Content (mcg)	Thyroid Equivalent (mg)
Euthroid®			
½ grain	30	7.5	30
1 grain	60	15	60
2 grain	120	30	120
3 grain	180	45	180
Thyrolar®			
¼ grain	12.5	3.1	15
½ grain	25	6.25	30
1 grain	50	12.5	60
2 grain	100	25	120
3 grain	150	37.5	180

Dosage Forms Tablet: 15 mg, 30 mg, 60 mg, 120 mg, 180 mg [thyroid equivalent]

- ♦ **Lipancreatin** *see* Pancrelipase *on page 883*
- ♦ **Lipid-Lowering Agents** *see page 1327*
- ♦ **Lipitor®** *see* Atorvastatin *on page 108*
- ♦ **Liposyn®** *see* Fat Emulsion *on page 469*
- ♦ **Liquaemin®** *see* Heparin *on page 560*
- ♦ **Liquibid®** *see* Guaifenesin *on page 549*
- ♦ **Liqui-Char® [OTC]** *see* Charcoal *on page 233*
- ♦ **Liquid Antidote** *see* Charcoal *on page 233*
- ♦ **Liquid Pred®** *see* Prednisone *on page 963*
- ♦ **Liquiprin® [OTC]** *see* Acetaminophen *on page 19*

Lisinopril *(lyse IN oh pril)*

Related Information

Angiotensin Agents *on page 1291*

Drug-Drug Interactions With ACEIs *on page 1295*

Heart Failure: Management of Patients With Left-Ventricular Systolic Dysfunction *on page 1472*

U.S. Brand Names Prinivil®; Zestril®

Canadian Brand Names Apo®-Lisinopril

Therapeutic Category Angiotensin-Converting Enzyme (ACE) Inhibitor; Antihypertensive Agent

Use Treatment of hypertension, either alone or in combination with other antihypertensive agents; adjunctive therapy in treatment of CHF (afterload reduction); treatment of hemodynamically stable patients within 24 hours of acute myocardial infarction, to improve survival

Pregnancy Risk Factor C (1st trimester); D (2nd and 3rd trimester)

Pregnancy/Breast-Feeding Implications
Clinical effects on the fetus: No data available on crossing the placenta. Cranial defects, hypocalvaria/acalvaria, oligohydramnios, persistent anuria following delivery, hypotension, renal defects, renal dysgenesis/dysplasia, renal failure, pulmonary hypoplasia, limb contractures secondary to oligohydramnios and stillbirth reported. ACE inhibitors should be avoided during pregnancy.

Breast-feeding/lactation: Crosses into breast milk. American Academy of Pediatrics considers **compatible** with breast-feeding.

Contraindications
Hypersensitivity to lisinopril or any component or other ACE inhibitors

Warnings/Precautions
Use with caution and modify dosage in patients with renal impairment (decrease dosage) (especially renal artery stenosis), severe congestive heart failure, or with coadministered diuretic therapy; experience in children is limited. Severe hypotension may occur in patients who are sodium and/or volume depleted, initiate lower doses and monitor closely when starting therapy in these patients.

Adverse Reactions
1% to 10%:
Cardiovascular: Hypotension (1% to 5%)
Central nervous system: Dizziness (6%), headache (5%), fatigue (3%)
Dermatologic: Rash (1.5%)
Gastrointestinal: Diarrhea/vomiting/nausea (1% to 3%)
Renal: Increased BUN/serum creatinine (transient)
Respiratory: Upper respiratory symptoms, cough (3% to 5%)
<1%: Chest discomfort (~1%), flushing, myocardial infarction, angina pectoris, orthostatic hypotension, rhythm disturbances, tachycardia, peripheral edema, vasculitis, palpitations, syncope, fever, malaise, depression, somnolence, insomnia, urticaria, pruritus, angioedema, gout, pancreatitis, abdominal pain, anorexia, constipation, flatulence, xerostomia, neutropenia, bone marrow suppression, hepatitis, arthralgia, shoulder pain, blurred vision, bronchitis, sinusitis, pharyngeal pain, diaphoresis

Overdosage/Toxicology
Mild hypotension has been the only toxic effect seen with acute overdose. Bradycardia may also occur; hyperkalemia occurs even with therapeutic doses, especially in patients with renal insufficiency and those taking NSAIDs

Following initiation of essential overdose management, toxic symptom treatment and supportive treatment should be initiated. Hypotension usually responds to I.V. fluids or Trendelenburg positioning.

Drug Interactions
Increased toxicity:
Probenecid increases blood levels of captopril
Captopril and diuretics have additive hypotensive effects
Increased toxicity: See Drug-Drug Interactions With ACEIs *on page 1295*

Mechanism of Action
Competitive inhibitor of angiotensin-converting enzyme (ACE); prevents conversion of angiotensin I to angiotensin II, a potent vasoconstrictor; results in lower levels of angiotensin II which causes an increase in plasma renin activity and a reduction in aldosterone secretion; a CNS mechanism may also be involved in hypotensive effect as angiotensin II increases adrenergic outflow from CNS; vasoactive kallikreins may be decreased in conversion to active hormones by ACE inhibitors, thus reducing blood pressure

Pharmacodynamics/Kinetics
Peak hypotensive effect: Oral: Within 6 hours
Absorption: Well absorbed; unaffected by food
Protein binding: 25%
Half-life: 11-12 hours
Elimination: Almost entirely excreted in urine as unchanged drug

Usual Dosage
Hypertension:
Adults: Initial: 10 mg/day; increase doses 5-10 mg/day at 1- to 2-week intervals; maximum daily dose: 40 mg
Elderly: Initial: 2.5-5 mg/day; increase doses 2.5-5 mg/day at 1- to 2-week intervals; maximum daily dose: 40 mg
Patients taking diuretics should have them discontinued 2-3 days prior to initiating lisinopril if possible; restart diuretic after blood pressure is stable if needed; if diuretic cannot be discontinued prior to therapy, begin with 5 mg with close supervision until stable blood pressure; in patients with hyponatremia (<130 mEq/L), start dose at 2.5 mg/day

Congestive heart failure: Adults: 5 mg initially with diuretics and digitalis; usual maintenance: 5-20 mg/day as a single dose

Acute myocardial infarction (within 24 hours in hemodynamically stable patients): Oral: 5 mg immediately, then 5 mg at 24 hours, 10 mg at 48 hours, and 10 mg every day thereafter for 6 weeks; patients should continue to receive standard treatments such as thrombolytics, aspirin, and beta-blockers

Dosing adjustment in renal impairment:
Cl_{cr} 10-50 mL/minute: Administer 50% to 75% of normal dose
Cl_{cr} <10 mL/minute: Administer 25% to 50% of normal dose
Hemodialysis: Dialyzable (50%)

Monitoring Parameters
Serum calcium levels, BUN, serum creatinine, renal function, WBC, and potassium

Test Interactions
May cause false-positive results in urine acetone determinations using sodium nitroprusside reagent; $\uparrow$ potassium (S); $\uparrow$ serum creatinine/BUN

Patient Information
Notify physician if vomiting, diarrhea, excessive perspiration, or dehydration should occur; also if swelling of face, lips, tongue or difficulty in breathing (Continued)

Lisinopril *(Continued)*

occurs or if persistent cough develops; do not stop therapy without the advise of the prescriber; do not add a salt substitute (potassium) without physician advice

Nursing Implications May cause depression in some patients; discontinue if angioedema of the face, extremities, lips, tongue, or glottis occurs; watch for hypotensive effects within 1-3 hours of first dose or new higher dose

Dosage Forms Tablet: 2.5 mg, 5 mg, 10 mg, 20 mg, 40 mg

Lisinopril and Hydrochlorothiazide

(lyse IN oh pril & hye droe klor oh THYE a zide)

U.S. Brand Names Prinzide®; Zestoretic®

Therapeutic Category Angiotensin-Converting Enzyme (ACE) Inhibitor Combination; Antihypertensive Agent, Combination

Dosage Forms Tablet:

Lisinopril 10 mg and hydrochlorothiazide 12.5 mg

[12.5]-Lisinopril 20 mg and hydrochlorothiazide 12.5 mg

[25]-Lisinopril 20 mg and hydrochlorothiazide 25 mg

♦ **Listermint® with Fluoride [OTC]** *see Fluoride on page 498*

♦ **Lithane®** *see Lithium on this page*

Lithium (LITH ee um)

Related Information

Antacid Drug Interactions *on page 1296*

U.S. Brand Names Eskalith®; Eskalith CR®; Lithane®; Lithobid®; Lithonate®; Lithotabs®

Synonyms Lithium Carbonate; Lithium Citrate

Therapeutic Category Antidepressant, Miscellaneous; Antimanic Agent

Use Management of acute manic episodes, bipolar disorders, and depression

Pregnancy Risk Factor D

Contraindications Hypersensitivity to lithium or any component; severe cardiovascular or renal disease

Warnings/Precautions Lithium toxicity is closely related to serum levels and can occur at therapeutic doses; serum lithium determinations are required to monitor therapy. Use with caution in patients with cardiovascular or thyroid disease, severe debilitation, dehydration or sodium depletion, or in patients receiving diuretics. Some elderly patients may be extremely sensitive to the effects of lithium; see dosage and therapeutic levels.

Adverse Reactions

>10%:

Endocrine & metabolic: Polydipsia, stress

Gastrointestinal: Nausea, diarrhea, abnormal taste

Neuromuscular & skeletal: Trembling

1% to 10%:

Central nervous system: Fatigue

Dermatologic: Rash

Gastrointestinal: Bloated feeling, weight gain

Neuromuscular & skeletal: Muscle twitching, weakness

<1%: Lethargy, dizziness, vertigo, pseudotumor cerebri, eruptions, hypothyroidism, goiter, acneiform, diabetes insipidus, anorexia, xerostomia, nonspecific nephron atrophy, renal tubular acidosis, leukocytosis, cogwheel rigidity, chronic movements of the limbs, tremor, vision problems, discoloration of fingers and toes

Overdosage/Toxicology

Symptoms of overdose include sedation, confusion, tremors, joint pain, visual changes, seizures, coma

There is no specific antidote for lithium poisoning. In the acute ingestion following initiation of essential overdose management, correction of fluid and electrolyte imbalances should be commenced. Hemodialysis and whole bowel irrigation is the treatment of choice for severe intoxications; charcoal is ineffective.

Drug Interactions

Decreased effect with xanthines (eg, theophylline, caffeine)

Increased effect/toxicity of CNS depressants, alfentanil, iodide salts increased hypothyroid effect

Increased toxicity with thiazide diuretics (dose may need to be reduced by 30%), NSAIDs, haloperidol, phenothiazines (neurotoxicity), neuromuscular blockers, carbamazepine, fluoxetine, ACE inhibitors

Mechanism of Action Alters cation transport across cell membrane in nerve and muscle cells and influences reuptake of serotonin and/or norepinephrine

Pharmacodynamics/Kinetics

Distribution: V_d: Initial: 0.3-0.4 L/kg; V_{dss}: 0.7-1 L/kg; crosses the placenta; appears in breast milk at 35% to 50% the concentrations in serum

Half-life: 18-24 hours; can increase to more than 36 hours in elderly or patients with renal impairment

Time to peak serum concentration (nonsustained release product): Within 0.5-2 hours following oral absorption

Elimination: 90% to 98% of dose excreted in urine as unchanged drug; other excretory routes include feces (1%) and sweat (4% to 5%)

Usual Dosage Oral: Monitor serum concentrations and clinical response (efficacy and toxicity) to determine proper dose

Children 6-12 years: 15-60 mg/kg/day in 3-4 divided doses; dose not to exceed usual adult dosage

Adults: 300-600 mg 3-4 times/day; usual maximum maintenance dose: 2.4 g/day or 450-900 mg of sustained release twice daily

Elderly: Initial dose: 300 mg twice daily; increase weekly in increments of 300 mg/day, monitoring levels; rarely need >900-1200 mg/day

Dosing adjustment in renal impairment:
Cl_{cr} 10-50 mL/minute: Administer 50% to 75% of normal dose
Cl_{cr} <10 mL/minute: Administer 25% to 50% of normal dose
Hemodialysis: Dialyzable (50% to 100%)

Administration Administer with meals to decrease GI upset

Monitoring Parameters Serum lithium every 3-4 days during initial therapy; draw lithium serum concentrations 8-12 hours postdose; renal, hepatic, thyroid, and cardiovascular function; fluid status; serum electrolytes; CBC with differential, urinalysis; monitor for signs of toxicity

Reference Range Levels should be obtained twice weekly until both patient's clinical status and levels are stable then levels may be obtained every 1-2 months

Timing of serum samples: Draw trough just before next dose

Therapeutic levels:

Acute mania: 0.6-1.2 mEq/L (SI: 0.6-1.2 mmol/L)

Protection against future episodes in most patients with bipolar disorder: 0.8-1 mEq/L (SI: 0.8-1.0 mmol/L); a higher rate of relapse is described in subjects who are maintained at <0.4 mEq/L (SI: 0.4 mmol/L)

Elderly patients can usually be maintained at lower end of therapeutic range (0.6-0.8 mEq/L)

Toxic concentration: >2 mEq/L (SI: >2 mmol/L)

Adverse effect levels:

GI complaints/tremor: 1.5-2 mEq/L

Confusion/somnolence: 2-2.5 mEq/L

Seizures/death: >2.5 mEq/L

Test Interactions ↑ calcium (S), glucose, magnesium, potassium (S); ↓ thyroxine (S)

Patient Information Avoid tasks requiring psychomotor coordination until the CNS effects are known, blood level monitoring is required to determine the proper dose; maintain a steady salt and fluid intake especially during the summer months; do not crush or chew slow or extended release dosage form, swallow whole

Nursing Implications Avoid dehydration

Additional Information
Lithium citrate: Cibalith-S®
Lithium carbonate: Eskalith®, Lithane®, Lithobid®, Lithonate®, Lithotabs®

Dosage Forms
Capsule, as carbonate: 150 mg, 300 mg, 600 mg
Syrup, as citrate: 300 mg/5 mL (5 mL, 10 mL, 480 mL)
Tablet, as carbonate: 300 mg
Tablet:
Controlled release, as carbonate: 450 mg
Slow release, as carbonate: 300 mg

- **Lithium Carbonate** *see* Lithium *on previous page*
- **Lithium Citrate** *see* Lithium *on previous page*
- **Lithobid®** *see* Lithium *on previous page*
- **Lithonate®** *see* Lithium *on previous page*
- **Lithotabs®** *see* Lithium *on previous page*
- **Livostin®** *see* Levocabastine *on page 671*
- **LKV-Drops® [OTC]** *see* Vitamins, Multiple *on page 1226*
- **8-L-Lysine Vasopressin** *see* Lypressin *on page 703*
- **LMD®** *see* Dextran *on page 341*
- **LoCHOLEST®** *see* Cholestyramine Resin *on page 254*
- **LoCHOLEST® Light** *see* Cholestyramine Resin *on page 254*
- **Locoid®** *see* Hydrocortisone *on page 579*
- **Lodine®** *see* Etodolac *on page 458*
- **Lodine® XL** *see* Etodolac *on page 458*
- **Lodosyn®** *see* Carbidopa *on page 192*

Lodoxamide Tromethamine (loe DOKS a mide troe METH a meen)

U.S. Brand Names Alomide® Ophthalmic

Therapeutic Category Antiallergic, Ophthalmic

Use Treatment of vernal keratoconjunctivitis, vernal conjunctivitis, and vernal keratitis

Pregnancy Risk Factor B

Contraindications Hypersensitivity to any component of product

Warnings/Precautions Safety and efficacy in children <2 years of age have not been established; not for injection; not for use in patients wearing soft contact lenses during treatment

Adverse Reactions
>10%: Local: Transient burning, stinging, discomfort
1% to 10%:
Central nervous system: Headache
Ocular: Blurred vision, corneal erosion/ulcer, eye pain, corneal abrasion, blepharitis
<1%: Dizziness, somnolence, rash, nausea, stomach discomfort, sneezing, dry nose

(Continued)

Lodoxamide Tromethamine *(Continued)*

Overdosage/Toxicology Symptoms include feeling of warmth of flushing, headache, dizziness, fatigue, sweating, nausea, loose stools, and urinary frequency/urgency; consider emesis in the event of accidental ingestion

Mechanism of Action Mast cell stabilizer that inhibits the *in vivo* type I immediate hypersensitivity reaction to increase cutaneous vascular permeability associated with IgE and antigen-mediated reactions

Pharmacodynamics/Kinetics Absorption: Topical: Very small and undetectable

Usual Dosage Children >2 years and Adults: Instill 1-2 drops in eye(s) 4 times/day for up to 3 months

Dosage Forms Solution, ophthalmic: 0.1% (10 mL)

- ♦ **Loestrin**® *see Ethinyl Estradiol and Norethindrone on page 451*
- ♦ **Lofene**® *see Diphenoxylate and Atropine on page 371*
- ♦ **Logen**® *see Diphenoxylate and Atropine on page 371*
- ♦ **Lomanate**® *see Diphenoxylate and Atropine on page 371*

Lomefloxacin *(loe me FLOKS a sin)*

U.S. Brand Names Maxaquin®

Synonyms Lomefloxacin Hydrochloride

Therapeutic Category Antibiotic, Quinolone

Use Lower respiratory infections, acute bacterial exacerbation of chronic bronchitis, skin infections, sexually transmitted diseases, and urinary tract infections caused by *E. coli*, *K. pneumoniae*, *P. mirabilis*, *P. aeruginosa*; also has gram-positive activity including *S. pneumoniae* and some staphylococci

Pregnancy Risk Factor C

Contraindications Hypersensitivity to lomefloxacin or other members of the quinolone group such as nalidixic acid, oxolinic acid, cinoxacin, norfloxacin, and ciprofloxacin; avoid use in children <18 years of age due to association of other quinolones with transient arthropathies

Warnings/Precautions Use with caution in patients with epilepsy or other CNS diseases which could predispose them to seizures

Adverse Reactions

1% to 10%:

Central nervous system: Headache, dizziness

Dermatologic: Photosensitivity

Gastrointestinal: Nausea

<1%: Flushing, chest pain, hypotension, hypertension, edema, syncope, tachycardia, bradycardia, arrhythmia, extrasystoles, cyanosis, cardiac failure, angina pectoris, myocardial infarction, facial edema, fatigue, malaise, chills, convulsions, vertigo, coma, purpura, rash, gout, hypoglycemia, abdominal pain, vomiting, flatulence, constipation, xerostomia, discoloration of tongue, abnormal taste, urinary disorders, dysuria, thrombocytopenia, increased fibrinolysis, back pain, hyperkinesia, tremor, paresthesias, leg cramps, myalgia, weakness, earache, hematuria, anuria, dyspnea, cough, epistaxis, diaphoresis (increased), allergic reaction, flu-like symptoms, decreased heat tolerance, thirst

Overdosage/Toxicology

Symptoms of overdose include acute renal failure, seizures

GI decontamination and supportive care; diazepam for seizures; not removed by peritoneal or hemodialysis

Drug Interactions

Decreased effect: Decreased absorption with antacids containing aluminum, magnesium, and/or calcium (by up to 98% if given at the same time)

Increased toxicity/serum levels: Quinolones cause increased levels of caffeine, warfarin, cyclosporine, and theophylline; cimetidine, probenecid increase quinolone levels

Mechanism of Action Inhibits DNA-gyrase in susceptible organisms thereby inhibits relaxation of supercoiled DNA and promotes breakage of DNA strands. DNA gyrase (topoisomerase II), is an essential bacterial enzyme that maintains the superhelical structure of DNA and is required for DNA replication and transcription, DNA repair, recombination, and transposition.

Pharmacodynamics/Kinetics

Absorption: Well absorbed

Distribution: V_d: 2.4-3.5 L/kg; distributed well into bronchus, prostatic tissue, and urine

Protein binding: 20%

Half-life, elimination: 5-7.5 hours

Elimination: Primarily unchanged in urine

Usual Dosage

Lower respiratory and urinary tract infections (UTI): Adults: Oral: 400 mg once daily for 10-14 days

Urinary tract infection (UTI) due to susceptible organisms:

Uncomplicated cystitis caused by *Escherichia coli*: Adult female: Oral: 400 mg once daily for 3 successive days

Uncomplicated cystitis caused by *Klebsiella pneumoniae*, *Proteus mirabilis*, or *Staphylococcus saprophyticus*: Adult female: 400 mg once daily for 10 successive days

Complicated UTI caused by *Eschericia coli*, *Klebsiella penumoniae*, *Proteus mirabilis*, or *Pseudomonas aeruginosa*: Adults: Oral: 400 mg once daily for 14 successive days

Surgical prophylaxis: 400 mg 2-6 hours before surgery

Uncomplicated gonorrhea: 400 mg as a single dose
No dosage adjustment is needed for elderly patients with normal renal function
Dosing adjustment in renal impairment:
Cl_{cr} 11-39 mL/minute: Loading dose: 400 mg; then 200 mg every day
Hemodialysis: Same as above
Dietary Considerations May be taken without regard to meals
Dosage Forms Tablet, as hydrochloride: 400 mg

♦ **Lomefloxacin Hydrochloride** see Lomefloxacin on previous page

♦ **Lomodix®** see Diphenoxylate and Atropine on page 371

♦ **Lomotil®** see Diphenoxylate and Atropine on page 371

Lomustine (loe MUS teen)

Related Information
Cancer Chemotherapy Regimens on page 1263
Toxicities of Chemotherapeutic Agents on page 1288
U.S. Brand Names CeeNU®
Synonyms CCNU
Therapeutic Category Antineoplastic Agent, Alkylating Agent (Nitrosourea)
Use Treatment of brain tumors and Hodgkin's disease, non-Hodgkin's lymphoma, melanoma, renal carcinoma, lung cancer, colon cancer
Pregnancy Risk Factor D
Contraindications Hypersensitivity to lomustine or any component
Warnings/Precautions The U.S. Food and Drug Administration (FDA) currently recommends that procedures for proper handling and disposal for antineoplastic agents be considered. Bone marrow suppression, notably thrombocytopenia and leukopenia, may lead to bleeding and overwhelming infections in an already compromised patient; will last for at least 6 weeks after a dose, do not administer courses more frequently than every 6 weeks because the toxicity is cumulative. Use with caution in patients with depressed platelet, leukocyte or erythrocyte counts, liver function abnormalities.

Adverse Reactions
>10%:
Gastrointestinal: Nausea and vomiting occur 3-6 hours after oral administration; this is due to a centrally mediated mechanism, not a direct effect on the GI lining; if vomiting occurs, it is not necessary to replace the dose unless it occurs immediately after drug administration
Emetic potential:
<60 mg: Moderately high (60% to 90%)
≥60 mg: High (>90%)
Time course of nausea/vomiting: Onset: 2-6 hours; Duration: 4-6 hours
Hematologic: Myelosuppression: Anemia; effects occur 4-6 weeks after a dose and may persist for 1-2 weeks
WBC: Moderate
Platelets: Severe
Onset (days): 14
Nadir (weeks): 4-5
Recovery (weeks): 6
1% to 10%:
Central nervous system: Neurotoxicity
Dermatologic: Skin rash
Gastrointestinal: Stomatitis, diarrhea
Hematologic: Anemia
<1%: Disorientation, lethargy, ataxia, alopecia, hepatotoxicity, dysarthria, pulmonary fibrosis with cumulative doses >600 mg, renal failure

Overdosage/Toxicology
Symptoms of overdose include nausea, vomiting, leukopenia; there are no known antidotes
Treatment is primarily symptomatic and supportive
Drug Interactions CYP2D6 enzyme inhibitor
Decreased effect with phenobarbital, resulting in decreased efficacy of both drugs
Increased toxicity with cimetidine, reported to cause bone marrow suppression or to potentiate the myelosuppressive effects of lomustine
Stability Refrigerate (<40°C/<104°F)
Mechanism of Action Inhibits DNA and RNA synthesis via carbamylation of DNA polymerase, alkylation of DNA, and alteration of RNA, proteins, and enzymes
Pharmacodynamics/Kinetics
Absorption: Complete from GI tract; appears in plasma within 3 minutes after administration
Distribution: Crosses blood-brain barrier to a greater degree than BNCU and CNS concentrations are equal to that of plasma
Protein binding: 50%
Metabolism: Rapid in the liver by hydroxylation produces at least 2 active metabolites
Half-life: Parent drug: 16-72 hours
Active metabolite: Terminal half-life: 1.3-2 days
Time to peak serum concentration: Active metabolite: Within 3 hours
Elimination: Enterohepatically recycled; excreted in the urine, feces (<5%), and in the expired air (<10%)
(Continued)

Lomustine *(Continued)*

Usual Dosage Oral (refer to individual protocols):

Children: 75-150 mg/m^2 as a single dose every 6 weeks; subsequent doses are readjusted after initial treatment according to platelet and leukocyte counts

Adults: 100-130 mg/m^2 as a single dose every 6 weeks; readjust after initial treatment according to platelet and leukocyte counts

With compromised marrow function: Initial dose: 100 mg/m^2 as a single dose every 6 weeks

Repeat courses should only be administered after adequate recovery: WBC >4000 and platelet counts >100,000

Subsequent dosing adjustment based on nadir:

Leukocytes 2000-2900/mm^3, platelets 25,000-74,999/mm^3: Administer 70% of prior dose

Leukocytes <2000/mm^3, platelets <25,000/mm^3: Administer 50% of prior dose

Dosage adjustment in renal impairment:

Cl$_{cr}$ 10-50 mL/minute: Administer 75% of normal dose

Cl$_{cr}$ <10 mL/minute: Administer 50% of normal dose

Hemodialysis: Supplemental dose is not necessary

Peritoneal dialysis: Significant drug removal is unlikely based on physiochemical characteristics

Monitoring Parameters CBC with differential and platelet count, hepatic and renal function tests, pulmonary function tests

Test Interactions Liver function tests

Patient Information Take with fluids on an empty stomach; no food or drink for 2 hours after administration; notify physician if unusual or persistent fever, sore throat, bleeding, bruising, or fatigue occur; contraceptive measures are recommended during therapy

Dosage Forms

Capsule: 10 mg, 40 mg, 100 mg

Dose Pack: 10 mg (2s); 100 mg (2s); 40 mg (2s)

♦ **Loniten**® *see Minoxidil on page 783*

♦ **Lonox**® *see Diphenoxylate and Atropine on page 371*

♦ **Lo/Ovral**® *see Ethinyl Estradiol and Norgestrel on page 454*

Loperamide *(loe PER a mide)*

U.S. Brand Names Diar-aid® [OTC]; Imodium®; Imodium® A-D [OTC]; Kaopectate® II [OTC]; Pepto® Diarrhea Control [OTC]

Canadian Brand Names PMS-Loperamine

Synonyms Loperamide Hydrochloride

Therapeutic Category Antidiarrheal

Use Treatment of acute diarrhea and chronic diarrhea associated with inflammatory bowel disease; chronic functional diarrhea (idiopathic); chronic diarrhea caused by bowel resection or organic lesions; to decrease the volume of ileostomy discharge

Unlabeled use: Treatment of traveler's diarrhea in combination with trimethoprim-sulfamethoxazole (co-trimoxazole) (3 days therapy)

Pregnancy Risk Factor B

Contraindications Patients who must avoid constipation, diarrhea resulting from some infections, or in patients with pseudomembranous colitis, hypersensitivity to specific drug or component, bloody diarrhea

Warnings/Precautions Large first-pass metabolism, use with caution in hepatic dysfunction; should not be used if diarrhea accompanied by high fever, blood in stool

Adverse Reactions Percentage unknown:

Central nervous system: Sedation, fatigue, dizziness, drowsiness

Dermatologic: Rash

Gastrointestinal: Nausea, vomiting, constipation, abdominal cramping, xerostomia, abdominal distention

Overdosage/Toxicology

Symptoms of overdose include CNS and respiratory depression, gastrointestinal cramping, constipation, GI irritation, nausea, vomiting; overdosage is noted when daily doses approximate 60 mg of loperamide

Treatment of overdose: Gastric lavage followed by 100 g activated charcoal through a nasogastric tube. Monitor for signs of CNS depression; if they occur, administer naloxone 2 mg I.V. (0.01 mg/kg for children) with repeat administration as necessary up to a total of 10 mg.

Drug Interactions Increased toxicity: CNS depressants, phenothiazines, tricyclic antidepressants may potentiate the adverse effects

Mechanism of Action Acts directly on intestinal muscles to inhibit peristalsis and prolongs transit time enhancing fluid and electrolyte movement through intestinal mucosa; reduces fecal volume, increases viscosity, and diminishes fluid and electrolyte loss; demonstrates antisecretory activity; exhibits peripheral action

Pharmacodynamics/Kinetics

Onset of action: Oral: Within 0.5-1 hour

Absorption: Oral: <40%; levels in breast milk expected to be very low

Protein binding: 97%

Metabolism: Hepatic (>50%) to inactive compounds

Half-life: 7-14 hours

Elimination: Fecal and urinary (1%) excretion of metabolites and unchanged drug (30% to 40%)

Usual Dosage Oral:

Children:

Acute diarrhea: Initial doses (in first 24 hours):

2-6 years: 1 mg 3 times/day

6-8 years: 2 mg twice daily

8-12 years: 2 mg 3 times/day

Maintenance: After initial dosing, 0.1 mg/kg doses after each loose stool, but not exceeding initial dosage

Chronic diarrhea: 0.08-0.24 mg/kg/day divided 2-3 times/day, maximum: 2 mg/dose

Adults: Initial: 4 mg (2 capsules), followed by 2 mg after each loose stool, up to 16 mg/day (8 capsules)

Patient Information Do not take more than 8 capsules or 80 mL in 24 hours; may cause drowsiness; if acute diarrhea lasts longer than 48 hours, consult physician

Nursing Implications Therapy for chronic diarrhea should not exceed 10 days

Dosage Forms

Caplet, as hydrochloride: 2 mg

Capsule, as hydrochloride: 2 mg

Liquid, oral, as hydrochloride: 1 mg/5 mL (60 mL, 90 mL, 120 mL)

Tablet, as hydrochloride: 2 mg

♦ **Loperamide Hydrochloride** see Loperamide on previous page

♦ **Lopid®** see Gemfibrozil on page 532

♦ **Lopressor®** see Metoprolol on page 768

♦ **Loprox®** see Ciclopirox on page 258

♦ **Lorabid™** see Loracarbef on this page

Loracarbef (lor a KAR bef)

Related Information

Cephalosporins by Generation on page 1373

U.S. Brand Names Lorabid™

Therapeutic Category Antibiotic, Carbacephem

Use Infections caused by susceptible organisms involving the respiratory tract, acute otitis media, sinusitis, skin and skin structure, bone and joint, and urinary tract and gynecologic

Pregnancy Risk Factor B

Contraindications Patients with a history of hypersensitivity to loracarbef or cephalosporins

Warnings/Precautions Modify dosage in patients with severe renal impairment; prolonged use may result in superinfection; use with caution in patients with a previous history of hypersensitivity to other beta-lactam antibiotics (eg, penicillins, cephalosporins)

Adverse Reactions

>1%: Gastrointestinal: Diarrhea

<1%: Seizures (with high doses and renal dysfunction), headache, nervousness, rash, urticaria, pruritus, Stevens-Johnson syndrome, nausea, vomiting, pseudomembranous colitis, eosinophilia, hemolytic anemia, neutropenia, positive Coombs' test, thrombocytopenia, cholestatic jaundice, slightly increased AST/ALT, arthralgia, nephrotoxicity with transient elevations of BUN/creatinine, interstitial nephritis, serum sickness, candidiasis

Overdosage/Toxicology

Symptoms of overdose include abdominal discomfort, diarrhea

Supportive care only

Drug Interactions

Increased effect: Probenecid may decrease cephalosporin elimination

Increased toxicity: Furosemide, aminoglycosides may be a possible additive to nephrotoxicity

Stability Suspension may be kept at room temperature for 14 days

Mechanism of Action Inhibits bacterial cell wall synthesis by binding to one or more of the penicillin binding proteins (PBPs); inhibits the final transpeptidation step of peptidoglycan synthesis in bacterial cell walls, thus inhibiting cell wall biosynthesis. It is thought that beta-lactam antibiotics inactivate transpeptidase via acylation of the enzyme with cleavage of the CO-N bond of the beta-lactam ring. Upon exposure to beta-lactam antibiotics, bacteria eventually lyse due to ongoing activity of cell wall autolytic enzymes (autolysins and murein hydrolases) while cell wall assembly is arrested.

Pharmacodynamics/Kinetics

Absorption: Oral: Rapid

Half-life, elimination: ~1 hour

Time to peak serum concentration: Oral: Within 1 hour

Elimination: Plasma clearance: ~200-300 mL/minute

Usual Dosage Oral:

Children:

Acute otitis media: 15 mg/kg twice daily for 10 days

Pharyngitis and impetigo: 7.5-15 mg/kg twice daily for 10 days

Adults:

Uncomplicated urinary tract infections: 200 mg once daily for 7 days

Skin and soft tissue: 200-400 mg every 12-24 hours

Uncomplicated pyelonephritis: 400 mg every 12 hours for 14 days

Upper/lower respiratory tract infection: 200-400 mg every 12-24 hours for 7-14 days

(Continued)

Loracarbef *(Continued)*

Dosing comments in renal impairment:
Cl$_{cr}$ 10-49 mL/minute: 50% of usual dose at usual interval or usual dose given half as often

Cl$_{cr}$ <10 mL/minute: Administer usual dose every 3-5 days

Hemodialysis: Doses should be administered after dialysis sessions

Patient Information Take on an empty stomach at least 1 hour before or 2 hours after meals; finish all medication

Dosage Forms
Capsule: 200 mg, 400 mg

Suspension, oral: 100 mg/5 mL (50 mL, 100 mL); 200 mg/5 mL (50 mL, 100 mL)

Loratadine *(lor AT a deen)*

U.S. Brand Names Claritin®

Therapeutic Category Antihistamine, Nonsedating

Use Relief of nasal and non-nasal symptoms of seasonal allergic rhinitis

Pregnancy Risk Factor B

Contraindications Patients hypersensitive to loratadine or any of its components

Warnings/Precautions Patients with liver impairment should start with a lower dose (10 mg every other day), since their ability to clear the drug will be reduced; use with caution in lactation, safety in children <12 years of age has not been established

Adverse Reactions
>10%:

Central nervous system: Headache, somnolence, fatigue

Gastrointestinal: Xerostomia

1% to 10%:

Cardiovascular: Hypotension, hypertension, palpitations, tachycardia

Central nervous system: Anxiety, depression

Endocrine & metabolic: Breast pain

Neuromuscular & skeletal: Hyperkinesia, arthralgias

Respiratory: Nasal dryness, pharyngitis, dyspnea

Miscellaneous: Diaphoresis

Overdosage/Toxicology
Symptoms of overdose include somnolence, tachycardia, headache

No specific antidote is available, treatment is first decontamination, then symptomatic and supportive; loratadine is not eliminated by dialysis

Drug Interactions CYP2D6 and 3A3/4 enzyme substrate

Increased plasma concentrations of loratadine and its active metabolite with ketoconazole; erythromycin increases the AUC of loratadine and its active metabolite; no change in QT$_c$ interval was seen

Increased toxicity: Procarbazine, other antihistamines, alcohol

Mechanism of Action Long-acting tricyclic antihistamine with selective peripheral histamine H$_1$-receptor antagonistic properties

Pharmacodynamics/Kinetics
Onset of action: Within 1-3 hours

Peak effect: 8-12 hours

Duration: >24 hours

Absorption: Rapid

Metabolism: Extensive to an active metabolite

Half-life: 12-15 hours

Elimination: Significant excretion into breast milk

Usual Dosage Children ≥6 years and Adults: Oral: 10 mg/day on an empty stomach

Dosing interval in hepatic impairment: 10 mg every other day to start

Patient Information Drink plenty of water; may cause dry mouth, sedation, drowsiness, and can impair judgment and coordination

Dosage Forms
Syrup: 1 mg/mL (480 mL)

Tablet: 10 mg

Rapid-disintegrating tablets: 10 mg (RediTabs®)

Loratadine and Pseudoephedrine *(lor AT a deen & soo doe e FED rin)*

U.S. Brand Names Claritin-D®; Claritin-D® 24-Hour

Therapeutic Category Antihistamine/Decongestant Combination

Dosage Forms
Tablet: Loratadine 5 mg and pseudoephedrine sulfate 120 mg

Tablet, extended release: Loratadine 10 mg and pseudoephedrine sulfate 240 mg

Lorazepam *(lor A ze pam)*

Related Information
Benzodiazepines Comparison *on page 1310*

Convulsive Status Epilepticus *on page 1470*

U.S. Brand Names Ativan®

Canadian Brand Names Apo®-Lorazepam; Novo-Lorazepam; Nu-Loraz; PMS-Lorazepam; Pro-Lorazepam®

Therapeutic Category Antianxiety Agent; Anticonvulsant; Antiemetic; Benzodiazepine; Sedative

Use Management of anxiety, status epilepticus, preoperative sedation, for desired amnesia, and as an antiemetic adjunct

Unapproved uses: Alcohol detoxification, insomnia, psychogenic catatonia, partial complex seizures

Restrictions C-IV

Pregnancy Risk Factor D

Pregnancy/Breast-Feeding Implications

Clinical effects on the fetus: Crosses the placenta. Respiratory depression or hypotonia if administered near time of delivery.

Breast-feeding/lactation: Crosses into breast milk and no data on clinical effects on the infant. American Academy of Pediatrics states MAY BE OF CONCERN.

Contraindications Hypersensitivity to lorazepam or any component; there may be a cross-sensitivity with other benzodiazepines; do not use in a comatose patient, those with pre-existing CNS depression, narrow-angle glaucoma, severe uncontrolled pain, severe hypotension

Warnings/Precautions Use caution in patients with renal or hepatic impairment, organic brain syndrome, myasthenia gravis, or Parkinson's disease. Dilute injection prior to I.V. use with equal volume of compatible diluent (D_5W, 0.9% sodium chloride, sterile water for injection); do **not** inject intra-arterially, arteriospasm and gangrene may occur; injection contains benzyl alcohol 2%, polyethylene glycol and propylene glycol, which may be toxic to newborns in high doses, may reduce effectiveness of ECT; oral doses >0.09 mg/kg produced increased ataxia without increased sedative benefit versus lower doses

Adverse Reactions

>10%:

Cardiovascular: Tachycardia, chest pain

Central nervous system: Drowsiness, confusion, ataxia, amnesia, slurred speech, paradoxical excitement, rage, headache, depression, anxiety, fatigue, lightheadedness, insomnia

Dermatologic: Rash

Endocrine & metabolic: Decreased libido

Gastrointestinal: Xerostomia, constipation, diarrhea, nausea, vomiting, increased or decreased appetite, decreased salivation

Local: Phlebitis, pain with injection

Neuromuscular & skeletal: Dysarthria

Ocular: Blurred vision, diplopia

Miscellaneous: Diaphoresis

1% to 10%:

Cardiovascular: Cardiac arrest, hypotension, bradycardia, cardiovascular collapse, syncope

Central nervous system: Confusion, nervousness, dizziness, akathisia

Neuromuscular & skeletal: Rigidity, tremor, muscle cramps

Dermatologic: Dermatitis

Gastrointestinal: Weight gain or loss

Otic: Tinnitus

Respiratory: Nasal congestion, hyperventilation

<1%: Menstrual irregularities, increased salivation, blood dyscrasias, reflex slowing, physical and psychological dependence with prolonged use

Overdosage/Toxicology

Symptoms of overdose include confusion, coma, hypoactive reflexes, dyspnea, labored breathing

Treatment for benzodiazepine overdose is supportive. Rarely is mechanical ventilation required. Flumazenil has been shown to selectively block the binding of benzodiazepines to CNS receptors, resulting in a reversal of benzodiazepine-induced CNS depression but not respiratory depression. Treatment requires support of blood pressure and respiration until drug effects subside.

Drug Interactions

Decreased effect with oral contraceptives (combination products), cigarette smoking; decreased effect of levodopa

Increased effect with morphine

Increased toxicity with alcohol, CNS depressants, MAO inhibitors, loxapine, TCAs

Stability

Intact vials should be refrigerated, protected from light; do not use discolored or precipitate containing solutions

May be stored at room temperature for up to 60 days

Stability of parenteral admixture at room temperature (25°C): 24 hours

Standard diluent: 1 mg/100 mL D_5W

I.V. is **incompatible** when administered in the same line with foscarnet, ondansetron, sargramostim

Mechanism of Action Depresses all levels of the CNS, including the limbic and reticular formation, probably through the increased action of gamma-aminobutyric acid (GABA), which is a major inhibitory neurotransmitter in the brain

Pharmacodynamics/Kinetics

Onset of hypnosis: I.M.: 20-30 minutes

Duration: 6-8 hours

Absorption: Oral, I.M.: Prompt following administration

Distribution: Crosses the placenta; appears in breast milk

V_d:

Neonates: 0.76 L/kg

Adults: 1.3 L/kg

Protein binding: 85%, free fraction may be significantly higher in elderly

Metabolism: In the liver to inactive compounds

(Continued)

Lorazepam *(Continued)*

Half-life:
Neonates: 40.2 hours
Older Children: 10.5 hours
Adults: 12.9 hours
Elderly: 15.9 hours
End-stage renal disease: 32-70 hours
Elimination: Urinary excretion and minimal fecal clearance

Usual Dosage
Antiemetic:
Children 2-15 years: I.V.: 0.05 mg/kg (up to 2 mg/dose) prior to chemotherapy
Adults: Oral, I.V.: 0.5-2 mg every 4-6 hours as needed
Anxiety and sedation:
Infants and Children: Oral, I.V.: Usual: 0.05 mg/kg/dose (range: 0.02-0.09 mg/kg) every 4-8 hours
Adults: Oral: 1-10 mg/day in 2-3 divided doses; usual dose: 2-6 mg/day in divided doses
Insomnia: Adults: Oral: 2-4 mg at bedtime
Preoperative: Adults:
I.M.: 0.05 mg/kg administered 2 hours before surgery; maximum: 4 mg/dose
I.V.: 0.044 mg/kg 15-20 minutes before surgery; usual maximum: 2 mg/dose
Operative amnesia: Adults: I.V.: Up to 0.05 mg/kg; maximum: 4 mg/dose
Status epilepticus: I.V.:
Infants and Children: 0.1 mg/kg slow I.V. over 2-5 minutes, do not exceed 4 mg/single dose; may repeat second dose of 0.05 mg/kg slow I.V. in 10-15 minutes if needed
Adolescents: 0.07 mg/kg slow I.V. over 2-5 minutes; maximum: 4 mg/dose; may repeat in 10-15 minutes
Adults: 4 mg/dose given slowly over 2-5 minutes; may repeat in 10-15 minutes; usual maximum dose: 8 mg

Dietary Considerations Alcohol: Additive CNS depression has been reported with benzodiazepines; avoid or limit alcohol

Administration
Lorazepam may be administered by I.M. or I.V.
I.M.: Should be administered deep into the muscle mass
I.V.: Do not exceed 2 mg/minute or 0.05 mg/kg over 2-5 minutes
Dilute I.V. dose with equal volume of compatible diluent (D_5W, NS, SWI)
Injection must be made slowly with repeated aspiration to make sure the injection is not intra-arterial and that perivascular extravasation has not occurred

Monitoring Parameters Respiratory and cardiovascular status, blood pressure, heart rate, symptoms of anxiety

Reference Range Therapeutic: 50-240 ng/mL (SI: 156-746 nmol/L)

Test Interactions May increase the results of liver function tests

Patient Information Advise patient of potential for physical and psychological dependence with chronic use; advise patient of possible retrograde amnesia after I.V. or I.M. use; will cause drowsiness, impairment of judgment or coordination

Nursing Implications Keep injectable form in the refrigerator; **inadvertent intra-arterial injection may produce arteriospasm resulting in gangrene which may require amputation;** emergency resuscitative equipment should be available when administering by I.V. use; prior to I.V. use, lorazepam injection must be diluted with an equal amount of compatible diluent; injection must be made slowly with repeated aspiration to make sure the injection is not intra-arterial and that perivascular extravasation has not occurred; provide safety measures (ie, side rails, night light, and call button); supervise ambulation

Dosage Forms
Injection: 2 mg/mL (1 mL, 10 mL); 4 mg/mL (1 mL, 10 mL)
Solution, oral concentrated, alcohol and dye free: 2 mg/mL (30 mL)
Tablet: 0.5 mg, 1 mg, 2 mg

♦ **Lorcet®-HD** *see* Hydrocodone and Acetaminophen *on page 575*
♦ **Lorcet® Plus** *see* Hydrocodone and Acetaminophen *on page 575*
♦ **Lortab®** *see* Hydrocodone and Acetaminophen *on page 575*
♦ **Lortab® ASA** *see* Hydrocodone and Aspirin *on page 576*

Losartan *(loe SAR tan)*

Related Information
Angiotensin Agents *on page 1291*

U.S. Brand Names Cozaar®

Synonyms DuP 753; Losartan Potassium; MK594

Therapeutic Category Angiotensin II Antagonist; Antihypertensive Agent

Use Treatment of hypertension with or without concurrent use of thiazide diuretics; may prolong survival in heart failure; recommended for patients unable to tolerated ACE inhibitors

Pregnancy Risk Factor C (1st trimester); D (2nd and 3rd trimester)

Pregnancy/Breast-Feeding Implications Breast-feeding/lactation: Avoid use in the nursing mother, if possible, since it is postulated that losartan is excreted in breast milk

Contraindications Hypersensitivity to losartan or any components; pregnancy

Warnings/Precautions Avoid use or use a much smaller dose in patients who are intravascularly volume-depleted; use caution in patients with unilateral or bilateral renal artery stenosis to avoid a decrease in renal function; AUCs of losartan (not the active metabolite) are about 50% greater in patients with Cl_{cr} <30 mL/minute and are doubled in hemodialysis patients

Adverse Reactions

1% to 10%:

Cardiovascular: Hypotension without reflex tachycardia

Central nervous system: Dizziness, insomnia

Endocrine & metabolic: Hyperkalemia

Gastrointestinal: Diarrhea, dyspepsia

Hematologic: Slight decreases in hemoglobin and hematocrit

Neuromuscular & skeletal: Back/leg pain, myalgia

Renal: Hypouricemia (with large doses)

Respiratory: Cough (less than ACE inhibitors), nasal congestion, sinus disorders, sinusitis

<1%: Orthostatic effects, angina, second degree A-V block, CVA, palpitations, sinus bradycardia, tachycardia, flushing, facial edema, anxiety, ataxia, confusion, depression, dream abnormality, migraine headache, sleep disorders, vertigo, fever, alopecia, dermatitis, dry skin, bruising, erythema, photosensitivity, pruritus, rash, urticaria, gout, anorexia, constipation, flatulence, vomiting, abnormal taste, gastritis, impotence, decreased libido, polyuria, nocturia, slightly elevated LFTs and bilirubin, paresthesia, tremor; arm, hip, shoulder, and knee pain, joint edema, fibromyalgia, muscle weakness, blurred vision, burning and stinging eyes, conjunctivitis, decreased visual acuity, tinnitus, urinary tract infection, nocturia, mild increases in BUN/creatinine, dyspnea, bronchitis, pharyngeal discomfort, epistaxis, rhinitis, respiratory congestion, diaphoresis

Overdosage/Toxicology

Symptoms may occur with very significant overdosages including hypotension and tachycardia

Treatment should be supportive

Drug Interactions CYP2C9 and 3A3/4 enzyme substrate

Decreased effect: Phenobarbital, troleandomycin, sulfaphenazole

Increased effect: Cimetidine

Mechanism of Action As a selective and competitive, nonpeptide angiotensin II receptor antagonist, losartan blocks the vasoconstrictor and aldosterone-secreting effects of angiotensin II; losartan interacts reversibly at the AT1 and AT2 receptors of many tissues and has slow dissociation kinetics; its affinity for the AT1 receptor is 1000 times greater than the AT2 receptor. Angiotensin II receptor antagonists may induce a more complete inhibition of the renin-angiotensin system than ACE inhibitors, they do not affect the response to bradykinin, and are less likely to be associated with nonrenin-angiotensin effects (eg, cough and angioedema). Losartan increases urinary flow rate and in addition to being natriuretic and kaliuretic, increases excretion of chloride, magnesium, uric acid, calcium, and phosphate.

Pharmacodynamics/Kinetics

Onset of effect: 6 hours

Distribution: Does not cross the blood brain barrier; V_d: Losartan: 34 L; E-3174: 12 L

Protein binding: Highly bound to plasma proteins

Metabolism: 14% of an orally administered dose is metabolized by cytochrome P-450 enzymes to an active metabolite E-3174 (40 times more potent than losartan); undergoes substantial first-pass metabolism

Bioavailability: 25% to 33%; AUC of E-3174 is 4 times greater than that of losartan

Half-life: Losartan: 1.5-2 hours; E-3174: 6-9 hours

Time to peak: Peak serum levels of losartan: 1 hour; metabolite, E-3174: 3-4 hours

Elimination: 3% to 8% excreted in urine as unchanged parent or as E-3174; ~35% of a dose is recovered in urine and 60% in feces; total plasma clearance of losartan: 600 mL/minute: its active metabolite: 50 mL/minute

Usual Dosage

Oral: The usual starting dose is 50 mg once daily; can be administered once or twice daily with total daily doses ranging from 25 mg to 100 mg

Usual initial doses in patients receiving diuretics or those with intravascular volume depletion: 25 mg

Patients not receiving diuretics: 50 mg

Dosing adjustment in renal impairment: None necessary

Dosing adjustment in hepatic impairment or geriatric patients: Reduce the initial dose to 25 mg; divide dosage intervals into two

Not removed via hemodialysis

Monitoring Parameters Supine blood pressure, electrolytes, serum creatinine, BUN, urinalysis, symptomatic hypotension and tachycardia, CBC

Patient Information Use caution standing or rising abruptly following a dosage increase; report any symptoms of difficulty breathing, swallowing, swelling of face, lips, extremities, or tongue immediately, as well as symptoms of fever or sore throat; do not use if pregnant

Nursing Implications Observe for symptomatic hypotension and tachycardia especially in patients with CHF; hyponatremia, high-dose diuretics, or severe volume depletion

Additional Information Losartan's effect in African-American patients was notably less than in non-African Americans; and while dosage adjustments are not needed, plasma levels are twice as high in female hypertensives as male hypertensives; if the antihypertensive effect measured at trough using once-a-day dosing is inadequate, a twice-a-day regimen at the same total daily dose or an increase in dose may give a more satisfactory response

(Continued)

Losartan *(Continued)*

Dosage Forms Tablet, film coated, as potassium: 25 mg, 50 mg

Losartan and Hydrochlorothiazide

(loe SAR tan & hye droe klor oh THYE a zide)

U.S. Brand Names Hyzaar®

Therapeutic Category Angiotensin II Antagonist Combination; Antihypertensive Agent, Combination

Dosage Forms Tablet: Losartan potassium 50 mg and hydrochlorothiazide 12.5 mg

- ♦ **Losartan Potassium** see Losartan *on page 696*
- ♦ **Losec®** see Omeprazole *on page 861*
- ♦ **Losec®** see Omeprazole *on page 861*
- ♦ **Lotemax®** see Loteprednol *on this page*
- ♦ **Lotensin®** see Benazepril *on page 131*
- ♦ **Lotensin® HCT** see Benazepril and Hydrochlorothiazide *on page 132*

Loteprednol (loe te PRED nol)

U.S. Brand Names Alrex™; Lotemax®

Synonyms Loteprednol Etabonate

Therapeutic Category Corticosteroid, Ophthalmic

Use

0.2% suspension (Alrex™): Temporary relief of signs and symptoms of seasonal allergic conjunctivitis

0.5% suspension (Lotemax®): Inflammatory conditions (treatment of steroid-responsive inflammatory conditions of the palpebral and bulbar conjunctiva, cornea, and anterior segment of the globe such as allergic conjunctivitis, acne rosacea, superficial punctate keratitis, herpes zoster keratitis, iritis, cyclitis, selected infective conjunctivitis, when the inherent hazard of steroid use is accepted to obtain an advisable diminution in edema and inflammation) and treatment of postoperative inflammation following ocular surgery

Pregnancy Risk Factor C

Contraindications Viral diseases of the cornea and conjunctiva; mycobacterial infection of the eye; fungal diseases of ocular structures; hypersensitivity to loteprednol and any ingredients; hypersensitivity to other corticosteroids

Warnings/Precautions For ophthalmic use only; patients should be re-evaluated if symptoms fail to improve after 2 days. Intraocular pressure should be monitored if this product is used >10 days. Prolonged use may result in glaucoma and injury to the optic nerve. Visual defects in acuity and field of vision may occur. Posterior subcapsular cataracts may form after long-term use. Use with caution in presence of glaucoma (steroids increase intraocular pressure). Perforation may occur with topical steroids in diseases which thin the cornea or sclera. Steroids may mask infection or enhance existing infection. Steroid use may delay healing after cataract surgery.

Adverse Reactions

10% to 15%:

Central nervous system: Headache

Respiratory: Rhinitis, pharyngitis

5% to 10%: Ocular: Abnormal vision/blurring, burning on instillation, chemosis, dry eyes, itching, injection

<5%: Ocular: Conjunctivitis/irritation, corneal abnormalities, eyelid erythema, papillae uveitis

<1%: Ocular: Increased intraocular pressure, changes in visual acuity and/or field defects, cataract formation, secondary ocular infection, global perforation in disease which thins cornea or sclera

Mechanism of Action Corticosteroids inhibit the inflammatory response including edema, capillary dilation, leukocyte migration, and scar formation. Loteprednol is highly lipid soluble and penetrates cells readily to induce the production of lipocortins. These proteins modulate the activity of prostaglandins and leukotrienes.

Pharmacodynamics/Kinetics Plasma levels following intraocular administration were not detectable

Usual Dosage Adults: Ophthalmic:

0.2% suspension (Alrex™): Instill 1 drop into affected eye(s) 4 times/day

0.5% suspension (Lotemax®):

Inflammatory conditions: Apply 1-2 drops into the conjunctival sac of the affected eye(s) 4 times/day. During the initial treatment within the first week, the dosing may be increased up to 1 drop every hour. Advise patients not to discontinue therapy prematurely. If signs and symptoms fail to improve after 2 days, re-evaluate the patient.

Postoperative inflammation: Apply 1-2 drops into the conjunctival sac of the operated eye(s) 4 times/day beginning 24 hours after surgery and continuing throughout the first 2 weeks of the postoperative period

Administration Shake well before using

Monitoring Parameters Intraocular pressure (if >10 days)

Dosage Forms Suspension, ophthalmic, as etabonate:

0.2% (Alrex™): 5 mL, 10 mL

0.5% (Lotemax®): 2.5 mL, 5 mL, 10 mL, 15 mL

- ♦ **Loteprednol Etabonate** see Loteprednol *on this page*

- **Lotrel**® *see* Amlodipine and Benazepril *on page 66*
- **Lotrimin**® *see* Clotrimazole *on page 287*
- **Lotrimin**® **AF Cream [OTC]** *see* Clotrimazole *on page 287*
- **Lotrimin**® **AF Lotion [OTC]** *see* Clotrimazole *on page 287*
- **Lotrimin**® **AF Powder [OTC]** *see* Miconazole *on page 775*
- **Lotrimin**® **AF Solution [OTC]** *see* Clotrimazole *on page 287*
- **Lotrimin**® **AF Spray Liquid [OTC]** *see* Miconazole *on page 775*
- **Lotrimin**® **AF Spray Powder [OTC]** *see* Miconazole *on page 775*
- **Lotrisone**® *see* Betamethasone and Clotrimazole *on page 142*

Lovastatin (LOE va sta tin)

Related Information
Lipid-Lowering Agents *on page 1327*
U.S. Brand Names Mevacor®
Canadian Brand Names Apo®-Lovastatin
Synonyms Mevinolin; Monacolin K
Therapeutic Category Antilipemic Agent; HMG-CoA Reductase Inhibitor
Use Adjunct to dietary therapy to decrease elevated serum total and LDL cholesterol concentrations in primary hypercholesterolemia
Pregnancy Risk Factor X
Contraindications Pregnancy; active liver disease, hypersensitivity to lovastatin or any component
Warnings/Precautions May elevate aminotransferases; LFTs should be performed before and every 4- 6 weeks during the first 12-15 months of therapy and periodically thereafter; can also cause myalgia and rhabdomyolysis; use with caution in patients who consume large quantities of alcohol or who have a history of liver disease
Adverse Reactions
1% to 10%:
Central nervous system: Headache, dizziness
Dermatologic: Rash, pruritus
Gastrointestinal: Flatulence, abdominal pain, cramps, diarrhea, pancreatitis, constipation, nausea, dyspepsia, heartburn
Neuromuscular & skeletal: Myalgia, increased CPK
<1%: Abnormal taste, gynecomastia, blurred vision, myositis, lenticular opacities
Overdosage/Toxicology Very few adverse events; treatment is symptomatic
Drug Interactions CYP3A3/4 and 3A5-7 enzyme substrate
Increased toxicity: Gemfibrozil (musculoskeletal effects such as myopathy, myalgia, and/ or muscle weakness accompanied by markedly elevated CK concentrations, rash, and/or pruritus); clofibrate, niacin (myopathy), erythromycin, cyclosporine, oral anticoagulants (elevated PT)
Increased effect/toxicity of lovastatin (20-fold increase in serum levels) with concurrent itraconazole or ketoconazole; interactions may also occur with simvastatin
Increased effect/toxicity of levothyroxine
Concurrent use of erythromycin and lovastatin may result in elevated lovastatin levels and rhabdomyolysis
Mechanism of Action Lovastatin acts by competitively inhibiting 3-hydroxyl-3-methylglutaryl-coenzyme A (HMG-CoA) reductase, the enzyme that catalyzes the rate-limiting step in cholesterol biosynthesis
Pharmacodynamics/Kinetics
Onset of effect: 3 days of therapy required for LDL cholesterol concentration reductions
Absorption: Oral: 30%
Protein binding: 95%
Half-life: 1.1-1.7 hours
Time to peak serum concentration: Oral: 2-4 hours
Elimination: ~80% to 85% of dose excreted in feces and 10% in urine following liver hydrolysis
Usual Dosage Adults: Oral: Initial: 20 mg with evening meal, then adjust at 4-week intervals; maximum dose: 80 mg/day; before initiation of therapy, patients should be placed on a standard cholesterol-lowering diet for 3-6 months and the diet should be continued during drug therapy
Administration Administer with meals
Monitoring Parameters Plasma triglycerides, cholesterol, and liver function tests
Test Interactions ↑ liver transaminases (S), altered thyroid function tests
Patient Information Promptly report any unexplained muscle pain, tenderness or weakness, especially if accompanied by malaise or fever; do not interrupt, increase, or decrease dose without advice of physician; take with meals
Nursing Implications Urge patient to adhere to cholesterol-lowering diet
Dosage Forms Tablet: 10 mg, 20 mg, 40 mg

- **Lovenox**® **Injection** *see* Enoxaparin *on page 412*
- **Low Potassium Diet** *see page 1513*
- **Low-Quel**® *see* Diphenoxylate and Atropine *on page 371*
- **Loxapac**® *see* Loxapine *on this page*

Loxapine (LOKS a peen)

Related Information
Antipsychotic Agents Comparison *on page 1305*
(Continued)

Loxapine *(Continued)*

U.S. Brand Names Loxitane®; Loxitane® C; Loxitane® I.M.

Canadian Brand Names Loxapac®

Synonyms Loxapine Hydrochloride; Loxapine Succinate; Oxilapine Succinate

Therapeutic Category Antipsychotic Agent

Use Management of psychotic disorders

Pregnancy Risk Factor C

Contraindications Hypersensitivity to chlorpromazine or any component, cross-sensitivity with other phenothiazines may exist; avoid use in patients with narrow-angle glaucoma, bone marrow suppression, severe liver or cardiac disease, severe CNS depression, coma

Warnings/Precautions Watch for hypotension when administering I.M.; safety in children <6 months of age has not been established; use with caution in patients with cardiovascular disease or seizures; benefits of therapy must be weighed against risks of therapy; should not be given I.V.

Adverse Reactions

>10%:
    Cardiovascular: Orthostatic hypotension
    Central nervous system: Drowsiness, extrapyramidal effects (parkinsonian), confusion, persistent tardive dyskinesia
    Gastrointestinal: Xerostomia
    Ocular: Blurred vision

1% to 10%:
    Dermatologic: Rash
    Endocrine & metabolic: Enlargement of breasts
    Gastrointestinal: Constipation, nausea, vomiting

<1%: Tachycardia, arrhythmias, abnormal T-waves with prolonged ventricular repolarization, neuroleptic malignant syndrome (NMS), sedation, restlessness, anxiety, seizures, altered central temperature regulation, hyperpigmentation, pruritus, photosensitivity, galactorrhea, amenorrhea, gynecomastia, weight gain, adynamic ileus, urinary retention, overflow incontinence, priapism, sexual dysfunction, agranulocytosis (more often in women between fourth and tenth week of therapy), leukopenia (usually in patients with large doses for prolonged periods), cholestatic jaundice, retinal pigmentation

Overdosage/Toxicology

Symptoms of overdose include deep sleep, dystonia, agitation, dysrhythmias, extrapyramidal symptoms, hypotension, seizures

Following initiation of essential overdose management, toxic symptom treatment and supportive treatment should be initiated. Hypotension usually responds to I.V. fluids or Trendelenburg positioning. If unresponsive to these measures, the use of a parenteral inotrope may be required (eg, norepinephrine 0.1-0.2 mcg/kg/minute titrated to response). Seizures commonly respond to diazepam (I.V. 5-10 mg bolus in adults every 15 minutes if needed up to a total of 30 mg; I.V. 0.25-0.4 mg/kg/dose up to a total of 10 mg in children) or to phenytoin or phenobarbital. Critical cardiac arrhythmias often respond to I.V. phenytoin (15 mg/kg up to 1 g), while other antiarrhythmics can be used. Neuroleptics often cause extrapyramidal symptoms (eg, dystonic reactions) requiring management with diphenhydramine 1-2 mg/kg (adults) up to a maximum of 50 mg I.M. or I.V. slow push followed by a maintenance dose for 48-72 hours. When these reactions are unresponsive to diphenhydramine, benztropine mesylate I.V. 1-2 mg (adults) may be effective. These agents are generally effective within 2-5 minutes.

Drug Interactions

Decreased effect of guanethidine, phenytoin

Increased toxicity with CNS depressants, metrizamide (increased seizure potential), guanabenz, MAO inhibitors

Mechanism of Action Unclear, thought to be similar to chlorpromazine

Pharmacodynamics/Kinetics

Onset of neuroleptic effect: Oral: Within 20-30 minutes
Peak effect: 1.5-3 hours
Duration: ~12 hours
Metabolism: Hepatic to glucuronide conjugates
Half-life, biphasic: Initial: 5 hours; Terminal: 12-19 hours
Elimination: In urine, and to a smaller degree, feces

Usual Dosage Adults:

Oral: 10 mg twice daily, increase dose until psychotic symptoms are controlled; usual dose range: 60-100 mg/day in divided doses 2-4 times/day; dosages >250 mg/day are not recommended

I.M.: 12.5-50 mg every 4-6 hours or longer as needed and change to oral therapy as soon as possible

Dietary Considerations Alcohol: Additive CNS effect, avoid use

Administration Injectable is for I.M. use only

Test Interactions False-positives for phenylketonuria, amylase, uroporphyrins, urobilinogen, ↑ liver function tests

Patient Information May cause drowsiness; avoid alcoholic beverages; may impair judgment or coordination; may cause photosensitivity; avoid excessive sunlight; do not stop taking without consulting physician

Additional Information

Loxapine hydrochloride: Loxitane® C oral concentrate, Loxitane® IM
Loxapine succinate: Loxitane® capsule

Dosage Forms
Capsule, as succinate: 5 mg, 10 mg, 25 mg, 50 mg
Concentrate, oral, as hydrochloride: 25 mg/mL (120 mL dropper bottle)
Injection, as hydrochloride: 50 mg/mL (1 mL)

Lyme Disease Vaccine (LIME dee seas vak SEEN)

U.S. Brand Names LYMErix®
Synonyms Lyme Disease Vaccine (Recombinant OspA)
Therapeutic Category Vaccine
Use Active immunization against Lyme disease in individuals between 15-70 years of age. Individuals most at risk are those who live, work, or travel to *B. burgdorfi*-infected, tick-infested, grassy/wooded areas.

Pregnancy Risk Factor C

Pregnancy/Breast-Feeding Implications It is not known whether Lyme disease vaccine is excreted in human milk. Because many drugs are excreted in milk, caution should be exercised when the vaccine is given to nursing mothers. Healthcare professionals are encouraged to register pregnant women who receive the vaccine with the SKB vaccination pregnancy registry (1-800-8900, ext 5231).

Contraindications Known hypersensitivity to any component of the vaccine. Vaccination should be postponed during acute moderate to severe febrile illness (minor illness is generally not a contraindication). Safety and efficacy in patients <15 years of age have not been established.

Warnings/Precautions Do not administer to patients with treatment-resistant Lyme arthritis. Will not prevent disease in patients with prior infection and offers no protection against other tick-borne diseases. Immunosuppressed patients or those receiving immunosuppressive therapy (vaccine may not be effective) - defer vaccination until 3 months after therapy. Avoid in patients receiving anticoagulant therapy (due to intramuscular injection). The physician should take all known precautions for prevention of allergic or other reactions. Administer with caution to patients with known or suspected latex allergy (applies only to the LMErix Tip-Lok™ syringe, vaccine vial does not contain natural rubber). Duration of immunity has not been established.

Adverse Reactions (Limited to overall self-reported events occurring within 30 days following a dose)
>10%: Local: Injection site pain (21.9%)
1% to 10%:
  Central nervous system: Headache (5.6%), fatigue (3.9%), fever (2.6%), chills (2%), dizziness (1%)
  Dermatologic: Rash (1.4%)
  Gastrointestinal: Nausea (1.1%)
  Neuromuscular & skeletal: Arthralgia (6.8%), myalgia (4.8%), muscle aches (2.8%), back pain (1.9%), stiffness (1%)
  Respiratory: Upper respiratory tract infection (4.4%), sinusitis (3.2%), pharyngitis (2.5%), rhinitis (2.4%), cough (1.5%), bronchitis (1.1%)
  Miscellaneous: Viral infection (2.8%), flu-like syndrome (2.5%)
(Continued)

Lyme Disease Vaccine *(Continued)*

Solicited adverse event rates were higher than unsolicited event rates (above). These included local reactions of soreness (93.5%), redness (41.8%), and swelling (29.9%). In addition, general systemic symptoms included fatigue (40.8%), headache (38.6%), arthralgia (25.6%), rash (11.7%), and fever (3.5%)

Patients with a history of Lyme disease were noted to experience a higher frequency of early musculoskeletal reactions. Other differences in the observed rate of adverse reactions were not significantly different between vaccine and placebo recipients.

Drug Interactions No data available

Stability Store between 2°C and 8°C (36°F and 46°F)

Mechanism of Action Lyme disease vaccine is a recombinant, noninfectious lipoprotein (OspA) derived from the outer surface of *Borrelia burgdorfi*, the causative agent of Lyme disease. Vaccination stimulates production of antibodies directed against this organism, including antibodies against the LA-2 epitope, which have bactericidal activity. Since OspA expression is down-regulated after inoculation into the human host, at least part of the vaccine's efficacy may be related to neutralization of bacteria within the midgut of the tick vector, preventing transmission to the human host.

Usual Dosage Adults: I.M.: Vaccination with 3 doses of 30 mcg (0.5 mL), administered at 0, 1, and 12 months, is recommended for optimal protection

Administration Intramuscular injection into the deltoid region is recommended. Do not administer intravenously, intradermally, or subcutaneously. The vaccine should be used as supplied without dilution. Shake well before withdrawal and use.

Test Interactions Vaccination will result in a positive *B. burgdorferi* IgG via ELISA (Western blot testing is recommended)

Patient Information Vaccination consists of a series of three injections over 12 months. Failure to complete the sequence may result in suboptimal protection. The vaccine may not provide 100% protection against Lyme disease, nor does it protect against other tick-borne disease. Individuals at risk should continue to use standard protective measures.

Dosage Forms Injection:
Vial: 30 mcg/0.5 mL
Prefilled syringe (Tip-Lok™): 30 mcg/0.5 mL

♦ **Lyme Disease Vaccine (Recombinant OspA)** *see* Lyme Disease Vaccine *on previous page*

♦ **LYMErix®** *see* Lyme Disease Vaccine *on previous page*

Lymphocyte Immune Globulin (LIM foe site i MYUN GLOB yoo lin)

U.S. Brand Names Atgam®

Synonyms Antithymocyte Globulin (Equine); Antithymocyte Immunoglobulin; ATG; Horse Antihuman Thymocyte Gamma Globulin

Therapeutic Category Immunosuppressant Agent

Use Prevention and treatment of acute renal and other solid organ allograft rejection; treatment of moderate to severe aplastic anemia in patients not considered suitable candidates for bone marrow transplantation; prevention of graft-versus-host disease following bone marrow transplantation

Pregnancy Risk Factor C

Contraindications Known hypersensitivity to ATG, thimerosal, or other equine gamma globulins; severe, unremitting leukopenia and/or thrombocytopenia

Warnings/Precautions Must be administered via central line due to chemical phlebitis; should only be used by physicians experienced in immunosuppressive therapy or management of solid organ or bone marrow transplant patients; adequate laboratory and supportive medical resources must be readily available in the facility for patient management; rash, dyspnea, hypotension, or anaphylaxis precludes further administration of the drug. Dose must be administered over at least 4 hours; patient may need to be pretreated with an antipyretic, antihistamine, and/or corticosteroid. Intradermal skin testing is recommended prior to first-dose administration.

Adverse Reactions
>10%:
Central nervous system: Fever, chills
Dermatologic: Rash
Hematologic: Leukopenia, thrombocytopenia
Miscellaneous: Systemic infection
1% to 10%:
Cardiovascular: Hypotension, hypertension, tachycardia, edema, chest pain
Central nervous system: Headache, malaise, pain
Gastrointestinal: Diarrhea, nausea, stomatitis, GI bleeding
Respiratory: Dyspnea
Local: Edema or redness at injection site, thrombophlebitis
Neuromuscular & skeletal: Myalgia, back pain, arthralgia
Renal: Abnormal renal function tests
Miscellaneous: Sensitivity reactions: Anaphylaxis may be indicated by hypotension, respiratory distress; serum sickness, viral infection
<1%: Seizures, pruritus, urticaria, hemolysis, anemia, arthralgia, weakness, acute renal failure, lymphadenopathy

Stability
Ampuls must be refrigerated
Dose must be diluted in 0.45% or 0.9% sodium chloride

Diluted solution is stable for 12 hours (including infusion time) at room temperature and 24 hours (including infusion time) at refrigeration

The use of dextrose solutions is not recommended (precipitation may occur)

Standard diluent: Dose/1000 mL NS or 0.45% sodium chloride

Minimum volume: Concentration should not exceed 1 mg/mL for a peripheral line or 4 mg/mL for a central line

Mechanism of Action May involve elimination of antigen-reactive T-lymphocytes (killer cells) in peripheral blood or alteration of T-cell function

Pharmacodynamics/Kinetics

Distribution: Poorly distributed into lymphoid tissues; binds to circulating lymphocytes, granulocytes, platelets, bone marrow cells

Half-life, plasma: 1.5-12 days

Elimination: ~1% of dose excreted in urine

Usual Dosage An intradermal skin test is recommended prior to administration of the initial dose of ATG; use 0.1 mL of a 1:1000 dilution of ATG in normal saline. A positive skin reaction consists of a wheal ≥10 mm in diameter. If a positive skin test occurs, the first infusion should be administered in a controlled environment with intensive life support immediately available. A systemic reaction precludes further administration of the drug. The absence of a reaction does **not** preclude the possibility of an immediate sensitivity reaction.

First dose: Premedicate with diphenhydramine 50 mg orally 30 minutes prior to and hydrocortisone 100 mg I.V. 15 minutes prior to infusion and acetaminophen 650 mg 2 hours after start of infusion

Children: I.V.:

Aplastic anemia protocol: 10-20 mg/kg/day for 8-14 days; then administer every other day for 7 more doses; addition doses may be given every other day for 21 total doses in 28 days

Renal allograft: 5-25 mg/kg/day

Adults: I.V.:

Aplastic anemia protocol: 10-20 mg/kg/day for 8-14 days, then administer every other day for 7 more doses

Renal allograft:

Rejection prophylaxis: 15 mg/kg/day for 14 days followed by 14 days of alternative day therapy at the same dose; the first dose should be administered within 24 hours before or after transplantation

Rejection treatment: 10-15 mg/kg/day for 14 days, then administer every other day for 10-14 days up to 21 doses in 28 days

Administration For I.V. use only; administer via central line; use of high flow veins will minimize the occurrence of phlebitis and thrombosis; administer by slow I.V. infusion through an inline filter with pore size of 0.2-1 micrometer over 4-8 hours at a final concentration not to exceed 4 mg ATG/mL

Monitoring Parameters Lymphocyte profile, CBC with differential and platelet count, vital signs during administration

Nursing Implications For I.V. use only; mild itching and erythema can be treated with antihistamines; infuse dose over at least 4 hours; any severe systemic reaction to the skin test such as generalized rash, tachycardia, dyspnea, hypotension, or anaphylaxis should preclude further therapy; **epinephrine and resuscitative equipment should be nearby.** Patient may need to be pretreated with an antipyretic, antihistamine, and/or corticosteroid.

Dosage Forms Injection: 50 of equine IgG/mL (5 mL)

♦ **Lyphocin®** see Vancomycin on page 1207

Lypressin (lye PRES in)

U.S. Brand Names Diapid® Nasal Spray

Synonyms 8-L-Lysine Vasopressin

Therapeutic Category Antidiuretic Hormone Analog; Pituitary Hormone; Vasopressin Analog

Use Controls or prevents signs and complications of neurogenic diabetes insipidus

Pregnancy Risk Factor C

Contraindications Known hypersensitivity to lypressin

Warnings/Precautions Use with caution in patients with coronary artery disease

Adverse Reactions

1% to 10%:

Cardiovascular: Chest tightness

Central nervous system: Dizziness, headache

Endocrine & metabolic: Water intoxication

Gastrointestinal: Abdominal cramping, increased bowel movements

Local: Irritation or burning

Respiratory: Coughing, dyspnea, rhinorrhea, nasal congestion

<1%: Inadvertent inhalation

Overdosage/Toxicology Symptoms of overdose include drowsiness, headache, confusion, weight gain, hypertension; systemic toxicity is unlikely to occur from the nasal spray

Drug Interactions Increased effect: Chlorpropamide, clofibrate, carbamazepine → prolongation of antidiuretic effects

Mechanism of Action Increases cyclic adenosine monophosphate (cAMP) which increases water permeability at the renal tubule resulting in decreased urine volume and increased osmolality; causes peristalsis by directly stimulating the smooth muscle in the GI tract

(Continued)

Lypressin *(Continued)*

Pharmacodynamics/Kinetics
Onset of antidiuretic effect: Intranasal spray: Within 0.5-2 hours
Duration: 3-8 hours
Metabolism: In the liver and kidneys
Half-life: 15-20 minutes
Elimination: Urinary excretion

Usual Dosage Children and Adults: Instill 1-2 sprays into one or both nostrils whenever frequency of urination increases or significant thirst develops; usual dosage is 1-2 sprays 4 times/day; range: 1 spray/day at bedtime to 10 sprays each nostril every 3-4 hours

Patient Information To control nocturia, an additional dose may be given at bedtime; notify physician if drowsiness, fatigue, headache, shortness of breath, abdominal cramps, or severe nasal irritation occurs

Additional Information Approximately 2 USP posterior pituitary pressor units per spray

Dosage Forms Spray: 0.185 mg/mL (equivalent to 50 USP posterior pituitary units/mL) (8 mL)

- ♦ **Lysatec-rt-PA®** *see* Alteplase *on page 49*
- ♦ **Lysodren®** *see* Mitotane *on page 787*
- ♦ **Macrobid®** *see* Nitrofurantoin *on page 843*
- ♦ **Macrodantin®** *see* Nitrofurantoin *on page 843*
- ♦ **Macrodex®** *see* Dextran *on page 341*

Mafenide *(MA fe nide)*

Related Information
Sulfonamide Derivatives *on page 1337*

U.S. Brand Names Sulfamylon® Topical

Synonyms Mafenide Acetate

Therapeutic Category Antibacterial, Topical; Antibiotic, Topical

Use Adjunct in the treatment of second and third degree burns to prevent septicemia caused by susceptible organisms such as *Pseudomonas aeruginosa*; prevention of graft loss of meshed autografts on excised burn wounds

Pregnancy Risk Factor C

Contraindications Hypersensitivity to mafenide, sulfites, or any component

Warnings/Precautions Use with caution in patients with renal impairment and in patients with G-6-PD deficiency; prolonged use may result in superinfection

Adverse Reactions
>10%:
   Central nervous system: Pain
   Local: Burning sensation, excoriation
1% to 10%:
   Cardiovascular: Facial edema
   Dermatologic: Rash
   Miscellaneous: Dyspnea
<1%: Erythema, hyperchloremia, metabolic acidosis, bone marrow suppression, hemolytic anemia, bleeding, porphyria, hyperventilation, tachypnea, hypersensitivity

Mechanism of Action Interferes with bacterial folic acid synthesis through competitive inhibition of para-aminobenzoic acid

Pharmacodynamics/Kinetics
Absorption: Diffuses through devascularized areas and is rapidly absorbed from burned surface
Metabolism: To para-carboxybenzene sulfonamide which is a carbonic anhydrase inhibitor
Time to peak serum concentration: Topical: 2-4 hours
Elimination: In urine as metabolites

Usual Dosage Children and Adults: Topical: Apply once or twice daily with a sterile gloved hand; apply to a thickness of approximately 16 mm; the burned area should be covered with cream at all times

Monitoring Parameters Acid base balance

Patient Information Discontinue and call physician immediately if rash, blisters, or swelling appear while using cream; discontinue if condition persists or worsens while using this product; for external use only

Dosage Forms
Cream, topical, as acetate: 85 mg/g (56.7 g, 113.4 g, 411 g)
Powder, topical: 5% (50 g)

- ♦ **Mafenide Acetate** *see* Mafenide *on this page*
- ♦ **Magnesia Magma** *see* Magnesium Hydroxide *on next page*
- ♦ **Magnesium Chloride** *see* Magnesium Salts (Other) *on page 707*

Magnesium Citrate *(mag NEE zhum SIT rate)*

Related Information
Laxatives, Classification and Properties *on page 1326*

U.S. Brand Names Evac-Q-Mag® [OTC]

Synonyms Citrate of Magnesia

Therapeutic Category Laxative, Saline

Use Evacuation of bowel prior to certain surgical and diagnostic procedures or overdose situations

Pregnancy Risk Factor B

Contraindications Renal failure, appendicitis, abdominal pain, intestinal impaction, obstruction or perforation, diabetes mellitus, complications in gastrointestinal tract, patients with colostomy, ileostomy, ulcerative colitis or diverticulitis

Warnings/Precautions Use with caution in patients with impaired renal function, especially if Cl_{cr} <30 mL/minute (accumulation of magnesium which may lead to magnesium intoxication); use with caution in digitalized patients (may alter cardiac conduction leading to heart block); use with caution in patients with lithium administration; use with caution with neuromuscular blocking agents, CNS depressants

Adverse Reactions 1% to 10%:
Cardiovascular: Hypotension
Endocrine & metabolic: Hypermagnesemia
Gastrointestinal: Abdominal cramps, diarrhea, gas formation
Respiratory: Respiratory depression

Overdosage/Toxicology
Serious, potentially life-threatening electrolyte disturbances may occur with long-term use or overdosage due to diarrhea; hypermagnesemia may occur. CNS depression, confusion, hypotension, muscle weakness, blockage of peripheral neuromuscular transmission.

Serum level >4 mEq/L (4.8 mg/dL): Deep tendon reflexes may be depressed

Serum level ≥10 mEq/L (12 mg/dL): Deep tendon reflexes may disappear, respiratory paralysis may occur, heart block may occur

I.V. calcium (5-10 mEq) will reverse respiratory depression or heart block; in extreme cases, peritoneal dialysis or hemodialysis may be required.

Serum level >12 mEq/L may be fatal, serum level ≥10 mEq/L may cause complete heart block

Mechanism of Action Promotes bowel evacuation by causing osmotic retention of fluid which distends the colon with increased peristaltic activity

Pharmacodynamics/Kinetics
Absorption: Oral: 15% to 30%
Elimination: Renal

Usual Dosage Cathartic: Oral:
Children:
<6 years: 0.5 mL/kg up to a maximum of 200 mL repeated every 4-6 hours until stools are clear
6-12 years: 100-150 mL
Adults ≥12 years: $1/2$ to 1 full bottle (120-300 mL)

Reference Range Serum magnesium:
Children: 1.5-1.9 mg/dL ~1.2-1.6 mEq/L
Adults: 2.2-2.8 mg/dL ~1.8-2.3 mEq/L

Test Interactions ↑ magnesium; ↓ protein, ↓ calcium (S), ↓ potassium (S)

Patient Information Take with a glass of water, fruit juice, or citrus flavored carbonated beverage to improve taste, chill before using; report severe abdominal pain to physician

Nursing Implications To increase palatability, manufacturer suggests chilling the solution prior to administration

Additional Information Magnesium content of 5 mL: 3.85-4.71 mEq

Dosage Forms Solution, oral: 300 mL

♦ **Magnesium Gluconate** see Magnesium Salts (Other) on page 707

Magnesium Hydroxide (mag NEE zhum hye DROKS ide)

Related Information
Laxatives, Classification and Properties on page 1326

U.S. Brand Names Phillips'® Milk of Magnesia [OTC]

Synonyms Magnesia Magma; Milk of Magnesia; MOM

Therapeutic Category Antacid; Laxative; Saline; Magnesium Salt

Use Short-term treatment of occasional constipation and symptoms of hyperacidity, magnesium replacement therapy

Pregnancy Risk Factor B

Contraindications Patients with colostomy or an ileostomy, intestinal obstruction, fecal impaction, renal failure, appendicitis, hypersensitivity to any component

Warnings/Precautions Use with caution in patients with severe renal impairment, (especially when doses are >50 mEq magnesium/day); hypermagnesemia and toxicity may occur due to decreased renal clearance of absorbed magnesium. Decreased renal function (Cl_{cr} <30 mL/minute) may result in toxicity; monitor for toxicity.

Adverse Reactions
>10%: Gastrointestinal: Diarrhea
1% to 10%:
Cardiovascular: Hypotension
Endocrine & metabolic: Hypermagnesemia
Gastrointestinal: Abdominal cramps
Neuromuscular & skeletal: Muscle weakness
Respiratory: Respiratory depression

Overdosage/Toxicology
Magnesium antacids are also laxative and may cause diarrhea and hypokalemia; in patients with renal failure, magnesium may accumulate to toxic levels.
I.V. calcium (5-10 mEq) will reverse respiratory depression or heart block; in extreme cases, peritoneal dialysis or hemodialysis may be required.

(Continued)

Magnesium Hydroxide *(Continued)*

Drug Interactions Decreased effect: Decreased absorption of tetracyclines, digoxin, indomethacin, or iron salts

Mechanism of Action Promotes bowel evacuation by causing osmotic retention of fluid which distends the colon with increased peristaltic activity; reacts with hydrochloric acid in stomach to form magnesium chloride

Pharmacodynamics/Kinetics

Onset of laxative action: 4-8 hours

Elimination: Absorbed magnesium ions (up to 30%) are usually excreted by kidneys, unabsorbed drug is excreted in feces

Usual Dosage Oral:

Average daily intakes of dietary magnesium have declined in recent years due to processing of food; the latest estimate of the average American dietary intake was 349 mg/day

Laxative:

<2 years: 0.5 mL/kg/dose

2-5 years: 5-15 mL/day or in divided doses

6-12 years: 15-30 mL/day or in divided doses

≥12 years: 30-60 mL/day or in divided doses

Antacid:

Children: 2.5-5 mL as needed up to 4 times/day

Adults: 5-15 mL up to 4 times/day as needed

Dosing in renal impairment: Patients in severe renal failure should not receive magnesium due to toxicity from accumulation. Patients with a Cl_{cr} <25 mL/minute receiving magnesium should be monitored by serum magnesium levels.

Reference Range Serum magnesium:

Children: 1.5-1.9 mg/dL (1.2-1.6 mEq/L)

Adults: 1.5-2.5 mg/dL (1.2-2.0 mEq/L)

Test Interactions ↑ magnesium; ↓ protein, calcium (S), ↓ potassium (S)

Patient Information Dilute dose in water or juice, shake well

Nursing Implications MOM concentrate is 3 times as potent as regular strength product

Additional Information Magnesium content of 30 mL: 1.05 g (87 mEq)

Dosage Forms

Liquid: 390 mg/5 mL (10 mL, 15 mL, 20 mL, 30 mL, 100 mL, 120 mL, 180 mL, 360 mL, 720 mL)

Liquid, concentrate: 10 mL equivalent to 30 mL milk of magnesia USP

Suspension, oral: 2.5 g/30 mL (10 mL, 15 mL, 30 mL)

Tablet: 300 mg, 600 mg

Magnesium Oxide *(mag NEE zhum OKS ide)*

U.S. Brand Names Maox®

Therapeutic Category Antacid; Electrolyte Supplement, Oral; Laxative, Saline; Magnesium Salt

Use Short-term treatment of occasional constipation and symptoms of hyperacidity

Pregnancy Risk Factor B

Contraindications Patients with colostomy or an ileostomy, appendicitis, ulcerative colitis, diverticulitis, heart block, myocardial damage, serious renal impairment, hepatitis, Addison's disease, hypersensitivity to any component

Warnings/Precautions Hypermagnesemia and toxicity may occur due to decreased renal clearance (Cl_{cr} <30 mL/minute) of absorbed magnesium; monitor serum magnesium level, respiratory rate, deep tendon reflex, renal function when $MgSO_4$ is administered parenterally; use with caution in digitalized patients (may alter cardiac conduction leading to heart block); use with caution in patients with lithium administration; elderly, due to disease or drug therapy, may be predisposed to diarrhea; diarrhea may result in electrolyte imbalance; monitor for toxicity

Adverse Reactions

>10%: Gastrointestinal: Diarrhea

1% to 10%:

Cardiovascular: Hypotension, EKG changes

Central nervous system: Mental depression, coma

Gastrointestinal: Nausea, vomiting

Respiratory: Respiratory depression

Overdosage/Toxicology

Magnesium antacids are also laxative and may cause diarrhea and hypokalemia. In patients with renal failure, magnesium may accumulate to toxic levels.

I.V. calcium (5-10 mEq) will reverse respiratory depression or heart block; in extreme cases, peritoneal dialysis or hemodialysis may be required.

Drug Interactions Decreased effect: Tetracyclines, digoxin, indomethacin, iron salts, isoniazid, quinolones

Mechanism of Action Promotes bowel evacuation by causing osmotic retention of fluid which distends the colon with increased peristaltic activity

Pharmacodynamics/Kinetics

Onset of laxative action: 4-8 hours

Elimination: Absorbed magnesium ions (up to 30%) are usually excreted by kidneys, unabsorbed drug is excreted in feces

Usual Dosage Adults: Oral:

Dietary supplement: 20-40 mEq (1-2 tablets) 2-3 times

Antacid: 140 mg 3-4 times/day **or** 400-840 mg/day

Laxative: 2-4 g at bedtime with full glass of water

Dosing in renal impairment: Patients in severe renal failure should not receive magnesium due to toxicity from accumulation. Patients with a Cl_{cr} <25 mL/minute should be monitored by serum magnesium levels.

Note: Oral magnesium is not generally adequate for repletion in patients with serum magnesium concentrations <1.5 mEq/L

Reference Range Serum magnesium:

Children: 1.5-1.9 mg/dL (1.2-1.6 mEq/L)

Adults: 1.5-2.5 mg/dL (1.2-2.0 mEq/L)

Test Interactions ↑ magnesium; ↓ protein, calcium (S), ↓ potassium (S)

Patient Information Chew tablets before swallowing; take with full glass of water; notify physician if relief not obtained or if any signs of bleeding occur (black tarry stools, "coffee ground" vomit)

Additional Information 60% elemental magnesium; 49.6 mEq magnesium/g; 25 mmol magnesium/g

Dosage Forms

Capsule: 140 mg

Tablet: 400 mg, 425 mg

Magnesium Salts (Other)

Related Information

Antiarrhythmic Drugs Comparison *on page 1297*

U.S. Brand Names Almora® (Gluconate); Magonate® (Gluconate) [OTC]; Magtrate® (Gluconate); Slow-Mag® (Chloride)

Synonyms Magnesium Chloride; Magnesium Gluconate

Therapeutic Category Magnesium Salt

Use Dietary supplement for treatment of magnesium deficiencies

Contraindications Patients with heart block, severe renal disease

Warnings/Precautions Use with caution in patients with impaired renal function; hypermagnesemia and toxicity may occur due to decreased renal clearance of absorbed magnesium

Adverse Reactions

1% to 10%: Gastrointestinal: Diarrhea (excessive dose)

<1%: Hypotension, hypermagnesemia, abdominal cramps, muscle weakness, respiratory depression

Overdosage/Toxicology

Hypermagnesemia rarely occurs after acute or chronic overexposure except in patients with renal insufficiency or massive overdose; moderate toxicity causes nausea, vomiting, weakness, and cutaneous flushing; larger doses cause cardiac conduction abnormalities, hypotension, severe muscle weakness, and lethargy; very high levels cause coma, respiratory arrest, and asystole.

Treatment includes replacing fluid and electrolyte losses caused by excessive catharsis; while there is no specific antidote and treatment is supportive, administration of I.V. calcium may temporarily alleviate respiratory depression; hemodialysis rapidly removes magnesium and is the only route of elimination in anuric patients (hemoperfusion and repeat-dose charcoal are not effective).

Drug Interactions

Increased effect of nondepolarizing neuromuscular blockers

Decreased absorption of aminoquinolones, digoxin, nitrofurantoin, penicillamine, and tetracyclines may occur with magnesium salts

Mechanism of Action Magnesium is important as a cofactor in many enzymatic reactions in the body involving protein synthesis and carbohydrate metabolism, (at least 300 enzymatic reactions require magnesium). Actions on lipoprotein lipase have been found to be important in reducing serum cholesterol and on sodium/potassium ATPase in promoting polarization (ie, neuromuscular functioning).

Pharmacodynamics/Kinetics

Absorption: Oral: 15% to 30%

Elimination: Renal

Usual Dosage Oral:

Average daily intakes of dietary magnesium have declined in recent years due to processing of food; the latest estimate of the average American dietary intake was 349 mg/day

Adequate intakes:

Infants:

0-6 months: 30 mg

7-12 months: 75 mg

Recommended dietary allowance:

Children:

1-3 years: 80 mg/day

4-8 years: 130 mg/day

Male:

9-13 years: 240 mg/day

14-18 years: 130 mg/day

19-30 years: 400 mg/day

≥31 years: 420 mg/day

Female:

9-13 years: 240 mg/day

14-18 years: 360 mg/day

19-30 years: 310 mg/day

(Continued)

Magnesium Salts (Other) *(Continued)*

≥31 years: 320 mg/day
Female: Pregnancy:
  ≤18 years: 400 mg/day
  19-30 years: 350 mg/day
  31-50 years: 360 mg/day
Female: Lactation:
  ≤18 years: 360 mg/day
  19-30 years: 310 mg/day
  31-50 years: 320 mg/day
Hypomagnesemia: There are no specific dosage recommendations for this product in replacement of magnesium. Extrapolation from dosage recommendations of magnesium sulfate are as follows:
  Children: 10-20 mg/kg/dose **elemental** magnesium 4 times/day
  Adults: 300 mg **elemental** magnesium 4 times/day

The recommended dietary allowance (RDA) of magnesium is 4.5 mg/kg which is a total daily allowance of 350-400 mg for adult men and 280-300 mg for adult women. During pregnancy the RDA is 300 mg and during lactation the RDA is 355 mg.

Dietary supplement: Oral:
  Children: 3-6 mg/kg/day in divided doses 3-4 times/day; maximum: 400 mg/day
  Adults: 54-483 mg/day in divided doses; refer to product labeling

Dosing in renal impairment: Patients in severe renal failure should not receive magnesium due to toxicity from accumulation. Patients with a Cl$_{cr}$ <25 mL/minute receiving magnesium should be monitored by serum magnesium levels.

Reference Range Serum magnesium:
  Children: 1.5-1.9 mg/dL ~1.2-1.6 mEq/L
  Adults: 2.2-2.8 mg/dL ~1.8-2.3 mEq/L

Additional Information Note: 1 g magnesium = 83.3 mEq (4.11 mmol)

Dosage Forms
Gluconate:
  Liquid: 54 mg/5 mL as magnesium
  Tablet: 500 mg (elemental magnesium 27 mg)
Chloride: Tablet, sustained release: 535 mg (64 mg magnesium)
Amino acids chelate: Tablet: 500 mg (100 mg magnesium)

Magnesium Sulfate *(mag NEE zhum SUL fate)*

Related Information
Adult ACLS Algorithm, V. Fib and Pulseless V. Tach *on page 1447*
Extravasation Treatment of Other Drugs *on page 1287*

Synonyms Epsom Salts

Therapeutic Category Antacid; Antiarrhythmic Agent, Miscellaneous; Anticonvulsant; Electrolyte Supplement, Parenteral; Laxative, Saline; Magnesium Salt

Use Treatment and prevention of hypomagnesemia and in seizure prevention in severe pre-eclampsia or eclampsia, pediatric acute nephritis; also used as short-term treatment of constipation, postmyocardial infarction, and torsade de pointes

Pregnancy Risk Factor B

Contraindications Heart block, serious renal impairment, myocardial damage, hepatitis, Addison's disease

Warnings/Precautions Use with caution in patients with impaired renal function (accumulation of magnesium which may lead to magnesium intoxication); use with caution in digitalized patients (may alter cardiac conduction leading to heart block); monitor serum magnesium level, respiratory rate, deep tendon reflex, renal function when MgSO$_4$ is administered parenterally

Adverse Reactions 1% to 10%:
Serum magnesium levels >3 mg/dL:
  Central nervous system: Depressed CNS
  Gastrointestinal: Diarrhea
  Neuromuscular & skeletal: Blocked peripheral neuromuscular transmission leading to anticonvulsant effects
Serum magnesium levels >5 mg/dL:
  Cardiovascular: Flushing
  Central nervous system: Somnolence
Serum magnesium levels >12.5 mg/dL:
  Cardiovascular: Complete heart block
  Respiratory: Respiratory paralysis

Overdosage/Toxicology
Symptoms of overdose usually present with serum level >4 mEq/L
  Serum magnesium >4: Deep tendon reflexes may be depressed
  Serum magnesium ≥10: Deep tendon reflexes may disappear, respiratory paralysis may occur, heart block may occur
  Serum level >12 mEq/L may be fatal, serum level ≥10 mEq/L may cause complete heart block
I.V. calcium (5-10 mEq) 1-2 g calcium gluconate will reverse respiratory depression or heart block; in extreme cases, peritoneal dialysis or hemodialysis may be required

Drug Interactions
Decreased effect: Nifedipine decreased blood pressure and neuromuscular blockade

Increased toxicity: Aminoglycosides increased neuromuscular blockade; CNS depressants increased CNS depression; neuromuscular antagonists, betamethasone (pulmonary edema), ritodrine increased cardiotoxicity

Stability Refrigeration of intact ampuls may result in precipitation or crystallization

Stability of parenteral admixture at room temperature (25°C): 60 days

I.V. is **incompatible** when mixed with fat emulsion (flocculation), calcium gluceptate, clindamycin, dobutamine, hydrocortisone (same syringe), nafcillin, polymyxin B, procaine hydrochloride, tetracyclines, thiopental

Mechanism of Action Promotes bowel evacuation by causing osmotic retention of fluid which distends the colon with increased peristaltic activity when taken orally; parenterally, decreases acetylcholine in motor nerve terminals and acts on myocardium by slowing rate of S-A node impulse formation and prolonging conduction time

Pharmacodynamics/Kinetics

Oral: Onset of cathartic action: Within 1-2 hours

I.M.: Onset of action: 1 hour; Duration: 3-4 hours

I.V.: Onset of action: Immediate; Duration: 30 minutes

Elimination: Primarily in feces; absorbed magnesium is rapidly eliminated by the kidneys

Usual Dosage The recommended dietary allowance (RDA) of magnesium is 4.5 mg/kg which is a total daily allowance of 350-400 mg for adult men and 280-300 mg for adult women. During pregnancy the RDA is 300 mg and during lactation the RDA is 355 mg. Average daily intakes of dietary magnesium have declined in recent years due to processing of food. The latest estimate of the average American dietary intake was 349 mg/day. Dose represented as $MgSO_4$ unless stated otherwise.

Note: Serum magnesium is poor reflection of repletional status as the majority of magnesium is intracellular; serum levels may be transiently normal for a few hours after a dose is given, therefore, aim for consistently high normal serum levels in patients with normal renal function for most efficient repletion

Hypomagnesemia:

Neonates: I.V.: 25-50 mg/kg/dose (0.2-0.4 mEq/kg/dose) every 8-12 hours for 2-3 doses

Children: I.M., I.V.: 25-50 mg/kg/dose (0.2-0.4 mEq/kg/dose) every 4-6 hours for 3-4 doses, maximum single dose: 2000 mg (16 mEq), may repeat if hypomagnesemia persists (higher dosage up to 100 mg/kg/dose $MgSO_4$ I.V. has been used); maintenance: I.V.: 30-60 mg/kg/day (0.25-0.5 mEq/kg/day)

Adults:

Oral: 3 g every 6 hours for 4 doses as needed

I.M., I.V.: 1 g every 6 hours for 4 doses; for severe hypomagnesemia: 8-12 g $MgSO_4$/day in divided doses has been used

Management of seizures and hypertension: Children: I.M., I.V.: 20-100 mg/kg/dose every 4-6 hours as needed; in severe cases doses as high as 200 mg/kg/dose have been used

Eclampsia, pre-eclampsia: Adults:

I.M.: 1-4 g every 4 hours

I.V.: Initial: 4 g, then switch to I.M. or 1-4 g/hour by continuous infusion

Maximum dose should not exceed 30-40 g/day; maximum rate of infusion: 1-2 g/hour

Maintenance electrolyte requirements:

Daily requirements: 0.2-0.5 mEq/kg/24 hours or 3-10 mEq/1000 kcal/24 hours

Maximum: 8-16 mEq/24 hours

Cathartic: Oral:

Children: 0.25 g/kg every 4-6 hours

Adults: 10-15 g in a glass of water

Dosing adjustment/comments in renal impairment: Cl_{cr} <25 mL/minute: Do not administer or monitor serum magnesium levels carefully

Administration

Magnesium sulfate may be administered I.M. or I.V.

I.M.: A 25% or 50% concentration may be used for adults and a 20% solution is recommended for children

I.V.: Magnesium may be administered IVP, IVPB or I.V. infusion in an auxiliary medication infusion solution (eg, TPN); when giving I.V. push, must dilute first and should not be given any faster than 150 mg/minute

Maximal rate of infusion: 2 g/hour to avoid hypotension; doses of 4 g/hour have been given in emergencies (eclampsia, seizures); optimally, should add magnesium to I.V. fluids or to IVH, but bolus doses are also effective

For I.V., a concentration <20% (200 mg/mL) should be used and the rate of injection should not exceed 1.5 mL of a 10% solution (or equivalent) per minute (150 mg/minute)

Monitoring Parameters Monitor blood pressure when administering $MgSO_4$ I.V.; serum magnesium levels should be monitored to avoid overdose; monitor for diarrhea; monitor for arrhythmias, hypotension, respiratory and CNS depression during rapid I.V. administration

Reference Range Serum magnesium:

Children: 1.5-1.9 mg/dL (1.2-1.6 mEq/L)

Adults: 1.5-2.5 mg/dL (1.2-2.0 mEq/L)

Note: Serum magnesium is poor reflection of repletional status as the majority of magnesium is intracellular; serum levels may be transiently normal for a few hours after a dose is given, therefore, aim for consistently high normal serum levels in patients with normal renal function for most efficient repletion

Test Interactions ↑ magnesium; ↓ protein, calcium (S), ↓ potassium (S)

(Continued)

Magnesium Sulfate *(Continued)*

Additional Information 10% elemental magnesium; 8.1 mEq magnesium/g; 4 mmol magnesium/g
500 mg MgSO₄ = 4.06 mEq magnesium = 49.3 mg elemental magnesium

Dosage Forms
Granules: ~40 mEq magnesium/5 g (240 g)
Injection: 100 mg/mL (20 mL); 125 mg/mL (8 mL); 250 mg/mL (150 mL); 500 mg/mL (2 mL, 5 mL, 10 mL, 30 mL, 50 mL)
Solution, oral: 50% [500 mg/mL] (30 mL)

◆ **Magonate® (Gluconate) [OTC]** *see* Magnesium Salts (Other) *on page 707*

◆ **Magtrate® (Gluconate)** *see* Magnesium Salts (Other) *on page 707*

◆ **Malaria Treatment** *see page 1425*

◆ **Malatal®** *see* Hyoscyamine, Atropine, Scopolamine, and Phenobarbital *on page 592*

Malathion *(mal a THYE on)*

U.S. Brand Names Ovide™

Therapeutic Category Pediculocide

Use Treatment of head lice and their ova

Pregnancy Risk Factor B

Contraindications Known hypersensitivity to malathion

Usual Dosage Sprinkle Ovide™ lotion on dry hair and rub gently until the scalp is thoroughly moistened; pay special attention to the back of the head and neck. Allow to dry naturally - use no heat and leave uncovered. After 8-12 hours, the hair should be washed with a nonmedicated shampoo; rinse and use a fine-toothed comb to remove dead lice and eggs. If required, repeat with second application in 7-9 days. Further treatment is generally not necessary. Other family members should be evaluated to determine if infested and if so, receive treatment.

Patient Information Topical use only

Dosage Forms Lotion: 0.5% (59 mL)

◆ **Mallamint® [OTC]** *see* Calcium Carbonate *on page 174*

◆ **Mallisol® [OTC]** *see* Povidone-Iodine *on page 955*

◆ **Malotuss® [OTC]** *see* Guaifenesin *on page 549*

◆ **Management of Healthcare Worker Exposures to HIV** *see page 1374*

◆ **Management of Overdosages** *see page 1486*

◆ **Mandelamine®** *see* Methenamine *on page 747*

◆ **Mandol®** *see* Cefamandole *on page 205*

◆ **Mandrake** *see* Podophyllum Resin *on page 940*

Manganese *(MAN ga nees)*

U.S. Brand Names Chelated Manganese® [OTC]

Synonyms Manganese Chloride; Manganese Sulfate

Therapeutic Category Trace Element; Trace Element, Parenteral

Use Trace element added to TPN (total parenteral nutrition) solution to prevent manganese deficiency; orally as a dietary supplement

Pregnancy Risk Factor C

Contraindications High manganese levels; patients with severe liver dysfunction or cholestasis (conjugated bilirubin >2 mg/dL) due to reduced biliary excretion

Overdosage/Toxicology Acute poisoning due to ingestion of manganese or manganese salts is rare owing to poor absorption of manganese. The main symptoms of chronic poisoning, either from injection or usually inhalation of manganese dust or fumes in air, include extrapyramidal symptoms that can lead to progressive deterioration in the central nervous system.

Stability Compatible with electrolytes usually present in amino acid/dextrose solution used for TPN solutions

Mechanism of Action Cofactor in many enzyme systems, stimulates synthesis of cholesterol and fatty acids in liver, and influences mucopolysaccharide synthesis

Pharmacodynamics/Kinetics
Distribution: Concentrated in mitochondria of pituitary gland, pancreas, liver, kidney, and bone
Elimination: Mainly in bile, urinary excretion is negligible

Usual Dosage
Infants: I.V.: 2-10 mcg/kg/day usually administered in TPN solutions
Adults:
Oral: 20-50 mg/day
RDA: 2-5 mg/day
I.V.: 150-800 mcg/day usually administered in TPN solutions

Administration Do not administer I.M. or by direct I.V. injection since the acidic pH of the solution may cause tissue irritations and it is hypotonic

Monitoring Parameters Periodic manganese plasma level

Reference Range 4-14 µg/L

Dosage Forms
Injection, as chloride: 0.1 mg/mL (10 mL)
Injection, as sulfate: 0.1 mg/mL (10 mL, 30 mL)
Tablet: 20 mg, 50 mg

◆ **Manganese Chloride** *see* Manganese *on this page*

♦ **Manganese Sulfate** *see* Manganese *on previous page*

Mannitol (MAN i tole)

U.S. Brand Names Osmitrol® Injection; Resectisol® Irrigation Solution

Synonyms D-Mannitol

Therapeutic Category Diuretic, Osmotic

Use Reduction of increased intracranial pressure associated with cerebral edema; promotion of diuresis in the prevention and/or treatment of oliguria or anuria due to acute renal failure; reduction of increased intraocular pressure; promoting urinary excretion of toxic substances; genitourinary irrigant in transurethral prostatic resection or other transurethral surgical procedures

Pregnancy Risk Factor C

Contraindications Severe renal disease (anuria), dehydration, or active intracranial bleeding, severe pulmonary edema or congestion, hypersensitivity to any component

Warnings/Precautions Should not be administered until adequacy of renal function and urine flow is established; cardiovascular status should also be evaluated; do not administer electrolyte-free mannitol solutions with blood

Adverse Reactions

>10%:

Central nervous system: Headache

Gastrointestinal: Nausea, vomiting

Genitourinary: Polyuria

1% to 10%:

Central nervous system: Dizziness

Dermatologic: Rash

Ocular: Blurred vision

<1%: Circulatory overload, congestive heart failure, convulsions, headache, chills, fluid and electrolyte imbalance, water intoxication, dehydration and hypovolemia secondary to rapid diuresis, xerostomia, dysuria, tissue necrosis, pulmonary edema, allergic reactions

Overdosage/Toxicology

Symptoms of overdose include polyuria, hypotension, cardiovascular collapse, pulmonary edema, hyponatremia, hypokalemia, oliguria, seizures

Increased electrolyte excretion and fluid overload can occur; hemodialysis will clear mannitol and reduce osmolality

Stability Should be stored at room temperature (15°C to 30°C) and protected from freezing; crystallization may occur at low temperatures; do not use solutions that contain crystals, heating in a hot water bath and vigorous shaking may be utilized for resolubilization; cool solutions to body temperature before using

Mechanism of Action Increases the osmotic pressure of glomerular filtrate, which inhibits tubular reabsorption of water and electrolytes and increases urinary output

Pharmacodynamics/Kinetics

Onset of diuresis: Injection: Within 1-3 hours

Onset of reduction in intracerebral pressure: Within 15 minutes

Duration of reduction in intracerebral pressure: 3-6 hours

Distribution: Remains confined to extracellular space (except in extreme concentrations) and does not penetrate the blood-brain barrier

Metabolism: Minimal amounts metabolized in the liver to glycogen

Half-life: 1.1-1.6 hours

Elimination: Primarily excreted unchanged in urine by glomerular filtration

Usual Dosage I.V.:

Children:

Test dose (to assess adequate renal function): 200 mg/kg over 3-5 minutes to produce a urine flow of at least 1 mL/kg for 1-3 hours

Initial: 0.5-1 g/kg

Maintenance: 0.25-0.5 g/kg given every 4-6 hours

Adults:

Test dose (to assess adequate renal function): 12.5 g (200 mg/kg) over 3-5 minutes to produce a urine flow of at least 30-50 mL of urine per hour over the next 2-3 hours

Initial: 0.5-1 g/kg

Maintenance: 0.25-0.5 g/kg every 4-6 hours; usual adult dose: 20-200 g/24 hours

Intracranial pressure: Cerebral edema: 1.5-2 g/kg/dose I.V. as a 15% to 20% solution over ≥30 minutes; maintain serum osmolality 310-320 mOsm/kg

Preoperative for neurosurgery: 1.5-2 g/kg administered 1-1.5 hours prior to surgery

Transurethral irrigation: Use urogenital solution as required for irrigation

Administration In-line 5-micron filter set should always be used for mannitol infusion with concentrations ≥20%; administer test dose (for oliguria) I.V. push over 3-5 minutes; for cerebral edema or elevated ICP, administer over 20-30 minutes

Monitoring Parameters Renal function, daily fluid I & O, serum electrolytes, serum and urine osmolality; for treatment of elevated intracranial pressure, maintain serum osmolality 310-320 mOsm/kg

Nursing Implications Avoid extravasation; crenation and agglutination of red blood cells may occur if administered with whole blood

Additional Information May autoclave or heat to redissolve crystals; mannitol 20% has an approximate osmolarity of 1100 mOsm/L and mannitol 25% has an approximate osmolarity of 1375 mOsm/L

(Continued)

711

Mannitol *(Continued)*

Dosage Forms
Injection: 5% [50 mg/mL] (1000 mL); 10% [100 mg/mL] (500 mL, 1000 mL); 15% [150 mg/mL] (150 mL, 500 mL); 20% [200 mg/mL] (150 mL, 250 mL, 500 mL); 25% [250 mg/mL] (50 mL)
Solution, urogenital: 0.54% [5.4 mg/mL] (2000 mL)

- ◆ **Mantoux** *see* Tuberculin Purified Protein Derivative *on page 1194*
- ◆ **Mantoux** *see* Tuberculin Tests *on page 1194*
- ◆ **Maox®** *see* Magnesium Oxide *on page 706*
- ◆ **Mapap® [OTC]** *see* Acetaminophen *on page 19*

Maprotiline *(ma PROE ti leen)*

Related Information
Antidepressant Agents Comparison *on page 1301*
U.S. Brand Names Ludiomil®
Therapeutic Category Antidepressant, Tetracyclic
Use Treatment of depression and anxiety associated with depression
Pregnancy Risk Factor B
Contraindications Narrow-angle glaucoma, hypersensitivity to maprotiline or any component
Drug Interactions CYP1A2 and 2D6 enzyme substrate
Usual Dosage Oral:
Children 6-14 years: 10 mg/day, increase to a maximum daily dose of 75 mg
Adults: 75 mg/day to start, increase by 25 mg every 2 weeks up to 150-225 mg/day; given in 3 divided doses or in a single daily dose
Elderly: Initial: 25 mg at bedtime, increase by 25 mg every 3 days for inpatients and weekly for outpatients if tolerated; usual maintenance dose: 50-75 mg/day, higher doses may be necessary in nonresponders
Additional Information Complete prescribing information for this medication should be consulted for additional detail
Dosage Forms Tablet, as hydrochloride: 25 mg, 50 mg, 75 mg

- ◆ **Maranox® [OTC]** *see* Acetaminophen *on page 19*
- ◆ **Marax®** *see* Theophylline, Ephedrine, and Hydroxyzine *on page 1125*
- ◆ **Marazide®** *see* Benzthiazide *on page 135*
- ◆ **Marbaxin®** *see* Methocarbamol *on page 749*
- ◆ **Marcaine®** *see* Bupivacaine *on page 160*
- ◆ **Marcillin®** *see* Ampicillin *on page 79*
- ◆ **Margesic® H** *see* Hydrocodone and Acetaminophen *on page 575*
- ◆ **Marinol®** *see* Dronabinol *on page 399*
- ◆ **Marnal®** *see* Butalbital Compound *on page 165*
- ◆ **Marpres®** *see* Hydralazine, Hydrochlorothiazide, and Reserpine *on page 573*
- ◆ **Marthritic®** *see* Salsalate *on page 1047*

Masoprocol *(ma SOE pro kole)*

U.S. Brand Names Actinex® Topical
Therapeutic Category Topical Skin Product, Acne
Use Treatment of actinic keratosis
Pregnancy Risk Factor B
Contraindications Hypersensitivity to masoprocol or any component
Warnings/Precautions Occlusive dressings should not be used; for external use only
Adverse Reactions
>10%:
Dermatologic: Erythema, flaking, dryness, itching
Local: Burning
1% to 10%:
Dermatologic: Soreness, rash
Neuromuscular & skeletal: Paresthesia
Ocular: Eye irritation
<1%: Blistering, excoriation, skin roughness, wrinkling
Mechanism of Action Antiproliferative activity against keratinocytes
Pharmacodynamics/Kinetics Absorption: Topical: <1% to 2%
Usual Dosage Adults: Topical: Wash and dry area; gently massage into affected area every morning and evening for 28 days
Patient Information For external use only; may stain clothing or fabrics; avoid eyes and mucous membranes; do not use occlusive dressings; transient local burning sensation may occur immediately after application; contact physician if oozing or blistering occurs; wash hands immediately after use.
Dosage Forms Cream: 10% (30 g)

- ◆ **Massengill® Medicated Douche w/Cepticin [OTC]** *see* Povidone-Iodine *on page 955*
- ◆ **Matulane®** *see* Procarbazine *on page 972*
- ◆ **Mavik®** *see* Trandolapril *on page 1166*
- ◆ **Maxair™ Autohaler™** *see* Pirbuterol *on page 934*
- ◆ **Maxair™ Inhalation Aerosol** *see* Pirbuterol *on page 934*

Measles and Rubella Vaccines, Combined

(MEE zels & roo BEL a vak SEENS, kom BINED)

Related Information

Adverse Events and Vaccination *on page 1369*

Immunization Recommendations *on page 1358*

U.S. Brand Names M-R-VAX® II

Synonyms Rubella and Measles Vaccines, Combined

Therapeutic Category Vaccine

Use Simultaneous immunization against measles and rubella

Note: Trivalent measles - mumps - rubella (MMR) vaccine is the preferred immunizing agent for most children and many adults. Adults born before 1957 are generally considered to be immune and need not be revaccinated.

Pregnancy Risk Factor C

Contraindications Immune deficiency condition, pregnancy

Warnings/Precautions Immunocompromised persons, history of anaphylactic reaction following receipt of neomycin

Adverse Reactions All serious adverse reactions must be reported to the U.S. Department of Health and Human Services (DHHS) Vaccine Adverse Event Reporting System (VAERS) 1-800-822-7967.

>10%:

Cardiovascular: Edema

Central nervous system: Fever (<100°F)

Local: Burning or stinging, induration

1% to 10%:

Central nervous system: Fever between 100°F and 103°F usually between 5th and 12th days postvaccination

Dermatologic: Rash (rarely generalized)

<1%: Fatigue, convulsions, encephalitis, confusion, severe headache, fever (>103°F - prolonged), palsies, Guillain-Barré syndrome, ataxia, urticaria, itching, reddening of skin (especially around ears and eyes), erythema multiforme, vomiting, sore throat, diarrhea, thrombocytopenic purpura, diplopia, stiff neck, dyspnea, cough, rhinitis, lymphadenopathy, coryza, allergic reactions

Drug Interactions Whole blood, interferon immune globulin, radiation therapy, and immunosuppressive drugs (eg, corticosteroids) may result in insufficient response to immunization. DTP, OPV, MMR, Hib, and hepatitis B may be given concurrently; other virus vaccine administration should be separated by ≥1 month from measles.

Stability Refrigerate prior to use, use as soon as possible; discard if not used within 8 hours of reconstitution

Mechanism of Action Promotes active immunity to measles and rubella by inducing specific antibodies including measles-specific IgG and IgM and rubella hemagglutination-inhibiting antibodies.

Usual Dosage Children at 15 months and Adults: S.C.: Inject 0.5 mL into outer aspect of upper arm; no routine booster for rubella

Administration Not for I.V. administration

Test Interactions May temporarily depress tuberculin skin test sensitivity and reduce the seroconversion.

Patient Information Parents should monitor children closely for fever 5-11 days after vaccination; females should not become pregnant within 3 months of vaccination

Additional Information Federal law requires that the date of administration, the vaccine manufacturer, lot number of vaccine, and the administering person's name, title and address be entered into the patient's permanent medical record

Adults born before 1957 are generally considered to be immune to measles; all born in or after 1957 without documentation of live vaccine on or after first birthday, physician-

(Continued)

Measles and Rubella Vaccines, Combined *(Continued)*

diagnosed measles, or laboratory evidence of immunity should be vaccinated with two doses separated by or less than 1 month. For those previously vaccinated with one dose of measles vaccine, revaccination is indicated for students entering institutions of higher learning, for healthcare workers at time of employment, and for travelers to endemic areas. Guidelines for rubella vaccination are the same with the exception of birth year. All adults should be vaccinated against rubella. A booster dose of rubella vaccine is not necessary. Women who are pregnant when vaccinated or become pregnant within 3 months of vaccination should be consulted on the risks to the fetus; although the risks appear negligible. MMR is the vaccine of choice if recipients are likely to be susceptible to mumps as well as measles and rubella.

Dosage Forms Injection: 1000 $TCID_{50}$ each of live attenuated measles virus vaccine and live rubella virus vaccine

Measles, Mumps, and Rubella Vaccines, Combined
(MEE zels, mumpz & roo BEL a vak SEENS, kom BINED)

Related Information

Adverse Events and Vaccination *on page 1369*

Guidelines for the Prevention of Opportunistic Infections in Persons with HIV *on page 1388*

Immunization Recommendations *on page 1358*

Recommendations of the Advisory Committee on Immunization Practices (ACIP) *on page 1360*

Recommended Childhood Immunization Schedule - US - January-December, 1999 *on page 1359*

Recommended Immunization Schedule for HIV-Infected Children *on page 1363*

U.S. Brand Names M-M-R® II

Synonyms MMR; Mumps, Measles and Rubella Vaccines, Combined; Rubella, Measles and Mumps Vaccines, Combined

Therapeutic Category Vaccine

Use Measles, mumps, and rubella prophylaxis

Pregnancy Risk Factor C

Pregnancy/Breast-Feeding Implications Clinical effects on the fetus: It is not known whether the drug can cause fetal harm or affect reproduction capacity (contracting natural measles during pregnancy can increase fetal risk)

Contraindications Blood dyscrasias, cancers affecting the bone marrow or lymphatic systems, known hypersensitivity to measles, mumps and rubella vaccine, known hypersensitivity to neomycin, acute infections, and respiratory illness, pregnancy; known hypersensitivity to eggs, chicken or chicken feathers, severely immunocompromised persons

Warnings/Precautions

Females should not become pregnant within 3 months of vaccination

MMR vaccine should not be given within 3 months of immune globulin or whole blood

Have epinephrine available during and after administration

MMR vaccine should not be administered to severely immunocompromised persons with the exception of asymptomatic children with HIV (ACIP and AAP recommendation)

Severely immunocompromised patients and symptomatic HIV-infected patients who are exposed to measles should receive immune globulin, regardless of prior vaccination status

The immunogenicity of measles virus vaccine is decreased if vaccine is administered <6 months after immune globulin

Defer immunization during any acute illness

Adverse Reactions All serious adverse reactions must be reported to the U.S. Department of Health and Human Services (DHHS) Vaccine Adverse Event Reporting System (VAERS) 1-800-822-7967.

>10%:
Cardiovascular: Edema
Central nervous system: Fever (<100°F)
Local: Burning or stinging, induration

1% to 10%:
Central nervous system: Fever between 100°F and 103°F usually between 5th and 12th days postvaccination
Dermatologic: Rash (rarely generalized)

<1%: Fatigue, convulsions, encephalitis, confusion, severe headache, fever (>103°F - prolonged), palsies, Guillain-Barré syndrome, ataxia, urticaria, itching, reddening of skin (especially around ears and eyes), erythema multiforme, vomiting, sore throat, diarrhea, thrombocytopenic purpura, diplopia, stiff neck, dyspnea, cough, rhinitis, lymphadenopathy, coryza, allergic reactions

Drug Interactions Whole blood, interferon immune globulin, radiation therapy, and immunosuppressive drugs (eg, corticosteroids) may result in insufficient response to immunization. DTP, OPV, MMR, Hib, and hepatitis B may be given concurrently; other virus vaccine administration should be separated by ≥1 month from measles.

Stability Refrigerate, protect from light prior to reconstitution; use as soon as possible; discard 8 hours after reconstitution

Usual Dosage

Infants <12 months of age: If there is risk of exposure to measles, single-antigen measles vaccine should be administered at 6-11 months of age with a second dose (of MMR) at >12 months of age

Administer S.C. in outer aspect of the upper arm to children ≥15 months of age:
0.5 mL at 15 months of age and then repeated at 4-6 years* of age
In some areas, MMR vaccine may be given at 12 months
*Many experts recommend that this dose of MMR be given at entry to middle school or junior high school

Administration Not for I.V. administration

Test Interactions Temporary suppression of TB skin test reactivity with onset approximately 3 days after administration

Patient Information Females should not become pregnant within 3 months of vaccination

Additional Information Live, attenuated vaccine. Federal law requires that the date of administration, the vaccine manufacturer, lot number of vaccine, and the administering person's name, title and address be entered into the patient's permanent medical record

Adults born before 1957 are generally considered to be immune to measles and mumps; all born in or after 1957 without documentation of live vaccine on or after first birthday, physician-diagnosed measles or mumps, or laboratory evidence of immunity should be vaccine with two doses separated by no less than 1 month; for those previously vaccinated with one dose of measles vaccine, revaccination is indicated for students entering institutions of higher learning, healthcare workers at time of employment, and for travelers to endemic areas. Guidelines for rubella vaccination are the same with the exception of birth year; all adults should be vaccinated against rubella. Booster doses of mumps and rubella are not necessary; women who are pregnant when vaccinated or become pregnant within 3 months should be counseled on the risks to the fetus; although the risks appear negligible.

Dosage Forms Injection: 1000 $TCID_{50}$ each of measles virus vaccine and rubella virus vaccine, 5000 $TCID_{50}$ mumps virus vaccine

Measles Virus Vaccine, Live, Attenuated

(MEE zels VYE rus vak SEEN, live)

Related Information

Adverse Events and Vaccination *on page 1369*
Immunization Recommendations *on page 1358*
Prophylaxis for Patients Exposed to Common Communicable Diseases *on page 1384*

U.S. Brand Names Attenuvax®

Synonyms More Attenuated Enders Strain; Rubeola Vaccine

Therapeutic Category Vaccine, Live Virus

Use Adults born before 1957 are generally considered to be immune. All those born in or after 1957 without documentation of live vaccine on or after first birthday, physician-diagnosed measles, or laboratory evidence of immunity should be vaccinated, ideally with two doses of vaccine separated by no less than 1 month. For those previously vaccinated with one dose of measles vaccine, revaccination is recommended for students entering colleges and other institutions of higher education, for healthcare workers at the time of employment, and for international travelers who visit endemic areas.

MMR is the vaccine of choice if recipients are likely to be susceptible to rubella and/or mumps as well as measles. Persons vaccinated between 1963 and 1967 with a killed measles vaccine, followed by live vaccine within 3 months, or with a vaccine of unknown type should be revaccinated with live measles virus vaccine.

Pregnancy Risk Factor C

Contraindications Pregnant females, known anaphylactoid reaction to eggs, known hypersensitivity to neomycin, acute respiratory infections, activated tuberculosis, immunosuppressed patients

Warnings/Precautions Avoid use in immunocompromised patients; defer administration in presence of acute respiratory or other active infections or inactive, untreated tuberculosis; avoid pregnancy for 3 months following vaccination; history of febrile seizures, hypersensitivity reactions may occur

Adverse Reactions All serious adverse reactions must be reported to the U.S. Department of Health and Human Services (DHHS) Vaccine Adverse Event Reporting System (VAERS) 1-800-822-7967.

>10%:
Cardiovascular: Edema
Central nervous system: Fever (<100°F)
Local: Burning or stinging, induration

1% to 10%:
Central nervous system: Fever between 100°F and 103°F usually between 5th and 12th days postvaccination
Dermatologic: Rash (rarely generalized)

<1%: Fatigue, convulsions, encephalitis, confusion, severe headache, fever (>103°F - prolonged), palsies, Guillain-Barré syndrome, ataxia, urticaria, itching, reddening of skin (especially around ears and eyes), erythema multiforme, vomiting, sore throat, diarrhea, thrombocytopenic purpura, diplopia, stiff neck, dyspnea, cough, rhinitis, lymphadenopathy, coryza, allergic reactions

Drug Interactions Whole blood, interferon immune globulin, radiation therapy, and immunosuppressive drugs (eg, corticosteroids) may result in insufficient response to immunization. DTP, OPV, MMR, Hib, and hepatitis B may be given concurrently; other virus vaccine administration should be separated by ≥1 month from measles.

Stability Refrigerate at 2°C to 8°C (36°F to 46°F); discard if left at room temperature for over 8 hours; protect from light

(Continued)

Measles Virus Vaccine, Live, Attenuated *(Continued)*

Mechanism of Action Promotes active immunity to measles virus by inducing specific measles IgG and IgM antibodies.

Usual Dosage Children ≥15 months and Adults: S.C.: 0.5 mL in outer aspect of the upper arm, no routine boosters

Administration Vaccine should not be given I.V.; S.C. injection preferred

Test Interactions May temporarily depress tuberculin skin test sensitivity

Patient Information Parents should monitor children closely for fever for 5-11 days after vaccination; females should not become pregnant within 3 months of vaccination

Additional Information Federal law requires that the date of administration, the vaccine manufacturer, lot number of vaccine, and the administering person's name, title and address be entered into the patient's permanent medical record

Dosage Forms Injection: 1000 TCID$_{50}$ per dose

♦ **Mebaral**® *see* Mephobarbital *on page 730*

Mebendazole (me BEN da zole)

U.S. Brand Names Vermox®

Therapeutic Category Anthelmintic

Use Treatment of pinworms (*Enterobius vermicularis*), whipworms (*Trichuris trichiura*), roundworms (*Ascaris lumbricoides*), and hookworms (*Ancylostoma duodenale*)

Pregnancy Risk Factor C

Contraindications Hypersensitivity to mebendazole or any component

Warnings/Precautions Pregnancy and children <2 years of age are relative contraindications since safety has not been established; not effective for hydatid disease

Adverse Reactions
1% to 10%: Gastrointestinal: Abdominal pain, diarrhea, nausea, vomiting
<1%: Fever, dizziness, headache, rash, angioedema, seizures, itching, alopecia (with high doses), neutropenia (sore throat, unusual fatigue), unusual weakness

Overdosage/Toxicology
Symptoms of overdose include abdominal pain, altered mental status
GI decontamination and supportive care

Drug Interactions Decreased effect: Anticonvulsants such as carbamazepine and phenytoin may increase metabolism of mebendazole

Mechanism of Action Selectively and irreversibly blocks glucose uptake and other nutrients in susceptible adult intestine-dwelling helminths

Pharmacodynamics/Kinetics
Absorption: Only 2% to 10%
Distribution: Distributed to serum, cyst fluid, liver, omental fat, and pelvic, pulmonary, and hepatic cysts; highest concentrations found in liver; relatively high concentrations also found in muscle-encysted *Trichinella spiralis* larvae; crosses placenta
Protein binding: High, 95%
Metabolism: Extensive in the liver
Half-life: 1-11.5 hours
Time to peak serum concentration: Within 2-4 hours
Elimination: Primarily excreted in feces with 5% to 10% eliminated in urine

Usual Dosage Children and Adults: Oral:
Pinworms: 100 mg as a single dose; may need to repeat after 2 weeks; treatment should include family members in close contact with patient
Whipworms, roundworms, hookworms: One tablet twice daily, morning and evening on 3 consecutive days; if patient is not cured within 3-4 weeks, a second course of treatment may be administered
Capillariasis: 200 mg twice daily for 20 days
Dosing adjustment in hepatic impairment: Dosage reduction may be necessary in patients with liver dysfunction
Hemodialysis: Not dialyzable (0% to 5%)

Monitoring Parameters Check for helminth ova in feces within 3-4 weeks following the initial therapy

Patient Information Tablets may be chewed, swallowed whole, or crushed and mixed with food; hygienic precautions should be taken to prevent reinfection such as wearing shoes and washing hands

Dosage Forms Tablet, chewable: 100 mg

Mecamylamine (mek a MIL a meen)

U.S. Brand Names Inversine®

Synonyms Mecamylamine Hydrochloride

Therapeutic Category Antihypertensive Agent; Ganglionic Blocking Agent

Use Treatment of moderately severe to severe hypertension and in uncomplicated malignant hypertension

Pregnancy Risk Factor C

Contraindications Coronary insufficiency, pyloric stenosis, glaucoma, uremia, recent myocardial infarction, unreliable, uncooperative patients

Warnings/Precautions Use with caution in patients receiving sulfonamides or antibiotics that cause neuromuscular blockade; use with caution in patients with impaired renal function, previous CNS abnormalities, prostatic hypertrophy, bladder obstruction, or urethral strictive; do not abruptly discontinue

Adverse Reactions Percentage unknown:
Cardiovascular: Postural hypotension

Central nervous system: Drowsiness, convulsions, confusion, mental depression

Endocrine & metabolic: Decreased sexual ability

Gastrointestinal: Xerostomia, loss of appetite, nausea, vomiting, bloating, frequent stools, followed by severe constipation

Genitourinary: Dysuria

Neuromuscular & skeletal: Uncontrolled movements of hands, arms, legs, or face, trembling

Ocular: Blurred vision, enlarged pupils

Respiratory: Shortness of breath

Overdosage/Toxicology

Symptoms of overdose include hypotension, nausea, vomiting, urinary retention, constipation. Signs and symptoms are a direct result of ganglionic blockade.

Treatment is supportive; pressor amines may be used to correct hypotension; use caution as patients will be unusually sensitive to these agents.

Drug Interactions Increased effect with sulfonamides and antibiotics that cause neuromuscular blockade; action of mecamylamine may be increased by anesthesia, other antihypertensives, and alcohol

Mechanism of Action Mecamylamine is a ganglionic blocker. This agent inhibits acetylcholine at the autonomic ganglia, causing a decrease in blood pressure. Mecamylamine also blocks central nicotinic cholinergic receptors, which inhibits the effects of nicotine and may suppress the desire to smoke.

Usual Dosage Adults: Oral: 2.5 mg twice daily after meals for 2 days; increased by increments of 2.5 mg at intervals ≥2 days until desired blood pressure response is achieved; average daily dose: 25 mg (usually in 3 divided doses)

Note: Reduce dosage of other antihypertensives when combined with mecamylamine with exception of thiazide diuretics which may be maintained at usual dose while decreasing mecamylamine by 50%

Dosing adjustment/comments in renal impairment: Use with caution, if at all, although no specific guidelines are available

Patient Information Take after meals at the same time each day; notify physician immediately if frequent loose bowel movements occur; rise slowly from sitting or lying for prolonged periods; do not restrict salt intake

Nursing Implications Check frequently for orthostatic hypotension; aid with ambulation

Dosage Forms Tablet, as hydrochloride: 2.5 mg

♦ **Mecamylamine Hydrochloride** *see* Mecamylamine *on previous page*

Mechlorethamine (me klor ETH a meen)

Related Information

Cancer Chemotherapy Regimens *on page 1263*

Extravasation Management of Chemotherapeutic Agents *on page 1285*

U.S. Brand Names Mustargen® Hydrochloride

Synonyms HN$_2$; Mechlorethamine Hydrochloride; Mustine; Nitrogen Mustard

Therapeutic Category Antineoplastic Agent, Alkylating Agent; Antineoplastic Agent, Nitrogen Mustard; Vesicant

Use Combination therapy of Hodgkin's disease and malignant lymphomas; non-Hodgkin's lymphoma; palliative treatment of bronchogenic, breast and ovarian carcinoma; may be used by intracavitary injection for treatment of metastatic tumors; pleural and other malignant effusions; topical treatment of mycosis fungoides

Pregnancy Risk Factor D

Contraindications Hypersensitivity to mechlorethamine or any component; pre-existing profound myelosuppression or infection

Warnings/Precautions The U.S. Food and Drug Administration (FDA) currently recommends that procedures for proper handling and disposal of antineoplastic agents be considered. Extravasation of the drug into subcutaneous tissues results in painful inflammation and induration; sloughing may occur. Patients with lymphomas should receive prophylactic allopurinol 2-3 days prior to therapy to prevent complications resulting from tumor lysis.

Adverse Reactions

>10%:

Gastrointestinal: Nausea and vomiting usually occur in nearly 100% of patients and onset is within 30 minutes to 2 hours after administration

Emetic potential: High (>90%)

Time course of nausea/vomiting: Onset: 1-3 hours; duration 2-8 hours

Hematologic: Myelosuppressive: Leukopenia and thrombocytopenia can be severe; caution should be used with patients who are receiving radiotherapy, secondary leukemia

WBC: Severe

Platelets: Severe

Onset (days): 4-7

Nadir (days): 14

Recovery (days): 21

Endocrine & metabolic: Delayed menses, oligomenorrhea, temporary or permanent amenorrhea, impaired spermatogenesis; spermatogenesis may return in patients in remission several years after the discontinuation of chemotherapy, chromosomal abnormalities

Genitourinary: Azoospermia

Otic: Ototoxicity

Miscellaneous: Precipitation of herpes zoster

(Continued)

Mechlorethamine *(Continued)*

1% to 10%:
Central nervous system: Fever, vertigo
Dermatologic: Alopecia
Endocrine & metabolic: Hyperuricemia
Gastrointestinal: Diarrhea, anorexia, metallic taste
Local: Thrombophlebitis/extravasation: May cause local vein discomfort which may be relieved by warm soaks and pain medication. A brown discoloration of veins may occur. Mechlorethamine is a strong vesicant and can cause tissue necrosis and sloughing.
Vesicant chemotherapy
Secondary malignancies: Have been reported after several years in 1% to 6% of patients treated
Neuromuscular & skeletal: Weakness
Otic: Tinnitus
Miscellaneous: Hypersensitivity, anaphylaxis
<1%: Vertigo, rash, peptic ulcer, myelosuppression, hemolytic anemia, hepatotoxicity, peripheral neuropathy

Overdosage/Toxicology
Suppression of all formed elements of the blood, uric acid crystals, nausea, vomiting, diarrhea
Sodium thiosulfate is the specific antidote for nitrogen mustard extravasations; treatment of systemic overdose is supportive

Stability
Store intact vials at room temperature.
Dilute powder with 10 mL SWI to a final concentration of 1 mg/mL; **solution is highly unstable** - should be administered within 15 minutes of dilution
May be diluted in up to 100 mL NS for intracavitary administration

Standard I.V. dilution:
I.V. push: Dose/syringe (concentration is 1 mg/mL)
Maximum syringe for IVP is 30 mL and syringe should be ≤75% full
Must be prepared fresh; solution is stable for only 1 hour after dilution and must be administered within that time period

Mechanism of Action Alkylating agent that inhibits DNA and RNA synthesis via formation of carbonium ions; cross-links strands of DNA, causing miscoding, breakage, and failure of replication; produces interstrand and intrastrand cross-links in DNA resulting in miscoding, breakage, and failure of replication

Pharmacodynamics/Kinetics
Absorption: Incomplete absorption into bloodstream following intracavitary administration secondary to rapid deactivation by body fluids
Metabolism: Following I.V. administration, drug undergoes rapid chemical transformation; unchanged drug is undetectable in the blood within a few minutes
Half-life: <1 minute
Elimination: <0.01% of unchanged drug is recovered in urine

Usual Dosage Refer to individual protocols. Dosage should be based on ideal dry weight; the presence of edema or ascites must be considered so that dosage will be based on actual weight unaugmented by these conditions

Children and Adults: MOPP: I.V.: 6 mg/m² on days 1 and 8 of a 28-day cycle
Adults:
I.V.: 0.4 mg/kg **OR** 12-16 mg/m² for one dose **OR** divided into 0.1 mg/kg/day for 4 days, repeated at 4- to 6-week intervals
Intracavitary: 10-20 mg diluted in 10 mL of SWI or 0.9% sodium chloride
Intrapericardially: 0.2-0.4 mg/kg diluted in up to 100 mL of 0.9% sodium chloride
Hemodialysis: Not removed; supplemental dosing is not required
Peritoneal dialysis: Not removed; supplemental dosing is not required
Topical mechlorethamine has been used in the treatment of cutaneous lesions of mycosis fungoides. A skin test should be performed prior to treatment with the topical preparation to detect sensitivity and possible irritation (use fresh mechlorethamine 0.1 mg/mL and apply over a 3 x 5 cm area of normal skin).

Administration Administer I.V. push through a free flowing I.V. over 1-3 minutes at a concentration not to exceed 1 mg/mL

Monitoring Parameters CBC with differential, hemoglobin, and platelet count

Patient Information Protect skin from contact, will burn and irritate. Any signs of infection, easy bruising or bleeding, shortness of breath, or painful or burning urination should be brought to physician's attention. Nausea, vomiting, or hair loss sometimes occurs. The drug may cause permanent sterility and may cause birth defects. The drug may be excreted in breast milk, therefore, an alternative form of feeding your baby should be used. Contraceptive measures are recommended during therapy.

Nursing Implications Use within 1 hour of preparation; avoid extravasation since mechlorethamine is a potent vesicant

Extravasation treatment: Sodium thiosulfate ⅛ molar solution is the specific antidote for nitrogen mustard extravasations and should be used as follows: Mix 4 mL of 10% sodium thiosulfate with 6 mL of sterile water for injection; inject 5-6 mL of this solution into the existing I.V. line; remove the needle; inject 2-3 mL of the solution S.C. clockwise into the infiltrated area using a 25-gauge needle; change the needle with each new injection; apply ice immediately for 6-12 hours.

Dosage Forms Powder for injection, as hydrochloride: 10 mg

♦ **Mechlorethamine Hydrochloride** *see Mechlorethamine on page 717*

♦ **Meclan® Topical** *see Meclocycline on this page*

Meclizine (MEK li zeen)

U.S. Brand Names Antivert®; Antrizine®; Bonine® [OTC]; Dizmiss® [OTC]; Dramamine® II [OTC]; Meni-D®; Nico-Vert® [OTC]; Ru-Vert-M®; Vergon® [OTC]

Canadian Brand Names Bonamine®

Synonyms Meclizine Hydrochloride; Meclozine Hydrochloride

Therapeutic Category Antiemetic; Antihistamine, H₁ Blocker

Use Prevention and treatment of symptoms of motion sickness; management of vertigo with diseases affecting the vestibular system

Pregnancy Risk Factor B

Pregnancy/Breast-Feeding Implications

Clinical effects on the fetus: No data available on crossing the placenta. Probably no effect on the fetus (insufficient data). Available evidence suggests safe use during pregnancy.

Breast-feeding/lactation: No data available

Contraindications Hypersensitivity to meclizine or any component; pregnancy

Warnings/Precautions Use with caution in patients with angle-closure glaucoma, prostatic hypertrophy, pyloric or duodenal obstruction, or bladder neck obstruction; use with caution in hot weather, and during exercise; elderly may be at risk for anticholinergic side effects such as glaucoma, prostatic hypertrophy, constipation, gastrointestinal obstructive disease; if vertigo does not respond in 1-2 weeks, it is advised to discontinue use

Adverse Reactions

>10%:

Central nervous system: Slight to moderate drowsiness

Respiratory: Thickening of bronchial secretions

1% to 10%:

Central nervous system: Headache, fatigue, nervousness, dizziness

Gastrointestinal: Appetite increase, weight gain, nausea, diarrhea, abdominal pain, xerostomia

Neuromuscular & skeletal: Arthralgia

Respiratory: Pharyngitis

<1%: Palpitations, hypotension, depression, sedation, photosensitivity, rash, angioedema, urinary retention, hepatitis, myalgia, tremor, paresthesia, blurred vision, bronchospasm, epistaxis

Overdosage/Toxicology

Symptoms of overdose include CNS depression, confusion, nervousness, hallucinations, dizziness, blurred vision, nausea, vomiting, hyperthermia

There is no specific treatment for an antihistamine overdose, however, most of its clinical toxicity is due to anticholinergic effects. For anticholinergic overdose with severe life-threatening symptoms, physostigmine 1-2 mg (0.5 mg or 0.02 mg/kg for children) I.V., slowly may be given to reverse these effects.

Drug Interactions Increased toxicity: CNS depressants, neuroleptics, anticholinergics

Mechanism of Action Has central anticholinergic action by blocking chemoreceptor trigger zone; decreases excitability of the middle ear labyrinth and blocks conduction in the middle ear vestibular-cerebellar pathways

Pharmacodynamics/Kinetics

Onset of action: Oral: Within 1 hour

Duration: 8-24 hours

Metabolism: Reportedly in the liver

Half-life: 6 hours

Elimination: As metabolites in urine and as unchanged drug in feces

Usual Dosage Children >12 years and Adults: Oral:

Motion sickness: 12.5-25 mg 1 hour before travel, repeat dose every 12-24 hours if needed; doses up to 50 mg may be needed

Vertigo: 25-100 mg/day in divided doses

Dietary Considerations Alcohol: Additive CNS effect, avoid use

Patient Information Take after meals; do not discontinue drug abruptly; notify physician if adverse GI effects, fever, or heat intolerance occurs; may cause drowsiness; avoid alcohol; adequate fluid intake, sugar free gum or hard candy may help dry mouth; adequate fluid and exercise may help constipation

Dosage Forms

Capsule, as hydrochloride: 15 mg, 25 mg, 30 mg

Tablet, as hydrochloride: 12.5 mg, 25 mg, 50 mg

Tablet, as hydrochloride:

Chewable: 25 mg

Film coated: 25 mg

♦ **Meclizine Hydrochloride** *see Meclizine on this page*

Meclocycline (me kloe SYE kleen)

U.S. Brand Names Meclan® Topical

Synonyms Meclocycline Sulfosalicylate

Therapeutic Category Antibiotic, Topical; Topical Skin Product, Acne

Use Topical treatment of inflammatory acne vulgaris

Pregnancy Risk Factor B

Contraindications Known hypersensitivity to tetracyclines or any component

(Continued)

Meclocycline *(Continued)*

Warnings/Precautions Use with caution in patients allergic to formaldehyde; for external use only

Adverse Reactions
>10%: Topical: Follicular staining, yellowing of the skin, burning/stinging feeling
1% to 10%: Topical: Pain, redness, skin irritation, dermatitis

Mechanism of Action Inhibits bacterial protein synthesis by binding with the 30S and possibly the 50S ribosomal subunit(s) of susceptible bacteria; may also cause alterations in the cytoplasmic membrane

Pharmacodynamics/Kinetics Absorption: Topical: Very little

Usual Dosage Children >11 years and Adults: Topical: Apply generously to affected areas twice daily

Patient Information Apply generously until skin is wet; avoid contact with eyes, nose, and mouth; stinging may occur with application, but soon stops; if skin is discolored yellow, washing will remove the color

Dosage Forms Cream, topical, as sulfosalicylate: 1% (20 g, 45 g)

♦ **Meclocycline Sulfosalicylate** *see Meclocycline on previous page*

Meclofenamate *(me kloe fen AM ate)*

Related Information
Nonsteroidal Anti-Inflammatory Agents Comparison *on page 1335*

U.S. Brand Names Meclomen®

Synonyms Meclofenamate Sodium

Therapeutic Category Analgesic, Nonsteroidal Anti-inflammatory Drug; Anti-inflammatory Agent; Nonsteroidal Anti-inflammatory Drug (NSAID), Oral

Use Treatment of inflammatory disorders

Pregnancy Risk Factor B (D if used in the 3rd trimester)

Contraindications Active GI bleeding, ulcer disease, hypersensitivity to aspirin, meclofenamate, or other NSAIDs

Warnings/Precautions May have adverse effects on fetus

Adverse Reactions
>10%:
Central nervous system: Dizziness
Dermatologic: Rash
Gastrointestinal: Abdominal cramps, heartburn, indigestion, nausea
1% to 10%:
Central nervous system: Headache, nervousness
Dermatologic: Itching
Endocrine & metabolic: Fluid retention
Gastrointestinal: Vomiting
Otic: Tinnitus
<1%: Congestive heart failure, hypertension, arrhythmia, tachycardia, confusion, hallucinations, aseptic meningitis, mental depression, drowsiness, insomnia, urticaria, erythema multiforme, toxic epidermal necrolysis, Stevens-Johnson syndrome, angioedema, polydipsia, hot flashes, gastritis, GI ulceration, cystitis, polyuria, agranulocytosis, anemia, hemolytic anemia, bone marrow suppression, leukopenia, thrombocytopenia, hepatitis, peripheral neuropathy, toxic amblyopia, blurred vision, conjunctivitis, dry eyes, decreased hearing, acute renal failure, allergic rhinitis, shortness of breath, epistaxis

Overdosage/Toxicology
Symptoms of overdose include drowsiness, lethargy, nausea, vomiting, seizures, paresthesia, headache, dizziness, GI bleeding, cerebral edema, cardiac arrest, tinnitus
Management of a nonsteroidal anti-inflammatory drug (NSAID) intoxication is primarily supportive and symptomatic. Fluid therapy is commonly effective in managing the hypotension that may occur following an acute NSAID overdose, except when this is due to an acute blood loss. Seizures tend to be very short-lived and often do not require drug treatment. Although, recurrent seizures should be treated with I.V. diazepam. Since many of the NSAID undergo enterohepatic cycling, multiple doses of charcoal may be needed to reduce the potential for delayed toxicities.

Drug Interactions
Decreased effect with aspirin; decreased effect of diuretics, antihypertensives
Increased effect/toxicity of warfarin, methotrexate

Mechanism of Action Inhibits prostaglandin synthesis by decreasing the activity of the enzyme, cyclo-oxygenase, which results in decreased formation of prostaglandin precursors

Pharmacodynamics/Kinetics
Duration of action: 2-4 hours
Distribution: Crosses the placenta
Protein binding: 99%
Half-life: 2-3.3 hours
Time to peak serum concentration: Within 0.5-1.5 hours
Elimination: Principally in urine and in feces as glucuronide conjugates

Usual Dosage Children >14 years and Adults: Oral:
Mild to moderate pain: 50 mg every 4-6 hours, not to exceed 400 mg/day
Rheumatoid arthritis/osteoarthritis: 200-400 mg/day in 3-4 equal doses

Test Interactions ↑ chloride (S), ↑ sodium (S)

Patient Information Take with food, milk, or with antacids

Nursing Implications Should be used for short-term only (<7 days); advise patient to report persistent GI discomfort, sore throat, fever, or malaise

Dosage Forms Capsule, as sodium: 50 mg, 100 mg

- ◆ **Meclofenamate Sodium** see Meclofenamate on previous page
- ◆ **Meclomen®** see Meclofenamate on previous page
- ◆ **Meclozine Hydrochloride** see Meclizine on page 719
- ◆ **Mectizan®** see Ivermectin on page 644
- ◆ **Medicinal Carbon** see Charcoal on page 233
- ◆ **Medicinal Charcoal** see Charcoal on page 233
- ◆ **Medigesic®** see Butalbital Compound on page 165
- ◆ **Medihaler-Iso®** see Isoproterenol on page 635
- ◆ **Medilium®** see Chlordiazepoxide on page 239
- ◆ **Medimet®** see Methyldopa on page 758
- ◆ **Medipain 5®** see Hydrocodone and Acetaminophen on page 575
- ◆ **Medipren® [OTC]** see Ibuprofen on page 593
- ◆ **Medi-Quick® Topical Ointment [OTC]** see Bacitracin, Neomycin, and Polymyxin B on page 123
- ◆ **Meditran®** see Meprobamate on page 731
- ◆ **Medi-Tuss® [OTC]** see Guaifenesin on page 549
- ◆ **Medralone® Injection** see Methylprednisolone on page 762
- ◆ **Medrol® Oral** see Methylprednisolone on page 762

Medroxyprogesterone Acetate

(me DROKS ee proe JES te rone AS e tate)

U.S. Brand Names Amen®; Curretab®; Cycrin®; Depo-Provera® Injection; Provera®

Canadian Brand Names Novo-Medrone

Synonyms Acetoxymethylprogesterone; Methylacetoxyprogesterone

Therapeutic Category Contraceptive, Parenteral (Progestin); Progestin

Use Endometrial carcinoma or renal carcinoma as well as secondary amenorrhea or abnormal uterine bleeding due to hormonal imbalance; prevention of pregnancy

Pregnancy Risk Factor X

Contraindications Pregnancy, thrombophlebitis; hypersensitivity to medroxyprogesterone or any component; cerebral apoplexy, undiagnosed vaginal bleeding, liver dysfunction

Warnings/Precautions Use with caution in patients with depression, diabetes, epilepsy, asthma, migraines, renal or cardiac dysfunction; pretreatment exams should include PAP smear, physical exam of breasts and pelvic areas. May increase serum cholesterol, LDL, decrease HDL and triglycerides; use of any progestin during the first 4 months of pregnancy is not recommended; monitor patient closely for loss of vision, sudden onset of proptosis, diplopia, migraine, and signs and symptoms of thromboembolic disorders.

Adverse Reactions

>10%:

Cardiovascular: Edema

Endocrine & metabolic: Breakthrough bleeding, spotting, changes in menstrual flow, amenorrhea

Gastrointestinal: Anorexia

Local: Pain at injection site

Neuromuscular & skeletal: Weakness

1% to 10%:

Cardiovascular: Embolism, central thrombosis

Central nervous system: Mental depression, fever, insomnia

Dermatologic: Melasma or chloasma, allergic rash with or without pruritus

Endocrine & metabolic: Changes in cervical erosion and secretions, increased breast tenderness

Gastrointestinal: Weight gain or loss

Hepatic: Cholestatic jaundice

Local: Thrombophlebitis

Overdosage/Toxicology

Toxicity is unlikely following single exposures of excessive doses

Supportive treatment is adequate in most cases

Drug Interactions Decreased effect: Aminoglutethimide may decrease effects by increasing hepatic metabolism

Mechanism of Action Inhibits secretion of pituitary gonadotropins, which prevents follicular maturation and ovulation, stimulates growth of mammary tissue

Pharmacodynamics/Kinetics

Absorption: I.M.: Slow

Bioavailability: 0.6% to 10%

Protein binding: 90%

Metabolism: Oral: In the liver

Half-life: 30 days

Elimination: Oral: In urine and feces

Usual Dosage

Adolescents and Adults: Oral:

Amenorrhea: 5-10 mg/day for 5-10 days or 2.5 mg/day

Abnormal uterine bleeding: 5-10 mg for 5-10 days starting on day 16 or 21 of cycle

(Continued)

Medroxyprogesterone Acetate *(Continued)*

Accompanying cyclic estrogen therapy, postmenopausal: 2.5-10 mg the last 10-13 days of estrogen dosing each month

Adults: I.M.:

Endometrial or renal carcinoma: 400-1000 mg/week

Contraception: 150 mg every 3 months

Dosing adjustment in hepatic impairment: Dose needs to be lowered in patients with alcoholic cirrhosis

Monitoring Parameters Monitor patient closely for loss of vision, sudden onset of proptosis, diplopia, migraine, and signs and symptoms of thromboembolic disorders

Test Interactions Altered thyroid and liver function tests

Patient Information Take this medicine only as directed; do not take more of it and do not take it for a longer period of time; if you suspect you may have become pregnant, stop taking this medicine; notify physician if sudden loss of vision or migraine headache occurs; may cause photosensitivity, wear protective clothing or sunscreen

Nursing Implications Patients should receive a copy of the patient labeling for the drug

Dosage Forms

Injection, suspension: 100 mg/mL (5 mL); 150 mg/mL (1 mL); 400 mg/mL (1 mL, 2.5 mL, 10 mL)

Tablet: 2.5 mg, 5 mg, 10 mg

Medrysone (ME dri sone)

U.S. Brand Names HMS Liquifilm®

Therapeutic Category Anti-inflammatory Agent, Ophthalmic; Corticosteroid, Ophthalmic

Use Treatment of allergic conjunctivitis, vernal conjunctivitis, episcleritis, ophthalmic epinephrine sensitivity reaction

Pregnancy Risk Factor C

Contraindications Fungal, viral, or untreated pus-forming bacterial ocular infections; not for use in iritis and uveitis

Warnings/Precautions Prolonged use has been associated with the development of corneal or scleral perforation and posterior subcapsular cataracts; may mask or enhance the establishment of acute purulent untreated infections of the eye; effectiveness and safety have not been established in children. Medrysone is a synthetic corticosteroid, structurally related to progesterone; if no improvement after several days of treatment, discontinue medrysone and institute other therapy; duration of therapy: 3-4 days to several weeks dependent on type and severity of disease; taper dose to avoid disease exacerbation.

Adverse Reactions

1% to 10%: Ocular: Temporary mild blurred vision

<1%: Stinging, burning eyes, corneal thinning, increased intraocular pressure, glaucoma, damage to the optic nerve, defects in visual activity, cataracts, secondary ocular infection

Overdosage/Toxicology Systemic toxicity is unlikely from the ophthalmic preparation

Mechanism of Action Decreases inflammation by suppression of migration of polymorphonuclear leukocytes and reversal of increased capillary permeability

Pharmacodynamics/Kinetics

Absorption: Through aqueous humor

Metabolism: Any drug absorbed is metabolized in the liver

Elimination: By the kidneys and feces

Usual Dosage Children and Adults: Ophthalmic: Instill 1 drop in conjunctival sac 2-4 times/day up to every 4 hours; may use every 1-2 hours during first 1-2 days

Monitoring Parameters Intraocular pressure and periodic examination of lens (with prolonged use)

Patient Information Shake well before using, do not touch dropper to the eye

Dosage Forms Solution, ophthalmic: 1% (5 mL, 10 mL)

Mefenamic Acid (me fe NAM ik AS id)

Related Information

Nonsteroidal Anti-Inflammatory Agents Comparison *on page 1335*

U.S. Brand Names Ponstel®

Canadian Brand Names Apo®-Mefenamic; Ponstan®

Therapeutic Category Analgesic, Nonsteroidal Anti-inflammatory Drug; Anti-inflammatory Agent; Nonsteroidal Anti-inflammatory Drug (NSAID), Oral

Use Short-term relief of mild to moderate pain including primary dysmenorrhea

Pregnancy Risk Factor C

Contraindications Known hypersensitivity to mefenamic acid or other NSAIDs

Warnings/Precautions May have adverse effects on fetus

Adverse Reactions

>10%:

Central nervous system: Dizziness

Dermatologic: Rash

Gastrointestinal: Abdominal cramps, heartburn, indigestion, nausea

1% to 10%:

Central nervous system: Headache, nervousness

Dermatologic: Itching

Endocrine & metabolic: Fluid retention

Gastrointestinal: Vomiting

Otic: Tinnitus

<1%: Congestive heart failure, hypertension, arrhythmias, tachycardia, confusion, hallucinations, aseptic meningitis, mental depression, drowsiness, insomnia, urticaria, erythema multiforme, toxic epidermal necrolysis, Stevens-Johnson syndrome, angioedema, polydipsia, hot flashes, gastritis, GI ulceration, cystitis, polyuria, agranulocytosis, anemia, hemolytic anemia, bone marrow suppression, leukopenia, thrombocytopenia, hepatitis, peripheral neuropathy, toxic amblyopia, blurred vision, conjunctivitis, dry eyes, decreased hearing, acute renal failure, shortness of breath, allergic rhinitis, epistaxis

Overdosage/Toxicology
Symptoms of overdose include CNS stimulation, agitation, seizures

Management of a nonsteroidal anti-inflammatory drug (NSAID) intoxication is primarily supportive and symptomatic. Fluid therapy is commonly effective in managing the hypotension that may occur following an acute NSAIDs overdose, except when this is due to an acute blood loss. Seizures tend to be very short-lived and often do not require drug treatment. Although, recurrent seizures should be treated with I.V. diazepam. Since many of the NSAID undergo enterohepatic cycling, multiple doses of charcoal may be needed to reduce the potential for delayed toxicities.

Drug Interactions CYP2C9 enzyme substrate

Decreased effect of diuretics, antihypertensives; decreased effect with aspirin

Increased effect/toxicity with oral anticoagulants, methotrexate

Mechanism of Action Inhibits prostaglandin synthesis by decreasing the activity of the enzyme, cyclo-oxygenase, which results in decreased formation of prostaglandin precursors

Pharmacodynamics/Kinetics
Peak effect: Oral: Within 2-4 hours

Duration of action: Up to 6 hours

Protein binding: High

Metabolism: Conjugated in the liver

Half-life: 3.5 hours

Elimination: In urine (50%) and feces as unchanged drug and metabolites

Usual Dosage Children >14 years and Adults: Oral: 500 mg to start then 250 mg every 4 hours as needed; maximum therapy: 1 week

Dosing adjustment/comments in renal impairment: Not recommended for use

Test Interactions ↑ chloride (S), ↑ sodium (S), positive Coombs' [direct], false-positive urinary bilirubin

Patient Information Take with food, milk, or with antacids; extended release capsules must be swallowed intact

Dosage Forms Capsule: 250 mg

Mefloquine (ME floe kwin)
Related Information
Malaria Treatment *on page 1425*

Prevention of Malaria *on page 1372*

U.S. Brand Names Lariam®

Synonyms Mefloquine Hydrochloride

Therapeutic Category Antimalarial Agent

Use Treatment of acute malarial infections and prevention of malaria

Pregnancy Risk Factor C

Contraindications Hypersensitivity to any component

Warnings/Precautions Caution is warranted with lactation; discontinue if unexplained neuropsychiatric disturbances occur, caution in epilepsy patients or in patients with significant cardiac disease. If mefloquine is to be used for a prolonged period, periodic evaluations including liver function tests and ophthalmic examinations should be performed. (Retinal abnormalities have not been observed with mefloquine in humans; however, it has with long-term administration to rats.) In cases of life-threatening, serious, or overwhelming malaria infections due to *Plasmodium falciparum*, patients should be treated with intravenous antimalarial drug. Mefloquine may be given orally to complete the course. Caution should be exercised with regard to driving, piloting airplanes, and operating machines since dizziness, disturbed sense of balance; neuropsychiatric reactions have been reported with mefloquine.

Adverse Reactions
1% to 10%:

Central nervous system: Difficulty concentrating, headache, insomnia, lightheadedness, vertigo

Gastrointestinal: Vomiting (3%), diarrhea, stomach pain, nausea

Ocular: Visual disturbances

Otic: Tinnitus

<1%: Bradycardia, extrasystoles, syncope, anxiety, dizziness, confusion, seizures, hallucinations, mental depression, psychosis

Overdosage/Toxicology
Symptoms of overdose include vomiting, diarrhea; cardiotoxic

Following GI contamination supportive care only

Drug Interactions
Decreased effect of valproic acid

Increased toxicity of beta-blockers; chloroquine, quinine, and quinidine (hold treatment until at least 12 hours after these later drugs)

(Continued)

Mefloquine *(Continued)*

Mechanism of Action Mefloquine is a quinoline-methanol compound structurally similar to quinine; mefloquine's effectiveness in the treatment and prophylaxis of malaria is due to the destruction of the asexual blood forms of the malarial pathogens that affect humans, *Plasmodium falciparum, P. vivax, P. malariae, P. ovale*

Pharmacodynamics/Kinetics

Absorption: Oral: Well absorbed

Distribution: V_d: 19 L/kg; concentrates in erythrocytes; appears in breast milk; distributed to blood, urine, CSF, and tissues; concentrates in erythrocytes

Protein binding: 98%

Half-life: 21-22 days

Elimination: ~1.5% to 9% of dose excreted unchanged in urine

Usual Dosage Oral:

Children: Malaria prophylaxis:

15-19 kg: 1/4 tablet

20-30 kg: 1/2 tablet

31-45 kg: 3/4 tablet

>45 kg: 1 tablet

Administer weekly starting 1 week before travel, continuing weekly during travel and for 4 weeks after leaving endemic area

Adults:

Treatment of mild to moderate malaria infection: 5 tablets (1250 mg) as a single dose with at least 8 oz of water

Malaria prophylaxis: 1 tablet (250 mg) weekly starting 1 week before travel, continuing weekly during travel and for 4 weeks after leaving endemic area

Monitoring Parameters LFTS; ocular examination

Patient Information Begin therapy before trip and continue after; do not take drug on empty stomach; take with food and at least 8 oz of water; women of childbearing age should use reliable contraception during prophylaxis treatment and for 2 months after the last dose; be aware of signs and symptoms of malaria when traveling to an endemic area. Caution should be exercised with regard to driving, piloting airplanes, and operating machines since dizziness, disturbed sense of balance, or neuropsychiatric reactions have been reported with mefloquine.

Dosage Forms Tablet, as hydrochloride: 250 mg

- ◆ **Mefloquine Hydrochloride** *see Mefloquine on previous page*
- ◆ **Mefoxin®** *see Cefoxitin on page 216*
- ◆ **Mega-B®** [OTC] *see Vitamins, Multiple on page 1226*
- ◆ **Megace®** *see Megestrol Acetate on this page*
- ◆ **Megacillin® Susp** *see Penicillin G Benzathine, Parenteral on page 895*

Megestrol Acetate *(me JES trole AS e tate)*

U.S. Brand Names Megace®

Therapeutic Category Antineoplastic Agent, Hormone; Progestin

Use Palliative treatment of breast and endometrial carcinomas, appetite stimulation, and promotion of weight gain in cachexia

Pregnancy Risk Factor X

Contraindications Hypersensitivity to megestrol or any component; pregnancy

Warnings/Precautions The U.S. Food and Drug Administration (FDA) currently recommends that procedures for proper handling and disposal of antineoplastic agents be considered. Use during the first few months of pregnancy is not recommended. Use with caution in patients with a history of thrombophlebitis. Elderly females may have vaginal bleeding or discharge and need to be forewarned of this side effect and inconvenience.

Adverse Reactions

>10%:

Cardiovascular: Edema

Endocrine & metabolic: Breakthrough bleeding and amenorrhea, spotting, changes in menstrual flow

Neuromuscular & skeletal: Weakness

1% to 10%:

Central nervous system: Insomnia, depression, fever, headache

Dermatologic: Allergic rash with or without pruritus, melasma or chloasma, rash, and rarely alopecia

Endocrine & metabolic: Changes in cervical erosion and secretions, increased breast tenderness, changes in vaginal bleeding pattern, edema, fluid retention, hyperglycemia

Gastrointestinal: Weight gain (not attributed to edema or fluid retention), nausea, vomiting, stomach cramps

Hepatic: Cholestatic jaundice, hepatotoxicity

Hematologic: Myelosuppressive:

WBC: None

Platelets: None

Local: Thrombophlebitis

Neuromuscular & skeletal: Carpal tunnel syndrome

Respiratory: Hyperpnea

Overdosage/Toxicology Toxicity is unlikely following simple exposures of excessive doses

Mechanism of Action A synthetic progestin with antiestrogenic properties which disrupt the estrogen receptor cycle. Megace® interferes with the normal estrogen cycle and results in a lower LH titer. May also have a direct effect on the endometrium. Megestrol is an antineoplastic progestin thought to act through an antileutenizing effect mediated via the pituitary.

Pharmacodynamics/Kinetics
Onset of action: At least 2 months of continuous therapy is necessary
Absorption: Oral: Well absorbed
Metabolism: Completely metabolized in the liver to free steroids and glucuronide conjugates
Time to peak serum concentration: Oral: Within 1-3 hours
Half-life, elimination: 15-20 hours
Elimination: In urine as steroid metabolites and inactive compound, some in feces and bile

Usual Dosage Adults: Oral (refer to individual protocols):
Female:
Breast carcinoma: 40 mg 4 times/day
Endometrial: 40-320 mg/day in divided doses; use for 2 months to determine efficacy; maximum doses used have been up to 800 mg/day
Uterine bleeding: 40 mg 2-4 times/day
Male/Female: HIV-related cachexia: Initial dose: 800 mg/day; daily doses of 400 and 800 mg/day were found to be clinically effective
Dosing adjustment in renal impairment: No data available; however, the urinary excretion of megestrol acetate administered in doses of 4-90 mg ranged from 56% to 78% within 10 days
Hemodialysis: Megestrol acetate has not been tested for dialyzability; however, due to its low solubility, it is postulated that dialysis would not be an effective means of treating an overdose

Monitoring Parameters Monitor for tumor response; observe for signs of thromboembolic phenomena; monitor for thromboembolism

Test Interactions Altered thyroid and liver function tests

Patient Information Exposure to megestrol during the first 4 months of pregnancy may pose risks to the fetus; notify physician if sudden loss of vision, double vision, migraine headache occur, or if pain in calves with warmth and tenderness develops; may cause photosensitivity, wear protective clothing or sunscreen

Dosage Forms
Suspension, oral: 40 mg/mL with alcohol 0.06% (236.6 mL)
Tablet: 20 mg, 40 mg

♦ **Melanex**® *see Hydroquinone on page 584*
♦ **Mellaril**® *see Thioridazine on page 1135*
♦ **Mellaril-S**® *see Thioridazine on page 1135*
♦ **Melpaque HP**® *see Hydroquinone on page 584*

Melphalan (MEL fa lan)
Related Information
Cancer Chemotherapy Regimens *on page 1263*
Toxicities of Chemotherapeutic Agents *on page 1288*
U.S. Brand Names Alkeran®
Synonyms L-PAM; L-Sarcolysin; Phenylalanine Mustard
Therapeutic Category Antineoplastic Agent, Alkylating Agent; Antineoplastic Agent, Nitrogen Mustard
Use Palliative treatment of multiple myeloma and nonresectable epithelial ovarian carcinoma; neuroblastoma, rhabdomyosarcoma, breast cancer
Pregnancy Risk Factor D
Contraindications Hypersensitivity to melphalan or any component; severe bone marrow suppression; patients whose disease was resistant to prior therapy
Warnings/Precautions The U.S. Food and Drug Administration (FDA) currently recommends that procedures for proper handling and disposal for antineoplastic agents be considered. Is potentially mutagenic, carcinogenic, and teratogenic; produces amenorrhea. Reduce dosage or discontinue therapy if leukocyte count <3000/mm³ or platelet count <100,000/mm³; use with caution in patients with bone marrow suppression, impaired renal function, or who have received prior chemotherapy or irradiation; will cause amenorrhea. Toxicity to immunosuppressives is increased in elderly. Start with lowest recommended adult doses. Signs of infection, such as fever and WBC rise, may not occur. Lethargy and confusion may be more prominent signs of infection.
Adverse Reactions
>10%:
Hematologic: Myelosuppressive: Leukopenia and thrombocytopenia are the most common effects of melphalan. Irreversible bone marrow failure has been reported.
WBC: Moderate
Platelets: Moderate
Onset (days): 7
Nadir (days): 8-10 and 27-32
Recovery (days): 42-50
Second malignancies: Reported are melphalan more frequently
1% to 10%:
Cardiovascular: Vasculitis
Dermatologic: Vesiculation of skin, alopecia, pruritus, rash
(Continued)

Melphalan *(Continued)*

Endocrine & metabolic: SIADH, sterility and amenorrhea

Gastrointestinal: Nausea and vomiting are mild; stomatitis and diarrhea are infrequent

Genitourinary: Bladder irritation, hemorrhagic cystitis

Hematologic: Anemia, agranulocytosis, hemolytic anemia

Respiratory: Pulmonary fibrosis, interstitial pneumonitis

Miscellaneous: Hypersensitivity

Overdosage/Toxicology Symptoms of overdose include hypocalcemia, pulmonary fibrosis, nausea and vomiting, bone marrow suppression

Drug Interactions

Decreased effect: Cimetidine and other H_2-antagonists: The reduction in gastric pH has been reported to decrease bioavailability of melphalan by 30%

Increased toxicity: Cyclosporine: Increased incidence of nephrotoxicity

Stability

Tablets/injection: Protect from light, store at room temperature (15°C to 30°C)

The time between reconstitution/dilution and administration of parenteral melphalan must be kept to a minimum (<60 minutes) because reconstituted and diluted solutions are unstable

Injection: Preparation:

Dissolve powder initially with 10 mL of diluent to a concentration of 5 mg/mL. This solution is chemically and physically stable for at least 90 minutes when stored at 25°C (77°F).

Immediately dilute dose in 0.9% sodium chloride to a concentration of 0.1-0.45 mg/mL. This solution is physically and chemically stable for at least 60 minutes at 25°C (77°F). HIGHLY UNSTABLE SOLUTION - administration should occur within one hour of dissolution. Do not refrigeration solution - precipitation occurs.

Standard I.V. dilution:

Dose/250-500 mL NS (concentration of 0.1-0.45 mg/mL)

MUST BE PREPARED FRESH - solution is stable for 1 hour after dilution and must be administered within that time period

Mechanism of Action Alkylating agent which is a derivative of mechlorethamine that inhibits DNA and RNA synthesis via formation of carbonium ions; cross-links strands of DNA

Pharmacodynamics/Kinetics

Absorption: Oral: Variable and incomplete from the GI tract; food interferes with absorption

Distribution: V_d: 0.5-0.6 L/kg throughout total body water

Bioavailability: Unpredictable, decreasing from 85% to 58% with repeated doses

Half-life, terminal: 1.5 hours

Time to peak serum concentration: Reportedly within 2 hours

Elimination: 10% to 30% of a dose excreted unchanged in the urine; 20% to 50% excreted in the stool after oral administration

Usual Dosage

Oral (refer to individual protocols); dose should always be adjusted to patient response and weekly blood counts:

Children: 4-20 mg/m^2/day for 1-21 days

Adults:

Multiple myeloma: 6 mg/day initially adjusted as indicated **or** 0.15 mg/kg/day for 7 days **or** 0.25 mg/kg/day for 4 days; repeat at 4- to 6-week intervals

Ovarian carcinoma: 0.2 mg/kg/day for 5 days, repeat every 4-5 weeks

Intravenous (refer to individual protocols):

Children:

Pediatric rhabdomyosarcoma: 10-35 mg/m^2/dose every 21-28 days

High-dose melphalan with bone marrow transplantation for neuroblastoma: 70-100 mg/m^2/day on day 7 and 6 before BMT **or** 140-220 mg/m^2 single dose before BMT **or** 50 mg/m^2/day for 4 days **or** 70 mg/m^2/day for 3 days

Adults:

Multiple myeloma: 16 mg/m^2 administered at 2-week intervals for 4 doses, then repeat monthly as per protocol for multiple myeloma

Dosing adjustment in renal impairment:

Cl_{cr} 10-50 mL/minute: Administer at 75% of normal dose

Cl_{cr} <10 mL/minute: Administer at 50% of normal dose

or

BUN >30 mg/dL: Reduce dose by 50%

Serum creatinine >1.5 mg/dL: Reduce dose by 50%

Hemodialysis: Unknown

CAPD effects: Unknown

CAVH effects: Unknown

Administration

Oral: Administer on an empty stomach

Parenteral: Due to limited stability, complete administration of I.V. dose should occur within 60 minutes of reconstitution

I.V. infusion: I.V. dose is FDA-approved for administration as a single infusion over 15-20 minutes

I.V. bolus: I.V. may be administered via central line and via peripheral vein as a rapid I.V. bolus; there have not been any unexpected or serious adverse events specifically related to rapid I.V. bolus administration; the most common adverse events were transient mild symptoms of hot flush and tingling sensation over the body

Central line: I.V. bolus doses of 17-200 mg/m^2 (reconstituted and not diluted) have been infused over 2-20 minutes

Peripheral line: I.V. bolus doses of 2-23 mg/m^2 (reconstituted and not diluted) have been infused over 1-4 minutes

Monitoring Parameters CBC with differential and platelet count, serum electrolytes, serum uric acid

Test Interactions False-positive Coombs' test [direct]

Patient Information Any signs of infection, easy bruising or bleeding, shortness of breath, or painful or burning urination should be brought to physician's attention. Nausea, vomiting, or hair loss sometimes occur. The drug may cause permanent sterility and may cause birth defects. The drug may be excreted in breast milk, therefore, an alternative form of feeding your baby should be used.

Nursing Implications Avoid skin contact with I.V. formulation

Dosage Forms

Powder for injection: 50 mg

Tablet: 2 mg

♦ **Melquin HP®** *see* Hydroquinone *on page 584*

♦ **Menadol® [OTC]** *see* Ibuprofen *on page 593*

♦ **Menest®** *see* Estrogens, Esterified *on page 438*

♦ **Meni-D®** *see* Meclizine *on page 719*

Meningococcal Polysaccharide Vaccine, Groups A, C, Y, and W-135

(me NIN joe kok al pol i SAK a ride vak SEEN groops aye, see, why & dubl yoo won thur tee fyve)

Related Information

Immunization Recommendations *on page 1358*

U.S. Brand Names Menomune®-A/C/Y/W-135

Therapeutic Category Vaccine, Inactivated Bacteria

Use

Immunization of persons 2 years of age and above in epidemic or endemic areas as might be determined in a population delineated by neighborhood, school, dormitory, or other reasonable boundary. The prevalent serogroup in such a situation should match a serogroup in the vaccine. Individuals at particular high-risk include persons with terminal component complement deficiencies and those with anatomic or functional asplenia.

Travelers visiting areas of a country that are recognized as having hyperendemic or epidemic meningococcal disease

Vaccinations should be considered for household or institutional contacts of persons with meningococcal disease as an adjunct to appropriate antibiotic chemoprophylaxis as well as medical and laboratory personnel at risk of exposure to meningococcal disease

Pregnancy Risk Factor C

Contraindications Children <2 years of age

Warnings/Precautions Patients who undergo splenectomy secondary to trauma or nonlymphoid tumors respond well; however, those asplenic patients with lymphoid tumors who receive either chemotherapy or irradiation respond poorly; pregnancy, unless there is substantial risk of infection.

Adverse Reactions All serious adverse reactions must be reported to the U.S. Department of Health and Human Services (DHHS) Vaccine Adverse Event Reporting System (VAERS) 1-800-822-7967.

>10%:

Central nervous system: Pain (17.5% to 24%)

Dermatologic: Erythema (0.8% to 31.7%), induration (4.8% to 8.3%)

Local: Tenderness (24% to 29%)

1% to 10%: Central nervous system: Headache (1.2% to 4.1%), malaise (≤2.6%), fever (0.4% to 3.1%), chills (≤1.7%)

Drug Interactions Decreased effect with administration of immunoglobulin within 1 month

Stability Discard remainder of vaccine within 5 days after reconstitution; store reconstituted vaccine in refrigerator

Mechanism of Action Induces the formation of bactericidal antibodies to meningococcal antigens; the presence of these antibodies is strongly correlated with immunity to meningococcal disease caused by *Neisseria meningitidis* groups A, C, Y and W-135.

Pharmacodynamics/Kinetics

Onset: Antibody levels are achieved within 10-14 days after administration

Duration: Antibodies against group A and C polysaccharides decline markedly (to prevaccination levels) over the first 3 years following a single dose of vaccine, especially in children <4 years of age

Usual Dosage One dose S.C. (0.5 mL); the need for booster is unknown

Nursing Implications Epinephrine 1:1000 should be available to control allergic reaction

Dosage Forms Injection: 10 dose, 50 dose

♦ **Menomune®-A/C/Y/W-135** *see* Meningococcal Polysaccharide Vaccine, Groups A, C, Y, and W-135 *on this page*

Menotropins (men oh TROE pins)

U.S. Brand Names Humegon™; Pergonal®; Repronex™

Therapeutic Category Gonadotropin; Ovulation Stimulator

(Continued)

Menotropins *(Continued)*

Use Sequentially with hCG to induce ovulation and pregnancy in the infertile woman with functional anovulation; used with hCG in men to stimulate spermatogenesis in those with primary hypogonadotropic hypogonadism

Pregnancy Risk Factor X

Contraindications Primary ovarian failure, overt thyroid and adrenal dysfunction, abnormal bleeding, pregnancy, men with normal urinary gonadotropin concentrations, elevated gonadotropin levels indicating primary testicular failure

Warnings/Precautions Advise patient of frequency and potential hazards of multiple pregnancy; to minimize the hazard of abnormal ovarian enlargement, use the lowest possible dose

Adverse Reactions
Male:
>10%: Endocrine & metabolic: Gynecomastia
1% to 10%: Erythrocytosis (shortness of breath, dizziness, anorexia, syncope, epistaxis)
Female:
>10%:
Endocrine & metabolic: Ovarian enlargement
Gastrointestinal: Abdominal distention
Local: Pain/rash at injection site
1% to 10%: Ovarian hyperstimulation syndrome
<1%: Thromboembolism, pain, febrile reactions

Overdosage/Toxicology Symptoms of overdose include ovarian hyperstimulation

Stability Lyophilized powder may be refrigerated or stored at room temperature; after reconstitution inject immediately, discard any unused portion

Mechanism of Action Actions occur as a result of both follicle stimulating hormone (FSH) effects and luteinizing hormone (LH) effects; menotropins stimulate the development and maturation of the ovarian follicle (FSH), cause ovulation (LH), and stimulate the development of the corpus luteum (LH); in males it stimulates spermatogenesis (LH)

Pharmacodynamics/Kinetics Elimination: ~10% of dose is excreted in the urine unchanged

Usual Dosage Adults: I.M.:
Male: Following pretreatment with hCG, 1 ampul 3 times/week and hCG 2000 units twice weekly until sperm is detected in the ejaculate (4-6 months) then may be increased to 2 ampuls of menotropins (150 units FSH/150 units LH) 3 times/week
Female: 1 ampul/day (75 units of FSH and LH) for 9-12 days followed by 10,000 units hCG 1 day after the last dose; repeated at least twice at same level before increasing dosage to 2 ampuls (150 units FSH/150 units LH)

Administration I.M. administration only

Patient Information Multiple ovulations resulting in plural gestations have been reported

Dosage Forms Injection:
Follicle stimulating hormone activity 75 units and luteinizing hormone activity 75 units per 2 mL ampul
Follicle stimulating hormone activity 150 units and luteinizing hormone activity 150 units per 2 mL ampul

♦ **Mentax®** *see* Butenafine *on page 167*

♦ **Mepergan®** *see* Meperidine and Promethazine *on page 730*

Meperidine *(me PER i deen)*

Related Information
Adult ACLS Algorithm, Electrical Conversion *on page 1453*
Narcotic Agonists Comparison *on page 1328*

U.S. Brand Names Demerol®

Synonyms Isonipecaine Hydrochloride; Meperidine Hydrochloride; Pethidine Hydrochloride

Therapeutic Category Analgesic, Narcotic

Use Management of moderate to severe pain; adjunct to anesthesia and preoperative sedation

Restrictions C-II

Pregnancy Risk Factor B (D if used for prolonged periods or in high doses at term)

Contraindications Hypersensitivity to meperidine or any component; patients receiving MAO inhibitors presently or in the past 14 days

Warnings/Precautions Use with caution in patients with pulmonary, hepatic, renal disorders, or increased intracranial pressure; use with caution in patients with renal failure or seizure disorders or those receiving high-dose meperidine; normeperidine (an active metabolite and CNS stimulant) may accumulate and precipitate twitches, tremors, or seizures; some preparations contain sulfites which may cause allergic reaction; not recommended as a drug of first choice for the treatment of chronic pain in the elderly due to the accumulation of normeperidine; for acute pain, its use should be limited to 1-2 doses; tolerance or drug dependence may result from extended use

Adverse Reactions
>10%:
Cardiovascular: Hypotension
Central nervous system: Fatigue, drowsiness, dizziness
Gastrointestinal: Nausea, vomiting, constipation
Neuromuscular & skeletal: Weakness

Miscellaneous: Histamine release

1% to 10%:

Central nervous system: Nervousness, headache, restlessness, malaise, confusion

Gastrointestinal: Anorexia, stomach cramps, xerostomia, biliary spasm

Genitourinary: Ureteral spasms, decreased urination

Local: Pain at injection site

Respiratory: Dyspnea, shortness of breath

<1%: Mental depression, hallucinations, paradoxical CNS stimulation, increased intra-cranial pressure, rash, urticaria, paralytic ileus, physical and psychological dependence

Overdosage/Toxicology

Symptoms of overdose include CNS depression, respiratory depression, mydriasis, bradycardia, pulmonary edema, chronic tremors, CNS excitability, seizures

Treatment of an overdose includes support of the patient's airway, establishment of an I.V. line, and administration of naloxone 2 mg I.V. (0.01 mg/kg for children) with repeat administration as necessary up to a total of 10 mg.

Drug Interactions CYP2D6 enzyme substrate

Decreased effect: Phenytoin may decrease the analgesic effects

Increased toxicity: May aggravate the adverse effects of isoniazid; MAO inhibitors, fluoxetine, and other serotonin uptake inhibitors greatly potentiate the effects of meperidine; acute opioid overdose symptoms can be seen, including severe toxic reactions; CNS depressants, tricyclic antidepressants, phenothiazines may potentiate the effects of meperidine

Stability Meperidine injection should be stored at room temperature and protected from light and freezing; protect oral dosage forms from light

Incompatible with aminophylline, heparin, phenobarbital, phenytoin, and sodium bicarbonate

Mechanism of Action Binds to opiate receptors in the CNS, causing inhibition of ascending pain pathways, altering the perception of and response to pain; produces generalized CNS depression

Pharmacodynamics/Kinetics

Oral, S.C., I.M.:

Onset of analgesic effect: Within 10-15 minutes

Peak effect: Within 1 hour

Duration: 2-4 hours

I.V.: Onset of effects: Within 5 minutes

Distribution: Crosses the placenta; appears in breast milk

Protein binding: 65% to 75%

Metabolism: In the liver

Bioavailability: ~50% to 60%; increased with liver disease

Half-life:

Parent drug: Terminal phase: Neonates: 23 hours; range: 12-39 hours; Adults: 2.5-4 hours; Adults with liver disease: 7-11 hours

Normeperidine (active metabolite): 15-30 hours; is dependent on renal function and can accumulate with high doses or in patients with decreased renal function

Usual Dosage Doses should be titrated to appropriate analgesic effect; when changing route of administration, note that oral doses are about half as effective as parenteral dose

Children: Oral, I.M., I.V., S.C.: 1-1.5 mg/kg/dose every 3-4 hours as needed; 1-2 mg/kg as a single dose preoperative medication may be used; maximum 100 mg/dose

Adults: Oral, I.M., I.V.: S.C.: 50-150 mg/dose every 3-4 hours as needed

Elderly:

Oral: 50 mg every 4 hours

I.M.: 25 mg every 4 hours

Dosing adjustment in renal impairment:

Cl_{cr} 10-50 mL/minute: Administer at 75% of normal dose

Cl_{cr} <10 mL/minute: Administer at 50% of normal dose

Dosing adjustment/comments in hepatic disease: Increased narcotic effect in cirrhosis; reduction in dose more important for oral than I.V. route

Dietary Considerations

Alcohol: Additive CNS effects, avoid or limit alcohol; watch for sedation

Food: Glucose may cause hyperglycemia; monitor blood glucose concentrations

Administration

Meperidine may be administered I.M. (preferably), S.C., or I.V.

I.V. push should be given slowly, use of a 10 mg/mL concentration has been recommended

Monitoring Parameters Pain relief, respiratory and mental status, blood pressure; observe patient for excessive sedation, CNS depression, seizures, respiratory depression

Reference Range Therapeutic: 70-500 ng/mL (SI: 283-2020 nmol/L); Toxic: >1000 ng/mL (SI: >4043 nmol/L)

Test Interactions ↑ amylase (S), ↑ BSP retention, ↑ CPK (I.M. injections)

Patient Information Avoid alcohol, may cause drowsiness

Dosage Forms

Injection, as hydrochloride:

Multiple-dose vials: 50 mg/mL (30 mL); 100 mg/mL (20 mL)

Single-dose: 10 mg/mL (5 mL, 10 mL, 30 mL); 25 mg/dose (0.5 mL, 1 mL); 50 mg/dose (1 mL); 75 mg/dose (1 mL, 1.5 mL); 100 mg/dose (1 mL)

Syrup, as hydrochloride: 50 mg/5 mL (500 mL)

(Continued)

Meperidine *(Continued)*

Tablet, as hydrochloride: 50 mg, 100 mg

Meperidine and Promethazine (me PER i deen & proe METH a zeen)

U.S. Brand Names Mepergan®
Therapeutic Category Analgesic, Narcotic
Dosage Forms

Capsule: Meperidine hydrochloride 50 mg and promethazine hydrochloride 25 mg
Injection: Meperidine hydrochloride 25 mg and promethazine hydrochloride 25 per mL (2 mL, 10 mL)

♦ **Meperidine Hydrochloride** *see Meperidine on page 728*

Mephobarbital (me foe BAR bi tal)

U.S. Brand Names Mebaral®
Synonyms Methylphenobarbital
Therapeutic Category Anticonvulsant; Barbiturate; Sedative
Use Sedative; treatment of grand mal and petit mal epilepsy
Restrictions C-IV
Pregnancy Risk Factor D
Contraindications Hypersensitivity to mephobarbital, other barbiturates, or any component; pre-existing CNS depression; respiratory depression; severe uncontrolled pain; history of porphyria
Drug Interactions CYP2C, 2C8, and 2C19 enzyme substrate
Usual Dosage Oral:

Epilepsy:
Children: 6-12 mg/kg/day in 2-4 divided doses
Adults: 200-600 mg/day in 2-4 divided doses
Sedation:
Children:
<5 years: 16-32 mg 3-4 times/day
>5 years: 32-64 mg 3-4 times/day
Adults: 32-100 mg 3-4 times/day

Dosing adjustment in renal or hepatic impairment: Use with caution and reduce dosages
Additional Information Complete prescribing information for this medication should be consulted for additional detail
Dosage Forms Tablet: 32 mg, 50 mg, 100 mg

♦ **Mephyton® Oral** *see Phytonadione on page 926*

Mepivacaine (me PIV a kane)

U.S. Brand Names Carbocaine®; Isocaine® HCl; Polocaine®
Synonyms Mepivacaine Hydrochloride
Therapeutic Category Local Anesthetic, Injectable
Use Local anesthesia by nerve block; infiltration in dental procedures; **not** for use in spinal anesthesia
Pregnancy Risk Factor C
Contraindications Hypersensitivity to mepivacaine or any component or other amide anesthetics, allergy to sodium bisulfate
Warnings/Precautions Use with caution in patients with cardiac disease, renal disease, and hyperthyroidism; convulsions due to systemic toxicity leading to cardiac arrest have been reported presumably due to intravascular injection
Adverse Reactions <1%: Bradycardia, myocardial depression, hypotension, cardiovascular collapse, edema, anxiety, restlessness, disorientation, confusion, seizures, drowsiness, unconsciousness, chills, urticaria, nausea, vomiting, transient stinging or burning at injection site, tremors, blurred vision, tinnitus, respiratory arrest, anaphylactoid reactions, shivering
Overdosage/Toxicology

Symptoms of overdose include dizziness, cyanosis, tremors, bronchial spasm
Treatment is primarily symptomatic and supportive. Termination of anesthesia by pneumatic tourniquet inflation should be attempted when the agent is administered by infiltration or regional injection. Seizures commonly respond to diazepam, while hypotension responds to I.V. fluids and Trendelenburg positioning. Bradyarrhythmias (when the heart rate is <60) can be treated with I.V., I.M., or S.C. atropine 15 mcg/kg. With the development of metabolic acidosis, I.V. sodium bicarbonate 0.5-2 mEq/kg and ventilatory assistance should be instituted.

Mechanism of Action Mepivacaine is an amino amide local anesthetic similar to lidocaine; like all local anesthetics, mepivacaine acts by preventing the generation and conduction of nerve impulses
Pharmacodynamics/Kinetics

Onset of action: Epidural: Within 7-15 minutes
Duration: 2-2.5 hours; similar onset and duration is seen following infiltration
Protein binding: 70% to 85%
Metabolism: Chiefly in the liver by N-demethylation, hydroxylation, and glucuronidation
Half-life: 1.9 hours
Elimination: Urinary excretion (95% as metabolites)

Usual Dosage Children and Adults: Injectable local anesthetic: Varies with procedure, degree of anesthesia needed, vascularity of tissue, duration of anesthesia required, and physical condition of patient

Nursing Implications Before injecting, withdraw syringe plunger to ensure injection is not into vein or artery

Additional Information
Peripheral nerve block, caudal/epidural, therapeutic block: 1% or 2% solution
Transvaginal, paracervical block: 1% solution
Infiltration: 0.5% solution
Dental procedures: 2% or 3% solution with levonordefrin

Dosage Forms Injection, as hydrochloride: 1% [10 mg/mL] (30 mL, 50 mL); 1.5% [15 mg/mL] (30 mL); 2% [20 mg/mL] (20 mL, 50 mL); 3% [30 mg/mL] (1.8 mL)

♦ **Mepivacaine Hydrochloride** see Mepivacaine *on previous page*

Meprobamate (me proe BA mate)

U.S. Brand Names Equanil®; Miltown®; Neuramate®

Canadian Brand Names Apo®-Meprobamate; Meditran®; Novo-Mepro

Therapeutic Category Antianxiety Agent

Use Management of anxiety disorders; insomnia; preprocedure sedation and relaxation
Unlabeled use: Demonstrated value for muscle contraction, headache, premenstrual tension, external sphincter spasticity, muscle rigidity, opisthotonos-associated with tetanus

Restrictions C-IV

Pregnancy Risk Factor D

Contraindications Acute intermittent porphyria; hypersensitivity to meprobamate or any component; do not use in patients with pre-existing CNS depression, narrow-angle glaucoma, or severe uncontrolled pain

Warnings/Precautions Physical and psychological dependence and abuse may occur; not recommended in children <6 years of age; allergic reaction may occur in patients with history of dermatological condition (usually by fourth dose); use with caution in patients with renal or hepatic impairment, or with a history of seizures

Adverse Reactions
>10%: Central nervous system: Drowsiness, ataxia
1% to 10%:
Central nervous system: Dizziness
Dermatologic: Rashes
Gastrointestinal: Diarrhea, vomiting
Ocular: Blurred vision
Respiratory: Wheezing
<1%: Syncope, peripheral edema, paradoxical excitement, confusion, slurred speech, headache, euphoria, chills, purpura, dermatitis, Stevens-Johnson syndrome, stomatitis, thrombocytopenia, leukopenia, renal failure, dyspnea, bronchospasm

Overdosage/Toxicology
Symptoms of overdose include drowsiness, lethargy, ataxia, coma, hypotension, shock, death

Treatment is supportive following attempts to enhance drug elimination. Hypotension should be treated with I.V. fluids and/or Trendelenburg positioning. Dialysis and hemoperfusion have not demonstrated significant reductions in blood drug concentrations.

Drug Interactions Increased toxicity: CNS depressants may increase CNS depression

Mechanism of Action Precise mechanism is not yet clear, but many effects have been ascribed to its central depressant actions

Pharmacodynamics/Kinetics
Onset of sedation: Oral: Within 1 hour
Distribution: Crosses the placenta; appears in breast milk
Metabolism: Promptly in the liver
Half-life: 10 hours
Elimination: In urine (8% to 20% as unchanged drug) and feces (10% as metabolites)

Usual Dosage Oral:
Children 6-12 years: 100-200 mg 2-3 times/day
Sustained release: 200 mg twice daily
Adults: 400 mg 3-4 times/day, up to 2400 mg/day
Sustained release: 400-800 mg twice daily
Dosing interval in renal impairment:
Cl_{cr} 10-50 mL/minute: Administer every 9-12 hours
Cl_{cr} <10 mL/minute: Administer every 12-18 hours
Hemodialysis: Moderately dialyzable (20% to 50%)
Dosing adjustment in hepatic impairment: Probably necessary in patients with liver disease

Dietary Considerations Alcohol: Additive CNS effect, avoid use

Monitoring Parameters Mental status

Reference Range Therapeutic: 6-12 µg/mL (SI: 28-55 µmol/L); Toxic: >60 µg/mL (SI: >275 µmol/L)

Patient Information May cause drowsiness; avoid alcoholic beverages

Dosage Forms
Capsule, sustained release: 200 mg, 400 mg
Tablet: 200 mg, 400 mg, 600 mg

♦ **Mepron™** see Atovaquone *on page 109*

Mercaptopurine (mer kap toe PYOOR een)

Related Information
Cancer Chemotherapy Regimens *on page 1263*
Toxicities of Chemotherapeutic Agents *on page 1288*

U.S. Brand Names Purinethol®

Synonyms 6-Mercaptopurine; 6-MP

Therapeutic Category Antineoplastic Agent, Antimetabolite (Purine)

Use Treatment of acute leukemias (ALL or AML) maintenance therapy

Pregnancy Risk Factor D

Contraindications Hypersensitivity to mercaptopurine or any component; patients whose disease showed prior resistance to mercaptopurine or thioguanine; severe liver disease, severe bone marrow suppression

Warnings/Precautions The U.S. Food and Drug Administration (FDA) currently recommends that procedures for proper handling and disposal of antineoplastic agents be considered. Mercaptopurine may cause birth defects; potentially carcinogenic; adjust dosage in patients with renal impairment or hepatic failure; use with caution in patients with prior bone marrow suppression; patients may be at risk for pancreatitis. Toxicity to immunosuppressives is increased in elderly. Start with lowest recommended adult doses. Signs of infection, such as fever and WBC rise, may not occur. Lethargy and confusion may be more prominent signs of infection.

Adverse Reactions
>10%: Hepatic: 6-MP can cause an intrahepatic cholestasis and focal centrilobular necrosis manifested as hyperbilirubinemia, increased alkaline phosphatase, and increased AST. This may be dose related, occurring more frequently at doses >2.5 mg/kg/day; jaundice is noted 1-2 months into therapy, but has ranged from 1 week to 8 years.

1% to 10%:
Dermatologic: Hyperpigmentation, rash
Endocrine & metabolic: Hyperuricemia
Gastrointestinal: Nausea, vomiting, diarrhea, stomatitis, anorexia, stomach pain, and mucositis may require parenteral nutrition and dose reduction; 6-TG is less GI toxic than 6-MP
Hematologic: Leukopenia, thrombocytopenia, anemia may occur at high doses
Myelosuppressive:
WBC: Moderate
Platelets: Moderate
Onset (days): 7-10
Nadir (days): 14
Recovery (days): 21
Renal: Renal toxicity
<1%: Drug fever, dry and scaling rash, glossitis, tarry stools, eosinophilia

Overdosage/Toxicology Symptoms of overdose include:
Immediate: Nausea, vomiting
Delayed: Bone marrow suppression, hepatic necrosis, gastroenteritis

Drug Interactions
Decreased effect: Warfarin: 6-MP inhibits the anticoagulation effect of warfarin by an unknown mechanism
Increased toxicity:
Allopurinol: Can cause increased levels of 6-MP by inhibition of xanthine oxidase; decrease dose of 6-MP by 75% when both drugs are used concomitantly; seen only with oral 6-MP usage, not with I.V.; may potentiate effect of bone marrow suppression (reduce 6-MP to 25% of dose)
Doxorubicin: Synergistic liver toxicity with 6-MP in >50% of patients, which resolved with discontinuation of the 6-MP
Hepatotoxic drugs: Any agent which could potentially alter the metabolic function of the liver could produce higher drug levels and greater toxicities from either 6-MP or 6-TG

Stability Store at room temperature

Mechanism of Action Purine antagonist which inhibits DNA and RNA synthesis; acts as false metabolite and is incorporated into DNA and RNA, eventually inhibiting their synthesis. 6-MP is substituted for hypoxanthine; must be metabolized to active nucleotides once inside the cell.

Pharmacodynamics/Kinetics
Absorption: Variable and incomplete (16% to 50%)
Distribution: V_d = total body water; CNS penetration is poor
Protein binding: 30%
Metabolism: Undergoes first-pass metabolism in the GI mucosa and liver; metabolized in the liver by xanthine oxidase and methylation to sulfate conjugates, 6-thiouric acid and other inactive compounds
Half-life: Age dependent: Children: 21 minutes; Adults: 47 minutes
Time to peak serum concentration: Within 2 hours
Elimination: Prompt excretion in the urine; with high doses of I.V. 6-MP, the renal excretion of unchanged drug is 20% to 40% and can produce hematuria and crystalluria; at conventional doses renal elimination is minor

Usual Dosage Oral (refer to individual protocols):
Children: Maintenance: 75 mg/m²/day given once daily
Adults:
Induction: 2.5-5 mg/kg/day (100-200 mg)

Maintenance: 1.5-2.5 mg/kg/day **OR** 80-100 mg/m²/day given once daily

Elderly: Due to renal decline with age, start with lower recommended doses for adults

Dosing adjustment in renal or hepatic impairment: Dose should be reduced to avoid accumulation, but specific guidelines are not available

Hemodialysis: Removed; supplemental dosing is usually required

Monitoring Parameters CBC with differential and platelet count, liver function tests, uric acid, urinalysis

Patient Information Should not be taken with meals. Nausea and vomiting are rare with usual doses. Any signs of infection, easy bruising or bleeding, shortness of breath, or painful or burning urination should be brought to physician's attention. Nausea, vomiting, or hair loss sometimes occurs. The drug may cause permanent sterility and may cause birth defects. Contraceptive measures are recommended during therapy. The drug may be excreted in breast milk, therefore, an alternative form of feeding your baby should be used. Contraceptive measures are recommended during therapy.

Dosage Forms Tablet, scored: 50 mg

Extemporaneous Preparations A 50 mg/mL oral suspension was made by crushing the tablets, mixing with a volume of Cologel® suspending agent equal to ¹/₃ the final volume, and adding a 2:1 mixture of simple syrup and cherry syrup to make the final volume; stable for 14 days when stored in an amber glass bottle at room temperature

Dressman JB and Poust RI, "Stability of Allopurinol and of Five Antineoplastics in Suspension," *Am J Hosp Pharm*, 1983, 40:616-8.

♦ **6-Mercaptopurine** *see* Mercaptopurine *on previous page*

♦ **Mercapturic Acid** *see* Acetylcysteine *on page 26*

♦ **Meridia**® *see* Sibutramine *on page 1059*

♦ **Meronem**® *see* Meropenem *on this page*

Meropenem (mer oh PEN em)

Related Information
Antimicrobial Drugs of Choice *on page 1404*
Community-Acquired Pneumonia in Adults *on page 1419*

U.S. Brand Names Meronem®; Merrem® I.V.

Therapeutic Category Antibiotic, Anaerobic; Antibiotic, Carbapenem

Use Intra-abdominal infections (complicated appendicitis and peritonitis) caused by viridans group streptococci, *E. coli*, *K. pneumoniae*, *P. aeruginosa*, *B. fragilis*, *B. thetaiotaomicron*, and *Peptostreptococcus* sp; also indicated for bacterial meningitis in pediatric patients >3 months of age caused by *S. pneumoniae*, *H. influenzae*, and *N. meningitidis*; meropenem has also been used to treat soft tissue infections, febrile neutropenia, and urinary tract infections

Pregnancy Risk Factor B

Pregnancy/Breast-Feeding Implications Although no teratogenic or infant harm has been found in studies, excretion in breast milk is not known and this drug should be used during pregnancy and lactation only if clearly indicated

Contraindications Patients with known hypersensitivity to meropenem, any component, or other carbapenems (eg, imipenem); patients who have experienced anaphylactic reactions to other beta-lactams

Warnings/Precautions Pseudomembranous colitis and hypersensitivity reactions have occurred and often require immediate drug discontinuation; thrombocytopenia has been reported in patients with significant renal dysfunction; seizures have occurred in patients with underlying neurologic disorders (less frequent than with Primaxin®); safety and efficacy have not been established for children <3 months of age; superinfection possible with long courses of therapy

Adverse Reactions
1% to 10%:
Central nervous system: Headache (2.8%)
Dermatologic: Rash, pruritus (1% to 2%)
Gastrointestinal: Diarrhea (5%), nausea/vomiting (4%), constipation (1.2%)
Local: Pain at injection site (3%), phlebitis, thrombophlebitis (1%)
Respiratory: Apnea (1.2%)
<1%: Hypotension, heart failure (MI and arrhythmias), tachycardia, hypertension, edema, seizures, insomnia, agitation, confusion, hallucinations, depression, seizures, fever, urticaria, anorexia, flatulence, ileus, oral moniliasis, glossitis, dysuria, RBCs in urine, cholestatic jaundice, hepatic failure, increase LFTs, anemia, hypo- and hypercytosis, bleeding events (epistaxis, melena, etc), paresthesia, whole body pain, renal failure, increased creatinine/BUN

Overdosage/Toxicology
No cases of acute overdosage are reported which have resulted in symptoms
Supportive therapy recommended; meropenem and metabolite are removable by dialysis

Drug Interactions Increased effect: Probenecid competes with meropenem for active tubular secretion and inhibits the renal excretion of meropenem (half-life increased by 38%)

Stability Store at room temperature; when vials are reconstituted with NaCl/D₅W, they are stable for 2 hours/1 hour at room temperature or for 18 hours/8 hours when refrigerated; when diluted in minibags, they are stable for up to 24 hours refrigerated in NaCl and 6 hours in D₅W

Mechanism of Action Inhibits bacterial cell wall synthesis by binding to several of the penicillin-binding proteins, which in turn inhibit the final transpeptidation step of peptidoglycan synthesis in bacterial cell walls, thus inhibiting cell wall biosynthesis; bacteria (Continued)

Meropenem *(Continued)*

eventually lyse due to ongoing activity of cell wall autolytic enzymes (autolysins and murein hydrolases) while cell wall assembly is arrested

Pharmacodynamics/Kinetics

Distribution: V_d: ~0.3 L/kg in adults (0.4-0.5 L/kg in children); penetrates well into most body fluids and tissues; CSF concentrations approximate those of the plasma

Protein binding: 2%

Metabolism: Hepatic; metabolizes to open beta-lactam form (inactive); not metabolized by same enzyme as imipenem which results in toxic metabolite

Half-life:

Normal renal function: 1-1.5 hours

Cl_{cr} 30-80 mL/minute: 1.9-3.3 hours

Cl_{cr} 2-30 mL/minute: 3.82-5.7 hours

Time to peak tissue concentration: 1 hour following infusion

Elimination: Renal, ~25% as the inactive metabolite

Usual Dosage I.V.:

Neonates:

Preterm: 20 mg/kg/dose every 12 hours (may be increased to 40 mg/kg/dose if treating a highly resistant organism such as *Pseudomonas aeruginosa*)

Full-term (<3 months of age): 20 mg/kg/dose every 8 hours (may be increased to 40 mg/kg/dose if treating a highly resistant organism such as *Pseudomonas aeruginosa*)

Children >3 months (<50 kg):

Intra-abdominal infections: 20 mg/kg every 8 hours (maximum dose: 1 g every 8 hours)

Meningitis: 40 mg/kg every 8 hours (maximum dose: 2 g every 8 hours)

Children >50 kg:

Intra-abdominal infections: 1 g every 8 hours

Meningitis: 2 g every 8 hours

Adults: 1 g every 8 hours

Dosing adjustment in renal impairment: Adults:

Cl_{cr} 26-50 mL/minute: Administer 1 g every 12 hours

Cl_{cr} 10-25 mL/minute: Administer 500 mg every 12 hours

Cl_{cr} <10 mL/minute: Administer 500 mg every 24 hours

Dialysis: Meropenem and its metabolites are readily dialyzable

Continuous arteriovenous or venovenous hemodiafiltration (CAVH) effects: Dose as Cl_{cr} 10-50 mL/minute

Administration Administer I.V. infusion over 15-30 minutes; I.V. bolus injection over 3-5 minutes

Monitoring Parameters Monitor for signs of anaphylaxis during first dose

Additional Information 1 g of meropenem contains 90.2 mg of sodium as sodium carbonate (3.92 mEq)

Dosage Forms

Infusion: 500 mg (100 mL); 1 g (100 mL)

Infusion, ADD-vantage®: 500 mg (15 mL); 1 g (15 mL)

Injection: 25 mg/mL (20 mL); 33.3 mg/mL (30 mL)

♦ **Merrem® I.V.** *see* Meropenem *on previous page*

♦ **Meruvax® II** *see* Rubella Virus Vaccine, Live *on page 1043*

Mesalamine *(me SAL a meen)*

U.S. Brand Names Asacol® Oral; Pentasa® Oral; Rowasa® Rectal

Synonyms 5-Aminosalicylic Acid; 5-ASA; Fisalamine; Mesalazine

Therapeutic Category 5-Aminosalicylic Acid Derivative; Anti-inflammatory Agent, Rectal

Use

Oral: Remission and treatment of mildly to moderately active ulcerative colitis

Rectal: Treatment of active mild to moderate distal ulcerative colitis, proctosigmoiditis, or proctitis

Pregnancy Risk Factor B

Contraindications Known hypersensitivity to mesalamine, sulfasalazine, sulfites, or salicylates

Warnings/Precautions Pericarditis should be considered in patients with chest pain; pancreatitis should be considered in any patient with new abdominal complaints. Elderly may have difficulty administering and retaining rectal suppositories. Given renal function decline with aging, monitor serum creatinine often during therapy. Use caution in patients with impaired hepatic function.

Adverse Reactions

>10%:

Central nervous system: Headache, malaise

Gastrointestinal: Abdominal pain, cramps, flatulence, gas

1% to 10%: Dermatologic: Alopecia, rash

<1%: Anal irritation, acute intolerance syndrome (bloody diarrhea, severe abdominal cramps, severe headache)

Overdosage/Toxicology

Symptoms of overdose include decreased motor activity, diarrhea, vomiting, renal function impairment

Treatment is supportive; emesis, gastric lavage, and follow with activated charcoal slurry

Drug Interactions Decreased effect: Decreased digoxin bioavailability

Stability Unstable in presence of water or light; once foil has been removed, unopened bottles have an expiration of 1 year following the date of manufacture

Mechanism of Action Mesalamine (5-aminosalicylic acid) is the active component of sulfasalazine; the specific mechanism of action of mesalamine is unknown; however, it is thought that it modulates local chemical mediators of the inflammatory response, especially leukotrienes; action appears topical rather than systemic

Pharmacodynamics/Kinetics

Absorption: Rectal: ~15%; variable and dependent upon retention time, underlying GI disease, and colonic pH

Metabolism: In the liver by acetylation to acetyl-5-aminosalicylic acid (active) and to glucuronide conjugates; intestinal metabolism may also occur

Half-life: 5-ASA: 0.5-1.5 hours; Acetyl 5-ASA: 5-10 hours

Time to peak serum concentration: Within 4-7 hours

Elimination: Most metabolites are excreted in urine with <2% appearing in feces

Usual Dosage Adults (usual course of therapy is 3-6 weeks):

Oral:

Capsule: 1 g 4 times/day

Tablet: 800 mg 3 times/day

Retention enema: 60 mL (4 g) at bedtime, retained overnight, approximately 8 hours

Rectal suppository: Insert 1 suppository in rectum twice daily

Some patients may require rectal and oral therapy concurrently

Patient Information Retain enemas for 8 hours or as long as practical; shake bottle well; do not chew or break oral tablets; for suppositories, remove foil wrapper, avoid excessive handling

Nursing Implications Provide patient with copy of mesalamine administration instructions

Dosage Forms

Capsule, controlled release (Pentasa®): 250 mg

Suppository, rectal (Rowasa®): 500 mg

Suspension, rectal (Rowasa®): 4 g/60 mL (7s)

Tablet, enteric coated (Asacol®): 400 mg

- ◆ **Mesalazine** *see Mesalamine on previous page*
- ◆ **M-Eslon®** *see Morphine Sulfate on page 797*

Mesna (MES na)

Related Information

Cancer Chemotherapy Regimens *on page 1263*

U.S. Brand Names Mesnex™

Synonyms Sodium 2-Mercaptoethane Sulfonate

Therapeutic Category Antidote, Cyclophosphamide-induced Hemorrhagic Cystitis; Antidote, Ifosfamide-induced Hemorrhagic Cystitis

Use Detoxifying agent used as a protectant against hemorrhagic cystitis induced by ifosfamide and cyclophosphamide

Pregnancy Risk Factor B

Contraindications Hypersensitivity to mesna or other thiol compounds

Warnings/Precautions Examine morning urine specimen for hematuria prior to ifosfamide or cyclophosphamide treatment; if hematuria (>50 RBC/HPF) develops, reduce the ifosfamide/cyclophosphamide dose or discontinue the drug; will not prevent or alleviate other toxicities associated with ifosfamide or cyclophosphamide and will not prevent hemorrhagic cystitis in all patients. Allergic reactions have been reported in patients with autoimmune disorders. Symptoms ranged from mild hypersensitivity to systemic anaphylactic reactions.

Adverse Reactions

1% to 10%:

Cardiovascular: Hypotension

Central nervous system: Malaise, headache

Gastrointestinal: Diarrhea, nausea, vomiting, bad taste in mouth, soft stools

Neuromuscular & skeletal: Limb pain

<1%: Skin rash, itching

Drug Interactions

Decreased effect: Warfarin: Questionable alterations in coagulation control

Stability Diluted solutions are chemically and physically stable for 24 hours at room temperature; polypropylene syringes are stable for 9 days at refrigeration or room temperature; injection diluted for oral administration is stable 24 hours at refrigeration

Standard dose: Dose/100-1,000 mL D₅W or NS to a final concentration of 1-20 mg/mL

Incompatible with cisplatin

Compatible with bleomycin, cyclophosphamide, dexamethasone, etoposide, lorazepam, potassium chloride

Mechanism of Action Binds with and detoxifies acrolein and other urotoxic metabolites of ifosfamide and cyclophosphamide; detoxifying agent used to prevent hemorrhagic cystitis induced by ifosfamide and cyclophosphamide. In the kidney, mesna is reduced to a free thiol compound which reacts chemically with the acrolein and 4-hydroxy-ifosfamide resulting in detoxification.

Pharmacodynamics/Kinetics

Absorption: From the GI tract

Peak plasma levels: 2-3 hours after administration

Distribution: No tissue penetration; following glomerular filtration, mesna disulfide is reduced in renal tubules back to mesna

(Continued)

CNS depressants; do not alter dosage or discontinue without consulting physician; avoid excessive sunlight, yearly ophthalmic examinations are necessary

Dosage Forms

Injection, as besylate: 25 mg/mL (1 mL)

Liquid, oral, as besylate: 25 mg/mL (118 mL)

Tablet, as besylate: 10 mg, 25 mg, 50 mg, 100 mg

- ◆ **Mesoridazine Besylate** *see Mesoridazine on previous page*
- ◆ **Mestatin®** *see Nystatin on page 856*
- ◆ **Mestinon®** *see Pyridostigmine on page 997*
- ◆ **Mestinon®-SR** *see Pyridostigmine on page 997*
- ◆ **Mestinon Time-Span®** *see Pyridostigmine on page 997*

Mestranol and Norethindrone (MES tra nole & nor eth IN drone)

U.S. Brand Names Genora® 1/50; Nelova™ 1/50M; Norethin™ 1/50M; Norinyl® 1+50; Ortho-Novum™ 1/50

Synonyms Norethindrone and Mestranol

Therapeutic Category Contraceptive, Oral (Low Potency Estrogen, Low Potency Progestin); Contraceptive, Oral (Monophasic); Estrogen Derivative, Oral; Progestin

Use Prevention of pregnancy; treatment of hypermenorrhea, endometriosis, female hypogonadism [monophasic oral contraceptive]

Pregnancy Risk Factor X

Contraindications Known or suspected breast cancer, undiagnosed abnormal vaginal bleeding, carcinoma of the breast, estrogen-dependent tumor, pregnancy

Warnings/Precautions Use with caution in patients with a history of thromboembolism, stroke, myocardial infarction, liver tumor, hypertension, cardiac, renal or hepatic insufficiency; use of any progestin during the first 4 months of pregnancy is not recommended; risk of cardiovascular side effects increases in those women who smoke cigarettes and in women >35 years of age

Adverse Reactions

>10%:

Cardiovascular: Peripheral edema

Central nervous system: Headache

Endocrine: Enlargement of breasts, breast tenderness, increased libido

Achieving Proper Hormonal Balance in an Oral Contraceptive

Estrogen		Progestin	
Excess	Deficiency	Excess	Deficiency
Nausea, bloating	Early or midcycle breakthrough bleeding	Increased appetite	Late breakthrough bleeding
Cervical mucorrhea, polyposis	Increased spotting	Weight gain	Amenorrhea
Melasma	Hypomenorrhea	Tiredness, fatigue	Hypermenorrhea
Migraine headache		Hypomenorrhea	
Breast fullness or tenderness		Acne, oily scalp*	
Edema		Hair loss, hirsutism*	
Hypertension		Depression	
		Monilial vaginitis	
		Breast regression	

*Result of androgenic activity of progestins.

(Continued)

Restrictions C-II

Pregnancy Risk Factor C

Contraindications Known hypersensitivity to methamphetamine

Warnings/Precautions Cardiovascular disease, nephritis, angina pectoris, hypertension, glaucoma, patients with a history of drug abuse, known hypersensitivity to amphetamine

Adverse Reactions

>10%:

Cardiovascular: Arrhythmia

Central nervous system: False feeling of well being, nervousness, restlessness, insomnia

1% to 10%:

Cardiovascular: Hypertension

Central nervous system: Mood or mental changes, dizziness, lightheadedness, headache

Endocrine & metabolic: Changes in libido

Gastrointestinal: Diarrhea, nausea, vomiting, stomach cramps, constipation, anorexia, weight loss, xerostomia

Ocular: Blurred vision

Miscellaneous: Diaphoresis (increased)

<1%: Chest pain, CNS stimulation (severe), Tourette's syndrome, hyperthermia, seizures, paranoia, rash, urticaria, tolerance and withdrawal with prolonged use

Overdosage/Toxicology

Symptoms of overdose include seizures, hyperactivity, coma, hypertension

There is no specific antidote for amphetamine intoxication and the bulk of the treatment is supportive. Hyperactivity and agitation usually respond to reduced sensory input, however with extreme agitation haloperidol (2-5 mg I.M. for adults) may be required.

(Continued)

Mesna *(Continued)*

Metabolism: Rapidly oxidized intravascularly to mesna disulfide; mesna disulfide is reduced in renal tubules back to mesna following glomerular filtration.

Half-life: Parent drug: 24 minutes; Mesna disulfide: 72 minutes

Elimination: Unchanged drug and metabolite are excreted primarily in the urine; time it takes for maximum urinary mesna excretion: 1 hour after I.V. and 2-3 hours after an oral mesna dose

Usual Dosage Children and Adults (refer to individual protocols); oral dose is approximately equivalent to 2 times the I.V. dose

I.V.:

Ifosamide: 20% W/W of ifosfamide dose 15 minutes before ifosfamide administration and 4 and 8 hours after each dose of ifosfamide; **total daily dose is 60% to 100% of ifosfamide**; for high dose ifosfamide: 20% W/W 15 minutes before ifosfamide administration, and every 3 hours for 3-6 doses, some regimens use up to 160% of the total ifosfamide dose

Cyclophosphamide: 20% W/W of cyclophosphamide dose 15 minutes prior to cyclophosphamide administration and 4 and 8 hours after each dose of cyclophosphamide; **total daily dose = 60% to 200% of cyclophosphamide dose**

Oral: 40% W/W of the ifosfamide or cyclophosphamide agent dose in 3 doses at 4-hour intervals OR 20 mg/kg/dose every 4 hours x 3 (oral mesna is not recommended for the first dose before ifosfamide or cyclophosphamide)

Administration For oral administration, injection may be diluted in 1:1, 1:2, 1:10, 1:100 concentrations in carbonated beverages (cola, ginger ale, Pepsi®, Sprite®, Dr Pepper®, etc), juices (apple or orange), or whole milk (chocolate or white), and is stable 24 hours at refrigeration; used in conjunction with ifosfamide; examine morning urine specimen for hematuria prior to ifosfamide or cyclophosphamide treatment

Administer by I.V. infusion over 15-30 minutes or per protocol; mesna can be diluted in D₅W or NS to a final concentration of 1-20 mg/mL

Monitoring Parameters Urinalysis

Test Interactions False-positive urinary ketones with Multistix® or Labstix®

Dosage Forms Injection: 100 mg/mL (2 mL, 4 mL, 10 mL)

♦ **Mesnex™** *see Mesna on previous page*

Mesoridazine *(mez oh RID a zeen)*

Related Information

Antipsychotic Agents Comparison *on page 1305*

U.S. Brand Names Serentil®

Synonyms Mesoridazine Besylate

Therapeutic Category Antipsychotic Agent; Phenothiazine Derivative

Use Symptomatic management of psychotic disorders, including schizophrenia, behavioral problems, alcoholism as well as reducing anxiety and tension occurring in neurosis

Pregnancy Risk Factor C

Contraindications Hypersensitivity to mesoridazine or any component, cross-sensitivity with other phenothiazines may exist

Warnings/Precautions Safety in children <6 months of age has not been established; use with caution in patients with cardiovascular disease or seizures; benefits of therapy must be weighed against risks of therapy; doses >1 g/day frequently cause pigmentary retinopathy; some products contain sulfites and/or tartrazine; use with caution in patients with narrow-angle glaucoma, bone marrow suppression, severe liver disease

---

Methacholine *(Continued)*

units by multiplying number of breaths by concentration given. Total cumulative units is the sum of cumulative units for each concentration given. See table.

Methacholine

Vial	Serial Concentration (mg/mL)	No. of Breaths	Cumulative Units per Concentration	Total Cumulative Units
E	0.025	5	0.125	0.125
D	0.25	5	1.25	1.375
C	2.5	5	12.5	13.88
B	10	5	50	63.88
A	25	5	125	188.88

Determine FEV_1 within 5 minutes of challenge, a positive challenge is a 20% reduction in FEV_1

Dosage Forms Powder for reconstitution, inhalation, as chloride: 100 mg/5 mL

♦ **Methacholine Chloride** *see Methacholine on previous page*

Methadone *(METH a done)*

Related Information

Narcotic Agonists Comparison *on page 1328*

U.S. Brand Names Dolophine®

Canadian Brand Names Methadose®

Synonyms Methadone Hydrochloride

Methenamine *(Continued)*

Tablet, as mandelate, enteric coated: 500 mg, 1 g

♦ **Methenamine Hippurate** *see Methenamine on previous page*

♦ **Methenamine Mandelate** *see Methenamine on previous page*

♦ **Methergine®** *see Methylergonovine on page 760*

Methicillin *(meth i SIL in)*

U.S. Brand Names Staphcillin®

Synonyms Dimethoxyphenyl Penicillin Sodium; Methicillin Sodium; Sodium Methicillin

Therapeutic Category Antibiotic, Penicillin

Use Treatment of susceptible bacterial infections such as osteomyelitis, septicemia, endocarditis, and CNS infections due to penicillinase-producing strains of *Staphylococcus*; other antistaphylococcal penicillins are usually preferred

Pregnancy Risk Factor B

Contraindications Known hypersensitivity to methicillin or any penicillin

Warnings/Precautions Elimination rate will be slow in neonates; modify dosage in patients with renal impairment and in the elderly; use with caution in patients with cephalosporin hypersensitivity

Adverse Reactions

1% to 10%:

Dermatologic: Rash

Renal: Acute interstitial nephritis

<1%: Fever, rash, hemorrhagic cystitis, eosinophilia, anemia, leukopenia, neutropenia, thrombocytopenia, phlebitis, serum sickness-like reactions

Overdosage/Toxicology

Symptoms of penicillin overdose include neuromuscular hypersensitivity (agitation, hallucinations, asterixis, encephalopathy, confusion, and seizures) and electrolyte imbalance with potassium or sodium salts, especially in renal failure

Hemodialysis may be helpful to aid in the removal of the drug from the blood, otherwise most treatment is supportive or symptom directed

Drug Interactions

Decreased effect: Efficacy of oral contraceptives may be reduced

Increased effect: Disulfiram, probenecid may increase penicillin levels, increased effect of anticoagulants

Stability Reconstituted solution is stable for 24 hours at room temperature and 4 days when refrigerated; discard solutions if it has a distinctive hydrogen sulfide odor and/or color turns to a deep orange; **incompatible** with aminoglycosides and tetracyclines

Mechanism of Action Inhibits bacterial cell wall synthesis by binding to one or more of the penicillin binding proteins (PBPs); which in turn inhibits the final transpeptidation step of peptidoglycan synthesis in bacterial cell walls, thus inhibiting cell wall biosynthesis. Bacteria eventually lyse due to ongoing activity of cell wall autolytic enzymes (autolysins and murein hydrolases) while cell wall assembly is arrested.

Pharmacodynamics/Kinetics

Distribution: Crosses the placenta; distributes into milk

Protein binding: 40%

Metabolism: Only partially

Half-life (with normal renal function):

Neonates: <2 weeks: 2-3.9 hours; >2 weeks: 0.9-3.3 hours

Children 2-16 years: 0.8 hour

Adults: 0.4-0.5 hour

Time to peak serum concentration: I.M.: 0.5-1 hour; I.V. infusion: Within 5 minutes

Elimination: ~60% to 70% of dose eliminated unchanged in urine within 4 hours by tubular secretion and glomerular filtration

Usual Dosage I.M., I.V.:

Infants:

>7 days and >2000 g: 100 mg/kg/day in divided doses every 6 hours (for meningitis: 200 mg/kg/day)

>7 days and >2000 g: 75 mg/kg/day in divided doses every 8 hours (for meningitis: 150 mg/kg/day)

<7 days and >2000 g: Same as above

<7 days and <2000 g: 50 mg/kg/day in divided doses every 12 hours (for meningitis: 100 mg/kg/day)

Children: 100-300 mg/kg/day in divided doses every 4-6 hours

Adults: 4-12 g/day in divided doses every 4-6 hours

Dosing interval in renal impairment:

Cl_{cr} 10-50 mL/minute: Administer every 6-8 hours

Cl_{cr} <10 mL/minute: Administer every 8-12 hours

Hemodialysis: Not dialyzable (0% to 5%)

Administration Can be administered IVP at a rate not to exceed 200 mg/minute or intermittent infusion over 20-30 minutes; final concentration for administration should not exceed 20 mg/mL

Monitoring Parameters Observe for signs and symptoms of anaphylaxis during first dose

Test Interactions Interferes with tests for urinary and serum proteins, uric acid, urinary steroids; may cause false-positive Coombs' test; may inactivate aminoglycosides *in vitro*

Additional Information Sodium content of 1 g injection: 59.8-71.3 mg (2.6-3.1 mEq)

Dosage Forms Powder for injection, as sodium: 1 g, 4 g, 6 g, 10 g

◆ **Methicillin Sodium** see Methicillin *on previous page*

Methimazole (meth IM a zole)
U.S. Brand Names Tapazole®
Synonyms Thiamazole
Therapeutic Category Antithyroid Agent
Use Palliative treatment of hyperthyroidism, return the hyperthyroid patient to a normal metabolic state prior to thyroidectomy, and to control thyrotoxic crisis that may accompany thyroidectomy. The use of antithyroid thioamides is as effective in elderly as they are in younger adults; however, the expense, potential adverse effects, and inconvenience (compliance, monitoring) make them undesirable. The use of radioiodine due to ease of administration and less concern for long-term side effects and reproduction problems (some older males) makes it a more appropriate therapy.
Pregnancy Risk Factor D
Contraindications Hypersensitivity to methimazole or any component, nursing mothers
Warnings/Precautions Use with extreme caution in patients receiving other drugs known to cause myelosuppression particularly agranulocytosis, patients >40 years of age; avoid doses >40 mg/day (↑ myelosuppression); may cause acneiform eruptions or worsen the condition of the thyroid
Adverse Reactions
>10%:
Central nervous system: Fever
Hematologic: Leukopenia
1% to 10%:
Central nervous system: Dizziness
Gastrointestinal: Nausea, vomiting, stomach pain, abnormal taste
Hematologic: Agranulocytosis
Miscellaneous: SLE-like syndrome
<1%: Edema, drowsiness, vertigo, headache, rash, urticaria, pruritus, alopecia, goiter, constipation, weight gain, nephrotic syndrome, thrombocytopenia, aplastic anemia, cholestatic jaundice, arthralgia, paresthesia, swollen salivary glands
Overdosage/Toxicology
Symptoms of overdose include nausea, vomiting, epigastric distress, headache, fever, arthralgia, pruritus, edema, pancytopenia, and signs of hypothyroidism
Management of overdose is supportive
Drug Interactions Increased toxicity: Iodinated glycerol, lithium, potassium iodide; anticoagulant activity increased
Stability Protect from light
Mechanism of Action Inhibits the synthesis of thyroid hormones by blocking the oxidation of iodine in the thyroid gland, blocking iodine's ability to combine with tyrosine to form thyroxine and triiodothyronine (T_3), does not inactivate circulating T_4 and T_3
Pharmacodynamics/Kinetics
Onset of antithyroid effect: Oral: 12-18 hours
Duration: 36-72 hours
Distribution: Concentrated in the thyroid gland; crosses the placenta; appears in breast milk (1:1)
Protein binding, plasma: None
Metabolism: In the liver
Bioavailability: 80% to 95%
Half-life: 4-13 hours
Elimination: 80% renal
Usual Dosage Oral: Administer in 3 equally divided doses at approximately 8-hour intervals
Children: Initial: 0.4 mg/kg/day in 3 divided doses; maintenance: 0.2 mg/kg/day in 3 divided doses up to 30 mg/24 hours maximum
Alternatively: Initial: 0.5-0.7 mg/kg/day **or** 15-20 mg/m²/day in 3 divided doses
Maintenance: $1/3$ to $2/3$ of the initial dose beginning when the patient is euthroid
Maximum: 30 mg/24 hours
Adults: Initial: 15 mg/day for mild hyperthyroidism; 30-40 mg/day in moderately severe hyperthyroidism; 60 mg/day in severe hyperthyroidism; maintenance: 5-15 mg/day
Adjust dosage as required to achieve and maintain serum T_3, T_4, and TSH levels in the normal range. An elevated T_3 may be the sole indicator of inadequate treatment. An elevated TSH indicates excessive antithyroid treatment.
Dosing adjustment in renal impairment: Adjustment is not necessary
Monitoring Parameters Monitor for signs of hypothyroidism, hyperthyroidism, T_4, T_3; CBC with differential, liver function (baseline and as needed), serum thyroxine, free thyroxine index
Patient Information Take with meals, take at regular intervals around-the-clock; notify physician if persistent fever, sore throat, fatigue, unusual bleeding or bruising occurs
Dosage Forms Tablet: 5 mg, 10 mg

Methocarbamol (meth oh KAR ba mole)
U.S. Brand Names Delaxin®; Marbaxin®; Robaxin®; Robomol®
Therapeutic Category Skeletal Muscle Relaxant
Use Treatment of muscle spasm associated with acute painful musculoskeletal conditions, supportive therapy in tetanus
Pregnancy Risk Factor C
(Continued)

Methocarbamol *(Continued)*

Contraindications Renal impairment, hypersensitivity to methocarbamol or any component

Warnings/Precautions Rate of injection should not exceed 3 mL/minute; solution is hypertonic; avoid extravasation; use with caution in patients with a history of seizures

Adverse Reactions

>10%: Central nervous system: Drowsiness, dizziness, lightheadedness

1% to 10%:

Cardiovascular: Flushing of face, bradycardia

Dermatologic: Allergic dermatitis

Gastrointestinal: Nausea, vomiting

Ocular: Nystagmus

Respiratory: Nasal congestion

<1%: Syncope, convulsion, leukopenia, pain at injection site, thrombophlebitis, blurred vision, renal impairment, allergic manifestations

Overdosage/Toxicology

Symptoms of overdose include cardiac arrhythmias, nausea, vomiting, drowsiness, coma

Treatment is supportive following attempts to enhance drug elimination. Hypotension should be treated with I.V. fluids and/or Trendelenburg positioning. Dialysis and hemoperfusion and osmotic diuresis have all been useful in reducing serum drug concentrations. The patient should be observed for possible relapses due to incomplete gastric emptying.

Drug Interactions Increased effect/toxicity with CNS depressants

Mechanism of Action Causes skeletal muscle relaxation by reducing the transmission of impulses from the spinal cord to skeletal muscle

Pharmacodynamics/Kinetics

Onset of muscle relaxation: Oral: Within 30 minutes

Metabolism: In the liver

Half-life: 1-2 hours

Time to peak serum concentration: ~2 hours

Elimination: Metabolites renally excreted

Usual Dosage

Children: Recommended **only** for use in tetanus I.V.: 15 mg/kg/dose or 500 mg/m^2/dose, may repeat every 6 hours if needed; maximum dose: 1.8 g/m^2/day for 3 days only

Adults: Muscle spasm:

Oral: 1.5 g 4 times/day for 2-3 days, then decrease to 4-4.5 g/day in 3-6 divided doses

I.M., I.V.: 1 g every 8 hours if oral not possible

Dosing adjustment/comments in renal impairment: Do not administer parenteral formulation to patients with renal dysfunction

Dietary Considerations Alcohol: Additive CNS effect, avoid use

Administration Maximum rate: 3 mL/minute

Patient Information May cause drowsiness, impair judgment or coordination; avoid alcohol or other CNS depressants; may turn urine brown, black, or green; notify physician of rash, itching, or nasal congestion

Nursing Implications Monitor closely for extravasation of I.V. injection

Dosage Forms

Injection: 100 mg/mL in polyethylene glycol 50% (10 mL)

Tablet: 500 mg, 750 mg

Methocarbamol and Aspirin *(meth oh KAR ba mole & AS pir in)*

U.S. Brand Names Robaxisal®

Therapeutic Category Skeletal Muscle Relaxant

Dosage Forms Tablet: Methocarbamol 400 mg and aspirin 325 mg

Methohexital *(meth oh HEKS i tal)*

Related Information

Adult ACLS Algorithm, Electrical Conversion *on page 1453*

U.S. Brand Names Brevital® Sodium

Canadian Brand Names Brietal® Sodium

Synonyms Methohexital Sodium

Therapeutic Category Barbiturate; General Anesthetic

Use Induction and maintenance of general anesthesia for short procedures

Can be used in pediatric patients >1 month of age as follows: For rectal or intramuscular induction of anesthesia prior to the use of other general anesthetic agents, as an adjunct to subpotent inhalational anesthetic agents for short surgical procedures, or for short surgical, diagnostic, or therapeutic procedures associated with minimal painful stimuli

Restrictions C-IV

Pregnancy Risk Factor C

Contraindications Porphyria, hypersensitivity to methohexital or any component

Warnings/Precautions Use with extreme caution in patients with liver impairment, asthma, cardiovascular instability

Adverse Reactions

>10%: Local: Pain on I.M. injection

1% to 10%: Gastrointestinal: Cramping, diarrhea, rectal bleeding

<1%: Hypotension, peripheral vascular collapse, seizures, headache, nausea, vomiting, hemolytic anemia, thrombophlebitis, tremor, twitching, rigidity, involuntary muscle movement, radial nerve palsy, apnea, respiratory depression, laryngospasm, coughing, hiccups

Overdosage/Toxicology
Symptoms of overdose include apnea, tachycardia, hypotension
Treatment is primarily supportive with mechanical ventilation if needed

Drug Interactions CNS depressants worsen CNS depression

Stability Do not dilute with solutions containing bacteriostatic agents; solutions are alkaline (pH 9.5-11) and **incompatible** with acids (eg, atropine sulfate, succinylcholine, silicone), also **incompatible** with phenol-containing solutions and silicone

Mechanism of Action Ultra short-acting I.V. barbiturate anesthetic

Usual Dosage Doses must be titrated to effect
Children 3-12 years:
    I.M.: Preop: 5-10 mg/kg/dose
    I.V.: Induction: 1-2 mg/kg/dose
    Rectal: Preop/induction: 20-35 mg/kg/dose; usual 25 mg/kg/dose; administer as 10% aqueous solution
Adults: I.V.: Induction: 50-120 mg to start; 20-40 mg every 4-7 minutes
    Dosing adjustment/comments in hepatic impairment: Lower dosage and monitor closely

Nursing Implications Avoid extravasation or intra-arterial administration

Dosage Forms Injection, as sodium: 500 mg, 2.5 g, 5 g

♦ **Methohexital Sodium** see Methohexital *on previous page*

Methotrexate (meth oh TREKS ate)

Related Information
Cancer Chemotherapy Regimens *on page 1263*
Toxicities of Chemotherapeutic Agents *on page 1288*

U.S. Brand Names Folex® PFS; Rheumatrex®

Synonyms Amethopterin; Methotrexate Sodium; MTX

Therapeutic Category Antineoplastic Agent, Antimetabolite; Antineoplastic Agent, Folate Antagonist; Antineoplastic Agent, Irritant; Immunosuppressant Agent

Use Treatment of trophoblastic neoplasms; leukemias; psoriasis; rheumatoid arthritis; breast, head and neck, and lung carcinomas; osteosarcoma; sarcomas; carcinoma of gastric, esophagus, testes; lymphomas

Pregnancy Risk Factor D

Contraindications Hypersensitivity to methotrexate or any component; severe renal or hepatic impairment; pre-existing profound bone marrow suppression in patients with psoriasis or rheumatoid arthritis, alcoholic liver disease, AIDS, pre-existing blood dyscrasias

Warnings/Precautions The U.S. Food and Drug Administration (FDA) currently recommends that procedures for proper handling and disposal of antineoplastic agents be considered

May cause photosensitivity type reaction. Reduce dosage in patients with renal or hepatic impairment; drain ascites and pleural effusions prior to treatment; use with caution in patients with peptic ulcer disease, ulcerative colitis, pre-existing bone marrow suppression. Monitor closely for pulmonary disease; use with caution in the elderly.

Because of the possibility of severe toxic reactions, fully inform patient of the risks involved. Do not use in women of childbearing age unless benefit outweighs risks; may cause hepatotoxicity, fibrosis, and cirrhosis, along with marked bone marrow depression. Death from intestinal perforation may occur.

Patients should receive 1-2 L of I.V. fluid prior to initiation of high-dose methotrexate. Patients should receive sodium bicarbonate to alkalinize their urine during and after high-dose methotrexate (urine SG <1.010 and pH >7 should be maintained for at least 24 hours after infusion).

Toxicity to methotrexate or any immunosuppressive is increased in elderly; must monitor carefully. For rheumatoid arthritis and psoriasis, immunosuppressive therapy should only be used when disease is active and less toxic, traditional therapy is ineffective. Recommended doses should be reduced when initiating therapy in elderly due to possible decreased metabolism, reduced renal function, and presence of interacting diseases and drugs.

Methotrexate penetrates slowly into 3rd space fluids, such as pleural effusions or ascites, and exits slowly from these compartments (slower than from plasma).

Adverse Reactions
>10%:
    Central nervous system (with I.T. administration only):
        Arachnoiditis: Acute reaction manifested as severe headache, nuchal rigidity, vomiting, and fever; may be alleviated by reducing the dose
        Subacute toxicity: 10% of patients treated with 12-15 mg/m^2 of I.T. MTX may develop this in the second or third week of therapy; consists of motor paralysis of extremities, cranial nerve palsy, seizures, or coma. This has also been seen in pediatric cases receiving very high-dose I.V. MTX (when enough MTX can get across into the CSF).
        Demyelinating encephalopathy: Seen months or years after receiving MTX; usually in association with cranial irradiation or other systemic chemotherapy

(Continued)

Methotrexate *(Continued)*

Dermatologic: Reddening of skin

Endocrine & metabolic: Hyperuricemia, defective oogenesis or spermatogenesis

Gastrointestinal: Ulcerative stomatitis, glossitis, gingivitis, nausea, vomiting, diarrhea, anorexia, intestinal perforation, mucositis (dose-dependent; appears in 3-7 days after therapy, resolving within 2 weeks)

Emetic potential:

<100 mg: Moderately low (10% to 30%)

≥100 mg or <250 mg: Moderate (30% to 60%)

≥250 mg: Moderately high (60% to 90%)

Hematologic: Leukopenia, thrombocytopenia

Renal: Renal failure, azotemia, nephropathy

Respiratory: Pharyngitis

1% to 10%:

Cardiovascular: Vasculitis

Central nervous system: Dizziness, malaise, encephalopathy, seizures, fever, chills

Dermatitis: Alopecia, rash, photosensitivity, depigmentation or hyperpigmentation of skin

Endocrine & metabolic: Diabetes

Genitourinary: Cystitis

Hematologic: Hemorrhage

Myelosuppressive: This is the primary dose-limiting factor (along with mucositis) of MTX; occurs about 5-7 days after MTX therapy, and should resolve within 2 weeks

WBC: Mild

Platelets: Moderate

Onset (days): 7

Nadir (days): 10

Recovery (days): 21

Hepatic: Cirrhosis and portal fibrosis have been associated with chronic MTX therapy; acute elevation of liver enzymes are common after high-dose MTX, and usually resolve within 10 days

Neuromuscular & skeletal: Arthralgia

Ocular: Blurred vision

Renal: Renal dysfunction: Manifested by an abrupt rise in serum creatinine and BUN and a fall in urine output; more common with high-dose MTX, and may be due to precipitation of the drug. The best treatment is prevention: Aggressively hydrate with 3 L/m^2/day starting 12 hours before therapy and continue for 24-36 hours; alkalinize the urine by adding 50 mEq of bicarbonate to each liter of fluid; keep urine flow >100 mL/hour and urine pH >7.

Respiratory: Pneumonitis: Associated with fever, cough, and interstitial pulmonary infiltrates; treatment is to withhold MTX during the acute reaction

Miscellaneous: Anaphylaxis, decreased resistance to infection

Overdosage/Toxicology

Symptoms of overdose include nausea, vomiting, alopecia, melena, renal failure

Antidote: Leucovorin; administer as soon as toxicity is seen; administer 10 mg/m^2 orally or parenterally; follow with 10 mg/m^2 orally every 6 hours for 72 hours. After 24 hours following methotrexate administration, if the serum creatinine is ≥50% premethotrexate serum creatinine, increase leucovorin dose to 100 mg/m^2 every 3 hours until serum MTX level is $<5 \times 10^{-8}$M. Hydration and alkalinization may be used to prevent precipitation of MTX or MTX metabolites in the renal tubules. Toxicity in low dose range is negligible, but may present mucositis and mild bone marrow suppression; severe bone marrow toxicity can result from overdose. Neither peritoneal nor hemodialysis have been shown to ↑ elimination. Leucovorin should be administered intravenously, never intrathecally, for over doses of intrathecal methotrexate.

Drug Interactions

Decreased effect:

Corticosteroids: Reported to decrease uptake of MTX into leukemia cells. Administration of these drugs should be separated by 12 hours. Dexamethasone has been reported to not affect methotrexate influx into cells.

Decreases phenytoin, 5-FU

Increased toxicity:

Live virus vaccines → vaccinia infections

Vincristine: Inhibits MTX efflux from the cell, leading to increased and prolonged MTX levels in the cell; the dose of VCR needed to produce this effect is not achieved clinically

Organic acids: Salicylates, sulfonamides, probenecid, and high doses of penicillins compete with MTX for transport and reduce renal tubular secretion. Salicylates and sulfonamides may also displace MTX from plasma proteins, ↑ MTX levels.

Ara-C: Increases formation of the Ara-C nucleotide can occur when MTX precedes Ara-C, thus promoting the action of Ara-C

Cyclosporine: CSA and MTX interfere with each others renal elimination, which may result in increased toxicity

Nonsteroidal anti-inflammatory drugs (NSAIDs): Should not be used during moderate or high-dose methotrexate due to increased and prolonged methotrexate levels may increase toxicity

Stability

Store intact vials at room temperature (15°C to 25°C) and protect from light

Use preservative-free preparations for high-dose and intrathecal administration

Dilute powder with D_5W or NS to a concentration of ≤25 mg/mL (20 mg and 50 mg vials) and 50 mg/mL (1 g vial) as follows; solution is stable for 7 days at room temperature

20 mg = 20 mL (1 mg/mL)
50 mg = 5 mL (10 mg/mL)
1 g = 19.4 mL (50 mg/mL)

Further dilution in D_5W or NS is stable for 24 hours at room temperature (21°C to 25°C)

Standard I.V. dilution:
Maximum syringe size for IVP is a 30 mL syringe and syringe should be ≤75% full

Doses <149 mg: Administer slow I.V. push
Dose/syringe (concentration ≤25 mg/mL)

Doses of 150-499 mg: Administer IVPB over 20-30 minutes
Dose/50 mL D_5W or NS

Doses of 500-1500 mg: Administer IVPB over ≥60 minutes
Dose/250 mL D_5W or NS

Doses of >1500 mg: Administer IVPB over 1-6 hours
Dose/1000 mL D_5W or NS

Standard I.M. dilution: Dose/syringe (concentration = 25 mg/mL)
I.V. dilutions are stable for 8 days at room temperature (25°C)

Intrathecal solutions in 3-20 mL LR are stable for 7 days at room temperature (30°C); compatible with cytarabine and hydrocortisone in LR or NS for 7 days at room temperature (25°C)

Standard intrathecal dilution: Dose/3-5 mL LR +/- methotrexate (12 mg) +/- hydrocortisone (15-25 mg)

Intrathecal dilutions are stable for 7 days at room temperature (25°C) but due to sterility issues, use within 24 hours

Mechanism of Action An antimetabolite that inhibits DNA synthesis and cell reproduction in malignant cells

Folates must be in the reduced form (FH_4) to be active
Folates are activated by dihydrofolate reductase (DHFR)
DHFR is inhibited by MTX (by binding irreversibly), causing an increase in the intracellular dihydrofolate pool (the inactive cofactor) and inhibition of both purine and thymidylate synthesis (TS)
MTX enters the cell through an energy-dependent and temperature-dependent process which is mediated by an intramembrane protein; this carrier mechanism is also used by naturally occurring reduced folates, including folinic acid (leucovorin), making this a competitive process
At high drug concentrations (>20 μM), MTX enters the cell by a second mechanism which is not shared by reduced folates; the process may be passive diffusion or a specific, saturable process, and provides a rationale for high-dose MTX
A small fraction of MTX is converted intracellularly to polyglutamates, which leads to a prolonged inhibition of DHFR

The MOA in the treatment of rheumatoid arthritis is unknown, but may affect immune function

In psoriasis, methotrexate is thought to target rapidly proliferating epithelial cells in the skin

Pharmacodynamics/Kinetics
Absorption:
Oral: Rapid; well absorbed orally at low doses (<30 mg/m^2), incomplete absorption after large doses
I.M. injection: Completely absorbed
Distribution: Drug penetrates slowly into 3rd space fluids, such as pleural effusions or ascites, and exits slowly from these compartments (slower than from plasma); crosses the placenta with small amounts appearing in breast milk; does not achieve therapeutic concentrations in the CSF and must be given intrathecally if given for CNS prophylaxis or treatment; sustained concentrations are retained in the kidney and liver
Protein binding: 50%
Metabolism: <10% metabolized; degraded by intestinal flora to DAMPA by carboxypeptidase; aldehyde oxidase in the liver converts MTX to 7-OH MTX; polyglutamates are produced intracellularly and are just as potent as MTX; their production is dose and duration dependent and are slowly eliminated by the cell once they are formed
Half-life: 8-12 hours with high doses and 3-10 hours with low doses
Time to peak serum concentration: Oral: 1-2 hours; Parenteral: 30-60 minutes
Elimination: Small amounts excreted in the feces; primarily excreted in the urine (44% to 100%) via glomerular filtration and active transport
Miscellaneous: Cytotoxicity is determined by both drug concentration and duration of cell exposure; extracellular drug concentrations of 1 x 10^{-8}M are required to inhibit thymidylate synthesis; reduced folates are able to rescue cells and reverse MTX toxicity if given within 48 hours of the MTX dose; at concentrations of >10 μM MTX, reduced folates are no longer effective

Usual Dosage Refer to individual protocols. May be administered orally, I.M., intra-arterially, intrathecally, or I.V.

Leucovorin may be administered concomitantly or within 24 hours of methotrexate - refer to Leucovorin Calcium *on page 666* for details
(Continued)

Methotrexate *(Continued)*

Children:
Dermatomyositis: Oral: 15-20 mg/m^2/week as a single dose once weekly or 0.3-1 mg/kg/dose once weekly

Juvenile rheumatoid arthritis: Oral, I.M.: 5-15 mg/m^2/week as a single dose **or** as 3 divided doses given 12 hours apart

Antineoplastic dosage range:
Oral, I.M.: 7.5-30 mg/m^2/week **or** every 2 weeks
I.V.: 10-18,000 mg/m^2 bolus dosing **or** continuous infusion over 6-42 hours

Methotrexate Dosing Schedules

Dose	Route	Frequency
Conventional		
15-20 mg/m^2	P.O.	Twice weekly
30-50 mg/m^2	P.O., I.V.	Weekly
15 mg/day for 5 days	P.O., I.M.	Every 2-3 weeks
Intermediate		
50-150 mg/m^2	I.V. push	Every 2-3 weeks
240 mg/m^{2*}	I.V. infusion	Every 4-7 days
0.5-1 g/m^{2*}	I.V. infusion	Every 2-3 weeks
High		
1-12 g/m^{2*}	I.V. infusion	Every 1-3 weeks

*Followed with leucovorin rescue - refer to Leucovorin monograph for details.

Pediatric solid tumors (high-dose): I.V.:
<12 years: 12 g/m^2 (dosage range: 12-18 g)
≥12 years: 8 g/m^2 (maximum: 18 g)

Acute lymphocytic leukemia (intermediate-dose): I.V.: Loading: 100 mg/m^2 over 1 hour, followed by a 35-hour infusion of 900 mg/m^2/day

Meningeal leukemia: I.T.: 10-15 mg/m^2 (maximum dose: 15 mg) **or**
≤3 months: 3 mg/dose
4-11 months: 6 mg/dose
1 year: 8 mg/dose
2 years: 10 mg/dose
≥3 years: 12 mg/dose

I.T. doses are prepared with preservative-free MTX only. Hydrocortisone may be added to the I.T. preparation; total volume should range from 3-6 mL. Doses should be repeated at 2- to 5-day intervals until CSF counts return to normal followed by a dose once weekly for 2 weeks then monthly thereafter.

Adults: I.V.: Range is wide from 30-40 mg/m^2/week to 100-12,000 mg/m^2 with leucovorin rescue

Doses **not** requiring leucovorin rescue range from 30-40 mg/m^2 I.V. or I.M. repeated weekly, or oral regimens of 10 mg/m^2 twice weekly

High-dose MTX is considered to be >100 mg/m^2 and can be as high as 1500-7500 mg/m^2. These doses **require** leucovorin rescue. Patients receiving doses ≥1000 mg/m^2 should have their urine alkalinized with bicarbonate or Bicitra® prior to and following MTX therapy.

Trophoblastic neoplasms: Oral, I.M.: 15-30 mg/day for 5 days; repeat in 7 days for 3-5 courses

Head and neck cancer: Oral, I.M., I.V.: 25-50 mg/m^2 once weekly

Rheumatoid arthritis: Oral: 7.5 mg once weekly **OR** 2.5 mg every 12 hours for 3 doses/week; not to exceed 20 mg/week

Psoriasis: Oral: 2.5-5 mg/dose every 12 hours for 3 doses given weekly or Oral, I.M.: 10-25 mg/dose given once weekly

Ectopic pregnancy: I.M./I.V.: 50 mg/m^2 single-dose without leucovorin rescue

Elderly: Rheumatoid arthritis/psoriasis: Oral: Initial: 5 mg once weekly; if nausea occurs, split dose to 2.5 mg every 12 hours for the day of administration; dose may be increased to 7.5 mg/week based on response, not to exceed 20 mg/week

Dosing adjustment in renal impairment:
Cl$_{cr}$ 61-80 mL/minute: Reduce dose to 75% of usual dose
Cl$_{cr}$ 51-60 mL/minute: Reduce dose to 70% of usual dose
Cl$_{cr}$ 10-50 mL/minute: Reduce dose to 30% to 50% of usual dose
Cl$_{cr}$ <10 mL/minute: Avoid use

Hemodialysis: Not dialyzable (0% to 5%); supplemental dose is not necessary
Peritoneal dialysis: Supplemental dose is not necessary

Dosage adjustment in hepatic impairment:
Bilirubin 3.1-5 mg/dL OR AST >180 units: Administer 75% of usual dose
Bilirubin >5 mg/dL: Do not use

Dietary Considerations Alcohol: Avoid use

Administration
Methotrexate may be administered I.M., I.V., or I.T.; refer to Stability section for I.V. administration recommendations based on dosage

I.V. administration rates:
Doses <149 mg: Administer slow I.V. push
Doses of 150-499 mg: Administer IVPB over 20-30 minutes
Doses of 500-1500 mg: Administer IVPB over ≥60 minutes

Doses of >1500 mg: Administer IVPB over 1-6 hours

Specific dosing schemes vary, but high dose should be followed by leucovorin calcium 24-36 hours after initiation of therapy to prevent toxicity

Renal toxicity can be minimized/prevented by alkalinizing the urine (with sodium bicarbonate) and increasing urine flow (hydration therapy)

Monitoring Parameters For prolonged use (especially rheumatoid arthritis, psoriasis) a baseline liver biopsy, repeated at each 1-1.5 g cumulative dose interval, should be performed; WBC and platelet counts every 4 weeks; CBC and creatinine, LFTs every 3-4 months; chest x-ray

Reference Range Refer to chart in Leucovorin Calcium monograph. Therapeutic levels: Variable; Toxic concentration: Variable; therapeutic range is dependent upon therapeutic approach.

High-dose regimens produce drug levels between 10^{-6}Molar and 10^{-7}Molar 24-72 hours after drug infusion

10^{-6} **Molar unit = 1 microMolar unit**

Toxic: Low-dose therapy: >9.1 ng/mL; high-dose therapy: >454 ng/mL

Patient Information Any signs of infection, easy bruising or bleeding, shortness of breath, or painful or burning urination should be brought to physician's attention. Nausea, vomiting or hair loss sometimes occur. The drug may cause permanent sterility and may cause birth defects; contraceptive measures are recommended during therapy. Pregnancy should be avoided for a minimum of 3 months after completion of therapy in male patients, and at least one ovulatory cycle in female patients. The drug may be excreted in breast milk, therefore, an alternative form of feeding your baby should be used. Food may decrease absorption, therefore, take on an empty stomach; avoid alcohol; avoid prolonged exposure to sun.

Additional Information
Sodium content of 100 mg injection: 20 mg (0.86 mEq)
Sodium content of 100 mg (low sodium) injection: 15 mg (0.65 mEq)
Latex-free products: 50 mg/2 mL, 100 mg/4 mL, and 250 mg/10 mL vials with and without preservatives by Immunex

Dosage Forms
Injection, as sodium: 2.5 mg/mL (2 mL); 25 mg/mL (2 mL, 4 mL, 8 mL, 10 mL)
Injection, as sodium, preservative free: 25 mg (2 mL, 4 mL, 8 mL, 10 mL)
Powder, for injection: 20 mg, 25 mg, 50 mg, 100 mg, 250 mg, 1 g
Tablet, as sodium: 2.5 mg
Tablet, as sodium, dose pack: 2.5 mg (4 cards with 2, 3, 4, 5, or 6 tablets each)

♦ **Methotrexate Sodium** see Methotrexate on page 751

Methoxamine (meth OKS a meen)
U.S. Brand Names Vasoxyl®
Synonyms Methoxamine Hydrochloride
Therapeutic Category Adrenergic Agonist Agent; Alpha-Adrenergic Agonist; Sympathomimetic
Use Treatment of hypotension occurring during general anesthesia; to terminate episodes of supraventricular tachycardia; treatment of shock
Pregnancy Risk Factor C
Contraindications Hypersensitivity to methoxamine or any component
Adverse Reactions
1% to 10%:
Cardiovascular: Hypertension (severe)
Gastrointestinal: Vomiting
<1%: Ventricular ectopic beats, fetal bradycardia, headache, urinary urgency, diaphoresis
Overdosage/Toxicology Symptoms of hypertension and bradycardia
Mechanism of Action Direct-acting sympathomimetic amine with similar actions as phenylephrine; causes vasoconstriction primarily via alpha-adrenergic stimulation
Pharmacodynamics/Kinetics
Adrenergic effect:
Onset of action: I.M.: Within 15 minutes
Duration: I.M.: 1.5 hours; I.V.: ~1 hour
Pressor activity:
Onset of action: I.M.: 15-20 minutes; I.V.: Within 1-2 minutes
Duration: ~1-1.5 hours
Elimination: Not well defined
Usual Dosage Adults:
Emergencies: I.V.: 3-5 mg
Supraventricular tachycardia: I.V.: 10 mg
During spinal anesthesia: I.M.: 10-20 mg
Dosage Forms Injection, as hydrochloride: 20 mg/mL (1 mL)

♦ **Methoxamine Hydrochloride** see Methoxamine on this page

Methoxsalen (meth OKS a len)
U.S. Brand Names 8-MOP®; Oxsoralen® Topical; Oxsoralen-Ultra® Oral
Synonyms Methoxypsoralen; 8-Methoxpsoralen; 8-MOP
Therapeutic Category Psoralen
(Continued)

Methoxsalen *(Continued)*

Use

Oral: Symptomatic control of severe, recalcitrant disabling psoriasis, not responsive to other therapy when to diagnosis has been supported by biopsy. Administer only in conjunction with a schedule of controlled doses of long wave ultraviolet (UV) radiation; also used with long wave ultraviolet (UV) radiation for repigmentation of idiopathic vitiligo.

Topical: Repigmenting agent in vitiligo, used in conjunction with controlled doses of UVA or sunlight

Pregnancy Risk Factor C

Contraindications
Diseases associated with photosensitivity, cataract, invasive squamous cell cancer, known hypersensitivity to methoxsalen (psoralens), and children <12 years of age

Warnings/Precautions
Family history of sunlight allergy or chronic infections; lotion should only be applied under direct supervision of a physician and should not be dispensed to the patient; for use only if inadequate response to other forms of therapy, serious burns may occur from UVA or sunlight even through glass if dose and or exposure schedule is not maintained; some products may contain tartrazine; use caution in patients with hepatic or cardiac disease

Adverse Reactions

>10%:

Dermatologic: Itching

Gastrointestinal: Nausea

1% to 10%:

Cardiovascular: Severe edema, hypotension

Central nervous system: Nervousness, vertigo, depression

Dermatologic: Painful blistering, burning, and peeling of skin; pruritus, freckling, hypopigmentation, rash, cheilitis, erythema

Neuromuscular & skeletal: Loss of muscle coordination

Overdosage/Toxicology
Symptoms of overdose include nausea, severe burns; follow accepted treatment of severe burns; keep room darkened until reaction subsides (8-24 hours or more)

Drug Interactions
Increased toxicity: Concomitant therapy with other photosensitizing agents such as anthralin, coal tar, griseofulvin, phenothiazines, nalidixic acid, sulfanilamides, tetracyclines, thiazides

Mechanism of Action
Bonds covalently to pyrimidine bases in DNA, inhibits the synthesis of DNA, and suppresses cell division. The augmented sunburn reaction involves excitation of the methoxsalen molecule by radiation in the long-wave ultraviolet light (UVA), resulting in transference of energy to the methoxsalen molecule producing an excited state ("triplet electronic state"). The molecule, in this "triplet state", then reacts with cutaneous DNA.

Pharmacodynamics/Kinetics

Metabolism: In the liver with >90% of dose appearing in urine as metabolites

Bioavailability: May be less with the capsule than with the liquid-encapsulated preparation

Time to peak serum concentration: Oral: 2-4 hours

Usual Dosage

Psoriasis: Adults: Oral: 10-70 mg 1½-2 hours before exposure to ultraviolet light, 2-3 times at least 48 hours apart; dosage is based upon patient's body weight and skin type

Vitiligo: Children >12 years and Adults:

Oral: 20 mg 2-4 hours before exposure to UVA light or sunlight; limit exposure to 15-40 minutes based on skin basic color and exposure

Topical: Apply lotion 1-2 hours before exposure to UVA light, no more than once weekly

Patient Information
To reduce nausea, oral drug can be taken with food or milk or in 2 divided doses 30 minutes apart. If burning or blistering or intractable pruritus occurs, discontinue therapy until effects subside. Do not sunbathe for at least 24 hours prior to therapy or 48 hours after PUVA therapy. Avoid direct and indirect sunlight for 8 hours after oral and 12-48 hours after topical therapy. **If sunlight cannot be avoided, protective clothing and/or sunscreens must be worn.** Following oral therapy, wraparound sunglasses with UVA-absorbing properties must be worn for 24 hours. Avoid furocoumarin-containing foods (limes, figs, parsley, celery, cloves, lemon, mustard, carrots); do not exceed prescribed dose or exposure times.

Dosage Forms

Capsule: 10 mg

Lotion: 1% (30 mL)

Solution: 20 mcg/mL

♦ **Methoxypsoralen** *see Methoxsalen on previous page*
♦ **8-Methoxypsoralen** *see Methoxsalen on previous page*

Methsuximide *(meth SUKS i mide)*

Related Information

Epilepsy Treatment *on page 1468*

U.S. Brand Names Celontin®

Canadian Brand Names Celontin®

Therapeutic Category Anticonvulsant

Use Control of absence (petit mal) seizures; useful adjunct in refractory, partial complex (psychomotor) seizures

Pregnancy Risk Factor C

Contraindications Known hypersensitivity to methsuximide

Usual Dosage Oral:

Children: Initial: 10-15 mg/kg/day in 3-4 divided doses; increase weekly up to maximum of 30 mg/kg/day

Adults: 300 mg/day for the first week; may increase by 300 mg/day at weekly intervals up to 1.2 g/day in 2-4 divided doses/day

Additional Information Complete prescribing information for this medication should be consulted for additional detail

Dosage Forms Capsule: 150 mg, 300 mg

Methyclothiazide (meth i kloe THYE a zide)

Related Information

Sulfonamide Derivatives on page 1337

U.S. Brand Names Aquatensen®; Enduron®

Therapeutic Category Antihypertensive Agent; Diuretic, Thiazide

Use Management of mild to moderate hypertension; treatment of edema in congestive heart failure and nephrotic syndrome

Pregnancy Risk Factor B

Contraindications Hypersensitivity to methyclothiazide, other thiazides or sulfonamides, or any component, anuria

Warnings/Precautions Use with caution in renal disease, hepatic disease, gout, lupus erythematosus, diabetes mellitus; some products may contain tartrazine

Adverse Reactions

1% to 10%: Endocrine & metabolic: Hypokalemia

<1%: Hypotension, drowsiness, photosensitivity, rash, fluid and electrolyte imbalances (hypocalcemia, hypomagnesemia, hyponatremia), hyperglycemia, nausea, vomiting, anorexia, polyuria, rarely blood dyscrasias, aplastic anemia, hemolytic anemia, leukopenia, agranulocytosis, thrombocytopenia, hepatitis, paresthesia, prerenal azotemia, uremia

Overdosage/Toxicology

Symptoms of overdose include hypermotility, diuresis, lethargy

GI decontamination and supportive care; fluids for hypovolemia

Drug Interactions

Decreased effect:

Thiazides may decrease the effect of anticoagulants, antigout agents, sulfonylureas

Bile acid sequestrants, methenamine, and NSAIDs may decrease the effect of the thiazides

Increased effect: Thiazides may increase the toxicity of allopurinol, anesthetics, antineoplastics, calcium salts, diazoxide, digitalis, lithium, loop diuretics, methyldopa, nondepolarizing muscle relaxants, vitamin D; amphotericin B and anticholinergics may increase the toxicity of thiazides

Mechanism of Action Inhibits sodium reabsorption in the distal tubules causing increased excretion of sodium and water, as well as, potassium and hydrogen ions

Pharmacodynamics/Kinetics

Onset of diuresis: Oral: 2 hours

Peak effect: 6 hours

Duration: ~1 day

Distribution: Crosses the placenta; appears in breast milk

Elimination: Unchanged in urine

Usual Dosage Adults: Oral:

Edema: 2.5-10 mg/day

Hypertension: 2.5-5 mg/day; may add another antihypertensive if 5 mg is not adequate after a trial of 8-12 weeks of therapy

Monitoring Parameters Blood pressure, fluids, weight loss, serum potassium

Patient Information May be taken with food or milk; take early in day to avoid nocturia; take the last dose of multiple doses no later than 6 PM unless instructed otherwise. A few people who take this medication become more sensitive to sunlight and may experience skin rash, redness, itching, or severe sunburn, especially if sun block SPF ≥15 is not used on exposed skin areas.

Nursing Implications Assess weight, I & O reports daily to determine fluid loss; take blood pressure with patient lying down and standing

Dosage Forms Tablet: 2.5 mg, 5 mg

Methyclothiazide and Deserpidine

(meth i kloe THYE a zide & de SER pi deen)

U.S. Brand Names Enduronyl®; Enduronyl® Forte

Therapeutic Category Antihypertensive Agent, Combination

Dosage Forms Tablet: Methyclothiazide 5 mg and deserpidine 0.25 mg; methyclothiazide 5 mg and deserpidine 0.5 mg

Methyclothiazide and Pargyline (meth i kloe THYE a zide & PAR gi leen)

U.S. Brand Names Eutron®

Therapeutic Category Antihypertensive Agent, Combination

Dosage Forms Tablet: Methyclothiazide 5 mg and pargyline hydrochloride 25 mg

♦ **Methylacetoxyprogesterone** see Medroxyprogesterone Acetate on page 721

Methyldopa (meth il DOE pa)

Related Information
Depression Disorders and Treatments *on page 1465*
Hypertension Therapy *on page 1479*

U.S. Brand Names Aldomet®

Canadian Brand Names Apo®-Methyldopa; Dopamet®; Medimet®; Novo-Medopa®; Nu-Medopa

Synonyms Methyldopate Hydrochloride

Therapeutic Category Alpha-Adrenergic Inhibitor; Antihypertensive Agent

Use Management of moderate to severe hypertension

Pregnancy Risk Factor B (oral); C (I.V.)

Pregnancy/Breast-Feeding Implications
Clinical effects on the fetus: Crosses the placenta. Hypotension reported. A large amount of clinical experience with the use of these drugs for the management of hypertension during pregnancy is available. Available evidence suggests safe use during pregnancy and breast-feeding.

Breast-feeding/lactation: Crosses into breast milk at extremely low levels. American Academy of Pediatrics considers **compatible** with breast-feeding.

Contraindications Hypersensitivity to methyldopa or any component; (oral suspension contains benzoic acid and sodium bisulfite; injection contains sodium bisulfite); liver disease, pheochromocytoma, coadministration with MAO inhibitors

Warnings/Precautions May rarely produce hemolytic anemia and liver disorders; positive Coombs' test occurs in 10% to 20% of patients (perform periodic CBCs); sedation usually transient may occur during initial therapy or whenever the dose is increased. Use with caution in patients with previous liver disease or dysfunction, the active metabolites of methyldopa accumulate in uremia. Patients with impaired renal function may respond to smaller doses. Elderly patients may experience syncope (avoid by giving smaller doses). Tolerance may occur usually between the second and third month of therapy. Adding a diuretic or increasing the dosage of methyldopa frequently restores blood pressure control. Because of its CNS effects, methyldopa is not considered a drug of first choice in the elderly.

Adverse Reactions
Percentage unknown:
Cardiovascular: Peripheral edema, orthostatic hypotension, bradycardia (sinus)
Central nervous system: Drug fever, mental depression, anxiety, nightmares, drowsiness, headache, fever, chills, sedation, vertigo, depression, memory lapse
Dermatologic: Rash
Endocrine & metabolic: Sodium retention, sexual dysfunction, gynecomastia, hyperprolactinemia
Gastrointestinal: Xerostomia, colitis, pancreatitis, diarrhea, nausea, vomiting, "black" tongue
Genitourinary: Decreased libido
Hepatic: Cholestasis or hepatitis and heptocellular injury, increased liver enzymes, jaundice, cirrhosis
Neuromuscular & skeletal: Paresthesias, weakness
Respiratory: Dyspnea <po]{ Miscellaneous: SLE-like syndrome
>10%: Hematologic: Positive Coombs' test (20% to 43%)
<1%: Thrombocytopenia, hemolytic anemia (0.1% to 0.2%), leukopenia, transient leukopenia or granulocytopenia

Overdosage/Toxicology
Symptoms of overdose include hypotension, sedation, bradycardia, dizziness, constipation or diarrhea, flatus, nausea, vomiting
Hypotension usually responds to I.V. fluids, Trendelenburg positioning, or vasoconstrictors. Treatment is primarily supportive and symptomatic; can be removed by hemodialysis.

Drug Interactions
Decreased effect: Iron supplements can interact and cause a significant **increase** in blood pressure; reduced effects of methyldopa may occur with barbiturates and tricyclic antidepressants; hypertension, sometimes severe, may occur with beta-blockers, MAO inhibitors, phenothiazines, and sympathomimetics
Increased toxicity: Methyldopa may increase lithium toxicity; tolbutamide, haloperidol, anesthetic, and levodopa effects/toxicity increased with methyldopa

Stability Injectable dosage form is most stable at acid to neutral pH; stability of parenteral admixture at room temperature (25°C): 24 hours; stability of parenteral admixture at refrigeration temperature (4°C): 4 days; standard diluent: 250-500 mg/100 mL D_5W

Mechanism of Action Stimulation of central alpha-adrenergic receptors by a false transmitter that results in a decreased sympathetic outflow to the heart, kidneys, and peripheral vasculature

Pharmacodynamics/Kinetics
Peak hypotensive effect: Oral, parenteral: Within 3-6 hours
Duration: 12-24 hours
Distribution: Crosses the placenta; appears in breast milk
Protein binding: <15%
Metabolism: Intestinally and in the liver
Half-life: 75-80 minutes; End-stage renal disease: 6-16 hours
Elimination: Most (85%) metabolites appearing in the urine within 24 hours

Usual Dosage

Children:

Oral: Initial: 10 mg/kg/day in 2-4 divided doses; increase every 2 days as needed to maximum dose of 65 mg/kg/day; do not exceed 3 g/day

I.V.: 5-10 mg/kg/dose every 6-8 hours up to a total dose of 65 mg/kg/24 hours or 3 g/24 hours

Adults:

Oral: Initial: 250 mg 2-3 times/day; increase every 2 days as needed; usual dose 1-1.5 g/day in 2-4 divided doses; maximum dose: 3 g/day

I.V.: 250-500 mg every 6-8 hours; maximum dose: 1 g every 6 hours

Dosing interval in renal impairment:

Cl_{cr} >50 mL/minute: Administer every 8 hours

Cl_{cr} 10-50 mL/minute: Administer every 8-12 hours

Cl_{cr} <10 mL/minute: Administer every 12-24 hours

Hemodialysis: Slightly dialyzable (5% to 20%)

Administration When methyldopa is given with antihypertensives other than thiazides, limit initial doses to 500 mg/day

Monitoring Parameters Blood pressure, standing and sitting/lying down, CBC, liver enzymes, Coombs' test (direct); blood pressure monitor required during I.V. administration

Test Interactions Methyldopa interferes with the following laboratory tests: urinary uric acid, serum creatinine (alkaline picrate method), AST (colorimetric method), and urinary catecholamines (falsely high levels)

Patient Information May cause transient drowsiness; may cause urine discoloration; notify physician of unexplained prolonged general tiredness, fever, or jaundice; rise slowly from prolonged sitting or lying position

Nursing Implications Transient sedation or depression may be common for first 72 hours of therapy; usually disappears over time; infuse over 30 minutes; assist with ambulation

Dosage Forms

Injection, as methyldopate hydrochloride: 50 mg/mL (5 mL, 10 mL)

Suspension, oral: 250 mg/5 mL (5 mL, 473 mL)

Tablet: 125 mg, 250 mg, 500 mg

Methyldopa and Hydrochlorothiazide

(meth il DOE pa & hye droe klor oh THYE a zide)

U.S. Brand Names Aldoril®

Therapeutic Category Antihypertensive Agent, Combination

Dosage Forms Tablet:

15: Methyldopa 250 mg and hydrochlorothiazide 15 mg

25: Methyldopa 250 mg and hydrochlorothiazide 25 mg

D30: Methyldopa 500 mg and hydrochlorothiazide 30 mg

D50: Methyldopa 500 mg and hydrochlorothiazide 50 mg

♦ **Methyldopate Hydrochloride** see Methyldopa on previous page

Methylene Blue (METH i leen bloo)

U.S. Brand Names Urolene Blue®

Therapeutic Category Antidote, Cyanide; Antidote, Drug-induced Methemoglobinemia

Use Antidote for cyanide poisoning and drug-induced methemoglobinemia, indicator dye, chronic urolithiasis.

Unlabeled use: Has been used topically (0.1% solutions) in conjunction with polychromatic light to photoinactivate viruses such as herpes simplex; has been used alone or in combination with vitamin C for the management of chronic urolithiasis

Pregnancy Risk Factor C (D if injected intra-amniotically)

Contraindications Renal insufficiency, hypersensitivity to methylene blue or any component, intraspinal injection

Warnings/Precautions Do not inject S.C. or intrathecally; use with caution in young patients and in patients with G-6-PD deficiency; continued use can cause profound anemia

Adverse Reactions

>10%:

Gastrointestinal: Fecal discoloration (blue-green)

Genitourinary: Discoloration of urine (blue-green)

1% to 10%: Hematologic: Anemia

<1%: Hypertension, precordial pain, dizziness, mental confusion, headache, fever, stains skin, nausea, vomiting, abdominal pain, bladder irritation, diaphoresis

Overdosage/Toxicology

Symptoms of overdose include nausea, vomiting, precordial pain, hypertension, methemoglobinemia, cyanosis; overdosage has resulted in methemoglobinemia and cyanosis

Treatment is symptomatic and supportive

Mechanism of Action Weak germicide in low concentrations, hastens the conversion of methemoglobin to hemoglobin; has opposite effect at high concentrations by converting ferrous ion of reduced hemoglobin to ferric ion to form methemoglobin; in cyanide toxicity, it combines with cyanide to form cyanmethemoglobin preventing the interference of cyanide with the cytochrome system

Pharmacodynamics/Kinetics

Absorption: Oral: 53% to 97%

(Continued)

Methylene Blue *(Continued)*

Elimination: In bile, feces, and urine

Usual Dosage

Children: NADPH-methemoglobin reductase deficiency: Oral: 1-1.5 mg/kg/day (maximum: 300 mg/day) given with 5-8 mg/kg/day of ascorbic acid

Children and Adults: Methemoglobinemia: I.V.: 1-2 mg/kg or 25-50 mg/m^2 over several minutes; may be repeated in 1 hour if necessary

Adults: Genitourinary antiseptic: Oral: 65-130 mg 3 times/day with a full glass of water (maximum: 390 mg/day)

Administration Administer I.V. undiluted by direct I.V. injection over several minutes

Patient Information May discolor urine and feces blue-green; take oral formulation after meals with a glass of water; skin stains may be removed using a hypochlorite solution

Additional Information Skin stains may be removed using a hypochlorite solution

Dosage Forms

Injection: 10 mg/mL (1 mL, 10 mL)

Tablet: 65 mg

♦ **Methylergometrine Maleate** *see* Methylergonovine *on this page*

Methylergonovine (meth il er goe NOE veen)

U.S. Brand Names Methergine®

Synonyms Methylergometrine Maleate; Methylergonovine Maleate

Therapeutic Category Ergot Alkaloid and Derivative

Use Prevention and treatment of postpartum and postabortion hemorrhage caused by uterine atony or subinvolution

Pregnancy Risk Factor C

Contraindications Induction of labor, threatened spontaneous abortion, hypertension, toxemia, hypersensitivity to methylergonovine or any component, pregnancy

Warnings/Precautions Use caution in patients with sepsis, obliterative vascular disease, hepatic, or renal involvement; hypertension; administer with extreme caution if using I.V.

Adverse Reactions

>10%: Cardiovascular: Hypertension

1% to 10%: Gastrointestinal: Nausea, vomiting

<1%: Temporary chest pain, palpitations, hallucinations, dizziness, seizures, headache, water intoxication, diarrhea, thrombophlebitis, leg cramps, tinnitus, hematuria, dyspnea, nasal congestion, diaphoresis, foul taste

Overdosage/Toxicology

Symptoms include vasospastic effects, nausea, vomiting, lassitude, impaired mental function, hypotension, hypertension, unconsciousness, seizures, shock, and death

Treatment includes general supportive therapy, gastric lavage, or induction of emesis, activated charcoal, saline cathartic; keep extremities warm. Activated charcoal is effective at binding certain chemicals, and this is especially true for ergot alkaloids; treatment is symptomatic with heparin, vasodilators (nitroprusside); vasodilators should be used with caution to avoid exaggerating any pre-existing hypotension.

Drug Interactions Augmented effects may occur with concurrent use of methylergonovine and vasoconstrictors or ergot alkaloids

Mechanism of Action Similar smooth muscle actions as seen with ergotamine; however, it affects primarily uterine smooth muscles producing sustained contractions and thereby shortens the third stage of labor

Pharmacodynamics/Kinetics

Onset of oxytocic effect: Oral: 5-10 minutes; I.M.: 2-5 minutes; I.V.: Immediately

Duration of action: Oral: ~3 hours; I.M.: ~3 hours; I.V.: 45 minutes

Absorption: Rapid

Distribution: Rapidly distributed primarily to plasma and extracellular fluid following I.V. administration; distribution to tissues also occurs rapidly

Metabolism: In the liver

Half-life (biphasic): Initial: 1-5 minutes; Terminal: 30 minutes to 2 hours

Time to peak serum concentration: Within 30 minutes to 3 hours

Elimination: In urine and feces

Usual Dosage Adults:

Oral: 0.2 mg 3-4 times/day for 2-7 days

I.M.: 0.2 mg after delivery of anterior shoulder, after delivery of placenta, or during puerperium; may be repeated as required at intervals of 2-4 hours

I.V.: Same dose as I.M., but should not be routinely administered I.V. because of possibility of inducing sudden hypertension and cerebrovascular accident

Administration Administer over no less than 60 seconds

Patient Information May cause nausea, vomiting, dizziness, increased blood pressure, headache, ringing in the ears, chest pain, or shortness of breath

Nursing Implications Ampuls containing discolored solution should not be used

Dosage Forms

Injection, as maleate: 0.2 mg/mL (1 mL)

Tablet, as maleate: 0.2 mg

♦ **Methylergonovine Maleate** *see* Methylergonovine *on this page*

♦ **Methylmorphine** *see* Codeine *on page 291*

♦ **Methylone®** *see* Methylprednisolone *on page 762*

Methylphenidate (meth il FEN i date)

U.S. Brand Names Ritalin®; Ritalin-SR®

Canadian Brand Names PMS-Methylphenidate; Riphenidate

Synonyms Methylphenidate Hydrochloride

Therapeutic Category Central Nervous System Stimulant, Nonamphetamine

Use Treatment of attention deficit disorder and symptomatic management of narcolepsy; many unlabeled uses

Restrictions C-II

Pregnancy Risk Factor C

Contraindications Hypersensitivity to methylphenidate or any components; glaucoma, motor tics, Tourette's syndrome, patients with marked agitation, tension, and anxiety

Warnings/Precautions Use with caution in patients with hypertension, dementia (may worsen agitation or confusion) seizures; has high potential for abuse. Treatment should include "drug holidays" or periodic discontinuation in order to assess the patient's requirements and to decrease tolerance and limit suppression of linear growth and weight; it is often useful in treating elderly patients who are discouraged, withdrawn, apathetic, or disinterested in their activities. In particular, it is useful in patients who are starting a rehabilitation program but have resigned themselves to fail; these patients may not have a major depressive disorder; will not improve memory or cognitive function.

Adverse Reactions
> 10%:
  Cardiovascular: Tachycardia
  Central nervous system: Nervousness, insomnia
  Gastrointestinal: Anorexia
1% to 10%:
  Central nervous system: Dizziness, drowsiness
  Gastrointestinal: Stomach pain
  Miscellaneous: Hypersensitivity reactions
<1%: Hypertension, hypotension, palpitations, cardiac arrhythmias, movement disorders, precipitation of Tourette's syndrome, and toxic psychosis (rare), fever, headache, convulsions, rash, nausea, weight loss, vomiting, growth retardation, thrombocytopenia, anemia, leukopenia, blurred vision

Overdosage/Toxicology
Symptoms of overdose include vomiting, agitation, tremors, hyperpyrexia, muscle twitching, hallucinations, tachycardia, mydriasis, sweating, palpitations

There is no specific antidote for methylphenidate intoxication and the bulk of the treatment is supportive. Hyperactivity and agitation usually respond to reduced sensory input or benzodiazepines, however, with extreme agitation haloperidol (2-5 mg I.M. for adults) may be required. Hyperthermia is best treated with external cooling measures, or when severe or unresponsive, muscle paralysis with pancuronium may be needed. Hypertension is usually transient and generally does not require treatment unless severe. For diastolic blood pressures >110 mm Hg, a nitroprusside infusion should be initiated. Seizures usually respond to diazepam I.V. and/or phenytoin maintenance regimens.

Drug Interactions
Decreased effect: Effects of guanethidine, bretylium may be antagonized by methylphenidate
Increased toxicity: May increase serum concentrations of tricyclic antidepressants, warfarin, phenytoin, phenobarbital, and primidone; MAO inhibitors may potentiate effects of methylphenidate

Mechanism of Action Blocks the reuptake mechanism of dopaminergic neurons; appears to stimulate the cerebral cortex and subcortical structures similar to amphetamines

Pharmacodynamics/Kinetics
Immediate release tablet:
  Peak cerebral stimulation effect: Within 2 hours
  Duration: 3-6 hours
Sustained release tablet:
  Peak effect: Within 4-7 hours
  Duration: 8 hours
Absorption: Slow and incomplete from GI tract
Metabolism: In liver via hydroxylation to ritolinic acid
Half-life: 2-4 hours
Elimination: In urine as metabolites and unchanged drug with 45% to 50% excreted in feces via bile

Usual Dosage Oral: (Discontinue periodically to re-evaluate or if no improvement occurs within 1 month)

Children ≥6 years: Attention deficit disorder: Initial: 0.3 mg/kg/dose or 2.5-5 mg/dose given before breakfast and lunch; increase by 0.1 mg/kg/dose or by 5-10 mg/day at weekly intervals; usual dose: 0.5-1 mg/kg/day; maximum dose: 2 mg/kg/day or 60 mg/day

Adults:
Narcolepsy: 10 mg 2-3 times/day, up to 60 mg/day
Depression: Initial: 2.5 mg every morning before 9 AM; dosage may be increased by 2.5-5 mg every 2-3 days as tolerated to a maximum of 20 mg/day; may be divided (ie, 7 AM and 12 noon), but should not be given after noon; do not use sustained release product

(Continued)

Methylphenidate *(Continued)*

Patient Information Last daily dose should be given several hours before retiring; do not abruptly discontinue; prolonged use may cause dependence

Nursing Implications Do not crush or allow patient to chew sustained release dosage form; to effectively avoid insomnia, dosing should be completed by noon

Dosage Forms
Tablet, as hydrochloride: 5 mg, 10 mg, 20 mg
Tablet, as hydrochloride, sustained release: 20 mg

- **Methylphenidate Hydrochloride** *see* Methylphenidate *on previous page*
- **Methylphenobarbital** *see* Mephobarbital *on page 730*
- **Methylphenyl Isoxazolyl Penicillin** *see* Oxacillin *on page 869*
- **Methylphytyl Napthoquinone** *see* Phytonadione *on page 926*

Methylprednisolone (meth il pred NIS oh lone)

Related Information
Cancer Chemotherapy Regimens *on page 1263*
Contrast Media Reactions, Premedication for Prophylaxis *on page 1464*
Corticosteroids Comparison *on page 1319*

U.S. Brand Names Adlone® Injection; A-methaPred® Injection; depMedalone® Injection; Depoject® Injection; Depo-Medrol® Injection; Depopred® Injection; D-Med® Injection; Duralone® Injection; Medralone® Injection; Medrol® Oral; Methylone®; M-Prednisol® Injection; Solu-Medrol® Injection

Synonyms 6-α-Methylprednisolone; Methylprednisolone Acetate; Methylprednisolone Sodium Succinate

Therapeutic Category Anti-inflammatory Agent; Corticosteroid; Corticosteroid, Systemic; Glucocorticoid

Use Primarily as an anti-inflammatory or immunosuppressant agent in the treatment of a variety of diseases including those of hematologic, allergic, inflammatory, neoplastic, and autoimmune origin. Prevention and treatment of graft-versus-host disease following allogeneic bone marrow transplantation.

Pregnancy Risk Factor C

Contraindications Serious infections, except septic shock or tuberculous meningitis; known hypersensitivity to methylprednisolone; viral, fungal, or tubercular skin lesions; administration of live virus vaccines. Methylprednisolone formulations containing benzyl alcohol preservative are contraindicated in infants.

Warnings/Precautions Use with caution in patients with hyperthyroidism, cirrhosis, nonspecific ulcerative colitis, hypertension, osteoporosis, thromboembolic tendencies, CHF, convulsive disorders, myasthenia gravis, thrombophlebitis, peptic ulcer, diabetes; because of the risk of adverse effects, systemic corticosteroids should be used cautiously in the elderly, in the smallest possible dose, and for the shortest possible time

Acute adrenal insufficiency may occur with abrupt withdrawal after long-term therapy or with stress; young pediatric patients may be more susceptible to adrenal axis suppression from topical therapy

Adverse Reactions
>10%:
 Central nervous system: Insomnia, nervousness
 Gastrointestinal: Increased appetite, indigestion
1% to 10%:
 Dermatologic: Hirsutism
 Endocrine & metabolic: Diabetes mellitus, adrenal suppression, hyperlipidemia
 Hematologic: Transient leukocytosis
 Neuromuscular & skeletal: Arthralgia
 Ocular: Cataracts, glaucoma
 Miscellaneous: Infections
<1%: Edema, hypertension, vertigo, seizures, psychoses, pseudotumor cerebri, headache, mood swings, delirium, hallucinations, euphoria, acne, skin atrophy, bruising, hyperpigmentation, Cushing's syndrome, pituitary-adrenal axis suppression, growth suppression, glucose intolerance, hypokalemia, alkalosis, amenorrhea, sodium and water retention, hyperglycemia, peptic ulcer, nausea, vomiting, abdominal distention, ulcerative esophagitis, pancreatitis, muscle weakness, osteoporosis, fractures, hypersensitivity reactions, arrhythmias, avascular necrosis, secondary malignancy, intractable hiccups

Overdosage/Toxicology Arrhythmias and cardiovascular collapse are possible with rapid intravenous infusion of high dose methylprednisolone. Symptoms of overdose include cushingoid appearance (systemic), muscle weakness (systemic), osteoporosis (systemic) all with long-term use only. When consumed in excessive quantities for prolonged periods, systemic hypercorticism and adrenal suppression may occur; in those cases, discontinuation and withdrawal of the corticosteroid should be done judiciously.

Drug Interactions CYP3A enzyme inducer

Decreased effect:
 Phenytoin, phenobarbital, rifampin increase clearance of methylprednisolone
 Potassium depleting diuretics enhance potassium depletion
Increased toxicity:
 Skin test antigens, immunizations decrease response and increase potential infections
 Methylprednisolone may increase circulating glucose levels and may need adjustments of insulin or oral hypoglycemics

Stability

Intact vials of methylprednisolone sodium succinate should be stored at controlled room temperature

Reconstituted solutions of methylprednisolone sodium succinate should be stored at room temperature (15°C to 30°C) and used within 48 hours

Stability of parenteral admixture at room temperature (25°C) and at refrigeration temperature (4°C): 48 hours

Standard diluent (Solu-Medrol®): 40 mg/50 mL D_5W; 125 mg/50 mL D_5W

Minimum volume (Solu-Medrol®): 50 mL D_5W

Mechanism of Action In a tissue-specific manner, corticosteroids regulate gene expression subsequent to binding specific intracellular receptors and translocation into the nucleus. Corticosteroids exert a wide array of physiologic effects including modulation of carbohydrate, protein, and lipid metabolism and maintenance of fluid and electrolyte homeostasis. Moreover cardiovascular, immunologic, musculoskeletal, endocrine, and neurologic physiology are influenced by corticosteroids. Decreases inflammation by suppression of migration of polymorphonuclear leukocytes and reversal of increased capillary permeability.

Pharmacodynamics/Kinetics

Time to obtain peak effect and the duration of these effects is dependent upon the route of administration; see table.

Methylprednisolone

Route	Peak Effect	Duration
P.O.	1-2 h	30-36 h
I.M.	4-8 d	1-4 wk
Intra-articular	1 wk	1-5 wk

Distribution: V_d: 0.7-1.5 L/kg

Half-life: 3-3.5 hours, clearance is reduced obese patients

Methylprednisolone sodium succinate is highly soluble and has a rapid effect by I.M. and I.V. routes; methylprednisolone acetate has a low solubility and has a sustained I.M. effect

Usual Dosage Dosing should be based on the lesser of ideal body weight or actual body weight

Only sodium succinate may be given I.V.; methylprednisolone sodium succinate is highly soluble and has a rapid effect by I.M. and I.V. routes. Methylprednisolone acetate has a low solubility and has a sustained I.M. effect.

Children:

Anti-inflammatory or immunosuppressive: Oral, I.M., I.V. (sodium succinate): 0.5-1.7 mg/kg/day or 5-25 mg/m²/day in divided doses every 6-12 hours; "Pulse" therapy: 15-30 mg/kg/dose over ≥30 minutes given once daily for 3 days

Status asthmaticus: I.V. (sodium succinate): Loading dose: 2 mg/kg/dose, then 0.5-1 mg/kg/dose every 6 hours for up to 5 days

Acute spinal cord injury: I.V. (sodium succinate): 30 mg/kg over 15 minutes, followed in 45 minutes by a continuous infusion of 5.4 mg/kg/hour for 23 hours

Lupus nephritis: I.V. (sodium succinate): 30 mg/kg over ≥30 minutes every other day for 6 doses

High-dose therapy for acute spinal cord injury: I.V. bolus: 30 mg/kg over 15 minutes, followed 45 minutes later by an infusion of 5.4 mg/kg/hour for 23 hours

Adults:

Anti-inflammatory or immunosuppressive: Oral: 2-60 mg/day in 1-4 divided doses to start, followed by gradual reduction in dosage to the lowest possible level consistent with maintaining an adequate clinical response

I.M. (sodium succinate): 10-80 mg/day once daily

I.M. (acetate): 10-80 mg every 1-2 weeks

I.V. (sodium succinate): 10-40 mg over a period of several minutes and repeated I.V. or I.M. at intervals depending on clinical response; when high dosages are needed, administer 30 mg/kg over a period of ≥30 minutes and may be repeated every 4-6 hours for 48 hours

Status asthmaticus: I.V. (sodium succinate): Loading dose: 2 mg/kg/dose, then 0.5-1 mg/kg/dose every 6 hours for up to 5 days

High-dose therapy for acute spinal cord injury: I.V. bolus: 30 mg/kg over 15 minutes, followed 45 minutes later by an infusion of 5.4 mg/kg/hour for 23 hours

Lupus nephritis: High-dose "pulse" therapy: I.V. (sodium succinate): 1 g/day for 3 days

Aplastic anemia: I.V. (sodium succinate): 1 mg/kg/day or 40 mg/day (whichever dose is higher), for 4 days. After 4 days, change to oral and continue until day 10 or until symptoms of serum sickness resolve, then rapidly reduce over approximately 2 weeks.

Hemodialysis: Slightly dialyzable (5% to 20%); administer dose posthemodialysis

Intra-articular (acetate): Administer every 1-5 weeks

Large joints: 20-80 mg

Small joints: 4-10 mg

Intralesional (acetate): 20-60 mg every 1-5 weeks

Administration

Oral: Administer after meals or with food or milk

Parenteral: Methylprednisolone sodium succinate may be administered I.M. or I.V.; I.V. administration may be IVP over one to several minutes or IVPB or continuous I.V. infusion

(Continued)

Methylprednisolone *(Continued)*

I.V.: Succinate:
Low dose: ≤1.8 mg/kg or ≤125 mg/dose: I.V. push over 3-15 minutes
Moderate dose: ≥2 mg/kg or 250 mg/dose: I.V. over 15-30 minutes
High dose: 15 mg/kg or ≥500 mg/dose: I.V. over ≥30 minutes
Doses >1 g: Administer over 1 hour

Do **not** administer high-dose I.V. push; hypotension, cardiac arrhythmia, and sudden death have been reported in patients given high-dose methylprednisolone I.V. push over <20 minutes; intermittent infusion over 15-60 minutes; maximum concentration: I.V. push 125 mg/mL

Monitoring Parameters Blood pressure, blood glucose, electrolytes

Test Interactions Interferes with skin tests

Patient Information Do not discontinue or decreasing the drug without contacting your physician; carry an identification card or bracelet advising that you are on steroids; may take with meals to decrease GI upset

Nursing Implications Acetate salt should not be given I.V.

Additional Information Sodium content of 1 g sodium succinate injection: 2.01 mEq; 53 mg of sodium succinate salt is equivalent to 40 mg of methylprednisolone base
Methylprednisolone acetate: Depo-Medrol®
Methylprednisolone sodium succinate: Solu-Medrol®

Dosage Forms
Injection, as acetate: 20 mg/mL (5 mL, 10 mL); 40 mg/mL (1 mL, 5 mL, 10 mL); 80 mg/mL (1 mL, 5 mL)
Injection, as sodium succinate: 40 mg (1 mL, 3 mL); 125 mg (2 mL, 5 mL); 500 mg (1 mL, 4 mL, 8 mL, 20 mL); 1000 mg (1 mL, 8 mL, 50 mL); 2000 mg (30.6 mL)
Tablet: 2 mg, 4 mg, 8 mg, 16 mg, 24 mg, 32 mg
Tablet, dose pack: 4 mg (21s)

♦ **6-α-Methylprednisolone** *see* Methylprednisolone *on page 762*
♦ **Methylprednisolone Acetate** *see* Methylprednisolone *on page 762*
♦ **Methylprednisolone Sodium Succinate** *see* Methylprednisolone *on page 762*
♦ **4-Methylpyrazole** *see* Fomepizole *on page 516*
♦ **Methylrosaniline Chloride** *see* Gentian Violet *on page 536*

Methyltestosterone *(meth il tes TOS te rone)*

U.S. Brand Names Android®; Metandren®; Oreton® Methyl; Testred®; Virilon®

Therapeutic Category Androgen

Use
Male: Hypogonadism; delayed puberty; impotence and climacteric symptoms
Female: Palliative treatment of metastatic breast cancer; postpartum breast pain and/or engorgement

Restrictions C-III

Pregnancy Risk Factor X

Contraindications Hypersensitivity to methyltestosterone or any component, known or suspected carcinoma of the breast or the prostate, pregnancy

Warnings/Precautions Use with extreme caution in patients with liver or kidney disease or serious heart disease; may accelerate bone maturation without producing compensatory gain in linear growth

Adverse Reactions
>10%:
Cardiovascular: Edema
Males: Virilism, priapism
Females: Virilism, menstrual problems (amenorrhea), breast soreness
Dermatologic: Acne
1% to 10%:
Males: Prostatic hypertrophy, prostatic carcinoma, impotence, testicular
Females: Hirsutism (increase in pubic hair growth) atrophy
Gastrointestinal: GI irritation, nausea, vomiting
Hepatic: Hepatic dysfunction
<1%: Gynecomastia, amenorrhea, hypercalcemia, leukopenia, polycythemia, hepatic necrosis, cholestatic hepatitis, hypersensitivity reactions

Overdosage/Toxicology Abnormal liver function tests

Drug Interactions Decreased effect: Oral anticoagulant effect or decrease insulin requirements

Mechanism of Action Stimulates receptors in organs and tissues to promote growth and development of male sex organs and maintains secondary sex characteristics in androgen-deficient males

Pharmacodynamics/Kinetics
Absorption: From GI tract and oral mucosa
Metabolism: Hepatic
Elimination: In urine

Usual Dosage Adults (buccal absorption produces twice the androgenic activity of oral tablets):
Male:
Hypogonadism, male climacteric and impotence: Oral: 10-40 mg/day
Androgen deficiency:
Oral: 10-50 mg/day
Buccal: 5-25 mg/day

Postpubertal cryptorchidism: Oral: 30 mg/day
Female:
Breast pain/engorgement:
Oral: 80 mg/day for 3-5 days
Buccal: 40 mg/day for 3-5 days
Breast cancer:
Oral: 50-200 mg/day
Buccal: 25-100 mg/day
Patient Information Men should report overly frequent or persistent penile erections; women should report menstrual irregularities; all patients should report persistent GI distress, diarrhea, or jaundice; buccal tablet should not be chewed or swallowed
Nursing Implications In prepubertal children, perform radiographic examination of the hand and wrist every 6 months to determine the rate of bone maturation and to assess the effect of treatment on the epiphyseal centers
Dosage Forms
Capsule: 10 mg
Tablet: 10 mg, 25 mg
Tablet, buccal: 5 mg, 10 mg

Methysergide (meth i SER jide)
U.S. Brand Names Sansert®
Therapeutic Category Ergot Alkaloid and Derivative
Use Prophylaxis of vascular headache
Pregnancy Risk Factor X
Contraindications Peripheral vascular disease, severe arteriosclerosis, pulmonary disease, severe hypertension, phlebitis, serious infections, pregnancy
Usual Dosage Adults: Oral: 4-8 mg/day with meals; if no improvement is noted after 3 weeks, drug is unlikely to be beneficial; must not be given continuously for longer than 6 months, and a drug-free interval of 3-4 weeks must follow each 6-month course
Additional Information Complete prescribing information for this medication should be consulted for additional detail
Dosage Forms Tablet, as maleate: 2 mg

♦ **Meticorten®** see Prednisone on page 963
♦ **Metimyd® Ophthalmic** see Sulfacetamide Sodium and Prednisolone on page 1091

Metipranolol (met i PRAN oh lol)
Related Information
Glaucoma Drug Therapy Comparison on page 1322
U.S. Brand Names OptiPranolol® Ophthalmic
Synonyms Metipranolol Hydrochloride
Therapeutic Category Beta-Adrenergic Blocker, Ophthalmic
Use Agent for lowering intraocular pressure in patients with chronic open-angle glaucoma
Pregnancy Risk Factor C
Contraindications Bronchial asthma, sinus bradycardia, second and third degree A-V block, cardiac failure, cardiogenic shock, hypersensitivity to betaxolol or any component, pregnancy
Warnings/Precautions Use with caution in patients with cardiac failure or diabetes mellitus, asthma, bradycardia, or A-V block
Adverse Reactions
>10%: Ocular: Mild ocular stinging and discomfort, eye irritation
1% to 10%: Ocular: Blurred vision, browache
<1%: Bradycardia, A-V block, congestive heart failure, erythema, weakness, conjunctivitis, blepharitis, tearing, itching eyes, keratitis, photophobia, decreased corneal sensitivity, bronchospasm
Overdosage/Toxicology
Symptoms of overdose include bradycardia, hypotension, A-V block
Sympathomimetics (eg, epinephrine or dopamine), glucagon or a pacemaker can be used to treat the toxic bradycardia, asystole, and/or hypotension; initially, fluids may be the best treatment for toxic hypotension
Mechanism of Action Beta-adrenoceptor-blocking agent; lacks intrinsic sympathomimetic activity and membrane-stabilizing effects and possesses only slight local anesthetic activity; mechanism of action of metipranolol in reducing intraocular pressure appears to be via reduced production of aqueous humor. This effect may be related to a reduction in blood flow to the iris root-ciliary body. It remains unclear if the reduction in intraocular pressure observed with beta-blockers is actually secondary to beta-adrenoceptor blockade
Pharmacodynamics/Kinetics
Onset of action: ≤30 minutes
Maximum effects: ~2 hours
Duration of action: Intraocular pressure reduction has persisted for 24 hours following ocular instillation
Metabolism: Rapid and complete to deacetyl metipranolol, an active metabolite
Half-life, elimination: ~3 hours
Usual Dosage Ophthalmic: Adults: Instill 1 drop in the affected eye(s) twice daily
Patient Information Intended for twice daily dosing; keep eye open and do not blink for 30 seconds after instillation; wear sunglasses to avoid photophobic discomfort
Nursing Implications Monitor for systemic effect of beta-blockade
Dosage Forms Solution, ophthalmic, as hydrochloride: 0.3% (5 mL, 10 mL)

♦ **Metipranolol Hydrochloride** see Metipranolol on previous page

Metoclopramide (met oh kloe PRA mide)

U.S. Brand Names Clopra®; Maxolon®; Octamide®; Reglan®

Canadian Brand Names Apo®-Metoclop; Maxeran®

Therapeutic Category Antiemetic; Gastroprokinetic Agent

Use Symptomatic treatment of diabetic gastric stasis, gastroesophageal reflux; prevention of nausea associated with chemotherapy or postsurgery and facilitates intubation of the small intestine

Pregnancy Risk Factor B

Pregnancy/Breast-Feeding Implications

Clinical effects on the fetus: Crosses the placenta. Available evidence suggests safe use during pregnancy and breast-feeding.

Breast-feeding/lactation: Crosses into breast milk

Clinical effects on the infant: Increased milk production; 2 reports of mild intestinal discomfort; American Academy of Pediatrics states MAY BE OF CONCERN

Contraindications Hypersensitivity to metoclopramide or any component; GI obstruction, perforation or hemorrhage, pheochromocytoma, history of seizure disorder

Warnings/Precautions Use with caution in patients with Parkinson's disease and in patients with a history of mental illness; dosage and/or frequency of administration should be modified in response to degree of renal impairment; extrapyramidal reactions, depression; may exacerbate seizures in seizure patients; to prevent extrapyramidal reactions, patients may be pretreated with diphenhydramine; elderly are more likely to develop dystonic reactions than younger adults; use lowest recommended doses initially

Adverse Reactions

>10%:

Central nervous system: Restlessness, drowsiness

Gastrointestinal: Diarrhea

Neuromuscular & skeletal: Weakness

1% to 10%:

Central nervous system: Insomnia, depression

Dermatologic: Rash

Endocrine & metabolic: Breast tenderness, prolactin stimulation

Gastrointestinal: Nausea, xerostomia

<1%: Tachycardia, hypertension or hypotension, extrapyramidal reactions*, tardive dyskinesia, fatigue, anxiety, agitation, constipation, methemoglobinemia

*Note: A recent study suggests the incidence of extrapyramidal reactions due to metoclopramide may be as high as 34% and the incidence appears more often in the elderly

Overdosage/Toxicology

Symptoms of overdose include drowsiness, ataxia, extrapyramidal reactions, seizures, methemoglobinemia (in infants); disorientation, muscle hypertonia, irritability, and agitation are common

Metoclopramide often causes extrapyramidal symptoms (eg, dystonic reactions) requiring management with diphenhydramine 1-2 mg/kg (adults) up to a maximum of 50 mg I.M. or I.V. slow push followed by a maintenance dose for 48-72 hours. When these reactions are unresponsive to diphenhydramine, benztropine mesylate I.V. 1-2 mg (adults) may be effective. These agents are generally effective within 2-5 minutes.

Drug Interactions CYP1A2 and 2D6 enzyme substrate

Decreased effect: Anticholinergic agents antagonize metoclopramide's actions

Increased toxicity: Opiate analgesics may increase CNS depression

Stability Injection is a clear, colorless solution and should be stored at controlled room temperature and protected from freezing; injection is photosensitive and should be protected from light during storage; dilutions do not require light protection if used within 24 hours

Stability of parenteral admixture at room temperature (25°C) and at refrigeration temperature (4°C): 24 hours

Standard diluent: 10-150 mg/50 mL D$_5$W or NS

Minimum volume: 50 mL D$_5$W or NS; send 10 mg unmixed to nursing unit

Compatible with diphenhydramine

Mechanism of Action Blocks dopamine receptors in chemoreceptor trigger zone of the CNS; enhances the response to acetylcholine of tissue in upper GI tract causing enhanced motility and accelerated gastric emptying without stimulating gastric, biliary, or pancreatic secretions

Pharmacodynamics/Kinetics

Onset of effect: Oral: Within 0.5-1 hour; I.V.: Within 1-3 minutes

Duration of therapeutic effect: 1-2 hours, regardless of route administered

Distribution: Crosses the placenta; appears in breast milk

Protein binding: 30%

Half-life, normal renal function: 4-7 hours (may be dose-dependent)

Elimination: Primarily as unchanged drug in urine and feces

Usual Dosage

Children:

Gastroesophageal reflux: Oral: 0.1-0.2 mg/kg/dose up to 4 times/day; efficacy of continuing metoclopramide beyond 12 weeks in reflux has not been determined; total daily dose should not exceed 0.5 mg/kg/day

Gastrointestinal hypomotility (gastroparesis): Oral, I.M., I.V.: 0.1 mg/kg/dose up to 4 times/day, not to exceed 0.5 mg/kg/day

    Antiemetic (chemotherapy-induced emesis): I.V.: 1-2 mg/kg 30 minutes before chemotherapy and every 2-4 hours
    Facilitate intubation: I.V.:
        <6 years: 0.1 mg/kg
        6-14 years: 2.5-5 mg
  Adults:
    Gastroesophageal reflux: Oral: 10-15 mg/dose up to 4 times/day 30 minutes before meals or food and at bedtime; single doses of 20 mg are occasionally needed for provoking situations; efficacy of continuing metoclopramide beyond 12 weeks in reflux has not been determined
    Gastrointestinal hypomotility (gastroparesis):
      Oral: 10 mg 30 minutes before each meal and at bedtime for 2-8 weeks
      I.V. (for severe symptoms): 10 mg over 1-2 minutes; 10 days of I.V. therapy may be necessary for best response
    Antiemetic (chemotherapy-induced emesis): I.V.: 1-2 mg/kg 30 minutes before chemotherapy and every 2-4 hours to every 4-6 hours (and usually given with diphenhydramine 25-50 mg I.V./oral)
    Postoperative nausea and vomiting: I.M.: 10 mg near end of surgery; 20 mg doses may be used
    Facilitate intubation: I.V.: 10 mg
  Elderly:
    Gastroesophageal reflux: Oral: 5 mg 4 times/day (30 minutes before meals and at bedtime); increase dose to 10 mg 4 times/day if no response at lower dose
    Gastrointestinal hypomotility:
      Oral: Initial: 5 mg 30 minutes before meals and at bedtime for 2-8 weeks; increase if necessary to 10 mg doses
      I.V.: Initiate at 5 mg over 1-2 minutes; increase to 10 mg if necessary
    Postoperative nausea and vomiting: I.M.: 5 mg near end of surgery; may repeat dose if necessary
  Dosing adjustment in renal impairment:
    Cl_{cr} 10-40 mL/minute: Administer at 50% of normal dose
    Cl_{cr} <10 mL/minute: Administer at 25% of normal dose
  Hemodialysis: Not dialyzable (0% to 5%); supplemental dose is not necessary

Dietary Considerations Alcohol: Additive CNS effect, avoid use

Administration Lower doses of metoclopramide can be given I.V. push undiluted over 1-2 minutes; parenteral doses of up to 10 mg should be given I.V. push; higher doses to be given IVPB; infuse over at least 15 minutes

Monitoring Parameters Periodic renal function test; monitor for dystonic reactions; monitor for signs of hypoglycemia in patients using insulin and those being treated for gastroparesis; monitor for agitation and irritable confusion

Test Interactions ↑ aminotransferase [ALT (SGPT)/AST (SGOT)] (S), ↑ amylase (S)

Patient Information May impair mental alertness or physical coordination; avoid alcohol, barbiturates or other CNS depressants; take 30 minutes before meals; notify physician if involuntary movements occur

Dosage Forms
  Injection: 5 mg/mL (2 mL, 10 mL, 30 mL, 50 mL, 100 mL)
  Solution, oral, concentrated: 10 mg/mL (10 mL, 30 mL)
  Syrup, sugar free: 5 mg/5 mL (10 mL, 480 mL)
  Tablet: 5 mg, 10 mg

Metolazone (me TOLE a zone)

Related Information
  Heart Failure: Management of Patients With Left-Ventricular Systolic Dysfunction *on page 1472*
  Sulfonamide Derivatives *on page 1337*

U.S. Brand Names Mykrox®; Zaroxolyn®

Therapeutic Category Antihypertensive Agent; Diuretic, Miscellaneous

Use Management of mild to moderate hypertension; treatment of edema in congestive heart failure and nephrotic syndrome, impaired renal function

Pregnancy Risk Factor D

Contraindications Hypersensitivity to metolazone or any component, other thiazides, and sulfonamide derivatives; patients with hepatic coma, anuria

Warnings/Precautions Use with caution in renal disease, hepatic disease, gout, lupus erythematosus, diabetes mellitus; some products may contain tartrazine. **Mykrox® is not bioequivalent to Zaroxolyn® and should not be interchanged for one another.**

Adverse Reactions
  1% to 10%:
    Cardiovascular: Chest pain (3% with fast-acting product)
    Central nervous system: Dizziness (10%), headache (9%)
    Endocrine & metabolic: Hypokalemia
    Neuromuscular & skeletal: Muscle cramps/spasms (6%)
  <1%: Hypotension, drowsiness, photosensitivity, rash, fluid and electrolyte imbalances (hypocalcemia, hypomagnesemia, hyponatremia), hyperglycemia, nausea, vomiting, anorexia, polyuria, rarely blood dyscrasias, aplastic anemia, hemolytic anemia, leukopenia, agranulocytosis, thrombocytopenia, hepatitis, paresthesia, prerenal azotemia, uremia

Overdosage/Toxicology
  Symptoms of overdose include hypermotility, diuresis, lethargy, confusion, muscle weakness
  (Continued)

767

Metolazone *(Continued)*

Following GI decontamination, therapy is supportive with I.V. fluids, electrolytes, and I.V. pressors if needed

Drug Interactions

Decreased effect:

Thiazides may decrease the effect of anticoagulants, antigout agents, sulfonylureas
Bile acid sequestrants, methenamine, and NSAIDs may decrease the effect of the thiazides

Increased effect: Thiazides may increase the toxicity of allopurinol, anesthetics, antineoplastics, calcium salts, diazoxide, digitalis, lithium, loop diuretics, methyldopa, nondepolarizing muscle relaxants, vitamin D; amphotericin B and anticholinergics may increase the toxicity of thiazides

Mechanism of Action Inhibits sodium reabsorption in the distal tubules causing increased excretion of sodium and water, as well as, potassium and hydrogen ions

Pharmacodynamics/Kinetics Same for all routes:

Onset of diuresis: Within 60 minutes

Duration: 12-24 hours

Absorption: Oral: Incomplete

Distribution: Crosses the placenta; appears in breast milk

Protein binding: 95%

Bioavailability: Mykrox® reportedly has highest

Half-life: 6-20 hours, renal function dependent

Elimination: Enterohepatic recycling; 80% to 95% excreted in urine

Usual Dosage Adults: Oral:

Edema: 5-20 mg/dose every 24 hours

Hypertension: 2.5-5 mg/dose every 24 hours

Hypertension (Mykrox®): 0.5 mg/day; if response is not adequate, increase dose to maximum of 1 mg/day

Dialysis: Not dialyzable (0% to 5%) via hemo- or peritoneal dialysis; supplemental dose is not necessary

Monitoring Parameters Serum electrolytes (potassium, sodium, chloride, bicarbonate), renal function, blood pressure (standing, sitting/supine)

Patient Information May be taken with food or milk; take early in day to avoid nocturia; take the last dose of multiple doses no later than 6 PM unless instructed otherwise. A few people who take this medication become more sensitive to sunlight and may experience skin rash, redness, itching, or severe sunburn, especially if sun block SPF ≥15 is not used on exposed skin areas.

Nursing Implications Assess weight, I & O reports daily to determine fluid loss; take blood pressure with patient lying down and standing

Dosage Forms Tablet:

Zaroxolyn®: 2.5 mg, 5 mg, 10 mg

Mykrox®: 0.5 mg

Extemporaneous Preparations A 1 mg/mL suspension can be made by crushing twenty-four 5 mg tablets. Add a small amount of distilled water. Add 30 mL Cologel® and mix well. Add a sufficient amount of 2:1 simple syrup/cherry syrup mixture to make a final volume of 120 mL. Label "shake well". Stability is 2 weeks refrigerated.

Handbook on Extemporaneous Formulations, Bethesda MD: American Society of Hospital Pharmacists, 1987.

Metoprolol *(me toe PROE lole)*

Related Information

Antiarrhythmic Drugs Comparison *on page 1297*

Beta-Blockers Comparison *on page 1311*

Extravasation Treatment of Other Drugs *on page 1287*

U.S. Brand Names Lopressor®; Toprol XL®

Canadian Brand Names Apo®-Metoprolol (Type L); Betaloc®; Betaloc® Durules®; Novo-Metoprolol; Nu-Metop

Synonyms Metoprolol Succinate; Metoprolol Tartrate

Therapeutic Category Antihypertensive Agent; Beta-Adrenergic Blocker

Use Treatment of hypertension and angina pectoris; prevention of myocardial infarction, atrial fibrillation, flutter, symptomatic treatment of hypertrophic subaortic stenosis

Unlabeled use: Treatment of ventricular arrhythmias, atrial ectopy, migraine prophylaxis, essential tremor, aggressive behavior

Pregnancy Risk Factor C

Pregnancy/Breast-Feeding Implications

Clinical effects on the fetus: Crosses the placenta. None; mild IUGR probably secondary to maternal hypertension. Available evidence suggests safe use during pregnancy and breast-feeding. Monitor breast-fed infant for symptoms of beta-blockade.

Breast-feeding/lactation: Crosses into breast milk. American Academy of Pediatrics considers **compatible** with breast-feeding.

Contraindications Hypersensitivity to beta-blocking agents, uncompensated congestive heart failure; cardiogenic shock; bradycardia (heart rate <45 bpm) or heart block; sinus node dysfunction; A-V conduction abnormalities, systolic blood pressure <100 mm Hg; diabetes mellitus. Although metoprolol primarily blocks beta$_1$-receptors, high doses can result in beta$_2$-receptor blockage; therefore, use with caution in elderly with bronchospastic lung disease.

Warnings/Precautions Use with caution in patients with inadequate myocardial function; those undergoing anesthesia, patients with CHF, myasthenia gravis, impaired hepatic or renal function, severe peripheral vascular disease, bronchospastic disease, diabetes mellitus or hyperthyroidism. Abrupt withdrawal of the drug should be avoided (may result in an exaggerated cardiac beta-adrenergic response, tachycardia, hypertension, ischemia, angina, myocardial infarction, and sudden death), drug should be discontinued over 1-2 weeks; do not use in pregnant or nursing women; may potentiate hypoglycemia in a diabetic patient and mask signs and symptoms; sweating will continue.

Adverse Reactions
>10%:
Central nervous system: Fatigue/dizziness (10%)
Neuromuscular & skeletal: Weakness
1% to 10%:
Cardiovascular: Bradycardia (3%), arrhythmia, hypotension/reduced peripheral circulation (1%)
Central nervous system: Mental depression (5%)
Dermatologic: Pruritus/rash (5%)
Gastrointestinal: Heartburn (1%), diarrhea (5%), nausea (1%), xerostomia, abdominal pain (1%)
Respiratory: Wheezing (1%), dyspnea (3%)
<1%: Chest pain, heart failure, Raynaud's phenomenon, insomnia, nightmares, confusion, headache, memory loss, decreased sexual activity, constipation, vomiting, stomach discomfort, impotence, cold extremities

Overdosage/Toxicology
Symptoms of intoxication include cardiac disturbances, CNS toxicity, bronchospasm, hypoglycemia and hyperkalemia. The most common cardiac symptoms include hypotension and bradycardia; atrioventricular block, intraventricular conduction disturbances, cardiogenic shock, and asystole may occur with severe overdose, especially with membrane-depressant drugs (eg, propranolol); CNS effects include convulsions, coma, and respiratory arrest.
Treatment includes symptomatic treatment of seizures, hypotension, hyperkalemia and hypoglycemia; bradycardia and hypotension resistant to atropine, isoproterenol or pacing, may respond to glucagon; wide QRS defects caused by the membrane-depressant poisoning may respond to hypertonic sodium bicarbonate; repeat-dose charcoal, hemoperfusion, or hemodialysis may be helpful in removal of only those beta-blockers with a small V_d, long half-life or low intrinsic clearance (acebutolol, atenolol, nadolol, sotalol)

Drug Interactions
CYP2D6 enzyme substrate
Decreased effect of beta-blockers with aluminum salts, barbiturates, calcium salts, cholestyramine, colestipol, NSAIDs, penicillins (ampicillin), rifampin, salicylates and sulfinpyrazone due to decreased bioavailability and plasma levels; thyroid hormones, when hypothyroid patient is converted to euthyroid state
Beta-blockers may decrease the effect of sulfonylureas
Increased effect/toxicity of beta-blockers with calcium blockers (diltiazem, felodipine, nicardipine), oral contraceptives, flecainide, H_2-antagonists (cimetidine, possibly ranitidine), hydralazine, MAO inhibitors, phenothiazines, propafenone, quinidine (in extensive metabolizers), ciprofloxacin
Beta-blockers may increase the effect/toxicity of flecainide, hydralazine, benzodiazepines (not atenolol), clonidine (hypertensive crisis after or during withdrawal of either agent), epinephrine (initial hypertensive episode followed by bradycardia), nifedipine, verapamil, lidocaine, ergots (peripheral ischemia), prazosin (postural hypotension)
Beta-blockers may affect the action or levels of ethanol, disopyramide, nondepolarizing muscle relaxants and theophylline although the effects are difficult to predict

Mechanism of Action
Selective inhibitor of beta$_1$-adrenergic receptors; competitively blocks beta$_1$-receptors, with little or no effect on beta$_2$-receptors at doses <100 mg; does not exhibit any membrane stabilizing or intrinsic sympathomimetic activity

Pharmacodynamics/Kinetics
Peak antihypertensive effect: Oral: Within 1.5-4 hours
Duration: 10-20 hours
Absorption: 95%
Protein binding: 8%
Metabolism: Significant first-pass metabolism; extensively metabolized in the liver
Bioavailability: Oral: 40% to 50%
Half-life: 3-4 hours; End-stage renal disease: 2.5-4.5 hours
Elimination: In urine (3% to 10% as unchanged drug)

Usual Dosage
Children: Oral: 1-5 mg/kg/24 hours divided twice daily; allow 3 days between dose adjustments
Adults:
Oral: 100-450 mg/day in 2-3 divided doses, begin with 50 mg twice daily and increase doses at weekly intervals to desired effect
Extended release: Same daily dose administered as a single dose
I.V.: 5 mg every 2 minutes for 3 doses in early treatment of myocardial infarction; thereafter administer 50 mg orally every 6 hours 15 minutes after last I.V. dose and continue for 48 hours; then administer a maintenance dose of 100 mg twice daily
Elderly: Oral: Initial: 25 mg/day; usual range: 25-300 mg/day
Hemodialysis: Administer dose posthemodialysis or administer 50 mg supplemental dose; supplemental dose is not necessary following peritoneal dialysis
Dosing adjustment/comments in hepatic disease: Reduced dose probably necessary
(Continued)

Metoprolol *(Continued)*

Monitoring Parameters Blood pressure, apical and radial pulses, fluid I & O, daily weight, respirations, mental status, and circulation in extremities before and during therapy

Patient Information Do not discontinue medication abruptly, sudden stopping of medication may precipitate or cause angina; consult pharmacist or physician before taking with other adrenergic drugs (eg, cold medications); use with caution while driving or performing tasks requiring alertness; may mask signs of hypoglycemia in diabetics; may be taken without regard to meals

Dosage Forms

Injection, as tartrate: 1 mg/mL (5 mL)

Tablet, as tartrate: 50 mg, 100 mg

Tablet, as succinate [equivalent to tartrate], sustained release: 50 mg, 100 mg, 200 mg

Extemporaneous Preparations A mixture of metoprolol 10 mg/mL plus hydrochlorothiazide 5 mg/mL was found to be stable for 60 days in a refrigerator in a 1:1 preparation of Ora-Sweet® and Ora-Plus®, in Ora-Sweet® SF and Ora-Plus®, and in cherry syrup

Allen LV and Erickson III MA, "Stability of Labetalol Hydrochloride, Metoprolol Tartrate, Verapamil Hydrochloride, and Spironolactone With Hydrochlorothiazide in Extemporaneously Compounded Oral Liquids," *Am J Health Syst Pharm*, 1996, 53:2304-9.

♦ **Metoprolol Succinate** *see* Metoprolol *on page 768*

♦ **Metoprolol Tartrate** *see* Metoprolol *on page 768*

♦ **Metreton® Ophthalmic** *see* Prednisolone *on page 961*

♦ **MetroGel® Topical** *see* Metronidazole *on this page*

♦ **MetroGel®-Vaginal** *see* Metronidazole *on this page*

♦ **Metro I.V.® Injection** *see* Metronidazole *on this page*

Metronidazole *(me troe NI da zole)*

Related Information

Antimicrobial Drugs of Choice *on page 1404*

Community-Acquired Pneumonia in Adults *on page 1419*

Helicobacter pylori Treatment *on page 1473*

Treatment of Sexually Transmitted Diseases *on page 1429*

U.S. Brand Names Flagyl ER® Oral; Flagyl® Oral; MetroGel® Topical; MetroGel®-Vaginal; Metro I.V.® Injection; Noritate® Cream; Protostat® Oral

Canadian Brand Names Apo®-Metronidazole; Novo-Nidazol

Synonyms Metronidazole Hydrochloride

Therapeutic Category Amebicide; Antibiotic, Anaerobic; Antibiotic, Topical; Antiprotozoal

Use Treatment of susceptible anaerobic bacterial and protozoal infections in the following conditions: amebiasis, symptomatic and asymptomatic trichomoniasis; skin and skin structure infections; intra-abdominal infections; CNS infections; systemic anaerobic infections; topically for the treatment of acne rosacea; treatment of antibiotic-associated pseudomembranous colitis (AAPC), bacterial vaginosis; used in combination with other agents (eg, tetracycline, bismuth subsalicylate, and an H_2-antagonist) to treat duodenal ulcer disease due to *Helicobacter pylori*; also used in Crohn's disease and hepatic encephalopathy

Pregnancy Risk Factor B

Contraindications Hypersensitivity to metronidazole or any component, 1st trimester of pregnancy since found to be carcinogenic in rats

Warnings/Precautions Use with caution in patients with liver impairment due to potential accumulation, blood dyscrasias; history of seizures, congestive heart failure, or other sodium retaining states; reduce dosage in patients with severe liver impairment, CNS disease, and severe renal failure (Cl_{cr} <10 mL/minute); if *H. pylori* is not eradicated in patients being treated with metronidazole in a regimen, it should be assumed that metronidazole-resistance has occurred and it should not again be used; seizures and neuropathies have been reported especially with increased doses and chronic treatment; if this occurs, discontinue therapy

Adverse Reactions

>10%:

Central nervous system: Dizziness, headache

Gastrointestinal (12%): Nausea, diarrhea, loss of appetite, vomiting

<1%: Ataxia, seizures, disulfiram-type reaction with alcohol, pancreatitis, xerostomia, metallic taste, furry tongue, vaginal candidiasis, leukopenia, thrombophlebitis, neuropathy, hypersensitivity, change in taste sensation, dark urine

Overdosage/Toxicology

Symptoms of overdose include nausea, vomiting, ataxia, seizures, peripheral neuropathy

Treatment is symptomatic and supportive

Drug Interactions CYP2C9 enzyme substrate; CYP2C9, 3A3/4, and 3A5-7 enzyme inhibitor

Decreased effect: Phenytoin, phenobarbital may decrease metronidazole half-life

Increased toxicity: Alcohol or disulfiram results in disulfiram-like reactions; metronidazole increases P-T prolongation with warfarin and increases lithium levels/toxicity; cimetidine may increase metronidazole levels

Stability

Metronidazole injection should be stored at 15°C to 30°C and protected from light

Product may be refrigerated but crystals may form; crystals redissolve on warming to room temperature

Prolonged exposure to light will cause a darkening of the product. However, short-term exposure to normal room light does not adversely affect metronidazole stability. Direct sunlight should be avoided.

Stability of parenteral admixture at room temperature (25°C): Out of overwrap stability: 30 days

Standard diluent: 500 mg/100 mL NS

Mechanism of Action Reduced to a product which interacts with DNA to cause a loss of helical DNA structure and strand breakage resulting in inhibition of protein synthesis and cell death in susceptible organisms

Pharmacodynamics/Kinetics

Absorption:

Oral: Well absorbed

Topical: Concentrations achieved systemically after application of 1 g topically are 10 times less than those obtained after a 250 mg oral dose

Distribution: To saliva, bile, seminal fluid, breast milk, bone, liver, and liver abscesses, lung and vaginal secretions; crosses placenta and blood-brain barrier; appears in breast milk

Ratio of CSF to blood level (%): Normal meninges: 16-43; Inflamed meninges: 100

Protein binding: <20%

Metabolism: 30% to 60% in the liver

Half-life:

Neonates: 25-75 hours

Others: 6-8 hours, increases with hepatic impairment

End-stage renal disease: 21 hours

Time to peak serum concentration: Within 1-2 hours

Elimination: Final excretion via the urine (20% to 40% as unchanged drug) and feces (6% to 15%)

Usual Dosage

Neonates: Anaerobic infections: Oral, I.V.:

0-4 weeks: <1200 g: 7.5 mg/kg/dose every 48 hours

Postnatal age <7 days:

1200-2000 g: 7.5 mg/kg/day every 24 hours

>2000 g: 15 mg/kg/day in divided doses every 12 hours

Postnatal age >7 days:

1200-2000 g: 15 mg/kg/day in divided doses every 12 hours

>2000 g: 30 mg/kg/day in divided doses every 12 hours

Infants and Children:

Amebiasis: Oral: 35-50 mg/kg/day in divided doses every 8 hours for 10 days

Trichomoniasis: Oral: 15-30 mg/kg/day in divided doses every 8 hours for 7 days

Anaerobic infections:

Oral: 15-35 mg/kg/day in divided doses every 8 hours

I.V.: 30 mg/kg/day in divided doses every 6 hours

Clostridium difficile (antibiotic-associated colitis): Oral: 20 mg/kg/day divided every 6 hours

Maximum dose: 2 g/day

Adults:

Amebiasis: Oral: 500-750 mg every 8 hours for 5-10 days

Trichomoniasis: Oral: 250 mg every 8 hours for 7 days or 2 g as a single dose

Anaerobic infections: Oral, I.V.: 500 mg every 6-8 hours, not to exceed 4 g/day

Antibiotic-associated pseudomembranous colitis: Oral: 250-500 mg 3-4 times/day for 10-14 days

H. pylori: 1 capsule with meals and at bedtime for 14 days in combination with other agents (eg, tetracycline, bismuth subsalicylate, and H_2-antagonist)

Vaginosis: 1 applicatorful (~37.5 mg metronidazole) intravaginally once or twice daily for 5 days; apply once in morning and evening if using twice daily, if daily, use at bedtime

Elderly: Use lower end of dosing recommendations for adults, do not administer as a single dose

Topical (acne rosacea therapy): Apply and rub a thin film twice daily, morning and evening, to entire affected areas after washing. Significant therapeutic results should be noticed within 3 weeks. Clinical studies have demonstrated continuing improvement through 9 weeks of therapy.

Dosing adjustment in renal impairment: Cl_{cr} <10 mL/minute: Administer every 12 hours

Hemodialysis: Extensively removed by hemodialysis and peritoneal dialysis (50% to 100%); administer dose posthemodialysis

Peritoneal dialysis: Dose as for Cl_{cr} <10 mL/minute

Continuous arteriovenous or venovenous hemofiltration (CAVH/CAVHD): Administer usual dose

Dosing adjustment/comments in hepatic disease: Unchanged in mild liver disease; reduce dosage in severe liver disease

Dietary Considerations

Alcohol: A disulfiram-like reaction characterized by flushing, headache, nausea, vomiting, sweating or tachycardia; patients should be warned to avoid alcohol during and 72 hours after therapy

Food: Peak antibiotic serum concentration lowered and delayed, but total drug absorbed not affected. Take on an empty stomach. Drug may cause GI upset; if GI upset occurs, take with food.

Test Interactions May interfere with AST, ALT, triglycerides, glucose, and LDH testing (Continued)

Metronidazole (Continued)

Patient Information Urine may be discolored to a dark or reddish-brown; do not take alcohol for at least 24 hours after the last dose; avoid beverage alcohol or any topical products containing alcohol during therapy; may cause metallic taste; may be taken with food to minimize stomach upset; notify physician if numbness or tingling in extremities; avoid contact of the topical product with the eyes; cleanse areas to be treated well before application

Nursing Implications No Antabuse®-like reactions have been reported after **topical** application, although metronidazole can be detected in the blood; avoid contact between the drug and aluminum in the infusion set

Additional Information Sodium content of 500 mg (I.V.): 322 mg (14 mEq)

Dosage Forms
Capsule: 375 mg
Gel, topical: 0.75% [7.5 mg/mL] (30 g)
Gel, vaginal: 0.75% (5 g applicator delivering 37.5 mg; 70 g tube)
Injection, ready to use: 5 mg/mL (100 mL)
Powder for injection, as hydrochloride: 500 mg
Tablet: 250 mg, 500 mg
Tablet, extended release: 750 mg

Extemporaneous Preparations To prepare metronidazole suspension 50 mg/mL, pulverize ten 250 mg tablets; levigate with a small amount of distilled water; add 10 mL Cologel® and levigate; add sufficient quantity of cherry syrup to total 50 mL and levigate until a uniform mixture is obtained; stable for 30 days if refrigerated

Committee on Extemporaneous Formulations, ASHP Special Interest Group (SIG) on Pediatric Pharmacy Practice, *Handbook on Extemporaneous Formulations*, 1987.

♦ **Metronidazole Hydrochloride** see Metronidazole on page 770

Metyrosine (me TYE roe seen)

U.S. Brand Names Demser®

Synonyms AMPT; OGMT

Therapeutic Category Tyrosine Hydroxylase Inhibitor

Use Short-term management of pheochromocytoma before surgery, long-term management when surgery is contraindicated or when malignant

Pregnancy Risk Factor C

Contraindications Hypertension of unknown etiology, known hypersensitivity to metyrosine

Warnings/Precautions Maintain fluid volume during and after surgery; use with caution in patients with impaired renal or hepatic function

Adverse Reactions
>10%:
Central nervous system: Drowsiness, extrapyramidal symptoms
Gastrointestinal: Diarrhea
1% to 10%:
Endocrine & metabolic: Galactorrhea, edema of the breasts
Gastrointestinal: Nausea, vomiting, xerostomia
Genitourinary: Impotence
Respiratory: Nasal congestion
<1%: Lower extremity edema, depression, hallucinations, disorientation, parkinsonism, urticaria, urinary problems, anemia, eosinophilia, hematuria, hyperstimulation after withdrawal

Overdosage/Toxicology Signs of overdose include sedation, fatigue, tremor; reducing dose or discontinuation of therapy usually results in resolution of symptoms

Mechanism of Action Blocks the rate-limiting step in the biosynthetic pathway of catecholamines. It is a tyrosine hydroxylase inhibitor, blocking the conversion of tyrosine to dihydroxyphenylalanine. This inhibition results in decreased levels of endogenous catecholamines. Catecholamine biosynthesis is reduced by 35% to 80% in patients treated with metyrosine 1-4 g/day.

Pharmacodynamics/Kinetics
Half-life: 7.2 hours
Elimination: Following oral absorption, excreted primarily unchanged in urine

Usual Dosage Children >12 years and Adults: Oral: Initial: 250 mg 4 times/day, increased by 250-500 mg/day up to 4 g/day; maintenance: 2-3 g/day in 4 divided doses; for preoperative preparation, administer optimum effective dosage for 5-7 days

Dosing adjustment in renal impairment: Adjustment should be considered

Dietary Considerations Alcohol: Additive CNS effect, avoid use

Patient Information Take plenty of fluids each day; may cause drowsiness, impair coordination and judgment; notify physician if drooling, tremors, speech difficulty, or diarrhea occurs; avoid alcohol and central nervous system depressants

Dosage Forms Capsule: 250 mg

♦ **Mevacor®** see Lovastatin on page 699
♦ **Meval®** see Diazepam on page 345
♦ **Mevinolin** see Lovastatin on page 699

Mexiletine (MEKS i le teen)

Related Information
Antiarrhythmic Drugs Comparison on page 1297

U.S. Brand Names Mexitil®

Therapeutic Category Antiarrhythmic Agent, Class I-B

Use Management of serious ventricular arrhythmias; use with lesser arrhythmias is generally not recommended

Unlabeled use: Diabetic neuropathy, reduction of ventricular tachycardia and other arrhythmias in the acute phase of myocardial infarction (mortality may not be reduced)

Pregnancy Risk Factor C

Contraindications Cardiogenic shock, second or third degree heart block, hypersensitivity to mexiletine or any component

Warnings/Precautions Exercise extreme caution in patients with pre-existing sinus node dysfunction; mexiletine can worsen CHF, bradycardias, and other arrhythmias; mexiletine, like other antiarrhythmic agents, is proarrhythmic; CAST study indicates a trend toward increased mortality with antiarrhythmics in the face of cardiac disease (myocardial infarction); elevation of AST/ALT; hepatic necrosis reported; leukopenia, agranulocytopenia, and thrombocytopenia; seizures; alterations in urinary pH may change urinary excretion; electrolyte disturbances (hypokalemia, hyperkalemia, etc) after drug response

Adverse Reactions

>10%:

Central nervous system: Lightheadedness (10.5%), dizziness (20% to 25%), nervousness (5% to 10%), incoordination (10.2%)

Gastrointestinal: GI distress (41%), nausea/vomiting (40%)

Neuromuscular & skeletal: Trembling, unsteady gait, tremor (12.6%)

1% to 10%:

Cardiovascular: Chest pain (2.5% to 7.5%), premature ventricular contractions (1% to 2%), palpitations (4% to 8%)

Central nervous system: Confusion, headache, insomnia (5% to 7%)

Dermatologic: Rash (3.8% to 4.2%)

Gastrointestinal: Constipation or diarrhea (4% to 5%), xerostomia (2.8%), abdominal pain (1.2%)

Neuromuscular & skeletal: Weakness, numbness of fingers or toes (2% to 4%)

Ocular: Blurred vision (5% to 7%)

Otic: Tinnitus (2% to 2.5%)

Respiratory: Shortness of breath

<1%: Leukopenia, agranulocytosis, thrombocytopenia, positive antinuclear antibody, increased LFTs, diplopia

Overdosage/Toxicology

Has a narrow therapeutic index and severe toxicity may occur slightly above the therapeutic range, especially with other antiarrhythmic drugs; acute ingestion of twice the daily therapeutic dose is potentially life-threatening; symptoms of overdose includes sedation, confusion, coma, seizures, respiratory arrest and cardiac toxicity (sinus arrest, A-V block, asystole, and hypotension); the QRS and Q-T intervals are usually normal, although they may be prolonged after massive overdose; other effects include dizziness, paresthesias, tremor, ataxia, and GI disturbance.

Treatment is supportive, using conventional therapies (fluids, positioning, vasopressors, antiarrhythmics, anticonvulsants); sodium bicarbonate may reverse the QRS prolongation, bradyarrhythmias and hypotension; enhanced elimination with dialysis, hemoperfusion or repeat charcoal is not effective.

Drug Interactions CYP2D6 enzyme substrate; CYP1A2 enzyme inhibitor

Decreased plasma levels: Phenobarbital, phenytoin, rifampin, and other hepatic enzyme inducers, cimetidine and drugs which make the urine acidic

Increased effect: Allopurinol

Increased toxicity/levels of caffeine and theophylline

Mechanism of Action Class IB antiarrhythmic, structurally related to lidocaine, which inhibits inward sodium current, decreases rate of rise of phase 0, increases effective refractory period/action potential duration ratio

Pharmacodynamics/Kinetics

Absorption: Elderly have a slightly slower rate of absorption but extent of absorption is the same as young adults

Distribution: V_d: 5-7 L/kg

Protein binding: 50% to 70%

Metabolism: Low first-pass metabolism

Half-life: Adults: 10-14 hours (average: 14.4 hours elderly, 12 hours in younger adults); increase in half-life with hepatic or heart failure

Time to peak: Peak levels attained in 2-3 hours

Elimination: 10% to 15% excreted unchanged in urine; urinary acidification increases excretion, alkalinization decreases excretion

Usual Dosage Adults: Oral: Initial: 200 mg every 8 hours (may load with 400 mg if necessary); adjust dose every 2-3 days; usual dose: 200-300 mg every 8 hours; maximum dose: 1.2 g/day (some patients respond to every 12-hour dosing); patients with hepatic impairment or CHF may require dose reduction; when switching from another antiarrhythmic, initiate a 200 mg dose 6-12 hours after stopping former agents, 3-6 hours after stopping procainamide

Administration Administer around-the-clock rather than 3 times/day to promote less variation in peak and trough serum levels; administer with food and antacids

Reference Range Therapeutic range: 0.5-2 µg/mL; potentially toxic: >2 µg/mL

Test Interactions Abnormal liver function test, positive ANA, thrombocytopenia

(Continued)

Mexiletine *(Continued)*

Patient Information Take with food or antacid; notify physician of severe or persistent abdominal pain, nausea, vomiting, yellowing of eyes or skin, pale stools, dark urine, or if persistent fever, sore throat, bleeding, or bruising occurs

Dosage Forms Capsule: 150 mg, 200 mg, 250 mg

- ◆ **Mexitil®** *see Mexiletine on page 772*
- ◆ **Mezlin®** *see Mezlocillin on this page*

Mezlocillin *(mez loe SIL in)*

Related Information

Antimicrobial Drugs of Choice *on page 1404*
Community-Acquired Pneumonia in Adults *on page 1419*

U.S. Brand Names Mezlin®

Synonyms Mezlocillin Sodium

Therapeutic Category Antibiotic, Penicillin

Use Treatment of infections caused by susceptible gram-negative aerobic bacilli (*Klebsiella, Proteus, Escherichia coli, Enterobacter, Pseudomonas aeruginosa, Serratia*) involving the skin and skin structure, bone and joint, respiratory tract, urinary tract, gastrointestinal tract, as well as, septicemia

Pregnancy Risk Factor B

Contraindications Hypersensitivity to mezlocillin, any component, or penicillins

Warnings/Precautions If bleeding occurs during therapy, mezlocillin should be discontinued; dosage modification required in patients with impaired renal function; use with caution in patients with renal impairment or biliary obstruction, or history of allergy to cephalosporins

Adverse Reactions

1% to 10%: Gastrointestinal: Nausea, diarrhea

<1%: Fever, seizures, dizziness, headache, rash, exfoliative dermatitis, hypokalemia, hypernatremia, vomiting, eosinophilia, leukopenia, neutropenia, thrombocytopenia, agranulocytosis, hemolytic anemia, prolonged bleeding time, positive Coombs' [direct], hepatotoxicity, elevated liver enzymes, hematuria, elevated BUN/serum creatinine, interstitial nephritis, serum sickness-like reactions

Overdosage/Toxicology

Symptoms of penicillin overdose include neuromuscular hypersensitivity (agitation, hallucinations, asterixis, encephalopathy, confusion, and seizures) and electrolyte imbalance with potassium or sodium salts, especially in renal failure

Hemodialysis may be helpful to aid in the removal of the drug from the blood, otherwise most treatment is supportive or symptom directed

Drug Interactions Aminoglycosides (synergy), probenecid (decreased clearance), vecuronium (increased duration of neuromuscular blockade), heparin (increased risk of bleeding); possible decrease in effectiveness of oral contraceptives; bacteriostatic action of tetracycline may impair bactericidal effects of the penicillins

Stability Reconstituted solution is stable for 48 hours at room temperature and 7 days when refrigerated; for I.V. infusion in NS or D_5W solution is stable for 48 hours at room temperature, 7 days when refrigerated or 28 days when frozen; after freezing, thawed solution is stable for 48 hours at room temperature or 7 days when refrigerated; if precipitation occurs under refrigeration, warm in water bath (37°C) for 20 minutes and shake well

Mechanism of Action Inhibits bacterial cell wall synthesis by binding to one or more of the penicillin binding proteins (PBPs); which in turn inhibits the final transpeptidation step of peptidoglycan synthesis in bacterial cell walls, thus inhibiting cell wall biosynthesis. Bacteria eventually lyse due to ongoing activity of cell wall autolytic enzymes (autolysins and murein hydrolases) while cell wall assembly is arrested.

Pharmacodynamics/Kinetics

Absorption: I.M.: 63%

Distribution: Into bile, heart, peritoneal fluid, sputum, bone; does not cross the blood-brain barrier well unless meninges are inflamed; crosses the placenta; distributes into breast milk at low concentrations

Protein binding: 30%

Metabolism: Minimal

Half-life: Dose dependent:

Neonates: <7 days: 3.7-4.4 hours; >7 days: 2.5 hours

Children 2-19 years: 0.9 hour

Adults: 50-70 minutes, increased in renal impairment

Time to peak serum concentration:

I.M.: 45-90 minutes after administration

I.V. infusion: Within 5 minutes

Elimination: Principally as unchanged drug in urine, also excreted via bile

Usual Dosage I.M., I.V.:

Infants:

≤7 days, ≤2000 g: 75 mg/kg every 12 hours

≤7 days, >2000 g: Same as above

>7 days, ≤2000 g: 75 mg/kg every 8 hours

>7 days, >2000 g: 75 mg/kg every 6 hours

Children: 300 mg/kg/day divided every 4-6 hours; maximum: 24 g/day

Adults: Usual: 3-4 g every 4-6 hours

Uncomplicated urinary tract infection: 1.5-2 g every 6 hours

Serious infections: 200-300 mg/kg/day in 4-6 divided doses

Dosing interval in renal impairment:
Cl$_{cr}$ 10-30 mL/minute: Administer every 6-8 hours
Cl$_{cr}$ <10 mL/minute: Administer every 8 hours
Hemodialysis: Moderately dialyzable (20% to 50%)
Dosing adjustment in hepatic impairment: Reduce dose by 50%
Administration Administer I.M. injections in large muscle mass, not more than 2 g/injection. I.M. injections given over 12-15 seconds will be less painful.
Monitoring Parameters Observe for signs and symptoms of anaphylaxis during first dose
Test Interactions False-positive direct Coombs'; false-positive urinary or serum protein; may inactivate aminoglycosides *in vitro*
Nursing Implications Administer at least 1 hour prior to aminoglycosides
Additional Information Minimum volume: 50 mL D$_5$W (concentration should not exceed 1 g/10 mL); sodium content of 1 g: 42.6 mg (1.85 mEq)
Dosage Forms Powder for injection, as sodium: 1 g, 2 g, 3 g, 4 g, 20 g

♦ **Mezlocillin Sodium** *see Mezlocillin on previous page*

♦ **Miacalcin® Injection** *see Calcitonin on page 171*

♦ **Miacalcin® Nasal Spray** *see Calcitonin on page 171*

♦ **Micanol® Cream** *see Anthralin on page 87*

♦ **Micardis®** *see Telmisartan on page 1110*

♦ **Micatin® Topical [OTC]** *see Miconazole on this page*

Miconazole (mi KON a zole)
Related Information
Antifungal Agents Comparison *on page 1303*
Treatment of Sexually Transmitted Diseases *on page 1429*
U.S. Brand Names Absorbine® Antifungal Foot Powder [OTC]; Breezee® Mist Antifungal [OTC]; Femizol-M® [OTC]; Fungoid® Creme; Fungoid® Tincture; Lotrimin® AF Powder [OTC]; Lotrimin® AF Spray Liquid [OTC]; Lotrimin® AF Spray Powder [OTC]; Maximum Strength Desenex® Antifungal Cream [OTC]; Micatin® Topical [OTC]; Monistat-Derm™ Topical; Monistat i.v.™ Injection; Monistat™ Vaginal; M-Zole® 7 Dual Pack [OTC]; Ony-Clear® Spray; Prescription Strength Desenex® [OTC]; Zeasorb-AF® Powder [OTC]
Canadian Brand Names Monazole-7®
Synonyms Miconazole Nitrate
Therapeutic Category Antifungal Agent, Imidazole Derivative; Antifungal Agent, Systemic; Antifungal Agent, Topical; Antifungal Agent, Vaginal
Use
I.V.: Treatment of severe systemic fungal infections and fungal meningitis that are refractory to standard treatment
Topical: Treatment of vulvovaginal candidiasis and a variety of skin and mucous membrane fungal infections
Pregnancy Risk Factor C
Contraindications Hypersensitivity to miconazole, fluconazole, ketoconazole, polyoxyl 35 castor oil, or any component; concomitant administration with cisapride
Warnings/Precautions Administer I.V. with caution to patients with hepatic insufficiency; the safety of miconazole in patients <1 year of age has not been established; cardiorespiratory and anaphylaxis have occurred with excessively rapid administration
Adverse Reactions
>10%:
Central nervous system: Fever, chills (10%)
Dermatologic: Rash, itching, pruritus (21%)
Gastrointestinal: Anorexia, diarrhea, nausea (18%), vomiting (7%)
Local: Pain at injection site
1% to 10%: Dermatologic: Rash (9%)
<1%: Flushing of face or skin, drowsiness, anemia, thrombocytopenia
Overdosage/Toxicology
Symptoms of overdose include nausea, vomiting, drowsiness
Following GI decontamination, supportive care only
Drug Interactions CYP3A3/4 enzyme substrate; CYP2C enzyme inhibitor, CYP3A3/4 enzyme inhibitor (moderate), and CYP3A5-7 enzyme inhibitor
Warfarin (increased anticoagulant effect), oral sulfonylureas, amphotericin B (decreased antifungal effect of both agents), phenytoin (levels may be increased)
Increased risk of significant cardiotoxicity with concurrent administration of cisapride - concomitant administration is contraindicated (see interactions associated with ketoconazole)
Stability Protect from heat; darkening of solution indicates deterioration; stability of parenteral admixture at room temperature (25°C): 2 days
Mechanism of Action Inhibits biosynthesis of ergosterol, damaging the fungal cell wall membrane, which increases permeability causing leaking of nutrients
Pharmacodynamics/Kinetics
Absorption: Negligible from topical dosage forms
Distribution: Appears to be widely distributed to body tissues; penetrates well into inflamed joints, vitreous humor of eye, and peritoneal cavity, but poorly into saliva and sputum; crosses blood-brain barrier but only to a small extent
Protein binding: 91% to 93%
Metabolism: In the liver
(Continued)

Miconazole *(Continued)*

Half-life, multiphasic: Initial: 40 minutes; Secondary: 126 minutes; Terminal phase: 24 hours

Elimination: ~50% excreted in feces and <1% in urine as unchanged drug

Usual Dosage

Children:

<1 year: 15-30 mg/kg/day

1-12 years:

I.V.: 20-40 mg/kg/day divided every 8 hours (do not exceed 15 mg/kg/dose)

Topical: Apply twice daily for up to 1 month

Adults:

Topical: Apply twice daily for up to 1 month

I.T.: 20 mg every 1-2 days

I.V.: Initial: 200 mg, then 0.6-3.6 g/day divided every 8 hours for up to 20 weeks

Bladder candidal infections: 200 mg diluted solution instilled in the bladder

Vaginal: Insert contents of 1 applicator of vaginal cream (100 mg) or 100 mg suppository at bedtime for 7 days, or 200 mg suppository at bedtime for 3 days

Hemodialysis: Not dialyzable (0% to 5%)

Administration Administer I.V. dose over 2 hours

Test Interactions ↑ protein

Patient Information Avoid contact with the eyes; for vaginal product, insert high into vagina and complete full course of therapy; notify physician if itching or burning occur; refrain from intercourse to prevent reinfection

Nursing Implications Observe patient closely during first I.V. dose for allergic reactions

Additional Information

Miconazole: Monistat i.v.™

Miconazole nitrate: Micatin®, Monistat™, Monistat-Derm™

Dosage Forms

Cream:

Topical, as nitrate: 2% (15 g, 30 g, 56.7 g, 85 g)

Vaginal, as nitrate: 2% (45 g is equivalent to 7 doses)

Dual pack: Vaginal suppositories and external vulvar cream 2%

Injection: 1% [10 mg/mL] (20 mL)

Lotion, as nitrate: 2% (30 mL, 60 mL)

Powder, topical: 2% (45 g, 90 g, 113 g)

Spray, topical: 2% (105 mL)

Suppository, vaginal, as nitrate: 100 mg (7s); 200 mg (3s)

Tincture: 2% with alcohol (7.39 mL, 29.57 mL)

◆ **Miconazole Nitrate** *see* Miconazole *on previous page*

◆ **MICRhoGAM™** *see* Rh₀(D) Immune Globulin (Intramuscular) *on page 1019*

Microfibrillar Collagen Hemostat

(mye kro FI bri lar KOL la jen HEE moe stat)

U.S. Brand Names Avitene®; Helistat®; Hemotene®

Synonyms Collagen; MCH

Therapeutic Category Hemostatic Agent

Use Adjunct to hemostasis when control of bleeding by ligature is ineffective or impractical

Pregnancy Risk Factor C

Contraindications Closure of skin incisions, contaminated wounds

Warnings/Precautions Fragments of MCH may pass through filters of blood scavenging systems, avoid reintroduction of blood from operative sites treated with MCH; after several minutes remove excess material

Adverse Reactions 1% to 10%: Miscellaneous: Potentiation of infection, allergic reaction, adhesion formation

Mechanism of Action Microfibrillar collagen hemostat is an absorbable topical hemostatic agent prepared from purified bovine corium collagen and shredded into fibrils. Physically, microfibrillar collagen hemostat yields a large surface area. Chemically, it is collagen with hydrochloric acid noncovalently bound to some of the available amino groups in the collagen molecules. When in contact with a bleeding surface, microfibrillar collagen hemostat attracts platelets which adhere to its fibrils and undergo the release phenomenon. This triggers aggregation of the platelets into thrombi in the interstices of the fibrous mass, initiating the formation of a physiologic platelet plug.

Pharmacodynamics/Kinetics Absorption: By animal tissue in 3 months

Usual Dosage Apply dry directly to source of bleeding

Dosage Forms

Fibrous: 1 g, 5 g

Nonwoven web: 70 mm x 70 mm x 1 mm; 70 mm x 35 mm x 1 mm

Sponge: 1" x 2" (10s); 3" x 4" (10s); 9" x 10" (5s)

◆ **Micro-K® 10** *see* Potassium Chloride *on page 949*

◆ **Micro-K® Extencaps®** *see* Potassium Chloride *on page 949*

◆ **Micro-K® LS®** *see* Potassium Chloride *on page 949*

◆ **Micronase®** *see* Glyburide *on page 540*

◆ **microNefrin®** *see* Epinephrine *on page 415*

◆ **Microsulfon®** *see* Sulfadiazine *on page 1092*

◆ **Microzide™** *see* Hydrochlorothiazide *on page 574*

◆ **Midamor®** *see* Amiloride *on page 56*

Midazolam (MID aye zoe lam)

Related Information

Adult ACLS Algorithm, Electrical Conversion *on page 1453*
Benzodiazepines Comparison *on page 1310*

U.S. Brand Names Versed®

Synonyms Midazolam Hydrochloride

Therapeutic Category Benzodiazepine; Hypnotic; Sedative

Use Preoperative sedation and provides conscious sedation prior to diagnostic or radiographic procedures

Unlabeled use: Anxiety, status epilepticus

Restrictions C-IV

Pregnancy Risk Factor D

Contraindications Hypersensitivity to midazolam or any component (cross-sensitivity with other benzodiazepines may occur); uncontrolled pain; existing CNS depression; shock; narrow-angle glaucoma

Warnings/Precautions Use with caution in patients with congestive heart failure, renal impairment, pulmonary disease, hepatic dysfunction, the elderly, and those receiving concomitant narcotics; midazolam may cause respiratory depression/arrest; deaths and hypoxic encephalopathy have resulted when these were not promptly recognized and treated appropriately. Serious respiratory reactions have occurred after midazolam syrup, most often when used in combination with other CNS depressants. It should only be used in hospital or ambulatory care settings that are equipped with the capabilities to monitor cardiac and respiratory function.

Adverse Reactions

>10%:

Local: Pain and local reactions at injection site (severity less than diazepam)

Miscellaneous: Hiccups

1% to 10%:

Cardiovascular: Cardiac arrest, hypotension, bradycardia

Central nervous system: Drowsiness, ataxia, amnesia, dizziness, paradoxical excitement, sedation, headache

Gastrointestinal: Nausea, vomiting

Ocular: Blurred vision, diplopia

Respiratory: Respiratory depression, apnea, laryngospasm, bronchospasm

Miscellaneous: Physical and psychological dependence with prolonged use

<1%: Tachycardia, delirium, rash, wheezing

Overdosage/Toxicology

Symptoms of overdose include respiratory depression, hypotension, coma, stupor, confusion, apnea

Treatment for benzodiazepine overdose is supportive. Rarely is mechanical ventilation required. Flumazenil has been shown to selectively block the binding of benzodiazepines to CNS receptors, resulting in a reversal of benzodiazepine-induced CNS depression; respiratory reaction to hypoxia may not be restored.

Drug Interactions CYP3A3/4 enzyme substrate

Decreased effect: Theophylline may antagonize the sedative effects of midazolam

Increased toxicity: CNS depressants, may increase sedation and respiratory depression; doses of anesthetic agents should be reduced when used in conjunction with midazolam; cimetidine may increase midazolam serum concentrations

If narcotics or other CNS depressants are administered concomitantly, the midazolam dose should be reduced by 30%, if <65 years of age or by at least 50%, if >65 years of age.

Stability Stable for 24 hours at room temperature/refrigeration; admixtures do not require protection from light for short-term storage; **compatible** with NS, D$_5$W

Standardized dose for continuous infusion: 100 mg/250 mL D$_5$W or NS; maximum concentration: 0.5 mg/mL

Mechanism of Action Depresses all levels of the CNS, including the limbic and reticular formation, probably through the increased action of gamma-aminobutyric acid (GABA), which is a major inhibitory neurotransmitter in the brain

Pharmacodynamics/Kinetics

I.M.:

Onset of sedation: Within 15 minutes

Peak effect: 0.5-1 hour

Duration: 2 hours mean, up to 6 hours

I.V.: Onset of action: Within 1-5 minutes

Absorption: Oral: Rapid

Distribution: V$_d$: 0.8-2.5 L/kg; increased with congestive heart failure (CHF) and chronic renal failure

Protein binding: 95%

Metabolism: Extensively in the liver (microsomally)

Bioavailability: 45% mean

Half-life, elimination: 1-4 hours, increased with cirrhosis, CHF, obesity, elderly

Elimination: As glucuronide conjugated metabolites in urine, ~2% to 10% excreted in feces

Usual Dosage The dose of midazolam needs to be individualized based on the patient's age, underlying diseases, and concurrent medications. Decrease dose (by ~30%) if narcotics or other CNS depressants are administered concomitantly. **Personnel and equipment needed for standard respiratory resuscitation should be immediately available during midazolam administration.**

(Continued)

Midazolam *(Continued)*

Neonates: Conscious sedation during mechanical ventilation: I.V. continuous infusion: 0.15-1 mcg/kg/minute. Use smallest dose possible; use lower doses (up to 0.5 mcg/kg/minute) for preterm neonates

Infants <2 months and Children: Status epilepticus refractory to standard therapy: I.V.: Loading dose: 0.15 mg/kg followed by a continuous infusion of 1 mcg/kg/minute; titrate dose upward very 5 minutes until clinical seizure activity is controlled; mean infusion rate required in 24 children was 2.3 mcg/kg/minute with a range of 1-18 mcg/kg/minute

Children:

Preoperative sedation:

Oral: Single dose preprocedure: 0.25-0.5 mg/kg, up to a maximum of 20 mg, depending on the status of the patient and desired effect; patients between 6 months and younger than 6 years, or less cooperative patients may require as much as 0.1 mg/kg as a single dose

I.M.: 0.07-0.08 mg/kg 30-60 minutes presurgery

I.V.: 0.035 mg/kg/dose, repeat over several minutes as required to achieve the desired sedative effect up to a total dose of 0.1-0.2 mg/kg

Conscious sedation during mechanical ventilation: I.V.: Loading dose: 0.05-0.2 mg/kg then follow with initial continuous infusion: 1-2 mcg/kg/minute; titrate to the desired effect; usual range: 0.4-6 mcg/kg/minute

Conscious sedation for procedures:

Oral, Intranasal: 0.2-0.4 mg/kg (maximum: 15 mg) 30-45 minutes before the procedure

I.V.: 0.05 mg/kg 3 minutes before procedure

Adolescents >12 years: I.V.: 0.5 mg every 3-4 minutes until effect achieved

Adults:

Preoperative sedation: I.M.: 0.07-0.08 mg/kg 30-60 minutes presurgery; usual dose: 5 mg

Conscious sedation: I.V.: Initial: 0.5-2 mg slow I.V. over at least 2 minutes; slowly titrate to effect by repeating doses every 2-3 minutes if needed; usual total dose: 2.5-5 mg; use decreased doses in elderly

Healthy Adults <60 years: Some patients respond to doses as low as 1 mg; no more than 2.5 mg should be administered over a period of 2 minutes. Additional doses of midazolam may be administered after a 2-minute waiting period and evaluation of sedation after each dose increment. A total dose >5 mg is generally not needed. If narcotics or other CNS depressants are administered concomitantly, the midazolam dose should be reduced by 30%.

Elderly: I.V.: Conscious sedation: Initial: 0.5 mg slow I.V.; give no more than 1.5 mg in a 2-minute period; if additional titration is needed, give no more than 1 mg over 2 minutes, waiting another 2 or more minutes to evaluate sedative effect; a total dose of >3.5 mg is rarely necessary

Sedation in mechanically intubated patients: I.V. continuous infusion: 100 mg in 250 mL D$_5$W or NS, (if patient is fluid-restricted, may concentrate up to a maximum of 0.5 mg/mL); initial dose: 0.01-0.05 mg/kg (~0.5-4 mg for a typical adult) initially and either repeated at 10-15 minute intervals until adequate sedation is achieved or continuous infusion rates of 0.02-0.1 mg/kg/hour (1-7 mg/hour) and titrate to reach desired level of sedation

Hemodialysis: Supplemental dose is not necessary

Peritoneal dialysis: Significant drug removal is unlikely based on physiochemical characteristics

Monitoring Parameters Respiratory and cardiovascular status, blood pressure, blood pressure monitor required during I.V. administration

Nursing Implications Midazolam is a short-acting benzodiazepine; recovery occurs within 2 hours in most patients, however, may require up to 6 hours in some cases

Additional Information Sodium content of 1 mL: 0.14 mEq

Dosage Forms

Injection, as hydrochloride: 1 mg/mL (2 mL, 5 mL, 10 mL); 5 mg/mL (1 mL, 2 mL, 5 mL, 10 mL)

Syrup: 2 mg/mL (118 mL)

♦ **Midazolam Hydrochloride** *see* Midazolam *on previous page*

♦ **Midchlor®** *see* Acetaminophen, Isometheptene, and Dichloralphenazone *on page 22*

Midodrine *(MI doe dreen)*

U.S. Brand Names ProAmatine®

Synonyms Midodrine Hydrochloride

Therapeutic Category Alpha-Adrenergic Agonist

Use Treatment of symptomatic orthostatic hypotension

Investigational: Management of urinary incontinence

Pregnancy Risk Factor C

Pregnancy/Breast-Feeding Implications Clinical effects on the fetus: No studies are available; use during pregnancy and lactation should be avoided unless the potential benefit outweighs the risk to the fetus

Contraindications Severe organic heart disease, urinary retention, pheochromocytoma, thyrotoxicosis, persistent and significant supine hypertension; hypersensitivity to midodrine or any component; concurrent use of fludrocortisone

Warnings/Precautions Only indicated for patients for whom orthostatic hypotension significantly impairs their daily life. Use is not recommended with supine hypertension and caution should be exercised in patients with diabetes, visual problems, urinary retention (reduce initial dose) or hepatic dysfunction; monitor renal and hepatic function prior to and periodically during therapy; safety and efficacy has not been established in children; discontinue and re-evaluate therapy if signs of bradycardia occur.

Adverse Reactions

>10%:
  Dermatologic: Piloerection (13%), pruritus (12%)
  Genitourinary: Urinary urgency, retention, or polyuria, dysuria (up to 13%)
  Neuromuscular & skeletal: Paresthesia (18.3%)

1% to 10%:
  Cardiovascular: Supine hypertension, (7%) facial flushing
  Central nervous system: Confusion, anxiety, dizziness, chills (5%)
  Dermatologic: Rash, dry skin (2%)
  Gastrointestinal: Xerostomia, nausea, abdominal pain
  Neuromuscular & skeletal: Pain (5%)

<1%: Flushing, headache, insomnia, flatulence, leg cramps, visual changes

Overdosage/Toxicology

Symptoms of overdose include hypertension, piloerection, urinary retention

Treatment is symptomatic following gastric decontamination; alpha-sympatholytics and/ or dialysis may be helpful

Drug Interactions Increased effect: Concomitant fludrocortisone results in hyperna-tremia or an increase in intraocular pressure and glaucoma; bradycardia may be accen-tuated with concomitant administration of cardiac glycosides, psychotherapeutics, and beta-blockers; alpha-agonists may increase the pressure effects and alpha-antagonists may negate the effects of midodrine

Mechanism of Action Midodrine forms an active metabolite, desglymidodrine, that is an alpha$_1$-agonist. This agent increases arteriolar and venous tone resulting in a rise in standing, sitting, and supine systolic and diastolic blood pressure in patients with ortho-static hypotension.

Causes of Orthostatic Hypotension

Primary Autonomic Causes
Pure autonomic failure (Bradbury-Eglleston syndrome, idiopathic orthostatic hypotension)
Autonomic failure with multiple system atrophy (Shy-Drager syndrome)
Familial dysautonomia (Riley-Day syndrome)
Dopamine beta-hydroxylase deficiency
Secondary Autonomic Causes
Chronic alcoholism
Parkinson's disease
Diabetes mellitus
Porphyria
Amyloidosis
Various carcinomas
Vitamin B$_1$ or B$_{12}$ deficiency
Nonautonomic Causes
Hypovolemia (such as associated with hemorrhage, burns, or hemodialysis) and dehydration
Diminished homeostatic regulation (such as associated with aging, pregnancy, fever, or prolonged best rest)
Medications (eg, antihypertensives, insulin, tricyclic antidepressants)

Pharmacodynamics/Kinetics

Absorption: Rapid

Distribution: V$_d$ (desglymidodrine): <1.6 L/kg; poorly distributed across membrane (eg, blood brain barrier)

Protein binding: Minimal

Metabolism: Rapid deglycination to desglymidodrine occurs in many tissues and plasma; further metabolism in the liver

Bioavailability: Absolute, 93%

Half-life: ~3-4 hours (active drug); 25 minutes (prodrug)

Time to peak serum concentration: 1-2 hours (active drug); 30 minutes (prodrug)

Elimination: Renal, minimal (2% to 4%); clearance of desglymidodrine: 385 mL/minute (predominantly by renal secretion)

Usual Dosage Adults: Oral: 10 mg 3 times/day during daytime hours (every 3-4 hours) when patient is upright (maximum: 40 mg/day)

  Dosing adjustment in renal impairment: 2.5 mg 3 times/day, gradually increasing as tolerated

Monitoring Parameters Blood pressure, renal and hepatic parameters

Patient Information Use caution with over-the-counter medications which may affect blood pressure (cough and cold, diet, stay-awake medications); avoid taking a particular dose if you are to be supine for any length of time; take your last daily dose 3-4 hours before bedtime to minimize nighttime supine hypertension

Nursing Implications Doses may be given in approximately 3- to 4-hour intervals (eg, shortly before or upon rising in the morning, at midday, in the late afternoon not later than 6 PM); avoid dosing after the evening meal or within 4 hours of bedtime; continue therapy only in patients who appear to attain symptomatic improvement during initial

(Continued)

Midodrine *(Continued)*

treatment; standing systolic blood pressure may be elevated 15-30 mm Hg at 1 hour after a 10 mg dose; some effect may persist for 2-3 hours

Dosage Forms Tablet, as hydrochloride: 2.5 mg, 5 mg

♦ **Midodrine Hydrochloride** *see* Midodrine *on page 778*

♦ **Midol® 200 [OTC]** *see* Ibuprofen *on page 593*

♦ **Midrin®** *see* Acetaminophen, Isometheptene, and Dichloralphenazone *on page 22*

Miglitol (MIG li tol)

Related Information

Hypoglycemic Drugs, Comparison of Oral Agents *on page 1325*

U.S. Brand Names Glyset®

Therapeutic Category Alpha-Glucosidase Inhibitor; Hypoglycemic Agent, Oral

Use

Noninsulin-dependent diabetes mellitus (NIDDM)

Monotherapy adjunct to diet to improve glycemic control in patients with NIDDM whose hyperglycemia cannot be managed with diet alone

Combination therapy with a sulfonylurea when diet plus either miglitol or a sulfonylurea alone do not result in adequate glycemic control. The effect of miglitol to enhance glycemic control is additive to that of sulfonylureas when used in combination.

Pregnancy Risk Factor B

Contraindications Diabetic ketoacidosis, inflammatory bowel disease, colonic ulceration, partial intestinal obstruction, patients predisposed to intestinal obstruction, chronic intestinal diseases associated with marked disorders of digestion or absorption or with conditions that may deteriorate as a result of increased gas formation in the intestine; hypersensitivity to drug or any of its components

Warnings/Precautions GI symptoms are the most common reactions. The incidence of abdominal pain and diarrhea tend to diminish considerably with continued treatment. Long-term clinical trials in diabetic patients with significant renal dysfunction (serum creatinine >2 mg/dL) have not been conducted. Treatment of these patients is not recommended. Because of its mechanism of action, miglitol administered alone should not cause hypoglycemia in the fasting of postprandial state. In combination with a sulfonylurea will cause a further lowering of blood glucose and may increase the hypoglycemic potential of the sulfonylurea.

Adverse Reactions

>10%: Gastrointestinal: Flatulence (41.5%), diarrhea (28.7%), abdominal pain (11.7%)

1% to 10%: Dermatologic: Rash

Overdosage/Toxicology An overdose of miglitol will not result in hypoglycemia. An overdose may result in transient increases in flatulence, diarrhea, and abdominal discomfort. No serious systemic reactions are expected in the event of an overdose.

Drug Interactions Decreased effect:

Miglitol may decrease the absorption and bioavailability of digoxin, propranolol, ranitidine

Digestive enzymes (amylase, pancreatin, charcoal) may reduce the effect of miglitol and should **not** be taken concomitantly

Mechanism of Action In contrast to sulfonylureas, miglitol does not enhance insulin secretion; the antihyperglycemic effect of miglitol results from a reversible inhibition of membrane-bound intestinal alpha-glucosidases which hydrolyze oligosaccharides and disaccharides to glucose and other monosaccharides in the brush border of the small intestine; in diabetic patients, this enzyme inhibition results in delayed glucose absorption and lowering of postprandial hyperglycemia

Pharmacodynamics/Kinetics

Absorption: Saturable at high doses: 25% mg dose: Completely absorbed; 100 mg dose: 50% to 70% absorbed; Peak concentrations within 2-3 hours

Distribution: V_d: 0.18 L/kg

Protein binding: Negligible (<4%)

Metabolism: Not metabolized

Half-life, elimination: ~2 hours

Elimination: Renal as unchanged drug

Usual Dosage Adults: Oral: 25 mg 3 times/day with the first bite of food at each meal; the dose may be increased to 50 mg 3 times/day after 4-8 weeks; maximum recommended dose: 100 mg 3 times/day

Dosing adjustment in renal impairment: Miglitol is primarily excreted by the kidneys; there is little information of miglitol in patients with Cl_{cr} <25 mL/minute

Dosing adjustment in hepatic impairment: No adjustment necessary

Administration Should be taken orally at the start (with the first bite) of each main meal

Monitoring Parameters Monitor therapeutic response by periodic blood glucose tests; measurement of glycosylated hemoglobin is recommended for the monitoring of long-term glycemic control

Reference Range Target range: Adults:

Fasting blood glucose: <120 mg/dL

Glycosylated hemoglobin: <7%

Patient Information Take orally 3 times/day with the first bite of each main meal. It is important to continue to adhere to dietary instructions, a regular exercise program, and regular testing of urine or blood glucose. If side effects occur, they usually develop during the first few weeks of therapy. They are most commonly mild-to-moderate dose-related GI effects, such as flatulence, soft stools, diarrhea, or abdominal discomfort, and they generally diminish in frequency and intensity with time. Discontinuation of drug usually results in rapid resolution of these GI symptoms.

Dosage Forms Tablet: 25 mg, 50 mg, 100 mg

+ **Migranal® Nasal Spray** see Dihydroergotamine on page 363
+ **Migratine®** see Acetaminophen, Isometheptene, and Dichloralphenazone on page 22
+ **Miles Nervine® Caplets [OTC]** see Diphenhydramine on page 369
+ **Milk of Magnesia** see Magnesium Hydroxide on page 705
+ **Milophene®** see Clomiphene on page 280

Milrinone (MIL ri none)

Related Information
Adrenergic Agonists, Cardiovascular Comparison on page 1290

U.S. Brand Names Primacor®

Synonyms Milrinone Lactate

Therapeutic Category Phosphodiesterase (Type 5) Enzyme Inhibitor

Use Short-term I.V. therapy of congestive heart failure; used for calcium antagonist intoxication

Pregnancy Risk Factor C

Contraindications Hypersensitivity to drug or amrinone

Warnings/Precautions Severe obstructive aortic or pulmonic valvular disease, history of ventricular arrhythmias; atrial fibrillation, flutter; renal dysfunction. Life-threatening arrhythmias were infrequent and have been associated with pre-existing arrhythmias, metabolic abnormalities, abnormal digoxin levels, and catheter insertion

Adverse Reactions
>10%: Cardiovascular: Ventricular arrhythmias (12.1%)
1% to 10%:
  Cardiovascular: Supraventricular arrhythmias, hypotension (2.9%), angina/chest pain (1.2), ventricular tachycardia (1% to 3%)
  Central nervous system: Headache (3%)
<1%: Ventricular fibrillation, hypokalemia, thrombocytopenia, tremor

Overdosage/Toxicology Hypotension should respond to I.V. fluids and Trendelenburg position; use of vasopressors may be required

Stability Colorless to pale yellow solution; store at room temperature and protect from light; stable at 0.2 mg/mL in 0.9% sodium chloride or D_5W for 72 hours at room temperature in normal light

Incompatible with furosemide and procainamide; **compatible** with atropine, calcium chloride, digoxin, epinephrine, lidocaine, morphine, propranolol, and sodium bicarbonate

Standardized dose: 20 mg in 80 mL of 0.9% sodium chloride or D_5W (0.2 mg/mL)

Mechanism of Action Phosphodiesterase inhibitor resulting in vasodilation

Pharmacodynamics/Kinetics
Serum level: I.V.: Following a 125 mcg/kg dose, peak plasma concentrations of ~1000 ng/mL were observed at 2 minutes postinjection, decreasing to <100 ng/mL in 2 hours
Therapeutic effect: Oral: Following doses of 7.5-15 mg, peak hemodynamic effects occurred at 90 minutes
Drug concentration levels:
  Therapeutic:
    Serum levels of 166 ng/mL, achieved during I.V. infusions of 0.25-1 mcg/kg/minute, were associated with sustained hemodynamic benefit in severe congestive heart failure patients over a 24-hour period
    Maximum beneficial effects on cardiac output and pulmonary capillary wedge pressure following I.V. infusion have been associated with plasma milrinone concentrations of 150-250 ng/mL
  Toxic: Serum concentrations >250-300 ng/mL have been associated with marked reductions in mean arterial pressure and tachycardia; however, more studies are required to determine the toxic serum levels for milrinone
Distribution: Not known if distributed into breast milk
  V_d at steady-state following I.V. administration as a single bolus: 0.32 L/kg; not significantly bound to tissues
  In patients with severe congestive heart failure (CHF), V_d has been 0.33-0.47 L/kg
Protein binding: ~70% in plasma
Metabolism: 12% hepatic
Half-life, elimination: I.V.: 136 minutes in patients with CHF; patients with severe CHF have a more prolonged half-life, with values ranging from 1.7-2.7 hours. Patients with CHF have a reduction in the systemic clearance of milrinone, resulting in a prolonged elimination half-life. Alternatively, one study reported that 1 month of therapy with milrinone did not change the pharmacokinetic parameters for patients with CHF despite improvement in cardiac function.
Elimination: Following I.V. administration, 85% of dose excreted unchanged in urine within 24 hours; active tubular secretion is a major elimination pathway for milrinone; bolus doses of I.V. milrinone produced systemic clearance values of 25.9±5.7 L/hour (0.37 L/hour/kg); however, in patients with severe congestive heart failure, the clearance is reduced to 0.11-0.13 L/hour/kg. The reduction in clearance may be a result of reduced renal function. Creatinine clearance values were ½ those reported for healthy adults in patients with severe congestive heart failure (52 vs 119 mL/minute).

Usual Dosage Adults: I.V.: Loading dose: 50 mcg/kg administered over 10 minutes followed by a maintenance dose titrated according to the hemodynamic and clinical response, see table.
(Continued)

Milrinone *(Continued)*

Maintenance Dosage	Dose Rate (mcg/kg/min)	Total Dose (mg/kg/24 h)
Minimum	0.375	0.59
Standard	0.500	0.77
Maximum	0.750	1.13

Dosing adjustment in renal impairment:
Cl_{cr} 50 mL/minute/1.73 m^2: Administer 0.43 mcg/kg/minute
Cl_{cr} 40 mL/minute/1.73 m^2: Administer 0.38 mcg/kg/minute
Cl_{cr} 30 mL/minute/1.73 m^2: Administer 0.33 mcg/kg/minute
Cl_{cr} 20 mL/minute/1.73 m^2: Administer 0.28 mcg/kg/minute
Cl_{cr} 10 mL/minute/1.73 m^2: Administer 0.23 mcg/kg/minute
Cl_{cr} 5 mL/minute/1.73 m^2: Administer 0.2 mcg/kg/minute

Monitoring Parameters Cardiac monitor and blood pressure monitor required; serum potassium
  Therapeutic: Patients should be monitored for improvement in the clinical signs and symptoms of congestive heart failure
  Toxic: Patients should be monitored for ventricular arrhythmias and exacerbation of anginal symptoms; during I.V. therapy with milrinone, blood pressure and heart rate should be monitored

Nursing Implications Monitor closely, titrate to blood pressure cardiac index

Dosage Forms Injection, as lactate: 1 mg/mL (5 mL, 10 mL, 20 mL)

- **Milrinone Lactate** *see Milrinone on previous page*
- **Miltown®** *see Meprobamate on page 731*
- **Minidyne® [OTC]** *see Povidone-Iodine on page 955*
- **Mini-Gamulin® Rh** *see Rh$_o$(D) Immune Globulin (Intramuscular) on page 1019*
- **Minims® Pilocarpine** *see Pilocarpine on page 927*
- **Minipress®** *see Prazosin on page 959*
- **Minitran® Patch** *see Nitroglycerin on page 845*
- **Minizide®** *see Prazosin and Polythiazide on page 960*
- **Minocin® IV Injection** *see Minocycline on this page*
- **Minocin® Oral** *see Minocycline on this page*

Minocycline *(mi noe SYE kleen)*

Related Information
  Antimicrobial Drugs of Choice *on page 1404*
  Community-Acquired Pneumonia in Adults *on page 1419*

U.S. Brand Names Dynacin® Oral; Minocin® IV Injection; Minocin® Oral

Canadian Brand Names Apo®-Minocycline; Syn-Minocycline

Synonyms Minocycline Hydrochloride

Therapeutic Category Antibiotic, Tetracycline Derivative

Use Treatment of susceptible bacterial infections of both gram-negative and gram-positive organisms; acne, meningococcal carrier state

Pregnancy Risk Factor D

Contraindications Hypersensitivity to minocycline, other tetracyclines, or any component; children <8 years of age

Warnings/Precautions Should be avoided in renal insufficiency, children ≤8 years of age, pregnant and nursing women; photosensitivity reactions can occur with minocycline

Adverse Reactions
  >10%: Miscellaneous: Discoloration of teeth in children
  1% to 10%:
    Dermatologic: Photosensitivity
    Gastrointestinal: Nausea, diarrhea
  <1%: Pericarditis, increased intracranial pressure, bulging fontanels in infants, dermatologic effects, pruritus, exfoliative dermatitis, rash, pigmentation of nails, diabetes insipidus syndrome, vomiting, esophagitis, anorexia, abdominal cramps, paresthesia, acute renal failure, azotemia, superinfections, anaphylaxis

Overdosage/Toxicology
  Symptoms of overdose include diabetes insipidus, nausea, anorexia, diarrhea
  Following GI decontamination, supportive care only; fluid support may be required

Drug Interactions
  Decreased effect with antacids (aluminum, calcium, zinc, or magnesium), bismuth salts, sodium bicarbonate, barbiturates, carbamazepine, hydantoins; decreased effect of oral contraceptives
  Increased effect of warfarin

Mechanism of Action Inhibits bacterial protein synthesis by binding with the 30S and possibly the 50S ribosomal subunit(s) of susceptible bacteria; cell wall synthesis is not affected

Pharmacodynamics/Kinetics
  Absorption: Well absorbed
  Distribution: Crosses placenta; appears in breast milk; majority of a dose deposits for extended periods in fat
  Protein binding: 70% to 75%

Half-life: 15 hours
Elimination: Eventually cleared renally

Usual Dosage
Children >8 years: Oral, I.V.: Initial: 4 mg/kg followed by 2 mg/kg/dose every 12 hours
Adults:
Infection: Oral, I.V.: 200 mg stat, 100 mg every 12 hours not to exceed 400 mg/24 hours
Acne: Oral: 50 mg 1-3 times/day
Hemodialysis: Not dialyzable (0% to 5%)

Administration
Infuse I.V. minocycline over 1 hour

Patient Information
Avoid unnecessary exposure to sunlight; do not take with antacids, iron products, or dairy products; finish all medication; do not skip doses; take 1 hour before or 2 hours after meals

Dosage Forms
Capsule:
As hydrochloride: 50 mg, 100 mg
As hydrochloride (Dynacin®, Vectrin®): 50 mg, 100 mg
Pellet-filled, as hydrochloride (Minocin®): 50 mg, 100 mg
Injection, as hydrochloride (Minocin® IV): 100 mg
Suspension, oral, as hydrochloride (Minocin®)50 mg/5 mL (60 mL)

♦ **Minocycline Hydrochloride** see Minocycline *on previous page*

Minoxidil (mi NOKS i dil)
Related Information
Hypertension Therapy *on page 1479*

U.S. Brand Names Loniten®; Rogaine® Extra Strength for Men [OTC]; Rogaine® for Men [OTC]; Rogaine® for Women [OTC]

Canadian Brand Names Apo-Gain®; Gen-Minoxidil®

Therapeutic Category Antihypertensive Agent; Vasodilator

Use Management of severe hypertension (usually in combination with a diuretic and beta-blocker); treatment of male pattern baldness (alopecia androgenetica)

Pregnancy Risk Factor C

Contraindications Pheochromocytoma, hypersensitivity to minoxidil or any component

Warnings/Precautions Note: Minoxidil can cause pericardial effusion, occasionally progressing to tamponade and it can exacerbate angina pectoris; use with caution in patients with pulmonary hypertension, significant renal failure, or congestive heart failure; use with caution in patients with coronary artery disease or recent myocardial infarction; renal failure or dialysis patients may require smaller doses; usually used with a beta-blocker (to treat minoxidil-induced tachycardia) and a diuretic (for treatment of water retention/edema); may take 1-6 months for hypertrichosis to totally reverse after minoxidil therapy is discontinued.

Adverse Reactions
>10%:
Cardiovascular: EKG changes (60%), tachycardia, congestive heart failure
Dermatologic: Hypertrichosis (commonly occurs within 1-2 months of therapy)
Hematologic: Transient hematocrit/hemoglobin decrease
1% to 10%:
Cardiovascular: Edema (7%)
Endocrine & metabolic: Fluid and electrolyte imbalance
<1%: Angina, pericardial effusion tamponade, dizziness, breast tenderness, rashes, headache, coarsening facial features, dermatologic reactions, Stevens-Johnson syndrome, sunburn, weight gain, thrombocytopenia, leukopenia

Overdosage/Toxicology
Symptoms of overdose include hypotension, tachycardia, headache, nausea, dizziness, weakness syncope, warm flushed skin and palpitations; lethargy and ataxia may occur in children
Hypotension usually responds to I.V. fluids, Trendelenburg positioning or vasoconstrictor; treatment is primarily supportive and symptomatic

Drug Interactions
Increased toxicity:
Concurrent administration with guanethidine may cause profound orthostatic hypotensive effects
Additive hypotensive effects with other hypotensive agents or diuretics

Mechanism of Action Produces vasodilation by directly relaxing arteriolar smooth muscle, with little effect on veins; effects may be mediated by cyclic AMP; stimulation of hair growth is secondary to vasodilation, increased cutaneous blood flow and stimulation of resting hair follicles

Pharmacodynamics/Kinetics
Onset of hypotensive effect: Oral: Within 30 minutes
Peak effect: Within 2-8 hours
Duration: Up to 2-5 days
Protein binding: None
Metabolism: 88% primarily via glucuronidation
Bioavailability: Oral: 90%
Half-life: Adults: 3.5-4.2 hours
Elimination: 12% excreted unchanged in urine
(Continued)

Minoxidil *(Continued)*

Usual Dosage
Children <12 years: Hypertension: Oral: Initial: 0.1-0.2 mg/kg once daily; maximum: 5 mg/day; increase gradually every 3 days; usual dosage: 0.25-1 mg/kg/day in 1-2 divided doses; maximum: 50 mg/day

Children >12 years and Adults:
Hypertension: Oral: Initial: 5 mg once daily, increase gradually every 3 days; usual dose: 10-40 mg/day in 1-2 divided doses; maximum: 100 mg/day
Alopecia: Topical: Apply twice daily; 4 months of therapy may be necessary for hair growth

Elderly: Initial: 2.5 mg once daily; increase gradually

Note: Dosage adjustment is needed when added to concomitant therapy

Dialysis: Supplemental dose is not necessary via hemo- or peritoneal dialysis

Monitoring Parameters
Blood pressure, standing and sitting/supine; fluid and electrolyte balance and body weight should be monitored

Patient Information
Topical product must be used every day. Hair growth usually takes 4 months. Notify physician if any of the following occur: Heart rate ≥20 beats per minute over normal; rapid weight gain >5 lb (2 kg); unusual swelling of extremities, face, or abdomen; breathing difficulty, especially when lying down; rise slowly from prolonged lying or sitting; new or aggravated angina symptoms (chest, arm, or shoulder pain); severe indigestion; dizziness, lightheadedness, or fainting; nausea or vomiting may occur. Do not make up for missed doses.

Nursing Implications
May cause hirsutism or hypertrichosis; observe for fluid retention and orthostatic hypotension

Dosage Forms
Solution, topical: 2% [20 mg/metered dose] (60 mL); 5% [50 mg/metered dose] (60 mL)
Tablet: 2.5 mg, 10 mg

- **Mintezol®** *see* Thiabendazole *on page 1130*
- **Minute-Gel®** *see* Fluoride *on page 498*
- **Miochol-E®** *see* Acetylcholine *on page 25*
- **Miostat® Intraocular** *see* Carbachol *on page 188*
- **Miradon®** *see* Anisotropine *on page 86*
- **Mirapex®** *see* Pramipexole *on page 957*
- **Mireze®** *see* Nedocromil Sodium *on page 821*

Mirtazapine *(mir TAZ a peen)*

Related Information
Antidepressant Agents Comparison *on page 1301*

U.S. Brand Names Remeron®

Therapeutic Category Antidepressant, Tetracyclic

Use Treatment of depression

Pregnancy Risk Factor C

Contraindications Patients with a known hypersensitivity to mirtazapine, use during or within 14 days of monoamine oxidase inhibitor therapy

Warnings/Precautions Hepatic or renal dysfunction, predisposition to conditions that could be exacerbated by hypotension, history of mania or hypomania, seizure disorders, immunocompromized patients, the elderly, or during pregnancy or nursing

Adverse Reactions
>10%:
Central nervous system: Somnolence
Endocrine & metabolic: Increased cholesterol
Gastrointestinal: Constipation, xerostomia, increased appetite, weight gain

1% to 10%:
Cardiovascular: Hypertension, vasodilatation, peripheral edema, edema
Central nervous system: Dizziness, abnormal dreams, abnormal thoughts, confusion, malaise
Endocrine & metabolic: Increased triglycerides
Gastrointestinal: Vomiting, anorexia, eructation, glossitis, cholecystitis
Genitourinary: Polyuria
Neuromuscular & skeletal: Myalgia, back pain, arthralgia, tremor, weakness
Respiratory: Dyspnea
Miscellaneous: Flu-like symptoms, thirst

<1%: Orthostatic hypotension, seizures (1 case reported), dehydration, weight loss, agranulocytosis, neutropenia, lymphadenopathy, increased LFTs

Drug Interactions CYP1A2, 2C9, 2D6, and 3A3/4 enzyme substrate
Increased toxicity: Impairment of cognitive and motor skills are additive with those produced by alcohol, benzodiazepines, and other CNS depressants; possibly serious or fatal reactions can occur when given with or when given within 14 days of a monoamine oxidase inhibitor.

Mechanism of Action Mirtazapine is a tetracyclic antidepressant that works by its central presynaptic alpha$_2$-adrenergic antagonist effects, which results in increased release of norepinephrine and serotonin. It is also a potent antagonist of 5-HT$_2$ and 5-HT$_3$ serotonin receptors and H$_1$ histamine receptors and a moderate peripheral alpha$_1$-adrenergic and muscarinic antagonist; it does not inhibit the reuptake of norepinephrine or serotonin.

Pharmacodynamics/Kinetics
Protein binding: 85%

Metabolism: Extensive by cytochrome P-450 enzymes in the liver

Bioavailability: 50%

Half-life: 20-40 hours

Time to peak serum concentration: 2 hours

Elimination: Extensive hepatic metabolism via demethylation and hydroxylation, metabolites eliminated primarily renally (75%) and some via the feces (15%); elimination is hampered with renal dysfunction or hepatic dysfunction.

Usual Dosage Adults: Oral: Initial: 15 mg nightly, titrate up to 15-45 mg/day with dose increases made no more frequently than every 1-2 weeks

Dietary Considerations Alcohol: Additive CNS effect, avoid use

Monitoring Parameters Patients should be monitored for signs of agranulocytosis or severe neutropenia such as sore throat, stomatitis or other signs of infection or a low WBC; monitor for improvement in clinical signs and symptoms of depression, improvement may be observed within 1-4 weeks after initiating therapy

Patient Information Be aware of the risk of developing agranulocytosis; contact physician if any indication of infection occurs (ie, fever, chills, sore throat, mucous membrane ulceration, and especially flu-like symptoms); may impair judgment, thinking, and particularly motor skills; may impair ability to drive, use machinery, or perform tasks that require you remain alert; avoid concurrent alcohol use

Dosage Forms Tablet: 15 mg, 30 mg

Misoprostol (mye soe PROST ole)

U.S. Brand Names Cytotec®

Therapeutic Category Prostaglandin

Use Prevention of NSAID-induced gastric ulcers

Pregnancy Risk Factor X

Contraindications Pregnancy; hypersensitivity to misoprostol or any component

Warnings/Precautions Safety and efficacy have not been established in children <18 years of age; use with caution in patients with renal impairment and the elderly; not to be used in pregnant women or women of childbearing potential unless woman is capable of complying with effective contraceptive measures; therapy is normally begun on the second or third day of next normal menstrual period

Adverse Reactions

>10%: Gastrointestinal: Diarrhea, abdominal pain

1% to 10%:

Central nervous system: Headache

Gastrointestinal: Constipation, flatulence

<1%: Nausea, vomiting, uterine stimulation, vaginal bleeding

Overdosage/Toxicology Symptoms of overdose include sedation, tremor, convulsions, dyspnea, abdominal pain, diarrhea, hypotension, bradycardia

Mechanism of Action Misoprostol is a synthetic prostaglandin E_1 analog that replaces the protective prostaglandins consumed with prostaglandin-inhibiting therapies eg, nonsteroidal anti-inflammatory drugs

Pharmacodynamics/Kinetics

Absorption: Oral: Rapid

Metabolism: Rapidly de-esterified to misoprostol acid

Half-life (parent and metabolite combined): 1.5 hours

Time to peak serum concentration (active metabolite): Within 15-30 minutes

Elimination: In urine (64% to 73% in 24 hours) and feces (15% in 24 hours)

Usual Dosage Adults: Oral: 200 mcg 4 times/day with food; if not tolerated, may decrease dose to 100 mcg 4 times/day with food or 200 mcg twice daily with food

Patient Information May cause diarrhea when first being used; take after meals and at bedtime; avoid taking with magnesium-containing antacids

Nursing Implications Incidence of diarrhea may be lessened by having patient take dose right after meals

Dosage Forms Tablet: 100 mcg, 200 mcg

♦ **Mithracin®** see Plicamycin on page 937

♦ **Mithramycin** see Plicamycin on page 937

Mitomycin (mye toe MYE sin)

Related Information

Cancer Chemotherapy Regimens on page 1263

Extravasation Management of Chemotherapeutic Agents on page 1285

Toxicities of Chemotherapeutic Agents on page 1288

U.S. Brand Names Mutamycin®

Synonyms Mitomycin-C; MTC

Therapeutic Category Antineoplastic Agent, Antibiotic; Antineoplastic Agent, Vesicant; Vesicant

Use Therapy of disseminated adenocarcinoma of stomach or pancreas in combination with other approved chemotherapeutic agents; bladder cancer, colorectal cancer

Pregnancy Risk Factor C

Contraindications Platelet counts <75,000/mm³; leukocyte counts <3,000/mm³ or serum creatinine >1.7 mg/dL; thrombocytopenia, hypersensitivity to mitomycin or any component

Warnings/Precautions The U.S. Food and Drug Administration (FDA) currently recommends that procedures for proper handling and disposal of antineoplastic agents be considered. Use with caution in patients with impaired renal or hepatic function, myelosuppression. Follow hemoglobin, hematocrit, BUN, and creatinine closely after therapy (Continued)

Mitomycin *(Continued)*

especially after second and subsequent cycles. Bone marrow suppression, notably thrombocytopenia and leukopenia, may contribute to the development of a secondary infection; hemolytic uremic syndrome, a serious and often fatal syndrome, has occurred in patients receiving long-term therapy and is correlated with total dose and total duration of therapy; mitomycin is potentially carcinogenic and teratogenic.

Adverse Reactions

>10%:

Gastrointestinal: **Nausea and vomiting (mild to moderate) seen in almost 100% of patients;** usually begins 1-2 hours after treatment and persists for 3 hours to 4 days; other toxicities include stomatitis, hepatotoxicity, diarrhea, anorexia

Emetic potential: Moderate (30% to 60%)

Time course of nausea/vomiting: Onset: 1-2 hours; Duration: 48-72 hours

Local: Extravasation: May cause severe tissue irritation if infiltrated; can progress to cellulitis, ulceration, and sloughing of tissue. Refer to institutional policy for treatment.

Vesicant chemotherapy

Hematologic: Myelosuppressive: Dose-related toxicity and may be cumulative; related to both total dose (incidence higher at doses >50 mg) and schedule, may occur at anytime within 8 weeks of treatment.

WBC: Moderate

Platelets: Severe

Onset (days): 21

Nadir (days): 36

Recovery (days): 42-56

1% to 10%:

Dermatologic: Discolored fingernails (violet), alopecia

Neuromuscular & skeletal: Extremity paresthesia

Renal: Elevation of creatinine seen in 2% of patients; hemolytic uremic syndrome observed in <10% of patients and is dose-dependent (doses ≥60 mg or >50 mg/m^2 have higher risk)

Respiratory: Interstitial pneumonitis or pulmonary fibrosis have been noticed in 7% of patients, and it occurs independent of dosing. Manifested as dry cough and progressive dyspnea; usually is responsive to steroid therapy.

<1%: Cardiac failure (in patients treated with doses >30 mg/m^2), malaise, fever, pruritus, rash, mouth ulcers, bone marrow suppression (leukopenia, thrombocytopenia), microangiopathic hemolytic anemia, thrombophlebitis, paresthesia, weakness

Overdosage/Toxicology
Symptoms of overdose include bone marrow suppression, nausea, vomiting, alopecia

Drug Interactions

Increased toxicity:

Vinca alkaloids → acute shortness of breath or bronchospasm

Doxorubicin may enhance cardiac toxicity

Stability

Store intact vials of lyophilized powder at room temperature

Dilute powder with SWI to a concentration of 0.5 mg/mL as follows: Solution is stable for 7 days at room temperature and 14 days at refrigeration if protected from light

5 mg = 10 mL

20 mg = 40 mL

Further dilution in NS is stable for 24 hours at room temperature

Standard I.V. dilution:

I.V. push: Dose/syringe (concentration = 0.5 mg/mL)

Maximum syringe size for IVP is a 30 mL syringe and syringe should be ≤75% full

Syringe is stable for 7 days at room temperature and 14 days at refrigeration if protected from light

IVPB: Dose/100 mL NS

IVPB solution is stable for 24 hours at room temperature

Mechanism of Action
Isolated from *Streptomyces caespitosus*; acts primarily as an alkylating agent and produces DNA cross-linking (primarily with guanine and cytosine pairs); cell-cycle nonspecific; inhibits DNA and RNA synthesis by alkylation and cross-linking the strands of DNA

Pharmacodynamics/Kinetics

Absorption: Fairly well from the GI tract

Distribution: V_d: 22 L/m^2; high drug concentrations found in kidney, tongue, muscle, heart, and lung tissue; probably not distributed into the CNS

Metabolism: Hepatic

Half-life: 23-78 minutes; Terminal: 50 minutes

Elimination: Primarily in metabolism, followed by urinary excretion (<10% as unchanged drug) and to a small extent biliary excretion

Usual Dosage
Refer to individual protocols

Children and Adults: I.V.:

Single-agent therapy: 20 mg/m^2 every 6-8 weeks

Note: Doses >20 mg/m^2 have not been shown to be more effective, and are more toxic.

Combination therapy: 10 mg/m^2 every 6-8 weeks

Bone marrow transplant:

40-50 mg/m^2

2-40 mg/m^2/day for 3 days

Total cumulative dose should not exceed 50 mg/m^2; see table.

Mitomycin

Nadir After Prior Dose per mm^3		% of Prior Dose to Be Given
Leukocytes	Platelets	
4000	>100,000	100
3000-3999	75,000-99,999	100
2000-2999	25,000-74,999	70
2000	<25,000	50

Dosing adjustment in renal impairment:
Cl$_{cr}$ <10 mL/minute: Administer 75% of normal dose
   or
Serum creatinine 1.6-2.4 mg/dL: Administer 50% of the dose
Serum creatinine >2.4 mg/dL: Do not administer
Hemodialysis: Unknown
CAPD effects: Unknown
CAVH effects: Unknown
Dosing adjustment in hepatic impairment:
Bilirubin 1.5-3 mg/dL OR BSP retention 9% to 16%: Administer 50% of the dose
Bilirubin >3.1 mg/dL OR BSP retention >Administer 25% of the dose
   or
Bilirubin >3.0 mg/dL OR hepatitic enzymes >3 times normal: Administer 50% of the dose
Intravesicular instillations for bladder carcinoma: 20-40 mg/dose (1 mg/mL in sterile aqueous solution) instilled into the bladder for 3 hours repeated up to 3 times/week for up to 20 procedures per course

Administration
Administer slow I.V. push by **central line only**
Administer mitomycin doses of 10 mg/m^2 over 5-10 minutes
Administer mitomycin doses of 10-20 mg/m^2 over 10-20 minutes
Avoid extravasation; severe local tissue necrosis occurs. Flush with 5-10 mL of I.V. solution before and after drug administration; IVPB infusions should be closely monitored for adequate vein patency.

Monitoring Parameters Platelet count, CBC with differential, hemoglobin, prothrombin time, renal and pulmonary function tests

Patient Information Any signs of infection, easy bruising or bleeding, shortness of breath, or painful or burning urination should be brought to physician's attention. Nausea, vomiting, or hair loss sometimes occur. The drug may cause permanent sterility and may cause birth defects. The drug may be excreted in breast milk, therefore, an alternative form of feeding your baby should be used. Contraceptive measures are recommended during therapy.

Nursing Implications
Extravasation management:
Care should be taken to avoid extravasation. If extravasation occurs, the site should be observed closely; these injuries frequently cause necrosis; a plastic surgery consult may be required.
Few agents have been effective as antidotes, but there are reports in the literature of some benefit with dimethylsulfoxide (DMSO). Delayed dermal reactions with mitomycin are possible, even in patients who are asymptomatic at time of drug administration.

Dosage Forms Powder for injection: 5 mg, 20 mg, 40 mg

♦ **Mitomycin-C** see Mitomycin on page 785

Mitotane (MYE toe tane)
Related Information
Toxicities of Chemotherapeutic Agents on page 1288
U.S. Brand Names Lysodren®
Synonyms o,p'-DDD
Therapeutic Category Antiadrenal Agent; Antineoplastic Agent, Miscellaneous
Use Treatment of inoperable adrenal cortical carcinoma
Pregnancy Risk Factor C
Contraindications Known hypersensitivity to mitotane
Warnings/Precautions The U.S. Food and Drug Administration (FDA) currently recommends that procedures for proper handling and disposal of antineoplastic agents be considered. Patients should be hospitalized when mitotane therapy is initiated until a stable dose regimen is established. Discontinue temporarily following trauma or shock since the prime action of mitotane is adrenal suppression; exogenous steroids may be indicated since adrenal function may not start immediately. Administer with care to patients with severe hepatic impairment; observe patients for neurotoxicity with prolonged (2 years) use.
Adverse Reactions
>10%:
Central nervous system: Vertigo, mental depression, dizziness; all are reversible with discontinuation of the drug and can occur in 15% to 26% of patients
(Continued)

Mitotane *(Continued)*

Dermatologic: Rash (15%) which may subside without discontinuation of therapy, hyperpigmentation

Gastrointestinal: 75% to 80% will experience nausea, vomiting, and anorexia; diarrhea can occur in 20% of patients

Ocular: Diplopia, visual disturbances, blurred vision (reversible with discontinuation)

1% to 10%:

Cardiovascular: Orthostatic hypotension

Endocrine & metabolic: Flushing of skin

Genitourinary: Hemorrhagic cystitis

Neuromuscular & skeletal: Myalgia

<1%: Adrenal insufficiency may develop and may require steroid replacement; hypertension, flushing, lethargy, somnolence, mental depression, irritability, confusion, fatigue, headache, fever, hyperpyrexia, hypercholesterolemia, tremor, weakness, lens opacities, toxic retinopathy, hypouricemia, hematuria, albuminuria, shortness of breath, wheezing

Myelosuppressive:

WBC: None

Platelets: None

Overdosage/Toxicology Symptoms of overdose include diarrhea, vomiting, numbness of limbs, weakness

Drug Interactions

Decreased effect:

Barbiturates, warfarin may be accelerated by induction of the hepatic microsomal enzyme system

Spironolactone has resulted in negation of mitotane's effect

Phenytoin may increase clearance of these drugs by microsomal enzyme stimulation by mitotane

Increased toxicity: CNS depressants may increase CNS depression

Stability Protect from light, store at room temperature

Mechanism of Action Causes adrenal cortical atrophy; drug affects mitochondria in adrenal cortical cells and decreases production of cortisol; also alters the peripheral metabolism of steroids

Pharmacodynamics/Kinetics

Absorption: Oral: ~35% to 40%

Time to peak serum concentration: Within 3-5 hours

Distribution: Stored mainly in fat tissue but is found in all body tissues

Metabolism: Primarily in the liver by hydroxylation and oxidation and other tissues

Half-life: 18-159 days

Elimination: Metabolites excreted in urine and bile

Usual Dosage Oral:

Children: 0.1-0.5 mg/kg or 1-2 g/day in divided doses increasing gradually to a maximum of 5-7 g/day

Adults: Start at 1-6 g/day in divided doses, then increase incrementally to 8-10 g/day in 3-4 divided doses; dose is changed on basis of side effect with aim of giving as high a dose as tolerated; maximum daily dose: 18 g

Dosing adjustment in hepatic impairment: Dose may need to be decreased in patients with liver disease

Dietary Considerations Alcohol: Additive CNS effect, avoid use

Patient Information Patients should be warned that mitotane may impair ability to operate hazardous equipment or drive; avoid alcohol and other CNS depressants; notify physician if rash or darkening of skin, severe nausea, vomiting, depression, flushing, or fever occurs; contraceptive measures are recommended during therapy

Dosage Forms Tablet, scored: 500 mg

Mitoxantrone *(mye toe ZAN trone)*

Related Information

Cancer Chemotherapy Regimens *on page 1263*

Toxicities of Chemotherapeutic Agents *on page 1288*

U.S. Brand Names Novantrone®

Synonyms DHAD; Mitoxantrone Hydrochloride

Therapeutic Category Antineoplastic Agent, Anthracycline; Antineoplastic Agent, Antibiotic; Antineoplastic Agent, Irritant; Vesicant

Use Treatment of acute nonlymphocytic leukemia (ANLL) in adults in combination with other agents; very active against various leukemias, lymphoma, and breast cancer, and moderately active against pediatric sarcoma

Pregnancy Risk Factor D

Contraindications Hypersensitivity to mitoxantrone or any component

Warnings/Precautions The FDA currently recommends that procedures for proper handling and disposal of antineoplastic agents be considered. Dosage should be reduced in patients with impaired hepatobiliary function; use with caution in patients with pre-existing myelosuppression. Predisposing factors for mitoxantrone-induced cardiotoxicity include prior anthracycline therapy, prior cardiovascular disease, and mediastinal irradiation. The risk of developing cardiotoxicity is <3% when the cumulative doses are <100-120 mg/m^2 in patients with predisposing factors and <160 mg/m^2 in patients with no predisposing factors.

Adverse Reactions

>10%:

Central nervous system: Headache

Dermatologic: Alopecia

Gastrointestinal: Nausea, vomiting, diarrhea, abdominal pain, mucositis, stomatitis, GI bleeding

Emetic potential: Moderate (31% to 72%)

Genitourinary: Discoloration of urine (blue-green)

Hepatic: Abnormal LFTs

Respiratory: Coughing, shortness of breath

1% to 10%:

Cardiac toxicity: Much reduced compared to doxorubicin and has been reported primarily in patients who have received prior anthracycline therapy, congestive heart failure, hypotension

Central nervous system: Seizures, fever

Dermatologic: Pruritus, skin desquamation

Hematologic: Myelosuppressive effects of chemotherapy:

WBC: Mild

Platelets: Mild

Onset (days): 7-10

Nadir (days): 14

Recovery (days): 21

Hepatic: Transient elevation of liver enzymes, jaundice

Ocular: Conjunctivitis

Renal: Renal failure

<1%: Pain or redness at injection site; **irritant chemotherapy** with blue skin discoloration

Overdosage/Toxicology

Symptoms of overdose include leukopenia, tachycardia, marrow hypoplasia

No known antidote

Stability

Store intact vials at room temperature or refrigeration

Dilute in at least 50 mL of NS or D_5W; solution is stable for 7 days at room temperature or refrigeration

Incompatible with heparin and hydrocortisone

Standard I.V. dilution:

IVPB: Dose/100 mL D_5W or NS

Solution is stable for 7 days at room temperature and refrigeration

Mechanism of Action Analogue of the anthracyclines, but different in mechanism of action, cardiac toxicity, and potential for tissue necrosis; mitoxantrone does intercalate DNA; binds to nucleic acids and inhibits DNA and RNA synthesis by template disordering and steric obstruction; replication is decreased by binding to DNA topoisomerase II (enzyme responsible for DNA helix supercoiling); active throughout entire cell cycle; does not appear to produce free radicals

Pharmacodynamics/Kinetics

Absorption: Oral: Poor

Distribution: V_d: 14 L/kg; distributes into pleural fluid, kidney, thyroid, liver, heart, and red blood cells

Protein binding: 78%

Albumin binding: 76%

Metabolism: In the liver

Half-life: Terminal: 37 hours; may be prolonged with liver impairment

Elimination: Slowly excreted in urine (6% to 11%) and bile as unchanged drug and metabolites

Usual Dosage Refer to individual protocols. I.V. (may dilute in D_5W or NS):

ANLL leukemias:

Children ≤2 years: 0.4 mg/kg/day once daily for 3-5 days

Children >2 years and Adults: 12 mg/m²/day once daily for 3 days; acute leukemia in relapse: 8-12 mg/m²/day once daily for 4-5 days

Solid tumors:

Children: 18-20 mg/m² every 3-4 weeks **OR** 5-8 mg/m² every week

Adults: 12-14 mg/m² every 3-4 weeks **OR** 2-4 mg/m²/day for 5 days

Maximum total dose: 80-120 mg/m² in patients with predisposing factor and <160 mg in patients with no predisposing factor

Hemodialysis: Supplemental dose is not necessary

Peritoneal dialysis: Supplemental dose is not necessary

Dosing adjustment in hepatic impairment: Official dosage adjustment recommendations have not been established

Moderate dysfunction (bilirubin 1.5-3 mg/dL): Some clinicians recommend a 50% dosage reduction

Severe dysfunction (bilirubin >3.0 mg/dL) have a lower total body clearance and may require a dosage adjustment to 8 mg/m²; some clinicians recommend a dosage reduction to 25% of dose

Dose modifications based on degree of leukopenia or thrombocytopenia; see table on following page

Administration

MUST BE DILUTED prior to administration

Do **not** administer I.V. bolus over <3 minutes; can be administered I.V. intermittent infusion over 15-30 minutes

(Continued)

Mitoxantrone (Continued)

Avoid extravasation; although has not generally been proven to be a vesicant

Granulocyte Count Nadir (cells/mm²)	Platelet Count Nadir (cells/mm²)	Total Bilirubin (mg/dL)	Dose Adjustment
>2000	>150,000	<1.5	Increase by 1 mg/m²
1000-2000	75,000-150,000	<1.5	Maintain same dose
<1000	<75,000	1.5-3	Decrease by 1 mg/m²

Monitoring Parameters CBC, serum uric acid, liver function tests, ECHO

Patient Information May impart a blue-green color to the urine for 24 hours after administration, and patients should be advised to expect this during therapy. Bluish discoloration of the sclera may also occur. Patients should be advised of the signs and symptoms of myelosuppression; report to physician if persistent fever, malaise, sore throat, fatigue, or unusual bleeding or bruising. Contraceptive measures are recommended during therapy.

Nursing Implications Vesicant; avoid extravasation

Mitoxantrone is excreted in human milk and significant concentrations (180 mg/mL) have been reported for 28 days after the last administration. Because of the potential for serious adverse reactions in infants from mitoxantrone, breast-feeding should be discontinued before starting treatment.

Dosage Forms Injection, as base: 2 mg/mL (10 mL, 12.5 mL, 15 mL)

♦ **Mitoxantrone Hydrochloride** see Mitoxantrone on page 788

♦ **Mitran® Oral** see Chlordiazepoxide on page 239

♦ **Mivacron®** see Mivacurium on this page

Mivacurium (mye va KYOO ree um)

Related Information

Neuromuscular Blocking Agents Comparison on page 1331

U.S. Brand Names Mivacron®

Synonyms Mivacurium Chloride

Therapeutic Category Neuromuscular Blocker Agent, Nondepolarizing; Skeletal Muscle Relaxant

Use Short-acting nondepolarizing neuromuscular blocking agent; an adjunct to general anesthesia; facilitates endotracheal intubation; provides skeletal muscle relaxation during surgery or mechanical ventilation

Pregnancy Risk Factor C

Contraindications Hypersensitivity to mivacurium chloride or other benzylisoquinolinium agents; pre-existing tachycardia

Adverse Reactions

>10%: Cardiovascular: Flushing of face

1% to 10%: Cardiovascular: Hypotension

<1%: Bradycardia, tachycardia, dizziness, cutaneous erythema, rash, injection site reaction, muscle spasms, bronchospasm, wheezing, hypoxemia, endogenous histamine release

Drug Interactions Prolonged neuromuscular blockade: Inhaled anesthetics; local anesthetics; calcium channel blockers; antiarrhythmics (eg, quinidine or procainamide); antibiotics (eg, aminoglycosides, tetracyclines, vancomycin, clindamycin); immunosuppressants (eg, cyclosporine)

Mechanism of Action Mivacurium is a short-acting, nondepolarizing, neuromuscular-blocking agent. Like other nondepolarizing drugs, mivacurium antagonizes acetylcholine by competitively binding to cholinergic sites on motor endplates in skeletal muscle. This inhibits contractile activity in skeletal muscle leading to muscle paralysis. This effect is reversible with cholinesterase inhibitors such as edrophonium, neostigmine, and physostigmine.

Pharmacodynamics/Kinetics

Onset of neuromuscular blockade effect: I.V.: Within 2-3 minutes

Peak effect: 1.5-8 minutes

Duration of action: Short due to rapid hydrolysis by plasma cholinesterases; recovery from muscular paralysis occurs within 15-30 minutes

Usual Dosage Continuous infusion requires an infusion pump; dose should be based on ideal body weight

Children 2-12 years (duration of action is shorter and dosage requirements are higher): 200 mcg/kg I.V. bolus; 5-31 mcg/kg/minute I.V. infusion

Adults: Initial: I.V.: 0.15 mg/kg bolus; for prolonged neuromuscular block, infusions of 1-15 mcg/kg/minute are used

Dosing adjustment in renal impairment: 150 mcg/kg I.V. bolus; duration of action of blockade: 1.5 times longer in ESRD, may decrease infusion rates by as much as 50%, dependent on degree of renal impairment

Dosing adjustment in hepatic impairment: 150 mcg/kg I.V. bolus; duration of blockade: 3 times longer in ESLD, may decrease rate of infusion by as much as 50% in ESLD, dependent on the degree of impairment

Administration Children require higher mivacurium infusion rates than adults; during opioid/nitrous oxide/oxygen anesthesia, the infusion rate required to maintain 89% to 99% neuromuscular block averages 14 mcg/kg/minute (range: 5-31). For adults and children, the amount of infusion solution required per hour depends upon the clinical requirements of the patient, the concentration of mivacurium in the infusion solution, and the patient's weight. The contribution of the infusion solution to the fluid requirements of the patient must be considered.

Nursing Implications Use with caution in patients in whom histamine release would be detrimental (eg, patients with severe cardiovascular disease or asthma)

Dosage Forms

Infusion, as chloride, in D_5W: 0.5 mg/mL (50 mL)

Injection, as chloride: 2 mg/mL (5 mL, 10 mL)

- **Mivacurium Chloride** see Mivacurium on previous page
- **MK 383** see Tirofiban on page 1148
- **MK 462** see Rizatriptan on page 1037
- **MK 594** see Losartan on page 696
- **MMR** see Measles, Mumps, and Rubella Vaccines, Combined on page 714
- **M-M-R® II** see Measles, Mumps, and Rubella Vaccines, Combined on page 714
- **Moban®** see Molindone on page 793
- **Mobenol®** see Tolbutamide on page 1155

Modafinil (moe DAF i nil)

U.S. Brand Names Provigil®

Canadian Brand Names Alertec®

Therapeutic Category Central Nervous System Stimulant, Nonamphetamine

Use Improve wakefulness in patients with excessive daytime sleepiness associated with narcolepsy

Restrictions C-IV

Pregnancy Risk Factor C

Pregnancy/Breast-Feeding Implications Currently, there are no studies in humans evaluating its teratogenicity. Embryotoxicity of modafinil has been observed in animal models at dosages above those employed therapeutically. As a result, it should be used cautiously during pregnancy and should be used only when the potential risk of drug therapy is outweighed by the drug's benefits. It remains unknown if modafinil is secreted into human milk and, therefore, should be used cautiously in nursing women.

Contraindications Hypersensitivity to modafinil or any component

Warnings/Precautions History of angina, ischemic EKG changes, left ventricular hypertrophy, or clinically significant mitral valve prolapse in association with CNS stimulant use; caution should be exercised when modafinil is given to patients with a history of psychosis, recent history of myocardial infarction, and because it has not yet been adequately studied in patients with hypertension, periodic monitoring of hypertensive patients receiving modafinil may be appropriate; caution is warranted when operating machinery or driving, although functional impairment has not been demonstrated with modafinil, all CNS-active agents may alter judgment, thinking and/or motor skills. Efficacy of oral contraceptives may be reduced, therefore, use of alternative contraception should be considered.

Adverse Reactions Limited to reports that were equal to or greater than placebo-related events:

<10%:

Cardiovascular: Chest pain (2%), hypertension (2%), hypotension (2%), vasodilation (1%), arrhythmia (1%), syncope (1%)

Central nervous system: Headache (50%, compared to 40% with placebo), nervousness (8%), dizziness (5%), depression (4%), anxiety (4%), cataplexy (3%), insomnia (3%), chills (2%), fever (1%), confusion (1%), amnesia (1%), emotional lability (1%), ataxia (1%)

Dermatologic: Dry skin (1%)

Endocrine & metabolic: Hyperglycemia (1%), albuminuria (1%)

Gastrointestinal: Diarrhea (8%), nausea (13%, compared to 4% with placebo), xerostomia (5%), anorexia (5%), vomiting (1%), mouth ulceration (1%), gingivitis (1%)

Genitourinary: Abnormal urine (1%), urinary retention (1%), ejaculatory disturbance (1%)

Hematologic: Eosinophilia (1%)

Hepatic: Abnormal LFTs (3%)

Neuromuscular & skeletal: Paresthesias (3%), dyskinesia (2%), neck pain (2%), hypertonia (2%), neck rigidity (1%), joint disorder (1%), tremor (1%)

Ocular: Amblyopia (2%), abnormal vision (2%)

Respiratory: Pharyngitis (6%), rhinitis (11%, compared to 8% with placebo), lung disorder (4%), dyspnea (2%), asthma (1%), epistaxis (1%)

Overdosage/Toxicology Signs and symptoms of an overdose include agitation, irritability, aggressiveness, confusion, nervousness, tremor, sleep disturbance, palpitations, decreased prothrombin time, and slight to moderate elevations of hemodynamic parameters; treatment is symptomatic and supportive, there is no data to suggest the utility of dialysis or urinary pH alteration to enhance elimination; cardiac monitoring is warranted

Drug Interactions Modafinil may interact with drugs that inhibit, induce, or are metabolized by cytochrome P-450 isoenzymes; specifically modafinil is a 3A4 isoenzyme substrate and induces CYP1A2, CYP2B6, and CYP3A4 isoenzymes, as a result modafinil may decrease serum concentrations of 3A4 metabolized drugs such as oral contraceptives, cyclosporine, and to a lesser degree, theophylline; agents that induce CYP3A4, including phenobarbital, carbamazepine, and rifampin may result in decreased modafinil levels; there is evidence to suggest that modafinil may induce its own metabolism.

(Continued)

Modafinil *(Continued)*

Increased effects: As a result of its inhibition of CYP2C19 isoenzymes, serum concentrations of drugs metabolized by this enzyme can be increased, these agents include diazepam, mephenytoin, phenytoin, and propranolol and due to modafinil's potential inhibition of the CYP2C9 isoenzyme, warfarin and phenytoin levels may be increased; in populations deficient in the CYP2D6 isoenzyme, where CYP2C19 acts as a secondary metabolic pathway, concentrations of tricyclic antidepressants and selective serotonin reuptake inhibitors may be increased during coadministration

Mechanism of Action The exact mechanism of action is unclear, it does not appear to alter the release of dopamine or norepinephrine, it may exert its stimulant effects by decreasing GABA-mediated neurotransmission, although this theory has not yet been fully evaluated; several studies also suggest that an intact central alpha-adrenergic system is required for modafinil's activity; the drug increases high-frequency alpha waves while decreasing both delta and theta wave activity, and these effects are consistent with generalized increases in mental alertness

Pharmacodynamics/Kinetics Modafinil is a racemic compound (10% *d*-isomer and 90% *l*-isomer at steady state), whose enantiomers have different pharmacokinetics

Distribution: V_d: 0.9 L/kg
Protein binding: 60%, mostly to albumin
Metabolism: In the liver; multiple pathways including the cytochrome P-450 system
Half-life: Effective half-life: 15 hours; time to steady-state: 2-4 days
Time to peak serum concentration: 2-4 hours
Elimination: Renal, as metabolites (<10% excreted unchanged)

Usual Dosage
Narcolepsy: Initial: 200 mg as a single daily dose in the morning
Doses of 400 mg/day, given as a single dose, have been well tolerated, but there is no consistent evidence that this dose confers additional benefit
Dosing adjustment in elderly: Elimination of modafinil and its metabolites may be reduced as a consequence of aging and as a result, lower doses should be considered.
Dosing adjustment in renal impairment: Inadequate data to determine safety and efficacy in severe renal impairment
Dosing adjustment in hepatic impairment: Dose should be reduced to one-half of that recommended for patients with normal liver function

Patient Information Take during the day to avoid insomnia; may cause dependence with prolonged use; patients should be reminded to notify their physician if they become pregnant, intend to become pregnant, or are breast-feeding an infant; patients should be advised that combined use with alcohol has not been studied and that it is prudent to avoid this combination. Patients should notify their physician and/or pharmacist of any concomitant medications they are taking, due to the drug interaction potential this might represent.

Dosage Forms Tablet: 100 mg, 200 mg

♦ **Modane® Bulk [OTC]** *see Psyllium on page 994*
♦ **Modane® Soft [OTC]** *see Docusate on page 384*
♦ **Modecate®** *see Fluphenazine on page 504*
♦ **Modecate® Enanthate** *see Fluphenazine on page 504*
♦ **Modicon™** *see Ethinyl Estradiol and Norethindrone on page 451*
♦ **Modified Dakin's Solution** *see Sodium Hypochlorite Solution on page 1070*
♦ **Modified Shohl's Solution** *see Sodium Citrate and Citric Acid on page 1069*
♦ **Moditen® Hydrochloride** *see Fluphenazine on page 504*
♦ **Moduretic®** *see Amiloride and Hydrochlorothiazide on page 57*

Moexipril *(mo EKS i pril)*

Related Information
Angiotensin Agents *on page 1291*
Drug-Drug Interactions With ACEIs *on page 1295*

U.S. Brand Names Univasc®

Synonyms Moexipril Hydrochloride

Therapeutic Category Angiotensin-Converting Enzyme (ACE) Inhibitor; Antihypertensive Agent

Use Treatment of hypertension, alone or in combination with thiazide diuretics in a once daily dosing regimen

Pregnancy Risk Factor C (1st trimester); D (2nd and 3rd trimester)

Contraindications Hypersensitivity to moexipril, moexiprilat, or component; hypersensitivity or allergic reactions or angioedema related to an ACE inhibitor

Warnings/Precautions Do not administer in pregnancy; use with caution and modify dosage in patients with renal impairment especially renal artery stenosis, severe congestive heart failure, or with coadministered diuretic therapy; experience in children is limited. Severe hypotension may occur in patients who are sodium and/or volume depleted; initiate lower doses and monitor closely when starting therapy in these patients; ACE inhibitors may be preferred agents in elderly patients with congestive heart failure and diabetes mellitus (diabetic proteinuria is reduced, minimal CNS effects, and enhanced insulin sensitivity), however due to decreased renal function, tolerance must be carefully monitored; if possible, discontinue the diuretic 2-3 days prior to initiating moexipril in patients receiving them to reduce the risk of symptomatic hypotension.

Adverse Reactions
1% to 10%:
Central nervous system: Headache, dizziness, fatigue
Dermatologic: Rash, pruritus, alopecia, flushing
Endocrine & metabolic: Hyperkalemia
Gastrointestinal: Diarrhea
Genitourinary: Polyuria
Renal: Oliguria, reversible increases in creatinine or BUN
Respiratory: Nonproductive cough (6%), pharyngitis, upper respiratory infections, rhinitis
Miscellaneous: Flu-like symptoms
<1%: Symptomatic hypotension, chest pain, angina, peripheral edema, myocardial infarction, palpitations, arrhythmias, sleep disturbances, anxiety, mood changes, angioedema, photosensitivity, pemphigus, hypercholesterolemia, abdominal pain, taste disturbance, constipation, vomiting, xerostomia, changes in appetite, pancreatitis, abnormal taste, neutropenia, elevated LFTs, myalgia, arthralgia, proteinuria, bronchospasm, dyspnea

Overdosage/Toxicology
Mild hypotension has been the only toxic effect seen with acute overdose; bradycardia may also occur; hyperkalemia occurs even with therapeutic doses, especially in patients with renal insufficiency and those taking NSAIDs
Following initiation of essential overdose management, toxic symptom treatment and supportive treatment should be initiated; hypotension usually responds to I.V. fluids or Trendelenburg positioning.

Drug Interactions Increased toxicity: See Drug-Drug Interactions With ACEIs *on page 1295*

Mechanism of Action Competitive inhibitor of angiotensin-converting enzyme (ACE); prevents conversion of angiotensin I to angiotensin II, a potent vasoconstrictor; results in lower levels of angiotensin II which causes an increase in plasma renin activity and a reduction in aldosterone secretion

Pharmacodynamics/Kinetics
Absorption: Food decreases bioavailability (AUC decreased by ~40%)
Distribution: V_d (moexiprilat): 180 L
Protein binding (plasma): Moexipril: 90%; Moexiprilat: 50% to 70%
Metabolism: Parent drug is metabolized in liver and small intestine to moexiprilat, the 1000 times more potent diacid metabolite; both parent
Bioavailability (moexiprilat): 13%
Half-life: Moexipril: 1 hour; Moexiprilat: 2-10 hours
Time to peak: 1.5 hours
Elimination: 50% appears in the feces

Usual Dosage Adults: Oral: Initial: 7.5 mg once daily (in patients **not** receiving diuretics), one hour prior to a meal **or** 3.75 mg once daily (when combined with thiazide diuretics); maintenance dose: 7.5-30 mg/day in 1 or 2 divided doses one hour before meals

Dosing adjustment in renal impairment: Cl_{cr} ≤40 mL/minute: Patients may be cautiously placed on 3.75 mg once daily, then upwardly titrated to a maximum of 15 mg/day

Monitoring Parameters Blood pressure, heart rate, electrolytes, CBC, symptoms of hypotension

Test Interactions Increases BUN, creatinine, potassium, positive Coombs' [direct]; decreases cholesterol (S); may cause false-positive results in urine acetone determinations using sodium nitroprusside reagent

Patient Information Food may delay and reduce peak serum levels; take on an empty stomach, if possible. Report swelling of the face, mouth, or tongue, rash, or difficulty breathing to your physician immediately; bothersome side effects such as cough, dizziness, diarrhea, tiredness, rash, headache, irregular heartbeat, anxiety, and flu-like symptoms should also be reported; avoid use of this medication if you are pregnant or have had a previous reaction to other ACE inhibitors.

Nursing Implications Observe for symptoms of severe hypotension, especially within the first 2 hours following the initial dose or subsequent increases in dose as well as for signs of hyperkalemia or cough; administer on an empty stomach

Dosage Forms Tablet, as hydrochloride: 7.5 mg, 15 mg

Moexipril and Hydrochlorothiazide
(mo EKS i pril & hye droe klor oh THYE a zide)
U.S. Brand Names Uniretic™
Therapeutic Category Angiotensin-Converting Enzyme (ACE) Inhibitor; Antihypertensive Agent, Combination; Diuretic, Thiazide
Dosage Forms Tablet: Moexipril hydrochloride 7.5 mg and hydrochlorothiazide 12.5 mg; moexipril hydrochloride 15 mg and hydrochlorothiazide 25 mg

♦ **Moexipril Hydrochloride** *see Moexipril on previous page*

Molindone (moe LIN done)
Related Information
Antipsychotic Agents Comparison *on page 1305*
U.S. Brand Names Moban®
Synonyms Molindone Hydrochloride
Therapeutic Category Antipsychotic Agent
Use Management of psychotic disorder
(Continued)

Molindone *(Continued)*

Pregnancy Risk Factor C

Contraindications Narrow-angle glaucoma, hypersensitivity to molindone or any component

Warnings/Precautions Use with caution in patients with cardiovascular disease or seizures, CNS depression, or hepatic impairment

Adverse Reactions

>10%:

Cardiovascular: Orthostatic hypotension

Central nervous system: Akathisia, extrapyramidal effects, persistent tardive dyskinesia

Gastrointestinal: Constipation, xerostomia

Ocular: Blurred vision

Miscellaneous: Diaphoresis (decreased)

1% to 10%:

Central nervous system: Mental depression, altered central temperature regulation

Endocrine & metabolic: Change in menstrual periods, edema of the breasts

<1%: Tachycardia, arrhythmias, sedation, drowsiness, restlessness, anxiety, seizures, neuroleptic malignant syndrome (NMS), hyperpigmentation, pruritus, rash, photosensitivity, galactorrhea, gynecomastia, weight gain, urinary retention, agranulocytosis (more often in women between fourth and tenth weeks of therapy), leukopenia (usually in patients with large doses for prolonged periods), retinal pigmentation

Overdosage/Toxicology

Symptoms of overdose include deep sleep, extrapyramidal symptoms, cardiac arrhythmias, seizures, hypotension

Following initiation of essential overdose management, toxic symptom treatment and supportive treatment should be initiated. Hypotension usually responds to I.V. fluids or Trendelenburg positioning. If unresponsive to these measures, the use of a parenteral inotrope may be required (eg, norepinephrine 0.1-0.2 mcg/kg/minute titrated to response). Seizures commonly respond to diazepam (I.V. 5-10 mg bolus in adults every 15 minutes if needed up to a total of 30 mg; I.V. 0.25-0.4 mg/kg/dose up to a total of 10 mg in children) or to phenytoin or phenobarbital. Critical cardiac arrhythmias often respond to I.V. phenytoin (15 mg/kg up to 1 g), while other antiarrhythmics can be used. Neuroleptics often cause extrapyramidal symptoms (eg, dystonic reactions) requiring management with diphenhydramine 1-2 mg/kg (adults) up to a maximum of 50 mg I.M. or I.V. slow push followed by a maintenance dose for 48-72 hours. When these reactions are unresponsive to diphenhydramine, benztropine mesylate I.V. 1-2 mg (adults) may be effective. These agents are generally effective within 2-5 minutes.

Drug Interactions CYP2D6 enzyme substrate

Increased toxicity: CNS depressants, antihypertensives, anticonvulsants

Mechanism of Action Mechanism of action mimics that of chlorpromazine; however, it produces more extrapyramidal effects and less sedation than chlorpromazine

Pharmacodynamics/Kinetics

Metabolism: In the liver

Half-life: 1.5 hours

Time to peak serum concentration: Oral: Within 1.5 hours

Elimination: Principally in urine and feces (90% within 24 hours)

Usual Dosage Oral:

Children:

3-5 years: 1-2.5 mg/day divided into 4 doses

5-12 years: 0.5-1 mg/kg/day in 4 divided doses

Adults: 50-75 mg/day increase at 3- to 4-day intervals up to 225 mg/day

Dietary Considerations Alcohol: Avoid use

Monitoring Parameters Monitor blood pressure and pulse rate prior to and during initial therapy evaluate mental status; monitor weight

Patient Information Dry mouth may be helped by sips of water, sugarless gum or hard candy; avoid alcohol; very important to maintain established dosage regimen; photosensitivity to sunlight can occur, do not discontinue abruptly; full effect may not occur for 3-4 weeks; full dosage may be taken at bedtime to avoid daytime sedation; report to physician any involuntary movements or feelings of restlessness

Nursing Implications May increase appetite and possibly a craving for sweets; recognize signs of neuroleptic malignant syndrome and tardive dyskinesia

Dosage Forms

Concentrate, oral, as hydrochloride: 20 mg/mL (120 mL)

Tablet, as hydrochloride: 5 mg, 10 mg, 25 mg, 50 mg, 100 mg

- ◆ **Molindone Hydrochloride** *see* Molindone *on previous page*
- ◆ **Mol-Iron® [OTC]** *see* Ferrous Sulfate *on page 480*
- ◆ **Mollifene® Ear Wax Removing Formula [OTC]** *see* Carbamide Peroxide *on page 190*
- ◆ **MOM** *see* Magnesium Hydroxide *on page 705*

Mometasone Furoate *(moe MET a sone FYOOR oh ate)*

Related Information

Corticosteroids Comparison *on page 1319*

U.S. Brand Names Elocon® Topical

Canadian Brand Names Elocom

Therapeutic Category Corticosteroid, Topical (Medium Potency)

Use Relief of the inflammatory and pruritic manifestations of corticosteroid-responsive dermatoses (medium potency topical corticosteroid)

Pregnancy Risk Factor C

Contraindications Hypersensitivity to mometasone or any component; fungal, viral, or tubercular skin lesions, herpes simplex or zoster

Warnings/Precautions Adverse systemic effects may occur when used on large areas of the body, denuded areas, for prolonged periods of time, with an occlusive dressing, and/or in infants or small children

Adverse Reactions <1%: Acne, hypopigmentation, allergic dermatitis, maceration of the skin, skin atrophy, striae, miliaria, itching, folliculitis, hypertrichosis, HPA suppression, Cushing's syndrome, growth retardation, burning, irritation, dryness, secondary infection

Mechanism of Action May depress the formation, release, and activity of endogenous chemical mediators of inflammation (kinins, histamine, liposomal enzymes, prostaglandins). Leukocytes and macrophages may have to be present for the initiation of responses mediated by the above substances. Inhibits the margination and subsequent cell migration to the area of injury, and also reverses the dilatation and increased vessel permeability in the area resulting in decreased access of cells to the sites of injury.

Usual Dosage Adults: Topical: Apply sparingly to area once daily, do not use occlusive dressings

Patient Information Before applying, gently wash area to reduce risk of infection; apply a thin film to cleansed area and rub in gently and thoroughly until medication vanishes; avoid exposure to sunlight, severe sunburn may occur

Nursing Implications For external use only; do not use on open wounds; should not be used in the presence of open or weeping lesions; use sparingly

Dosage Forms
Cream: 0.1% (15 g, 45 g)
Lotion: 0.1% (30 mL, 60 mL)
Ointment, topical: 0.1% (15 g, 45 g)

- **Monacolin K** see Lovastatin on page 699
- **Monafed®** see Guaifenesin on page 549
- **Monafed® DM** see Guaifenesin and Dextromethorphan on page 550
- **Monazole-7®** see Miconazole on page 775
- **Monistat-Derm™ Topical** see Miconazole on page 775
- **Monistat i.v.™ Injection** see Miconazole on page 775
- **Monistat™ Vaginal** see Miconazole on page 775
- **Monitan®** see Acebutolol on page 18
- **Monocid®** see Cefonicid on page 211
- **Monoclate-P®** see Antihemophilic Factor (Human) on page 88
- **Monoclonal Antibody** see Muromonab-CD3 on page 802
- **Monoclonal Antibody Purified** see Factor IX, Purified (Human) on page 466
- **Mono-Gesic®** see Salsalate on page 1047
- **Monoket®** see Isosorbide Mononitrate on page 639
- **Mononine®** see Factor IX, Purified (Human) on page 466
- **Monopril®** see Fosinopril on page 522

Montelukast (mon te LOO kast)

U.S. Brand Names Singulair®

Synonyms Montelukast Sodium

Therapeutic Category Leukotriene Receptor Antagonist

Use Prophylaxis and chronic treatment of asthma in adults and children ≥6 years

Pregnancy Risk Factor B

Contraindications Hypersensitivity to any component

Warnings/Precautions Montelukast is not indicated for use in the reversal of bronchospasm in acute asthma attacks, including status asthmaticus. Should not be used as monotherapy for the treatment and management of exercise-induced bronchospasm. Advise patients to have appropriate rescue medication available. Appropriate clinical monitoring and caution are recommended when systemic corticosteroid reduction is considered in patients receiving montelukast. Inform phenylketonuric patients that the chewable tablet contains phenylalanine 0.842 mg/5 mg chewable tablet.

In rare cases, patients on therapy with montelukast may present with systemic eosinophilia, sometimes presenting with clinical features of vasculitis consistent with Churg-Strauss syndrome, a condition which is often treated with systemic corticosteroid therapy. See Adverse Reactions.

Adverse Reactions
>10%: Central nervous system: Headache
1% to 10%:
Central nervous system: Dizziness, fatigue, fever
Dermatologic: Rash
Gastrointestinal: Dyspepsia, dental pain, gastroenteritis, diarrhea, nausea, abdominal pain
Neuromuscular & skeletal: Weakness
Respiratory: Cough, nasal congestion, laryngitis, pharyngitis
Miscellaneous: Flu-like symptoms, trauma

In rare cases, patients on therapy with montelukast may present with systemic eosinophilia, sometimes presenting with clinical features of vasculitis consistent with Churg-
(Continued)

Montelukast *(Continued)*

Strauss syndrome, a condition which is often treated with systemic corticosteroid therapy. Physicians should be alert to eosinophilia, vasculitic rash, worsening pulmonary symptoms, cardiac complications, and/or neuropathy presenting in their patients. A casual association between montelukast and these underlying conditions has not been established.

Overdosage/Toxicology No specific antidote

Remove unabsorbed material from the GI tract, employ clinical monitoring and institute supportive therapy if required

Drug Interactions CYP2A6, and 2C9, 3A3/4, enzyme substrate

Decreased effect: Phenobarbital, rifampin induce hepatic metabolism and decrease the AUC of montelukast

Mechanism of Action Selective leukotriene receptor antagonist that inhibits the cysteinyl leukotriene receptor. Cysteinyl leukotrienes and leukotriene receptor occupation have been correlated with the pathophysiology of asthma, including airway edema, smooth muscle contraction, and altered cellular activity associated with the inflammatory process, which contribute to the signs and symptoms of asthma.

Pharmacodynamics/Kinetics

Distribution: V_d: 8-11 L

Protein binding, plasma: >99%

Metabolism: Extensively by cytochrome P-450 3A4 and 2C9

Bioavailability: Oral: Mean: 64% for 10 mg tablet and 63% to 73% for 5 mg tablet

Half-life, plasma: Mean: 2.7-5.5 hours

Time to peak serum concentration: 3-4 hours for 10 mg tablet and 2-2.5 hours for 5 mg tablet

Elimination: Almost exclusively in the bile; fecal (86%), urine (<0.2%)

Usual Dosage Oral:

Children:

<6 years: Safety and efficacy have not been established

6 to 14 years: Chew one 5 mg chewable tablet/day, taken in the evening

Children ≥15 years and Adults: 10 mg/day, taken in the evening

Dosing adjustment in hepatic impairment: Mild moderate: No adjustment necessary

Patient Information Advise patients to take montelukast daily as prescribed, even when they are symptomatic, as well as during periods of worsening asthma, and to contact physician if the asthma is not well controlled. Advise patients that oral tablets of montelukast are not for the treatment of acute asthma attacks. Patients should have appropriate short-acting inhaled beta-agonist medication available to treat asthma exacerbations.

Advise patients using montelukast to seek medical attention if short-acting inhaled bronchodilators are needed more often than usual or if more than the maximum number of inhalations of short-acting bronchodilator treatment prescribed for a 24-hour period are needed. Instruct patients receiving montelukast not to decrease the dose or to stop taking any other antiasthma medications unless instructed by a physician.

Instruct patients who have exacerbations of asthma after exercise to continue to use their usual regimen of inhaled beta-agonists as prophylaxis unless otherwise instructed by a physician. All patients should have a short-acting inhaled beta-agonist available for rescue.

Additional Information 5 mg chewable tablet contains 0.842 mg phenylalanine

Dosage Forms

Tablet, as sodium: 10 mg

Tablet, chewable (cherry), as sodium: 5 mg

- ◆ **Montelukast Sodium** see Montelukast on previous page
- ◆ **Monurol™** see Fosfomycin on page 521
- ◆ **8-MOP** see Methoxsalen on page 755
- ◆ **8-MOP®** see Methoxsalen on page 755
- ◆ **More Attenuated Enders Strain** see Measles Virus Vaccine, Live, Attenuated on page 715
- ◆ **More-Dophilus®** [OTC] see Lactobacillus acidophilus and Lactobacillus bulgaricus on page 655

Moricizine *(mor I siz een)*

Related Information

Antiarrhythmic Drugs Comparison on page 1297

U.S. Brand Names Ethmozine®

Synonyms Moricizine Hydrochloride

Therapeutic Category Antiarrhythmic Agent, Class I-C

Use Treatment of ventricular tachycardia and life-threatening ventricular arrhythmias

Unlabeled use: PVCs, complete and nonsustained ventricular tachycardia

Pregnancy Risk Factor B

Contraindications Pre-existing second or third degree A-V block and in patients with right bundle-branch block when associated with left hemiblock, unless pacemaker is present; cardiogenic shock; known hypersensitivity to the drug

Warnings/Precautions Considering the known proarrhythmic properties and lack of evidence of improved survival for any antiarrhythmic drug in patients without life-threatening arrhythmias, it is prudent to reserve the use for patients with life-threatening ventricular arrhythmias; CAST II trial demonstrated a trend towards decreased survival for patients treated with moricizine; proarrhythmic effects occur as with other antiarrhythmic agents; hypokalemia, hyperkalemia, hypomagnesemia may effect response to class I agents; use with caution in patients with sick-sinus syndrome, hepatic, and renal impairment

Adverse Reactions

>10%: Central nervous system: Dizziness (15%)

1% to 10%:
Cardiovascular: Proarrhythmia, palpitations (5.8%), cardiac death (2% to 5%), EKG abnormalities (1.6%), congestive heart failure (1%)
Central nervous system: Headache (8%), fatigue (6%), insomnia (2% to 5%)
Gastrointestinal: Nausea (3% to 9%), diarrhea (2% to 5%)
Ocular: Blurred vision (2% to 5%)
Respiratory: Dyspnea (6%)

<1%: Ventricular tachycardia, cardiac chest pain, hypotension or hypertension, syncope, supraventricular arrhythmias, myocardial infarction, anxiety, drug fever, confusion, loss of memory, vertigo, anorexia, rash, dry skin, GI upset, vomiting, dyspepsia, flatulence, bitter taste, urinary retention, urinary incontinence, impotence, tremor, tinnitus, apnea, diaphoresis

Overdosage/Toxicology

Has a narrow therapeutic index and severe toxicity may occur slightly above the therapeutic range, especially if combined with other antiarrhythmic drugs. (Acute single ingestion of twice the daily therapeutic dose is life-threatening). Symptoms of overdose include increases in P-R, QRS, Q-T intervals and amplitude of the T wave, A-V block, bradycardia, hypotension, ventricular arrhythmias (monomorphic or polymorphic ventricular tachycardia), and asystole; other symptoms include dizziness, blurred vision, headache, and GI upset.

Treatment is supportive, using conventional treatment (fluids, positioning, anticonvulsants, antiarrhythmics). **Note:** Type Ia antiarrhythmic agents should not be used to treat cardiotoxicity caused by type 1c drugs; sodium bicarbonate may reverse QRS prolongation, bradycardia and hypotension; ventricular pacing may be needed.

Drug Interactions

Decreased levels of theophylline (50%) with moricizine due to increased clearance
Increased levels of moricizine with concomitant cimetidine (50%)
Diltiazem increases moricizine levels resulting in an increased incidence of side effects
Moricizine decreases diltiazem plasma levels and decreases its half-life
Digoxin and moricizine concurrent administration may result in additive prolongation of the PR interval (but not rate of second and third degree A-V block)

Mechanism of Action Class I antiarrhythmic agent; reduces the fast inward current carried by sodium ions, shortens Phase I and Phase II repolarization, resulting in decreased action potential duration and effective refractory period

Pharmacodynamics/Kinetics

Protein binding, plasma: 95%
Metabolism: Undergoes significant first-pass metabolism absolute
Bioavailability: 38%
Half-life: Normal patients: 3-4 hours; Cardiac disease patients: 6-13 hours
Elimination: Some enterohepatic recycling occurs; 56% is excreted in feces and 39% in urine

Usual Dosage Adults: Oral: 200-300 mg every 8 hours, adjust dosage at 150 mg/day at 3-day intervals. See table for dosage recommendations of transferring from other antiarrhythmic agents to Ethmozine®.

Moricizine

Transferred From	Start Ethmozine®
Encainide, propafenone, tocainide, or mexiletine	8-12 hours after last dose
Flecainide	12-24 hours after last dose
Procainamide	3-6 hours after last dose
Quinidine, disopyramide	6-12 hours after last dose

Dosing interval in renal or hepatic impairment: Start at 600 mg/day or less

Patient Information Take as directed; do not change dose except from advice of your physician; report any chest pain and irregular heartbeats

Nursing Implications Administering 30 minutes after a meal delays the rate of absorption, resulting in lower peak plasma concentrations

Dosage Forms Tablet, as hydrochloride: 200 mg, 250 mg, 300 mg

♦ **Moricizine Hydrochloride** *see Moricizine on previous page*

♦ **Morning After Pill** *see Ethinyl Estradiol and Norgestrel on page 454*

♦ **Morphine-HP®** *see Morphine Sulfate on this page*

Morphine Sulfate (MOR feen SUL fate)

Related Information

Adult ACLS Algorithm, Electrical Conversion *on page 1453*
Narcotic Agonists Comparison *on page 1328*

U.S. Brand Names Astramorph™ PF Injection; Duramorph® Injection; Infumorph™ Injection; Kadian™; MS Contin® Oral; MSIR® Oral; MS/L®; MS/S®; OMS® Oral; Oramorph SR™ Oral; RMS® Rectal; Roxanol™ Oral; Roxanol Rescudose®; Roxanol SR™ Oral (Continued)

Morphine Sulfate *(Continued)*

Canadian Brand Names Epimorph®; M-Eslon®; Morphine-HP®; MS-IR®; MST Continus; Statex®

Synonyms MS

Therapeutic Category Analgesic, Narcotic

Use Relief of moderate to severe acute and chronic pain; pain of myocardial infarction; relieves dyspnea of acute left ventricular failure and pulmonary edema; preanesthetic medication

Restrictions C-II

Pregnancy Risk Factor B (D if used for prolonged periods or in high doses at term)

Contraindications Known hypersensitivity to morphine sulfate; increased intracranial pressure; severe respiratory depression

Warnings/Precautions Some preparations contain sulfites which may cause allergic reactions; infants <3 months of age are more susceptible to respiratory depression, use with caution and generally in reduced doses in this age group; use with caution in patients with impaired respiratory function or severe hepatic dysfunction and in patients with hypersensitivity reactions to other phenanthrene derivative opioid agonists (codeine, hydrocodone, hydromorphone, levorphanol, oxycodone, oxymorphone). Morphine shares the toxic potential of opiate agonists and usual precautions of opiate agonist therapy should be observed; may cause hypotension in patients with acute myocardial infarction. Tolerance or drug dependence may result from extended use.

Elderly may be particularly susceptible to the CNS depressant and constipating effects of narcotics

Adverse Reactions

Percentage unknown: Flushing, CNS depression, drowsiness, sedation, increased intracranial pressure, antidiuretic hormone release, physical and psychological dependence, diaphoresis

>10%:
Cardiovascular: Palpitations, hypotension, bradycardia
Central nervous system: Dizziness
Gastrointestinal: Nausea, vomiting, constipation, xerostomia
Local: Pain at injection site
Neuromuscular & skeletal: Weakness
Miscellaneous: Histamine release

1% to 10%:
Central nervous system: Restlessness, headache, false feeling of well being, confusion
Gastrointestinal: Anorexia, GI irritation, paralytic ileus
Genitourinary: Decreased urination
Neuromuscular & skeletal: Trembling
Ocular: Vision problems
Respiratory: Respiratory depression, shortness of breath

<1%: Peripheral vasodilation, insomnia, mental depression, hallucinations, paradoxical CNS stimulation, increased intracranial pressure, pruritus, biliary tract spasm, urinary tract spasm, muscle rigidity, miosis, increased liver function tests

Overdosage/Toxicology

Symptoms of overdose include respiratory depression, miosis, hypotension, bradycardia, apnea, pulmonary edema

Treatment of an overdose includes support of the patient's airway, establishment of an I.V. line, and administration of naloxone 2 mg I.V. (0.01 mg/kg for children) with repeat administration as necessary up to a total of 10 mg. Primary attention should be directed to ensuring adequate respiratory exchange.

Drug Interactions CYP2D6 enzyme substrate

Decreased effect: Phenothiazines may antagonize the analgesic effect of morphine and other opiate agonists

Increased toxicity: CNS depressants, tricyclic antidepressants may potentiate the effects of morphine and other opiate agonists; dextroamphetamine may enhance the analgesic effect of morphine and other opiate agonists

Stability Refrigerate suppositories; do not freeze; degradation depends on pH and presence of oxygen; relatively stable in pH ≤4; darkening of solutions indicate degradation; usual concentration for continuous I.V. infusion = 0.1-1 mg/mL in D_5W

Morphine Sulfate

Dosage Form/Route	Analgesia	
	Peak	Duration
Tablets	1 h	4-5 h
Oral solution	1 h	4-5 h
Extended release tablets	1 h	8-12 h
Suppository	20-60 min	3-7 h
Subcutaneous injection	50-90 min	4-5 h
I.M. injection	30-60 min	4-5 h
I.V. injection	20 min	4-5 h

Mechanism of Action Binds to opiate receptors in the CNS, causing inhibition of ascending pain pathways, altering the perception of and response to pain; produces generalized CNS depression

Pharmacodynamics/Kinetics

Absorption: Oral: Variable

Metabolism: In the liver via glucuronide conjugation

Half-life: Neonates: 4.5-13.3 hours (mean 7.6 hours); Adults: 2-4 hours

Elimination: Unchanged in urine; see table.

Usual Dosage Doses should be titrated to appropriate effect; when changing routes of administration in chronically treated patients, please note that oral doses are approximately one-half as effective as parenteral dose

Infants and Children:

Oral: Tablet and solution (prompt release): 0.2-0.5 mg/kg/dose every 4-6 hours as needed; tablet (controlled release): 0.3-0.6 mg/kg/dose every 12 hours

I.M., I.V., S.C.: 0.1-0.2 mg/kg/dose every 2-4 hours as needed; usual maximum: 15 mg/dose; may initiate at 0.05 mg/kg/dose

I.V., S.C. continuous infusion: Sickle cell or cancer pain: 0.025-2 mg/kg/hour; postoperative pain: 0.01-0.04 mg/kg/hour

Sedation/analgesia for procedures: I.V.: 0.05-0.1 mg/kg 5 minutes before the procedure

Adolescents >12 years: Sedation/analgesia for procedures: I.V.: 3-4 mg and repeat in 5 minutes if necessary

Adults:

Oral: Prompt release: 10-30 mg every 4 hours as needed; controlled release: 15-30 mg every 8-12 hours

I.M., I.V., S.C.: 2.5-20 mg/dose every 2-6 hours as needed; usual: 10 mg/dose every 4 hours as needed

I.V., S.C. continuous infusion: 0.8-10 mg/hour; may increase depending on pain relief/adverse effects; usual range: up to 80 mg/hour

Epidural: Initial: 5 mg in lumbar region; if inadequate pain relief within 1 hour, administer 1-2 mg, maximum dose: 10 mg/24 hours

Intrathecal ($^{1}/_{10}$ of epidural dose): 0.2-1 mg/dose; repeat doses **not** recommended

Rectal: 10-20 mg every 4 hours

Dosing adjustment in renal impairment:

Cl_{cr} 10-50 mL/minute: Administer at 75% of normal dose

Cl_{cr} <10 mL/minute: Administer at 50% of normal dose

Dosing adjustment/comments in hepatic disease: Unchanged in mild liver disease; substantial extrahepatic metabolism may occur; excessive sedation may occur in cirrhosis

Dietary Considerations

Alcohol: Additive CNS effects, avoid or limit alcohol; watch for sedation

Food:

Glucose may cause hyperglycemia; monitor blood glucose concentrations

Administration of oral morphine solution with food may increase bioavailability (ie, a report of 34% increase in morphine AUC when morphine oral solution followed a high-fat meal). Morphine may cause GI upset. Be consistent when taking morphine with or without meals. Take with food if GI upset.

Administration When giving morphine I.V. push, it is best to first dilute in 4-5 mL of sterile water, and then to administer slowly (eg, 15 mg over 3-5 minutes)

Monitoring Parameters Pain relief, respiratory and mental status, blood pressure

Reference Range Therapeutic: Surgical anesthesia: 65-80 ng/mL (SI: 227-280 nmol/L); Toxic: 200-5000 ng/mL (SI: 700-17,500 nmol/L)

Patient Information Avoid alcohol, may cause drowsiness, impaired judgment or coordination; may cause physical and psychological dependence with prolonged use

Nursing Implications Do not crush controlled release drug product, observe patient for excessive sedation, respiratory depression; implement safety measures, assist with ambulation; use preservative-free solutions for intrathecal or epidural use

Dosage Forms

Capsule (MSIR®): 15 mg, 30 mg

Capsule, sustained release (Kadian™): 20 mg, 50 mg, 100 mg

Injection: 0.5 mg/mL (10 mL); 1 mg/mL (10 mL, 30 mL, 60 mL); 2 mg/mL (1 mL, 2 mL, 60 mL); 3 mg/mL (50 mL); 4 mg/mL (1 mL, 2 mL); 5 mg/mL (1 mL, 30 mL); 8 mg/mL (1 mL, 2 mL); 10 mg/mL (1 mL, 2 mL, 10 mL); 15 mg/mL (1 mL, 2 mL, 20 mL); 25 mg/mL (4 mL, 10 mL, 20 mL, 40 mL); 50 mg/mL (10 mL, 20 mL, 40 mL)

Injection:

Preservative free (Astramorph™ PF, Duramorph®): 0.5 mg/mL (2 mL, 10 mL); 1 mg/mL (2 mL, 10 mL); 10 mg/mL (10 mL, 20 mL); 25 mg/mL (20 mL)

I.V. via PCA pump: 1 mg/mL (10 mL, 30 mL, 60 mL); 5 mg/mL (30 mL)

I.V. infusion preparation: 25 mg/mL (4 mL, 10 mL, 20 mL)

Solution, oral: 10 mg/5 mL (5 mL, 10 mL, 100 mL, 120 mL, 500 mL); 20 mg/5 mL (5 mL, 100 mL, 120 mL, 500 mL)

MSIR®: 10 mg/5 mL (5 mL, 120 mL, 500 mL); 20 mg/5 mL (5 mL 120 mL, 500 mL); 20 mg/mL (30 mL, 120 mL)

MS/L®: 100 mg/5 mL (120 mL) 20 mg/5 mL

OMS®: 20 mg/mL (30 mL, 120 mL)

Roxanol™: 10 mg/2.5 mL (2.5 mL); 20 mg/mL (1 mL, 1.5 mL, 30 mL, 120 mL, 240 mL)

Suppository, rectal: 5 mg, 10 mg, 20 mg, 30 mg

MS/S®, RMS®, Roxanol™: 5 mg, 10 mg, 20 mg, 30 mg

Tablet: 15 mg, 30 mg

(Continued)

Morphine Sulfate (Continued)

MSIR®: 15 mg, 30 mg
Controlled release:
  MS Contin®: 15 mg, 30 mg, 60 mg, 100 mg, 200 mg
  Roxanol™ SR: 30 mg
Soluble: 10 mg, 15 mg, 30 mg
Sustained release (Oramorph SR™): 30 mg, 60 mg, 100 mg

Morrhuate Sodium (MOR yoo ate SOW dee um)

U.S. Brand Names Scleromate™

Therapeutic Category Sclerosing Agent

Use Treatment of small, uncomplicated varicose veins of the lower extremities

Contraindications Arterial disease, thrombophlebitis, hypersensitivity to morrhuate sodium or any component

Warnings/Precautions Sloughing and necrosis of tissue may occur following extravasation; anaphylactoid and allergic reactions have occurred; this drug should only be administered by a physician familiar with proper injection techniques; a test dose of 0.25-5 mL of a 5% injection should be given 24 hours before full-dose treatment

Adverse Reactions

>10%:
  Cardiovascular: Thrombosis, valvular incompetency
  Dermatologic: Urticaria
  Local: Burning at the site of injection, severe extravasation effects
<1%: Vascular collapse, drowsiness, headache, dizziness, nausea, vomiting, weakness, asthma, anaphylaxis

Stability Refrigerate

Mechanism of Action Both varicose veins and esophageal varices are treated by the thrombotic action of morrhuate sodium. By causing inflammation of the vein's intima, a thrombus is formed. Occlusion secondary to the fibrous tissue and the thrombus results in the obliteration of the vein.

Pharmacodynamics/Kinetics

Onset of action: ~5 minutes
Absorption: Most of the dose stays at the site of injection
Distribution: After treatment of esophageal varices, ~20% of dose distributes to the lungs

Usual Dosage Adults: I.V.: 50-250 mg, repeated at 5- to 7-day intervals (50-100 mg for small veins, 150-250 mg for large veins)

Administration For I.V. use only

Nursing Implications Avoid extravasation; use only clear solutions, solution should become clear when warmed

Dosage Forms Injection: 50 mg/mL (5 mL)

Mumps Virus Vaccine, Live (mumpz VYE rus vak SEEN, live)

Related Information

Immunization Recommendations *on page 1358*
Skin Tests *on page 1353*

U.S. Brand Names Mumpsvax®

Therapeutic Category Vaccine, Live Virus

Use Mumps prophylaxis by promoting active immunity

Note: Trivalent measles-mumps-rubella (MMR) vaccine is the preferred agent for most children and many adults; persons born prior to 1957 are generally considered immune and need not be vaccinated

Pregnancy Risk Factor C

Pregnancy/Breast-Feeding Implications Although mumps virus can infect the placenta and fetus, there is not good evidence that it causes congenital malformations

Warnings/Precautions Pregnancy, immunocompromised persons, history of anaphylactic reaction following egg ingestion or receipt of neomycin

Adverse Reactions All serious adverse reactions must be reported to the U.S. Department of Health and Human Services (DHHS) Vaccine Adverse Event Reporting System (VAERS) 1-800-822-7967.

>10%: Local: Burning or stinging at injection site

1% to 10%:

Central nervous system: Fever ($\leq$100°F)

Dermatologic: Rash

Endocrine & metabolic: Parotitis

<1%: Convulsions, confusion, severe or continuing headache, fever (>103°F), orchitis in postpubescent and adult males, thrombocytopenic purpura, anaphylactic reactions

Drug Interactions Whole blood, interferon immune globulin, radiation therapy, and immunosuppressive drugs (eg, corticosteroids) may result in insufficient response to immunization; may temporarily depress tuberculin skin test sensitivity and reduce the seroconversion. DTP, OPV, MMR, Hib, and hepatitis B may be given concurrently; other virus vaccine administration should be separated by $\geq$1 month.

Stability Refrigerate, protect from light, discard within 8 hours after reconstitution

Mechanism of Action Promotes active immunity to mumps virus by inducing specific antibodies.

Usual Dosage Children $\geq$15 months and Adults: 0.5 mL S.C. in outer aspect of the upper arm, no booster

Administration Reconstitute only with diluent provided; administer only S.C. on outer aspect of upper arm

Test Interactions Temporary suppression of tuberculosis skin test

Patient Information Pregnancy should be avoided for 3 months following vaccination; a little swelling of the glands in the cheeks and under the jaw may occur that lasts for a few days; this could happen from 1-2 weeks after getting the mumps vaccine; this happens rarely

Additional Information Federal law requires that the date of administration, the vaccine manufacturer, lot number of vaccine, and the administering person's name, title and address be entered into the patient's permanent medical record; all adults without documentation of live vaccine on or after the first birthday or physician-diagnosed mumps, or laboratory evidence or immunity (particularly males and young adults who work in or congregate in hospitals, colleges, and on military bases) should be vaccinated. It is reasonable to consider persons born before 1957 immune, but there is no contraindication to vaccination of older persons. Susceptible travelers should be vaccinated.

Dosage Forms Injection: Single dose

Mupirocin (myoo PEER oh sin)

U.S. Brand Names Bactroban®; Bactroban® Nasal

Synonyms Mupirocin Calcium; Pseudomonic Acid A

Therapeutic Category Antibiotic, Topical

Use Topical treatment of impetigo due to *Staphylococcus aureus*, beta-hemolytic *Streptococcus*, and *S. pyogenes*

Pregnancy Risk Factor B

Contraindications Known hypersensitivity to mupirocin or polyethylene glycol

Warnings/Precautions Potentially toxic amounts of polyethylene glycol contained in the vehicle may be absorbed percutaneously in patients with extensive burns or open wounds; prolonged use may result in over growth of nonsusceptible organisms; for external use only; not for treatment of pressure sores

Adverse Reactions 1% to 10%:

Dermatologic: Pruritus, rash, erythema, dry skin

Local: Burning, stinging, tenderness, edema, pain

Stability Do not mix with Aquaphor®, coal tar solution, or salicylic acid

Mechanism of Action Binds to bacterial isoleucyl transfer-RNA synthetase resulting in the inhibition of protein and RNA synthesis

Pharmacodynamics/Kinetics

Absorption: Topical: Penetrates the outer layers of the skin; systemic absorption minimal through intact skin

Protein binding: 95%

Metabolism: Extensively to monic acid, principally in the liver and skin

Half-life: 17-36 minutes

Elimination: In urine

(Continued)

Mupirocin *(Continued)*

Usual Dosage
Topical: Children and Adults: Apply small amount to affected area 2-5 times/day for 5-14 days

Nasal: In adults (12 years of age and older), approximately one-half of the ointment from the single-use tube should be applied into one nostril and the other half into the other nostril twice daily for 5 days

Patient Information For topical use only; do not apply into the eye; discontinue if rash, itching, or irritation occurs; improvement should be seen in 5 days

Additional Information Not for treatment of pressure sores in elderly; contains polyethylene glycol vehicle

Dosage Forms Ointment, as calcium:
Intranasal: 2% (1 g single use tube)
Topical: 2% (15 g, 30 g)

- ◆ **Mupirocin Calcium** *see Mupirocin on previous page*
- ◆ **Murine® Ear Drops [OTC]** *see Carbamide Peroxide on page 190*
- ◆ **Muro 128® Ophthalmic [OTC]** *see Sodium Chloride on page 1067*
- ◆ **Murocoll-2® Ophthalmic** *see Phenylephrine and Scopolamine on page 919*

Muromonab-CD3 *(myoo roe MOE nab see dee three)*

U.S. Brand Names Orthoclone® OKT3

Synonyms Monoclonal Antibody; OKT3

Therapeutic Category Immunosuppressant Agent

Use Treatment of acute allograft rejection in renal transplant patients; treatment of acute hepatic, kidney, and pancreas rejection episodes resistant to conventional treatment. Acute graft-versus-host disease following bone marrow transplantation resistant to conventional treatment.

Pregnancy Risk Factor C

Contraindications Hypersensitivity to OKT3 or any murine product; patients in fluid overload or those with >3% weight gain within 1 week prior to start of mouse antibody titers >1:1000

Warnings/Precautions It is imperative, especially prior to the first few doses, that there be no clinical evidence of volume overload, uncontrolled hypertension, or uncompensated heart failure, including a clear chest x-ray and weight restriction of ≤3% above the patient's minimum weight during the week prior to injection.

May result in an increased susceptibility to infection; dosage of concomitant immunosuppressants should be reduced during OKT3 therapy; cyclosporine should be decreased to 50% usual maintenance dose and maintenance therapy resumed about 4 days before stopping OKT3.

Severe pulmonary edema has occurred in patients with fluid overload.

First dose effect (flu-like symptoms, anaphylactic-type reaction): may occur within 30 minutes to 6 hours up to 24 hours after the first dose and may be minimized by using the recommended regimens. See table.

Suggested Prevention/Treatment of Muromonab-CD3 First-Dose Effects

Adverse Reaction	Effective Prevention or Palliation	Supportive Treatment
Severe pulmonary edema	Clear chest x-ray within 24 hours preinjection; weight restriction to ≤3% gain over 7 days preinjection	Prompt intubation and oxygenation 24 hours close observation
Fever, chills	15 mg/kg methylprednisolone sodium succinate 1 hour preinjection; fever reduction to <37.8°C (100°F) 1 hour preinjection; acetaminophen (1 g orally) and diphenhydramine (50 mg orally) 1 hour preinjection	Cooling blanket Acetaminophen prn
Respiratory effects	100 mg hydrocortisone sodium succinate 30 minutes postinjection	Additional 100 mg hydrocortisone sodium succinate prn for wheezing; if respiratory distress, give epinephrine 1:1000 (0.3 mL S.C.)

Cardiopulmonary resuscitation may be needed. If the patient's temperature is >37.8°C, reduce before administering OKT3

Adverse Reactions
>10%:

"First-dose" (cytokine release) effects: Onset: 1-3 hours after the dose; duration: 12-16 hours. Severity is mild to life-threatening. Signs and symptoms include fever, chilling, dyspnea, wheezing, chest pain, chest tightness, nausea, vomiting, and diarrhea. Hypervolemic pulmonary edema, nephrotoxicity, meningitis, and encephalopathy are possible. Reactions tend to decrease with repeated doses.

Cardiovascular: Tachycardia (including ventricular)

Central nervous system: Dizziness, faintness

Gastrointestinal: Diarrhea, nausea, vomiting

Hematologic: Transient lymphopenia
Neuromuscular & skeletal: Trembling
Respiratory: Shortness of breath
1% to 10%:
Central nervous system: Headache
Neuromuscular & skeletal: Stiff neck
Ocular: Photophobia
Respiratory: Pulmonary edema
<1%: Hypertension, hypotension, chest pain, tightness, aseptic meningitis, seizures, fatigue, confusion, coma, hallucinations, pyrexia, pruritus, rash, arthralgia, tremor, increased BUN and creatinine, dyspnea, wheezing. Sensitivity reactions: Anaphylactic-type reactions, flu-like symptoms (ie, fever, chills), infection, pancytopenia, secondary lymphoproliferative disorder or lymphoma, thrombosis of major vessels in renal allograft.

Drug Interactions Decreased effect: Immunosuppressive drugs; it is recommended to decrease dose of azathioprine to 1 mg/kg and decrease dose of cyclosporine by 50% until 4 days prior to stopping OKT3

Stability Refrigerate; do not shake or freeze; stable in Becton Dickinson syringe for 16 hours at room temperature or refrigeration

Mechanism of Action Reverses graft rejection by binding to T cells and interfering with their function by binding T-cell receptor-associated CD3 glycoprotein

Pharmacodynamics/Kinetics
Absorption: I.V.: Immediate
Time to steady-state: Trough level: 3-14 days; pretreatment levels are restored within 7 days after treatment is terminated

Usual Dosage I.V. (refer to individual protocols):
Children <30 kg: 2.5 mg/day once daily for 7-14 days
Children >30 kg: 5 mg/day once daily for 7-14 days
OR
Children <12 years: 0.1 mg/kg/day once daily for 10-14 days
Children ≥12 years and Adults: 5 mg/day once daily for 10-14 days
Hemodialysis: Molecular size of OKT3 is 150,000 daltons; not dialyzed by most standard dialyzers; however, may be dialyzed by high flux dialysis; OKT3 will be removed by plasmapheresis; administer following dialysis treatments
Peritoneal dialysis: Significant drug removal is unlikely based on physiochemical characteristics

Administration Filter each dose through a low protein-binding 0.22 micron filter (Millex GV) before administration; administer I.V. push over <1 minute at a final concentration of 1 mg/mL

Children and Adults:
Methylprednisolone sodium succinate 15 mg/kg I.V. given prior to first muromonab-CD3 administration and I.V. hydrocortisone sodium succinate 50-100 mg given 30 minutes after administration are strongly recommended to decrease the incidence of reactions to the first dose
Patient temperature should not exceed 37.8°C (100°F) at time of administration

Monitoring Parameters Chest x-ray, weight gain, CBC with differential, temperature, vital signs (blood pressure, temperature, pulse, respiration); immunologic monitoring of T cells, serum levels of OKT3

Reference Range
OKT3 serum concentrations:
Serum level monitoring should be performed in conjunction with lymphocyte subset determinations; Trough concentration sampling best correlates with clinical outcome. Serial monitoring may provide a better early indicator of inadequate dosing during induction or rejection.
Mean serum trough levels rise during the first 3 days, then average 0.9 mcg/mL on days 3-14
Circulating levels ≥0.8 mcg/mL block the function of cytotoxic T cells *in vitro* and *in vivo*
Several recent analysis have suggested appropriate dosage adjustments of OKT3 induction course are better determined with OKT3 serum levels versus lymphocyte subset determination; however, no prospective controlled trials have been performed to validate the equivalency of these tests in predicting clinical outcome.

Lymphocyte subset monitoring: CD3+ cells: Trough sample measurement is preferable and reagent utilized defines reference range.
OKT3-FITC: <10-50 cells/mm³ or <3% to 5%
CD3(IgG1)-FITC: similar to OKT3-FITC
Leu-4a: Higher number of CD3+ cells appears acceptable
Dosage adjustments should be made in conjunction with clinical response and based upon trends over several consecutive days

Patient Information Inform patient of expected first dose effects which are markedly reduced with subsequent treatments

Nursing Implications Do not administer I.M., monitor patient closely for 24 hours after the first dose; drugs and equipment for treating pulmonary edema and anaphylaxis should be on hand

Dosage Forms Injection: 5 mg/5 mL

- **Mustargen® Hydrochloride** see Mechlorethamine on page 717
- **Mustine** see Mechlorethamine on page 717
- **Mutamycin®** see Mitomycin on page 785
- **M.V.I.®** see Vitamins, Multiple on page 1226
- **M.V.I.®-12** see Vitamins, Multiple on page 1226
- **M.V.I.® Concentrate** see Vitamins, Multiple on page 1226
- **M.V.I.® Pediatric** see Vitamins, Multiple on page 1226
- **Myambutol®** see Ethambutol on page 444
- **Mycelex®** see Clotrimazole on page 287
- **Mycelex®-7** see Clotrimazole on page 287
- **Mycelex®-G** see Clotrimazole on page 287
- **Mycifradin® Sulfate** see Neomycin on page 824
- **Mycinettes® [OTC]** see Benzocaine on page 133
- **Mycitracin® Topical [OTC]** see Bacitracin, Neomycin, and Polymyxin B on page 123
- **Mycobutin®** see Rifabutin on page 1022
- **Mycogen II Topical** see Nystatin and Triamcinolone on page 857
- **Mycolog®-II Topical** see Nystatin and Triamcinolone on page 857
- **Myconel® Topical** see Nystatin and Triamcinolone on page 857

Mycophenolate (mye koe FEN oh late)

Related Information
Antacid Drug Interactions on page 1296

U.S. Brand Names CellCept®

Synonyms Mycophenolate Mofetil

Therapeutic Category Immunosuppressant Agent

Use Immunosuppressant used with corticosteroids and cyclosporine to prevent organ rejection in patients receiving allogenic renal and cardiac transplants; treatment of rejection in liver transplant patients unable to tolerate tacrolimus or cyclosporine due to neurotoxicity; mild rejection in heart transplant patients; treatment of moderate-severe psoriasis

Intravenous formulation is an alternative dosage form to oral capsules and tablets

Pregnancy Risk Factor C

Contraindications Hypersensitivity to mycophenolate mofetil, mycophenolic acid or any ingredient; intravenous is contraindicated in patients who are allergic to polysorbate 80

Warnings/Precautions Increased risk for infection and development of lymphoproliferative disorders. Patients should be monitored appropriately and given supportive treatment should these conditions occur. Increased toxicity in patients with renal impairment. Should be used with caution in patients with active peptic ulcer disease.

Because mycophenolate mofetil has demonstrated teratogenic effects in rats and rabbits, tablets should not be crushed and capsules should not be opened or crushed. Avoid inhalation or direct contact with skin or mucous membranes of the powder contained in the capsules. Caution should be exercised in the handling and preparation of solutions of intravenous mycophenolate. Avoid skin contact with the solution. If such contact occurs, wash thoroughly with soap and water, rinse eyes with plain water.

Adverse Reactions 1% to 10%: Thrombophlebitis and thrombosis (4%) with intravenous administration
See table.

Drug Interactions
Decreased effect: Antacids decrease C_{max} and AUC, **do not administer together**; cholestyramine decreases AUC, **do not administer together**
Increased toxicity: Acyclovir and ganciclovir levels may increase due to competition for tubular secretion of these drugs; probenecid may increase mycophenolate levels due to inhibition of tubular secretion; salicylates: high doses may increase free fraction of mycophenolic acid

Stability Tablets/capsules should be stored at room temperature (15°C to 39°C/59°F to 86°F). Tablets should also be protected from light. Intact vials of injection should be stored at room temperature (15°C to 30°C/59°F to 86°F).

Mycophenolate injection does not contain an antibacterial preservative; therefore, reconstitution and dilution of the product must be done under aseptic conditions. Preparation of intravenous formulation should take place in a vertical laminar flow hood with the same precautions as antineoplastic agents.

Preparation procedure:
Step 1:
  a. Two vials of mycophenolate injection are used for preparing a 1 g dose, whereas 3 vials are needed for each 1.5 g dose. Reconstitute the contents of each vial by injecting 14 mL of 5% dextrose injection.
  b. Gently shake the vial to dissolve the drug
  c. Inspect the resulting slightly yellow solution for particulate matter and discoloration prior to further dilution. Discard the vial if particulate matter or discoloration is observed.
Step 2:
  a. To prepare a 1 g dose, further dilute the contents of the two reconstituted vials into 140 mL of 5% dextrose in water. To prepare a 1.5 g dose, further dilute the contents of the three reconstituted vials into 210 mL of 5% dextrose in water. The final

concentration of both solutions is 6 mg mycophenolate mofetil per mL.
b. Inspect the infusion solution for particulate matter or discoloration. Discard the infusion solution if particulate matter or discoloration is observed.

Stability of the infusion solution: 4 hours from reconstitution and dilution of the product. Store solutions at 15°C to 30°C (59°F to 86°F)

Mechanism of Action Inhibition of purine synthesis of human lymphocytes and proliferation of human lymphocytes

Pharmacodynamics/Kinetics

Absorption: Mycophenolate mofetil is hydrolyzed to mycophenolic acid in the liver and gastrointestinal tract; food does not alter the extent of absorption, but the maximum concentration is decreased

Mycophenolate Adverse Reactions Reported in >10%

Adverse Reaction	MM 2 g/day	MM 3 g/day
Body as a Whole		
Pain	33	31.2
Abdominal pain	12.1-24.7	11.9-27.6
Fever	20.4	23.3
Headache	20.1	16.1
Infection	12.7-18.2	15.6-20.9
Sepsis	17.6-20.8	17.5-19.7
Asthenia	13.7	16.1
Chest pain	13.4	13.3
Back pain	11.6	12.1
Hypertension	17.6-32.4	16.9-28.2
Central Nervous System		
Tremor	11	11.8
Insomnia	8.9	11.8
Dizziness	5.7	11.2
Dermatologic		
Acne	10.1	9.7
Rash	7.7	6.4
Gastrointestinal		
Diarrhea	16.4-31	18.8-36.1
Constipation	21.9	18.5
Nausea	19.9	23.6
Dyspepsia	17.6	13.6
Vomiting	12.5	13.6
Nausea & vomiting	10.4	9.7
Oral moniliasis	10.1	12.1
Hemic/Lymphatic		
Anemia	25.6	25.8
Leukopenia	11.5-23.2	16.3-34.5
Thrombocytopenia	10.1	8.2
Hypochromic anemia	7.4	11.5
Leukocytosis	7.1	10.9
Metabolic/Nutritional		
Peripheral edema	28.6	27
Hypercholesterolemia	12.8	8.5
Hypophosphatemia	12.5	15.8
Edema	12.2	11.8
Hypokalemia	10.1	10
Hyperkalemia	8.9	10.3
Hyperglycemia	8.6	12.4
Respiratory		
Infection	15.8-21	13.1-23.9
Dyspnea	15.5	17.3
Cough increase	15.5	13.3
Pharyngitis	9.5	11.2
Bronchitis	8.5	11.9
Pneumonia	3.6	10.6
Urogenital		
UTI	37.2-45.5	37-44.4
Hematuria	14	12.1
Kidney tubular necrosis	6.3	10
Urinary tract disorder	6.7	10.6

(Continued)

Mycophenolate *(Continued)*

Protein binding: 97%

Metabolism: Mycophenolate mofetil is metabolized to the acid form which is pharmacologically active; mycophenolic acid is glucuronidated to an inactive form; enterohepatic cycling of mycophenolic acid may occur.

Elimination: Mycophenolic acid glucuronide is excreted in the urine and bile. 87% of mycophenolic acid dose has been recovered in urine as inactive glucuronide metabolite.

Half-life: 18 hours

Serum concentrations: Correlation of toxicity or efficacy is still being developed, however, one study indicated that 12-hour AUCs of >40 mcg/mL/hour were correlated with efficacy and decreased episodes of rejection

Usual Dosage

Oral:

Children: 600 mg/m²/dose twice daily; **Note:** Limited information regarding mycophenolate use in pediatric patients is currently available in the literature: 32 pediatric patients (14 underwent living donor and 18 receiving cadaveric donor renal transplants) received mycophenolate 8-30 mg/kg/dose orally twice daily with cyclosporine, prednisone, and Atgam® induction; however, pharmacokinetic studies suggest that doses of mycophenolate adjusted to body surface area resulted in AUCs which better approximated those of adults versus doses adjusted for body weight which resulted in lower AUCs in pediatric patients

Adults: 1 g twice daily within 72 hours of transplant (although 3 g daily has been given in some clinical trials, there was decreased tolerability and no efficacy advantage)

Dosing adjustment in renal impairment: Doses >2 g/day are not recommended in these patients because of the possibility for enhanced immunosuppression as well as toxicities

Dosing adjustment in severe chronic renal impairment: Cl_{cr} <25 mL/minute/1.73 m²: Doses of >1 g administered twice daily should be avoided; patients should also be carefully observed; no dose adjustments are needed in renal transplant patients experiencing delayed graft function postoperatively

Hemodialysis: Not removed; supplemental dose is not necessary

Peritoneal dialysis: Supplemental dose is not necessary

Dosing adjustment for neutropenia: ANC <1.3 x 10^3/µL: Dosing should be interrupted or the dose reduced, appropriate diagnostic tests performed and patients managed appropriately

Administration Intravenous should be administered within 24 hours following transplantation. Intravenous can be administered for up to 14 days; patients should be switched to oral as soon as they can tolerate oral medication. Administer intravenous as a slow infusion over a period of **no less than 2 hours** by either peripheral or central vein. The same precautions utilized with antineoplastic agents should be followed with mycophenolate administration.

Patient Information Take on an empty stomach

Dosage Forms

Capsule, as mofetil: 250 mg
Injection: 500 mg
Tablet, film coated: 500 mg

- **Mycophenolate Mofetil** *see* Mycophenolate *on page 804*
- **Mycostatin®** *see* Nystatin *on page 856*
- **Myco-Triacet® II** *see* Nystatin and Triamcinolone *on page 857*
- **Mydfrin® Ophthalmic Solution** *see* Phenylephrine *on page 918*
- **Mydriacyl®** *see* Tropicamide *on page 1192*
- **Mykrox®** *see* Metolazone *on page 767*
- **Mylanta® Gelcaps®** *see* Calcium Carbonate and Magnesium Carbonate *on page 176*
- **Myleran®** *see* Busulfan *on page 163*
- **Myotonachol™** *see* Bethanechol *on page 143*
- **Myphetane DC®** *see* Brompheniramine, Phenylpropanolamine, and Codeine *on page 156*
- **Mysoline®** *see* Primidone *on page 966*
- **Mytrex® F Topical** *see* Nystatin and Triamcinolone *on page 857*
- **Mytussin® [OTC]** *see* Guaifenesin *on page 549*
- **Mytussin® AC** *see* Guaifenesin and Codeine *on page 550*
- **Mytussin® DAC** *see* Guaifenesin, Pseudoephedrine, and Codeine *on page 551*
- **Mytussin® DM [OTC]** *see* Guaifenesin and Dextromethorphan *on page 550*
- **M-Zole® 7 Dual Pack [OTC]** *see* Miconazole *on page 775*

Nabumetone (na BYOO me tone)

Related Information

Nonsteroidal Anti-Inflammatory Agents Comparison *on page 1335*

U.S. Brand Names Relafen®

Therapeutic Category Analgesic, Nonsteroidal Anti-inflammatory Drug; Anti-inflammatory Agent; Nonsteroidal Anti-inflammatory Drug (NSAID), Oral

Use Management of osteoarthritis and rheumatoid arthritis

Unlabeled use: Sunburn, mild to moderate pain

Pregnancy Risk Factor C

Contraindications Hypersensitivity to nabumetone; should not be administered to patients with active peptic ulceration and those with severe hepatic impairment or in patients in whom nabumetone, aspirin, or other NSAIDs have induced asthma, urticaria, or other allergic-type reactions; fatal asthmatic reactions have occurred following NSAID administration

Warnings/Precautions Elderly patients may sometimes require lower doses; patients with impaired renal function may need a dose reduction; use with caution in patients with severe hepatic impairment

Adverse Reactions
>10%:
Central nervous system: Dizziness
Dermatologic: Rash
Gastrointestinal: Abdominal cramps, heartburn, indigestion, nausea
1% to 10%:
Central nervous system: Headache, nervousness
Dermatologic: Itching
Endocrine & metabolic: Fluid retention
Gastrointestinal: Vomiting
Otic: Tinnitus
<1%: Congestive heart failure, hypertension, arrhythmia, tachycardia, confusion, halluci-nations, aseptic meningitis, mental depression, drowsiness, insomnia, angioedema, urticaria, erythema multiforme, toxic epidermal necrolysis, Stevens-Johnson syndrome, polydipsia, hot flashes, gastritis, GI ulceration, cystitis, polyuria, agranulo-cytosis, anemia, hemolytic anemia, bone marrow suppression, leukopenia, thrombocy-topenia, hepatitis, peripheral neuropathy, toxic amblyopia, blurred vision, conjunctivitis, dry eyes, decreased hearing, acute renal failure, allergic rhinitis, shortness of breath, epistaxis

Mechanism of Action Nabumetone is a nonacidic, nonsteroidal anti-inflammatory drug that is rapidly metabolized after absorption to a major active metabolite, 6-methoxy-2-naphthylacetic acid. As found with previous nonsteroidal anti-inflammatory drugs, nabumetone's active metabolite inhibits the cyclo-oxygenase enzyme which is indirectly responsible for the production of inflammation and pain during arthritis by way of enhancing the production of endoperoxides and prostaglandins E_2 and I_2 (prostacyclin). The active metabolite of nabumetone is felt to be the compound primarily responsible for therapeutic effect. Comparatively, the parent drug is a poor inhibitor of prostaglandin synthesis.

Pharmacodynamics/Kinetics
Distribution: Diffusion occurs readily into synovial fluid with peak concentrations in 4-12 hours
Protein binding: >99%
Metabolism: A prodrug being rapidly metabolized to an active metabolite (6-methoxy-2-naphthylacetic acid); extensive first-pass hepatic metabolism
Half-life, elimination: Major metabolite: 24 hours
Time to peak serum concentration: Metabolite: Oral: Within 3-6 hours
Elimination: 80% recovered in urine and 10% in feces, with very little excreted as unchanged compound

Usual Dosage Adults: Oral: 1000 mg/day; an additional 500-1000 mg may be needed in some patients to obtain more symptomatic relief; may be administered once or twice daily

Dosing adjustment in renal impairment: None necessary; however, adverse effects due to accumulation of inactive metabolites of nabumetone that are renally excreted have not been studied and should be considered

Dietary Considerations
Alcohol: May add to irritant action in the stomach, avoid use if possible
Food: Increases the rate but not the extent of oral absorption. Take without regard to meals OR take with food or milk to minimize GI upset.

Patient Information Take this medication at meal times or with food or milk to minimize gastric irritation; inform your physician if you develop stomach disturbances, blurred vision, or other eye symptoms, rash, weight gain, or edema; inform your physician if you pass dark-colored or tarry stools; concomitant use of alcohol should be avoided, if possible, since it may add to the irritant action of nabumetone in the stomach; aspirin should be avoided

Dosage Forms Tablet: 500 mg, 750 mg

♦ **NAC** see Acetylcysteine on page 26
♦ **N-Acetylcysteine** see Acetylcysteine on page 26
♦ **N-Acetyl-L-cysteine** see Acetylcysteine on page 26
♦ **N-Acetyl-P-Aminophenol** see Acetaminophen on page 19
♦ **NaCl** see Sodium Chloride on page 1067

Nadolol (nay DOE lole)

Related Information
Beta-Blockers Comparison on page 1311
U.S. Brand Names Corgard®
Canadian Brand Names Apo®-Nadol; Syn-Nadolol
Therapeutic Category Antianginal Agent; Antihypertensive Agent; Antimigraine Agent; Beta-Adrenergic Blocker
Use Treatment of hypertension and angina pectoris; prevention of myocardial infarction; prophylaxis of migraine headaches
(Continued)

Nadolol *(Continued)*

Pregnancy Risk Factor C

Pregnancy/Breast-Feeding Implications

Clinical effects on the fetus: No data available on crossing the placenta. Bradycardia, hypotension, hypoglycemia, respiratory depression, hypothermia, IUGR reported. IUGR probably related to maternal hypertension. Alternative beta-blockers are preferred for use during pregnancy due to limited data. Monitor breast-fed infant for symptoms of beta-blockade.

Breast-feeding/lactation: Crosses into breast milk. American Academy of Pediatrics considers **compatible** with breast-feeding.

Contraindications Uncompensated congestive heart failure, cardiogenic shock, bradycardia or heart block, hypersensitivity to any component, bronchial asthma, bronchospasms, diabetes mellitus

Warnings/Precautions Increase dosing interval in patients with renal dysfunction; abrupt withdrawal of beta-blockers may result in an exaggerated cardiac beta-adrenergic responsiveness; symptomatology has included reports of tachycardia, hypertension, ischemia, angina, myocardial infarction, and sudden death; it is recommended that patients be tapered gradually off of beta-blockers over a period of 1-2 weeks rather than via abrupt discontinuation; use with caution in patients with bronchial asthma, bronchospasms, CHF, or diabetes mellitus

Adverse Reactions

>5%:

Central nervous system: Nightmares

Neuromuscular & skeletal: Paresthesia of toes and fingers

1% to 5%:

Cardiovascular: Bradycardia, reduced peripheral circulation, congestive heart failure, chest pain, orthostatic hypotension, Raynaud's syndrome, edema

Central nervous system: Mental depression, dizziness, drowsiness, vivid dreams, insomnia, lethargy, fatigue (2%), confusion, headache

Dermatologic: Itching, rash

Endocrine & metabolic: Decreased sexual ability

Gastrointestinal: Constipation, vomiting, stomach discomfort, diarrhea, nausea

Genitourinary: Impotence

Hematologic: Thrombocytopenia

Neuromuscular & skeletal: Weakness

Ocular: Dry eyes

Respiratory: Dyspnea, wheezing, nasal congestion

Miscellaneous: Cold extremities

Overdosage/Toxicology

Symptoms of intoxication include cardiac disturbances, CNS toxicity, bronchospasm, hypoglycemia and hyperkalemia. The most common cardiac symptoms include hypotension and bradycardia; atrioventricular block, intraventricular conduction disturbances, cardiogenic shock, and asystole may occur with severe overdose, especially with membrane-depressant drugs (eg, propranolol); CNS effects include convulsions, coma, and respiratory arrest (commonly seen with propranolol and other membrane-depressant and lipid-soluble drugs).

Treatment includes symptomatic treatment of seizures, hypotension, hyperkalemia, and hypoglycemia; bradycardia and hypotension resistant to atropine, isoproterenol, or pacing may respond to glucagon; wide QRS defects caused by the membrane-depressant poisoning may respond to hypertonic sodium bicarbonate; repeat-dose charcoal, hemoperfusion, or hemodialysis may be helpful in removal of only those beta-blockers with a small V_d, long half-life, or low intrinsic clearance (acebutolol, atenolol, nadolol, sotalol)

Drug Interactions

Decreased effect of beta-blockers with aluminum salts, barbiturates, calcium salts, cholestyramine, colestipol, NSAIDs, penicillins (ampicillin), rifampin, salicylates and sulfinpyrazone due to decreased bioavailability and plasma levels

Beta-blockers may decrease the effect of sulfonylureas, beta agonists

Increased effect/toxicity of beta-blockers with calcium blockers (diltiazem, felodipine, nicardipine), contraceptives, flecainide, MAO inhibitors, quinidine (in extensive metabolizers), ciprofloxacin

Beta-blockers may increase the effect/toxicity of flecainide, phenothiazines, acetaminophen, clonidine (hypertensive crisis after or during withdrawal of either agent), epinephrine (initial hypertensive episode followed by bradycardia), nifedipine and verapamil, lidocaine, ergots (peripheral ischemia), prazosin (postural hypotension)

Beta-blockers may affect the action or levels of ethanol, disopyramide, nondepolarizing muscle relaxants and theophylline although the effects are difficult to predict

Mechanism of Action Competitively blocks response to beta$_1$- and beta$_2$-adrenergic stimulation; does not exhibit any membrane stabilizing or intrinsic sympathomimetic activity

Pharmacodynamics/Kinetics

Duration of effect: 24 hours

Absorption: Oral: 30% to 40%

Time to peak serum concentration: Within 2-4 hours persisting for 17-24 hours

Distribution: Concentration in human breast milk is 4.6 times higher than serum

Protein binding: 28%

Half-life: Adults: 10-24 hours; increased half-life with decreased renal function

End-stage renal disease: 45 hours

Elimination: Renally unchanged

Usual Dosage Oral:

Adults: Initial: 40 mg/day, increase dosage gradually by 40-80 mg increments at 3- to 7-day intervals until optimum clinical response is obtained with profound slowing of heart rate; doses up to 160-240 mg/day in angina and 240-320 mg/day in hypertension may be necessary

Elderly: Initial: 20 mg/day; increase doses by 20 mg increments at 3- to 7-day intervals; usual dosage range: 20-240 mg/day

Dosing adjustment in renal impairment:

Cl_{cr} 31-40 mL/minute: Administer every 24-36 hours or administer 50% of normal dose

Cl_{cr} 10-30 mL/minute: Administer every 24-48 hours or administer 50% of normal dose

Cl_{cr} <10 mL/minute: Administer every 40-60 hours or administer 25% of normal dose

Hemodialysis: Moderately dialyzable (20% to 50%); administer dose postdialysis or administer 40 mg supplemental dose

Peritoneal dialysis: Supplemental dose is not necessary

Dosing adjustment/comments in hepatic disease: Reduced dose probably necessary

Patient Information Adhere to dosage regimen; watch for postural hypotension; abrupt withdrawal of the drug should be avoided; take at the same time each day; may mask symptoms of diabetes; sweating will continue

Nursing Implications Patient's therapeutic response may be evaluated by looking at blood pressure, apical and radial pulses

Dosage Forms Tablet: 20 mg, 40 mg, 80 mg, 120 mg, 160 mg

◆ **Nadopen-V®** see Penicillin V Potassium on page 898

◆ **Nadostine®** see Nystatin on page 856

Nafarelin (NAF a re lin)

U.S. Brand Names Synarel®

Synonyms Nafarelin Acetate

Therapeutic Category Hormone, Posterior Pituitary; Luteinizing Hormone-Releasing Hormone Analog

Use Treatment of endometriosis, including pain and reduction of lesions; treatment of central precocious puberty (gonadotropin-dependent precocious puberty) in children of both sexes

Pregnancy Risk Factor X

Contraindications Hypersensitivity to GnRH, GnRH-agonist analogs or any components of this product; undiagnosed abnormal vaginal bleeding; pregnancy; lactation

Warnings/Precautions Use with caution in patients with risk factors for decreased bone mineral content, nafarelin therapy may pose an additional risk; hypersensitivity reactions occur in 0.2% of the patients; safety and efficacy in children have not been established

Adverse Reactions

>10%:

Central nervous system: Headache, emotional lability

Dermatologic: Acne

Endocrine & metabolic: Hot flashes, decreased libido, decreased breast size

Genitourinary: Vaginal dryness

Neuromuscular & skeletal: Myalgia

Respiratory: Nasal irritation

1% to 10%:

Cardiovascular: Edema, chest pain

Central nervous system: Insomnia

Dermatologic: Urticaria, rash, pruritus, seborrhea

Respiratory: Shortness of breath

<1%: Increased libido, weight loss

Stability Store at room temperature; protect from light

Mechanism of Action Potent synthetic decapeptide analogue of gonadotropin-releasing hormone (GnRH; LHRH) which is approximately 200 times more potent than GnRH in terms of pituitary release of luteinizing hormone (LH) and follicle-stimulating hormone (FSH). Effects on the pituitary gland and sex hormones are dependent upon its length of administration. After acute administration, an initial stimulation of the release of LH and FSH from the pituitary is observed; an increase in androgens and estrogens subsequently follows. Continued administration of nafarelin, however, suppresses gonadotrope responsiveness to endogenous GnRH resulting in reduced secretion of LH and FSH and, secondarily, decreased ovarian and testicular steroid production.

Pharmacodynamics/Kinetics

Absorption: Not absorbed from GI tract

Maximum serum concentration: 10-45 minutes

Protein binding: 80% bound to plasma proteins

Usual Dosage

Endometriosis: Adults: Female: 1 spray (200 mcg) in 1 nostril each morning and the other nostril each evening starting on days 2-4 of menstrual cycle for 6 months

Central precocious puberty: Children: Males/Females: 2 sprays (400 mcg) into each nostril in the morning 2 sprays (400 mcg) into each nostril in the evening. If inadequate suppression, may increase dose to 3 sprays (600 mcg) into alternating nostrils 3 times/day.

Patient Information Begin treatment between days 2 and 4 of menstrual cycle; usually menstruation will stop (as well as ovulation), but is not a reliable contraceptive, use of a nonhormonal contraceptive is suggested; full compliance with taking the medicine is very important; do not use nasal decongestant for at least 30 minutes after using nafarelin spray; notify physician if regular menstruation persists

(Continued)

Nafarelin *(Continued)*

Nursing Implications Do not administer to pregnant or breast-feeding patients; topical nasal decongestant should be used at least 30 minutes after nafarelin use

Additional Information Each spray delivers 200 mcg

Dosage Forms Solution, nasal, as acetate: 2 mg/mL (10 mL)

♦ **Nafarelin Acetate** *see Nafarelin on previous page*

♦ **Nafazair®** *see Naphazoline on page 817*

♦ **Nafcil™ Injection** *see Nafcillin on this page*

Nafcillin *(naf SIL in)*

Related Information

Antibiotic Treatment of Adults With Infective Endocarditis *on page 1401*
Community-Acquired Pneumonia in Adults *on page 1419*
Extravasation Treatment of Other Drugs *on page 1287*

U.S. Brand Names Nafcil™ Injection; Nallpen® Injection; Unipen® Injection; Unipen® Oral

Synonyms Ethoxynaphthamido Penicillin Sodium; Nafcillin Sodium; Sodium Nafcillin

Therapeutic Category Antibiotic, Penicillin

Use Treatment of infections such as osteomyelitis, septicemia, endocarditis, and CNS infections caused by susceptible strains of staphylococci species

Pregnancy Risk Factor B

Contraindications Hypersensitivity to nafcillin or any component or penicillins

Warnings/Precautions Extravasation of I.V. infusions should be avoided; modification of dosage is necessary in patients with both severe renal and hepatic impairment; elimination rate will be slow in neonates; use with caution in patients with cephalosporin hypersensitivity

Adverse Reactions Percentage unknown: Fever, pain, rash, nausea, diarrhea, neutropenia, thrombophlebitis; oxacillin (less likely to cause phlebitis) is often preferred in pediatric patients, acute interstitial nephritis, hypersensitivity reactions

Overdosage/Toxicology

Symptoms of penicillin overdose include neuromuscular hypersensitivity (agitation, hallucinations, asterixis, encephalopathy, confusion, and seizures) and electrolyte imbalance with potassium or sodium salts, especially in renal failure

Hemodialysis may be helpful to aid in the removal of the drug from the blood, otherwise most treatment is supportive or symptom directed

Drug Interactions

Decreased effect: Efficacy of oral contraceptives may be reduced; warfarin/anticoagulants

Increased effect: Disulfiram, probenecid may increase penicillin levels

Stability Refrigerate oral solution after reconstitution; discard after 7 days; reconstituted parenteral solution is stable for 3 days at room temperature and 7 days when refrigerated or 12 weeks when frozen; for I.V. infusion in NS or D_5W, solution is stable for 24 hours at room temperature and 96 hours when refrigerated

Mechanism of Action Interferes with bacterial cell wall synthesis during active multiplication, causing cell wall death and resultant bactericidal activity against susceptible bacteria

Pharmacodynamics/Kinetics

Absorption: Oral: Poor and erratic

Distribution: Widely distributed; CSF penetration is poor but enhanced by meningeal inflammation; crosses the placenta

Metabolism: Primarily in the liver; it undergoes enterohepatic circulation

Half-life:

Neonates: <3 weeks: 2.2-5.5 hours; 4-9 weeks: 1.2-2.3 hours

Children 3 months to 14 years: 0.75-1.9 hours

Adults: 30 minutes to 1.5 hours, with normal renal and hepatic function

Time to peak serum concentration: Oral: Within 2 hours; I.M.: Within 30-60 minutes

Elimination: Primarily eliminated in bile, 10% to 30% in urine as unchanged drug; undergoes enterohepatic recycling

Usual Dosage

Neonates:

<2000 g, <7 days: 50 mg/kg/day divided every 12 hours

<2000 g, >7 days: 75 mg/kg/day divided every 8 hours

>2000 g, <7 days: 50 mg/kg/day divided every 8 hours

>2000 g, >7 days: 75 mg/kg/day divided every 6 hours

Children:

Oral: 25-50 mg/kg/day in 4 divided doses

I.M.: 25 mg/kg twice daily

I.V.:

Mild to moderate infections: 50-100 mg/kg/day in divided doses every 6 hours

Severe infections: 100-200 mg/kg/day in divided doses every 4-6 hours

Maximum dose: 12 g/day

Adults:

Oral: 250-500 mg (up to 1 g) every 4-6 hours

I.M.: 500 mg every 4-6 hours

I.V.: 500-2000 mg every 4-6 hours

Dosing adjustment in renal impairment: Not necessary

Dialysis: Not dializable (0% to 5%) via hemodialysis; supplemental dosage not necessary with hemo- or peritoneal dialysis or continuous arteriovenous or venovenous hemofiltration (CAVH/CAVHD)

Monitoring Parameters Periodic CBC, urinalysis, BUN, serum creatinine, AST and ALT; observe for signs and symptoms of anaphylaxis during first dose

Test Interactions Positive Coombs' test (direct), false-positive urinary and serum proteins; may inactivate aminoglycosides *in vitro*

Nursing Implications

Extravasation: Use cold packs

Hyaluronidase (Wydase®): Add 1 mL NS to 150 unit vial to make 150 units/mL of concentration; mix 0.1 mL of above with 0.9 mL NS in 1 mL syringe to make final concentration = 15 units/mL

Additional Information Sodium content of 1 g: 66.7 mg (2.9 mEq); other penicillinase-resistant penicillins (ie, dicloxacillin or cloxacillin) are preferred for oral therapy

Dosage Forms

Capsule, as sodium: 250 mg

Powder for injection, as sodium: 500 mg, 1 g, 2 g, 4 g, 10 g

Solution, as sodium: 250 mg/5 mL (100 mL)

Tablet, as sodium: 500 mg

♦ **Nafcillin Sodium** see Nafcillin on previous page

Naftifine (NAF ti feen)

U.S. Brand Names Naftin®

Synonyms Naftifine Hydrochloride

Therapeutic Category Antifungal Agent, Topical

Use Topical treatment of tinea cruris (jock itch), tinea corporis (ringworm), and tinea pedis (athlete's foot)

Pregnancy Risk Factor B

Contraindications Hypersensitivity to any component

Warnings/Precautions For external use only

Adverse Reactions

>10%: Local: Burning, stinging

1% to 10%:

Dermatologic: Erythema, itching

Local: Dryness, irritation

Mechanism of Action Synthetic, broad-spectrum antifungal agent in the allylamine class; appears to have both fungistatic and fungicidal activity. Exhibits antifungal activity by selectively inhibiting the enzyme squalene epoxidase in a dose-dependent manner which results in the primary sterol, ergosterol, within the fungal membrane not being synthesized.

Pharmacodynamics/Kinetics

Absorption: Systemic, 6% for cream, ≤4% for gel

Half-life: 2-3 days

Elimination: Metabolites excreted in urine and feces

Usual Dosage Adults: Topical: Apply cream once daily and gel twice daily (morning and evening) for up to 4 weeks

Patient Information External use only; avoid eyes, mouth, and other mucous membranes; do not use occlusive dressings unless directed to do so; discontinue if irritation or sensitivity develops; wash hands after application

Dosage Forms

Cream, as hydrochloride: 1% (15 g, 30 g, 60 g)

Gel, topical, as hydrochloride: 1% (20 g, 40 g, 60 g)

♦ **Naftifine Hydrochloride** see Naftifine on this page

♦ **Naftin®** see Naftifine on this page

♦ **NaHCO₃** see Sodium Bicarbonate on page 1066

Nalbuphine (NAL byoo feen)

Related Information

Narcotic Agonists Comparison on page 1328

U.S. Brand Names Nubain®

Synonyms Nalbuphine Hydrochloride

Therapeutic Category Analgesic, Narcotic

Use Relief of moderate to severe pain; preoperative analgesia, postoperative and surgical anesthesia, and obstetrical analgesia during labor and delivery

Pregnancy Risk Factor B (D if used for prolonged periods or in high doses at term)

Contraindications Hypersensitivity to nalbuphine or any component, including sulfites

Warnings/Precautions Use with caution in patients with recent myocardial infarction, biliary tract surgery, or sulfite sensitivity; may produce respiratory depression; use with caution in women delivering premature infants; use with caution in patients with a history of drug dependence, head trauma or increased intracranial pressure, decreased hepatic or renal function, or pregnancy; tolerance or drug dependence may result from extended use

Adverse Reactions

>10%:

Central nervous system: Drowsiness, CNS depression, narcotic withdrawal

Miscellaneous: Histamine release

(Continued)

Nalbuphine (Continued)

1% to 10%:
- Cardiovascular: Hypotension, flushing
- Central nervous system: Dizziness, headache
- Dermatologic: Urticaria, rash
- Gastrointestinal: Nausea, vomiting, anorexia, xerostomia
- Local: Pain at injection site
- Neuromuscular & skeletal: Weakness
- Respiratory: Pulmonary edema

<1%: Hypertension, tachycardia, mental depression, hallucinations, confusion, paradoxical CNS stimulation, nervousness, restlessness, nightmares, insomnia GI irritation, biliary spasm, decreased urination, toxic megacolon, ureteral spasm, blurred vision, shortness of breath, respiratory depression

Overdosage/Toxicology
Symptoms of overdose include CNS depression, respiratory depression, miosis, hypotension, bradycardia

Treatment of an overdose includes support of the patient's airway, establishment of an I.V. line and administration of naloxone 2 mg I.V. (0.01 mg/kg for children) with repeat administration as necessary up to a total of 10 mg.

Drug Interactions Increased toxicity: Barbiturate anesthetics may increase CNS depression

Mechanism of Action Binds to opiate receptors in the CNS, causing inhibition of ascending pain pathways, altering the perception of and response to pain; produces generalized CNS depression

Pharmacodynamics/Kinetics
Peak effect: I.M.: 30 minutes; I.V.: 1-3 minutes
Metabolism: In the liver
Half-life: 3.5-5 hours
Elimination: Metabolites excreted primarily in feces (via bile) and in urine (~7%)

Usual Dosage I.M., I.V., S.C.:
Children 10 months to 14 years: Premedication: 0.2 mg/kg; maximum: 20 mg/dose
Adults: 10 mg/70 kg every 3-6 hours; maximum single dose: 20 mg; maximum daily dose: 160 mg
Dosing adjustment/comments in hepatic impairment: Use with caution and reduce dose

Dietary Considerations Alcohol: Additive CNS effects, avoid or limit alcohol; watch for sedation

Monitoring Parameters Relief of pain, respiratory and mental status, blood pressure

Patient Information Avoid alcohol, may cause drowsiness, impaired judgment or coordination; may cause physical and psychological dependence with prolonged use; will cause withdrawal in patients currently dependent on narcotics

Nursing Implications Observe patient for excessive sedation, respiratory depression, implement safety measures, assist with ambulation; observe for narcotic withdrawal

Dosage Forms Injection, as hydrochloride: 10 mg/mL (1 mL, 10 mL); 20 mg/mL (1 mL, 10 mL)

- **Nalbuphine Hydrochloride** see Nalbuphine on previous page
- **Naldecon®** see Chlorpheniramine, Phenyltoloxamine, Phenylpropanolamine, and Phenylephrine on page 247
- **Naldecon® Senior DX [OTC]** see Guaifenesin and Dextromethorphan on page 550
- **Naldecon® Senior EX [OTC]** see Guaifenesin on page 549
- **Naldelate®** see Chlorpheniramine, Phenyltoloxamine, Phenylpropanolamine, and Phenylephrine on page 247
- **Nalfon®** see Fenoprofen on page 473
- **Nalgest®** see Chlorpheniramine, Phenyltoloxamine, Phenylpropanolamine, and Phenylephrine on page 247

Nalidixic Acid (nal i DIKS ik AS id)

U.S. Brand Names NegGram®
Synonyms Nalidixinic Acid
Therapeutic Category Antibiotic, Quinolone
Use Treatment of urinary tract infections
Pregnancy Risk Factor B
Contraindications Hypersensitivity to nalidixic acid or any component; infants <3 months of age
Warnings/Precautions Use with caution in patients with impaired hepatic or renal function and prepubertal children; has been shown to cause cartilage degeneration in immature animals; may induce hemolysis in patients with G-6-PD deficiency
Adverse Reactions
>10%: Central nervous system: Dizziness, drowsiness, headache
1% to 10%: Gastrointestinal: Nausea, vomiting
<1%: Increased intracranial pressure, malaise, vertigo, confusion, toxic psychosis, convulsions, fever, chills, rash, urticaria, photosensitivity reactions, metabolic acidosis, leukopenia, thrombocytopenia, hepatotoxicity, visual disturbances
Overdosage/Toxicology
Symptoms of overdose include nausea, vomiting, toxic psychosis, convulsions, increased intracranial pressure, metabolic acidosis; severe overdose, intracranial hypertension, increased pressure, and seizures have occurred

After GI decontamination, treatment is symptomatic
Drug Interactions
Decreased effect with antacids
Increased effect of warfarin
Mechanism of Action Inhibits DNA polymerization in late stages of chromosomal replication
Pharmacodynamics/Kinetics
Distribution: Crosses the placenta; appears in breast milk; achieves significant antibacterial concentrations only in the urinary tract
Protein binding: 90%
Metabolism: Partly in the liver
Half-life: 6-7 hours; increases significantly with renal impairment
Time to peak serum concentration: Oral: Within 1-2 hours
Elimination: In urine as unchanged drug and 80% as metabolites; small amounts appear in feces
Usual Dosage Oral:
Children 3 months to 12 years: 55 mg/kg/day divided every 6 hours; suppressive therapy is 33 mg/kg/day divided every 6 hours
Adults: 1 g 4 times/day for 2 weeks; then suppressive therapy of 500 mg 4 times/day
Dosing comments in renal impairment: Cl_{cr} <50 mL/minute: Avoid use
Test Interactions False-positive urine glucose with Clinitest®, false increase in urinary VMA
Patient Information Avoid undue exposure to direct sunlight or use a sunscreen; take 1 hour before meals, but can take with food to decrease GI upset, finish all medication, do not skip doses; if persistent cough occurs, notify physician
Dosage Forms
Suspension, oral (raspberry flavor): 250 mg/5 mL (473 mL)
Tablet: 250 mg, 500 mg, 1 g

♦ **Nalidixinic Acid** see Nalidixic Acid on previous page
♦ **Nallpen® Injection** see Nafcillin on page 810
♦ **N-allylnoroxymorphine Hydrochloride** see Naloxone on next page

Nalmefene (NAL me feen)

U.S. Brand Names Revex®
Synonyms Nalmefene Hydrochloride
Therapeutic Category Antidote for Narcotic Agonists
Use Complete or partial reversal of opioid drug effects, including respiratory depression induced by natural or synthetic opioids; reversal of postoperative opioid depression; management of known or suspected opioid overdose (if opioid dependence is suspected, nalmefene should only be used in opioid overdose if the likelihood of overdose is high based on history or the clinical presentation of respiratory depression with concurrent pupillary constriction is present)
Pregnancy Risk Factor B
Pregnancy/Breast-Feeding Implications Limited information available; do not use in pregnant or lactating women if possible
Contraindications Hypersensitivity to nalmefene, naltrexone, or components
Warnings/Precautions May induce symptoms of acute withdrawal in opioid-dependent patients; recurrence of respiratory depression is possible if the opioid involved is long-acting; observe patients until there is no reasonable risk of recurrent respiratory depression; dosage may need to be decreased in renal and hepatic impairment; safety and efficacy have not been established in children; avoid abrupt reversal of opioid effects in patients of high cardiovascular risk or who have received potentially cardiotoxic drugs; animal studies indicate nalmefene may not completely reverse buprenorphine-induced respiratory depression
Adverse Reactions
>10%: Gastrointestinal: Nausea (18%)
1% to 10%:
Cardiovascular: Tachycardia/hypertension (5%)
Central nervous system: Fever/dizziness (3%)
Gastrointestinal: Vomiting (9%)
Miscellaneous: Postoperative pain (4%)
<1%: Hypotension, vasodilation, arrhythmia, bradycardia, headache, chills, nervousness, confusion, somnolence, depression, pruritus, diarrhea, xerostomia, urinary retention, increased AST, tremor, myoclonus, pharyngitis, withdrawal syndrome
Overdosage/Toxicology No known symptoms in significant overdose; large doses of opioids administered to overcome a full blockade of opioid antagonists, however, has resulted in adverse respiratory and circulatory reactions
Drug Interactions Increased effect: Potential increased risk of seizures exists with use of flumazenil and nalmefene coadministration
Mechanism of Action As a 6-methylene analog of naltrexone, nalmefene acts as a competitive antagonist at opioid receptor sites, preventing or reversing the respiratory depression, sedation, and hypotension induced by opiates; no pharmacologic activity of its own (eg, opioid agonist activity) has been demonstrated
Pharmacodynamics/Kinetics
Onset of action: I.M., S.C.: 5-15 minutes
Distribution: V_d: 8.6 L/kg; rapid
Protein binding: 45%
Metabolism: Hepatic by glucuronide conjugation to metabolites with little or no activity
(Continued)

Nalmefene *(Continued)*

Bioavailability: I.M., I.V., S.C.: 100%

T_{max}: I.M.: 2.3 hours; I.V.: <2 minutes; S.C.: 1.5 hours

Half-life: 10.8 hours

Time to peak serum concentration: 2.3 hours

Elimination: <5% excreted unchanged in urine, 17% in feces; clearance: 0.8 L/hour/kg

Usual Dosage

Reversal of postoperative opioid depression: Blue labeled product (100 mcg/mL): Titrate to reverse the undesired effects of opioids; initial dose for nonopioid dependent patients: 0.25 mcg/kg followed by 0.25 mcg/kg incremental doses at 2- to 5-minute intervals; after a total dose of >1 mcg/kg, further therapeutic response is unlikely

Management of known/suspected opioid overdose: Green labeled product (1000 mcg/mL): Initial dose: 0.5 mg/70 kg; may repeat with 1 mg/70 kg in 2-5 minutes; further increase beyond a total dose of 1.5 mg/70 kg will not likely result in improved response and may result in cardiovascular stress and precipitated withdrawal syndrome. (If opioid dependency is suspected, administer a challenge dose of 0.1 mg/70 kg; if no withdrawal symptoms are observed in 2 minutes, the recommended doses can be administered.)

Dosing adjustment in renal or hepatic impairment: Not necessary with single uses, however, slow administration (over 60 seconds) of incremental doses is recommended to minimize hypertension and dizziness

Administration Dilute drug (1:1) with diluent and use smaller doses in patients known to be at increased cardiovascular risk; may be administered via I.M. or S.C. routes if I.V. access is not feasible

Nursing Implications Check dosage strength carefully before use to avoid error; monitor patients for signs of withdrawal, especially those physically dependent who are in pain or at high cardiovascular risk

Additional Information Proper steps should be used to prevent use of the incorrect dosage strength; the goal of treatment in the postoperative setting is to achieve reversal of excessive opioid effects without inducing a complete reversal and acute pain

Dosage Forms Injection, as hydrochloride: 100 mcg/mL [blue label] (1 mL); 1000 mcg/mL [green label] (2 mL)

♦ **Nalmefene Hydrochloride** *see Nalmefene on previous page*

Naloxone *(nal OKS one)*

Related Information

Narcotic Agonists Comparison *on page 1328*

U.S. Brand Names Narcan® Injection

Synonyms *N*-allylnoroxymorphine Hydrochloride; Naloxone Hydrochloride

Therapeutic Category Antidote for Narcotic Agonists

Use Reverses CNS and respiratory depression in suspected narcotic overdose; neonatal opiate depression; coma of unknown etiology

Investigational: Shock, PCP and alcohol ingestion

Pregnancy Risk Factor B

Contraindications Hypersensitivity to naloxone or any component

Warnings/Precautions Use with caution in patients with cardiovascular disease; excessive dosages should be avoided after use of opiates in surgery, because naloxone may cause an increase in blood pressure and reversal of anesthesia; may precipitate withdrawal symptoms in patients addicted to opiates, including pain, hypertension, sweating, agitation, irritability, shrill cry, failure to feed

Adverse Reactions 1% to 10%:

Cardiovascular: Hypertension, hypotension, tachycardia, ventricular arrhythmias

Central nervous system: Insomnia, irritability, anxiety, narcotic withdrawal

Dermatologic: Rash

Gastrointestinal: Nausea, vomiting

Ocular: Blurred vision

Miscellaneous: Diaphoresis

Overdosage/Toxicology Naloxone is the drug of choice for respiratory depression that is known or suspected to be caused by an overdose of an opiate or opioid

Caution: Naloxone's effects are due to its action on narcotic reversal, not due to any direct effect upon opiate receptors. Therefore, adverse events occur secondarily to reversal (withdrawal) of narcotic analgesia and sedation, which can cause severe reactions.

Drug Interactions Decreased effect of narcotic analgesics

Stability Protect from light; stable in 0.9% sodium chloride and D_5W at 4 mcg/mL for 24 hours; do not mix with alkaline solutions

Mechanism of Action Competes and displaces narcotics at narcotic receptor sites

Pharmacodynamics/Kinetics

Onset of effect: Endotracheal, I.M., S.C.: Within 2-5 minutes; I.V.: Within 2 minutes

Duration: 20-60 minutes; since shorter than that of most opioids, repeated doses are usually needed

Distribution: Crosses the placenta

Metabolism: Primarily by glucuronidation in the liver

Half-life: Neonates: 1.2-3 hours; Adults: 1-1.5 hours

Elimination: In urine as metabolites

Usual Dosage I.M., I.V. (preferred), intratracheal, S.C.:

Postanesthesia narcotic reversal: Infants and Children: 0.01 mg/kg; may repeat every 2-3 minutes as needed based on response

Opiate intoxication:

Birth (including premature infants) to 5 years or <20 kg: 0.1 mg/kg; repeat every 2-3 minutes if needed; may need to repeat doses every 20-60 minutes

>5 years or ≥20 kg: 2 mg/dose; if no response, repeat every 2-3 minutes; may need to repeat doses every 20-60 minutes

Continuous infusion: I.V.: Children and Adults: If continuous infusion is required, calculate dosage/hour based on effective intermittent dose used and duration of adequate response seen, titrate dose 0.04-0.16 mg/kg/hour for 2-5 days in children, up to 0.8 mg/kg/hour in adults; alternatively, continuous infusion utilizes $2/3$ of the initial naloxone bolus on an hourly basis; add 10 times this dose to each liter of D_5W and infuse at a rate of 100 mL/hour; $1/2$ of the initial bolus dose should be readministered 15 minutes after initiation of the continuous infusion to prevent a drop in naloxone levels; increase infusion rate as needed to assure adequate ventilation

Narcotic overdose: Adults: I.V.: 0.4-2 mg every 2-3 minutes as needed; may need to repeat doses every 20-60 minutes, if no response is observed after 10 mg, question the diagnosis. **Note:** Use 0.1-0.2 mg increments in patients who are opioid dependent and in postoperative patients to avoid large cardiovascular changes

Monitoring Parameters Respiratory rate, heart rate, blood pressure

Nursing Implications The use of neonatal naloxone (0.02 mg/mL) is no longer recommended because unacceptable fluid volumes will result, especially to small neonates; the 0.4 mg/mL preparation is available and can be accurately dosed with appropriately sized syringes (1 mL)

Dosage Forms

Injection, as hydrochloride: 0.4 mg/mL (1 mL, 2 mL, 10 mL); 1 mg/mL (2 mL, 10 mL)

Injection, neonatal, as hydrochloride: 0.02 mg/mL (2 mL)

♦ **Naloxone Hydrochloride** see Naloxone on previous page

♦ **Nalspan®** see Chlorpheniramine, Phenyltoloxamine, Phenylpropanolamine, and Phenylephrine on page 247

Naltrexone (nal TREKS one)

U.S. Brand Names ReVia®

Synonyms Naltrexone Hydrochloride

Therapeutic Category Antidote for Narcotic Agonists

Use Adjunct to the maintenance of an opioid-free state in detoxified individual; alcoholism

Pregnancy Risk Factor C

Contraindications Acute hepatitis, liver failure, known hypersensitivity to naltrexone

Warnings/Precautions Dose-related hepatocellular injury is possible; the margin of separation between the apparent safe and hepatotoxic doses appear to be only fivefold or less

Adverse Reactions

>10%:

Central nervous system: Insomnia, nervousness, headache

Gastrointestinal: Abdominal cramping, nausea, vomiting

Neuromuscular & skeletal: Arthralgia

1% to 10%:

Central nervous system: Dizziness

Dermatologic: Rash

Endocrine & metabolic: Polydipsia

Gastrointestinal: Anorexia

Respiratory: Sneezing

<1%: Insomnia, irritability, anxiety, narcotic withdrawal, thrombocytopenia, agranulocytosis, hemolytic anemia, blurred vision

Overdosage/Toxicology Symptoms of overdose include clonic-tonic convulsions, respiratory failure; patients receiving up to 800 mg/day for 1 week have shown no toxicity; seizures and respiratory failure have been seen in animals

Mechanism of Action Naltrexone is a cyclopropyl derivative of oxymorphone similar in structure to naloxone and nalorphine (a morphine derivative); it acts as a competitive antagonist at opioid receptor sites

Pharmacodynamics/Kinetics

Duration of action:

50 mg: 24 hours

100 mg: 48 hours

150 mg: 72 hours

Absorption: Oral: Almost completely

Distribution: V_d: 19 L/kg; distributed widely throughout the body but considerable inter-individual variation exists

Protein binding: 21%

Metabolism: Undergoes extensive first-pass metabolism to 6-β-naltrexol

Half-life: 4 hours; 6-β-naltrexol: 13 hours

Time to peak serum concentration: Within 60 minutes

Elimination: Principally in urine as metabolites and unchanged drug

Usual Dosage Do not give until patient is opioid-free for 7-10 days as required by urine analysis; Adults: Oral:

(Continued)

Naltrexone *(Continued)*

25 mg; if no withdrawal signs within 1 hour give another 25 mg; maintenance regimen is flexible, variable and individualized (50 mg/day to 100-150 mg 3 times/week)

Adjunct in the management of alcoholism: A flexible approach to dosing is recommended by the manufacturer; the following are acceptable regimens:
50 mg once daily
50 mg once daily on weekdays and 100 mg on Saturdays
100 mg every other day
150 mg every third day

Administration Naltrexone is administered orally; to minimize adverse gastrointestinal effects, give with food or antacids or after meals; advise patient not to self-administer opiates while receiving naltrexone therapy

Patient Information Will cause narcotic withdrawal; serious overdose can occur after attempts to overcome the blocking effect of naltrexone

Nursing Implications Monitor for narcotic withdrawal

Dosage Forms Tablet, as hydrochloride: 50 mg

♦ **Naltrexone Hydrochloride** *see Naltrexone on previous page*

Nandrolone *(NAN droe lone)*

U.S. Brand Names Anabolin® Injection; Androlone®-D Injection; Androlone® Injection; Deca-Durabolin® Injection; Durabolin® Injection; Hybolin™ Decanoate Injection; Hybolin™ Improved Injection; Neo-Durabolic Injection

Synonyms Nandrolone Decanoate; Nandrolone Phenpropionate

Therapeutic Category Anabolic Steroid; Androgen

Use Control of metastatic breast cancer; management of anemia of renal insufficiency

Restrictions C-III

Pregnancy Risk Factor X

Contraindications Carcinoma of breast or prostate, nephrosis, pregnancy and infants, hypersensitivity to any component

Warnings/Precautions Monitor diabetic patients carefully; anabolic steroids may cause peliosis hepatis, liver cell tumors, and blood lipid changes with increased risk of arteriosclerosis; use with caution in elderly patients, they may be at greater risk for prostatic hypertrophy; use with caution in patients with cardiac, renal, or hepatic disease or epilepsy

Adverse Reactions

Male:
Postpubertal:
>10%:
Dermatologic: Acne
Endocrine & metabolic: Gynecomastia
Genitourinary: Bladder irritability, priapism
1% to 10%:
Central nervous system: Insomnia, chills
Endocrine & metabolic: Decreased libido, hepatic dysfunction
Gastrointestinal: Nausea, diarrhea
Genitourinary: Prostatic hypertrophy (elderly)
Hematologic: Iron deficiency anemia, suppression of clotting factors
<1%: Hepatic necrosis, hepatocellular carcinoma
Prepubertal:
>10%:
Dermatologic: Acne
Endocrine & metabolic: Virilism
1% to 10%:
Central nervous system: Chills, insomnia
Dermatologic: Hyperpigmentation
Gastrointestinal: Diarrhea, nausea
Hematologic: Iron deficiency anemia, suppression of clotting
<1%: Hepatocellular carcinoma, necrosis

Female:
>10%: Endocrine & metabolic: Virilism
1% to 10%:
Central nervous system: Chills, insomnia
Endocrine & metabolic: Hypercalcemia
Gastrointestinal: Nausea, diarrhea
Hematologic: Iron deficiency anemia, suppression of clotting factors
Hepatic: Hepatic dysfunction
<1%: Hepatic necrosis, hepatocellular carcinoma

Drug Interactions Increased toxicity: Oral anticoagulants, insulin, oral hypoglycemic agents, adrenal steroids, ACTH

Mechanism of Action Promotes tissue-building processes, increases production of erythropoietin, causes protein anabolism; increases hemoglobin and red blood cell volume

Pharmacodynamics/Kinetics
Onset: 3-6 months
Duration: Up to 30 days
Absorption: 77% intramuscularly
Metabolism: In the liver

Elimination: Renal

Usual Dosage Deep I.M. (into gluteal muscle):

Children 2-13 years: (decanoate): 25-50 mg every 3-4 weeks

Adults:

Male:

Breast cancer (phenpropionate): 50-100 mg/week

Anemia of renal insufficiency (decanoate): 100-200 mg/week

Female: 50-100 mg/week

Breast cancer (phenpropionate): 50-100 mg/week

Anemia of renal insufficiency (decanoate): 50-100 mg/week

Administration Inject deeply I.M., preferably into the gluteal muscle

Test Interactions Altered glucose tolerance tests

Patient Information Virilization may occur in female patients; report menstrual irregularities; male patients report persistent penile erections; all patients should report persistent GI distress, diarrhea, dark urine, pale stools, yellow coloring of skin or sclera; diabetic patients should monitor glucose closely

Additional Information Both phenpropionate and decanoate are Injections in oil

Dosage Forms

Injection, as phenpropionate, in oil: 25 mg/mL (5 mL); 50 mg/mL (2 mL)

Injection, as decanoate, in oil: 50 mg/mL (1 mL, 2 mL); 100 mg/mL (1 mL, 2 mL); 200 mg/mL (1 mL)

Injection, repository, as decanoate: 50 mg/mL (2 mL); 100 mg/mL (2 mL); 200 mg/mL (2 mL)

♦ **Nandrolone Decanoate** see Nandrolone on previous page

♦ **Nandrolone Phenpropionate** see Nandrolone on previous page

Naphazoline (naf AZ oh leen)

U.S. Brand Names AK-Con®; Albalon® Liquifilm®; Allerest® Eye Drops [OTC]; Clear Eyes® [OTC]; Comfort® [OTC]; Degest® 2 [OTC]; Estivin® II [OTC]; I-Naphline®; Muro's Opcon®; Nafazair®; Naphcon® [OTC]; Naphcon Forte®; Opcon®; Privine®; VasoClear® [OTC]; Vasocon Regular®

Synonyms Naphazoline Hydrochloride

Therapeutic Category Adrenergic Agonist Agent, Ophthalmic; Decongestant, Nasal; Nasal Agent, Vasoconstrictor; Ophthalmic Agent, Vasoconstrictor

Use Topical ocular vasoconstrictor; will temporarily relieve congestion, itching, and minor irritation, and to control hyperemia in patients with superficial corneal vascularity; treatment of nasal congestion; adjunct for sinusitis

Pregnancy Risk Factor C

Contraindications Hypersensitivity to naphazoline or any component, narrow-angle glaucoma, prior to peripheral iridectomy (in patients susceptible to angle block)

Warnings/Precautions Rebound congestion may occur with extended use; use with caution in the presence of hypertension, diabetes, hyperthyroidism, heart disease, coronary artery disease, cerebral arteriosclerosis, or long-standing bronchial asthma

Adverse Reactions 1% to 10%:

Cardiovascular: Systemic cardiovascular stimulation

Central nervous system: Dizziness, headache, nervousness

Gastrointestinal: Nausea

Local: Transient stinging, nasal mucosa irritation, dryness, rebound congestion

Ocular: Mydriasis, increased intraocular pressure, blurring of vision

Respiratory: Sneezing

Overdosage/Toxicology

Symptoms of overdose include CNS depression, hypothermia, bradycardia, cardiovascular collapse, apnea, coma

Following initiation of essential overdose management, toxic symptoms should be treated. The patient should be kept warm and monitored for alterations in vital functions. Seizures commonly respond to diazepam (5-10 mg I.V. bolus in adults every 15 minutes if needed up to a total of 30 mg; I.V. 0.25-0.4 mg/kg/dose up to a total of 10 mg for children) or to phenytoin or phenobarbital. Hypotension should be treated with fluids.

Drug Interactions Increased toxicity: Anesthetics (discontinue mydriatic prior to use of anesthetics that sensitize the myocardium to sympathomimetics, ie, cyclopropane, halothane), MAO inhibitors, tricyclic antidepressants → hypertensive reactions

Stability Store in tight, light-resistant containers

Mechanism of Action Stimulates alpha-adrenergic receptors in the arterioles of the conjunctiva and the nasal mucosa to produce vasoconstriction

Pharmacodynamics/Kinetics

Onset of decongestant action: Topical: Within 10 minutes

Duration: 2-6 hours

Elimination: Not well defined

Usual Dosage

Nasal:

Children:

<6 years: Intranasal: Not recommended (especially infants) due to CNS depression

6-12 years: 1 spray of 0.05% into each nostril every 6 hours if necessary; therapy should not exceed 3-5 days

Children >12 years and Adults: 0.05%, instill 1-2 drops or sprays every 6 hours if needed; therapy should not exceed 3-5 days

(Continued)

Naphazoline *(Continued)*

Ophthalmic:

Children <6 years: Not recommended for use due to CNS depression (especially in infants)

Children >6 years and Adults: Instill 1-2 drops into conjunctival sac of affected eye(s) every 3-4 hours; therapy generally should not exceed 3-4 days

Patient Information Do not use discolored solutions; discontinue eye drops if visual changes or ocular pain occur; notify physician of insomnia, tremor, or irregular heartbeat; stinging, burning, or drying of the nasal mucosa may occur; do not use beyond 72 hours

Nursing Implications Rebound congestion can result with continued use

Dosage Forms Solution, as hydrochloride:

Nasal:

Drops: 0.05% (20 mL)

Spray: 0.05% (15 mL)

Ophthalmic: 0.012% (7.5 mL, 30 mL); 0.02% (15 mL); 0.03% (15 mL); 0.1% (15 mL)

♦ **Naphazoline Hydrochloride** *see Naphazoline on previous page*

♦ **Naphcon®** [OTC] *see Naphazoline on previous page*

♦ **Naphcon Forte®** *see Naphazoline on previous page*

♦ **Naprelan®** *see Naproxen on this page*

♦ **Naprosyn®** *see Naproxen on this page*

Naproxen *(na PROKS en)*

Related Information

Antacid Drug Interactions *on page 1296*

Nonsteroidal Anti-Inflammatory Agents Comparison *on page 1335*

U.S. Brand Names Aleve® [OTC]; Anaprox®; Naprelan®; Naprosyn®

Canadian Brand Names Apo®-Naproxen; Naxen®; Novo-Naprox; Nu-Naprox

Synonyms Naproxen Sodium

Therapeutic Category Analgesic, Nonsteroidal Anti-inflammatory Drug; Anti-inflammatory Agent; Antimigraine Agent; Antipyretic; Nonsteroidal Anti-inflammatory Drug (NSAID), Oral

Use Management of inflammatory disease and rheumatoid disorders (including juvenile rheumatoid arthritis); acute gout; mild to moderate pain; dysmenorrhea; fever, migraine headache

Pregnancy Risk Factor B (D if used in the 3rd trimester or near delivery)

Contraindications Hypersensitivity to naproxen, aspirin, or other nonsteroidal anti-inflammatory drugs (NSAIDs)

Warnings/Precautions Use with caution in patients with GI disease (bleeding or ulcers), cardiovascular disease (CHF, hypertension), renal or hepatic impairment, and patients receiving anticoagulants; perform ophthalmologic evaluation for those who develop eye complaints during therapy (blurred vision, diminished vision, changes in color vision, retinal changes); NSAIDs may mask signs/symptoms of infections; photosensitivity reported; elderly are at especially high-risk for adverse effects

Adverse Reactions

>10%:

Central nervous system: Dizziness

Dermatologic: Pruritus, rash

Gastrointestinal: Abdominal discomfort, nausea, heartburn, constipation, GI bleeding, ulcers, perforation, indigestion

1% to 10%:

Central nervous system: Headache, nervousness

Dermatologic: Itching

Endocrine & metabolic: Fluid retention

Gastrointestinal: Vomiting

Otic: Tinnitus

<1%: Edema, congestive heart failure, arrhythmias, tachycardia, hypertension, confusion, hallucinations, mental depression, fatigue, drowsiness, insomnia, aseptic meningitis, urticaria, erythema multiforme, toxic epidermal necrolysis, Stevens-Johnson syndrome, angioedema, polydipsia, hot flashes, gastritis, GI ulceration, cystitis, renal dysfunction, polyuria, anemia, hemolytic anemia, bone marrow suppression, leukopenia, thrombocytopenia, inhibits platelet aggregation, prolongs bleeding time, agranulocytosis, hepatitis, peripheral neuropathy, toxic amblyopia, blurred vision, conjunctivitis, dry eyes, decreased hearing, acute renal failure, shortness of breath, epistaxis, allergic rhinitis

Overdosage/Toxicology

Symptoms of overdose include drowsiness, heartburn, vomiting, CNS depression, leukocytosis, renal failure

Management of a nonsteroidal anti-inflammatory drug (NSAID) intoxication is primarily supportive and symptomatic; fluid therapy is commonly effective in managing the hypotension that may occur following an acute NSAID overdose, except when this is due to an acute blood loss. Seizures tend to be very short-lived and often do not require drug treatment; although, recurrent seizures should be treated with I.V. diazepam; since many of the NSAIDs undergo enterohepatic cycling, multiple doses of charcoal may be needed to reduce the potential for delayed toxicities.

Drug Interactions CYP2C8, 2C9, and 2C18 enzyme substrate

Decreased effect of furosemide

Increased toxicity:

Naproxen could displace other highly protein bound drugs, such as oral anticoagulants, hydantoins, salicylates, sulfonamides, and sulfonylureas

Naproxen and warfarin may cause a slight increase in free warfarin

Naproxen and probenecid may cause increased plasma half-life of naproxen

Naproxen and methotrexate may significantly increase and prolong blood methotrexate concentration, which may be severe or fatal

Mechanism of Action Inhibits prostaglandin synthesis by decreasing the activity of the enzyme, cyclo-oxygenase, which results in decreased formation of prostaglandin precursors

Pharmacodynamics/Kinetics

Analgesia: Onset of action: 1 hour; Duration: Up to 7 hours

Anti-inflammatory: Onset of action: Within 2 weeks; Peak: 2-4 weeks

Absorption: Oral: Almost 100%

Time to peak serum concentration: Within 1-2 hours and persisting for up to 12 hours

Protein binding: Highly protein bound (>90%); increased free fraction in elderly

Half-life:

Normal renal function: 12-15 hours

End-stage renal disease: Unchanged

Usual Dosage Oral:

Children >2 years:

Fever: 2.5-10 mg/kg/dose; maximum: 10 mg/kg/day

Juvenile arthritis: 10 mg/kg/day in 2 divided doses

Adults:

Rheumatoid arthritis, osteoarthritis, and ankylosing spondylitis: 500-1000 mg/day in 2 divided doses; may increase to 1.5 g/day of naproxen base for limited time period

Mild to moderate pain or dysmenorrhea: Initial: 500 mg, then 250 mg every 6-8 hours; maximum: 1250 mg/day naproxen base

Dosing adjustment in hepatic impairment: Reduce dose to 50%

Dietary Considerations

Alcohol: Additive impairment of mental alertness and physical coordination, avoid or limit use

Food: Food may decrease the rate but not the extent of oral absorption. Drug may cause GI upset, bleeding, ulceration, perforation; take with food or milk to minimize GI upset.

Administration Administer with food, milk, or antacids to decrease GI adverse effects

Monitoring Parameters Occult blood loss, periodic liver function test, CBC, BUN, serum creatinine

Patient Information Serious gastrointestinal bleeding can occur as well as ulceration and perforation. Pain may or may not be present. Avoid aspirin and aspirin-containing products while taking this medication. If gastric upset occurs, take with food, milk, or antacid. If gastric adverse effects persist, contact physician. May cause drowsiness, dizziness, blurred vision, and confusion. Use caution when performing tasks which require alertness (eg, driving). Do not take for more than 3 days for fever or 10 days for pain without physician's advice.

Additional Information Naproxen: Naprosyn®; naproxen sodium: Anaprox®; 275 mg of Anaprox® equivalent to 250 mg of Naprosyn®

Dosage Forms

Suspension, oral: 125 mg/5 mL (15 mL, 30 mL, 480 mL)

Tablet, as sodium:

220 mg (200 mg base)

Anaprox®: 220 mg (200 mg base); 275 mg (250 mg base); 550 mg (500 mg base)

Tablet:

Aleve®: 200 mg

Naprosyn®: 250 mg, 375 mg, 500 mg

Tablet, controlled release (Naprelan®): 375 mg, 500 mg

♦ **Naproxen Sodium** see Naproxen on previous page

♦ **Naqua®** see Trichlormethiazide on page 1179

Naratriptan (NAR a trip tan)

Related Information

Antimigraine Drugs: Pharmacokinetic Differences on page 1304

U.S. Brand Names Amerge®

Therapeutic Category Antimigraine Agent; Serotonin Agonist

Use Treatment of acute migraine headache with or without aura

Pregnancy Risk Factor C

Contraindications Hypersensitivity to naratriptan or any component; cerebrovascular, peripheral vascular disease (ischemic bowel disease), ischemic heart disease (angina pectoris, history of myocardial infarction, or proven silent ischemia); or in patients with symptoms consistent with ischemic heart disease, coronary artery vasospasm, or Prinzmetal's variant angina; uncontrolled hypertension or patients who have received within 24 hours another 5-HT agonist (sumatriptan, zolmitriptan) or ergotamine-containing product; patients with known risk factors associated with coronary artery disease; patients with severe hepatic or renal disease (Cl$_{cr}$ <15 mL/minute); do not administer naratriptan to patients with hemiplegic or basilar migraine

Warnings/Precautions Use only if there is a clear diagnosis of migraine. Patients who are at risk of CAD but have had a satisfactory cardiovascular evaluation may receive naratriptan but with extreme caution (ie, in a physician's office where there are adequate precautions in place to protect the patient). Blood pressure may increase with the (Continued)

Naratriptan *(Continued)*

administration of naratriptan. Monitor closely, especially with the first administration of the drug. If the patient does not respond to the first dose, re-evaluate the diagnosis of migraine before trying a second dose.

Adverse Reactions

1% to 10%:

Central nervous system: Dizziness, drowsiness, malaise/fatigue

Gastrointestinal: Nausea, vomiting

Neuromuscular & skeletal: Paresthesias

Miscellaneous: Pain or pressure in throat or neck

<1% (Limited to important or life-threatening symptoms): Coronary artery vasospasm, transient myocardial ischemia, myocardial infarction, ventricular tachycardia, ventricular fibrillation, palpitations, hypertension, EKG changes (PR prolongation, QT_c prolongation, premature ventricular contractions, atrial flutter, or atrial fibrillation) hypotension, heart murmurs, bradycardia, hyperlipidemia, hypercholesterolemia, hypothyroidism, hyperglycemia, glycosuria, ketonuria, eye hemorrhage, abnormal liver function tests, abnormal bilirubin tests, convulsions, allergic reaction, panic, hallucinations

Drug Interactions

Decreased effect: Smoking increases the clearance of naratriptan

Increased effect/toxicity: Ergot-containing drugs (dihydroergotamine or methysergide) may cause vasospastic reactions when taken with naratriptan. Avoid concomitant use with ergots; separate dose of naratriptan and ergots by at least 24 hours. Oral contraceptives taken with naratriptan reduced the clearance of naratriptan +30% which may contribute to adverse effects. Selective serotonin reuptake inhibitors (SSRIs) (eg, fluoxetine, fluvoxamine, paroxetine, sertraline) may cause lack of coordination, hyperreflexia, or weakness and should be avoided when taking naratriptan.

Mechanism of Action The therapeutic effect for migraine is due to serotonin agonist activity

Pharmacodynamics/Kinetics

Protein binding, plasma: 28% to 31%

Metabolism: Liver, cytochrome P-450 isoenzymes

Bioavailability: 70%

Time to peak: 2-3 hours

Elimination: Urine

Usual Dosage

Adults: Oral: 1-2.5 mg at the onset of headache; it is recommended to use the lowest possible dose to minimize adverse effects. If headache returns or does not fully resolve, the dose may be repeated after 4 hours; do not exceed 5 mg in 24 hours.

Elderly: Not recommended for use in the elderly

Dosing in renal impairment:

Cl_{cr}: 18-39 mL/minute: Initial: 1 mg; do not exceed 2.5 mg in 24 hours

Cl_{cr}: <15 mL/minute: Do not use

Dosing in hepatic impairment: Contraindicated in patients with severe liver failure; maximum dose: 2.5 mg in 24 hours for patients with mild or moderate liver failure; recommended starting dose: 1 mg

Patient Information Do not crush or chew tablet; swallow whole with water. This drug is to be used to reduce migraine, not to prevent or reduce the number of attacks. If headache returns or is not fully resolved, the dose may be repeated after 4 hours. If patient has no relief with first dose, do not take a second dose without consulting prescriber. Do not exceed 5 mg in 24 hours. Do not take within 24 hours of any other migraine medication without first consulting prescriber. Patient may experience some dizziness, fatigue, or drowsiness; use caution when driving or engaging in tasks that require alertness. Frequent mouth care and sucking on lozenges may relieve dry mouth. Patient should report immediately any chest pain, heart throbbing, tightness in throat, skin rash or hives, hallucinations, anxiety, or panic. Inform prescriber if they are or intend to become pregnant. Breast-feeding is not recommended.

Dosage Forms Tablet: 1 mg, 2.5 mg

Natamycin (na ta MYE sin)

U.S. Brand Names Natacyn® Ophthalmic

Synonyms Pimaricin

Therapeutic Category Antifungal Agent, Ophthalmic

Use Treatment of blepharitis, conjunctivitis, and keratitis caused by susceptible fungi (*Aspergillus*, *Candida*), *Cephalosporium*, *Curvularia*, *Fusarium*, *Penicillium*, *Microsporum*, *Epidermophyton*, *Blastomyces dermatitidis*, *Coccidioides immitis*, *Cryptococcus neoformans*, *Histoplasma capsulatum*, *Sporothrix schenckii*, and *Trichomonas vaginalis*

Pregnancy Risk Factor C

Contraindications Known hypersensitivity to natamycin or any component

Warnings/Precautions Failure to improve (keratitis) after 7-10 days of administration suggests infection caused by a microorganism not susceptible to natamycin; inadequate as a single agent in fungal endophthalmitis

Adverse Reactions <1%: Blurred vision, photophobia, eye pain, eye irritation not present before therapy

Drug Interactions Increased toxicity: Topical corticosteroids (concomitant use contraindicated)

Stability Store at room temperature (8°C to 24°C/46°F to 75°F); protect from excessive heat and light; do not freeze

Mechanism of Action Increases cell membrane permeability in susceptible fungi

Pharmacodynamics/Kinetics
Absorption: Ophthalmic: <2% systemically absorbed
Distribution: Adheres to cornea and is retained in the conjunctival fornices

Usual Dosage Adults: Ophthalmic: Instill 1 drop in conjunctival sac every 1-2 hours, after 3-4 days reduce to one drop 6-8 times/day; usual course of therapy is 2-3 weeks.

Patient Information Shake well before using, do not touch dropper to eye; notify physician if condition worsens or does not improve after 3-4 days

Dosage Forms Suspension, ophthalmic: 5% (15 mL)

- Natural Lung Surfactant see Beractant on page 139
- Navane® see Thiothixene on page 1138
- Navelbine® see Vinorelbine on page 1221
- Naxen® see Naproxen on page 818
- Nebcin® Injection see Tobramycin on page 1150
- NebuPent™ Inhalation see Pentamidine on page 900

Nedocromil Sodium (ne doe KROE mil SOW dee um)

Related Information
Asthma, Guidelines for the Diagnosis and Management of on page 1456

U.S. Brand Names Tilade® Inhalation Aerosol

Canadian Brand Names Mireze®

Therapeutic Category Antihistamine, Inhalation

Use Maintenance therapy in patients with mild to moderate bronchial asthma

Pregnancy Risk Factor B

Contraindications Hypersensitivity to nedocromil or other ingredients in the preparation

Warnings/Precautions Safety and efficacy in children <12 years of age have not been established; if systemic or inhaled steroid therapy is at all reduced, monitor patients carefully; nedocromil is **not** a bronchodilator and, therefore, should not be used for reversal of acute bronchospasm

Adverse Reactions 1% to 10%:
Cardiovascular: Chest pain
Central nervous system: Dizziness, dysphonia, headache, fatigue
Dermatologic: Rash
Gastrointestinal: Nausea, vomiting, dyspepsia, diarrhea, abdominal pain, xerostomia, unpleasant taste
Hepatic: Increased ALT
Neuromuscular & skeletal: Arthritis, tremor
Respiratory: Cough, pharyngitis, rhinitis, bronchitis, upper respiratory infection, bronchospasm, increased sputum production

Stability Store at 2°C to 30°C/36°F to 86°F; do not freeze

Mechanism of Action Inhibits the activation of and mediator release from a variety of inflammatory cell types associated with asthma including eosinophils, neutrophils, macrophages, mast cells, monocytes, and platelets; it inhibits the release of histamine, leukotrienes, and slow-reacting substance of anaphylaxis; it inhibits the development of early and late bronchoconstriction responses to inhaled antigen

Pharmacodynamics/Kinetics
Duration of therapeutic effect: 2 hours
Protein binding, plasma: 89%
Bioavailability: Systemic: 7% to 9% absorption
Half-life: 1.5-2 hours
Elimination: Excreted unchanged in urine

Usual Dosage Children >12 years and Adults: Inhalation: 2 inhalations 4 times/day; may reduce dosage to 2-3 times/day once desired clinical response to initial dose is observed

Additional Information Has no known therapeutic systemic activity when delivered by inhalation

Dosage Forms Aerosol: 1.75 mg/activation (16.2 g)

- N.E.E.® 1/35 see Ethinyl Estradiol and Norethindrone on page 451

Nefazodone (nef AY zoe done)

Related Information

Antidepressant Agents Comparison *on page 1301*

U.S. Brand Names Serzone®

Synonyms Nefazodone Hydrochloride

Therapeutic Category Antidepressant, Miscellaneous

Use Treatment of depression

Pregnancy Risk Factor C

Contraindications Hypersensitivity to nefazodone or any component; concomitant use of any MAO inhibitors, astemizole, or terfenadine

Warnings/Precautions Safety and efficacy in children <18 years of age have not been established; monitor closely and use with extreme caution in patients with cardiac disease, cerebrovascular disease or seizures; very sedating and can be dehydrating; therapeutic effects may take up to 4 weeks to occur; therapy is normally maintained for several months and optimum response is reached to prevent recurrence of depression, discontinue therapy and re-evaluate if priapism occurs

Adverse Reactions

>10%:

    Central nervous system: Headache, drowsiness, insomnia, agitation, dizziness, confusion

    Gastrointestinal: Xerostomia, nausea

    Neuromuscular & skeletal: Tremor

1% to 10%:

    Cardiovascular: Postural hypotension

    Gastrointestinal: Constipation, vomiting

    Neuromuscular & skeletal: Weakness

    Ocular: Blurred vision, amblyopia

<1%: Diarrhea, prolonged priapism

Overdosage/Toxicology

Symptoms of overdose include drowsiness, vomiting, hypotension, tachycardia, incontinence, coma

Following initiation of essential overdose management, toxic symptoms should be treated. Ventricular arrhythmias often respond to lidocaine 1.5 mg/kg bolus followed by 2 mg/minute infusion with concurrent systemic alkalinization (sodium bicarbonate 0.5-2 mEq/kg I.V.). Seizures usually respond to diazepam I.V. boluses (5-10 mg for adults up to 30 mg or 0.25-0.4 mg/kg/dose for children up to 10 mg/dose). If seizures are unresponsive or recur, phenytoin or phenobarbital may be required. Hypotension is best treated by I.V. fluids and by placing the patient in the Trendelenburg position.

Drug Interactions CYP3A3/4 enzyme substrate; CYP3A3/4 enzyme inhibitor

Decreased effect: Clonidine, methyldopa, diuretics, oral hypoglycemics, anticoagulants

Increased toxicity: Terfenadine, astemizole, and cisapride (increased concentrations have been associated with serious ventricular arrhythmias and death), fluoxetine, triazolam (reduce triazolam dose by 75%), alprazolam (reduce alprazolam dose by 50%), haloperidol, phenytoin, MAO inhibitors (allow 14 days after MAO inhibitors are stopped or 7 days after nefazodone is stopped); carbamazepine (40% increase); digoxin

Mechanism of Action Inhibits serotonin (5-HT) reuptake and is a potent antagonist at type 2 serotonin (5-HT) receptors; minimal affinity for cholinergic, histaminic, or alpha$_1$-adrenergic receptors

Pharmacodynamics/Kinetics

Onset of effect: Therapeutic effects take at least 2 weeks to appear

Metabolism: In the liver to 3 active metabolites; triazoledione, hydroxynefazodone and m-chlorophenylpiperazine (mCPP)

Half-life: 2-4 hours (parent compound), active metabolites persist longer

Time to peak serum concentration: 30 minutes, prolonged in presence of food

Elimination: Primarily as metabolites in urine and secondarily in feces

Usual Dosage Oral: Adults: 200 mg/day, administered in two divided doses initially, with a range of 300-600 mg/day in two divided doses thereafter

Dietary Considerations Alcohol: Additive CNS effect, avoid use

Reference Range Therapeutic plasma levels have not yet been defined

Patient Information Take shortly after a meal or light snack; can be given at bedtime if drowsiness occurs; optimum effect may take 2-4 weeks to be achieved; avoid alcohol; may cause painful erections (contact physician if this should occur); avoid sudden changes in position

Nursing Implications Dosing after meals may decrease lightheadedness and postural hypotension, but may also decrease absorption and therefore effectiveness; use side rails on bed if administered to the elderly; observe patient's activity and compare with admission level; assist with ambulation; sitting and standing blood pressure and pulse

Dosage Forms Tablet, as hydrochloride: 50 mg, 100 mg, 150 mg, 200 mg, 250 mg

♦ **Nefazodone Hydrochloride** *see Nefazodone on this page*

♦ **NegGram®** *see Nalidixic Acid on page 812*

Nelfinavir (nel FIN a veer)

Related Information

Antiretroviral Agents *on page 1306*

Antiretroviral Therapy for HIV Infection *on page 1410*

Management of Healthcare Worker Exposures to HIV *on page 1374*

U.S. Brand Names Viracept®

Therapeutic Category Antiretroviral Agent, Protease Inhibitor; Protease Inhibitor

Use In combination with other antiretroviral therapy in the treatment of HIV infection

Pregnancy Risk Factor B

Pregnancy/Breast-Feeding Implications Breast-feeding/lactation: Animal studies suggest that nelfinavir may be excreted in human milk; the CDC advises against breast-feeding by HIV-infected mothers to avoid postnatal transmission of the virus to the infant

Contraindications Hypersensitivity to nelfinavir or product components; phenylketo-nuria; concurrent therapy with terfenadine, astemizole, cisapride, triazolam, or midazolam

Warnings/Precautions Avoid use of powder in phenylketonurics since contains phenylalanine; use extreme caution when administered to patients with hepatic insufficiency since nelfinavir is metabolized in the liver and excreted predominantly in the feces; avoid use, if possible, with terfenadine, astemizole, cisapride, triazolam, or midazolam. Concurrent use with some anticonvulsants may significantly limit nelfinavir's effectiveness.

Adverse Reactions Protease inhibitors cause dyslipidemia which includes elevated cholesterol and triglycerides and a redistribution of body fat centrally to cause "protease paunch", buffalo hump, facial atrophy, and breast enlargement. These agents also cause hyperglycemia.

>10%: Gastrointestinal: Diarrhea (19%)

1% to 10%:
Central nervous system: Decreased concentration
Dermatologic: Rash
Gastrointestinal: Nausea, flatulence, abdominal pain
Neuromuscular & skeletal: Weakness

<1%: Anxiety, depression, dizziness, emotional lability, hyperkinesia, insomnia, migraine, seizures, sleep disorder, somnolence, suicide ideation, fever, headache, malaise, dermatitis, pruritus, urticaria, increased LFTs, hyperlipemia, hyperuricemia, hypoglycemia, anorexia, dyspepsia, epigastric pain, mouth ulceration, GI bleeding, pancreatitis, vomiting, kidney calculus, sexual dysfunction, anemia, leukopenia, thrombocytopenia, hepatitis, arthralgia, arthritis, cramps, myalgia, myasthenia, myopathy, paresthesia, back pain, dyspnea, pharyngitis, rhinitis, sinusitis, diaphoresis, allergy

Overdosage/Toxicology No data available; however, unabsorbed drug should be removed via gastric lavage and activated charcoal; significant symptoms beyond gastrointestinal disturbances are likely following acute overdose; hemodialysis will not be effective due to high protein binding of nelfinavir

Drug Interactions CYP3A3/4 enzyme substrate; CYP3A3/4 enzyme inducer; CYP3A3/4 enzyme inhibitor

Increased effect:
Nelfinavir inhibits the metabolism of cisapride and astemizole and should, therefore, not be administered concurrently due to risk of life-threatening cardiac arrhythmias.
A 20% increase in rifabutin plasma AUC has been observed when coadministered with nelfinavir (decrease rifabutin's dose by 50%).
An increase in midazolam and triazolam serum levels may occur resulting in significant oversedation when administered with nelfinavir. These drugs should not be administered together.
Indinavir and ritonavir may increase nelfinavir plasma concentrations resulting in potential increases in side effects (the safety of these combinations have not been established).

Decreased effect:
Rifampin decreases nelfinavir's plasma AUC by ~82%; the two drugs should not be administered together.
Serum levels of the hormones in oral contraceptives may decrease significantly with administration of nelfinavir. Patients should use alternative methods of contraceptives during nelfinavir therapy.
Phenobarbital, phenytoin, and carbamazepine may decrease serum levels and consequently effectiveness of nelfinavir.
Nelfinavir's effectiveness may be decreased with concomitant nevirapine

Mechanism of Action Inhibits the HIV-1 protease; inhibition of the viral protease prevents cleavage of the gag-pol polyprotein resulting in the production of immature, noninfectious virus

Pharmacodynamics/Kinetics

Absorption: Food increases plasma concentration-time curve (AUC) by two- to threefold

Distribution: V_d: 2-7 L/kg

Metabolism: Via multiple cytochrome P-450 isoforms (eg, CYP3A); major metabolite has activity comparable to the parent drug

Protein binding: 98%

Half-life: 3.5-5 hours

Time to peak serum concentration: 2-4 hours

Elimination: 98% to 99% excreted in the feces (78% as metabolites and 22% as unchanged nelfinavir); 1% to 2% excreted in the urine

Usual Dosage Oral:

Children 2-13 years: 20-30 mg/kg 3 times/day with a meal or light snack; if tablets are unable to be taken, use oral powder in small amount of water, milk, formula, or dietary supplements; do not use acidic food/juice or store for >6 hours

Adults: 750 mg 3 times/day with meals

Dosing adjustment in renal impairment: No adjustment needed

(Continued)

Nelfinavir *(Continued)*

Dosing adjustment in hepatic impairment: Use caution when administering to patients with hepatic impairment since eliminated predominantly by the liver

Monitoring Parameters LFTs, viral load, CD4 count, triglycerides, cholesterol, glucose

Patient Information Nelfinavir should be taken with food to increase its absorption; it is not a cure for HIV infection and the long-term effects of the drug are unknown at this time; the drug has not demonstrated a reduction in the risk of transmitting HIV to others. Take the drug as prescribed; if you miss a dose, take it as soon as possible and then return to your usual schedule (never double a dose, however). If tablets are unable to be taken, use oral powder in small amount of water, milk, formula, or dietary supplement; do not use acidic food/juice of store dilution for >6 hours. Use an alternative method of contraception from birth control pills during nelfinavir therapy.

Nursing Implications If diarrhea occurs, it may be treated with OTC antidiarrheals

Dosage Forms

Powder, oral: 50 mg/g (contains 11.2 mg phenylalanine)

Tablet: 250 mg

♦ **Nelova™ 0.5/35E** *see Ethinyl Estradiol and Norethindrone on page 451*

♦ **Nelova™ 1/50M** *see Mestranol and Norethindrone on page 737*

♦ **Nelova™ 10/11** *see Ethinyl Estradiol and Norethindrone on page 451*

♦ **Nembutal®** *see Pentobarbital on page 902*

♦ **Neo-Calglucon® [OTC]** *see Calcium Glubionate on page 177*

♦ **Neo-Codema®** *see Hydrochlorothiazide on page 574*

♦ **Neo-Cortef®** *see Neomycin and Hydrocortisone on next page*

♦ **NeoDecadron® Ophthalmic** *see Neomycin and Dexamethasone on next page*

♦ **NeoDecadron® Topical** *see Neomycin and Dexamethasone on next page*

♦ **Neo-Dexameth® Ophthalmic** *see Neomycin and Dexamethasone on next page*

♦ **Neo-Durabolic Injection** *see Nandrolone on page 816*

♦ **Neo-Estrone®** *see Estrogens, Esterified on page 438*

♦ **Neo-Estrone®** *see Estrone on page 439*

♦ **Neofed® [OTC]** *see Pseudoephedrine on page 993*

♦ **Neo-fradin® Oral** *see Neomycin on this page*

♦ **Neomixin® Topical [OTC]** *see Bacitracin, Neomycin, and Polymyxin B on page 123*

Neomycin *(nee oh MYE sin)*

Related Information

Prevention of Wound Infection & Sepsis in Surgical Patients *on page 1381*

U.S. Brand Names Mycifradin® Sulfate Oral; Mycifradin® Sulfate Topical; Neo-fradin® Oral; Neo-Tabs® Oral

Synonyms Neomycin Sulfate

Therapeutic Category Ammonium Detoxicant; Antibiotic, Aminoglycoside; Antibiotic, Irrigation; Antibiotic, Topical

Use Orally to prepare GI tract for surgery; topically to treat minor skin infections; treat diarrhea caused by *E. coli*; adjunct in the treatment of hepatic encephalopathy

Pregnancy Risk Factor C

Contraindications Hypersensitivity to neomycin or any component, or other aminoglycosides; patients with intestinal obstruction

Warnings/Precautions Use with caution in patients with renal impairment, pre-existing hearing impairment, neuromuscular disorders; neomycin is more toxic than other aminoglycosides when given parenterally; **do not administer parenterally**; topical neomycin is a contact sensitizer with sensitivity occurring in 5% to 15% of patients treated with the drug; symptoms include itching, reddening, edema, and failure to heal; **do not use as peritoneal lavage** due to significant systemic adsorption of the drug

Adverse Reactions

1% to 10%:

Dermatologic: Dermatitis, rash, urticaria, erythema

Local: Burning

Ocular: Contact conjunctivitis

<1%: Nausea, vomiting, diarrhea, neuromuscular blockade, ototoxicity, nephrotoxicity

Overdosage/Toxicology

Symptoms of overdose (rare due to poor oral bioavailability) include ototoxicity, nephrotoxicity, and neuromuscular toxicity

The treatment of choice following a single acute overdose appears to be the maintenance of good urine output of at least 3 mL/kg/hour. Dialysis is of questionable value in the enhancement of aminoglycoside elimination. If required, hemodialysis is preferred over peritoneal dialysis in patients with normal renal function. Chelation with penicillin may be of benefit.

Drug Interactions

Decreased effect: May decrease GI absorption of digoxin and methotrexate

Increased effect: Synergistic effects with penicillins

Increased toxicity:

Oral neomycin may potentiate the effects of oral anticoagulants

Increased adverse effects with other neurotoxic, ototoxic, or nephrotoxic drugs

Stability Use reconstituted parenteral solutions within 7 days of mixing, when refrigerated

Mechanism of Action Interferes with bacterial protein synthesis by binding to 30S ribosomal subunits

Pharmacodynamics/Kinetics
  Absorption: Oral, percutaneous: Poor (3%)
  Distribution: V_d: 0.36 L/kg
  Metabolism: Slight hepatic
  Half-life: 3 hours (age and renal function dependent)
  Time to peak serum concentration: Oral: 1-4 hours; I.M.: Within 2 hours
  Elimination: In urine (30% to 50% as unchanged drug); 97% of an oral dose eliminated
    unchanged in feces

Usual Dosage
  Children: Oral:
    Preoperative intestinal antisepsis: 90 mg/kg/day divided every 4 hours for 2 days; or 25
      mg/kg at 1 PM, 2 PM, and 11 PM on the day preceding surgery as an adjunct to
      mechanical cleansing of the intestine and in combination with erythromycin base
    Hepatic coma: 50-100 mg/kg/day in divided doses every 6-8 hours or 2.5-7 g/m²/day
      divided every 4-6 hours for 5-6 days not to exceed 12 g/day
  Children and Adults: Topical: Apply ointment 1-4 times/day; topical solutions containing
    0.1% to 1% neomycin have been used for irrigation
  Adults: Oral:
    Preoperative intestinal antisepsis: 1 g each hour for 4 doses then 1 g every 4 hours for
      5 doses; or 1 g at 1 PM, 2 PM, and 11 PM on day preceding surgery as an adjunct to
      mechanical cleansing of the bowel and oral erythromycin; or 6 g/day divided every 4
      hours for 2-3 days
    Hepatic coma: 500-2000 mg every 6-8 hours or 4-12 g/day divided every 4-6 hours for
      5-6 days
    Chronic hepatic insufficiency: 4 g/day for an indefinite period
  Hemodialysis: Dialyzable (50% to 100%)

Monitoring Parameters Renal function tests, audiometry in symptomatic patients

Patient Information Notify physician if redness, burning, itching, ringing in the ears,
hearing impairment, or dizziness occurs of if condition does not improve in 3-4 days

Dosage Forms
  Cream, as sulfate: 0.5% (15 g)
  Injection, as sulfate: 500 mg
  Ointment, topical, as sulfate: 0.5% (15 g, 30 g, 120 g)
  Solution, oral, as sulfate: 125 mg/5 mL (480 mL)
  Tablet, as sulfate: 500 mg [base 300 mg]

Neomycin and Dexamethasone (nee oh MYE sin & deks a METH a sone)
  U.S. Brand Names AK-Neo-Dex® Ophthalmic; NeoDecadron® Ophthalmic;
  NeoDecadron® Topical; Neo-Dexameth® Ophthalmic

  Therapeutic Category Antibiotic/Corticosteroid, Ophthalmic; Antibiotic/Corticosteroid,
  Topical

  Dosage Forms
    Cream: Neomycin sulfate 0.5% [5 mg/g] and dexamethasone 0.1% [1 mg/g] (15 g, 30 g)
    Ointment, ophthalmic: Neomycin sulfate 0.35% [3.5 mg/g] and dexamethasone 0.05%
      [0.5 mg/g] (3.5 g)
    Solution, ophthalmic: Neomycin sulfate 0.35% [3.5 mg/mL] and dexamethasone 0.1% [1
      mg/mL] (5 mL)

Neomycin and Hydrocortisone (nee oh MYE sin & hye droe KOR ti sone)
  U.S. Brand Names Neo-Cortef®

  Therapeutic Category Antibiotic/Corticosteroid, Ophthalmic; Antibiotic/Corticosteroid,
  Topical

  Dosage Forms
    Cream: Neomycin sulfate 0.5% and hydrocortisone 1% (20 g)
    Ointment, topical: Neomycin sulfate 0.5% and hydrocortisone 0.5% (20 g); neomycin
      sulfate 0.5% and hydrocortisone 1% (20 g)
    Solution, ophthalmic: Neomycin sulfate 0.5% and hydrocortisone 0.5% (5 mL)

Neomycin and Polymyxin B (nee oh MYE sin & pol i MIKS in bee)
  U.S. Brand Names Neosporin® Cream [OTC]; Neosporin® G.U. Irrigant

  Synonyms Polymyxin B and Neomycin

  Therapeutic Category Antibiotic, Topical; Antibiotic, Urinary Irrigation

  Use Short-term as a continuous irrigant or rinse in the urinary bladder to prevent bacteri-
  uria and gram-negative rod septicemia associated with the use of indwelling catheters; to
  help prevent infection in minor cuts, scrapes, and burns

  Pregnancy Risk Factor C (D G.U. irrigant)

  Contraindications Known hypersensitivity to neomycin or polymyxin B or any component; ophthalmic use for topical cream

  Warnings/Precautions Use with caution in patients with impaired renal function, infants
  with diaper rash involving large area of abraded skin, dehydrated patients, burn patients,
  and patients receiving a high-dose for prolonged periods; topical neomycin is a contact
  sensitizer; contains methylparaben

  Adverse Reactions 1% to 10%:
    Dermatologic: Contact dermatitis, erythema, rash, urticaria
    Genitourinary: Bladder irritation
    Local: Burning
    Neuromuscular & skeletal: Neuromuscular blockade
    Otic: Ototoxicity
    Renal: Nephrotoxicity
    (Continued)

Neomycin and Polymyxin B *(Continued)*

Overdosage/Toxicology Refer to individual monographs for Neomycin and Polymyxin B

Stability Store irrigation solution in refrigerator; aseptic prepared dilutions (1 mL/1 L) should be stored in the refrigerator and discarded after 48 hours

Mechanism of Action Refer to individual monographs for Neomycin and Polymyxin

Pharmacodynamics/Kinetics Absorption: Topical: Not absorbed following application to intact skin; absorbed through denuded or abraded skin, peritoneum, wounds, or ulcers

Usual Dosage Children and Adults:

Bladder irrigation: **Not for injection**; add 1 mL irrigant to 1 liter isotonic saline solution and connect container to the inflow of lumen of 3-way catheter. Continuous irrigant or rinse in the urinary bladder for up to a maximum of 10 days with administration rate adjusted to patient's urine output; usually no more than 1 L of irrigant is used per day.

Topical: Apply cream 1-4 times/day to affected area

Monitoring Parameters Urinalysis

Patient Information Notify physician if condition worsens or if rash or irritation develops

Nursing Implications Do not inject irrigant solution; connect irrigation container to the inflow lumen of a 3-way catheter to permit continuous irrigation of the urinary bladder

Dosage Forms

Cream: Neomycin sulfate 3.5 mg and polymyxin B sulfate 10,000 units per g (0.94 g, 15 g)

Solution, irrigant: Neomycin sulfate 40 mg and polymyxin B sulfate 200,000 units per mL (1 mL, 20 mL)

Neomycin, Polymyxin B, and Dexamethasone

(nee oh MYE sin, pol i MIKS in bee, & deks a METH a sone)

U.S. Brand Names AK-Trol®; Dexacidin®; Dexasporin®; Maxitrol®

Therapeutic Category Antibiotic, Ophthalmic; Corticosteroid, Ophthalmic

Use Steroid-responsive inflammatory ocular conditions in which a corticosteroid is indicated and where bacterial infection or a risk of bacterial infection exists

Pregnancy Risk Factor C

Contraindications Hypersensitivity to dexamethasone, polymyxin B, neomycin or any component; herpes simplex, vaccinia, and varicella

Warnings/Precautions Prolonged use may result in glaucoma, defects in visual acuity, posterior subcapsular cataract formation, and secondary ocular infections

Adverse Reactions 1% to 10%:

Dermatologic: Contact dermatitis, delayed wound healing

Ocular: Cutaneous sensitization, eye pain, development of glaucoma, cataract, increased intraocular pressure, optic nerve damage

Overdosage/Toxicology Refer to individual monographs for Neomycin, Polymyxin B, and Dexamethasone

Mechanism of Action Refer to individual monographs for Neomycin Sulfate, Polymyxin B Sulfate, and Dexamethasone

Pharmacodynamics/Kinetics Refer to individual monographs for Neomycin Sulfate, Polymyxin B Sulfate, and Dexamethasone

Usual Dosage Children and Adults: Ophthalmic:

Ointment: Place a small amount (~½") in the affected eye 3-4 times/day or apply at bedtime as an adjunct with drops

Solution: Instill 1-2 drops into affected eye(s) every 3-4 hours; in severe disease, drops may be used hourly and tapered to discontinuation

Monitoring Parameters Intraocular pressure with use >10 days

Patient Information For the eye; shake well before using; tilt head back, place medication in conjunctival sac, and close eyes; do not touch dropper to eye; apply finger pressure on lacrimal sac for 1 minute following instillation; notify physician if condition worsens or does not improve in 3-4 days

Dosage Forms Ophthalmic:

Ointment: Neomycin sulfate 3.5 mg, polymyxin B sulfate 10,000 units and dexamethasone 0.1% per g (3.5 g, 5 g)

Suspension: Neomycin sulfate 3.5 mg, polymyxin B sulfate 10,000 units and dexamethasone 0.1% per mL (5 mL, 10 mL)

Neomycin, Polymyxin B, and Gramicidin

(nee oh MYE sin, pol i MIKS in bee, & gram i SYE din)

U.S. Brand Names AK-Spore® Ophthalmic Solution; Neosporin® Ophthalmic Solution; Ocutricin® Ophthalmic Solution

Therapeutic Category Antibiotic, Ophthalmic

Use Treatment of superficial ocular infection, infection prophylaxis in minor skin abrasions

Pregnancy Risk Factor C

Contraindications Hypersensitivity to neomycin, polymyxin B, gramicidin or any component

Warnings/Precautions Symptoms of neomycin sensitization include itching, reddening, edema, failure to heal; prolonged use may result in glaucoma, defects in visual acuity, posterior subcapsular cataract formation, and secondary ocular infections

Adverse Reactions 1% to 10%:

Cardiovascular: Edema

Dermatologic: Itching

Local: Reddening, failure to heal

Ocular: Low grade conjunctivitis

Mechanism of Action Interferes with bacterial protein synthesis by binding to 30S ribosomal subunits; binds to phospholipids, alters permeability, and damages the bacterial cytoplasmic membrane permitting leakage of intracellular constituents

Usual Dosage Children and Adults: Ophthalmic: Instill 1-2 drops 4-6 times/day or more frequently as required for severe infections

Patient Information Tilt head back, place medication in conjunctival sac, and close eyes; apply finger pressure on lacrimal sac for 1 minute following instillation

Dosage Forms Solution, ophthalmic: Neomycin sulfate 1.75 mg, polymyxin B sulfate 10,000 units, and gramicidin 0.025 mg per mL (2 mL, 10 mL)

Neomycin, Polymyxin B, and Hydrocortisone
(nee oh MYE sin, pol i MIKS in bee, & hye droe KOR ti sone)

U.S. Brand Names AK-Spore H.C.® Ophthalmic Suspension; AK-Spore H.C.® Otic; AntibiOtic® Otic; Bacticort® Otic; Cortatrigen® Otic; Cortisporin® Ophthalmic Suspension; Cortisporin® Otic; Cortisporin® Topical Cream; Drotic® Otic; Ear-Eze® Otic; LazerSporin-C® Otic; Octicair® Otic; Otic-Care® Otic; OtiTricin® Otic; Otocort® Otic; Otomycin-HPN® Otic; Otosporin® Otic; PediOtic® Otic; UAD® Otic

Therapeutic Category Antibiotic, Ophthalmic; Antibiotic, Otic; Antibiotic, Topical; Anti-inflammatory Agent; Corticosteroid, Ophthalmic; Corticosteroid, Otic; Corticosteroid, Topical (Low Potency)

Use Steroid-responsive inflammatory condition for which a corticosteroid is indicated and where bacterial infection or a risk of bacterial infection exists

Pregnancy Risk Factor C

Contraindications Known hypersensitivity to hydrocortisone, polymyxin B sulfate or neomycin sulfate; otic use when drum is perforated; herpes simplex, vaccinia, and varicella

Warnings/Precautions Prolonged use can lead to skin thinning, atrophy, sensitization, and development of resistant infections; neomycin may cause cutaneous and conjunctival sensitization; children are more susceptible to topical corticosteroid-induced hypothalamic - pituitary - adrenal axis suppression and Cushing's syndrome. Otic suspension is the preferred otic preparation; otic suspension can be used for the treatment of infections of mastoidectomy and fenestration cavities caused by susceptible organisms; otic solution is used **only** for superficial infections of the external auditory canal (ie, swimmer's ear).

Adverse Reactions
>10%: Hypersensitivity
1% to 10%:
 Dermatologic: Contact dermatitis, erythema, rash, urticaria, itching
 Genitourinary: Bladder irritation
 Local: Burning, pain, edema, stinging
 Neuromuscular & skeletal: Neuromuscular blockade
 Ocular: Elevation of intraocular pressure, glaucoma, cataracts, conjunctival erythema
 Otic: Ototoxicity
 Renal: Nephrotoxicity
 Miscellaneous: Sensitization to neomycin, secondary infections

Overdosage/Toxicology Refer to individual monographs for Neomycin, Polymyxin B, and Hydrocortisone

Mechanism of Action Refer to individual monographs for Neomycin, Polymyxin B, and Hydrocortisone

Usual Dosage Duration of use should be limited to 10 days unless otherwise directed by the physician

Otic solution is used **only** for swimmer's ear (infections of external auditory canal)
Otic:
 Children: Instill 3 drops into affected ear 3-4 times/day
 Adults: Instill 4 drops 3-4 times/day; otic suspension is the preferred otic preparation
Children and Adults:
 Ophthalmic: Drops: Instill 1-2 drops 2-4 times/day, or more frequently as required for severe infections; in acute infections, instill 1-2 drops every 15-30 minutes gradually reducing the frequency of administration as the infection is controlled
 Topical: Apply a thin layer 1-4 times/day

Patient Information
Ophthalmic: May cause sensitivity to bright light; may cause temporary blurring of vision or stinging following administration, but discontinue product and consult physician if problems persist or increase; to use, tilt head back and place medication in conjunctival sac and close eyes; apply light pressure on lacrimal sac for 1 minute

Otic: Hold container in hand to warm; if drops are in suspension form, shake well for approximately 10 seconds, lie on your side with affected ear up; for adults hold the ear lobe up and back, for children hold the ear lobe down and back; instill drops in ear without inserting dropper into ear; maintain tilted ear for 2 minutes

Dosage Forms
Cream, topical: Neomycin sulfate 5 mg, polymyxin B sulfate 10,000 units, and hydrocortisone 10 mg per mL (7.5 g)
Solution, otic: Neomycin sulfate 5 mg, polymyxin B sulfate 10,000 units, and hydrocortisone 10 mg per mL (10 mL)
Suspension:
 Ophthalmic: Neomycin sulfate 5 mg, polymyxin B sulfate 10,000 units, and hydrocortisone 10 mg per mL (7.5 mL)

(Continued)

Neomycin, Polymyxin B, and Hydrocortisone *(Continued)*

Otic: Neomycin sulfate 5 mg, polymyxin B sulfate 10,000 units, and hydrocortisone 10 mg per mL (10 mL)

Neomycin, Polymyxin B, and Prednisolone

(nee oh MYE sin, pol i MIKS in bee, & pred NIS oh lone)

U.S. Brand Names Poly-Pred® Ophthalmic Suspension

Therapeutic Category Antibiotic, Ophthalmic; Corticosteroid, Ophthalmic

Use Steroid-responsive inflammatory ocular condition in which bacterial infection or a risk of bacterial ocular infection exists

Pregnancy Risk Factor C

Contraindications Known hypersensitivity to neomycin, polymyxin B, or prednisolone; dendritic keratitis, viral disease of the cornea and conjunctiva, mycobacterial infection of the eye, fungal disease of the ocular structure, or after uncomplicated removal of a corneal foreign body

Warnings/Precautions Prolonged use may result in overgrowth of nonsusceptible organisms, glaucoma, damage to the optic nerve, defects in visual acuity, and cataract formation; symptoms of neomycin sensitization include itching, reddening, edema, or failure to heal

Adverse Reactions 1% to 10%:

Dermatologic: Cutaneous sensitization, rash, delayed wound healing

Ocular: Increased intraocular pressure, glaucoma, optic nerve damage, cataracts, conjunctival sensitization

Overdosage/Toxicology Refer to individual monographs for Neomycin, Polymyxin B, and Prednisolone

Mechanism of Action Refer to individual monographs for Neomycin, Polymyxin B, and Prednisolone

Pharmacodynamics/Kinetics Refer to individual monographs for Neomycin Sulfate, Polymyxin B Sulfate, and Prednisolone

Usual Dosage Children and Adults: Ophthalmic: Instill 1-2 drops every 3-4 hours; acute infections may require every 30-minute instillation initially with frequency of administration reduced as the infection is brought under control. To treat the lids: Instill 1-2 drops every 3-4 hours, close the eye and rub the excess on the lids and lid margins.

Patient Information Ophthalmic: May cause sensitivity to bright light; may cause temporary blurring of vision or stinging following administration, but discontinue product and consult physician if problems persist or increase; to use, tilt head back and place medication in conjunctival sac and close eyes; apply light pressure on lacrimal sac for 1 minute

Nursing Implications Shake suspension before using

Dosage Forms Suspension, ophthalmic: Neomycin sulfate 0.35%, polymyxin B sulfate 10,000 units, and prednisolone acetate 0.5% per mL (5 mL, 10 mL)

- **Neomycin Sulfate** *see* Neomycin *on page 824*
- **Neopap® [OTC]** *see* Acetaminophen *on page 19*
- **Neoral® Oral** *see* Cyclosporine *on page 308*
- **Neosar® Injection** *see* Cyclophosphamide *on page 305*
- **Neosporin® Cream [OTC]** *see* Neomycin and Polymyxin B *on page 825*
- **Neosporin® G.U. Irrigant** *see* Neomycin and Polymyxin B *on page 825*
- **Neosporin® Ophthalmic Ointment** *see* Bacitracin, Neomycin, and Polymyxin B *on page 123*
- **Neosporin® Ophthalmic Solution** *see* Neomycin, Polymyxin B, and Gramicidin *on page 826*
- **Neosporin® Topical Ointment [OTC]** *see* Bacitracin, Neomycin, and Polymyxin B *on page 123*

Neostigmine (nee oh STIG meen)

U.S. Brand Names Prostigmin®

Synonyms Neostigmine Bromide; Neostigmine Methylsulfate

Therapeutic Category Antidote, Neuromuscular Blocking Agent; Cholinergic Agent; Diagnostic Agent, Myasthenia Gravis

Use Diagnosis and treatment of myasthenia gravis and prevent and treat postoperative bladder distention and urinary retention; reversal of the effects of nondepolarizing neuromuscular blocking agents after surgery

Pregnancy Risk Factor C

Contraindications Hypersensitivity to neostigmine, bromides or any component; GI or GU obstruction

Warnings/Precautions Does **not** antagonize and may prolong the phase I block of depolarizing muscle relaxants (eg, succinylcholine); use with caution in patients with epilepsy, asthma, bradycardia, hyperthyroidism, cardiac arrhythmias, or peptic ulcer; adequate facilities should be available for cardiopulmonary resuscitation when testing and adjusting dose for myasthenia gravis; have atropine and epinephrine ready to treat hypersensitivity reactions; overdosage may result in cholinergic crisis, this must be distinguished from myasthenic crisis; anticholinesterase insensitivity can develop for brief or prolonged periods

Adverse Reactions

>10%:

Gastrointestinal: Hyperperistalsis, nausea, vomiting, salivation, diarrhea, stomach cramps

Miscellaneous: Diaphoresis (increased)

1% to 10%:

Genitourinary: Urge to urinate

Ocular: Small pupils, lacrimation

Respiratory: Increased bronchial secretions

<1%: A-V block, bradycardia, hypotension, bradyarrhythmias, asystole, dysphoria, restlessness, agitation, seizures, headache, drowsiness, thrombophlebitis, muscle spasms, tremor, weakness, fasciculations, diplopia, miosis, laryngospasm, respiratory paralysis, hypersensitivity, hyper-reactive cholinergic responses, bronchoconstriction

Overdosage/Toxicology

Symptoms of overdose include muscle weakness, blurred vision, excessive sweating, tearing and salivation, nausea, vomiting, diarrhea, hypertension, bradycardia, muscle weakness, paralysis

Atropine sulfate injection should be readily available as an antagonist for the effects of neostigmine

Drug Interactions

Decreased effect: Antagonizes effects of nondepolarizing muscle relaxants (eg, pancuronium, tubocurarine); atropine antagonizes the muscarinic effects of neostigmine

Increased effect: Neuromuscular blocking agents effects are increased

Mechanism of Action Inhibits destruction of acetylcholine by acetylcholinesterase which facilitates transmission of impulses across myoneural junction

Pharmacodynamics/Kinetics

Onset of effect: I.M.: Within 20-30 minutes; I.V.: Within 1-20 minutes

Duration: I.M.: 2.5-4 hours; I.V.: 1-2 hours

Absorption: Oral: Poor, <2%

Metabolism: In the liver

Half-life: Normal renal function: 0.5-2.1 hours; End-stage renal disease: Prolonged

Elimination: 50% excreted renally as unchanged drug

Usual Dosage

Myasthenia gravis: Diagnosis: I.M.:

Children: 0.04 mg/kg as a single dose

Adults: 0.02 mg/kg as a single dose

Myasthenia gravis: Treatment:

Children:

Oral: 2 mg/kg/day divided every 3-4 hours

I.M., I.V., S.C.: 0.01-0.04 mg/kg every 2-4 hours

Adults:

Oral: 15 mg every 3-4 hours up to 375 mg/day maximum

I.M., I.V., S.C.: 0.5-2.5 mg every 1-3 hours up to 10 mg/24 hours maximum

Reversal of nondepolarizing neuromuscular blockade after surgery in conjunction with atropine: I.V.:

Infants: 0.025-0.1 mg/kg/dose

Children: 0.025-0.08 mg/kg/dose

Adults: 0.5-2.5 mg; total dose not to exceed 5 mg

Bladder atony: Adults: I.M., S.C.:

Prevention: 0.25 mg every 4-6 hours for 2-3 days

Treatment: 0.5-1 mg every 3 hours for 5 doses after bladder has emptied

Dosing adjustment in renal impairment:

Cl$_{cr}$ 10-50 mL/minute: Administer 50% of normal dose

Cl$_{cr}$ <10 mL/minute: Administer 25% of normal dose

Test Interactions ↑ aminotransferase [ALT (SGPT)/AST (SGOT)] (S), ↑ amylase (S)

Patient Information Side effects are generally due to exaggerated pharmacologic effects; most common are salivation and muscle fasciculations; notify physician if nausea, vomiting, muscle weakness, severe abdominal pain, or difficulty breathing occurs

Nursing Implications In the diagnosis of myasthenia gravis, all anticholinesterase medications should be discontinued for at least 8 hours before administering neostigmine

Additional Information

Neostigmine bromide: Prostigmin® tablet

Neostigmine methylsulfate: Prostigmin® injection

Dosage Forms

Injection, as methylsulfate: 0.25 mg/mL (1 mL); 0.5 mg/mL (1 mL, 10 mL); 1 mg/mL (10 mL)

Tablet, as bromide: 15 mg

- **Nephronex**® see Nitrofurantoin on page 843
- **Nephrox Suspension [OTC]** see Aluminum Hydroxide on page 50
- **Neptazane**® see Methazolamide on page 746
- **Nervocaine**® see Lidocaine on page 679
- **Nesacaine**® see Chloroprocaine on page 241
- **Nesacaine**®-MPF see Chloroprocaine on page 241
- **Nestrex**® see Pyridoxine on page 998
- **1-N-Ethyl Sisomicin** see Netilmicin on this page

Netilmicin (ne til MYE sin)

U.S. Brand Names Netromycin®
Canadian Brand Names Netromicina®
Synonyms 1-N-Ethyl Sisomicin
Therapeutic Category Antibiotic, Aminoglycoside
Use Short-term treatment of serious or life-threatening infections including septicemia, peritonitis, intra-abdominal abscess, lower respiratory tract infections, urinary tract infections; skin, bone, and joint infections caused by susceptible organisms; active against *Pseudomonas aeruginoasa*, *E. coli*, *Proteus*, *Klebsiella*, *Serratia*, *Enterobacter*, *Citrobacter*, and other gram-negative bacilli
Pregnancy Risk Factor D
Contraindications Known hypersensitivity to netilmicin (aminoglycosides, bisulfites)
Warnings/Precautions Use with caution in patients with pre-existing renal insufficiency, vestibular or cochlear impairment, myasthenia gravis, hypocalcemia, conditions which depress neuromuscular transmission. Parenteral aminoglycosides are associated with nephrotoxicity or ototoxicity; the ototoxicity may be proportional to the amount of drug given and the duration of treatment; tinnitus or vertigo are indications of vestibular injury and impending hearing loss; renal damage is usually reversible.
Adverse Reactions
>10%:
  Central nervous system: Neurotoxicity
  Otic: Ototoxicity (auditory), ototoxicity (vestibular)
  Renal: Nephrotoxicity, decreased creatinine clearance
1% to 10%: Dermatologic: Skin itching, redness, rash, swelling
<1%: Difficulty in breathing, drowsiness, weakness, headache, tremors, muscle cramps, pseudomotor cerebri, anorexia, nausea, vomiting, weight loss, increased salivation, enterocolitis, granulocytopenia, agranulocytosis, thrombocytopenia, photosensitivity, erythema, burning, stinging
Overdosage/Toxicology
  Serum levels monitoring is recommended. Signs and symptoms of overdose include ototoxicity, nephrotoxicity, and neuromuscular toxicity.
  Treatment of choice following a single acute overdose appears to be the maintenance of good urine output of at least 3 mL/kg/hour. Dialysis is of questionable value in the enhancement of aminoglycoside elimination. If required, hemodialysis is preferred over peritoneal dialysis in patients with normal renal function. Careful hydration may be all that is required to promote diuresis and therefore the enhancement of the drug's elimination. Chelation with penicillins is experimental.
Drug Interactions
  Increased/prolonged effect of depolarizing and nondepolarizing neuromuscular blocking agents
  Increased toxicity: Concurrent use of amphotericin, vancomycin, ethacrynic acid, furosemide and other nephrotoxic agents may increase nephrotoxicity
Mechanism of Action Interferes with protein synthesis in bacterial cell by binding to 30S ribosomal subunits
Pharmacodynamics/Kinetics
  Absorption: I.M.: Well absorbed
  Distribution: To extracellular fluid including serum, abscesses, ascitic, pericardial, pleural, synovial, lymphatic, and peritoneal fluids; high concentrations in urine; crosses placenta
  Half-life: 2-3 hours (age and renal function dependent)
  Time to peak serum concentration: I.M.: Within 30-60 minutes
  Elimination: Excreted by glomerular filtration
Usual Dosage Individualization is critical because of the low therapeutic index. Use of ideal body weight (IBW) for determining the mg/kg/dose appears to be more accurate than dosing on the basis of total body weight (TBW). In morbid obesity, dosage requirement may best be estimated using a dosing weight of IBW + 0.4 (TBW - IBW). Peak and trough plasma drug levels should be determined, particularly in critically ill patients with serious infections or in disease states known to significantly alter aminoglycoside pharmacokinetics (eg, cystic fibrosis, burns, or major surgery).

I.M., I.V.:
  Neonates <6 weeks: 2-3.25 mg/kg/dose every 12 hours
  Children 6 weeks to 12 years: 1-2.5 mg/kg/dose every 8 hours
  Children >12 years and Adults: 1.5-2 mg/kg/dose every 8-12 hours
Some clinicians suggest a daily dose of 4-7 mg/kg for all patients with normal renal function. This dose is at least as efficacious with similar, if not less, toxicity than conventional dosing.
Dosing adjustment in renal impairment: Initial dose:
  All patients should receive a loading dose of at least 2 mg/kg (subsequent dosing should be base on serum concentrations)

Cl$_{cr}$ ≥60 mL/minute: Administer every 8 hours
Cl$_{cr}$ 40-60 mL/minute: Administer every 12 hours
Cl$_{cr}$ 20-40 mL/minute: Administer every 24 hours
Continuous arteriovenous or venovenous hemodiafiltration (CAVH) effects: Dose as for Cl$_{cr}$ 10-40 mL/minute and follow levels

Reference Range Therapeutic: Peak: 4-10 µg/mL (SI: 8-21 µmol/L); Trough: <2 µg/mL (SI: 4 µmol/L); Toxic: Peak: >10 µg/mL (SI: >21 µmol/L); Trough: >2 µg/mL (SI: >4.2 µmol/L)

Test Interactions Penicillins may decrease aminoglycoside serum concentrations *in vitro*

Patient Information Report any dizziness or sensations of ringing or fullness in ears

Nursing Implications Peak levels are drawn 30 minutes after the end of a 30-minute infusion; trough levels are drawn within 30 minutes before the next dose; give other antibiotic drugs at least 1 hour before or after gentamicin, if possible.

Dosage Forms
Injection, as sulfate: 100 mg/mL (1.5 mL)
Injection, as sulfate:
Neonatal: 10 mg/mL (2 mL)
Pediatric: 25 mg/mL (2 mL)

♦ **Netromicina®** *see Netilmicin on previous page*
♦ **Netromycin®** *see Netilmicin on previous page*
♦ **Neucalm®** *see Hydroxyzine on page 589*
♦ **Neumega®** *see Oprelvekin on page 865*
♦ **Neupogen® Injection** *see Filgrastim on page 482*
♦ **Neuramate®** *see Meprobamate on page 731*
♦ **Neuromuscular Blocking Agents Comparison** *see page 1331*
♦ **Neurontin®** *see Gabapentin on page 527*
♦ **Neut® Injection** *see Sodium Bicarbonate on page 1066*
♦ **Neutra-Phos®** *see Potassium Phosphate and Sodium Phosphate on page 955*
♦ **Neutra-Phos®-K** *see Potassium Phosphate on page 953*
♦ **Neutrexin® Injection** *see Trimetrexate Glucuronate on page 1185*

Nevirapine (ne VYE ra peen)

Related Information
Antiretroviral Agents *on page 1306*
Antiretroviral Therapy for HIV Infection *on page 1410*

U.S. Brand Names Viramune®

Therapeutic Category Antiretroviral Agent, Reverse Transcriptase Inhibitor; Reverse Transcriptase Inhibitor

Use In combination therapy with other antiretroviral agents for the treatment of HIV-1 in adults

Pregnancy Risk Factor C

Pregnancy/Breast-Feeding Implications
Clinical effects on the fetus: Administer nevirapine during pregnancy only if benefits to the mother outweigh the risk to the fetus
Breast-feeding/lactation: Avoid use during lactation, if possible

Contraindications Previous hypersensitivity to nevirapine or its components; concurrent use with oral contraceptives and protease inhibitors (indinavir, nelfinavir, ritonavir, saquinavir)

Warnings/Precautions Consider alteration of antiretroviral therapies if disease progression occurs while patients are receiving nevirapine. Resistant HIV virus emerges rapidly and uniformly when nevirapine is administered as monotherapy. Therefore, always administer in combination with at least 1 additional antiretroviral agent. Severe skin reactions (eg, Stevens-Johnson syndrome) have occurred, usually within 6 weeks. Therapy should be discontinued if any rash which develops does not resolve; mild to moderate alterations in LFTs are not uncommon, however, severe hepatotoxic reactions may occur rarely, and if abnormalities reoccur after temporarily discontinuing therapy, treatment should be permanently halted. Safety and efficacy have not been established in children.

Adverse Reactions
>10%:
Central nervous system: Headache (11%), fever (8% to 11%)
Dermatologic: Rash (15% to 20%)
Gastrointestinal: Diarrhea (15% to 20%)
Hematologic: Neutropenia (10% to 11%)
1% to 10%:
Gastrointestinal: Ulcerative stomatitis (4%), nausea, abdominal pain (2%)
Hematologic: Anemia
Hepatic: Hepatitis, increased LFTs (2% to 4%)
Neuromuscular & skeletal: Peripheral neuropathy, paresthesia (2%), myalgia
<1%: Thrombocytopenia, Stevens-Johnson syndrome, hepatotoxicity, hepatic necrosis

Overdosage/Toxicology No toxicities have been reported with acute ingestions of large sums of tablets

Drug Interactions CYP3A3/4 enzyme substrate; CYP3A3/4 enzyme inducer; CYP3A3/4 enzyme inhibitor
Decreased effect: Rifampin and rifabutin may decrease nevirapine trough concentrations due to induction of CYP3A; since nevirapine may decrease concentrations of protease inhibitors, they should not be administered concomitantly or doses should be *(Continued)*

Nevirapine *(Continued)*

increased; nevirapine may decrease the effectiveness of oral contraceptives - suggest alternate method of birth control; decreased effect of ketoconazole

Increased effect/toxicity with cimetidine, macrolides, ketoconazole

Mechanism of Action As a non-nucleoside reverse transcriptase inhibitor, nevirapine has activity against HIV-1 by binding to reverse transcriptase. It consequently blocks the RNA-dependent and DNA-dependent DNA polymerase activities including HIV-1 replication. It does not require intracellular phosphorylation for antiviral activity.

Pharmacodynamics/Kinetics

Absorption: Oral: >90%

Distribution: V_d: 1.2-1.4 L/kg; widely distributed; distributes well into breast milk and crosses the placenta; CSF penetration approximates 50% of that found in the plasma

Protein binding, plasma: 50% to 60%

Metabolism: Extensively metabolized via cytochrome P-450 system (hydroxylation to inactive compounds); may undergo enterohepatic recycling

Half-life: Decreases over 2- to 4-week time with chronic dosing due to autoinduction (ie, half-life = 45 hours initially and decreases to 23 hours)

Time to peak serum concentration: 2-4 hours

Elimination: Renal elimination of metabolites; <3% of parent compound excreted in urine

Usual Dosage Adults: Oral:

Initial: 200 mg once daily for 14 days

Maintenance: 200 mg twice daily (in combination with an additional antiretroviral agent)

Monitoring Parameters Liver function tests periodically throughout therapy; observe for CNS side effects

Patient Information Report any right upper quadrant pain, jaundice, or rash to your physician immediately

Nursing Implications May be given with food, antacids, or didanosine; if a therapy is interrupted for >7 days, the dose should be decreased to the initial regimen and increased after 14 days

Additional Information Potential compliance problems, frequency of administration and adverse effects should be discussed with patients before initiating therapy to help prevent the emergence of resistance.

Dosage Forms

Suspension, oral: 50 mg/5 mL (240 mL)

Tablet: 200 mg

♦ **New Decongestant®** *see* Chlorpheniramine, Phenyltoloxamine, Phenylpropanolamine, and Phenylephrine *on page 247*

♦ **N.G.T.® Topical** *see* Nystatin and Triamcinolone *on page 857*

Niacin *(NYE a sin)*

Related Information

Lipid-Lowering Agents *on page 1327*

U.S. Brand Names Nicobid® [OTC]; Nicolar® [OTC]; Nicotinex [OTC]; Slo-Niacin® [OTC]

Synonyms Nicotinic Acid; Nicotinamide; Vitamin B_3

Therapeutic Category Antilipemic Agent; Vitamin, Water Soluble

Use Adjunctive treatment of hyperlipidemias; peripheral vascular disease and circulatory disorders; treatment of pellagra; dietary supplement

Pregnancy Risk Factor A (C if used in doses greater than RDA suggested doses)

Contraindications Liver disease, peptic ulcer, severe hypotension, arterial hemorrhaging, hypersensitivity to niacin

Warnings/Precautions Monitor liver function tests, blood glucose; may elevate uric acid levels; use with caution in patients predisposed to gout; large doses should be administered with caution to patients with gallbladder disease, jaundice, liver disease, or diabetes; some products may contain tartrazine

Adverse Reactions

1% to 10%:

Cardiovascular: Generalized flushing

Central nervous system: Headache

Gastrointestinal: Bloating, flatulence, nausea

Hepatic: Abnormalities of hepatic function tests, jaundice

Neuromuscular & skeletal: Paresthesia in extremities

Miscellaneous: Increased sebaceous gland activity, sensation of warmth

<1%: Tachycardia, syncope, vasovagal attacks, dizziness, rash, liver damage (dose-related incidence), blurred vision, wheezing

Overdosage/Toxicology

Symptoms of acute overdose include flushing, GI distress, pruritus; chronic excessive use has been associated with hepatitis

Antihistamines may relieve niacin-induced histamine release; otherwise treatment is symptomatic

Drug Interactions

Decreased effect of oral hypoglycemics; may inhibit uricosuric effects of sulfinpyrazone and probenecid

Decreased toxicity (flush) with aspirin

Increased toxicity with lovastatin (myopathy) and possibly with other HMG-CoA reductase inhibitors; adrenergic blocking agents → additive vasodilating effect and postural hypotension

Mechanism of Action Component of two coenzymes which is necessary for tissue respiration, lipid metabolism, and glycogenolysis; inhibits the synthesis of very low density lipoproteins

Pharmacodynamics/Kinetics

Peak serum concentrations: Oral: Within 45 minutes

Metabolism: Depending upon the dose, niacin converts to niacinamide; following this conversion, niacinamide is 30% metabolized in the liver

Half-life: 45 minutes

Elimination: In urine; with larger doses, a greater percentage is excreted unchanged in urine

Usual Dosage Administer I.M., I.V., or S.C. only if oral route is unavailable and use only for vitamin deficiencies (not for hyperlipidemia)

Children: Oral:

Pellagra: 50-100 mg/dose 3 times/day

Recommended daily allowances:

0-0.5 years: 5 mg/day

0.5-1 year: 6 mg/day

1-3 years: 9 mg/day

4-6 years: 12 mg/day

7-10 years: 13 mg/day

Children and Adolescents: Oral: Recommended daily allowances:

Male:

11-14 years: 17 mg/day

15-18 years: 20 mg/day

19-24 years: 19 mg/day

Female: 11-24 years: 15 mg/day

Adults: Oral:

Recommended daily allowances:

Male: 25-50 years: 19 mg/day; >51 years: 15 mg/day

Female: 25-50 years: 15 mg/day; >51 years: 13 mg/day

Hyperlipidemia: 1.5-6 g/day in 3 divided doses with or after meals

Pellagra: 50-100 mg 3-4 times/day, maximum: 500 mg/day

Niacin deficiency: 10-20 mg/day, maximum: 100 mg/day

Administration Administer with food

Monitoring Parameters Blood glucose, liver function tests (with large doses or prolonged therapy), serum cholesterol

Test Interactions False elevations in some fluorometric determinations of urinary catecholamines; false-positive urine glucose (Benedict's reagent)

Patient Information May experience transient cutaneous flushing and sensation of warmth, especially of face and upper body; itching or tingling, and headache may occur, these adverse effects may be decreased by increasing the dose slowly or by taking aspirin or a NSAID 30 minutes to 1 hour prior to taking niacin; may cause GI upset, take with food; if dizziness occurs, avoid sudden changes in posture; report any persistent nausea, vomiting, abdominal pain, dark urine, or pale stools to the physician; do not crush sustained release capsule

Nursing Implications Monitor closely for signs of hepatotoxicity and myositis; avoid sudden changes in posture

Dosage Forms

Capsule, timed release: 125 mg, 250 mg, 300 mg, 400 mg, 500 mg

Elixir: 50 mg/5 mL (473 mL, 4000 mL)

Injection: 100 mg/mL (30 mL)

Tablet: 25 mg, 50 mg, 100 mg, 250 mg, 500 mg

Tablet:

Timed release: 150 mg, 250 mg, 500 mg, 750 mg

Extended release: 500 mg, 750 mg, 1000 mg

Niacinamide (nye a SIN a mide)

Synonyms Nicotinamide; Vitamin B_3

Therapeutic Category Vitamin, Water Soluble

Use Prophylaxis and treatment of pellagra

Pregnancy Risk Factor A (C if used in doses greater than RDA suggested doses)

Contraindications Liver disease, peptic ulcer, known hypersensitivity to niacin

Warnings/Precautions Large doses should be administered with caution to patients with gallbladder disease or diabetes; monitor blood glucose; may elevate uric acid levels; use with caution in patients predisposed to gout; some products may contain tartrazine

Adverse Reactions Percentage unknown

Cardiovascular: Tachycardia

Dermatologic: Rash

Gastrointestinal: Bloating, flatulence, nausea

Neuromuscular & skeletal: Paresthesia in extremities

Ocular: Blurred vision

Respiratory: Wheezing

Miscellaneous: Increased sebaceous gland activity

Overdosage/Toxicology

Symptoms of overdose include GI distress

Treatment is supportive

(Continued)

Niacinamide *(Continued)*

Mechanism of Action Used by the body as a source of niacin; is a component of two coenzymes which is necessary for tissue respiration, lipid metabolism, and glycogenolysis; inhibits the synthesis of very low density lipoproteins; does not have hypolipidemia or vasodilating effects

Pharmacodynamics/Kinetics
Absorption: Rapid from GI tract
Metabolism: In the liver
Half-life: 45 minutes
Time to peak serum concentration: 20-70 minutes
Elimination: In urine

Usual Dosage Oral:
Children: Pellagra: 100-300 mg/day in divided doses
Adults: 50 mg 3-10 times/day
Pellagra: 300-500 mg/day
Recommended daily allowance: 13-19 mg/day

Test Interactions False elevations of urinary catecholamines in some fluorometric determinations

Dosage Forms Tablet: 50 mg, 100 mg, 125 mg, 250 mg, 500 mg

Nicardipine *(nye KAR de peen)*

Related Information
Calcium Channel Blockers Comparison *on page 1315*
Hypertension Therapy *on page 1479*

U.S. Brand Names Cardene®; Cardene® SR; Cardene® I.V.

Canadian Brand Names Ridene

Synonyms Nicardipine Hydrochloride

Therapeutic Category Antianginal Agent; Antihypertensive Agent; Antimigraine Agent; Calcium Channel Blocker

Use Chronic stable angina (immediate-release product only); management of essential hypertension (immediate and sustained release; parenteral only for short time that oral treatment is not feasible), migraine prophylaxis
Unlabeled use: Congestive heart failure

Pregnancy Risk Factor C

Pregnancy/Breast-Feeding Implications
Clinical effects on the fetus: Crosses the placenta; may exhibit tocolytic effect
Breast-feeding/lactation: No data available

Contraindications Contraindicated in severe hypotension or second and third degree heart block, sinus bradycardia, advanced heart block, ventricular tachycardia, cardiogenic shock, atrial fibrillation or flutter associated with accessory conduction pathways, CHF; hypersensitivity to nicardipine or any component, calcium channel blockers, and adenosine; not to be given within a few hours of I.V. beta-blocking agents

Warnings/Precautions Use with caution in titrating dosages for impaired renal or hepatic function patients; may increase frequency, severity, and duration of angina during initiation of therapy; do not abruptly withdraw (chest pain); may have a greater hypotensive effect in the elderly

Adverse Reactions
1% to 10%:
Cardiovascular: Flushing (6% to 10%), palpitations, tachycardia (1% to 3.4%), peripheral edema (7% to 8%), syncope (3% to 4%)
Central nervous system: Headache (6.4% to 8%), dizziness (4% to 7%), somnolence (4.2% to 6%)
Gastrointestinal: Nausea (1.9% to 2.2%), abdominal pain (0.8% to 1.5%)
Neuromuscular & skeletal: Weakness (4.2% to 6%)
<1%: Abnormal EKG, insomnia, malaise, abnormal dreams, rash, vomiting, constipation, dyspepsia, xerostomia, nocturia, tremor

Overdosage/Toxicology The primary cardiac symptoms of calcium blocker overdose include hypotension and bradycardia. The hypotension is caused by peripheral vasodilation, myocardial depression, and bradycardia. Bradycardia results from sinus bradycardia, second- or third-degree atrioventricular block, or sinus arrest with junctional rhythm. Intraventricular conduction is usually not affected so QRS duration is normal (verapamil does prolong the P-R interval and bepridil prolongs the Q-T and may cause ventricular arrhythmias, including torsade de pointes).

The noncardiac symptoms include confusion, stupor, nausea, vomiting, metabolic acidosis and hyperglycemia. Following initial gastric decontamination, if possible, repeated calcium administration may promptly reverse the depressed cardiac contractility (but not sinus node depression or peripheral vasodilation); glucagon, epinephrine, and amrinone may treat refractory hypotension; glucagon and epinephrine also increase the heart rate (outside the U.S., 4-aminopyridine may be available as an antidote); dialysis and hemoperfusion are not effective in enhancing elimination although repeat-dose activated charcoal may serve as an adjunct with sustained-release preparations.

In a few reported cases, overdose with calcium channel blockers has been associated with hypotension and bradycardia, initially refractory to atropine but becoming more responsive to this agent when larger doses (approaching 1 g/hour for more than 24 hours) of calcium chloride was administered.

Drug Interactions CYP3A3/4 enzyme substrate

Increased toxicity/effect/levels:

Nicardipine and H$_2$ blockers (cimetidine, ranitidine) may increase bioavailability of nicardipine

Nicardipine and propranolol or metoprolol (and possibly other beta-blockers) may increase cardiac depressant effects on A-V conduction

Nicardipine and cyclosporine may increase cyclosporine levels

Stability Compatible with D$_5$W, D$_5$^{1}/$_2$NS, D$_5$NS, and D$_5$W with 40 mEq potassium chloride; 0.45% and 0.9% NS; **do not** mix with 5% sodium bicarbonate and lactated Ringer's solution; store at room temperature; protect from light; stable for 24 hours at room temperature

Mechanism of Action Inhibits calcium ion from entering the "slow channels" or select voltage-sensitive areas of vascular smooth muscle and myocardium during depolarization, producing a relaxation of coronary vascular smooth muscle and coronary vasodilation; increases myocardial oxygen delivery in patients with vasospastic angina

Pharmacodynamics/Kinetics

Absorption: Oral: Well absorbed, ~100%

Protein binding: 95%

Metabolism: Extensive first-pass metabolism; only metabolized in the liver

Bioavailability: Absolute, 35%

Half-life: 2-4 hours

Time to peak: Peak serum levels occur within 20-120 minutes and an onset of hypotension occurs within 20 minutes

Elimination: As metabolites in urine

Usual Dosage Adults:

Oral:

Immediate release: Initial: 20 mg 3 times/day; usual: 20-40 mg 3 times/day (allow 3 days between dose increases)

Sustained release: Initial: 30 mg twice daily, titrate up to 60 mg twice daily

I.V. (dilute to 0.1 mg/mL): Initial: 5 mg/hour increased by 2.5 mg/hour every 15 minutes to a maximum of 15 mg/hour

Dosing adjustment in renal impairment: Titrate dose beginning with 20 mg 3 times/day (immediate release) or 30 mg twice daily (sustained release)

Dosing adjustment in hepatic impairment: Starting dose: 20 mg twice daily (immediate release) with titration

Equivalent Oral vs I.V. Infusion Doses

Oral Dose	Equivalent I.V. Infusion
20 mg q8h	0.5 mg/h
30 mg q8h	1.2 mg/h
40 mg q8h	2.2 mg/h

Dietary Considerations Alcohol: Avoid use

Administration The total daily dose of immediate-release product may not automatically be equivalent to the daily sustained-release dose; use caution in converting

Patient Information Sustained release products should be taken with food (not fatty meal); do not crush; limit caffeine intake; avoid alcohol; notify physician if angina pain is not reduced when taking this drug, irregular heartbeat, shortness of breath, swelling, dizziness, constipation, nausea, or hypotension occur; do not stop therapy without advice of physician

Nursing Implications Monitor closely for orthostasis; ampuls must be diluted before use; do not crush sustained release product; to assess adequacy of blood pressure response, measure blood pressure 8 hours after dosing

Additional Information Although there is some initial data which may show increased risk of myocardial infarction following treatment of hypertension with calcium antagonists, controlled trials (eg, ALL-HAT) are ongoing to examine the long-term effects of not only calcium antagonists but other antihypertensives in preventing heart disease. Until these studies are completed, patients taking calcium antagonists should be encouraged to continue with prescribed antihypertensive regimens although a switch from high-dose, short-acting agents to sustained release products may be warranted.

Dosage Forms

Capsule, as hydrochloride: 20 mg, 30 mg

Capsule, as hydrochloride, sustained release: 30 mg, 45 mg, 60 mg

Injection, as hydrochloride: 2.5 mg/mL (10 mL)

♦ **Nicardipine Hydrochloride** *see Nicardipine on previous page*

♦ **N'ice® Vitamin C Drops [OTC]** *see Ascorbic Acid on page 99*

♦ **Niclocide®** *see Niclosamide on this page*

Niclosamide (ni KLOE sa mide)

U.S. Brand Names Niclocide®

Therapeutic Category Anthelmintic

Use Treatment of intestinal beef and fish tapeworm infections and dwarf tapeworm infections

Pregnancy Risk Factor B

Contraindications Known hypersensitivity to niclosamide

Warnings/Precautions Affects cestodes of the intestine only; it is without effect in cysticercosis

(Continued)

Niclosamide *(Continued)*

Adverse Reactions

1% to 10%:

Central nervous system: Drowsiness, dizziness, headache

Gastrointestinal: Nausea, vomiting, loss of appetite, diarrhea

<1%: Rash, pruritus ani, oral irritation, fever, rectal bleeding, weakness, bad taste in mouth, diaphoresis, palpitations, constipation, alopecia, edema in the arm, backache

Overdosage/Toxicology

Signs and symptoms of overdose include nausea, vomiting, anorexia

In the event of an overdose, do not administer ipecac

Mechanism of Action Inhibits the synthesis of ATP through inhibition of oxidative phosphorylation in the mitochondria of cestodes

Pharmacodynamics/Kinetics

Absorption: Oral: Not significantly absorbed

Metabolism: Not appreciably metabolized by mammalian host, but may be metabolized in GI tract by the worm

Elimination: Excreted in feces

Usual Dosage Oral:

Beef and fish tapeworm:

Children:

11-34 kg: 1 g (2 tablets) as a single dose

>34 kg: 1.5 g (3 tablets) as a single dose

Adults: 2 g (4 tablets) in a single dose

May require a second course of treatment 7 days later

Dwarf tapeworm:

Children:

11-34 g: 1 g (2 tablets) chewed thoroughly in a single dose the first day, then 500 mg/day (1 tablet) for next 6 days

>34 g: 1.5 g (3 tablets) in a single dose the first day, then 1 g/day for 6 days

Adults: 2 g (4 tablets) in a single daily dose for 7 days

Monitoring Parameters Stool cultures

Patient Information Chew tablets thoroughly; tablets can be pulverized and mixed with water to form a paste for administration to children; can be taken with food; a mild laxative can be used for constipation

Nursing Implications Administer a laxative 2-3 hours after the niclosamide dose if treating *Taenia solium* infections to prevent the development of cysticercosis

Additional Information Not available in the U.S.

Dosage Forms Tablet, chewable (vanilla flavor): 500 mg

♦ **Nicobid® [OTC]** *see Niacin on page 832*

♦ **Nicoderm® Patch** *see Nicotine on this page*

♦ **Nicolar® [OTC]** *see Niacin on page 832*

♦ **Nicorette®** *see Nicotine on this page*

♦ **Nicorette® DS Gum** *see Nicotine on this page*

♦ **Nicorette® Gum** *see Nicotine on this page*

♦ **Nicorette® Plus** *see Nicotine on this page*

♦ **Nicotinamide** *see Niacinamide on page 833*

Nicotine *(nik oh TEEN)*

Related Information

Nicotine Products Comparison *on page 1333*

U.S. Brand Names Habitrol™ Patch; Nicoderm® Patch; Nicorette® DS Gum; Nicorette® Gum; Nicotrol® NS Nasal Spray; Nicotrol® Patch [OTC]; ProStep® Patch

Canadian Brand Names Nicorette®; Nicorette® Plus

Therapeutic Category Smoking Deterrent

Use Treatment aid to smoking cessation while participating in a behavioral modification program under medical supervision

Pregnancy Risk Factor D (transdermal)/X (chewing gum)

Contraindications Nonsmokers, patients with a history of hypersensitivity or allergy to nicotine or any components used in the transdermal system, pregnant or nursing women, patients who are smoking during the postmyocardial infarction period, patients with life-threatening arrhythmias, or severe or worsening angina pectoris, active temporo-romandibular joint disease (gum)

Warnings/Precautions Use with caution in oropharyngeal inflammation and in patients with history of esophagitis, peptic ulcer, coronary artery disease, vasospastic disease, angina, hypertension, hyperthyroidism, diabetes, and hepatic dysfunction; nicotine is known to be one of the most toxic of all poisons; while the gum is being used to help the patient overcome a health hazard, it also must be considered a hazardous drug vehicle. Nicotine nasal spray: Fatal dose: 40 mg

Adverse Reactions

Chewing gum:

>10%:

Cardiovascular: Tachycardia

Central nervous system: Headache (mild)

Gastrointestinal: Nausea, vomiting, indigestion, excessive salivation, belching, increased appetite, mouth or throat soreness

Neuromuscular & skeletal: Jaw muscle ache

1% to 10%:
   Central nervous system: Insomnia, dizziness, nervousness
   Endocrine & metabolic: Dysmenorrhea
   Gastrointestinal: GI distress, eructation
   Neuromuscular & skeletal: Myalgia
   Respiratory: Hoarseness
   Miscellaneous: Hiccups
<1%: Atrial fibrillation, erythema, itching, hypersensitivity reactions

Transdermal systems:
>10%:
   Cardiovascular: Tachycardia
   Central nervous system: Headache (mild)
   Dermatologic: Pruritus, erythema
   Gastrointestinal: Increased appetite
1% to 10%:
   Central nervous system: Insomnia, nervousness
   Endocrine & metabolic: Dysmenorrhea
   Neuromuscular & skeletal: Myalgia
<1%: Atrial fibrillation, itching, hypersensitivity reactions

Overdosage/Toxicology
   Symptoms of overdose include nausea, vomiting, abdominal pain, mental confusion, diarrhea, salivation, tachycardia, respiratory and cardiovascular collapse
   Treatment after decontamination is symptomatic and supportive; remove patch, rinse area with water and dry, do not use soap as this may increase absorption.

Drug Interactions CYP2A6, 2B6 enzyme substrate; CYP1A2 enzyme inducer

Mechanism of Action Nicotine is one of two naturally-occurring alkaloids which exhibit their primary effects via autonomic ganglia stimulation. The other alkaloid is lobeline which has many actions similar to those of nicotine but is less potent. Nicotine is a potent ganglionic and central nervous system stimulant, the actions of which are mediated via nicotine-specific receptors. Biphasic actions are observed depending upon the dose administered. The main effect of nicotine in small doses is stimulation of all autonomic ganglia; with larger doses, initial stimulation is followed by blockade of transmission. Biphasic effects are also evident in the adrenal medulla; discharge of catecholamines occurs with small doses, whereas prevention of catecholamines release is seen with higher doses as a response to splanchnic nerve stimulation. Stimulation of the central nervous system (CNS) is characterized by tremors and respiratory excitation. However, convulsions may occur with higher doses, along with respiratory failure secondary to both central paralysis and peripheral blockade to respiratory muscles.

Pharmacodynamics/Kinetics Intranasal nicotine may more closely approximate the time course of plasma nicotine levels observed after cigarette smoking than other dosage forms

   Duration of action: Transdermal: 24 hours
   Absorption: Transdermal: Slow
   Metabolism: In the liver, primarily to cotinine, which is $\frac{1}{5}$ as active.
   Half-life, elimination: 4 hours
   Time to peak serum concentration: Transdermal: 8-9 hours
   Elimination: Via the kidneys; renal clearance is pH-dependent

Usual Dosage Patients should be advised to completely stop smoking upon initiation of therapy
   Gum: Chew 1 piece of gum when urge to smoke, up to 30 pieces/day; most patients require 10-12 pieces of gum/day
   Transdermal patch: Apply new patch every 24 hours to nonhairy, clean, dry skin on the upper body or upper outer arm; each patch should be applied to a different site
   24-hour patches (some 24-hour duration patches may be worn for 16 hours/day and then removed at bedtime):
      Initial starting dose: 21 mg/day for 4-8 weeks for most patients
      First weaning dose: 14 mg/day for 2-4 weeks
      Second weaning dose: 7 mg/day for 2-4 weeks
      Initial starting dose for patients <100 pounds, smoke <10 cigarettes/day, have a history of cardiovascular disease: 14 mg/day for 4-8 weeks followed by 7 mg/day for 2-4 weeks
      In patients who are receiving >600 mg/day of cimetidine: Decrease to the next lower patch size
   16-hour patches:
      One patch worn for 16 hours daily (remove at bedtime) for 6 weeks, then discontinue; these patches are not intended for lighter smokers
   Benefits of use of nicotine transdermal patches beyond 3 months have not been demonstrated
   Spray: 1-2 sprays/hour; do not exceed more than 5 doses (10 sprays) per hour; each dose (2 sprays) contains 1 mg of nicotine. **Warning:** A dose of 40 mg can cause fatalities.
   Inhaler: Patients may self-titrate doses; most patients use between 6 and 16 cartridges daily during the first 3 months of therapy and then gradually reduce their daily dose over the ensuing 6-12 weeks; no tapering strategy has been shown to be superior to any other; the best clinical effects are seen with frequent continuous inhaler puffing (20 minutes). The recommended duration of treatment is 3 months and some patients may require up to 6 months of therapy.
(Continued)

Nicotine *(Continued)*

Patient Information Instructions for the proper use of the patch should be given to the patient; notify physician if persistent rash, itching, or burning may occur with the patch; do not smoke while wearing patches

Nursing Implications Patients should be instructed to chew slowly to avoid jaw ache and to maximize benefit; patches cannot be cut; use of an aerosol corticosteroid may diminish local irritation under patches

Dosage Forms
Inhaler: Each inhaler cartridge delivers 4 mg of nicotine

Patch, transdermal:
  Habitrol™: 21 mg/day; 14 mg/day; 7 mg/day (30 systems/box)
  Nicoderm®: 21 mg/day; 14 mg/day; 7 mg/day (14 systems/box)
  Nicotrol® [OTC]: 15 mg/day (gradually released over 16 hours)
  ProStep®: 22 mg/day; 11 mg/day (7 systems/box)

Pieces, chewing gum, as polacrilex: 2 mg/square [OTC] (96 pieces/box); 4 mg/square (96 pieces/box)

Spray, nasal: 0.5 mg/actuation [10 mg/mL (200 actuations)] (10 mL)

- ◆ **Nicotine Products Comparison** *see page 1333*
- ◆ **Nicotinex [OTC]** *see Niacin on page 832*
- ◆ **Nicotinic Acid** *see Niacin on page 832*
- ◆ **Nicotiramide** *see Niacin on page 832*
- ◆ **Nicotrol® NS Nasal Spray** *see Nicotine on page 836*
- ◆ **Nicotrol® Patch [OTC]** *see Nicotine on page 836*
- ◆ **Nico-Vert® [OTC]** *see Meclizine on page 719*

Nifedipine *(nye FED i peen)*

Related Information
Calcium Channel Blockers Comparison *on page 1315*

U.S. Brand Names Adalat®; Adalat® CC; Procardia®; Procardia XL®

Canadian Brand Names Adalat PA®; Apo®-Nifed; Gen-Nifedipine; Novo-Nifedin; Nu-Nifedin

Therapeutic Category Antianginal Agent; Antihypertensive Agent; Antimigraine Agent; Calcium Channel Blocker

Use Angina, hypertrophic cardiomyopathy, hypertension (sustained release only), pulmonary hypertension; Raynaud's disease, migraine headaches.

Pregnancy Risk Factor C

Pregnancy/Breast-Feeding Implications
Clinical effects on the fetus: Use in pregnancy only when clearly needed and when the benefits outweigh the potential hazard to the fetus. No data on crossing the placenta. Hypotension, IUGR reported. IUGR probably related to maternal hypertension. May exhibit tocolytic effects. Available evidence suggests safe use during pregnancy and breast-feeding.

Breast-feeding/lactation: Crosses into breast milk. American Academy of Pediatrics considers **compatible** with breast-feeding.

Contraindications Known hypersensitivity to nifedipine or any other calcium channel blocker and adenosine; sick-sinus syndrome, 2nd or 3rd degree A-V block, hypotension (<90 mm Hg systolic); advanced aortic stenosis; acute myocardial infarction

Warnings/Precautions The routine use of short-acting nifedipine capsules in hypertensive emergencies and pseudoemergencies is not recommended. **The FDA has concluded that the use of sublingual short-acting nifedipine in hypertensive emergencies is neither safe or effective and SHOULD BE ABANDONED!** Serious adverse events (cerebrovascular ischemia, syncope, heart block, stroke, sinus arrest, severe hypotension, acute myocardial infarction, ECG changes, and fetal distress) have been reported in relation to the administration of short-acting nifedipine in hypertensive emergencies.

Increased angina may be seen upon starting or increasing doses; may increase frequency, duration, and severity of angina during initiation of therapy; use with caution in patients with congestive heart failure or aortic stenosis (especially with concomitant beta-adrenergic blocker); severe left ventricular dysfunction, hepatic or renal impairment, hypertrophic cardiomyopathy (especially obstructive), concomitant therapy with beta-blockers or digoxin, edema

Mild and transient elevations in liver function enzymes may be apparent within 8 weeks of therapy initiation.

Therapeutic potential of sustained-release formulation (elementary osmotic pump, gastrointestinal therapeutic system [GITS]) may be decreased in patients with certain GI disorders that accelerate intestinal transit time (eg, short bowel syndrome, inflammatory bowel disease, severe diarrhea).

Note: Elderly patients may experience a greater hypotensive response and the use of the immediate release formulation in patients >71 years of age has been associated with a nearly fourfold increased risk for all-cause mortality when compared to β-blockers, ACE inhibitors, or other classes of calcium channel blockers

Adverse Reactions
>10%:
  Cardiovascular: Flushing (3% to 25%), peripheral edema (10% to 30%)
  Central nervous system: Dizziness/lightheadedness (4% to 27%), giddiness, headache (10% to 23%)

Gastrointestinal: Nausea (3% to 11%), heartburn
Neuromuscular & skeletal: Weakness/jitteriness (≤12%)
Miscellaneous: Heat sensation
1% to 10%:
Cardiovascular: Congestive heart failure (2% to 7%), palpitations (≤7%), hypotension (<5%), myocardial infarction (4% to 7%)
Central nervous system: Nervousness (<7%), mood changes, somnolence(<3%)
Dermatologic: Rash/urticaria (≤3%)
Gastrointestinal: Sore throat, diarrhea (<3%), constipation (~3%), abdominal discomfort/flatulence (≤3%)
Neuromuscular & skeletal: Muscle cramps (<8%), arthritis (≤3%), paresthesia/weakness (<3%)
Respiratory: Dyspnea (≤8%), cough (6%), nasal congestion (≤6%), pulmonary edema (7%)
<1%: Tachycardia, syncope, fever, chills, dermatitis, urticaria, purpura, gingival hyperplasia, thrombocytopenia, leukopenia, anemia, joint stiffness, arthritis with increased ANA, blurred vision, transient blindness, diaphoresis

Overdosage/Toxicology The primary cardiac symptoms of calcium blocker overdose include hypotension and bradycardia. The hypotension is caused by peripheral vasodilation, myocardial depression, and bradycardia. Bradycardia results from sinus bradycardia, second- or third-degree atrioventricular block, or sinus arrest with junctional rhythm. Intraventricular conduction is usually not affected so QRS duration is normal.

The noncardiac symptoms include confusion, stupor, nausea, vomiting, metabolic acidosis and hyperglycemia. Following initial gastric decontamination, if possible, repeated calcium administration may promptly reverse the depressed cardiac contractility (but not sinus node depression or peripheral vasodilation); glucagon, epinephrine, and amrinone may treat refractory hypotension; glucagon and epinephrine also increase the heart rate (outside the U.S., 4-aminopyridine may be available as an antidote); dialysis and hemoperfusion are not effective in enhancing elimination although repeated-dose activated charcoal may serve as an adjunct with sustained-release preparations.

In a few reported cases, overdose with calcium channel blockers has been associated with hypotension and bradycardia, initially refractory to atropine but becoming more responsive to this agent when larger doses (approaching 1 g/hour for more than 24 hours) of calcium chloride was administered.

Drug Interactions CYP3A3/4 and 3A5-7 enzyme substrate
Decreased toxicity:
Nifedipine and phenobarbital may decrease nifedipine levels as observed with other calcium antagonists
Nifedipine and quinidine may decrease quinidine levels
Nifedipine and rifampin may result in decreased nifedipine levels as with verapamil
Increased toxicity:
Nifedipine and beta-blockers may increase cardiovascular adverse effects
Nifedipine and H_2-antagonists (cimetidine) increase bioavailability and may increase nifedipine serum concentration
Nifedipine and quinidine may increase nifedipine levels and toxicity
Nifedipine and theophylline may increase theophylline levels
Nifedipine and vincristine may increase vincristine levels
Nifedipine and digoxin may increase digoxin levels
Nifedipine rarely increases PT time with concomitant warfarin administration
Neuromuscular blockade and hypotension may occur with coadministration of nifedipine and parenteral magnesium sulfate
Severe hypotension and fluid volume requirements may increase with concomitant fentanyl

Mechanism of Action Inhibits calcium ion from entering the "slow channels" or select voltage-sensitive areas of vascular smooth muscle and myocardium during depolarization, producing a relaxation of coronary vascular smooth muscle and coronary vasodilation; increases myocardial oxygen delivery in patients with vasospastic angina

Pharmacodynamics/Kinetics
Onset of action: Oral: Within 20 minutes; S.L.: Within 1-5 minutes
Protein binding: 92% to 98% (concentration-dependent)
Metabolism: In the liver to inactive metabolites
Bioavailability: Capsules: 45% to 75%; Sustained release: 65% to 86%
Half-life: Adults, normal: 2-5 hours; Adults with cirrhosis: 7 hours
Elimination: In urine

Usual Dosage Oral or "bite and swallow" (eg, patient bites capsule to release liquid contents and then swallows): **Note:** Doses are usually titrated upward at 7- to 14-day intervals; may increase every 3 days if clinically necessary

Children: Hypertrophic cardiomyopathy: 0.6-0.9 mg/kg/24 hours in 3-4 divided doses
Adolescents and Adults: (note: when switching from immediate release to sustained release formulations, total daily dose will start the same)
Initial: 10 mg 3 times/day as capsules or 30 mg once daily as sustained release
Usual dose: 10-30 mg 3 times/day as capsules or 30-60 mg once daily as sustained release
Maximum dose: 120-180 mg/day
Increase sustained release at 7- to 14-day intervals
Hemodialysis: Supplemental dose is not necessary
Peritoneal dialysis effects: Supplemental dose is not necessary
(Continued)

Nifedipine *(Continued)*

Dosing adjustment in hepatic impairment: Reduce oral dose by 50% to 60% in patients with cirrhosis

Dietary Considerations Alcohol: Avoid use

Monitoring Parameters Heart rate, blood pressure, signs and symptoms of CHF, peripheral edema

Patient Information Sustained release products should not be crushed or chewed; Adalat® CC should be taken on an empty stomach; limit caffeine intake; avoid alcohol; notify physician if angina pain is not reduced when taking this drug, irregular heartbeat, shortness of breath, swelling, dizziness, constipation, nausea, or hypotension occurs; do not stop therapy without advice of physician; the shell of the sustained-release tablet may appear intact in the stool, this is no cause for concern

Nursing Implications May cause some patients to urinate frequently at night; may cause inflamed gums; capsule may be punctured and drug solution administered sublingually or orally to reduce blood pressure in recumbent patient

Additional Information Although there is some initial data which may show increased risk of myocardial infarction with the treatment of hypertension with calcium antagonists, controlled trial (eg, ALL-HAT) are ongoing to examine the long-term effects of not only these agents but other antihypertensives in preventing heart disease. Until these studies are completed, patients taking calcium antagonists should be encouraged to continue with the prescribed antihypertensive regimens although a switch from high-dose short-acting products to sustained release agents may be warranted. Adalat® and Procardia® contain 0.34 mL of liquid per capsule. UDL Laboratory generic formulation contains 0.312 mL of liquid per capsule. Purepac generic formulation contains 0.37 mL per 15 mg capsule and 0.498 mL per 20 mg capsule.

Dosage Forms
Capsule, liquid-filled (Adalat®, Procardia®): 10 mg, 20 mg
Tablet, extended release (Adalat® CC): 30 mg, 60 mg, 90 mg
Tablet, sustained release (Procardia XL®): 30 mg, 60 mg, 90 mg

◆ **Niferex®-PN** *see* Vitamins, Multiple *on page 1226*
◆ **Nilandron™** *see* Nilutamide *on this page*
◆ **Nilstat®** *see* Nystatin *on page 856*

Nilutamide *(ni LU ta mide)*

Related Information
Cancer Chemotherapy Regimens *on page 1263*

U.S. Brand Names Nilandron™

Canadian Brand Names Anandron®

Therapeutic Category Antiandrogen; Antineoplastic Agent, Miscellaneous

Use In combination with surgical castration in treatment of metastatic prostatic carcinoma (Stage D_2); for maximum benefit, nilutamide treatment must begin on the same day as or on the day after surgical castration

Pregnancy Risk Factor C

Contraindications Severe hepatic impairment; severe respiratory insufficiency; hypersensitivity to nilutamide or any component of this preparation

Warnings/Precautions The U.S. Food and Drug Administration (FDA) currently recommends that procedures for proper handling and disposal of antineoplastic agents be considered.

Interstitial pneumonitis has been reported in 2% of patients exposed to nilutamide. Patients typically experienced progressive exertional dyspnea, and possibly cough, chest pain and fever. X-rays showed interstitial or alveolo-interstitial changes. The suggestive signs of pneumonitis most often occurred within the first 3 months of nilutamide treatment.

Hepatitis or marked increases in liver enzymes leading to drug discontinuation occurred in 1% of nilutamide patients. There has been a report of elevated hepatic enzymes followed by death in a 65 year old patient treated with nilutamide.

Foreign postmarketing surveillance has revealed isolated cases of aplastic anemia in which a causal relationship with nilutamide could not be ascertained.

13% to 57% of patients receiving nilutamide reported a delay in adaptation to the dark, ranging from seconds to a few minutes. This effect sometimes does not abate as drug treatment is continued. Caution patients who experience this effect about driving at night or through tunnels. This effect can be alleviated by wearing tinted glasses.

Adverse Reactions
>10%:
Central nervous system: Pain, headache, insomnia
Gastrointestinal: Nausea, constipation, anorexia
Genitourinary: Impotence, testicular atrophy, gynecomastia
Endocrine & metabolic: Loss of libido, hot flashes
Neuromuscular & skeletal: Weakness
Ocular: Impaired adaption to dark
1% to 10%:
Cardiovascular: Hypertension
Central nervous system: Flu syndrome, fever, dizziness, depression, hypesthesia
Dermatologic: Alopecia, dry skin, rash
Gastrointestinal: Dyspepsia, vomiting, abdominal pain
Genitourinary: Urinary tract infection, hematuria, urinary tract disorder, nocturia

Ocular: Chromatopsia, impaired adaption to light, abnormal vision

Respiratory: Dyspnea, upper respiratory infection, pneumonia

Miscellaneous: Diaphoresis

Overdosage/Toxicology

One case of massive overdosage has been published. A 79-year old man attempted suicide by ingesting 13 g of nilutamide. There were no clinical signs or symptoms or changes in parameters such as transaminases or chest x-ray. Maintenance treatment (150 mg/day) was resumed 30 days later.

Management is supportive, dialysis not of benefit; induce vomiting if the patient is alert, general supportive care (including frequent monitoring of the vital signs and close observation of the patient)

Stability Store at room temperature (15°C to 30°C/59°F to 86°F); protect from light

Mechanism of Action Nonsteroidal antiandrogen that inhibits androgen uptake or inhibits binding of androgen in target tissues

Pharmacodynamics/Kinetics

Absorption: Rapid and complete

Distribution: Moderately binds to plasma proteins and low binding to erythrocytes.

Metabolism: Extensive

Half-life: 38-59 hours

Elimination: All metabolites excreted primarily in urine

Usual Dosage Adults: Oral: 6 tablets (50 mg each) once a day for a total daily dose of 300 mg for 30 days followed thereafter by 3 tablets (50 mg each) once a day for a total daily dose of 150 mg

Dietary Considerations Food: Can be taken without regard to food

Monitoring Parameters

Perform routine chest x-rays before treatment, and tell patients to report immediately any dyspnea or aggravation of pre-existing dyspnea. At the onset of dyspnea or worsening of pre-existing dyspnea any time during therapy, interrupt nilutamide until it can be determined if respiratory symptoms are drug-related. Obtain a chest x-ray, and if there are findings suggestive of interstitial pneumonitis, discontinue treatment with nilutamide. The pneumonitis is almost always reversible when treatment is discontinued. If the chest x-ray appears normal, perform pulmonary function tests.

Measure serum hepatic enzyme levels at baseline and at regular intervals (3 months); if transaminases increase over 2-3 times the upper limit of normal, discontinue treatment. Perform appropriate laboratory testing at the first symptom/sign of liver injury (eg, jaundice, dark urine, fatigue, abdominal pain or unexplained GI symptoms) and nilutamide treatment must be discontinued immediately if transaminases exceed 3 times the upper limit of normal.

Dosage Forms Tablet: 50 mg

♦ **Nimbex®** see Cisatracurium on page 266

Nimodipine (nye MOE di peen)

Related Information

Calcium Channel Blockers Comparison on page 1315

U.S. Brand Names Nimotop®

Therapeutic Category Calcium Channel Blocker

Use Improvement of neurological deficits due to spasm following subarachnoid hemorrhage from ruptured congenital intracranial aneurysms in patients who are in good neurological condition postictus

Pregnancy Risk Factor C

Pregnancy/Breast-Feeding Implications

Clinical effects on the fetus: Use in pregnancy only when clearly needed and when the benefits outweigh the potential hazard to the fetus. Teratogenic and embryotoxic effects have been demonstrated in small animals. No well controlled studies have been conducted in pregnant women.

Breast milk/lactation: Appears in breast milk at levels higher than maternal plasma levels; no recommendations are currently available on breast-feeding

Contraindications Hypersensitivity to nimodipine or any component

Warnings/Precautions Use with caution and titrate dosages for patients with impaired renal or hepatic function; use caution when treating patients with congestive heart failure, sick-sinus syndrome, PVCs, severe left ventricular dysfunction, hypertrophic cardiomyopathy (especially obstructive, IHSS), concomitant therapy with beta-blockers or digoxin, edema, or increased intracranial pressure with cranial tumors; do not abruptly withdraw (may cause chest pain); elderly may experience hypotension and constipation more readily

Adverse Reactions

1% to 10%:

Cardiovascular: Reductions in systemic blood pressure (1.2% to 8.1%)

Central nervous system: Headache (1.4% to 4.1%)

Dermatologic: Rash (0.6% to 2.4%)

Gastrointestinal: Diarrhea (1.7% to 4.2%), abdominal discomfort (2%)

<1%: Edema (0.4% to 1.2%), EKG abnormalities (0.6% to 1.4%), tachycardia, bradycardia, depression, acne, nausea (0.6% to 1.4%), hemorrhage, hepatitis, muscle cramps (0.2% to 1.4%), dyspnea

(Continued)

Nimodipine *(Continued)*

Overdosage/Toxicology The primary cardiac symptoms of calcium blocker overdose include hypotension and bradycardia. The hypotension is caused by peripheral vasodilation, myocardial depression, and bradycardia. Bradycardia results from sinus bradycardia, second- or third-degree atrioventricular block, or sinus arrest with junctional rhythm. Intraventricular conduction is usually not affected so QRS duration is normal.

The noncardiac symptoms include confusion, stupor, nausea, vomiting, metabolic acidosis and hyperglycemia. Following initial gastric decontamination, if possible, repeated calcium administration may promptly reverse the depressed cardiac contractility (but not sinus node depression or peripheral vasodilation); glucagon, epinephrine, and amrinone may treat refractory hypotension; glucagon and epinephrine also increase the heart rate (outside the U.S., 4-aminopyridine may be available as an antidote); dialysis and hemoperfusion are not effective in enhancing elimination although repeat-dose activated charcoal may serve as an adjunct with sustained-release preparations.

In a few reported cases, overdose with calcium channel blockers has been associated with hypotension and bradycardia, initially refractory to atropine but becoming more responsive to this agent when larger doses (approaching 1 g/hour for more than 24 hours) of calcium chloride was administered.

Drug Interactions CYP3A3/4 enzyme substrate
Increased toxicity/effect/levels:
Nimodipine and cimetidine may increase bioavailability of nimodipine as with other calcium blockers
Nimodipine and omeprazole may increase bioavailability of nimodipine
Nimodipine, propranolol, and other beta-blockers may have minimal increase of depressant effects on A-V conduction

Mechanism of Action Nimodipine shares the pharmacology of other calcium channel blockers; animal studies indicate that nimodipine has a greater effect on cerebral arterials than other arterials; this increased specificity may be due to the drug's increased lipophilicity and cerebral distribution as compared to nifedipine; inhibits calcium ion from entering the "slow channels" or select voltage sensitive areas of vascular smooth muscle and myocardium during depolarization

Pharmacodynamics/Kinetics
Metabolism: Extensive in the liver
Half-life: 3 hours, increases with reduced renal function
Protein binding: >95%
Bioavailability: 13%
Time to peak serum concentration: Oral: Within 1 hour
Elimination: In feces (32%) and in urine (50% within 4 days)

Usual Dosage Adults: Oral: 60 mg every 4 hours for 21 days, start therapy within 96 hours after subarachnoid hemorrhage

Dialysis: Not removed by hemo- or peritoneal dialysis; supplemental dose is not necessary
Dosing adjustment in hepatic impairment: Reduce dosage to 30 mg every 4 hours in patients with liver failure

Nursing Implications If the capsules cannot be swallowed, the liquid may be removed by making a hole in each end of the capsule with an 18-gauge needle and extracting the contents into a syringe; if given via NG tube, follow with a flush of 30 mL NS

Dosage Forms Capsule, liquid-filled: 30 mg

♦ **Nimotop®** *see Nimodipine on previous page*
♦ **Nipent™ Injection** *see Pentostatin on page 904*

Nisoldipine *(NYE sole di peen)*

Related Information
Calcium Channel Blockers Comparison *on page 1315*
U.S. Brand Names Sular®
Therapeutic Category Antihypertensive Agent; Calcium Channel Blocker
Use Management of hypertension, may be used alone or in combination with other antihypertensive agents
Pregnancy Risk Factor C
Contraindications Hypersensitivity to nisoldipine or any component or other dihydropyridine calcium channel blocker
Warnings/Precautions Increased angina and/or myocardial infarction in patients with coronary artery disease
Adverse Reactions
Cardiovascular: Peripheral edema, tachycardia
Central nervous system: Dizziness, headache
Overdosage/Toxicology The primary cardiac symptoms of calcium blocker overdose include hypotension and bradycardia. The hypotension is caused by peripheral vasodilation, myocardial depression, and bradycardia. Bradycardia results from sinus bradycardia, second- or third-degree atrioventricular block, or sinus arrest with junctional rhythm. Intraventricular conduction is usually not affected so QRS duration is normal.

The noncardiac symptoms include confusion, stupor, nausea, vomiting, metabolic acidosis and hyperglycemia. Following initial gastric decontamination, if possible, repeated calcium administration may promptly reverse the depressed cardiac contractility (but not sinus node depression or peripheral vasodilation); glucagon, epinephrine, and amrinone may treat refractory hypotension; glucagon and epinephrine also increase the heart rate (outside the U.S., 4-aminopyridine may be available as an antidote); dialysis and hemoperfusion are not effective in enhancing elimination although repeat-dose activated charcoal may serve as an adjunct with sustained release preparations.

In a few reported cases, overdose with calcium channel blockers has been associated with hypotension and bradycardia, initially refractory to atropine but becoming more responsive to this agent when larger doses (approaching 1 g/hour for more than 24 hours) of calcium chloride was administered.

Drug Interactions CYP3A3/4 enzyme substrate
Increased toxicity:
Nisoldipine and digoxin may increase digoxin effect
Nisoldipine, propranolol, and other beta-blockers may increase cardiovascular adverse effects
Nisoldipine and H_2-antagonists (cimetidine) increase bioavailability and may increase nisoldipine serum concentration
Nisoldipine and omeprazole increase bioavailability and may increase nisoldipine serum concentration

Mechanism of Action As a dihydropyridine calcium channel blocker, structurally similar to nifedipine, nisoldipine impedes the movement of calcium ions into vascular smooth muscle and cardiac muscle. Dihydropyridines are potent vasodilators and are not as likely to suppress cardiac contractility and slow cardiac conduction as other calcium antagonists such as verapamil and diltiazem; nisoldipine is 5-10 times as potent a vasodilator as nifedipine.

Pharmacodynamics/Kinetics
Absorption: Well absorbed
Metabolism: Extensive presystemic metabolism in the intestinal wall and the liver; hepatically metabolized to inactive metabolites
Half-life: 7-12 hours
Bioavailability: 5%; T_{max}: 6-12 hours
Elimination: In the urine

Usual Dosage Adults: Oral: Initial: 20 mg once daily, then increase by 10 mg/week (or longer intervals) to attain adequate control of blood pressure; doses >60 mg once daily are not recommended. A starting dose not exceeding 10 mg/day is recommended for the elderly and those with hepatic impairment.

Dietary Considerations Avoid grapefruit products before and after dosing

Patient Information Avoid grapefruit products before and after dosing; administration with a high fat meal can lead to excessive peak drug concentrations and should be avoided

Nursing Implications Administer at the same time each day to ensure minimal fluctuation of serum levels

Additional Information Initial data indicate that once daily doses of 10-40 mg are about as effective as hydrochlorothiazide, lisinopril, or amlodipine; doses of 20-60 mg are about as effective as twice daily verapamil in lowering blood pressure in patients with mild to moderate hypertension; although there is some initial data which may show increased risk of myocardial infarction following treatment of hypertension with calcium channel blockers, controlled trials (eg, ALL-HAT) are ongoing to examine the long-term effects of not only the calcium channel blockers, but also other antihypertensives in preventing heart disease. Until done, patients taking these agents should be encouraged to continue with prescribed antihypertension regimens although a switch from high-dose, short-acting agents to sustained release products may be warranted. Most practitioners agree to avoid calcium channel blockers as primary treatment for hypertension unless diuretics or beta-blockers are contraindicated.

Dosage Forms Tablet, extended release: 10 mg, 20 mg, 30 mg, 40 mg

◆ **Nitalapram** see Citalopram on page 270
◆ **Nitrates Comparison** see page 1334
◆ **Nitrek® Patch** see Nitroglycerin on page 845
◆ **Nitro-Bid® I.V. Injection** see Nitroglycerin on page 845
◆ **Nitro-Bid® Ointment** see Nitroglycerin on page 845
◆ **Nitrodisc® Patch** see Nitroglycerin on page 845
◆ **Nitro-Dur® Patch** see Nitroglycerin on page 845
◆ **Nitrofural** see Nitrofurazone on next page

Nitrofurantoin (nye troe fyoor AN toyn)

Related Information
Antacid Drug Interactions on page 1296
Antimicrobial Drugs of Choice on page 1404

U.S. Brand Names Furadantin®; Furalan®; Furan®; Furanite®; Macrobid®; Macrodantin®

Canadian Brand Names Apo®-Nitrofurantoin; Nephronex®; Novo-Furan

Therapeutic Category Antibiotic, Miscellaneous

Use Prevention and treatment of urinary tract infections caused by susceptible gram-negative and some gram-positive organisms; *Pseudomonas*, *Serratia*, and most species of *Proteus* are generally resistant to nitrofurantoin

Pregnancy Risk Factor B

Contraindications Hypersensitivity to nitrofurantoin or any component; renal impairment; infants <1 month (due to the possibility of hemolytic anemia)

Warnings/Precautions Use with caution in patients with G-6-PD deficiency, patients with anemia, vitamin B deficiency, diabetes mellitus or electrolyte abnormalities; therapeutic concentrations of nitrofurantoin are not attained in urine of patients with Cl_{cr} <40
(Continued)

Nitrofurantoin *(Continued)*

mL/minute (elderly); use with caution if prolonged therapy is anticipated due to possible pulmonary toxicity; acute, subacute, or chronic (usually after 6 months of therapy) pulmonary reactions have been observed in patients treated with nitrofurantoin; if these occur, discontinue therapy; monitor closely for malaise, dyspnea, cough, fever, radiologic evidence of diffuse interstitial pneumonitis or fibrosis

Adverse Reactions Percentage unknown: Chest pains, chills, fever, fatigue, drowsiness, headache, dizziness, rash, itching, lupus-like syndrome, exfoliative dermatitis, stomach upset, diarrhea, loss of appetite/vomiting/nausea (most common), sore throat, hemolytic anemia, hepatitis, hypersensitivity, increased LFTs, weakness, paresthesia, numbness, arthralgia, cough, dyspnea, hypersensitivity, *C. difficile*-colitis

Overdosage/Toxicology
Symptoms of overdose include vomiting
Supportive care only

Drug Interactions
Decreased effect: Antacids, especially magnesium salts, decrease absorption of nitrofurantoin; nitrofurantoin may antagonize effects of norfloxacin
Increased toxicity: Probenecid (decreases renal excretion of nitrofurantoin); anticholinergic drugs increase absorption of nitrofurantoin

Mechanism of Action Inhibits several bacterial enzyme systems including acetyl coenzyme A interfering with metabolism and possibly cell wall synthesis

Pharmacodynamics/Kinetics
Absorption: Well absorbed from GI tract; the macrocrystalline form is absorbed more slowly due to slower dissolution, but causes less GI distress
Distribution: V_d: 0.8 L/kg; crosses the placenta; appears in breast milk
Protein binding: ~40%
Metabolism: 60% of drug metabolized by body tissues throughout the body, with exception of plasma, to inactive metabolites
Bioavailability: Increased by presence of food
Half-life: 20-60 minutes; prolonged with renal impairment
Elimination: As metabolites and unchanged drug (40%) in urine and small amounts in bile; renal excretion via glomerular filtration and tubular secretion

Usual Dosage Oral:
Children >1 month: 5-7 mg/kg/day in divided doses every 6 hours; maximum: 400 mg/day
Chronic therapy: 1-2 mg/kg/day in divided doses every 12-24 hours; maximum dose: 100 mg/day
Adults: 50-100 mg/dose every 6 hours
Macrocrystal/monohydrate: 100 mg twice daily
Prophylaxis or chronic therapy: 50-100 mg/dose at bedtime
Dosing adjustment in renal impairment: Cl_{cr} <50 mL/minute: Avoid use
Avoid use in hemo and peritoneal dialysis and continuous arteriovenous or venovenous hemofiltration (CAVH/CAVHD)

Dietary Considerations Alcohol: Avoid use

Administration Administer with meals to slow the rate of absorption and decrease adverse effects; suspension may be mixed with water, milk, fruit juice, or infant formula

Monitoring Parameters Signs of pulmonary reaction, signs of numbness or tingling of the extremities, periodic liver function tests

Test Interactions Causes false-positive urine glucose with Clinitest®

Patient Information Take with food or milk; may discolor urine to a dark yellow or brown color; notify physician if fever, chest pain, persistent, nonproductive cough, or difficulty breathing occurs; avoid alcohol

Additional Information Nitrofurantoin macrocrystal/monohydrate is Macrobid®

Dosage Forms
Capsule: 50 mg, 100 mg
Capsule:
Macrocrystal: 25 mg, 50 mg, 100 mg
Macrocrystal/monohydrate: 100 mg
Suspension, oral: 25 mg/5 mL (470 mL)

Nitrofurazone *(nye troe FYOOR a zone)*

U.S. Brand Names Furacin® Topical

Synonyms Nitrofural

Therapeutic Category Antibacterial, Topical

Use Antibacterial agent in second and third degree burns and skin grafting

Pregnancy Risk Factor C

Contraindications Hypersensitivity to nitrofurazone or any component

Warnings/Precautions Use with caution in patients with renal impairment and patients with G-6-PD deficiency

Adverse Reactions Women should inform their physicians if signs or symptoms of any of the following occur thromboembolic or thrombotic disorders including sudden severe headache or vomiting, disturbance of vision or speech, loss of vision, numbness or weakness in an extremity, sharp or crushing chest pain, calf pain, shortness of breath, severe abdominal pain or mass, mental depression or unusual bleeding

Women should discontinue taking the medication if they suspect they are pregnant or become pregnant. Notify physician if area under dermal patch becomes irritated or a rash develops.

Drug Interactions Decreased effect: Sutilains decrease activity of nitrofurazone

Stability Avoid exposure to direct sunlight; excessive heat, strong fluorescent lighting, and alkaline materials

Mechanism of Action A broad antibacterial spectrum; it acts by inhibiting bacterial enzymes involved in carbohydrate metabolism; effective against a wide range of gram-negative and gram-positive organisms; bactericidal against most bacteria commonly causing surface infections including *Staphylococcus aureus*, *Streptococcus*, *Escherichia coli*, *Enterobacter cloacae*, *Clostridium perfringens*, *Aerobacter aerogenes*, and *Proteus* sp; not particularly active against most *Pseudomonas aeruginosa* strains and does not inhibit viruses or fungi. Topical preparations of nitrofurazone are readily soluble in blood, pus, and serum and are nonmacerating.

Usual Dosage Children and Adults: Topical: Apply once daily or every few days to lesion or place on gauze

Patient Information Notify physician if condition worsens or if irritation develops

Dosage Forms
Cream: 0.2% (28 g)
Ointment, soluble dressing, topical: 0.2% (28 g, 56 g, 454 g, 480 g)
Solution, topical: 0.2% (480 mL, 4000 mL)

♦ **Nitrogard® Buccal** *see* Nitroglycerin *on this page*

♦ **Nitrogen Mustard** *see* Mechlorethamine *on page 717*

Nitroglycerin (nye troe GLI ser in)

Related Information
Adrenergic Agonists, Cardiovascular Comparison *on page 1290*
Adult ACLS Algorithm, Hypotension, Shock *on page 1454*
Hypertension Therapy *on page 1479*
Nitrates Comparison *on page 1334*

U.S. Brand Names Deponit® Patch; Minitran® Patch; Nitrek® Patch; Nitro-Bid® I.V. Injection; Nitro-Bid® Ointment; Nitrodisc® Patch; Nitro-Dur® Patch; Nitrogard® Buccal; Nitroglyn® Oral; Nitrolingual® Translingual Spray; Nitrol® Ointment; Nitrong® Oral Tablet; Nitrostat® Sublingual; Nitro-Time® Capsules; Transdermal-NTG® Patch; Transderm-Nitro® Patch; Tridil® Injection

Synonyms Glyceryl Trinitrate; Nitroglycerol; NTG

Therapeutic Category Antianginal Agent; Antihypertensive Agent; Nitrate; Vasodilator; Vasodilator, Coronary

Use Treatment and prevention of angina pectoris; I.V. for congestive heart failure (especially when associated with acute myocardial infarction); pulmonary hypertension; hypertensive emergencies occurring perioperatively (especially during cardiovascular surgery)

Pregnancy Risk Factor C

Contraindications Hypersensitivity to nitroglycerin or any component; pericardial tamponade, restrictive cardiomyopathy, or constrictive pericarditis; allergy to adhesive (transdermal), uncorrected hypovolemia (I.V.); transdermal NTG is not effective for immediate relief of angina

Warnings/Precautions Do not use extended release preparations in patients with GI hypermotility or malabsorptive syndrome; use with caution in patients with hepatic impairment, CHF, or acute myocardial infarction; available preparations of I.V. nitroglycerin differ in concentration or volume; pay attention to dilution and dosage; I.V. preparations contain alcohol and/or propylene glycol; avoid loss of nitroglycerin in standard PVC tubing; dosing instructions must be followed with care when the appropriate infusion sets are used

Hypotension may occur, use with caution in patients who are volume-depleted, are hypotensive, have inadequate circulation; nitrate therapy may aggravate angina caused by hypertrophic cardiomyopathy

Adverse Reactions
>10% Central nervous system: Headache (especially at higher doses, may be recurrent with each daily dose), lightheadedness
1% to 10%:
Cardiovascular: Reflex tachycardia, hypotension, syncope, angina, rebound hypertension, bradycardia
Dermatologic: Contact dermatitis, fixed drug eruptions (with ointments or patches)
<1%: Hematologic: Methemoglobinemia (very rare)

Overdosage/Toxicology
Symptoms of overdose include hypotension, flushing, syncope, throbbing headache with reflex tachycardia, methemoglobinemia with extremely large overdoses; I.V. overdose may be additionally associated with increased intracranial pressure, confusion, vertigo, palpitation, nausea, vomiting, dyspnea, diaphoresis, heartblock, bradycardia, coma, seizures, and death

After gastric decontamination, treatment is supportive and symptomatic; hypotension is treated with positioning, fluids, and careful use of low-dose pressors, if needed; methylene blue may treat methemoglobinemia

Drug Interactions
Decreased effect: I.V. nitroglycerin may antagonize the anticoagulant effect of heparin, monitor closely; may need to decrease heparin dosage when nitroglycerin is discontinued

Increased toxicity: Alcohol, other vasodilators (eg, calcium channel blockers) may enhance nitroglycerin's hypotensive effect

Stability Doses should be made in glass bottles, Excell® or PAB® containers; adsorption occurs to soft plastic (ie, PVC)

(Continued)

Nitroglycerin *(Continued)*

Nitroglycerin diluted in D_5W or NS in glass containers is physically and chemically stable for 48 hours at room temperature and 7 days under refrigeration; in D_5W or NS in Excell®/PAB® containers is physically and chemically stable for 24 hours at room temperature and 14 days under refrigeration

Premixed bottles are stable according to the manufacturer's expiration dating

Standard diluent: 50 mg/250 mL D_5W; 50 mg/500 mL D_5W

Minimum volume: 100 mg/250 mL D_5W; concentration should not exceed 400 mcg/mL

Store sublingual tablets and ointment in tightly closed containers at 15°C to 30°C

Mechanism of Action Reduces cardiac oxygen demand by decreasing left ventricular pressure and systemic vascular resistance; dilates coronary arteries and improves collateral flow to ischemic regions

Pharmacodynamics/Kinetics

Onset and duration of action is dependent upon dosage form administered; see table.

Nitroglycerin

Dosage Form	Onset of Effect	Peak Effect	Duration
Sublingual tablet	1-3 min	4-8 min	30-60 min
Translingual spray	2 min	4-10 min	30-60 min
Buccal tablet	2-5 min	4-10 min	2 h
Sustained release	20-45 min	45-120 min	4-8 h
Topical	15-60 min	30-120 min	2-12 h
Transdermal	40-60 min	60-180 min	18-24 h
I.V. drip	Immediate	Immediate	3-5 min

Protein binding: 60%

Metabolism: Extensive first-pass metabolism

Half-life: 1-4 minutes

Elimination: Excretion of inactive metabolites in urine

Usual Dosage Note: Hemodynamic and antianginal tolerance often develop within 24-48 hours of continuous nitrate administration

Children: Pulmonary hypertension: Continuous infusion: Start 0.25-0.5 mcg/kg/minute and titrate by 1 mcg/kg/minute at 20- to 60-minute intervals to desired effect; usual dose: 1-3 mcg/kg/minute; maximum: 5 mcg/kg/minute

Adults:

Buccal: Initial: 1 mg every 3-5 hours while awake (3 times/day); titrate dosage upward if angina occurs with tablet in place

Oral: 2.5-9 mg 2-4 times/day (up to 26 mg 4 times/day)

I.V.: 5 mcg/minute, increase by 5 mcg/minute every 3-5 minutes to 20 mcg/minute; if no response at 20 mcg/minute increase by 10 mcg/minute every 3-5 minutes, up to 200 mcg/minute

Ointment: ½" upon rising and ½" 6 hours later; the dose may be doubled and even doubled again as needed

Patch, transdermal: Initial: 0.2-0.4 mg/hour, titrate to doses of 0.4-0.8 mg/hour; tolerance is minimized by using a patch-on period of 12-14 hours and patch-off period of 10-12 hours

Sublingual: 0.2-0.6 mg every 5 minutes for maximum of 3 doses in 15 minutes; may also use prophylactically 5-10 minutes prior to activities which may provoke an attack

Translingual: 1-2 sprays into mouth under tongue every 3-5 minutes for maximum of 3 doses in 15 minutes, may also be used 5-10 minutes prior to activities which may provoke an attack prophylactically

Hemodialysis: Supplemental dose is not necessary

Peritoneal dialysis: Supplemental dose is not necessary

May need to use nitrate-free interval (10-12 hours/day) to avoid tolerance development; gradually decrease dose in patients receiving NTG for prolonged period to avoid withdrawal reaction

Monitoring Parameters Blood pressure, heart rate

Patient Information Go to hospital if no relief after 3 sublingual doses; do not swallow or chew sublingual form; do not change brands without notifying your physician or pharmacist; take oral nitrates on an empty stomach; keep tablets and capsules in original container; keep tightly closed; use spray only when lying down; highly flammable; do not inhale spray; do not chew sustained release products; a treatment-free interval of 8-12 hours is recommended each day; take 3 times/day rather than every 8 hours

Nursing Implications I.V. must be prepared in glass bottles and use special sets intended for nitroglycerin; transdermal patches labeled as mg/hour; do not crush sublingual drug product; NTG infusions should be administered only via a pump that can maintain a constant infusion rate

Dosage Forms

Capsule, sustained release: 2.5 mg, 6.5 mg, 9 mg, 13 mg

Injection: 0.5 mg/mL (10 mL); 0.8 mg/mL (10 mL); 5 mg/mL (1 mL, 5 mL, 10 mL, 20 mL); 10 mg/mL (5 mL, 10 mL)

Injection, solution in D_5W: 25 mg (250 mL); 50 mg (250 mL, 500 mL), 100 mg (250 mL), 200 mg (500 mL)

Ointment, topical (Nitrol®): 2% [20 mg/g] (30 g, 60 g)

Patch, transdermal, topical: Systems designed to deliver 2.5, 5, 7.5, 10, or 15 mg NTG over 24 hours

Spray, translingual: 0.4 mg/metered spray (13.8 g)

Tablet:

Buccal, controlled release: 1 mg, 2 mg, 3 mg

Sublingual (Nitrostat®): 0.3 mg, 0.4 mg, 0.6 mg ━━━

Sustained release: 2.6 mg, 6.5 mg, 9 mg

- ◆ **Nitroglycerol** see Nitroglycerin on page 845
- ◆ **Nitroglyn® Oral** see Nitroglycerin on page 845
- ◆ **Nitrolingual® Translingual Spray** see Nitroglycerin on page 845
- ◆ **Nitrol® Ointment** see Nitroglycerin on page 845
- ◆ **Nitrong® Oral Tablet** see Nitroglycerin on page 845
- ◆ **Nitropress®** see Nitroprusside on this page

Nitroprusside (nye troe PRUS ide)

Related Information

Adrenergic Agonists, Cardiovascular Comparison on page 1290

Adult ACLS Algorithm, Hypotension, Shock on page 1454

Hypertension Therapy on page 1479

U.S. Brand Names Nitropress®

Synonyms Nitroprusside Sodium; Sodium Nitroferricyanide; Sodium Nitroprusside

Therapeutic Category Antihypertensive Agent; Vasodilator

Use Management of hypertensive crises; congestive heart failure; used for controlled hypotension to reduce bleeding during surgery

Pregnancy Risk Factor C

Contraindications Hypersensitivity to nitroprusside or components; decreased cerebral perfusion; arteriovenous shunt or coarctation of the aorta (ie, compensatory hypertension)

Warnings/Precautions Use with caution in patients with increased intracranial pressure (head trauma, cerebral hemorrhage); severe renal impairment, hepatic failure, hypothyroidism; use only as an infusion with 5% dextrose in water; continuously monitor patient's blood pressure; excessive amounts of nitroprusside can cause cyanide toxicity (usually in patients with decreased liver function) or thiocyanate toxicity (usually in patients with decreased renal function, or in patients with normal renal function but prolonged nitroprusside use)

Adverse Reactions

<10%:

Cardiovascular: Excessive hypotensive response, palpitations, substernal distress

Central nervous system: Disorientation, psychosis, headache, restlessness

Endocrine & metabolic: Thyroid suppression

Gastrointestinal: Nausea, vomiting

Neuromuscular & skeletal: Weakness, muscle spasm

Otic: Tinnitus

Respiratory: Hypoxia

Miscellaneous: Diaphoresis, thiocyanate toxicity

<1%: Methemoglobinemia (in high-dose and prolonged infusions)

Overdosage/Toxicology

Symptoms of overdose include hypotension, vomiting, hyperventilation, tachycardia, muscular twitching, hypothyroidism, cyanide or thiocyanate toxicity. Thiocyanate toxicity includes psychosis, hyper-reflexia, confusion, weakness, tinnitus, seizures, and coma; cyanide toxicity includes acidosis (decreased HCO_3, decreased pH, increased lactate), increase in mixed venous blood oxygen tension, tachycardia, altered consciousness, coma, convulsions, and almond smell on breath.

Nitroprusside has been shown to release cyanide in vivo with hemoglobin. Cyanide toxicity does not usually occur because of the rapid uptake of cyanide by erythrocytes and its eventual incorporation into cyanocobalamin. However, prolonged administration of nitroprusside or its reduced elimination can lead to cyanide intoxication. In these situations, airway support with oxygen therapy is germane, followed closely with antidotal therapy of amyl nitrate perles, sodium nitrate 300 mg I.V. (6 mg/kg for children) and sodium thiosulfate 12.5 g I.V. (1.5 mL/kg for children); nitrates should not be administered to neonates and small children. Thiocyanate is dialyzable. May be mixed with sodium thiosulfate in I.V. to prevent cyanide toxicity.

Stability

Nitroprusside sodium should be reconstituted freshly by diluting 50 mg in 250-1000 mL of D_5W

Use only clear solutions; solutions of nitroprusside exhibit a color described as brownish, brown, brownish-pink, light orange, and straw. Solutions are highly sensitive to light. Exposure to light causes decomposition, resulting in a highly colored solution of orange, dark brown or blue. **A blue color indicates almost complete degradation and breakdown to cyanide.**

Solutions should be wrapped with aluminum foil or other opaque material to protect from light (do as soon as possible)

Stability of parenteral admixture at room temperature (25°C) and at refrigeration temperature (4°C): 24 hours

Mechanism of Action Causes peripheral vasodilation by direct action on venous and arteriolar smooth muscle, thus reducing peripheral resistance; will increase cardiac output by decreasing afterload; reduces aortal and left ventricular impedance

(Continued)

Nitroprusside (Continued)

Pharmacodynamics/Kinetics

Onset of hypotensive effect: <2 minutes

Duration: Within 1-10 minutes following discontinuation of therapy, effects cease

Metabolism: Nitroprusside is converted to cyanide ions in the bloodstream; decomposes to prussic acid which in the presence of sulfur donor is converted to thiocyanate (liver and kidney rhodanase systems)

Half-life: Parent drug: <10 minutes; Thiocyanate: 2.7-7 days

Elimination: Thiocyanate renally eliminated

Usual Dosage
Administration requires the use of an infusion pump. Average dose: 5 mcg/kg/minute

Children: Pulmonary hypertension: I.V.: Initial: 1 mcg/kg/minute by continuous I.V. infusion; increase in increments of 1 mcg/kg/minute at intervals of 20-60 minutes; titrating to the desired response; usual dose: 3 mcg/kg/minute, rarely need >4 mcg/kg/minute; maximum: 5 mcg/kg/minute.

Adults: I.V. Initial: 0.3-0.5 mcg/kg/minute; increase in increments of 0.5 mcg/kg/minute, titrating to the desired hemodynamic effect or the appearance of headache or nausea; usual dose: 3 mcg/kg/minute; rarely need >4 mcg/kg/minute; maximum: 10 mcg/kg/minute. When >500 mcg/kg is administered by prolonged infusion of faster than 2 mcg/kg/minute, cyanide is generated faster than an unaided patient can handle.

Administration
I.V. infusion only, not for direct injection

Monitoring Parameters
Blood pressure, heart rate; monitor for cyanide and thiocyanate toxicity; monitor acid-base status as acidosis can be the earliest sign of cyanide toxicity; monitor thiocyanate levels if requiring prolonged infusion (>3 days) or dose ≥4 mcg/kg/minute or patient has renal dysfunction; monitor cyanide blood levels in patients with decreased hepatic function; cardiac monitor and blood pressure monitor required

Reference Range
Monitor thiocyanate levels if requiring prolonged infusion (>4 days) or ≥4 µg/mL/minute; not to exceed 100 µg/mL (or 10 mg/dL) plasma thiocyanate

Thiocyanate:
Therapeutic: 6-29 µg/mL
Toxic: 35-100 µg/mL
Fatal: >200 µg/mL
Cyanide: Normal <0.2 µg/mL; normal (smoker): <0.4 µg/mL
Toxic: >2 µg/mL
Potentially lethal: >3 µg/mL

Nursing Implications
Brownish solution is usable, discard if bluish in color

Dosage Forms
Injection, as sodium: 10 mg/mL (5 mL); 25 mg/mL (2 mL)

- ◆ **Nitroprusside Sodium** see Nitroprusside on previous page
- ◆ **Nitrostat® Sublingual** see Nitroglycerin on page 845
- ◆ **Nitro-Time® Capsules** see Nitroglycerin on page 845
- ◆ **Nix™ Creme Rinse** see Permethrin on page 908

Nizatidine (ni ZA ti deen)

U.S. Brand Names Axid® AR [OTC]; Axid®

Canadian Brand Names Apo®-Nizatidine

Therapeutic Category Antihistamine, H_2 Blocker; Histamine H_2 Antagonist

Use Treatment and maintenance of duodenal ulcer; treatment of gastroesophageal reflux disease (GERD); OTC tablet used for the prevention of meal-induced heartburn, acid indigestion, and sour stomach

Pregnancy Risk Factor C

Contraindications Hypersensitivity to nizatidine or any component of the preparation; hypersensitivity to other H_2-antagonists since a cross-sensitivity has been observed with this class of drugs

Warnings/Precautions Use with caution in children <12 years of age; use with caution in patients with liver and renal impairment; dosage modification required in patients with renal impairment

Adverse Reactions

1% to 10%:
Central nervous system: Dizziness, headache
Gastrointestinal: Constipation, diarrhea
<1%: Bradycardia, tachycardia, palpitations, hypertension, fever, fatigue, seizures, insomnia, drowsiness, acne, pruritus, urticaria, dry skin, abdominal discomfort, flatulence, belching, anorexia, agranulocytosis, neutropenia, thrombocytopenia, increased AST/ALT, paresthesia, weakness, increased BUN/creatinine, proteinuria, bronchospasm, allergic reaction

Overdosage/Toxicology

Symptoms of overdose include muscular tremors, vomiting, rapid respiration

LD_{50} ~80 mg/kg; treatment is primarily symptomatic and supportive

Mechanism of Action Nizatidine is an H_2-receptor antagonist. In healthy volunteers, nizatidine has been effective in suppressing gastric acid secretion induced by pentagastrin infusion or food. Nizatidine reduces gastric acid secretion by 29.4% to 78.4%. This compares with a 60.3% reduction by cimetidine. Nizatidine 100 mg is reported to provide equivalent acid suppression as cimetidine 300 mg.

Usual Dosage Adults: Oral:
Active duodenal ulcer:
Treatment: 300 mg at bedtime or 150 mg twice daily

Maintenance: 150 mg/day

Meal-induced heartburn, acid indigestion, and sour stomach:
   75 mg tablet [OTC] twice daily, 30 to 60 minutes prior to consuming food or beverages

Dosing adjustment in renal impairment:
   Cl_{cr} 50-80 mL/minute: Administer 75% of normal dose
   Cl_{cr} 10-50 mL/minute: Administer 50% of normal dose or 150 mg/day for active treatment and 150 mg every other day for maintenance treatment
   Cl_{cr} <10 mL/minute: Administer 25% of normal dose or 150 mg every other day for treatment and 150 mg every 3 days for maintenance treatment

Test Interactions False-positive urine protein using Multistix®, gastric acid secretion test, skin tests allergen extracts, serum creatinine and serum transaminase concentrations, urine protein test

Patient Information May take several days before medication begins to relieve stomach pain; antacids may be taken with nizatidine unless physician has instructed you not to use them; wait 30-60 minutes between taking the antacid and nizatidine; avoid aspirin, cough and cold preparations; avoid use of black pepper, caffeine, alcohol, and harsh spices; may cause drowsiness or impair coordination and judgment

Nursing Implications Giving dose at 6 PM may better suppress nocturnal acid secretion than 10 PM

Dosage Forms
   Capsule: 150 mg, 300 mg
   Tablet [OTC]: 75 mg

+ **Nizoral®** *see* Ketoconazole *on page 649*
+ **N-Methylhydrazine** *see* Procarbazine *on page 972*
+ **Nobesine®** *see* Diethylpropion *on page 354*
+ **Nolamine®** *see* Chlorpheniramine, Phenindamine, and Phenylpropanolamine *on page 246*
+ **Nolvadex®** *see* Tamoxifen *on page 1106*
+ **Nonsteroidal Anti-Inflammatory Agents Comparison** *see page 1335*
+ **Noradrenaline** *see* Norepinephrine *on this page*
+ **Noradrenaline Acid Tartrate** *see* Norepinephrine *on this page*
+ **Norcet®** *see* Hydrocodone and Acetaminophen *on page 575*
+ **Norcuron®** *see* Vecuronium *on page 1212*
+ **Nordeoxyguanosine** *see* Ganciclovir *on page 529*
+ **Nordette®** *see* Ethinyl Estradiol and Levonorgestrel *on page 449*
+ **Norditropin® Injection** *see* Human Growth Hormone *on page 569*
+ **Nordryl® Injection** *see* Diphenhydramine *on page 369*
+ **Nordryl® Oral** *see* Diphenhydramine *on page 369*

Norepinephrine (nor ep i NEF rin)

Related Information
   Adrenergic Agonists, Cardiovascular Comparison *on page 1290*
   Adult ACLS Algorithm, Hypotension, Shock *on page 1454*
   Extravasation Treatment of Other Drugs *on page 1287*

U.S. Brand Names Levophed® Injection

Synonyms Levarterenol Bitartrate; Noradrenaline; Noradrenaline Acid Tartrate; Norepinephrine Bitartrate

Therapeutic Category Adrenergic Agonist Agent; Sympathomimetic

Use Treatment of shock which persists after adequate fluid volume replacement

Pregnancy Risk Factor D

Contraindications Hypersensitivity to norepinephrine or sulfites

Warnings/Precautions Blood/volume depletion should be corrected, if possible, before norepinephrine therapy; extravasation may cause severe tissue necrosis, administer into a large vein. The drug should not be given to patients with peripheral or mesenteric vascular thrombosis because ischemia may be increased and the area of infarct extended; use with caution during cyclopropane and halothane anesthesia; use with caution in patients with occlusive vascular disease; some products may contain sulfites

Adverse Reactions
   1% to 10%:
      Central nervous system: Dizziness, anxiety, headache, insomnia
      Endocrine & metabolic: Thyroid gland enlargement
      Neuromuscular & skeletal: Trembling
   <1%: Cardiac arrhythmias, palpitations, bradycardia, tachycardia, hypertension, chest pain, pallor, gangrene of extremities, vomiting, uterine contractions, sloughing at the infusion site, photophobia, respiratory distress, diaphoresis

Overdosage/Toxicology
   Symptoms of overdose include hypertension, sweating, cerebral hemorrhage, convulsions
   Treatment of extravasation: Infiltrate area of extravasation with phentolamine 5-10 mg in 10-15 mL of saline solution

Drug Interactions
   Increased effect with tricyclic antidepressants, MAO inhibitors, antihistamines (diphenhydramine, tripelennamine), guanethidine, ergot alkaloids, and methyldopa
   Atropine sulfate may block the reflex bradycardia caused by norepinephrine and enhances the pressor response
   (Continued)

Norepinephrine *(Continued)*

Stability Readily oxidized, protect from light, do not use if brown coloration; dilute with D_5W or DS/NS, but not recommended to dilute in normal saline; not stable with alkaline solutions; stability of parenteral admixture at room temperature (25°C): 24 hours

Mechanism of Action Stimulates beta₁-adrenergic receptors and alpha-adrenergic receptors causing increased contractility and heart rate as well as vasoconstriction, thereby increasing systemic blood pressure and coronary blood flow; clinically alpha effects (vasoconstriction) are greater than beta effects (inotropic and chronotropic effects)

Pharmacodynamics/Kinetics
Onset of action: I.V.: Very rapid-acting
Duration: Limited
Metabolism: By catechol-o-methyltransferase (COMT) and monoamine oxidase (MAO)
Elimination: In urine (84% to 96% as inactive metabolites)

Usual Dosage Administration requires the use of an infusion pump!
Note: Norepinephrine dosage is stated in terms of norepinephrine base and intravenous formulation is norepinephrine bitartrate
Norepinephrine bitartrate 2 mg = Norepinephrine base 1 mg
Continuous I.V. infusion:
Children: Initial: 0.05-0.1 mcg/kg/minute; titrate to desired effect; maximum dose: 1-2 mcg/kg/minute
Adults: Initial: 4 mcg/minute and titrate to desired response; 8-12 mcg/minute is usual range; ACLS dosing range: 0.5-30 mcg/minute

Administration Administer into large vein to avoid the potential for extravasation; potent drug, must be diluted prior to use. Rate (mL/hour) = dose (mcg/kg/minute) x weight (kg) x 60 minutes/hour divided by concentration (mcg/mL)

To prepare for infusion:

$$\frac{6 \times weight\ (kg) \times desired\ dose\ (mcg/kg/min)}{I.V.\ infusion\ rate\ (mL/h)} = \begin{array}{l} mg\ of\ drug\ to\ be\ added\ to \\ 100\ mL\ of\ I.V.\ fluid \end{array}$$

"Rule of 6" method for infusion preparation:
Simplified equation: 0.6 x weight (kg) = amount (mg) of drug to be added to 100 mL of I.V. fluid
When infused at 1 mL/hour, then it will deliver the drug at a rate of 0.1 mcg/kg/minute
Complex equation: 6 x desired dose (mcg/kg/minute) x body weight (kg) divided by desired rate (mL/hour) is the mg added to make 100 mL of solution

Nursing Implications Central line administration required; do not administer $NaHCO_3$ through an I.V. line containing norepinephrine; administer into large vein to avoid the potential for extravasation; potent drug, must be diluted prior to use

Extravasation: Use phentolamine as antidote; mix 5 mg with 9 mL of NS; inject a small amount of this dilution into extravasated area; blanching should reverse immediately. Monitor site; if blanching should recur, additional injections of phentolamine may be needed.

Dosage Forms Injection, as bitartrate: 1 mg/mL (4 mL)

♦ **Norepinephrine Bitartrate** *see Norepinephrine on previous page*
♦ **Norethin™ 1/35E** *see Ethinyl Estradiol and Norethindrone on page 451*
♦ **Norethin™ 1/50M** *see Mestranol and Norethindrone on page 737*
♦ **Norethindrone Acetate and Ethinyl Estradiol** *see Ethinyl Estradiol and Norethindrone on page 451*
♦ **Norethindrone and Mestranol** *see Mestranol and Norethindrone on page 737*
♦ **Norflex™** *see Orphenadrine on page 867*

Norfloxacin *(nor FLOKS a sin)*

U.S. Brand Names Chibroxin™ Ophthalmic; Noroxin® Oral
Therapeutic Category Antibiotic, Ophthalmic; Antibiotic, Quinolone
Use Uncomplicated urinary tract infections and cystitis caused by susceptible gram-negative and gram-positive bacteria; sexually transmitted disease (eg, uncomplicated urethral and cervical gonorrhea) caused by *N. gonorrhoeae*; prostatitis due to *E. coli*; ophthalmic solution for conjunctivitis
Pregnancy Risk Factor C
Contraindications Known hypersensitivity to quinolones
Warnings/Precautions Not recommended in children <18 years of age; other quinolones have caused transient arthropathy in children; CNS stimulation may occur which may lead to tremor, restlessness, confusion, and very rarely to hallucinations or convulsive seizures; use with caution in patients with known or suspected CNS disorders; has rarely caused ruptured tendons (discontinue immediately with signs of inflammation or tendon pain)
Adverse Reactions
1% to 10%:
Central nervous system: Headache (2.7%), dizziness (1.8%), fatigue
Gastrointestinal: Nausea (2.8%)
<1%: Somnolence, depression, insomnia, fever, pruritus, hyperhidrosis, erythema, rash, abdominal pain, dyspepsia, constipation, flatulence, heartburn, xerostomia, diarrhea, vomiting, loose stools, anorexia, bitter taste, GI bleeding, increased liver enzymes, back pain, ruptured tendons, weakness, increased serum creatinine/BUN, acute renal failure

Overdosage/Toxicology
Symptoms of overdose include acute renal failure, seizures
Following GI decontamination, use supportive measures
Drug Interactions CYP1A2 and 3A3/4 enzyme inhibitor
Decreased effect: Decreased absorption with antacids containing aluminum, magnesium, and/or calcium (by up to 98% if given at the same time); decreased serum levels of fluoroquinolones by antineoplastics; nitrofurantoin may antagonize effects of norfloxacin; phenytoin serum levels may be decreased by fluoroquinolones
Increased toxicity/serum levels: Quinolones cause increased levels or toxicity of digoxin, caffeine, warfarin, cyclosporine, and possibly theophylline. Cimetidine and probenecid increase quinolone levels.
Mechanism of Action Norfloxacin is a DNA gyrase inhibitor. DNA gyrase is an essential bacterial enzyme that maintains the superhelical structure of DNA. DNA gyrase is required for DNA replication and transcription, DNA repair, recombination, and transposition; bactericidal
Pharmacodynamics/Kinetics
Absorption: Oral: Rapid, up to 40%
Distribution: Crosses the placenta; small amounts appear in breast milk
Protein binding: 15%
Metabolism: In the liver
Half-life: 4.8 hours (can be higher with reduced glomerular filtration rates)
Time to peak serum concentration: Within 1-2 hours
Elimination: In urine and feces (30%)
Usual Dosage
Ophthalmic: Children >1 year and Adults: Instill 1-2 drops in affected eye(s) 4 times/day for up to 7 days
Oral: Adults:
Urinary tract infections: 400 mg twice daily for 3-21 days depending on severity of infection or organism sensitivity; maximum: 800 mg/day
Uncomplicated gonorrhea: 800 mg as a single dose (CDC recommends as an alternative regimen to ciprofloxacin or ofloxacin)
Prostatitis: 400 mg every 12 hours for 4 weeks
Dosing interval in renal impairment:
Cl_{cr} 10-30 mL/minute: Administer every 24 hours
Cl_{cr} <10 mL/minute: Do not use
Patient Information Tablets should be taken at least 1 hour before or at least 2 hours after a meal with a glass of water; patients receiving norfloxacin should be well hydrated; take all the medication, do not skip doses; do not take with antacids; contact your physician immediately with inflammation or tendon pain
Nursing Implications Hold antacids, sucralfate for 3-4 hours after giving
Dosage Forms
Solution, ophthalmic: 0.3% [3 mg/mL] (5 mL)
Tablet: 400 mg

♦ **Norgesic™** see Orphenadrine, Aspirin, and Caffeine on page 868

♦ **Norgesic™ Forte** see Orphenadrine, Aspirin, and Caffeine on page 868

♦ **Norgestimate and Ethinyl Estradiol** see Ethinyl Estradiol and Norgestimate on page 453

Norgestrel (nor JES trel)
U.S. Brand Names Ovrette®
Therapeutic Category Contraceptive, Oral (Progestin); Progestin
Use Prevention of pregnancy; **progestin only products have higher risk of failure in contraceptive use**
Pregnancy Risk Factor X
Contraindications Known hypersensitivity to norgestrel; thromboembolic disorders, severe hepatic disease, breast cancer, undiagnosed vaginal bleeding, pregnancy
Warnings/Precautions Discontinue if sudden loss of vision or if diplopia or proptosis occur; use with caution in patients with a history of mental depression; use of any progestin during the first 4 months of pregnancy is not recommended
Adverse Reactions
>10%:
Cardiovascular: Edema
Endocrine & metabolic: Breakthrough bleeding, spotting, changes in menstrual flow, amenorrhea
Gastrointestinal: Anorexia
Neuromuscular & skeletal: Weakness
1% to 10%:
Cardiovascular: Embolism, central thrombosis
Central nervous system: Mental depression, fever, insomnia
Dermatologic: Melasma or chloasma, allergic rash with or without pruritus
Endocrine & metabolic: Changes in cervical erosion and secretions, increased breast tenderness
Gastrointestinal: Weight gain or loss
Hepatic: Cholestatic jaundice
Local: Thrombophlebitis
Overdosage/Toxicology
Toxicity is unlikely following single exposures of excessive doses
Supportive treatment is adequate in most cases
(Continued)

Norgestrel *(Continued)*

Drug Interactions Decreased effect: Aminoglutethimide may decrease effects by increasing hepatic metabolism

Mechanism of Action Inhibits secretion of pituitary gonadotropin (LH) which prevents follicular maturation and ovulation

Pharmacodynamics/Kinetics
Absorption: Oral: Readily absorbed
Protein binding: >90%
Metabolism: Primarily hepatic
Half-life: ~20 hours

Usual Dosage Administer daily, starting the first day of menstruation, take 1 tablet at the same time each day, every day of the year. If one dose is missed, take as soon as remembered, then next tablet at regular time; if two doses are missed, take 1 tablet and discard the other, then take daily at usual time; if three doses are missed, use an additional form of birth control until menses or pregnancy is ruled out.

Test Interactions Thyroid function tests, metyrapone test, liver function tests

Patient Information Take this medicine only as directed; do not take more of it and do not take it for a longer period of time; if you suspect you may have become pregnant, stop taking this medicine; report any loss of vision or vision changes immediately; avoid excessive exposure to sunlight

Nursing Implications Patients should receive a copy of the patient labeling

Dosage Forms Tablet: 0.075 mg

◆ **Norgestrel and Ethinyl Estradiol** *see* Ethinyl Estradiol and Norgestrel *on page 454*

◆ **Norinyl® 1+35** *see* Ethinyl Estradiol and Norethindrone *on page 451*

◆ **Norinyl® 1+50** *see* Mestranol and Norethindrone *on page 737*

◆ **Norisodrine®** *see* Isoproterenol *on page 635*

◆ **Noritate® Cream** *see* Metronidazole *on page 770*

◆ **Normal Human Serum Albumin** *see* Albumin *on page 34*

◆ **Normal Saline** *see* Sodium Chloride *on page 1067*

◆ **Normal Serum Albumin (Human)** *see* Albumin *on page 34*

◆ **Normiflo®** *see* Ardeparin *on page 96*

◆ **Normodyne®** *see* Labetalol *on page 653*

◆ **Noroxin® Oral** *see* Norfloxacin *on page 850*

◆ **Norpace®** *see* Disopyramide *on page 379*

◆ **Norplant® Implant** *see* Levonorgestrel *on page 675*

◆ **Norpramin®** *see* Desipramine *on page 333*

◆ **Nor-tet® Oral** *see* Tetracycline *on page 1122*

Nortriptyline *(nor TRIP ti leen)*

Related Information
Antidepressant Agents Comparison *on page 1301*

U.S. Brand Names Aventyl® Hydrochloride; Pamelor®

Canadian Brand Names Apo®-Nortriptyline

Synonyms Nortriptyline Hydrochloride

Therapeutic Category Antidepressant, Tricyclic

Use Treatment of various forms of depression, often in conjunction with psychotherapy. Maximum antidepressant effect may not be seen for 2 or more weeks after initiation of therapy; has also demonstrated effectiveness for chronic pain.

Pregnancy Risk Factor D

Contraindications Narrow-angle glaucoma, avoid use during pregnancy and lactation, hypersensitivity to tricyclic antidepressants

Warnings/Precautions Use with caution in patients with cardiac conduction disturbances, history of hyperthyroid; should not be abruptly discontinued in patients receiving high doses for prolonged periods; use with caution with renal or hepatic impairment

Adverse Reactions
>10%:
Central nervous system: Dizziness, drowsiness, headache
Gastrointestinal: Xerostomia, constipation, increased appetite, nausea, unpleasant taste, weight gain
Neuromuscular & skeletal: Weakness
1% to 10%:
Cardiovascular: Postural hypotension, arrhythmias, tachycardia, sudden death
Central nervous system: Confusion, delirium, hallucinations, nervousness, restlessness, parkinsonian syndrome, insomnia
Endocrine & metabolic: Sexual dysfunction
Gastrointestinal: Diarrhea, heartburn, constipation
Genitourinary: Dysuria, urinary retention
Ocular: Blurred vision, eye pain, increased intraocular pressure
Neuromuscular & skeletal: Fine muscle tremors
Miscellaneous: Diaphoresis (excessive)
<1%: Anxiety, seizures, alopecia, photosensitivity, breast enlargement, galactorrhea, SIADH, trouble with gums, decreased lower esophageal sphincter tone may cause GE reflux, testicular edema, leukopenia, rarely agranulocytosis, eosinophilia, increased liver enzymes, cholestatic jaundice, increased intraocular pressure, tinnitus, allergic reactions

Overdosage/Toxicology

Symptoms of overdose include agitation, confusion, hallucinations, urinary retention, hypothermia, hypotension, seizures, ventricular tachycardia

Following initiation of essential overdose management, toxic symptoms should be treated. Sodium bicarbonate is indicated when QRS interval is >0.10 seconds or QT_c >0.42 seconds. Ventricular arrhythmias and EKG changes (QRS widening) often respond to phenytoin 15-20 mg/kg (adults) with concurrent systemic alkalinization (sodium bicarbonate 0.5-2 mEq/kg I.V.). Arrhythmias unresponsive to this therapy may respond to lidocaine 1 mg/kg I.V. followed by a titrated infusion. Physostigmine (1-2 mg I.V. slowly for adults or 0.5 mg I.V. slowly for children) may be indicated in reversing cardiac arrhythmias that are life-threatening. Seizures usually respond to diazepam I.V. boluses (5-10 mg for adults up to 30 mg or 0.25-0.4 mg/kg/dose for children up to 10 mg/dose). If seizures are unresponsive or recur, phenytoin or phenobarbital may be required.

Drug Interactions CYP1A2 and 2D6 enzyme substrate

Blocks the uptake of guanethidine and thus prevents the hypotensive effect of guanethidine; may be additive with or may potentiate the action of other CNS depressants such as sedatives or hypnotics; potentiates the pressor and cardiac effects of sympathomimetic agents such as isoproterenol, epinephrine, etc

With MAO inhibitors, hyperpyrexia, hypertension, tachycardia, confusion, seizures, and death have been reported

Additive anticholinergic effect seen with other anticholinergic agents

Cimetidine reduces the metabolism of nortriptyline

May increase prothrombin time in patients stabilized on warfarin

Stability Protect from light

Mechanism of Action Traditionally believed to increase the synaptic concentration of serotonin and/or norepinephrine in the central nervous system by inhibition of their reuptake by the presynaptic neuronal membrane. However, additional receptor effects have been found including desensitization of adenyl cyclase, down regulation of beta-adrenergic receptors, and down regulation of serotonin receptors.

Pharmacodynamics/Kinetics

Onset of action: 1-3 weeks before therapeutic effects are seen

Distribution: V_d: 21 L/kg

Protein binding: 93% to 95%

Metabolism: Undergoes significant first-pass metabolism; primarily detoxified in the liver

Half-life: 28-31 hours

Time to peak serum concentration: Oral: Within 7-8.5 hours

Elimination: As metabolites and small amounts of unchanged drug in urine; small amounts of biliary elimination occur

Usual Dosage Oral:

Nocturnal enuresis:

Children:

6-7 years (20-25 kg): 10 mg/day

8-11 years (25-35 kg): 10-20 mg/day

>11 years (35-54 kg): 25-35 mg/day

Depression:

Adolescents: 30-50 mg/day in divided doses

Adults: 25 mg 3-4 times/day up to 150 mg/day

Elderly:

Initial: 10-25 mg at bedtime

Dosage can be increased by 25 mg every 3 days for inpatients and weekly for outpatients if tolerated

Usual maintenance dose: 75 mg as a single bedtime dose, however, lower or higher doses may be required to stay within the therapeutic window

Dosing adjustment in hepatic impairment: Lower doses and slower titration dependent on individualization of dosage is recommended

Dietary Considerations Alcohol: Additive CNS effect, avoid use

Monitoring Parameters Monitor blood pressure and pulse rate prior to and during initial therapy; evaluate mental status; monitor weight

Reference Range

Plasma levels do not always correlate with clinical effectiveness

Therapeutic: 50-150 ng/mL (SI: 190-570 nmol/L)

Toxic: >500 ng/mL (SI: >1900 nmol/L)

Test Interactions ↑ glucose

Patient Information Avoid alcohol ingestion; do not discontinue medication abruptly; may cause urine to turn blue-green; may cause drowsiness; full effect may not occur for 3-6 weeks; dry mouth may be helped by sips of water, sugarless gum, or hard candy

Nursing Implications May increase appetite and possibly a craving for sweets

Dosage Forms

Capsule, as hydrochloride: 10 mg, 25 mg, 50 mg, 75 mg

Solution, as hydrochloride: 10 mg/5 mL (473 mL)

- **Novambarb**® *see* Amobarbital *on page 67*
- **Novamoxin**® *see* Amoxicillin *on page 69*
- **Novantrone**® *see* Mitoxantrone *on page 788*
- **Nova Rectal**® *see* Pentobarbital *on page 902*
- **Novasen** *see* Aspirin *on page 102*
- **Novo-Alprazol** *see* Alprazolam *on page 45*
- **Novo-Atenol** *see* Atenolol *on page 106*
- **Novo-AZT** *see* Zidovudine *on page 1235*
- **Novo-Butamide** *see* Tolbutamide *on page 1155*
- **Novocain**® **Injection** *see* Procaine *on page 971*
- **Novo-Captopril** *see* Captopril *on page 185*
- **Novo-Carbamaz** *see* Carbamazepine *on page 188*
- **Novo-Chlorhydrate** *see* Chloral Hydrate *on page 235*
- **Novo-Chlorpromazine** *see* Chlorpromazine *on page 248*
- **Novo-Cimetine** *see* Cimetidine *on page 261*
- **Novo-Clobetasol** *see* Clobetasol *on page 277*
- **Novo-Clonidine** *see* Clonidine *on page 283*
- **Novo-Clopate** *see* Clorazepate *on page 286*
- **Novo-Cloxin** *see* Cloxacillin *on page 288*
- **Novo-Cromolyn** *see* Cromolyn Sodium *on page 300*
- **Novo-Cycloprine** *see* Cyclobenzaprine *on page 304*
- **Novo-Difenac**® *see* Diclofenac *on page 348*
- **Novo-Difenac**®**-SR** *see* Diclofenac *on page 348*
- **Novo-Diflunisal** *see* Diflunisal *on page 356*
- **Novo-Digoxin** *see* Digoxin *on page 359*
- **Novo-Diltazem** *see* Diltiazem *on page 365*
- **Novo-Dipam** *see* Diazepam *on page 345*
- **Novo-Dipiradol** *see* Dipyridamole *on page 377*
- **Novo-Doxepin** *see* Doxepin *on page 392*
- **Novo-Doxylin** *see* Doxycycline *on page 397*
- **Novo-Famotidine** *see* Famotidine *on page 469*
- **Novo-Fibrate** *see* Clofibrate *on page 279*
- **Novo-Flupam** *see* Flurazepam *on page 506*
- **Novo-Flurprofen** *see* Flurbiprofen *on page 507*
- **Novo-Flutamide** *see* Flutamide *on page 508*
- **Novo-Folacid** *see* Folic Acid *on page 512*
- **Novo-Furan** *see* Nitrofurantoin *on page 843*
- **Novo-Gesic-C8** *see* Acetaminophen and Codeine *on page 21*
- **Novo-Gesic-C15** *see* Acetaminophen and Codeine *on page 21*
- **Novo-Gesic-C30** *see* Acetaminophen and Codeine *on page 21*
- **Novo-Glyburide** *see* Glyburide *on page 540*
- **Novo-Hexidyl** *see* Trihexyphenidyl *on page 1182*
- **Novo-Hydrazide** *see* Hydrochlorothiazide *on page 574*
- **Novo-Hydroxyzin** *see* Hydroxyzine *on page 589*
- **Novo-Hylazin** *see* Hydralazine *on page 572*
- **Novo-Keto-EC** *see* Ketoprofen *on page 650*
- **Novo-Lexin** *see* Cephalexin *on page 228*
- **Novolin**® **70/30** *see* Insulin Preparations *on page 613*
- **Novolin**® **L** *see* Insulin Preparations *on page 613*
- **Novolin**® **N** *see* Insulin Preparations *on page 613*
- **Novolin**® **R** *see* Insulin Preparations *on page 613*
- **Novo-Lorazepam** *see* Lorazepam *on page 694*
- **Novo-Medopa**® *see* Methyldopa *on page 758*
- **Novo-Medrone** *see* Medroxyprogesterone Acetate *on page 721*
- **Novo-Mepro** *see* Meprobamate *on page 731*
- **Novo-Metformin** *see* Metformin *on page 741*
- **Novo-Methacin** *see* Indomethacin *on page 609*
- **Novo-Metoprolol** *see* Metoprolol *on page 768*
- **Novo-Mucilax** *see* Psyllium *on page 994*
- **Novo-Naprox** *see* Naproxen *on page 818*
- **Novo-Nidazol** *see* Metronidazole *on page 770*
- **Novo-Nifedin** *see* Nifedipine *on page 838*
- **Novo-Oxazepam** *see* Oxazepam *on page 872*
- **Novo-Pen-VK**® *see* Penicillin V Potassium *on page 898*
- **Novo-Pindol** *see* Pindolol *on page 929*
- **Novo-Piroxicam** *see* Piroxicam *on page 935*
- **Novo-Poxide** *see* Chlordiazepoxide *on page 239*
- **Novo-Pramine** *see* Imipramine *on page 601*
- **Novo-Prazin** *see* Prazosin *on page 959*
- **Novo-Prednisolone** *see* Prednisolone *on page 961*

- **Novo-Prednisone** see Prednisone on page 963
- **Novo-Profen**® see Ibuprofen on page 593
- **Novo-Propamide** see Chlorpropamide on page 250
- **Novo-Propoxyn** see Propoxyphene on page 985
- **Novo-Purol** see Allopurinol on page 44
- **Novo-Pyrazone** see Sulfinpyrazone on page 1096
- **Novo-Ranidine** see Ranitidine Hydrochloride on page 1011
- **Novo-Reserpine** see Reserpine on page 1016
- **Novo-Ridazine** see Thioridazine on page 1135
- **Novo-Rythro Encap** see Erythromycin on page 427
- **Novo-Salmol** see Albuterol on page 35
- **Novo-Secobarb** see Secobarbital on page 1053
- **Novo-Selegiline** see Selegiline on page 1053
- **Novo-Semide** see Furosemide on page 525
- **Novo-Seven**® see Factor VIIa, Recombinant on page 467
- **Novo-Soxazole** see Sulfisoxazole on page 1097
- **Novo-Spiroton** see Spironolactone on page 1078
- **Novo-Sucralate** see Sucralfate on page 1088
- **Novo-Sundac** see Sulindac on page 1099
- **Novo-Tamoxifen** see Tamoxifen on page 1106
- **Novo-Tetra** see Tetracycline on page 1122
- **Novo-Thalidone** see Chlorthalidone on page 251
- **Novo-Timol** see Timolol on page 1146
- **Novo-Tolmetin** see Tolmetin on page 1158
- **Novo-Triamzide** see Hydrochlorothiazide and Triamterene on page 575
- **Novo-Trimel** see Co-Trimoxazole on page 299
- **Novo-Triolam** see Triazolam on page 1178
- **Novo-Tripramine** see Trimipramine on page 1186
- **Novo-Tryptin** see Amitriptyline on page 62
- **Novo-Veramil** see Verapamil on page 1214
- **Novo-Zolamide** see Acetazolamide on page 22
- **NP-27**® [OTC] see Tolnaftate on page 1159
- **NPH Iletin**® I see Insulin Preparations on page 613
- **NPH Insulin** see Insulin Preparations on page 613
- **NPH-N** see Insulin Preparations on page 613
- **NSC 125066** see Bleomycin on page 149
- **NTG** see Nitroglycerin on page 845
- **Nu-Alprax** see Alprazolam on page 45
- **Nu-Amoxi** see Amoxicillin on page 69
- **Nu-Ampi Trihydrate** see Ampicillin on page 79
- **Nu-Atenol** see Atenolol on page 106
- **Nubain**® see Nalbuphine on page 811
- **Nu-Capto** see Captopril on page 185
- **Nu-Carbamazepine** see Carbamazepine on page 188
- **Nu-Cephalex** see Cephalexin on page 228
- **Nu-Cimet** see Cimetidine on page 261
- **Nu-Clonidine** see Clonidine on page 283
- **Nu-Cloxi** see Cloxacillin on page 288
- **Nucofed**® see Guaifenesin, Pseudoephedrine, and Codeine on page 551
- **Nucofed**® **Pediatric Expectorant** see Guaifenesin, Pseudoephedrine, and Codeine on page 551
- **Nu-Cotrimox** see Co-Trimoxazole on page 299
- **Nucotuss**® see Guaifenesin, Pseudoephedrine, and Codeine on page 551
- **Nu-Diclo** see Diclofenac on page 348
- **Nu-Diflunisal** see Diflunisal on page 356
- **Nu-Diltiaz** see Diltiazem on page 365
- **Nu-Doxycycline** see Doxycycline on page 397
- **Nu-Famotidine** see Famotidine on page 469
- **Nu-Flurprofen** see Flurbiprofen on page 507
- **Nu-Gemfibrozil** see Gemfibrozil on page 532
- **Nu-Glyburide** see Glyburide on page 540
- **Nu-Hydral** see Hydralazine on page 572
- **Nu-Ibuprofen** see Ibuprofen on page 593
- **Nu-Indo** see Indomethacin on page 609
- **Nu-Ketoprofen** see Ketoprofen on page 650
- **Nu-Ketoprofen-E** see Ketoprofen on page 650
- **Nu-Loraz** see Lorazepam on page 694
- **NuLytely**® see Polyethylene Glycol-Electrolyte Solution on page 942
- **Nu-Medopa** see Methyldopa on page 758
- **Nu-Metop** see Metoprolol on page 768

- **Numorphan®** *see* Oxymorphone *on page 877*
- **Numzitdent®** **[OTC]** *see* Benzocaine *on page 133*
- **Numzit Teething®** **[OTC]** *see* Benzocaine *on page 133*
- **Nu-Naprox** *see* Naproxen *on page 818*
- **Nu-Nifedin** *see* Nifedipine *on page 838*
- **Nu-Pen-VK** *see* Penicillin V Potassium *on page 898*
- **Nu-Pindol** *see* Pindolol *on page 929*
- **Nu-Pirox** *see* Piroxicam *on page 935*
- **Nu-Prazo** *see* Prazosin *on page 959*
- **Nuprin®** **[OTC]** *see* Ibuprofen *on page 593*
- **Nu-Prochlor** *see* Prochlorperazine *on page 973*
- **Nu-Propranolol** *see* Propranolol *on page 986*
- **Nuquin HP®** *see* Hydroquinone *on page 584*
- **Nu-Ranit** *see* Ranitidine Hydrochloride *on page 1011*
- **Nuromax® Injection** *see* Doxacurium *on page 390*
- **Nu-Sulfinpyrazone** *see* Sulfinpyrazone *on page 1096*
- **Nu-Tetra** *see* Tetracycline *on page 1122*
- **Nu-Timolol** *see* Timolol *on page 1146*
- **Nutracort®** *see* Hydrocortisone *on page 579*
- **Nutraplus® Topical [OTC]** *see* Urea *on page 1199*
- **Nu-Triazide** *see* Hydrochlorothiazide and Triamterene *on page 575*
- **Nu-Triazo** *see* Triazolam *on page 1178*
- **Nutrilipid®** *see* Fat Emulsion *on page 469*
- **Nu-Trimipramine** *see* Trimipramine *on page 1186*
- **Nutropin® AQ Injection** *see* Human Growth Hormone *on page 569*
- **Nutropin® Injection** *see* Human Growth Hormone *on page 569*
- **Nu-Verap** *see* Verapamil *on page 1214*
- **Nyaderm** *see* Nystatin *on this page*
- **Nydrazid®** *see* Isoniazid *on page 633*

Nystatin (nye STAT in)

Related Information
Antifungal Agents Comparison *on page 1303*
Guidelines for the Prevention of Opportunistic Infections in Persons with HIV *on page 1388*

U.S. Brand Names Mycostatin®; Nilstat®; Nystat-Rx®; Nystex®; O-V Staticin®

Canadian Brand Names Mestatin®; Nadostine®; Nyaderm; PMS-Nystatin

Therapeutic Category Antifungal Agent, Oral Nonabsorbed; Antifungal Agent, Topical; Antifungal Agent, Vaginal

Use Treatment of susceptible cutaneous, mucocutaneous, and oral cavity fungal infections normally caused by the *Candida* species

Pregnancy Risk Factor B/C (oral)

Contraindications Hypersensitivity to nystatin or any component

Adverse Reactions
Percentage unknown: Contact dermatitis, Stevens-Johnson syndrome
1% to 10%: Gastrointestinal: Nausea, vomiting, diarrhea, stomach pain
<1%: Hypersensitivity reactions

Overdosage/Toxicology
Symptoms of overdose include nausea, vomiting, diarrhea
Treatment is supportive

Stability Keep vaginal inserts in refrigerator; protect from temperature extremes, moisture, and light

Mechanism of Action Binds to sterols in fungal cell membrane, changing the cell wall permeability allowing for leakage of cellular contents

Pharmacodynamics/Kinetics
Absorption: Not absorbed through mucous membranes or intact skin; poorly absorbed from the GI tract
Elimination: In feces as unchanged drug

Usual Dosage
Oral candidiasis:
Suspension (swish and swallow orally):
Premature infants: 100,000 units 4 times/day
Infants: 200,000 units 4 times/day or 100,000 units to each side of mouth 4 times/day
Children and Adults: 400,000-600,000 units 4 times/day
Troche: Children and Adults: 200,000-400,000 units 4-5 times/day
Powder for compounding: Children and Adults: 1/8 teaspoon (500,000 units) to equal approximately 1/2 cup of water; give 4 times/day
Mucocutaneous infections: Children and Adults: Topical: Apply 2-3 times/day to affected areas; very moist topical lesions are treated best with powder
Intestinal infections: Adults: Oral tablets: 500,000-1,000,000 units every 8 hours
Vaginal infections: Adults: Vaginal tablets: Insert 1 tablet/day at bedtime for 2 weeks

Patient Information The oral suspension should be swished about the mouth and retained in the mouth for as long as possible (several minutes) before swallowing. For neonates and infants, paint nystatin suspension into recesses of the mouth. Troches must be allowed to dissolve slowly and should not be chewed or swallowed whole. If topical irritation occurs, discontinue; for external use only; do not discontinue therapy even if symptoms are gone

Dosage Forms
Cream: 100,000 units/g (15 g, 30 g)
Ointment, topical: 100,000 units/g (15 g, 30 g)
Powder, for preparation of oral suspension: 50 million units, 1 billion units, 2 billion units, 5 billion units
Powder, topical: 100,000 units/g (15 g)
Suspension, oral: 100,000 units/mL (5 mL, 60 mL, 480 mL)
Tablet:
Oral: 500,000 units
Vaginal: 100,000 units (15 and 30/box with applicator)
Troche: 200,000 units

Nystatin and Triamcinolone (nye STAT in & trye am SIN oh lone)

U.S. Brand Names Mycogen II Topical; Mycolog®-II Topical; Myconel® Topical; Myco-Triacet® II; Mytrex® F Topical; N.G.T.® Topical; Tri-Statin® II Topical
Synonyms Triamcinolone and Nystatin
Therapeutic Category Antifungal Agent, Topical; Corticosteroid, Topical (Medium Potency)
Use Treatment of cutaneous candidiasis
Pregnancy Risk Factor C
Contraindications Known hypersensitivity to nystatin or triamcinolone
Warnings/Precautions Avoid use of occlusive dressings; limit therapy to least amount necessary for effective therapy, pediatric patients may be more susceptible to HPA axis suppression due to larger BSA to weight ratio
Adverse Reactions 1% to 10%:
Dermatologic: Dryness, folliculitis, hypertrichosis, acne, hypopigmentation, allergic dermatitis, maceration of the skin, skin atrophy, itching
Local: Burning, irritation
Miscellaneous: Increased incidence of secondary infection
Overdosage/Toxicology Refer to individual monographs for Nystatin and Triamcinolone
Mechanism of Action Refer to individual monographs for Nystatin and Triamcinolone
Pharmacodynamics/Kinetics Refer to individual monographs for Nystatin and Triamcinolone
Usual Dosage Children and Adults: Topical: Apply sparingly 2-4 times/day
Patient Information Before applying, gently wash area to reduce risk of infection; apply a thin film to cleansed area and rub in gently and thoroughly until medication vanishes; avoid exposure to sunlight, severe sunburn may occur
Nursing Implications External use only; do not use on open wounds; apply sparingly to occlusive dressings; should not be used in the presence of open or weeping lesions
Dosage Forms
Cream: Nystatin 100,000 units and triamcinolone acetonide 0.1% (1.5 g, 15 g, 30 g, 60 g, 120 g)
Ointment, topical: Nystatin 100,000 units and triamcinolone acetonide 0.1% (15 g, 30 g, 60 g, 120 g)

- **Nystat-Rx®** see Nystatin on previous page
- **Nystex®** see Nystatin on previous page
- **Nytol® Extra Strength** see Diphenhydramine on page 369
- **Nytol® Oral [OTC]** see Diphenhydramine on page 369
- **Occlucort®** see Betamethasone on page 141
- **Ocean Nasal Mist [OTC]** see Sodium Chloride on page 1067
- **OCL®** see Polyethylene Glycol-Electrolyte Solution on page 942
- **Octamide®** see Metoclopramide on page 766
- **Octicair® Otic** see Neomycin, Polymyxin B, and Hydrocortisone on page 827
- **Octocaine®** see Lidocaine on page 679
- **Octocaine® With Epinephrine** see Lidocaine and Epinephrine on page 681
- **Octostim®** see Desmopressin Acetate on page 334

Octreotide Acetate (ok TREE oh tide AS e tate)

U.S. Brand Names Sandostatin®; Sandostatin LAR® Depot
Therapeutic Category Antidiarrheal; Antisecretory Agent; Somatostatin Analog
Use Control of symptoms in patients with metastatic carcinoid and vasoactive intestinal peptide-secreting tumors (VIPomas); pancreatic tumors, gastrinoma, secretory diarrhea, acromegaly
Unlabeled use: AIDS-associated secretory diarrhea, control of bleeding of esophageal varices, breast cancer, cryptosporidiosis, Cushing's syndrome, insulinomas, small bowel fistulas, postgastrectomy dumping syndrome, chemotherapy-induced diarrhea, graft-versus-host disease (GVHD) induced diarrhea, Zollinger-Ellison syndrome
Pregnancy Risk Factor B
Contraindications Known hypersensitivity to octreotide or any component
Warnings/Precautions Dosage adjustment may be required to maintain symptomatic control; insulin requirements may be reduced as well as sulfonylurea requirements; monitor patients for cholelithiasis, hyper- or hypoglycemia; use with caution in patients with renal impairment
(Continued)

Octreotide Acetate *(Continued)*

Adverse Reactions

1% to 10%:

Cardiovascular: Flushing, edema

Central nervous system: Fatigue, headache, dizziness, vertigo, anorexia, depression

Endocrine & metabolic: Hypoglycemia or hyperglycemia (1%), hypothyroidism, galactorrhea

Gastrointestinal: Nausea, vomiting, diarrhea, constipation, abdominal pain, cramping, discomfort, fat malabsorption, loose stools, flatulence

Hepatic: Jaundice, hepatitis, increase LFTs, cholelithiasis has occurred, presumably by altering fat absorption and decreasing the motility of the gallbladder

Local: Pain at injection site (dose-related)

Neuromuscular & skeletal: Weakness

<1%: Chest pain, hypertensive reaction, anxiety, fever, hyperesthesia, alopecia, wheal/erythema, rash, thrombophlebitis, leg cramps, Bell's palsy, muscle cramping, burning eyes, throat discomfort, rhinorrhea, shortness of breath

Overdosage/Toxicology
Symptoms of overdose include hypo- or hyperglycemia, blurred vision, dizziness, drowsiness, loss of motor function; well tolerated bolus doses up to 1000 mcg have failed to produce adverse effects

Drug Interactions
CYP2D6 (high dose) and 3A enzyme inhibitor

Decreased effect: Cyclosporine (case report of a transplant rejection due to reduction of serum cyclosporine levels)

Stability
Octreotide is a clear solution and should be stored under refrigeration; ampuls may be stored at room temperature for up to 14 days when protected from light

Stability of parenteral admixture in NS at room temperature (25°C) and at refrigeration temperature (4°C): 48 hours

Common diluent: 50-100 mcg/50 mL NS; common diluent for continuous I.V. infusion: 1200 mcg/250 mL NS

Minimum volume: 50 mL NS

Mechanism of Action
Mimics natural somatostatin by inhibiting serotonin release, and the secretion of gastrin, VIP, insulin, glucagon, secretin, motilin, and pancreatic polypeptide

Pharmacodynamics/Kinetics

Duration of action: 6-12 hours (S.C.)

Absorption: Oral: Absorbed but still under study; S.C.: Rapid

Bioavailability: S.C.: 100%

Distribution: V_d: 14 L; 65% bound to lipoproteins

Metabolism: Extensive by the liver

Half-life: 60-110 minutes

Elimination: 32% by the kidney

Usual Dosage
Adults: S.C.: Initial: 50 mcg 1-2 times/day and titrate dose based on patient tolerance and response

Carcinoid: 100-600 mcg/day in 2-4 divided doses

VIPomas: 200-300 mcg/day in 2-4 divided doses

Diarrhea: Initial: I.V.: 50-100 mcg every 8 hours; increase by 100 mcg/dose at 48-hour intervals; maximum dose: 500 mcg every 8 hours

Esophageal varices bleeding: I.V. bolus: 25-50 mcg followed by continuous I.V. infusion of 25-50 mcg/hour

Acromegaly, carcinoid tumors, and VIPomas (depot injection): Patients must be stabilized on subcutaneous octreotide for at least 2 weeks before switching to the long-acting depot: Upon switch: 20 mg I.M. intragluteally every 4 weeks for 2-3 months, then the dose may be modified based upon response

Dosage adjustment for acromegaly: After 3 months of depot injections the dosage may be continued or modified as follows:

GH ≤2.5 ng/mL, IGF-1 is normal, symptoms are controlled: Maintain octreotide LAR® at 20 mg I.M. every 4 weeks

GH >2.5 ng/mL, IGF-1 is elevated, or symptoms: Increase octreotide LAR® to 10 mg I.M. every 4 weeks

GH ≤1 ng/mL, IGF-1 is normal, symptoms controlled: Reduce octreotide LAR® to 10 mg I.M. every 4 weeks

Dosages >40 mg are not recommended

Dosage adjustment for carcinoid tumors and VIPomas: After 2 months of depot injections the dosage may be continued or modified as follows:

Increase to 30 mg I.M. every 4 weeks if symptoms are inadequately controlled

Decrease to 10 mg I.M. every 4 weeks, for a trial period, if initially responsive to 20 mg dose

Dosage >30 mg is not recommended

Administration

Administer S.C. or I.V.

I.V. administration may be IVP, IVPB, or continuous I.V. infusion

IVP should be administered undiluted over 3 minutes

IVPB should be administered over 15-30 minutes

Continuous I.V. infusion rates have ranged from 25-50 mcg/hour for the treatment of esophageal variceal bleeding

Do not use if solution contains particles or is discolored

Depot form: Administer I.M. intragluteal; must be administered immediately after mixing

Reference Range
Vasoactive intestinal peptide: <75 ng/L; levels vary considerably between laboratories

Nursing Implications
Do not use if solution contains particles or is discolored

Dosage Forms
Injection: 0.05 mg/mL (1 mL); 0.1 mg/mL (1 mL); 0.2 mg/mL (5 mL); 0.5 mg/mL (1 mL); 1 mg/mL (5 mL)

Injection, suspension, depot: 10 mg (5 mL); 20 mg (5 mL); 30 mg (5 mL)

- ◆ **Ocu-Carpine® Ophthalmic** see Pilocarpine on page 927
- ◆ **Ocu-Dex®** see Dexamethasone on page 337
- ◆ **Ocufen® Ophthalmic** see Flurbiprofen on page 507
- ◆ **Ocuflox™ Ophthalmic** see Ofloxacin on this page
- ◆ **Oculinum®** see Botulinum Toxin Type A on page 151
- ◆ **Ocumycin®** see Gentamicin on page 533
- ◆ **Ocupress® Ophthalmic** see Carteolol on page 199
- ◆ **Ocusert Pilo-20® Ophthalmic** see Pilocarpine on page 927
- ◆ **Ocusert Pilo-40® Ophthalmic** see Pilocarpine on page 927
- ◆ **Ocusulf-10® Ophthalmic** see Sulfacetamide Sodium on page 1091
- ◆ **Ocutricin® Ophthalmic Solution** see Neomycin, Polymyxin B, and Gramicidin on page 826
- ◆ **Ocutricin® Topical Ointment** see Bacitracin, Neomycin, and Polymyxin B on page 123
- ◆ **Ocu-Tropine® Ophthalmic** see Atropine on page 111
- ◆ **Oestrilin®** see Estrone on page 439

Ofloxacin (oh FLOKS a sin)

Related Information
Antimicrobial Drugs of Choice on page 1404
Treatment of Sexually Transmitted Diseases on page 1429
Tuberculosis Treatment Guidelines on page 1432

U.S. Brand Names Floxin®; Ocuflox™ Ophthalmic

Therapeutic Category Antibiotic, Quinolone

Use
Quinolone antibiotic for skin and skin structure, lower respiratory and urinary tract infections and sexually transmitted diseases. Active against many gram-positive and gram-negative aerobic bacteria.

Ophthalmic: Treatment of superficial ocular infections involving the conjunctiva or cornea due to strains of susceptible organisms

Pregnancy Risk Factor C

Contraindications Hypersensitivity to ofloxacin or other members of the quinolone group such as nalidixic acid, oxolinic acid, cinoxacin, norfloxacin, and ciprofloxacin

Warnings/Precautions Use with caution in patients with epilepsy or other CNS diseases which could predispose seizures; use with caution in patients with renal impairment; failure to respond to an ophthalmic antibiotic after 2-3 days may indicate the presence of resistant organisms, or another causative agent; use caution with systemic preparation in children <18 years of age due to association of other quinolones with transient arthropathy; has rarely caused ruptured tendons (discontinue immediately with signs of inflammation or tendon pain)

Adverse Reactions
1% to 10%:
Cardiovascular: Chest pain (1% to 3%)
Central nervous system: Headache (1% to 9%), insomnia (3% to 7%), dizziness (1% to 5%), fatigue (1% to 3%), somnolence (1% to 3%), sleep disorders, nervousness (1% to 3%), pyrexia (1% to 3%), pain
Dermatologic: Rash/pruritus (1% to 3%)
Gastrointestinal: Diarrhea (1% to 4%), vomiting (1% to 3%), GI distress, cramps, abdominal cramps (1% to 3%), flatulence (1% to 3%), abnormal taste (1% to 3%), xerostomia (1% to 3%), decreased appetite, nausea (3% to 10%)
Genitourinary: Vaginitis (1% to 3%), external genital pruritus in women
Local: Pain at injection site
Ocular: Superinfection (ophthalmic), photophobia, lacrimation, dry eyes, stinging, visual disturbances (1% to 3%)
Miscellaneous: Trunk pain
<1%: Syncope, vasculitis, edema, hypertension, palpitations, vasodilation, anxiety, cognitive change, depression, dream abnormality, euphoria, hallucinations, vertigo, chills, malaise, extremity pain, weight loss, paresthesia, ruptured tendons, Tourette's syndrome, weakness, photophobia, photosensitivity, hepatitis, decreased hearing acuity, tinnitus, cough, thirst

Overdosage/Toxicology
Symptoms of overdose include acute renal failure, seizures, nausea, vomiting
Treatment includes GI decontamination, if possible, and supportive care

Drug Interactions
Decreased effect: Decreased absorption with antacids containing aluminum, magnesium, and/or calcium (by up to 98% if given at the same time); fluoroquinolones may be decreased by antineoplastic agents
Increased toxicity/serum levels: Quinolones cause increased caffeine, warfarin, cyclosporine, procainamide, and possibly theophylline levels. Cimetidine and probenecid increase quinolone levels.

Mechanism of Action Ofloxacin is a DNA gyrase inhibitor. DNA gyrase is an essential bacterial enzyme that maintains the superhelical structure of DNA. DNA gyrase is required for DNA replication and transcription, DNA repair, recombination, and transposition; bactericidal

(Continued)

Ofloxacin *(Continued)*

Pharmacodynamics/Kinetics

Absorption: Well absorbed; administration with food causes only minor alterations in absorption

Distribution: V_d: 2.4-3.5 L/kg

Protein binding: 20%

Half-life, elimination 5-7.5 hours

Elimination: Primarily unchanged in urine

Usual Dosage

Children >1 year and Adults: Ophthalmic: Instill 1-2 drops in affected eye(s) every 2-4 hours for the first 2 days, then use 4 times/day for an additional 5 days

Adults:

Lower respiratory tract infection: 400 mg every 12 hours for 10 days

Gonorrhea: 400 mg as a single dose

Cervicitis due to *C. trachomatis* and/or *N. gonorrhoeae*: 300 mg every 12 hours for 7 days

Skin/skin structure: 400 mg every 12 hours for 10 days

Urinary tract infection: 200-400 mg every 12 hours for 3-10 days

Prostatitis: 300 mg every 12 hours for 6 weeks

Dosing adjustment/interval in renal impairment: Adults: I.V., Oral:

Cl_{cr} 10-50 mL/minute: Administer 200-400 mg every 24 hours

Cl_{cr} <10 mL/minute: Administer 100-200 mg every 24 hours

Continuous arteriovenous or venovenous hemodiafiltration (CAVH) effects: Administer 300 mg every 24 hours

Patient Information Report any skin rash or other allergic reactions; avoid excessive sunlight; do not take with food; do not take within 2 hours of any products including antacids which contain zinc, magnesium, or aluminum; contact your physician immediately with signs of inflammation or tendon pain

Dosage Forms

Injection: 200 mg (50 mL); 400 mg (10 mL, 20 mL, 100 mL)

Solution, ophthalmic: 0.3% (5 mL)

Tablet: 200 mg, 300 mg, 400 mg

- ◆ **Ogen® Oral** *see* Estropipate *on page 440*
- ◆ **Ogen® Vaginal** *see* Estropipate *on page 440*
- ◆ **OGMT** *see* Metyrosine *on page 772*
- ◆ **OKT3** *see* Muromonab-CD3 *on page 802*

Olanzapine *(oh LAN za peen)*

Related Information

Antipsychotic Agents Comparison *on page 1305*

U.S. Brand Names Zyprexa™

Synonyms LY170053

Therapeutic Category Antipsychotic Agent

Use Treatment of the manifestations of psychotic disorders

Pregnancy Risk Factor C

Warnings/Precautions Use with caution in patients with cardiovascular disease, cerebrovascular disease, hypovolemia, dehydration, seizure disorders, Alzheimer's disease, hepatic impairment, prostatic hypertrophy, narrow-angle glaucoma, history of paralytic ileus or a history of breast cancer, the elderly, and in pregnancy or with nursing patients

Adverse Reactions

>10%: Central nervous system: Headache, somnolence, insomnia, agitation, nervousness, hostility, dizziness

1% to 10%:

Central nervous system: Dystonic reactions, parkinsonian events, akathisia, anxiety, personality changes, fever

Gastrointestinal: Xerostomia, constipation, abdominal pain, weight gain

Neuromuscular & skeletal: Arthralgia

Ocular: Amblyopia

Respiratory: Rhinitis, cough, pharyngitis

<1%: Peripheral edema, tardive dyskinesia, neuroleptic malignant syndrome

Drug Interactions CYP1A2 enzyme substrate, CYP2C19 enzyme substrate (minor), and CYP2D6 enzyme substrate (minor)

Decreased effect: Cigarette smoking, levodopa, pergolide, bromocriptine, charcoal, and reduction of effects may be seen with cytochrome P-450 enzyme inducers such as rifampin, omeprazole, carbamazepine

Increased effect: Effects may be potentiated with CYP1A2 inhibitors such as fluvoxamine

Increased toxicity: Increased sedation with alcohol or other CNS depressants, increased risk of hypotension and orthostatic hypotension with antihypertensives

Mechanism of Action Olanzapine is a thienobenzodiazepine neuroleptic; thought to work by antagonizing dopamine and serotonin activities. It is a selective monoaminergic antagonist with high affinity binding to serotonin 5-HT$_{2A}$ and 5-HT$_{2C}$, dopamine D$_{1-4}$, muscarinic M$_{1-5}$, histamine H$_1$ and alpha$_1$-adrenergic receptor sites.

Pharmacodynamics/Kinetics

Onset of effect: ≥1 week

Absorption: Oral: Readily absorbed

Protein binding: 93%

Metabolism: Extensive in the liver

Half-life: 21-54 hours

Elimination: 40% removed via first-pass metabolism, 57% eliminated renally, and 30% in feces

Usual Dosage Adults >18 years: Oral: Usual starting dose: 5-10 mg once daily; increase to 10 mg once daily within 5-7 days, thereafter adjust by 5 mg/day at 1-week intervals, up to a maximum of 20 mg/day

Dosage Forms Tablet: 2.5 mg, 5 mg, 7.5 mg, 10 mg

♦ **Oleovitamin A** see Vitamin A on page 1223

Olsalazine (ole SAL a zeen)

U.S. Brand Names Dipentum®

Synonyms Olsalazine Sodium

Therapeutic Category 5-Aminosalicylic Acid Derivative; Anti-inflammatory Agent

Use Maintenance of remission of ulcerative colitis in patients intolerant to sulfasalazine

Pregnancy Risk Factor C

Contraindications Hypersensitivity to salicylates

Warnings/Precautions Diarrhea is a common adverse effect of olsalazine; use with caution in patients with hypersensitivity to salicylates, sulfasalazine, or mesalamine

Adverse Reactions

>10%: Gastrointestinal: Diarrhea, cramps, abdominal pain

1% to 10%:

Central nervous system: Headache, fatigue, depression

Dermatologic: Rash, itching

Gastrointestinal: Nausea, dyspepsia, bloating, anorexia

Neuromuscular & skeletal: Arthralgia

<1%: Fever, bloody diarrhea, blood dyscrasias, hepatitis

Overdosage/Toxicology Symptoms of overdose include decreased motor activity, diarrhea

Mechanism of Action The mechanism of action appears to be topical rather than systemic

Pharmacodynamics/Kinetics

Absorption: <3%; very little intact olsalazine is systemically absorbed

Protein binding: High

Metabolism: Mostly by colonic bacteria to the active drug, 5-aminosalicylic acid

Half-life, elimination: 56 minutes or 55 hours depending on the analysis used.

Elimination: Primarily in feces

Usual Dosage Adults: Oral: 1 g/day in 2 divided doses

Test Interactions ↑ ALT, AST (S)

Patient Information Take with food in evenly divided doses; report any sign of allergic reaction including rash

Dosage Forms Capsule, as sodium: 250 mg

♦ **Olsalazine Sodium** see Olsalazine on this page

Omeprazole (oh ME pray zol)

Related Information

Helicobacter pylori Treatment on page 1473

Replaces Losec®

U.S. Brand Names Prilosec™

Canadian Brand Names Losec®

Therapeutic Category Gastric Acid Secretion Inhibitor; Proton Pump Inhibitor

Use Short-term (4-8 weeks) treatment of severe erosive esophagitis (grade 2 or above), diagnosed by endoscopy and short-term treatment of symptomatic gastroesophageal reflux disease (GERD) poorly responsive to customary medical treatment; pathological hypersecretory conditions; peptic ulcer disease; gastric ulcer therapy; approved for combination use in the eradication of *H. pylori* in patients with active duodenal ulcer.

Unlabeled use: Healing NSAID-induced ulcers

Pregnancy Risk Factor C

Pregnancy/Breast-Feeding Implications

Clinical effects on the fetus: Crosses the placenta

Breast-feeding/lactation: No data available. American Academy of Pediatrics makes NO RECOMMENDATION.

Contraindications Known hypersensitivity to omeprazole

Warnings/Precautions In long-term (2-year) studies in rats, omeprazole produced a dose-related increase in gastric carcinoid tumors. While available endoscopic evaluations and histologic examinations of biopsy specimens from human stomachs have not detected a risk from short-term exposure to omeprazole, further human data on the effect of sustained hypochlorhydria and hypergastrinemia are needed to rule out the possibility of an increased risk for the development of tumors in humans receiving long-term therapy. Bioavailability may be increased in the elderly.

Adverse Reactions

1% to 10%:

Cardiovascular: Angina, tachycardia, bradycardia, edema

Central nervous system: Headache (7%), dizziness

Dermatologic: Rash, urticaria, pruritus, dry skin, purpura, petechiae

Gastrointestinal: Diarrhea, nausea, abdominal pain, vomiting, constipation, anorexia, irritable colon, fecal discoloration, esophageal candidiasis, xerostomia, abnormal taste

(Continued)

Omeprazole *(Continued)*

Genitourinary: Testicular pain, urinary tract infection, polyuria

Neuromuscular & skeletal: Back pain, muscle cramps, myalgia, arthralgia, leg pain, weakness occurred in more frequently than 1% of patients

Renal: Pyuria, proteinuria, hematuria, glycosuria

Respiratory: Cough

<1%: Chest pain, fever, fatigue, malaise, apathy, somnolence, nervousness, anxiety, pain, abdominal swelling, anaphylaxis (rare)

Overdosage/Toxicology

Symptoms of overdose include hypothermia, sedation, convulsions, decreased respiratory rate demonstrated in animals only

Treatment is supportive; not dialyzable

Drug Interactions CYP2C8, 2C9, 2C18, 2C19, and 3A3/4 enzyme substrate; CYP1A2 enzyme inducer; CYP2C19, 2C8, 2C9, and 2C19 enzyme inhibitor, CYP3A3/4 enzyme inhibitor (weak)

Decreased effect: Decreased ketoconazole; decreased itraconazole

Increased toxicity: Diazepam may increase half-life; increased digoxin, increased phenytoin, increased warfarin

Stability Omeprazole stability is a function of pH; it is rapidly degraded in acidic media, but has acceptable stability under alkaline conditions. Prilosec™ is supplied as capsules for oral administration; each capsule contains omeprazole in the form of enteric coated granules to inhibit omeprazole degradation by gastric acidity; therefore, the manufacturer recommends against extemporaneously preparing it in an oral liquid form for administration via an NG tube.

Mechanism of Action Suppresses gastric acid secretion by inhibiting the parietal cell H+/K+ ATP pump

Pharmacodynamics/Kinetics

Onset of antisecretory action: Oral: Within 1 hour

Peak effect: 2 hours

Duration: 72 hours

Protein binding: 95%

Metabolism: Extensive in the liver

Half-life: 30-90 minutes

Usual Dosage Adults: Oral:

Active duodenal ulcer: 20 mg/day for 4-8 weeks

GERD or severe erosive esophagitis: 20 mg/day for 4-8 weeks

Pathological hypersecretory conditions: 60 mg once daily to start; doses up to 120 mg 3 times/day have been administered; administer daily doses >80 mg in divided doses

Helicobacter pylori: Combination therapy with bismuth subsalicylate, tetracycline, clarithromycin, and H₂-antagonist; or with clarithromycin. Adult dose: Oral: 20 mg twice daily

Gastric ulcers: 40 mg/day for 4-8 weeks

Administration Omeprazole has been administered via a nasogastric (NG) tube for the prevention of stress-related mucosal damage in ventilated, critically ill patients. The contents of one or two 20 mg omeprazole capsules were poured into a syringe; 10-20 mL of an 8.4% sodium bicarbonate solution was withdrawn in the syringe; 30 minutes were allowed for the enteric-coated omeprazole granules to break down. The resulting milky substance was shaken prior to administration. The NG tube was then flushed with 5-10 mL of water then clamped for at least 1 hour. Patients received omeprazole 40 mg once, then 40 mg 6-8 hours later, then 20 mg once daily using this technique.

Another study used a different technique. The omeprazole capsule (20 mg or 40 mg) was opened; then the intact granules were poured into a container holding 30 mL of water. With the plunger removed, ⅓ to ½ of the granules were then poured into a 30 mL syringe which was attached to a nasogastric tube (NG). The plunger was replaced with 1 cm of air between the granules and the plunger top while the plunger was depressed. This process was repeated until all the granules were flushed, then a final 15 mL of water was flushed through the tube. Patients who received omeprazole 40 mg in this manner had a more predictable increase in intragastric pH than patients who received omeprazole 20 mg.

Patient Information Take before eating; do not chew, crush, or open capsule

Nursing Implications Capsule should be swallowed whole; not chewed, crushed, or opened

Dosage Forms Capsule, delayed release: 10 mg, 20 mg, 40 mg

Ondansetron *(on DAN se tron)*

U.S. Brand Names Iofran ODT®; Zofran®

Synonyms Ondansetron Hydrochloride

Therapeutic Category Antiemetic, Serotonin Antagonist; 5-HT₃ Receptor Antagonist; Serotonin Antagonist

Use May be prescribed for patients who are refractory to or have severe adverse reactions to standard antiemetic therapy. Ondansetron may be prescribed for young patients (ie, <45 years of age who are more likely to develop extrapyramidal reactions to high-dose metoclopramide) who are to receive highly emetogenic chemotherapeutic agents as listed:

Ondansetron should not be prescribed for chemotherapeutic agents with a low emetogenic potential (eg, bleomycin, busulfan, cyclophosphamide <1000 mg, etoposide, 5-fluorouracil, vinblastine, vincristine)

Pregnancy Risk Factor B

Pregnancy/Breast-Feeding Implications

Clinical effects on the fetus: No data available on crossing the placenta; no effects on the fetus from 2 case reports

Breast-feeding/lactation: No data available. American Academy of Pediatrics has NO RECOMMENDATION.

Contraindications Hypersensitivity to ondansetron or any component

Warnings/Precautions Ondansetron should be used on a scheduled basis, not as an "as needed" (PRN) basis, since data supports the use of this drug in the prevention of nausea and vomiting and not in the rescue of nausea and vomiting. Ondansetron should only be used in the first 24-48 hours of receiving chemotherapy. Data does not support any increased efficacy of ondansetron in delayed nausea and vomiting.

Adverse Reactions

>10%:

Central nervous system: Headache, fever

Gastrointestinal: Constipation, diarrhea

1% to 10%:

Central nervous system: Dizziness

Gastrointestinal: Abdominal cramps, xerostomia

Hepatic: AST/ALT elevations (5%)

Neuromuscular & skeletal: Weakness

<1%: Tachycardia, lightheadedness, seizures, rash, hypokalemia, transient elevations in serum levels of aminotransferases and bilirubin, bronchospasm, shortness of breath, wheezing, angina

Drug Interactions CYP1A2, 2D6, 2E1, and 3A3/4 enzyme substrate

Decreased effect: Metabolized by the hepatic cytochrome P-450 enzymes; therefore, the drug's clearance and half-life may be changed with concomitant use of cytochrome P-450 inducers (eg, barbiturates, carbamazepine, rifampin, phenytoin, and phenylbutazone)

Increased toxicity: Inhibitors (eg, cimetidine, allopurinol, and disulfiram)

Stability Injection may be stored between 36°F and 86°F; stable when mixed in 5% dextrose or 0.9% sodium chloride for 48 hours at room temperature; does not need protection from light

Mechanism of Action Selective 5-HT$_3$-receptor antagonist, blocking serotonin, both peripherally on vagal nerve terminals and centrally in the chemoreceptor trigger zone

Pharmacodynamics/Kinetics

Plasma protein binding: 70% to 76%

Metabolism: Extensively by hydroxylation, followed by glucuronide or sulfate conjugation

Half-life: Children <15 years: 2-3 hours; Adults: 4 hours

Elimination: In urine and feces; <10% of parent drug recovered unchanged in urine

Usual Dosage

Chemotherapy-induced emesis: Oral:

Children 4-11 years: 4 mg 30 minutes before chemotherapy; repeat 4 and 8 hours after initial dose, then 4 mg every 8 hours for 1-2 days after chemotherapy completed

Children >11 years and Adults: 8 mg every 8 hours for 2 doses beginning 30 minutes before chemotherapy, then 8 mg every 12 hours for 1-2 days after chemotherapy completed

Total body irradiation: Adults: 8 mg 1-2 hours before each fraction of radiotherapy administered each day

Single high-dose fraction radiotherapy to abdomen: 8 mg 1-2 hours before irradiation, then 8 mg every 8 hours after first dose for 1-2 days after completion of radiotherapy

Daily fractionated radiotherapy to abdomen: 8 mg 1-2 hours before irradiation, then 8 mg every 8 hours after first dose for each day of radiotherapy

Prophylaxis with moderate-emetogenic chemotherapy (not FDA-approved): 8 mg twice daily has been shown to be as effective as doses given 3 times/day

I.V.: Administer either three 0.15 mg/kg doses or a single 32 mg dose; with the 3-dose regimen, the initial dose is given 30 minutes prior to chemotherapy with subsequent doses administered 4 and 8 hours after the first dose. With the single-dose regimen 32 mg is infused over 15 minutes beginning 30 minutes before the start of emetogenic chemotherapy. Dosage should be calculated based on weight:

Children: Pediatric dosing should follow the manufacturer's guidelines for 0.15 mg/kg/dose administered 30 minutes prior to chemotherapy, 4 and 8 hours after the first dose. While not as yet FDA-approved, literature supports the day's total dose administered as a single dose 30 minutes prior to chemotherapy.

Adults:

>80 kg: 12 mg IVPB

45-80 kg: 8 mg IVPB

<45 kg: 0.15 mg/kg/dose IVPB

(Continued)

Ondansetron *(Continued)*

Postoperative emesis: I.V.:

Children >2 years: 0.1 mg/kg I.V. slow push; if over 40 kg weight, administer 4 mg IVP over 2-5 minutes (no faster than 30 seconds); give I.V. as s single dose immediately before induction of anesthesia or shortly following procedure if vomiting occurs

Adults (infuse in not less than 30 seconds, preferably over 2-5 minutes, as undiluted drug): 4 mg as a single dose immediately before induction of anesthesia; or shortly following procedure if vomiting occurs

Dosing in hepatic impairment: Maximum daily dose: 8 mg in cirrhotic patients with severe liver disease

Dietary Considerations

Food: Increases the extent of absorption. The C_{max} and T_{max} does not change much; take without regard to meals

Potassium: Hypokalemia; monitor potassium serum concentration

Nursing Implications First dose should be given 30 minutes prior to beginning chemotherapy

Dosage Forms

Injection, as hydrochloride: 2 mg/mL (20 mL); 32 mg (single-dose vials)

Solution, as hydrochloride: 4 mg/5 mL

Tablet, as hydrochloride: 4 mg, 8 mg

Tablet, as hydrochloride, orally disentegrating: 4 mg, 8 mg

Extemporaneous Preparations A 0.8 mg/mL syrup may be made by crushing ten 8 mg tablets; flaking of the tablet coating occurs. Mix thoroughly with 50 mL of the suspending vehicle, Ora-Plus® (Paddock), in 5 mL increments. Add sufficient volume of any of the following syrups: Cherry syrup USP, Syrpalta® (Humco), Ora-Sweet® (Paddock), or Ora-Sweet® Sugar-Free (Paddock) to make a final volume of 100 mL. Stability is 42 days refrigerated.

Trissel LA, "Trissel's Stability of Compounded Formulations," American Pharmaceutical Association, 1996.

+ **Ondansetron Hydrochloride** *see Ondansetron on page 862*
+ **Ony-Clear® Spray** *see Miconazole on page 775*
+ **Onyvul®** *see Urea on page 1199*
+ **OPC13013** *see Cilostazol on page 260*
+ **OPC-17116** *see Grepafloxacin on page 547*
+ **Opcon®** *see Naphazoline on page 817*
+ **o,p'-DDD** *see Mitotane on page 787*
+ **Operand® [OTC]** *see Povidone-Iodine on page 955*
+ **Ophthetic®** *see Proparacaine on page 982*
+ **Ophthifluor®** *see Fluorescein Sodium on page 497*
+ **Ophtho-Dipivefrin™** *see Dipivefrin on page 376*
+ **Opium and Belladonna** *see Belladonna and Opium on page 130*

Opium Tincture *(OH pee um TING chur)*

Synonyms Deodorized Opium Tincture; DTO

Therapeutic Category Analgesic, Narcotic; Antidiarrheal

Use Treatment of diarrhea or relief of pain

Restrictions C-II

Pregnancy Risk Factor B (D if used for prolonged periods or in high doses at term)

Contraindications Increased intracranial pressure, severe respiratory depression, severe liver or renal insufficiency, known hypersensitivity to morphine sulfate

Warnings/Precautions Opium shares the toxic potential of opiate agonists, and usual precautions of opiate agonist therapy should be observed; some preparations contain sulfites which may cause allergic reactions; infants <3 months of age are more susceptible to respiratory depression, use with caution and generally in reduced doses in this age group; this is **not** paregoric, dose accordingly

Adverse Reactions

>10%:

Cardiovascular: Palpitations, hypotension, bradycardia

Central nervous system: Drowsiness, dizziness

Neuromuscular & skeletal: Weakness

1% to 10%:

Central nervous system: Restlessness, headache, malaise

Genitourinary: Decreased urination

Miscellaneous: Histamine release

<1%: Peripheral vasodilation, CNS depression, increased intracranial pressure, insomnia, mental depression, nausea, vomiting, constipation, anorexia, stomach cramps, biliary tract spasm, urinary tract spasm, miosis, respiratory depression, physical and psychological dependence

Overdosage/Toxicology Primary attention should be directed to ensuring adequate respiratory exchange; opiate agonist-induced respiratory depression may be reversed with parenteral naloxone hydrochloride

Naloxone 2 mg I.V. (0.01 mg/kg for children) with repeat administration as necessary up to a total of 10 mg

Drug Interactions

Decreased effect: Phenothiazines may antagonize the analgesic effect of opiate agonists

Increased toxicity: CNS depressants, MAO inhibitors, tricyclic antidepressants may potentiate the effects of opiate agonists; dextroamphetamine may enhance the analgesic effect of opiate agonists

Mechanism of Action Contains many narcotic alkaloids including morphine; its mechanism for gastric motility inhibition is primarily due to this morphine content; it results in a decrease in digestive secretions, an increase in GI muscle tone, and therefore a reduction in GI propulsion

Pharmacodynamics/Kinetics
Duration of effect: 4-5 hours
Absorption: Variable from GI tract
Metabolism: In the liver
Elimination: Urine

Usual Dosage Oral:
Children:
Diarrhea: 0.005-0.01 mL/kg/dose every 3-4 hours for a maximum of 6 doses/24 hours
Analgesia: 0.01-0.02 mL/kg/dose every 3-4 hours
Adults:
Diarrhea: 0.3-1 mL/dose every 2-6 hours to maximum of 6 mL/24 hours
Analgesia: 0.6-1.5 mL/dose every 3-4 hours

Dietary Considerations Alcohol: Additive CNS effect, avoid use

Monitoring Parameters Observe patient for excessive sedation, respiratory depression, implement safety measures, assist with ambulation

Test Interactions ↑ aminotransferase [ALT (SGPT)/AST (SGOT)] (S)

Patient Information Avoid alcohol, may cause drowsiness, impair judgment, or coordination; may cause physical and psychological dependence with prolonged use

Dosage Forms Liquid: 10% [0.6 mL equivalent to morphine 6 mg]

Oprelvekin (oh PREL ve kin)

U.S. Brand Names Neumega®

Synonyms IL-11; Interleukin-11; Recombinant Human Interleukin-11; Recombinant Interleukin-11; rhIL-11; rIL-11

Therapeutic Category Biological Response Modulator; Human Growth Factor; Interleukin

Use Prevention of severe thrombocytopenia and the reduction of the need for platelet transfusions following myelosuppressive chemotherapy in patients with nonmyeloid malignancies who are at high risk of severe thrombocytopenia.

Pregnancy Risk Factor C

Contraindications Hypersensitivity to oprelvekin, or any component

Warnings/Precautions Oprelvekin should be used cautiously in patients with conditions where expansion of plasma volume should be avoided (eg, left ventricular dysfunction, congestive heart failure, hypertension); cardiac arrhythmias or conduction defects, respiratory disease; history of thromboembolic problems; hepatic or renal dysfunction; not indicated following myeloablative chemotherapy

Adverse Reactions
>10%:
Cardiovascular: Tachycardia (19% to 30%), palpitations (14% to 24%), atrial arrhythmias (12%), peripheral edema (60% to 75%)
Central nervous system: Headache (41%), dizziness (38%), insomnia (33%), fatigue (30%), fever (36%)
Dermatologic: Rash (25%)
Endocrine & metabolic: Fluid retention
Gastrointestinal: Nausea (50% to 77%), vomiting, anorexia
Hematologic: Anemia (100%), probably a dilutional phenomena; appears within 3 days of initiation of therapy, resolves in about 2 weeks after cessation of oprelvekin
Neuromuscular & skeletal: Arthralgia, myalgias
Respiratory: Dyspnea (48%), pleural effusions (10%)
1% to 10%:
Cardiovascular: Syncope (6% to 13%)
Gastrointestinal: Weight gain (5%)

Overdosage/Toxicology Doses of oprelvekin >50 mcg/kg may be associated with an increased incidence of cardiovascular events. If an overdose is administered, discontinue oprelvekin and closely observe patient for signs of toxicity. Base reinstitution of therapy on individual patient factors (evidence of toxicity and continued need for therapy).

Stability Store vials of lyophilized oprelvekin and diluent under refrigeration (2°C to 8°C/36°F to 46°F); do not freeze.

Reconstitute oprelvekin with 1 mL of sterile water for injection, USP (without preservative). Direct at the side of vial and swirl the contents gently. Avoid excessive or vigorous agitation. Reconstituted solution contains 5 mg/mL of oprelvekin. Use reconstituted oprelvekin within 3 hours of reconstitution and store in the vial at either 2°C to 8°C/36°F to 46°F or room temperature (≤25°C/70°F). Do not freeze or shake reconstituted solution.

Mechanism of Action Oprelvekin stimulates multiple stages of megakaryocytopoiesis and thrombopoiesis, resulting in proliferation of megakaryocyte progenitors and megakaryocyte maturation

Pharmacodynamics/Kinetics
Metabolism: Uncertain
Half-life: Terminal: 5-8 hours
(Continued)

Oprelvekin *(Continued)*

Time to peak serum concentration: 1-6 hours

Elimination: Renal, primarily as metabolites

Usual Dosage S.C.:

Children: 75-100 mcg/kg once daily for 10-21 days (until postnadir platelet count ≥50,000 cells/μL)

Adults: 50 mcg/kg once daily for 10-21 days (until postnadir platelet count ≥50,000 cells/μL)

Administration Subcutaneously in either the abdomen, thigh, or hip (or upper arm if not self-injected). Initiate dosing 6-24 hours after the completion of chemotherapy. Discontinue treatment with oprelvekin ≥2 days before starting the next planned cycle of chemotherapy.

Monitoring Parameters Monitor fluid balance during therapy, appropriate medical management is advised. If a diuretic is used, carefully monitor fluid and electrolyte balance. Obtain a CBC prior to chemotherapy and at regular intervals during therapy. Monitor platelet counts during the time of the expected nadir and until adequate recovery has occurred (postnadir counts ≥50,000 cells/μL).

Test Interactions Decrease in hemoglobin concentration, serum concentration of albumin and other proteins (result of expansion of plasma volume)

Patient Information Report any swelling in the arms or legs (peripheral edema), shortness of breath (congestive failure, anemia), irregular heartbeat, headaches

Dosage Forms Powder for injection, lyophilized: 5 mg

- ◆ **Opticrom®** *see Cromolyn Sodium on page 300*
- ◆ **Opticyl®** *see Tropicamide on page 1192*
- ◆ **Optimine®** *see Azatadine on page 115*
- ◆ **OptiPranolol® Ophthalmic** *see Metipranolol on page 765*
- ◆ **OPV** *see Polio Vaccines on page 940*
- ◆ **Orabase®-B [OTC]** *see Benzocaine on page 133*
- ◆ **Orabase® HCA** *see Hydrocortisone on page 579*
- ◆ **Orabase®-O [OTC]** *see Benzocaine on page 133*
- ◆ **Oracit®** *see Sodium Citrate and Citric Acid on page 1069*
- ◆ **Orafen** *see Ketoprofen on page 650*
- ◆ **Orajel® Brace-Aid Oral Anesthetic [OTC]** *see Benzocaine on page 133*
- ◆ **Orajel® Maximum Strength [OTC]** *see Benzocaine on page 133*
- ◆ **Orajel® Mouth-Aid [OTC]** *see Benzocaine on page 133*
- ◆ **Orajel® Perioseptic [OTC]** *see Carbamide Peroxide on page 190*
- ◆ **Oramorph SR™ Oral** *see Morphine Sulfate on page 797*
- ◆ **Orap™** *see Pimozide on page 928*
- ◆ **Orasept® [OTC]** *see Benzocaine on page 133*
- ◆ **Orasol® [OTC]** *see Benzocaine on page 133*
- ◆ **Orasone®** *see Prednisone on page 963*
- ◆ **Oratect™ [OTC]** *see Benzocaine on page 133*
- ◆ **Orazinc® [OTC]** *see Zinc Supplements on page 1239*
- ◆ **Orbenin®** *see Cloxacillin on page 288*
- ◆ **Orciprenaline Sulfate** *see Metaproterenol on page 739*
- ◆ **Ordrine AT® Extended Release Capsule** *see Caramiphen and Phenylpropanolamine on page 188*
- ◆ **Oretic®** *see Hydrochlorothiazide on page 574*
- ◆ **Oreton® Methyl** *see Methyltestosterone on page 764*
- ◆ **Orfenace** *see Orphenadrine on next page*
- ◆ **ORG 946** *see Rocuronium on page 1038*
- ◆ **Organidin®** *see Iodinated Glycerol on page 622*
- ◆ **Organidin® NR** *see Guaifenesin on page 549*
- ◆ **Orgaran®** *see Danaparoid on page 320*
- ◆ **ORG NC 45** *see Vecuronium on page 1212*
- ◆ **Orimune®** *see Polio Vaccines on page 940*
- ◆ **Orinase® Diagnostic Injection** *see Tolbutamide on page 1155*
- ◆ **Orinase® Oral** *see Tolbutamide on page 1155*
- ◆ **ORLAAM®** *see Levomethadyl Acetate Hydrochloride on page 675*

Orlistat *(OR li stat)*

U.S. Brand Names Xenical®

Therapeutic Category Lipase Inhibitor

Use Management of obesity, including weight loss and weight management when used in conjunction with a reduced-calorie diet; reduce the risk of weight regain after prior weight loss; indicated for obese patients with an initial body mass index (BMI) ≥30 kg/m² or ≥27 kg/m² in the presence of other risk factors; see table

Pregnancy Risk Factor B

Pregnancy/Breast-Feeding Implications There are no adequate and well-controlled studies of orlistat in pregnant women. Because animal reproductive studies are not always predictive of human response, orlistat is not recommended for use during pregnancy. Teratogenicity studies were conducted in rats and rabbits at doses up to 800 mg/kg/day. Neither study showed embryotoxicity or teratogenicity. This dose is 23 and 47 times the daily human dose calculated on a body surface area basis for rats and rabbits, respectively. It is not know if orlistat is secreted in human milk. Therefore, it should not be taken by nursing women.

Body Mass Index (BMI), kg/m²
Height (feet, inches)

Weight (lb)	5'0"	5'3"	5'6"	5'9"	6'0"	6'3"
140	27	25	23	21	19	18
150	29	27	24	22	20	19
160	31	28	26	24	22	20
170	33	30	28	25	23	21
180	35	32	29	27	25	23
190	37	34	31	28	26	24
200	39	36	32	30	27	25
210	41	37	34	31	29	26
220	43	39	36	33	30	28
230	45	41	37	34	31	29
240	47	43	39	36	33	30
250	49	44	40	37	34	31

Contraindications Chronic malabsorption syndrome or cholestasis; hypersensitivity to orlistat or any component

Warnings/Precautions Patients should be advised to adhere to dietary guidelines; gastrointestinal adverse events may increase if taken with a diet high in fat (>30% total daily calories from fat). The daily intake of fat should be distributed over three main meals. If taken with any one meal very high in fat, the possibility of gastrointestinal effects increases. Patients should be counseled to take a multivitamin supplement that contains fat-soluble vitamins to ensure adequate nutrition because orlistat has been shown to reduce the absorption of some fat-soluble vitamins and beta-carotene. The supplement should be taken once daily at least 2 hours before or after the administration of orlistat (ie, bedtime). Some patients may develop increased levels of urinary oxalate following treatment; caution should be exercised when prescribing it to patients with a history of hyperoxaluria or calcium oxalate nephrolithiasis. As with any weight-loss agent, the potential exists for misuse in appropriate patient populations (eg, patients with anorexia nervosa or bulimia).

Adverse Reactions
Central nervous system: Headache, dizziness, sleep disorder, anxiety, depression
Dermatitis: Dry skin, rash
Gastrointestinal: Oily spotting, flatus with discharge, fecal urgency, fatty/oily stool, oily evacuation, increased defecation, fecal incontinence
Neuromuscular & skeletal: Back pain, pain of lower extremities, arthritis, myalgia, joint disorder, tendonitis
Otic: Otitis
Respiratory: Influenza; respiratory tract infection; ear, nose, and throat symptoms

Overdosage/Toxicology Single doses of 800 mg and multiple doses of up to 400 mg 3 times daily for 15 days have been studied in normal weight and obese patients without significant adverse findings; in case of significant overdose, it is recommended that the patient be observed for 24 hours

Drug Interactions Decreased effect: Vitamin K absorption may be decreased when taken with orlistat

Usual Dosage 120 mg 3 times daily with each main meal containing fat (during or up to 1 hour after the meal); omit dose if meal is occasionally missed or contains no fat

Monitoring Parameters Changes in coagulation parameters

Patient Information Patient should be on a nutritionally balanced, reduced-calorie diet that contains approximately 30% of calories from fat; daily intake of fat, carbohydrate, and protein should be distributed over the three main meals

Dosage Forms Capsule: 120 mg

♦ **Ormazine** see Chlorpromazine on page 248
♦ **Ornidyl®** see Eflornithine on page 408

Orphenadrine (or FEN a dreen)

U.S. Brand Names Norflex™

Canadian Brand Names Disipal™; Orfenace

Synonyms Orphenadrine Citrate

Therapeutic Category Skeletal Muscle Relaxant

Use Treatment of muscle spasm associated with acute painful musculoskeletal conditions; supportive therapy in tetanus

Pregnancy Risk Factor C

Contraindications Glaucoma, GI obstruction, cardiospasm, myasthenia gravis, hypersensitivity to orphenadrine or any component

Warnings/Precautions Use with caution in patients with CHF or cardiac arrhythmias; some products contain sulfites

(Continued)

Orphenadrine *(Continued)*

Adverse Reactions
>10%:
 Central nervous system: Drowsiness, dizziness
 Ocular: Blurred vision
1% to 10%:
 Cardiovascular: Flushing of face, tachycardia, syncope
 Dermatologic: Rash
 Gastrointestinal: Nausea, vomiting, constipation
 Genitourinary: Decreased urination
 Neuromuscular & skeletal: Weakness
 Ocular: Nystagmus, increased intraocular pressure
 Respiratory: Nasal congestion
<1%: Hallucinations, aplastic anemia

Overdosage/Toxicology
Symptoms of overdose include blurred vision, tachycardia, confusion, seizures, respiratory arrest, dysrhythmias

There is no specific treatment for an antihistamine overdose, however, most of its clinical toxicity is due to anticholinergic effects. Anticholinesterase inhibitors may be useful by reducing acetylcholinesterase. Anticholinesterase inhibitors include physostigmine, neostigmine, pyridostigmine and edrophonium. For anticholinergic overdose with severe life-threatening symptoms, physostigmine 1-2 mg (0.5 mg or 0.02 mg/kg for children) I.V., slowly may be given to reverse these effects. Lethal dose is 2-3 g; treatment is symptomatic.

Drug Interactions CYP2B6, 2D6, and 3A3/4 enzyme substrate; CYP2B6 enzyme inhibitor

Mechanism of Action Indirect skeletal muscle relaxant thought to work by central atropine-like effects; has some euphorigenic and analgesic properties

Pharmacodynamics/Kinetics
Peak effect: Oral: Within 2-4 hours
Duration: 4-6 hours
Protein binding: 20%
Metabolism: Extensive
Half-life: 14-16 hours
Elimination: Primarily in urine (8% as unchanged drug)

Usual Dosage Adults:
Oral: 100 mg twice daily
I.M., I.V.: 60 mg every 12 hours

Dietary Considerations Alcohol: Additive CNS effect, avoid use

Patient Information May cause drowsiness; swallow whole, do not crush or chew sustained release product; avoid alcohol, may impair coordination and judgment

Nursing Implications Do not crush sustained release drug product; raise bed rails, institute safety measures, assist with ambulation

Dosage Forms
Injection, as citrate: 30 mg/mL (2 mL, 10 mL)
Tablet, as citrate: 100 mg
Tablet, as citrate, sustained release: 100 mg

Orphenadrine, Aspirin, and Caffeine
(or FEN a dreen, AS pir in, & KAF een)

U.S. Brand Names Norgesic™; Norgesic™ Forte

Therapeutic Category Skeletal Muscle Relaxant

Dosage Forms
Tablet: Orphenadrine citrate 25 mg, aspirin 385 mg, and caffeine 30 mg
Tablet (Norgesic® Forte): Orphenadrine citrate 50 mg, aspirin 770 mg, and caffeine 60 mg

- **Otic Domeboro**® *see* Aluminum Acetate and Acetic Acid *on page 50*
- **OtiTricin**® **Otic** *see* Neomycin, Polymyxin B, and Hydrocortisone *on page 827*
- **Otobiotic**® **Otic** *see* Polymyxin B and Hydrocortisone *on page 944*
- **Otocalm**® **Ear** *see* Antipyrine and Benzocaine *on page 91*
- **Otocort**® **Otic** *see* Neomycin, Polymyxin B, and Hydrocortisone *on page 827*
- **Otomycin-HPN**® **Otic** *see* Neomycin, Polymyxin B, and Hydrocortisone *on page 827*
- **Otosporin**® **Otic** *see* Neomycin, Polymyxin B, and Hydrocortisone *on page 827*
- **Ovcon**® **35** *see* Ethinyl Estradiol and Norethindrone *on page 451*
- **Ovcon**® **50** *see* Ethinyl Estradiol and Norethindrone *on page 451*
- **Over-the-Counter Products** *see page 1515*
- **Ovide**™ *see* Malathion *on page 710*
- **Ovral**® *see* Ethinyl Estradiol and Norgestrel *on page 454*
- **Ovrette**® *see* Norgestrel *on page 851*
- **O-V Staticin**® *see* Nystatin *on page 856*

Oxacillin (oks a SIL in)
Related Information
Antibiotic Treatment of Adults With Infective Endocarditis *on page 1401*
Community-Acquired Pneumonia in Adults *on page 1419*
U.S. Brand Names Bactocill®; Prostaphlin®
Synonyms Methylphenyl Isoxazolyl Penicillin; Oxacillin Sodium
Therapeutic Category Antibiotic, Penicillin
Use Treatment of infections such as osteomyelitis, septicemia, endocarditis, and CNS infections caused by susceptible strains of *Staphylococcus*
Pregnancy Risk Factor B
Contraindications Hypersensitivity to oxacillin or other penicillins or any component
Warnings/Precautions Elimination rate will be slow in neonates; modify dosage in patients with renal impairment and in the elderly; use with caution in patients with cephalosporin hypersensitivity
Adverse Reactions
1% to 10%: Gastrointestinal: Nausea, diarrhea
<1%: Fever, rash, vomiting, eosinophilia, leukopenia, neutropenia, thrombocytopenia, agranulocytosis, hepatotoxicity, increased AST, hematuria, acute interstitial nephritis, serum sickness-like reactions
Overdosage/Toxicology
Symptoms of penicillin overdose include neuromuscular hypersensitivity (agitation, hallucinations, asterixis, encephalopathy, confusion, and seizures) and electrolyte imbalance with potassium or sodium salts, especially in renal failure
Hemodialysis may be helpful to aid in the removal of the drug from the blood, otherwise most treatment is supportive or symptom directed
Drug Interactions
Decreased effect: Efficacy of oral contraceptives may be reduced; effects of penicillins may be impaired by tetracycline
Increased effect: Disulfiram, probenecid may increase penicillin levels, increased effect of anticoagulants are possible with large I.V. doses
Stability Reconstituted parenteral solution is stable for 3 days at room temperature and 7 days when refrigerated; for I.V. infusion in NS or D$_5$W, solution is stable for 24 hours at room temperature
Mechanism of Action Inhibits bacterial cell wall synthesis by binding to one or more of the penicillin binding proteins (PBPs); which in turn inhibits the final transpeptidation step of peptidoglycan synthesis in bacterial cell walls, thus inhibiting cell wall biosynthesis. Bacteria eventually lyse due to ongoing activity of cell wall autolytic enzymes (autolysins and murein hydrolases) while cell wall assembly is arrested.
Pharmacodynamics/Kinetics
Absorption: Oral: 35% to 67%
Distribution: Into bile, synovial and pleural fluids, bronchial secretions; also distributes to peritoneal and pericardial fluids; crosses the placenta and appears in breast milk; penetrates the blood-brain barrier only when meninges are inflamed
Metabolism: In the liver to active metabolites
Half-life: Children 1 week to 2 years: 0.9-1.8 hours; Adults: 23-60 minutes (prolonged with reduced renal function and in neonates)
Time to peak serum concentration: Oral: Within 2 hours; I.M.: Within 30-60 minutes
Elimination: By kidneys and to small degree the bile as parent drug and metabolites
Usual Dosage
Neonates: I.M., I.V.:
  Postnatal age <7 days:
    <2000 g: 25 mg/kg/dose every 12 hours
    >2000 g: 25 mg/kg/dose every 8 hours
  Postnatal age >7 days:
    <1200 g: 25 mg/kg/dose every 12 hours
    1200-2000 g: 30 mg/kg/dose every 8 hours
    >2000 g: 37.5 mg/kg/dose every 6 hours
Infants and Children:
  Oral: 50-100 mg/kg/day divided every 6 hours
  I.M., I.V.: 150-200 mg/kg/day in divided doses every 6 hours; maximum dose: 12 g/day
Adults:
  Oral: 500-1000 mg every 4-6 hours for at least 5 days
(Continued)

Oxacillin *(Continued)*

I.M., I.V.: 250 mg to 2 g/dose every 4-6 hours

Dosing adjustment in renal impairment: Cl_{cr} <10 mL/minute: Use lower range of the usual dosage

Hemodialysis: Not dialyzable (0% to 5%)

Monitoring Parameters Observe for signs and symptoms of anaphylaxis during first dose

Test Interactions May interfere with urinary glucose tests using cupric sulfate (Benedict's solution, Clinitest®); may inactivate aminoglycosides *in vitro*; false-positive urinary and serum proteins

Patient Information Take orally on an empty stomach 1 hour before meals or 2 hours after meals; take all medication, do not skip doses

Additional Information Sodium content of 1 g: 64.4-71.3 mg (2.8-3.1 mEq)

Dosage Forms

Capsule, as sodium: 250 mg, 500 mg

Powder:

For injection, as sodium: 250 mg, 500 mg, 1 g, 2 g, 4 g, 10 g

For oral solution, as sodium: 250 mg/5 mL (100 mL)

♦ **Oxacillin Sodium** *see Oxacillin on previous page*

Oxamniquine (oks AM ni kwin)

U.S. Brand Names Vansil™

Therapeutic Category Anthelmintic

Use Treatment of all stages of *Schistosoma mansoni* infection

Pregnancy Risk Factor C

Warnings/Precautions Rare epileptiform convulsions have been observed within the first few hours of administration, especially in patients with a history of CNS pathology

Adverse Reactions

>10%: Central nervous system: Dizziness, drowsiness, headache

<10%:

Central nervous system: Insomnia, malaise, hallucinations, behavior changes

Gastrointestinal: GI effects, orange/red discoloration of urine

Hepatic: Elevated LFTs

Dermatologic: Rash, urticaria, pruritus

Renal: Proteinuria

Drug Interactions May be synergistic with praziquantel

Mechanism of Action Not fully elucidated; causes worms to dislodge from their usual site of residence (mesenteric veins to the liver) by paralysis and contraction of musculature and subsequently phagocytized

Pharmacodynamics/Kinetics

Absorption: Oral: Well absorbed

Metabolism: Extensive in the GI tract via oxidation

Half-life: 1-2.5 hours

Time to peak: 1-3 hours

Elimination: <2% unchanged in urine; up to 75% of metabolites excreted in urine

Usual Dosage Oral:

Children <30 kg: 20 mg/kg in 2 divided doses of 10 mg/kg at 2- to 8-hour intervals

Adults: 12-15 mg/kg as a single dose

Test Interactions May interfere with spectrometric or color reaction urinalysis

Patient Information Take with food

Additional Information Strains other than from the western hemisphere may require higher doses

Dosage Forms Capsule: 250 mg

♦ **Oxandrin®** *see Oxandrolone on this page*

Oxandrolone (oks AN droe lone)

U.S. Brand Names Oxandrin®

Therapeutic Category Androgen

Use Adjunctive therapy to promote weight gain after weight loss following extensive surgery, chronic infections, or severe trauma, and in some patients who, without definite pathophysiologic reasons, fail to gain or to maintain normal weight

Restrictions C-III

Pregnancy Risk Factor X

Contraindications Nephrosis, carcinoma of breast or prostate, pregnancy, hypersensitivity to oxandrolone or any component

Warnings/Precautions May stunt bone growth in children; anabolic steroids may cause peliosis hepatis, liver cell tumors, and blood lipid changes with increased risk of arteriosclerosis; monitor diabetic patients carefully; use with caution in elderly patients, they may be at greater risk for prostatic hypertrophy; use with caution in patients with cardiac, renal, or hepatic disease or epilepsy

Adverse Reactions

Male:

Postpubertal:

>10%:

Dermatologic: Acne

Endocrine & metabolic: Gynecomastia

Genitourinary: Bladder irritability, priapism

1% to 10%:
Central nervous system: Insomnia, chills
Endocrine & metabolic: Decreased libido, hepatic dysfunction
Gastrointestinal: Nausea, diarrhea
Genitourinary: Prostatic hypertrophy (elderly)
Hematologic: Iron deficiency anemia, suppression of clotting factors
<1%: Hepatic necrosis, hepatocellular carcinoma
Prepubertal:
>10%:
Dermatologic: Acne
Endocrine & metabolic: Virilism
1% to 10%:
Central nervous system: Chills, insomnia,
Dermatologic: Hyperpigmentation
Gastrointestinal: Diarrhea, nausea
Hematologic: Iron deficiency anemia, suppression of clotting factors
<1%: Hepatic necrosis, hepatocellular carcinoma

Female:
>10%: Endocrine & metabolic: Virilism
1% to 10%:
Central nervous system: Chills, insomnia
Endocrine & metabolic: Hypercalcemia
Gastrointestinal: Nausea, diarrhea
Hematologic: Iron deficiency anemia, suppression of clotting factors
Hepatic: Hepatic dysfunction
<1%: Hepatic necrosis, hepatocellular carcinoma

Drug Interactions Increased toxicity: ACTH, adrenal steroids may increase risk of edema and acne; stanozolol enhances the hypoprothrombinemic effects of oral anticoagulants; enhances the hypoglycemic effects of insulin and sulfonylureas (oral hypoglycemics)

Mechanism of Action Synthetic testosterone derivative with similar androgenic and anabolic actions

Pharmacodynamics/Kinetics
Onset: 1 month
Absorption: Oral absorption is high
Distribution: V_d: 0.578 L/kg
Protein binding, plasma: 94% to 97%
Metabolism: In an analogous fashion to testosterone in the liver
Excretion: 60% renal; 3% feces

Usual Dosage
Children: Total daily dose: ≤0.1 mg/kg or ≤0.045 mg/lb
Adults: 2.5 mg 2-4 times/day; however, since the response of individuals to anabolic steroids varies, a daily dose of as little as 2.5 mg or as much as 20 mg may be required to achieve the desired response. A course of therapy of 2-4 weeks is usually adequate. This may be repeated intermittently as needed.
Dosing adjustment in renal impairment: Caution is recommended because of the propensity of oxandrolone to cause edema and water retention
Dosing adjustment in hepatic impairment: Caution is advised but there are not specific guidelines for dosage reduction

Patient Information High protein, high caloric diet is suggested, restrict salt intake; glucose tolerance may be altered in diabetics

Dosage Forms Tablet: 2.5 mg

Oxaprozin (oks a PROE zin)

Related Information
Nonsteroidal Anti-Inflammatory Agents Comparison on page 1335

U.S. Brand Names Daypro™

Therapeutic Category Anti-inflammatory Agent; Nonsteroidal Anti-inflammatory Drug (NSAID), Oral

Use Acute and long-term use in the management of signs and symptoms of osteoarthritis and rheumatoid arthritis

Pregnancy Risk Factor C

Contraindications Aspirin allergy, 3rd trimester pregnancy or allergy to oxaprozin, history of GI disease, renal or hepatic dysfunction, bleeding disorders, cardiac failure, elderly, debilitated, nursing mothers

Adverse Reactions
1% to 10%:
Central nervous system: CNS inhibition, disturbance of sleep
Dermatologic: Rash
Gastrointestinal: Nausea, dyspepsia, abdominal pain, anorexia, flatulence, vomiting
Genitourinary: Dysuria or frequency
<1%: Anaphylaxis, serum sickness, edema, change in blood pressure, peptic ulcer and/or GI bleed, LFT abnormalities, stomatitis, rectal bleeding, pancreatitis, anemia, thrombocytopenia, leukopenia, ecchymosis, agranulocytosis, pancytopenia, weight gain, weight loss, weakness, malaise, symptoms of upper respiratory infection, pruritus, urticaria, photosensitivity, exfoliative dermatitis, erythema multiforme, Stevens-Johnson syndrome, blurred vision, conjunctivitis, acute interstitial nephritis, nephrotic syndrome, hematuria, renal insufficiency, acute renal failure, decreased menstrual flow
(Continued)

Oxaprozin *(Continued)*

Overdosage/Toxicology

Symptoms of overdose include acute renal failure, vomiting, drowsiness, leukocytes

Management of a nonsteroidal anti-inflammatory drug (NSAID) intoxication is primarily supportive and symptomatic. Fluid therapy is commonly effective in managing the hypotension that may occur following an acute NSAID overdose, except when this is due to an acute blood loss. Seizures tend to be very short-lived and often do not require drug treatment. Although, recurrent seizures should be treated with I.V. diazepam. Since many of the NSAID undergo enterohepatic cycling, multiple doses of charcoal may be needed to reduce the potential for delayed toxicities.

Drug Interactions Increased toxicity: Aspirin, oral anticoagulants, diuretics

Mechanism of Action Inhibits prostaglandin synthesis by decreasing the activity of the enzyme, cyclo-oxygenase, which results in decreased formation of prostaglandin precursors

Pharmacodynamics/Kinetics

Absorption: Almost completely

Protein binding: >99%

Half-life: 40-50 hours

Time to peak: 2-4 hours

Usual Dosage Adults: Oral (individualize dosage to lowest effective dose to minimize adverse effects):

Osteoarthritis: 600-1200 mg once daily

Rheumatoid arthritis: 1200 mg once daily

Maximum dose: 1800 mg/day or 26 mg/kg (whichever is lower) in divided doses

Monitoring Parameters Monitor blood, hepatic, renal, and ocular function

Dosage Forms Tablet: 600 mg

Oxazepam *(oks A ze pam)*

Related Information

Benzodiazepines Comparison *on page 1310*

U.S. Brand Names Serax®

Canadian Brand Names Apo®-Oxazepam; Novo-Oxazepam; Oxpam®; PMS-Oxazepam; Zapex®

Therapeutic Category Antianxiety Agent; Anticonvulsant; Benzodiazepine

Use Treatment of anxiety and management of alcohol withdrawal; may also be used as an anticonvulsant in management of simple partial seizures

Restrictions C-IV

Pregnancy Risk Factor D

Contraindications Hypersensitivity to oxazepam or any component, cross-sensitivity with other benzodiazepines may exist

Warnings/Precautions Avoid using in patients with pre-existing CNS depression, severe uncontrolled pain, or narrow-angle glaucoma; use with caution in patients using other CNS depressants and in the elderly

Adverse Reactions

>10%:

Cardiovascular: Tachycardia, chest pain

Central nervous system: Drowsiness, fatigue, ataxia, lightheadedness, memory impairment, insomnia, anxiety, depression, headache

Dermatologic: Rash

Endocrine & metabolic: Decreased libido

Gastrointestinal: Xerostomia, constipation, diarrhea, decreased salivation, nausea, vomiting, increased or decreased appetite

Neuromuscular & skeletal: Dysarthria

Miscellaneous: Diaphoresis

1% to 10%:

Cardiovascular: Syncope, hypotension

Central nervous system: Confusion, nervousness, dizziness, akathisia

Dermatologic: Dermatitis

Gastrointestinal: Increased salivation, weight gain or loss

Neuromuscular & skeletal: Rigidity, tremor, muscle cramps

Ocular: Blurred vision

Otic: Tinnitus

Respiratory: Nasal congestion, hyperventilation

<1%: Menstrual irregularities, blood dyscrasias, reflex slowing, drug dependence

Overdosage/Toxicology

Symptoms of overdose include somnolence, confusion, coma, hypoactive reflexes, dyspnea, hypotension, slurred speech, impaired coordination

Treatment for benzodiazepine overdose is supportive. Rarely is mechanical ventilation required. Flumazenil has been shown to selectively block the binding of benzodiazepines to CNS receptors, resulting in a reversal of benzodiazepine-induced CNS depression but not the respiratory depression due to toxicity.

Drug Interactions Increased toxicity with CNS depressants (eg, barbiturates, MAO inhibitors, TCAs, alcohol, narcotics, phenothiazines, and other sedative-hypnotics)

Mechanism of Action Benzodiazepine anxiolytic sedative that produces CNS depression at the subcortical level, except at high doses, whereby it works at the cortical level

Pharmacodynamics/Kinetics

Absorption: Oral: Almost completely

Protein binding: 86% to 99%

Metabolism: In the liver to inactive compounds (primarily as glucuronides)
Half-life: 2.8-5.7 hours
Time to peak serum concentration: Within 2-4 hours
Elimination: Excretion of unchanged drug (50%) and metabolites; excreted without need for liver metabolism

Usual Dosage Oral:
Children: 1 mg/kg/day has been administered
Adults:
Anxiety: 10-30 mg 3-4 times/day
Alcohol withdrawal: 15-30 mg 3-4 times/day
Hypnotic: 15-30 mg
Hemodialysis: Not dialyzable (0% to 5%)

Dietary Considerations Alcohol: Additive CNS effect, avoid use
Monitoring Parameters Respiratory and cardiovascular status
Reference Range Therapeutic: 0.2-1.4 µg/mL (SI: 0.7-4.9 µmol/L)
Patient Information Avoid alcohol and other CNS depressants; avoid activities needing good psychomotor coordination until CNS effects are known; drug may cause physical or psychological dependence; avoid abrupt discontinuation after prolonged use
Nursing Implications Provide safety measures (ie, side rails, night light, and call button); remove smoking materials from area; supervise ambulation
Dosage Forms
Capsule: 10 mg, 15 mg, 30 mg
Tablet: 15 mg

Oxiconazole (oks i KON a zole)

U.S. Brand Names Oxistat®
Synonyms Oxiconazole Nitrate
Therapeutic Category Antifungal Agent, Topical
Use Treatment of tinea pedis (athlete's foot), tinea cruris (jock itch), and tinea corporis (ringworm)
Pregnancy Risk Factor B
Contraindications Hypersensitivity to this agent; not for ophthalmic use
Warnings/Precautions May cause irritation during therapy; if a sensitivity to oxiconazole occurs, therapy should be discontinued; avoid contact with eyes or vagina
Adverse Reactions 1% to 10%:
Dermatologic: Itching, erythema
Local: Transient burning, local irritation, stinging, dryness
Drug Interactions CYP3A3/4 enzyme inhibitor
Mechanism of Action The cytoplasmic membrane integrity of fungi is destroyed by oxiconazole which exerts a fungicidal activity through inhibition of ergosterol synthesis. Effective for treatment of tinea pedis, tinea cruris, and tinea corporis. Active against *Trichophyton rubrum*, *Trichophyton mentagrophytes*, *Trichophyton violaceum*, *Microsporum canis*, *Microsporum audouini*, *Microsporum gypseum*, *Epidermophyton floccosum*, *Candida albicans*, and *Malassezia furfur*.
Pharmacodynamics/Kinetics
Absorption: In each layer of the dermis; very little is absorbed systemically after one topical dose
Distribution: To each layer of the dermis; excreted in breast milk
Elimination: <0.3% excreted in urine
Usual Dosage Children and Adults: Topical: Apply once to twice daily to affected areas for 2 weeks (tinea corporis/tinea cruris) to 1 month (tinea pedis)
Patient Information External use only; discontinue if sensitivity or chemical irritation occurs, contact physician if condition fails to improve in 3-4 days
Dosage Forms
Cream, as nitrate: 1% (15 g, 30 g, 60 g)
Lotion, as nitrate: 1% (30 mL)

Oxybutynin (oks i BYOO ti nin)

U.S. Brand Names Ditropan®; Ditropan XL®
Canadian Brand Names Albert® Oxybutynin
Synonyms Oxybutynin Chloride
Therapeutic Category Antispasmodic Agent, Urinary
Use Antispasmodic for neurogenic bladder (urgency, frequency, urge incontinence) and uninhibited bladder
Pregnancy Risk Factor B
Contraindications Glaucoma, myasthenia gravis, partial or complete GI obstruction, GU obstruction, ulcerative colitis, hypersensitivity to drug or specific component, intestinal atony, megacolon, toxic megacolon
(Continued)

Oxybutynin *(Continued)*

Warnings/Precautions Use with caution in patients with urinary tract obstruction, angle-closure glaucoma, hyperthyroidism, reflux esophagitis, heart disease, hepatic or renal disease, prostatic hypertrophy, autonomic neuropathy, ulcerative colitis (may cause ileus and toxic megacolon), hypertension, hiatal hernia. Caution should be used in elderly due to anticholinergic activity (eg, confusion, constipation, blurred vision, and tachycardia).

Adverse Reactions
>10%:
  Central nervous system: Drowsiness
  Gastrointestinal: Xerostomia, constipation
  Miscellaneous: Diaphoresis (decreased)
1% to 10%:
  Cardiovascular: Tachycardia, palpitations
  Central nervous system: Dizziness, insomnia, fever, headache
  Dermatologic: Rash
  Endocrine & metabolic: Decreased flow of breast milk, decreased sexual ability, hot flashes
  Gastrointestinal: Nausea, vomiting
  Genitourinary: Urinary hesitancy or retention
  Neuromuscular & skeletal: Weakness
  Ocular: Blurred vision, mydriatic effect
<1%: Increased intraocular pressure, allergic reaction

Overdosage/Toxicology
Symptoms of overdose include hypotension, circulatory failure, psychotic behavior, flushing, respiratory failure, paralysis, tremor, irritability, seizures, delirium, hallucinations, coma
Symptomatic and supportive treatment; induce emesis or perform gastric lavage followed by charcoal and a cathartic; physostigmine may be required; treat hyperpyrexia with cooling techniques (ice bags, cold applications, alcohol sponges)

Drug Interactions Increased toxicity:
Additive sedation with CNS depressants and alcohol
Additive anticholinergic effects with antihistamines and anticholinergic agents

Mechanism of Action Direct antispasmodic effect on smooth muscle, also inhibits the action of acetylcholine on smooth muscle (exhibits $^1/_5$ the anticholinergic activity of atropine, but is 4-10 times the antispasmodic activity); does not block effects at skeletal muscle or at autonomic ganglia; increases bladder capacity, decreases uninhibited contractions, and delays desire to void; therefore, decreases urgency and frequency

Pharmacodynamics/Kinetics
Onset of effect: Oral: 30-60 minutes
Peak effect: 3-6 hours
Duration: 6-10 hours
Absorption: Oral: Rapid and well absorbed
Metabolism: In the liver
Half-life: 1-2.3 hours
Time to peak serum concentration: Within 60 minutes
Elimination: In urine

Usual Dosage Oral:
Children:
  1-5 years: 0.2 mg/kg/dose 2-4 times/day
  >5 years: 5 mg twice daily, up to 5 mg 4 times/day maximum
Adults: 5 mg 2-3 times/day up to 5 mg 4 times/day maximum
  Extended release: Initial: 5 mg once daily, may increase in 5-10 mg increments; maximum: 30 mg daily
Elderly: 2.5-5 mg twice daily; increase by 2.5 mg increments every 1-2 days
Note: Should be discontinued periodically to determine whether the patient can manage without the drug and to minimize any resistance to the drug

Monitoring Parameters Incontinence episodes, postvoid residual (PVR)

Test Interactions May suppress the wheal and flare reactions to skin test antigens

Patient Information May impair ability to perform activities requiring mental alertness or physical coordination; alcohol or other sedating drugs may enhance drowsiness; swallow extended release tablets whole, do not crush, chew, or break

Nursing Implications Raise bed rails, institute safety measures, assist with ambulation

Dosage Forms
Syrup, as chloride: 5 mg/5 mL (473 mL)
Tablet, as chloride: 5 mg
Tablet, as chloride, extended release: 5 mg, 10 mg

♦ **Oxybutynin Chloride** *see Oxybutynin on previous page*
♦ **Oxycocet** *see Oxycodone and Acetaminophen on next page*
♦ **Oxycodan** *see Oxycodone and Aspirin on page 876*

Oxycodone *(oks i KOE done)*

U.S. Brand Names OxyContin®; OxyIR™; Percolone™; Roxicodone™
Canadian Brand Names Supeudol®
Synonyms Dihydrohydroxycodeinone; Oxycodone Hydrochloride
Therapeutic Category Analgesic, Narcotic
Use Management of moderate to severe pain, normally used in combination with non-narcotic analgesics

Restrictions C-II

Pregnancy Risk Factor B (D if used for prolonged periods or in high doses at term)

Contraindications Hypersensitivity to oxycodone or any component

Warnings/Precautions Use with caution in patients with hypersensitivity reactions to other phenanthrene derivative opioid agonists (morphine, hydrocodone, hydromorphone, levorphanol, oxycodone, oxymorphone); respiratory diseases including asthma, emphysema, COPD, or severe liver or renal insufficiency; some preparations contain sulfites which may cause allergic reactions; dextromethorphan has equivalent antitussive activity but has much lower toxicity in accidental overdose; tolerance or drug dependence may result from extended use

Adverse Reactions

>10%:
Cardiovascular: Hypotension
Central nervous system: Fatigue, drowsiness, dizziness
Gastrointestinal: Nausea, vomiting
Neuromuscular & skeletal: Weakness

1% to 10%:
Central nervous system: Nervousness, headache, restlessness, malaise, confusion
Gastrointestinal: Anorexia, stomach cramps, xerostomia, constipation, biliary spasm
Genitourinary: Ureteral spasms, decreased urination
Local: Pain at injection site
Respiratory: Dyspnea, shortness of breath

<1%: Mental depression, hallucinations, paradoxical CNS stimulation, increased intracranial pressure, skin rash, urticaria, paralytic ileus, histamine release, physical and psychological dependence

Overdosage/Toxicology
Symptoms of overdose include CNS depression, respiratory depression, miosis
Treatment: Naloxone 2 mg I.V. (0.01 mg/kg for children) with repeat administration as necessary up to a total of 10 mg

Drug Interactions CYP2D6 enzyme substrate
Decreased effect: Phenothiazines may antagonize the analgesic effect of opiate agonists
Increased toxicity: CNS depressants, monoamine oxidase inhibitors, general anesthetics, and tricyclic antidepressants may potentiate the effects of opiate agonists; dextroamphetamine may enhance the analgesic effect of opiate agonists

Mechanism of Action Binds to opiate receptors in the CNS, causing inhibition of ascending pain pathways, altering the perception of and response to pain; produces generalized CNS depression

Pharmacodynamics/Kinetics
Onset of pain relief: Oral: Within 10-15 minutes
Peak effect: 0.5-1 hour
Duration: 4-5 hours
Metabolism: In the liver
Elimination: In urine

Usual Dosage Oral:
Immediate release:
Children:
6-12 years: 1.25 mg every 6 hours as needed
>12 years: 2.5 mg every 6 hours as needed
Adults: 5 mg every 6 hours as needed
Controlled release: Adults: 10 mg every 12 hours around-the-clock
Dosing adjustment in hepatic impairment: Reduce dosage in patients with severe liver disease

Dietary Considerations Alcohol: Additive CNS effect, avoid use

Monitoring Parameters Pain relief, respiratory and mental status, blood pressure

Reference Range Blood level of 5 mg/L associated with fatality

Patient Information Avoid alcohol; may cause drowsiness, impaired judgment or coordination; may be addicting if used for prolonged periods; do not crush or chew the controlled-release product

Nursing Implications Observe patient for excessive sedation, respiratory depression, implement safety measures, assist with ambulation

Additional Information Prophylactic use of a laxative should be considered

Dosage Forms
Capsule, as hydrochloride, immediate release (OxyIR™): 5 mg
Liquid, oral, as hydrochloride: 5 mg/5 mL (500 mL)
Solution, oral concentrate, as hydrochloride: 20 mg/mL (30 mL)
Tablet, as hydrochloride: 5 mg
Roxicodone™: 10 mg, 30 mg
Percolone™: 5 mg
Tablet, controlled release, as hydrochloride (OxyContin®): 10 mg, 20 mg, 40 mg, 80 mg

Oxycodone and Acetaminophen (oks i KOE done & a seet a MIN oh fen)

Related Information
Narcotic Agonists Comparison on page 1328

U.S. Brand Names Percocet®; Roxicet® 5/500; Roxilox®; Tylox®

Canadian Brand Names Endocet®; Oxycocet; Percocet®-Demi

Synonyms Acetaminophen and Oxycodone

Therapeutic Category Analgesic, Narcotic

Restrictions C-II

(Continued)

Oxycodone and Acetaminophen *(Continued)*

Dosage Forms

Caplet: Oxycodone hydrochloride 5 mg and acetaminophen 500 mg

Capsule: Oxycodone hydrochloride 5 mg and acetaminophen 500 mg

Solution, oral: Oxycodone hydrochloride 5 mg and acetaminophen 325 mg per 5 mL (5 mL, 500 mL)

Tablet: Oxycodone hydrochloride 5 mg and acetaminophen 325 mg

Oxycodone and Aspirin (oks i KOE done & AS pir in)

Related Information

Narcotic Agonists Comparison *on page 1328*

U.S. Brand Names Codoxy®; Percodan®; Percodan®-Demi; Roxiprin®

Canadian Brand Names Endodan®; Oxycodan

Therapeutic Category Analgesic, Narcotic

Restrictions C-II

Dosage Forms Tablet:

Percodan®: Oxycodone hydrochloride 4.5 mg, oxycodone terephthalate 0.38 mg, and aspirin 325 mg

Percodan®-Demi: Oxycodone hydrochloride 2.25 mg, oxycodone terephthalate 0.19 mg, and aspirin 325 mg

♦ **Oxycodone Hydrochloride** *see Oxycodone on page 874*

♦ **OxyContin®** *see Oxycodone on page 874*

♦ **Oxydess® II** *see Dextroamphetamine on page 342*

♦ **OxyIR™** *see Oxycodone on page 874*

Oxymetholone (oks i METH oh lone)

U.S. Brand Names Anadrol®

Canadian Brand Names Anapolon®

Therapeutic Category Anabolic Steroid; Androgen

Use Anemias caused by the administration of myelotoxic drugs

Restrictions C-III

Pregnancy Risk Factor X

Contraindications Carcinoma of breast or prostate, nephrosis, pregnancy, hypersensitivity to any component

Warnings/Precautions Anabolic steroids may cause peliosis hepatis, liver cell tumors, and blood lipid changes with increased risk of arteriosclerosis; monitor diabetic patients carefully; use with caution in elderly patients, they may be at greater risk for prostatic hypertrophy; use with caution in patients with cardiac, renal, or hepatic disease or epilepsy

Adverse Reactions

Male:

Postpubertal:

>10%:

Dermatologic: Acne

Endocrine & metabolic: Gynecomastia

Genitourinary: Bladder irritability, priapism

1% to 10%:

Central nervous system: Insomnia, chills

Endocrine & metabolic: Decreased libido

Gastrointestinal: Nausea, diarrhea

Genitourinary: Prostatic hypertrophy (elderly)

Hematologic: Iron deficiency anemia, suppression of clotting factors

Hepatic: Hepatic dysfunction

<1%: Hepatic necrosis, hepatocellular carcinoma

Prepubertal:

>10%:

Dermatologic: Acne

Endocrine & metabolic: Virilism

1% to 10%:

Central nervous system: Chills, insomnia

Dermatologic: Hyperpigmentation

Gastrointestinal: Diarrhea, nausea

Hematologic: Iron deficiency anemia, suppression of clotting factors

<1%: Hepatic necrosis, hepatocellular carcinoma

Female:

>10%: Endocrine & metabolic: Virilism

1% to 10%:

Central nervous system: Chills, insomnia

Endocrine & metabolic: Hypercalcemia

Gastrointestinal: Nausea, diarrhea

Hematologic: Iron deficiency anemia, suppression of clotting factors

Hepatic: Hepatic dysfunction

<1%: Hepatic necrosis, hepatocellular carcinoma

Overdosage/Toxicology Abnormal liver function test

Drug Interactions Increased toxicity: Increased oral anticoagulants, insulin requirements may be decreased

Mechanism of Action Stimulates receptors in organs and tissues to promote growth and development of male sex organs and maintains secondary sex characteristics in androgen-deficient males

Pharmacodynamics/Kinetics
Onset: 2-6 months
Half-life: 9 hours
Elimination: Renal, 20% to 25%

Usual Dosage Adults: Erythropoietic effects: Oral: 1-5 mg/kg/day in one daily dose; usual effective dose: 1-2 mg/kg/day; give for a minimum trial of 3-6 months because response may be delayed

Dosing adjustment in hepatic impairment:
Mild to moderate hepatic impairment: Oxymetholone should be used with caution in patients with liver dysfunction because of it's hepatotoxic potential
Severe hepatic impairment: Oxymetholone should **not** be used

Monitoring Parameters Liver function tests

Test Interactions Altered glucose tolerance tests, altered thyroid function tests, altered metyrapone tests

Dosage Forms Tablet: 50 mg

Oxymorphone (oks i MOR fone)

Related Information
Narcotic Agonists Comparison *on page 1328*

U.S. Brand Names Numorphan®

Synonyms Oxymorphone Hydrochloride

Therapeutic Category Analgesic, Narcotic

Use Management of moderate to severe pain and preoperatively as a sedative and a supplement to anesthesia

Restrictions C-II

Pregnancy Risk Factor B (D if used for prolonged periods or in high doses at term)

Contraindications Hypersensitivity to oxymorphone or any component, increased intracranial pressure; severe respiratory depression

Warnings/Precautions Some preparations contain sulfites which may cause allergic reactions; infants <3 months of age are more susceptible to respiratory depression, use with caution and generally in reduced doses in this age group; use with caution in patients with impaired respiratory function or severe hepatic dysfunction and in patients with hypersensitivity reactions to other phenanthrene derivative opioid agonists (codeine, hydrocodone, hydromorphone, levorphanol, oxycodone, oxymorphone); tolerance or drug dependence may result from extended use

Adverse Reactions
>10%:
Cardiovascular: Hypotension
Central nervous system: Fatigue, drowsiness, dizziness
Gastrointestinal: Nausea, vomiting, constipation
Neuromuscular & skeletal: Weakness
Miscellaneous: Histamine release
1% to 10%:
Central nervous system: Nervousness, headache, restlessness, malaise, confusion
Gastrointestinal: Anorexia, stomach cramps, xerostomia, biliary spasm
Genitourinary: Decreased urination, ureteral spasms
Local: Pain at injection site
Respiratory: Dyspnea, shortness of breath
<1%: Mental depression, hallucinations, paradoxical CNS stimulation, increased intracranial pressure, rash, urticaria, paralytic ileus, histamine release, physical and psychological dependence

Overdosage/Toxicology
Symptoms of overdose include respiratory depression, miosis, hypotension, bradycardia, apnea, pulmonary edema
Treatment of an overdose includes support of the patient's airway, establishment of an I.V. line and administration of naloxone 2 mg I.V. (0.01 mg/kg for children) with repeat administration as necessary up to a total of 10 mg.

Drug Interactions
Decreased effect with phenothiazines
Increased effect/toxicity with CNS depressants, TCAs, dextroamphetamine

Stability Refrigerate suppository

Mechanism of Action Oxymorphone hydrochloride (Numorphan®) is a potent narcotic analgesic with uses similar to those of morphine. The drug is a semisynthetic derivative of morphine (phenanthrene derivative) and is closely related to hydromorphone chemically (Dilaudid®).

Pharmacodynamics/Kinetics
Onset of analgesia: I.V., I.M., S.C.: Within 5-10 minutes; Rectal: Within 15-30 minutes
Duration of analgesia: Parenteral, rectal: 3-4 hours
Metabolism: Conjugated with glucuronic acid
Elimination: In urine

Usual Dosage Adults:
I.M., S.C.: 0.5 mg initially, 1-1.5 mg every 4-6 hours as needed
I.V.: 0.5 mg initially
Rectal: 5 mg every 4-6 hours

Dietary Considerations Alcohol: Additive CNS effect, avoid use
(Continued)

Oxymorphone *(Continued)*

Monitoring Parameters Respiratory rate, heart rate, blood pressure, CNS activity

Patient Information Avoid alcohol, may cause drowsiness, impaired judgment or coordination; may cause physical and psychological dependence with prolonged use

Nursing Implications Observe patient for excessive sedation, respiratory depression, implement safety measures, assist with ambulation

Dosage Forms

Injection, as hydrochloride: 1 mg (1 mL); 1.5 mg/mL (1 mL, 10 mL)

Suppository, rectal, as hydrochloride: 5 mg

♦ **Oxymorphone Hydrochloride** *see* Oxymorphone *on previous page*

Oxytetracycline (oks i tet ra SYE kleen)

U.S. Brand Names Terramycin® I.M. Injection; Terramycin® Oral; Uri-Tet® Oral

Synonyms Oxytetracycline Hydrochloride

Therapeutic Category Antibiotic, Tetracycline Derivative

Use Treatment of susceptible bacterial infections; both gram-positive and gram-negative, as well as, *Rickettsia* and *Mycoplasma* organisms

Pregnancy Risk Factor D

Contraindications Hypersensitivity to tetracycline or any component

Warnings/Precautions Avoid in children ≤8 years of age, pregnant and nursing women; photosensitivity can occur with oxytetracycline

Adverse Reactions

>10%: Miscellaneous: Discoloration of teeth and enamel hypoplasia (infants)

1% to 10%:

Dermatologic: Photosensitivity

Gastrointestinal: Nausea, diarrhea

<1%: Pericarditis, increased intracranial pressure, bulging fontanels in infants, pseudotumor cerebri, pruritus, exfoliative dermatitis, dermatologic effects, diabetes insipidus syndrome, vomiting, esophagitis, anorexia, abdominal cramps, antibiotic-associated pseudomembranous colitis, staphylococcal enterocolitis, hepatotoxicity, thrombophlebitis, paresthesia, renal damage, acute renal failure, azotemia, superinfections, anaphylaxis, pigmentation of nails, hypersensitivity reactions, candidal superinfection

Overdosage/Toxicology

Symptoms of overdose include nausea, anorexia, diarrhea

Following GI decontamination, supportive care only

Drug Interactions

Decreased effect with antacids containing aluminum, calcium or magnesium

Iron and bismuth subsalicylate may decrease doxycycline bioavailability

Barbiturates, phenytoin, and carbamazepine decrease doxycycline's half-life

Increased effect of warfarin

Mechanism of Action Inhibits bacterial protein synthesis by binding with the 30S and possibly the 50S ribosomal subunit(s) of susceptible bacteria, cell wall synthesis is not affected

Pharmacodynamics/Kinetics

Absorption: Oral: Adequate (~75%); I.M.: Poor

Distribution: Crosses the placenta

Metabolism: Small amounts in the liver

Half-life: 8.5-9.6 hours (increases with renal impairment)

Time to peak serum concentration: Within 2-4 hours

Elimination: In urine, while much higher amounts can be found in bile

Usual Dosage

Oral:

Children >8 years: 40-50 mg/kg/day in divided doses every 6 hours (maximum: 2 g/24 hours)

Adults: 250-500 mg/dose every 6-12 hours depending on severity of the infection

I.M.:

Children >8 years: 15-25 mg/kg/day (maximum: 250 mg/dose) in divided doses every 8-12 hours

Adults: 250 mg every 24 hours or 300 mg/day divided every 8-12 hours

Syphilis: 30-40 g in divided doses over 10-15 days

Gonorrhea: 1.5 g, then 500 mg every 6 hours for total of 9 g

Uncomplicated chlamydial infections: 500 mg every 6 hours for 7 days

Severe acne: 1 g/day then decrease to 125-500 mg/day

Dosing interval in renal impairment:

Cl$_{cr}$ <10 mL/minute: Administer every 24 hours or avoid use if possible

Dosing adjustment/comments in hepatic impairment: Avoid use in patients with severe liver disease

Administration Injection for intramuscular use only; do not administer with antacids, iron products, or dairy products; administer 1 hour before or 2 hours after meals

Patient Information Avoid unnecessary exposure to sunlight; do not take with antacids, iron products, or dairy products; finish all medication; do not skip doses; take 1 hour before or 2 hours after meals

Dosage Forms

Capsule, as hydrochloride: 250 mg

Injection, as hydrochloride, with lidocaine 2%: 5% [50 mg/mL] (2 mL, 10 mL); 12.5% [125 mg/mL] (2 mL)

Oxytetracycline and Hydrocortisone
(oks i tet ra SYE kleen & hye droe KOR ti sone)
U.S. Brand Names Terra-Cortril® Ophthalmic Suspension
Therapeutic Category Antibiotic/Corticosteroid, Ophthalmic
Dosage Forms Suspension, ophthalmic: Oxytetracycline hydrochloride 0.5% and hydro-
cortisone 0.5% (5 mL)

Oxytetracycline and Polymyxin B
(oks i tet ra SYE kleen & pol i MIKS in bee)
U.S. Brand Names Terak® Ophthalmic Ointment; Terramycin® Ophthalmic Ointment;
Terramycin® w/Polymyxin B Ophthalmic Ointment
Therapeutic Category Antibiotic, Ophthalmic
Dosage Forms
Ointment, ophthalmic/otic: Oxytetracycline hydrochloride 5 mg and polymyxin B 10,000
units per g (3.5 g)
Tablet, vaginal: Oxytetracycline hydrochloride 100 mg and polymyxin B 100,000 units
(10s)

♦ **Oxytetracycline Hydrochloride** *see* Oxytetracycline *on previous page*

Oxytocin (oks i TOE sin)
U.S. Brand Names Pitocin® Injection; Syntocinon® Injection; Syntocinon® Nasal Spray
Canadian Brand Names Toesen®
Synonyms Pit
Therapeutic Category Oxytocic Agent
Use Induces labor at term; controls postpartum bleeding; nasal preparation used to
promote milk letdown in lactating females
Pregnancy Risk Factor X
Contraindications Hypersensitivity to oxytocin or any component; significant cephalo-
pelvic disproportion, unfavorable fetal positions, fetal distress, hypertonic or hyperactive
uterus, contraindicated vaginal delivery, prolapse, total placenta previa, and vasa previa
Warnings/Precautions To be used for medical rather than elective induction of labor;
may produce antidiuretic effect (ie, water intoxication and excess uterine contractions);
high doses or hypersensitivity to oxytocin may cause uterine hypertonicity, spasm,
tetanic contraction, or rupture of the uterus; severe water intoxication with convulsions,
coma, and death is associated with a slow oxytocin infusion over 24 hours
Adverse Reactions
Fetal: <1%: Bradycardia, arrhythmias, intracranial hemorrhage, brain damage, neonatal
jaundice, hypoxia, death
Maternal: <1%: Cardiac arrhythmias, premature ventricular contractions, hypotension,
tachycardia, arrhythmias, seizures, coma, SIADH with hyponatremia, nausea,
vomiting, pelvic hematoma, postpartum hemorrhage, increased uterine motility, fatal
afibrinogenemia, increased blood loss, death, anaphylactic reactions
Overdosage/Toxicology
Symptoms of overdose include tetanic uterine contractions, impaired uterine blood flow,
amniotic fluid embolism, uterine rupture, SIADH, seizures
Treat SIADH via fluid restriction, diuresis, saline administration, and anticonvulsants, if
needed
Drug Interactions Sympathomimetic pressor effects may be increased by oxytocin
resulting in postpartum hypertension
Stability Oxytocin should be stored at room temperature (15°C to 30°C) and protected
from freezing; **incompatible** with norepinephrine, prochlorperazine
Mechanism of Action Produces the rhythmic uterine contractions characteristic to
delivery and stimulates breast milk flow during nursing
Pharmacodynamics/Kinetics
Onset of uterine contractions: I.V.: Within 1 minute
Duration: <30 minutes
Metabolism: Rapid in the liver and plasma (by oxytocinase) and to a smaller degree the
mammary gland
Half-life: 1-5 minutes
Elimination: Renal
Usual Dosage I.V. administration requires the use of an infusion pump
Adults:
Induction of labor: I.V.: 0.001-0.002 units/minute; increase by 0.001-0.002 units every
15-30 minutes until contraction pattern has been established; maximum dose should
not exceed 20 milliunits/minute
Postpartum bleeding:
I.M.: Total dose of 10 units after delivery
I.V.: 10-40 units by I.V. infusion in 1000 mL of intravenous fluid at a rate sufficient to
control uterine atony
Promotion of milk letdown: Intranasal: 1 spray or 3 drops in one or both nostrils 2-3
minutes before breast-feeding
Monitoring Parameters Fluid intake and output during administration; fetal monitoring
Additional Information Sodium chloride 0.9% (NS) and dextrose 5% in water (D_5W)
have been recommended as diluents; dilute 10-40 units to 1 L in NS, LR, or D_5W
Dosage Forms
Injection: 10 units/mL (1 mL, 10 mL)
Solution, nasal: 40 units/mL (2 mL, 5 mL)

- **Oyst-Cal 500 [OTC]** *see* Calcium Carbonate *on page 174*
- **Oystercal® 500** *see* Calcium Carbonate *on page 174*
- **P-071** *see* Cetirizine *on page 233*
- **Pacerone®** *see* Amiodarone *on page 60*

Paclitaxel (PAK li taks el)

Related Information
Cancer Chemotherapy Regimens *on page 1263*
Toxicities of Chemotherapeutic Agents *on page 1288*

U.S. Brand Names Taxol®

Therapeutic Category Antineoplastic Agent, Antimicrotubular; Antineoplastic Agent, Miscellaneous

Use Treatment of metastatic carcinoma of the ovary in combination with cisplatin; treatment of metastatic breast cancer

Pregnancy Risk Factor D

Contraindications History of hypersensitivity to any component

Warnings/Precautions Severe hypersensitivity reactions have been reported with the first or later infusions. Current evidence indicates that prolongation of the infusion (to ≥6 hours) plus premedication may minimize this effect.

Adverse Reactions Irritant chemotherapy
>10%:
  Cardiovascular: Hypotension, abnormal EKG
  Dermatologic: Alopecia
  Gastrointestinal: Nausea, vomiting, diarrhea, mucositis
  Hematologic: Bleeding, neutropenia, leukopenia, thrombocytopenia, anemia, neutropenia is increased with longer infusions
  Hepatic: Abnormal LFTs
  Neuromuscular & skeletal: Peripheral neuropathy, myalgia
  Miscellaneous: Hypersensitivity reactions, infections
1% to 10%: Cardiovascular: Bradycardia, severe cardiovascular events
<1%: Rare reports of radiation pneumonitis have been received in patients receiving concurrent radiotherapy; rare reports of skin abnormalities related to radiation recall as well as reports of maculopapular rash and pruritus have been received

Drug Interactions CYP2C8 and 3A3/4 substrate
Increased toxicity:
  In phase I trials, myelosuppression was more profound when given after cisplatin than with alternative sequence; pharmacokinetic data demonstrates a decrease in clearance of ~33% when administered following cisplatin
  Possibility of an inhibition of metabolism in patients treated with ketoconazole

Stability Store intact vials at room temperature or refrigeration (2°C to 36°C/36°F to 77°F)

Further dilution in NS or D₅W to a concentration of 0.3-1.2 mg/mL is stable for up to 27 hours at room temperature (25°C) and ambient light conditions

Paclitaxel should be administered in either glass or Excel™/PAB™ containers. Should also use **nonpolyvinyl** (non-PVC) tubing (eg, polyethylene) to minimize leaching. Formulated in a vehicle known as Cremophor® EL (polyoxyethylated castor oil). Cremophor® EL has been found to leach the plasticizer DEHP from polyvinyl chloride infusion bags or administration sets. Contact of the undiluted concentrate with plasticized polyvinyl chloride (PVC) equipment or devices is not recommended. Administer through I.V. tubing containing an in-line (NOT >0.22 µ) filter; administration through IVEX-2® filters (which incorporate short inlet and outlet polyvinyl chloride-coated tubing) has not resulted in significant leaching of DEHP.

Visually **compatible** via Y-site: Acyclovir, amikacin, bleomycin, calcium chloride, carboplatin, ceftazidime, ceftriaxone, cimetidine, cisplatin, cyclophosphamide, cytarabine, dexamethasone sodium phosphate, diphenhydramine hydrochloride, doxorubicin, etoposide, famotidine, fluconazole, fluorouracil, ganciclovir, gentamicin, haloperidol lactate, heparin, hydrocortisone sodium succinate, hydrocortisone phosphate hydromorphone, lorazepam, magnesium sulfate, mannitol, meperidine, mesna, methotrexate sodium, metoclopramide hydrochloride, morphine sulfate, ondansetron, potassium chloride, prochlorperazine edisylate, ranitidine hydrochloride, sodium bicarbonate, vancomycin hydrochloride

Visually/chemically **incompatible** via Y-site: amphotericin B, chlorpromazine, hydroxyzine, methylprednisolone, mitoxantrone

Standard I.V. dilution: IVPB: Dose/500-1,000 mL D₅W or NS
Solutions are stable for 27 hours at room temperature (25°C)

Mechanism of Action Paclitaxel exerts its effects on microtubules and their protein subunits, tubulin dimers. Microtubules serve as facilitators of intracellular transport and maintain the integrity and function of cells. Paclitaxel promotes microtubule assembly by enhancing the action of tubulin dimers, stabilizing existing microtubules, and inhibiting their disassembly. Maintaining microtubule assembly inhibits mitosis and cell death. The G₂- and M-phases of the cell cycle are affected. In addition, the drug can distort mitotic spindles, resulting in the breakage of chromosomes.

Pharmacodynamics/Kinetics Administered by I.V. infusion and exhibits a biphasic decline in plasma concentrations
Distribution: Initial rapid decline represents distribution to the peripheral compartment and significant elimination of the drug; later phase is due to a relatively slow efflux of paclitaxel from the peripheral compartment; mean steady state: 42-162 L/m², indicating extensive extravascular distribution and/or tissue binding

Protein binding: 89% to 98% bound to human serum proteins at concentrations of 0.1-50 mcg/mL

Metabolism: In the liver in animals and evidence suggests hepatic metabolism in humans

Half-life, mean, terminal: 5.3-17.4 hours after 1- and 6-hour infusions at dosing levels of 15-275 mg/m^2

Elimination: Urinary recovery of unchanged drug: 1.3% to 12.6% following 1-, 6-, and 24-hour infusions of 15-275 mg/m^2

Mean total body clearance range:
    After 1- and 6-hour infusions: 5.8-16.3 L/hour/m^2
    After 24-hour infusions: 14.2-17.2 L/hour/m^2

Usual Dosage Premedication with dexamethasone (20 mg orally or I.V. at 12 and 6 hours **or** 14 and 7 hours before the dose), diphenhydramine (50 mg I.V. 30-60 minutes prior to the dose), and cimetidine, famotidine or ranitidine (I.V. 30-60 minutes prior to the dose) is recommended

Adults: I.V. infusion: Refer to individual protocol
    Ovarian carcinoma: 135-175 mg/m^2 over 1-24 hours administered every 3 weeks
    Metastatic breast cancer: Treatment is still undergoing investigation; most protocols have used doses of 175-250 mg/m^2 over 1-24 hours every 3 weeks

Hemodialysis: Significant drug removal is unlikely based on physiochemical characteristics

Peritoneal dialysis: Significant drug removal is unlikely based on physiochemical characteristics

Dosage adjustment in hepatic impairment:
    Total bilirubin ≤1.5 mg/dL and AST >2 X normal limits: Total dose <135 mg/m^2
    Total bilirubin 1.6-3.0 mg/dL: Total dose ≤75 mg/m^2
    Total bilirubin ≥3.1 mg/dL: Total dose ≤50 mg/m^2

Administration

Anaphylactoid-like reactions have been reported: Corticosteroids (dexamethasone), H$_1$-antagonists (diphenhydramine), and H$_2$-antagonists (famotidine), should be administered prior to paclitaxel administration to minimize potential for anaphylaxis

Administer I.V. infusion over 1-24 hours; use of a 0.22 micron in-line filter is recommended during the infusion

Monitoring Parameters Monitor for hypersensitivity reactions

Reference Range Mean maximum serum concentrations: 435-802 ng/mL following 24-hour infusions of 200-275 mg/m^2 and were approximately 10% to 30% of those following 6-hour infusions of equivalent doses

Patient Information Alopecia occurs in almost all patients. Contraceptive measures are recommended during therapy. It's important to take dexamethasone prior to therapy secondary to potential hypersensitivity reactions. Notify physician if any signs or symptoms of hypersensitivity reactions.

Dosage Forms Injection: 6 mg/mL (5 mL, 16.7 mL)

♦ **Palafer®** see Ferrous Fumarate on page 478

Palivizumab (pah li VIZ u mab)

U.S. Brand Names Synagis®

Therapeutic Category Monoclonal Antibody

Use Prevention of serious lower respiratory tract disease caused by respiratory syncytial virus (RSV) in pediatric patients at high risk of RSV disease; safety and efficacy were established in infants with bronchopulmonary dysplasia (BPD) and infants with a history of prematurity ≤35 weeks gestational age

Pregnancy Risk Factor C

Pregnancy/Breast-Feeding Implications Animal reproduction studies have not been conducted; it is not known whether palivizumab can cause fetal harm when administered to a pregnant woman or could affect reproductive capacity

Contraindications Patients with a history of severe prior reaction to palivizumab or other components of the product

Warnings/Precautions Anaphylactoid reactions have not been observed following palivizumab administration; however, can occur after administration of proteins. Safety and efficacy of palivizumab have not been demonstrated in the treatment of established RSV disease.

Adverse Reactions The incidence of adverse events was similar between the palivizumab and placebo groups

>1%:
    Central nervous system: Nervousness
    Dermatologic: Fungal dermatitis, eczema, seborrhea
    Gastrointestinal: Diarrhea, vomiting, gastroenteritis
    Hematologic: Anemia
    Hepatic: ALT increase, abnormal LFTs
    Local: Injection site reaction
    Ocular: Conjunctivitis
    Respiratory: Cough, wheezing, bronchiolitis, pneumonia, bronchitis, asthma, croup, dyspnea, sinusitis, apnea
    Miscellaneous: Oral moniliasis, failure to thrive, viral infection, flu syndrome

Overdosage/Toxicology No data from clinical studies are available

Drug Interactions No formal drug interaction studies have been conducted

Stability Store in refrigerator at a temperature between 2°C to 8°C (35.6°F to 46.4°F) in original container; do not freeze

(Continued)

Palivizumab *(Continued)*

Use aseptic technique when reconstituting; add 1 mL of sterile water for injection to a 100 mg vial; swirl vial gently for 30 seconds to avoid foaming. Do not shake vial. Allow to stand at room temperature for 20 minutes until the solution clarifies; solution should be administered with in 6 hours of reconstitution.

Mechanism of Action Exhibits neutralizing and fusion-inhibitory activity against RSV; these activities inhibit RSV replication in laboratory and clinical studies

Pharmacodynamics/Kinetics Half-life: ~18 days

Usual Dosage Children: I.M.: 15 mg/kg of body weight, monthly throughout RSV season (First dose administered prior to commencement of RSV season)

Administration Injection should (preferably) be in the anterolateral aspect of the thigh; gluteal muscle should not be used routinely; injection volume over 1 mL should be given as divided doses

Dose per month equals patient weight in cubagrams x 15 mg/kg divided by 100 mg/mL of palivizumab

Dosage Forms Injection, lyophilized: 100 mg

♦ **Palmitate-A® 5000 [OTC]** *see* Vitamin A *on page 1223*

♦ **2-PAM** *see* Pralidoxime *on page 956*

♦ **Pamelor®** *see* Nortriptyline *on page 852*

Pamidronate *(pa mi DROE nate)*

U.S. Brand Names Aredia™

Synonyms Pamidronate Disodium

Therapeutic Category Antidote, Hypercalcemia; Bisphosphonate Derivative

Use Treatment of hypercalcemia associated with malignancy; treatment of osteolytic bone lesions associated with multiple myeloma or metastatic breast cancer; moderate to severe Paget's disease of bone

Pregnancy Risk Factor C

Contraindications Previous hypersensitivity to pamidronate or other biphosphonates

Warnings/Precautions Use caution in patients with renal impairment as nephropathy was seen in animal studies. However, in contrast to reports of renal failure with other biphosphonates, impairment of renal function has not been reported with pamidronate in studies to date. However, further experience is needed to assess the nephrotoxic potential with higher doses and prolonged administration. Use caution in patients who are pregnant or in the breast-feeding period; leukopenia has been observed with oral pamidronate and monitoring of white blood cell counts is suggested. Vein irritation and thrombophlebitis may occur with infusions. Has not been studied exclusively in the elderly; monitor serum electrolytes periodically since elderly are often receiving diuretics which can result in decreases in serum calcium, potassium, and magnesium.

Adverse Reactions

1% to 10%:
Central nervous system: Malaise, fever, convulsions
Endocrine & metabolic: Hypomagnesemia, hypocalcemia, hypokalemia, fluid overload, hypophosphatemia
Gastrointestinal: GI symptoms, nausea, diarrhea, constipation, anorexia
Hepatic: Abnormal hepatic function
Neuromuscular & skeletal: Bone pain
Respiratory: Dyspnea
<1%: Pain, angioedema, skin rash, occult blood in stools, abnormal taste, leukopenia, increased risk of fractures, nephrotoxicity, hypersensitivity reactions

Overdosage/Toxicology

Symptoms of overdose include hypocalcemia, EKG changes, seizures, bleeding, paresthesia, carpopedal spasm, fever
Treat with I.V. calcium gluconate, general supportive care; fever and hypotension can be treated with corticosteroids

Stability

Reconstitute by adding 10 mL of sterile water for injection to each 30 mg vial of lyophilized pamidronate disodium powder, the resulting solution will be 30 mg/10 mL
Pamidronate is **incompatible** with calcium-containing infusion solutions such as Ringer's injection
Pamidronate may be further diluted in 250-1000 mL of 0.45% or 0.9% sodium chloride or 5% dextrose; pamidronate should not be mixed with calcium-containing solutions (eg, Ringer's solution)
Pamidronate [reconstituted solution and infusion solution] is stable at room temperature and under refrigeration (36°F to 46°F or 2°C to 8°C) for 24 hours

Mechanism of Action A biphosphonate which inhibits bone resorption via actions on osteoclasts or on osteoclast precursors. Does not appear to produce any significant effects on renal tubular calcium handling and is poorly absorbed following oral administration (high oral doses have been reported effective); therefore, I.V. therapy is preferred.

Pharmacodynamics/Kinetics

Onset of effect: 24-48 hours
Maximum effect: 5-7 days
Absorption: Poorly from the GI tract; pharmacokinetic studies are lacking
Half-life, unmetabolized: 2.5 hours
Distribution half-life: 1.6 hours
Urinary (elimination) half-life: 2.5 hours
Bone half-life: 300 days

Elimination: Biphasic; ~50% excreted unchanged in urine within 72 hours

Usual Dosage Drug must be diluted properly before administration and infused intravenously slowly (over at least 1 hour). Adults: I.V.:

Hypercalcemia of malignancy:

Moderate cancer-related hypercalcemia (corrected serum calcium: 12-13 mg/dL): 60-90 mg given as a slow infusion over 2-24 hours

Severe cancer-related hypercalcemia (corrected serum calcium: >13.5 mg/dL): 90 mg as a slow infusion over 2-24 hours

A period of 7 days should elapse before the use of second course; repeat infusions every 2-3 weeks have been suggested, however, could be administered every 2-3 months according to the degree and of severity of hypercalcemia and/or the type of malignancy

Osteolytic bone lesions with multiple myeloma: 90 mg in 500 mL D_5W, 0.45% NaCl or 0.9% NaCl administered over 4 hours on a monthly basis

Osteolytic bone lesions with metastatic breast cancer: 90 mg in 250 mL D_5W, 0.45% NaCl or 0.9% NaCl administered over 2 hours, repeated every 3-4 weeks

Paget's disease: 30 mg in 500 mL 0.45% NaCl, 0.9% NaCl or D_5W administered over 4 hours for 3 consecutive days

Dosing adjustment in renal impairment: Adjustment is not necessary

Monitoring Parameters Serum electrolytes, monitor for hypocalcemia for at least 2 weeks after therapy; serum calcium, phosphate, magnesium, potassium, serum creatinine, CBC with differential

Reference Range Calcium (total): Adults: 9.0-11.0 mg/dL (SI: 2.05-2.54 mmol/L), may slightly decrease with aging; Phosphorus: 2.5-4.5 mg/dL (SI: 0.81-1.45 mmol/L)

Patient Information Maintain adequate intake of calcium and vitamin D; report any fever, sore throat, or unusual bleeding to your physician

Dosage Forms Powder for injection, lyophilized, as disodium: 30 mg, 60 mg, 90 mg

◆ **Pamidronate Disodium** see Pamidronate on previous page

◆ **p-Aminoclonidine** see Apraclonidine on page 94

◆ **Pamprin IB® [OTC]** see Ibuprofen on page 593

◆ **Panadol® [OTC]** see Acetaminophen on page 19

◆ **Panasal® 5/500** see Hydrocodone and Aspirin on page 576

◆ **Pan-B Antibodies** see Rituximab on page 1035

◆ **Pancrease®** see Pancrelipase on this page

◆ **Pancrease® MT 4** see Pancrelipase on this page

◆ **Pancrease® MT 10** see Pancrelipase on this page

◆ **Pancrease® MT 16** see Pancrelipase on this page

◆ **Pancrease® MT 20** see Pancrelipase on this page

Pancrelipase (pan kre LI pase)

U.S. Brand Names Cotazym®; Cotazym-S®; Creon 10®; Creon 20®; Ilozyme®; Ku-Zyme® HP; Pancrease®; Pancrease® MT 4; Pancrease® MT 10; Pancrease® MT 16; Pancrease® MT 20; Protilase®; Ultrase® MT12; Ultrase® MT20; Viokase®; Zymase®

Synonyms Lipancreatin

Therapeutic Category Enzyme, Pancreatic; Pancreatic Enzyme

Use Replacement therapy in symptomatic treatment of malabsorption syndrome caused by pancreatic insufficiency

Pregnancy Risk Factor C

Contraindications Hypersensitivity to pancrelipase or any component, pork protein

Warnings/Precautions Pancrelipase is inactivated by acids; use microencapsulated products whenever possible, since these products permit better dissolution of enzymes in the duodenum and protect the enzyme preparations from acid degradation in the stomach

Adverse Reactions

1% to 10%: High doses:

Endocrine & metabolic: Hyperuricemia

Gastrointestinal: Nausea, cramps, constipation, diarrhea

Genitourinary: Hyperuricosuria

Ocular: Lacrimation

Respiratory: Sneezing, bronchospasm

<1%: Rash, shortness of breath, bronchospasm, irritation of the mouth

Overdosage/Toxicology Symptoms of overdose include diarrhea, other transient intestinal upset, hyperuricosuria, hyperuricemia

Drug Interactions

Decreased effect: Calcium carbonate, magnesium hydroxide

Increased effect: H_2-antagonists (eg, ranitidine, cimetidine)

Mechanism of Action Replaces endogenous pancreatic enzymes to assist in digestion of protein, starch and fats

Pharmacodynamics/Kinetics

Absorption: Not absorbed, acts locally in GI tract

Elimination: In feces

Usual Dosage Oral:

Powder: Actual dose depends on the digestive requirements of the patient

Children <1 year: Start with $1/8$ teaspoonful with feedings

Adults: 0.7 g with meals

(Continued)

Pancrelipase *(Continued)*

Enteric coated microspheres and microtablets: The following dosage recommendations are only an approximation for initial dosages. The actual dosage will depend on the digestive requirements of the individual patient.

Children:
<1 year: 2000 units of lipase with meals
1-6 years: 4000-8000 units of lipase with meals and 4000 units with snacks
7-12 years: 4000-12,000 units of lipase with meals and snacks

Adults: 4000-16,000 units of lipase with meals and with snacks or 1-3 tablets/capsules before or with meals and snacks; in severe deficiencies, dose may be increased to 8 tablets/capsules

Occluded feeding tubes: One tablet of Viokase® crushed with one 325 mg tablet of sodium bicarbonate (to activate the Viokase®) in 5 mL of water can be instilled into the nasogastric tube and clamped for 5 minutes; then, flushed with 50 mL of tap water

Patient Information Do not chew capsules, microspheres, or microtablets; take before or with meals; avoid inhaling powder dosage form

Dosage Forms

Capsule:
Cotazym®: Lipase 8000 units, protease 30,000 units, amylase 30,000 units
Ku-Zyme® HP: Lipase 8000 units, protease 30,000 units, amylase 30,000 units
Ultrase® MT12: Lipase 12,000 units, protease 39,000 units, amylase 39,000 units
Ultrase® MT20: Lipase 20,000 units, protease 65,000 units, amylase 65,000 units
Enteric coated microspheres (Pancrease®): Lipase 4000 units, protease 25,000 units, amylase 20,000 units

Enteric coated microtablets:
Pancrease® MT 4: Lipase 4500 units, protease 12,000 units, amylase 12,000 units
Pancrease® MT 10: Lipase 10,000 units, protease 30,000 units, amylase 30,000 units
Pancrease® MT 16: Lipase 16,000 units, protease 48,000 units, amylase 48,000 units
Pancrease® MT 20: Lipase 20,000 units, protease 44,000 units, amylase 56,000 units

Enteric coated spheres:
Cotazym-S®: Lipase 5000 units, protease 20,000 units, amylase 20,000 units
Pancrelipase, Protilase®: Lipase 4000 units, protease 25,000 units, amylase 20,000 units
Zymase®: Lipase 12,000 units, protease 24,000 units, amylase 24,000 units

Delayed release:
Creon® 10: Lipase 10,000 units, protease 37,500 units, amylase 33,200 units
Creon® 20: Lipase 20,000 units, protease 75,000 units, amylase 66,400 units

Powder (Viokase®): Lipase 16,800 units, protease 70,000 units, amylase 70,000 units per 0.7 g

Tablet:
Ilozyme®: Lipase 11,000 units, protease 30,000 units, amylase 30,000 units
Viokase®: Lipase 8000 units, protease 30,000 units, amylase 30,000 units

Pancuronium *(pan kyoo ROE nee um)*

Related Information
Neuromuscular Blocking Agents Comparison *on page 1331*

U.S. Brand Names Pavulon®

Synonyms Pancuronium Bromide

Therapeutic Category Neuromuscular Blocker Agent, Nondepolarizing; Skeletal Muscle Relaxant

Use Drug of choice for neuromuscular blockade except in patients with renal failure, hepatic failure, or cardiovascular instability; produce skeletal muscle relaxation during surgery after induction of general anesthesia, increase pulmonary compliance during assisted respiration, facilitate endotracheal intubation, preferred muscle relaxant for neonatal cardiac patients, must provide artificial ventilation

Pregnancy Risk Factor C

Contraindications Hypersensitivity to pancuronium, bromide, or any component

Warnings/Precautions Ventilation must be supported during neuromuscular blockade. Electrolyte imbalance alters blockade. Use with caution in patients with myasthenia gravis or other neuromuscular diseases, pre-existing pulmonary, hepatic, renal disease, and in the elderly.

Adverse Reactions

1% to 10%:
Cardiovascular: Elevation in pulse rate, elevated blood pressure, tachycardia, hypertension
Dermatologic: Rash, itching
Gastrointestinal: Excessive salivation
<1%: Skin flushing, edema, erythema, burning sensation along the vein, profound muscle weakness, wheezing, circulatory collapse, bronchospasm, hypersensitivity reaction

Causes of prolonged neuromuscular blockade:
Excessive drug administration
Cumulative drug effect, decreased metabolism/excretion (hepatic and/or renal impairment)
Accumulation of active metabolites

Electrolyte imbalance (hypokalemia, hypocalcemia, hypermagnesemia, hypernatremia)

Hypothermia

Drug interactions

Increased sensitivity to muscle relaxants (eg, neuromuscular disorders such as myasthenia gravis or polymyositis)

Overdosage/Toxicology Symptoms of overdose include apnea, respiratory depression, cardiovascular collapse; pyridostigmine, neostigmine, or edrophonium in conjunction with atropine will usually antagonize the action of pancuronium

Drug Interactions

Increased toxicity: Magnesium sulfate, furosemide can increase or decrease neuromuscular blockade (dose-dependent)

Prolonged neuromuscular blockade:

Inhaled anesthetics

Local anesthetics

Calcium channel blockers

Antiarrhythmics (eg, quinidine or procainamide)

Antibiotics (eg, aminoglycosides, tetracyclines, vancomycin, clindamycin)

Immunosuppressants (eg, cyclosporine)

Stability Refrigerate; however, is stable for up to 6 months at room temperature; I.V. form is **incompatible** when mixed with diazepam at a Y-site injection

Mechanism of Action Blocks neural transmission at the myoneural junction by binding with cholinergic receptor sites

Pharmacodynamics/Kinetics

Peak effect: I.V.: Within 2-3 minutes

Duration: 40-60 minutes (dose dependent)

Metabolism: 30% to 45% in the liver

Half-life: 110 minutes

Elimination: In urine (55% to 70% as unchanged drug)

Usual Dosage Based on ideal body weight in obese patients. **I.V.:**

Infants >1 month, Children, and Adults: Initial: 0.04-0.1 mg/kg; maintenance dose: 0.02-0.1 mg/kg/dose every 30 minutes to 3 hours as needed

Continuous I.V. infusions are not recommended due to case reports of prolonged paralysis

Dosing adjustment in renal impairment: Elimination half-life is doubled, plasma clearance is reduced and rate of recovery is sometimes much slower

Cl$_{cr}$ 10-50 mL/minute: Administer 50% of normal dose

Cl$_{cr}$ <10 mL/minute: Do not use

Dosing adjustment/comments in hepatic disease: Elimination half-life is doubled, plasma clearance is doubled, recovery time is prolonged, volume of distribution is increased (50%) and results in a slower onset, higher total dosage and prolongation of neuromuscular blockade

Patients with liver disease may develop slow resistance to nondepolarizing muscle relaxant; large doses may be required and problems may arise in antagonism

Monitoring Parameters Heart rate, blood pressure, assisted ventilation status; cardiac monitor, blood pressure monitor, and ventilator required

Dosage Forms Injection, as bromide: 1 mg/mL (10 mL); 2 mg/mL (2 mL, 5 mL)

♦ **Pancuronium Bromide** see Pancuronium on previous page

♦ **Pandel®** see Hydrocortisone on page 579

♦ **Panmycin® Oral** see Tetracycline on page 1122

♦ **Panretin®** see Alitretinoin on page 43

♦ **Panthoderm® [OTC]** see Dexpanthenol on page 340

♦ **Pantothenyl Alcohol** see Dexpanthenol on page 340

Papaverine (pa PAV er een)

U.S. Brand Names Genabid®; Pavabid®; Pavatine®

Synonyms Papaverine Hydrochloride

Therapeutic Category Vasodilator

Use Oral: Relief of peripheral and cerebral ischemia associated with arterial spasm and myocardial ischemia complicated by arrhythmias

Investigational: Parenteral: Various vascular spasms associated with muscle spasms as in myocardial infarction, angina, peripheral and pulmonary embolism, peripheral vascular disease, angiospastic states, and visceral spasm (ureteral, biliary, and GI colic); testing for impotence

Pregnancy Risk Factor C

Contraindications Hypersensitivity to papaverine or its components

Warnings/Precautions Use with caution in patients with glaucoma; administer I.V. cautiously since apnea and arrhythmias may result; may, in large doses, depress A-V and intraventricular cardiac conduction leading to serious arrhythmias (eg, premature beats, paroxysmal tachycardia); chronic hepatitis noted with jaundice, eosinophilia, and abnormal LFTs

Adverse Reactions <1%: Flushing of the face, tachycardias, mild hypertension, vertigo, drowsiness, sedation, lethargy, headache, nausea, constipation, abdominal distress, anorexia, diarrhea, hepatic hypersensitivity, chronic hepatitis

Overdosage/Toxicology

Symptoms of acute overdose include nausea, vomiting weakness, gastric distress, ataxia, drowsiness, nystagmus, diplopia, incoordination, lethargy, and coma with cyanosis, and respiratory depression

(Continued)

Papaverine (Continued)

After gastric decontamination, treatment is supportive with conventional therapy (ie, fluids, positioning and vasopressors for hypotension)

Drug Interactions CYP2D6 enzyme substrate

Decreased effect: Papaverine decreases the effects of levodopa

Increased toxicity: Additive effects with CNS depressants

Stability Protect from heat or freezing; refrigerate injection at 2°C to 8°C (35°F to 46°F); solutions should be clear to pale yellow; precipitates with lactated Ringer's

Mechanism of Action Smooth muscle spasmolytic producing a generalized smooth muscle relaxation including: vasodilatation, gastrointestinal sphincter relaxation, bronchiolar muscle relaxation, and potentially a depressed myocardium (with large doses); muscle relaxation may occur due to inhibition or cyclic nucleotide phosphodiesterase, increasing cyclic AMP; muscle relaxation is unrelated to nerve innervation; papaverine increases cerebral blood flow in normal subjects; oxygen uptake is unaltered

Pharmacodynamics/Kinetics

Onset of action: Oral: Rapid

Protein binding: 90%

Metabolism: Rapidly in the liver

Half-life: 0.5-1.5 hours

Elimination: Primarily as metabolites in urine

Usual Dosage Adults: Oral, sustained release: 150-300 mg every 12 hours; in difficult cases: 150 mg every 8 hours

Patient Information May cause dizziness, flushing, headache, diarrhea, sweating, tiredness, anorexia, jaundice, constipation; caution when driving or performing tasks needing alertness; if side effects become bothersome, consult your physician

Dosage Forms Capsule, sustained release, as hydrochloride: 150 mg

- **Papaverine Hydrochloride** see Papaverine on previous page
- **Para-Aminosalicylate Sodium** see Aminosalicylate Sodium on page 59
- **Paracetamol** see Acetaminophen on page 19
- **Paraflex®** see Chlorzoxazone on page 252
- **Parafon Forte™ DSC** see Chlorzoxazone on page 252
- **Paraplatin®** see Carboplatin on page 193
- **Par Decon®** see Chlorpheniramine, Phenyltoloxamine, Phenylpropanolamine, and Phenylephrine on page 247

Paregoric (par e GOR ik)

Synonyms Camphorated Tincture of Opium

Therapeutic Category Analgesic, Narcotic; Antidiarrheal

Use Treatment of diarrhea or relief of pain; neonatal opiate withdrawal

Restrictions C-III

Pregnancy Risk Factor B (D when used long-term or in high doses)

Contraindications Hypersensitivity to opium or any component; diarrhea caused by poisoning until the toxic material has been removed

Warnings/Precautions Use with caution in patients with respiratory, hepatic or renal dysfunction, severe prostatic hypertrophy, or history of narcotic abuse; opium shares the toxic potential of opiate agonists, and usual precautions of opiate agonist therapy should be observed; some preparations contain sulfites which may cause allergic reactions; infants <3 months of age are more susceptible to respiratory depression, use with caution and generally in reduced doses in this age group; tolerance or drug dependence may result from extended use

Adverse Reactions

>10%:

Cardiovascular: Hypotension

Central nervous system: Drowsiness, dizziness

Gastrointestinal: Constipation

Neuromuscular & skeletal: Weakness

1% to 10%:

Central nervous system: Restlessness, headache, malaise

Genitourinary: Ureteral spasms, decreased urination

Miscellaneous: Histamine release

<1%: Peripheral vasodilation, insomnia, CNS depression, mental depression, increased intracranial pressure, anorexia, stomach cramps, nausea, vomiting, biliary tract spasm, urinary tract spasm, miosis, respiratory depression, physical and psychological dependence, increased liver function tests

Overdosage/Toxicology

Symptoms of overdose include hypotension, drowsiness, seizures, respiratory depression

Naloxone 2 mg I.V. (0.01 mg/kg for children) with repeat administration as necessary up to a total of 10 mg

Drug Interactions Increased effect/toxicity with CNS depressants (eg, alcohol, narcotics, benzodiazepines, TCAs, MAO inhibitors, phenothiazine)

Stability Store in light-resistant, tightly closed container

Mechanism of Action Increases smooth muscle tone in GI tract, decreases motility and peristalsis, diminishes digestive secretions

Pharmacodynamics/Kinetics In terms of opium

Metabolism: In the liver

Elimination: In urine, primarily as morphine glucuronide conjugates and as parent compound (morphine, codeine, papaverine, etc)

Usual Dosage Oral:

Neonatal opiate withdrawal: Instill 3-6 drops every 3-6 hours as needed, or initially 0.2 mL every 3 hours; increase dosage by approximately 0.05 mL every 3 hours until withdrawal symptoms are controlled; it is rare to exceed 0.7 mL/dose. Stabilize withdrawal symptoms for 3-5 days, then gradually decrease dosage over a 2- to 4-week period.

Children: 0.25-0.5 mL/kg 1-4 times/day

Adults: 5-10 mL 1-4 times/day

Dietary Considerations Alcohol: Additive CNS effect, avoid use

Patient Information Avoid alcohol, may cause drowsiness, impaired judgment or coordination; may cause physical and psychological dependence with prolonged use

Nursing Implications Observe patient for excessive sedation, respiratory depression, implement safety measures, assist with ambulation

Additional Information Contains morphine 0.4 mg/mL and alcohol 45%

Dosage Forms Liquid: 2 mg morphine equivalent/5 mL [equivalent to 20 mg opium powder] (5 mL, 60 mL, 473 mL, 4000 mL)

- ◆ **Paremyd® Ophthalmic** see Hydroxyamphetamine and Tropicamide on page 585
- ◆ **Parenteral Multiple Vitamin** see Vitamins, Multiple on page 1226
- ◆ **Parenteral Nutrition, Calculations for Therapy - Adult Patients** see page 1442
- ◆ **Parepectolin®** see Kaolin and Pectin With Opium on page 647
- ◆ **Par Glycerol®** see Iodinated Glycerol on page 622

Paricalcitol (par eh CAL ci tol)

U.S. Brand Names Zemplar™

Therapeutic Category Vitamin D Analog

Use Prevention and treatment of secondary hyperparathyroidism associated with chronic renal failure. Has been evaluated only in hemodialysis patients.

Pregnancy Risk Factor C

Contraindications Should not be given to patients with evidence of vitamin D toxicity, hypercalcemia, or hypersensitivity to any of the ingredients of this product

Warnings/Precautions The most frequently reported adverse reactions with paricalcitol include nausea, vomiting, and edema. Chronic administration can place patients at risk of hypercalcemia, elevated calcium-phosphorus product and metastatic calcification; it should not be used in patients with evidence of hypercalcemia or vitamin D toxicity.

Adverse Reactions The three most frequently reported events in clinical studies were nausea, vomiting, and edema, which are commonly seen in hemodialysis patients.

>10%: Gastrointestinal: Nausea (13%)

1% to 10%:

Cardiovascular: Palpitations, peripheral edema (7%)

Central nervous system: Chills, malaise, fever, lightheadedness (5%)

Gastrointestinal: Vomiting (8%), GI bleeding (5%), xerostomia (3%)

Respiratory: Pneumonia (5%)

Miscellaneous: Flu-like symptoms, sepsis

Overdosage/Toxicology Acute overdose may cause hypercalcemia; monitor serum calcium and phosphorus closely during titration of paricalcitol; dosage reduction/interruption may be required if hypercalcemia develops; chronic use may predispose to metastatic calcification; bone lesions may develop if parathyroid hormone is suppressed below normal

Drug Interactions Phosphate or vitamin D-related compounds should not be taken concurrently; digitalis toxicity is potentiated by hypercalcemia

Mechanism of Action Synthetic vitamin D analog which has been shown to reduce PTH serum concentrations

Pharmacodynamics/Kinetics

Protein binding: >99%

Elimination: Hepatobiliary excretion (74%) in healthy subjects; urinary excretion (16%), metabolites represent 51% to 59%

Kinetics have not been investigated in geriatric, pediatric, or hepatically impaired patients

Usual Dosage Adults: I.V.: 0.04-0.1 mcg/kg (2.8-7 mcg) given as a bolus dose no more frequently than every other day at any time during dialysis; doses as high as 0.24 mcg/kg (16.8 mcg) have been administered safely; usually start with 0.04 mcg/kg 3 times/week by I.V. bolus, increased by 0.04 mcg/kg every 2 weeks; the dose of paricalcitol should be adjusted based on serum PTH levels

Serum PTH Levels

PTH Level	Paricalcitol Dose
Same or increasing	Increase
Decreased by <30%	Increase
Decreased by <30% and <60%	Maintain
Decreased by >60%	Decrease
1.5-3 times upper limit of normal	Maintain

(Continued)

Paricalcitol (Continued)

Monitoring Parameters Serum calcium and phosphorus should be monitored closely (eg, twice weekly) during dose titration; monitor for signs and symptoms of vitamin D intoxication; serum PTH; in trials, a mean PTH level reduction of 30% was achieved within 6 weeks

Patient Information To ensure effectiveness of therapy, it is important to adhere to a dietary regimen of calcium supplementation and phosphorous restriction; avoid excessive use of aluminum-containing compounds

Dosage Forms Injection: 5 mcg/mL (1 mL, 2 mL, 5 mL)

♦ **Parkinson's Disease, Dosing of Drugs Used for Treatment of** see page 1336

♦ **Parlodel®** see Bromocriptine on page 155

♦ **Parnate®** see Tranylcypromine on page 1168

Paromomycin (par oh moe MYE sin)

U.S. Brand Names Humatin®

Synonyms Paromomycin Sulfate

Therapeutic Category Amebicide

Use Treatment of acute and chronic intestinal amebiasis; preoperatively to suppress intestinal flora; tapeworm infestations; treatment of *Cryptosporidium*

Pregnancy Risk Factor C

Contraindications Intestinal obstruction, renal failure, known hypersensitivity to paromomycin or components

Warnings/Precautions Use with caution in patients with impaired renal function or possible or proven ulcerative bowel lesions

Adverse Reactions
1% to 10%: Gastrointestinal: Diarrhea, abdominal cramps, nausea, vomiting, heartburn
<1%: Headache, vertigo, exanthema, rash, pruritus, steatorrhea, secondary enterocolitis, eosinophilia, ototoxicity

Overdosage/Toxicology
Symptoms of overdose include nausea, vomiting, diarrhea
Following GI decontamination, if possible; care is supportive and symptomatic

Drug Interactions
Decreased effect of digoxin, vitamin A, and methotrexate
Increased effect of oral anticoagulants, neuromuscular blockers, and polypeptide antibiotics

Mechanism of Action Acts directly on ameba; has antibacterial activity against normal and pathogenic organisms in the GI tract; interferes with bacterial protein synthesis by binding to 30S ribosomal subunits

Pharmacodynamics/Kinetics
Absorption: Not absorbed via oral route
Elimination: 100% unchanged in feces

Usual Dosage Oral:
Intestinal amebiasis: Children and Adults: 25-35 mg/kg/day in 3 divided doses for 5-10 days
Dientamoeba fragilis: Children and Adults: 25-30 mg/kg/day in 3 divided doses for 7 days
Cryptosporidium: Adults with AIDS: 1.5-2.25 g/day in 3-6 divided doses for 10-14 days (occasionally courses of up to 4-8 weeks may be needed)
Tapeworm (fish, dog, bovine, porcine):
Children: 11 mg/kg every 15 minutes for 4 doses
Adults: 1 g every 15 minutes for 4 doses
Hepatic coma: Adults: 4 g/day in 2-4 divided doses for 5-6 days
Dwarf tapeworm: Children and Adults: 45 mg/kg/dose every day for 5-7 days

Patient Information Take full course of therapy; do not skip doses; notify physician if ringing in ears, hearing loss, or dizziness occurs

Dosage Forms Capsule, as sulfate: 250 mg

♦ **Paromomycin Sulfate** see Paromomycin on this page

Paroxetine (pa ROKS e teen)

Related Information
Antidepressant Agents Comparison on page 1301

U.S. Brand Names Paxil™

Therapeutic Category Antidepressant, Serotonin Reuptake Inhibitor

Use Treatment of depression; treatment of panic disorder and obsessive-compulsive disorder

Pregnancy Risk Factor C

Contraindications Do not use within 14 days of MAO inhibitors

Warnings/Precautions Use cautiously in patients with a history of seizures, mania, renal disease, cardiac disease, suicidal patients, children, or during breast-feeding in lactating women

Adverse Reactions
>10%:
Central nervous system: Headache, somnolence, dizziness, insomnia
Gastrointestinal: Nausea, xerostomia, constipation, diarrhea
Genitourinary: Ejaculatory disturbances
Neuromuscular & skeletal: Weakness
Miscellaneous: Diaphoresis

1% to 10%:
Cardiovascular: Palpitations, vasodilation, postural hypotension
Central nervous system: Nervousness, anxiety
Endocrine & metabolic: Decreased libido
Gastrointestinal: Anorexia, flatulence, vomiting
Neuromuscular & skeletal: Tremor, paresthesia
<1%: Bradycardia, hypotension, migraine, akinesia, alopecia, amenorrhea, gastritis, anemia, leukopenia, arthritis, eye pain, ear pain, asthma, bruxism, thirst

Overdosage/Toxicology
Symptoms of overdose include nausea, vomiting, drowsiness, sinus tachycardia, and dilated pupils
There are no specific antidotes, following attempts at decontamination, treatment is supportive and symptomatic; forced diuresis, dialysis, and hemoperfusion are unlikely to be beneficial

Drug Interactions CYP2D6 enzyme substrate (minor); CYP1A2, 2D6, and 3A3/4 enzyme inhibitor

Decreased effect: Phenobarbital, phenytoin
Increased toxicity: Alcohol, cimetidine, MAO inhibitors (hyperpyrexic crisis); increased effect/toxicity of TCAs, fluoxetine, sertraline, phenothiazines, class 1C antiarrhythmics, warfarin

Mechanism of Action Paroxetine is a selective serotonin reuptake inhibitor, chemically unrelated to tricyclic, tetracyclic, or other antidepressants; presumably, the inhibition of serotonin reuptake from brain synapse stimulated serotonin activity in the brain

Pharmacodynamics/Kinetics
Metabolism: Extensive following absorption by cytochrome P-450 enzymes
Half-life: 21 hours
Elimination: Metabolites are excreted in bile and urine

Usual Dosage Adults: Oral:
Depression: 20 mg once daily (maximum: 60 mg/day), preferably in the morning; in elderly, debilitated, or patients with hepatic or renal impairment, start with 10 mg/day (maximum: 40 mg/day); adjust doses at 7-day intervals
Panic disorder and obsessive compulsive disorder: Recommended average daily dose: 40 mg, this dosage should be given after an adequate trial on 20 mg/day and then titrating upward

Monitoring Parameters Hepatic and renal function tests, blood pressure, heart rate
Test Interactions ↑ LFTs
Dosage Forms
Suspension, oral: 10 mg/5 mL
Tablet: 10 mg, 20 mg, 30 mg, 40 mg

- ◆ **PAS** see Aminosalicylate Sodium on page 59
- ◆ **Pathocil®** see Dicloxacillin on page 350
- ◆ **Pavabid®** see Papaverine on page 885
- ◆ **Pavatine®** see Papaverine on page 885
- ◆ **Paveral Stanley Syrup With Codeine Phosphate** see Codeine on page 291
- ◆ **Pavulon®** see Pancuronium on page 884
- ◆ **Paxil™** see Paroxetine on previous page
- ◆ **Paxipam®** see Halazepam on page 556
- ◆ **PBZ®** see Tripelennamine on page 1187
- ◆ **PBZ-SR®** see Tripelennamine on page 1187
- ◆ **PCA** see Procainamide on page 968
- ◆ **PCE®** see Erythromycin on page 427
- ◆ **PediaCare® Oral** see Pseudoephedrine on page 993
- ◆ **Pediacof®** see Chlorpheniramine, Phenylephrine, and Codeine on page 246
- ◆ **Pediaflor®** see Fluoride on page 498
- ◆ **Pediapred® Oral** see Prednisolone on page 961
- ◆ **PediaProfen™** see Ibuprofen on page 593
- ◆ **Pediatric ALS Algorithm, Asystole and Pulseless Arrest** see page 1445
- ◆ **Pediatric ALS Algorithm, Bradycardia** see page 1444
- ◆ **Pediatric Triban®** see Trimethobenzamide on page 1183
- ◆ **Pediatrix** see Acetaminophen on page 19
- ◆ **Pediazole®** see Erythromycin and Sulfisoxazole on page 429
- ◆ **Pedi-Cort V® Creme** see Clioquinol and Hydrocortisone on page 277
- ◆ **PediOtic® Otic** see Neomycin, Polymyxin B, and Hydrocortisone on page 827
- ◆ **Pedituss®** see Chlorpheniramine, Phenylephrine, and Codeine on page 246
- ◆ **PedvaxHIB™** see Haemophilus b Conjugate Vaccine on page 554

Pegademase Bovine (peg A de mase BOE vine)
U.S. Brand Names Adagen™
Therapeutic Category Enzyme, Replacement Therapy
Use Enzyme replacement therapy for adenosine deaminase (ADA) deficiency in patients with severe combined immunodeficiency disease (SCID) who can not benefit from bone marrow transplant; not a cure for SCID, unlike bone marrow transplants, injections must be used the rest of the child's life, therefore is not really an alternative
Pregnancy Risk Factor C
(Continued)

Pegademase Bovine *(Continued)*

Contraindications Hypersensitivity to pegademase bovine; not to be used as preparatory or support therapy for bone marrow transplantation

Warnings/Precautions Use with caution in patients with thrombocytopenia

Adverse Reactions <1%: Headache, pain at injection site

Drug Interactions Decreased effect: Vidarabine

Stability Refrigerate at 2°C to 8°C (36°F to 46°F); do not freeze

Mechanism of Action Adenosine deaminase is an enzyme that catalyzes the deamination of both adenosine and deoxyadenosine. Hereditary lack of adenosine deaminase activity results in severe combined immunodeficiency disease, a fatal disorder of infancy characterized by profound defects of both cellular and humoral immunity. It is estimated that 25% of patients with the autosomal recessive form of severe combined immunodeficiency lack adenosine deaminase.

Pharmacodynamics/Kinetics

Plasma adenosine deaminase activity generally normalizes after 2-3 weeks of weekly I.M. injections

Absorption: Rapid

Half-life: 48-72 hours

Usual Dosage Children: I.M.: Dose given every 7 days, 10 units/kg the first dose, 15 units/kg the second dose, and 20 units/kg the third dose; maintenance dose: 20 units/kg/week is recommended depending on patient's ADA level; maximum single dose: 30 units/kg

Patient Information Not a cure for SCID; unlike bone marrow transplants, injections must be used the rest of the child's life; frequent blood tests are necessary to monitor effect and adjust the dose as needed

Dosage Forms Injection: 250 units/mL (1.5 mL)

Pegaspargase *(peg AS par jase)*

Related Information

Cancer Chemotherapy Regimens *on page 1263*

U.S. Brand Names Oncaspar®

Synonyms PEG-L-asparaginase

Therapeutic Category Antineoplastic Agent, Protein Synthesis Inhibitor

Use Patients with acute lymphoblastic leukemia (ALL) who require asparaginase in their treatment regimen, but have developed hypersensitivity to the native forms of asparaginase. Use as a single agent should only be undertaken when multiagent chemotherapy is judged to be inappropriate for the patient.

Pregnancy Risk Factor C

Pregnancy/Breast-Feeding Implications Clinical effects on the fetus: Based on limited reports in humans, the use of asparaginase does not seem to pose a major risk to the fetus when used in the 2nd and 3rd trimesters, or when exposure occurs prior to conception in either females or males. Because of the teratogenicity observed in animals and the lack of human data after 1st trimester exposure, asparaginase should be used cautiously, if at all, during this period.

Contraindications Pancreatitis or a history of pancreatitis; patients who have had significant hemorrhagic events associated with prior asparaginase therapy; previous serious allergic reactions, such as generalized urticaria, bronchospasm, laryngeal edema, hypotension, or other unacceptable adverse reactions to pegaspargase.

Warnings/Precautions

The U.S. Food and Drug Administration (FDA) currently recommends that procedures for proper handling and disposal of antineoplastic agents be considered

Hypersensitivity reactions to pegaspargase, including life-threatening anaphylaxis, may occur during therapy, especially in patients with known hypersensitivity to the other forms of asparaginase. As a routine precaution, keep patients under observation for 1 hour with resuscitation equipment and other agents necessary to treat anaphylaxis (eg, epinephrine, oxygen, I.V. steroids) available.

Use caution when treating patients with pegaspargase in combination with hepatotoxic agents, especially when liver dysfunction is present

Adverse Reactions

Overall, the adult patients had a somewhat higher incidence of asparaginase toxicities, except for hypersensitivity reactions, than the pediatric patients

>10%:

Cardiovascular: Edema

Central nervous system: Pain

Dermatologic: Urticaria, erythema

Gastrointestinal: Pancreatitis, (sometimes fulminant and fatal); increased serum amylase and lipase

Hepatic: Elevations of AST/ALT and bilirubin (direct and indirect); jaundice, ascites and hypoalbuminemia, fatty changes in the liver, liver failure

Local: Induration, tenderness

Neuromuscular & skeletal: Arthralgia

Respiratory: Bronchospasm, dyspnea

Miscellaneous: Hypersensitivity: Acute or delayed anaphylaxis, edema of the lips

>5%:

Central nervous system: Fever, chills, malaise

Dermatologic: Rash

Gastrointestinal: Emetic potential: Mild (>5%)

Hepatic: ALT increase

Respiratory: Dyspnea or bronchospasm

1% to 5%:

Cardiovascular: Hypotension, tachycardia, thrombosis

Central nervous system: Chills

Dermatologic: Lip edema

Endocrine & metabolic: Hyperglycemia requiring insulin (3%)

Gastrointestinal: Abdominal pain, pancreatitis (1%)

Hematologic: Decreased anticoagulant effect, disseminated intravascular coagulation, decreased fibrinogen, hemolytic anemia, leukopenia, pancytopenia, thrombocytopenia, increased thromboplastin

Myelosuppressive effects:

WBC: Mild

Platelets: Mild

Onset (days): 7

Nadir (days): 14

Recovery (days): 21

Local: Injection site hypersensitivity

Respiratory: Dyspnea

Overdosage/Toxicology Symptoms of overdose include nausea, diarrhea

Drug Interactions

Decreased effect: Methotrexate: Asparaginase terminates methotrexate action by inhibition of protein synthesis and prevention of cell entry into the S phase

Increased toxicity:

Aspirin, dipyridamole, heparin, warfarin, NSAIDs: Imbalances in coagulation factors have been noted with the use of pegaspargase - use with caution

Vincristine and prednisone: An increase in toxicity has been noticed when asparaginase is administered with VCR and prednisone

Cyclophosphamide (decreases metabolism)

Mercaptopurine (increases hepatotoxicity)

Vincristine (increases neuropathy)

Prednisone (increases hyperglycemia)

Stability Avoid excessive agitation; do **not** shake; refrigerate at 2°C to 8°C (36°F to 46°F); single-use vial; discard unused portions

Do not use if cloudy or if precipitate is present; do not use if stored at room temperature for >48 hours; do **not** freeze; do not use product if it is known to have been frozen

Standard I.M. dilution: Usually no >2 mL/injection site

Standard I.V. dilution: Dose/100 mL NS or D_5W; stable for 48 hours at room temperature

Mechanism of Action Pegaspargase is a modified version of the enzyme L-asparaginase; the L-asparaginase used in the manufacture of pegaspargase is derived from *Escherichia coli*

Some malignant cells (ie, lymphoblastic leukemia cells and those of lymphocyte derivation) must acquire the amino acid asparagine from surrounding fluid such as blood, whereas normal cells can synthesize their own asparagine. Asparaginase is an enzyme that deaminates asparagine to aspartic acid and ammonia in the plasma and extracellular fluid and therefore deprives tumor cells of the amino acid for protein synthesis.

Pharmacodynamics/Kinetics

Distribution: V_d: 4-5 L/kg; 70% to 80% of plasma volume; does not penetrate the CSF

Metabolism: Systemically degraded, only trace amounts are found in the urine

Half-life: 5.73 days

Elimination: Clearance unaffected by age, renal function, or hepatic function; asparaginase was measurable for at least 15 days following initial treatment with pegaspargase

Usual Dosage Refer to individual protocols; dose must be individualized based upon clinical response and tolerance of the patient

I.M. administration is **preferred** over I.V. administration; I.M. administration may decrease the incidence of hepatotoxicity, coagulopathy, and GI and renal disorders

Children: I.M., I.V.:

Body surface area <0.6 m²: 82.5 international units/kg every 14 days

Body surface area ≥0.6 m²: 2500 international units/m² every 14 days

Adults: I.M., I.V.: 2500 international units/m² every 14 days

Hemodialysis: Significant drug removal is unlikely based on physiochemical characteristics

Peritoneal dialysis: Significant drug removal is unlikely based on physiochemical characteristics

Administration

I.M.: Must only be given as a deep intramuscular injection into a large muscle; limit the volume of a single injection site to 2 mL; if the volume to be administered is >2 mL, use multiple injection sites

I.V.: Administer over a period of 1-2 hours in 100 mL of 0.9% sodium chloride or dextrose 5% in water, through an infusion that is already running

Monitoring Parameters Vital signs during administration, CBC, urinalysis, amylase, liver enzymes, prothrombin time, renal function tests, urine dipstick for glucose, blood glucose

Patient Information

Inform patients of the possibility of hypersensitivity reactions, including immediate anaphylaxis

Instruct patients that the simultaneous use of pegaspargase with other drugs that may increase the risk of bleeding should be avoided

Patients should notify their physician of adverse reactions that occur

(Continued)

Pegaspargase *(Continued)*

Nursing Implications Do not filter solution; appropriate agents for maintenance of an adequate airway and treatment of a hypersensitivity reaction (antihistamine, epinephrine, oxygen, I.V. corticosteroids) should be readily available. Be prepared to treat anaphylaxis at each administration; monitor for onset of abdominal pain and mental status changes.

Dosage Forms Injection, preservative free: 750 units/mL

♦ **PEG-L-asparaginase** *see* Pegaspargase *on page 890*

♦ **Peglyte™** *see* Polyethylene Glycol-Electrolyte Solution *on page 942*

Pemoline *(PEM oh leen)*

U.S. Brand Names Cylert®

Synonyms Phenylisohydantoin; PIO

Therapeutic Category Central Nervous System Stimulant, Nonamphetamine

Use Treatment of attention deficit/hyperactivity disorder (ADHD); narcolepsy

Restrictions C-IV

Pregnancy Risk Factor B

Contraindications Liver disease; hypersensitivity to pemoline or any component; children <6 years of age; Tourette's syndrome, psychoses

Warnings/Precautions Use with caution in patients with renal dysfunction, hypertension, or a history of abuse

Adverse Reactions

>10%:
  Central nervous system: Insomnia
  Gastrointestinal: Anorexia, weight loss

1% to 10%:
  Central nervous system: Dizziness, drowsiness, mental depression
  Dermatologic: Rash
  Gastrointestinal: Stomach pain, nausea

<1%: Seizures, precipitation of Tourette's syndrome, hallucination, headache, movement disorders, growth reaction, diarrhea, increased liver enzymes (usually reversible upon discontinuation), hepatitis, jaundice

Overdosage/Toxicology

Symptoms of overdose include tachycardia, hallucinations, agitation

There is no specific antidote for intoxication and the bulk of the treatment is supportive. Hyperactivity and agitation usually respond to reduced sensory input or benzodiazepines, however, with extreme agitation haloperidol (2-5 mg I.M. for adults) may be required. Hyperthermia is best treated with external cooling measures, or when severe or unresponsive, muscle paralysis with pancuronium may be needed.

Drug Interactions

Decreased effect of insulin

Increased effect/toxicity with CNS depressants, CNS stimulants, sympathomimetics

Mechanism of Action Blocks the reuptake mechanism of dopaminergic neurons, appears to act at the cerebral cortex and subcortical structures; CNS and respiratory stimulant with weak sympathomimetic effects; actions may be mediated via increase in CNS dopamine

Pharmacodynamics/Kinetics

Peak effect: 4 hours
Duration: 8 hours
Protein binding: 50%
Metabolism: Partially by the liver
Half-life: Children: 7-8.6 hours; Adults: 12 hours
Time to peak serum concentration: Oral: Within 2-4 hours
Elimination: In urine; only negligible amounts can be detected in feces

Usual Dosage Children ≥6 years: Oral: Initial: 37.5 mg given once daily in the morning, increase by 18.75 mg/day at weekly intervals; usual effective dose range: 56.25-75 mg/day; maximum: 112.5 mg/day; dosage range: 0.5-3 mg/kg/24 hours; significant benefit may not be evident until third or fourth week of administration

Dosing adjustment/comments in renal impairment: Cl_{cr} <50 mL/minute: Avoid use

Dietary Considerations Alcohol: Additive CNS effect, avoid use

Monitoring Parameters Liver enzymes

Patient Information Avoid caffeine; avoid alcoholic beverages; last daily dose should be given several hours before retiring; do not abruptly discontinue; prolonged use may cause dependence

Nursing Implications Administer medication in the morning

Dosage Forms

Tablet: 18.75 mg, 37.5 mg, 75 mg
Tablet, chewable: 37.5 mg

Penciclovir *(pen SYE kloe veer)*

U.S. Brand Names Denavir™

Therapeutic Category Antiviral Agent, Topical

Use Topical treatment of herpes simplex labialis (cold sores); potentially used for Epstein-Barr virus infections

Pregnancy Risk Factor B

Contraindications Previous and significant adverse reactions to famciclovir; hypersensitivity to the product or any of its components

Warnings/Precautions Penciclovir should only be used on herpes labialis on the lips and face; because no data are available, application to mucous membranes is not recommended. Avoid application in or near eyes since it may cause irritation. The effect of penciclovir has not been established in immunocompromised patients.

Adverse Reactions

Central nervous system: Headache (5.3%)

Dermatologic: Mild erythema (50%), local anesthesia (0.9%)

Mechanism of Action In cells infected with HSV-1 or HSV-2, viral thymidine kinase phosphorylates penciclovir to a monophosphate form which, in turn, is converted to penciclovir triphosphate by cellular kinases. Penciclovir triphosphate inhibits HSV polymerase competitively with deoxyguanosine triphosphate. Consequently, herpes viral DNA synthesis and, therefore, replication are selectively inhibited

Pharmacodynamics/Kinetics Measurable penciclovir concentrations were not detected in plasma or urine of health male volunteers following single or repeat application of the 1% cream at a dose of 180 mg penciclovir daily (approximately 67 times the usual clinical dose)

Usual Dosage Apply cream at the first sign or symptom of cold sore (eg, tingling, swelling); apply every 2 hours during waking hours for 4 days

Monitoring Parameters Reduction in virus shedding, negative cultures for herpes virus; resolution of pain and healing of cold sore lesion

Patient Information Inform your physician if you experience significant burning, itching, stinging, or redness when using this medication

Additional Information Penciclovir is the active metabolite of the prodrug famciclovir. Penciclovir is an alternative to topical acyclovir for HSV-1 and HSV-2 infections. Neither drug will prevent recurring HSV attacks.

Dosage Forms Cream: 1% [10 mg/g] (2 g)

- ♦ **Penecort®** see Hydrocortisone on page 579
- ♦ **Penetrex™** see Enoxacin on page 412
- ♦ **Penglobe®** see Bacampicillin on page 121

Penicillamine (pen i SIL a meen)

Related Information

Antacid Drug Interactions on page 1296

U.S. Brand Names Cuprimine®; Depen®

Synonyms D-3-Mercaptovaline; β,β-Dimethylcysteine; D-Penicillamine

Therapeutic Category Antidote, Copper Toxicity; Antidote, Lead Toxicity; Chelating Agent, Oral

Use Treatment of Wilson's disease, cystinuria, adjunct in the treatment of rheumatoid arthritis; lead, mercury, copper, and possibly gold poisoning. **(Note:** Oral DMSA is preferable for lead or mercury poisoning); primary biliary cirrhosis; as adjunctive therapy following initial treatment with calcium EDTA or BAL

Pregnancy Risk Factor D

Contraindications Hypersensitivity to penicillamine or components; renal insufficiency; patients with previous penicillamine-related aplastic anemia or agranulocytosis; concomitant administration with other hematopoietic-depressant drugs (eg, gold, immunosuppressants, antimalarials, phenylbutazone)

Warnings/Precautions Cross-sensitivity with penicillin is possible; therefore, should be used cautiously in patients with a history of penicillin allergy. Patients on penicillamine for Wilson's disease or cystinuria should receive pyridoxine supplementation 25 mg/day; once instituted for Wilson's disease or cystinuria, continue treatment on a daily basis; interruptions of even a few days have been followed by hypersensitivity with reinstitution of therapy. Penicillamine has been associated with fatalities due to agranulocytosis, aplastic anemia, thrombocytopenia, Goodpasture's syndrome, and myasthenia gravis; patients should be warned to report promptly any symptoms suggesting toxicity; approximately 33% of patients will experience an allergic reaction; since toxicity may be dose related, it is recommended not to exceed 750 mg/day in elderly.

Adverse Reactions

>10%:

Dermatologic: Rash, urticaria, itching (44% to 50%)

Gastrointestinal: Hypogeusia (25% to 33%)

Neuromuscular & skeletal: Arthralgia

1% to 10%:

Cardiovascular: Edema of the face, feet, or lower legs

Central nervous system: Fever, chills

Gastrointestinal: Weight gain, sore throat

Genitourinary: Bloody or cloudy urine

Hematologic: Aplastic or hemolytic anemia, leukopenia (2%), thrombocytopenia (4%)

Miscellaneous: White spots on lips or mouth, positive ANA

<1%: Fatigue, toxic epidermal necrolysis, pemphigus, increased friability of the skin, iron deficiency, nausea, vomiting, anorexia, pancreatitis, cholestatic jaundice, hepatitis, myasthenia gravis syndrome, weakness, optic neuritis, tinnitus, nephrotic syndrome, coughing, wheezing, SLE-like syndrome, spitting of blood, allergic reactions, lymphadenopathy

Overdosage/Toxicology

Symptoms of overdose include nausea and vomiting

Following GI decontamination, treatment is supportive

(Continued)

Penicillamine *(Continued)*

Drug Interactions

Decreased effect with iron and zinc salts, antacids (magnesium, calcium, aluminum) and food

Decreased effect/levels of digoxin

Increased effect of gold, antimalarials, immunosuppressants, phenylbutazone (hematologic, renal toxicity)

Stability Store in tight, well-closed containers

Mechanism of Action Chelates with lead, copper, mercury and other heavy metals to form stable, soluble complexes that are excreted in urine; depresses circulating IgM rheumatoid factor, depresses T-cell but not B-cell activity; combines with cystine to form a compound which is more soluble, thus cystine calculi are prevented

Pharmacodynamics/Kinetics

Absorption: Oral: 40% to 70%

Metabolism: Small amounts of hepatic metabolism

Protein binding: 80% bound to albumin

Half-life: 1.7-3.2 hours

Time to peak serum concentration: Within 2 hours

Elimination: Primarily (30% to 60%) in urine as unchanged drug

Usual Dosage Oral:

Rheumatoid arthritis:

Children: Initial: 3 mg/kg/day (≤250 mg/day) for 3 months, then 6 mg/kg/day (≤500 mg/day) in divided doses twice daily for 3 months to a maximum of 10 mg/kg/day in 3-4 divided doses

Adults: 125-250 mg/day, may increase dose at 1- to 3-month intervals up to 1-1.5 g/day

Wilson's disease (doses titrated to maintain urinary copper excretion >1 mg/day):

Infants <6 months: 250 mg/dose once daily

Children <12 years: 250 mg/dose 2-3 times/day

Adults: 250 mg 4 times/day

Cystinuria:

Children: 30 mg/kg/day in 4 divided doses

Adults: 1-4 g/day in divided doses every 6 hours

Lead poisoning (continue until blood lead level is <60 μg/dL): Children and Adults: 25-35 mg/kg/d, administered in 3-4 divided doses; initiating treatment at 25% of this dose and gradually increasing to the full dose over 2-3 weeks may minimize adverse reactions

Primary biliary cirrhosis: 250 mg/day to start, increase by 250 mg every 2 weeks up to a maintenance dose of 1 g/day, usually given 250 mg 4 times/day

Arsenic poisoning: Children: 100 mg/kg/day in divided doses every 6 hours for 5 days; maximum: 1 g/day

Dosing adjustment/comments in renal impairment: Cl_{cr} <50 mL/minute: Avoid use

Administration Administer on an empty stomach (1 hour before meals and at bedtime)

Monitoring Parameters Urinalysis, CBC with differential, platelet count, liver function tests; weekly measurements of urinary and blood concentration of the intoxicating metal is indicated (3 months has been tolerated)

CBC: WBC <3500/mm^3, neutrophils <2000/mm^3 or monocytes >500/mm^3 indicate need to stop therapy immediately; quantitative 24-hour urine protein at 1- to 2-week intervals initially (first 2-3 months); urinalysis, LFTs occasionally; platelet counts <100,000/mm^3 indicate need to stop therapy until numbers of platelets increase

Patient Information Take at least 1 hour before a meal on an empty stomach; patients with cystinuria should drink copious amounts of water; notify physician if unusual bleeding or bruising, or persistent fever, sore throat, or fatigue occurs; report any unexplained cough, shortness of breath, or rash; loss of taste may occur; do not skip or miss doses or discontinue without notifying physician

Nursing Implications For patients who cannot swallow, contents of capsules may be administered in 15-30 mL of chilled puréed fruit or fruit juice; patients should be warned to report promptly any symptoms suggesting toxicity

Dosage Forms

Capsule: 125 mg, 250 mg

Tablet: 250 mg

Extemporaneous Preparations A 50 mg/mL suspension may be made by mixing twenty 250 mg capsules with 1 g carboxymethylcellulose, 50 g sucrose, 100 mg citric acid, parabens, and purified water to a total volume of 100 mL; cherry flavor may be added. Stability is 30 days refrigerated.

Nahata MC and Hipple TF, *Pediatric Drug Formulations*, 1st ed, Cincinnati, OH: Harvey Whitney Books Co, 1990.

Penicillin G Benzathine and Procaine Combined

(pen i SIL in jee BENZ a theen & PROE kane KOM bined)

U.S. Brand Names Bicillin® C-R; Bicillin® C-R 900/300

Synonyms Penicillin G Procaine and Benzathine Combined

Therapeutic Category Antibiotic, Penicillin

Use May be used in specific situations in the treatment of streptococcal infections

Pregnancy Risk Factor B

Contraindications Known hypersensitivity to penicillin or any component

Warnings/Precautions Use with caution in patients with impaired renal function, impaired cardiac function or seizure disorder

Overdosage/Toxicology
Many beta-lactam-containing antibiotics have the potential to cause neuromuscular hyperirritability or convulsive seizures

Hemodialysis may be helpful to aid in the removal of the drug from the blood, otherwise most treatment is supportive or symptom directed

Drug Interactions Probenecid, tetracyclines, methotrexate, aminoglycosides

Stability Store in the refrigerator

Mechanism of Action Inhibits bacterial cell wall synthesis by binding to one or more of the penicillin binding proteins (PBPs); which in turn inhibits the final transpeptidation step of peptidoglycan synthesis in bacterial cell walls, thus inhibiting cell wall biosynthesis. Bacteria eventually lyse due to ongoing activity of cell wall autolytic enzymes (autolysins and murein hydrolases) while cell wall assembly is arrested.

Usual Dosage I.M.:
Children:
<30 lb: 600,000 units in a single dose
30-60 lb: 900,000 units to 1.2 million units in a single dose
Children >60 lb and Adults: 2.4 million units in a single dose

Monitoring Parameters Observe for signs and symptoms for anaphylaxis during first dose

Test Interactions May interfere with urinary glucose tests using cupric sulfate (Benedict's solution, Clinitest®); may inactivate aminoglycosides *in vitro*; positive Coombs' [direct], increased protein

Nursing Implications Administer by deep I.M. injection in the upper outer quadrant of the buttock

Dosage Forms
Injection:
300,000 units [150,000 units each of penicillin g benzathine and penicillin g procaine] (10 mL)
600,000 units [300,000 units each penicillin g benzathine and penicillin g procaine] (1 mL)
1,200,000 units [600,000 units each penicillin g benzathine and penicillin g procaine] (2 mL)
2,400,000 units [1,200,000 units each penicillin g benzathine and penicillin g procaine] (4 mL)
Injection: Penicillin g benzathine 900,000 units and penicillin g procaine 300,000 units per dose (2 mL)

Penicillin G Benzathine, Parenteral
(pen i SIL in jee BENZ a theen, pa REN ter al)

Related Information
Treatment of Sexually Transmitted Diseases *on page 1429*

U.S. Brand Names Bicillin® L-A; Permapen®

Canadian Brand Names Megacillin® Susp

Synonyms Benzathine Benzylpenicillin; Benzathine Penicillin G; Benzylpenicillin Benzathine

Therapeutic Category Antibiotic, Penicillin

Use Active against some gram-positive organisms, few gram-negative organisms such as *Neisseria gonorrhoeae*, and some anaerobes and spirochetes; used in the treatment of syphilis; used only for the treatment of mild to moderately severe infections caused by organisms susceptible to low concentrations of penicillin G or for prophylaxis of infections caused by these organisms

Pregnancy Risk Factor B

Contraindications Known hypersensitivity to penicillin or any component

Warnings/Precautions Use with caution in patients with impaired renal function, seizure disorder, or history of hypersensitivity to other beta-lactams; CDC and AAP do not currently recommend the use of penicillin G benzathine to treat congenital syphilis or neurosyphilis due to reported treatment failures and lack of published clinical data on its efficacy

Adverse Reactions
1% to 10%: Local: Pain
<1%: Convulsions, confusion, drowsiness, fever, rash, electrolyte imbalance, hemolytic anemia, positive Coombs' reaction, thrombophlebitis, myoclonus, acute interstitial nephritis, Jarisch-Herxheimer reaction, hypersensitivity reactions, anaphylaxis

Overdosage/Toxicology
Symptoms of penicillin overdose include neuromuscular hypersensitivity (agitation, hallucinations, asterixis, encephalopathy, confusion, and seizures) and electrolyte imbalance with potassium or sodium salts, especially in renal failure

Hemodialysis may be helpful to aid in the removal of the drug from the blood, otherwise most treatment is supportive or symptom directed

Drug Interactions
Decreased effect: Tetracyclines may decrease penicillin effectiveness; decreased oral contraceptive effect is possible
Increased effect:
Probenecid may increase penicillin levels
Aminoglycosides → synergistic efficacy; heparin and parenteral penicillins may result in increased bleeding

Stability Store in refrigerator
(Continued)

Penicillin G Benzathine, Parenteral *(Continued)*

Mechanism of Action Interferes with bacterial cell wall synthesis during active multiplication, causing cell wall death and resultant bactericidal activity against susceptible bacteria

Pharmacodynamics/Kinetics

Absorption: I.M.: Slow

Time to peak serum concentration: Within 12-24 hours; serum levels are usually detectable for 1-4 weeks depending on the dose; larger doses result in more sustained levels rather than higher levels

Usual Dosage I.M.: Administer undiluted injection; higher doses result in more sustained rather than higher levels. Use a penicillin G benzathine-penicillin G procaine combination to achieve early peak levels in acute infections.

Infants and Children:

Group A streptococcal upper respiratory infection: 25,000-50,000 units/kg as a single dose; maximum: 1.2 million units

Prophylaxis of recurrent rheumatic fever: 25,000-50,000 units/kg every 3-4 weeks; maximum: 1.2 million units/dose

Early syphilis: 50,000 units/kg as a single injection; maximum: 2.4 million units

Syphilis of more than 1-year duration: 50,000 units/kg every week for 3 doses; maximum: 2.4 million units/dose

Adults:

Group A streptococcal upper respiratory infection: 1.2 million units as a single dose

Prophylaxis of recurrent rheumatic fever: 1.2 million units every 3-4 weeks or 600,000 units twice monthly

Early syphilis: 2.4 million units as a single dose in 2 injection sites

Syphilis of more than 1-year duration: 2.4 million units in 2 injection sites once weekly for 3 doses

Not indicated as single drug therapy for neurosyphilis, but may be given 1 time/week for 3 weeks following I.V. treatment (refer to Penicillin G monograph for dosing)

Administration Administer by deep I.M. injection in the upper outer quadrant of the buttock do **not** administer I.V., intra-arterially, or S.C.; in children <2 years of age, I.M. injections should be made into the midlateral muscle of the thigh, not the gluteal region; when doses are repeated, rotate the injection site

Monitoring Parameters Observe for signs and symptoms of anaphylaxis during first dose

Test Interactions Positive Coombs' [direct], false-positive urinary and/or serum proteins; false-positive or negative urinary glucose using Clinitest®

Patient Information Report any rash

Dosage Forms Injection: 300,000 units/mL (10 mL); 600,000 units/mL (1 mL, 2 mL, 4 mL)

Penicillin G, Parenteral, Aqueous

(pen i SIL in jee, pa REN ter al, AYE kwee us)

Related Information

Antibiotic Treatment of Adults With Infective Endocarditis *on page 1401*

Antimicrobial Drugs of Choice *on page 1404*

Community-Acquired Pneumonia in Adults *on page 1419*

Desensitization Protocols *on page 1347*

Treatment of Sexually Transmitted Diseases *on page 1429*

U.S. Brand Names Pfizerpen®

Synonyms Benzylpenicillin Potassium; Benzylpenicillin Sodium; Crystalline Penicillin; Penicillin G Potassium; Penicillin G Sodium

Therapeutic Category Antibiotic, Penicillin

Use Active against some gram-positive organisms, generally not *Staphylococcus aureus*; some gram-negative organisms such as *Neisseria gonorrhoeae*, and some anaerobes and spirochetes

Pregnancy Risk Factor B

Contraindications Known hypersensitivity to penicillin or any component

Warnings/Precautions Avoid intra-arterial administration or injection into or near major peripheral nerves or blood vessels since such injections may cause severe and/or permanent neurovascular damage; use with caution in patients with renal impairment (dosage reduction required), pre-existing seizure disorders, or with a history of hypersensitivity to cephalosporins

Adverse Reactions <1%: Convulsions, confusion, drowsiness, fever, rash, electrolyte imbalance, hemolytic anemia, positive Coombs' reaction, thrombophlebitis, myoclonus, acute interstitial nephritis, Jarisch-Herxheimer reaction, hypersensitivity reactions, anaphylaxis

Overdosage/Toxicology

Symptoms of penicillin overdose include neuromuscular hypersensitivity (agitation, hallucinations, asterixis, encephalopathy, confusion, and seizures) and electrolyte imbalance with potassium or sodium salts, especially in renal failure

Hemodialysis may be helpful to aid in the removal of the drug from the blood, otherwise most treatment is supportive or symptom directed

Drug Interactions

Decreased effect: Tetracyclines may decrease penicillin effectiveness; decreased oral contraceptive effect is possible

Increased effect:

Probenecid may increase penicillin levels

Aminoglycosides may result in synergistic efficacy; heparin and parenteral penicillins may result in increased bleeding

Stability

Penicillin G potassium is stable at room temperature

Reconstituted parenteral solution is stable for 7 days when refrigerated (2°C to 15°C)

Penicillin G potassium for I.V. infusion in NS or D_5W, solution is stable for 24 hours at room temperature

Incompatible with aminoglycosides; inactivated in acidic or alkaline solutions

Mechanism of Action Interferes with bacterial cell wall synthesis during active multiplication, causing cell wall death and resultant bactericidal activity against susceptible bacteria

Pharmacodynamics/Kinetics

Distribution: Crosses the placenta; appears in breast milk; penetration across the blood-brain barrier is poor, despite inflamed meninges

Relative diffusion of antimicrobial agents from blood into cerebrospinal fluid (CSF): Good only with inflammation (exceeds usual MICs)

Ratio of CSF to blood level (%): Normal meninges: <1; Inflamed meninges: 3-5

Protein binding: 65%

Metabolism: In the liver (30%) to penicilloic acid

Half-life:

Neonates: <6 days: 3.2-3.4 hours; 7-13 days: 1.2-2.2 hours; >14 days: 0.9-1.9 hours

Children and adults with normal renal function: 20-50 minutes

End-stage renal disease: 3.3-5.1 hours

Time to peak serum concentration: I.M.: Within 30 minutes; I.V. Within 1 hour

Elimination: In urine

Usual Dosage I.M., I.V.:

Infants:

>7 days, >2000 g: 100,000 units/kg/day in divided doses every 6 hours

>7 days, <2000 g: 75,000 units/kg/day in divided doses every 8 hours

<7 days, >2000 g: 50,000 units/kg/day in divided doses every 8 hours

<7 days, <2000 g: 50,000 units/kg/day in divided doses every 12 hours

Infants and Children (sodium salt is preferred in children): 100,000-250,000 units/kg/day in divided doses every 4 hours

Severe infections: Up to 400,000 units/kg/day in divided doses every 4 hours; maximum dose: 24 million units/day

Adults: 2-24 million units/day in divided doses every 4 hours depending on sensitivity of the organism and severity of the infection

Congenital syphilis:

Newborns: 50,000 units/kg/day I.V. every 8-12 hours for 10-14 days

Infants: 50,000 units/kg every 4-6 hours for 10-14 days

Disseminated gonococcal infections or gonococcus ophthalmia (if organism proven sensitive): 100,000 units/kg/day in 2 equal doses (4 equal doses/day for infants >1 week)

Gonococcal meningitis: 150,000 units/kg in 2 equal doses (4 doses/day for infants >1 week)

Dosing interval in renal impairment:

Cl_{cr} 30-50 mL/minute: Administer every 6 hours

Cl_{cr} 10-30 mL/minute: Administer every 8 hours

Cl_{cr} <10 mL/minute: Administer every 12 hours

Hemodialysis: Moderately dialyzable (20% to 50%)

Continuous arteriovenous or venovenous hemodiafiltration (CAVH) effects: Dose as for Cl_{cr} 10-50 mL/minute

Administration Administer I.M. by deep injection in the upper outer quadrant of the buttock

Monitoring Parameters Observe for signs and symptoms of anaphylaxis during first dose

Test Interactions False-positive or negative urinary glucose determination using Clinitest®; positive Coombs' [direct]; false-positive urinary and/or serum proteins

Patient Information Report any rash or shortness of breath

Nursing Implications Dosage modification required in patients with renal insufficiency

Additional Information 1 million units is approximately equal to 625 mg

Penicillin G potassium: 1.7 mEq of potassium and 0.3 mEq of sodium per 1 million units of penicillin G

Penicillin G sodium: 2 mEq of sodium per 1 million units of penicillin G

Dosage Forms

Injection, as sodium: 5 million units

Injection:

Frozen premixed, as potassium: 1 million units, 2 million units, 3 million units

Powder, as potassium: 1 million units, 5 million units, 10 million units, 20 million units

♦ **Penicillin G Potassium** see Penicillin G, Parenteral, Aqueous on previous page

Penicillin G Procaine (pen i SIL in jee PROE kane)

Related Information

Treatment of Sexually Transmitted Diseases on page 1429

U.S. Brand Names Crysticillin® A.S.; Wycillin®

Canadian Brand Names Ayercillin®

Synonyms APPG; Aqueous Procaine Penicillin G; Procaine Benzylpenicillin; Procaine Penicillin G

(Continued)

Penicillin G Procaine *(Continued)*

Therapeutic Category Antibiotic, Penicillin

Use Moderately severe infections due to *Treponema pallidum* and other penicillin G-sensitive microorganisms that are susceptible to low but prolonged serum penicillin concentrations

Pregnancy Risk Factor B

Contraindications Known hypersensitivity to penicillin or any component; also contraindicated in patients hypersensitive to procaine

Warnings/Precautions May need to modify dosage in patients with severe renal impairment, seizure disorders, or history of hypersensitivity to cephalosporins; avoid I.V., intravascular, or intra-arterial administration of penicillin G procaine since severe and/or permanent neurovascular damage may occur

Adverse Reactions
>10%: Local: Pain at injection site
<1%: Myocardial depression, vasodilation, conduction disturbances, CNS stimulation, seizures, confusion, drowsiness, hemolytic anemia, positive Coombs' reaction, sterile abscess at injection site, myoclonus, interstitial nephritis, pseudoanaphylactic reactions, Jarisch-Herxheimer reaction, hypersensitivity reactions

Overdosage/Toxicology
Symptoms of penicillin overdose include neuromuscular hypersensitivity (agitation, hallucinations, asterixis, encephalopathy, confusion, and seizures) and electrolyte imbalance with potassium or sodium salts, especially in renal failure
Hemodialysis may be helpful to aid in the removal of the drug from the blood, otherwise most treatment is supportive or symptom directed

Drug Interactions
Decreased effect: Tetracyclines may decrease penicillin effectiveness; decreased oral contraceptive effect is possible
Increased effect:
Probenecid may increase penicillin levels
Aminoglycosides may result in synergistic efficacy; heparin and parenteral penicillins may result in increased bleeding

Stability Store in refrigerator

Mechanism of Action Inhibits bacterial cell wall synthesis by binding to one or more of the penicillin binding proteins (PBPs); which in turn inhibits the final transpeptidation step of peptidoglycan synthesis in bacterial cell walls, thus inhibiting cell wall biosynthesis. Bacteria eventually lyse due to ongoing activity of cell wall autolytic enzymes (autolysins and murein hydrolases) while cell wall assembly is arrested.

Pharmacodynamics/Kinetics
Absorption: I.M.: Slowly absorbed
Distribution: Penetration across the blood-brain barrier is poor, despite inflamed meninges; appears in breast milk
Protein binding: 65%
Metabolism: ~30% of a dose is inactivated in the liver
Time to peak serum concentration: Within 1-4 hours; can persist within the therapeutic range for 15-24 hours
Elimination: Renal clearance is delayed in neonates, young infants, and patients with impaired renal function; 60% to 90% of the drug is excreted unchanged via renal tubular excretion

Usual Dosage I.M.:
Children: 25,000-50,000 units/kg/day in divided doses 1-2 times/day; not to exceed 4.8 million units/24 hours
Congenital syphilis: 50,000 units/kg/day for 10-14 days
Adults: 0.6-4.8 million units/day in divided doses every 12-24 hours
Endocarditis caused by susceptible viridans *Streptococcus* (when used in conjunction with an aminoglycoside): 1.2 million units every 6 hours for 2-4 weeks
Neurosyphilis: I.M.: 2-4 million units/day with 500 mg probenecid by mouth 4 times/day for 10-14 days; **penicillin G aqueous I.V. is the preferred agent**
Hemodialysis: Moderately dialyzable (20% to 50%)

Administration Procaine suspension for deep I.M. injection only; rotate the injection site; **do not administer I.V.**

Monitoring Parameters Periodic renal and hematologic function tests with prolonged therapy; fever, mental status, WBC count

Test Interactions Positive Coombs' [direct], false-positive urinary and/or serum proteins

Patient Information Notify physician if skin rash, itching, hives, or severe diarrhea occurs

Nursing Implications Renal and hematologic systems should be evaluated periodically during prolonged therapy; do not inject in gluteal muscle in children <2 years of age

Dosage Forms Injection, suspension: 300,000 units/mL (10 mL); 500,000 units/mL (1.2 mL); 600,000 units/mL (1 mL, 2 mL, 4 mL)

♦ **Penicillin G Procaine and Benzathine Combined** *see* Penicillin G Benzathine and Procaine Combined *on page 894*
♦ **Penicillin G Sodium** *see* Penicillin G, Parenteral, Aqueous *on page 896*

Penicillin V Potassium *(pen i SIL in vee poe TASS ee um)*

Related Information
Animal and Human Bites Guidelines *on page 1399*
Antimicrobial Drugs of Choice *on page 1404*
Community-Acquired Pneumonia in Adults *on page 1419*

Desensitization Protocols *on page 1347*

U.S. Brand Names Beepen-VK®; Betapen®-VK; Pen.Vee® K; Robicillin® VK; V-Cillin K®; Veetids®

Canadian Brand Names Apo®-Pen VK; Nadopen-V®; Novo-Pen-VK®; Nu-Pen-VK; PVF® K

Synonyms Pen VK; Phenoxymethyl Penicillin

Therapeutic Category Antibiotic, Penicillin

Use Treatment of infections caused by susceptible organisms involving the respiratory tract, otitis media, sinusitis, skin, and urinary tract; prophylaxis in rheumatic fever

Pregnancy Risk Factor B

Contraindications Known hypersensitivity to penicillin or any component

Warnings/Precautions Use with caution in patients with severe renal impairment (modify dosage), history of seizures, or hypersensitivity to cephalosporins

Adverse Reactions

>10%: Gastrointestinal: Mild diarrhea, vomiting, nausea, oral candidiasis

<1%: Convulsions, fever, hemolytic anemia, positive Coombs' reaction, acute interstitial nephritis, hypersensitivity reactions, anaphylaxis

Overdosage/Toxicology

Symptoms of penicillin overdose include neuromuscular hypersensitivity (agitation, hallucinations, asterixis, encephalopathy, confusion, and seizures) and electrolyte imbalance with potassium or sodium salts, especially in renal failure

Hemodialysis may be helpful to aid in the removal of the drug from the blood, otherwise most treatment is supportive or symptom directed

Drug Interactions

Decreased effect: Tetracyclines may decrease penicillin effectiveness; decreased oral contraceptive effect is possible

Increased effect:

Probenecid may increase penicillin levels

Aminoglycosides may result in synergistic efficacy; heparin and parenteral penicillins may result in increased bleeding

Stability Refrigerate suspension after reconstitution; discard after 14 days

Mechanism of Action Inhibits bacterial cell wall synthesis by binding to one or more of the penicillin binding proteins (PBPs); which in turn inhibits the final transpeptidation step of peptidoglycan synthesis in bacterial cell walls, thus inhibiting cell wall biosynthesis. Bacteria eventually lyse due to ongoing activity of cell wall autolytic enzymes (autolysins and murein hydrolases) while cell wall assembly is arrested.

Pharmacodynamics/Kinetics

Absorption: Oral: 60% to 73% from GI tract

Distribution: Appears in breast milk

Plasma protein binding: 80%

Half-life: 0.5 hours; prolonged in patients with renal impairment

Time to peak serum concentration: Oral: Within 0.5-1 hour

Elimination: Penicillin V and its metabolites are excreted in urine mainly by tubular secretion

Usual Dosage Oral:

Systemic infections:

Children <12 years: 25-50 mg/kg/day in divided doses every 6-8 hours; maximum dose: 3 g/day

Children ≥12 years and Adults: 125-500 mg every 6-8 hours

Prophylaxis of pneumococcal infections:

Children <5 years: 125 mg twice daily

Children ≥5 years and Adults: 250 mg twice daily

Prophylaxis of recurrent rheumatic fever:

Children <5 years: 125 mg twice daily

Children ≥5 years and Adults: 250 mg twice daily

Dosing interval in renal impairment: Cl_{cr} <10 mL/minute: Administer 250 mg every 6 hours

Dietary Considerations Food: Decreases drug absorption rate; decreases drug serum concentration. Take on an empty stomach 1 hour before or 2 hours after meals.

Administration Administer on an empty stomach to increase oral absorption

Monitoring Parameters Periodic renal and hematologic function tests during prolonged therapy; monitor for signs of anaphylaxis during first dose

Test Interactions False-positive or negative urinary glucose determination using Clinitest®; positive Coombs' [direct]; false-positive urinary and/or serum proteins

Patient Information Take on an empty stomach 1 hour before or 2 hours after meals, take until gone, do not skip doses, report any rash or shortness of breath; shake liquid well before use

Additional Information 0.7 mEq of potassium per 250 mg penicillin V; 250 mg equals 400,000 units of penicillin

Dosage Forms 250 mg = 400,000 units

Powder for oral solution: 125 mg/5 mL (3 mL, 100 mL, 150 mL, 200 mL); 250 mg/5 mL (100 mL, 150 mL, 200 mL)

Tablet: 125 mg, 250 mg, 500 mg

♦ **Penicilloyl-polylysine** *see* Benzylpenicilloyl-polylysine *on page 137*

♦ **Pentacarinat® Injection** *see* Pentamidine *on next page*

♦ **Pentam-300® Injection** *see* Pentamidine *on next page*

Pentamidine (pen TAM i deen)

Related Information

Guidelines for the Prevention of Opportunistic Infections in Persons with HIV *on page 1388*

U.S. Brand Names NebuPent™ Inhalation; Pentacarinat® Injection; Pentam-300® Injection

Synonyms Pentamidine Isethionate

Therapeutic Category Antibiotic, Miscellaneous

Use Treatment and prevention of pneumonia caused by *Pneumocystis carinii*; treatment of trypanosomiasis and visceral leishmaniasis

Pregnancy Risk Factor C

Contraindications Hypersensitivity to pentamidine isethionate or any component (inhalation and injection)

Warnings/Precautions Use with caution in patients with diabetes mellitus, renal or hepatic dysfunction; hypertension or hypotension; leukopenia, thrombocytopenia, asthma, hypo/hyperglycemia

Adverse Reactions Injection (I); Aerosol (A)

>10%:
Cardiovascular: Chest pain (A - 10% to 23%)
Central nervous system: Fatigue (A - 50% to 70%); dizziness (A - 31% to 47%)
Dermatologic: Rash (31% to 47%)
Endocrine & metabolic: Hyperkalemia
Gastrointestinal: Anorexia (A - 50% to 70%), nausea (A - 10% to 23%)
Local: Local reactions at injection site
Renal: Increased creatinine (I - 23%)
Respiratory: Wheezing (A - 10% to 23%), dyspnea (A - 50% to 70%), coughing (A - 31% to 47%), pharyngitis (10% to 23%)

1% to 10%:
Cardiovascular: Hypotension (I - 4%)
Central nervous system: Confusion/hallucinations (1% to 2%), headache (A - 1% to 5%)
Dermatologic: Rash (I - 3.3%)
Endocrine & metabolic: Hypoglycemia <25 mg/dL (I - 2.4%)
Gastrointestinal: Nausea/anorexia (I - 6%), diarrhea (A - 1% to 5%), vomiting
Hematologic: Severe leukopenia (I - 2.8%), thrombocytopenia <20,000/mm^3 (I - 1.7%), anemia (A - 1% to 5%)
Hepatic: Increased LFTs (I - 8.7%)

<1%: Hypotension <60 mm Hg systolic (I - 0.9%), tachycardia, arrhythmias, dizziness (I), fever, fatigue (I), hyperglycemia or hypoglycemia, hypocalcemia, pancreatitis, megaloblastic anemia, granulocytopenia, leukopenia, renal insufficiency, extrapulmonary pneumocystosis, irritation of the airway, pneumothorax, Jarisch-Herxheimer-like reaction, mild renal or hepatic injury

Overdosage/Toxicology

Symptoms of overdose include hypotension, hypoglycemia, cardiac arrhythmias
Treatment is supportive

Drug Interactions CYP2C19 enzyme substrate

Stability Do not refrigerate due to the possibility of crystallization; do not use NS as a diluent, NS is **incompatible** with pentamidine; reconstituted solutions (60-100 mg/mL) are stable for 48 hours at room temperature and do not require light protection; diluted solutions (1-2.5 mg/mL) in D_5W are stable for at least 24 hours at room temperature

Mechanism of Action Interferes with RNA/DNA, phospholipids and protein synthesis, through inhibition of oxidative phosphorylation and/or interference with incorporation of nucleotides and nucleic acids into RNA and DNA, in protozoa

Pharmacodynamics/Kinetics

Absorption: I.M.: Well absorbed
Distribution: Systemic accumulation of pentamidine does not appear to occur following inhalation therapy
Half-life, terminal: 6.4-9.4 hours; may be prolonged in patients with severe renal impairment
Elimination: 33% to 66% excreted in urine as unchanged drug

Usual Dosage

Children:
Treatment: I.M., I.V. (I.V. preferred): 4 mg/kg/day once daily for 10-14 days
Prevention:
I.M., I.V.: 4 mg/kg monthly or every 2 weeks
Inhalation (aerosolized pentamidine in children ≥5 years): 300 mg/dose given every 3-4 weeks via Respirgard® II inhaler (8 mg/kg dose has also been used in children <5 years)
Treatment of trypanosomiasis: I.V.: 4 mg/kg/day once daily for 10 days
Adults:
Treatment: I.M., I.V. (I.V. preferred): 4 mg/kg/day once daily for 14-21 days
Prevention: Inhalation: 300 mg every 4 weeks via Respirgard® II nebulizer
Dialysis: Not removed by hemo or peritoneal dialysis or continuous arteriovenous or venovenous hemofiltration (CAVH/CAVHD); supplemental dosage is not necessary
Dosing adjustment in renal impairment: Adults: I.V.:
Cl_{cr} 10-50 mL/minute: Administer 4 mg/kg every 24-36 hours
Cl_{cr} <10 mL/minute: Administer 4 mg/kg every 48 hours

Administration Infuse I.V. slowly over a period of at least 60 minutes or administer deep I.M.; patients receiving I.V. or I.M. pentamidine should be lying down and blood pressure should be monitored closely during administration of drug and several times thereafter until it is stable

Monitoring Parameters Liver function tests, renal function tests, blood glucose, serum potassium and calcium, EKG, blood pressure

Patient Information PCP pneumonia may still occur despite pentamidine use; notify physician of fever, shortness of breath, or coughing up blood; maintain adequate fluid intake

Nursing Implications Virtually indetectable amounts are transferred to healthcare personnel during aerosol administration; **do not use NS as a diluent**

Dosage Forms

Inhalation, as isethionate: 300 mg

Powder for injection, as isethionate, lyophilized: 300 mg

- ♦ **Pentamidine Isethionate** see Pentamidine on previous page
- ♦ **Pentamycetin®** see Chloramphenicol on page 238
- ♦ **Pentasa® Oral** see Mesalamine on page 734

Pentazocine (pen TAZ oh seen)

Related Information

Depression Disorders and Treatments on page 1465

Narcotic Agonists Comparison on page 1328

U.S. Brand Names Talwin®; Talwin® NX

Synonyms Pentazocine Hydrochloride; Pentazocine Lactate

Therapeutic Category Analgesic, Narcotic; Sedative

Use Relief of moderate to severe pain; has also been used as a sedative prior to surgery and as a supplement to surgical anesthesia

Restrictions C-IV

Pregnancy Risk Factor B (D if used for prolonged periods or in high doses at term)

Contraindications Hypersensitivity to pentazocine or any component, increased intracranial pressure (unless the patient is mechanically ventilated)

Warnings/Precautions Use with caution in seizure-prone patients, acute myocardial infarction, patients undergoing biliary tract surgery, patients with renal and hepatic dysfunction, head trauma, increased intracranial pressure, and patients with a history of prior opioid dependence or abuse; pentazocine may precipitate opiate withdrawal symptoms in patients who have been receiving opiates regularly; injection contains sulfites which may cause allergic reaction; tolerance or drug dependence may result from extended use

Adverse Reactions

>10%:

Central nervous system: Euphoria, drowsiness

Gastrointestinal: Nausea, vomiting

Neuromuscular & skeletal: Weakness

1% to 10%:

Cardiovascular: Hypotension

Central nervous system: Malaise, headache, restlessness, nightmares

Dermatologic: Rash

Gastrointestinal: Xerostomia

Genitourinary: Ureteral spasm

Ocular: Blurred vision

Respiratory: Dyspnea

<1%: Insomnia, CNS depression, sedation, hallucinations, confusion, disorientation, seizures may occur in seizure-prone patients, increased intracranial pressure, palpitations, bradycardia, peripheral vasodilation, pruritus, antidiuretic hormone release, GI irritation, constipation, biliary tract spasm, urinary tract spasm, tissue damage and irritation with I.M./S.C. use, miosis, histamine release, physical and psychological dependence

Overdosage/Toxicology

Symptoms of overdose include drowsiness, sedation, respiratory depression, coma

Naloxone 2 mg I.V. (0.01 mg/kg for children) with repeat administration as necessary up to a total of 10 mg

Drug Interactions CYP2D6 enzyme substrate

May potentiate or reduce analgesic effect of opiate agonist, (eg, morphine) depending on patients tolerance to opiates can precipitate withdrawal in narcotic addicts

Increased effect/toxicity with tripelennamine (can be lethal), CNS depressants (phenothiazines, tranquilizers, anxiolytics, sedatives, hypnotics, or alcohol)

Stability Store at room temperature, protect from heat and from freezing; I.V. form is **incompatible** with aminophylline, amobarbital (and all other I.V. barbiturates), glycopyrrolate (same syringe), heparin (same syringe), nafcillin (Y-site)

Mechanism of Action Binds to opiate receptors in the CNS, causing inhibition of ascending pain pathways, altering the perception of and response to pain; produces generalized CNS depression; partial agonist-antagonist

Pharmacodynamics/Kinetics

Onset of action: Oral, I.M., S.C.: Within 15-30 minutes; I.V.: Within 2-3 minutes

Duration: Oral: 4-5 hours; Parenteral: 2-3 hours

Protein binding: 60%

Metabolism: Large first-pass effect; metabolized in liver via oxidative and glucuronide conjugation pathways

Bioavailability, oral: ~20%; increased to 60% to 70% in patients with cirrhosis

Half-life: 2-3 hours; increased with decreased hepatic function

(Continued)

Pentazocine *(Continued)*

Elimination: Smaller amounts excreted unchanged in urine

Usual Dosage
Children: I.M., S.C.:
  5-8 years: 15 mg
  8-14 years: 30 mg
Children >12 years and Adults: Oral: 50 mg every 3-4 hours; may increase to 100 mg/dose if needed, but should not exceed 600 mg/day
Adults:
  I.M., S.C.: 30-60 mg every 3-4 hours, not to exceed total daily dose of 360 mg
  I.V.: 30 mg every 3-4 hours
Dosing adjustment in renal impairment:
  Cl$_{cr}$ 10-50 mL/minute: Administer 75% of normal dose
  Cl$_{cr}$ <10 mL/minute: Administer 50% of normal dose
Dosing adjustment in hepatic impairment: Reduce dose or avoid use in patients with liver disease

Dietary Considerations Alcohol: Additive CNS effect, avoid use

Administration Rotate injection site for I.M., S.C. use; avoid intra-arterial injection

Monitoring Parameters Relief of pain, respiratory and mental status, blood pressure

Patient Information Avoid alcohol, may cause drowsiness, impaired judgment or coordination; may cause physical and psychological dependence with prolonged use; will cause withdrawal in patients currently dependent on narcotics

Nursing Implications Observe patient for excessive sedation, respiratory depression, implement safety measures, assist with ambulation; observe for narcotic withdrawal

Additional Information Pentazocine hydrochloride: Talwin® NX tablet (with naloxone); naloxone is used to prevent abuse by dissolving tablets in water and using as injection

Dosage Forms
Injection, as lactate: 30 mg/mL (1 mL, 1.5 mL, 2 mL, 10 mL)
Tablet: Pentazocine hydrochloride 50 mg and naloxone hydrochloride 0.5 mg

♦ **Pentazocine Hydrochloride** *see* Pentazocine *on previous page*
♦ **Pentazocine Lactate** *see* Pentazocine *on previous page*

Pentobarbital *(pen toe BAR bi tal)*

U.S. Brand Names Nembutal®

Canadian Brand Names Nova Rectal®

Synonyms Pentobarbital Sodium

Therapeutic Category Anticonvulsant; Barbiturate; Sedative

Use Short-term treatment of insomnia; preoperative sedation; high-dose barbiturate coma for treatment of increased intracranial pressure or status epilepticus unresponsive to other therapy

Restrictions C-II (capsules, injection); C-III (suppositories)

Pregnancy Risk Factor D

Contraindications Marked liver function impairment or latent porphyria; hypersensitivity to barbiturates or any component

Warnings/Precautions Tolerance to hypnotic effect can occur; do not use for >2 weeks to treat insomnia; taper dose to prevent withdrawal; loading doses of 15-35 mg/kg (given over 1-2 hours) have been utilized in pediatric patients to induce pentobarbital coma, but these higher loading doses often cause hypotension requiring vasopressor therapy. Use of this agent as a hypnotic in the elderly is not recommended due to its long half-life and potential for physical and psychological dependence. Use with caution in patients with hypovolemic shock, congestive heart failure, hepatic impairment, respiratory dysfunction or depression, previous addiction to the sedative/hypnotic group, chronic or acute pain, renal dysfunction; tolerance or psychological and physical dependence may occur with prolonged use.

Adverse Reactions
Renal: Oliguria
>10%:
  Cardiovascular: Cardiac arrhythmias, bradycardia, hypotension, arterial spasm
  Central nervous system: Drowsiness, lethargy, CNS excitation or depression, impaired judgment, "hangover" effect
  Local: Pain at injection site, thrombophlebitis with I.V. use
  Miscellaneous: Gangrene with inadvertent intra-arterial injection
1% to 10%:
  Central nervous system: Confusion, mental depression, unusual excitement, nervousness, faint feeling, headache, insomnia, nightmares
  Gastrointestinal: Nausea, vomiting, constipation
<1%: Hallucinations, hypothermia, rash, exfoliative dermatitis, Stevens-Johnson syndrome, agranulocytosis, thrombocytopenia, megaloblastic anemia, thrombophlebitis, laryngospasm, respiratory depression, apnea (especially with rapid I.V. use)

Overdosage/Toxicology
Symptoms of overdose include unsteady gait, slurred speech, confusion, jaundice, hypothermia, hypotension, respiratory depression, coma

If hypotension occurs, administer I.V. fluids and place the patient in the Trendelenburg position. If unresponsive, an I.V. vasopressor (eg, dopamine, epinephrine) may be required. Forced alkaline diuresis is of no value in the treatment of intoxications with short-acting barbiturates. Charcoal hemoperfusion or hemodialysis may be useful in the harder to treat intoxications, especially in the presence of very high serum barbiturate levels when the patient is in a coma, shock, or renal failure.

Drug Interactions
Decreased effect: Decreased chloramphenicol; decreased doxycycline effects
Increased toxicity: Increased CNS depressants, cimetidine; may increase pentobarbital

Stability Protect from light; aqueous solutions are not stable, commercially available vehicle (containing propylene glycol) is more stable; low pH may cause precipitate; use only clear solution

Mechanism of Action Short-acting barbiturate with sedative, hypnotic, and anticonvulsant properties

Pharmacodynamics/Kinetics
Onset of action: Oral, rectal: 15-60 minutes; I.M.: Within 10-15 minutes; I.V.: Within 1 minute
Duration: Oral, rectal: 1-4 hours; I.V.: 15 minutes
Distribution: V_d: Children: 0.8 L/kg; Adults: 1 L/kg
Protein binding: 35% to 55%
Metabolism: Extensively in liver via hydroxylation and oxidation pathways
Half-life, terminal: Children: 25 hours; Adults, normal: 22 hours; range: 35-50 hours
Elimination: <1% excreted unchanged renally

Usual Dosage
Children:
Sedative: Oral: 2-6 mg/kg/day divided in 3 doses; maximum: 100 mg/day
Hypnotic: I.M.: 2-6 mg/kg; maximum: 100 mg/dose
Rectal:
2 months to 1 year (10-20 lb): 30 mg
1-4 years (20-40 lb): 30-60 mg
5-12 years (40-80 lb): 60 mg
12-14 years (80-110 lb): 60-120 mg
or
<4 years: 3-6 mg/kg/dose
>4 years: 1.5-3 mg/kg/dose
Preoperative/preprocedure sedation: ≥6 months:
Oral, I.M., rectal: 2-6 mg/kg; maximum: 100 mg/dose
I.V.: 1-3 mg/kg to a maximum of 100 mg until asleep
Children 5-12 years: Conscious sedation prior to a procedure: I.V.: 2 mg/kg 5-10 minutes before procedures, may repeat one time
Adolescents: Conscious sedation: Oral, I.V.: 100 mg prior to a procedure
Adults:
Hypnotic:
Oral: 100-200 mg at bedtime or 20 mg 3-4 times/day for daytime sedation
I.M.: 150-200 mg
I.V.: Initial: 100 mg, may repeat every 1-3 minutes up to 200-500 mg total dose
Rectal: 120-200 mg at bedtime
Preoperative sedation: I.M.: 150-200 mg
Children and Adults: Barbiturate coma in head injury patients: I.V.: Loading dose: 5-10 mg/kg given slowly over 1-2 hours; monitor blood pressure and respiratory rate; Maintenance infusion: Initial: 1 mg/kg/hour; may increase to 2-3 mg/kg/hour; maintain burst suppression on EEG
Dosing adjustment in hepatic impairment: Reduce dosage in patients with severe liver dysfunction

Dietary Considerations Alcohol: Additive CNS effect, avoid use

Administration Pentobarbital may be administered by deep I.M. or slow I.V. injection. I.M.: No more than 5 mL (250 mg) should be injected at any one site because of possible tissue irritation I.V. push doses can be given undiluted, but should be administered no faster than 50 mg/minute; parenteral solutions are highly alkaline; avoid extravasation; avoid rapid I.V. administration >50 mg/minute; avoid intra-arterial injection

Monitoring Parameters Respiratory status (for conscious sedation, includes pulse oximetry), cardiovascular status, CNS status; cardiac monitor and blood pressure monitor required

Reference Range
Therapeutic:
Hypnotic: 1-5 µg/mL (SI: 4-22 µmol/L)
Coma: 10-50 µg/mL (SI: 88-221 µmol/L)
Toxic: >10 µg/mL (SI: >44 µmol/L)

Test Interactions ↑ ammonia (B); ↓ bilirubin (S)

Patient Information Avoid the use of alcohol and other CNS depressants; avoid driving and other hazardous tasks; avoid abrupt discontinuation; may cause physical and psychological dependence; do not alter dose without notifying physician

Nursing Implications Avoid extravasation; institute safety measures to avoid injuries; has many incompatibilities when given I.V.

Additional Information Pentobarbital: Nembutal® elixir pentobarbital sodium: Nembutal® capsule, injection, and suppository
Sodium content of 1 mL injection: 5 mg (0.2 mEq)

Dosage Forms
Capsule, as sodium (C-II): 50 mg, 100 mg
Elixir (C-II): 18.2 mg/5 mL (473 mL, 4000 mL)
Injection, as sodium (C-II): 50 mg/mL (1 mL, 2 mL, 20 mL, 50 mL)
Suppository, rectal (C-III): 30 mg, 60 mg, 120 mg, 200 mg

♦ **Pentobarbital Sodium** see Pentobarbital on previous page

Pentosan Polysulfate Sodium (PEN toe san pol i SUL fate SOW dee um)

U.S. Brand Names Elmiron®

Synonyms PPS

Therapeutic Category Analgesic, Urinary

Use Relief of bladder pain or discomfort due to interstitial cystitis

Pregnancy Risk Factor B

Contraindications Hypersensitivity to pentosan polysulfate sodium or any component

Warnings/Precautions Pentosan polysulfate is a low-molecular weight heparin-like compound with anticoagulant and fibrinolytic effects, therefore, bleeding complications such as ecchymosis, epistaxis and gum bleeding, may occur; patients with the following diseases should be carefully evaluated before initiating therapy: aneurysm, thrombocytopenia, hemophilia, gastrointestinal ulcerations, polyps, diverticula, or hepatic insufficiency; patients undergoing invasive procedures or having signs or symptoms of underlying coagulopathies or other increased risk of bleeding (eg, receiving heparin, warfarin, thrombolytics, or high dose aspirin) should be evaluated for hemorrhage; elevations in transaminases and alopecia can occur

Adverse Reactions

1% to 10%:
  Central nervous system: Headache, dizziness
  Dermatologic: Alopecia, rash
  Gastrointestinal: Diarrhea, nausea, dyspepsia, abdominal pain
  Hepatic: Liver function test abnormalities

<1%: Pruritus, urticaria, photosensitivity, bruising, vomiting, mouth ulcer, colitis, esophagitis, gastritis, flatulence, constipation, anorexia, gum bleeding, anemia, prolonged PT, increased partial thromboplastin time, leukopenia, thrombocytopenia, conjunctivitis, optic neuritis, amblyopia, retinal hemorrhage, tinnitus, pharyngitis, rhinitis, epistaxis, dyspnea, allergic reactions

Overdosage/Toxicology

Overdosage has not been reported; based on the pharmacodynamics, toxicity is likely to include anticoagulation, bleeding, thrombocytopenia, liver function abnormalities and gastric distress

Gastric lavage along with symptomatic and supportive therapy is recommended

Drug Interactions Although there is no information about potential drug interactions, it is expected that pentosan polysulfate sodium would have at least additive anticoagulant effects when administered with anticoagulant drugs such as warfarin or heparin, and possible similar effects when administered with aspirin or thrombolytics

Mechanism of Action Although pentosan polysulfate sodium is a low-molecular weight heparinoid, it is not known whether these properties play a role in its mechanism of action in treating interstitial cystitis; the drug appears to adhere to the bladder wall mucosa where it may act as a buffer to protect the tissues from irritating substances in the urine.

Pharmacodynamics/Kinetics

Absorption: ~3%
Metabolism: In the liver and spleen
Half-life: 4.8 hours
Elimination: In urine, 3% unchanged drug

Usual Dosage Adults: Oral: 100 mg 3 times/day taken with water 1 hour before or 2 hours after meals

Patients should be evaluated at 3 months and may be continued an additional 3 months if there has been no improvement and if there are no therapy-limiting side effects. **The risks and benefits of continued use beyond 6 months in patients who have not responded is not yet known.**

Patient Information Patients should be advised to take the medication as prescribed and no more frequently; tell patients about the slight anticoagulant effects and the potential for increased bleeding; until more is known about drug interactions, carefully monitor the medication profile of patients receiving pentosan polysulfate sodium for drugs that might increase the anticoagulant effects

Dosage Forms Capsule: 100 mg

Pentostatin (PEN toe stat in)

U.S. Brand Names Nipent™ Injection

Synonyms DCF; Deoxycoformycin; 2'-deoxycoformycin

Therapeutic Category Antineoplastic Agent, Antimetabolite (Purine)

Use Treatment of adult patients with alpha-interferon-refractory hairy cell leukemia; non-Hodgkin's lymphoma, cutaneous T-cell lymphoma

Pregnancy Risk Factor D

Contraindications Limited or severely compromised bone marrow reserves (white blood cell count <3000 cells/mm^3)

Warnings/Precautions The FDA currently recommends that procedures for proper handling and disposal of antineoplastic agents be considered. Pregnant women or women of childbearing age should be apprised of the potential risk to the fetus; use extreme caution in the presence of renal insufficiency; use with caution in patients with signs or symptoms of impaired hepatic function.

Adverse Reactions

>10%:
  Central nervous system: Headache, neurologic disorder, fever, fatigue, chills, pain
  Dermatologic: Rash
  Gastrointestinal: Vomiting, nausea, anorexia, diarrhea

Hematologic: Leukopenia, anemia, thrombocytopenia
Hepatic: Hepatic disorder, abnormal LFTs
Neuromuscular & skeletal: Myalgia
Respiratory: Coughing
Miscellaneous: Allergic reaction
1% to 10%:
Cardiovascular: Chest pain, arrhythmia, peripheral edema
Central nervous system: Anxiety, confusion, depression, dizziness, insomnia, lethargy, coma, seizures, malaise
Dermatologic: Dry skin, eczema, pruritus
Gastrointestinal: Constipation, flatulence, stomatitis, weight loss
Genitourinary: Dysuria
Hematologic: Myelosuppression
Hepatic: Liver dysfunction
Local: Thrombophlebitis
Neuromuscular & skeletal: Arthralgia, paresthesia, back pain, weakness
Ocular: Abnormal vision, eye pain, keratoconjunctivitis
Otic: Ear pain
Renal: Renal failure, hematuria
Respiratory: Bronchitis, dyspnea, lung edema, pneumonia
Miscellaneous: Death, opportunistic infections, diaphoresis

Overdosage/Toxicology
Symptoms of overdose include severe renal, hepatic, pulmonary, and CNS toxicity
Supportive therapy

Drug Interactions Increased toxicity: Vidarabine, fludarabine, allopurinol

Stability Vials are stable under refrigeration at 2°C to 8°C; reconstituted vials, or further dilutions, may be stored at room temperature exposed to ambient light; diluted solutions are stable for 24 hours in D_5W or 48 hours in NS or lactated Ringer's at room temperature; infusion with 5% dextrose injection USP or 0.9% sodium chloride injection USP does not interact with PVC-containing administration sets or containers

Mechanism of Action An antimetabolite inhibiting adenosine deaminase (ADA), prevents ADA from controlling intracellular adenosine levels through the irreversible deamination of adenosine and deoxyadenosine. ADA is found to exhibit the highest activity in lymphoid tissue. Patients receiving pentostatin accumulate deoxyadenosine (dAdo) and deoxyadenosine 5'-triphosphate (dATP); accumulation of dATP results in cell death, probably through inhibiting DNA or RNA synthesis. Following a single dose, pentostatin has the ability to inhibit ADA for periods exceeding 1 week.

Pharmacodynamics/Kinetics
Distribution: I.V.: V_d: 36.1 L (20.1 L/m²); distributes rapidly to body tissues and may obtain plasma concentrations ranging from 12-36 ng following doses of 250 mcg/kg for 4-5 days
Half-life, terminal: 5-15 hours
Elimination: ~50% to 96% is recovered in urine within 24 hours

Usual Dosage Refractory hairy cell leukemia: Adults (refer to individual protocols): 4 mg/m² every other week; I.V. bolus over ≥3-5 minutes in D_5W or NS at concentrations ≥2 mg/mL

Dosing interval in renal impairment:
Cl_{cr} <60 mL/minute: Use extreme caution
Cl_{cr} 50-60 mL/minute: 2 mg/m²/dose

Dosage Forms Powder for injection: 10 mg/vial

♦ **Pentothal® Sodium** see Thiopental on page 1134

Pentoxifylline (pen toks I fi leen)

U.S. Brand Names Trental®
Canadian Brand Names Albert® Pentoxifylline; Apo®-Pentoxifylline SR
Synonyms Oxpentifylline
Therapeutic Category Blood Viscosity Reducer Agent; Hemorheologic Agent
Use Symptomatic management of peripheral vascular disease, mainly intermittent claudication

Unapproved use: AIDS patients with increased TNF, CVA, cerebrovascular diseases, diabetic atherosclerosis, diabetic neuropathy, gangrene, hemodialysis shunt thrombosis, vascular impotence, cerebral malaria, septic shock, sickle cell syndromes, and vasculitis

Pregnancy Risk Factor C
Contraindications Hypersensitivity to pentoxifylline or any component and other xanthine derivatives; patients with recent cerebral and/or retinal hemorrhage
Warnings/Precautions Use with caution in patients with renal impairment
Adverse Reactions
1% to 10%:
Central nervous system: Dizziness, headache
Gastrointestinal: Dyspepsia, nausea, vomiting
<1%: Mild hypotension, angina, agitation, blurred vision, earache

Overdosage/Toxicology
Symptoms of overdose include hypotension, flushing, convulsions, deep sleep, agitation, bradycardia, A-V block
Treatment is supportive; seizures can be treated with diazepam 5-10 mg (0.25-0.4 mg/kg in children); arrhythmias respond to lidocaine
(Continued)

Pentoxifylline *(Continued)*

Drug Interactions
Increased effect/toxic potential with cimetidine (increased levels) and other H$_2$-antagonists, warfarin; increased effect of antihypertensives

Increased toxicity with theophylline

Mechanism of Action Mechanism of action remains unclear; is thought to reduce blood viscosity and improve blood flow by altering the rheology of red blood cells

Pharmacodynamics/Kinetics
Absorption: Oral: Well absorbed

Metabolism: Undergoes first-pass metabolism in the liver

Half-life: Parent drug: 24-48 minutes; Metabolites: 60-96 minutes

Time to peak serum concentration: Within 2-4 hours

Elimination: Mainly in urine

Usual Dosage Adults: Oral: 400 mg 3 times/day with meals; may reduce to 400 mg twice daily if GI or CNS side effects occur

Test Interactions ↓ calcium (S), ↓ magnesium (S), false-positive theophylline levels

Patient Information Take with food or meals; if GI or CNS side effects continue, contact physician; while effects may be seen in 2-4 weeks, continue treatment for at least 8 weeks

Dosage Forms Tablet, controlled release: 400 mg

- **Pen.Vee® K** see Penicillin V Potassium *on page 898*
- **Pen VK** see Penicillin V Potassium *on page 898*
- **Pepcid®** see Famotidine *on page 469*
- **Pepcid® AC Acid Controller [OTC]** see Famotidine *on page 469*
- **Pepto-Bismol® [OTC]** see Bismuth *on page 145*
- **Pepto® Diarrhea Control [OTC]** see Loperamide *on page 692*
- **Peptol®** see Cimetidine *on page 261*
- **Percocet®** see Oxycodone and Acetaminophen *on page 875*
- **Percocet®-Demi** see Oxycodone and Acetaminophen *on page 875*
- **Percodan®** see Oxycodone and Aspirin *on page 876*
- **Percodan®-Demi** see Oxycodone and Aspirin *on page 876*
- **Percolone™** see Oxycodone *on page 874*
- **Perdiem® Plain [OTC]** see Psyllium *on page 994*

Pergolide *(PER go lide)*

Related Information
Parkinson's Disease, Dosing of Drugs Used for Treatment of *on page 1336*

U.S. Brand Names Permax®

Synonyms Pergolide Mesylate

Therapeutic Category Anti-Parkinson's Agent; Ergot Alkaloid and Derivative

Use Adjunctive treatment to levodopa/carbidopa in the management of Parkinson's Disease

Pregnancy Risk Factor B

Contraindications Known hypersensitivity to pergolide mesylate or other ergot derivatives

Warnings/Precautions Symptomatic hypotension occurs in 10% of patients; use with caution in patients with a history of cardiac arrhythmias, hallucinations, or mental illness

Adverse Reactions
>10%:

Central nervous system: Dizziness, somnolence, insomnia, confusion, hallucinations, anxiety, dystonia

Gastrointestinal: Nausea, constipation

Neuromuscular & skeletal: Dyskinesia

Respiratory: Rhinitis

1% to 10%:

Cardiovascular: Myocardial infarction, postural hypotension, syncope, arrhythmias, peripheral edema, vasodilation, palpitations, chest pain

Central nervous system: Chills

Gastrointestinal: Diarrhea, abdominal pain, vomiting, xerostomia, anorexia, weight gain

Neuromuscular & skeletal: Weakness

Ocular: Abnormal vision

Respiratory: Dyspnea

Miscellaneous: Flu syndrome

Overdosage/Toxicology
Symptoms of overdose include vomiting, hypotension, agitation, hallucinations, ventricular extrasystoles, possible seizures; data on overdose is limited

Treatment is supportive and may require antiarrhythmias and/or neuroleptics for agitation; hypotension, when unresponsive to I.V. fluids or Trendelenburg positioning, often responds to norepinephrine infusions started at 0.1-0.2 mcg/kg/minute followed by a titrated infusion. If signs of CNS stimulation are present, a neuroleptic may be indicated; antiarrhythmics may be indicated, monitor EKG; activated charcoal is useful to prevent further absorption and to hasten elimination.

Drug Interactions
Decreased effect: Dopamine antagonists, metoclopramide

Increased toxicity: Highly plasma protein bound drugs

Mechanism of Action Pergolide is a semisynthetic ergot alkaloid similar to bromocriptine but stated to be more potent and longer-acting; it is a centrally-active dopamine agonist stimulating both D_1 and D_2 receptors

Pharmacodynamics/Kinetics
Absorption: Oral: Well absorbed
Protein binding: Plasma 90%
Metabolism: Extensive in the liver (on first-pass)
Half-life: 27 hours
Elimination: ~50% excreted in urine and 50% in feces

Usual Dosage When adding pergolide to levodopa/carbidopa, the dose of the latter can usually and should be decreased. Patients no longer responsive to bromocriptine may benefit by being switched to pergolide.

Adults: Oral: Start with 0.05 mg/day for 2 days, then increase dosage by 0.1 or 0.15 mg/day every 3 days over next 12 days, increase dose by 0.25 mg/day every 3 days until optimal therapeutic dose is achieved, up to 5 mg/day maximum; usual dosage range: 2-3 mg/day in 3 divided doses

Monitoring Parameters Blood pressure (both sitting/supine and standing), symptoms of parkinsonism, dyskinesias, mental status

Patient Information Take with food or milk; rise slowly from sitting or lying down; report any confusion or change in mental status

Nursing Implications Monitor closely for orthostasis and other adverse effects; raise bed rails and institute safety measures; aid patient with ambulation, may cause postural hypotension and drowsiness

Dosage Forms Tablet, as mesylate: 0.05 mg, 0.25 mg, 1 mg

- **Pergolide Mesylate** see Pergolide on previous page
- **Pergonal®** see Menotropins on page 727
- **Periactin®** see Cyproheptadine on page 311
- **Peridex® Oral Rinse** see Chlorhexidine Gluconate on page 240
- **Peridol** see Haloperidol on page 558

Perindopril Erbumine (per IN doe pril er BYOO meen)
Related Information
Angiotensin Agents on page 1291
Drug-Drug Interactions With ACEIs on page 1295

U.S. Brand Names Aceon®

Therapeutic Category Angiotensin-Converting Enzyme (ACE) Inhibitor; Antihypertensive Agent

Use Treatment of stage I or II hypertension and congestive heart failure

Pregnancy Risk Factor D (especially during 2nd and 3rd trimester)

Pregnancy/Breast-Feeding Implications Breast-feeding/lactation: Only small amounts are excreted in breast milk

Contraindications Hypersensitivity to perindopril, perindoprilat, other ACE inhibitors, or any component; pregnancy; history of angioedema with other ACE inhibitors

Warnings/Precautions Use with caution and modify dosage in patients with renal impairment (especially renal artery stenosis), severe congestive heart failure, or with coadministered diuretic therapy, valvular stenosis, hyperkalemia (>5.7 mEq/L); experience in children is limited. Severe hypotension may occur in patients who are sodium and/or volume depleted; initiate lower doses and monitor closely when starting therapy in these patients.

Adverse Reactions
1% to 10%:
Central nervous system: Headache, dizziness, mood and sleep disorders, fatigue
Dermatologic: Rash, pruritus
Gastrointestinal: Nausea, epigastric pain, diarrhea, vomiting
Neuromuscular & skeletal: Muscle cramps
Respiratory: Cough (incidence is greater in women, 3:1)
<1%: Hypotension, angioedema, psoriasis, hyperkalemia, taste disturbances, impotence, agranulocytosis for all ACE inhibitors (especially in patients with renal impairment or collagen vascular disease), possibly neutropenia, dry eyes, blurred vision, optic phosphenes, decreases in creatinine clearance in some elderly hypertensive patients or those with chronic renal failure, worsening of renal function in patients with bilateral renal artery stenosis, or furosemide therapy; proteinuria

Overdosage/Toxicology
Mild hypotension has been the only toxic effect seen with acute overdose. Bradycardia may also occur; hyperkalemia occurs even with therapeutic doses, especially in patients with renal insufficiency and those taking NSAIDs.
Following initiation of essential overdose management, toxic symptom treatment and supportive treatment should be initiated. Hypotension usually responds to I.V. fluids or Trendelenburg positioning.

Drug Interactions Increased toxicity: See Drug-Drug Interactions With ACEIs on page 1295

Mechanism of Action Competitive inhibitor of angiotensin-converting enzyme (ACE); prevents conversion of angiotensin I to angiotensin II, a potent vasoconstrictor; results in lower levels of angiotensin II which, in turn, causes an increase in plasma renin activity and a reduction in aldosterone secretion

Pharmacodynamics/Kinetics
Distribution: Small amounts of the drug are excreted into breast milk
(Continued)

Perindopril Erbumine *(Continued)*

Protein binding: Perindopril: 10% to 20%; Perindoprilat: 60%

Metabolism: Perindopril is hydrolyzed in liver to active metabolite, perindoprilat (~17% to 20% of a dose) and other inactive metabolites

Bioavailability: Perindopril: 65% to 95%

Half-life: Parent drug: 1.5-3 hours; Metabolite: 25-30 hours

Time to peak: Occurs in 1 and 3-4 hours for perindopril and perindoprilat, respectively after chronic therapy; (maximum perindoprilat serum levels are 2-3 times higher and T_{max} is shorter following chronic therapy); in CHF, the peak of perindoprilat is prolonged to 6 hours

Elimination: 75% of an oral dose is recovered in urine (10% as unchanged drug)

Usual Dosage Adults: Oral:

Congestive heart failure: 4 mg once daily

Hypertension: Initial: 4 mg/day but may be titrated to response; usual range: 4-8 mg/day, maximum: 16 mg/day

Dosing adjustment in renal impairment:

Cl_{cr} >60 mL/minute: 4 mg/day

Cl_{cr} 30-60 mL/minute: 2 mg/day

Cl_{cr} 15-29 mL/minute: 2 mg every other day

Cl_{cr} <15 mL/minute: 2 mg on the day of dialysis

Hemodialysis: Perindopril and its metabolites are dialyzable

Dosing adjustment in hepatic impairment: None needed

Dosing adjustment in geriatric patients: Due to greater bioavailability and lower renal clearance of the drug in elderly subjects, dose reduction of 50% is recommended

Monitoring Parameters Serum creatinine, electrolytes, and WBC with differential initially and repeated at 2-week intervals for at least 90 days

Patient Information Avoid taking with food since the efficacy of the drug may be reduced; immediately report signs of infection (sore throat, fever) perioral swelling, significant orthostatic hypotension, difficulty swallowing/breathing, or signs of anaphylaxis or allergy; inform your physician if you are pregnant or have a history of kidney disease

Nursing Implications A reduction in clinical signs of congestive heart failure (dyspnea, orthopnea, cough) and an improvement in exercise duration are indicative of therapeutic response; a reduction of supine diastolic blood pressure of 10 mm Hg or to 90 mm Hg is indicative of excellent therapeutic response in patients with hypertension; observe for cough, difficulty breathing/swallowing, perioral swelling and signs and symptoms of agranulocytosis; monitor for 6 hours after initial dosing for profound hypotension or first-dose phenomenon

Dosage Forms Tablet: 2 mg, 4 mg, 8 mg

♦ **PerioChip®** *see* Chlorhexidine Gluconate *on page 240*

♦ **PerioGard®** *see* Chlorhexidine Gluconate *on page 240*

♦ **Periostat™** *see* Doxycycline *on page 397*

♦ **Permapen®** *see* Penicillin G Benzathine, Parenteral *on page 895*

♦ **Permax®** *see* Pergolide *on page 906*

Permethrin *(per METH rin)*

U.S. Brand Names Acticin® Cream; Elimite™ Cream; Nix™ Creme Rinse

Therapeutic Category Antiparasitic Agent, Topical; Scabicidal Agent; Shampoos

Use Single application treatment of infestation with *Pediculus humanus capitis* (head louse) and its nits or *Sarcoptes scabiei* (scabies); indicated for prophylactic use during epidemics of lice

Pregnancy Risk Factor B

Contraindications Known hypersensitivity to pyrethyroid, pyrethrin, or chrysanthemums

Warnings/Precautions Treatment may temporarily exacerbate the symptoms of itching, redness, swelling; for external use only; use during pregnancy only if clearly needed

Adverse Reactions 1% to 10%:

Dermatologic: Pruritus, erythema, rash of the scalp

Local: Burning, stinging, tingling, numbness or scalp discomfort, edema

Mechanism of Action Inhibits sodium ion influx through nerve cell membrane channels in parasites resulting in delayed repolarization and thus paralysis and death of the pest

Pharmacodynamics/Kinetics

Absorption: Topical: Minimal (<2%)

Metabolism: In the liver by ester hydrolysis to inactive metabolites

Elimination: In urine

Usual Dosage Topical: Children >2 months and Adults:

Head lice: After hair has been washed with shampoo, rinsed with water, and towel dried, apply a sufficient volume of topical liquid to saturate the hair and scalp. Leave on hair for 10 minutes before rinsing off with water; remove remaining nits; may repeat in 1 week if lice or nits still present.

Scabies: Apply cream from head to toe; leave on for 8-14 hours before washing off with water; for infants, also apply on the hairline, neck, scalp, temple, and forehead; may reapply in 1 week if live mites appear

Permethrin 5% cream was shown to be safe and effective when applied to an infant <1 month of age with neonatal scabies; time of application was limited to 6 hours before rinsing with soap and water

Patient Information Avoid contact with eyes and mucous membranes during application; shake well before using; notify physician if irritation persists; clothing and bedding should be washed in hot water or dry cleaned to kill the scabies mite

Dosage Forms
Cream: 5% (60 g)
Liquid, topical: 1% (60 mL)

♦ **Permitil® Oral** see Fluphenazine on page 504

Perphenazine (per FEN a zeen)

Related Information
Antipsychotic Agents Comparison on page 1305

U.S. Brand Names Trilafon®

Canadian Brand Names Apo®-Perphenazine; PMS-Perphenazine

Therapeutic Category Antipsychotic Agent; Phenothiazine Derivative

Use Management of manifestations of psychotic disorders, depressive neurosis, alcohol withdrawal, nausea and vomiting, nonpsychotic symptoms associated with dementia in elderly, Tourette's syndrome, Huntington's chorea, spasmodic torticollis and Reye's syndrome

Pregnancy Risk Factor C

Contraindications Hypersensitivity to perphenazine or any component, cross-sensitivity with other phenothiazines may exist; avoid use in patients with narrow-angle glaucoma, bone marrow suppression, severe liver or cardiac disease; subcortical brain damage; circulatory collapse; severe hypotension or hypertension

Warnings/Precautions Safety in children <6 months of age has not been established; use with caution in patients with cardiovascular disease or seizures, bone marrow suppression, severe liver or cardiac disease

Adverse Reactions
>10%:
Cardiovascular: Hypotension, orthostatic hypotension
Central nervous system: Pseudoparkinsonism, akathisia, dystonias, tardive dyskinesia (persistent), dizziness
Gastrointestinal: Constipation
Ocular: Pigmentary retinopathy
Respiratory: Nasal congestion
Miscellaneous: Diaphoresis (decreased)
1% to 10%:
Dermatologic: Increased sensitivity to sun, rash
Endocrine & metabolic: Changes in menstrual cycle, changes in libido, breast pain
Gastrointestinal: Weight gain, vomiting, stomach pain, nausea
Genitourinary: Dysuria, ejaculatory disturbances
Neuromuscular & skeletal: Trembling of fingers
<1%: Neuroleptic malignant syndrome (NMS), impairment of temperature regulation, lowering of seizures threshold, discoloration of skin (blue-gray), galactorrhea, priapism, agranulocytosis, leukopenia, cholestatic jaundice, hepatotoxicity, cornea and lens changes

Overdosage/Toxicology
Symptoms of overdose include deep sleep, dystonia, agitation, coma, abnormal involuntary muscle movements, hypotension, arrhythmias
Following initiation of essential overdose management, toxic symptom treatment and supportive treatment should be initiated. Hypotension usually responds to I.V. fluids or Trendelenburg positioning. If unresponsive to these measures, the use of a parenteral inotrope may be required (eg, norepinephrine 0.1-0.2 mcg/kg/minute titrated to response). Seizures commonly respond to diazepam (I.V. 5-10 mg bolus in adults every 15 minutes if needed up to a total of 30 mg; I.V. 0.25-0.4 mg/kg/dose up to a total of 10 mg in children) or to phenytoin or phenobarbital. Extrapyramidal symptoms (eg, dystonic reactions) may be managed with diphenhydramine. When these reactions are unresponsive to diphenhydramine, benztropine mesylate may be effective.

Drug Interactions CYP2D6 enzyme substrate; CYP2D6 enzyme inhibitor
Decreased effect: Anticholinergics, anticonvulsants; decreased effect of guanethidine, epinephrine
Increased toxicity: CNS depressants; increased effect/toxicity of anticonvulsants

Mechanism of Action Blocks postsynaptic mesolimbic dopaminergic receptors in the brain; exhibits a strong alpha-adrenergic blocking effect and depresses the release of hypothalamic and hypophyseal hormones

Pharmacodynamics/Kinetics
Absorption: Oral: Well absorbed
Distribution: Crosses the placenta
Metabolism: In the liver
Half-life: 9 hours
Time to peak serum concentration: Within 4-8 hours
Elimination: In urine and bile

Usual Dosage
Children:
Psychoses: Oral:
1-6 years: 4-6 mg/day in divided doses
6-12 years: 6 mg/day in divided doses
>12 years: 4-16 mg 2-4 times/day
I.M.: 5 mg every 6 hours
(Continued)

Perphenazine *(Continued)*

Nausea/vomiting: I.M.: 5 mg every 6 hours

Adults:

Psychoses:

Oral: 4-16 mg 2-4 times/day not to exceed 64 mg/day

I.M.: 5 mg every 6 hours up to 15 mg/day in ambulatory patients and 30 mg/day in hospitalized patients

Nausea/vomiting:

Oral: 8-16 mg/day in divided doses up to 24 mg/day

I.M.: 5-10 mg every 6 hours as necessary up to 15 mg/day in ambulatory patients and 30 mg/day in hospitalized patients

I.V. (severe): 1 mg at 1- to 2-minute intervals up to a total of 5 mg

Hemodialysis: Not dialyzable (0% to 5%)

Dosing adjustment in hepatic impairment: Dosage reductions should be considered in patients with liver disease although no specific guidelines are available

Dietary Considerations Alcohol: Additive CNS effect, avoid use

Administration Dilute oral concentration to at least 2 oz with water, juice, or milk; for I.V. use, injection should be diluted to at least 0.5 mg/mL with NS and given at a rate of 1 mg/minute; observe for tremor and abnormal movements or posturing

Reference Range 2-6 nmol/L

Test Interactions ↑ cholesterol (S), ↑ glucose; ↓ uric acid (S)

Patient Information May cause drowsiness, impair judgment and coordination; report any feelings of restlessness or any involuntary movements; avoid alcohol and other CNS depressants; do not alter dose or discontinue without consulting physician

Nursing Implications Monitor for hypotension when administering I.M. or I.V. during the first 3-5 days after initiating therapy or making a dosage adjustment

Dosage Forms

Concentrate, oral: 16 mg/5 mL (118 mL)

Injection: 5 mg/mL (1 mL)

Tablet: 2 mg, 4 mg, 8 mg, 16 mg

- ◆ **Persantine®** *see Dipyridamole on page 377*
- ◆ **Pethidine Hydrochloride** *see Meperidine on page 728*
- ◆ **PFA** *see Foscarnet on page 519*
- ◆ **Pfizerpen®** *see Penicillin G, Parenteral, Aqueous on page 896*
- ◆ **PGE₁** *see Alprostadil on page 46*
- ◆ **PGE₂** *see Dinoprostone on page 368*
- ◆ **PGI₂** *see Epoprostenol on page 421*
- ◆ **PGX** *see Epoprostenol on page 421*
- ◆ **Phanatuss® Cough Syrup [OTC]** *see Guaifenesin and Dextromethorphan on page 550*
- ◆ **Pharmacal®** *see Calcium Carbonate on page 174*
- ◆ **Pharmaflur®** *see Fluoride on page 498*
- ◆ **Phenadex® Senior [OTC]** *see Guaifenesin and Dextromethorphan on page 550*
- ◆ **Phenahist-TR®** *see Chlorpheniramine, Phenylephrine, Phenylpropanolamine, and Belladonna Alkaloids on page 247*
- ◆ **Phenameth® DM** *see Promethazine and Dextromethorphan on page 980*
- ◆ **Phenaphen® With Codeine** *see Acetaminophen and Codeine on page 21*
- ◆ **Phenazine®** *see Promethazine on page 979*
- ◆ **Phenazo** *see Phenazopyridine on this page*
- ◆ **Phenazodine®** *see Phenazopyridine on this page*

Phenazopyridine *(fen az oh PEER i deen)*

U.S. Brand Names Azo-Standard® [OTC]; Baridium® [OTC]; Geridium®; Phenazodine®; Prodium® [OTC]; Pyridiate®; Pyridium®; Urodine®; Urogesic®

Canadian Brand Names Phenazo; Pyronium®; Vito Reins®

Synonyms Phenazopyridine Hydrochloride; Phenylazo Diamino Pyridine Hydrochloride

Therapeutic Category Analgesic, Urinary; Local Anesthetic, Urinary

Use Symptomatic relief of urinary burning, itching, frequency and urgency in association with urinary tract infection or following urologic procedures

Pregnancy Risk Factor B

Contraindications Hypersensitivity to phenazopyridine or any component; kidney or liver disease

Warnings/Precautions Does not treat infection, acts only as an analgesic; drug should be discontinued if skin or sclera develop a yellow color; use with caution in patients with renal impairment. Use of this agent in the elderly is limited since accumulation of phenazopyridine can occur in patients with renal insufficiency. It should not be used in patients with a Cl_{cr} <50 mL/minute.

Adverse Reactions

1% to 10%:

Central nervous system: Headache, dizziness

Gastrointestinal: Stomach cramps

<1%: Vertigo, skin pigmentation, rash, methemoglobinemia, hemolytic anemia, hepatitis, acute renal failure

Overdosage/Toxicology

Symptoms of overdose include methemoglobinemia, hemolytic anemia, skin pigmentation, renal and hepatic impairment

Antidote is methylene blue 1-2 mg/kg I.V. for methemoglobinemia

Mechanism of Action An azo dye which exerts local anesthetic or analgesic action on urinary tract mucosa through an unknown mechanism

Pharmacodynamics/Kinetics

Metabolism: In the liver and other tissues

Elimination: In urine (where it exerts its action); renal excretion (as unchanged drug) is rapid and accounts for 65% of the drug's elimination

Usual Dosage Oral:

Children: 12 mg/kg/day in 3 divided doses administered after meals for 2 days

Adults: 100-200 mg 3 times/day after meals for 2 days when used concomitantly with an antibacterial agent

Dosing interval in renal impairment:

Cl_{cr} 50-80 mL/minute: Administer every 8-16 hours

Cl_{cr} <50 mL/minute: Avoid use

Test Interactions Phenazopyridine may cause delayed reactions with glucose oxidase reagents (Clinistix®, Tes-Tape®); occasional false-positive tests occur with Tes-Tape®; cupric sulfate tests (Clinitest®) are not affected; interference may also occur with urine ketone tests (Acetest®, Ketostix®) and urinary protein tests; tests for urinary steroids and porphyrins may also occur

Patient Information Take after meals; tablets may color urine orange or red and may stain clothing

Dosage Forms Tablet, as hydrochloride:

Azo-Standard®, Prodium®: 95 mg

Baridium®, Geridium®, Pyridiate®, Pyridium®, Urodine®, Urogesic®: 100 mg

Geridium®, Phenazodine®, Pyridium®, Urodine®: 200 mg

Extemporaneous Preparations A 10 mg/mL suspension may be made by crushing three 200 mg tablets. Mix with a small amount of distilled water or glycerin. Add 20 mL Cologel® and levigate until a uniform mixture is obtained. Add sufficient 2:1 simple syrup/cherry syrup mixture to make a final volume of 60 mL. Store in an amber container. Label "shake well". Stability is 60 days refrigerated.

Handbook on Extemporaneous Formulations, Bethesda MD: American Society of Hospital Pharmacists, 1987.

- ◆ **Phenazopyridine Hydrochloride** *see* Phenazopyridine *on previous page*
- ◆ **Phenchlor® S.H.A.** *see* Chlorpheniramine, Phenylephrine, Phenylpropanolamine, and Belladonna Alkaloids *on page 247*
- ◆ **Phendry® Oral [OTC]** *see* Diphenhydramine *on page 369*

Phenelzine (FEN el zeen)

Related Information

Antidepressant Agents Comparison *on page 1301*

Tyramine Content of Foods *on page 1525*

U.S. Brand Names Nardil®

Synonyms Phenelzine Sulfate

Therapeutic Category Antidepressant, Monoamine Oxidase Inhibitor

Use Symptomatic treatment of atypical, nonendogenous or neurotic depression. The MAO inhibitors are usually reserved for patients who do not tolerate or respond to the traditional "cyclic" or "second generation" antidepressants. The brain activity of monoamine oxidase increases with age and even more so in patients with Alzheimer's disease. Therefore, the MAO inhibitors may have an increased role in patients with Alzheimer's disease who are depressed. Phenelzine is less stimulating than tranylcypromine.

Pregnancy Risk Factor C

Contraindications Pheochromocytoma, hepatic or renal disease, cerebrovascular defect, cardiovascular disease, hypersensitivity to phenelzine or any component, do not use within 5 weeks of fluoxetine or 2 weeks of sertraline or paroxetine discontinuance

Warnings/Precautions Safety in children <16 years of age has not been established; use with caution in patients who are hyperactive, hyperexcitable, or who have glaucoma; avoid use of meperidine within 2 weeks of phenelzine use. Hypertensive crisis may occur with tyramine. See Tyramine Content of Foods *on page 1525* in Appendix.

The MAO inhibitors are effective and generally well tolerated by older patients. It is the potential interactions with tyramine or tryptophan-containing foods and other drugs, and their effects on blood pressure that have limited their use.

Adverse Reactions

>10%:

Cardiovascular: Orthostatic hypotension

Central nervous system: Drowsiness

Endocrine & metabolic: Decreased sexual ability

Neuromuscular & skeletal: Trembling, weakness

Ocular: Blurred vision

1% to 10%:

Cardiovascular: Tachycardia, peripheral edema

Central nervous system: Nervousness, chills

Gastrointestinal: Diarrhea, anorexia, xerostomia, constipation

<1%: Parkinsonism syndrome, leukopenia, hepatitis

(Continued)

Phenelzine *(Continued)*

Overdosage/Toxicology

Symptoms of overdose include tachycardia, palpitations, muscle twitching, seizures, insomnia, restlessness, transient hypertension, hypotension, drowsiness, hyperpyrexia, coma

Competent supportive care is the most important treatment for an overdose with a monoamine oxidase (MAO) inhibitor. Both hypertension or hypotension can occur with intoxication. Hypotension may respond to I.V. fluids or vasopressors and hypertension usually responds to an alpha-adrenergic blocker. While treating the hypertension, care is warranted to avoid sudden drops in blood pressure, since this may worsen the MAO inhibitor toxicity. Muscle irritability and seizures often respond to diazepam, while hyperthermia is best treated antipyretics and cooling blankets. Cardiac arrhythmias are best treated with phenytoin or procainamide.

Drug Interactions

Increased effect/toxicity of barbiturates, psychotropics, rauwolfia alkaloids, CNS depressants

Increased toxicity with disulfiram (seizures), fluoxetine and other serotonin active agents (increased cardiac effect), tricyclic antidepressants (increased cardiovascular instability), meperidine (increased cardiovascular instability), phenothiazine (hypertensive crisis), sympathomimetics (hypertensive crisis), levodopa (hypertensive crisis), tyramine-containing foods (increased blood pressure), dextroamphetamine

Stability Protect from light

Mechanism of Action Thought to act by increasing endogenous concentrations of epinephrine, norepinephrine, dopamine and serotonin through inhibition of the enzyme (monoamine oxidase) responsible for the breakdown of these neurotransmitters

Pharmacodynamics/Kinetics

Onset of action: Within 2-4 weeks

Absorption: Oral: Well absorbed

Duration: May continue to have a therapeutic effect and interactions 2 weeks after discontinuing therapy

Elimination: In urine primarily as metabolites and unchanged drug

Usual Dosage Oral:

Adults: 15 mg 3 times/day; may increase to 60-90 mg/day during early phase of treatment, then reduce to dose for maintenance therapy slowly after maximum benefit is obtained; takes 2-4 weeks for a significant response to occur

Elderly: Initial: 7.5 mg/day; increase by 7.5-15 mg/day every 3-4 days as tolerated; usual therapeutic dose: 15-60 mg/day in 3-4 divided doses

Dietary Considerations

Alcohol: Additive CNS effect, avoid use

Food: Avoid tyramine-containing foods

Monitoring Parameters Blood pressure, heart rate, diet, weight, mood (if depressive symptoms)

Test Interactions ↓ glucose

Patient Information Avoid tyramine-containing foods: Red wine, cheese (except cottage, ricotta, and cream), smoked or pickled fish, beef or chicken liver, dried sausage, fava or broad bean pods, yeast vitamin supplements; do not begin any prescription or OTC medications without consulting your physician or pharmacist; may take as long as 3 weeks to see effects; report any severe headaches, irregular heartbeats, skin rash, insomnia, sedation, changes in strength; sensations of pain, burning, touch, or vibration; or any other unusual symptoms to your physician; avoid alcohol; get up slowly from chair or bed

Nursing Implications Watch for postural hypotension; monitor blood pressure carefully, especially at therapy onset or if other CNS drugs or cardiovascular drugs are added; check for dietary and drug restriction

Dosage Forms Tablet, as sulfate: 15 mg

♦ **Phenelzine Sulfate** *see* Phenelzine *on previous page*

♦ **Phenerbel-S®** *see* Belladonna, Phenobarbital, and Ergotamine Tartrate *on page 131*

♦ **Phenergan®** *see* Promethazine *on page 979*

♦ **Phenergan® VC Syrup** *see* Promethazine and Phenylephrine *on page 980*

♦ **Phenergan® VC With Codeine** *see* Promethazine, Phenylephrine, and Codeine *on page 980*

♦ **Phenergan® With Codeine** *see* Promethazine and Codeine *on page 980*

♦ **Phenergan® With Dextromethorphan** *see* Promethazine and Dextromethorphan *on page 980*

♦ **Phenhist® Expectorant** *see* Guaifenesin, Pseudoephedrine, and Codeine *on page 551*

Pheniramine, Phenylpropanolamine, and Pyrilamine

(fen EER a meen, fen il proe pa NOLE a meen, & peer IL a meen)

U.S. Brand Names Triaminic® Oral Infant Drops

Therapeutic Category Antihistamine/Decongestant Combination

Dosage Forms Drops: Pheniramine maleate 10 mg, phenylpropanolamine hydrochloride 20 mg, and pyrilamine maleate 10 mg per mL (15 mL)

Phenobarbital (fee noe BAR bi tal)

Related Information

Anticonvulsants by Seizure Type *on page 1300*

Convulsive Status Epilepticus *on page 1470*

Epilepsy Treatment *on page 1468*
Febrile Seizures *on page 1469*

U.S. Brand Names Barbita®; Luminal®; Solfoton®

Canadian Brand Names Barbilixir®

Synonyms Phenobarbital Sodium; Phenobarbitone; Phenylethylmalonylurea

Therapeutic Category Anticonvulsant; Barbiturate; Hypnotic; Sedative

Use Management of generalized tonic-clonic (grand mal) and partial seizures; neonatal seizures; febrile seizures in children; sedation; may also be used for prevention and treatment of neonatal hyperbilirubinemia and lowering of bilirubin in chronic cholestasis

Restrictions C-IV

Pregnancy Risk Factor D

Pregnancy/Breast-Feeding Implications

Clinical effects on the fetus: Crosses the placenta. Cardiac defect reported; hemorrhagic disease of newborn due to fetal vitamin K depletion may occur; may induce maternal folic acid deficiency; withdrawal symptoms observed in infant following delivery. Epilepsy itself, number of medications, genetic factors, or a combination of these probably influence the teratogenicity of anticonvulsant therapy. Benefit:risk ratio usually favors continued use during pregnancy and breast-feeding.

Breast-feeding/Lactation: Crosses into breast milk

Clinical effects on the infant: Sedation; withdrawal with abrupt weaning reported. American Academy of Pediatrics recommends USE WITH CAUTION.

Contraindications Hypersensitivity to phenobarbital or any component; pre-existing CNS depression, severe uncontrolled pain, porphyria, severe respiratory disease with dyspnea or obstruction

Warnings/Precautions Use with caution in patients with hypovolemic shock, congestive heart failure, hepatic impairment, respiratory dysfunction or depression, previous addiction to the sedative/hypnotic group, chronic or acute pain, renal dysfunction, and the elderly, due to its long half-life and risk of dependence, phenobarbital is not recommended as a sedative in the elderly; tolerance or psychological and physical dependence may occur with prolonged use. **Abrupt withdrawal in patients with epilepsy may precipitate status epilepticus.**

Adverse Reactions

\>10%:

Cardiovascular: Cardiac arrhythmias, bradycardia, arterial spasm

Central nervous system: Dizziness, lightheadedness, "hangover" effect, drowsiness, lethargy, CNS excitation or depression, impaired judgment

Local: Pain at injection site, thrombophlebitis with I.V. use

Miscellaneous: Gangrene with inadvertent intra-arterial injection

1% to 10%:

Central nervous system: Confusion, mental depression, unusual excitement, nervousness, faint feeling, headache, insomnia, nightmares

Gastrointestinal: Nausea, vomiting, constipation

<1%: Hypotension, hallucinations, hypothermia, exfoliative dermatitis, Stevens-Johnson syndrome, rash, agranulocytosis, megaloblastic anemia, thrombocytopenia, laryngospasm, respiratory depression, apnea (especially with rapid I.V. use)

Overdosage/Toxicology

Symptoms of overdose include unsteady gait, slurred speech, confusion, jaundice, hypothermia, hypotension, respiratory depression, coma

If hypotension occurs, administer I.V. fluids and place the patient in the Trendelenburg position. If unresponsive, an I.V. vasopressor (eg, dopamine, epinephrine) may be required.

Repeated oral doses of activated charcoal significantly reduce the half-life of phenobarbital resulting from an enhancement of nonrenal elimination. The usual dose is 0.1-1 g/kg every 4-6 hours for 3-4 days unless the patient has no bowel movement causing the charcoal to remain in the GI tract. Assure adequate hydration and renal function. Urinary alkalinization with I.V. sodium bicarbonate also helps to enhance elimination. Hemodialysis or hemoperfusion is of uncertain value. Patients in stage IV coma due to high serum barbiturate levels may require charcoal hemoperfusion.

Drug Interactions CYP1A2, 2B6, 2C, 2C8, 2C9, 2C18, 2C19, 2D6, 3A3/4, and 3A5-7 enzyme inducer

Decreased effect: Phenothiazines, haloperidol, quinidine, cyclosporine, tricyclic antidepressants, corticosteroids, theophylline, ethosuximide, warfarin, oral contraceptives, chloramphenicol, griseofulvin, doxycycline, beta-blockers

Increased toxicity: Propoxyphene, benzodiazepines, CNS depressants, valproic acid, methylphenidate, chloramphenicol

Stability Protect elixir from light; not stable in aqueous solutions; use only clear solutions; do not add to acidic solutions, precipitation may occur; I.V. form is **incompatible** with benzquinamide (in syringe), cephalothin, chlorpromazine, hydralazine, hydrocortisone, hydroxyzine, insulin, levorphanol, meperidine, methadone, morphine, norepinephrine, pentazocine, prochlorperazine, promazine, promethazine, ranitidine (in syringe), vancomycin

Mechanism of Action Interferes with transmission of impulses from the thalamus to the cortex of the brain resulting in an imbalance in central inhibitory and facilitatory mechanisms

Pharmacodynamics/Kinetics

Oral:

Onset of hypnosis: Within 20-60 minutes

Duration: 6-10 hours

(Continued)

913

Phenobarbital (Continued)

I.V.:
Onset of action: Within 5 minutes
Peak effect: Within 30 minutes
Duration: 4-10 hours
Absorption: Oral: 70% to 90%
Protein binding: 20% to 45%, decreased in neonates
Metabolism: In the liver via hydroxylation and glucuronide conjugation
Half-life: Neonates: 45-500 hours; Infants: 20-133 hours; Children: 37-73 hours; Adults: 53-140 hours
Time to peak serum concentration: Oral: Within 1-6 hours
Elimination: 20% to 50% excreted unchanged in urine

Usual Dosage

Children:
Sedation: Oral: 2 mg/kg 3 times/day
Hypnotic: I.M., I.V., S.C.: 3-5 mg/kg at bedtime
Preoperative sedation: Oral, I.M., I.V.: 1-3 mg/kg 1-1.5 hours before procedure
Anticonvulsant: Status epilepticus: **Loading dose:** I.V.:
Infants and Children: 10-20 mg/kg in a single or divided dose; in select patients may administer additional 5 mg/kg/dose every 15-30 minutes until seizure is controlled or a total dose of 40 mg/kg is reached
Adults: 300-800 mg initially followed by 120-240 mg/dose at 20-minute intervals until seizures are controlled or a total dose of 1-2 g
Anticonvulsant maintenance dose: Oral, I.V.:
Infants: 5-8 mg/kg/day in 1-2 divided doses
Children:
1-5 years: 6-8 mg/kg/day in 1-2 divided doses
5-12 years: 4-6 mg/kg/day in 1-2 divided doses
Children >12 years and Adults: 1-3 mg/kg/day in divided doses or 50-100 mg 2-3 times/day
Adults:
Sedation: Oral, I.M.: 30-120 mg/day in 2-3 divided doses
Hypnotic: Oral, I.M., I.V., S.C.: 100-320 mg at bedtime
Preoperative sedation: I.M.: 100-200 mg 1-1.5 hours before procedure
Dosing interval in renal impairment: Cl$_{cr}$ <10 mL/minute: Administer every 12-16 hours
Hemodialysis: Moderately dialyzable (20% to 50%)
Dosing adjustment/comments in hepatic disease: Increased side effects may occur in severe liver disease; monitor plasma levels and adjust dose accordingly

Dietary Considerations

Alcohol: Additive CNS effect, avoid use
Food:
Protein-deficient diets: Increases duration of action of barbiturates. Should not restrict or delete protein from diet unless discussed with physician. Be consistent with protein intake during therapy with barbiturates.
Fresh fruits containing vitamin C: Displaces drug from binding sites, resulting in increased urinary excretion of barbiturate. Educate patients regarding the potential for a decreased anticonvulsant effect of barbiturates with consumption of foods high in vitamin C.
Vitamin D: Loss in vitamin D due to malabsorption; increase intake of foods rich in vitamin D. Supplementation of vitamin D may be necessary.

Administration Avoid rapid I.V. administration >50 mg/minute; avoid intra-arterial injection

Monitoring Parameters Phenobarbital serum concentrations, mental status, CBC, LFTs, seizure activity

Reference Range

Therapeutic:
Infants and children: 15-30 µg/mL (SI: 65-129 µmol/L)
Adults: 20-40 µg/mL (SI: 86-172 µmol/L)
Toxic: >40 µg/mL (SI: >172 µmol/L)
Toxic concentration: Slowness, ataxia, nystagmus: 35-80 µg/mL (SI: 150-344 µmol/L)
Coma with reflexes: 65-117 µg/mL (SI: 279-502 µmol/L)
Coma without reflexes: >100 µg/mL (SI: >430 µmol/L)

Test Interactions ↑ ammonia (B); ↓ bilirubin (S), ↑ copper (S), assay interference of LDH, ↑ LFTs

Patient Information Avoid use of alcohol and other CNS depressants; avoid driving and other hazardous tasks; avoid abrupt discontinuation; may cause physical and psychological dependence; do not alter dose without notifying physician

Nursing Implications Parenteral solutions are highly alkaline; avoid extravasation; institute safety measures to avoid injuries; observe patient for excessive sedation and respiratory depression

Additional Information Injectable solutions contain propylene glycol
Sodium content of injection (65 mg, 1 mL): 6 mg (0.3 mEq)
Phenobarbital: Barbita®, Solfoton®
Phenobarbital sodium: Luminal®

Dosage Forms

Capsule: 16 mg
Elixir: 15 mg/5 mL (5 mL, 10 mL, 20 mL); 20 mg/5 mL (3.75 mL, 5 mL, 7.5 mL, 120 mL, 473 mL, 946 mL, 4000 mL)

Injection, as sodium: 30 mg/mL (1 mL); 60 mg/mL (1 mL); 65 mg/mL (1 mL); 130 mg/mL (1 mL)

Powder for injection: 120 mg

Tablet: 8 mg, 15 mg, 16 mg, 30 mg, 32 mg, 60 mg, 65 mg, 100 mg

♦ **Phenobarbital Sodium** see Phenobarbital on page 912

♦ **Phenobarbitone** see Phenobarbital on page 912

♦ **Phenoxine® [OTC]** see Phenylpropanolamine on page 919

Phenoxybenzamine (fen oks ee BEN za meen)

U.S. Brand Names Dibenzyline®

Synonyms Phenoxybenzamine Hydrochloride

Therapeutic Category Alpha-Adrenergic Blocking Agent, Oral; Antihypertensive Agent

Use Symptomatic management of pheochromocytoma; treatment of hypertensive crisis caused by sympathomimetic amines

   Unlabeled use: Micturition problems associated with neurogenic bladder, functional outlet obstruction, and partial prostate obstruction

Pregnancy Risk Factor C

Contraindications Conditions in which a fall in blood pressure would be undesirable (eg, shock)

Warnings/Precautions Use with caution in patients with renal impairment, cerebral, or coronary arteriosclerosis, can exacerbate symptoms of respiratory tract infections. Because of the risk of adverse effects, avoid the use of this medication in the elderly if possible.

Adverse Reactions
>10%:
   Cardiovascular: Postural hypotension, tachycardia, syncope
   Ocular: Miosis
   Respiratory: Nasal congestion
1% to 10%:
   Cardiovascular: Shock
   Central nervous system: Lethargy, headache, confusion, fatigue
   Gastrointestinal: Vomiting, nausea, diarrhea, xerostomia
   Genitourinary: Inhibition of ejaculation
   Neuromuscular & skeletal: Weakness

Overdosage/Toxicology
Symptoms of overdose include hypotension, tachycardia, lethargy, dizziness, shock
Hypotension and shock should be treated with fluids and by placing the patient in the Trendelenburg position; only alpha-adrenergic pressors such as norepinephrine should be used; mixed agents such as epinephrine, may cause more hypotension

Drug Interactions
Decreased effect: Alpha agonists
Increased toxicity: Beta-blockers (hypotension, tachycardia)

Mechanism of Action Produces long-lasting noncompetitive alpha-adrenergic blockade of postganglionic synapses in exocrine glands and smooth muscle; relaxes urethra and increases opening of the bladder

Pharmacodynamics/Kinetics
Onset of action: Oral: Within 2 hours
Peak effect: Within 4-6 hours
Duration: Can continue for 4 or more days
Half-life: 24 hours
Elimination: Primarily in urine and feces

Usual Dosage Oral:
   Children: Initial: 0.2 mg/kg (maximum: 10 mg) once daily, increase by 0.2 mg/kg increments; usual maintenance dose: 0.4-1.2 mg/kg/day every 6-8 hours, higher doses may be necessary
   Adults: Initial: 10 mg twice daily, increase by 10 mg every other day until optimum dose is achieved; usual range: 20-40 mg 2-3 times/day

Dietary Considerations Alcohol: Avoid use

Monitoring Parameters Blood pressure, pulse, urine output, orthostasis

Patient Information Avoid alcoholic beverages; if dizziness occurs, avoid sudden changes in posture; may cause nasal congestion and constricted pupils; may inhibit ejaculation; avoid cough, cold or allergy medications containing sympathomimetics

Nursing Implications Monitor for orthostasis; assist with ambulation

Dosage Forms Capsule, as hydrochloride: 10 mg

♦ **Phenoxybenzamine Hydrochloride** see Phenoxybenzamine on this page

♦ **Phenoxymethyl Penicillin** see Penicillin V Potassium on page 898

Phentermine (FEN ter meen)

U.S. Brand Names Adipex-P®; Fastin®; Ionamin®; Zantryl®

Synonyms Phentermine Hydrochloride

Therapeutic Category Anorexiant

Use Short-term adjunct in exogenous obesity in patients with an initial body mass index (BMI) ≥30 kg/m^2 or a BMI ≥27 kg/m^2 when other risk factors are present (eg, hypertension, diabetes, hyperlipidemia)

Restrictions C-IV

Pregnancy Risk Factor C

Contraindications Known hypersensitivity to phentermine

(Continued)

Phentermine (Continued)

Body Mass Index (BMI), kg/m^2
Height (feet, inches)

Weight (lb)	5'0"	5'3"	5'6"	5'9"	6'0"	6'3"
140	27	25	23	21	19	18
150	29	27	24	22	20	19
160	31	28	26	24	22	20
170	33	30	28	25	23	21
180	35	32	29	27	25	23
190	37	34	31	28	26	24
200	39	36	32	30	27	25
210	41	37	34	31	29	26
220	43	39	36	33	30	28
230	45	41	37	34	31	29
240	47	43	39	36	33	30
250	49	44	40	37	34	31

Warnings/Precautions Do not use in children ≤16 years of age. Use with caution in patients with diabetes mellitus, cardiovascular disease, nephritis, angina pectoris, hypertension, glaucoma, patients with a history of drug abuse. **Primary pulmonary hypertension (PPH)**, a rare and frequently fatal pulmonary disease, has been reported to occur in patients receiving a combination of phentermine and fenfluramine or dexfenfluramine. The possibility of an association between PPH and the use of phentermine alone cannot be ruled out.

Adverse Reactions
>10%:
Cardiovascular: Hypertension
Central nervous system: Euphoria, nervousness, insomnia
1% to 10%:
Central nervous system: Confusion, mental depression, restlessness
Gastrointestinal: Nausea, vomiting, constipation
Endocrine & metabolic: Changes in libido
Neuromuscular & skeletal: Tremor
Ocular: Blurred vision
<1%: Tachycardia, arrhythmias, depression, headache, alopecia, diarrhea, abdominal cramps, dysuria, polyuria, myalgia, tremor, dyspnea, diaphoresis (increased)

Overdosage/Toxicology
Symptoms of overdose include hyperactivity, agitation, hyperthermia, hypertension, seizures
There is no specific antidote for phentermine intoxication and the bulk of the treatment is supportive. Hyperactivity and agitation usually respond to reduced sensory input, however with extreme agitation haloperidol (2-5 mg I.M. for adults) may be required. Hyperthermia is best treated with external cooling measures, or when severe or unresponsive, muscle paralysis with pancuronium may be needed. Hypertension is usually transient and generally does not require treatment unless severe. For diastolic blood pressures >110 mm Hg, a nitroprusside infusion should be initiated. Seizures usually respond to diazepam IVP and/or phenytoin maintenance regimens.

Drug Interactions
Decreased effect of guanethidine; decreased effect with CNS depressants
Increased effect/toxicity with MAO inhibitors (hypertensive crisis), sympathomimetics, CNS stimulants

Mechanism of Action Phentermine is structurally similar to dextroamphetamine and is comparable to dextroamphetamine as an appetite suppressant, but is generally associated with a lower incidence and severity of CNS side effects. Phentermine, like other anorexiants, stimulates the hypothalamus to result in decreased appetite; anorexiant effects are most likely mediated via norepinephrine and dopamine metabolism. However, other CNS effects or metabolic effects may be involved.

Pharmacodynamics/Kinetics
Absorption: Well absorbed; resin absorbed slower and produces more prolonged clinical effects
Half-life: 20 hours
Elimination: Primarily unchanged in urine

Usual Dosage Oral:
Children 3-15 years: 5-15 mg/day for 4 weeks
Adults: 8 mg 3 times/day 30 minutes before meals or food or 15-37.5 mg/day before breakfast or 10-14 hours before retiring

Monitoring Parameters CNS

Patient Information Take during day to avoid insomnia; do not discontinue abruptly, may cause physical and psychological dependence with prolonged use

Nursing Implications Dose should not be given in evening or at bedtime

Dosage Forms
Capsule, as hydrochloride: 15 mg, 18.75 mg, 30 mg, 37.5 mg
Capsule, resin complex, as hydrochloride: 15 mg, 30 mg

Tablet, as hydrochloride: 8 mg, 37.5 mg

♦ **Phentermine Hydrochloride** *see* Phentermine *on page 915*

Phentolamine (fen TOLE a meen)

Related Information
Extravasation Treatment of Other Drugs *on page 1287*
Hypertension Therapy *on page 1479*

U.S. Brand Names Regitine®

Canadian Brand Names Rogitine®

Synonyms Phentolamine Mesylate

Therapeutic Category Alpha-Adrenergic Blocking Agent, Parenteral; Antidote, Extravasation; Antihypertensive Agent; Diagnostic Agent, Pheochromocytoma

Use Diagnosis of pheochromocytoma and treatment of hypertension associated with pheochromocytoma or other caused by excess sympathomimetic amines; as treatment of dermal necrosis after extravasation of drugs with alpha-adrenergic effects (norepinephrine, dopamine, epinephrine, dobutamine)

Pregnancy Risk Factor C

Contraindications Hypersensitivity to phentolamine or any component; renal impairment; coronary or cerebral arteriosclerosis

Warnings/Precautions Myocardial infarction, cerebrovascular spasm and cerebrovascular occlusion have occurred following administration; use with caution in patients with gastritis or peptic ulcer, tachycardia, or a history of cardiac arrhythmias

Adverse Reactions
>10%:
  Cardiovascular: Hypotension, tachycardia, arrhythmias, reflex tachycardia, anginal pain, orthostatic hypotension
  Gastrointestinal: Nausea, vomiting, diarrhea, exacerbation of peptic ulcer, abdominal pain
  Respiratory: Nasal congestion
1% to 10%:
  Cardiovascular: Flushing of face, syncope
  Central nervous system: Dizziness
  Neuromuscular & skeletal: Weakness
  Respiratory: Nasal congestion
<1%: Myocardial infarction, severe headache

Overdosage/Toxicology
Symptoms of overdose include tachycardia, shock, vomiting, dizziness
Hypotension and shock should be treated with fluids and by placing the patient in the Trendelenburg position; only alpha-adrenergic pressors such as norepinephrine should be used; mixed agents such as epinephrine, may cause more hypotension. Take care not to cause so much swelling of the extremity or digit that a compartment syndrome occurs.

Drug Interactions
Decreased effect: Epinephrine, ephedrine
Increased toxicity: Ethanol (disulfiram reaction)

Stability Reconstituted solution is stable for 48 hours at room temperature and 1 week when refrigerated

Mechanism of Action Competitively blocks alpha-adrenergic receptors to produce brief antagonism of circulating epinephrine and norepinephrine to reduce hypertension caused by alpha effects of these catecholamines; also has a positive inotropic and chronotropic effect on the heart

Pharmacodynamics/Kinetics
Onset of action: I.M.: Within 15-20 minutes; I.V.: Immediate
Duration: I.M.: 30-45 minutes; I.V.: 15-30 minutes
Metabolism: In the liver
Half-life: 19 minutes
Elimination: Urine (10% as unchanged drug)

Usual Dosage
Treatment of alpha-adrenergic drug extravasation: S.C.:
  Children: 0.1-0.2 mg/kg diluted in 10 mL 0.9% sodium chloride infiltrated into area of extravasation within 12 hours
  Adults: Infiltrate area with small amount of solution made by diluting 5-10 mg in 10 mL 0.9% sodium chloride within 12 hours of extravasation
  If dose is effective, normal skin color should return to the blanched area within 1 hour
Diagnosis of pheochromocytoma: I.M., I.V.:
  Children: 0.05-0.1 mg/kg/dose, maximum single dose: 5 mg
  Adults: 5 mg
Surgery for pheochromocytoma: Hypertension: I.M., I.V.:
  Children: 0.05-0.1 mg/kg/dose given 1-2 hours before procedure; repeat as needed every 2-4 hours until hypertension is controlled; maximum single dose: 5 mg
  Adults: 5 mg given 1-2 hours before procedure and repeated as needed every 2-4 hours
Hypertensive crisis: Adults: 5-20 mg

Administration Infiltrate the area of dopamine extravasation with multiple small injections using only 27- or 30-gauge needles and changing the needle between each skin entry; take care not to cause so much swelling of the extremity or digit that a compartment syndrome occurs

Monitoring Parameters Blood pressure, heart rate

(Continued)

Phentolamine *(Continued)*

Test Interactions ↑ LFTs rarely
Nursing Implications Monitor patient for orthostasis; assist with ambulation
Dosage Forms Injection, as mesylate: 5 mg/mL (1 mL)

♦ **Phentolamine Mesylate** *see Phentolamine on previous page*
♦ **Phenylalanine Mustard** *see Melphalan on page 725*
♦ **Phenylazo Diamino Pyridine Hydrochloride** *see Phenazopyridine on page 910*
♦ **Phenyldrine® [OTC]** *see Phenylpropanolamine on next page*

Phenylephrine *(fen il EF rin)*

Related Information
Adrenergic Agonists, Cardiovascular Comparison *on page 1290*
Extravasation Treatment of Other Drugs *on page 1287*
U.S. Brand Names AK-Dilate® Ophthalmic Solution; AK-Nefrin® Ophthalmic Solution; Alconefrin® Nasal Solution [OTC]; Doktors® Nasal Solution [OTC]; I-Phrine® Ophthalmic Solution; Isopto® Frin Ophthalmic Solution; Mydfrin® Ophthalmic Solution; Neo-Synephrine® Nasal Solution [OTC]; Neo-Synephrine® Ophthalmic Solution; Nostril® Nasal Solution [OTC]; Prefrin™ Ophthalmic Solution; Relief® Ophthalmic Solution; Rhinall® Nasal Solution [OTC]; Sinarest® Nasal Solution [OTC]; St. Joseph® Measured Dose Nasal Solution [OTC]; Vicks® Sinex® Nasal Solution [OTC]
Canadian Brand Names Dionephrine; Novahistine® Decongestant; Prefrin™ Liquifilm®
Synonyms Phenylephrine Hydrochloride
Therapeutic Category Adrenergic Agonist Agent; Adrenergic Agonist Agent, Ophthalmic; Alpha-Adrenergic Agonist; Nasal Agent, Vasoconstrictor; Ophthalmic Agent, Mydriatic; Sympathomimetic
Use Treatment of hypotension, vascular failure in shock; as a vasoconstrictor in regional analgesia; symptomatic relief of nasal and nasopharyngeal mucosal congestion; as a mydriatic in ophthalmic procedures and treatment of wide-angle glaucoma; supraventricular tachycardia
Pregnancy Risk Factor C
Contraindications Pheochromocytoma, severe hypertension, bradycardia, ventricular tachyarrhythmias; hypersensitivity to phenylephrine or any component; narrow-angle glaucoma (ophthalmic preparation), acute pancreatitis, hepatitis, peripheral or mesenteric vascular thrombosis, myocardial disease, severe coronary disease
Warnings/Precautions Injection may contain sulfites which may cause allergic reaction in some patients; do not use if solution turns brown or contains a precipitate; use with extreme caution in elderly patients, patients with hyperthyroidism, bradycardia, partial heart block, myocardial disease, or severe arteriosclerosis; infuse into large veins to help prevent extravasation which may cause severe necrosis; the 10% ophthalmic solution has caused increased blood pressure in elderly patients and its use should, therefore, be avoided
Adverse Reactions
Nasal:
>10%: Burning, rebound congestion, sneezing
1% to 10%: Stinging, dryness
Ophthalmic:
>10%: Transient stinging
1% to 10%:
Central nervous system: Headache, browache
Ocular: Blurred vision, photophobia, lacrimation
Systemic:
>10%: Neuromuscular & skeletal: Tremor
1% to 10%:
Cardiovascular: Peripheral vasoconstriction hypertension, angina, reflex bradycardia, arrhythmias
Central nervous system: Restlessness, excitability
Overdosage/Toxicology
Symptoms of overdose include vomiting, hypertension, palpitations, paresthesia, ventricular extrasystoles
Treatment is supportive; in extreme cases, I.V. phentolamine may be used
Drug Interactions
Decreased effect: With alpha- and beta-adrenergic blocking agents
Increased effect: With oxytocic drugs
Increased toxicity: With sympathomimetics, tachycardia or arrhythmias may occur; with MAO inhibitors, actions may be potentiated
Stability Is stable for 48 hours in 5% dextrose in water at pH 3.5-7.5; do not use brown colored solutions
Mechanism of Action Potent, direct-acting alpha-adrenergic stimulator with weak beta-adrenergic activity; causes vasoconstriction of the arterioles of the nasal mucosa and conjunctiva; activates the dilator muscle of the pupil to cause contraction; produces vasoconstriction of arterioles in the body; produces systemic arterial vasoconstriction
Pharmacodynamics/Kinetics
Onset of effect: I.M., S.C.: Within 10-15 minutes; I.V.: Immediate
Duration: I.M.: 30 minutes to 2 hours; I.V.: 15-30 minutes; S.C.: 1 hour
Metabolism: To phenolic conjugates; metabolized in liver and intestine by monoamine oxidase
Half-life: 2.5 hours

Elimination: Urine (90%)

Usual Dosage

Ophthalmic procedures:

Infants <1 year: Instill 1 drop of 2.5% 15-30 minutes before procedures

Children and Adults: Instill 1 drop of 2.5% or 10% solution, may repeat in 10-60 minutes as needed

Nasal decongestant: (therapy should not exceed 5 continuous days)

Children:

2-6 years: Instill 1 drop every 2-4 hours of 0.125% solution as needed

6-12 years: Instill 1-2 sprays or instill 1-2 drops every 4 hours of 0.25% solution as needed

Children >12 years and Adults: Instill 1-2 sprays or instill 1-2 drops every 4 hours of 0.25% to 0.5% solution as needed; 1% solution may be used in adult in cases of extreme nasal congestion; do not use nasal solutions more than 3 days

Hypotension/shock:

Children:

I.M., S.C.: 0.1 mg/kg/dose every 1-2 hours as needed (maximum: 5 mg)

I.V. bolus: 5-20 mcg/kg/dose every 10-15 minutes as needed

I.V. infusion: 0.1-0.5 mcg/kg/minute

Adults:

I.M., S.C.: 2-5 mg/dose every 1-2 hours as needed (initial dose should not exceed 5 mg)

I.V. bolus: 0.1-0.5 mg/dose every 10-15 minutes as needed (initial dose should not exceed 0.5 mg)

I.V. infusion: 10 mg in 250 mL D_5W or NS (1:25,000 dilution) (40 mcg/mL); start at 100-180 mcg/minute (2-5 mL/minute; 50-90 drops/minute) initially; when blood pressure is stabilized, maintenance rate: 40-60 mcg/minute (20-30 drops/minute)

Paroxysmal supraventricular tachycardia: I.V.:

Children: 5-10 mcg/kg/dose over 20-30 seconds

Adults: 0.25-0.5 mg/dose over 20-30 seconds

Administration Concentration and rate of infusion can be calculated using the following formulas: Dilute 0.6 mg x weight (kg) to 100 mL; then the dose in mcg/kg/minute = 0.1 x the infusion rate in mL/hour

Monitoring Parameters Blood pressure, heart rate, arterial blood gases, central venous pressure

Patient Information Nasal decongestant should not be used for >3 days in a row, hereby reducing problems of rebound congestion; notify physician of insomnia, dizziness, tremor, or irregular heartbeat; if symptoms do not improve within 7 days or are accompanied by signs of infection, consult physician

Nursing Implications May cause necrosis or sloughing tissue if extravasation occurs during I.V. administration or S.C. administration

Extravasation: Use phentolamine as antidote; mix 5 mg with 9 mL of NS; inject a small amount of this dilution into extravasated area; blanching should reverse immediately. Monitor site; if blanching should recur, additional injections of phentolamine may be needed.

Dosage Forms

Injection, as hydrochloride (Neo-Synephrine®): 1% [10 mg/mL] (1 mL)

Nasal solution, as hydrochloride:

Drops:

Neo-Synephrine®: 0.125% (15 mL)

Alconefrin® 12: 0.16% (30 mL)

Alconefrin® 25, Neo-Synephrine®, Children's Nostril®, Rhinall®: 0.25% (15 mL, 30 mL, 40 mL)

Alconefrin®, Neo-Synephrine®: 0.5% (15 mL, 30 mL)

Spray:

Alconefrin® 25, Neo-Synephrine®, Rhinall®: 0.25% (15 mL, 30 mL, 40 mL)

Neo-Synephrine®, Nostril®, Sinex®: 0.5% (15 mL, 30 mL)

Neo-Synephrine®: 1% (15 mL)

Ophthalmic solution, as hydrochloride:

AK-Nefrin®, Prefrin™ Liquifilm®, Relief®: 0.12% (0.3 mL, 15 mL, 20 mL)

AK-Dilate®, Mydfrin®, Neo-Synephrine®, Phenoptic®: 2.5% (2 mL, 3 mL, 5 mL, 15 mL)

AK-Dilate®, Neo-Synephrine®, Neo-Synephrine® Viscous: 10% (1 mL, 2 mL, 5 mL, 15 mL)

Phenylephrine and Scopolamine (fen il EF rin & skoe POL a meen)

U.S. Brand Names Murocoll-2® Ophthalmic

Therapeutic Category Anticholinergic/Adrenergic Agonist

Dosage Forms Solution, ophthalmic: Phenylephrine hydrochloride 10% and scopolamine hydrobromide 0.3% (7.5 mL)

- **Phenylephrine Hydrochloride** *see* Phenylephrine *on previous page*
- **Phenylethylmalonylurea** *see* Phenobarbital *on page 912*
- **Phenylisohydantoin** *see* Pemoline *on page 892*

Phenylpropanolamine (fen il proe pa NOLE a meen)

U.S. Brand Names Acutrim® 16 Hours [OTC]; Acutrim® II, Maximum Strength [OTC]; Acutrim® Late Day [OTC]; Control® [OTC]; Dexatrim® Pre-Meal [OTC]; Maximum Strength Dex-A-Diet® [OTC]; Maximum Strength Dexatrim® [OTC]; Phenoxine® [OTC]; Phenyldrine® [OTC]; Prolamine® [OTC]; Propagest® [OTC]; Rhindecon®; Unitrol® [OTC] (Continued)

Phenylpropanolamine *(Continued)*

Synonyms *dl*-Norephedrine Hydrochloride; Phenylpropanolamine Hydrochloride; PPA

Therapeutic Category Adrenergic Agonist Agent; Anorexiant; Decongestant; Sympathomimetic

Use Anorexiant; nasal decongestant

Pregnancy Risk Factor C

Contraindications Known hypersensitivity to drug

Warnings/Precautions Use with caution in patients with high blood pressure, tachyarrhythmias, pheochromocytoma, bradycardia, cardiac disease, arteriosclerosis; do not use for more than 3 weeks for weight loss

Adverse Reactions
>10%: Cardiovascular: Hypertension, palpitations
1% to 10%:
    Central nervous system: Insomnia, restlessness, dizziness
    Gastrointestinal: Xerostomia, nausea
<1%: Tightness in chest, bradycardia, arrhythmias, angina, severe headache, anxiety, nervousness, restlessness, dysuria

Overdosage/Toxicology
Symptoms of overdose include vomiting, hypertension, palpitations, paresthesia, excitation, seizures
Treatment is supportive; diazepam 5-10 mg I.V. (0.25-0.4 mg/kg for children) may be used for excitation and seizures

Drug Interactions
Decreased effect of antihypertensives
Increased effect/toxicity with MAO inhibitors (hypertensive crisis), beta-blockers (increased pressor effects)

Mechanism of Action Releases tissue stores of epinephrine and thereby produces an alpha- and beta-adrenergic stimulation; this causes vasoconstriction and nasal mucosa blanching; also appears to depress central appetite centers

Pharmacodynamics/Kinetics
Absorption: Oral: Well absorbed
Metabolism: In the liver to norephedrine
Bioavailability: Close to 100%
Half-life: 4.6-6.6 hours
Elimination: In urine primarily as unchanged drug (80% to 90%)

Usual Dosage Oral:
Children: Decongestant:
    2-6 years: 6.25 mg every 4 hours
    6-12 years: 12.5 mg every 4 hours not to exceed 75 mg/day
Adults:
    Decongestant: 25 mg every 4 hours or 50 mg every 8 hours, not to exceed 150 mg/day
    Anorexic: 25 mg 3 times/day 30 minutes before meals or 75 mg (timed release) once daily in the morning
    Precision release: 75 mg after breakfast

Monitoring Parameters Blood pressure, heart rate

Patient Information Should not be used more than 3 consecutive weeks for weight loss; contact physician for insomnia, tremor, or irregular heartbeat

Nursing Implications Administer dose early in day to prevent insomnia; observe for signs of nervousness, excitability

Dosage Forms
Capsule, as hydrochloride: 37.5 mg
Capsule, as hydrochloride, timed release: 25 mg, 75 mg
Tablet, as hydrochloride: 25 mg, 50 mg
Tablet, as hydrochloride:
    Precision release: 75 mg
    Timed release: 75 mg

♦ **Phenylpropanolamine Hydrochloride** *see* Phenylpropanolamine *on previous page*

Phenyltoloxamine, Phenylpropanolamine, and Acetaminophen

(fen il tol OKS a meen, fen il proe pa NOLE a meen, & a seet a MIN oh fen)

U.S. Brand Names Sinubid®

Therapeutic Category Antihistamine/Decongestant/Analgesic

Dosage Forms Tablet: Phenyltoloxamine citrate 22 mg, phenylpropanolamine hydrochloride 25 mg, and acetaminophen 325 mg

Phenyltoloxamine, Phenylpropanolamine, Pyrilamine, and Pheniramine

(fen il tol OKS a meen, fen il proe pa NOLE a meen, peer IL a meen, & fen IR a meen)

U.S. Brand Names Poly-Histine-D® Capsule

Therapeutic Category Cold Preparation

Dosage Forms Capsule: Phenyltoloxamine citrate 16 mg, phenylpropanolamine hydrochloride 50 mg, pyrilamine maleate 16 mg, and pheniramine maleate 16 mg

Phenytoin (FEN i toyn)

Related Information

Antacid Drug Interactions *on page 1296*
Anticonvulsants by Seizure Type *on page 1300*
Convulsive Status Epilepticus *on page 1470*
Epilepsy Treatment *on page 1468*
Extravasation Treatment of Other Drugs *on page 1287*
Fosphenytoin and Phenytoin, Parenteral Comparison *on page 1321*

U.S. Brand Names Dilantin®; Diphenylan Sodium®

Canadian Brand Names Tremytoine®

Synonyms Diphenylhydantoin; DPH; Phenytoin Sodium; Phenytoin Sodium, Extended; Phenytoin Sodium, Prompt

Therapeutic Category Antiarrhythmic Agent, Class I-B; Anticonvulsant

Use Management of generalized tonic-clonic (grand mal), simple partial and complex partial seizures; prevention of seizures following head trauma/neurosurgery; ventricular arrhythmias, including those associated with digitalis intoxication, prolonged Q-T interval and surgical repair of congenital heart diseases in children; also used for epidermolysis bullosa

Pregnancy Risk Factor D

Pregnancy/Breast-Feeding Implications

Clinical effects on the fetus: Crosses the placenta. Cardiac defects and multiple other malformations reported; characteristic pattern of malformations called "fetal hydantoin syndrome"; hemorrhagic disease of newborn due to fetal vitamin K depletion, maternal folic acid deficiency may occur. Epilepsy itself, number of medications, genetic factors, or a combination of these probably influence the teratogenicity of anticonvulsant therapy. Benefit:risk ratio usually favors continued use during pregnancy and breast-feeding.

Breast-feeding/lactation: Crosses into breast milk

Clinical effects on the infant: Methemoglobinemia, drowsiness and decreased sucking reported in 1 case. American Academy of Pediatrics considers **compatible** with breast-feeding.

Contraindications Hypersensitivity to phenytoin, other hydantoins, or any component; heart block, sinus bradycardia

Warnings/Precautions May increase frequency of petit mal seizures; I.V. form may cause hypotension, skin necrosis at I.V. site; avoid I.V. administration in small veins; use with caution in patients with porphyria; discontinue if rash or lymphadenopathy occurs; use with caution in patients with hepatic dysfunction, sinus bradycardia, S-A block, A-V block, or hepatic impairment; elderly may have reduced hepatic clearance and low albumin levels, which will increase the free fraction of phenytoin in the serum and, therefore, the pharmacologic response

Adverse Reactions I.V. effects: Hypotension, bradycardia, cardiac arrhythmias, cardiovascular collapse (especially with rapid I.V. use), venous irritation and pain, thrombophlebitis

Effects not related to plasma phenytoin concentrations: Hypertrichosis, gingival hypertrophy, thickening of facial features, carbohydrate intolerance, folic acid deficiency, peripheral neuropathy, vitamin D deficiency, osteomalacia, systemic lupus erythematosus

Dose-related effects: Nystagmus, blurred vision, diplopia, ataxia, slurred speech, dizziness, drowsiness, lethargy, coma, rash, fever, nausea, vomiting, gum tenderness, confusion, mood changes, folic acid depletion, osteomalacia, hyperglycemia

Related to elevated concentrations:
>20 mcg/mL: Far lateral nystagmus
>30 mcg/mL: 45° lateral gaze nystagmus and ataxia
>40 mcg/mL: Decreased mentation
>100 mcg/mL: Death

>10%:
Central nervous system: Psychiatric changes, slurred speech, dizziness, drowsiness
Gastrointestinal: Constipation, nausea, vomiting, gingival hyperplasia
Neuromuscular & skeletal: Trembling
1% to 10%:
Central nervous system: Headache, insomnia
Dermatologic: Rash
Gastrointestinal: Anorexia, weight loss
Hematologic: Leukopenia
Hepatic: Hepatitis
Renal: Increase in serum creatinine
<1%: Hypotension, bradycardia, cardiac arrhythmias, cardiovascular collapse, confusion, fever, ataxia, thrombophlebitis, peripheral neuropathy, paresthesia, diplopia, nystagmus, blurred vision, SLE-like syndrome, lymphadenopathy, hepatitis, Stevens-Johnson syndrome, blood dyscrasias, dyskinesias, pseudolymphoma, lymphoma, venous irritation and pain

Overdosage/Toxicology

Symptoms of overdose include unsteady gait, slurred speech, confusion, nausea, hypothermia, fever, hypotension, respiratory depression, coma

Treatment is supportive for hypotension; treat with I.V. fluids and place patient in Trendelenburg position; seizures may be controlled with diazepam 5-10 mg (0.25-0.4 mg/kg in children)

(Continued)

Phenytoin *(Continued)*

Drug Interactions CYP2C9 and 2C19 enzyme substrate; CYP1A2, 2B6, 2C, 2C9, 2C18, 2C19, 2D6, 3A3/4, and 3A5-7 enzyme inducer

Decreased effect: Phenytoin with rifampin, cisplatin, vinblastine, bleomycin, folic acid, theophylline, and continuous NG feedings. Phenytoin may decrease the effect of oral contraceptives, itraconazole, mebendazole, methadone, oral midazolam, valproic acid, cyclosporine, theophylline, doxycycline, quinidine, mexiletine, disopyramide.

Amiodarone or disulfiram decreases metabolism of phenytoin.

Increased toxicity: Isoniazid, chloramphenicol, or fluconazole may increase phenytoin serum concentrations. Valproic acid may increase, decrease or have no effect on phenytoin serum concentrations. Phenytoin may increase the effect of dopamine (enhanced hypotension), warfarin (enhanced anticoagulation), increase the rate of conversion of primidone to phenobarbital resulting in increased phenobarbital serum concentrations. Ticlopidine increases serum phenytoin concentrations to increase toxicity of phenytoin

Stability

Phenytoin is stable as long as it remains free of haziness and precipitation

Use only clear solutions; parenteral solution may be used as long as there is no precipitate and it is not hazy, slightly yellowed solution may be used

Refrigeration may cause precipitate, sometimes the precipitate is resolved by allowing the solution to reach room temperature again

Drug may precipitate at a pH <11.5

May dilute with normal saline for I.V. infusion; stability is concentration dependent

Standard diluent: Dose/100 mL NS

Minimum volume: Concentration should be maintained at 1-10 mg/mL secondary to stability problems (stable for 4 hours)

Comments: Maximum rate of infusion: 50 mg/minute

IVPB dose should be administered via an in-line 0.22-5 micron filter because of high potential for precipitation I.V. form is highly **incompatible** with many drugs and solutions such as dextrose in water, some saline solutions, amikacin, bretylium, cephapirin, dobutamine, heparin, insulin, levorphanol, lidocaine, meperidine, metaraminol, morphine, norepinephrine, potassium chloride, vitamin B complex with C

Mechanism of Action Stabilizes neuronal membranes and decreases seizure activity by increasing efflux or decreasing influx of sodium ions across cell membranes in the motor cortex during generation of nerve impulses; prolongs effective refractory period and suppresses ventricular pacemaker automaticity, shortens action potential in the heart

Pharmacodynamics/Kinetics

Absorption: Oral: Slow

Distribution: V_d:

Neonates:

Premature: 1-1.2 L/kg

Full-term: 0.8-0.9 L/kg

Infants: 0.7-0.8 L/kg

Children: 0.7 L/kg

Adults: 0.6-0.7 L/kg

Protein binding:

Neonates: Up to 20% free

Infants: Up to 15% free

Adults: 90% to 95%

Others: Increased free fraction (decreased protein binding)

Patients with hyperbilirubinemia, hypoalbuminemia, uremia **(see table)**

Metabolism: Follows dose-dependent capacity-limited (Michaelis-Menten) pharmacokinetics with increased V_{max} in infants >6 months of age and children versus adults

Bioavailability: Dependent upon formulation administered

Time to peak serum concentration (dependent upon formulation administered): Oral:

Extended-release capsule: Within 4-12 hours

Immediate release preparation: Within 2-3 hours

Elimination: Highly variable clearance dependent upon intrinsic hepatic function and dose administered; increased clearance and decreased serum concentrations with febrile illness; <5% excreted unchanged in urine; major metabolite (via oxidation) HPPA undergoes enterohepatic recycling and elimination in urine as glucuronides

Disease States Resulting in a Decrease in Serum Albumin Concentration	Disease States Resulting in an Apparent Decrease in Affinity of Phenytoin for Serum Albumin
Burns Hepatic cirrhosis Nephrotic syndrome Pregnancy Cystic fibrosis	Renal failure Jaundice (severe) Other drugs (displacers) Hyperbilirubinemia (total bilirubin >15 mg/dL) Cl_{cr} <25 mL/min (unbound fraction is increased 2- to 3-fold in uremia)

Usual Dosage

Status epilepticus: I.V.:

Infants and Children: Loading dose: 15-20 mg/kg in a single or divided dose; maintenance dose: Initial: 5 mg/kg/day in 2 divided doses, usual doses:

6 months to 3 years: 8-10 mg/kg/day

4-6 years: 7.5-9 mg/kg/day

7-9 years: 7-8 mg/kg/day

10-16 years: 6-7 mg/kg/day, some patients may require every 8 hours dosing

Adults: Loading dose: 15-20 mg/kg in a single or divided dose, followed by 100-150 mg/dose at 30-minute intervals up to a maximum of 1500 mg/24 hours; maintenance dose: 300 mg/day or 5-6 mg/kg/day in 3 divided doses or 1-2 divided doses using extended release

Anticonvulsant: Children and Adults: Oral:

Loading dose: 15-20 mg/kg; based on phenytoin serum concentrations and recent dosing history; administer oral loading dose in 3 divided doses given every 2-4 hours to decrease GI adverse effects and to ensure complete oral absorption; maintenance dose: same as I.V.

Dosing adjustment/comments in renal impairment or hepatic disease: Safe in usual doses in mild liver disease; clearance may be substantially reduced in cirrhosis and plasma level monitoring with dose adjustment advisable. Free phenytoin levels should be monitored closely.

Dietary Considerations

Alcohol: Additive CNS depression has been reported with hydantoins

Alcohol (acute use): Inhibits metabolism of phenytoin; avoid or limit use; watch for sedation

Alcohol (chronic use): Stimulates metabolism of phenytoin; avoid or limit use

Food:

Folic acid: Low erythrocyte and CSF folate concentrations. Phenytoin may decrease mucosal uptake of folic acid; to avoid folic acid deficiency and megaloblastic anemia, some clinicians recommend giving patients on anticonvulsants prophylactic doses of folic acid and cyanocobalamin.

Calcium: Hypocalcemia has been reported in patients taking prolonged high-dose therapy with an anticonvulsant. Phenytoin may decrease calcium absorption. Monitor calcium serum concentration and for bone disorders (eg, rickets, osteomalacia). Some clinicians have given an additional 4,000 Units/week of vitamin D (especially in those receiving poor nutrition and getting no sun exposure) to prevent hypocalcemia.

Fresh fruits containing vitamin C: Displaces drug from binding sites, resulting in increased urinary excretion of hydantoin. Educate patients regarding the potential for a decreased anticonvulsant effect of hydantoins with consumption of foods high in vitamin C.

Vitamin D: Phenytoin interferes with vitamin D metabolism and osteomalacia may result; may need to supplement with vitamin D

Glucose: Hyperglycemia and glycosuria may occur in patients receiving high-dose therapy. Monitor blood glucose concentration, especially in patients with impaired renal function.

Tube feedings: Tube feedings decrease phenytoin bioavailability; to avoid decreased serum levels with continuous NG feeds, hold feedings for 2 hours prior to and 2 hours after phenytoin administration, if possible. There is a variety of opinions on how to administer phenytoin with enteral feedings. BE CONSISTENT throughout therapy.

Administration

Phenytoin may be administered by IVP or IVPB administration

I.M. administration is not recommended due to erratic absorption, pain on injection and precipitation of drug at injection site

S.C. administration is not recommended because of the possibility of local tissue damage

The maximum rate of I.V. administration is 50 mg/minute; highly sensitive patients (eg, elderly, patients with pre-existing cardiovascular conditions) should receive phenytoin more slowly (eg, 20 mg/minute)

An in-line 0.22-5 micron filter is recommended for IVPB solutions due to the high potential for precipitation of the solution; avoid extravasation; following I.V. administration, NS should be injected through the same needle or I.V. catheter to prevent irritation

Monitoring Parameters Blood pressure, vital signs (with I.V. use), plasma phenytoin level, CBC, liver function tests

Reference Range Timing of serum samples: Because it is slowly absorbed, peak blood levels may occur 4-8 hours after ingestion of an oral dose. The serum half-life varies with the dosage and the drug follows Michaelis-Menten kinetics. The average adult half-life is about 24 hours. Steady-state concentrations are reached in 5-10 days.

Neonates: 8-15 µg/mL total phenytoin; 1-2 µg/mL free phenytoin

Children and Adults: Toxicity is measured clinically, and some patients require levels outside the suggested therapeutic range

Toxic: 30-50 µg/mL;

Lethal: >100 µg/mL

Therapeutic range:

Total phenytoin: 10-20 µg/mL (children and adults), 8-15 µg/mL (neonates)

Concentrations of 5-10 µg/mL may be therapeutic for some patients but concentrations <5 µg/mL are not likely to be effective

50% of patients show decreased frequency of seizures at concentrations >10 µg/mL

86% of patients show decreased frequency of seizures at concentrations >15 µg/mL

Add another anticonvulsant if satisfactory therapeutic response is not achieved with a phenytoin concentration of 20 µg/mL

Free phenytoin: 1-2.5 µg/mL

(Continued)

Phenytoin *(Continued)*

Toxic: <30-50 µg/mL (SI: <120-200 µmol/L)
Lethal: >100 µg/mL (SI: >400 µmol/L)
When to draw levels: This is dependent on the disease state being treated and the clinical condition of the patient
Key points:
  Slow absorption minimizes fluctuations between peak and trough concentrations, timing of sampling not crucial
  Trough concentrations are generally recommended for routine monitoring. Daily levels are not necessary and may result in incorrect dosage adjustments. If it is determined essential to monitor free phenytoin concentrations, concomitant monitoring of total phenytoin concentrations is not necessary and expensive.
After a loading dose: Draw level within 48-96 hours
Rapid achievement: Draw within 2-3 days of therapy initiation to ensure that the patient's metabolism is not remarkably different from that which would be predicted by average literature-derived pharmacokinetic parameters; early levels should be used cautiously in design of new dosing regimens
Second concentration: Draw within 6-7 days with subsequent doses of phenytoin adjusted accordingly
If plasma concentrations have not changed over a 3- to 5-day period, monitoring interval may be increased to once weekly in the acute clinical setting
In stable patients requiring long-term therapy, generally monitor levels at 3- to 12-month intervals

Adjustment of Serum Concentration in Patients With Low Serum Albumin

Measured Total Phenytoin Concentration (mcg/mL)	Patient's Serum Albumin (g/dL)			
	3.5	3	2.5	2
	Adjusted Total Phenytoin Concentration (mcg/mL)*			
5	6	7	8	10
10	13	14	17	20
15	19	21	25	30

*Adjusted concentration = measured total concentration + [(0.2 x albumin) + 0.1].

Adjustment of Serum Concentration in Patients With Renal Failure (Cl_cr ≤10 mL/min)

Measured Total Phenytoin Concentration (mcg/mL)	Patient's Serum Albumin (g/dL)				
	4	3.5	3	2.5	2
	Adjusted Total Phenytoin Concentration (mcg/mL)*				
5	10	11	13	14	17
10	20	22	25	29	33
15	30	33	38	43	50

*Adjusted concentration = measured total concentration + [(0.1 x albumin) + 0.1].

Test Interactions ↑ glucose, alkaline phosphatase (S); ↓ thyroxine (S), calcium (S)
Patient Information Shake oral suspension well prior to each dose; do not change brand or dosage form without consulting physician; do not skip doses, may cause drowsiness, dizziness, ataxia, loss of coordination or judgment; take with food; maintain good oral hygiene; do not crush or open extended capsules
Additional Information
Phenytoin: Dilantin® chewable tablet and oral suspension
Phenytoin sodium, extended: Dilantin® Kapseal®
Phenytoin sodium, prompt: Diphenylan Sodium® capsule
Sodium content of 1 g injection: 88 mg (3.8 mEq)
Dosage Forms
Capsule, as sodium:
  Extended: 30 mg, 100 mg
  Prompt: 30 mg, 100 mg
Injection, as sodium: 50 mg/mL (2 mL, 5 mL)
Suspension, oral: 30 mg/5 mL (5 mL, 240 mL); 125 mg/5 mL (5 mL, 240 mL)
Tablet, chewable: 50 mg

- ◆ **pHisoHex®** *see* Hexachlorophene *on page 567*
- ◆ **Phos-Ex® 125** *see* Calcium Acetate *on page 173*
- ◆ **Phos-Flur®** *see* Fluoride *on page 498*
- ◆ **PhosLo®** *see* Calcium Acetate *on page 173*
- ◆ **Phosphate, Potassium** *see* Potassium Phosphate *on page 953*
- ◆ **Phospholine Iodide® Ophthalmic** *see* Echothiophate Iodide *on page 402*
- ◆ **Phosphonoformate** *see* Foscarnet *on page 519*
- ◆ **Phosphonoformic Acid** *see* Foscarnet *on page 519*
- ◆ **3-Phosphoryloxymethyl Phenytoin Disodium** *see* Fosphenytoin *on page 523*
- ◆ **Photofrin®** *see* Porfimer *on page 945*
- ◆ **Phrenilin®** *see* Butalbital Compound *on page 165*
- ◆ **Phrenilin® Forte** *see* Butalbital Compound *on page 165*
- ◆ **p-Hydroxyampicillin** *see* Amoxicillin *on page 69*
- ◆ **Phyllocontin®** *see* Theophylline Salts *on page 1125*
- ◆ **Phylloquinone** *see* Phytonadione *on next page*

Physostigmine (fye zoe STIG meen)

Related Information
Depression Disorders and Treatments *on page 1465*
Glaucoma Drug Therapy Comparison *on page 1322*

U.S. Brand Names Antilirium®; Isopto® Eserine

Synonyms Eserine Salicylate; Physostigmine Salicylate; Physostigmine Sulfate

Therapeutic Category Antidote, Anticholinergic Agent; Antidote, Belladonna Alkaloids; Cholinergic Agent; Cholinergic Agent, Ophthalmic; Ophthalmic Agent, Miotic

Use Reverse toxic CNS effects caused by anticholinergic drugs; used as miotic in treatment of glaucoma

Pregnancy Risk Factor C

Contraindications Hypersensitivity to physostigmine or any component; GI or GU obstruction; physostigmine therapy of drug intoxications should be used with extreme caution in patients with asthma, gangrene, severe cardiovascular disease, or mechanical obstruction of the GI tract or urogenital tract. In these patients, physostigmine should be used only to treat life-threatening conditions.

Warnings/Precautions Use with caution in patients with epilepsy, asthma, diabetes, gangrene, cardiovascular disease, bradycardia. Discontinue if excessive salivation or emesis, frequent urination or diarrhea occur. Reduce dosage if excessive sweating or nausea occurs. Administer I.V. slowly or at a controlled rate not faster than 1 mg/minute. Due to the possibility of hypersensitivity or overdose/cholinergic crisis, atropine should be readily available; ointment may delay corneal healing, may cause loss of dark adaptation; not intended as a first-line agent for anticholinergic toxicity or Parkinson's disease.

Adverse Reactions
Ophthalmic:
>10%:
Ocular: Lacrimation, marked miosis, blurred vision, eye pain
Miscellaneous: Diaphoresis
1% to 10%:
Central nervous system: Headache, browache
Dermatologic: Burning, redness
Systemic:
>10%:
Gastrointestinal: Nausea, salivation, diarrhea, stomach pains
Ocular: Lacrimation
Miscellaneous: Diaphoresis
1% to 10%:
Cardiovascular: Palpitations, bradycardia
Central nervous system: Restlessness, nervousness, hallucinations, seizures
Genitourinary: Frequent urge to urinate
Neuromuscular & skeletal: Muscle twitching
Ocular: Miosis
Respiratory: Dyspnea, bronchospasm, respiratory paralysis, pulmonary edema

Overdosage/Toxicology
Symptoms of overdose include muscle weakness, blurred vision, excessive sweating, tearing and salivation, nausea, vomiting, bronchospasm, seizures
If physostigmine is used in excess or in the absence of an anticholinergic overdose, patients may manifest signs of cholinergic toxicity. At this point a cholinergic agent (eg, atropine 0.015-0.05 mg/kg) may be necessary.

Drug Interactions Increased toxicity: Bethanechol, methacholine, succinylcholine may increase neuromuscular blockade with systemic administration

Stability Do not use solution if cloudy or dark brown

Mechanism of Action Inhibits destruction of acetylcholine by acetylcholinesterase which facilitates transmission of impulses across myoneural junction and prolongs the central and peripheral effects of acetylcholine

Pharmacodynamics/Kinetics
Onset of action: Ophthalmic instillation: Within 2 minutes; Parenteral: Within 5 minutes
Absorption: I.M., ophthalmic, S.C.: Readily absorbed
Distribution: Crosses the blood-brain barrier readily and reverses both central and peripheral anticholinergic effects
Duration: Ophthalmic: 12-48 hours; Parenteral: 0.5-5 hours
(Continued)

925

Physostigmine *(Continued)*

Metabolism: In the liver
Half-life: 15-40 minutes
Elimination: Via hydrolysis by cholinesterases

Usual Dosage

Children: Anticholinergic drug overdose: Reserve for life-threatening situations only: I.V.: 0.01-0.03 mg/kg/dose, (maximum: 0.5 mg/minute); may repeat after 5-10 minutes to a maximum total dose of 2 mg or until response occurs or adverse cholinergic effects occur

Adults: Anticholinergic drug overdose:
I.M., I.V., S.C.: 0.5-2 mg to start, repeat every 20 minutes until response occurs or adverse effect occurs
Repeat 1-4 mg every 30-60 minutes as life-threatening signs (arrhythmias, seizures, deep coma) recur; maximum I.V. rate: 1 mg/minute

Ophthalmic:
Ointment: Instill a small quantity to lower fornix up to 3 times/day
Solution: Instill 1-2 drops into eye(s) up to 4 times/day

Test Interactions ↑ aminotransferase [ALT (SGPT)/AST (SGOT)] (S), ↑ amylase (S)

Patient Information Burning or stinging may occur with application; may cause loss of dark adaptation; notify physician if abdominal cramps, sweating, salivation, or cramps occur

Dosage Forms

Injection, as salicylate: 1 mg/mL (2 mL)
Ointment, ophthalmic, as sulfate: 0.25% (3.5 g, 3.7 g)

- ◆ **Physostigmine Salicylate** *see Physostigmine on previous page*
- ◆ **Physostigmine Sulfate** *see Physostigmine on previous page*
- ◆ **Phytomenadione** *see Phytonadione on this page*

Phytonadione *(fye toe na DYE one)*

U.S. Brand Names AquaMEPHYTON® Injection; Konakion® Injection; Mephyton® Oral

Synonyms Methylphytyl Napthoquinone; Phylloquinone; Phytomenadione; Vitamin K₁

Therapeutic Category Vitamin, Fat Soluble

Use Prevention and treatment of hypoprothrombinemia caused by drug-induced or anticoagulant-induced vitamin K deficiency, hemorrhagic disease of the newborn; phytonadione is more effective and is preferred to other vitamin K preparations in the presence of impending hemorrhage; oral absorption depends on the presence of bile salts

Pregnancy Risk Factor C

Contraindications Hypersensitivity to phytonadione or any component

Warnings/Precautions Severe reactions resembling anaphylaxis or hypersensitivity have occurred rarely during or immediately after I.V. administration (even with proper dilution and rate of administration); restrict I.V. administration for emergency use only; ineffective in hereditary hypoprothrombinemia, hypoprothrombinemia caused by severe liver disease; severe hemolytic anemia has been reported rarely in neonates following large doses (10-20 mg) of phytonadione

Adverse Reactions <1%: Transient flushing reaction, rarely hypotension, cyanosis, dizziness (rarely), pain, abnormal taste, GI upset (oral), hemolysis in neonates and in patients with G-6-PD deficiency, tenderness at injection site, dyspnea, diaphoresis, anaphylaxis, hypersensitivity reactions

Drug Interactions Decreased effect: Warfarin sodium, dicumarol, anisindione effects antagonized by phytonadione; mineral oil may decrease GI absorption of vitamin K

Stability Protect injection from light at all times; may be autoclaved

Mechanism of Action Promotes liver synthesis of clotting factors (II, VII, IX, X); however, the exact mechanism as to this stimulation is unknown. Menadiol is a water soluble form of vitamin K; phytonadione has a more rapid and prolonged effect than menadione; menadiol sodium diphosphate (K₄) is half as potent as menadione (K₃).

Pharmacodynamics/Kinetics

Onset of increased coagulation factors: Oral: Within 6-12 hours; Parenteral: Within 1-2 hours; prothrombin may become normal after 12-14 hours
Absorption: Oral: Absorbed from the intestines in the presence of bile
Metabolism: In the liver rapidly
Elimination: In bile and urine

Usual Dosage I.V. route should be restricted for emergency use only

Minimum daily requirement: Not well established
Infants: 1-5 mcg/kg/day
Adults: 0.03 mcg/kg/day
Hemorrhagic disease of the newborn:
Prophylaxis: I.M.: 0.5-1 mg within 1 hour of birth
Treatment: I.M., S.C.: 1-2 mg/dose/day
Oral anticoagulant overdose:
Infants: I.M., S.C.: 1-2 mg/dose every 4-8 hours
Children and Adults: Oral, I.M., I.V., S.C.: 2.5-10 mg/dose; rarely up to 25-50 mg has been used; may repeat in 6-8 hours if given by I.M., I.V., S.C. route; may repeat 12-48 hours after oral route
Vitamin K deficiency: Due to drugs, malabsorption or decreased synthesis of vitamin K
Infants and Children:
Oral: 2.5-5 mg/24 hours
I.M., I.V.: 1-2 mg/dose as a single dose

Adults:
Oral: 5-25 mg/24 hours
I.M., I.V.: 10 mg

Administration I.V. administration: Dilute in normal saline, D$_5$W or D$_5$NS and infuse slowly; rate of infusion should not exceed 1 mg/minute. **This route should be used only if administration by another route is not feasible.** The parenteral preparation has been administered orally to neonates. I.V. administration should not exceed 1 mg/minute; for I.V. infusion, dilute in PF (preservative free) D$_5$W or normal saline.

Monitoring Parameters PT

Additional Information Injection contains benzyl alcohol 0.9% as preservative

Dosage Forms
Injection:
Aqueous colloidal: 2 mg/mL (0.5 mL); 10 mg/mL (1 mL, 2.5 mL, 5 mL)
Aqueous (I.M. only): 2 mg/mL (0.5 mL); 10 mg/mL (1 mL)
Tablet: 5 mg

Extemporaneous Preparations A 1 mg/mL oral suspension was stable for only 3 days when refrigerated when compounded as follows:
Triturate six 5 mg tablets in a mortar, reduce to a fine powder, then add 5 mL each of water and methylcellulose 1% while mixing; then transfer to a graduate and qs to 30 mL with sorbitol
Shake well before using and keep in refrigerator

Nahata MC and Hipple TF, *Pediatric Drug Formulations*, 3rd ed, Cincinnati, OH: Harvey Whitney Books Co, 1997.

♦ **Pilagan® Ophthalmic** *see* Pilocarpine *on this page*
♦ **Pilocar® Ophthalmic** *see* Pilocarpine *on this page*

Pilocarpine (pye loe KAR peen)

Related Information
Glaucoma Drug Therapy Comparison *on page 1322*

U.S. Brand Names Adsorbocarpine® Ophthalmic; Akarpine® Ophthalmic; Isopto® Carpine Ophthalmic; Ocu-Carpine® Ophthalmic; Ocusert Pilo-20® Ophthalmic; Ocusert Pilo-40® Ophthalmic; Pilagan® Ophthalmic; Pilocar® Ophthalmic; Pilopine HS® Ophthalmic; Piloptic® Ophthalmic; Pilostat® Ophthalmic; Salagen® Oral

Canadian Brand Names Minims® Pilocarpine

Synonyms Pilocarpine Hydrochloride; Pilocarpine Nitrate

Therapeutic Category Cholinergic Agent; Cholinergic Agent, Ophthalmic; Ophthalmic Agent, Miotic

Use
Ophthalmic: Management of chronic simple glaucoma, chronic and acute angle-closure glaucoma; counter effects of cycloplegics
Oral: Symptomatic treatment of xerostomia caused by salivary gland hypofunction resulting from radiotherapy for cancer of the head and neck

Pregnancy Risk Factor C

Contraindications Acute inflammatory disease of anterior chamber, hypersensitivity to pilocarpine or any component

Warnings/Precautions Use with caution in patients with corneal abrasion, CHF, asthma, peptic ulcer, urinary tract obstruction, Parkinson's disease, or narrow-angle glaucoma

Adverse Reactions
>10%: Ocular: Blurred vision, miosis
1% to 10%:
Central nervous system: Headache
Genitourinary: Polyuria
Local: Stinging, burning
Ocular: Ciliary spasm, retinal detachment, browache, photophobia, acute iritis, lacrimation, conjunctival and ciliary congestion early in therapy
Miscellaneous: Hypersensitivity reactions
<1%: Hypertension, tachycardia, nausea, vomiting, diarrhea, salivation, diaphoresis

Overdosage/Toxicology
Symptoms of overdose include bronchospasm, bradycardia, involuntary urination, vomiting, hypotension, tremors
Atropine is the treatment of choice for intoxications manifesting with significant muscarinic symptoms. Atropine I.V. 2-4 mg every 3-60 minutes (or 0.04-0.08 mg I.V. every 5-60 minutes if needed for children) should be repeated to control symptoms and then continued as needed for 1-2 days following the acute ingestion. Epinephrine 0.1-1 mg S.C. may be useful in reversing severe cardiovascular or pulmonary sequel.

Stability Refrigerate gel; store solution at room temperature of 8°C to 30°C (46°F to 86°F) and protect from light

Mechanism of Action Directly stimulates cholinergic receptors in the eye causing miosis (by contraction of the iris sphincter), loss of accommodation (by constriction of ciliary muscle), and lowering of intraocular pressure (with decreased resistance to aqueous humor outflow)

Pharmacodynamics/Kinetics
Ophthalmic instillation:
Miosis: Onset of effect: Within 10-30 minutes; Duration: 4-8 hours
Intraocular pressure reduction: Onset of effect: 1 hour required; Duration: 4-12 hours
Ocusert® Pilo application:
Miosis: Onset of effect: 1.5-2 hours
(Continued)

Pilocarpine *(Continued)*

Reduced intraocular pressure: Onset: Within 1.5-2 hours; miosis within 10-30 minutes; Duration: ~1 week

Usual Dosage Adults:

Ophthalmic:

Nitrate solution: Shake well before using; instill 1-2 drops 2-4 times/day

Hydrochloride solution:

Instill 1-2 drops up to 6 times/day; adjust the concentration and frequency as required to control elevated intraocular pressure

To counteract the mydriatic effects of sympathomimetic agents: Instill 1 drop of a 1% solution in the affected eye

Gel: Instill 0.5" ribbon into lower conjunctival sac once daily at bedtime

Ocular systems: Systems are labeled in terms of mean rate of release of pilocarpine over 7 days; begin with 20 mcg/hour at night and adjust based on response

Oral: 5 mg 3 times/day, titration up to 10 mg 3 times/day may be considered for patients who have not responded adequately

Monitoring Parameters Intraocular pressure, funduscopic exam, visual field testing

Patient Information May sting on instillation; notify physician of sweating, urinary retention; usually causes difficulty in dark adaptation; advise patients to use caution while night driving or performing hazardous tasks in poor illumination; after topical instillation, finger pressure should be applied to lacrimal sac to decrease drainage into the nose and throat and minimize possible systemic absorption

Nursing Implications Usually causes difficulty in dark adaptation; advise patients to use caution while night driving or performing hazardous tasks in poor illumination; finger pressure should be applied to lacrimal sac for 1-2 minutes after instillation to decrease risk of absorption and systemic reactions. Assure the patient or a caregiver can adequately administer ophthalmic medication dosage form.

Additional Information

Ocusert® 20 mcg is approximately equivalent to 0.5% or 1% drops

Ocusert® 40 mcg is approximately equivalent to 2% or 3% drops

Oral: Avoid administering with high fat meal; fat decreases the rate of absorption, maximum concentration and increases the time it takes to reach maximum concentration

Dosage Forms Tablet: 5 mg

See table.

Pilocarpine

Dosage Form	Strength %	1 mL	2 mL	15 mL	30 mL	3.5 g
Gel	4					x
Solution as hydrochloride	0.25			x		
	0.5			x	x	
	1	x	x	x	x	
	2	x	x	x	x	
	3			x	x	
	4	x	x	x	x	
	6			x	x	
	8		x			
	10			x		
Solution as nitrate	1			x		
	2			x		
	4			x		

Ocusert® Pilo-20: Releases 20 mcg/hour for 1 week

Ocusert® Pilo-40: Releases 40 mcg/hour for 1 week

Pilocarpine and Epinephrine *(pye loe KAR peen & ep i NEF rin)*

U.S. Brand Names E-Pilo-x® Ophthalmic; P₁E₁® Ophthalmic

Therapeutic Category Cholinergic Agent

Dosage Forms Solution, ophthalmic: Epinephrine bitartrate 1% and pilocarpine hydrochloride 1%, 2%, 3%, 4%, 6% (15 mL)

♦ **Pilocarpine Hydrochloride** *see* Pilocarpine *on previous page*

♦ **Pilocarpine Nitrate** *see* Pilocarpine *on previous page*

♦ **Pilopine HS® Ophthalmic** *see* Pilocarpine *on previous page*

♦ **Piloptic® Ophthalmic** *see* Pilocarpine *on previous page*

♦ **Pilostat® Ophthalmic** *see* Pilocarpine *on previous page*

♦ **Pima®** *see* Potassium Iodide *on page 952*

♦ **Pimaricin** *see* Natamycin *on page 821*

Pimozide *(PI moe zide)*

Related Information

Antipsychotic Agents Comparison *on page 1305*

U.S. Brand Names Orap™

Therapeutic Category Neuroleptic Agent

Use Suppression of severe motor and phonic tics in patients with Tourette's disorder

Pregnancy Risk Factor C

Contraindications Simple tics other than Tourette's, history of cardiac dysrhythmias, known hypersensitivity to pimozide; use in patients receiving macrolide antibiotics such as clarithromycin, erythromycin, azithromycin, and dirithromycin

Adverse Reactions

>10%:

Cardiovascular: Tachycardia, orthostatic hypotension

Central nervous system: Akathisia, akinesia, extrapyramidal effects, drowsiness

Dermatologic: Rash

Endocrine & metabolic: Edema of the breasts

Gastrointestinal: Constipation, xerostomia

1% to 10%:

Cardiovascular: Facial edema

Central nervous system: Tardive dyskinesia, mental depression

Gastrointestinal: Diarrhea, anorexia

<1%: Neuroleptic malignant syndrome (NMS), blood dyscrasias, jaundice

Overdosage/Toxicology

Symptoms of overdose include hypotension, respiratory depression, EKG abnormalities, extrapyramidal symptoms

Following attempts at decontamination, treatment is supportive and symptomatic; seizures can be treated with diazepam, phenytoin, or phenobarbital

Drug Interactions CYP3A3/4 enzyme substrate

Increased effect/toxicity of alfentanil, CNS depressants, guanabenz (increased sedation), MAO inhibitors

Mechanism of Action A potent centrally-acting dopamine-receptor antagonist resulting in its characteristic neuroleptic effects

Pharmacodynamics/Kinetics

Absorption: Oral: 50%

Protein binding: 99%

Metabolism: In the liver with significant first-pass decay

Half-life: 50 hours

Time to peak serum concentration: Within 6-8 hours

Elimination: In urine

Usual Dosage Children >12 years and Adults: Oral: Initial: 1-2 mg/day, then increase dosage as needed every other day; range is usually 7-16 mg/day, maximum dose: 20 mg/day or 0.3 mg/kg/day should not be exceeded

Dosing adjustment in hepatic impairment: Reduction of dose is necessary in patients with liver disease

Test Interactions ↑ prolactin (S)

Patient Information Treatment with pimozide exposes the patient to serious risks; a decision to use pimozide chronically in Tourette's disorder is one that deserves full consideration by the patient (or patient's family) as well as by the treating physician. Because the goal of treatment is symptomatic improvement, the patient's view of the need for treatment and assessment of response are critical in evaluating the impact of therapy and weighing its benefits against the risks.

Dosage Forms Tablet: 2 mg

Pindolol (PIN doe lole)

Related Information

Beta-Blockers Comparison *on page 1311*

U.S. Brand Names Visken®

Canadian Brand Names Apo®-Pindol; Gen-Pindolol; Novo-Pindol; Nu-Pindol; Syn-Pindol®

Therapeutic Category Antihypertensive Agent; Beta-Adrenergic Blocker

Use Management of hypertension

Unlabeled use: Ventricular arrhythmias/tachycardia, antipsychotic-induced akathisia, situational anxiety; aggressive behavior associated with dementia

Pregnancy Risk Factor B

Contraindications Uncompensated congestive heart failure, cardiogenic shock, bradycardia or heart block, asthma, COPD; hypersensitivity to any component

Warnings/Precautions Use with caution in patients with inadequate myocardial function, undergoing anesthesia, bronchospastic disease, diabetes mellitus, hyperthyroidism, impaired hepatic function; abrupt withdrawal of the drug should be avoided (may exacerbate symptoms; discontinue over 1-2 weeks); do not use in pregnant or nursing women; may potentiate hypoglycemia in a diabetic patient and mask signs and symptoms

Adverse Reactions

1% to 10%:

Cardiovascular: Chest pain (3%), edema (6%)

Central nervous system: Insomnia (10%), nightmares/vivid dreams (5%), dizziness (9%), fatigue (8%), nervousness (7%), anxiety (<2%)

Dermatologic: Rash, itching (4%)

Gastrointestinal: Diarrhea, nausea (5%), vomiting, abdominal discomfort (4%)

Neuromuscular & skeletal: Back pain/myalgia (10%), weakness (4%), paresthesia (3%), arthralgia (7%)

Respiratory: Dyspnea (5%)

<1%: Bradycardia, CHF, palpitations, claudication, hypotension, confusion, mental depression, hallucinations, impotence, thrombocytopenia, dry eyes, wheezing

(Continued)

Pindolol *(Continued)*

Overdosage/Toxicology

Symptoms of intoxication include cardiac disturbances, CNS toxicity, bronchospasm, hypoglycemia and hyperkalemia. The most common cardiac symptoms include hypotension and bradycardia; atrioventricular block, intraventricular conduction disturbances, cardiogenic shock, and asystole may occur with severe overdose, especially with membrane-depressant drugs (eg, propranolol); CNS effects include convulsions, coma, and respiratory arrest (commonly seen with propranolol and other membrane-depressant and lipid-soluble drugs).

Treatment includes symptomatic treatment of seizures, hypotension, hyperkalemia and hypoglycemia; bradycardia and hypotension resistant to atropine, isoproterenol or pacing may respond to glucagon; wide QRS defects caused by the membrane-depressant poisoning may respond to hypertonic sodium bicarbonate; repeat-dose charcoal, hemoperfusion, or hemodialysis may be helpful in removal of only those beta-blockers with a small V_d, long half-life or low intrinsic clearance (acebutolol, atenolol, nadolol, sotalol).

Drug Interactions CYP2D6 enzyme substrate

Decreased effect of beta-blockers with aluminum salts, barbiturates, calcium salts, cholestyramine, colestipol, NSAIDs, penicillins (ampicillin), rifampin, salicylates and sulfinpyrazone due to decreased bioavailability and plasma levels

Beta-blockers may decrease the effect of sulfonylureas

Increased effect/toxicity of beta-blockers with calcium blockers (diltiazem, felodipine, nicardipine), contraceptives, flecainide, quinidine (in extensive metabolizers), ciprofloxacin

Beta-blockers may increase the effect/toxicity of flecainide, acetaminophen, clonidine (hypertensive crisis after or during withdrawal of either agent), epinephrine (initial hypertensive episode followed by bradycardia), nifedipine and verapamil lidocaine, ergots (peripheral ischemia), prazosin (postural hypotension)

Beta-blockers may affect the action or levels of ethanol, disopyramide, nondepolarizing muscle relaxants and theophylline although the effects are difficult to predict

Mechanism of Action Blocks both beta$_1$- and beta$_2$-receptors and has mild intrinsic sympathomimetic activity; pindolol has negative inotropic and chronotropic effects and can significantly slow A-V nodal conduction

Pharmacodynamics/Kinetics

Absorption: Oral: Rapid, 50% to 95%

Protein binding: 50%

Metabolism: In the liver (60% to 65%) to conjugates

Half-life: 2.5-4 hours; increased with renal insufficiency, age, and cirrhosis

Time to peak serum concentration: Within 1-2 hours

Elimination: In urine (35% to 50% unchanged drug)

Usual Dosage

Adults: Initial: 5 mg twice daily, increase as necessary by 10 mg/day every 3-4 weeks; maximum daily dose: 60 mg

Elderly: Initial: 5 mg once daily, increase as necessary by 5 mg/day every 3-4 weeks

Dosing adjustment in renal and hepatic impairment: Reduction is necessary in severely impaired

Monitoring Parameters Blood pressure, standing and sitting/supine, pulse, respiratory function

Patient Information Adhere to dosage regimen; watch for postural hypotension; abrupt withdrawal of the drug should be avoided; take at the same time each day; may mask diabetes symptoms; do not discontinue medication abruptly; consult pharmacist or physician before taking over-the-counter cold preparations

Nursing Implications Evaluate blood pressure, apical and radial pulses; do not discontinue abruptly

Dosage Forms Tablet: 5 mg, 10 mg

- ♦ **Pink Bismuth® [OTC]** *see* Bismuth *on page 145*
- ♦ **Pin-Rid® [OTC]** *see* Pyrantel Pamoate *on page 995*
- ♦ **Pin-X® [OTC]** *see* Pyrantel Pamoate *on page 995*
- ♦ **PIO** *see* Pemoline *on page 892*

Pipecuronium *(pi pe kur OH nee um)*

Related Information

Neuromuscular Blocking Agents Comparison *on page 1331*

U.S. Brand Names Arduan®

Synonyms Pipecuronium Bromide

Therapeutic Category Neuromuscular Blocker Agent, Nondepolarizing; Skeletal Muscle Relaxant

Use Adjunct to general anesthesia, to provide skeletal muscle relaxation during surgery and to provide skeletal muscle relaxation for endotracheal intubation; recommended only for procedures anticipated to last 90 minutes or longer

Pregnancy Risk Factor C

Contraindications Hypersensitivity to pipecuronium or bromide

Warnings/Precautions Use with caution in patients with renal impairment, obesity, cardiovascular disease, myasthenia gravis, myasthenic syndrome, and in the elderly

Adverse Reactions

1% to 10%: Cardiovascular: Hypotension, bradycardia

<1%: Atrial fibrillation, myocardial ischemia, thrombosis, hypertension, ventricular extra-systole, CNS depression, urticaria, hypoglycemia, hyperkalemia, muscle atrophy, anuria, respiratory depression, dyspnea

Overdosage/Toxicology Support ventilation by artificial means; paralysis including cessation of respiration

Drug Interactions Increased effect with enflurane, halothane, isoflurane, ketorolac, quinidine, succinylcholine

Mechanism of Action Pipecuronium bromide is a nondepolarizing neuromuscular blocking agent structurally related to pancuronium and vecuronium. Studies in adult patients have demonstrated that pipecuronium is ~20% to 50% more potent than pancuronium as a neuromuscular blocking agent. The neuromuscular effects and pharmacokinetics of pipecuronium appears to lack vagolytic or autonomic activity and produces minimal cardiovascular effects.

Pharmacodynamics/Kinetics
Onset of action: Effective neuromuscular blockade is generally observed within 2-3 minutes
Metabolism: In the liver primarily to 3-desacetyl-pipecuronium
Half-life, elimination: 2-2.5 hours
Elimination: Renally (40% unchanged drug)

Usual Dosage I.V.:
Children:
3 months to 1 year: Adult dosage
1-14 years: May be less sensitive to effects
Adults: Dose is individualized based on ideal body weight, ranges are 85-100 mcg/kg initially to a maintenance dose of 5-25 mcg/kg
Dosing adjustment in renal impairment:
Cl_{cr} 61-80 mL/minute: 70 mcg/kg
Cl_{cr} 41-60 mL/minute: 55 mcg/kg
Cl_{cr} <40 mL/minute: 50 mcg/kg
Extended duration should be expected

Administration Not recommended for dilution into or administration from large volume I.V. solutions

Dosage Forms Injection, as bromide: 10 mg (10 mL)

♦ **Pipecuronium Bromide** see Pipecuronium on previous page

Piperacillin (pi PER a sil in)

Related Information
Antimicrobial Drugs of Choice on page 1404
Community-Acquired Pneumonia in Adults on page 1419

U.S. Brand Names Pipracil®

Synonyms Piperacillin Sodium

Therapeutic Category Antibiotic, Penicillin

Use Treatment of susceptible infections such as septicemia, acute and chronic respiratory tract infections, skin and soft tissue infections, and urinary tract infections due to susceptible strains of Pseudomonas, Proteus, and Escherichia coli and Enterobacter; active against some streptococci and some anaerobic bacteria

Pregnancy Risk Factor B

Contraindications Hypersensitivity to piperacillin or any component or penicillins

Warnings/Precautions Dosage modification required in patients with impaired renal function; history of seizure activity; use with caution in patients with a history of beta-lactam allergy

Adverse Reactions Percentage unknown: Convulsions, confusion, drowsiness, fever, rash, electrolyte imbalance, hemolytic anemia, positive Coombs' reaction, abnormal platelet aggregation and prolonged PT (high doses), thrombophlebitis, myoclonus, acute interstitial nephritis, hypersensitivity reactions, anaphylaxis, Jarisch-Herxheimer reaction

Overdosage/Toxicology
Symptoms of penicillin overdose include neuromuscular hypersensitivity (agitation, hallucinations, asterixis, encephalopathy, confusion, and seizures) and electrolyte imbalance with potassium or sodium salts, especially in renal failure
Hemodialysis may be helpful to aid in the removal of the drug from the blood, otherwise most treatment is supportive or symptom directed

Drug Interactions
Decreased effect: Tetracyclines may decrease penicillin effectiveness; aminoglycosides → physical inactivation of aminoglycosides in the presence of high concentrations of piperacillin and potential toxicity in patients with mild to moderate renal dysfunction; decreased efficacy of oral contraceptives is possible
Increased effect:
Probenecid may increase penicillin levels
Neuromuscular blockers may increase duration of blockade
Aminoglycosides → synergistic efficacy
Heparin with high-dose parenteral penicillins may result in increased risk of bleeding

Stability Reconstituted solution is stable (I.V. infusion) in NS or D_5W for 24 hours at room temperature, 7 days when refrigerated or 4 weeks when frozen; after freezing, thawed solution is stable for 24 hours at room temperature or 48 hours when refrigerated; 40 g bulk vial should **not** be frozen after reconstitution; **incompatible** with aminoglycosides

Mechanism of Action Inhibits bacterial cell wall synthesis by binding to one or more of the penicillin binding proteins (PBPs); which in turn inhibits the final transpeptidation step of peptidoglycan synthesis in bacterial cell walls, thus inhibiting cell wall biosynthesis. (Continued)

Piperacillin *(Continued)*

Bacteria eventually lyse due to ongoing activity of cell wall autolytic enzymes (autolysins and murein hydrolases) while cell wall assembly is arrested.

Pharmacodynamics/Kinetics

Absorption: I.M.: 70% to 80%

Distribution: Crosses the placenta; distributes into milk at low concentrations

Protein binding: 22%

Half-life: Dose-dependent; prolonged with moderately severe renal or hepatic impairment:

Neonates: 1-5 days: 3.6 hours; >6 days: 2.1-2.7 hours

Children: 1-6 months: 0.79 hour; 6 months to 12 years: 0.39-0.5 hour

Adults: 36-80 minutes

Time to peak serum concentration: I.M.: Within 30-50 minutes

Elimination: Principally in urine and partially in feces (via bile)

Usual Dosage

Neonates: 100 mg/kg every 12 hours

Infants and Children: I.M., I.V.: 200-300 mg/kg/day in divided doses every 4-6 hours

Higher doses have been used in cystic fibrosis: 350-500 mg/kg/day in divided doses every 4-6 hours

Adults: I.M., I.V.:

Moderate infections (urinary tract infections): 2-3 g/dose every 6-12 hours; maximum: 2 g I.M./site

Serious infections: 3-4 g/dose every 4-6 hours; maximum: 24 g/24 hours

Uncomplicated gonorrhea: 2 g I.M. in a single dose accompanied by 1 g probenecid 30 minutes prior to injection

Dosing adjustment in renal impairment: Adults: I.V.:

Cl_{cr} 20-40 mL/minute: Administer 3-4 g every 8 hours

Cl_{cr} <20 mL/minute: Administer 3-4 g every 12 hours

Moderately dialyzable (20% to 50%)

Continuous arteriovenous or venovenous hemodiafiltration (CAVH) effects: Dose as for Cl_{cr} 10-50 mL/minute

Administration Administer at least 1 hour apart from aminoglycosides

Monitoring Parameters Observe for signs and symptoms for anaphylaxis during first dose

Test Interactions May interfere with urinary glucose tests using cupric sulfate (Benedict's solution, Clinitest®); may inactivate aminoglycosides *in vitro*; false-positive urinary and serum proteins, positive Coombs' test [direct]

Additional Information Sodium content of 1 g: 1.85 mEq

Dosage Forms Powder for injection, as sodium: 2 g, 3 g, 4 g, 40 g

Piperacillin and Tazobactam Sodium

(pi PER a sil in & ta zoe BAK tam SOW dee um)

Related Information

Antimicrobial Drugs of Choice *on page 1404*

U.S. Brand Names Zosyn™

Therapeutic Category Antibiotic, Penicillin; Antibiotic, Penicillin & Beta-lactamase Inhibitor

Use Treatment of infections of lower respiratory tract, urinary tract, skin and skin structures, gynecologic, bone and joint infections, and septicemia caused by susceptible organisms. Tazobactam expands activity of piperacillin to include beta-lactamase producing strains of *S. aureus*, *H. influenzae*, *Bacteroides*, and other gram-negative bacteria.

Pregnancy Risk Factor B

Pregnancy/Breast-Feeding Implications Breast-feeding/lactation: Use by the breast-feeding mother may result in diarrhea, candidiasis, or allergic response in the infant

Contraindications Hypersensitivity to penicillins, beta-lactamase inhibitors, or any component

Warnings/Precautions Due to sodium load and to the adverse effects of high serum concentrations of penicillins, dosage modification is required in patients with impaired or underdeveloped renal function; use with caution in patients with seizures or in patients with history of beta-lactam allergy; safety and efficacy have not been established in children <12 years of age

Adverse Reactions

>10%: Gastrointestinal: Diarrhea (11.3%)

1% to 10%:

Cardiovascular: Hypertension (1.6%)

Central nervous system: Insomnia (6.7%), headache (7% to 8%), agitation (2%), fever (2.4%), dizziness (1.4%)

Dermatologic: Rash (4%), pruritus (3%)

Gastrointestinal: Constipation (7% to 8%), nausea (6.9%), vomiting/dyspepsia (3.3%)

Respiratory: Rhinitis/dyspnea (~1%)

Miscellaneous: Serum sickness-like reaction

<1%: Hypotension, edema, confusion, pseudomembranous colitis, bronchospasm

Several laboratory abnormalities have rarely been associated with piperacillin/tazobactam including reversible eosinophilia, and neutropenia (associated most often with prolonged therapy), positive direct Coombs' test, prolonged PT and PTT, transient elevations of LFT, increases in creatinine

Overdosage/Toxicology
Symptoms of penicillin overdose include neuromuscular hypersensitivity (agitation, hallucinations, asterixis, encephalopathy, confusion, and seizures) and electrolyte imbalance with potassium or sodium salts, especially in renal dysfunction
Hemodialysis may be helpful to aid in the removal of the drug from the blood, otherwise most treatment is supportive or symptom directed

Drug Interactions
Decreased effect: Tetracyclines may decrease penicillin effectiveness; aminoglycosides → physical inactivation of aminoglycosides in the presence of high concentrations of piperacillin and potential toxicity in patients with mild to moderate renal dysfunction; decreased efficacy of oral contraceptives is possible
Increased effect:
Probenecid may increase penicillin levels
Neuromuscular blockers may increase duration of blockade
Aminoglycosides → synergistic efficacy
Heparin with high-dose parenteral penicillins may result in increased risk of bleeding

Stability Store at controlled room temperature; after reconstitution, solution is stable in NS or D_5W for 24 hours at room temperature and 7 days when refrigerated; use single dose vials immediately after reconstitution (discard unused portions after 24 hours at room temperature and 48 hours if refrigerated)

Mechanism of Action Inhibits bacterial cell wall synthesis by binding to one or more of the penicillin binding proteins (PBPs); which in turn inhibits the final transpeptidation step of peptidoglycan synthesis in bacterial cell walls, thus inhibiting cell wall biosynthesis. Bacteria eventually lyse due to ongoing activity of cell wall autolytic enzymes (autolysins and murein hydrolases) while cell wall assembly is arrested. Tazobactam inhibits many beta-lactamases, including staphylococcal penicillinase and Richmond and Sykes types II, III, IV, and V, including extended spectrum enzymes; it has only limited activity against class I beta-lactamases other than class Ic types.

Pharmacodynamics/Kinetics Both AUC and peak concentrations are dose proportional
Distribution: Distributes well into lungs, intestinal mucosa, skin, muscle, uterus, ovary, prostate, gallbladder, and bile; penetration into CSF is low in subject with noninflamed meninges
Metabolism: Piperacillin: 6% to 9%; Tazobactam: ~26%
Protein binding: Piperacillin: ~26% to 33%; Tazobactam: 31% to 32%
Half-life: Piperacillin: 1 hour; Metabolite: 1-1.5 hours; Tazobactam: 0.7-0.9 hour
Elimination: Both piperacillin and tazobactam are directly proportional to renal function
Piperacillin: 50% to 70% eliminated unchanged in urine, 10% to 20% excreted in bile
Tazobactam: Found in urine at 24 hours, with 26% as the inactive metabolite
Hemodialysis removes 30% to 40% of piperacillin and tazobactam; peritoneal dialysis removes 11% to 21% of tazobactam and 6% of piperacillin; hepatic impairment does not affect the kinetics of piperacillin or tazobactam significantly

Usual Dosage
Children <12 years: Not recommended due to lack of data
Children ≥12 years and Adults:
Severe infections: I.V.: Piperacillin/tazobactam 4/0.5 g every 8 hours or 3/0.375 g every 6 hours
Moderate infections: I.M.: Piperacillin/tazobactam 2/0.25 g every 6-8 hours; treatment should be continued for ≥7-10 days depending on severity of disease (Note: I.M. route not FDA-approved)
Dosing interval in renal impairment:
Cl_{cr} 20-40 mL/minute: Administer 2/0.25 g every 6 hours
Cl_{cr} <20 mL/minute: Administer 2/0.25 g every 8 hours
Hemodialysis: Administer 2/0.25 g every 8 hours with an additional dose of 0.75 g after each dialysis
Continuous arteriovenous or venovenous hemodiafiltration (CAVH) effects: Dose as for Cl_{cr} 10-50 mL/minute

Administration Administer by I.V. infusion over 30 minutes; reconstitute with 5 mL of diluent per 1 g of piperacillin and then further dilute; **compatible** diluents include NS, SW, dextran 6%, D_5W, D_5W with potassium chloride 40 mEq, bacteriostatic saline and water; **incompatible** with lactated Ringer's solution

Monitoring Parameters LFTs, creatinine, BUN, CBC with differential, serum electrolytes, urinalysis, PT, PTT; monitor for signs of anaphylaxis during first dose

Test Interactions Positive Coombs' [direct] test 3.8%, ALT, AST, bilirubin, and LDH

Nursing Implications Discontinue primary infusion, if possible, during infusion and administer aminoglycosides separately from Zosyn™

Additional Information Sodium content of 1 g injection: 54 mg (2.35 mEq)

Dosage Forms Injection: Piperacillin sodium 2 g and tazobactam sodium 0.25 g; piperacillin sodium 3 g and tazobactam sodium 0.375 g; piperacillin sodium 4 g and tazobactam sodium 0.5 g (vials at an 8:1 ratio of piperacillin sodium/tazobactam sodium)

♦ **Piperacillin Sodium** see Piperacillin on page 931

Piperazine (PI per a zeen)
U.S. Brand Names Vermizine®
Therapeutic Category Anthelmintic
Use Treatment of pinworm and roundworm infections (used as an alternative to first-line agents, mebendazole, or pyrantel pamoate)
Pregnancy Risk Factor B
(Continued)

Piperazine *(Continued)*

Contraindications Seizure disorders, liver or kidney impairment, hypersensitivity to piperazine or any component

Warnings/Precautions Use with caution in patients with anemia or malnutrition; avoid prolonged use especially in children

Adverse Reactions <1%: Dizziness, vertigo, weakness, seizures, EEG changes, headache, nausea, vomiting, diarrhea, hemolytic anemia, visual impairment, hypersensitivity reactions, bronchospasms

Drug Interactions Pyrantel pamoate (antagonistic mode of action)

Mechanism of Action Causes muscle paralysis of the roundworm by blocking the effects of acetylcholine at the neuromuscular junction

Pharmacodynamics/Kinetics
Absorption: Well absorbed from GI tract
Time to peak serum concentration: 1 hour
Elimination: Excreted in urine as metabolites and unchanged drug

Usual Dosage Oral:
Pinworms: Children and Adults: 65 mg/kg/day (not to exceed 2.5 g/day) as a single daily dose for 7 days; in severe infections, repeat course after a 1-week interval
Roundworms:
Children: 75 mg/kg/day as a single daily dose for 2 days; maximum: 3.5 g/day
Adults: 3.5 g/day for 2 days (in severe infections, repeat course, after a 1-week interval)

Monitoring Parameters Stool exam for worms and ova

Patient Information Take on empty stomach; if severe or persistent headache, loss of balance or coordination, dizziness, vomiting, diarrhea, or rash occurs, contact physician. If used for pinworm infections, all members of the family should be treated.

Dosage Forms
Syrup, as citrate: 500 mg/5 mL (473 mL, 4000 mL)
Tablet, as citrate: 250 mg

♦ **Piperazine Estrone Sulfate** *see* Estropipate *on page 440*

Pipobroman (pi poe BROE man)

U.S. Brand Names Vercyte®

Therapeutic Category Antineoplastic Agent, Alkylating Agent

Use Treat polycythemia vera; chronic myelocytic leukemia (in patients refractory to busulfan)

Pregnancy Risk Factor D

Contraindications Pre-existing bone marrow suppression, hypersensitivity to any component

Warnings/Precautions The U.S. Food and Drug Administration (FDA) currently recommends that procedures for proper handling and disposal of antineoplastic agents be considered; bone marrow suppression may not occur for 4 weeks

Adverse Reactions 1% to 10%:
Dermatologic: Rash
Gastrointestinal: Vomiting, diarrhea, nausea, abdominal cramps
Hematologic: Leukopenia, thrombocytopenia, anemia

Overdosage/Toxicology
Symptoms of overdose include severe marrow suppression
Supportive therapy is required

Mechanism of Action An alkylating agent considered to be cell-cycle nonspecific and capable of killing tumor cells in any phase of the cell cycle. Alkylating agents form covalent cross-links with DNA thereby resulting in cytotoxic, mutagenic, and carcinogenic effects. The end result of the alkylation process results in the misreading of the DNA code and the inhibition of DNA, RNA, and protein synthesis in rapidly proliferating tumor cells.

Usual Dosage Children >15 years and Adults: Oral:
Polycythemia: 1 mg/kg/day for 30 days; may increase to 1.5-3 mg/kg until hematocrit reduced to 50% to 55%; maintenance: 0.1-0.2 mg/kg/day
Myelocytic leukemia: 1.5-2.5 mg/kg/day until WBC drops to 10,000/mm^3 then start maintenance 7-175 mg/day; stop if WBC falls to <3000/mm^3 or platelets fall to <150,000/mm^3

Monitoring Parameters CBC, liver and renal function tests

Patient Information Notify physician if nausea, vomiting, diarrhea, or rash become severe or if unusual bleeding or bruising, sore throat, or fatigue occur; contraceptives are recommended during therapy

Dosage Forms Tablet: 25 mg

♦ **Pipracil®** *see* Piperacillin *on page 931*

Pirbuterol (peer BYOO ter ole)

Related Information
Bronchodilators, Comparison of Inhaled and Sympathomimetic *on page 1314*

U.S. Brand Names Maxair™ Autohaler™; Maxair™ Inhalation Aerosol

Synonyms Pirbuterol Acetate

Therapeutic Category Beta$_2$-Adrenergic Agonist Agent; Bronchodilator

Use Prevention and treatment of reversible bronchospasm including asthma

Pregnancy Risk Factor C

Contraindications Hypersensitivity to pirbuterol or albuterol

Warnings/Precautions Excessive use may result in tolerance; some adverse reactions may occur more frequently in children 2-5 years of age; use with caution in patients with hyperthyroidism, diabetes mellitus; cardiovascular disorders including coronary insufficiency or hypertension or sensitivity to sympathomimetic amines

Adverse Reactions

>10%:

Central nervous system: Nervousness, restlessness

Neuromuscular & skeletal: Trembling

1% to 10%:

Central nervous system: Headache, dizziness

Gastrointestinal: Taste changes, vomiting, nausea

<1%: Hypertension, arrhythmias, chest pain, insomnia, bruising, anorexia, numbness in hands, weakness, paradoxical bronchospasm

Overdosage/Toxicology

Symptoms of overdose include hypertension, tachycardia, angina, hypokalemia

In cases of overdose, supportive therapy should be instituted, and prudent use of a cardioselective beta-adrenergic blocker (eg, atenolol or metoprolol) should be considered, keeping in mind the potential for induction of bronchoconstriction in an asthmatic individual. Dialysis has not been shown to be of value in the treatment of an overdose with this agent.

Drug Interactions

Decreased effect with beta-blockers

Increased toxicity with other beta agonists, MAO inhibitors, TCAs

Mechanism of Action Pirbuterol is a beta$_2$-adrenergic agonist with a similar structure to albuterol, specifically a pyridine ring has been substituted for the benzene ring in albuterol. The increased beta$_2$ selectivity of pirbuterol results from the substitution of a tertiary butyl group on the nitrogen of the side chain, which additionally imparts resistance of pirbuterol to degradation by monoamine oxidase and provides a lengthened duration of action in comparison to the less selective previous beta-agonist agents.

Pharmacodynamics/Kinetics

Peak therapeutic effect: Oral: 2-3 hours with peak serum concentration of 6.2-9.8 mcg/L; Inhalation: 0.5-1 hour

Half-life: 2-3 hours

Metabolism: In the liver

Elimination: 10% kidney excretion as unchanged drug

Usual Dosage Children >12 years and Adults: 2 inhalations every 4-6 hours for prevention; two inhalations at an interval of at least 1-3 minutes, followed by a third inhalation in treatment of bronchospasm, not to exceed 12 inhalations/day

Monitoring Parameters Respiratory rate, heart rate, and blood pressure

Patient Information Patient instructions are available with product. Do not exceed recommended dosage; rinse mouth with water following each inhalation to help with dry throat and mouth.

Nursing Implications Before using, the inhaler must be shaken well; assess lung sounds, pulse, and blood pressure before administration and during peak of medication; observe patient for wheezing after administration, if this occurs, call physician

Dosage Forms

Aerosol, oral, as acetate: 0.2 mg per actuation (25.6 g)

Aerosol (Autohaler™): 0.2 mg per actuation (2.8 g - 80 inhalations, 14 g - 400 inhalations)

♦ **Pirbuterol Acetate** see Pirbuterol on previous page

Piroxicam (peer OKS i kam)

Related Information

Nonsteroidal Anti-Inflammatory Agents Comparison on page 1335

U.S. Brand Names Feldene®

Canadian Brand Names Apo®-Piroxicam; Novo-Piroxicam; Nu-Pirox; Pro-Piroxicam®

Therapeutic Category Analgesic, Nonsteroidal Anti-inflammatory Drug; Anti-inflammatory Agent; Nonsteroidal Anti-inflammatory Drug (NSAID), Oral

Use Management of inflammatory disorders; symptomatic treatment of acute and chronic rheumatoid arthritis, osteoarthritis, and ankylosing spondylitis; also used to treat sunburn

Pregnancy Risk Factor B (D if used in the 3rd trimester)

Contraindications Hypersensitivity to piroxicam, any component, aspirin or other nonsteroidal anti-inflammatory drugs (NSAIDs); active GI bleeding

Warnings/Precautions Use with caution in patients with impaired cardiac function, hypertension, impaired renal function, GI disease (bleeding or ulcers) and patients receiving anticoagulants; elderly have increased risk for adverse reactions to NSAIDs

Adverse Reactions

>10%:

Central nervous system: Dizziness

Dermatologic: Rash

Gastrointestinal: Abdominal cramps, heartburn, indigestion, nausea

1% to 10%:

Central nervous system: Headache, nervousness

Dermatologic: Itching

Endocrine & metabolic: Fluid retention

Gastrointestinal: Vomiting

Otic: Tinnitus

(Continued)

Piroxicam *(Continued)*

<1%: Congestive heart failure, hypertension, arrhythmias, tachycardia, confusion, hallucinations, aseptic meningitis, mental depression, drowsiness, insomnia, urticaria, erythema multiforme, toxic epidermal necrolysis, Stevens-Johnson syndrome, angioedema, polydipsia, hot flashes, gastritis, GI ulceration, cystitis, polyuria, agranulocytosis, anemia, hemolytic anemia, bone marrow suppression, leukopenia, thrombocytopenia, hepatitis, peripheral neuropathy, toxic amblyopia, blurred vision, conjunctivitis, dry eyes, decreased hearing, acute renal failure, allergic rhinitis, shortness of breath, epistaxis

Overdosage/Toxicology

Symptoms of overdose include nausea, epigastric distress, CNS depression, leukocytosis, renal failure

Management of a nonsteroidal anti-inflammatory drug (NSAID) intoxication is primarily supportive and symptomatic. Fluid therapy is commonly effective in managing the hypotension that may occur following an acute NSAID overdose, except when this is due to an acute blood loss.

Seizures tend to be very short-lived and often do not require drug treatment; although, recurrent seizures should be treated with I.V. diazepam

Since many of the NSAIDs undergo enterohepatic cycling, multiple doses of charcoal may be needed to reduce the potential for delayed toxicities

Drug Interactions CYP2C9 and 2C18 enzyme substrate

Decreased effect of diuretics, beta-blockers; decreased effect with aspirin, antacids, cholestyramine

Increased effect/toxicity of lithium, warfarin, methotrexate (controversial)

Mechanism of Action

Inhibits prostaglandin synthesis, acts on the hypothalamus heat-regulating center to reduce fever, blocks prostaglandin synthetase action which prevents formation of the platelet-aggregating substance thromboxane A_2; decreases pain receptor sensitivity. Other proposed mechanisms of action for salicylate anti-inflammatory action are lysosomal stabilization, kinin and leukotriene production, alteration of chemotactic factors, and inhibition of neutrophil activation. This latter mechanism may be the most significant pharmacologic action to reduce inflammation.

Pharmacodynamics/Kinetics

Onset of analgesia: Oral: Within 1 hour

Peak effect: 3-5 hours

Protein binding: 99%

Metabolism: In the liver

Half-life: 45-50 hours

Elimination: As unchanged drug (5%) and metabolites primarily in urine and to a small degree in feces

Usual Dosage Oral:

Children: 0.2-0.3 mg/kg/day once daily; maximum dose: 15 mg/day

Adults: 10-20 mg/day once daily; although associated with increase in GI adverse effects, doses >20 mg/day have been used (ie, 30-40 mg/day)

Dosing adjustment in hepatic impairment: Reduction of dosage is necessary

Monitoring Parameters

Occult blood loss, hemoglobin, hematocrit, and periodic renal and hepatic function tests; periodic ophthalmologic exams with chronic use

Test Interactions ↑ chloride (S), ↑ sodium (S), ↑ bleeding time

Patient Information Take with food, may cause drowsiness or dizziness

Dosage Forms Capsule: 10 mg, 20 mg

♦ *p*-Isobutylhydratropic Acid *see Ibuprofen on page 593*

♦ Pit *see Oxytocin on page 879*

♦ Pitocin® Injection *see Oxytocin on page 879*

♦ Pitressin® Injection *see Vasopressin on page 1211*

♦ Pitrex® *see Tolnaftate on page 1159*

♦ Placidyl® *see Ethchlorvynol on page 445*

Plague Vaccine *(plaig vak SEEN)*

Therapeutic Category Vaccine, Inactivated Bacteria

Use

Selected travelers to countries reporting cases for whom avoidance of rodents and fleas is impossible; all laboratory and field personnel working with *Yersinia pestis* organisms possibly resistant to antimicrobials; those engaged in *Yersinia pestis* aerosol experiments or in field operations in areas with enzootic plague where regular exposure to potentially infected wild rodents, rabbits, or their fleas cannot be prevented. Prophylactic antibiotics may be indicated following definite exposure, whether or not the exposed persons have been vaccinated.

Pregnancy Risk Factor C

Contraindications

Persons with known hypersensitivity to any of the vaccine constituents (see manufacturer's label); patients who have had severe local or systemic reactions to a previous dose; defer immunization in patients with a febrile illness until resolved

Warnings/Precautions

Pregnancy, unless there is substantial and unavoidable risk of exposure; the expected immune response may not be obtained if plague vaccine is administered to immunosuppressed persons or patients receiving immunosuppressive therapy; be prepared with epinephrine injection (1:1000) in cases of anaphylaxis

Adverse Reactions

All serious adverse reactions must be reported to the U.S. Department of Health and Human Services (DHHS) Vaccine Adverse Event Reporting System (VAERS) 1-800-822-7967.

1% to 10%:
Central nervous system: Malaise (10%), fever, headache (7% to 20%)
Dermatologic: Tenderness (20% to 80%)
<1%: Tachycardia, nausea (3% to 13%), vomiting, local erythema (4.5%), sterile abscess

Drug Interactions Decreased effect with immunoglobulin, other live vaccine used within 1 month; accentuated side effects may occur if given on the same occasion as cholera vaccine or AKD or H-P typhoid vaccine

Mechanism of Action Promotes active immunity to plague in high-risk individuals.

Usual Dosage Three I.M. doses: First dose 1 mL, second dose (0.2 mL) 1 month later, third dose (0.2 mL) 5 months after the second dose; booster doses (0.2 mL) at 1- to 2-year intervals if exposure continues

Administration I.M. into deltoid muscle

Test Interactions Temporary suppression of tuberculosis skin test

Additional Information Federal law requires that the date of administration, the vaccine manufacturer, lot number of vaccine, and the administering person's name, title and address be entered into the patient's permanent medical record

Dosage Forms Injection: 2 mL, 20 mL

- ♦ **Plantago Seed** see Psyllium on page 994
- ♦ **Plantain Seed** see Psyllium on page 994
- ♦ **Plaquenil®** see Hydroxychloroquine on page 585
- ♦ **Plasbumin®** see Albumin on page 34
- ♦ **Platinol®** see Cisplatin on page 267
- ♦ **Platinol®-AQ** see Cisplatin on page 267
- ♦ **Plavix®** see Clopidogrel on page 285
- ♦ **Plendil®** see Felodipine on page 470
- ♦ **Pletal®** see Cilostazol on page 260

Plicamycin (plye kay MYE sin)

Related Information
Cancer Chemotherapy Regimens on page 1263

U.S. Brand Names Mithracin®

Synonyms Mithramycin

Therapeutic Category Antidote, Hypercalcemia; Antineoplastic Agent, Vesicant; Antineoplastic Agent, Miscellaneous; Vesicant

Use Malignant testicular tumors, in the treatment of hypercalcemia and hypercalciuria of malignancy not responsive to conventional treatment; Paget's disease

Pregnancy Risk Factor X

Contraindications Thrombocytopenia, bleeding diatheses, coagulation disorders; bone marrow function impairment; or hypocalcemia

Warnings/Precautions The U.S. Food and Drug Administration (FDA) currently recommends that procedures for proper handling and disposal of antineoplastic agents be considered. Use with caution in patients with hepatic or renal impairment; reduce dosage in patients with renal impairment; discontinue if bleeding or epistaxis occurs. Plicamycin may cause permanent sterility and may cause birth defects.

Adverse Reactions
>10%: Gastrointestinal: Anorexia, stomatitis, nausea, vomiting, diarrhea
Nausea and vomiting occur in almost 100% of patients within the first 6 hours after treatment; incidence increases with rapid injection; stomatitis has also occurred
Time course for nausea/vomiting: Onset 4-6 hours; Duration: 4-24 hours
1% to 10%:
Cardiovascular: Facial flushing
Central nervous system: Fever, headache, depression, drowsiness
Endocrine & metabolic: Hypocalcemia
Hematologic: Myelosuppressive: Mild leukopenia and thrombocytopenia
WBC: Moderate, but uncommon
Platelets: Moderate, rapid onset
Onset (days): 7-10
Nadir (days): 14
Recovery (days): 21
Clotting disorders: May also depress hepatic synthesis of clotting factors, leading to a form of coagulopathy; petechiae, prolonged PT, epistaxis, and thrombocytopenia may be seen and may require discontinuation of the drug. Epistaxis is frequently the first sign of this bleeding disorder.
Hepatic: Hepatotoxicity
Local: Pain at injection site
Extravasation: Is an irritant; may produce local tissue irritation or cellulitis if infiltrated; if extravasation occurs, follow hospital procedure, discontinue I.V., and apply ice for 24 hours
Irritant chemotherapy
Renal: Azotemia, nephrotoxicity
Miscellaneous: Hemorrhagic diathesis

Overdosage/Toxicology
Symptoms of overdose include bone marrow suppression, bleeding syndrome, thrombocytopenia
(Continued)

937

Plicamycin *(Continued)*

Supportive therapy; treatment of hemorrhagic episodes should include transfusion of fresh whole blood or packed red blood cells and fresh frozen plasma, vitamin K, and corticosteroids

Drug Interactions
Increased toxicity: Calcitonin, etidronate, glucagon, → additive hypoglycemic effects

Stability Store intact vials under refrigeration (2°C to 8°C); vials are stable at room temperature (<25°C) for up to 3 months. Dilute powder in 4.9 mL SWI to result in a concentration of 500 mcg/mL which is stable for 24 hours at room temperature (25°C) and 48 hours under refrigeration (4°C). Further dilution in 1000 mL D_5W or NS is stable for 24 hours at room temperature.

Standard I.V. dilution: Dose/1000 mL D_5W or NS; solution is stable for 24 hours at room temperature (25°C)

Mechanism of Action Potent osteoclast inhibitor; may inhibit parathyroid hormone effect on osteoclasts; inhibits bone resorption; forms a complex with DNA in the presence of magnesium or other divalent cations inhibiting DNA-directed RNA synthesis

Pharmacodynamics/Kinetics
Decreasing calcium levels:
  Onset of action: Within 24 hours
  Peak effect: 48-72 hours
  Duration: 5-15 days
Distribution: Crosses blood-brain barrier in low concentrations
Protein binding: 0%
Half-life, plasma: 1 hour
Elimination: 90% of dose excreted in urine within the first 24 hours

Usual Dosage Refer to individual protocols. Dose should be diluted in 1 L of D_5W or NS and administered over 4-6 hours. Dosage should be based on the patient's body weight. If a patient has abnormal fluid retention (ie, edema, hydrothorax or ascites), the patient's ideal weight rather than actual body weight should be used to calculate the dose.

Adults: I.V.:
  Testicular cancer: 25-30 mcg/kg/day for 8-10 days
  Blastic chronic granulocytic leukemia: 25 mcg/kg over 2-4 hours every other day for 3 weeks
  Paget's disease: 15 mcg/kg/day once daily for 10 days
  Hypercalcemia:
    25 mcg/kg single dose which may be repeated in 48 hours if no response occurs
    OR 25 mcg/kg/day for 3-4 days
    OR 25-50 mcg/kg/dose every other day for 3-8 doses

Dosing adjustment in renal impairment:
  Cl_{cr} 10-50 mL/minute: Decrease dosage to 75% of normal dose
  Cl_{cr} <10 mL/minute: Decrease dosage to 50% of normal dose
Hemodialysis: Unknown
CAPD effects: Unknown
CAVH effects: Unknown

Dosing in hepatic impairment: In the treatment of hypercalcemia in patients with hepatic dysfunction: Reduce dose to 12.5 mcg/kg/day

Administration
Administer I.V. infusion over 4-7 hours via central line
Avoid extravasation; local tissue irritation and cellulitis has been reported

Monitoring Parameters Hepatic and renal function tests, CBC, platelet count, prothrombin time, serum electrolytes

Patient Information Any signs of infection, easy bruising or bleeding, shortness of breath, or painful or burning urination should be brought to physician's attention. Nausea, vomiting, or hair loss sometimes occur. The drug may cause permanent sterility and may cause birth defects. The drug may be excreted in breast milk, therefore, an alternative form of feeding your baby should be used.

Nursing Implications Rapid I.V. infusion has been associated with an increased incidence of nausea and vomiting; an antiemetic given prior to and during plicamycin infusion may be helpful. Avoid extravasation since plicamycin is a strong vesicant.

Dosage Forms Powder for injection: 2.5 mg

Pneumococcal Polysaccharide Vaccine, Polyvalent

(noo moe KOK al poly SACK ride vak SEEN, poly VAY lent)

Related Information

Guidelines for the Prevention of Opportunistic Infections in Persons with HIV on page 1388

Immunization Recommendations on page 1358

U.S. Brand Names Pneumovax® 23; Pnu-Imune® 23

Synonyms Pneumococcal Polysaccharide Vaccine

Therapeutic Category Vaccine, Inactivated Bacteria

Use Children >2 years of age and adults who are at increased risk of pneumococcal disease and its complications because of underlying health conditions; older adults, including all those ≥65 years of age

Pregnancy Risk Factor C

Pregnancy/Breast-Feeding Implications The safety of vaccine in pregnant women has not been evaluated; it should not be given during pregnancy unless the risk of infection is high

Contraindications Active infections, Hodgkin's disease patients, <2 years of age, pregnancy, hypersensitivity to pneumococcal vaccine or any component; <10 days prior to or during treatment with immunosuppressive drugs or radiation; (children <5 years of age do not respond satisfactorily to the capsular types of 23 capsular pneumococcal vaccine; the safety of vaccine in pregnant women has not been evaluated; it should not be given during pregnancy unless the risk of infection is high)

Warnings/Precautions Epinephrine injection (1:1000) must be immediately available in the case of anaphylaxis; use caution in individuals who have had episodes of pneumococcal infection within the preceding 3 years (pre-existing pneumococcal antibodies may result in increased reactions to vaccine); may cause relapse in patients with stable idiopathic thrombocytopenia purpura

Adverse Reactions All serious adverse reactions must be reported to the U.S. Department of Health and Human Services (DHHS) Vaccine Adverse Event Reporting System (VAERS) 1-800-822-7967.

>10%: Local: Induration and soreness at the injection site (~72%) (2-3 days)

<1%: Guillain-Barré syndrome, low-grade fever, erythema, rash, paresthesias, myalgia, arthralgia, anaphylaxis

Drug Interactions Decreased effect with immunosuppressive agents, immunoglobulin, other live vaccines within 1 month

Stability Refrigerate

Mechanism of Action Although there are more than 80 known pneumococcal capsular types, pneumococcal disease is mainly caused by only a few types of pneumococci. Pneumococcal vaccine contains capsular polysaccharides of 23 pneumococcal types which represent at least 98% of pneumococcal disease isolates in the United States and Europe. The pneumococcal vaccine with 23 pneumococcal capsular polysaccharide types became available in 1983. The 23 capsular pneumococcal vaccine contains purified capsular polysaccharides of pneumococcal types 1, 2, 3, 4, 5, 8, 9, 12, 14, 17, 19, 20, 22, 23, 26, 34, 43, 51, 56, 57, 67, 70 (American Classification). These are the main pneumococcal types associated with serious infections in the United States.

Usual Dosage Children >2 years and Adults: I.M., S.C.: 0.5 mL

Revaccination should be considered:

1. If ≥6 years since initial vaccination has elapsed, or

(Continued)

Pneumococcal Polysaccharide Vaccine, Polyvalent
(Continued)

2. In patients who received 14-valent pneumococcal vaccine and are at highest risk (asplenic) for fatal infection or
3. At ≥6 years in patients with nephrotic syndrome, renal failure, or transplant recipients, or
4. 3-5 years in children with nephrotic syndrome, asplenia, or sickle cell disease

Administration Do not inject I.V., avoid intradermal, administer S.C. or I.M. (deltoid muscle or lateral midthigh)

Additional Information Federal law requires that the date of administration, the vaccine manufacturer, lot number of vaccine, and the administering person's name, title and address be entered into the patient's permanent medical record; inactivated bacteria vaccine

Dosage Forms Injection: 25 mcg each of 23 polysaccharide isolates/0.5 mL dose (0.5 mL, 1 mL, 5 mL)

- ◆ **Pneumomist®** see Guaifenesin on page 549
- ◆ **Pneumovax® 23** see Pneumococcal Polysaccharide Vaccine, Polyvalent on previous page
- ◆ **Pnu-Imune® 23** see Pneumococcal Polysaccharide Vaccine, Polyvalent on previous page
- ◆ **Pod-Ben-25®** see Podophyllum Resin on this page
- ◆ **Podocon-25™** see Podophyllum Resin on this page
- ◆ **Podofilm®** see Podophyllum Resin on this page
- ◆ **Podofin®** see Podophyllum Resin on this page
- ◆ **Podophyllin** see Podophyllum Resin on this page

Podophyllin and Salicylic Acid (po DOF fil um & sal i SIL ik AS id)
U.S. Brand Names Verrex-C&M®
Therapeutic Category Keratolytic Agent
Dosage Forms Solution, topical: Podophyllum 10% and salicylic acid 30% with penederm 0.5% (7.5 mL)

Podophyllum Resin (po DOF fil um REZ in)
U.S. Brand Names Pod-Ben-25®; Podocon-25™; Podofin®
Canadian Brand Names Podofilm®
Synonyms Mandrake; May Apple; Podophyllin
Therapeutic Category Keratolytic Agent
Use Topical treatment of benign growths including external genital and perianal warts, papillomas, fibroids; compound benzoin tincture generally is used as the medium for topical application
Pregnancy Risk Factor X
Contraindications Not to be used on birthmarks, moles, or warts with hair growth; cervical, urethral, oral warts; not to be used by diabetic patient or patient with poor circulation; pregnant women
Warnings/Precautions Use of large amounts of drug should be avoided; avoid contact with the eyes as it can cause severe corneal damage; do not apply to moles, birthmarks, or unusual warts; to be applied by a physician only; for external use only; 25% solution should not be applied to or near mucous membranes
Adverse Reactions
1% to 10%:
  Dermatologic: Pruritus
  Gastrointestinal: Nausea, vomiting, abdominal pain, diarrhea
<1%: Confusion, lethargy, hallucinations, leukopenia, thrombocytopenia, hepatotoxicity, peripheral neuropathy, renal failure
Mechanism of Action Directly affects epithelial cell metabolism by arresting mitosis through binding to a protein subunit of spindle microtubules (tubulin)
Usual Dosage Topical:
  Children and Adults: 10% to 25% solution in compound benzoin tincture; apply drug to dry surface, use 1 drop at a time allowing drying between drops until area is covered; total volume should be limited to <0.5 mL per treatment session
  Condylomata acuminatum: 25% solution is applied daily; use a 10% solution when applied to or near mucous membranes
  Verrucae: 25% solution is applied 3-5 times/day directly to the wart
Patient Information Notify physician if undue skin irritation develops; should be applied by a physician
Nursing Implications Shake well before using; solution should be washed off within 1-4 hours for genital and perianal warts and within 1-2 hours for accessible meatal warts; use protective occlusive dressing around warts to prevent contact with unaffected skin
Dosage Forms Liquid, topical: 25% in benzoin (5 mL, 7.5 mL, 30 mL)

- ◆ **Point-Two®** see Fluoride on page 498
- ◆ **Poladex®** see Dexchlorpheniramine on page 339
- ◆ **Polaramine®** see Dexchlorpheniramine on page 339
- ◆ **Poliomyelitis Vaccine** see Polio Vaccines on this page

Polio Vaccines (POE lee oh vak SEENS)
Related Information
Adverse Events and Vaccination on page 1369

U.S. Brand Names IPOL™; Orimune®

Synonyms E-IPV; Enhanced-potency Inactivated Poliovirus Vaccine; OPV; Poliomyelitis Vaccine; Poliovirus Vaccine, Live, Trivalent; Sabin; Salk; TOPV

Therapeutic Category Vaccine, Live Virus and Inactivated Virus

Use

American Academy of Pediatrics recommends three poliomyelitis vaccines schedules: OPV-only, IPV-only and sequential IPV-OPV.

Inactivated poliovirus vaccine contains three types of poliovirus grown either in monkey kidney or human diploid cells and inactivated with formaldehyde. IPV is of enhanced potency and is highly immunogenic.

OPV schedule ONLY is recommended: when parents or providers who prefer not to have the child receive the additional injections needed if IPV were to be used, for infants and children starting vaccination regimens after 6 months of age in whom an accelerated schedule is necessary to complete immunizations, an OPV-only regimen will minimize the number of injections required at each visit. In populations with low vaccination rates, OPV may be preferred in order to expedite implementation of the routine childhood immunization schedule.

IPV schedule ONLY is recommended: for immunocompromised persons and their household contacts (OPV would be contraindicated); for infants and children in which an adult household member is know to be inadequately vaccinated against poliomyelitis, because unimmunized adults are at increased risk of vaccine-associated paralytic poliomyelitis (VAPP); when the number of injections is not likely to decrease compliance and when IPV is preferred by health care providers or parents or other caregivers.

IPV Primary immunization is also recommended for unvaccinated adults because the risk of VAPP after OPV is slightly higher in adults than in children.

Sequential IPV/OPV schedule is recommended to reduce the total number of injections required to reduce the risk of VAPP while maintaining optimal intestinal immunity, especially for travelers to areas where poliovirus is still endemic. The rationale of sequential use of IPV and OPV is that two doses of IPV induce sufficient humoral immunity to prevent VAPP in recipients from subsequent administration of OPV, given to induce optimal intestinal immunity as well as to sustain humoral immunity.

Pregnancy Risk Factor C

Contraindications

Oral: Leukemia, lymphoma, or other generalized malignancies; diseases in which cellular immunity is absent or suppressed (hypogammaglobulinemia, agammaglobulinemia); immunosuppressive therapy; diarrhea; parenteral administration

Parenteral: Hypersensitivity to any component including neomycin, streptomycin, or polymyxin B; defer vaccination for persons with acute febrile illness until recovery

Warnings/Precautions Although there is no convincing evidence documenting adverse effects of either OPV or E-IPV on the pregnant woman or developing fetus, it is prudent on theoretical grounds to avoid vaccinating pregnant women. However, if immediate protection against poliomyelitis is needed, OPV is recommended. OPV should not be given to immunocompromised individuals or to persons with known or possibly immunocompromised family members; E-IPV is recommended in such situations.

Adverse Reactions All serious adverse reactions must be reported to the U.S. Department of Health and Human Services (DHHS) Vaccine Adverse Event Reporting System (VAERS) 1-800-822-7967.

1% to 10%:

Central nervous system: Fever (>101.3°F)

Dermatologic: Rash

Local: Tenderness or pain at injection site

<1%: Fatigue, fussiness, sleepiness, crying, Guillain-Barré, reddening of skin, erythema, decreased appetite, weakness, dyspnea

Drug Interactions Decreased effect with immunosuppressive agents, immune globulin, cholera vaccine; separate by 1 month if possible; may temporarily suppress tuberculin skin test sensitivity (4-6 weeks); DTP, MMR, Hib, and hepatitis B vaccines may be given concurrently if at different sites

Usual Dosage

Oral:

Infants:

Primary series: 0.5 mL at 6-12 weeks of age, second dose 6-8 weeks after first dose (commonly at 4 months), and third dose 8-12 months after second dose (commonly at 18 months)

Booster: All children who have received primary immunization series, should receive a single follow-up dose and all children who have not should complete primary series

Children (older) and Adults (adolescents through 18 years of age): Two 0.5 mL doses 6-8 weeks apart and a third dose of 0.5 mL 6-12 months after second dose

Subcutaneous: **Enhanced-potency inactivated poliovirus vaccine (E-IPV) is preferred for primary vaccination of adults,** two doses S.C. 4-8 weeks apart, a third dose 6-12 months after the second. For adults with a completed primary series and for

(Continued)

Polio Vaccines *(Continued)*

whom a booster is indicated, either OPV or E-IPV can be given (E-IPV preferred). If immediate protection is needed, either OPV or E-IPV is recommended.

Administration Do not administer I.V.

Additional Information Federal law requires that the date of administration, the vaccine manufacturer, lot number of vaccine, and the administering person's name, title and address be entered into the patient's permanent medical record

Dosage Forms

Injection (IPOL™, E-IPV, Enhanced-potency Inactivated Poliovirus Vaccine, Poliomyelitis Vaccine, Salk): Suspension of three types of poliovirus (Types 1, 2 and 3) grown in human diploid cell cultures (0.5 mL)

Solution, oral (Orimune®, OPV, Poliovirus Vaccine, Live, Trivalent, Sabin, TOPV): Mixture of type 1, 2, and 3 viruses in monkey kidney tissue (0.5 mL)

- ◆ **Poliovirus Vaccine, Live, Trivalent** *see* Polio Vaccines *on page 940*
- ◆ **Polocaine®** *see* Mepivacaine *on page 730*
- ◆ **Polycillin®** *see* Ampicillin *on page 79*
- ◆ **Polycillin-N®** *see* Ampicillin *on page 79*
- ◆ **Polycitra®** *see* Sodium Citrate and Potassium Citrate Mixture *on page 1069*
- ◆ **Polycitra®-K** *see* Potassium Citrate and Citric Acid *on page 951*
- ◆ **Polydine®** [OTC] *see* Povidone-Iodine *on page 955*

Polyestradiol *(pol i es tra DYE ole)*

Synonyms Polyestradiol Phosphate

Therapeutic Category Antineoplastic Agent, Hormone; Estrogen Derivative

Use Palliative treatment of advanced, inoperable carcinoma of the prostate

Pregnancy Risk Factor X

Contraindications Known or suspected estrogen-dependent neoplasm, carcinoma of the breast, active thromboembolic disorders, hypersensitivity to estrogens or any component, pregnancy

Warnings/Precautions Use with caution in patients with migraine, diabetes, cardiac, or renal impairment

Adverse Reactions

>10%:

Cardiovascular: Peripheral edema

Endocrine & metabolic: Enlargement of breasts (female and male), breast tenderness

Gastrointestinal: Nausea, anorexia, bloating

1% to 10%:

Central nervous system: Headache

Endocrine & metabolic: Increased libido (female), decrease libido (male)

Gastrointestinal: Vomiting, diarrhea

<1%: Hypertension, thromboembolism, myocardial infarction, edema, depression, dizziness, anxiety, stroke, chloasma, melasma, rash, amenorrhea, alterations in frequency and flow of menses, decreased glucose tolerance, increased triglycerides and LDL, nausea, GI distress, cholestatic jaundice, intolerance to contact lenses, increased susceptibility to *Candida* infection, breast tumors

Overdosage/Toxicology

Toxicity is unlikely following single exposures of excessive doses

Any treatment following emesis and charcoal administration should be supportive and symptomatic

Stability After reconstitution, solution is stable for 10 days at room temperature and protected from direct light

Mechanism of Action Estrogens exert their primary effects on the interphase DNA-protein complex (chromatin) by binding to a receptor (usually located in the cytoplasm of a target cell) and initiating translocation of the hormone-receptor complex to the nucleus

Pharmacodynamics/Kinetics

90% of injected dose leaves bloodstream within 24 hours

Passive storage in reticuloendothelial system

Increasing the dose prolongs duration of action

Usual Dosage Adults: Deep I.M.: 40 mg every 2-4 weeks or less frequently; maximum dose: 80 mg

Dosage Forms Powder for injection, as phosphate: 40 mg

- ◆ **Polyestradiol Phosphate** *see* Polyestradiol *on this page*

Polyethylene Glycol-Electrolyte Solution

(pol i ETH i leen GLY kol ee LEK troe lite soe LOO shun)

Related Information

Laxatives, Classification and Properties *on page 1326*

U.S. Brand Names Colovage®; Colyte®; GoLYTELY®; NuLytely®; OCL®

Canadian Brand Names Klean-Prep®; Peglyte™

Synonyms Electrolyte Lavage Solution

Therapeutic Category Cathartic; Laxative, Bowel Evacuant

Use Bowel cleansing prior to GI examination or following toxic ingestion

Pregnancy Risk Factor C

Contraindications Gastrointestinal obstruction, gastric retention, bowel perforation, toxic colitis, megacolon

Warnings/Precautions Safety and efficacy not established in children; do not add flavorings as additional ingredients before use; observe unconscious or semiconscious patients with impaired gag reflex or those who are otherwise prone to regurgitation or aspiration during administration; use with caution in ulcerative colitis, caution against the use of hot loop polypectomy

Adverse Reactions
>10%: Gastrointestinal: Nausea, abdominal fullness, bloating
1% to 10%: Gastrointestinal: Abdominal cramps, vomiting, anal irritation
<1%: Rash

Drug Interactions Oral medications should not be administered within 1 hour of start of therapy

Stability Use within 48 hours of preparation; refrigerate reconstituted solution; tap water may be used for preparation of the solution; shake container vigorously several times to ensure dissolution of powder

Mechanism of Action Induces catharsis by strong electrolyte and osmotic effects

Pharmacodynamics/Kinetics Onset of effect: Oral: Within 1-2 hours

Usual Dosage The recommended dose for adults is 4 L of solution prior to gastrointestinal examination, as ingestion of this dose produces a satisfactory preparation in >95% of patients. Ideally the patient should fast for approximately 3-4 hours prior to administration, but in no case should solid food be given for at least 2 hours before the solution is given. The solution is usually administered orally, but may be given via nasogastric tube to patients who are unwilling or unable to drink the solution.

Children: Oral: 25-40 mL/kg/hour for 4-10 hours
Adults:
Oral: At a rate of 240 mL (8 oz) every 10 minutes, until 4 liters are consumed or the rectal effluent is clear; rapid drinking of each portion is preferred to drinking small amounts continuously
Nasogastric tube: At a rate of 20-30 mL/minute (1.2-1.8 L/hour); the first bowel movement should occur approximately 1 hour after the start of administration

Monitoring Parameters Electrolytes, serum glucose, BUN, urine osmolality

Patient Information Chilled solution is often more palatable

Nursing Implications Rapid drinking of each portion is preferred over small amounts continuously; first bowel movement should occur in 1 hour; chilled solution often more palatable; do not add flavorings as additional ingredients before use

Dosage Forms Powder, for oral solution: PEG 3350 236 g, sodium sulfate 22.74 g, sodium bicarbonate 6.74 g, sodium chloride 5.86 g and potassium chloride 2.97 g (2000 mL, 4000 mL, 4800 mL, 6000 mL)

♦ **Polygam®** see Immune Globulin, Intravenous on page 604

♦ **Polygam® S/D** see Immune Globulin, Intravenous on page 604

♦ **Poly-Histine CS®** see Brompheniramine, Phenylpropanolamine, and Codeine on page 156

♦ **Poly-Histine-D® Capsule** see Phenyltoloxamine, Phenylpropanolamine, Pyrilamine, and Pheniramine on page 920

♦ **Polymox®** see Amoxicillin on page 69

Polymyxin B (pol i MIKS in bee)

Synonyms Polymyxin B Sulfate

Therapeutic Category Antibiotic, Irrigation; Antibiotic, Miscellaneous

Use
Topical: Wound irrigation and bladder irrigation against *Pseudomonas aeruginosa*; used occasionally for gut decontamination
Parenteral use of polymyxin B has mainly been replaced by less toxic antibiotics; it is reserved for life-threatening infections caused by organisms resistant to the preferred drugs (eg, pseudomonal meningitis - intrathecal administration)

Pregnancy Risk Factor B

Contraindications Concurrent use of neuromuscular blockers

Warnings/Precautions Use with caution in patients with impaired renal function, (modify dosage); polymyxin B-induced nephrotoxicity may be manifested by albuminuria, cellular casts, and azotemia. Discontinue therapy with decreasing urinary output and increasing BUN; neurotoxic reactions are usually associated with high serum levels, often in patients with renal dysfunction. Avoid concurrent or sequential use of other nephrotoxic and neurotoxic drugs (eg, aminoglycosides). The drug's neurotoxicity can result in respiratory paralysis from neuromuscular blockade, especially when the drug is given soon after anesthesia or muscle relaxants. Polymyxin B sulfate is most toxic when given parenterally; avoid parenteral use whenever possible.

Adverse Reactions <1%: Facial flushing, neurotoxicity (irritability, drowsiness, ataxia, perioral paresthesia, numbness of the extremities, and blurring of vision); drug fever, urticarial rash, hypocalcemia, hyponatremia, hypokalemia, hypochloremia, pain at injection site, neuromuscular blockade, weakness, nephrotoxicity, respiratory arrest, anaphylactoid reaction, meningeal irritation with intrathecal administration

Overdosage/Toxicology
Symptoms of overdose include respiratory paralysis, ototoxicity, nephrotoxicity
Supportive care is indicated as treatment; ventilatory support may be necessary

Drug Interactions Polymyxin may increase/prolong effect of neuromuscular blocking agents; aminoglycosides may increase polymyxin's risk of respiratory paralysis and renal dysfunction
(Continued)

Polymyxin B *(Continued)*

Stability Discard any unused solution after 72 hours. **Incompatible** with strong acids/alkalies, calcium, magnesium, cephalothin, cefazolin, chloramphenicol, heparin, penicillins.

Mechanism of Action Binds to phospholipids, alters permeability, and damages the bacterial cytoplasmic membrane permitting leakage of intracellular constituents

Pharmacodynamics/Kinetics

Absorption: Well absorbed from the peritoneum; minimal absorption from the GI tract (except in neonates) from mucous membranes or intact skin

Distribution: Minimal distribution into the CSF; crosses the placenta

Half-life: 4.5-6 hours, increased with reduced renal function

Time to peak serum concentration: I.M.: Within 2 hours

Elimination: Primarily as unchanged drug (>60%) in urine via glomerular filtration

Usual Dosage

Otic: 1-2 drops, 3-4 times/day; should be used sparingly to avoid accumulation of excess debris

Infants <2 years:

I.M.: Up to 40,000 units/kg/day divided every 6 hours (not routinely recommended due to pain at injection sites)

I.V.: Up to 40,000 units/kg/day by continuous I.V. infusion

Intrathecal: 20,000 units/day for 3-4 days, then 25,000 units every other day for at least 2 weeks after CSF cultures are negative and CSF (glucose) has returned to within normal limits

Children ≥2 years and Adults:

I.M.: 25,000-30,000 units/kg/day divided every 4-6 hours (not routinely recommended due to pain at injection sites)

I.V.: 15,000-25,000 units/kg/day divided every 12 hours or by continuous infusion

Intrathecal: 50,000 units/day for 3-4 days, then every other day for at least 2 weeks after CSF cultures are negative and CSF (glucose) has returned to within normal limits

Total daily dose should not exceed 2,000,000 units/day

Bladder irrigation: Continuous irrigant or rinse in the urinary bladder for up to 10 days using 20 mg (equal to 200,000 units) added to 1 L of normal saline; usually no more than 1 L of irrigant is used per day unless urine flow rate is high; administration rate is adjusted to patient's urine output

Topical irrigation or topical solution: 500,000 units/L of normal saline; topical irrigation should not exceed 2 million units/day in adults

Gut sterilization: Oral: 15,000-25,000 units/kg/day in divided doses every 6 hours

Clostridium difficile enteritis: Oral: 25,000 units every 6 hours for 10 days

Ophthalmic: A concentration of 0.1% to 0.25% is administered as 1-3 drops every hour, then increasing the interval as response indicates to 1-2 drops 4-6 times/day

Dosing adjustment/interval in renal impairment:

Cl$_{cr}$ 20-50 mL/minute: Administer 75% to 100% of normal dose every 12 hours

Cl$_{cr}$ 5-20 mL/minute: Administer 50% of normal dose every 12 hours

Cl$_{cr}$ <5 mL/minute: Administer 15% of normal dose every 12 hours

Administration Dissolve 500,000 units in 300-500 mL D$_5$W for continuous I.V. drip; dissolve 500,000 units in 2 mL water for injection, saline, or 1% procaine solution for I.M. injection; dissolve 500,000 units in 10 mL physiologic solution for intrathecal administration

Monitoring Parameters Neurologic symptoms and signs of superinfection; renal function (decreasing urine output and increasing BUN may require discontinuance of therapy)

Reference Range Serum concentrations >5 µg/mL are toxic in adults

Patient Information Report any dizziness or sensations of ringing in the ear, loss of hearing, or any muscle weakness

Nursing Implications Parenteral use is indicated only in life-threatening infections caused by organisms not susceptible to other agents

Additional Information 1 mg = 10,000 units

Dosage Forms

Injection: 500,000 units (20 mL)

Solution (otic): 10,000 units of polymyxin B per mL in combination with hydrocortisone 0.5% solution (eg, Otobiotic®)

Suspension (otic): 10,000 units of polimixin B per mL in combination with hydrocortisone 1% and neomycin sulfate 0.5% (eg, PediOtic®)

Also available in a variety of other combination products for ophthalmic and otic use.

Polymyxin B and Hydrocortisone

(pol i MIKS in bee & hye droe KOR ti sone)

U.S. Brand Names Otobiotic® Otic

Therapeutic Category Antibiotic/Corticosteroid, Otic

Dosage Forms Solution, otic: Polymyxin B sulfate 10,000 units and hydrocortisone 0.5% [5 mg/mL] per mL (10 mL, 15 mL)

♦ **Polymyxin B and Neomycin** *see* Neomycin and Polymyxin B *on page 825*

♦ **Polymyxin B Sulfate** *see* Polymyxin B *on previous page*

♦ **Polymyxin E** *see* Colistin *on page 295*

♦ **Poly-Pred® Ophthalmic Suspension** *see* Neomycin, Polymyxin B, and Prednisolone *on page 828*

♦ **Polysporin® Ophthalmic** *see* Bacitracin and Polymyxin B *on page 122*

♦ **Polysporin® Topical** *see* Bacitracin and Polymyxin B *on page 122*

Polythiazide (pol i THYE a zide)
Related Information
 Sulfonamide Derivatives *on page 1337*
U.S. Brand Names Renese®
Therapeutic Category Antihypertensive Agent; Diuretic, Thiazide
Use Adjunctive therapy in treatment of edema and hypertension
Pregnancy Risk Factor D
Contraindications Anuria; hypersensitivity to polythiazide or any other sulfonamide derivatives
Usual Dosage Adults: Oral:
 Edema: 1-4 mg/day
 Hypertension: 2-4 mg/day
Additional Information Complete prescribing information for this medication should be consulted for additional detail
Dosage Forms Tablet: 1 mg, 2 mg, 4 mg

♦ **Polytopic** *see* Bacitracin and Polymyxin B *on page 122*
♦ **Polytrim® Ophthalmic** *see* Trimethoprim and Polymyxin B *on page 1185*
♦ **Poly-Vi-Flor®** *see* Vitamins, Multiple *on page 1226*
♦ **Poly-Vi-Sol® [OTC]** *see* Vitamins, Multiple *on page 1226*
♦ **Ponstan®** *see* Mefenamic Acid *on page 722*
♦ **Ponstel®** *see* Mefenamic Acid *on page 722*
♦ **Pontocaine®** *see* Tetracaine *on page 1121*
♦ **Pontocaine® With Dextrose Injection** *see* Tetracaine and Dextrose *on page 1122*
♦ **Porcelana® [OTC]** *see* Hydroquinone *on page 584*
♦ **Porcelana® Sunscreen [OTC]** *see* Hydroquinone *on page 584*

Porfimer (POR fi mer)
U.S. Brand Names Photofrin®
Synonyms Porfimer Sodium
Therapeutic Category Antineoplastic Agent, Miscellaneous
Use Esophageal cancer: Photodynamic therapy (PDT) with porfimer for palliation of patients with completely obstructing esophageal cancer, or of patients with partially obstructing esophageal cancer who cannot be satisfactorily treated with Nd:YAG laser therapy
Pregnancy Risk Factor C
Contraindications Porphyria or in patients with known allergies to porphyrins; existing tracheoesophageal or bronchoesophageal fistula; tumors eroding into a major blood vessel
Warnings/Precautions The U.S. Food and Drug Administration (FDA) currently recommends that procedures for proper handling and disposal of antineoplastic agents be considered. If the esophageal tumor is eroding into the trachea or bronchial tree, the likelihood of tracheoesophageal or bronchoesophageal fistula resulting from treatment is sufficiently high that PDT is not recommended. All patients who receive porfimer sodium will be photosensitive and must observe precautions to avoid exposure of skin and eyes to direct sunlight or bright indoor light for 30 days. The photosensitivity is due to residual drug which will be present in all parts of the skin. Exposure of the skin to ambient indoor light is, however, beneficial because the remaining drug will be inactivated gradually and safely through a photobleaching reaction. Patients should not stay in a darkened room during this period and should be encouraged to expose their skin to ambient indoor light. Ocular discomfort has been reported; for 30 days, when outdoors, patients should wear dark sunglasses which have an average white light transmittance of <4%.
Adverse Reactions
 >10%:
  Cardiovascular: Atrial fibrillation, chest pain
  Central nervous system: Fever, pain, insomnia
  Dermatologic: Photosensitivity reaction
  Gastrointestinal: Abdominal pain, constipation, dysphagia, nausea, vomiting
  Hematologic: Anemia
  Neuromuscular & skeletal: Back pain
  Respiratory: Dyspnea, pharyngitis, pleural effusion, pneumonia, respiratory insufficiency
 1% to 10%:
  Cardiovascular: Hypertension, hypotension, edema, cardiac failure, tachycardia, chest pain (substernal)
  Central nervous system: Anxiety, confusion
  Endocrine & metabolic: Dehydration
  Gastrointestinal: Diarrhea, dyspepsia, eructation, esophageal edema, esophageal tumor bleeding, esophageal stricture, esophagitis, hematemesis, melena, weight loss, anorexia
  Genitourinary: Urinary tract infection
  Neuromuscular & skeletal: Weakness
  Respiratory: Coughing, tracheoesophageal fistula
  Miscellaneous: Moniliasis, surgical complication
 (Continued)

Porfimer (Continued)

Overdosage/Toxicology

Overdose of laser light following porfimer injection: Increased symptoms and damage to normal tissue might be expected following an overdose of light

Treatment: Effects of overdosage on the duration of photosensitivity are unknown. Laser treatment should not be given if an overdose of porfimer is administered. In the event of an overdose, patients should protect their eyes and skin from direct sunlight or bright indoor lights for 30 days. At this time, patients should test for residual photosensitivity. Porfimer is not dialyzable.

Drug Interactions

Decreased effect: Compounds that quench active oxygen species or scavenge radicals (eg, dimethyl sulfoxide, beta-carotene, ethanol, mannitol) would be expected to decrease PDT activity; allopurinol, calcium channel blockers and some prostaglandin synthesis inhibitors could interfere with porfimer; drugs that decrease clotting, vasoconstriction or platelet aggregation could decrease the efficacy of PDT; glucocorticoid hormones may decrease the efficacy of the treatment

Increased toxicity: Concomitant administration of other photosensitizing agents (eg, tetracyclines, sulfonamides, phenothiazines, sulfonylureas, thiazide diuretics, griseofulvin) could increase the photosensitivity reaction

Stability Store intact vials at controlled room temperature of 20°C to 25°C/68°F to 77°F

Reconstitute each vial of porfimer with 31.8 mL of either 5% dextrose injection or 0.9% sodium chloride injection resulting in a final concentration of 2.5 mg/mL and a pH of 7-8. Shake well until dissolved. Do not mix porfimer with other drugs in the same solution. Protect the reconstituted product from bright light and use immediately. Reconstituted porfimer is an opaque solution in which detection of particulate matter by visual inspection is extremely difficult.

Mechanism of Action Photosensitizing agent used in the photodynamic therapy (PDT) of tumors: cytotoxic and antitumor actions of porfimer are light and oxygen dependent. Cellular damage caused by porfimer PDT is a consequence of the propagation of radical reactions.

Pharmacodynamics/Kinetics

Distribution: Steady state V_d: 0.49 L/kg

Protein binding, plasma: 90%

Half-life: 250 hours

Time to peak serum concentration: Within 2 hours

Elimination: Total plasma clearance: 0.051 mL/minute/kg

Usual Dosage I.V. (refer to individual protocols):

Children: Safety and efficacy have not been established

Adults: I.V.: 2 mg/kg over 3-5 minutes

Photodynamic therapy is a two-stage process requiring administration of both drug and light. The first stage of PDT is the I.V. injection of porfimer. Illumination with laser light 40-50 hours following the injection with porfimer constitutes the second stage of therapy. A second laser light application may be given 90-120 hours after injection, preceded by gentle debridement of residual tumor.

Patients may receive a second course of PDT a minimum of 30 days after the initial therapy; up to three courses of PDT (each separated by a minimum of 30 days) can be given. Before each course of treatment, evaluate patients for the presence of a tracheoesophageal or bronchoesophageal fistula.

Administration Administer slow I.V. injection over 3-5 minutes; avoid extravasation; if extravasation occurs, take care to protect to protect the area from light. There is no known benefit from injecting the extravasation site with another substance. Wipe up spills with a damp cloth. Avoid skin and eye contact due to the potential for photosensitivity reactions upon exposure to light; use of rubber gloves and eye protection is recommended.

Patient Information Avoid exposure of skin and eyes to direct sunlight or bright indoor light (eg, examination lamps, including dental lamps, operating room lamps, unshaded light bulbs at close proximity) for 30 days after exposure. Exposure of skin to ambient indoor light is beneficial, however, because the remaining drug will be inactivated gradually and safely through a photobleaching reaction. Patients should wear dark sunglasses which have an average white light transmittance of <4% when outdoors.

Dosage Forms Powder for injection, as sodium: 75 mg

- ◆ **Porfimer Sodium** see Porfimer on previous page
- ◆ **Pork NPH Iletin® II** see Insulin Preparations on page 613
- ◆ **Pork Regular Iletin® II** see Insulin Preparations on page 613
- ◆ **Postexposure Prophylaxis for Hepatitis B** see page 1383
- ◆ **Potasalan®** see Potassium Chloride on page 949

Potassium Acetate (poe TASS ee um AS e tate)

Therapeutic Category Electrolyte Supplement, Parenteral; Potassium Salt; Vesicant

Use Potassium deficiency; to avoid chloride when high concentration of potassium is needed, source of bicarbonate

Pregnancy Risk Factor C

Contraindications Severe renal impairment, hyperkalemia

Warnings/Precautions Use with caution in patients with renal disease, hyperkalemia, cardiac disease, metabolic alkalosis; must be administered in patients with adequate urine flow

Adverse Reactions
>10%: Gastrointestinal: Diarrhea, nausea, stomach pain, flatulence, vomiting (oral)
1% to 10%:
Cardiovascular: Bradycardia
Endocrine & metabolic: Hyperkalemia
Neuromuscular & skeletal: Weakness
Respiratory: Dyspnea
Local: Local tissue necrosis with extravasation
<1%: Chest pain, mental confusion, alkalosis, abdominal pain, throat pain, phlebitis, paresthesias, paralysis

Overdosage/Toxicology
Symptoms of overdose include muscle weakness, paralysis, peaked T waves, flattened P waves, prolongation of chloride. QRS complex, ventricular arrhythmias
Removal of potassium can be accomplished by various means; removal through the GI tract with Kayexalate® administration; by way of the kidney through diuresis, mineralocorticoid administration or increased sodium intake; by hemodialysis or peritoneal dialysis; or by shifting potassium back into the cells by insulin and glucose infusion or administration of sodium bicarbonate; calcium chloride will reverse cardiac effects.

Drug Interactions Increased effect/levels with potassium-sparing diuretics, salt substitutes, ACE inhibitors

Mechanism of Action Potassium is the major cation of intracellular fluid and is essential for the conduction of nerve impulses in heart, brain, and skeletal muscle; contraction of cardiac, skeletal and smooth muscles; maintenance of normal renal function, acid-base balance, carbohydrate metabolism, and gastric secretion

Pharmacodynamics/Kinetics
Absorption: Absorbed well from upper GI tract
Distribution: Enters cells via active transport from extracellular fluid
Elimination: Largely by the kidneys, but also small amount via the skin and feces, with most intestinal potassium being reabsorbed

Usual Dosage I.V. doses should be incorporated into the patient's maintenance I.V. fluids, intermittent I.V. potassium administration should be reserved for severe depletion situations and requires EKG monitoring; doses listed as mEq of potassium

Treatment of hypokalemia: I.V.:
Children: 2-5 mEq/kg/day
Adults: 40-100 mEq/day
I.V. intermittent infusion (must be diluted prior to administration):
Children: 0.5-1 mEq/kg/dose (maximum: 30 mEq/dose) to infuse at 0.3-0.5 mEq/kg/hour (maximum: 1 mEq/kg/hour)
Adults: 5-10 mEq/dose (maximum: 40 mEq/dose) to infuse over 2-3 hours (maximum: 40 mEq over 1 hour)

Note: Continuous cardiac monitor recommended for rates >0.5 mEq/hour

Potassium Dosage/Rate of Infusion Guidelines

Serum Potassium	Maximum Infusion Rate	Maximum Concentration	Maximum 24-Hour Dose
>2.5 mEq/L	10 mEq/h	40 mEq/L	200 mEq
<2.5 mEq/L	40 mEq/h	80 mEq/L	400 mEq

Administration Injections must be diluted for I.V. infusions

Nursing Implications Supplements usually not needed with adequate diet; EKG should be monitored continuously during the course of highly concentrate potassium solutions

Additional Information 1 mEq of acetate is equivalent to the alkalinizing effect of 1 mEq of bicarbonate

Dosage Forms Injection: 2 mEq/mL (20 mL, 50 mL, 100 mL); 4 mEq/mL (50 mL)

Potassium Acetate, Potassium Bicarbonate, and Potassium Citrate
(poe TASS ee um AS e tate, poe TASS ee um bye KAR bun ate, & poe TASS ee um SIT rate)

U.S. Brand Names Tri-K®

Therapeutic Category Electrolyte Supplement

Dosage Forms Solution, oral: 45 mEq/15 mL from potassium acetate 1500 mg, potassium bicarbonate 1500 mg, and potassium citrate 1500 mg per 15 mL

Potassium Acid Phosphate (poe TASS ee um AS id FOS fate)

U.S. Brand Names K-Phos® Original

Therapeutic Category Potassium Salt; Urinary Acidifying Agent

Use Acidifies urine and lowers urinary calcium concentration; reduces odor and rash caused by ammoniacal urine; increases the antibacterial activity of methenamine

Pregnancy Risk Factor C

Contraindications Severe renal impairment, hyperkalemia, hyperphosphatemia, and infected magnesium ammonium phosphate stones

Warnings/Precautions Use with caution in patients receiving other potassium supplementation and in patients with renal insufficiency, or severe tissue breakdown (eg, chemotherapy or hemodialysis)

Adverse Reactions
>10%: Gastrointestinal: Diarrhea, nausea, stomach pain, flatulence, vomiting
(Continued)

Potassium Acid Phosphate *(Continued)*

1% to 10%:
Cardiovascular: Bradycardia
Endocrine & metabolic: Hyperkalemia
Local: Local tissue necrosis with extravasation
Neuromuscular & skeletal: Weakness
Respiratory: Dyspnea
<1%: Chest pain, arrhythmia, edema, mental confusion, tetany, pain of extremities, hyperphosphatemia, hypocalcemia, alkalosis, abdominal pain, weight gain, throat pain, decreased urine output, phlebitis, paresthesias, paralysis, bone pain, arthralgia, weakness of extremities, shortness of breath, thirst

Overdosage/Toxicology
Symptoms of overdose include muscle weakness, paralysis, peaked T waves, flattened P waves, prolongation of QRS complex, ventricular arrhythmias
Removal of potassium can be accomplished by various means; removal through the GI tract with Kayexalate® administration; by way of the kidney through diuresis, mineralocorticoid administration or increased sodium intake; by hemodialysis or peritoneal dialysis; or by shifting potassium back into the cells by insulin and glucose infusion or sodium bicarbonate; calcium chloride will reverse cardiac effects.

Drug Interactions
Increased effect/levels with potassium-sparing diuretics, salt substitutes, salicylates, ACE inhibitors
Decreased effect with antacids containing magnesium, calcium or aluminum (bind phosphate and decreased its absorption)

Mechanism of Action The principal intracellular cation; involved in transmission of nerve impulses, muscle contractions, enzyme activity, and glucose utilization

Pharmacodynamics/Kinetics
Absorption: Absorbed well from upper GI tract
Distribution: Enters cells via active transport from extracellular fluid
Elimination: Largely by the kidneys, but also small amount via the skin and feces, with most intestinal potassium being reabsorbed

Usual Dosage Adults: Oral: 1000 mg dissolved in 6-8 oz of water 4 times/day with meals and at bedtime; for best results, soak tablets in water for 2-5 minutes, then stir and swallow

Monitoring Parameters Serum potassium, sodium, phosphate, calcium; serum salicylates (if taking salicylates)

Test Interactions ↓ ammonia (B)

Patient Information Dissolve tablets completely before drinking; avoid taking magnesium, calcium, or aluminum antacids at the same time; patients may pass old kidney stones when starting therapy; notify physician if experiencing nausea, vomiting, or abdominal pain

Dosage Forms Tablet, sodium free: 500 mg [potassium 3.67 mEq]

Potassium Bicarbonate and Potassium Chloride, Effervescent

(poe TASS ee um bye KAR bun ate & poe TASS ee um KLOR ide, ef er VES ent)
U.S. Brand Names Klorvess® Effervescent; K/Lyte/CL®
Therapeutic Category Electrolyte Supplement
Dosage Forms
Granules for oral solution, effervescent (Klorvess®): 20 mEq per packet
Tablet for oral solution, effervescent
Klorvess®: 20 mEq per packet
K/Lyte/Cl®: 25 mEq, 50 mEq per packet

Potassium Bicarbonate and Potassium Citrate, Effervescent

(poe TASS ee um bye KAR bun ate & poe TASS ee um SIT rate, ef er VES ent)
U.S. Brand Names Effer-K™; K-Ide®; Klor-Con®/EF; K-Lyte®; K-Vescent®
Synonyms Potassium Citrate and Potassium Bicarbonate, Effervescent
Therapeutic Category Potassium Salt
Use Treatment or prevention of hypokalemia
Pregnancy Risk Factor C
Contraindications Severe renal impairment, hyperkalemia
Warnings/Precautions Use with caution in patients with renal disease, cardiac disease
Adverse Reactions
>10%: Gastrointestinal: Diarrhea, nausea, stomach pain, flatulence, vomiting
1% to 10%:
Cardiovascular: Bradycardia
Endocrine & metabolic: Hyperkalemia
Local: Local tissue necrosis with extravasation
Neuromuscular & skeletal: Weakness
Respiratory: Dyspnea
<1%: Chest pain, mental confusion, alkalosis, abdominal pain, throat pain, phlebitis, paresthesias, paralysis

Overdosage/Toxicology
Symptoms of overdose include muscle weakness, paralysis, peaked T waves, flattened P waves, prolongation of QRS complex, ventricular arrhythmias

Removal of potassium can be accomplished by various means; removal through the GI tract with Kayexalate® administration; by way of the kidney through diuresis, mineralo-corticoid administration or increased sodium intake; by hemodialysis or peritoneal dialysis; or by shifting potassium back into the cells by insulin and glucose infusion or sodium bicarbonate; calcium chloride will reverse cardiac effects.

Drug Interactions Increased effect/levels with potassium-sparing diuretics, salt substitutes, ACE inhibitors

Mechanism of Action Needed for the conduction of nerve impulses in heart, brain, and skeletal muscle; contraction of cardiac, skeletal and smooth muscles; maintenance of normal renal function

Pharmacodynamics/Kinetics

Absorption: Absorbed well from upper GI tract

Distribution: Enters cells via active transport from extracellular fluid

Elimination: Largely by the kidneys, but also small amount via the skin and feces, with most intestinal potassium being reabsorbed

Usual Dosage Oral:

Children: 1-4 mEq/kg/24 hours in divided doses as required to maintain normal serum potassium

Adults:

Prevention: 16-24 mEq/day in 2-4 divided doses

Treatment: 40-100 mEq/day in 2-4 divided doses

Monitoring Parameters Serum potassium

Test Interactions ↓ ammonia (B)

Patient Information Dissolve completely in 3-8 oz cold water, juice, or other suitable beverage and drink slowly

Dosage Forms

Capsule, extended release: 8 mEq, 10 mEq

Powder for oral solution: 15 mEq/packet; 20 mEq/packet; 25 mEq/packet

Tablet, effervescent: 25 mEq, 50 mEq

Potassium Bicarbonate, Potassium Chloride, and Potassium Citrate

(poe TASS ee um bye KAR bun ate, poe TASS ee um KLOR ide & poe TASS ee um SIT rate)

U.S. Brand Names Kaochlor-Eff®

Therapeutic Category Electrolyte Supplement

Dosage Forms Tablet for oral solution: 20 mEq from potassium bicarbonate 1 g, potassium chloride 600 mg, and potassium citrate 220 mg

Potassium Chloride (poe TASS ee um KLOR ide)

Related Information

Extravasation Treatment of Other Drugs *on page 1287*

U.S. Brand Names Cena-K®; Gen-K®; K+ 10®; Kaochlor®; Kaochlor® SF; Kaon-Cl®; Kaon Cl-10®; Kay Ciel®; K+ Care®; K-Dur® 10; K-Dur® 20; K-Lease®; K-Lor™; Klor-Con®; Klor-Con® 8; Klor-Con® 10; Klor-Con/25®; Klorvess®; Klotrix®; K-Lyte/Cl®; K-Norm®; K-Tab®; Micro-K® 10; Micro-K® Extencaps®; Micro-K® LS®; Potasalan®; Rum-K®; Slow-K®; Ten-K®

Synonyms KCl

Therapeutic Category Electrolyte Supplement, Oral; Electrolyte Supplement, Parenteral; Potassium Salt; Vesicant

Use Treatment or prevention of hypokalemia

Pregnancy Risk Factor A

Contraindications Severe renal impairment, untreated Addison's disease, heat cramps, hyperkalemia, severe tissue trauma; solid oral dosage forms are contraindicated in patients in whom there is a structural, pathological, and/or pharmacologic cause for delay or arrest in passage through the GI tract; an oral liquid potassium preparation should be used in patients with esophageal compression or delayed gastric emptying time

Warnings/Precautions Use with caution in patients with cardiac disease, severe renal impairment, hyperkalemia

Adverse Reactions

>10%: Gastrointestinal: Diarrhea, nausea, stomach pain, flatulence, vomiting (oral)

1% to 10%:

Cardiovascular: Bradycardia

Endocrine & metabolic: Hyperkalemia

Local: Local tissue necrosis with extravasation, pain at the site of injection

Neuromuscular & skeletal: Weakness

Respiratory: Dyspnea

<1%: Chest pain, arrhythmias, heart block, hypotension, mental confusion, alkalosis, abdominal pain, throat pain, phlebitis, paresthesias, paralysis

Overdosage/Toxicology

Symptoms of overdose include muscle weakness, paralysis, peaked T waves, flattened P waves, prolongation of QRS complex, ventricular arrhythmias

Removal of potassium can be accomplished by various means; removal through the GI tract with Kayexalate® administration; by way of the kidney through diuresis, mineralo-corticoid administration or increased sodium intake; by hemodialysis or peritoneal dialysis; or by shifting potassium back into the cells by insulin and glucose infusion or sodium bicarbonate; calcium chloride reverses cardiac effects.

(Continued)

Potassium Chloride *(Continued)*

Drug Interactions Increased effect/levels with potassium-sparing diuretics, salt substitutes, ACE inhibitors

Stability Store at room temperature, protect from freezing; use only clear solutions; use admixtures within 24 hours

Mechanism of Action Potassium is the major cation of intracellular fluid and is essential for the conduction of nerve impulses in heart, brain, and skeletal muscle; contraction of cardiac, skeletal and smooth muscles; maintenance of normal renal function, acid-base balance, carbohydrate metabolism, and gastric secretion

Pharmacodynamics/Kinetics
Absorption: Absorbed well from upper GI tract
Distribution: Enters cells via active transport from extracellular fluid
Elimination: Largely by the kidneys, but also small amount via the skin and feces, with most intestinal potassium being reabsorbed

Usual Dosage I.V. doses should be incorporated into the patient's maintenance I.V. fluids; intermittent I.V. potassium administration should be reserved for severe depletion situations in patients undergoing EKG monitoring.

Normal daily requirements: Oral, I.V.:
Premature infants: 2-6 mEq/kg/24 hours
Term infants 0-24 hours: 0-2 mEq/kg/24 hours
Infants >24 hours: 1-2 mEq/kg/24 hours
Children: 2-3 mEq/kg/day
Adults: 40-80 mEq/day
Prevention during diuretic therapy: Oral:
Children: 1-2 mEq/kg/day in 1-2 divided doses
Adults: 20-40 mEq/day in 1-2 divided doses
Treatment of hypokalemia: Children:
Oral: 1-2 mEq/kg initially, then as needed based on frequently obtained lab values. If deficits are severe or ongoing losses are great, I.V. route should be considered.
I.V.: 1 mEq/kg over 1-2 hours initially, then repeated as needed based on frequently obtained lab values; severe depletion or ongoing losses may require >200% of normal limit needs
I.V. intermittent infusion: Dose should not exceed 1 mEq/kg/hour, or 40 mEq/hour; if it exceeds 0.5 mEq/kg/hour, physician should be at bedside and patient should have continuous EKG monitoring; usual pediatric maximum: 3 mEq/kg/day or 40 mEq/m^2/day
Treatment of hypokalemia: Adults:
I.V. intermittent infusion: 5-10 mEq/hour (continuous cardiac monitor recommended for rates >5 mEq/hour), not to exceed 40 mEq/hour; usual adult maximum per 24 hours: 400 mEq/day. See table.

Potassium Dosage/Rate of Infusion Guidelines

Serum Potassium	Maximum Infusion Rate	Maximum Concentration	Maximum 24-Hour Dose
>2.5 mEq/L	10 mEq/h	40 mEq/L	200 mEq
<2.5 mEq/L	40 mEq/h	80 mEq/L	400 mEq

Potassium >2.5 mEq/L:
Oral: 60-80 mEq/day plus additional amounts if needed
I.V.: 10 mEq over 1 hour with additional doses if needed
Potassium <2.5 mEq/L:
Oral: Up to 40-60 mEq initial dose, followed by further doses based on lab values
I.V.: Up to 40 mEq over 1 hour, with doses based on frequent lab monitoring; deficits at a plasma level of 2 mEq/L may be as high as 400-800 mEq of potassium

Administration Maximum concentration (peripheral line): 80 mEq/L; usual maximum: 30-40 mEq/L; most guidelines recommend maximal infusion rates of 5 mEq/hour if patient is **not** on a cardiac monitor and 10 mEq/hour (children: 0.3 mEq/kg/hour) if monitored; may not be given I.V. push or I.V. retrograde; oral liquid potassium supplements should be diluted with water or fruit juice during administration

Monitoring Parameters Serum potassium, glucose, chloride, pH, urine output (if indicated), cardiac monitor (if intermittent infusion or potassium infusion rates >0.25 mEq/kg/hour)

Patient Information Sustained release and wax matrix tablets should be swallowed whole, do not crush or chew; effervescent tablets must be dissolved in water before use; take with food; liquid and granules can be diluted or dissolved in water or juice

Nursing Implications Wax matrix tablets must be swallowed and not allowed to dissolve in mouth

Dosage Forms
Capsule, controlled release (microcapsulated): 600 mg [8 mEq]; 750 mg [10 mEq]
Micro-K® Extencaps®: 600 mg [8 mEq]
K-Lease®, K-Norm®, Micro-K® 10: 750 mg [10 mEq]
Liquid: 10% [20 mEq/15 mL] (480 mL, 4000 mL); 20% [40 mEq/15 mL] (480 mL, 4000 mL)
Cena-K®, Kaochlor®, Kaochlor® SF, Kay Ciel®, Klorvess®, Potasalan®: 10% [20 mEq/15 mL] (480 mL, 4000 mL)
Rum-K®: 15% [30 mEq/15 mL] (480 mL, 4000 mL)
Cena-K®, Kaon-Cl® 20%: 20% [40 mEq/15 mL]

Crystals for oral suspension, extended release (Micro-K® LS®): 20 mEq per packet
Powder: 20 mEq per packet (30s, 100s)
    K+ Care®, K-Lor™: 15 mEq per packet (30s, 100s)
    Gen-K®, Kay Ciel®, K+ Care®, K-Lor®, Klor-Con®: 20 mEq per packet (30s, 100s)
    K+ Care®, Klor-Con/25®: 25 mEq per packet (30s, 100s)
    K-Lyte/Cl®: 25 mEq per dose (30s)
Infusion, concentrate: 0.1 mEq/mL, 0.2 mEq/mL, 0.3 mEq/mL, 0.4 mEq/mL
Injection, concentrate: 1.5 mEq/mL, 2 mEq/mL, 3 mEq/mL
Tablet, controlled release (microencapsulated)
    K-Dur® 10, Ten-K®: 750 mg [10 mEq]
    K-Dur® 20: 1500 mg [20 mEq]
Tablet, controlled release (wax matrix): 600 mg [8 mEq]; 750 mg [10 mEq]
    Kaon-Cl®: 500 mg [6.7 mEq]
    Klor-Con® 8, Slow-K®: 600 mg [8 mEq]
    K+ 10®, Kaon-Cl-10®, Klor-Con® 10, Klotrix®, K-Tab®: 750 mg [10 mEq]

Potassium Chloride and Potassium Gluconate
(poe TASS ee um KLOR ide & poe TASS ee um GLOO coe nate)
U.S. Brand Names Kolyum®
Therapeutic Category Electrolyte Supplement
Dosage Forms Solution, oral: Potassium 20 mEq/15 mL

Potassium Citrate and Citric Acid
(poe TASS ee um SIT rate & SI trik AS id)
U.S. Brand Names Polycitra®-K
Therapeutic Category Alkalinizing Agent, Oral
Dosage Forms
Crystals for reconstitution: Potassium citrate 3300 mg and citric acid 1002 mg per packet
Solution, oral: Potassium citrate 1100 mg and citric acid 334 mg per 5 mL

♦ **Potassium Citrate and Potassium Bicarbonate, Effervescent** *see* Potassium Bicarbonate and Potassium Citrate, Effervescent *on page 948*

Potassium Citrate and Potassium Gluconate
(poe TASS ee um SIT rate & poe TASS ee um GLOO coe nate)
U.S. Brand Names Twin-K®
Therapeutic Category Electrolyte Supplement
Dosage Forms Solution, oral: 20 mEq/5 mL from potassium citrate 170 mg and potassium gluconate 170 mg per 5 mL

Potassium Gluconate (poe TASS ee um GLOO coe nate)
U.S. Brand Names Kaon®; Kaylixir®; K-G®
Therapeutic Category Potassium Salt
Use Treatment or prevention of hypokalemia
Pregnancy Risk Factor A
Contraindications Severe renal impairment, untreated Addison's disease, heat cramps, hyperkalemia, severe tissue trauma; solid oral dosage forms are contraindicated in patients in whom there is a structural, pathological, and/or pharmacologic cause for delay or arrest in passage through the GI tract; an oral liquid potassium preparation should be used in patients with esophageal compression or delayed gastric emptying time
Warnings/Precautions Use with caution in patients with cardiac disease, severe renal impairment, hyperkalemia; patients must be on a cardiac monitor during intermittent infusions
Adverse Reactions
>10%: Gastrointestinal: Diarrhea, nausea, stomach pain, flatulence, vomiting (oral)
1% to 10%:
    Cardiovascular: Bradycardia
    Endocrine & metabolic: Hyperkalemia
    Neuromuscular & skeletal: Weakness
    Respiratory: Dyspnea
<1%: Chest pain, mental confusion, alkalosis, throat pain, phlebitis, paresthesias, paralysis
Overdosage/Toxicology
Symptoms of overdose include muscle weakness, paralysis, peaked T waves, flattened P waves, prolongation of QRS complex, ventricular arrhythmias
Removal of potassium can be accomplished by various means; removal through the GI tract with Kayexalate® administration; by way of the kidney through diuresis, mineralocorticoid administration or increased sodium intake; by hemodialysis or peritoneal dialysis; or by shifting potassium back into the cells by insulin, glucose infusion, or sodium bicarbonate; calcium chloride reverses cardiac effects
Drug Interactions Increased effect/levels with potassium-sparing diuretics, salt substitutes, ACE inhibitors; increased effect of digitalis
Stability Store at room temperature, protect from freezing; use only clear solutions
Mechanism of Action Potassium is the major cation of intracellular fluid and is essential for the conduction of nerve impulses in heart, brain, and skeletal muscle; contraction of cardiac, skeletal and smooth muscles; maintenance of normal renal function, acid-base balance, carbohydrate metabolism, and gastric secretion
(Continued)

Potassium Gluconate *(Continued)*

Pharmacodynamics/Kinetics

Absorption: Absorbed well from upper GI tract

Distribution: Enters cells via active transport from extracellular fluid

Elimination: Largely by the kidneys, but also small amount via the skin and feces, with most intestinal potassium being reabsorbed

Usual Dosage Oral (doses listed as mEq of potassium):

Normal daily requirement:

Children: 2-3 mEq/kg/day

Adults: 40-80 mEq/day

Prevention of hypokalemia during diuretic therapy:

Children: 1-2 mEq/kg/day in 1-2 divided doses

Adults: 16-24 mEq/day in 1-2 divided doses

Treatment of hypokalemia:

Children: 2-5 mEq/kg/day in 2-4 divided doses

Adults: 40-100 mEq/day in 2-4 divided doses

Monitoring Parameters Serum potassium, chloride, glucose, pH, urine output (if indicated)

Test Interactions ↓ ammonia (B)

Patient Information Take with food, water, or fruit juice; swallow tablets whole; do not crush or chew

Nursing Implications Do not administer liquid full strength, must be diluted in 2-6 parts of water or juice

Additional Information 9.4 g potassium gluconate is approximately equal to 40 mEq potassium (4.3 mEq potassium/g salt)

Dosage Forms

Elixir: 20 mEq/15 mL

K-G®, Kaon®, Kaylixir®: 20 mEq/15 mL

Tablet:

Glu-K®: 2 mEq

Kaon®: 5 mEq

Potassium Iodide *(poe TASS ee um EYE oh dide)*

U.S. Brand Names Pima®; SSKI®; Thyro-Block®

Synonyms KI; Lugol's Solution; Strong Iodine Solution

Therapeutic Category Antithyroid Agent; Cough Preparation; Expectorant

Use Facilitate bronchial drainage and cough; reduce thyroid vascularity prior to thyroidectomy and management of thyrotoxic crisis; block thyroidal uptake of radioactive isotopes of iodine in a radiation emergency

Pregnancy Risk Factor D

Contraindications Known hypersensitivity to iodine; hyperkalemia, pulmonary tuberculosis, pulmonary edema, bronchitis, impaired renal function

Warnings/Precautions Prolonged use can lead to hypothyroidism; cystic fibrosis patients have an exaggerated response; can cause acne flare-ups, can cause dermatitis, some preparations may contain sodium bisulfite (allergy); use with caution in patients with a history of thyroid disease, patients with renal failure, or GI obstruction

Adverse Reactions 1% to 10%:

Central nervous system: Fever, headache

Dermatologic: Urticaria, acne, angioedema, cutaneous hemorrhage

Endocrine & metabolic: Goiter with hypothyroidism

Gastrointestinal: Metallic taste, GI upset, soreness of teeth and gums

Hematologic: Eosinophilia, hemorrhage (mucosal)

Neuromuscular & skeletal: Arthralgia

Respiratory: Rhinitis

Miscellaneous: Lymph node enlargement

Overdosage/Toxicology

Symptoms of overdose include angioedema, laryngeal edema in patients with hypersensitivity; muscle weakness, paralysis, peaked T waves, flattened P waves, prolongation of QRS complex, ventricular arrhythmias

Removal of potassium can be accomplished by various means; removal through the GI tract with Kayexalate® administration; by way of the kidney through diuresis, mineralocorticoid administration or increased sodium intake; by hemodialysis or peritoneal dialysis; or by shifting potassium back into the cells by insulin and glucose infusion.

Drug Interactions Increased toxicity: Lithium → additive hypothyroid effects

Stability Store in tight, light-resistant containers at temperature <40°C; freezing should be avoided

Mechanism of Action Reduces viscosity of mucus by increasing respiratory tract secretions; inhibits secretion of thyroid hormone, fosters colloid accumulation in thyroid follicles

Pharmacodynamics/Kinetics

Onset of action: 24-48 hours

Peak effect: 10-15 days after continuous therapy

Duration: May persist for up to 6 weeks

Elimination: In euthyroid patient, renal clearance rate is 2 times that of the thyroid

Usual Dosage Oral:

Adults: RDA: 130 mcg

Expectorant:

Children: 60-250 mg every 6-8 hours; maximum single dose: 500 mg

Adults: 300-650 mg 2-3 times/day
Preoperative thyroidectomy: Children and Adults: 50-250 mg (1-5 drops SSKI®) 3 times/day or 0.1-0.3 mL (3-5 drops) of strong iodine (Lugol's solution) 3 times/day; administer for 10 days before surgery
Thyrotoxic crisis:
Infants <1 year: 150-250 mg (3-5 drops SSKI®) 3 times/day
Children and Adults: 300-500 mg (6-10 drops SSKI®) 3 times/day or 1 mL strong iodine (Lugol's solution) 3 times/day
Sporotrichosis:
Initial:
Preschool: 50 mg/dose 3 times/day
Children: 250 mg/dose 3 times/day
Adults: 500 mg/dose 3 times/day
Oral increase 50 mg/dose daily
Maximum dose:
Preschool: 500 mg/dose 3 times/day
Children and Adults: 1-2 g/dose 3 times/day
Continue treatment for 4-6 weeks after lesions have completely healed
Monitoring Parameters Thyroid function tests
Patient Information Take after meals with food or milk or dilute with a large quantity of water, fruit juice, milk, or broth; discontinue use if stomach pain, skin rash, metallic taste, or nausea and vomiting occurs
Nursing Implications Must be diluted before administration of 240 mL of water, fruit juice, milk, or broth
Additional Information 10 drops of SSKI® = potassium iodide 500 mg
Dosage Forms
Solution, oral:
SSKI®: 1 g/mL (30 mL, 240 mL, 473 mL)
Lugol's solution, strong iodine: 100 mg/mL with iodine 50 mg/mL (120 mL)
Syrup: 325 mg/5 mL
Tablet: 130 mg

Potassium Phosphate (poe TASS ee um FOS fate)

U.S. Brand Names Neutra-Phos®-K
Synonyms Phosphate, Potassium
Therapeutic Category Electrolyte Supplement, Oral; Electrolyte Supplement, Parenteral; Phosphate Salt; Potassium Salt; Vesicant
Use Treatment and prevention of hypophosphatemia or hypokalemia
Pregnancy Risk Factor C
Contraindications Hyperphosphatemia, hyperkalemia, hypocalcemia, hypomagnesemia, renal failure
Warnings/Precautions Use with caution in patients with renal insufficiency, cardiac disease, metabolic alkalosis; admixture of phosphate and calcium in I.V. fluids can result in calcium phosphate precipitation
Adverse Reactions
>10%: Gastrointestinal: Diarrhea, nausea, stomach pain, flatulence, vomiting
1% to 10%:
Cardiovascular: Bradycardia
Endocrine & metabolic: Hyperkalemia
Neuromuscular & skeletal: Weakness
Respiratory: Dyspnea
<1%: Chest pain, mental confusion, alkalosis, hypocalcemia tetany (with large doses of phosphate), abdominal pain, throat pain, phlebitis, paresthesias, paralysis, acute renal failure
Overdosage/Toxicology
Symptoms of overdose include muscle weakness, paralysis, peaked T waves, flattened P waves, prolongation of QRS complex, ventricular arrhythmias, tetany, calcium-phosphate precipitation
Removal of potassium can be accomplished by various means; removal through the GI tract with Kayexalate® administration; by way of the kidney through diuresis, mineralocorticoid administration or increased sodium intake; by hemodialysis or peritoneal dialysis; or by shifting potassium back into the cells by insulin, glucose infusion, or sodium bicarbonate; calcium chloride reverses cardiac effects.
Drug Interactions
Decreased effect/levels with aluminum and magnesium-containing antacids or sucralfate which can act as phosphate binders
Increased effect/levels with potassium-sparing diuretics, salt substitutes, or ACE-inhibitors; increased effect of digitalis
Stability Store at room temperature, protect from freezing; use only clear solutions; up to 10-15 mEq of calcium may be added per liter before precipitate may occur

Stability of parenteral admixture at room temperature (25°C): 24 hours

Phosphate salts may precipitate when mixed with calcium salts; solubility is improved in amino acid parenteral nutrition solutions; check with a pharmacist to determine compatibility
Usual Dosage I.V. doses should be incorporated into the patient's maintenance I.V. fluids; intermittent I.V. infusion should be reserved for severe depletion situations in patients undergoing continuous EKG monitoring. It is difficult to determine total body phosphorus deficit; the following dosages are empiric guidelines:
(Continued)

Potassium Phosphate *(Continued)*

Normal requirements elemental phosphorus: Oral:

0-6 months: 240 mg

6-12 months: 360 mg

1-10 years: 800 mg

>10 years: 1200 mg

Pregnancy lactation: Additional 400 mg/day

Adults: 800 mg

Treatment: It is difficult to provide concrete guidelines for the treatment of severe hypophosphatemia because the extent of total body deficits and response to therapy are difficult to predict. Aggressive doses of phosphate may result in a transient serum elevation followed by redistribution into intracellular compartments or bone tissue. It is recommended that repletion of severe hypophosphatemia (<1 mg/dL in adults) be done I.V. because large doses of oral phosphate may cause diarrhea and intestinal absorption may be unreliable

Pediatric I.V. phosphate repletion:

Children: 0.25-0.5 mmol/kg **administer over 4-6 hours and repeat if symptomatic hypophosphatemia persists**; to assess the need for further phosphate administration, obtain serum inorganic phosphate after administration of the first dose and base further doses on serum levels and clinical status

Adult I.V. phosphate repletion:

Initial dose: 0.08 mmol/kg if recent uncomplicated hypophosphatemia

Initial dose: 0.16 mmol/kg if prolonged hypophosphatemia with presumed total body deficits; increase dose by 25% to 50% if patient symptomatic with severe hypophosphatemia

Do not exceed 0.24 mmol/kg/day; administer over 6 hours by I.V. infusion

With orders for I.V. phosphate, there is considerable confusion associated with the use of millimoles (mmol) versus milliequivalents (mEq) to express the phosphate requirement. Because inorganic phosphate exists as monobasic and dibasic anions, with the mixture of valences dependent on pH, ordering by mEq amounts is unreliable and may lead to large dosing errors. In addition, I.V. phosphate is available in the sodium and potassium salt; therefore, the content of these cations must be considered when ordering phosphate. The most reliable method of ordering I.V. phosphate is by millimoles, then specifying the potassium or sodium salt. For example, an order for 15 mmol of phosphate as potassium phosphate in one liter of normal saline The dosing of phosphate should be 0.2-0.3 mmol/kg with a usual daily requirement of 30-60 mmol/day or 15 mmol of phosphate per liter of TPN or 15 mmol phosphate per 1000 calories of dextrose. Would also provide 22 mEq of potassium.

Maintenance:

I.V. solutions:

Children: 0.5-1.5 mmol/kg/24 hours I.V. or 2-3 mmol/kg/24 hours orally in divided doses

Adults: 15-30 mmol/24 hours I.V. or 50-150 mmol/24 hours orally in divided doses

Oral:

Children <4 years: 1 capsule (250 mg phosphorus/8 mmol) 4 times/day; dilute as instructed

Children >4 years and Adults: 1-2 capsules (250-500 mg phosphorus/8-16 mmol) 4 times/day; dilute as instructed

Administration Injection must be diluted in appropriate I.V. solution and volume prior to administration and administered over a minimum of 4 hours

Monitoring Parameters Serum potassium, calcium, phosphate, sodium, cardiac monitor (when intermittent infusion or high-dose I.V. replacement needed)

Test Interactions ↓ ammonia (B)

	Elemental Phosphorus (mg)	Phosphate (mmol)	Na (mEq)	K (mEq)
Oral				
Whole cow's milk per mL		0.29	0.025	0.035
Neutra-Phos®				
capsule				
powder concentrate per 75 mL	250	8	7.1	7.1
Neutra-Phos®-K				
capsule				
powder	250	8		14.2
K-Phos® Neutral tablets	250	8	13	1.1
K-Phos® MF tablets	125.6	4	2.9	1.1
K-Phos® No. 2	250	8	5.8	2.3
K-Phos® Original tablets	114	3.6		3.7
Uro-KP-Neutral® tablets	250	8	10.8	1.3
Intravenous				
K phosphate per mL		3		4.4

Patient Information Do not swallow the capsule; empty contents of capsule into 75 mL (2.5 oz) of water before taking; take with food to reduce the risk of diarrhea

Nursing Implications Capsule must be emptied into 3-4 oz of water before administration

Dosage Forms See table.

Potassium Phosphate and Sodium Phosphate
(poe TASS ee um FOS fate & SOW dee um FOS fate)

U.S. Brand Names K-Phos® Neutral; Neutra-Phos®; Uro-KP-Neutral®

Synonyms Sodium Phosphate and Potassium Phosphate

Therapeutic Category Phosphate Salt; Potassium Salt

Use Treatment of conditions associated with excessive renal phosphate loss or inadequate GI absorption of phosphate; to acidify the urine to lower calcium concentrations; to increase the antibacterial activity of methenamine; reduce odor and rash caused by ammonia in urine

Pregnancy Risk Factor C

Contraindications Addison's disease, hyperkalemia, hyperphosphatemia, infected urolithiasis or struvite stone formation, patients with severely impaired renal function

Warnings/Precautions Use with caution in patients with renal disease, hyperkalemia, cardiac disease and metabolic alkalosis

Adverse Reactions

>10%: Gastrointestinal: Diarrhea, nausea, stomach pain, flatulence, vomiting

1% to 10%:
Cardiovascular: Bradycardia
Endocrine & metabolic: Hyperkalemia
Neuromuscular & skeletal: Weakness
Respiratory: Dyspnea

<1%: Arrhythmia, chest pain, edema, mental confusion, tetany (with large doses of phosphate), alkalosis, weight gain, throat pain, decreased urine output, phlebitis, paresthesias, paralysis, pain/weakness of extremities, bone pain, arthralgia, acute renal failure, shortness of breath, thirst

Overdosage/Toxicology

Symptoms of overdose include muscle weakness, paralysis, peaked T waves, flattened P waves, prolongation of QRS complex, ventricular arrhythmias, tetany, calcium phosphate precipitation

Removal of potassium can be accomplished by various means; removal through the GI tract with Kayexalate® administration; by way of the kidney through diuresis, mineralocorticoid administration or increased sodium intake; by hemodialysis or peritoneal dialysis; or by shifting potassium back into the cells by insulin and glucose infusion; calcium chloride reverses cardiac effects.

Drug Interactions

Decreased effect/levels with aluminum and magnesium-containing antacids or sucralfate which can act as phosphate binders

Increased effect/levels with potassium-sparing diuretics or ACE inhibitors; salicylates

Usual Dosage All dosage forms to be mixed in 6-8 oz of water prior to administration

Children: 2-3 mmol phosphate/kg/24 hours given 4 times/day **or** 1 capsule 4 times/day

Adults: 1-2 capsules (250-500 mg phosphorus/8-16 mmol) 4 times/day after meals and at bedtime

Monitoring Parameters Serum potassium, sodium, calcium, phosphate, EKG

Patient Information Do not swallow, open capsule and dissolve in 6-8 oz of water; powder packets are to be mixed in 6-8 oz of water; tablets should be crushed and mixed in 6-8 oz of water

Nursing Implications Tablets may be crushed and stirred vigorously to speed dissolution

Dosage Forms See table in Potassium Phosphate monograph

Povidone-Iodine (POE vi done EYE oh dyne)

U.S. Brand Names ACU-dyne® [OTC]; Aerodine® [OTC]; Betadine® [OTC]; Betagan® [OTC]; Biodine [OTC]; Efodine® [OTC]; Iodex® [OTC]; Iodex-p® [OTC]; Isodine® [OTC]; Mallisol® [OTC]; Massengill® Medicated Douche w/Cepticin [OTC]; Minidyne® [OTC]; Operand® [OTC]; Polydine® [OTC]; Summer's Eve® Medicated Douche [OTC]; Yeast-Gard® Medicated Douche

Therapeutic Category Antibacterial, Topical; Antifungal Agent, Topical; Antiviral Agent, Topical; Shampoos

Use External antiseptic with broad microbicidal spectrum against bacteria, fungi, viruses, protozoa, and yeasts

Pregnancy Risk Factor D

Contraindications Hypersensitivity to iodine

Warnings/Precautions Highly toxic if ingested; sodium thiosulfate is the most effective chemical antidote; avoid contact with eyes

Adverse Reactions

1% to 10%:
Dermatologic: Rash, pruritus
Local: Local edema

<1%: Systemic absorption in extensive burns causing iododerma, metabolic acidosis, and renal impairment

(Continued)

Povidone-Iodine *(Continued)*

Mechanism of Action Povidone-iodine is known to be a powerful broad spectrum germicidal agent effective against a wide range of bacteria, viruses, fungi, protozoa, and spores.

Pharmacodynamics/Kinetics Absorption: In normal individuals, topical application results in very little systemic absorption; with vaginal administration, however, absorption is rapid and serum concentrations of total iodine and inorganic iodide are increased significantly

Usual Dosage

Shampoo: Apply 2 teaspoons to hair and scalp, lather and rinse; repeat application 2 times/week until improvement is noted, then shampoo weekly

Topical: Apply as needed for treatment and prevention of susceptible microbial infections

Patient Information Do not swallow; avoid contact with eyes

Dosage Forms

Aerosol: 5% (88.7 mL, 90 mL)

Antiseptic gauze pads: 10% (3" x 9")

Cleanser:

Skin: 7.5% (30 mL, 118 mL)

Skin, foam: 7.5% (170 g)

Topical: 60 mL, 240 mL

Concentrate, whirlpool: 3,840 mL

Cream: 5% (14 g)

Douche (10%): 0.5 oz/packet (6 packets/box), 240 mL

Foam, topical (10%): 250 g

Gel:

Lubricating: 5% (5 g)

Vaginal (10%): 18 g, 90 g

Liquid: 473 mL

Mouthwash (0.5%): 177 mL

Ointment, topical: 10% (0.94 g, 3.8 g, 28 g, 30 g, 454 g); 1 g, 1.2 g, 2.7 g packets

Perineal wash concentrate: 1% (240 mL); 10% (236 mL)

Scrub, surgical: 7.5% (15 mL, 473 mL, 946 mL)

Shampoo: 7.5% (118 mL)

Solution:

Ophthalmic sterile prep: 5% (50 mL)

Prep: 30 mL, 60 mL, 240 mL, 473 mL, 1000 mL, 4000 mL

Swab aid: 1%

Swabsticks: 4"

Topical: 10% (15 mL, 30 mL, 120 mL, 237 mL, 473 mL, 480 mL, 1000 mL, 4000 mL)

Suppositories, vaginal: 10%

♦ **PPA** *see* Phenylpropanolamine *on page 919*

♦ **PPD** *see* Tuberculin Purified Protein Derivative *on page 1194*

♦ **PPD** *see* Tuberculin Tests *on page 1194*

♦ **PPL** *see* Benzylpenicilloyl-polylysine *on page 137*

♦ **PPS** *see* Pentosan Polysulfate Sodium *on page 904*

Pralidoxime *(pra li DOKS eem)*

U.S. Brand Names Protopam®

Synonyms 2-PAM; Pralidoxime Chloride; 2-Pyridine Aldoxime Methochloride

Therapeutic Category Antidote, Ambenonium; Antidote, Anticholinesterase; Antidote, Neostigmine; Antidote, Organophosphate Poisoning; Antidote, Pyridostigmine

Use Reverse muscle paralysis with toxic exposure to organophosphate anticholinesterase pesticides and chemicals; control of overdose of drugs used to treat myasthenia gravis (ambenonium, neostigmine, pyridostigmine)

Pregnancy Risk Factor C

Contraindications Hypersensitivity to pralidoxime or any component; poisonings due to phosphorus, inorganic phosphates, or organic phosphates without anticholinesterase activity

Warnings/Precautions Use with caution in patients with myasthenia gravis; dosage modification required in patients with impaired renal function may not be effective for treating carbamate intoxication; use with caution in patients receiving theophylline, succinylcholine, phenothiazines, respiratory depressants (eg, narcotics, barbiturates)

Adverse Reactions

>10%: Local: Pain at injection site after I.M. administration

1% to 10%:

Cardiovascular: Tachycardia, hypertension

Central nervous system: Dizziness, headache, drowsiness

Dermatologic: Rash

Gastrointestinal: Nausea

Neuromuscular & skeletal: Muscle rigidity, weakness

Ocular: Blurred vision, diplopia

Respiratory: Hyperventilation, laryngospasm

Overdosage/Toxicology

Symptoms of overdose include blurred vision, nausea, tachycardia, dizziness

Supportive therapy, mechanical ventilation may be required

Drug Interactions
Decreased effect: Atropine, although often used concurrently with pralidoxime to offset muscarinic stimulation, these effects can occur earlier than anticipated
Increased effect: Barbiturates (potentiated)
Increased toxicity: Avoid morphine, theophylline, succinylcholine, reserpine and phenothiazines in patients with organophosphate poisoning

Mechanism of Action Reactivates cholinesterase that had been inactivated by phosphorylation due to exposure to organophosphate pesticides by displacing the enzyme from its receptor sites; removes the phosphoryl group from the active site of the inactivated enzyme

Pharmacodynamics/Kinetics
Absorption: Slowly from GI tract
Metabolism: In the liver, not bound to plasma proteins
Half-life: 0.8-2.7 hours
Time to peak serum concentration: I.V.: Within 5-15 minutes
Elimination: 80% to 90% quickly excreted in urine, as metabolites and unchanged drug

Usual Dosage Poisoning: I.M. (use in conjunction with atropine; atropine effects should be established before pralidoxime is administered), I.V.:
Children: 20-50 mg/kg/dose; repeat in 1-2 hours if muscle weakness has not been relieved, then at 10- to 12-hour intervals if cholinergic signs recur
Adults: 1-2 g; repeat in 1-2 hours if muscle weakness has not been relieved, then at 10- to 12-hour intervals if cholinergic signs recur
Treatment of acetylcholinesterase inhibitor toxicity: Initial: 1-2 g followed by increments of 250 mg every 5 minutes until response is observed
Dosing adjustment in renal impairment: Dose should be reduced

Administration Infuse over 15-30 minutes at a rate not to exceed 200 mg/minute; may administer I.M. or S.C. if I.V. is not accessible; reconstitute with 20 mL sterile water (preservative free) resulting in 50 mg/mL solution; dilute in normal saline 20 mg/mL and infuse over 15-30 minutes; if a more rapid onset of effect is desired or in a fluid-restricted situation, the maximum concentration is 50 mg/mL; the maximum rate of infusion is over 5 minutes

Monitoring Parameters Heart rate, respiratory rate, blood pressure, continuous EKG; cardiac monitor and blood pressure monitor required for I.V. administration

Dosage Forms
Injection: 20 mL vial containing 1 g each pralidoxime chloride with one 20 mL ampul diluent, disposable syringe, needle, and alcohol swab
Injection, as chloride: 300 mg/mL (2 mL)

♦ **Pralidoxime Chloride** see Pralidoxime on previous page

♦ **Pramet® FA** see Vitamins, Multiple on page 1226

♦ **Pramilet® FA** see Vitamins, Multiple on page 1226

Pramipexole (pra mi PEX ole)

Related Information
Parkinson's Disease, Dosing of Drugs Used for Treatment of on page 1336

U.S. Brand Names Mirapex®

Therapeutic Category Anti-Parkinson's Agent

Use Treatment of the signs and symptoms of idiopathic Parkinson's Disease; has been evaluated for use in the treatment of depression with positive results

Pregnancy Risk Factor C

Contraindications Patients with known hypersensitivity to pramipexole or any of the product's ingredients

Warnings/Precautions Caution should be taken in patients with renal insufficiency and in patients with pre-existing dyskinesias. Pathologic degeneration and loss of photoreceptor cells were observed in the retinas of albino rats during studies, however, similar changes have not been observed in the retinas of pigmented rats, mice, monkeys, or minipigs. The significance of these data for humans remains unestablished.

Adverse Reactions
1% to 10%:
Cardiovascular: Edema, postural hypotension, syncope, tachycardia, chest pain
Central nervous system: Malaise, fever, dizziness, somnolence, insomnia, hallucinations, confusion, amnesia, dystonias, akathisia, thinking abnormalities, myoclonus, headache
Endocrine & metabolic: Decreased libido
Gastrointestinal: Nausea, constipation, anorexia, dysphagia, xerostomia
Genitourinary: Urinary frequency (up to 3%)
Neuromuscular & skeletal: Weakness, muscle twitching, leg cramps
Ocular: Vision abnormalities (3%)
<1%: Elevated liver transaminase levels

Drug Interactions Increased effect/toxicity: Cimetidine increases pramipexole AUC and half-life; levodopa levels are increased with concurrent use of pramipexole

Mechanism of Action Pramipexole is a nonergot dopamine agonist with specificity for the D_2 dopamine receptor, but has also been shown to bind to D_3 and D_4 receptors. By binding to these receptors, it is thought that pramipexole can stimulate dopamine activity on the nerves of the striatum and substantia nigra.

Pharmacodynamics/Kinetics
Protein binding: 15%
Bioavailability: 90%
Half-life: ~8 hours (12-14 hours in the elderly)
(Continued)

Pramipexole *(Continued)*

Time to peak serum concentration: Within 2 hours

Elimination: Urine, 90% recovered as unmetabolized drug

Usual Dosage Adults: Oral: Initial: 0.375 mg/day given in 3 divided doses, increase gradually by 0.125 mg/dose every 5-7 days; range: 1.5-4.5 mg/day

Dietary Considerations Food intake does not affect the extent of drug absorption, although the time to maximal plasma concentration is delayed by 60 minutes when taken with a meal

Administration Doses should be titrated gradually in all patients to avoid the onset of intolerable side effects. The dosage should be increased to achieve a maximum therapeutic effect, balanced against the side effects of dyskinesia, hallucinations, somnolence, and dry mouth.

Monitoring Parameters Monitor for improvement in symptoms of Parkinson's disease (eg, mentation, behavior, daily living activities, motor examinations), blood pressure, body weight changes, and heart rate

Patient Information Ask your physician or pharmacist before taking any other medicine, including over-the-counter products; especially important are other medicines that could make you sleepy such as sleeping pills, tranquilizers, some cold and allergy medicines, narcotic pain killers, or medicines that relax muscles. Tell your physician if you drink alcohol as this may increase the potential for drowsiness or sedation.

Dosage Forms Tablet: 0.125 mg, 0.25 mg, 1 mg, 1.5 mg

♦ **Pramosone**® *see Pramoxine and Hydrocortisone on this page*

Pramoxine and Hydrocortisone *(pra MOKS een & hye droe KOR ti sone)*

U.S. Brand Names Enzone®; Pramosone®; Proctofoam®-HC; Zone-A Forte®

Therapeutic Category Anesthetic/Corticosteroid

Dosage Forms

Cream, topical: Pramoxine hydrochloride 1% and hydrocortisone acetate 0.5% (30 g); pramoxine hydrochloride 1% and hydrocortisone acetate 1%

Foam, rectal: Pramoxine hydrochloride 1% and hydrocortisone acetate 1% (10 g)

Lotion, topical: Pramoxine hydrochloride 1% and hydrocortisone 0.25%; pramoxine hydrochloride 1% and hydrocortisone 2.5%; pramoxine hydrochloride 2.5% and hydrocortisone 1% (37.5 mL, 120 mL, 240 mL)

♦ **Prandin**® *see Repaglinide on page 1014*

♦ **Pravachol**® *see Pravastatin on this page*

Pravastatin *(PRA va stat in)*

Related Information

Lipid-Lowering Agents *on page 1327*

U.S. Brand Names Pravachol®

Synonyms Pravastatin Sodium

Therapeutic Category Antilipemic Agent; HMG-CoA Reductase Inhibitor

Use

"Primary prevention" in hypercholesterolemic patients without clinically-evident coronary heart disease to reduce the risk of myocardial infarction, reduce the risk of undergoing myocardial revascularization procedures, reduce the risk of cardiovascular mortality with no increase in death from noncardiovascular causes

"Secondary prevention" in hypercholesterolemic patients with clinically-evident coronary artery disease, including prior myocardial infarction, to slow the progression of coronary atherosclerosis, and reduce the risk of acute coronary events

"Secondary prevention" in patients with previous myocardial infarction, and normal cholesterol levels; to reduce the risk of recurrent myocardial infarction; reduce the risk of undergoing myocardial revascularization procedures; and reduce the risk of stroke or transient ischemic attack (TI)

Adjunct to diet to reduce elevated total cholesterol, LDL-cholesterol, and triglyceride levels in patients with primary hypercholesterolemia and mixed dyslipidemia (Fredrickson type IIa and IIb)

Pregnancy Risk Factor X

Contraindications Previous hypersensitivity, active liver disease, or persistent, unexplained liver function enzyme elevations; specifically contraindicated in pregnant or lactating females

Warnings/Precautions May elevate aminotransferases; LFTs should be performed before and every 4-6 weeks during the first 12-15 months of therapy and periodically thereafter; can also cause myalgia and rhabdomyolysis; use with caution in patients who consume large quantities of alcohol or who have a history of liver disease

Adverse Reactions

1% to 10%:

Central nervous system: Headache, dizziness

Dermatologic: Rash

Gastrointestinal: Flatulence, abdominal cramps, diarrhea, constipation, nausea, dyspepsia, heartburn

Neuromuscular & skeletal: Myalgia, increased CPK

<1%: Abnormal taste, lenticular opacities, blurred vision

Overdosage/Toxicology Very little adverse events; treatment is symptomatic

Drug Interactions CYP3A3/4 enzyme substrate

Increased effect with cholestyramine

Increased toxicity with gemfibrozil, clofibrate

Concurrent use of erythromycin and HMG-CoA reductase inhibitors may result in rhabdomyolysis

Mechanism of Action Pravastatin is a competitive inhibitor of 3-hydroxy-3-methylglu-taryl coenzyme A (HMG-CoA) reductase, which is the rate-limiting enzyme involved in *de novo* cholesterol synthesis.

Pharmacodynamics/Kinetics
Absorption: Poor
Metabolism: In the liver to at least two metabolites
Bioavailability: 17%
Half-life, elimination: ~2-3 hours
Time to peak serum concentration: 1-1.5 hours
Elimination: Up to 20% excreted in urine (8% unchanged)

Usual Dosage Adults: Oral: 10-20 mg once daily at bedtime, may increase to 40 mg/day at bedtime

Monitoring Parameters Creatine phosphokinase due to possibility of myopathy

Patient Information Promptly report any unexplained muscle pain, tenderness or weakness, especially if accompanied by malaise or fever

Nursing Implications Liver enzyme elevations may be observed during therapy with pravastatin; diet, weight reduction, and exercise should be attempted prior to therapy with pravastatin

Dosage Forms Tablet, as sodium: 10 mg, 20 mg, 40 mg

♦ **Pravastatin Sodium** *see Pravastatin on previous page*

Praziquantel (pray zi KWON tel)

U.S. Brand Names Biltricide®

Therapeutic Category Anthelmintic

Use All stages of schistosomiasis caused by all *Schistosoma* species pathogenic to humans; clonorchiasis and opisthorchiasis

Unlabeled use: Cysticercosis, flukes, and many intestinal tapeworms

Pregnancy Risk Factor B

Contraindications Ocular cysticercosis, known hypersensitivity to praziquantel

Warnings/Precautions Use caution in patients with severe hepatic disease; patients with cerebral cysticercosis require hospitalization

Adverse Reactions
1% to 10%:
Central nervous system: Dizziness, drowsiness, headache, malaise
Gastrointestinal: Abdominal pain, loss of appetite, nausea, vomiting
Miscellaneous: Diaphoresis
<1%: CSF reaction syndrome in patients being treated for neurocysticercosis, fever, rash, urticaria, itching, diarrhea

Overdosage/Toxicology
Symptoms of overdose include dizziness, drowsiness, headache, liver function impairment

Treatment is supportive following GI decontamination; administer fast-acting laxative

Drug Interactions Hydantoins may decrease praziquantel levels causing treatment failures

Mechanism of Action Increases the cell permeability to calcium in schistosomes, causing strong contractions and paralysis of worm musculature leading to detachment of suckers from the blood vessel walls and to dislodgment

Pharmacodynamics/Kinetics
Absorption: Oral: ~80%; CSF concentration is 14% to 20% of plasma concentration
Distribution: CSF concentration is 14% to 20% of plasma concentration; appears in breast milk
Protein binding: ~80%
Metabolism: Extensive first-pass metabolism
Half-life: Parent drug: 0.8-1.5 hours; Metabolites: 4.5 hours
Time to peak serum concentration: Within 1-3 hours
Elimination: Urinary excretion (99% as metabolites)

Usual Dosage Children >4 years and Adults: Oral:
Schistosomiasis: 20 mg/kg/dose 2-3 times/day for 1 day at 4- to 6-hour intervals
Flukes: 25 mg/kg/dose every 8 hours for 1-2 days
Cysticercosis: 50 mg/kg/day divided every 8 hours for 14 days
Tapeworms: 10-20 mg/kg as a single dose (25 mg/kg for *Hymenolepis nana*)
Clonorchiasis/opisthorchiasis: 3 doses of 25 mg/kg as a 1-day treatment

Patient Information Do not chew tablets due to bitter taste; take with food; caution should be used when performing tasks requiring mental alertness, may impair judgment and coordination

Nursing Implications Tablets can be halved or quartered

Dosage Forms Tablet, tri-scored: 600 mg

Prazosin (PRA zoe sin)

Related Information
Depression Disorders and Treatments *on page 1465*

U.S. Brand Names Minipress®

Canadian Brand Names Apo®-Prazo; Novo-Prazin; Nu-Prazo

Synonyms Furazosin; Prazosin Hydrochloride

Therapeutic Category Alpha-Adrenergic Blocking Agent, Oral; Antihypertensive Agent
(Continued)

Prazosin (Continued)

Use Treatment of hypertension, severe refractory congestive heart failure (in conjunction with diuretics and cardiac glycosides); may reduce mortality in stable postmyocardial patients with left ventricular dysfunction (ejection fraction ≤40%)

Unlabeled use: Symptoms of benign prostatic hypertrophy, Raynaud's vasospasm

Pregnancy Risk Factor C

Contraindications Hypersensitivity to prazosin or any component

Warnings/Precautions Marked orthostatic hypotension, syncope, and loss of consciousness may occur with first dose ("first dose phenomenon") occurs more often in patients receiving beta-blockers, diuretics, low sodium diets, or larger first doses (ie, >1 mg/dose in adults); avoid rapid increase in dose; use with caution in patients with renal impairment

Adverse Reactions

> 10%: Central nervous system: Dizziness (10.3%), lightheadedness

1% to 10%:

Cardiovascular: Edema, palpitations (5%)

Central nervous system: Nervousness, drowsiness (7.6%), headache (7.8%), orthostatic hypotension

Gastrointestinal: Xerostomia, nausea (5%)

Genitourinary: Urinary incontinence

Neuromuscular & skeletal: Weakness (7%)

<1%: Angina, nightmares, hypothermia, rash, sexual dysfunction, priapism, polyuria, dyspnea, nasal congestion

Overdosage/Toxicology

Symptoms of overdose include hypotension, drowsiness

Hypotension usually responds to I.V. fluids, Trendelenburg positioning or vasoconstrictors; treatment is otherwise supportive and symptomatic

Drug Interactions

Decreased effect (antihypertensive) with NSAIDs (eg, indomethacin); clonidine's antihypertensive effect may be decreased

Increased effect (hypotensive) with diuretics and antihypertensive medications (especially beta-blockers); verapamil may increase serum prazosin levels and sensitivity to postural hypotension

Mechanism of Action Competitively inhibits postsynaptic alpha-adrenergic receptors which results in vasodilation of veins and arterioles and a decrease in total peripheral resistance and blood pressure

Pharmacodynamics/Kinetics

Onset of hypotensive effect: Within 2 hours

Maximum decrease: 2-4 hours

Duration: 10-24 hours

Distribution: V_d: 0.5 L/kg (hypertensive adults)

Protein binding: 92% to 97%

Metabolism: Extensively in the liver

Bioavailability: Oral: 43% to 82%

Half-life: 2-4 hours; increased with congestive heart failure

Elimination: 6% to 10% excreted renally as unchanged drug

Usual Dosage Oral:

Children: Initial: 5 mcg/kg/dose (to assess hypotensive effects); usual dosing interval: every 6 hours; increase dosage gradually up to maximum of 25 mcg/kg/dose every 6 hours

Adults:

CHF, hypertension: Initial: 1 mg/dose 2-3 times/day; usual maintenance dose: 3-15 mg/day in divided doses 2-4 times/day; maximum daily dose: 20 mg

Hypertensive urgency: 10-20 mg once, may repeat in 30 minutes

Raynaud's: 0.5-3 mg twice daily

Benign prostatic hypertrophy: 2 mg twice daily

Dietary Considerations Alcohol: Avoid use

Monitoring Parameters Blood pressure, standing and sitting/supine

Test Interactions Increased urinary UMA 17%, norepinephrine metabolite 42%

Patient Information Rise from sitting/lying carefully; take first dose at bedtime; may cause dizziness; report if painful, persistent erection occurs; avoid alcohol

Nursing Implications Syncope may occur (usually within 90 minutes of the initial dose)

Dosage Forms Capsule, as hydrochloride: 1 mg, 2 mg, 5 mg

Prazosin and Polythiazide (PRA zoe sin & pol i THYE a zide)

U.S. Brand Names Minizide®

Therapeutic Category Antihypertensive Agent, Combination

Dosage Forms Capsule:

1: Prazosin 1 mg and polythiazide 0.5 mg

2: Prazosin 2 mg and polythiazide 0.5 mg

5: Prazosin 5 mg and polythiazide 0.5 mg

♦ **Prazosin Hydrochloride** see Prazosin on previous page

♦ **Precose®** see Acarbose on page 17

♦ **Predair®** see Prednisolone on next page

♦ **Predaject®** see Prednisolone on next page

♦ **Predalone T.B.A.®** see Prednisolone on next page

♦ **Predcor®** see Prednisolone on next page

♦ **Predcor-TBA**® see Prednisolone on this page
♦ **Pred Forte**® **Ophthalmic** see Prednisolone on this page
♦ **Pred-G**® **Ophthalmic** see Prednisolone and Gentamicin on page 963
♦ **Pred Mild**® **Ophthalmic** see Prednisolone on this page

Prednicarbate (PRED ni kar bate)
U.S. Brand Names Dermatop®
Therapeutic Category Corticosteroid, Topical (Medium Potency)
Use Relief of the inflammatory and pruritic manifestations of corticosteroid-responsive dermatoses (medium potency topical corticosteroid)
Pregnancy Risk Factor C
Contraindications Hypersensitivity to prednicarbate or any component; fungal, viral, or tubercular skin lesions, herpes simplex or zoster
Warnings/Precautions Systemic absorption of topical corticosteroids has produced reversible HPA axis suppression. This is more likely to occur when the preparation is used on large surface or denuded areas for prolonged periods of time or with an occlusive dressing.
Adverse Reactions
1% to 10%: Dermatologic: Skin atrophy, shininess, thinness, mild telangiectasia
<1%: Pruritus, edema, urticaria, burning, allergic contact dermatitis and rash, folliculitis, acneiform eruptions, hypopigmentation, perioral dermatitis, secondary infection, striae, miliaria, paresthesia
Mechanism of Action Topical corticosteroids have anti-inflammatory, antipruritic, vasoconstrictive, and antiproliferative actions
Usual Dosage Adults: Topical: Apply a thin film to affected area twice daily
Monitoring Parameters Relief of symptoms
Patient Information Use only as prescribed and for no longer than the period prescribed; apply sparingly in a thin film and rub in lightly; avoid contact with eyes; do not apply to the face, underarms, or groin areas; notify physician if condition persists or worsens
Nursing Implications Use sparingly
Additional Information Has been shown that the atrophic activity of prednicarbate is many times less than agents with similar clinical potency, nevertheless, avoid prolonged use on the face
Dosage Forms Cream: 0.1% (15 g, 60 g)

♦ **Prednicen-M**® see Prednisone on page 963

Prednisolone (pred NIS oh lone)
Related Information
Corticosteroids Comparison on page 1319
U.S. Brand Names AK-Pred® Ophthalmic; Articulose-50® Injection; Delta-Cortef® Oral; Econopred® Ophthalmic; Econopred® Plus Ophthalmic; Inflamase® Forte Ophthalmic; Inflamase® Mild Ophthalmic; Key-Pred® Injection; Key-Pred-SP® Injection; Metreton® Ophthalmic; Pediapred® Oral; Predair®; Predaject®; Predalone T.B.A.®; Predcor®; Predcor-TBA®; Pred Forte® Ophthalmic; Pred Mild® Ophthalmic; Prednisol® TBA Injection; Prelone® Oral
Canadian Brand Names Novo-Prednisolone
Synonyms Deltahydrocortisone; Metacortandralone; Prednisolone Acetate; Prednisolone Acetate, Ophthalmic; Prednisolone Sodium Phosphate; Prednisolone Sodium Phosphate, Ophthalmic; Prednisolone Tebutate
Therapeutic Category Anti-inflammatory Agent; Anti-inflammatory Agent, Ophthalmic; Corticosteroid; Corticosteroid, Ophthalmic; Corticosteroid, Systemic; Glucocorticoid
Use Treatment of palpebral and bulbar conjunctivitis; corneal injury from chemical, radiation, thermal burns, or foreign body penetration; endocrine disorders, rheumatic disorders, collagen diseases, dermatologic diseases, allergic states, ophthalmic diseases, respiratory diseases, hematologic disorders, neoplastic diseases, edematous states, and gastrointestinal diseases; useful in patients with inability to activate prednisone (liver disease)
Pregnancy Risk Factor C
Contraindications Acute superficial herpes simplex keratitis; systemic fungal infections; varicella; hypersensitivity to prednisolone or any component
Warnings/Precautions Use with caution in patients with hyperthyroidism, cirrhosis, nonspecific ulcerative colitis, hypertension, osteoporosis, thromboembolic tendencies, CHF, convulsive disorders, myasthenia gravis, thrombophlebitis, peptic ulcer, diabetes; acute adrenal insufficiency may occur with abrupt withdrawal after long-term therapy or with stress; young pediatric patients may be more susceptible to adrenal axis suppression from topical therapy. Because of the risk of adverse effects, systemic corticosteroids should be used cautiously in the elderly, in the smallest possible dose, and for the shortest possible time.
Adverse Reactions
>10%:
Central nervous system: Insomnia, nervousness
Gastrointestinal: Increased appetite, indigestion
1% to 10%:
Dermatologic: Hirsutism
Endocrine & metabolic: Diabetes mellitus
Neuromuscular & skeletal: Arthralgia
Ocular: Cataracts, glaucoma
(Continued)

Prednisolone *(Continued)*

Respiratory: Epistaxis

<1%: Edema, hypertension, vertigo, seizures, psychoses, pseudotumor cerebri, headache, mood swings, delirium, hallucinations, euphoria, acne, skin atrophy, bruising, hyperpigmentation, Cushing's syndrome, pituitary-adrenal axis suppression, growth suppression, glucose intolerance, hypokalemia, alkalosis, amenorrhea, sodium and water retention, hyperglycemia, nausea, vomiting, abdominal distention, ulcerative esophagitis, pancreatitis, muscle weakness, osteoporosis, fractures, muscle wasting, hypersensitivity reactions

Overdosage/Toxicology When consumed in excessive quantities for prolonged periods, systemic hypercorticism and adrenal suppression may occur, in those cases discontinuation and withdrawal of the corticosteroid should be done judiciously.

Drug Interactions CYP3A enzyme substrate; inducer of cytochrome P-450 enzymes

Decreased effect:
Barbiturates, phenytoin, rifampin decrease corticosteroid effectiveness
Decreases salicylates
Decreases vaccines
Decreases toxoids effectiveness

Mechanism of Action Decreases inflammation by suppression of migration of polymorphonuclear leukocytes and reversal of increased capillary permeability; suppresses the immune system by reducing activity and volume of the lymphatic system

Pharmacodynamics/Kinetics

Protein binding: 65% to 91% (concentration dependent)

Metabolism: Primarily in the liver, but also metabolized in most tissues, to inactive compounds

Half-life: 3.6 hours; Biological: 18-36 hours; End-stage renal disease: 3-5 hours

Elimination: In urine principally as glucuronides, sulfates, and unconjugated metabolites

Usual Dosage Dose depends upon condition being treated and response of patient; dosage for infants and children should be based on severity of the disease and response of the patient rather than on strict adherence to dosage indicated by age, weight, or body surface area. Consider alternate day therapy for long-term therapy. Discontinuation of long-term therapy requires gradual withdrawal by tapering the dose.

Children:
Acute asthma:
Oral: 1-2 mg/kg/day in divided doses 1-2 times/day for 3-5 days
I.V. (sodium phosphate salt): 2-4 mg/kg/day divided 3-4 times/day
Anti-inflammatory or immunosuppressive dose: Oral, I.V., I.M. (sodium phosphate salt): 0.1-2 mg/kg/day in divided doses 1-4 times/day
Nephrotic syndrome: Oral:
Initial (first 3 episodes): 2 mg/kg/day **or** 60 mg/m^2/day (maximum: 80 mg/day) in divided doses 3-4 times/day until urine is protein free for 3 consecutive days (maximum: 28 days); followed by 1-1.5 mg/kg/dose **or** 40 mg/m^2/dose given every other day for 4 weeks
Maintenance (long-term maintenance dose for frequent relapses): 0.5-1 mg/kg/dose given every other day for 3-6 months

Adults:
Oral, I.V., I.M. (sodium phosphate salt): 5-60 mg/day
Multiple sclerosis (sodium phosphate): Oral: 200 mg/day for 1 week followed by 80 mg every other day for 1 month
Rheumatoid arthritis: Oral: Initial: 5-7.5 mg/day; adjust dose as necessary

Elderly: Use lowest effective dose

Dosing adjustment in hyperthyroidism: Prednisolone dose may need to be increased to achieve adequate therapeutic effects

Hemodialysis: Slightly dialyzable (5% to 20%); administer dose posthemodialysis

Peritoneal dialysis: Supplemental dose is not necessary

Intra-articular, intralesional, soft-tissue administration:
Tebutate salt: 4-40 mg/dose
Sodium phosphate salt: 2-30 mg/dose

Ophthalmic suspension/solution: Children and Adults: Instill 1-2 drops into conjunctival sac every hour during day, every 2 hours at night until favorable response is obtained, then use 1 drop every 4 hours

Administration Administer oral formulation with food or milk to decrease GI effects

Monitoring Parameters Blood pressure, blood glucose, electrolytes

Test Interactions Response to skin tests

Patient Information Notify surgeon or dentist before surgical repair; may cause GI upset, take orally with food; notify physician if any sign of infection occurs; avoid abrupt withdrawal when on long-term therapy

Nursing Implications Do not administer acetate or tebutate salt I.V.

Additional Information

Sodium phosphate injection: For I.V., I.M., intra-articular, intralesional, or soft tissue administration

Tebutate injection: For intra-articular, intralesional, or soft tissue administration only

Dosage Forms

Injection:
As acetate (for I.M., intralesional, intra-articular, or soft tissue administration only): 25 mg/mL (10 mL, 30 mL); 50 mg/mL (30 mL)
As sodium phosphate (for I.M., I.V., intra-articular, intralesional, or soft tissue administration): 20 mg/mL (2 mL, 5 mL, 10 mL)

As tebutate (for intra-articular, intralesional, soft tissue administration only): 20 mg/mL (1 mL, 5 mL, 10 mL)

Liquid, oral, as sodium phosphate: 5 mg/5 mL (120 mL)

Solution, ophthalmic, as sodium phosphate: 0.125% (5 mL, 10 mL, 15 mL); 1% (5 mL, 10 mL, 15 mL)

Suspension, ophthalmic, as acetate: 0.12% (5 mL, 10 mL); 0.125% (5 mL, 10 mL, 15 mL); 1% (1 mL, 5 mL, 10 mL, 15 mL)

Syrup: 15 mg/5 mL (240 mL)

Tablet: 5 mg

- ♦ **Prednisolone Acetate** *see Prednisolone on page 961*
- ♦ **Prednisolone Acetate, Ophthalmic** *see Prednisolone on page 961*

Prednisolone and Gentamicin (pred NIS oh lone & jen ta MYE sin)
U.S. Brand Names Pred-G® Ophthalmic
Therapeutic Category Antibiotic/Corticosteroid, Ophthalmic
Dosage Forms
Ointment, ophthalmic: Prednisolone acetate 0.6% and gentamicin sulfate 0.3% (3.5 g)

Suspension, ophthalmic: Prednisolone acetate 1% and gentamicin sulfate 0.3% (2 mL, 5 mL, 10 mL)

- ♦ **Prednisolone Sodium Phosphate** *see Prednisolone on page 961*
- ♦ **Prednisolone Sodium Phosphate, Ophthalmic** *see Prednisolone on page 961*
- ♦ **Prednisolone Tebutate** *see Prednisolone on page 961*
- ♦ **Prednisol® TBA Injection** *see Prednisolone on page 961*

Prednisone (PRED ni sone)
Related Information
Anticonvulsants by Seizure Type *on page 1300*
Cancer Chemotherapy Regimens *on page 1263*
Contrast Media Reactions, Premedication for Prophylaxis *on page 1464*
Corticosteroids Comparison *on page 1319*
U.S. Brand Names Deltasone®; Liquid Pred®; Meticorten®; Orasone®; Prednicen-M®; Sterapred®
Canadian Brand Names Apo®-Prednisone; Jaa-Prednisone®; Novo-Prednisone; Winpred
Synonyms Deltacortisone; Deltadehydrocortisone
Therapeutic Category Anti-inflammatory Agent; Corticosteroid; Corticosteroid, Systemic; Glucocorticoid
Use Treatment of a variety of diseases including adrenocortical insufficiency, hypercalcemia, rheumatic, and collagen disorders; dermatologic, ocular, respiratory, gastrointestinal, and neoplastic diseases; organ transplantation and a variety of diseases including those of hematologic, allergic, inflammatory, and autoimmune in origin; not available in injectable form, prednisolone must be used

Investigational: Prevention of postherpetic neuralgia and relief of acute pain in the early stages

Pregnancy Risk Factor B
Pregnancy/Breast-Feeding Implications
Clinical effects on the fetus: Crosses the placenta. Immunosuppression reported in 1 infant exposed to high-dose prednisone plus azathioprine throughout gestation. One report of congenital cataracts. Available evidence suggests safe use during pregnancy.

Breast-feeding/lactation: Crosses into breast milk. No data on clinical effects on the infant. American Academy of Pediatrics considers **compatible** with breast-feeding.

Contraindications Serious infections, except septic shock or tuberculous meningitis; systemic fungal infections; hypersensitivity to prednisone or any component; varicella
Warnings/Precautions Withdraw therapy with gradual tapering of dose, may retard bone growth; use with caution in patients with hypothyroidism, cirrhosis, hypertension, congestive heart failure, ulcerative colitis, thromboembolic disorders, and patients at increased risk for peptic ulcer disease. Because of the risk of adverse effects, systemic corticosteroids should be used cautiously in the elderly, in the smallest possible dose, and for the shortest possible time.
Adverse Reactions
>10%:
Central nervous system: Insomnia, nervousness
Gastrointestinal: Increased appetite, indigestion

1% to 10%:
Dermatologic: Hirsutism
Endocrine & metabolic: Diabetes mellitus
Ocular: Cataracts, glaucoma
Neuromuscular & skeletal: Arthralgia
Respiratory: Epistaxis

<1%: Edema, hypertension, vertigo, seizures, psychoses, pseudotumor cerebri, headache, mood swings, delirium, hallucinations, euphoria, acne, skin atrophy, bruising, hyperpigmentation, Cushing's syndrome, pituitary-adrenal axis suppression, growth suppression, glucose intolerance, hypokalemia, alkalosis, amenorrhea, sodium and water retention, hyperglycemia, peptic ulcer, nausea, vomiting, abdominal distention, ulcerative esophagitis, pancreatitis, muscle weakness, osteoporosis, fractures, muscle wasting, hypersensitivity reactions

(Continued)

Prednisone *(Continued)*

Overdosage/Toxicology When consumed in excessive quantities for prolonged periods, systemic hypercorticism and adrenal suppression may occur; in those cases, discontinuation and withdrawal of the corticosteroid should be done judiciously.

Drug Interactions CYP3A3/4 enzyme substrate
Decreased effect:
Barbiturates, phenytoin, rifampin decrease corticosteroid effectiveness
Decreases salicylates
Decreases vaccines
Decreases toxoids effectiveness

Mechanism of Action Decreases inflammation by suppression of migration of polymorphonuclear leukocytes and reversal of increased capillary permeability; suppresses the immune system by reducing activity and volume of the lymphatic system; suppresses adrenal function at high doses. Antitumor effects may be related to inhibition of glucose transport, phosphorylation, or induction of cell death in immature lymphocytes. Antiemetic effects are thought to occur due to blockade of cerebral innervation of the emetic center via inhibition of prostaglandin synthesis.

Pharmacodynamics/Kinetics Refer to Prednisolone monograph for complete pharmacokinetic information
Metabolism: Converted rapidly to prednisolone (active)
Prednisone is inactive and must be metabolized to prednisolone which may be impaired in patients with impaired liver function
Half-life: Normal renal function: 2.5-3.5 hours

Usual Dosage Oral: Dose depends upon condition being treated and response of patient; dosage for infants and children should be based on severity of the disease and response of the patient rather than on strict adherence to dosage indicated by age, weight, or body surface area. Consider alternate day therapy for long-term therapy. Discontinuation of long-term therapy requires gradual withdrawal by tapering the dose.

Children:
Anti-inflammatory or immunosuppressive dose: 0.05-2 mg/kg/day divided 1-4 times/day
Acute asthma: 1-2 mg/kg/day in divided doses 1-2 times/day for 3-5 days
Alternatively (for 3- to 5-day "burst"):
<1 year: 10 mg every 12 hours
1-4 years: 20 mg every 12 hours
5-13 years: 30 mg every 12 hours
>13 years: 40 mg every 12 hours
Asthma long-term therapy (alternative dosing by age):
<1 year: 10 mg every other day
1-4 years: 20 mg every other day
5-13 years: 30 mg every other day
>13 years: 40 mg every other day
Nephrotic syndrome: Initial (first 3 episodes): 2 mg/kg/day **or** 60 mg/m²/day (maximum: 80 mg/day) in divided doses 3-4 times/day until urine is protein free for 3 consecutive days (maximum: 28 days); followed by 1-1.5 mg/kg/dose **or** 40 mg/m²/dose given every other day for 4 weeks
Maintenance dose (long-term maintenance dose for frequent relapses): 0.5-1 mg/kg/dose given every other day for 3-6 months
Children and Adults: Physiologic replacement: 4-5 mg/m²/day
Adults: 5-60 mg/day in divided doses 1-4 times/day
Elderly: Use the lowest effective dose

Dosing adjustment in hepatic impairment: Prednisone is inactive and must be metabolized by the liver to prednisolone. This conversion may be impaired in patients with liver disease, however, prednisolone levels are observed to be higher in patients with severe liver failure than in normal patients. Therefore, compensation for the inadequate conversion of prednisone to prednisolone occurs.

Dosing adjustment in hyperthyroidism: Prednisone dose may need to be increased to achieve adequate therapeutic effects
Hemodialysis: Supplemental dose is not necessary
Peritoneal dialysis: Supplemental dose is not necessary

Administration Administer with meals to decrease gastrointestinal upset

Monitoring Parameters Blood pressure, blood glucose, electrolytes

Test Interactions Response to skin tests

Patient Information Notify surgeon or dentist before surgical repair; may cause GI upset, take with food; notify physician if any sign of infection occurs; avoid abrupt withdrawal when on long-term therapy; do not discontinue or decrease drug without contacting physician, carry an identification card or bracelet advising that you are on steroids

Nursing Implications Withdraw therapy with gradual tapering of dose

Dosage Forms
Solution, oral: Concentrate (30% alcohol): 5 mg/mL (30 mL); Nonconcentrate (5% alcohol): 5 mg/5 mL (5 mL, 500 mL)
Syrup: 5 mg/5 mL (120 mL, 240 mL)
Tablet: 1 mg, 2.5 mg, 5 mg, 10 mg, 20 mg, 50 mg

♦ **Prefrin™ Liquifilm®** *see* Phenylephrine *on page 918*

♦ **Prefrin™ Ophthalmic Solution** *see* Phenylephrine *on page 918*

♦ **Pregnenedione** *see* Progesterone *on page 976*

- **Pregnyl®** see Chorionic Gonadotropin on page 258
- **Prelone® Oral** see Prednisolone on page 961
- **Premarin®** see Estrogens, Conjugated on page 436
- **Premarin® With Methyltestosterone** see Estrogens and Methyltestosterone on page 436
- **Premphase™** see Estrogens and Medroxyprogesterone on page 436
- **Prempro™** see Estrogens and Medroxyprogesterone on page 436
- **Prenatal Vitamins** see Vitamins, Multiple on page 1226
- **Prenavite® [OTC]** see Vitamins, Multiple on page 1226
- **Pre-Par®** see Ritodrine on page 1032
- **Pre-Pen®** see Benzylpenicilloyl-polylysine on page 137
- **Prepidil® Vaginal Gel** see Dinoprostone on page 368
- **Prepulsid®** see Cisapride on page 265
- **Prescription Strength Desenex® [OTC]** see Miconazole on page 775
- **Pressyn®** see Vasopressin on page 1211
- **Pretz® [OTC]** see Sodium Chloride on page 1067
- **Pretz-D® [OTC]** see Ephedrine on page 414
- **Prevacid®** see Lansoprazole on page 659
- **Prevalite®** see Cholestyramine Resin on page 254
- **Prevention of Bacterial Endocarditis** see page 1377
- **Prevention of Hepatitis A Through Active or Passive Immunization** see page 1370
- **Prevention of Malaria** see page 1372
- **Prevention of Wound Infection & Sepsis in Surgical Patients** see page 1381
- **PreviDent®** see Fluoride on page 498
- **Priftin®** see Rifapentine on page 1026
- **Prilosec™** see Omeprazole on page 861
- **Primaclone** see Primidone on next page
- **Primacor®** see Milrinone on page 781
- **Primaquine and Chloroquine** see Chloroquine and Primaquine on page 242

Primaquine Phosphate (PRIM a kween FOS fate)

Related Information
Malaria Treatment on page 1425
Prevention of Malaria on page 1372

Synonyms Prymaccone

Therapeutic Category Antimalarial Agent

Use Provides radical cure of *P. vivax* or *P. ovale* malaria after a clinical attack has been confirmed by blood smear or serologic titer and postexposure prophylaxis

Pregnancy Risk Factor C

Contraindications Acutely ill patients who have a tendency to develop granulocytopenia (rheumatoid arthritis, SLE); patients receiving other drugs capable of depressing the bone marrow (eg, quinacrine and primaquine)

Warnings/Precautions Use with caution in patients with G-6-PD deficiency, NADH methemoglobin reductase deficiency, acutely ill patients who have a tendency to develop granulocytopenia; patients receiving other drugs capable of depressing the bone marrow; do not exceed recommended dosage

Adverse Reactions
>10%:
 Gastrointestinal: Abdominal pain, nausea, vomiting
 Hematologic: Hemolytic anemia in G-6-PD deficiency
1% to 10%: Hematologic: Methemoglobinemia in NADH-methemoglobin reductase-deficient individuals
<1%: Arrhythmias, headache, pruritus, leukopenia, agranulocytosis, leukocytosis, interference with visual accommodation

Overdosage/Toxicology
Symptoms of acute overdose include abdominal cramps, vomiting, cyanosis, methemoglobinemia (possibly severe), leukopenia, acute hemolytic anemia (often significant), granulocytopenia; with chronic overdose, symptoms include ototoxicity and retinopathy
Following GI decontamination, treatment is supportive (fluids, anticonvulsants, blood transfusions, methylene blue if methemoglobinemia severe - 1-2 mg/kg over several minutes)

Drug Interactions Quinacrine may potentiate the toxicity of antimalarial compounds which are structurally related to primaquine

Mechanism of Action Eliminates the primary tissue exoerythrocytic forms of *P. falciparum*; disrupts mitochondria and binds to DNA

Pharmacodynamics/Kinetics
Absorption: Oral: Well absorbed
Metabolism: Liver metabolism to carboxyprimaquine, an active metabolite
Half-life: 3.7-9.6 hours
Time to peak serum concentration: Within 1-2 hours
Elimination: Only a small amount of unchanged drug excreted in urine

Usual Dosage Oral:
Children: 0.3 mg base/kg/day once daily for 14 days (not to exceed 15 mg/day) or 0.9 mg base/kg once weekly for 8 weeks not to exceed 45 mg base/week
Adults: 15 mg/day (base) once daily for 14 days or 45 mg base once weekly for 8 weeks
(Continued)

965

Primaquine Phosphate (Continued)

CDC treatment recommendations: Begin therapy during last 2 weeks of, or following a course of, suppression with chloroquine or a comparable drug

Monitoring Parameters Periodic CBC, visual color check of urine, glucose, electrolytes; if hemolysis suspected - CBC, haptoglobin, peripheral smear, urinalysis dipstick for occult blood

Patient Information Take with meals to decrease adverse GI effects; drug has a bitter taste; notify physician if a darkening of urine occurs or if shortness of breath, weakness or skin discoloration (chocolate cyanosis) occurs; complete full course of therapy

Dosage Forms Tablet: 26.3 mg [15 mg base]

♦ **Primatene® Mist [OTC]** see Epinephrine on page 415

♦ **Primaxin®** see Imipenem and Cilastatin on page 600

Primidone (PRI mi done)

Related Information
Epilepsy Treatment on page 1468
U.S. Brand Names Mysoline®
Canadian Brand Names Apo®-Primidone; Sertan®
Synonyms Desoxyphenobarbital; Primaclone
Therapeutic Category Anticonvulsant; Barbiturate
Use Management of grand mal, complex partial, and focal seizures
Unlabeled use: Benign familial tremor (essential tremor)
Pregnancy Risk Factor D
Pregnancy/Breast-Feeding Implications
Clinical effects on the fetus: Crosses the placenta. Dysmorphic facial features; hemorrhagic disease of newborn due to fetal vitamin K depletion, maternal folic acid deficiency may occur. Epilepsy itself, number of medications, genetic factors, or a combination of these probably influence the teratogenicity of anticonvulsant therapy. Benefit:risk ratio usually favors continued use during pregnancy and breast-feeding.
Breast-feeding/lactation: Crosses into breast milk
Clinical effects on the infant: Sedation; feeding problems reported. American Academy of Pediatrics recommends USE WITH CAUTION.
Contraindications Hypersensitivity to primidone, phenobarbital, or any component; porphyria
Warnings/Precautions Use with caution in patients with renal or hepatic impairment, pulmonary insufficiency; abrupt withdrawal may precipitate status epilepticus
Adverse Reactions
>10%: Central nervous system: Drowsiness, vertigo, ataxia, lethargy, behavior change, sedation, headache
1% to 10%:
Gastrointestinal: Nausea, vomiting, anorexia
Genitourinary: Impotence
<1%: Behavior change, rash, leukopenia, malignant lymphoma-like syndrome, megaloblastic anemia, diplopia, nystagmus, systemic lupus-like syndrome
Overdosage/Toxicology
Symptoms of overdose include unsteady gait, slurred speech, confusion, jaundice, hypothermia, fever, hypotension, coma, respiratory arrest
Assure adequate hydration and renal function. Urinary alkalinization with I.V. sodium bicarbonate also helps to enhance elimination. Repeated oral doses of activated charcoal significantly reduces the half-life of primidone resulting from an enhancement of nonrenal elimination. The usual dose is 0.1-1 g/kg every 4-6 hours for 3-4 days unless the patient has no bowel movement causing the charcoal to remain in the GI tract. Hemodialysis or hemoperfusion is of uncertain value. Patients in stage IV coma due to high serum drug levels may require charcoal hemoperfusion.
Drug Interactions CYP1A2, 2B6, 2C, 2C8, 3A3/4, and 3A5-7 enzyme inducer

Decreased effect: Primidone may decrease serum concentrations of ethosuximide, valproic acid, griseofulvin; phenytoin may decrease primidone serum concentrations
Increased toxicity: Methylphenidate may increase primidone serum concentrations; valproic acid may increase phenobarbital concentrations derived from primidone
Stability Protect from light
Mechanism of Action Decreases neuron excitability, raises seizure threshold similar to phenobarbital; primidone has two active metabolites, phenobarbital and phenylethylmalonamide (PEMA); PEMA may enhance the activity of phenobarbital
Pharmacodynamics/Kinetics
Distribution: V_d: 2-3 L/kg in adults
Protein binding: 99%
Metabolism: In the liver to phenobarbital (active) and phenylethylmalonamide (PEMA)
Bioavailability: 60% to 80%
Half-life (age dependent): Primidone: 10-12 hours; PEMA: 16 hours; Phenobarbital: 52-118 hours
Time to peak serum concentration: Oral: Within 4 hours
Elimination: Urinary excretion of both active metabolites and unchanged primidone (15% to 25%)
Usual Dosage Oral:
Children <8 years: Initial: 50-125 mg/day given at bedtime; increase by 50-125 mg/day increments every 3-7 days; usual dose: 10-25 mg/kg/day in divided doses 3-4 times/day

Children >8 years and Adults: Initial: 125-250 mg/day at bedtime; increase by 125-250 mg/day every 3-7 days; usual dose: 750-1500 mg/day in divided doses 3-4 times/day with maximum dosage of 2 g/day

Dosing interval in renal impairment:
Cl$_{cr}$ 50-80 mL/minute: Administer every 8 hours
Cl$_{cr}$ 10-50 mL/minute: Administer every 8-12 hours
Cl$_{cr}$ <10 mL/minute: Administer every 12-24 hours
Hemodialysis: Moderately dialyzable (20% to 50%); administer dose postdialysis or administer supplemental 30% dose

Dietary Considerations
Food:
Folic acid: Low erythrocyte and CSF folate concentrations. Megaloblastic anemia has been reported. To avoid folic acid deficiency and megaloblastic anemia, some clinicians recommend giving patients on anticonvulsants prophylactic doses of folic acid and cyanocobalamin.
Protein-deficient diets: Increases duration of action of primidone. Should not restrict or delete protein from diet unless discussed with physician. Be consistent with protein intake during primidone therapy.
Fresh fruits containing vitamin C: Displaces drug from binding sites, resulting in increased urinary excretion of primidone. Educate patients regarding the potential for decreased primidone effect with consumption of foods high in vitamin C.

Monitoring Parameters Serum primidone and phenobarbital concentration, CBC, neurological status. Due to CNS effects, monitor closely when initiating drug in elderly. Monitor CBC at 6-month intervals to compare with baseline obtained at start of therapy. Since elderly metabolize phenobarbital at a slower rate than younger adults, it is suggested to measure both primidone and phenobarbital levels together.

Reference Range Therapeutic: Children <5 years: 7-10 µg/mL (SI: 32-46 µmol/L); Adults: 5-12 µg/mL (SI: 23-55 µmol/L); toxic effects rarely present with levels <10 µg/mL (SI: 46 µmol/L) if phenobarbital concentrations are low. Dosage of primidone is adjusted with reference mostly to the phenobarbital level; Toxic: >15 µg/mL (SI: >69 µmol/L)

Test Interactions ↑ alkaline phosphatase (S); ↓ calcium (S)

Patient Information May cause drowsiness, impair judgment and coordination; do not abruptly discontinue or change dosage without notifying physician; can take with food to avoid GI upset

Nursing Implications Observe patient for excessive sedation; institute safety measures

Dosage Forms
Suspension, oral: 250 mg/5 mL (240 mL)
Tablet: 50 mg, 250 mg

♦ **Principen®** see Ampicillin on page 79
♦ **Prinivil®** see Lisinopril on page 686
♦ **Prinzide®** see Lisinopril and Hydrochlorothiazide on page 688
♦ **Priscoline®** see Tolazoline on page 1155
♦ **Privine®** see Naphazoline on page 817
♦ **ProAmatine®** see Midodrine on page 778
♦ **Pro-Amox®** see Amoxicillin on page 69
♦ **Pro-Ampi® Trihydrate** see Ampicillin on page 79
♦ **Proaqua®** see Benzthiazide on page 135
♦ **Probalan®** see Probenecid on this page
♦ **Pro-Banthine®** see Propantheline on page 982

Probenecid (proe BEN e sid)

Related Information
Treatment of Sexually Transmitted Diseases on page 1429

U.S. Brand Names Benemid®; Probalan®

Canadian Brand Names Benuryl™

Therapeutic Category Uricosuric Agent

Use Prevention of gouty arthritis; hyperuricemia; prolongation of beta-lactam effect (ie, serum levels)

Pregnancy Risk Factor B

Contraindications Hypersensitivity to probenecid or any component; high-dose aspirin therapy; moderate to severe renal impairment; children <2 years of age

Warnings/Precautions Use with caution in patients with peptic ulcer; use extreme caution in the use of probenecid with penicillin in patients with renal insufficiency; probenecid may not be effective in patients with a creatinine clearance <30 to 50 mL/minute; may cause exacerbation of acute gouty attack

Adverse Reactions
>10%:
Central nervous system: Headache
Gastrointestinal: Anorexia, nausea, vomiting
Neuromuscular & skeletal: Gouty arthritis (acute)
1% to 10%:
Cardiovascular: Flushing of face
Central nervous system: Dizziness
Dermatologic: Rash, itching
Gastrointestinal: Sore gums
Genitourinary: Painful urination
Renal: Renal calculi
(Continued)

Probenecid *(Continued)*

<1%: Leukopenia, hemolytic anemia, aplastic anemia, hepatic necrosis, urate nephropathy, nephrotic syndrome, anaphylaxis

Overdosage/Toxicology

Symptoms of overdose include nausea, vomiting, tonic-clonic seizures, coma

Activated charcoal is especially effective at binding probenecid, for GI decontamination

Drug Interactions

Decreased effect:

Salicylates (high dose) may decrease uricosuria

Nitrofurantoin may decrease efficacy

Increased toxicity:

Increases methotrexate toxic potential; combination with diflunisal has resulted in 40% decrease in its clearance and as much as a 65% increase in plasma concentrations due to inhibition of diflunisal metabolism

Probenecid decreases clearance of beta-lactams such as penicillins and cephalosporins; increases levels/toxicity of acyclovir, thiopental, clofibrate, dyphylline, pantothenic acid, benzodiazepines, rifampin, sulfonamide, dapsone, sulfonylureas, and zidovudine

Avoid concomitant use with ketorolac (and other NSAIDs) since its half-life is increased twofold and levels and toxicity are significantly increased

Allopurinol readministration may be beneficial by increasing the uric acid lowering effect

Pharmacologic effects of penicillamine may be attenuated

Mechanism of Action Competitively inhibits the reabsorption of uric acid at the proximal convoluted tubule, thereby promoting its excretion and reducing serum uric acid levels; increases plasma levels of weak organic acids (penicillins, cephalosporins, or other beta-lactam antibiotics) by competitively inhibiting their renal tubular secretion

Pharmacodynamics/Kinetics

Onset of action: Effect on penicillin levels reached in about 2 hours

Absorption: Rapid and complete from GI tract

Metabolism: In the liver

Half-life: Normal renal function: 6-12 hours and is dose dependent

Time to peak serum concentration: 2-4 hours

Elimination: In urine

Usual Dosage Oral:

Children:

<2 years: Not recommended

2-14 years: Prolong penicillin serum levels: 25 mg/kg starting dose, then 40 mg/kg/day given 4 times/day

Gonorrhea: <45 kg: 25 mg/kg x 1 (maximum: 1 g/dose) 30 minutes before penicillin, ampicillin or amoxicillin

Adults:

Hyperuricemia with gout: 250 mg twice daily for one week; increase to 250-500 mg/day; may increase by 500 mg/month, if needed, to maximum of 2-3 g/day (dosages may be increased by 500 mg every 6 months if serum urate concentrations are controlled)

Prolong penicillin serum levels: 500 mg 4 times/day

Gonorrhea: 1 g 30 minutes before penicillin, ampicillin, procaine, or amoxicillin

Pelvic inflammatory disease: Cefoxitin 2 g I.M. plus probenecid 1 g orally as a single dose

Neurosyphilis: Aqueous procaine penicillin 2.4 units/day I.M. plus probenecid 500 mg 4 times/day for 10-14 days

Dosing adjustment in renal impairment: Cl_{cr} <50 mL/minute: Avoid use

Dietary Considerations Food: Drug may cause GI upset; take with food if GI upset. Drink plenty of fluids.

Monitoring Parameters Uric acid, renal function, CBC

Test Interactions False-positive glucosuria with Clinitest®, a falsely high determination of theophylline has occurred and the renal excretion of phenolsulfonphthalein 17-ketosteroids and bromsulfophthalein (BSP) may be inhibited

Patient Information Take with food or antacids; drink plenty of fluids to reduce the risk of uric acid stones; the frequency of acute gouty attacks may increase during the first 6-12 months of therapy; avoid taking large doses of aspirin or other salicylates

Nursing Implications An alkaline urine is recommended to avoid crystallization of urates; use of sodium bicarbonate or potassium citrate is suggested until serum uric acid normalizes and tophaceous deposits disappear

Dosage Forms Tablet: 500 mg

Procainamide *(proe kane A mide)*

Related Information

Adult ACLS Algorithm, Tachycardia *on page 1450*

Adult ACLS Algorithm, V. Fib and Pulseless V. Tach *on page 1447*

Antiarrhythmic Drugs Comparison *on page 1297*

Depression Disorders and Treatments *on page 1465*

U.S. Brand Names Procanbid™; Promine®; Pronestyl®; Rhythmin®

Canadian Brand Names Apo®-Procainamide

Synonyms PCA; Procainamide Hydrochloride; Procaine Amide Hydrochloride

Therapeutic Category Antiarrhythmic Agent, Class I-A

Use Treatment of ventricular tachycardia, premature ventricular contractions, paroxysmal atrial tachycardia, and atrial fibrillation; to prevent recurrence of ventricular tachycardia, paroxysmal supraventricular tachycardia, atrial fibrillation or flutter

Pregnancy Risk Factor C

Contraindications Complete heart block; second or third degree heart block without pacemaker; "torsade de pointes"; hypersensitivity to the drug or procaine, or related drugs; SLE; concurrent use of sparfloxacin. Due to results of the CAST study, procainamide and other antiarrhythmic drugs with potentially proarrhythmic effects should be reserved only for documented ventricular arrhythmias which are life-threatening.

Warnings/Precautions Use with caution in patients with marked A-V conduction disturbances, myasthenia gravis, bundle-branch block, or severe cardiac glycoside intoxication, ventricular arrhythmias with organic heart disease or coronary occlusion, CHF supraventricular tachyarrhythmias unless adequate measures are taken to prevent marked increases in ventricular rates; concurrent therapy with other class IA drugs may accumulate in patients with renal or hepatic dysfunction; some tablets contain tartrazine; injection may contain bisulfite (allergens). Long-term administration leads to the development of a positive antinuclear antibody (ANA) test in 50% of patients which may result in a lupus erythematosus-like syndrome (in 20% to 30% of patients); discontinue procainamide with SLE symptoms and choose an alternative agent; elderly have reduced clearance and frequent drug interactions. Potentially fatal blood dyscrasias have occurred with therapeutic doses; close monitoring is recommended during the first 3 months of therapy.

Adverse Reactions

>1%:

Dermatologic: Rash

Gastrointestinal: Diarrhea (3% to 4%), nausea, vomiting, GI complaints (3% to 4%)

<1%:

Cardiovascular: Tachycardia, Q-T prolongation, hypotension, second degree heart block

Central nervous system: Dizziness, lightheadedness, confusion, hallucinations, mental depression, disorientation, fever, drug fever

Hematologic: Hemolytic anemia, agranulocytosis, neutropenia, thrombocytopenia (0.5%), positive Coombs' test

Neuromuscular & skeletal: Arthralgia, myalgia (<0.5%)

Respiratory: Pleural effusion

Miscellaneous: SLE-like syndrome (increased incidence with long-term therapy)

Overdosage/Toxicology

Has a low toxic:therapeutic ratio and may easily produce fatal intoxication (acute toxic dose: 5 g in adults); symptoms of overdose include sinus bradycardia, sinus node arrest or asystole, P-R, QRS or Q-T interval prolongation, torsade de pointes (polymorphous ventricular tachycardia) and depressed myocardial contractility, which along with alpha-adrenergic or ganglionic blockade, may result in hypotension and pulmonary edema; other effects are seizures, coma, and respiratory arrest.

Treatment is primarily symptomatic and effects usually respond to conventional therapies (fluids, positioning, vasopressors, anticonvulsants, antiarrhythmics). **Note:** Do not use other type 1a or 1c antiarrhythmic agents to treat ventricular tachycardia; sodium bicarbonate may treat wide QRS intervals or hypotension; markedly impaired conduction or high degree A-V block, unresponsive to bicarbonate, indicates consideration of a pacemaker is needed.

Drug Interactions

Increased plasma/NAPA concentrations with cimetidine, ranitidine, beta-blockers, amiodarone, trimethoprim, and quinidine

Increased procainamide levels with ofloxacin (21% increase in peak plasma concentrations and 24% increase in AUC) due to inhibition of tubular secretion of procainamide; contraindicated with sparfloxacin due to increased risk of cardiotoxicity

Increased effect of skeletal muscle relaxants, quinidine and lidocaine and neuromuscular blockers (succinylcholine); additive cardiodepressant action occurs with lidocaine

Stability Procainamide may be stored at room temperature up to 27°C; however, refrigeration retards oxidation, which causes color formation. The solution is initially colorless but may turn slightly yellow on standing. Injection of air into the vial causes the solution to darken. Solutions darker than a light amber should be discarded.

Minimum volume: 1 g/250 mL NS/D₅W

Stability of admixture at room temperature in D₅W or NS: 24 hours

Some information indicates that procainamide may be subject to greater decomposition in D₅W unless the admixture is refrigerated or the pH is adjusted. Procainamide is believed to form an association complex with dextrose - the bioavailability of procainamide in this complex is not known and the complex formation is reversible.

Mechanism of Action Decreases myocardial excitability and conduction velocity and may depress myocardial contractility, by increasing the electrical stimulation threshold of ventricle, HIS-Purkinje system and through direct cardiac effects

Pharmacodynamics/Kinetics

Onset of action: I.M. 10-30 minutes

Distribution: V_d: Children: 2.2 L/kg; Adults: 2 L/kg; Congestive heart failure of shock: Decreased V_d

Protein binding: 15% to 20%

Metabolism: By acetylation in the liver to produce N-acetyl procainamide (NAPA) (active metabolite)

Bioavailability: Oral: 75% to 95%

(Continued)

Procainamide *(Continued)*

Half-life:
  Procainamide: (Dependent upon hepatic acetylator, phenotype, cardiac function, and renal function):
    Children: 1.7 hours
    Adults: 2.5-4.7 hours
    Anephric: 11 hours
  NAPA: (Dependent upon renal function):
    Children: 6 hours
    Adults: 6-8 hours
    Anephric: 42 hours
Time to peak serum concentration: Capsule: Within 45 minutes to 2.5 hours; I.M.: 15-60 minutes
Elimination: Urinary excretion (25% as NAPA)

Usual Dosage Must be titrated to patient's response
Children:
  Oral: 15-50 mg/kg/24 hours divided every 3-6 hours
  I.M.: 50 mg/kg/24 hours divided into doses of $1/8$ to $1/4$ every 3-6 hours in divided doses until oral therapy is possible
  I.V. (infusion requires use of an infusion pump):
  Load: 3-6 mg/kg/dose over 5 minutes not to exceed 100 mg/dose; may repeat every 5-10 minutes to maximum of 15 mg/kg/load
  Maintenance as continuous I.V. infusion: 20-80 mcg/kg/minute; maximum: 2 g/24 hours
Adults:
  Oral: 250-500 mg/dose every 3-6 hours or 500 mg to 1 g every 6 hours sustained release; usual dose: 50 mg/kg/24 hours; maximum: 4 g/24 hours (**Note:** Twice daily dosing approved for Procanbid™)
  I.M.: 0.5-1 g every 4-8 hours until oral therapy is possible
  I.V. (infusion requires use of an infusion pump): Loading dose: 15-18 mg/kg administered as slow infusion over 25-30 minutes or 100-200 mg/dose repeated every 5 minutes as needed to a total dose of 1 g; maintenance dose: 1-6 mg/minute by continuous infusion
  Infusion rate: 2 g/250 mL D_5W/NS (I.V. infusion requires use of an infusion pump):
    1 mg/minute: 7 mL/hour
    2 mg/minute: 15 mL/hour
    3 mg/minute: 21 mL/hour
    4 mg/minute: 30 mL/hour
    5 mg/minute: 38 mL/hour
    6 mg/minute: 45 mL/hour
  Refractory ventricular fibrillation: 30 mg/minute, up to a total of 17 mg/kg; I.V. maintenance infusion: 1-4 mg/minute; monitor levels and do not exceed 3 mg/minute for >24 hours in adults with renal failure
  ACLS guidelines: I.V.: Infuse 20 mg/minute until arrhythmia is controlled, hypotension occurs, QRS complex widens by 50% of its original width, or total of 17 mg/kg is given

Dosing interval in renal impairment:
  Cl_{cr} 10-50 mL/minute: Administer every 6-12 hours
  Cl_{cr} <10 mL/minute: Administer every 8-24 hours
Dialysis:
  Procainamide: Moderately hemodialyzable (20% to 50%): 200 mg supplemental dose posthemodialysis is recommended
  N-acetylprocainamide: Not dialyzable (0% to 5%)
  Procainamide/N-acetylprocainamide: Not peritoneal dialyzable (0% to 5%)
  Procainamide/N-acetylprocainamide: Replace by blood level during continuous arteriovenous or venovenous hemofiltration (CAVH/CAVHD)
  Dosing adjustment in hepatic impairment: Reduce dose 50%

Administration Dilute I.V. with D_5W; maximum rate: 50 mg/minute; administer around-the-clock rather than 4 times/day to promote less variation in peak and trough serum levels

Monitoring Parameters EKG, blood pressure, CBC with differential, platelet count; cardiac monitor and blood pressure monitor required during I.V. administration

Reference Range
  Timing of serum samples: Draw trough just before next oral dose; draw 6-12 hours after I.V. infusion has started; half-life is 2.5-5 hours
  Therapeutic levels: Procainamide: 4-10 µg/mL; NAPA 15-25 µg/mL; Combined: 10-30 µg/mL
  Toxic concentration: Procainamide: >10-12 µg/mL

Patient Information Do not discontinue therapy unless instructed by physician; notify physician or pharmacist if soreness of mouth, throat or gums, unexplained fever, or symptoms of upper respiratory tract infection occur. Do not chew sustained release tablets; some sustained release tablets contain a wax core that slowly releases the drug; when this process is complete, the empty, nonabsorbable wax core is eliminated and may be visible in feces; some sustained release tablets may be broken in half.

Nursing Implications Do not crush sustained release drug product

Dosage Forms
  Capsule, as hydrochloride: 250 mg, 375 mg, 500 mg
  Injection, as hydrochloride: 100 mg/mL (10 mL); 500 mg/mL (2 mL)
  Tablet, as hydrochloride: 250 mg, 375 mg, 500 mg

Tablet, as hydrochloride, sustained release: 250 mg, 500 mg, 750 mg, 1000 mg
Tablet, as hydrochloride, sustained release (Procanbid™): 500 mg, 1000 mg

Extemporaneous Preparations Note: Several formulations have been described, some being more complex; for all formulations, the pH must be 4-6 to prevent degradation; some preparations require adjustment of pH; shake well before use

A suspension of 50 mg/mL can be made with the capsules, distilled water, and a 2:1 simple syrup/cherry syrup mixture; stability 2 weeks under refrigeration; (ASHP, 1987)

Concentrations of 5, 50, and 100 mg/mL oral liquid preparations, (made with the capsules, sterile water for irrigation and cherry syrup) stored at 4°C to 6°C (pH 6) were stable for at least 6 months (Metras, 1992).

A sucrose-based syrup (procainamide 50 mg/mL) made with capsules, distilled water, simple syrup, parabens, and cherry flavoring had a calculated stability of 456 days at 25°C and measured stability of 42 days at 40°C (pH ~5) while a maltitol-based syrup (procainamide 50 mg/mL) made with capsules, distilled water, Lycasin® (a syrup vehicle with 75% w/w maltitol), parabens, sodium bisulfate, saccharin, sodium acetate, pineapple and apricot flavoring, FD & C yellow number 6, (pH adjusted to 5 with glacial acetic acid) had a calculated stability of 97 days at 25°C and a measured stability of 94 days at 40°C. The maltitol-based syrup was more stable than the sucrose-based syrup when temperature was >37°C, but the sucrose-based syrup was more stable at temperatures <37°C (Alexander, 1993).

Alexander KS, Pudipeddi M, and Parker GA, "Stability of Procainamide Hydrochloride Syrups Compounded From Capsules," *Am J Hosp Pharm*, 1993, 50(4):693-8.

Handbook in Extemporaneous Formulations, Bethesda, MD: American Society of Hospital Pharmacists, 1987.

Metras JI, Swenson CF, and MacDermott MP, "Stability of Procainamide Hydrochloride in an Extemporaneously Compounded Oral Liquid," *Am J Hosp Pharm*, 1992, 49(7):1720-4.

Swenson CF, "Importance of Following Instructions When Compounding," *Am J Hosp Pharm*, 1993, 50(2):261.

♦ **Procainamide Hydrochloride** *see Procainamide on page 968*

Procaine (PROE kane)

U.S. Brand Names Novocain® Injection
Synonyms Procaine Hydrochloride
Therapeutic Category Local Anesthetic, Injectable
Use Produces spinal anesthesia and epidural and peripheral nerve block by injection and infiltration methods
Pregnancy Risk Factor C
Contraindications Known hypersensitivity to procaine, PABA, parabens, or other ester local anesthetics
Warnings/Precautions Patients with cardiac diseases, hyperthyroidism, or other endocrine diseases may be more susceptible to toxic effects of local anesthetics; some preparations contain metabisulfite
Adverse Reactions
1% to 10%: Local: Burning sensation at site of injection, tissue irritation, pain at injection site
<1%: Aseptic meningitis resulting in paralysis can occur, CNS stimulation followed by CNS depression, chills, discoloration of skin, nausea, vomiting, miosis, tinnitus, anaphylactoid reaction
Overdosage/Toxicology Treatment is primarily symptomatic and supportive. Termination of anesthesia by pneumatic tourniquet inflation should be attempted when the agent is administered by infiltration or regional injection. Seizures commonly respond to diazepam, while hypotension responds to I.V. fluids and Trendelenburg positioning. Bradyarrhythmias (heart rate <60) can be treated with I.V., I.M., or S.C. atropine 15 mcg/kg. With the development of metabolic acidosis, I.V. sodium bicarbonate 0.5-2 mEq/kg and ventilatory assistance should be instituted.
Drug Interactions
Decreased effect of sulfonamides with the PABA metabolite of procaine, chloroprocaine, and tetracaine
Decreased/increased effect of vasopressors, ergot alkaloids, and MAO inhibitors on blood pressure when using anesthetic solutions with a vasoconstrictor
Mechanism of Action Blocks both the initiation and conduction of nerve impulses by decreasing the neuronal membrane's permeability to sodium ions, which results in inhibition of depolarization with resultant blockade of conduction
Pharmacodynamics/Kinetics
Onset of effect: Injection: Within 2-5 minutes
Duration: 0.5-1.5 hours (dependent upon patient, type of block, concentration, and method of anesthesia)
Metabolism: Rapidly hydrolyzed by plasma enzymes to para-aminobenzoic acid and diethylaminoethanol (80% conjugated before elimination)
Half-life: 7.7 minutes
Elimination: In urine as metabolites and some unchanged drug
Usual Dosage Dose varies with procedure, desired depth, and duration of anesthesia, desired muscle relaxation, vascularity of tissues, physical condition, and age of patient
Nursing Implications Prior to instillation of anesthetic agent, withdraw plunger to ensure needle is not in artery or vein; resuscitative equipment should be available when local anesthetics are administered
(Continued)

Procaine *(Continued)*

Dosage Forms Injection, as hydrochloride: 1% [10 mg/mL] (2 mL, 6 mL, 30 mL, 100 mL); 2% [20 mg/mL] (30 mL, 100 mL); 10% (2 mL)

- ◆ **Procaine Amide Hydrochloride** *see* Procainamide *on page 968*
- ◆ **Procaine Benzylpenicillin** *see* Penicillin G Procaine *on page 897*
- ◆ **Procaine Hydrochloride** *see* Procaine *on previous page*
- ◆ **Procaine Penicillin G** *see* Penicillin G Procaine *on page 897*
- ◆ **Pro-Cal-Sof® [OTC]** *see* Docusate *on page 384*
- ◆ **Procanbid™** *see* Procainamide *on page 968*

Procarbazine *(proe KAR ba zeen)*

Related Information
Cancer Chemotherapy Regimens *on page 1263*
Toxicities of Chemotherapeutic Agents *on page 1288*
Tyramine Content of Foods *on page 1525*

U.S. Brand Names Matulane®

Synonyms Ibenzmethyzin; N-Methylhydrazine; Procarbazine Hydrochloride

Therapeutic Category Antineoplastic Agent, Alkylating Agent

Use Treatment of Hodgkin's disease, non-Hodgkin's lymphoma, brain tumor, bronchogenic carcinoma

Pregnancy Risk Factor D

Contraindications Hypersensitivity to procarbazine or any component, or pre-existing bone marrow aplasia, alcohol ingestion

Warnings/Precautions The U.S. Food and Drug Administration (FDA) currently recommends that procedures for proper handling and disposal of antineoplastic agents be considered; use with caution in patients with pre-existing renal or hepatic impairment; modify dosage in patients with renal or hepatic impairment, or marrow disorders; reduce dosage with serum creatinine >2 mg/dL or total bilirubin >3 mg/dL; procarbazine possesses MAO inhibitor activity. Procarbazine is a carcinogen which may cause acute leukemia; procarbazine may cause infertility.

Adverse Reactions
>10%:
    Central nervous system: Mental depression, manic reactions, hallucinations, dizziness, headache, nervousness, insomnia, nightmares, ataxia, disorientation, confusion, seizure, CNS stimulation
    Gastrointestinal: Severe nausea and vomiting occur frequently and may be dose-limiting; anorexia, abdominal pain, stomatitis, dysphagia, diarrhea, and constipation; use a nonphenothiazine antiemetic, when possible
        Emetic potential: Moderately high (60% to 90%)
        Time course of nausea/vomiting: Onset: 24-27 hours; Duration: variable
    Hematologic: Thrombocytopenia, hemolytic anemia
    Myelosuppressive: May be dose-limiting toxicity; procarbazine should be discontinued if leukocyte count is <4000/mm³ or platelet count <100,000/mm³
        WBC: Moderate
        Platelets: Moderate
        Onset (days): 14
        Nadir (days): 21
        Recovery (days): 28
    Neuromuscular & skeletal: Weakness, paresthesia, neuropathies, decreased reflexes, foot drop, tremors
    Ocular: Nystagmus
    Respiratory: Pleural effusion, cough
1% to 10%:
    Dermatologic: Hyperpigmentation
    Hepatic: Hepatotoxicity
    Neuromuscular & skeletal: Peripheral neuropathy
<1%: Orthostatic hypotension, hypertensive crisis, irritability, somnolence, dermatitis, alopecia, pruritus, hypersensitivity rash, disulfiram-like reaction, cessation of menses, jaundice, arthralgia, myalgia, diplopia, photophobia, pneumonitis, hoarseness, secondary malignancy, allergic reactions, flu-like syndrome

Overdosage/Toxicology
Symptoms of overdose include arthralgia, alopecia, paresthesia, bone marrow suppression, hallucinations, nausea, vomiting, diarrhea, seizures, coma
Treatment is supportive, adverse effects such as marrow toxicity may begin as late as 2 weeks after exposure

Drug Interactions Increased toxicity:
Procarbazine exhibits weak monoamine oxidase (MAO) inhibitor activity; foods containing high amounts of tyramine should, therefore, be avoided (ie, beer, yogurt, yeast, wine, cheese, pickled herring, chicken liver, and bananas). When a MAO inhibitor is given with food high in tyramine, a hypertensive crisis, intracranial bleeding, and headache have been reported.
Sympathomimetic amines (epinephrine and amphetamines) and antidepressants (tricyclics) should be used cautiously with procarbazine.
Barbiturates, narcotics, phenothiazines, and other CNS depressants can cause somnolence, ataxia, and other symptoms of CNS depression
Alcohol has caused a disulfiram-like reaction with procarbazine; may result in headache, respiratory difficulties, nausea, vomiting, sweating, thirst, hypotension, and flushing

Stability Protect from light

Mechanism of Action Mechanism of action is not clear, methylating of nucleic acids; inhibits DNA, RNA, and protein synthesis; may damage DNA directly and suppresses mitosis; metabolic activation required by host

Pharmacodynamics/Kinetics

Absorption: Oral: Rapid and complete

Distribution: Crosses the blood-brain barrier and distributes into CSF

Metabolism: In the liver and kidney

Half-life: 1 hour

Elimination: In urine and through respiratory tract (<5% as unchanged drug) and 70% as metabolites

Usual Dosage Refer to individual protocols. Dose based on patient's ideal weight if the patient is obese or has abnormal fluid retention. Oral:

Children:

BMT aplastic anemia conditioning regimen: 12.5 mg/kg/dose every other day for 4 doses

Hodgkin's disease: MOPP/IC-MOPP regimens: 100 mg/m^2/day for 14 days and repeated every 4 weeks

Neuroblastoma and medulloblastoma: Doses as high as 100-200 mg/m^2/day once daily have been used

Adults: Initial: 2-4 mg/kg/day in single or divided doses for 7 days then increase dose to 4-6 mg/kg/day until response is obtained or leukocyte count decreased <4000/mm^3 or the platelet count decreased <100,000/mm^3; maintenance: 1-2 mg/kg/day

In MOPP, 100 mg/m^2/day on days 1-14 of a 28-day cycle

Dosing in renal/hepatic impairment: Use with caution, may result in increased toxicity

Dietary Considerations

Alcohol: Avoid use, including alcohol-containing products

Food: Avoid foods with high tyramine content

Monitoring Parameters CBC with differential, platelet and reticulocyte count, urinalysis, liver function test, renal function test.

Patient Information Avoid food with high tyramine content; obtain a list from your physician or pharmacist; do not take any new prescription or OTC drug without consulting your physician or pharmacist; avoid alcohol and alcohol containing products including topicals; notify physician of persistent fever, sore throat, bleeding, or bruising; may impair judgment and coordination; avoid prolonged exposure to sunlight

Dosage Forms Capsule, as hydrochloride: 50 mg

- ◆ **Procarbazine Hydrochloride** see Procarbazine on previous page
- ◆ **Procardia**® see Nifedipine on page 838
- ◆ **Procardia XL**® see Nifedipine on page 838
- ◆ **Procetofene** see Fenofibrate on page 472

Prochlorperazine (proe klor PER a zeen)

U.S. Brand Names Compazine®

Canadian Brand Names Nu-Prochlor; PMS-Prochlorperazine; Prorazin®; Stemetil®

Synonyms Prochlorperazine Edisylate; Prochlorperazine Maleate

Therapeutic Category Antiemetic; Antipsychotic Agent; Phenothiazine Derivative

Use Management of nausea and vomiting; acute and chronic psychosis

Pregnancy Risk Factor C

Pregnancy/Breast-Feeding Implications

Clinical effects on the fetus: Crosses the placenta. Isolated reports of congenital anomalies, however some included exposures to other drugs. Available evidence with use of occasional low doses suggests safe use during pregnancy.

Breast-feeding/lactation: No data available. American Academy of Pediatrics considers **compatible** with breast-feeding.

Contraindications Hypersensitivity to prochlorperazine or any component; cross-sensitivity with other phenothiazines may exist; avoid use in patients with narrow-angle glaucoma; bone marrow suppression; severe liver or cardiac disease

Warnings/Precautions Injection contains sulfites which may cause allergic reactions; may impair ability to perform hazardous tasks requiring mental alertness or physical coordination; some products contain tartrazine dye, avoid use in sensitive individuals

Tardive dyskinesia: Prevalence rate may be 40% in elderly; development of the syndrome and the irreversible nature are proportional to duration and total cumulative dose over time. May be reversible if diagnosed early in therapy.

High incidence of extrapyramidal reactions, especially in children or the elderly, so reserve use in children <5 years of age to those who are unresponsive to other antiemetics; incidence of extrapyramidal reactions is increased with acute illnesses such as chicken pox, measles, CNS infections, gastroenteritis, and dehydration

Drug-induced **Parkinson's syndrome** occurs often. **Akathisia** is the most common extrapyramidal reaction in elderly.

Increased confusion, memory loss, psychotic behavior, and agitation frequently occur as a consequence of anticholinergic effects

Lowers seizure threshold, use cautiously in patients with seizure history

Orthostatic hypotension is due to alpha-receptor blockade, the elderly are at greater risk for orthostatic hypotension

Antipsychotic associated sedation in nonpsychotic patients is extremely unpleasant due to feelings of depersonalization, derealization, and dysphoria

Life-threatening arrhythmias have occurred at therapeutic doses of antipsychotics

(Continued)

Prochlorperazine *(Continued)*

Adverse Reactions Incidence of extrapyramidal reactions are higher with prochlorperazine than chlorpromazine

Percentage unknown:

Central nervous system: Sedation, drowsiness, restlessness, anxiety, extrapyramidal reactions, parkinsonian signs and symptoms, seizures, altered central temperature regulation

Dermatologic: Photosensitivity, hyperpigmentation, pruritus, rash

Endocrine & metabolic: Amenorrhea, gynecomastia

Gastrointestinal: Weight gain, GI upset

Miscellaneous: Anaphylactoid reactions

>10%:

Cardiovascular: Hypotension (especially with I.V. use), orthostatic hypotension, tachycardia, arrhythmias

Central nervous system: Pseudoparkinsonism, akathisia, tardive dyskinesia (persistent), dizziness, dystonias

Gastrointestinal: Xerostomia, constipation

Genitourinary: Urinary retention

Ocular: Pigmentary retinopathy, blurred vision

Respiratory: Nasal congestion

Miscellaneous: Diaphoresis (decreased)

1% to 10%:

Dermatologic: Increased sensitivity to sun, rash

Endocrine & metabolic: Changes in menstrual cycle, breast pain, changes in libido

Gastrointestinal: Nausea, vomiting, stomach pain

Genitourinary: Dysuria, ejaculatory disturbances

Neuromuscular & skeletal: Trembling of fingers

<1%: Neuroleptic malignant syndrome (NMS), impairment of temperature regulation, lowering of seizures threshold, discoloration of skin (blue-gray), galactorrhea, priapism, agranulocytosis, leukopenia, thrombocytopenia, cholestatic jaundice, hepatotoxicity, cornea and lens changes

Overdosage/Toxicology

Symptoms of overdose include deep sleep, coma, extrapyramidal symptoms, abnormal involuntary muscle movements, hypotension

Following initiation of essential overdose management, toxic symptom treatment and supportive treatment should be initiated. Hypotension usually responds to I.V. fluids or Trendelenburg positioning. If unresponsive to these measures, the use of a parenteral inotrope may be required (eg, norepinephrine 0.1-0.2 mcg/kg/minute titrated to response). Seizures commonly respond to diazepam (I.V. 5-10 mg bolus in adults every 15 minutes if needed up to a total of 30 mg; I.V. 0.25-0.4 mg/kg/dose up to a total of 10 mg in children) or to phenytoin or phenobarbital. Critical cardiac arrhythmias often respond to I.V. phenytoin (15 mg/kg up to 1 g), while other antiarrhythmics can be used. Extrapyramidal symptoms (eg, dystonic reactions) may require management with diphenhydramine 1-2 mg/kg (adults) up to a maximum of 50 mg I.M. or I.V. slow push followed by a maintenance dose for 48-72 hours. When these reactions are unresponsive to diphenhydramine, benztropine mesylate I.V. 1-2 mg (adults) may be effective. These agents are generally effective within 2-5 minutes.

Drug Interactions Increased toxicity: Additive effects with other CNS depressants; anticonvulsants; epinephrine may cause hypotension

Stability Protect from light; clear or slightly yellow solutions may be used; **incompatible** when mixed with aminophylline, amphotericin B, ampicillin, calcium salts, cephalothin, foscarnet (Y-site), furosemide, hydrocortisone, hydromorphone, methohexital, midazolam, penicillin G, pentobarbital, phenobarbital, thiopental

Mechanism of Action Blocks postsynaptic mesolimbic dopaminergic D_1 and D_2 receptors in the brain, including the medullary chemoreceptor trigger zone; exhibits a strong alpha-adrenergic and anticholinergic blocking effect and depresses the release of hypothalamic and hypophyseal hormones; believed to depress the reticular activating system, thus affecting basal metabolism, body temperature, wakefulness, vasomotor tone and emesis

Pharmacodynamics/Kinetics

Onset of effect: Oral: Within 30-40 minutes; I.M.: Within 10-20 minutes; Rectal: Within 60 minutes

Duration: Persists longest with I.M. and oral extended-release doses (12 hours); shortest following rectal and immediate release oral administration (3-4 hours)

Distribution: Crosses the placenta; appears in breast milk

Metabolism: Hepatic

Half-life: 23 hours

Elimination: Primarily by hepatic metabolism

Usual Dosage

Antiemetic: Children:

Oral, rectal:

>10 kg: 0.4 mg/kg/24 hours in 3-4 divided doses; **or**

9-14 kg: 2.5 mg every 12-24 hours as needed; maximum: 7.5 mg/day

14-18 kg: 2.5 mg every 8-12 hours as needed; maximum: 10 mg/day

18-39 kg: 2.5 mg every 8 hours or 5 mg every 12 hours as needed; maximum: 15 mg/day

I.M.: 0.1-0.15 mg/kg/dose; usual: 0.13 mg/kg/dose; change to oral as soon as possible

I.V.: Not recommended in children <10 kg or <2 years

Antiemetic: Adults:
Oral: 5-10 mg 3-4 times/day; usual maximum: 40 mg/day
I.M.: 5-10 mg every 3-4 hours; usual maximum: 40 mg/day
I.V.: 2.5-10 mg; maximum 10 mg/dose or 40 mg/day; may repeat dose every 3-4 hours as needed
Rectal: 25 mg twice daily
Antipsychotic:
Children 2-12 years:
Oral, rectal: 2.5 mg 2-3 times/day; increase dosage as needed to maximum daily dose of 20 mg for 2-5 years and 25 mg for 6-12 years
I.M.: 0.13 mg/kg/dose; change to oral as soon as possible
Adults:
Oral: 5-10 mg 3-4 times/day; doses up to 150 mg/day may be required in some patients for treatment of severe disturbances
I.M.: 10-20 mg every 4-6 hours may be required in some patients for treatment of severe disturbances; change to oral as soon as possible
Dementia behavior (nonpsychotic): Elderly: Initial: 2.5-5 mg 1-2 times/day; increase dose at 4- to 7-day intervals by 2.5-5 mg/day; increase dosing intervals (twice daily, 3 times/day, etc) as necessary to control response or side effects; maximum daily dose should probably not exceed 75 mg in elderly; gradual increases (titration) may prevent some side effects or decrease their severity
Hemodialysis: Not dialyzable (0% to 5%)
Administration Prochlorperazine may be administered I.M. or I.V.
I.M. should be administered into the upper outer quadrant of the buttock
I.V. may be administered IVP or IVPB
IVP should be administered at a concentration of 1 mg/mL at a rate of 1 mg/minute
Test Interactions False-positives for phenylketonuria, urinary amylase, uroporphyrins, urobilinogen
Patient Information May cause drowsiness, impair judgment and coordination; may cause photosensitivity; avoid excessive sunlight; notify physician of involuntary movements or feelings of restlessness
Nursing Implications Avoid skin contact with oral solution or injection, contact dermatitis has occurred; observe for extrapyramidal symptoms
Additional Information
Prochlorperazine: Compazine® suppository
Prochlorperazine edisylate: Compazine® oral solution and injection
Prochlorperazine maleate: Compazine® capsule and tablet
Dosage Forms
Capsule, sustained action, as maleate: 10 mg, 15 mg, 30 mg
Injection, as edisylate: 5 mg/mL (2 mL, 10 mL)
Suppository, rectal: 2.5 mg, 5 mg, 25 mg (12/box)
Syrup, as edisylate: 5 mg/5 mL (120 mL)
Tablet, as maleate: 5 mg, 10 mg, 25 mg

◆ **Prochlorperazine Edisylate** see Prochlorperazine on page 973
◆ **Prochlorperazine Maleate** see Prochlorperazine on page 973
◆ **Procort® [OTC]** see Hydrocortisone on page 579
◆ **Procrit®** see Epoetin Alfa on page 418
◆ **Proctocort™** see Hydrocortisone on page 579
◆ **Proctofene** see Fenofibrate on page 472
◆ **Proctofoam®-HC** see Pramoxine and Hydrocortisone on page 958
◆ **Procyclid** see Procyclidine on this page

Procyclidine (proe SYE kli deen)

U.S. Brand Names Kemadrin®
Canadian Brand Names PMS-Procyclidine; Procyclid
Synonyms Procyclidine Hydrochloride
Therapeutic Category Anticholinergic Agent; Anti-Parkinson's Agent
Use Relieves symptoms of parkinsonian syndrome and drug-induced extrapyramidal symptoms
Pregnancy Risk Factor C
Contraindications Angle-closure glaucoma; safe use in children not established
Warnings/Precautions Use with caution in hot weather or during exercise. Elderly patients frequently develop increased sensitivity and require strict dosage regulation - side effects may be more severe in elderly patients with atherosclerotic changes. Use with caution in patients with tachycardia, cardiac arrhythmias, hypertension, hypotension, prostatic hypertrophy (especially in the elderly) or any tendency toward urinary retention, liver or kidney disorders and obstructive disease of the GI or GU tract. When given in large doses or to susceptible patients, may cause weakness and inability to move particular muscle groups.
Adverse Reactions
>10%:
Dermatologic: Dry skin
Gastrointestinal: Constipation, xerostomia, dry throat
Respiratory: Dry nose
Miscellaneous: Diaphoresis (decreased)
1% to 10%:
Dermatologic: Increased sensitivity to light
Endocrine & metabolic: Decreased flow of breast milk
(Continued)

Procyclidine (Continued)

Gastrointestinal: Dysphagia

<1%: Orthostatic hypotension, ventricular fibrillation, tachycardia, palpitations, confusion, drowsiness, headache, loss of memory, fatigue, ataxia, rash, bloated feeling, nausea, vomiting, dysuria, weakness, increased intraocular pain, blurred vision

Overdosage/Toxicology

Symptoms of overdose include disorientation, hallucinations, delusions, blurred vision, dysphagia, absent bowel sounds, hyperthermia, hypertension, urinary retention

Anticholinergic toxicity is caused by strong binding of the drug to cholinergic receptors. Anticholinesterase inhibitors reduce acetylcholinesterase, the enzyme that breaks down acetylcholine and thereby allows acetylcholine to accumulate and compete for receptor binding with the offending anticholinergic. For anticholinergic overdose with severe life-threatening symptoms, physostigmine 1-2 mg (0.5 mg or 0.02 mg/kg for children) S.C. or I.V., slowly may be given to reverse these effects.

Drug Interactions

Decreased effect of psychotropics

Increased toxicity with phenothiazines, meperidine, TCAs

Mechanism of Action Thought to act by blocking excess acetylcholine at cerebral synapses; many of its effects are due to its pharmacologic similarities with atropine

Pharmacodynamics/Kinetics

Onset of effect: Oral: Within 30-40 minutes

Duration: 4-6 hours

Usual Dosage Adults: Oral: 2.5 mg 3 times/day after meals; if tolerated, gradually increase dose, maximum of 20 mg/day if necessary

Dosing adjustment in hepatic impairment: Decrease dose to a twice daily dosing regimen

Dietary Considerations Alcohol: Avoid use

Patient Information Take after meals; do not discontinue drug abruptly; notify physician if adverse GI effects, fever or heat intolerance occurs; may cause drowsiness; avoid alcohol; adequate fluid intake or sugar free gum or hard candy may help dry mouth; adequate fluid and exercise may help constipation

Dosage Forms Tablet, as hydrochloride: 5 mg

- ◆ **Procyclidine Hydrochloride** see Procyclidine on previous page
- ◆ **Procytox®** see Cyclophosphamide on page 305
- ◆ **Prodiem® Plain** see Psyllium on page 994
- ◆ **Prodium® [OTC]** see Phenazopyridine on page 910
- ◆ **Profasi® HP** see Chorionic Gonadotropin on page 258
- ◆ **Profenal®** see Suprofen on page 1101
- ◆ **Profilate® OSD** see Antihemophilic Factor (Human) on page 88
- ◆ **Profilate® SD** see Antihemophilic Factor (Human) on page 88
- ◆ **Profilnine® SD** see Factor IX Complex (Human) on page 464
- ◆ **Progestasert®** see Progesterone on this page

Progesterone (proe JES ter one)

Related Information

Depression Disorders and Treatments on page 1465

U.S. Brand Names Crinone™ Vaginal Gel; Progestasert®

Canadian Brand Names PMS-Progesterone; Progesterone Oil

Synonyms Pregnenedione; Progestin

Therapeutic Category Progestin

Use Intrauterine contraception in women who have had at least 1 child, are in a stable, mutually monogamous relationship, and have no history of pelvic inflammatory disease; amenorrhea; functional uterine bleeding; replacement therapy

Pregnancy Risk Factor X

Contraindications Pregnancy, thrombophlebitis, undiagnosed vaginal bleeding, hypersensitivity to progesterone or any component, carcinoma of the breast, cerebral apoplexy

Warnings/Precautions Use with caution in patients with impaired liver function, depression, diabetes, and epilepsy; use of any progestin during the first 4 months of pregnancy is not recommended; monitor closely for loss of vision, proptosis, diplopia, migraine, and signs and symptoms of embolic disorders. Not a progestin of choice in the elderly for hormonal cycling.

Adverse Reactions

Intrauterine device:

>10%:

Cardiovascular: Edema

Endocrine & metabolic: Breakthrough bleeding, spotting, changes in menstrual flow, amenorrhea

Gastrointestinal: Anorexia

Neuromuscular & skeletal: Weakness

1% to 10%:

Cardiovascular: Embolism, central thrombosis

Central nervous system: Mental depression, fever, insomnia

Dermatologic: Melasma or chloasma, allergic rash with or without pruritus

Endocrine: Changes in cervical erosion and secretions, increased breast tenderness

Gastrointestinal: Weight gain or loss

Hepatic: Cholestatic jaundice

Injection (I.M.):
>10% Local: Pain at injection site
1% to 10%: Local: Thrombophlebitis

Overdosage/Toxicology
Toxicity is unlikely following single exposures of excessive doses
Supportive treatment is adequate in most cases

Drug Interactions CYP3A3/4 enzyme substrate; CYP3A3/4 enzyme inducer
Decreased effect: Aminoglutethimide may decrease effect by increasing hepatic metabolism

Mechanism of Action Natural steroid hormone that induces secretory changes in the endometrium, promotes mammary gland development, relaxes uterine smooth muscle, blocks follicular maturation and ovulation, and maintains pregnancy

Pharmacodynamics/Kinetics
Duration of action: 24 hours
Protein binding: 96% to 99%
Metabolism: Liver
Half-life: 5 minutes
Elimination: 50% to 60% renal; ~10% bile and feces

Usual Dosage Adults:
Amenorrhea: I.M.: 5-10 mg/day for 6-8 consecutive days
Functional uterine bleeding: I.M.: 5-10 mg/day for 6 doses
Contraception: Female: Intrauterine device: Insert a single system into the uterine cavity; contraceptive effectiveness is retained for 1 year and system must be replaced 1 year after insertion
Replacement therapy: Gel: Administer 90 mg once daily in women who require progesterone supplementation

Monitoring Parameters Before starting therapy, a physical exam including the breasts and pelvis are recommended, also a PAP smear; signs or symptoms of depression, glucose in diabetics

Test Interactions Thyroid function, metyrapone, liver function, coagulation tests, endocrine function tests

Patient Information Notify physician if sudden loss of vision or migraine headache occur or if you suspect you may have become pregnant; may cause photosensitivity, wear protective clothing or sunscreen

Nursing Implications Patients should receive a copy of the patient labeling for the drug; administer deep I.M. only; monitor patient closely for loss of vision, sudden onset of proptosis, diplopia, migraine, and signs and symptoms of embolic disorders

Dosage Forms
Gel, vaginal: 8% (90 mg) Single-use disposable applicator
Injection, in oil: 50 mg/mL (10 mL)
Intrauterine system, reservoir: 38 mg in silicone fluid

♦ **Progesterone Oil** see Progesterone on previous page

♦ **Progestin** see Progesterone on previous page

♦ **Proglycem® Oral** see Diazoxide on page 347

♦ **Prograf®** see Tacrolimus on page 1103

♦ **ProHIBiT®** see Haemophilus b Conjugate Vaccine on page 554

♦ **Pro-Indo®** see Indomethacin on page 609

♦ **Prolamine® [OTC]** see Phenylpropanolamine on page 919

♦ **Proleukin®** see Aldesleukin on page 37

♦ **Prolixin Decanoate® Injection** see Fluphenazine on page 504

♦ **Prolixin Enanthate® Injection** see Fluphenazine on page 504

♦ **Prolixin® Injection** see Fluphenazine on page 504

♦ **Prolixin® Oral** see Fluphenazine on page 504

♦ **Proloprim®** see Trimethoprim on page 1184

♦ **Pro-Lorazepam®** see Lorazepam on page 694

Promazine (PROE ma zeen)

Related Information
Antipsychotic Agents Comparison on page 1305

U.S. Brand Names Sparine®

Synonyms Promazine Hydrochloride

Therapeutic Category Antiemetic; Antipsychotic Agent; Phenothiazine Derivative

Use Management of manifestations of psychotic disorders; depressive neurosis; alcohol withdrawal; nausea and vomiting; nonpsychotic symptoms associated with dementia in elderly; Tourette's syndrome; Huntington's chorea; spasmodic torticollis and Reye's syndrome

Pregnancy Risk Factor C

Contraindications Hypersensitivity to promazine or any component; severe CNS depression, cross-sensitivity to other phenothiazines may exist; avoid use in patients with narrow-angle glaucoma, blood dyscrasias, severe liver or cardiac disease; subcortical brain damage; circulatory collapse; severe hypotension or hypertension

Warnings/Precautions
Tardive dyskinesia: Prevalence rate may be 40% in elderly; development of the syndrome and the irreversible nature are proportional to duration and total cumulative dose over time. May be reversible if diagnosed early in therapy.
(Continued)

Promazine *(Continued)*

Extrapyramidal reactions are more common in elderly with up to 50% developing these reactions after 60 years of age. These reactions may be more common in dementia patients.

Drug-induced **Parkinson's syndrome** occurs often. **Akathisia** is the most common extrapyramidal reaction in elderly.

Increased confusion, memory loss, psychotic behavior, and agitation frequently occur as a consequence of anticholinergic effects

Orthostatic hypotension is due to alpha-receptor blockade, the elderly are at greater risk for orthostatic hypotension

Antipsychotic associated sedation in nonpsychotic patients is extremely unpleasant due to feelings of depersonalization, derealization, and dysphoria

Life-threatening arrhythmias have occurred at therapeutic doses of antipsychotics; use with caution in patients with narrow-angle glaucoma, severe liver disease or severe cardiac disease

Adverse Reactions

>10%:

Cardiovascular: Hypotension, orthostatic hypotension

Central nervous system: Pseudoparkinsonism, akathisia, dystonias, tardive dyskinesia (persistent), dizziness

Gastrointestinal: Constipation

Respiratory: Nasal congestion

Miscellaneous: Diaphoresis (decreased)

1% to 10%:

Dermatologic: Increased sensitivity to sun, rash

Endocrine & metabolic: Changes in menstrual cycle, changes in libido, breast pain

Gastrointestinal: Weight gain, nausea, vomiting, stomach pain

Genitourinary: Dysuria, ejaculatory disturbances

Neuromuscular & skeletal: Trembling of fingers

<1%: Neuroleptic malignant syndrome (NMS), impairment of temperature regulation, lowering of seizures threshold, discoloration of skin (blue-gray), galactorrhea, priapism, agranulocytosis, leukopenia, cholestatic jaundice, hepatotoxicity, cornea and lens changes, pigmentary retinopathy

Overdosage/Toxicology

Symptoms of overdose include deep sleep, coma, extrapyramidal symptoms, abnormal involuntary muscle movements, hypotension

Following initiation of essential overdose management, toxic symptom treatment and supportive treatment should be initiated. Hypotension usually responds to I.V. fluids or Trendelenburg positioning. If unresponsive to these measures, the use of a parenteral inotrope may be required (eg, norepinephrine 0.1-0.2 mcg/kg/minute titrated to response). Seizures commonly respond to diazepam (I.V. 5-10 mg bolus in adults every 15 minutes if needed up to a total of 30 mg; I.V. 0.25-0.4 mg/kg/dose up to a total of 10 mg in children) or to phenytoin or phenobarbital. Critical cardiac arrhythmias often respond to I.V. phenytoin (15 mg/kg up to 1 g), while other antiarrhythmics can be used. Neuroleptics often cause extrapyramidal symptoms (eg, dystonic reactions) requiring management with diphenhydramine 1-2 mg/kg (adults) up to a maximum of 50 mg I.M. or I.V. slow push followed by a maintenance dose for 48-72 hours. When these reactions are unresponsive to diphenhydramine, benztropine mesylate I.V. 1-2 mg (adults) may be effective. These agents are generally effective within 2-5 minutes.

Stability Protect all dosage forms from light, clear or slightly yellow solutions may be used; should be dispensed in amber or opaque vials/bottles. Solutions may be diluted or mixed with fruit juices or other liquids, but must be administered immediately after mixing

Injection: **Incompatible** when mixed with aminophylline, dimenhydrinate, methohexital, nafcillin, penicillin G, pentobarbital, phenobarbital, sodium bicarbonate, thiopental

Mechanism of Action Blocks postsynaptic mesolimbic dopaminergic D_1 and D_2 receptors in the brain; exhibits a strong alpha-adrenergic blocking and anticholinergic effect, depresses the release of hypothalamic and hypophyseal hormones; believed to depress the reticular activating system thus affecting basal metabolism, body temperature, wakefulness, vasomotor tone, and emesis

Pharmacodynamics/Kinetics The specific pharmacokinetics of promazine are poorly established but probably resemble those of other phenothiazines.

Absorption: Phenothiazines are only partially absorbed; great variability in plasma levels resulting from a given dose

Metabolism: Extensively in the liver

Half-life: Most phenothiazines have long half-lives in the range of 24 hours or more

Usual Dosage Oral, I.M.:

Children >12 years: Antipsychotic: 10-25 mg every 4-6 hours

Adults:

Psychosis: 10-200 mg every 4-6 hours not to exceed 1000 mg/day

Antiemetic: 25-50 mg every 4-6 hours as needed

Hemodialysis: Not dialyzable (0% to 5%)

Administration I.M. injections should be deep injections; if giving I.V., dilute to at least 25 mg/mL and administer slowly

Test Interactions ↑ cholesterol (S), ↑ glucose; ↓ uric acid (S)

Patient Information May cause drowsiness, impair judgment and coordination; may cause photosensitivity; avoid excessive sunlight; notify physician of involuntary movements or feelings of restlessness

Nursing Implications Watch for hypotension

Dosage Forms
Injection, as hydrochloride: 25 mg/mL (10 mL); 50 mg/mL (1 mL, 2 mL, 10 mL)
Tablet, as hydrochloride: 25 mg, 50 mg, 100 mg

♦ **Promazine Hydrochloride** *see* Promazine *on page 977*

♦ **Prometa®** *see* Metaproterenol *on page 739*

Promethazine (proe METH a zeen)

U.S. Brand Names Anergan®; Phenazine®; Phenergan®; Prorex®

Synonyms Promethazine Hydrochloride

Therapeutic Category Antihistamine, H₁ Blocker; Phenothiazine Derivative; Sedative

Use Symptomatic treatment of various allergic conditions, antiemetic, motion sickness, and as a sedative

Pregnancy Risk Factor C

Pregnancy/Breast-Feeding Implications
Clinical effects on the fetus: Crosses the placenta. Possible respiratory depression if drug is administered near time of delivery; behavioral changes, EEG alterations, impaired platelet aggregation reported with use during labor. Available evidence with use of occasional low doses suggests safe use during pregnancy.
Breast-feeding/lactation: No data available. American Academy of Pediatrics makes NO RECOMMENDATION.

Contraindications Hypersensitivity to promethazine or any component; narrow-angle glaucoma

Warnings/Precautions Do not administer S.C. or intra-arterially, necrotic lesions may occur; injection may contain sulfites which may cause allergic reactions in some patients; use with caution in patients with cardiovascular disease, impaired liver function, asthma, sleep apnea, seizures. Rapid I.V. administration may produce a transient fall in blood pressure, rate of administration should not exceed 25 mg/minute; slow I.V. administration may produce a slightly elevated blood pressure. Because promethazine is a phenothiazine (and can, therefore, cause side effects such as extrapyramidal symptoms), it is not considered an antihistamine of choice in the elderly.

Adverse Reactions
>10%:
Central nervous system: Slight to moderate drowsiness
Respiratory: Thickening of bronchial secretions
1% to 10%:
Central nervous system: Headache, fatigue, nervousness, dizziness
Gastrointestinal: Xerostomia, abdominal pain, nausea, diarrhea, increased appetite, weight gain
Neuromuscular & skeletal: Arthralgia
Respiratory: Pharyngitis
<1%: Thrombocytopenia, jaundice, tachycardia, bradycardia, palpitations, hypotension, sedation (pronounced), confusion, excitation, extrapyramidal reactions with high doses, dystonia, faintness with I.V. administration, depression, insomnia, photosensitivity, rash, angioedema, urinary retention, hepatitis, tremor, paresthesia, myalgia, blurred vision, irregular respiration, bronchospasm, epistaxis, allergic reactions

Overdosage/Toxicology
Symptoms of overdose include CNS depression, respiratory depression, possible CNS stimulation, dry mouth, fixed and dilated pupils, hypotension
Following initiation of essential overdose management, toxic symptom treatment and supportive treatment should be initiated. Hypotension usually responds to I.V. fluids or Trendelenburg positioning. If unresponsive to these measures, norepinephrine 0.1-0.2 mcg/kg/minute titrated to response may be tried. Seizures commonly respond to diazepam (I.V. 5-10 mg bolus in adults every 15 minutes if needed up to a total of 30 mg; I.V. 0.25-0.4 mg/kg/dose up to a total of 10 mg in children) or to phenytoin or phenobarbital. Critical cardiac arrhythmias often respond to I.V. phenytoin (15 mg/kg up to 1 g), while other antiarrhythmics can be used. Neuroleptics often cause extrapyramidal symptoms (eg, dystonic reactions) requiring management with diphenhydramine 1-2 mg/kg (adults) up to a maximum of 50 mg I.M. or I.V. slow push followed by a maintenance dose for 48-72 hours. When these reactions are unresponsive to diphenhydramine, benztropine mesylate I.V. 1-2 mg (adults) may be effective. These agents are generally effective within 2-5 minutes.

Drug Interactions CYP2D6 enzyme substrate
Increased toxicity: Epinephrine should not be used together with promethazine since blood pressure may decrease further; additive effects with other CNS depressants

Stability Protect from light and from freezing; **compatible** (when comixed in the same syringe) with atropine, chlorpromazine, diphenhydramine, droperidol, fentanyl, glycopyrrolate, hydromorphone, hydroxyzine hydrochloride, meperidine, midazolam, nalbuphine, pentazocine, prochlorperazine, scopolamine; **incompatible** when mixed with aminophylline, cefoperazone (Y-site), chloramphenicol, dimenhydrinate (same syringe), foscarnet (Y-site), furosemide, heparin, hydrocortisone, methohexital, penicillin G, pentobarbital, phenobarbital, thiopental

Mechanism of Action Blocks postsynaptic mesolimbic dopaminergic receptors in the brain; exhibits a strong alpha-adrenergic blocking effect and depresses the release of hypothalamic and hypophyseal hormones; competes with histamine for the H₁-receptor; reduces stimuli to the brainstem reticular system

Pharmacodynamics/Kinetics
Onset of effect: I.V.: Within 20 minutes (3-5 minutes with I.V. injection)
Duration: 2-6 hours
(Continued)

979

Promethazine *(Continued)*

Metabolism: In the liver

Elimination: Principally as inactive metabolites in urine and in feces

Usual Dosage

Children:

Antihistamine: Oral, rectal: 0.1 mg/kg/dose every 6 hours during the day and 0.5 mg/kg/dose at bedtime as needed

Antiemetic: Oral, I.M., I.V., rectal: 0.25-1 mg/kg 4-6 times/day as needed

Motion sickness: Oral, rectal: 0.5 mg/kg/dose 30 minutes to 1 hour before departure, then every 12 hours as needed

Sedation: Oral, I.M., I.V., rectal: 0.5-1 mg/kg/dose every 6 hours as needed

Adults:

Antihistamine (including allergic reactions to blood or plasma):

Oral, rectal: 12.5 mg 3 times/day and 25 mg at bedtime

I.M., I.V.: 25 mg, may repeat in 2 hours when necessary; switch to oral route as soon as feasible

Antiemetic: Oral, I.M., I.V., rectal: 12.5-25 mg every 4 hours as needed

Motion sickness: Oral, rectal: 25 mg 30-60 minutes before departure, then every 12 hours as needed

Sedation: Oral, I.M., I.V., rectal: 25-50 mg/dose

Hemodialysis: Not dialyzable (0% to 5%)

Administration Avoid I.V. use; if necessary, may dilute to a maximum concentration of 25 mg/mL and infuse at a maximum rate of 25 mg/minute; rapid I.V. administration may produce a transient fall in blood pressure

Test Interactions Alters the flare response in intradermal allergen tests

Patient Information May cause drowsiness, impair judgment and coordination; may cause photosensitivity; avoid excessive sunlight; notify physician of involuntary movements or feelings of restlessness

Dosage Forms

Injection, as hydrochloride: 25 mg/mL (1 mL, 10 mL); 50 mg/mL (1 mL, 10 mL)

Suppository, rectal, as hydrochloride: 12.5 mg, 25 mg, 50 mg

Syrup, as hydrochloride: 6.25 mg/5 mL (5 mL, 120 mL, 240 mL, 480 mL, 4000 mL); 25 mg/5 mL (120 mL, 480 mL, 4000 mL)

Tablet, as hydrochloride: 12.5 mg, 25 mg, 50 mg

Promethazine and Codeine *(proe METH a zeen & KOE deen)*

U.S. Brand Names Phenergan® With Codeine; Pherazine® With Codeine; Prothazine-DC®

Therapeutic Category Antihistamine/Antitussive

Dosage Forms Syrup: Promethazine hydrochloride 6.25 mg and codeine phosphate 10 mg per 5 mL (120 mL, 180 mL, 473 mL)

Promethazine and Dextromethorphan

(proe METH a zeen & deks troe meth OR fan)

U.S. Brand Names Phenameth® DM; Phenergan® With Dextromethorphan; Pherazine® w/DM

Therapeutic Category Antihistamine/Antitussive

Dosage Forms Syrup: Promethazine hydrochloride 6.25 mg and dextromethorphan hydrobromide 15 mg per 5 mL with alcohol 7% (120 mL, 480 mL, 4000 mL)

Promethazine and Phenylephrine *(proe METH a zeen & fen il EF rin)*

U.S. Brand Names Phenergan® VC Syrup; Promethazine VC Plain Syrup; Promethazine VC Syrup; Prometh VC Plain Liquid

Therapeutic Category Antihistamine/Decongestant Combination

Dosage Forms Liquid: Promethazine hydrochloride 6.25 mg and phenylephrine hydrochloride 5 mg per 5 mL (120 mL, 240 mL, 473 mL)

♦ **Promethazine Hydrochloride** *see* Promethazine *on previous page*

Promethazine, Phenylephrine, and Codeine

(proe METH a zeen, fen il EF rin, & KOE deen)

U.S. Brand Names Phenergan® VC With Codeine; Pherazine® VC w/ Codeine; Promethist® With Codeine; Prometh® VC With Codeine

Therapeutic Category Antihistamine/Decongestant/Antitussive

Dosage Forms Liquid: Promethazine hydrochloride 6.25 mg, phenylephrine hydrochloride 5 mg, and codeine phosphate 10 mg per 5 mL with alcohol 7% (120 mL, 240 mL, 480 mL, 4000 mL)

♦ **Promethazine VC Plain Syrup** *see* Promethazine and Phenylephrine *on this page*

♦ **Promethazine VC Syrup** *see* Promethazine and Phenylephrine *on this page*

♦ **Promethist® With Codeine** *see* Promethazine, Phenylephrine, and Codeine *on this page*

♦ **Prometh VC Plain Liquid** *see* Promethazine and Phenylephrine *on this page*

♦ **Prometh® VC With Codeine** *see* Promethazine, Phenylephrine, and Codeine *on this page*

♦ **Promine®** *see* Procainamide *on page 968*

♦ **Promit®** *see* Dextran 1 *on page 342*

♦ **Pronestyl®** *see* Procainamide *on page 968*

♦ **Pronto® Shampoo [OTC]** *see* Pyrethrins *on page 996*

♦ **Propacet®** *see* Propoxyphene and Acetaminophen *on page 986*

♦ **Propaderm®** *see* Beclomethasone *on page 128*

Propafenone (proe pa FEEN one)

Related Information
Antiarrhythmic Drugs Comparison *on page 1297*

U.S. Brand Names Rythmol®

Synonyms Propafenone Hydrochloride

Therapeutic Category Antiarrhythmic Agent, Class I-C

Use Life-threatening ventricular arrhythmias

Unlabeled use: Supraventricular tachycardias, including those patients with Wolff-Parkinson-White syndrome

Pregnancy Risk Factor C

Contraindications Hypersensitivity to propafenone or any component; uncontrolled congestive heart failure; bronchospastic disorders; cardiogenic shock, conduction disorders (A-V block, sick-sinus syndrome), bradycardia

Warnings/Precautions Until evidence to the contrary, propafenone should be considered acceptable only for the treatment of life-threatening arrhythmias; propafenone may cause new or worsened arrhythmias, worsen CHF, decrease A-V conduction and alter pacemaker thresholds; use with caution in patients with recent myocardial infarction, congestive heart failure, hepatic or renal dysfunction; elderly may be at greater risk for toxicity

Adverse Reactions
>10%: Central nervous system: Dizziness (6.5%), drowsiness

1% to 10%:
Cardiovascular: A-V block (first (4.5%) and second (1.2%) degree), cardiac conduction disturbances (eg, bundle-branch block (1.2%)), palpitations (2% to 4%), congestive heart failure, angina (1.2%), bradycardia

Central nervous system: Headache (4.5%), anxiety (2%), loss of balance (1.2%)

Gastrointestinal: Abnormal taste (7.3%), constipation (4%), nausea (1.2%), vomiting (2.8%), abdominal pain, dyspepsia, anorexia (1.6%), flatulence (1.2%), diarrhea (1.2%), xerostomia (2%)

Ocular: Blurred vision (2%)

Respiratory: Dyspnea (2%)

<1%: New or worsened arrhythmias (proarrhythmic effect), bundle-branch block, abnormal speech, vision, or dreams; leukopenia, thrombocytopenia, agranulocytosis, paresthesias, numbness, (+) ANA titers

Overdosage/Toxicology
Has a narrow therapeutic index and severe toxicity may occur slightly above the therapeutic range, especially if combined with other antiarrhythmic drugs. Acute single ingestion of twice the daily therapeutic dose is life-threatening. Symptoms of overdose include increases in P-R, QRS, Q-T intervals and amplitude of the T wave, A-V block, bradycardia, hypotension, ventricular arrhythmias (monomorphic or polymorphic ventricular tachycardia), and asystole; other symptoms include dizziness, blurred vision, headache, and GI upset.

Treatment is supportive, using conventional treatment (fluids, positioning, anticonvulsants, antiarrhythmics). **Note:** Type Ia antiarrhythmic agents should not be used to treat cardiotoxicity caused by type 1c drugs; sodium bicarbonate may reverse QRS prolongation, bradycardia and hypotension; ventricular pacing may be needed; hemodialysis only of possible benefit for tocainide or flecainide overdose in patients with renal failure.

Drug Interactions CYP1A2, 2D6, 3A3/4 enzyme substrate; CYP2D6 enzyme inhibitor
Decreased levels with rifampin

Increased levels/toxicity with cimetidine, quinidine, and beta-blockers; avoid use with ritonavir due to increased risk of propafenone toxicity especially cardiotoxicity

Increased effect/levels of warfarin, beta-blockers metabolized by the liver, local anesthetics, cyclosporine, and digoxin (**Note:** Reduce dose of digoxin by 25%)

Mechanism of Action Propafenone is a 1C antiarrhythmic agent which possesses local anesthetic properties, blocks the fast inward sodium current, and slows the rate of increase of the action potential. prolongs conduction and refractoriness in all areas of the myocardium, with a slightly more pronounced effect on intraventricular conduction; it prolongs effective refractory period, reduces spontaneous automaticity and exhibits some beta-blockade activity.

Pharmacodynamics/Kinetics
Absorption: Well absorbed

Metabolism: Two genetically determined metabolism groups exist: fast or slow metabolizers; 10% of Caucasians are slow metabolizers

Half-life after a single dose (100-300 mg): 2-8 hours; half-life after chronic dosing ranges from 10-32 hours

Time to peak: Peak levels occur in 2 hours with a 150 mg dose and 3 hours after a 300 mg dose; this agent exhibits nonlinear pharmacokinetics; when dose is increased from 300 mg to 900 mg/day, serum concentrations increase tenfold; this nonlinearity is thought to be due to saturable first-pass hepatic enzyme metabolism

Usual Dosage Adults: Oral: 150 mg every 8 hours, increase at 3- to 4-day intervals up to 300 mg every 8 hours. **Note:** Patients who exhibit significant widening of QRS complex or second or third degree A-V block may need dose reduction.

Dosing adjustment in hepatic impairment: Reduction is necessary
(Continued)

Propafenone *(Continued)*

Monitoring Parameters EKG, blood pressure, pulse (particularly at initiation of therapy)

Patient Information Take dose the same way each day, either with or without food; do not double the next dose if present dose is missed; do not discontinue drug or change dose without advice of physician; report any severe or persistent fatigue, sore throat, or any unusual bleeding or bruising; may cause drowsiness and impair coordination and judgment

Nursing Implications Patients should be on a cardiac monitor during initiation of therapy or when dosage is increased; monitor heart sounds and pulses for rate, rhythm and quality

Dosage Forms Tablet, as hydrochloride: 150 mg, 225 mg, 300 mg

♦ **Propafenone Hydrochloride** *see* Propafenone *on previous page*

♦ **Propagest® [OTC]** *see* Phenylpropanolamine *on page 919*

♦ **Propanthel™** *see* Propantheline *on this page*

Propantheline *(proe PAN the leen)*

U.S. Brand Names Pro-Banthine®

Canadian Brand Names Propanthel™

Therapeutic Category Anticholinergic Agent; Antispasmodic Agent, Gastrointestinal; Antispasmodic Agent, Urinary

Use Adjunctive treatment of peptic ulcer, irritable bowel syndrome, pancreatitis, ureteral and urinary bladder spasm; reduce duodenal motility during diagnostic radiologic procedures

Pregnancy Risk Factor C

Contraindications Narrow-angle glaucoma, known hypersensitivity to propantheline; ulcerative colitis; toxic megacolon; obstructive disease of the GI or urinary tract

Usual Dosage Oral:

Antisecretory:

Children: 1-2 mg/kg/day in 3-4 divided doses

Adults: 15 mg 3 times/day before meals or food and 30 mg at bedtime

Elderly: 7.5 mg 3 times/day before meals and at bedtime

Antispasmodic:

Children: 2-3 mg/kg/day in divided doses every 4-6 hours and at bedtime

Adults: 15 mg 3 times/day before meals or food and 30 mg at bedtime

Additional Information Complete prescribing information for this medication should be consulted for additional detail

Dosage Forms Tablet, as bromide: 7.5 mg, 15 mg

Proparacaine *(proe PAR a kane)*

U.S. Brand Names AK-Taine®; Alcaine®; I-Paracaine®; Ophthetic®

Canadian Brand Names Diocaine

Synonyms Proparacaine Hydrochloride; Proxymetacaine

Therapeutic Category Local Anesthetic, Ophthalmic

Use Anesthesia for tonometry, gonioscopy; suture removal from cornea; removal of corneal foreign body; cataract extraction, glaucoma surgery; short operative procedure involving the cornea and conjunctiva

Pregnancy Risk Factor C

Contraindications Known hypersensitivity to proparacaine

Warnings/Precautions Use with caution in patients with cardiac disease, hyperthyroidism; for typical ophthalmic use only; prolonged use not recommended

Adverse Reactions

1% to 10%: Local: Burning, stinging, redness

<1%: Arrhythmias, CNS depression, allergic contact dermatitis, irritation, sensitization, lacrimation, keratitis, iritis, erosion of the corneal epithelium, conjunctival congestion and hemorrhage, corneal opacification, blurred vision, diaphoresis (increased)

Drug Interactions Increased effect of phenylephrine, tropicamide

Stability Store in tight, light-resistant containers

Mechanism of Action Prevents initiation and transmission of impulse at the nerve cell membrane by decreasing ion permeability through stabilizing

Pharmacodynamics/Kinetics

Onset of action: Within 20 seconds of instillation

Duration: 15-20 minutes

Usual Dosage Children and Adults:

Ophthalmic surgery: Instill 1 drop of 0.5% solution in eye every 5-10 minutes for 5-7 doses

Tonometry, gonioscopy, suture removal: Instill 1-2 drops of 0.5% solution in eye just prior to procedure

Patient Information May slow wound healing; use sparingly, avoid touching or rubbing the eye until anesthesia has worn off

Nursing Implications Do not use if discolored; protect eye from irritating chemicals, foreign bodies, and blink reflex; use eye patch if necessary

Dosage Forms Ophthalmic, solution, as hydrochloride: 0.5% (2 mL, 15 mL)

Proparacaine and Fluorescein (proe PAR a kane & FLURE e seen)

U.S. Brand Names Fluoracaine® Ophthalmic

Therapeutic Category Diagnostic Agent, Ophthalmic Dye; Local Anesthetic, Ester Derivative (Ophthalmic); Local Anesthetic, Ophthalmic

Use Anesthesia for tonometry, gonioscopy; suture removal from cornea; removal of corneal foreign body; cataract extraction, glaucoma surgery

Pregnancy Risk Factor C

Contraindications Known hypersensitivity to proparacaine or fluorescein or any component or ester-type local anesthetics

Warnings/Precautions Use with caution in patients with cardiac disease, hyperthyroidism; for topical ophthalmic use only; prolonged use not recommended

Adverse Reactions

1% to 10%: Local: Burning, stinging of eye

<1%: Allergic contact dermatitis, irritation, sensitization, erosion of the corneal epithelium, conjunctival congestion and hemorrhage, keratitis, iritis, corneal opacification

Stability Store in tight, light-resistant containers

Mechanism of Action Prevents initiation and transmission of impulse at the nerve cell membrane by decreasing ion permeability through stabilizing

Pharmacodynamics/Kinetics

Onset of action: Within 20 seconds of instillation

Duration: 15-20 minutes

Usual Dosage

Ophthalmic surgery: Children and Adults: Instill 1 drop in each eye every 5-10 minutes for 5-7 doses

Tonometry, gonioscopy, suture removal: Adults: Instill 1-2 drops in each eye just prior to procedure

Patient Information May slow wound healing; use sparingly, avoid touching or rubbing the eye until anesthesia has worn off

Nursing Implications Do not use if discolored; protect eye from irritating chemicals, foreign bodies, and blink reflex; use eye patch if necessary

Dosage Forms Solution: Proparacaine hydrochloride 0.5% and fluorescein sodium 0.25% (2 mL, 5 mL)

◆ **Proparacaine Hydrochloride** see Proparacaine on previous page

◆ **Propecia**® see Finasteride on page 484

◆ **Prophylaxis for Patients Exposed to Common Communicable Diseases** see page 1384

◆ **Propine**® **Ophthalmic** see Dipivefrin on page 376

◆ **Pro-Piroxicam**® see Piroxicam on page 935

◆ **Proplex**® **T** see Factor IX Complex (Human) on page 464

Propofol (PROE po fole)

U.S. Brand Names Diprivan®

Therapeutic Category General Anesthetic; Sedative

Use Induction or maintenance of anesthesia for inpatient or outpatient surgery; may be used (for patients >18 years of age who are intubated and mechanically ventilated) as an alternative to benzodiazepines for the treatment of agitation in the intensive care unit; pain should be treated with analgesic agents, propofol must be titrated separately from the analgesic agent; has demonstrated antiemetic properties in the postoperative setting

Pregnancy Risk Factor B

Contraindications

Absolute contraindications:

Patients with a hypersensitivity to propofol

Patients with a hypersensitivity to propofol's emulsion which contains soybean oil, egg phosphatide, and glycerol or any of the components

Patients who are not intubated or mechanically ventilated

Patients who are pregnant or nursing: Propofol is not recommended for obstetrics, including cesarian section deliveries. Propofol crosses the placenta and, therefore, may be associated with neonatal depression.

Relative contraindications:

Pediatric Intensive Care Unit patients: Safety and efficacy of propofol is not established

Patients with severe cardiac disease (ejection fraction <50%) or respiratory disease - propofol may have more profound adverse cardiovascular responses

Patients with a history of epilepsy or seizures

Patients with increased intracranial pressure or impaired cerebral circulation - substantial decreases in mean arterial pressure and subsequent decreases in cerebral perfusion pressure may occur

Patients with hyperlipidemia as evidenced by increased serum triglyceride levels or serum turbidity

Patients who are hypotensive, hypovolemic, or hemodynamically unstable

Warnings/Precautions Use slower rate of induction in the elderly; transient local pain may occur during I.V. injection; perioperative myoclonia has occurred; do not administer with blood or blood products through the same I.V. catheter; not for obstetrics, including cesarean section deliveries. Safety and effectiveness has not been established in children. Abrupt discontinuation prior to weaning or daily wake up assessments should be avoided. Abrupt discontinuation can result in rapid awakening, anxiety, agitation, and resistance to mechanical ventilation; not for use in neurosurgical anesthesia.

(Continued)

Propofol *(Continued)*

Adverse Reactions

>10%:

Cardiovascular: Hypotension, intravenous propofol produces a dose-related degree of hypotension and decrease in systemic vascular resistance which is not associated with a significant increase in heart rate or decrease in cardiac output

Local: Pain at injection site occurs at an incidence of 28.5% when administered into smaller veins of hand versus 6% when administered into antecubital veins

Respiratory: Apnea (incidence occurs in 50% to 84% of patients and may be dependent on premedication, speed of administration, dose and presence of hyperventilation and hyperoxia)

1% to 10%:

Anaphylaxis: Several cases of anaphylactic reactions have been reported with propofol

Central nervous system: Dizziness, fever, headache; although propofol has demonstrated anticonvulsant activity, several cases of propofol-induced seizures with opisthotonos have occurred

Gastrointestinal: Nausea, vomiting, abdominal cramps

Respiratory: Cough, apnea

Neuromuscular & skeletal: Twitching

Miscellaneous: Hiccups

Overdosage/Toxicology

Symptoms of overdose include hypotension, bradycardia, cardiovascular collapse

Treatment is symptomatic and supportive; hypotension usually responds to I.V. fluids and/or Trendelenburg positioning; parenteral inotropes may be needed

Drug Interactions

Increased toxicity:

Neuromuscular blockers:

Atracurium: Anaphylactoid reactions (including bronchospasm) have been reported in patients who have received concomitant atracurium and propofol

Vecuronium: Propofol may potentiate the neuromuscular blockade of vecuronium

Central nervous system depressants: Additive CNS depression and respiratory depression may necessitate dosage reduction when used with: Anesthetics, benzodiazepines, opiates, ethanol, narcotics, phenothiazines

Decreased effect: Theophylline: May antagonize the effect of propofol, requiring dosage increases

Stability

Do not use if there is evidence of separation of phases of emulsion

Store at room temperature 4°C to 22°C (40°F to 72°F), refrigeration is not recommended; protect from light

Propofol may be further diluted in dextrose 5% in water to a concentration ≥2 mg/mL and is stable for 8 hours at room temperature

Y-site **compatible** with D5LR, D5NS, D5W, LR, lidocaine

Soybean fat emulsion is used as a vehicle for propofol. This soybean fat emulsion contains no preservatives. **Strict aseptic technique must be maintained in handling because this vehicle is capable of supporting rapid bacterial growth.**

Mechanism of Action Propofol is a hindered phenolic compound with intravenous general anesthetic properties. The drug is unrelated to any of the currently used barbiturate, opioid, benzodiazepine, arylcyclohexylamine, or imidazole intravenous anesthetic agents.

Pharmacodynamics/Kinetics

Onset of anesthesia: Within 9-51 seconds (average 30 seconds) after bolus infusion (dose dependent)

Duration: 3-10 minutes depending on the dose and the rate of administration

Distribution: V_d: 2-6 mcg/mL during anesthesia; 1-2 mcg/mL upon awakening; large volume of distribution; highly lipophilic

Protein binding: 97% to 99%

Half-life, elimination (biphasic): Initial: 40 minutes; Terminal: 1-3 days

Metabolism: In the liver to water-soluble sulfate and glucuronide conjugates; total body clearance exceeds liver blood flow

Elimination: ~88% of a propofol dose is recovered in the urine as metabolites (40% as glucuronide metabolite) and <2% of a propofol dose is excreted in the feces

Usual Dosage Dosage must be individualized based on total body weight and titrated to the desired clinical effect; however, as a general guideline:

No pediatric dose has been established; however, induction for children 1-12 years 2-2.8 mg/kg has been used

Induction: I.V.:

Adults ≤55 years, and/or ASA I or II patients: 2-2.5 mg/kg of body weight (approximately 40 mg every 10 seconds until onset of induction)

Elderly, debilitated, hypovolemic, and/or ASA III or IV patients: 1-1.5 mg/kg of body weight (approximately 20 mg every 10 seconds until onset of induction)

Maintenance: I.V. infusion:

Adults ≤55 years, and/or ASA I or II patients: 0.1-0.2 mg/kg of body weight/minute (6-12 mg/kg of body weight/hour)

Elderly, debilitated, hypovolemic, and/or ASA III or IV patients: 0.05-0.1 mg/kg of body weight/minute (3-6 mg/kg of body weight/hour)

I.V. intermittent: 25-50 mg increments, as needed

ICU sedation: Rapid bolus injection should be avoided. Bolus injection can result in hypotension, oxyhemoglobin desaturation, apnea, airway obstruction, and oxygen desaturation. The preferred route of administration is slow infusion. Doses are based on individual need and titrated to response.

Recommended starting dose: 5 mcg/kg/minute (0.3-0.6 mg/kg/hour) over 5-10 minutes may be used until the desired level of sedation is achieved; infusion rate should be increased by increments of 5-10 mcg/kg/minute (0.3-0.6 mg/kg/hour) until the desired level of sedation is achieved; most adult patients require maintenance rates of 5-50 mcg/kg/minute (0.3-3 mg/kg/hour) or higher

Adjustments in dose can occur at 3- to 5-minute intervals. An 80% reduction in dose should be considered in elderly, debilitated, and ASA II or IV patients. Once sedation is established, the dose should be decreased for the maintenance infusion period and adjusted to response.

Monitoring Parameters Cardiac monitor, blood pressure monitor, and ventilator required; serum triglyceride levels should be obtained prior to initiation of therapy (ICU setting) and every 3-7 days, thereafter

Vital signs: Blood pressure, heart rate, cardiac output, pulmonary capillary wedge pressure should be monitored

Test Interactions ↓ cholesterol (S); ↑ porphyrin (U); ↓ cortisol (S), but does not appear to inhibit adrenal responsiveness to ACTH

Nursing Implications Changes urine color to green; abrupt discontinuation of infusion may result in rapid awakening of the patient associated with anxiety, agitation, and resistance to mechanical ventilation, making weaning from mechanical ventilation difficult; use a light level of sedation throughout the weaning process until 10-15 minutes before extubation; titrate the infusion rate so the patient awakens slowly. Tubing and any unused portions of propofol vials should be discarded after 12 hours.

Dosage Forms Injection: 10 mg/mL (20 mL, 50 mL, 100 mL)

Propoxyphene (proe POKS i feen)

Related Information

Narcotic Agonists Comparison *on page 1328*

U.S. Brand Names Darvon®; Darvon-N®; Dolene®

Canadian Brand Names Novo-Propoxyn; 624® Tablets

Synonyms Dextropropoxyphene; Propoxyphene Hydrochloride; Propoxyphene Napsylate

Therapeutic Category Analgesic, Narcotic

Use Management of mild to moderate pain

Restrictions C-IV

Pregnancy Risk Factor C (D if used for prolonged periods)

Contraindications Hypersensitivity to propoxyphene or any component

Warnings/Precautions Administer with caution in patients dependent on opiates, substitution may result in acute opiate withdrawal symptoms, use with caution in patients with severe renal or hepatic dysfunction; when given in excessive doses, either alone or in combination with other CNS depressants or propoxyphene products, propoxyphene is a major cause of drug-related deaths; **do not exceed recommended dosage**; tolerance or drug dependence may result from extended use

Adverse Reactions

Percentage unknown: Increased liver enzymes, may increase LFTs; may decrease glucose, urinary 17-OHCS

>10%:
Cardiovascular: Hypotension
Central nervous system: Dizziness, lightheadedness, sedation, paradoxical excitement and insomnia, fatigue, drowsiness
Gastrointestinal: Nausea, vomiting, constipation
Neuromuscular & skeletal: Weakness

1% to 10%:
Central nervous system: Nervousness, headache, restlessness, malaise, confusion
Gastrointestinal: Anorexia, stomach cramps, xerostomia, biliary spasm
Genitourinary: Decreased urination, ureteral spasms
Respiratory: Dyspnea, shortness of breath

<1%: Mental depression hallucinations, paradoxical CNS stimulation, increased intracranial pressure, rash, urticaria, paralytic ileus, psychologic and physical dependence with prolonged use, histamine release

Overdosage/Toxicology

Symptoms of overdose include CNS, respiratory depression, hypotension, pulmonary edema, seizures

Treatment of an overdose includes support of the patient's airway; establishment of an I.V. line and administration of naloxone 2 mg I.V. (0.01 mg/kg for children) with repeat administration as necessary up to a total of 10 mg; emesis is not indicated as overdose may cause seizures; charcoal is very effective (>95%) at binding propoxyphene

Drug Interactions CYP3A3/4 enzyme inhibitor

Decreased effect with charcoal, cigarette smoking

Increased toxicity: CNS depressants may potentiate pharmacologic effects; propoxyphene may inhibit the metabolism and increase the serum concentrations of carbamazepine, phenobarbital, MAO inhibitors, tricyclic antidepressants, and warfarin

Mechanism of Action Binds to opiate receptors in the CNS, causing inhibition of ascending pain pathways, altering the perception of and response to pain; produces generalized CNS depression

(Continued)

Propoxyphene *(Continued)*

Pharmacodynamics/Kinetics
Onset of effect: Oral: Within 0.5-1 hour
Duration: 4-6 hours
Metabolism: First-pass effect; metabolized in the liver to an active metabolite (norpropoxyphene) and inactive metabolites
Bioavailability: Oral: 30% to 70%
Half-life: Adults: Parent drug: 8-24 hours (mean: ~15 hours); Norpropoxyphene: 34 hours
Elimination: 20% to 25% excreted in urine

Usual Dosage Oral:
Children: Doses for children are not well established; doses of the hydrochloride of 2-3 mg/kg/d divided every 6 hours have been used
Adults:
Hydrochloride: 65 mg every 3-4 hours as needed for pain; maximum: 390 mg/day
Napsylate: 100 mg every 4 hours as needed for pain; maximum: 600 mg/day
Dosing comments in renal impairment: Cl_{cr} <10 mL/minute: Avoid use
Hemodialysis: Not dialyzable (0% to 5%)
Dosing adjustment in hepatic impairment: Reduced doses should be used

Dietary Considerations
Alcohol: Additive CNS effects, avoid or limit alcohol; watch for sedation
Food: May decrease rate of absorption, but may slightly increase bioavailability
Glucose may cause hyperglycemia; monitor blood glucose concentrations

Monitoring Parameters Pain relief, respiratory and mental status, blood pressure

Reference Range
Therapeutic: Ranges published vary between laboratories and may not correlate with clinical effect
Therapeutic concentration: 0.1-0.4 µg/mL (SI: 0.3-1.2 µmol/L)
Toxic: >0.5 µg/mL (SI: >1.5 µmol/L)

Test Interactions False-positive methadone test

Patient Information May cause drowsiness, dizziness, or blurring of vision; avoid alcohol and other sedatives; may take with food; can impair judgment and coordination

Additional Information 100 mg of napsylate = 65 mg of hydrochloride
Propoxyphene hydrochloride: Darvon®
Propoxyphene napsylate: Darvon-N®

Dosage Forms
Capsule, as hydrochloride: 65 mg
Tablet, as napsylate: 100 mg

Propoxyphene and Acetaminophen
(proe POKS i feen & a seet a MIN oh fen)

Related Information
Acetaminophen *on page 19*
Propoxyphene *on previous page*

U.S. Brand Names Darvocet-N®; Darvocet-N® 100; Genagesic®; Propacet®; Wygesic®

Synonyms Propoxyphene Hydrochloride and Acetaminophen; Propoxyphene Napsylate and Acetaminophen

Therapeutic Category Analgesic, Narcotic

Restrictions C-IV

Dosage Forms Tablet:
Darvocet-N®: Propoxyphene napsylate 50 mg and acetaminophen 325 mg
Darvocet-N® 100: Propoxyphene napsylate 100 mg and acetaminophen 650 mg
Genagesic®, Wygesic®: Propoxyphene hydrochloride 65 mg and acetaminophen 650 mg

Propoxyphene and Aspirin (proe POKS i feen & AS pir in)

U.S. Brand Names Bexophene®; Darvon® Compound-65 Pulvules®

Therapeutic Category Analgesic, Narcotic

Dosage Forms
Capsule: Propoxyphene hydrochloride 65 mg and aspirin 389 mg with caffeine 32.4 mg
Tablet (Darvon-N® with A.S.A.): Propoxyphene napsylate 100 mg and aspirin 325 mg

♦ **Propoxyphene Hydrochloride** *see* Propoxyphene *on previous page*

♦ **Propoxyphene Hydrochloride and Acetaminophen** *see* Propoxyphene and Acetaminophen *on this page*

♦ **Propoxyphene Napsylate** *see* Propoxyphene *on previous page*

♦ **Propoxyphene Napsylate and Acetaminophen** *see* Propoxyphene and Acetaminophen *on this page*

Propranolol (proe PRAN oh lole)

Related Information
Antiarrhythmic Drugs Comparison *on page 1297*
Beta-Blockers Comparison *on page 1311*
Depression Disorders and Treatments *on page 1465*

U.S. Brand Names Betachron E-R®; Inderal®; Inderal® LA

Canadian Brand Names Apo®-Propranolol; Detensol®; Nu-Propranolol

Synonyms Propranolol Hydrochloride

Therapeutic Category Antianginal Agent; Antiarrhythmic Agent, Class II; Antihypertensive Agent; Antimigraine Agent; Beta-Adrenergic Blocker

Use Management of hypertension, angina pectoris, pheochromocytoma, essential tremor, tetralogy of Fallot cyanotic spells, and arrhythmias (such as atrial fibrillation and flutter, A-V nodal re-entrant tachycardias, and catecholamine-induced arrhythmias); prevention of myocardial infarction, migraine headache; symptomatic treatment of hypertrophic subaortic stenosis

Unlabeled use: Tremor due to Parkinson's disease, alcohol withdrawal, aggressive behavior, antipsychotic-induced akathisia, esophageal varices bleeding, anxiety, schizophrenia, acute panic, and gastric bleeding in portal hypertension

Pregnancy Risk Factor C

Pregnancy/Breast-Feeding Implications

Clinical effects on the fetus: Crosses the placenta. IUGR, hypoglycemia, bradycardia, respiratory depression, hyperbilirubinemia, polycythemia, polydactyly reported. IUGR probably related to maternal hypertension. Preterm labor has been reported. Available evidence suggests safe use during pregnancy and breast-feeding. Monitor breast-fed infant for symptoms of beta-blockade.

Breast-feeding/lactation: Crosses into breast milk. American Academy of Pediatrics considers **compatible** with breast-feeding.

Contraindications Uncompensated congestive heart failure, cardiogenic shock, bradycardia or heart block, pulmonary edema, severe hyperactive airway disease or chronic obstructive lung disease, Raynaud's disease, hypersensitivity to beta-blockers

Warnings/Precautions Safety and efficacy in children have not been established; administer very cautiously to patients with CHF, asthma, diabetes mellitus, hyperthyroidism. Abrupt withdrawal of the drug should be avoided, drug should be discontinued over 1-2 weeks; do not use in pregnant or nursing women; may potentiate hypoglycemia in a diabetic patient and mask signs and symptoms.

Adverse Reactions

>10%:
Cardiovascular: Bradycardia
Central nervous system: Mental depression
Endocrine & metabolic: Decreased sexual ability

1% to 10%:
Cardiovascular: Congestive heart failure, reduced peripheral circulation
Central nervous system: Confusion, hallucinations, dizziness, insomnia, fatigue
Dermatologic: Rash
Gastrointestinal: Diarrhea, nausea, vomiting, stomach discomfort
Neuromuscular & skeletal: Weakness
Respiratory: Wheezing

<1%: Chest pain, hypotension, impaired myocardial contractility, worsening of A-V conduction disturbances, nightmares, vivid dreams, lethargy, red, scaling, or crusted skin; hypoglycemia, hyperglycemia, GI distress, leukopenia, thrombocytopenia, agranulocytosis, bronchospasm, cold extremities

Overdosage/Toxicology

Symptoms of intoxication include cardiac disturbances, CNS toxicity, bronchospasm, hypoglycemia and hyperkalemia. The most common cardiac symptoms include hypotension and bradycardia; atrioventricular block, intraventricular conduction disturbances, cardiogenic shock, and asystole may occur with severe overdose, especially with membrane-depressant drugs (eg, propranolol); CNS effects include convulsions, coma, and respiratory arrest is commonly seen with propranolol and other membrane-depressant and lipid-soluble drugs.

Treatment includes symptomatic treatment of seizures, hypotension, hyperkalemia and hypoglycemia; bradycardia and hypotension resistant to atropine, isoproterenol or pacing may respond to glucagon; wide QRS defects caused by the membrane-depressant poisoning may respond to hypertonic sodium bicarbonate; repeat-dose charcoal, hemoperfusion, or hemodialysis may be helpful in removal of only those beta-blockers with a small V_d, long half-life or low intrinsic clearance (acebutolol, atenolol, nadolol, sotalol)

Drug Interactions CYP1A2, 2C18, 2C19, and 2D6 enzyme substrate

Decreased effect:

Aluminum salts, barbiturates, calcium salts, cholestyramine, colestipol, NSAIDs, penicillins (ampicillin), rifampin, salicylates and sulfinpyrazone decrease effect of beta-blockers due to decreased bioavailability and plasma levels

Beta-blockers may decrease the effect of sulfonylureas

Ascorbic acid decreases propranolol Cp_{max} and AUC and increases the T_{max} significantly resulting in a greater decrease in the reduction of heart rate, possibly due to decreased absorption and first pass metabolism (n=5)

Nefazodone decreased peak plasma levels and AUC of propranolol and increases time to reach steady state; monitoring of clinical response is recommended

Increased effect:

Increased effect/toxicity of beta-blockers with calcium blockers (diltiazem, felodipine, nicardipine), contraceptives, flecainide, haloperidol (hypotensive effects), H_2-antagonists (cimetidine, possibly ranitidine), hydralazine, loop diuretics, possibly MAO inhibitors, phenothiazines, propafenone, quinidine (in extensive metabolizers), ciprofloxacin, thyroid hormones (metoprolol, propranolol, when hypothyroid patient is converted to euthyroid state)

Beta-blockers may increase the effect/toxicity of flecainide, haloperidol (hypotensive effects), hydralazine, phenothiazines, acetaminophen, anticoagulants (warfarin), benzodiazepines, clonidine (hypertensive crisis after or during withdrawal of either agent), epinephrine (initial hypertensive episode followed by bradycardia), nifedipine

(Continued)

Propranolol (Continued)

and verapamil lidocaine, ergots (peripheral ischemia), prazosin (postural hypotension)

Beta-blockers may affect the action or levels of ethanol, disopyramide, nondepolarizing muscle relaxants and theophylline although the effects are difficult to predict

Stability Compatible in saline, **incompatible** with HCO_3^-; protect injection from light; solutions have maximum stability at pH of 3 and decompose rapidly in alkaline pH; propranolol is stable for 24 hours at room temperature in D_5W or NS

Mechanism of Action Nonselective beta-adrenergic blocker (class II antiarrhythmic); competitively blocks response to beta$_1$- and beta$_2$-adrenergic stimulation which results in decreases in heart rate, myocardial contractility, blood pressure, and myocardial oxygen demand

Pharmacodynamics/Kinetics

Onset of beta-blockade: Oral: Within 1-2 hours

Duration: ~6 hours

Distribution: V_d: 3.9 L/kg in adults; crosses the placenta; small amounts appear in breast milk

Protein binding: Newborns: 68%; Adults: 93%

Metabolism: Extensive first-pass effect; metabolized in the liver to active and inactive compounds

Bioavailability: 30% to 40%; oral bioavailability may be increased in Down syndrome children

Half-life: Neonates and Infants: Possible increased half-life; Children: 3.9-6.4 hours; Adults: 4-6 hours

Elimination: Primarily in urine (96% to 99%)

Usual Dosage

Tachyarrhythmias:

Oral:

Children: Initial: 0.5-1 mg/kg/day in divided doses every 6-8 hours; titrate dosage upward every 3-7 days; usual dose: 2-4 mg/kg/day; higher doses may be needed; do not exceed 16 mg/kg/day or 60 mg/day

Adults: 10-30 mg/dose every 6-8 hours

Elderly: Initial: 10 mg twice daily; increase dosage every 3-7 days; usual dosage range: 10-320 mg given in 2 divided doses

I.V.:

Children: 0.01-0.1 mg/kg slow IVP over 10 minutes; maximum dose: 1 mg

Adults: 1 mg/dose slow IVP; repeat every 5 minutes up to a total of 5 mg

Hypertension: Oral:

Children: Initial: 0.5-1 mg/kg/day in divided doses every 6-12 hours; increase gradually every 3-7 days; maximum: 2 mg/kg/24 hours

Adults: Initial: 40 mg twice daily; increase dosage every 3-7 days; usual dose: ≤320 mg divided in 2-3 doses/day; maximum daily dose: 640 mg

Migraine headache prophylaxis: Oral:

Children: 0.6-1.5 mg/kg/day **or**

≤35 kg: 10-20 mg 3 times/day

>35 kg: 20-40 mg 3 times/day

Adults: Initial: 80 mg/day divided every 6-8 hours; increase by 20-40 mg/dose every 3-4 weeks to a maximum of 160-240 mg/day given in divided doses every 6-8 hours; if satisfactory response not achieved within 6 weeks of starting therapy, drug should be withdrawn gradually over several weeks

Tetralogy spells: Children:

Oral: 1-2 mg/kg/day every 6 hours as needed, may increase by 1 mg/kg/day to a maximum of 5 mg/kg/day, or if refractory may increase slowly to a maximum of 10-15 mg/kg/day

I.V.: 0.15-0.25 mg/kg/dose slow IVP; may repeat in 15 minutes

Thyrotoxicosis:

Adolescents and Adults: Oral: 10-40 mg/dose every 6 hours

Adults: I.V.: 1-3 mg/dose slow IVP as a single dose

Adults: Oral:

Angina: 80-320 mg/day in doses divided 2-4 times/day

Pheochromocytoma: 30-60 mg/day in divided doses

Myocardial infarction prophylaxis: 180-240 mg/day in 3-4 divided doses

Hypertrophic subaortic stenosis: 20-40 mg 3-4 times/day

Essential tremor: 40 mg twice daily initially; maintenance doses: usually 120-320 mg/day

Dosing adjustment in renal impairment:

Cl_{cr} 31-40 mL/minute: Administer every 24-36 hours or administer 50% of normal dose

Cl_{cr} 10-30 mL/minute: Administer every 24-48 hours or administer 50% of normal dose

Cl_{cr} <10 mL/minute: Administer every 40-60 hours or administer 25% of normal dose

Hemodialysis: Not dialyzable (0% to 5%); supplemental dose is not necessary

Peritoneal dialysis: Supplemental dose is not necessary

Dosing adjustment/comments in hepatic disease: Marked slowing of heart rate may occur in cirrhosis with conventional doses; low initial dose and regular heart rate monitoring

Administration I.V. administration should not exceed 1 mg/minute; I.V. dose much smaller than oral dose

Monitoring Parameters Blood pressure, EKG, heart rate, CNS and cardiac effects

Reference Range Therapeutic: 50-100 ng/mL (SI: 190-390 nmol/L) at end of dose interval

Test Interactions ↑ thyroxine (S)

Patient Information Do not discontinue abruptly; notify physician if CHF symptoms become worse or side effects develop; take at the same time each day; may mask diabetes symptoms; consult pharmacist or physician before taking with other adrenergic drugs (eg, cold medications); use with caution while driving or performing tasks requiring alertness

Nursing Implications Patient's therapeutic response may be evaluated by looking at blood pressure, apical and radial pulses, fluid I & O, daily weight, respirations, and circulation in extremities before and during therapy

Dosage Forms
Capsule, as hydrochloride, sustained action: 60 mg, 80 mg, 120 mg, 160 mg
Injection, as hydrochloride: 1 mg/mL (1 mL)
Solution, oral, as hydrochloride (strawberry-mint flavor): 4 mg/mL (5 mL, 500 mL); 8 mg/mL (5 mL, 500 mL)
Solution, oral, concentrate, as hydrochloride: 80 mg/mL (30 mL)
Tablet, as hydrochloride: 10 mg, 20 mg, 40 mg, 60 mg, 80 mg

Propranolol and Hydrochlorothiazide

(proe PRAN oh lole & hye droe klor oh THYE a zide)
U.S. Brand Names Inderide®
Therapeutic Category Antihypertensive Agent, Combination
Dosage Forms
Capsule, long-acting (Inderide® LA):
80/50 Propranolol hydrochloride 80 mg and hydrochlorothiazide 50 mg
120/50 Propranolol hydrochloride 120 mg and hydrochlorothiazide 50 mg
160/50 Propranolol hydrochloride 160 mg and hydrochlorothiazide 50 mg
Tablet (Inderide®):
40/25 Propranolol hydrochloride 40 mg and hydrochlorothiazide 25 mg
80/25 Propranolol hydrochloride 80 mg and hydrochlorothiazide 25 mg

♦ **Propranolol Hydrochloride** see Propranolol on page 986

♦ **Propulsid®** see Cisapride on page 265

♦ **2-Propylpentanoic Acid** see Valproic Acid and Derivatives on page 1203

Propylthiouracil (proe pil thye oh YOOR a sil)

Canadian Brand Names Propyl-Thyracil®
Synonyms PTU
Therapeutic Category Antithyroid Agent
Use Palliative treatment of hyperthyroidism as an adjunct to ameliorate hyperthyroidism in preparation for surgical treatment or radioactive iodine therapy and in the management of thyrotoxic crisis. The use of antithyroid thioamides is as effective in elderly as they are in younger adults; however, the expense, potential adverse effects, and inconvenience (compliance, monitoring) make them undesirable. The use of radioiodine, due to ease of administration and less concern for long-term side effects and reproduction problems, makes it a more appropriate therapy.
Pregnancy Risk Factor D
Contraindications Hypersensitivity to propylthiouracil or any component
Warnings/Precautions Use with caution in patients >40 years of age because PTU may cause hypoprothrombinemia and bleeding, use with extreme caution in patients receiving other drugs known to cause agranulocytosis; may cause agranulocytosis, thyroid hyperplasia, thyroid carcinoma (usage >1 year); breast-feeding (enters breast milk)
Adverse Reactions
>10%:
Central nervous system: Fever
Dermatologic: Skin rash
Hematologic: Leukopenia
1% to 10%:
Central nervous system: Dizziness
Gastrointestinal: Nausea, vomiting, loss of taste perception, stomach pain
Hematologic: Agranulocytosis
Miscellaneous: SLE-like syndrome
<1%: Edema, cutaneous vasculitis, drowsiness, vertigo, headache, drug fever, urticaria, pruritus, exfoliative dermatitis, alopecia, goiter, constipation, weight gain, swollen salivary glands, thrombocytopenia, bleeding, aplastic anemia, cholestatic jaundice, hepatitis, arthralgia, paresthesia, neuritis, nephritis
Overdosage/Toxicology
Symptoms of overdose include nausea, vomiting, epigastric pain, headache, fever, arthralgia, pruritus, edema, pancytopenia, epigastric distress, headache, fever, CNS stimulation or depression
Treatment is supportive; monitor bone marrow response, forced diuresis, peritoneal and hemodialysis, as well as charcoal hemoperfusion
Drug Interactions Increased effect: Increases anticoagulant activity
Mechanism of Action Inhibits the synthesis of thyroid hormones by blocking the oxidation of iodine in the thyroid gland; blocks synthesis of thyroxine and triiodothyronine
Pharmacodynamics/Kinetics
Onset of action: For significant therapeutic effects 24-36 hours are required
Peak effect: Remissions of hyperthyroidism do not usually occur before 4 months of continued therapy
(Continued)

Propylthiouracil *(Continued)*

Distribution: Concentrated in the thyroid gland
Protein binding: 75% to 80%
Metabolism: Hepatic
Bioavailability: 80% to 95%
Half-life: 1.5-5 hours; End-stage renal disease: 8.5 hours
Time to peak serum concentration: Oral: Within 1 hour; persists for 2-3 hours
Elimination: 35% excreted in urine

Usual Dosage Oral: Administer in 3 equally divided doses at approximately 8-hour intervals. Adjust dosage to maintain T_3, T_4, and TSH levels in normal range; elevated T_3 may be sole indicator of inadequate treatment. Elevated TSH indicates excessive antithyroid treatment.

Children: Initial: 5-7 mg/kg/day **or** 150-200 mg/m^2/day in divided doses every 8 hours
or
6-10 years: 50-150 mg/day
>10 years: 150-300 mg/day
Maintenance: Determined by patient response **or** $1/3$ to $2/3$ of the initial dose in divided doses every 8-12 hours. This usually begins after 2 months on an effective initial dose.
Adults: Initial: 300 mg/day in divided doses every 8 hours. In patients with severe hyperthyroidism, very large goiters, or both, the initial dosage is usually 450 mg/day; an occasional patient will require 600-900 mg/day; maintenance: 100-150 mg/day in divided doses every 8-12 hours
Elderly: Use lower dose recommendations; Initial: 150-300 mg/day
Withdrawal of therapy: Therapy should be withdrawn gradually with evaluation of the patient every 4-6 weeks for the first 3 months then every 3 months for the first year after discontinuation of therapy to detect any reoccurrence of a hyperthyroid state.

Dosing adjustment in renal impairment: Adjustment is not necessary

Monitoring Parameters CBC with differential, prothrombin time, liver function tests, thyroid function tests (TSH, T_3, T_4); periodic blood counts are recommended chronic therapy

Reference Range See table.

Laboratory Ranges

	Normal Values
Total T_4	5-12 µg/dL
Serum T_3	90-185 ng/dL
Free thyroxine index (FT_4I)	6-10.5
TSH	0.5-4.0 µIU/mL

Patient Information Do not exceed prescribed dosage; take at regular intervals around-the-clock; notify physician or pharmacist if fever, sore throat, unusual bleeding or bruising, headache, or general malaise occurs

Additional Information The use of antithyroid thioamides is as effective in elderly as in younger adults; however, the expense, potential adverse effects, and inconvenience (compliance, monitoring) make them undesirable. The use of radioiodine, due to ease of administration and less concern for long-term side effects and reproduction problems, makes it a more appropriate therapy.

Dosage Forms Tablet: 50 mg

Extemporaneous Preparations A 5 mg/mL oral suspension was stable for 10 days when refrigerated when compounded as follows:
Triturate six 50 mg tablets in a mortar, reduce to a fine powder, add 30 mL of carboxymethylcellulose 1.5%, transfer to a graduate and qs to 60 mL
Shake well before using and keep in refrigerator; protect from light

Nahata MC and Hipple TF, *Pediatric Drug Formulations*, 3rd ed, Cincinnati, OH: Harvey Whitney Books Co, 1997.

Protamine Sulfate (PROE ta meen SUL fate)

Therapeutic Category Antidote, Heparin

Use Treatment of heparin overdosage; neutralize heparin during surgery or dialysis procedures

Pregnancy Risk Factor C

Contraindications Hypersensitivity to protamine or any component

Warnings/Precautions May not be totally effective in some patients following cardiac surgery despite adequate doses; may cause hypersensitivity reaction in patients with a history of allergy to fish (have epinephrine 1:1000 available) and in patients sensitized to protamine (via protamine zinc insulin); too rapid administration can cause severe hypotensive and anaphylactoid-like reactions. Heparin rebound associated with anticoagulation and bleeding has been reported to occur occasionally; symptoms typically occur 8-9 hours after protamine administration, but may occur as long as 18 hours later.

Adverse Reactions

>10%:
  Cardiovascular: Sudden fall in blood pressure, bradycardia
  Respiratory: Dyspnea
1% to 10%: Hematologic: Hemorrhage
<1%: Hypotension, flushing, lassitude, nausea, vomiting, pulmonary hypertension, hypersensitivity reactions

Overdosage/Toxicology Symptoms of overdose include hypertension; may cause hemorrhage; doses exceeding 100 mg may cause paradox anticoagulation

Stability Refrigerate, avoid freezing; remains stable for at least 2 weeks at room temperature; **incompatible** with cephalosporins and penicillins; preservative-free formulation does not require refrigeration

Mechanism of Action Combines with strongly acidic heparin to form a stable complex (salt) neutralizing the anticoagulant activity of both drugs

Pharmacodynamics/Kinetics Onset of effect: I.V. injection: Heparin neutralization occurs within 5 minutes

Usual Dosage Protamine dosage is determined by the dosage of heparin; 1 mg of protamine neutralizes 90 USP units of heparin (lung) and 115 USP units of heparin (intestinal); maximum dose: 50 mg

In the situation of heparin overdosage, since blood heparin concentrations decrease rapidly **after** administration, adjust the protamine dosage depending upon the duration of time since heparin administration as follows:

Time Elapsed	Dose of Protamine (mg) to Neutralize 100 units of Heparin
Immediate	1-1.5
30-60 min	0.5-0.75
>2 h	0.25-0.375

If heparin administered by deep S.C. injection, use 1-1.5 mg protamine per 100 units heparin; this may be done by a portion of the dose (eg, 25-50 mg) given slowly I.V. followed by the remaining portion as a continuous infusion over 8-16 hours (the expected absorption time of the S.C. heparin dose)

Administration For I.V. use only; **incompatible** with cephalosporins and penicillins; administer slow IVP (50 mg over 10 minutes); rapid I.V. infusion causes hypotension; reconstitute vial with 5 mL sterile water; if using protamine in neonates, reconstitute with preservative-free sterile water for injection; resulting solution equals 10 mg/mL; inject without further dilution over 1-3 minutes; maximum of 50 mg in any 10-minute period

Monitoring Parameters Coagulation test, APTT or ACT, cardiac monitor and blood pressure monitor required during administration

Dosage Forms Injection: 10 mg/mL (5 mL, 10 mL, 25 mL)

♦ **Prothazine-DC®** see Promethazine and Codeine on page 980
♦ **Prothrombin Concentrate** see Factor IX Complex (Human) on page 464
♦ **Protilase®** see Pancrelipase on page 883
♦ **Protopam®** see Pralidoxime on page 956
♦ **Protostat® Oral** see Metronidazole on page 770
♦ **Pro-Trin®** see Co-Trimoxazole on page 299

Protriptyline (proe TRIP ti leen)

Related Information
  Antidepressant Agents Comparison on page 1301

U.S. Brand Names Vivactil®

Canadian Brand Names Triptil®

Synonyms Protriptyline Hydrochloride

Therapeutic Category Antidepressant, Tricyclic

Use Treatment of various forms of depression, often in conjunction with psychotherapy

Pregnancy Risk Factor C

Contraindications Narrow-angle glaucoma, hypersensitivity to protriptyline or any component

Warnings/Precautions Use with caution in patients with cardiac conduction disturbances, history of hyperthyroid, seizure disorders, or decreased renal function; safe use of tricyclic antidepressants in children <12 years of age has not been established; (Continued)

Protriptyline *(Continued)*

protriptyline should not be abruptly discontinued in patients receiving high doses for prolonged periods

Adverse Reactions

>10%:

Central nervous system: Dizziness, drowsiness, headache

Gastrointestinal: Xerostomia, constipation, unpleasant taste, weight gain, increased appetite, nausea

Neuromuscular & skeletal: Weakness

1% to 10%:

Cardiovascular: Arrhythmias, hypotension

Central nervous system: Confusion, delirium, hallucinations, nervousness, restlessness, parkinsonian syndrome, insomnia

Gastrointestinal: Diarrhea, heartburn

Genitourinary: Dysuria, sexual dysfunction

Neuromuscular & skeletal: Fine muscle tremors

Ocular: Blurred vision, eye pain

Miscellaneous: Diaphoresis (excessive)

<1%: Anxiety, seizures, alopecia, photosensitivity, breast enlargement, galactorrhea, SIADH, trouble with gums, decreased lower esophageal sphincter tone may cause GE reflux, testicular edema, agranulocytosis, leukopenia, eosinophilia, cholestatic jaundice, increased liver enzymes, increased intraocular pressure, tinnitus, allergic reactions

Overdosage/Toxicology

Symptoms of overdose include confusion, hallucinations, urinary retention, hypotension, tachycardia, seizures, hyperthermia

Following initiation of essential overdose management, toxic symptoms should be treated. Sodium bicarbonate is indicated when QRS interval is >0.10 seconds or QT$_c$ >0.42 seconds. Ventricular arrhythmias often respond to systemic alkalinization (sodium bicarbonate 0.5-2 mEq/kg I.V.). Arrhythmias unresponsive to this therapy may respond to lidocaine 1 mg/kg I.V. followed by a titrated infusion. Physostigmine (1-2 mg I.V. slowly for adults or 0.5 mg I.V. slowly for children) may be indicated in reversing cardiac arrhythmias that are life-threatening.

Seizures usually respond to diazepam I.V. boluses (5-10 mg for adults up to 30 mg or 0.25-0.4 mg/kg/dose for children up to 10 mg/dose). If seizures are unresponsive or recur, phenytoin or phenobarbital may be required.

Drug Interactions

Decreased effect of guanethidine; decreased effect with barbiturates, carbamazepine, phenytoin

Increased toxicity of alcohol, MAO inhibitors, sympathomimetics, CNS depressants, anticholinergics (paralytic ileus and hyperpyrexia); increased toxicity with MAO inhibitors (hyperpyretic crisis, convulsions, and death), cimetidine (increased drug levels)

Mechanism of Action Increases the synaptic concentration of serotonin and/or norepinephrine in the central nervous system by inhibition of their reuptake by the presynaptic neuronal membrane

Pharmacodynamics/Kinetics

Maximum antidepressant effect: 2 weeks of continuous therapy is commonly required

Distribution: Crosses the placenta

Protein binding: 92%

Metabolism: Undergoes first-pass metabolism (10% to 25%); extensively metabolized in the liver by N-oxidation, hydroxylation and glucuronidation

Half-life: 54-92 hours, averaging 74 hours

Time to peak serum concentration: Oral: Within 24-30 hours

Elimination: In urine

Usual Dosage Oral:

Adolescents: 15-20 mg/day

Adults: 15-60 mg in 3-4 divided doses

Elderly: 15-20 mg/day

Reference Range Therapeutic: 70-250 ng/mL (SI: 266-950 nmol/L); Toxic: >500 ng/mL (SI: >1900 nmol/L)

Test Interactions ↑ glucose

Patient Information Avoid unnecessary exposure to sunlight; do not discontinue abruptly; take dose in morning to avoid insomnia

Nursing Implications Offer patient sugarless hard candy or gum for dry mouth

Dosage Forms Tablet, as hydrochloride: 5 mg, 10 mg

♦ **Protriptyline Hydrochloride** *see* Protriptyline *on previous page*

♦ **Protropin® Injection** *see* Human Growth Hormone *on page 569*

♦ **Proventil®** *see* Albuterol *on page 35*

♦ **Proventil® HFA** *see* Albuterol *on page 35*

♦ **Provera®** *see* Medroxyprogesterone Acetate *on page 721*

♦ **Provigil®** *see* Modafinil *on page 791*

♦ **Provisc®** *see* Sodium Hyaluronate *on page 1069*

♦ **Provocholine®** *see* Methacholine *on page 743*

♦ **Proxigel® Oral [OTC]** *see* Carbamide Peroxide *on page 190*

♦ **Proxymetacaine** *see* Proparacaine *on page 982*

♦ **Prozac®** *see* Fluoxetine *on page 502*

♦ **PRP-D** *see* Haemophilus b Conjugate Vaccine *on page 554*

+ **Prymaccone** *see* Primaquine Phosphate *on page 965*
+ **Pseudo-Car® DM** *see* Carbinoxamine, Pseudoephedrine, and Dextromethorphan *on page 193*

Pseudoephedrine (soo doe e FED rin)

U.S. Brand Names Actifed® Allergy Tablet (Day) [OTC]; Afrin® Tablet [OTC]; Cenafed® [OTC]; Children's Silfedrine® [OTC]; Decofed® Syrup [OTC]; Drixoral® Non-Drowsy [OTC]; Efidac/24® [OTC]; Neofed® [OTC]; PediaCare® Oral; Sudafed® [OTC]; Sudafed® 12 Hour [OTC]; Sufedrin® [OTC]; Triaminic® AM Decongestant Formula [OTC]

Canadian Brand Names Balminil® Decongestant; Eltor®; PMS-Pseudoephedrine; Robidrine®

Synonyms *d*-Isoephedrine Hydrochloride; Pseudoephedrine Hydrochloride; Pseudoephedrine Sulfate

Therapeutic Category Adrenergic Agonist Agent; Decongestant; Sympathomimetic

Use Temporary symptomatic relief of nasal congestion due to common cold, upper respiratory allergies, and sinusitis; also promotes nasal or sinus drainage

Pregnancy Risk Factor C

Contraindications Hypersensitivity to pseudoephedrine or any component; MAO inhibitor therapy

Warnings/Precautions Use with caution in patients >60 years of age; administer with caution to patients with hypertension, hyperthyroidism, diabetes mellitus, cardiovascular disease, ischemic heart disease, increased intraocular pressure, or prostatic hypertrophy. Elderly patients are more likely to experience adverse reactions to sympathomimetics. Overdosage may cause hallucinations, seizures, CNS depression, and death.

Adverse Reactions

>10%:
  Cardiovascular: Tachycardia, palpitations, arrhythmias
  Central nervous system: Nervousness, transient stimulation, insomnia, excitability, dizziness, drowsiness
  Neuromuscular & skeletal: Tremor

1% to 10%:
  Central nervous system: Headache
  Neuromuscular & skeletal: Weakness
  Miscellaneous: Diaphoresis

<1%: Convulsions, hallucinations, nausea, vomiting, dysuria, shortness of breath, dyspnea

Overdosage/Toxicology

Symptoms of overdose include seizures, nausea, vomiting, cardiac arrhythmias, hypertension, agitation

There is no specific antidote for pseudoephedrine intoxication; the bulk treatment is supportive. Hyperactivity and agitation usually respond to reduced sensory input; however, with extreme agitation, haloperidol (2-5 mg I.M. for adults) may be required. Hyperthermia is best treated with external cooling measures; or when severe or unresponsive, muscle paralysis with pancuronium may be needed. Hypertension is usually transient and generally does not require treatment unless severe. For diastolic blood pressures >110 mm Hg, a nitroprusside infusion should be initiated. Seizures usually respond to diazepam I.V. and/or phenytoin maintenance regimens.

Drug Interactions

Decreased effect of methyldopa, reserpine

Increased toxicity: MAO inhibitors may increase blood pressure effects of pseudoephedrine; propranolol, sympathomimetic agents may increase toxicity

Mechanism of Action Directly stimulates alpha-adrenergic receptors of respiratory mucosa causing vasoconstriction; directly stimulates beta-adrenergic receptors causing bronchial relaxation, increased heart rate and contractility

Pharmacodynamics/Kinetics

Onset of decongestant effect: Oral: 15-30 minutes
Duration: 4-6 hours (up to 12 hours with extended release formulation administration)
Metabolism: Partially in the liver
Half-life: 9-16 hours
Elimination: 70% to 90% of dose excreted in urine as unchanged drug and 1% to 6% as norpseudoephedrine (active); renal elimination is dependent on urine pH and flow rate; alkaline urine decreases renal elimination of pseudoephedrine

Usual Dosage Oral:
Children:
  <2 years: 4 mg/kg/day in divided doses every 6 hours
  2-5 years: 15 mg every 6 hours; maximum: 60 mg/24 hours
  6-12 years: 30 mg every 6 hours; maximum: 120 mg/24 hours
Adults: 30-60 mg every 4-6 hours, sustained release: 120 mg every 12 hours; maximum: 240 mg/24 hours

Dosing adjustment in renal impairment: Reduce dose

Test Interactions Interferes with urine detection of amphetamine (false-positive)

Patient Information Do not exceed recommended dosage and do not use for more than 3-5 days; may cause wakefulness or nervousness; take last dose 4-6 hours before bedtime; do not crush sustained release product; consult pharmacist or physician before using

Nursing Implications Do not crush extended release drug product; elderly patients should be counseled about the proper use of over-the-counter cough and cold preparations

(Continued)

Pseudoephedrine *(Continued)*

Additional Information
Pseudoephedrine hydrochloride: Cenafed® syrup [OTC], Decofed® syrup [OTC], Neofed® [OTC], Sudafed® [OTC], Sudafed® 12 Hour [OTC], Sudafed® tablet [OTC], Sufedrin® [OTC]

Pseudoephedrine sulfate: Afrinol® [OTC]

Dosage Forms
Capsule: 60 mg

Capsule, timed release, as hydrochloride: 120 mg

Drops, oral, as hydrochloride: 7.5 mg/0.8 mL (15 mL)

Liquid, as hydrochloride: 15 mg/5 mL (120 mL); 30 mg/5 mL (120 mL, 240 mL, 473 mL)

Syrup, as hydrochloride: 15 mg/5 mL (118 mL)

Tablet, as hydrochloride: 30 mg, 60 mg

Tablet:

Timed release, as hydrochloride: 120 mg

Extended release, as sulfate: 120 mg, 240 mg

+ **Pseudoephedrine and Acrivastine** *see* Acrivastine and Pseudoephedrine *on page 27*

+ **Pseudoephedrine Hydrochloride** *see* Pseudoephedrine *on previous page*

+ **Pseudoephedrine Sulfate** *see* Pseudoephedrine *on previous page*

+ **Pseudomonic Acid A** *See* Mupirocin *on page 801*

+ **Psorcon™** *see* Diflorasone *on page 356*

+ **Psorion® Cream** *see* Betamethasone *on page 141*

Psyllium *(SIL i yum)*

Related Information
Laxatives, Classification and Properties *on page 1326*

U.S. Brand Names Effer-Syllium® [OTC]; Fiberall® Powder [OTC]; Fiberall® Wafer [OTC]; Hydrocil® [OTC]; Konsyl-D® [OTC]; Konsyl® [OTC]; Metamucil® [OTC]; Metamucil® Instant Mix [OTC]; Modane® Bulk [OTC]; Perdiem® Plain [OTC]; Reguloid® [OTC]; Serutan® [OTC]; Syllact® [OTC]; V-Lax® [OTC]

Canadian Brand Names Fibrepur®; Novo-Mucilax; Prodiem® Plain

Synonyms Plantago Seed; Plantain Seed; Psyllium Hydrophilic Mucilloid

Therapeutic Category Laxative, Bulk-Producing

Use Treatment of chronic atonic or spastic constipation and in constipation associated with rectal disorders; management of irritable bowel syndrome

Pregnancy Risk Factor C

Contraindications Fecal impaction, GI obstruction, hypersensitivity to psyllium or any component

Warnings/Precautions May contain aspartame which is metabolized in the GI tract to phenylalanine which is contraindicated in individuals with phenylketonuria; use with caution in patients with esophageal strictures, ulcers, stenosis, or intestinal adhesions; elderly may have insufficient fluid intake which may predispose them to fecal impaction and bowel obstruction.

Adverse Reactions 1% to 10%:

Gastrointestinal: Esophageal or bowel obstruction, diarrhea, constipation, abdominal cramps

Respiratory: Bronchospasm

Miscellaneous: Anaphylaxis upon inhalation in susceptible individuals, rhinoconjunctivitis

Overdosage/Toxicology Symptoms of overdose include abdominal pain, diarrhea, constipation

Drug Interactions Decreased effect of warfarin, digitalis, potassium-sparing diuretics, salicylates, tetracyclines, nitrofurantoin

Mechanism of Action Adsorbs water in the intestine to form a viscous liquid which promotes peristalsis and reduces transit time

Pharmacodynamics/Kinetics

Onset of action: 12-24 hour, but full effect may take 2-3 days

Peak effect: May take 2-3 days

Absorption: Oral: Generally not absorbed following administration, small amounts of grain extracts present in the preparation have been reportedly absorbed following colonic hydrolysis

Usual Dosage Oral (administer at least 3 hours before or after drugs):

Children 6-11 years: (Approximately 1/2 adult dosage) 1/2 to 1 rounded teaspoonful in 4 oz glass of liquid 1-3 times/day

Adults: 1-2 rounded teaspoonfuls or 1-2 packets or 1-2 wafers in 8 oz glass of liquid 1-3 times/day

Patient Information Must be mixed in a glass of water or juice; drink a full glass of liquid with each dose; do not use for longer than 1 week without the advice of a physician

Nursing Implications Inhalation of psyllium dust may cause sensitivity to psyllium (runny nose, watery eyes, wheezing)

Additional Information 3.4 g psyllium hydrophilic mucilloid per 7 g powder is equivalent to a rounded teaspoonful or one packet

Sodium content of Metamucil® Instant Mix (orange): 6 mg (0.27 mEq)

Dosage Forms

Granules: 4.03 g per rounded teaspoon (100 g, 250 g); 2.5 g per rounded teaspoon

Powder: Psyllium 50% and dextrose 50% (6.5 g, 325 g, 420 g, 480 g, 500 g)

Powder:
Effervescent: 3 g/dose (270 g, 480 g); 3.4 g/dose (single-dose packets)
Psyllium hydrophilic: 3.4 g per rounded teaspoon (210 g, 300 g, 420 g, 630 g)
Squares, chewable: 1.7 g, 3.4 g
Wafers: 3.4 g

Pyrantel Pamoate (pi RAN tel PAM oh ate)

U.S. Brand Names Antiminth® [OTC]; Pin-Rid® [OTC]; Pin-X® [OTC]; Reese's® Pinworm Medicine [OTC]

Therapeutic Category Anthelmintic

Use Treatment of pinworms (*Enterobius vermicularis*), whipworms (*Trichuris trichiura*), roundworms (*Ascaris lumbricoides*), and hookworms (*Ancylostoma duodenale*)

Pregnancy Risk Factor C

Contraindications Known hypersensitivity to pyrantel pamoate

Warnings/Precautions Use with caution in patients with liver impairment, anemia, malnutrition, or pregnancy. Since pinworm infections are easily spread to others, treat all family members in close contact with the patient.

Adverse Reactions
1% to 10%: Gastrointestinal: Anorexia, nausea, vomiting, abdominal cramps, diarrhea
<1%: Dizziness, drowsiness, insomnia, headache, rash, elevated liver enzymes, tenesmus, weakness

Overdosage/Toxicology
Symptoms of overdose include anorexia, nausea, vomiting, cramps, diarrhea, ataxia
Treatment is supportive following GI decontamination

Drug Interactions Decreased effect with piperazine

Stability Protect from light

Mechanism of Action Causes the release of acetylcholine and inhibits cholinesterase; acts as a depolarizing neuromuscular blocker, paralyzing the helminths

Pharmacodynamics/Kinetics
Absorption: Oral: Poor
Metabolism: Undergoes partial hepatic metabolism
Time to peak serum concentration: Within 1-3 hours
Elimination: In feces (50% as unchanged drug) and urine (7% as unchanged drug)

Usual Dosage Children and Adults (purgation is not required prior to use): Oral:
Roundworm, pinworm, or trichostrongyliasis: 11 mg/kg administered as a single dose; maximum dose: 1 g. **(Note:** For pinworm infection, dosage should be repeated in 2 weeks and all family members should be treated).
Hookworm: 11 mg/kg administered once daily for 3 days

Monitoring Parameters Stool for presence of eggs, worms, and occult blood, serum AST and ALT

Patient Information May mix drug with milk or fruit juice; strict hygiene is essential to prevent reinfection

Nursing Implications Shake well before pouring to assure accurate dosage; protect from light

Dosage Forms
Capsule: 180 mg
Liquid: 50 mg/mL (30 mL); 144 mg/mL (30 mL)
Suspension, oral (caramel-currant flavor): 50 mg/mL (60 mL)

Pyrazinamide (peer a ZIN a mide)

Related Information
Antimicrobial Drugs of Choice *on page 1404*
Tuberculosis Treatment Guidelines *on page 1432*

Canadian Brand Names PMS-Pyrazinamide; Tebrazid

Synonyms Pyrazinoic Acid Amide

Therapeutic Category Antitubercular Agent

Use Adjunctive treatment of tuberculosis in combination with other antituberculosis agents

Pregnancy Risk Factor C

Contraindications Severe hepatic damage; hypersensitivity to pyrazinamide or any component; acute gout

Warnings/Precautions Use with caution in patients with renal failure, chronic gout, diabetes mellitus, or porphyria

(Continued)

Pyrazinamide *(Continued)*

Adverse Reactions
1% to 10%:
Central nervous system: Malaise
Gastrointestinal: Nausea, vomiting, anorexia
Neuromuscular & skeletal: Arthralgia, myalgia
<1%: Fever, rash, itching, acne, photosensitivity, gout, dysuria, porphyria, thrombocytopenia, hepatotoxicity, interstitial nephritis

Overdosage/Toxicology
Symptoms of overdose include gout, gastric upset, hepatic damage (mild)
Treatment following GI decontamination is supportive

Mechanism of Action Converted to pyrazinoic acid in susceptible strains of *Mycobacterium* which lowers the pH of the environment; exact mechanism of action has not been elucidated

Pharmacodynamics/Kinetics Bacteriostatic or bactericidal depending on the drug's concentration at the site of infection

Absorption: Oral: Well absorbed
Distribution: Widely distributed into body tissues and fluids including the liver, lung, and CSF
Relative diffusion of antimicrobial agents from blood into cerebrospinal fluid (CSF): Adequate with or without inflammation (exceeds usual MICs)
Ratio of CSF to blood level (%): Inflamed meninges: 100
Protein binding: 50%
Metabolism: In the liver
Half-life: 9-10 hours
Time to peak serum concentration: Within 2 hours
Elimination: In urine (4% as unchanged drug)

Usual Dosage Oral (calculate dose on ideal body weight rather than total body weight):
Note: A four-drug regimen (isoniazid, rifampin, pyrazinamide, and either streptomycin or ethambutol) is preferred for the initial, empiric treatment of TB. When the drug susceptibility results are available, the regimen should be altered as appropriate.

Children and Adults:
Daily therapy: 15-30 mg/kg/day (maximum: 2 g/day)
Directly observed therapy (DOT): Twice weekly: 50-70 mg/kg (maximum: 4 g)
DOT: 3 times/week: 50-70 mg/kg (maximum: 3 g)
Elderly: Start with a lower daily dose (15 mg/kg) and increase as tolerated
Dosing adjustment in renal impairment: Cl_{cr} <50 mL/minute: Avoid use or reduce dose to 12-20 mg/kg/day
Dosing adjustment in hepatic impairment: Reduce dose

Monitoring Parameters Periodic liver function tests, serum uric acid, sputum culture, chest x-ray 2-3 months into treatment and at completion

Test Interactions Reacts with Acetest® and Ketostix® to produce pinkish-brown color

Patient Information Notify physician if fever, loss of appetite, malaise, nausea, vomiting, darkened urine, pale stools occur; do not stop taking without consulting a physician

Dosage Forms Tablet: 500 mg

Extemporaneous Preparations Pyrazinamide suspension can be compounded with simple syrup or 0.5% methylcellulose with simple syrup at a concentration of 100 mg/mL; the suspension is stable for 2 months at 4°C or 25°C when stored in glass or plastic bottles

To prepare pyrazinamide suspension in 0.5% methylcellulose with simple syrup: Crush 200 pyrazinamide 500 mg tablets and mix with a suspension containing 500 mL of 1% methylcellulose and 500 mL simple syrup. Add to this a suspension containing 140 crushed pyrazinamide tablets in 350 mL of 1% methylcellulose and 350 mL of simple syrup to make 1.7 L of suspension containing pyrazinamide 100 mg/mL in 0.5% methylcellulose with simple syrup.

Nahata MC, Morosco RS, and Peritre SP, "Stability of Pyrazinamide in Two Suspensions," *Am J Health Syst Pharm*, 1995, 52:1558-60.

♦ **Pyrazinoic Acid Amide** *see* Pyrazinamide *on previous page*

Pyrethrins *(pye RE thrins)*
U.S. Brand Names A-200™ Shampoo [OTC]; Barc™ Liquid [OTC]; End Lice® Liquid [OTC]; Lice-Enz® Shampoo [OTC]; Pronto® Shampoo [OTC]; Pyrinex® Pediculicide Shampoo [OTC]; Pyrinyl II® Liquid [OTC]; Pyrinyl Plus® Shampoo [OTC]; R & C® Shampoo [OTC]; RID® Shampoo [OTC]; Tisit® Blue Gel [OTC]; Tisit® Liquid [OTC]; Tisit® Shampoo [OTC]; Triple X® Liquid [OTC]

Therapeutic Category Antiparasitic Agent, Topical; Pediculocide; Shampoo, Pediculocide

Use Treatment of *Pediculus humanus* infestations (head lice, body lice, pubic lice and their eggs)

Pregnancy Risk Factor C

Contraindications Known hypersensitivity to pyrethrins, ragweed, or chrysanthemums

Warnings/Precautions For external use only; do not use in eyelashes or eyebrows

Adverse Reactions 1% to 10%:
Dermatologic: Pruritus
Local: Burning, stinging, irritation with repeat use

Mechanism of Action Pyrethrins are derived from flowers that belong to the chrysanthemum family. The mechanism of action on the neuronal membranes of lice is similar to that of DDT. Piperonyl butoxide is usually added to pyrethrin to enhance the product's activity by decreasing the metabolism of pyrethrins in arthropods.

Pharmacodynamics/Kinetics

Onset of action: ~30 minutes

Absorption: Topical into the system is minimal

Metabolism: By ester hydrolysis and hydroxylation

Usual Dosage Application of pyrethrins: Topical:

Apply enough solution to completely wet infested area, including hair

Allow to remain on area for 10 minutes

Wash and rinse with large amounts of warm water

Use fine-toothed comb to remove lice and eggs from hair

Shampoo hair to restore body and luster

Treatment may be repeated if necessary once in a 24-hour period

Repeat treatment in 7-10 days to kill newly hatched lice

Patient Information For external use only; avoid touching eyes, mouth, or other mucous membranes; contact physician if irritation occurs or if condition does not improve in 2-3 days

Dosage Forms

Gel, topical: 0.3% (30 g)

Liquid, topical: 0.18% (60 mL); 0.2% (60 mL, 120 mL); 0.3% (60 mL, 118 mL, 120 mL, 177 mL, 237 mL, 240 mL)

Shampoo: 0.3% (59 mL, 60 mL, 118 mL, 120 mL, 240 mL); 0.33% (60 mL, 120 mL)

◆ **Pyribenzamine®** see Tripelennamine on page 1187

◆ **Pyridiate®** see Phenazopyridine on page 910

◆ **2-Pyridine Aldoxime Methochloride** see Pralidoxime on page 956

◆ **Pyridium®** see Phenazopyridine on page 910

Pyridostigmine (peer id oh STIG meen)

U.S. Brand Names Mestinon®; Mestinon Time-Span®; Regonol® Injection

Canadian Brand Names Mestinon®-SR

Synonyms Pyridostigmine Bromide

Therapeutic Category Antidote, Neuromuscular Blocking Agent; Cholinergic Agent

Use Symptomatic treatment of myasthenia gravis; also used as an antidote for nondepolarizing neuromuscular blockers; not a cure; patient may develop resistance to the drug

Pregnancy Risk Factor C

Contraindications Hypersensitivity to pyridostigmine, bromides, or any component; GI or GU obstruction

Warnings/Precautions Use with caution in patients with epilepsy, asthma, bradycardia, hyperthyroidism, cardiac arrhythmias, or peptic ulcer; adequate facilities should be available for cardiopulmonary resuscitation when testing and adjusting dose for myasthenia gravis; have atropine and epinephrine ready to treat hypersensitivity reactions; overdosage may result in cholinergic crisis, this must be distinguished from myasthenic crisis; anticholinesterase insensitivity can develop for brief or prolonged periods

Adverse Reactions

>10%:

Gastrointestinal: Diarrhea, nausea, stomach cramps, mouth watering

Miscellaneous: Diaphoresis (increased)

1% to 10%:

Genitourinary: Urge to urinate

Ocular: Small pupils, lacrimation

Respiratory: Increased bronchial secretions

<1%: Bradycardia, A-V block, seizures, headache, dysphoria, drowsiness, thrombophlebitis, muscle spasms, weakness, miosis, diplopia, laryngospasm, respiratory paralysis, hypersensitivity, hyper-reactive cholinergic responses

Overdosage/Toxicology

Symptoms of overdose include muscle weakness, blurred vision, excessive sweating, tearing and salivation, nausea, vomiting, diarrhea, hypertension, bradycardia, paralysis

Atropine is the treatment of choice for intoxications manifesting with significant muscarinic symptoms. Atropine I.V. 2-4 mg every 3-60 minutes (or 0.04-0.08 mg I.V. every 5-60 minutes if needed for children) should be repeated to control symptoms and then continued as needed for 1-2 days following the acute ingestion.

Drug Interactions

Increased effect of depolarizing neuromuscular blockers (succinylcholine)

Increased toxicity with edrophonium

Stability Protect from light

Mechanism of Action Inhibits destruction of acetylcholine by acetylcholinesterase which facilitates transmission of impulses across myoneural junction

Pharmacodynamics/Kinetics

Onset of action: Oral, I.M.: Within 15-30 minutes; I.V. injection: Within 2-5 minutes

Absorption: Oral: Very poor (10% to 20%) from GI tract

Metabolism: In the liver

Usual Dosage Normally, sustained release dosage form is used at bedtime for patients who complain of morning weakness

(Continued)

Pyridostigmine *(Continued)*

Myasthenia gravis:
Oral:
Children: 7 mg/kg/day in 5-6 divided doses
Adults: Initial: 60 mg 3 times/day with maintenance dose ranging from 60 mg to 1.5 g/day; sustained release formulation should be dosed at least every 6 hours (usually 12-24 hours)
I.M., I.V.:
Children: 0.05-0.15 mg/kg/dose (maximum single dose: 10 mg)
Adults: 2 mg every 2-3 hours or 1/30th of oral dose
Reversal of nondepolarizing neuromuscular blocker: I.M., I.V.:
Children: 0.1-0.25 mg/kg/dose preceded by atropine
Adults: 10-20 mg preceded by atropine

Test Interactions ↑ aminotransferase [ALT (SGPT)/AST (SGOT)] (S), ↑ amylase (S)

Patient Information Side effects are generally due to exaggerated pharmacologic effects; most common side effects are salivation and muscle fasciculations; notify physician if nausea, vomiting, muscle weakness, severe abdominal pain, or difficulty breathing occurs

Nursing Implications Do not crush sustained release drug product; observe for cholinergic reactions, particularly when administered I.V.

Dosage Forms
Injection, as bromide: 5 mg/mL (2 mL, 5 mL)
Syrup, as bromide (raspberry flavor): 60 mg/5 mL (480 mL)
Tablet, as bromide: 60 mg
Tablet, as bromide, sustained release: 180 mg

♦ **Pyridostigmine Bromide** *see* Pyridostigmine *on previous page*

Pyridoxine (peer i DOKS een)

Related Information
Epilepsy Treatment *on page 1468*
Guidelines for the Prevention of Opportunistic Infections in Persons with HIV *on page 1388*

U.S. Brand Names Nestrex®

Synonyms Pyridoxine Hydrochloride; Vitamin B_6

Therapeutic Category Antidote, Cycloserine Toxicity; Antidote, Hydralazine Toxicity; Antidote, Isoniazid Toxicity; Vitamin, Water Soluble

Use Prevents and treats vitamin B_6 deficiency, pyridoxine-dependent seizures in infants, adjunct to treatment of acute toxicity from isoniazid, cycloserine, or hydralazine overdose

Pregnancy Risk Factor A (C if dose exceeds RDA recommendation)

Pregnancy/Breast-Feeding Implications
Clinical effects on the fetus: Crosses the placenta; available evidence suggests safe use during pregnancy and breast-feeding
Breast-feeding/lactation: Crosses into breast milk; possible inhibition of lactation at doses >600 mg/day. American Academy of Pediatrics considers **compatible** with breast-feeding.

Contraindications Hypersensitivity to pyridoxine or any component

Warnings/Precautions Dependence and withdrawal may occur with doses >200 mg/day

Adverse Reactions <1%: Sensory neuropathy, seizures have occurred following I.V. administration of very large doses, headache, nausea, decreased serum folic acid secretions, increased AST, paresthesia, allergic reactions have been reported

Overdosage/Toxicology Ataxia, sensory neuropathy with doses of 50 mg to 2 g daily over prolonged periods; acute doses of 70-357 mg/kg have been well tolerated

Drug Interactions Decreased serum levels of levodopa, phenobarbital, and phenytoin

Stability Protect from light

Mechanism of Action Precursor to pyridoxal, which functions in the metabolism of proteins, carbohydrates, and fats; pyridoxal also aids in the release of liver and muscle-stored glycogen and in the synthesis of GABA (within the central nervous system) and heme

Pharmacodynamics/Kinetics
Absorption: Enteral, parenteral: Well absorbed from GI tract
Metabolism: Metabolized in 4-pyridoxic acid (active form), and other metabolites
Half-life: 15-20 days

Usual Dosage
Recommended daily allowance (RDA):
Children:
1-3 years: 0.9 mg
4-6 years: 1.3 mg
7-10 years: 1.6 mg
Adults:
Male: 1.7-2.0 mg
Female: 1.4-1.6 mg
Pyridoxine-dependent Infants:
Oral: 2-100 mg/day
I.M., I.V., S.C.: 10-100 mg
Dietary deficiency: Oral:
Children: 5-25 mg/24 hours for 3 weeks, then 1.5-2.5 mg/day in multiple vitamin product

Adults: 10-20 mg/day for 3 weeks

Drug-induced neuritis (eg, isoniazid, hydralazine, penicillamine, cycloserine): Oral:
Children:
Treatment: 10-50 mg/24 hours
Prophylaxis: 1-2 mg/kg/24 hours
Adults:
Treatment: 100-200 mg/24 hours
Prophylaxis: 25-100 mg/24 hours

Treatment of seizures and/or coma from acute isoniazid toxicity, a dose of pyridoxine hydrochloride equal to the amount of INH ingested can be given I.M./I.V. in divided doses together with other anticonvulsants; if the amount INH ingested is not known, administer 5 g I.V. pyridoxine

Treatment of acute hydralazine toxicity, a pyridoxine dose of 25 mg/kg in divided doses I.M./I.V. has been used

Reference Range Over 50 ng/mL (SI: 243 nmol/L) (varies considerably with method). A broad range is ~25-80 ng/mL (SI: 122-389 nmol/L). HPLC method for pyridoxal phosphate has normal range of 3.5-18 ng/mL (SI: 17-88 nmol/L).

Test Interactions Urobilinogen

Patient Information Dietary sources of pyridoxine include red meats, bananas, potatoes, yeast, lima beans, whole grain cereals; do not exceed recommended doses

Nursing Implications Burning may occur at the injection site after I.M. or S.C. administration; seizures have occurred following I.V. administration of very large doses

Dosage Forms
Injection, as hydrochloride: 100 mg/mL (10 mL, 30 mL)
Tablet, as hydrochloride: 25 mg, 50 mg, 100 mg
Tablet, as hydrochloride, extended release: 100 mg

Extemporaneous Preparations A 1 mg/mL oral solution was stable for 30 days when refrigerated when compounded as follows:
Withdraw 100 mg (1 mL of a 100 mg/mL injection) from a vial with a needle and syringe, add to 99 mL of simple syrup in an amber bottle
Keep in refrigerator

Nahata MC and Hipple TF, *Pediatric Drug Formulations*, 3rd ed, Cincinnati, OH: Harvey Whitney Books Co, 1997.

♦ **Pyridoxine Hydrochloride** *see Pyridoxine on previous page*

Pyrimethamine (peer i METH a meen)

Related Information
Guidelines for the Prevention of Opportunistic Infections in Persons with HIV *on page 1388*
Malaria Treatment *on page 1425*
Prevention of Malaria *on page 1372*

U.S. Brand Names Daraprim®

Therapeutic Category Antimalarial Agent

Use Prophylaxis of malaria due to susceptible strains of plasmodia; used in conjunction with quinine and sulfadiazine for the treatment of uncomplicated attacks of chloroquine-resistant *P. falciparum* malaria; used in conjunction with fast-acting schizonticide to initiate transmission control and suppression cure; synergistic combination with sulfonamide in treatment of toxoplasmosis

Pregnancy Risk Factor C

Contraindications Megaloblastic anemia secondary to folate deficiency; known hypersensitivity to pyrimethamine, chloroguanide; resistant malaria

Warnings/Precautions When used for more than 3-4 days, it may be advisable to administer leucovorin to prevent hematologic complications; monitor CBC and platelet counts every 2 weeks; use with caution in patients with impaired renal or hepatic function or with possible G-6-PD

Adverse Reactions
1% to 10%:
Gastrointestinal: Anorexia, abdominal cramps, vomiting
Hematologic: Megaloblastic anemia, leukopenia, thrombocytopenia, agranulocytosis
<1%: Insomnia, lightheadedness, fever, malaise, seizures, depression, rash, dermatitis, Stevens-Johnson syndrome, erythema multiforme, anaphylaxis, abnormal skin pigmentation, diarrhea, xerostomia, atrophic glossitis, pulmonary eosinophilia

Overdosage/Toxicology
Symptoms of overdose include megaloblastic anemia, leukopenia, thrombocytopenia, anorexia, CNS stimulation, seizures, nausea, vomiting, hematemesis
Following GI decontamination, leucovorin should be administered in a dosage of 5-15 mg/day I.M., I.V., or oral for 5-7 days or as required to reverse symptoms of folic acid deficiency; diazepam 0.1-0.25 mg/kg can be used to treat seizures

Drug Interactions
Decreased effect: Pyrimethamine effectiveness decreased by acid
Increased effect: Sulfonamides (synergy), methotrexate, TMP/SMX may increase the risk of bone marrow suppression; mild hepatotoxicity with lorazepam

Stability Pyrimethamine tablets may be crushed to prepare oral suspensions of the drug in water, cherry syrup, or sucrose-containing solutions at a concentration of 1 mg/mL; stable at room temperature for 5-7 days

Mechanism of Action Inhibits parasitic dihydrofolate reductase, resulting in inhibition of vital tetrahydrofolic acid synthesis
(Continued)

Pyrimethamine *(Continued)*

Pharmacodynamics/Kinetics

Absorption: Oral: Well absorbed

Distribution: Widely distributed ; mainly concentrated in blood cells, kidneys, lungs, liver, and spleen; crosses into CSF; crosses placenta; appears in breast milk

Metabolism: Hepatic

Half-life: 80-95 hours

Time to peak serum concentration: Within 1.5-8 hours

Elimination: 20% to 30% excreted unchanged in urine

Usual Dosage

Malaria chemoprophylaxis (for areas where chloroquine-resistant *P. falciparum* exists): Begin prophylaxis 2 weeks before entering endemic area:

Children: 0.5 mg/kg once weekly; not to exceed 25 mg/dose

or

Children:

    <4 years: 6.25 mg once weekly

    4-10 years: 12.5 mg once weekly

Children >10 years and Adults: 25 mg once weekly

Dosage should be continued for all age groups for at least 6-10 weeks after leaving endemic areas

Chloroquine-resistant *P. falciparum* malaria (when used in conjunction with quinine and sulfadiazine):

Children:

    <10 kg: 6.25 mg/day once daily for 3 days

    10-20 kg: 12.5 mg/day once daily for 3 days

    20-40 kg: 25 mg/day once daily for 3 days

Adults: 25 mg twice daily for 3 days

Toxoplasmosis:

Infants for congenital toxoplasmosis: Oral: 1 mg/kg once daily for 6 months with sulfadiazine then every other month with sulfa, alternating with spiramycin.

Children: Loading dose: 2 mg/kg/day divided into 2 equal daily doses for 1-3 days (maximum: 100 mg/day) followed by 1 mg/kg/day divided into 2 doses for 4 weeks; maximum: 25 mg/day

With sulfadiazine or trisulfapyrimidines: 2 mg/kg/day divided every 12 hours for 3 days followed by 1 mg/kg/day once daily or divided twice daily for 4 weeks given with trisulfapyrimidines or sulfadiazine

Adults: 50-75 mg/day together with 1-4 g of a sulfonamide for 1-3 weeks depending on patient's tolerance and response, then reduce dose by 50% and continue for 4-5 weeks **or** 25-50 mg/day for 3-4 weeks

In HIV, life-long suppression is necessary to prevent relapse; leucovorin (5-10 mg/day) is given concurrently

Monitoring Parameters CBC, including platelet counts

Patient Information Take with meals to minimize vomiting; begin malaria prophylaxis at least 1-2 weeks prior to departure; discontinue at first sign of skin rash; notify physician if persistent fever, sore throat, bleeding or bruising occurs; regular blood work may be necessary in patients taking high doses

Dosage Forms Tablet: 25 mg

Extemporaneous Preparations Pyrimethamine tablets may be crushed to prepare oral suspensions of the drug in water, cherry syrup or sucrose-containing solutions at a concentration of 1 mg/mL; stable at room temperature for 5-7 days

McEvoy G, ed. AHFS Drug Information 96. Bethesda, MD: American Society of Health-System Pharmacists, 1996.

♦ **Pyrinex® Pediculicide Shampoo [OTC]** *see* Pyrethrins *on page 996*

♦ **Pyrinyl II® Liquid [OTC]** *see* Pyrethrins *on page 996*

♦ **Pyrinyl Plus® Shampoo [OTC]** *see* Pyrethrins *on page 996*

♦ **Pyronium®** *see* Phenazopyridine *on page 910*

♦ **Quaternium-18 Bentonite** *see* Bentoquatam *on page 132*

Quazepam *(KWAY ze pam)*

Related Information

Benzodiazepines Comparison *on page 1310*

U.S. Brand Names Doral®

Therapeutic Category Benzodiazepine; Hypnotic; Sedative

Use Treatment of insomnia; more likely than triazolam to cause daytime sedation and fatigue; is classified as a long-acting benzodiazepine hypnotic (like flurazepam - Dalmane®), this long duration of action may prevent withdrawal symptoms when therapy is discontinued

Restrictions C-IV

Pregnancy Risk Factor X

Contraindications Narrow-angle glaucoma, pregnancy, known hypersensitivity to quazepam

Usual Dosage Adults: Oral: Initial: 15 mg at bedtime, in some patients the dose may be reduced to 7.5 mg after a few nights

Dosing adjustment in hepatic impairment: Dose reduction may be necessary

Additional Information Complete prescribing information for this medication should be consulted for additional detail

Dosage Forms Tablet: 7.5 mg, 15 mg

- ♦ **Quelicin® Injection** *see* Succinylcholine *on page 1087*
- ♦ **Queltuss®** *see* Guaifenesin and Dextromethorphan *on page 550*
- ♦ **Questran®** *see* Cholestyramine Resin *on page 254*
- ♦ **Questran® Light** *see* Cholestyramine Resin *on page 254*

Quetiapine (kwe TYE a peen)

U.S. Brand Names Seroquel®

Synonyms Quetiapine Fumarate

Therapeutic Category Antipsychotic Agent

Use Treatment of acute exacerbations of schizophrenia or other psychotic disorders. Like other atypical antipsychotics, quetiapine is probably best tried in cases for which typical antipsychotic drugs have proven ineffective.

Pregnancy Risk Factor C

Contraindications Known hypersensitivity to this drug or any of its ingredients

Warnings/Precautions May induce orthostatic hypotension associated with dizziness, tachycardia, and, in some cases, syncope, especially during the initial dose titration period. Should be used with particular caution in patients with known cardiovascular disease (history of MI or ischemic heart disease, heart failure, or conduction abnormalities), cerebrovascular disease, or conditions that predispose to hypotension. Development of cataracts has been observed in animal studies, therefore, lens examinations should be made upon initiation of therapy and every 6 months thereafter.

Neuroleptic malignant syndrome (NMS) is a potentially fatal symptom complex that has been reported in association with administration of antipsychotic drugs. Clinical manifestations of NMS are hyperpyrexia, muscle rigidity, altered mental status, and evidence of autonomic instability (irregular pulse or blood pressure, tachycardia, diaphoresis, and cardiac dysrhythmia). Management of NMS should include immediate discontinuation of antipsychotic drugs and other drugs not essential to concurrent therapy, intensive symptomatic treatment and medication monitoring, and treatment of any concomitant medical problems for which specific treatment are available.

Tardive dyskinesia; caution in patients with a history of seizures, decreases in total free thyroxine, pre-existing hyperprolactinemia, elevations of liver enzymes, cholesterol levels and/or triglyceride increases.

Adverse Reactions

>2%:

Cardiovascular: Postural hypotension (4% to 14%)

Central nervous system: Agitation (6% to 28%), somnolence (6% to 39%), headache (5% to 31%), insomnia (4% to 15%), dizziness (2% to 11%)

Gastrointestinal: Xerostomia (8% to 19%)

Hepatic: Serum ALT increases (5% to 17%)

<2%: Tachycardia, dyspepsia, constipation, weight gain, increases in total cholesterol and triglycerides; hypothyroidism developed in a small number of patients. Treatment-related extrapyramidal symptoms were not observed in animal studies and lens changes have been observed in patients receiving long-term therapy.

Drug Interactions CYP2D6 and 3A3/4enzyme substrate

Caution with other centrally acting drugs; avoid alcohol. May enhance effects of antihypertensive agents; may antagonize levodopa, dopamine agonists. Increased clearance when given with phenytoin or thioridazine, caution with other liver enzyme inducers (carbamazepine, barbiturates, rifampin, glucocorticoids); although data is not yet available, caution is advised with inhibitors of cytochrome P-450 (eg, ketoconazole, erythromycin); reduces the clearance of lorazepam.

Mechanism of Action Mechanism of action of quetiapine, as with other antipsychotic drugs, is unknown. However, it has been proposed that this drug's antipsychotic activity is mediated through a combination of dopamine type 2 (D_2) and serotonin type 2 (5-HT_2) antagonism. However, it is an antagonist at multiple neurotransmitter receptors in the brain: serotonin 5-HT_{1A} and 5-HT_2, dopamine D_1 and D_2, histamine H_1, and adrenergic alpha$_1$- and alpha$_2$-receptors; but appears to have no appreciable affinity at cholinergic muscarinic and benzodiazepine receptors.

Antagonism at receptors other than dopamine and 5-HT_2 with similar receptor affinities may explain some of the other effects of quetiapine. The drug's antagonism of histamine H_1 receptors may explain the somnolence observed with it. The drug's antagonism of adrenergic alpha$_1$-receptors may explain the orthostatic hypotension observed with it.

Pharmacodynamics/Kinetics

Absorption: Accumulation is predictable upon multiple dosing

Distribution: Steady-state concentrations are expected to be achieved within 2 days of dosing; unlikely to interfere with the metabolism of drugs metabolized by cytochrome P-450 enzymes

Metabolism: Both metabolites are pharmacologically inactive

Half-life, mean terminal: ~6 hours

Time to peak plasma concentrations: 1.5 hours

Elimination: Mainly via hepatic metabolism

Usual Dosage Adults: Oral: 25-100 mg 2-3 times/day; usual starting dose: 25 mg twice daily and then increased in increments of 25-50 mg 2-3 times/day on the second or third day; by day 4, the dose should be in the range of 300-400 mg/day in 2-3 divided doses. Make further adjustments as needed at intervals of at least 2 days in adjustments of 25-50 mg twice daily. The usual maintenance range is 150-750 mg/day; maximum dose: 800 mg/day.

(Continued)

Quetiapine *(Continued)*

Dosing comments in geriatric patients: 40% lower mean oral clearance of quetiapine in adults >65 years of age; higher plasma levels expected and, therefore, dosage adjustment may be needed

Dosing comments in hepatic insufficiency: 30% lower mean oral clearance of quetiapine than normal subjects; higher plasma levels expected in hepatically impaired subjects; dosage adjustment may be needed

Dietary Considerations In healthy volunteers, administration of quetiapine with food resulted in an increase in the peak serum concentration and AUC (each by ~150%) compared to the fasting state. The clinical relevance of these data requires qualification in further studies.

Monitoring Parameters Patients should have eyes checked every 6 months for cataracts while on this medication

Patient Information May cause headache, drowsiness, dizziness, and/or lightheadedness, especially when the patient stands up or gets up from lying down. If this happens, the patient should sit or lie down immediately. This agent might increase the risk of cataracts; avoid alcohol, overheating, dehydration.

Additional Information Quetiapine has a very low incidence of extrapyramidal symptoms such as restlessness and abnormal movement, and is at least as effective as conventional antipsychotics

Dosage Forms Tablet: 25 mg, 100 mg, 200 mg

- ◆ **Quetiapine Fumarate** *see Quetiapine on previous page*
- ◆ **Quibron®** *see Theophylline and Guaifenesin on page 1125*
- ◆ **Quibron®-T** *see Theophylline Salts on page 1125*
- ◆ **Quibron®-T/SR** *see Theophylline Salts on page 1125*
- ◆ **Quiess®** *see Hydroxyzine on page 589*
- ◆ **Quinaglute® Dura-Tabs®** *see Quinidine on next page*
- ◆ **Quinalan®** *see Quinidine on next page*
- ◆ **Quinalbarbitone Sodium** *see Secobarbital on page 1053*

Quinapril *(KWIN a pril)*

Related Information
Angiotensin Agents *on page 1291*
Drug-Drug Interactions With ACEIs *on page 1295*
Heart Failure: Management of Patients With Left-Ventricular Systolic Dysfunction *on page 1472*

U.S. Brand Names Accupril®

Synonyms Quinapril Hydrochloride

Therapeutic Category Angiotensin-Converting Enzyme (ACE) Inhibitor; Antihypertensive Agent

Use Management of hypertension and treatment of congestive heart failure; increase circulation in Raynaud's phenomenon; idiopathic edema; believed to improve survival in heart failure

Unlabeled use: Hypertensive crisis, diabetic nephropathy, rheumatoid arthritis, diagnosis of anatomic renal artery stenosis, hypertension secondary to scleroderma renal crisis, diagnosis of aldosteronism, Bartter's syndrome, postmyocardial infarction for prevention of ventricular failure

Pregnancy Risk Factor C (1st trimester); D (2nd and 3rd trimester)

Contraindications Hypersensitivity to quinapril or history of angioedema induced by other ACE inhibitors

Warnings/Precautions Use with caution in patients with renal insufficiency, autoimmune disease, renal artery stenosis; excessive hypotension may be more likely in volume-depleted patients, the elderly, and following the first dose (first dose phenomenon); quinapril should be discontinued if laryngeal stridor or angioedema of the face, tongue, or glottis is observed

Adverse Reactions
1% to 10%:
Cardiovascular: Hypotension
Central nervous system: Dizziness (3.9%), headache (5.6%), fatigue (2.6%)
Gastrointestinal: Vomiting/nausea (1.4%)
Renal: Increased BUN/serum creatinine (transient)
Respiratory: Upper respiratory symptoms, cough (2%)
<1%: Chest discomfort, flushing, myocardial infarction, angina pectoris, orthostatic hypotension, rhythm disturbances, tachycardia, peripheral edema, vasculitis, palpitations, syncope, fever, malaise, depression, somnolence, insomnia, urticaria, pruritus, angioedema, gout, pancreatitis, abdominal pain, anorexia, constipation, flatulence, xerostomia, neutropenia, bone marrow suppression, hepatitis, arthralgia, shoulder pain, blurred vision, bronchitis, sinusitis, pharyngeal pain, diaphoresis

Overdosage/Toxicology
Mild hypotension has been the only toxic effect seen with acute overdose. Bradycardia may also occur; hyperkalemia occurs even with therapeutic doses, especially in patients with renal insufficiency and those taking NSAIDs.
Following initiation of essential overdose management, toxic symptom treatment and supportive treatment should be initiated. Hypotension usually responds to I.V. fluids or Trendelenburg positioning.

Drug Interactions See Drug-Drug Interactions With ACEIs *on page 1295*

Stability Store at room temperature; unstable in aqueous solutions; to prepare solution for oral administration, mix prior to administration and use within 10 minutes

Mechanism of Action Competitive inhibitor of angiotensin-converting enzyme (ACE); prevents conversion of angiotensin I to angiotensin II, a potent vasoconstrictor; results in lower levels of angiotensin II which causes an increase in plasma renin activity and a reduction in aldosterone secretion; a CNS mechanism may also be involved in hypotensive effect as angiotensin II increases adrenergic outflow from CNS; vasoactive kallikreins may be decreased in conversion to active hormones by ACE inhibitors, thus reducing blood pressure

Pharmacodynamics/Kinetics

Metabolism: Rapidly hydrolyzed to quinaprilat, the active metabolite

Half-life, elimination: Quinapril: 0.8 hours; Quinaprilat: 2 hours

Time to peak serum concentration: Quinapril: 1 hour; Quinaprilat: ~2 hours

Elimination: 50% to 60% of quinapril excreted in urine primarily as quinaprilat

Usual Dosage

Adults: Oral: Initial: 10 mg once daily, adjust according to blood pressure response at peak and trough blood levels; in general, the normal dosage range is 20-80 mg/day for hypertension and 20-40 mg/day for edema in single or divided doses

Elderly: Initial: 2.5-5 mg/day; increase dosage at increments of 2.5-5 mg at 1- to 2-week intervals

Dosing adjustment in renal impairment:

Cl_{cr} >60 mL/minute: Administer 10 mg/day

Cl_{cr} 30-60 mL/minute: 5 mg/day

Cl_{cr} 10-30 mL/minute: 2.5 mg/day

Dosing comments in hepatic impairment: In patients with alcoholic cirrhosis, hydrolysis of quinapril to quinaprilat is impaired; however, the subsequent elimination of quinaprilat is unaltered

Patient Information Do not discontinue medication without advice of physician; notify physician if sore throat, swelling, palpitations, cough, chest pains, difficulty swallowing, swelling of face, eyes, tongue, lips; hoarseness, sweating, vomiting, or diarrhea occurs; may cause dizziness, lightheadedness during first few days; may also cause changes in taste perception

Nursing Implications May cause depression in some patients; discontinue if angioedema of the face, extremities, lips, tongue, or glottis occurs; watch for hypotensive effects within 1-3 hours of first dose or new higher dose

Dosage Forms Tablet, as hydrochloride: 5 mg, 10 mg, 20 mg, 40 mg

♦ **Quinapril Hydrochloride** *see Quinapril on previous page*

Quinethazone (kwin ETH a zone)

Related Information

Sulfonamide Derivatives *on page 1337*

U.S. Brand Names Hydromox®

Therapeutic Category Antihypertensive Agent; Diuretic, Thiazide

Use Adjunctive therapy in treatment of edema and hypertension

Pregnancy Risk Factor D

Contraindications Anuria; hypersensitivity to sulfonamide-derived drugs

Usual Dosage Adults: Oral: 50-100 mg once daily; usual maximum: 200 mg/day

Additional Information Complete prescribing information for this medication should be consulted for additional detail

Dosage Forms Tablet: 50 mg

♦ **Quinidex® Extentabs®** *see Quinidine on this page*

Quinidine (KWIN i deen)

Related Information

Adult ACLS Algorithm, Tachycardia *on page 1450*

Antacid Drug Interactions *on page 1296*

Antiarrhythmic Drugs Comparison *on page 1297*

Malaria Treatment *on page 1425*

U.S. Brand Names Cardioquin®; Quinaglute® Dura-Tabs®; Quinalan®; Quinidex® Extentabs®; Quinora®

Synonyms Quinidine Gluconate; Quinidine Polygalacturonate; Quinidine Sulfate

Therapeutic Category Antiarrhythmic Agent, Class I-A

Use Prophylaxis after cardioversion of atrial fibrillation and/or flutter to maintain normal sinus rhythm; also used to prevent reoccurrence of paroxysmal supraventricular tachycardia, paroxysmal A-V junctional rhythm, paroxysmal ventricular tachycardia, paroxysmal atrial fibrillation, and atrial or ventricular premature contractions; also has activity against *Plasmodium falciparum* malaria

Pregnancy Risk Factor C

Contraindications Patients with complete A-V block with an A-V junctional or idioventricular pacemaker; patients with intraventricular conduction defects (marked widening of QRS complex); patients with cardiac-glycoside induced A-V conduction disorders; hypersensitivity to the drug or cinchona derivatives; concurrent use of sparfloxacin or ritonavir

Warnings/Precautions Use with caution in patients with myocardial depression, sick-sinus syndrome, incomplete A-V block, hepatic and/or renal insufficiency, myasthenia gravis; hemolysis may occur in patients with G-6-PD (glucose-6-phosphate dehydrogenase) deficiency; quinidine-induced hepatotoxicity, including granulomatous hepatitis

(Continued)

Quinidine (Continued)

can occur, increased serum AST and alkaline phosphatase concentrations, and jaundice may occur; use with caution in nursing women and elderly

Adverse Reactions

>10%: Gastrointestinal: Bitter taste, diarrhea, anorexia, nausea, vomiting, stomach cramping

1% to 10%:

Cardiovascular: Hypotension, syncope

Central nervous system: Lightheadedness, severe headache

Dermatologic: Rash

Ocular: Blurred vision

Otic: Tinnitus

Respiratory: Wheezing

<1%: Tachycardia, heart block, ventricular fibrillation, vascular collapse, confusion, delirium, fever, vertigo, angioedema, anemia, thrombocytopenic purpura, blood dyscrasias, impaired hearing, respiratory depression, pneumonitis, bronchospasm

Overdosage/Toxicology

Has a low toxic:therapeutic ratio and may easily produce fatal intoxication (acute toxic dose: 1 g in adults); symptoms of overdose include sinus bradycardia, sinus node arrest or asystole, P-R, QRS or Q-T interval prolongation, torsade de pointes (polymorphous ventricular tachycardia) and depressed myocardial contractility, which along with alpha-adrenergic or ganglionic blockade, may result in hypotension and pulmonary edema; other effects are anticholinergic (dry mouth, dilated pupils, and delirium) as well as seizures, coma and respiratory arrest.

Treatment is primarily symptomatic and effects usually respond to conventional therapies (fluids, positioning, vasopressors, anticonvulsants, antiarrhythmics). **Note:** Do not use other type 1a or 1c antiarrhythmic agents to treat ventricular tachycardia; sodium bicarbonate may treat wide QRS intervals or hypotension; markedly impaired conduction or high degree A-V block, unresponsive to bicarbonate, indicates consideration of a pacemaker is needed.

Drug Interactions CYP3A3/4 and 3A5-7 enzyme substrate; CYP2D6 and 3A3/4 enzyme inhibitor

Decreased effect: Phenobarbital, phenytoin, and rifampin may decrease quinidine serum concentrations (rifampin may decrease quinidine half-life by 50%, probably by inducing the CYP3A isozyme)

Increased toxicity:

Quinidine potentiates nondepolarizing and depolarizing muscle relaxants; quinidine may increase plasma concentration of digoxin, procainamide, propafenone, tricyclic antidepressants, closely monitor digoxin concentrations, digoxin dosage may need to be reduced (by one-half) when quinidine is initiated; quinidine may enhance coumarin anticoagulants

Beta-blockers + quinidine may increase bradycardia

Verapamil, amiodarone, alkalinizing agents, and cimetidine may increase quinidine serum concentrations

Avoid use with sparfloxacin due to increased risk of cardiotoxicity

Contraindicated with ritonavir due to increased risk of quinidine toxicity, especially cardiotoxicity

Increased disopyramide or decreased quinidine levels can occur when administered concurrently

Stability Do not use discolored parenteral solution

Mechanism of Action Class 1A antiarrhythmic agent; depresses phase O of the action potential; decreases myocardial excitability and conduction velocity, and myocardial contractility by decreasing sodium influx during depolarization and potassium efflux in repolarization; also reduces calcium transport across cell membrane

Pharmacodynamics/Kinetics

Distribution: V_d: Adults: 2-3.5 L/kg, decreased with congestive heart failure, malaria; increased with cirrhosis; crosses the placenta; appears in breast milk

Protein binding:

Newborns: 60% to 70%; decreased protein binding with cyanotic congenital heart disease, cirrhosis, or acute myocardial infarction

Adults: 80% to 90%

Metabolism: Extensively in the liver (50% to 90%) to inactive compounds

Bioavailability: Sulfate: 80%; Gluconate: 70%

Plasma half-life: Children: 2.5-6.7 hours; Adults: 6-8 hours; increased half-life with elderly, cirrhosis, and congestive heart failure

Elimination: In urine (15% to 25% as unchanged drug)

Usual Dosage Dosage expressed in terms of the salt: 267 mg of quinidine gluconate = 200 mg of quinidine sulfate

Children: Test dose for idiosyncratic reaction (sulfate, oral or gluconate, I.M.): 2 mg/kg or 60 mg/m²

Oral (quinidine sulfate): 15-60 mg/kg/day in 4-5 divided doses or 6 mg/kg every 4-6 hours; usual 30 mg/kg/day or 900 mg/m²/day given in 5 daily doses

I.V. not recommended (quinidine gluconate): 2-10 mg/kg/dose given at a rate ≤10 mg/minute every 3-6 hours as needed

Adults: Test dose: Oral, I.M.: 200 mg administered several hours before full dosage (to determine possibility of idiosyncratic reaction)

Oral (for malaria):
Sulfate: 100-600 mg/dose every 4-6 hours; begin at 200 mg/dose and titrate to desired effect (maximum daily dose: 3-4 g)
Gluconate: 324-972 mg every 8-12 hours
I.M.: 400 mg/dose every 2-6 hours; initial dose: 600 mg (gluconate)
I.V.: 200-400 mg/dose diluted and given at a rate ≤10 mg/minute; may require as much as 500-750 mg

Dosing adjustment in renal impairment: Cl$_{cr}$ <10 mL/minute: Administer 75% of normal dose
Hemodialysis: Slightly hemodialyzable (5% to 20%); 200 mg supplemental dose posthemodialysis is recommended
Peritoneal dialysis: Not dialyzable (0% to 5%)

Dosing adjustment/comments in hepatic impairment: Larger loading dose may be indicated, reduce maintenance doses by 50% and monitor serum levels closely

Administration When injecting I.M., aspirate carefully to avoid injection into a vessel; administer around-the-clock to promote less variation in peak and trough serum levels; maximum I.V. infusion rate: 10 mg/minute

Monitoring Parameters Cardiac monitor required during I.V. administration; CBC, liver and renal function tests, should be routinely performed during long-term administration

Reference Range Therapeutic: 2-5 µg/mL (SI: 6.2-15.4 µmol/L). Patient dependent therapeutic response occurs at levels of 3-6 µg/mL (SI: 9.2-18.5 µmol/L). Optimal therapeutic level is method dependent; >6 µg/mL (SI: >18 µmol/L).

Patient Information Do not crush sustained release preparations. Patients should notify their physician if rash, fever, unusual bleeding or bruising, ringing in the ears, visual disturbances, or syncope occurs; seek emergency help if palpitations occur.

Nursing Implications Do not crush sustained release drug product

Additional Information
Quinidine gluconate: Duraquin®, Quinaglute® Dura-Tabs®, Quinalan®, Quinatime®
Quinidine polygalacturonate: Cardioquin®
Quinidine sulfate: Cin-Quin®, Quinidex® Extentabs®, Quinora®

Dosage Forms
Injection, as gluconate: 80 mg/mL (10 mL)
Tablet, as polygalacturonate: 275 mg
Tablet, as sulfate: 200 mg, 300 mg
Tablet:
Sustained action, as sulfate: 300 mg
Sustained release, as gluconate: 324 mg

Extemporaneous Preparations A 10 mg/mL quinidine sulfate solution made with six 200 mg capsules, 15 mL alcohol USP, and citric acid syrup USP qs ad to a total amount of 120 mL is stable for 30 days under refrigeration

Nahata MC and Hipple TF, *Pediatric Drug Formulations*, 2nd ed, Cincinnati, OH: Harvey Whitney Books Co, 1992.

♦ **Quinidine Gluconate** *see* Quinidine *on page 1003*
♦ **Quinidine Polygalacturonate** *see* Quinidine *on page 1003*
♦ **Quinidine Sulfate** *see* Quinidine *on page 1003*

Quinine (KWYE nine)

Related Information
Malaria Treatment *on page 1425*

U.S. Brand Names Formula Q®

Synonyms Quinine Sulfate

Therapeutic Category Antimalarial Agent

Use In conjunction with other antimalarial agents, suppression or treatment of chloroquine-resistant *P. falciparum* malaria; treatment of *Babesia microti* infection in conjunction with clindamycin; prevention and treatment of nocturnal recumbency leg muscle cramps

Pregnancy Risk Factor X

Contraindications Tinnitus, optic neuritis, G-6-PD deficiency, hypersensitivity to quinine or any component, history of black water fever, and thrombocytopenia with quinine or quinidine

Warnings/Precautions Use with caution in patients with cardiac arrhythmias (quinine has quinidine-like activity) and in patients with myasthenia gravis

Adverse Reactions
Percentage unknown: Cinchonism (risk of cinchonism is directly related to dose and duration of therapy): Severe headache, nausea, vomiting, diarrhea, blurred vision, tinnitus
<1%: Flushing of the skin, anginal symptoms, fever, rash, pruritus, hypoglycemia, epigastric pain, hemolysis in G-6-PD deficiency, thrombocytopenia, hepatitis, nightblindness, diplopia, optic atrophy, impaired hearing, hypersensitivity reactions

Overdosage/Toxicology
Symptoms of mild toxicity include nausea, vomiting, and cinchonism; severe intoxication may cause ataxia, obtundation, convulsions, coma, and respiratory arrest; with massive intoxication quinidine-like cardiotoxicity (hypotension, QRS and Q-T interval prolongation, A-V block, and ventricular arrhythmias) may be fatal; retinal toxicity occurs 9-10 hours after ingestion (blurred vision, impaired color perception, constriction of visual fields and blindness); other toxic effects include hypokalemia, hypoglycemia, hemolysis and congenital malformations when taken during pregnancy.
Treatment includes symptomatic therapy with conventional agents (anticonvulsants, fluids, positioning, vasoconstrictors, antiarrhythmics). **Note:** Avoid type 1a and 1c (Continued)

Quinine *(Continued)*

antiarrhythmic drugs; treat cardiotoxicity with sodium bicarbonate; dialysis and hemo-perfusion procedures are ineffective in enhancing elimination.

Drug Interactions CYP3A3/4 enzyme substrate; CYP3A3/4 enzyme inhibitor

Decreased effect: Phenobarbital, phenytoin, aluminum salt antacids, and rifampin may decrease quinine serum concentrations

Increased toxicity:

To avoid risk of seizures and cardiac arrest, delay mefloquine dosing at least 12 hours after last dose of quinine

Beta-blockers + quinine may increase bradycardia

Quinine may enhance coumarin anticoagulants and potentiate nondepolarizing and depolarizing muscle relaxants

Quinine may inhibit metabolism of astemizole resulting in toxic levels and potentially life-threatening cardiotoxicity

Quinine may increase plasma concentration of digoxin by as much as twofold; closely monitor digoxin concentrations and decrease digoxin dose with initiation of quinine by $\frac{1}{2}$

Verapamil, amiodarone, urinary alkalinizing agents, and cimetidine may increase quinine serum concentrations

Stability Protect from light

Mechanism of Action Depresses oxygen uptake and carbohydrate metabolism; interca-lates into DNA, disrupting the parasite's replication and transcription; affects calcium distribution within muscle fibers and decreases the excitability of the motor end-plate region; cardiovascular effects similar to quinidine

Pharmacodynamics/Kinetics

Absorption: Oral: Readily absorbed mainly from the upper small intestine

Protein binding: 70% to 95%

Metabolism: Primarily in the liver

Half-life: Children: 6-12 hours; Adults: 8-14 hours

Time to peak serum concentration: Within 1-3 hours

Elimination: In bile and saliva with <5% excreted unchanged in urine

Usual Dosage Oral:

Children:

Treatment of chloroquine-resistant malaria: 25-30 mg/kg/day in divided doses every 8 hours for 5-7 days in conjunction with another agent

Babesiosis: 25 mg/kg/day divided every 8 hours for 7 days

Adults:

Treatment of chloroquine-resistant malaria: 260-650 mg every 8 hours for 6-12 days in conjunction with another agent

Suppression of malaria: 325 mg twice daily and continued for 6 weeks after exposure

Babesiosis: 650 mg every 6-8 hours for 7 days

Leg cramps: 200-300 mg at bedtime

Dosing interval/adjustment in renal impairment:

Cl_{cr} 10-50 mL/minute: Administer every 8-12 hours or 75% of normal dose

Cl_{cr} <10 mL/minute: Administer every 24 hours or 30% to 50% of normal dose

Dialysis: Not removed

Peritoneal dialysis: Dose as for Cl_{cr} <10 mL/min

Continuous arteriovenous or venovenous hemodiafiltration (CAVH) effects: Dose for Cl_{cr} 10-50 mL/minute

Reference Range Toxic: >10 µg/mL

Test Interactions Positive Coombs' [direct]; false elevation of urinary steroids and cate-cholamines

Patient Information Do not crush sustained release preparations. Avoid use of aluminum-containing antacids because of drug absorption problems; swallow dose whole to avoid bitter taste; may cause night blindness. Patients should notify their physician if rash, fever, unusual bleeding or bruising, ringing in the ears, visual distur-bances, or syncope occur; seek emergency help if palpitations occur.

Dosage Forms

Capsule, as sulfate: 200 mg, 260 mg, 325 mg

Tablet, as sulfate: 260 mg

- ◆ **Quinine Sulfate** *see Quinine on previous page*
- ◆ **Quinol** *see Hydroquinone on page 584*
- ◆ **Quinora®** *see Quinidine on page 1003*
- ◆ **Quinsana Plus® [OTC]** *see Tolnaftate on page 1159*
- ◆ **QYS®** *see Hydroxyzine on page 589*
- ◆ **RabAvert™** *see Rabies Virus Vaccine on next page*

Rabies Immune Globulin (Human)

(RAY beez i MYUN GLOB yoo lin, HYU man)

Related Information

Immunization Recommendations *on page 1358*

U.S. Brand Names Hyperab®; Imogam®

Synonyms RIG

Therapeutic Category Immune Globulin

Use Part of postexposure prophylaxis of persons with rabies exposure who lack a history or pre-exposure or postexposure prophylaxis with rabies vaccine or a recently docu-mented neutralizing antibody response to previous rabies vaccination; although it is preferable to administer RIG with the first dose of vaccine, it can be given up to 8 days after vaccination

Pregnancy Risk Factor C

Contraindications Inadvertent I.V. administration; allergy to thimerosal or any component

Warnings/Precautions Use with caution in individuals with thrombocytopenia, bleeding disorders, or prior allergic reactions to immune globulins

Adverse Reactions

1% to 10%:

Central nervous system: Fever (mild)

Local: Soreness at injection site

<1%: Urticaria, angioedema, stiffness, soreness of muscles, anaphylactic shock

Drug Interactions Decreased effect: Live virus vaccines (eg, MMR, rabies) may have delayed or diminished antibody response with immune globulin administration; should not be administered within 3 months unless antibody titers dictate as appropriate

Stability Refrigerate

Mechanism of Action Rabies immune globulin is a solution of globulins dried from the plasma or serum of selected adult human donors who have been immunized with rabies vaccine and have developed high titers of rabies antibody. It generally contains 10% to 18% of protein of which not less than 80% is monomeric immunoglobulin G.

Usual Dosage Children and Adults: I.M.: 20 units/kg in a single dose (RIG should always be administered as part of rabies vaccine (HDCV)) regimen (as soon as possible after the first dose of vaccine, up to 8 days); infiltrate ½ of the dose locally around the wound; administer the remainder I.M.

Note: Persons known to have an adequate titer or who have been completely immunized with rabies vaccine should not receive RIG, only booster doses of HDCV

Administration Intramuscular injection only; injection should be made into the deltoid muscle or anterolateral aspect of the thigh

Nursing Implications Severe adverse reactions can occur if patient receives RIG I.V.

Dosage Forms Injection: 150 units/mL (2 mL, 10 mL)

Rabies Virus Vaccine (RAY beez VYE rus vak SEEN)

Related Information

Immunization Recommendations *on page 1358*

U.S. Brand Names Imovax® Rabies I.D. Vaccine; Imovax® Rabies Vaccine; RabAvert™

Synonyms HDCV; Human Diploid Cell Cultures Rabies Vaccine; Human Diploid Cell Cultures Rabies Vaccine (Intradermal use)

Therapeutic Category Vaccine, Inactivated Virus

Use Pre-exposure immunization: Vaccinate persons with greater than usual risk due occupation or avocation including veterinarians, rangers, animal handlers, certain laboratory workers, and persons living in or visiting countries for longer than 1 month where rabies is a constant threat.

Postexposure prophylaxis: If a bite from a carrier animal is unprovoked, if it is not captured and rabies is present in that species and area, administer rabies immune globulin (RIG) and the vaccine as indicated

The Food and Drug Administration has not approved the I.D. use of rabies vaccine for postexposure prophylaxis (only I.M.). The type of and schedule for postexposure prophylaxis depends upon the previous rabies vaccination status or the result of a previous or current serologic test for rabies antibody.

Pregnancy Risk Factor C

Contraindications Developing febrile illness (during pre-exposure therapy only); allergy to neomycin, gentamicin, or amphotericin B; life-threatening allergic reactions to rabies vaccine or its components (however, carefully consider a patient's risk of rabies before continuing therapy)

Warnings/Precautions Report serious reactions to the State Health Department or the manufacturer/distributor, an immune complex reaction is possible 2-21 days following booster doses of HDCV; hypersensitivity reactions may be treated with antihistamines or epinephrine, if severe.

Use care to administer Imovax® rabies vaccine human and rabies vaccine adsorbed (RDA) only by I.M. route. Diploid cell (HDCV) (in the **deltoid only**) and Imovax® rabies I.D. vaccine by I.D. route only

Adverse Reactions Mild systemic reactions occur at an incidence of ~8% to 10% with RVA and 20% with HDCV. **All serious adverse reactions must be reported to the U.S. Department of Health and Human Services (DHHS) Vaccine Adverse Event Reporting System (VAERS) 1-800-822-7967.**

Cardiovascular: Edema

Central nervous system: Dizziness, malaise, encephalomyelitis, transverse myelitis, fever, pain, headache, neuroparalytic reactions

Dermatologic: Itching, erythema

Gastrointestinal: Nausea, abdominal pain

Local: Local discomfort, pain at injection site

Neuromuscular & skeletal: Myalgia

Note: Serum sickness reaction is much less frequent with RVA (<1%) vs the HDCV (6%)

Drug Interactions Decreased effect with immunosuppressive agents, corticosteroids, antimalarial drugs (ie, chloroquine); persons on these drugs should receive RIG (3 doses/1 mL each) by the I.M. route

(Continued)

Rabies Virus Vaccine *(Continued)*

Stability Refrigerate dried vaccine; HDCV can presumably tolerate 30 days at room temperature; reconstituted vaccine should be used immediately

Mechanism of Action Rabies vaccine is an inactivated virus vaccine which promotes immunity by inducing an active immune response. The production of specific antibodies requires about 7-10 days to develop. Rabies immune globulin or antirabies serum, equine (ARS) is given in conjunction with rabies vaccine to provide immune protection until an antibody response can occur.

Pharmacodynamics/Kinetics
Onset of effect: I.M.: Rabies antibody appears in the serum within 7-10 days
Peak effect: Within 30-60 days and persists for at least 1 year

Usual Dosage
Pre-exposure prophylaxis: 1 mL I.M. or 0.1 mL I.D. on days 0, 7, and 21 to 28. **Note:** Prolonging the interval between doses does not interfere with immunity achieved after the concluding dose of the basic series.

Postexposure prophylaxis: All postexposure treatment should begin with immediate cleansing of the wound with soap and water
Persons not previously immunized as above: Rabies immune globulin 20 units/kg body weight, half infiltrated at bite site if possible, remainder I.M.; and 5 doses of rabies vaccine, 1 mL I.M., one each on days 0, 3, 7, 14, 28
Persons who have previously received postexposure prophylaxis with rabies vaccine, received a recommended I.M. pre-exposure series of rabies vaccine or have a previously documented rabies antibody titer considered adequate: 1 mL of either vaccine I.M. only on days 0 and 3; do not administer RIG
Booster (for occupational or other continuing risk): 1 mL I.M. or 0.1 mL I.D. every 2-5 years or based on antibody titers

Administration HDCV may be given I.M. or I.D. (I.M. for postexposure prophylaxis); RVA may be given I.M. only; give I.M. injections in the deltoid muscle, not the gluteal, in adults and older children; for younger children, use the outer aspect of the thigh. I.D. injections are best given in the lateral aspect of the upper arm; travelers to endemic areas may receive the vaccine by the I.D. route if the 3-dose series can be completed >30 days before departure, otherwise give I.M.

Reference Range Antibody titers ≥115 as determined by rapid fluorescent-focus inhibition test are indicative of adequate response; collect titers on day 28 postexposure

Additional Information Federal law requires that the date of administration, the vaccine manufacturer, lot number of vaccine, and the administering person's name, title and address be entered into the patient's permanent medical record

Dosage Forms Injection:
Human diploid cell vaccine (HDCV): Rabies antigen 2.5 units/mL (1 mL)
Imovax® rabies I.D. vaccine: Rabies antigen 0.25 units/0.1 mL (1 mL)
Rabies vaccine (adsorbed): 1 mL

- **Racemic Amphetamine Sulfate** *see* Amphetamine *on page 72*
- **Racemic Epinephrine** *see* Epinephrine *on page 415*
- **Radiostol®** *see* Ergocalciferol *on page 424*

Raloxifene (ral OX i feen)

U.S. Brand Names Evista®

Synonyms Keoxifene

Therapeutic Category Selective Estrogen Receptor Modulator (SERM)

Use Prevention of osteoporosis in postmenopausal women

Pregnancy Risk Factor X

Pregnancy/Breast-Feeding Implications Raloxifene should not be used by pregnant women or by women planning to become pregnant in the immediate future

Contraindications Pregnancy; prior hypersensitivity to raloxifene; active thromboembolic disorder; not intended for use in premenopausal women

Warnings/Precautions History of venous thromboembolism/pulmonary embolism; patients with cardiovascular disease; history of cervical/uterine carcinoma; renal/hepatic insufficiency (however, pharmacokinetic data are lacking); concurrent use of estrogens

Adverse Reactions ≥2%:
Cardiovascular: Chest pain
Central nervous system: Migraine, depression, insomnia, fever
Dermatologic: Rash
Endocrine & metabolic: Hot flashes
Gastrointestinal: Nausea, dyspepsia, vomiting, flatulence, gastroenteritis, weight gain
Genitourinary: Vaginitis, urinary tract infection, cystitis, leukorrhea
Neuromuscular & skeletal: Leg cramps, arthralgia, myalgia, arthritis
Respiratory: Sinusitis, pharyngitis, cough, pneumonia, laryngitis
Miscellaneous: Infection, flu syndrome, diaphoresis

Overdosage/Toxicology Incidence of overdose in humans has not been reported. In an 8-week study of postmenopausal women, a dose of raloxifene 600 mg/day was safely tolerated. No mortality was seen after a single oral dose in rats or mice at 810 times the human dose for rats and 405 times the human dose for mice. There is no specific antidote for raloxifene.

Drug Interactions Decreased effects: Ampicillin and cholestyramine decreases raloxifene absorption

Mechanism of Action A selective estrogen receptor modulator, meaning that it affects some of the same receptors that estrogen does, but not all, and in some instances, it antagonizes or blocks estrogen; it acts like estrogen to prevent bone loss and improve lipid profiles, but it has the potential to block some estrogen effects such as those that lead to breast cancer and uterine cancer

Pharmacodynamics/Kinetics
Onset of action: 8 weeks
Distribution: 2348 L/kg
Protein binding: >95% to albumin and α-glycoprotein
Metabolism: Extensive first pass metabolism
Bioavailability: ~2%
Half-life: 27.7-32.5 hours
Elimination: Primarily in the feces and 0.2% renal

Usual Dosage Adults: Female: Oral: 60 mg/day which may be administered any time of the day without regard to meals

Monitoring Parameters Radiologic evaluation of bone mineral density (BMD) is the best measure of the treatment of osteoporosis; to monitor for the potential toxicities of raloxifene, complete blood counts should be evaluated periodically.

Additional Information The decrease in estrogen-related adverse effects with the selective estrogen-receptor modulators in general and raloxifene in particular should improve compliance and decrease the incidence of cardiovascular events and fractures while not increasing breast cancer

Dosage Forms Tablet, as hydrochloride: 60 mg

Ramipril (ra MI pril)

Related Information
Angiotensin Agents *on page 1291*
Heart Failure: Management of Patients With Left-Ventricular Systolic Dysfunction *on page 1472*

U.S. Brand Names Altace™

Therapeutic Category Angiotensin-Converting Enzyme (ACE) Inhibitor; Antihypertensive Agent

Use Treatment of hypertension, alone or in combination with thiazide diuretics; treatment of congestive heart failure within the first few days after myocardial infarction (**Note:** This indication is based on a study involving 2006 patients; a decrease by 26% in all-cause mortality was observed when ramipril was administered 3-10 days after a myocardial infarction)

Pregnancy Risk Factor C (1st trimester); D (2nd and 3rd trimester)

Contraindications Hypersensitivity to ramipril or ramiprilat, or history of angioedema with any other angiotensin-converting enzyme inhibitors

Warnings/Precautions Use with caution and modify dosage in patients with renal impairment (especially renal artery stenosis), severe congestive heart failure; severe hypotension may occur in the elderly and patients who are sodium and/or volume depleted, initiate lower doses and monitor closely when starting therapy in these patients; should be discontinued if laryngeal stridor or angioedema of the face, tongue, or glottis is observed

Adverse Reactions
>10% Respiratory: Cough (12%)
<1%: Hypotension, syncope, arrhythmia, angina, palpitations, myocardial infarction, headache, dizziness, fatigue, insomnia, drowsiness, depression, malaise, nervousness, vertigo, amnesia, convulsions, rash, pruritus, alopecia, photosensitivity, angioedema rash, dermatitis, hyperkalemia (small increase in patients with renal dysfunction), abdominal pain (rarely occurs but may with enzyme changes which suggest pancreatitis), vomiting, nausea, diarrhea, dysgeusia, anorexia, constipation, dyspepsia, xerostomia, dysphagia, increased salivation, weight gain, impotence, neutropenia, eosinophilia, decreased hemoglobin (rare), muscle cramps, myalgia, arthritis, arthralgia, paresthesia, tremor, neuralgia, neuropathy, tinnitus, proteinuria, transient increases BUN/serum creatinine, epistaxis, dyspnea, flu-like symptoms, diaphoresis

Overdosage/Toxicology
Mild hypotension has been the only toxic effect seen with acute overdose. Bradycardia may also occur; mild hyperkalemia may occur even with therapeutic doses, especially in patients with renal insufficiency and those taking NSAIDs.

Following initiation of essential overdose management, toxic symptom treatment and supportive treatment should be initiated. Hypotension usually responds to I.V. fluids or Trendelenburg positioning.

Drug Interactions See table.

Drug-Drug Interactions With ACEIs

Precipitant Drug	Drug (Category) and Effect	Description
Ramipril	Lithium: increased	Increased serum lithium levels and symptoms of toxicity may occur.
Ramipril	Potassium preps/ potassium-sparing diuretics increased	Coadministration may result in elevated potassium levels.
Rampiril	Diuretics	Additive hypotensive effects, especially with initiation of therapy or increased dose

(Continued)

Ramipril *(Continued)*

Mechanism of Action Ramipril is an angiotensin-converting enzyme (ACE) inhibitor which prevents the formation of angiotensin II from angiotensin I and exhibits pharmacologic effects that are similar to captopril. Ramipril must undergo enzymatic saponification by esterases in the liver to its biologically active metabolite, ramiprilat. The pharmacodynamic effects of ramipril result from the high-affinity, competitive, reversible binding of ramiprilat to angiotensin-converting enzyme thus preventing the formation of the potent vasoconstrictor angiotensin II. This isomerized enzyme-inhibitor complex has a slow rate of dissociation, which results in high potency and a long duration of action; a CNS mechanism may also be involved in the hypotensive effect as angiotensin II increases adrenergic outflow from CNS; vasoactive kallikreins may be decreased in conversion to active hormones by ACE inhibitors, thus reducing blood pressure

Pharmacodynamics/Kinetics

Absorption: Well absorbed from GI tract (50% to 60%)

Distribution: Plasma levels decline in a triphasic fashion; rapid decline is a distribution phase to peripheral compartment, plasma protein and tissue ACE (half-life 2-4 hours); 2nd phase is an apparent elimination phase representing the clearance of free ramiprilat (half-life: 9-18 hours); and final phase is the terminal elimination phase representing the equilibrium phase between tissue binding and dissociation (half-life: >50 hours)

Metabolism: Hepatic to the active form, ramiprilat

Half-life: Ramiprilat: >50 hours

Time to peak serum concentration: ~1 hour

Elimination: Ramipril and its metabolites are eliminated primarily through the kidneys (60%) and feces (40%)

Usual Dosage Adults: Oral:

Hypertension: 2.5-5 mg once daily, maximum: 20 mg/day

Heart failure postmyocardial infarction: Initial: 2.5 mg twice daily titrated upward, if possible, to 5 mg twice daily

Note: The dose of any concomitant diuretic should be reduced; if the diuretic cannot be discontinued, initiate therapy with 1.25 mg; after the initial dose, the patient should be monitored carefully until blood pressure has stabilized

Dosing adjustment in renal impairment:

Cl_{cr} <40 mL/minute: Administer 25% of normal dose

Renal failure and hypertension: 1.25 mg once daily, titrated upward as possible

Renal failure and heart failure: 1.25 mg once daily, increasing to 1.25 mg twice daily up to 2.5 mg twice daily as tolerated

Test Interactions Increases BUN, creatinine, potassium, positive Coombs' [direct]; decreases cholesterol (S); may cause false-positive results in urine acetone determinations using sodium nitroprusside reagent

Patient Information Notify physician if vomiting, diarrhea, excessive perspiration, or dehydration should occur; also if sore throat, fever, swelling of face, lips, tongue, or difficulty in breathing occurs or if persistent cough develops; may cause lightheadedness during first few days of therapy; if a cough develops which is bothersome, consult a physician. Capsule is usually swallowed whole but may be sprinkled on applesauce or mixed in water or juice.

Nursing Implications May cause depression in some patients; discontinue if angioedema of the face, extremities, lips, tongue, or glottis occurs; watch for hypotensive effects within 1-3 hours of first dose or new higher dose; may be mixed in water, apple juice, or applesauce and will remain stable for 48 hours if refrigerated or 24 hours at room temperature

Dosage Forms Capsule: 1.25 mg, 2.5 mg, 5 mg, 10 mg

Ranitidine Bismuth Citrate *(ra NI ti deen BIZ muth SIT rate)*

Related Information

Helicobacter pylori Treatment *on page 1473*

U.S. Brand Names Tritec®

Synonyms GR1222311X; RBC

Therapeutic Category Histamine H_2 Antagonist

Use In combination with clarithromycin for the treatment of active duodenal ulcer associated with *H. pylori* infection; not to be used as monotherapy

Pregnancy Risk Factor C

Contraindications Hypersensitivity to ranitidine or bismuth compounds or components; acute porphyria

Warnings/Precautions Avoid use in patients with Cl_{cr} <25 mL/minute; do not use for maintenance therapy or for >16 weeks/year

Adverse Reactions

>1%:

Central nervous system: Headache (14%), dizziness (1% to 2%)

Gastrointestinal: Diarrhea (5%), nausea/vomiting (3%), constipation (2%), abdominal pain, gastric upset (<10%), darkening of the tongue and/or stool (60% to 70%), taste disturbance (11%)

Miscellaneous: Flu-like symptoms (2%)

<1%: Rash, pruritus, anemia, thrombocytopenia, elevated LFTs

Drug Interactions See individual monographs

Increased effect: Optimal antimicrobial effects of ranitidine bismuth citrate occur when the drug is taken with food

Mechanism of Action As a complex of ranitidine and bismuth citrate, gastric acid secretion is inhibited by histamine-blocking activity at the parietal cell and the structural integrity of *H. pylori* organisms is disrupted; additionally bismuth reduces the adherence of *H. pylori* to epithelial cells of the stomach and may exert a cytoprotectant effect, inhibiting pepsin, as well. Adequate eradication of *Helicobacter pylori* is achieved with the combination of clarithromycin.

Pharmacodynamics/Kinetics See individual monographs

Absorption: Bismuth: Minimal systemic absorption (≤1%); Ranitidine: 50% to 60% (dose-dependent)

Distribution: Ranitidine: 1.7 L/kg

Protein binding: Bismuth: 90%; Ranitidine: 15%

Metabolism: Ranitidine: Metabolized to N-oxide, S-oxide, and N-desmethyl metabolites

Half-life: Complex: 5-8 days; Bismuth: 11-28 days; Ranitidine: 3 hours

Time to peak serum concentration: Bismuth: 1-2 hours; Ranitidine: 0.5-5 hours; Time to peak effect of complex: 1 week

Elimination: Bismuth: Clearance: 50 mL/minute; Ranitidine: Clearance: 530 mL/minute; ~30% of ranitidine and <1% of bismuth is excreted in the urine

Usual Dosage Adults: Oral: 400 mg twice daily for 4 weeks with clarithromycin 500 mg 2 times/day for first 2 week

Dosing adjustment in renal impairment: Not recommended with Cl_{cr} <25 mL/minute

Dosing adjustment in hepatic impairment: No dosage change necessary

Note: Most patients not eradicated of *H. pylori* following an adequate course of therapy that includes clarithromycin will have clarithromycin-resistant isolates and should be treated with an alternative multiple drug regimen

Dietary Considerations May be taken without regard to food

Monitoring Parameters (13) C-urea breath tests to detect *H. pylori*, endoscopic evidence of ulcer healing, CBCs, LFTs, renal function tests

Patient Information Inform your physician immediately if signs of allergy occur; take medication with food, if possible

Dosage Forms Tablet: 400 mg (ranitidine 162 mg, trivalent bismuth 128 mg, and citrate 110 mg)

Ranitidine Hydrochloride (ra NI ti deen hye droe KLOR ide)

Related Information

Antacid Drug Interactions *on page 1296*

U.S. Brand Names Zantac®; Zantac® 75 [OTC]

Canadian Brand Names Apo®-Ranitidine; Novo-Ranidine; Nu-Ranit

Therapeutic Category Antihistamine, H_2 Blocker; Histamine H_2 Antagonist

Use Short-term treatment of active duodenal ulcers and benign gastric ulcers; long-term prophylaxis of duodenal ulcer and gastric hypersecretory states, gastroesophageal reflux, recurrent postoperative ulcer, upper GI bleeding, prevention of acid-aspiration pneumonitis during surgery, and prevention of stress-induced ulcers; causes fewer interactions than cimetidine

Pregnancy Risk Factor B

Contraindications Hypersensitivity to ranitidine or any component

Warnings/Precautions Use with caution in children <12 years of age; use with caution in patients with liver and renal impairment; dosage modification required in patients with renal impairment; long-term therapy may cause vitamin B_{12} deficiency

Adverse Reactions

1% to 10%:

Central nervous system: Dizziness, sedation, malaise, headache, drowsiness

Dermatologic: Rash

Gastrointestinal: Constipation, nausea, vomiting, diarrhea

<1%: Gynecomastia, hepatitis, arthralgia, bradycardia, tachycardia, fever, confusion, thrombocytopenia, neutropenia, agranulocytosis, bronchospasm

Overdosage/Toxicology

Symptoms of overdose include muscular tremors, vomiting, rapid respiration, renal failure, CNS depression

Treatment is primarily symptomatic and supportive

Drug Interactions CYP2D6 and 3A3/4 enzyme inhibitor

Decreased effect: Variable effects on warfarin; antacids may decrease absorption of ranitidine; ketoconazole and itraconazole absorptions are decreased; may produce altered serum levels of procainamide and ferrous sulfate; decreased effect of nondepolarizing muscle relaxants, cefpodoxime, cyanocobalamin (decreased absorption), diazepam, oxaprozin

Decreased toxicity of atropine

Increased toxicity of cyclosporine (increased serum creatinine), gentamicin (neuromuscular blockade), glipizide, glyburide, midazolam (increased concentrations), metoprolol, pentoxifylline, phenytoin, quinidine

Stability Ranitidine injection should be stored at 4°C to 30°C and protected from light; injection solution is a clear, colorless to yellow solution; slight darkening does not affect potency

Stability at room temperature:

Prepared bags: 2 days

Premixed bags: Manufacturer expiration dating and out of overwrap stability: 15 days

Stability of prepared bags at refrigeration temperature (4°C): 10 days

Solution for I.V. infusion in NS or D_5W is stable for 30 days when frozen; I.V. form is **incompatible** with amphotericin B, clindamycin, diazepam (same syringe), hetastarch

(Continued)

Ranitidine Hydrochloride *(Continued)*

(Y-line), hydroxyzine (same syringe), midazolam (same syringe), pentobarbital (same syringe), phenobarbital (same syringe)

Mechanism of Action Competitive inhibition of histamine at H_2-receptors of the gastric parietal cells, which inhibits gastric acid secretion, gastric volume and hydrogen ion concentration reduced

Pharmacodynamics/Kinetics

Absorption: Oral: 50% to 60%

Distribution: Minimally penetrates the blood-brain barrier; appears in breast milk

Protein binding: 15%

Metabolism: In the liver (<10%)

Half-life: Children 3.5-16 years: 1.8-2 hours; Adults: 2-2.5 hours; End-stage renal disease: 6-9 hours

Time to peak serum concentration: Oral: Within 1-3 hours and persisting for 8 hours

Elimination: Primarily in urine (35% as unchanged drug) and in feces

Usual Dosage Giving oral dose at 6 PM may be better than 10 PM bedtime, the highest acid production usually starts at approximately 7 PM, thus giving at 6 PM controls acid secretion better

Children:

Oral: 1.25-2.5 mg/kg/dose every 12 hours; maximum: 300 mg/day

I.M., I.V.: 0.75-1.5 mg/kg/dose every 6-8 hours, maximum daily dose: 400 mg

Continuous infusion: 0.1-0.25 mg/kg/hour (preferred for stress ulcer prophylaxis in patients with concurrent maintenance I.V.s or TPNs)

Adults:

Short-term treatment of ulceration: 150 mg/dose twice daily or 300 mg at bedtime

Prophylaxis of recurrent duodenal ulcer: Oral: 150 mg at bedtime

Gastric hypersecretory conditions:

Oral: 150 mg twice daily, up to 600mg/day

I.M., I.V.: 50 mg/dose every 6-8 hours (dose not to exceed 400 mg/day)

I.V.: 50 mg/dose IVPB every 6-8 hours (dose not to exceed 400 mg/day)

or

Continuous I.V. infusion: Initial: 50 mg IVPB, followed by 6.25 mg/hour titrated to gastric pH >4.0 for prophylaxis or >7.0 for treatment; **continuous I.V. infusion is preferred in patients with active bleeding**

Gastric hypersecretory conditions: Doses up to 2.5 mg/kg/hour (220 mg/hour) have been used

Dosing adjustment in renal impairment:

Cl_{cr} 10-50 mL/minute: Administer at 75% of normal dose or administer every 18-24 hours

Cl_{cr} <10 mL/minute: Administer at 50% of normal dose or administer every 18-24 hours

Hemodialysis: Slightly dialyzable (5% to 20%)

Dosing adjustment/comments in hepatic disease: Unchanged

Administration Ranitidine injection may be administered I.M. or I.V.

I.M.: Injection is given undiluted

I.V. must be diluted and may be administered IVP or IVPB or continuous I.V. infusion

IVP: Ranitidine (usually 50 mg) should be diluted to a total of 20 mL with NS or D_5W and administered over at least 5 minutes

IVPB: administer over 15-20 minutes

Continuous I.V. infusion: Administer at 6.25 mg/hour and titrate dosage based on gastric pH by continuous infusion over 24 hours

Monitoring Parameters AST, ALT, serum creatinine; when used to prevent stress-related GI bleeding, measure the intragastric pH and try to maintain pH >4; signs and symptoms of peptic ulcer disease, occult blood with GI bleeding, monitor renal function to correct dose; monitor for side effects

Test Interactions False-positive urine protein using Multistix®, gastric acid secretion test, skin test allergen extracts, serum creatinine and serum transaminase concentrations, urine protein test

Patient Information It may take several days before this medicine begins to relieve stomach pain; antacids may be taken with ranitidine unless your physician has told you not to use them; wait 30-60 minutes between taking the antacid and ranitidine; may cause drowsiness, impair judgment, or coordination

Nursing Implications I.M. solution does not need to be diluted before use; monitor creatinine clearance for renal impairment; observe caution in patients with renal function impairment and hepatic function impairment

Dosage Forms

Capsule (GELdose™): 150 mg, 300 mg

Granules, effervescent (EFFERdose™): 150 mg

Infusion, preservative free, in NaCl 0.45%: 1 mg/mL (50 mL)

Injection: 25 mg/mL (2 mL, 10 mL, 40 mL)

Syrup (peppermint flavor): 15 mg/mL (473 mL)

Tablet: 75 mg [OTC]; 150 mg, 300 mg

Tablet, effervescent (EFFERdose™): 150 mg

♦ **Raxar®** *see* Grepafloxacin *on page 547*

♦ **RBC** *see* Ranitidine Bismuth Citrate *on page 1010*

♦ **R & C® Shampoo [OTC]** *see* Pyrethrins *on page 996*

♦ **Reactine™** *see* Cetirizine *on page 233*

♦ **Rea-Lo® [OTC]** *see* Urea *on page 1199*

- **Rebetol®** see Ribavirin on page 1021
- **Rebetron™** see Interferon Alfa-2b and Ribavirin Combination Pack on page 619
- **Recombinant Human Deoxyribonuclease** see Dornase Alfa on page 388
- **Recombinant Human Follicle Stimulating Hormone** see Follitropins on page 513
- **Recombinant Human Interleukin-11** see Oprelvekin on page 865
- **Recombinant Human Platelet-Derived Growth Factor B** see Becaplermin on page 127
- **Recombinant Interleukin-11** see Oprelvekin on page 865
- **Recombinant plasminogen activator** see Reteplase on page 1018
- **Recombinate®** see Antihemophilic Factor (Human) on page 88
- **Recombivax HB®** see Hepatitis B Vaccine on page 565
- **Recommendations for Preventing the Spread of Vancomycin Resistance** see page 1426
- **Recommendations of the Advisory Committee on Immunization Practices (ACIP)** see page 1360
- **Recommended Childhood Immunization Schedule - US - January-December, 1999** see page 1359
- **Recommended Immunization Schedule for HIV-Infected Children** see page 1363
- **Redisol®** see Cyanocobalamin on page 302
- **Redoxon®** see Ascorbic Acid on page 99
- **Redutemp®** [OTC] see Acetaminophen on page 19
- **Reese's®** Pinworm Medicine [OTC] see Pyrantel Pamoate on page 995
- **Reference Values for Adults and Children** see page 1436
- **Refludan™** see Lepirudin on page 663
- **Regitine®** see Phentolamine on page 917
- **Reglan®** see Metoclopramide on page 766
- **Regonol® Injection** see Pyridostigmine on page 997
- **Regranex®** see Becaplermin on page 127
- **Regular (Concentrated) Iletin® II U-500** see Insulin Preparations on page 613
- **Regular Iletin® I** see Insulin Preparations on page 613
- **Regular Insulin** see Insulin Preparations on page 613
- **Regular Purified Pork Insulin** see Insulin Preparations on page 613
- **Regular Strength Bayer® Enteric 500 Aspirin** [OTC] see Aspirin on page 102
- **Regulax SS®** [OTC] see Docusate on page 384
- **Regulex®** see Docusate on page 384
- **Reguloid®** [OTC] see Psyllium on page 994
- **Rela®** see Carisoprodol on page 196
- **Relafen®** see Nabumetone on page 806
- **Relaxadon®** see Hyoscyamine, Atropine, Scopolamine, and Phenobarbital on page 592
- **Relief® Ophthalmic Solution** see Phenylephrine on page 918
- **Remeron®** see Mirtazapine on page 784
- **Remicade™** see Infliximab on page 610

Remifentanil (rem i FEN ta nil)

Related Information
  Narcotic Agonists Comparison on page 1328
U.S. Brand Names Ultiva™
Synonyms GI87084B
Therapeutic Category Analgesic, Narcotic
Use Analgesic for use during general anesthesia for continued analgesia
Pregnancy Risk Factor C
Contraindications Not for intrathecal or epidural administration, due to the presence of glycine in the formulation, it is also contraindicated in patients with a known hypersensitivity to remifentanil, fentanyl or fentanyl analogs; interruption of an infusion will result in offset of effects within 5-10 minutes; the discontinuation of remifentanil infusion should be preceded by the establishment of adequate postoperative analgesia orders, especially for patients in whom postoperative pain is anticipated
Warnings/Precautions Remifentanil is not recommended as the sole agent in general anesthesia, because the loss of consciousness cannot be assured and due to the high incidence of apnea, hypotension, tachycardia and muscle rigidity; it should be administered by individuals specifically trained in the use of anesthetic agents and should not be used in diagnostic or therapeutic procedures outside the monitored anesthesia setting; resuscitative and intubation equipment should be readily available
Adverse Reactions
  >10%: Gastrointestinal: Nausea, vomiting
  1% to 10%:
    Cardiovascular: Hypotension, bradycardia, tachycardia, hypertension
    Central nervous system: Dizziness, headache, agitation, fever
    Dermatologic: Pruritus
    Ocular: Visual disturbances
    Respiratory: Respiratory depression, apnea, hypoxia
    Miscellaneous: Shivering, postoperative pain
Overdosage/Toxicology
  Symptoms of overdose include apnea, chest wall rigidity, seizures, hypoxemia, hypotension and bradycardia
  (Continued)

1013

Remifentanil *(Continued)*

Support of patient's airway, establish an I.V. line, administer intravenous fluids and administer naloxone 2 mg I.V. (0.01 mg/kg for children) with repeat administration as needed up to a total of 10 mg; glycopyrrolate or atropine may be useful for the treatment of bradycardia or hypotension

Mechanism of Action Binds with stereospecific mu-opioid receptors at many sites within the CNS, increases pain threshold, alters pain reception, inhibits ascending pain pathways

Pharmacodynamics/Kinetics

Onset of effect: I.V.: 1-3 minutes

Protein binding: 92%

Metabolism: Rapid by blood and tissue esterases

Half-life: 10 minutes (dose-dependent)

Elimination: Renal

Usual Dosage Adults: I.V. continuous infusion:

During induction: 0.5-1 mcg/kg/minute

During maintenance:

With nitrous oxide (66%): 0.4 mcg/kg/minute (range: 0.1-2 mcg/kg/min)

With isoflurane: 0.25 mcg/kg/minute (range: 0.05-2 mcg/kg/min)

With propofol: 0.25 mcg/kg/minute (range: 0.05-2 mcg/kg/min)

Continuation as an analgesic in immediate postoperative period: 0.1 mcg/kg/minute (range: 0.025-0.2 mcg/kg/min)

Monitoring Parameters Respiratory and cardiovascular status, blood pressure, heart rate

Dosage Forms Powder for injection, lyophilized: 1 mg/3 mL vial, 2 mg/5 mL vial, 5 mg/10 mL vial

♦ **Renagel**® see Sevelamer *on page 1058*

♦ **Renedil**® see Felodipine *on page 470*

♦ **Renese**® see Polythiazide *on page 945*

♦ **Renova**™ see Tretinoin, Topical *on page 1173*

♦ **Rentamine**® see Chlorpheniramine, Ephedrine, Phenylephrine, and Carbetapentane *on page 246*

♦ **ReoPro**® see Abciximab *on page 15*

Repaglinide *(re PAG li nide)*

Related Information

Hypoglycemic Drugs, Comparison of Oral Agents *on page 1325*

U.S. Brand Names Prandin®

Therapeutic Category Antidiabetic Agent, Oral; Hypoglycemic Agent, Oral; Meglitinide

Use Management of noninsulin-dependent diabetes mellitus (type II)

An adjunct to diet and exercise to lower the blood glucose in patients with type 2 diabetes mellitus whose hyperglycemia cannot be controlled satisfactorily by diet and exercise alone

In combination with metformin to lower blood glucose in patients whose hyperglycemia cannot be controlled by exercise, diet and either agent alone

Pregnancy Risk Factor C

Pregnancy/Breast-Feeding Implications Clinical effects on the fetus: Safety in pregnant women has not been established. Use during pregnancy only if clearly needed. Insulin is the drug of choice for the control of diabetes mellitus during pregnancy. It is not known whether repaglinide is excreted in breast milk. Because the potential for hypoglycemia in nursing infants may exist, decide whether to discontinue repaglinide or discontinue breast-feeding. If repaglinide is discontinued and if diet alone is inadequate for controlling blood glucose, consider insulin therapy.

Contraindications Diabetic ketoacidosis, with or without coma (treat with insulin); type 1 diabetes; hypersensitivity to the drug or its inactive ingredients

Warnings/Precautions Use with caution in patients with hepatic impairment. The administration of oral hypoglycemic drugs is associated with increased cardiovascular mortality as compared with treatment with diet alone or diet plus insulin. All oral hypoglycemic agents are capable of producing hypoglycemia. Proper patient selection, dosage, and instructions to the patients are important to avoid hypoglycemic episodes. It may be necessary to discontinue repaglinide and administer insulin if the patient is exposed to stress (fever, trauma, infection, surgery).

Adverse Reactions

>10%:

Central nervous system: Headache

Endocrine & metabolic: Hyperglycemia, hypoglycemia, related symptoms

1% to 10%:

Cardiovascular: Chest pain

Gastrointestinal: Nausea, epigastric fullness, heartburn, constipation, diarrhea, anorexia, tooth disorder

Genitourinary: Urinary tract infection

Neuromuscular: Arthralgia, back pain, paresthesia

Miscellaneous: Allergy

Overdosage/Toxicology

Symptoms of overdose include severe hypoglycemia, seizures, cerebral damage, tingling of lips and tongue, nausea, yawning, confusion, agitation, tachycardia, sweating, convulsions, stupor, and coma

Intoxications are best managed with glucose administration (oral for milder hypoglycemia or by injection in more severe forms) and symptomatic management

Drug Interactions CYP3A4 enzyme substrate

Decreased effect: Drugs that induce cytochrome P-450 3A4 may increase metabolism of repaglinide (troglitazone rifampin, barbiturates, carbamazepine). Certain drugs (thiazides, diuretics, corticosteroids, phenothiazines, thyroid products, estrogens, oral contraceptives, phenytoin, nicotinic acid, sympathomimetics, calcium channel blockers, isoniazid) tend to produce hyperglycemia and may lead to loss of glycemic control.

Increased effect: Agents that inhibit cytochrome P-450 3A4 (ketoconazole, miconazole) and antibacterial agents (erythromycin) may increase repaglinide concentrations

Increased toxicity: Since this agent is highly protein bound, the toxic potential is increased when given concomitantly with other highly protein bound drugs (ie, phenylbutazone, oral anticoagulants, hydantoins, salicylates, NSAIDs, sulfonamides) - increase hypoglycemic effect

Mechanism of Action Nonsulfonylurea hypoglycemic agent of the meglitinide class (the nonsulfonylurea moiety of glyburide) used in the management of type 2 diabetes mellitus; stimulates insulin release from the pancreatic beta cells

Pharmacodynamics/Kinetics

Onset of action: Oral: Insulin levels in the serum begin to increase within 15-60 minutes after a single dose

Duration: Up to 24 hours

Absorption: Rapidly and completely from the GI tract with peak plasma drug levels within 1 hour

Distribution: V_d: 31 L

Protein binding, plasma: >98%

Metabolism: Completely metabolized by oxidative biotransformation and direct conjugation with glucuronic acid. The cytochrome P-450 enzyme system (specifically 3A4) is involved in metabolism (inactive metabolites)

Bioavailability, mean absolute: ~56%

Elimination: ~90% in the feces and ~8% within 96 hours

Usual Dosage Adults: Oral: Should be taken within 15 minutes of the meal, but time may vary from immediately preceding the meal to as long as 30 minutes before the meal

Initial: For patients not previously treated or whose Hb A_{1c} is <8%, the starting dose is 0.5 mg. For patients previously treated with blood glucose-lowering agents whose Hb A_{1c} is ≥8%, the initial dose is 1 or 2 mg before each meal.

Dose adjustment: Determine dosing adjustments by blood glucose response, usually fasting blood glucose. Double the preprandial dose up to 4 mg until satisfactory blood glucose response is achieved. At least 1 week should elapse to assess response after each dose adjustment.

Dose range: 0.5-4 mg taken with meals. Repaglinide may be dosed preprandial 2, 3 or 4 times/day in response to changes in the patient's meal pattern. Maximum recommended daily dose: 16 mg.

Patients receiving other oral hypoglycemic agents: When repaglinide is used to replace therapy with other oral hypoglycemic agents, it may be started the day after the final dose is given. Observe patients carefully for hypoglycemia because of potential overlapping of drug effects. When transferred from longer half-life sulfonylureas (eg, chlorpropamide), close monitoring may be indicated for up to ≥1 week.

Combination therapy: If repaglinide monotherapy does not result in adequate glycemic control, metformin may be added. Or, if metformin therapy does not provide adequate control, repaglinide may be added. The starting dose and dose adjustments for combination therapy are the same as repaglinide monotherapy. Carefully adjust the dose of each drug to determine the minimal dose required to achieve the desired pharmacologic effect. Failure to do so could result in an increase in the incidence of hypoglycemic episodes. Use appropriate monitoring of FPG and Hb A_{1c} measurements to ensure that the patient is not subjected to excessive drug exposure or increased probability of secondary drug failure. If glucose is not achieved after a suitable trial of combination therapy, consider discontinuing these drugs and using insulin.

Dosing adjustment/comments in renal impairment: Initial dosage adjustment does not appear to be necessary, but make subsequent increases carefully in patients with renal function impairment or renal failure requiring hemodialysis

Dosing adjustment in hepatic impairment: Use conservative initial and maintenance doses and avoid use in severe disease

Dietary Considerations

Food: When given with food, the AUC of repaglinide is decreased; administer repaglinide before meals

Glucose: Decreases blood glucose concentration. Hypoglycemia may occur. Educate patients how to detect and treat hypoglycemia. Monitor for signs and symptoms of hypoglycemia. Administer glucose if necessary. Evaluate patient's diet and exercise regimen. May need to decrease or discontinue dose of sulfonylurea.

Monitoring Parameters Periodically monitor fasting blood glucose and glycosylated hemoglobin (Hb A_{1c}) levels with a goal of decreasing these levels towards the normal range. During dose adjustment, fasting glucose can be used to determine response.

Reference Range Target range: Adults:

Fasting blood glucose: <120 mg/dL

Glycosylated hemoglobin: <7%

Patient Information Inform patients about the importance of adherence to dietary instructions, of a regular exercise program, and of regular testing of blood glucose and Hb A_{1c}

(Continued)

Repaglinide *(Continued)*

Explain the risks of hypoglycemia, its symptoms and treatment, and conditions that predispose to its development and concomitant administration of other glucose-lowering drugs to patients and responsible family members

Instruct patients to take repaglinide before meals (2, 3, or 4 times/day preprandial). Doses are usually taken within 15 minutes of the meal, but time may vary from immediately preceding the meal to as long as 30 minutes before the meal. Instruct patients who skip a meal (or add an extra meal) to skip (or add) a dose for that meal.

Nursing Implications Patients who are anorexic or NPO, may need to have their dose held to avoid hypoglycemia

Dosage Forms Tablet : 0.5 mg, 1 mg, 2 mg

◆ **Repan®** see Butalbital Compound *on page 165*

◆ **Reposans-10® Oral** see Chlordiazepoxide *on page 239*

◆ **Repronex™** see Menotropins *on page 727*

◆ **Requip™** see Ropinirole *on page 1039*

◆ **Resa®** see Reserpine *on this page*

◆ **Rescaps-D® S.R. Capsule** see Caramiphen and Phenylpropanolamine *on page 188*

◆ **Rescriptor®** see Delavirdine *on page 330*

◆ **Resectisol® Irrigation Solution** see Mannitol *on page 711*

Reserpine *(re SER peen)*

Related Information
Depression Disorders and Treatments *on page 1465*
Hypertension Therapy *on page 1479*
U.S. Brand Names Resa®; Serpalan®; Serpasil®; Serpatabs®

Canadian Brand Names Novo-Reserpine

Therapeutic Category Antihypertensive Agent; Rauwolfia Alkaloid

Use Management of mild to moderate hypertension

Unlabeled use: Management of tardive dyskinesia

Pregnancy Risk Factor C

Contraindications Any ulcerative condition, mental depression, hypersensitivity to reserpine or any component

Warnings/Precautions Discontinue reserpine 7 days before electroshock therapy; use with caution in patients with impaired renal function or peptic ulcer disease, gallstones, and the elderly; at high doses, significant mental depression may occur; some products may contain tartrazine

Adverse Reactions

Percentage unknown:

Cardiovascular: Peripheral edema, arrhythmias, bradycardia, chest pain, hypotension

Central nervous system: Dizziness, headache, drowsiness, fatigue, parkinsonism

Dermatologic: Rash

Endocrine & metabolic: Sodium and water retention

Gastrointestinal: Anorexia, diarrhea, xerostomia, nausea, vomiting, black stools, increased gastric acid secretion

Genitourinary: Impotence, dysuria

Neuromuscular & skeletal: Trembling of hands/fingers

Respiratory: Nasal congestion

Miscellaneous: Bloody vomit

>10%: Mental depression (6% to 30%)

Overdosage/Toxicology

Symptoms of overdose include hypotension, bradycardia, CNS depression, sedation, coma, hypothermia, miosis, tremors, diarrhea, vomiting

Hypotension usually responds to I.V. fluids or Trendelenburg positioning. If unresponsive to these measures, the use of a parenteral inotrope may be required (eg, norepinephrine 0.1-0.2 mcg/kg/minute titrated to response). Anticholinergic agents may be useful in reducing the parkinsonian effects and bradycardia.

Drug Interactions

Decreased effect of indirect-acting sympathomimetics (ie, ephedrine, tyramine, amphetamines)

Increased effect/toxicity of MAO inhibitors (avoid use or use extreme caution), direct-acting sympathomimetics (ie, epinephrine, isoproterenol, phenylephrine, metaraminol), and tricyclic antidepressants; cardiac arrhythmias have occurred with digoxin

Stability Protect oral dosage forms from light

Mechanism of Action Reduces blood pressure via depletion of sympathetic biogenic amines (norepinephrine and dopamine); this also commonly results in sedative effects

Pharmacodynamics/Kinetics

Onset of antihypertensive effect: Within 3-6 days

Duration: 2-6 weeks

Absorption: Oral: ~40%

Distribution: Crosses the placenta; appears in breast milk

Protein binding: 96%

Metabolism: Extensively in the liver, >90%

Half-life: 50-100 hours

Elimination: Principal excretion in feces (30% to 60%) and small amounts in urine (10%)

Usual Dosage Oral (full antihypertensive effects may take as long as 3 weeks):
Children: 0.01-0.02 mg/kg/24 hours divided every 12 hours; maximum dose: 0.25 mg/day (not recommended in children)
Adults:
Hypertension: 0.1-0.25 mg/day in 1-2 doses; initial: 0.5 mg/day for 1-2 weeks; maintenance: reduce to 0.1-0.25 mg/day
Psychiatric: Initial: 0.5 mg/day; usual range: 0.1-1 mg
Elderly: Initial: 0.05 mg once daily, increasing by 0.05 mg every week as necessary
Dosing adjustment in renal impairment: Cl$_{cr}$ <10 mL/minute: Avoid use
Dialysis: Not removed by hemo or peritoneal dialysis; supplemental dose is not necessary

Monitoring Parameters Blood pressure, standing and sitting/supine
Test Interactions ↓ catecholamines (U)
Patient Information Take with food or milk; impotency is reversible; notify physician if a weight gain of more than 5 lb has taken place during therapy; may cause drowsiness, may impair judgment and coordination
Nursing Implications Observe for mental depression and alert family members to report any symptoms
Dosage Forms Tablet: 0.1 mg, 0.25 mg

♦ **Respa-DM®** see Guaifenesin and Dextromethorphan on page 550
♦ **Respa-GF®** see Guaifenesin on page 549
♦ **Respbid®** see Theophylline Salts on page 1125
♦ **RespiGam™** see Respiratory Syncytial Virus Immune Globulin (Intravenous) on this page

Respiratory Syncytial Virus Immune Globulin (Intravenous)
(RES peer rah tor ee sin SISH al VYE rus i MYUN GLOB yoo lin in tra VEE nus)
U.S. Brand Names RespiGam™
Synonyms RSV-IGIV
Therapeutic Category Immune Globulin
Use Prevention of serious lower respiratory infection caused by respiratory syncytial virus (RSV) in children <24 months of age with bronchopulmonary dysplasia (BPD) or a history of premature birth (≤35 weeks gestation)
Pregnancy Risk Factor C
Contraindications Selective IgA deficiency; history of severe prior reaction to any immunoglobulin preparation
Warnings/Precautions Use caution to avoid fluid overload in patients, particularly infants with bronchopulmonary dysplasia (BPD), when administering RSV-IGIV; hypersensitivity including anaphylaxis or angioneurotic edema may occur; keep epinephrine 1:1000 readily available during infusion; rare occurrences of aseptic meningitis syndrome have been associated with IGIV treatment, particularly with high doses; observe carefully for signs and symptoms of such and treat promptly
Adverse Reactions
1% to 10%:
Dermatologic: Rash (1%)
Cardiovascular: Tachycardia (1%), hypertension (1%), hypotension
Central nervous system: Fever (6%)
Endocrine & metabolic: Fluid overload (1%)
Gastrointestinal: Vomiting (2%), diarrhea (1%), gastroenteritis (1%)
Local: Injection site inflammation (1%)
Respiratory: Respiratory distress (2%), wheezing (2%), rales, hypoxia (1%), tachypnea (1%)
<1%: Edema, pallor, heart murmur, cyanosis, flushing, palpitations, chest tightness, dizziness, anxiety, eczema, pruritus, abdominal cramps, myalgia, arthralgia, cough, rhinorrhea, dyspnea
Overdosage/Toxicology
Likely symptoms of overdose include those associated with fluid overload
Treatment is supportive (eg, diuretics)
Drug Interactions
Decreased toxicity: Antibodies present in IVIG preparations may interfere with the immune response to live virus vaccines (eg, MMR); reimmunization is recommended if such vaccines are administered within 10 months following RSV-IVIG treatment; additionally, it is advised that booster doses of oral polio, DPT, and HIB be considered 3-4 months after the last dose of RSV-IVIG in order to ensure immunity
Stability Store between 2°C and 8°C; do not freeze or shake vial; avoid foaming; discard after single use since it is preservative free
Mechanism of Action RSV-IGIV is a sterile liquid immunoglobulin G containing neutralizing antibody to respiratory syncytial virus. It is effective in reducing the incidence and duration of RSV hospitalization and the severity of RSV illness in high risk infants.
Usual Dosage I.V.: 750 mg/kg/month according to the following infusion schedule:
1.5 mL/kg/hour for 15 minutes, then at 3 mL/kg/hour for the next 15 minutes if the clinical condition does not contraindicate a higher rate, and finally, administer at 6 mL/kg/hour until completion of dose
Monitoring Parameters Monitor for symptoms of allergic reaction; check vital signs; cardiopulmonary status after each rate increase and thereafter at 30-minute intervals until 30 minutes following completion of the infusion
Nursing Implications Begin infusion within 6 hours and complete within 12 hours after entering vial. Observe for signs of intolerance during and after infusion; administer
(Continued)

Respiratory Syncytial Virus Immune Globulin (Intravenous)
(Continued)

through an I.V. line using a constant infusion pump and through a separate I.V. line, if possible; begin infusion within 6 hours and complete within 12 hours after entering the vial; if needed, RSV-IGIV may be "piggy-backed" into dextrose with or without saline solutions, avoiding dilutions >2:1 with such line configurations. Filters are not necessary, but an in-line filter with a pore size >15 micrometers may be used.

Monitor vital signs frequently; adverse reactions may be related to the rate of administration; RSV-IGIV is made from human plasma and carries the possibility for transmission of blood-borne pathogenic agents

Additional Information Each vial contains 1 to 1.5 mEq sodium

Dosage Forms Injection: 2500 mg RSV immunoglobulin/50 mL vial

- ♦ **Restoril®** see Temazepam on page 1111
- ♦ **Retavase™** see Reteplase on this page

Reteplase (RE ta plase)
U.S. Brand Names Retavase™

Synonyms Recombinant plasminogen activator; r-PA

Therapeutic Category Thrombolytic Agent

Use Improvement of ventricular function following acute myocardial infarction, for the reduction of the incidence of CHF and the reduction of mortality associated with acute myocardial infarction

Pregnancy Risk Factor C

Contraindications Active internal bleeding, history of cerebrovascular accident, recent intracranial or intraspinal surgery or trauma, intracranial neoplasm, arteriovenous malformations or aneurysm, known bleeding diathesis, severe uncontrolled hypertension, history of severe allergic reactions to reteplase, alteplase, anistreplase or streptokinase

Adverse Reactions
>10%:
  Cardiovascular: Hypotension, arrhythmias, trauma arrhythmias
  Hematologic: Bleeding
1% to 10%: Hematologic: Anemia, genitourinary bleeding, gastrointestinal bleeding, injection site bleeding
<1%: Intracranial hemorrhage, allergic reactions, anaphylaxis

Overdosage/Toxicology Symptoms of overdose include increased incidence of intracranial bleeding

Drug Interactions Increased effect: Anticoagulants, aspirin, ticlopidine, dipyridamole, abciximab and heparin are at least additive

Stability Dosage kits should be stored at 2°C to 25°C (36°F to 77°F) and remain sealed until use in order to protect from light

Mechanism of Action Reteplase is a nonglycosylated form of tPA produced by recombinant DNA technology using *E. coli*; it initiates local fibrinolysis by binding to fibrin in a thrombus (clot) and converts entrapped plasminogen to plasmin

Pharmacodynamics/Kinetics
Onset: 30-90 minutes
Half-life: 13-16 minutes
Elimination: Hepatic and renal, cleared from the plasma at a rate of 250-450 mL/minute

Usual Dosage
Children: Not recommended
Adults: 10 units I.V. over 2 minutes, followed by a second dose 30 minutes later of 10 units I.V. over 2 minutes
  Withhold second dose if serious bleeding or anaphylaxis occurs

Administration Reteplase should be reconstituted using the diluent, syringe, needle and dispensing pin provided with each kit and the each reconstituted dose should be given I.V. over 2 minutes; no other medication should be added to the injection solution

Monitoring Parameters Monitor for signs of bleeding (hematuria, GI bleeding, gingival bleeding)

Additional Information The dosage of reteplase in clinical trials was expressed in terms of million unit (MU); however, reteplase is being marketed in units (U) with 1 unit equivalent to 1 million units, reteplase units are expressed using a reference standard specific for reteplase and are not comparable with units used for other thrombolytic agents, 10 units is equivalent to 17.4 mg

Dosage Forms
Injection: Powder in vials, each vial contains reteplase 10.8 units; supplied with 2 mL diluent (preservative free)

- ♦ **Retin-A™ Micro Topical** see Tretinoin, Topical on page 1173
- ♦ **Retin-A™ Topical** see Tretinoin, Topical on page 1173
- ♦ **Retinoic Acid** see Tretinoin, Topical on page 1173
- ♦ **Retisol-A®** see Tretinoin, Topical on page 1173
- ♦ **Retrovir®** see Zidovudine on page 1235
- ♦ **Reversol® Injection** see Edrophonium on page 405
- ♦ **Revex®** see Nalmefene on page 813
- ♦ **Rēv-Eyes™** see Dapiprazole on page 324
- ♦ **ReVia®** see Naltrexone on page 815
- ♦ **Revitalose-C-1000®** see Ascorbic Acid on page 99

- **Rezine®** *see* Hydroxyzine *on page 589*
- **Rezulin®** *see* Troglitazone *on page 1188*
- **rFSH-alpha** *see* Follitropins *on page 513*
- **rFSH-beta** *see* Follitropins *on page 513*
- **rFVIIa** *see* Factor VIIa, Recombinant *on page 467*
- **R-Gen®** *see* Iodinated Glycerol *on page 622*
- **R-Gene®** *see* Arginine *on page 98*
- **rGM-CSF** *see* Sargramostim *on page 1049*
- **Rheomacrodex®** *see* Dextran *on page 341*
- **Rheumatrex®** *see* Methotrexate *on page 751*
- **rhFSH-alpha** *see* Follitropins *on page 513*
- **rhFSH-beta** *see* Follitropins *on page 513*
- **rhIL-11** *see* Oprelvekin *on page 865*
- **Rhinalar®** *see* Flunisolide *on page 494*
- **Rhinall® Nasal Solution [OTC]** *see* Phenylephrine *on page 918*
- **Rhinaris®-F** *see* Flunisolide *on page 494*
- **Rhinatate® Tablet** *see* Chlorpheniramine, Pyrilamine, and Phenylephrine *on page 247*
- **Rhindecon®** *see* Phenylpropanolamine *on page 919*
- **Rhinocort®** *see* Budesonide *on page 157*
- **Rhinosyn-DMX® [OTC]** *see* Guaifenesin and Dextromethorphan *on page 550*

$Rh_o(D)$ Immune Globulin (Intramuscular)

(ar aych oh (dee) i MYUN GLOB yoo lin)

U.S. Brand Names Gamulin® Rh; HypRho®-D; HypRho®-D Mini-Dose; MICRhoGAM™; Mini-Gamulin® Rh; RhoGAM™

Therapeutic Category Immune Globulin

Use Prevention of isoimmunization in Rh-negative individuals exposed to Rh-positive blood during delivery of an Rh-positive infant, as a result of an abortion, following amniocentesis or abdominal trauma, or following a transfusion accident; prevention of hemolytic disease of the newborn if there is a subsequent pregnancy with an Rh-positive fetus

Pregnancy Risk Factor C

Contraindications $Rh_o(D)$-positive patient; known hypersensitivity to immune globulins or to thimerosal; transfusion of $Rh_o(D)$-positive blood in previous 3 months; prior sensitization to $Rh_o(D)$

Warnings/Precautions Use with caution in patients with thrombocytopenia or bleeding disorders, patients with IgA deficiency; do not inject I.V.; do not administer to neonates

Adverse Reactions <1%: Lethargy, splenomegaly, elevated bilirubin, pain at the injection site, myalgia, temperature elevation

Stability Reconstituted solution should be refrigerated and will remain stable for 30 days; solution that have been frozen should be discarded

Mechanism of Action Suppresses the immune response and antibody formation of Rh-negative individuals to Rh-positive red blood cells

Pharmacodynamics/Kinetics

Distribution: Appears in breast milk; however, not absorbed by the nursing infant

Half-life: 23-26 days

Usual Dosage Adults (administered I.M. to mothers **not** to infant) I.M.:

Obstetrical usage: 1 vial (300 mcg) prevents maternal sensitization if fetal packed red blood cell volume that has entered the circulation is <15 mL; if it is more, give additional vials. The number of vials = RBC volume of the calculated fetomaternal hemorrhage divided by 15 mL

Postpartum prophylaxis: 300 mcg within 72 hours of delivery

Antepartum prophylaxis: 300 mcg at approximately 26-28 weeks gestation; followed by 300 mcg within 72 hours of delivery if infant is Rh-positive

Following miscarriage, abortion, or termination of ectopic pregnancy at up to 13 weeks of gestation: 50 mcg ideally within 3 hours, but may be given up to 72 hours after; if pregnancy has been terminated at 13 or more weeks of gestation, administer 300 mcg

Administration Administer I.M. in deltoid muscle; do **not** administer I.V.; the total volume can be given in divided doses at different sites at one time or may be divided and given at intervals, provided the total dosage is given within 72 hours of the fetomaternal hemorrhage or transfusion.

Patient Information Acetaminophen may be taken to ease minor discomfort after vaccination

Dosage Forms

Injection: Each package contains one single dose 300 mcg of Rh_o (D) immune globulin

Injection, microdose: Each package contains one single dose of microdose, 50 mcg of Rh_o (D) immune globulin

$Rh_o(D)$ Immune Globulin (Intravenous-Human)

(ar aych oh (dee) i MYUN GLOB yoo lin in tra VEE nus HYU man)

U.S. Brand Names WinRho SD®

Synonyms RhoIGIV

Therapeutic Category Immune Globulin

Use

Prevention of Rh isoimmunization in nonsensitized $Rh_o(D)$ antigen-negative women within 72 hours after spontaneous or induced abortion, amniocentesis, chorionic villus

(Continued)

Rho(D) Immune Globulin (Intravenous-Human) (Continued)

sampling, ruptured tubal pregnancy, abdominal trauma, transplacental hemorrhage, or in the normal course of pregnancy unless the blood type of the fetus or father is known to be Rho(D) antigen-negative.

Suppression of Rh isoimmunization in Rho(D) antigen-negative female children and female adults in their childbearing years transfused with Rho(D) antigen-positive RBCs or blood components containing Rho(D) antigen-positive RBCs

Treatment of idiopathic thrombocytopenic purpura (ITP) in nonsplenectomized Rho(D) antigen-positive patients

Pregnancy Risk Factor C

Contraindications Hypersensitivity to immune globulin or any component, IgA deficiency

Warnings/Precautions Anaphylactic hypersensitivity reactions can occur; studies indicate that there is no discernible risk of transmitting HIV or hepatitis B; do not administer by S.C. route; use only the I.V. route when treating ITP

Adverse Reactions 1% to 10%:

Central nervous system: Headache (2%), fever (1%), chills (<2%)

Hematologic: Hemolysis (Hgb decrease of >2 g/dL in 5% to 10% of ITP patients)

Local: Slight edema and pain at the injection site

Overdosage/Toxicology

No symptoms are likely, however, high doses have been associated with a mild, transient hemolytic anemia

Treatment is supportive

Drug Interactions Increased toxicity: Live virus, vaccines (measles, mumps, rubella); do not administer within 3 months after administration of these vaccines

Stability Store at 2°C to 8°C; do not freeze; if not used immediately, store the product at room temperature for 4 hours; do not freeze the reconstituted product; use within 4 hours; discard unused portions

Mechanism of Action The Rho(D) antigen is responsible for most cases of Rh sensitization, which occurs when Rh-positive fetal RBCs enter the maternal circulation of an Rh-negative woman. Injection of anti-D globulin results in opsonization of the fetal RBCs, which are then phagocytized in the spleen, preventing immunization of the mother. Injection of anti-D into an Rh-positive patient with ITP coats the patient's own D-positive RBCs with antibody and, as they are cleared by the spleen, they saturate the capacity of the spleen to clear antibody-coated cells, sparing antibody-coated platelets. Other proposed mechanisms involve the generation of cytokines following the interaction between antibody-coated RBCs and macrophages.

Pharmacodynamics/Kinetics

Time to peak serum concentration: I.V.: 2 hours; I.M.: 5-10 days

Half-life: I.V.: 24 days; I.M.: 30 days

Usual Dosage

Prevention of Rh isoimmunization: I.V.: 1500 units (300 mcg) at 28 weeks gestation or immediately after amniocentesis if before 34 weeks gestation or after chorionic villus sampling; repeat this dose every 12 weeks during the pregnancy. Administer 600 units (120 mcg) at delivery (within 72 hours) and after invasive intrauterine procedures such as abortion, amniocentesis, or any other manipulation if at >34 weeks gestation. **Note:** If the Rh status of the baby is not known at 72 hours, administer Rho(D) immune globulin to the mother at 72 hours after delivery. If >72 hours have elapsed, do not withhold Rho(D) immune globulin, but administer as soon as possible, up to 28 days after delivery.

I.M.: Reconstitute vial with 1.25 mL and administer as above

Transfusion: Administer within 72 hours after exposure for treatment of incompatible blood transfusions or massive fetal hemorrhage as follows:

I.V.: 3000 units (600 mcg) every 8 hours until the total dose is administered (45 units [9 mcg] of Rh-positive blood/mL blood; 90 units [18 mcg] Rh-positive red cells/mL cells)

I.M.: 6000 units [1200 mcg] every 12 hours until the total dose is administered (60 units [12 mcg] of Rh-positive blood/mL blood; 120 units [24 mcg] Rh-positive red cells/mL cells)

Treatment of ITP: I.V.: Initial: 25-50 mcg/kg depending on the patient's Hgb concentration; maintenance: 25-60 mcg/kg depending on the clinical response

Administration The product should not be shaken when reconstituting or transporting; reconstitute the product shortly before use with NS, according to the manufacturer's guidelines; do not administer with other products

Nursing Implications Increasing the time of infusion from 1-3 minutes to 15-20 minutes may also help; pretreatment with acetaminophen, diphenhydramine, or prednisone can prevent the fever/chill reaction

Additional Information Rho(D) is IgA-depleted and is unlikely to cause an anaphylactic reaction in women with IgA deficiency and anti-IgA antibodies. Although immune globulins for I.M. use, manufactured in the U.S. have never been found to transmit any viral infection, Rho(D) is the only Rho(D) preparation treated with highly effective solvent detergent method of viral inactivation for hepatitis C, HIV, and hepatitis B; treatment of ITP in Rh-positive patients with an intact spleen appears to be about as effective as IVIG

Dosage Forms Injection: 600 units [120 mcg], 1500 units [300 mcg] with 2.5 mL diluent

- **Rhodis™** see Ketoprofen on page 650
- **Rhodis-EC™** see Ketoprofen on page 650
- **RhoGAM™** see Rho(D) Immune Globulin (Intramuscular) on previous page
- **RhoIGIV** see Rho(D) Immune Globulin (Intravenous-Human) on previous page
- **Rhoprolene** see Betamethasone on page 141

- **Rhoprosone** *see* Betamethasone *on page 141*
- **Rhotral** *see* Acebutolol *on page 18*
- **Rhotrimine®** *see* Trimipramine *on page 1186*
- **rHuEPO-α** *see* Epoetin Alfa *on page 418*
- **Rhulicaine® [OTC]** *see* Benzocaine *on page 133*
- **Rhythmin®** *see* Procainamide *on page 968*

Ribavirin (rye ba VYE rin)

U.S. Brand Names Rebetol®; Virazole® Aerosol

Synonyms RTCA; Tribavirin

Therapeutic Category Antiviral Agent, Inhalation Therapy

Use Inhalation: Treatment of patients with respiratory syncytial virus (RSV) infections; may also be used in other viral infections including influenza A and B and adenovirus; specially indicated for treatment of severe lower respiratory tract RSV infections in patients with an underlying compromising condition (prematurity, bronchopulmonary dysplasia and other chronic lung conditions, congenital heart disease, immunodeficiency, immunosuppression), and recent transplant recipients

Oral capsules: The combination therapy of oral ribavirin with interferon alfa-2b, recombinant (Intron® A) injection is indicated for the treatment of chronic hepatitis C in patients with compensated liver disease who have relapsed after alpha interferon therapy.

Pregnancy Risk Factor X

Contraindications Females of childbearing age; hypersensitivity to ribavirin; patients with autoimmune hepatitis

Warnings/Precautions Use with caution in patients requiring assisted ventilation because precipitation of the drug in the respiratory equipment may interfere with safe and effective patient ventilation; monitor carefully in patients with COPD and asthma for deterioration of respiratory function. Ribavirin is potentially mutagenic, tumor-promoting, and gonadotoxic. Anemia has been observed in patients receiving the interferon/ribavirin combination. Severe psychiatric events have also occurred including depression and suicidal behavior during combination therapy; avoid use in patients with a psychiatric history.

Adverse Reactions

Inhalation:

1% to 10%:

Central nervous system: Fatigue, headache, insomnia

Gastrointestinal: Nausea, anorexia

Hematologic: Anemia

<1%: Hypotension, cardiac arrest, digitalis toxicity, rash, skin irritation, conjunctivitis, mild bronchospasm, worsening of respiratory function, apnea

Note: Incidence of adverse effects in healthcare workers approximate 51% headache; 32% conjunctivitis; 10% to 20% rhinitis, nausea, rash, dizziness, pharyngitis, and lacrimation

Oral: (All adverse reactions are documented while receiving combination therapy with interferon alpha-2b)

>10%:

Cardiovascular: Chest pain

Central nervous system: Dizziness, headache, fatigue, fever, insomnia, irritability, depression, emotional lability, impaired concentration

Dermatologic: Alopecia, rash, pruritus

Gastrointestinal: Nausea, anorexia, dyspepsia, vomiting

Hematologic: Decreased hemoglobin and WBC

Neuromuscular & skeletal: Myalgia, arthralgia, musculoskeletal pain, weakness, rigors

Respiratory: Dyspnea, sinusitis

Miscellaneous: Flu-like syndrome

1% to 10%:

Central nervous system: Nervousness

Endocrine & metabolic: Thyroid function test abnormalities

Gastrointestinal: Taste perversion

Drug Interactions Decreased effect of zidovudine

Stability Do not use any water containing an antimicrobial agent to reconstitute drug; reconstituted solution is stable for 24 hours at room temperature

Mechanism of Action Inhibits replication of RNA and DNA viruses; inhibits influenza virus RNA polymerase activity and inhibits the initiation and elongation of RNA fragments resulting in inhibition of viral protein synthesis

Pharmacodynamics/Kinetics

Absorption: Absorbed systemically from the respiratory tract following nasal and oral inhalation; absorption is dependent upon respiratory factors and method of drug delivery; maximal absorption occurs with the use of the aerosol generator via an endotracheal tube; highest concentrations are found in the respiratory tract and erythrocytes

Metabolism: Occurs intracellularly and may be necessary for drug action

Half-life, plasma:

Children: 6.5-11 hours

Adults: 24 hours, much longer in the erythrocyte (16-40 days), which can be used as a marker for intracellular metabolism

Time to peak serum concentration: Inhalation: Within 60-90 minutes

(Continued)

Ribavirin *(Continued)*

Elimination: Hepatic metabolism is major route of elimination with 40% of the drug cleared renally as unchanged drug and metabolites

Usual Dosage Infants, Children, and Adults:

Aerosol inhalation: Use with Viratek® small particle aerosol generator (SPAG-2) at a concentration of 20 mg/mL (6 g reconstituted with 300 mL of sterile water without preservatives)

Aerosol only: 12-18 hours/day for 3 days, up to 7 days in length

Monitoring Parameters Respiratory function, CBC, reticulocyte count, I & O

Patient Information Do not use if pregnant

Nursing Implications Keep accurate I & O record, discard solutions placed in the SPAG-2 unit at least every 24 hours and before adding additional fluid; healthcare workers who are pregnant or who may become pregnant should be advised of the potential risks of exposure and counseled about risk reduction strategies including alternate job responsibilities; ribavirin may adsorb to contact lenses

Dosage Forms

Capsule: 200 mg; available only in Rebetron® combination package

Powder for aerosol: 6 g (100 mL)

Riboflavin *(RYE boe flay vin)*

U.S. Brand Names Riobin®

Synonyms Lactoflavin; Vitamin B_2; Vitamin G

Therapeutic Category Vitamin, Water Soluble

Use Prevent riboflavin deficiency and treat ariboflavinosis

Pregnancy Risk Factor A (C if dose exceeds RDA recommendation)

Warnings/Precautions Riboflavin deficiency often occurs in the presence of other B vitamin deficiencies

Drug Interactions Decreased absorption with probenecid

Mechanism of Action Component of flavoprotein enzymes that work together, which are necessary for normal tissue respiration; also needed for activation of pyridoxine and conversion of tryptophan to niacin

Pharmacodynamics/Kinetics

Absorption: Readily via GI tract, however, food increases extent of GI absorption; GI absorption is decreased in patients with hepatitis, cirrhosis, or biliary obstruction

Metabolism: Metabolic fate unknown

Half-life, biologic: 66-84 minutes

Elimination: 9% excreted unchanged in urine

Usual Dosage Oral:

Riboflavin deficiency:

Children: 2.5-10 mg/day in divided doses

Adults: 5-30 mg/day in divided doses

Recommended daily allowance:

Children: 0.4-1.8 mg

Adults: 1.2-1.7 mg

Test Interactions Large doses may interfere with urinalysis based on spectrometry; may cause false elevations in fluorometric determinations of catecholamines and urobilinogen

Patient Information Take with food; large doses may cause bright yellow or orange urine

Additional Information Dietary sources of riboflavin include liver, kidney, dairy products, green vegetables, eggs, whole grain cereals, yeast, mushroom

Dosage Forms Tablet: 25 mg, 50 mg, 100 mg

◆ **Rid-A-Pain® [OTC]** see Benzocaine *on page 133*

◆ **Ridaura®** see Auranofin *on page 112*

◆ **Ridene** see Nicardipine *on page 834*

◆ **Ridenol® [OTC]** see Acetaminophen *on page 19*

◆ **RID® Shampoo [OTC]** see Pyrethrins *on page 996*

Rifabutin *(rif a BYOO tin)*

Related Information

Antimicrobial Drugs of Choice *on page 1404*

Guidelines for the Prevention of Opportunistic Infections in Persons with HIV *on page 1388*

Tuberculosis Prophylaxis *on page 1386*

U.S. Brand Names Mycobutin®

Synonyms Ansamycin

Therapeutic Category Antibiotic, Miscellaneous; Antitubercular Agent

Use Prevention of disseminated *Mycobacterium avium* complex (MAC) in patients with advanced HIV infection; also utilized in multiple drug regimens for treatment of MAC

Pregnancy Risk Factor B

Contraindications Hypersensitivity to rifabutin or any other rifamycins; rifabutin is contraindicated in patients with a WBC <1000/mm³ or a platelet count <50,000/mm³; concurrent use with ritonavir

Warnings/Precautions Rifabutin as a single agent must not be administered to patients with active tuberculosis since its use may lead to the development of tuberculosis that is resistant to both rifabutin and rifampin; rifabutin should be discontinued in patients with AST >500 units/L or if total bilirubin is >3 mg/dL. Use with caution in patients with liver impairment; modification of dosage should be considered in patients with renal impairment.

Adverse Reactions
>10%:
Dermatologic: Rash (11%)
Genitourinary: Discolored urine (30%)
Hematologic: Neutropenia (25%), leukopenia (17%)
1% to 10%:
Central nervous system: Headache (3%)
Gastrointestinal: Vomiting/nausea (3%), abdominal pain (4%), diarrhea (3%), anorexia (2%), flatulence (2%), eructation (3%)
Hematologic: Anemia, thrombocytopenia (5%)
Hepatic: Increased AST/ALT (7% to 9%)
Neuromuscular & skeletal: Myalgia
<1%: Chest pain, fever, insomnia, dyspepsia, taste perversion, uveitis

Overdosage/Toxicology
Symptoms of overdose include nausea, vomiting, hepatotoxicity, lethargy, CNS depression
Treatment is supportive; hemodialysis will remove rifabutin, its effect on outcome is unknown

Drug Interactions CYP3A3/4 enzyme inducer
Decreased plasma concentration (due to induction of liver enzymes) of verapamil, methadone, digoxin, cyclosporine, corticosteroids, oral anticoagulants, theophylline, barbiturates, chloramphenicol, ketoconazole, oral contraceptives, quinidine, halothane, protease inhibitors, non-nucleoside reverse transcriptase inhibitors, and perhaps clarithromycin
Increased concentration by indinavir; reduce to 1/2 standard dose when used with indinavir
Increased risk of rifabutin-induced hematologic and ocular toxicity (uveitis) with concurrent administration of drug that inhibits CYP450 enzymes such as protease inhibitors, erythromycin, clarithromycin, ketoconazole, and itraconazole

Mechanism of Action Inhibits DNA-dependent RNA polymerase at the beta subunit which prevents chain initiation

Pharmacodynamics/Kinetics
Absorption: Oral: Readily absorbed 53%
Distribution: V_d: 9.32 L/kg; distributes to body tissues including the lungs, liver, spleen, eyes, and kidneys
Protein binding: 85%
Metabolism: To active and inactive metabolites
Bioavailability: Absolute, 20% in HIV patients
Half-life, terminal: 45 hours (range: 16-69 hours)
Peak serum level: Within 2-4 hours
Elimination: Renal and biliary clearance of unchanged drugs is 10%; 30% excreted in feces; 53% in urine as metabolites

Usual Dosage Oral:
Children: Efficacy and safety of rifabutin have not been established in children; a limited number of HIV-positive children with MAC have been given rifabutin for MAC prophylaxis; doses of 5 mg/kg/day have been useful
Adults: 300 mg once daily; for patients who experience gastrointestinal upset, rifabutin can be administered 150 mg twice daily with food

Monitoring Parameters Periodic liver function tests, CBC with differential, platelet count

Patient Information May discolor urine, tears, sweat, or other body fluids to a red-orange color; take 1 hour before or 2 hours after a meal on an empty stomach; soft contact lenses may be permanently stained; report to physician any severe or persistent flu-like symptoms, nausea, vomiting, dark urine or pale stools, unusual bleeding or bruising, or any eye problems; can be taken with meals or sprinkled on applesauce

Dosage Forms Capsule: 150 mg

- **Rifadin®** see Rifampin on this page
- **Rifadin® Injection** see Rifampin on this page
- **Rifadin® Oral** see Rifampin on this page
- **Rifamate®** see Rifampin and Isoniazid on page 1025
- **Rifampicin** see Rifampin on this page

Rifampin (RIF am pin)

Related Information
Antibiotic Treatment of Adults With Infective Endocarditis on page 1401
Antimicrobial Drugs of Choice on page 1404
Community-Acquired Pneumonia in Adults on page 1419
Desensitization Protocols on page 1347
Guidelines for the Prevention of Opportunistic Infections in Persons with HIV on page 1388
Prophylaxis for Patients Exposed to Common Communicable Diseases on page 1384
Tuberculosis Prophylaxis on page 1386
Tuberculosis Treatment Guidelines on page 1432

U.S. Brand Names Rifadin® Injection; Rifadin® Oral; Rimactane® Oral
Canadian Brand Names Rifadin®; Rimactane®; Rofact™
Synonyms Rifampicin
Therapeutic Category Antibiotic, Miscellaneous; Antitubercular Agent
(Continued)

1023

Rifampin *(Continued)*

Use Management of active tuberculosis in combination with other agents; eliminate meningococci from asymptomatic carriers; prophylaxis of *Haemophilus influenzae* type b infection; used in combination with other anti-infectives in the treatment of staphylococcal infections

Pregnancy Risk Factor C

Pregnancy/Breast-Feeding Implications Clinical effects on the fetus: Teratogenicity has occurred in rodents given many times the adult human dose

Contraindications Hypersensitivity to any rifamycins or any component

Warnings/Precautions Use with caution and modify dosage in patients with liver impairment; observe for hyperbilirubinemia; discontinue therapy if this in conjunction with clinical symptoms or any signs of significant hepatocellular damage develop; since rifampin has enzyme-inducing properties, porphyria exacerbation is possible; use with caution in patients with porphyria; do not use for meningococcal disease, only for short-term treatment of asymptomatic carrier states

Monitor for compliance and effects including hypersensitivity, decreased thrombocytopenia in patients on intermittent therapy; urine, feces, saliva, sweat, tears, and CSF may be discolored to red/orange; do not administer I.V. form via I.M. or S.C. routes; restart infusion at another site if extravasation occurs; remove soft contact lenses during therapy since permanent staining may occur; regimens of 600 mg once or twice weekly have been associated with a high incidence of adverse reactions including a flu-like syndrome

Adverse Reactions

Percentage unknown: Flushing, edema headache, drowsiness, dizziness, confusion, numbness, behavioral changes, pruritus, urticaria, pemphigoid reaction, eosinophilia, leukopenia, hemolysis, hemolytic anemia, thrombocytopenia (especially with high-dose therapy), hepatitis (rare), ataxia, myalgia, weakness, osteomalacia, visual changes, exudative conjunctivitis

1% to 10%:

Dermatologic: Rash (1% to 5%)

Gastrointestinal: (1% to 2%): Epigastric distress, anorexia, nausea, vomiting, diarrhea, cramps, pseudomembranous colitis, pancreatitis

Hepatic: Increased LFTs (up to 14%)

Overdosage/Toxicology

Symptoms of overdose include nausea, vomiting, hepatotoxicity

Treatment is supportive; lavage with activated charcoal is preferred to ipecac as emesis is frequently present with overdose; hemodialysis will remove rifampin, its effect on outcome is unknown

Drug Interactions CYP3A3/4 enzyme substrate; CYP1A2, 2C9, 2C18, 2C19, 2D6, 3A3/4, and 3A5-7 enzyme inducer

Decreased effect: Rifampin induces liver enzymes which may decrease the plasma concentration of calcium channel blockers (verapamil, diltiazem, nifedipine), methadone, digitalis, cyclosporine, corticosteroids, oral anticoagulants, haloperidol, theophylline, barbiturates, chloramphenicol, imidazole antifungals, oral or systemic hormonal contraceptives, acetaminophen, benzodiazepines, hydantoins, sulfa drugs, enalapril, beta-blockers, chloramphenicol, clofibrate, dapsone, antiarrhythmics (disopyramide, mexiletine, quinidine, tocainide), diazepam, doxycycline, fluoroquinolones, levothyroxine, nortriptyline, progestins, tacrolimus, zidovudine, protease inhibitors, and nonnucleoside reverse transcriptase inhibitors

Coadministration with INH or halothane may result in additive hepatotoxicity; probenecid and co-trimoxazole may increase rifampin levels while antacids may decrease its absorption

Stability Rifampin powder is reddish brown. Intact vials should be stored at room temperature and protected from excessive heat and light. Reconstituted vials are stable for 24 hours at room temperature

Stability of parenteral admixture at room temperature (25°C) is 4 hours for D_5W and 24 hours for NS

Mechanism of Action Inhibits bacterial RNA synthesis by binding to the beta subunit of DNA-dependent RNA polymerase, blocking RNA transcription

Pharmacodynamics/Kinetics

Absorption: Oral: Well absorbed

Time to peak serum concentration: Oral: 2-4 hours and persisting for up to 24 hours; food may delay or slightly reduce

Distribution: Crosses the blood-brain barrier well

Relative diffusion of antimicrobial agents from blood into cerebrospinal fluid (CSF): Adequate with or without inflammation (exceeds usual MICs)

Ratio of CSF to blood level (%): Inflamed meninges: 25

Protein binding: 80%

Metabolism: Highly lipophilic; metabolized in the liver, undergoes enterohepatic recycling

Half-life: 3-4 hours, prolonged with hepatic impairment

End-stage renal disease: 1.8-11 hours

Elimination: Undergoes enterohepatic recycling; principally excreted unchanged in the feces (60% to 65%) and urine (~30%); excreted unchanged: 15% to 30%; plasma rifampin concentrations are not significantly affected by hemodialysis or peritoneal dialysis

Usual Dosage Oral (I.V. infusion dose is the same as for the oral route):
Tuberculosis therapy:
Note: A four-drug regimen (isoniazid, rifampin, pyrazinamide, and either streptomycin or ethambutol) is preferred for the initial, empiric treatment of TB. When the drug susceptibility results are available, the regimen should be altered as appropriate.
Infants and Children <12 years:
Daily therapy: 10-20 mg/kg/day usually as a single dose (maximum: 600 mg/day)
Directly observed therapy (DOT): Twice weekly: 10-20 mg/kg (maximum: 600 mg); 3 times/week: 10-20 mg/kg (maximum: 600 mg)
Adults:
Daily therapy: 10 mg/kg/day (maximum: 600 mg/day)
Directly observed therapy (DOT): Twice weekly: 10 mg/kg (maximum: 600 mg); 3 times/week: 10 mg/kg (maximum: 600 mg)
H. influenzae prophylaxis:
Infants and Children: 20 mg/kg/day every 24 hours for 4 days, not to exceed 600 mg/dose
Adults: 600 mg every 24 hours for 4 days
Meningococcal prophylaxis:
<1 month: 10 mg/kg/day in divided doses every 12 hours for 2 days
Infants and Children: 20 mg/kg/day in divided doses every 12 hours for 2 days
Adults: 600 mg every 12 hours for 2 days
Nasal carriers of *Staphylococcus aureus*:
Children: 15 mg/kg/day divided every 12 hours for 5-10 days in combination with other antibiotics
Adults: 600 mg/day for 5-10 days in combination with other antibiotics
Synergy for *Staphylococcus aureus* infections: Adults: 300-600 mg twice daily with other antibiotics
Dosing adjustment in hepatic impairment: Dose reductions may be necessary to reduce hepatotoxicity
Dietary Considerations Food: Rifampin is best taken on an empty stomach since food decreases the extent of absorption
Administration Administer on an empty stomach (ie, 1 hour prior to, or 2 hours after meals or antacids) to increase total absorption
Monitoring Parameters Periodic (baseline and every 2-4 weeks during therapy) monitoring of liver function (AST, ALT, bilirubin BSD), CBC; hepatic status and mental status, sputum culture, chest x-ray 2-3 months into treatment
Test Interactions Positive Coombs' reaction [direct], rifampin inhibits standard assay's ability to measure serum folate and B_{12}; transient increase in LFTs and decreased biliary excretion of contrast media
Patient Information May discolor urine, tears, sweat, or other body fluids to a red-orange color; take 1 hour before or 2 hours after a meal on an empty stomach; soft contact lenses may be permanently stained; report to physician any severe or persistent flu-like symptoms, nausea, vomiting, dark urine or pale stools, or unusual bleeding or bruising; utilize an alternate form from oral/other systemic contraceptives during therapy; compliance and completion with course of therapy is very important; if you are a diabetic taking oral medications or if you regularly take oral anticoagulant therapy, your medication may need special and careful adjustment.
Dosage Forms
Capsule: 150 mg, 300 mg
Injection: 600 mg
Extemporaneous Preparations For pediatric and adult patients with difficulty swallowing or where lower doses are needed, the package insert lists an extemporaneous liquid suspension as follows:

Rifampin 1% w/v suspension (10 mg/mL) can be compounded using one of four syrups (Syrup NF, simple syrup, Syrpalta® syrup, or raspberry syrup)
Empty contents of four 300 mg capsules or eight 150 mg capsules onto a piece of weighing paper
If necessary, crush contents to produce a fine powder
Transfer powder blend to a 4 oz amber glass or plastic prescription bottle
Rinse paper and spatula with 20 mL of syrup and add the rinse to bottle; shake vigorously
Add 100 mL of syrup to the bottle and shake vigorously
This compounding procedure results in a 1% w/v suspension containing 10 mg rifampin/mL; stability studies indicate suspension is stable at room temperature (25°C ±3°C) or in refrigerator (2°C to 8°C) for 4 weeks; shake well prior to administration

Rifampin and Isoniazid (RIF am pin & eye soe NYE a zid)
U.S. Brand Names Rifamate®
Therapeutic Category Antibiotic, Miscellaneous
Dosage Forms Capsule: Rifampin 300 mg and isoniazid 150 mg

Rifampin, Isoniazid, and Pyrazinamide
(RIF am pin, eye soe NYE a zid, & peer a ZIN a mide)
U.S. Brand Names Rifater®
Therapeutic Category Antibiotic, Miscellaneous
Dosage Forms Tablet: Rifampin 120 mg, isoniazid 50 mg, and pyrazinamide 300 mg

Rifapentine (RIF a pen teen)

U.S. Brand Names Priftin®

Therapeutic Category Antitubercular Agent

Use Treatment of pulmonary tuberculosis (indication is based on the 6-month follow-up treatment outcome observed in controlled clinical trial). Rifapentine must always be used in conjunction with at least one other antituberculosis drug to which the isolate is susceptible; it may also be necessary to add a third agent (either streptomycin or ethambutol) until susceptibility is known.

Pregnancy Risk Factor C

Pregnancy/Breast-Feeding Implications Has been shown to be teratogenic in rats and rabbits. Rat offspring showed cleft palates, right aortic arch, and delayed ossification and increased number of ribs. Rabbits displayed ovarian agenesis, pes varus, arhinia, microphthalmia, and irregularities of the ossified facial tissues. Rat studies also show decreased fetal weight, increased number of stillborns, and decreased gestational survival. No adequate well-controlled studies in pregnant women are available. Rifapentine should be used during pregnancy only if the potential benefits justifies the potential risk to the fetus.

Contraindications Patients with a history of hypersensitivity to rifapentine, rifampin, rifabutin, and any rifamycin analog

Warnings/Precautions Compliance with dosing regimen is absolutely necessary for successful drug therapy. patients with abnormal liver tests and/or liver disease should only be given rifapentine when absolutely necessary and under strict medical supervision. Monitoring of liver function tests should be carried out prior to therapy and then every 2-4 weeks during therapy if signs of liver disease occur or worsen, rifapentine should be discontinued. Pseudomembranous colitis has been reported to occur with various antibiotics including other rifamycins. If this is suspected, rifapentine should be stopped and the patient treated with specific and supportive treatment. Experience in treating TB in HIV-infected patients is limited.

Rifapentine may produce a red-orange discoloration of body tissues/fluids including skin, teeth, tongue, urine, feces, saliva, sputum, tears, sweat, and cerebral spinal fluid. Contact lenses may become permanently stained. All patients treated with rifapentine should have baseline measurements of liver function tests and enzymes, bilirubin, and a complete blood count. patients should be seen monthly and specifically questioned regarding symptoms associated with adverse reactions. Routine laboratory monitoring in people with normal baseline measurements is generally not necessary.

Adverse Reactions

>10%: Endocrine & metabolic: Hyperuricemia (most likely due to pyrazinamide from initiation phase combination therapy)

1% to 10%:

Cardiovascular: Hypertension

Central nervous system: Headache, dizziness

Dermatologic: Rash, pruritus, acne

Gastrointestinal: Anorexia, nausea, vomiting, dyspepsia, diarrhea

Hematologic: Neutropenia, lymphopenia, anemia, leukopenia, thrombocytosis

Hepatic: Increased ALT/AST

Neuromuscular & skeletal: Arthralgia, pain

Renal: Pyuria, proteinuria, hematuria, urinary casts

Respiratory: Hemoptysis

<1%: Peripheral edema, aggressive reaction, fatigue, urticaria, skin discoloration, hyperkalemia, hypovolemia, increased alkaline phosphatase, increased LDH, constipation, esophagitis, gastritis, pancreatitis, thrombocytopenia, neutrophilia, leukocytosis, purpura, hematoma, bilirubinemia, hepatitis, gout, arthrosis

Overdosage/Toxicology There is no experience with treatment of acute overdose with rifapentine; experience with other rifamycins suggests that gastric lavage followed by activated charcoal may help adsorb any remaining drug from the GI tract. Hemodialysis or forced diuresis is not expected to enhance elimination of unchanged rifapentine in an overdose.

Drug Interactions CYP3A4 and 2C8/9 inducer. Rifapentine may increase the metabolism of coadministered drugs that are metabolized by these enzymes. Enzymes are induced within 4 days after the first dose and returned to baseline 14 days after discontinuation of rifapentine. The magnitude of enzyme induction is dose and frequency dependent. Rifampin has been shown to accelerate the metabolism and may reduce activity of the following drugs (therefore, rifapentine may also do the same): Phenytoin, disopyramide, mexiletine, quinidine, tocainide, chloramphenicol, clarithromycin, dapsone, doxycycline, fluoroquinolones, warfarin, fluconazole, itraconazole, ketoconazole, barbiturates, benzodiazepines, beta-blockers, diltiazem, nifedipine, verapamil, corticosteroids, cardiac glycoside preparations, clofibrate, oral or other systemic hormonal contraceptives, haloperidol, HIV protease inhibitors, sulfonylureas, cyclosporine, tacrolimus, levothyroxine, methadone, progestins, quinine, delavirdine, zidovudine, sildenafil, theophylline, amitriptyline, and nortriptyline.

Rifapentine should be used with extreme caution, if at all, in patients who are also taking protease inhibitors

Patients using oral or other systemic hormonal contraceptives should be advised to change to nonhormonal methods of birth control when receiving concomitant rifapentine.

Rifapentine metabolism is mediated by esterase activity, therefore, there is minimal potential for rifapentine metabolism to be affected by other drug therapy.

Stability Store at room temperature (15°C to 30°C; 59°F to 86°F); protect from excessive heat and humidity

Mechanism of Action Inhibits DNA-dependent RNA polymerase in susceptible strains of *Mycobacterium tuberculosis* (but not in mammalian cells). Rifapentine is bactericidal against both intracellular and extracellular MTB organisms. MTB resistant to other rifamycins including rifampin are likely to be resistant to rifapentine. Cross-resistance does not appear between rifapentine and other nonrifamycin antimycobacterial agents.

Pharmacodynamics/Kinetics

Absorption: Food increases AUC and C_{max} by 43% and 44% respectively.

Distribution: V_d: ~70.2 L

Metabolism: Hydrolyzed by an esterase and esterase enzyme to form the active metabolite 25-desacetyl rifapentine

Protein binding: Rifapentine and 25-desacetyl metabolite were 97.7% and 93.2% protein bound (mainly to albumin). Rifapentine and metabolite accumulate in human monocyte-derived macrophages with intracellular/extracellular ratios of 24:1 and 7:1 respectively

Half-life: Rifapentine: 14-17 hours; 25-desacetyl rifapentine: 13 hours

Bioavailability: ~70%

Time to peak serum concentration: 5-6 hours

Elimination: Extent of renal excretion is unknown; excreted as parent drug and metabolite; 17% of administered dose is excreted via the kidneys

Usual Dosage

Children: No dosing information available

Adults: **Rifapentine should not be used alone**; initial phase should include a 3- to 4-drug regimen

Intensive phase of short-term therapy: 600 mg (four 150 mg tablets) given weekly (every 72 hours); following the intensive phase, treatment should continue with rifapentine 600 mg once weekly for 4 months in combination with INH or appropriate agent for susceptible organisms

Dosing adjustment in renal or hepatic impairment: Unknown

Dietary Considerations Food increases AUC and maximum serum concentration by 43% and 44% respectively as compared to fasting conditions

Monitoring Parameters Patients with pre-existing hepatic problems should have liver function tests monitored every 2-4 weeks during therapy

Test Interactions Rifampin has been shown to inhibit standard microbiological assays for serum folate and vitamin B_{12}; this should be considered for rifapentine; therefore, alternative assay methods should be considered.

Patient Information May produce a reddish coloration of urine, sweat, sputum, tears, and contact lenses may be permanently stained. oral or other systemic hormonal contraceptives may not be effective while taking rifapentine; alternative contraceptive measures should be used. Administration of rifapentine with food may decrease GI intolerance. Notify physician if experiencing fever, decreased appetite, malaise, nausea/vomiting, darkened urine, yellowish discoloration of skin or eyes, and pain or swelling of the joints. Adherence with the full course of therapy is essential; no doses of therapy should be missed.

Additional Information Rifapentine has only been studied in patients with tuberculosis receiving a 6-month short-course intensive regimen approval; outcomes have been based on 6-month follow-up treatment observed in clinical trial 008 as a surrogate for the 2-year follow-up generally accepted as evidence for efficacy in the treatment of pulmonary tuberculosis

Dosage Forms Tablet, film-coated: 150 mg

- **Rifater®** see Rifampin, Isoniazid, and Pyrazinamide *on page 1025*
- **rIFN-A** see Interferon Alfa-2a *on page 616*
- **rIFN-b** see Interferon Beta-1a *on page 621*
- **RIG** see Rabies Immune Globulin (Human) *on page 1006*
- **rIL-11** see Oprelvekin *on page 865*
- **Rilutek®** see Riluzole *on this page*

Riluzole (RIL yoo zole)

U.S. Brand Names Rilutek®

Synonyms 2-Amino-6-Trifluoromethoxy-benzothiazole; RP54274

Therapeutic Category Amyotrophic Lateral Sclerosis (ALS) Agent; Antipsychotic Agent, Benzisoxazole

Use Amyotrophic lateral sclerosis (ALS): Treatment of patients with ALS; riluzole can extend survival or time to tracheostomy

Pregnancy Risk Factor C

Contraindications Severe hypersensitivity reactions to riluzole or any of the tablet components

Warnings/Precautions Among 4000 patients given riluzole for ALS, there were 3 cases of marked neutropenia (ANC <500/mm³), all seen within the first 2 months of treatment. Use with caution in patients with concomitant renal insufficiency. Use with caution in patients with current evidence or history of abnormal liver function. Monitor liver chemistries.

Adverse Reactions >10%:

Gastrointestinal: Nausea, abdominal pain, constipation

Hepatic: Increased ALT

Overdosage/Toxicology No specific antidote or treatment information available; treatment should be supportive and directed toward alleviating symptoms

(Continued)

Riluzole *(Continued)*

Drug Interactions CYP1A2 enzyme substrate

Decreased effect: Drugs that induce CYP 1A2 (eg, cigarette smoke, charbroiled food, rifampin, omeprazole) could increase the rate of riluzole elimination

Increased toxicity: Inhibitors of CYP 1A2 (eg, caffeine, theophylline, amitriptyline, quinolones) could decrease the rate of riluzole elimination

Stability Protect from bright light

Mechanism of Action Inhibitory effect on glutamate release, inactivation of voltage-dependent sodium channels; and ability to interfere with intracellular events that follow transmitter binding at excitatory amino acid receptors

Pharmacodynamics/Kinetics

Absorption: Well absorbed (90%); a high fat meal decreases absorption of riluzole (decreasing AUC by 20% and peak blood levels by 45%)

Protein binding: 96% bound to plasma proteins, mainly albumin and lipoproteins

Metabolism: Extensively to 6 major and a number of minor metabolites. Metabolism is mostly hepatic and consists of cytochrome P-450 dependent hydroxylation and glucuronidation; principle isozyme is CYP 1A2

Bioavailability: Oral: Absolute (50%)

Usual Dosage Adults: Oral: 50 mg every 12 hours; no increased benefit can be expected from higher daily doses, but adverse events are increased

Dosage adjustment in smoking: Cigarette smoking is known to induce CYP 1A2; patients who smoke cigarettes would be expected to eliminate riluzole faster. There is no information, however, on the effect of, or need for, dosage adjustment in these patients.

Dosage adjustment in special populations: Females and Japanese patients may possess a lower metabolic capacity to eliminate riluzole compared with male and Caucasian subjects, respectively

Dosage adjustment in renal impairment: Use with caution in patients with concomitant renal insufficiency

Dosage adjustment in hepatic impairment: Use with caution in patients with current evidence or history of abnormal liver function indicated by significant abnormalities in serum transaminase, bilirubin or GGT levels. Baseline elevations of several LFTs (especially elevated bilirubin) should preclude use of riluzole.

Monitoring Parameters Monitor serum aminotransferases including ALT levels before and during therapy. Evaluate serum ALT levels every month during the first 3 months of therapy, every 3 months during the remainder of the first year and periodically thereafter. Evaluate ALT levels more frequently in patients who develop elevations. Maximum increases in serum ALT usually occurred within 3 months after the start of therapy and were usually transient when <5 x ULN (upper limits of normal).

In trials, if ALT levels were <5 x ULN, treatment continued and ALT levels usually returned to below 2 x ULN within 2-6 months. Treatment in studies was discontinued, however, if ALT levels exceed 5 x ULN, so that there is no experience with continued treatment of ALS patients once ALT values exceed 5 x ULN.

If a decision is made to continue treatment in patients when the ALT exceeds 5 x ULN, frequent monitoring (at least weekly) of complete liver function is recommended. Discontinue treatment if ALT exceeds 10 x ULN or if clinical jaundice develops.

Patient Information Take at least 1 hour before or 2 hours after a meal to avoid decreased bioavailability. Report any febrile illness to your physician. Take riluzole at the same time of the day each day. If a dose is missed, take the next tablet as originally planned.

Nursing Implications Warn patients about the potential for dizziness, vertigo or somnolence and advise them not to drive or operate machinery until they have gained sufficient experience on riluzole to gauge whether or not it affects their mental or motor performance adversely. Whether alcohol increases the risk of serious hepatotoxicity with riluzole is unknown; discourage riluzole-treated patients from drinking alcohol in excess.

Additional Information May be obtained through Rhone-Poulenc Rorer Inc (Collegeville, PA) for compassionate use (through treatment IND process) by calling 800-727-6737 for treatment of amyotrophic lateral sclerosis; may be more effective for amyotrophic lateral sclerosis of bulbar onset; in animal models, riluzole was a potent inhibitor of seizures induced by ouabain

Dosage Forms Tablet: 50 mg

- **Rimactane®** *see Rifampin on page 1023*
- **Rimactane® Oral** *see Rifampin on page 1023*

Rimantadine *(ri MAN ta deen)*

Related Information

Community-Acquired Pneumonia in Adults *on page 1419*

Guidelines for the Prevention of Opportunistic Infections in Persons with HIV *on page 1388*

U.S. Brand Names Flumadine®

Synonyms Rimantadine Hydrochloride

Therapeutic Category Antiviral Agent, Oral

Use Prophylaxis (adults and children >1 year) and treatment (adults) of influenza A viral infection

Pregnancy Risk Factor C

Pregnancy/Breast-Feeding Implications
Clinical effects on the fetus: Embryotoxic in high dose rat studies
Breast-feeding/lactation: Avoid use in nursing mothers due to potential adverse effect in infants; rimantadine is concentrated in milk

Contraindications Hypersensitivity to drugs of the adamantine class, including rimantadine and amantadine

Warnings/Precautions Use with caution in patients with renal and hepatic dysfunction; avoid use, if possible, in patients with recurrent and eczematoid dermatitis, uncontrolled psychosis, or severe psychoneurosis. An increase in seizure incidence may occur in patients with seizure disorders; discontinue drug if seizures occur; consider the development of resistance during rimantadine treatment of the index case as likely if failure of rimantadine prophylaxis among family contact occurs and if index case is a child; viruses exhibit cross-resistance between amantadine and rimantadine.

Adverse Reactions 1% to 10%:
Cardiovascular: Orthostatic hypotension, edema
Central nervous system: Dizziness (1.9%), confusion, headache (1.4%), insomnia (2.1%), difficulty in concentrating, anxiety (1.3%), restlessness, irritability, hallucinations; incidence of CNS side effects may be less than that associated with amantadine
Gastrointestinal: Nausea (2.8%), vomiting (1.7%), xerostomia (1.5%), abdominal pain (1.4%), anorexia (1.6%)
Genitourinary: Urinary retention

Overdosage/Toxicology
Agitation, hallucinations, ventricular cardiac arrhythmias (torsade de pointes and PVCs), slurred speech, anticholinergic effects (dry mouth, urinary retention and mydriasis), ataxia, tremor, myoclonus, seizures and death have been reported with amantadine, a related drug
Treatment is symptomatic (do not use physostigmine); tachyarrhythmias may be treated with beta-blockers such as propranolol; dialysis is not recommended except possibly in renal failure

Drug Interactions
Acetaminophen: Reduction in AUC and peak concentration of rimantadine
Aspirin: Peak plasma and AUC concentrations of rimantadine are reduced
Cimetidine: Rimantadine clearance is decreased (~16%)

Mechanism of Action Exerts its inhibitory effect on three antigenic subtypes of influenza A virus (H1N1, H2N2, H3N3) early in the viral replicative cycle, possibly inhibiting the uncoating process; it has no activity against influenza B virus and is two- to eightfold more active than amantadine

Pharmacodynamics/Kinetics
Absorption: Tablet and syrup formulations are equally absorbed; T_{max}: 6 hours
Metabolism: Extensive in the liver
Half-life: 25.4 hours (increased in elderly)
Elimination: <25% of dose excreted in urine as unchanged drug; hemodialysis does not contribute to the clearance of rimantadine; no data exist establishing a correlation between plasma concentration and antiviral effect

Usual Dosage Oral:
Prophylaxis:
Children <10 years: 5 mg/kg once daily; maximum: 150 mg
Children >10 years and Adults: 100 mg twice daily; decrease to 100 mg/day in elderly or in patients with severe hepatic or renal impairment (Cl_{cr} ≤10 mL/minute)
Treatment: Adults: 100 mg twice daily; decrease to 100 mg/day in elderly or in patients with severe hepatic or renal impairment (Cl_{cr} ≤10 mL/minute)

Administration Initiation of rimantadine within 48 hours of the onset of influenza A illness halves the duration of illness and significantly reduces the duration of viral shedding and increased peripheral airways resistance; continue therapy for 5-7 days after symptoms begin

Monitoring Parameters Monitor for CNS or GI effects in elderly or patients with renal or hepatic impairment

Dosage Forms
Syrup, as hydrochloride: 50 mg/5 mL (60 mL, 240 mL, 480 mL)
Tablet, as hydrochloride: 100 mg

♦ **Rimantadine Hydrochloride** see Rimantadine on previous page

Rimexolone (ri MEKS oh lone)

U.S. Brand Names Vexol® Ophthalmic Suspension

Therapeutic Category Anti-inflammatory Agent, Ophthalmic; Corticosteroid, Ophthalmic

Use Treatment of inflammation after ocular surgery and the treatment of anterior uveitis

Pregnancy Risk Factor C

Contraindications Fungal, viral, or untreated pus-forming bacterial ocular infections; hypersensitivity to any component

Warnings/Precautions Prolonged use has been associated with the development of corneal or scleral perforation and posterior subcapsular cataracts; may mask or enhance the establishment of acute purulent untreated infections of the eye; effectiveness and safety have not been established in children

Adverse Reactions
1% to 10%: Ocular: Temporary mild blurred vision
(Continued)

Rimexolone *(Continued)*

<1%: Stinging, burning eyes, corneal thinning, increased intraocular pressure, glaucoma, damage to the optic nerve, defects in visual activity, cataracts, secondary ocular infection

Overdosage/Toxicology Systemic toxicity is unlikely from the ophthalmic preparation

Mechanism of Action Decreases inflammation by suppression of migration of polymorphonuclear leukocytes and reversal of increased capillary permeability

Pharmacodynamics/Kinetics
Absorption: Through aqueous humor
Metabolism: Any drug absorbed is metabolized in the liver
Elimination: By the kidneys and feces

Usual Dosage Adults: Ophthalmic: Instill 1 drop in conjunctival sac 2-4 times/day up to every 4 hours; may use every 1-2 hours during first 1-2 days

Monitoring Parameters Intraocular pressure and periodic examination of lens (with prolonged use)

Patient Information Shake well before using, do not touch dropper to the eye

Dosage Forms Suspension, ophthalmic: 1% (5 mL, 10 mL)

♦ Riobin® *see Riboflavin on page 1022*

♦ Riphenidate *see Methylphenidate on page 761*

Risedronate *(ris ED roe nate)*

U.S. Brand Names Actonel®

Synonyms Risedronate Sodium

Therapeutic Category Bisphosphonate Derivative

Use Paget's disease of the bone
Unlabeled use: Osteoporosis in postmenopausal women

Pregnancy Risk Factor C

Contraindications Hypersensitivity to risedronate, bisphosphonates, or any component; hypocalcemia; abnormalities of the esophagus which delay esophageal emptying such as stricture or achalasia; inability to stand or sit upright for at least 30 minutes

Warnings/Precautions Use caution in patients with renal impairment; concomitant hormone replacement therapy with alendronate for osteoporosis in postmenopausal women is not recommended; hypocalcemia must be corrected before therapy initiation with alendronate; ensure adequate calcium and vitamin D intake to provide for enhanced needs in patients with Paget's disease in whom the pretreatment rate of bone turnover may be greatly elevated.

Adverse Reactions
>10%:
Dermatological: Rash
Gastrointestinal: Abdominal pain, diarrhea
Neuromuscular & skeletal: Arthralgia
1% to 10%:
Cardiovascular: Chest pain
Central nervous system: Headache, dizziness
Gastrointestinal: Belching, colitis, constipation, nausea
Neuromuscular & skeletal: Bone pain, leg cramps, myasthenia
Respiratory: Bronchitis, rales/rhinitis

Overdosage/Toxicology
Symptoms of overdose include hypocalcemia, hypophosphatemia; upper GI adverse events (upset stomach, heartburn, esophagitis, gastritis, or ulcer)
Gastric lavage may remove unabsorbed drug; treat with milk or antacids to bind alendronate; dialysis would not be beneficial

Drug Interactions Decreased effect: Calcium supplements and antacids interfere with the absorption of risedronate

Food Interactions Mean oral bioavailability is decreased when given with food. Take ≥30 minutes before the first food or drink of the day other than water.

Mechanism of Action A bisphosphonate which inhibits bone resorption via actions on osteoclasts or on osteoclast precursors; decreases the rate of bone resorption direction, leading to an indirect decrease in bone formation

Pharmacodynamics/Kinetics
Absorption: Oral: Poorly absorbed from the gastrointestinal tract
Distribution: V_d: 6.3 L/kg
Protein binding: ~24%
Metabolism: Not metabolized
Bioavailability: ~0.54% to 0.75%
Half-life: Terminal: 220 hours
Elimination: Renal (up to 80%) with unabsorbed drug eliminated in feces

Usual Dosage Oral:
Adults (patients with Paget's disease should receive supplemental calcium and vitamin D if dietary intake is inadequate):
Paget's disease of bone: 30 mg once daily for 2 months
Elderly: No dosage adjustment is necessary

Dosage adjustment in renal impairment: Cl_{cr} <30 mL/minute: **Not** recommended

Administration It is imperative to administer risedronate 30-60 minutes before the patient takes any food, drink, or other medications orally to avoid interference with absorption. The patient should take alendronate on an empty stomach with a full glass (8

oz) of **plain water** (not mineral water) and avoid lying down for 30 minutes after swallowing tablet to help delivery to stomach.

Monitoring Parameters Alkaline phosphatase should be periodically measured; serum calcium, phosphorus, and possibly potassium due to its drug class; use of absorptiometry may assist in noting benefit in osteoporosis; monitor pain and fracture rate

Reference Range Calcium (total): Adults: 9.0-11.0 mg/dL (2.05-2.54 mmol/L), may slightly decrease with aging; phosphorus: 2.5-4.5 mg/dL (0.81-1.45 mmol/L)

Patient Information The expected benefits of risedronate may only be obtained when each tablet is taken with plain water the first thing in the morning and at least 30 minutes before the first food, beverage, or medication of the day. Wait >30 minutes to improve alendronate absorption. Even dosing with orange juice or coffee markedly reduces the absorption of risedronate.

Take alendronate with a full glass of water (6-8 oz 180-240 mL) and do not lie down (stay fully upright sitting or standing) for at least 30 minutes following administration to facilitate delivery to the stomach and reduce the potential for esophageal irritation.

Take supplemental calcium and vitamin D if dietary intake is inadequate. Consider weight-bearing exercise along with the modification of certain behavioral factors, such as excessive cigarette smoking or alcohol consumption if these factors exist.

Dosage Forms Tablet, as sodium: 30 mg

♦ **Risedronate Sodium** *see* Risedronate *on previous page*

♦ **Risperdal®** *see* Risperidone *on this page*

Risperidone (ris PER i done)

Related Information
Antipsychotic Agents Comparison *on page 1305*

U.S. Brand Names Risperdal®

Therapeutic Category Antipsychotic Agent

Use Management of psychotic disorders (eg, schizophrenia); nonpsychotic symptoms associated with dementia in elderly

Pregnancy Risk Factor C

Contraindications Known hypersensitivity to any component of the product

Adverse Reactions
1% to 10%:
  Cardiovascular: Hypotension (especially orthostatic), tachycardia, arrhythmias, abnormal T waves with prolonged ventricular repolarization; EKG changes, syncope
  Central nervous system: Sedation (occurs at daily doses ≥20 mg/day), headache, dizziness, restlessness, anxiety, extrapyramidal reactions, dystonic reactions, pseudoparkinson signs and symptoms, tardive dyskinesia, neuroleptic malignant syndrome, altered central temperature regulation
  Dermatologic: Photosensitivity (rare)
  Endocrine & metabolic: Amenorrhea, galactorrhea, gynecomastia sexual dysfunction (up to 60%)
  Gastrointestinal: Constipation, adynamic ileus, GI upset, xerostomia (problem for denture user), nausea and anorexia, weight gain
  Genitourinary: Urinary retention, overflow incontinence, priapism
  Hematologic: Agranulocytosis, leukopenia (usually in patients with large doses for prolonged periods)
  Hepatic: Cholestatic jaundice
  Ocular: Blurred vision, retinal pigmentation, decreased visual acuity (may be irreversible)
<1%: Seizures

Drug Interactions CYP2D6 enzyme substrate; CYP2D6 inhibitor (weak)
Increased toxicity: Quinidine, warfarin
May antagonize effects of levodopa; carbamazepine decreases risperidone serum concentrations; clozapine decreases clearance of risperidone

Mechanism of Action Risperidone is a benzisoxazole derivative, mixed serotonin-dopamine antagonist; binds to 5-HT₂-receptors in the CNS and in the periphery with a very high affinity; binds to dopamine-D₂ receptors with less affinity. The binding affinity to the dopamine-D₂ receptor is 20 times lower than the 5-HT₂ affinity. The addition of serotonin antagonism to dopamine antagonism (classic neuroleptic mechanism) is thought to improve negative symptoms of psychoses and reduce the incidence of extrapyramidal side effects.

Pharmacodynamics/Kinetics
Absorption: Oral: Rapid
Metabolism: Extensive by cytochrome P-450
Protein binding: Plasma: 90%
Half-life: 24 hours (risperidone and its active metabolite)
Time to peak: Peak plasma concentrations within 1 hour

Usual Dosage Recommended starting dose: 1 mg twice daily; slowly increase to the optimum range of 4-6 mg/day; daily dosages >6 mg does not appear to confer any additional benefit, and the incidence of extrapyramidal reactions is higher than with lower doses

Dosing adjustment in renal, hepatic impairment, and elderly: Starting dose of 0.5 mg twice daily is advisable

Administration Oral solution can be mixed with water, coffee, orange juice, or low-fat milk, but is not compatible with cola or tea
(Continued)

Risperidone *(Continued)*

Nursing Implications Monitor and observe for extrapyramidal effects, orthostatic blood pressure changes for 3-5 days after starting or increasing dose

Dosage Forms
Solution, oral: 1 mg/mL (100 mL)
Tablet: 1 mg, 2 mg, 3 mg, 4 mg

- ♦ **Ritalin®** *see* Methylphenidate *on page 761*
- ♦ **Ritalin-SR®** *see* Methylphenidate *on page 761*

Ritodrine *(RI toe dreen)*

U.S. Brand Names Pre-Par®; Yutopar®

Synonyms Ritodrine Hydrochloride

Therapeutic Category Adrenergic Agonist Agent; Beta$_2$-Adrenergic Agonist Agent; Sympathomimetic; Tocolytic Agent

Use Inhibits uterine contraction in preterm labor

Pregnancy Risk Factor B

Contraindications Do not use before 20th week of pregnancy, cardiac arrhythmias, pheochromocytoma

Warnings/Precautions Monitor hydration status and blood glucose concentrations; fatal maternal pulmonary edema has been reported, sometimes after delivery; fluid overload must be avoided, hydration levels should be monitored closely; if pulmonary edema occurs, the drug should be discontinued; use with caution in patients with moderate preeclampsia, diabetes, or migraine; some products may contain sulfites; maternal deaths have been reported in patients treated with ritodrine and concurrent corticosteroids (pulmonary edema)

Adverse Reactions
>10%:
Cardiovascular: Increases in maternal and fetal heart rates and maternal hypertension, palpitations
Endocrine & metabolic: Temporary hyperglycemia
Gastrointestinal: Nausea, vomiting
Neuromuscular & skeletal: Tremor
1% to 10%:
Cardiovascular: Chest pain
Central nervous system: Nervousness, anxiety, restlessness
<1%: Ketoacidosis, impaired LFTs, anaphylactic shock

Overdosage/Toxicology
Symptoms of overdose include tachycardia, palpitations, hypotension, nervousness, nausea, vomiting, tremor
Use an appropriate beta-blocker as an antidote

Drug Interactions
Decreased effect with beta-blockers
Increased effect/toxicity with meperidine, sympathomimetics, diazoxide, magnesium, betamethasone (pulmonary edema), potassium-depleting diuretics, general anesthetics

Stability Stable for 48 hours at room temperature after dilution in 500 mL of NS, D$_5$W, or LR I.V. solutions

Mechanism of Action Tocolysis due to its uterine beta$_2$-adrenergic receptor stimulating effects; this agent's beta$_2$ effects can also cause bronchial relaxation and vascular smooth muscle stimulation

Pharmacodynamics/Kinetics
Absorption: Oral: Rapid
Distribution: Crosses the placenta
Protein binding: 32%
Metabolism: In the liver
Half-life: 15 hours
Time to peak serum concentration: Within 0.5-1 hour
Elimination: In urine as unchanged drug and inactive conjugates

Usual Dosage Adults: I.V.: 50-100 mcg/minute; increase by 50 mcg/minute every 10 minutes; continue for 12 hours after contractions have stopped
Hemodialysis: Removed by hemodialysis

Administration Monitor amount of I.V. fluid administered to prevent fluid overload; place patient in left lateral recumbent position to reduce risk of hypotension; use microdrip chamber or I.V. pump to control infusion rate

Monitoring Parameters Hematocrit, serum potassium, glucose, colloidal osmotic pressure, heart rate, and uterine contractions

Patient Information Remain in bed during infusion

Dosage Forms
Infusion, in D$_5$W: 0.3 mL (500 mL)
Injection, as hydrochloride: 10 mg/mL (5 mL); 15 mg/mL (10 mL)

- ♦ **Ritodrine Hydrochloride** *see* Ritodrine *on this page*

Ritonavir *(rye TON a veer)*

Related Information
Antiretroviral Agents *on page 1306*
Antiretroviral Therapy for HIV Infection *on page 1410*

U.S. Brand Names Norvir®

Therapeutic Category Antiretroviral Agent, Protease Inhibitor; Protease Inhibitor

Use In combination with other antiretroviral agents; treatment of HIV infection when therapy is warranted

Pregnancy Risk Factor B

Pregnancy/Breast-Feeding Implications

Clinical effects on the fetus: Administer during pregnancy only if benefits to mother outweigh risks to the fetus

Breast-feeding/lactation: HIV-infected mothers are discouraged from breast-feeding to decrease postnatal transmission of HIV

Contraindications Patients with known hypersensitivity to ritonavir or any ingredients; see contraindicated medications table below

Contraindicated Medications and Potential Alternatives*

Contraindicated Medications†			Potential Alternatives‡ (these alternatives may not be therapeutically equivalent)		
Drug Class	Generic Name	Brand Name	Generic Name	Brand Name	Exposed Patients
Analgesic	Meperidine	Demerol®	Acetaminophen	Tylenol®	N=135
	Piroxicam	Feldene®	Aspirin		N=43
	Propoxyphene	Darvon®	Oxycodone	Percodan®	N=23
Cardiovascular (antiarrythmic)	Amiodarone Flecainide Propafenone Quinidine	Cordarone® Tambocor® Rythmol®	Very limited clinical experience		
Antimycobacterial	Rifabutin	Mycobutin®	Clarithromycin Ethambutol	Biaxin® Myambutol®	N=156§ N=66
Cardiovascular (calcium channel blocker)	Bepridil	Vascor®	Very limited clinical experience		
Cold and allergy (antihistamine)	Astemizole Terfenadine	Hismanal® Seldane®	Loratadine	Clarifin®	N=36
Ergot alkaloid (vasoconstrictor)	Dihydro-ergotamine Ergotamine	D.H.E. 45® various	Very limited clinical experience		
Gastrointestinal	Cisapride	Propulsid®	Very limited clinical experience		
Psychotropic (antidepressant)	Bupropion	Wellbutrin®	Desipramine	Norpramin®	¶
Psychotropic (neuroleptic)	Clozapine Pimozide	Clozaril® Orap™	Very limited clinical experience		
Psychotropic (sedative-hypnotic)	Alprazolam Clorazepate Diazepam Estazolam Flurazepam Midazolam Triazolam Zolpidem	Xanax® Tranxene® Valium® ProSom™ Dalmane® Versed® Halcion® Ambien®	Temazepam Lorazepam	Restoril® Ativan®	N=40 N=33

* During clinical trials, Norvir® was given to patients concomitantly taking a variety of medications. These medications were not evaluated in drug interaction studies. The number of Norvir®-treated patients exposed to each drug is provided in the last column.

† See Contraindications in the drug monograph.

‡ See Warnings/Precautions and Drug Interactions in the drug monograph.

§ Also evaluated in drug interaction study (N=22). See Results of Drug Interaction Studies table.

¶ No clinical experience with combination. Only evaluated in drug interaction study (N=14). See Results of Drug Interaction Studies table.

Warnings/Precautions Use caution in patients with hepatic insufficiency; safety and efficacy have not been established in children <16 years of age; use caution with benzodiazepines, antiarrhythmics (flecainide, encainide, bepridil, amiodarone, quinidine) and certain analgesics (meperidine, piroxicam, propoxyphene)

Adverse Reactions Protease inhibitors cause dyslipidemia which includes elevated cholesterol and triglycerides and a redistribution of body fat centrally to cause "protease paunch", buffalo hump, facial atrophy, and breast enlargement. These agents also cause hyperglycemia.

>10%:
Gastrointestinal: Diarrhea, nausea, vomiting, taste perversion
Endocrine & metabolic: Increased triglycerides
Hematologic: Anemia, decreased WBCs
Hepatic: Increased GGT
Neuromuscular & skeletal: Weakness

1% to 10%:
Cardiovascular: Vasodilation
Central nervous system: Fever, headache, malaise, dizziness, insomnia, somnolence, thinking abnormally
Dermatologic: Rash
Endocrine & metabolic: Hyperlipidemia, increased uric acid, increased glucose
Gastrointestinal: Abdominal pain, anorexia, constipation, dyspepsia, flatulence, local throat irritation
Hematologic: Neutropenia, eosinophilia, neutrophilia, prolonged PT, leukocytosis
Hepatic: Increased LFTs
Neuromuscular & skeletal: Increased CPK, myalgia, paresthesia

(Continued)

Ritonavir (Continued)

Respiratory: Pharyngitis

Miscellaneous: Diaphoresis, increased potassium, increased calcium,

Overdosage/Toxicology Human experience is limited; there is no specific antidote for overdose with ritonavir. Dialysis is unlikely to be beneficial in significant removal of the drug. Charcoal or gastric lavage may be useful to remove unabsorbed drug.

Drug Interactions CYP1A2, 2A6, 2C9, 2C19, 2E1, and 3A3/4 enzyme substrate, CYP2D6 enzyme substrate (minor); CYP1A2 and 2D6 enzyme inducer; CYP2A6, 2C9, 1A2, 2C19, 2D6, 2E1, and 3A3/4 inhibitor

Results of Drug Interaction Studies

Co-administered Drug	Finding
Amiodarone	Increased risk of amiodarone toxicity, including cardiotoxicity
Astemizole	Increased risk of toxicity
Benzodiazepines	Increased risk of prolonged sedation and respiratory depression
Bepridil	Increased risk of bepridil toxicity, including cardiotoxicity
Bupropion	Increased risk of bupropion toxicity, including seizures
Cisapride	Increased risk of cardiotoxicity
Clarithromycin	77% increase in clarithromycin AUC; no dosage reduction is necessary in patients with normal renal function; for patients with Cl_{cr} from 30-60 mL/minute, decrease dose by 50%; for patients with Cl_{cr}<30 mL/minute, decrease dose by 75%
Clozapine	Increased risk of clozapine toxicity, including agranulocytosis, EKG changes, and seizures
Desipramine	145% increase in desipramine AUC; dosage reduction should be considered
Didanosine (ddL)	13% decrease in didanosine AUC; no dosage adjustment is necessary
Ethinyl estradiol	40% decrease in ethinyl estradiol AUC; increase ethinyl estradiol dose or substitute with another contraceptive
Flecainide	Increased risk of flecainide toxicity, including cardiotoxicity
Fluconazole	15% increase in ritonavir AUC
Meperidine	Increased risk of meperidine toxicity, including CNS side effects, seizures, and cardiac arrhythmias
Nevirapine	Efficacy of ritonavir may be decreased
Piroxicam	Increased risk of piroxicam toxicity
Propafenone	Increased risk of propafenone, including cardiotoxicity
Propoxyphene	Increased risk of propoxyphene toxicity, including respiratory depression
Quinidine	Increased risk of quinidine toxicity, including cardiotoxicity
Rifabutin	Efficacy of ritonavir may be decreased while the risk of rifabutin-induced hematologic toxicity may be increased
Saquinavir	Greater than 20-fold increase in saquinavir AUC
Sulfamethoxazole	20% decrease is sulfamethoxazole AUC; no dosage adjustment is necessary
Terfenadine	Increased risk of cardiotoxicity
Theophylline	43% decrease in theophylline AUC; increase in theophylline dose may be required
Zidovudine (AZT)	25% decrease in zidovudine AUC; no dosage adjustment is necessary
Zolpidem	Increased risk of prolonged sedation and respiratory depression

Ritonavir may significantly increase the AUC of the following drugs: Alfentanil, fentanyl, methadone, lidocaine, erythromycin, carbamazepine, nefazodone, sertraline, itraconazole, ketoconazole, miconazole, loratadine, quinine, amlodipine, diltiazem, felodipine, isradipine, nicardipine, nifedipine, nimodipine, nisoldipine, nitrendipine, verapamil, tamoxifen, bromocriptine, indinavir, fluvastatin, lovastatin, simvastatin, cyclosporine, tacrolimus, dexamethasone

Stability Store both capsules and oral solution in refrigerator (36°F to 46°F; 2°C to 80°C); may be left out at room temperature if used within 30 days

Mechanism of Action Ritonavir inhibits HIV protease and renders the enzyme incapable of processing of polyprotein precursor which leads to production of noninfectious immature HIV particles

Pharmacodynamics/Kinetics

Absorption: Variable, with or without food

Distribution: High concentrations are produced in serum and lymph nodes

Protein binding: 98% to 99%

Metabolism: Hepatic; 5 metabolites, low concentration of an active metabolite achieved in plasma (oxidative); see Drug Interactions

Half-life: 3-5 hours

Elimination: Renal clearance is negligible

Usual Dosage Oral:

Children: 250 mg/m^2 twice daily; titrate dose upward to 400 mg/m^2 twice daily (maximum: 600 mg twice daily)

Adults: 600 mg twice daily; dose escalation tends to avoid nausea that many patients experience upon initiation of full dosing. Escalate the dose as follows: 300 mg twice daily for 1 day, 400 mg twice daily for 2 days, 500 mg twice daily for 1 day, then 600 mg twice daily. Ritonavir may be better tolerated when used in combination with other antiretrovirals by initiating the drug alone and subsequently adding the second agent within 2 weeks.

If used in combination with saquinavir, dose is 400 mg twice daily

Dosing adjustment in renal impairment: None necessary

Dosing adjustment in hepatic impairment: Not determined; caution advised with severe impairment

Monitoring Parameters Triglycerides, cholesterol, LFTs, CPK, uric acid, basic HIV monitoring, viral load, and CD4 count, glucose

Patient Information Take with food, if possible; many drugs interact with ritonavir, consult with physician or pharmacist before adding any drug therapy including over-the-counter medications. Ritonavir is not a cure for HIV infection; long-term effects of ritonavir are unknown at this time. Taste of oral ritonavir solution may be enhanced by mixing with chocolate milk, Ensure®, or Advera®. Refrigeration is necessary for both capsules and solution.

Additional Information Potential compliance problems, frequency of administration and adverse effects should be discussed with patients before initiating therapy to help prevent the emergence of resistance.

Dosage Forms

Capsule: 100 mg

Solution: 80 mg/mL (240 mL)

♦ **Rituxan®** see Rituximab on this page

Rituximab (ri TUK si mab)

U.S. Brand Names Rituxan®

Synonyms Anti-CD20 Monoclonal Antibodies; C2B8 Monoclonal Antibody; Pan-B Antibodies

Therapeutic Category Antineoplastic Agent, Monoclonal Antibody; Monoclonal Antibody

Use Non-Hodgkin's lymphoma: Treatment of patients with relapsed or refractory low-grade or follicular, CD20 positive, B-cell non-Hodgkin's lymphoma

Pregnancy Risk Factor C

Contraindications Type I hypersensitivity or anaphylactic reactions to murine proteins or to any component of this product

Warnings/Precautions Rituximab is associated with hypersensitivity reactions which may respond to adjustments in the infusion rate. Hypotension, bronchospasm, and angioedema have occurred as part of an infusion-related symptom complex. Interrupt rituximab infusion for severe reactions and resume at a 50% reduction in rate (eg, from 100 to 50 mg/hour) when symptoms have completely resolved. Treatment of these symptoms with diphenhydramine and acetaminophen is recommended; additional treatment with bronchodilators or I.V. saline may be indicated. In most cases, patients who have experienced nonlife-threatening reactions have been able to complete the full course of therapy. Medications for the treatment of hypersensitivity reactions (eg, epinephrine, antihistamines, corticosteroids) should be available for immediate use in the event of such a reaction during administration.

Discontinue infusions in the event of serious or life-threatening cardiac arrhythmias. Patients who develop clinically significant arrhythmias should undergo cardiac monitoring during and after subsequent infusions of rituximab. Patients with pre-existing cardiac conditions including arrhythmias and angina have had recurrences of these events during rituximab therapy; monitor these patients throughout the infusion and immediate postinfusion periods.

Adverse Reactions

>10%:

Central nervous system: Headache, fever, chills

Gastrointestinal: Nausea

Hematologic: Leukopenia

Neuromuscular & skeletal: Asthenia

Miscellaneous: Angioedema

Immunologic: Rituximab-induced B-cell depletion occurred in 70% to 80% of patients and was associated with decreased serum immunoglobulins in a minority of patients. The incidence of infections does not appear to be increased. During the treatment period, 50 patients in the pivotal trial developed infectious events, including six grade 3 events (there were no grade 4 events. The six serious events were not associated with neutropenia).

Infusion-related: An infusion-related symptom complex consisting of fever and chills/rigors occurred in the majority of patients during the first rituximab infusion. Other frequent infusion-related symptoms included nausea, urticaria, fatigue, headache, pruritus, bronchospasm, dyspnea, sensation of tongue or throat swelling (angioedema), rhinitis, vomiting, hypotension, flushing, and pain at disease sites. These reactions generally occurred within 30 minutes to 2 hours of beginning the first infusion, and resolved with slowing or interruption of the infusion and with supportive care (I.V. saline, diphenhydramine, and acetaminophen). The incidence of infusion related events decreased from 80% during the first to ~40% with subsequent infusions. Mild to moderate hypotension requiring interruption of rituximab infusion, with or without the administration of I.V. saline, occurred in 10%. Isolated occurrences of

(Continued)

Rituximab (Continued)

severe reactions requiring epinephrine have been reported in patients receiving rituximab for other indicators. Angioedema was reported in 13% and was serious in one patient.

1% to 10%:

Cardiovascular: Hypotension

Central nervous system: Myalgia, dizziness

Dermatologic: Pruritus, rash, urticaria

Gastrointestinal: Vomiting, abdominal pain

Hematologic: Thrombocytopenia, neutropenia; during the treatment period (up to 30 days following the last dose), the following occurred: Severe thrombocytopenia, severe neutropenia, and severe anemia

Respiratory: Bronchospasm occurred in 8%; 25% of these patients were treated with bronchodilators; rhinitis

Miscellaneous: Throat irritation

<1%:

Four patients developed arrhythmias during rituximab infusion. One of the four discontinued treatment based on ventricular tachycardia and supraventricular tachycardias. The other three patients experienced trigeminy and irregular pulses and did not require discontinuation of therapy. Angina was reported during infusion and myocardial infarction occurred 4 days postinfusion in one subject with a history of myocardial infarction.

A single occurrence of transient aplastic anemia (pure red-cell aplasia) and two occurrences of hemolytic anemia were reported.

Note: Twenty-one patients have received more than one course of rituximab. The percentage of patients reporting any adverse event upon retreatment was similar to the percentage of patients reporting adverse events upon initial exposure. The following adverse events were reported more frequently in retreated patients: Asthenia, throat irritation, flushing, tachycardia, anorexia, leukopenia, thrombocytopenia, anemia, peripheral edema, dizziness, depression, respiratory symptoms, night sweats, pruritus.

Stability

Store vials at refrigeration (2°C to 8°C/36°F to 46°F); protect vials from direct sunlight

Withdraw the necessary amount of rituximab and dilute to a final concentration of 1-4 mg/mL into an infusion bag containing either 0.9% sodium chloride or 5% dextrose in water. Gently invert the bag to mix the solution. Solutions for infusion are stable at 2°C to 8°C/36°F to 46°F for 24 hours and at room temperature for an additional 12 hours.

Mechanism of Action Genetically engineered chimeric murine/human monoclonal antibody directed against the CD20 antigen found on the surface of normal and malignant B lymphocytes. The antibody is an IgG_1 kappa immunoglobulin. It binds specifically to the antigen CD20. The antigen is also expressed on >90% of B-cell non-Hodgkin's lymphomas (NHL) but is not found on hematopoietic stem cells, pro-B cells, normal plasma cells, or other normal tissues. CD20 regulates an early step(s) in the activation process for cell-cycle initiation and differentiation, and possible functions as a calcium ion channel. CD20 is not shed from the cell surface and does not internalize upon antibody binding. The Fab domain of rituximab binds to the CD20 antigen on B-lymphocytes and the Fc domain recruits immune effector functions to mediate B-cell lysis *in vitro*. Possible mechanisms of cell lysis include complement-dependent cytotoxicity and antibody-dependent cellular cytotoxicity. The antibody induces apoptosis in the DHL-4 human B-cell lymphoma line.

Pharmacodynamics/Kinetics

Absorption: I.V.: Immediate and results in a rapid and sustained depletion of circulating and tissue-based B cells

Half-life, mean serum: 59.8 hours after the first infusion and 174 hours after the fourth infusion

Duration: Detectable in the serum of patients 3-6 months after completion of treatment. B-cell recovery began ~6 months following completion of treatment. Median B-cell levels returned to normal by 12 months following completion of treatment.

Usual Dosage Adults: I.V. (refer to individual protocols): **Do not administer I.V. push or bolus** (hypersensitivity reactions may occur). Consider premedication (consisting of acetaminophen and diphenhydramine) before each infusion of rituximab. Premedication may attenuate infusion-related events. Because transient hypotension may occur during infusion, give consideration to withholding antihypertensive medications 12 hours prior to rituximab infusion.

I.V. infusion: 375 mg/m² once weekly for 4 doses (days 1, 8, 15, and 22).

Administration Administer the first infusion at an initial rate of 50 mg/hour. If hypersensitivity or infusion-related events do not occur, escalate the infusion rate in 50 mg/hour increments every 30 minutes, to a maximum of 400 mg/hour. If hypersensitivity or an infusion-related event develops, temporarily slow or interrupt the infusion. The infusion can continue at one-half the previous rate upon improvement of patient symptoms. Subsequent rituximab infusion can be administered at an initial rate of 100 mg/hour and increased by 100 mg/hour increments at 30-minute intervals, to a maximum of 400 mg/hour as tolerated.

Monitoring Parameters Obtain complete blood counts and platelet counts at regular intervals during rituximab therapy and more frequently in patients who develop cytopenia. Human antimurine antibody (HAMA) was not detected in 57 patients evaluated. Less than 1% of patients evaluated for human antichimeric antibody (HACA) was positive. Patients who develop HAMA/HACA titers may have an allergic or hypersensitivity reaction when treated with this or other murine or chimeric monoclonal antibodies. Monitor peripheral CD20+ cells.

Reference Range Peripheral CD20+ cells: High level pretreatment (500-1600 cells/µL, malignant or normal) may indicate risk of more severe infusional reactions

Dosage Forms Injection, preservative free: 100 mg (10 mL); 500 mg (10 mL)

♦ **Rivastatin** see Cerivastatin on page 232

♦ **Rivotril®** see Clonazepam on page 282

Rizatriptan (rye za TRIP tan)

Related Information
Antimigraine Drugs: Pharmacokinetic Differences on page 1304

U.S. Brand Names Maxalt®; Maxalt-MLT™

Synonyms MK 462

Therapeutic Category Antimigraine Agent; Serotonin Agonist

Use Acute treatment of migraine with or without aura

Pregnancy Risk Factor C

Contraindications Prior hypersensitivity to rizatriptan; documented ischemic heart disease or Prinzmetal's angina; uncontrolled hypertension; basilar or hemiplegic migraine; during or within 2 weeks of MAO inhibitors

Warnings/Precautions Use only in patients with a clear diagnosis of migraine; use with caution in elderly or patients with hepatic or renal impairment, history of hypersensitivity to sumatriptan or adverse effects from sumatriptan, and in patients at risk of coronary artery disease. Do not use with ergotamines. May increase blood pressure transiently; may cause coronary vasospasm (less than sumatriptan); avoid in patients with signs/symptoms suggestive of reduced arterial flow (ischemic bowel, Raynaud's) which could be exacerbated by vasospasm. Phenylketonurics (tablets contain phenylalanine).

Patients who experience sensations of chest pain/pressure/tightness or symptoms suggestive of angina following dosing should be evaluated for coronary artery disease or Prinzmetal's angina before receiving additional doses.

Caution in dialysis patients or hepatically impaired. Reconsider diagnosis of migraine if no response to initial dose. Long-term effects on vision have not been evaluated.

Adverse Reactions
1% to 10%:
    Cardiovascular: Systolic/diastolic blood pressure increases (5-10 mm Hg), chest pain (5%)
    Central nervous system: Dizziness, drowsiness, fatigue (13% to 30% - dose related)
    Dermatologic: Skin flushing
    Endocrine & metabolic: Mild increase in growth hormone, hot flashes
    Gastrointestinal: Nausea, vomiting, abdominal pain, dry mouth (<5%)
    Respiratory: Dyspnea
<1%: Syncope, facial edema, tachycardia, palpitation, bradycardia, chills, hangover, decreased mental activity, neurological/psychiatric abnormalities, pruritus, neck pain/stiffness, muscle weakness, myalgia, arthralgia, blurred vision, dry eyes, eye pain, tinnitus, polyuria, nasopharyngeal irritation, heat sensitivity, diaphoresis

Drug Interactions
Use within 24 hours of another selective 5-HT$_1$ agonist or ergot-containing drug should be avoided due to possible additive vasoconstriction
Propranolol: Plasma concentration of rizatriptan increased 70%
SSRIs: Rarely, concurrent use results in weakness and incoordination; monitor closely
MAO inhibitors and nonselective MAO inhibitors increase concentration of rizatriptan

Stability Store in blister pack until administration

Mechanism of Action Selective agonist for serotonin (5-HT$_{1D}$ receptor) in cranial arteries to cause vasoconstriction and reduce sterile inflammation associated with antidromic neuronal transmission correlating with relief of migraine

Pharmacodynamics/Kinetics
Onset of action: Within 30 minutes
Duration: 14-16 hours
Protein binding: Minimal (14%)
Metabolism: Substantial nonrenal clearance by monoamine oxidase-A; undergoes first-pass metabolism
Bioavailability: 40% to 50%
Half-life: 2-3 hours
Time to peak concentration: 1-1.5 hours
Elimination: 8% to 16% excreted unchanged in urine; parent and metabolites eliminated (82%)

Usual Dosage Oral: 5-10 mg, repeat after 2 hours if significant relief is not attained; maximum: 30 mg in a 24-hour period (Use 5 mg dose in patients receiving propranolol with a maximum of 15 mg in 24 hours)

Dietary Considerations Food delays the absorption

Monitoring Parameters Headache severity, signs/symptoms suggestive of angina; consider monitoring blood pressure, heart rate, and/or EKG with first dose in patients with likelihood of unrecognized coronary disease, such as patients with significant hypertension, hypercholesterolemia, obese patients, diabetics, smokers with other risk factors or strong family history of coronary artery disease

Patient Information For orally disintegrating tablets: Do not remove blister from outer pouch until just before dosing; open blister with dry hands, place tablet on tongue and allow to dissolve. Dissolved tablet will be swallowed with saliva.
(Continued)

Rizatriptan (Continued)

For all dosage forms: May repeat dose anytime after 2 hours of the first dose. Do not take a second dose without first consulting your physician. Do not take more than 30 mg in a 24-hour period (15 mg maximum in 24 hours if taking propranolol).

Dosage Forms Tablet, as benzoate:

Maxalt®: 5 mg, 10 mg

Maxalt-MLT™ (orally disintegrating): 5 mg, 10 mg

- ◆ **rLFN-α2** see Interferon Alfa-2b on page 617
- ◆ **rIFN-b** see Interferon Beta-1b on page 621
- ◆ **RMS® Rectal** see Morphine Sulfate on page 797
- ◆ **Robafen® AC** see Guaifenesin and Codeine on page 550
- ◆ **Robafen DM® [OTC]** see Guaifenesin and Dextromethorphan on page 550
- ◆ **Robaxin®** see Methocarbamol on page 749
- ◆ **Robaxisal®** see Methocarbamol and Aspirin on page 750
- ◆ **Robicillin® VK** see Penicillin V Potassium on page 898
- ◆ **Robidrine®** see Pseudoephedrine on page 993
- ◆ **Robinul®** see Glycopyrrolate on page 542
- ◆ **Robinul® Forte** see Glycopyrrolate on page 542
- ◆ **Robitussin® [OTC]** see Guaifenesin on page 549
- ◆ **Robitussin® A-C** see Guaifenesin and Codeine on page 550
- ◆ **Robitussin®-DAC** see Guaifenesin, Pseudoephedrine, and Codeine on page 551
- ◆ **Robitussin®-DM [OTC]** see Guaifenesin and Dextromethorphan on page 550
- ◆ **Robomol®** see Methocarbamol on page 749
- ◆ **Rocaltrol®** see Calcitriol on page 172
- ◆ **Rocephin®** see Ceftriaxone on page 223

Rocuronium (roe kyoor OH nee um)

Related Information

Neuromuscular Blocking Agents Comparison on page 1331

U.S. Brand Names Zemuron™

Synonyms ORG 946; Rocuronium Bromide

Therapeutic Category Neuromuscular Blocker Agent, Nondepolarizing; Skeletal Muscle Relaxant

Use Inpatient and outpatient use as an adjunct to general anesthesia to facilitate both rapid-sequence and routine tracheal intubation, and to provide skeletal muscle relaxation during surgery or mechanical ventilation

Pregnancy Risk Factor B

Contraindications Known hypersensitivity to rocuronium or vecuronium

Warnings/Precautions Use with caution in patients with cardiovascular or pulmonary disease, hepatic impairment, neuromuscular disease, myasthenia gravis, dehydration (may alter neuromuscular blocking effects); respiratory acidosis, hypomagnesemia, hypokalemia, or hypocalcemia (may enhance actions) and the elderly; ventilation must be supported during neuromuscular blockade

Adverse Reactions

>1%: Cardiovascular: Transient hypotension and hypertension

<1%: Arrhythmias, abnormal EKG, tachycardia, edema, rash, injection site pruritus, nausea, vomiting, bronchospasm, wheezing, rhonchi, hiccups

Overdosage/Toxicology

Symptoms of overdose include prolonged skeletal muscle block, muscle weakness and apnea

Treatment is maintenance of a patent airway and controlled ventilation until recovery of normal neuromuscular block is observed, further recovery may be facilitated by administering an anticholinesterase agent (eg, neostigmine, edrophonium, or pyridostigmine) with atropine, to antagonize the skeletal muscle relaxation; support of the cardiovascular system with fluids and pressors may be necessary

Drug Interactions

Decreased effect: Chronic carbamazepine or phenytoin can shorten the duration of neuromuscular blockade; phenylephrine can severely inhibit neuromuscular blockade

Increased effect: Infusion requirements are reduced 35% to 40% during anesthesia with enflurane or isoflurane

Increased toxicity: Aminoglycosides, vancomycin, tetracyclines, bacitracin

Stability Store under refrigeration (2°C to 8°C), do not freeze; when stored at room temperature, it is stable for 30 days; unlike vecuronium, it is stable in 0.9% sodium chloride and 5% dextrose in water, this mixture should be used within 24 hours of preparation

Mechanism of Action Blocks acetylcholine from binding to receptors on motor endplate inhibiting depolarization

Pharmacodynamics/Kinetics

Onset: Good intubation conditions within 1-2 minutes; maximum neuromuscular blockade within 4 minutes

Duration: ~30 minutes (with standard doses, increases with higher doses)

Metabolism: Undergoes minimal hepatic metabolism

Elimination: Primarily through hepatic uptake and biliary excretion

Usual Dosage
Children:
Initial: 0.6 mg/kg under halothane anesthesia produce excellent to good intubating conditions within 1 minute and will provide a median time of 41 minutes of clinical relaxation in children 3 months to 1 year of age, and 27 minutes in children 1-12 years

Maintenance: 0.075-0.125 mg/kg administered upon return of T_1 to 25% of control provides clinical relaxation for 7-10 minutes

Adults:
Tracheal intubation: I.V.:
Initial: 0.6 mg/kg is expected to provide approximately 31 minutes of clinical relaxation under opioid/nitrous oxide/oxygen anesthesia with neuromuscular block sufficient for intubation attained in 1-2 minutes; lower doses (0.45 mg/kg) may be used to provide 22 minutes of clinical relaxation with median time to neuromuscular block of 1-3 minutes; maximum blockade is achieved in <4 minutes

Maximum: 0.9-1.2 mg/kg may be given during surgery under opioid/nitrous oxide/oxygen anesthesia without adverse cardiovascular effects and is expected to provide 58-67 minutes of clinical relaxation; neuromuscular blockade sufficient for intubation is achieved in <2 minutes with maximum blockade in <3 minutes

Maintenance: 0.1, 0.15, and 0.2 mg/kg administered at 25% recovery of control T_1 (defined as 3 twitches of train-of-four) provides a median of 12, 17, and 24 minutes of clinical duration under anesthesia

Rapid sequence intubation: 0.6-1.2 mg/kg in appropriately premedicated and anesthetized patients with excellent or good intubating conditions within 2 minutes

Continuous infusion: Initial: 0.01-0.012 mg/kg/minute only after early evidence of spontaneous recovery of neuromuscular function is evident

Dosing adjustment in hepatic impairment: Reductions are necessary in patients with liver disease

Administration Administer I.V. only

Monitoring Parameters Peripheral nerve stimulator measuring twitch response, heart rate, blood pressure, assisted ventilation status

Nursing Implications Concurrent sedation and analgesia are needed

Additional Information Dose based on actual body weight

Dosage Forms Injection, as bromide: 10 mg/mL (5 mL, 10 mL)

- ◆ **Rocuronium Bromide** see Rocuronium on previous page
- ◆ **Rofact™** see Rifampin on page 1023
- ◆ **Roferon-A®** see Interferon Alfa-2a on page 616
- ◆ **Rogaine® Extra Strength for Men [OTC]** see Minoxidil on page 783
- ◆ **Rogaine® for Men [OTC]** see Minoxidil on page 783
- ◆ **Rogaine® for Women [OTC]** see Minoxidil on page 783
- ◆ **Rogitine®** see Phentolamine on page 917
- ◆ **Rolaids® Calcium Rich [OTC]** see Calcium Carbonate on page 174
- ◆ **Rolatuss® Plain Liquid** see Chlorpheniramine and Phenylephrine on page 246
- ◆ **Romazicon™ Injection** see Flumazenil on page 493
- ◆ **Rondamine-DM® Drops** see Carbinoxamine, Pseudoephedrine, and Dextromethorphan on page 193
- ◆ **Rondec®-DM** see Carbinoxamine, Pseudoephedrine, and Dextromethorphan on page 193
- ◆ **Rondec® Drops** see Carbinoxamine and Pseudoephedrine on page 192
- ◆ **Rondec® Filmtab®** see Carbinoxamine and Pseudoephedrine on page 192
- ◆ **Rondec® Syrup** see Carbinoxamine and Pseudoephedrine on page 192
- ◆ **Rondec-TR®** see Carbinoxamine and Pseudoephedrine on page 192

Ropinirole (roe PIN i role)

Related Information
Parkinson's Disease, Dosing of Drugs Used for Treatment of on page 1336

U.S. Brand Names Requip™

Synonyms Ropinirole Hydrochloride

Therapeutic Category Anti-Parkinson's Agent; Dopaminergic Agent (Antiparkinson's)

Use Treatment of idiopathic Parkinson's disease; in patients with early Parkinson's disease who were not receiving concomitant levodopa therapy as well as in patients with advanced disease on concomitant levodopa

Pregnancy Risk Factor C

Contraindications Hypersensitivity to ropinirole

Warnings/Precautions Syncope, sometimes associated with bradycardia, was observed in association with ropinirole in both early Parkinson's disease (without L-dopa) patients and advanced Parkinson's disease (with L-dopa) patients. Dopamine agonists appear to impair the systemic regulation of blood pressure resulting in postural hypotension, especially during dose escalation. Parkinson's disease patients appear to have an impaired capacity to respond to a postural challenge. Parkinson's patients being treated with dopaminergic agonists ordinarily require careful monitoring for signs and symptoms of postural hypotension, especially during dose escalation, and should be informed of this risk. In patients with Parkinson's disease who were not treated with L-dopa, 5.2% of those treated with ropinirole reported hallucinations as compared to 1.4% on a placebo.

Adverse Reactions
Early Parkinson's disease:
Cardiovascular: Syncope, dependent/leg edema, orthostatic symptoms
(Continued)

Ropinirole *(Continued)*

Central nervous system: Dizziness, somnolence (40% vs 6% with placebo), headache, fatigue, pain, confusion, hallucinations

Gastrointestinal: Nausea (60% vs 22% with placebo), dyspepsia, constipation, abdominal pain

Genitourinary: Urinary tract infections

Neuromuscular & skeletal: Weakness

Ocular: Abnormal vision

Respiratory: Pharyngitis

Miscellaneous: Viral infection, diaphoresis (increased)

Advanced Parkinson's disease (with levodopa):

Cardiovascular: Hypotension (2%), syncope (3%)

Central nervous system: Dizziness (26% vs 16% with placebo), aggravated parkinsonism, somnolence (40%), headache (17% vs 12% with placebo), insomnia, hallucinations, confusion (9% vs 2% with placebo), pain (5% vs 3% with placebo), paresis (3%), amnesia (5%), anxiety (6%), abnormal dreaming (3%)

Gastrointestinal: Nausea (30% vs 18% with placebo), abdominal pain (9% vs 8% with placebo), vomiting (7% vs 4% with placebo), constipation (6%), diarrhea (5%), dysphagia (2%), flatulence (2%), increased salivation (2%), xerostomia, weight loss (2%)

Genitourinary: Urinary tract infections

Neuromuscular & skeletal: Dyskinesias (34% vs 13% with placebo), falls (10% vs 7% with placebo), hypokinesia (5%), paresthesia (5%), tremor (6%), arthralgia (7%), arthritis (3%)

Respiratory: Upper respiratory tract infection

Miscellaneous: Injury, increased diaphoresis (7%), viral infection

<1%: Hypoglycemia, increased LDH, hyperphosphatemia, hyperuricemia, diabetes mellitus, hypokalemia, hypercholesterolemia, hyperkalemia, acidosis, hyponatremia, dehydration, hypochloremia, weight increase, increased alkaline phosphatase, increased CPK, elevated BUN, glycosuria, thirst, increased lactate dehydrogenase (LDH)

Overdosage/Toxicology No reports of intentional overdose; symptoms reported with accidental overdosage were agitation, increased dyskinesia, sedation, orthostatic hypotension, chest pain, confusion, nausea, and vomiting. It is anticipated that the symptoms of overdose will be related to its dopaminergic activity. General supportive measures are recommended. Vital signs should be maintained, if necessary. Removal of any unabsorbed material (eg, by gastric lavage) should be considered.

Drug Interactions Ropinirole is metabolized by CYP1A2 so there is the potential for interaction when given with inhibitors or inducers of this enzyme

Ciprofloxacin increased C max and AUC of ropinirole

Estrogens decreased clearance of ropinirole

Decreased effect: Dopamine antagonists (phenothiazine, haloperidol, metoclopramide)

Mechanism of Action Ropinirole has a high relative *in vitro* specificity and full intrinsic activity at the D_2 and D_3 dopamine receptor subtypes, binding with higher affinity to D_3 than to D_2 or D_4 receptor subtypes. Although precise mechanism of action of ropinirole is unknown, it is believed to be due to stimulation of postsynaptic dopamine D_2-type receptors within the caudate-putamen in the brain.

Pharmacodynamics/Kinetics

Absorption: Not affected by food; T_{max} increased by 2.5 hours when drug taken with a meal; absolute bioavailability was 55%, indicating first-pass effect

Distribution: V_d: 525 L

Metabolism: Extensively by liver to inactive metabolites; CYP1A2 was the major enzyme responsible for metabolism of ropinirole

Half-life, elimination: ~6 hours

Time to peak concentration: ~1-2 hours

Clearance: Reduced by 30% in patients >65 years of age and removal of drug by hemodialysis is unlikely

Usual Dosage Adults: Oral: Dosage should be increased to achieve a maximum therapeutic effect, balanced against the principle side effects of nausea, dizziness, somnolence, and dyskinesia

Recommended starting dose: 0.25 mg 3 times/day; based on individual patient response, the dosage should be titrated with weekly increments as described below:

Week 1: 0.25 mg 3 times/day; total daily dose: 0.75 mg

Week 2: 0.5 mg 3 times/day; total daily dose: 1.5 mg

Week 3: 0.75 mg 3 times/day; total daily dose: 2.25 mg

Week 4: 1 mg 3 times/day; total daily dose: 3 mg

After week 4, if necessary, daily dosage may be increased by 1.5 mg/day on a weekly basis up to a dose of 9 mg/day, and then by up to 3 mg/day weekly to a total of 24 mg/day

Patient Information Ropinirole can be taken with or without food. Hallucinations can occur and elderly are at a higher risk than younger patients with Parkinson's disease. Postural hypotension may develop with or without symptoms such as dizziness, nausea, syncope, and sometimes sweating. Hypotension and/or orthostatic symptoms may occur more frequently during initial therapy or with an increase in dose at any time. Use caution when rising rapidly after sitting or lying down, especially after having done so for prolonged periods and especially at the initiation of treatment with ropinirole. Because of additive sedative effects, caution should be used when taking CNS depressants (eg, benzodiazepines, antipsychotics, antidepressants) in combination with ropinirole.

Dosage Forms Tablet: 0.25 mg, 0.5 mg, 1 mg, 2 mg, 5 mg

♦ **Ropinirole Hydrochloride** *see* Ropinirole *on page 1039*

Ropivacaine (roe PIV a kane)

U.S. Brand Names Naropin™

Synonyms Ropivacaine Hydrochloride

Therapeutic Category Local Anesthetic, Injectable

Use Local anesthetic (injectable) for use in surgery, postoperative pain management, and obstetrical procedures when local or regional anesthesia is needed. It can be administered via local infiltration, epidural block and epidural infusion, or intermittent bolus.

Pregnancy Risk Factor B

Contraindications Hypersensitivity to amide-type local anesthetics (eg, bupivacaine, mepivacaine, lidocaine); septicemia, severe hypotension and for spinal anesthesia, in the presence of complete heart block

Warnings/Precautions Use with caution in patients with liver disease, cardiovascular disease, neurological or psychiatric disorders; it is not recommended for use in emergency situations where rapid administration is necessary

Adverse Reactions

>10% (dose and route related):
Cardiovascular: Hypotension, bradycardia
Gastrointestinal: Nausea, vomiting
Neuromuscular & skeletal: Back pain
Miscellaneous: Shivering

1% to 10% (dose related):
Cardiovascular: Hypertension, tachycardia
Central nervous system: Headache, dizziness, anxiety, lightheadedness
Neuromuscular & skeletal: Hypoesthesia, paresthesia, circumoral paresthesia
Otic: Tinnitus
Respiratory: Apnea

Overdosage/Toxicology

Treatment is primarily symptomatic and supportive. Termination of anesthesia by pneumatic tourniquet inflation should be attempted when the agent is administered by infiltration or regional injection.

Seizures commonly respond to diazepam, while hypotension responds to I.V. fluids and Trendelenburg positioning

Bradyarrhythmias (when the heart rate is <60) can be treated with I.V., or S.C. atropine 15 mcg/kg

With the development of metabolic acidosis, I.V. sodium bicarbonate 0.5-2 mEq/kg and ventilatory assistance should be instituted

Methemoglobinemia should be treated with methylene blue 1-2 mg/kg in a 1% sterile aqueous solution I.V. push over 4-6 minutes repeated up to a total dose of 7 mg/kg

Drug Interactions CYP2D6 enzyme substrate

Increased effect: Other local anesthetics or agents structurally related to the amide-type anesthetics

Increased toxicity (possible but not yet reported): Drugs that decrease cytochrome P-450 1A enzyme function

Mechanism of Action Blocks both the initiation and conduction of nerve impulses by decreasing the neuronal membrane's permeability to sodium ions, which results in inhibition of depolarization with resultant blockade of conduction

Pharmacodynamics/Kinetics

Onset of anesthesia (dependent on route administered): Within 3-15 minutes generally
Duration of action (dependent on dose and route administered): 3-15 hours generally
Metabolism: In the liver
Half-life: Epidural: 5-7 hours; I.V.: 2.4 hours
Elimination: 86% of metabolites are excreted in urine

Usual Dosage Dose varies with procedure, onset and depth of anesthesia desired, vascularity of tissues, duration of anesthesia, and condition of patient

Adults:
Lumbar epidural for surgery: 15-30 mL of 0.5% to 1%
Lumbar epidural block for cesarean section: 20-30 mL of 0.5%
Thoracic epidural block for postoperative pain relief: 5-15 mL of 0.5%
Major nerve block: 35-50 mL dose of 0.5% (175-250 mg)
Field block: 1-40 mL dose of 0.5% (5-200 mg)
Lumbar epidural for labor pain: Initial: 10-20 mL 0.2%; continuous infusion dose: 6-14 mL/hour of 0.2% with incremental injections of 10-15 mL/hour of 0.2% solution

Dosage Forms

Infusion, as hydrochloride: 2 mg/mL (100 mL, 200 mL)
Injection, as hydrochloride (single dose): 2 mg/mL (20 mL); 5 mg/mL (30 mL); 7.5 mg/mL (10 mL, 20 mL); 10 mg/mL (10 mL, 20 mL)

♦ **Ropivacaine Hydrochloride** *see* Ropivacaine *on this page*

♦ **RotaShield®** *see* Rotavirus Vaccine *on this page*

Rotavirus Vaccine (RO ta tye rus vak SEEN)

U.S. Brand Names RotaShield®

Therapeutic Category Vaccine

Use Prevention of gastroenteritis caused by the rotavirus serotypes responsible for the majority of disease in infants and children in the U.S. (serotypes G 1,2,3 and 4)

(Continued)

Rotavirus Vaccine *(Continued)*

Pregnancy Risk Factor C

Contraindications Known hypersensitivity to any component of the vaccine (due to the method of preparation, rotavirus vaccine may include small amounts of an aminoglycoside antibiotic, monosodium glutamate, and amphotericin B). Contraindicated in patients with ongoing diarrhea or vomiting.

Immunocompromised patients may shed virus for prolonged periods. RotaShield® is contraindicated in patients with known or suspected immune deficiency states, or in patients receiving therapy with agents which may compromise immune function (alkylating agents, antimetabolites, radiation, or high-dose systemic corticosteroids). Use of steroids when administered topically, via inhalation aerosol, or by intra-articular, tendon, or bursal injection does not contraindicate therapy. Although antibodies to rotavirus may be present in breast milk, there is no evidence that the efficacy of the rotavirus vaccine is diminished when administered to breast-fed infants.

Warnings/Precautions Vaccine administration may be delayed due to current or recent severe to moderate febrile illness. Minor illness with or without low-grade fever is not generally a contraindication. Do not administer parenterally. Do not administer to immunocompromised infants. Administer with caution to patients with possible latex allergy. Close association with immunosuppressed or other high-risk individuals should be avoided whenever possible for up to 4 weeks after administration. Data concerning administration to premature infants are insufficient to establish safety or efficacy. Prior to administration, the physician should take all known precautions for prevention of allergic or other reactions. A careful history for possible sensitivity should be taken and agents to control immediate allergic reactions, including epinephrine (1:1000), should be readily available.

Adverse Reactions

>10%: Central nervous system: Fever (>38°C to <39°C) (11% to 21%), decreased appetite (11% to 17%), irritability (36% to 41%), decreased activity (10% to 20%)

1% to 10%: Central nervous system: Fever (≥39°C) (1% to 2%)

The incidence of fever is greater when administered to infants >6 months of age. The highest incidence of adverse effects was associated with the first dose of the vaccine. By the third dose, there were no significant differences in the incidence of adverse effects between vaccine and placebo.

Drug Interactions No drug interactions have been reported. No data have been reported with respect to administration of orally or intravenously administered immune globulin-containing products.

Stability Store lyophilized vaccine at room temperature below 25°C. Lyophilized vaccine (and diluent) may be refrigerated. Reconstituted vaccine is stable for 60 minutes at room temperature and 4 hours under refrigeration.

Mechanism of Action The live virus vaccine stimulates production of IgG and IgA antibodies which cross-react with human serotypes. The four serotypes which cause the majority of infections in humans are neutralized by these antibodies.

Usual Dosage For oral administration only

Children: Three 2.5 mL doses are administered. The recommended schedule for immunization is at 2, 4, and 6 months of age. The first dose may be administered as early as 6 weeks of age, with subsequent doses at least 3 weeks apart. The third dose has been administered to infants up to 33 weeks of age with no increase in adverse reactions. Initiation of vaccination after the age of 6 months is not currently recommended due to an increased risk of fever. RotaShield® does not diminish the efficacy of OPV, DTP, or Hib when administered concurrently. Repeat dosing of vaccine is not recommended if an infant should regurgitate a dose.

Adults: Not approved for administration to adults

Administration Reconstitute lyophilized vaccine by adding diluent from Dispette®, then withdraw reconstituted solution back into Dispette® (may reuse cap to store until administration). Must be administered within 60 minutes of reconstitution if stored at room temperature, or within 4 hours of reconstitution if refrigerated. Place tip of Dispette® into the infant's mouth and slowly squeeze out contents.

Test Interactions A positive stool test for rotavirus may occur for at least one week after administration due to the presence of vaccine virus

Patient Information Parents must be instructed as to the importance of completing the vaccination sequence

Dosage Forms Powder, lyophilized, for oral solution: 2.5 mL diluent (Dispette®); specialized diluent contains citric acid and sodium bicarbonate

- **R-Tannamine® Tablet** *see* Chlorpheniramine, Pyrilamine, and Phenylephrine *on page 247*
- **R-Tannate® Tablet** *see* Chlorpheniramine, Pyrilamine, and Phenylephrine *on page 247*
- **RTCA** *see* Ribavirin *on page 1021*
- **Rubella and Measles Vaccines, Combined** *see* Measles and Rubella Vaccines, Combined *on page 713*

Rubella and Mumps Vaccines, Combined
(rue BEL a & mumpz vak SEENS, kom BINED)

Related Information
Adverse Events and Vaccination *on page 1369*
Immunization Recommendations *on page 1358*

U.S. Brand Names Biavax®_II

Therapeutic Category Vaccine

Use Promote active immunity to rubella and mumps by inducing production of antibodies
Note: Routine vaccination with trivalent MMR is recommended by ACIP as children enter kindergarten or first grade. AAP recommends a routine second vaccination as children enter into middle or junior high school.

Pregnancy Risk Factor C

Pregnancy/Breast-Feeding Implications Women who are pregnant when vaccinated or who become pregnant within 3 months of vaccination should be counseled on the theoretical risks to the fetus. The risk of rubella-associated malformations in these women is so small as to be negligible. MMR is the vaccine of choice if recipients are likely to be susceptible to measles or mumps as well as to rubella.

Contraindications Known hypersensitivity to neomycin, eggs; children <1 year, pregnant women, primary immunodeficient patients, patients receiving immunosuppressant drugs except corticosteroids

Warnings/Precautions Women planning on becoming pregnant in the next 3 months should not be vaccinated

Adverse Reactions All serious adverse reactions must be reported to the U.S. Department of Health and Human Services (DHHS) Vaccine Adverse Event Reporting System (VAERS) 1-800-822-7967.
>10%:
Dermatologic: Local tenderness and erythema, urticaria, rash
Neuromuscular & skeletal: Arthralgia
1% to 10%:
Central nervous system: Malaise, moderate fever, headache
Gastrointestinal: Sore throat
Miscellaneous: Lymphadenopathy
<1%: High fever (>103°F), encephalitis, polyneuropathy, erythema multiforme, optic neuritis, hypersensitivity, allergic reactions to the vaccine

Drug Interactions Whole blood, interferon immune globulin, radiation therapy, and immunosuppressive drugs (eg, corticosteroids) may result in insufficient response to immunization; may temporarily depress tuberculin skin test sensitivity and reduce the seroconversion. DTP, OPV, MMR, Hib, and hepatitis B may be given concurrently; other virus vaccine administration should be separated by ≥1 month.

Stability Refrigerate, discard unused portion within 8 hours, protect from light

Usual Dosage Children >12 months (preferably at 15 months) and Adults: 1 vial (0.5 mL) in outer aspect of the upper arm; children vaccinated before 12 months of age should be revaccinated

Administration Administer S.C. only

Test Interactions Temporary suppression of TB skin test

Patient Information Patient may experience burning or stinging at the injection site; joint pain usually occurs 1-10 weeks after vaccination and persists 1-3 days

Nursing Implications Children immunized before 12 months of age should be reimmunized

Additional Information Federal law requires that the date of administration, the vaccine manufacturer, lot number of vaccine, and the administering person's name, title and address be entered into the patient's permanent medical record

Dosage Forms Injection (mixture of 2 viruses):
1. Wistar RA 27/3 strain of rubella virus
2. Jeryl Lynn (B level) mumps strain grown cell cultures of chick embryo

- **Rubella, Measles and Mumps Vaccines, Combined** *see* Measles, Mumps, and Rubella Vaccines, Combined *on page 714*

Rubella Virus Vaccine, Live (rue BEL a VYE rus vak SEEN, live)

Related Information
Adverse Events and Vaccination *on page 1369*
Immunization Recommendations *on page 1358*

U.S. Brand Names Meruvax® II

Synonyms German Measles Vaccine

Therapeutic Category Vaccine, Live Virus

Use Selective active immunization against rubella; vaccination is routinely recommended for persons from 12 months of age to puberty. All adults, both male and female, lacking documentation of live vaccine on or after first birthday, or laboratory evidence of immunity (particularly women of childbearing age and young adults who work in or congregate in hospitals, colleges, and on military bases) should be vaccinated. Susceptible travelers should be vaccinated.
(Continued)

Rubella Virus Vaccine, Live (Continued)

Note: Trivalent measles - mumps - rubella (MMR) vaccine is the preferred immunizing agent for most children and many adults.

Pregnancy Risk Factor C

Pregnancy/Breast-Feeding Implications Women who are pregnant when vaccinated or who become pregnant within 3 months of vaccination should be counseled on the theoretical risks to the fetus. The risk of rubella-associated malformations in these women is so small as to be negligible. MMR is the vaccine of choice if recipients are likely to be susceptible to measles or mumps as well as to rubella.

Warnings/Precautions Pregnancy, immunocompromised persons, history of anaphylactic reaction following receipt of neomycin; do not administer with other live vaccines

Adverse Reactions All serious adverse reactions must be reported to the U.S. Department of Health and Human Services (DHHS) Vaccine Adverse Event Reporting System (VAERS) 1-800-822-7967.

>10%:
  Dermatologic: Local tenderness and erythema
  Neuromuscular & skeletal: Arthralgia

1% to 10%:
  Central nervous system: Malaise, moderate fever, headache
  Dermatologic: Rash, urticaria
  Gastrointestinal: Sore throat
  Miscellaneous: Lymphadenopathy

<1%: High fever (>103°F), encephalitis, polyneuropathy, erythema multiforme, optic neuritis, hypersensitivity, allergic reactions to the vaccine

Drug Interactions Whole blood, interferon immune globulin, radiation therapy, and immunosuppressive drugs (eg, corticosteroids) may result in insufficient response to immunization; may temporarily depress tuberculin skin test sensitivity and reduce the seroconversion. DTP, OPV, MMR, Hib, and hepatitis B may be given concurrently; other virus vaccine administration should be separated by ≥1 month from measles.

Stability Refrigerate, discard reconstituted vaccine after 8 hours; store at 2°C to 8°C (36°F to 46°F); ship vaccine at 10°C; may use dry ice, protect from light

Mechanism of Action Rubella vaccine is a live attenuated vaccine that contains the Wistar Institute RA 27/3 strain, which is adapted to and propagated in human diploid cell culture. Promotes active immunity by inducing rubella hemagglutination-inhibiting antibodies.

Pharmacodynamics/Kinetics Onset of effect: Antibodies to the vaccine are detectable within 2-4 weeks following immunization

Usual Dosage Children ≥12 months and Adults: S.C.: 0.5 mL in outer aspect of upper arm; children vaccinated before 12 months of age should be revaccinated

Test Interactions May depress tuberculin skin test sensitivity

Patient Information Patient may experience burning or stinging at the injection site; joint pain usually occurs 1-10 weeks after vaccination and persists 1-3 days

Nursing Implications Reconstituted vaccine should be used within 8 hours; S.C. injection only

Additional Information Live virus vaccine: Federal law requires that the date of administration, the vaccine manufacturer, lot number of vaccine, and the administering person's name, title and address be entered into the patient's permanent record

Dosage Forms Injection, single dose: 1000 TCID$_{50}$ (Wistar RA 27/3 Strain)

- ♦ **Rubeola Vaccine** see Measles Virus Vaccine, Live, Attenuated on page 715
- ♦ **Rubex®** see Doxorubicin on page 393
- ♦ **Rubidomycin Hydrochloride** see Daunorubicin Hydrochloride on page 327
- ♦ **Rubramin** see Cyanocobalamin on page 302
- ♦ **Rubramin-PC®** see Cyanocobalamin on page 302
- ♦ **Rum-K®** see Potassium Chloride on page 949
- ♦ **Ru-Tuss®** see Chlorpheniramine, Phenylephrine, Phenylpropanolamine, and Belladonna Alkaloids on page 247
- ♦ **Ru-Tuss® Liquid** see Chlorpheniramine and Phenylephrine on page 246
- ♦ **Ru-Vert-M®** see Meclizine on page 719
- ♦ **Ryna-C® Liquid** see Chlorpheniramine, Pseudoephedrine, and Codeine on page 247
- ♦ **Rynacrom®** see Cromolyn Sodium on page 300
- ♦ **Ryna-CX®** see Guaifenesin, Pseudoephedrine, and Codeine on page 551
- ♦ **Rynatan® Pediatric Suspension** see Chlorpheniramine, Pyrilamine, and Phenylephrine on page 247
- ♦ **Rynatan® Tablet** see Chlorpheniramine, Pyrilamine, and Phenylephrine on page 247
- ♦ **Rynatuss® Pediatric Suspension** see Chlorpheniramine, Ephedrine, Phenylephrine, and Carbetapentane on page 246
- ♦ **Rythmol®** see Propafenone on page 981
- ♦ **Sabin** see Polio Vaccines on page 940
- ♦ **Sabulin** see Albuterol on page 35

Sacrosidase (sak RO se dase)

U.S. Brand Names Sucraid™

Therapeutic Category Enzyme, Gastrointestinal

Use Oral replacement therapy in sucrase deficiency, as seen in congenital sucrase-isomaltase deficiency (CSID)

Pregnancy Risk Factor C

Pregnancy/Breast-Feeding Implications Animal studies have not been conducted. Should be administered to a pregnant woman only when indicated; **compatible** with breast-feeding

Contraindications Hypersensitivity to yeast, yeast products, or glycerin

Warnings/Precautions Hypersensitivity reactions to sacrosidase, including broncho-spasm, have been reported. Administer initial doses in a setting where acute hypersensitivity reactions may be treated within a few minutes. Skin testing for hypersensitivity may be performed prior to administration to identify patients at risk.

Adverse Reactions

1% to 10%: Gastrointestinal: Abdominal pain, vomiting, nausea, diarrhea, constipation

<1%:

Central nervous system: Insomnia, headache, nervousness

Endocrine & metabolic: Dehydration

Respiratory: Bronchospasm

Miscellaneous: Hypersensitivity reaction

Overdosage/Toxicology Symptoms may include epigastric pain, drowsiness, lethargy, nausea, and vomiting; gastrointestinal bleeding may occur. Rare manifestations include hypertension, respiratory depression, coma, and acute renal failure. Treatment is symptomatic and supportive. Forced diuresis, hemodialysis, and/or urinary alkalinization are not likely to be useful.

Drug Interactions Drug-drug interactions have not been evaluated

Stability Store under refrigeration at 4°C to 8°C (36°F to 46°F); protect from heat or light

Mechanism of Action Sacrosidase is a naturally occurring gastrointestinal enzyme which breaks down the disaccharide sucrose to its monosaccharide components. Hydrolysis is necessary to allow absorption of these nutrients.

Pharmacodynamics/Kinetics Absorption: Sacrosidase is metabolized in the gastrointestinal tract to individual amino acids, which may be absorbed

Usual Dosage Oral:

Infants ≥5 months and Children <15 kg: 8500 int. units (1 mL) per meal or snack

Children >15 kg and Adults: 17,000 int. units (2 mL) per meal or snack

Doses should be diluted with 2-4 oz of water, milk, or formula with each meal or snack. Approximately one-half of the dose may be taken before, and the remainder of a dose taken at the completion of each meal or snack.

Dietary Considerations May be inactivated or denatured if administered with fruit juice, warm or hot food or liquids. Since isomaltase deficiency is not addressed by supplementation of sacrosidase, adherence to a low-starch diet may be required.

Administration Do not administer with fruit juices, warm or hot liquids; the solution is fully soluble with water, milk, or formula

Additional Information Oral solution contains 50% glycerol

Dosage Forms Solution, oral: 8500 int. units per mL

- ♦ **Safe Tussin® 30 [OTC]** see Guaifenesin and Dextromethorphan on page 550
- ♦ **Saizen® Injection** see Human Growth Hormone on page 569
- ♦ **Salagen® Oral** see Pilocarpine on page 927
- ♦ **Salazopyrin®** see Sulfasalazine on page 1095
- ♦ **Salazopyrin EN-Tabs®** see Sulfasalazine on page 1095
- ♦ **Salbutamol** see Albuterol on page 35
- ♦ **Saleto-200® [OTC]** see Ibuprofen on page 593
- ♦ **Saleto-400®** see Ibuprofen on page 593
- ♦ **Salflex®** see Salsalate on page 1047
- ♦ **Salgesic®** see Salsalate on page 1047
- ♦ **Salicylazosulfapyridine** see Sulfasalazine on page 1095

Salicylic Acid and Lactic Acid (sal i SIL ik AS id & LAK tik AS id)

U.S. Brand Names Duofilm® Solution

Therapeutic Category Keratolytic Agent

Dosage Forms Solution, topical: Salicylic acid 16.7% and lactic acid 16.7% in flexible collodion (15 mL)

Salicylic Acid and Propylene Glycol

(sal i SIL ik AS id & PROE pi leen GLYE cole)

U.S. Brand Names Keralyt® Gel

Therapeutic Category Keratolytic Agent

Dosage Forms Gel, topical: Salicylic acid 6% and propylene glycol 60% in ethyl alcohol 19.4% with hydroxypropyl methylcellulose and water (30 g)

- ♦ **Salicylsalicylic Acid** see Salsalate on page 1047
- ♦ **SalineX® [OTC]** see Sodium Chloride on page 1067
- ♦ **Salk** see Polio Vaccines on page 940

Salmeterol (sal ME te role)

Related Information

Bronchodilators, Comparison of Inhaled and Sympathomimetic on page 1314

U.S. Brand Names Serevent®; Serevent® Diskus®

Synonyms Salmeterol Xinafoate

Therapeutic Category Adrenergic Agonist Agent; Beta₂-Adrenergic Agonist Agent; Bronchodilator

(Continued)

Salmeterol (Continued)

Use Maintenance treatment of asthma and in prevention of bronchospasm in patients >12 years of age with reversible obstructive airway disease, including patients with symptoms of nocturnal asthma, who require regular treatment with inhaled, short-acting beta$_2$ agonists; prevention of exercise-induced bronchospasm; treatment of COPD-induced bronchospasm

Pregnancy Risk Factor C

Contraindications Hypersensitivity to salmeterol, adrenergic amines or any ingredients; need for acute bronchodilation; within 2 weeks of MAO inhibitor use

Warnings/Precautions Salmeterol is not meant to relieve acute asthmatic symptoms. Acute episodes should be treated with short-acting beta$_2$ agonist. Do not increase the frequency of salmeterol. Cardiovascular effects are not common with salmeterol when used in recommended doses. All beta agonists may cause elevation in blood pressure, heart rate, and result in excitement (CNS). Use with caution in patients with prostatic hypertrophy, diabetes, cardiovascular disorders, convulsive disorders, thyrotoxicosis, or others who are sensitive to the effects of sympathomimetic amines. Paroxysmal bronchospasm (which can be fatal) has been reported with this and other inhaled agents. If this occurs, discontinue treatment. The elderly may be at greater risk of cardiovascular side effects; safety and efficacy have not been established in children <12 years of age.

Adverse Reactions
>10%:
  Central nervous system: Headache
  Respiratory: Pharyngitis
1% to 10%:
  Cardiovascular: Tachycardia, palpitations, elevation or depression of blood pressure, cardiac arrhythmias
  Central nervous system: Nervousness, CNS stimulation, hyperactivity, insomnia, malaise, dizziness
  Gastrointestinal: GI upset, diarrhea, nausea
  Neuromuscular & skeletal: Tremors (may be more common in the elderly), myalgias, back pain, arthralgia
  Respiratory: Upper respiratory infection, cough, bronchitis
<1%: Immediate hypersensitivity reactions (rash, urticaria, bronchospasm)

Overdosage/Toxicology
  Decontaminate using lavage/activated charcoal
  Beta-blockers can be used for hyperadrenergic signs (use with caution in patients with bronchospasm)
  Prudent use of a cardioselective beta-adrenergic blocker (eg, atenolol or metoprolol); keep in mind the potential for induction of bronchoconstriction in an asthmatic. Dialysis has not been shown to be of value in the treatment of an overdose with this agent.

Drug Interactions CYP3A3/4 enzyme substrate
  Increased effect: Beta-adrenergic blockers (eg, propranolol)
  Increased toxicity (cardiovascular): MAO inhibitors, tricyclic antidepressants

Stability
  Aerosol: Store at 15°C to 30°C (59°F to 86°F); store cannister with nozzle down; shake well before each use
  Inhalation powder: Store at controlled room temperature 20°C to 25°C (68°F to 77°F) in a dry place away from direct heat or sunlight

Mechanism of Action Relaxes bronchial smooth muscle by selective action on beta$_2$-receptors with little effect on heart rate; because salmeterol acts locally in the lung, therapeutic effect is not predicted by plasma levels

Pharmacodynamics/Kinetics
  Onset of action: 5-20 minutes (average 10 minutes)
  Peak effect: 2-4 hours
  Duration: 12 hours
  Protein binding: 94% to 98%
  Metabolism: Hydroxylated in liver
  Half-life: 3-4 hours

Usual Dosage
  Inhalation: 42 mcg (2 puffs) twice daily (12 hours apart) for maintenance and prevention of symptoms of asthma
  Prevention of exercise-induced asthma: 42 mcg (2 puffs) 30-60 minutes prior to exercise; additional doses should not be used for 12 hours
  COPD: Adults: For maintenance treatment of bronchospasm associated with COPD (including chronic bronchitis and emphysema): 2 inhalations (42 mcg) twice daily (morning and evening - 12 hours apart); do not use a spacer with the inhalation powder

Monitoring Parameters Pulmonary function tests, blood pressure, pulse, CNS stimulation

Patient Information Do not use to treat acute symptoms; do not exceed the prescribed dose of salmeterol. Do not stop using inhaled or oral corticosteroids without medical advice even if you "feel better". Shake well before using; avoid spraying in eyes. Remove the canister and rinse the plastic case and cap under warm water and dry daily. Store canister with nozzle end down.

Nursing Implications Not to be used for the relief of acute attacks. Monitor lung sounds, pulse, blood pressure. Before using, the inhaler must be shaken well. Observe for wheezing after administration; if this occurs, call physician.

Dosage Forms
  Aerosol, oral, as xinafoate: 21 mcg/spray [60 inhalations] (6.5 g), [120 inhalations] (13 g)

Inhaler: 25 mcg/metered inhalation
Powder for inhalation, oral (Serevent® Diskus®): 50 mcg [46 mcg/inhalation] (60 doses)

♦ **Salmeterol Xinafoate** see Salmeterol on page 1045
♦ **Salmonine® Injection** see Calcitonin on page 171

Salsalate (SAL sa late)

U.S. Brand Names Argesic®-SA; Artha-G®; Disalcid®; Marthritic®; Mono-Gesic®; Salflex®; Salgesic®; Salsitab®

Synonyms Disalicylic Acid; Salicylsalicylic Acid

Therapeutic Category Analgesic, Salicylate; Anti-inflammatory Agent; Antipyretic; Nonsteroidal Anti-inflammatory Drug (NSAID), Oral; Salicylate

Use Treatment of minor pain or fever; arthritis

Pregnancy Risk Factor C

Contraindications GI ulcer or bleeding, known hypersensitivity to salsalate

Warnings/Precautions Use with caution in patients with platelet and bleeding disorders, renal dysfunction, erosive gastritis, or peptic ulcer disease, previous nonreaction does not guarantee future safe taking of medication; do not use aspirin in children <16 years of age for chickenpox or flu symptoms due to the association with Reye's syndrome

Adverse Reactions
>10%: Gastrointestinal: Nausea, heartburn, stomach pains, dyspepsia
1% to 10%:
Central nervous system: Fatigue
Dermatologic: Rash
Gastrointestinal: Gastrointestinal ulceration
Hematologic: Hemolytic anemia
Neuromuscular & skeletal: Weakness
Respiratory: Dyspnea
Miscellaneous: Anaphylactic shock
<1%: Insomnia, nervousness, jitters, leukopenia, thrombocytopenia, iron deficiency anemia, does not appear to inhibit platelet aggregation, occult bleeding, hepatotoxicity, impaired renal function, bronchospasm

Overdosage/Toxicology
Symptoms of overdose include respiratory alkalosis, hyperpnea, tachypnea, tinnitus, headache, hyperpyrexia, metabolic acidosis, hypoglycemia, coma. The "Done" nomogram is very helpful for estimating the severity of aspirin poisoning and directing treatment using serum salicylate levels.
Treatment can also be based upon symptomatology.

Salicylates

Toxic Symptoms	Treatment
Overdose	Induce emesis with ipecac, and/or lavage with saline, followed with activated charcoal
Dehydration	I.V. fluids with KCl (no D_5W only)
Metabolic acidosis (must be treated)	Sodium bicarbonate
Hyperthermia	Cooling blankets or sponge baths
Coagulopathy/hemorrhage	Vitamin K I.V.
Hypoglycemia (with coma, seizures, or change in mental status)	Dextrose 25 g I.V.
Seizures	Diazepam 5-10 mg I.V.

Drug Interactions
Decreased effect with urinary alkalinizers, antacids, corticosteroids; decreased effect of uricosurics, spironolactone
Increased effect/toxicity of oral anticoagulants, hypoglycemics, methotrexate

Mechanism of Action Inhibits prostaglandin synthesis, acts on the hypothalamus heat-regulating center to reduce fever, blocks prostaglandin synthetase action which prevents formation of the platelet-aggregating substance thromboxane A_2

Pharmacodynamics/Kinetics
Onset of action: Therapeutic effects occur within 3-4 days of continuous dosing
Absorption: Oral: Completely from the small intestine
Metabolism: Hydrolyzed in the liver to 2 moles of salicylic acid (active)
Half-life: 7-8 hours
Elimination: Almost totally excreted renally

Usual Dosage Adults: Oral: 3 g/day in 2-3 divided doses
Dosing comments in renal impairment: In patients with end-stage renal disease undergoing hemodialysis: 750 mg twice daily with an additional 500 mg after dialysis

Test Interactions False-negative results for glucose oxidase urinary glucose tests (Clinistix®); false-positives using the cupric sulfate method (Clinitest®); also, interferes with Gerhardt test, VMA determination; 5-HIAA, xylose tolerance test and T_3 and T_4

Patient Information Do not self-medicate with other drug products containing aspirin; use antacids to relieve upset stomach; watch for bleeding gums or any signs of GI bleeding; take with food or milk to minimize GI distress, notify physician if ringing in ears or persistent GI pain occurs

Dosage Forms
Capsule: 500 mg
Tablet: 500 mg, 750 mg

- **Salsitab**® *see* Salsalate *on previous page*
- **Salt** *see* Sodium Chloride *on page 1067*
- **Salt Poor Albumin** *see* Albumin *on page 34*
- **Saluron**® *see* Hydroflumethiazide *on page 582*
- **Salutensin**® *see* Hydroflumethiazide and Reserpine *on page 583*
- **Salutensin**®-**Demi** *see* Hydroflumethiazide and Reserpine *on page 583*
- **Sandimmune**® **Injection** *see* Cyclosporine *on page 308*
- **Sandimmune**® **Oral** *see* Cyclosporine *on page 308*
- **Sandoglobulin**® *see* Immune Globulin, Intravenous *on page 604*
- **Sandostatin**® *see* Octreotide Acetate *on page 857*
- **Sandostatin LAR**® **Depot** *see* Octreotide Acetate *on page 857*
- **Sang**® **CyA** *see* Cyclosporine *on page 308*
- **Sansert**® *see* Methysergide *on page 765*
- **Santyl**® *see* Collagenase *on page 295*

Saquinavir (sa KWIN a veer)

Related Information
Antiretroviral Agents *on page 1306*
Antiretroviral Therapy for HIV Infection *on page 1410*
Management of Healthcare Worker Exposures to HIV *on page 1374*

U.S. Brand Names Fortovase®; Invirase®

Synonyms Saquinavir Mesylate

Therapeutic Category Antiretroviral Agent, Protease Inhibitor; Protease Inhibitor

Use Treatment of HIV infection in selected patients; used in combination with other antiretroviral agents

Pregnancy Risk Factor B

Pregnancy/Breast-Feeding Implications
Clinical effects on the fetus: Administer saquinavir during pregnancy only if benefits to the mother outweigh the risk to the fetus
Breast-feeding/lactation: HIV-infected mothers are discouraged from breast-feeding to decrease postnatal transmission of HIV

Contraindications Hypersensitivity to saquinavir or any components; exposure to direct sunlight without sunscreen or protective clothing; coadministration with terfenadine, cisapride, astemizole, triazolam, midazolam, or ergot derivatives

Warnings/Precautions The indication for saquinavir for the treatment of HIV infection is based on changes in surrogate markers. At present, there are no results from controlled clinical trials evaluating its effect on patient survival or the clinical progression of HIV infection (ie, occurrence of opportunistic infections or malignancies); use caution in patients with hepatic insufficiency; safety and efficacy have not been established in children <16 years of age. May exacerbate pre-existing hepatic dysfunction; use with caution in patients with hepatitis B or C and in cirrhosis

Adverse Reactions Protease inhibitors cause dyslipidemia which includes elevated cholesterol and triglycerides and a redistribution of body fat centrally to cause "protease paunch", buffalo hump, facial atrophy, and breast enlargement. These agents also cause hyperglycemia.

1% to 10%:
Dermatologic: Rash
Endocrine & metabolic: Hyperglycemia
Gastrointestinal: Diarrhea, abdominal discomfort, nausea, abdominal pain, buccal mucosa ulceration
Neuromuscular & skeletal: Paresthesia, weakness, increased CPK
<1%: Headache, confusion, seizures, ataxia, pain, Stevens-Johnson syndrome, hypoglycemia, hyper- and hypokalemia, low serum amylase, upper quadrant abdominal pain, acute myeloblastic leukemia, hemolytic anemia, thrombocytopenia, jaundice, ascites, bullous skin eruption, polyarthritis, portal hypertension, exacerbation of chronic liver disease, elevated LFTs, altered AST/ALT, bilirubin, Hgb, thrombophlebitis

Drug Interactions CYP3A3/4 enzyme substrate; CYP3A3/4 enzyme inhibitor
Decreased effect: Rifampin may decrease saquinavir's plasma levels and AUC by 40% to 80%; other enzyme inducers may induce saquinavir's metabolism (eg, phenobarbital, phenytoin, dexamethasone, carbamazepine); may decrease delavirdine concentrations
Increased effect: Ketoconazole significantly increases plasma levels and AUC of saquinavir; as a known, although not potent inhibitor of the cytochrome P-450 system, saquinavir may decrease the metabolism of terfenadine and astemizole, as well as cisapride, ergot derivatives, midazolam, and triazolam (and result in rare but serious effects including cardiac arrhythmias); other drugs which may have increased adverse effects if coadministered with saquinavir include calcium channel blockers, clindamycin, dapsone, and quinidine. Both clarithromycin and saquinavir levels/effects may be increased with coadministration. Delavirdine may increase concentration; ritonavir may increase AUC >17-fold; concurrent administration of nelfinavir results in increase in nelfinavir (18%) and saquinavir (mean: 392%).

Mechanism of Action As an inhibitor of HIV protease, saquinavir prevents the cleavage of viral polyprotein precursors which are needed to generate functional proteins in and maturation of HIV-infected cells

Pharmacodynamics/Kinetics
Absorption: Poor, increased with high fat meal. Fortovase® has improved absorption over Invirase®

Distribution: V_d: 700 L; does not distribute into CSF
Protein binding: ~98% bound to plasma proteins
Metabolism: Widely metabolized undergoing extensive first pass metabolism
Bioavailability: ~4% (Invirase®); 12% to 15% (Fortovase®)

Usual Dosage Adults: Oral:

Fortovase®: Six 200 mg capsules (1200 mg) 3 times/day within 2 hours after a meal in combination with a nucleoside analog

Invirase®: Three 200 mg capsules (600 mg) 3 times/day within 2 hours after a full meal in combination with a nucleoside analog

Dose of either Fortovase® or Invirase® in combination with ritonavir: 400 mg twice daily

Monitoring Parameters Monitor viral load, CD4 count, triglycerides, cholesterol, glucose

Patient Information Saquinavir is not a cure for HIV infection nor has it been found to reduce the transmission of HIV; opportunistic infections and other illnesses associated with AIDS may still occur; take saquinavir within 2 hours after a full meal; avoid direct sunlight when taking saquinavir

Nursing Implications Observe for signs of opportunistic infections and other illnesses associated with HIV; administer on a full stomach, if possible

Additional Information The indication for saquinavir for the treatment of HIV infection is based on changes in surrogate markers. At present, there are no results from controlled clinical trials evaluating the effect of regimens containing saquinavir on patient survival or the clinical progression of HIV infection, such as the occurrence of opportunistic infections or malignancies; in cell culture, saquinavir is additive to synergistic with AZT, ddC, and DDI without enhanced toxicity. According to the manufacturer, Invirase® will be phased out over time and completely replaced by Fortovase®. Potential compliance problems, frequency of administration and adverse effects should be discussed with patients before initiating therapy to help prevent the emergence of resistance.

Dosage Forms

Capsule (hard) as mesylate (Invirase®): 200 mg
Capsule (soft) (Fortovase®): 200 mg

♦ **Saquinavir Mesylate** *see* Saquinavir *on previous page*

Sargramostim (sar GRAM oh stim)

Related Information

Filgrastim on page 482

U.S. Brand Names Leukine™

Synonyms GM-CSF; Granulocyte-Macrophage Colony Stimulating Factor; rGM-CSF

Therapeutic Category Colony Stimulating Factor

Use

Myeloid reconstitution after autologous bone marrow transplantation:
Non-Hodgkin's lymphoma (NHL)
Acute lymphoblastic leukemia (ALL)
Hodgkin's lymphoma
Metastatic breast cancer

Myeloid reconstitution after allogeneic bone marrow transplantation

Peripheral stem cell transplantation
Metastatic breast cancer
Non-Hodgkin's lymphoma
Hodgkin's lymphoma
Multiple myeloma

Acute myelogenous leukemia (AML) following induction chemotherapy in older adults to shorten time to neutrophil recovery and to reduce the incidence of severe and life-threatening infections and infections resulting in death

Bone marrow transplant (allogeneic or autologous) failure or engraftment delay
Safety and efficacy of GM-CSF given simultaneously with cytotoxic chemotherapy have not been established. Concurrent treatment may increase myelosuppression.

Pregnancy Risk Factor C

Pregnancy/Breast-Feeding Implications Clinical effects to the fetus: Animal reproduction studies have not been conducted. It is not known whether sargramostim can cause fetal harm when administered to a pregnant woman or can affect reproductive capability. Sargramostim should be given to a pregnant woman only if clearly needed.

Contraindications GM-CSF is contraindicated in the following instances:
Patients with excessive myeloid blasts (>10%) in the bone marrow or peripheral blood
Patients with known hypersensitivity to GM-CSF, yeast-derived products, or any known component of the product

Warnings/Precautions Simultaneous administration with cytotoxic chemotherapy or radiotherapy or administration 24 hours preceding or following chemotherapy is recommended. Use with caution in patients with pre-existing cardiac problems, hypoxia, fluid retention, pulmonary infiltrates or congestive heart failure, renal or hepatic impairment.

Rapid increase in peripheral blood counts: If ANC >20,000/mm^3 or platelets >500,000/mm^3, decrease dose by 50% or discontinue drug (counts will fall to normal within 3-7 days after discontinuing drug)

Growth factor potential: Use with caution with myeloid malignancies. Precaution should be exercised in the usage of GM-CSF in any malignancy with myeloid characteristics. GM-CSF can potentially act as a growth factor for any tumor type, particularly myeloid malignancies. Tumors of nonhematopoietic origin may have surface receptors for GM-CSF.

(Continued)

Sargramostim *(Continued)*

There is a "first-dose effect" (refer to Adverse Reactions for details) which is rarely seen with the first dose and does not usually occur with subsequent doses.

Adverse Reactions

>10%:
"First-dose" effects: Fever, hypotension, tachycardia, rigors, flushing, nausea, vomiting, dyspnea
Central nervous system: Neutropenic fever
Dermatologic: Alopecia
Endocrine & metabolic: Polydipsia
Gastrointestinal: Nausea, vomiting, diarrhea, stomatitis, GI hemorrhage, mucositis
Neuromuscular & skeletal: Bone pain, myalgia
1% to 10%:
Cardiovascular: Chest pain, peripheral edema, capillary leak syndrome
Central nervous system: Headache
Dermatologic: Rash
Endocrine & metabolic: Fluid retention
Gastrointestinal: Anorexia, sore throat, stomatitis, constipation
Hematologic: Leukocytosis
Local: Pain at injection site
Neuromuscular & skeletal: Weakness
Respiratory: Dyspnea, cough
<1%: Hypotension, flushing, pericardial effusion, transient supraventricular arrhythmias, pericarditis, malaise, thrombophlebitis, anaphylactic reaction

Overdosage/Toxicology The maximum amount that can be safely administered in single or multiple doses has not been determined
Symptoms include dyspnea, malaise, nausea, fever, rash, sinus tachycardia, headache, and chills; all of these adverse events were reversible after discontinuation of sargramostim
Treatment: Discontinue therapy and carefully monitor the patient for WBC increase and respiratory symptoms

Drug Interactions
Increased toxicity: Lithium, corticosteroids may potentiate myeloproliferative effects

Stability The manufacturer currently recommends that solutions which are reconstituted with sterile water should be used within 6 hours (due to a lack of a preservative) and that solution reconstituted with bacteriostatic water should be used within 20 days. The manufacturer recommends that further diluted solutions be discarded if not used within 6 hours
Sargramostim is available as a sterile, white, preservative-free, lyophilized powder
Sargramostim should be stored at 2°C to 8°C (36°F to 46°F)
Vials should not be frozen or shaken
Sargramostim is stable after dilution in 1 mL of bacteriostatic or nonbacteriostatic sterile water for injection for 30 days at 2°C to 8°C or 25°C
Sargramostim may also be further diluted in 0.9% sodium chloride to a concentration of ≥10 mcg/mL for I.V. infusion administration; this diluted solution is stable for 48 hours at room temperature and refrigeration
If the final concentration of sargramostim is <10 mcg/mL, human albumin should be added to the saline prior to the addition of sargramostim to prevent absorption of the components to the delivery system
It is recommended that 1 mg of human albumin/1 mL of 0.9% sodium chloride (eg, 1 mL of 5% human albumin/50 mL of 0.9% sodium chloride) be added
Standard diluent: Dose ≥250 mcg/25 mL NS
Incompatible with dextrose-containing solutions

Mechanism of Action Stimulates proliferation, differentiation and functional activity of neutrophils, eosinophils, monocytes, and macrophages; see table.

Proliferation/Differentiation	G-CSF (Filgrastim)	GM-CSF (Sargramostim)
Neutrophils	Yes	Yes
Eosinophils	No	Yes
Macrophages	No	Yes
Neutrophil migration	Enhanced	Inhibited

Pharmacodynamics/Kinetics
Onset of action: Increase in WBC in 7-14 days
Duration: WBC will return to baseline within 1 week after discontinuing drug
Half-life: 2 hours
Time to peak serum concentration: S.C.: Within 1-2 hours

Usual Dosage
Children and Adults: I.V. infusion over ≥2 hours or S.C.
Existing clinical data suggest that starting GM-CSF between 24 and 72 hours subsequent to chemotherapy may provide optimal neutrophil recover; continue therapy until the occurrence of an absolute neutrophil count of 10,000/μL after the neutrophil nadir
The available data suggest that rounding the dose to the nearest vial size may enhance patient convenience and reduce costs without clinical detriment
Myeloid reconstitution after peripheral stem cell, allogeneic or autologous bone marrow transplant: I.V.: 250 mcg/m²/day for 21 days to begin 2-4 hours after the

marrow infusion on day 0 of autologous bone marrow transplant or ≥24 hours after chemotherapy or 12 hours after last dose of radiotherapy

If a severe adverse reaction occurs, reduce or temporarily discontinue the dose until the reaction abates

If blast cells appear or progression of the underlying disease occurs, disrupt treatment

Interrupt or reduce the dose by half if ANC is >20,000 cells/mm^3

Patients should not receive sargramostim until the postmarrow infusion ANC is <500 cells/mm^3

Neutrophil recovery following chemotherapy in AML: I.V.: 250 mg/m^2/day over a 4-hour period starting ~day 11 or 4 days following the completion of induction chemotherapy, if day 10 bone marrow is hypoblastic with <5% blasts

If a second cycle of chemotherapy is necessary, administer ~4 days after the completion of chemotherapy if the bone marrow is hypoblastic with <5% blasts

Continue sargramostim until ANC is >1500 cells/mm^3 for consecutive days or a maximum of 42 days

Discontinue sargramostim immediately if leukemic regrowth occurs

If a severe adverse reaction occurs, reduce the dose by 50% or temporarily discontinue the dose until the reaction abates

Mobilization of peripheral blood progenitor cells: I.V.: 250 mcg/m^2/day over 24 hours or S.C. once daily

Continue the same dose through the period of PBPC collection

The optimal schedule for PBPC collection has not been established (usually begun by day 5 and performed daily until protocol specified targets are achieved)

If WBC >50,000 cells/mm^3, reduce the dose by 50%

If adequate numbers of progenitor cells are not collected, consider other mobilization therapy

Postperipheral blood progenitor cell transplantation: I.V.: 250 mcg/m^2/day over 24 hours or S.C. once daily beginning immediately following infusion of progenitor cells and continuing until ANC is >1500 for 3 consecutive days is attained

BMT failure or engraftment delay: I.V.: 250 mcg/m^2/day for 14 days as a 2-hour infusion

The dose can be repeated after 7 days off therapy if engraftment has not occurred

If engraftment still has not occurred, a third course of 500 mcg/m^2/day for 14 days may be tried after another 7 days off therapy; if there is still no improvement, it is unlikely that further dose escalation will be beneficial

If a severe adverse reaction occurs, reduce or temporarily discontinue the dose until the reaction abates

If blast cells appear or disease progression occurs, discontinue treatment

Administration Administer by S.C. (undiluted) or I.V. infusion; I.V. infusion should be over at least 2 hours; **incompatible** with dextrose-containing solutions

Monitoring Parameters Vital signs, weight, CBC with differential, platelets, renal/liver function tests, especially with previous dysfunction, WBC with differential, pulmonary function

Reference Range Excessive leukocytosis: ANC >20,000/mm^3 or WBC >50,000 cells/mm^3

Patient Information May cause bone pain and first dose reaction

Nursing Implications Can premedicate with analgesics and antipyretics; control bone pain with non-narcotic analgesics; do not shake solution; when administering GM-CSF subcutaneously, rotate injection sites

Additional Information

Reimbursement Hotline (Leukine™): 1-800-321-4669

Professional Services (IMMUNEX): 1-800-334-6273

Dosage Forms Injection: 250 mcg, 500 mcg

♦ **S.A.S™** *see* Sulfasalazine *on page 1095*

♦ **Scabene®** *see* Lindane *on page 682*

♦ **Scalpicin®** *see* Hydrocortisone *on page 579*

♦ **Sclavo-PPD Solution®** *see* Tuberculin Purified Protein Derivative *on page 1194*

♦ **Sclavo-PPD Solution®** *see* Tuberculin Tests *on page 1194*

♦ **Sclavo Test-PPD®** *see* Tuberculin Purified Protein Derivative *on page 1194*

♦ **Sclavo Test-PPD®** *see* Tuberculin Tests *on page 1194*

♦ **Scleromate™** *see* Morrhuate Sodium *on page 800*

♦ **Scopace™ Tablet** *see* Scopolamine *on this page*

Scopolamine (skoe POL a meen)

Related Information

Cycloplegic Mydriatics Comparison *on page 1321*

U.S. Brand Names Isopto® Hyoscine Ophthalmic; Scopace™ Tablet; Transderm Scop® Patch

Canadian Brand Names Transdermal-V®

Synonyms Hyoscine; Scopolamine Hydrobromide

Therapeutic Category Anticholinergic Agent; Anticholinergic Agent, Ophthalmic; Anticholinergic Agent, Transdermal; Ophthalmic Agent, Mydriatic

Use Preoperative medication to produce amnesia and decrease salivary and respiratory secretions; to produce cycloplegia and mydriasis; treatment of iridocyclitis; prevention of motion sickness; prevention of nausea/vomiting associated with anesthesia or opiate analgesia (patch); symptomatic treatment of postencephalitic parkinsonism and paralysis agitans (oral); inhibits excessive motility and hypertonus of the gastrointestinal tract in (Continued)

Scopolamine *(Continued)*

such conditions as the irritable colon syndrome, mild dysentery, diverticulitis, pylorospasm, and cardiospasm; it may also prevent motion sickness (oral)

Pregnancy Risk Factor C

Contraindications Hypersensitivity to scopolamine or any component; narrow-angle glaucoma; acute hemorrhage, gastrointestinal or genitourinary obstruction, thyrotoxicosis, tachycardia secondary to cardiac insufficiency, paralytic ileus

Warnings/Precautions Use with caution in hepatic or renal impairment since adverse CNS effects occur more often in these patients; use with caution in infants and children since they may be more susceptible to adverse effects of scopolamine; use with caution in patients with GI obstruction; anticholinergic agents are not well tolerated in the elderly and their use should be avoided when possible

Adverse Reactions

Ophthalmic:

>10%: Ocular: Blurred vision, photophobia

1% to 10%:

Ocular: Local irritation, increased intraocular pressure

Respiratory: Congestion

<1%: Vascular congestion, edema, drowsiness, eczematoid dermatitis, follicular conjunctivitis, exudate

Systemic:

>10%:

Dermatologic: Dry skin

Gastrointestinal: Constipation, xerostomia, dry throat

Local: Irritation at injection site

Respiratory: Dry nose

Miscellaneous: Diaphoresis (decreased)

1% to 10%:

Dermatologic: Increased sensitivity to light

Endocrine & metabolic: Decreased flow of breast milk

Gastrointestinal: Dysphagia

<1%: Orthostatic hypotension, ventricular fibrillation, tachycardia, palpitations, confusion, drowsiness, headache, loss of memory, ataxia, fatigue, rash, bloated feeling, nausea, vomiting, dysuria, weakness, increased intraocular pain, blurred vision

Note: Systemic adverse effects have been reported following ophthalmic administration

Overdosage/Toxicology

Symptoms of overdose include dilated pupils, flushed skin, tachycardia, hypertension, EKG abnormalities, CNS manifestations resemble acute psychosis; CNS depression, circulatory collapse, respiratory failure, and death can occur

Pure scopolamine intoxication is extremely rare. However, for a scopolamine overdose with severe life-threatening symptoms, physostigmine 1-2 mg (0.5 mg or 0.02 mg/kg for children) S.C. or I.V. slowly should be given to reverse the toxic effects.

Drug Interactions

Decreased effect of acetaminophen, levodopa, ketoconazole, digoxin, riboflavin, potassium chloride in wax matrix preparations

Increased toxicity: Additive adverse effects with other anticholinergic agents; GI absorption of the following drugs may be affected: acetaminophen, levodopa, ketoconazole, digoxin, riboflavin, potassium chloride wax-matrix preparations

Stability Avoid acid solutions, because hydrolysis occurs at pH <3; **physically compatible** when mixed in the same syringe with atropine, butorphanol, chlorpromazine, dimenhydrinate, diphenhydramine, droperidol, fentanyl, glycopyrrolate, hydromorphone, hydroxyzine, meperidine, metoclopramide, morphine, pentazocine, pentobarbital, perphenazine, prochlorperazine, promazine, promethazine, or thiopental

Mechanism of Action Blocks the action of acetylcholine at parasympathetic sites in smooth muscle, secretory glands and the CNS; increases cardiac output, dries secretions, antagonizes histamine and serotonin

Pharmacodynamics/Kinetics

Onset of effect: Oral, I.M.: 0.5-1 hour; I.V.: 10 minutes

Duration of effect: Oral, I.M.: 4-6 hours; I.V.: 2 hours

Peak effect: 20-60 minutes; it may take 3-7 days for full recovery

Absorption: Well absorbed by all routes of administration

Protein binding: Reversibly bound to plasma proteins

Metabolism: In the liver

Elimination: In urine

Usual Dosage

Preoperatively:

Children: I.M., S.C.: 6 mcg/kg/dose (maximum: 0.3 mg/dose) or 0.2 mg/m^2 may be repeated every 6-8 hours **or** alternatively:

4-7 months: 0.1 mg

7 months to 3 years: 0.15 mg

3-8 years: 0.2 mg

8-12 years: 0.3 mg

Adults:

I.M., I.V., S.C.: 0.3-0.65 mg; may be repeated every 4-6 hours

Transdermal patch: Apply 2.5 cm^2 patch to hairless area behind ear the night before surgery (the patch should be applied no sooner than 1 hour before surgery for best results)

Motion sickness: Transdermal: Children >12 years and Adults: Apply 1 disc behind the ear at least 4 hours prior to exposure and every 3 days as needed; effective if applied as soon as 2-3 hours before anticipated need, best if 12 hours before

Ophthalmic:

Refraction:

Children: Instill 1 drop of 0.25% to eye(s) twice daily for 2 days before procedure

Adults: Instill 1-2 drops of 0.25% to eye(s) 1 hour before procedure

Iridocyclitis:

Children: Instill 1 drop of 0.25% to eye(s) up to 3 times/day

Adults: Instill 1-2 drops of 0.25% to eye(s) up to 4 times/day

Oral: 0.4 to 0.8 mg as a range; the dosage may be cautiously increased in parkinsonism and spastic states.

Administration I.V.: Dilute with an equal volume of sterile water and administer by direct I.V. injection over 2-3 minutes

Patient Information Report any changes of vision; wait 5 minutes after instilling ophthalmic preparation before using any other drops, do not blink excessively, after instilling ophthalmic preparation, apply pressure to the side of the nose near the eye to minimize systemic absorption; put patch on day before traveling; once applied, do not remove the patch for 3 full days; may cause drowsiness, dizziness, and blurred vision; may impair coordination and judgment; report to physician any CNS effects; apply patch behind ear

Nursing Implications Topical disc is programmed to deliver *in vivo* 0.5 mg over 3 days; wash hands before and after applying the disc to avoid drug contact with eyes

Dosage Forms

Disc, transdermal: 1.5 mg/disc (4's)

Injection, as hydrobromide: 0.3 mg/mL (1 mL); 0.4 mg/mL (0.5 mL, 1 mL); 0.86 mg/mL (0.5 mL); 1 mg/mL (1 mL)

Solution, ophthalmic, as hydrobromide: 0.25% (5 mL, 15 mL)

Tablet: 0.4 mg

♦ **Scopolamine Hydrobromide** see Scopolamine on page 1051

♦ **Scot-Tussin®** [OTC] see Guaifenesin on page 549

♦ **Scot-Tussin® Senior Clear** [OTC] see Guaifenesin and Dextromethorphan on page 550

♦ **SeaMist®** [OTC] see Sodium Chloride on page 1067

♦ **Sebizon® Topical Lotion** see Sulfacetamide Sodium on page 1091

Secobarbital (see koe BAR bi tal)

U.S. Brand Names Seconal™ Injection

Canadian Brand Names Novo-Secobarb; Seconal™

Synonyms Quinalbarbitone Sodium; Secobarbital Sodium

Therapeutic Category Barbiturate; Hypnotic; Sedative

Use Short-term treatment of insomnia and as preanesthetic agent

Restrictions C-II

Pregnancy Risk Factor D

Contraindications CNS depression, uncontrolled pain, hypersensitivity to secobarbital or any component

Usual Dosage

Hypnotic:

Children: I.M.: 3-5 mg/kg/dose; maximum: 100 mg/dose

Adults:

I.M.: 100-200 mg/dose

I.V.: 50-250 mg/dose

Hemodialysis: Slightly dialyzable (5% to 20%)

Additional Information Complete prescribing information for this medication should be consulted for additional detail

Dosage Forms Injection, as sodium: 50 mg/mL (2 mL)

♦ **Secobarbital Sodium** see Secobarbital on this page

♦ **Seconal™** see Secobarbital on this page

♦ **Seconal™ Injection** see Secobarbital on this page

♦ **Secran®** see Vitamins, Multiple on page 1226

♦ **Sectral®** see Acebutolol on page 18

♦ **Sedapap-10®** see Butalbital Compound on page 165

♦ **Selax®** see Docusate on page 384

Selegiline (seh LEDGE ah leen)

Related Information

Parkinson's Disease, Dosing of Drugs Used for Treatment of on page 1336

Tyramine Content of Foods on page 1525

U.S. Brand Names Eldepryl®

Canadian Brand Names Apo®-Selegiline; Novo-Selegiline

Synonyms Deprenyl; L-Deprenyl; Selegiline Hydrochloride

Therapeutic Category Anti-Parkinson's Agent

Use Adjunct in the management of parkinsonian patients in which levodopa/carbidopa therapy is deteriorating

Unlabeled use: Early Parkinson's disease

Investigational: Alzheimer's disease

(Continued)

Selegiline *(Continued)*

Selegiline is also being studied in Alzheimer's disease. Small studies have shown some improvement in behavioral and cognitive performance in patients, however, further study is needed.

Pregnancy Risk Factor C

Contraindications Known hypersensitivity to selegiline, concomitant use of meperidine

Warnings/Precautions Increased risk of nonselective MAO inhibition occurs with doses >10 mg/day; is a monoamine oxidase inhibitor type "B", there should **not** be a problem with tyramine-containing products as long as the typical doses are employed

Adverse Reactions

>10%:
Central nervous system: Mood changes, dizziness
Gastrointestinal: Nausea, vomiting, xerostomia, abdominal pain
Neuromuscular & skeletal: Dyskinesias

1% to 10%:
Cardiovascular: Orthostatic hypotension, arrhythmias, hypertension
Central nervous system: Hallucinations, confusion, depression, insomnia, agitation, loss of balance
Neuromuscular & skeletal: Increased involuntary movements, bradykinesia, muscle twitches
Miscellaneous: Bruxism

Overdosage/Toxicology

Symptoms of overdose include tachycardia, palpitations, muscle twitching, seizures
Competent supportive care is the most important treatment; both hypertension or hypotension can occur with intoxication. Hypotension may respond to I.V. fluids or vasopressors, and hypertension usually responds to an alpha-adrenergic blocker. While treating the hypertension, care is warranted to avoid sudden drops in blood pressure, since this may worsen the MAO inhibitor toxicity. Muscle irritability and seizures often respond to diazepam, while hyperthermia is best treated antipyretics and cooling blankets. Cardiac arrhythmias are best treated with phenytoin or procainamide.

Drug Interactions CYP2D6 enzyme substrate

Increased toxicity: Meperidine in combination with selegiline has caused agitation, delirium, and death; it may be prudent to avoid other opioids as well; fluoxetine increases pressor effect

Mechanism of Action Potent monoamine oxidase (MAO) type-B inhibitor; MAO-B plays a major role in the metabolism of dopamine; selegiline may also increase dopaminergic activity by interfering with dopamine reuptake at the synapse

Pharmacodynamics/Kinetics

Onset of therapeutic effects: Within 1 hour
Duration: 24-72 hours
Half-life: 9 minutes
Metabolism: In the liver to amphetamine and methamphetamine

Usual Dosage Oral:

Adults: 5 mg twice daily with breakfast and lunch or 10 mg in the morning
Elderly: Initial: 5 mg in the morning, may increase to a total of 10 mg/day

Monitoring Parameters Blood pressure, symptoms of parkinsonism

Patient Information Do not exceed daily doses of 10 mg; report to physician any involuntary movements or CNS agitation; explain the tyramine reaction to patients and tell them to report severe headaches or other unusual symptoms to physician

Nursing Implications Monoamine oxidase inhibitor type "B"; there should **not** be a problem with tyramine-containing products as long as the typical doses are employed

Dosage Forms

Capsule, as hydrochloride (Eldepryl®): 5 mg
Tablet: 5 mg

♦ **Selegiline Hydrochloride** *see Selegiline on previous page*

Selenium *(se LEE nee um)*

U.S. Brand Names Sele-Pak®; Selepen®

Canadian Brand Names Versel®

Therapeutic Category Trace Element, Parenteral

Use Trace metal supplement

Pregnancy Risk Factor C

Contraindications Known hypersensitivity to selenium or any component

Adverse Reactions 1% to 10%:

Central nervous system: Lethargy
Dermatologic: Alopecia or hair discoloration
Gastrointestinal: Vomiting following long-term use on damaged skin; abdominal pain, garlic breath
Local: Irritation
Neuromuscular & skeletal: Tremor
Miscellaneous: Diaphoresis

Overdosage/Toxicology Symptoms of overdose include nausea, vomiting, diarrhea

Mechanism of Action Part of glutathione peroxidase which protects cell components from oxidative damage due to peroxidases produced in cellular metabolism

Pharmacodynamics/Kinetics Elimination: Urine, feces, lungs, skin

Usual Dosage I.V. in TPN solutions:

Children: 3 mcg/kg/day

Adults:
Metabolically stable: 20-40 mcg/day
Deficiency from prolonged TPN support: 100 mcg/day for 24 and 21 days
Dosage Forms Injection: 40 mcg/mL (10 mL, 30 mL)

Selenium Sulfide (se LEE nee um SUL fide)

U.S. Brand Names Exsel®; Head & Shoulders® Intensive Treatment [OTC]; Selsun®; Selsun Blue® [OTC]; Selsun Gold® for Women [OTC]

Therapeutic Category Antiseborrheic Agent, Topical; Shampoos

Use Treatment of itching and flaking of the scalp associated with dandruff, to control scalp seborrheic dermatitis; treatment of tinea versicolor

Pregnancy Risk Factor C

Contraindications Known hypersensitivity to selenium or any component

Warnings/Precautions Do not use on damaged skin to avoid any systemic toxicity; avoid topical use in very young children; safety of topical in infants has not been established

Adverse Reactions
>10%: Dermatologic: Unusual dryness or oiliness of scalp
1% to 10%:
Central nervous system: Lethargy
Dermatologic: Alopecia or hair discoloration
Gastrointestinal: Vomiting following long-term use on damaged skin, abdominal pain, garlic breath
Local: Irritation
Neuromuscular & skeletal: Tremor
Miscellaneous: Diaphoresis

Overdosage/Toxicology Symptoms of overdose include nausea, vomiting, diarrhea

Mechanism of Action May block the enzymes involved in growth of epithelial tissue

Pharmacodynamics/Kinetics
Absorption: Topical: Not absorbed through intact skin, but can be absorbed through damaged skin
Elimination: Urine, feces, lungs, skin

Usual Dosage Topical:
Dandruff, seborrhea: Massage 5-10 mL into wet scalp, leave on scalp 2-3 minutes, rinse thoroughly, and repeat application; shampoo twice weekly for 2 weeks initially, then use once every 1-4 weeks as indicated depending upon control
Tinea versicolor: Apply the 2.5% lotion to affected area and lather with small amounts of water; leave on skin for 10 minutes, then rinse thoroughly; apply every day for 7 days

Patient Information Topical formulations are for external use only; notify physician if condition persists or worsens; avoid contact with eyes; thoroughly rinse after application

Dosage Forms
Lotion: 2.5% (120 mL)
Shampoo: 1% (120 mL, 210 mL, 240 mL, 330 mL); 2.5% (120 mL)

♦ Sele-Pak® *see* Selenium *on previous page*

♦ Selepen® *see* Selenium *on previous page*

♦ Selsun® *see* Selenium Sulfide *on this page*

♦ Selsun Blue® [OTC] *see* Selenium Sulfide *on this page*

♦ Selsun Gold® for Women [OTC] *see* Selenium Sulfide *on this page*

♦ Semprex®-D *see* Acrivastine and Pseudoephedrine *on page 27*

♦ Sensorcaine® *see* Bupivacaine *on page 160*

♦ Sensorcaine®-MPF *see* Bupivacaine *on page 160*

♦ Septa® Topical Ointment [OTC] *see* Bacitracin, Neomycin, and Polymyxin B *on page 123*

♦ Septisol® *see* Hexachlorophene *on page 567*

♦ Septra® *see* Co-Trimoxazole *on page 299*

♦ Septra® DS *see* Co-Trimoxazole *on page 299*

♦ Ser-Ap-Es® *see* Hydralazine, Hydrochlorothiazide, and Reserpine *on page 573*

♦ Serax® *see* Oxazepam *on page 872*

♦ Serentil® *see* Mesoridazine *on page 736*

♦ Serevent® *see* Salmeterol *on page 1045*

♦ Serevent® Diskus® *see* Salmeterol *on page 1045*

Sermorelin Acetate (ser moe REL in AS e tate)

U.S. Brand Names Geref® Injection

Therapeutic Category Diagnostic Agent, Pituitary Function

Use For the evaluation of short children whose height is at least 2 standard deviations below the mean height for their chronological age and sex, presenting with low basal serum levels of IGF-1 and IGF-1-BP3. A single intravenous injection of sermorelin is indicated for evaluating the ability of the somatotroph of the pituitary gland to secrete growth hormone (GH). A normal plasma GH response demonstrates that the somatotroph is intact.
Orphan drug: Sermorelin has been designated an orphan product for use in the treatment of growth hormone deficiencies, AIDS-associated catabolism or weight loss, and as an adjunct to gonadotropin on ovulation induction.

Pregnancy Risk Factor C
(Continued)

Sermorelin Acetate *(Continued)*

Pregnancy/Breast-Feeding Implications Clinical effects on the fetus: Sermorelin has been shown to produce minor variations in fetuses of rats and rabbits when given in S.C. doses of 50, 150, and 500 mcg/kg. In the rat teratology study, external malformations (thin tail) were observed in the higher dose groups, and there was an increase in minor skeletal variants at the high dose. Some visceral malformations (hydroureter) were observed in all treatment groups, with the incidence greatest in the high-dose group. In rabbits, minor skeletal anomalies were significantly greater in the treated animals than in the controls. There are no adequate and well-controlled studies in pregnant women.

Contraindications Known hypersensitivity to sermorelin acetate, mannitol, or albumin

Warnings/Precautions Not used for the diagnosis of acromegaly; subnormal GH response may cause obesity, hyperglycemia, and elevated plasma fatty acids

Adverse Reactions 1% to 10%:
Cardiovascular: Tightness in the chest
Central nervous system: Headache
Dermatologic: Transient flushing of the face
Gastrointestinal: Nausea, vomiting
Local: Pain, redness, and/or swelling at the injection site

Overdosage/Toxicology Changes of heart rate and blood pressure have been reported with sermorelin in I.V. doses exceeding 10 mcg/kg. Cardiovascular collapse is a conceivable, but as of yet, unreported, complication of overdosage with sermorelin.

Drug Interactions The test should not be conducted in the presence of drugs that directly affect the pituitary secretion of somatotropin. These include preparations that contain or release somatostatin, insulin, glucocorticoids, or cyclo-oxygenase inhibitors such as ASA or indomethacin. Somatotropin levels may be transiently elevated by clonidine, levodopa, and insulin-induced hypoglycemia. Response to sermorelin may be blunted in patients who are receiving muscarinic antagonists (atropine) or who are hypothyroid or being treated with antithyroid medications such as propylthiouracil. Obesity, hyperglycemia, and elevated plasma fatty acids generally are associated with subnormal GH responses to sermorelin. Exogenous growth hormone therapy should be discontinued at least 1 week before administering the test.

Stability Lyophilized preparation must be stored in the refrigerator; use immediately after reconstitution; each ampul should be reconstituted with a minimum of 0.5 mL of the accompanying sterile diluent. Parenteral drug products should be inspected visually for particulate matter and discoloration prior to administration. Do not use the reconstituted solution if it appears cloudy, lumpy, or discolored.

Pharmacodynamics/Kinetics In a study of 71 children, the growth hormone peak plasma response to a bolus injection of sermorelin occurred at 30 ± 27 minutes; however, the response following subsequent injections is smaller and gradually diminishes; continuous infusion does not lead to sustained increases in growth hormone secretion

Usual Dosage I.V.: As a single dose in the morning following an overnight fast:
Children and Adults:
<50 kg: Draw venous blood samples for GH determinations 15 minutes before and immediately prior to administration, then administer 1 mcg/kg followed by a 3 mL normal saline flush, draw blood samples again for GH determinations
>50 kg: Determine the number of ampuls needed based on a dose of 1 mcg/kg, draw venous blood samples for GH determinations 15 minutes before and immediately prior to administration, then administer 1 mcg/kg followed by a 3 mL normal saline flush, draw blood samples again for GH determinations

Administration Venous blood samples for growth hormone determinations should be drawn 15 minutes before and immediately prior to sermorelin administration. Administer a bolus of 1 mcg/kg/body weight sermorelin I.V. over 1-3 minutes at a final concentration not to exceed 100 mcg/mL followed by a 3 mL normal saline flush. Draw venous blood samples for growth hormone determinations at 15, 30, 45, and 60 minutes after sermorelin administration.

Reference Range Peak growth hormone levels of >7-10 mcg/L are rarely achieved upon provocation in patients with classic growth hormone deficiency; a marked growth hormone response in these patients (>10-12 mcg/L) is strongly suggestive of hypothalamic dysfunction, as opposed to pituitary dysfunction

Test Interactions See Drug Interactions

Dosage Forms Powder for injection, lyophilized: 50 mcg

♦ **Seromycin® Pulvules®** *see* Cycloserine *on page 308*

♦ **Serophene®** *see* Clomiphene *on page 280*

♦ **Seroquel®** *see* Quetiapine *on page 1001*

♦ **Serostim® Injection** *see* Human Growth Hormone *on page 569*

♦ **Serovane™** *see* Sevoflurane *on page 1058*

♦ **Serpalan®** *see* Reserpine *on page 1016*

♦ **Serpasil®** *see* Reserpine *on page 1016*

♦ **Serpatabs®** *see* Reserpine *on page 1016*

♦ **Sertan®** *see* Primidone *on page 966*

Sertraline *(SER tra leen)*

Related Information
Antidepressant Agents Comparison *on page 1301*

U.S. Brand Names Zoloft™

Synonyms Sertraline Hydrochloride

Therapeutic Category Antidepressant, Serotonin Reuptake Inhibitor

Use Treatment of major depression; also being studied for use in obesity and obsessive-compulsive disorder

Pregnancy Risk Factor C

Contraindications Hypersensitivity to sertraline or any component

Warnings/Precautions Do not use in combination with monoamine oxidase inhibitor or within 14 days of discontinuing treatment or initiating treatment with a monoamine oxidase inhibitor due to the risk of serotonin syndrome; use with caution in patients with pre-existing seizure disorders, patients in whom weight loss is undesirable, patients with recent myocardial infarction, unstable heart disease, hepatic or renal impairment, patients taking other psychotropic medications, agitated or hyperactive patients as drug may produce or activate mania or hypomania; because the risk of suicide is inherent in depression, patient should be closely monitored until depressive symptoms remit and prescriptions should be written for minimum quantities to reduce the risk of overdose

Adverse Reactions 1% to 10%: In clinical trials, dizziness and nausea were two most frequent side effects that led to discontinuation of therapy

Cardiovascular: Palpitations

Central nervous system: Insomnia, agitation, dizziness, headache, somnolence, nervousness, fatigue, pain

Dermatologic: Dermatological reactions

Endocrine & metabolic: Sexual dysfunction in men

Gastrointestinal: Xerostomia, diarrhea or loose stools, nausea, constipation

Genitourinary: Urinary disorders

Neuromuscular & skeletal: Tremors

Ocular: Visual difficulty

Otic: Tinnitus

Miscellaneous: Diaphoresis

Overdosage/Toxicology

Symptoms of overdose include serious toxicity has not yet been reported, monitor cardiovascular, gastrointestinal, and hepatic functions

Establish and maintain an airway, ensure adequate oxygenation and ventilation. Activated charcoal with 70% sorbitol may be as or more effective than emesis or lavage. Monitoring of cardiac and vital signs is recommended along with general symptomatic and supportive measures. There is no specific antidote for sertraline. Treatment should be aimed at first decontamination, then symptomatic and supportive care; forced diuresis, dialysis, hemoperfusion and exchange transfusion are unlikely to enhance elimination due to sertraline's large volume of distribution.

Drug Interactions CYP3A3/4 enzyme substrate, CYP2D6 enzyme substrate (minor); CYP1A2 and 2D6 enzyme inhibitor (weak); CYP2C9, 2C18, 2C19 and 3A3/4 enzyme inhibitor

All serotonin reuptake inhibitors are capable of inhibiting CYP2D6 isoenzyme enzyme system. The drugs metabolized by this system include desipramine, dextromethorphan, encainide, haloperidol, imipramine, metoprolol, perphenazine, propafenone, and thioridazine

Increased toxicity:

MAO inhibitors and possibly with lithium or tricyclic antidepressants → **serotonin syndrome** serotonergic hyperstimulation with the following clinical features: mental status changes, restlessness, myoclonus, hyper-reflexia, diaphoresis, diarrhea, shivering, and tremor

May decrease metabolism/plasma clearance of some drugs (diazepam, tolbutamide) to result in increased duration and pharmacological effects

May displace highly plasma protein bound drugs from binding sites (eg, warfarin) to result in increased effect

Mechanism of Action Antidepressant with selective inhibitory effects on presynaptic serotonin (5-HT) reuptake

Pharmacodynamics/Kinetics

Absorption: Slow

Protein binding: High

Metabolism: Extensive

Half-life: Parent: 24 hours; Metabolites: 66 hours

Elimination: In both urine and feces

Usual Dosage Oral:

Adults: Start with 50 mg/day in the morning and increase by 50 mg/day increments every 2-3 days if tolerated to 100 mg/day; additional increases may be necessary; maximum dose: 200 mg/day. If somnolence is noted, administer at bedtime.

Elderly: Start treatment with 25 mg/day in the morning and increase by 25 mg/day increments every 2-3 days if tolerated to 75-100 mg/day; additional increases may be necessary; maximum dose: 200 mg/day

Hemodialysis: Not removed by hemodialysis

Dosage comments in hepatic impairment: Sertraline is extensively metabolized by the liver; caution should be used in patients with hepatic impairment

Test Interactions Minor ↑ triglycerides (S), ↑ LFTs, ↓ uric acid (S)

Patient Information If you are currently on another antidepressant drug, please notify your physician. Although sertraline has not been shown to increase the effects of alcohol, it is recommended that you refrain from drinking while on this medication. If you are pregnant or intend becoming pregnant while on this drug, please alert your physician to this fact. You may experience some weight loss, but it is usually minimal.

Dosage Forms Tablet, as hydrochloride: 25 mg, 50 mg, 100 mg

- **Sertraline Hydrochloride** *see Sertraline on page 1056*
- **Serutan®** [OTC] *see Psyllium on page 994*
- **Serzone®** *see Nefazodone on page 822*

Sevelamer (se VEL a mer)

U.S. Brand Names Renagel®

Synonyms Sevelamer Hydrochloride

Therapeutic Category Phosphate Binder

Use Reduction of serum phosphorous in patients with end-stage renal disease

Pregnancy Risk Factor C

Pregnancy/Breast-Feeding Implications It is not known whether sevelamer is excreted in human milk. Because sevelamer may cause a reduction in the absorption of some vitamins, it should be used with caution in pregnant and/or nursing women.

Contraindications Hypersensitivity to sevelamer or any component of the formulation, hypophosphatemia, or bowel obstruction

Warnings/Precautions Use with caution in patients with gastrointestinal disorders including dysphagia, swallowing disorders, severe gastrointestinal motility disorders, or major gastrointestinal surgery. May cause reductions in vitamin D, E, K, and folic acid absorption. Long-term studies of carcinogenic potential have not been completed. Capsules should not be taken apart or chewed.

Adverse Reactions

>10%:
  Cardiovascular: Hypotension (11%), thrombosis (10%)
  Central nervous system: Headache (10%)
  Endocrine and metabolic: Decreased absorption of vitamins D, E, K and folic acid
  Gastrointestinal: Diarrhea (16%), dyspepsia (5% to 11%), vomiting (12%)
  Neuromuscular and skeletal: Pain (13%)
  Miscellaneous: Infection (15%)

1% to 10%:
  Cardiovascular: Hypertension (9%)
  Gastrointestinal: Nausea (7%), flatulence (4%), diarrhea (4%), constipation (2%)
  Respiratory: Cough (4%)

Overdosage/Toxicology Sevelamer is not absorbed systemically. There are no reports of overdosage in patients.

Drug Interactions No formal drug interaction studies have been undertaken. Sevelamer may bind to some drugs in the gastrointestinal tract and decrease their absorption. When changes in absorption of oral medications may have significant clinical consequences (such as antiarrhythmic and antiseizure medications), these medications should be taken at least 1 hour before or 3 hours after a dose of sevelamer.

Stability Store at controlled room temperature

Mechanism of Action Sevelamer (a polymeric compound) binds phosphate within the intestinal lumen, limiting absorption and decreasing serum phosphate concentrations without altering calcium, aluminum, or bicarbonate concentrations

Pharmacodynamics/Kinetics
  Absorption: Not absorbed systemically
  Elimination: Feces

Usual Dosage Adults: Oral: 2-4 capsules 3 times/day with meals; the initial dose may be based on serum phosphorous:
  (Phosphorous: Initial Dose)
    >6.0 mg/dL and <7.5 mg/dL: 2 capsules 3 times/day
    >7.5 mg/dL and <9.0 mg/dL: 3 capsules 3 times/day
    ≥9.0 mg/dL: 4 capsules 3 times/day
  Dosage should be adjusted based on serum phosphorous concentration, with a goal of lowering to <6.0 mg/dL; maximum daily dose studied was 30 capsules/day.

Administration Must be administered with meals

Monitoring Parameters Serum phosphorus

Patient Information Take with meals; swallow capsule whole, do not open or chew capsules

Dosage Forms Capsule: 403 mg

- **Sevelamer Hydrochloride** *see Sevelamer on this page*

Sevoflurane (see voe FLOO rane)

U.S. Brand Names Ultane®

Canadian Brand Names Serovane™

Therapeutic Category General Anesthetic

Use General induction and maintenance of anesthesia (inhalation)

Pregnancy Risk Factor B

Contraindications Previous hypersensitivity to sevoflurane or other halogenated anesthetics

Warnings/Precautions Malignant hyperthermia has been reported in susceptible patients, due to its potential for fluoride nephropathy, renal function should be closely monitored, similar to isoflurane, sevoflurane has the potential to increase cerebral blood flow and intracranial pressure and therefore, must be used with caution in patients with pre-existing increases in CSF pressure.

Adverse Reactions >1%:
  Cardiovascular: Bradycardia, hypotension, tachycardia, hypertension

Central nervous system: Agitation, headache, somnolence, dizziness, fever, early emergence movement, hypothermia

Gastrointestinal: Nausea (25%) and vomiting (18%), increased salivation

Respiratory: Laryngospasm, airway obstruction, breath holding, increased cough, apnea

Miscellaneous: Shivering

Drug Interactions CYP2E1 enzyme substrate

Increased effect: Administration of 50% N_2O reduces the minimum alveolar concentration (MAC) equivalent dose of sevoflurane by 50% in adults and 25% in children; benzodiazepines and opioids also reduce the MAC of sevoflurane

Stability Store at controlled room temperature (15°C to 30°C); use cautiously in low-flow or closed-circuit systems, since sevoflurane is unstable potentially toxic breakdown products have been liberated

Pharmacodynamics/Kinetics Sevoflurane has a low blood/gas partition coefficient and therefore is associated with a rapid onset of anesthesia and recovery

Time to induction: Within 2 minutes

Emergence time: 4 to 14 minutes

Metabolism: In the liver to inorganic fluoride, hexafluoroisopropanol and hexafluoroisopropanol glucuronide

Usual Dosage

Induction: Usually administered in concentrations of 1.8% to 5% in N_2O/O_2. It has also been given via the vital capacity rapid inhalation technique as 4.5% in N_2O/O_2

Maintenance: Surgical levels of anesthesia can usually be obtained with concentrations of 0.75% to 3%

Monitoring Parameters Blood pressure, temperature, heart rate, neuromuscular function, oxygen saturation, end-tidal CO_2 and end-tidal sevoflurane concentrations should be monitored prior to and throughout anesthesia; the dose of sevoflurane may be adjusted by monitoring blood pressure, since the depth of anesthesia is inversely related to blood pressure in the absence of other complications

Dosage Forms Liquid for inhalation: 250 mL

Sibutramine (si BYOO tra meen)

U.S. Brand Names Meridia®

Synonyms Sibutramine Hydrochloride

Therapeutic Category Anorexiant

Use Management of obesity, including weight loss and maintenance of weight loss, and should be used in conjunction with a reduced calorie diet

Body Mass Index (BMI), kg/m²
Height (feet, inches)

Weight (lb)	5'0"	5'3"	5'6"	5'9"	6'0"	6'3"
140	27	25	23	21	19	18
150	29	27	24	22	20	19
160	31	28	26	24	22	20
170	33	30	28	25	23	21
180	35	32	29	27	25	23
190	37	34	31	28	26	24
200	39	36	32	30	27	25
210	41	37	34	31	29	26
220	43	39	36	33	30	28
230	45	41	37	34	31	29
240	47	43	39	36	33	30
250	49	44	40	37	34	31

Restrictions CIV; Recommended only for obese patients with a body mass index ≥30 kg/m² or ≥27 kg/m² in the presence of other risk factors such as hypertension, diabetes, and/or dyslipidemia

Pregnancy Risk Factor C

Contraindications During or within 2 weeks of MAO inhibitors (eg, phenelzine, selegiline) or concomitant centrally-acting appetite suppressants. Use is not recommended in patients with anorexia nervosa; uncontrolled or poorly controlled hypertension, congestive heart failure, coronary heart disease, conduction disorders (arrhythmias) or stroke.

Warnings/Precautions Use with caution in severe renal impairment or severe hepatic dysfunction, seizure disorder, hypertension, narrow-angle glaucoma, nursing mothers, elderly patients

Adverse Reactions ≥1%:

Cardiovascular: Hypertension, tachycardia, vasodilation, palpitations

Central nervous system: Insomnia, headache, migraine, dizziness, nervousness, depression, somnolence

Gastrointestinal: Xerostomia, GI upset, anorexia, constipation, increased appetite, nausea, vomiting

Ocular: Mydriasis

Overdosage/Toxicology There is no specific antidote; treatment should consist of general supportive measures employed in the management of overdosage. Cautious

(Continued)

Sibutramine *(Continued)*

use of beta-blockers to control elevated blood pressure and tachycardia may be indicated; the benefits of forced diuresis and hemodialysis remain unknown.

Drug Interactions CYP3A3/4 enzyme substrate

Caution with other CNS active agents, avoid concurrent use with other serotonergic agents such as venlafaxine, selective serotonin reuptake inhibitors (eg, fluoxetine, fluvoxamine, paroxetine, sertraline), sumatriptan, dihydroergotamine, lithium, tryptophan, some opioid/analgesics (eg, dextromethorphan, tramadol). Other drugs that can raise the blood pressure can worsen the possibility of sibutramine-associated cardiovascular complications (eg, decongestants, centrally acting weight loss products, amphetamines, and amphetamine-like compounds). Possible interaction with ketoconazole, erythromycin, and other agents metabolized by the CYP3A4 enzyme system.

Mechanism of Action Blocks the neuronal reuptake of norepinephrine and, to a lesser extent, serotonin and dopamine

Usual Dosage Adults ≥16 years: Initial: 10 mg once daily; after 4 weeks may titrate up to 15 mg once daily as needed and tolerated; doses >15 mg/day are not recommended

Dietary Considerations Avoid concurrent excess alcohol ingestion; sibutramine, as an appetite suppressant, is the most effective when combined with a low calorie diet and behavior modification counseling

Monitoring Parameters Do initial blood pressure and heart rate evaluation and then monitor regularly during therapy. If patient has sustained increases in either blood pressure or pulse rate, consider discontinuing or reducing the dose of the drug.

Patient Information Maintain proper medical follow-up and inform physician of any potential concomitant medications including over-the-counter products you are taking, especially weight loss products, antidepressants, antimigraine drugs, decongestants, lithium, tryptophan, antitussives, or ergot derivatives

Additional Information Physicians should carefully evaluate patients for history of drug abuse and follow such patients closely, observing them for signs of misuse or abuse (eg, development of tolerance, excessive increases of doses, drug seeking behavior)

Dosage Forms Capsule, as hydrochloride: 5 mg, 10 mg, 15 mg

♦ **Sibutramine Hydrochloride** *see* Sibutramine *on previous page*

♦ **Siladryl® Oral [OTC]** *see* Diphenhydramine *on page 369*

Sildenafil *(sil DEN a fil)*

U.S. Brand Names Viagra™

Therapeutic Category Infantile Spasms, Treatment

Use Treatment of erectile dysfunction

Pregnancy Risk Factor B

Contraindications In patients with a known hypersensitivity to any component of the tablet; has been shown to potentiate the hypotensive effects of nitrates, and its administration to patients who are concurrently using organic nitrates in any form is contraindicated

Warnings/Precautions There is a degree of cardiac risk associated with sexual activity; therefore, physicians may wish to consider the cardiovascular status of their patients prior to initiating any treatment for erectile dysfunction. Agents for the treatment of erectile dysfunction should be used with caution in patients with anatomical deformation of the penis (angulation, cavernosal fibrosis, or Peyronie's disease), or in patients who have conditions which may predispose them to priapism (sickle cell anemia, multiple myeloma, leukemia).

The safety and efficacy of sildenafil with other treatments for erectile dysfunction have not been studied and are, therefore, not recommended as combination therapy.

A minority of patients with retinitis pigmentosa have genetic disorders of retinal phosphodiesterases. There is no safety information on the administration of sildenafil to these patients and sildenafil should be administered with caution.

Adverse Reactions

>10%:

Central nervous system: Headache

Cardiovascular: Flushing

1% to 10%:

Central nervous system: Dizziness

Dermatologic: Rash

Gastrointestinal: Dyspepsia, diarrhea

Genitourinary: Urinary tract infection

Ocular: Abnormal vision

Respiratory: Nasal congestion

Overdosage/Toxicology In studies with healthy volunteers of single doses up to 800 mg, adverse events were similar to those seen at lower doses but incidence rates were increased

Drug Interactions CYP3A3/4 enzyme substrate (major); CYP2C9 enzyme substrate (minor)

Increased effect/toxicity: Cimetidine, erythromycin, ketoconazole, itraconazole, mibefradil

Decreased effect: Rifampin

Stability Store tables at controlled room temperature 15°C to 30°C (59°F to 86°F)

Mechanism of Action Does not directly cause penile erections, but affects the response to sexual stimulation. The physiologic mechanism of erection of the penis involves release of nitric oxide (NO) in the corpus cavernosum during sexual stimulation. NO then activates the enzyme guanylate cyclase, which results in increased levels of cyclic guanosine monophosphate (cGMP), producing smooth muscle relaxation and inflow of blood to the corpus cavernosum. Sildenafil enhances the effect of NO by inhibiting phosphodiesterase type 5 (PDE5), which is responsible for degradation of cGMP in the corpus cavernosum; when sexual stimulation causes local release of NO, inhibition of PDE5 by sildenafil causes increased levels of cGMP in the corpus cavernosum, resulting in smooth muscle relaxation and inflow of blood to the corpus cavernosum; at recommended doses, it has no effect in the absence of sexual stimulation.

Pharmacodynamics/Kinetics
Bioavailability: 40%
Protein binding: 96%
Half-life: 4 hours
Metabolism: Hepatic microsomal isoenzymes (CYP3A4 [major] and CYP2C9 [minor route])
Elimination: Feces (80%), urine (13%)

Usual Dosage Adults: Oral: For most patients, the recommended dose is 50 mg taken as needed, approximately 1 hour before sexual activity. However, sildenafil may be taken anywhere from 30 minutes to 4 hours before sexual activity. Based on effectiveness and tolerance, the dose may be increased to a maximum recommended dose of 100 mg or decreased to 25 mg. The maximum recommended dosing frequency is once daily.

Dosage adjustment for patients >65 years of age, hepatic impairment (cirrhosis), severe renal impairment (creatinine clearance <30 mL/minute), or concomitant use of potent cytochrome P-450 3A4 inhibitors (erythromycin, ketoconazole, itraconazole): Higher plasma levels have been associated which may result in increase in efficacy and adverse effects and a starting dose of 25 mg should be considered

Administration Administer 30 minutes to 4 hours before sexual activity (optimally 1 hour before)

Patient Information Discuss with your physician the contraindication of sildenafil citrate with concurrent organic nitrates. The use of sildenafil offers no protection against sexually transmitted diseases. Counseling of patients about the protective measures necessary to guard against transmitted diseases, including the human immunodeficiency virus (HIV), may be considered.

Dosage Forms Tablet, as citrate: 25 mg, 50 mg, 100 mg

◆ Silphen® Cough [OTC] *see* Diphenhydramine *on page 369*

◆ Siltussin® [OTC] *see* Guaifenesin *on page 549*

◆ Siltussin DM® [OTC] *see* Guaifenesin and Dextromethorphan *on page 550*

◆ Silvadene® *see* Silver Sulfadiazine *on next page*

Silver Nitrate (SIL ver NYE trate)

U.S. Brand Names Dey-Drop® Ophthalmic Solution

Synonyms AgNO₃

Therapeutic Category Antibiotic, Ophthalmic; Antibiotic, Topical; Cauterizing Agent, Topical; Topical Skin Product, Antibacterial

Use Prevention of gonococcal ophthalmia neonatorum; cauterization of wounds and sluggish ulcers, removal of granulation tissue and warts; aseptic prophylaxis of burns

Pregnancy Risk Factor C

Contraindications Not for use on broken skin or cuts; hypersensitivity to silver nitrate or any component

Warnings/Precautions Do not use applicator sticks on the eyes; repeated applications of the ophthalmic solution into the eye can cause cauterization of the cornea and blindness

Adverse Reactions
>10%:
Dermatologic: Burning and skin irritation
Ocular: Chemical conjunctivitis
1% to 10%:
Dermatologic: Staining of the skin
Hematologic: Methemoglobinemia
Ocular: Cauterization of the cornea, blindness

Overdosage/Toxicology
Symptoms of overdose include pain and burning of mouth, salivation, vomiting, diarrhea, shock, coma, convulsions, death; blackening of skin and mucous membranes; absorbed nitrate can cause methemoglobinemia
Fatal dose is as low as 2 g
Administer sodium chloride in water (10 g/L) to cause precipitation of silver

Drug Interactions Decreased effect: Sulfacetamide preparations are **incompatible**

Stability Must be stored in a dry place; exposure to light causes silver to oxidize and turn brown, dipping in water causes oxidized film to readily dissolve

Mechanism of Action Free silver ions precipitate bacterial proteins by combining with chloride in tissue forming silver chloride; coagulates cellular protein to form an eschar; silver ions or salts or colloidal silver preparations can inhibit the growth of both gram-positive and gram-negative bacteria. This germicidal action is attributed to the precipitation of bacterial proteins by liberated silver ions. Silver nitrate coagulates cellular protein to form an eschar, and this mode of action is the postulated mechanism for control of benign hematuria, rhinitis, and recurrent pneumothorax.
(Continued)

Silver Nitrate *(Continued)*

Pharmacodynamics/Kinetics

Absorption: Because silver ions readily combine with protein, there is minimal GI and cutaneous absorption of the 0.5% and 1% preparations

Elimination: Although the highest amounts of silver noted on autopsy have been in the kidneys, excretion in urine is minimal

Usual Dosage

Neonates: Ophthalmic: Instill 2 drops immediately after birth (no later than 1 hour after delivery) into conjunctival sac of each eye as a single dose, allow to sit for ≥30 seconds; do not irrigate eyes following instillation of eye drops

Children and Adults:

Ointment: Apply in an apertured pad on affected area or lesion for approximately 5 days

Sticks: Apply to mucous membranes and other moist skin surfaces only on area to be treated 2-3 times/week for 2-3 weeks

Topical solution: Apply a cotton applicator dipped in solution on the affected area 2-3 times/week for 2-3 weeks

Monitoring Parameters With prolonged use, monitor methemoglobin levels

Patient Information Discontinue topical preparation if redness or irritation develop

Nursing Implications Silver nitrate solutions stain skin and utensils

Additional Information Applicators are **not** for ophthalmic use

Dosage Forms

Applicator sticks: 75% with potassium nitrate 25% (6")

Ointment: 10% (30 g)

Solution:

Ophthalmic: 1% (wax ampuls)

Topical: 10% (30 mL); 25% (30 mL); 50% (30 mL)

Silver Sulfadiazine (SIL ver sul fa DYE a zeen)

Related Information

Sulfonamide Derivatives on page 1337

U.S. Brand Names Silvadene®; SSD® AF; SSD® Cream; Thermazene®

Canadian Brand Names Dermazin™; Flamazine®

Therapeutic Category Antibacterial, Topical

Use Prevention and treatment of infection in second and third degree burns

Pregnancy Risk Factor B

Contraindications Hypersensitivity to silver sulfadiazine or any component; premature infants or neonates <2 months of age because sulfonamides compete with bilirubin for protein binding sites which may displace bilirubin and cause kernicterus, pregnant women approaching or at term

Warnings/Precautions Use with caution in patients with G-6-PD deficiency, renal impairment, or history of allergy to other sulfonamides; sulfadiazine may accumulate in patients with impaired hepatic or renal function; fungal superinfection may occur; use of analgesic might be needed before application; systemic absorption is significant and adverse reactions may occur

Adverse Reactions

1% to 10%:

Dermatologic: Itching, rash, erythema multiforme, discoloration of skin

Hematologic: Hemolytic anemia, leukopenia, agranulocytosis, aplastic anemia

Hepatic: Hepatitis

Renal: Interstitial nephritis

Miscellaneous: Allergic reactions may be related to sulfa component

<1%: Photosensitivity

Drug Interactions Decreased effect: Topical proteolytic enzymes are inactivated

Stability Silvadene® cream will occasionally darken either in the jar or after application to the skin. This color change results from a light catalyzed reaction which is a common characteristic of all silver salts. A similar analogy is the oxidation of silverware. The product of this color change reaction is silver oxide which ranges in color from gray to black. Silver oxide has rarely been associated with permanent skin discoloration. Additionally, the antimicrobial activity of the product is not substantially diminished because the color change reaction involves such a small amount of the active drug and is largely a surface phenomenon.

Mechanism of Action Acts upon the bacterial cell wall and cell membrane. Bactericidal for many gram-negative and gram-positive bacteria and is effective against yeast. Active against *Pseudomonas aeruginosa, Pseudomonas maltophilia, Enterobacter* species, *Klebsiella* species, *Serratia* species, *Escherichia coli, Proteus mirabilis, Morganella morganii, Providencia rettgeri, Proteus vulgaris, Providencia* species, *Citrobacter* species, *Acinetobacter calcoaceticus, Staphylococcus aureus, Staphylococcus epidermidis, Enterococcus* species, *Candida albicans, Corynebacterium diphtheriae,* and *Clostridium perfringens*

Pharmacodynamics/Kinetics

Absorption: Significant percutaneous absorption of silver sulfadiazine can occur especially when applied to extensive burns

Half-life: 10 hours and is prolonged in patients with renal insufficiency

Time to peak serum concentration: Within 3-11 days of continuous therapy

Elimination: ~50% excreted unchanged in urine

Usual Dosage Children and Adults: Topical: Apply once or twice daily with a sterile-gloved hand; apply to a thickness of $^1/_{16}$"; burned area should be covered with cream at all times

Monitoring Parameters Serum electrolytes, urinalysis, renal function tests, CBC in patients with extensive burns on long-term treatment

Patient Information For external use only; bathe daily to aid in debridement (if not contraindicated); apply liberally to burned areas; for external use only; notify physician if condition persists or worsens

Nursing Implications Evaluate the development of granulation

Additional Information Contains methylparaben and propylene glycol

Dosage Forms Cream, topical: 1% [10 mg/g] (20 g, 50 g, 85 g, 400 g, 1000 g)

♦ Simron® [OTC] *see* Ferrous Gluconate *on page 479*

♦ Simulect® *see* Basiliximab *on page 125*

Simvastatin (SIM va stat in)

Related Information

Lipid-Lowering Agents *on page 1327*

U.S. Brand Names Zocor®

Therapeutic Category Antilipemic Agent; HMG-CoA Reductase Inhibitor

Use "Secondary prevention" in patients with coronary heart disease and hypercholesterolemia to reduce the risk of total mortality by reducing coronary death; reduce the risk of nonfatal myocardial infarction; reduce the risk of undergoing myocardial revascularization procedures; and reduce the risk of stroke or transient ischemic attack

Adjunct to diet to reduce elevated total cholesterol, LDL-cholesterol, apo-B and triglyceride levels in patients with primary hypercholesterolemia (heterozygous, familial, and nonfamilial), and mixed dyslipidemia (Fredrickson types IIa and IIb)

Pregnancy Risk Factor X

Contraindications Previous hypersensitivity to simvastatin or lovastatin or other HMG-CoA reductase inhibitors; active liver disease or unexplained elevations of serum transaminases; pregnancy and lactation

Adverse Reactions

1% to 10%:

Central nervous system: Headache (3.5%)

Gastrointestinal: Flatulence (1.9%), abdominal cramps (3.2%), diarrhea (1.9%), constipation (2.3%), nausea/vomiting (1.3%), dyspepsia/heartburn (1.1%)

Neuromuscular & skeletal: Myalgia, weakness (1.6%), increased CPK

Respiratory: Upper respiratory infection (2.1%)

<1%: Abnormal taste, lenticular opacities, blurred vision

Overdosage/Toxicology Very few adverse events; treatment is symptomatic

Drug Interactions CYP3A3/4 enzyme substrate

Increased effect of warfarin and digoxin possible with simvastatin or other HMG-CoA reductase inhibitors

Possibly increased toxicity of simvastatin with itraconazole since itraconazole increases lovastatin levels by as much as 20-fold

Concurrent use of erythromycin, gemfibrozil, cyclosporine, and niacin with HMG-CoA reductase inhibitors may result in rhabdomyolysis

Decreased antihyperlipidemic activity possible with rifampin, nicotinic acid (fluvastatin) and isradipine (lovastatin)

Stability Tablets should be stored in well closed containers at temperatures between 5°C to 30°C (41°F to 86°F)

Mechanism of Action Simvastatin is a methylated derivative of lovastatin that acts by competitively inhibiting 3-hydroxy-3-methylglutaryl-coenzyme A (HMG-CoA) reductase, the enzyme that catalyzes the rate-limiting step in cholesterol biosynthesis

Pharmacodynamics/Kinetics

Absorption: Oral: Although 85% is absorbed following administration, <5% reaches the general circulation due to an extensive first-pass effect

Time to peak concentrations: 1.3-2.4 hours

Protein binding: ~95%

Elimination: 13% excreted in urine and 60% in feces; the elimination half-life is unknown In patients with severe renal insufficiency, high systemic levels may occur

Usual Dosage Oral:

Adults:

Initial: 20 mg once daily in the evening; patients who require only a moderate reduction of LDL cholesterol may be started at 10 mg

Maintenance: Recommended dosing range: 5-80 mg/day as a single dose in the evening; doses should be individualized according to the baseline LDL-C levels, the recommended goal of therapy, and the patient's response

Adjustments: Should be made at intervals of 4 weeks or more

Patients with homozygous familial hypercholesteremia: Adults: 40 mg in the evening or 80 mg/day in 3 divided doses of 20 mg, 20 mg, and an evening dose of 40 mg

Elderly: Maximum reductions in LDL-cholesterol may be achieved with daily dose of ≤20 mg

Patients who are concomitantly receiving cyclosporine: Initial: 5 mg, should not exceed 10 mg/day

Patients receiving concomitant fibrates or niacin: Dose should **not** exceed 10 mg/day

Dosing adjustment/comments in renal impairment: Because simvastatin does not undergo significant renal excretion, modification of dose should not be necessary in patients with mild to moderate renal insufficiency

(Continued)

Simvastatin *(Continued)*

Severe renal impairment: Cl_{cr} <10 mL/minute: Initial: 5 mg/day with close monitoring

Monitoring Parameters Creatine phosphokinase levels due to possibility of myopathy; serum cholesterol (total and fractionated)

Patient Information Promptly report any unexplained muscle pain, tenderness or weakness, especially if accompanied by malaise or fever; follow prescribed diet; take with meals

Nursing Implications Liver enzyme elevations may be observed during simvastatin therapy; combination therapy with other hypolipidemic agents may be required to achieve optimal reductions of LDL cholesterol; diet, weight reduction, and exercise should be attempted to control hypercholesterolemia before the institution of simvastatin therapy

Dosage Forms Tablet: 5 mg, 10 mg, 20 mg, 40 mg, 80 mg

♦ **Sinarest® Nasal Solution [OTC]** *see* Phenylephrine *on page 918*
♦ **Sinemet®** *see* Levodopa and Carbidopa *on page 672*
♦ **Sinemet® CR** *see* Levodopa and Carbidopa *on page 672*
♦ **Sinequan® Oral** *see* Doxepin *on page 392*
♦ **Singulair®** *see* Montelukast *on page 795*
♦ **Sinubid®** *see* Phenyltoloxamine, Phenylpropanolamine, and Acetaminophen *on page 920*
♦ **Sinumist®-SR Capsulets®** *see* Guaifenesin *on page 549*
♦ **Sinupan®** *see* Guaifenesin and Phenylephrine *on page 551*
♦ **Sirdalud®** *see* Tizanidine *on page 1149*
♦ **SK and F 104864** *see* Topotecan *on page 1162*
♦ **Skelaxin®** *see* Metaxalone *on page 741*
♦ **Skelid®** *see* Tiludronate *on page 1145*
♦ **SKF 82526** *see* Fenoldopam *on page 472*
♦ **SKF 104864** *see* Topotecan *on page 1162*
♦ **SKF 104864-A** *see* Topotecan *on page 1162*

Skin Test Antigens, Multiple *(skin test AN tee gens, MUL ti pul)*

U.S. Brand Names Multitest CMI®

Therapeutic Category Diagnostic Agent, Hypersensitivity Skin Testing

Use Detection of nonresponsiveness to antigens by means of delayed hypersensitivity skin testing

Pregnancy Risk Factor C

Contraindications Infected or inflamed skin, known hypersensitivity to skin test antigens; do not apply at sites involving acneiform, infected or inflamed skin; although severe systemic reactions are rare to diphtheria and tetanus antigens, persons known to have a history of systemic reactions should be tested with this test only after the test heads containing these antigens have been removed

Warnings/Precautions Epinephrine should be available is case of severe reactions. Safety and effectiveness in children <17 years of age have not been established; discard applicator after use, do not reuse.

Adverse Reactions 1% to 10%: Local: Irritation

Drug Interactions Decreased effect: Drugs or procedures that suppress immunity such as corticosteroids, chemotherapeutic agents, antilymphocyte globulin and irradiation, may possibly cause a loss of reactivity

Stability Keep in refrigerator at 2°C to 8°C (35°F to 46°F)

Usual Dosage Select only test sites that permit sufficient surface area and subcutaneous tissue to allow adequate penetration of all eight points, avoid hairy areas. Press loaded unit into the skin with sufficient pressure to puncture the skin and allow adequate penetration of all points, maintain firm contact for at least 5 seconds, during application the device should not be "rocked" back and forth and side to side without removing any of the test heads from the skin sites.

If adequate pressure is applied it will be possible to observe:
1. The puncture marks of the nine tines on each of the eight test heads
2. An imprint of the circular platform surrounding each test head
3. Residual antigen and glycerin at each of the eight sites

If any of the above three criteria are not fully followed, the test results may not be reliable.

Reading should be done in good light, read the test sites at both 24 and 48 hours, the largest reaction recorded from the two readings at each test site should be used. If two readings are not possible, a single 48 hour is recommended. A positive reaction from any of the seven delayed hypersensitivity skin test antigens is **induration ≥2 mm** providing there is no induration at the negative control site. The size of the induration reactions with this test may be smaller than those obtained with other intradermal procedures.

Nursing Implications Patients should be informed of the types of test site reactions that may be expected. Remove tests from refrigeration approximately 1 hour before use; select only test sites that permit sufficient surface area and subcutaneous tissue to allow adequate penetration of all points on all eight test heads; avoid hairy areas when possible because interpretation of reactions will be more difficult

Additional Information Contains disposable plastic applicator consisting of eight sterile test heads preloaded with the following seven delayed hypersensitivity skin test antigens and glycerin negative control for percutaneous administration

Test Head No. 1 = Tetanus toxoid antigen

Test Head No. 2 = Diphtheria toxoid antigen
Test Head No. 3 = *Streptococcus* antigen
Test Head No. 4 = Tuberculin, old
Test Head No. 5 = Glycerin negative control
Test Head No. 6 = *Candida* antigen
Test Head No. 7 = *Trichophyton* antigen
Test Head No. 8 = *Proteus* antigen

Dosage Forms Individual carton containing one preloaded skin test antigen for cellular hypersensitivity

♦ **Skin Tests** *see page 1353*

♦ **Sleep-eze 3® Oral [OTC]** *see* Diphenhydramine *on page 369*

♦ **Sleepinal® [OTC]** *see* Diphenhydramine *on page 369*

♦ **Sleepwell 2-nite® [OTC]** *see* Diphenhydramine *on page 369*

♦ **Slim-Mint® [OTC]** *see* Benzocaine *on page 133*

♦ **Slo-bid™** *see* Theophylline Salts *on page 1125*

♦ **Slo-Niacin® [OTC]** *see* Niacin *on page 832*

♦ **Slo-Phyllin®** *see* Theophylline Salts *on page 1125*

♦ **Slo-Phyllin® GG** *see* Theophylline and Guaifenesin *on page 1125*

♦ **Slow FE® [OTC]** *see* Ferrous Sulfate *on page 480*

♦ **Slow-K®** *see* Potassium Chloride *on page 949*

♦ **Slow-Mag® (Chloride)** *see* Magnesium Salts (Other) *on page 707*

♦ **SMX-TMP** *see* Co-Trimoxazole *on page 299*

♦ **SMZ-TMP** *see* Co-Trimoxazole *on page 299*

♦ **Sodium 2-Mercaptoethane Sulfonate** *see* Mesna *on page 735*

Sodium Acetate (SOW dee um AS e tate)

Therapeutic Category Alkalinizing Agent, Parenteral; Electrolyte Supplement, Parenteral; Sodium Salt

Use Sodium source in large volume I.V. fluids to prevent or correct hyponatremia in patients with restricted intake; used to counter acidosis through conversion to bicarbonate

Pregnancy Risk Factor C

Contraindications Alkalosis, hypocalcemia, low sodium diets, edema, cirrhosis

Warnings/Precautions Avoid extravasation, use with caution in patients with hepatic failure

Adverse Reactions 1% to 10%:
Cardiovascular: Thrombosis, hypervolemia
Dermatologic: Chemical cellulitis at injection site (extravasation)
Endocrine & metabolic: Hypernatremia, dilution of serum electrolytes, overhydration, hypokalemia, metabolic alkalosis, hypocalcemia
Gastrointestinal: Gastric distension, flatulence
Local: Phlebitis
Respiratory: Pulmonary edema
Miscellaneous: Congestive conditions

Stability Protect from light, heat, and from freezing; **incompatible** with acids, acidic salts, alkaloid salts, calcium salts, catecholamines, atropine

Usual Dosage Sodium acetate is metabolized to bicarbonate on an equimolar basis outside the liver; administer in large volume I.V. fluids as a sodium source. Refer to Sodium Bicarbonate monograph.
Maintenance electrolyte requirements of sodium in parenteral nutrition solutions:
Daily requirements: 3-4 mEq/kg/24 hours or 25-40 mEq/1000 kcal/24 hours
Maximum: 100-150 mEq/24 hours

Additional Information Sodium and acetate content of 1 g: 7.3 mEq

Dosage Forms Injection: 2 mEq/mL (20 mL, 50 mL, 100 mL); 4 mEq/mL (50 mL, 100 mL)

♦ **Sodium Acid Carbonate** *see* Sodium Bicarbonate *on next page*

Sodium Ascorbate (SOW dee um a SKOR bate)

U.S. Brand Names Cenolate®

Therapeutic Category Urinary Acidifying Agent; Vitamin, Water Soluble

Use Prevention and treatment of scurvy and to acidify urine

Pregnancy Risk Factor C

Contraindications Large doses during pregnancy

Usual Dosage Oral, I.V., S.C.:
Infants:
Daily protective requirement: 30 mg
Treatment: 100-300 mg/day (75-100 mg in premature infants)
Children:
Scurvy: 100-300 mg/day in divided doses for at least 2 weeks
Urinary acidification: 500 mg every 6-8 hours
Dietary supplement: 35-45 mg/day
Adults:
Scurvy: 100-250 mg 1-2 times/day for at least 2 weeks
Urinary acidification: 4-12 g/day in divided doses
Dietary supplement: 50-60 mg/day (RDA: 60 mg)
Prevention and treatment of cold: 1-3 g/day
(Continued)

Sodium Ascorbate *(Continued)*

Additional Information Complete prescribing information for this medication should be consulted for additional detail

Dosage Forms

Crystals: 1020 mg per ¼ teaspoonful [ascorbic acid 900 mg]

Injection: 250 mg/mL [ascorbic acid 222 mg/mL] (30 mL); 562.5 mg/mL [ascorbic acid 500 mg/mL] (1 mL, 2 mL)

Tablet: 585 mg [ascorbic acid 500 mg]

Sodium Bicarbonate (SOW dee um bye KAR bun ate)

Related Information

Adult ACLS Algorithm, Asystole *on page 1449*

Adult ACLS Algorithm, Pulseless Electrical Activity *on page 1448*

Adult ACLS Algorithm, V. Fib and Pulseless V. Tach *on page 1447*

U.S. Brand Names Neut® Injection

Synonyms Baking Soda; NaHCO₃; Sodium Acid Carbonate; Sodium Hydrogen Carbonate

Therapeutic Category Alkalinizing Agent, Oral; Alkalinizing Agent, Parenteral; Antacid; Electrolyte Supplement, Oral; Electrolyte Supplement, Parenteral; Sodium Salt

Use Management of metabolic acidosis; gastric hyperacidity; as an alkalinization agent for the urine; treatment of hyperkalemia

Pregnancy Risk Factor C

Contraindications Alkalosis, hypernatremia, severe pulmonary edema, hypocalcemia, unknown abdominal pain

Warnings/Precautions Rapid administration in neonates and children <2 years of age has led to hypernatremia, decreased CSF pressure and intracranial hemorrhage. **Use of I.V. NaHCO₃ should be reserved for documented metabolic acidosis and for hyperkalemia-induced cardiac arrest.** Routine use in cardiac arrest is not recommended. Avoid extravasation, tissue necrosis can occur due to the hypertonicity of NaHCO₃. May cause sodium retention especially if renal function is impaired; not to be used in treatment of peptic ulcer; use with caution in patients with CHF, edema, cirrhosis, or renal failure. Not the antacid of choice for the elderly because of sodium content and potential for systemic alkalosis.

Adverse Reactions Percentage unknown:

Cardiovascular: Edema, cerebral hemorrhage, aggravation of congestive heart failure

Central nervous system: Tetany, intracranial acidosis

Endocrine & metabolic: Metabolic alkalosis, hypernatremia, hypokalemia, hypocalcemia, hyperosmolality

Gastrointestinal: Belching, gastric distension, flatulence (with oral)

Respiratory: Pulmonary edema

Miscellaneous: Increased affinity of hemoglobin for oxygen-reduced pH in myocardial tissue necrosis when extravasated; milk alkali syndrome (especially with renal dysfunction)

Overdosage/Toxicology

Symptoms of overdose include hypocalcemia, hypokalemia, hypernatremia, seizures

Seizures can be treated with diazepam 0.1-0.25 mg/kg; hypernatremia is resolved through the use of diuretics and free water replacement

Drug Interactions

Decreased effect/levels of lithium, chlorpropamide, methotrexate, tetracyclines, and salicylates due to urinary alkalinization

Increased toxicity/levels of amphetamines, anorexiants, mecamylamine, ephedrine, pseudoephedrine, flecainide, quinidine, quinine due to urinary alkalinization

Stability Store injection at room temperature; protect from heat and from freezing; use only clear solutions; Advise patient of milk-alkali syndrome if use is long-term; observe for extravasation when giving I.V.; **incompatible** with acids, acidic salts, alkaloid salts, atropine, calcium salts, catecholamines

Mechanism of Action Dissociates to provide bicarbonate ion which neutralizes hydrogen ion concentration and raises blood and urinary pH

Pharmacodynamics/Kinetics

Oral: Onset of action: Rapid; Duration: 8-10 minutes

I.V.: Onset of action: 15 minutes; Duration: 1-2 hours

Absorption: Oral: Well absorbed

Elimination: Reabsorbed by kidney and <1% is excreted by urine

Usual Dosage

Cardiac arrest: **Routine use of NaHCO₃ is not recommended and should be given only after adequate alveolar ventilation has been established and effective cardiac compressions are provided**

Infants and Children: I.V.: 0.5-1 mEq/kg/dose repeated every 10 minutes or as indicated by arterial blood gases; rate of infusion should not exceed 10 mEq/minute; neonates and children <2 years of age should receive 4.2% (0.5 mEq/mL) solution

Adults: I.V.: Initial: 1 mEq/kg/dose one time; maintenance: 0.5 mEq/kg/dose every 10 minutes or as indicated by arterial blood gases

Metabolic acidosis: Dosage should be based on the following formula if blood gases and pH measurements are available:

Infants and Children:

$HCO_3^-(mEq) = 0.3 \times weight (kg) \times base\ deficit (mEq/L)$ **or**

$HCO_3^-(mEq) = 0.5 \times weight (kg) \times [24 - serum\ HCO_3^- (mEq/L)]$

Adults:

$HCO_3^-(mEq) = 0.2$ x weight (kg) x base deficit (mEq/L) **or**

$HCO_3^-(mEq) = 0.5$ x weight (kg) x [24 - serum HCO_3^- (mEq/L)]

If acid-base status is not available: Dose for older Children and Adults: 2-5 mEq/kg I.V. infusion over 4-8 hours; subsequent doses should be based on patient's acid-base status

Chronic renal failure: Oral: Initiate when plasma HCO_3^- <15 mEq/L

Children: 1-3 mEq/kg/day

Adults: Start with 20-36 mEq/day in divided doses, titrate to bicarbonate level of 18-20 mEq/L

Renal tubular acidosis: Oral:

Distal:

Children: 2-3 mEq/kg/day

Adults: 0.5-2 mEq/kg/day in 4-5 divided doses

Proximal: Children: Initial: 5-10 mEq/kg/day; maintenance: Increase as required to maintain serum bicarbonate in the normal range

Urine alkalinization: Oral:

Children: 1-10 mEq (84-840 mg)/kg/day in divided doses every 4-6 hours; dose should be titrated to desired urinary pH

Adults: Initial: 48 mEq (4 g), then 12-24 mEq (1-2 g) every 4 hours; dose should be titrated to desired urinary pH; doses up to 16 g/day (200 mEq) in patients <60 years and 8 g (100 mEq) in patients >60 years

Antacid: Adults: Oral: 325 mg to 2 g 1-4 times/day

Patient Information Avoid chronic use as an antacid (<2 weeks)

Nursing Implications Advise patient of milk-alkali syndrome if use is long-term; observe for extravasation when giving I.V.

Additional Information

Sodium content of injection 50 mL, 8.4% = 1150 mg = 50 mEq; each 6 mg of $NaHCO_3$ contains 12 mEq sodium; 1 mEq $NaHCO_3$ = 84 mg

Each 84 mg of sodium bicarbonate provides 1 mEq of sodium and bicarbonate ions; each gram of sodium bicarbonate provides 12 mEq of sodium and bicarbonate ions

Dosage Forms

Injection: 4% [40 mg/mL = 2.4 mEq/5 mL] (5 mL); 4.2% [42 mg/mL = 5 mEq/10 mL] (10 mL); 7.5% [75 mg/mL = 8.92 mEq/10 mL] (10 mL, 50 mL); 8.4% [84 mg/mL = 10 mEq/10 mL] (10 mL, 50 mL)

Powder: 120 g, 480 g

Tablet: 300 mg [3.6 mEq]; 325 mg [3.8 mEq]; 520 mg [6.3 mEq]; 600 mg [7.3 mEq]; 650 mg [7.6 mEq]

Sodium Chloride (SOW dee um KLOR ide)

U.S. Brand Names Adsorbonac® Ophthalmic [OTC]; Afrin® Saline Mist [OTC]; AK-NaCl® [OTC]; Ayr® Saline [OTC]; Breathe Free® [OTC]; Dristan® Saline Spray [OTC]; HuMist® Nasal Mist [OTC]; Muro 128® Ophthalmic [OTC]; Muroptic-5® [OTC]; NāSal™ [OTC]; Nasal Moist® [OTC]; Ocean Nasal Mist [OTC]; Pretz® [OTC]; SalineX® [OTC]; SeaMist® [OTC]

Synonyms NaCl; Normal Saline; Salt

Therapeutic Category Electrolyte Supplement, Oral; Electrolyte Supplement, Parenteral; Lubricant, Ocular; Sodium Salt

Use Parenteral restoration of sodium ion in patients with restricted oral intake (especially hyponatremia states or low salt syndrome). In general, parenteral saline uses:

Normal saline: Restores water/sodium losses

Hypotonic sodium chloride: Hydrating solution

Hypertonic sodium chloride: For severe hyponatremia and hypochloremia

Bacteriostatic sodium chloride: Dilution or dissolving drugs for I.M./I.V./S.C. injections

Concentrated sodium chloride: Additive for parenteral fluid therapy

Pharmaceutical aid/diluent for infusion of compatible drug additives

Pregnancy Risk Factor C

Contraindications Hypertonic uterus, hypernatremia, fluid retention

Warnings/Precautions Use with caution in patients with congestive heart failure, renal insufficiency, liver cirrhosis, hypertension, edema; sodium toxicity is almost exclusively related to how fast a sodium deficit is corrected; both rate and magnitude are extremely important; do not use bacteriostatic sodium chloride in newborns since benzyl alcohol preservatives have been associated with toxicity

Adverse Reactions 1% to 10%:

Cardiovascular: Thrombosis, hypervolemia

Endocrine & metabolic: Hypernatremia, dilution of serum electrolytes, overhydration, hypokalemia

Local: Phlebitis

Respiratory: Pulmonary edema

Miscellaneous: Congestive conditions, extravasation

Overdosage/Toxicology

Symptoms of overdose include nausea, vomiting, diarrhea, abdominal cramps, hypocalcemia, hypokalemia, hypernatremia

Hypernatremia is resolved through the use of diuretics and free water replacement

Drug Interactions Decreased levels of lithium

Stability Store injection at room temperature; protect from heat and from freezing; use only clear solutions

Mechanism of Action Principal extracellular cation; functions in fluid and electrolyte balance, osmotic pressure control, and water distribution

(Continued)

Sodium Chloride (Continued)

Pharmacodynamics/Kinetics
Absorption: Oral, I.V.: Rapid
Distribution: Widely distributed
Elimination: Mainly in urine but also in sweat, tears, and saliva

Usual Dosage
Newborn electrolyte requirement:
  Premature: 2-8 mEq/kg/24 hours
  Term:
    0-48 hours: 0-2 mEq/kg/24 hours
    >48 hours: 1-4 mEq/kg/24 hours
  Children: I.V.: Hypertonic solutions (>0.9%) should only be used for the initial treatment of acute serious symptomatic hyponatremia; maintenance: 3-4 mEq/kg/day; maximum: 100-150 mEq/day; dosage varies widely depending on clinical condition
  Replacement: Determined by laboratory determinations mEq
    Sodium deficiency (mEq/kg) = [% dehydration (L/kg)/100 x 70 (mEq/L)] + [0.6 (L/kg) x (140 - serum sodium) (mEq/L)]
  Nasal: Use as often as needed
Adults:
  GU irrigant: 1-3 L/day by intermittent irrigation
  Heat cramps: Oral: 0.5-1 g with full glass of water, up to 4.8 g/day
  Replacement I.V.: Determined by laboratory determinations mEq
  Sodium deficiency (mEq/kg) = [% dehydration (L/kg)/100 x 70 (mEq/L)] + [0.6 (L/kg) x (140 - serum sodium) (mEq/L)]
  To correct acute, serious hyponatremia: mEq sodium = [desired sodium (mEq/L) - actual sodium (mEq/L)] x [0.6 x wt (kg)]; for acute correction use 125 mEq/L as the desired serum sodium; acutely correct serum sodium in 5 mEq/L/dose increments; more gradual correction in increments of 10 mEq/L/day is indicated in the asymptomatic patient
  Chloride maintenance electrolyte requirement in parenteral nutrition: 2-4 mEq/kg/24 hours or 25-40 mEq/1000 kcals/24 hours; maximum: 100-150 mEq/24 hours
  Sodium maintenance electrolyte requirement in parenteral nutrition: 3-4 mEq/kg/24 hours or 25-40 mEq/1000 kcals/24 hours; maximum: 100-150 mEq/24 hours. See table.

Approximate Deficits of Water and Electrolytes in Moderately Severe Dehydration

Condition	Water (mL/kg)	Sodium (mEq/kg)
Fasting and thirsting	100-120	5-7
Diarrhea		
isonatremic	100-120	8-10
hypernatremic	100-120	2-4
hyponatremic	100-120	10-12
Pyloric stenosis	100-120	8-10
Diabetic acidosis	100-120	9-10

*A negative deficit indicates total body excess prior to treatment.

Adapted from Behrman RE, Kleigman RM, Nelson WE, et al, eds, *Nelson Textbook of Pediatrics*, 14th ed, WB Saunders Co, 1992.

Ophthalmic:
  Ointment: Apply once daily or more often
  Solution: Instill 1-2 drops into affected eye(s) every 3-4 hours
Abortifacient: 20% (250 mL) administered by transabdominal intra-amniotic instillation

Monitoring Parameters Serum sodium, potassium, chloride, and bicarbonate levels; I & O, weight

Reference Range Serum/plasma sodium levels:
  Neonates:
  Full-term: 133-142 mEq/L
  Premature: 132-140 mEq/L
  Children ≥2 months to Adults: 135-145 mEq/L

Patient Information Blurred vision is common with ophthalmic ointment; may sting eyes when first applied

Nursing Implications Bacteriostatic NS should not be used for diluting or reconstituting drugs for administration in neonates; I.V. infusion of 3% or 5% sodium chloride should not exceed 100 mL/hour and should be administered in a central line only

Dosage Forms
Drops, nasal: 0.9% with dropper
Injection: 0.2% (3 mL); 0.45% (3 mL, 5 mL, 500 mL, 1000 mL); 0.9% (1 mL, 2 mL, 3 mL, 4 mL, 5 mL, 10 mL, 20 mL, 25 mL, 30 mL, 50 mL, 100 mL, 130 mL, 150 mL, 250 mL, 500 mL, 1000 mL); 3% (500 mL); 5% (500 mL); 20% (250 mL); 23.4% (30 mL, 100 mL)
Injection:
  Admixtures: 50 mEq (20 mL); 100 mEq (40 mL); 625 mEq (250 mL)
  Bacteriostatic: 0.9% (30 mL)
  Concentrated: 14.6% (20 mL, 40 mL, 200 mL); 23.4% (10 mL, 20 mL, 30 mL)

Irrigation: 0.45% (500 mL, 1000 mL, 1500 mL); 0.9% (250 mL, 500 mL, 1000 mL, 1500 mL, 2000 mL, 3000 mL, 4000 mL)

Ointment, ophthalmic: 5% (3.5 g)

Solution:

Irrigation: 0.9% (1000 mL, 2000 mL)

Nasal: 0.4% (15 mL, 50 mL); 0.6% (15 mL); 0.65% (20 mL, 45 mL, 50 mL)

Ophthalmic: 2% (15 mL); 5% (15 mL, 30 mL)

Tablet: 650 mg, 1 g, 2.25 g

Tablet:

Enteric coated: 1 g

Slow release: 600 mg

Sodium Citrate and Citric Acid (SOW dee um SIT rate & SI trik AS id)

U.S. Brand Names Bicitra®; Oracit®

Synonyms Modified Shohl's Solution

Therapeutic Category Alkalinizing Agent, Oral

Use Treatment of metabolic acidosis; alkalinizing agent in conditions where long-term maintenance of an alkaline urine is desirable

Pregnancy Risk Factor C

Contraindications Severe renal insufficiency, sodium-restricted diet

Warnings/Precautions Conversion to bicarbonate may be impaired in patients with hepatic failure, in shock, or who are severely ill

Adverse Reactions 1% to 10%:

Central nervous system: Tetany

Endocrine & metabolic: Metabolic alkalosis, hyperkalemia

Gastrointestinal: Diarrhea, nausea, vomiting

Overdosage/Toxicology

Symptoms of overdose include hypokalemia, hypernatremia, tetany, seizures

Hypernatremia is resolved through the use of diuretics and free water replacement

Drug Interactions

Decreased effect/levels of lithium, chlorpropamide, salicylates due to urinary alkalinization

Increased toxicity/levels of amphetamines, ephedrine, pseudoephedrine, flecainide, quinidine, quinine due to urinary alkalinization

Usual Dosage Oral:

Infants and Children: 2-3 mEq/kg/day in divided doses 3-4 times/day **or** 5-15 mL with water after meals and at bedtime

Adults: 15-30 mL with water after meals and at bedtime

Administration Administer after meals

Patient Information Palatability is improved by chilling solution, dilute each dose with 1-3 oz of water and follow with additional water; take after meals to prevent saline laxative effect

Nursing Implications May be ordered as modified Shohl's solution; dilute with 30-90 mL of chilled water to enhance taste

Additional Information 1 mL of Bicitra® contains 1 mEq of sodium and the equivalent of 1 mEq of bicarbonate

Dosage Forms Solution, oral:

Bicitra®: Sodium citrate 500 mg and citric acid 334 mg per 5 mL (15 mL unit dose, 480 mL)

Oracit®: Sodium citrate 490 mg and citric acid 640 mg per 5 mL

Polycitra®: Sodium citrate 500 mg and citric acid 334 mg with potassium citrate 550 mg per 5 mL

Sodium Citrate and Potassium Citrate Mixture

(SOW dee um SIT rate & poe TASS ee um SIT rate MIKS chur)

U.S. Brand Names Polycitra®

Therapeutic Category Alkalinizing Agent, Oral

Dosage Forms Syrup: Sodium citrate 500 mg, potassium citrate 550 mg, with citric acid 334 mg per 5 mL [sodium 1 mEq, potassium 1 mEq, bicarbonate 2 mEq]

♦ **Sodium Edetate** see Edetate Disodium on page 405

♦ **Sodium Etidronate** see Etidronate Disodium on page 457

♦ **Sodium Ferric Gluconate** see Ferric Gluconate on page 477

♦ **Sodium Fluoride** see Fluoride on page 498

Sodium Hyaluronate (SOW dee um hye al yoor ON ate)

U.S. Brand Names AMO Vitrax®; Amvisc®; Amvisc® Plus; Healon®; Healon® GV; Provisc®

Synonyms Hyaluronic Acid

Therapeutic Category Ophthalmic Agent, Viscoelastic

Use Surgical aid in cataract extraction, intraocular implantation, corneal transplant, glaucoma filtration, and retinal attachment surgery

Pregnancy Risk Factor C

Contraindications Hypersensitivity to hyaluronate

Warnings/Precautions Do not overfill the anterior chamber; carefully monitor intraocular pressure; risk of hypersensitivity exists

(Continued)

Sodium Hyaluronate *(Continued)*

Adverse Reactions 1% to 10%: Ocular: Postoperative inflammatory reactions (iritis, hypopyon), corneal edema, corneal decompensation, transient postoperative increase in IOP

Stability Store in refrigerator (2°C to 8°C); do not freeze

Mechanism of Action Functions as a tissue lubricant and is thought to play an important role in modulating the interactions between adjacent tissues. Sodium hyaluronate is a polysaccharide which is distributed widely in the extracellular matrix of connective tissue in man. (Vitreous and aqueous humor of the eye, synovial fluid, skin, and umbilical cord.) Sodium hyaluronate forms a viscoelastic solution in water (at physiological pH and ionic strength) which makes it suitable for aqueous and vitreous humor in ophthalmic surgery.

Pharmacodynamics/Kinetics
Absorption: Following intravitreous injection, diffusion occurs slowly
Elimination: By way of the Canal of Schlemm

Usual Dosage Depends upon procedure (slowly introduce a sufficient quantity into eye)

Monitoring Parameters Intraocular pressure

Dosage Forms Injection, intraocular:
Healon®: 10 mg/mL (0.4 mL, 0.55 mL, 0.85 mL, 2 mL)
Amvisc®: 12 mg/mL (0.5 mL, 0.8 mL)
Healon® GV: 14 mg/mL (0.55 mL, 0.85 mL)
Amvisc® Plus: 16 mg/mL (0.5 mL, 8 mL)
AMO Vitrax®: 30 mg/mL (0.65 mL)

♦ **Sodium Hyaluronate-Chrondroitin Sulfate** *see* Chondroitin Sulfate-Sodium Hyaluronate *on page 257*

♦ **Sodium Hydrogen Carbonate** *see* Sodium Bicarbonate *on page 1066*

Sodium Hypochlorite Solution
(SOW dee um hye poe KLOR ite soe LOO shun)

Synonyms Dakin's Solution; Modified Dakin's Solution

Therapeutic Category Disinfectant, Antibacterial (Topical)

Use Treatment of athlete's foot (0.5%); wound irrigation (0.5%); disinfect utensils and equipment (5%)

Pregnancy Risk Factor C

Contraindications Hypersensitivity

Warnings/Precautions For external use only; avoid eye or mucous membrane contact; do not use on open wounds

Adverse Reactions 1% to 10%:
Dermatologic: Irritating to skin
Hematologic: Dissolves blood clots, delays clotting

Stability Use prepared solution within 7 days

Usual Dosage Topical irrigation

Patient Information External use only

Nursing Implications Dakin's solution may hinder wound healing

Dosage Forms
Solution: 5% (4000 mL)
Solution (modified Dakin's solution):
Full strength: 0.5% (1000 mL)
Half strength: 0.25% (1000 mL)
Quarter strength: 0.125% (1000 mL)

♦ **Sodium L-Triiodothyronine** *see* Liothyronine *on page 683*

♦ **Sodium Methicillin** *see* Methicillin *on page 748*

♦ **Sodium Nafcillin** *see* Nafcillin *on page 810*

♦ **Sodium Nitroferricyanide** *see* Nitroprusside *on page 847*

♦ **Sodium Nitroprusside** *see* Nitroprusside *on page 847*

♦ **Sodium P.A.S.** *see* Aminosalicylate Sodium *on page 59*

Sodium Phenylacetate and Sodium Benzoate
(SOW dee um fen il AS e tate & SOW dee um BENZ oh ate)

U.S. Brand Names Ucephan®

Therapeutic Category Ammonium Detoxicant

Dosage Forms Solution: Sodium phenylacetate 100 mg and sodium benzoate 100 mg per mL (100 mL)

Sodium Phenylbutyrate (SOW dee um fen il BYOO ti rate)

U.S. Brand Names Buphenyl®

Synonyms Ammonapse

Therapeutic Category Urea Cycle Disorder (UCD) Treatment Agent

Use Adjunctive therapy in the chronic management of patients with urea cycle disorder involving deficiencies of carbamoylphosphate synthetase, ornithine transcarbamylase, or argininosuccinic acid synthetase

Contraindications Previous hypersensitivity to phenylbutyrate, severe hypertension, heart failure or renal dysfunction; phenylbutyrate is not indicated in the treatment of acute hyperammonemia

Warnings/Precautions Since no studies have been conducted in pregnant women, sodium phenylbutyrate should be used cautiously during pregnancy; each 1 gram of drug contains 125 mg of sodium and, therefore, should be used cautiously, if at all, in patients who must maintain a low sodium intake

Adverse Reactions
>10%: Endocrine & metabolic: Amenorrhea, menstrual dysfunction
1% to 10%:
Gastrointestinal: Anorexia, abnormal taste
Miscellaneous: Offensive body odor

Stability Store at room temperature (59°F to 86°F); after opening, containers should be kept tightly closed

Mechanism of Action Sodium phenylbutyrate is a prodrug that, when given orally, is rapidly converted to phenylacetate, which is in turn conjugated with glutamine to form the active compound phenylacetylglutamine; phenylacetylglutamine serves as a substitute for urea and is excreted in the urine whereby it carries with it 2 moles of nitrogen per mole of phenylacetylglutamine and can thereby assist in the clearance of nitrogenous waste in patients with urea cycle disorders

Usual Dosage
Powder: Patients weighing <20 kg: 450-600 mg/kg/day or 9.9-13 g/m^2/day, administered in equally divided amounts with each meal or feeding, four to six times daily; safety and efficacy of doses >20 g/day has not been established
Tablet: Children >20 kg and Adults: 450-600 mg/kg/day or 9.9-13 g/m^2/day, administered in equally divided amounts with each meal; safety and efficacy of doses >20 g/day have not been established

Patient Information It is important that patients understand and follow the dietary restrictions required when treating this disorder, the medication must be taken in strict accordance with the prescribed regimen and the patient should avoid altering the dosage without the prescriber's knowledge; the powder formulation has a very salty taste

Dosage Forms
Powder: 3.2 g [sodium phenylbutyrate 3 g] per teaspoon (500 mL, 950 mL); 9.1 g [sodium phenylbutyrate 8.6 g] per **tablespoon** (500 mL, 950 mL)
Tablet: 500 mg

♦ **Sodium Phosphate and Potassium Phosphate** see Potassium Phosphate and Sodium Phosphate on page 955

Sodium Polystyrene Sulfonate
(SOW dee um pol ee STYE reen SUL fon ate)

Related Information
Antacid Drug Interactions on page 1296

U.S. Brand Names Kayexalate®; SPS®

Therapeutic Category Antidote, Hyperkalemia; Antidote, Potassium

Use Treatment of hyperkalemia

Pregnancy Risk Factor C

Contraindications Hypernatremia, hypersensitivity to any component

Warnings/Precautions Use with caution in patients with severe congestive heart failure, hypertension, edema, or renal failure; avoid using the commercially available liquid product in neonates due to the preservative content; large oral doses may cause fecal impaction (especially in elderly); enema will reduce the serum potassium faster than oral administration, but the oral route will result in a greater reduction over several hours.

Adverse Reactions 1% to 10%:
Endocrine & metabolic: Hypokalemia, hypocalcemia, hypomagnesemia, sodium retention
Gastrointestinal: Fecal impaction, constipation, loss of appetite, nausea, vomiting

Overdosage/Toxicology
Symptoms of overdose include hypokalemia including cardiac dysrhythmias, confusion, irritability, EKG changes, muscle weakness, gastrointestinal effects
Treatment is supportive, limited to management of fluid and electrolytes

Drug Interactions Systemic alkalosis and seizure has occurred after cation-exchange resins were administered with nonabsorbable cation-donating antacids and laxatives (eg, magnesium hydroxide, aluminum carbonate)

Mechanism of Action Removes potassium by exchanging sodium ions for potassium ions in the intestine before the resin is passed from the body; exchange capacity is 1 mEq/g in vivo, and in vitro capacity is 3.1 mEq/g, therefore, a wide range of exchange capacity exists such that close monitoring of serum electrolytes is necessary

Pharmacodynamics/Kinetics
Onset of action: Within 2-24 hours
Absorption: Remains in GI tract
Elimination: Completely in feces (primarily as potassium polystyrene sulfonate)

Usual Dosage
Children:
Oral: 1 g/kg/dose every 6 hours
Rectal: 1 g/kg/dose every 2-6 hours (In small children and infants, employ lower doses by using the practical exchange ratio of 1 mEq K$^+$/g of resin as the basis for calculation)
Adults:
Oral: 15 g (60 mL) 1-4 times/day
Rectal: 30-50 g every 6 hours

Monitoring Parameters Serum electrolytes (potassium, sodium, calcium, magnesium), EKG

Reference Range Serum potassium: Adults: 3.5-5.2 mEq/L

(Continued)

Sodium Polystyrene Sulfonate *(Continued)*

Patient Information Mix well in full glass of liquid prior to drinking

Nursing Implications Administer oral (or NG) as ~25% sorbitol solution, never mix in orange juice; enema route is less effective than oral administration; retain enema in colon for at least 30-60 minutes and for several hours, if possible; chilling the oral mixture will increase palatability; enema should be followed by irrigation with normal saline to prevent necrosis

Additional Information 1 g of resin binds approximately 1 mEq of potassium; sodium content of 1 g: 31 mg (1.3 mEq)

Dosage Forms Oral or rectal:

Powder for suspension: 454 g

Suspension: 1.25 g/5 mL with sorbitol 33% and alcohol 0.3% (60 mL, 120 mL, 200 mL, 500 mL)

♦ **Sodium Sulamyd® Ophthalmic** *see* Sulfacetamide Sodium *on page 1091*

♦ **Sodium Sulfacetamide** *see* Sulfacetamide Sodium *on page 1091*

Sodium Tetradecyl Sulfate (SOW dee um tetra DEK il)

U.S. Brand Names Sotradecol®

Therapeutic Category Sclerosing Agent

Use Treatment of small, uncomplicated varicose veins of the lower extremities; endoscopic sclerotherapy in the management of bleeding esophageal varices

Pregnancy Risk Factor C

Contraindications Arterial disease, thrombophlebitis, hypersensitivity to sodium tetradecyl or any component, valvular or deep vein incompetence, phlebitis, migraines, cellulitis, acute infections; bedridden patients; patients with uncontrolled systemic disease such as diabetes, toxic hyperthyroidism, tuberculosis, asthma, neoplasm, sepsis, blood dyscrasias, and acute respiratory or skin diseases

Warnings/Precautions Buerger's disease, peripheral arteriosclerosis, avoid extravasation; observe for hypersensitivity/anaphylactic reaction

Adverse Reactions Percentage unknown: Headache, urticaria; sloughing and tissue necrosis following extravasation; nausea, vomiting, mucosal lesions, esophageal perforation, discoloration at the site of injection, ulceration at the site, pain at injection site, pulmonary edema, asthma

Drug Interactions Chemically **incompatible** with heparin

Stability Store at controlled room temperature in a well-closed container; protect from light

Mechanism of Action Acts by irritation of the vein intimal endothelium

Usual Dosage I.V.: Test dose: 0.5 mL given several hours prior to administration of larger dose; 0.5-2 mL in each vein, maximum: 10 mL per treatment session; 3% solution reserved for large varices

Patient Information Notify physician if chest pain, shortness of breath, or heat, pain, or tenderness in lower extremities

Nursing Implications Observe for signs and symptoms of embolism

Dosage Forms Injection: 1% [10 mg/mL] (2 mL); 3% [30 mg/mL] (2 mL)

Sodium Thiosulfate (SOW dee um thye oh SUL fate)

U.S. Brand Names Tinver® Lotion

Therapeutic Category Antidote, Arsenic Toxicity; Antidote, Cyanide; Antifungal Agent, Topical

Use

Parenteral: Used alone or with sodium nitrite or amyl nitrite in cyanide poisoning or arsenic poisoning; reduce the risk of nephrotoxicity associated with cisplatin therapy

Topical: Treatment of tinea versicolor

Pregnancy Risk Factor C

Contraindications Hypersensitivity to any component

Warnings/Precautions Safety in pregnancy has not been established; discontinue topical use if irritation or sensitivity occurs; rapid I.V. infusion has caused transient hypotension and EKG changes in dogs; can increase risk of thiocyanate intoxication

Adverse Reactions 1% to 10%:

Cardiovascular: Hypotension

Central nervous system: Coma, CNS depression secondary to thiocyanate intoxication, psychosis, confusion

Dermatologic: Contact dermatitis, local irritation

Neuromuscular & skeletal: Weakness

Otic: Tinnitus

Mechanism of Action

Cyanide toxicity: Increases the rate of detoxification of cyanide by the enzyme rhodanese by providing an extra sulfur

Cisplatin toxicity: Complexes with cisplatin to form a compound that is nontoxic to either normal or cancerous cells

Pharmacodynamics/Kinetics

Half-life: 0.65 hour

Elimination: 28.5% excreted unchanged in urine

Usual Dosage

Cyanide and nitroprusside antidote: I.V.:

Children <25 kg: 50 mg/kg after receiving 4.5-10 mg/kg sodium nitrite; a half dose of each may be repeated if necessary

Children >25 kg and Adults: 12.5 g after 300 mg of sodium nitrite; a half dose of each may be repeated if necessary

Cyanide poisoning: I.V.: Dose should be based on determination as with nitrite, at rate of 2.5-5 mL/minute to maximum of 50 mL. See table.

Variation of Sodium Nitrite and Sodium Thiosulfate Dose With Hemoglobin Concentration*

Hemoglobin (g/dL)	Initial Dose Sodium Nitrite (mg/kg)	Initial Dose Sodium Nitrite 3% (mL/kg)	Initial Dose Sodium Thiosulfate 25% (mL/kg)
7	5.8	0.19	0.95
8	6.6	0.22	1.10
9	7.5	0.25	1.25
10	8.3	0.27	1.35
11	9.1	0.30	1.50
12	10.0	0.33	1.65
13	10.8	0.36	1.80
14	11.6	0.39	1.95

*Adapted from Berlin DM Jr, "The Treatment of Cyanide Poisoning in Children," *Pediatrics*, 1970, 46:793.

Cisplatin rescue should be given before or during cisplatin administration: I.V. infusion (in sterile water): 12 g/m^2 over 6 hours or 9 g/m^2 I.V. push followed by 1.2 g/m^2 continuous infusion for 6 hours

Arsenic poisoning: I.V.: 1 mL first day, 2 mL second day, 3 mL third day, 4 mL fourth day, 5 mL on alternate days thereafter

Children and Adults: Topical: 20% to 25% solution: Apply a thin layer to affected areas twice daily

Administration I.V.: Inject slowly, over at least 10 minutes; rapid administration may cause hypotension

Monitoring Parameters Monitor for signs of thiocyanate toxicity

Patient Information Avoid topical application near the eyes, mouth, or other mucous membranes; notify physician if condition worsens or burning or irritation occurs; shake well before using

Dosage Forms
Injection: 100 mg/mL (10 mL); 250 mg/mL (50 mL)
Lotion: 25% with salicylic acid 1% and isopropyl alcohol 10% (120 mL, 180 mL)

- **Sodol®** see Carisoprodol on page 196
- **SoFlax™** see Docusate on page 384
- **Solaquin® [OTC]** see Hydroquinone on page 584
- **Solaquin Forte®** see Hydroquinone on page 584
- **Solarcaine® [OTC]** see Benzocaine on page 133
- **Solarcaine® Aloe Extra Burn Relief [OTC]** see Lidocaine on page 679
- **Solatene®** see Beta-Carotene on page 140
- **Solfoton®** see Phenobarbital on page 912
- **Solganal®** see Aurothioglucose on page 113
- **Solium®** see Chlordiazepoxide on page 239
- **Soluble Fluorescein** see Fluorescein Sodium on page 497
- **Solu-Cortef®** see Hydrocortisone on page 579
- **Solu-Medrol® Injection** see Methylprednisolone on page 762
- **Solurex L.A.®** see Dexamethasone on page 337
- **Soma®** see Carisoprodol on page 196
- **Soma® Compound** see Carisoprodol and Aspirin on page 197
- **Soma® Compound w/Codeine** see Carisoprodol, Aspirin, and Codeine on page 197
- **Somatrem** see Human Growth Hormone on page 569
- **Somatropin** see Human Growth Hormone on page 569
- **Sominex® Oral [OTC]** see Diphenhydramine on page 369
- **Somnol®** see Flurazepam on page 506
- **Som Pam®** see Flurazepam on page 506
- **Sopamycetin** see Chloramphenicol on page 238
- **Soprodol®** see Carisoprodol on page 196

Sorbitol (SOR bi tole)

Related Information
Laxatives, Classification and Properties on page 1326

Therapeutic Category Genitourinary Irrigant

Use Genitourinary irrigant in transurethral prostatic resection or other transurethral resection or other transurethral surgical procedures; diuretic; humectant; sweetening agent; hyperosmotic laxative; facilitate the passage of sodium polystyrene sulfonate through the intestinal tract

Contraindications Anuria

Warnings/Precautions Use with caution in patients with severe cardiopulmonary or renal impairment and in patients unable to metabolize sorbitol

Adverse Reactions 1% to 10%:
Cardiovascular: Edema
(Continued)

Sorbitol (Continued)

Endocrine & metabolic: Fluid and electrolyte losses, lactic acidosis

Gastrointestinal: Diarrhea, nausea, vomiting, abdominal discomfort, xerostomia

Overdosage/Toxicology

Symptoms of overdose include nausea, diarrhea, fluid and electrolyte loss

Treatment is supportive to ensure fluid and electrolyte balance

Mechanism of Action A polyalcoholic sugar with osmotic cathartic actions

Pharmacodynamics/Kinetics

Onset of action: About 0.25-1 hour

Absorption: Oral, rectal: Poor

Metabolism: Mainly in the liver to fructose

Usual Dosage Hyperosmotic laxative (as single dose, at infrequent intervals):

Children 2-11 years:

Oral: 2 mL/kg (as 70% solution)

Rectal enema: 30-60 mL as 25% to 30% solution

Children >12 years and Adults:

Oral: 30-150 mL (as 70% solution)

Rectal enema: 120 mL as 25% to 30% solution

Adjunct to sodium polystyrene sulfonate: 15 mL as 70% solution orally until diarrhea occurs (10-20 mL/2 hours) or 20-100 mL as an oral vehicle for the sodium polystyrene sulfonate resin

When administered with charcoal:

Oral:

Children: 4.3 mL/kg of 35% sorbitol with 1 g/kg of activated charcoal

Adults: 4.3 mL/kg of 70% sorbitol with 1 g/kg of activated charcoal every 4 hours until first stool containing charcoal is passed

Topical: 3% to 3.3% as transurethral surgical procedure irrigation

Nursing Implications Do not use unless solution is clear

Dosage Forms

Solution: 70%

Solution, genitourinary irrigation: 3% (1500 mL, 3000 mL); 3.3% (2000 mL)

- **Sorbitrate®** see Isosorbide Dinitrate on page 637
- **Soridol®** see Carisoprodol on page 196
- **Sotacor®** see Sotalol on this page

Sotalol (SOE ta lole)

Related Information

Antiarrhythmic Drugs Comparison on page 1297

Beta-Blockers Comparison on page 1311

U.S. Brand Names Betapace®

Canadian Brand Names Sotacor®

Synonyms Sotalol Hydrochloride

Therapeutic Category Antiarrhythmic Agent, Class III; Beta-Adrenergic Blocker

Use Treatment of documented ventricular arrhythmias, such as sustained ventricular tachycardia, that in the judgment of the physician are life-threatening

Unlabeled use: Supraventricular arrhythmias

Pregnancy Risk Factor B

Pregnancy/Breast-Feeding Implications Clinical effects on the fetus: Although there are no adequate and well controlled studies in pregnant women, sotalol has been shown to cross the placenta, and is found in amniotic fluid. There has been a report of subnormal birth weight with sotalol, therefore, sotalol should be used during pregnancy only if the potential benefit outweighs the potential risk.

Contraindications Bronchial asthma, sinus bradycardia, second and third degree A-V block (unless a functioning pacemaker is present), congenital or acquired long Q-T syndromes, cardiogenic shock, uncontrolled congestive heart failure, and previous evidence of hypersensitivity to sotalol; concurrent use with sparfloxacin

Warnings/Precautions Use with caution in patients with congestive heart failure, peripheral vascular disease, hypokalemia, hypomagnesemia, renal dysfunction, sick-sinus syndrome; abrupt withdrawal may result in return of life-threatening arrhythmias; sotalol can provoke new or worsening ventricular arrhythmias

Adverse Reactions

>10%:

Cardiovascular: Bradycardia (16%), chest pain (16%), palpitations (14%)

Central nervous system: Fatigue (20%), dizziness (20%)

Neuromuscular & skeletal: Weakness (13%)

Respiratory: Dyspnea (21%)

1% to 10%:

Cardiovascular: Congestive heart failure, reduced peripheral circulation (3%), edema (8%), abnormal EKG (7%), hypotension (6%), proarrhythmia (5%), syncope (5%)

Central nervous system: Mental confusion (6%), anxiety (4%), headache (8%), sleep problems (8%), depression (4%)

Dermatologic: Itching/rash (5%)

Endocrine & metabolic: Decreased sexual ability (3%)

Gastrointestinal: Diarrhea (7%), nausea/vomiting (10%), stomach discomfort (3% to 6%)

Hematologic: Bleeding (2%)

Neuromuscular & skeletal: Paresthesia (4%)

Ocular: Visual problems (5%)

Respiratory: Upper respiratory problems (5% to 8%), asthma (2%)

<1%: Raynaud's phenomenon, red, crusted skin, skin necrosis after extravasation; leukopenia, phlebitis, diaphoresis, cold extremities

Overdosage/Toxicology

Symptoms of intoxication include cardiac disturbances, CNS toxicity, bronchospasm, hypoglycemia and hyperkalemia. The most common cardiac symptoms include hypotension and bradycardia; atrioventricular block, intraventricular conduction disturbances, cardiogenic shock, and asystole may occur with severe overdose, especially with membrane-depressant drugs (eg, propranolol); CNS effects include convulsions, coma, and respiratory arrest is commonly seen with propranolol and other membrane-depressant and lipid-soluble drugs.

Treatment includes symptomatic treatment of seizures, hypotension, hyperkalemia and hypoglycemia; bradycardia and hypotension resistant to atropine, isoproterenol or pacing may respond to glucagon; wide QRS defects caused by the membrane-depressant poisoning may respond to hypertonic sodium bicarbonate; repeat-dose charcoal, hemoperfusion, or hemodialysis may be helpful in removal of only those beta-blockers with a small V_d, long half-life or low intrinsic clearance (acebutolol, atenolol, nadolol, sotalol)

Drug Interactions

Decreased effect of beta-blockers with aluminum salts, barbiturates, calcium salts, cholestyramine, colestipol, NSAIDs, penicillins (ampicillin), rifampin, salicylates and sulfinpyrazone due to decreased bioavailability and plasma levels

Beta-blockers may decrease the effect of sulfonylureas and beta agonists

Increased effect/toxicity of beta-blockers with calcium blockers (diltiazem, felodipine, nicardipine), contraceptives, flecainide, quinidine (in extensive metabolizers), ciprofloxacin

Beta-blockers may increase the effect/toxicity of digoxin, flecainide, and other antiarrhythmics (especially class Ia), haloperidol, phenothiazines, acetaminophen, clonidine (hypertensive crisis after or during withdrawal of either agent), epinephrine (initial hypertensive episode followed by bradycardia), nifedipine and verapamil, lidocaine, ergots (peripheral ischemia), prazosin (postural hypotension), and catecholamine-depleting agents (reserpine and guanethidine)

Beta-blockers may affect the action or levels of ethanol, disopyramide, nondepolarizing muscle relaxants and theophylline although the effects are difficult to predict

Avoid use of sotalol with sparfloxacin, terfenadine, and astemizole since risk of cardiotoxicity may be increased

Mechanism of Action

Beta-blocker which contains both beta-adrenoreceptor-blocking (Vaughan Williams Class II) and cardiac action potential duration prolongation (Vaughan Williams Class III) properties

Class II effects: Increased sinus cycle length, slowed heart rate, decreased A-V nodal conduction, and increased A-V nodal refractoriness

Class III effects: Prolongation of the atrial and ventricular monophasic action potentials, and effective refractory prolongation of atrial muscle, ventricular muscle, and atrioventricular accessory pathways in both the antegrade and retrograde directions

Sotalol is a racemic mixture of d- and l-sotalol; both isomers have similar Class III antiarrhythmic effects while the l-isomer is responsible for virtually all of the beta-blocking activity

Sotalol has both beta$_1$- and beta$_2$-receptor blocking activity

The beta-blocking effect of sotalol is a noncardioselective [half maximal at about 80 mg/day and maximal at doses of 320-640 mg/day]. Significant beta-blockade occurs at oral doses as low as 25 mg/day.

The Class III effects are seen only at oral doses ≥160 mg/day

Pharmacodynamics/Kinetics

Onset of action: Rapid, 1-2 hours

Peak effect: 2.5-4 hours

Absorption: Decreased 20% to 30% by meals compared to fasting

Bioavailability: 90% to 100%

Distribution: Low lipid solubility; sotalol is excreted in the milk of laboratory animals and is reported to be present in human milk

Metabolism: Sotalol is **not** metabolized

Protein binding: Not protein bound

Half-life: 12 hours

Elimination: Unchanged through kidney

Serum concentrations have not been systematically evaluated: Concentration-effect curves for the beta-blocking and antiarrhythmic agents of sotalol are different

Serum levels of 340-3,440 ng/mL have shown a 70% to 100% reduction in PVBs

Average serum concentrations associated with significant Q-T prolongation were 2,550 ng/mL

Average serum concentrations associated with maximum heart reduction by 50% was 804 ng/mL

Usual Dosage Sotalol should be initiated and doses increased in a hospital with facilities for cardiac rhythm monitoring and assessment. Proarrhythmic events can occur after initiation of therapy and with each upward dosage adjustment.

Children: Oral: The safety and efficacy of sotalol in children have not been established Supraventricular arrhythmias: 2-4 mg/kg/24 hours was given in 2 equal doses every 12 hours to 18 infants (≤2 months of age). All infants, except one with chaotic atrial tachycardia, were successfully controlled with sotalol. Ten infants discontinued (Continued)

Sotalol *(Continued)*

therapy between the ages of 7-18 months when it was no longer necessary. Median duration of treatment was 12.8 months.

Adults: Oral:

Initial: 80 mg twice daily

Dose may be increased (gradually allowing 2-3 days between dosing increments in order to attain steady-state plasma concentrations and to allow monitoring of Q-T intervals) to 240-320 mg/day

Most patients respond to a total daily dose of 160-320 mg/day in 2-3 divided doses

Some patients, with life-threatening refractory ventricular arrhythmias, may require doses as high as 480-640 mg/day; however, these doses should only be prescribed when the potential benefit outweighs the increased of adverse events

Elderly patients: Age does not significantly alter the pharmacokinetics of sotalol, but impaired renal function in elderly patients can increase the terminal half-life, resulting in increased drug accumulation

Dosing adjustment in renal impairment:

Cl_{cr} >60 mL/minute: Administer every 12 hours

Cl_{cr} 30-60 mL/minute: Administer every 24 hours

Cl_{cr} 10-30 mL/minute: Administer every 36-48 hours

Cl_{cr} <10 mL/minute: Individualize dose

Dialysis: Hemodialysis would be expected to reduce sotalol plasma concentrations because sotalol is not bound to plasma proteins and does not undergo extensive metabolism; administer dose postdialysis or administer supplemental 80 mg dose; peritoneal dialysis does not remove sotalol; supplemental dose is not necessary

Monitoring Parameters Serum magnesium, potassium, EKG

Patient Information Seek emergency help if palpitations occur; do not discontinue abruptly or change dose without notifying physician; take on an empty stomach

Nursing Implications Initiation of therapy and dose escalation should be done in a hospital with cardiac monitoring; lidocaine and other resuscitative measures should be available

Dosage Forms Tablet, as hydrochloride: 80 mg, 120 mg, 160 mg, 240 mg

- ◆ **Sotalol Hydrochloride** *see* Sotalol *on page 1074*
- ◆ **Sotradecol®** *see* Sodium Tetradecyl Sulfate *on page 1072*
- ◆ **Soyacal®** *see* Fat Emulsion *on page 469*
- ◆ **SPA** *see* Albumin *on page 34*
- ◆ **Spancap® No. 1** *see* Dextroamphetamine *on page 342*
- ◆ **Span-FF® [OTC]** *see* Ferrous Fumarate *on page 478*

Sparfloxacin *(spar FLOKS a sin)*

Related Information

Antimicrobial Drugs of Choice *on page 1404*

Community-Acquired Pneumonia in Adults *on page 1419*

U.S. Brand Names Zagam®

Therapeutic Category Antibiotic, Quinolone

Use Treatment of adults with community-acquired pneumonia caused by *C. pneumoniae, H. influenzae, H. parainfluenza, M. catarrhalis, M. pneumoniae* or *S. pneumoniae*; treatment of acute bacterial exacerbations of chronic bronchitis caused by *C. pneumoniae, E. cloacae, H. influenzae, H. parainfluenza, K. pneumoniae, M. catarrhalis, S. aureus* or *S. pneumoniae*

Pregnancy Risk Factor C

Pregnancy/Breast-Feeding Implications

Clinical effects on the fetus: Avoid use in pregnant women unless the benefit justifies the potential risk to the fetus

Breast-feeding/lactation: Quinolones are known to distribute well into breast milk; consequently use during lactation should be avoided if possible

Contraindications Hypersensitivity to sparfloxacin, any component, or other quinolones; a concurrent administration with drugs which increase the Q-T interval including: amiodarone, bepridil, bretylium, disopyramide, furosemide, procainamide, quinidine, sotalol, albuterol, astemizole, chloroquine, cisapride, halofantrine, phenothiazines, prednisone, terfenadine, and tricyclic antidepressants

Warnings/Precautions Not recommended in children <18 years of age, other quinolones have caused transient arthropathy in children; CNS stimulation may occur (tremor, restlessness, confusion, and very rarely hallucinations or seizures); use with caution in patients with known or suspected CNS disorder or renal dysfunction; prolonged use may result in superinfection; if an allergic reaction (itching, urticaria, dyspnea, pharyngeal or facial edema, loss of consciousness, tingling, cardiovascular collapse) occurs, discontinue the drug immediately; use caution to avoid possible photosensitivity reactions during and for several days following fluoroquinolone therapy; pseudomembranous colitis may occur and should be considered in patients who present with diarrhea

Adverse Reactions

>1%:

Central nervous system: Insomnia, agitation, sleep disorders, anxiety, delirium

Gastrointestinal: Diarrhea, abdominal pain, vomiting

Hematologic: Leukopenia, eosinophilia, anemia

Hepatic: Increased LFTs

<1%: Photosensitivity, rash, myalgia, arthralgia

Overdosage/Toxicology
Symptoms of overdose include acute renal failure, seizures
GI decontamination and supportive care; not removed by peritoneal or hemodialysis

Drug Interactions
Decreased effect: Decreased absorption with antacids containing aluminum, magnesium, and/or calcium and by products containing zinc and iron salts when administered concurrently; phenytoin serum levels may be reduced by quinolones; antineoplastic agents may also decrease serum levels of fluoroquinolones

Increased toxicity/serum levels: Quinolones cause increased levels of caffeine, warfarin, cyclosporine, and theophylline (although one study indicates that sparfloxacin may not affect theophylline metabolism), cimetidine and probenecid increase quinolone levels; an increased incidence of seizures may occur with foscarnet. Avoid use with drugs which increase Q-T interval as significant risk of cardiotoxicity may occur

Mechanism of Action Inhibits DNA-gyrase in susceptible organisms; inhibits relaxation of supercoiled DNA and promotes breakage of double-stranded DNA

Pharmacodynamics/Kinetics
Absorption: Oral absorption is unaffected by food or milk but can be reduced by approximately 50% by concurrent administration of aluminum- and magnesium-containing antacids

Distribution: Widely distributed throughout the body

Metabolism: Sparfloxacin is metabolized in the liver, but does not utilize the cytochrome P-450 system

Half-life: Mean terminal half-life: 20 hours (range: 16-30 hours)

Elimination: Equally excreted in both the urine and feces; ~10% of an oral dose is excreted unchanged in the urine

Usual Dosage Adults: Oral:
Loading dose: 2 tablets (400 mg) on day 1
Maintenance: 1 tablet (200 mg) daily for 10 days total therapy (total 11 tablets)
Dosing adjustment in renal impairment: Cl_{cr} <50 mL/minute: Administer 400 mg on day 1, then 200 mg every 48 hours for a total of 9 days of therapy (total 6 tablets)

Monitoring Parameters Evaluation of organ system functions (renal, hepatic, ophthalmologic, and hematopoietic) is recommended periodically during therapy; the possibility of crystalluria should be assessed; WBC and signs and symptoms of infection

Patient Information May take with or without food; drink with plenty of fluids; avoid exposure to direct sunlight during therapy and for several days following; do not take antacids within 4 hours before or 2 hours after dosing; contact your physician immediately if signs of allergy occur; do not discontinue therapy until your course has been completed; take a missed dose as soon as possible, unless it is almost time for your next dose

Dosage Forms Tablet: 200 mg

♦ **Sparine®** see Promazine on page 977

♦ **Spaslin®** see Hyoscyamine, Atropine, Scopolamine, and Phenobarbital on page 592

♦ **Spasmolin®** see Hyoscyamine, Atropine, Scopolamine, and Phenobarbital on page 592

♦ **Spasmophen®** see Hyoscyamine, Atropine, Scopolamine, and Phenobarbital on page 592

♦ **Spasquid®** see Hyoscyamine, Atropine, Scopolamine, and Phenobarbital on page 592

♦ **Spec-T® [OTC]** see Benzocaine on page 133

♦ **Spectam®** see Spectinomycin on this page

♦ **Spectazole™ Topical** see Econazole on page 403

Spectinomycin (spek ti noe MYE sin)

Related Information
Antimicrobial Drugs of Choice on page 1404
Treatment of Sexually Transmitted Diseases on page 1429

U.S. Brand Names Spectam®; Trobicin®

Synonyms Spectinomycin Hydrochloride

Therapeutic Category Antibiotic, Miscellaneous

Use Treatment of uncomplicated gonorrhea

Pregnancy Risk Factor B

Contraindications Hypersensitivity to spectinomycin or any component

Adverse Reactions <1%: Dizziness, headache, chills, urticaria, rash, pruritus, nausea, vomiting, pain at injection site

Overdosage/Toxicology Symptoms of overdose include paresthesia, dizziness, blurring of vision, ototoxicity, renal damage, nausea, sleeplessness, decrease in hemoglobin

Stability Use reconstituted solutions within 24 hours; reconstitute with supplied diluent only

Mechanism of Action A bacteriostatic antibiotic that selectively binds to the 30s subunits of ribosomes, and thereby inhibiting bacterial protein synthesis

Pharmacodynamics/Kinetics
Absorption: I.M.: Rapid and almost completely
Distribution: Concentrates in urine; does not distribute well into the saliva
Half-life: 1.7 hours
Elimination: Excreted almost entirely as unchanged drug in urine (70% to 100%)

Usual Dosage I.M.:
Children:
<45 kg: 40 mg/kg/dose 1 time (ceftriaxone preferred)
≥45 kg: See adult dose
(Continued)

Spectinomycin *(Continued)*

Children >8 years who are allergic to PCNS/cephalosporins may be treated with oral tetracycline

Adults:

Uncomplicated urethral endocervical or rectal gonorrhea: 2 g deep I.M. or 4 g where antibiotic resistance is prevalent 1 time; 4 g (10 mL) dose should be given as two 5 mL injections, followed by doxycycline 100 mg twice daily for 7 days

Disseminated gonococcal infection: 2 g every 12 hours

Dosing adjustment in renal impairment: None necessary

Hemodialysis: 50% removed by hemodialysis

Administration For I.M. use only

Dosage Forms Powder for injection: 2 g, 4 g

- **Spectinomycin Hydrochloride** *see Spectinomycin on previous page*
- **Spectrobid®** *see Bacampicillin on page 121*

Spironolactone *(speer on oh LAK tone)*

Related Information

Heart Failure: Management of Patients With Left-Ventricular Systolic Dysfunction *on page 1472*

U.S. Brand Names Aldactone®

Canadian Brand Names Novo-Spiroton

Therapeutic Category Antihypertensive Agent; Diuretic, Potassium Sparing

Use Management of edema associated with excessive aldosterone excretion; hypertension; primary hyperaldosteronism; hypokalemia; treatment of hirsutism; cirrhosis of liver accompanied by edema or ascites

Pregnancy Risk Factor D

Pregnancy/Breast-Feeding Implications

Clinical effects on the fetus: No data available on crossing the placenta. 1 report of oral cleft. Generally, use of diuretics during pregnancy is avoided due to risk of decreased placental perfusion.

Breast-feeding/lactation: Crosses into breast milk. American Academy of Pediatrics considers **compatible** with breast-feeding.

Contraindications Hypersensitivity to spironolactone or any components, hyperkalemia, renal failure, anuria, patients receiving other potassium-sparing diuretics or potassium supplements

Warnings/Precautions Use with caution in patients with dehydration, hepatic disease, hyponatremia, renal sufficiency; it is recommended the drug may be discontinued several days prior to adrenal vein catheterization; shown to be tumorigenic in toxicity studies using rats at 25-250 times the usual human dose

Adverse Reactions

Cardiovascular: Arrhythmia

Central nervous system: Confusion, nervousness, dizziness, drowsiness, lack of energy, unusual fatigue, headache, fever, chills, ataxia

Dermatologic: Skin rash

Endocrine & metabolic: Hyperkalemia, breast tenderness in females, deepening of voice in females, enlargement of breast in males, inability to achieve or maintain an erection, increased hair growth in females, decreased sexual ability, menstrual changes

Gastrointestinal: Diarrhea, nausea, vomiting, stomach cramps, dryness of mouth

Genitourinary: Painful urination, dysuria

Neuromuscular & skeletal: Weakness, numbness or paresthesia in hands, feet, or lips; lower back or side pain

Respiratory: Shortness of breath, dyspnea, cough or hoarseness

Miscellaneous: Increased thirst, diaphoresis

Overdosage/Toxicology

Symptoms of overdose include drowsiness, confusion, clinical signs of dehydration and electrolyte imbalance, hyperkalemia; ingestion of large amounts of potassium-sparing diuretics, may result in life-threatening hyperkalemia.

This can be treated with I.V. glucose, with concurrent regular insulin; sodium bicarbonate may also be used as a temporary measure. If needed, Kayexalate® oral or rectal solutions in sorbitol may also be used.

Drug Interactions

Decreased effect: Effects of anticoagulants may be decreased; diuretic effect of spironolactone may be decreased by salicylates

Increased toxicity: Potassium, potassium-sparing diuretics (eg, triamterene), indomethacin, angiotensin-converting enzymes inhibitors may increase serum potassium levels

Variable effects of digoxin have occurred with concurrent dosing

Stability Protect from light

Mechanism of Action Competes with aldosterone for receptor sites in the distal renal tubules, increasing sodium chloride and water excretion while conserving potassium and hydrogen ions; may block the effect of aldosterone on arteriolar smooth muscle as well

Pharmacodynamics/Kinetics

Protein binding: 91% to 98%

Metabolism: In the liver to multiple metabolites, including canrenone (active)

Half-life: 78-84 minutes

Time to peak serum concentration: Within 1-3 hours (primarily as the active metabolite)

Elimination: Urinary and biliary excretion

Usual Dosage Administration with food increases absorption. To reduce delay in onset of effect, a loading dose of 2 or 3 times the daily dose may be administered on the first day of therapy. Oral:

Neonates: Diuretic: 1-3 mg/kg/day divided every 12-24 hours

Children:

Diuretic, hypertension: 1.5-3.5 mg/kg/day **or** 60 mg/m²/day in divided doses every 6-24 hours

Diagnosis of primary aldosteronism: 125-375 mg/m²/day in divided doses

Vaso-occlusive disease: 7.5 mg/kg/day in divided doses twice daily (not FDA approved)

Adults:

Edema, hypertension, hypokalemia: 25-200 mg/day in 1-2 divided doses

Diagnosis of primary aldosteronism: 100-400 mg/day in 1-2 divided doses

Hirsutism in women: 50-200 mg/day in 1-2 divided doses

Elderly: Initial: 25-50 mg/day in 1-2 divided doses, increasing by 25-50 mg every 5 days as needed

Dosing interval in renal impairment:

Cl_{cr} 10-50 mL/minute: Administer every 12-24 hours

Cl_{cr} <10 mL/minute: Avoid use

Monitoring Parameters Blood pressure, serum electrolytes (potassium, sodium), renal function, I & O ratios and daily weight throughout therapy

Test Interactions May cause false elevation in serum digoxin concentrations measured by RIA

Patient Information Avoid hazardous activity such as driving, until response to drug is known; take with meals or milk; avoid excessive ingestion of foods high in potassium or use of salt substitutes

Nursing Implications Diuretic effect may be delayed 2-3 days and maximum hypertensive may be delayed 2-3 weeks; monitor I & O ratios and daily weight throughout therapy

Dosage Forms Tablet: 25 mg, 50 mg, 100 mg

Extemporaneous Preparations A 5 mg/mL suspension may be made by crushing tablets, levigating with a small amount of distilled water or glycerin; dilute with 1 part Cologel® and 2 parts simple syrup and/or cherry syrup to make the final concentration; spironolactone 5 mg/mL plus hydrochlorothiazide 5 mg/mL were found stable for 60 days in refrigerator in a 1:1 preparation in Ora-Sweet®/Ora-Plus®, in Ora-Sweet® SF/Ora-Plus®, and in cherry syrup

A 1 mg/mL suspension may be compounded by crushing ten 25 mg tablets, add a small amount of water and soak for 5 minutes; add 50 mL 1.5% carboxymethylcellulose, 100 mL syrup NF, and mix; use a sufficient quantity of purified water to a total volume of 250 mL; stable at room temperature or refrigerated for 3 months

Allen LV and Erickson III MA, "Stability of Labetalol Hydrochloride, Metoprolol Tartrate, Verapamil Hydrochloride, and Spironolactone With Hydrochlorothiazide in Extemporaneously Compounded Oral Liquids," *Am J Health Syst Pharm*, 1996, 53:2304-9.

Handbook on Extemporaneous Formulations, Bethesda, MD: American Society of Hospital Pharmacists, 1987.

Nahata MC, Morosco RS, and Hipple TF, "Stability of Spironolactone in an Extemporaneously Prepared Suspension at Two Temperatures," *Ann Pharmacother*, 1993, 27:1198-9.

Stanozolol (stan OH zoe lole)

U.S. Brand Names Winstrol®

Therapeutic Category Anabolic Steroid; Androgen

Use Prophylactic use against hereditary angioedema

Restrictions C-III

Pregnancy Risk Factor X

Contraindications Nephrosis, carcinoma of breast or prostate, pregnancy, hypersensitivity to any component

Warnings/Precautions May stunt bone growth in children; anabolic steroids may cause peliosis hepatis, liver cell tumors, and blood lipid changes with increased risk of arteriosclerosis; monitor diabetic patients carefully; use with caution in elderly patients, they may be at greater risk for prostatic hypertrophy; use with caution in patients with cardiac, renal, or hepatic disease or epilepsy

(Continued)

Stanozolol *(Continued)*

Adverse Reactions

Male:

Postpubertal:

>10%:

Dermatologic: Acne

Endocrine & metabolic: Gynecomastia

Genitourinary: Bladder irritability, priapism

1% to 10%:

Central nervous system: Insomnia, chills

Endocrine & metabolic: Decreased libido, hepatic dysfunction

Gastrointestinal: Nausea, diarrhea

Genitourinary: Prostatic hypertrophy (elderly)

Hematologic: Iron deficiency anemia, suppression of clotting factors

<1%: Hepatic necrosis, hepatocellular carcinoma

Prepubertal:

>10%:

Dermatologic: Acne

Endocrine & metabolic: Virilism

1% to 10%:

Central nervous system: Chills, insomnia, factors

Dermatologic: Hyperpigmentation

Gastrointestinal: Diarrhea, nausea

Hematologic: Iron deficiency anemia, suppression of clotting

<1%: Hepatic necrosis, hepatocellular carcinoma

Female:

>10%: Endocrine & metabolic: Virilism

1% to 10%:

Central nervous system: Chills, insomnia

Endocrine & metabolic: Hypercalcemia

Gastrointestinal: Nausea, diarrhea

Hematologic: Iron deficiency anemia, suppression of clotting factors

Hepatic: Hepatic dysfunction

<1%: Hepatic necrosis, hepatocellular carcinoma

Drug Interactions Increased toxicity: ACTH, adrenal steroids may increase risk of edema and acne; stanozolol enhances the hypoprothrombinemic effects of oral anticoagulants; enhances the hypoglycemic effects of insulin and sulfonylureas (oral hypoglycemics)

Mechanism of Action Synthetic testosterone derivative with similar androgenic and anabolic actions

Pharmacodynamics/Kinetics

Metabolism: In an analogous fashion to testosterone

Elimination: In an analogous fashion to testosterone

Usual Dosage

Children: Acute attacks:

<6 years: 1 mg/day

6-12 years: 2 mg/day

Adults: Oral: Initial: 2 mg 3 times/day, may then reduce to a maintenance dose of 2 mg/day or 2 mg every other day after 1-3 months

Dosing adjustment in hepatic impairment: Stanozolol is **not** recommended for patients with severe liver dysfunction

Patient Information High protein, high caloric diet is suggested, restrict salt intake; glucose tolerance may be altered in diabetics

Dosage Forms Tablet: 2 mg

♦ **Staphcillin**® *see* Methicillin *on page 748*

♦ **Statex**® *see* Morphine Sulfate *on page 797*

Stavudine *(STAV yoo deen)*

Related Information

Antiretroviral Agents *on page 1306*

Antiretroviral Therapy for HIV Infection *on page 1410*

U.S. Brand Names Zerit®

Synonyms d4T

Therapeutic Category Antiretroviral Agent, Reverse Transcriptase Inhibitor; Reverse Transcriptase Inhibitor

Use Treatment of adults with HIV infection in combination with other antiretroviral agents

Pregnancy Risk Factor C

Pregnancy/Breast-Feeding Implications

Clinical effects on the fetus: Administer during pregnancy only if benefits to mother outweigh risks to the fetus

Breast-feeding/lactation: HIV-infected mothers are discouraged from breast-feeding to decrease potential transmission of HIV

Contraindications Hypersensitivity to stavudine

Warnings/Precautions Use with caution in patients who demonstrate previous hypersensitivity to zidovudine, didanosine, zalcitabine, pre-existing bone marrow suppression, renal insufficiency, or peripheral neuropathy. Peripheral neuropathy may be the dose-limiting side effect. Zidovudine should not be used in combination with stavudine. Potentially fatal lactic acidosis and hepatomegaly have been reported, use with caution in patients at risk of hepatic disease

Adverse Reactions All adverse reactions reported below were similar to comparative agent, zidovudine, except for peripheral neuropathy, which was greater for stavudine.

>10%:
   Central nervous system: Headache, chills/fever, malaise, insomnia, anxiety, depression, pain
   Dermatologic: Rash
   Gastrointestinal: Nausea, vomiting, diarrhea, pancreatitis, abdominal pain
   Neuromuscular & skeletal: Peripheral neuropathy (15% to 21%)
1% to 10%:
   Hematologic: Neutropenia, thrombocytopenia
   Hepatic: Increased hepatic transaminases, increased bilirubin
   Neuromuscular & skeletal: Myalgia, back pain, weakness
<1%: Lactic acidosis, hepatomegaly, hepatic failure, anemia, pancreatitis

Mechanism of Action Stavudine is a thymidine analog which interferes with HIV viral DNA dependent DNA polymerase resulting in inhibition of viral replication; nucleoside reverse transcriptase inhibitor

Pharmacodynamics/Kinetics
Distribution: V_d: 0.5 L/kg
Peak serum level: 1 hour after administration
Bioavailability: 86.4%
Half-life: 1-1.6 hours
Elimination: Renal (40%)

Usual Dosage Oral:
Children: 2 mg/kg/day
Adults:
   ≥60 kg: 40 mg every 12 hours
   <60 kg: 30 mg every 12 hours
   Dose may be cut in half if symptoms of peripheral neuropathy occur
Dosing adjustment in renal impairment:
   Cl_{cr} >50 mL/minute:
      ≥60 kg: 40 mg every 12 hours
      <60 kg: 30 mg every 12 hours
   Cl_{cr} 26-50 mL/minute:
      ≥60 kg: 20 mg every 12 hours
      <60 kg: 15 mg every 12 hours
   Hemodialysis:
      ≥60 kg: 20 mg every 24 hours
      <60 kg: 15 mg every 24 hours

Monitoring Parameters Monitor liver function tests and signs and symptoms of peripheral neuropathy; monitor viral load and CD4 count

Patient Information Contact physician at first signs or symptoms of peripheral neuropathy

Additional Information Potential compliance problems, frequency of administration and adverse effects should be discussed with patients before initiating therapy to help prevent the emergence of resistance.

Dosage Forms
Capsule: 15 mg, 20 mg, 30 mg, 40 mg
Powder for oral solution: 1 mg/mL (200 mL)

♦ **S-T Cort®** see Hydrocortisone on page 579
♦ **Stelazine®** see Trifluoperazine on page 1180
♦ **Stemetil®** see Prochlorperazine on page 973
♦ **Sterapred®** see Prednisone on page 963
♦ **Stieva-A®** see Tretinoin, Topical on page 1173
♦ **Stieva-A® Forte** see Tretinoin, Topical on page 1173
♦ **Stilbestrol** see Diethylstilbestrol on page 355
♦ **Stilphostrol®** see Diethylstilbestrol on page 355
♦ **Stimate® Nasal** see Desmopressin Acetate on page 334
♦ **St Joseph® Adult Chewable Aspirin [OTC]** see Aspirin on page 102
♦ **St. Joseph® Measured Dose Nasal Solution [OTC]** see Phenylephrine on page 918
♦ **Stop® [OTC]** see Fluoride on page 498
♦ **Streptase®** see Streptokinase on this page

Streptokinase (strep toe KYE nase)

U.S. Brand Names Kabikinase®; Streptase®
Therapeutic Category Thrombolytic Agent
Use Thrombolytic agent used in treatment of recent severe or massive deep vein thrombosis, pulmonary emboli, myocardial infarction, and occluded arteriovenous cannulas
Pregnancy Risk Factor C
Contraindications Hypersensitivity to streptokinase or any component; recent streptococcal infection within the last 6 months; any internal bleeding; brain carcinoma; pregnancy; cerebrovascular accident or transient ischemic attack, gastrointestinal bleeding, trauma or surgery, prolonged external cardiac massage, intracranial or intraspinal surgery or trauma within 1 month; arteriovenous malformation or aneurysm; bleeding diathesis; severe hepatic or renal disease; subacute bacterial endocarditis; pericarditis; (Continued)

Streptokinase *(Continued)*

hemostatic defects; suspected aortic dissection, severe uncontrolled hypertension (BP systolic ≥180 mm Hg, BP diastolic ≥110 mm Hg)

Warnings/Precautions Avoid I.M. injections; use with caution in patients with a history of cardiac arrhythmias, major surgery within last 10 days, GI bleeding, recent trauma, or severe hypertension; antibodies to streptokinase remain for 3-6 months after initial dose, use another thrombolytic enzyme (ie, alteplase) if thrombolytic therapy is indicated in patients with prior streptokinase therapy

Adverse Reactions

>10%:

    Cardiovascular: Hypotension, arrhythmias, trauma arrhythmias

    Dermatologic: Angioneurotic edema

    Hematologic: Surface bleeding, internal bleeding, cerebral hemorrhage

    Ocular: Periorbital swelling

    Respiratory: Bronchospasm

<1%: Flushing, headache, chills, fever, rash, itching, nausea, vomiting, anemia, musculoskeletal pain, eye hemorrhage, epistaxis, diaphoresis, anaphylaxis

Overdosage/Toxicology

Symptoms of overdose include epistaxis, bleeding gums, hematoma, spontaneous ecchymoses, oozing at catheter site

If uncontrollable bleeding occurs, discontinue infusion; whole blood or blood products may be used to reverse bleeding

Drug Interactions

Decreased effect: Antifibrinolytic agents (aminocaproic acid) may decrease effectiveness

Increased toxicity: Anticoagulants, antiplatelet agents may increase risk of bleeding

Stability Streptokinase, a white lyophilized powder, may have a slight yellow color in solution due to the presence of albumin; intact vials should be stored at room temperature; reconstituted solutions should be refrigerated and are stable for 24 hours

Stability of parenteral admixture at room temperature (25°C): 8 hours; at refrigeration (4°C): 24 hours

Mechanism of Action Activates the conversion of plasminogen to plasmin by forming a complex, exposing plasminogen-activating site, and cleaving a peptide bond that converts plasminogen to plasmin; plasmin degrades fibrin, fibrinogen and other procoagulant proteins into soluble fragments; effective both outside and within the formed thrombus/embolus

Pharmacodynamics/Kinetics

Onset of action: Activation of plasminogen occurs almost immediately

Duration: Fibrinolytic effects last only a few hours, while anticoagulant effects can persist for 12-24 hours

Half-life: 83 minutes

Elimination: By circulating antibodies and via the reticuloendothelial system

Usual Dosage I.V.:

Children: Safety and efficacy not established; limited studies have used 3500-4000 units/kg over 30 minutes followed by 1000-1500 units/kg/hour

    Clotted catheter: 25,000 units, clamp for 2 hours then aspirate contents and flush with normal saline

Adults: Antibodies to streptokinase remain for at least 3-6 months after initial dose; Administration requires the use of an infusion pump

    An intradermal skin test of 100 units has been suggested to predict allergic response to streptokinase. If a positive reaction is not seen after 15-20 minutes, a therapeutic dose may be administered.

Guidelines for acute myocardial infarction (AMI): 1.5 million units over 60 minutes

Administration:

    Dilute two 750,000 unit vials of streptokinase with 5 mL dextrose 5% in water (D$_5$W) each, gently swirl to dissolve

    Add this dose of the 1.5 million units to 150 mL D$_5$W

    This should be infused over 60 minutes; an in-line filter ≥0.45 micron should be used

    Monitor for the first few hours for signs of anaphylaxis or allergic reaction. **Infusion should be slowed if lowering of 25 mm Hg in blood pressure or terminated if asthmatic symptoms appear.**

    Begin heparin 5000-10,000 unit bolus followed by 1000 units/hour approximately 3-4 hours after completion of streptokinase infusion or when PTT is <100 seconds

Guidelines for acute pulmonary embolism (APE): 3 million unit dose over 24 hours

Administration:

    Dilute four 750,000 unit vials of streptokinase with 5 mL dextrose 5% in water (D$_5$W) each, gently swirl to dissolve

    Add this dose of 3 million units to 250 mL D$_5$W, an in-line filter ≥0.45 micron should be used

    Administer 250,000 units (23 mL) over 30 minutes followed by 100,000 units/hour (9 mL/hour) for 24 hours

    Monitor for the first few hours for signs of anaphylaxis or allergic reaction. **Infusion should be slowed if blood pressure is lowered by 25 mm Hg or if asthmatic symptoms appear.**

    Begin heparin 1000 units/hour about 3-4 hours after completion of streptokinase infusion or when PTT is <100 seconds

    Monitor PT, PTT, and fibrinogen levels during therapy

    Thromboses: 250,000 units to start, then 100,000 units/hour for 24-72 hours depending on location

Cannula occlusion: 250,000 units into cannula, clamp for 2 hours, then aspirate contents and flush with normal saline

Administration Avoid I.M. injections

Monitoring Parameters Blood pressure, PT, APTT, platelet count, hematocrit, fibrinogen concentration, signs of bleeding

Reference Range

Partial thromboplastin time (PTT) activated: 20.4-33.2 seconds

Prothrombin time (PT): 10.9-13.7 seconds (same as control)

Fibrinogen: 200-400 mg/dL

Nursing Implications For I.V. or intracoronary use only; monitor for bleeding every 15 minutes for the first hour of therapy; do not mix with other drugs

Dosage Forms Powder for injection: 250,000 units (5 mL, 6.5 mL); 600,000 units (5 mL); 750,000 units (6 mL, 6.5 mL); 1,500,000 units (6.5 mL, 10 mL, 50 mL)

Streptomycin (strep toe MYE sin)

Related Information

Antimicrobial Drugs of Choice *on page 1404*

Tuberculosis Treatment Guidelines *on page 1432*

Therapeutic Category Antibiotic, Aminoglycoside; Antitubercular Agent

Use Part of combination therapy of active tuberculosis; used in combination with other agents for treatment of streptococcal or enterococcal endocarditis, mycobacterial infections, plague, tularemia, and brucellosis

Pregnancy Risk Factor D

Contraindications Hypersensitivity to streptomycin or any component

Warnings/Precautions Use with caution in patients with pre-existing vertigo, tinnitus, hearing loss, neuromuscular disorders, or renal impairment; modify dosage in patients with renal impairment; aminoglycosides are associated with significant nephrotoxicity or ototoxicity; the ototoxicity is directly proportional to the amount of drug given and the duration of treatment; tinnitus or vertigo are indications of vestibular injury and impending bilateral irreversible damage; renal damage is usually reversible

Adverse Reactions

1% to 10%:

Central nervous system: Neurotoxicity

Renal: Nephrotoxicity

Otic: Ototoxicity (auditory), ototoxicity (vestibular)

<1%: Skin rash, drug fever, headache, paresthesia, tremor, nausea, vomiting, eosinophilia, arthralgia, anemia, hypotension, difficulty in breathing, drowsiness, weakness

Overdosage/Toxicology

Symptoms of overdose include ototoxicity, nephrotoxicity, and neuromuscular toxicity

The treatment of choice following a single acute overdose appears to be the maintenance of good urine output of at least 3 mL/kg/hour. Dialysis is of questionable value in the enhancement of aminoglycoside elimination. If required, hemodialysis is preferred over peritoneal dialysis in patients with normal renal function. Careful hydration may be all that is required to promote diuresis and therefore the enhancement of the drug's elimination.

Drug Interactions

Increased/prolonged effect: Depolarizing and nondepolarizing neuromuscular blocking agents

Increased toxicity: Concurrent use of amphotericin may increase nephrotoxicity

Stability Depending upon manufacturer, reconstituted solution remains stable for 2-4 weeks when refrigerated; exposure to light causes darkening of solution without apparent loss of potency

Mechanism of Action Inhibits bacterial protein synthesis by binding directly to the 30S ribosomal subunits causing faulty peptide sequence to form in the protein chain

Pharmacodynamics/Kinetics

Absorption: I.M.: Absorbed well

Distribution: To extracellular fluid including serum, abscesses, ascitic, pericardial, pleural, synovial, lymphatic, and peritoneal fluids; crosses the placenta; small amounts appear in breast milk

Half-life: Newborns: 4-10 hours; Adults: 2-4.7 hours and is prolonged with renal impairment

Elimination: Almost completely (90%) excreted as unchanged drug in urine, with small amounts (1%) excreted in bile, saliva, sweat, and tears

Usual Dosage

Children:

Daily therapy: 20-30 mg/kg/day (maximum: 1 g/day)

Directly observed therapy (DOT): Twice weekly: 25-30 mg/kg (maximum: 1.5 g)

DOT: 3 times/week: 25-30 mg/kg (maximum: 1 g)

Adults:

Daily therapy: 15 mg/kg/day (maximum: 1 g)

Directly observed therapy (DOT): Twice weekly: 25-30 mg/kg (maximum: 1.5 g)

DOT: 3 times/week: 25-30 mg/kg (maximum: 1 g)

Enterococcal endocarditis: 1 g every 12 hours for 2 weeks, 500 mg every 12 hours for 4 weeks in combination with penicillin

Streptococcal endocarditis: 1 g every 12 hours for 1 week, 500 mg every 12 hours for 1 week

Tularemia: 1-2 g/day in divided doses for 7-10 days or until patient is afebrile for 5-7 days

Plague: 2-4 g/day in divided doses until the patient is afebrile for at least 3 days

(Continued)

Streptomycin *(Continued)*

Elderly: 10 mg/kg/day, not to exceed 750 mg/day; dosing interval should be adjusted for renal function; some authors suggest not to give more than 5 days/week or give as 20-25 mg/kg/dose twice weekly

Dosing interval in renal impairment:
Cl_{cr} 10-50 mL/minute: Administer every 24-72 hours
Cl_{cr} <10 mL/minute: Administer every 72-96 hours
Removed by hemo and peritoneal dialysis: Administer dose postdialysis

Administration Inject deep I.M. into large muscle mass; may be administered I.V. over 30-60 minutes

Monitoring Parameters Hearing (audiogram), BUN, creatinine; serum concentration of the drug should be monitored in all patients; eighth cranial nerve damage is usually preceded by high-pitched tinnitus, roaring noises, sense of fullness in ears, or impaired hearing and may persist for weeks after drug is discontinued

Reference Range Therapeutic: Peak: 20-30 µg/mL; Trough: <5 µg/mL; Toxic: Peak: >50 µg/mL; Trough: >10 µg/mL

Test Interactions False-positive urine glucose with Benedict's solution or Clinitest®; penicillin may decrease aminoglycoside serum concentrations *in vitro*

Patient Information Report any unusual symptom of hearing loss, dizziness, roaring noises, or fullness in ears

Additional Information Due to the critical supply of streptomycin, the drug is being released on a per patient basis at no cost; patient specific information will be required to obtain the drug from Pfizer Inc. For more information, call 1-800-254-4445.

Dosage Forms Injection, as sulfate: 400 mg/mL (2.5 mL)

Streptozocin *(strep toe ZOE sin)*

Related Information

Cancer Chemotherapy Regimens *on page 1263*
Toxicities of Chemotherapeutic Agents *on page 1288*

U.S. Brand Names Zanosar®

Therapeutic Category Antineoplastic Agent, Alkylating Agent; Vesicant

Use Treat metastatic islet cell carcinoma of the pancreas, carcinoid tumor and syndrome, Hodgkin's disease, palliative treatment of colorectal cancer

Pregnancy Risk Factor C

Warnings/Precautions The U.S. Food and Drug Administration (FDA) currently recommends that procedures for proper handling and disposal of antineoplastic agents be considered. Renal toxicity is dose-related and cumulative and may be severe or fatal; other major toxicities include liver dysfunction, diarrhea, nausea and vomiting. There may be an acute release of insulin during treatment. Keep syringe of $D_{50}W$ at bedside during administration.

Adverse Reactions

>10%:

Gastrointestinal: Nausea and vomiting in all patients usually 1-4 hours after infusion; diarrhea in 10% of patients; increased LFTs and hypoalbuminemia
Emetic potential: High (>90%)
Time course of nausea/vomiting: Onset 1-3 hours; Duration: 1-12 hours
Renal: Renal dysfunction occurs in 65% of patients; proteinuria, decreased Cl_{cr}, increased BUN, hypophosphatemia, and renal tubular acidosis; use caution with patients on other nephrotoxic agents; nephrotoxicity (25% to 75% of patients)

1% to 10%:

Gastrointestinal: Diarrhea
Endocrine & metabolic: Hypoglycemia: Seen in 6% of patients; may be prevented with the administration of nicotinamide
Local: Pain at injection site

<1%: Confusion, lethargy, depression, leukopenia, thrombocytopenia, liver dysfunction, secondary malignancy

Myelosuppressive:

WBC: Mild
Platelets: Mild
Onset (days): 7
Nadir (days): 14
Recovery (days): 21

Overdosage/Toxicology

Symptoms of overdose include bone marrow suppression, nausea, vomiting
Treatment of bone marrow suppression is supportive

Drug Interactions

Decreased effect: Phenytoin results in negation of streptozocin cytotoxicity
Increased toxicity: Doxorubicin prolongs half-life and thus prolonged leukopenia and thrombocytopenia

Stability

Store intact vials under refrigeration; vials are stable for one year at room temperature
Dilute powder with 9.5 mL SWI or NS to a concentration of 100 mg/mL which is stable for 48 hours at room temperature and 96 hours under refrigeration
Further dilution in D_5W or NS is stable for 48 hours at room temperature and 96 hours under refrigeration when protected from light

Standard I.V. dilution: IVPB: Dose/100-250 mL D_5W or NS
Solution is stable for 48 hours at room temperature and 96 hours under refrigeration when protected from light

Mechanism of Action Interferes with the normal function of DNA by alkylation and cross-linking the strands of DNA, and by possible protein modification

Pharmacodynamics/Kinetics

Distribution: Concentrates in the liver, intestine, pancreas, and kidney

Metabolism: Rapidly metabolized and disappears from serum in 4 hours

Half-life: 35-40 minutes

Elimination: Majority (60% to 70%) excreted in the urine as metabolites, and smaller amounts eliminated in bile (1%) and in expired air (5%)

Usual Dosage I.V. (refer to individual protocols):

Children and Adults:

Single agent therapy: 1-1.5 g/m^2 weekly for 6 weeks followed by a 4-week observation period

Combination therapy: 0.5-1 g/m^2 for 5 consecutive days followed by a 4- to 6-week observation period

Dosing adjustment in renal impairment:

Cl_{cr} 10-50 mL/minute: Administer 75% of dose

Cl_{cr} <10 mL/minute: Administer 50% of dose

Hemodialysis: Unknown

CAPD effects: Unknown

CAVH effects: Unknown

Dosing adjustment in hepatic impairment: Dose should be decreased in patients with severe liver disease

Administration

Administer by slow I.V. infusion over 15 minutes to 6 hours

Avoid extravasation

Monitoring Parameters Monitor renal function closely

Patient Information Avoid aspirin; use electric shaver; any signs of infection, easy bruising or bleeding, shortness of breath, or painful or burning urination should be brought to physician's attention. Nausea, vomiting or hair loss sometimes occur. The drug may cause permanent sterility and may cause birth defects. The drug may be excreted in breast milk, therefore, an alternative form of feeding your baby should be used.

Nursing Implications Wear gloves when preparing and administering; avoid extravasation

Dosage Forms Injection: 1 g

♦ **Stresstabs® 600 Advanced Formula Tablets [OTC]** *see* Vitamins, Multiple *on page 1226*

♦ **Stromectol®** *see* Ivermectin *on page 644*

♦ **Strong Iodine Solution** *see* Potassium Iodide *on page 952*

Strontium-89 (STRON shee um atey nine)

U.S. Brand Names Metastron®

Synonyms Strontium-89 Chloride

Therapeutic Category Radiopharmaceutical

Use Relief of bone pain in patients with skeletal metastases

Pregnancy Risk Factor D

Contraindications Patients with a history of hypersensitivity to any strontium-containing compounds, or any other component; pregnancy, lactation

Warnings/Precautions Use caution in patients with bone marrow compromise; incontinent patients may require urinary catheterization. Body fluids may remain radioactive up to one week after injection. Not indicated for use in patients with cancer not involving bone and should be used with caution in patients whose platelet counts fall <60,000 or whose white blood cell counts fall <2400. A small number of patients have experienced a transient increase in bone pain at 36-72 hours postdose; this reaction is generally mild and self-limiting. It should be handled cautiously, in a similar manner to other radioactive drugs. Appropriate safety measures to minimize radiation to personnel should be instituted.

Adverse Reactions Most severe reactions of marrow toxicity can be managed by conventional means

Percentage unknown:

Cardiovascular: Flushing (most common after rapid injection)

Central nervous system: Fever and chills (rare)

Hematologic: Thrombocytopenia, leukopenia

Neuromuscular & skeletal: An increase in bone pain may occur (10% to 20% of patients)

Stability Store vial and its contents inside its transportation container at room temperature

Usual Dosage Adults: I.V.: 148 megabecquerel (4 millicurie) administered by slow I.V. injection over 1-2 minutes or 1.5-2.2 megabecquerel (40-60 microcurie)/kg; repeated doses are generally not recommended at intervals <90 days; measure the patient dose by a suitable radioactivity calibration system immediately prior to administration

Monitoring Parameters Routine blood tests

Patient Information Eat and drink normally, there is no need to avoid alcohol or caffeine unless already advised to do so; may be advised to take analgesics until Metastron® begins to become effective; the effect lasts for several months, if pain returns before that, notify medical personnel

Nursing Implications During the first week after injection, strontium-89 will be present in the blood and urine, therefore, the following common sense precautions should be instituted:

(Continued)

Strontium-89 *(Continued)*

1. Where a normal toilet is available, use in preference to a urinal, flush the toilet twice
2. Wipe away any spilled urine with a tissue and flush it away
3. Have patient wash hands after using the toilet
4. Immediately wash any linen or clothes that become stained with blood or urine
5. Wash away any spilled blood if a cut occurs

Dosage Forms Injection, as chloride: 10.9-22.6 mg/mL [148 megabecquerel, 4 millicurie] (10 mL)

+ **Strontium-89 Chloride** *see Strontium-89 on previous page*
+ **Stuartnatal® 1 + 1** *see Vitamins, Multiple on page 1226*
+ **Stuart Prenatal® [OTC]** *see Vitamins, Multiple on page 1226*
+ **Sublimaze® Injection** *see Fentanyl on page 474*

Succimer *(SUKS i mer)*

U.S. Brand Names Chemet®

Therapeutic Category Antidote, Lead Toxicity; Chelating Agent, Oral

Use Treatment of lead poisoning in children with blood levels >45 µg/dL. It is not indicated for prophylaxis of lead poisoning in a lead-containing environment. Following oral administration, succimer is generally well tolerated and produces a linear dose-dependent reduction in serum lead concentrations. This agent appears to offer advantages over existing lead chelating agents.

Pregnancy Risk Factor C

Contraindications Known hypersensitivity to succimer

Warnings/Precautions Caution in patients with renal or hepatic impairment; adequate hydration should be maintained during therapy

Adverse Reactions

>10%:
    Central nervous system: Fever
    Gastrointestinal: Nausea, vomiting, diarrhea, appetite loss, hemorrhoidal symptoms, metallic taste
    Neuromuscular & skeletal: Back pain

1% to 10%:
    Central nervous system: Drowsiness, dizziness
    Dermatologic: Rash
    Endocrine & metabolic: Serum cholesterol
    Gastrointestinal: Sore throat
    Hepatic: Elevated AST/ALT, alkaline phosphatase
    Respiratory: Nasal congestion, cough
    Miscellaneous: Flu-like symptoms

<1%: Arrhythmias

Overdosage/Toxicology Symptoms of overdose include anorexia, vomiting, nephritis, hepatotoxicity, renal tubular necrosis, GI bleeding

Drug Interactions Not recommended for concomitant administration with edetate calcium disodium or penicillamine

Mechanism of Action Succimer is an analog of dimercaprol. It forms water soluble chelates with heavy metals which are subsequently excreted renally. Initial data have shown encouraging results in the treatment of mercury and arsenic poisoning. Succimer binds heavy metals; however, the chemical form of these chelates is not known.

Pharmacodynamics/Kinetics

Absorption: Rapid but incomplete
Metabolism: Rapidly and extensively to mixed succimer cysteine disulfides
Half-life, elimination: 2 days
Time to peak serum concentration: ~1-2 hours
Elimination: ~25% in urine with peak urinary excretion occurring between 2-4 hours after dosing; of the total amount of succimer eliminated in urine, 90% is eliminated as mixed succimer-cysteine disulfide conjugates; 10% is excreted unchanged; fecal excretion of succimer probably represents unabsorbed drug

Usual Dosage Children and Adults: Oral: 10 mg/kg/dose every 8 hours for an additional 5 days followed by 10 mg/kg/dose every 12 hours for 14 days

    Dosing adjustment in renal/hepatic impairment: Administer with caution and monitor closely

    Concomitant iron therapy has been reported in a small number of children without the formation of a toxic complex with iron (as seen with dimercaprol); courses of therapy may be repeated if indicated by weekly monitoring of blood lead levels; lead levels should be stabilized <15 µg/dL; 2 weeks between courses is recommended unless more timely treatment is indicated by lead levels

Monitoring Parameters Blood lead levels, serum aminotransferases

Test Interactions False-positive ketones (U) using nitroprusside methods, falsely elevated serum CPK; falsely decreased uric acid measurement

Patient Information Maintain adequate fluid intake; notify physician if rash occurs; capsules may be opened and contents sprinkled on food or put on a spoon

Nursing Implications Adequately hydrate patients; rapid rebound of serum lead levels can occur; monitor closely

Dosage Forms Capsule: 100 mg

Succinylcholine (suks in il KOE leen)

Related Information
Neuromuscular Blocking Agents Comparison *on page 1331*

U.S. Brand Names Anectine® Chloride Injection; Anectine® Flo-Pack®; Quelicin® Injection

Synonyms Succinylcholine Chloride; Suxamethonium Chloride

Therapeutic Category Cholinergic Agent; Neuromuscular Blocker Agent, Depolarizing; Skeletal Muscle Relaxant

Use Produces skeletal muscle relaxation in procedures of short duration such as endotracheal intubation or endoscopic exams

Pregnancy Risk Factor C

Contraindications Malignant hyperthermia, myopathies associated with elevated serum creatine phosphokinase (CPK) values, narrow-angle glaucoma, hyperkalemia, penetrating eye injuries, disorders of plasma pseudocholinesterase, hypersensitivity to succinylcholine or any component

Warnings/Precautions Use in pediatrics and adolescents; use with caution in patients with pre-existing hyperkalemia, paraplegia, extensive or severe burns, extensive denervation of skeletal muscle because of disease or injury to the CNS or with degenerative or dystrophic neuromuscular disease; may increase vagal tone

Adverse Reactions
>10%:
  Ocular: Increased intraocular pressure
  Miscellaneous: Postoperative stiffness
1% to 10%:
  Cardiovascular: Bradycardia, hypotension, cardiac arrhythmias, tachycardia
  Gastrointestinal: Intragastric pressure, salivation
<1%: Hypertension, rash, itching, erythema, hyperkalemia, myalgia, myoglobinuria, apnea, bronchospasm, circulatory collapse, malignant hyperthermia

Causes of prolonged neuromuscular blockade:
  Excessive drug administration
  Cumulative drug effect, decreased metabolism/excretion (hepatic and/or renal impairment)
  Accumulation of active metabolites
  Electrolyte imbalance (hypokalemia, hypocalcemia, hypermagnesemia, hypernatremia)
  Hypothermia
  Drug interactions
  Increased sensitivity to muscle relaxants (eg, neuromuscular disorders such as myasthenia gravis or polymyositis)

Overdosage/Toxicology
Symptoms of overdose include respiratory paralysis, cardiac arrest
Bradyarrhythmias can often be treated with atropine 0.1 mg (infants); do not treat with anticholinesterase drugs (eg, neostigmine, physostigmine) since this may worsen its toxicity by interfering with its metabolism

Drug Interactions
Increased toxicity: Anticholinesterase drugs (neostigmine, physostigmine, or pyridostigmine) in combination with succinylcholine can cause cardiorespiratory collapse; cyclophosphamide, oral contraceptives, lidocaine, thiotepa, pancuronium, lithium, magnesium salts, aprotinin, chloroquine, metoclopramide, terbutaline, and procaine enhance and prolong the effects of succinylcholine

Prolonged neuromuscular blockade:
  Inhaled anesthetics
  Local anesthetics
  Calcium channel blockers
  Antiarrhythmics (eg, quinidine or procainamide)
  Antibiotics (eg, aminoglycosides, tetracyclines, vancomycin, clindamycin)
  Immunosuppressants (eg, cyclosporine)

Stability
Refrigerate (2°C to 8°C/36°F to 46°F); however, remains stable for 14 days unrefrigerated; powder form does not require refrigeration
Stability of parenteral admixture at refrigeration temperature (4°C): 24 hours in D_5W or NS

I.V. form is **incompatible** when mixed with sodium bicarbonate, pentobarbital, thiopental

Mechanism of Action Acts similar to acetylcholine, produces depolarization of the motor endplate at the myoneural junction which causes sustained flaccid skeletal muscle paralysis produced by state of accommodation that developes in adjacent excitable muscle membranes

Pharmacodynamics/Kinetics
Onset of effect: I.M.: 2-3 minutes; I.V.: Complete muscular relaxation occurs within 30-60 seconds of injection
Duration: I.M.: 10-30 minutes; I.V.: 4-6 minutes with single administration
Metabolism: Rapidly hydrolyzed by plasma pseudocholinesterase

Usual Dosage I.M., I.V.:
Small Children: Intermittent: Initial: 2 mg/kg/dose one time; maintenance: 0.3-0.6 mg/kg/dose at intervals of 5-10 minutes as necessary
Older Children and Adolescents: Intermittent: Initial: 1 mg/kg/dose one time; maintenance: 0.3-0.6 mg/kg every 5-10 minutes as needed
Adults: 0.6 mg/kg (range: 0.3-1.1 mg/kg) over 10-30 seconds, up to 150 mg total dose
(Continued)

Succinylcholine *(Continued)*

Maintenance: 0.04-0.07 mg/kg every 5-10 minutes as needed

Continuous infusion: 2.5 mg/minute (or 0.5-10 mg/minute); dilute to concentration of 1-2 mg/mL in D_5W or NS

Note: Pretreatment with atropine may reduce occurrence of bradycardia

Dosing adjustment in hepatic impairment: Dose should be decreased in patients with severe liver disease

Administration I.M. injections should be made deeply, preferably high into deltoid muscle

Monitoring Parameters Cardiac monitor, blood pressure monitor, and ventilator required during administration; temperature, serum potassium and calcium, assisted ventilator status

Test Interactions ↑ potassium (S)

Dosage Forms

Injection, as chloride: 20 mg/mL (10 mL); 50 mg/mL (10 mL); 100 mg/mL (5 mL, 10 mL, 20 mL)

Powder for injection, as chloride: 100 mg, 500 mg, 1 g

♦ **Succinylcholine Chloride** *see Succinylcholine on previous page*

♦ **Sucraid™** *see Sacrosidase on page 1044*

Sucralfate *(soo KRAL fate)*

U.S. Brand Names Carafate®

Canadian Brand Names Novo-Sucralate; Sulcrate®; Sulcrate® Suspension Plus

Synonyms Aluminum Sucrose Sulfate, Basic

Therapeutic Category Gastrointestinal Agent, Miscellaneous

Use Short-term management of duodenal ulcers

Unlabeled use: Gastric ulcers; maintenance of duodenal ulcers; suspension may be used topically for treatment of stomatitis due to cancer chemotherapy and other causes of esophageal and gastric erosions; GERD, esophagitis; treatment of NSAID mucosal damage; prevention of stress ulcers; postsclerotherapy for esophageal variceal bleeding

Pregnancy Risk Factor B

Pregnancy/Breast-Feeding Implications

Clinical effects on the fetus: No data available; available evidence suggests safe use during pregnancy and breast-feeding

Breast-feeding/lactation: No data available. American Academy of Pediatrics has NO RECOMMENDATION.

Contraindications Hypersensitivity to sucralfate or any component

Warnings/Precautions Successful therapy with sucralfate should not be expected to alter the posthealing frequency of recurrence or the severity of duodenal ulceration; use with caution in patients with chronic renal failure who have an impaired excretion of absorbed aluminum. Because of the potential for sucralfate to alter the absorption of some drugs, separate administration (take other medication 2 hours before sucralfate) should be considered when alterations in bioavailability are believed to be critical

Adverse Reactions

1% to 10%: Gastrointestinal: Constipation

<1%: Dizziness, sleepiness, vertigo, insomnia, rash, pruritus, diarrhea, nausea, vomiting, gastric discomfort, indigestion, xerostomia, back pain

Overdosage/Toxicology Toxicity is minimal, may cause constipation

Drug Interactions Decreased effect: Digoxin, phenytoin (hydantoins), warfarin, ketoconazole, quinidine, ciprofloxacin, norfloxacin (quinolones), tetracycline, theophylline; because of the potential for sucralfate to alter the absorption of some drugs, separate administration (take other medications 2 hours before sucralfate) should be considered when alterations in bioavailability are believed to be critical

Note: When given with aluminum-containing antacids, may increase serum/body aluminum concentrations (see Warnings/Precautions)

Mechanism of Action Forms a complex by binding with positively charged proteins in exudates, forming a viscous paste-like, adhesive substance. This selectively forms a protective coating that protects the lining against peptic acid, pepsin, and bile salts.

Pharmacodynamics/Kinetics

Onset of action: Paste formation and ulcer adhesion occur within 1-2 hours

Duration: At least 6 hours

Absorption: Oral: <5%

Distribution: Acts locally at ulcer sites; unbound in the GI tract to aluminum and sucrose octasulfate

Metabolism: Not metabolized

Elimination: Small absorbed amounts are excreted in urine as unchanged compounds

Usual Dosage Oral:

Children: Dose not established, doses of 40-80 mg/kg/day divided every 6 hours have been used

Stomatitis: 2.5-5 mL (1 g/10 mL suspension), swish and spit or swish and swallow 4 times/day

Adults:

Stress ulcer prophylaxis: 1 g 4 times/day

Stress ulcer treatment: 1 g every 4 hours

Duodenal ulcer:
Treatment: 1 g 4 times/day on an empty stomach and at bedtime for 4-8 weeks, or alternatively 2 g twice daily; treatment is recommended for 4-8 weeks in adults, the elderly may require 12 weeks
Maintenance: Prophylaxis: 1 g twice daily
Stomatitis: 1 g/10 mL suspension, swish and spit or swish and swallow 4 times/day
Dosage comment in renal impairment: Aluminum salt is minimally absorbed (<5%), however, may accumulate in renal failure
Patient Information Take before meals or on an empty stomach; do not take antacids 30 minutes before or after taking sucralfate
Nursing Implications Monitor for constipation; administer other medications 2 hours before sucralfate
Dosage Forms
Suspension, oral: 1 g/10 mL (420 mL)
Tablet: 1 g

- Sucrets® [OTC] see Dyclonine on page 402
- Sudafed® [OTC] see Pseudoephedrine on page 993
- Sudafed® 12 Hour [OTC] see Pseudoephedrine on page 993
- Sufedrin® [OTC] see Pseudoephedrine on page 993
- Sufenta® see Sufentanil on this page

Sufentanil (soo FEN ta nil)

Related Information
Narcotic Agonists Comparison on page 1328
U.S. Brand Names Sufenta®
Synonyms Sufentanil Citrate
Therapeutic Category General Anesthetic
Use Analgesic supplement in maintenance of balanced general anesthesia
Restrictions C-II
Pregnancy Risk Factor C
Contraindications Hypersensitivity to sufentanil or any component
Warnings/Precautions Sufentanil can cause severely compromised respiratory depression; use with caution in patients with head injuries, hepatic or renal impairment or with pulmonary disease; sufentanil shares the toxic potential of opiate agonists, precaution of opiate agonist therapy should be observed; rapid I.V. infusion may result in skeletal muscle and chest wall rigidity → impaired ventilation → respiratory distress/arrest; inject slowly over 3-5 minutes; nondepolarizing skeletal muscle relaxant may be required
Adverse Reactions
>10%:
Cardiovascular: Bradycardia, hypotension
Central nervous system: Drowsiness
Gastrointestinal: Nausea, vomiting
Respiratory: Respiratory depression
1% to 10%:
Cardiovascular: Cardiac arrhythmias, orthostatic hypotension
Central nervous system: Confusion, CNS depression
Gastrointestinal: Biliary tract spasm
Ocular: Blurred vision
<1%: Circulatory depression, convulsions, dysesthesia, paradoxical CNS excitation or delirium; mental depression, dizziness, rash, urticaria, itching, urinary tract spasm, laryngospasm, bronchospasm; cold, clammy skin; physical and psychological dependence with prolonged use
Overdosage/Toxicology Naloxone 2 mg I.V. (0.01 mg/kg for children) with repeat administration as necessary up to a total of 10 mg; supportive care includes establishment of respiratory change; naloxone may be used to treat respiratory depression; muscular rigidity may also respond to opiate antagonist therapy or to neuromuscular blocking agents
Drug Interactions CYP3A3/4 enzyme substrate
Increased effect/toxicity with CNS depressants, beta-blockers
Mechanism of Action Binds with stereospecific receptors at many sites within the CNS, increases pain threshold, alters pain reception, inhibits ascending pain pathways; ultra short-acting narcotic
Pharmacodynamics/Kinetics
Onset of action: 1-3 minutes
Duration: Dose dependent
Metabolism: Primarily by the liver
Usual Dosage
Children <12 years: 10-25 mcg/kg with 100% O₂, maintenance: 25-50 mcg as needed
Adults: Dose should be based on body weight. **Note:** In obese patients (ie, >20% above ideal body weight), use lean body weight to determine dosage.
1-2 mcg/kg with N₂O/O₂ for endotracheal intubation; maintenance: 10-25 mcg as needed
2-8 mcg/kg with N₂O/O₂ more complicated major surgical procedures; maintenance: 10-50 mcg as needed
8-30 mcg/kg with 100% O₂ and muscle relaxant produces sleep; at doses ≥8 mcg/kg maintains a deep level of anesthesia; maintenance: 10-50 mcg as needed
Nursing Implications Patient may develop rebound respiratory depression postoperatively
(Continued)

Sufentanil *(Continued)*
Dosage Forms Injection, as citrate: 50 mcg/mL (1 mL, 2 mL, 5 mL)

♦ **Sufentanil Citrate** *see Sufentanil on previous page*

♦ **Sular®** *see Nisoldipine on page 842*

♦ **Sulbactam and Ampicillin** *see Ampicillin and Sulbactam on page 81*

Sulconazole (sul KON a zole)
U.S. Brand Names Exelderm®

Synonyms Sulconazole Nitrate

Therapeutic Category Antifungal Agent, Imidazole Derivative; Antifungal Agent, Topical

Use Treatment of superficial fungal infections of the skin, including tinea cruris (jock itch), tinea corporis (ringworm), tinea versicolor, and possibly tinea pedis (athlete's foot - cream only)

Pregnancy Risk Factor C

Contraindications Known hypersensitivity to sulconazole

Warnings/Precautions Use with caution in nursing mothers; for external use only

Adverse Reactions 1% to 10%:
Dermatologic: Itching
Local: Burning, stinging, redness

Mechanism of Action Substituted imidazole derivative which inhibits metabolic reactions necessary for the synthesis of ergosterol, an essential membrane component. The end result is usually fungistatic; however, sulconazole may act as a fungicide in *Candida albicans* and parapsilosis during certain growth phases.

Pharmacodynamics/Kinetics
Absorption: Topical: About 8.7% absorbed percutaneously
Elimination: Mostly in urine

Usual Dosage Adults: Topical: Apply a small amount to the affected area and gently massage once or twice daily for 3 weeks (tinea cruris, tinea corporis, tinea versicolor) to 4 weeks (tinea pedis).

Patient Information For external use only; avoid contact with eyes; if burning or irritation develops, notify physician

Dosage Forms
Cream, as nitrate: 1% (15 g, 30 g, 60 g)
Solution, as nitrate, topical: 1% (30 mL)

♦ **Sulconazole Nitrate** *see Sulconazole on this page*

♦ **Sulcrate®** *see Sucralfate on page 1088*

♦ **Sulcrate® Suspension Plus** *see Sucralfate on page 1088*

♦ **Sulf-10® Ophthalmic** *see Sulfacetamide Sodium on next page*

Sulfabenzamide, Sulfacetamide, and Sulfathiazole
(sul fa BENZ a mide, sul fa SEE ta mide & sul fa THYE a zole)

U.S. Brand Names Femguard®; Gyne-Sulf®; Sulfa-Gyn®; Sulfa-Trip®; Sultrin™; Trysul®; Vagilia®; V.V.S.®

Synonyms Triple Sulfa

Therapeutic Category Antibiotic, Vaginal

Use Treatment of *Haemophilus vaginalis* vaginitis

Pregnancy Risk Factor C

Contraindications Hypersensitivity to sulfabenzamide, sulfacetamide, sulfathiazole or any component, renal dysfunction

Warnings/Precautions Associated with Stevens-Johnson syndrome; if local irritation or systemic toxicity develops, discontinue therapy

Adverse Reactions
>10%: Local: Irritation, pruritus, urticaria
<1%: Allergic reactions, Stevens-Johnson syndrome

Mechanism of Action Interferes with microbial folic acid synthesis and growth via inhibition of para-aminobenzoic acid metabolism

Pharmacodynamics/Kinetics
Absorption: Absorption from the vagina is variable and unreliable
Metabolism: Primarily by acetylation
Elimination: By glomerular filtration into urine

Usual Dosage Adults:
Cream: Insert one applicatorful in vagina twice daily for 4-6 days; dosage may then be decreased to ½ to ¼ of an applicatorful twice daily
Tablet: Insert one intravaginally twice daily for 10 days

Patient Information Complete full course of therapy; notify physician if burning, irritation, or signs of a systemic allergic reaction occur

Dosage Forms
Cream, vaginal: Sulfabenzamide 3.7%, sulfacetamide 2.86%, and sulfathiazole 3.42% (78 g with applicator, 90 g, 120 g)
Tablet, vaginal: Sulfabenzamide 184 mg, sulfacetamide 143.75 mg, and sulfathiazole 172.5 mg (20 tablets/box with vaginal applicator)

Sulfacetamide Sodium (sul fa SEE ta mide SOW dee um)

U.S. Brand Names AK-Sulf® Ophthalmic; Bleph®-10 Ophthalmic; Cetamide® Ophthalmic; Isopto® Cetamide® Ophthalmic; Klaron® Lotion; Ocusulf-10® Ophthalmic; Sebizon® Topical Lotion; Sodium Sulamyd® Ophthalmic; Sulf-10® Ophthalmic

Synonyms Sodium Sulfacetamide

Therapeutic Category Antibiotic, Ophthalmic; Antibiotic, Sulfonamide Derivative

Use Treatment and prophylaxis of conjunctivitis due to susceptible organisms; corneal ulcers; adjunctive treatment with systemic sulfonamides for therapy of trachoma; topical application in scaling dermatosis (seborrheic); bacterial infections of the skin

Pregnancy Risk Factor C

Contraindications Hypersensitivity to sulfacetamide or any component, sulfonamides; infants <2 months of age

Warnings/Precautions Inactivated by purulent exudates containing PABA; use with caution in severe dry eye; ointment may retard corneal epithelial healing; sulfite in some products may cause hypersensitivity reactions; cross-sensitivity may occur with previous exposure to other sulfonamides given by other routes

Adverse Reactions

1% to 10%: Local: Irritation, stinging, burning

<1%: Headache, Stevens-Johnson syndrome, exfoliative dermatitis, toxic epidermal necrolysis, blurred vision, browache, hypersensitivity reactions

Drug Interactions Decreased effect: Silver, gentamicin (antagonism)

Stability Protect from light; discolored solution should not be used; **incompatible** with silver and zinc sulfate; sulfacetamide is inactivated by blood or purulent exudates

Mechanism of Action Interferes with bacterial growth by inhibiting bacterial folic acid synthesis through competitive antagonism of PABA

Pharmacodynamics/Kinetics

Half-life: 7-13 hours

Elimination: When absorbed, excreted primarily in urine as unchanged drug

Usual Dosage

Children >2 months and Adults: Ophthalmic:

Ointment: Apply to lower conjunctival sac 1-4 times/day and at bedtime

Solution: Instill 1-3 drops several times daily up to every 2-3 hours in lower conjunctival sac during waking hours and less frequently at night

Children >12 years and Adults: Topical:

Seborrheic dermatitis: Apply at bedtime and allow to remain overnight; in severe cases, may apply twice daily

Secondary cutaneous bacterial infections: Apply 2-4 times/day until infection clears

Monitoring Parameters Response to therapy

Patient Information Eye drops will burn upon instillation; wait at least 10 minutes before using another eye preparation; may sting eyes when first applied; do not touch container to eye, ointment will cause blurred vision; notify physician if condition does not improve in 3-4 days; may cause sensitivity to sunlight

Nursing Implications Assess whether patient can adequately instill drops or ointment

Dosage Forms

Lotion: 10% (59 mL, 85 mL)

Ointment, ophthalmic: 10% (3.5 g)

Solution, ophthalmic: 10% (1 mL, 2 mL, 2.5 mL, 5 mL, 15 mL); 15% (5 mL, 15 mL); 30% (15 mL)

Sulfacetamide Sodium and Fluorometholone

(sul fa SEE ta mide SOW dee um & flure oh METH oh lone)

U.S. Brand Names FML-S® Ophthalmic Suspension

Therapeutic Category Antibiotic/Corticosteroid, Ophthalmic

Dosage Forms Suspension, ophthalmic: Sulfacetamide sodium 10% and fluorometholone 0.1% (5 mL, 10 mL)

Sulfacetamide Sodium and Phenylephrine

(sul fa SEE ta mide SOW dee um & fen il EF rin)

U.S. Brand Names Vasosulf® Ophthalmic

Therapeutic Category Antibiotic, Ophthalmic

Dosage Forms Solution, ophthalmic: Sulfacetamide sodium 15% and phenylephrine hydrochloride 0.125% (5 mL, 15 mL)

Sulfacetamide Sodium and Prednisolone

(sul fa SEE ta mide SOW dee um & pred NIS oh lone)

Related Information

Prednisolone on page 961
Sulfacetamide Sodium on this page

U.S. Brand Names AK-Cide® Ophthalmic; Blephamide® Ophthalmic; Cetapred® Ophthalmic; Isopto® Cetapred® Ophthalmic; Metimyd® Ophthalmic; Vasocidin® Ophthalmic

Therapeutic Category Antibiotic, Ophthalmic; Anti-inflammatory Agent, Ophthalmic; Corticosteroid, Ophthalmic

Dosage Forms

Ointment, ophthalmic:

AK-Cide®, Metimyd®, Vasocidin®: Sulfacetamide sodium 10% and prednisolone acetate 0.5% (3.5 g)

Blephamide®: Sulfacetamide sodium 10% and prednisolone acetate 0.2% (3.5 g)

(Continued)

Sulfacetamide Sodium and Prednisolone *(Continued)*

Cetapred®: Sulfacetamide sodium 10% and prednisolone acetate 0.25% (3.5 g)

Suspension, ophthalmic: Sulfacetamide sodium 10% and prednisolone sodium phosphate 0.25% (5 mL)

Suspension, ophthalmic:

AK-Cide®, Metimyd®: Sulfacetamide sodium 10% and prednisolone acetate 0.5% (5 mL)

Blephamide®: Sulfacetamide sodium 10% and prednisolone acetate 0.2% (2.5 mL, 5 mL, 10 mL)

Isopto® Cetapred®: Sulfacetamide sodium 10% and prednisolone acetate 0.25% (5 mL, 15 mL)

Vasocidin®: Sulfacetamide sodium 10% and prednisolone sodium phosphate: 0.25% (5 mL, 10 mL)

♦ **Sulfacet-R® Topical** *see* Sulfur and Sulfacetamide Sodium *on page 1098*

Sulfadiazine (sul fa DYE a zeen)

Related Information

Guidelines for the Prevention of Opportunistic Infections in Persons with HIV *on page 1388*

Sulfonamide Derivatives *on page 1337*

U.S. Brand Names Microsulfon®

Canadian Brand Names Coptin®

Therapeutic Category Antibiotic, Sulfonamide Derivative

Use Treatment of urinary tract infections and nocardiosis, rheumatic fever prophylaxis; adjunctive treatment in toxoplasmosis; uncomplicated attack of malaria

Pregnancy Risk Factor B (D at term)

Contraindications Porphyria, hypersensitivity to any sulfa drug or any component, pregnancy at term, children <2 months of age unless indicated for the treatment of congenital toxoplasmosis, sunscreens containing PABA, nursing mothers

Warnings/Precautions Use with caution in patients with impaired hepatic function or impaired renal function, G-6-PD deficiency; dosage modification required in patients with renal impairment; fluid intake should be maintained ≥1500 mL/day, or administer sodium bicarbonate to keep urine alkaline; more likely to cause crystalluria because it is less soluble than other sulfonamides

Adverse Reactions

>10%:

Central nervous system: Fever, dizziness, headache

Dermatologic: Itching, rash, photosensitivity

Gastrointestinal: Anorexia, nausea, vomiting, diarrhea

1% to 10%:

Dermatologic: Lyell's syndrome, Stevens-Johnson syndrome

Hematologic: Granulocytopenia, leukopenia, thrombocytopenia, aplastic anemia, hemolytic anemia

Hepatic: Hepatitis

<1%: Thyroid function disturbance, crystalluria, jaundice, interstitial nephritis, acute nephropathy, hematuria, serum sickness-like reactions

Overdosage/Toxicology

Symptoms of overdose include drowsiness, dizziness, anorexia, abdominal pain, nausea, vomiting, hemolytic anemia, acidosis, jaundice, fever, agranulocytosis; doses of as little as 2-5 g/day may produce toxicity; the aniline radical is responsible for hematologic toxicity

High volume diuresis may aid in elimination and prevention of renal failure

Drug Interactions Decreased effect with PABA or PABA metabolites of drugs (eg, procaine, proparacaine, tetracaine, sunscreens); increased effect of oral anticoagulants and oral hypoglycemic agents

Stability Tablets may be crushed to prepare oral suspension of the drug in water or with a sucrose-containing solution; aqueous suspension with concentrations of 100 mg/mL should be stored in the refrigerator and used within 7 days

Mechanism of Action Interferes with bacterial growth by inhibiting bacterial folic acid synthesis through competitive antagonism of PABA

Pharmacodynamics/Kinetics

Absorption: Oral: Well absorbed

Distribution: Throughout body tissues and fluids including pleural, peritoneal, synovial, and ocular fluids; distributed throughout total body water; readily diffused into CSF; appears in breast milk

Metabolism: By N-acetylation

Half-life: 10 hours

Elimination: In urine as metabolites (15% to 40%) and as unchanged drug (43% to 60%)

Usual Dosage Oral:

Congenital toxoplasmosis:

Newborns and Children <2 months: 100 mg/kg/day divided every 6 hours in conjunction with pyrimethamine 1 mg/kg/day once daily and supplemental folinic acid 5 mg every 3 days for 6 months

Children >2 months: 25-50 mg/kg/dose 4 times/day

Toxoplasmosis:

Children >2 months: Loading dose: 75 mg/kg; maintenance dose: 120-150 mg/kg/day, maximum dose: 6 g/day; divided every 4-6 hours in conjunction with pyrimethamine

2 mg/kg/day divided every 12 hours for 3 days followed by 1 mg/kg/day once daily (maximum: 25 mg/day) with supplemental folinic acid

Adults: 2-4 g/day divided every 4-8 hours in conjunction with pyrimethamine 25 mg/day and with supplemental folinic acid

Prevention of recurrent attacks of rheumatic fever:

>30 kg: 1 g/day

<30 kg: 0.5 g/day

Patient Information Drink plenty of fluids; take on an empty stomach; avoid prolonged exposure to sunlight or wear protective clothing and sunscreen; notify physician if rash, difficulty breathing, severe or persistent fever, or sore throat occurs

Nursing Implications Maintain adequate hydration and monitor urine output

Dosage Forms Tablet: 500 mg

Sulfadiazine, Sulfamethazine, and Sulfamerazine

(sul fa DYE a zeen sul fa METH a zeen & sul fa MER a zeen)

Synonyms Multiple Sulfonamides; Trisulfapyrimidines

Therapeutic Category Antibiotic, Sulfonamide Derivative

Use Treatment of toxoplasmosis and other susceptible organisms, however, other agents are preferred

Pregnancy Risk Factor B (D at term)

Contraindications Porphyria, known hypersensitivity to any sulfa drug or any component

Mechanism of Action Interferes with microbial folic acid synthesis and growth via inhibition of para-aminobenzoic acid metabolism

Pharmacodynamics/Kinetics

Metabolism: By acetylation

Elimination: Excreted in urine via glomerular filtration

Usual Dosage Adults: Oral: 2-4 g to start, then 2-4 g/day in 3-6 divided doses

Test Interactions Increases cholesterol (S), protein, uric acid (S)

Patient Information Drink plenty of fluids

Dosage Forms Tablet: Sulfadiazine 167 mg, sulfamethazine 167 mg, and sulfamerazine 167 mg

Sulfadoxine and Pyrimethamine

(sul fa DOKS een & peer i METH a meen)

Therapeutic Category Antimalarial Agent

Use Treatment of *Plasmodium falciparum* malaria in patients in whom chloroquine resistance is suspected; malaria prophylaxis for travelers to areas where chloroquine-resistant malaria is endemic

Pregnancy Risk Factor C

Contraindications Known hypersensitivity to any sulfa drug, pyrimethamine, or any component; porphyria, megaloblastic anemia, severe renal insufficiency; children <2 months of age due to competition with bilirubin for protein binding sites

Warnings/Precautions Use with caution in patients with renal or hepatic impairment, patients with possible folate deficiency, and patients with seizure disorders, increased adverse reactions are seen in patients also receiving chloroquine; fatalities associated with sulfonamides, although rare, have occurred due to severe reactions including Stevens-Johnson syndrome, toxic epidermal necrolysis, hepatic necrosis, agranulocytosis, aplastic anemia and other blood dyscrasias; discontinue use at first sign of rash or any sign of adverse reaction; hemolysis occurs in patients with G-6-PD deficiency; leucovorin should be administered to reverse signs and symptoms of folic acid deficiency

Adverse Reactions

>10%:

Central nervous system: Ataxia, seizures, headache

Dermatologic: Photosensitivity

Gastrointestinal: Atrophic glossitis, vomiting, gastritis

Hematologic: Megaloblastic anemia, leukopenia, thrombocytopenia, pancytopenia

Neuromuscular & skeletal: Tremors

Miscellaneous: Hypersensitivity

1% to 10%:

Dermatologic: Stevens-Johnson syndrome

Hepatic: Hepatitis

<1%: Erythema multiforme, toxic epidermal necrolysis, rash, thyroid function dysfunction, anorexia, glossitis, crystalluria, hepatic necrosis, respiratory failure

Overdosage/Toxicology

Symptoms of overdose include anorexia, vomiting, CNS stimulation including seizures, megaloblastic anemia, leukopenia, thrombocytopenia, crystalluria

Leucovorin should be administered in a dosage of 3-9 mg/day for 3 days or as required to reverse symptoms of folic acid deficiency; doses of as little as 2-5 g/day may produce toxicity; the aniline radical is responsible for hematologic toxicity; high volume diuresis may aid in elimination and prevention of renal failure; diazepam can be used to control seizures

Drug Interactions

Decreased effect with PABA or PABA metabolites of local anesthetics

Increased toxicity with methotrexate, other sulfonamides, co-trimoxazole

Mechanism of Action Sulfadoxine interferes with bacterial folic acid synthesis and growth via competitive inhibition of para-aminiobenzoic acid; pyrimethamine inhibits microbial dihydrofolate reductase, resulting in inhibition of tetrahydrofolic acid synthesis

(Continued)

Sulfadoxine and Pyrimethamine *(Continued)*

Pharmacodynamics/Kinetics
Absorption: Oral: Well absorbed

Distribution:

Pyrimethamine: Widely distributed; mainly concentrated in blood cells, kidneys, lungs, liver, and spleen

Sulfadoxine: Well distributed like other sulfonamides

Metabolism: Pyrimethamine: Hepatic; Sulfadoxine: None

Half-life: Pyrimethamine: 80-95 hours; Sulfadoxine: 5-8 days

Time to peak serum concentration: Within 2-8 hours

Elimination: Excreted in urine as parent compounds and several unidentified metabolites

Usual Dosage Children and Adults: Oral:
Treatment of acute attack of malaria: A single dose of the following number of Fansidar® tablets is used in sequence with quinine or alone:

2-11 months: 1/4 tablet

1-3 years: 1/2 tablet

4-8 years: 1 tablet

9-14 years: 2 tablets

>14 years: 2-3 tablets

Malaria prophylaxis:

The first dose of Fansidar® should be taken 1-2 days before departure to an endemic area (CDC recommends that therapy be initiated 1-2 weeks before such travel), administration should be continued during the stay and for 4-6 weeks after return. Dose = pyrimethamine 0.5 mg/kg/dose and sulfadoxine 10 mg/kg/dose up to a maximum of 25 mg pyrimethamine and 500 mg sulfadoxine/dose weekly.

2-11 months: 1/8 tablet weekly **or** 1/4 tablet once every 2 weeks

1-3 years: 1/4 tablet once weekly **or** 1/2 tablet once every 2 weeks

4-8 years: 1/2 tablet once weekly **or** 1 tablet once every 2 weeks

9-14 years: 3/4 tablet once weekly **or** 1 1/2 tablets once every 2 weeks

>14 years: 1 tablet once weekly **or** 2 tablets once every 2 weeks

Monitoring Parameters
CBC, including platelet counts, and urinalysis should be performed periodically

Patient Information
Begin prophylaxis at least 2 days before departure; drink plenty of fluids; avoid prolonged exposure to the sun; notify physician if rash, sore throat, pallor, or glossitis occurs

Dosage Forms
Tablet: Sulfadoxine 500 mg and pyrimethamine 25 mg

- **Sulfa-Gyn®** see Sulfabenzamide, Sulfacetamide, and Sulfathiazole *on page 1090*
- **Sulfalax® [OTC]** see Docusate *on page 384*

Sulfamethoxazole *(sul fa meth OKS a zole)*

Related Information
Sulfonamide Derivatives *on page 1337*

U.S. Brand Names
Gantanol®; Urobak®

Canadian Brand Names
Apo®-Sulfamethoxazole

Therapeutic Category
Antibiotic, Sulfonamide Derivative

Use
Treatment of urinary tract infections, nocardiosis, toxoplasmosis, acute otitis media, and acute exacerbations of chronic bronchitis due to susceptible organisms

Pregnancy Risk Factor
B (D at term)

Contraindications
Porphyria, hypersensitivity to any sulfa drug or any component, pregnancy during 3rd trimester, children <2 months of age unless indicated for the treatment of congenital toxoplasmosis, sunscreens containing PABA

Warnings/Precautions
Maintain adequate fluid intake to prevent crystalluria; use with caution in patients with renal or hepatic impairment, and patients with G-6-PD deficiency; should not be used for group A beta-hemolytic streptococcal infections

Adverse Reactions
>10%:

Central nervous system: Fever, dizziness, headache

Dermatologic: Itching, rash, photosensitivity

Gastrointestinal: Anorexia, nausea, vomiting, diarrhea

1% to 10%:

Dermatologic: Lyell's syndrome, Stevens-Johnson syndrome

Hematologic: Granulocytopenia, leukopenia, thrombocytopenia, aplastic anemia, hemolytic anemia

Hepatic: Hepatitis

<1%: Vasculitis, thyroid function disturbance, crystalluria, jaundice, hematuria, acute nephropathy, interstitial nephritis, serum sickness-like reactions

Overdosage/Toxicology
Symptoms of overdose include drowsiness, dizziness, anorexia, abdominal pain, nausea, vomiting, hemolytic anemia, acidosis, jaundice, fever, agranulocytosis; the aniline radical is responsible for hematologic toxicity

High volume diuresis may aid in elimination and prevention of renal failure

Drug Interactions
Decreased effect with PABA or PABA metabolites of drugs (ie, procaine, proparacaine, tetracaine); cyclosporine levels may be decreased

Increased effect/toxicity of oral anticoagulants, oral hypoglycemic agents, hydantoins, uricosuric agents, methotrexate when administered with sulfonamides

Increased toxicity of sulfonamides with diuretics, indomethacin, methenamine, probenecid, and salicylates

Stability Protect from light

Mechanism of Action Interferes with bacterial growth by inhibiting bacterial folic acid synthesis through competitive antagonism of PABA

Pharmacodynamics/Kinetics

Absorption: Oral: 90%

Distribution: Crosses the placenta; readily enters the CSF

Protein binding: 70%

Metabolism: Primarily in the liver, with 10% to 20% as the N-acetylated form in the plasma

Half-life: 9-12 hours, prolonged with renal impairment

Time to peak serum concentration: Within 3-4 hours

Elimination: Unchanged drug (20%) and its metabolites are excreted in urine

Usual Dosage Oral:

Children >2 months: 50-60 mg/kg as single dose followed by 50-60 mg/kg/day divided every 12 hours; maximum: 3 g/24 hours or 75 mg/kg/day

Adults: Initial: 2 g, then 1 g 2-3 times/day; maximum: 3 g/24 hours

Dosing adjustment/interval in renal impairment:

Cl_{cr} 10-50 mL/minute: Administer every 12-24 hours

Cl_{cr} <10 mL/minute: Administer every 24 hours

Hemodialysis: Moderately dialyzable (20% to 50%)

Administration Administer around-the-clock to promote less variation in peak and trough serum levels

Monitoring Parameters Monitor urine output

Test Interactions May interfere with Jaffé alkaline picrate reaction assay for creatinine resulting in over-estimations of ~10% in the range of normal values; decreased effect with PABA or PABA metabolites of drugs (ie, procaine, proparacaine, tetracaine)

Patient Information Drink plenty of fluids; avoid prolonged exposure to sunlight or wear protective clothing; avoid aspirin and vitamin C products, notify physician if rash, unusual bleeding, difficulty breathing, severe or persistent fever, or sore throat occurs

Nursing Implications Maintain adequate hydration

Dosage Forms

Suspension, oral (cherry flavor): 500 mg/5 mL (480 mL)

Tablet: 500 mg

Sulfamethoxazole and Phenazopyridine

(sul fa meth OKS a zole & fen az oh PEER i deen)

Related Information

Phenazopyridine *on page 910*

Sulfamethoxazole *on previous page*

Therapeutic Category Sulfonamide

Dosage Forms Tablet: Sulfamethoxazole 500 mg and phenazopyridine 100 mg

♦ **Sulfamethoxazole and Trimethoprim** *see Co-Trimoxazole on page 299*

♦ **Sulfamylon® Topical** *see Mafenide on page 704*

Sulfanilamide (sul fa NIL a mide)

U.S. Brand Names AVC™ Cream; AVC™ Suppository; Vagitrol®

Therapeutic Category Antifungal Agent, Vaginal

Use Treatment of vulvovaginitis caused by *Candida albicans*

Pregnancy Risk Factor C; kernicterus possible in nursing newborn, avoid breast-feeding if possible

Contraindications Hypersensitivity to sulfanilamide or any component

Warnings/Precautions Since sulfonamides may be absorbed from vaginal mucosa, the same precaution for oral sulfonamides apply (eg, blood dyscrasias); if a rash develops, terminate therapy immediately. Use vaginal applicators very cautiously after the 7th month of pregnancy.

Adverse Reactions Percentage unknown: Rarely, systemic reactions occur; increased discomfort, burning, allergic reactions, Stevens-Johnson syndrome (infrequent)

Mechanism of Action Interferes with microbial folic acid synthesis and growth via inhibition of para-aminiobenzoic acid metabolism; exerts a bacteriostatic action

Usual Dosage Adults: Female: Insert one applicatorful intravaginally once or twice daily continued through 1 complete menstrual cycle or insert one suppository intravaginally once or twice daily for 30 days

Patient Information Complete full course of therapy; notify physician if burning or irritation become severe or persist or if allergic symptoms occur; insert high into vagina; use of an applicator is not recommended during pregnancy; avoid sexual intercourse during treatment

Dosage Forms

Cream, vaginal (AVC™, Vagitrol®): 15% [150 mg/g] (120 g with applicator)

Suppository, vaginal (AVC™): 1.05 g (16s)

Sulfasalazine (sul fa SAL a zeen)

Related Information

Sulfonamide Derivatives *on page 1337*

U.S. Brand Names Azulfidine®; Azulfidine® EN-tabs®

Canadian Brand Names Apo®-Sulfasalazine; PMS-Sulfasalazine; Salazopyrin®; Salazopyrin EN-Tabs®; S.A.S™

Synonyms Salicylazosulfapyridine

Therapeutic Category 5-Aminosalicylic Acid Derivative; Anti-inflammatory Agent

(Continued)

Sulfasalazine *(Continued)*

Use Management of ulcerative colitis; enteric coated tablets are used for for rheumatoid arthritis in patients who inadequately respond to analgesics and NSAIDs

Pregnancy Risk Factor B (D at term)

Contraindications Hypersensitivity to sulfasalazine, sulfa drugs, or any component; porphyria, GI or GU obstruction; hypersensitivity to salicylates; children <2 years of age

Warnings/Precautions Use with caution in patients with renal impairment; impaired hepatic function or urinary obstruction, blood dyscrasias severe allergies or asthma, or G-6-PD deficiency; may cause folate deficiency (consider providing 1 mg/day folate supplement)

Adverse Reactions
>10%:
    Central nervous system: Dizziness, headache (33%)
    Dermatologic: Photosensitivity
    Gastrointestinal: Anorexia, nausea, vomiting, diarrhea (33%)
    Genitourinary: Reversible oligospermia (33%)
<3%:
    Dermatologic: Urticaria/pruritus (<3%)
    Hematologic: Hemolytic anemia (<3%), Heinz body anemia (<3%)
<0.1%: Lyell's syndrome, Stevens-Johnson syndrome, thyroid function disturbance, crystalluria, granulocytopenia, leukopenia, thrombocytopenia, aplastic anemia, jaundice, interstitial nephritis, acute nephropathy, hematuria, serum sickness-like reactions

Overdosage/Toxicology
Symptoms of overdose include drowsiness, dizziness, anorexia, abdominal pain, nausea, vomiting, hemolytic anemia, acidosis, jaundice, fever, agranulocytosis; the aniline radical is responsible for hematologic toxicity
High volume diuresis may aid in elimination and prevention of renal failure

Drug Interactions
Decreased effect of iron, digoxin, folic acid, and like other sulfa drugs PABA or PABA metabolites of drugs (ie, procaine, proparacaine, tetracaine)
Increased effect of oral anticoagulants, methotrexate, and oral hypoglycemic agents as with other sulfa drugs

Stability Protect from light; shake suspension well

Mechanism of Action Acts locally in the colon to decrease the inflammatory response and systemically interferes with secretion by inhibiting prostaglandin synthesis

Pharmacodynamics/Kinetics
Absorption: 10% to 15% of dose is absorbed as unchanged drug from the small intestine
Distribution: Small amounts appear in feces and breast milk
Metabolism: Following absorption, both components are metabolized in the liver; split into sulfapyridine and 5-aminosalicylic acid (5-ASA) in the colon
Half-life: 5.7-10 hours
Elimination: Primary excretion in urine (as unchanged drug, components, and acetylated metabolites)

Usual Dosage Oral:
Children >2 years: Initial: 40-60 mg/kg/day in 3-6 divided doses; maintenance dose: 20-30 mg/kg/day in 4 divided doses
Adults: Initial: 1 g 3-4 times/day, 2 g/day maintenance in divided doses; may initiate therapy with 0.5-1 g/day enteric-coated tablets
Dosing interval in renal impairment:
Cl$_{cr}$ 10-30 mL/minute: Administer twice daily
Cl$_{cr}$ <10 mL/minute: Administer once daily
Dosing adjustment in hepatic impairment: Avoid use

Administration GI intolerance is common during the first few days of therapy (administer with meals)

Patient Information Maintain adequate fluid intake; take after meals; may cause orange-yellow discoloration of urine and skin; take after meals or with food; do not take with antacids; may permanently stain soft contact lenses yellow; avoid prolonged exposure to sunlight; shake well before using

Nursing Implications Drug commonly imparts an orange-yellow discoloration to urine and skin

Dosage Forms
Tablet: 500 mg
Tablet, enteric coated: 500 mg

♦ **Sulfatrim®** *see* Co-Trimoxazole *on page 299*

♦ **Sulfa-Trip®** *see* Sulfabenzamide, Sulfacetamide, and Sulfathiazole *on page 1090*

Sulfinpyrazone *(sul fin PEER a zone)*

U.S. Brand Names Anturane®

Canadian Brand Names Antazone®; Anturan®; Apo®-Sulfinpyrazone; Novo-Pyrazone; Nu-Sulfinpyrazone

Therapeutic Category Uricosuric Agent

Use Treatment of chronic gouty arthritis and intermittent gouty arthritis
Unlabeled use: To decrease the incidence of sudden death postmyocardial infarction

Pregnancy Risk Factor C

Contraindications Active peptic ulcers, hypersensitivity to sulfinpyrazone, phenylbutazone, or other pyrazoles, GI inflammation, blood dyscrasias

Warnings/Precautions Safety and efficacy not established in children <18 years of age, use with caution in patients with impaired renal function and urolithiasis

Adverse Reactions

1% to 10%: Gastrointestinal: Nausea, vomiting, stomach pain

<1%:

Cardiovascular: Flushing

Central nervous system: Dizziness, headache

Dermatologic: Dermatitis, rash

Hematologic: Anemia, leukopenia, increased bleeding time (decreased platelet aggregation)

Hepatic: Hepatic necrosis

Genitourinary: Polyuria

Renal: Nephrotic syndrome, uric acid stones

Overdosage/Toxicology

Symptoms of overdose include nausea, vomiting, ataxia, respiratory depression, seizures

Following GI decontamination, treatment is supportive only

Drug Interactions CYP2C and 3A3/4 enzyme inducer; CYP2C9 enzyme inhibitor

Decreased effect/levels of theophylline, verapamil; decreased uricosuric activity with salicylates, niacins

Increased effect of oral anticoagulants

Risk of acetaminophen hepatotoxicity is increased, but therapeutic effects may be reduced

Mechanism of Action Acts by increasing the urinary excretion of uric acid, thereby decreasing blood urate levels; this effect is therapeutically useful in treating patients with acute intermittent gout, chronic tophaceous gout, and acts to promote resorption of tophi; also has antithrombic and platelet inhibitory effects

Pharmacodynamics/Kinetics

Absorption: Complete and rapid

Metabolism: Hepatic to two active metabolites

Half-life, elimination: 2.7-6 hours

Time to peak serum concentration: 1.6 hours

Elimination: Renal excretion with 22% to 50% as unchanged drug

Usual Dosage Adults: Oral: 100-200 mg twice daily; maximum daily dose: 800 mg

Dosing adjustment in renal impairment: Cl$_{cr}$ <50 mL/minute: Avoid use

Monitoring Parameters Serum and urinary uric acid, CBC

Test Interactions ↓ uric acid (S)

Patient Information Take with food or antacids; drink plenty of fluids; avoid aspirin and other salicylate products

Dosage Forms

Capsule: 200 mg

Tablet: 100 mg

Sulfisoxazole (sul fi SOKS a zole)

Related Information

Antimicrobial Drugs of Choice on page 1404

Sulfonamide Derivatives on page 1337

Treatment of Sexually Transmitted Diseases on page 1429

Canadian Brand Names Novo-Soxazole; Sulfizole®

Synonyms Sulfisoxazole Acetyl; Sulphafurazole

Therapeutic Category Antibiotic, Sulfonamide Derivative

Use Treatment of urinary tract infections, otitis media, *Chlamydia*; nocardiosis; treatment of acute pelvic inflammatory disease in prepubertal children; often used in combination with trimethoprim

Pregnancy Risk Factor B (D at term)

Contraindications Hypersensitivity to any sulfa drug or any component, porphyria, pregnancy during 3rd trimester, infants <2 months of age (sulfas compete with bilirubin for protein binding sites), patients with urinary obstruction, sunscreens containing PABA

Warnings/Precautions Use with caution in patients with G-6-PD deficiency (hemolysis may occur), hepatic or renal impairment; dosage modification required in patients with renal impairment; risk of crystalluria should be considered in patients with impaired renal function

Adverse Reactions

>10%:

Central nervous system: Fever, dizziness, headache

Dermatologic: Itching, rash, photosensitivity

Gastrointestinal: Anorexia, nausea, vomiting, diarrhea

1% to 10%:

Dermatologic: Lyell's syndrome, Stevens-Johnson syndrome

Hematologic: Granulocytopenia, leukopenia, thrombocytopenia, aplastic anemia, hemolytic anemia

Hepatic: Hepatitis

<1%: Vasculitis, thyroid function disturbance, crystalluria, jaundice, hematuria, acute nephropathy, interstitial nephritis, serum sickness-like reactions

Overdosage/Toxicology

Symptoms of overdose include drowsiness, dizziness, anorexia, abdominal pain, nausea, vomiting, hemolytic anemia, acidosis, jaundice, fever, agranulocytosis; doses of as little as 2-5 g/day may produce toxicity; the aniline radical is responsible for hematologic toxicity

(Continued)

Sulfisoxazole *(Continued)*

High volume diuresis may aid in elimination and prevention of renal failure

Drug Interactions Decreased effect with PABA or PABA metabolites of drugs (ie, procaine, proparacaine, tetracaine); cyclosporine levels may be decreased

Increased effect/toxicity of oral anticoagulants, oral hypoglycemic agents, hydantoins, uricosuric agents, methotrexate when administered with sulfonamides

Increased toxicity of sulfonamides with diuretics, indomethacin, methenamine, probenecid, and salicylates

Stability Protect from light

Mechanism of Action Interferes with bacterial growth by inhibiting bacterial folic acid synthesis through competitive antagonism of PABA

Pharmacodynamics/Kinetics

Absorption: Sulfisoxazole acetyl is hydrolyzed in the GI tract to sulfisoxazole which is readily absorbed

Distribution: Crosses the placenta; excreted into breast milk

Ratio of CSF to blood level (%): Normal meninges: 50-80; Inflamed meninges: 80+

Protein binding: 85% to 88%

Metabolized: In the liver by acetylation and glucuronide conjugation to inactive compounds

Half-life: 4-7 hours, prolonged with renal impairment

Time to peak serum concentration: Within 2-3 hours

Elimination: Primarily in urine (95% within 24 hours), 40% to 60% as unchanged drug

Usual Dosage Not for use in patients <2 months of age:

Children >2 months: Oral: Initial: 75 mg/kg, followed by 120-150 mg/kg/day in divided doses every 4-6 hours; not to exceed 6 g/day

Pelvic inflammatory disease: 100 mg/kg/day in divided doses every 6 hours; used in combination with ceftriaxone

Chlamydia trachomatis: 100 mg/kg/day in divided doses every 6 hours

Adults: Oral: Initial: 2-4 g, then 4-8 g/day in divided doses every 4-6 hours

Pelvic inflammatory disease: 500 mg every 6 hours for 21 days; used in combination with ceftriaxone

Chlamydia trachomatis: 500 mg every 6 hours for 10 days

Dosing interval in renal impairment:

Cl_{cr} 10-50 mL/minute: Administer every 8-12 hours

Cl_{cr} <10 mL/minute: Administer every 12-24 hours

Hemodialysis: >50% removed by hemodialysis

Children and Adults: Ophthalmic:

Solution: Instill 1-2 drops to affected eye every 2-3 hours

Ointment: Apply small amount to affected eye 1-3 times/day and at bedtime

Monitoring Parameters CBC, urinalysis, renal function tests, temperature

Test Interactions False-positive protein in urine; false-positive urine glucose with Clinitest®

Patient Information Take with a glass of water on an empty stomach; avoid prolonged exposure to sunlight; report to physician any sore throat, mouth sores, rash, unusual bleeding, or fever; complete full course of therapy

Nursing Implications Maintain adequate fluid intake

Additional Information

Sulfisoxazole: Gantrisin® tablet

Sulfisoxazole acetyl: Gantrisin® pediatric syrup/suspension

Dosage Forms

Ointment, ophthalmic, as diolamine: 4% [40 mg/mL] (3.75 g)

Solution, ophthalmic, as diolamine: 4% [40 mg/mL] (15 mL)

Suspension, oral, pediatric, as acetyl (raspberry flavor): 500 mg/5 mL (480 mL)

Tablet: 500 mg

♦ **Sulfisoxazole Acetyl** *see Sulfisoxazole on previous page*
♦ **Sulfisoxazole and Erythromycin** *see Erythromycin and Sulfisoxazole on page 429*

Sulfisoxazole and Phenazopyridine

(sul fi SOKS a zole & fen az oh PEER i deen)

Related Information

Phenazopyridine *on page 910*
Sulfisoxazole *on previous page*

U.S. Brand Names Azo-Sulfisoxazole

Therapeutic Category Antibiotic, Sulfonamide Derivative; Local Anesthetic, Urinary

Dosage Forms Tablet: Sulfisoxazole 500 mg and phenazopyridine 50 mg

♦ **Sulfizole®** *see Sulfisoxazole on previous page*
♦ **Sulfonamide Derivatives** *see page 1337*

Sulfur and Sulfacetamide Sodium

(SUL fur & sul fa SEE ta mide SOW dee um)

U.S. Brand Names Novacet® Topical; Sulfacet-R® Topical

Therapeutic Category Antiseborrheic Agent, Topical

Dosage Forms Lotion, topical: Sulfur colloid 5% and sulfacetamide sodium 10% (30 mL)

Sulindac (sul IN dak)

Related Information
Nonsteroidal Anti-Inflammatory Agents Comparison *on page 1335*

U.S. Brand Names Clinoril®

Canadian Brand Names Apo®-Sulin; Novo-Sundac

Therapeutic Category Analgesic, Nonsteroidal Anti-inflammatory Drug; Anti-inflammatory Agent; Nonsteroidal Anti-inflammatory Drug (NSAID), Oral

Use Management of inflammatory disease, rheumatoid disorders; acute gouty arthritis; structurally similar to indomethacin but acts like aspirin; safest NSAID for use in mild renal impairment

Pregnancy Risk Factor B (D at term)

Contraindications Hypersensitivity to sulindac, any component, aspirin or other nonsteroidal anti-inflammatory drugs (NSAIDs)

Warnings/Precautions Use with caution in patients with peptic ulcer disease, GI bleeding, bleeding abnormalities, impaired renal or hepatic function, congestive heart failure, hypertension, and patients receiving anticoagulants

Adverse Reactions
>10%:
  Central nervous system: Dizziness
  Dermatologic: Rash
  Gastrointestinal: Abdominal cramps, heartburn, indigestion, nausea
1% to 10%:
  Central nervous system: Headache, nervousness
  Dermatologic: Itching
  Endocrine & metabolic: Fluid retention
  Gastrointestinal: Vomiting
  Otic: Tinnitus
<1%: Congestive heart failure, hypertension, arrhythmias, tachycardia, confusion, hallucinations, aseptic meningitis, mental depression, drowsiness, insomnia, urticaria, erythema multiforme, toxic epidermal necrolysis, Stevens-Johnson syndrome, angioedema, polydipsia, hot flashes, gastritis, GI ulceration, cystitis, polyuria, agranulocytosis, anemia, hemolytic anemia, bone marrow suppression, leukopenia, thrombocytopenia, hepatitis, peripheral neuropathy, toxic amblyopia, blurred vision, conjunctivitis, dry eyes, decreased hearing, acute renal failure, allergic rhinitis, shortness of breath, epistaxis

Overdosage/Toxicology
Symptoms of overdose include dizziness, vomiting, nausea, abdominal pain, hypotension, coma, stupor, metabolic acidosis, leukocytosis, renal failure
Management of a nonsteroidal anti-inflammatory drug (NSAID) intoxication is primarily supportive and symptomatic. Fluid therapy is commonly effective in managing the hypotension that may occur following an acute NSAID overdose, except when this is due to an acute blood loss. Seizures tend to be very short-lived and often do not require drug treatment; although, recurrent seizures should be treated with I.V. diazepam.

Drug Interactions
Decreased effect of diuretics, beta-blockers, hydralazine, captopril
Increased toxicity with probenecid, NSAIDs; increased toxicity of digoxin, methotrexate, lithium, aminoglycosides antibiotics (reported in neonates), cyclosporine (increased nephrotoxicity), potassium-sparing diuretics (hyperkalemia), anticoagulants

Mechanism of Action Inhibits prostaglandin synthesis by decreasing the activity of the enzyme, cyclo-oxygenase, which results in decreased formation of prostaglandin precursors

Pharmacodynamics/Kinetics
Absorption: 90%
Metabolism: Sulindac is a prodrug and, therefore, requires metabolic activation; requires hepatic metabolism to sulfide metabolite (active) for therapeutic effects; also metabolized in the liver to sulfone metabolites (inactive)
Half-life: Parent drug: 7 hours; Active metabolite: 18 hours
Elimination: Principally in urine (50%) with some biliary excretion (25%)

Usual Dosage Maximum therapeutic response may not be realized for up to 3 weeks
Oral:
  Children: Dose not established
  Adults: 150-200 mg twice daily or 300-400 mg once daily; not to exceed 400 mg/day
  Dosing adjustment in hepatic impairment: Dose reduction is necessary

Dietary Considerations Food: May decrease the rate but not the extent of oral absorption. Drug may cause GI upset, bleeding, ulceration, perforation; take with food or milk to minimize GI upset.

Monitoring Parameters Liver enzymes, BUN, serum creatinine, CBC, blood pressure

Test Interactions ↑ chloride (S), ↑ sodium (S), ↑ bleeding time

Patient Information Take with food or milk; inform dentist or surgeon because of prolonged bleeding time; do not take aspirin; may cause dizziness, drowsiness, impair coordination and judgment

Nursing Implications Observe for edema and fluid retention; monitor blood pressure

Dosage Forms Tablet: 150 mg, 200 mg

Extemporaneous Preparations A suspension of sulindac can be prepared by triturating 1000 mg sulindac (5 x 200 mg tablets) with 50 mg of kelco and 400 mg of Veegum® until a powder mixture is formed; then add 30 mL of sorbitol 35% (prepared
(Continued)

Sulindac *(Continued)*

from 70% sorbitol) to form a slurry; finally add a sufficient quantity of 35% sorbitol to make a final volume of 100 mL; the final suspension is 10 mg/mL and is stable for 7 days

♦ **Sulphafurazole** *see* Sulfisoxazole *on page 1097*

♦ **Sultrin™** *see* Sulfabenzamide, Sulfacetamide, and Sulfathiazole *on page 1090*

Sumatriptan Succinate (SOO ma trip tan SUKS i nate)

Related Information
Antimigraine Drugs: Pharmacokinetic Differences *on page 1304*

U.S. Brand Names Imitrex®

Therapeutic Category Antimigraine Agent; Serotonin Agonist

Use Acute treatment of migraine with or without aura
Sumatriptan injection: Acute treatment of cluster headache episodes

Pregnancy Risk Factor C

Contraindications Intravenous administration; use in patients with ischemic heart disease or Prinzmetal angina, patients with signs or symptoms of ischemic heart disease, uncontrolled HTN; use with ergotamine derivatives (within 24 hours of); use with in 24 hours of another 5-HT₁ agonist; concurrent administration or within 2 weeks of discontinuing an MAOI; hypersensitivity to any component; management of hemiplegic or basilar migraine

Warnings/Precautions
Sumatriptan is indicated only in patient populations with a clear diagnosis of migraine or cluster headache

Cardiac events (coronary artery vasospasm, transient ischemia, myocardial infarction, ventricular tachycardia/fibrillation, cardiac arrest and death) have been reported with 5-HT₁ agonist administration. Significant elevation in blood pressure, including hypertensive crisis, has also been reported on rare occasions in patients with and without a history of hypertension. Vasospasm-related reactions have been reported other than coronary artery vasospasm. Peripheral vascular ischemia and colonic ischemia with abdominal pain and bloody diarrhea have occurred.

Adverse Reactions
>10%:
  Central nervous system: Dizziness
  Endocrine & metabolic: Hot flashes
  Local: Injection site reaction
  Neuromuscular & skeletal: Paresthesia
1% to 10%:
  Cardiovascular: Tightness in chest
  Central nervous system: Drowsiness, headache
  Dermatologic: Burning sensation
  Gastrointestinal: Abdominal discomfort, mouth discomfort
  Neuromuscular & skeletal: Myalgia, numbness, weakness, neck pain, jaw discomfort
  Miscellaneous: Diaphoresis
<1%: Rashes, polydipsia, dehydration, dysmenorrhea, dysuria, renal calculus, dyspnea, thirst, hiccups

Drug Interactions Increased toxicity: Ergot-containing drugs, MAOIs, SSRIs can lead to symptoms of hyper-reflexia, weakness, and incoordination

Stability Store at 2°C to 20°C (36°F to 86°F); protect from light

Mechanism of Action Selective agonist for serotonin (5-HT₁D receptor) in cranial arteries to cause vasoconstriction and reduces sterile inflammation associated with antidromic neuronal transmission correlating with relief of migraine

Pharmacodynamics/Kinetics
Distribution: V_d: 2.4 L/kg
Protein binding: 14% to 21%
Bioavailability: 15%
Half-life: 2.5 hours
Time to peak serum concentration: 5-20 minutes
Elimination: In urine unchanged (22%), excreted as indole acetic acid metabolite (38%)

Usual Dosage Adults:
Oral: 25 mg (taken with fluids); maximum recommended dose is 100 mg. If a satisfactory response has not been obtained at 2 hours, a second dose of up to 100 mg may be given. Efficacy of this second dose has not been examined. If a headache returns, additional doses may be taken at intervals of at least 2 hours up to a daily maximum of 300 mg. There is no evidence that an initial dose of 100 mg provides substantially greater relief than 25 mg.

Intranasal: A single dose of 5, 10 or 20 mg administered in one nostril. A 10 mg dose may be achieved by administering a single 5 mg dose in each nostril. If headache returns, the dose maybe be repeated once after 2 hours not to exceed a total daily dose of 40 mg. The safety of treating an average of >4 headaches in a 30-day period has not been established.

S.C.: 6 mg; a second injection may be administered at least 1 hour after the initial dose, but not more than 2 injections in a 24-hour period. If side effects are dose-limiting, lower doses may be used.

Administration
Oral: Should be taken with fluids as soon as symptoms to appear
Do not administer I.V.; may cause coronary vasospasm

Patient Information If the patient has risk factors for heart disease (high blood pressure, high cholesterol, obesity, diabetes, smoking, strong family history of heart disease, postmenopausal woman or a male >40 years of age), tell physician

This agent is intended to relieve migraine, but not to prevent or reduce the number of attacks; use only to treat an actual migraine attack or cluster headache (injection only)

Do not use this agent if you are pregnant, think you may be pregnant, are trying to become pregnant or are not using adequate contraception, unless you have discussed this with your physician. Glaxo Wellcome maintains a Sumatriptan Pregnancy Registry. Register patients by calling 1-800-722-9292, extension 39441.

If pain or tightness in the chest or throat occurs when using this agent, discuss it with a physician before using more. If the chest pain is severe or does not go away, call physician immediately. If shortness of breath; wheezing; heart throbbing; swelling of eyelids, face or lips; skin rash, skin lumps or hives occur, tell physician immediately. Do not take any more unless the physician instructs you to do so. If feelings of tingling, heat, flushing (redness of face lasting a short time), heaviness, pressure, drowsiness, dizziness, tiredness, or sickness develop, tell your physician.

Oral: Take a single dose with fluids as soon as symptoms of migraine appear; a second dose may be taken if symptoms return, but no sooner than 2 hours following the first dose. For a given attack, if there is no response to the first tablet, do not take a second tablet without first consulting a physician. Do not take >300 mg in any 24-hour period.

Injection: Instruct patients who are advised to self-administer sumatriptan in medically-unsupervised situations on the proper use of the product prior to doing so for the first time, including loading the autoinjector and discarding the empty syringes. For adults, the usual dose is a single injection given just below the skin. Administer as soon as migraine symptoms appear, but it may be given any time during an attack. A second injection may be given if the symptoms of migraine return. Do not use >2 injections/24 hours, and allow ≥1 hour between each dose. The patient may experience pain or redness at the site of injection, but this usually lasts <1 hour.

Intranasal: For adults, the usual dose is a single nasal spray into one nostril. If headache returns, a second nasal spray may be given ≥2 hours after the first spray. For any attack where the patient has no response to the first nasal spray, do not use a second nasal spray without first consulting a physician. Do not administer >40 mg of nasal spray in any 24-hour period.

Nursing Implications Pain at injection site lasts <1 hour

Dosage Forms
Injection: 12 mg/mL (0.5 mL, 2 mL)
Spray, Intranasal: 5 mg (100 μL unit dose spray device), 20 mg (100 μL unit dose spray device)
Tablet: 25 mg, 50 mg

♦ **Summer's Eve® Medicated Douche [OTC]** see Povidone-Iodine on page 955
♦ **Sumycin® Oral** see Tetracycline on page 1122
♦ **Supeudol®** see Oxycodone on page 874
♦ **Supprelin™ Injection** see Histrelin on page 568
♦ **Suprax®** see Cefixime on page 209

Suprofen (soo PROE fen)

U.S. Brand Names Profenal®

Therapeutic Category Anti-inflammatory Agent; Nonsteroidal Anti-inflammatory Drug (NSAID), Ophthalmic

Use Inhibition of intraoperative miosis

Pregnancy Risk Factor C

Contraindications Previous hypersensitivity or intolerance to suprofen; epithelial herpes simplex keratitis; history of hypersensitivity reactions to aspirin or other nonsteroidal anti-inflammatory agents

Warnings/Precautions Use with caution in patients sensitive to acetylsalicylic acid and other NSAIDs; some systemic absorption occurs; use with caution in patients with bleeding tendencies; perform ophthalmic evaluation for those who develop eye complaints during therapy (blurred vision, diminished vision, changes in color vision, retinal changes)

Adverse Reactions
1% to 10%: Topical: Transient burning or stinging, redness, iritis
<1%: Chemosis, photophobia, discomfort, pain, punctate epithelial staining

Overdosage/Toxicology Not usually a problem; if accidental oral ingestion, dilute with fluids

Drug Interactions Decreased effect: When used concurrently with suprofen, acetylcholine chloride and carbachol may be ineffective

Mechanism of Action Inhibits prostaglandin synthesis, acts on the hypothalamus heat-regulating center to reduce fever, blocks prostaglandin synthetase action which prevents formation of the platelet-aggregating substance thromboxane A_2; decreases pain receptor sensitivity.

Pharmacodynamics/Kinetics
Protein binding: 99%
Metabolism: Occurs in the liver to one major inactive metabolite
Half-life, elimination: 2-4 hours
Time to peak serum concentration: ~1 hour
Elimination: <15% excreted unchanged in urine in 48 hours
(Continued)

Suprofen *(Continued)*

Usual Dosage Adults: On day of surgery, instill 2 drops in conjunctival sac at 3, 2, and 1 hour prior to surgery; or 2 drops in sac every 4 hours, while awake, the day preceding surgery

Patient Information Avoid aspirin and aspirin-containing products while taking this medication; get instructions on administration of eye drops

Nursing Implications In elderly, remove contact lenses before administering; assess ability to self-administer

Dosage Forms Solution, ophthalmic: 1% (2.5 mL)

- **Surfak® [OTC]** *see Docusate on page 384*
- **Surmontil®** *see Trimipramine on page 1186*
- **Survanta®** *see Beractant on page 139*
- **Susano®** *see Hyoscyamine, Atropine, Scopolamine, and Phenobarbital on page 592*
- **Sus-Phrine®** *see Epinephrine on page 415*
- **Sustaire®** *see Theophylline Salts on page 1125*
- **Sustiva™** *see Efavirenz on page 406*
- **Suxamethonium Chloride** *see Succinylcholine on page 1087*
- **Syllact® [OTC]** *see Psyllium on page 994*
- **Symadine®** *see Amantadine on page 51*
- **Symmetrel®** *see Amantadine on page 51*
- **Synacol® CF [OTC]** *see Guaifenesin and Dextromethorphan on page 550*
- **Synacort®** *see Hydrocortisone on page 579*
- **Synacthen** *see Cosyntropin on page 298*
- **Synagis®** *see Palivizumab on page 881*
- **Synalar®** *see Fluocinolone on page 496*
- **Synalar-HP®** *see Fluocinolone on page 496*
- **Synalgos®-DC** *see Dihydrocodeine Compound on page 362*
- **Synarel®** *see Nafarelin on page 809*
- **Syn-Captopril** *see Captopril on page 185*
- **Syn-Diltiazem** *see Diltiazem on page 365*
- **Synemol®** *see Fluocinolone on page 496*
- **Syn-Flunisolide** *see Flunisolide on page 494*
- **Syn-Minocycline** *see Minocycline on page 782*
- **Syn-Nadolol** *see Nadolol on page 807*
- **Synphasic®** *see Ethinyl Estradiol and Norethindrone on page 451*
- **Syn-Pindol®** *see Pindolol on page 929*
- **Synthetic Lung Surfactant** *see Colfosceril Palmitate on page 294*
- **Synthroid®** *see Levothyroxine on page 677*
- **Syntocinon® Injection** *see Oxytocin on page 879*
- **Syntocinon® Nasal Spray** *see Oxytocin on page 879*
- **Syprine®** *see Trientine on page 1179*
- **Syracol-CF® [OTC]** *see Guaifenesin and Dextromethorphan on page 550*
- **Sytobex®** *see Cyanocobalamin on page 302*
- **T₃ Sodium** *see Liothyronine on page 683*
- **T₃/T₄ Liotrix** *see Liotrix on page 685*
- **T₄** *see Levothyroxine on page 677*
- **222® Tablets** *see Aspirin and Codeine on page 105*
- **282® Tablets** *see Aspirin and Codeine on page 105*
- **292® Tablets** *see Aspirin and Codeine on page 105*
- **624® Tablets** *see Propoxyphene on page 985*
- **Tac™-3** *see Triamcinolone on page 1174*
- **Tac™-40** *see Triamcinolone on page 1174*
- **TACE®** *see Chlorotrianisene on page 245*

Tacrine *(TAK reen)*

U.S. Brand Names Cognex®

Synonyms Tacrine Hydrochloride; Tetrahydroaminoacrine; THA

Therapeutic Category Cholinergic Agent

Use Treatment of mild to moderate dementia of the Alzheimer's type

Pregnancy Risk Factor C

Contraindications Patients previously treated with the drug who developed jaundice and in those who are hypersensitive to tacrine or acridine derivatives

Warnings/Precautions The use of tacrine has been associated with elevations in serum transaminases; serum transaminases (specifically ALT) must be monitored throughout therapy; use extreme caution in patients with current evidence of a history of abnormal liver function tests; use caution in patients with bladder outlet obstruction, asthma, and sick-sinus syndrome (tacrine may cause bradycardia). Also, patients with cardiovascular disease, asthma, or peptic ulcer should use cautiously.

Overdosage/Toxicology

General supportive measures; can cause a cholinergic crisis characterized by severe nausea, vomiting, salivation, sweating, bradycardia, hypotension, collapse, and convulsions; increased muscle weakness is a possibility and may result in death if respiratory muscles are involved

Tertiary anticholinergics, such as atropine, may be used as an antidote for overdosage. I.V. atropine sulfate titrated to effect is recommended; initial dose of 1-2 mg I.V. with subsequent doses based upon clinical response. Atypical increases in blood pressure and heart rate have been reported with other cholinomimetics when coadministered with quaternary anticholinergics such as glycopyrrolate.

Drug Interactions CYP1A2 enzyme substrate; CYP1A2 inhibitor

Increased effect of theophylline, cimetidine, succinylcholine, cholinesterase inhibitors, or cholinergic agonists

Usual Dosage Adults: Initial: 10 mg 4 times/day; may increase by 40 mg/day adjusted every 6 weeks; maximum: 160 mg/day; best administered separate from meal times; see table.

Dose Adjustment Based Upon Transaminase Elevations

ALT	Regimen
≤3 x ULN*	Continue titration
>3 to ≤5 x ULN	Decrease dose by 40 mg/day, resume when ALT returns to normal
>5 x ULN	Stop treatment, may rechallenge upon return of ALT to normal

*ULN = upper limit of normal.

Patients with clinical jaundice confirmed by elevated total bilirubin (>3 mg/dL) should not be rechallenged with tacrine

Monitoring Parameters ALT (SGPT) levels and other liver enzymes weekly for at least the first 18 weeks, then monitor once every 3 months

Reference Range In clinical trials, serum concentrations >20 ng/mL were associated with a much higher risk of development of symptomatic adverse effects

Patient Information Effect of tacrine therapy is thought to depend upon its administration at regular intervals, as directed; possibility of adverse effects such as those occurring in close temporal association with the initiation of treatment or an increase in dose (ie, nausea, vomiting, loose stools, diarrhea) and those with a delayed onset (ie, rash, jaundice, changes in the color of stool); inform physician of the emergence of new events or any increase in the severity of existing adverse effects; abrupt discontinuation of the drug or a large reduction in total daily dose (80 mg/day or more) may cause a decline in cognitive function and behavioral disturbances; unsupervised increases in the dose may also have serious consequences; do not change dose without consulting physician

Dosage Forms Capsule, as hydrochloride: 10 mg, 20 mg, 30 mg, 40 mg

♦ **Tacrine Hydrochloride** see Tacrine on previous page

Tacrolimus (ta KROE li mus)

U.S. Brand Names Prograf®

Synonyms FK506

Therapeutic Category Immunosuppressant Agent

Use Potent immunosuppressive drug used in liver, kidney, heart, lung, small bowel transplant recipients; immunosuppressive drug for peripheral stem cell/bone marrow transplantation

Pregnancy Risk Factor C

Pregnancy/Breast-Feeding Implications

Tacrolimus crosses the placenta and reaches concentrations four times greater than maternal plasma concentrations

Tacrolimus concentrations in breast milk are equivalent to plasma concentrations; breast-feeding is not advised while therapy is ongoing

Contraindications Hypersensitivity to tacrolimus or any component; hypersensitivity to HCO-60 polyoxyl 60 hydrogenated castor oil (used in the parenteral dosage formulation) is a contraindication to parenteral tacrolimus therapy

Warnings/Precautions Increased susceptibility to infection and the possible development of lymphoma may occur after administration of tacrolimus; it should not be administered simultaneously with cyclosporine; since the pharmacokinetics show great inter- and intrapatient variability over time, monitoring of serum concentrations (trough for oral therapy) is essential to prevent organ rejection and reduce drug-related toxicity; tonic clonic seizures may have been triggered by tacrolimus. Injection contains small volume of ethanol.

Adverse Reactions

>10%:

Cardiovascular: Hypertension, peripheral edema

Central nervous system: Headache, insomnia, pain, fever

Dermatologic: Pruritus

Endocrine & metabolic: Hypo-/hyperkalemia, hyperglycemia, hypomagnesemia

Gastrointestinal: Diarrhea, nausea, anorexia, vomiting, abdominal pain

Hematologic: Anemia, leukocytosis

Hepatic: LFT abnormalities, ascites

Neuromuscular & skeletal: Tremors, paresthesias, back pain, weakness

Renal: Nephrotoxicity, increased BUN/creatinine

Respiratory: Pleural effusion, atelectasis, dyspnea

Miscellaneous: Infection

1% to 10%:

Central nervous system: Seizures

(Continued)

Tacrolimus (Continued)

    Dermatologic: Rash

    Endocrine & metabolic: Hyperphosphatemia, hyperuricemia, pancreatitis

    Gastrointestinal: Constipation

    Genitourinary: Urinary tract infection

    Hematologic: Thrombocytopenia

    Neuromuscular & skeletal: Myoclonus

    Renal: Oliguria

<1%: Hypertrophic cardiomyopathy, arthralgia, myalgia, hemolytic uremic syndrome, anaphylaxis, expressive aphasia, photophobia, secondary malignancy

Overdosage/Toxicology

Symptoms are extensions of pharmacologic activity and listed adverse effects

Symptomatic and supportive treatment required, hemodialysis is not effective

Drug Interactions CYP3A3/4 enzyme substrate

Decreased effect: Separate administration of antacids and Carafate® from tacrolimus by at least 2 hours

Increased effect: Cyclosporine is associated with synergistic immunosuppression and increased nephrotoxicity

Increased toxicity: Nephrotoxic antibiotics, NSAIDs and amphotericin B potentially increase nephrotoxicity

See table.

Drug Interactions With Tacrolimus

Drugs Which May INCREASE Tacrolimus Blood Levels		
Calcium Channel Blockers	Antibiotic/Antifungal Agents	Other Drugs
Diltiazem Nicardipine Verapamil	Clotrimazole Erythromycin Fluconazole Itraconazole Ketoconazole	Bromocriptine Cimetidine Clarithromycin Cyclosporine Danazol Methylprednisolone Metoclopramide Grapefruit juice
Drugs Which May DECREASE Tacrolimus Blood Levels		
Anticonvulsants	Antibiotics	
Carbamazepine Phenobarbital Phenytoin	Rifabutin Rifampin	

Stability Polyvinyl-containing sets (eg, Venoset®, Accuset®) adsorb significant amounts of the drug, and their use may lead to a lower dose being delivered to the patient; tacrolimus capsules should be stored at controlled room temperature (15°C to 30°C). FK506 admixtures prepared in 5% dextrose injection or 0.9% sodium chloride injection should be stored in polyolefin containers or glass bottles. Infusion of FK506 through PVC tubings did not result in decreased concentration of the drug, however, loss by absorption may be more important when lower concentrations of FK506 are used. Stable for 48 hours in D_5W or NS in glass or polyolefin containers.

Mechanism of Action Binds to 40 FK binding protein resulting in inhibition of calcium-dependent signal transduction pathway in T cells, thereby blocking the secretion of IL-2 and other cytokines

Pharmacodynamics/Kinetics

Absorption: Highly variable following oral administration; food may reduce absorption

    Peak serum concentrations 0.4-5.6 µg/mL after single oral dose of 0.15 mg/kg.

Distribution: Highly lipophilic and undergoes extensive tissue distribution; sequestered by erythrocytes which result in plasma concentrations 10- to 30-fold lower than whole blood concentrations

    V_d: ~17 L/kg

Protein binding, plasma: ~88%

Metabolism: Extensive in the liver by cytochrome P-450 isozymes IA and 3A4

Bioavailability: Oral: Ranges from 5% to 67% (mean: ~27%)

Half-life, elimination: ~8.7 hours (mean)

Plasma clearance following intravenous administration: ~143 L/hour (mean)

Elimination: <1% of the parent compound excreted in the bile and urine

Usual Dosage

Children: Patients without pre-existing renal or hepatic dysfunction have required and tolerated higher doses than adults to achieve similar blood concentrations. It is recommended that therapy be initiated at high end of the recommended adult I.V. and oral dosing ranges.

    Oral: 0.3 mg/kg/day divided every 12 hours; children generally require higher maintenance dosages than adults on a mg/kg basis than adults

    I.V. continuous infusion: 0.05-0.15 mg/kg/day

Adults:

    Oral (usually 3-4 times the I.V. dose): 0.15-0.30 mg/kg/day in two divided doses administered every 12 hours and given 8-12 hours after discontinuation of the I.V. infusion. Lower tacrolimus doses may be sufficient as maintenance therapy.

Solid organ transplantation: Oral: 0.15-0.30 mg/kg/day in two divided doses administered every 12 hours; lower tacrolimus doses may be sufficient as maintenance therapy

Peripheral stem cell/bone marrow transplantation: Oral (usually ~2-3 times the intravenous dose): 0.06-0.09 mg/kg/day (maximum: 0.12 mg/kg/day) in two divided doses administered every 12 hours and given 8-12 hours after discontinuation of the intravenous infusion; adjust doses based on trough serum concentrations

I.V.:

Solid organ transplantation: Initial (given at least 6 hours after transplantation): 0.05-0.10 mg/kg/day; corticosteroid therapy is advised to enhance immunosuppression. Patients should be switched to oral therapy as soon as possible (within 2-3 days).

Peripheral stem cell/bone marrow transplantation: Initial: 0.03 mg/kg/day as a continuous intravenous infusion

Dosing adjustment in renal impairment: Evidence suggests that lower doses should be used; patients should receive doses at the lowest value of the recommended I.V. and oral dosing ranges; further reductions in dose below these ranges may be required

Tacrolimus therapy should usually be delayed up to 48 hours or longer in patients with postoperative oliguria

Hemodialysis: Not removed by hemodialysis; supplemental dose is not necessary

Peritoneal dialysis: Significant drug removal is unlikely based on physiochemical characteristics

Dosing adjustment in hepatic impairment: Use of tacrolimus in liver transplant recipients experiencing post-transplant hepatic impairment may be associated with increased risk of developing renal insufficiency related to high whole blood levels of tacrolimus. The presence of moderate-to-severe hepatic dysfunction (serum bilirubin >2 mg/dL) appears to affect the metabolism of FK506. The half-life of the drug was prolonged and the clearance reduced after I.V. administration. The bioavailability of FK506 was also increased after oral administration. The higher plasma concentrations as determined by ELISA, in patients with severe hepatic dysfunction are probably due to the accumulation of FK506 metabolites of lower activity. These patients should be monitored closely and dosage adjustments should be considered. Some evidence indicates that lower doses could be used in these patients. See table.

Dosing Tacrolimus

Condition	Tacrolimus
Switch from I.V. to oral therapy	Threefold increase in dose
T-tube clamping	No change in dose
Pediatric patients	About 2 times higher dose compared to adults
Liver dysfunction	Decrease I.V. dose; decrease oral dose
Renal dysfunction	Does not affect kinetics; decrease dose to decrease levels if renal dysfunction is related to the drug
Dialysis	Not removed
Inhibitors of hepatic metabolism	Decrease dose
Inducers of hepatic metabolism	Monitor drug level; increase dose

Administration Administer I.V. by continuous infusion only (requires an infusion pump); tacrolimus must be diluted with 0.9% sodium chloride or 5% dextrose to a concentration of 0.004-0.02 mg/mL prior to administration. Diluted infusions should be stored in glass or polyethylene containers and discarded after 24 hours. The diluted solution should not be stored in polyvinyl chloride (PVC) containers due to a decreased stability and the potential for extraction of phthalates. Intravenous tacrolimus should not be infused with intravenous acyclovir or ganciclovir. The high pH of acyclovir and ganciclovir result in a significant chemical degradation of tacrolimus. If either acyclovir or ganciclovir are administered simultaneously via a multilumen central line, different ports should be used. Do **not** need to use nitroglycerin tubing to infuse intravenous tacrolimus.

Monitoring Parameters Renal function, hepatic function, serum electrolytes, glucose and blood pressure, hypersensitivity indicators, neurological responses, and other clinical parameters; monitoring of serum concentrations (trough for oral therapy), see Warnings/Precautions; measure 3 times/week for first few weeks, then gradually decrease frequency as patient stabilizes

Reference Range

Whole blood: Trough level: 7-20 ng/mL (ELISA). Plasma levels are generally 0.02-0.2 times whole blood levels; increased precision with whole blood levels.

Plasma: Trough levels: 0.5-2 ng/mL (ELISA, plasma, extracted at 37°C) for all transplant procedures (liver, heart, lung, kidney, small bowel) whole blood measurements produce concentration 5-40 times higher than those in serum due to high binding to RBCs (therapeutic range: 5-10 ng/mL, although levels >20 mg/mL may be desirable for short periods to prevent rejection)

Patient Information Separate administration with antacids by at least 2 hours

Nursing Implications For I.V. administration, tacrolimus is dispensed in a 50 mL glass container or nonpolyvinyl chloride container; it is intended to be infused over at least 12 hours; polyolefin administration sets should be used

Additional Information Each mL of injection contains polyoxyl 60 hydrogenated castor oil (HCO-60), 200 mg and dehydrated alcohol, USP, 80% v/v

(Continued)

Tacrolimus *(Continued)*

Dosage Forms
Capsule: 1 mg, 5 mg
Injection, with alcohol and surfactant: 5 mg/mL (1 mL)

Extemporaneous Preparations Tacrolimus oral suspension can be compounded at a concentration of 0.5 mg/mL; an extemporaneous suspension can be prepared by mixing the contents of six 5-mg tacrolimus capsules with equal amounts of Ora-Plus® and Simple Syrup, N.F., to make a final volume of 60 mL. The Suspension is stable for 56 days at room temperature in glass or plastic amber prescription bottles.

Esquivel C, So S, McDiarmid S, Andrews W, Colombani P. Suggested guidelines for the use of tacrolimus in pediatric liver transplant patients. *Transplantation* 1996, 61(5):847-8.

Foster JA, Jacobson PA, Johnson CE, et al. Stability of tacrolimus in an extemporaneously compounded oral liquid. (Abstract of Meeting Presentation) *American Society of Health-System Pharmacists Annual Meeting* 1996, 53:P-52(E).

♦ **Tagamet®** *see* Cimetidine *on page 261*
♦ **Tagamet® HB [OTC]** *see* Cimetidine *on page 261*
♦ **Talwin®** *see* Pentazocine *on page 901*
♦ **Talwin® NX** *see* Pentazocine *on page 901*
♦ **Tambocor™** *see* Flecainide *on page 486*
♦ **Tamofen®** *see* Tamoxifen *on this page*
♦ **Tamone®** *see* Tamoxifen *on this page*

Tamoxifen (ta MOKS i fen)

Related Information
Cancer Chemotherapy Regimens *on page 1263*
Toxicities of Chemotherapeutic Agents *on page 1288*

U.S. Brand Names Nolvadex®
Canadian Brand Names Alpha-Tamoxifen®; Apo®-Tamox; Novo-Tamoxifen; Tamofen®; Tamone®
Synonyms Tamoxifen Citrate
Therapeutic Category Antineoplastic Agent, Hormone Antagonist; Estrogen Receptor Antagonist
Use Palliative or adjunctive treatment of advanced breast cancer; reduce the incidence of breast cancer in women at high risk (taking into account age, number of first-degree relatives with breast cancer, previous breast biopsies, age at first live birth, age at first menstrual period, and a history of lobular carcinoma *in situ*)
Unlabeled use: Treatment of mastalgia, gynecomastia, male breast cancer, and pancreatic carcinoma. Studies have shown tamoxifen to be effective in the treatment of primary breast cancer in elderly women. Comparative studies with other antineoplastic agents in elderly women with breast cancer had more favorable survival rates with tamoxifen. Initiation of hormone therapy rather than chemotherapy is justified for elderly patients with metastatic breast cancer who are responsive.
Pregnancy Risk Factor D
Contraindications Hypersensitivity to tamoxifen
Warnings/Precautions Use with caution in patients with leukopenia, thrombocytopenia, or hyperlipidemias; ovulation may be induced; "hot flashes" may be countered by Bellergal-S® tablets; decreased visual acuity, retinopathy and corneal changes have been reported with use for more than 1 year at doses above recommended; hypercalcemia in patients with bone metastasis; hepatocellular carcinomas have been reported in animal studies; endometrial hyperplasia and polyps have occurred

Adverse Reactions
>10%:
Cardiovascular: Flushing
Dermatologic: Skin rash
Gastrointestinal: Little to mild nausea (10%), vomiting, weight gain
Hematologic: Myelosuppressive: Transient thrombocytopenia occurs in ~24% of patients receiving 10-20 mg/day; platelet counts return to normal within several weeks in spite of continued administration; leukopenia has also been reported and does resolve during continued administration; anemia has also been reported
WBC: Rare
Platelets: None
Hepatic: Hepatotoxicity
Neuromuscular & skeletal: Increased bone and tumor pain and local disease flare shortly after starting therapy; this will subside rapidly, but patients should be aware of this since many may discontinue the drug due to the side effects
1% to 10%:
Cardiovascular: Thromboembolism: Tamoxifen has been associated with the occurrence of venous thrombosis and pulmonary embolism; arterial thrombosis has also been described in a few case reports
Central nervous system: Lightheadedness, depression, dizziness, headache, lassitude, mental confusion
Dermatologic: Rash
Endocrine & metabolic: Hypercalcemia may occur in patients with bone metastases; galactorrhea and vitamin deficiency, menstrual irregularities

Genitourinary: Vaginal bleeding or discharge, endometriosis, priapism, possible endometrial cancer

Neuromuscular & skeletal: Weakness

Ocular: Ophthalmologic effects (visual acuity changes, cataracts, or retinopathy), corneal opacities

Overdosage/Toxicology

Symptoms of overdose include hypercalcemia, edema

General supportive care

Drug Interactions CYP1A2, 2A6, 2B6, 2C, 2D6, 2E1, and 3A3/4 enzyme substrate

Increased toxicity: Allopurinol results in exacerbation of allopurinol-induced hepatotoxicity; cyclosporine may result in increase in cyclosporine serum levels; warfarin results in significant enhancement of the anticoagulant effects of warfarin

Mechanism of Action Competitively binds to estrogen receptors on tumors and other tissue targets, producing a nuclear complex that decreases DNA synthesis and inhibits estrogen effects; nonsteroidal agent with potent antiestrogenic properties which compete with estrogen for binding sites in breast and other tissues; cells accumulate in the G_0 and G_1 phases; therefore, tamoxifen is cytostatic rather than cytocidal.

Pharmacodynamics/Kinetics

Absorption: Well absorbed from GI tract

Time to peak serum concentration: Oral: Within 4-7 hours

Distribution: High concentrations found in uterus, endometrial and breast tissue

Metabolism: In the liver

Half-life: 7 days

Elimination: Undergoes enterohepatic recycling; excreted in feces with only small amounts appearing in urine

Usual Dosage Oral (refer to individual protocols):

Adults: 10-20 mg twice daily in the morning and evening

High-dose therapy is under investigation

Monitoring Parameters Monitor WBC and platelet counts, tumor

Test Interactions T_4 elevations (no clinical evidence of hyperthyroidism)

Patient Information This drug will cause an initial "flare" of this disease (increased bone pain and hot flashes) which will subside. Report any vomiting that occurs after taking dose; women should be advised to notify their physician of vaginal bleeding, weakness, mental confusion.

Nursing Implications Increase of bone pain usually indicates a good therapeutic response

Dosage Forms Tablet, as citrate: 10 mg, 20 mg

♦ **Tamoxifen Citrate** *see Tamoxifen on previous page*

Tamsulosin (tam SOO loe sin)

U.S. Brand Names Flomax®

Therapeutic Category Alpha-Adrenergic Blocking Agent, Oral

Use Treatment of signs and symptoms of benign prostatic hyperplasia (BPH)

Pregnancy Risk Factor C

Warnings/Precautions Not intended for use as an antihypertensive drug; may cause orthostasis (ie, postural hypotension, dizziness, vertigo); patients should avoid situations where injury could result if syncope occurs; rule out the presence of carcinoma of prostate before beginning tamsulosin therapy

Adverse Reactions

Central nervous system: Headache, dizziness (0.4 mg: 14.9%; 0.8 mg: 17.1%), somnolence (0.4 mg: 3.0%; 0.8 mg: 4.3%), insomnia

Endocrine & metabolic: Decreased libido

Gastrointestinal: Diarrhea, nausea, tooth disorder

Genitourinary: Ejaculation disturbances

Neuromuscular & skeletal: Back pain, chest pain, asthenia

Ocular: Amblyopia

Respiratory: Rhinitis, pharyngitis, increased cough, sinusitis

Miscellaneous: Infections, allergic-type reactions such as skin rash, pruritus, angioedema, and urticaria have been reported upon drug rechallenge

Drug Interactions Use caution with concomitant administration of warfarin and tamsulosin; no dosage adjustments necessary if administered with atenolol, enalapril, or Procardia XL®; cimetidine resulted in a significant decrease (26%) in the clearance of tamsulosin which resulted in a moderate increase in tamsulosin AUC (44%); therefore, use with caution when used in combination with cimetidine (especially doses >0.4 mg); do not use in combination with other alpha-adrenergic blocking agents

Mechanism of Action An antagonist of alpha$_{1A}$ adrenoceptors in the prostate. Three subtypes identified: alpha$_{1A}$, alpha$_{1B}$, alpha$_{1D}$ have distribution that differs between human organs and tissue. Approximately 70% of the alpha$_1$-receptors in human prostate are of alpha$_{1A}$ subtype. The symptoms associated with benign prostatic hyperplasia (BPH) are related to bladder outlet obstruction, which is comprised of two underlying components: static and dynamic. Static is related to an increase in prostate size, partially caused by a proliferation of smooth muscle cells in the prostatic stroma. Severity of BPH symptoms and the degree of urethral obstruction do not correlate well with the size of the prostate. Dynamic is a function of an increase in smooth muscle tone in the prostate and bladder neck leading to constriction of the bladder outlet. Smooth muscle tone is mediated by the sympathetic nervous stimulation of alpha$_1$ adrenoceptors, which are abundant in the prostate, prostatic capsule, prostatic urethra, and bladder neck. Blockade of (Continued)

Tamsulosin (Continued)

these adrenoceptors can cause smooth muscles in the bladder neck and prostate to relax, resulting in an improvement in urine flow rate and a reduction in symptoms of BPH.

Pharmacodynamics/Kinetics

Absorption: >90%

Bioavailability: Fasting: 30% increase

Protein binding: Extensively to human plasma protein (94% to 99%), primarily alpha$_1$ acid glycoprotein (AAG); not affected by amitriptyline, diclofenac, glyburide, simvastatin plus simvastatin-hydroxy acid metabolite, warfarin, diazepam, propranolol, trichlormethazide, or chlormadinone, nor does tamsulosin effect extent of binding of these drugs

Metabolism: Cytochrome P-450 enzymes in the liver; profile of metabolites in humans has not been established

Steady-state: By the fifth day of once daily dosing

Peak concentrations: C_{max}: Fasting: 40% to 70% increase; T_{max}: Fasting: 4-5 hours; With food: 6-7 hours

Half-life: Healthy volunteers: 9-13 hours; Target population: 14-15 hours

Elimination: <10% excreted unchanged in urine; metabolites undergo extensive conjugation to glucuronide or sulfate prior to renal excretion

Usual Dosage Oral: Adults: 0.4 mg once daily approximately 30 minutes after the same meal each day

Dietary Considerations The time to maximum concentration (T_{max}) is reached by 4-5 hours under fasting conditions and by 6-7 hours when administered with food. Taking it under fasted conditions results in a 30% increase in bioavailability and 40% to 70% increase in peak concentrations (C_{max}) compared to fed conditions.

Patient Information Symptoms related to postural hypotension (ie, dizziness) may occur; do not drive, operate machinery, or perform hazardous activities; do not crush, chew, or open capsules

Dosage Forms Capsule, as hydrochloride: 0.4 mg

♦ **Tanac®** [OTC] see Benzocaine on page 133
♦ **Tanoral® Tablet** see Chlorpheniramine, Pyrilamine, and Phenylephrine on page 247
♦ **Tantaphen®** see Acetaminophen on page 19
♦ **Tao®** see Troleandomycin on page 1190
♦ **Tapazole®** see Methimazole on page 749
♦ **Tarka®** see Trandolapril and Verapamil on page 1167
♦ **Taro-Ampicillin® Trihydrate** see Ampicillin on page 79
♦ **Taro-Atenol®** see Atenolol on page 106
♦ **Taro-Cloxacillin®** see Cloxacillin on page 288
♦ **Taro-Sone®** see Betamethasone on page 141
♦ **Tasmar®** see Tolcapone on page 1157
♦ **TAT** see Tetanus Antitoxin on page 1119
♦ **Tavist®** see Clemastine on page 274
♦ **Tavist®-1** [OTC] see Clemastine on page 274
♦ **Tavist-D®** see Clemastine and Phenylpropanolamine on page 275
♦ **Taxol®** see Paclitaxel on page 880
♦ **Taxotere®** see Docetaxel on page 383

Tazarotene (taz AR oh teen)

U.S. Brand Names Tazorac®

Therapeutic Category Keratolytic Agent

Use Topical treatment of facial acne vulgaris; topical treatment of stable plaque psoriasis of up to 20% body surface area involvement

Pregnancy Risk Factor X

Contraindications Hypersensitivity to tazarotene and other retinoids or vitamin A derivatives (isotretinoin, tretinoin, etretinate); pregnancy

Warnings/Precautions Use with caution in patients who are breast-feeding. Use with caution in patients with eczema or open wounds (increased irritation and absorption may occur). Because of heightened burning susceptibility, exposure to sunlight should be avoided unless deemed medically necessary, and in such cases, exposure should be minimized during use of tazarotene. Administer with caution if the patient is also taking drugs known to be photosensitizers (thiazides, tetracyclines, fluoroquinolones, phenothiazines, sulfonamides) because of the increased possibility of augmented photosensitivity. Patients should be warned to use sunscreens (SPF minimum of 15) and protective clothing when using tazarotene. Application may cause a transitory feeling of burning or stinging. For external use only; avoid contact with eyes, eyelids, and mouth. The safety of use over >20% of body surface area has not been established.

Adverse Reactions

>10%: Local: Pruritus, burning/stinging, erythema, worsening of psoriasis, irritation, skin pain

1% to 10%: Dermatologic: Rash, desquamation, irritant contact dermatitis, skin inflammation, fissure, bleeding, dry skin, skin discoloration

Overdosage/Toxicology

Excessive topical use may lead to marked redness, peeling, or discomfort. Oral ingestion may lead to the same adverse effects as those associated with excessive oral intake of Vitamin A (hypervitaminosis A) or other retinoids.

Treatment: If oral ingestion occurs, monitor the patient and administer appropriate supportive measures as necessary

Stability Store gel at room temperature, away from heat and direct light; do not freeze

Mechanism of Action Synthetic, acetylenic retinoid which modulates differentiation and proliferation of epithelial tissue and exerts some degree of anti-inflammatory and immunological activity

Pharmacodynamics/Kinetics

Absorption: Minimal following cutaneous application of 0.05 or 0.1% gel (≤6% of dose)

Distribution: Retained in skin for prolonged periods after topical application. Therapeutic effects have been observed for up to 3 months after a 3-month course of topical treatment in patients with psoriasis.

Metabolism: Tazarotene is a prodrug which is rapidly metabolized by esterases to an active metabolite (tazarotenic acid) following topical application and systemic absorption. Tazarotenic acid is further metabolized in the liver.

Elimination: Primarily in the bile as tazarotene and tazarotenic acid

Usual Dosage Children >12 years and Adults: Topical:

Acne: Cleanse the face gently. After the skin is dry, apply a thin film of tazarotene (2 mg/cm^2) once daily, in the evening, to the skin where the acne lesions appear. Use enough to cover the entire affected area. Tazarotene was investigated ≤12 weeks during clinical trials for acne.

Psoriasis: Apply tazarotene once daily, in the evening, to psoriatic lesions using enough (2 mg/cm^2) to cover only the lesion with a thin film to no more than 20% of body surface area. If a bath or shower is taken prior to application, dry the skin before applying the gel. Because unaffected skin may be more susceptible to irritation, avoid application of tazarotene to these areas. Tazarotene was investigated for up to 12 months during clinical trials for psoriasis.

Monitoring Parameters Disease severity in plaque psoriasis during therapy (reduction in erythema, scaling, induration); routine blood chemistries (including transaminases) are suggested during long-term topical therapy

Patient Information Do not take this medication if you have had an allergic reaction to tazarotene. Do not use tazarotene if you are pregnant or planning to become pregnant. Tazarotene may cause birth defects or be harmful to an unborn baby if used during pregnancy. This may be more likely if the medicine is used on large areas of skin.

Your physician will tell you how much medicine to use and how often. Do not use more of the medication than your physician ordered. Using too much of the medication can cause red, peeling, or irritated skin. Wash your hands before and after using this medication (unless treating psoriasis lesions on your hands). Use this medication on your skin only. Do not put the medication in your eyes, eyelids, or in your mouth. If you do get the medication in your eyes, rinse them with large amounts of cool water. Tell your physician if you have eye pain or redness that does not go away.

Acne patients: Gently wash and dry your face. Apply a thin layer of medication to cover the acne. Your acne should start to clear up in about 4 weeks.

Psoriasis patients: If using the medication after bathing or showering, make sure your skin is completely dry before applying the medication. Apply a thin layer to lesions.

Wash off any medication that gets on skin areas that do not need to be treated. The medication can irritate skin that does not need treatment. Do not bandage or cover the treated skin. Ask your physician or pharmacist before taking any other medication, including over-the-counter products. Talk with your physician or pharmacist before using medicated cosmetics or shampoos, abrasive soaps or cleansers, products with alcohol, spice, or lime in them, other acne medicines, hair removal products, or products that dry your skin.

This medication may make your skin sensitive to sunlight and cause a rash or sunburn. Avoid spending long periods of time in direct sunlight and protect your skin with clothing and a strong sunscreen when you are outdoors. Do not use a sunlamp or tanning booth. Call your physician if you have blistering or crusting skin, severe redness, pain, or swelling on the areas that you use the medication.

Dosage Forms Gel, topical: 0.05% (30 g, 100 g), 0.1% (30 g, 100 g)

Telmisartan (tel mi SAR tan)

Related Information
Angiotensin Agents *on page 1291*

U.S. Brand Names Micardis®

Therapeutic Category Angiotensin II Antagonist; Antihypertensive Agent

Use Alone or in combination with other antihypertensive agents in treating essential hypertension

Pregnancy Risk Factor C (1st trimester); D (2nd and 3rd trimester)

Pregnancy/Breast-Feeding Implications Avoid use in the nursing mother, if possible, since telmisartan may be excreted in breast milk. The drug should be discontinued as soon as possible when pregnancy is detected. Drugs which act directly on renin-angiotensin can cause fetal and neonatal morbidity and death.

Contraindications Hypersensitivity to telmisartan or any component (telmisartan, sodium hydroxide, meglumine, povidone, sorbitol, magnesium stearate); sensitivity to other A-II receptor antagonists; pregnancy

Warnings/Precautions Avoid use or use smaller dose in volume-depleted patients. Drugs which alter renin-angiotensin system have been associated with deterioration in renal function, including oliguria, acute renal failure, and progressive azotemia. Use with caution in patients with renal artery stenosis (unilateral or bilateral) to avoid decrease in renal function; use caution in patients with pre-existing renal insufficiency (may decrease renal perfusion); the major route of elimination for telmisartan is via biliary elimination and as a result, patients with biliary obstruction can be expected to have reduced clearance and, therefore, telmisartan should be used with caution.

Adverse Reactions
1% to 10%:
Cardiovascular: Hypertension (1%), chest pain (1%), peripheral edema (1%)
Central nervous system: Headache (1%), dizziness (1%), pain (1%), fatigue (1%)
Gastrointestinal: Diarrhea (3%, compared to 2% with placebo), dyspepsia (1%), nausea (1%), abdominal pain (1%)
Genitourinary: Urinary tract infection (7%, compared to 6% with placebo)
Neuromuscular & skeletal: Back pain (3%, compared to 1% with placebo), myalgia (1%)
Respiratory: Upper respiratory infection (7%, compared to 6% with placebo), sinusitis (3%, compared to 2% with placebo), pharyngitis (1%), cough (1.6%, same as placebo)
Miscellaneous: Flu-like syndrome (1%)
<1%: Angioedema, allergic reaction, elevate liver enzymes, decreased hemoglobin, increased creatinine/BUN, impotence, sweating, flushing, fever, malaise, palpitations, angina, tachycardia, abnormal EKG, insomnia, anxiety, nervousness, migraine, vertigo, depression, somnolence, paresthesias, involuntary muscle contractions, constipation, flatulence, dry mouth, hemorrhoids, gastroenteritis, toothache, gout, hypercholesterolemia, diabetes mellitus, arthralgias, leg cramps, anxiety, depression, nervousness, infection, asthma, bronchitis, rhinitis, dyspnea, epistaxis, dermatitis, rash, eczema, pruritus, micturition frequency, cystitis, cerebrovascular disorder, abnormal vision, conjunctivitis, tinnitus, earache

Overdosage/Toxicology Signs and symptoms of overdose include hypotension, dizziness and tachycardia; treatment is supportive; vagal stimulation may result in bradycardia

Drug Interactions Not metabolized by cytochrome P-450
May increase serum digoxin levels (increased peak levels by a median of 49% and trough levels by 20%)
Has been associated with slight reductions in warfarin serum concentrations; however, this was not associated with a change in INR

Mechanism of Action Angiotensin II acts as a vasoconstrictor. In addition to causing direct vasoconstriction, angiotensin II also stimulates the release of aldosterone. Once aldosterone is released, sodium as well as water are reabsorbed. The end result is an elevation in blood pressure. Telmisartan is a nonpeptide AT1 angiotensin II receptor antagonist. This binding prevents angiotensin II from binding to the receptor thereby blocking the vasoconstriction and the aldosterone secreting effects of angiotensin II.

Pharmacodynamics/Kinetics Telmisartan does not require prodrug conversion prior to drug action
Onset of action: 1-2 hours
Time to peak: 0.5-1 hours
Duration: Up to 24 hours
Protein binding: >99.5%
Metabolism: Hepatic, via conjugation to inactive metabolites
Bioavailability: 42% to 58% (dose-dependent)
Half-life, terminal: 24 hours
Elimination: Total body clearance: 800 mL/minute; 97% of a dose is excreted in the feces via extensive biliary secretion

Usual Dosage Adults: Oral: Initial: 40 mg once daily; may be administered with or without food; usual maintenance dose range: 20-80 mg/day
Patients with volume depletion: Should be initiated on a lower dosage with close supervision or the condition should be corrected prior to initiating therapy or the use of an alternative ATII antagonist during initiation of therapy is warranted
Dosing in the elderly: No initial dose adjustment is required
Dosing in hepatic/biliary impairment: Supervise patients closely
Dosing in renal impairment: No initial dosing adjustment is necessary; patients on dialysis may develop orthostatic hypotension

Dietary Considerations May be administered without regard to food

Monitoring Parameters Supine blood pressure, electrolytes, serum creatinine, BUN, urinalysis, symptomatic hypotension, and tachycardia

Patient Information Patients of childbearing age should be informed about the consequences of 2nd- and 3rd-trimester exposure to drugs that act on the renin-angiotensin system, and that these consequences do not appear to have resulted from intrauterine drug exposure that has been limited to the 1st trimester. Patients should report pregnancy to their physician as soon as possible.

Dosage Forms Tablet: 40 mg, 80 mg

Temazepam (te MAZ e pam)

Related Information
Benzodiazepines Comparison *on page 1310*

U.S. Brand Names Restoril®

Canadian Brand Names Apo®-Temazepam

Therapeutic Category Benzodiazepine; Hypnotic; Sedative

Use Treatment of anxiety and as an adjunct in the treatment of depression; also may be used in the management of panic attacks; transient insomnia and sleep latency

Restrictions C-IV

Pregnancy Risk Factor X

Contraindications Hypersensitivity to temazepam or any component, severe uncontrolled pain, pre-existing CNS depression, or narrow-angle glaucoma; not to be used in pregnancy or lactation

Warnings/Precautions Safety and efficacy in children <18 years of age have not been established; do not use in pregnant women; may cause drug dependency; avoid abrupt discontinuance in patients with prolonged therapy or seizure disorders; use with caution in patients receiving other CNS depressants, in patients with hepatic dysfunction, and the elderly

Adverse Reactions
>10%:
Cardiovascular: Tachycardia, chest pain
Central nervous system: Drowsiness, fatigue, ataxia, lightheadedness, memory impairment, insomnia, anxiety, depression, headache
Dermatologic: Rash
Endocrine & metabolic: Decreased libido
Gastrointestinal: Xerostomia, constipation, diarrhea, decreased salivation, nausea, vomiting, increased or decreased appetite
Neuromuscular & skeletal: Dysarthria
Ocular: Blurred vision
Miscellaneous: Diaphoresis
1% to 10%:
Cardiovascular: Syncope, hypotension
Central nervous system: Confusion, nervousness, dizziness, akathisia
Dermatologic: Dermatitis
Gastrointestinal: Increased salivation, weight gain or loss
Neuromuscular & skeletal: Rigidity, tremor, muscle cramps
Otic: Tinnitus
Respiratory: Nasal congestion, hyperventilation
<1%: Menstrual irregularities, blood dyscrasias, reflex slowing, drug dependence

Overdosage/Toxicology
Symptoms of overdose include somnolence, confusion, coma, hypoactive reflexes, dyspnea, hypotension, slurred speech, impaired coordination
Treatment for benzodiazepine overdose is supportive. Rarely is mechanical ventilation required. Flumazenil has been shown to selectively block the binding of benzodiazepines to CNS receptors, resulting in a reversal of benzodiazepine-induced CNS depression.

Drug Interactions CYP3A3/4 enzyme substrate
Increased effect of CNS depressants

Mechanism of Action Benzodiazepine anxiolytic sedative that produces CNS depression at the subcortical level, except at high doses, whereby it works at the cortical level; causes minimal change in REM sleep patterns

Pharmacodynamics/Kinetics
Protein binding: 96%
Metabolism: In the liver
Half-life: 9.5-12.4 hours
Time to peak serum concentration: Within 2-3 hours
Elimination: 80% to 90% excreted in urine as inactive metabolites

Usual Dosage Adults: Oral: 15-30 mg at bedtime; 15 mg in elderly or debilitated patients

Dietary Considerations Alcohol: Additive CNS effect, avoid use

Monitoring Parameters Respiratory and cardiovascular status

Reference Range Therapeutic: 26 ng/mL after 24 hours

Patient Information Avoid alcohol and other CNS depressants; avoid activities needing good psychomotor coordination until CNS effects are known; drug may cause physical or psychological dependence; avoid abrupt discontinuation after prolonged use

Nursing Implications Provide safety measures (ie, side rails, night light, and call button); remove smoking materials from area; supervise ambulation

Dosage Forms Capsule: 7.5 mg, 15 mg, 30 mg

♦ Temovate® Topical *see Clobetasol on page 277*

♦ **Tempra® [OTC]** see Acetaminophen on page 19

♦ **Tenex®** see Guanfacine on page 552

Teniposide (ten i POE side)

Related Information

Extravasation Management of Chemotherapeutic Agents on page 1285

Toxicities of Chemotherapeutic Agents on page 1288

U.S. Brand Names Vumon® Injection

Synonyms EPT; VM-26

Therapeutic Category Antineoplastic Agent, Podophyllotoxin Derivative; Antineoplastic Agent, Vesicant

Use Treatment of acute lymphocytic leukemia, small cell lung cancer

Pregnancy Risk Factor D

Contraindications Hypersensitivity to teniposide or Cremophor EL (polyoxyethylated castor oil) any component

Warnings/Precautions The U.S. Food and Drug Administration (FDA) currently recommends that procedures for proper handling and disposal of antineoplastic agents be considered. Administer I.V. infusions over a period of at least 30-60 minutes, must be diluted, do not administer IVP. Teniposide contains benzyl alcohol, which has been associated with a fatal "gasping" syndrome in premature infants.

Adverse Reactions

>10%:

Gastrointestinal: Mucositis, nausea, vomiting, diarrhea

Hematologic: Myelosuppression, leukopenia, neutropenia, thrombocytopenia

Miscellaneous: Infection

1% to 10%:

Cardiovascular: Hypotension

Central nervous system: Fever

Dermatologic: Alopecia, rash

Hematologic: Hemorrhage

Miscellaneous: Hypersensitivity

<1%: Metabolic abnormalities, hepatic dysfunction, peripheral neurotoxicity, renal dysfunction

Overdosage/Toxicology

Symptoms of overdose include bone marrow suppression, leukopenia, thrombocytopenia, nausea, vomiting

Treatment is supportive

Drug Interactions CYP3A3/4 enzyme substrate; CYP2C19 enzyme inhibitor

Increased toxicity:

Methotrexate: Alteration of MTX transport has been found as a slow efflux of MTX and its polyglutamated form out of the cell, leading to intercellular accumulation of MTX

Sodium salicylate, sulfamethizole, tolbutamide: displace teniposide from protein-binding sites - could cause substantial increases in free drug levels, resulting in potentiation of toxicity

Stability Store ampuls in refrigerator at 2°C to 8°C (36°F to 46°F); reconstituted solutions are stable at room temperature for up to 24 hours after preparation. Teniposide must be diluted with either D_5W or 0.9% sodium chloride solutions to a final concentration of 0.1, 0.2, 0.4 or 1 mg/mL. In order to prevent extraction of the plasticizer DEHP, **solutions should be prepared in non-DEHP-containing containers such as glass or polyolefin containers.** The use of polyvinyl chloride (PVC) containers is not recommended. Administer 1 mg/mL solutions within 4 hours of preparation to reduce the potential for precipitation. Precipitation may occur at any concentration. **Incompatible with heparin.**

Mechanism of Action Inhibits mitotic activity; inhibits cells from entering mitosis

Pharmacodynamics/Kinetics

Distribution: V_d: 0.28 L/kg; distributed mainly into liver, kidneys, small intestine, and adrenals; crosses blood-brain barrier to a limited extent

V_d: 3-11 L (children); 8-44 L (adults)

Protein binding: 99.4%

Metabolism: Extensively in the liver

Half-life: 5 hours

Elimination: In urine (21% as unchanged drug); renal (44%) and fecal (≤10%)

Usual Dosage I.V.:

Children: 130 mg/m²/week, increasing to 150 mg/m² after 3 weeks and up to 180 mg/m² after 6 weeks

Adults: 50-180 mg/m² once or twice weekly for 4-6 weeks or 20-60 mg/m²/day for 5 days

Acute lymphoblastic leukemia (ALL): 165 mg/m² twice weekly for 8-9 doses **or** 250 mg/m² weekly for 4-8 weeks

Small cell lung cancer: 80-90 mg/m²/day for 5 days

Dosage adjustment in renal/hepatic impairment: Data is insufficient, but dose adjustments may be necessary in patient with significant renal or hepatic impairment

Dosage adjustment in Down syndrome patients: Reduce initial dosing; administer the first course at half the usual dose. Patients with both Down syndrome and leukemia may be especially sensitive to myelosuppressive chemotherapy.

Administration Do not use in-line filter during I.V. infusion; slow I.V. infusion over ≥30 minutes

Teniposide must be diluted with either D_5W or 0.9% sodium chloride solutions to a final concentration of 0.1, 0.2, 0.4, or 1 mg/mL. In order to prevent extraction of the plasticizer DEHP, solutions should be prepared in non-DEHP-containing containers such as glass or polyolefin containers. **The use of polyvinyl chloride (PVC) containers is not recommended.**

Patient Information Hair should grow back after treatment

Nursing Implications Monitor blood pressure during infusion; observe for chemical phlebitis at injection site

Additional Information May be available only through investigational protocols

Dosage Forms Injection: 10 mg/mL (5 mL)

♦ **Ten-K**® see Potassium Chloride on page 949
♦ **Tenoretic**® see Atenolol and Chlorthalidone on page 108
♦ **Tenormin**® see Atenolol on page 106
♦ **Tensilon**® **Injection** see Edrophonium on page 405
♦ **Tenuate**® see Diethylpropion on page 354
♦ **Tenuate**® **Dospan**® see Diethylpropion on page 354
♦ **Terak**® **Ophthalmic Ointment** see Oxytetracycline and Polymyxin B on page 879
♦ **Terazol**® **Vaginal** see Terconazole on page 1116

Terazosin (ter AY zoe sin)

U.S. Brand Names Hytrin®

Therapeutic Category Alpha-Adrenergic Blocking Agent, Oral; Antihypertensive Agent

Use Management of mild to moderate hypertension; used alone or in combination with other agents such as diuretics or beta-blockers; benign prostate hypertrophy

Pregnancy Risk Factor C

Contraindications Hypersensitivity to terazosin, other alpha-adrenergic antagonists, or any component

Warnings/Precautions Marked orthostatic hypotension, syncope, and loss of consciousness may occur with first dose ("first dose phenomenon"). This reaction is more likely to occur in patients receiving beta-blockers, diuretics, low sodium diets, or first doses >1 mg/dose in adults; avoid rapid increase in dose; use with caution in patients with renal impairment.

Adverse Reactions

>10%:
  Central nervous system: Dizziness (9% to 19%), headache (5% to 16%)
  Neuromuscular & skeletal: Weakness (7.4% to 11.3%)

1% to 10%:
  Cardiovascular: Peripheral edema (5.5%), palpitations (0.9% to 4.3%), postural hypotension (0.6% to 3.9%), tachycardia (1.9%)
  Central nervous system: Fatigue, nervousness (2.3%)
  Gastrointestinal: Xerostomia, nausea (4.4%), vomiting (1%), diarrhea/constipation (1%), abdominal pain (1%), flatulence (1%)
  Neuromuscular & skeletal: Paresthesia (2.9%)
  Respiratory: Dyspnea (1.7% to 3.1%), nasal congestion (1.9% to 5.9%)

<1%: Angina (~1%), syncope, depression, insomnia, rash, sexual dysfunction, decreased libido, priapism, polyuria, arthritis, myalgia, blurred vision, conjunctivitis, tinnitus, bronchospasm, epistaxis, pharyngitis, flu-like symptoms

Overdosage/Toxicology

Symptoms of overdose include hypotension, drowsiness, shock (but very unusual)

Hypotension usually responds to I.V. fluids or Trendelenburg positioning; if unresponsive to these measures, the use of a parenteral vasoconstrictor may be required; treatment is primarily supportive and symptomatic

Drug Interactions

Decreased antihypertensive response with NSAIDs and alpha$_1$-blockers; decreased clonidine effects

Increased hypotensive effect with diuretics and antihypertensive medications (especially beta-blockers)

Mechanism of Action Alpha$_1$-specific blocking agent with minimal alpha$_2$ effects; this allows peripheral postsynaptic blockade, with the resultant decrease in arterial tone, while preserving the negative feedback loop which is mediated by the peripheral presynaptic alpha$_2$-receptors; terazosin relaxes the smooth muscle of the bladder neck, thus reducing bladder outlet obstruction

Pharmacodynamics/Kinetics

Absorption: Oral: Rapid
Protein binding: 90% to 95%
Metabolism: Extensively in the liver
Half-life: 9.2-12 hours
Time to peak serum concentration: Within 1 hour
Elimination: Principally in feces (60%) and in urine (40%)

Usual Dosage Adults: Oral:

Hypertension: Initial: 1 mg at bedtime; slowly increase dose to achieve desired blood pressure, up to 20 mg/day; usual dose: 1-5 mg/day

Dosage reduction may be needed when adding a diuretic or other antihypertensive agent; if drug is discontinued for greater than several days, consider beginning with initial dose and retitrate as needed; dosage may be given on a twice daily regimen if response is diminished at 24 hours and hypotensive is observed at 2-4 hours following a dose

Benign prostatic hypertrophy: Initial: 1 mg at bedtime, increasing as needed; most patients require 10 mg day; if no response after 4-6 weeks of 10 mg/day, may increase to 20 mg/day

(Continued)

Terazosin (Continued)

Monitoring Parameters Standing and sitting/supine blood pressure, especially following the initial dose at 2-4 hours following the dose and thereafter at the trough point to ensure adequate control throughout the dosing interval; urinary symptoms

Patient Information Report any gain of body weight or painful, persistent erection; fainting sometimes occurs after the first dose; rise slowly from prolonged sitting or standing

Dosage Forms
Capsule: 1 mg, 2 mg, 5 mg, 10 mg
Tablet: 1 mg, 2 mg, 5 mg, 10 mg

Terbinafine (TER bin a feen)

U.S. Brand Names Daskil®; Lamisil®

Synonyms Terbinafine Hydrochloride

Therapeutic Category Antifungal Agent, Topical

Use Active against most strains of *Trichophyton mentagrophytes*, *Trichophyton rubrum*; may be effective for infections of *Microsporum gypseum* and *M. nanum*, *Trichophyton verrucosum*, *Epidermophyton floccosum*, *Candida albicans*, and *Scopulariopsis brevicaulis*

Oral: Onychomycosis of the toenail or fingernail due to susceptible dermatophytes

Topical: Antifungal for the treatment of tinea pedis (athlete's foot), tinea cruris (jock itch), and tinea corporis (ringworm)

Unlabeled use: Topical: Cutaneous candidiasis and pityriasis versicolor

Pregnancy Risk Factor B

Pregnancy/Breast-Feeding Implications
Clinical effects on the fetus: Avoid use in pregnancy since treatment of onychomycosis is postponable

Breast-feeding/lactation: Although minimal concentrations of terbinafine cross into breast milk after topical use, oral or topical treatment during lactation should be avoided

Contraindications Hypersensitivity to terbinafine, naftifine or any component; pre-existing liver or renal disease (≤50 mL/minute GFR)

Warnings/Precautions While rare, the following complications have been reported and may require discontinuation of therapy: Changes in the ocular lens and retina, pancytopenia, neutropenia, Stevens-Johnson syndrome, toxic epidermal necrolysis. Discontinue if symptoms or signs of hepatobiliary dysfunction or cholestatic hepatitis develop. If irritation/sensitivity develop with topical use, discontinue therapy.

Adverse Reactions
Oral: 1% to 10%:
Central nervous system: Headache, dizziness, vertigo
Dermatologic: Rash, pruritus, and alopecia with oral therapy
Gastrointestinal: Nausea, diarrhea, dyspepsia, abdominal pain, appetite decrease, taste disturbance
Hematologic: Neutropenia, lymphocytopenia
Hepatic: Cholestasis, jaundice, hepatitis, liver enzyme elevations
Ocular: Visual disturbance
Miscellaneous: Allergic reaction
Topical: 1% to 10%:
Dermatologic: Pruritus, contact dermatitis, irritation, burning, dryness
Local: Irritation, stinging

Drug Interactions
Decreased effect: Cyclosporine clearance is increased (~15%) with concomitant terbinafine; rifampin increases terbinafine clearance (100%)
Increased effect: Terbinafine clearance is decreased by cimetidine (33%) and terfenadine (16%); caffeine clearance is decreased by terfenadine (19%)

Stability Cream: Store at 5°C to 30°C/41°F to 86°F

Mechanism of Action Synthetic alkylamine derivative which inhibits squalene epoxidase, a key enzyme in sterol biosynthesis in fungi. This results in a deficiency in ergosterol within the fungal cell wall and results in fungal cell death.

Pharmacodynamics/Kinetics
Absorption: Topical: Limited (<5%); Oral: >70%
Distribution: V_d: 2000 L; distributed to sebum and skin predominantly
Protein binding, plasma: >99%
Metabolism: Hepatic; no active metabolites
Bioavailability: Oral: 80% although undergoes first-pass metabolism (40%); does not involve significant (<5%) of total cytochrome P-450 capacity of liver; peak plasma levels occur at 1-2 hours
Half-life: 22-26 hours; very slow release of drug from skin and adipose tissues occurs
Elimination: ~75% of dose excreted in urine; 3.5% of a topically administered dose excreted in urine and feces

Usual Dosage Adults:
Oral:
Superficial mycoses: Fingernail: 250 mg/day for up to 6 weeks; toenail: 250 mg/day for 12 weeks; doses may be given in two divided doses
Systemic mycosis: 250-500 mg/day for up to 16 months
Topical:
Athlete's foot: Apply to affected area twice daily for at least 1 week, not to exceed 4 weeks

Ringworm and jock itch: Apply to affected area once or twice daily for at least 1 week, not to exceed 4 weeks

Dosing adjustment in renal impairment: Although specific guidelines are not available, dose reduction in significant renal insufficiency (GFR <50 mL/minute) is recommended

Monitoring Parameters CBC and LFTs at baseline and repeated if use is for >6 weeks

Patient Information Topical: Avoid contact with eyes, nose, or mouth during treatment with cream; nursing mothers should not use on breast tissue; advise physician if eyes or skin becomes yellow or if irritation, itching, or burning develops. Do not use occlusive dressings concurrent with therapy. Full clinical effect may require several months due to the time required for a new nail to grow.

Nursing Implications Patients should not be considered therapeutic failures until they have been symptom-free for 2-4 weeks off following a course of treatment; GI complaints usually subside with continued administration

Additional Information A meta-analysis of efficacy studies for toenail infections revealed that weighted average mycological cure rates for continuous therapy were 36.7% (griseofulvin), 54.7% (itraconazole), and 77% (terbinafine). Cure rate for 4-month pulse therapy for itraconazole and terbinafine were 73.3% and 80%. Additionally, the final outcome measure of final costs per cured infections for continuous therapy was significantly lower for terbinafine.

Dosage Forms
Cream: 1% (15 g, 30 g)
Tablet: 250 mg

♦ **Terbinafine Hydrochloride** see Terbinafine on previous page

Terbutaline (ter BYOO ta leen)

Related Information
Bronchodilators, Comparison of Inhaled and Sympathomimetic on page 1314

U.S. Brand Names Brethaire® Inhalation Aerosol; Brethine® Injection; Brethine® Oral; Bricanyl® Injection; Bricanyl® Oral

Synonyms Terbutaline Sulfate

Therapeutic Category Beta$_2$-Adrenergic Agonist Agent; Bronchodilator; Sympathomimetic; Tocolytic Agent

Use Bronchodilator in reversible airway obstruction and bronchial asthma

Pregnancy Risk Factor B

Contraindications Hypersensitivity to terbutaline or any component, cardiac arrhythmias associated with tachycardia, tachycardia caused by digitalis intoxication

Warnings/Precautions Excessive or prolonged use may lead to tolerance; paradoxical bronchoconstriction may occur with excessive use; if it occurs, discontinue terbutaline immediately

Adverse Reactions
>10%:
    Central nervous system: Nervousness, restlessness
    Neuromuscular & skeletal: Trembling
1% to 10%:
    Cardiovascular: Tachycardia, hypertension
    Central nervous system: Dizziness, drowsiness, headache, insomnia
    Gastrointestinal: Xerostomia, nausea, vomiting, bad taste in mouth
    Neuromuscular & skeletal: Muscle cramps, weakness
    Miscellaneous: Diaphoresis
<1%: Chest pain, arrhythmias, paradoxical bronchospasm

Overdosage/Toxicology
Symptoms of overdose include seizures, nausea, vomiting, tachycardia, cardiac dysrhythmias, hypokalemia

In cases of overdose, supportive therapy should be instituted; prudent use of a cardioselective beta-adrenergic blocker (eg, atenolol or metoprolol) should be considered, keeping in mind the potential for induction of bronchoconstriction in an asthmatic individual. Dialysis has not been shown to be of value in the treatment of an overdose with this agent.

Drug Interactions
Decreased effect with beta-blockers
Increased toxicity with MAO inhibitors, TCAs

Stability Store injection at room temperature; protect from heat, light, and from freezing; use only clear solutions

Mechanism of Action Relaxes bronchial smooth muscle by action on beta$_2$-receptors with less effect on heart rate

Pharmacodynamics/Kinetics
Onset of action: Oral: 30-45 minutes; S.C.: Within 6-15 minutes
Protein binding: 25%
Metabolism: In the liver to inactive sulfate conjugates
Bioavailability: S.C. doses are more bioavailable than oral
Half-life: 11-16 hours
Elimination: In urine

Usual Dosage
Children <12 years:
    Oral: Initial: 0.05 mg/kg/dose 3 times/day, increased gradually as required; maximum: 0.15 mg/kg/dose 3-4 times/day or a total of 5 mg/24 hours
    S.C.: 0.005-0.01 mg/kg/dose to a maximum of 0.3 mg/dose every 15-20 minutes for 3 doses
(Continued)

Terbutaline *(Continued)*

    Nebulization: 0.01-0.03 mg/kg/dose every 4-6 hours
    Inhalation: 1-2 inhalations every 4-6 hours
  Children >12 years and Adults:
    Oral:
      12-15 years: 2.5 mg every 6 hours 3 times/day; not to exceed 7.5 mg in 24 hours
      >15 years: 5 mg/dose every 6 hours 3 times/day; if side effects occur, reduce dose
        to 2.5 mg every 6 hours; not to exceed 15 mg in 24 hours
    S.C.: 0.25 mg/dose repeated in 15-30 minutes for one time only; a total dose of 0.5 mg
      should not be exceeded within a 4-hour period
    Nebulization: 0.01-0.03 mg/kg/dose every 4-6 hours
    Inhalation: 2 inhalations every 4-6 hours; wait 1 minute between inhalations

Dosing adjustment/comments in renal impairment:
  Cl$_{cr}$ 10-50 mL/minute: Administer at 50% of normal dose
  Cl$_{cr}$ <10 mL/minute: Avoid use

Administration Injection with S.C. use; in oral administration administer around-the-clock to promote less variation in peak and trough serum levels

Monitoring Parameters Serum potassium, heart rate, blood pressure, respiratory rate

Patient Information Precede administration of aerosol adrenocorticoid by 15 minutes; report any decreased effectiveness of drug; do not exceed recommended dose or frequency; may take last dose at 6 PM to avoid insomnia

Dosage Forms
  Aerosol, oral, as sulfate: 0.2 mg/actuation (10.5 g)
  Injection, as sulfate: 1 mg/mL (1 mL)
  Tablet, as sulfate: 2.5 mg, 5 mg

Extemporaneous Preparations A 1 mg/mL suspension made from terbutaline tablets in simple syrup NF is stable 30 days when refrigerated

    Horner RK and Johnson CE, "Stability of An Extemporaneously Compounded Terbutaline Sulfate Oral Liquid," *Am J Hosp Pharm*, 1991, 48(2):293-5.

- ◆ **Terbutaline Sulfate** *see Terbutaline on previous page*

Terconazole *(ter KONE a zole)*

Related Information
  Treatment of Sexually Transmitted Diseases *on page 1429*
U.S. Brand Names Terazol® Vaginal
Synonyms Triaconazole
Therapeutic Category Antifungal Agent, Vaginal
Use Local treatment of vulvovaginal candidiasis
Pregnancy Risk Factor C
Contraindications Known hypersensitivity to terconazole or components of the vaginal cream or suppository
Warnings/Precautions Should be discontinued if sensitization or irritation occurs. Microbiological studies (KOH smear and/or cultures) should be repeated in patients not responding to terconazole in order to confirm the diagnosis and rule out other other pathogens.
Adverse Reactions 1% to 10%: Genitourinary: Vulvar/vaginal burning
Stability Room temperature (13°C to 30°C/59°F to 86°F)
Mechanism of Action Triazole ketal antifungal agent; involves inhibition of fungal cytochrome P-450. Specifically, terconazole inhibits cytochrome P-450-dependent 14-alpha-demethylase which results in accumulation of membrane disturbing 14-alpha-demethylsterols and ergosterol depletion.
Pharmacodynamics/Kinetics Absorption: Extent of systemic absorption after vaginal administration may be dependent on the presence of a uterus; 5% to 8% in women who had a hysterectomy versus 12% to 16% in nonhysterectomy women
Usual Dosage Adults: Female: Insert 1 applicatorful intravaginally at bedtime for 7 consecutive days
Patient Information Insert high into vagina; complete full course of therapy; contact physician if itching or burning occurs
Nursing Implications Watch for local irritation; assist patient in administration, if necessary; assess patient's ability to self-administer, may be difficult in patients with arthritis or limited range of motion
Dosage Forms
  Cream, vaginal: 0.4% (45 g); 0.8% (20 g)
  Suppository, vaginal: 80 mg (3s)

Terpin Hydrate and Codeine *(TER pin HYE drate & KOE deen)*

Therapeutic Category Antitussive/Expectorant
Dosage Forms Elixir: Terpin hydrate 85 mg and codeine 10 mg per 5 mL with alcohol 42.5%

- ◆ **Terra-Cortril® Ophthalmic Suspension** *see Oxytetracycline and Hydrocortisone on page 879*
- ◆ **Terramycin® I.M. Injection** *see Oxytetracycline on page 878*
- ◆ **Terramycin® Ophthalmic Ointment** *see Oxytetracycline and Polymyxin B on page 879*
- ◆ **Terramycin® Oral** *see Oxytetracycline on page 878*

♦ **Terramycin® w/Polymyxin B Ophthalmic Ointment** *see* Oxytetracycline and Polymyxin B *on page 879*

♦ **Teslac®** *see* Testolactone *on this page*

♦ **TESPA** *see* Thiotepa *on page 1136*

♦ **Tessalon® Perles** *see* Benzonatate *on page 134*

♦ **Testex®** *see* Testosterone *on this page*

♦ **Testoderm® Transdermal System** *see* Testosterone *on this page*

Testolactone (tes toe LAK tone)

U.S. Brand Names Teslac®

Therapeutic Category Antineoplastic Agent, Androgen

Use Palliative treatment of advanced disseminated breast carcinoma

Restrictions C-III

Pregnancy Risk Factor C

Contraindications In men for the treatment of breast cancer; known hypersensitivity to testolactone

Warnings/Precautions The U.S. Food and Drug Administration (FDA) currently recommends that procedures for proper handling and disposal of antineoplastic agents be considered. Use with caution in hepatic, renal, or cardiac disease; prolonged use may cause drug-induced hepatic disease; history or porphyria.

Adverse Reactions 1% to 10%:

Cardiovascular: Edema

Dermatologic: Maculopapular rash

Endocrine & metabolic: Hypercalcemia,

Gastrointestinal: Anorexia, diarrhea, nausea, edema of the tongue

Neuromuscular & skeletal: Paresthesias, peripheral neuropathies

Overdosage/Toxicology Increased toxicity: Increased effects of oral anticoagulants

Mechanism of Action Testolactone is a synthetic testosterone derivative without significant androgen activity. The drug inhibits steroid aromatase activity, thereby blocking the production of estradiol and estrone from androgen precursors such as testosterone and androstenedione. Unfortunately, the enzymatic block provided by testolactone is transient and is usually limited to a period of 3 months.

Pharmacodynamics/Kinetics

Absorption: Oral: Absorbed well

Metabolism: In the liver

Elimination: In urine

Usual Dosage Adults: Female: Oral: 250 mg 4 times/day for at least 3 months; desired response may take as long as 3 months

Monitoring Parameters Plasma calcium levels

Test Interactions Plasma estradiol concentrations by RIA

Patient Information Passive exercises should be maintained throughout therapy to keep patient mobile; notify physician if numbness of fingers, toes, or face occurs

Dosage Forms Tablet: 50 mg

♦ **Testopel® Pellet** *see* Testosterone *on this page*

Testosterone (tes TOS ter one)

U.S. Brand Names Androderm® Transdermal System; Andro-L.A.® Injection; Andropository® Injection; Delatest® Injection; Delatestryl® Injection; depAndro® Injection; Depotest® Injection; Depo®-Testosterone Injection; Duratest® Injection; Durathate® Injection; Everone® Injection; Histerone® Injection; Testex®; Testoderm® Transdermal System; Testopel® Pellet

Synonyms Aqueous Testosterone; Testosterone Cypionate; Testosterone Enanthate; Testosterone Propionate

Therapeutic Category Androgen

Use Androgen replacement therapy in the treatment of delayed male puberty; postpartum breast pain and engorgement; inoperable breast cancer; male hypogonadism

Restrictions C-III

Pregnancy Risk Factor X

Contraindications Severe renal or cardiac disease, benign prostatic hypertrophy with obstruction, undiagnosed genital bleeding, males with carcinoma of the breast or prostate; hypersensitivity to testosterone or any component; pregnancy

Warnings/Precautions Perform radiographic examination of the hand and wrist every 6 months to determine the rate of bone maturation; may accelerate bone maturation without producing compensating gain in linear growth; has both androgenic and anabolic activity, the anabolic action may enhance hypoglycemia

Adverse Reactions

>10%:

Dermatologic: Acne

Endocrine & metabolic: Menstrual problems (amenorrhea), virilism, breast soreness

Genitourinary: Epididymitis, priapism, bladder irritability

1% to 10%:

Cardiovascular: Flushing, edema

Central nervous system: Excitation, aggressive behavior, sleeplessness, anxiety, mental depression, headache

Dermatologic: Hirsutism (increase in pubic hair growth)

Gastrointestinal: Nausea, vomiting, GI irritation

(Continued)

Testosterone (Continued)

Genitourinary: Prostatic hypertrophy, prostatic carcinoma, impotence, testicular atrophy

Hepatic: Hepatic dysfunction

<1%: Gynecomastia, hypercalcemia, hypoglycemia, leukopenia, suppression of clotting factors, polycythemia, cholestatic hepatitis, hepatic necrosis, hypersensitivity reactions

Drug Interactions CYP3A3/4 and 3A5-7 enzyme substrate

Increased toxicity: Effects of oral anticoagulants may be enhanced

Mechanism of Action Principal endogenous androgen responsible for promoting the growth and development of the male sex organs and maintaining secondary sex characteristics in androgen-deficient males

Pharmacodynamics/Kinetics

Duration of effect: Based upon the route of administration and which testosterone ester is used; the cypionate and enanthate esters have the longest duration, up to 2-4 weeks after I.M. administration

Distribution: Crosses the placenta; appears in breast milk

Protein binding: 98% (to transcortin and albumin)

Metabolism: In the liver

Half-life: 10-100 minutes

Elimination: In urine (90%) and feces via bile (6%)

Usual Dosage

Children: I.M.:

Male hypogonadism:

Initiation of pubertal growth: 40-50 mg/m^2/dose (cypionate or enanthate ester) monthly until the growth rate falls to prepubertal levels

Terminal growth phase: 100 mg/m^2/dose (cypionate or enanthate ester) monthly until growth ceases

Maintenance virilizing dose: 100 mg/m^2/dose (cypionate or enanthate ester) twice monthly

Delayed puberty: 40-50 mg/m^2/dose monthly (cypionate or enanthate ester) for 6 months

Adults: Inoperable breast cancer: I.M.: 200-400 mg every 2-4 weeks

Male: Short-acting formulations: Testosterone Aqueous/Testosterone Propionate (in oil): I.M.:

Androgen replacement therapy: 10-50 mg 2-3 times/week

Male hypogonadism: 40-50 mg/m^2/dose monthly until the growth rate falls to prepubertal levels (~5 cm/year); during terminal growth phase: 100 mg/m^2/dose monthly until growth ceases; maintenance virilizing dose: 100 mg/m^2/dose twice monthly or 50-400 mg/dose every 2-4 weeks

Male: Long-acting formulations: Testosterone enthanate (in oil)/testosterone cypionate (in oil): I.M.:

Male hypogonadism: 50-400 mg every 2-4 weeks

Male with delayed puberty: 50-200 mg every 2-4 weeks for a limited duration

Male ≥18 years: Transdermal: Primary hypogonadism **or** hypogonadotropic hypogonadism:

Testoderm®: Apply 6 mg patch daily to scrotum (if scrotum is inadequate, use a 4 mg daily system)

Testoderm-TSS®: Apply 5 mg patch daily to clean, dry area of skin on the arm, back or upper buttocks

Do not apply Testoderm-TSS® to the scrotum

Androderm®: Apply 2 systems nightly to clean, dry area on the back, abdomen, upper arms or thighs for 24 hours for a total of 5 mg/day

Dosing adjustment/comments in hepatic disease: Reduce dose

Monitoring Parameters Periodic liver function tests, radiologic examination of wrist and hand every 6 months (when using in prepubertal children)

Reference Range Testosterone, urine: Male: 100-1500 ng/24 hours; Female: 100-500 ng/24 hours

Test Interactions May cause a decrease in creatinine and creatine excretion and an increase in the excretion of 17-ketosteroids, thyroid function tests

Patient Information Virilization may occur in female patients; report menstrual irregularities; male patients report persistent penile erections; all patients should report persistent GI distress, diarrhea, or jaundice

Nursing Implications Warm injection to room temperature and shaking vial will help redissolve crystals that have formed after storage; administer by deep I.M. injection into the upper outer quadrant of the gluteus maximus. Transdermal system should be applied on clean, dry, scrotal skin. Dry-shave scrotal hair for optimal skin contact. Do not use chemical depilatories.

Additional Information

Testosterone (aqueous): Andro®, Histerone®, Tesamone®

Testosterone cypionate: Andro-Cyp®, Andronate®, Depotest®, Depo®-Testosterone, Duratest®

Testosterone enanthate: Andro-L.A.®, Andropository®, Delatestryl®, Durathate®, Everone®, Testrin® P.A.

Testosterone propionate: Testex®

Dosage Forms

Injection:

Aqueous suspension: 25 mg/mL (10 mL, 30 mL); 50 mg/mL (10 mL, 30 mL); 100 mg/mL (10 mL, 30 mL)

In oil, as cypionate: 100 mg/mL (1 mL, 10 mL); 200 mg/mL (1 mL, 10 mL)
In oil, as enanthate: 100 mg/mL (1 mL, 5 mL, 10 mL); 200 mg/mL (1 mL, 5 mL, 10 mL)
In oil, as propionate: 100 mg/mL (10 mL, 30 mL)
Pellet: 75 mg (1 pellet per vial)
Transdermal system:
Androderm®: 2.5 mg/day; 5 mg/day
Testoderm®: 4 mg/day; 6 mg/day
Testoderm-TTS®: 5 mg/day

♦ **Testosterone Cypionate** *see* Testosterone *on page 1117*
♦ **Testosterone Enanthate** *see* Testosterone *on page 1117*
♦ **Testosterone Propionate** *see* Testosterone *on page 1117*
♦ **Testred®** *see* Methyltestosterone *on page 764*
♦ **Tetanus and Diphtheria Toxoid** *see* Diphtheria and Tetanus Toxoid *on page 372*

Tetanus Antitoxin (TET a nus an tee TOKS in)
Synonyms TAT
Therapeutic Category Antitoxin
Use Tetanus prophylaxis or treatment of active tetanus only when tetanus immune globulin (TIG) is not available; tetanus immune globulin (Hyper-Tet®) is the preferred tetanus immunoglobulin for the treatment of active tetanus; may be given concomitantly with tetanus toxoid adsorbed when immediate treatment is required, but active immunization is desirable
Pregnancy Risk Factor D
Contraindications Patients sensitive to equine-derived preparations
Warnings/Precautions Tetanus antitoxin is not the same as tetanus immune globulin; sensitivity testing should be conducted in all individuals regardless of clinical history; have epinephrine 1:1000 available
Adverse Reactions Skin eruptions, erythema, urticaria, local pain, numbness, arthralgia, serum sickness may develop up to several weeks after injection in 10% of patients, anaphylaxis
Stability Refrigerate, do not freeze
Mechanism of Action Provides passive immunization; solution of concentrated globulins containing antitoxic antibodies obtained from horse serum after immunization against tetanus toxin
Usual Dosage
Prophylaxis: I.M., S.C.:
Children <30 kg: 1500 units
Children and Adults ≥30 kg: 3000-5000 units
Treatment: Children and Adults: Inject 10,000-40,000 units into wound; administer 40,000-100,000 units
Nursing Implications All patients should have sensitivity testing prior to starting therapy with tetanus antitoxin
Dosage Forms Injection, equine: Not less than 400 units/mL (12.5 mL, 50 mL)

Tetanus Immune Globulin (Human)
(TET a nus i MYUN GLOB yoo lin HYU man)
Related Information
Adverse Events and Vaccination *on page 1369*
Immunization Recommendations *on page 1358*
U.S. Brand Names Hyper-Tet®
Synonyms TIG
Therapeutic Category Immune Globulin
Use Passive immunization against tetanus; tetanus immune globulin is preferred over tetanus antitoxin for treatment of active tetanus; part of the management of an unclean, wound in a person whose history of previous receipt of tetanus toxoid is unknown or who has received less than three doses of tetanus toxoid; elderly may require TIG more often than younger patients with tetanus infection due to declining antibody titers with age
Pregnancy Risk Factor C
Contraindications Hypersensitivity to tetanus immune globulin, thimerosal, or any immune globulin product or component; patients with IgA deficiency; I.V. administration
Warnings/Precautions Have epinephrine 1:1000 available for anaphylactic reactions; do not administer I.V.
Adverse Reactions
>10%: Local: Pain, tenderness, erythema at injection site
1% to 10%:
Central nervous system: Fever (mild)
Dermatologic: Urticaria, angioedema
Neuromuscular & skeletal: Muscle stiffness
Miscellaneous: Anaphylaxis reaction
<1%: Sensitization to repeated injections
Drug Interactions Never administer tetanus toxoid and TIG in same syringe (toxoid will be neutralized); toxoid may be given at a separate site; concomitant administration with Td may decrease its immune response, especially in individuals with low prevaccination antibody titers
Stability Refrigerate
Mechanism of Action Passive immunity toward tetanus
Pharmacodynamics/Kinetics Absorption: Well absorbed
(Continued)

1119

Tetanus Immune Globulin (Human) *(Continued)*

Usual Dosage I.M.:
Prophylaxis of tetanus:
Children: 4 units/kg; some recommend administering 250 units to small children
Adults: 250 units
Treatment of tetanus:
Children: 500-3000 units; some should infiltrate locally around the wound
Adults: 3000-6000 units

Administration Do not administer I.V.; I.M. use only

Additional Information Tetanus immune globulin (TIG) must not contain <50 units/mL. Protein makes up 10% to 18% of TIG preparations. The great majority of this (≥90%) is IgG. TIG has almost no color or odor and it is a sterile, nonpyrogenic, concentrated preparation of immunoglobulins that has been derived from the plasma of adults hyper-immunized with tetanus toxoid. The pooled material from which the immunoglobulin is derived may be from fewer than 1000 donors. This plasma has been shown to be free of hepatitis B surface antigen.

Dosage Forms Injection: 250 units/mL

Tetanus Toxoid, Adsorbed (TET a nus TOKS oyd, ad SORBED)

Related Information
Adverse Events and Vaccination *on page 1369*
Immunization Recommendations *on page 1358*
Skin Tests *on page 1353*

Therapeutic Category Toxoid

Use Selective induction of active immunity against tetanus in selected patients. **Note:** Tetanus and diphtheria toxoids for adult use (Td) is the preferred immunizing agent for most adults and for children after their seventh birthday. Young children should receive trivalent DTwP or DTaP (diphtheria/tetanus/pertussis - whole cell or acellular), as part of their childhood immunization program, unless pertussis is contraindicated, then TD is warranted.

Pregnancy Risk Factor C

Contraindications Hypersensitivity to tetanus toxoid or any component (may use the fluid tetanus toxoid to immunize the rare patient who is hypersensitive to aluminum adjuvant); avoid use with chloramphenicol or if neurological signs or symptoms occurred after prior administration; poliomyelitis outbreaks require deferral of immunizations; acute respiratory infections or other active infections may dictate deferral of administration of routine primary immunizing but not emergency doses

Warnings/Precautions Not equivalent to tetanus toxoid fluid; the tetanus toxoid adsorbed is the preferred toxoid for immunization and Td, TD or DTaP/DTwP are the preferred adsorbed forms; avoid injection into a blood vessel; have epinephrine (1:1000) available; not for use in treatment of tetanus infection nor for immediate prophylaxis of unimmunized individuals; immunosuppressive therapy or other immunodeficiencies may diminish antibody response, however it is recommended for routine immunization of symptomatic and asymptomatic HIV-infected patients; deferral of immunization until immunosuppression is discontinued or administration of an additional dose >1 month after treatment is recommended; allergic reactions may occur; epinephrine 1:1000 must be available; use in pediatrics should be deferred until >1 year of age when a history of a CNS disorder is present; elderly may not mount adequate antibody titers following immunization

Adverse Reactions
>10%: Local: Induration/redness at injection site
1% to 10%:
Central nervous system: Chills, fever
Local: Sterile abscess at injection site
Miscellaneous: Allergic reaction
<1%: Fever >103°F, malaise, neurological disturbances, blistering at injection site, Arthus-type hypersensitivity reactions

Drug Interactions Decreased response: If primary immunization is started in individuals receiving an immunosuppressive agent or corticosteroids, serologic testing may be needed to ensure adequate antibody response; concurrent use of TIG and tetanus toxoid may delay the development of active immunity by several days

Stability Refrigerate, do not freeze

Mechanism of Action Tetanus toxoid preparations contain the toxin produced by virulent tetanus bacilli (detoxified growth products of *Clostridium tetani*). The toxin has been modified by treatment with formaldehyde so that it has lost toxicity but still retains ability to act as antigen and produce active immunity; the aluminum salt, a mineral adjuvant, delays the rate of absorption and prolongs and enhances its properties; duration ~10 years.

Pharmacodynamics/Kinetics Duration of immunization following primary immunization: ~10 years

Usual Dosage Adults: I.M.:
Primary immunization: 0.5 mL; repeat 0.5 mL at 4-8 weeks after first dose and at 6-12 months after second dose
Routine booster doses are recommended only every 5-10 years

Administration Inject intramuscularly in the area of the vastus lateralis (midthigh laterally) or deltoid

Patient Information A nodule may be palpable at the injection site for a few weeks. DT, Td and T vaccines cause few problems; they may cause mild fever or soreness, swelling, and redness where the shot was given. These problems usually last 1-2 days, but this does not happen nearly as often as with DTP vaccine. Sometimes, adults who get these vaccines can have a lot of soreness and swelling where the shot was given.

Dosage Forms Injection, adsorbed:
Tetanus 5 Lf units per 0.5 mL dose (0.5 mL, 5 mL)
Tetanus 10 Lf units per 0.5 mL dose (0.5 mL, 5 mL)

Tetanus Toxoid, Fluid (TET a nus TOKS oyd FLOO id)

Related Information
Adverse Events and Vaccination on page 1369
Immunization Recommendations on page 1358
Skin Tests on page 1353

Synonyms Tetanus Toxoid Plain
Therapeutic Category Toxoid
Use Detection of delayed hypersensitivity and assessment of cell-mediated immunity; active immunization against tetanus in the rare adult or child who is allergic to the aluminum adjuvant (a product containing adsorbed tetanus toxoid is preferred)

Pregnancy Risk Factor C
Contraindications Hypersensitivity to tetanus toxoid or any product components
Warnings/Precautions Epinephrine 1:1000 should be readily available; skin test responsiveness may be delayed or reduced in elderly patients
Adverse Reactions Percentage unknown: Very hypersensitive persons may develop a local reaction at the injection site; urticaria, anaphylactic reactions, shock and death are possible

Drug Interactions Increased effect: Cimetidine may augment delayed hypersensitivity responses to skin test antigens
Stability Refrigerate
Mechanism of Action Tetanus toxoid preparations contain the toxin produced by virulent tetanus bacilli (detoxified growth products of Clostridium tetani). The toxin has been modified by treatment with formaldehyde so that is has lost toxicity but still retains ability to act as antigen and produce active immunity.

Usual Dosage
Anergy testing: Intradermal: 0.1 mL
Primary immunization (**Note:** Td, TD, DTaP/DTwP are recommended): Adults: Inject 3 doses of 0.5 mL I.M. or S.C. at 4- to 8-week intervals; administer fourth dose 6-12 months after third dose
Booster doses: I.M., S.C.: 0.5 mL every 10 years

Administration Must not be used I.V.; for skin testing, use 0.1 mL of 1:100 v/v or 0.02 mL of 1:10 v/v solution

Dosage Forms Injection, fluid:
Tetanus 4 Lf units per 0.5 mL dose (7.5 mL)
Tetanus 5 Lf units per 0.5 mL dose (0.5 mL, 7.5 mL)

♦ **Tetanus Toxoid Plain** see Tetanus Toxoid, Fluid on this page

Tetracaine (TET ra kane)

U.S. Brand Names Pontocaine®
Canadian Brand Names Ametop™
Synonyms Amethocaine Hydrochloride; Tetracaine Hydrochloride
Therapeutic Category Local Anesthetic, Ester Derivative; Local Anesthetic, Injectable; Local Anesthetic, Ophthalmic; Local Anesthetic, Oral; Local Anesthetic, Topical
Use Spinal anesthesia; local anesthesia in the eye for various diagnostic and examination purposes; topically applied to nose and throat for various diagnostic procedures; **approximately 10 times more potent than procaine**

Pregnancy Risk Factor C
Contraindications Hypersensitivity to tetracaine or any component; ophthalmic secondary bacterial infection, patients with liver disease, CNS disease, meningitis (if used for epidural or spinal anesthesia), myasthenia gravis
Warnings/Precautions No pediatric dosage recommendations; ophthalmic preparations may delay wound healing; use with caution in patients with cardiac disease and hyperthyroidism

Adverse Reactions
1% to 10%: Dermatologic: Contact dermatitis, burning, stinging, angioedema
<1%: Tenderness, urticaria, urethritis, methemoglobinemia in infants

Overdosage/Toxicology Maximum dose is 50 mg

Treatment of overdose is primarily symptomatic and supportive. Termination of anesthesia by pneumatic tourniquet inflation should be attempted when the agent is administered by infiltration or regional injection. Seizures commonly respond to diazepam, while hypotension responds to I.V. fluids and Trendelenburg positioning. Bradyarrhythmias (when the heart rate is less than 60) can be treated with I.V., I.M. or S.C. atropine 15 mcg/kg. With the development of metabolic acidosis, I.V. sodium bicarbonate 0.5-2 mEq/kg and ventilatory assistance should be instituted.

Drug Interactions Decreased effect: Aminosalicylic acid, sulfonamides effects may be antagonized
Stability Store solution in the refrigerator
Mechanism of Action Ester local anesthetic blocks both the initiation and conduction of nerve impulses by decreasing the neuronal membrane's permeability to sodium ions, which results in inhibition of depolarization with resultant blockade of conduction
(Continued)

Tetracaine *(Continued)*

Pharmacodynamics/Kinetics
Onset of anesthetic effect:
  Ophthalmic instillation: Within 60 seconds
  Topical or spinal injection: Within 3-8 minutes after applied to mucous membranes or when saddle block administered for spinal anesthesia
Duration of action: Topical: 1.5-3 hours
Metabolism: By the liver
Elimination: Renal

Usual Dosage Maximum adult dose: 50 mg
Children: Safety and efficacy have not been established
Adults:
  Ophthalmic (not for prolonged use):
    Ointment: Apply ½" to 1" to lower conjunctival fornix
    Solution: Instill 1-2 drops
  Spinal anesthesia:
    High, medium, low, and saddle blocks: 0.2% to 0.3% solution
    Prolonged (2-3 hours): 1% solution
    Subarachnoid injection: 5-20 mg
    Saddle block: 2-5 mg; a 1% solution should be diluted with equal volume of CSF before administration
  Topical mucous membranes (2% solution): Apply as needed; dose should not exceed 20 mg
  Topical for skin: Ointment/cream: Apply to affected areas as needed

Patient Information
Report any rashes; keep refrigerated; may cause transient burning or stinging of eyes upon instillation; do not touch or rub eye until anesthesia (if ophthalmic) has worn off

Nursing Implications
Store the solutions in the refrigerator; before injection, withdraw syringe plunger to make sure injection is not into vein or artery

Dosage Forms
Cream, as hydrochloride: 1% (28 g)
Injection, as hydrochloride: 1% [10 mg/mL] (2 mL)
Injection, as hydrochloride, with dextrose 6%: 0.2% [2 mg/mL] (2 mL); 0.3% [3 mg/mL] (5 mL)
Ointment, as hydrochloride:
  Ophthalmic: 0.5% [5 mg/mL] (3.75 g)
  Topical: 0.5% [5 mg/mL] (28 g)
Powder for injection, as hydrochloride: 20 mg
Solution, as hydrochloride:
  Ophthalmic: 0.5% [5 mg/mL] (1 mL, 2 mL, 15 mL, 59 mL)
  Topical: 2% [20 mg/mL] (30 mL, 118 mL)

Tetracaine and Dextrose *(TET ra kane & DEKS trose)*
U.S. Brand Names Pontocaine® With Dextrose Injection
Therapeutic Category Local Anesthetic
Dosage Forms Injection: Tetracaine hydrochloride 0.2% and dextrose 6% (2 mL); tetracaine hydrochloride 0.3% and dextrose 6% (5 mL)

♦ **Tetracaine Hydrochloride** *see* Tetracaine *on previous page*

♦ **Tetracap® Oral** *see* Tetracycline *on this page*

♦ **Tetracosactide** *see* Cosyntropin *on page 298*

Tetracycline *(tet ra SYE kleen)*
Related Information
Antacid Drug Interactions *on page 1296*
Antimicrobial Drugs of Choice *on page 1404*
Helicobacter pylori Treatment *on page 1473*
U.S. Brand Names Achromycin® Ophthalmic; Achromycin® Topical; Nor-tet® Oral; Panmycin® Oral; Sumycin® Oral; Tetracap® Oral; Topicycline® Topical
Canadian Brand Names Apo®-Tetra; Novo-Tetra; Nu-Tetra
Synonyms TCN; Tetracycline Hydrochloride
Therapeutic Category Acne Products; Antibiotic, Ophthalmic; Antibiotic, Tetracycline Derivative; Antibiotic, Topical
Use Treatment of susceptible bacterial infections of both gram-positive and gram-negative organisms; also infections due to *Mycoplasma, Chlamydia,* and *Rickettsia;* indicated for acne, exacerbations of chronic bronchitis, and treatment of gonorrhea and syphilis in patients that are allergic to penicillin; used concomitantly with metronidazole, bismuth subsalicylate and an H_2-antagonist for the treatment of duodenal ulcer disease induced by *H. pylori*
Pregnancy Risk Factor D; B (topical)
Pregnancy/Breast-Feeding Implications Breast-feeding/lactation: Excreted in breast milk; avoid use if possible in lactating mothers
Contraindications Hypersensitivity to tetracycline or any component; do not administer to children ≤8 years of age
Warnings/Precautions Use of tetracyclines during tooth development may cause permanent discoloration of the teeth and enamel, hypoplasia and retardation of skeletal development and bone growth with risk being the greatest for children <4 years and those receiving high doses; use with caution in patients with renal or hepatic impairment

(eg, elderly) and in pregnancy; dosage modification required in patients with renal impairment since it may increase BUN as an antianabolic agent; pseudotumor cerebri has been reported with tetracycline use (usually resolves with discontinuation); outdated drug can cause nephropathy; superinfection possible; use protective measure to avoid photosensitivity

Adverse Reactions

>10%: Gastrointestinal: Discoloration of teeth and enamel hypoplasia (young children)

1% to 10%:

Dermatologic: Photosensitivity

Gastrointestinal: Nausea, diarrhea

<1%: Pericarditis, increased intracranial pressure, bulging fontanels in infants, pseudotumor cerebri, dermatologic effects, pruritus, pigmentation of nails, exfoliative dermatitis, diabetes insipidus syndrome, vomiting, esophagitis, anorexia, abdominal cramps, antibiotic-associated pseudomembranous colitis, staphylococcal enterocolitis, hepatotoxicity, thrombophlebitis, paresthesia, acute renal failure, azotemia, renal damage, superinfections, anaphylaxis, hypersensitivity reactions, candidal superinfection

Overdosage/Toxicology

Symptoms of overdose include nausea, anorexia, diarrhea; following GI decontamination Supportive care only

Drug Interactions

Decreased effect: Calcium, magnesium or aluminum-containing antacids, oral contraceptives, iron, zinc, sodium bicarbonate, penicillins, cimetidine may decrease tetracycline absorption

Although no clinical evidence exists, may bind with bismuth or calcium carbonate, an excipient in bismuth subsalicylate, during treatment for *H. pylori*

Increased toxicity: Methoxyflurane anesthesia when concurrent with tetracycline may cause fatal nephrotoxicity; warfarin with tetracyclines may result in increased anticoagulation; tetracyclines may rarely increase digoxin serum levels

Stability Outdated tetracyclines have caused a Fanconi-like syndrome; protect oral dosage forms from light

Mechanism of Action Inhibits bacterial protein synthesis by binding with the 30S and possibly the 50S ribosomal subunit(s) of susceptible bacteria; may also cause alterations in the cytoplasmic membrane

Pharmacodynamics/Kinetics

Absorption: Oral: 75%

Distribution: Small amount appears in bile

Relative diffusion of antimicrobial agents from blood into cerebrospinal fluid (CSF): Good only with inflammation (exceeds usual MICs)

Ratio of CSF to blood level (%): Inflamed meninges: 25

Protein binding: 20% to 60%

Half-life:

Normal renal function: 8-11 hours

End-stage renal disease: 57-108 hours

Time to peak serum concentration: Oral: Within 2-4 hours

Elimination: Primary route is the kidney, with 60% of a dose excreted as unchanged drug in the urine; concentrated by liver in bile and feces in biologically active form

Usual Dosage

Children >8 years: Oral: 25-50 mg/kg/day in divided doses every 6 hours

Children >8 years and Adults:

Ophthalmic:

Ointment: Instill every 2-12 hours

Suspension: Instill 1-2 drops 2-4 times/day or more often as needed

Topical: Apply to affected areas 1-4 times/day

Adults: Oral: 250-500 mg/dose every 6 hours

Helicobacter pylori: Clinically effective treatment regimens include triple therapy with amoxicillin or tetracycline, metronidazole, and bismuth subsalicylate; amoxicillin, metronidazole, and H_2-receptor antagonist; or double therapy with amoxicillin and omeprazole. Adult dose: 850 mg 3 times/day to 500 mg 4 times/day

Dosing interval in renal impairment:

Cl_{cr} 50-80 mL/minute: Administer every 8-12 hours

Cl_{cr} 10-50 mL/minute: Administer every 12-24 hours

Cl_{cr} <10 mL/minute: Administer every 24 hours

Dialysis: Slightly dialyzable (5% to 20%) via hemo- and peritoneal dialysis nor via continuous arteriovenous or venovenous hemofiltration (CAVH/CAVHD); no supplemental dosage necessary

Dosing adjustment in hepatic impairment: Avoid use or maximum dose is 1 g/day

Dietary Considerations Food: Dairy products decrease effect of tetracycline

Administration Oral should be given on an empty stomach (ie, 1 hour prior to, or 2 hours after meals) to increase total absorption. Administer at least 1-2 hours prior to, or 4 hours after antacid because aluminum and magnesium cations may chelate with tetracycline and reduce its total absorption.

Monitoring Parameters Renal, hepatic, and hematologic function test, temperature, WBC, cultures and sensitivity, appetite, mental status

Test Interactions False-negative urine glucose with Clinistix®

Patient Information Take 1 hour before or 2 hours after meals with adequate amounts of fluid; avoid prolonged exposure to sunlight or sunlamps; avoid taking antacids, iron, or dairy products within 2 hours of taking tetracyclines; report persistent nausea, vomiting, yellow coloring of skin or eyes, dark urine, or pale stools; ophthalmic may cause transient burning or itching; topical is for external use only and may stain skin yellow

(Continued)

Tetracycline *(Continued)*

Additional Information
Tetracycline: Sumycin® syrup

Tetracycline hydrochloride: Nor-tet® capsule, Panmycin® capsule, Sumycin® capsule and tablet, Tetracyn® capsule

Dosage Forms
Capsule, as hydrochloride: 100 mg, 250 mg, 500 mg

Ointment:
Ophthalmic: 1% [10 mg/mL] (3.5 g)
Topical, as hydrochloride: 3% [30 mg/mL] (14.2 g, 30 g)

Solution, topical: 2.2 mg/mL (70 mL)

Suspension:
Ophthalmic: 1% [10 mg/mL] (0.5 mL, 1 mL, 4 mL)
Oral, as hydrochloride: 125 mg/5 mL (60 mL, 480 mL)

Tablet, as hydrochloride: 250 mg, 500 mg

- **Tetracycline Hydrochloride** *see* Tetracycline *on page 1122*
- **Tetrahydroaminoacrine** *see* Tacrine *on page 1102*
- **Tetrahydrocannabinol** *see* Dronabinol *on page 399*
- **Tetramune®** *see* Diphtheria, Tetanus Toxoids, Whole-Cell Pertussis, and *Haemophilus influenzae* Type b Conjugate Vaccines *on page 375*
- **TG** *see* Thioguanine *on page 1133*
- **6-TG** *see* Thioguanine *on page 1133*
- **T-Gen®** *see* Trimethobenzamide *on page 1183*
- **T-Gesic®** *see* Hydrocodone and Acetaminophen *on page 575*
- **THA** *see* Tacrine *on page 1102*
- **Thalidomid®** *see* Thalidomide *on this page*

Thalidomide *(tha LI doe mide)*

U.S. Brand Names Thalidomid®

Therapeutic Category Immunosuppressant Agent

Use Treatment of erythema nodosum leprosum

Orphan status: Crohn's disease

Investigational: Treatment or prevention of graft-versus-host reactions after bone marrow transplantation; in aphthous ulceration in HIV-positive patients; Langerhans cell histocytosis, Behçet's syndrome; hypnotic agent; also may be effective in rheumatoid arthritis, discoid lupus, and erythema multiforme; useful in type 2 lepra reactions, but not type 1; can assist in healing mouth ulcers in AIDS patients

Pregnancy Risk Factor X

Pregnancy/Breast-Feeding Implications Embryotoxic with limb defects noted from the 27th to 40th gestational day of exposure; all cases of phocomelia occur from the 27th to 42nd gestational day; fetal cardiac, gastrointestinal, and genitourinary tract abnormalities have also been described

Contraindications Pregnancy or women in childbearing years, neuropathy (peripheral), thalidomide hypersensitivity

Warnings/Precautions Liver, hepatic, neurological disorders, constipation, congestive heart failure, hypertension

Adverse Reactions Percentage unknown: Tachycardia, sinus tachycardia, dizziness, headache, irritability, lethargy, fever, edema, alopecia, pruritus, amenorrhea, sexual dysfunction, nausea, vomiting, xerostomia, constipation, leukopenia, sensory neuropathy (peripheral) (after prolonged therapy due to neuronal degeneration), clonus, myoclonus

Mechanism of Action A derivative of glutethimide; mode of action for immunosuppression is unclear; inhibition of neutrophil chemotaxis and decreased monocyte phagocytosis may occur; may cause 50% to 80% reduction of tumor necrosis factor - alpha

Pharmacodynamics/Kinetics
Distribution: V_d: 120 L
Metabolism: Hepatic
Half-life: 8.7 hours
Peak plasma levels: 2-6 hours

Usual Dosage
Leprosy: Up to 400 mg/day; usual maintenance dose: 50-100 mg/day

Behçet's syndrome: 100-400 mg/day

Graft-vs-host reactions:
Children: 3 mg/kg 4 times/day
Adults: 100-1600 mg/day; usual initial dose: 200 mg 4 times/day for use up to 700 days

AIDS-related aphthous stomatitis: 200 mg twice daily for 5 days, then 200 mg/day for up to 8 weeks

Discoid lupus erythematosus: 100-400 mg/day; maintenance dose: 25-50 mg

Reference Range Therapeutic plasma thalidomide levels in graft-vs-host reactions are 5-8 µg/mL, although it has been suggested that lower plasma levels (0.5-1.5 µg/mL) may be therapeutic; peak serum thalidomide level after a 200 mg dose: 1.2 µg/mL

Additional Information Must be obtained via "STEPS Program" through Boston University

- **Thalitone®** *see* Chlorthalidone *on page 251*
- **THAM-E® Injection** *see* Tromethamine *on page 1191*
- **THAM® Injection** *see* Tromethamine *on page 1191*

- **THC** *see Dronabinol on page 399*
- **Theo-24®** *see Theophylline Salts on this page*
- **Theobid®** *see Theophylline Salts on this page*
- **Theochron®** *see Theophylline Salts on this page*
- **Theoclear® L.A.** *see Theophylline Salts on this page*
- **Theo-Dur®** *see Theophylline Salts on this page*
- **Theo-Dur® Sprinkle** *see Theophylline Salts on this page*
- **Theolair™** *see Theophylline Salts on this page*
- **Theon®** *see Theophylline Salts on this page*
- **Theophylline** *see Theophylline Salts on this page*

Theophylline and Guaifenesin (thee OF i lin & gwye FEN e sin)
U.S. Brand Names Bronchial®; Glycerol-T®; Quibron®; Slo-Phyllin® GG
Therapeutic Category Theophylline Derivative
Dosage Forms
Capsule: Theophylline 150 mg and guaifenesin 90 mg; theophylline 300 mg and guaifenesin 180 mg
Elixir: Theophylline 150 mg and guaifenesin 90 mg per 15 mL (480 mL)

Theophylline, Ephedrine, and Hydroxyzine
(thee OF i lin, e FED rin, & hye DROKS i zeen)
U.S. Brand Names Hydrophed®; Marax®
Therapeutic Category Theophylline Derivative
Dosage Forms
Syrup, dye free: Theophylline 32.5 mg, ephedrine 6.25 mg, and hydroxyzine 2.5 mg per 5 mL
Tablet: Theophylline 130 mg, ephedrine 25 mg, and hydroxyzine 10 mg

Theophylline, Ephedrine, and Phenobarbital
(thee OF i lin, e FED rin, & fee noe BAR bi tal)
U.S. Brand Names Tedral®
Therapeutic Category Theophylline Derivative
Dosage Forms
Suspension: Theophylline 65 mg, ephedrine sulfate 12 mg, and phenobarbital 4 mg per 5 mL
Tablet: Theophylline 118 mg, ephedrine sulfate 25 mg, and phenobarbital 11 mg; theophylline 130 mg, ephedrine sulfate 24 mg, and phenobarbital 8 mg

Theophylline Salts (thee OFF i lin salts)
Related Information
Asthma, Guidelines for the Diagnosis and Management of *on page 1456*
U.S. Brand Names Aerolate®; Aerolate III®; Aerolate JR®; Aerolate SR®; Aminophyllin™; Aquaphyllin®; Asmalix®; Bronkodyl®; Choledyl®; Constant-T®; Duraphyl™; Elixophyllin®; Elixophyllin® SR; LaBID®; Phyllocontin®; Quibron®-T; Quibron®-T/SR; Respbid®; Slobid™; Slo-Phyllin®; Sustaire®; Theo-24®; Theobid®; Theochron®; Theoclear® L.A.; Theo-Dur®; Theo-Dur® Sprinkle; Theolair™; Theon®; Theospan®-SR; Theovent®; Truphylline®
Synonyms Aminophylline; Choline Theophyllinate; Ethylenediamine; Oxtriphylline; Theophylline
Therapeutic Category Bronchodilator; Theophylline Derivative
Use Bronchodilator in reversible airway obstruction due to asthma, chronic bronchitis, and emphysema; for neonatal apnea/bradycardia
Pregnancy Risk Factor C
Pregnancy/Breast-Feeding Implications
Clinical effects on the fetus: Crosses the placenta. Transient tachycardia, irritability, vomiting in newborn especially if maternal serum concentrations >20 mcg/mL. Apneic spells attributed to withdrawal in newborn exposed throughout gestation period. Available evidence suggests safe use during pregnancy.
Breast-feeding/lactation: Crosses into breast milk
Clinical effects on the infant: Irritability reported in infants. American Academy of Pediatrics considers **compatible** with breast-feeding.
Contraindications Uncontrolled arrhythmias, hyperthyroidism, peptic ulcers, uncontrolled seizure disorders, hypersensitivity to xanthines or any component
Warnings/Precautions Use with caution in patients with peptic ulcer, hyperthyroidism, hypertension, tachyarrhythmias, and patients with compromised cardiac function; do not inject I.V. solution faster than 25 mg/minute; elderly, acutely ill, and patients with severe respiratory problems, pulmonary edema, or liver dysfunction are at greater risk of toxicity because of reduced drug clearance

Although there is a great intersubject variability for half-lives of methylxanthines (2-10 hours), elderly as a group have slower hepatic clearance. Therefore, use lower initial doses and monitor more closely for response and adverse reactions. Additionally, elderly are at greater risk for toxicity due to concomitant disease (eg, CHF, arrhythmias), and drug use (eg, cimetidine, ciprofloxacin, etc).
Adverse Reactions See table.
Uncommon at serum theophylline concentrations ≤20 mcg/mL
1% to 10%:
Cardiovascular: Tachycardia
Central nervous system: Nervousness, restlessness
(Continued)

Theophylline Salts *(Continued)*

Gastrointestinal: Nausea, vomiting

<1%: Allergic reactions, insomnia, irritability, seizures, rash, gastric irritation, tremor

Theophylline Serum Levels (mcg/mL)*	Adverse Reactions
15-25	GI upset, diarrhea, N/V, abdominal pain, nervousness, headache, insomnia, agitation, dizziness, muscle cramp, tremor
25-35	Tachycardia, occasional PVC
>35	Ventricular tachycardia, frequent PVC, seizure

*Adverse effects do not necessarily occur according to serum levels. Arrhythmia and seizure can occur without seeing the other adverse effects.

Overdosage/Toxicology

Symptoms of overdose include tachycardia, extrasystoles, nausea, vomiting, anorexia, tonic-clonic seizures, insomnia, circulatory failure; agitation, irritability, headache

If seizures have not occurred, induce vomiting; ipecac syrup is preferred. Do not induce emesis in the presence of impaired consciousness. Repeated doses of charcoal have been shown to be effective in enhancing the total body clearance of theophylline. Do not repeat charcoal doses if an ileus is present. Charcoal hemoperfusion may be considered if the serum theophylline level exceed 40 mcg/mL, the patient is unable to tolerate repeat oral charcoal administrations, or if severe toxic symptoms are present. Clearance with hemoperfusion is better than clearance from hemodialysis. Administer a cathartic, especially if sustained release agents were used. Phenobarbital administered prophylactically may prevent seizures.

Drug Interactions CYP1A2 and 3A3/4 enzyme substrate, CYP2E enzyme substrate (minor)

Cytochrome P-450 1A2 enzyme substrate and cytochrome P-450 2E1 enzyme substrate (minor)

Decreased effect/increased toxicity: Changes in diet may affect the elimination of theophylline; charcoal-broiled foods may increase elimination, reducing half-life by 50%; see table for factors affecting serum levels.

Factors Reported to Affect Theophylline Serum Levels

Decreased Theophylline Level	Increased Theophylline Level
Aminoglutethimide	Allopurinol (>600 mg/d)
Barbiturates	Beta-blockers
Carbamazepine	Calcium channel blockers
Charcoal	Carbamazepine
High protein/low carbohydrate diet	CHF
Hydantoins	Cimetidine
Isoniazid	Ciprofloxacin
I.V. isoproterenol	Cor pulmonale
Ketoconazole	Corticosteroids
Loop diuretics	Disulfiram
Phenobarbital	Ephedrine
Phenytoin	Erythromycin
Rifampin	Fever/viral illness
Smoking (cigarettes, marijuana)	Hepatic cirrhosis
Sulfinpyrazone	Influenza virus vaccine
Sympathomimetics	Interferon
	Isoniazid
	Loop diuretics
	Macrolides
	Mexiletine
	Oral contraceptives
	Propranolol
	Quinolones
	Thiabendazole
	Thyroid hormones
	Troleandomycin

Stability

Theophylline injection should be stored at room temperature and protected from freezing

Stability of parenteral admixture at room temperature (25°C): manufacturer expiration dating; out of overwrap stability: 30 days

Standard diluent: 400 mg theophylline/500 mL D_5W (premixed); 800 mg theophylline/1000 mL D_5W (premixed)

Aminophylline injection [content = 80% theophylline] should be stored at room temperature and protected from freezing and light

Stability of parenteral admixture at room temperature (25°C): 24 hours

Standard diluent: 250 mg aminophylline/100 mL D_5W ; 500 mg aminophylline/100 mL D_5W

Mechanism of Action Causes bronchodilatation, diuresis, CNS and cardiac stimulation, and gastric acid secretion by blocking phosphodiesterase which increases tissue concentrations of cyclic adenine monophosphate (cAMP) which in turn promotes cate-cholamine stimulation of lipolysis, glycogenolysis, and gluconeogenesis and induces release of epinephrine from adrenal medulla cells

Pharmacodynamics/Kinetics

Absorption: Oral: 100% of a dose is absorbed, depending upon the formulation used

Distribution: V_d: 0.45 L/kg; distributes into breast milk (approximates serum concentration); crosses the placenta

Metabolism: In the liver by demethylation and oxidation

Half-life: Highly variable and dependent upon age, liver function, cardiac function, lung disease, and smoking history

Aminophylline

Patient Group	Approximate Half-Life (h)
Neonates	
Premature	30
Normal newborn	24
Infants	
4-52 weeks	4-30
Children/Adolescents	
1-9 years	2-10 (4 avg)
9-16 years	4-16
Adults	
Nonsmoker	4-16 (8.7 avg)
Smoker	4.4
Cardiac compromised, liver failure	20-30

Dosage Form	Time to Peak	Dosing Interval
Uncoated tablet/syrup	2 h	6 h
Enteric coated tablet	5 h	12 h
Chewable tablet	1-1.5 h	6 h
Extended release	4-7 h	12 h
Intravenous	<30 min	

Elimination: In the urine; adults excrete 10% in urine as unchanged drug; neonates excrete a greater percentage of the dose unchanged in the urine (up to 50%)

Usual Dosage Use ideal body weight for obese patients

Neonates:

Apnea of prematurity: Oral, I.V.: Loading dose: 4 mg/kg (theophylline); 5 mg/kg (aminophylline)

There appears to be a delay in theophylline elimination in infants <1 year of age, especially neonates; both the initial dose and maintenance dosage should be conservative

I.V.: Initial: Maintenance infusion rates:

Neonates:

≤24 days: 0.08 mg/kg/hour theophylline

>24 days: 0.12 mg/kg/hour theophylline

Infants 6-52 weeks: 0.008 (age in weeks) + 0.21 mg/kg/hour theophylline

Children >1 year and Adults:

Treatment of acute bronchospasm: I.V.: Loading dose (in patients not currently receiving aminophylline or theophylline): 6 mg/kg (based on aminophylline) given I.V. over 20-30 minutes; administration rate should not exceed 25 mg/minute (aminophylline). See table.

Approximate I.V. Theophylline Dosage for Treatment of Acute Bronchospasm

Group	Dosage for Next 12 h*	Dosage After 12 h*
Infants 6 wk - 6 mo	0.5 mg/kg/h	
Children 6 mo - 1 y	0.6-0.7 mg/kg/h	
Children 1-9 y	0.95 mg/kg/h (1.2 mg/kg/h)	0.79 mg/kg/h (1 mg/kg/h)
Children 9-16 y and young adult smokers	0.79 mg/kg/h (1 mg/kg/h)	0.63 mg/kg/h (0.8 mg/kg/h)
Healthy, nonsmoking adults	0.55 mg/kg/h (0.7 mg/kg/h)	0.39 mg/kg/h (0.5 mg/kg/h)
Older patients and patients with cor pulmonale	0.47 mg/kg/h (0.6 mg/kg/h)	0.24 mg/kg/h (0.3 mg/kg/h)
Patients with congestive heart failure or liver failure	0.39 mg/kg/h (0.5 mg/kg/h)	0.08-0.16 mg/kg/h (0.1-0.2 mg/kg/h)

*Equivalent hydrous aminophylline dosage indicated in parentheses.

(Continued)

Theophylline Salts *(Continued)*

Approximate I.V. maintenance dosages are based upon continuous infusions; bolus dosing (often used in children <6 months of age) may be determined by multiplying the hourly infusion rate by 24 hours and dividing by the desired number of doses/day; see table.

Maintenance Dose for Acute Symptoms

Population Group	Oral Theophylline (mg/kg/day)	I.V. Aminophylline
Premature infant or newborn - 6 wk (for apnea/bradycardia)	4	5 mg/kg/day
6 wk - 6 mo	10	12 mg/kg/day or continuous I.V. infusion*
Infants 6 mo - 1 y	12-18	15 mg/kg/day or continuous I.V. infusion*
Children 1-9 y	20-24	1 mg/kg/h
Children 9-12 y, and adolescent daily smokers of cigarettes or marijuana, and otherwise healthy adult smokers <50 y	16	0.9 mg/kg/h
Adolescents 12-16 y (nonsmokers)	13	0.7 mg/kg/h
Otherwise healthy nonsmoking adults (including elderly patients)	10 (not to exceed 900 mg/day)	0.5 mg/kg/h
Cardiac decompensation, cor pulmonale and/or liver dysfunction	5 (not to exceed 400 mg/day)	0.25 mg/kg/h

*For continuous I.V. infusion divide total daily dose by 24 = mg/kg/h.

Dosage should be adjusted according to serum level measurements during the first 12- to 24-hour period; see table.

Dosage Adjustment After Serum Theophylline Measurement

Serum Theophylline		Guidelines
Within normal limits	10-20 mcg/mL	Maintain dosage if tolerated. Recheck serum theophylline concentration at 6- to 12-month intervals.*
Too high	20-25 mcg/mL	Decrease doses by about 10%. Recheck serum theophylline concentration after 3 days and then at 6- to 12-month intervals.*
	25-30 mcg/mL	Skip next dose and decrease subsequent doses by about 25%. Recheck serum theophylline.
	>30 mcg/mL	Skip next 2 doses and decrease subsequent doses by 50%. Recheck serum theophylline.
Too low	7.5-10 mcg/mL	Increase dose by about 25%.† Recheck serum theophylline concentration after 3 days and then at 6- to 12-month intervals.*
	5-7.5 mcg/mL	Increase dose by about 25% to the nearest dose increment† and recheck serum theophylline for guidance in further dosage adjustment (another increase will probably be needed, but this provides a safety check).

*Finer adjustments in dosage may be needed for some patients.

†Dividing the daily dose into 3 doses administered at 8-hour intervals may be indicated if symptoms occur repeatedly at the end of a dosing interval.

From Weinberger M and Hendeles L, "Practical Guide to Using Theophylline," *J Resp Dis*, 1981,2:12-27.

Oral theophylline: Initial dosage recommendation: Loading dose (to achieve a serum level of about 10 mcg/mL; loading doses should be given using a rapidly absorbed oral product **not** a sustained release product):

If no theophylline has been administered in the previous 24 hours: 4-6 mg/kg theophylline

If theophylline has been administered in the previous 24 hours: administer ½ loading dose or 2-3 mg/kg theophylline can be given in emergencies when serum levels are not available

On the average, for every 1 mg/kg theophylline given, blood levels will rise 2 mcg/mL

Ideally, defer the loading dose if a serum theophylline concentration can be obtained rapidly. However, if this is not possible, exercise clinical judgment. If the patient is not experiencing theophylline toxicity, this is unlikely to result in dangerous adverse effects.

See table.

Oral Theophylline Dosage for Bronchial Asthma*

Age	Initial 3 Days	Second 3 Days	Steady-State Maintenance
<1 y	0.2 x (age in weeks) + 5		0.3 x (age in weeks) + 8
1-9 y	16 up to a maximum of 400 mg/24 h	20	22
9-12 y	16 up to a maximum of 400 mg/24 h	16 up to a maximum of 600 mg/24 h	20 up to a maximum of 800 mg/24 h
12-16 y	16 up to a maximum of 400 mg/24 h	16 up to a maximum of 600 mg/24 h	18 up to a maximum of 900 mg/24 h
Adults	400 mg/24 h	600 mg/24 h	900 mg/24 h

*Dose in mg/kg/24 hours of theophylline.

Increasing dose: The dosage may be increased in approximately 25% increments at 2- to 3-day intervals so long as the drug is tolerated or until the maximum dose is reached

Maintenance dose: In newborns and infants, a fast-release oral product can be used. The total daily dose can be divided every 12 hours in newborns and every 6-8 hours in infants. In children and healthy adults, a slow-release product can be used. The total daily dose can be divided every 8-12 hours.

These recommendations, based on mean clearance rates for age or risk factors, were calculated to achieve a serum level of 10 mcg/mL (5 mcg/mL for newborns with apnea/bradycardia)

Dosage should be adjusted according to serum level

Oral oxtriphylline:

Children 1-9 years: 6.2 mg/kg/dose every 6 hours

Children 9-16 years and Adult smokers: 4.7 mg/kg/dose every 6 hours

Adult nonsmokers: 4.7 mg/kg/dose every 8 hours

Dose should be further adjusted based on serum levels

Dosing adjustment/comments in hepatic disease: Higher incidence of toxic effects including seizures in cirrhosis; plasma levels should be monitored closely during long-term administration in cirrhosis and during acute hepatitis, with dose adjustment as necessary

Hemodialysis: Administer dose posthemodialysis or administer supplemental 50% dose

Peritoneal dialysis: Supplemental dose is not necessary

Continuous arteriovenous or venovenous hemodiafiltration (CAVH/CAVHD) effects: Supplemental dose is not necessary

Administration Administer oral and I.V. administration around-the-clock to promote less variation in peak and trough serum levels; theophylline injection may be administered by continuous I.V. infusion (requires an infusion pump) or IVPB; maximum rate of I.V. administration of theophylline is 20-25 mg per minute

Monitoring Parameters Heart rate, CNS effects (insomnia, irritability); respiratory rate (COPD patients often have resting controlled respiratory rates in low 20s), serum theophylline level, arterial or capillary blood gases (if applicable)

Reference Range

Sample size: 0.5-1 mL serum (red top tube)

Saliva levels are approximately equal to 60% of plasma levels

Therapeutic levels: 10-20 µg/mL
Neonatal apnea 6-13 µg/mL
Pregnancy: 3-12 µg/mL
Toxic concentration: >20 µg/mL

Timing of serum samples: If toxicity is suspected, draw a level any time during a continuous I.V. infusion, or 2 hours after an oral dose; if lack of therapeutic is effected, draw a trough immediately before the next oral dose; see table.

Guidelines for Drawing Theophylline Serum Levels

Dosage Form	Time to Draw Level
I.V. bolus	30 min after end of 30 min infusion
I.V. continuous infusion	12-24 h after initiation of infusion
P.O. liquid, fast-release tab	Peak: 1 h postdose after at least 1 day of therapy Trough: Just before a dose after at least one day of therapy
P.O. slow-release product	Peak: 4 h postdose after at least 1 day of therapy Trough: Just before a dose after at least one day of therapy

Test Interactions May elevate uric acid levels

Patient Information Oral preparations should be taken with a full glass of water; capsule forms may be opened and sprinkled on soft foods; do not chew beads; notify physician if nausea, vomiting, severe GI pain, restlessness, or irregular heartbeat occurs; do not drink or eat large quantities of caffeine-containing beverages or food (colas, coffee, chocolate); remain in bed for 15-20 minutes after inserting suppository; do not chew or crush enteric coated or sustained release products; take at regular intervals; notify (Continued)

Theophylline Salts *(Continued)*

physician if insomnia, nervousness, irritability, palpitations, seizures occur; do not change brands or doses without consulting physician

Nursing Implications Do not crush sustained release drug products; do not crush enteric coated drug product; encourage patient to drink adequate fluids (2 L/day) to decrease mucous viscosity

Additional Information See table for theophylline content.

Salt	% Theophylline Content
Theophylline anhydrous (eg, most oral solids)	100%
Theophylline monohydrate (eg, oral solutions)	91%
Aminophylline (theophylline) (eg, injection)	80% (79% to 86%)
Oxtriphylline (choline theophylline) (eg, Choledyl®)	64%

Dosage Forms

Aminophylline (79% theophylline):
  Injection: 25 mg/mL (10 mL, 20 mL); 250 mg (equivalent to 187 mg theophylline) per 10 mL; 500 mg (equivalent to 394 mg theophylline) per 20 mL
  Liquid, oral: 105 mg (equivalent to 90 mg theophylline) per 5 mL (240 mL, 500 mL)
  Suppository, rectal: 250 mg (equivalent to 198 mg theophylline); 500 mg (equivalent to 395 mg theophylline)
  Tablet: 100 mg (equivalent to 79 mg theophylline); 200 mg (equivalent to 158 mg theophylline)
  Tablet, controlled release: 225 mg (equivalent to 178 mg theophylline)
Oxtriphylline (64% theophylline):
  Elixir: 100 mg (equivalent to 64 mg theophylline)/5 mL (5 mL, 10 mL, 473 mL)
  Syrup: 50 mg (equivalent to 32 mg theophylline)/5 mL (473 mL)
  Tablet: 100 mg (equivalent to 64 mg theophylline); 200 mg (equivalent to 127 mg theophylline)
  Tablet, sustained release: 400 mg (equivalent to 254 mg theophylline); 600 mg (equivalent to 382 mg theophylline)
Theophylline:
  Capsule:
    Immediate release: 100 mg, 200 mg
    Sustained release (8-12 hours): 50 mg, 60 mg, 65 mg, 75 mg, 100 mg, 125 mg, 130 mg, 200 mg, 250 mg, 260 mg, 300 mg
    Timed release (12 hours): 50 mg, 75 mg, 125 mg, 130 mg, 200 mg, 250 mg, 260 mg
    Timed release (24 hours): 100 mg, 200 mg, 300 mg
  Injection: Theophylline in 5% dextrose: 200 mg/container (50 mL, 100 mL); 400 mg/container (100 mL, 250 mL, 500 mL, 1000 mL); 800 mg/container (250 mL, 500 mL, 1000 mL)
  Elixir, oral: 80 mg/15 mL (15 mL, 30 mL, 500 mL, 4000 mL)
  Solution, oral: 80 mg/15 mL (15 mL, 18.75 mL, 30 mL, 120 mL, 500 mL, 4000 mL); 150 mg/15 mL (480 mL)
  Syrup, oral: 80 mg/15 mL (5 mL, 15 mL, 30 mL, 120 mL, 500 mL, 4000 mL); 150 mg/15 mL (480 mL)
  Tablet:
    Immediate release: 100 mg, 125 mg, 200 mg, 250 mg, 300 mg
    Timed release (8-12 hours): 100 mg, 200 mg, 250 mg, 300 mg, 500 mg
    Timed release (8-24 hours): 100 mg, 200 mg, 300 mg, 450 mg
    Timed release (12-24 hours): 100 mg, 200 mg, 300 mg
    Timed release (24 hours): 400 mg

- **Theospan®-SR** *see* Theophylline Salts *on page 1125*
- **Theovent®** *see* Theophylline Salts *on page 1125*
- **Therabid®** [OTC] *see* Vitamins, Multiple *on page 1226*
- **TheraCys®** *see* BCG Vaccine *on page 126*
- **Thera-Flur®** *see* Fluoride *on page 498*
- **Thera-Flur-N®** *see* Fluoride *on page 498*
- **Theragran®** [OTC] *see* Vitamins, Multiple *on page 1226*
- **Theragran® Hematinic®** *see* Vitamins, Multiple *on page 1226*
- **Theragran® Liquid** [OTC] *see* Vitamins, Multiple *on page 1226*
- **Theragran-M®** [OTC] *see* Vitamins, Multiple *on page 1226*
- **Therapeutic Multivitamins** *see* Vitamins, Multiple *on page 1226*
- **Thermazene®** *see* Silver Sulfadiazine *on page 1062*

Thiabendazole *(thye a BEN da zole)*

U.S. Brand Names Mintezol®

Synonyms Tiabendazole

Therapeutic Category Anthelmintic

Use Treatment of strongyloidiasis, cutaneous larva migrans, visceral larva migrans, dracunculiasis, trichinosis, and mixed helminthic infections

Pregnancy Risk Factor C

Contraindications Known hypersensitivity to thiabendazole

Warnings/Precautions Use with caution in patients with renal or hepatic impairment, malnutrition or anemia, or dehydration

Adverse Reactions
>10%:

Central nervous system: Seizures, hallucinations, delirium, dizziness, drowsiness, headache

Gastrointestinal: Anorexia, diarrhea, nausea, vomiting, drying of mucous membranes

Neuromuscular & skeletal: Numbness

Otic: Tinnitus

1% to 10%: Dermatologic: Rash, Stevens-Johnson syndrome

<1%: Chills, malodor of urine, leukopenia, hepatotoxicity, blurred or yellow vision, nephrotoxicity, lymphadenopathy, hypersensitivity reactions

Overdosage/Toxicology
Symptoms of overdose include altered mental status, visual problems

Supportive care only following GI decontamination

Drug Interactions Increased levels of theophylline and other xanthines

Mechanism of Action Inhibits helminth-specific mitochondrial fumarate reductase

Pharmacodynamics/Kinetics
Absorption: Rapid and well from GI tract

Metabolism: Rapid

Half-life: 1.2 hours

Elimination: Excreted in feces (5%) and urine (87%), primarily as conjugated metabolites

Usual Dosage Purgation is not required prior to use; drinking of fruit juice aids in expulsion of worms by removing the mucous to which the intestinal tapeworms attach themselves.

Children and Adults: Oral: 50 mg/kg/day divided every 12 hours (if >68 kg: 1.5 g/dose); maximum dose: 3 g/day

Strongyloidiasis, ascariasis, uncinariasis, trichuriasis: For 2 consecutive days

Cutaneous larva migrans: For 2-5 consecutive days

Visceral larva migrans: For 5-7 consecutive days

Trichinosis: For 2-4 consecutive days

Dracunculosis: 50-75 mg/kg/day divided every 12 hours for 3 days

Dosing comments in renal/hepatic impairment: Use with caution

Patient Information Take after meals, chew chewable tablet well; may decrease alertness, avoid driving or operating machinery; drinking of fruit juice aids in expulsion of worms by removing the mucous to which the intestinal tapeworms attach themselves

Dosage Forms
Suspension, oral: 500 mg/5 mL (120 mL)

Tablet, chewable (orange flavor): 500 mg

♦ **Thiamazole** see Methimazole on page 749

♦ **Thiamilate®** see Thiamine on this page

Thiamine (THYE a min)

U.S. Brand Names Thiamilate®

Canadian Brand Names Betaxin®; Bewon®

Synonyms Aneurine Hydrochloride; Thiamine Hydrochloride; Thiaminium Chloride Hydrochloride; Vitamin B_1

Therapeutic Category Vitamin, Water Soluble

Use Treatment of thiamine deficiency including beriberi, Wernicke's encephalopathy syndrome, and peripheral neuritis associated with pellagra, alcoholic patients with altered sensorium; various genetic metabolic disorders

Pregnancy Risk Factor A (C if dose exceeds RDA recommendation)

Contraindications Hypersensitivity to thiamine or any component

Warnings/Precautions Use with caution with parenteral route (especially I.V.) of administration

Adverse Reactions <1%: Cardiovascular collapse and death, warmth, rash, angioedema, paresthesia

Stability Protect oral dosage forms from light; **incompatible** with alkaline or neutral solutions and with oxidizing or reducing agents

Mechanism of Action An essential coenzyme in carbohydrate metabolism by combining with adenosine triphosphate to form thiamine pyrophosphate

Pharmacodynamics/Kinetics
Absorption: Oral: Adequate; I.M.: Rapid and complete

Elimination: Renally as unchanged drug, and as pyrimidine after body storage sites become saturated

Usual Dosage
Recommended daily allowance:

<6 months: 0.3 mg

6 months to 1 year: 0.4 mg

1-3 years: 0.7 mg

4-6 years: 0.9 mg

7-10 years: 1 mg

11-14 years: 1.1-1.3 mg

>14 years: 1-1.5 mg

Thiamine deficiency (beriberi):

Children: 10-25 mg/dose I.M. or I.V. daily (if critically ill), or 10-50 mg/dose orally every day for 2 weeks, then 5-10 mg/dose orally daily for 1 month

Adults: 5-30 mg/dose I.M. or I.V. 3 times/day (if critically ill); then orally 5-30 mg/day in single or divided doses 3 times/day for 1 month

(Continued)

Thiamine *(Continued)*

Wernicke's encephalopathy: Adults: Initial: 100 mg I.V., then 50-100 mg/day I.M. or I.V. until consuming a regular, balanced diet

Dietary supplement (depends on caloric or carbohydrate content of the diet):
Infants: 0.3-0.5 mg/day
Children: 0.5-1 mg/day
Adults: 1-2 mg/day
Note: The above doses can be found in multivitamin preparations
Metabolic disorders: Oral: Adults: 10-20 mg/day (dosages up to 4 g/day in divided doses have been used)

Administration Parenteral form may be administered by I.M. or slow I.V. injection

Reference Range Therapeutic: 1.6-4 mg/dL

Test Interactions False-positive for uric acid using the phosphotungstate method and for urobilinogen using the Ehrlich's reagent; large doses may interfere with the spectrophotometric determination of serum theophylline concentration

Patient Information Dietary sources include legumes, pork, beef, whole grains, yeast, fresh vegetables; a deficiency state can occur in as little 3 weeks following total dietary absence

Nursing Implications Single vitamin deficiency is rare; look for other deficiencies

Additional Information Dietary sources include legumes, pork, beef, whole grains, yeast, fresh vegetables; a deficiency state can occur in as little as 3 weeks following total dietary absence

Dosage Forms
Injection, as hydrochloride: 100 mg/mL (1 mL, 2 mL, 10 mL, 30 mL); 200 mg/mL (30 mL)
Tablet, as hydrochloride: 50 mg, 100 mg, 250 mg, 500 mg
Tablet, as hydrochloride, enteric coated: 20 mg

- ◆ **Thiamine Hydrochloride** *see* Thiamine *on previous page*
- ◆ **Thiaminium Chloride Hydrochloride** *see* Thiamine *on previous page*

Thiethylperazine *(thye eth il PER a zeen)*

U.S. Brand Names Norzine®; Torecan®

Synonyms Thiethylperazine Maleate

Therapeutic Category Antiemetic; Phenothiazine Derivative

Use Relief of nausea and vomiting
Unlabeled use: Treatment of vertigo

Pregnancy Risk Factor X

Contraindications Comatose states, hypersensitivity to thiethylperazine or any component; pregnancy, cross-sensitivity to other phenothiazines may exist

Warnings/Precautions Reduce or discontinue if extrapyramidal effects occur; safety and efficacy in children <12 years of age have not been established; postural hypotension may occur after I.M. injection; the injectable form contains sulfite which may cause allergic reactions in some patients; use caution in patients with narrow-angle glaucoma

Adverse Reactions
>10%:
Central nervous system: Drowsiness, dizziness
Gastrointestinal: Xerostomia
Respiratory: Dry nose
1% to 10%:
Cardiovascular: Tachycardia, orthostatic hypotension
Central nervous system: Confusion, convulsions, extrapyramidal effects, tardive dyskinesia, fever, headache
Hematologic: Agranulocytosis
Hepatic: Cholestatic jaundice
Otic: Tinnitus

Overdosage/Toxicology
Symptoms of overdose include deep sleep, coma, extrapyramidal symptoms, abnormal involuntary muscle movements, hypotension
Following initiation of essential overdose management, toxic symptom treatment and supportive treatment should be initiated. Hypotension usually responds to I.V. fluids or Trendelenburg positioning. If unresponsive to these measures, use of a parenteral inotrope may be required (eg, norepinephrine 0.1-0.2 mcg/kg/minute titrated to response); avoid epinephrine for thiethylperazine-induced hypotension. Seizures commonly respond to diazepam (I.V. 5-10 mg bolus in adults every 15 minutes if needed up to a total of 30 mg; I.V. 0.25-0.4 mg/kg/dose up to a total of 10 mg in children) or to phenytoin or phenobarbital. Critical cardiac arrhythmias often respond to I.V. phenytoin (15 mg/kg up to 1 g), while other antiarrhythmics can be used. Neuroleptics often cause extrapyramidal symptoms (eg, dystonic reactions) requiring management with diphenhydramine 1-2 mg/kg (adults) up to a maximum of 50 mg I.M. or I.V. slow push followed by a maintenance dose for 48-72 hours. When these reactions are unresponsive to diphenhydramine, benztropine mesylate I.V. 1-2 mg (adults) may be effective. These agents are generally effective within 2-5 minutes.

Drug Interactions Increased effect/toxicity with CNS depressants (eg, anesthetics, opiates, tranquilizers, alcohol), lithium, atropine, epinephrine, MAO inhibitors, TCAs

Mechanism of Action Blocks postsynaptic mesolimbic dopaminergic receptors in the brain; exhibits a strong alpha-adrenergic blocking effect and depresses the release of hypothalamic and hypophyseal hormones; acts directly on chemoreceptor trigger zone and vomiting center

Pharmacodynamics/Kinetics
Onset of antiemetic effect: Within 30 minutes
Duration of action: ~4 hours

Usual Dosage Children >12 years and Adults:
Oral, I.M., rectal: 10 mg 1-3 times/day as needed
I.V. and S.C. routes of administration are not recommended
Hemodialysis: Not dialyzable (0% to 5%)
Dosing comments in hepatic impairment: Use with caution

Administration Inject I.M. deeply into large muscle mass, patient should be lying down and remain so for at least 1 hour after administration

Patient Information May cause drowsiness, impair judgment and coordination; may cause photosensitivity; avoid excessive sunlight; notify physician of involuntary movements or feelings of restlessness

Nursing Implications Assist with ambulation, observe for extrapyramidal symptoms
Dosage Forms
Injection, as maleate: 5 mg/mL (2 mL)
Suppository, rectal, as maleate: 10 mg
Tablet, as maleate: 10 mg

♦ **Thiethylperazine Maleate** *see Thiethylperazine on previous page*

Thioguanine (thye oh GWAH neen)
Related Information
Cancer Chemotherapy Regimens *on page 1263*

Synonyms 2-Amino-6-Mercaptopurine; TG; 6-TG; 6-Thioguanine; Tioguanine
Therapeutic Category Antineoplastic Agent, Antimetabolite (Purine)
Use Remission induction, consolidation, and maintenance therapy of acute myelogenous (nonlymphocytic) leukemia; treatment of chronic myelogenous leukemia and granulocytic leukemia

Pregnancy Risk Factor D

Contraindications History of previous therapy resistance with either thioguanine or mercaptopurine (there is usually complete cross resistance between these two); hypersensitivity to thioguanine or any component

Warnings/Precautions The U.S. Food and Drug Administration (FDA) currently recommends that procedures for proper handling and disposal of antineoplastic agents be considered. Use with caution and reduce dose of thioguanine in patients with renal or hepatic impairment; thioguanine is potentially carcinogenic and teratogenic; myelosuppression may be delayed.

Adverse Reactions
>10%:
Hematologic: Myelosuppressive:
WBC: Moderate
Platelets: Moderate
Onset (days): 7-10
Nadir (days): 14
Recovery (days): 21
1% to 10%:
Dermatologic: Skin rash
Endocrine & metabolic: Hyperuricemia
Gastrointestinal: Mild nausea or vomiting, anorexia, stomatitis, diarrhea
Emetic potential: Low (<10%)
Neuromuscular & skeletal: Unsteady gait
<1%: Neurotoxicity, photosensitivity, hepatitis, jaundice, veno-occlusive hepatic disease

Overdosage/Toxicology
Symptoms of overdose include bone marrow suppression, nausea, vomiting, malaise, hypertension, sweating
Treatment is supportive; dialysis is not useful

Drug Interactions
Increased toxicity:
Allopurinol can be used in full doses with 6 TG unlike 6-MP
Busulfan → hepatotoxicity and esophageal varices

Mechanism of Action Purine analog that is incorporated into DNA and RNA resulting in the blockage of synthesis and metabolism of purine nucleotides

Pharmacodynamics/Kinetics
Absorption: Oral: 30%
Distribution: Crosses placenta
Metabolism: Rapidly and extensively in the liver to 2-amino-6-methylthioguanine (active) and inactive compounds
Half-life, terminal: 11 hours
Time to peak serum concentration: Within 8 hours
Elimination: In urine

Usual Dosage Total daily dose can be given at one time; offers little advantage over mercaptopurine; is sometimes ordered as 6-thioguanine, with 6 being part of the drug name and not a unit or strength

Oral (refer to individual protocols):
Infants and Children <3 years: Combination drug therapy for acute nonlymphocytic leukemia: 3.3 mg/kg/day in divided doses twice daily for 4 days
Children and Adults: 2-3 mg/kg/day calculated to nearest 20 mg or 75-200 mg/m²/day in 1-2 divided doses for 5-7 days or until remission is attained
(Continued)

Thioguanine (Continued)

Dosing comments in renal or hepatic impairment: Reduce dose

Monitoring Parameters CBC with differential and platelet count, liver function tests, hemoglobin, hematocrit, serum uric acid

Patient Information Avoid exposure to persons with infections. Drink plenty of fluids while taking the drug. May cause diarrhea, fever and weakness. Notify physician if these become pronounced. Notify physician if fever, chills, nausea, vomiting, sore throat, unusual bleeding or bruising, yellow discoloration of the skin or eyes, swelling of the feet or legs, or abdominal, joint, or flank pain occurs. Any signs of infection, easy bruising or bleeding, shortness of breath, or painful or burning urination should be brought to physician's attention. Hair loss sometimes occur. The drug may cause permanent sterility and may cause birth defects. The drug may be excreted in breast milk, therefore, an alternative form of feeding your baby should be used.

Dosage Forms Tablet, scored: 40 mg

Extemporaneous Preparations A 40 mg/mL oral suspension compounded from tablets which were crushed, mixed with a volume of Cologel® suspending agent equal to $^1/_3$ the final volume, and brought to the final volume with a 2:1 mixture of simple syrup and cherry syrup was stable for 84 days when stored in an amber bottle at room temperature

Dressman JB and Poust RI, "Stability of Allopurinol and Five Antineoplastics in Suspension," *Am J Hosp Pharm*, 1983, 40:616-8.

♦ **6-Thioguanine** see Thioguanine *on previous page*

Thiopental (thye oh PEN tal)

U.S. Brand Names Pentothal® Sodium

Synonyms Thiopental Sodium

Therapeutic Category Anticonvulsant; Barbiturate; General Anesthetic; Sedative

Use Induction of anesthesia; adjunct for intubation in head injury patients; control of convulsive states; treatment of elevated intracranial pressure

Restrictions C-III

Pregnancy Risk Factor C

Contraindications Porphyria (variegate or acute intermittent); known hypersensitivity to thiopental or other barbiturates

Warnings/Precautions Use with caution in patients with asthma, unstable aneurysms, severe cardiovascular disease, hepatic or renal disease, laryngospasm or bronchospasms which can occur; hypotension; extravasation or intra-arterial injection causes necrosis due to pH of 10.6, ensure patient has intravenous access

Adverse Reactions

>10%: Local: Pain on I.M. injection

1% to 10%: Gastrointestinal: Cramping, diarrhea, rectal bleeding

<1%: Hypotension, peripheral vascular collapse, myocardial depression, cardiac arrhythmias, circulatory depression, seizures, headache, emergence delirium, prolonged somnolence and recovery, anxiety, erythema, pruritus, urticaria, nausea, vomiting, hemolytic anemia, thrombophlebitis, tremor, involuntary muscle movement, twitching, rigidity, radial nerve palsy, respiratory depression, coughing, rhinitis, apnea, laryngospasm, bronchospasm, sneezing, dyspnea, hiccups, anaphylactic reactions

Overdosage/Toxicology

Symptoms of overdose include respiratory depression, hypotension, shock

Hypotension should respond to I.V. fluids and placement of patient in Trendelenburg position; if necessary, pressors such as norepinephrine may be used; patient may require ventilatory support

Drug Interactions Increased toxicity with CNS depressants (especially narcotic analgesics and phenothiazines), salicylates, sulfisoxazole

Stability Reconstituted solutions remain stable for 3 days at room temperature and 7 days when refrigerated; solutions are alkaline and **incompatible** with drugs with acidic pH, such as succinylcholine, atropine sulfate, etc. I.V. form is **incompatible** when mixed with amikacin, benzquinamide, chlorpromazine, codeine, dimenhydrinate, diphenhydramine, glycopyrrolate, hydromorphone, insulin, levorphanol, meperidine, metaraminol, morphine, norepinephrine, penicillin G, prochlorperazine, succinylcholine, tetracycline

Mechanism of Action Interferes with transmission of impulses from the thalamus to the cortex of the brain resulting in an imbalance in central inhibitory and facilitatory mechanisms

Pharmacodynamics/Kinetics

Onset of action: I.V.: Anesthesia occurs in 30-60 seconds

Duration: 5-30 minutes

Distribution: V_d: 1.4 L/kg

Protein binding: 72% to 86%

Metabolism: In the liver primarily to inactive metabolites but pentobarbital is also formed

Half-life: 3-11.5 hours, decreased in children vs adults

Usual Dosage I.V.:

Induction anesthesia:

Infants: 5-8 mg/kg

Children 1-12 years: 5-6 mg/kg

Adults: 3-5 mg/kg

Maintenance anesthesia:

Children: 1 mg/kg as needed

Adults: 25-100 mg as needed

Increased intracranial pressure: Children and Adults: 1.5-5 mg/kg/dose; repeat as needed to control intracranial pressure

Seizures:

Children: 2-3 mg/kg/dose, repeat as needed

Adults: 75-250 mg/dose, repeat as needed

Rectal administration: (Patient should be NPO for no less than 3 hours prior to administration)

Suggested initial doses of thiopental rectal suspension are:

<3 months: 15 mg/kg/dose

>3 months: 25 mg/kg/dose

Note: The age of a premature infant should be adjusted to reflect the age that the infant would have been if full-term (eg, an infant, now age 4 months, who was 2 months premature should be considered to be a 2-month old infant).

Doses should be rounded downward to the nearest 50 mg increment to allow for accurate measurement of the dose

Inactive or debilitated patients and patients recently medicated with other sedatives, (eg, chloral hydrate, meperidine, chlorpromazine, and promethazine), may require smaller doses than usual

If the patient is not sedated within 15-20 minutes, a single repeat dose of thiopental can be given. The single repeat doses are:

<3 months: <7.5 mg/kg/dose

>3 months: 15 mg/kg/dose

Adults weighing >90 kg should not receive >3 g as a total dose (initial plus repeat doses)

Children weighing >34 kg should not receive >1 g as a total dose (initial plus repeat doses)

Neither adults nor children should receive more than one course of thiopental rectal suspension (initial dose plus repeat dose) per 24-hour period

Dosing adjustment in renal impairment: Cl_{cr} <10 mL/minute: Administer at 75% of normal dose

Note: Accumulation may occur with chronic dosing due to lipid solubility; prolonged recovery may result from redistribution of thiopental from fat stores

Monitoring Parameters Respiratory rate, heart rate, blood pressure

Reference Range Therapeutic: Hypnotic: 1-5 µg/mL (SI: 4.1-20.7 µmol/L); Coma: 30-100 µg/mL (SI: 124-413 µmol/L); Anesthesia: 7-130 µg/mL (SI: 29-536 µmol/L); Toxic: >10 µg/mL (SI: >41 µmol/L)

Test Interactions ↑ potassium (S)

Nursing Implications Monitor vital signs every 3-5 minutes; monitor for respiratory distress; place patient in Sim's position if vomiting, to prevent from aspirating vomitus; avoid extravasation, necrosis may occur

Additional Information Sodium content of 1 g (injection) : 86.8 mg (3.8 mEq)

Dosage Forms

Injection, as sodium: 250 mg, 400 mg, 500 mg, 1 g, 2.5 g, 5 g

Suspension, rectal, as sodium: 400 mg/g (2 g)

♦ **Thiopental Sodium** see Thiopental on previous page

♦ **Thiophosphoramide** see Thiotepa on next page

Thioridazine (thye oh RID a zeen)

Related Information

Antipsychotic Agents Comparison on page 1305

U.S. Brand Names Mellaril®; Mellaril-S®

Canadian Brand Names Apo®-Thioridazine; Novo-Ridazine; PMS-Thioridazine

Synonyms Thioridazine Hydrochloride

Therapeutic Category Antipsychotic Agent; Phenothiazine Derivative

Use Management of manifestations of psychotic disorders; depressive neurosis; alcohol withdrawal; dementia in elderly; behavioral problems in children

Pregnancy Risk Factor C

Contraindications Severe CNS depression, hypersensitivity to thioridazine or any component; cross-sensitivity to other phenothiazines may exist

Warnings/Precautions Oral formulations may cause stomach upset; may cause thermoregulatory changes; use caution in patients with narrow-angle glaucoma, severe liver or cardiac disease; doses of 1 g/day frequently cause pigmentary retinopathy

Adverse Reactions

>10%:

Central nervous system: Pseudoparkinsonism, akathisia, dystonias, tardive dyskinesia (persistent), dizziness

Cardiovascular: Hypotension, orthostatic hypotension

Gastrointestinal: Constipation

Ocular: Pigmentary retinopathy

Respiratory: Nasal congestion

Miscellaneous: Diaphoresis (decreased)

1% to 10%:

Dermatologic: Increased sensitivity to sun, rash

Endocrine & metabolic: Changes in menstrual cycle, changes in libido, breast pain

Gastrointestinal: Weight gain, nausea, vomiting, stomach pain

Genitourinary: Dysuria, ejaculatory disturbances

Neuromuscular & skeletal: Trembling of fingers

(Continued)

Thioridazine (Continued)

<1%: Neuroleptic malignant syndrome (NMS), impairment of temperature regulation, lowering of seizures threshold, discoloration of skin (blue-gray), galactorrhea, priapism, agranulocytosis, leukopenia, cholestatic jaundice, hepatotoxicity, cornea and lens changes

Overdosage/Toxicology

Symptoms of overdose include deep sleep, coma, extrapyramidal symptoms, abnormal involuntary muscle movements, hypotension, arrhythmias

Following initiation of essential overdose management, toxic symptom treatment and supportive treatment should be initiated. Hypotension usually responds to I.V. fluids or Trendelenburg positioning. If unresponsive to these measures, the use of a parenteral inotrope may be required (eg, norepinephrine 0.1-0.2 mcg/kg/minute titrated to response); do not use epinephrine. Seizures commonly respond to diazepam (I.V. 5-10 mg bolus in adults every 15 minutes if needed up to a total of 30 mg; I.V. 0.25-0.4 mg/kg/dose up to a total of 10 mg in children) or to phenytoin or phenobarbital. Neuroleptics often cause extrapyramidal symptoms (eg, dystonic reactions) requiring management with diphenhydramine 1-2 mg/kg (adults) up to a maximum of 50 mg I.M. or I.V. slow push followed by a maintenance dose for 48-72 hours. When these reactions are unresponsive to diphenhydramine, benztropine mesylate I.V. 1-2 mg (adults) may be effective. These agents are generally effective within 2-5 minutes.

Drug Interactions CYP1A2 and 2D6 enzyme substrate; CYP2D6 enzyme inhibitor

Decreased effect with anticholinergics
Decreased effect of guanethidine
Increased toxicity with CNS depressants, epinephrine (hypotension), lithium (rare), TCA (cardiotoxicity), propranolol, pindolol

Stability Protect all dosage forms from light

Mechanism of Action Blocks postsynaptic mesolimbic dopaminergic receptors in the brain; exhibits a strong alpha-adrenergic blocking effect and depresses the release of hypothalamic and hypophyseal hormones

Pharmacodynamics/Kinetics

Duration of action: 4-5 days
Half-life: 21-25 hours
Time to peak serum concentration: Within 1 hour

Usual Dosage Oral:

Children >2 years: Range: 0.5-3 mg/kg/day in 2-3 divided doses; usual: 1 mg/kg/day; maximum: 3 mg/kg/day

Behavior problems: Initial: 10 mg 2-3 times/day, increase gradually
Severe psychoses: Initial: 25 mg 2-3 times/day, increase gradually

Adults:
Psychoses: Initial: 50-100 mg 3 times/day with gradual increments as needed and tolerated; maximum: 800 mg/day in 2-4 divided doses; if >65 years, initial dose: 10 mg 3 times/day

Depressive disorders, dementia: Initial: 25 mg 3 times/day; maintenance dose: 20-200 mg/day

Hemodialysis: Not dialyzable (0% to 5%)

Dietary Considerations Alcohol: Additive CNS effect, avoid use

Administration Dilute oral concentrate with water or juice before administration

Monitoring Parameters For patients on prolonged therapy: CBC, ophthalmologic exam, blood pressure, liver function tests

Reference Range Therapeutic: 1.0-1.5 µg/mL (SI: 2.7-4.1 µmol/L); Toxic: >10 µg/mL (SI: >27 µmol/L)

Test Interactions False-positives for phenylketonuria, urinary amylase, uroporphyrins, urobilinogen

Patient Information Oral concentrate must be diluted in 2-4 oz of liquid (water, fruit juice, carbonated drinks, milk, or pudding); do not take antacid within 1 hour of taking drug; avoid excess sun exposure; may cause drowsiness, restlessness, avoid alcohol and other CNS depressants; do not alter dosage or discontinue without consulting physician; yearly eye exams are necessary; might discolor urine (pink or reddish brown)

Nursing Implications Avoid skin contact with oral suspension or solution; may cause contact dermatitis

Additional Information

Thioridazine: Mellaril-S® oral suspension
Thioridazine hydrochloride: Mellaril® oral solution and tablet

Dosage Forms

Concentrate, oral: 30 mg/mL (120 mL); 100 mg/mL (3.4 mL, 120 mL)
Suspension, oral: 25 mg/5 mL (480 mL); 100 mg/5 mL (480 mL)
Tablet: 10 mg, 15 mg, 25 mg, 50 mg, 100 mg, 150 mg, 200 mg

♦ **Thioridazine Hydrochloride** see Thioridazine on previous page

Thiotepa (thye oh TEP a)

Related Information

Cancer Chemotherapy Regimens on page 1263

Synonyms TESPA; Thiophosphoramide; Triethylenethiophosphoramide; TSPA

Therapeutic Category Antineoplastic Agent, Alkylating Agent

Use Treatment of superficial tumors of the bladder; palliative treatment of adenocarcinoma of breast or ovary; lymphomas and sarcomas; controlling intracavitary effusions caused by metastatic tumors; I.T. use: CNS leukemia/lymphoma

Pregnancy Risk Factor D

Contraindications Hypersensitivity to thiotepa or any component; severe myelosuppression with leukocyte count <3000/mm^3 or platelet count <150,000 mm^3, except in stem cell transplant

Warnings/Precautions The U.S. Food and Drug Administration (FDA) currently recommends that procedures for proper handling and disposal of antineoplastic agents be considered. The drug is potentially mutagenic, carcinogenic, and teratogenic. Reduce dosage in patients with hepatic, renal, or bone marrow damage.

Adverse Reactions

>10%:

Hematopoietic: Dose-limiting toxicity which is dose-related and cumulative; moderate to severe leukopenia and severe thrombocytopenia have occurred. Anemia and pancytopenia may become fatal, so careful hematologic monitoring is required; intravesical administration may cause bone marrow suppression as well.

Hematologic: Myelosuppressive:

WBC: Moderate

Platelets: Severe

Onset (days): 7-10

Nadir (days): 14

Recovery (days): 28

Local: Pain at injection site

1% to 10%:

Central nervous system: Dizziness, fever, headache

Dermatologic: Alopecia, rash, pruritus, hyperpigmentation with high-dose therapy

Endocrine & metabolic: Hyperuricemia

Gastrointestinal: Anorexia, nausea and vomiting rarely occur

Emetic potential: Low (<10%)

Genitourinary: Hemorrhagic cystitis

Renal: Hematuria

Miscellaneous: Tightness of the throat, allergic reactions

<1%: Stomatitis, anaphylaxis; like other alkylating agents, this drug is carcinogenic

Overdosage/Toxicology

Symptoms of overdose include nausea, vomiting, precipitation of uric acid in kidney tubules, bone marrow suppression, bleeding

Therapy is supportive only; thiotepa is dialyzable; transfusions of whole blood or platelets have been proven beneficial

Drug Interactions

Decreased effect:

Clofibrate, phenobarbital may increase clearance of thiotepa

Increased toxicity:

Other alkylating agents or irradiation concomitantly with thiotepa intensifies toxicity rather than enhancing therapeutic response

Prolonged muscular paralysis and respiratory depression may occur when neuromuscular blocking agents are administered

Succinylcholine and other neuromuscular blocking agents' action can be prolonged due to thiotepa inhibiting plasma pseudocholinesterase

Stability

Store intact vials under refrigeration (2°C to 8°C) and protect from light. **Not stable** at room temperature for any duration of time.

Dilute powder 1.5 mL SWI to a concentration of 10.4 mg/mL which is stable for 8 hours at refrigeration

Further dilution in NS: Thiotepa is stable for 24 hours at a concentration of 5 mg/mL in NS at 8°C and 23°C; however, stability decreases significantly at concentrations of ≤0.5 mg/mL (< 8 hours); concentrations of 1-3 mg/mL are stable 48 hours at 8°C and 24 hours at 23°C

Standard I.V. dilution:

I.V. push: Dose/syringe (concentration = 10 mg/mL)

IVPB: Dose/100-150 mL NS for a final concentration of 1.5-3.5 mg/mL

Standard intravesicular dilution: 60 mg/30-60 mL NS; solution is placed via catheter and retained for two hours for maximum effect.

Standard intrathecal dilution: Intrathecal doses of 1-10 mg/m^2 should be diluted to 1-5 mg/mL in preservative-free NS or LR or 1 mg/mL in preservative-free SWI

ALL solutions should be **prepared fresh** and administered within one hour of preparation

Mechanism of Action Alkylating agent that reacts with DNA phosphate groups to produce cross-linking of DNA strands leading to inhibition of DNA, RNA, and protein synthesis; mechanism of action has not been explored as thoroughly as the other alkylating agents, it is presumed that the aziridine rings open and react as nitrogen mustard; reactivity is enhanced at a lower pH

Pharmacodynamics/Kinetics

Absorption: Following intracavitary instillation, the drug is unreliably absorbed (10% to 100%) through the bladder mucosa; variable I.M. absorption

Metabolism: Extensively in the liver

Half-life, terminal: 109 minutes with dose-dependent clearance

Elimination: As metabolites and unchanged drug in urine

Usual Dosage Refer to individual protocols; dosing must be based on the clinical and hematologic response of the patient

Children: Sarcomas: I.V.: 25-65 mg/m^2 as a single dose every 21 days

(Continued)

Thiotepa (Continued)

Adults:

I.M., I.V., S.C.: 30-60 mg/m^2 once per week

I.V. doses of 0.3-0.4 mg/kg by rapid I.V. administration every 1-4 weeks, or 0.2 mg/kg or 6-8 mg/m^2/day for 4-5 days every 2-4 weeks

High-dose therapy for bone marrow transplant: I.V.: 500 mg/m^2; up to 900 mg/m^2

I.M. doses of 15-30 mg in various schedules have been given

Intracavitary: 0.6-0.8 mg/kg

Intrapericardial dose: Usually 15-30 mg

Dosing comments/adjustment in renal impairment: Use with extreme caution, reduced dose may be warranted. Less than 3% of alkylating species are detected in the urine in 24 hours.

Intrathecal: Doses of 1-10 mg/m^2 administered 1-2 times/week in concentrations of 1 mg/mL diluted with preservative-free sterile water for injection

Intravesical: Used for treatment of carcinoma of the bladder; patients should be dehydrated for 8-12 hours prior to treatment; instill 60 mg (in 30-60 mL of NS) into the bladder and retain for a minimum of 2 hours. Patient should be positioned every 15 minutes for maximal area exposure. Instillations usually once a week for 4 weeks. Monitor for bone marrow suppression.

Intratumor: Use a 22-gauge needle to inject thiotepa directly into the tumor. Initial dose: 0.6-0.8 mg/kg (diluted to 10 mg/mL) are used every 1-4 weeks; maintenance dose: 0.07-0.8 mg/kg are administered at 1- to 4-week intervals

Ophthalmic: 0.05% solution in LR has been instilled into the eye every 3 hours for 6-8 weeks for the prevention of pterygium recurrence

Administration Administer I.V., I.M., S.C., intracavitary, and intrathecally; solutions should be filtered through a 0.22 micron filter prior to administration

Monitoring Parameters CBC with differential and platelet count, uric acid, urinalysis

Patient Information Any signs of infection, easy bruising or bleeding, shortness of breath, or painful or burning urination should be brought to physician's attention. Nausea, vomiting, or hair loss sometimes occur. The drug may cause permanent sterility and may cause birth defects. The drug may be excreted in breast milk, therefore, an alternative form of feeding your baby should be used. Contraceptive measures are recommended during therapy.

Nursing Implications Not a vesicant

Dosage Forms Powder for injection: 15 mg

Thiothixene (thye oh THIKS een)

Related Information

Antipsychotic Agents Comparison on page 1305

U.S. Brand Names Navane®

Synonyms Tiotixene

Therapeutic Category Antipsychotic Agent; Phenothiazine Derivative

Use Management of psychotic disorders

Pregnancy Risk Factor C

Contraindications Hypersensitivity to thiothixene or any component; cross-sensitivity with other phenothiazines may exist, lactation

Warnings/Precautions Watch for hypotension when administering I.M. or I.V.; safety in children <6 months of age has not been established; use with caution in patients with narrow-angle glaucoma, bone marrow suppression, severe liver or cardiac disease, seizures

Adverse Reactions

>10%:

Cardiovascular: Hypotension, orthostatic hypotension

Central nervous system: Pseudoparkinsonism, akathisia, dystonias, tardive dyskinesia (persistent), dizziness

Gastrointestinal: Constipation

Respiratory: Nasal congestion

Miscellaneous: Diaphoresis (decreased)

1% to 10%:

Dermatologic: Increased sensitivity to sun, rash

Endocrine & metabolic: Changes in menstrual cycle, changes in libido, breast pain

Gastrointestinal: Weight gain, nausea, vomiting, stomach pain

Genitourinary: Dysuria, ejaculatory disturbances

Neuromuscular & skeletal: Trembling of fingers

Ocular: Pigmentary retinopathy

<1%: Neuroleptic malignant syndrome (NMS), impairment of temperature regulation, lowering of seizures threshold, discoloration of skin (blue-gray), galactorrhea, priapism, agranulocytosis, leukopenia, cholestatic jaundice, hepatotoxicity, cornea and lens changes

Overdosage/Toxicology

Symptoms of overdose include muscle twitching, drowsiness, dizziness, rigidity, tremor, hypotension, cardiac arrhythmias

Following initiation of essential overdose management, toxic symptom treatment and supportive treatment should be initiated. Hypotension usually responds to I.V. fluids or Trendelenburg positioning. If unresponsive to these measures, the use of a parenteral inotrope may be required (eg, norepinephrine 0.1-0.2 mcg/kg/minute titrated to response). Seizures commonly respond to diazepam (I.V. 5-10 mg bolus in adults every 15 minutes if needed up to a total of 30 mg; I.V. 0.25-0.4 mg/kg/dose up to a total of 10 mg in children) or to phenytoin or phenobarbital. Neuroleptics often cause extrapyramidal symptoms (eg, dystonic reactions) requiring management with diphenhydramine 1-2 mg/kg (adults) up to a maximum of 50 mg I.M. or I.V. slow push followed by a maintenance dose for 48-72 hours. When these reactions are unresponsive to diphenhydramine, benztropine mesylate I.V. 1-2 mg (adults) may be effective. These agents are generally effective within 2-5 minutes.

Drug Interactions CYP1A2 enzyme substrate

Decreased effect of guanethidine

Increased toxicity with CNS depressants, anticholinergics, alcohol

Stability Refrigerate

Mechanism of Action Elicits antipsychotic activity by postsynaptic blockade of CNS dopamine receptors resulting in inhibition of dopamine-mediated effects; also has alpha-adrenergic blocking activity

Pharmacodynamics/Kinetics

Metabolism: Extensive in the liver

Half-life: >24 hours with chronic use

Usual Dosage

Children <12 years: Oral: 0.25 mg/kg/24 hours in divided doses (dose not well established)

Children >12 years and Adults: Mild to moderate psychosis:

Oral: 2 mg 3 times/day, up to 20-30 mg/day; more severe psychosis: Initial: 5 mg 2 times/day, may increase gradually, if necessary; maximum: 60 mg/day

I.M.: 4 mg 2-4 times/day, increase dose gradually; usual: 16-20 mg/day; maximum: 30 mg/day; change to oral dose as soon as able

Hemodialysis: Not dialyzable (0% to 5%)

Dietary Considerations Alcohol: Additive CNS effect, avoid use

Monitoring Parameters Liver function tests; for patients on prolonged therapy: CBC, ophthalmologic exam

Test Interactions ↑ cholesterol (S), ↑ glucose (S); ↓ uric acid (S); may cause false-positive pregnancy test

Patient Information May cause drowsiness, restlessness, avoid alcohol and other CNS depressants; do not alter dosage or discontinue without consulting physician

Nursing Implications Observe for extrapyramidal effects; concentrate should be mixed in juice before administration

Dosage Forms

Capsule: 1 mg, 2 mg, 5 mg, 10 mg, 20 mg

Powder for injection, as hydrochloride: 5 mg/mL (2 mL)

- ◆ **Thorazine®** see Chlorpromazine on page 248
- ◆ **Thrombate III™** see Antithrombin III on page 91
- ◆ **Thymoglobulin®** see Antithymocyte Globulin (Rabbit) on page 92
- ◆ **Thyrar®** see Thyroid on this page
- ◆ **Thyro-Block®** see Potassium Iodide on page 952
- ◆ **Thyrogen®** see Thyrotropin Alpha on next page

Thyroid (THYE royd)

U.S. Brand Names Armour® Thyroid; S-P-T; Thyrar®; Thyroid Strong®

Synonyms Desiccated Thyroid; Thyroid Extract

Therapeutic Category Thyroid Hormone; Thyroid Product

Use Replacement or supplemental therapy in hypothyroidism; pituitary TSH suppressants (thyroid nodules, thyroiditis, multinodular goiter, thyroid cancer), thyrotoxicosis, diagnostic suppression tests

Dosage Forms

Capsule, pork source in soybean oil (S-P-T): 60 mg, 120 mg, 180 mg, 300 mg

Tablet:

Armour® Thyroid: 15 mg, 30 mg, 60 mg, 90 mg, 120 mg, 180 mg, 240 mg, 300 mg

Thyrar® (bovine source): 30 mg, 60 mg, 120 mg

Thyroid Strong® (60 mg is equivalent to 90 mg thyroid USP):

Regular: 30 mg, 60 mg, 120 mg

Sugar coated: 30 mg, 60 mg, 120 mg, 180 mg

Thyroid USP: 15 mg, 30 mg, 60 mg, 120 mg, 180 mg, 300 mg

- ◆ **Thyroid Extract** see Thyroid on this page
- ◆ **Thyroid Stimulating Hormone** see Thyrotropin on this page
- ◆ **Thyroid Strong®** see Thyroid on this page
- ◆ **Thyrolar®** see Liotrix on page 685
- ◆ **Thyrotropic Hormone** see Thyrotropin on this page

Thyrotropin (thye roe TROE pin)

U.S. Brand Names Thytropar®

Synonyms Thyroid Stimulating Hormone; Thyrotropic Hormone; TSH

Therapeutic Category Diagnostic Agent, Hypothyroidism; Diagnostic Agent, Thyroid Function

Use Diagnostic aid to differentiate thyroid failure; diagnosis of decreased thyroid reserve, to differentiate between primary and secondary hypothyroidism and between primary hypothyroidism and euthyroidism in patients receiving thyroid replacement

Pregnancy Risk Factor C

(Continued)

Thyrotropin (Continued)

Contraindications Coronary thrombosis, untreated Addison's disease, hypersensitivity to thyrotropin or any component

Warnings/Precautions Use with caution in patients with angina pectoris or cardiac failure, patients with hypopituitarism, adrenal cortical suppression as may be seen with corticosteroid therapy; may cause thyroid hyperplasia

Adverse Reactions <1%: Tachycardia, fever, headache, menstrual irregularities, nausea, vomiting, increased bowel motility, anaphylaxis with repeated administration

Overdosage/Toxicology

Symptoms of overdose include weight loss, nervousness, sweating, tachycardia, insomnia, heat intolerance, menstrual irregularities, headache, angina pectoris, CHF

Acute massive overdose may require cardiac glycosides for CHF; fever should be controlled with the help of acetaminophen; antiadrenergic agents, particularly propranolol 1-3 mg I.V. every 6 hours or 80-160 mg/day, can be used to treat increased sympathetic activity.

Stability Refrigerate at 2°C to 8°C (36°F to 46°F) after reconstitution; use within 2 weeks

Mechanism of Action Stimulates formation and secretion of thyroid hormone, increases uptake of iodine by thyroid gland

Pharmacodynamics/Kinetics

Half-life: 35 minutes, dependent upon thyroid state

Elimination: Rapidly by the kidney in the urine

Usual Dosage Adults: I.M., S.C.: 10 units/day for 1-3 days; follow by a radioiodine study 24 hours past last injection, no response in thyroid failure, substantial response in pituitary failure

Dosage Forms Injection: 10 units

Thyrotropin Alpha (thye roe TROE pin AL fa)

U.S. Brand Names Thyrogen®

Synonyms Human Thyroid Stimulating Hormone; TSH

Therapeutic Category Diagnostic Agent

Use As an adjunctive diagnostic tool for serum thyroglobulin (Tg) testing with or without radioiodine imaging in the follow-up of patients with well-differentiated thyroid cancer

Potential clinical uses:

1. Patients with an undetectable Tg on thyroid hormone suppressive therapy to exclude the diagnosis of residual or recurrent thyroid cancer
2. Patients requiring serum Tg testing and radioiodine imaging who are unwilling to undergo thyroid hormone withdrawal testing and whose treating physician believes that use of a less sensitive test is justified
3. Patients who are either unable to mount an adequate endogenous TSH response to thyroid hormone withdrawal or in whom withdrawal is medically contraindicated

Pregnancy Risk Factor C

Contraindications Hypersensitivity to any component

Warnings/Precautions Caution should be exercised when administered to patients who have been previously treated with bovine TSH and, in particular, to those patients who have experienced hypersensitivity reactions to bovine TSH

Considerations in the use of thyrogen:

1. There remains a meaningful risk of a diagnosis of thyroid cancer or of an underestimating the extent of disease when thyrogen-stimulated Tg testing is performed and in combination with radioiodine imaging
2. Thyrogen® Tg levels are generally lower than, and do not correlate with, Tg levels after thyroid hormone withdrawal
3. Newly detectable Tg level or a Tg level rising over time after Thyrogen® or a high index of suspicion of metastatic disease, even in the setting of a negative or low-stage Thyrogen® radioiodine scan, should prompt further evaluation such as thyroid hormone withdrawal to definitively establish the location and extent of thyroid cancer.
4. Decision to perform a Thyrogen® radioiodine scan in conjunction with a Thyrogen® serum Tg test and whether or when to withdraw a patient from thyroid hormones are complex. Pertinent factors in this decision include the sensitivity of the Tg assay used, the Thyrogen® Tg level obtained, and the index of suspicion of recurrent or persistent local or metastatic disease.
5. Thyrogen® is not recommended to stimulate radioiodine uptake for the purposes of ablative radiotherapy of thyroid cancer
6. The signs and symptoms of hypothyroidism which accompany thyroid hormone withdrawal are avoided with Thyrogen® use

Adverse Reactions 1% to 10%:

Central nervous system: Headache, chills, fever, flu-like syndrome, dizziness

Gastrointestinal: Nausea, vomiting

Neuromuscular & skeletal: Weakness, paresthesia

Overdosage/Toxicology There has been no reported experience of overdose in humans

Stability Store intact vials at 2°C to 8°C/36°F to 46°F; reconstitute each vial with 1.0 mL of sterile water for injection - each vial should be reconstituted immediately prior to use with diluent provided. If necessary, the reconstituted solution can be stored for up to 24 hours at 2°C to 8°C

Mechanism of Action An exogenous source of human TSH that offers an additional diagnostic tool in the follow-up of patients with a history of well-differentiated thyroid cancer. Binding of thyrotropin alpha to TSH receptors on normal thyroid epithelial cells or on well-differentiated thyroid cancer tissue stimulates iodine uptake and organification and synthesis and secretion of thyroglobulin, triiodothyronine, and thyroxine.

Pharmacodynamics/Kinetics
Mean peak concentrations: 3-24 hours after injection
Half-life, elimination: 25 ± 10 hours

Usual Dosage Children >16 years and Adults: I.M.: 0.9 mg every 24 hours for 2 doses or every 72 hours for 3 doses. For radioiodine imaging, radioiodine administration should be given 24 hours following the final Thyrogen® injection. Scanning should be performed 48 hours after raidoiodine administration (72 hours after the final injection of Thyrogen®).

Administration I.M. injection into the buttock

Dosage Forms Kits containing two 1.1 mg vials (>4 int. units) of thyrogen® and two 10 mL vials of sterile water for injection

♦ **Thytropar**® *see* Thyrotropin *on page 1139*

♦ **Tiabendazole** *see* Thiabendazole *on page 1130*

Tiagabine (tye AG a bene)

Related Information
Anticonvulsants by Seizure Type *on page 1300*
U.S. Brand Names Gabitril®
Therapeutic Category Anticonvulsant
Use Adjunctive therapy in adults and children ≥12 years of age in the treatment of partial seizures

Pregnancy Risk Factor C

Contraindications Patients who have demonstrated hypersensitivity to the drug or any of its ingredients

Warnings/Precautions Anticonvulsants should not be discontinued abruptly because of the possibility of increasing seizure frequency; tiagabine should be withdrawn gradually to minimize the potential of increased seizure frequency, unless safety concerns require a more rapid withdrawal

Adverse Reactions All adverse effects are dose-related
>1%
Central nervous system: Dizziness, headache, somnolence, CNS depression, memory disturbance, ataxia, confusion
Neuromuscular & skeletal: Tremors, weakness, myalgia

Drug Interactions CYP2D6 and 3A3/4 enzyme substrate
The clearance of tiagabine is affected by the coadministration of hepatic enzyme-inducing antiepilepsy drugs; tiagabine is cleared more rapidly in patients who have been treated with carbamazepine, phenytoin, primidone, and phenobarbital than in patients who have not received these drugs

Mechanism of Action The exact mechanism by which tiagabine exerts antiseizure activity is not definitively known; however, *in vitro* experiments demonstrate that it enhances the activity of gamma aminobutyric acid (GABA), the major neuroinhibitory transmitter in the nervous system. It is thought that binding to the GABA uptake carrier inhibits the uptake of GABA into presynaptic neurons, allowing an increased amount of GABA to be available to postsynaptic neurons. Based on *in vitro* studies, tiagabine does not inhibit the uptake of dopamine, norepinephrine, serotonin, glutamate, or choline.

Pharmacodynamics/Kinetics
Absorption: Rapid (within 1 hour); food prolongs absorption
Protein binding: 96%
Half-life: 6.7 hours

Usual Dosage Take with food; Oral:
Children 12-18 years: 4 mg once daily for 1 week; may increase to 8 mg daily in 2 divided doses for 1 week; then may increase by 4-8 mg weekly to response or up to 32 mg daily in 2-4 divided doses
Adults: 4 mg once daily for 1 week; may increase by 4-8 mg weekly to response or up to 56 mg daily in 2-4 divided doses

Monitoring Parameters A reduction in seizure frequency is indicative of therapeutic response to tiagabine in patients with partial seizures. Complete blood counts, renal function tests, liver function tests, and routine blood chemistry should be monitored periodically during therapy.

Reference Range Maximal plasma level after a 24 mg/dose: 552 ng/mL

Patient Information Use exactly as directed; take orally with food, usually beginning at 4 mg once daily, and usually in addition to other antiepilepsy drugs. The dose will be increased based on age and medical condition, up to 2-4 times/day. Do not interrupt or discontinue treatment without consulting your physician or pharmacist. If told to stop this medication, it should be discontinued gradually.

Dosage Forms Tablet: 4 mg, 12 mg, 16 mg, 20 mg

♦ **Tiamate**® *see* Diltiazem *on page 365*

♦ **Tiamol**® *see* Fluocinonide *on page 496*

♦ **Tiazac**™ *see* Diltiazem *on page 365*

♦ **Ticar**® *see* Ticarcillin *on this page*

Ticarcillin (tye kar SIL in)

Related Information
Antimicrobial Drugs of Choice *on page 1404*
Community-Acquired Pneumonia in Adults *on page 1419*
U.S. Brand Names Ticar®
(Continued)

Ticarcillin *(Continued)*

Synonyms Ticarcillin Disodium

Therapeutic Category Antibiotic, Penicillin

Use Treatment of susceptible infections such as septicemia, acute and chronic respiratory tract infections, skin and soft tissue infections, and urinary tract infections due to susceptible strains of *Pseudomonas*, and other gram-negative bacteria

Pregnancy Risk Factor B

Contraindications Hypersensitivity to ticarcillin or any component or penicillins

Warnings/Precautions Due to sodium load and adverse effects (anemia, neuropsychological changes), use with caution and modify dosage in patients with renal impairment; serious and occasionally severe or fatal hypersensitivity (anaphylactoid) reactions have been reported in patients on penicillin therapy (especially with a history of beta-lactam hypersensitivity and/or a history of sensitivity to multiple allergens); use with caution in patients with seizures

Adverse Reactions Percentage unknown: Convulsions, confusion, drowsiness, fever, rash, electrolyte imbalance, hemolytic anemia, positive Coombs' reaction, eosinophilia, bleeding, thrombophlebitis, myoclonus, acute interstitial nephritis, hypersensitivity reactions, anaphylaxis, Jarisch-Herxheimer reaction

Overdosage/Toxicology

Symptoms of penicillin overdose include neuromuscular hypersensitivity (agitation, hallucinations, asterixis, encephalopathy, confusion, and seizures) and electrolyte imbalance with potassium or sodium salts, especially in renal failure

Hemodialysis may be helpful to aid in the removal of the drug from the blood, otherwise most treatment is supportive or symptom directed

Drug Interactions

Decreased effect:

Tetracyclines may decrease penicillin effectiveness

Aminoglycosides → physical inactivation of aminoglycosides in the presence of high concentrations of ticarcillin

Decreased effectiveness of oral contraceptives

Increased effect:

Probenecid may increase penicillin levels

Neuromuscular blockers may increase duration of blockade

Potential toxicity in patients with mild to moderate renal dysfunction

Aminoglycosides → synergistic efficacy

Increased bleeding risk with large I.V. doses and anticoagulants

Stability Reconstituted solution is stable for 72 hours at room temperature and 14 days when refrigerated; for I.V. infusion in NS or D_5W solution is stable for 72 hours at room temperature, 14 days when refrigerated or 30 days when frozen; after freezing, thawed solution is stable for 72 hours at room temperature or 14 days when refrigerated; **incompatible** with aminoglycosides

Mechanism of Action Inhibits bacterial cell wall synthesis by binding to one or more of the penicillin binding proteins (PBPs); which in turn inhibits the final transpeptidation step of peptidoglycan synthesis in bacterial cell walls, thus inhibiting cell wall biosynthesis. Bacteria eventually lyse due to ongoing activity of cell wall autolytic enzymes (autolysins and murein hydrolases) while cell wall assembly is arrested.

Pharmacodynamics/Kinetics

Absorption: I.M.: 86%

Distribution: In blister fluid, lymph tissue, and gallbladder; crosses placenta; distributed into milk at low concentrations

Protein binding: 45% to 65%

Half-life:

Neonates: <1 week: 3.5-5.6 hours; 1-8 weeks: 1.3-2.2 hours

Children 5-13 years: 0.9 hour

Adults: 66-72 minutes, prolonged with renal impairment and/or hepatic impairment

Peak serum levels: I.M.: Within 30-75 minutes

Elimination: Almost entirely in urine as unchanged drug and its metabolites with small amounts excreted in feces (3.5%)

Usual Dosage Ticarcillin is generally given I.V., I.M. injection is only for the treatment of uncomplicated urinary tract infections and dose should not exceed 2 g/injection when administered I.M.

Neonates: I.M., I.V.:

Postnatal age <7 days:

<2000 g: 75 mg/kg/dose every 12 hours

>2000 g: 75 mg/kg/dose every 8 hours

Postnatal age >7 days:

<1200 g: 75 mg/kg/dose every 12 hours

1200-2000 g: 75 mg/kg/dose every 8 hours

>2000 g: 75 mg/kg/dose every 6 hours

Infants and Children:

Systemic infections: I.V.: 200-300 mg/kg/day in divided doses every 4-6 hours

Urinary tract infections: I.M., I.V.: 50-100 mg/kg/day in divided doses every 6-8 hours

Maximum dose: 24 g/day

Adults: I.M., I.V.: 1-4 g every 4-6 hours, usual dose: 3 g I.V. every 4-6 hours

Dosing adjustment in renal impairment: Adults:

Cl_{cr} 30-60 mL/minute: 2 g every 4 hours or 3 g every 8 hours

Cl_{cr} 10-30 mL/minute: 2 g every 8 hours or 3 g every 12 hours

Cl_{cr} <10 mL/minute: 2 g every 12 hours

Moderately dialyzable (20% to 50%)

Continuous arteriovenous or venovenous hemodiafiltration (CAVH) effects: Dose as for Cl_{cr} 10-50 mL/minute

Administration Administer 1 hour apart from aminoglycosides

Monitoring Parameters Serum electrolytes, bleeding time, and periodic tests of renal, hepatic, and hematologic function; monitor for signs of anaphylaxis during first dose

Test Interactions May interfere with urinary glucose tests using cupric sulfate (Benedict's solution, Clinitest®); may inactivate aminoglycosides *in vitro*; false-positive urinary or serum protein

Nursing Implications Draw sample for culture and sensitivity before administering first dose, if possible

Additional Information Sodium content of 1 g: 119.6-149.5 mg (5.2-6.5 mEq)

Dosage Forms Powder for injection, as disodium: 1 g, 3 g, 6 g, 20 g, 30 g

Ticarcillin and Clavulanate Potassium

(tye kar SIL in & klav yoo LAN ate poe TASS ee um)

Related Information

Antimicrobial Drugs of Choice *on page 1404*

U.S. Brand Names Timentin®

Synonyms Ticarcillin and Clavulanic Acid

Therapeutic Category Antibiotic, Penicillin; Antibiotic, Penicillin & Beta-lactamase Inhibitor

Use Treatment of infections of lower respiratory tract, urinary tract, skin and skin structures, bone and joint, and septicemia caused by susceptible organisms. Clavulanate expands activity of ticarcillin to include beta-lactamase producing strains of *S. aureus, H. influenzae, Bacteroides* species, and some other gram-negative bacilli

Pregnancy Risk Factor B

Contraindications Known hypersensitivity to ticarcillin, clavulanate, or any penicillin

Warnings/Precautions Not approved for use in children <12 years of age; use with caution and modify dosage in patients with renal impairment; use with caution in patients with a history of allergy to cephalosporins and in patients with CHF due to high sodium load

Adverse Reactions Percentage unknown: Convulsions, confusion, drowsiness, fever, rash, electrolyte imbalance, hemolytic anemia, positive Coombs' reaction, bleeding, thrombophlebitis, myoclonus, acute interstitial nephritis, hypersensitivity reactions, anaphylaxis, Jarisch-Herxheimer reaction

Overdosage/Toxicology

Symptoms of overdose include neuromuscular hypersensitivity, seizures

Many beta-lactam containing antibiotics have the potential to cause neuromuscular hyperirritability or convulsive seizures. Hemodialysis may be helpful to aid in the removal of the drug from the blood, otherwise most treatment is supportive or symptom directed.

Drug Interactions

Decreased effect:

Tetracyclines may decrease penicillin effectiveness

Aminoglycosides → physical inactivation of aminoglycosides in the presence of high concentrations of ticarcillin

Decreased effectiveness of oral contraceptives

Increased effect:

Probenecid may increase penicillin levels

Neuromuscular blockers may increase duration of blockade

Potential toxicity in patients with with mild to moderate renal dysfunction

Aminoglycosides → synergistic efficacy

Increased bleeding risk with large I.V. doses and anticoagulants

Stability Reconstituted solution is stable for 6 hours at room temperature and 72 hours when refrigerated; for I.V. infusion in NS is stable for 24 hours at room temperature, 7 days when refrigerated or 30 days when frozen; after freezing, thawed solution is stable for 8 hours at room temperature; for I.V. infusion in D_5W solution is stable for 24 hours at room temperature, 3 days when refrigerated or 7 days when frozen; after freezing, thawed solution is stable for 8 hours at room temperature; darkening of drug indicates loss of potency of clavulanate potassium; **incompatible** with sodium bicarbonate, aminoglycosides

Mechanism of Action Inhibits bacterial cell wall synthesis by binding to one or more of the penicillin binding proteins (PBPs); which in turn inhibits the final transpeptidation step of peptidoglycan synthesis in bacterial cell walls, thus inhibiting cell wall biosynthesis. Bacteria eventually lyse due to ongoing activity of cell wall autolytic enzymes (autolysins and murein hydrolases) while cell wall assembly is arrested.

Pharmacodynamics/Kinetics

Distribution: Low concentrations of ticarcillin distribute into the CSF and increase when meninges are inflamed, otherwise widely distributed

Protein binding:

Ticarcillin: 45% to 65%

Clavulanic acid: 9% to 30% removed by hemodialysis

Metabolism: Clavulanic acid is metabolized in the liver

Half-life:

Clavulanate: 66-90 minutes

Ticarcillin: 66-72 minutes in patients with normal renal function; clavulanic acid does not affect the clearance of ticarcillin

(Continued)

Ticarcillin and Clavulanate Potassium *(Continued)*

Elimination: 45% excreted unchanged in urine, whereas 60% to 90% of ticarcillin excreted unchanged in urine

Usual Dosage I.V.:

Children and Adults <60 kg: 200-300 mg of ticarcillin component/kg/day in divided doses every 4-6 hours

Children >60 kg and Adults: 3.1 g (ticarcillin 3 g plus clavulanic acid 0.1 g) every 4-6 hours; maximum: 24 g/day

Urinary tract infections: 3.1 g every 6-8 hours

Dosing adjustment in renal impairment:

Cl_{cr} 30-60 mL/minute: Administer 2 g every 4 hours or 3.1 g every 8 hours

Cl_{cr} 10-30 mL/minute: Administer 2 g every 8 hours or 3.1 g every 12 hours

Cl_{cr} <10 mL/minute: Administer 2 g every 12 hours

Moderately dialyzable (20% to 50%)

Continuous arteriovenous or venovenous hemodiafiltration (CAVH) effects: Dose as for Cl_{cr} 10-50 mL/minute

Administration Infuse over 30 minutes; administer 1 hour apart from aminoglycosides

Monitoring Parameters Observe signs and symptoms of anaphylaxis during first dose

Test Interactions Positive Coombs' test, false-positive urinary proteins

Nursing Implications Draw sample for culture and sensitivity prior to first dose if possible

Additional Information Sodium content of 1 g: 4.75 mEq; potassium content of 1 g: 0.15 mEq

Dosage Forms

Infusion, premixed (frozen): Ticarcillin disodium 3 g and clavulanate potassium 0.1 g (100 mL)

Powder for injection: Ticarcillin disodium 3 g and clavulanate potassium 0.1 g (3.1 g, 31 g)

- ◆ **Ticarcillin and Clavulanic Acid** *see* Ticarcillin and Clavulanate Potassium *on previous page*
- ◆ **Ticarcillin Disodium** *see* Ticarcillin *on page 1141*
- ◆ **TICE® BCG** *see* BCG Vaccine *on page 126*
- ◆ **Ticlid®** *see* Ticlopidine *on this page*

Ticlopidine *(tye KLOE pi deen)*

U.S. Brand Names Ticlid®

Synonyms Ticlopidine Hydrochloride

Therapeutic Category Antiplatelet Agent

Use Platelet aggregation inhibitor that reduces the risk of thrombotic stroke in patients who have had a stroke or stroke precursors

Unlabeled use: Protection of aortocoronary bypass grafts, diabetic microangiopathy, ischemic heart disease, prevention of postoperative DVT, reduction of graft loss following renal transplant; reduction of postoperative reocclusion in patients receiving PTCA with stents

Pregnancy Risk Factor B

Contraindications Hypersensitivity to ticlopidine; active bleeding disorders; neutropenia or thrombocytopenia; severe liver impairment

Warnings/Precautions Patients predisposed to bleeding such as those with gastric or duodenal ulcers; patients with underlying hematologic disorders; patients receiving oral anticoagulant therapy or nonsteroidal anti-inflammatory agents (including aspirin); liver disease; patients undergoing lumbar puncture or surgical procedure. Ticlopidine should be discontinued if the absolute neutrophil count falls to <1200/mm³ or if the platelet count falls to <80,000/mm³. If possible, ticlopidine should be discontinued 10-14 days prior to surgery. Use caution when phenytoin or propranolol is used concurrently.

Adverse Reactions

>1%:

Dermatologic: Rash

Hematologic: Thrombotic thrombocytopenic purpura (TTP)

<1%: Bruising, diarrhea, nausea, vomiting, GI pain, neutropenia, thrombocytopenia, increased LFTs, tinnitus, hematuria, epistaxis

Overdosage/Toxicology

Symptoms of overdose include ataxia, seizures, vomiting, abdominal pain, hematologic abnormalities; specific treatments are lacking; after decontamination

Treatment is symptomatic and supportive

Drug Interactions CYP2C19 inhibitor

Decreased effect with antacids (decreased absorption), corticosteroids; decreased effect of digoxin, cyclosporine

Increased effect/toxicity of aspirin, anticoagulants, antipyrine, theophylline, cimetidine (increased levels), NSAIDs

Mechanism of Action Ticlopidine is an inhibitor of platelet function with a mechanism which is different from other antiplatelet drugs. The drug significantly increases bleeding time. This effect may not be solely related to ticlopidine's effect on platelets. The prolongation of the bleeding time caused by ticlopidine is further increased by the addition of aspirin in *ex vivo* experiments. Although many metabolites of ticlopidine have been found, none have been shown to account for *in vivo* activity.

Pharmacodynamics/Kinetics

Onset of action: Within 6 hours

Peak: Achieved after 3-5 days of oral therapy; serum levels do not correlate with clinical antiplatelet activity

Metabolism: Extensively in the liver and has at least one active metabolite

Half-life, elimination: 24 hours

Usual Dosage Adults: Oral: 1 tablet twice daily with food

Monitoring Parameters Signs of bleeding; CBC with differential every 2 weeks starting the second week through the third month of treatment; more frequent monitoring is recommended for patients whose absolute neutrophil counts have been consistently declining or are 30% less than baseline values. Liver function tests (alkaline phosphatase and transaminases) should be performed in the first 4 months of therapy if liver dysfunction is suspected.

Test Interactions ↑ cholesterol (S), ↑ alkaline phosphatase, ↑ transaminases (S)

Dosage Forms Tablet, as hydrochloride: 250 mg

♦ **Ticlopidine Hydrochloride** see Ticlopidine on previous page
♦ **Ticon®** see Trimethobenzamide on page 1183
♦ **TIG** see Tetanus Immune Globulin (Human) on page 1119
♦ **Tigan®** see Trimethobenzamide on page 1183
♦ **Tilade® Inhalation Aerosol** see Nedocromil Sodium on page 821

Tiludronate (tye LOO droe nate)

U.S. Brand Names Skelid®

Synonyms Tiludronate Disodium

Therapeutic Category Bisphosphonate Derivative

Use Treatment of Paget's disease of the bone (1) who have a level of serum alkaline phosphatase (SAP) at least twice the upper limit of normal, (2) or who are symptomatic, (3) or who are at risk for future complications of their disease

Pregnancy Risk Factor C

Contraindications Hypersensitivity to biphosphonates or any component of the product

Warnings/Precautions Not recommended in patients with severe renal impairment (Cl_{cr} <30 mL/minute). Use with caution in patients with active upper GI problems (eg, dysphagia, symptomatic esophageal diseases, gastritis, duodenitis, ulcers).

Adverse Reactions 1% to 10%:
Cardiovascular: Flushing
Central nervous system: Vertigo, involuntary muscle contractions, anxiety, nervousness
Dermatologic: Pruritus, increased sweating, Stevens-Johnson type syndrome (rare)
Gastrointestinal: Xerostomia, gastritis
Genitourinary: Urinary tract infection
Neuromuscular & skeletal: Weakness, pathological fracture
Respiratory: Bronchitis
Miscellaneous: Increased diaphoresis

Overdosage/Toxicology Hypocalcemia is a potential consequence of tiludronate overdose. No specific information on overdose treatment is available; dialysis would not be beneficial. Standard medical practices may be used to manage renal insufficiency or hypocalcemia, if signs of these occur.

Drug Interactions
Decreased effect:
Calcium supplements, antacids interfere with the bioavailability (decreased 60%) when administered 1 hour before tiludronate
Aspirin decreases the bioavailability of tiludronate by up to 50% when taken 2 hours after tiludronate
Increased effect/toxicity: Indomethacin increases the bioavailability of tiludronate two- to fourfold

Stability Do not remove tablets from the foil strips until they are to be used

Mechanism of Action Inhibition of normal and abnormal bone resorption. Inhibits osteoclasts through at least two mechanisms: disruption of the cytoskeletal ring structure, possibly by inhibition of protein-tyrosine-phosphatase, thus leading to the detachment of osteoclasts from the bone surface area and the inhibition of the osteoclast proton pump.

Pharmacodynamics/Kinetics
Metabolism: Little, if any
Bioavailability: Oral: 6%; reduced by food
Peak plasma concentrations: Within 2 hours

Usual Dosage Tiludronate should be taken with 6-8 oz of plain water and not taken within 2 hours of food
Adults: Oral: 400 mg (2 tablets of tiludronic acid) daily for a period of 3 months; allow an interval of 3 months to assess response
Dosing adjustment in renal impairment: Cl_{cr} <30 mL/minute: **Not recommended**
Dosing adjustment in hepatic impairment: Adjustment is not necessary

Dietary Considerations In single-dose studies, the bioavailability of tiludronate was reduced by 90% when an oral dose was administered with, or 2 hours after, a standard breakfast compared to the same dose administered after an overnight fast and 4 hours before a standard breakfast; therefore, do not take within 2 hours of food

Administration Administer as a single oral dose, take with 6-8 oz of plain water. Beverages other than plain water (including mineral water), food, and some medications (see Drug Interactions) are likely to reduce the absorption of tiludronate. Do not take within 2 hours of food. Take calcium or mineral supplements at least 2 hours before or after tiludronate. Take aluminum- or magnesium-containing antacids at least 2 hours after taking tiludronate. Do not take tiludronate within 2 hours of indomethacin.
(Continued)

Tiludronate *(Continued)*

Patient Information Take tiludronate with 6-8 oz of plain water. Do not take within 2 hours of food. Maintain adequate vitamin D and calcium intake. Do not take calcium supplements, aspirin, and indomethacin within 2 hours before or after tiludronate. Take aluminum- or magnesium-containing antacids, if needed, at least 2 hours after tiludronate.

Dosage Forms Tablet, as disodium: 240 mg [tiludronic acid 200 mg]; dosage is expressed in terms of tiludronic acid.

♦ **Tiludronate Disodium** see Tiludronate *on previous page*

♦ **Timentin®** see Ticarcillin and Clavulanate Potassium *on page 1143*

Timolol *(TYE moe lole)*

Related Information
Antiarrhythmic Drugs Comparison *on page 1297*
Beta-Blockers Comparison *on page 1311*
Glaucoma Drug Therapy Comparison *on page 1322*

U.S. Brand Names Betimol® Ophthalmic; Blocadren® Oral; Timoptic® OcuDose®; Timoptic® Ophthalmic; Timoptic-XE® Ophthalmic

Canadian Brand Names Apo®-Timol; Apo®-Timop; Gen-Timolol; Novo-Timol; Nu-Timolol

Synonyms Timolol Hemihydrate; Timolol Maleate

Therapeutic Category Antianginal Agent; Antihypertensive Agent; Antimigraine Agent; Beta-Adrenergic Blocker; Beta-Adrenergic Blocker, Ophthalmic

Use Ophthalmic dosage form used to treat elevated intraocular pressure such as glaucoma or ocular hypertension; orally for treatment of hypertension and angina and reduce mortality following myocardial infarction and prophylaxis of migraine

Pregnancy Risk Factor C

Contraindications Uncompensated congestive heart failure, cardiogenic shock, bradycardia or heart block, severe chronic obstructive pulmonary disease, asthma, hypersensitivity to beta-blockers

Warnings/Precautions Some products contain sulfites which can cause allergic reactions; tachyphylaxis may develop; use with a miotic in angle-closure glaucoma; use with caution in patients with decreased renal or hepatic function (dosage adjustment required); severe CNS, cardiovascular and respiratory adverse effects have been seen following ophthalmic use; patients with a history of asthma, congestive heart failure, or bradycardia appear to be at a higher risk

Adverse Reactions
Ophthalmic:
1% to 10%:
Dermatologic: Alopecia
Ocular: Burning, stinging of eyes
<1%: Rash, blepharitis, conjunctivitis, keratitis, vision disturbances
Oral:
>10%: Endocrine & metabolic: Decreased sexual ability
1% to 10%:
Cardiovascular: Bradycardia, arrhythmia, reduced peripheral circulation
Central nervous system: Dizziness, fatigue
Dermatologic: Itching
Neuromuscular & skeletal: Weakness
Ocular: Burning eyes, stinging of eyes
Respiratory: Dyspnea
<1%: Chest pain, congestive heart failure, hallucinations, mental depression, anxiety, nightmares, skin rash, diarrhea, nausea, vomiting, stomach discomfort, numbness in toes and fingers, dry sore eyes

Overdosage/Toxicology
Symptoms of intoxication include cardiac disturbances, CNS toxicity, bronchospasm, hypoglycemia and hyperkalemia. The most common cardiac symptoms include hypotension and bradycardia; atrioventricular block, intraventricular conduction disturbances, cardiogenic shock, and asystole may occur with severe overdose, especially with membrane-depressant drugs (eg, propranolol); CNS effects include convulsions, coma, and respiratory arrest is commonly seen with propranolol and other membrane-depressant and lipid-soluble drugs.

Treatment includes symptomatic treatment of seizures, hypotension, hyperkalemia and hypoglycemia; bradycardia and hypotension resistant to atropine, isoproterenol or pacing may respond to glucagon; wide QRS defects caused by the membrane-depressant poisoning may respond to hypertonic sodium bicarbonate; repeat-dose charcoal, hemoperfusion, or hemodialysis may be helpful in removal of only those beta-blockers with a small V_d, long half-life or low intrinsic clearance (acebutolol, atenolol, nadolol, sotalol).

Drug Interactions CYP2D6 enzyme substrate
Decreased effect of beta-blockers with aluminum salts, barbiturates, calcium salts, cholestyramine, colestipol, NSAIDs, penicillins (ampicillin), rifampin, salicylates and sulfinpyrazone due to decreased bioavailability and plasma levels
Beta-blockers may decrease the effect of sulfonylureas
Increased effect/toxicity of beta-blockers with calcium blockers (diltiazem, felodipine, nicardipine), contraceptives, flecainide, propafenone (metoprolol, propranolol), quinidine (in extensive metabolizers), ciprofloxacin

Beta-blockers may increase the effect/toxicity of flecainide, phenothiazines, acetaminophen, clonidine (hypertensive crisis after or during withdrawal of either agent), epinephrine (initial hypertensive episode followed by bradycardia), nifedipine and verapamil lidocaine, ergots (peripheral ischemia), prazosin (postural hypotension)

Beta-blockers may affect the action or levels of ethanol, disopyramide, nondepolarizing muscle relaxants and theophylline although the effects are difficult to predict

Mechanism of Action Blocks both beta$_1$- and beta$_2$-adrenergic receptors, reduces intraocular pressure by reducing aqueous humor production or possibly outflow; reduces blood pressure by blocking adrenergic receptors and decreasing sympathetic outflow, produces a negative chronotropic and inotropic activity through an unknown mechanism

Pharmacodynamics/Kinetics

Onset of hypotensive effect: Oral: Within 15-45 minutes

Peak effect: Within 0.5-2.5 hours

Duration of action: ~4 hours; intraocular effects persist for 24 hours after ophthalmic instillation

Protein binding: 60%

Metabolism: Extensive first-pass effect; extensively metabolized in the liver

Half-life: 2-2.7 hours; prolonged with reduced renal function

Elimination: Urinary excretion (15% to 20% as unchanged drug)

Usual Dosage

Children and Adults: Ophthalmic: Initial: 0.25% solution, instill 1 drop twice daily; increase to 0.5% solution if response not adequate; decrease to 1 drop/day if controlled; do not exceed 1 drop twice daily of 0.5% solution

Adults: Oral:

Hypertension: Initial: 10 mg twice daily, increase gradually every 7 days, usual dosage: 20-40 mg/day in 2 divided doses; maximum: 60 mg/day

Prevention of myocardial infarction: 10 mg twice daily initiated within 1-4 weeks after infarction

Migraine headache: Initial: 10 mg twice daily, increase to maximum of 30 mg/day

Monitoring Parameters Blood pressure, apical and radial pulses, fluid I & O, daily weight, respirations, mental status, and circulation in extremities before and during therapy

Patient Information Apply gentle pressure to lacrimal sac during and immediately following instillation (1 minute) to avoid systemic absorption; stop drug if breathing difficulty occurs

Nursing Implications Monitor for systemic effect of beta-blockade even when administering ophthalmic product

Dosage Forms

Gel, as maleate, ophthalmic (Timoptic-XE®): 0.25% (2.5 mL, 5 mL); 0.5% (2.5 mL, 5 mL)

Solution, as hemihydrate, ophthalmic (Betimol®): 0.25% (2.5 mL, 5 mL, 10 mL, 15 mL); 0.5% (2.5 mL, 5 mL, 10 mL, 15 mL)

Solution, as maleate, ophthalmic (Timoptic®): 0.25% (2.5 mL, 5 mL, 10 mL, 15 mL); 0.5% (2.5 mL, 5 mL, 10 mL, 15 mL)

Solution, as maleate, ophthalmic, preservative free, single use (Timoptic® OcuDose®): 0.25%, 0.5%

Tablet, as maleate, (Blocadren®): 5 mg, 10 mg, 20 mg

- **Timolol Hemihydrate** see Timolol on previous page
- **Timolol Maleate** see Timolol on previous page
- **Timoptic® OcuDose®** see Timolol on previous page
- **Timoptic® Ophthalmic** see Timolol on previous page
- **Timoptic-XE® Ophthalmic** see Timolol on previous page
- **Tinactin® [OTC]** see Tolnaftate on page 1159
- **Tinactin® for Jock Itch [OTC]** see Tolnaftate on page 1159
- **Tindal®** see Acetophenazine on page 25
- **Tine Test** see Tuberculin Purified Protein Derivative on page 1194
- **Tine Test** see Tuberculin Tests on page 1194
- **Tine Test PPD** see Tuberculin Purified Protein Derivative on page 1194
- **Tine Test PPD** see Tuberculin Tests on page 1194
- **Ting® [OTC]** see Tolnaftate on page 1159
- **Tinver® Lotion** see Sodium Thiosulfate on page 1072

Tioconazole (tye oh KONE a zole)

Related Information

Treatment of Sexually Transmitted Diseases on page 1429

U.S. Brand Names Vagistat® Vaginal

Therapeutic Category Antifungal Agent, Imidazole Derivative; Antifungal Agent, Vaginal

Use Local treatment of vulvovaginal candidiasis

Pregnancy Risk Factor C

Contraindications Known hypersensitivity to tioconazole

Warnings/Precautions Not effective when applied to the scalp; may interact with condoms and vaginal contraceptive diaphragms; avoid these products for 3 days following treatment

Adverse Reactions

1% to 10%: Genitourinary: Vulvar/vaginal burning

<1%: Vulvar itching, soreness, edema, or discharge; polyuria

(Continued)

Tioconazole *(Continued)*

Mechanism of Action A 1-substituted imidazole derivative with a broad antifungal spectrum against a wide variety of dermatophytes and yeasts, usually at a concentration ≤6.25 mg/L; has been demonstrated to be at least as active *in vitro* as other imidazole antifungals. *In vitro*, tioconazole has been demonstrated 2-8 times as potent as miconazole against common dermal pathogens including *Trichophyton mentagrophytes*, *T. rubrum*, *T. erinacei*, *T. tonsurans*, *Microsporum canis*, *Microsporum gypseum*, and *Candida albicans*. Both agents appear to be similarly effective against *Epidermophyton floccosum*.

Pharmacodynamics/Kinetics
  Absorption: Intravaginal: Following application small amounts of drug are absorbed systemically (25%) within 2-8 hours; therapeutic levels persist for 3-5 days after single dose
  Half-life: 21-24 hours
  Elimination: Urine and feces in approximate equal amounts

Usual Dosage Adults: Vaginal: Insert 1 applicatorful in vagina, just prior to bedtime, as a single dose; therapy may extend to 7 days

Patient Information Insert high into vagina; contact physician if itching or burning continues; Vagistat®-1 may interact with condoms and vaginal contraceptive diaphragms (ie, weaken latex); do not rely on these products for 3 days following treatment

Dosage Forms Cream, vaginal: 6.5% with applicator (4.6 g)

◆ **Tioguanine** *see* Thioguanine *on page 1133*

◆ **Tiotixene** *see* Thiothixene *on page 1138*

Tirofiban *(tye roe FYE ban)*

Related Information
  Glycoprotein Antagonists *on page 1323*

U.S. Brand Names Aggrastat®

Synonyms MK 383

Therapeutic Category Antiplatelet Agent; Glycoprotein IIb/IIIa Inhibitor, Reversible; Platelet Aggregation Inhibitor

Use In combination with heparin, is indicated for the treatment of acute coronary syndrome, including patients who are to be managed medically and those undergoing PTCA or atherectomy. In this setting, it has been shown to decrease the rate of a combined endpoint of death, new myocardial infarction or refractory ischemia/repeat cardiac procedure.

Pregnancy Risk Factor B

Contraindications Hypersensitivity to any component; history of intracranial/hemorrhagic intracranial neoplasm, A-V malformation or aneurysm; history of stroke in last 30 days, any history of hemorrhagic stroke, major surgery/trauma in last 30 days; history, symptoms, or findings which suggest aortic dissection; severe hypertension, acute pericarditis, concurrent use of other GP IIb/IIIa inhibitor, active bleeding (internal or history of bleeding diathesis); history of thrombocytopenia following prior exposure to tirofiban

Warnings/Precautions Bleeding is the most common complication encountered during this therapy; most major bleeding occurs at the arterial access site for cardiac catheterization. Caution in patients with platelets <150,000/mm³; patients with hemorrhagic retinopathy; when used in combination with other drugs impacting on coagulation. To minimize bleeding complications, care must be taken in sheath insertion/removal. Sheath hemostasis should be achieved at least 4 hours before hospital discharge. Other trauma and vascular punctures should be minimized. Avoid obtaining vascular access through a noncompressible site (eg, subclavian or jugular vein). Patients with severe renal insufficiency require dosage reduction.

Adverse Reactions Bleeding is the major drug-related adverse effect. Major bleeding was reported in 1.4% to 2.2%, minor bleeding in 10.5% to 12%, transfusion was required in 4.0% to 4.3%.

  >1% (nonbleeding adverse events):
    Cardiovascular: Bradycardia (4%), coronary artery dissection (5%), edema (2%)
    Central nervous system: Dizziness (3%), fever (>1%), headache (>1%), vasovagal reaction (2%)
    Gastrointestinal: Nausea (>1%)
    Genitourinary: Pelvic pain (6%)
    Hematologic: Thrombocytopenia: <90,000/mm³ (1.5%)
    Neuromuscular & skeletal: Leg pain (3%)
    Miscellaneous: Diaphoresis (2%)
  <1%: Intracranial bleeding (0.0% to 0.1%), GI bleeding (0.1% to 0.2%), retroperitoneal bleeding (0.0% to 0.6%), GU bleeding (0.0% to 0.1%), thrombocytopenia: <50,000/mm³ (0.3%)

Overdosage/Toxicology Most frequent manifestation of overdose is bleeding; treatment is cessation of therapy and assessment of transfusion. Tirofiban has a relatively short half-life and its platelet effects dissipate rather quickly. However, when immediate reversal is required, platelet transfusions can be useful. Tirofiban is dialyzable.

Drug Interactions Use with aspirin and heparin is associated with an increase in bleeding over aspirin and heparin alone. However, the concurrent use of aspirin and heparin has also improved the efficacy of tirofiban. Caution is warranted when used with other drugs that affect hemostasis - thrombolytics, oral anticoagulants, nonsteroidal antiinflammatory drugs, dipyridamole, ticlopidine, and clopidogrel. Avoid concomitant use of other injectable glycoprotein IIb/IIIa antagonists (see Contraindications). Levothyroxine and omeprazole increase tirofiban clearance; however, the clinical significance of this interaction remains to be demonstrated.

Stability Store at 25°C (77°F); do not freeze. Protect from light during storage.

Mechanism of Action A reversible antagonist of fibrinogen binding to the GP IIb/IIIa receptor, the major platelet surface receptor involved in platelet aggregation. When administered intravenously, it inhibits *ex vivo* platelet aggregation in a dose- and concentration-dependent manner. When given according to the recommended regimen, >90% inhibition is attained by the end of the 30-minute infusion. Platelet aggregation inhibition is reversible following cessation of the infusion.

Pharmacodynamics/Kinetics

Distribution: 35% unbound

Metabolism: Minimal

Elimination: Primarily unchanged drug; 65% in urine, 25% in feces; clearance is reduced in elderly patients by 19% to 26%

Usual Dosage Adults: I.V.: Initial rate of 0.4 mcg/kg/minute for 30 minutes and then continued at 0.1 mcg/kg/minute; dosing should be continued through angiography and for 12-24 hours after angioplasty or atherectomy; see table

Tirofiban Dosing

Patient Weight (kg)	Patients With Normal Renal Function		Patients With Renal Dysfunction	
	30-Min Loading Infusion Rate (mL/h)	Maintenance Infusion Rate (mL/h)	30-Min Loading Infusion Rate (mL/h)	Maintenance Infusion Rate (mL/h)
30-37	16	4	8	2
38-45	20	5	10	3
46-54	24	6	12	3
55-62	28	7	14	4
63-70	32	8	16	4
71-79	36	9	18	5
80-87	40	10	20	5
88-95	44	11	22	6
96-104	48	12	24	6
105-112	52	13	26	7
113-120	56	14	28	7
121-128	60	15	30	8
128-137	64	16	32	8
138-145	68	17	34	9
146-153	72	18	36	8

Dosing adjustment in severe renal impairment: Cl_{cr} <30 mL/minute: Reduce dose to 50% of normal rate

Administration Intended for intravenous delivery using sterile equipment and technique. Do not add other drugs or remove solution directly from the bag with a syringe. Do not use plastic containers in series connections; such use can result in air embolism by drawing air from the first container if it is empty of solution. Discard unused solution 24 hours following the start of infusion. May be administered through the same catheter as heparin. Tirofiban injection must be diluted to a concentration of 50 mcg/mL (premixed solution does not require dilution).

Monitoring Parameters Platelet count, persistent reductions <90,000/mm³ may require interruption or discontinuation of infusion. Hemoglobin and hematocrit should be monitored prior to treatment, within 6 hours following loading infusion, and at least daily thereafter during therapy. Because tirofiban requires concurrent heparin therapy, aPTT levels should also be followed. Monitor vital signs and laboratory results prior to, during, and after therapy. Assess infusion insertion site during and after therapy (every 15 minutes or as institutional policy). Observe and teach patient bleeding precautions (avoid invasive procedures and activities that could result in injury). Monitor closely for signs of unusual or excessive bleeding (eg, CNS changes, blood in urine, stool, or vomitus, unusual bruising or bleeding). Breast-feeding is contraindicated.

Dosage Forms Injection: 50 mcg/mL (500 mL); 250 mcg/mL (50 mL)

♦ **Tisit® Blue Gel [OTC]** *see Pyrethrins on page 996*
♦ **Tisit® Liquid [OTC]** *see Pyrethrins on page 996*
♦ **Tisit® Shampoo [OTC]** *see Pyrethrins on page 996*

Tizanidine (tye ZAN i deen)

U.S. Brand Names Zanaflex®

Synonyms Sirdalud®

Therapeutic Category Alpha₂-Adrenergic Agonist Agent

Use Skeletal muscle relaxant used for treatment of muscle spasticity; although not approved for these indications it has been shown to be effective for tension headaches, low back pain and trigeminal neuralgia in a limited number of trials

Pregnancy Risk Factor C

Contraindications Previous hypersensitivity to tizanidine

(Continued)

Tizanidine *(Continued)*

Warnings/Precautions Reduce dose in patients with liver or renal disease; use with caution in patients with hypotension or cardiac disease. Tizanidine clearance is reduced by more than 50% in elderly patients with renal insufficiency (Cl_{cr} <25 mL/minute) compared to healthy elderly subjects; this may lead to a longer duration of effects and, therefore, should be used with caution in renally impaired patients.

Adverse Reactions
>10%:
  Cardiovascular: Hypotension
  Central nervous system: Sedation, daytime drowsiness, somnolence
  Gastrointestinal: Xerostomia
1% to 10%:
  Cardiovascular: Bradycardia, syncope
  Central nervous system: Fatigue, dizziness, anxiety, nervousness, insomnia
  Dermatologic: Pruritus, skin rash
  Gastrointestinal: Nausea, vomiting, dyspepsia, constipation, diarrhea
  Hepatic: Elevation of liver enzymes
  Neuromuscular & skeletal: Muscle weakness, tremor
<1%: Palpitations, ventricular extrasystoles, psychotic-like symptoms, visual hallucinations, delusions, hepatic failure

Overdosage/Toxicology
Symptoms of overdose include dry mouth, bradycardia, hypotension
Treatment: Lavage (within 2 hours of ingestion) with activated charcoal; benzodiazepines for seizure control; atropine can be given for treatment of bradycardia; flumazenil has been used to reverse coma successfully; forced diuresis is not helpful; multiple dosing of activated charcoal may be helpful. Following attempts to enhance drug elimination, hypotension should be treated with I.V. fluids and/or Trendelenburg positioning.

Drug Interactions
Increased effect: Oral contraceptives
Increased toxicity: Additive hypotensive effects may be seen with diuretics, other alpha adrenergic agonists, or antihypertensives; CNS depression with alcohol, baclofen or other CNS depressants

Mechanism of Action An alpha$_2$-adrenergic agonist agent which decreases excitatory input to alpha motor neurons; an imidazole derivative chemically-related to clonidine, which acts as a centrally acting muscle relaxant with alpha$_2$-adrenergic agonist properties; acts on the level of the spinal cord

Pharmacodynamics/Kinetics
Duration: 3-6 hours
Bioavailability: 40%
Half-life: 2.5 hours
Time to peak serum concentration: 1-5 hours

Usual Dosage
Adults: 2-4 mg 3 times/day
  Usual initial dose: 4 mg, may increase by 2-4 mg as needed for satisfactory reduction of muscle tone every 6-8 hours to a maximum of three doses in any 24 hour period
  Maximum dose: 36 mg/day
  Dosing adjustment in renal/hepatic impairment: May require dose reductions or less frequent dosing

Monitoring Parameters Monitor liver function (aminotransferases) at baseline, 1, 3, 6 months and then periodically thereafter; monitor ophthalmic function

Dosage Forms Tablet: 4 mg

♦ **TMP** *see* Trimethoprim *on page 1184*
♦ **TMP-SMX** *see* Co-Trimoxazole *on page 299*
♦ **TMP-SMZ** *see* Co-Trimoxazole *on page 299*
♦ **TOBI™ Inhalation Solution** *see* Tobramycin *on this page*
♦ **TobraDex® Ophthalmic** *see* Tobramycin and Dexamethasone *on page 1152*

Tobramycin *(toe bra MYE sin)*

Related Information
  Antimicrobial Drugs of Choice *on page 1404*
  Prevention of Wound Infection & Sepsis in Surgical Patients *on page 1381*
U.S. Brand Names AKTob® Ophthalmic; Nebcin® Injection; TOBI™ Inhalation Solution; Tobrex® Ophthalmic

Synonyms Tobramycin Sulfate

Therapeutic Category Antibiotic, Aminoglycoside; Antibiotic, Ophthalmic

Use Treatment of documented or suspected infections caused by susceptible gram-negative bacilli including *Pseudomonas aeruginosa*; topically used to treat superficial ophthalmic infections caused by susceptible bacteria

Pregnancy Risk Factor C

Contraindications Hypersensitivity to tobramycin or other aminoglycosides or components

Warnings/Precautions Use with caution in patients with renal impairment; pre-existing auditory or vestibular impairment; and in patients with neuromuscular disorders; dosage modification required in patients with impaired renal function; (I.M. & I.V.) Aminoglycosides are associated with significant nephrotoxicity or ototoxicity; the ototoxicity is directly proportional to the amount of drug given and the duration of treatment; tinnitus or vertigo are indications of vestibular injury; ototoxicity is often irreversible; renal damage is usually reversible

Adverse Reactions
1% to 10%:
Renal: Nephrotoxicity
Neuromuscular & skeletal: Neurotoxicity (neuromuscular blockade)
Otic: Ototoxicity (auditory), ototoxicity (vestibular)
<1%: Hypotension, drug fever, headache, drowsiness, rash, nausea, vomiting, eosinophilia, anemia, paresthesia, tremor, arthralgia, weakness, lacrimation, itching eyes, edema of the eyelid, keratitis, dyspnea

Overdosage/Toxicology
Symptoms of overdose include ototoxicity, nephrotoxicity, and neuromuscular toxicity
The treatment of choice following a single acute overdose appears to be the maintenance of good urine output of at least 3 mL/kg/hour. Dialysis is of questionable value in the enhancement of aminoglycoside elimination. If required, hemodialysis is preferred over peritoneal dialysis in patients with normal renal function. Careful hydration may be all that is required to promote diuresis and therefore the enhancement of the drug's elimination.

Drug Interactions
Increased effect: Extended spectrum penicillins (synergistic)
Increased toxicity:
Neuromuscular blockers increase neuromuscular blockade
Amphotericin B, cephalosporins, loop diuretics, and vancomycin may increase risk of nephrotoxicity

Stability
Tobramycin is stable at room temperature both as the clear, colorless solution and as the dry powder; reconstituted solutions remain stable for 24 hours at room temperature and 96 hours when refrigerated
Stability of parenteral admixture at room temperature (25°C) and at refrigeration temperature (4°C): 48 hours
Standard diluent: Dose/100 mL NS
Minimum volume: 50 mL NS
Incompatible with penicillins

Mechanism of Action
Interferes with bacterial protein synthesis by binding to 30S and 50S ribosomal subunits resulting in a defective bacterial cell membrane

Pharmacodynamics/Kinetics
Absorption: I.M.: Rapid and complete
Time to peak serum concentration: I.M.: Within 30-60 minutes; I.V.: Within 30 minutes
Distribution: To extracellular fluid including serum, abscesses, ascitic, pericardial, pleural, synovial, lymphatic, and peritoneal fluids; crosses the placenta; poor penetration into CSF, eye, bone, prostate
V_d: 0.2-0.3 L/kg; Pediatric patients: 0.2-0.7 L/kg
Protein binding: <30%
Half-life:
Neonates: ≤1200 g: 11 hours; >1200 g: 2-9 hours
Adults: 2-3 hours, directly dependent upon glomerular filtration rate
Adults with impaired renal function: 5-70 hours
Elimination: With normal renal function, about 90% to 95% of a dose is excreted in the urine within 24 hours

Usual Dosage
Individualization is critical because of the low therapeutic index

Use of ideal body weight (IBW) for determining the mg/kg/dose appears to be more accurate than dosing on the basis of total body weight (TBW)

In morbid obesity, dosage requirement may best be estimated using a dosing weight of IBW + 0.4 (TBW - IBW)

Initial and periodic peak and trough plasma drug levels should be determined, particularly in critically ill patients with serious infections or in disease states known to significantly alter aminoglycoside pharmacokinetics (eg, cystic fibrosis, burns, or major surgery). Two to three serum level measurements should be obtained after the initial dose to measure the half-life in order to determine the frequency of subsequent doses.

Once daily dosing: Higher peak serum drug concentration to MIC ratios, demonstrated aminoglycoside postantibiotic effect, decreased renal cortex drug uptake, and improved cost-time efficiency are supportive reasons for the use of once daily dosing regimens for aminoglycosides. Current research indicates these regimens to be as effective for nonlife-threatening infections, with no higher incidence of nephrotoxicity, than those requiring multiple daily doses. Doses are determined by calculating the entire day's dose via usual multiple dose calculation techniques and administering this quantity as a single dose. Doses are then adjusted to maintain mean serum concentrations above the MIC(s) of the causative organism(s). (Example: 2.5-5 mg/kg as a single dose; expected Cp_{max}: 10-20 mcg/mL and Cp_{min}: <1 mcg/mL). Further research is needed for universal recommendation in all patient populations and gram-negative disease; exceptions may include those with known high clearance (eg, children, patients with cystic fibrosis, or burns who may require shorter dosage intervals) and patients with renal function impairment for whom longer than conventional dosage intervals are usually required.

Some clinicians suggest a daily dose of 4-7 mg/kg for all patients with normal renal function. This dose is at least as efficacious with similar, if not less, toxicity than conventional dosing.

Infants and Children <5 years: I.M., I.V.: 2.5 mg/kg/dose every 8 hours
(Continued)

Tobramycin *(Continued)*

Children >5 years: 1.5-2.5 mg/kg/dose every 8 hours

Note: Some patients may require larger or more frequent doses if serum levels document the need (ie, cystic fibrosis or febrile granulocytopenic patients).

Adults: I.M., I.V.:
Severe life-threatening infections: 2-2.5 mg/kg/dose
Urinary tract infection: 1.5 mg/kg/dose
Synergy (for gram-positive infections): 1 mg/kg/dose

Children and Adults: Ophthalmic: Instill 1-2 drops of solution every 4 hours; apply ointment 2-3 times/day; for severe infections apply ointment every 3-4 hours, or solution 2 drops every 30-60 minutes initially, then reduce to less frequent intervals

Inhalation:
Standard aerosolized tobramycin:
Children: 40-80 mg 2-3 times/day
Adults: 60-80 mg 3 times/day
High-dose regimen: Children ≥6 years and Adults: 300 mg every 12 hours (do not administer doses less than 6 hours apart); administer in repeated cycles of 28 days on drug followed by 28 days off drug

Dosing interval in renal impairment:
Cl_{cr} ≥60 mL/minute: Administer every 8 hours
Cl_{cr} 40-60 mL/minute: Administer every 12 hours
Cl_{cr} 20-40 mL/minute: Administer every 24 hours
Cl_{cr} 10-20 mL/minute: Administer every 48 hours
Cl_{cr} <10 mL/minute: Administer every 72 hours

Hemodialysis: Dialyzable; 30% removal of aminoglycosides occurs during 4 hours of HD - administer dose after dialysis and follow levels

Continuous arteriovenous or venovenous hemofiltration (CAVH/CAVHD): Dose as for Cl_{cr} of 10-40 mL/minute and follow levels

Administration in CAPD fluid:
Gram-negative infection: 4-8 mg/L (4-8 mcg/mL) of CAPD fluid
Gram-positive infection (ie, synergy): 3-4 mg/L (3-4 mcg/mL) of CAPD fluid
Administration IVPB/I.M.: Dose as for Cl_{cr} <10 mL/minute and follow levels

Dosing adjustment/comments in hepatic disease: Monitor plasma concentrations

Dietary Considerations Calcium, magnesium, potassium: Renal wasting may cause hypocalcemia, hypomagnesemia, and/or hypokalemia

Monitoring Parameters Urinalysis, urine output, BUN, serum creatinine, peak and trough plasma tobramycin levels; be alert to ototoxicity; hearing should be tested before and during treatment

Reference Range

Timing of serum samples: Draw peak 30 minutes after 30-minute infusion has been completed or 1 hour following I.M. injection or beginning of infusion; draw trough immediately before next dose

Therapeutic levels:
Peak:
Serious infections: 6-8 µg/mL (SI: 12-17 mg/L)
Life-threatening infections: 8-10 µg/mL (SI: 17-21 mg/L)
Urinary tract infections: 4-6 µg/mL (SI: 7-12 mg/L)
Synergy against gram-positive organisms: 3-5 µg/mL
Trough:
Serious infections: 0.5-1 µg/mL
Life-threatening infections: 1-2 µg/mL
Monitor serum creatinine and urine output; obtain drug levels after the third dose unless otherwise directed

Patient Information Report symptoms of superinfection; for eye drops - no other eye drops 5-10 minutes before or after tobramycin; report any dizziness or sensations of ringing or fullness in ears

Nursing Implications Eye solutions: Allow 5 minutes between application of "multiple-drop" therapy; obtain drug levels after the third dose; peak levels are drawn 30 minutes after the end of a 30-minute infusion or 1 hour after initiation of infusion or I.M. injection; the trough is drawn just before the next dose; administer penicillins or cephalosporins at least 1 hour apart from tobramycin

Dosage Forms

Injection, as sulfate (Nebcin®): 10 mg/mL (2 mL); 40 mg/mL (1.5 mL, 2 mL)
Ointment, ophthalmic (Tobrex®): 0.3% (3.5 g)
Powder for injection (Nebcin®): 40 mg/mL (1.2 g vials)
Solution, inhalation (TOBI™): 60 mg/mL (5 mL)
Solution, ophthalmic: 0.3% (5 mL)
AKTob®, Tobrex®: 0.3% (5 mL)

Tobramycin and Dexamethasone

(toe bra MYE sin & deks a METH a sone)

Related Information

Dexamethasone *on page 337*
Tobramycin *on page 1150*

U.S. Brand Names TobraDex® Ophthalmic

Synonyms Dexamethasone and Tobramycin

Therapeutic Category Antibiotic, Ophthalmic; Corticosteroid, Ophthalmic

Dosage Forms
Ointment, ophthalmic: Tobramycin 0.3% and dexamethasone 0.1% (3.5 g)
Suspension, ophthalmic: Tobramycin 0.3% and dexamethasone 0.1% (2.5 mL, 5 mL)

- **Tobramycin Sulfate** *see* Tobramycin *on page 1150*
- **Tobrex® Ophthalmic** *see* Tobramycin *on page 1150*

Tocainide (toe KAY nide)
Related Information
Antiarrhythmic Drugs Comparison *on page 1297*
U.S. Brand Names Tonocard®
Synonyms Tocainide Hydrochloride
Therapeutic Category Antiarrhythmic Agent, Class I-B
Use Suppress and prevent symptomatic life-threatening ventricular arrhythmias
   Unlabeled use: Trigeminal neuralgia
Pregnancy Risk Factor C
Contraindications Second or third degree A-V block without a pacemaker, hypersensitivity to tocainide, amide-type anesthetics, or any component
Warnings/Precautions May exacerbate some arrhythmias (ie, atrial fibrillation/flutter); use with caution in CHF patients; administer with caution in patients with pre-existing bone marrow failure, cytopenia, severe renal or hepatic disease
Adverse Reactions
>10%:
   Central nervous system: Dizziness (8% to 15%)
   Gastrointestinal: Nausea (14% to 15%)
1% to 10%:
   Cardiovascular: Tachycardia (3%), bradycardia/angina/palpitations (0.5% to 1.8%)
   Central nervous system: Nervousness (0.5% to 1.5%), confusion (2% to 3%)
   Dermatologic: Rash (0.5% to 8.4%)
   Gastrointestinal: Vomiting, diarrhea (4% to 5%), anorexia (1% to 2%)
   Neuromuscular & skeletal: Paresthesia (3.5% to 9%), tremor (2.9% to 8.4%)
   Ocular: Blurred vision (~1.5%)
<1%: Ataxia, agranulocytosis, anemia, leukopenia, neutropenia, respiratory arrest, diaphoresis
Overdosage/Toxicology
Has a narrow therapeutic index and severe toxicity may occur slightly above the therapeutic range, especially with other antiarrhythmic drugs; and acute ingestion of twice the daily therapeutic dose is potentially life-threatening; symptoms of overdose include sedation, confusion, coma, seizures, respiratory arrest and cardiac toxicity (sinus arrest, A-V block, asystole, and hypotension); the QRS and Q-T intervals are usually normal, although they may be prolonged after massive overdose; other effects include dizziness, paresthesias, tremor, ataxia, and GI disturbance.
Treatment is supportive, using conventional therapies (fluids, positioning, vasopressors, antiarrhythmics, anticonvulsants); sodium bicarbonate may reverse the QRS prolongation (if present), bradyarrhythmias, and hypotension; enhanced elimination with dialysis, hemoperfusion or repeat charcoal is not effective.
Drug Interactions
Decreased plasma levels: Phenobarbital, phenytoin, rifampin, and other hepatic enzyme inducers, cimetidine and drugs which make the urine acidic
Increased toxicity/levels of caffeine and theophylline
Increased effects with metoprolol
Mechanism of Action Class 1B antiarrhythmic agent; suppresses automaticity of conduction tissue, by increasing electrical stimulation threshold of ventricle, HIS-Purkinje system, and spontaneous depolarization of the ventricles during diastole by a direct action on the tissues; blocks both the initiation and conduction of nerve impulses by decreasing the neuronal membrane's permeability to sodium ions, which results in inhibition of depolarization with resultant blockade of conduction
Pharmacodynamics/Kinetics
Absorption: Oral: Extensive, 99% to 100%
Distribution: V_d: 1.62-3.2 L/kg
Protein binding: 10% to 20%
Metabolism: In the liver to inactive metabolites; first-pass effect is negligible
Half-life: 11-14 hours, prolonged with renal and hepatic impairment with half-life increased to 23-27 hours
Time to peak: Peak serum levels occur within 30-160 minutes
Elimination: In urine (40% to 50% as unchanged drug)
Usual Dosage Adults: Oral: 1200-1800 mg/day in 3 divided doses, up to 2400 mg/day
   Dosing adjustment in renal impairment: Cl_{cr} <30 mL/minute: Administer 50% of normal dose or 600 mg once daily
   Hemodialysis: Moderately dialyzable (20% to 50%)
   Dosing adjustment in hepatic impairment: Maximum daily dose: 1200 mg
Reference Range Therapeutic: 5-12 µg/mL (SI: 22-52 µmol/L)
Patient Information Report any unusual bleeding, fever, sore throat, or any breathing difficulties; do not discontinue or alter dose without notifying physician; may cause drowsiness, dizziness, impair judgment, and coordination
Nursing Implications Monitor for tremor; titration of dosing and initiation of therapy require cardiac monitoring
Dosage Forms Tablet, as hydrochloride: 400 mg, 600 mg

- **Tocainide Hydrochloride** see Tocainide on previous page
- **Toesen®** see Oxytocin on page 879
- **Tofranil®** see Imipramine on page 601
- **Tofranil-PM®** see Imipramine on page 601

Tolazamide (tole AZ a mide)

Related Information
  Hypoglycemic Drugs, Comparison of Oral Agents on page 1325
  Sulfonamide Derivatives on page 1337

U.S. Brand Names Tolinase®

Therapeutic Category Antidiabetic Agent, Oral; Hypoglycemic Agent, Oral; Sulfonylurea Agent

Use Adjunct to diet for the management of mild to moderately severe, stable, noninsulindependent (type II) diabetes mellitus

Pregnancy Risk Factor D

Contraindications Type I diabetes therapy (IDDM), hypersensitivity to sulfonylureas, diabetes complicated by ketoacidosis

Warnings/Precautions False-positive response has been reported in patients with liver disease, idiopathic hypoglycemia of infancy, severe malnutrition, acute pancreatitis, renal dysfunction. Transferring a patient from one sulfonylurea to another does not require a priming dose; doses >1000 mg/day normally do not improve diabetic control. Has not been studied in older patients; however, except for drug interactions, it appears to have a safe profile and decline in renal function does not affect its pharmacokinetics. How "tightly" an elderly patient's blood glucose should be controlled is controversial; however, a fasting blood sugar <150 mg/dL is now an accepted end point. Such a decision should be based on the patient's functional and cognitive status, how well they recognize hypoglycemic or hyperglycemic symptoms, and how to respond to them and their other disease states.

Adverse Reactions
  >10%:
    Central nervous system: Headache, dizziness
    Gastrointestinal: Anorexia, nausea, vomiting, diarrhea, constipation, heartburn, epigastric fullness
  1% to 10%: Dermatologic: Rash, urticaria, photosensitivity
  <1%: Hypoglycemia, aplastic anemia, hemolytic anemia, bone marrow suppression, thrombocytopenia, agranulocytosis, cholestatic jaundice, diuretic effect

Overdosage/Toxicology
  Symptoms of overdose include low blood sugar, tingling of lips and tongue, nausea, yawning, confusion, agitation, tachycardia, sweating, convulsions, stupor, and coma
  Intoxications with sulfonylureas can cause hypoglycemia and are best managed with glucose administration (oral for milder hypoglycemia or by injection in more severe forms)

Drug Interactions
  Increased toxicity: Monitor patient closely; large number of drugs interact with sulfonylureas including salicylates, anticoagulants, H_2-antagonists, TCAs, MAO inhibitors, betablockers, thiazides

Mechanism of Action Stimulates insulin release from the pancreatic beta cells; reduces glucose output from the liver; insulin sensitivity is increased at peripheral target sites

Pharmacodynamics/Kinetics
  Onset of action: Oral: Within 4-6 hours
  Duration: 10-24 hours
  Protein binding: >98% ionic/nonionic
  Metabolism: Extensively in the liver to one active and three inactive metabolites
  Half-life: 7 hours
  Elimination: Renal

Usual Dosage Oral (doses >1000 mg/day normally do not improve diabetic control):
  Adults:
    Initial: 100-250 mg/day with breakfast or the first main meal of the day
      Fasting blood sugar <200 mg/dL: 100 mg/day
      Fasting blood sugar >200 mg/dL: 250 mg/day
      Patient is malnourished, underweight, elderly, or not eating properly: 100 mg/day
    Adjust dose in increments of 100-250 mg/day at weekly intervals to response. If >500 mg/day is required, give in divided doses twice daily; maximum daily dose: 1 g (doses >1 g/day are not likely to improve control)
    Conversion from insulin → tolazamide
      10 units day = 100 mg/day
      20-40 units/day = 250 mg/day
      >40 units/day = 250 mg/day and 50% of insulin dose
    Doses >500 mg/day should be given in 2 divided doses
  Dosing adjustment in renal impairment: Conservative initial and maintenance doses are recommended because tolazamide is metabolized to active metabolites, which are eliminated in the urine
  Dosing comments in hepatic impairment: Conservative initial and maintenance doses and careful monitoring of blood glucose are recommended

Dietary Considerations Alcohol: Avoid use

Monitoring Parameters Signs and symptoms of hypoglycemia, (fatigue, sweating, numbness of extremities); urine for glucose and ketones; fasting blood glucose; hemoglobin A_{1c} or fructosamine

Reference Range Target range:
Fasting blood glucose:
  Adults: 80-140 mg/dL
  Geriatrics: 100-150 mg/dL
Glycosylated hemoglobin: <7%
Patient Information Tablets may be crushed; take drug at the same time each day; avoid alcohol; recognize signs and symptoms of hyper- and hypoglycemia; report any persistent or severe sore throat, fever, malaise, unusual bleeding, or bruising; can take with food; do not skip meals; carry a quick sugar source; medical alert bracelet
Nursing Implications Patients who are anorexic or NPO may need to have their dose held to avoid hypoglycemia
Dosage Forms Tablet: 100 mg, 250 mg, 500 mg

Tolazoline (tole AZ oh leen)

U.S. Brand Names Priscoline®
Synonyms Benzazoline Hydrochloride; Tolazoline Hydrochloride
Therapeutic Category Alpha-Adrenergic Blocking Agent, Parenteral
Use Treatment of persistent pulmonary vasoconstriction and hypertension of the newborn (persistent fetal circulation), peripheral vasospastic disorders
Pregnancy Risk Factor C
Contraindications Hypersensitivity to tolazoline; known or suspected coronary artery disease
Warnings/Precautions Stimulates gastric secretion and may activate stress ulcers; therefore, use with caution in patients with gastritis, peptic ulcer; use with caution in patients with mitral stenosis
Adverse Reactions 1% to 10%:
Cardiovascular: Hypotension, peripheral vasodilation, tachycardia, hypertension, arrhythmias
Endocrine & metabolic: Hypochloremic alkalosis
Gastrointestinal: GI bleeding, abdominal pain, nausea, diarrhea
Hematologic: Thrombocytopenia, increased agranulocytosis, pancytopenia
Local: Burning at injection site
Neuromuscular & skeletal: Increased pilomotor activity
Ocular: Mydriasis
Renal: Acute renal failure, oliguria
Respiratory: Pulmonary hemorrhage
Miscellaneous: Increased secretions
Overdosage/Toxicology
Symptoms of overdose include hypotension, shock, flushing
I.V. fluids and Trendelenburg position for hypotension; if pressors are required, use direct-acting alpha agonists (norepinephrine)
Drug Interactions
Decreased effect (vasopressor) of epinephrine followed by a rebound increase in blood pressure
Increased toxicity: Disulfiram reaction may possibly be seen with concomitant ethanol use
Stability Compatible in D_5W, $D_{10}W$, and saline solutions
Mechanism of Action Competitively blocks alpha-adrenergic receptors to produce brief antagonism of circulating epinephrine and norepinephrine; reduces hypertension caused by catecholamines and causes vascular smooth muscle relaxation (direct action); results in peripheral vasodilation and decreased peripheral resistance
Pharmacodynamics/Kinetics
Half-life: Neonates: 3-10 hours, increased half-life with decreased renal function, oliguria
Time to peak serum concentration: Within 30 minutes
Elimination: Excreted rapidly in urine primarily as unchanged drug
Usual Dosage
Neonates: Initial: I.V.: 1-2 mg/kg over 10-15 minutes via scalp vein or upper extremity; maintenance: 1-2 mg/kg/hour; use lower maintenance doses in patients with decreased renal function. Also used in neonates for acute vasospasm "cath toes" at 0.25 mg/kg/hour (no load); maximum dose: 6-8 mg/kg/hour.
  Dosing interval in renal impairment in newborns: Urine output <0.9 mL/kg/hour: Decrease dose to 0.08 mg/kg/hour for every 1 mg/kg of loading dose
Adults: Peripheral vasospastic disorder: I.M., I.V., S.C.: 10-50 mg 4 times/day
Dietary Considerations Alcohol: Avoid use
Monitoring Parameters Vital signs, blood gases, cardiac monitor
Patient Information Side effects decrease with continued therapy; avoid alcohol
Nursing Implications Dilute in D_5W; monitor blood pressure for hypotension; observe limbs for change in color; do not mix with any other drug in syringe or bag
Dosage Forms Injection, as hydrochloride: 25 mg/mL (4 mL)

♦ Tolazoline Hydrochloride see Tolazoline on this page

Tolbutamide (tole BYOO ta mide)

Related Information
Hypoglycemic Drugs, Comparison of Oral Agents on page 1325
Sulfonamide Derivatives on page 1337
U.S. Brand Names Orinase® Diagnostic Injection; Orinase® Oral
Canadian Brand Names Apo®-Tolbutamide; Mobenol®; Novo-Butamide
Synonyms Tolbutamide Sodium
(Continued)

Tolbutamide (Continued)

Therapeutic Category Antidiabetic Agent, Oral; Diagnostic Agent, Hypoglycemia; Diagnostic Agent, Insulinoma; Hypoglycemic Agent, Oral; Sulfonylurea Agent

Use Adjunct to diet for the management of mild to moderately severe, stable, noninsulin-dependent (type II) diabetes mellitus

Pregnancy Risk Factor D

Contraindications Diabetes complicated by ketoacidosis, therapy of IDDM, hypersensitivity to sulfonylureas

Warnings/Precautions False-positive response has been reported in patients with liver disease, idiopathic hypoglycemia of infancy, severe malnutrition, acute pancreatitis. Because of its low potency and short duration, it is a useful agent in the elderly if drug interactions can be avoided. How "tightly" an elderly patient's blood glucose should be controlled is controversial; however, a fasting blood sugar <150 mg/dL is now an acceptable end point. Such a decision should be based on the patient's functional and cognitive status, how well they recognize hypoglycemic or hyperglycemic symptoms, and how to respond to them and their other disease states.

Adverse Reactions

>10%:
    Central nervous system: Headache, dizziness
    Gastrointestinal: Constipation, diarrhea, heartburn, anorexia, epigastric fullness
1% to 10%: Dermatologic: Rash, urticaria, photosensitivity
<1%: Venospasm, SIADH, disulfiram-type reactions, thrombocytopenia, agranulocytosis, hypoglycemia, leukopenia, aplastic anemia, hemolytic anemia, bone marrow suppression, cholestatic jaundice, thrombophlebitis, tinnitus, hypersensitivity reaction

Overdosage/Toxicology

Symptoms of overdose include low blood sugar, tingling of lips and tongue, nausea, yawning, confusion, agitation, tachycardia, sweating, convulsions, stupor, and coma
Treatment: I.V. glucose (12.5-25 g), epinephrine for anaphylaxis

Drug Interactions CYP2C8, 2C9, 2C18, and 2C19 enzyme substrate; CYP2C19 enzyme inhibitor

Increased effects with salicylates, probenecid, MAO inhibitors, chloramphenicol, insulin, phenylbutazone, antidepressants, metformin, H_2-antagonists, and others
Decreased effects:
    Hypoglycemic effects may be decreased by beta-blockers, cholestyramine, hydantoins, thiazides, rifampin, and others
    Ethanol may decrease the half-life of tolbutamide

Stability Use parenteral formulation within 1 hour following reconstitution

Mechanism of Action Stimulates insulin release from the pancreatic beta cells; reduces glucose output from the liver; insulin sensitivity is increased at peripheral target sites, suppression of glucagon may also contribute

Pharmacodynamics/Kinetics

Peak hypoglycemic action: Oral: 1-3 hours; I.V.: 30 minutes
Duration: Oral: 6-24 hours; I.V.: 3 hours
Time to peak serum concentration: 3-5 hours
Absorption: Oral: Rapid
Distribution: V_d: 6-10 L
Protein binding: 95% to 97% (principally to albumin) ionic/nonionic
Metabolism/Elimination: Hepatic metabolism to hydroxymethyltolbutamide (mildly active) and carboxytolbutamide (inactive) both rapidly excreted renally, less 2% excreted in the urine unchanged; metabolism does not appear to be affected by age
Increased plasma concentrations and volume of distribution secondary to decreased albumin concentrations and less protein binding have been reported.
Half-life: Plasma: 4-25 hours; Elimination: 4-9 hours

Usual Dosage Divided doses may increase gastrointestinal side effects

Adults:
    Oral: Initial: 1-2 g/day as a single dose in the morning or in divided doses throughout the day. Total doses may be taken in the morning; however, divided doses may allow increased gastrointestinal tolerance. Maintenance dose: 0.25-3 g/day; however, a maintenance dose >2 g/day is seldom required.
    I.V. bolus: 1 g over 2-3 minutes
Elderly: Oral: Initial: 250 mg 1-3 times/day; usual: 500-2000 mg; maximum: 3 g/day
Dosing adjustment in renal impairment: Adjustment is not necessary
Hemodialysis: Not dialyzable (0% to 5%)
Dosing adjustment in hepatic impairment: Reduction of dose may be necessary in patients with impaired liver function

Dietary Considerations Alcohol: Avoid use

Monitoring Parameters Fasting blood glucose, hemoglobin A_{1c} or fructosamine

Reference Range Target range:

Fasting blood glucose: <120 mg/dL
    Adults: 80-140 mg/dL
    Geriatrics: 100-150 mg/dL
Glycosylated hemoglobin: <7%

Patient Information Tablets may be crushed; take drug at the same time each day; avoid alcohol; recognize signs and symptoms of hyper- and hypoglycemia; report any persistent or severe sore throat, fever, malaise, unusual bleeding, or bruising; can take with food

Nursing Implications Patients who are anorexic or NPO may need to have their dose held to avoid hypoglycemia

Additional Information Sodium content of 1 g vial: 3.5 mEq

Dosage Forms

Injection, diagnostic, as sodium: 1 g (20 mL)

Tablet: 250 mg, 500 mg

♦ **Tolbutamide Sodium** see Tolbutamide on page 1155

Tolcapone (TOLE ka pone)

Related Information

Parkinson's Disease, Dosing of Drugs Used for Treatment of on page 1336

U.S. Brand Names Tasmar®

Therapeutic Category Anti-Parkinson's Agent; Reverse COMT Inhibitor

Use An adjunct to levodopa/carbidopa for the treatment of signs and symptoms of Parkinson's disease

Pregnancy Risk Factor C

Contraindications Hypersensitivity to tolcapone or other ingredients, including tolcapone, lactose monohydrate, cellulose, povidone, sodium starch glycolate, talc, and/or magnesium stearate; patients with liver disease or who had increased LFTs on tolcapone; patients with a history of nontraumatic rhabdomyolysis or hyperpyrexia and confusion possibly related to medication

Warnings/Precautions Note: Due to reports of fatal liver injury associated with use of this drug, the manufacturer is advising that tolcapone be reserved for use only in patients who do not have severe movement abnormalities and who do not respond to or who are not appropriate candidates for other available treatments. Before initiating therapy with tolcapone, the risks should be discussed with the patient, and the patient can provide written informed consent (form available from Roche).

It is not recommended that patients receive tolcapone concomitantly with nonselective MAO inhibitors (see Drug Interactions). Selegiline is a selective MAO-B inhibitor and can be taken with tolcapone.

Patients receiving tolcapone are predisposed to orthostatic hypotension, diarrhea (usually within the first 6-12 weeks of therapy), transient hallucinations (most commonly within the first 2 weeks of therapy), and new onset or worsened dyskinesia. Use with caution in patients with severe renal failure. Tolcapone is secreted into maternal milk in rats and may be excreted into human milk; until more is known, tolcapone should be considered **incompatible** with breast-feeding.

Adverse Reactions Patients receiving tolcapone are predisposed to orthostatic hypotension. Inform the patient and explain methods to manage the symptoms. Patients may experience diarrhea, most commonly 6-12 weeks after tolcapone is started. Diarrhea is sometimes associated with anorexia. Patients may experience hallucinations shortly after starting therapy, most commonly within the first 2 weeks. Hallucinations may diminish or resolve with a decrease in the levodopa dose. Hallucinations commonly accompany confusion and sometimes insomnia or excessive dreaming. Tolcapone may exacerbate or induce dyskinesia; lowering the levodopa dose may help. Use tolcapone with caution in patients with severe renal or hepatic failure.

>10%:

Cardiovascular: Orthostasis

Central nervous system: Sleep disorder, excessive dreaming, headache, dizziness, somnolence, confusion

Gastrointestinal: Nausea, anorexia, diarrhea

Neuromuscular & skeletal: Dyskinesia, dystonia, muscle cramps

1% to 10%:

Cardiovascular: Hypotension, chest pain, syncope

Central nervous system: Hallucination, fatigue

Gastrointestinal: Vomiting, constipation, dry mouth, dyspepsia, abdominal pain, flatulence

Genitourinary: Urine discoloration

Neuromuscular & skeletal: Hyperkinesia, stiffness, arthritis

Respiratory: Dyspnea

<1%: Fatal liver injury, bradycardia, coronary artery disorder, heart arrest, angina pectoris, myocardial infarct, myocardial ischemia, arteriosclerosis, thrombosis, hypertension, vasodilation, amnesia, extrapyramidal syndrome, manic reaction, cerebrovascular accident, psychosis, myoclonus, delirium, encephalopathy, meningitis, cellulitis, hypercholesteremia, gastrointestinal hemorrhage, colitis, duodenal ulcer, uterine hemorrhage, anemia, leukemia, thrombocytopenia, cholecystitis, neuralgia, hemiplegia, hematuria, bronchitis, epistaxis, hyperventilation, allergic reaction

Drug Interactions Theoretically, nonselective MAO inhibitors (phenelzine and tranylcypromine) taken with tolcapone may inhibit the major metabolic pathways of catecholamines, which may result in excessive adverse effects possibly due to levodopa accumulation. Concomitant therapy is not recommended.

Mechanism of Action A reversible inhibitor of catechol-O-methyltransferase (COMT). COMT is the major route of metabolism for levodopa. When tolcapone is taken with levodopa the pharmacokinetics are altered, resulting in more sustained levodopa serum levels compared to levodopa taken alone. The resulting levels of levodopa provide for increased concentrations available for absorption across the blood-brain barrier, thereby providing for increased CNS levels of dopamine, the active metabolite of levodopa.

Pharmacodynamics/Kinetics

Protein binding: >99.0%

Bioavailability: 65%

(Continued)

Tolcapone *(Continued)*

Half-life: 2-3 hours
Time to peak: Within 2 hours
Metabolism: Glucuronidation
Elimination: In urine and feces (40%)

Usual Dosage Oral: 100 mg 3 times/day always given as an adjunct to levodopa/carbidopa. The first dose of the day should be given with the first dose of the day of levodopa/carbidopa, and then administer the next 2 doses 6 and 12 hours later. Because increased liver enzymes occur more frequently with 200 mg 3 times/day, only increase to 200 mg if clinically justified.

Note: Many patients will require a decrease in levodopa dosage to avoid increased dopaminergic side effects

Dosing adjustment in renal impairment: Generally, no adjustment necessary; however, in patients with severe renal failure, treat with caution and do not exceed 100 mg 3 times/day

Dosing adjustment in hepatic impairment: Do not use if the patient has evidence of active liver disease or the AST or ALT are greater than the upper limit of normal

Dietary Considerations Tolcapone taken with food within 1 hour before or 2 hours after the dose decreases bioavailability by 10% to 20%

Monitoring Parameters Blood pressure, symptoms of Parkinson's disease, liver enzymes at baseline and then every 2 weeks for the first year of therapy, every 4 weeks for the next 6 months, then every 8 weeks thereafter. If the dose is increased to 200 mg 3 times/day, reinitiate LFT monitoring at the previous frequency. Discontinue therapy if the ALT or AST exceeds the upper limit of normal or if the clinical signs and symptoms suggest the onset of liver failure.

Patient Information Take exactly as directed (may be prescribed in conjunction with levodopa/carbidopa); do not change dosage or discontinue without consulting prescriber.

Therapeutic effects may take several weeks or months to achieve and you may need frequent monitoring during first weeks of therapy.

Best to take 2 hours before or after a meal; however, may be taken with meals if GI upset occurs. Take at same time each day. Maintain adequate hydration (2-3 L/day). Do not use alcohol, prescription or OTC sedatives, or CNS depressants without consulting prescriber.

Urine or perspiration may appear darker. You may experience drowsiness, dizziness, confusion, or vision changes (use caution when driving, climbing stairs, or engaging in hazardous tasks). Orthostatic hypotension (use caution when changing position - rising to standing from sitting or lying); increased susceptibility to heat stroke, decreased perspiration (use caution in hot weather - maintain adequate fluids and reduce exercise activity); constipation (increased exercise, fluids, or dietary fruit and fiber may help); dry skin or nasal passages (consult prescriber for appropriate relief); nausea, vomiting, loss of appetite, or stomach discomfort (small frequent meals, chewing gum, or sucking on lozenges may help).

Report unresolved constipation or vomiting; chest pain or irregular heartbeat; difficulty breathing; acute headache or dizziness; CNS changes (hallucination, loss of memory, nervousness, etc); painful or difficult urination; abdominal pain or blood in stool; increased muscle spasticity, rigidity, or involuntary movements; skin rash; or significant worsening of condition. Inform prescriber if you are or intend to be pregnant. Do not breast-feed.

Dosage Forms Tablet: 100 mg, 200 mg

♦ **Tolectin® 200** see Tolmetin *on this page*
♦ **Tolectin® 400** see Tolmetin *on this page*
♦ **Tolectin® DS** see Tolmetin *on this page*
♦ **Tolinase®** see Tolazamide *on page 1154*

Tolmetin *(TOLE met in)*

Related Information

Antacid Drug Interactions *on page 1296*
Nonsteroidal Anti-Inflammatory Agents Comparison *on page 1335*

U.S. Brand Names Tolectin® 200; Tolectin® 400; Tolectin® DS

Canadian Brand Names Novo-Tolmetin

Synonyms Tolmetin Sodium

Therapeutic Category Analgesic, Nonsteroidal Anti-inflammatory Drug; Anti-inflammatory Agent; Nonsteroidal Anti-inflammatory Drug (NSAID), Oral

Use Treatment of rheumatoid arthritis and osteoarthritis, juvenile rheumatoid arthritis

Pregnancy Risk Factor C (D at term)

Contraindications Known hypersensitivity to tolmetin or any component, aspirin, or other nonsteroidal anti-inflammatory drugs (NSAIDs)

Warnings/Precautions Use with caution in patients with upper GI disease, impaired renal function, congestive heart failure, hypertension, and patients receiving anticoagulants; if GI upset occurs with tolmetin, take with antacids other than sodium bicarbonate

Adverse Reactions

>10%:
Central nervous system: Dizziness
Dermatologic: Rash
Gastrointestinal: Abdominal cramps, heartburn, indigestion, nausea

1% to 10%:
Central nervous system: Headache, nervousness
Dermatologic: Itching
Endocrine & metabolic: Fluid retention
Gastrointestinal: Vomiting
Otic: Tinnitus

<1%: Congestive heart failure, hypertension, arrhythmias, tachycardia, confusion, hallu-
cinations, aseptic meningitis, mental depression, drowsiness, insomnia, urticaria,
erythema multiforme, toxic epidermal necrolysis, Stevens-Johnson syndrome, angioedema, polydipsia, hot flashes, gastritis, GI ulceration, cystitis, polyuria, agranulocytosis, anemia, hemolytic anemia, bone marrow suppression, leukopenia,
thrombocytopenia, hepatitis, peripheral neuropathy, toxic amblyopia, blurred vision,
conjunctivitis, dry eyes, decreased hearing, acute renal failure, allergic rhinitis, shortness of breath, epistaxis

Overdosage/Toxicology
Symptoms of overdose include lethargy, mental confusion, dizziness, leukocytosis, renal
failure

Management of a nonsteroidal anti-inflammatory drug (NSAID) intoxication is primarily
supportive and symptomatic. Fluid therapy is commonly effective in managing the
hypotension that may occur following an acute NSAID overdose, except when this is
due to an acute blood loss. Seizures tend to be very short-lived and often do not
require drug treatment; although, recurrent seizures should be treated with I.V. diazepam. Since many of the NSAID undergo enterohepatic cycling, multiple doses of
charcoal may be needed to reduce the potential for delayed toxicities.

Drug Interactions
Decreased effect with aspirin; decreased effect of thiazides, furosemide

Increased toxicity of digoxin, methotrexate, cyclosporine, lithium, insulin, sulfonylureas,
potassium-sparing diuretics, aspirin

Mechanism of Action Inhibits prostaglandin synthesis by decreasing the activity of the
enzyme, cyclo-oxygenase, which results in decreased formation of prostaglandin precursors

Pharmacodynamics/Kinetics
Absorption: Oral: Well absorbed
Bioavailability: Food/milk decreases total bioavailability by 16%
Time to peak serum concentration: Within 30-60 minutes

Usual Dosage Oral:
Children ≥2 years:
Anti-inflammatory: Initial: 20 mg/kg/day in 3 divided doses, then 15-30 mg/kg/day in 3
divided doses
Analgesic: 5-7 mg/kg/dose every 6-8 hours
Adults: 400 mg 3 times/day; usual dose: 600 mg to 1.8 g/day; maximum: 2 g/day

Monitoring Parameters Occult blood loss, CBC, liver enzymes, BUN, serum creatinine,
periodic liver function test

Patient Information Take with food, milk, or water; may cause drowsiness, impair
judgment or coordination

Additional Information Sodium content of 200 mg: 0.8 mEq

Dosage Forms
Capsule, as sodium (Tolectin® DS): 400 mg
Tablet, as sodium (Tolectin®): 200 mg, 600 mg

♦ **Tolmetin Sodium** see Tolmetin on previous page

Tolnaftate (tole NAF tate)

U.S. Brand Names Absorbine® Antifungal [OTC]; Absorbine® Jock Itch [OTC]; Absorbine
Jr.® Antifungal [OTC]; Aftate® for Athlete's Foot [OTC]; Aftate® for Jock Itch [OTC]; Blis-
To-Sol® [OTC]; Breezee® Mist Antifungal [OTC]; Dr Scholl's Athlete's Foot [OTC]; Dr
Scholl's Maximum Strength Tritin [OTC]; Genaspor® [OTC]; NP-27® [OTC]; Quinsana
Plus® [OTC]; Tinactin® [OTC]; Tinactin® for Jock Itch [OTC]; Ting® [OTC]; Zeasorb-AF®
Powder [OTC]

Canadian Brand Names Pitrex®

Therapeutic Category Antifungal Agent, Topical

Use Treatment of tinea pedis, tinea cruris, tinea corporis, tinea manuum, tinea versicolor
infections

Pregnancy Risk Factor C

Contraindications Known hypersensitivity to tolnaftate; nail and scalp infections

Warnings/Precautions Cream is not recommended for nail or scalp infections; keep
from eyes; if no improvement within 4 weeks, treatment should be discontinued. Usually
not effective alone for the treatment of infections involving hair follicles or nails.

Adverse Reactions 1% to 10%:
Dermatologic: Pruritus, contact dermatitis
Local: Irritation, stinging

Mechanism of Action Distorts the hyphae and stunts mycelial growth in susceptible
fungi

Pharmacodynamics/Kinetics Onset of action: 24-72 hours

Usual Dosage Children and Adults: Topical: Wash and dry affected area; apply 1-3 drops
of solution or a small amount of cream or powder and rub into the affected areas 2-3
times/day for 2-4 weeks
(Continued)

Tolnaftate *(Continued)*

Patient Information Avoid contact with the eyes; apply to clean dry area; consult the physician if a skin irritation develops or if the skin infection worsens or does not improve after 10 days of therapy; does not stain skin or clothing

Nursing Implications Itching, burning, and soreness are usually relieved within 24-72 hours

Dosage Forms
Aerosol, topical:
    Liquid: 1% (59.2 mL, 90 mL, 120 mL)
    Powder: 1% (56.7 g, 100 g, 105 g, 150 g)
Cream: 1% (15 g, 30 g)
Gel, topical: 1% (15 g)
Powder, topical: 1% (45 g, 90 g)
Solution, topical: 1% (10 mL)

Tolterodine *(tole TER oh dine)*

U.S. Brand Names Detrol™

Therapeutic Category Anticholinergic Agent

Use Treatment of patients with an overactive bladder with symptoms of urinary frequency, urgency, or urge incontinence

Pregnancy Risk Factor C

Contraindications Urinary retention or gastric retention; uncontrolled narrow-angle glaucoma; demonstrated hypersensitivity to tolterodine or ingredients

Warnings/Precautions Caution in patients with bladder flow obstruction, pyloric stenosis or other GI obstruction, narrow-angle glaucoma (controlled), reduced hepatic/renal function

Adverse Reactions
>10%: Central nervous system: Headache
1% to 10%:
    Cardiovascular: Chest pain, hypertension (1.5%)
    Central nervous system: Vertigo (8.6%), nervousness (1.1%), somnolence (3.0%)
    Dermatologic: Pruritus (1.3%), rash (1.9%), dry skin (1.7%)
    Gastrointestinal: Abdominal pain (7.6%), constipation (6.5%), diarrhea (4.0%), dyspepsia (5.9%), flatulence (1.3%), nausea (4.2%), vomiting (1.7%), weight gain (1.5%)
    Genitourinary: Dysuria (2.5%), polyuria (1.1%), urinary retention (1.7%), urinary tract infection (5.5%)
    Neuromuscular & skeletal: Back pain, falling (1.3%), paresthesia (1.1%)
    Ocular: Vision abnormalities (4.7%), dry eyes (3.8%)
    Respiratory: Bronchitis (2.1%), cough (2.1%), pharyngitis (1.5%), rhinitis (1.1%), sinusitis (1.1%), upper respiratory infection (5.9%)
    Miscellaneous: Flu-like symptoms (4.4%), infection (2.1%)

Overdosage/Toxicology Overdosage with tolterodine can potentially result in severe central anticholinergic effects and should be treated accordingly. EKG monitoring is recommended in the event of overdosage.

Drug Interactions CYP3A3/4 substrate; CYP2D6 substrate
Increased toxicity: Macrolide antibiotics/azole antifungal agents may inhibit the metabolism of tolterodine. Doses of tolterodine >1 mg twice daily should not be exceeded.

Fluoxetine, which inhibits cytochrome P-450 2D6, increases concentration 4.8 times. Other drugs which inhibit this isoenzyme may also interact. Studies with inhibitors of cytochrome isoenzyme 3A4 have not been performed.

Mechanism of Action Tolterodine is a competitive antagonist of muscarinic receptors. In animal models, tolterodine demonstrates selectivity for urinary bladder receptors over salivary receptors. Urinary bladder contraction is mediated by muscarinic receptors. Tolterodine increases residual urine volume and decreases detrusor muscle pressure.

Pharmacodynamics/Kinetics
Distribution: V_d: 113 ±27 L; highly bound to alpha$_1$-acid glycoprotein
Metabolism: Extensive hepatic metabolism primarily by hepatic cytochrome P-450 isoenzyme 2D6 (some metabolites share activity). Metabolism via isoenzyme 3A4 is a minor pathway in most patients. In patients with a genetic deficiency of isoenzyme 2D6, metabolism via isoenzyme 3A4 predominates.
Bioavailability: 77%; C_{max}: 1-2 hours after dose; food increases bioavailability
Elimination: Primarily urinary excretion of parent drug and metabolites; <1% excreted unchanged

Usual Dosage Adults: Oral: Initial: 2 mg twice daily; the dose may be lowered to 1 mg twice daily based on individual response and tolerability
Dosing adjustment in patients concurrently taking cytochrome P-450 3A4 inhibitors: 1 mg twice daily
Dosing adjustment in renal impairment: Use with caution
Dosing adjustment in hepatic impairment: Administer 1 mg twice daily

Dietary Considerations Food increases bioavailability (~53% increase)

Patient Information Inform patients that antimuscarinic agents such as tolterodine may produce blurred vision

Dosage Forms Tablet, as tartrate: 1 mg, 2 mg

♦ **Tolu-Sed® DM [OTC]** *see* Guaifenesin and Dextromethorphan *on page 550*

♦ **Tonocard®** *see* Tocainide *on page 1153*

♦ **Topactin®** *see* Fluocinonide *on page 496*

Topiramate (toe PYE ra mate)

Related Information
Anticonvulsants by Seizure Type *on page 1300*

U.S. Brand Names Topamax®

Therapeutic Category Anticonvulsant

Use Adjunctive therapy for partial onset seizures in adults
Orphan drug: Topiramate has also been granted orphan drug status for the treatment of Lennox-Gastaut syndrome

Pregnancy Risk Factor C

Pregnancy/Breast-Feeding Implications
Breast-feeding/lactation: In studies of rats topiramate has been shown to be secreted in milk; however, it has not been studied in humans

Contraindications
Patients with a known hypersensitivity to any components of this drug

Warnings/Precautions
Avoid abrupt withdrawal of topiramate therapy, it should be withdrawn slowly to minimize the potential of increased seizure frequency; the risk of kidney stones is about 2-4 times that of the untreated population, the risk of this event may be reduced by increasing fluid intake; use cautiously in patients with hepatic or renal impairment, during pregnancy or in nursing mothers.

Adverse Reactions
>10%:
Central nervous system: Fatigue, dizziness, ataxia, somnolence, psychomotor slowing, nervousness, memory difficulties, speech problems
Gastrointestinal: Nausea
Neuromuscular & skeletal: Paresthesia, tremor
Ocular: Nystagmus
Respiratory: Upper respiratory infections
1% to 10%:
Cardiovascular: Chest pain, edema
Central nervous system: Language problems, abnormal coordination, confusion, depression, difficulty concentrating, hypoesthesia
Endocrine & metabolic: Hot flashes
Gastrointestinal: Dyspepsia, abdominal pain, anorexia, constipation, xerostomia, gingivitis, weight loss
Neuromuscular & skeletal: Myalgia, weakness, back pain, leg pain, rigors
Otic: Decreased hearing
Renal: Nephrolithiasis
Respiratory: Pharyngitis, sinusitis, epistaxis
Miscellaneous: Flu-like symptoms

Overdosage/Toxicology
Activated charcoal has not been shown to adsorb topiramate and is, therefore, not recommended; hemodialysis can remove drug, however, most cases do not require removal and instead is best treated with supportive measures

Drug Interactions
CYP2C19 enzyme substrate; CYP2C19 enzyme inhibitor
Decreased effect: Phenytoin can decrease topiramate levels by as much as 48%, carbamazepine reduces it by 40% and valproic acid reduces topiramate by 14%; digoxin levels and norethindrone blood levels are decreased when coadministered with topiramate
Increased toxicity: Concomitant administration with other CNS depressants will increase its sedative effects; coadministration with other carbonic anhydrase inhibitors may increase the chance of nephrolithiasis

Mechanism of Action
Mechanism is not fully understood, it is thought to decrease seizure frequency by blocking sodium channels in neurons, enhancing GABA activity and by blocking glutamate activity

Pharmacodynamics/Kinetics
Absorption: Good; unaffected by food
Protein binding: 13% to 17%
Metabolism: Minimal, primarily eliminated unchanged in urine (~70% of administered dose)
Bioavailability: 80%
Half-life: Mean: 21 hours in adults
Time to peak serum concentration: ~2-4 hours
Elimination: Primarily eliminated unchanged in the urine
Dializable: ~30%

Usual Dosage
Adults: Initial: 50 mg/day; titrate by 50 mg/day at 1-week intervals to target dose of 200 mg twice daily; usual maximum dose: 1600 mg/day
Dosing adjustment in renal impairment: Cl$_{cr}$ <70 mL/minute: Administer 50% dose and titrate more slowly
Dosing adjustment in hepatic impairment: Clearance may be minimally reduced

Dosage Forms
Capsule (Topamax® Sprinkles): 15 mg, 25 mg
Tablet: 25 mg, 100 mg, 200 mg

♦ **TOPO** *see* Topotecan *on this page*
♦ **Toposar® Injection** *see* Etoposide *on page 459*

Topotecan (toe poe TEE kan)
U.S. Brand Names Hycamtin™
Synonyms Hycamptamine; SK and F 104864; SKF 104864; SKF 104864-A; TOPO; Topotecan Hydrochloride; TPT
Therapeutic Category Antineoplastic Agent, Antibiotic
Use Treatment of metastatic carcinoma of the ovary after failure of initial or subsequent chemotherapy; second-line treatment of small cell lung cancer
  Unlabeled use: Under investigation for the treatment of nonsmall cell lung cancer, sarcoma (pediatrics)
Pregnancy Risk Factor D
Contraindications Hypersensitivity to any component, pregnancy, breast-feeding
Warnings/Precautions The U.S. Food and Drug Administration (FDA) currently recommends that procedures for proper handling and disposal of antineoplastic agents be considered; monitor bone marrow function
Adverse Reactions
>10%:
  Central nervous system: Headache
  Dermatologic: Alopecia (reversible)
  Gastrointestinal: Nausea, vomiting, diarrhea
    Emetic potential: Moderately low (10% to 30%)
    Hematologic: Myelosuppressive: Principle dose-limiting toxicity; white blood cell count nadir is 8-11 days after administration and is more frequent than thrombocytopenia (at lower doses); recover is usually within 21 days and cumulative toxicity has not been noted
    WBC: Mild to severe
    Platelets: Mild (at low doses)
    Nadir (days): 8-11
    Recovery (days): 14-21
1% to 10%:
  Neuromuscular & skeletal: Paresthesia
  Respiratory: Dyspnea
<1%: Mild erythema and bruising
Drug Interactions Increased toxicity: Filgrastim (G-CSF): Prolonged/severe neutropenia and thrombocytopenia; concomitant administration with other antineoplastics has been associated with increased morbidity/mortality - not recommended (eg, cisplatin)
Stability
  Store intact vials of lyophilized powder for injection at room temperature and protected from light. Topotecan should be initially reconstituted with 4 mL SWI. This solution is stable for 24 hours at room temperature. Topotecan should be further diluted in 100 mL D_5W. This solution is stable for 24 hours at room temperature.
  Standard I.V. dilution: Dose/100 mL D_5W; stability is pH dependent; although topotecan may be further diluted in 0.9% NaCl, stability is longer in D_5W
Mechanism of Action Inhibits topoisomerase I (an enzyme which relaxes torsionally strained-coiled duplex DNA) to prevent DNA replication and translocation; topotecan acts in S phase
Pharmacodynamics/Kinetics
  Absorption: Oral: ~30%
  Distribution: V_{dss} of the lactone is high (mean: 87.3 L/mm^2; range: 25.6-186 L/mm^2), suggesting wide distribution and/or tissue sequestering
  Metabolism: Topotecan (TPT) undergoes a rapid, pH-dependent opening of the lactone ring to yield a relatively inactive hydroxy acid in plasma.
  Half-life: 3 hours
  Protein binding: 35%
  Elimination: Primarily renal, with 30% of dose eliminated within 24 hours
Usual Dosage Refer to individual protocols:
  Adults:
    Metastatic ovarian cancer and small cell lung cancer: IVPB: 1.5 mg/m^2/day for 5 days; repeated every 21 days (neutrophil count should be >1500/mm^3 and platelet count should be >100,000/mm^3)
    Dosage adjustment for hematological effects: If neutrophil count <1500/mm^3, reduce dose by 0.25 mg/m^2/day for 5 days for next cycle
  Dosing adjustment in renal impairment:
    Cl$_{cr}$ 20-39 mL/minute: Administer 50% of normal dose
    Cl$_{cr}$ <20 mL/minute: Do not use, insufficient data available
  Hemodialysis: Supplemental dose is not necessary
    CAPD effects: Unknown
    CAVH effects: Unknown
  Dosing adjustment in hepatic impairment: Bilirubin 1.5-10 mg/dL: Adjustment is not necessary
Administration Administer lower doses IVPB over 30 minutes
Monitoring Parameters CBC with differential and platelet count and renal function tests
Test Interactions None known
Patient Information Any signs of infection, easy bruising or bleeding, shortness of breath, painful or burning urination should be brought to the physician's attention. Nausea, vomiting, or hair loss sometimes occur. The drug may cause permanent sterility

and may cause birth defects. The drug may be excreted in breast milk, therefore, an alternative form of feeding your baby should be used.

Dosage Forms Powder for injection, as hydrochloride, lyophilized: 4 mg (base)

- ♦ **Topotecan Hydrochloride** see Topotecan on previous page
- ♦ **Toprol XL**® see Metoprolol on page 768
- ♦ **Topsyn**® see Fluocinonide on page 496
- ♦ **TOPV** see Polio Vaccines on page 940
- ♦ **Toradol**® **Injection** see Ketorolac Tromethamine on page 651
- ♦ **Toradol**® **Oral** see Ketorolac Tromethamine on page 651
- ♦ **Torecan**® see Thiethylperazine on page 1132

Toremifene (TORE em i feen)

U.S. Brand Names Fareston®

Synonyms Toremifene Citrate

Therapeutic Category Antineoplastic Agent, Hormone Antagonist; Estrogen Receptor Antagonist

Use Treatment of metastatic breast cancer in postmenopausal women with estrogen-receptor (ER) positive or ER unknown tumors

Pregnancy Risk Factor D

Contraindications Hypersensitivity to toremifene

Warnings/Precautions Hypercalcemia and tumor flare have been reported in some breast cancer patients with bone metastases during the first weeks of treatment. Tumor flare is a syndrome of diffuse musculoskeletal pain and erythema with increased size of tumor lesions that later regress. It is often accompanied by hypercalcemia. Tumor flare does not imply treatment failure or represent tumor progression. Institute appropriate measures if hypercalcemia occurs, and if severe, discontinue treatment. Drugs that decrease renal calcium excretion (eg, thiazide diuretics) may increase the risk of hypercalcemia in patients receiving toremifene.

Patients with a history of thromboembolic disease should generally not be treated with toremifene

Adverse Reactions

>10%:

Endocrine & metabolic: Vaginal discharge, hot flashes

Gastrointestinal: Nausea

Miscellaneous: Diaphoresis

1% to 10%:

Cardiovascular: Thromboembolism: Tamoxifen has been associated with the occurrence of venous thrombosis and pulmonary embolism; arterial thrombosis has also been described in a few case reports; cardiac failure, myocardial infarction, edema

Central nervous system: Dizziness

Endocrine & metabolic: Hypercalcemia may occur in patients with bone metastases; galactorrhea and vitamin D deficiency, menstrual irregularities

Gastrointestinal: Vomiting

Genitourinary: Vaginal bleeding or discharge, endometriosis, priapism, possible endometrial cancer

Ocular: Ophthalmologic effects (visual acuity changes, cataracts, or retinopathy), corneal opacities, dry eyes

Overdosage/Toxicology

Theoretically, overdose may be manifested as an increase of antiestrogenic effects such as hot flashes; estrogenic effects such as vaginal bleeding; or nervous system disorders such as vertigo, dizziness, ataxia and nausea

No specific antidote exists and treatment is symptomatic

Drug Interactions CYP3A3/4 enzyme substrate

Decreased effect: CYP3A4 enzyme inducers: Phenobarbital, phenytoin and carbamazepine increase the rate of toremifene metabolism and lower the steady state concentration in serum

Increased toxicity:

CYP3A4-6 enzyme inhibitors (ketoconazole, erythromycin) inhibit the metabolism of toremifene

Warfarin results in significant enhancement of the anticoagulant effects of warfarin; has been speculated that a decrease in antitumor effect of tamoxifen may also occur due to alterations in the percentage of active tamoxifen metabolites

Mechanism of Action Nonsteroidal, triphenylethylene derivative. Competitively binds to estrogen receptors on tumors and other tissue targets, producing a nuclear complex that decreases DNA synthesis and inhibits estrogen effects. Nonsteroidal agent with potent antiestrogenic properties which compete with estrogen for binding sites in breast and other tissues; cells accumulate in the G_0 and G_1 phases; therefore, tamoxifen is cytostatic rather than cytocidal.

Pharmacodynamics/Kinetics

Absorption: Well absorbed from GI tract

Distribution: V_d: 580 L

Protein binding: Plasma: Extensive, >99.5%, mainly to albumin

Metabolism: Extensively, principally by cytochrome P-450 3A4 to N-demethyltoremifene, which is also antiestrogenic but with weak in vivo antitumor potency

Half-life: ~5 days

Time to peak serum concentration: Oral: Within 3 hours

(Continued)

Toremifene *(Continued)*

Elimination: Primarily in the feces with about 10% excreted in the urine during a 1-week period

Usual Dosage Refer to individual protocols

Adults: Oral: 60 mg once daily, generally continued until disease progression is observed

Dosage adjustment in renal impairment: No dosage adjustment necessary

Dosage adjustment in hepatic impairment: Toremifene is extensively metabolized in the liver and dosage adjustments may be indicated in patients with liver disease; however, no specific guidelines have been developed

Monitoring Parameters Obtain periodic complete blood counts, calcium levels, and liver function tests. Closely monitor patients with bone metastases for hypercalcemia during the first few weeks of treatment. Leukopenia and thrombocytopenia have been reported rarely; monitor leukocyte and platelet counts during treatment.

Patient Information This drug will cause an initial "flare" of this disease (increased bone pain and hot flashes) which will subside. Report any vomiting that occurs after taking dose; women should be advised to notify their physician of vaginal bleeding, weakness, mental confusion.

Nursing Implications Increase of bone pain usually indicates a good therapeutic response

Dosage Forms Tablet: 60 mg

- ◆ **Toremifene Citrate** *see* Toremifene *on previous page*
- ◆ **Tornalate®** *see* Bitolterol *on page 148*

Torsemide *(TOR se mide)*

Related Information

Sulfonamide Derivatives *on page 1337*

U.S. Brand Names Demadex®

Therapeutic Category Antihypertensive Agent; Diuretic, Loop

Use Management of edema associated with congestive heart failure and hepatic or renal disease; used alone or in combination with antihypertensives in treatment of hypertension; I.V. form is indicated when rapid onset is desired

Pregnancy Risk Factor B

Pregnancy/Breast-Feeding Implications Clinical effect on the fetus: A decrease in fetal weight, an increase in fetal resorption, and delayed fetal ossification has occurred in animal studies

Contraindications Anuria; hypersensitivity to torsemide or any component, or other sulfonylureas; safety in children <18 years has not been established

Warnings/Precautions Excessive diuresis may result in dehydration, acute hypotensive or thromboembolic episodes and cardiovascular collapse; rapid injection, renal impairment, or excessively large doses may result in ototoxicity; SLE may be exacerbated; sudden alterations in electrolyte balance may precipitate hepatic encephalopathy and coma in patients with hepatic cirrhosis and ascites; monitor carefully for signs of fluid or electrolyte imbalances, especially hypokalemia in patients at risk for such (eg, digitalis therapy, history of ventricular arrhythmias, elderly, etc), hyperuricemia, hypomagnesemia, or hypocalcemia; use caution with exposure to ultraviolet light.

Adverse Reactions

>10%: Cardiovascular: Orthostatic hypotension

1% to 10%:

Central nervous system: Headache, dizziness, vertigo, pain

Dermatologic: Photosensitivity, urticaria

Endocrine & metabolic: Electrolyte imbalance, dehydration, hyperuricemia

Gastrointestinal: Diarrhea, loss of appetite, stomach cramps

Ocular: Blurred vision

<1%: Rash, gout, pancreatitis, nausea, hepatic dysfunction, agranulocytosis, leukopenia, anemia, thrombocytopenia, redness at injection site, ototoxicity, nephrocalcinosis, prerenal azotemia, interstitial nephritis

Overdosage/Toxicology

Symptoms include electrolyte depletion, volume depletion, hypotension, dehydration, circulatory collapse; electrolyte depletion may be manifested by weakness, dizziness, mental confusion, anorexia, lethargy, vomiting, and cramps

Following GI decontamination, treatment is supportive; hypotension responds to fluids and Trendelenburg position

Drug Interactions CYP2C9 enzyme substrate

Aminoglycosides: Ototoxicity may be increased; anticoagulant activity is enhanced

Beta-blockers: Plasma concentrations of beta-blockers may be increased with furosemide

Cisplatin: Ototoxicity may be increased

Digitalis: Arrhythmias may occur with diuretic-induced electrolyte disturbances

Lithium: Plasma concentrations of lithium may be increased

NSAIDs: Torsemide efficacy may be decreased

Probenecid: Torsemide action may be reduced

Salicylates: Diuretic action may be impaired in patients with cirrhosis and ascites

Sulfonylureas: Glucose tolerance may be decreased

Thiazides: Synergistic effects may result

Chloral hydrate: Transient diaphoresis, hot flashes, hypertension may occur

Stability If torsemide is to be administered via continuous infusion, stability has been demonstrated through 24 hours at room temperature in plastic containers for the following fluids and concentrations:

200 mg torsemide (10 mg/mL) added to 250 mL D5W, 250 mL NS or 500 mL 0.45% sodium chloride

50 mg torsemide (10 mg/mL) added to 500 mL D5W, 250 mL NS or 500 mL 0.45% sodium chloride

Mechanism of Action Inhibits reabsorption of sodium and chloride in the ascending loop of Henle and distal renal tubule, interfering with the chloride-binding cotransport system, thus causing increased excretion of water, sodium, chloride, magnesium, and calcium; does not alter GFR, renal plasma flow, or acid-base balance

Pharmacodynamics/Kinetics
Onset of diuresis: 30-60 minutes
Peak effect: 1-4 hours
Duration: ~6 hours
Absorption: Oral: Rapid
Protein binding: Plasma: ~97% to 99%
Metabolism: Hepatic by cytochrome P-450, 80%
Bioavailability: 80% to 90%
Half-life: 2-4; 7-8 hours in cirrhosis (dose modification appears unnecessary)
Elimination: 20% eliminated unchanged in urine; hemodialysis does not accelerate removal

Usual Dosage Adults: Oral, I.V.:
Congestive heart failure: 10-20 mg once daily; may increase gradually for chronic treatment by doubling dose until the diuretic response is apparent (for acute treatment, I.V. dose may be repeated every 2 hours with double the dose as needed)
Chronic renal failure: 20 mg once daily; increase as described above
Hepatic cirrhosis: 5-10 mg once daily with an aldosterone antagonist or a potassium-sparing diuretic; increase as described above
Hypertension: 5 mg once daily; increase to 10 mg after 4-6 weeks if an adequate hypotensive response is not apparent; if still not effective, an additional antihypertensive agent may be added

Administration I.V. injections should be given over ≥2 minutes; the oral form may be given regardless of meal times; patients may be switched from the I.V. form to the oral and vice-versa with no change in dose; no dosage adjustment is needed in the elderly or patients with hepatic impairment
To administer as a continuous infusion: 50 mg or 200 mg torsemide should be diluted in 250 mL or 500 mL of compatible solution in plastic containers

Monitoring Parameters Renal function, electrolytes, and fluid status (weight and I & O), blood pressure

Patient Information May be taken with food or milk; rise slowly from a lying or sitting position to minimize dizziness, lightheadedness or fainting; also use extra care when exercising, standing for long periods of time, and during hot weather; take dose in the morning or early in the evening to prevent nocturia; use caution with exposure to ultraviolet light

Additional Information 10-20 mg torsemide is approximately equivalent to furosemide 40 mg or bumetanide 1 mg

Dosage Forms
Injection: 10 mg/mL (2 mL, 5 mL)
Tablet: 5 mg, 10 mg, 20 mg, 100 mg

♦ **Totacillin®** see Ampicillin on page 79
♦ **Totacillin®-N** see Ampicillin on page 79
♦ **Touro Ex®** see Guaifenesin on page 549
♦ **Toxicities of Chemotherapeutic Agents** see page 1288
♦ **Toxicology Information** see page 1491
♦ **Toxidromes** see page 1499
♦ **t-PA** see Alteplase on page 49
♦ **TPT** see Topotecan on page 1162
♦ **Tracrium®** see Atracurium on page 110

Tramadol (TRA ma dole)

U.S. Brand Names Ultram®
Synonyms Tramadol Hydrochloride
Therapeutic Category Analgesic, Miscellaneous
Use Relief of moderate to moderately severe pain
Pregnancy Risk Factor C
Contraindications Previous hypersensitivity to tramadol or any components; do not give to opioid-dependent patients; concurrent use of monoamine oxidase inhibitors; acute alcohol intoxication; concurrent use of centrally acting analgesics, opioids, or psychotropic drugs
Warnings/Precautions Elderly patients and patients with chronic respiratory disorders may be at greater risk of adverse events; liver disease; patients with myxedema, hypothyroidism, or hypoadrenalism should use tramadol with caution and at reduced dosages; not recommended during pregnancy or in nursing mothers; increased incidence of seizures may occur in patients receiving concurrent tricyclic antidepressants; tolerance or drug dependence may result from extended use
Adverse Reactions
>1%:
Central nervous system: Dizziness, headache, somnolence, stimulation, restlessness
Gastrointestinal: Nausea, diarrhea, constipation, vomiting, dyspepsia
(Continued)

Tramadol *(Continued)*

Neuromuscular & skeletal: Weakness
Miscellaneous: Diaphoresis
<1%: Palpitations, seizures, respiratory depression, suicidal tendency

Overdosage/Toxicology
Symptoms of overdose include CNS and respiratory depression, gastrointestinal cramping, constipation
Naloxone 2 mg I.V. (0.01 mg/kg children) with repeat administration as needed up to 18 mg

Drug Interactions CYP2D6 enzyme substrate
Decreased effects: Carbamazepine (decreases half-life by 33% to 50%)
Increased toxicity: Monoamine oxidase inhibitors and tricyclic antidepressants (seizures); quinidine (inhibits CYP2D6, thereby increases tramadol serum concentrations); cimetidine (tramadol half-life increased 20% to 25%)

Mechanism of Action Binds to μ-opiate receptors in the CNS causing inhibition of ascending pain pathways, altering the perception of and response to pain; also inhibits the reuptake of norepinephrine and serotonin, which also modifies the ascending pain pathway

Usual Dosage Adults: Oral: 50-100 mg every 4-6 hours, not to exceed 400 mg/day
Initiation of low dose followed by titration in increments of 50 mg/day every 3 days to effective dose (not >400 mg/day) may minimize dizziness and vertigo

Monitoring Parameters Monitor patient for pain, respiratory rate, and look for signs of tolerance and, therefore, abuse potential; monitor blood pressure and pulse rate, especially in patients on higher doses

Reference Range 100-300 ng/mL; however, serum level monitoring is not required

Patient Information Avoid driving or operating machinery until the effect of drug wears off; tramadol has not been fully evaluated for its abuse potential, report cravings to your physician immediately

Dosage Forms Tablet, as hydrochloride: 50 mg

♦ **Tramadol Hydrochloride** *see Tramadol on previous page*
♦ **Trandate®** *see Labetalol on page 653*

Trandolapril *(tran DOE la pril)*

Related Information
Angiotensin Agents *on page 1291*

U.S. Brand Names Mavik®

Therapeutic Category Angiotensin-Converting Enzyme (ACE) Inhibitor; Antihypertensive Agent

Use Treatment of hypertension (alone or in combination with other antihypertensive medications such as hydrochlorothiazide). For stable patients who have evidence of left-ventricular systolic dysfunction (identified by wall motion abnormalities) or who are symptomatic from CHF within the first few days after sustaining acute myocardial infarction. Administration to Caucasians decreases the risk of death (principally cardiovascular death) and decreases the risk of heart failure-related admissions.

Pregnancy Risk Factor C (1st trimester); D (2nd and 3rd trimesters)

Contraindications Hypersensitivity to trandolapril, other ACE inhibitors, in patients with a history of angioedema related to previous treatment with an ACE inhibitor, or any component

Warnings/Precautions Neutropenia, agranulocytosis, angioedema, decreased renal function (hypertension, renal artery stenosis, CHF), hepatic dysfunction (elimination, activation), proteinuria, first-dose hypotension (hypovolemia, CHF, dehydrated patients at risk, eg, diuretic use, elderly), elderly (due to renal function changes); use with caution and modify dosage in patients with renal impairment; use with caution in patients with collagen vascular disease, CHF, hypovolemia, valvular stenosis, hyperkalemia (>5.7 mEq/L), anesthesia

Patients taking diuretics are at risk for developing hypotension on initial dosing; to prevent this, discontinue diuretics 2-3 days prior to initiating trandolapril; may restart diuretics if blood pressure is not controlled by trandolapril alone

Adverse Reactions
1% to 10%:
Cardiovascular: Chest pain, hypotension, syncope
Central nervous system: Fatigue
Gastrointestinal: Dyspepsia
Neuromuscular & skeletal: Myalgia
Respiratory: Cough (1.9% to 35%)
≤1%: Palpitations, flushing, insomnia, sleep disturbances, vertigo, anxiety, pruritus, rash, angioedema, decreased libido, abdominal pain, vomiting, diarrhea, constipation, pancreatitis, urinary tract infection, impotence, paresthesia, muscle cramps, dyspnea, upper respiratory infection

Overdosage/Toxicology
Symptoms include hypotension, vertigo, dizziness
Following initiation of essential overdose management, toxic symptom treatment and supportive treatment should be initiated. Hypotension usually responds to I.V. fluids or Trendelenburg positioning. If unresponsive to these measures, the use of a parenteral inotrope may be required (eg, norepinephrine 0.1-0.2 mcg/kg/minute titrated to response). Seizures commonly respond to diazepam (I.V. 5-10 mg bolus in adults every 15 minutes if needed up to a total of 30 mg) or to phenytoin or phenobarbital.

Drug Interactions
ACE inhibitors (trandolapril) and potassium-sparing diuretics may have additive hyperkalemic effect

ACE inhibitors (trandolapril) and indomethacin or nonsteroidal anti-inflammatory agents may reduce antihypertensive response to ACE inhibitors (trandolapril)

Allopurinol and trandolapril → neutropenia

Antacids and ACE inhibitors may decrease absorption of ACE inhibitors

Phenothiazines and ACE inhibitors may increase ACE inhibitor effect

Probenecid and ACE inhibitors (trandolapril) may increase ACE inhibitors (trandolapril) levels

Rifampin and ACE inhibitors (trandolapril) may decrease ACE inhibitor effect

Digoxin and ACE inhibitors may increase serum digoxin levels

Lithium and ACE inhibitors may increase lithium serum levels

Tetracycline and ACE inhibitors (trandolapril) may decrease tetracycline absorption (up to 37%)

Food decreases trandolapril absorption; rate, but not extent, of ramipril and fosinopril is reduced by concomitant administration with food; food does not reduce absorption of enalapril, lisinopril, or benazepril; trandolapril has a decreased rate and extent (25% to 30%) of absorption when taken with a high fat meal

Mechanism of Action Trandolapril is an angiotensin-converting enzyme (ACE) inhibitor which prevents the formation of angiotensin II from angiotensin I. Trandolapril must undergo enzymatic hydrolysis, mainly in liver, to its biologically active metabolite, trandolaprilat. A CNS mechanism may also be involved in the hypotensive effect as angiotensin II increases adrenergic outflow from the CNS. Vasoactive kallikrein's may be decreased in conversion to active hormones by ACE inhibitors, thus, reducing blood pressure.

Pharmacodynamics/Kinetics
Peak reduction in blood pressure: 6 hours postdose
Peak levels: 6 hours

Trandolaprilat (active metabolite) is very lipophilic in comparison to other ACE inhibitors which may contribute to its prolonged duration of action (72 hours after a single dose)
Absorption: Rapid
Metabolism: Hydrolyzed, mainly in liver, to the active metabolite, trandolaprilat
Half-life: 24 hours
Elimination: As metabolites in urine; reduce dose in renal failure; creatinine clearances ≤30 mL/minute result in accumulation of active metabolite

Usual Dosage Adults: Oral:
Hypertension: Initial dose in patients not receiving a diuretic: 1 mg/day (2 mg/day in black patients). Adjust dosage according to the blood pressure response. Make dosage adjustments at intervals of ≥1 week. Most patients have required dosages of 2-4 mg/day. There is a little experience with doses >8 mg/day. Patients inadequately treated with once daily dosing at 4 mg may be treated with twice daily dosing. If blood pressure is not adequately controlled with trandolapril monotherapy, a diuretic may be added.

Heart failure postmyocardial infarction or left-ventricular dysfunction postmyocardial infarction: Initial: 1 mg/day; titrate patients (as tolerated) towards the target dose of 4 mg/day. If a 4 mg dose is not tolerated, patients can continue therapy with the greatest tolerated dose.

Dosing adjustment in renal impairment: Cl_{cr} ≤30 mL/minute: Recommended starting dose: 0.5 mg/day

Dosing adjustment in hepatic impairment: Cirrhosis: Recommended starting dose: 0.5 mg/day

Monitoring Parameters Serum potassium, renal function, serum creatinine, BUN, CBC

Patient Information Do not discontinue medication without advice of physician; notify physician if sore throat, swelling, palpitations, cough, chest pains, difficulty swallowing, swelling of face, eyes, tongue, lips, hoarseness, sweating, vomiting, or diarrhea occurs; may cause dizziness, lightheadedness during first few days; may also cause changes in taste perception; do not use salt substitutes containing potassium without consulting a physician

Nursing Implications May cause depression in some patients; discontinue if angioedema of the face, extremities, lips, tongue, or glottis occurs; watch for hypotensive effects within 1-3 hours of first dose or new higher dose

Dosage Forms Tablet: 1 mg, 2 mg, 4 mg

Trandolapril and Verapamil (tran DOE la pril & ver AP a mil)
U.S. Brand Names Tarka®
Therapeutic Category Angiotensin-Converting Enzyme (ACE) Inhibitor Combination; Antihypertensive Agent, Combination
Dosage Forms Tablet:
Trandolapril 1 mg and verapamil hydrochloride 240 mg
Trandolapril 2 mg and verapamil hydrochloride 180 mg
Trandolapril 2 mg and verapamil hydrochloride 240 mg
Trandolapril 4 mg and verapamil hydrochloride 240 mg

Tranexamic Acid (tran eks AM ik AS id)
U.S. Brand Names Cyklokapron®
Therapeutic Category Antihemophilic Agent
Use Short-term use (2-8 days) in hemophilia patients during and following tooth extraction to reduce or prevent hemorrhage, has also been used as an alternative to aminocaproic acid for subarachnoid hemorrhage
Pregnancy Risk Factor B
(Continued)

Tranexamic Acid *(Continued)*

Contraindications Acquired defective color vision, active intravascular clotting

Warnings/Precautions Dosage modification required in patients with renal impairment; ophthalmic exam before and during therapy required if patient is treated beyond several days; caution in patients with cardiovascular, renal, or cerebrovascular disease; when used for subarachnoid hemorrhage, ischemic complications may occur

Adverse Reactions
>10%: Gastrointestinal: Nausea, diarrhea, vomiting
1% to 10%:
  Cardiovascular: Hypotension, thrombosis
  Ocular: Blurred vision
<1%: Unusual menstrual discomfort

Stability Incompatible with solutions containing penicillin

Mechanism of Action Forms a reversible complex that displaces plasminogen from fibrin resulting in inhibition of fibrinolysis; it also inhibits the proteolytic activity of plasmin

Pharmacodynamics/Kinetics
Half-life: 2-10 hours
Elimination: Primarily as unchanged drug (>90%) in urine

Usual Dosage Children and Adults: I.V.: 10 mg/kg immediately before surgery, then 25 mg/kg/dose orally 3-4 times/day for 2-8 days

Alternatively:
  Oral: 25 mg/kg 3-4 times/day beginning 1 day prior to surgery
  I.V.: 10 mg/kg 3-4 times/day in patients who are unable to take oral
  Dosing adjustment/interval in renal impairment:
    Cl_{cr} 50-80 mL/minute: Administer 50% of normal dose or 10 mg/kg twice daily I.V. or 15 mg/kg twice daily orally
    Cl_{cr} 10-50 mL/minute: Administer 25% of normal dose or 10 mg/kg/day I.V. or 15 mg/kg/day orally
    Cl_{cr} <10 mL/minute: Administer 10% of normal dose or 10 mg/kg/dose every 48 hours I.V. or 15 mg/kg/dose every 48 hours orally

Administration Use plastic syringe only for I.V. push

Reference Range 5-10 µg/mL is required to decrease fibrinolysis

Patient Information Report any signs of bleeding or myopathy, changes in vision; GI upset usually disappears when dose is reduced

Nursing Implications Dosage modification required in patients with renal impairment

Dosage Forms
Injection: 100 mg/mL (10 mL)
Tablet: 500 mg

♦ **Transamine Sulphate** *see* Tranylcypromine *on this page*
♦ **Transdermal-NTG® Patch** *see* Nitroglycerin *on page 845*
♦ **Transdermal-V®** *see* Scopolamine *on page 1051*
♦ **Transderm-Nitro® Patch** *see* Nitroglycerin *on page 845*
♦ **Transderm Scop® Patch** *see* Scopolamine *on page 1051*
♦ *trans*-Retinoic Acid *see* Tretinoin, Topical *on page 1173*
♦ **Tranxene®** *see* Clorazepate *on page 286*

Tranylcypromine *(tran il SIP roe meen)*

Related Information
Antidepressant Agents Comparison *on page 1301*
Tyramine Content of Foods *on page 1525*

U.S. Brand Names Parnate®

Synonyms Transamine Sulphate; Tranylcypromine Sulfate

Therapeutic Category Antidepressant, Monoamine Oxidase Inhibitor

Use Symptomatic treatment of depressed patients refractory to or intolerant to tricyclic antidepressants or electroconvulsive therapy; has a more rapid onset of therapeutic effect than other MAO inhibitors, but causes more severe hypertensive reactions

Pregnancy Risk Factor C

Contraindications Uncontrolled hypertension, known hypersensitivity to tranylcypromine, pheochromocytoma, cardiovascular disease, severe renal or hepatic impairment, pheochromocytoma

Warnings/Precautions Safety in children <16 years of age has not been established; use with caution in patients who are hyperactive, hyperexcitable, or who have glaucoma, suicidal tendencies, diabetes, elderly

Adverse Reactions
1% to 10%: Cardiovascular: Orthostatic hypotension
<1%: Edema, hypertensive crises, drowsiness, hyperexcitability, headache, rash, photosensitivity, xerostomia, constipation, urinary retention, hepatitis, blurred vision

Overdosage/Toxicology
Symptoms of overdose include tachycardia, palpitations, muscle twitching, seizures, insomnia, transient hypotension, hypertension, hyperpyrexia, coma
Competent supportive care is the most important treatment for an overdose with a monoamine oxidase (MAO) inhibitor. Both hypertension or hypotension can occur with intoxication. Hypotension may respond to I.V. fluids or vasopressors, and hypertension usually responds to an alpha-adrenergic blocker. While treating the hypertension, care is warranted to avoid sudden drops in blood pressure, since this may worsen the MAO inhibitor toxicity. Muscle irritability and seizures often respond to diazepam, while

hyperthermia is best treated antipyretics and cooling blankets. Cardiac arrhythmias are best treated with phenytoin or procainamide.

Drug Interactions CYP2A6 and 2C19 enzyme inhibitor

Decreased effect of antihypertensives

Increased toxicity with disulfiram (seizures), fluoxetine and other serotonin-active agents (eg, paroxetine, sertraline), TCAs (cardiovascular instability), meperidine (cardiovascular instability), phenothiazine (hypertensive crisis), sympathomimetics (hypertensive crisis), sumatriptan (hypothetical), CNS depressants, levodopa (hypertensive crisis), tyramine-containing foods (eg, aged foods), dextroamphetamine (psychosis)

Mechanism of Action Inhibits the enzymes monoamine oxidase A and B which are responsible for the intraneuronal metabolism of norepinephrine and serotonin and increasing their availability to postsynaptic neurons; decreased firing rate of the locus ceruleus, reducing norepinephrine concentration in the brain; agonist effects of serotonin

Pharmacodynamics/Kinetics

Onset of action: 2-3 weeks are required of continued dosing to obtain full therapeutic effect

Half-life: 90-190 minutes

Time to peak serum concentration: Within 2 hours

Elimination: In urine

Usual Dosage Adults: Oral: 10 mg twice daily, increase by 10 mg increments at 1- to 3-week intervals; maximum: 60 mg/day

Dosing comments in hepatic impairment: Use with care and monitor plasma levels and patient response closely

Dietary Considerations

Alcohol: Avoid use

Food: Avoid tyramine-containing foods

Monitoring Parameters Blood pressure, blood glucose

Test Interactions ↓ glucose

Patient Information Tablets may be crushed; avoid alcohol; do not discontinue abruptly; avoid foods high in tyramine (eg, aged cheeses, Chianti wine, raisins, liver, bananas, chocolate, yogurt, sour cream); discuss list of drugs and foods to avoid with pharmacist or physician; arise slowly from prolonged sitting or lying

Nursing Implications Assist with ambulation during initiation of therapy; monitor blood pressure closely, patients should be cautioned against eating foods high in tyramine or tryptophan (cheese, wine, beer, pickled herring, dry sausage)

Dosage Forms Tablet, as sulfate: 10 mg

♦ **Tranylcypromine Sulfate** *see* Tranylcypromine *on previous page*

Trastuzumab (tras TU zoo mab)

U.S. Brand Names Herceptin®

Therapeutic Category Antineoplastic Agent, Monoclonal Antibody; Monoclonal Antibody

Use

Single agent for the treatment of patients with metastatic breast cancer whose tumors overexpress the HER2/neu protein and who have received one or more chemotherapy regimens for their metastatic disease

Combination therapy with paclitaxel for the treatment of patients with metastatic breast cancer whose tumors overexpress the HER2/neu protein and who have not received chemotherapy for their metastatic disease

Note: HER2/neu protein overexpression or amplification has been noted in ovarian, gastric, colorectal, endometrial, lung, bladder, prostate, and salivary gland tumors. It is not yet known whether trastuzumab may be effective in these other carcinomas which overexpress HER2/neu protein.

Pregnancy Risk Factor B

Pregnancy/Breast-Feeding Implications It is not known whether trastuzumab is secreted in human milk; because many immunoglobulins are secreted in milk, and the potential for serious adverse reactions exists, patients should discontinue nursing during treatment and for 6 months after the last dose

Contraindications None known

Warnings/Precautions Congestive heart failure associated with trastuzumab may be severe and has been associated with disabling cardiac failure, death, mural thrombus, and stroke. Left ventricular function should be evaluated in all patients prior to and during treatment with trastuzumab. Discontinuation should be strongly considered in patients who develop a clinically significant decrease in ejection fraction during therapy. Combination therapy which includes anthracyclines and cyclophosphamide increases the incidence and severity of cardiac dysfunction. Extreme caution should be used when treating patients with pre-existing cardiac disease or dysfunction, and in patients with previous exposure to anthracyclines. Advanced age may also predispose to cardiac toxicity. Hypersensitivity to hamster ovary cell proteins or any component of this product.

Adverse Reactions

>10%:

Central nervous system: Pain (47%), fever (36%), chills (32%), headache (26%)

Dermatologic: Rash (18%)

Neuromuscular & skeletal: Weakness (42%), back pain (22%)

Gastrointestinal: Nausea (33%), diarrhea (25%), vomiting (23%), abdominal pain (22%), anorexia (14%)

Respiratory: Cough (26%), dyspnea (22%), rhinitis (14%), pharyngitis (12%)

Miscellaneous: Infection (20%)

(Continued)

Trastuzumab *(Continued)*

1% to 10%:

Cardiovascular: Peripheral edema (10%), congestive heart failure (7%), tachycardia (5%)

Central nervous system: Insomnia (14%), dizziness (13%), paresthesia (9%), depression (6%), peripheral neuritis (2%), neuropathy (1%)

Dermatologic: Herpes simplex (2%), acne (2%)

Gastrointestinal: Nausea and vomiting (8%)

Genitourinary: Urinary tract infection (5%)

Hematologic: Anemia (4%), leukopenia (3%)

Neuromuscular & skeletal: Bone pain (7%), arthralgia (6%)

Respiratory: Sinusitis (9%)

Miscellaneous: Flu syndrome (10%), accidental injury (6%), allergic reaction (3%)

<1%: Vascular thrombosis, pericardial effusion, cardiac arrest, hypotension, hemorrhage, shock, arrhythmia, syncope, cellulitis, hypothyroidism, gastroenteritis, hematemesis, ileus, intestinal obstruction, colitis, esophageal ulcer, stomatitis, pancreatitis, pancytopenia, acute leukemia, coagulopathy, lymphangitis, ascites, hydrocephalus, hepatic failure, hepatitis, amblyopia, deafness, anaphylactoid reaction, radiation injury

Overdosage/Toxicology There is no experience with overdosage in human trials; single doses >500 mg have not been tested

Drug Interactions Increased effect: Paclitaxel may result in a decrease in clearance of trastuzumab, increasing serum concentrations

Stability Store intact vials under refrigeration (2°C to 8°C/36°F to 46°F) prior to reconstitution. Reconstituted each vial with 20 mL of bacteriostatic sterile water for injection. This solution results in a concentration of 21 mg/mL and is stable for 28 days from the date of reconstitution under refrigeration. If the patient has a known hypersensitivity to benzyl alcohol, trastuzumab may be reconstituted with sterile water for injection which must be used immediately.

Determine the dose of trastuzumab and further dilute to an infusion bag containing 0.9% sodium chloride. **Dextrose 5% solution CANNOT BE used.** This solution is stable for 24 hours at room temperature. However, since diluted trastuzumab contains no effective preservative, the reconstituted and diluted solution should be stored under refrigeration (2° to 8°C).

Mechanism of Action Trastuzumab is a monoclonal antibody which binds to the extracellular domain of the human epidermal growth factor receptor 2 protein (HER2); it mediates antibody-dependent cellular cytotoxicity against cells which overproduce HER2

Pharmacodynamics/Kinetics

Distribution: V_d: 44 mL/kg

Half-life: Mean: 5.8 days (range: 1-32 days)

Usual Dosage I.V. infusion:

Adults:

Initial loading dose: 4 mg/kg intravenous infusion over 90 minutes

Maintenance dose: 2 mg/kg intravenous infusion over 90 minutes (can be administered over 30 minutes if prior infusions are well tolerated) weekly until disease progression

Dosing adjustment in renal impairment: Data suggest that the disposition of trastuzumab is not altered based on age or serum creatinine (up to 2 mg/dL); however, no formal interaction studies have been performed

Dosing adjustment in hepatic impairment: No data is currently available

Administration Administer initial infusion over 90 minutes. Subsequent weekly infusions may be administered over 30 minutes if prior infusions are well tolerated. During the first infusion with trastuzumab, a complex of symptoms most commonly consisting of chills, and/or fever were observed in ~ 40% of patients. These symptoms were usually mild to moderate in severity and were treated with acetaminophen, diphenhydramine and meperidine (with or without reduction in the rate of trastuzumab infusion). These symptoms occurred infrequently with subsequent trastuzumab infusions.

Monitoring Parameters Signs and symptoms of cardiac dysfunction

Dosage Forms Injection: Vial, 440 mg, with vial of bacteriostatic water for injection

♦ **Trasylol®** see Aprotinin *on page 95*

Trazodone *(TRAZ oh done)*

Related Information

Antidepressant Agents Comparison *on page 1301*

U.S. Brand Names Desyrel®

Synonyms Trazodone Hydrochloride

Therapeutic Category Antidepressant, Miscellaneous

Use Treatment of depression

Pregnancy Risk Factor C

Contraindications Hypersensitivity to trazodone or any component

Warnings/Precautions Safety and efficacy in children <18 years of age have not been established; monitor closely and use with extreme caution in patients with cardiac disease or arrhythmias. Very sedating, but little anticholinergic effects; therapeutic effects may take up to 4 weeks to occur; therapy is normally maintained for several months after optimum response is reached to prevent recurrence of depression.

Adverse Reactions

>10%:

Central nervous system: Dizziness, headache, confusion

Gastrointestinal: Nausea, bad taste in mouth, xerostomia
Neuromuscular & skeletal: Muscle tremors
1% to 10%:
Gastrointestinal: Diarrhea, constipation
Neuromuscular & skeletal: Weakness
Ocular: Blurred vision
<1%: Hypotension, tachycardia, bradycardia, agitation, seizures, extrapyramidal reactions, rash, prolonged priapism, urinary retention, hepatitis

Overdosage/Toxicology
Symptoms of overdose include drowsiness, vomiting, hypotension, tachycardia, incontinence, coma, priapism

Following initiation of essential overdose management, toxic symptoms should be treated. Ventricular arrhythmias often respond to lidocaine 1.5 mg/kg bolus followed by 2 mg/minute infusion with concurrent systemic alkalinization (sodium bicarbonate 0.5-2 mEq/kg I.V.). Seizures usually respond to diazepam I.V. boluses (5-10 mg for adults up to 30 mg or 0.25-0.4 mg/kg/dose for children up to 10 mg/dose). If seizures are unresponsive or recur, phenytoin or phenobarbital may be required. Hypotension is best treated by I.V. fluids and by placing the patient in the Trendelenburg position.

Drug Interactions CYP2D6 and 3A3/4 enzyme substrate
Decreased effect: Clonidine, methyldopa, anticoagulants
Increased toxicity: Fluoxetine; increased effect/toxicity of phenytoin, CNS depressants, MAO inhibitors; digoxin serum levels increase

Mechanism of Action Inhibits reuptake of serotonin and norepinephrine by the presynaptic neuronal membrane and desensitization of adenyl cyclase, down regulation of beta-adrenergic receptors, and down regulation of serotonin receptors

Pharmacodynamics/Kinetics
Onset of effect: Therapeutic effects take 1-3 weeks to appear
Protein binding: 85% to 95%
Metabolism: In the liver
Half-life: 4-7.5 hours, 2 compartment kinetics
Time to peak serum concentration: Within 30-100 minutes, prolonged in the presence of food (up to 2.5 hours)
Elimination: Primarily in urine and secondarily in feces

Usual Dosage Oral: Therapeutic effects may take up to 4 weeks to occur; therapy is normally maintained for several months after optimum response is reached to prevent recurrence of depression

Children 6-18 years: Initial: 1.5-2 mg/kg/day in divided doses; increase gradually every 3-4 days as needed; maximum: 6 mg/kg/day in 3 divided doses
Adolescents: Initial: 25-50 mg/day; increase to 100-150 mg/day in divided doses
Adults: Initial: 150 mg/day in 3 divided doses (may increase by 50 mg/day every 3-7 days); maximum: 600 mg/day
Elderly: 25-50 mg at bedtime with 25-50 mg/day dose increase every 3 days for inpatients and weekly for outpatients, if tolerated; usual dose: 75-150 mg/day

Dietary Considerations Alcohol: Avoid use

Reference Range
Plasma levels do not always correlate with clinical effectiveness
Therapeutic: 0.5-2.5 μg/mL
Potentially toxic: >2.5 μg/mL
Toxic: >4 μg/mL

Patient Information Take shortly after a meal or light snack, can be given as bedtime dose if drowsiness occurs; avoid alcohol; be aware of possible photosensitivity reaction; report any prolonged or painful erection

Nursing Implications Dosing after meals may decrease lightheadedness and postural hypotension; use side rails on bed if administered to the elderly; observe patient's activity and compare with admission level; assist with ambulation; sitting and standing blood pressure and pulse

Dosage Forms Tablet, as hydrochloride: 50 mg, 100 mg, 150 mg, 300 mg

♦ **Trazodone Hydrochloride** see Trazodone on previous page
♦ **Treatment of Sexually Transmitted Diseases** see page 1429
♦ **Trecator®-SC** see Ethionamide on page 455
♦ **Tremytoine®** see Phenytoin on page 921
♦ **Trendar® [OTC]** see Ibuprofen on page 593
♦ **Trental®** see Pentoxifylline on page 905

Tretinoin, Oral (TRET i noyn, oral)

U.S. Brand Names Vesanoid®
Synonyms All-trans-Retinoic Acid; ATRA
Therapeutic Category Antineoplastic Agent, Miscellaneous; Retinoic Acid Derivative; Vitamin A Derivative; Vitamin, Fat Soluble
Use Acute promyelocytic leukemia (APL): Induction of remission in patients with APL, French American British (FAB) classification M3 (including the M3 variant), characterized by the presence of the t(15;17) translocation or the presence of the PML/RARα gene who are refractory to or who have relapsed from anthracycline chemotherapy, or for whom anthracycline-based chemotherapy is contraindicated. Tretinoin is for the induction of remission only. All patients should receive an accepted form of remission consolidation or maintenance therapy for APL after completion of induction therapy with tretinoin.
(Continued)

Tretinoin, Oral *(Continued)*

Pregnancy Risk Factor D

Contraindications Sensitivity to parabens, vitamin A, or other retinoids

Warnings/Precautions Patients with acute promyelocytic leukemia (APL) are at high risk and can have severe adverse reactions to tretinoin. Administer under the supervision of a physician who is experienced in the management of patients with acute leukemia and in a facility with laboratory and supportive services sufficient to monitor drug tolerance and to protect and maintain a patient compromised by drug toxicity, including respiratory compromise.

About 25% of patients with APL, who have been treated with tretinoin, have experienced a syndrome called the retinoic acid-APL (RA-APL) syndrome which is characterized by fever, dyspnea, weight gain, radiographic pulmonary infiltrates and pleural or pericardial effusions. This syndrome has occasionally been accompanied by impaired myocardial contractility and episodic hypotension. It has been observed with or without concomitant leukocytosis. Endotracheal intubation and mechanical ventilation have been required in some cases due to progressive hypoxemia, and several patients have expired with multiorgan failure. The syndrome usually occurs during the first month of treatment, with some cases reported following the first dose.

Management of the syndrome has not been defined, but high-dose steroids given at the first suspicion of RA-APL syndrome appear to reduce morbidity and mortality. At the first signs suggestive of the syndrome, immediately initiate high-dose steroids (dexamethasone 10 mg I.V.) every 12 hours for 3 days or until resolution of symptoms, regardless of the leukocyte count. The majority of patients do not require termination of tretinoin therapy during treatment of the RA-APL syndrome.

During treatment, ~40% of patients will develop rapidly evolving leukocytosis. Rapidly evolving leukocytosis is associated with a higher risk of life-threatening complications.

If signs and symptoms of the RA-APL syndrome are present together with leukocytosis, initiate treatment with high-dose steroids immediately. Consider adding full-dose chemotherapy (including an anthracycline, if not contraindicated) to the tretinoin therapy on day 1 or 2 for patients presenting with a WBC count of >5 x 10^9/L or immediately, for patients presenting with a WBC count of <5 x 10^9/L, if the WBC count reaches ≥6 x 10^9/L by day 5, or ≥10 x 10^9/L by day 10 or ≥15 x 10^9/L by day 28.

Not to be used in women of childbearing potential unless the woman is capable of complying with effective contraceptive measures; therapy is normally begun on the second or third day of next normal menstrual period; two reliable methods of effective contraception must be used during therapy and for 1 month after discontinuation of therapy, unless abstinence is the chosen method. Within one week prior to the institution of tretinoin therapy, the patient should have blood or urine collected for a serum or urine pregnancy test with a sensitivity of at least 50 mIU/L. When possible, delay tretinoin therapy until a negative result from this test is obtained. When a delay is not possible, place the patient on two reliable forms of contraception. Repeat pregnancy testing and contraception counseling monthly throughout the period of treatment.

Initiation of therapy with tretinoin may be based on the morphological diagnosis of APL. Confirm the diagnosis of APL by detection of the t(15;17) genetic marker by cytogenetic studies. If these are negative, PML/RARα fusion should be sought using molecular diagnostic techniques. The response rate of other AML subtypes to tretinoin has not been demonstrated.

Retinoids have been associated with pseudotumor cerebri (benign intracranial hypertension), especially in children. Early signs and symptoms include papilledema, headache, nausea, vomiting and visual disturbances.

Up to 60% of patients experienced hypercholesterolemia or hypertriglyceridemia, which were reversible upon completion of treatment.

Elevated liver function test results occur in 50% to 60% of patients during treatment. Carefully monitor liver function test results during treatment and give consideration to a temporary withdrawal of tretinoin if test results reach >5 times the upper limit of normal.

Adverse Reactions Virtually all patients experience some drug-related toxicity, especially headache, fever, weakness and fatigue. These adverse effects are seldom permanent or irreversible nor do they usually require therapy interruption

>10%:

Cardiovascular: Arrhythmias, flushing, hypotension, hypertension, peripheral edema, chest discomfort, edema

Central nervous system: Dizziness, anxiety, insomnia, depression, confusion, malaise, pain

Dermatologic: Burning, redness, cheilitis, inflammation of lips, dry skin, pruritus, photosensitivity

Endocrine & metabolic: Increased serum concentration of triglycerides

Gastrointestinal: GI hemorrhage, abdominal pain, other GI disorders, diarrhea, constipation, dyspepsia, abdominal distention, weight gain or loss, xerostomia

Hematologic: Hemorrhage, disseminated intravascular coagulation

Local: Phlebitis, injection site reactions

Neuromuscular & skeletal: Bone pain, arthralgia, myalgia, paresthesia

Ocular: Itching of eye

Renal: Renal insufficiency

Respiratory: Upper respiratory tract disorders, dyspnea, respiratory insufficiency, pleural effusion, pneumonia, rales, expiratory wheezing, dry nose

Miscellaneous: Infections, shivering

1% to 10%:

Cardiovascular: Cardiac failure, cardiac arrest, myocardial infarction, enlarged heart, heart murmur, ischemia, stroke, myocarditis, pericarditis, pulmonary hypertension, secondary cardiomyopathy, cerebral hemorrhage, pallor

Central nervous system: Intracranial hypertension, agitation, hallucination, agnosia, aphasia, cerebellar edema, cerebellar disorders, convulsions, coma, CNS depression, encephalopathy, hypotaxia, no light reflex, neurologic reaction, spinal cord disorder, unconsciousness, dementia, forgetfulness, somnolence, slow speech, hypothermia

Dermatologic: Skin peeling on hands or soles of feet, rash, cellulitis

Endocrine & metabolic: Fluid imbalance, acidosis

Gastrointestinal: Hepatosplenomegaly, ulcer

Genitourinary: Dysuria, polyuria, enlarged prostate

Hepatic: Ascites, hepatitis

Neuromuscular & skeletal: Tremor, leg weakness, hyporeflexia, dysarthria, facial paralysis, hemiplegia, flank pain, asterixis, abnormal gait

Ocular: Dry eyes, photophobia

Renal: Acute renal failure, renal tubular necrosis

Respiratory: Lower respiratory tract disorders, pulmonary infiltration, bronchial asthma, pulmonary/larynx edema, unspecified pulmonary disease

Miscellaneous: Face edema, lymph disorders

<1%: Mood changes, pseudomotor cerebri, alopecia, hyperuricemia, anorexia, nausea, vomiting, inflammatory bowel syndrome, bleeding of gums, increase in erythrocyte sedimentation rate, decrease in hemoglobin and hematocrit, conjunctivitis, corneal opacities, optic neuritis, cataracts

Overdosage/Toxicology The maximum tolerated dose in adult patients with myelodysplastic syndrome in solid tumors was 195 mg/m^2/day; the maximum tolerated dose in pediatric patients was lower at 60 mg/m^2/day. Overdosage with other retinoids has been associated with transient headache, facial flushing, cheilosis, abdominal pain, dizziness, and ataxia. These symptoms resolved quickly without residual effects.

Drug Interactions CYP3A3/4 enzyme substrate

Metabolized by the hepatic cytochrome P-450 system; therefore, all drugs that induce or inhibit this system would be expected to interact with tretinoin CYP2C9 substrate

Increased toxicity: Ketoconazole increases the mean plasma AUC of tretinoin

Mechanism of Action Retinoid that induces maturation of acute promyelocytic leukemia (APL) cells in cultures; induces cytodifferentiation and decreased proliferation of APL cells

Pharmacodynamics/Kinetics

Protein binding: >95%

Metabolism: In the liver via cytochrome P-450 enzymes

Half-life, terminal: Parent drug: 0.5-2 hours

Time to peak serum concentration: Within 1-2 hours

Elimination: Equally in urine and feces

Usual Dosage Oral:

Children: There are limited clinical data on the pediatric use of tretinoin. Of 15 pediatric patients (age range: 1-16 years) treated with tretinoin, the incidence of complete remission was 67%. Safety and efficacy in pediatric patients <1 year of age have not been established. Some pediatric patients experience severe headache and pseudotumor cerebri, requiring analgesic treatment and lumbar puncture for relief. Increased caution is recommended. Consider dose reduction in children experiencing serious or intolerable toxicity; however, the efficacy and safety of tretinoin at doses <45 mg/m^2/day have not been evaluated.

Adults: 45 mg/m^2/day administered as two evenly divided doses until complete remission is documented. Discontinue therapy 30 days after achievement of complete remission or after 90 days of treatment, whichever occurs first. If after initiation of treatment the presence of the t(15;17) translocation is not confirmed by cytogenetics or by polymerase chain reaction studies and the patient has not responded to tretinoin, consider alternative therapy.

Note: Tretinoin is for the induction of remission only. Optimal consolidation or maintenance regimens have not been determined. All patients should therefore receive a standard consolidation or maintenance chemotherapy regimen for APL after induction therapy with tretinoin unless otherwise contraindicated.

Dietary Considerations Absorption of retinoids has been shown to be enhanced when taken with food

Monitoring Parameters Monitor the patient's hematologic profile, coagulation profile, liver function test results and triglyceride and cholesterol levels frequently

Patient Information Avoid pregnancy during therapy; effective contraceptive measures must be used since this drug may harm the fetus; there is information from manufacturers about this product that you should receive; discontinue therapy if visual difficulties, abdominal pain, rectal bleeding, diarrhea; avoid use of other vitamin A products; decreased tolerance to contact lenses may occur; loss of night vision may occur, avoid prolonged exposure to sunlight

Dosage Forms Capsule: 10 mg

Tretinoin, Topical (TRET i noyn, TOP i kal)

U.S. Brand Names Avita®; Renova™; Retin-A™ Micro Topical; Retin-A™ Topical

Canadian Brand Names Retisol-A®; Stieva-A®; Stieva-A® Forte

Synonyms Retinoic Acid; trans-Retinoic Acid; Vitamin A Acid

(Continued)

Tretinoin, Topical *(Continued)*

Therapeutic Category Acne Products; Retinoic Acid Derivative; Vitamin A Derivative; Vitamin, Topical

Use Treatment of acne vulgaris, photodamaged skin, and some skin cancers

Pregnancy Risk Factor C

Pregnancy/Breast-Feeding Implications Clinical effects on the fetus: Oral tretinoin is teratogenic and fetotoxic in rats at doses 1000 and 500 times the topical human dose, respectively; however, tretinoin does not appear to be teratogenic when used topically since it is rapidly metabolized by the skin

Contraindications Hypersensitivity to tretinoin or any component; sunburn

Warnings/Precautions Use with caution in patients with eczema; avoid excessive exposure to sunlight and sunlamps; avoid contact with abraded skin, mucous membranes, eyes, mouth, angles of the nose

Adverse Reactions 1% to 10%:

Cardiovascular: Edema

Dermatologic: Excessive dryness, erythema, scaling of the skin, hyperpigmentation or hypopigmentation, photosensitivity, initial acne flare-up

Local: Stinging, blistering

Overdosage/Toxicology

Toxic signs of an overdose commonly respond to drug discontinuation, and generally return to normal spontaneously within a few days to weeks.

When confronted with signs of increased intracranial pressure, treatment with mannitol (0.25 g/kg I.V./dose repeated every 5 minutes as needed), dexamethasone (1.5 mg/kg I.V. load followed with 0.375 mg/kg every 6 hours for 5 days), and/or hyperventilation should be employed.

Drug Interactions CYP3A3/4 enzyme substrate

Increased toxicity: Sulfur, benzoyl peroxide, salicylic acid, resorcinol (potentiates adverse reactions seen with tretinoin)

Mechanism of Action Keratinocytes in the sebaceous follicle become less adherent which allows for easy removal; inhibits microcomedone formation and eliminates lesions already present

Pharmacodynamics/Kinetics

Absorption: Topical: Minimum absorption occurs

Metabolism: Of the small amount absorbed, metabolism occurs in the liver

Elimination: In bile and urine

Usual Dosage Children >12 years and Adults: Topical: Begin therapy with a weaker formulation of tretinoin (0.025% cream or 0.01% gel) and increase the concentration as tolerated; apply once daily before retiring or on alternate days; if stinging or irritation develop, decrease frequency of application

Patient Information Thoroughly wash hands after applying; avoid hydration of skin immediately before application; minimize exposure to sunlight; avoid washing face more frequently than 2-3 times/day; if severe irritation occurs, discontinue medication temporarily and adjust dose when irritation subsides; avoid using topical preparations with high alcoholic content during treatment period; do not exceed prescribed dose

Nursing Implications Observe for signs of hypersensitivity, blistering, excessive dryness; do not apply to mucous membranes

Dosage Forms

Cream:

Retin-A™: 0.025% (20 g, 45 g); 0.05% (20 g, 45 g); 0.1% (20 g, 45 g)

Avita®: 0.025% (20 g, 45 g)

Renova™: 0.05% emollient cream

Gel, topical:

Retin-A™: 0.01% (15 g, 45 g); 0.025% (15 g, 45 g)

Retin-A™ Micro: 0.1% (20 g, 45 g)

Liquid, topical (Retin-A™): 0.05% (28 mL)

♦ **Triacet™** *see* Triamcinolone *on this page*

♦ **Triacetyloleandomycin** *see* Troleandomycin *on page 1190*

♦ **Triacin-C®** *see* Triprolidine, Pseudoephedrine, and Codeine *on page 1188*

♦ **Triaconazole** *see* Terconazole *on page 1116*

♦ **Triadapin®** *see* Doxepin *on page 392*

♦ **Triam-A®** *see* Triamcinolone *on this page*

Triamcinolone *(trye am SIN oh lone)*

Related Information

Asthma, Guidelines for the Diagnosis and Management of *on page 1456*

Corticosteroids Comparison *on page 1319*

Estimated Clinical Comparability of Doses for Inhaled Corticosteroids *on page 1463*

U.S. Brand Names Amcort®; Aristocort®; Aristocort A; Aristocort® Forte; Aristocort® Intralesional; Aristospan® Intra-Articular; Aristospan® Intralesional; Atolone®; Azmacort™; Delta-Tritex®; Flutex®; Kenacort®; Kenaject-40®; Kenalog®; Kenalog-10®; Kenalog-40®; Kenalog® H; Kenalog® in Orabase®; Kenonel®; Nasacort®; Nasacort® AQ; Tac™-3; Tac™-40; Triacet™; Triam-A®; Triam Forte®; Triderm®; Tri-Kort®; Trilog®; Trilone®; Tristoject®

Synonyms Triamcinolone Acetonide, Aerosol; Triamcinolone Acetonide, Parenteral; Triamcinolone Diacetate, Oral; Triamcinolone Diacetate, Parenteral; Triamcinolone Hexacetonide; Triamcinolone, Oral

Therapeutic Category Anti-inflammatory Agent; Anti-inflammatory Agent, Inhalant; Corticosteroid, Inhalant; Corticosteroid, Intranasal; Corticosteroid, Systemic; Corticosteroid, Topical (Medium Potency); Corticosteroid, Topical (High Potency); Glucocorticoid

Use

Inhalation: Control of bronchial asthma and related bronchospastic conditions.

Systemic: Adrenocortical insufficiency, rheumatic disorders, allergic states, respiratory diseases, systemic lupus erythematosus, and other diseases requiring anti-inflammatory or immunosuppressive effects

Topical: Inflammatory dermatoses responsive to steroids

Pregnancy Risk Factor C

Pregnancy/Breast-Feeding Implications

Clinical effects on the fetus: No data on crossing the placenta or effect on fetus

Breast-feeding/lactation: No data on crossing into breast milk or clinical effects on the infant

Contraindications Known hypersensitivity to triamcinolone; systemic fungal infections; serious infections (except septic shock or tuberculous meningitis); primary treatment of status asthmaticus

Warnings/Precautions Fatalities have occurred due to adrenal insufficiency in asthmatic patients during and after transfer from systemic corticosteroids to aerosol steroids; several months may be required for recovery from this syndrome; during this period, aerosol steroids do **not** provide the increased systemic steroid requirement needed to treat patients having trauma, surgery or infections; avoid using higher than recommended dose

Use with caution in patients with hypothyroidism, cirrhosis, nonspecific ulcerative colitis and patients at increased risk for peptic ulcer disease; do not use occlusive dressings on weeping or exudative lesions and general caution with occlusive dressings should be observed; discontinue if skin irritation or contact dermatitis should occur; do not use in patients with decreased skin circulation; avoid the use of high potency steroids on the face

Because of the risk of adverse effects, systemic corticosteroids should be used cautiously in the elderly, in the smallest possible dose, and for the shortest possible time. Azmacort™ (metered dose inhaler) comes with its own spacer device attached and may be easier to use in older patients. Controlled clinical studies have shown that inhaled and intranasal corticosteroids may cause a reduction in growth velocity in pediatric patients. Growth velocity provides a means of comparing the rate of growth among children of the same age.

In studies involving inhaled corticosteroids, the average reduction in growth velocity was approximately 1 cm (about 1/3 of an inch) per year. It appears that the reduction is related to dose and how long the child takes the drug.

FDA's Pulmonary and Allergy Drugs and Metabolic and Endocrine Drugs advisory committees discussed this issue at a July 1998 meeting. They recommended that the agency develop class-wide labeling to inform healthcare providers so they would understand this potential side effect and monitor growth routinely in pediatric patients who are treated with inhaled corticosteroids, intranasal corticosteroids or both.

Long-term effects of this reduction in growth velocity on final adult height are unknown. Likewise, it also has not yet been determined whether patients' growth will "catch up" if treatment in discontinued. Drug manufacturers will continue to monitor these drugs to learn more about long-term effects. Children are prescribed inhaled corticosteroids to treat asthma. Intranasal corticosteroids are generally used to prevent and treat allergy-related nasal symptoms.

Patients are advised not to stop using their inhaled or intranasal corticosteroids without first speaking to their healthcare providers about the benefits of these drugs compared to their risks.

Adverse Reactions

>10%:

Central nervous system: Insomnia, nervousness

Gastrointestinal: Increased appetite, indigestion

1% to 10%:

Ocular: Cataracts

Endocrine & metabolic: Diabetes mellitus, hirsutism

Neuromuscular & skeletal: Arthralgia

Respiratory: Epistaxis

<1%: Fatigue, seizures, mood swings, headache, delirium, hallucinations, euphoria, itching, hypertrichosis, skin atrophy, hyperpigmentation, hypopigmentation, acne, bruising, amenorrhea, sodium and water retention, Cushing's syndrome, hyperglycemia, bone growth suppression, oral candidiasis, dry throat, xerostomia, peptic ulcer, abdominal distention, ulcerative esophagitis, pancreatitis, burning, osteoporosis, muscle wasting, hoarseness, wheezing, cough, hypersensitivity reactions

Overdosage/Toxicology When consumed in excessive quantities, systemic hypercorticism and adrenal suppression may occur, in those cases discontinuation and withdrawal of the corticosteroid should be done judiciously

Drug Interactions

Decreased effect: Barbiturates, phenytoin, rifampin ↑ metabolism of triamcinolone; vaccine and toxoid effects may be reduced

Increased toxicity: Salicylates may increase risk of GI ulceration

(Continued)

Triamcinolone *(Continued)*

Mechanism of Action Decreases inflammation by suppression of migration of polymorphonuclear leukocytes and reversal of increased capillary permeability; suppresses the immune system by reducing activity and volume of the lymphatic system; suppresses adrenal function at high doses

Pharmacodynamics/Kinetics
Duration of action: Oral: 8-12 hours
Absorption: Topical: Systemic absorption may occur
Time to peak: I.M.: Within 8-10 hours
Half-life, biologic: 18-36 hours

Usual Dosage In general, single I.M. dose of 4-7 times oral dose will control patient from 4-7 days up to 3-4 weeks

Children 6-12 years:
Oral inhalation: 1-2 inhalations 3-4 times/day, not to exceed 12 inhalations/day
I.M. (acetonide or hexacetonide): 0.03-0.2 mg/kg at 1- to 7-day intervals
Intra-articular, intrabursal, or tendon-sheath injection: 2.5-15 mg, repeated as needed
Children >12 years and Adults:
Intranasal: 2 sprays in each nostril once daily; may increase after 4-7 days up to 4 sprays once daily or 1 spray 4 times/day in each nostril
Topical: Apply a thin film 2-3 times/day
Oral: 4-48 mg/day
I.M. (acetonide or hexacetonide): 60 mg (of 40 mg/mL), additional 20-100 mg doses (usual: 40-80 mg) may be given when signs and symptoms recur, best at 6-week intervals to minimize HPA suppression
Intra-articular (hexacetonide): 2-20 mg every 3-4 weeks
Intralesional (diacetate or acetonide - use 10 mg/mL): 1 mg/injection site, may be repeated one or more times/week depending upon patient's response; maximum: 30 mg at any one time; may use multiple injections if there are more than 1 cm apart
Intra-articular, intrasynovial, and soft-tissue (diacetate or acetonide - use 10 mg/mL or 40 mg/mL) 2.5-40 mg depending upon location, size of joints, and degree of inflammation; repeat when signs and symptoms recur
Sublesionally (as acetonide): Up to 1 mg per injection site and may be repeated one or more times weekly; multiple sites may be injected if they are 1 cm or more apart, not to exceed 30 mg
See table.

Triamcinolone Dosing

	Acetonide	Diacetate	Hexacetonide
Intrasynovial	2.5-40 mg	5-40 mg	
Intralesional	2.5-40 mg	5-48 mg	Up to 0.5 mg/sq inch affected area
Sublesional	1-30 mg		
Systemic I.M.	2.5-60 mg/d	~40 mg/wk	20-100 mg
Intra-articular		5-40 mg	2-20 mg average
large joints	5-15 mg		10-20 mg
small joints	2.5-5 mg		2-6 mg
Tendon sheaths	10-40 mg		
Intradermal	1 mg/site		

Oral inhalation: 2 inhalations 3-4 times/day, not to exceed 16 inhalations/day

Patient Information
Inhaler: Rinse mouth and throat after use to prevent candidiasis
Topical: Apply sparingly to affected area, rub in until drug disappears, do not use on open skin
Report any change in body weight; do not discontinue or decrease the drug without contacting your physician; carry an identification card or bracelet advising that you are on steroids; may take with meals to decrease GI upset

Nursing Implications Once daily doses should be given in the morning; evaluate clinical response and mental status; may mask signs and symptoms of infection; inject I.M. dose deep in large muscle mass, avoid deltoid; avoid S.C. dose; a thin film is effective topically and avoid topical application on the face; do not occlude area unless directed

Additional Information 16 mg triamcinolone is equivalent to 100 mg cortisone (no mineralocorticoid activity)

Dosage Forms
Aerosol:
Oral inhalation: 100 mcg/metered spray (20 g)
Topical, as acetonide: 0.2 mg/2 second spray (23 g, 63 g)
Cream, as acetonide: 0.025% (15 g, 30 g, 60 g, 80 g, 120 g, 240 g); 0.1% (15 g, 20 g, 30 g, 60 g, 80 g, 90 g, 120 g, 240 g); 0.5% (15 g, 20 g, 30 g, 120 g, 240 g)
Injection, as acetonide: 3 mg/mL (5 mL); 10 mg/mL (5 mL); 40 mg/mL (1 mL, 5 mL, 10 mL)
Injection, as diacetate: 25 mg/mL (5 mL); 40 mg/mL (1 mL, 5 mL)
Injection, as hexacetonide: 5 mg/mL (5 mL); 20 mg/mL (1 mL, 5 mL)
Lotion, as acetonide: 0.025% (60 mL); 0.1% (15 mL, 60 mL)
Ointment, topical, as acetonide: 0.025% (15 g, 28 g, 30 g, 57 g, 80 g, 113 g, 240 g); 0.1% (15 g, 28 g, 57 g, 60 g, 80 g, 113 g, 240 g, 454 g); 0.5% (15 g, 28 g, 57 g, 113 g, 240 g)
Spray, intranasal acetonide: 55 mcg per actuation (100 sprays/canister) (15 mg canister)

Syrup: 4 mg/5 mL (120 mL)
Tablet: 1 mg, 2 mg, 4 mg, 8 mg

- ♦ **Triamcinolone Acetonide, Aerosol** *see* Triamcinolone *on page 1174*
- ♦ **Triamcinolone Acetonide, Parenteral** *see* Triamcinolone *on page 1174*
- ♦ **Triamcinolone and Nystatin** *see* Nystatin and Triamcinolone *on page 857*
- ♦ **Triamcinolone Diacetate, Oral** *see* Triamcinolone *on page 1174*
- ♦ **Triamcinolone Diacetate, Parenteral** *see* Triamcinolone *on page 1174*
- ♦ **Triamcinolone Hexacetonide** *see* Triamcinolone *on page 1174*
- ♦ **Triamcinolone, Oral** *see* Triamcinolone *on page 1174*
- ♦ **Triam Forte®** *see* Triamcinolone *on page 1174*
- ♦ **Triaminic® AM Decongestant Formula [OTC]** *see* Pseudoephedrine *on page 993*
- ♦ **Triaminic® Oral Infant Drops** *see* Pheniramine, Phenylpropanolamine, and Pyrilamine *on page 912*

Triamterene (trye AM ter een)

Related Information
Heart Failure: Management of Patients With Left-Ventricular Systolic Dysfunction *on page 1472*

U.S. Brand Names Dyrenium®

Therapeutic Category Antihypertensive Agent; Diuretic, Potassium Sparing

Use Alone or in combination with other diuretics to treat edema and hypertension; decreases potassium excretion caused by kaliuretic diuretics

Pregnancy Risk Factor B

Pregnancy/Breast-Feeding Implications
Clinical effects on the fetus: No data available. Generally, use of diuretics during pregnancy is avoided due to risk of decreased placental perfusion.
Breast-feeding/lactation: No data available

Contraindications Hyperkalemia, renal impairment, diabetes, hypersensitivity to triamterene or any component; do not administer to patients receiving spironolactone, amiloride, or potassium supplementation unless the patient has documented evidence of hypokalemia unresponsive to either agent alone

Warnings/Precautions Use with caution in patients with severe hepatic encephalopathy, patients with diabetes, renal dysfunction, a history of renal stones, or those receiving potassium supplements, potassium-containing medications, blood or ACE inhibitors

Adverse Reactions
1% to 10%:
Cardiovascular: Hypotension, edema, congestive heart failure, bradycardia
Central nervous system: Dizziness, headache, fatigue
Dermatologic: Rash
Gastrointestinal: Constipation, nausea
Respiratory: Dyspnea
<1%: Flushing, hyperkalemia, dehydration, hyponatremia, gynecomastia, hyperchloremic metabolic acidosis, postmenopausal bleeding, inability to achieve or maintain an erection

Overdosage/Toxicology
Symptoms of overdose include drowsiness, confusion, clinical signs of dehydration, electrolyte imbalance, and hypotension; chronic or acute ingestion of large amounts of potassium-sparing diuretics, may result in life-threatening hyperkalemia especially with decreased renal function.
If the EKG shows no widening of the QRS or an arrhythmia, discontinue triamterene and any potassium supplement and substitute a thiazide. Consider Kayexalate® to increase potassium excretion. If an abnormal cardiac status is obvious, treat with calcium or sodium bicarbonates as needed, pacing dialysis and/or Kayexalate®. Infusions of glucose and insulin are also useful.

Drug Interactions
Increased risk of hyperkalemia if given together with amiloride, spironolactone, angiotensin-converting enzyme (ACE) inhibitors; use of indomethacin may result in renal failure; avoid concurrent use if possible; cimetidine may increase bioavailability and decrease clearance of triamterene
Increased toxicity of amantadine (possibly by decreasing its renal excretion)

Mechanism of Action Interferes with potassium/sodium exchange (active transport) in the distal tubule, cortical collecting tubule and collecting duct by inhibiting sodium, potassium-ATPase; decreases calcium excretion; increases magnesium loss

Pharmacodynamics/Kinetics
Onset of action: Diuresis occurs within 2-4 hours
Duration: 7-9 hours
Absorption: Oral: Unreliable

Usual Dosage Adults: Oral: 100-300 mg/day in 1-2 divided doses; maximum dose: 300 mg/day
Dosing comments in renal impairment: Cl_{cr} <10 mL/minute: Avoid use
Dosing adjustment in hepatic impairment: Dose reduction is recommended in patients with cirrhosis

Monitoring Parameters Blood pressure, serum electrolytes (especially potassium), renal function, weight, I & O

Test Interactions Interferes with fluorometric assay of quinidine
(Continued)

Triamterene (Continued)

Patient Information Take in the morning; take the last dose of multiple doses no later than 6 PM unless instructed otherwise; take after meals; notify physician if weakness, headache or nausea occurs; avoid excessive ingestion of food high in potassium or use of salt substitute; may increase blood glucose; may impart a blue fluorescence color to urine

Nursing Implications Observe for hyperkalemia; assess weight and I & O daily to determine weight loss; if ordered once daily, dose should be given in the morning

Dosage Forms Capsule: 50 mg, 100 mg

♦ **Triapin®** see Butalbital Compound on page 165

♦ **Triavil®** see Amitriptyline and Perphenazine on page 64

Triazolam (trye AY zoe lam)

Related Information
Benzodiazepines Comparison on page 1310

U.S. Brand Names Halcion®

Canadian Brand Names Apo®-Triazo; Gen-Triazolam; Novo-Triolam; Nu-Triazo

Therapeutic Category Benzodiazepine; Hypnotic; Sedative

Use Short-term treatment of insomnia

Restrictions C-IV

Pregnancy Risk Factor X

Contraindications Hypersensitivity to triazolam, or any component, cross-sensitivity with other benzodiazepines may occur; severe uncontrolled pain; pre-existing CNS depression; narrow-angle glaucoma; not to be used in pregnancy or lactation

Warnings/Precautions May cause drug dependency; avoid abrupt discontinuance in patients with prolonged therapy or seizure disorders; not considered a drug of choice in the elderly

Adverse Reactions
>10%:
  Cardiovascular: Tachycardia, chest pain
  Central nervous system: Drowsiness, fatigue, ataxia, lightheadedness, memory impairment, insomnia, anxiety, depression, headache
  Dermatologic: Rash
  Endocrine & metabolic: Decreased libido
  Gastrointestinal: Xerostomia, decreased salivation, constipation, nausea, vomiting, diarrhea, increased or decreased appetite
  Neuromuscular & skeletal: Dysarthria
  Ocular: Blurred vision
  Miscellaneous: Diaphoresis
1% to 10%:
  Cardiovascular: Syncope, hypotension
  Central nervous system: Confusion, nervousness, dizziness, akathisia
  Dermatologic: Dermatitis
  Gastrointestinal: Weight gain or loss, increased salivation, muscle cramps
  Neuromuscular & skeletal: Rigidity, tremor
  Otic: Tinnitus
  Respiratory: Nasal congestion, hyperventilation
<1%: Menstrual irregularities, blood dyscrasias, reflex slowing, drug dependence

Overdosage/Toxicology
Symptoms of overdose include somnolence, confusion, coma, diminished reflexes, dyspnea, and hypotension
Treatment for benzodiazepine overdose is supportive. Rarely is mechanical ventilation required. Flumazenil has been shown to selectively block the binding of benzodiazepines to CNS receptors, resulting in a reversal of benzodiazepine-induced CNS depression but not always respiratory depression.

Drug Interactions CYP3A3/4 and 3A5-7 enzyme substrate

Decreased effect with phenytoin, phenobarbital
Increased effect/toxicity with CNS depressants, cimetidine, erythromycin, nefazodone

Mechanism of Action Depresses all levels of the CNS, including the limbic and reticular formation, probably through the increased action of gamma-aminobutyric acid (GABA), which is a major inhibitory neurotransmitter in the brain

Pharmacodynamics/Kinetics
Onset of hypnotic effect: Within 15-30 minutes
Duration: 6-7 hours
Distribution: V_d: 0.8-1.8 L/kg
Protein binding: 89%
Metabolism: Extensively in the liver
Half-life: 1.7-5 hours
Elimination: In urine as unchanged drug and metabolites

Usual Dosage Onset of action is rapid, patient should be in bed when taking medication
Oral:
  Children <18 years: Dosage not established
  Adults: 0.125-0.25 mg at bedtime
  Dosing adjustment/comments in hepatic impairment: Reduce dose or avoid use in cirrhosis

Dietary Considerations Alcohol: Additive CNS effect, avoid use

Monitoring Parameters Respiratory and cardiovascular status

Patient Information Avoid alcohol and other CNS depressants; avoid activities needing good psychomotor coordination until CNS effects are known; drug may cause physical or psychological dependence; avoid abrupt discontinuation after prolonged use

Nursing Implications Patients may require assistance with ambulation; lower doses in the elderly are usually effective; institute safety measures

Dosage Forms Tablet: 0.125 mg, 0.25 mg

♦ **Triban®** see Trimethobenzamide on page 1183

♦ **Tribavirin** see Ribavirin on page 1021

Trichlormethiazide (trye klor meth EYE a zide)

Related Information

Sulfonamide Derivatives on page 1337

U.S. Brand Names Metahydrin®; Naqua®

Therapeutic Category Antihypertensive Agent; Diuretic, Thiazide

Use Management of mild to moderate hypertension; treatment of edema in congestive heart failure and nephrotic syndrome

Pregnancy Risk Factor D

Contraindications Hypersensitivity to trichlormethiazide, other thiazides and sulfonamides, or any component

Warnings/Precautions Use with caution in renal disease, hepatic disease, gout, lupus erythematosus, diabetes mellitus; some products may contain tartrazine

Adverse Reactions

1% to 10%:

Endocrine & metabolic: Hypokalemia

Respiratory: Dyspnea (<5%)

<1%: Hypotension, photosensitivity, lichenoid dermatitis, fluid and electrolyte imbalances (hypocalcemia, hypomagnesemia, hyponatremia); hyperglycemia, rarely blood dyscrasias, prerenal azotemia

Overdosage/Toxicology

Symptoms of overdose include hypotension, dizziness, electrolyte abnormalities, lethargy, confusion, muscle weakness

Following GI decontamination, therapy is supportive with I.V. fluids, electrolytes, and I.V. pressors if needed; dialysis is unlikely to be effective

Drug Interactions

Decreased effect:

Thiazides may decrease the effect of anticoagulants, antigout agents, sulfonylureas Bile acid sequestrants, methenamine, and NSAIDs may decrease the effect of the thiazides

Increased effect: Thiazides may increase the toxicity of allopurinol, anesthetics, antineoplastics, calcium salts, diazoxide, digitalis, lithium, loop diuretics, methyldopa, nondepolarizing muscle relaxants, vitamin D; amphotericin B and anticholinergics may increase the toxicity of thiazides

Mechanism of Action The diuretic mechanism of action of the thiazides is primarily inhibition of sodium, chloride, and water reabsorption in the renal distal tubules, thereby producing diuresis with a resultant reduction in plasma volume. The antihypertensive mechanism of action of the thiazides is unknown. It is known that doses of thiazides produce greater reduction in blood pressure than equivalent diuretic doses of loop diuretics. There has been speculation that the thiazides may have some influence on vascular tone mediated through sodium depletion, but this remains to be proven.

Pharmacodynamics/Kinetics

Onset of of diuretic effect: Within 2 hours

Peak: 4 hours

Duration: 12-24 hours

Usual Dosage Adults: Oral: 1-4 mg/day; initially doses may be given twice daily

Dosing adjustment in renal impairment: Reduced dosage is necessary

Test Interactions ↑ ammonia (B), ↑ amylase (S), ↑ calcium (S), ↑ chloride (S), ↑ cholesterol (S), ↑ glucose, ↑ uric acid (S); ↓ chloride (S), ↓ magnesium, ↓ potassium (S), ↓ sodium (S)

Patient Information May be taken with food or milk; take early in day to avoid nocturia; take the last dose of multiple doses no later than 6 PM unless instructed otherwise. A few people who take this medication become more sensitive to sunlight and may experience skin rash, redness, itching, or severe sunburn, especially if sun block SPF ≥15 is not used on exposed skin areas.

Nursing Implications Assess weight, I & O reports daily to determine fluid loss; take blood pressure with patient lying down and standing

Dosage Forms Tablet: 2 mg, 4 mg

♦ **Trichloroacetaldehyde Monohydrate** see Chloral Hydrate on page 235

♦ **TriCor™** see Fenofibrate on page 472

♦ **Tricosal®** see Choline Magnesium Trisalicylate on page 254

♦ **Tri-Cyclen®** see Ethinyl Estradiol and Norgestimate on page 453

♦ **Triderm®** see Triamcinolone on page 1174

♦ **Tridesilon® Topical** see Desonide on page 335

♦ **Tridil® Injection** see Nitroglycerin on page 845

Trientine (TRYE en teen)

Replaces Cuprid®

U.S. Brand Names Syprine®

(Continued)

Trientine *(Continued)*

Synonyms Trientine Hydrochloride

Therapeutic Category Antidote, Copper Toxicity; Chelating Agent, Oral

Use Treatment of Wilson's disease in patients intolerant to penicillamine

Pregnancy Risk Factor C

Contraindications Rheumatoid arthritis, biliary cirrhosis, cystinuria, known hypersensitivity to trientine

Warnings/Precautions May cause iron deficiency anemia; monitor closely; use with caution in patients with reactive airway disease

Adverse Reactions Percentage unknown: Malaise, iron deficiency, heartburn, epigastric pain, anemia, tenderness, thickening and fissuring of skin, muscle cramps, systemic lupus erythematosus (SLE)

Overdosage/Toxicology
Overdosage is unknown; a single 30 g ingestion resulted in no toxicity
Following GI decontamination, treatment is supportive

Drug Interactions Decreased effect with iron and possibly other mineral supplements

Mechanism of Action Trientine hydrochloride is an oral chelating agent structurally dissimilar from penicillamine and other available chelating agents; an effective oral chelator of copper used to induce adequate cupriuresis

Usual Dosage Oral (administer on an empty stomach):
Children <12 years: 500-750 mg/day in divided doses 2-4 times/day; maximum: 1.5 g/day
Adults: 750-1250 mg/day in divided doses 2-4 times/day; maximum dose: 2 g/day

Patient Information Take 1 hour before or 2 hours after meals and at least 1 hour apart from any drug, food, or milk; do not chew capsule, swallow whole followed by a full glass of water; notify physician of any fever or skin changes; any skin exposed to the contents of a capsule should be promptly washed with water

Dosage Forms Capsule, as hydrochloride: 250 mg

♦ **Trientine Hydrochloride** *see Trientine on previous page*

Triethanolamine Polypeptide Oleate-Condensate
(trye eth a NOLE a meen pol i PEP tide OH lee ate-KON den sate)

U.S. Brand Names Cerumenex® Otic

Therapeutic Category Otic Agent, Cerumenolytic

Use Removal of ear wax (cerumen)

Pregnancy Risk Factor C

Contraindications Perforated tympanic membrane or otitis media, hypersensitivity to product or any component

Warnings/Precautions Avoid undue exposure to peridural skin during administration and the flushing out of ear canal; discontinue if sensitization or irritation occurs

Adverse Reactions <1%: Mild erythema and pruritus, severe eczematoid reactions, localized dermatitis

Mechanism of Action Emulsifies and disperses accumulated cerumen

Pharmacodynamics/Kinetics Onset of effect: Produces slight disintegration of very hard ear wax by 24 hours

Usual Dosage Children and Adults: Otic: Fill ear canal, insert cotton plug; allow to remain 15-30 minutes; flush ear with lukewarm water as a single treatment; if a second application is needed for unusually hard impactions, repeat the procedure

Monitoring Parameters Evaluate hearing before and after instillation of medication

Patient Information For external use in the ear only; warm to body temperature before using to improve effect; avoid touching dropper to any surface; hold ear lobe up and back; lie on your side or tilt the affected ear up for ease of administration; fill ear canal, let stand for 15-30 minutes, then flush

Nursing Implications Warm solution to body temperature before using; avoid undue exposure of the drug to the periauricular skin

Dosage Forms Solution, otic: 6 mL, 12 mL

♦ **Triethylenethiophosphoramide** *see Thiotepa on page 1136*

♦ **Trifed-C®** *see Triprolidine, Pseudoephedrine, and Codeine on page 1188*

Trifluoperazine *(trye floo oh PER a zeen)*

Related Information
Antipsychotic Agents Comparison *on page 1305*

U.S. Brand Names Stelazine®

Synonyms Trifluoperazine Hydrochloride

Therapeutic Category Antianxiety Agent; Antipsychotic Agent; Phenothiazine Derivative

Use Treatment of psychoses and management of nonpsychotic anxiety

Pregnancy Risk Factor C

Contraindications Hypersensitivity to trifluoperazine or any component, cross-sensitivity with other phenothiazines may exist, coma, circulatory collapse, history of blood dyscrasias

Warnings/Precautions Safety in children <6 months of age has not been established; use with caution in patients with cardiovascular disease, seizures, hepatic dysfunction, narrow-angle glaucoma, or bone marrow suppression; watch for hypotension when administering I.M. or I.V.; use with caution in patients with myasthenia gravis or Parkinson's disease

Adverse Reactions

>10%:

Cardiovascular: Hypotension, orthostatic hypotension

Central nervous system: Pseudoparkinsonism, akathisia, dystonias, tardive dyskinesia (persistent), dizziness

Gastrointestinal: Constipation

Ocular: Pigmentary retinopathy

Respiratory: Nasal congestion

Miscellaneous: Diaphoresis (decreased)

1% to 10%:

Dermatologic: Increased sensitivity to sun, rash

Endocrine & metabolic: Changes in menstrual cycle, changes in libido, breast pain

Gastrointestinal: Weight gain, nausea, vomiting, stomach pain

Genitourinary: Dysuria, ejaculatory disturbances

Neuromuscular & skeletal: Trembling of fingers

<1%: Neuroleptic malignant syndrome (NMS), impairment of temperature regulation, lowering of seizures threshold, discoloration of skin (blue-gray), galactorrhea, priapism, agranulocytosis, leukopenia, cholestatic jaundice, hepatotoxicity, cornea and lens changes

Overdosage/Toxicology

Symptoms of overdose include deep sleep, coma, extrapyramidal symptoms, abnormal involuntary muscle movements, hypo- or hypertension, cardiac arrhythmias

Following initiation of essential overdose management, toxic symptom treatment and supportive treatment should be initiated. Hypotension usually responds to I.V. fluids or Trendelenburg positioning. If unresponsive to these measures, the use of a parenteral inotrope may be required (eg, norepinephrine 0.1-0.2 mcg/kg/minute titrated to response). Seizures commonly respond to diazepam (I.V. 5-10 mg bolus in adults every 15 minutes if needed up to a total of 30 mg; I.V. 0.25-0.4 mg/kg/dose up to a total of 10 mg in children) or to phenytoin or phenobarbital. Neuroleptics often cause extrapyramidal symptoms (eg, dystonic reactions) requiring management with diphenhydramine 1-2 mg/kg (adults) up to a maximum of 50 mg I.M. or I.V. slow push followed by a maintenance dose for 48-72 hours. When these reactions are unresponsive to diphenhydramine, benztropine mesylate I.V. 1-2 mg (adults) may be effective. These agents are generally effective within 2-5 minutes. Cardiac arrhythmias are treated with lidocaine 1-2 mg/kg bolus followed by a maintenance infusion.

Drug Interactions CYP1A2 enzyme substrate

Decreased effect of anticonvulsants (increases requirements), guanethidine, anticoagulants; decreased effect with anticholinergics

Increased effect/toxicity with CNS depressants, metrizamide (increases seizures), propranolol, lithium (rare encephalopathy)

Stability Store injection at room temperature; protect from heat and from freezing; use only clear or slightly yellow solutions

Mechanism of Action Blocks postsynaptic mesolimbic dopaminergic receptors in the brain; exhibits a strong alpha-adrenergic blocking effect and depresses the release of hypothalamic and hypophyseal hormones

Pharmacodynamics/Kinetics

Metabolism: Extensive in the liver

Half-life: >24 hours with chronic use

Usual Dosage

Children 6-12 years: Psychoses:

Oral: Hospitalized or well supervised patients: Initial: 1 mg 1-2 times/day, gradually increase until symptoms are controlled or adverse effects become troublesome; maximum: 15 mg/day

I.M.: 1 mg twice daily

Adults:

Psychoses:

Outpatients: Oral: 1-2 mg twice daily

Hospitalized or well supervised patients: Initial: 2-5 mg twice daily with optimum response in the 15-20 mg/day range; do not exceed 40 mg/day

I.M.: 1-2 mg every 4-6 hours as needed up to 10 mg/24 hours maximum

Nonpsychotic anxiety: Oral: 1-2 mg twice daily; maximum: 6 mg/day; therapy for anxiety should not exceed 12 weeks; do not exceed 6 mg/day for longer than 12 weeks when treating anxiety; agitation, jitteriness, or insomnia may be confused with original neurotic or psychotic symptoms

Hemodialysis: Not dialyzable (0% to 5%)

Administration Administer I.M. injection deep in upper outer quadrant of buttock

Reference Range Therapeutic response and blood levels have not been established

Test Interactions ↑ cholesterol (S), ↑ glucose; ↓ uric acid (S)

Patient Information This drug usually requires several weeks for a full therapeutic response to be seen. Avoid excessive exposure to sunlight tanning lamps; concentrate must be diluted in 2-4 oz of liquid (water, carbonated drinks, fruit juices, tomato juice, milk, or pudding); wash hands if undiluted concentrate is spilled on skin to prevent contact dermatosis

Nursing Implications Watch for hypotension when administering I.M. or I.V.; observe for extrapyramidal effects

Dosage Forms

Concentrate, oral, as hydrochloride: 10 mg/mL (60 mL)

Injection, as hydrochloride: 2 mg/mL (10 mL)

Tablet, as hydrochloride: 1 mg, 2 mg, 5 mg, 10 mg

♦ **Trifluoperazine Hydrochloride** *see* Trifluoperazine *on page 1180*
♦ **Trifluorothymidine** *see* Trifluridine *on this page*

Trifluridine (trye FLURE i deen)
U.S. Brand Names Viroptic® Ophthalmic
Synonyms F_3T; Trifluorothymidine
Therapeutic Category Antiviral Agent, Ophthalmic
Use Treatment of primary keratoconjunctivitis and recurrent epithelial keratitis caused by herpes simplex virus types I and II
Pregnancy Risk Factor C
Contraindications Known hypersensitivity to trifluridine or any component
Warnings/Precautions Mild local irritation of conjunctival and cornea may occur when instilled but usually transient effects
Adverse Reactions
  1% to 10%: Local: Burning, stinging
  <1%: Hyperemia, palpebral edema, epithelial keratopathy, keratitis, stromal edema, increased intraocular pressure, hypersensitivity reactions
Stability Refrigerate at 2°C to 8°C (36°F to 46°F); storage at room temperature may result in a solution altered pH which could result in ocular discomfort upon administration and/or decreased potency
Mechanism of Action Interferes with viral replication by incorporating into viral DNA in place of thymidine, inhibiting thymidylate synthetase resulting in the formation of defective proteins
Pharmacodynamics/Kinetics Absorption: Ophthalmic instillation: Systemic absorption is negligible, while corneal penetration is adequate
Usual Dosage Adults: Instill 1 drop into affected eye every 2 hours while awake, to a maximum of 9 drops/day, until re-epithelialization of corneal ulcer occurs; then use 1 drop every 4 hours for another 7 days; do **not** exceed 21 days of treatment; if improvement has not taken place in 7-14 days, consider another form of therapy
Patient Information Notify physician if improvement is not seen after 7 days, condition worsens, or if irritation occurs; do not discontinue without notifying the physician, do not exceed recommended dosage
Dosage Forms Solution, ophthalmic: 1% (7.5 mL)

♦ **Trihexy®** *see* Trihexyphenidyl *on this page*
♦ **Trihexyphen®** *see* Trihexyphenidyl *on this page*

Trihexyphenidyl (trye heks ee FEN i dil)
U.S. Brand Names Artane®; Trihexy®
Canadian Brand Names Apo®-Trihex; Novo-Hexidyl; PMS-Trihexyphenidyl; Trihexyphen®
Synonyms Benzhexol Hydrochloride; Trihexyphenidyl Hydrochloride
Therapeutic Category Anticholinergic Agent; Anti-Parkinson's Agent
Use Adjunctive treatment of Parkinson's disease; also used in treatment of drug-induced extrapyramidal effects and acute dystonic reactions
Pregnancy Risk Factor C
Contraindications Hypersensitivity to trihexyphenidyl or any component, patients with narrow-angle glaucoma; pyloric or duodenal obstruction, stenosing peptic ulcers; bladder neck obstructions; achalasia; myasthenia gravis
Warnings/Precautions Use with caution in hot weather or during exercise. Elderly patients require strict dosage regulation. Use with caution in patients with tachycardia, cardiac arrhythmias, hypertension, hypotension, prostatic hypertrophy or any tendency toward urinary retention, liver or kidney disorders, and obstructive disease of the GI or GU tract. May exacerbate mental symptoms when used to treat extrapyramidal reactions When given in large doses or to susceptible patients, may cause weakness.
Adverse Reactions
  >10%:
    Dermatologic: Dry skin
    Gastrointestinal: Constipation, xerostomia, dry throat
    Respiratory: Dry nose
    Miscellaneous: Diaphoresis (decreased)
  1% to 10%:
    Dermatologic: Increased sensitivity to light
    Endocrine & metabolic: Decreased flow of breast milk
    Gastrointestinal: Dysphagia
  <1%: Orthostatic hypotension, ventricular fibrillation, tachycardia, palpitations, confusion, drowsiness, headache, loss of memory, fatigue, ataxia, rash, bloated feeling, nausea, vomiting, dysuria, weakness, increased intraocular pain, blurred vision
Overdosage/Toxicology
  Symptoms of overdose include blurred vision, urinary retention, tachycardia
  Anticholinergic toxicity is caused by strong binding of the drug to cholinergic receptors. Anticholinesterase inhibitors reduce acetylcholinesterase; for anticholinergic overdose with severe life-threatening symptoms, physostigmine 1-2 mg (0.5 mg or 0.02 mg/kg for children) S.C. or I.V., slowly may be given to reverse these effects
Drug Interactions
  Decreased effect of levodopa
  Increased toxicity with narcotic analgesics, phenothiazines, TCAs, quinidine, levodopa; anticholinergics

Mechanism of Action Thought to act by blocking excess acetylcholine at cerebral synapses; many of its effects are due to its pharmacologic similarities with atropine

Pharmacodynamics/Kinetics
Peak effect: Within 1 hour
Half-life: 3.3-4.1 hours
Time to peak serum concentration: Within 1-1.5 hours
Elimination: Primarily in urine

Usual Dosage Adults: Oral: Initial: 1-2 mg/day, increase by 2 mg increments at intervals of 3-5 days; usual dose: 5-15 mg/day in 3-4 divided doses

Dietary Considerations Alcohol: Additive CNS effect, avoid use

Monitoring Parameters IOP monitoring and gonioscopic evaluations should be performed periodically

Patient Information Take after meals or with food if GI upset occurs; do not discontinue drug abruptly; notify physician if adverse GI effects, rapid or pounding heartbeat, confusion, eye pain, rash, fever or heat intolerance occurs. Observe caution when performing hazardous tasks or those that require alertness such as driving, as may cause drowsiness. Avoid alcohol and other CNS depressants. May cause dry mouth - adequate fluid intake or hard sugar free candy may relieve. Difficult urination or constipation may occur - notify physician if effects persist; may increase susceptibility to heat stroke.

Nursing Implications Tolerated best if given in 3 daily doses and with food; high doses may be divided into 4 doses, at meal times and at bedtime; patients may be switched to sustained-action capsules when stabilized on conventional dosage forms

Dosage Forms
Capsule, as hydrochloride, sustained release: 5 mg
Elixir, as hydrochloride: 2 mg/5 mL (480 mL)
Tablet, as hydrochloride: 2 mg, 5 mg

◆ **Trihexyphenidyl Hydrochloride** *see* Trihexyphenidyl *on previous page*

◆ **TriHIBit®** *see* Diphtheria, Tetanus Toxoids, and Acellular Pertussis Vaccine *on page 373*

◆ **TriHIBIT®** *see* Haemophilus b Conjugate Vaccine *on page 554*

◆ **Tri-Immunol®** *see* Diphtheria, Tetanus Toxoids, and Whole-Cell Pertussis Vaccine, Adsorbed *on page 374*

◆ **Tri-K®** *see* Potassium Acetate, Potassium Bicarbonate, and Potassium Citrate *on page 947*

◆ **Tri-Kort®** *see* Triamcinolone *on page 1174*

◆ **Trilafon®** *see* Perphenazine *on page 909*

◆ **Tri-Levlen®** *see* Ethinyl Estradiol and Levonorgestrel *on page 449*

◆ **Trilisate®** *see* Choline Magnesium Trisalicylate *on page 254*

◆ **Trilog®** *see* Triamcinolone *on page 1174*

◆ **Trilone®** *see* Triamcinolone *on page 1174*

◆ **Trimazide®** *see* Trimethobenzamide *on this page*

Trimethobenzamide (trye meth oh BEN za mide)

U.S. Brand Names Arrestin®; Pediatric Triban®; Tebamide®; T-Gen®; Ticon®; Tigan®; Triban®; Trimazide®

Synonyms Trimethobenzamide Hydrochloride

Therapeutic Category Antiemetic

Use Control of nausea and vomiting (especially for long-term antiemetic therapy); less effective than phenothiazines but may be associated with fewer side effects

Pregnancy Risk Factor C

Contraindications Hypersensitivity to trimethobenzamide, benzocaine, or any component; injection contraindicated in children and suppositories are contraindicated in premature infants or neonates

Warnings/Precautions May mask emesis due to Reye's syndrome or mimic CNS effects of Reye's syndrome in patients with emesis of other etiologies; use in patients with acute vomiting should be avoided

Adverse Reactions
>10%: Central nervous system: Drowsiness
1% to 10%:
Cardiovascular: Hypotension
Central nervous system: Dizziness, headache
Gastrointestinal: Diarrhea
Neuromuscular & skeletal: Muscle cramps
<1%: Mental depression, convulsions, opisthotonus, hypersensitivity skin reactions, blood dyscrasias, hepatic impairment

Overdosage/Toxicology
Symptoms of overdose include hypotension, seizures, CNS depression, cardiac arrhythmias, disorientation, confusion

Following initiation of essential overdose management, toxic symptom treatment and supportive treatment should be initiated. Hypotension usually responds to I.V. fluids or Trendelenburg positioning. If unresponsive to these measures, the use of a parenteral inotrope may be required (eg, norepinephrine 0.1-0.2 mcg/kg/minute titrated to response). Seizures commonly respond to diazepam (I.V. 5-10 mg bolus in adults every 15 minutes, if needed, up to a total of 30 mg; I.V. 0.25-0.4 mg/kg/dose up to a total of 10 mg in children) or to phenytoin or phenobarbital. Critical cardiac arrhythmias often respond to lidocaine 1-2 mg/kg bolus followed by a maintenance infusion. Extrapyramidal symptoms (eg, dystonic reactions) may be managed with diphenhydramine 1-2 mg/kg (adults) up to a maximum of 50 mg I.M. or I.V. slow push followed by a (Continued)

Trimethobenzamide *(Continued)*

maintenance dose for 48-72 hours. When these reactions are unresponsive to diphenhydramine, benztropine mesylate I.V. 1-2 mg (adults) may be effective. These agents are generally effective within 2-5 minutes.

Drug Interactions Antagonism of oral anticoagulants may occur

Stability Store injection at room temperature; protect from heat and from freezing; use only clear solutions

Mechanism of Action Acts centrally to inhibit the medullary chemoreceptor trigger zone

Pharmacodynamics/Kinetics
Onset of antiemetic effect: Oral: Within 10-40 minutes; I.M.: Within 15-35 minutes
Duration: 3-4 hours
Absorption: Rectal: ~60%

Usual Dosage Rectal use is contraindicated in neonates and premature infants
Children:
Rectal: <14 kg: 100 mg 3-4 times/day
Oral, rectal: 14-40 kg: 100-200 mg 3-4 times/day
Adults:
Oral: 250 mg 3-4 times/day
I.M., rectal: 200 mg 3-4 times/day

Patient Information May cause drowsiness, impair judgment and coordination; report any restlessness or involuntary movements to physician

Nursing Implications Use only clear solution; observe for extrapyramidal and anticholinergic effects

Dosage Forms
Capsule, as hydrochloride: 100 mg, 250 mg
Injection, as hydrochloride: 100 mg/mL (2 mL, 20 mL)
Suppository, rectal, as hydrochloride: 100 mg, 200 mg

♦ **Trimethobenzamide Hydrochloride** *see* Trimethobenzamide *on previous page*

Trimethoprim *(trye METH oh prim)*

U.S. Brand Names Proloprim®; Trimpex®

Synonyms TMP

Therapeutic Category Antibiotic, Miscellaneous

Use Treatment of urinary tract infections due to susceptible strains of *E. coli, P. mirabilis, K. pneumoniae, Enterobacter* sp and coagulase-negative *Staphylococcus* including *S. saprophyticus;* acute otitis media in children; acute exacerbations of chronic bronchitis in adults; in combination with other agents for treatment of toxoplasmosis, *Pneumocystis carinii;* treatment of superficial ocular infections involving the conjunctiva and cornea

Pregnancy Risk Factor C

Contraindications Hypersensitivity to trimethoprim or any component, megaloblastic anemia due to folate deficiency

Warnings/Precautions Use with caution in patients with impaired renal or hepatic function or with possible folate deficiency

Adverse Reactions
1% to 10%:
Dermatologic: Rash (3% to 7%), pruritus
Hematologic: Megaloblastic anemia (with chronic high doses)
<1%: Fever, exfoliative dermatitis, nausea, vomiting, epigastric distress, thrombocytopenia, neutropenia, leukopenia, hyperkalemia, cholestatic jaundice, increased LFTs, elevated BUN/serum creatinine

Overdosage/Toxicology
Symptoms of acute toxicity includes: nausea, vomiting, confusion, dizziness; chronic overdose results in bone marrow suppression
Treatment of acute overdose is supportive following GI decontamination; treatment of chronic overdose is use of oral leucovorin 5-15 mg/day

Drug Interactions Increased effect/toxicity/levels of phenytoin; increased myelosuppression with methotrexate; may increase levels of digoxin

Mechanism of Action Inhibits folic acid reduction to tetrahydrofolate, and thereby inhibits microbial growth

Pharmacodynamics/Kinetics
Absorption: Oral: Readily and extensive
Protein binding: 42% to 46%
Metabolism: Partially in the liver
Half-life: 8-14 hours, prolonged with renal impairment
Time to peak serum concentration: Within 1-4 hours
Elimination: Significantly in urine (60% to 80% as unchanged drug)

Usual Dosage Oral:
Children: 4 mg/kg/day in divided doses every 12 hours
Adults: 100 mg every 12 hours or 200 mg every 24 hours; in the treatment of *Pneumocystis carinii* pneumonia; dose may be as high as 15-20 mg/kg/day in 3-4 divided doses
Dosing interval in renal impairment: Cl_cr 15-30 mL/minute: Administer 50 mg every 12 hours
Hemodialysis: Moderately dialyzable (20% to 50%)

Reference Range Therapeutic: Peak: 5-15 mg/L; Trough: 2-8 mg/L

Patient Information Take with milk or food; report any skin rash, persistent or severe fatigue, fever, sore throat, or unusual bleeding or bruising; complete full course of therapy

Dosage Forms Tablet: 100 mg, 200 mg

Trimethoprim and Polymyxin B (trye METH oh prim & pol i MIKS in bee)

U.S. Brand Names Polytrim® Ophthalmic

Therapeutic Category Antibiotic, Ophthalmic

Dosage Forms Solution, ophthalmic: Trimethoprim sulfate 1 mg and polymyxin B sulfate 10,000 units per mL (10 mL)

♦ **Trimethoprim and Sulfamethoxazole** see Co-Trimoxazole on page 299

♦ **Trimethylpsoralen** see Trioxsalen on page 1187

Trimetrexate Glucuronate (tri me TREKS ate gloo KYOOR oh nate)

Related Information

Toxicities of Chemotherapeutic Agents on page 1288

U.S. Brand Names Neutrexin® Injection

Therapeutic Category Antineoplastic Agent, Folate Antagonist

Use Alternative therapy for the treatment of moderate-to-severe *Pneumocystis carinii* pneumonia (PCP) in immunocompromised patients, including patients with acquired immunodeficiency syndrome (AIDS), who are intolerant of, or are refractory to, co-trimoxazole therapy or for whom co-trimoxazole and pentamidine are contraindicated. **Concurrent folinic acid (leucovorin) must always be administered.**

Pregnancy Risk Factor D

Contraindications Previous hypersensitivity to trimetrexate or methotrexate, severe existing myelosuppression

Warnings/Precautions Must be administered with concurrent leucovorin to avoid potentially serious or life-threatening toxicities; leucovorin therapy must extend for 72 hours past the last dose of trimetrexate; use with caution in patients with mild myelosuppression, severe hepatic or renal dysfunction, hypoproteinemia, hypoalbuminemia, or previous extensive myelosuppressive therapies

Adverse Reactions 1% to 10%:

Central nervous system: Seizures, fever

Dermatologic: Rash

Gastrointestinal: Stomatitis, nausea, vomiting

Hematologic: Neutropenia, thrombocytopenia, anemia

Hepatic: Elevated LFTs

Neuromuscular & skeletal: Peripheral neuropathy

Renal: Increased serum creatinine

Miscellaneous: Flu-like illness, hypersensitivity reactions

Drug Interactions

Decreased effect of pneumococcal vaccine

Increased toxicity (infection rates) of yellow fever vaccine

Stability Reconstituted I.V. solution is stable for 24 hours at room temperature or 7 days when refrigerated; intact vials should be refrigerated at 2°C to 8°C

Mechanism of Action Exerts an antimicrobial effect through potent inhibition of the enzyme dihydrofolate reductase (DHFR)

Pharmacodynamics/Kinetics

Distribution: V_d: 0.62 L/kg

Metabolism: Extensive in the liver

Half-life: 15-17 hours

Usual Dosage Adults: I.V.: 45 mg/m² once daily over 60 minutes for 21 days; it is necessary to reduce the dose in patients with liver dysfunction, although no specific recommendations exist; concurrent folinic acid 20 mg/m² every 6 hours orally or I.V. for 24 days

Administration Reconstituted solution should be filtered (0.22 μM) prior to further dilution; final solution should be clear, hue will range from colorless to pale yellow; trimetrexate forms a precipitate instantly upon contact with chloride ion or leucovorin, therefore it should not be added to solutions containing sodium chloride or other anions; trimetrexate and leucovorin solutions **must** be administered separately; intravenous lines should be flushed with at least 10 mL of D₅W between trimetrexate and leucovorin

Monitoring Parameters Check and record patient's temperature daily; absolute neutrophil counts (ANC), platelet count, renal function tests (serum creatinine, BUN), hepatic function tests (ALT, AST, alkaline phosphatase)

Patient Information Report promptly any fever, rash, flu-like symptoms, numbness or tingling in the extremities, nausea, vomiting, abdominal pain, mouth sores, increased bruising or bleeding, black tarry stools

Nursing Implications Notify primary physician if there is fever ≥103°F, generalized rash, seizures, bleeding from any site, uncontrolled nausea/vomiting; laboratory abnormalities which warrant dose modification; any other clinical adverse event or laboratory abnormality occurring in therapy which is judged as serious for that patient or which causes unexplained effects or concern; initiate "Bleeding Precautions" for platelet counts ≤50,000/mm³; initiate "Infection Control Measures" for absolute neutrophil counts (ANC) ≤1000/mm³

Must administer folinic acid 20 mg/m² orally or I.V. every 6 hours for 24 days

Additional Information Not a vesicant; methotrexate derivative

Dosage Forms Powder for injection: 25 mg

Trimipramine (trye MI pra meen)

Related Information
Antidepressant Agents Comparison *on page 1301*
U.S. Brand Names Surmontil®
Canadian Brand Names Apo®-Trimip; Novo-Tripramine; Nu-Trimipramine; Rhotrimine®
Synonyms Trimipramine Maleate
Therapeutic Category Antidepressant, Tricyclic
Use Treatment of various forms of depression, often in conjunction with psychotherapy
Pregnancy Risk Factor C
Contraindications Narrow-angle glaucoma; avoid use during pregnancy and lactation
Warnings/Precautions Use with caution in patients with cardiovascular disease, conduction disturbances, seizure disorders, urinary retention, hyperthyroidism or those receiving thyroid replacement; avoid use during lactation; use with caution in pregnancy; do not discontinue abruptly in patients receiving chronic high-dose therapy

Adverse Reactions
>10%:
Central nervous system: Dizziness, drowsiness, headache
Gastrointestinal: Xerostomia, constipation, increased appetite, nausea, unpleasant taste, weight gain
Neuromuscular & skeletal: Weakness
1% to 10%:
Cardiovascular: Arrhythmias, hypotension
Central nervous system: Confusion, delirium, hallucinations, nervousness, restlessness, parkinsonian syndrome, insomnia
Endocrine & metabolic: Sexual dysfunction
Gastrointestinal: Diarrhea, heartburn
Genitourinary: Dysuria
Neuromuscular & skeletal: Fine muscle tremors
Ocular: Blurred vision, eye pain
Miscellaneous: Diaphoresis (excessive)
<1%: Anxiety, seizures, alopecia, photosensitivity, breast enlargement, galactorrhea, SIADH, trouble with gums, decreased lower esophageal sphincter tone may cause GE reflux, testicular edema, agranulocytosis, leukopenia, eosinophilia, cholestatic jaundice, increased liver enzymes, increased intraocular pressure, tinnitus, allergic reactions

Overdosage/Toxicology
Symptoms of overdose include agitation, confusion, hallucinations, urinary retention, hypothermia, hypotension, tachycardia, cardiac arrhythmias
Following initiation of essential overdose management, toxic symptoms should be treated. Sodium bicarbonate is indicated when QRS interval is >0.10 seconds or QT_c >0.42 seconds. Ventricular arrhythmias and EKG changes (QRS widening) often respond to systemic alkalinization (sodium bicarbonate 0.5-2 mEq/kg I.V.). Arrhythmias unresponsive to this therapy may respond to lidocaine 1 mg/kg I.V. followed by a titrated infusion. Physostigmine (1-2 mg I.V. slowly for adults or 0.5 mg I.V. slowly for children) may be indicated in reversing cardiac arrhythmias that are life-threatening. Seizures usually respond to diazepam I.V. boluses (5-10 mg for adults up to 30 mg or 0.25-0.4 mg/kg/dose for children up to 10 mg/dose). If seizures are unresponsive or recur, phenytoin or phenobarbital may be required.

Drug Interactions CYP2D6 enzyme substrate
Decreased effect of guanethidine, clonidine; decreased effect with barbiturates, carbamazepine, phenytoin
Increased effect/toxicity with MAO inhibitors (hyperpyretic crises), CNS depressants, alcohol (CNS depression), methylphenidate (increased levels), cimetidine (decreased clearance), anticholinergics

Mechanism of Action Increases the synaptic concentration of serotonin and/or norepinephrine in the central nervous system by inhibition of their reuptake by the presynaptic neuronal membrane

Pharmacodynamics/Kinetics
Therapeutic plasma levels: Oral: Occurs within 6 hours
Protein binding: 95%
Metabolism: Undergoes significant first-pass metabolism; metabolized in the liver
Half-life: 20-26 hours
Elimination: In urine

Usual Dosage Adults: Oral: 50-150 mg/day as a single bedtime dose up to a maximum of 200 mg/day outpatient and 300 mg/day inpatient

Dietary Considerations Alcohol: Avoid use

Monitoring Parameters Blood pressure and pulse rate prior to and during initial therapy; evaluate mental status; monitor weight

Test Interactions ↑ glucose

Patient Information Avoid unnecessary exposure to sunlight; avoid alcohol ingestion; do not discontinue medication abruptly; may cause urine to turn blue-green; may cause drowsiness; can use sugarless gum or hard candy for dry mouth; full effect may not occur for 4-6 weeks

Nursing Implications May increase appetite; may cause drowsiness, raise bed rails, institute safety precautions

Dosage Forms Capsule, as maleate: 25 mg, 50 mg, 100 mg

♦ **Trimipramine Maleate** see Trimipramine *on this page*

- **Trimox**® see Amoxicillin on page 69
- **Trimpex**® see Trimethoprim on page 1184
- **Trinalin**® see Azatadine and Pseudoephedrine on page 115
- **Tri-Norinyl**® see Ethinyl Estradiol and Norethindrone on page 451
- **Triostat™ Injection** see Liothyronine on page 683
- **Triotann**® **Tablet** see Chlorpheniramine, Pyrilamine, and Phenylephrine on page 247

Trioxsalen (trye OKS a len)

U.S. Brand Names Trisoralen®

Synonyms Trimethylpsoralen

Therapeutic Category Psoralen

Use In conjunction with controlled exposure to ultraviolet light or sunlight for repigmentation of idiopathic vitiligo; increasing tolerance to sunlight with albinism; enhance pigmentation

Pregnancy Risk Factor C

Contraindications Hypersensitivity to psoralens, melanoma, a history of melanoma, or other diseases associated with photosensitivity; porphyria, acute lupus erythematosus; patients <12 years of age

Warnings/Precautions Serious burns from UVA or sunlight can occur if dosage or exposure schedules are exceeded; patients must wear protective eye wear to prevent cataracts; use with caution in patients with severe hepatic or cardiovascular disease

Adverse Reactions
>10%:
    Dermatologic: Itching
    Gastrointestinal: Nausea
1% to 10%:
    Central nervous system: Dizziness, headache, mental depression, insomnia, nervousness
    Dermatologic: Severe burns from excessive sunlight or ultraviolet exposure
    Gastrointestinal: Gastric discomfort

Mechanism of Action Psoralens are thought to form covalent bonds with pyrimidine bases in DNA which inhibit the synthesis of DNA. This reaction involves excitation of the trioxsalen molecule by radiation in the long-wave ultraviolet light (UVA) resulting in transference of energy to the trioxsalen molecule producing an excited state. Binding of trioxsalen to DNA occurs only in the presence of ultraviolet light. The increase in skin pigmentation produced by trioxsalen and UVA radiation involves multiple changes in melanocytes and interaction between melanocytes and keratinocytes. In general, melanogenesis is stimulated but the size and distribution of melanocytes is unchanged.

Pharmacodynamics/Kinetics
Peak photosensitivity: 2 hours
Duration: Skin sensitivity to light remains for 8-12 hours
Absorption: Rapid
Half-life, elimination: ~2 hours

Usual Dosage Children >12 years and Adults: Oral: 10 mg/day as a single dose, 2-4 hours before controlled exposure to UVA (for 15-35 minutes) or sunlight; do not continue for longer than 14 days

Patient Information To minimize gastric discomfort, tablets may be taken with milk or after a meal; wear sunglasses during exposure and a light-screening lipstick; do not exceed dose or exposure duration

Dosage Forms Tablet: 5 mg

- **Tripedia**® see Diphtheria, Tetanus Toxoids, and Acellular Pertussis Vaccine on page 373
- **Tripedia/ActHIB**® see Diphtheria, Tetanus Toxoids, Whole-Cell Pertussis, and Haemophilus influenzae Type b Conjugate Vaccines on page 375

Tripelennamine (tri pel EN a meen)

U.S. Brand Names PBZ®; PBZ-SR®

Canadian Brand Names Pyribenzamine®

Synonyms Tripelennamine Citrate; Tripelennamine Hydrochloride

Therapeutic Category Antihistamine, H₁ Blocker

Use Perennial and seasonal allergic rhinitis and other allergic symptoms including urticaria

Pregnancy Risk Factor B

Contraindications Hypersensitivity to tripelennamine or any component

Warnings/Precautions Use with caution in patients with narrow-angle glaucoma, bladder neck obstruction, symptomatic prostate hypertrophy, asthmatic attacks, and stenosing peptic ulcer

Adverse Reactions
>10%:
    Central nervous system: Slight to moderate drowsiness
    Respiratory: Thickening of bronchial secretions
1% to 10%:
    Central nervous system: Headache, fatigue, nervousness, dizziness
    Gastrointestinal: Appetite increase, weight gain, nausea, diarrhea, abdominal pain, xerostomia
    Neuromuscular & skeletal: Arthralgia
    Respiratory: Pharyngitis
(Continued)

Tripelennamine (Continued)

<1%: Edema, palpitations, hypotension, depression, sedation, paradoxical excitement, insomnia, angioedema, photosensitivity, rash, urinary retention, hepatitis, myalgia, paresthesia, tremor, blurred vision, bronchospasm, epistaxis

Overdosage/Toxicology
Symptoms of overdose include CNS stimulation or depression; flushed skin, mydriasis, ataxia, athetosis, dry mouth
There is no specific treatment for an antihistamine overdose, however, most of its clinical toxicity is due to anticholinergic effects. For anticholinergic overdose with severe life-threatening symptoms, physostigmine 1-2 mg (0.5 mg or 0.02 mg/kg for children) I.V., slowly may be given to reverse these effects.

Drug Interactions Increased effect/toxicity with alcohol, CNS depressants, MAO inhibitors

Mechanism of Action Competes with histamine for H_1-receptor sites on effector cells in the gastrointestinal tract, blood vessels, and respiratory tract

Pharmacodynamics/Kinetics
Onset of antihistaminic effect: Within 15-30 minutes
Duration: 4-6 hours (up to 8 hours with PBZ-SR®)
Metabolism: Almost completely in the liver
Elimination: In urine

Usual Dosage Oral:
Infants and Children: 5 mg/kg/day in 4-6 divided doses, up to 300 mg/day maximum
Adults: 25-50 mg every 4-6 hours, extended release tablets 100 mg morning and evening up to 100 mg every 8 hours

Dietary Considerations Alcohol: Additive CNS effect, avoid use

Patient Information Do not crush extended release tablets; urinary hesitancy can be reduced if patient voids just prior to taking drug; may cause drowsiness; swallow whole, do not crush or chew sustained release product; avoid alcohol, may impair coordination and judgment

Nursing Implications Raise bed rails, institute safety measures, assist with ambulation

Dosage Forms
Elixir, as citrate: 37.5 mg/5 mL [equivalent to 25 mg hydrochloride] (473 mL)
Tablet, as hydrochloride: 25 mg, 50 mg
Tablet, extended release, as hydrochloride: 100 mg

- **Tripelennamine Citrate** see Tripelennamine on previous page
- **Tripelennamine Hydrochloride** see Tripelennamine on previous page
- **Triphasil®** see Ethinyl Estradiol and Levonorgestrel on page 449
- **Tri-Phen-Chlor®** see Chlorpheniramine, Phenyltoloxamine, Phenylpropanolamine, and Phenylephrine on page 247
- **Triple Antibiotic® Topical** see Bacitracin, Neomycin, and Polymyxin B on page 123
- **Triple Sulfa** see Sulfabenzamide, Sulfacetamide, and Sulfathiazole on page 1090
- **Triple X® Liquid [OTC]** see Pyrethrins on page 996

Triprolidine, Pseudoephedrine, and Codeine
(trye PROE li deen, soo doe e FED rin, & KOE deen)

U.S. Brand Names Actagen-C®; Allerfrin® w/Codeine; Aprodine® w/C; Triacin-C®; Trifed-C®

Therapeutic Category Antihistamine/Decongestant/Antitussive

Dosage Forms Syrup: Triprolidine hydrochloride 1.25 mg, pseudoephedrine hydrochloride 30 mg, and codeine phosphate 10 mg per 5 mL with alcohol 4.3%

- **Triptil®** see Protriptyline on page 991
- **Tris Buffer** see Tromethamine on page 1191
- **Tris(hydroxymethyl)aminomethane** see Tromethamine on page 1191
- **Trisoralen®** see Trioxsalen on previous page
- **Tri-Statin® II Topical** see Nystatin and Triamcinolone on page 857
- **Tristoject®** see Triamcinolone on page 1174
- **Trisulfa®** see Co-Trimoxazole on page 299
- **Trisulfapyrimidines** see Sulfadiazine, Sulfamethazine, and Sulfamerazine on page 1093
- **Trisulfa-S®** see Co-Trimoxazole on page 299
- **Tri-Tannate Plus®** see Chlorpheniramine, Ephedrine, Phenylephrine, and Carbetapentane on page 246
- **Tri-Tannate® Tablet** see Chlorpheniramine, Pyrilamine, and Phenylephrine on page 247
- **Tritec®** see Ranitidine Bismuth Citrate on page 1010
- **Tri-Vi-Flor®** see Vitamins, Multiple on page 1226
- **Trobicin®** see Spectinomycin on page 1077
- **Trocaine® [OTC]** see Benzocaine on page 133

Troglitazone (TROE gli to zone)

Related Information
Hypoglycemic Drugs, Comparison of Oral Agents on page 1325

U.S. Brand Names Rezulin®

Therapeutic Category Antidiabetic Agent, Oral; Hypoglycemic Agent, Oral

Use Type II diabetes: For use in patients with type II diabetes currently on insulin therapy whose hyperglycemia is inadequately controlled (Hb A_{1c} >8.5%) despite insulin therapy >30 units/day given as multiple injections.

Management of type II diabetes should include diet control. Caloric restriction, weight loss and exercise are essential for the proper treatment of the diabetic patient. This is important not only the primary treatment of type II diabetes but in maintaining the efficacy of drug therapy. Prior to initiation of troglitazone therapy, investigate secondary causes of poor glycemic control (eg, infection or poor injection technique).

Either monotherapy or combination therapy with sulfonylureas, for patients with type II diabetes

Investigational: A study showed troglitazone may be beneficial in the productive and metabolic consequences of polycystic ovary syndrome (PCOS) (400 mg/day) and less essential hypertension with NIDDM, but more studies are needed.

Pregnancy Risk Factor B

Contraindications Hypersensitivity to troglitazone or any component

Warnings/Precautions Patients with New York Heart Association (NYHA) Class III and IV cardiac status were not studied during clinical trials. Heart enlargement without microscopic changes has been observed in rodents at exposures exceeding 14 times the AUC of the 400 mg human dose. Caution is advised during the administration of troglitazone to patients with NYHA Class III or IV cardiac status.

A total of 150 adverse event reports postmarketing have been reported to the FDA including 3 deaths from liver failure linked to the use of troglitazone. Approximately 600,000 patients in the U.S. and 200,000 patients in Japan have been treated with troglitazone.

Patients on troglitazone who develop jaundice or whose laboratory results indicate liver injury should stop taking the drug. Approximately 2% of patients can expect to stop taking the drug because of elevated liver enzymes.

Because of its mechanism of action, troglitazone is active only in the presence of insulin. Therefore, do not use in type I diabetes or for the treatment of diabetic ketoacidosis.

Patients receiving troglitazone in combination with insulin may be at risk for hypoglycemia, and a reduction in the dose of insulin may be necessary. Hypoglycemia has not been observed during the administration of troglitazone as monotherapy and would not be expected based on the mechanism of action.

Across all clinical studies, hemoglobin declined by 3% to 4% in troglitazone-treated patients compared with 1% to 2% with placebo. White blood cell counts also declined slightly in troglitazone-treated patients compared with those treated with placebo. These changes occurred within the first 4-8 weeks of therapy. Levels stabilized and remained unchanged for ≤2 years of continuing therapy. These changes may be due to the dilutional effects of increased plasma volume and have not been associated with any significant hematologic clinical effects.

Adverse Reactions
>10%:
Central nervous system: Headache, pain
Miscellaneous: Infection
1% to 10%:
Cardiovascular: Peripheral edema
Central nervous system: Dizziness
Gastrointestinal: Nausea, diarrhea, pharyngitis
Genitourinary: Urinary tract infection
Neuromuscular & skeletal: Neck pain, weakness
Respiratory: Rhinitis

Drug Interactions CYP3A3/4 enzyme substrate; CYP3A3/4 enzyme inducer; CYP2C9, 2C19, and 3A3/4 enzyme inhibitor
Decreased effects:
Cholestyramine: Concomitant administration of cholestyramine with troglitazone reduces the absorption of troglitazone by 70%; COADMINISTRATION OF CHOLESTYRAMINE AND TROGLITAZONE IS NOT RECOMMENDED.
Oral contraceptives: Administration of troglitazone with an oral contraceptive containing ethinyl estradiol and norethindrone reduced the plasma concentrations of both by 30%. These changes could result in loss of contraception.
Terfenadine: Coadministration of troglitazone with terfenadine decreases plasma concentrations of terfenadine and its active metabolite by 50% to 70% and may reduce the effectiveness of terfenadine
Increased toxicity:
Sulfonylureas (glyburide): Coadministration of troglitazone with glyburide may further decrease plasma glucose levels

Mechanism of Action Thiazolidinedione antidiabetic agent that lowers blood glucose by improving target cell response to insulin, without increasing pancreatic insulin secretion. It has a unique mechanism of action that is dependent on the presence of insulin for activity. Troglitazone decreases hepatic glucose output and increases insulin-dependent glucose disposal in skeletal muscle and possible liver and adipose tissue.

Pharmacodynamics/Kinetics
Absorption: Food increases absorption by 30% to 85%
Distribution: V_d:10.5-26.5 L/kg
Protein binding: >99%, to serum albumin
Metabolism: Extensive; troglitazone does induce cytochrome P-450 3A4 metabolism; the inhibitory effect on P-450 isozymes (especially 3A4, 2C9, and 2C19) is believed to not be clinically important and associated with troglitazone concentrations of 11 mcg/mL.
NOTE: Concentrations of 1-3 mcg/mL are obtained at 600 mg/day of troglitazone (ie, the maximum adult dosage).
(Continued)

Troglitazone *(Continued)*

Bioavailability: Absolute
Half-life, plasma elimination: 16-34 hours
Time to peak plasma concentrations: 2-3 hours
Elimination: 85% in feces and 3% in urine

Usual Dosage Oral (take with meals):
Adults:
Combination therapy with insulin: Continue the current insulin dose upon initiation of troglitazone therapy
Initiate therapy at 200 mg once daily in patients on insulin therapy. For patients not responding adequately, increase the dose after 2-4 weeks. The usual dose is 400 mg/day; maximum recommended dose: 600 mg/day.
It is recommended that the insulin dose be decreased by 10% to 25% when fasting plasma glucose concentrations decrease to <120 mg/dL in patients receiving concomitant insulin and troglitazone. Individualize further adjustments based on glucose-lowering response.
Monotherapy: Initial: 400 mg once daily with a meal. For patients not responding to 400 mg/day, the troglitazone dose should be increased to 600 mg after 1 month. For patients not responding adequately to 600 mg after 1 month, troglitazone should be discontinued and alternate therapeutic options should be pursued.
Elderly: Steady-state pharmacokinetics of troglitazone and metabolites in healthy elderly subjects were comparable to those seen in young adults

Dosing adjustment/comments in renal impairment: Dose adjustment is not necessary

Dosing adjustment in hepatic impairment: Troglitazone should **not** be initiated if the patient exhibits clinical evidence of active liver disease or increased serum transaminase levels (ALT >1.5 times the upper limit of normal).

Monitoring Parameters Urine for glucose and ketones, fasting blood glucose, hemoglobin A_{1c}, and fructosamine. **Serum transaminase levels should be monitored at the start of therapy, monthly for the first 8 months of treatment, every other month for the remainder of the first year, and periodically thereafter.** Additionally, liver function tests should be performed on any patient on troglitazone who develops symptoms of liver dysfunction, such as nausea, vomiting, abdominal pain, fatigue, loss of appetite, or dark urine.

Reference Range Target range: Adults:
Fasting blood glucose: <120 mg/dL
Glycosylated hemoglobin: <7%

Patient Information Notify physician if symptoms of liver dysfunction such as nausea, vomiting, abdominal pain, fatigue, loss of appetite, or dark urine occur. Blood will be drawn to check liver function at the start of therapy, monthly for the first 8 months of therapy, every 2 months for the remainder of the first year of troglitazone therapy, and periodically thereafter.

Take troglitazone with meals. If the dose is missed at the usual meal, take it at the next meal. If the dose is missed on one day, do not double the dose the following day.

It is important to adhere to dietary instructions and to have blood glucose and glycosylated hemoglobin tested regularly. During periods of stress such as fever, trauma, infection or surgery, insulin requirements may change and patients should seek the advice of their physician.

When using combination therapy with insulin, explain the risks of hypoglycemia, its symptoms, treatment and predisposing conditions to patients and their family members.

Nursing Implications Patients who are NPO may need to have their dose held to avoid hypoglycemia

Dosage Forms Tablet: 200 mg, 400 mg

Troleandomycin (troe lee an doe MYE sin)

U.S. Brand Names Tao®
Synonyms Triacetyloleandomycin
Therapeutic Category Antibiotic, Macrolide
Use Adjunct in the treatment of corticosteroid-dependent asthma due to its steroid-sparing properties; antibiotic with spectrum of activity similar to erythromycin
Pregnancy Risk Factor C
Contraindications Hypersensitivity to troleandomycin, other macrolides, or any component; concurrent use with cisapride
Warnings/Precautions Use with caution in patients with impaired hepatic function; chronic hepatitis may occur in patients with long or repetitive courses
Adverse Reactions
>10%: Gastrointestinal: Abdominal cramping and discomfort (dose-related)
1% to 10%:
Dermatologic: Urticaria, rashes
Gastrointestinal: Nausea, vomiting, diarrhea
<1%: Rectal burning, cholestatic jaundice
Overdosage/Toxicology
Symptoms of overdose include nausea, vomiting, diarrhea, hearing loss
Following GI decontamination, treatment is supportive
Drug Interactions CYP3A3/4 enzyme substrate; CYP3A3/4 and 3A5-7 enzyme inhibitor
Increased effect/toxicity/levels of carbamazepine, ergot alkaloids, methylprednisolone, oral contraceptives, theophylline, and triazolam; contraindicated with terfenadine,

astemizole, cisapride, and pimozide due to decreased metabolism of this agent and resultant risk of cardiac arrhythmias and death

Mechanism of Action Decreases methylprednisolone clearance from a linear first order decline to a nonlinear decline in plasma concentration. Troleandomycin also has an undefined action independent of its effects on steroid elimination. Inhibits RNA-dependent protein synthesis at the chain elongation step; binds to the 50S ribosomal subunit resulting in blockage of transpeptidation.

Pharmacodynamics/Kinetics

Time to peak serum concentration: Within 2 hours

Elimination: 10% to 25% of dose excreted in urine as active drug; also excreted in feces via bile

Usual Dosage Oral:

Children 7-13 years: 25-40 mg/kg/day divided every 6 hours (125-250 mg every 6 hours)

Adjunct in corticosteroid-dependent asthma: 14 mg/kg/day in divided doses every 6-12 hours not to exceed 250 mg every 6 hours; dose is tapered to once daily then alternate day dosing

Adults: 250-500 mg 4 times/day

Monitoring Parameters Hepatic function tests

Patient Information Complete full course of therapy; notify physician if persistent or severe abdominal pain, nausea, vomiting, jaundice, darkened urine, or fever occurs

Dosage Forms Capsule: 250 mg

Tromethamine (troe METH a meen)

U.S. Brand Names THAM-E® Injection; THAM® Injection

Synonyms Tris Buffer; Tris(hydroxymethyl)aminomethane

Therapeutic Category Alkalinizing Agent, Parenteral

Use Correction of metabolic acidosis associated with cardiac bypass surgery or cardiac arrest; to correct excess acidity of stored blood that is preserved with acid citrate dextrose; to prime the pump-oxygenator during cardiac bypass surgery; indicated in infants needing alkalinization after receiving maximum sodium bicarbonate (8-10 mEq/kg/24 hours); (advantage of Tham® is that it alkalinizes without increasing pCO_2 and sodium)

Pregnancy Risk Factor C

Contraindications Uremia or anuria; chronic respiratory acidosis

Warnings/Precautions Reduce dose and monitor pH carefully in renal impairment; drug should not be given for a period of longer than 24 hours unless for a life-threatening situation

Adverse Reactions

1% to 10%:

Cardiovascular: Venospasm

Local: Tissue irritation, necrosis with extravasation

<1%: Hyperosmolality of serum, hyperkalemia, hypoglycemia (transient), increased blood coagulation time, liver cell destruction from direct contact with THAM®, apnea, respiratory depression

Overdosage/Toxicology

Symptoms of overdose include alkalosis, hypokalemia, respiratory depression, hypoglycemia

Supportive therapy is required to correct electrolyte, osmolality, and abnormalities

Mechanism of Action Acts as a proton acceptor, which combines with hydrogen ions to form bicarbonate buffer, to correct acidosis

Pharmacodynamics/Kinetics

Absorption: 30% of dose is not ionized

Elimination: Rapidly eliminated by kidneys (>75% in 3 hours)

Usual Dosage Dose depends on buffer base deficit; when deficit is known: tromethamine (mL of 0.3 M solution) = body weight (kg) x base deficit (mEq/L); when base deficit is not known: 3-6 mL/kg/dose I.V. (1-2 mEq/kg/dose)

Metabolic acidosis with cardiac arrest:

I.V.: 3.5-6 mL/kg (1-2 mEq/kg/dose) into large peripheral vein; 500-1000 mL if needed in adults

I.V. continuous drip: Infuse slowly by syringe pump over 3-6 hours

Acidosis associated with cardiac bypass surgery: Average dose: 9 mL/kg (2.7 mEq/kg); 500 mL is adequate for most adults; maximum dose: 500 mg/kg in ≤1 hour

Excess acidity of acid citrate dextrose priming blood: 14-70 mL of 0.3 molar solution added to each 500 mL of blood

Dosing comments in renal impairment: Use with caution and monitor for hyperkalemia and EKG

Administration May administer undiluted; infuse into as large a vein as possible; not effective if given orally

Monitoring Parameters Serum electrolytes, arterial blood gases, serum pH, blood sugar, EKG monitoring, renal function tests

Reference Range Blood pH: 7.35-7.45

Nursing Implications If extravasation occurs, aspirate as much fluid as possible, then infiltrate area with procaine 1% to which hyaluronidase has been added

Additional Information 1 mM = 120 mg = 3.3 mL = 1 mEq of Tham®

Dosage Forms Injection:

Tham®: 18 g [0.3 molar] (500 mL)

Tham-E®: 36 g with sodium 30 mEq, potassium 5 mEq, and chloride 35 mEq (1000 mL)

♦ **Tropicacyl®** see Tropicamide on this page

Tropicamide (troe PIK a mide)
Related Information
    Cycloplegic Mydriatics Comparison on page 1321
U.S. Brand Names Mydriacyl®; Opticyl®; Tropicacyl®
Synonyms Bistropamide
Therapeutic Category Ophthalmic Agent, Mydriatic
Use Short-acting mydriatic used in diagnostic procedures; as well as preoperatively and postoperatively; treatment of some cases of acute iritis, iridocyclitis, and keratitis
Pregnancy Risk Factor C
Contraindications Glaucoma, hypersensitivity to tropicamide or any component
Warnings/Precautions Use with caution in infants and children since tropicamide may cause potentially dangerous CNS disturbances; tropicamide may cause an increase in intraocular pressure
Adverse Reactions 1% to 10%:
    Cardiovascular: Tachycardia, vascular congestion, edema
    Central nervous system: Parasympathetic stimulations, drowsiness, headache
    Dermatologic: Eczematoid dermatitis
    Gastrointestinal: Xerostomia
    Local: Transient stinging
    Ocular: Blurred vision, photophobia with or without corneal staining, increased intraocular pressure, follicular conjunctivitis
Overdosage/Toxicology
    Symptoms of overdose include blurred vision, urinary retention, tachycardia, cardiorespiratory collapse
    Antidote is physostigmine, pilocarpine; anticholinergic toxicity is caused by strong binding of the drug to cholinergic receptors. For anticholinergic overdose with severe life-threatening symptoms, physostigmine 1-2 mg (0.5 mg or 0.02 mg/kg for children) S.C. or I.V., slowly may be given to reverse systemic effects.
Stability Store in tightly closed containers
Mechanism of Action Prevents the sphincter muscle of the iris and the muscle of the ciliary body from responding to cholinergic stimulation
Pharmacodynamics/Kinetics
    Onset of mydriasis: ~20-40 minutes Duration: ~6-7 hours;
    Onset of cycloplegia: Within 30 minutes; Duration: <6 hours
Usual Dosage Children and Adults (individuals with heavily pigmented eyes may require larger doses):
    Cycloplegia: Instill 1-2 drops (1%); may repeat in 5 minutes
        Exam must be performed within 30 minutes after the repeat dose; if the patient is not examined within 20-30 minutes, instill an additional drop
    Mydriasis: Instill 1-2 drops (0.5%) 15-20 minutes before exam; may repeat every 30 minutes as needed
Monitoring Parameters Ophthalmic exam
Patient Information If irritation persists or increases, discontinue use, may cause blurred vision and increased light sensitivity
Nursing Implications Finger pressure should be applied on the lacrimal sac for 1-2 minutes following topical instillation of the solution
Dosage Forms Solution, ophthalmic: 0.5% (2 mL, 15 mL); 1% (2 mL, 3 mL, 15 mL)

Trovafloxacin (TROE va flox a sin)
Related Information
    Antimicrobial Drugs of Choice on page 1404
    Community-Acquired Pneumonia in Adults on page 1419
U.S. Brand Names Trovan™
Synonyms Alatrovafloxacin Mesylate; CP-99,219-27
Therapeutic Category Antibiotic, Quinolone
Use Treatment of nosocomial pneumonia, community-acquired pneumonia, acute exacerbation of chronic bronchitis, acute sinusitis, intra-abdominal infections, gynecologic/pelvic infections, skin and skin structure infections, urinary tract infections, pelvic inflammatory disease, cervicitis, and gonorrhea.

Trovafloxacin is active against most aerobic gram-negative bacilli including Pseudomonas aeruginosa and many gram-positive cocci including staphylococcal sp and streptococcal sp (including S. pneumoniae). Trovafloxacin also has activity against many anaerobes including Bacteroides fragilis.
Pregnancy Risk Factor C
Contraindications History of hypersensitivity to trovafloxacin, alatrofloxacin, quinolone antimicrobial agents or any other components of these products
Warnings/Precautions May alter GI flora resulting in pseudomembranous colitis due to Clostridium difficile; use with caution in patients with seizure disorders or severe cerebral atherosclerosis; discontinue if skin rash or pain, inflammation, or rupture of a tendon; photosensitivity; CNS stimulation may occur which may lead to tremor, restlessness, confusion, hallucinations, paranoia, depression, nightmares, insomnia, or lightheadedness. May cause liver enzyme abnormalities, hepatitis, or liver failure
Adverse Reactions <10%:
    Central nervous system: Dizziness, lightheadedness, headache
    Dermatologic: Rash, pruritus
    Gastrointestinal: Nausea, vomiting, diarrhea, abdominal pain

Genitourinary: Vaginitis

Hepatic: Increased LFTs

Local: Injection site reaction, pain, or inflammation

<1%: Anaphylaxis, hepatic necrosis, pancreatitis, Stevens-Johnson syndrome

Overdosage/Toxicology Empty the stomach by vomiting or gastric lavage. Observe carefully and give symptomatic and supportive treatment; maintain adequate hydration.

Drug Interactions Decreased effect of oral trovafloxacin:

Antacids containing magnesium or aluminum, sucralfate, citric acid buffered with sodium citrate, and metal cations: Administer oral trovafloxacin doses at least 2 hours before or 2 hours after

Morphine: Administer I.V. morphine at least 2 hours after oral trovafloxacin in the fasting state and at least 4 hours after oral trovafloxacin when taken with food

Stability Trovan™ I.V. should not be diluted with 0.9% sodium chloride injection, USP (normal saline), alone or in combination with other diluents. A precipitate may form under these conditions. In addition, Trovan® I.V. should not be diluted with lactated Ringer's, USP.

Mechanism of Action Inhibits DNA-gyrase in susceptible organisms; inhibits relaxation of supercoiled DNA and promotes breakage of double-stranded DNA

Pharmacodynamics/Kinetics

Distribution: Concentration in most tissues greater than plasma or serum

Protein binding: 76%

Metabolism: Hepatic conjugation

Bioavailability: 88%

Half-life: 9-12 hours

Elimination: 50% excreted unchanged (43% feces, 6% urine)

Usual Dosage Adults:

Nosocomial pneumonia: I.V.: 300 mg single dose followed by 200 mg/day orally for a total duration of 10-14 days

Community-acquired pneumonia: Oral, I.V.: 200 mg/day for 7-14 days

Acute bacterial exacerbation of chronic bronchitis: Oral: 100 mg/day for 7-10 days

Acute sinusitis: Oral: 200 mg/day for 10 days

Complicated intra-abdominal infections, including postsurgical infections/gynecologic and pelvic infections: I.V.: 300 mg as a single dose followed by 200 mg/day orally for a total duration of 7-14 days

Surgical prophylaxis (elective colorectal surgery, elective and abdominal and vaginal hysterectomy): Oral, I.V.: 200 mg as a single dose within 30 minutes to 4 hours before surgery

Skin and skin structure infections: Oral: 100 mg/day for 7-10 days

Skin and skin structure infections, complicated, including diabetic foot infections: Oral, I.V.: 200 mg/day for 10-14 days

Uncomplicated UTI (cystitis): Oral: 100 mg/day for 3 days

Chronic bacterial prostatitis: Oral: 200 mg/day for 28 days

Uncomplicated urethral gonorrhea in males; endocervical/rectal gonorrhea in females: Oral: 100 mg single dose

Cervicitis caused by *Chlamydia trachomatis*: Oral: 200 mg/day for 5 days

Pelvic inflammatory disease (mild to moderate): Oral: 200 mg for 14 days

Dosage adjustment in renal impairment: No adjustment is necessary

Dosage adjustment for hemodialysis: None required; trovafloxacin not sufficiently removed by hemodialysis

Dosage adjustment in hepatic impairment:

Mild to moderate cirrhosis:

Initial dose for normal hepatic function: 300 mg I.V.; 200 mg I.V. or oral; 100 mg oral

Reduced dose: 200 mg I.V.; 100 mg I.V. or oral; 100 mg oral

Severe cirrhosis: No data available

Dietary Considerations Dairy products such as milk and yogurt reduce the absorption of oral trovafloxacin - avoid concurrent use. The bioavailability may also be decreased by enteral feedings.

Administration Administer IVPB over 60 minutes

Monitoring Parameters Periodic assessment of liver function tests should be considered

Patient Information Drink fluids liberally; do not take antacids containing magnesium or aluminum or products containing iron or zinc simultaneously or within 4 hours before or 2 hours after taking dose. May cause dizziness or lightheadedness; observe caution while driving or performing other tasks requiring alertness, coordination, or physical dexterity. CNS stimulation may occur (eg, tremor, restlessness, confusion). Avoid excessive sunlight/artificial ultraviolet light; discontinue drug if phototoxicity occurs. Avoid re-exposure to ultraviolet light. Reactions may recur up to several weeks after stopping therapy.

Dosage Forms

Injection, as mesylate (alatrofloxacin): 5 mg/mL (40 mL, 60 mL)

Tablet, as mesylate (trovafloxacin): 100 mg, 200 mg

♦ **Trovan**™ see Trovafloxacin on previous page

♦ **Truphylline**® see Theophylline Salts on page 1125

♦ **Trusopt**® see Dorzolamide on page 389

Trypsin, Balsam Peru, and Castor Oil

(TRIP sin, BAL sam pe RUE, & KAS tor oyl)

U.S. Brand Names Granulex

Therapeutic Category Protectant, Topical

(Continued)

Trypsin, Balsam Peru, and Castor Oil *(Continued)*

Dosage Forms Aerosol, topical: Trypsin 0.1 mg, balsam Peru 72.5 mg, and castor oil 650 mg per 0.82 mL (60 g, 120 g)

♦ **Trysul®** *see* Sulfabenzamide, Sulfacetamide, and Sulfathiazole *on page 1090*

♦ **TSH** *see* Thyrotropin *on page 1139*

♦ **TSH** *see* Thyrotropin Alpha *on page 1140*

♦ **TSPA** *see* Thiotepa *on page 1136*

♦ **TST** *see* Tuberculin Purified Protein Derivative *on this page*

♦ **TST** *see* Tuberculin Tests *on this page*

♦ **Tubasal®** *see* Aminosalicylate Sodium *on page 59*

Tuberculin Purified Protein Derivative *(too BER kyoo lin tests)*

U.S. Brand Names Aplisol®; Aplitest®; Sclavo-PPD Solution®; Sclavo Test-PPD®; Tine Test PPD; Tubersol®

Synonyms Mantoux; PPD; Tine Test; TST; Tuberculin Skin Test

Therapeutic Category Diagnostic Agent, Skin Test

Use Skin test in diagnosis of tuberculosis, cell-mediated immunodeficiencies

Pregnancy Risk Factor C

Contraindications 250 TU strength should not be used for initial testing

Warnings/Precautions Do not administer I.V. or S.C.; epinephrine (1:1000) should be available to treat possible allergic reactions

Adverse Reactions 1% to 10%:
Dermatologic: Ulceration, necrosis, vesiculation
Local: Pain at injection site

Drug Interactions Decreased effect: Reaction may be suppressed in patients receiving systemic corticosteroids, aminocaproic acid, or within 4-6 weeks following immunization with live or inactivated viral vaccines

Stability Refrigerate; Tubersol™ opened vials are stable for up to 24 hours at <75°F

Mechanism of Action Tuberculosis results in individuals becoming sensitized to certain antigenic components of the *M. tuberculosis* organism. Culture extracts called tuberculins are contained in tuberculin skin test preparations. Upon intracutaneous injection of these culture extracts, a classic delayed (cellular) hypersensitivity reaction occurs. This reaction is characteristic of a delayed course (peak occurs >24 hours after injection, induration of the skin secondary to cell infiltration, and occasional vesiculation and necrosis). Delayed hypersensitivity reactions to tuberculin may indicate infection with a variety of nontuberculosis mycobacteria, or vaccination with the live attenuated mycobacterial strain of *M. bovis* vaccine, BCG, in addition to previous natural infection with *M. tuberculosis*.

Pharmacodynamics/Kinetics
Onset of action: Delayed hypersensitivity reactions to tuberculin usually occur within 5-6 hours following injection
Peak effect: Become maximal at 48-72 hours
Duration: Reactions subside over a few days

Usual Dosage Children and Adults: Intradermal: 0.1 mL about 4" below elbow; use ¼" to ½" or 26- or 27-gauge needle; significant reactions are ≥5 mm in diameter
Interpretation of induration of tuberculin skin test injections: Positive: ≥10 mm; inconclusive: 5-9 mm; negative: <5 mm
Interpretation of induration of Tine test injections: Positive: >2 mm and vesiculation present; inconclusive: <2 mm (give patient Mantoux test of 5 TU/0.1 mL - base decisions on results of Mantoux test); negative: <2 mm or erythema of any size (no need for retesting unless person is a contact of a patient with tuberculosis or there is clinical evidence suggestive of the disease)

Patient Information Return to physician for reaction interpretation at 48-72 hours

Nursing Implications Test dose: 0.1 mL intracutaneously; store in refrigerator; examine site at 48-72 hours after administration; whenever tuberculin is administered, a record should be made of the administration technique (Mantoux method, disposable multiple-puncture device), tuberculin used (OT or PPD), manufacturer and lot number of tuberculin used, date of administration, date of test reading, and the size of the reaction in millimeters (mm).

Dosage Forms Injection:
First test strength: 1 TU/0.1 mL (1 mL)
Intermediate test strength: 5 TU/0.1 mL (1 mL, 5 mL, 10 mL)
Second test strength: 250 TU/0.1 mL (1 mL)
Tine: 5 TU each test

♦ **Tuberculin Purified Protein Derivative** *see* Tuberculin Tests *on this page*

♦ **Tuberculin Skin Test** *see* Tuberculin Purified Protein Derivative *on this page*

♦ **Tuberculin Skin Test** *see* Tuberculin Tests *on this page*

Tuberculin Tests *(too BER kyoo lin tests)*

U.S. Brand Names Aplisol®; Aplitest®; Sclavo-PPD Solution®; Sclavo Test-PPD®; Tine Test PPD; Tubersol®

Synonyms Mantoux; PPD; Tine Test; TST; Tuberculin Purified Protein Derivative; Tuberculin Skin Test

Therapeutic Category Diagnostic Agent, Skin Test

Use Skin test in diagnosis of tuberculosis, cell-mediated immunodeficiencies

Pregnancy Risk Factor C

Contraindications 250 TU strength should not be used for initial testing

Warnings/Precautions Do not administer I.V. or S.C.; epinephrine (1:1000) should be available to treat possible allergic reactions

Adverse Reactions 1% to 10%:
Dermatologic: Ulceration, vesiculation
Local: Pain at injection site
Miscellaneous: Necrosis

Drug Interactions Decreased effect: Reaction may be suppressed in patients receiving systemic corticosteroids, aminocaproic acid, or within 4-6 weeks following immunization with live or inactivated viral vaccines

Stability Refrigerate; Tubersol™ opened vials are stable for up to 24 hours at <75°F

Mechanism of Action Tuberculosis results in individuals becoming sensitized to certain antigenic components of the *M. tuberculosis* organism. Culture extracts called tuberculins are contained in tuberculin skin test preparations. Upon intracutaneous injection of these culture extracts, a classic delayed (cellular) hypersensitivity reaction occurs. This reaction is characteristic of a delayed course (peak occurs >24 hours after injection, induration of the skin secondary to cell infiltration, and occasional vesiculation and necrosis). Delayed hypersensitivity reactions to tuberculin may indicate infection with a variety of nontuberculosis mycobacteria, or vaccination with the live attenuated mycobacterial strain of *M. bovis* vaccine, BCG, in addition to previous natural infection with *M. tuberculosis*.

Pharmacodynamics/Kinetics
Onset of action: Delayed hypersensitivity reactions to tuberculin usually occur within 5-6 hours following injection
Peak effect: Become maximal at 48-72 hours
Duration: Reactions subside over a few days

Usual Dosage Children and Adults: Intradermal: 0.1 mL about 4" below elbow; use ¼" to ½" or 26- or 27-gauge needle; significant reactions are ≥5 mm in diameter
Interpretation of induration of tuberculin skin test injections: Positive: ≥10 mm; inconclusive: 5-9 mm; negative: <5 mm
Interpretation of induration of Tine test injections: Positive: >2 mm and vesiculation present; inconclusive: <2 mm (give patient Mantoux test of 5 TU/0.1 mL - base decisions on results of Mantoux test); negative: <2 mm or erythema of any size (no need for retesting unless person is a contact of a patient with tuberculosis or there is clinical evidence suggestive of the disease)

Patient Information Return to physician for reaction interpretation at 48-72 hours

Nursing Implications Test dose: 0.1 mL intracutaneously; store in refrigerator; examine site at 48-72 hours after administration; whenever tuberculin is administered, a record should be made of the administration technique (Mantoux method, disposable multiple-puncture device), tuberculin used (OT or PPD), manufacturer and lot number of tuberculin used, date of administration, date of test reading, and the size of the reaction in millimeters (mm).

Dosage Forms Injection:
First test strength: 1 TU/0.1 mL (1 mL)
Intermediate test strength: 5 TU/0.1 mL (1 mL, 5 mL, 10 mL)
Second test strength: 250 TU/0.1 mL (1 mL)
Tine: 5 TU each test

♦ **Tuberculosis Prophylaxis** *see page 1386*
♦ **Tuberculosis Treatment Guidelines** *see page 1432*
♦ **Tubersol®** *see Tuberculin Purified Protein Derivative on previous page*
♦ **Tubersol®** *see Tuberculin Tests on previous page*

Tubocurarine (too boe kyoor AR een)

Related Information
Neuromuscular Blocking Agents Comparison *on page 1331*

Synonyms *d*-Tubocurarine Chloride; Tubocurarine Chloride

Therapeutic Category Neuromuscular Blocker Agent, Nondepolarizing; Skeletal Muscle Relaxant

Use Adjunct to anesthesia to induce skeletal muscle relaxation

Pregnancy Risk Factor C

Contraindications Hypersensitivity to tubocurarine or any component; patients in whom histamine release is a definite hazard

Warnings/Precautions Use with caution in patients with renal impairment, respiratory depression, impaired hepatic or endocrine function, myasthenia gravis, and the elderly; ventilation must be supported during neuromuscular blockade; rapid administration may cause histamine release resulting in respiratory depression and bronchospasm

Adverse Reactions
1% to 10%: Cardiovascular: Hypotension
<1%: Edema, circulatory collapse, cardiac arrhythmias, increased heart rate or bradycardia, skin flushing, rash, itching, erythema, increased salivation, decreased GI motility, bronchospasm, hypersensitivity reactions, allergic reactions

Overdosage/Toxicology
Symptoms of overdose include prolonged skeletal muscle weakness and apnea, cardiovascular collapse
Use neostigmine, edrophonium or pyridostigmine with atropine to antagonize skeletal muscle relaxation; support of ventilation and the cardiovascular system through mechanical means, fluids, and pressors may be necessary.

(Continued)

Tubocurarine *(Continued)*

Drug Interactions Increased effect/toxicity with aminoglycosides, ketamine, magnesium sulfate, verapamil, quinidine, clindamycin, furosemide

Stability Refrigerate; **incompatible** with barbiturates

Mechanism of Action Blocks acetylcholine from binding to receptors on motor endplate inhibiting depolarization

Pharmacodynamics/Kinetics Elimination: ~33% to 75% of parenteral dose is excreted unchanged in urine in 24 hours; ~10% excreted in bile

Usual Dosage I.V.:

Children and Adults: 0.2-0.4 mg/kg as a single dose; maintenance: 0.04-0.2 mg/kg/dose as needed to maintain paralysis

Alternative adult dose: 6-9 mg once daily, then 3-4.5 mg as needed to maintain paralysis

Dosing adjustment/comments in renal impairment: May accumulate with multiple doses and reductions in subsequent doses is recommended

Cl_{cr} 50-80 mL/minute: Administer 75% of normal dose

Cl_{cr} 10-50 mL/minute: Administer 50% of normal dose

Cl_{cr} <10 mL/minute: Avoid use

Dosing comments in hepatic impairment: Larger doses may be necessary

Administration May also administer I.M.; administer I.V. undiluted over 60-90 seconds and flush I.V. cannula with NS or D_5W

Monitoring Parameters Mean arterial pressure, heart rate, respiratory status, serum potassium

Dosage Forms Injection, as chloride: 3 mg/mL [3 units/mL] (5 mL, 10 mL, 20 mL)

- **Tubocurarine Chloride** *see* Tubocurarine *on previous page*
- **Tuinal®** *see* Amobarbital and Secobarbital *on page 68*
- **Tums® [OTC]** *see* Calcium Carbonate *on page 174*
- **Tums® E-X Extra Strength Tablet [OTC]** *see* Calcium Carbonate *on page 174*
- **Tums® Extra Strength Liquid [OTC]** *see* Calcium Carbonate *on page 174*
- **Tusibron® [OTC]** *see* Guaifenesin *on page 549*
- **Tusibron-DM® [OTC]** *see* Guaifenesin and Dextromethorphan *on page 550*
- **Tussafed® Drops** *see* Carbinoxamine, Pseudoephedrine, and Dextromethorphan *on page 193*
- **Tussafin® Expectorant** *see* Hydrocodone, Pseudoephedrine, and Guaifenesin *on page 579*
- **Tuss-Allergine® Modified T.D. Capsule** *see* Caramiphen and Phenylpropanolamine *on page 188*
- **Tussar® SF Syrup** *see* Guaifenesin, Pseudoephedrine, and Codeine *on page 551*
- **Tuss-DM® [OTC]** *see* Guaifenesin and Dextromethorphan *on page 550*
- **Tussigon®** *see* Hydrocodone and Homatropine *on page 577*
- **Tussionex®** *see* Hydrocodone and Chlorpheniramine *on page 577*
- **Tussi-Organidin® DM NR** *see* Guaifenesin and Dextromethorphan *on page 550*
- **Tussi-Organidin® NR** *see* Guaifenesin and Codeine *on page 550*
- **Tussogest® Extended Release Capsule** *see* Caramiphen and Phenylpropanolamine *on page 188*
- **Tusstat® Syrup** *see* Diphenhydramine *on page 369*
- **Twilite® Oral [OTC]** *see* Diphenhydramine *on page 369*
- **Twin-K®** *see* Potassium Citrate and Potassium Gluconate *on page 951*
- **Two-Dyne®** *see* Butalbital Compound *on page 165*
- **Tylenol® [OTC]** *see* Acetaminophen *on page 19*
- **Tylenol® Extended Relief [OTC]** *see* Acetaminophen *on page 19*
- **Tylenol® With Codeine** *see* Acetaminophen and Codeine *on page 21*
- **Tylox®** *see* Oxycodone and Acetaminophen *on page 875*
- **Typhim Vi®** *see* Typhoid Vaccine *on this page*

Typhoid Vaccine *(TYE foid vak SEEN)*

Related Information

Immunization Recommendations *on page 1358*

U.S. Brand Names Typhim Vi®; Vivotif Berna™ Oral

Synonyms Typhoid Vaccine Live Oral Ty21a

Therapeutic Category Vaccine, Inactivated Bacteria

Use

Parenteral: Promotes active immunity to typhoid fever for patients intimately exposed to a typhoid carrier or foreign travel to a typhoid fever endemic area

Oral: For immunization of children >6 years and adults who expect intimate exposure of or household contact with typhoid fever, travelers to areas of world with risk of exposure to typhoid fever, and workers in microbiology laboratories with expected frequent contact with *S. typhi*

Typhoid vaccine: Live, attenuated Ty21a typhoid vaccine should not be administered to immunocompromised persons, including those known to be infected with HIV. Parenteral inactivated vaccine is a theoretically safer alternative for this group.

Pregnancy Risk Factor C

Contraindications Acute respiratory or other active infections, previous sensitivity to typhoid vaccine, congenital or acquired immunodeficient state, acute febrile illness, acute GI illness, other active infection, persistent diarrhea or vomiting

Warnings/Precautions Postpone use in presence of acute infection; use during pregnancy only when clearly needed, immune deficiency conditions; not all recipients of typhoid vaccine will be fully protected against typhoid fever. Travelers should take all necessary precautions to avoid contact or ingestion of potentially contaminated food or water sources. Unless a complete immunization schedule is followed, an optimum immune response may not be achieved.

Adverse Reactions All serious adverse reactions must be reported to the U.S. Department of Health and Human Services (DHHS) Vaccine Adverse Event Reporting System (VAERS) 1-800-822-7967.

Oral:
1% to 10%:
Dermatologic: Rash
Gastrointestinal: Abdominal discomfort, stomach cramps, diarrhea, nausea, vomiting
<1%: Anaphylactic reaction
Injection:
>10%:
Central nervous system: Headache (9% to 30%), fever
Dermatologic: Local tenderness, erythema, induration (6% to 40%)
Neuromuscular & skeletal: Myalgia (14% to 29%)
<1%: Hypotension

Drug Interactions Simultaneous administration with other vaccines which cause local or systemic adverse effects should be avoided
Decreased effect with concurrent use of sulfonamides or other antibiotics

Stability Refrigerate, do not freeze; potency is not harmed if mistakenly placed in freezer; however, remove from freezer as soon as possible and place in refrigerator; can still be used if exposed to temperature ≤80°F

Mechanism of Action Virulent strains of *Salmonella typhi* cause disease by penetrating the intestinal mucosa and entering the systemic circulation via the lymphatic vasculature. One possible mechanism of conferring immunity may be the provocation of a local immune response in the intestinal tract induced by oral ingesting of a live strain with subsequent aborted infection. The ability of *Salmonella typhi* to produce clinical disease (and to elicit an immune response) is dependent on the bacteria having a complete lipopolysaccharide. The live attenuate Ty21a strain lacks the enzyme UDP-4-galactose epimerase so that lipopolysaccharide is only synthesized under conditions that induce bacterial autolysis. Thus, the strain remains avirulent despite the production of sufficient lipopolysaccharide to evoke a protective immune response. Despite low levels of lipopolysaccharide synthesis, cells lyse before gaining a virulent phenotype due to the intracellular accumulation of metabolic intermediates.

Pharmacodynamics/Kinetics
Oral: Onset of immunity to *Salmonella typhi*: Within about 1 week; Duration: ~5 years
Parenteral: Duration of immunity: ~3 years

Usual Dosage
S.C. (AKD and H-P):
Children 6 months to 10 years: 0.25 mL; repeat in ≥4 weeks (total immunization is 2 doses)
Children >10 years and Adults: 0.5 mL; repeat dose in ≥4 weeks (total immunization is 2 doses)
Booster: 0.25 mL every 3 years for children 6 months to 10 years and 0.5 mL every 3 years for children >10 years and adults; see Administration comments
Oral: Adults:
Primary immunization: 1 capsule on alternate days (day 1, 3, 5, and 7)
Booster immunization: Repeat full course of primary immunization every 5 years

Administration Only the H-P vaccine may be given intradermally and only for booster doses. The AKD vaccine may be given by jet injection; Typhim Vi® may be given I.M. and is indicated for children ≥2 years of age, give as a single 0.5 mL (25 mcg) injection in deltoid muscle

Patient Information Oral capsule should be taken 1 hour before a meal with cold or lukewarm drink, do not chew, swallow whole; systemic adverse effects may persist for 1-2 days. Take all 4 doses exactly as directed on alternate days to obtain a maximal response.

Nursing Implications The doses of vaccine are different between S.C. and intradermal; S.C. injection only should be used

Additional Information Inactivated bacteria vaccine; federal law requires that the date of administration, the vaccine manufacturer, lot number of vaccine, and the administering person's name, title and address be entered into the patient's permanent medical record

Dosage Forms
Capsule, enteric coated (Vivotif Berna™): Viable *S. typhi* Ty21a Colony-forming units 2-6 x 10^9 and nonviable *S. typhi* Ty21a Colony-forming units 50 x 10^9 with sucrose, ascorbic acid, amino acid mixture, lactose and magnesium stearate
Injection, suspension (H-P): Heat- and phenol-inactivated, killed Ty-2 strain of *S. typhi* organisms; provides 8 units/mL, ≤1 billion/mL and ≤35 mcg nitrogen/mL (5 mL, 10 mL)
Injection (Typhim Vi®): Purified Vi capsular polysaccharide 25 mcg/0.5 mL (0.5 mL)
Powder for suspension (AKD): 8 units/mL ≤1 billion/mL, acetone inactivated dried (50 doses)

♦ **Typhoid Vaccine Live Oral Ty21a** see Typhoid Vaccine *on previous page*
♦ **Tyramine Content of Foods** see page 1525
♦ **Tyrodone® Liquid** see Hydrocodone and Pseudoephedrine *on page 579*

- U-90152S *see* Delavirdine *on page 330*
- UAD® Otic *see* Neomycin, Polymyxin B, and Hydrocortisone *on page 827*
- UCB-P071 *see* Cetirizine *on page 233*
- Ucephan® *see* Sodium Phenylacetate and Sodium Benzoate *on page 1070*
- U-Cort™ *see* Hydrocortisone *on page 579*
- Ultane® *see* Sevoflurane *on page 1058*
- Ultiva™ *see* Remifentanil *on page 1013*
- Ultracef® *see* Cefadroxil *on page 204*
- Ultram® *see* Tramadol *on page 1165*
- Ultra Mide® Topical *see* Urea *on next page*
- Ultraquin™ *see* Hydroquinone *on page 584*
- Ultrase® MT12 *see* Pancrelipase *on page 883*
- Ultrase® MT20 *see* Pancrelipase *on page 883*
- Ultravate™ Topical *see* Halobetasol *on page 557*
- Unasyn® *see* Ampicillin and Sulbactam *on page 81*
- Unguentine® [OTC] *see* Benzocaine *on page 133*
- Uni-Ace® [OTC] *see* Acetaminophen *on page 19*
- Uni-Bent® Cough Syrup *see* Diphenhydramine *on page 369*
- Unicap® [OTC] *see* Vitamins, Multiple *on page 1226*
- Uni-Decon® *see* Chlorpheniramine, Phenyltoloxamine, Phenylpropanolamine, and Phenylephrine *on page 247*
- Unipen® Injection *see* Nafcillin *on page 810*
- Unipen® Oral *see* Nafcillin *on page 810*
- Uni-Pro® [OTC] *see* Ibuprofen *on page 593*
- Uniretic™ *see* Moexipril and Hydrochlorothiazide *on page 793*
- Unitrol® [OTC] *see* Phenylpropanolamine *on page 919*
- Uni-Tussin® [OTC] *see* Guaifenesin *on page 549*
- Uni-tussin® DM [OTC] *see* Guaifenesin and Dextromethorphan *on page 550*
- Univasc® *see* Moexipril *on page 792*
- Unna's Boot *see* Zinc Gelatin *on page 1238*
- Unna's Paste *see* Zinc Gelatin *on page 1238*
- Urabeth® *see* Bethanechol *on page 143*

Uracil Mustard (YOOR a sil MUS tard)

Therapeutic Category Antineoplastic Agent, Alkylating Agent; Antineoplastic Agent, Nitrogen Mustard

Use Palliative treatment in symptomatic chronic lymphocytic leukemia; non-Hodgkin's lymphomas, chronic myelocytic leukemia, mycosis fungoides, thrombocytosis, polycythemia vera, ovarian carcinoma

Pregnancy Risk Factor X

Contraindications Severe leukopenia, thrombocytopenia, aplastic anemia; in patients whose bone marrow is infiltrated with malignant cells; hypersensitivity to any component; pregnancy

Warnings/Precautions The U.S. Food and Drug Administration (FDA) currently recommends that procedures for proper handling and disposal of antineoplastic agents be considered. Impaired kidney or liver function. The drug should be discontinued if intractable vomiting or diarrhea, precipitous falls in leukocyte or platelet count, or myocardial ischemia occurs. Use with caution in patients who have had high-dose pelvic radiation or previous use of alkylating agents. Patient should be hospitalized during initial course of therapy; may impair fertility in men and women; use with caution in patients with pre-existing marrow suppression.

Adverse Reactions
>10%:
Gastrointestinal: Nausea, vomiting, diarrhea
Hematologic: Myelosuppressive; leukopenia and thrombocytopenia nadir: 2-4 weeks, anemia
1% to 10%:
Central nervous system: Mental depression, nervousness
Dermatologic: Hyperpigmentation, alopecia
Endocrine & metabolic: Hyperuricemia
<1%: Pruritus, stomatitis, hepatotoxicity

Overdosage/Toxicology
Symptoms of overdose include diarrhea, vomiting, severe marrow suppression
No specific antidote to marrow toxicity is available

Mechanism of Action Polyfunctional alkylating agent. The basic reaction of uracil mustard, like that of any alkylating agent, is the replacement of the hydrogen in a reacting chemical with an alkyl group; cell cycle-phase nonspecific antineoplastic agent; exact site of drug action within the cell is not known, but the nucleoproteins of the cell nucleus are believed to be involved.

Pharmacodynamics/Kinetics
Absorption: Oral
Elimination: <1% detected in urine

Usual Dosage Oral (do not administer until 2-3 weeks after maximum effect of any previous x-ray or cytotoxic drug therapy of the bone marrow is obtained):

Children: 0.3 mg/kg in a single weekly dose for 4 weeks

Adults: 0.15 mg/kg in a single weekly dose for 4 weeks
Thrombocytosis: 1-2 mg/day for 14 days
Patient Information Notify physician of persistent or severe nausea, diarrhea, fever, sore throat, chills, bleeding, or bruising
Dosage Forms Capsule: 1 mg

♦ **Urasal®** *see* Methenamine *on page 747*

Urea *(yoor EE a)*

U.S. Brand Names Amino-Cerv™ Vaginal Cream; Aquacare® Topical [OTC]; Carmol® Topical [OTC]; Gormel® Creme [OTC]; Lanaphilic® Topical [OTC]; Nutraplus® Topical [OTC]; Rea-Lo® [OTC]; Ultra Mide® Topical; Ureacin®-20 Topical [OTC]; Ureacin®-40; Ureaphil® Injection

Canadian Brand Names Onyvul®; Uremol™; Urisec®; Velvelan®

Synonyms Carbamide

Therapeutic Category Diuretic, Osmotic; Keratolytic Agent; Topical Skin Product

Use Reduces intracranial pressure and intraocular pressure; topically promotes hydration and removal of excess keratin in hyperkeratotic conditions and dry skin; mild cervicitis

Pregnancy Risk Factor C

Contraindications Severely impaired renal function, hepatic failure; active intracranial bleeding, sickle cell anemia, topical use in viral skin disease

Warnings/Precautions Urea should not be used near the eyes; use with caution if applied to face, broken, or inflamed skin; use with caution in patients with mild hepatic or renal impairment

Adverse Reactions 1% to 10%:
Central nervous system: Headache
Endocrine & metabolic: Electrolyte imbalance
Gastrointestinal: Nausea, vomiting
Local: Transient stinging, local irritation, tissue necrosis from extravasation of I.V. preparation

Overdosage/Toxicology Increased BUN, decreased renal function; treatment is supportive

Drug Interactions Decreased effect/toxicity/levels of lithium

Mechanism of Action Elevates plasma osmolality by inhibiting tubular reabsorption of water, thus enhancing the flow of water into extracellular fluid

Pharmacodynamics/Kinetics
Onset of therapeutic effect: I.V.: Maximum effects within 1-2 hours
Duration: 3-6 hours (diuresis can continue for up to 10 hours)
Distribution: Crosses the placenta; appears in breast milk
Half-life: 1 hour
Elimination: Excreted unchanged in urine

Usual Dosage
Children: I.V. slow infusion:
<2 years: 0.1-0.5 g/kg
>2 years: 0.5-1.5 g/kg
Adults:
I.V. infusion: 1-1.5 g/kg by slow infusion (1-2½ hours); maximum: 120 g/24 hours
Topical: Apply 1-3 times/day
Vaginal: Insert 1 applicatorful in vagina at bedtime for 2-4 weeks

Patient Information Moisturizing effect is enhanced by applying to the skin while it is still moist after washing or bathing; for external use only

Nursing Implications Do not infuse into leg veins; injection dosage form may be used orally, mix with carbonated beverages, jelly or jam, to mask unpleasant flavor

Dosage Forms
Cream:
Topical: 2% [20 mg/mL] (75 g); 10% [100 mg/mL] (75 g, 90 g, 454 g); 20% [200 mg/mL] (45 g, 75 g, 90 g, 454 g); 30% [300 mg/mL] (60 g, 454 g); 40% (30 g)
Vaginal: 8.34% [83.4 mg/g] (82.5 g)
Injection: 40 g/150 mL
Lotion: 2% (240 mL); 10% (180 mL, 240 mL, 480 mL); 15% (120 mL, 480 mL); 25% (180 mL)

Urea and Hydrocortisone *(yoor EE a & hye droe KOR ti sone)*

U.S. Brand Names Carmol-HC® Topical

Therapeutic Category Corticosteroid, Topical

Dosage Forms Cream, topical: Urea 10% and hydrocortisone acetate 1% in a water-washable vanishing cream base (30 g)

♦ **Ureacin®-20 Topical [OTC]** *see* Urea *on this page*

♦ **Ureacin®-40** *see* Urea *on this page*

♦ **Urea Peroxide** *see* Carbamide Peroxide *on page 190*

♦ **Ureaphil® Injection** *see* Urea *on this page*

♦ **Urecholine®** *see* Bethanechol *on page 143*

♦ **Uremol™** *see* Urea *on this page*

♦ **Urex®** *see* Methenamine *on page 747*

♦ **Uridon®** *see* Chlorthalidone *on page 251*

♦ **Urisec®** *see* Urea *on this page*

♦ **Urispas®** *see* Flavoxate *on page 485*

Urokinase (yoor oh KIN ase)

U.S. Brand Names Abbokinase® Injection

Therapeutic Category Thrombolytic Agent

Use Thrombolytic agent used in treatment of recent severe or massive deep vein thrombosis, pulmonary emboli, myocardial infarction, and occluded arteriovenous cannulas; not useful on thrombi over 1 week old

Pregnancy Risk Factor B

Contraindications Active internal bleeding, history of a cerebrovascular accident, recent intracranial or intraspinal surgery (within prior two months), recent trauma including cardiopulmonary resuscitation, intracranial neoplasm, AV malformation or aneurysm, known bleeding diathesis, or severe uncontrolled arterial hypertension; hypersensitivity to urokinase or any component

Warnings/Precautions Use with caution in patients with recent (within 10 days) major surgery, obstetrical delivery, organ biopsy, previous puncture of noncompressible vessels, recent serious GI bleeding, high likelihood of left heart thrombus (eg, mitral stenosis with A-fib), subacute bacterial endocarditis, hemostatic defects including those secondary to severe hepatic or renal disease, pregnancy, cerebrovascular disease, diabetic hemorrhagic retinopathy, or any other condition in which bleeding might constitute a significant hazard or be particularly difficult to manage because of its location

The FDA is recommending (1/25/99) that Abbokinase® be reserved for only those situations where a physician has considered the alternatives and has determined that the use of urokinase is critical to the care of a specific patient in a specific situation; Abbokinase® is produced from primary cultures of kidney cells harvested postmortem from human neonates. Products manufactured from human source materials have the potential to transmit infectious agents. While some procedures to help control such risks in products of human source are in place, recent manufacturing inspections revealed deficiencies in some of the procedures used by Abbott and its supplier of the human neonatal kidney cells that could increase the risk of transmitting infectious agents. In considering this risk, the prescriber should be aware of the following information regarding currently available lots of urokinase; the kidney cells used in the manufacture of this product were harvested postmortem from human neonates from a population at high risk for a variety of infectious diseases, including tropical diseases. The screening of potential donors did not include the questioning of the mothers to determine infectious disease status or specific risk factors for infectious diseases; neither the mothers nor the neonate donors were tested for hepatitis C virus (HCV) infection; Abbott has recently instituted a test for HCV in the kidney cells used in the manufacture of Abbokinase® and negative test results have been obtained for currently available lots; however, Abbott has not validated this test; prior to use in the manufacture of Abbokinase®, the human kidney cells were harvested, stored and handled in a manner which may have permitted contamination with infectious agents; the FDA is not aware of any cases of infectious diseases that can be attributed to the use of Abbokinase®; however, the likelihood that cases of infectious diseases caused by Abbokinase®, if any, would have been recognized as such and reported to FDA is probably very low; therefore, the actual risk to patients of developing an infectious disease as a result of using Abbokinase® is unknown; for each setting in which the use of Abbokinase® is being contemplated, we encourage you to consider the appropriateness of other treatment options; FDA approved indications for Abbokinase® are: pulmonary embolism, coronary artery thrombosis, and I.V. catheter clearance; it should also be noted that the FDA has not approved the use of Abbokinase® for clearance of peripheral venous and arterial obstructions or for clearance of arteriovenous cannulas; other thrombolytic products on the U.S. market with well-described experience in multiple indications include Streptase® (Streptokinase), Kabikinase® (Streptokinase), Activase® (Alteplase), Eminase® (Anistreplase), and Retavase™ (Reteplase). We encourage all physicians to consider the appropriateness of other treatment options

Adverse Reactions

>10%:

Cardiovascular: Hypotension, arrhythmias

Hematologic: Bleeding, especially at sites of percutaneous trauma

Ocular: Periorbital swelling

Respiratory: Dyspnea

<1%: Headache, chills, rash, nausea, vomiting, anemia, eye hemorrhage, bronchospasm, epistaxis, diaphoresis, anaphylaxis

Overdosage/Toxicology

Symptoms of overdose include epistaxis, bleeding gums, hematoma, spontaneous ecchymoses, oozing at catheter site

In case of overdose, stop infusion, reverse bleeding with blood products that contain clotting factors

Drug Interactions Increased toxicity (increased bleeding) with anticoagulants, antiplatelet drugs, aspirin, indomethacin, dextran

Stability Store in refrigerator; reconstitute by gently rolling and tilting; do not shake; contains no preservatives, should not be reconstituted until immediately before using, discard unused portion; stable at room temperature for 24 hours after reconstitution

Mechanism of Action Promotes thrombolysis by directly activating plasminogen to plasmin, which degrades fibrin, fibrinogen, and other procoagulant plasma proteins

Pharmacodynamics/Kinetics
Onset of action: I.V.: Fibrinolysis occurs rapidly
Duration: 4 or more hours
Half-life: 10-20 minutes
Elimination: Cleared by the liver with a small amount excreted in urine and bile

Usual Dosage
Children and Adults: Deep vein thrombosis: I.V.: Loading: 4400 units/kg over 10 minutes, then 4400 units/kg/hour for 12 hours
Adults:
Myocardial infarction: Intracoronary: 750,000 units over 2 hours (6000 units/minute over up to 2 hours)
Occluded I.V. catheters:
5000 units (use only Abbokinase® Open Cath) in each lumen over 1-2 minutes, leave in lumen for 1-4 hours, then aspirate; may repeat with 10,000 units in each lumen if 5000 units fails to clear the catheter; **do not infuse into the patient**; volume to instill into catheter is equal to the volume of the catheter
I.V. infusion: 200 units/kg/hour in each lumen for 12-48 hours at a rate of at least 20 mL/hour
Dialysis patients: 5000 units is administered in each lumen over 1-2 minutes; leave urokinase in lumen for 1-2 days, then aspirate
Clot lysis (large vessel thrombi): Loading: I.V.: 4400 units/kg over 10 minutes, increase to 6000 units/kg/hour; maintenance: 4400-6000 units/kg/hour adjusted to achieve clot lysis or patency of affected vessel; doses up to 50,000 units/kg/hour have been used. **Note:** Therapy should be initiated as soon as possible after diagnosis of thrombi and continued until clot is dissolved (usually 24-72 hours).
Acute pulmonary embolism: Three treatment alternatives: 3 million unit dosage
Alternative 1: 12-hour infusion: 4400 units/kg (2000 units/lb) bolus over 10 minutes followed by 4400 units/kg/hour (2000 units/lb); begin heparin 1000 units/hour approximately 3-4 hours after completion of urokinase infusion or when PTT is <100 seconds
Alternative 2: 2-hour infusion: 1 million unit bolus over 10 minutes followed by 2 million units over 110 minutes; begin heparin 1000 units/hour approximately 3-4 hours after completion of urokinase infusion or when PTT is <100 seconds
Alternative 3: Bolus dose only: 15,000 units/kg over 10 minutes; begin heparin 1000 units/hour approximately 3-4 hours after completion of urokinase infusion or when PTT is <100 seconds

Administration Use 0.22 or 0.45 micron filter during I.V. therapy

Monitoring Parameters CBC, reticulocyte count, platelet count, DIC panel (fibrinogen, plasminogen, FDP, D-dimer, PT, PTT), thrombosis panel (AT-III, protein C), urinalysis, ACT

Dosage Forms
Powder for injection: 250,000 units (5 mL)
Powder for injection, catheter clear: 5000 units (1 mL)

♦ **Uro-KP-Neutral®** see Potassium Phosphate and Sodium Phosphate on page 955
♦ **Urolene Blue®** see Methylene Blue on page 759
♦ **Urozide®** see Hydrochlorothiazide on page 574
♦ **Ursodeoxycholic Acid** see Ursodiol on this page

Ursodiol (ER soe dye ole)

U.S. Brand Names Actigall™
Synonyms Ursodeoxycholic Acid
Therapeutic Category Gallstone Dissolution Agent
Use Gallbladder stone dissolution
Pregnancy Risk Factor B
Contraindications Not to be used with cholesterol, radiopaque, bile pigment stones, or stones >20 mm in diameter; allergy to bile acids
Warnings/Precautions Gallbladder stone dissolution may take several months of therapy; complete dissolution may not occur and recurrence of stones within 5 years has been observed in 50% of patients; use with caution in patients with a nonvisualizing gallbladder and those with chronic liver disease; not recommended for children

Adverse Reactions
1% to 10%: Gastrointestinal: Diarrhea
<1%: Fatigue, headache, pruritus, rash, nausea, vomiting, dyspepsia, metallic taste, abdominal pain, biliary pain, constipation

Overdosage/Toxicology
Symptoms of overdose include diarrhea
No specific therapy for diarrhea and for overdose

Drug Interactions Decreased effect with aluminum-containing antacids, cholestyramine, colestipol, clofibrate, oral contraceptives (estrogens)

Mechanism of Action Decreases the cholesterol content of bile and bile stones by reducing the secretion of cholesterol from the liver and the fractional reabsorption of cholesterol by the intestines
(Continued)

Ursodiol *(Continued)*

Pharmacodynamics/Kinetics

Metabolism: Undergoes extensive enterohepatic recycling; following hepatic conjugation and biliary secretion, the drug is hydrolyzed to active ursodiol, where it is recycled or transformed to lithocholic acid by colonic microbial flora

Half-life: 100 hours

Elimination: In feces via bile

Usual Dosage Adults: Oral: 8-10 mg/kg/day in 2-3 divided doses; use beyond 24 months is not established; obtain ultrasound images at 6-month intervals for the first year of therapy; 30% of patients have stone recurrence after dissolution

Monitoring Parameters ALT, AST, sonogram

Patient Information Frequent blood work necessary to follow drug effects; report any persistent nausea, vomiting, abdominal pain

Dosage Forms Capsule: 300 mg

Extemporaneous Preparations A 60 mg/mL ursodiol suspension may be made by opening twelve 300 mg capsules and wetting with sufficient glycerin and triturating to make a fine paste; gradually add 45 mL of simple syrup in three steps:

1. Add 15 mL to paste, triturate well and transfer to 2 oz amber bottle
2. Rinse mortar with 10 mL simple syrup and add to amber bottle
3. Repeat step 2 with sufficient syrup to make 60 mL final volume; label "Shake Well and Store in Refrigerator"; 35-day stability

- ♦ Utradol™ *see* Etodolac *on page 458*
- ♦ Vagilia® *see* Sulfabenzamide, Sulfacetamide, and Sulfathiazole *on page 1090*
- ♦ Vagistat® Vaginal *see* Tioconazole *on page 1147*
- ♦ Vagitrol® *see* Sulfanilamide *on page 1095*

Valacyclovir *(val ay SYE kloe veer)*

U.S. Brand Names Valtrex®

Therapeutic Category Antiviral Agent, Oral

Use Treatment of herpes zoster (shingles) in immunocompetent patients; episodic treatment or prophylaxis of recurrent genital herpes in immunocompetent patients; for first episode genital herpes

Pregnancy Risk Factor B

Pregnancy/Breast-Feeding Implications

Clinical effects on the fetus: Teratogenicity registry, thus far, has shown no increased rate of birth defects than that of the general population; however, the registry is small and use during pregnancy is only warranted if the potential benefit to the mother justifies the risk of the fetus

Breast-feeding/lactation: Avoid use in breast-feeding, if possible, since the drug distributes in high concentrations in breast milk

Contraindications Hypersensitivity to the drug or any component

Warnings/Precautions Thrombotic thrombocytopenic purpura/hemolytic uremic syndrome has occurred in immunocompromised patients; use caution and adjust the dose in elderly patients or those with renal insufficiency; safety and efficacy in children have not been established

Adverse Reactions

>10%:

Central nervous system: Headache (13% to 17%)

Gastrointestinal: Nausea (8% to 16%)

1% to 10%:

Central nervous system: Dizziness (2% to 4%)

Dermatologic: Pruritus

Gastrointestinal: Diarrhea (4% to 5%), constipation (1% to 5%), abdominal pain (2% to 3%), anorexia (≤3%), vomiting (≤7%)

Neuromuscular & skeletal: Weakness (2% to 4%)

Ocular: Photophobia

Overdosage/Toxicology

Symptoms of overdose include elevated serum creatinine, renal failure, and encephalitis, precipitation in renal tubules

Hemodialysis has resulted in up to 60% reduction in serum acyclovir levels after administration of acyclovir

Drug Interactions Decreased toxicity: Cimetidine and/or probenecid has decreased the rate but not the extent of valacyclovir conversion to acyclovir

Mechanism of Action Valacyclovir is rapidly and nearly completely converted to acyclovir by intestinal and hepatic metabolism. Acyclovir is converted to acyclovir monophosphate by virus-specific thymidine kinase then further converted to acyclovir triphosphate by other cellular enzymes. Acyclovir triphosphate inhibits DNA synthesis and viral replication by competing with deoxyguanosine triphosphate for viral DNA polymerase and being incorporated into viral DNA.

Pharmacodynamics/Kinetics

Distribution: Acyclovir is widely distributed throughout the body including brain, kidney, lungs, liver, spleen, muscle, uterus, vagina, and CSF

Protein binding: Valacyclovir is 13.5% to 17.9% bound to human plasma proteins

Metabolism: Valacyclovir is rapidly and nearly completely converted to acyclovir and elvalene by first pass intestinal and/or hepatic metabolism; acyclovir is hepatically metabolized to a very small extent

Bioavailability: After administration of valacyclovir, bioavailability of acyclovir is ~55%

Half-life: Normal renal function: Adults: 2.5-3.3 hours (acyclovir), approximately 30 minutes (valacyclovir); half-life of acyclovir in end-stage renal disease: 14-20 hours
Elimination: Primary route of acyclovir is the kidney
Usual Dosage Oral: Adults:
Shingles: 1 g 3 times/day for 7 days
Genital herpes:
Episodic treatment: 500 mg twice daily for 5 days
Prophylaxis: 500-1000 mg once daily
Dosing interval in renal impairment:
Cl_{cr} 30-49 mL/minute: 1 g every 12 hours
Cl_{cr} 10-29 mL/minute: 1 g every 24 hours
Cl_{cr} <10 mL/minute: 500 mg every 24 hours
Hemodialysis: 33% removed during 4-hour session
Monitoring Parameters Urinalysis, BUN, serum creatinine, liver enzymes, and CBC
Patient Information Take with plenty of water
Herpes zoster: Therapy is most effective when started within 48 hours of onset of zoster rash
Recurrent genital herpes: Therapy should be initiated within 24 hours after the onset of signs or symptoms
Nursing Implications Observe for CNS changes; avoid dehydration; begin therapy at the earliest sign of zoster infection (within 48 hours of the rash)
Dosage Forms Caplets: 500 mg

♦ **Valergen® Injection** see Estradiol on page 433
♦ **Valertest No.1® Injection** see Estradiol and Testosterone on page 435
♦ **Valisone®** see Betamethasone on page 141
♦ **Valium® Injection** see Diazepam on page 345
♦ **Valium® Oral** see Diazepam on page 345
♦ **Valpin® 50** see Anisotropine on page 86
♦ **Valproate Semisodium** see Valproic Acid and Derivatives on this page
♦ **Valproate Sodium** see Valproic Acid and Derivatives on this page
♦ **Valproic Acid** see Valproic Acid and Derivatives on this page

Valproic Acid and Derivatives (val PROE ik AS id & dah RIV ah tives)
Related Information
Anticonvulsants by Seizure Type on page 1300
Epilepsy Treatment on page 1468
Febrile Seizures on page 1469
U.S. Brand Names Depacon®; Depakene®; Depakote®
Canadian Brand Names Deproic
Synonyms Dipropylacetic Acid; Divalproex Sodium; DPA; 2-Propylpentanoic Acid; 2-Propylvaleric Acid; Valproate Semisodium; Valproate Sodium; Valproic Acid
Therapeutic Category Anticonvulsant; Antimigraine Agent
Use Management of simple and complex absence seizures; mixed seizure types; myoclonic and generalized tonic-clonic (grand mal) seizures; may be effective in partial seizures, infantile spasms, bipolar disorder; prevention of migraine headaches
Pregnancy Risk Factor D
Pregnancy/Breast-Feeding Implications
Clinical effects on the fetus: Crosses the placenta. Neural tube, cardiac, facial (characteristic pattern of dysmorphic facial features), skeletal, multiple other defects reported. Epilepsy itself, number of medications, genetic factors, or a combination of these probably influence the teratogenicity of anticonvulsant therapy. Risk of neural tube defects with use during first 30 days of pregnancy warrants discontinuation prior to pregnancy and through this period of possible.
Breast-feeding/lactation: Crosses into breast milk. American Academy of Pediatrics considers compatible with breast-feeding.
Contraindications Hypersensitivity to valproic acid or derivatives or any component; hepatic dysfunction
Warnings/Precautions Hepatic failure resulting in fatalities has occurred in patients; children <2 years of age are at considerable risk; monitor patients closely for appearance of malaise, weakness, facial edema, anorexia, jaundice, and vomiting; may cause severe thrombocytopenia, bleeding; hepatotoxicity has been reported after 3 days to 6 months of therapy; tremors may indicate overdosage; use with caution in patients receiving other anticonvulsants
Adverse Reactions
1% to 10%:
Endocrine & metabolic: Change in menstrual cycle
Gastrointestinal: Abdominal cramps, anorexia, diarrhea, nausea, vomiting, weight gain
<1%: Drowsiness, ataxia, irritability, confusion, restlessness, hyperactivity, headache, malaise, alopecia, erythema multiforme, hyperammonemia, pancreatitis, thrombocytopenia, prolongation of bleeding time, transient increased liver enzymes, liver failure, tremor, nystagmus, spots before eyes
Overdosage/Toxicology
Symptoms of overdose include coma, deep sleep, motor restlessness, visual hallucinations
Supportive treatment is necessary; naloxone has been used to reverse CNS depressant effects, but may block action of other anticonvulsants
(Continued)

Valproic Acid and Derivatives *(Continued)*

Drug Interactions CYP2C19 enzyme substrate; CYP2C9 and 2D6 enzyme inhibitor, CYP3A3/4 enzyme inhibitor (weak)

Decreased effects of phenytoin

Decreased effects with carbamazepine, lamotrigine, possibly clonazepam (increased absence seizures have been reported)

Increased effects/toxicity of diazepam, CNS depressants, alcohol

Increased effects/toxicity with aspirin (increase valproic acid levels)

Mechanism of Action Causes increased availability of gamma-aminobutyric acid (GABA), an inhibitory neurotransmitter, to brain neurons or may enhance the action of GABA or mimic its action at postsynaptic receptor sites

Pharmacodynamics/Kinetics

Protein binding: 80% to 90% (dose dependent)

Metabolism: Extensively in the liver

Half-life (increased in neonates and patients with liver disease): Children: 4-14 hours; Adults: 8-17 hours

Time to peak serum concentration: Within 1-4 hours; 3-5 hours after divalproex (enteric coated)

Elimination: 2% to 3% excreted unchanged in urine

Usual Dosage Children and Adults:

Oral: Initial: 10-15 mg/kg/day in 1-3 divided doses; increase by 5-10 mg/kg/day at weekly intervals until therapeutic levels are achieved; maintenance: 30-60 mg/kg/day in 2-3 divided doses

Children receiving more than 1 anticonvulsant (ie, polytherapy) may require doses up to 100 mg/kg/day in 3-4 divided doses

I.V.: Administer as a 60 minute infusion (≤20 mg/min) with the same frequency as oral products; switch patient to oral products as soon as possible

Rectal: Dilute syrup 1:1 with water for use as a retention enema; loading dose: 17-20 mg/kg one time; maintenance: 10-15 mg/kg/dose every 8 hours

Not dialyzable (0% to 5%)

Dosing adjustment/comments in hepatic impairment: Reduce dose

Dietary Considerations

Alcohol: Additive CNS depression, avoid or limit alcohol

Food:

Valproic acid may cause GI upset; take with large amount of water or food to decrease GI upset. May need to split doses to avoid GI upset.

Food may delay but does not affect the extent of absorption

Coated particles of divalproex sodium may be mixed with semisolid food (eg, applesauce or pudding) in patients having difficulty swallowing; particles should be swallowed and not chewed

Valproate sodium oral solution will generate valproic acid in carbonated beverages and may cause mouth and throat irritation; do not mix valproate sodium oral solution with carbonated beverages

Milk: No effect on absorption; may take with milk

Sodium: SIADH and water intoxication; monitor fluid status. May need to restrict fluid.

Monitoring Parameters Liver enzymes, CBC with platelets

Reference Range Therapeutic: 50-100 µg/mL (SI: 350-690 µmol/L); Toxic: >200 µg/mL (SI: >1390 µmol/L). Seizure control may improve at levels >100 µg/mL (SI: 690 µmol/L), but toxicity may occur at levels of 100-150 µg/mL (SI: 690-1040 µmol/L).

Test Interactions False-positive result for urine ketones

Patient Information Take with food or milk; do not chew, break, or crush the tablet or capsule; do not administer with carbonated drinks; report any sore throat, fever or fatigue, bleeding or bruising that is severe or that persists; may cause drowsiness, impair judgment or coordination

Nursing Implications Do not crush enteric coated drug product or capsules

Additional Information Sodium content of valproate sodium syrup (5 mL): 23 mg (1 mEq)

Divalproex sodium: Depakote®

Valproate sodium: Depakene® syrup

Valproic acid: Depakene® capsule

Dosage Forms

Capsule, sprinkle, as divalproex sodium (Depakote® Sprinkle®): 125 mg

Capsule, as valproic acid (Depakene®): 250 mg

Injection, as sodium valproate (Depacon™): 100 mg/mL (5 mL)

Syrup, as sodium valproate (Depakene®): 250 mg/5 mL (5 mL, 50 mL, 480 mL)

Tablet, delayed release, as divalproex sodium (Depakote®): 125 mg, 250 mg, 500 mg

Valrubicin *(val ru BYE cin)*

U.S. Brand Names Valstar™

Therapeutic Category Antineoplastic Agent, Monoclonal Antibody

Use Intravesical therapy of BCG-refractory carcinoma *in situ* of the urinary bladder

Pregnancy Risk Factor C

Pregnancy/Breast-Feeding Implications It is not known whether valrubicin is secreted in human milk. Because many drugs are secreted in milk, and the potential for serious adverse reactions exists, a decision should be made whether to discontinue nursing or discontinue the drug, taking into account the importance of the drug to the mother.

Contraindications Known hypersensitivity to anthracyclines, Cremophor® EL, or any component of this product; concurrent urinary tract infection or small bladder capacity (unable to tolerate a 75 mL instillation)

Warnings/Precautions Complete response observed in only 1 of 5 patients, delay of cystectomy may lead to development of metastatic bladder cancer, which is lethal. If complete response is not observed after 3 months or disease recurs, cystectomy must be reconsidered. Do not administer if mucosal integrity of bladder has been compromised or bladder perforation is present. Following TURP, status of bladder mucosa should be evaluated prior to initiation of therapy. Administer under the supervision of a physician experienced in the use of intravesical chemotherapy. Aseptic technique must be used during administration. All patients of reproductive age should use an effective method of contraception during the treatment period. Irritable bladder symptoms may occur during instillation and retention. Caution in patients with severe irritable bladder symptoms. Do not clamp urinary catheter. Red-tinged urine is typical for the first 24 hours after instillation. Prolonged symptoms or discoloration should prompt contact with the physician.

Valrubicin preparation should be performed in a class II laminar flow biologic safety cabinet. Personnel should be wearing surgical gloves and a closed front surgical gown with knit cuffs. Appropriate safety equipment is recommended for preparation, administration, and disposal of antineoplastics. If valrubicin contacts the skin, wash and flush thoroughly with water.

Adverse Reactions
>10%: Genitourinary: Frequency (61%), dysuria (56%), urgency (57%), bladder spasm (31%), hematuria (29%), bladder pain (28%), urinary incontinence (22%), cystitis (15%), urinary tract infection (15%)
1% to 10%:
Cardiovascular: Chest pain (2%), vasodilation (2%), peripheral edema (1%)
Central nervous system: Headache (4%), malaise (4%), dizziness (3%), fever (2%)
Dermatologic: Rash (3%)
Endocrine & metabolic: Hyperglycemia (1%)
Gastrointestinal: Abdominal pain (5%), nausea (5%), diarrhea (3%), vomiting (2%), flatulence (1%)
Genitourinary: Nocturia (7%), burning symptoms (5%), urinary retention (4%), urethral pain (3%), pelvic pain (1%), hematuria (microscopic) (3%)
Hematologic: Anemia (2%)
Neuromuscular & skeletal: Weakness (4%), back pain (3%), myalgia (1%)
Respiratory: Pneumonia (1%)
<1%: Tenesmus, pruritus, taste disturbance, skin irritation, decreased urine flow, urethritis

Overdosage/Toxicology Inadvertent paravenous extravasation was not associated with skin ulceration or necrosis. Myelosuppression is possible following inadvertent systemic administration or following significant systemic absorption from intravesical instillation.

Drug Interactions No specific drug interactions studies have been performed; the systemic exposure to valrubicin is negligible, and interactions are unlikely

Stability Store unopened vials under refrigeration at 2°C to 8°C (36°F to 48°F); stable for 12 hours when diluted in 0.9% sodium chloride

Mechanism of Action Blocks function of DNA topoisomerase II; inhibits DNA synthesis, causes extensive chromosomal damage, and arrests cell development

Pharmacodynamics/Kinetics
Absorption: Well absorbed into bladder tissue, negligible systemic absorption. Trauma to mucosa may increase absorption, and perforation greatly increases absorption with significant systemic myelotoxicity.
Metabolism: Negligible after intravesical instillation and 2 hour retention
Elimination: In urine, when expelled from urinary bladder

Usual Dosage Adults: Intravesical: 800 mg once weekly for 6 weeks
Dosing adjustment in renal impairment: No specific adjustment recommended
Dosing adjustment in hepatic impairment: No specific adjustment recommended

Administration Withdraw contents of 4 vials, each containing 200 mg in 5 mL (allowed to warm to room temperature without heating), and dilute with 55 mL of 0.9% sodium chloride injection, USP. Instill slowly via gravity flow through a urinary catheter (following sterile insertion). Withdraw the catheter and allow patient to retain solution for 2 hours. After 2 hours, the patient should void.

Monitoring Parameters Cystoscopy, biopsy, and urine cytology every 3 months for recurrence or progression

Patient Information Complete response observed in only 1 of 5 patients, delay of cystectomy may lead to development of metastatic bladder cancer, which is lethal. If complete response is not observed after 3 months or disease recurs, cystectomy must be reconsidered. Irritable bladder symptoms may occur during instillation and retention. Red-tinged urine is typical for the first 24 hours after instillation. Prolonged symptoms or discoloration should prompt contact with the physician. Maintain adequate hydration following treatment. Do not become pregnant or cause pregnancy (males) during treatment. Do not breast-feed during treatment period.

Dosage Forms Injection: 200 mg/5mL

Valsartan (val SAR tan)
Related Information
Angiotensin Agents on page 1291
U.S. Brand Names Diovan™
(Continued)

Valsartan *(Continued)*

Therapeutic Category Angiotensin II Antagonist; Antihypertensive Agent

Use Alone or in combination with other antihypertensive agents in treating essential hypertension; may have an advantage over losartan due to minimal metabolism requirements and consequent use in mild to moderate hepatic impairment

Pregnancy Risk Factor C (1st trimester); D (2nd and 3rd trimesters)

Pregnancy/Breast-Feeding Implications Breast-feeding/lactation: Although no human data exist, valsartan is known to be excreted in animal breast milk and should be avoided in lactating mothers if possible

Contraindications Hypersensitivity to valsartan or any components, pregnancy, severe hepatic insufficiency, biliary cirrhosis or biliary obstruction, primary hyperaldosteronism, bilateral renal artery stenosis

Warnings/Precautions Use extreme caution with concurrent administration of potassium-sparing diuretics or potassium supplements, in patients with mild to moderate hepatic dysfunction (adjust dose), in those who may be sodium/water depleted (eg, on high-dose diuretics), and in the elderly; avoid use in patients with congestive heart failure, unilateral renal artery stenosis, aortic/mitral valve stenosis, coronary artery disease, or hypertrophic cardiomyopathy, if possible

Adverse Reactions Similar incidence to placebo; independent of race, age, and gender

>1%:

Central nervous system: Headache, dizziness, drowsiness, ataxia

Endocrine & metabolic: Decreased libido

Gastrointestinal: Diarrhea, abdominal pain, nausea, abnormal taste

Genitourinary: Polyuria

Hematologic: Neutropenia

Hepatic: Increased LFTs

Neuromuscular & skeletal: Arthralgia

Respiratory: Cough, upper respiratory infection, rhinitis, sinusitis, pharyngitis

<1%: Anemia, increased creatinine

Overdosage/Toxicology

Only mild toxicity (hypotension, bradycardia, hyperkalemia) has been reported with large overdoses (up to 5 g of captopril and 300 mg of enalapril); no fatalities have been reported

Treatment is symptomatic (eg, fluids)

Drug Interactions

Decreased effect: Phenobarbital, ketoconazole, troleandomycin, sulfaphenazole

Increased effect: Cimetidine, moxonidine

Mechanism of Action As a prodrug, valsartan produces direct antagonism of the angiotensin II (AT2) receptors, unlike the angiotensin-converting enzyme inhibitors. It displaces angiotensin II from the AT1 receptor and produces its blood pressure lowering effects by antagonizing AT1-induced vasoconstriction, aldosterone release, catecholamine release, arginine vasopressin release, water intake, and hypertrophic responses. This action results in more efficient blockade of the cardiovascular effects of angiotensin II and fewer side effects than the ACE inhibitors.

Pharmacodynamics/Kinetics

Distribution: V_d: 17 L (adults)

Protein binding: 94% to 97%

Metabolism: Metabolized to an inactive metabolite

Bioavailability: 23%

Half-life: 9 hours

Time to peak serum concentration: 2 hours (maximal effect: 4-6 hours)

Elimination: 13% and 83% excreted as unchanged drug in urine and feces, respectively

Usual Dosage Adults: 80 mg/day; may be increased to 160 mg if needed (maximal effects observed in 4-6 weeks)

Dosing adjustment in renal impairment: No dosage adjustment necessary if Cl_{cr} >10 mL/minute

Dosing adjustment in hepatic impairment (mild - moderate): ≤80 mg/day

Dialysis: Not significantly removed

Monitoring Parameters Baseline and periodic electrolyte panels, renal and liver function tests, urinalysis; symptoms of hypotension or hypersensitivity

Patient Information Do not stop taking this medication unless instructed by a physician, do not take this medication during pregnancy or lactation; take a missed dose as soon as possible unless it is almost time for your next dose; call your physician immediately if you have symptoms of allergy or develop side effects including headache and dizziness

Dosage Forms Capsule: 80 mg, 160 mg

Valsartan and Hydrochlorothiazide

(val SAR tan & hye droe klor oh THYE a zide)

U.S. Brand Names Diovan™ HCT

Therapeutic Category Angiotensin II Antagonist Combination; Antihypertensive Agent, Combination

Dosage Forms Tablet: Valsartan 80 mg and hydrochlorothiazide 12.5 mg; valsartan 160 mg and hydrochlorothiazide 12.5 mg

♦ **Valstar™** *see Valrubicin on page 1204*

♦ **Valtrex®** *see Valacyclovir on page 1202*

♦ **Vamate®** *see Hydroxyzine on page 589*

♦ **Vancenase® AQ Inhaler** *see Beclomethasone on page 128*

♦ **Vancenase® Nasal Inhaler** *see* Beclomethasone *on page 128*
♦ **Vanceril® Oral Inhaler** *see* Beclomethasone *on page 128*
♦ **Vancocin®** *see* Vancomycin *on this page*
♦ **Vancocin® CP** *see* Vancomycin *on this page*
♦ **Vancoled®** *see* Vancomycin *on this page*

Vancomycin (van koe MYE sin)

Related Information

Antibiotic Treatment of Adults With Infective Endocarditis *on page 1401*
Antimicrobial Drugs of Choice *on page 1404*
Community-Acquired Pneumonia in Adults *on page 1419*
Prevention of Bacterial Endocarditis *on page 1377*
Prevention of Wound Infection & Sepsis in Surgical Patients *on page 1381*
Recommendations for Preventing the Spread of Vancomycin Resistance *on page 1426*

U.S. Brand Names Lyphocin®; Vancocin®; Vancoled®
Canadian Brand Names Vancocin® CP
Synonyms Vancomycin Hydrochloride
Therapeutic Category Antibiotic, Miscellaneous
Use Treatment of patients with infections caused by staphylococcal species and streptococcal species; used orally for staphylococcal enterocolitis or for antibiotic-associated pseudomembranous colitis produced by *C. difficile*
Pregnancy Risk Factor C
Contraindications Hypersensitivity to vancomycin or any component; avoid in patients with previous severe hearing loss
Warnings/Precautions Use with caution in patients with renal impairment or those receiving other nephrotoxic or ototoxic drugs; dosage modification required in patients with impaired renal function (especially elderly)

Adverse Reactions

Oral:
>10%: Gastrointestinal: Bitter taste, nausea, vomiting
1% to 10%:
Central nervous system: Chills, drug fever
Hematologic: Eosinophilia
<1%: Vasculitis, thrombocytopenia, ototoxicity, renal failure, interstitial nephritis
Parenteral:
>10%:
Cardiovascular: Hypotension accompanied by flushing
Dermatologic: Erythematous rash on face and upper body (red neck or red man syndrome - infusion rate related)
1% to 10%:
Central nervous system: Chills, drug fever
Dermatologic: Rash
Hematologic: Eosinophilia, reversible neutropenia
<1%: Vasculitis, Stevens-Johnson syndrome, ototoxicity (especially with large doses), thrombocytopenia, renal failure (especially with renal dysfunction or pre-existing hearing loss)

Overdosage/Toxicology

Symptoms of overdose include ototoxicity, nephrotoxicity
There is no specific therapy for an overdosage with vancomycin. Care is symptomatic and supportive in nature. Peritoneal filtration and hemofiltration (not dialysis) have been shown to reduce the serum concentration of vancomycin; high flux dialysis may remove up to 25%.

Drug Interactions Increased toxicity: Anesthetic agents; other ototoxic or nephrotoxic agents

Stability

Vancomycin reconstituted intravenous solutions are stable for 14 days at room temperature or refrigeration
Stability of parenteral admixture at room temperature (25°C) or refrigeration temperature (4°C): 7 days
Standard diluent: 500 mg/150 mL D_5W; 750 mg/250 mL D_5W; 1 g/250 mL D_5W
Minimum volume: Maximum concentration is 5 mg/mL to minimize thrombophlebitis
Incompatible with heparin, phenobarbital
After the oral solution is reconstituted, it should be refrigerated and used within 2 weeks

Mechanism of Action Inhibits bacterial cell wall synthesis by blocking glycopeptide polymerization through binding tightly to D-alanyl-D-alanine portion of cell wall precursor

Pharmacodynamics/Kinetics

Absorption:
Oral: Poor
I.M.: Erratic
Intraperitoneal: Can result in 38% absorption systemically
Distribution: Widely distributed in body tissues and fluids except for CSF
Relative diffusion of antimicrobial agents from blood into cerebrospinal fluid (CSF): Good only with inflammation (exceeds usual MICs)
Ratio of CSF to blood level (%): Normal meninges: Nil; Inflamed meninges: 20-30
Protein binding: 10%-50%
Half-life (biphasic): Terminal:
Newborns: 6-10 hours
(Continued)

Vancomycin *(Continued)*

Infants and Children 3 months to 4 years: 4 hours
Children >3 years: 2.2-3 hours
Adults: 5-11 hours, prolonged significantly with reduced renal function
End-stage renal disease: 200-250 hours
Time to peak serum concentration: I.V.: Within 45-65 minutes
Elimination: As unchanged drug in the urine via glomerular filtration (80% to 90%); oral doses are excreted primarily in the feces

Usual Dosage Initial dosage recommendation: I.V.:

Neonates:

Postnatal age ≤7 days:
<1200 g: 15 mg/kg/dose every 24 hours
1200-2000 g: 10 mg/kg/dose every 12 hours
>2000 g: 15 mg/kg/dose every 12 hours
Postnatal age >7 days:
<1200 g: 15 mg/kg/dose every 24 hours
≥1200 g: 10 mg/kg/dose divided every 8 hours

Infants >1 month and Children:
40 mg/kg/day in divided doses every 6 hours
Prophylaxis for bacterial endocarditis:
Dental, oral, or upper respiratory tract surgery: 20 mg/kg 1 hour prior to the procedure
GI/GU procedure: 20 mg/kg plus gentamicin 2 mg/kg 1 hour prior to surgery
Infants >1 month and Children with staphylococcal central nervous system infection: 60 mg/kg/day in divided doses every 6 hours

Adults:
With normal renal function: 1 g **or** 10-15 mg/kg/dose every 12 hours
Prophylaxis for bacterial endocarditis:
Dental, oral, or upper respiratory tract surgery: 1 g 1 hour before surgery
GI/GU procedure: 1 g plus 1.5 mg/kg gentamicin 1 hour prior to surgery

Dosing interval in renal impairment (vancomycin levels should be monitored in patients with any renal impairment):
Cl_{cr} >60 mL/minute: Start with 1 g or 10-15 mg/kg/dose every 12 hours
Cl_{cr} 40-60 mL/minute: Start with 1 g or 10-15 mg/kg/dose every 24 hours
Cl_{cr} <40 mL/minute: Will need longer intervals; determine by serum concentration monitoring

Hemodialysis: Not dialyzable (0% to 5%); generally not removed; exception minimal-moderate removal by some of the newer high-flux filters; dose may need to be administered more frequently; monitor serum concentrations
Continuous ambulatory peritoneal dialysis (CAPD): Not significantly removed; administration via CAPD fluid: 15-30 mg/L (15-30 mcg/mL) of CAPD fluid
Continuous arteriovenous hemofiltration: Dose as for Cl_{cr} 10-40 mL/minute

Antibiotic lock technique (for catheter infections): 2 mg/mL in SWI/NS or D_5W; instill 3-5 mL into catheter port as a flush solution instead of heparin lock (**Note:** Do not mix with any other solutions)

Intrathecal: Vancomycin is available as a powder for injection and may be diluted to 1-5 mg/mL concentration in preservative-free 0.9% sodium chloride for administration into the CSF
Neonates: 5-10 mg/day
Children: 5-20 mg/day
Adults: Up to 20 mg/day

Oral: Pseudomembranous colitis produced by *C. difficile*:
Neonates: 10 mg/kg/day in divided doses
Children: 40 mg/kg/day in divided doses, added to fluids
Adults: 125 mg 4 times/day for 10 days

Monitoring Parameters Periodic renal function tests, urinalysis, serum vancomycin concentrations, WBC, audiogram

Reference Range
Timing of serum samples: Draw peak 1 hour after 1-hour infusion has completed; draw trough just before next dose
Therapeutic levels: Peak: 25-40 µg/mL; Trough: 5-12 µg/mL
Toxic: >80 µg/mL (SI: >54 µmol/L)

Patient Information Report pain at infusion site, dizziness, fullness or ringing in ears with I.V. use; nausea or vomiting with oral use

Nursing Implications Obtain drug levels after the third dose unless otherwise directed; peaks are drawn 1 hour after the completion of a 1- to 2-hour infusion; troughs are obtained just before the next dose; slow I.V. infusion rate if maculopapular rash appears on face, neck, trunk, and upper extremities (Red man reaction)

Dosage Forms
Capsule, as hydrochloride: 125 mg, 250 mg
Powder for oral solution, as hydrochloride: 1 g, 10 g
Powder for injection, as hydrochloride: 500 mg, 1 g, 2 g, 5 g, 10 g

♦ **Vancomycin Hydrochloride** *see* Vancomycin *on previous page*
♦ **Vanoxide-HC®** *see* Benzoyl Peroxide and Hydrocortisone *on page 135*
♦ **Vansil™** *see* Oxamniquine *on page 870*
♦ **Vantin®** *see* Cefpodoxime *on page 217*
♦ **Vapocet®** *see* Hydrocodone and Acetaminophen *on page 575*
♦ **Vapo-Iso®** *see* Isoproterenol *on page 635*

♦ **Vaponefrin**® *see* Epinephrine *on page 415*
♦ **VAQTA**® *see* Hepatitis A Vaccine *on page 563*

Varicella Virus Vaccine (var i SEL a VYE rus vak SEEN)

Related Information
Immunization Recommendations *on page 1358*
Recommendations of the Advisory Committee on Immunization Practices (ACIP) *on page 1360*
Recommended Childhood Immunization Schedule - US - January-December, 1999 *on page 1359*

U.S. Brand Names Varivax®

Synonyms Chicken Pox Vaccine; Varicella-Zoster Virus (VZV) Vaccine

Therapeutic Category Vaccine, Live Virus

Use
The American Association of Pediatrics recommends that the chickenpox vaccine should be given to all healthy children between 12 months and 18 years; children between 12 months and 13 years who have not been immunized or who have not had chickenpox should receive 1 vaccination while children 13-18 years of age require 2 vaccinations 4-8 weeks apart; the vaccine has been added to the childhood immunization schedule for infants 12-28 months of age and children 11-12 years of age who have not been vaccinated previously or who have not had the disease; it is recommended to be given with the measles, mumps, and rubella (MMR) vaccine

Pregnancy Risk Factor C

Pregnancy/Breast-Feeding Implications
Clinical effects on the fetus: Varivax® should not be administered to pregnant females and pregnancy should be avoided for 3 months following vaccination
Breast-feeding/lactation: Use during breast-feeding should be avoided

Contraindications
Hypersensitivity to any component of the vaccine, including gelatin; a history of anaphylactoid reaction to neomycin; individuals with blood dyscrasias, leukemia, lymphomas, or other malignant neoplasms affecting the bone marrow or lymphatic systems; those receiving immunosuppressive therapy; primary and acquired immunodeficiency states; a family history of congenital or hereditary immunodeficiency; active untreated tuberculosis; febrile illness; pregnancy; I.V. injection

Warnings/Precautions
Children and adolescents with acute lymphoblastic leukemia in remission can receive the vaccine under an investigational protocol (215-283-0897); no clinical data are available or efficacy in children <12 months of age
Immediate treatment for anaphylactoid reaction should be available during vaccine use; defer vaccination for at least 5 months following blood or plasma transfusions, immune globulin (IgG), or VZIG (avoid IgG or IVIG use for 2 months following vaccination); salicylates should be avoided for 5 weeks after vaccination; vaccinated individuals should not have close association with susceptible high risk individuals (newborns, pregnant women, immunocompromised persons) following vaccination

Adverse Reactions All serious adverse reactions must be reported to the U.S. Department of Health and Human Services (DHHS) Vaccine Adverse Event Reporting System (VAERS) 1-800-822-7967.

Percentages are listed for children ≤12 years of age
>10%:
Central nervous system: Fever (14.7%)
Local: Induration/stiffness at the injection site (19.3%)
1% to 10%:
Central nervous system: Pain, irritability/nervousness, fatigue, disturbed sleep, headache, malaise, chills
Dermatologic: Redness, rash (at injection site - 3.4%), pruritus, generalized varicella-like rash (generalized - 3.8%)
Gastrointestinal: Diarrhea, loss of appetite, vomiting, abdominal pain, nausea
Hematologic: Hematoma
Neuromuscular & skeletal: Myalgia, arthralgia
Otic: Otitis
Respiratory: Upper respiratory illness, cough
Miscellaneous: Lymphadenopathy, allergic reactions
<1%: Febrile seizures (causality not established), pneumonitis

Drug Interactions
Clinical studies show that Varivax® can be administered concomitantly with MMR and limited data indicate that DTP and PedvaxHIB™ may also be administered together (using separate sites and syringes)
Decreased effect: The effect of the vaccine may be decreased and the risk of varicella disease in individuals who are receiving immunosuppressant drugs may be increased
Increased effect: Salicylates may increase the risk of Reye's following varicella vaccination

Stability
Store in freezer (-15°C), store diluent separately at room temperature or in refrigerator; discard if reconstituted vaccine is not used within 30 minutes

Mechanism of Action
As a live, attenuated vaccine, varicella virus vaccine offers active immunity to disease caused by the varicella-zoster virus

Pharmacodynamics/Kinetics
Onset of action: Approximately 4-6 weeks postvaccination
Duration: Lowest breakthrough rates (0.2% to 2.9%) exist in the first 2 years following postvaccination, with slightly higher rates in the third through the fifth year

Usual Dosage S.C.:
Children 12 months to 12 years: 0.5 mL
Children 12 years to Adults: 2 doses of 0.5 mL separated by 4-8 weeks
(Continued)

Varicella Virus Vaccine *(Continued)*

Administration Inject S.C. into the outer aspect of the upper arm, if possible

Monitoring Parameters Rash, fever

Patient Information Report any adverse reactions to the healthcare provider or Vaccine Adverse Event Reporting System (1-800-822-7967); avoid pregnancy for 3 months following vaccination; avoid salicylates for 5 weeks after vaccination; avoid close association with susceptible high risk individuals following vaccination

Nursing Implications Obtain the previous immunization history (including allergic reactions) to previous vaccines; do not inject into a blood vessel; use the supplied diluent only for reconstitution; inject immediately after reconstitution

Additional Information Minimum potency level: 1350 plaque forming units (PFU)/0.5 mL

Dosage Forms Powder for injection, lyophilized powder, preservative free: 1350 plaque forming units (PFU)/0.5 mL (0.5 mL single-dose vials)

Varicella-Zoster Immune Globulin (Human)

(var i SEL a- ZOS ter i MYUN GLOB yoo lin HYU man)

Related Information

Adverse Events and Vaccination *on page 1369*

Guidelines for the Prevention of Opportunistic Infections in Persons with HIV *on page 1388*

Immunization Recommendations *on page 1358*

Prophylaxis for Patients Exposed to Common Communicable Diseases *on page 1384*

Synonyms VZIG

Therapeutic Category Immune Globulin

Use Passive immunization of susceptible immunodeficient patients after exposure to varicella; most effective if begun within 96 hours of exposure; there is no evidence VZIG modifies established varicella-zoster infections.

Restrict administration to those patients meeting the following criteria:

Neoplastic disease (eg, leukemia or lymphoma)

Congenital or acquired immunodeficiency

Immunosuppressive therapy with steroids, antimetabolites or other immunosuppressive treatment regimens

Newborn of mother who had onset of chickenpox within 5 days before delivery or within 48 hours after delivery

Premature (≥28 weeks gestation) whose mother has no history of chickenpox

Premature (<28 weeks gestation or ≤1000 g VZIG) regardless of maternal history

One of the following types of exposure to chickenpox or zoster patient(s) may warrant administration:

Continuous household contact

Playmate contact (>1 hour play indoors)

Hospital contact (in same 2-4 bedroom or adjacent beds in a large ward or prolonged face-to-face contact with an infectious staff member or patient)

Susceptible to varicella-zoster

Age <15 years; administer to immunocompromised adolescents and adults and to other older patients on an individual basis

An acceptable alternative to VZIG prophylaxis is to treat varicella, if it occurs, with high-dose I.V. acyclovir

Age is the most important risk factor for reactivation of varicella zoster; persons <50 years of age have incidence of 2.5 cases per 1000, whereas those 60-79 have 6.5 cases per 1000 and those >80 years have 10 cases per 1000

Pregnancy Risk Factor C

Contraindications Not for prophylactic use in immunodeficient patients with history of varicella, unless patient's immunosuppression is associated with bone marrow transplantation; **not** recommended for nonimmunodeficient patients, including pregnant women, because the severity of chickenpox is much less than in immunosuppressed patients; allergic response to gamma globulin or anti-immunoglobulin; sensitivity to thimerosal; persons with IgA deficiency; do not administer to patients with thrombocytopenia or coagulopathies

Warnings/Precautions VZIG is not indicated for prophylaxis or therapy of normal adults who are exposed to or who develop varicella; it is not indicated for treatment of herpes zoster. Do not inject I.V.

Adverse Reactions

1% to 10%: Local: Discomfort at the site of injection (pain, redness, edema)

<1%: Malaise, headache, rash, angioedema, GI symptoms, respiratory symptom, anaphylactic shock

Drug Interactions Decreased effect: Live virus vaccines (do not administer within 3 months of immune globulin administration)

Stability Refrigerate at 2°C to 8°C (36°F to 46°F)

Mechanism of Action The exact mechanism has not been clarified but the antibodies in varicella-zoster immune globulin most likely neutralize the varicella-zoster virus and prevent its pathological actions

Usual Dosage High risk susceptible patients who are exposed again more than 3 weeks after a prior dose of VZIG should receive another full dose; there is no evidence VZIG modifies established varicella-zoster infections.

I.M.: Administer by deep injection in the gluteal muscle or in another large muscle mass. Inject 125 units/10 kg (22 lb); maximum dose: 625 units (5 vials); minimum dose: 125 units; do not administer fractional doses. Do not inject I.V. See table.

VZIG Dose Based on Weight

Weight of Patient		Dose	
kg	lb	Units	No. of Vials
0-10	0-22	125	1
10.1-20	22.1-44	250	2
20.1-30	44.1-66	375	3
30.1-40	66.1-88	500	4
>40	>88	625	5

Administration Do not inject I.V.; administer deep I.M. into the gluteal muscle or other large muscle mass. For patients ≤10 kg, administer 1.25 mL at a single site; for patients >10 kg, administer no more than 2.5 mL at a single site. Administer entire contents of each vial

Dosage Forms Injection: 125 units of antibody in single dose vials

♦ **Varicella-Zoster Virus (VZV) Vaccine** see Varicella Virus Vaccine on page 1209
♦ **Varivax®** see Varicella Virus Vaccine on page 1209
♦ **Vascor®** see Bepridil on page 137
♦ **Vaseretic® 10-25** see Enalapril and Hydrochlorothiazide on page 411
♦ **Vasocidin® Ophthalmic** see Sulfacetamide Sodium and Prednisolone on page 1091
♦ **VasoClear® [OTC]** see Naphazoline on page 817
♦ **Vasocon Regular®** see Naphazoline on page 817
♦ **Vasodilan®** see Isoxsuprine on page 641

Vasopressin (vay soe PRES in)

U.S. Brand Names Pitressin® Injection
Canadian Brand Names Pressyn®
Synonyms ADH; Antidiuretic Hormone; 8-Arginine Vasopressin; Vasopressin Tannate
Therapeutic Category Antidiuretic Hormone Analog; Hormone, Posterior Pituitary; Vesicant
Use Treatment of diabetes insipidus; prevention and treatment of postoperative abdominal distention; differential diagnosis of diabetes insipidus
Unlabeled use: Adjunct in the treatment of GI hemorrhage and esophageal varices
Pregnancy Risk Factor B
Contraindications Hypersensitivity to vasopressin or any component
Warnings/Precautions Use with caution in patients with seizure disorders, migraine, asthma, vascular disease, renal disease, cardiac disease; chronic nephritis with nitrogen retention. Goiter with cardiac complications, arteriosclerosis; I.V. infiltration may lead to severe vasoconstriction and localized tissue necrosis; also, gangrene of extremities, tongue, and ischemic colitis. Elderly patients should be cautioned not to increase their fluid intake beyond that sufficient to satisfy their thirst in order to avoid water intoxication and hyponatremia; under experimental conditions, the elderly have shown to have a decreased responsiveness to vasopressin with respect to its effects on water homeostasis
Adverse Reactions
  1% to 10%:
    Cardiovascular: Increased blood pressure, bradycardia, arrhythmias, venous thrombosis, vasoconstriction with higher doses, angina
    Central nervous system: Pounding in the head, fever, vertigo
    Dermatologic: Urticaria, circumoral pallor
    Gastrointestinal: Flatulence, abdominal cramps, nausea, vomiting
    Neuromuscular & skeletal: Tremor
    Miscellaneous: Diaphoresis
  <1%: Myocardial infarction, water intoxication, allergic reaction
Overdosage/Toxicology
  Symptoms of overdose include drowsiness, weight gain, confusion, listlessness, water intoxication
  Water intoxication requires withdrawal of the drug; severe intoxication may require osmotic diuresis and loop diuretics
Drug Interactions
  Decreased effect: Lithium, epinephrine, demeclocycline, heparin, and alcohol block antidiuretic activity to varying degrees
  Increased effect: Chlorpropamide, phenformin, urea and fludrocortisone potentiate antidiuretic response
Stability Store injection at room temperature; protect from heat and from freezing; use only clear solutions
Mechanism of Action Increases cyclic adenosine monophosphate (cAMP) which increases water permeability at the renal tubule resulting in decreased urine volume and increased osmolality; causes peristalsis by directly stimulating the smooth muscle in the GI tract
Pharmacodynamics/Kinetics
  Nasal: Onset of action: 1 hour; Duration: 3-8 hours
  (Continued)

Vasopressin *(Continued)*

Parenteral: Duration of action: I.M., S.C.: 2-8 hours

Absorption: Destroyed by trypsin in GI tract, must be administered parenterally or intranasally

Nasal:
Metabolism: In the liver, kidneys
Half-life: 15 minutes
Elimination: In urine

Parenteral:
Metabolism: Most of dose metabolized by liver and kidneys
Half-life: 10-20 minutes
Elimination: 5% of S.C. dose (aqueous) excreted unchanged in urine after 4 hours

Usual Dosage

Diabetes insipidus (highly variable dosage; titrated based on serum and urine sodium and osmolality in addition to fluid balance and urine output):

I.M., S.C.:
Children: 2.5-10 units 2-4 times/day as needed
Adults: 5-10 units 2-4 times/day as needed (dosage range 5-60 units/day)

Continuous I.V. infusion: Children and Adults: 0.5 milliunit/kg/hour (0.0005 unit/kg/hour); double dosage as needed every 30 minutes to a maximum of 0.01 unit/kg/hour

Intranasal: Administer on cotton pledget or nasal spray

Abdominal distention (aqueous): Adults: I.M.: 5 mg stat, 10 mg every 3-4 hours

GI hemorrhage: I.V. infusion: Dilute aqueous in NS or D_5W to 0.1-1 unit/mL
Children: Initial: 0.002-0.005 units/kg/minute; titrate dose as needed; maximum: 0.01 unit/kg/minute; continue at same dosage (if bleeding stops) for 12 hours, then taper off over 24-48 hours
Adults: Initial: 0.2-0.4 unit/minute, then titrate dose as needed, if bleeding stops; continue at same dose for 12 hours, taper off over 24-48 hours

Dosing adjustment in hepatic impairment: Some patients respond to much lower doses with cirrhosis

Administration

I.V. infusion administration requires the use of an infusion pump and should be administered in a peripheral line to minimize adverse reactions on coronary arteries

Infusion rates: 100 units (aqueous) in 500 mL D_5W rate
0.1 unit/minute: 30 mL/hour
0.2 unit/minute: 60 mL/hour
0.3 unit/minute: 90 mL/hour
0.4 unit/minute: 120 mL/hour
0.5 unit/minute: 150 mL/hour
0.6 unit/minute: 180 mL/hour

Monitoring Parameters Serum and urine sodium, urine output, fluid input and output, urine specific gravity, urine and serum osmolality

Reference Range Plasma: 0-2 pg/mL (SI: 0-2 ng/L) if osmolality <285 mOsm/L; 2-12 pg/mL (SI: 2-12 ng/L) if osmolality >290 mOsm/L

Patient Information Side effects such as abdominal cramps and nausea may be reduced by drinking a glass of water with each dose

Nursing Implications Watch for signs of I.V. infiltration and gangrene; elderly patients should be cautioned not to increase their fluid intake beyond that sufficient to satisfy their thirst in order to avoid water intoxication and hyponatremia; under experimental conditions, the elderly have shown to have a decreased responsiveness to vasopressin with respect to its effects on water homeostasis

Dosage Forms Injection, aqueous: 20 pressor units/mL (0.5 mL, 1 mL)

♦ **Vasopressin Tannate** *see Vasopressin on previous page*

♦ **Vasosulf® Ophthalmic** *see Sulfacetamide Sodium and Phenylephrine on page 1091*

♦ **Vasotec®** *see Enalapril on page 409*

♦ **Vasotec® I.V.** *see Enalapril on page 409*

♦ **Vasoxyl®** *see Methoxamine on page 755*

♦ **V-Cillin K®** *see Penicillin V Potassium on page 898*

♦ **VCR** *see Vincristine on page 1219*

Vecuronium *(ve KYOO roe nee um)*

Related Information
Neuromuscular Blocking Agents Comparison *on page 1331*

U.S. Brand Names Norcuron®

Synonyms ORG NC 45

Therapeutic Category Neuromuscular Blocker Agent, Nondepolarizing; Skeletal Muscle Relaxant

Use Adjunct to anesthesia, to facilitate intubation, and provide skeletal muscle relaxation during surgery or mechanical ventilation

Pregnancy Risk Factor C

Contraindications Known hypersensitivity to vecuronium

Warnings/Precautions Use with caution in patients with hepatic impairment, neuromuscular disease, myasthenia gravis, and the elderly; ventilation must be supported during neuromuscular blockade

Adverse Reactions <1%: Tachycardia, flushing, edema, hypotension, circulatory collapse, bradycardia, rash, itching, hypersensitivity reaction

Overdosage/Toxicology

Symptoms of overdose include prolonged skeletal muscle weakness and apnea cardiovascular collapse

Use neostigmine, edrophonium, or pyridostigmine with atropine to antagonize skeletal muscle relaxation; support of ventilation and the cardiovascular system through mechanical means, fluids, and pressors may be necessary

Drug Interactions Increased toxicity/effect with aminoglycosides, ketamine, magnesium sulfate, verapamil, quinidine, clindamycin, furosemide

Stability Stable for 5 days at room temperature when reconstituted with bacteriostatic water; stable for 24 hours at room temperature when reconstituted with preservative-free sterile water (avoid preservatives in neonates); do not mix with alkaline drugs

Mechanism of Action Blocks acetylcholine from binding to receptors on motor endplate inhibiting depolarization

Pharmacodynamics/Kinetics

Good intubation conditions within 2.5-3 minutes; maximum neuromuscular blockade within 3-5 minutes

Elimination: Vecuronium bromide and its metabolite(s) appear to be excreted principally in feces via biliary eliminations; the drug and its metabolite(s) are also excreted in urine

Usual Dosage I.V. (do not administer I.M.):

Infants >7 weeks to 1 year: Initial: 0.08-0.1 mg/kg/dose; maintenance: 0.05-0.1 mg/kg/ every hour as needed

Children >1 year and Adults: Initial: 0.08-0.1 mg/kg/dose; maintenance: 0.05-0.1 mg/kg/ every hour as needed; may be administered with caution as a continuous infusion at 0.075 mg/kg/hour (concern has been raised of drug-induced myopathies in ICU setting)

Note: Children (1-10 years) may require slightly higher initial doses and slightly more frequent supplementation

Dosing adjustment in hepatic impairment: Dose reductions are necessary in patients with liver disease

Administration Administer undiluted I.V. injection as a single bolus

Monitoring Parameters Blood pressure, heart rate

Dosage Forms Powder for injection: 10 mg (5 mL, 10 mL)

♦ **Veetids®** see Penicillin V Potassium on page 898
♦ **Velban®** see Vinblastine on page 1217
♦ **Velosef®** see Cephradine on page 231
♦ **Velosulin® Human** see Insulin Preparations on page 613
♦ **Velvelan®** see Urea on page 1199

Venlafaxine (VEN la faks een)

Related Information

Antidepressant Agents Comparison on page 1301

U.S. Brand Names Effexor®; Effexor® XR

Therapeutic Category Antidepressant, Miscellaneous

Use Treatment of depression in adults

Unapproved use: Obsessive-compulsive disorder

Pregnancy Risk Factor C

Contraindications Do not use concomitantly with MAO inhibitors, contraindicated in patients with hypersensitivity to venlafaxine or other components

Warnings/Precautions Venlafaxine is associated with sustained increases in blood pressure (10-15 mm Hg SDBP); venlafaxine may actuate mania or hypomania and seizures. Concurrent therapy with a monoamine oxidase inhibitor may result in serious or fatal reactions; at least 14 days should elapse between treatment with an MAO inhibitor and venlafaxine. Patients with cardiovascular disorders or a recent myocardial infarction probably should only receive venlafaxine if the benefits of therapy outweigh the risks.

Adverse Reactions

≥10%:

Central nervous system: Headache, somnolence, dizziness, insomnia, nervousness

Gastrointestinal: Nausea, xerostomia, constipation

Genitourinary: Abnormal ejaculation

Neuromuscular & skeletal: Weakness, neck pain

Miscellaneous: Diaphoresis

1% to 10%:

Cardiovascular: Palpitations, hypertension, sinus tachycardia

Central nervous system: Anxiety

Gastrointestinal: Weight loss, anorexia, vomiting, diarrhea, dysphagia

Genitourinary: Impotence

Neuromuscular & skeletal: Tremor

Ocular: Blurred vision

<1%: Seizures, ear pain

Overdosage/Toxicology

Symptoms of overdose include somnolence and occasionally tachycardia

Most overdoses resolve with only supportive treatment. Use of activated charcoal, induction of emesis, or gastric lavage should be considered for acute ingestion; forced diuresis, dialysis, and hemoperfusion not effective due to large volume of distribution

Drug Interactions CYP2D6, 2E1, and 3A3/4 enzyme substrate; CYP2D6 enzyme inhibitor (weak)

Increased toxicity: Cimetidine MAO inhibitors (hyperpyrexic crisis); TCAs, fluoxetine, sertraline, phenothiazine, class 1C antiarrhythmics, warfarin; venlafaxine is a weak

(Continued)

Venlafaxine *(Continued)*

inhibitor of CYP2D6, which is responsible for metabolizing antipsychotics, antiarrhythmics, TCAs, and beta-blockers. Therefore, interactions with these agents are possible, however, less likely than with more potent enzyme inhibitors such as the SSRIs.

Mechanism of Action Venlafaxine and its active metabolite o-desmethylvenlafaxine (ODV) are potent inhibitors of neuronal serotonin and norepinephrine reuptake and weak inhibitors of dopamine reuptake; causes beta-receptor down regulation and reduces adenylcyclase coupled beta-adrenergic systems in the brain

Pharmacodynamics/Kinetics

Absorption: Oral: 92% to 100%

Protein binding: Bound to human plasma 27% to 30%; steady-state achieved within 3 days of multiple dose therapy

Metabolism: In the liver by cytochrome P-450 enzyme system to active metabolite, O-desmyethyl-venlafaxine (ODV)

Half-life: 3-7 hours (venlafaxine) and 11-13 hours (ODV)

Time to peak: 1-2 hours

Elimination: Primarily by renal route

Usual Dosage Adults: Oral:

Immediate-release tablets: 75 mg/day, administered in 2 or 3 divided doses, taken with food; dose may be increased in 75 mg/day increments at intervals of at least 4 days, up to 225-375 mg/day

Extended-release capsules: 75 mg once daily taken with food; for some new patients, it may be desirable to start at 37.5 mg/day for 4-7 days before increasing to 75 mg once daily; dose may be increased by up to 75 mg/day increments every 4 days as tolerated, up to a maximum of 225 mg/day

Dosing adjustment in renal impairment: Cl_{cr} 10-70 mL/minute: Decrease dose by 25%; decrease total daily dose by 50% if dialysis patients; dialysis patients should receive dosing after completion of dialysis

Dosing adjustment in moderate hepatic impairment: Reduce total daily dosage by 50%

Dietary Considerations

Alcohol: Additive CNS effect, avoid use

Food: May be taken without regard to food

Monitoring Parameters Blood pressure should be regularly monitored, especially in patients with a high baseline blood pressure

Reference Range Peak serum level of 163 ng/mL (325 ng/mL of ODV metabolite) obtained after a 150 mg oral dose

Test Interactions ↑ thyroid, ↑ uric acid, ↑ glucose, ↑ potassium, ↑ AST, ↑ cholesterol (S)

Patient Information Avoid use of alcohol; use caution when operating hazardous machinery; if a rash or shortness of breath occurs while using venlafaxine, contact physician immediately

Nursing Implications Causes mean increase in heart rate of 4 beats/minute; tapering to minimize symptoms of discontinuation is recommended when the drug is discontinued; tapering should be over a 2-week period if the patient has received it longer than 6 weeks

Dosage Forms

Capsule, extended release: 37.5 mg, 75 mg, 150 mg

Tablet: 25 mg, 37.5 mg, 50 mg, 75 mg, 100 mg

♦ **Venoglobulin®-I** *see* Immune Globulin, Intravenous *on page 604*

♦ **Venoglobulin®-S** *see* Immune Globulin, Intravenous *on page 604*

♦ **Ventolin®** *see* Albuterol *on page 35*

♦ **Ventolin® Rotocaps®** *see* Albuterol *on page 35*

♦ **VePesid® Injection** *see* Etoposide *on page 459*

♦ **VePesid® Oral** *see* Etoposide *on page 459*

Verapamil *(ver AP a mil)*

Related Information

Adult ACLS Algorithm, Tachycardia *on page 1450*

Antiarrhythmic Drugs Comparison *on page 1297*

Calcium Channel Blockers Comparison *on page 1315*

Hypertension Therapy *on page 1479*

U.S. Brand Names Calan®; Calan® SR; Covera-HS®; Isoptin®; Isoptin® SR; Verelan®

Canadian Brand Names Apo®-Verap; Novo-Veramil; Nu-Verap

Synonyms Iproveratril Hydrochloride; Verapamil Hydrochloride

Therapeutic Category Antianginal Agent; Antiarrhythmic Agent, Class IV; Antihypertensive Agent; Calcium Channel Blocker

Use Orally used for treatment of angina pectoris (vasospastic, chronic stable, unstable) and hypertension; I.V. for supraventricular tachyarrhythmias (PSVT, atrial fibrillation, atrial flutter); only Covera-HS® is approved for both hypertension and angina as a sustained release product

Pregnancy Risk Factor C

Pregnancy/Breast-Feeding Implications

Clinical effects on the fetus: Use in pregnancy only when clearly needed and when the benefits outweigh the potential hazard to the fetus. Crosses the placenta. 1 report of suspected heart block when used to control fetal supraventricular tachycardia. May exhibit tocolytic effects.

Breast-feeding/lactation: Crosses into breast milk. American Academy of Pediatrics considers **compatible** with breast-feeding.

Contraindications Sinus bradycardia; advanced heart block; ventricular tachycardia; cardiogenic shock; hypersensitivity to verapamil or any component; atrial fibrillation or flutter associated with accessory conduction pathways

Warnings/Precautions Use with caution in sick-sinus syndrome, severe left ventricular dysfunction, hepatic or renal impairment, hypertrophic cardiomyopathy (especially obstructive), abrupt withdrawal may cause increased duration and frequency of chest pain; avoid I.V. use in neonates and young infants due to severe apnea, bradycardia, or hypotensive reactions; elderly may experience more constipation and hypotension. Monitor EKG and blood pressure closely in patients receiving I.V. therapy particularly in patients with supraventricular tachycardia.

Adverse Reactions O (oral); I.V. (intravenous):

1% to 10%:

 Cardiovascular: Bradycardia; first, second, or third degree A-V block; congestive heart failure (1.8%), hypotension (O - 2.5%; I.V. - 1.5%), peripheral edema (2.1%)

 Central nervous system: Dizziness/lightheadedness (O - 3.5%; I.V. - 1.2%), fatigue, headache (O - 2.2%; I.V. - 1.2%)

 Dermatologic: Rash (1.2%)

 Gastrointestinal: Constipation (7.3%), nausea (O - 2.7%; I.V. - 0.9%)

 Neuromuscular & skeletal: Weakness

<1%: Chest pain, hypotension (excessive), tachycardia, flushing, galactorrhea, gingival hyperplasia

Overdosage/Toxicology The primary cardiac symptoms of calcium blocker overdose include hypotension and bradycardia. The hypotension is caused by peripheral vasodilation, myocardial depression, and bradycardia. Bradycardia results from sinus bradycardia, second- or third-degree atrioventricular block, or sinus arrest with junctional rhythm. Intraventricular conduction is usually not affected so QRS duration is normal (verapamil does prolong the P-R interval and bepridil prolongs the Q-T and may cause ventricular arrhythmias, including torsade de pointes).

The noncardiac symptoms include confusion, stupor, nausea, vomiting, metabolic acidosis and hyperglycemia.

Following initial gastric decontamination, if possible, repeated calcium administration may promptly reverse the depressed cardiac contractility (but not sinus node depression or peripheral vasodilation); glucagon, epinephrine, and amrinone may treat refractory hypotension; glucagon and epinephrine also increase the heart rate (outside the U.S., 4-aminopyridine may be available as an antidote); dialysis and hemoperfusion are not effective in enhancing elimination although repeat-dose activated charcoal may serve as an adjunct with sustained-release preparations.

In a few reported cases, overdose with calcium channel blockers has been associated with hypotension and bradycardia, initially refractory to atropine but becoming more responsive to this agent when larger doses (approaching 1 g/hour for more than 24 hours) of calcium chloride was administered.

Drug Interactions CYP1A2 and 3A3/4 enzyme substrate; CYP3A3/4 inhibitor

Decreased effect: Phenobarbital, hydantoins, vitamin D, sulfinpyrazone, and rifampin may decrease verapamil serum concentrations by increased hepatic metabolism

Increased effect of quinidine with verapamil

Increased toxicity:

 Verapamil and alcohol may increase blood alcohol levels and prolong its effects

 Verapamil and amiodarone may increase cardiotoxicity

 Verapamil and aspirin may cause bruising

 Verapamil and cimetidine may cause increased bioavailability of verapamil

 Verapamil and beta-blockers may cause increased cardiac depressant effects on A-V conduction

 Verapamil and carbamazepine may cause increased carbamazepine levels

 Verapamil and cyclosporine may cause increased cyclosporine levels

 Verapamil and digoxin may cause increased digoxin levels

 Verapamil and doxorubicin may cause increased doxorubicin levels

 Verapamil and lithium has reportedly increased the patient's sensitivity to the effects of lithium (neurotoxicity)

 Verapamil and theophylline may cause increased pharmacologic actions of theophylline secondary to decreased clearance of theophylline

 Verapamil and vecuronium may cause increased vecuronium levels

 Dantrolene and verapamil may result in hyperkalemia and myocardial depression

Disopyramide: Avoid combination with disopyramide, discontinue disopyramide 48 hours before starting therapy, do not restart until 24 hours after verapamil has been discontinued

Stability Store injection at room temperature; protect from heat and from freezing; use only clear solutions; **compatible** in solutions of pH of 3-6, but may precipitate in solutions having a pH ≥6

Mechanism of Action Inhibits calcium ion from entering the "slow channels" or select voltage-sensitive areas of vascular smooth muscle and myocardium during depolarization; produces a relaxation of coronary vascular smooth muscle and coronary vasodilation; increases myocardial oxygen delivery in patients with vasospastic angina; slows automaticity and conduction of A-V node.

Pharmacodynamics/Kinetics

Oral (nonsustained tablets): Peak effect: 2 hours; Duration: 6-8 hours

I.V.: Peak effect: 1-5 minutes; Duration: 10-20 minutes

(Continued)

Verapamil *(Continued)*

Protein binding: 90%

Metabolism: In the liver; extensive first-pass effect

Bioavailability: Oral: 20% to 30%

Half-life: Infants: 4.4-6.9 hours; Adults: Single dose: 2-8 hours, increased up to 12 hours with multiple dosing; increased half-life with hepatic cirrhosis

Elimination: 70% of dose excreted in urine (3% to 4% as unchanged drug) and 16% in feces

Usual Dosage

Children: SVT:

I.V.:

<1 year: 0.1-0.2 mg/kg over 2 minutes; repeat every 30 minutes as needed

1-15 years: 0.1-0.3 mg/kg over 2 minutes; maximum: 5 mg/dose, may repeat dose in 15 minutes if adequate response not achieved; maximum for second dose: 10 mg/dose

Oral (dose not well established):

1-5 years: 4-8 mg/kg/day in 3 divided doses **or** 40-80 mg every 8 hours

>5 years: 80 mg every 6-8 hours

Adults:

SVT: I.V.: 5-10 mg (approximately 0.075-0.15 mg/kg), second dose of 10 mg (~0.15 mg/kg) may be given 15-30 minutes after the initial dose if patient tolerates, but does not respond to initial dose

Angina: Oral: Initial dose: 80-120 mg 3 times/day (elderly or small stature: 40 mg 3 times/day); range: 240-480 mg/day in 3-4 divided doses

Hypertension: 80 mg 3 times/day or 240 mg/day (sustained release); range: 240-480 mg/day; 120 mg/day in the elderly or small patients (no evidence of additional benefit in doses >360 mg/day)

Note: One time per day dosing is recommended at bedtime with Covera-HS®

Dosing adjustment in renal impairment: Cl_{cr} <10 mL/minute: Administer at 50% to 75% of normal dose

Dialysis: Not dialyzable (0% to 5 %) via hemo or peritoneal dialysis; supplemental dose is not necessary

Dosing adjustment/comments in hepatic disease: Reduce dose in cirrhosis, reduce dose to 20% to 50% of normal and monitor EKG

Administration Administer around-the-clock to promote less variation in peak and trough serum levels; I.V. rate of infusion: Over 2 minutes

Monitoring Parameters Monitor blood pressure closely

Reference Range Therapeutic: 50-200 ng/mL (SI: 100-410 nmol/L) for parent; under normal conditions norverapamil concentration is the same as parent drug. Toxic: >90 µg/mL

Patient Information Sustained release products should be taken with food and not crushed; limit caffeine intake; notify physician if angina pain is not reduced when taking this drug, or if irregular heartbeat or shortness of breath occurs

Nursing Implications Do not crush sustained release drug product

Additional Information Although there is some initial data which may show increased risk of myocardial infarction with the treatment of hypertension with calcium antagonists, controlled trial (eg, ALL-HAT) are ongoing to examine the long-term effects of not only these agents but other antihypertensives in preventing heart disease. Until these studies are completed, patients taking calcium antagonists should be encouraged to continue with the prescribed antihypertensive regimen although a switch from high-dose short-acting products to sustained release agents may be warranted.

Dosage Forms

Capsule, , as hydrochloride, sustained release (Verelan®): 120 mg, 180 mg, 240 mg, 360 mg

Injection, as hydrochloride: 2.5 mg/mL (2 mL, 4 mL)

Isoptin®: 2.5 mg/mL (2 mL, 4 mL)

Tablet, as hydrochloride: 40 mg, 80 mg, 120 mg

Calan®, Isoptin®: 40 mg, 80 mg, 120 mg

Tablet, as hydrochloride, sustained release: 180 mg, 240 mg

Calan® SR, Isoptin® SR: 120 mg, 180 mg, 240 mg

Covera-HS®: 180 mg, 240 mg

Extemporaneous Preparations A 50 mg/mL oral suspension may be made using twenty 80 mg verapamil tablets, 3 mL of purified water USP, 8 mL of methylcellulose 1% and simple syrup qs ad to 32 mL; the expected stability is 30 days under refrigeration; shake well before use. A mixture of verapamil 50 mg/mL plus hydrochlorothiazide 5 mg/mL was stable 60 days in refrigerator in a 1:1 preparation of Ora-Sweet® and Ora-Plus®, of Ora-Sweet® SF and Ora-Plus®, and of cherry syrup.

Allen LV and Erickson III MA, "Stability of Labetalol Hydrochloride, Metoprolol Tartrate, Verapamil Hydrochloride, and Spironolactone With Hydrochlorothiazide in Extemporaneously Compounded Oral Liquids," *Am J Health Syst Pharm,* 1996, 53:304-9.

Nahata MC and Hipple TF, *Pediatric Drug Formulations,* 2nd ed, Cincinnati, OH: Harvey Whitney Books Co, 1992.

- **Vermizine®** *see* Piperazine *on page 933*
- **Vermox®** *see* Mebendazole *on page 716*
- **Verrex-C&M®** *see* Podophyllin and Salicylic Acid *on page 940*
- **Versed®** *see* Midazolam *on page 777*
- **Versel®** *see* Selenium *on page 1054*
- **Vesanoid®** *see* Tretinoin, Oral *on page 1171*
- **Vexol® Ophthalmic Suspension** *see* Rimexolone *on page 1029*
- **Viagra™** *see* Sildenafil *on page 1060*
- **Vibazine®** *see* Buclizine *on page 156*
- **Vibramycin®** *see* Doxycycline *on page 397*
- **Vibramycin® IV** *see* Doxycycline *on page 397*
- **Vibra-Tabs®** *see* Doxycycline *on page 397*
- **Vicks® 44E [OTC]** *see* Guaifenesin and Dextromethorphan *on page 550*
- **Vicks® Children's Chloraseptic® [OTC]** *see* Benzocaine *on page 133*
- **Vicks® Chloraseptic® Sore Throat [OTC]** *see* Benzocaine *on page 133*
- **Vicks® Pediatric Formula 44E [OTC]** *see* Guaifenesin and Dextromethorphan *on page 550*
- **Vicks® Sinex® Nasal Solution [OTC]** *see* Phenylephrine *on page 918*
- **Vicodin®** *see* Hydrocodone and Acetaminophen *on page 575*
- **Vicodin® ES** *see* Hydrocodone and Acetaminophen *on page 575*
- **Vicodin® HP** *see* Hydrocodone and Acetaminophen *on page 575*
- **Vicon Forte®** *see* Vitamins, Multiple *on page 1226*
- **Vicon® Plus [OTC]** *see* Vitamins, Multiple *on page 1226*
- **Vicoprofen®** *see* Hydrocodone and Ibuprofen *on page 578*

Vidarabine (vye DARE a been)

U.S. Brand Names Vira-A® Ophthalmic

Synonyms Adenine Arabinoside; Ara-A; Arabinofuranosyladenine; Vidarabine Monohydrate

Therapeutic Category Antiviral Agent, Ophthalmic

Use Treatment of acute keratoconjunctivitis and epithelial keratitis due to herpes simplex virus type 1 and 2; superficial keratitis caused by herpes simplex virus

Pregnancy Risk Factor C

Contraindications Hypersensitivity to vidarabine or any component; sterile trophic ulcers

Warnings/Precautions Not effective against RNA virus, adenoviral ocular infections, bacterial fungal or chlamydial infections of the cornea, or trophic ulcers; temporary visual haze may be produced; neoplasia has occurred with I.M. vidarabine-treated animals; although *in vitro* studies have been inconclusive, they have shown mutagenesis

Adverse Reactions Percentage unknown: Burning eyes, lacrimation, keratitis, photophobia, foreign body sensation, uveitis

Overdosage/Toxicology No untoward effects anticipated with ingestion

Mechanism of Action Inhibits viral DNA synthesis by blocking DNA polymerase

Usual Dosage Children and Adults: Ophthalmic: Keratoconjunctivitis: Instill ½" of ointment in lower conjunctival sac 5 times/day every 3 hours while awake until complete re-epithelialization has occurred, then twice daily for an additional 7 days

Patient Information Do not use eye make-up when on this medication for ophthalmic infection; use sunglasses if photophobic reaction occurs; may cause blurred vision; notify physician if improvement not seen after 7 days or if condition worsens

Dosage Forms Ointment, ophthalmic, as monohydrate: 3% [30 mg/mL = 28 mg/mL base] (3.5 g)

- **Vidarabine Monohydrate** *see* Vidarabine *on this page*
- **Vi-Daylin® [OTC]** *see* Vitamins, Multiple *on page 1226*
- **Vi-Daylin/F®** *see* Vitamins, Multiple *on page 1226*
- **Videx®** *see* Didanosine *on page 352*

Vinblastine (vin BLAS teen)

Related Information

Cancer Chemotherapy Regimens *on page 1263*
Extravasation Management of Chemotherapeutic Agents *on page 1285*
Toxicities of Chemotherapeutic Agents *on page 1288*

U.S. Brand Names Alkaban-AQ®; Velban®

Synonyms Vinblastine Sulfate; Vincaleukoblastine; VLB

Therapeutic Category Antineoplastic Agent, Vesicant; Antineoplastic Agent, Vinca Alkaloid; Vesicant

Use Treatment of Hodgkin's and non-Hodgkin's lymphoma, testicular, lung, head and neck, breast, and renal carcinomas, Mycosis fungoides, Kaposi's sarcoma, histiocytosis, choriocarcinoma, and idiopathic thrombocytopenic purpura

Pregnancy Risk Factor D

Contraindications For I.V. use only; **I.T. use may result in death;** severe bone marrow suppression or presence of bacterial infection not under control prior to initiation of therapy

Warnings/Precautions The U.S. Food and Drug Administration (FDA) currently recommends that procedures for proper handling and disposal of antineoplastic agents be considered. Avoid extravasation; dosage modification required in patients with impaired liver function and neurotoxicity. Using small amounts of drug daily for long periods may (Continued)

Vinblastine (Continued)

increase neurotoxicity and is therefore not advised. For I.V. use only. **Intrathecal administration may result in death.** Use with caution in patients with cachexia or ulcerated skin; monitor closely for shortness of breath or bronchospasm in patients receiving mitomycin C.

Adverse Reactions

>10%:

Dermatologic: Alopecia

Gastrointestinal: Nausea and vomiting are most common and are easily controlled with standard antiemetics; constipation, diarrhea (less common), stomatitis, abdominal cramps, anorexia, metallic taste

Emetic potential: Moderate (30% to 60%)

Hematologic: May cause severe bone marrow suppression and is the dose-limiting toxicity of VLB (unlike vincristine); severe granulocytopenia and thrombocytopenia may occur following the administration of VLB and nadir 7-10 days after treatment

Myelosuppressive:

WBC: Moderate - severe

Platelets: Moderate - severe

Onset (days): 4-7

Nadir (days): 4-10

Recovery (days): 17

1% to 10%:

Cardiovascular: Hypertension, Raynaud's phenomenon

Central nervous system: Depression, malaise, headache, seizures

Dermatologic: Rash, photosensitivity, dermatitis

Endocrine & metabolic: Hyperuricemia

Extravasation: VLB is a vesicant and can cause tissue irritation and necrosis if infiltrated; if extravasation occurs, follow institutional policy, which may include hyaluronidase and hot compresses

Gastrointestinal: Paralytic ileus, stomatitis

Genitourinary: Urinary retention

Local: **Vesicant chemotherapy**

Neuromuscular & skeletal: Jaw pain, myalgia, paresthesia

Respiratory: Bronchospasm

<1%: VLB rarely produces neurotoxicity at clinical doses; however, neurotoxicity may be seen, especially at high doses; if it occurs, symptoms are similar to VCR toxicity (ie, peripheral neuropathy, loss of deep tendon reflexes, headache, weakness, urinary retention, and GI symptoms, tachycardia, orthostatic hypotension, convulsions); hemorrhagic colitis

Overdosage/Toxicology

Symptoms of overdose include bone marrow suppression, mental depression, paresthesia, loss of deep reflexes, neurotoxicity

There is no information regarding the effectiveness of dialysis. There are no antidotes for vinblastine; treatment is supportive and symptomatic, including fluid restriction or hypertonic saline (3% sodium chloride) for drug-induced secretion of inappropriate antidiuretic hormone (SIADH), diazepam or phenytoin for seizures, laxatives for constipation, and antiemetics for toxic emesis

Drug Interactions CYP3A3/4 and 3A5-7 enzyme substrate; CYP2D6 enzyme inhibitor

Decreased effect:

Phenytoin plasma levels may be reduced with concomitant combination chemotherapy with vinblastine

Alpha-interferon enhances interferon toxicity; phenytoin may decrease plasma levels

Increased toxicity:

Previous or simultaneous use with mitomycin-C has resulted in acute shortness of breath and severe bronchospasm within minutes or several hours after vinca alkaloid injection and may occur up to 2 weeks after the dose of mitomycin

Mitomycin-C in combination with administration of VLB may cause acute shortness of breath and severe bronchospasm, onset may be within minutes or several hours after VLB injection

Stability

Store intact vials under refrigeration (2°C to 8°C) and protect from light; stable for 24 hours at room temperature

Further dilution in D_5W or NS is stable for 21 days at room temperature (25°C) and refrigeration (4°C)

Standard I.V. dilution:

I.V. push: Dose/syringe (concentration = 1 mg/mL)

Maximum syringe size for IVP is a 30 mL syringe and syringe should be ≤75% full

CIV: Dose/250-1000 mL D_5W or NS

Protect from light

Mechanism of Action VLB binds to tubulin and inhibits microtubule formation, therefore, arresting the cell at metaphase by disrupting the formation of the mitotic spindle; it is specific for the M and S phases; binds to microtubular protein of the mitotic spindle causing metaphase arrest

Pharmacodynamics/Kinetics

Absorption: Not reliably absorbed from the GI tract and must be given I.V.

Distribution: V_d: 27.3 L/kg; binds extensively to tissues; does not penetrate CNS or other fatty tissues; distributes to the liver

Protein binding: 99% rapidly

Metabolism: Hepatic metabolism to an active metabolite
Half-life (biphasic): Initial 0.164 hours; Terminal: 25 hours
Elimination: Biliary excretion (95%); <1% eliminated unchanged in urine

Usual Dosage Refer to individual protocols. Varies depending upon clinical and hematological response. Give at intervals of at least 14 days and only after leukocyte count has returned to at least 4000/mm³; maintenance therapy should be titrated according to leukocyte count. Dosage should be reduced in patients with recent exposure to radiation therapy or chemotherapy; single doses in these patients should not exceed 5.5 mg/m².

Children and Adults: I.V.: 4-20 mg/m² (0.1-0.5 mg/kg) every 7-10 days **or** 5-day continuous infusion of 1.5-2 mg/m²/day **or** 0.1-0.5 mg/kg/week

Dosing adjustment in hepatic impairment:
Serum bilirubin 1.5-3.0 mg/dL or AST 60-180 units: Administer 50% of normal dose
Serum bilirubin 3.0-5.0 mg/dL: Administer 25% of dose
Serum bilirubin >5.0 mg/dL or AST >180 units: Omit dose

Administration
FATAL IF GIVEN INTRATHECALLY
IVP over at least one minute is desired route of administration because of potential for extravasation. However, has also been administered CIV - **CENTRAL LINE ONLY** for CIV administration.

Avoid extravasation
Protect from light

Monitoring Parameters CBC with differential and platelet count, serum uric acid, hepatic function tests

Patient Information Hair may be lost during treatment but will regrow to its pretreatment extent even with continued treatment. Report any bleeding; examine mouth daily and report soreness to a physician; jaw pain or pain in the organs containing tumor tissue; avoid constipation. Any signs of infection, easy bruising or bleeding, shortness of breath, or painful or burning urination should be brought to physician's attention. Nausea, vomiting, or hair loss sometimes occurs. The drug may cause permanent sterility and may cause birth defects. Contraceptive measures are recommended during therapy. The drug may be excreted in breast milk, therefore, an alternative form of feeding your baby should be used.

Nursing Implications May be administered by I.V. push or into a free flowing I.V.; monitor for life-threatening bronchospasm (most likely to occur if patient is also taking mitomycin). Maintain adequate hydration; allopurinol may be given to prevent uric acid nephropathy; may cause sloughing upon extravasation.

Extravasation treatment:
Mix 250 units hyaluronidase with 6 mL of NS
Inject the hyaluronidase solution subcutaneously through 6 clockwise injections into the infiltrated area using a 25-gauge needle; change the needle with each new injection
Apply heat immediately for 1 hour; repeat 4 times/day for 3-5 days
Application of cold or hydrocortisone is contraindicated

Dosage Forms
Injection, as sulfate: 1 mg/mL (10 mL)
Powder for injection, as sulfate: 10 mg

♦ **Vinblastine Sulfate** see Vinblastine on page 1217
♦ **Vincaleukoblastine** see Vinblastine on page 1217
♦ **Vincasar® PFS™ Injection** see Vincristine on this page

Vincristine (vin KRIS teen)
Related Information
Cancer Chemotherapy Regimens on page 1263
Extravasation Management of Chemotherapeutic Agents on page 1285
Toxicities of Chemotherapeutic Agents on page 1288
U.S. Brand Names Oncovin® Injection; Vincasar® PFS™ Injection
Synonyms LCR; Leurocristine; VCR; Vincristine Sulfate
Therapeutic Category Antineoplastic Agent, Vesicant; Antineoplastic Agent, Vinca Alkaloid; Vesicant
Use Treatment of leukemias, Hodgkin's disease, non-Hodgkin's lymphomas, Wilms' tumor, neuroblastoma, rhabdomyosarcoma
Pregnancy Risk Factor D
Contraindications Hypersensitivity to vincristine or any component; **for I.V. use only, fatal if given intrathecally**; patients with demyelinating form of Charcot-Marie-Tooth syndrome
Warnings/Precautions The U.S. Food and Drug Administration (FDA) currently recommends that procedures for proper handling and disposal of antineoplastic agents be considered. Dosage modification required in patients with impaired hepatic function or who have pre-existing neuromuscular disease; avoid extravasation; use with caution in the elderly; avoid eye contamination; observe closely for shortness of breath, bronchospasm, especially in patients treated with mitomycin C. For I.V. use only; **intrathecal administration results in death**; administer allopurinol to prevent uric acid nephropathy; not to be used with radiation.
Adverse Reactions
>10%:
Dermatologic: Alopecia occurs in 20% to 70% of patients
(Continued)

Vincristine (Continued)

Extravasation: VCR is a vesicant and can cause tissue irritation and necrosis if infiltrated; if extravasation occurs, follow institutional policy, which may include hyaluronidase and hot compresses

Vesicant chemotherapy

1% to 10%:

Cardiovascular: Orthostatic hypotension or hypertension, hypertension, hypotension

Central nervous system: Motor difficulties, seizures, headache, CNS depression, cranial nerve paralysis, fever

Dermatologic: Rash

Endocrine & metabolic: Hyperuricemia

SIADH: Rarely occurs, but may be related to the neurologic toxicity; may cause symptomatic hyponatremia with seizures; the increase in serum ADH concentration usually subsides within 2-3 days after onset

Gastrointestinal: Constipation and possible paralytic ileus secondary to neurologic toxicity; oral ulceration, abdominal cramps, anorexia, metallic taste, bloating, nausea, vomiting, weight loss, diarrhea

Emetic potential: Low (<10%)

Local: Phlebitis

Neurologic: Alterations in mental status such as depression, confusion, or insomnia; constipation, paralytic ileus, and urinary tract disturbances may occur. All patients should be on a prophylactic bowel management regimen. Cranial nerve palsies, headaches, jaw pain, optic atrophy with blindness have been reported. Intrathecal administration of VCR has uniformly caused death; VCR should **never** be administered by this route. Neurologic effects of VCR may be additive with those of other neurotoxic agents and spinal cord irradiation.

Neuromuscular & skeletal: Jaw pain, leg pain, myalgia, cramping, numbness, weakness

Peripheral neuropathy: Frequently the dose-limiting toxicity of VCR. Most frequent in patients >40 years of age; occurs usually after an average of 3 weekly doses, but may occur after just one dose. Manifested as loss of the deep tendon reflexes in the lower extremities, numbness, tingling, pain, paresthesias of the fingers and toes (stocking glove sensation), and "foot drop" or "wrist drop"

Ocular: Photophobia

<1%: Stomatitis

Myelosuppressive: Occasionally mild leukopenia and thrombocytopenia may occur

WBC: Rare

Platelets: Rare

Onset (days): 7

Nadir (days): 10

Recovery (days): 21

Overdosage/Toxicology

Symptoms of overdose include bone marrow suppression, mental depression, paresthesia, loss of deep reflexes, alopecia, nausea, severe symptoms may occur with 3-4 mg/m^2

There are no antidotes for vincristine; treatment is supportive and symptomatic, including fluid restriction or hypertonic saline (3% sodium chloride) for drug-induced secretion of inappropriate antidiuretic hormone (SIADH), diazepam or phenytoin for seizures, laxatives for constipation, and antiemetics for toxic emesis; case reports suggest that folinic acid may be helpful in treating vincristine overdose; it is suggested that 100 mg folinic acid be given I.V. every 3 hours for 24 hours, then every 6 hours for 48 hours; this is in addition to supportive care; the use of pyridoxine, leucovorin factor, cyanocobalamin or thiamine have been used with little success for drug-induced peripheral neuropathy

Drug Interactions CYP3A3/4 and 3A5-7 enzyme substrate; CYP2D6 enzyme inhibitor

Decreased effect: Phenytoin levels may decrease with combination chemotherapy

Increased toxicity:

Digoxin plasma levels and renal excretion may decrease with combination chemotherapy including vincristine

Vincristine should be given 12-24 hours before asparaginase to minimize toxicity (may decrease the hepatic clearance of vincristine)

Acute pulmonary reactions may occur with mitomycin-C. Previous or simultaneous use with mitomycin-C has resulted in acute shortness of breath and severe bronchospasm within minutes or several hours after vinca alkaloid injection and may occur up to 2 weeks after the dose of mitomycin.

Stability

Store intact vials at refrigeration (2°C to 8°C); stable for one month at room temperature

Further dilution in NS or D$_5$W is stable for 21 days at room temperature (25°C) and refrigeration (4°C)

Compatible with bleomycin, cytarabine, doxorubicin, fluorouracil, methotrexate, metoclopramide

Standard I.V. dilution:

I.V. push: Dose/syringe (concentration = 1 mg/mL)

Maximum syringe size for IVP is 30 mL syringe and syringe should be ≤75% full

IVPB: Dose/50 mL D$_5$W

Mechanism of Action Binds to microtubular protein of the mitotic spindle causing metaphase arrest; cell-cycle phase specific in the M and S phases

Pharmacodynamics/Kinetics
Absorption: Oral: Poor
Distribution: Poor penetration into the CSF; rapidly removed from the bloodstream and tightly bound to tissues; penetrates blood-brain barrier poorly
Protein binding: 75%
Metabolism: Extensively in the liver
Half-life: Terminal: 24 hours
Elimination: Primarily in the bile (~80%); <1% excreted unchanged in urine

Usual Dosage Refer to individual protocols as dosages vary with protocol used; adjustments are made depending upon clinical and hematological response and upon adverse reactions

Children ≤10 kg or BSA <1 m^2: Initial therapy: 0.05 mg/kg once weekly then titrate dose; maximum single dose: 2 mg
Children >10 kg or BSA ≥1 m^2: 1-2 mg/m^2, may repeat once weekly for 3-6 weeks; maximum single dose: 2 mg
Neuroblastoma: I.V. continuous infusion with doxorubicin: 1 mg/m^2/day for 72 hours
Adults: I.V.: 0.4-1.4 mg/m^2 (up to 2 mg maximum in most patients); may repeat every week

Dosing adjustment in hepatic impairment:
Serum bilirubin 1.5-3.0 mg/dL or AST 60-180 units: Administer 50% of normal dose
Serum bilirubin 3.0-5.0 mg/dL: Administer 25% of dose
Serum bilirubin >5.0 mg/dL or AST >180 units: Omit dose
The average total dose per course of treatment should be around 2-2.5 mg; some recommend capping the dose at 2 mg maximum to reduce toxicity; however, it is felt that this measure can reduce the efficacy of the drug

Administration
FATAL IF GIVEN INTRATHECALLY
IVP over at least one minute is desired route of administration because of potential for extravasation. However, has also been administered IVPB over 15 minutes - **CENTRAL LINE ONLY** for IVPB administration.
Avoid extravasation
Protect from light

Monitoring Parameters Serum electrolytes (sodium), hepatic function tests, neurologic examination, CBC, serum uric acid

Patient Information Maintain adequate fluid intake; rinse mouth with water 3-4 times/day, brush teeth with soft brush and floss with waxed floss. Loss of hair occurs in ~70% of patients; report any nerve effects to physician. Stool softener should be used for constipation prophylaxis; report to physician any persistent or severe fever, sore throat, bleeding, or bruising; shortness of breath. Contraceptive measures are recommended during therapy.

Nursing Implications Observe for life-threatening bronchospasm after administration; use of rectal thermometer or rectal tubing should be avoided to prevent injury to rectal mucosa

Extravasation treatment:
Mix 250 units hyaluronidase with 6 mL of NS
Inject the hyaluronidase solution subcutaneously through 6 clockwise injections into the infiltrated area using a 25-gauge needle; change the needle with each new injection
Apply heat immediately for 1 hour; repeat 4 times/day for 3-5 days
Application of cold or hydrocortisone is contraindicated

Dosage Forms Injection, as sulfate: 1 mg/mL (1 mL, 2 mL, 5 mL)

♦ **Vincristine Sulfate** see Vincristine on page 1219

Vinorelbine (vi NOR el been)

Related Information
Cancer Chemotherapy Regimens on page 1263
Extravasation Management of Chemotherapeutic Agents on page 1285
Toxicities of Chemotherapeutic Agents on page 1288

U.S. Brand Names Navelbine®

Synonyms Vinorelbine Tartrate

Therapeutic Category Antineoplastic Agent, Vesicant; Antineoplastic Agent, Vinca Alkaloid; Vesicant

Use Treatment of nonsmall cell lung cancer (as a single agent or in combination with cisplatin)
Unlabeled use: Breast cancer, ovarian carcinoma (cisplatin-resistant), Hodgkin's disease

Pregnancy Risk Factor D

Contraindications For I.V. use only; **I.T. use may result in death**; severe bone marrow suppression (granulocyte counts <1000 cells/mm^3) or presence of bacterial infection not under control prior to initiation of therapy

Warnings/Precautions The U.S. Food and Drug Administration (FDA) currently recommends that procedures for proper handling and disposal of antineoplastic agents be considered. Avoid extravasation; dosage modification required in patients with impaired liver function and neurotoxicity. Frequently monitor patients for myelosuppression both during and after therapy. Granulocytopenia is dose-limiting. **Intrathecal administration may result in death**. Use with caution in patients with cachexia or ulcerated skin.
(Continued)

Vinorelbine *(Continued)*

Adverse Reactions

>10%:

Dermatologic: Alopecia (12%)

Gastrointestinal: Nausea and vomiting are most common and are easily controlled with standard antiemetics; constipation, diarrhea, stomatitis, abdominal cramps, anorexia, metallic taste

Emetic potential: Moderate (30% to 60%)

Hematologic: May cause severe bone marrow suppression and is the dose-limiting toxicity of vinorelbine; severe granulocytopenia may occur following the administration of vinorelbine

Myelosuppressive:

WBC: Moderate - severe

Onset (days): 4-7

Nadir (days): 7-10

Recovery (days): 14-21

Neuromuscular and skeletal: Peripheral neuropathy (20% to 25%)

1% to 10%:

Central nervous system: Fatigue

Extravasation: Vesicant and can cause tissue irritation and necrosis if infiltrated; if extravasation occurs, follow institutional policy, which may include hyaluronidase and hot compresses

Vesicant chemotherapy

Neuromuscular & skeletal: Mild to moderate peripheral neuropathy manifested by paresthesia and hyperesthesia, loss of deep tendon reflexes; myalgia, arthralgia, jaw pain

<1%: Hemorrhagic colitis, severe peripheral neuropathy (generally reversible)

Overdosage/Toxicology

Symptoms of overdose include bone marrow suppression, mental depression, paresthesia, loss of deep reflexes, neurotoxicity. Overdoses involving quantities of up to 10 times the recommended dose (30 mg/m^2) have been reported. The toxicities described were consistent with those listed in the adverse reactions section including paralytic ileus, stomatitis, and esophagitis. Bone marrow aplasia, sepsis, and paresis have also been reported. Fatalities have occurred following overdose of vinorelbine.

There are no antidotes for vinorelbine. Treatment is supportive and symptomatic, including fluid restriction or hypertonic saline (3% sodium chloride) for drug-induced secretion of inappropriate antidiuretic hormone (SIADH), diazepam or phenytoin for seizures, laxatives for constipation, blood transfusions, growth factors, antibiotics, and antiemetics for toxic emesis.

Drug Interactions CYP2D6 enzyme inhibitor

Increased toxicity:

Previous or simultaneous use with mitomycin-C has resulted in acute shortness of breath and severe bronchospasm within minutes or several hours after vinca alkaloid injection and may occur up to 2 weeks after the dose of mitomycin

Cisplatin: Incidence of granulocytopenia is significantly higher than with single-agent vinorelbine

Stability

Store intact vials under refrigeration (2°C to 8°C) and protect from light; vials are stable at room temperature for up to 72 hours

Further dilution in D$_5$W or NS is stable for 24 hours at room temperature

Standard I.V. dilution:

I.V. push: Dose/syringe (concentration = 1.5-3 mg/mL)

Maximum syringe size for IVP is a 30 mL syringe and syringe should be ≤75% full

IVPB: Dose/50-250 mL D$_5$W or NS (concentration = 0.5-2 mg/mL)

Solutions are stable for 24 hours at room temperature

Mechanism of Action Semisynthetic vinca alkaloid which binds to tubulin and inhibits microtubule formation, therefore, arresting the cell at metaphase by disrupting the formation of the mitotic spindle; it is specific for the M and S phases; binds to microtubular protein of the mitotic spindle causing metaphase arrest

Pharmacodynamics/Kinetics

Absorption: Not reliably absorbed from the GI tract and must be given I.V.

Distribution: V$_d$: 25.4-40.1 L/kg; binds extensively to human platelets and lymphocytes (79.6% to 91.2%)

Metabolism: Extensive hepatic metabolism to an active metabolite (deacetylvinorelbine)

Half-life (triphasic): Terminal: 27.7-43.6 hours; Mean plasma clearance: 0.97-1.26 L/hour/kg

Elimination: Feces (46%) and urine (18%)

Usual Dosage Refer to individual protocols; varies depending upon clinical and hematological response

Adults: I.V.: 30 mg/m^2 every 7 days

Dosage adjustment in hematological toxicity: Granulocyte counts should be ≥1000 cells/mm^3 prior to the administration of vinorelbine. Adjustments in the dosage of vinorelbine should be based on granulocyte counts obtained on the day of treatment as follows:

Granulocytes ≥1500 cells/mm^3 on day of treatment: Administer 30 mg/m^2

Granulocytes 1000-1499 cells/mm^3 on day of treatment: Administer 15 mg/m^2

Granulocytes <1000 cells/mm³ on day of treatment: Do not administer. Repeat granulocyte count in one week; if 3 consecutive doses are held because granulocyte count is <1000 cells/mm³, discontinue vinorelbine

For patients who, during treatment, have experienced fever and/or sepsis while granulocytopenic or had 2 consecutive weekly doses held due to granulocytopenia, subsequent doses of vinorelbine should be:

22.5 mg/m² for granulocytes ≥1500 cells/mm³

11.25 mg/m² for granulocytes 1000-1499 cells/mm³

Dosage adjustment in renal impairment: No dose adjustments are required for renal insufficiency. If moderate or severe neurotoxicity develops, discontinue vinorelbine.

Dosage adjustment in hepatic impairment: Vinorelbine should be administered with caution in patients with hepatic insufficiency. In patients who develop hyperbilirubinemia during treatment with vinorelbine, the dose should be adjusted for total bilirubin as follows:

Serum bilirubin ≤2 mg/dL: Administer 30 mg/m²

Serum bilirubin 2.1-3 mg/dL: Administer 15 mg/m²

Serum bilirubin >3 mg/dL: Administer 7.5 mg/m²

Dosing adjustment in patients with concurrent hematologic toxicity and hepatic impairment: Administer the lower doses determined from the above recommendations

Administration

FATAL IF GIVEN INTRATHECALLY

Administer IVPB over 20-30 minutes or I.V. push over 6-10 minutes

CENTRAL LINE ONLY for IVPB administration

Avoid extravasation

Monitoring Parameters CBC with differential and platelet count, serum uric acid, hepatic function tests

Patient Information Hair may be lost during treatment but will regrow to its pretreatment extent even with continued treatment. Report any bleeding; examine mouth daily and report soreness to a physician; jaw pain or pain in the organs containing tumor tissue; avoid constipation. Any signs of infection, easy bruising or bleeding, shortness of breath, or painful or burning urination should be brought to physician's attention. Nausea, vomiting, or hair loss sometimes occurs. The drug may cause permanent sterility and may cause birth defects. Contraceptive measures are recommended during therapy. The drug may be excreted in breast milk, therefore, an alternative form of feeding your baby should be used.

Nursing Implications

Extravasation treatment:

Mix 250 units hyaluronidase with 6 mL of NS

Inject the hyaluronidase solution subcutaneously through 6 clockwise injections into the infiltrated area using a 25-gauge needle; change the needle with each new injection

Apply heat immediately for 1 hour; repeat 4 times/day for 3-5 days

Application of cold or hydrocortisone is contraindicated.

Monitor for life-threatening bronchospasm (most likely to occur if patient is also taking mitomycin). Maintain adequate hydration; allopurinol may be given to prevent uric acid nephropathy; may cause sloughing upon extravasation.

Dosage Forms Injection, as tartrate: 10 mg/mL (1 mL, 5 mL)

Vitamin A (VYE ta min aye)

U.S. Brand Names Aquasol A®; Del-Vi-A®; Palmitate-A® 5000 [OTC]

Synonyms Oleovitamin A

Therapeutic Category Vitamin, Fat Soluble

Use Treatment and prevention of vitamin A deficiency

Pregnancy Risk Factor A (X if dose exceeds RDA recommendation)

(Continued)

Vitamin A *(Continued)*

Pregnancy/Breast-Feeding Implications Clinical effect on the fetus: Excessive use of vitamin A shortly before and during pregnancy could be harmful to babies

Contraindications Hypervitaminosis A, hypersensitivity to vitamin A or any component; pregnancy if dose exceeds RDA recommendations

Warnings/Precautions Evaluate other sources of vitamin A while receiving this product; patients receiving >25,000 units/day should be closely monitored for toxicity

Adverse Reactions 1% to 10%:

Central nervous system: Irritability, vertigo, lethargy, malaise, fever, headache

Dermatologic: Drying or cracking of skin

Endocrine & metabolic: Hypercalcemia

Gastrointestinal: Weight loss

Ocular: Visual changes

Miscellaneous: Hypervitaminosis A

Overdosage/Toxicology

Symptoms of acute ingestion of >12,000 international units/kg or chronic overdose (eg, adults: 25,000 units/day for 2-3 weeks) include increased intracranial pressure (headache, altered mental status, blurred vision), bulging fontanelles in infants, jaundice, ascites, cutaneous desquamation; symptoms of acute overdose (12,000 units/kg) include nausea, vomiting, and diarrhea; toxic signs of an overdose commonly respond to drug discontinuation and generally return to normal spontaneously within a few days to weeks.

Treat intracranial hypertension from chronic exposure, if needed; for acute exposure, use gut decontamination and treat symptomatically

Drug Interactions

Decreased effect: Cholestyramine decreases absorption of vitamin A; neomycin and mineral oil may also interfere with vitamin A absorption

Increased toxicity: Retinoids may have additive adverse effects

Stability Protect from light

Mechanism of Action Needed for bone development, growth, visual adaptation to darkness, testicular and ovarian function, and as a cofactor in many biochemical processes

Pharmacodynamics/Kinetics

Absorption: Vitamin A in dosages **not** exceeding physiologic replacement is well absorbed after oral administration; water miscible preparations are absorbed more rapidly than oil preparations; large oral doses, conditions of fat malabsorption, low protein intake, or hepatic or pancreatic disease reduces oral absorption

Distribution: Following oral absorption, large amounts concentrate for storage in the liver; appears in breast milk

Metabolism: Conjugated with glucuronide, undergoes enterohepatic circulation

Elimination: In feces via biliary elimination

Usual Dosage

RDA:

<1 year: 375 mcg

1-3 years: 400 mcg

4-6 years: 500 mcg*

7-10 years: 700 mcg*

>10 years: 800-1000 mcg*

Male: 1000 mcg

Female: 800 mcg

* mcg retinol equivalent (0.3 mcg retinol = 1 unit vitamin A)

Vitamin A supplementation in measles (recommendation of the World Health Organization): Children: Oral: Administer as a single dose; repeat the next day and at 4 weeks for children with ophthalmologic evidence of vitamin A deficiency:

6 months to 1 year: 100,000 units

>1 year: 200,000 units

Note: Use of vitamin A in measles is recommended only for patients 6 months to 2 years of age hospitalized with measles and its complications **or** patients >6 months of age who have any of the following risk factors and who are not already receiving vitamin A: immunodeficiency, ophthalmologic evidence of vitamin A deficiency including night blindness, Bitot's spots or evidence of xerophthalmia, impaired intestinal absorption, moderate to severe malnutrition including that associated with eating disorders, or recent immigration from areas where high mortality rates from measles have been observed

Note: Monitor patients closely; dosages >25,000 units/kg have been associated with toxicity

Severe deficiency with xerophthalmia: Oral:

Children 1-8 years: 5000-10,000 units/kg/day for 5 days or until recovery occurs

Children >8 years and Adults: 500,000 units/day for 3 days, then 50,000 units/day for 14 days, then 10,000-20,000 units/day for 2 months

Deficiency (without corneal changes): Oral:

Infants <1 year: 100,000 units every 4-6 months

Children 1-8 years: 200,000 units every 4-6 months

Children >8 years and Adults: 100,000 units/day for 3 days then 50,000 units/day for 14 days

Malabsorption syndrome (prophylaxis): Children >8 years and Adults: Oral: 10,000-50,000 units/day of water miscible product

Dietary supplement: Oral:

Infants up to 6 months: 1500 units/day

Children:

  6 months to 3 years: 1500-2000 units/day

  4-6 years: 2500 units/day

  7-10 years: 3300-3500 units/day

Children >10 years and Adults: 4000-5000 units/day

Reference Range 1 RE = 1 retinol equivalent; 1 RE = 1 µg retinol or 6 µg beta-carotene; Normal levels of Vitamin A in serum = 80-300 units/mL

Patient Information Avoid use of mineral oil when taking drug; take with food; notify physician if nausea, vomiting, anorexia, malaise, drying or cracking of skin or lips, irritability, headache, or loss of hair occurs

Nursing Implications Do not administer by I.V. push; patients receiving >25,000 units/day should be closely monitored for toxicity

Additional Information 1 mg equals 3333 units

Dosage Forms

Capsule: 10,000 units [OTC], 25,000 units, 50,000 units

Drops, oral (water miscible) [OTC]: 5000 units/0.1 mL (30 mL)

Injection: 50,000 units/mL (2 mL)

Tablet [OTC]: 5000 units

♦ **Vitamin A Acid** see Tretinoin, Topical on page 1173

♦ **Vitamin B$_1$** see Thiamine on page 1131

♦ **Vitamin B$_2$** see Riboflavin on page 1022

♦ **Vitamin B$_3$** see Niacin on page 832

♦ **Vitamin B$_3$** see Niacinamide on page 833

♦ **Vitamin B$_6$** see Pyridoxine on page 998

♦ **Vitamin B$_{12}$** see Cyanocobalamin on page 302

♦ **Vitamin B$_{12}$** see Hydroxocobalamin on page 585

Vitamin B Complex With Vitamin C and Folic Acid

(VYE ta min bee KOM pleks with VYE ta min see & FOE lik AS id)

U.S. Brand Names Berocca®; Nephrocaps®

Therapeutic Category Vitamin, Water Soluble

Dosage Forms Capsule

♦ **Vitamin C** see Ascorbic Acid on page 99

♦ **Vitamin D$_2$** see Ergocalciferol on page 424

Vitamin E (VYE ta min ee)

U.S. Brand Names Amino-Opti-E® [OTC]; Aquasol E® [OTC]; E-Complex-600® [OTC]; E-Vitamin® [OTC]; Vita-Plus® E Softgels® [OTC]; Vitec® [OTC]; Vite E® Creme [OTC]

Synonyms d-Alpha Tocopherol; dl-Alpha Tocopherol

Therapeutic Category Vitamin, Fat Soluble; Vitamin, Topical

Use Prevention and treatment hemolytic anemia secondary to vitamin E deficiency, dietary supplement

Investigational: To reduce the risk of bronchopulmonary dysplasia or retrolental fibroplasia in infants exposed to high concentrations of oxygen

Pregnancy Risk Factor A (C if dose exceeds RDA recommendation)

Contraindications Hypersensitivity to drug or any components; I.V. route

Warnings/Precautions May induce vitamin K deficiency; necrotizing enterocolitis has been associated with oral administration of large dosages (eg, >200 units/day) of a hyperosmolar vitamin E preparation in low birth weight infants

Adverse Reactions <1%: Headache, fatigue, contact dermatitis with topical preparation, nausea, diarrhea, intestinal cramps, weakness, blurred vision, gonadal dysfunction

Drug Interactions

Decreased absorption with mineral oil

Delayed absorption of iron

Increased effect of oral anticoagulants

Stability Protect from light

Mechanism of Action Prevents oxidation of vitamin A and C; protects polyunsaturated fatty acids in membranes from attack by free radicals and protects red blood cells against hemolysis

Pharmacodynamics/Kinetics

Absorption: Oral: Depends upon the presence of bile; absorption is reduced in conditions of malabsorption, in low birth weight premature infants, and as dosage increases; water miscible preparations are better absorbed than oil preparations

Distribution: Distributes to all body tissues, especially adipose tissue, where it is stored

Metabolism: In the liver to glucuronides

Elimination: In feces and bile

Usual Dosage One unit of vitamin E = 1 mg dl-alpha-tocopherol acetate. Oral:

Vitamin E deficiency:

Children (with malabsorption syndrome): 1 unit/kg/day of water miscible vitamin E (to raise plasma tocopherol concentrations to the normal range within 2 months and to maintain normal plasma concentrations)

Adults: 60-75 units/day

Prevention of vitamin E deficiency: Adults: 30 units/day

(Continued)

Vitamin E *(Continued)*

Prevention of retinopathy of prematurity or BPD secondary to O_2 therapy: (American Academy of Pediatrics considers this use investigational and routine use is not recommended):

Retinopathy prophylaxis: 15-30 units/kg/day to maintain plasma levels between 1.5-2 µg/mL (may need as high as 100 units/kg/day)

Cystic fibrosis, beta-thalassemia, sickle cell anemia may require higher daily maintenance doses:

Cystic fibrosis: 100-400 units/day

Beta-thalassemia: 750 units/day

Sickle cell: 450 units/day

Recommended daily allowance:

Premature infants ≤3 months: 17 mg (25 units)

Infants:

≤6 months: 3 mg (4.5 units)

6-12 months: 4 mg (6 units)

Children:

1-3 years: 6 mg (9 units)

4-10 years: 7 mg (10.5 units)

Children >11 years and Adults:

Male: 10 mg (15 units)

Female: 8 mg (12 units)

Topical: Apply a thin layer over affected area

Reference Range Therapeutic: 0.8-1.5 mg/dL (SI: 19-35 µmol/L), some method variation

Patient Information Drops can be given directly in the mouth or mixed with cereal, fruit juice, or other food; take only the prescribed dose. Vitamin E toxicity appears as blurred vision, diarrhea, dizziness, flu-like symptoms, nausea, headache; swallow capsules whole, do not crush or chew

Additional Information 1 mg dl-alpha tocopherol acetate = 1 international unit

Dosage Forms

Capsule: 100 units, 200 units, 330 mg, 400 units, 500 units, 600 units, 1000 units

Capsule, water miscible: 73.5 mg, 147 mg, 165 mg, 330 mg, 400 units

Cream: 50 mg/g (15 g, 30 g, 60 g, 75 g, 120 g, 454 g)

Drops, oral: 50 mg/mL (12 mL, 30 mL)

Liquid, topical: 10 mL, 15 mL, 30 mL, 60 mL

Lotion: 120 mL

Oil: 15 mL, 30 mL, 60 mL

Ointment, topical: 30 mg/g (45 g, 60 g)

Tablet: 200 units, 400 units

♦ **Vitamin G** *see Riboflavin on page 1022*

♦ **Vitamin K₁** *see Phytonadione on page 926*

♦ **Vitamin K Content in Selected Foods** *see page 1526*

♦ **Vitamin, Multiple, Prenatal** *see Vitamins, Multiple on this page*

♦ **Vitamin, Multiple, Therapeutic** *see Vitamins, Multiple on this page*

♦ **Vitamin, Multiple With Iron** *see Vitamins, Multiple on this page*

Vitamins, Multiple *(VYE ta mins, MUL ti pul)*

U.S. Brand Names Adeflor®; Allbee® With C; Becotin® Pulvules®; Cefol® Filmtab®; Chromagen® OB [OTC]; Eldercaps® [OTC]; Filibon® [OTC]; Florvite®; Iberet-Folic-500®; LKV-Drops® [OTC]; Mega-B® [OTC]; Multi Vit® Drops [OTC]; M.V.I.®; M.V.I.®-12; M.V.I.® Concentrate; M.V.I.® Pediatric; Natabec® [OTC]; Natabec® FA [OTC]; Natabec® Rx; Natalins® [OTC]; Natalins® Rx; NeoVadrin® [OTC]; Niferex®-PN; Poly-Vi-Flor®; Poly-Vi-Sol® [OTC]; Pramet® FA; Pramilet® FA; Prenavite® [OTC]; Secran®; Stresstabs® 600 Advanced Formula Tablets [OTC]; Stuartnatal® 1 + 1; Stuart Prenatal® [OTC]; Therabid® [OTC]; Theragran® [OTC]; Theragran® Hematinic®; Theragran® Liquid [OTC]; Theragran-M® [OTC]; Tri-Vi-Flor®; Unicap® [OTC]; Vicon Forte®; Vicon® Plus [OTC]; Vi-Daylin® [OTC]; Vi-Daylin/F®

Synonyms B Complex; B Complex With C; Children's Vitamins; Hexavitamin; Multiple Vitamins; Multivitamins/Fluoride; Parenteral Multiple Vitamin; Prenatal Vitamins; Therapeutic Multivitamins; Vitamin, Multiple, Prenatal; Vitamin, Multiple, Therapeutic; Vitamin, Multiple With Iron

Therapeutic Category Vitamin

Use Dietary supplement

Pregnancy Risk Factor A (C if used in doses above RDA recommendation)

Contraindications Hypersensitivity to product components

Warnings/Precautions RDA values are not requirements, but are recommended daily intakes of certain essential nutrients; periodic dental exams should be performed to check for dental fluorosis; use with caution in patients with severe renal or liver failure

Adverse Reactions 1% to 10%: Hypervitaminosis; refer to individual vitamin entries for individual reactions

Usual Dosage

Infants 1.5-3 kg: I.V.: 3.25 mL/24 hours (M.V.I.® Pediatric)

Children:

Oral:

≤2 years: Drops: 1 mL/day (premature infants may get 0.5-1 mL/day)

>2 years: Chew 1 tablet/day

≥4 years: 5 mL/day liquid

I.V.: >3 kg and <11 years: 5 mL/24 hours (M.V.I.® Pediatric)

Multivitamin Products Comparison

Product	Content Given Per	A IU	D IU	E IU	C mg	FA mg	B₁ mg	B₂ mg	B₃ mg	B₆ mg	B₁₂ mcg	Other
Theragran®	5 mL liquid	10,000	400		200		10	10	100	4.1	5	B₅ 21.4 mg
Vi-Daylin®	1 mL drops	1500	400	4.1	35		0.5	0.6	8	0.4	1.5	Alcohol <0.5%
Vi-Daylin® Iron	1 mL	1500	400	4.1	35		0.5	0.6	8	0.4		Fe 10 mg
Albee® with C	tablet				300		15	10.2		5		Niacinamide 50 mg, pantothenic acid 10 mg
Vitamin B complex	tablet						1.5	1.7		2	6	Niacinamide 20 mg
Hexavitamin	cap/tab	5000	400		75	400 mcg	2	3	20			
Iberet-Folic-500®	tablet				500	0.8	6	6	30	5	25	B₅ 10 mg, Fe 105 mg
Stuartnatal® 1+1	tablet	4000	400	11	120	1	1.5	3	20	10	12	Cu, Zn 25 mg, Fe 65 mg, Ca 200 mg
Theragran-M®	tablet	5000	400	30	90	0.4	3	3.4	30	3	9	Cl, Cr, I, K, B₅ 10 mg, Mg, Mn, Mo, P, Se, Zn 15 mg, Fe 27 mg, biotin 30 mcg, beta-carotene 1250 IU
Vi-Daylin®	tablet	2500	400	15	60	0.3	1.05	1.2	13.5	1.05	4.5	
M.V.I.®-12 injection	5 mL	3300	200	10	100	0.4	3	3.6	40	4	5	B₅ 15 mg, biotin 60 mcg
M.V.I.®-12 unit vial	20 mL											
M.V.I.® pediatric powder	5 mL	2300	400	7	80	0.14	1.2	1.4	17	1	1	B₅ 5 mg, biotin 20 mcg, vitamin K 200 mcg

Vitamins, Multiple (Continued)

Adults:
Oral: 1 tablet/day or 5 mL/day liquid
I.V.: >11 years: 5 mL of vials 1 and 2 (M.V.I.®-12)/one TPN bag/day
I.V. solutions: 10 mL/24 hours (M.V.I.®-12)

Reference Range Recommended daily allowances are published by Food and Nutrition Board, National Research Council - National Academy of Sciences and are revised periodically. RDA quantities apply only to healthy persons and are not intended to cover therapeutic nutrition requirements in disease or other abnormal states (ie, metabolic disorders, weight reduction, chronic disease, drug therapy).

Patient Information Take only amount prescribed

Nursing Implications Doses may be higher for burn or cystic fibrosis patients

Dosage Forms See table.

- ♦ **Vita-Plus® E Softgels® [OTC]** see Vitamin E on page 1225
- ♦ **Vitec® [OTC]** see Vitamin E on page 1225
- ♦ **Vite E® Creme [OTC]** see Vitamin E on page 1225
- ♦ **Vito Reins®** see Phenazopyridine on page 910
- ♦ **Vitrasert®** see Ganciclovir on page 529
- ♦ **Vitravene™** see Fomivirsen on page 518
- ♦ **Vivactil®** see Protriptyline on page 991
- ♦ **Vivelle® Transdermal** see Estradiol on page 433
- ♦ **Vivol®** see Diazepam on page 345
- ♦ **Vivotif Berna™ Oral** see Typhoid Vaccine on page 1196
- ♦ **V-Lax® [OTC]** see Psyllium on page 994
- ♦ **VLB** see Vinblastine on page 1217
- ♦ **VM-26** see Teniposide on page 1112
- ♦ **Volmax®** see Albuterol on page 35
- ♦ **Voltaren® Ophthalmic** see Diclofenac on page 348
- ♦ **Voltaren® Oral** see Diclofenac on page 348
- ♦ **Voltaren Rapide®** see Diclofenac on page 348
- ♦ **Voltaren-XR® Oral** see Diclofenac on page 348
- ♦ **VōSol®** see Acetic Acid on page 24
- ♦ **VōSol® HC Otic** see Acetic Acid, Propylene Glycol Diacetate, and Hydrocortisone on page 25
- ♦ **Voxsuprine®** see Isoxsuprine on page 641
- ♦ **VP-16** see Etoposide on page 459
- ♦ **VP-16-213** see Etoposide on page 459
- ♦ **Vumon® Injection** see Teniposide on page 1112
- ♦ **V.V.S.®** see Sulfabenzamide, Sulfacetamide, and Sulfathiazole on page 1090
- ♦ **Vytone® Topical** see Iodoquinol and Hydrocortisone on page 623
- ♦ **VZIG** see Varicella-Zoster Immune Globulin (Human) on page 1210

Warfarin (WAR far in)

U.S. Brand Names Coumadin®

Canadian Brand Names Warfilone®

Synonyms Warfarin Sodium

Therapeutic Category Anticoagulant

Use Prophylaxis and treatment of venous thrombosis, pulmonary embolism and thromboembolic disorders; atrial fibrillation with risk of embolism and as an adjunct in the prophylaxis of systemic embolism after myocardial infarction

Unlabeled use: Prevention of recurrent transient ischemic attacks and to reduce risk of recurrent myocardial infarction

Pregnancy Risk Factor D

Pregnancy/Breast-Feeding Implications

Clinical effects on the fetus: Oral anticoagulants cross the placenta and produce fetal abnormalities. Warfarin should not be used during pregnancy because of significant risks. Adjusted-dose heparin can be given safely throughout pregnancy in patients with venous thromboembolism.

Breast-feeding/lactation: Warfarin does not pass into breast milk and can be given to nursing mothers

Contraindications Hypersensitivity to warfarin or any component; severe liver or kidney disease; open wounds; uncontrolled bleeding; GI ulcers; neurosurgical procedures; malignant hypertension, pregnancy

Warnings/Precautions

Do not switch brands once desired therapeutic response has been achieved

Use with caution in patients with active tuberculosis or diabetes

Concomitant use with vitamin K may decrease anticoagulant effect; monitor carefully

Concomitant use with NSAIDs or aspirin may cause severe GI irritation and also increase the risk of bleeding due to impaired platelet function

Salicylates may further increase warfarin's effect by displacing it from plasma protein binding sites

Patients with protein C or S deficiency are at increased risk of skin necrosis syndrome

Before committing an elderly patient to long-term anticoagulation therapy, their risk for bleeding complications secondary to falls, drug interactions, living situation, and cognitive status should be considered. The risk for bleeding complications decreases with the duration of therapy and may increase with advancing age.

If a patient is to undergo an invasive surgical procedure (dental to actual minor/major surgery), warfarin should be stopped 3 days before the scheduled surgery date and the INR/PT should be checked prior to the procedure

Adverse Reactions

1% to 10%:

Dermatologic: Skin lesions, alopecia, skin necrosis

Gastrointestinal: Anorexia, nausea, vomiting, stomach cramps, diarrhea

Hematologic: Hemorrhage, leukopenia, unrecognized bleeding sites (eg, colon cancer) may be uncovered by anticoagulation

Respiratory: Hemoptysis

<1%: Fever, rash, anorexia, agranulocytosis, hepatotoxicity, renal damage, mouth ulcers, discolored toes (blue or purple)

Overdosage/Toxicology See table. Symptoms of overdose include internal or external hemorrhage and hematuria. Avoid emesis and lavage to avoid possible trauma and incidental bleeding. When an overdose occurs, the drug should be immediately discontinued and vitamin K_1 (phytonadione) may be administered, up to 25 mg I.V. for adults. When hemorrhage occurs, fresh frozen plasma transfusions can help control bleeding by replacing clotting factors. In urgent bleeding, prothrombin complex concentrates may be needed.

Management of Elevated INR

INR	Patient Situation	Action
>3 and ≤6	No bleeding or need for rapid reversal (ie, no need for surgery)	Omit next few warfarin doses and restart at lower dose when INR ≤3.0
>6 and <10.0	No bleeding but in need of rapid reversal for surgery	Stop warfarin and give phytonadione 0.5-1 mg I.V.; repeat 0.5 mg phytonadione I.V. if INR >3 after 24 hours; restart warfarin at a lower dose; oral vitamin K (1-2.5mg) can be given in place of parenteral phytonadione when a more gradual reversal is acceptable
>10.0 and <20.0	No bleeding	Stop warfarin, give phytonadione 3-5 mg I.V.; check INR every 6-12 hours; repeat phytonadione if needed; reassess need and dose of warfarin
>20.0	Serious bleeding or warfarin overdose	Stop warfarin, give phytonadione 10 mg I.V.; check INR every 6 hours, if needed, repeat phytonadione every 12 hours and give plasma transfusion or factor concentrate; consider giving heparin if warfarin still indicated

Drug Interactions CYP1A2 enzyme substrate (minor), CYP2C8, 2C9, 2C18, 2C19, and 3A3/4 enzyme substrate; CYP2C9 enzyme inhibitor

Decreased Anticoagulant Effects

Induction of Enzymes		Increased Procoagulant Factors	Decreased Drug Absorption	Other
Barbiturates Carbamazepine Glutethimide Griseofulvin	Nafcillin Phenytoin Rifampin	Estrogens Oral contraceptives Vitamin K (including nutritional supplements)	Aluminum hydroxide Cholestyramine* Colestipol*	Ethchlorvynol Griseofulvin Spironolactone† Sucralfate

Decreased anticoagulant effect may occur when these drugs are administered with oral anticoagulants.

*Cholestyramine and colestipol may increase the anticoagulant effect by binding vitamin K in the gut; yet, the decreased drug absorption appears to be of more concern.

†Diuretic-induced hemoconcentration with subsequent concentration of clotting factors has been reported to decrease the effects of oral anticoagulants.

Increased Bleeding Tendency

Inhibit Platelet Aggregation	Inhibit Procoagulant Factors	Ulcerogenic Drugs
Cephalosporins Dipyridamole Indomethacin Oxyphenbutazone Penicillin, parenteral Phenylbutazone Salicylates Sulfinpyrazone	Antimetabolites Quinidine Quinine Salicylates	Adrenal corticosteroids Indomethacin Oxyphenbutazone Phenylbutazone Potassium products Salicylates

Use of these agents with oral anticoagulants may increase the chances of hemorrhage.

Stability Protect from light; injection is stable for 4 hours at room temperature after reconstitution with 2.7 mL of sterile water

(Continued)

Warfarin *(Continued)*

Enhanced Anticoagulant Effects

Decrease Vitamin K	Displace Anticoagulant	Inhibit Metabolism	Other
Oral antibiotics Can ↑ or ↓ INR Check INR 3 days after patient begins antibiotics to see the INR value and adjust the warfarin dose accordingly	Chloral hydrate Clofibrate Diazoxide Ethacrynic acid Miconazole Nalidixic acid Phenylbutazone Salicylates Sulfonamides Sulfonylureas Triclofos	Alcohol (acute ingestion)* Allopurinol Amiodarone Chloramphenicol Chlorpropamide Cimetidine Co-trimoxazole Disulfiram Metronidazole Phenylbutazone Phenytoin Propoxyphene Sulfinpyrazone Sulfonamides Tolbutamide	Acetaminophen Anabolic steroids Clofibrate Danazol Erythromycin Gemfibrozil Glucagon Influenza vaccine Ketoconazole Propranolol Ranitidine Sulindac Thyroid drugs

* The hypoprothrombinemic effect of oral anticoagulants has been reported to be both increased and decreased during chronic and excessive alcohol ingestion. Data are insufficient to predict the direction of this interaction in alcoholic patients.

Mechanism of Action Interferes with hepatic synthesis of vitamin K-dependent coagulation factors (II, VII, IX, X)

Pharmacodynamics/Kinetics
Onset of anticoagulation effect: Oral: Within 36-72 hours
Peak effect: Within 5-7 days
Absorption: Oral: Rapid
Metabolism: In the liver
Half-life: 42 hours, highly variable among individuals

Usual Dosage
Oral:
Infants and Children: 0.05-0.34 mg/kg/day; infants <12 months of age may require doses at or near the high end of this range; consistent anticoagulation may be difficult to maintain in children <5 years of age
Adults: 5-15 mg/day for 2-5 days, then adjust dose according to results of prothrombin time; usual maintenance dose ranges from 2-10 mg/day
I.V. (administer as a slow bolus injection): 2-5 mg/day
Dosing adjustment/comments in hepatic disease: Monitor effect at usual doses; the response to oral anticoagulants may be markedly enhanced in obstructive jaundice (due to reduced vitamin K absorption) and also in hepatitis and cirrhosis (due to decreased production of vitamin K-dependent clotting factors); prothrombin index should be closely monitored

Dietary Considerations
Alcohol: Chronic use of alcohol inhibits warfarin metabolism; avoid or limit use
Food:
Vitamin K: Foods high in vitamin K (eg, beef liver, pork liver, green tea and leafy green vegetables) inhibit anticoagulant effect. Do not change dietary habits once stabilized on warfarin therapy; a balanced diet with a consistent intake of vitamin K is essential; avoid large amounts of alfalfa, asparagus, broccoli, Brussels sprouts, cabbage, cauliflower, green teas, kale, lettuce, spinach, turnip greens, watercress. It is recommended that the diet contain a CONSISTENT vitamin K content of 70-140 mcg/day. Check with physician before changing diet.
Vitamin E: May increase warfarin effect; do not change dietary habits or vitamin supplements once stabilized on warfarin therapy

Administration Administer as a slow bolus injection over 1-2 minutes; avoid all I.M. injections

Monitoring Parameters Prothrombin time, hematocrit, INR

Reference Range
Therapeutic: 2-5 μg/mL (SI: 6.5-16.2 μmol/L)
Prothrombin time should be 1½ to 2 times the control or INR should be ↑ 2 to 3 times based upon indication
Normal prothrombin time: 10-13 seconds

INR Ranges Based Upon Indication

Diagnosis	Desired INR Range
Atrial fibrillation	2.0-3.0
Venous thromboembolism (DVT, PE)	2.0-3.0
TIA and stroke	2.0-3.0
Bioprosthetic heart valve	2.0-3.0
Acute myocardial infarction with risk factors*	2.5-3.5
Mechanical heart valve (bileaflet, tilting disk)	2.5-3.5
Mechanical heart valve (caged ball, caged disk)	3.0-4.0

*Anterior Q-wave infarction, severe left-ventricular dysfunction, mural thrombus on 2D echo, atrial fibrillation, history of systemic or pulmonary embolism, congestive heart failure

Warfarin levels are not used for monitoring degree of anticoagulation. They may be useful if a patient with unexplained coagulopathy is using the drug surreptitiously or if it is unclear whether clinical resistance is due to true drug resistance or lack of drug intake.

Normal prothrombin time (PT): 10.9-12.9 seconds. Healthy premature newborns have prolonged coagulation test screening results (eg, PT, APTT, TT) which return to normal adult values at approximately 6 months of age. Healthy prematures, however, do not develop spontaneous hemorrhage or thrombotic complications because of a balance between procoagulants and inhibitors

The World Health Organization (WHO), in cooperation with other regulatory-advisory bodies, has developed system of standardizing the reporting of PT values through the determination of the International Normalized Ratio (INR). The INR involves the standardization of the PT by the generation of two pieces of information: the PT ratio and the International Sensitivity Index (ISI)

Therapeutic ranges are now available or being developed to assist practicing physicians in their treatment of patients with a wide variety of thrombotic disorders

Test Interactions Warfarin ↑ PTT

Patient Information

Call your physician or nurse immediately if you have any of the following:
A fever or developing illness, including vomiting, diarrhea, or infection
Pain, swelling, discomfort or any other unusual symptoms
Prolonged bleeding from cuts, nosebleeds
Unusual bleeding from gums when brushing teeth
Increased menstrual flow or vaginal bleeding
Red or dark brown urine
Red or tarry-black stools
Unusual bruising for unknown reasons
Pregnancy or planned pregnancy

Call your physician immediately if you have serious fall or trauma.

Discuss any new medications with your physician or pharmacist - talk to your physician before starting, changing, or discontinuing any medication (including OTC medications).

Notify you physician immediately with any severe diarrhea (alters absorption of vitamin K) to discuss the need to check INR.

Try to keep the same general diet and avoid excessive amounts of alcohol.

Carry Medi-Alert® ID identifying drug usage.

If you forget to take a pill one day, let your physician know. DO NOT TAKE ANOTHER PILL TO "CATCH UP".

Consult physician before undergoing dental work or elective surgery.

Concomitant use of aspirin or nonsteroidal anti-inflammatory medicine, such as Motrin® or Advil®, is NOT RECOMMENDED unless discussed with your physician.

It is important to strictly adhere to the prescribed dosing schedule. Dosage is highly individual and may need to be adjusted several times based on lab test results.

Nursing Implications Should not be given in close proximity to other drugs because absorption may be decreased. Administer warfarin at least 1-2 hours prior to, or 6 hours after, cholestyramine or sucralfate, because cholestyramine or sucralfate may bind warfarin and decrease its total absorption; avoid all I.M. injections.

Additional Information

Food-Drug Interaction Education Required: Maintain consistent intake of foods high in vitamin K content.

Dosage Forms
Powder for injection, as sodium, lyophilized: 2 mg, 5 mg
Tablet, as sodium: 1 mg, 2 mg, 2.5 mg, 3 mg, 4 mg, 5 mg, 6 mg, 7.5 mg, 10 mg

- **Xenical**® *see* Orlistat *on page 866*
- **Xylocaine**® *see* Lidocaine *on page 679*
- **Xylocaine**® **With Epinephrine** *see* Lidocaine and Epinephrine *on page 681*
- **Xylocard**® *see* Lidocaine *on page 679*
- **Yeast-Gard**® **Medicated Douche** *see* Povidone-Iodine *on page 955*

Yellow Fever Vaccine (YEL oh FEE ver vak SEEN)

Related Information
Immunization Recommendations *on page 1358*

U.S. Brand Names YF-VAX®

Therapeutic Category Vaccine, Live Virus

Use Induction of active immunity against yellow fever virus, primarily among persons traveling or living in areas where yellow fever infection exists. (Some countries require a valid international Certification of Vaccination showing receipt of vaccine; if a pregnant woman is to be vaccinated only to satisfy an international requirement, efforts should be made to obtain a waiver letter.) The WHO requires revaccination every 10 years to maintain traveler's vaccination certificate.

Pregnancy Risk Factor D

Contraindications Sensitivity to egg or chick embryo protein; pregnant women, children <6 months of age unless in high risk area

Warnings/Precautions Do not use in immunodeficient persons or patients receiving immunosuppressants (eg, steroids, radiation); have epinephrine available in persons with previous history of egg allergy if the vaccine must be used. Avoid use in infants <6 months and pregnant women unless travel to high-risk areas are unavoidable; avoid use in infants <4 months of age.

Adverse Reactions All serious adverse reactions must be reported to the U.S. Department of Health and Human Services (DHHS) Vaccine Adverse Event Reporting System (VAERS) 1-800-822-7967.
>10%: Central nervous system: Fever, malaise (7-14 days after administration - ~10%)
1% to 10%:
    Central nervous system: Headache (2% to 5%)
    Neuromuscular & skeletal: Myalgia (2% to 5%)
<1%: Encephalitis in very young infants (rare), anaphylaxis

Drug Interactions Administer yellow fever vaccine at least 1 month apart from other live virus vaccines; defer vaccination for 3 weeks following immune globulin; concurrent cholera and yellow fever and concurrent hepatitis B vaccine and yellow fever vaccines may decrease immune response; separate vaccinations by 1 month, if possible; defer vaccination for 8 weeks following blood or plasma transfusion

Stability Yellow fever vaccine is shipped with dry ice; do not use vaccine unless shipping case contains some dry ice on arrival; maintain vaccine continuously at a temperature between 0°C to 5°C (32°F to 41°F)

Usual Dosage One dose (0.5 mL) S.C. 10 days to 10 years before travel, booster every 10 years; see Warnings/Precautions

Administration Do not reconstitute the powder for injection with a diluent that has preservatives since they may inactivate the live virus

Patient Information Immunity develops by the tenth day and **WHO** requires revaccination every 10 years to maintain travelers' vaccination certificates

Nursing Implications Sterilize and discard all unused rehydrated vaccine and containers after 1 hour; avoid vigorous shaking

Additional Information Federal law requires that the date of administration, the vaccine manufacturer, lot number of vaccine, and the administering person's name, title and address be entered into the patient's permanent medical record

Dosage Forms Injection: Not less than 5.04 Log$_{10}$ Plaque Forming Units (PFU) per 0.5 mL

- **YF-VAX**® *see* Yellow Fever Vaccine *on this page*
- **Yodoxin**® *see* Iodoquinol *on page 623*
- **Yutopar**® *see* Ritodrine *on page 1032*

Zafirlukast (za FIR loo kast)

Related Information
Asthma, Guidelines for the Diagnosis and Management of *on page 1456*

U.S. Brand Names Accolate®

Therapeutic Category Leukotriene Receptor Antagonist

Use Prophylaxis and chronic treatment of asthma in adults and children ≥12 years of age

Pregnancy Risk Factor B

Pregnancy/Breast-Feeding Implications
Clinical effects on the fetus: At 2,000 mg/kg/day in rats, maternal toxicity and deaths were seen with increased incidence of early fetal resorption. Spontaneous abortions occurred in cynomolgus monkeys at a maternally toxic dose of 2,000 mg/kg/day orally. There are no adequate and well controlled trials in pregnant women.
Breast-feeding/lactation: Zafirlukast is excreted in breast milk; do not administer to nursing women

Contraindications Hypersensitivity to zafirlukast or any of its inactive ingredients

Warnings/Precautions The clearance of zafirlukast is reduced in patients with stable alcoholic cirrhosis such that the C_{max} and AUC are approximately 50% to 60% greater than those of normal adults.

Zafirlukast is not indicated for use in the reversal of bronchospasm in acute asthma attacks, including status asthmaticus. Therapy with zafirlukast can be continued during acute exacerbations of asthma.

An increased proportion of zafirlukast patients >55 years old reported infections as compared to placebo-treated patients. these infections were mostly mild or moderate in intensity and predominantly affected the respiratory tract. Infections occurred equally in both sexes, were dose-proportional to total milligrams of zafirlukast exposure and were associated with coadministration of inhaled corticosteroids.

Although the frequency of hepatic transaminase elevations was comparable between zafirlukast and placebo-treated patients, a single case of symptomatic hepatitis and hyperbilirubinemia, without other attributable cause, occurred in patient who had received 40 mg/day of zafirlukast for 100 days. In this patient, the liver enzymes returned to normal within 3 months of stopping zafirlukast.

Adverse Reactions
>10%: Central nervous system: Headache (12.9%)
1% to 10%:
Central nervous system: Dizziness, pain, fever
Gastrointestinal: Nausea, diarrhea, abdominal pain, vomiting, dyspepsia
Neuromuscular & skeletal: Myalgia, weakness

Overdosage/Toxicology
There is no experience to date with zafirlukast overdose in humans
Use supportive treatment measures

Drug Interactions CYP2C9 enzyme substrate; CYP2C9 and 3A3/4 enzyme inhibitor
Decreased effect:
Erythromycin: Coadministration of a single dose of zafirlukast with erythromycin to steady state results in decreased mean plasma levels of zafirlukast by 40% due to a decrease in zafirlukast bioavailability.
Terfenadine: Coadministration of zafirlukast with terfenadine to steady state results in a decrease in the mean C_{max} (66%) and AUC (54%) of zafirlukast. No effect of zafirlukast on terfenadine plasma concentrations or EKG parameters was seen.
Theophylline: Coadministration of zafirlukast at steady state with a single dose of liquid theophylline preparations results in decreased mean plasma levels of zafirlukast by 30%, but no effects on plasma theophylline levels were observed.
Increased effect: Aspirin: Coadministration of zafirlukast with aspirin results in mean increased plasma levels of zafirlukast by 45%
Increased toxicity: Warfarin: Coadministration of zafirlukast with warfarin results in a clinically significant increase in prothrombin time (PT). Closely monitor prothrombin times of patients on oral warfarin anticoagulant therapy and zafirlukast, and adjust anticoagulant dose accordingly.

Stability Store tablets at controlled room temperature (20°C to 25°C; 68°F to 77°F); protect from light and moisture; dispense in original airtight container

Mechanism of Action Zafirlukast is a selectively and competitive leukotriene-receptor antagonist (LTRA) of leukotriene D4 and E4 (LTD4 and LTE4), components of slow-reacting substance of anaphylaxis (SRSA). Cysteinyl leukotriene production and receptor occupation have been correlated with the pathophysiology of asthma, including airway edema, smooth muscle constriction and altered cellular activity associated with the inflammatory process, which contribute to the signs and symptoms of asthma.

Pharmacodynamics/Kinetics
Absorption: Food reduces bioavailability by 40%
Protein binding: >99%, predominantly albumin
Metabolism: extensively metabolized by liver via cytochrome P-450 2C9 enzyme pathway.
Half-life: 10 hours
Time to peak serum concentration: 3 hours
Elimination: Urinary excretion (10%) and feces

Usual Dosage Oral:
Children <12 years: Safety and effectiveness has not been established
Adults: 20 mg twice daily
Elderly: The mean dose (mg/kg) normalized AUC and C_{max} increase and plasma clearance decreases with increasing age. In patients >65 years of age, there is an 2-3 fold greater C_{max} and AUC compared to younger adults.
Dosing adjustment in renal impairment: There are no apparent differences in the pharmacokinetics between renally impaired patients and normal subjects.
Dosing adjustment in hepatic impairment: In patients with hepatic impairment (ie, biopsy-proven cirrhosis), there is a 50% to 60% greater C_{max} and AUC compared to normal subjects.

Administration Take at least 1 hour before or 2 hours after a meal

Patient Information Take regularly as prescribed, even during symptom-free periods. Do not use to treat acute episodes of asthma. Do not decrease the dose or stop taking any other antiasthma medications unless instructed by a physician. Nursing women should not take zafirlukast.

Dosage Forms Tablet: 20 mg

♦ Zagam® see Sparfloxacin on page 1076

Zalcitabine (zal SITE a been)
Related Information
Antiretroviral Agents on page 1306
Antiretroviral Therapy for HIV Infection on page 1410
(Continued)

Zalcitabine (Continued)

U.S. Brand Names Hivid®

Synonyms ddC; Dideoxycytidine

Therapeutic Category Antiretroviral Agent, Reverse Transcriptase Inhibitor; Antiviral Agent, Oral; Reverse Transcriptase Inhibitor

Use In combination with at least two other antiretrovirals in the treatment of patients with HIV infection; it is not recommended that zalcitabine be given in combination with didanosine, stavudine, or lamivudine due to overlapping toxicities, virologic interactions, or lack of clinical data

Pregnancy Risk Factor C

Pregnancy/Breast-Feeding Implications
Clinical effects on the fetus: Administer during pregnancy only if benefits to mother outweigh risks to the fetus
Breast-feeding/lactation: HIV-infected mothers are discouraged from breast-feeding to decrease potential transmission of HIV

Contraindications Hypersensitivity to zalcitabine or any component

Warnings/Precautions Careful monitoring of pancreatic enzymes and liver function tests in patients with a history of pancreatitis, increased amylase, those on parenteral nutrition or with a history of ethanol abuse; discontinue use immediately if pancreatitis is suspected; lactic acidosis and severe hepatomegaly and failure have rarely occurred with zalcitabine resulting in fatality; some cases may possibly be related to underlying hepatitis B; use with caution in patients on digitalis, congestive heart failure, renal failure, hyperphosphatemia; zalcitabine can cause severe peripheral neuropathy; avoid use, if possible, in patients with pre-existing neuropathy

Adverse Reactions
>10%:
Central nervous system: Fever (5% to 17%), malaise (2% to 13%)
Neuromuscular & skeletal: Peripheral neuropathy (28.3%)
1% to 10%:
Central nervous system: Headache (2.1%), dizziness (1.1%), fatigue (3.8%), seizures (1.3%)
Endocrine & metabolic: Hypoglycemia (1.8% to 6.3%), hyponatremia (3.5%), hyperglycemia (1% to 6%)
Hematologic: Anemia (occurs as early as 2-4 weeks), granulocytopenia (usually after 6-8 weeks)
Dermatologic: Rash (2% to 11%), pruritus (3% to 5%)
Gastrointestinal: Nausea (3%), dysphagia (1% to 4%), anorexia (3.9%), abdominal pain (3% to 8%), vomiting (1% to 3%), diarrhea (0.4% to 9.5%), weight loss, oral ulcers (3% to 7%), increased amylase (3% to 8%)
Hepatic: Abnormal hepatic function (8.9%), hyperbilirubinemia (2% to 5%)
Neuromuscular & skeletal: Myalgia (1% to 6%), foot pain
Respiratory: Pharyngitis (1.8%), cough (6.3%), nasal discharge (3.5%)
<1%: Edema, hypertension, palpitations, syncope, atrial fibrillation, tachycardia, heart racing, chest pain, night sweats, pain, hypocalcemia, constipation, pancreatitis, jaundice, hepatitis, hepatomegaly, hepatic failure, myositis, weakness, epistaxis

Overdosage/Toxicology
Symptoms of overdose include delayed peripheral neurotoxicity; following oral decontamination
Treatment is supportive

Drug Interactions
Decreased effect: Magnesium/aluminum-containing antacids and metoclopramide may reduce zalcitabine absorption
Increased toxicity:
Amphotericin, foscarnet, cimetidine, probenecid, and aminoglycosides may potentiate the risk of developing peripheral neuropathy or other toxicities associated with zalcitabine by interfering with the renal elimination of zalcitabine
Other drugs associated with peripheral neuropathy which should be avoided, if possible, include chloramphenicol, cisplatin, dapsone, disulfiram, ethionamide, glutethimide, didanosine, gold, hydralazine, iodoquinol, isoniazid, metronidazole, nitrofurantoin, phenytoin, ribavirin, and vincristine
It is not recommended that zalcitabine be given in combination with didanosine, stavudine, or lamivudine due to overlapping toxicities, virologic interactions, or lack of clinical data

Stability Tablets should be stored in tightly closed bottles at 59°F to 86°F

Mechanism of Action Purine nucleoside analogue, zalcitabine or 2',3'-dideoxycytidine (ddC) is converted to active metabolite ddCTP; lack the presence of the 3'-hydroxyl group necessary for phosphodiester linkages during DNA replication. As a result viral replication is prematurely terminated. ddCTP acts as a competitor for binding sites on the HIV-RNA dependent DNA polymerase (reverse transcriptase) to further contribute to inhibition of viral replication.

Pharmacodynamics/Kinetics
Absorption: Well but variably absorbed from GI tract; food decreases absorption by 39%
Distribution: Minimal data available; CSF penetration is variable
Protein binding: Minimal, <4%
Metabolism: Intracellularly to active triphosphorylated agent
Bioavailability: >80%
Half-life: 2.9 hours, may be prolonged to 8.5 hours in patients with renal impairment
Elimination: Mainly renal, >70% unchanged

Usual Dosage Oral:
Children <13 years: Safety and efficacy have not been established
Adults: Daily dose: 0.75 mg every 8 hours
Dosing adjustment in renal impairment: Adults:
Cl_{cr} 10-40 mL/minute: 0.75 mg every 12 hours
Cl_{cr} <10 mL/minute: 0.75 mg every 24 hours
Moderately dialyzable (20% to 50%)

Dietary Considerations Food: Extent and rate of absorption may be decreased with food

Monitoring Parameters Renal function, viral load, liver function tests, CD4 counts, CBC, serum amylase, triglycerides, calcium

Patient Information Zalcitabine is not a cure; if numbness or tingling occurs, or if persistent, severe abdominal pain, nausea, or vomiting occur, notify physician. Women of childbearing age should use effective contraception while on zalcitabine; take on an empty stomach, if possible.

Additional Information Potential compliance problems, frequency of administration and adverse effects should be discussed with patients before initiating therapy to help prevent the emergence of resistance.

Dosage Forms Tablet: 0.375 mg, 0.75 mg

Zidovudine (zye DOE vyoo deen)

Related Information
Antiretroviral Agents on page 1306
Antiretroviral Therapy for HIV Infection on page 1410
Management of Healthcare Worker Exposures to HIV on page 1374

U.S. Brand Names Retrovir®

Canadian Brand Names Apo®-Zidovudine; Novo-AZT

Synonyms Azidothymidine; AZT; Compound S

Therapeutic Category Antiretroviral Agent, Reverse Transcriptase Inhibitor; Reverse Transcriptase Inhibitor

Use Management of patients with HIV infections in combination with at least two other antiretroviral agents; for prevention of maternal/fetal HIV transmission as monotherapy

Pregnancy Risk Factor C

Pregnancy/Breast-Feeding Implications
Clinical effect on the fetus: Administer during pregnancy only if benefits to mother outweigh risks to the fetus
Breast-feeding/lactation: HIV-infected mothers are discouraged from breast-feeding to decrease potential transmission of HIV

Contraindications Life-threatening hypersensitivity to zidovudine or any component

Warnings/Precautions Often associated with hematologic toxicity including granulocytopenia and severe anemia requiring transfusions; zidovudine has been shown to be carcinogenic in rats and mice

Adverse Reactions
>10%:
Central nervous system: Severe headache (42%), fever (16%)
Dermatologic: Rash (17%)
Gastrointestinal: Nausea (46% to 61%), anorexia (11%), diarrhea (17%), pain (20%), vomiting (6% to 25%)
Hematologic: Anemia (23% in children), leukopenia, granulocytopenia (39% in children)
Neuromuscular & skeletal: Weakness (19%)
1% to 10%:
Central nervous system: Malaise (8%), dizziness (6%), insomnia (5%), somnolence (8%)
Dermatologic: Hyperpigmentation of nails (bluish-brown)
Gastrointestinal: Dyspepsia (5%)
(Continued)

Zidovudine (Continued)

Hematologic: Changes in platelet count

Neuromuscular & skeletal: Paresthesia (6%)

<1%: Neurotoxicity, confusion, mania, seizures, bone marrow suppression, granulocytopenia, thrombocytopenia, pancytopenia, hepatotoxicity, cholestatic jaundice, tenderness, myopathy

Overdosage/Toxicology

Symptoms of overdose include nausea, vomiting, ataxia, granulocytopenia

Erythropoietin, thymidine, and cyanocobalamin have been used experimentally to treat zidovudine-induced hematopoietic toxicity, yet none are presently specified as the agent of choice. Treatment is supportive.

Drug Interactions

Decreased effect: Acetaminophen may decrease AUC of zidovudine as can the rifamycins

Increased toxicity: Coadministration with drugs that are nephrotoxic (amphotericin b), cytotoxic (flucytosine, Adriamycin®, vincristine, vinblastine, doxorubicin, interferon), inhibit glucuronidation or excretion (acetaminophen, cimetidine, indomethacin, lorazepam, probenecid, aspirin), or interfere with RBC/WBC number or function (acyclovir, ganciclovir, pentamidine, dapsone); although the AUC was unaffected, the rate of absorption and peak plasma concentrations were increased significantly when zidovudine was administered with clarithromycin (n=18); valproic acid increased AZT's AUC by 80% and decreased clearance by 38% (believed due to inhibition first pass metabolism); fluconazole may increase zidovudine's AUC and half-life, concomitant interferon alfa may increase hematologic toxicities and phenytoin, trimethoprim, and interferon beta-1b may increase zidovudine levels

Stability After dilution to ≤4 mg/mL, the solution is physically and chemically stable for 24 hours at room temperature and 48 hours if refrigerated; attempt to administer diluted solution within 8 hours, if stored at room temperature or 24 hours if refrigerated to minimize potential for microbially contaminated solutions; store undiluted vials at room temperature and protect from light

Mechanism of Action Zidovudine is a thymidine analog which interferes with the HIV viral RNA dependent DNA polymerase resulting in inhibition of viral replication; nucleoside reverse transcriptase inhibitor

Pharmacodynamics/Kinetics

Absorption: Oral: Well absorbed (66% to 70%)

Distribution: Significant penetration into the CSF; crosses the placenta

Relative diffusion of antimicrobial agents from blood into cerebrospinal fluid (CSF): Adequate with or without inflammation (exceeds usual MICs)

Ratio of CSF to blood level (%): Normal meninges: ~60

Protein binding: 25% to 38%

Metabolism: Extensive first-pass metabolism; metabolized in the liver via glucuronidation to inactive metabolites

Half-life: Terminal: 60 minutes

Time to peak serum concentration: Within 30-90 minutes

Elimination: Urinary excretion (63% to 95%); following oral administration, 72% to 74% of the drug excreted in urine as metabolites and 14% to 18% as unchanged drug; following I.V. administration, 45% to 60% excreted in urine as metabolites and 18% to 29% as unchanged drug

Usual Dosage

Prevention of maternal-fetal HIV transmission:

Neonatal: Oral: 2 mg/kg/dose every 6 hours for 6 weeks beginning 8-12 hours after birth; infants unable to receive oral dosing may receive 1.5 mg/kg I.V. infused over 30 minutes every 6 hours

Maternal (>14 weeks gestation): Oral: 100 mg 5 times/day until the start of labor; during labor and delivery, administer zidovudine I.V. at 2 mg/kg over 1 hour followed by a continuous I.V. infusion of 1 mg/kg/hour until the umbilical cord is clamped

Children 3 months to 12 years for HIV infection:

Oral: 160 mg/m²/dose every 8 hours; dosage range: 90 mg/m²/dose to 180 mg/m²/dose every 6-8 hours; some Working Group members use a dose of 180 mg/m² every 12 hours when using in drug combinations with other antiretroviral compounds, but data on this dosing in children is limited

I.V. continuous infusion: 20 mg/m²/hour

I.V. intermittent infusion: 120 mg/m²/dose every 6 hours

Adults:

Oral: 300 mg twice daily or 200 mg 3 times/day

I.V.: 1-2 mg/kg/dose (infused over 1 hour) administered every 4 hours around-the-clock (6 doses/day)

Prevention of HIV following needlesticks: 200 mg 3 times/day plus lamivudine 150 mg twice daily; a protease inhibitor (eg, indinavir) may be added for high risk exposures; begin therapy within 2 hours of exposure if possible

Patients should receive I.V. therapy only until oral therapy can be administered

Dosing interval in renal impairment: Cl$_{cr}$ <10 mL/minute: May require minor dose adjustment

Hemodialysis: At least partially removed by hemo- and peritoneal dialysis; administer dose after hemodialysis or administer 100 mg supplemental dose; during CAPD, dose as for Cl$_{cr}$ <10 mL/minute

Continuous arteriovenous or venovenous hemodiafiltration (CAVH) effects: Administer 100 mg every 8 hours

Dosing adjustment in hepatic impairment: Reduce dose by 50% or double dosing interval in patients with cirrhosis

Dietary Considerations Food: Administration with a fatty meal decreased zidovudine's AUC and peak plasma concentration

Monitoring Parameters Monitor CBC and platelet count at least every 2 weeks, MCV, serum creatinine kinase, viral load, and CD4 cell count; observe for appearance of opportunistic infections

Patient Information Take 30 minutes before or 1 hour after a meal with a glass of water; take zidovudine exactly as prescribed; take around-the-clock; limit acetaminophen-containing analgesics; report all side effects to you physician; zidovudine therapy has not been shown to reduce the risk of transmission of HIV to others nor will is cure HIV infections; opportunistic infections and other illnesses may still occur; maternal/fetal transmission may appear in some cases despite therapy; transfusion, dose modifications and even drug discontinuation may be needed if blood disorders such as anemia occur.

Additional Information Potential compliance problems, frequency of administration and adverse effects should be discussed with patients before initiating therapy to help prevent the emergence of resistance.

Dosage Forms
Capsule: 100 mg
Injection: 10 mg/mL (20 mL)
Syrup (strawberry flavor): 50 mg/5 mL (240 mL)
Tablet: 300 mg

Zidovudine and Lamivudine (zye DOE vyoo deen & la MI vyoo deen)

Related Information
Antiretroviral Agents on page 1306
Lamivudine on page 657
Zidovudine on page 1235

U.S. Brand Names Combivir®

Synonyms AZT + 3TC

Therapeutic Category Antiretroviral Agent, Reverse Transcriptase Inhibitor; Reverse Transcriptase Inhibitor

Dosage Forms Tablet: Zidovudine 300 mg and lamivudine 150 mg

♦ **Zilactin-B® Medicated [OTC]** see Benzocaine on page 133

♦ **Zilactin-L® [OTC]** see Lidocaine on page 679

Zileuton (zye LOO ton)

Related Information
Asthma, Guidelines for the Diagnosis and Management of on page 1456

U.S. Brand Names Zyflo™

Therapeutic Category Leukotriene Receptor Antagonist

Use Prophylaxis and chronic treatment of asthma in adults and children ≥12 years of age

Pregnancy Risk Factor C

Pregnancy/Breast-Feeding Implications
Clinical effects on the fetus: Developmental studies indicated adverse effects (reduced body weight and increased skeletal variations) in rats at an oral dose of 300 mg/kg/day. There are no adequate and well controlled studies in pregnant women.
Breast-feeding/lactation: Zileuton and its metabolites are excreted in rat milk; it is not known if zileuton is excreted in breast milk

Contraindications Active liver disease or transaminase elevations greater than or equal to three times the upper limit of normal (≥3 x ULN), hypersensitivity to zileuton or any of its active ingredients

Warnings/Precautions Elevations of one or more liver function tests may occur during therapy. These laboratory abnormalities may progress, remain unchanged or resolve with continued therapy. Use with caution in patients who consume substantial quantities of alcohol or have a past history of liver disease. Zileuton is not indicated for use in the reversal of bronchospasm in acute asthma attacks, including status asthmaticus. Zileuton can be continued during acute exacerbations of asthma.

Adverse Reactions
>10%:
Central nervous system: Headache (24.6%)
Hepatic: Increased ALT (12%)
1% to 10%:
Cardiovascular: Chest pain
Central nervous system: Pain, dizziness, fever, insomnia, malaise, nervousness, somnolence
Gastrointestinal: Dyspepsia, nausea, abdominal pain, constipation, flatulence
Hematologic: Low white blood cell count
Neuromuscular & skeletal: Myalgia, arthralgia, weakness
Ocular: Conjunctivitis

Overdosage/Toxicology
Symptoms of overdose: Human experience is limited. Oral minimum lethal doses in mice and rats were 500-1000 and 300-1000 mg/kg, respectively (providing >3 and 9 times the systemic exposure achieved at the maximum recommended human daily oral dose, respectively). No deaths occurred, but nephritis was reported in dogs at an oral dose of 1000 mg/kg.

(Continued)

Zileuton *(Continued)*

Treat symptomatically; institute supportive measures as required. If indicated, achieve elimination of unabsorbed drug by emesis or gastric lavage; observe usual precautions to maintain the airway. Zileuton is NOT removed by dialysis.

Drug Interactions CYP1A2, 2C9, and 3A3/4 enzyme substrate; CYP1A2 and 3A3/4 inhibitor

Increased toxicity:

Propranolol: Doubling of propranolol AUC and consequent increased beta-blocker activity

Terfenadine: Decrease in clearance of terfenadine leading to increase in AUC

Theophylline: Doubling of serum theophylline concentrations - reduce theophylline dose and monitor serum theophylline concentrations closely.

Warfarin: Clinically significant increases in prothrombin time (PT) - monitor PT closely

Mechanism of Action Specific inhibitor of 5-lipoxygenase and thus inhibits leukotriene (LTB1, LTC1, LTD1 and LTE1) formation. Leukotrienes are substances that induce numerous biological effects including augmentation of neutrophil and eosinophil migration, neutrophil and monocyte aggregation, leukocyte adhesion, increased capillary permeability and smooth muscle contraction.

Pharmacodynamics/Kinetics

Absorption: Oral: Rapidly absorbed

Distribution: 1.2 L/kg

Protein binding: 93%

Metabolism: Several metabolites in plasma and urine; metabolized by the cytochrome P-450 isoenzymes 1A2, 2C9 and 3A4

Bioavailability: Absolute bioavailability is unknown

Half-life: 2.5 hours

Time to peak serum concentration: 1.7 hours

Elimination: Predominantly via metabolism

Dialyzable: Not removed (>0.5%)

Usual Dosage Oral:

Adults: 600 mg 4 times/day with meals and at bedtime

Elderly: Zileuton pharmacokinetics were similar in healthy elderly subjects (>65 years) compared with healthy younger adults (18-40 years)

Dosing adjustment in renal impairment: Dosing adjustment is not necessary in renal impairment or renal failure (even during dialysis)

Dosing adjustment in hepatic impairment: Contraindicated in patients with active liver disease

Administration Can be administered without regard to meals (ie, with or without food)

Monitoring Parameters Evaluate hepatic transaminases at initiation of and during therapy with zileuton. Monitor serum ALT before treatment begins, once-a-month for the first 3 months, every 2-3 months for the remainder of the first year, and periodically thereafter for patients receiving long-term zileuton therapy. If symptoms of liver dysfunction (right upper quadrant pain, nausea, fatigue, lethargy, pruritus, jaundice or "flu-like" symptoms) develop or transaminase elevations >5 times the ULN occur, discontinue therapy and follow transaminase levels until normal.

Patient Information Inform patients that zileuton is indicated for the chronic treatment of asthma and to take regularly as prescribed even during symptom-free periods. Zileuton is not a bronchodilator; do not use to treat acute episodes of asthma. When taking zileuton, do not decrease the dose or stop taking any other antiasthma medications unless instructed by a physician.

While using zileuton, seek medical attention if short-acting bronchodilators are needed more often than usual or if more than the maximum number of inhalations of short-acting bronchodilator treatment prescribed for a 24-period are needed.

The most serious side effect of zileuton is elevation of liver enzyme tests. While taking zileuton, patients must have liver enzyme tests monitored on a regular basis. If patients experience signs or symptoms of liver dysfunction (right upper quadrant pain, nausea, fatigue, lethargy, pruritus, jaundice, or "flu-like" symptoms), contact a physician immediately.

Zileuton can interact with other drugs. While taking zileuton, consult a physician before starting or stopping any prescription or nonprescription medicines.

Dosage Forms Tablet: 600 mg

- **Zinacef® Injection** *see* Cefuroxime *on page 224*
- **Zinca-Pak®** *see* Zinc Supplements *on next page*
- **Zincate®** *see* Zinc Supplements *on next page*
- **Zinc Chloride** *see* Zinc Supplements *on next page*

Zinc Gelatin *(zingk JEL ah tin)*

U.S. Brand Names Gelucast®

Synonyms Dome Paste Bandage; Unna's Boot; Unna's Paste; Zinc Gelatin Boot

Therapeutic Category Topical Skin Product

Use As a protectant and to support varicosities and similar lesions of the lower limbs

Contraindications Hypersensitivity to any component

Adverse Reactions 1% to 10%: Local: Irritation

Usual Dosage Apply externally as an occlusive boot

Nursing Implications After a period of about 2 weeks, the dressing is removed by soaking in warm water

Dosage Forms Bandage: 3" x 10 yards, 4" x 10 yards

* **Zinc Gelatin Boot** see Zinc Gelatin on previous page
* **Zinc Gluconate** see Zinc Supplements on this page
* **Zinc Sulfate** see Zinc Supplements on this page

Zinc Supplements (zink SUP la ments)

U.S. Brand Names Eye-Sed® [OTC]; Orazinc® [OTC]; Verazinc® [OTC]; Zinca-Pak®; Zincate®

Synonyms Zinc Chloride; Zinc Gluconate; Zinc Sulfate

Therapeutic Category Mineral, Oral; Mineral, Parenteral; Trace Element

Use Cofactor for replacement therapy to different enzymes helps maintain normal growth rates, normal skin hydration and senses of taste and smell; zinc supplement (oral and parenteral); may improve wound healing in those who are deficient. May be useful to promote wound healing in patients with pressure sores.

Pregnancy Risk Factor C

Contraindications Hypersensitivity to any component

Warnings/Precautions Do not take undiluted by direct injection into a peripheral vein because of potential for phlebitis, tissue irritation, and potential to increase renal loss of minerals from a bolus injection; administration of zinc in absence of copper may decrease plasma levels; excessive dose may increase HDL and impair immune system function

Adverse Reactions <1%: Hypotension, indigestion, nausea, vomiting, neutropenia, leukopenia, jaundice, pulmonary edema

Overdosage/Toxicology

Symptoms of overdose include hypotension, pulmonary edema, diarrhea, vomiting, oliguria, nausea, gastric ulcers, restlessness, dizziness, profuse sweating, decreased consciousness, blurred vision, tachycardia, hypothermia, hyperamylasemia, jaundice.

This agent is corrosive and emesis or gastric lavage should be avoided, instead dilute rapidly with milk or water. Calcium disodium edetate or dimercaprol can be very effective at binding zinc. Supportive care should always be instituted.

Drug Interactions

Decreased effect: Decreased penicillamine, decreased tetracycline effect reduced, iron decreased uptake of zinc, bran products, dairy products reduce absorption of zinc

Mechanism of Action Provides for normal growth and tissue repair, is a cofactor for more than 70 enzymes; ophthalmic astringent and weak antiseptic due to precipitation of protein and clearing mucus from outer surface of the eye

Pharmacodynamics/Kinetics

Absorption: Poor from gastrointestinal tract (20% to 30%)

Elimination: In feces with only traces appearing in urine

Usual Dosage Clinical response may not occur for up to 6-8 weeks

Zinc sulfate:

RDA: Oral:

Birth to 6 months: 3 mg elemental zinc/day

6-12 months: 5 mg elemental zinc/day

1-10 years: 10 mg elemental zinc/day (44 mg zinc sulfate)

≥11 years: 15 mg elemental zinc/day (65 mg zinc sulfate)

Zinc deficiency: Oral:

Infants and Children: 0.5-1 mg elemental zinc/kg/day divided 1-3 times/day; somewhat larger quantities may be needed if there is impaired intestinal absorption or an excessive loss of zinc

Adults: 110-220 mg zinc sulfate (25-50 mg elemental zinc)/dose 3 times/day

Parenteral: TPN: I.V. infusion (chloride or sulfate): Supplemental to I.V. solutions (clinical response may not occur for up to 6-8 weeks):

Premature Infants <1500 g, up to 3 kg: 300 mcg/kg/day

Full-term Infants and Children ≤5 years: 100 mcg/kg/day

or

Premature Infants: 400 mcg/kg/day

Term <3 months: 250 mcg/kg/day

Term >3 months: 100 mcg/kg/day

Children: 50 mcg/kg/day

Adults:

Stable with fluid loss from small bowel: 12.2 mg zinc/liter TPN or 17.1 mg zinc/kg (added to 1000 mL I.V. fluids) of stool or ileostomy output

Metabolically stable: 2.5-4 mg/day, add 2 mg/day for acute catabolic states

Dietary Considerations Food: Avoid foods high in calcium or phosphorus

Administration Administer oral formulation with food if GI upset occurs

Monitoring Parameters Patients on TPN therapy should have periodic serum copper and serum zinc levels, skin integrity

Reference Range

Serum: 50-150 µg/dL (<20 µg/dL as solid test with dermatitis followed by alopecia)

Therapeutic: 66-110 µg/dL (SI: 10-16.8 µmol/L)

Patient Information Take with food if GI upset occurs, but avoid foods high in calcium, phosphorous, or phytate; do not exceed recommended dose; if irritation persists or continues with ophthalmic use, notify physician

Nursing Implications Do not administer undiluted by direct injection into a peripheral vein because of potential for phlebitis, tissue irritation, and potential to increase renal loss of minerals from a bolus injection

(Continued)

Zinc Supplements *(Continued)*

Dosage Forms
Zinc carbonate, complex: Liquid: 15 mg/mL (30 mL)

Zinc chloride: Injection: 1 mg/mL (10 mL)

Zinc gluconate (14.3% zinc): Tablet: 10 mg (elemental zinc 1.4 mg), 15 mg (elemental zinc 2 mg), 50 mg (elemental zinc 7 mg), 78 mg (elemental zinc 11 mg)

Zinc sulfate (23% zinc):
Capsule: 110 mg (elemental zinc 25 mg), 220 mg (elemental zinc 50 mg)

Injection: 1 mg/mL (10 mL, 30 mL); 4 mg/mL (10 mL); 5 mg/mL (5 mL, 10 mL)

Tablet: 66 mg (elemental zinc 15 mg), 110 mg (elemental zinc 25 mg), 200 mg (elemental zinc 45 mg)

♦ **Zinecard®** see Dexrazoxane *on page 340*

♦ **Zithromax™** see Azithromycin *on page 118*

♦ **Zocor®** see Simvastatin *on page 1063*

♦ **Zofran®** see Ondansetron *on page 862*

♦ **Zoladex® Implant** see Goserelin *on page 545*

♦ **Zolicef®** see Cefazolin *on page 206*

Zolmitriptan (zohl mi TRIP tan)

Related Information
Antimigraine Drugs: Pharmacokinetic Differences *on page 1304*

U.S. Brand Names Zomig®

Therapeutic Category Antimigraine Agent; Serotonin Agonist

Use Acute treatment of migraine with or without auras

Pregnancy Risk Factor C

Contraindications
Use in patients with ischemic heart disease or Prinzmetal angina, patients with signs or symptoms of ischemic heart disease, uncontrolled hypertension; use in patients with symptomatic Wolff-Parkinson-White syndrome or arrhythmias associated with other cardiac accessory conduction pathway disorders

Use with ergotamine derivatives (within 24 hours of); use within 24 hours of another 5-HT₁ agonist; concurrent administration or within 2 weeks of discontinuing an MAOI; hypersensitivity to any component; management of hemiplegic or basilar migraine

Warnings/Precautions Zolmitriptan is indicated only in patient populations with a clear diagnosis of migraine. Cardiac events (coronary artery vasospasm, transient ischemia, myocardial infarction, ventricular tachycardia/fibrillation, cardiac arrest, and death) have been reported with 5-HT₁ agonist administration. Significant elevation in blood pressure, including hypertensive crisis, has also been reported on rare occasions in patients with and without a history of hypertension. Vasospasm-related reactions have been reported other than coronary artery vasospasm. Peripheral vascular ischemia and colonic ischemia with abdominal pain and bloody diarrhea have occurred. Use with caution in patients with hepatic impairment.

Adverse Reactions
>10%:
Central nervous system: Dizziness

Endocrine & metabolic: Hot flashes

Neuromuscular & skeletal: Paresthesia

1% to 10%:
Cardiovascular: Tightness in chest

Central nervous system: Drowsiness, headache

Dermatologic: Burning sensation

Gastrointestinal: Abdominal discomfort, mouth discomfort

Neuromuscular & skeletal: Myalgia, numbness, weakness, neck pain, jaw discomfort

Miscellaneous: Diaphoresis

<1%: Rashes, polydipsia, dehydration, dysmenorrhea, dysuria, renal calculus, dyspnea, thirst, hiccups

Drug Interactions Increased toxicity: Ergot-containing drugs, MAOIs, cimetidine, oral contraceptives, SSRIs

Mechanism of Action Selective agonist for serotonin (5-HT₁ᵦ and 5-HT₁ᴅ receptors) in cranial arteries to cause vasoconstriction and reduce sterile inflammation associated with antidromic neuronal transmission correlating with relief of migraine

Pharmacodynamics/Kinetics
Distribution: V_d: 7 L/kg

Protein binding: 25%

Metabolism: Converted to an active N-desmethyl metabolite which is 2-6 times more potent than zolmitriptan

Half-life: 2.8-3.7 hours

Bioavailability, absolute: 49%

Time to peak serum concentrations: 2-3.5 hours

Elimination: Urine (~60% to 65% of the total dose) and feces (30% to 40%)

Usual Dosage Adults:
Oral: Initial recommended dose: 2.5 mg or lower (achieved by manually breaking a 2.5 mg tablet in half). If the headache returns, the dose may be repeated after 2 hours, not to exceed 10 mg within a 24-hour period. Response is greater following the 2.5 or 5 mg dose compared with 1 mg, with little added benefit and increased side effects associated with the 5 mg dose.

Dosage adjustment in hepatic impairment: Administer with caution in patients with liver disease, generally using doses <2.5 mg. Patients with moderate-to-severe hepatic impairment may have decreased clearance of zolmitriptan, and significant elevation in blood pressure was observed in some patients.

Patient Information Take a single dose with fluids as soon as symptoms of migraine appear; a second dose may be taken if symptoms return, but no sooner than 2 hours following the first dose. For a given attack, if there is no response to the first tablet, do not take a second tablet without first consulting a physician. Do not take >10 mg in any 24-hour period.

If the patient has risk factors for heart disease (high blood pressure, high cholesterol, obesity, diabetes, smoking, strong family history of heart disease, postmenopausal woman, or a male >40 years of age), tell physician

This agent is intended to relieve migraine, but not to prevent or reduce the number of attacks. Use only to treat an actual migraine attack.

Do not use this agent if you are pregnant, think you may be pregnant, are trying to become pregnant, or are not using adequate contraception, unless you have discussed this with your physician

If pain or tightness in the chest or throat occurs when using this agent, discuss with physician before using more. If the chest pain is severe or does not go away, call physician immediately. If shortness of breath; wheezing; heart throbbing; swelling of eyelids, face or lips; skin rash, skin lumps or hives occur, tell physician immediately. Do not take any more unless the physician instructs you to do so. If feelings of tingling, heat, flushing (redness of face lasting a short time), heaviness, pressure, drowsiness, dizziness, tiredness, or sickness develop, tell your physician.

Dosage Forms Tablet: 2.5 mg, 5 mg

♦ **Zoloft™** see Sertraline on page 1056

Zolpidem (zole PI dem)

U.S. Brand Names Ambien™
Synonyms Zolpidem Tartrate
Therapeutic Category Hypnotic; Sedative
Use Short-term treatment of insomnia
Restrictions C-IV
Pregnancy Risk Factor B
Contraindications Lactation
Warnings/Precautions Closely monitor elderly or debilitated patients for impaired cognitive or motor performance; not recommended for use in children <18 years of age
Adverse Reactions
1% to 10%:
Central nervous system: Headache, drowsiness, dizziness
Gastrointestinal: Nausea, diarrhea
Neuromuscular & skeletal: Myalgia
<1%: Amnesia, confusion, vomiting, falls, tremor
Overdosage/Toxicology
Symptoms of overdose include coma and hypotension
Treatment for overdose is supportive. Rarely is mechanical ventilation required. Flumazenil has been shown to selectively block binding to CNS receptors, resulting in a reversal of CNS depression but not always respiratory depression.
Drug Interactions CYP3A3/4 enzyme substrate
Increased effect/toxicity with alcohol, CNS depressants
Mechanism of Action Structurally dissimilar to benzodiazepine, however, has much or all of its actions explained by its effects on benzodiazepine (BZD) receptors, especially the omega-1 receptor; retains hypnotic and much of the anxiolytic properties of the BZD, but has reduced effects on skeletal muscle and seizure threshold.
Pharmacodynamics/Kinetics
Onset of action: 30 minutes
Duration: 6-8 hours
Absorption: Rapid
Distribution: Very low amounts secreted into breast milk
Protein binding: 92%
Metabolism: Hepatic to inactive metabolites
Half-life: 2-2.6 hours, in cirrhosis increased to 9.9 hours
Usual Dosage Duration of therapy should be limited to 7-10 days
Adults: Oral: 10 mg immediately before bedtime; maximum dose: 10 mg
Elderly: 5 mg immediately before bedtime
Hemodialysis: Not dialyzable
Dosing adjustment in hepatic impairment: Decrease dose to 5 mg
Dietary Considerations Alcohol: Additive CNS effect, avoid use
Monitoring Parameters Respiratory, cardiac and mental status
Reference Range 80-150 ng/mL
Patient Information Avoid alcohol and other CNS depressants while taking this medication; for fastest onset, take on an empty stomach; may cause drowsiness
Nursing Implications Patients may require assistance with ambulation; lower doses in the elderly are usually effective; institute safety measures
Dosage Forms Tablet, as tartrate: 5 mg, 10 mg

♦ **Zolpidem Tartrate** see Zolpidem on this page

ALPHABETICAL LISTING OF DRUGS

- **Zomig®** *see* Zolmitriptan *on page 1240*
- **Zonalon® Topical Cream** *see* Doxepin *on page 392*
- **Zone-A Forte®** *see* Pramoxine and Hydrocortisone *on page 958*
- **ZORprin®** *see* Aspirin *on page 102*
- **Zosyn™** *see* Piperacillin and Tazobactam Sodium *on page 932*
- **Zovia®** *see* Ethinyl Estradiol and Ethynodiol Diacetate *on page 447*
- **Zovirax®** *see* Acyclovir *on page 28*
- **Zyban™** *see* Bupropion *on page 161*
- **Zydone®** *see* Hydrocodone and Acetaminophen *on page 575*
- **Zyflo™** *see* Zileuton *on page 1237*
- **Zyloprim®** *see* Allopurinol *on page 44*
- **Zymase™** *see* Pancrelipase *on page 883*
- **Zyprexa®** *see* Olanzapine *on page 860*
- **Zyrtec®** *see* Cetirizine *on page 233*

APPENDIX TABLE OF CONTENTS

APPENDIX TABLE OF CONTENTS *(Continued)*

ABBREVIATIONS, ACRONYMS, AND SYMBOLS

Abbreviation	Meaning
aa, āā	of each
AA	Alcoholics Anonymous
ac	before meals or food
ad	to, up to
a.d.	right ear
ADHD	attention-deficit/hyperactivity disorder
ADLs	activities of daily living
ad lib	at pleasure
AIMS	Abnormal Involuntary Movement Scale
a.l.	left ear
AM	morning
amp	ampul
amt	amount
aq	water
aq. dest.	distilled water
a.s.	left ear
ASAP	as soon as possible
a.u.	each ear
AUC	area under the curve
BDI	Beck Depression Inventory
bid	twice daily
bm	bowel movement
bp	blood pressure
BPRS	Brief Psychiatric Rating Scale
BSA	body surface area
c	a gallon
c̄	with
cal	calorie
cap	capsule
CBT	cognitive behavioral therapy
cc	cubic centimeter
CGI	Clinical Global Impression
cm	centimeter
CIV	continuous I.V. infusion
comp	compound
cont	continue
CT	computed tomography
d	day
d/c	discontinue
dil	dilute
disp	dispense
div	divide
DSM-IV	Diagnostic and Statistical Manual
DTs	delirium tremens
dtd	give of such a dose
ECT	electroconvulsive therapy
EEG	electroencephalogram
elix, el	elixir
emp	as directed
EPS	extrapyramidal side effects
et	and
ex aq	in water
f, ft	make, let be made
FDA	Food and Drug Administration
g	gram
GA	Gamblers Anonymous
GAD	generalized anxiety disorder
GAF	Global Assessment of Functioning Scale

Abbreviation	Meaning
GABA	gamma-aminobutyric acid
GITS	gastrointestinal therapeutic system
gr	grain
gtt	a drop
h	hour
HAM-A	Hamilton Anxiety Scale
HAM-D	Hamilton Depression Scale
hs	at bedtime
I.M.	intramuscular
IU	international unit
I.V.	intravenous
kcal	kilocalorie
kg	kilogram
KIU	kallikrein inhibitor unit
L	liter
LAMM	L-α-acetyl methadol
liq	a liquor, solution
M	mix
MADRS	Montgomery Asbery Depression Rating Scale
MAOIs	monamine oxidase inhibitors
mcg	microgram
MDEA	3,4-methylene-dioxy amphetamine
m. dict	as directed
MDMA	3,4-methylene-dioxy methamphetamine
mEq	milliequivalent
mg	milligram
mixt	a mixture
mL	milliliter
mm	millimeter
MMSE	Mini-Mental State Examination
MPPP	l-methyl-4-proprionoxy-4-phenyl pyridine
MR	mental retardation
MRI	magnetic resonance imaging
NF	National Formulary
NMS	neuroleptic malignant syndrome
no.	number
noc	in the night
non rep	do not repeat, no refills
NPO	nothing by mouth
O, Oct	a pint
OCD	obsessive-compulsive disorder
o.d.	right eye
o.l.	left eye
o.s.	left eye
o.u.	each eye
PANSS	Positive and Negative Symptom Scale
pc, post cib	after meals
PCP	phencyclidine
per	through or by
PM	afternoon or evening
P.O.	by mouth
P.R.	rectally
prn	as needed
PTSD	post-traumatic stress disorder
pulv	a powder
q	every
qad	every other day
qd	every day
qh	every hour
qid	four times a day
qod	every other day

ABBREVIATIONS, ACRONYMS, AND SYMBOLS *(Continued)*

Abbreviation	Meaning
qs	a sufficient quantity
qs ad	a sufficient quantity to make
qty	quantity
qv	as much as you wish
REM	rapid eye movement
Rx	take, a recipe
rep	let it be repeated
s̄	without
sa	according to art
sat	saturated
S.C.	subcutaneous
sig	label, or let it be printed
sol	solution
solv	dissolve
s̄s̄	one-half
sos	if there is need
SSRIs	selective serotonin reuptake inhibitors
stat	at once, immediately
supp	suppository
syr	syrup
tab	tablet
tal	such
TCA	tricyclic antidepressant
TD	tardive dyskinesia
tid	three times a day
tr, tinct	tincture
trit	triturate
tsp	teaspoonful
ULN	upper limits of normal
ung	ointment
USAN	United States Adopted Names
USP	United States Pharmacopeia
u.d., ut dict	as directed
v.o.	verbal order
w.a.	while awake
x3	3 times
x4	4 times
YBOC	Yale Brown Obsessive-Compulsive Scale
YMRS	Young Mania Rating Scale

APOTHECARY/METRIC EQUIVALENTS

Approximate Liquid Measures

Basic equivalent: 1 fluid ounce = 30 mL

Examples:

1 gallon	3800 mL	1 gallon	128 fluid ounces
1 quart	960 mL	1 quart	32 fluid ounces
1 pint	480 mL	1 pint	16 fluid ounces
8 fluid oz	240 mL	15 minims	1 mL
4 fluid oz	120 mL	10 minims	0.6 mL

Approximate Household Equivalents

1 teaspoonful	5 mL	1 tablespoonful	15 mL

Weights

Basic equivalents:

1 oz	30 g	15 gr	1 g

Examples:

4 oz	120 g	1 gr	60 mg
2 oz	60 g	1/100 gr	600 mcg
10 gr	600 mg	1/150 gr	400 mcg
7½ gr	500 mg	1/200 gr	300 mcg
16 oz	1 lb		

Metric Conversions

Basic equivalents:

1 g	1000 mg	1 mg	1000 mcg

Examples:

5 g	5000 mg	5 mg	5000 mcg
0.5 g	500 mg	0.5 g	500 mcg
0.05 g	50 mg	0.05 mg	50 mcg

Exact Equivalents

1 g	=	15.43 gr	0.1 mg	=	1/600 gr
1 mL	=	16.23 minims	0.12 mg	=	1/500 gr
1 minim	=	0.06 mL	0.15 mg	=	1/400 gr
1 gr	=	64.8 mg	0.2 mg	=	1/300 gr
1 pint (pt)	=	473.2 mL	0.3 mg	=	1/200 gr
1 oz	=	28.35 g	0.4 mg	=	1/150 gr
1 lb	=	453.6 g	0.5 mg	=	1/120 gr
1 kg	=	2.2 lbs	0.6 mg	=	1/100 gr
1 qt	=	946.4 mL	0.8 mg	=	1/80 gr
			1 mg	=	1/65 gr

Solids*

¼ grain	=	15 mg
½ grain	=	30 mg
1 grain	=	60 mg
1½ grains	=	90 mg
5 grains	=	300 mg
10 grains	=	600 mg

*Use exact equivalents for compounding and calculations requiring a high degree of accuracy.

AVERAGE WEIGHTS AND SURFACE AREAS

Average Weight and Surface Area of Preterm Infants, Term Infants, and Children

Age	Average Weight (kg)*	Approximate Surface Area (m²)
Weeks Gestation		
26	0.9-1	0.1
30	1.3-1.5	0.12
32	1.6-2	0.15
38	2.9-3	0.2
40	3.1-4	0.25
(term infant at birth)		
Months		
3	5	0.29
6	7	0.38
9	8	0.42
Year		
1	10	0.49
2	12	0.55
3	15	0.64
4	17	0.74
5	18	0.76
6	20	0.82
7	23	0.90
8	25	0.95
9	28	1.06
10	33	1.18
11	35	1.23
12	40	1.34
Adults	70	1.73

*Weights from age 3 months and older are rounded off to the nearest kilogram.

BODY SURFACE AREA OF ADULTS AND CHILDREN

Calculating Body Surface Area in Children

In a child of average size, find weight and corresponding surface area on the boxed scale to the left; or, use the nomogram to the right. Lay a straightedge on the correct height and weight points for the child, then read the intersecting point on the surface area scale.

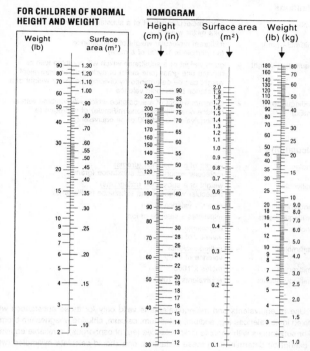

FOR CHILDREN OF NORMAL HEIGHT AND WEIGHT

NOMOGRAM

Height (cm) (in) — Surface area (m²) — Weight (lb) (kg)

BODY SURFACE AREA FORMULA
(Adult and Pediatric)

$$BSA\ (m^2) = \sqrt{\frac{Ht\ (in) \times Wt\ (lb)}{3131}} \quad \text{or, in metric: } BSA\ (m^2) = \sqrt{\frac{Ht\ (cm) \times Wt\ (kg)}{3600}}$$

References

Lam TK and Leung DT, "More on Simplified Calculation of Body Surface Area," *N Engl J Med*, 1988, 318(17):1130 (Letter).

Mosteller RD, "Simplified Calculation of Body Surface Area", *N Engl J Med*, 1987, 317(17):1098 (Letter).

IDEAL BODY WEIGHT CALCULATION

Adults (18 years and older) (IBW is in kg)

IBW (male) = 50 + (2.3 x height in inches over 5 feet)

IBW (female) = 45.5 + (2.3 x height in inches over 5 feet)

Children (IBW is in kg; height is in cm)

a. 1-18 years

$$IBW = \frac{(height^2 \times 1.65)}{1000}$$

b. 5 feet and taller

IBW (male) = 39 + (2.27 x height in inches over 5 feet)

IBW (female) = 42.2 + (2.27 x height in inches over 5 feet)

MILLIEQUIVALENT AND MILLIMOLE CALCULATIONS & CONVERSIONS

DEFINITIONS & CALCULATIONS

Definitions

mole	=	gram molecular weight of a substance (aka molar weight)
millimole (mM)	=	milligram molecular weight of a substance (a millimole is 1/1000 of a mole)
equivalent weight	=	gram weight of a substance which will combine with or replace one gram (one mole) of hydrogen; an equivalent weight can be determined by dividing the molar weight of a substance by its ionic valence
milliequivalent (mEq)	=	milligram weight of a substance which will combine with or replace one milligram (one millimole) of hydrogen (a milliequivalent is 1/1000 of an equivalent)

Calculations

moles	=	$\dfrac{\text{weight of a substance (grams)}}{\text{molecular weight of that substance (grams)}}$
millimoles	=	$\dfrac{\text{weight of a substance (milligrams)}}{\text{molecular weight of that substance (milligrams)}}$
equivalents	=	moles x valence of ion
milliequivalents	=	millimoles x valence of ion
moles	=	$\dfrac{\text{equivalents}}{\text{valence of ion}}$
millimoles	=	$\dfrac{\text{milliequivalents}}{\text{valence of ion}}$
millimoles	=	moles x 1000
milliequivalents	=	equivalents x 1000

Note: Use of equivalents and milliequivalents is valid only for those substances which have fixed ionic valences (eg, sodium, potassium, calcium, chlorine, magnesium bromine, etc). For substances with variable ionic valences (eg, phosphorous), a reliable equivalent value cannot be determined. In these instances, one should calculate millimoles (which are fixed and reliable) rather than milliequivalents.

MILLIEQUIVALENT CONVERSIONS

To convert mg/100 mL to mEq/L the following formula may be used:

$$\frac{\text{(mg/100 mL) x 10 x valence}}{\text{atomic weight}} = \text{mEq/L}$$

To convert mEq/L to mg/100 mL the following formula may be used:

$$\frac{\text{(mEq/L) x atomic weight}}{\text{10 x valence}} = \text{mg/100 mL}$$

To convert mEq/L to volume of percent of a gas the following formula may be used:

$$\frac{\text{(mEq/L) x 22.4}}{10} = \text{volume percent}$$

Valences and Atomic Weights of Selected Ions

Substance	Electrolyte	Valence	Molecular Wt
Calcium	Ca^{++}	2	40
Chloride	Cl^-	1	35.5
Magnesium	Mg^{++}	2	24
Phosphate	HPO_4^{--} (80%)	1.8	96*
pH = 7.4	$H_2PO_4^-$ (20%)	1.8	96*
Potassium	K^+	1	39
Sodium	Na^+	1	23
Sulfate	SO_4^{--}	2	96*

*The molecular weight of phosphorus only is 31, and sulfur only is 32.

Approximate Milliequivalents — Weights of Selected Ions

Salt	mEq/g Salt	Mg Salt/mEq
Calcium carbonate ($CaCO_3$)	20	50
Calcium chloride ($CaCl_2 - 2H_2O$)	14	73
Calcium gluconate (Ca gluconate$_2 - 1H_2O$)	4	224
Calcium lactate (Ca lactate$_2 - 5H_2O$)	6	154
Magnesium sulfate ($MgSO_4$)	16	60
Magnesium sulfate ($MgSO_4 - 7H_2O$)	8	123
Potassium acetate (K acetate)	10	98
Potassium chloride (KCl)	13	75
Potassium citrate (K_3 citrate $- 1H_2O$)	9	108
Potassium iodide (KI)	6	166
Sodium bicarbonate ($NaHCO_3$)	12	84
Sodium chloride (NaCl)	17	58
Sodium citrate (Na_3 citrate $- 2H_2O$)	10	98
Sodium iodine (NaI)	7	150
Sodium lactate (Na lactate)	9	112

CORRECTED SODIUM

Corrected Na^+ = measured Na^+ + [1.5 x (glucose − 150 divided by 100)]

Note: Do not correct for glucose <150.

WATER DEFICIT

Water deficit = 0.6 x body weight [1 − (140 divided by Na^+)]

Note: Body weight is estimated weight in kg when fully hydrated; **Na⁺** is serum or plasma sodium. Use corrected Na^+ if necessary. Consult medical references for recommendations for replacement of deficit.

TOTAL SERUM CALCIUM CORRECTED FOR ALBUMIN LEVEL

[(Normal albumin − patient's albumin) x 0.8] + patient's measured total calcium

ACID-BASE ASSESSMENT

Henderson-Hasselbalch Equation

$$pH = 6.1 + \log (HCO_3^-/ (0.03) (pCO_2))$$

MILLIEQUIVALENT AND MILLIMOLE CALCULATIONS & CONVERSIONS *(Continued)*

Alveolar Gas Equation

PIO_2 = FiO_2 x (total atmospheric pressure − vapor pressure of H_2O at 37°C)

= FiO_2 x (760 mm Hg − 47 mm Hg)

PAO_2 = PIO_2 − $PACO_2$ / R

Alveolar/arterial oxygen gradient = PAO_2 − PaO_2

Normal ranges:

	Children	15-20 mm Hg
	Adults	20-25 mm Hg

where:

PIO_2 = Oxygen partial pressure of inspired gas (mm Hg) (150 mm Hg in room air at sea level)

FiO_2 = Fractional pressure of oxygen in inspired gas (0.21 in room air)

PAO_2 = Alveolar oxygen partial pressure

$PACO_2$ = Alveolar carbon dioxide partial pressure

PaO_2 = Arterial oxygen partial pressure

R = Respiratory exchange quotient (typically 0.8, increases with high carbohydrate diet, decreases with high fat diet)

Acid-Base Disorders

Acute metabolic acidosis (<12 h duration):

$$PaCO_2 \text{ expected} = 1.5 (HCO_3^-) + 8 \pm 2$$

or

expected change in pCO = (1-1.5) x change in HCO_3^-

Acute metabolic alkalosis (<12 h duration):

expected change in pCO_2 = (0.5-1) x change in HCO_3^-

Acute respiratory acidosis (<6 h duration):

expected change in HCO_3^- = 0.1 x pCO_2

Acute respiratory acidosis (>6 h duration):

expected change in HCO_3^- = 0.4 x change in pCO_2

Acute respiratory alkalosis (<6 h duration):

expected change in HCO_3^- = 0.2 x change in pCO_2

Acute respiratory alkalosis (>6 h duration):

expected change in HCO_3^- = 0.5 x change in pCO_2

ACID-BASE EQUATION

H^+ (in mEq/L) = (24 x $PaCO_2$) divided by HCO_3^-

Aa GRADIENT

Aa gradient [(713)(FiO_2 − ($PaCO_2$ divided by 0.8))] − PaO_2

Aa gradient	=	alveolar-arterial oxygen gradient
FiO_2	=	inspired oxygen (expressed as a fraction)
$PaCO_2$	=	arterial partial pressure carbon dioxide (mm Hg)
PaO_2	=	arterial partial pressure oxygen (mm Hg)

OSMOLALITY

Definition: The summed concentrations of all osmotically active solute particles.

Predicted serum osmolality =
2 Na^+ + glucose (mg/dL) / 18 + BUN (mg/dL) / 2.8

The normal range of serum osmolality is 285-295 mOsm/L.

Differential diagnosis of increased serum osmolal gap (>10 mOsm/L)

Medications and toxins
Alcohols (ethanol, methanol, isopropanol, glycerol, ethylene glycol)
Mannitol
Paraldehyde

Calculated Osm

Osmolal gap = measured Osm − calculated Osm

> 0 to +10: Normal
> >10: Abnormal
> <0: Probable lab or calculation error

For drugs causing increased osmolar gap, see "Toxicology Information" section in this Appendix.

BICARBONATE DEFICIT

HCO_3^- deficit = (0.4 x wt in kg) x (HCO_3^- desired − HCO_3^- measured)

Note: In clinical practice, the calculated quantity may differ markedly from the actual amount of bicarbonate needed or that which may be safely administered.

ANION GAP

Definition: The difference in concentration between unmeasured cation and anion equivalents in serum.

Anion gap = $Na^+ − Cl^− − HCO_3^-$
(The normal anion gap is 10-14 mEq/L)

Differential Diagnosis of Increased Anion Gap Acidosis

Organic anions

Lactate (sepsis, hypovolemia, seizures, large tumor burden)
Pyruvate
Uremia
Ketoacidosis (β-hydroxybutyrate and acetoacetate)
Amino acids and their metabolites
Other organic acids

Inorganic anions

Hyperphosphatemia
Sulfates
Nitrates

Differential Diagnosis of Decreased Anion Gap

Organic cations

Hypergammaglobulinemia

Inorganic cations

Hyperkalemia
Hypercalcemia
Hypermagnesemia

Medications and toxins

Lithium

Hypoalbuminemia

RETICULOCYTE INDEX

(% retic divided by 2) x (patient's Hct divided by normal Hct) or (% retic divided by 2) x (patient's Hgb divided by normal Hgb)

Normal index: 1.0
Good marrow response: 2.0-6.0

PEDIATRIC DOSAGE ESTIMATIONS

Dosage Estimations Based on Weight:

Augsberger's rule:

$$\frac{(1.5 \times \text{weight in kg} + 10)}{\% \text{ of adult dose}} = \text{child's approximate dose}$$

Clark's rule:

$$\frac{\text{weight (in pounds)}}{150} \times \text{adult dose} = \text{child's approximate dose}$$

Dosage Estimations Based on Age:

Augsberger's rule:

$$\frac{(4 \times \text{age in years} + 20)}{\% \text{ of adult dose}} = \text{child's approximate dose}$$

Bastedo's rule:

$$\frac{\text{age in years} + 3}{30} \times \text{adult dose} = \text{child's approximate dose}$$

Cowling's rule:

$$\frac{\text{age at next birthday (in years)}}{24} \times \text{adult dose} = \text{child's approximate dose}$$

Dilling's rule:

$$\frac{\text{age (in years)}}{20} \times \text{adult dose} = \text{child's approximate dose}$$

Fried's rule for infants (younger than 1 year):

$$\frac{\text{age (in months)}}{150} \times \text{adult dose} = \text{infant's approximate dose}$$

Young's rule:

$$\frac{\text{age (in years)}}{\text{age} + 12} \times \text{adult dose} = \text{child's approximate dose}$$

POUNDS/KILOGRAMS CONVERSION

1 pound = 0.45359 kilograms
1 kilogram = 2.2 pounds

lb	=	kg	lb	=	kg	lb	=	kg
1		0.45	70		31.75	140		63.50
5		2.27	75		34.02	145		65.77
10		4.54	80		36.29	150		68.04
15		6.80	85		38.56	155		70.31
20		9.07	90		40.82	160		72.58
25		11.34	95		43.09	165		74.84
30		13.61	100		45.36	170		77.11
35		15.88	105		47.63	175		79.38
40		18.14	110		49.90	180		81.65
45		20.41	115		52.16	185		83.92
50		22.68	120		54.43	190		86.18
55		24.95	125		56.70	195		88.45
60		27.22	130		58.91	200		90.72
65		29.48	135		61.24			

TEMPERATURE CONVERSION

Celsius to Fahrenheit = (°C x 9/5) + 32 = °F
Fahrenheit to Celsius = (°F -32) x 5/9 = °C

°C	=	°F	°C	=	°F	°C	=	°F
100.0		212.0	39.0		102.2	36.8		98.2
50.0		122.0	38.8		101.8	36.6		97.9
41.0		105.8	38.6		101.5	36.4		97.5
40.8		105.4	38.4		101.1	36.2		97.2
40.6		105.1	38.2		100.8	36.0		96.8
40.4		104.7	38.0		100.4	35.8		96.4
40.2		104.4	37.8		100.1	35.6		96.1
40.0		104.0	37.6		99.7	35.4		95.7
39.8		103.6	37.4		99.3	35.2		95.4
39.6		103.3	37.2		99.0	35.0		95.0
39.4		102.9	37.0		98.6	0		32.0
39.2		102.6						

LIVER DISEASE

Pugh's Modification of Child's Classification for Severity

Parameter	Points for Increasing Abnormality		
	1	2	3
Encephalopathy	None	1 or 2	3 or 4
Ascites	Absent	Slight	Moderate
Bilirubin (mg/dL)	<2.9	2.9-5.8	>5.8
Albumin (g/dL)	>3.5	2.8-3.5	<2.8
Prothrombin time (seconds over control)	1-4	4-6	>6

Scores:

Mild hepatic impairment = <6 points.
Moderate hepatic impairment = 6-10 points.
Severe hepatic impairment = >10 points.

Considerations for Drug Dose Adjustment

Extent of Change in Drug Dose	Conditions or Requirements to Be Satisfied
No or minor change	Mild liver disease
	Extensive elimination of drug by kidneys and no renal dysfunction
	Elimination by pathways of metabolism spared by liver disease
	Drug is enzyme-limited and given acutely
	Drug is flow/enzyme-sensitive and only given acutely by I.V. route
	No alteration in drug sensitivity
Decrease in dose up to 25%	Elimination by the liver does not exceed 40% of the dose; no renal dysfunction
	Drug is flow-limited and given by I.V. route, with no large change in protein binding
	Drug is flow/enzyme-limited and given acutely by oral route
	Drug has a large therapeutic ratio
>25% decrease in dose	Drug metabolism is affected by liver disease; drug administered chronically
	Drug has a narrow therapeutic range; protein binding altered significantly
	Drug is flow-limited and given orally
	Drug is eliminated by kidneys and renal function severely affected
	Altered sensitivity to drug due to liver disease

Reference

Arns PA, Wedlund PJ, and Branch RA, "Adjustment of Medications in Liver Failure," *The Pharmacologic Approach to the Critically Ill Patient*, 2nd ed, Chernow B, ed, Baltimore, MD: Williams & Wilkins, 1988, 85-111.

CREATININE CLEARANCE ESTIMATING METHODS IN PATIENTS WITH STABLE RENAL FUNCTION

These formulas provide an acceptable estimate of the patient's creatinine clearance **except** in the following instances.

- Patient's serum creatinine is changing rapidly (either up or down).
- Patients are markedly emaciated.

In above situations, certain assumptions have to be made.

- In patients with rapidly rising serum creatinines (ie, >0.5-0.7 mg/dL/day), it is best to assume that the patient's creatinine clearance is probably <10 mL/minute.

- In emaciated patients, although their actual creatinine clearance is less than their calculated creatinine clearance (because of decreased creatinine production), it is not possible to easily predict how much less.

Infants

Estimation of creatinine clearance using serum creatinine and body length (to be used when an adequate timed specimen cannot be obtained). **Note:** This formula may not provide an accurate estimation of creatinine clearance for infants younger than 6 months of age and for patients with severe starvation or muscle wasting.

$$Cl_{cr} = K \times L/S_{cr}$$

where:

Cl_{cr}	=	creatinine clearance in mL/minute/1.73 m^2
K	=	constant of proportionality that is age specific

Age	K
Low birth weight ≤1 y	0.33
Full-term ≤1 y	0.45
2-12 y	0.55
13-21 y female	0.55
13-21 y male	0.70

L	=	length in cm
S_{cr}	=	serum creatinine concentration in mg/dL

Reference

Schwartz GJ, Brion LP, and Spitzer A, "The Use of Plasma Creatinine Concentration for Estimating Glomerular Filtration Rate in Infants, Children and Adolescents," *Ped Clin N Amer*, 1987, 34:571-90.

Children (1-18 years)

Method 1: (Traub SL, Johnson CE, *Am J Hosp Pharm*, 1980, 37:195-201)

$$Cl_{cr} = \frac{0.48 \times (height) \times BSA}{S_{cr} \times 1.73}$$

where:

BSA	=	body surface area in m^2
Cl_{cr}	=	creatinine clearance in mL/min
S_{cr}	=	serum creatinine in mg/dL
Height	=	in cm

CREATININE CLEARANCE ESTIMATING METHODS IN PATIENTS WITH STABLE RENAL FUNCTION *(Continued)*

<u>Method 2:</u> Nomogram (Traub SL and Johnson CE, *Am J Hosp Pharm*, 1980, 37:195-201)

Children 1-18 Years

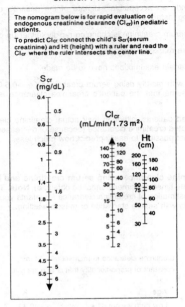

> The nomogram below is for rapid evaluation of endogenous creatinine clearance (Cl_{cr}) in pediatric patients.
>
> To predict Cl_{cr} connect the child's S_{cr} (serum creatinine) and Ht (height) with a ruler and read the Cl_{cr} where the ruler intersects the center line.

Adults (18 years and older)

<u>Method:</u> (Cockroft DW and Gault MH, *Nephron*, 1976, 16:31-41)

Estimated creatinine clearance (Cl_{cr}) (mL/min):

$$\text{Male} = \frac{(140 - \text{age})\ \text{IBW (kg)}}{72 \times S_{cr}}$$

$$\text{Female} = \text{estimated } Cl_{cr} \text{ male} \times 0.85$$

Note: The use of the patient's ideal body weight (IBW) is recommended for the above formula except when the patient's actual body weight is less than ideal. Use of the IBW is especially important in obese patients.

RENAL FUNCTION TESTS

Endogenous creatinine clearance vs age (timed collection)

Creatinine clearance (mL/min/1.73 m^2) = (Cr$_u$V/Cr$_s$T) (1.73/A)

where:

Cr$_u$	=	urine creatinine concentration (mg/dL)
V	=	total urine collected during sampling period (mL)
Cr$_s$	=	serum creatinine concentration (mg/dL)
T	=	duration of sampling period (min) (24 h = 1440 min)
A	=	body surface area (m^2)

Age-specific normal values

5-7 d	50.6 ± 5.8 mL/min/1.73 m^2
1-2 mo	64.6 ± 5.8 mL/min/1.73 m^2
5-8 mo	87.7 ± 11.9 mL/min/1.73 m^2
9-12 mo	86.9 ± 8.4 mL/min/1.73 m^2
≥18 mo	
male	124 ± 26 mL/min/1.73 m^2
female	109 ± 13.5 mL/min/1.73 m^2
Adults	
male	105 ± 14 mL/min/1.73 m^2
female	95 ± 18 mL/min/1.73 m^2

Note: In patients with renal failure (creatinine clearance <25 mL/min), creatinine clearance may be elevated over GFR because of tubular secretion of creatinine.

Calculation of Creatinine Clearance From a 24-Hour Urine Collection

Equation 1:

$$Cl_{cr} = \frac{U \times V}{P}$$

where:

Cl$_{cr}$	=	creatinine clearance
U	=	urine concentration of creatinine
V	=	total urine volume in the collection
P	=	plasma creatinine concentration

Equation 2:

$$Cl_{cr} = \frac{(\text{total urine volume [mL]}) \times (\text{urine Cr concentration [mg/dL]})}{(\text{serum creatinine [mg/dL]}) \times (\text{time of urine collection [minutes]})}$$

Occasionally, a patient will have a 12- or 24-hour urine collection done for direct calculation of creatinine clearance. Although a urine collection for 24 hours is best, it is difficult to do since many urine collections occur for a much shorter period. A 24-hour urine collection is the desired duration of urine collection because the urine excretion of creatinine is diurnal and thus the measured creatinine clearance will vary throughout the day as the creatinine in the urine varies. When the urine collection is less than 24 hours, the total excreted creatinine will be affected by the time of the day during which the collection is performed. A 24-hour urine collection is sufficient to be able to accurately average the diurnal creatinine excretion variations. If a patient has 24 hours of urine collected for creatinine clearance, equation 1 can be used for calculating the creatinine clearance. To use equation 1 to calculate the creatinine clearance, it will be necessary to know the duration of urine collection, the urine collection volume, the urine creatinine concentration, and the serum creatinine value that reflects the urine collection period. In most cases, a serum creatinine concentration is drawn anytime during the day, but it is best to have the value drawn halfway through the collection period.

Amylase/Creatinine Clearance Ratio*

$$\frac{\text{Amylase}_u \times \text{creatinine}_p}{\text{Amylase}_p \times \text{creatinine}_u} \times 100$$

u = urine; p = plasma

RENAL FUNCTION TESTS (Continued)

Serum BUN/Serum Creatinine Ratio

Serum BUN (mg/dL:serum creatinine (mg/dL))

Normal BUN:creatinine ratio is 10-15

BUN:creatinine ratio >20 suggests prerenal azotemia (also seen with high urea-generation states such as GI bleeding)

BUN:creatinine ratio <5 may be seen with disorders affecting urea biosynthesis such as urea cycle enzyme deficiencies and with hepatitis.

Fractional Sodium Excretion

Fractional sodium secretion (FENa) = Na_uCr_s/Na_sCr_u x 100%

where:

$$Na_u = \text{urine sodium (mEq/L)}$$
$$Na_s = \text{serum sodium (mEq/L)}$$
$$Cr_u = \text{urine creatinine (mg/dL)}$$
$$Cr_s = \text{serum creatinine (mg/dL)}$$

FENa <1% suggests prerenal failure

FENa >2% suggest intrinsic renal failure
(for newborns, normal FENa is approximately 2.5%)

Note: Disease states associated with a falsely elevated FENa include severe volume depletion (>10%), early acute tubular necrosis and volume depletion in chronic renal disease. Disorders associated with a lowered FENa include acute glomerulonephritis, hemoglobinuric or myoglobinuric renal failure, nonoliguric acute tubular necrosis and acute urinary tract obstruction. In addition, FENa may be <1% in patients with acute renal failure **and** a second condition predisposing to sodium retention (eg, burns, congestive heart failure, nephrotic syndrome).

Urine Calcium/Urine Creatinine Ratio (spot sample)

Urine calcium (mg/dL): urine creatinine (mg/dL)

Normal values <0.21 (mean values 0.08 males, 0.06 females)

Premature infants show wide variability of calcium:creatinine ratio, and tend to have lower thresholds for calcium loss than older children. Prematures without nephrolithiasis had mean Ca:Cr ratio of 0.75 ± 0.76. Infants with nephrolithiasis had mean Ca:Cr ratio of 1.32 ± 1.03 (Jacinto, et al, *Pediatrics*, vol 81, p 31.)

Urine Protein/Urine Creatinine Ratio (spot sample)

P_u/Cr_u	Total Protein Excretion (mg/m^2/d)
0.1	80
1	800
10	8000

where:

P_u = urine protein concentration (mg/dL)
Cr_u = urine creatinine concentration (mg/dL)

CANCER CHEMOTHERAPY REGIMENS

ADULT REGIMENS

Adenocarcinoma – Unknown Primary

Carbo-Tax

Paclitaxel, I.V., 135 mg/m^2 over 24 hours, day 1, followed by
Carboplatin dose targeted by Calvert equation to AUC 7.5 I.V.

Repeat cycle every 21 days

EP

Cisplatin, I.V., 60-100 mg/m^2, day 1
Etoposide, I.V., 80-100 mg/m^2, days 1-3

Repeat cycle every 21 days

FAM

Fluorouracil, I.V., 600 mg/m^2, days 1, 8, 29, 36
Doxorubicin, I.V., 30 mg/m^2, days 1, 29
Mitomycin, I.V., 10 mg/m^2, day 1

Repeat cycle every 8 weeks

Paclitaxel/Carboplatin/Etoposide

Paclitaxel, I.V., 200 mg/m^2 over 1 hour, day 1, followed by
Carboplatin dose targeted by Calvert equation to AUC 6 I.V.
Etoposide, P.O., 50 mg/day alternated with 100 mg/day, days 1-10

Repeat cycle every 21 days

Breast Cancer

Standard adjuvant chemotherapy includes 4 cycles of AC or
6 cycles of CMF (d$_1$/d$_8$ variety)

AC

Doxorubicin, I.V., 60 mg/m^2, day 1
Cyclophosphamide, I.V., 400-600 mg/m^2, day 1

Repeat cycle every 21 days

ACe

Doxorubicin, I.V., 40 mg/m^2, day 1
Cyclophosphamide, P.O., 200 mg/m^2/day, days 1-3 or 3-6

Repeat cycle every 21-28 days

CAF

Cyclophosphamide, P.O., 100 mg/m^2, days 1-14 or 600 mg/m^2 I.V., day 1
Doxorubicin, I.V., 25 mg/m^2, days 1, 8 or 60 mg/m^2 I.V., day 1
Fluorouracil, I.V., 500-600 mg/m^2, days 1, 8

Repeat cycle every 28 days

or

Cyclophosphamide, I.V., 500 mg/m^2, day 1
Doxorubicin, I.V., 50 mg/m^2, day 1
Fluorouracil, I.V., 500 mg/m^2, day 1

Repeat cycle every 21 days

CFM

Cyclophosphamide, I.V., 500-600 mg/m^2, day 1
Fluorouracil, I.V., 500-600 mg/m^2, day 1
Mitoxantrone, I.V., 10-12 mg/m^2, day 1

Repeat cycle every 21 days

CFPT

Cyclophosphamide, I.V., 150 mg/m^2, days 1-5
Fluorouracil, I.V., 300 mg/m^2, days 1-5
Prednisone, P.O., 10 mg tid, days 1-7
Tamoxifen, P.O., 10 mg bid, days 1-42

Repeat cycle every 42 days

CMF

Cyclophosphamide, P.O., 100 mg/m^2, days 1-14 or 600 mg/m^2 I.V., days 1, 8
Methotrexate, I.V., 40 mg/m^2, days 1, 8
Fluorouracil, I.V., 600 mg/m^2, days 1, 8

Repeat cycle every 28 days

or

Cyclophosphamide, I.V., 600 mg/m^2, day 1
Methotrexate, I.V., 40 mg/m^2, day 1
Fluorouracil, I.V., 400-600 mg/m^2, day 1

Repeat cycle every 21 days

CANCER CHEMOTHERAPY REGIMENS (Continued)

CMFP

Cyclophosphamide, P.O., 100 mg/m^2, days 1-14
Methotrexate, I.V., 40-60 mg/m^2, days 1, 8
Fluorouracil, I.V., 600-700 mg/m^2, days 1, 8
Prednisone, P.O., 40 mg (first 3 cycles only), days 1-14

Repeat cycle every 28 days

FAC

Fluorouracil, I.V., 500 mg/m^2, days 1, 8
Doxorubicin, I.V., 50 mg/m^2, day 1
Cyclophosphamide, I.V., 500 mg/m^2, day 1

Repeat cycle every 21 days

IMF

Ifosfamide, I.V., 1.5 g/m^2, days 1, 8
Mesna, I.V., 20% of ifosfamide dose, give immediately before and 4 and 8 hours after ifosfamide infusion, days 1, 8
Methotrexate, I.V., 40 mg/m^2, days 1, 8
Fluorouracil, I.V., 600 mg/m^2, days 1, 8

Repeat cycle every 28 days

NFL

Mitoxantrone, I.V., 12 mg/m^2, day 1
Fluorouracil, I.V., 350 mg/m^2, days 1-3, given after leucovorin calcium
Leucovorin calcium, I.V., 300 mg/m^2, days 1-3
or
Mitoxantrone, I.V., 10 mg/m^2, day 1
Fluorouracil, I.V., 1000 mg/m^2 continuous infusion, given after leucovorin calcium, days 1-3
Leucovorin calcium, I.V., 100 mg/m^2, days 1-3

Repeat cycle every 21 days

Sequential Dox-CMF

Doxorubicin, I.V., 75 mg/m^2, every 21 days for 4 cycles followed by 21- or 28-day CMF for 8 cycles

Vinorelbine/Doxorubicin

Vinorelbine, I.V., 25 mg/m^2, days 1, 8
Doxorubicin, I.V., 50 mg/m^2, day 1

Repeat cycle every 21 days

VATH

Vinblastine, I.V., 4.5 mg/m^2, day 1
Doxorubicin, I.V., 45 mg/m^2, day 1
Thiotepa, I.V., 12 mg/m^2, day 1
Fluoxymesterone, P.O., 10 mg tid, days 1-21

Repeat cycle every 21 days

Single-Agent Regimens

Anastrozole, P.O., 1 mg qd

Capecitabine, P.O., 2500 mg/m^2/day, bid regimen, days 1-14, repeat cycle every 21 days

Docetaxel, I.V., 60-100 mg/m^2 over 1 hour; patient must be premedicated with dexamethasone 8 mg bid P.O. for 5 days, start 1 day before docetaxel; repeat cycle every 3 weeks

Gemcitabine, I.V., 725 mg/m^2 over 30 minutes, weekly for 3 weeks, followed by 1-week rest, repeat cycle every 28 days

Letrozole, P.O., 2.5 mg qd

Megestrol, P.O., 40 mg qid

Paclitaxel, I.V., 175 mg/m^2 over 3 hours, every 21 days or 250 mg/m^2 over 3-24 hours, every 21 days
Patient must be premedicated with:
Dexamethasone 20 mg P.O., 12 and 6 hours prior
Diphenhydramine 50 mg I.V., 30 minutes prior
Cimetidine 300 mg I.V., or ranitidine 50 mg I.V., 30 minutes prior

Tamoxifen, P.O., 20 mg qd

Toremifene citrate, P.O., 60 mg qd

Vinorelbine, I.V., 30 mg/m^2, every 7 days

Cervical Cancer

CLD-BOMP

> Bleomycin, I.V., 5 mg continuous infusion, days 1-7
> Cisplatin, I.V., 10 mg/m^2, day 1, 22
> Vincristine, I.V., 0.7 mg/m^2, day 7
> Mitomycin-C. I.V., 7 mg/m^2, day 7
>
> Repeat cycle every 21 days

MOBP

> Bleomycin, I.V., 30 units/day continuous infusion, days 1, 4
> Vincristine, I.V., 0.5 mg/m^2, days 1, 4
> Mitomycin-C. I.V., 10 mg/m^2, day 1
> Cisplatin, I.V., 50 mg/m^2, days 1, 22
>
> Repeat cycle every 28 days

Single-Agent Regimen

> Cisplatin, I.V., 50-100 mg/m^2, every 21 days

Colon Cancer

F-CL

> Fluorouracil, I.V., 375 mg/m^2, days 1-5
> Leucovorin calcium, I.V., 200 mg/m^2, days 1-5
>
> Repeat cycle every 28 days
>
> or
>
> Fluorouracil, I.V., 500 mg/m^2/week 1 hour after initiating the calcium leuco-
> vorin infusion for 6 weeks
> Leucovorin calcium, I.V., 500 mg/m^2, over 2 hours, weekly for 6 weeks
> 2-week break, then repeat cycle

FLe

> Fluorouracil, I.V., 450 mg/m^2 for 5 days, then, after a pause of 4 weeks, 450
> mg/m^2/week for 48 weeks
> Levamisole, P.O., 50 mg tid for 3 days, repeated every 2 weeks for 1 year

FMV

> Fluorouracil, I.V., 10 mg/kg/day, days 1-5
> Methyl-CCNU, P.O., 175 mg/m^2, day 1
> Vincristine, I.V., 1 mg/m^2 (max: 2 mg), day 1
>
> Repeat cycle every 35 days

FU/LV

> Fluorouracil, I.V., 370-400 mg/m^2/day, days 1-5
> Leucovorin calcium, I.V., 200 mg/m^2/day, commence infusion 15 minutes
> prior to fluorouracil infusion, days 1-5
>
> Repeat cycle every 21 days
>
> or
>
> Fluorouracil, I.V., 1000 mg/m^2/day by continuous infusion, days 1-4
> Leucovorin calcium, I.V., 200 mg/m^2/day, days 1-4
>
> Repeat cycle every 28 days

Weekly 5FU/LV

> Fluorouracil, I.V., 600 mg/m^2 over 1 hour given after leucovorin, repeat
> weekly x 6 then 2-week rest period = 1 cycle, days 1, 8, 15, 22, 29, 36
> Leucovorin calcium, I.V., 500 mg/m^2 over 2 hours, days 1, 8, 15, 22, 29, 36
> Repeat cycle every 56 days

5FU/LDLF

> Fluorouracil, I.V., 425 mg/m^2/day, days 1-5
> Leucovorin calcium, I.V., 20-25 mg/m^2/day, days 1-5
>
> Repeat cycle every 28 days

Single-Agent Regimens

> 5-FU, I.V., 1000 mg/m^2/day, continuous infusion, days 1-5
> Repeat cycle every 21-28 days
>
> Irinotecan, I.V., 125 mg/m^2 over 90 minutes every 7 days for 4 cycles or 350
> mg/m^2 over 30 minutes
>
> Repeat cycle every 21 days

Endometrial Cancer

AP

> Doxorubicin, I.V., 60 mg/m^2, day 1
> Cisplatin, I.V., 60 mg/m^2, day 1
>
> Repeat cycle every 21 days

Single-Agent Regimens

> Doxorubicin, I.V., 40-60 mg/m^2, day 1
>
> Repeat cycle every 21-28 days
>
> Medroxyprogesterone, P.O., 200 mg/day

CANCER CHEMOTHERAPY REGIMENS *(Continued)*

Gastric Cancer

EAP

Etoposide, I.V., 120 mg/m^2, days 4, 5, 6
Doxorubicin, I.V., 20 mg/m^2, days 1, 7
Cisplatin, I.V., 40 mg/m^2, days 2, 8

Repeat cycle every 28 days

ELF

Leucovorin calcium, I.V., 300 mg/m^2, days 1-3 followed by
Etoposide, I.V., 120 mg/m^2, days 1-3 followed by
Fluorouracil, I.V., 500 mg/m^2, days 1-3

Repeat cycle every 21-28 days

FAM

Fluorouracil, I.V., 600 mg/m^2, days 1, 8, 29, 36
Doxorubicin, I.V., 30 mg/m^2, days 1, 29
Mitomycin C, I.V., 10 mg/m^2, day 1

Repeat cycle every 8 weeks

FAME

Fluorouracil, I.V., 350 mg/m^2, days 1-5, 36-40
Doxorubicin, I.V., 40 mg/m^2, days 1, 36
Methyl-CCNU, P.O., 150 mg/m^2, day 1

Repeat cycle every 70 days

FAMTX

Methotrexate, IVPB, 1500 mg/m^2, day 1
Fluorouracil, IVPB, 1500 mg/m^2 1 hour after methotrexate, day 1
Leucovorin calcium, P.O., 15 mg/m^2 q6h x 48 hours, 24 hours after metho-
   trexate, day 2
Doxorubicin, IVPB, 30 mg/m^2, day 15

Repeat cycle every 28 days

FCE

Fluorouracil, I.V., 900 mg/m^2/day continuous infusion, days 1-5
Cisplatin, I.V., 20 mg/m^2, days 1-5
Etoposide, I.V., 90 mg/m^2, days 1, 3, 5

Repeat cycle every 21 days

PFL

Cisplatin, I.V., 25 mg/m^2 continuous infusion, days 1-5
Fluorouracil, I.V., 800 mg/m^2 continuous infusion, days 2-5
Leucovorin calcium, I.V., 500 mg/m^2 continuous infusion, days 1-5

Repeat cycle every 28 days

Single-Agent Regimens

Irinotecan, I.V., over 90 minutes: 125 mg/m^2/week; repeat weekly for 4
   weeks, then 2-week rest period
or
Irinotecan, I.V. over 30-90 minutes: 350 mg/m^2; repeat every 21 days

Genitourinary Cancer
Bladder

CAP

Cyclophosphamide, I.V., 400 mg/m^2, day 1
Doxorubicin, I.V., 40 mg/m^2, day 1
Cisplatin, I.V., 60 mg/m^2, day 1

Repeat cycle every 21 days

CISCA

Cisplatin, I.V., 70-100 mg/m^2, day 2
Cyclophosphamide, I.V., 650 mg/m^2, day 1
Doxorubicin, I.V., 50 mg/m^2, day 1

Repeat cycle every 21-28 days

CMV

Cisplatin, I.V., 100 mg/m^2 over 4 hours, start 12 hours after MTX, day 2
Methotrexate, I.V., 30 mg/m^2, days 1, 8
Vinblastine, I.V., 4 mg/m^2, days 1, 8

Repeat cycle every 21 days

m-PFL

Methotrexate, I.V., 60 mg/m^2, day 1
Cisplatin, I.V., 25 mg/m^2 continuous infusion, days 2-6
Fluorouracil, I.V., 800 mg/m^2 continuous infusion, days 2-6
Leucovorin calcium, I.V., 500 mg/m^2 continuous infusion, days 2-6

Repeat cycle every 28 days for 4 cycles

MVAC

Methotrexate, I.V., 30 mg/m^2, days 1, 15, 22
Vinblastine, I.V., 3 mg/m^2, days 2, 15, 22
Doxorubicin, I.V., 30 mg/m^2, day 2
Cisplatin, I.V., 70 mg/m^2, day 2

Repeat cycle every 28 days

PC

Paclitaxel, I.V., 200 mg/m^2 or 225 mg/m^2 over 3 hours, day 1
Carboplatin, I.V., dose targeted by Calvert equation to AUC 5 or 6 after
paclitaxel, day 1

Repeat cycle every 21 days

Single-Agent Regimens

Gemcitabine, I.V., 1200 mg/m^2, days 1, 8, 15

Repeat cycle every 28 days

Paclitaxel, I.V., 250 mg/m^2 over 24 hours, day 1

Repeat cycle every 21 days

Ovarian, Epithelial

Carbo-Tax

Paclitaxel, I.V., 135 mg/m^2 over 24 hours, day 1
or
175 mg/m^2 over 3 hours, day 1, followed by
Carboplatin dose targeted by Calvert equation to AUC 7.5 I.V.

Repeat cycle every 21 days

CC

Carboplatin, I.V., dose targeted by Calvert equation to AUC 6-7
Cyclophosphamide, I.V., 600 mg/m^2, day 1

Repeat cycle every 28 days

CP

Cyclophosphamide, I.V., 750 mg/m^2, day 1
Cisplatin, I.V., 75 mg/m^2, day 1

Repeat cycle every 21 days

CT

Paclitaxel, I.V., 135 mg/m^2 over 24 hours, day 1
or
175 mg/m^2 over 3 hours, day 1, followed by
Cisplatin, I.V., 75 mg/m^2

Repeat cycle every 21 days

PAC (CAP)

Cisplatin, I.V., 50 mg/m^2, day 1
Doxorubicin, I.V., 50 mg/m^2, day 1
Cyclophosphamide, I.V., 750 mg/m^2, day 1

Repeat cycle every 21 days x 8 cycles

Single-Agent Regimens

Altretamine, P.O., 260 mg/m^2/day, qid for 14-21 days

Repeat cycle every 28 days

Etoposide, I.V., 50-60 mg/m^2/day, days 1-21

Repeat cycle every 28 days

Liposomal doxorubicin, I.V., 50 mg/m^2, 1-hour infusion, day 1

Repeat cycle every 21 days

Paclitaxel, I.V., 135 mg/m^2, over 3 or 24 hours, day 1

Repeat cycle every 21 days

Topotecan, I.V., 1.5 mg/m^2, over 30 minutes, days 1-5

Repeat cycle every 21 days

Ovarian, Germ Cell

BEP

Bleomycin, I.V., 30 units, days 2, 9, 16
Etoposide, I.V., 100 mg/m^2, days 1-5
Cisplatin, I.V., 20 mg/m^2, days 1-5

VAC

Vincristine, I.V., 1.2-1.5 mg/m^2 (max: 2 mg) weekly for 10-12 weeks, or every
2 weeks for 12 doses
Dactinomycin, I.V., 0.3-0.4 mg/m^2, days 1-5
Cyclophosphamide, I.V., 150 mg/m^2, days 1-5

Repeat every 28 days

CANCER CHEMOTHERAPY REGIMENS *(Continued)*

Prostate

EV

> Estramustine, P.O., 200 mg tid, days 1-42
> Vinblastine, I.V., 4 mg/m²/week, begin day 1
>
> Repeat cycle every 6 weeks

FL

> Flutamide, P.O., 250 mg tid, days 1-28
> Leuprolide acetate, S.C., 1 mg qd, days 1-28
>
> Repeat cycle every 28 days
>
> or
>
> Flutamide, P.O., 250 mg tid, days 1-28
> Leuprolide acetate depot, I.M., 7.5 mg, day 1
>
> Repeat cycle every 28 days

FZ

> Flutamide, P.O., 250 mg tid
> Goserelin acetate, S.C., 3.6 mg implant, every 28 days or goserelin S.C.,
> 10.8 mg depot every 12 weeks

L-VAM

> Leuprolide acetate, S.C., 1 mg qd, days 1-28
> Vinblastine, I.V., 1.5 mg/m²/day continuous infusion, days 2-7
> Doxorubicin, I.V., 50 mg/m² continuous infusion, day 1
> Mitomycin C, I.V., 10 mg/m², day 2
>
> Repeat cycle every 28 days

Mitoxantrone/Prednisone

> Mitoxantrone, I.V., 12 mg/m², day 1
> Prednisone, P.O., 5 mg bid
>
> Repeat cycle every 21 days

No Known Acronym

> Bicalutamide, P.O., 50 mg/day
> Leuprolide acetate depot, I.M., 7.5 mg or goserelin S.C. 3.6 mg implant every
> 28 days

PE

> Paclitaxel, I.V., 120 mg/m², days 1-4
> Estramustine, P.O., 600 mg qd, 24 hours before paclitaxel
>
> Repeat cycle every 21 days

Single-Agent Regimens

> Estramustine, P.O., 14 mg/kg/day, tid or qid
>
> Goserelin acetate implant, S.C., 3.6 mg every 28 days or 10.8 mg every 12
> weeks
>
> Nilutamide, P.O., 300 mg qd, days 1-30, then 150 mg qd in combination with
> surgical castration; begin on same day or day after castration
>
> Prednisone, P.O., 5 mg bid

Renal

> Interleukin-2 (rIL-2), S.C.
> 20 million units/m², days 3-5, weeks 1, 4
> 5 million units/m², days 1, 3, 5, weeks 2, 3, 5, 6
>
> or
>
> Interferon alfa (rIFNα2), S.C.
> 6 million units/m², day 1, weeks 1, 4;
> 6 million units/m², days 1, 3, 5, weeks 2, 3, 5, 6
>
> Repeat cycle every 8 weeks

Single-Agent Regimen

> Interleukin-2:
> High dose: I.V. bolus over 15 minutes, 600,000-720,000 units/kg q8h
> until toxicity or 14 days; administer 2 courses separated by 7-10 days
> Low dose: S.C., 18 million units/day for 5 days, then 9 million units/day
> for 2 days, then 18 million units/day 3 days/week for 6 weeks
>
> or
>
> 3 million units/m²/day for 5 days/week, every 2 weeks for 1 month, then
> every 4 weeks

Testicular

EP

> Etoposide, I.V., 100 mg/m², days 1-5
> Cisplatin, I.V., 20 mg/m², days 1-5
>
> Repeat cycle every 21 days

Testicular, Induction, Good Risk

BEP

Bleomycin, I.V., 30 units, days 2, 9, 16
Etoposide, I.V., 100 mg/m^2, days 1-5
Cisplatin, I.V., 20 mg/m^2, days 1-5

Repeat cycle every 21 days

PVB

Cisplatin, I.V., 20 mg/m^2, days 1-5
Vinblastine, I.V., 0.15 mg/kg, days 1, 2
Bleomycin, I.V., 30 units, days 2, 9, 16

Repeat cycle every 21 days

Testicular, Induction, Poor Risk

VIP

Etoposide, I.V., 75 mg/m^2, days 1-5
Ifosfamide, I.V., 1.2 g/m^2, days 1-5
Cisplatin, I.V., 20 mg/m^2, days 1-5
Mesna, I.V., 400 mg/m^2, then 1200 mg/m^2/day continuous infusion, days 1-5

Repeat cycle every 21 days

VIP (Einhorn)

Vinblastine, I.V., 0.11 mg/kg, days 1-2
Ifosfamide, I.V., 1200 mg/m^2, days 1-5
Cisplatin, I.V., 20 mg/m^2, days 1-5
Mesna, I.V., 400 mg/m^2, then 1200 mg/m^2/day continuous infusion, days 1-5

Repeat cycle every 21 days

Testicular, Induction, Salvage

VAB VI

Vinblastine, I.V., 4 mg/m^2, day 1
Dactinomycin, I.V., 1 mg/m^2, day 1
Bleomycin, I.V., 30 units push day 1, then 20 units/m^2/day continuous infusion, days 1-3
Cisplatin, I.V., 120 mg/m^2, day 4
Cyclophosphamide, I.V., 600 mg/m^2, day 1

Repeat cycle every 21 days

VBP (PVB)

Vinblastine, I.V., 6 mg/m^2, days 1, 2
Bleomycin, I.V., 30 units, days 1, 8, 15, (22)
Cisplatin, I.V., 20 mg/m^2, days 1-5

Repeat cycle every 21-28 days

Gestational Trophoblastic Cancer

DMC

Dactinomycin, I.V., 0.37 mg/m^2, days 1-5
Methotrexate, I.V., 11 mg/m^2, days 1-5
Cyclophosphamide, I.V., 110 mg/m^2, days 1-5

Repeat cycle every 21 days

Head and Neck Cancer

CAP

Cyclophosphamide, I.V., 500 mg/m^2, day 1
Doxorubicin, I.V., 50 mg/m^2, day 1
Cisplatin, I.V., 50 mg/m^2, day 1

Repeat cycle every 28 days

CF

Cisplatin, I.V., 100 mg/m^2, day 1
Fluorouracil, I.V., 1000 mg/m^2/day continuous infusion, days 1-5

Repeat cycle every 21-28 days

CF

Carboplatin, I.V., 400 mg/m^2, day 1
Fluorouracil, I.V., 1000 mg/m^2/day continuous infusion, days 1-5

Repeat cycle every 21-28 days

COB

Cisplatin, I.V., 100 mg/m^2, day 1
Vincristine, I.V., 1 mg/m^2, days 2, 5
Bleomycin, I.V., 30 units/day continuous infusion, days 2-5

Repeat cycle every 21 days

CANCER CHEMOTHERAPY REGIMENS *(Continued)*

5-FU HURT

Hydroxyurea, P.O., 1000 mg q12h x 11 doses; start PM of admission, give 2 hours prior to radiation therapy, days 0-5

Fluorouracil, I.V., 800 mg/m^2/day continuous infusion, start AM after admission, days 1-5

Paclitaxel, I.V., 5-25 mg/m^2/day continuous infusion, start AM after admission; dose escalation study – refer to protocol, days 1-5

G-CSF, S.C., 5 mcg/kg/day, days 6-12, start ≥12 hours after completion of 5-FU infusion

5-7 cycles may be administered

PFL

Cisplatin, I.V., 100 mg/m^2, day 1

Fluorouracil, I.V., 600-800 mg/m^2/day continuous infusion, days 1-5

Leucovorin calcium, I.V., 200-300 mg/m^2/day, days 1-5

Repeat cycle every 21 days

PFL+IFN

Cisplatin, I.V., 100 mg/m^2, day 1

Fluorouracil, I.V., 640 mg/m^2/day continuous infusion, days 1-5

Leucovorin calcium, P.O., 100 mg q4h, days 1-5

Interferon alfa-2b, S.C., 2 x 10^6 units/m^2, days 1-6

TIP

Paclitaxel, I.V., 175 mg/m^2 3-hour infusion, day 1

Ifosfamide, I.V., 1000 mg/m^2 2-hour infusion, days 1-3

Mesna, I.V., 400 mg/m^2 before ifosfamide and 200 mg/m^2 I.V., 4 hours after ifosfamide

Cisplatin, I.V., 60 mg/m^2, day 1

Repeat cycle every 21-28 days

Single-Agent Regimens

Carboplatin, I.V., 300-400 mg/m^2, over 2 hours every 21-28 days

Methotrexate, I.V., 40 mg/m^2, every week, escalating day 14 by 5 mg/m^2/week as tolerated

Cisplatin I.V., 100 mg/m^2, every 28 days divided into 1, 2, or 4 equal doses per month

Vinorelbine, I.V., 25-30 mg/m^2, repeat weekly

Leukemias

Acute Lymphoblastic, Induction

VAD

Vincristine, I.V., 0.4 mg continuous infusion, days 1-4

Doxorubicin, I.V., 12 mg/m^2 continuous infusion, days 1-4

Dexamethasone, P.O., 40 mg, days 1-4, 9-12, 17-20

VP

Vincristine, I.V., 2 mg/m^2/week for 4-6 weeks (max: 2 mg)

Prednisone, P.O., 60 mg/m^2/day in divided doses for 4 weeks, taper weeks 5-7

VP-L-Asparaginase

Vincristine, I.V., 2 mg/m^2/week for 4-6 weeks (max: 2 mg)

Prednisone, P.O., 60 mg/m^2/day for 4-6 weeks, then taper

L-asparaginase, I.V., 10,000 units/m^2/day

No Known Acronym

Cyclophosphamide, I.V., 1200 mg/m^2, day 1

Daunorubicin, I.V., 45 mg/m^2, days 1-3

Prednisone, P.O., 60 mg/m^2, days 1-21

Vincristine, I.V., 2 mg/m^2/week

L-asparaginase, I.V., 6000 units/m^2, 3 times/week

or

Pegaspargase, I.M./I.V., 2500 units/m^2, every 14 days if patient develops hypersensitivity to native L-asparaginase

Acute Lymphoblastic, Maintenance

MM

Mercaptopurine, P.O., 50-75 mg/m^2, days 1-7

Methotrexate, P.O./I.V., 20 mg/m^2, day 1

Repeat cycle every 7 days

MMC (MTX + MP + CTX)*
>> Methotrexate, I.V., 20 mg/m^2/week
>> Mercaptopurine, P.O., 50 mg/m^2/day
>> Cyclophosphamide, I.V., 200 mg/m^2/week

>> *Continue all 3 drugs until relapse of disease or after 3 years of remission.

Acute Lymphoblastic, Relapse

AVDP
>> Asparaginase, I.V., 15,000 units/m^2, days 1-5, 8-12, 15-19, 22-26
>> Vincristine, I.V., 2 mg/m^2 (max: 2 mg), days 8, 15, 22
>> Daunorubicin, I.V., 30-60 mg/m^2, days 8, 15, 22
>> Prednisone, P.O., 40 mg/m^2, days 8-12, 15-19, 22-26

Acute Myeloid Leukemia, Induction

7+3
>> Cytarabine, I.V., 100-200 mg/m^2/day continuous infusion, days 1-7
>> **with**
>> Daunorubicin, I.V., 45 mg/m^2, days 1-3
>> **or**
>> Idarubicin, I.V., 12 mg/m^2, days 1-3
>> **or**
>> Mitoxantrone, I.V., 12 mg/m^2, days 1-3

5+2*
>> Cytarabine, I.V., 100-200 mg/m^2/day continuous infusion, days 1-5
>> **with**
>> Daunorubicin, I.V., 45 mg/m^2, days 1-2
>> **or**
>> Mitoxantrone, I.V., 12 mg/m^2, days 1-2
>> *For reinduction

D-3+7
>> Daunorubicin, I.V., 45 mg/m^2, days 1-3
>> Cytarabine, I.V., 100-200 mg/m^2 continuous infusion, days 1-7

DAT/DCT
>> Daunorubicin, I.V., 60 mg/m^2/day, days 1-3
>> Cytarabine, I.V., 200 mg/m^2/day continuous infusion, days 1-5
>> Thioguanine, P.O., 100 mg/m^2 q12h, days 1-5

>> *Modified DAT (considerations in elderly patients)*
>> Daunorubicin, I.V., 50 mg/m^2, day 1
>> Cytarabine, S.C., 100 mg/m^2/day q12h, days 1-5
>> Thioguanine, P.O., 100 mg/m^2 q12h, days 1-5

EMA-86
>> Etoposide, I.V., 200 mg/m^2/day continuous infusion, days 8-10
>> Mitoxantrone, I.V., 12 mg/m^2/day, days 1-3
>> Cytarabine, I.V., 500 mg/m^2/day continuous infusion, days 1-3, 8-10

I-3+7
>> Idarubicin, I.V., 12 mg/m^2, days 1-3
>> Cytarabine, I.V., 100 mg/m^2 continuous infusion, days 1-7

IC
>> Idarubicin, I.V., 12 mg/m^2/day, days 1-3
>> Cytarabine, I.V., 100-200 mg/m^2/day continuous infusion, days 1-7

LDAC
>> *Considerations in Elderly Patients*
>> Cytarabine, S.C., 10 mg/m^2 bid, days 10-21

MC
>> Mitoxantrone, I.V., 12 mg/m^2/day, days 1-3
>> Cytarabine, I.V., 100-200 mg/m^2/day continuous infusion, days 1-7

>> *Consolidation*
>> Mitoxantrone, I.V., 12 mg/m^2, days 1-2
>> Cytarabine, I.V., 100 mg/m^2 continuous infusion, days 1-5
>> Repeat cycle every 28 days

MV
>> Mitoxantrone, I.V., 10 mg/m^2/day, days 1-5
>> Etoposide, I.V., 100 mg/m^2/day, days 1-3

Single-Agent Regimen

>> All transrelincic acid (ATRA), P.O., 45 mg/m^2/day (1 or 2 divided doses) with
>> or without 7+3 induction regimen

CANCER CHEMOTHERAPY REGIMENS *(Continued)*

Acute Myeloid Leukemia, Postremission

Single-Agent Regimens

Cytarabine, I.V., 100 mg/m^2/day continuous infusion, days 1-5*; repeat cycle every 28 days

*For patients >60 years of age

Cytarabine (HiDAC), I.V. 3000 mg/m^2 over 1-3 hours, every 12 hours, days 1-6

or

3000 mg/m^2 over 1-3 hours, every 12 hours, days 1, 3, 5. Administer with saline, methylcellulose, or steroid eyedrops OU, every 2-4 hours, beginning with cytarabine and continuing 48-72 hours after last cytarabine dose

Repeat cycle every 28 days

Acute Nonlymphoblastic, Consolidation

CD

Cytarabine, I.V., 3000 mg/m^2 q12h, days 1-6
Daunorubicin, I.V., 30 mg/m^2/day, days 7-9

Chronic Lymphocytic Leukemia

CHL + PRED

Chlorambucil, P.O., 0.4 mg/kg for 1 day every other week
Prednisone, P.O., 100 mg/day for 2 days every other week; adjust dosage according to blood counts every 2 weeks prior to therapy; increase initial dose of 0.4 mg/kg by 0.1 mg/kg every 2 weeks until toxicity or disease control is achieved

CVP

Cyclophosphamide, P.O., 400 mg/m^2/day, days 1-5
Vincristine, I.V., 1.4 mg/m^2 (max: 2 mg), day 1
Prednisone, P.O., 100 mg/m^2, days 1-5

Repeat cycle every 21 days

Single-Agent Regimens

Chlorambucil, P.O., 0.1-0.2 mg/kg/day for 3-6 weeks

or

Chlorambucil, P.O., 20-30 mg/m^2, day 1

Repeat cycle every 14-28 days

Cladribine, I.V., 0.1 mg/kg/day continuous infusion, days 1-5 or 1-7

Repeat cycle every 28-35 days

Cyclophosphamide, P.O., 2-4 mg/kg, days 1-10

Repeat cycle every 21-28 days

Fludarabine, I.V., 25-30 mg/m^2, days 1-5

Repeat cycle every 28 days

Prednisone,* P.O., 30-60 mg/m^2, days 1-5 or 1-7

*Use if patient symptomatic with autoimmune thrombocytopenia or hemolytic anemia.

Chronic Myelogenous Leukemia

Single-Agent Regimens

Busulfan, P.O., 4-8 mg/day

Hydroxyurea, P.O., 2-5 g/day

Interferon alfa-2a, S.C., 3-5 million units/day

Hairy-Cell Leukemia

Single-Agent Regimens

Cladribine, I.V., 0.1 mg/kg/day continuous infusion, days 1-7

Administer one cycle

Interferon alfa-2a, S.C., 3 million units, 3 times/week

Pentostatin, I.V., 4 mg/m^2, day 1

Repeat cycle every 14 days

Lung Cancer
Small Cell

CAV/VAC

Cyclophosphamide, I.V., 750-1000 mg/m^2, day 1
Doxorubicin, I.V., 50 mg/m^2, day 1
Vincristine, I.V., 1.4 mg/m^2 (max: 2 mg), day 1

Repeat cycle every 3 weeks

CAVE

Cyclophosphamide, I.V., 750 mg/m^2, day 1
Doxorubicin, I.V., 50 mg/m^2, day 1
Vincristine, I.V., 1.4 mg/m^2 (max: 2 mg), day 1
Etoposide, I.V., 60-100 mg/m^2, days 1-3

Repeat cycle every 21 days

EC

Etoposide, I.V., 100-120 mg/m^2, days 1-3
Carboplatin, I.V., 325-400 mg/m^2, day 1

Repeat cycle every 28 days

EP/PE

Etoposide, I.V., 120 mg/m^2, days 1-3
Cisplatin, I.V., 60-120 mg/m^2, day 1

Repeat cycle every 21-28 days

Single-Agent Regimen

Etoposide, P.O., 50 mg/m^2, days 1-21

Repeat cycle every 28 days

Topotecan, I.V., 1.5 mg/m^2/day, over 30 minutes, days 1-5

Repeat cycle every 21 days

Nonsmall Cell

Carbo-Tax

Paclitaxel, I.V., 135 mg/m^2 over 24 hours, day 1 **or**
175 mg/m^2 over 3 hours, day 1, followed by
Carboplatin dose targeted by Calvert equation to AUC 7.5 I.V.

Repeat cycle every 21 days

EC

Etoposide, I.V., 100-120 mg/m^2, days 1-3
with
Carboplatin, I.V., 300-325 mg/m^2, day 1

Repeat cycle every 21-28 days

EP

Etoposide, I.V., 80 mg/m^2, days 1-3
Cisplatin, I.V., 60-100 mg/m^2, day 1

Repeat cycle every 21-28 days

Gemcitabine-Cis

Gemcitabine, I.V., 1000 mg/m^2, days 1, 8, 15
Cisplatin, I.V., 100 mg/m^2, day 2 or 15

Repeat cycle every 28 days

PC

Paclitaxel, I.V., 175 mg/m^2, 3-hour infusion, day 1
Cisplatin, I.V., 80 mg/m^2, day 1

Repeat cycle every 21 days

Vinorelbine-Cis

Vinorelbine, I.V., 30 mg/m^2, every 7 days
Cisplatin, I.V., 120 mg/m^2, day 1, 29, then every 6 weeks

Single-Agent Regimens

Topotecan, I.V., 1.5 mg/m^2/day, over 30 minutes, days 1-5

Repeat cycle every 21 days

Vinorelbine, I.V., 30 mg/m^2, every 7 days

Lymphoma
Hodgkin's

ABVD

Doxorubicin, I.V., 25 mg/m^2, days 1, 15
Bleomycin, I.V., 10 units/m^2, days 1, 15
Vinblastine, I.V., 6 mg/m^2, days 1, 15
Dacarbazine, I.V., 150 mg/m^2, days 1-5
or
Dacarbazine, I.V., 350-375 mg/m^2, days 1, 15

Repeat cycle every 28 days

1273

CANCER CHEMOTHERAPY REGIMENS *(Continued)*

ChlVPP

    Chlorambucil, P.O., 6 mg/m^2 (max: 10 mg/day), days 1-14
    Vinblastine, I.V., 6 mg/m^2 (max: 10 mg dose), days 1, 8
    Procarbazine, P.O., 100 mg/m^2 (max: 150 mg/day), days 1-14
    Prednisone, P.O., 40 mg/day, days 1-14

                                         Repeat cycle every 28 days

CVPP

    Lomustine, P.O., 75 mg/m^2, day 1
    Vinblastine, I.V., 4 mg/m^2, days 1, 8
    Procarbazine, P.O., 100 mg/m^2, days 1-14
    Prednisone, P.O., 30 mg/m^2, days 1-14 (cycles 1 and 4 only)

                                         Repeat cycle every 28 days

DHAP

    Dexamethasone, P.O./I.V., 40 mg, days 1-4
    Cytarabine, I.V., 2 g/m^2, q12h for 2 doses, day 2
    Cisplatin, I.V., 100 mg/m^2 continuous infusion, day 1

                                      Repeat cycle every 3-4 weeks

EVA

    Etoposide, I.V., 100 mg/m^2, days 1-3
    Vinblastine, I.V., 6 mg/m^2, day 1
    Doxorubicin, I.V., 50 mg/m^2, day 1

                                      Repeat cycle every 28 days

MOPP

    Mechlorethamine, I.V., 6 mg/m^2, days 1, 8
    Vincristine, I.V., 1.4 mg/m^2 (max: 2.5 mg), days 1, 8
    Procarbazine, P.O., 100 mg/m^2, days 1-14
    Prednisone, P.O., 40 mg/m^2 (cycles 1 and 4 only), days 1-14

                                      Repeat cycle every 28 days

MOPP/ABV Hybrid

    Mechlorethamine, I.V., 6 mg/m^2, day 1
    Vincristine, I.V., 1.4 mg/m^2 (max: 2 mg), day 1
    Procarbazine, P.O., 100 mg/m^2, days 1-7
    Prednisone, P.O., 40 mg/m^2, days 1-14
    Doxorubicin, I.V., 35 mg/m^2, day 8
    Bleomycin, I.V., 10 units/m^2, day 8
    Vinblastine, I.V., 6 mg/m^2, day 8

                                      Repeat cycle every 28 days

MVPP

    Mechlorethamine, I.V., 6 mg/m^2, days 1, 8
    Vinblastine, I.V., 6 mg/m^2, days 1, 8
    Procarbazine, P.O., 100 mg/m^2, days 1-14
    Prednisone, P.O., 40 mg/m^2, days 1-14

                                      Repeat cycle every 42 days

NOVP

    Mitoxantrone, I.V., 10 mg/m^2, day 1
    Vincristine, I.V., 2 mg, day 8
    Vinblastine, I.V., 6 mg/m^2, day 1
    Prednisone, P.O., 100 mg/m^2, days 1-5

                                      Repeat cycle every 21 days

Stanford V*

    Mechlorethamine, I.V., 6 mg/m^2, day 1
    Doxorubicin, I.V., 25 mg/m^2, days 1, 15
    Vinblastine, I.V., 6 mg/m^2, days 1, 15
    Vincristine, I.V., 1.4 mg/m^2, days 8, 22
    Bleomycin, I.V., 5 units/m^2, days 8, 22
    Etoposide, I.V., 60 mg/m^2, days 15, 16
    Prednisone, P.O., 40 mg/m^2/day, dose tapered over the last 15 days

                                      Repeat cycle every 28 days

    *In patients older than 50 years of age, vinblastine dose decreased to 4 mg/m^2 and vincristine dose decreased to 1 mg/m^2 on weeks 9-12. Concomitant trimethoprim/sulfamethoxazole DS P.O. bid; acyclovir 200 mg P.O. tid; ketoconazole 200 mg P.O. qd and stool softeners used.

Non-Hodgkin's

BACOP

    Bleomycin, I.V., 5 units/m^2, days 15, 22
    Doxorubicin, I.V., 25 mg/m^2, days 1, 8
    Cyclophosphamide, I.V., 650 mg/m^2, days 1, 8
    Vincristine, I.V., 1.4 mg/m^2 (max: 2 mg), days 1, 8
    Prednisone, P.O., 60 mg/m^2, days 15-28

                                      Repeat cycle every 28 days

CHOP

Cyclophosphamide, I.V., 750 mg/m^2, day 1
Doxorubicin, I.V., 50 mg/m^2, day 1
Vincristine, I.V., 1.4 mg/m^2 (max: 2 mg), day 1
Prednisone, P.O., 100 mg, days 1-5

Repeat cycle every 21 days

CHOP-Bleo

Cyclophosphamide, I.V., 750 mg/m^2, day 1
Doxorubicin, I.V., 50 mg/m^2, day 1
Vincristine, I.V., 2 mg, days 1, 5
Prednisone, P.O., 100 mg, days 1-5
Bleomycin, I.V., 15 units, days 1, 5

Repeat cycle every 21-28 days

CNOP

Cyclophosphamide, I.V., 750 mg/m^2, day 1
Mitoxantrone, I.V., 10 mg/m^2, day 1
Vincristine, I.V., 1.4 mg/m^2, day 1
Prednisone, P.O., 50 mg/m^2, days 1-5

Repeat cycle every 21 days

COMLA

Cyclophosphamide, I.V., 1500 mg/m^2, day 1
Vincristine, I.V., 1.4 mg/m^2 (max: 2.5 mg), days 1, 8, 15
Methotrexate, I.V., 120 mg/m^2, days 22, 29, 36, 43, 50, 57, 64, 71
Leucovorin calcium rescue, P.O., 25 mg/m^2, q6h for 4 doses, beginning 24
hours after each methotrexate dose
Cytarabine, I.V., 300 mg/m^2, days 22, 29, 36, 43, 50, 57, 64, 71

Repeat cycle every 21 days

COP

Cyclophosphamide, I.V., 800 mg/m^2, day 1
Vincristine, I.V., 1.4 mg/m^2 (max: 2 mg), day 1
Prednisone, P.O., 60 mg/m^2, days 1-5

Repeat cycle every 21 days

COP-BLAM

Cyclophosphamide, I.V., 400 mg/m^2, day 1
Vincristine, I.V., 1 mg/m^2, day 1
Prednisone, P.O., 40 mg/m^2, days 1-10
Bleomycin, I.V., 15 mg, day 14
Doxorubicin, I.V., 40 mg/m^2, day 1
Procarbazine, P.O., 100 mg/m^2, days 1-10

COPP (or "C" MOPP)

Cyclophosphamide, I.V., 400-650 mg/m^2, days 1, 8
Vincristine, I.V., 1.4-1.5 mg/m^2 (max: 2 mg), days 1, 8
Procarbazine, P.O., 100 mg/m^2, days 1-14
Prednisone, P.O., 40 mg/m^2, days 1-14

Repeat cycle every 28 days

CVP

Cyclophosphamide, P.O., 400 mg/m^2, days 1-5
Vincristine, I.V., 1.4 mg/m^2 (max: 2 mg), day 1
Prednisone, P.O., 100 mg/m^2, days 1-5

Repeat cycle every 21 days

DHAP*

Dexamethasone, I.V., 10 mg q6h, days 1-4
Cytarabine, I.V., 2 g/m^2 q12h x 2 doses, day 2
Cisplatin, I.V., 100 mg/m^2 continuous infusion, day 1

Repeat cycle every 21-28 days

*Administer with saline, methylcellulose, or steroid eyedrops OU, every 2-4
hours, beginning with cytarabine and continuing 48-72 hours after last
cytarabine dose.

ESHAP*

Etoposide, I.V., 60 mg/m^2, days 1-4
Cisplatin, I.V., 25 mg/m^2 continuous infusion, days 1-4
Cytarabine, I.V., 2 g/m^2, immediately following completion of etoposide and
cisplatin therapy
Methylprednisolone, I.V., 500 mg/day, days 1-4

Repeat cycle every 21-28 days

*Administer with saline, methylcellulose, or steroid eyedrops OU, every 2-4
hours, beginning with cytarabine and continuing 48-72 hours after last
cytarabine dose.

CANCER CHEMOTHERAPY REGIMENS *(Continued)*

IMVP-16

Ifosfamide, I.V., 4 g/m^2 continuous infusion over 24 hours, day 1
Mesna, I.V., 800 mg/m^2 bolus prior to ifosfamide, then 4 g/m^2 continuous infusion over 12 hours concurrent w/ifosfamide; then 2.4 g/m^2 continuous infusion over 12 hours after ifosfamide infusion, day 1
Methotrexate, I.V., 30 mg/m^2, days 3, 10
Etoposide, I.V., 100 mg/m^2, days 1-3

Repeat cycle every 21-28 days

MACOP-B

Methotrexate, I.V., 400 mg/m^2, weeks 2, 6, 10
Doxorubicin, I.V., 50 mg/m^2, weeks 1, 3, 5, 7, 9, 11
Cyclophosphamide, I.V., 350 mg/m^2, weeks 1, 3, 5, 7, 9, 11
Vincristine, I.V., 1.4 mg/m^2 (max: 2 mg), weeks 2, 4, 8, 10, 12
Bleomycin, I.V., 10 units/m^2, weeks 4, 8, 12
Prednisone, P.O., 75 mg/day tapered over 15 d, days 1-15
Leucovorin calcium, P.O., 15 mg/m^2, q6h x 6 doses 24 hours after methotrexate, weeks 2, 6, 10
Trimethoprim/sulfamethoxazole DS, P.O., tablet, bid, for 12 weeks
Ketoconazole, P.O., 200 mg/day

Administer one cycle

m-BACOD

Methotrexate, I.V., 200 mg/m^2, days 8, 15
Leucovorin calcium, P.O., 10 mg/m^2 q6h x 8 doses beginning 24 hours after each methotrexate dose, days 8, 15
Bleomycin, I.V., 4 units/m^2, day 1
Doxorubicin, I.V., 45 mg/m^2, day 1
Cyclophosphamide, I.V., 600 mg/m^2, day 1
Vincristine, I.V., 1 mg/m^2, day 1
Dexamethasone, P.O., 6 mg/m^2, days 1-5

Repeat cycle every 21 days

m-BACOS

Methotrexate, I.V., 1 g/m^2, day 2
Bleomycin, I.V., 10 units/m^2, day 1
Doxorubicin, I.V., 50 mg/m^2 continuous infusion, day 1
Cyclophosphamide, I.V., 750 mg/m^2, day 1
Vincristine, I.V., 1.4 mg/m^2 (max: 2 mg), day 1
Leucovorin calcium rescue, P.O., 15 mg q6h for 8 doses, starting 24 hours after methotrexate
Methylprednisolone, I.V., 500 mg, days 1-3

Repeat cycle every 21-25 days

MINE

Mesna, I.V., 1.33 g/m^2/day concurrent with ifosfamide dose, then 500 mg P.O. 4 hours after each ifosfamide infusion, days 1-3
Ifosfamide, I.V., 1.33 g/m^2/day, days 1-3
Mitoxantrone, I.V., 8 mg/m^2, day 1
Etoposide, I.V., 65 mg/m^2/day, days 1-3

Repeat cycle every 28 days

MINE-ESHAP

Mesna, I.V., 1.33 g/m^2, administered at same time as ifosfamide, then 500 mg P.O., 4 hours after ifosfamide, days 1-3
Ifosfamide, I.V., 1.33 g/m^2, over 1 hour, days 1-3
Mitoxantrone, I.V., 8 mg/m^2, day 1
Etoposide, I.V., 65 mg/m^2, days 1-3
Repeat cycle every 21 days for 6 cycles, followed by 3-6 cycles of ESHAP

NOVP

Mitoxantrone, I.V., 10 mg/m^2, day 1
Vinblastine, I.V., 6 mg/m^2, day 1
Prednisone, P.O., 100 mg, days 1-5
Vincristine, I.V., 2 mg, day 8

Repeat cycle every 21 days

Pro-MACE

Prednisone, P.O., 60 mg/m^2, days 1-14
Methotrexate, I.V., 1.5 g/m^2, day 14
Leucovorin calcium, I.V., 50 mg/m^2 q6h x 5 doses beginning 24 hours after methotrexate dose, day 14
Doxorubicin, I.V., 25 mg/m^2, days 1, 8
Cyclophosphamide, I.V., 650 mg/m^2, days 1, 8
Etoposide, I.V., 120 mg/m^2, days 1, 8

Repeat cycle every 28 days

Pro-MACE-CytaBOM

Prednisone, P.O., 60 mg/m², days 1-14
Doxorubicin, I.V., 25 mg/m², day 1
Cyclophosphamide, I.V., 650 mg/m², day 1
Etoposide, I.V., 120 mg/m², day 1
Cytarabine, I.V., 300 mg/m², day 8
Bleomycin, I.V., 5 units/m², day 8
Vincristine, I.V., 1.4 mg/m² (max: 2 mg), day 8
Methotrexate, I.V., 120 mg/m², day 8
Leucovorin calcium, P.O., 25 mg/m² q6h x 4 doses, day 9
Concomitant trimethoprim/sulfamethoxazole DS, P.O., bid

Repeat cycle every 21-28 days

Single-Agent Regimens

CDA cladribine, S.C., 0.1 mg/kg/day for 5 days or 0.1 mg/kg/day I.V., for 7 days

Repeat cycle every 28 days

Rituximab, I.V., 375 mg/m², days 1, 8, 15, 22

Malignant Melanoma

CVD

Cisplatin, I.V., 20 mg/m², days 1-5
Vinblastine, I.V., 1.6 mg/m², days 1-5
Dacarbazine, I.V., 800 mg/m², day 1

Repeat cycle every 21 days

CVD + IL-21

Cisplatin, I.V., 20 mg/m²/day, days 1-4
Vinblastine, I.V., 1.6 mg/m²/day, days 1-4
Dacarbazine, I.V., 800 mg/m², day 1
IL-2, I.V., 9 million units/m² continuous infusion, days 1-4
Interferon alfa, S.C., 5 million units/m², every day, days 1-5, 7, 9, 11, 13

Repeat cycle every 21 days

Dacarbazine/Tamoxifen

Dacarbazine, I.V., 250 mg/m², days 1-5, every 21 days
Tamoxifen,* P.O., 20 mg/day

No Known Acronym

Dacarbazine, I.V., 220 mg/m², days 1-3, every 21-28 days
Carmustine, I.V., 150 mg/m², day 1, every 42-56 days
Cisplatin, I.V., 25 mg/m², days 1-3, every 21-28 days
Tamoxifen,* P.O., 20 mg/day

*Use of tamoxifen is optional.

Single-Agent Regimens

Interferon alfa-2b adjuvant therapy, I.M., 20 million units/m², days 1-30, **then**
10 million units/m² S.C., 3 times/week for 48 weeks

Interferon alfa-2a, I.M., 20 million units/m² 3 times/week for 12 weeks

Multiple Myeloma

EDAP

Etoposide, I.V., 100-200 mg/m², days 1-4
Dexamethasone, P.O./I.V., 40 mg/m², days 1-5
Cytarabine, 1000 mg, day 5
Cisplatin, I.V., 20 mg continuous infusion, days 1-4

MP

Melphalan, P.O., 8-10 mg/m², days 1-4
Prednisone, P.O., 40-60 mg/m²/day, days 1-4

Repeat cycle every 28-42 days

M-2

Vincristine, I.V., 0.03 mg/kg (max: 2 mg), day 1
Carmustine, I.V., 0.5-1 mg/kg, day 1
Cyclophosphamide, I.V., 10 mg/kg, day 1
Melphalan, P.O., 0.25 mg/kg, days 1-4 or 0.1 mg/kg, days 1-7 or 1-10
Prednisone, P.O., 1 mg/kg/day, days 1-7

Repeat cycle every 35-42 days

VAD

Vincristine, I.V., 0.4 mg/day continuous infusion, days 1-4
Doxorubicin, I.V., 9 mg/m²/day continuous infusion, days 1-4
Dexamethasone, P.O., 40 mg, days 1-4, 9-12, 17-20

Repeat cycle every 28-35 days

VAD induction therapy followed by maintenance
Interferon alfa, S.C., 3 million units/m², 3 times/week
Prednisone, P.O., 50 mg, 3 times/week, after interferon

CANCER CHEMOTHERAPY REGIMENS (Continued)

VBAP

Vincristine, I.V., 1 mg, day 1
Carmustine, I.V., 30 mg/m^2, day 1
Doxorubicin, I.V., 30 mg/m^2, day 1
Prednisone, P.O., 100 mg, days 1-4

Repeat cycle every 21 days

VBMCP

Vincristine, I.V., 1.2 mg/m^2, day 1
Carmustine, I.V., 20 mg/m^2, day 1
Melphalan, P.O., 8 mg/m^2, days 1-4
Cyclophosphamide, I.V., 400 mg/m^2, day 1
Prednisone, P.O., 40 mg/m^2, days 1-7 all cycles, and 20 mg/m^2, days 8-14
first 3 cycles only

Repeat cycle every 35 days

VCAP

Vincristine, I.V., 1 mg, day 1
Cyclophosphamide, P.O., 100 mg/m^2, days 1-4
Doxorubicin, I.V., 25 mg/m^2, day 2
Prednisone, P.O., 60 mg/m^2, days 1-4

Repeat cycle every 28 days

Single-Agent Regimens

Aldesleukin, 600,000-700,000 int. units/kg every 8 hours x 14 doses
Repeat cycle every 14 days

Dexamethasone, P.O., 20 mg/m^2 for 4 days beginning on days 1-4, 9-12, and
17-20

Repeat cycle every 35 days

Interferon alfa-2b, S.C., 2 million units/m^2, 3 times/week for maintenance
therapy in selected patients with significant response to initial chemotherapy treatment

Melphalan, I.V., 90-140 mg/m^2

Administer one cycle

Pancreatic Cancer

FAM

Fluorouracil, I.V., 600 mg/m^2, days 1, 8, 29, 36
Doxorubicin, I.V., 30 mg/m^2, days 1, 29
Mitomycin, I.V., 10 mg/m^2, day 1

Repeat cycle every 72 days

SMF

Streptozocin, I.V., 1000 mg/m^2, days 1, 8, 29, 36
Mitomycin, I.V., 10 mg/m^2, day 1
Fluorouracil, I.V., 600 mg/m^2, days 1, 8, 29, 36

Repeat cycle every 72 days

Single-Agent Regimens

Gemcitabine, I.V., 1000 mg/m^2 over 30 minutes once weekly for 7 weeks,
followed by a 1-week rest period; subsequent cycles once weekly for 3
consecutive weeks out of every 4 weeks

Sarcoma

AC

Doxorubicin, I.V., 75-90 mg/m^2 96-hour continuous infusion
Cisplatin, I.A./I.V., 90-120 mg/m^2, 6 days

Repeat cycle every 28 days

AD

Doxorubicin, I.V., 22.5 mg/m^2/day continuous infusion, days 1-4
Dacarbazine, I.V., 225 mg/m^2/day continuous infusion, days 1-4

Repeat cycle every 21 days

CYVADIC

Cyclophosphamide, I.V., 500 mg/m^2, day 1
Vincristine, I.V., 1.4 mg/m^2, days 1, 5
Doxorubicin, I.V., 50 mg/m^2, day 1
Dacarbazine, I.V., 250 mg/m^2, days 1-5

Repeat cycle every 21 days

DI

Doxorubicin, I.V., 50 mg/m² bolus, day 1

Ifosfamide, I.V., 5000 mg/m²/day continuous infusion, following doxorubicin, day 1

Mesna, I.V., 600 mg/m², bolus before ifosfamide, followed by 2500 mg/m²/day, continuous infusion, for 36 hours

Repeat cycle every 21 days

HDMTX

Methotrexate, I.V., 8-12 g/m²

Leucovorin calcium, P.O./I.V., 15-25 mg q6h for at least 10 doses beginning 24 hours after methotrexate dose; courses repeated weekly for 2-4 weeks, alternating with various cancer chemotherapy combination regimens

IE

Etoposide, I.V., 100 mg/m², days 1-5

Ifosfamide, I.V., 1800 mg/m², days 1-5

Mesna, I.V., at 20% of ifosfamide dose prior to and 4 and 8 hours after ifosfamide administration

Repeat cycle every 21-28 days

MAID

Mesna, I.V., 2500 mg/m²/day continuous infusion, days 1-4

Doxorubicin, I.V., 15 mg/m²/day continuous infusion, days 1-4

Ifosfamide, I.V., 2500 mg/m²/day continuous infusion, days 1-3

Dacarbazine, I.V., 250 mg/m²/day continuous infusion, days 1-4

Repeat cycle every 21-28 days

VAC

Vincristine, I.V., 2 mg/m²/week (max: 2 mg), during weeks 1-12

Dactinomycin, I.V., 0.015 mg/kg (max: 0.5 mg) every 3 months for 5-6 courses, days 1-5

Cyclophosphamide, P.O., 2.5 mg/kg/day for 2 years

Single-Agent Regimens

Doxorubicin, I.V., 75 mg/m², day 1

Repeat cycle every 21 days

PEDIATRIC REGIMENS

Small patients have a large body surface area relative to their kg weight and could possibly be overdosed if a m² dosing regimen is applied. Therefore, for calculating pediatric doses of chemotherapy agents, as a general rule a child who weighs 30 kg is ~1 m². **For children weighing <15 kg or with surface area <0.6 m², the dose per m² of an agent listed herein should be divided by 30 and multiplied by the weight of the child (in kg) to obtain the correct dose.**

ALL, Consolidation

IDMTX/6-MP

Methotrexate, I.V. push, 200 mg/m², then 800 mg/m² as a 24-hour infusion

Mercaptopurine, I.V., 200 mg/m² over 20 minutes, then 800 mg/m² as an 8-hour infusion

Leucovorin, P.O./I.V., 15 mg/m² q6h x 9; begin 24 hours after end of methotrexate

ALL, Continuation

MTX/6-MP

Methotrexate, I.M., 20 mg/m²/week, during weeks 25-130

Mercaptopurine, P.O., 50 mg/m²/day, during weeks 25-130

MTX/6-MP/VP

Methotrexate, P.O., 20 mg/m²/week

Mercaptopurine, P.O., 75 mg/m²/day

Vincristine, I.V., 1.5 mg/m² x 1 each month

Prednisone, P.O., 40 mg/m² x 5 days each month

ALL, Induction

PVD

Prednisone, P.O., 40 mg/m²/day x 28 days

Vincristine, I.V., 1.5 mg/m²/week x 4

Asparaginase, I.M., 5000 int. units/m² on days 2, 5, 8, 12, 15, 18

CANCER CHEMOTHERAPY REGIMENS *(Continued)*

PVDA

Prednisone, P.O., 40 mg/m², days 1-28
Vincristine, I.V., 1.5 mg/m², days 2, 8, 15, 22
Daunorubicin, I.V., 25 mg/m², days 2, 8, 15, 22
Asparaginase, I.M., 5000 int. units/m² on days 2, 5, 8, 12, 15, 19

TIT (CNS Prophylaxis)

Methotrexate: 1 y: 10 mg; 2 y: 12.5 mg; ≥3 y: 15 mg
Cytarabine: 1 y: 20 mg; 2 y: 25 mg; ≥3 y: 30 mg
Hydrocortisone: 1 y: 10 mg; 2 y: 12.5 mg; ≥3 y: 15 mg

AML, Induction

CA

Cytarabine, I.V., 3 g/m², q12h for 4 doses
Asparaginase, I.M., 6000 int. units/m² 3 hours after last dose of cytarabine

DA

Daunorubicin, I.V., 45 mg/m², days 1-3
Cytarabine, I.V., 100 mg/m²/day, continuous infusion, days 1-7

DAT

Daunorubicin, I.V., 45 mg/m²/day continuous infusion, days 1-3
Cytarabine, I.V., 100 mg/m²/day continuous infusion, days 1-7
Thioguanine, P.O., 100 mg/m², days 1-7

DAV

Daunorubicin, I.V., 60 mg/m², days 3, 4, 5
Cytarabine, I.V., 100 mg/m² continuous infusion, days 1-2, then 30-minute
infusion q12h on days 3-8
Etoposide, I.V., 150 mg/m², days 6, 7, 8

HI-CDAZE

Daunorubicin, I.V., 30 mg/m², days 1-3
Cytarabine, I.V., 3 g/m², q12h, days 1-4
Etoposide, I.V., 200 mg/m², days 1-3, 6-8
Azacytidine, I.V., 150 mg/m², days 3-5, 8-10

Brain Tumors

CDDP/VP

Cisplatin, I.V., 90 mg/m², day 1
Etoposide, I.V., 150 mg/m², days 3, 4

Repeat cycle every 21 days

CDDP/VP-16

Cisplatin, I.V., 90 mg/m², day 1
Etoposide, I.V., 150 mg/m², days 3, 4

Repeat cycle every 21 days

COPE or "Baby Brain I"

Cycle A:
Vincristine, I.V., 0.065 mg/kg (max: 1.5 mg), days 1, 8
Cyclophosphamide, I.V., 65 mg/kg, day 1
Cycle B:
Cisplatin, I.V., 4 mg/m², day 1
Etoposide, I.V., 6.5 mg/kg, days 3, 4
Regimens given in alternating 28-day cycles in the sequence AABAAB

MOP

Mechlorethamine (nitrogen mustard), I.V., 6 mg/m², days 1, 8
Vincristine, I.V., 1.4 mg/m², days 1, 8
Procarbazine, P.O., 100 mg/m², days 1-14

MOPP

Mechlorethamine (nitrogen mustard), I.V., 3 mg/m², days 1, 8
Vincristine, I.V., 1.4 mg/m², days 1, 8
Procarbazine, P.O., 50 mg on day 1, 100 mg on day 2, then 100 mg/m² on
days 3-10
Prednisone, P.O., 40 mg/m², days 1-10

Repeat cycle every 28 days

PCV

Procarbazine, P.O., 60 mg/m², days 18-21
Methyl-CCNU, P.O., 110 mg/m², day 1
Vincristine, I.V., 1.4 mg/m², days 8 and 29

POC

Prednisone, P.O., 40 mg/m², days 1-14
CCNU, P.O., 100 mg/m², day 1
Vincristine, I.V., 1.5 mg/m², days 1, 8, 15

"8 in 1"

Methylprednisolone, P.O., 300 mg/m^2 for 3 doses q6h
Vincristine, I.V., 1.5 mg/m^2
Lomustine, P.O., 100 mg/m^2
Procarbazine, P.O., 75 mg/m^2
Hydroxyurea, P.O., 3000 mg/m^2
Cisplatin, I.V., 90 mg/m^2
Cytarabine, I.V., 300 mg/m^2
Dacarbazine, I.V., 150 mg/m^2

Repeat cycle every 14 days

Single-Agent Regimen

Carboplatin, I.V., 560 mg/m^2, every 4 weeks

Lymphomas

ABVD

Doxorubicin, I.V., 25 mg/m^2, days 1, 15
Bleomycin, I.V., 10 units/m^2, days 1, 15
Vinblastine, I.V., 6 mg/m^2, days 1, 15
Dacarbazine (DTIC), I.V., 375 mg/m^2, days 1, 15

Repeat cycle every 28 days

COMP

Cyclophosphamide, I.V., 1.2 g/m^2, day 1
Vincristine, I.V., 2 mg/m^2, days 3, 10, 17, 24
Methotrexate, I.V., 300 mg/m^2, day 12
Prednisone, P.O., 60 mg/m^2, days 3-30, then taper for 7 days (max: 60 mg)

COPP

Cyclophosphamide, I.V., 500 mg/m^2, days 1, 8
Vincristine, I.V., 1.5 mg/m^2, days 1, 8
Procarbazine, P.O., 100 mg/m^2 (max: 150 mg), days 1-14
Prednisone, P.O., 40 mg/m^2, days 1-14

MOPP

Mechlorethamine (nitrogen mustard), I.V., 6 mg/m^2, days 1, 8
Vincristine, I.V., 1.4 mg/m^2, days 1, 8
Procarbazine, P.O., 50 mg, day 1, then 100 mg/m^2, days 2-14
Prednisone, P.O., 40 mg/m^2, days 1-14 in courses 1 and 4 only

OPA

Vincristine, I.V., 1.5 mg/m^2, days 1, 8, 15
Prednisone, P.O., 60 mg/m^2, days 1-15
Doxorubicin, I.V., 40 mg/m^2, days 1, 15

OPPA

Vincristine, I.V., 1.5 mg/m^2, days 1, 8, 15
Procarbazine, P.O., 100 mg/m^2, days 1-15
Prednisone, P.O., 60 mg/m^2, days 1-15
Doxorubicin, I.V., 40 mg/m^2, days 1, 15

Repeat cycle every 28 days

Burkitt's Lymphoma

Advanced Stage Burkitt's/B-cell ALL

Methotrexate, I.T., 10 mg/m^2 at hour 0
Cytarabine, I.T., 50 mg/m^2 at hour 0
Cyclophosphamide, I.V., 300 mg/m^2 q12h x 6 at hours 0-60
Vincristine, I.V., 1.5 mg/m^2 at hour 72
Doxorubicin, I.V., 50 mg/m^2 at hour 72

Followed after hematopoietic recovery by:

Methotrexate, I.T., 12 mg/m^2 at hour 0
Methotrexate, I.V. push, 200 mg/m^2, then 800 mg/m^2 as a 24-hour infusion from hours 0-24
Cytarabine, I.T., 50 mg/m^2 at hour 24
Cytarabine, I.V., 400 mg/m^2 over 48 hours from hours 24-72, with escalating doses in succeeding courses
Leucovorin, I.V., 30 mg/m^2 at hours 36 and 42, then 3 mg/m^2 at hours 54, 66, 78

CANCER CHEMOTHERAPY REGIMENS *(Continued)*

Neuroblastoma

Cy/A

Cyclophosphamide, P.O., 150 mg/m^2/day x 7 days
Doxorubicin, I.V., 35 mg/m^2 on day 8

Pt/VM

Cisplatin, I.V., 90 mg/m^2 over 6 hours
Teniposide, I.V., 100 mg/m^2, 48 hours after completion of cisplatin

Osteosarcoma

HDMTX

Methotrexate, I.V., 12 g/m^2/week for 2-12 weeks
Leucovorin calcium rescue, P.O./I.V., 15 mg/m^2 q6h for 10 doses beginning
30 hours after the beginning of the 4-hour methotrexate infusion
(serum methotrexate levels must be monitored)

IFoVP

Ifosfamide, I.V., 1800 mg/m^2, days 1-5
Etoposide, I.V., 100 mg/m^2, days 1-5
Mesna uroprotection, I.V., 2880 mg/m^2, days 1-5
Repeat cycle every 21 days

MTX-CDDPAdr

Methotrexate, I.V., 12 g/m^2/week for 2 weeks
Leucovorin calcium rescue, I.V., 20 mg/m^2 q3h for 8 doses beginning 16
hours after completion of methotrexate, then q6h P.O. for 8 doses
alternating with
Cisplatin, I.V., 75 mg/m^2, day 15 of cycles 1-7, then 120 mg/m^2 for cycles 8-
10
Doxorubicin, I.V., 25 mg/m^2, days 15, 16, 17 of cycles 1-7

Sarcomas (Bony and Soft Tissue)

ICE

Ifosfamide, I.V., 1500 mg/m^2, days 1-3 (with mesna uroprotection)
Carboplatin, I.V., 635 mg/m^2, day 3
Etoposide, I.V., 100 mg/m^2, days 1, 2, 3

Topo/CTX

Cyclophosphamide, I.V., 250 mg/m^2 on days 1-5, followed by
Topotecan, I.V., 0.75 mg/m^2 on days 1-5

VACAdr

Vincristine, I.V., 1.5 mg/m^2/week for 6 weeks
Cyclophosphamide, I.V., 500 mg/m^2/week for 6 weeks
Doxorubicin, I.V., 60 mg/m^2, week 6
6-week rest period, then
Dactinomycin, I.V., 15 mcg/kg/day, for 5 days, followed 9 days later by
Vincristine + cyclophosphamide as above, given weekly for 5 weeks, and
with
Doxorubicin given with the last treatment
or
Vincristine, I.V., 1.4 mg/m^2, day 1
Doxorubicin, I.V., 50 mg/m^2, day 1
Cyclophosphamide, I.V., 750 mg/m^2, day 1

VAC

Vincristine, I.V., 2 mg/m^2, day 1
Dactinomycin, I.V., 1 mg/m^2, day 1
Cyclophosphamide, I.V., 600 mg/m^2, day 1
or
Vincristine, I.V., 1.5 mg/m^2, day 1
Dactinomycin, I.V., 25 mcg/kg, day 1
Cyclophosphamide, I.V., 1.5 g/m^2, day 1
Repeat cycle every 21 days

VACAdr-IfoVP

Vincristine, I.V., 1.5 mg/m^2 (max: 2 mg), weekly
Dactinomycin, I.V., 1.5 mg/m^2 (max: 2 mg), every other week
Doxorubicin, I.V., 60 mg/m^2 continuous infusion over 24 hours
Cyclophosphamide, I.V., 1-1.5 g/m^2
Ifosfamide, I.V., 1.6-2 g/m^2, days 1-5
Etoposide, I.V., 150 mg/m^2, days 1-5

VAdrC

Vincristine, I.V., 1.5 mg/m^2 (max: 2 mg)
Doxorubicin, I.V., 35-60 mg/m^2
Cyclophosphamide, I.V., 500-1500 mg/m^2

Wilms' Tumor

VAD

Vincristine, I.V., 1.5 mg/m^2/week for 10 weeks, then every 3 weeks
Dactinomycin, I.V., 1.5 mg/m^2, every 3 weeks, alternating with
Doxorubicin, I.V., 40 mg/m^2, every 3 weeks

or

Vincristine, I.V., 1.5 mg/m^2, every 6 weeks
Dactinomycin, I.V., 15 mcg/kg x 5

or

60 mcg/kg I.V. x 1 every 6 weeks ± (add if stage III or IV)
Doxorubicin, I.V., 20 mg/m^2, every 6 weeks

CANCER PAIN MANAGEMENT

(Adapted from the Agency for Healthcare Policy and Research, Publication No. 94-0593, March, 1994)

Recommended Clinical Approach

A. **Ask** about pain regularly. **Assess** pain systematically.

B. **Believe** the patient and family in their reports of pain and what relieves it.

C. **Choose** pain control options appropriate for the patient, family, and setting.

D. **Deliver** interventions in a timely, logical, coordinated fashion.

E. **Empower** patients and their families. **Enable** patients to control their course to the greatest extent possible.

Who Three-Step Analgesic Ladder

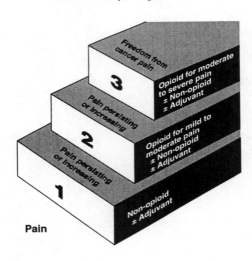

EXTRAVASATION MANAGEMENT OF CHEMOTHERAPEUTIC AGENTS

Risk Factors for Extravasation

- Vascular disease
- Elderly patients
- Vascular obstruction
- Vascular ischemia
- Prior radiation
- Small vessel diameter
- Venous spasms
- Traumatic catheter or needle insertion
- Decreased lymphatic drainage in mastectomy patients

Purpose

To minimize harm caused to the patient by the extravasation of vesicant chemotherapeutic agents through prompt detection and treatment.

Procedure

1. Stop administration of the chemotherapeutic agent.

2. Leave the needle in place.

3. Aspirate any residual drug and blood in the I.V. tubing, needle, and suspected extravasation site.

4. For all drugs except mechlorethamine (nitrogen mustard), remove the needle.

5. Apply cold pack if the extravasated drug is amsacrine, doxorubicin, daunorubicin, or mechlorethamine. Apply a hot pack if the extravasated drug is etoposide, teniposide, navelbine, vinblastine, vincristine, or vindesine. Refer to individual drug in Alphabetical Listing of Drugs for appropriate management.

6. Notify the physician who ordered the chemotherapy of the suspected extravasation. Institute the attached recommended interventions unless countermanded by the physician.

7. Document the date, time, needle size and type, insertion site, drug sequence, drug administration technique, approximate amount of drug extravasated, management, patient complaints, appearance of site, physician notification, and follow-up measures.

8. The extravasation site should be evaluated by the physician as soon as possible after the extravasation and periodically thereafter as indicated by symptoms.

9. For inpatients, assess the site every day for pain, erythema, induration, or skin breakdown. For outpatients, contact the patient daily for 3 days for assessment of the site, and weekly thereafter until the problem is resolved.

10. The plastic surgery service should be consulted by the physician if pain and/or tissue breakdown occur.

Amsacrine/Daunorubicin/Doxorubicin/Epirubicin/Idarubicin

1. Apply cold pack immediately for 1 hour; repeat qid for 3-5 days.[1,2]

2. Dimethyl sulfoxide (DMSO) 50% to 99% (w/v) solution: Apply 1.5 mL to site every 6 hours for 14 days; allow to air dry, do not cover.[3]

3. Injection of sodium bicarbonate is contraindicated.[4]

4. Injection of hydrocortisone is of doubtful benefit.[4,5]

EXTRAVASATION MANAGEMENT OF CHEMOTHERAPEUTIC AGENTS *(Continued)*

Mechlorethamine (nitrogen mustard)

1. Mix 4 mL of 10% sodium thiosulfate with 6 mL of sterile water for injection.
2. Inject 4 mL of this solution into the existing I.V. line.
3. Remove the needle.
4. Inject 2-3 mL of the solution subcutaneously clockwise into the infiltrated area using a 25-gauge needle. Change the needle with each new injection.
5. Apply ice immediately for 6-12 hours.

Mitomycin

1. Data is not currently available regarding potential antidotes and the application of heat or cold.
2. The site should be observed closely. These injuries frequently cause necrosis. A plastic surgery consult may be required.
3. Dimethyl sulfoxide (DMSO) 50% to 99% (w/v) solution: Apply 1.5 mL to site every 6 hours for 14 days; allow to air dry, do not cover.[3]

Etoposide/Teniposide/Vinblastine/Vincristine/Vindesine/Vinorelbine[6]

1. Inject 3-5 mL of hyaluronidase (150 units/mL) subcutaneously clockwise into the infiltrated area using a 25-gauge needle. Change the needle with each injection.
2. Apply heat immediately for 1 hour; repeat qid for 3-5 days.
3. Application of cold is contraindicated.
4. Injection of hydrocortisone is contraindicated.

Footnotes

1. Dorr RT, Alberts DS, and Stone A, "Cold Protection and Heat Enhancement of Doxorubicin Skin Toxicity in the Mouse," *Cancer Treat Rep*, 1985, 69:431-7.
2. Larson D, "What Is the Appropriate Management of Tissue Extravasation by Antitumor Agents?" *Plastic & Reconstr Surg*, 1985, 75:397-402.
3. Oliver IW, Aisner J, Hament A, et al, "A Prospective Study of Topical Dimethyl Sulfoxide for Treating Anthracycline Extravasation," *J Clin Onc*, 1988, 6:1732-5.
4. Dorr RT, Alberts DS, and Chen HS, "Limited Role of Corticosteroids in Ameliorating Experimental Doxorubicin Skin Toxicity in the Mouse," *Canc Chemother and Pharmacol*, 1980, 5:17-20.
5. Coleman JJ, Walker AP, and Didolkar MS, "Treatment of Adriamycin Induced Skin Ulcers: A Prospective Controlled Study," *J Surg Oncol*, 1983, 22:129-35.
6. Dorr RT and Alberts DS, "Vinca Alkaloid Skin Toxicity Antidote and Drug Disposition Studies in the Mouse," *JNCI*, 1985, 74:113-20.

EXTRAVASATION TREATMENT OF OTHER DRUGS

Medication Extravasated	Cold/ WarmPack	Antidote
Vasopressors		
Dobutamine Dopamine Epinephrine Norepinephrine Phenylephrine	None	Phentolamine (Regitine®) Mix 5 mg with 9 mL of NS Inject a small amount of this dilution into extravasated area. Blanching should reverse immediately. Monitor site. If blanching should recur, additional injections of phentolamine may be needed.
I.V. Fluids and Other Medications		
Aminophylline Calcium Dextrose, 10% Electrolyte solutions Esmolol Magnesium sulfate Metoprolol Nafcillin Parenteral nutrition preparations Phenytoin Potassium Radiocontrast media Sodium solutions	Cold	Hyaluronidase (Wydase®) 1. Add 1 mL NS to 150-unit vial to make 150 units/mL 2. Mix 0.1 mL of above with 0.9 mL NS in 1 mL syringe to make final concentration = 15 units/mL 3. Inject 5 injections of 0.2 mL each with a 25-gauge needle into area of extravasation

TOXICITIES OF CHEMOTHERAPEUTIC AGENTS

Drug	Radiation-Recall Reactions	Ocular Toxicity	Pulmonary Toxicity	Cardiotoxicity	Hepatotoxicity	Cumulative Myelosuppression	Peripheral Neuropathy	Neurotoxicity	Alopecia
Altretamine							x		
Azathioprine		x	x		x				x
BCNU (carmustine)		x	x			x		x	x
Bleomycin			x	x	x				
Busulfan		x	x	x	x			x†	x
Carboplatin					x	x	x	x	
CCNU (lomustine)			x†		x		x	x	
Chlorambucil		x	x		x		x	x	
Cisplatin		x		x	x		x		
Cladribine				x		x		x	
Corticosteroids		x							
Cyclophosphamide		x	x	x*	x			x	x
Cytarabine		x	x	x	x			x	x
Dactinomycin	x		x		x				x
Daunomycin				x†					
2'-Deoxycoformycin							x		
Docetaxel (Taxotere®)	x	x	x	x†	x				x
Doxorubicin				x	x		x		x
Etoposide			x	x	x				x
Floxuridine		x		x	x			x	x
Fludarabine			x	x	x	x		x	x
Fluorouracil		x		x‡	x				x
Gemcitabine					x			x	x
Hydroxyurea	x			x†					x
Idarubicin				x				x	x
Ifosfamide			x	x	x			x	x
Interferon		x	x	x	x				
Irinotecan			x						x
L-asparaginase					x			x	

Drug	Radiation-Recall Reactions	Ocular Toxicity	Pulmonary Toxicity	Cardiotoxicity	Hepatotoxicity	Cumulative Myelosuppression	Peripheral Neuropathy	Neurotoxicity	Alopecia
Melphalan			x	x		x			x
Mercaptopurine									
Methotrexate	x	x	x	x	x			x	
Methyl-CCNU (semustine)			x		x			x	x
Mithramycin		x				x			
Mitomycin-C		x	x	x	x			x	
Mitotane		x	x			x	x	x	
Mitoxantrone		x		x†					
Nitrogen mustard		x					x	x	x
Nitrosoureas		x			x			x	x
Paclitaxel (Taxol®)				x			x		x
Procarbazine		x	x	x	x		x	x	x
Streptozocin					x	x		x	
Tamoxifen		x			x			x	
Teniposide			x		x			x	
Topotecan									
Trimetrexate	x				x				x
Vinblastine		x	x	x	x		x	x	
Vincristine		x		x			x	x	x
Vinorelbine							x	x	x

Adapted from Patterson W and Perry MC, "Chemotherapeutic Toxicities: A Comprehensive Overview," *Contemporary Oncology*, 1993, 3(7):58-61.

*At high dose; †Dose-related; ‡idiosyncratic

ADRENERGIC AGONISTS, CARDIOVASCULAR

Drug	Hemodynamic Effects			
	CO	TPR	Mean BP	Renal Perfusion
Amrinone	↑	↓	<–>	↑
Dobutamine	↑	↓	↑	<–>
Dopamine	↑	+/–*	<–>/↑*	↑*
Epinephrine	↑	↓	↑	↓
Isoproterenol	↑	↓	↓	+/–†
Metaraminol	↓	↑	↑	↓
Milrinone	↑	↓	<–>	↑
Norepinephrine	<–>/↓	↑	↑	↓
Phenylephrine	↓	↑	↑	↓

↑ = increase ↓ = decrease, <–> = no change, * = dose dependent

†In patients with cardiogenic or septic shock, renal perfusion commonly increases; however, in the normal patient, renal perfusion may be reduced with isoproterenol.

Drug	Hemodynamic Effects			
	α1	β1	β2	Dopamine
Dobutamine (Dobutrex®)	+	++++	++	0
Dopamine (Inotropin®)	++++	++++	++	++
Epinephrine (Adrenalin®)	++++	++++	++	++
Isoproterenol (Isuprel®)	0	++++	++++	0
Norepinephrine (Levophed®)	++++	++++	0	0

Usual Hemodynamic Effects of Intravenous Agents Commonly Used for the Treatment of Acute/Severe Heart Failure

Drug	Dose	HR	MAP	PCWP	CO	SVR
Amrinone	5-10 mcg/kg/min	0/↑	0/↓	↓	↑	↓
Dobutamine	2.5-20 mcg/kg/min	0/↑	0/↑	↓	↑	↓
Dopamine	1-3 mcg/kg/min	0	0	0	0/↑	↓
	3-10 mcg/kg/min	↑	↑	0	↑	0
	>10 mcg/kg/min	↑	↑	↑	↑	↑
Furosemide	20-80 mg, repeated as needed up to 4-6 times/ day	0	0	↓	0	0
Milrinone	0.375-0.75 mcg/kg/min	0/↑	0/↓	↓	↑	↓
Nitroglycerin	0.1-2 mcg/kg/min	0/↑	0/↓	↓	0/↑	0/↓
Nitroprusside	0.25-3 mcg/kg/min	0/↑	0/↓	↓	↑	↓

HR = heart rate, MAP = mean arterial pressure, PCWP = pulmonary capillary wedge pressure, CO = cardiac output, SVR = systemic vascular resistance

↑ = increase, ↓ = decrease, 0 = no change

ANGIOTENSIN AGENTS

Comparisons of Indications and Adult Dosages

Drug	Hypertension	CHF	Renal Dysfunction	Dialyzable	Strengths (mg)
Benazepril	20-80 mg qd qd-bid Maximum: 80 mg qd	Not FDA approved	Cl$_{cr}$ <30 mL/min: 5 mg/day initially Maximum: 40 mg qd	Yes	Tablets 5, 10, 20, 40
Candesartan	8-32 mg qd qd-bid Maximum: 32 mg qd	Not approved	No adjustment necessary	No	Tablets 4, 8, 16, 32
Captopril	25-150 mg qd bid-tid Maximum: 450 mg qd	6.25-100 mg tid Maximum: 450 mg qd	Cl$_{cr}$ 10-50 mL/min: 75% of usual dose Cl$_{cr}$ <10 mL/min: 50% of usual dose	Yes	Tablets 12.5, 25, 50, 100
Enalapril	5-40 mg qd qd-bid Maximum: 40 mg qd	2.5-20 mg bid Maximum: 20 mg bid	Cl$_{cr}$ 30-80 mL/min: 5 mg/day initially Cl$_{cr}$ <30 mL/min: 2.5 mg/day initially	Yes	Tablets 2.5, 5, 10, 20
(Enalaprilat*)	(0.625 mg, 1.25 mg, 2.5 mg q6h) Maximum: 5 mg q6h	(Not FDA approved)	Cl$_{cr}$ <30 mL/min: 0.625 mg)	(Yes)	(2.5 mg/2 mL vial)
Fosinopril	10-40 mg qd Maximum: 80 mg qd	10-40 mg qd	No dosage reduction necessary	Not well dialyzed	Tablets 10, 20
Irbesartan†	150 mg qd Maximum: 300 mg qd	Not FDA approved	No dosage reduction necessary	No	Tablets 75, 150, 300
Lisinopril	10-40 mg qd Maximum: 80 mg qd	5-20 mg qd	Cl$_{cr}$ 10-30 mL/min: 5 mg/day initially Cl$_{cr}$ <10 mL/min: 2.5 mg/day initially	Yes	Tablets 5, 10, 20, 40
Losartan†	25-100 mg qd or bid		No adjustment needed	No	Tablets 25, 50
Moexipril	7.5-30 mg qd qd-bid Maximum: 30 mg qd	Not FDA approved	Cl$_{cr}$ <30 mL/min: 3.75 mg/day initially Maximum: 15 mg/day	Unknown	Tablets 7.5, 15
Quinapril	10-80 mg qd qd-bid	5-20 mg bid	Cl$_{cr}$ 30-60 mL/min: 5 mg/day initially Cl$_{cr}$ <10 mL/min: 2.5 mg qd initially	Not well dialyzed	Tablets 5, 10, 20, 40
Ramipril	2.5-20 mg qd qd-bid	2.5-20 mg qd	Cl$_{cr}$ <40 mL/min: 1.25 mg/day Maximum: 5 mg qd	Unknown	Capsules 1.25, 2.5, 5
Telmisartan	20-80 mg qd	Not FDA approved	No dosage reduction necessary	No	Tablets 40, 80

ANGIOTENSIN AGENTS (Continued)

Comparisons of Indications and Adult Dosages (continued)

Drug	Hypertension	CHF	Renal Dysfunction	Dialyzable	Strengths (mg)
Trandolapril	2-4 mg qd maximum: 8 mg/d qd-bid	Not FDA approved	Cl_{cr} <30 mL/min: 0.5 mg/day initially	No	Tablets 1 mg, 2 mg, 4 mg
Valsartan†	80-160 mg qd	Not FDA approved	Decrease dose only if Cl_{cr} <10 mL/minute	No	Capsules 80, 160

*Enalaprilat is the only available ACEI in a parenteral formulation.
†Angiotensin II antagonist
Dosage is based on 70 kg adult with normal hepatic and renal function.

Comparative Pharmacokinetics

Drug	Prodrug	Lipid Solubility	Absorption (%)	Serum $t_{1/2}$ (h)	Serum Protein Binding (%)	Elimination	Onset of Hypotensive Action (h)	Peak Hypotensive Effects (h)	Duration of Hypotensive Effects (h)
Benazepril	Yes	No data	37	10-12	>95	Primarily renal, some biliary	0.5-1	0.5-1	24
Benazeprilat									
Captopril	No	Not very lipophilic	75	<2	25-30	Metabolism to disulfide, then renally	0.25-0.5	0.5-1.5	6-12
Enalapril	Yes	Lipophilic	60 (53-73)	1.3	50-60	Renal	1	4-6	24
Enalaprilat				11			0.25	3-4	~6
Fosinopril	Yes	Very lipophilic	36	12	>95	Renal 50% Hepatic 50%	1	~3	24
Fosinoprilat									
Lisinopril	No	Very hydrophilic	25 (6-60)	12	0	Renal	1	~7	24
Moexipril	Yes	No data		2-9	≥50	Urine 13% Feces 53%	1		24
Perindopril	Yes		65-95	1.5-3	10-20	Hepatic/Renal		1	
Perindoprilat				25-30	60			3-4	
Quinapril	Yes	No data	60	0.8	97	Renal 61% Hepatic 37%	1	1	24
Quinaprilat				2					
Ramipril	Yes	Somewhat lipophilic	50-100	1-2	73	Renal	1-2	1	24
Ramiprilat				13-17	56				
Trandolapril	Yes	Very lipophilic	10-70	0.6-1.1	80	Hepatic/Renal	0.5	2-4	≥24
Trandolaprilat			40-60	16-24	94				

ANGIOTENSIN AGENTS *(Continued)*

Comparative Pharmacokinetics of Angiotensin II Receptor Antagonists

	Candesartan	Irbesartan	Losartan	Telmisartan	Valsartan
Prodrug	Yes*	No	Yes†	No	No
Time to peak (h)	3-4	1.5-2	1 / 2-4†	0.5-1	2-4
Bioavailability (%)	15	60-80	33	42-58	25
Food - Area-under-the-curve	No effect	No effect	9% to 10%	9.6% to 20%	9% to 40%
Elimination half-life (h)	9	11-15	2 / 6-9†	24	6
Elimination altered in renal dysfunction	Yes‡	No	No	No	No
Precautions in severe renal dysfunction	Yes	Yes	Yes	Yes	Yes
Elimination altered in hepatic dysfunction	No	No	Yes	Yes	Yes
Precautions in hepatic dysfunction	No	No	No	Yes	No
Protein binding (%)	>99	90	~99	>99.5	95

*Candesartan cilexetil: Active metabolite candesartan

†Losartan: Active metabolite EXP3174

‡Dosage adjustments are not necessary

Drug-Drug Interactions With ACEIs

Precipitant Drug	Drug (Category) and Effect	Description
Antacids	ACEIs: decreased	Decreased bioavailability of ACEIs. May be more likely with captopril. Separate administration times by 1-2 hours.
NSAIDs (indomethacin)	ACEIs: decreased	Reduced hypotensive effects of ACEIs. More prominent in low renin or volume dependent hypertensive patients.
ACEIs	Allopurinol: increased	Higher risk of hypersensitivity reaction possible when given concurrently. Three case reports of Stevens-Johnson syndrome with captopril.
ACEIs	Digoxin: increased	Increased plasma digoxin levels.
ACEIs	Lithium: increased	Increased serum lithium levels and symptoms of toxicity may occur.
ACEIs	Potassium preps/ potassium-sparing diuretics increased	Coadministration may result in elevated potassium levels.
Rifampin	Enalapril decreased	Effects decreased by rifampin
ACEIs	Probenecid	Increased captopril levels and decreased clearance have occurred
ACEIs	Diuretics	Additive hypotensive effects

ANTACID DRUG INTERACTIONS

Drug	Antacid				
	Al Salts	Ca Salts	Mg Salts	NaHCO$_3$	Mg/Al
Allopurinol	↓				
Anorexiants				↑	
Atorvastatin	↓		↓		
Benzodiazepines	↑		↓	↓	↓
Calcitriol			x*		x*
Captopril					↓
Cimetidine	↓		↓		↓
Corticosteroids	↓		↓		↓
Digoxin	↓		↓		
Flecainide				↑	
Indomethacin	↓		↓		↓
Iron	↓	↓	↓	↓	↓
Isoniazid	↓				
Itraconazole	↓	↓	↓	↓	↓
Ketoconazole				↓	↓
Levodopa					↑
Lithium				↓	
Mycophenolate	↓		↓		
Naproxen	↑		↑	↓	↑
Nitrofurantoin			↓		
Penicillamine	↓		↓		↓
Phenothiazines	↓		↓		↓
Phenytoin		↓			↓
Quinidine		↑	↑		↑
Quinolones	↓	↓	↓		↓
Ranitidine	↓				↓
Salicylates				↓	↓
Sodium polystyrene sulfonate	x†		x†		x†
Sulfonylureas				↑	
Sympathomimetics				↑	
Tetracyclines	↓	↓	↓	↓	↓
Tolmetin				x‡	

Pharmacologic effect increased (↑) or decreased (↓) by antacids.

*Concomitant use in patients on chronic renal dialysis may lead to hypermagnesemia.

†Concomitant use may cause metabolic alkalosis in patients with renal failure.

‡Concomitant use not recommended by manufacturer.

ANTIARRHYTHMIC DRUGS

Vaughan Williams Classification of Antiarrhythmic Drugs Based on Cardiac Effects

Type	Drug(s)	Conduction Velocity*	Refractory Period	Automaticity
Ia	Disopyramide Procainamide Quinidine	↓	↑	↓
Ib	Lidocaine Mexiletine Moricizine† Tocainide	0/↓	↓	↓
Ic	Flecainide Indecainide Propafenone‡	↓↓	0	↓
II	Beta-blockers	0	0	↓
III	Amiodarone Bretylium Ibutilide Sotalol‡	0	↑↑	0
IV	Diltiazem Verapamil§	↓	↑	↓

*Variables for normal tissue models in ventricular tissue.

†Also has type Ia action to decrease conduction velocity more than most type Ib.

‡Also has type II, beta-blocking action.

§Variables for SA and AV nodal tissue only.

ANTIARRHYTHMIC DRUGS *(Continued)*

Vaughan Williams Classification of Antiarrhythmic Agents and Their Indications/Adverse Effects

Type	Drug(s)	Indication	Route of Administration	Adverse Effects
Ia	Disopyramide	AF, VT	P.O.	Anticholinergic effects, CHF
	Procainamide	AF, VT, WPW	P.O./I.V.	GI, CNS, lupus, fever, hematological, anticholinergic effects
	Quinidine	AF, PSVT, VT, WPW	P.O./I.V.	Hypotension, GI, thrombocytopenia, cinchonism
Ib	Lidocaine	VT, VF, PVC	I.V.	CNS, GI
	Mexiletine	VT	P.O.	GI, CNS
	Tocainide	VT	P.O.	GI, CNS, pulmonary, agranulocytosis
Ic	Flecainide	VT	P.O.	CHF, GI, CNS, blurred vision
	Propafenone	VT	P.O.	GI, blurred vision, dizziness
	Moricizine	VT	P.O.	Dizziness, nausea, rash, seizures
II	Esmolol	VT, SVT	I.V.	CHF, CNS, lupus-like syndrome, hypotension, bradycardia, bronchospasm
	Propranolol	SVT, VT, PVC, digoxin toxicity	P.O./I.V.	CHF, bradycardia, hypotension, CNS, fatigue
III	Amiodarone	VT	P.O.	CNS, GI, thyroid, pulmonary fibrosis, liver, corneal deposits
	Bretylium	VT, VF	I.V.	GI, orthostatic hypotension, CNS
	Ibutilide	VT, VF	I.V.	Torsade de pointes, hypotension, branch bundle block, AV block, nausea, headache
	Sotalol	VT	P.O.	Bradycardia, hypotension, CHF, CNS, fatigue
IV	Diltiazem	AF, PSVT	P.O./I.V.	Hypotension, GI, liver
	Verapamil	AF, PSVT	P.O./I.V.	Hypotension, CHF, bradycardia, vertigo, constipation
Miscellaneous	Adenosine	SVT, PSVT	I.V.	Flushing, dizziness, bradycardia, syncope
	Digoxin	AF, PSVT	P.O./I.V.	GI, CNS, arrhythmias
	Magnesium	VT, VF	I.V.	Hypotension, CNS, hypothermia, myocardial depression

AF = atrial fibrillation; PSVT = paroxysmal supraventricular tachycardia; VT = ventricular tachycardia; WPW = Wolf-Parkinson-White arrhythmias; VF = ventricular fibrillation; SVT = supraventricular tachycardia.

Comparative Pharmacokinetic Properties of Antiarrhythmic Agents

Type	Drug(s)	Bioavailability (%)	Primary Route of Elimination	Volume of Distribution (L/kg)	Protein Binding (%)	Half-Life	Therapeutic Range (mcg/mL)
Ia	Disopyramide	70-95	Hepatic/Renal	0.8-2	50-80	4-8 h	2-6
	Procainamide	75-95	Hepatic/Renal	1.5-3	10-20	2.5-5 h	4-15
	Quinidine	70-80	Hepatic	2-3.5	80-90	5-9 h	2-6
Ib	Lidocaine	20-40	Hepatic	1-2	65-75	60-180 min	1.5-5
	Mexiletine	80-95	Hepatic	5-12	60-75	6-12 h	0.75-2
	Tocainide	90-95	Hepatic	1.5-3	10-30	12-15 h	4-10
Ic	Flecainide	90-95	Hepatic/Renal	8-10	35-45	12-30 h	0.3-2.5
	Propafenone*	11-39	Hepatic	2.5-4	85-95	12-32 h / 2-10 h	—
	Moricizine	34-38	Hepatic	6-11	92-95	1-6 h	—
II	Esmolol			Refer to Beta-Blocker Comparison Chart			
	Propranolol			Refer to Beta-Blocker Comparison Chart			
III	Amiodarone	22-28	Hepatic	70-150	95-97	15-100 d	1-2.5
	Bretylium	15-20	Renal	4-8	Negligible	5-10 h	0.5-2
	Ibutilide	NA	Hepatic	11	40	2-12 h	—
	Sotalol	90-95	Renal	1.6-2.4	Negligible	12-15 h	—
IV	Diltiazem	80-90	Hepatic/Renal	1.7	77-85	4-6 h	0.05-0.2
	Verapamil	20-40	Hepatic	1.5-5	95-99	4-12 h	>50 ng/mL

*Top numbers reflect **poor** metabolizers and **bottom** numbers reflect **extensive** metabolizers

ANTICONVULSANTS BY SEIZURE TYPE

Seizure Type	Age	Commonly Used	Alternatives
Primarily generalized tonic-clonic seizures	1-12 mo	Carbamazepine Phenytoin Phenobarbital	Valproate
	1-6 y	Carbamazepine Phenytoin Phenobarbital	Valproate
	6-11 y	Carbamazepine	Valproate Phenytoin Phenobarbital Lamotrigine†
Primarily generalized tonic-clonic seizures with absence or with myoclonic seizures	1 mo - 18 y	Valproate	Phenytoin‡ Phenobarbital‡ Carbamazepine‡
Absence seizures	Any age	Ethosuximide	Valproate Clonazepam Diamox Lamotrigine†
Myoclonic seizures	Any age	Valproate Clonazepam	Phenytoin† Phenobarbital†
Tonic and atonic seizures	Any age	Valproate	Phenytoin† Clonazepam Phenobarbital†
Partial seizures	1-12 mo	Phenobarbital	Carbamazepine Phenytoin
	1-6 y	Carbamazepine	Phenytoin Phenobarbital Valproate† Lamotrigine† Gabapentin
	6-18 y	Carbamazepine	Lamotrigine Phenytoin Phenobarbital Tiagabine Topiramate Valproate†
Infantile spasms		Corticotropin (ACTH)	Prednisone† Valproate† Clonazepam† Diazepam†

†Not FDA approved for this indication.
‡Phenytoin, phenobarbital, carbamazepine will not treat absence seizures. Addition of another anticonvulsant (ie, ethosuximide) would be needed.

ANTIDEPRESSANT AGENTS

Comparison of Usual Dosage, Mechanism of Action, and Adverse Effects of Antidepressants

Drug	Usual Dosage (mg/d)	Reuptake Inhibition		Adverse Effects					
		N	S	ACH	Drowsiness	Orthostatic Hypotension	Cardiac Arrhythmias	GI Distress	Weight Gain
First-Generation Antidepressants *Tricyclic Antidepressants*									
Amitriptyline (Elavil®, Endep®)	100–300	Moderate	High	4+	4+	4+	3+	0	4+
Clomipramine† (Anafranil®)	100–250	Moderate	High	4+	4+	2+	3+	1+	4+
Desipramine (Norpramin®, Pertofrane®)	100–300	High	Low	1+	2+	2+	2+	0	1+
Doxepin (Adapin®, Sinequan®)	100–300	Low	Moderate	3+	4+	2+	2+	0	4+
Imipramine (Janimine®, Tofranil®)	100–300	Moderate	Moderate	3+	3+	4+	3+	1+	4+
Nortriptyline (Aventyl®, Pamelor®)	50–200	Moderate	Low	2+	2+	1+	2+	0	1+
Protriptyline (Vivactil®)	15–60	Moderate	Low	2+	1+	2+	3+	0	0
Trimipramine (Surmontil®)	100–300	Low	Low	4+	4+	3+	3+	0	4+
Monoamine Oxidase Inhibitors									
Phenelzine (Nardil®)	15–90	—	—	2+	2+	2+	1+	1+	3+
Tranylcypromine (Parnate®)	10–40	—	—	2+	1+	2+	1+	1+	2+
Second-Generation Antidepressants *Older Second-Generation Antidepressants*									
Amoxapine (Asendin®)	100–400	Moderate	Low	2+	2+	2+	2+	0	2+
Maprotiline (Ludiomil®)	100–225	Moderate	Low	2+	3+	2+	2+	0	2+
Trazodone (Desyrel®)	150–500	Very low	Moderate	0	4+	3+	1+	1+	2+
Newer Second-Generation Antidepressants									
Bupropion (Wellbutrin®)	300–450‡	Very low§	Very low§	0	0	0	1+	1+	0
Third-Generation Antidepressants *Selective Serotonin Reuptake Inhibitors*									
Citalopram (Celexa®)	20–60	Very low	Very high	0	0	0	0	3+¶	0
Fluoxetine (Prozac®)	10–40	Very low	High	0	0	0	0	3+¶	0
Fluvoxamine (Luvox®)	100–300	Very low	Very high	0	0	0	0	3+¶	0
Paroxetine (Paxil®)	20–50	Very low	Very high	1+	1+	0	0	3+¶	1+
Sertraline (Zoloft®)	50–150	Very low	Very high	0	0	0	0	3+¶	0

ANTIDEPRESSANT AGENTS (Continued)

Comparison of Usual Dosage, Mechanism of Action, and Adverse Effects of Antidepressants (continued)

Drug	Usual Dosage (mg/d)	Reuptake Inhibition			Adverse Effects				
		N	S	ACH	Drowsiness	Orthostatic Hypotension	Cardiac Arrhythmias	GI Distress	Weight Gain
		Serotonin/Norepinephrine Reuptake Inhibitors							
Venlafaxine# (Effexor®)	75–375	Very high	Very high	1+	1+	0	1+	3+¶	0
		Atypical Antidepressants with 5HT2 Receptor Antagonist Properties							
Mirtazapine (Remeron®)**	15–45	Very low	Very low	1+	2+	0	0	3+	0
Nefazodone (Serzone®)**	300–600	Very low	High	1+	1+	0	0	1+	0

Key: N = norepinephrine; S = serotonin; ACH = anticholinergic effects (dry mouth, blurred vision, urinary retention, constipation); 0 - 4+ = absent or rare - relatively common.

†Not approved by FDA for depression

‡Not to exceed 150 mg/dose to minimize seizure risk

§Norepinephrine and serotonin reuptake inhibition is minimal, but inhibits dopamine reuptake

¶Nausea is usually mild and transient

Comparative studies evaluating the adverse effects of venlafaxine in relation to other antidepressants have not been performed

** These agents work primarily through antagonizing the postsynaptic 5HT2 receptor.

ANTIFUNGAL AGENTS

Activities of Various Agents Against Specific Fungi

Fungus	Itraconazole	Flucytosine*	Amphotericin B	Miconazole	Ketoconazole	Nystatin	Fluconazole	Griseofulvin
Aspergillus	x	–	x	–	–	–	?	–
Blastomyces	x	–	x	–	x	–	?	–
Candida	x	x	x	x	x	x	x	–
Chromomycosis	x	–	–	–	–	–	?	–
Coccidioides	x	–	x	x	x	–	x	–
Cryptococcus	x	x	x	x	x	–	x	–
Epidermophyton	–	–	–	–	x	–	–	x
Histoplasma	x	–	x	–	x	–	x	–
Microsporum	–	–	–	–	x	–	x	–
Mucor	–	–	x	–	x	–	–	x
Paracoccidioides	–	–	–	–	x	–	–	–
Phialophora	–	–	–	x	x	–	–	–
Pseudoallescheria	–	–	–	x	x	–	–	–
Rhodotorula	–	–	x	–	–	–	–	–
Sporothrix	x	–	x	–	–	–	?	–
Trichophyton	x	–	–	–	x	–	–	x

ANTIMIGRAINE DRUGS

5-HT₁ Receptor Agonists: Pharmacokinetic Differences

Pharmacokinetic Parameter	Naratriptan Oral	Rizatriptan Tablets	Rizatriptan Disintegrating Tablets	Zolmitriptan Oral (5 mg)	Zolmitriptan Oral (10 mg)	Sumatriptan Subcutaneous (6 mg)	Sumatriptan Oral (100 mg)	Sumatriptan Nasal (20 mg)
Time to peak serum concentration (min)	2-4	1-1.5	1.6-2.5	1.5	2-3.5	5-20	1.5-2.5	1
Average bioavailability (%)	70	45	—	40-46	46-49	96	14	17
Volume of distribution (L)	170	110-140	110-140	—	402	170	170	NA
Half-life (h)	6	2-3	2-3	2.8-3.4	2.5-3.7	2	2-2.5*	2
Fraction excreted unchanged in urine (%)	50	14	14	8	8	22	22	—

*With extended dosing the half-life extends to 7 hours.

ANTIPSYCHOTIC AGENTS

Antipsychotic Agent	Equivalent Dosages (approx) (mg)	Usual Adult Daily Maintenance Dose (mg)	Sedation (Incidence)	Extrapyramidal Side Effects	Anticholinergic Side Effects	Cardiovascular Side Effects
Acetophenazine	20	60-120	Moderate	High	Low	Low
Chlorpromazine	100	200-1000	High	Moderate	Moderate	Moderate/high
Chlorprothixene	100	75-600	High	Moderate	Moderate	Moderate
Clozapine	50	300-900	High	Low	High	High
Fluphenazine	2	0.5-40	Low	High	Low	Low
Haloperidol	2	1-15	Low	High	Low	Low
Loxapine	10	25-250	Moderate	High	Low	Low
Mesoridazine	50	30-400	High	Low	High	Moderate
Molindone	15	15-225	Low	High	Low	Low
Olanzapine	NA	10-15	High	Low	High	High
Perphenazine	10	16-48	Low	High	Low	Low
Pimozide	0.3-0.5	1-10	Moderate	High	Moderate	Low
Promazine	200	40-1200	Moderate	Moderate	High	Moderate
Risperidone	NA	4-16	Low	Low	Low	Low
Thioridazine	100	200-800	High	Low	High	Moderate/high
Thiothixene	5	5-40	Low	High	Low	Low/moderate
Trifluoperazine	5	2-40	Low	High	Low	Low

NA = not available.

ANTIRETROVIRAL AGENTS

Renal Dosing Adjustment, Dosage Forms, and Adverse Reactions

Chemical and Generic Names	Brand Name (company)	Dose (renal adjustment)	Dosage Forms	Adverse Reaction
NRTIs (Nucleoside Reverse Transcriptase Inhibitors)				
Zidovudine (AZT)	Retrovir® (Glaxo-Wellcome)	200 mg tid or 300 mg bid on empty stomach (ESRD: 100 mg q6-8 h)	Tablet: 300 mg Capsule: 100 mg Syrup: 50 mg/mL (240 mL) Injection: 10 mg/mL (20 mL)	Anemia, neutropenia, thrombocytopenia, headache, nausea, vomiting, myopathy, hepatitis, hyperpigmentation of nails
Zidovudine/ lamivudine	Combivir® (Glaxo-Wellcome)	1 tablet bid (see lamivudine for dose adjustment)	Tablet: 300 mg zidovudine, 150 mg lamivudine	See individual agents
Didanosine (ddl)	Videx® (Bristol-Myers Squibb)	≥60 kg: 200 mg bid on empty stomach <60 kg: 125 mg bid (adjust for Cl_{cr} <60)	Tablet, chewable: 25 mg, 50 mg, 100 mg, 150 mg Powder, oral: 100 mg, 167 mg, 250 mg, 375 mg Powder, pediatric: 2 g, 4 g	Peripheral neuropathy, pancreatitis, abdominal pain, nausea, diarrhea, retinal depigmentation, anxiety, insomnia
Zalcitabine (ddC)	Hivid® (Roche)	0.75 mg tid on empty stomach Cl_{cr} 10-40: bid Cl_{cr} <10: qd	Tablet: 0.375 mg, 0.75 mg	Peripheral neuropathy, oral/esophageal ulceration, rash, nausea, vomiting, diarrhea, abdominal pain, myalgia, pancreatitis
Stavudine (d4T)	Zerit® (Bristol-Myers Squibb)	≥60 kg: 40 mg bid Cl_{cr} 26-50: 20 mg bid Cl_{cr} 10-25: 20 mg qd <60 kg: 30 mg bid Cl_{cr} 26-50: 15 mg bid Cl_{cr} 10-25: 15 mg qd	Capsule: 15 mg, 20 mg, 30 mg, 40 mg Solution, oral: 1 mg/mL (200 mL)	Peripheral neuropathy, headache, abdominal or back pain, asthenia, nausea, vomiting, diarrhea, myalgia, anxiety, depression, pancreatitis, less frequently hepatotoxicity
Lamivudine (3TC)	Epivir® (Glaxo-Wellcome)	≥50 kg: 150 mg bid <50 kg: 2 mg/kg bid Cl_{cr} 30-49: 150 mg qd Cl_{cr} 15-29: 150 mg first dose, then 100 mg qd Cl_{cr} 5-14: 150 mg first dose, then 50 mg qd Cl_{cr} <5: 50 mg first dose, then 25 mg qd	Tablet: 150 mg Solution, oral: 10 mg/mL (240 mL)	Headache, insomnia, nausea, vomiting, diarrhea, abdominal pain, myalgia, arthralgia, pancreatitis in children
Abacavir	Ziagen® (Glaxo-Wellcome)	300 mg bid	Tablet: 300 mg Solution, oral: 20 mg/mL (240 mL)	Hypersensitivity syndrome (fever, fatigue, GI symptoms, ↑rash); **do not restart abacavir in patients who have experienced this;** GI symptoms
NNRTIs (Non-nucleoside Reverse Transcriptase Inhibitors)				
Nevirapine	Viramune® (Roxane)	200 mg qd for 14 days, then 200 mg bid	Tablet: 200 mg	Rash (severe), abnormal liver function tests, fever, nausea, headache
Delavirdine	Rescriptor® (Pharmacia/Upjohn)	400 mg tid	Tablet: 100 mg	Rash
Efavirenz	Sustiva™ (DuPont)	600 mg qd	Capsule: 50 mg, 100 mg, 200 mg	Dizziness, psychiatric symptoms (hallucinations, confusion, depersonalization, others), agitation, vivid dreams, rash, GI intolerance

Renal Dosing Adjustment, Dosage Forms, and Adverse Reactions *(continued)*

Chemical and Generic Names	Brand Name (company)	Dose (renal adjustment)	Dosage Forms	Adverse Reaction
		PIs (Protease Inhibitors)		
Saquinavir	Invirase® (Roche) Fortavase® (Roche)	600 mg tid with a full meal 1200 mg tid with a full meal	Capsule: 200 mg Gelcap: 200 mg	Diarrhea, abdominal discomfort, nausea, headache, hyperglycemia/diabetes, dyslipidemia
Ritonavir	Norvir® (Abbott)	600 mg bid with food (titrate)	Capsule: 100 mg Solution, oral: 80 mg/mL (240 mL)	Asthenia, nausea, diarrhea, vomiting, anorexia, abdominal pain, circumoral and peripheral paresthesia, taste perversion, headache, hyperglycemia/diabetes, dyslipidemia
Indinavir	Crixivan® (Merck)	800 mg q8h with water (Hepatic insufficiency: 600 mg tid)	Capsule: 200 mg, 400 mg	Hyperbilirubinemia, nephrolithiasis, elevated AST/ALT, abdominal pain, nausea, vomiting, diarrhea, taste perversion, hyperglycemia/diabetes, dyslipidemia
Nelfinavir	Viracept® (Agouron)	750 mg tid with food	Tablet: 250 mg Powder, oral: 50 mg/g (144 g)	Diarrhea, nausea, hyperglycemia/diabetes, dyslipidemia
Amprenavir	Agenerase (Glaxo-Wellcome)	1200 mg bid (avoid high fat meal)	Capsule: 150 mg Solution, oral: 15 mg/mL (240 mL)	Rash (life-threatening), paresthesias (perioral), depression, nausea, diarrhea, vomiting, hyperglycemia/diabetes, dyslipidemia

ANTIRETROVIRAL AGENTS (Continued)

Antiretroviral Drug Interactions

Antiretroviral Agent	Interacting Agent	Severity*	Additional Comments
Abacavir	Ethanol	3	Increased abacavir AUC
Amprenavir	Astemizole, rifampin, midazolam, bepridil, dihydroergotamine, ergotamine, cisapride	1	Contraindicated. Avoid concomitant use.
	Abacavir, clarithromycin, indinavir, ritonavir?, cimetidine?	2	Increased amprenavir C_{max} and AUC
	Saquinavir	1	Decreased amprenavir AUC and C_{max}
	Rifabutin	1	Increased rifabutin AUC by 193%; administer one-half usual rifabutin dose
	Amiodarone, lidocaine, quinidine, warfarin, tricyclic antidepressants	1	Increased toxic effect of these agents; must have concentration monitoring
	HMGCoA reductase inhibitors, diltiazem, nicardipine, nifedipine, nimodipine, alprozolam, clarzepate, diazepam, flurazepam, itraconazole, dapsone, erythromycin, loratadine, silfenafil, carbamazepine, pimozide	2	Increased serum concentrations of these agents, potential for increased toxic effects
	Oral contraceptives	1	Decreased oral contraceptive concentrations
Delavirdine	Protease inhibitors	2	Increased levels of protease inhibitors; start indinavir at 600 mg every 8 hours; nelfinavir may decrease delavirdine levels by 50%
	Terfenadine, astemizole, cisapride, alprazolam, midazolam, triazolam	1	Delavirdine may significantly increase concentrations of these drugs
	Dihydropyridine calcium channel blockers, ergot derivatives, quinidine	2	Delavirdine may increase concentrations of these drugs
	Warfarin	2	Delavirdine may increase warfarin concentrations
	Rifampin/rifabutin, phenytoin, carbamazepine	1	Avoid concomitant use; decreased delavirdine concentration
	Antacids, H_2-antagonists, didanosine	2	Decreased delavirdine absorption; administer antacids or didanosine at least 1 hour apart from delavirdine
	Clarithromycin, dapsone	2	Delavirdine may increase levels of these drugs; clarithromycin may increase delavirdine levels
	Ketoconazole, fluoxetine	3	May increase delavirdine concentration by 50%
Didanosine	Tetracycline, itraconazole, ketoconazole, indinavir	2	Decreased absorption with didanosine
	Dapsone	3	Administer 2 hours before didanosine
	Ciprofloxacin/norfloxacin (quinolones)	2	Administer didanosine 6 hours before or 2 hours after quinolone
Efavirenz	Astemizole, cisapride, ergot derivatives, midazolam, triazolam	1	Contraindicated. Avoid concomitant use.
	Indinavir	2	Decreased indinavir AUC by 31% and Cp_{max} by 16%. Increase indinavir dose to 1000 mg every 8 hours.
	Ritonavir	3	Increased AUC by ~20% for each drug
	Saquinavir	2	Decreased saquinavir AUC by 62% and Cp_{max} by 50%. Not recommended as sole protease inhibitor with efavirenz.
	Rifampin	2	Decreased efavirenz AUC by 26% and Cp_{max} by 20%
	Clarithromycin	2	Decreased clarithromycin AUC by 39% and Cp_{max} by 49%; increased hydroxy metabolite of clarithromycin AUC by 34% and Cp_{max} by 49%
	Ethinyl estradiol	2	Increased ethinyl estradiol AUC by 37%
	Warfarin	2	Decreased or increased warfarin effects
Indinavir	Rifabutin	1	Increased rifabutin AUC by 204%; decrease rifabutin dose to one-half
	Ketoconazole	2	Increased indinavir AUC by 68%; decrease indinavir dose to 600 mg every 8 hours
	Didanosine	2	Decreased indinavir absorption; administer 1 hour apart on an empty stomach
	Rifampin	1	Avoid concomitant use due to decreased indinavir concentration
	Terfenadine/astemizole, cisapride, triazolam/midazolam	1	Indinavir may increase toxicity of these drugs; avoid concomitant use
Lamivudine	Trimethoprim/sulfamethoxazole	3	Increased lamivudine AUC by 44%
	Zidovudine	3	Increased zidovudine C_{max} by 39%

1308

Antiretroviral Drug Interactions (continued)

Antiretroviral Agent	Interacting Agent	Severity*	Additional Comments
Nelfinavir	Astemizole, cisapride, midazolam, rifampin, terfenadine, triazolam	1	Contraindicated. Avoid concomitant use.
	Rifabutin	2	Increased rifabutin concentrations; reduce rifabutin dose
	Anticonvulsants	1	May decrease nelfinavir concentrations
	Oral contraceptives	1	Decreased oral contraceptive concentrations
	Delavirdine	2	Nelfinavir concentration doubled; delavirdine level decreased by 50%
Nevirapine	Oral contraceptives	1	Decreased oral contraceptives concentration
	Protease inhibitors	1	Decreased concentrations of protease inhibitors; avoid concomitant use
	Rifabutin/rifampin	2	Decreased nevirapine concentrations
Ritonavir	Meperidine	1	Contraindicated. Alternative: Acetaminophen
	Piroxicam	1	Contraindicated. Alternative: Aspirin
	Propoxyphene	1	Contraindicated. Alternative: Oxycodone
	Amiodarone, encainide, flecainide, propafenone, quinidine/quinine	1	Contraindicated
	Rifabutin	1	Contraindicated. Alternatives: Clarithromycin, ethambutol
	Bepridil	1	Contraindicated
	Astemizole/terfenadine	1	Contraindicated. Alternatives: Loratadine
	Cisapride	1	Contraindicated
	Bupropion	1	Contraindicated. Alternative: Fluoxetine, desipramine
	Clozapine	1	Contraindicated
	Alprazolam, clorazepate, diazepam, estazolam, flurazepam, midazolam, triazolam, zolpidem	1	Contraindicated. Alternatives: Temazepam, lorazepam
	Clarithromycin	2	Increased clarithromycin AUC by 77%; decrease dose of clarithromycin by 50% if Cl_{cr} is 30-60 mL/minute and by 75% if Cl_{cr} is <30 mL/minute
	Erythromycin	2	>3 times increase in AUC of erythromycin
	Desipramine	2	Increased desipramine AUC by 145%
	Disulfiram/metronidazole	2	Disulfiram-like reaction
	Oral contraceptives	1	Decreased ethinyl estradiol AUC by 40%
	Theophylline	2	Decreased theophylline AUC by 43%
	Antiarrhythmics, anticoagulants, anticonvulsants, tricyclic antidepressants, neuroleptics	2	1.5 to >3 times increase in AUC of interacting drug
	Phenytoin, phenobarbital, rifampin/rifabutin	2	May decrease ritonavir levels
Saquinavir	Carbamazepine, dexmethasone, phenobarbital, phenytoin	2	May decrease saquinavir levels
	Rifampin	1	Decreased saquinavir level by 80%
	Rifabutin	2	Decreased saquinavir level by 40%
Stavudine	None		
Zalcitabine	Antacids (aluminum-, magnesium-containing)	2	Decreased zalcitabine absorption by 25%; do not administer simultaneously
	Pentamidine	2	Increased risk of pancreatitis; avoid concomitant use
Zidovudine	Ganciclovir	1	Increased toxicity (hematologic)
	Interferon	2	Dose reduction or interruption may be necessary or change to foscarnet
	Probenecid	2	Increased zidovudine levels

*Severity: 1 = major; 2 = moderate; 3 = minor.

BENZODIAZEPINES

Agent	Peak Blood Levels (oral) (h)	Protein Binding (%)	Volume of Distribution (L/kg)	Major Active Metabolite	Half-Life (parent) (h)	Half-Life* (metabolite) (h)	Adult Oral Dosage Range
Anxiolytic							
Alprazolam (Xanax®)	1-2	80	1.1	No	12-15	—	0.75-4 mg/d
Chlordiazepoxide (Librium®)	2-4	90-98	0.3	Yes	5-30	24-96	15-100 mg/d
Diazepam (Valium®)	0.5-2	96	1.1	Yes	20-80	50-100	4-40 mg/d
Lorazepam (Ativan®)	1-6	88-92	1.3	No	10-20	—	2-4 mg/d
Oxazepam (Serax®)	2-4	86-96	0.6-2	No	5-20	—	30-120 mg/d
Sedative/Hypnotic							
Estazolam (ProSom™)	2	93	—	No	10-24	—	1-2 mg
Flurazepam (Dalmane®)	0.5-2	97	—	Yes	Not significant	40-114	15-60 mg
Quazepam (Doral®)	2	>95	5	Yes	25-41	28-114	7.5-15 mg
Temazepam (Restoril®)	2-3	96	1.4	No	10-15	—	15-30 mg
Triazolam (Halcion®)	1	89-94	0.8-1.3	No	2.3	—	0.125-0.25 mg
Miscellaneous							
Clonazepam (Klonopin®)	1-2	86	1.8-4	No	18-50 h	—	1.5-20 mg/d
Clorazepate (Tranxene®)	1-2	80-95	—	Yes	Not significant	50-100 h	15-60 mg
Midazolam (Versed®)	0.4-0.7†	>95	0.8-6.6	No	2-5 h	—	NA

* = significant metabolite.
† = I.V. only.
NA = not available.

BETA-BLOCKERS

Beta-Blockers Comparison

Agent	Adrenergic Receptor Blocking Activity	Lipid Solubility	Protein Bound (%)	Half-Life (h)	Bioavailability (%)	Primary (Secondary) Route of Elimination	Indications	Usual Dosage
Acebutolol (Sectral®)	beta₁	Low	15-25	3-4	40 7-fold*	Hepatic (renal)	Hypertension, arrhythmias	P.O.: 400-1200 mg/d
Atenolol (Tenormin®)	beta₁	Low	<5-10	6-9†	50-60 4-fold*	Renal (hepatic)	Hypertension, angina pectoris, acute MI	P.O.: 50-200 mg/d I.V.: 5 mg x 2 doses
Betaxolol (Kerlone®)	beta₁	Low	50-55	14-22	84-94	Hepatic (renal)	Hypertension	P.O.: 10-20 mg/d
Bisoprolol (Zebeta®)	beta₁	Low	26-33	9-12	80	Renal (hepatic)	Hypertension	P.O.: 2.5-5 mg
Carteolol (Cartrol®)	beta₁ beta₂	Low	20-30	6	80-85	Renal	Hypertension	P.O.: 2.5-10 mg/d
Carvedilol (Coreg™)				7-10	25-35	Bile into feces	Hypertension	P.O.: 6.25 mg twice daily
Esmolol (Brevibloc®)	beta₁	Low	55	0.15	NA 5-fold*	Red blood cell	Supraventricular tachycardia, sinus tachycardia	I.V. infusion: 25-300 mcg/kg/min
Labetalol (Trandate®, Normodyne®)	alpha₁ beta₁ beta₂	Moderate	50	5.5-8	18-30 10-fold*	Renal (hepatic)	Hypertension	P.O.: 200-2400 mg/d I.V.: 20-80 mg at 10-min intervals up to a maximum of 300 mg or continuous infusion of 2 mg/min
Metoprolol (Lopressor®)	beta₁	Moderate	10-12	3-7	50 10-fold*	Hepatic/renal	Hypertension, angina pectoris, acute MI	P.O.: 100-450 mg/d I.V.: Post-MI 15 mg Angina: 15 mg then 2-5 mg/hour Arrhythmias: 0.2 mg/kg
Nadolol (Corgard®)	beta₁ beta₂	Low	25-30	20-24	30 5-8 fold*	Renal	Hypertension, angina pectoris	P.O.: 40-320 mg/d
Penbutolol (Levatol™)	beta₁ beta₂	High	80-98	5	≅100	Hepatic (renal)	Hypertension	P.O.: 20-80 mg/d
Pindolol (Visken®)	beta₁ beta₂	Moderate	57	3-4†	90 4-fold*	Hepatic (renal)	Hypertension	P.O.: 20-60 mg/d
Propranolol (Inderal®, various)	beta₁ beta₂	High	90	3-5†	30 20-fold*	Hepatic	Hypertension, angina pectoris, arrhythmias	P.O.: 40-480 mg/d I.V.: Reflex tachycardia 1-10 mg

BETA-BLOCKERS *(Continued)*

Beta-Blockers Comparison *(continued)*

Agent	Adrenergic Receptor Blocking Activity	Lipid Solubility	Protein Bound (%)	Half-Life (h)	Bioavailability (%)	Primary (Secondary) Route of Elimination	Indications	Usual Dosage
Propranolol long-acting (Inderal-LA®)	beta₁ beta₂	High	90	9-18	20-30 fold*	Hepatic	Hypertrophic subaortic stenosis, prophylaxis (post-MI)	P.O.: 180-240 mg/d
Sotalol (Betapace® Oral)	beta₁ beta₂	Low	0	12	90-100	Renal	Ventricular arrhythmias/ tachyarrhythmias	P.O. 160-320 mg/d
Timolol (Blocadren®)	beta₁ beta₂	Low to moderate	<10	4	75 7-fold*	Hepatic (renal)	Hypertension, prophylaxis (post-MI)	P.O.: 20-60 mg/d P.O.: 20 mg/d

Dosage is based on 70 kg adult with normal hepatic and renal function

Note: All beta₁-selective agents will inhibit beta₂ receptors at higher doses.

*Interpatient variations in plasma levels.

†Half-life increased to 16-27 h in creatinine clearance of 15-35 mL/min and >27 h in creatinine clearances <15 mL/min.

Selected Properties of Beta-Adrenergic Blocking Drugs

Drug	Relative Beta, Selectivity	Beta-Blockade Potency Ratio*	ISA	MSA
Acebutolol	+	0.3	+	+
Atenolol	+	1	–	–
Betaxolol	+		0	+
Bisoprolol	+		0	0
Carteolol	–		++	0
Esmolol	+	0.02	–	–
Labetalol	–		0	0
Metoprolol	+	1	–	–
Nadolol	–	2-9	–	–
Penbutolol	–		+++	+
Pindolol	–	6	++	+
Propranolol	–	1	–	++
Sotalol	–	0.3	–	–
Timolol	–	6	–	–

*Propranolol = 1
ISA = intrinsic sympathomimetic activity, MSA = membrane stabilizing activity.

BRONCHODILATORS

Comparison of Inhaled Sympathomimetic Bronchodilators

Generic (Brand)	Adrenergic Receptor	Onset (min)	Duration Activity (h)
Albuterol (Proventil®)	$Beta_1 < Beta_2$	<5	3-8
Bitolterol (Tornalate®)	$Beta_1 < Beta_2$	3-4	5 > 8
Epinephrine (Bronkaid®)	Alpha and $Beta_1$ and $Beta_2$	1-5	1-3
Isoetharine (Bronkometer®)	$Beta_1 < Beta_2$	<5	1-3
Isoproterenol (Isuprel®)	$Beta_1$ and $Beta_2$	2-5	0.5-2
Metaproterenol (Alupent®)	$Beta_1 < Beta_2$	5-30	2-6
Pirbuterol (Maxair®)	$Beta_1 < Beta_2$	<5	5
Salmeterol (Serevent®)	$Beta_1 < Beta_2$	5-14	12
Terbutaline (Brethaire®)	$Beta_1 < Beta_2$	5-30	3-6

CALCIUM CHANNEL BLOCKERS

Calcium Channel Blockers: Comparative Actions

Agent	A-V Conduction Node	SA Node Automaticity	Contractility	Heart Rate	Cardiac Output	Peripheral Vascular Resistance
DIHYDROPYRIDINES						
Nifedipine (Procardia®)	NE	0	0-SD†	0-SI	MI	PD
Amlodipine (Norvasc®)	0	0	0-SI	NE	SI	PD
Felodipine (Plendil®)	0	0	0-SI	0-SI	SI	PD
Isradipine (DynaCirc®)	0	0	0-SI	NE	SI	PD
Nicardipine (Cardene®)	0-SI	0	0-SI	0-SI	MI	PD
Nimodipine (Nimotop®)	NA	NA	NA	NA	NA	NA
Nisoldipine (Sular™)	0	0	0	SE	0	PD
PHENYLALKYLAMINES						
Verapamil (Calan®, Isoptin®)	NE	MD	MD	SE	SE	MD
BENZOTHIAZEPINES						
Diltiazem (Cardizem®)	NE	SD	SD	SD	SE	SD
MISCELLANEOUS						
Bepridil (Vascor®)	NE	SD	SD	SD	0	SD

†Drug may worsen symptoms of congestive heart failure due to systolic dysfunction (ejection fraction <40%).

MD = moderate decrease, MI = moderate increase, NE = negligible effect, NA = not available, PD = pronounced decrease, SD = slight decrease, SE = slight effect (increase or decrease), SI = slight increase.

CALCIUM CHANNEL BLOCKERS (Continued)

Calcium Channel Blockers: Comparative Dosages

Agent	Initial Dose	Usual Dose	Maximum Dose
DIHYDROPYRIDINES			
Nifedipine (prototype) (Adalat®, Procardia®/Adalat CC®, Procardia XL®	10 mg tid XL®: 30 mg/d	10-20 mg tid XL®: 30-60 mg/d	120-180 mg/d
Amlodipine (Norvasc®)	2.5-5 mg/d	5-10 mg/d	10 mg/d
Felodipine (Plendil®)	5 mg/d	5-10 mg bid	20 mg/d
Isradipine (DynaCirc®)	2.5 mg bid	2.5-5 mg bid	20 mg/d
Nicardipine (Cardene®/Cardene® SR)	20 mg tid SR: 30 mg bid	20-40 mg tid SR: 30-60 mg bid	120 mg/d
Nimodipine (Nimotop®)	Not applicable	60 mg q4h for 21 days	60 mg qd
Nisoldipine (Sular™)	20 mg qd	20-40 mg qd	
PHENYLALKYLAMINES			
Verapamil (prototype) (Calan®/Calan® SR, Isoptin®/Isoptin® SR, Verelan®)	Angina: 80-120 mg tid Arrhythmias: 240-320 mg/d in 3-4 divided doses Hypertension: 40-80 mg tid SR: 120-240 mg/d	Angina: 40-120 mg tid Arrhythmias: 240-480 mg/d in 3-4 divided doses Hypertension: 360-480 mg/d in 3 divided doses SR: 240 mg/d	480 mg/d
BENZOTHIAZEPINES			
Diltiazem (prototype) (Cardizem®/Cardizem® CD, Dilacor® XR)	30 mg qid (CD/XR): 120-240 mg/d	180-360 mg/d in 3-4 divided doses (CD): 240-360 mg/d (XR): 180-480 mg/d	Immediate release (CD): 360 mg/d (XR): 540 mg/d
MISCELLANEOUS			
Bepridil (Vascor®)	200 mg/d	300 mg/d	400 mg/d

Calcium Channel Blockers: Comparative Pharmacokinetics

Agent	Bioavailability (%)	Protein Binding (%)	Onset (min)	Peak (h)	Half-Life (h)	Volume of Distribution	Route of Metabolism	Route of Excretion
DIHYDROPYRIDINES								
Nifedipine (prototype) (Adalat®, Procardia®/Procardia XL®)	Immediate/sustained release 45-70/86	92-98	20	Immediate/sustained release 0.5/6	2-5	ND	Liver, inactive metabolites	60%-80% urine, feces, bile
Amlodipine (Norvasc®)	52-88	97	6 h	6-9	33.8	21 L/kg	Liver, inactive metabolites, not a significant first-pass metabolism/presystemic metabolism	Bile, gut wall
Felodipine (Plendil®)	10-25	>99	3-5 h	2.5-5	10-36	10.3 L/kg	Liver, inactive metabolites, extensive metabolism by several pathways including cytochrome P-450, extensive first-pass metabolism/presystemic metabolism	70% urine, 10% feces
Isradipine (DynaCirc®)	15-24	97	120	0.5-2.5	8	2.9 L/kg	Liver, inactive metabolites, extensive first-pass metabolism	90% urine, 10% feces
Nicardipine (Cardene®)	35	>95	20	0.5-2	2-4	ND	Liver, saturable first-pass metabolism	60% urine, 35% feces
Nimodipine (Nimotop®)	13	>95	ND	≤1	1-2	0.43 L/kg	Liver, inactive metabolites, high first-pass metabolism	Urine
Nisoldipine (Sular™)	4-8	>99	ND	6-12	7-12	4-5 L/kg	Liver, 1 active metabolite (10%), presystemic metabolism	70%-75% kidney, 6%-12% feces
PHENYLALKYLAMINES								
Verapamil (prototype) (Calan®/Calan® SR, Isoptin®/Isoptin® SR, Verelan®)	20-35	83-92	30	1-2.2	3-7	4.5-7 L/kg	Liver	70% urine, 16% feces
BENZOTHIAZEPINES								
Diltiazem (prototype) (Cardizem®/Cardizem® CD, Dilacor® XR)	40-67	70-80	30-60	Immediate/sustained release 2-3/6-11	Immediate/sustained release 3.5-6/5-7	ND	Liver; drugs which inhibit/induce hepatic microsomal enzymes may alter disposition	Urine
MISCELLANEOUS								
Bepridil (Vascor®)	59	>99	60	2-3	24	ND	Liver	70% urine, 22% feces

CALCIUM CHANNEL BLOCKERS (Continued)

Calcium Channel Blockers: FDA-Approved Indications

Agent	Hypertension	Subarachnoid Hemorrhage	Arrhythmias	Angina
DIHYDROPYRIDINES				
Nifedipine (prototype) (Adalat®, Procardia®/Procardia XL®)	X Sustained release only			Vasospastic and chronic stable
Amlodipine (Norvasc®)	X			Vasospastic and chronic stable
Felodipine (Plendil®)	X			
Isradipine (DynaCirc®)	X			
Nicardipine (Cardene®)	X	X		Chronic stable
Nimodipine (Nimotop®)		X		
Nisoldipine (Sular™)	X			
PHENYLALKYLAMINES				
Verapamil (prototype) (Calan®/Calan® SR, Isoptin®/Isoptin® SR, Verelan®)	X		X I.V. — supraventricular arrhythmias	Unstable, vasospastic, and chronic stable
BENZOTHIAZEPINES				
Diltiazem (prototype) (Cardizem®/Cardizem® CD, Dilacor® XR)	X Sustained release only		X I.V. — supraventricular arrhythmias	Vasospastic (SR only) and chronic stable
MISCELLANEOUS				
Bepridil (Vascor®)				Chronic stable

CORTICOSTEROIDS

Corticosteroids, Systemic Equivalencies

Glucocorticoid	Pregnancy Category	Approximate Equivalent Dose (mg)	Routes of Administration	Relative Anti-Inflammatory Potency	Relative Mineralocorticoid Potency	Protein Binding (%)	Half-life Plasma (min)	Half-life Biologic (h)
Short-Acting								
Cortisone	D	25	P.O., I.M.	0.8	2	90	30	8-12
Hydrocortisone	C	20	I.M., I.V.	1	2	90	80-118	8-12
Intermediate-Acting								
Methylprednisolone*	—	4	P.O., I.M., I.V.	5	0	—	78-188	18-36
Prednisolone	B	5	P.O., I.M., I.V., intra-articular, intradermal, soft tissue injection	4	1	90-95	115-212	18-36
Prednisone	B	5	P.O.	4	1	70	60	18-36
Triamcinolone*	C	4	P.O., I.M., intra-articular, intradermal, intrasynovial, soft tissue injection	5	0	—	200+	18-36
Long-Acting								
Betamethasone	C	0.6-0.75	P.O., I.M., intra-articular, intradermal, intrasynovial, soft tissue injection	25	0	64	300+	36-54
Dexamethasone	C	0.75	P.O., I.M., I.V., intra-articular, intradermal, soft tissue injection	25-30	0	—	110-210	36-54
Mineralocorticoids								
Fludrocortisone	C	—	P.O.	10	125	42	210+	18-36

*May contain propylene glycol as an excipient in injectable forms.

CORTICOSTEROIDS *(Continued)*

Corticosteroids, Topical

Steroid		Vehicle
Very High Potency		
0.05%	Augmented betamethasone dipropionate	Ointment
0.05%	Clobetasol propionate	Cream, ointment
0.05%	Diflorasone diacetate	Gel, ointment
0.05%	Halobetasol propionate	Cream, ointment
High Potency		
0.1%	Amcinonide	Cream, ointment
0.05%	Betamethasone dipropionate	Cream, ointment, lotion
0.25%	Desoximetasone	Cream, ointment
0.2%	Fluocinolone	Cream
0.05%	Fluocinonide	Cream, ointment
0.1%	Halcinonide	Cream, ointment, solution
0.5%	Triamcinolone acetonide	Cream, ointment
Intermediate Potency		
0.025%	Betamethasone benzoate	Cream, gel, lotion
0.1%	Betamethasone valerate	Cream, ointment, lotion
0.05%	Desoximetasone	Cream
0.025%	Fluocinolone acetonide	Cream, ointment
0.05%	Flurandrenolide	Cream, ointment, lotion
0.05%	Fluticasone propionate	Cream
0.025%	Halcinonide	Cream, ointment
0.1%	Mometasone furoate	Cream, ointment, lotion
0.1%	Triamcinolone acetonide	Cream, ointment
Low Potency		
0.01%	Betamethasone valerate	Cream
0.1%	Clocortolone†	Cream
0.01%	Fluocinolone acetonide	Cream, solution, shampoo, oil
0.025%	Flurandrenolide	Cream, ointment
0.2%	Hydrocortisone valerate†	Cream
0.025%	Triamcinolone acetonide	Cream, ointment
Lowest Potency (may be ineffective for some indications)		
0.05%	Alclometasone	Cream, ointment
0.1%	Betamethasone	Cream
0.2%	Betamethasone	Cream
0.05%	Desonide†	Cream, ointment, lotion
0.04%	Dexamethasone	Aerosol
0.1%	Dexamethasone	Cream
1%	Hydrocortisone†	Cream, ointment, lotion
2.5%	Hydrocortisone†	Cream, ointment
0.25%	Methylprednisolone acetate†	Ointment
1%	Methylprednisolone acetate†	Ointment

†Fluorinated.

CYCLOPLEGIC MYDRIATICS

Agent	Peak Mydriasis	Peak Cycloplegia	Time to Recovery
Atropine	30-40 min	1-3 h	>14 d
Cyclopentolate	25-75 min	25-75 min	24 h
Homatropine	30-90 min	30-90 min	6 h-4 d
Scopolamine	20-30 min	30 min-1 h	5-7 d
Tropicamide	20-40 min	20-35 min	1-6 h

FOSPHENYTOIN AND PHENYTOIN

Comparison of Parenteral Fosphenytoin and Phenytoin

	Fosphenytoin (Cerebyx®)	Phenytoin (Dilantin®)
Parenteral dosage forms available	50 mg PE/mL in 2 mL and 10 mL vials	50 mg phenytoin sodium/mL in 2 mL and 5 mL vials
Intravenous Administration	Recommended	Recommended
Loading dose	10-20 mg PE*/kg	10-15 mg/kg
Maintenance dose	4-7 mg/kg/day	100 mg I.V. q6-8h (oral form available)
Maximum infusion rate	Up to 150 mg PE/min	Up to 50 mg/min
Minimum infusion time for 1000 mg	6.7 min	20 min
Compatible with saline	Yes	Yes
Compatible with D_5W	Yes	No
Saline flush recommended after infusion	No	Yes
Intramuscular Administration	Recommended	Not recommended
Loading dose	10-20 mg PE/kg	10-15 mg/kg
Maintenance dose	4-7 mg/kg	Not recommended

*PE = phenytoin equivalents. See Fosphenytoin monograph for more details.

GLAUCOMA DRUG THERAPY

Ophthalmic Agent	Reduces Aqueous Humor Production	Increases Aqueous Humor Outflow*	Average Duration of Action	Strengths Available
Cholinesterase inhibitors		Miotics*		
Demecarium	No data	Significant	7 d	0.125%–0.25%
Echothiophate	No data	Significant	2 wk	0.03%–0.25%
Isoflurophate	No data	Significant	2 wk	0.025%
Physostigmine	No data	Significant	24 h	0.25%
Direct-acting				
Acetylcholine	Some activity	Significant	14 min	Injection 1%
Carbachol	Some activity	Significant	8 h	0.75%–3%
Pilocarpine	Some activity	Significant	5 h	0.5%, 1%, 2%, 3%, 4%
		Mydriatics		
Sympathomimetics				
Dipivefrin	Some activity	Moderate	12 h	0.1%
Epinephrine	Some activity	Moderate	18 h	0.25%–2%
		Miscellaneous		
Beta Blockers				
Betaxolol	Significant	Some activity	12 h	0.5%
Levobunolol	Significant	Some activity	18 h	0.5%
Metipranolol	Significant	Some activity	18 h	0.3%
Timolol	Significant	Some activity	18 h	0.25%, 0.5%
Carbonic Anhydrase Inhibitors				
Acetazolamide	Significant	No data	10 h	250 mg tab, 500 mg cap
Carteolol	Yes	No	12 h	1%
Dorzolamide	Yes	No	8 h	2%
Latanoprost		Yes	8–12 h	0.005%
Methazolamide	Significant	No data	14 h	50 mg

*All miotic drugs significantly affect accommodation.

GLYCOPROTEIN ANTAGONISTS

Comparison of Glycoprotein IIb/IIIa Receptor Antagonists

	Abciximab	Tirofiban	Eptifibatide
Brand name	ReoPro®	Aggrastat®	Integrelin®
Type	Monoclonal antibody	Nonpeptide	Peptide
Mechanism of action	Steric hindrance and conformational changes	Mimics native protein sequence in receptor	Mimics native protein sequence in receptor
Biologic half-life	12-24 h	4-8 h	4-8 h
Reversible with platelet infusions	Yes	No (effect dissipates within 4-8 h)	No (effect dissipates within 4-8 h)
Speed of reversibility (return of platelet function)	Slow (>48 h)	Fast (2 h)	Fast (2 h)
Vitronectin activity	Yes	No	No
FDA-approved labeling			
Percutaneous coronary intervention (PCI)	Yes	No	Yes
Coronary stents	Yes	No	No
Unstable angina pre-PCI	When PCI planned	When PCI planned	When PCI planned
Unstable angina, medical stabilization	No	Yes	Yes
FDA-approved dosing for percutaneous coronary intervention	0.25 mg/kg bolus followed by 0.125 mcg/kg/min infusion (max: 10 mcg/min) x 12 h	Not approved for use in planned PCI	135 mcg/kg bolus followed by 0.5 mcg/kg/min infusion for 20-24 h
FDA-approved dosing for unstable angina stabilization	0.25 mg/kg bolus followed by 10 mcg/min infusion x 18-24 h, concluding 1 h post-PCI	0.4 mcg/kg/min x 30 min followed by 0.1 mcg/kg/min infusion through angiography or 12-24 h after subsequent PCI	180 mcg/kg/bolus followed by 2 mcg/kg/min infusion until discharge, CABG procedure or up to 72 h
How supplied – volume of injectable (total drug contents/vial)	5 mL vial (10 mg)	10 mL vial (20 mg) 100 mL vial (75 mg)	50 mL vial (12.5 mg) 500 mL premixed solution (25 mg)
Storage requirements	Refrigerate, do not freeze and do not shake	Can store at room temperature, do not freeze, protect from light during storage	Refrigerate and protect from light until administered

HEPARINS

Product	Method of Preparation	Average Molecular Weight (daltons)	Half-life (min)	Anti-Xa to IIa Ratio	Availability
Heparin (various)	Unfractionated mixture	3000-30,000	60-120	1.0	1000 units in 1 mL; 5000 units in 1 mL; 10,000 units in 1 mL; 20,000 units in 1 mL; 40,000 units in 1 mL
Ardeparin (Normiflo®)	Perioxidative depolymerization	6000	200	1.9	5000 units in 0.5 mL; 10,000 units in 0.5 mL
Dalteparin (Fragmin®)	Nitrous acid depolymerization	5000	119-139	2.7	Antifactor Xa 2500 units per 0.2 mL; antifactor Xa 5000 units per 0.2 mL
Enoxaparin (Lovenox®)	Benzylation and alkaline depolymerization	4200	129-180	3.8	30 mg per 0.3 mL; 40 mg per 0.4 mL; 60 mg per 0.6 mL; 80 mg per 0.8 mL; 100 mg per 1 mL
Danaparoid (Orgaron®)	From porcine intestinal mucosa; heparan, dermatan, and chondroitin	5500-6000	24 h	22-90	750 units per 0.6 mL

HYPOGLYCEMIC DRUGS

Contraindications to Therapy and Potential Adverse Effects of Oral Antidiabetic Agents

	Sulfonylureas/ Meglitinide	Metformin	Acarbose/ Miglitol	Troglitazone
CONTRAINDICATIONS				
Insulin dependency	A	A	A*	
Pregnancy/lactation	A	A	A	
Hypersensitivity to the agent	A	A	A	A
Hepatic impairment	R	A	R	
Renal impairment	R	A	R	
Congestive heart failure		A		R
Chronic lung disease		A		
Peripheral vascular disease		A		
Steroid-induced diabetes	R	R		
Inflammatory bowel disease		A	A	
Major recurrent illness	R	A		
Surgery	R	A		
Alcoholism	R	A		
ADVERSE EFFECTS				
Hypoglycemia	Yes	No	No	N
Body weight gain	Yes	No	No	N
Hypersensitivity	Yes	No	No	
Drug interactions	Yes	No	No	Y
Lactic acidosis	No	Yes	No	
Gastrointestinal disturbances	No	Yes	No	N

*Can be used in conjunction with insulin. A = absolute; R = relative.

Comparative Pharmacokinetics

Drug	Duration of Action (h)	Dose and Frequency (mg)	Metabolism
Sulfonylureas – First Generation Agents			
Acetohexamide	12-24	250-1500 bid	Hepatic (60%) with active metabolite
Chlorpropamide	24-72	100-500 qd	Renal excretion (30%) and hepatic metabolism with active metabolites
Tolazamide	10-24	100-1000 qd or bid	Hepatic with active metabolites
Tolbutamide	6-24	500-3000 qd-tid	Hepatic
Sulfonylureas – Second Generation Agents			
Glimepiride	24	1-4 mg qd	Hepatic
Glipizide	12-24	2.5-40 qd or bid	Hepatic
Glipizide GITS	24	5-10 qd	Hepatic
Glyburide	16-24	1.25-20 qd or bid	Hepatic with active metabolites
Thiazolidinedione			
Troglitazone	8 wk	200-600 mg qd	Hepatic
Meglitinides			
Repaglinide	<4 hours (single dose)	0.4-4 mg administered with meals 2, 3, or 4 times/day	Hepatic to inactive metabolites

LAXATIVES, CLASSIFICATION AND PROPERTIES

Laxative	Onset of Action	Site of Action	Mechanism of Action
Saline			
Magnesium citrate (Citroma®) Magnesium hydroxide (Milk of Magnesia)	30 min to 3 h	Small and large intestine	Attract/retain water in intestinal lumen increasing intraluminal pressure; cholecystokinin release
Sodium phosphate/ biphosphate enema (Fleet® Enema)	2-15 min	Colon	
Irritant/Stimulant			
Cascara Casanthranol Senna (Senokot®)	6-10 h	Colon	Direct action on intestinal mucosa; stimulate myenteric plexus; alter water and electrolyte secretion
Bisacodyl (Dulcolax®) tablets, suppositories	15 min to 1 h	Colon	
Castor oil	2-6 h	Small intestine	
Cascara aromatic fluid extract	6-10 h	Colon	
Bulk-Producing			
Methylcellulose Psyllium (Metamucil®) Malt soup extract (Maltsupex®) Calcium polycarbophil (Mitrolan®, FiberCon®)	12-24 h (up to 72 h)	Small and large intestine	Holds water in stool; mechanical distention; malt soup extract reduces fecal pH
Lubricant			
Mineral oil	6-8 h	Colon	Lubricates intestine; retards colonic absorption of fecal water; softens stool
Surfactants/Stool Softener			
Docusate sodium (Colace®) Docusate calcium (Surfak®) Docusate potassium (Dialose®)	24-72 h	Small and large intestine	Detergent activity; facilitates admixture of fat and water to soften stool
Miscellaneous and Combination Laxatives			
Glycerin suppository	15-30 min	Colon	Local irritation; hyperosmotic action
Lactulose (Cephulac®)	24-48 h	Colon	Delivers osmotically active molecules to colon
Docusate/casanthranol (Peri-Colace®)	8-12 h	Small and large intestine	Casanthranol – mild stimulant; docusate – stool softener
Polyethylene glycol-electrolyte solution (GoLYTELY®)	30-60 min	Small and large intestine	Nonabsorbable solution which acts as an osmotic agent
Sorbitol 70%	24-48 h	Colon	Delivers osmotically active molecules to colon

LIPID-LOWERING AGENTS

Effects on Lipoproteins

Drug	Total Cholesterol (%)	LDLC (%)	HDLC (%)	TG (%)
Bile-acid resins	↓20-25	↓20-35	→	↑5-20
Fibric acid derivatives	↓10	↓10 (↑)	↑10-25	↓40-55
HMG-CoA RI (statins)	↓15-35	↓20-40	↑2-15	↓7-25
Nicotinic acid	↓25	↓20	↑20	↓40
Probucol	↓10-15	↓<10	↓30	→

Comparative Dosages of Agents Used to Treat Hyperlipidemia

Antilipemic Agent*	Usual Daily Dose	Average Dosing Interval
Fibric Acid Derivatives		
Clofibrate	2000 mg	qid
Gemfibrozil	1200 mg	bid
Miscellaneous Agents		
Niacin	6 g	tid
Bile Acid Sequestrants		
Colestipol	max: 30 g	bid
Cholestyramine	max: 24 g	tid-qid

Dosage is based on 70 kg adult with normal hepatic and renal function.

Recommended Liver Function Monitoring for HMG-CoA Reductase Inhibitors

Agent	Initial and After Elevation in Dose	6 Weeks*	12 Weeks*	Semiannually
Atorvastatin	x	x	x	x
Cerivastatin	x	x	x	x
Fluvastatin	x	x	x	x
Lovastatin	x	x	x	x
Pravastatin	x		x	
Simvastatin	x			x

*After initiation of therapy or any elevation in dose.

Comparative Dosages of HMG-CoA Reductase Inhibitors

Agent	Daily Dosage
Atorvastatin (Lipitor®)	10 mg
Fluvastatin (Lescol®)	20 mg (dose recommended by manufacturer, but appears to be less effective than the recommended doses of atorvastatin, lovastatin, pravastatin, and simvastatin)
Lovastatin (Mevacor®)	20 mg
Pravastatin (Pravachol®)	20 mg
Simvastatin (Zocor®)	10 mg

NARCOTIC AGONISTS

Comparative Pharmacokinetics

Drug	Onset (min)	Peak (h)	Duration (h)	Half-Life (h)	Average Dosing Interval (h)	Equianalgesic Doses* (mg) I.M.	Equianalgesic Doses* (mg) Oral
Alfentanil	Immediate	ND	ND	1-2	—	ND	NA
Buprenorphine	15	1	4-8	2-3	—	0.4	—
Butorphanol	I.M.: 30-60 I.V.: 4-5	0.5-1	3-5	2.5-3.5	3 (3-6)	2	—
Codeine	P.O.: 30-60 I.M.: 10-30	0.5-1	4-6	3-4	3 (3-6)	120	200
Fentanyl	I.M.: 7-15 I.V.: Immediate	ND	1-2	1.5-6	1 (0.5-2)	0.1	NA
Hydrocodone	ND	ND	4-8	3.3-4.4	6 (4-8)	ND	ND
Hydromorphone	P.O.: 15-30	0.5-1	4-6	2-4	4 (3-6)	1.5	7.5
Levorphanol	P.O.: 10-60	0.5-1	4-8	12-16	6 (6-24)	2	4
Meperidine	P.O./I.M./S.C.: 10-15 I.V.: ≤5	0.5-1	2-4	3-4	3 (2-4)	75	300
Methadone	P.O.: 30-60 I.V.: 10-20	0.5-1	4-6 (acute) >8 (chronic)	15-30	8 (6-12)	10	20
Morphine	P.O.: 15-60 I.V.: ≤5	P.O./I.M./ S.C.: 0.5-1 I.V.: 0.3	3-6	2-4	4 (3-6)	10	60# (acute) 30 (chronic)
Nalbuphine	I.M.: 30 I.V.: 1-3	1	3-6	5	—	10	—
Naloxone†	2-5	0.5-2	0.5-1	0.5-1.5	—	—	—
Oxycodone	P.O.: 10-15	0.5-1	4-6	3-4	4 (3-6)	NA	30
Oxymorphone	5-15	0.5-1	3-6		1	1	10‡
Pentazocine	15-20	0.25-1	3-4	2-3	3 (3-6)		

Comparative Pharmacokinetics *(continued)*

Drug	Onset (min)	Peak (h)	Duration (h)	Half-Life (h)	Average Dosing Interval (h)		Equianalgesic Doses* (mg)	
							I.M.	Oral
Propoxyphene	P.O.: 30-60	2-2.5	4-6	3.5-15	6	(4-8)	ND	130§-200¶
Remifentanil	1-3	<0.3	0.1-0.2	0.15-0.3	—	—	ND	ND
Sufentanil	1.3-3	ND	ND	2.5-3	—	—	0.02	NA

ND = no data available. NA = not applicable.

*Based on acute, short-term use. Chronic administration may alter pharmacokinetics and decrease the oral parenteral dose ratio. The morphine oral-parenteral ratio decreases to ~1.5-2.5:1 upon chronic dosing.

#Extensive survey data suggest that the relative potency of I.M.:P.O. morphine of 1:6 changes to 1:2-3 with chronic dosing.

†Narcotic antagonist

‡Rectal.

§HCl salt.

¶Napsylate salt.

NARCOTIC AGONISTS *(Continued)*

Comparative Pharmacology

Drug	Analgesic	Antitussive	Constipation	Respiratory Depression	Sedation	Emesis
Phenanthrenes						
Codeine	+	+++	+	+	+	+
Hydrocodone	+	+++		+		
Hydromorphone	++	+++	+	++	+	+
Levorphanol	++	++	++	++	++	+
Morphine	++	+++	++	++	++	++
Oxycodone	++	+++	++	++	++	++
Oxymorphone	++	+	++	+++		+++
Phenylpiperidines						
Alfentanil	++					
Fentanyl	++			+		+
Meperidine	++	+	+	++	+	
Sufentanil	+++					
Diphenylheptanes						
Methadone	++	++	++	++	+	+
Propoxyphene	+			+	+	+
Agonist/Antagonist						
Buprenorphine	++	N/A	+++	+++	++	++
Butorphanol	++	N/A	+++	+++	++	+
Dezocine	++	N/A	+	++	+	++
Nalbuphine	++	N/A	+++	+++	++	++
Pentazocine	++	N/A	+	++	++ or stimulation	++

NEUROMUSCULAR BLOCKING AGENTS

Comparative Dosages*

Agent	Comparative Dosages (mcg/kg)	Recommended Bolus Dose	Recommended I.V. Infusion Rates
Short-Acting Agents			
Mivacurium (Mivacron®)	80-90	150 mcg/kg	1-15 mcg/kg/min
Rocuronium (Zemuron®)	300	0.6-1.2 mg/kg	10-40 mcg/kg/min
Succinylcholine	300	25-75 mg (1-2 mg/kg)	2.5 mg/min
Intermediate-Acting Agents			
Atracurium (Tracrium®)	225	400-500 mcg/kg	2-15 mcg/kg/min
Cisatracurium (Nimbex®)	100	150-200 mcg/kg	1-5 mcg/kg/minute
Pancuronium (Pavulon®)	60	40-100 mcg/kg	50-100 mcg/kg/h
Vecuronium (Norcuron®)	50-60	80-100 mcg/kg	0.8-1.2 mcg/kg/min
Long-Acting Agents			
Doxacurium (Nuromax®)	25-30	50 mcg/kg	Not applicable
Pipecuronium (Arduan®)	45	50-100 mcg/kg	Not applicable
Tubocurarine	500	100-600 mcg/kg	Not applicable

*Dosages in a 70 kg adult patient with normal renal and hepatic function.

NEUROMUSCULAR BLOCKING AGENTS *(Continued)*

Comparative Pharmacokinetic Parameters in Adult Patients With Normal Renal and Hepatic Function

Agent	Volume of Distribution (central compartment)	Onset of Action	Duration of Action	Half-Life	Body Clearance
Short-Acting Agents		**1-2 min**	**10-20 min**		
Mivacurium (Mivacron®)	0.15-0.25 L/kg	2 min	17 min	16.9 min	3.3 L/kg/h 55 mL/kg/min
Rocuronium (Zemuron®)	0.22-0.25 L/kg	0.7-1 min	31-67 min	84-90 min	2.7 L/kg/min
Succinylcholine	Unknown	1-1.5 min	5-10 min	Unknown	Unknown
Intermediate-Acting Agents		**2-3 min**	**40-60 min**		
Atracurium (Tracrium®)	0.16-0.18 L/kg (0.04-0.06 L/kg)	2 min	30 min	20-21 min	5.3-6.1 mL/kg/min
Cisatracurium (Nimbex®)	0.133 L/kg	2 min	30 min	22-31 min	4.5-5.7 mL/kg/min
Pancuronium (Pavulon®)	0.26-0.28 L/kg (0.05-0.12 L/kg)	1-5.2 min	60 min	114-140 min	1.8-1.9 mL/kg/min
Vecuronium (Norcuron®)	0.19-0.25 L/kg (0.05-0.11 L/kg)	1.5 min	30 min	58-80 min	3.0-5.2 mL/kg/min
Long-Acting Agents		**4-6 min**	**90-180 min**		
Doxacurium (Nuromax®)	0.22±0.11 L/kg	6 min	83 min	99±54 min	2.67±0.09 mL/kg/min
Pipecuronium (Arduan®)	0.31±0.1 L/kg	3-5 min	70 min	137±68 min	2.3±0.04 mL/kg/min
Tubocurarine	0.22-0.39 L/kg	6 min	80 min	3.9 h	Unknown

NICOTINE PRODUCTS

Dosage Form	Brand Name	Dosing	Recommended Treatment Duration	Strengths Available
Chewing gum	Nicorette®	Chew 1 piece q1-2h for 6 wks, then decrease to 1 piece q2-4h for 3 wks, then 1 piece q4-8h for 3 wks, then discontinue	~12 wks	2 mg, 4 mg
Transdermal	Habitrol®	One 21 mg/d patch qd for 4-8 wks, then one 14 mg/d patch qd for 2-4 wks, then one 7 mg/d patch qd for 2-4 wks, then discontinue Low-dose Regimen[1]: One 14 mg/d patch qd for 6 wks, then one 7 mg/d patch qd for 2-4 wks, then discontinue	~12 wks	Patch: 21 mg/d 14 mg/d 7 mg/d
	Nicoderm CQ®	One 21 mg/d patch qd for 6 wks, then one 14 mg/d patch qd for 2 wks, then one 7 mg/d patch qd for 2 wks, then discontinue Low-dose Regimen[1]: One 14 mg/d patch qd for 6 wks, then one 7 mg/d patch qd for 2 wks, then discontinue	~10 wks	Patch: 21 mg/d 14 mg/d 7 mg/d
	Nicotrol®	One 15 mg patch qd, worn for 16 h/d and removed for 8 h/d for a total of 6 wks, then discontinue	~6 wks	15 mg/16 h patch
Nasal spray	Nicotrol® NS	One dose is 2 sprays (1 spray in each nostril) Initial dose: 1-2 sprays q1h, should not exceed 10 sprays (5 doses)/h or 80 sprays (40 doses)/d	~12 wks	10 mL spray 0.5/mg spray (200 actuations)
Inhaler	Nicotrol®	Inhaler releases 4 mg nicotine (the equivalent of 2 cigarettes smoked) for 20 min of active inhaler puffing Usual dose: 6-16 cartridges/d for up to 12 wks, then reduce dose gradually over ensuing 12 wks, then discontinue	~18-24 wks	10 mg/cartridge: releases 4 mg/cartridge

[1]Transdermal low-dose regimens are intended for patients <100 lbs, smoke <10 cigarettes/d, and/or have a history of cardiovascular disease.

NITRATES

Nitrates*	Dosage Form	Onset (min)	Duration
Nitroglycerin	I.V.	1-2	3-5 min
	Sublingual	1-3	30-60 min
	Translingual spray	2	30-60 min
	Oral, sustained release	40	4-8 h
	Topical ointment	20-60	2-12 h
	Transdermal	40-60	18-24 h
Isosorbide dinitrate	Sublingual and chewable	2-5	1-2 h
	Oral	20-40	4-6 h
	Oral, sustained release	Slow	8-12 h
Isosorbide mononitrate	Oral	60-120	5-12 h

Adapted from Corwin S and Reiffel JA, "Nitrate Therapy for Angina Pectoris," *Arch Intern Med*, 1985, 145:538-43 and Franciosa JA, "Nitroglycerin and Nitrates in Congestive Heart Failure," *Heart and Lung*, 1980, 9(5):873-82.

*Hemodynamic and antianginal tolerance often develops within 24-48 hours of continuous nitrate administration.

NONSTEROIDAL ANTI-INFLAMMATORY AGENTS

Comparative Dosages and Pharmacokinetics

Drug	Maximum Recommended Daily Dose (mg)	Time to Peak Levels (h)*	Half-life (h)
Propionic Acids			
Fenoprofen (Nalfon®)	3200	1-2	2-3
Flurbiprofen (Ansaid®)	300	1.5	5.7
Ibuprofen	3200	1-2	1.8-2.5
Ketoprofen (Orudis®)	300	0.5-2	2-4
Naproxen (Naprosyn®)	1500	2-4	12-15
Naproxen sodium (Anaprox®)	1375	1-2	12-13
Oxaprozin	1800	3-5	42-50
Acetic Acids			
Diclofenac sodium delayed release (Voltaren®)	225	2-3	1-2
Diclofenac potassium immediate release (Cataflam®)	200	1	1-2
Etodolac (Lodine®)	1200	1-2	7.3
Indomethacin (Indocin®)	200	1-2	4.5
Indomethacin SR	150	2-4	4.5-6
Ketorolac (Toradol®)	I.M.: 120† P.O.: 40	0.5-1	3.8-8.6
Sulindac (Clinoril®)	400	2-4	7.8 (16.4)‡
Tolmetin (Tolectin®)	2000	0.5-1	1-1.5
Fenamates (Anthranilic Acids)			
Meclofenamate (Meclomen®)	400	0.5-1	2 (3.3)§
Mefenamic acid (Ponstel®)	1000	2-4	2-4
Nonacidic Agent			
Nabumetone (Relafen®)	2000	3-6	24
Oxicam			
Piroxicam (Feldene®)	20	3-5	30-86

Dosage is based on 70 kg adult with normal hepatic and renal function.

*Food decreases the rate of absorption and may delay the time to peak levels.

†150 mg on the first day.

‡Half-life of active sulfide metabolite.

§Half-life with multiple doses.

PARKINSON'S DISEASE DOSING

Dosing of Drugs Used for the Treatment of Parkinson's Disease

Generic Drug (Brand Name)	Receptor Affinity	Initial Dose	Titration Schedule	Usual Daily Dosage Range	Recommended Dosing Schedule
Amantadine (Symmetrel®)	NMDA receptor antagonist and inhibits neuronal reuptake of dopamine	100 mg every other day	100 mg/dose every week, up to 300 mg 3 times/d	100-200 mg	Twice daily
Benztropine (Cogentin®)	Cholinegic receptors, also has antihistmine effects	0.5-2 mg/d in 1-4 divided doses	0.5 mg/dose every 5-6 d	2-6 mg	1-2 times/d
Bromocriptine (Parlodel®)	Moderate affinity for D_2 and D_3 dopamine receptors	1.25 mg twice daily	2.5 mg/d every 2-4 wks	2.5-100 mg	3 times/d
Cabergoline (Dostinex)*	Selective to D_2 dopamine receptors	0.5 mg once daily	0.25-0.5 mg/d every 4 wks	0.5-5 mg	Once daily
Levodopa/carbidopa (Sinemet® CR)	Converts to dopamine; binds to all CNS dopamine receptors	10/100-25/100 mg 2-4 times/d	One-half to 1 tablet (10/100 or 25/100) every 1-2 d	50/200 to 200/2000 mg (3-8 tablets)	3 times/d or twice daily (for controlled release)
Pergolide (Permax®)	Low affinity for D_1 and maximal affinity for D_2 and D_3 dopamine receptors	0.05 mg/night	0.1-0.15 mg/d every 3 d for 12 d, then 0.25 mg/d every 3 d	0.05-5 mg	3 times/d
Pramipexole (Mirapex®)	High affinity for D_2 and D_3 dopamine receptors	0.125 mg 3 times/d	0.125 mg/dose every 5-7 d	1.5-4.5 mg	3 times/d
Ropinirole (Requip®)	High affinity for D_2 and D_3 dopamine receptors	0.25 mg 3 times/d	0.25 mg/dose weekly for 4 wks, then 1.5 mg/d every week up to 9 mg/d; 3 mg/d up to a max of 24 mg/d	0.75-24 mg	3 times/d
Selegiline (Eldepryl®)	No receptor effects, inhibits monoamine oxidase	5-10 mg twice daily	Titrate down the doses of levodopa/carbidopa as required	5-10 mg	Twice daily
Tolcapone (Tasmar®)	COMT enzyme inhibitor	100 mg 3 times/d	Titrate down the doses of levodopa/carbidopa as required	300-600 mg	3 times/d

*Cabergoline is not FDA approved for the treatment of Parkinson's disease.

SULFONAMIDE DERIVATIVES

The following table lists commonly prescribed drugs which are either sulfonamide derivatives or are structurally similar to sulfonamides. Please note that the list may not be all inclusive.

Commonly Prescribed Drugs

Classification	Specific Drugs
Antimicrobial Agents	Mafenide acetate (Sulfamylon®) Silver sulfadiazine (Silvadene®) Sodium sulfacetamide (Sodium Sulamyd®) Sulfadiazine Sulfamethizole Sulfamethoxazole (ie, Bactrim™ and co-trimoxazole) Sulfisoxazole (Gantrisin®)
Diuretics, Carbonic Anhydrase Inhibitors	Acetazolamide (Diamox®) Dichlorphenamide (Daranide®) Methazolamide (Neptazane®)
Diuretics, Loop	Bumetanide (Bumex®) Furosemide (Lasix®) Torsemide (Demadex®)
Diuretics, Thiazide	Bendroflumethiazide Benzthiazide Chlorothiazide (Diuril®) Chlorthalidone (Hygroton®) Cyclothiazide (Anhydron®) Hydrochlorothiazide (Dyazide®, HydroDIURIL®, Maxzide®) Hydroflumethiazide Indapamide (Lozol®) Methyclothiazide (Enduron®) Metolazone (Diulo®, Zaroxolyn®) Polythiazide Quinethazone Trichlormethiazide
Hypoglycemic Agents, Oral	Acetohexamide (Dymelor®) Chlorpropamide (Diabinese®) Glipizide (Glucotrol®) Glyburide (DiaBeta®, Micronase®) Tolazamide (Tolinase®) Tolbutamide (Orinase®)
Other Agents	Sulfasalazine (Azulfidine®)

CYTOCHROME P-450 ENZYMES AND DRUG METABOLISM

Background

There are five distinct groups of drug metabolizing which account for the majority of drug metabolism in humans. These enzymes "families", known as isoenzymes, are localized primarily in the liver. The nomenclature of this system has been standardized. Isoenzyme families are identified as a cytochrom (CYP prefix), followed by their numerical designation (eg, 1A2).

Enzymes may be inhibited (slowing metabolism through this pathway) or induced (increased in activity or number). Individual drugs metabolized by a specific enzyme are identified as substrates for the isoenzyme. Considerable effort has been expended in recent years to classify drugs metabolized by this system as either an inhibitor, inducer, or substrate of a specific isoenzyme. It should be noted that a drug may demonstrate complex activity within this scheme, acting as an inhibitor of one isoenzyme while serving as a substrate for another.

By recognizing that a substrate's metabolism may be dramatically altered by concurrent therapy with either an inducer or inhibitor, potential interactions may be identified and addressed. For example, a drug which inhibits CYP1A2 is likely to block metabolism of theophylline (a substrate for this isoenzyme). Because of this interaction, the dose of theophylline required to maintain a consistent level in the patient should be reduced when an inhibitor is added. Failure to make this adjustment may lead to supratherapeutic theophylline concentrations and potential toxicity.

This approach does have limitations. For example, the metabolism of specific drugs may have primary and secondary pathways. The contribution of secondary pathways to the overall metabolism may limit the impact of any given inhibitor. In addition, there may be up to a tenfold variation in the concentration of an isoenzyme across the broad population. In fact, a complete absence of an isoenzyme may occur in some genetic subgroups. Finally, the relative potency of inhibition, relative to the affinity of the enzyme for its substrate, demonstrates a high degree of variability. These issues make it difficult to anticipate whether a theoretical interaction will have a clinically relevant impact in a specific patient.

The details of this enzyme system continue to be investigated, and information is expanding daily. However, to be complete, it should be noted that other enzyme systems also influence a drug's pharmacokinetic profile. For example, a key enzyme system regulating the absorption of drugs is the p-glycoprotein system. Recent evidence suggests that some interaction originally attributed to the cytochrome system may, in fact, have been the result of inhibition of this enzyme.

The following tables represent an attempt to detail the available information with respect to isoenzyme activities. Within certain limits, they may be used to identify potential interactions. Of particular note, an effort has been made in each drug monograph to identify involvement of a particular isoenzyme in the drug's metabolism. These tables are intended to supplement the limited space available to list drug interactions in the monograph. Consequently, they may be used to define a greater range of both actual and potential drug interactions.

DRUGS CAUSING INHIBITORY AND INDUCTIVE INTERACTION

INHIBITORY (Enhancement of Interacting Drug Effect)	INDUCTIVE (Impairment of Interacting Drug Effect)
Amiodarone (Cordarone®)	Anticonvulsants
Cimetidine (Tagamet®)	Chronic ethanol use
Contraceptives, oral	Cigarette smoking
Erythromycin	Rifampin (Rifadin®, Rimactane®)
Ethanol intoxication	
Fluconazole	
Isoniazid (Laniazid®, Nydrazid®)	
Itraconazole	
Ketoconazole	
Neuroleptics	
Psoralen dermatologics	
Quinidine	
Quinolone antibiotics	
SSRIs	
Tricyclic antidepressants	

LOW THERAPEUTIC INDEX DRUGS

Hepatic Oxidation (Cytochrome P-450 Mediated Clearance)
Antiarrhythmic drugs
Anticoagulants, oral
Anticonvulsants
Antineoplastic/immunosuppressive drugs
Theophylline

CYTOCHROME P-450 ENZYMES AND RESPECTIVE METABOLIZED DRUGS

CYP1A2

Substrates

Acetaminophen	Mirtazapine (hydroxylation)
Acetanilid	Nortriptyline
Aminophylline	Olanzapine (demethylation, hydroxylation)
Amitriptyline (demethylation)	Ondansetron
Antipyrine	Phenacetin
Betaxolol	Phenothiazines
Caffeine	Propafenone
Chlorpromazine	Propranolol
Clomipramine (demethylation)	Riluzole
Clozapine	Ritonavir
Cyclobenzaprine (demethylation)	Ropinirole
Desipramine (demethylation)	Ropivacaine
Diazepam	Tacrine
Estradiol	Tamoxifen
Fluvoxamine	Theophylline
Grepafloxacin	Thioridazine
Haloperidol	Thiothixene
Imipramine (demethylation)	Trifluoperazine
Levopromazine	Verapamil
Maprotiline	Warfarin (R-warfarin, minor pathway)
Methadone	Zileuton
Metoclopramide	Zopiclone

Inducers

Carbamazepine	Omeprazole
Charbroiled foods	Phenobarbital
Cigarette smoke	Phenytoin
Cruciferous vegetables (cabbage, brussels sprouts, broccoli, cauliflower)	Primidone
	Rifampin
Nicotine	Ritonavir

Inhibitors

Anastrozole	Isoniazid
Cimetidine	Ketoconazole
Ciprofloxacin	Levofloxacin
Citalopram (weak)	Mexiletine
Clarithromycin	Mibefradil
Diethyldithiocarbamate	Norfloxacin
Diltiazem	Paroxetine (high dose)
Enoxacin	Ritonavir
Erythromycin	Sertraline (weak)
Ethinyl estradiol	Tacrine
Fluvoxamine	Tertiary TCAs
Fluoxetine (high dose)	Zileuton
Grapefruit juice	

CYTOCHROME P-450 ENZYMES AND DRUG METABOLISM
(Continued)

CYP2A6

Substrates

Letrozole
Montelukast
Nicotine

Ritonavir
Tamoxifen

Inducers

Barbiturates

Inhibitors

Diethyldithiocarbamate
Letrozole

Ritonavir
Tranylcypromine

CYP2B6

Substrates

Antipyrine
Bupropion (hydroxylation)
Cyclophosphamide
Ifosfamide

Nicotine
Orphenadrine
Tamoxifen

Inducers

Phenobarbital
Phenytoin

Primidone

Inhibitors

Diethyldithiocarbamate

Orphenadrine

CYP2C
(Specific isozyme has not been identified)

Substrates

Antipyrine
Carvedilol
Clozapine (minor)
Mestranol

Mephobarbital
Tamoxifen
Ticrynafen

Inducers

Carbamazepine
Phenobarbital
Phenytoin

Primidone
Sulfinpyrazone

Inhibitors

Isoniazid
Ketoconazole

Ketoprofen

CYP2C8

Substrates

Carbamazepine
Diazepam
Diclofenac
Ibuprofen
Mephobarbital
Naproxen (5-hydroxylation)

Omeprazole
Paclitaxel
Retinoic acid
Tolbutamide
Warfarin (S-warfarin)

Inducers

Phenobarbital

Primidone

Inhibitors

Anastrozole

Omeprazole

CYP2C9

Substrates

Amitriptyline (demethylation)
Clomipramine
Dapsone
Diazepam
Diclofenac
Flurbiprofen
Fluvastatin
Glimepiride
Hexobarbital
Ibuprofen
Imipramine (demethylation)
Indomethacin
Irbesartan
Losartan
Mefenamic acid
Metronidazole

Mirtazapine
Montelukast
Naproxen (5-hydroxylation)
Omeprazole
Phenytoin
Piroxicam
Ritonavir
Sildenafil citrate
Tenoxicam
Tetrahydrocannabinol
Tolbutamide
Torsemide
Warfarin (S-warfarin)
Zafirlukast (hydroxylation)
Zileuton

Inducers

Carbamazepine
Fluconazole
Fluoxetine

Phenobarbital
Phenytoin
Rifampin

Inhibitors

Amiodarone
Anastrozole
Chloramphenicol
Cimetidine
Diclofenac
Disulfiram
Flurbiprofen
Fluoxetine
Fluvastatin
Fluvoxamine (potent)
Isoniazid
Ketoconazole (weak)
Ketoprofen

Metronidazole
Omeprazole
Phenylbutazone
Ritonavir
Sertraline
Sulfamethoxazole-trimethoprim
Sulfaphenazole
Sulfinpyrazone
Sulfonamides
Troglitazone
Valproic acid
Warfarin (R-warfarin)
Zafirlukast

CYP2C18

Substrates

Amitriptyline
Clomipramine
Dronabinol
Imipramine
Naproxen
Omeprazole

Piroxicam
Proguanil
Propranolol
Retinoic acid
Tolbutamide
Warfarin

Inducers

Carbamazepine
Phenobarbital

Phenytoin
Rifampin

Inhibitors

Cimetidine
Fluconazole
Fluoxetine
Fluvastatin

Ketoconazole (weak)

Isoniazid

Sertraline

CYTOCHROME P-450 ENZYMES AND DRUG METABOLISM
(Continued)

CYP2C19

Substrates

Amitriptyline (demethylation)
Barbiturates
Carisoprodol
Citalopram
Clomipramine (demethylation)
Desmethyldiazepam
Diazepam (N-demethylation, minor
    pathway)
Divalproex sodium
Hexobarbital
Imipramine (demethylation)
Lansoprazole
Mephenytoin
Mephobarbital
Moclobemide
Olanzapine (minor)
Omeprazole
Pentamidine
Phenytoin
Proguanil
Propranolol
Ritonavir
Tolbutamide
Topiramate
Valproic acid
Warfarin (R-warfarin)

Inducers

Carbamazepine
Phenobarbital
Phenytoin
Rifampin

Inhibitors

Cimetidine
Citalopram (weak)
Felbamate
Fluconazole
Fluoxetine
Fluvastatin
Fluvoxamine
Isoniazid
Ketoconazole (weak)
Letrozole
Omeprazole
Proguanil
Ritonavir
Sertraline
Teniposide
Tolbutamide
Topiramate
Tranylcypromine
Troglitazone

CYP2D6

Substrates

Amitriptyline (hydroxylation)
Amphetamine
Betaxolol
Bisoprolol
Brofaromine
Bufurolol
Bupropion
Captopril
Carvedilol
Chlorpheniramine
Chlorpromazine
Cinnarizine
Clomipramine (hydroxylation)
Clozapine (minor pathway)
Codeine (hydroxylation, o-demethylation)
Cyclobenzaprine (hydroxylation)
Cyclophosphamide
Debrisoquin
Delavirdine
Desipramine
Dexfenfluramine
Dextromethorphan (o-demethylation)
Dihydrocodeine
Diphenhydramine
Dolasetron
Donepezil
Doxepin
Encainide
Fenfluramine
Flecainide
Fluoxetine (minor pathway)
Fluphenazine
Halofantrine
Haloperidol (minor pathway)
Hydrocodone
Hydrocortisone
Hydroxyamphetamine
Imipramine (hydroxylation)
Labetalol
Loratadine
Maprotiline
m-Chlorophenylpiperazine (m-CPP)
Meperidine
Methadone
Methamphetamine
Metoclopramide
Metoprolol
Mexiletine
Mianserin
Mirtazapine (hydroxylation)
Molindone
Morphine
Nortriptyline (hydroxylation)
Olanzapine (minor, hydroxymethylation)
Ondansetron
Orphenadrine
Oxycodone
Papaverine
Paroxetine (minor pathway)
Penbutolol
Pentazocine
Perhexiline
Perphenazine
Phenformin
Pindolol
Promethazine
Propafenone
Propranolol

Quetiapine
Remoxipride
Risperidone
Ritonavir (minor)
Ropivacaine
Selegiline
Sertindole
Sertraline (minor pathway)
Sparteine
Tamoxifen

Thioridazine
Tiagabine
Timolol
Tolterodine
Tramadol
Trazodone
Trimipramine
Tropisetron
Venlafaxine (o-desmethylation)
Yohimbine

Inducers

Carbamazepine
Phenobarbital
Phenytoin

Rifampin
Ritonavir

Inhibitors

Amiodarone
Chloroquine
Chlorpromazine
Cimetidine
Citalopram
Clomipramine
Codeine
Delavirdine
Desipramine
Dextropropoxyphene
Diltiazem
Doxorubicin
Fluoxetine
Fluphenazine
Fluvoxamine
Haloperidol
Labetalol
Lobeline
Lomustine
Methadone

Mibefradil
Moclobemide
Norfluoxetine
Paroxetine
Perphenazine
Propafenone
Quinacrine
Quinidine
Ranitidine
Risperidone (weak)
Ritonavir
Sertindole
Sertraline (weak)
Thioridazine
Valproic acid
Venlafaxine (weak)
Vinblastine
Vincristine
Vinorelbine
Yohimbine

CYP2E1

Substrates

Acetaminophen
Acetone
Aniline
Benzene
Caffeine
Chlorzoxazone
Clozapine
Dapsone
Dextromethorphan
Enflurane
Ethanol
Halothane

Isoflurane
Isoniazid
Methoxyflurane
Nitrosamine
Ondansetron
Phenol
Ritonavir
Sevoflurane
Styrene
Tamoxifen
Theophylline
Venlafaxine

Inducers

Ethanol

Isoniazid

Inhibitors

Diethyldithiocarbamate (disulfiram
    metabolite)
Dimethyl sulfoxide

Disulfiram
Ritonavir

CYP3A3/4

Substrates

Acetaminophen
Alfentanil
Alprazolam**
Amiodarone
Amitriptyline (minor)
Amlodipine
Anastrozole
Androsterone

Antipyrine
Astemizole**
Atorvastatin
Benzphetamine
Bepridil
Budesonide
Bupropion (minor)
Buspirone

CYTOCHROME P-450 ENZYMES AND DRUG METABOLISM
(Continued)

Busulfan
Bromazepam
Bromocriptine
Busulfan
Caffeine
Cannabinoids
Carbamazepine
Cerivastatin
Chlorpromazine
Cimetidine
Cisapride**
Citalopram
Clarithromycin
Clindamycin
Clomipramine
Clonazepam
Clozapine
Cocaine
Codeine (demethylation)
Cortisol
Cortisone
Cyclobenzaprine (demethylation)
Cyclophosphamide
Cyclosporine
Dapsone
Dehydroepiandrostendione
Delavirdine
Desmethyldiazepam
Dexamethasone
Dextromethorphan (minor,
   N-demethylation)
Diazepam (minor; hydroxylation,
   N-demethylation)
Digitoxin
Diltiazem
Disopyramide
Docetaxel
Dolasetron
Donepezil
Doxorubicin
Doxycycline
Dronabinol
Enalapril
Erythromycin
Estradiol
Ethinyl estradiol
Ethosuximide
Etoposide
Felodipine
Fentanyl
Fexofenadine
Finasteride
Fluoxetine
Flutamide
Glyburide
Granisetron
Halofantrine
Hydrocortisone
Hydroxyarginine
Ifosfamide
Imipramine
Indinavir
Isradipine
Itraconazole
Ketoconazole
Lansoprazole (minor)
Letrozole
Lidocaine
Loratadine
Losartan
Lovastatin

Methadone
Mibefradil
Miconazole
Midazolam
Mifepristone
Mirtazapine (N-demethylation)
Montelukast
Navelbine
Nefazodone
Nelfinavir**
Nevirapine
Nicardipine
Nifedipine
Niludipine
Nimodipine
Nisoldipine
Nitrendipine
Omeprazole (sulfonation)
Ondansetron
Oral contraceptives
Orphenadrine
Paclitaxel
Pimozide**
Pravastatin
Prednisone
Progesterone
Proguanil
Propafenone
Quercetin
Quetiapine
Quinidine
Quinine
Repaglinide
Retinoic acid
Rifampin
Ritonavir**
Salmeterol
Saquinavir
Sertindole
Sertraline
Sibutramine##
Sildenafil citrate
Simvastatin
Sufentanil
Tacrolimus
Tamoxifen
Temazepam
Teniposide
Terfenadine**
Testosterone
Tetrahydrocannabinol
Theophylline
Tiagabine
Tolterodine
Toremifene
Trazodone
Tretinoin
Triazolam**
Troglitazone
Troleandomycin
Venlafaxine (N-demethylation)
Verapamil
Vinblastine
Vincristine
Warfarin (R-warfarin)
Yohimbine
Zatoestron
Zileuton
Ziprasidone
Zolpidem**
Zonisamide

Inducers

Carbamazepine
Dexamethasone
Ethosuximide
Glucocorticoids
Griseofulvin
Nafcillin
Nelfinavir
Nevirapine
Phenobarbital

Phenylbutazone
Phenytoin
Primidone
Progesterone
Rifabutin
Rifampin
Sulfadimidine
Sulfinpyrazone
Troglitazone

Inhibitors

Amiodarone
Anastrozole
Azithromycin
Cannabinoids
Cimetidine
Clarithromycin**
Clotrimazole
Cyclosporine
Danazol
Delavirdine
Dexamethasone
Diethyldithiocarbamate
Diltiazem
Dirithromycin
Disulfiram
Erythromycin**
Ethinyl estradiol
Fluconazole (weak)
Fluoxetine
Fluvoxamine**
Gestodene
Grapefruit juice
Indinavir
Isoniazid
Itraconazole**
Ketoconazole**

Metronidazole
Mibefradil**
Miconazole (moderate)
Nefazodone**
Nelfinavir
Nevirapine
Norfloxacin
Norfluoxetine
Omeprazole (weak)
Oxiconazole
Paroxetine (weak)
Propoxyphene
Quinidine
Quinine**
Ranitidine
Ritonavir**
Saquinavir
Sertindole
Sertraline
Troglitazone
Troleandomycin
Valproic acid (weak)
Verapamil
Zafirlukast
Zileuton

Contraindications:

Terfenadine, astemizole, cisapride, and triazolam contraindicated with nefazodone
Pimozide contraindicated with macrolide antibiotics
Alprazolam and triazolam contraindicated with ketoconazole and itraconazole
Terfenadine, astemizole, and cisapride contraindicated with fluvoxamine
Terfenadine contraindicated with mibefradil, ketoconazole, erythromycin, clarithromycin, troleandomycin
Ritonavir contraindicated with triazolam, zolpidem, astemizole, rifabutin, quinine, clarithromycin, troleandomycin
Mibefradil contraindicated with astemizole
Nelfinavir contraindicated with rifabutin

##Do not use with SSRIs, sumatriptan, lithium, meperidine, fentanyl, dextromethorphan, or pentazocine within 2 weeks of a MAOI.

CYP3A5-7

Substrates

Cortisol
Ethinyl estradiol
Lovastatin
Nifedipine
Quinidine

Terfenadine
Testosterone
Triazolam
Vinblastine
Vincristine

Inducers

Phenobarbital
Phenytoin

Primidone
Rifampin

Inhibitors

Clotrimazole
Ketoconazole
Metronidazole

Miconazole
Troleandomycin

CYTOCHROME P-450 ENZYMES AND DRUG METABOLISM
(Continued)

References

Baker GB, Urichuk CJ, and Coutts RT, "Drug Metabolism and Metabolic Drug-Drug Interactions in Psychiatry," *Child Adolescent Psychopharm News (Suppl)*.

DeVane CL, "Pharmacogenetics and Drug Metabolism of Newer Antidepressant Agents," *J Clin Psychiatry*, 1994, 55(Suppl 12):38-45.

Drug Interactions Analysis and Management. Cytochrome (CYP) 450 Isozyme Drug Interactions, Vancouver, WA: Applied Therapeutics, Inc, 523-7.

Ereshefsky L, "Drug-Drug Interactions Involving Antidepressants: Focus on Venlafaxine," *J Clin Psychopharmacol*, 1996, 16(3 Suppl 2):375-535.

Ereshefsky L, *Psychiatr Annal*, 1996, 26:342-50.

Fleishaker JC and Hulst LK, "A Pharmacokinetic and Pharmacodynamic Evaluation of the Combined Administration of Alprazolam and Fluvoxamine," *Eur J Clin Pharmacol*, 1994, 46(1):35-9.

Flockhart DA, et al, *Clin Pharmacol Ther*, 1996, 59:189.

Ketter TA, Flockhart DA, Post RM, et al, "The Emerging Role of Cytochrome P-450 3A in Psychopharmacology," *J Clin Psychopharmacol*, 1995, 15(6):387-98.

Michalets EL, "Update: Clinically Significant Cytochrome P-450 Drug Interactions," *Pharmacotherapy*, 1998, 18(1):84-112.

Nemeroff CB, DeVane CL, and Pollock BG, "Newer Antidepressants and the Cytochrome P450 System," *Am J Psychiatry*, 1996, 153(3):311-20.

Pollock BG, "Recent Developments in Drug Metabolism of Relevance to Psychiatrists," *Harv Rev Psychiatry*, 1994, 2(4):204-13.

Richelson E, "Pharmacokinetic Drug Interactions of New Antidepressants: A Review of the Effects on the Metabolism of Other Drugs," *Mayo Clin Proc*, 1997, 72(9):835-47.

Riesenman C, "Antidepressant Drug Interactions and the Cytochrome P450 System: A Critical Appraisal," *Pharmacotherapy*, 1995, 15(6 Pt 2):84S-99S.

Schmider J, Greenblatt DJ, von Moltke LL, et al, "Relationship of *In Vitro* Data on Drug Metabolism to *In Vivo* Pharmacokinetics and Drug Interactions: Implications for Diazepam Disposition in Humans," *J Clin Psychopharmacol*, 1996, 16(4):267-72.

Slaughter RL, *Pharm Times*, 1996, 7:6-16.

Watkins PB, "Role of Cytochrome P450 in Drug Metabolism and Hepatotoxicity," *Semin Liver Dis*, 1990, 10(4):235-50.

DESENSITIZATION PROTOCOLS

PENICILLIN DESENSITIZATION PROTOCOL: MUST BE DONE BY PHYSICIAN!

Acute penicillin desensitization should only be performed in an intensive care setting. Any remedial risk factor should be corrected. All β-adrenergic antagonists such as propranolol or even timolol ophthalmic drops should be discontinued. Asthmatic patients should be under optimal control. An intravenous line should be established, baseline electrocardiogram (EKG) and spirometry should be performed, and continuous EKG monitoring should be instituted. Premedication with antihistamines or steroids is not recommended, as these drugs have not proven effective in suppressing severe reactions but may mask early signs of reactivity that would otherwise result in a modification of the protocol.

Protocols have been developed for penicillin desensitization using both the oral and parenteral route. As of 1987 there were 93 reported cases of oral desensitization, 74 of which were done by Sullivan and his collaborators. Of these 74 patients, 32% experienced a transient allergic reaction either during desensitization (one-third) or during penicillin treatment after desensitization (two-thirds). These reactions were usually mild and self-limited in nature. Only one IgE-mediated reaction (wheezing and bronchospasm) required discontinuation of the procedure before desensitization could be completed. It has been argued that oral desensitization may be safer than parenteral desensitization, but most patients can also be safely desensitized by parenteral route.

During desensitization any dose that causes mild systemic reactions such as pruritus, fleeting urticaria, rhinitis, or mild wheezing should be repeated until the patient tolerates the dose without systemic symptoms or signs. More serious reactions such as hypotension, laryngeal edema, or asthma require appropriate treatment, and if desensitization is continued, the dose should be decreased by at least 10-fold and withheld until the patient is stable.

Once desensitized, the patient's treatment with penicillin must not lapse or the risk of an allergic reaction increases. If the patient requires a β-lactam antibiotic in the future and still remains skin test-positive to penicillin reagents, desensitization would be required again.

Several patients have been maintained on long-term, low-dose penicillin therapy (usually bid-tid) to sustain a chronic state of desensitization. Such individuals usually require chronic desensitization because of continuous occupationally related exposure to β-lactam drugs.

Order for placement/availability at the bedside in the event of a hypersensitivity reaction during scratch/skin testing and desensitization:

Hydrocortisone: 100 mg IVP
Diphenhydramine: 50 mg IVP
Epinephrine: 1:1000 S.C.

Several investigators have demonstrated that penicillin can be administered to history positive, skin test positive patients if initially small but gradually increasing doses are given. However, patients with a history of exfoliative dermatitis secondary to penicillin should not be re-exposed to the drug, even by desensitization.

Desensitization is a potentially dangerous procedure and should be only performed in an area where immediate access to emergency drugs and equipment can be assured.

Begin between 8-10 AM in the morning.

Follow desensitization as indicated for penicillin G or ampicillin.

AMPICILLIN
Oral Desensitization Protocol

1. Begin 0.03 mg of ampicillin

2. Double the dose administered every 30 minutes until complete

3. Example of oral dosing regimen:

Dose #	Ampicillin (mg)
1	0.03
2	0.06
3	0.12
4	0.23
5	0.47
6	0.94
7	1.87
8	3.75
9	7.5
10	15
11	30
12	60
13	125
14	250
15	500

DESENSITIZATION PROTOCOLS (Continued)

PENICILLIN G PARENTERAL
Desensitization Protocol: Typical Schedule

Injection No.	Benzylpenicillin Concentration (units/mL)	Volume and Route (mL)*
1†	100	0.1 I.D.
2	↓	0.2 S.C.
3		0.4 S.C.
4		0.8 S.C.
5†	1,000	0.1 I.D.
6	↓	0.3 S.C.
7		0.6 S.C.
8†	10,000	0.1 I.D.
9	↓	0.2 S.C.
10		0.4 S.C.
11		0.8 S.C.
12†	100,000	0.1 I.D.
13	↓	0.3 S.C.
14		0.6 S.C.
15†	1,000,000	0.1 I.D.
16	↓	0.2 S.C.
17		0.2 I.M.
18		0.4 I.M.
19	Continuous I.V. infusion (1,000,000 units/h)	

*Administer progressive doses at intervals of not less than 20 minutes.

†Observe and record skin wheal and flare response to intradermal dose.

Abbreviations: I.D. = intradermal, S.C. = subcutaneous, I.M. = intramuscular, I.V. = intravenous.

PENICILLIN
Oral Desensitization Protocol

Step*	Phenoxymethyl Penicillin (units/mL)	Amount (mL)	Dose (units)	Cumulative Dosage (units)
1	1000	0.1	100	100
2	1000	0.2	200	300
3	1000	0.4	400	700
4	1000	0.8	800	1500
5	1000	1.6	1600	3100
6	1000	3.2	3200	6300
7	1000	6.4	6400	12,700
8	10,000	1.2	12,000	24,700
9	10,000	2.4	24,000	48,700
10	10,000	4.8	48,000	96,700
11	80,000	1	80,000	176,700
12	80,000	2	160,000	336,700
13	80,000	4	320,000	656,700
14	80,000	8	640,000	1,296,700
	Observe patient for 30 minutes			
Change to benzylpenicillin G I.V.				
15	500,000	0.25	125,000	
16	500,000	0.50	250,000	
17	500,000	1	500,000	
18	500,000	2.25	1,125,000	

*Interval between steps, 15 min

ALLOPURINOL
Successful Desensitization for Treatment of a Fixed Drug Eruption

	Oral Dose of Allopurinol
Days 1-3	50 mcg/day
Days 4-6	100 mcg/day
Days 7-9	200 mcg/day
Days 10-12	500 mcg/day
Days 13-15	1 mg/day
Days 16-18	5 mg/day
Days 19-21	10 mg/day
Days 22-24	25 mg/day
Days 25-27	50 mg/day
Day 28	100 mg/day

Prednisone 10 mg/day through desensitization and 1 month after reaching dose of 100 mg allopurinol

Modified from J Allergy Clin Immunol, 1996, 97:1171-2.

AMPHOTERICIN B

Challenge and Desensitization Protocol

1. Procedure supervised by physician

2. Epinephrine, 1:1000 wt/vol, multidose vial at bedside

3. Premixed albuterol solution at bedside for nebulization

4. Endotracheal intubation supplies at bedside with anesthesiologist on standby

5. Continuous cardiac telemetry with electronic monitoring of blood pressure

6. Continuous pulse oximetry

7. Premedication with methylprednisolone, 60 mg, I.V. and diphenhydramine, 25 mg I.V.

8. Amphotericin B (Fungizone®)* administration schedule

   a. 10^{-6} dilution, infused over 10 minutes

   b. 10^{-5} dilution, infused over 10 minutes

   c. 10^{-4} dilution, infused over 10 minutes

   d. 10^{-3} dilution, infused over 10 minutes

   e. 10^{-2} dilution, infused over 10 minutes

   f. 10^{-1} dilution (1 mg), infused over 30 minutes

   g. 30 mg in 250 mL 5% dextrose, infused over 4 hours

From Kemp SF and Lockey RF, "Amphotericin B: Emergency Challenge in a Neutropenic, Asthmatic Patient With Fungal Sepsis," *J Allergy Clin Immunol*, 1995, 96(3):425-7.

*Mixtures were prepared in 10 mL 5% dextrose by hospital intensive care unit pharmacy, unless otherwise noted.

BACTRIM™ ORAL DESENSITIZATION PROTOCOL

(Adapted from Gluckstein D and Ruskin J, "Rapid Oral Desensitization to Trimethoprim-Sulfamethoxazole (TMP-SMZ): Use in Prophylaxis for *Pneumocystis carinii* Pneumonia in Patients With AIDS Who Were Previously Intolerant to TMP-SMZ," *Clin Infect Dis*, 1995, 20:849-53.)

Please read the directions carefully before starting the protocol!

1. There must be a clear cut need for a sulfa drug or a sulfa drug combination product such as Bactrim™. The decision to use sulfa must be made prior to skin testing.

2. Informed consent from the patient or an appropriate relative must have been obtained.

3. A trained individual, physician, nurse, or aide, **must be with the patient** at all times.

4. A physician **must** be on the floor at all times.

5. Injectable epinephrine 0.3 mL 1:1000, diphenhydramine (Benadryl®) 50 mg, corticosteroids and oral ibuprofen 400 mg solution should be drawn up and available at the bedside.

6. Appropriate resuscitative equipment must be available.

7. All dilution of oral Bactrim™ should be made up prior to beginning procedure.

8. Patient should drink 180 mL of water after each Bactrim™ dose.

Dilution for Bactrim™ Desensitization

Final Concentration	Bottle #	Procedure
Oral Bactrim™ 40/200 mg/5 mL	A	Conventional oral Bactrim™ suspension 5 mL = 40/200 mg
Oral Bactrim™ 0.4/2 mg/mL	B	1. Add 5 mL conventional oral Bactrim™ suspension or A (concentration = 40/200 mg/5 mL) to 95 mL of sterile water 2. Shake well. This will give 100 mL of 40/200 mg Bactrim™; each mL = 0.4/2 mg Bactrim™. 3. Dispense 20 mL for use
Oral Bactrim™ 0.004/0.02 mg/mL	C	1. Add 1 mL of the 0.4/2 mg/mL Bactrim™ or B to 99 mL of sterile water 2. Shake well. This will give 100 mL of 0.4/2 mg Bactrim™; each mL = 0.004/0.02 mg Bactrim™. 3. Dispense 20 mL for use

Adverse Reactions and Response During the Protocol

Types of Reactions	Alteration of Protocol
Mild reactions (rash, fever, nausea)	I.V. diphenhydramine (Benadryl®) 50 mg and oral ibuprofen suspension 400 mg
Urticaria, dyspnea, severe vomiting, or hypotension	**STOP** the protocol IMMEDIATELY

• If patient tolerates up to Bactrim™ DS, he/she is desensitized.

• Assuming that there was no complications, the procedure will take up to 6 hours.

DESENSITIZATION PROTOCOLS *(Continued)*

Sample Bactrim™ Desensitization Flow Sheet

Patient Name _____ Age _____ Gender _____ Physician _____ Pager _____ Hospital # _____

Diagnosis _____ History of sulfa reaction _____

# Hour	Actual Time	Suggested Dose	Form	Suggested Volume	Actual Dose	Form	Actual Volume	Reaction/Notes	Initial
0		Bactrim™ 0.004/0.02 mg (use **0.004/0.02 mg/mL** bottle or bottle C)	Susp (C)	1 mL					
1		Bactrim™ 0.04/0.2 mg (use 0.004/0.02 mg/mL bottle or bottle C)	Susp (C)	10 mL					
2		Bactrim™ 0.4/2 mg (use **0.4/2 mg/mL bottle** or bottle B)	Susp (B)	1 mL					
3		Bactrim™ 4/20 mg (use 0.4/2 mg/mL bottle or bottle B)	Susp (B)	10 mL					
4		Bactrim™ 40/200 mg (use **40/200 mg/5 mL unit dose** Bactrim™ or A)	Susp (A)	5 mL					
5		Bactrim™ 80/400 mg (use 40/200 mg/5 mL unit dose Bactrim™ or A)	Susp (A)	10 mL					
6		Bactrim™ DS tablet	Tablet	1 DS pill					

Note: Drink 180 mL of water after each Bactrim™ dose.

CIPROFLOXACIN

Modified from *J Allergy Clin Immunol*, 1996, 97:1426-7.

Premedicated with diphenhydramine hydrochloride, ranitidine, and prednisone 1 hour before the desensitization.

The individual doses were administered at 15-minute intervals. Because the patient was intubated in the intensive care unit, vital signs were continually monitored. The patient's skin was inspected for development of urticaria, and his chest was auscultated for wheezing every 10 minutes. No rash, hypotension, or wheezing developed during desensitization. The procedure took 4 hours, and once finished, the patient had received an equivalent to his first scheduled dose (400 mg twice daily). The second dose was given 4 hours later, followed by routine administration of 400 mg every 12 hours, with a small dose (25 mg intravenously) between therapeutic doses to maintain a drug level in the blood. The patient subsequently received 4 weeks of ciprofloxacin treatment without difficulty.

Desensitization Regimen for Ciprofloxacin

Ciprofloxacin Concentration (mg/mL)	Volume Given (mL)	Absolute Amount (mg)	Cumulative Total Dose (mg)
0.1	0.1	0.01	0.01
0.1	0.2	0.02	0.03
0.1	0.4	0.04	0.07
0.1	0.8	0.08	0.15
1	0.16	0.16	0.31
1	0.32	0.32	0.63
1	0.64	0.64	1.27
2	0.6	1.2	2.47
2	1.2	2.4	4.87
2	2.4	4.8	9.67
2	5	10	19.67
2	10	20	39.67
2	20	40	79.67
2	40	80	159.67
2	120	240	399.67

Drug volumes <1 mL were mixed with normal saline solution to a final volume of 3 mL and then slowly infused; the other doses were administered over 10 minutes, except the last dose (240 mg in 120 mL), which was given with an infusion pump over 20 minutes.

DESENSITIZATION PROTOCOLS *(Continued)*

INSULIN

Lilly's appropriate diluting fluid, sterile saline, or distilled water, to which 1 mL of the patient's blood or the addition of 1 mL of 1% serum albumin (making a 0.1% solution) for each 10 mL of stock diluent, is a satisfactory diluent. The albumin in the blood or serum albumin solution is necessary to retain the integrity of the higher dilutions by preventing adsorption to glass or plastic. Dilution is stable 30 days under refrigeration or room temperature, but should be used within 24 hours due to a lack of preservative.

1. Make a 1:1 dilution of single species (beef, pork, or human) insulin (50 units/mL).

2. Add 0.5 mL of the above dilution to 4.5 mL of diluent (5 units/mL).

3. Add 0.5 mL of the 5 units/mL dilution to 4.5 mL of diluent (0.5 unit/mL).

4. Add 0.5 mL of the 0.5 unit/mL dilution to 4.5 mL of diluent (0.05 unit/mL).

5. Add 0.5 mL of the 0.05 unit/mL dilution to 4.5 mL of diluent (0.005 unit/mL).

The 5 vials containing 50, 5, 0.5, 0.05, and 0.005 units/mL are ready for skin testing or desensitization procedures.

One may start desensitization by giving 0.02 mL of 0.05 unit/mL concentration (1/1000 unit) intradermally. If no reaction occurs, administer 0.04 and 0.08 mL of the same concentration at 30-minute intervals.

The procedure continues proceeding to the next greater concentration (0.5 unit/mL) and giving 0.02, 0.04, and 0.08 mL at 30-minute intervals.

In the same manner proceed through the 5 units/mL and 50 units/mL concentrations with the exception that these injections should be given subcutaneously.

Note: If a reaction is noted, back up 2 steps and try to proceed forward again.

If the patient reacts to the initial injection, it will be necessary to utilize the lower concentration (0.005 units/mL) to initiate the procedure.

It is essential that manifestations of allergic reactions not be obscured. Therefore, antihistamines or steroids should not be used during desensitization except to treat severe allergic reactions. The use of these agents may obscure mild to moderate reactions to the lower doses and result in more severe reactions as doses increase, leading to failure of the desensitization program.

RIFAMPIN and ETHAMBUTOL
Oral Desensitization in Mycobacterial Disease

Time from Start (h:min)	Rifampin (mg)	Ethambutol (mg)
0	0.1	0.1
00:45	0.5	0.5
01:30	1	1
02:15	2	2
03:00	4	4
03:45	8	8
04:30	16	16
05:15	32	32
06:00	50	50
06:45	100	100
07:30	150	200
11:00	300	400
Next day		
6:30 AM	300 twice daily	400 three times/day

From *Am J Respir Crit Care Med*, 1994, 149:815-7.

SKIN TESTS

Delayed Hypersensitivity (Anergy)

Delayed cutaneous hypersensitivity (DCH) is a cell-mediated immunological response which has been used diagnostically to assess previous infection (eg, purified protein derivative (PPD), histoplasmin, and coccidioidin) or as an indicator of the status of the immune system by using mumps, *Candida*, tetanus toxoid, or trichophyton to test for anergy. Anergy is a defect in cell-mediated immunity that is characterized by an impaired response, or lack of a response to DCH testing with injected antigens. Anergy has been associated with several disease states, malnutrition, and immunosuppressive therapy, and has been correlated with increased risk of infection, morbidity, and mortality.

Many of the skin test antigens have not been approved by the FDA as tests for anergy, and so the directions for use and interpretation of reactions to these products may differ from that of the product labeling. There is also disagreement in the published literature as to the selection and interpretation of these tests for anergy assessment, leading to different recommendations for use of these products.

General Guidelines

Read these guidelines before using any skin test.

Administration

1. Use a separate sterile TB syringe for each antigen. Immediately after the antigen is drawn up, make the injection intradermally in the flexor surface of the forearm.
2. A small bleb 6-10 mm in diameter will form if the injection is made at the correct depth. If a bleb does not form or if the antigen solution leaks from the site, the injection must be repeated.
3. When applying more than one skin test, make the injections at least 5 cm apart.
4. Do any serologic blood tests before testing or wait 48-96 hours.

Reading

1. Read all tests at 24, 48, and 72 hours. Reactions occurring before 24 hours are indicative of an immediate rather than a delayed hypersensitivity.
2. Measure the diameter of the induration in two directions (at right angles) with a ruler and record each diameter in millimeters. Ballpoint pen method of measurement is the most accurate.
3. Test results should be recorded by the nurse in the Physician's Progress Notes section of the chart, and should include the millimeters of induration present, and a picture of the arm showing the location of the test(s).

Factors Causing False-Negative Reactions

1. Improper administration, interpretation, or use of outdated antigen
2. Test is applied too soon after exposure to the antigen (DCH takes 2-20 weeks to develop.)
3. Concurrent viral illnesses (eg, rubeola, influenza, mumps, and probably others) or recent administration of live attenuated virus vaccines (eg, measles)
4. Anergy may be associated with:
   a. Immune suppressing chronic illnesses such as diabetes, uremia, sarcoidosis, metastatic carcinomas, Hodgkin's, acute lymphocytic leukemia, hypothyroidism, chronic hepatitis, and cirrhosis.
   b. Some antineoplastic agents, radiation therapy, and corticosteroids. If possible, discontinue steroids at least 48 hours prior to DCH skin testing.
   c. Congenital immune deficiencies.
   d. Malnutrition, shock, severe burns, and trauma.
   e. Severe disseminated infections (miliary or cavitary TB, cocci granuloma, and other disseminated mycotic infections, gram-negative bacillary septicemia).
   f. Leukocytosis (>15,000 cells/mm^3).

Factors Causing False-Positive Reactions

1. Improper interpretation
2. Patient sensitivity to minor ingredients in the antigen solutions such as the phenol or thimerosal preservatives
3. Cross-reactions between similar antigens

Candida 1:1000

Dose = 0.1 mL intradermally (30% of children <18 months of age and 50% >18 months of age respond)
Can be used as a control antigen

Coccidioidin 1:1000

Dose = 0.1 mL intradermally (apply with PPD **and** a control antigen)
Mercury derivative used as a preservative for spherulin.

Histoplasmin 1:1000

Dose = 0.1 mL intradermally (yeast derived)

Multitest CMI (**candida, diphtheria toxoid, tetanus toxoid, *Streptococcus*, old tuberculin, *Trichophyton*, *Proteus* antigen, and negative control**)

Press loaded unit into the skin with sufficient pressure to puncture the skin and allow adequate penetration of all points.

Mumps 40 cfu per mL

Dose = 0.1 mL intradermally (contraindicated in patients allergic to eggs, egg products, or thimerosal)

SKIN TESTS (Continued)

Dosage as Part of Disease Diagnosis

Tuberculin Testing

Purified Protein Derivative (PPD)

Preparation	Dilution	Units/0.1 mL
First strength	1:10,000	1
Intermediate strength	1:2000	5
Second strength	1:100	250

The usual initial dose is 0.1 mL of the intermediate strength. The first strength should be used in the individuals suspected of being highly sensitive. The second strength is used only for individuals who fail to respond to a previous injection of the first or intermediate strengths.

A positive reaction is 10 mm induration or greater except in HIV-infected individuals where a positive reaction is 5 mm or greater of induration.

Adverse Reactions

In patients who are highly sensitive, or when higher than recommended doses are used, exaggerated local reactions may occur, including erythema, pain, blisters, necrosis, and scarring. Although systemic reactions are rare, a few cases of lymph node enlargement, fever, malaise, and fatigue have been reported.

To prevent severe local reactions, never use second test strengths as the initial agent. Use diluted first strengths in patients with known or suspected hypersensitivity to the antigen.

Have epinephrine and antihistamines on hand to treat severe allergic reactions that may occur.

Treatment of Adverse Reactions

Severe reactions to intradermal skin tests are rare and treatment consists of symptomatic care.

Skin Testing

All skin tests are given intradermally into the flexor surface of one arm.

Purified protein derivative (PPD) is used most often in the diagnosis of tuberculosis. *Candida, Trichophyton*, and mumps skin tests are used most often as controls for anergy.

Dose: The usual skin test dose is as follows:

Antigen		Standard Dose	Concentration
PPD	1 TU	0.1 mL	1 TU — highly sensitive patients
	5 TU	0.1 mL	5 TU — standard dose
	250 TU	0.1 mL	250 TU — anergic patients in whom TB is suspected
Candida		0.02 mL	
Histoplasmin		0.1 mL	Seldom used. Serology is preferred method to diagnose histoplasmosis.
Mumps		0.1 mL	
Trichophyton		0.02 mL	

Interpretation:

Skin Test	Reading Time	Positive Reaction
PPD	48-72 h	**≥5 mm considered positive for:** • close contacts to an infectious case • persons with abnormal chest x-ray indicating old healed TB • persons with known or suspected HIV infection **≥10 mm considered positive for:** • other medical risk factors • foreign born from high prevalence areas • medically underserved, low income populations • alcoholics and intravenous drug users • residents of long-term care facilities (including correctional facilities and nursing homes) • staff in settings where disease would pose a hazard to large number of susceptible persons **≥15 mm considered positive for:** • persons without risk factors for TB
Candida	24-72 h	5 mm induration or greater
Histoplasmin	24-72 h	5 mm or greater
Mumps	24-36 h	5 mm or greater
Trichophyton	24-72 h	5 mm induration or greater

Recommended Interpretation of Skin Test Reactions

Reaction	Local Reaction	
	After Intradermal Injections of Antigens	**After Dinitrochlorobenzene**
1+	Erythema >10 mm and/or induration >1-5 mm	Erythema and/or induration covering <½ area of dose site
2+	Induration 6-10 mm	Induration covering >½ area of dose site
3+	Induration 11-20 mm	Vesiculation and induration at dose site or spontaneous flare at days 7-14 at the site
4+	Induration >20 mm	Bulla or ulceration at dose site or spontaneous flare at days 7-14 at the site

Penicillin Allergy

The recommended battery of major and minor determinants used in penicillin skin testing will disclose those individuals with circulating IgE antibodies. This procedure is therefore useful to identify patients at risk for immediate or accelerated reactions. Skin tests are of no value in predicting the occurrence of non-IgE-mediated hypersensitivity reactions to penicillin such as delayed exanthem, drug fever, hemolytic anemia, interstitial nephritis, or exfoliative dermatitis. Based on large scale trials, skin testing solutions have been standardized.

Antihistamines, tricyclic antidepressants, and adrenergic drugs, all of which may inhibit skin test results, should be discontinued at least 24 hours prior to skin testing. Antihistamines with long half-lives (hydroxyzine, terfenadine, astemizole, etc) may attenuate skin test results up to a week, or longer after discontinuation.

When properly performed with due consideration for preliminary scratch tests and appropriate dilutions, skin testing with penicillin reagents can almost always be safely accomplished. Systemic reactions accompany about 1% of positive skin tests; these are usually mild but can be serious. **Therefore skin tests should be done in the presence of a physician and with immediate access to medications and equipment needed to treat anaphylaxis.**

SKIN TESTS *(Continued)*

History of Penicillin Allergy

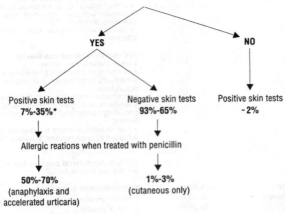

YES

NO

Positive skin tests
7%-35%*

Negative skin tests
93%-65%

Positive skin tests
~ 2%

Allergic reations when treated with penicillin

50%-70%
(anaphylaxis and
accelerated urticaria)

1%-3%
(cutaneous only)

*One study found 65% positive

Prevalence of positive and negative skin tests and subsequent allergic
reactions in patients treated with penicillin (based on studies using both
penicilloyl-polylysine and minor determinant mixture as skin test reagents).

Penicillin Skin Testing Protocol

Skin tests evaluate the patient for the presence of penicillin IgE — sensitive mast cells
which are responsible for anaphylaxis and other immediate hypersensitivity reactions.
Local or systemic allergic reactions rarely occur due to skin testing, therefore, a tourniquet,
I.V., and epinephrine should be at the bedside. The breakdown products of penicillin
provide the antigen which is responsible for the allergy. Testing is performed with
benzylpenicilloyl-polylysine (Pre-Pen®), the major determinant, penicillin G which provides
the minor determinants and the actual penicillin which will be administered.

Controls are important if the patient is extremely ill or is taking antihistamines, codeine, or
morphine. Normal saline is the negative control. Morphine sulfate, a mast cell degranu-
lator, can be used as a positive control, if the patient is not on morphine or codeine.
Histamine is the preferred positive control, however, is not manufactured in a pharmaceutical formulation anymore. A false-positive or false-negative will make further skin testing
invalid.

Control Solutions

Normal saline = negative control
Morphine sulfate (10 mg/100 mL 0.9% NaCl, 0.1 mg/mL) = positive control

Test Solutions

Order the necessary solutions as 0.5 mL in a tuberculin syringe. **Note:** May need to order
2 syringes of each — one for scratch testing and one for intradermal skin testing.

I. **Pre-Pen®: Benzylpenicilloyl-polylysine (0.25 mL ampul) = MAJOR DETERMI-
NANT**

    A. Undiluted Pre-Pen®

    B. 1:100 concentration
       To make: Dilute 0.1 mL of Pre-Pen® in 10 mL of 0.9% NaCl

    C. 1:10,000 concentration
       (Only necessary in patients with a history of anaphylaxis)
       To make: Dilute 1 mL of the 1:100 solution in 100 mL of 0.9% NaCl

II. **Penicillin G sodium/potassium = MINOR DETERMINANT**

    A. 5000 units/mL concentration

    B. 5 units/mL concentration
       (Only necessary in patients with a history of anaphylaxis)
       To make: Dilute 0.1 mL of a 5000 units/mL solution in 100 mL of 0.9% NaCl

III. **Penicillin product to be administered — if not penicillin G**

    A. **Ampicillin** 2.5 mg/mL concentration
       To make: Dilute 250 mg in 100 mL of 0.9% NaCl

    B. **Nafcillin** 2.5 mg/mL concentration
       To make: Dilute 250 mg in 100 mL of 0.9% NaCl

Order for placement/availability at the bedside in the event of a hypersensitivity reaction during scratch/skin testing and desensitization:

Hydrocortisone: 100 mg IVP
Diphenhydramine: 50 mg IVP
Epinephrine: 1:1000 S.C.

Scratch/Skin Testing Protocol: Must Be Done by Physician!

1. Begin with the control solutions (ie, normal saline and morphine).

2. Administer **scratch tests** in the following order (beginning with the most dilute solution):

Pre-Pen®	Syringes: C,B,A
Penicillin G	Syringes: E,D
Ampicillin/Nafcillin	Syringe: F

The inner volar surface of the forearm is usually used.

A nonbleeding scratch of 3-5 mm in length is made in the epidermis with a 20-gauge needle.

If bleeding occurs, another site should be selected and another scratch made using less pressure.

A small drop of the test solution is then applied and rubbed gently into the scratch using an applicator, toothpick, or the side of the needle.

The scratch test site should be observed for the appearance of a wheal, erythema, and pruritis.

A positive reaction is signified by the appearance within 15 minutes of a pale wheal (usually with pseudopods) ranging from 5-15 mm or more in diameter.

As soon as a positive response is elicited, or 15 minutes has elapsed, the solution should be wiped off the scratch.

If the scratch test is negative or equivocal (ie, a wheal of <5 mm in diameter with little or no erythema or itching appears), an intradermal test may be performed.

If significant reaction, treat and proceed to desensitization.

3. Administer **intradermal tests** in the following order (beginning with the most dilute solution):

Pre-Pen®	Syringes: C,B,A
Penicillin G	Syringes: E,D
Ampicillin/Nafcillin	Syringe: F

Intradermal tests are usually performed on a sterilized area of the upper outer arm at a sufficient distance below the deltoid muscle to permit proximal application of a tourniquet if a severe reaction occurs.

Using a tuberculin syringe with a $3/8$-$5/8$ inch 26- to 30-gauge needle, an amount of each test solution sufficient to raise the smallest perceptible bleb (usually 0.01-0.02 mL) is injected immediately under the surface of the skin.

A separate needle and syringe must be used for each solution.

Each test and control site should be at least 15 cm apart.

Positive reactions are manifested as a wheal at the test site with a diameter at least 5 mm larger than the saline control, often accompanied by itching and a marked increase in the size of the bleb.

Skin responses to penicillin testing will develop within 15 minutes.

If no significant reaction, may challenge patient with reduced dosage of the penicillin to be administered.

Physician should be at the bedside during this challenge dose!

If significant reaction, treat and begin desensitization.

IMMUNIZATION RECOMMENDATIONS

Standards for Pediatric Immunization Practices

Standard 1.	Immunization services are readily available.
Standard 2.	There are no barriers or unnecessary prerequisites to the receipt of vaccines.
Standard 3.	Immunization services are available free or for a minimal fee.
Standard 4.	Providers utilize all clinical encounters to screen and, when indicated, immunize children.
Standard 5.	Providers educate parents and guardians about immunizations in general terms.
Standard 6.	Providers question parents or guardians about contraindications and, before immunizing a child, inform them in specific terms about the risks and benefits of the immunizations their child is to receive.
Standard 7.	Providers follow only true contraindications.
Standard 8.	Providers administer simultaneously all vaccine doses for which a child is eligible at the time of each visit.
Standard 9.	Providers use accurate and complete recording procedures.
Standard 10.	Providers co-schedule immunization appointments in conjunction with appointments for other child health services.
Standard 11.	Providers report adverse events following immunization promptly, accurately, and completely.
Standard 12.	Providers operate a tracking system.
Standard 13.	Providers adhere to appropriate procedures for vaccine management.
Standard 14.	Providers conduct semiannual audits to assess immunization coverage levels and to review immunization records in the patient populations they serve.
Standard 15.	Providers maintain up-to-date, easily retrievable medical protocols at all locations where vaccines are administered.
Standard 16.	Providers operate with patient-oriented and community-based approaches.
Standard 17.	Vaccines are administered by properly trained individuals.
Standard 18.	Providers receive ongoing education and training on current immunization recommendations.

Recommended by the National Vaccine Advisory Committee, April 1992.

Approved by the United States Public Health Service, May 1992.

Endorsed by the American Academy of Pediatrics, May 1992.

The Standards represent the consensus of the National Vaccine Advisory Committee (NVAC) and of a broad group of medical and public health experts about what constitutes the most desirable immunization practices. It is recognized by the NVAC that not all of the current immunization practices of public and private providers are in compliance with the Standards. Nevertheless, the Standards are expected to be useful as a means of helping providers to identify needed changes, to obtain resources if necessary, and to actually implement the desirable immunization practices in the future.

Recommended Childhood Immunization Schedule
United States, January - December 1999

Vaccines [1] are listed under the routinely recommended ages. [Bars] indicate range of recommended ages for immunization. Any dose not given at the recommended age should be given as a "catch up" immunization at any subsequent visit when indicated and feasible.

(Ovals) indicate vaccines to be given if previously recommended doses were missed or given earlier than the recommended minimum age.

Age ► Vaccine ▼	Birth	1 mo	2 mo	4 mo	6 mo	12 mo	15 mo	18 mo	4-6 y	11-12 y	14-16 y
Hepatitis B [2]	Hep B	Hep B			Hep B					(Hep B)	
Diphtheria, Tetanus, Pertussis [3]			DTaP	DTaP	DTaP		DTaP[3]		DTaP	Td	
H. influenzae type b [4]			Hib	Hib	Hib	Hib					
Polio [5]			IPV	IPV	Polio[5]				Polio		
Rotavirus [6]			Rv[6]	Rv[6]	Rv[6]						
Measles, Mumps, Rubella [7]						MMR			MMR[7]	(MMR[7])	
Varicella [8]						Var				Var[8]	

[1] This schedule indicates the recommended ages for routine administration of currently licensed childhood vaccines. Combination vaccines may be used whenever any components of the combination are indicated and its other components are not contraindicated. Providers should consult the manufacturers' package inserts for detailed recommendations.

[2] Infants born to HBsAg-negative mothers should receive the 2nd dose of hepatitis B vaccine at least 1 month after the 1st dose. The 3rd dose should be administered at least 4 months after the 1st dose and at least 2 months after the 2nd dose, but not before 6 months of age for infants.

Infants born to HBsAg-positive mothers should receive hepatitis B vaccine and 0.5 mL hepatitis B immune globulin (HBIG) within 12 hours of birth at separate sites. The 2nd dose is recommended at 1-2 months of age and the 3rd dose at 6 months of age.

Infants born to mothers whose HBsAg status is unknown should receive hepatitis B vaccine within 12 hours of birth. Maternal blood should be drawn at the time of delivery to determine the mother's HBsAg status; if the HBsAg test is positive, the infant should receive HBIG as soon as possible (no later than 1 week of age).

All children and adolescents (through 18 years of age) who have not been immunized against hepatitis B may begin the series during any visit. Special efforts should be made to immunize children who were born in or whose parents were born in areas of the world with moderate or high endemicity of HBV infection.

[3] DTaP (diphtheria and tetanus toxoids and acellular pertussis vaccine) is the preferred vaccine for all doses in the immunization series, including completion of the series in children who have received 1 or more doses of whole-cell DTP vaccine. Whole-cell DTP is an acceptable alternative to DTaP. The 4th dose (DTP or DTaP) may be administered as early as 12 months of age, provided 6 months have elapsed since the 3rd dose and if the child is unlikely to return at age 15-18 months. Td (tetanus and diphtheria toxoids) is recommended at 11-12 years of age if at least 5 years have elapsed since the last dose of DTP, DTaP, or DT. Subsequent routine Td boosters are recommended every 10 years.

[4] Three H. influenzae type b (Hib) conjugate vaccines are licensed for infant use. If PRP-OMP (PedvaxHIB and COMVAX [Merck]) is administered at ages 2 and 4 months, a dose at 6 months is not required. Because clinical studies in infants have demonstrated that using some combination products may induce a lower immune response to the Hib vaccine component, DTaP/Hib combination products should not be used for primary immunization in infants at 2, 4, or 6 months of age, unless FDA-approved for these ages.

[5] Two poliovirus vaccines currently are licensed in the United States: Inactivated poliovirus vaccine (IPV) and oral poliovirus vaccine (OPV). The ACIP, AAP, and AAFP now recommend that the first two doses of poliovirus vaccine should be IPV. The ACIP continues to recommend a sequential schedule of two doses of IPV administered at ages 2 and 4 months, followed by two doses of OPV at 12-18 months and 4-6 years. Use of IPV for all doses also is acceptable and is recommended for immunocompromised persons and their household contacts. OPV is no longer recommended for the first two doses of the schedule and is acceptable only for special circumstances such as: Children of parents who do not accept the recommended number of injections, late initiation of immunization which would require an unacceptable number of injections, and imminent travel to polio-endemic areas. OPV remains the vaccine of choice for mass immunization campaigns to control outbreaks due to wild poliovirus.

[6] Rotavirus vaccine (Rv) is italicized to indicate: 1) Health care providers may require time and resources to incorporate this new vaccine into practice; and 2) the AAFP feels that the decision to use rotavirus vaccine should be made by the parent or guardian in consultation with their physician or other health care provider. The first dose of Rv vaccine should not be administered before 6 weeks of age, and the minimum interval between doses is 3 weeks. The Rv vaccine series should not be initiated at 7 months of age or older, and all doses should be completed by the first birthday.

[7] The 2nd dose of measles, mumps, and rubella vaccine (MMR) is recommended routinely at 4-6 years of age but may be administered during any visit, provided at least 4 weeks have elapsed since receipt of the 1st dose and that both doses are administered beginning at or after 12 months of age. Those who have not previously received the second dose should complete the schedule by the 11- to 12-year-old visit.

[8] Varicella vaccine is recommended at any visit on or after the first birthday for susceptible children, ie, those who lack a reliable history of chickenpox (as judged by a health care provider) and who have not been immunized. Susceptible persons 13 years of age or older should receive 2 doses, given at least 4 weeks apart.

Adapted from Advisory Committee on Immunization Practices (ACIP), the American Academy of Pediatrics (AAP), and the American Academy of Family Physicians (AAFP).

IMMUNIZATION RECOMMENDATIONS *(Continued)*

RECOMMENDATIONS OF THE ADVISORY COMMITTEE ON IMMUNIZATION PRACTICES (ACIP)

Recommended Poliovirus Vaccination Schedules for Children

Vaccine	Child's Age			
	2 mo	4 mo	12-18 mo	4-6 y
Sequential IPV*/OPV*/ OPV†	IPV	IPV	OPV	OPV
OPV*	OPV	OPV	OPV‡	OPV
IPV†	IPV	IPV	IPV	OPV

*Inactivated poliovirus vaccine.

†Live, oral poliovirus vaccine.

‡For children who receive only OPV, the third dose of OPV may be administered as early as 6 months of age.

Adapted from *MMWR Morb Mortal Wkly Rep*, "Poliomyelitis Prevention in the United States: Introduction of a Sequential Vaccination Schedule of Inactivated Poliovirus Vaccine Followed by Oral Poliovirus Vaccine" 1997, 46(RR-3).

Recommendations for Measles Vaccination*

Category	Recommendations
Unvaccinated, no history of measles (12-15 mo)	A 2-dose schedule (with MMR) is recommended if born after 1956. The first dose is recommended at 12-15 mo; the second is recommended at 4-6 y
Children 12 mo in areas of recurrent measles transmission	Vaccinate; a second dose is indicated at 4-6 y (at school entry)
Children 6-11 mo in epidemic situations†	Vaccinate (with monovalent measles vaccine or, if not available, MMR); revaccination (with MMR) at 12-15 mo is necessary and a third dose is indicated at 4-6 y
Children 11-12 y who have received 1 dose of measles vaccine at ≥12 mo	Revaccinate (1 dose)
Students in college and other posthigh school institutions who have received 1 dose of measles vaccine at ≥12 mo	Revaccinate (1 dose)
History of vaccination before the first birthday	Consider susceptible and vaccinate (2 doses)
Unknown vaccine, 1963-1967	Consider susceptible and vaccinate (2 doses)
Further attenuated or unknown vaccine given with IG	Consider susceptible and vaccinate (2 doses)
Egg allergy	Vaccinate; no reactions likely
Neomycin allergy, nonanaphylactic	Vaccinate; no reactions likely
Tuberculosis	Vaccinate; vaccine does not exacerbate infection
Measles exposure	Vaccinate or give IG, depending on circumstances
HIV-infected	Vaccinate (2 doses) unless severely compromised
Immunoglobulin or blood product received	Vaccinate at the appropriate interval

*See text for details. MMR indicates measles-mumps-rubella vaccine; IG, immune globulin.

†See Outbreak Control.

Adapted from "Report of the Committee on Infectious Diseases," *1997 Red Book*, 24th ed.

Recommended Immunization Schedules for Children Not Immunized in the First Year of Life*

Recommended Time/Age	Immunization(s)[1,2,3]	Comments
Younger Than 7 Years		
First visit	DTaP (or DTP), Hib, HBV, MMR, OPV[3]	If indicated, tuberculin testing may be done at same visit. If child is ≥5 y of age, Hib is not indicated in most circumstances.
Interval after first visit		
1 mo (4 wk)	DTaP (or DTP), HBV, Var[4]	The second dose of OPV may be given if accelerated poliomyelitis vaccination is necessary, such as for travelers to areas where polio is endemic.
2 mo	DTaP (or DTP), Hib, OPV[3]	Second dose of Hib is indicated only if the first dose was received when <15 mo.
≥8 mo	DTaP (or DTP), HBV, OPV[3]	OPV and HBV are not given if the third doses were given earlier.
Age 4-6 y (at or before school entry)	DTaP (or DTP), OPV,[3] MMR[5]	DTaP (or DTP) is not necessary if the fourth dose was given after the fourth birthday; OPV is not necessary if the third dose was given after the fourth birthday.
Age 11-12 y	See Childhood Immunization Schedule	
7-12 Years		
First visit	HBV, MMR, Td, OPV[3]	
Interval after first visit		
2 mo (8 wk)	HBV, MMR,[5] Var,[4] Td, OPV[3]	OPV also may be given 1 mo after the first visit if accelerated poliomyelitis vaccination is necessary.
8-14 mo	HBV,[6] Td, OPV[3]	OPV is not given if the third dose was given earlier.
Age 11-12 y	See Childhood Immunization Schedule	

*Table is not completely consistent with all package inserts. For products used, also consult manufacturer's package insert for instructions on storage, handling, dosage, and administration. Biologics prepared by different manufacturers may vary, and package inserts of the same manufacturer may change from time to time. Therefore, the physician should be aware of the contents of the current package insert.

Vaccine abbreviations: HBV indicates hepatitis B virus vaccine; Var, varicella vaccine; DTP, diphtheria and tetanus toxoids and pertussis vaccine; DTaP, diphtheria and tetanus toxoids and acellular pertussis vaccine; Hib, *Haemophilus influenzae* type b conjugate vaccine; OPV, oral poliovirus vaccine; IPV, inactivated poliovirus vaccine; MMR, live measles-mumps-rubella vaccine; Td, adult tetanus toxoid (full dose) and diphtheria toxoid (reduced dose), for children ≥7 years and adults.

[1] If all needed vaccines cannot be administered simultaneously, priority should be given to protecting the child against those diseases that pose the greatest immediate risk. In the United States, these diseases for children <2 years usually are measles and *Haemophilus influenzae* type b infection; for children >7 years, they are measles, mumps, and rubella. Before 13 years of age, immunity against hepatitis B and varicella should be ensured.

[2] DTaP, HBV, Hib, MMR, and Var can be given simultaneously at separate sites if failure of the patient to return for future immunizations is a concern.

[3] IPV is also acceptable. However, for infants and children starting vaccination late (ie, after 6 months of age), OPV is preferred in order to complete an accelerated schedule with a minimum number of injections.

[4] Varicella vaccine can be administered to susceptible children any time after 12 months of age. Unvaccinated children who lack a reliable history of chickenpox should be vaccinated before their 13th birthday.

[5] Minimal interval between doses of MMR is 1 month (4 weeks).

[6] HBV may be given earlier in a 0-, 2-, and 4-month schedule.

Adapted from "Report of the Committee on Infectious Diseases," *1997 Red Book*®, 24th ed.

IMMUNIZATION RECOMMENDATIONS (Continued)

Minimum Age for Initial Vaccination and Minimum Interval Between Vaccine Doses, by Type of Vaccine

Vaccine	Minimum Age for First Dose*	Minimum Interval From Dose 1 to 2*	Minimum Interval From Dose 2 to 3*	Minimum Interval From Dose 3 to 4*
DTP (DT)†	6 wk‡	4 wk	4 wk	6 mo
Combined DTP-Hib	6 wk	1 mo	1 mo	6 mo
DTaP*	6 wk			6 mo
Hib (primary series)				
HbOC	6 wk	1 mo	1 mo	§
PRP-T	6 wk	1 mo	1 mo	§
PRP-OMP	6 wk	1 mo	§	
OPV			6 wk	
IPV¶	6 wk	4 wk	6 mo#	
MMR	12 mo•	1 mo		
Hepatitis B	Birth	1 mo	2 mo♦	
Varicella-zoster	12 mo	4 wk		

DTP = diphtheria-tetanus-pertussis.

DTaP = diphtheria-tetanus-acellular pertussis.

Hib = *Haemophilus influenzae* type b conjugate.

IPV = inactivated poliovirus vaccine.

MMR = measles-mumps-rubella.

OPV = poliovirus vaccine, live oral, trivalent.

Modified from *MMWR Morb Mortal Wkly Rep*, 1994, 43(RR-1).

*These minimum acceptable ages and intervals may not correspond with the optimal recommended ages and intervals for vaccination. See tables for the current recommended routine and accelerated vaccination schedules.

†DTaP can be used in place of the fourth (and fifth) dose of DTP for children who are at least 15 months of age. Children who have received all four primary vaccination doses before their fourth birthday should receive a fifth dose of DTP (DT) or DTaP at 4-6 years of age before entering kindergarten or elementary school **and** at least 6 months after the fourth dose. The total number of doses of diphtheria and tetanus toxoids should not exceed six each before the seventh birthday.

‡The American Academy of Pediatrics permits DTP to be administered as early as 4 weeks of age in areas with high endemicity and during outbreaks.

§The booster dose of Hib vaccine which is recommended following the primary vaccination series should be administered no earlier than 12 months of age **and** at least 2 months after the previous dose of Hib vaccine.

¶See text to differentiate conventional inactivated poliovirus vaccine from enhanced-potency IPV.

#For unvaccinated adults at increased risk of exposure to poliovirus with <3 months but >2 months available before protection is needed, three doses of IPV should be administered at least 1 month apart.

•Although the age for measles vaccination may be as young as 6 months in outbreak areas where cases are occurring in children <1 year of age, children initially vaccinated before the first birthday should be revaccinated at 12-15 months of age and an additional dose of vaccine should be administered at the time of school entry or according to local policy. Doses of MMR or other measles-containing vaccines should be separated by at least 1 month.

♦This final dose is recommended no earlier than 4 months of age.

Recommended Immunization Schedule For HIV-Infected Children[1]

Age ▶ Vaccine ▼	Birth	1 mo	2 mo	4 mo	6 mo	12 mo	15 mo	18 mo	24 mo	4-6 y	11-12 y	14-16 y
◀ Recommendations for these vaccines are the same as those for immunocompetent children ◀												
Hepatitis B[2]		HepB-1									Hep B[3]	
			Hep B-2			Hep B-3						
Diphtheria, Tetanus, Pertussis[4]			DTaP or DTP	DTaP or DTP	DTaP or DTP		DTaP or DTP[4]			DTaP or DTP	Td	
Haemophilus influenzae type b[5]			Hib	Hib	Hib	Hib						
◀ Recommendations for these vaccines differ from those for immunocompetent children ◀												
Polio[6]			IPV	IPV		IPV				IPV		
Measles, Mumps, Rubella[7]						MMR			MMR			
Influenza[8]						Influenza (a dose is required every year)						
Streptococcus pneumoniae[9]									pneumo-coccal			
Varicella									**CONTRAINDICATED in all HIV-infected persons**			

Note: Modified from the immunization schedule for immunocompetent children. This schedule also applies to children born to HIV-infected mothers whose HIV infection status has not been determined. Once a child is known not to be HIV-infected, the schedule for immunocompetent children applies. This schedule indicates the recommended age for routine administration of currently licensed childhood vaccines. Some combination vaccines are available and may be used whenever administration of all components of the vaccine is indicated. Providers should consult the manufacturers' package inserts for detailed recommendations.

1 Vaccines are listed under the routinely recommended ages. [Bars] indicate range of acceptable ages for vaccination. [Shaded bars] indicate catch-up vaccination: at 11-12 years of age, hepatitis B vaccine should be administered to children not previously vaccinated.

2 **Infants born to HB$_s$Ag-negative mothers** should receive 2.5 mcg of Merch vaccine (Recombivax HB®) or 10 mcg of Smith Kline Beecham (SB) vaccine (Engerix-B®). The 2nd dose should be administered >1 mo after the 1st dose.

Infants born to HB$_s$Ag-positive mothers should receive 0.5 mL of hepatitis B immune globulin (HBIG) within 12 h of birth and either 5 mcg of Merck vaccine (Recombivax HB®) or 10 mcg of SB vaccine (Engerix-B®) at a separate site. The 2nd dose is recommended at 1-2 months of age and the 3rd dose at 6 months of age.

Infants born to mothers whose HB$_s$Ag status is unknown should receive either 5 mcg of Merck vaccine (Recombivax HB®) or 10 mcg of SB vaccine (Engerix-B®) within 12 hours of birth. The 2nd dose of vaccine is recommended at 1 month of age and the 3rd dose at 6 months of age. Blood should be drawn at the time of delivery to determine the mother's HB$_s$Ag status; if it is positive, the infant should receive HBIG as soon as possible (no later than 1 week of age). The dosage and timing of subsequent vaccine doses should be based upon the mother's HB$_s$Ag status.

3 Children and adolescents who have not been vaccinated against hepatitis B in infancy may begin the series during any childhood visit. Those who have not previously received 3 doses of hepatitis B vaccine should initiate or complete the series during the 11- to 12-year old visit. The 2nd dose should be administered at least 1 month after the 1st dose and at least 2 months after the 2nd dose.

4 DTaP (diphtheria and tetanus toxoids and acellular pertusssis vaccine) is the preferred vaccine for all doses in the vaccination series, including completion of the series in children who have received >1 dose of whole-cell DTP vaccine. Whole-cell DTP is an acceptable alternative to DTaP. The 4th dose of DTaP may be administered as early as 12 months of age, provided 6 months have elapsed since the 3rd dose, and if the child is considered unlikely to return at 15-18 months of age. Td (tetanus and diphtheria toxoids, absorbed for adult use) is recommended at 11-12 years of age if at least 5 years have elapsed since the last dose of DTP, DTaP, or DT. Subsequent routine Td boosters are recommended every 10 years.

5 Three *H. influenzae* type b (Hib) conjugate vaccines are licensed for infant use. If PRP-OMP (PedvaxHIB® [Merck]) is administered at 2 and 4 months of age, a dose at 6 months is not required. After the primary series has been completed, any Hib conjugate vaccine may be used as a booster.

6 Inactivated poliovirus vaccine (IPV) is the only polio vaccine recommended for HIV-infected persons and their household contacts. Although the third dose of IPV is generally administered at 12-18 months of age, the 3rd dose of IPV has been approved to be administered as early as 6 months of age. Oral poliovirus vaccine (OPV) should NOT be administered to HIV-infected persons or their household contacts.

7 MMR should not be administered to severely immunocompromised children. HIV-infected children without severe immunosuppression should routinely receive their first dose of MMR as soon as possible upon reaching the first birthday. Consideration should be given to administering the 2nd dose of MMR vaccine as soon as 1 month (ie, minimum 28 days) after the 1st dose, rather than waiting until school entry.

8 Influenza virus vaccine should be administered to all HIV-infected children >6 months of age each year. Children 6 months to 8 years of age who are receiving influenza vaccine for the first time should receive 2 doses of split virus vaccine separated by at least 1 month. In subsequent years, a single dose should be administered each year. The dose of vaccine for children aged 6-35 months is 0.25 mL; the dose for children ≥3 years of age is 0.5 mL.

9 The 23-valent pneumococcal vaccine should be administered to HIV-infected children at 24 months of age. Revaccination should generally be offered to HIV-infected children vaccinated 3-5 years (children ≤10 years of age) or >5 years (children >10 years of age) earlier.

Adapted from the American Academy of Pediatrics and American Academy of Family Practice Physicians, Advisory Committee on Immunization Practices and the Centers for Disease Control.

IMMUNIZATION RECOMMENDATIONS *(Continued)*

Licensed Vaccines and Toxoids Available in the United States, by Type and Recommended Routes of Administration

	Type	Route
Adenovirus*	Live virus	Oral
Anthrax†	Inactivated bacteria	Subcutaneous
Bacillus of Calmette and Guerin (BCG)	Live bacteria	Intradermal/percutaneous
Cholera	Inactivated bacteria	Subcutaneous, intramuscular, or intradermal‡
Diphtheria-tetanus-pertussis (DTP)	Toxoids and inactivated whole bacteria	Intramuscular
DTP-*Haemophilus influenzae* type b conjugate (DTP-Hib)	Toxoids, inactivated whole bacteria, and bacterial polysaccharide conjugated to protein	Intramuscular
Diphtheria-tetanus-acellular pertussis (DTaP)	Toxoids and inactivated bacterial components	Intramuscular
Hepatitis A	Inactivated virus	Intramuscular
Hepatitis B	Purified viral antigen	Intramuscular
Haemophilus influenzae type b conjugate (Hib)§	Bacterial polysaccharide conjugated to protein	Intramuscular
Influenza	Inactivated virus or viral components	Intramuscular
Japanese encephalitis	Inactivated virus	Subcutaneous
Measles	Live virus	Subcutaneous
Measles-mumps-rubella (MMR)	Live virus	Subcutaneous
Meningococcal	Bacterial polysaccharides of serotypes A/C/Y/W-135	Subcutaneous
Mumps	Live virus	Subcutaneous
Pertussis†	Inactivated whole bacteria	Intramuscular
Plague	Inactivated bacteria	Intramuscular
Pneumococcal	Bacterial polysaccharides of 23 pneumococcal types	Intramuscular or subcutaneous
Poliovirus vaccine		
Inactivated (IPV)	Inactivated viruses of all 3 serotypes	Subcutaneous
Oral (OPV)	Live viruses of all 3 serotypes	Oral
Rabies	Inactivated virus	Intramuscular or intradermal¶
Rubella	Live virus	Subcutaneous
Tetanus	Inactivated toxin (toxoid)	Intramuscular#
Tetanus-diphtheria (Td or DT)•	Inactivated toxins (toxoids)	Intramuscular#
Typhoid		
Parenteral	Inactivated bacteria	Subcutaneous♦
Ty21a oral	Live bacteria	Oral
Varicella	Live virus	Subcutaneous
Yellow fever	Live virus	Subcutaneous

Modified from *MMWR Morb Mortal Wkly Rep*, 1994, 43(RR-1).

*Available only to the U.S. Armed Forces.

†Distributed by the Division of Biologic Products, Michigan Department of Public Health.

‡The intradermal dose is lower than the subcutaneous dose.

§The recommended schedule for infants depends on the vaccine manufacturer; consult the package insert and ACIP recommendations for specific products.

¶The intradermal dose of rabies vaccine, human diploid cell (HDCV), is lower than the intramuscular dose and is used only for pre-exposure vaccination. **Rabies vaccine, adsorbed (RVA) should not be used intradermally.**

#Preparations with adjuvants should be administered intramuscularly.

•Td-tetanus and diphtheria toxoids for use among persons ≥7 years of age. Td contains the same amount of tetanus toxoid as DTP or DT, but contains a smaller dose of diphtheria toxoid. DT = tetanus and diphtheria toxoids for use among children <7 years of age.

♦Booster doses may be administered intradermally unless vaccine that is acetone-killed and dried is used.

Immune Globulins and Antitoxins* Available in the United States, by Type of Antibodies and Indications for Use

Immunobiologic	Type	Indication(s)
Botulinum antitoxin	Specific equine antibodies	Treatment of botulism
Cytomegalovirus immune globulin, intravenous (CMV-IGIV)	Specific human antibodies	Prophylaxis for bone marrow and kidney transplant recipients
Diphtheria antitoxin	Specific equine antibodies	Treatment of respiratory diphtheria
Immune globulin (IG)	Pooled human antibodies	Hepatitis A pre- and postexposure prophylaxis; measles postexposure prophylaxis
Immune globulin, intravenous (IGIV)	Pooled human antibodies	Replacement therapy for antibody deficiency disorders; immune thrombocytopenic purpura (ITP); hypogammaglobulinemia in chronic lymphocytic leukemia; Kawasaki disease
Hepatitis B immune globulin (HBIG)	Specific human antibodies	Hepatitis B postexposure prophylaxis
Rabies immune globulin (HRIG)†	Specific human antibodies	Rabies postexposure management of persons not previously immunized with rabies vaccine
Tetanus immune globulin (TIG)	Specific human antibodies	Tetanus treatment; postexposure prophylaxis of persons not adequately immunized with tetanus toxoid
Vaccinia immune globulin (VIG)	Specific human antibodies	Treatment of eczema vaccinatum, vaccinia necrosum, and ocular vaccinia
Varicella-zoster immune globulin (VZIG)	Specific human antibodies	Postexposure prophylaxis of susceptible immunocompromised persons, certain susceptible pregnant women, and perinatally exposed newborn infants

Modified from *MMWR Morb Mortal Wkly Rep*, 1994, 43(RR-1).

*Immune globulin preparations and antitoxins are administered intramuscularly unless otherwise indicated.

†HRIG is administered around the wounds in addition to the intramuscular injection.

IMMUNIZATION RECOMMENDATIONS (Continued)

Suggested Intervals Between Administration of Immune Globulin Preparations for Various Indications and Vaccines Containing Live Measles Virus*

Indication	Dose (including mg IgG/kg)	Time Interval (mo) Before Measles Vaccination
Tetanus (TIG) prophylaxis	I.M.: 250 units (10 mg IgG/kg)	3
Hepatitis A (IG) prophylaxis		
Contact prophylaxis	I.M.: 0.02 mL/kg (3.3 mg IgG/kg)	3
International travel	I.M.: 0.06 mL/kg (10 mg IgG/kg)	3
Hepatitis B prophylaxis (HBIG)	I.M.: 0.06 mL/kg (10 mg IgG/kg)	3
Rabies immune globulin (HRIG)	I.M.: 20 IU/kg (22 mg IgG/kg)	4
Varicella prophylaxis (VZIG)	I.M.: 125 units/10 kg (20-40 mg IgG/kg) (max: 625 units)	5
Measles prophylaxis (IG) Standard (ie, nonimmunocompromised contact)	I.M.: 0.25 mL/kg (40 mg IgG/kg)	5
Immunocompromised contact	I.M.: 0.50 mL/kg (80 mg IgG/kg)	6
Blood transfusion		
RBCs, washed	I.V.: 10 mL/kg (negligible IgG/kg)	0
RBCs, adenine-saline added	I.V.: 10 mL/kg (10 mg IgG/kg)	3
Packed RBCs (Hct 65%)†	I.V.: 10 mL/kg (60 mg IgG/kg)	6
Whole blood cells (Hct 35%-50%)†	I.V.: 10 mL/kg (80-100 mg IgG/kg)	6
Plasma/platelet products	I.V.: 10 mL/kg (160 mg IgG/kg)	7
Replacement therapy for immune deficiencies	I.V.: 300-400 mg/kg (as IGIV)‡	8
Treatment of Immune thrombocytopenic purpura§	I.V.: 400 mg/kg (as IGIV)	8
Immune thrombocytopenic purpura§	I.V.: 1000 mg/kg (as IGIV)	10
Kawasaki disease	I.V.: 2 g/kg (as IGIV)	11

*This table is not intended for determining the correct indications and dosage for the use of immune globulin preparations. Unvaccinated persons may not be fully protected against measles during the entire suggested time interval, and additional doses of immune globulin and/or measles vaccine may be indicated after measles exposure. The concentration of measles antibody in a particular immune globulin preparation can vary by lot. The rate of antibody clearance after receipt of an immune globulin preparation also can vary. The recommended time intervals are extrapolated from an estimated half-life of 30 days of passively acquired antibody and an observed interference with the immune response to measles vaccine for 5 months after a dose of 80 mg IgG/kg.

†Assumes a serum IgG concentration of 16 mg/mL.

‡Measles vaccination is recommended for most HIV-infected children who do not have evidence of severe immunosuppression, but it is contraindicated for patients who have congenital disorders of the immune system.

§Formerly referred to as idiopathic thrombocytopenic purpura.

Modified from MMWR Morb Mortal Wkly Rep, 1996, 45(RR-12).

HAEMOPHILUS INFLUENZAE VACCINATION

Recommendations for *Haemophilus influenzae* Type b Conjugate Vaccination in Children Immunized Beginning at 2-6 Months of Age

Vaccine Product at Initiation*	Total No. of Doses to Be Administered	Currently Recommended Vaccine Regimens
HbOC or PRP-T	4	3 doses at 2-month intervals When feasible, same vaccine for doses 1-3 Fourth dose at 12-15 months of age Any conjugate vaccine for dose 4
PRP-OMP	3	2 doses at 2-month intervals When feasible, same vaccine for doses 1 and 2 Third dose at 12-15 months of age Any conjugate vaccine for dose 3†

Adapted from "Report of the Committee on Infectious Diseases," *1994 Red Book*®, 23rd ed, Montvale, NJ: Medical Economics Co, Inc.

*See text. The HbOC, PRP-T, or PRP-OMP should be given in a separate syringe and at a separate site from other immunizations unless specific combinations are approved by the FDA. HbOC is also available as a combination vaccine with DTP (HbOC-DTP). This combination can be used in infants scheduled to receive separate injections of DTP and HbOC. PRP-T may be reconstituted with DTP, made by Connaught Laboratories; other licensed formulations of DTP may not be used for this purpose.

†The safety and efficacy of PRP-OMP, PRP-D, PRP-T, and HbOC are likely to be equivalent in children 12 months and older.

Recommendations for *Haemophilus influenzae* Type b Conjugate Vaccination in Children in Whom Initial Vaccination Is Delayed Until 7 Months of Age or Older

Age at Initiation of Immunization (mo)	Vaccine Product at Initiation	Total No. of Doses to Be Administered	Currently Recommended Vaccine Regimens*
7-11	HbOC, PRP-T, or PRP-OMP	3	2 doses at 2-month intervals† When feasible, same vaccine for doses 1 and 2 Third dose at 12-18 months, given at least 2 months after dose 2 Any conjugate vaccine for dose 3‡
12-14	HbOC, PRP-T, PRP-OMP, or PRP-D	2	2-month interval between doses† Any conjugate vaccine for dose 2‡
15-59	HbOC, PRP-T, PRP-OMP, or PRP-D	1	Any conjugate vaccine
60 and older§	HbOC, PRP-T, PRP-OMP, or PRP-D	1 or 2¶	Any conjugate vaccine

Adapted from "Report of the Committee on Infectious Diseases," *1994 Red Book*®, 23rd ed, Montvale, NJ: Medical Economics Co, Inc.

*See text. HbOC, PRP-T, or PRP-OMP should be given in a separate syringe and at a separate site from other immunizations unless specific combinations are approved by the FDA. HbOC is also available as a combination vaccine with DTP (HbOC-DTP). This combination can be used in infants scheduled to receive separate injections of DTP and HbOC. PRP-T may be reconstituted with DTP, made by Connaught Laboratories; other licensed formulations of DTP may not be used for this purpose. In children 15 months or older eligible to receive DTaP (containing acellular pertussis vaccine), however, separate injections of conjugate vaccine and DTaP are acceptable because of the lower rate of febrile, minor local and systemic reactions associated with DTaP.

†For "catch up," a minimum of a 1-month interval between doses may be used.

‡The safety and efficacy of PRP-OMP, PRP-D, PRP-T, and HbOC are likely to be equivalent for use as a booster dose in children 12 months or older.

§Only for children with chronic illness known to be associated with an increased risk for *H. influenzae* type b disease (see text).

¶Two doses separated by 2 months are recommended by some experts for children with certain underlying diseases associated with increased risk of disease and impaired antibody responses to *H. influenzae* type conjugate vaccination (see text).

IMMUNIZATION RECOMMENDATIONS *(Continued)*

Recommendations for *Haemophilus influenzae* Type b Conjugate Vaccination in Children With a Lapse in Vaccination

Age at Presentation (mo)	Previous Vaccination History	Recommended Regimen
7-11	1 dose*	1 dose of conjugate at 7-11 months, with a booster dose given at least 2 months later, at 12-15 months†
	2 doses of HbOC or PRP-T	Same as above
12-14	2 doses before 12 months*	A single dose of any licensed conjugate‡
	1 dose before 12 months*	2 additional doses of any licensed conjugate, separated by 2 months‡
15-59	Any incomplete schedule	A single dose of any licensed conjugate‡

Adapted from "Report of the Committee on Infectious Diseases," *1994 Red Book®*, 23rd ed, Montvale, NJ: Medical Economics Co, Inc.

*PRP-OMP, PRP-T, or HbOC. HbOC is also available as a combination vaccine with DTP (HbOC-DTP), which may be used in infants scheduled to receive separate injections of DTP and HbOC. PRP-T may be reconstituted with DTP, made by Connaught Laboratories; other licensed formulations of DTP may not be used for this purpose. In children 15 months or older eligible to receive DTaP (containing acellular pertussis), however, separate injections of conjugate vaccine and DTaP may be given because of the lower rate of febrile, minor local and systemic reactions associated with DTaP.

†For the dose given at 7-11 months, when feasible, the same vaccine should be given as was used for the dose given at 2-6 months. For the dose given at 12-15 months, any licensed conjugate can be used.

‡The Academy considers that safety and efficacy of PRP-OMP, PRP-D, PRP-T, or HbOC are likely to be equivalent when used in children 12 months or older.

ADVERSE EVENTS AND VACCINATION

Reportable Events Following Vaccination*

These events are reportable by law to the Vaccine Adverse Event Reporting System (VAERS). In addition, individuals are encouraged to report any clinically significant or unexpected events (even if uncertain whether the vaccine caused the event) for any vaccine, whether or not it is listed in the table. Manufacturers also are required to report to the VAERS program all adverse events made known to them for any vaccine.

Vaccine/Toxoid		Event	Interval From Vaccination
Tetanus in any combination; DTaP, DTP, DTP-Hib, DT, Td, TT	A.	Anaphylaxis or anaphylactic shock	7 d
	B.	Briachial neuritis	28 d
	C.	Any sequela (including death) of above	No limit
	D.	Events described in manufacturer's package events insert as contraindications to additional doses of vaccine	See package insert
Pertussis in any combination; DTaP, DTP, DTP-Hib, P	A.	Anaphylaxis or anaphylactic shock	7 d
	B.	Encephalopathy (or encephalitis)	7 d
	C.	Any sequela (including death) of above events	No limit
	D.	Events described in manufacturer's package insert as contraindications to additional doses of vaccine	See package insert
Measles, mumps, and rubella in any combination; MMR, MR, M, R	A.	Anaphylaxis or anaphylactic shock	7 d
	B.	Encephalopathy (or encephalitis)	15 d
	C.	Any sequela (including death) of above events	No limit
	D.	Events described in manufacturer's package insert as contraindications to additional doses of vaccine	See package insert
Rubella in any combination; MMR, MR, R	A.	Chronic arthritis	42 d
	B.	Any sequela (including death) of above events	No limit
	C.	Events described in manufacturer's package insert as contraindications to additional doses of vaccine	See package insert
Measles in any combination; MMR, MR, M	A.	Thrombocytopenic purpura	30 d
	B.	Vaccine-strain measles viral infection in an immunodeficient recipient	6 mo
	C.	Any sequela (including death) of above events	No limit
	D.	Events described in manufacturer's package insert as contraindications to additional doses of vaccine	See package insert
Oral polio (OPV)	A.	Paralytic polio	
		• in a nonimmunodeficient recipient	30 d
		• in an immunodeficient recipient	6 mo
		• in a vaccine-associated community case	No limit
	B.	Vaccine-strain polio viral infection	
		• in a nonimmunodeficient recipient	30 d
		• in an immunodeficient recipient	6 mo
		• in a vaccine-associated community case	No limit
	C.	Any sequela (including death) of above events	No limit
	D.	Events described in manufacturer's package insert as contraindications to additional doses of vaccine	See package insert
Inactivated polio (IPV)	A.	Anaphylaxis or anaphylactic shock	7 d
	B.	Any sequela (including death) of above events	No limit
	C.	Events described in manufacturer's package insert as contraindications to additional doses of vaccine	See package insert
Hepatitis B	A.	Anaphylaxis or anaphylactic shock	7 d
	B.	Any sequela (including death) of above events	No limit
	C.	Events described in manufacturer's package insert as contraindications to additional doses of vaccine	See package insert
Haemophilus influenzae type b	A.	Early onset Hib disease	7 d
	B.	Any sequela (including death) of above events	No limit
	C.	Events described in manufacturer's package insert as contraindications to additional doses of vaccine	See package insert
Varicella	A.	No condition specified for compensation	Not applicable
	B.	Events described in manufacturer's package insert as contraindications to additional doses of vaccine	See package insert

*Effective March 24, 1997.

Adapted from "Report of the Committee on Infectious Diseases," *1997 Red Book*®, 24th ed.

IMMUNIZATION RECOMMENDATIONS *(Continued)*

PREVENTION OF HEPATITIS A THROUGH ACTIVE OR PASSIVE IMMUNIZATION

Recommendations of the Advisory Committee on Immunization Practices (ACIP)

December 27, 1996, Vol. 45, No. RR-15

PROPHYLAXIS AGAINST HEPATITIS A VIRUS INFECTION

Recommended Doses of Immune Globulin (IG) for Hepatitis A Pre-exposure and Postexposure Prophylaxis

Setting	Duration of Coverage	IG Dose*
Pre-exposure	Short-term (1-2 months)	0.02 mL/kg
	Long-term (3-5 months)	0.06 mL/kg†
Postexposure	—	0.02 mL/kg

*IG should be administered by intramuscular injection into either the deltoid or gluteal muscle. For children <24 months of age, IG can be administered in the anterolateral thigh muscle.

†Repeat every 5 months if continued exposure to HAV occurs.

Recommended Dosages of Havrix®*

Vaccinee's Age (y)	Dose (EL.U.)†	Volume (mL)	No. Doses	Schedule (mo)‡
2-18	720	0.5	2	0, 6-12
>18	1440	1.0	2	0, 6-12

*Hepatitis A vaccine, inactivated, SmithKline Beecham Biologicals

†ELISA units

‡0 months represents timing of the initial dose; subsequent numbers represent months after the initial dose.

Recommended Dosages of VAQTA®*

Vaccinee's Age (y)	Dose (units)	Volume (mL)	No. Doses	Schedule (mo)†
2-17	25	0.5	2	0, 6-18
>17	50	1.0	2	0, 6

*Hepatitis A vaccine, inactivated, Merck & Company, Inc.

†0 months represents timing of the initial dose; subsequent numbers represent months after the initial dose.

RECOMMENDATIONS FOR TRAVELERS

Recommended Immunizations for Travelers to Developing Countries*

Immunizations	Length of Travel[1]		
	Brief, <2 wk	Intermediate, 2 wk - 3 mo	Long-term Residential, >3 mo
Review and complete age-appropriate childhood schedule	+	+	+
• DTaP (or DTP) may be given at 4 wk intervals[2]			
• Poliovirus vaccine may be given at 4-8 wk intervals[2]			
• Measles: extra dose given if 6-11 mo old at 1st dose			
• Varicella			
• Hepatitis B[3]			
Yellow fever[4]	+	+	+
Typhoid fever[5]	±	+	+
Meningococcal meningitis[6]	±	+	+
Rabies[7]	+	+	±
Japanese encephalitis[4]	−	±	+

*See disease-specific chapters for details. For further sources of information, see text.

[1] + indicates recommended; ± consider; and −, not recommended.

[2] If necessary to complete the recommended schedule before departure.

[3] If insufficient time to complete 6-month primary series, accelerated series can be given (see Red Book® for details).

[4] For endemic regions see *Health Information for International Travel*, page 2 of *Red Book®*.

[5] Indicated for travelers who will consume food at nontourist facilities.

[6] For endemic regions of central Africa and during local epidemics.

[7] Indicated for persons with high risk of wild animal exposure and for spelunkers.

Adapted from "Report of the Committee on Infectious Diseases," *1997 Red Book®*, 24th ed.

Recommendations for Pre-exposure Immunoprophylaxis of Hepatitis A Infection for Travelers*

Age (y)	Likely Exposure (mo)	Recommended Prophylaxis
<2	<3	IG 0.02 mL/kg†
	3-5	IG 0.06 mL/kg†
	Long term	IG 0.06 mL/kg at departure and every 5 mo thereafter†
≥2	<3‡	HAV vaccine§¶
		or
		IG 0.02 mL/kg†
	3-5‡	HAV vaccine§¶
		or
		IG 0.06 mL/kg†
		HAV vaccine§¶

*HAV, hepatitis A virus; IG, immune globulin.

†IG should be administered deep into a large muscle mass. Ordinarily no more than 5 mL should be administered in one site in an adult or large child; lesser amounts (maximum 3 mL) should be given to small children and infants.

‡Vaccine is preferable, but IG is an acceptable alternative.

§To ensure protection in travelers whose departure is imminent, IG also may be given (see text).

¶Dose and schedule of HAV vaccine as recommended according to age.

Adapted from "Report of the Committee on Infectious Diseases," *1997 Red Book®*, 24th ed.

IMMUNIZATION RECOMMENDATIONS *(Continued)*

Prevention of Malaria*

Drug†	Adult Dosage	Pediatric Dosage
Chloroquine-Sensitive Areas		
Chloroquine phosphate	P.O.: 300 mg base (500 mg salt), once/week beginning 1 week before exposure, and continuing for 4 weeks after last exposure	5 mg/kg base (8.3 mg/kg salt) once/week (maximum 300 mg base)
Chloroquine-Resistant Areas		
Mefloquine‡	P.O.: 250 mg salt (228 mg base), once/week, beginning 1 week before travel and continuing for 4 weeks after last exposure	15-19 kg: $^1/_4$ tablet/wk 20-30 kg: $^1/_2$ tablet/wk 31-45 kg: $^3/_4$ tablet/wk >45 kg: 1 tablet/wk
Alternatives		
Doxycycline§	100 mg/d, starting 1-2 days before exposure and continuing for 4 weeks after last exposure	>8 y: P.O.: 2 mg/kg/d (maximum 100 mg/d)
or		
Chloroquine phosphate	Same as above	Same as above
with or without		
Proguanil#	200 mg daily during exposure and for 4 weeks after last exposure	<2 y: 50 mg/d 2-6 y: 100 mg/d 7-10 y: 150 mg/d >10 y: 200 mg/d
plus		
Pyrimethamine-sulfadoxine (Fansidar®) for presumptive treatment¶	Carry a single dose (3 tablets) for self-treatment of febrile illness when medical care is not immediately available	Used as for adults in the following doses: <1 y: $^1/_4$ tablet 1-3 y: $^1/_2$ tablet 4-8 y: 1 tablet 9-14 y: 2 tablets >14 y: 3 tablets

*Currently, no drug regimen guarantees protection against malaria. Travelers to countries with risk of malaria should be advised to avoid mosquito bites by using personal protective measures (see text).

†All drugs should be continued for 4 weeks after last exposure.

‡Mefloquine is not licensed by the Food and Drug Administration for children weighing <15 kg, but recent recommendations from the Centers for Disease Control and Prevention allow use of the drug to be considered in children without weight restrictions when travel to chloroquine-resistant *P. falciparum* areas cannot be avoided. Mefloquine is **contraindicated** for use by travelers with a known hypersensitivity to mefloquine and travelers with a history of epilepsy or severe psychiatric disorders. A review of available data suggests that a mefloquine may be administered to persons concurrently receiving β-blockers if they have no underlying arrhythmia. However, mefloquine is not recommended for persons with cardiac conduction abnormalities until additional data are available. Caution may be advised for persons involved in tasks requiring fine coordination and spatial discrimination, such as airline pilots. Quinidine or quinine may exacerbate the known side effects or mefloquine; patients not responding to mefloquine therapy or failing mefloquine prophylaxis should be closely monitored if they are treated with quinidine or quinine.

§Physicians who prescribe doxycycline as malaria chemoprophylaxis should advise patients to limit the exposure to direct sunlight to minimize the possibility of photosensitivity reaction. Use of doxycycline is contraindicated in pregnant women and usually in children <8 years. Physicians must weight the benefits of doxycycline therapy against the possibility of dental staining in children <8 years (see Antimicrobial and Related Therapy).

#Proguanil (chloroguanide hydrochloride) is not available in the United States but is widely available overseas. It is recommended primarily for use in Africa south of the Sahara. Failures in prophylaxis with chloroquine and chloroguanide have been reported commonly, however, as they are only 40% to 60% effective.

¶Use of Fansidar®, which contains 25 mg pyrimethamine and 500 mg sulfadoxine per tablet, is contraindicated in patients with a history of sulfonamide or pyrimethamine intolerance, in infants <2 months, and in pregnant women at term. Resistance to pyrimethamine-sulfadoxine has been reported from Southeast Asia and the Amazon Basin and therefore should not be used for treatment of malaria acquired in these area.

Adapted from "Report of the Committee on Infectious Diseases," *1997 Red Book®,* 24th ed.

CEPHALOSPORINS BY GENERATION

First Generation	2nd Generation	3rd Generation	4th Generation
Cefadroxil	Cefaclor	Cefdinir	Cefepime
(Duricef®)*	(Ceclor®)*	(Omnicef®)	(Maxipime®)†
Cefazolin	Cefamandole	Cefixime	
(Ancef®)	(Mandol®)	(Suprax®)*	
Cephalexin	Cefmetazole	Cefoperazone	
(Keflex®)*	(Zefazone®)	(Cefobid®)†	
Cephalothin	Cefonicid	Cefotaxime	
(Keflin®)	(Monocid®)	(Claforan®)	
Cephapirin	Ceforanide	Cefpodoxime	
(Cefadryl®)	(Precef®)	(Vantin®)*	
Cephradine	Cefotetan	Ceftizoxime	
(Anspor®)*	(Cefotan®)	(Cefizox®)	
	Cefoxitin	Ceftriaxone	
	(Mefoxin®)	(Rocephin®)	
	Cefprozil	Ceftazidime	
	(Cefzil®)*	(Fortaz)†	
	Cefuroxime		
	(Zinacef®)*		
	Cefuroxime axetil		
	(Ceftin®)		
	Loracarbef		
	(Lorabid®)		

*Oral dosage form available

†Anti-pseudomonal activity notable

Note: Other brand names or generic products may be available

MANAGEMENT OF HEALTHCARE WORKER EXPOSURES TO HIV

RECOMMENDATIONS FOR POSTEXPOSURE PROPHYLAXIS

Adapted from "Public Health Service Guidelines for the Management of Health-Care Worker Exposures to HIV and Recommendations for Postexposure Prophylaxis," *MMWR Morb Mortal Wkly Rep*, 1998, 47(RR-7)

**Determining the Need for HIV Postexposure Prophylaxis (PEP)
After an Occupational Exposure***

Step 1: Determine the Exposure Code (EC)

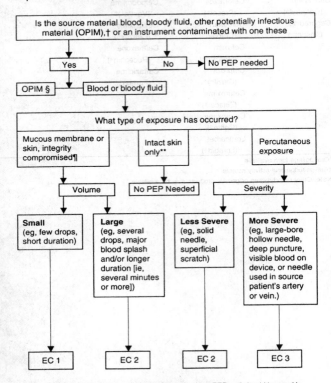

* This algorithm is intended to guide initial decisions about PEP and should be used in conjunction with other guidance provided in this report.

† Semen or vaginal secretions; cerebrospinal, synovial, pleural, peritoneal, pericardial, or amniotic fluids; or tissue

§ Exposure to OPIM must be evaluated on a case-by-case basis. In general, these body substances are considered a low risk for transmission in health-care settings. Any unprotected contact to concentrated HIV in a research laboratory or production facility is considered an occupational exposure that requires clinical evaluation to determine the need for PEP.

¶ Skin integrity is considered compromised if there is evidence of chapped skin, dermatitis, abrasion, or open wound.

** Contact with intact skin is not normally considered a risk for HIV transmission. However, if the exposure was to blood, and the circumstance suggests a higher volume exposure (eg, an extensive area of skin was exposed or there was prolonged contact with blood), the risk for HIV transmission should be considered.

†† The combination of these severity factors (eg, large-bore, hollow needle and deep puncture) contribute to an elevated risk for transmission if the source person is HIV-

Determining the need for HIV postexposure prophylaxis (PEP) after an occupational exposure* — Continued

Step 2: Determine the HIV Status Code (HIV SC)

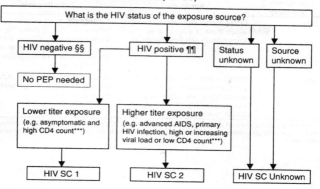

§§ A source is considered negative for HIV infection if there is laboratory documentation of a negative HIV antibody, HIV polymerase chain reaction (PCR), or HIV p24 antigen test result from a specimen collected at or near the time of exposure and there is no clinical evidence of recent retroviral-like illness.

¶¶ A source is considered infected with HIV (HIV positive) if there has been a positive laboratory result for HIV antibody, HIV PCR, or HIV p24 antigen or physician-diagnosed AIDS.

*** Examples are used as surrogates to estimates the HIV titer in an exposure source for purposes of considering PEP regimens and do not reflect all clinical situations that may be observed. Although a high HIV titer (HIV SC 2) in an exposure source has been associated with an increased risk for transmission, the possibility of transmission from a source with a low HIV titer also must be considered.

Step 3: Determine the PEP Recommendation

EC	HIV SC	PEP recommendation
1	1	PEP may not be warranted. Exposure type does not pose a known risk for HIV transmission. Whether the risk for drug toxicity outweighs the benefit of PEP should be decided by the exposed HCW and treating clinician.
1	2	Consider basic regimen. ††† Exposure type poses a negligible risk for HIV transmission. A high HIV titer in the source may justify consideration of PEP. Whether the risk for drug toxicity outweighs the benefit of PEP should be decided by the exposed HCW and treating clinician.
2	1	Recommended basic regimen. Most HIV exposures are in thes category; no increased risk for HIV transmission has been observed but use of PEP is appropriate.
2	1	Recommended expanded regimen. §§§ Exposure type represents an increased HIV transmission risk.
3	1 or 2	Recommended expanded regimen. Exposure type represents an increased HIV transmission risk.

††† Basic regimen is four weeks of zidovudine, 600 mg per day in two or three divided doses, and lamivudine, 150 mg twice daily.

§§§ Expanded regimen is the basic regimen plus either indinavir, 800 mg every 8 hours, or nelfinavir, 750 mg three times a day.

MANAGEMENT OF HEALTHCARE WORKER EXPOSURES TO HIV (Continued)

Basic and Expanded Postexposure Prophylaxis Regimens

Regimen Category	Application	Drug Regimen
Basic	Occupational HIV exposures for which there is a recognized transmission risk (see Figure 1)	4 weeks (28 days) of both zidovudine 600 mg every day in divided doses (ie, 300 mg 2 times/day, 200 mg 3 times/day, or 100 mg every 4 h) and lamivudine 150 mg 2 times/d.
Expanded	Occupational HIV exposures that pose an increased risk for transmission (eg, larger volume of blood and/or higher virus titer in blood; see Figure 1)	Basic regimen plus either indinavir 800 mg every 8 h or nelfinavir 750 mg 3 times/d*

*Indinavir should be taken on an empty stomach (ie, without food or with a light meal) and with increased fluid consumption (ie, drinking six 8 oz glasses of water throughout the day); nelfinavir should be taken with meals.

PREVENTION OF BACTERIAL ENDOCARDITIS

Recommendations by the American Heart Association
(*JAMA*, 1997, 277:1794-801)

Consensus Process - The recommendations were formulated by the writing group after specific therapeutic regimens were discussed. The consensus statement was subsequently reviewed by outside experts not affiliated with the writing group and by the Science Advisory and Coordinating Committee of the American Heart Association. These guidelines are meant to aid practitioners but are not intended as the standard of care or as a substitute for clinical judgment.

Table 1. Cardiac Conditions*

Endocarditis Prophylaxis Recommended

High-risk Category

    Prosthetic cardiac valves, including bioprosthetic and homograft valves

    Previous bacterial endocarditis

    Complex cyanotic congenital heart disease (eg, single ventricle states, transposition of the great arteries, tetralogy of Fallot)

    Surgically constructed systemic pulmonary shunts or conduits

Moderate-risk Category

    Most other congenital cardiac malformations (other than above and below)

    Acquired valvar dysfunction (eg, rheumatic heart disease)

    Hypertrophic cardiomyopathy

    Mitral valve prolapse with valvar regurgitation and/or thickened leaflets

Endocarditis Prophylaxis Not Recommended

Negligible-risk Category (no greater risk than the general population)

    Isolated secundum atrial septal defect

    Surgical repair of atrial septal defect, ventricular septal defect, or patent ductus arteriosus (without residua beyond 6 months)

    Previous coronary artery bypass graft surgery

    Mitral valve prolapse without valvar regurgitation†

    Physiologic, functional, or innocent heart murmurs

    Previous Kawasaki disease without valvar dysfunction

    Previous rheumatic fever without valvar dysfunction

    Cardiac pacemakers (intravascular and epicardial) and implanted defibrillators

---

*This table lists selected conditions but is not meant to be all-inclusive.

PREVENTION OF BACTERIAL ENDOCARDITIS *(Continued)*

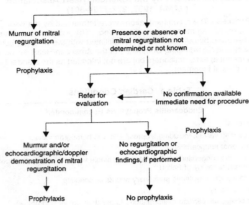

Patient With Suspected Mitral Valve Prolapse

Table 2. Dental Procedures and Endocarditis Prophylaxis

Endocarditis Prophylaxis Recommended*

Dental extractions

Periodontal procedures including surgery, scaling and root planing, probing, and recall maintenance

Dental implant placement and reimplantation of avulsed teeth

Endodontic (root canal) instrumentation or surgery only beyond the apex

Subgingival placement of antibiotic fibers or strips

Initial placement of orthodontic bands but not brackets

Intraligamentary local anesthetic injections

Prophylactic cleaning of teeth or implants where bleeding is anticipated

Endocarditis Prophylaxis Not Recommended

Restorative dentistry† (operative and prosthodontic) with or without retraction cord‡

Local anesthetic injections (nonintraligamentary)

Intracanal endodontic treatment; post placement and buildup

Placement of rubber dams

Postoperative suture removal

Placement of removable prosthodontic or orthodontic appliances

Taking of oral impressions

Fluoride treatments

Taking of oral radiographs

Orthodontic appliance adjustment

Shedding of primary teeth

*Prophylaxis is recommended for patients with high- and moderate-risk cardiac conditions.

†This includes restoration of decayed teeth (filling cavities) and replacement of missing teeth.

‡Clinical judgment may indicate antibiotic use in selected circumstances that may create significant bleeding.

Table 3. Recommended Standard Prophylactic Regimen for Dental, Oral, or Upper Respiratory Tract Procedures in Patients Who Are at Risk*

Endocarditis Prophylaxis Recommended

Respiratory Tract
  Tonsillectomy and/or adenoidectomy
  Surgical operations that involve respiratory mucosa
  Bronchoscopy with a rigid bronchoscope
Gastrointestinal Tract*
  Sclerotherapy for esophageal varices
  Esophageal stricture dilation
  Endoscopic retrograde cholangiography with biliary obstruction
  Biliary tract surgery
  Surgical operations that involve intestinal mucosa
Genitourinary Tract
  Prostatic surgery
  Cystoscopy
  Urethral dilation

Endocarditis Prophylaxis Not Recommended

Respiratory Tract
  Endotracheal intubation
  Bronchoscopy with a flexible bronchoscope, with or without biopsy†
  Tympanostomy tube insertion
Gastrointestinal Tract
  Transesophageal echocardiography†
  Endoscopy with or without gastrointestinal biopsy†
Genitourinary Tract
  Vaginal hysterectomy†
  Vaginal delivery†
  Cesarean section
  In uninfected tissues:
    Urethral catheterization
    Uterine dilatation and curettage
    Therapeutic abortion
    Sterilization procedures
    Insertion or removal of intrauterine devices
Other
  Cardiac catheterization, including balloon angioplasty
  Implanted cardiac pacemakers, implanted defibrillators, and coronary stents
  Incision or biopsy or surgically scrubbed skin
  Circumcision

*Prophylaxis is recommended for high-risk patients, optional for medium-risk patients.
†Prophylaxis is optional for high-risk patients.

PREVENTION OF BACTERIAL ENDOCARDITIS (Continued)

Table 4. Prophylactic Regimens for Dental, Oral, Respiratory Tract, or Esophageal Procedures

Situation	Agent	Regimen* Adults	Children
Standard general prophylaxis	Amoxicillin	2 g P.O. 1 h before procedure	50 mg/kg P.O. 1 h before procedure
Unable to take oral medications	Ampicillin	2 g I.M./I.V. within 30 min before procedure	50 mg/kg I.M./I.V. within 30 min before procedure
Allergic to penicillin	Clindamycin or	600 mg P.O. 1 h before procedure	20 mg/kg P.O. 1 h before procedure
	Cephalexin† or cefadroxil† or	2 g P.O 1 h before procedure	50 mg/kg P.O. 1 h before procedure
	Azithromycin or clarithromycin	500 mg P.O. 1 h before procedure	15 mg/kg P.O. 1 h before procedure
Allergic to penicillin and unable to take oral medications	Clindamycin or	600 mg I.V. within 30 min before procedure	20 mg/kg I.V. within 30 min before procedure
	Cefazolin†	1 g I.M./I.V. within 30 min before procedure	25 mg/kg I.M./I.V. within 30 min before procedure

*Total children's dose should not exceed adult dose.

†Cephalosporins should not be used in individuals with immediate-type hypersensitivity reaction (urticaria, angioedema, or anaphylaxis) to penicillins

Table 5. Prophylactic Regimens for Genitourinary/Gastrointestinal (Excluding Esophageal) Procedures*

Situation	Agents*	Regimen† Adults	Children
High-risk‡ patients	Ampicillin plus gentamicin	Ampicillin 2 g I.M. or I.V. plus gentamicin 1.5 mg/kg (not to exceed 120 mg) within 30 min of starting the procedure; 6 h later, ampicillin 1 g I.M./I.V. or amoxicillin 1 g orally	Ampicillin 50 mg/kg I.M./I.V. (not to exceed 2 g) plus gentamicin 1.5 mg/kg within 30 min of starting the procedure; 6 h later, ampicillin 25 mg/kg I.M./I.V. or amoxicillin 25 mg/kg orally
High-risk‡ patients allergic to ampicillin/ amoxicillin	Vancomycin plus gentamicin	Vancomycin 1 g I.V. over 1-2 h plus gentamicin 1.5 mg/kg I.M./I.V. (not to exceed 120 mg); complete injection/infusion within 30 min of starting the procedure	Vancomycin 20 mg/kg I.V. over 1-2 h plus gentamicin 1.5 mg/kg I.M./I.V.; complete injection/infusion within 30 min of starting the procedure
Moderate-risk§ patients	Amoxicillin or ampicillin	Amoxicillin 2 g orally 1 h before procedure, or ampicillin 2 g I.M./I.V within 30 min of starting the procedure	Amoxicillin 50 mg/kg orally 1 h before procedure, or ampicillin 50 mg/kg I.M./I.V. within 30 min of starting the procedure
Moderate-risk§ patients allergic to ampicillin/amoxicillin	Vancomycin	Vancomycin 1 g I.V. over 1-2 h; complete infusion within 30 min of starting the procedure	Vancomycin 20 mg/kg I.V. over 1-2 h; complete infusion within 30 min of starting the procedure

*Total children's dose should not exceed adult dose

†No second dose of vancomycin or gentamicin is recommended

‡High-risk: Patients are those who have prosthetic valves, a previous history of endocarditis (even in the absence of other heart disease, complex cyanotic congenital heart disease, or surgically constructed systemic pulmonary shunts or conduits).

§Moderate-risk: Individuals with certain other underlying cardiac defects. Congenital cardiac conditions include the following uncorrected conditions: Patent ductus arteriosus, ventricular septal defect, ostium primum atrial septal defect, coarctation of the aorta, and bicuspid aortic valve. Acquired valvar dysfunction and hypertrophic cardiomyopathy are also moderate risk conditions.

PREVENTION OF WOUND INFECTION AND SEPSIS IN SURGICAL PATIENTS

Nature of Operation	Likely Pathogens	Recommended Drugs	Adult Dosage Before Surgery[1]
Cardiac			
Prosthetic valve, coronary artery bypass, other open-heart surgery, pacemaker or defibrillator implant	S. epidermidis, S. aureus, Corynebacterium, enteric gram-negative bacilli	Cefazolin or cefuroxime or vancomycin[3]	1-2 g I.V.[2] 1-2 g I.V.[2] 1 g I.V.
Gastrointestinal			
Esophageal, gastroduodenal	Enteric gram-negative bacilli, gram-positive cocci	High risk[4] only: cefazolin	1-2 g I.V.
Biliary tract	Enteric gram-negative bacilli, enterococci, clostridia	High risk[5] only: cefazolin	1-2 g I.V.
Colorectal	Enteric gram-negative bacilli, anaerobes, enterococci	Oral: neomycin + erythromycin base[6]	1-2 g I.V.
		Parenteral:	
		Cefoxitin	1-2 g I.V.
		or cefotetan	1-2 g I.V.
Appendectomy, nonperforated	Enteric gram-negative bacilli, anaerobes, enterococci	Cefoxitin	1-2 g I.V.
		or cefotetan	1-2 g I.V.
Genitourinary	Enteric gram-negative bacilli, enterococci	High risk[7] only: Ciprofloxacin	500 mg P.O. or 400 mg I.V.
Gynecologic and Obstetric			
Vaginal or abdominal hysterectomy	Enteric gram-negatives, anaerobes, group B streptococci, enterococci	Cefazolin or cefotetan or cefoxitin	1-2 g I.V. 1-2 g I.V. 1 g I.V.
Cesarean section	Same as for hysterectomy	High risk[8] only: Cefazolin	1 g I.V. after cord clamping
Abortion	Same as for hysterectomy	First trimester, high-risk[9] only: Aqueous penicillin G	2 mill units I.V.
		or doxycycline	300 mg P.O.[10]
		Second trimester: Cefazolin	1 g I.V.
Head and Neck			
Entering oral cavity or pharynx	S. aureus, streptococci, oral anaerobes	Cefazolin	1-2 g I.V.
		or clindamycin	600-900 mg I.V.
		± gentamicin	1.5 mg/kg I.V.
Neurosurgery			
Craniotomy	S. aureus, S. epidermidis	Cefazolin	1-2 g I.V.
		or vancomycin[3]	1 g I.V.
Ophthalmic	S. aureus, S. epidermidis, streptococci, enteric gram-negative bacilli, Pseudomonas	Gentamicin or tobramycin or neomycin-gramicidin-polymyxin B	Multiple drops topically over 2-24 h
		Cefazolin	100 mg subconjunctivally at end of procedure
Orthopedic			
Total joint replacement, internal fixation of fractures	S. aureus, S. epidermidis	Cefazolin	1-2 g I.V.
		or vancomycin[3]	1 g I.V.
Thoracic (Noncardiac)	S. aureus, S. epidermidis, streptococci, enteric gram-negative bacilli	Cefazolin	1-2 g I.V.
		or cefuroxime	1-2 g I.V.
		or vancomycin[3]	1 g I.V.
Vascular			
Arterial surgery involving the abdominal aorta, a prosthesis, or a groin incision	S. aureus, S. epidermidis, enteric gram-negative bacilli	Cefazolin	1-2 g I.V.
		or vancomycin[3]	1 g I.V.
Lower extremity amputation for ischemia	S. aureus, S. epidermidis, enteric gram-negative bacilli, clostridia	Cefazolin	1-2 g I.V.
		or vancomycin[3]	1 g I.V.

PREVENTION OF WOUND INFECTION AND SEPSIS IN SURGICAL PATIENTS (Continued)

Nature of Operation	Likely Pathogens	Recommended Drugs	Adult Dosage Before Surgery[1]
CONTAMINATED SURGERY[11]			
Ruptured viscus	Enteric gram-negative bacilli, anaerobes, enterococci	Cefoxitin	1-2 g I.V. q6h
		or cefotetan	1-2 g I.V. q12h
		± gentamicin	1.5 mg/kg I.V. q8h
		or clindamycin	600 mg I.V. q6h
		+ gentamicin	1.5 mg/kg I.V. q8h
Traumatic wound	S. aureus, Group A strep, clostridia	Cefazolin[12]	1-2 g I.V. q8h

[1]Parenteral prophylactic antimicrobials can be given as a single intravenous dose just before the operation. For prolonged operations, additional intraoperative doses should be given every 4-8 hours for the duration of the procedure.

[2]Some consultants recommend an additional dose when patients are removed from bypass during open-heart surgery.

[3]For hospitals in which methicillin-resistant S. aureus and S. epidermidis are a frequent cause of postoperative wound infection, or for patients allergic to penicillins or cephalosporin. Rapid I.V. administration may cause hypotension, which could be especially dangerous during induction of anesthesia. Even if the drug is given over 60 minutes, hypotension may occur; treatment with diphenhydramine (Benadryl® and others) and further slowing of the infusion rate may be helpful (Maki DG et al, J Thorac Cardiovasc Surg, 1992, 104:1423). For procedures in which enteric gram-negative bacilli are likely pathogens, such as vascular surgery involving a groin incision, cefazolin should be included in the prophylaxis regimen for patients not allergic to cephalosporins.

[4]Morbid obesity, esophageal obstruction, decreased gastric acidity or gastrointestinal motility.

[5]Age >70 years, acute cholecystitis, nonfunctioning gall bladder, obstructive jaundice or common duct stones.

[6]After appropriate diet and catharsis, 1 g of each at 1 PM, 2 PM, and 11 PM the day before an 8 AM operation.

[7]Urine culture positive or unavailable, preoperataive catheter.

[8]Active labor or premature rupture of membranes.

[9]Patients with previous pelvic inflammatory disease, previous gonorrhea or multiple sex partners.

[10]Divided into 100 mg one hour before the abortion and 200 mg one half hour after.

[11]For contaminated or "dirty" surgery, therapy should usually be continued for about 5 days.

[12]For bite wounds, in which likely pathogens may also include oral anaerobes, Eikenella corrodens (human) and Pasteurella multocida (dog and cat), some Medical Letter consultants recommend use of amoxicillin/clavulanic acid (Augmentin®) or ampicillin/sulbactam (Unasyn®)

Adapted with permission from The Medical Letter, 1997, 39(Issue 1012).

POSTEXPOSURE PROPHYLAXIS FOR HEPATITIS B*

Exposure	Hepatitis B Immune Globulin	Hepatitis B Vaccine
Perinatal	0.5 mL I.M. within 12 h of birth	0.5 mL† I.M. within 12 h of birth (no later than 7 d), and at 1 and 6 mo‡; test for HB$_s$Ag and anti-HB$_s$ at 12-15 mo
Sexual	0.06 mL/kg I.M. within 14 d of sexual contact; a second dose should be given if the index patient remains HB$_s$Ag-positive after 3 mo and hepatitis B vaccine was not given initially	1 mL I.M. at 0, 1, and 6 mo for homosexual and bisexual men and regular sexual contacts of persons with acute and chronic hepatitis B
Percutaneous; exposed person unvaccinated		
Source known HB$_s$Ag-positive	0.06 mL/kg I.M. within 24 h	1 mL I.M. within 7 d, and at 1 and 6 mo§
Source known, HB$_s$Ag status not known	Test source for HB$_s$Ag; if source is positive, give exposed person 0.06 mL/kg I.M. once within 7 d	1 mL I.M. within 7 d, and at 1 and 6 mo§
Source not tested or unknown	Nothing required	1 mL I.M. within 7 d, and at 1 and 6 mo
Percutaneous; exposed person vaccinated		
Source known HB$_s$Ag-positive	Test exposed person for anti-HB$_s$¶. If titer is protective, nothing is required; if titer is not protective, give 0.06 mL/kg within 24 h	Review vaccination status#
Source known, HB$_s$Ag status not known	Test source for HB$_s$Ag and exposed person for anti-HB$_s$. If source is HB$_s$Ag-negative, or if source is HB$_s$Ag-positive but anti-HB$_s$ titer is protective, nothing is required. If source is HB$_s$Ag-positive and anti-HB$_s$ titer is not protective or if exposed person is a known nonresponder, give 0.06 mL/kg I.M. within 24 h. A second dose of hepatitis B immune globulin can be given 1 mo later if a booster dose of hepatitis B vaccine is not given.	Review vaccination status#
Source not tested or unknown	Test exposed person for anti-HB$_s$. If anti-HB$_s$ titer is protective, nothing is required. If anti-HB$_s$ titer is not protective, 0.06 mL/kg may be given along with a booster dose of hepatitis B vaccine	Review vaccination status#

*HB$_s$Ag = hepatitis B surface antigen; anti-HB$_s$ = antibody to hepatitis B surface antigen; I.M. = intramuscularly; SRU = standard ratio units.

†Each 0.5 mL dose of plasma-derived hepatitis B vaccine contains 10 μg of HB$_s$Ag; each 0.5 mL dose of recombinant hepatitis B vaccine contains 5 μg (Merck Sharp & Dohme) or 10 μg (SmithKline Beecham) of HB$_s$Ag.

‡If hepatitis B immune globulin and hepatitis B vaccine are given simultaneously, they should be given at separate sites.

§If hepatitis B vaccine is not given, a second dose of hepatitis B immune globulin should be given 1 month later.

¶Anti-HB$_s$ titers <10 SRU by radioimmunoassay or negative by enzyme immunoassay indicate lack of protection. Testing the exposed person for anti-HB$_s$ is not necessary if a protective level of antibody has been shown within the previous 24 months.

#If the exposed person has not completed a three-dose series of hepatitis B vaccine, the series should be completed. Test the exposed person for anti-HB$_s$. If the antibody level is protective, nothing is required. If an adequate antibody response in the past is shown on retesting to have declined to an inadequate level, a booster dose (1 mL) of hepatitis B vaccine should be given. If the exposed person has inadequate antibody or is a known nonresponder to vaccination, a booster dose can be given along with one dose of hepatitis B immune globulin.

PROPHYLAXIS FOR PATIENTS EXPOSED TO COMMON COMMUNICABLE DISEASES

Disease	Exposure	Prophylaxis/Management
Invasive *Haemophilus influenzae* disease	Close contact with an infected child for more than 4 hours	Give rifampin 20 mg/kg orally once daily for 4 days (600 mg maximum daily dose) to entire family with at least one household contact less than 48 months old. Contraindication: Pregnant contacts.
Hepatitis A	Direct contact with an infected child, or sharing of food or utensils	Give 0.02 mL/kg immune globulin (IG) within 7 days of exposure.
Hepatitis B	Needlestick (used needle) Mucous membrane exposure with blood or body fluid Direct inoculation of blood or body fluid into open cut, lesion, or laceration	**Known source and employee status unknown: Test patient for HB,Ag and employee for anti-HB,.** If patient is HB,Ag negative and the patient does not have non-A, non-B hepatitis, do nothing. If patient is HB,Ag negative and has non-A, non-B hepatitis, **offer** ISG (optional). If patient is HB,Ag positive, give HBIG and hepatitis B vaccine within 48 hours of exposure. Employee antibody status may not be available for up to a week, so the above should be given as soon as patient's antigen status is known. Occasionally, the patient's antigen status will be unavailable for more than 24 hours. In these cases, HBIG should be given if the patient is high risk (ie, Asian immigrants, institutionalized patients, homosexuals, intravenous drug abusers, hemodialysis patients, patients with a history of hepatitis). If the employee is anti-HB, negative, give the second and third doses of hepatitis B vaccine. **Known source and employee documented anti-HB, positive:** If source has non-A, non-B hepatitis, **offer** ISG (optional). If employee is believed to be anti-HB, positive due to vaccination, has received 3 doses of vaccine, and has not had an anti-HB, test done, draw serum for anti-HB,.
Measles	15 minutes or more in the same room with a child with measles from 2 days before the onset of symptoms to 4 days after the appearance of the rash	Children who have not been vaccinated and have not had natural infection should be isolated from the 7th through the 18th day after exposure and/or for 4 days after the rash appears. Those who have not been vaccinated should be vaccinated within 72 hours of exposure if no contraindication exists, or receive immune globulin (IG) 0.25 mL/kg I.M. for immunocompetent individuals and 0.5 mL/kg (maximum: 15 mL) for immunosuppressed individuals. Children who are younger than 15 months of age should be revaccinated at 15 months of age but at least 3 months after receipt of vaccine or IG. Older individuals who have received IG should be vaccinated 3 months later.
Meningococcal disease	Household contact or direct contact with secretions	Household, day care center, and nursery school children should receive rifampin prophylaxis for 2 days. Dosages are given every 12 hours for a total of 4 doses. Dosage is 10 mg/kg/dose for children ages 1 month to 12 years (maximum: 600 mg/dose), 5 mg/kg/dose for infants less than 1 month of age, and 600 mg/dose for adults. Contraindication: Pregnant contacts. **Because prophylaxis is not always effective, exposed children should be monitored for symptoms.** **Employee exposure: Anyone who develops a febrile illness should receive prompt medical evaluation. If indicated, antimicrobial therapy should be administered.**
Pertussis	Housed in the same room with an infected child or spent 15 minutes in the playroom with the infected child	**Prophylaxis:** Contacts less than 7 years old who have had at least 4 doses of pertussis vaccine should receive a booster dose of DTP, unless a dose has been given within the past 3 years, and should receive erythromycin 40-50 mg/kg/day orally for 14 days. Contacts less than 7 years old who are not immunized or who have received less than 4 doses of DTP should have DTP immunization initiated or continued according to the recommended schedule. Children who have received their third dose 6 months or more before exposure should be given their fourth dose at this time. Erythromycin should also be given for 14 days. Contacts 7 years of age and above should receive prophylactic erythromycin (maximum: 1 g/day) for 10-14 days. All exposed patients should be watched closely for respiratory symptoms for 14 days after exposure has stopped because immunity conferred by the vaccine is not absolute and the efficacy of erythromycin in prophylaxis has not been established.

Disease	Exposure	Prophylaxis/Management
Tuberculosis	Housed in the same room with a child with contagious tuberculosis (tuberculosis is contagious if the child has a cough plus AFB seen on smear plus cavitation on CXR)	Place PPD immediately and 10 weeks after exposure. Start on INH. Consult Infectious Diseases if seroconversion occurs.
Varicella-zoster	1 hour or more in the same room with a contagious child from 24 hours before vesicles appear to when all vesicles are crusted, which is usually 5 to 7 days after vesicles appear. In household exposure, communicability is 48 hours before vesicles appear.	**Immunocompetent** children who have not been vaccinated or had natural infection, should have titers drawn only if they will still be hospitalized for more than 10 days after exposure. If titers are negative, they should be isolated from 10 to 21 days after exposure and/or until all lesions are crusted and dry. If VZIG was given the child should be isolated from 10 to 28 days after exposure. **Immunocompromised** children who have not been vaccinated or had natural infection should first have titers drawn, and then receive VZIG (varicella-zoster immune globulin) **1 vial/10 kg I.M.** up to a maximum of 5 vials as soon as possible but at most 96 hours after exposure. Fractional doses are not recommended. If titers are positive, nothing further need be done. If titers are negative, the child should be isolated from 10 to 28 days after exposure and should be monitored very carefully for the appearance of vesicles so that treatment can be initiated. VZIG is available from the Blood Bank.

TUBERCULOSIS

Tuberculin Skin Test Recommendations*

Children for whom immediate skin testing is indicated:

- Contacts of persons with confirmed or suspected infectious tuberculosis (contact investigation); this includes children identified as contacts of family members or associates in jail or prison in the last 5 years

- Children with radiographic or clinical findings suggesting tuberculosis

- Children immigrating from endemic countries (eg, Asia, Middle East, Africa, Latin America)

- Children with travel histories to endemic countries and/or significant contact with indigenous persons from such countries

Children who should be tested annually for tuberculosis†:

- Children infected with HIV or living in household with HIV-infected persons

- Incarcerated adolescents

Children who should be tested every 2-3 years†:

- Children exposed to the following individuals: HIV-infected, homeless, residents of nursing homes, institutionalized adolescents or adults, users of illicit drugs, incarcerated adolescents or adults, and migrant farm workers. Foster children with exposure to adults in the preceding high-risk groups are included.

Children who should be considered for tuberculin skin testing at ages 4-6 and 11-16 years:

- Children whose parents immigrated (with unknown tuberculin skin test status) from regions of the world with high prevalence of tuberculosis; continued potential exposure by travel to the endemic areas and/or household contact with persons from the endemic areas (with unknown tuberculin skin test status) should be an indication for repeat tuberculin skin testing

- Children without specific risk factors who reside in high-prevalence areas; in general, a high-risk neighborhood or community does not mean an entire city is at high risk; rates in any area of the city may vary by neighborhood, or even from block to block; physicians should be aware of these patterns in determining the likelihood of exposure; public health officials or local tuberculosis experts should help clinicians identify areas that have appreciable tuberculosis rates

Children at increased risk of progression of infection to disease: Those with other medical risk factors, including diabetes mellitus, chronic renal failure, malnutrition, and congenital or acquired immunodeficiencies deserve special consideration. Without recent exposure, these persons are not at increased risk of acquiring tuberculosis infection. Underlying immune deficiencies associated with these conditions theoretically would enhance the possibility for progression to severe disease. Initial histories of potential exposure to tuberculosis should be included on all of these patients. If these histories or local epidemiologic factors suggest a possibility of exposure, immediate and periodic tuberculin skin testing should be considered. An initial Mantoux tuberculin skin test should be performed before initiation of immunosuppressive therapy in any child with an underlying condition that necessitates immunosuppressive therapy.

---

*BCG immunization is not a contraindication to tuberculin skin testing.

†Initial tuberculin skin testing is at the time of diagnosis or circumstance, beginning as early as at age 3 months.

Tuberculosis Therapy

Specific Circumstances/ Organism	Comments	Regimen
Category I. Exposure		
(Household members and other close contacts of potentially infectious cases) (Exposee tuberculin test negative)*		
Neonate	Rx essential	INH (10 mg/kg/d) for 3 months, then repeat tuberculin test (TBnT). If mother's smear negative and infant's TBnT negative and chest x-ray (CXR) are normal, stop INH. In the United Kingdom, BCG is then given (*Lancet*, 1990, 2:1479), unless mother is HIV-positive. If infants repeat TBnT is positive and/or CXR abnormal (hilar adenopathy and/or infiltrate), administer INH + RIF (10-20 mg/kg/d) (or streptomycin) for a total of 6 months. If mother is being treated, separation from mother is not indicated.*
Children <5 y	Rx indicated	As for neonate first 3 months. If repeat TBnT is negative, stop. If repeat TBnT is positive, continue INH for a total of 9 months. If INH is not given initially, repeat TBnT at 3 months; if positive, treat with INH for 9 months (see Category II below).
Older children and adults	No Rx	Repeat TBnT at 3 months, if positive, treat with INH for 6 months (see Category II below)
Category II. Infection Without Disease		
(Positive tuberculin test)*		
Regardless of age (see INH Preventive Therapy)	Rx indicated	INH (5 mg/kg/d, maximum: 300 mg/d for adults, 10 mg/kg/d not to exceed 300 mg/d for children). Results with 6 months of treatment are nearly as effective as 12 months (65% vs 75% reduction in disease). *Am Thoracic Society* (6 months), *Am Acad Pediatrics*, 1991 (9 months). If CXR is abnormal, treat for 12 months. In HIV-positive patient, treatment for a minimum of 12 months, some suggest longer. Monitor transaminases monthly (*MMWR Morb Mortal Wkly Rep* 1989, 38:247).
Age <35 y	Rx indicated	Reanalysis of earlier studies favors INH prophylaxis for 6 months (if INH-related hepatitis case fatality rate is <1% and TB case fatality is ≥6.7%, which appears to be the case, monitor transaminases monthly (*Arch Int Med*, 1990, 150:2517).
INH-resistant organisms likely	Rx indicated	Data on efficacy of alternative regimens is currently lacking. Regimens include ETB + RIF daily for 6 months. PZA + RIF daily for 2 months, then INH + RIF daily until sensitivities from index case (if available) known, then if INH-CR, discontinue INH and continue RIF for 9 months, otherwise INH + RIF for 9 months (this latter is *Am Acad Pediatrics*, 1991 recommendation).
INH + RIF resistant organisms likely	Rx indicated	Efficacy of alternative regimens is unknown; PZA (25-30 mg/kg/d P.O.) + ETB (15-25 mg/kg/d P.O.) (at 25 mg/kg ETB, monitoring for retrobulbar neuritis required), for 6 months unless HIV-positive, then 12 months; PZA + ciprofloxacin (750 mg P.O. bid) or ofloxacin (400 mg P.O. bid) x 6-12 months (*MMWR Morb Mortal Wkly Rep*, 1992, 41(RR11):68).

INH = isoniazid; RIF = rifampin; KM = kanamycin; ETB = ethambutol

SM = streptomycin; CXR = chest x-ray; Rx = treatment

See also guidelines for interpreting PPD in "Skin Testing for Delayed Hypersensitivity" in the Appendix.

*Tuberculin test (TBnT). The standard is the Mantoux test, 5 TU PPD in 0.1 mL diluent stabilized with Tween 80. Read at 48-72 hours measuring maximum diameter of induration. A reaction ≥5 mm is defined as positive in the following: positive HIV or risk factors, recent close case contacts, CXR consistent with healed TBc. ≥10 mm is positive in foreign-born in countries of high prevalence, injection drug users, low income populations, nursing home residents, patients with medical conditions which increase risk (see above, preventive treatment). ≥15 mm is positive in all others (*Am Rev Resp Dis*, 1990, 142:725). Two-stage TBnT: Use in individuals to be tested regularly (ie, healthcare workers). TBn reactivity may decrease over time but be boosted by skin testing. If unrecognized, individual may be incorrectly diagnosed as recent converter. If first TBnT is reactive but <10 mm, repeat 5 TU in 1 week, if then ≥10 mm = positive, not recent conversion (*Am Rev Resp Dis*, 1979, 119:587).

USPHS/IDSA GUIDELINES FOR THE PREVENTION OF OPPORTUNISTIC INFECTIONS IN PERSONS INFECTED WITH HIV

(*MMWR Morb Mortal Wkly Rep*, 1997, 46(RR-12))

DRUG REGIMENS FOR ADULTS AND ADOLESCENTS

Prophylaxis for First Episode of Opportunistic Disease in HIV-Infected Adults and Adolescents

Pathogen	Indication	Preventive Regimens	
		First Choice	Alternatives
I. Strongly Recommended as Standard of Care			
Pneumocystis carinii*	CD4+ count <200/µL *or* oropharyngeal candidiasis *or* unexplained fever for ≥2 weeks	TMP-SMZ, 1 DS P.O. once daily (AI); TMP-SMZ, 1 SS P.O. once daily (AI)	TMP-SMZ, 1 DS P.O. 3 times/week (BIII); dapsone, 50 mg P.O. twice daily *or* 100 mg P.O. once daily (BI); dapsone, 50 mg P.O. once daily *plus* leucovorin, 25 mg P.O. once a week (BI); dapsone, 200 mg P.O. *plus* pyrimethamine, 75 mg P.O. *plus* leucovorin, 25 mg P.O. once a week (BI); aerosolized pentamidine, 300 mg once a month via Respirgard II™ nebulizer (BI)
Mycobacterium tuberculosis			
Isoniazid-sensitive†	TST reaction ≥5 mm *or* prior positive TST result without treatment *or* contact with case of active tuberculosis	Isoniazid, 300 mg P.O. *plus* pyridoxine, 50 mg P.O. once daily x 12 months (AI) *or* isoniazid, 900 mg P.O. twice a week *plus* pyridoxine, 50 mg P.O. twice a week x 12 months (BIII)	Rifampin, 600 mg P.O. once daily x 12 months (BII)
Isoniazid-resistant	Same; high probability of exposure to isoniazid-resistant tuberculosis	Rifampin, 600 mg P.O. once daily x 12 months (BII)	Rifabutin, 300 mg P.O. once daily x 12 months (CIII)
Multidrug (isoniazid and rifampin)-resistant	Same; high probability of exposure to multidrug-resistant tuberculosis	Choice of drugs requires consultation with public health authorities	None
Toxoplasma gondii§	IgG antibody to *Toxoplasma* and CD4+ count <100/µL	TMP-SMZ, 1 DS P.O. once daily (AII)	TMP-SMZ, 1 SS P.O. once daily (BIII); dapsone, 50 mg P.O. once daily *plus* pyrimethamine, 50 mg P.O. once a week *plus* leucovorin, 25 mg P.O. once a week (BI)
Mycobacterium avium complex¶	CD4+ count <50/µL	Clarithromycin, 500 mg P.O. twice daily (AI) or azithromycin, 1200 mg P.O. once a week (AI)	Rifabutin, 300 mg P.O. once daily (BI); azithromycin, 1200 mg P.O. once a week *plus* rifabutin, 300 mg P.O. once daily (CI)
Streptococcus pneumoniae**	All patients	Pneumococcal vaccine, 0.5 mL I.M. x 1 (CD4+ ≥200/µL, AII; CD4+ <200/µL, CIII)	None

Prophylaxis for First Episode of Opportunistic Disease in HIV-Infected Adults and Adolescents (continued)

Pathogen	Indication	Preventive Regimens	
		First Choice	Alternatives
Varicella-zoster virus (VZV)	Significant exposure to chickenpox or shingles for patients who have no history of either condition or, if available, negative antibody to VZV	Varicella-zoster immune globulin (VZIG), 5 vials (1.25 mL each) I.M., administered ≤96 hours after exposure, ideally within 48 hours (AIII)	Acyclovir, 800 mg P.O. 5 times/day for 3 weeks (CIII)

II. Generally Recommended

Pathogen	Indication	First Choice	Alternatives
Hepatitis B virus††	All susceptible (anti-HBc-negative) patients	Engerix B®, 20 µg I.M. x 3 (BII); or Recombivax HB®, 10 µg I.M. x 3 (BII)	None
Influenza virus††	All patients (annually, before influenza season)	Whole or split virus, 0.5 mL/year I.M. (BIII)	Rimantadine, 100 mg P.O. twice daily (CIII) or amantadine, 100 mg P.O. once daily (CIII)

III. Not Recommended for Most Patients; Indicated for Use Only in Unusual Circumstances

Pathogen	Indication	First Choice	Alternatives
Candida species	CD4+ count <50/µL	Fluconazole, 100-200 mg P.O. once daily (CI)	None
Bacteria	Neutropenia	Granulocyte-colony-stimulating factor (G-CSF), 5-10 µg/kg S.C. once daily x 2-4 weeks or granulocyte-macrophage colony-stimulating factor (GM-CSF), 250 µg/m² I.V. over 2 hours once daily x 2-4 weeks (CIII)	None
Cryptococcus neoformans§§	CD4+ count <50/µL	Fluconazole, 100-200 mg P.O. once daily (CI)	Itraconazole, 200 mg P.O. once daily (CIII)
Histoplasma capsulatum§§	CD4+ count <100/µL, endemic geographic area	Itraconazole, 200 mg P.O. once daily (CI)	None
Cytomegalovirus¶¶	CD4+ count <50/µL and CMV antibody positivity	Oral ganciclovir, 1 g P.O. 3 times/day (CI)	None

Note: Information included in these guidelines may not represent Food and Drug Administration (FDA) approval or approved labeling for the particular products or indications in question. Specifically, the terms "safe" and "effective" may not be synonymous with the FDA-defined legal standards for product approval. Anti-HBc = antibody to hepatitis B core antigen; CMV = cytomegalovirus; DS = double-strength tablet; SS = single-strength tablet; TMP-SMZ = trimethoprim-sulfamethoxazole; and TST = tuberculin skin test. The Respirgard II™ nebulizer is manufactured by Marquest, Englewood, CO; Engerix-B® by SmithKline Beecham, Rixensart, Belgium; and Recombivax HB® by Merck & Co., West Point, PA. Letters and Roman numerals in parentheses after regimens indicate the strength of the recommendation and the quality of evidence supporting it (see tables 1 and 2 in preface).

*Patients receiving dapsone should be tested for glucose-6-phosphate dehydrogenase deficiency. A dosage of 50 mg once daily is probably less effective than that of 100 mg once daily. The efficacy of parenteral pentamidine (eg, 4 mg/[kg • mol]) is uncertain. Inadequate data are available regarding efficacy or safety of atovaquone or clindamycin-primaquine. Fansidar (sulfadoxine-pyrimethamine) is rarely used because of severe hypersensitivity reactions. TMP-SMZ reduces the frequency of some bacterial infections. Patients who are being administered therapy for toxoplasmosis with sulfadiazine-pyrimethamine as protected against *Pneumocystis carinii* pneumonia and do not need TMP-SMZ.

†Directly observed therapy required for isoniazid (INH), 900 mg twice a week; INH regimens should include pyridoxine to prevent peripheral neuropathy. Rifampin should not be administered concurrently with protease inhibitors. Rifabutin, which may be administered at a reduced dose with indinavir or nelfinavir, is an option; consult an expert. Exposure to multidrug-resistant tuberculosis may require prophylaxis with two drugs; consult public health authorities. Possible regimens include pyrazinamide plus either ethambutol or a fluoroquinolone.

§Protection against *Toxoplasma* is provided by the preferred anti-*Pneumocystis* regimens. Pyrimethamine alone probably provides little, if any, protection.

¶Rifabutin should not be administered concurrently with the protease inhibitors saquinavir or ritonavir; however, it may be administered at half the dose (150 mg once daily) with indinavir or nelfinavir.

**Vaccination should be offered to persons who have a CD4+ T-lymphocyte count <200 cells/µL, although the efficacy may be diminished. Some authorities are concerned that immunizations may

USPHS/IDSA GUIDELINES FOR THE PREVENTION OF OPPORTUNISTIC INFECTIONS IN PERSONS INFECTED WITH HIV *(Continued)*

stimulate the replication of HIV. However, one study showed no adverse effect of pneumococcal vaccination on patient survival. Revaccination ≥5 years after the first dose is considered optional.

††These immunizations or chemoprophylactic regimens do not target pathogens traditionally classified as opportunistic but should be considered for use in HIV-infected patients. Data are inadequate concerning clinical benefit of these vaccines in this population, although it is logical to assume that those patients who develop antibody responses will derive some protection. Some authorities are concerned that immunizations may stimulate HIV replication, although, for influenza vaccination, a large observational study of HIV-infected persons in clinical care showed no adverse effect of this vaccine, including multiple doses, on patient survival (J. Ward, CDC, personal communication). Hepatitis B vaccine has been recommended for all children and adolescents and for all adults with risk factors for hepatitis B infection. Rimantadine/amantadine is appropriated during outbreaks of influenza A. Because of the theoretical concern that increases in HIV plasma RNA following vaccination during pregnancy might increase the risk of perinatal transmission of HIV, providers may wish to defer vaccination until after antiretroviral therapy is initiated.

§§There may be a few unusual occupational or other circumstances under which to consider prophylaxis: consult a specialist.

¶¶Acyclovir is not protective against CMV. Valaciclovir is not recommended because of an unexplained trend toward increased mortality observed in persons who have AIDS who were being administered this drug for prevention of CMV disease.

Prophylaxis for Recurrence of Opportunistic Disease (After Chemotherapy for Acute Disease) in HIV-Infected Adults and Adolescents

Pathogen	Indication	Preventive Regimens	
		First Choice	Alternatives
I. Recommended for Life as Standard of Care			
Pneumocystis carinii	Prior *P. carinii* pneumonia	TMP-SMZ, 1 DS P.O. once daily (AI); TMP-SMZ 1 SS P.O. once daily (AII)	TMP-SMZ, 1 DS P.O. three times a week (CIII); dapsone, 50 mg P.O. twice daily *or* 100 mg P.O. once daily (BII); dapsone, 50 mg P.O. once daily *plus* pyrimethamine, 50 mg P.O. weekly *plus* leucovorin, 25 mg P.O. weekly (BI); dapsone, 200 mg P.O. *plus* pyrimethamine, 75 mg P.O. *plus* leucovorin, 25 mg P.O. weekly (BI); aerosolized pentamidine, 300 mg monthly via Respirgard II™ nebulizer (BI)
*Toxoplasma gondii**	Prior toxoplasmic encephalitis	Sulfadiazine 500-1000 mg P.O. 4 times a day *plus* pyrimethamine 25-75 mg P.O. once daily *plus* leucovorin 10 mg P.O. once daily (AI)	Clindamycin, 300-450 mg P.O. every 6-8 hours *plus* pyrimethamine, 25-75 mg P.O. once daily *plus* leucovorin, 10-25 mg P.O. once to four times a day (BI)
Mycobacterium avium complex†	Documented disseminated disease	Clarithromycin, 500 mg P.O. twice daily (AI) *plus* one or more of the following: ethambutol, 15 mg/kg P.O. once daily (AII); rifabutin, 300 mg P.O. once daily (AII)	Azithromycin, 500 mg P.O. once daily (AII) *plus* one or more of the following: ethambutol, 15 mg/kg P.O. once daily (AII); rifabutin, 300 mg P.O. once daily (AII)
Cytomegalovirus	Prior end-organ disease	Ganciclovir, 5-6 mg/kg I.V. 5-7 days/week *or* 1000 mg P.O. 3 times/day (AI); *or* foscarnet, 90-120 mg/kg I.V. once daily (AI); *or* cidofovir, 5 mg/kg I.V. every other week (AI); *or* (for retinitis) ganciclovir sustained-release implant every 6-9 months (AI)	
Cryptococcus neoformans	Documented disease	Fluconazole, 200 mg P.O. once daily (AI)	Amphotericin B, 0.6-1 mg/kg I.V. weekly to 3 times/week (AI); itraconazole, 200 mg P.O. once daily (BI)

Prophylaxis for Recurrence of Opportunistic Disease (After Chemotherapy for Acute Disease) in HIV-Infected Adults and Adolescents *(continued)*

Pathogen	Indication	Preventive Regimens	
		First Choice	Alternatives
Histoplasma capsulatum	Documented disease	Itraconazole, 200 mg P.O. twice daily (AII)	Amphotericin B, 1 mg/kg I.V. weekly (AII); fluconazole, 400 mg P.O. once daily (CII)
Coccidioides immitis	Documented disease	Fluconazole, 400 mg P.O. once daily (AII)	Amphotericin B, 1 mg/kg I.V. weekly (AI); itraconazole, 200 mg P.O. twice daily (AII)
Salmonella species (non-typhi)§	Bacteremia	Ciprofloxacin, 500 mg P.O. twice daily for several months (BII)	None
II. Recommended Only if Subsequent Episodes Are Frequent or Severe			
Herpes simplex virus	Frequent/ severe recurrences	Acyclovir, 200 mg P.O. 3 times/day or 400 mg P.O. twice daily (AI)	
Candida (oral, vaginal, or esophageal)	Frequent/ severe recurrences	Fluconazole, 100-200 mg P.O. once daily (AI)	Ketoconazole, 200 mg P.O. once daily (CIII); itraconazole, 200 mg P.O. once daily (CIII)

Note: Information included in these guidelines may not represent Food and Drug Administration (FDA) approval or approved labeling for the particular products or indications in question. Specifically, the terms "safe" and "effective" may not be synonymous with the FDA-defined legal standards for product approval. DS = double-strength tablet; SS = single-strength tablet; and TMP-SMZ = trimethoprim-sulfamethoxazole. The Respirgard II™ nebulizer is manufactured by Marquest, Englewood, CO. Letters and Roman numerals in parentheses after regimens indicate the strength of the recommendation and the quality of the evidence supporting it.

*Pyrimethamine/sulfadiazine confers protection against PCP as well as toxoplasmosis; clindamycin-pyrimethamine does not.

†Many multiple-drug regimens are poorly tolerated. Drug interactions (eg, those seen with clarithromycin/ rifabutin) can be problematic; rifabutin has been associated with uveitis, especially when administered at daily doses of >300 mg or concurrently with fluconazole or clarithromycin. Rifabutin should not be administered concurrently with the protease inhibitors saquinavir or ritonavir, but it can be administered at half dose (150 mg once daily) with indinavir or nelfinavir.

§The efficacy of eradication of *Salmonella* has been demonstrated only for ciprofloxacin.

USPHS/IDSA GUIDELINES FOR THE PREVENTION OF OPPORTUNISTIC INFECTIONS IN PERSONS INFECTED WITH HIV (Continued)

DRUG REGIMENS FOR INFANTS AND CHILDREN

Prophylaxis for First Episode of Opportunistic Disease in HIV-Infected Infants and Children

Pathogen	Indication	Preventive Regimens	
		First Choice	Alternatives
I. Strongly Recommended as Standard of Care			
*Pneumocystis carinii**	HIV-infected or HIV-indeterminate infants aged 1-12 months; HIV-infected children aged 1-5 years old with CD4+ count <500/µL or CD4+ percentage <15%; HIV-infected children aged 6-12 years of age with CD4+ count <200/µL or CD4+ percentage <15%	TMP-SMZ, 150/750 mg/m²/d in 2 divided doses P.O. 3 times a week on consecutive days (AII); Acceptable alternative dosage schedules: (AII) Single dose P.O. 3 times a week on consecutive days; 2 divided doses P.O. once daily; 2 divided doses P.O. 3 times a week on alternate days	Aerosolized pentamidine (children aged ≥5 years of age, 300 mg monthly via Respirgard II™ nebulizer (CIII); dapsone (children aged ≥1 month), 2 mg/kg (max: 100 mg) P.O. once daily (CIII); I.V. pentamidine, 4 mg/kg every 2-4 weeks (CIII)
Mycobacterium tuberculosis			
Isoniazid-sensitive	TST reaction ≥5 mm or prior positive TST result without treatment or contact with case of active tuberculosis	Isoniazid 10-15 mg/kg (max: 300 mg) P.O. or I.M. once daily x 12 months (AI) or 20-30 mg/kg (max: 900 mg) P.O. twice a week x 12 months (BIII)	Rifampin, 10-20 mg/kg (max: 600 mg) P.O. or I.V. once daily x 12 months (BII)
Isoniazid-resistant	Same as above; high probability of exposure to isoniazid-resistant tuberculosis	Rifampin, 10-20 mg/kg (max: 600 mg) P.O. or I.V. once daily x 12 months (BII)	Uncertain
Multidrug (isoniazid and rifampin)-resistant	Same as above; high probability of exposure to multidrug-resistant tuberculosis	Choice of drug requires consultation with public health authorities	None
Mycobacterium avium complex	For children aged ≥6 years, CD4+ count <50/µL; aged 2-6 years, CD4+ count <75/µL; aged 1-2 years, CD4+ count <500/µL; aged <1 year, CD4+ count <750/µL	Clarithromycin, 7.5 mg/kg (max: 500 mg) P.O. twice daily (AII), or azithromycin, 20 mg/kg (max: 1200 mg) P.O. weekly (AII)	Children aged ≥6 years, rifabutin, 300 mg P.O. once daily (BII); children aged <6 years, 5 mg/kg P.O. once daily when suspension becomes available (BI); azithromycin, 5 mg/kg (max: 250 mg) P.O. once daily (AII)
Varicella-zoster virus†	Significant exposure to varicella with no history of chickenpox or shingles	Varicella-zoster immune globulin (VZIG), 1 vial (1.25 mL)/10 kg (max: 5 vials) I.M., administered ≤96 hours after exposure, ideally within 48 hours (AII)	None
Vaccine-preventable pathogens§	HIV exposure/infection	Routine immunizations	None
II. Generally Recommended			
Toxoplasma gondii¶	IgG antibody *Toxoplasma* and severe immunosuppression	TMP-SMZ, 150/750 mg/m²/d in 2 divided doses P.O. once daily (BIII)	Dapsone (children aged ≥1month), 2 mg/kg or 15 mg/m²(max: 25 mg) P.O. once daily plus pyrimethamine, 1 mg/kg P.O. once daily plus leucovorin, 5 mg P.O. every 3 days (BIII)

Prophylaxis for First Episode of Opportunistic Disease in HIV-Infected Infants and Children (continued)

Pathogen	Indication	Preventive Regimens	
		First Choice	Alternatives
III. Not Recommended for Most Patients; Indicated for Use Only in Unusual Circumstances			
Invasive bacterial infections**	Hypogamma-globulinemia	IVIG (400 mg/kg/month) (AI)	None
Candida species	Severe immunosuppression	Nystatin (100,000 U/mL), 4-6 mL P.O. every 6 hours (CIII) or topical clotrimazole, 10 mg P.O. 5 times/day (CIII)	None
Cryptococcus neoformans	Severe immunosuppression	Fluconazole, 3-6 mg/kg P.O. once daily (CII)	Itraconazole, 2-5 mg/kg P.O. every 12-24 hours (CIII)
Histoplasma capsulatum	Severe immunosuppression, endemic geographic area	Itraconazole, 2-5 mg/kg P.O. every 12-24 hours (CII)	None
Cytomegalovirus (CMV)††	CMV antibody positivity and severe immunosuppression	Children aged 6-12 years; oral ganciclovir under investigation	None

Note: Information included in these guidelines may not represent Food and Drug Administration (FDA) approval or approved labeling for the particular products or indications in question. Specifically, the terms "safe" and "effective" may not be synonymous with the FDA-defined legal standards for product approval. CMV = cytomegalovirus; IVIG = intravenous immune globulin; TMP-SMZ = trimethoprim-sulfamethoxazole; and VZIG = varicella-zoster immune globulin. The Respirgard II™ nebulizer is manufactured by Marquest, Englewood, CO. Letters and Roman numerals in parentheses after regimens indicate the strength of the recommendation and the quality of the evidence supporting it.

*The efficacy of parenteral pentamidine (eg, 4 mg/kg/month) is controversial. TMP-SMZ, dapsone-pyrimethamine, and possibly dapsone alone appear to protect against toxoplasmosis, although data have not been prospectively collected. Daily TMP-SMZ reduces the frequency of some bacterial infections. Patients receiving therapy for toxoplasmosis with sulfadiazine-pyrimethamine are protected against Pneumocystits carinii pneumonia (PCP) and do not need TMP-SMZ.

†Children routinely being administered intravenous immune globulin (IVIG) should receive VZIG if the last dose of IVIG was administered >21 days before exposure.

§HIV-infected and HIV-exposed children should be immunized according to the following childhood immunization schedule, which has been adapted fromt he January-December 1997 schedule recommended for immunocompetent children by the Advisory committee on Immunization Practices, the American Academy of Pediatrics, and the American Academy of Family Physicians. This schedule differs from that for immunocompetent children by the IPV replaces OPV, vaccination against S. pneumoniae (AII) and influenza (BIII) should be offered, and vaccination against varicella is contraindicated (EIII). MMR should not be administered to severly immunocompromised children (DIII). Once an HIV-exposed child is determined not to be HIV-infected, the schedule for immunocompetent children applies.

¶Protection against Toxoplasma is provided by the preferred antipneumocystis regimens. Pyrimethamine alone probably provides little, if any, protection.

**Respiratory syncytial virus (RSV) IVIG may be substituted for IVIG during the RSV season.

††Data on oral ganciclovir are still being evaluated; durability of effect is unclear. Acyclovir is not protective against CMV.

USPHS/IDSA GUIDELINES FOR THE PREVENTION OF OPPORTUNISTIC INFECTIONS IN PERSONS INFECTED WITH HIV *(Continued)*

Prophylaxis for Recurrence of Opportunistic Disease (After Chemotherapy for Acute Disease) in HIV-Infected Infants and Children

Pathogen	Indication	Preventive Regimens	
		First Choice	Alternatives
I. Recommended for Life as Standard of Care			
Pneumocystis carinii	Prior *P.carinii* pneumonia	TMP-SMZ, 150/750 mg/m²/d in 2 divided doses P.O. three times a week on consecutive days (AII); acceptable alternative schedules for same dosage (AII)	Aerosolized pentamidine (children ≥5 years of age), 300 mg every month via Respirgard II™ nebulizer (CIII); dapsone (children ≥1 month old), 2 mg/kg (max: 100 mg) P.O. once daily (CIII)
		Single dose P.O. three times a week on consecutive days; 2 divided doses P.O. once daily; 2 divided doses P.O. three times a week on alternate days	I.V. pentamidine, 4 mg/kg every 2-4 weeks (CIII)
Toxoplasma gondii*	Prior toxoplasmic encephalitis	Sulfadiazine, 85-120 mg/kg/d in 2-4 divided doses P.O. once daily *plus* pyrimethamine, 1 mg/kg *or* 15 mg/m² (max: 25 mg) P.O. once daily *plus* leucovorin, 5 mg P.O. every 3 days (AI)	Clindamycin, 20-30 mg/kg/d in 4 divided doses P.O. once daily *plus* pryimethamine, 1 mg/kg P.O. once daily *plus* leucovorin, 5 mg P.O. every 3 days (BI)
Mycobacterium avium complex	Prior disease	Clarithromycin, 7.5 mg/kg (max: 500 mg) P.O. twice daily (AII) *plus* at least one of the following: ethambutol, 15 mg/kg (max: 900 mg) P.O. once daily (AII); rufabutin, 5 mg/kg (max: 300 mg) P.O. once daily (AII)	None
Cryptococcus neoformans	Documented disease	Fluconazole, 3-6 mg/kg P.O. once daily (AII)	Itraconazole, 2-5 mg/kg P.O. every 12-14 hours (BII); amphotericin B, 0.5-1.5 mg/kg I.V. 1-3 times/week (AI)
Histoplasma capsulatum	Documented disease	Itraconazole, 2-5 mg/kg P.O. every 12-48 hours (AIII)	Fluconazole, 3-6 mg/kg P.O. once daily (CIII); amphotericin B, 1 mg/kg I.V. weekly (AIII)
Coccidioides immitis	Documented disease	Fluconazole, 6 mg/kg P.O. once daily (AIII)	Amphotericin B, 1 mg/kg I.V. weekly (AII)
Cytomegalovirus	Prior end-organ disease	Ganciclovir, 5 mg/kg I.V. once daily; *or* foscarnet, 90-120 mg/kg I.V. once daily (AI); *or* (for retinitis) ganciclovir sustained-release implant (AI)	None
Salmonella species (non-typhi)†	Bacteremia	TMP-SMZ, 150/750 mg/m² in 2 divided doses P.O. once daily for several months (CIII)	Antibiotic chemoprophylaxis with antoher active agent (CIII)

Prophylaxis for Recurrence of Opportunistic Disease (After Chemotherapy for Acute Disease) in HIV-Infected Infants and Children (continued)

Pathogen	Indication	Preventive Regimens	
		First Choice	Alternatives
II. Recommended Only if Subsequent Episodes Are Frequent or Severe			
Invasive bacterial infections§	>2 infections in 1-year period	TMP-SMZ, 150/750 mg/m² divided doses P.O. once daily (BI); or IVIG, 400 mg/kg monthly (BI)	Antibiotic chemoprophylaxis with another active agent (BIII)
Herpes simplex virus	Frequent/ severe recurrences	Acyclovir, 80 mg/kg/d in 3-4 divided doses P.O. once daily (AII)	
Candida species	Frequent/ severe recurrences	Fluconazole, 3-6 mg/kg P.O. once daily (AII); or ketoconazole, 5-10 mg/kg P.O. every 12-24 hours (CIII)	

Note: Information included in these guidelines may not represent Food and Drug Administration (FDA) approval or approved labeling for the particular products or indications in question. Specifically, the terms "safe" and "effective" may not be synonymous with the FDA-defined legal standards for product approval. IVIG = intravenous immune globulin and TMP-SMZ = trimethoprim-sulfamethoxazole. The Respirgard II™ nebulizer is manufactured by Marquest, Englewood, CO. Letters and Roman numerals in parentheses after regimens indicate the strength of the recommendations and the quality of the evidence supporting it.

*Only pyrimethamine plus sulfadiazine confers protection against PCP. Although the clindamycin plus pyrimethamine regimen is the preferred alternative in adults, it has not been tested in children. However, these drugs are safe and are used for other infections.

†Drug should be determined by susceptibilities of the organism isolated. Alternatives to TMP-SMZ include ampicillin, chloramphenicol, or ciprofloxacin. However, ciprofloxacin is not approved for use in persons aged <18 years; therefore, it should be used in children with caution and only if no alternatives exist.

§Antimicrobial prophylaxis should be chosen based on the microorganism and antibiotic sensitivities. TMP-SMZ, if used, should be administered daily. Providers should be cautious about using antibiotics solely for this purpose because of the potential for development of drug-resistant microorganisms. IVIG may not provide additional benefit to children receiving daily TMP-SMZ. Choice of antibiotic prophylaxis vs. IVIG should also involve consideration of adherence, ease of intravenous access, and cost. If IVIG is used, RSV-IVIG may be substituted for IVIG during the RSV season.

INTERPRETATION OF GRAM'S STAIN RESULTS GUIDELINES

These guidelines are not definitive but presumptive for the identification of organisms on Gram's stain. Treatment will depend on the quality of the specimen and appropriate clinical evaluation.

	Example
Gram-Negative Bacilli (GNB)	
Enterobacteriaceae	*Escherichia coli*
	Serratia sp
	Klebsiella sp
	Enterobacter sp
	Citrobacter sp
Nonfermentative GNB	*Xanthomonas maltophilia*
Pseudomonas aeruginosa	
Bacteroides fragilis group	
If fusiform (long and pointed)	*Capnocytophaga* sp
	Fusobacterium sp
Gram-Negative Cocci (GNC)	
Diplococci, pairs	*Moraxella (Branhamella) catarrhalis*
	Neisseria gonorrhoeae
	Neisseria meningitidis
Coccobacilli	*Acinetobacter* sp
	Haemophilus influenzae
Gram-Positive Bacilli (GPB)	
Diphtheroids (small pleomorphic)	*Corynebacterium* sp
	Propionibacterium
Large, with spores	*Bacillus* sp
	Clostridium sp
Branching, beaded, rods	*Actinomyces* sp
	Nocardia sp
Other	*Lactobacillus* sp
	Listeria sp
Gram-Positive Cocci (GPC)	
Pairs, chains, clusters	*Enterococcus* sp
	Staphylococcus sp
	Streptococcus sp
Pairs, lancet-shaped	*Streptococcus pneumoniae*

KEY CHARACTERISTICS OF SELECTED BACTERIA

Gram-Negative Bacilli (GNB)	**Example**
Lactose-positive	*Citrobacter* sp* (Enterobacteriaceae)
	Enterobacter sp* (Enterobacteriaceae)
	Escherichia coli (Enterobacteriaceae)
	Klebsiella pneumoniae (Enterobacteriaceae)
Lactose-negative/oxidase-negative	*Acinetobacter* sp
	Morganella morganii
	Proteus mirabilis: indole-negative
	Proteus vulgaris: indole-positive
	Providencia sp
	Salmonella sp
	Serratia sp† (Enterobacteriaceae)
	Shigella sp
	Xanthomonas maltophilia
Lactose-negative/oxidase-positive	*Aeromonas hydrophila* (may be lactose positive)
	Alcaligenes sp
	Flavobacterium sp
	Moraxella sp‡
	Pseudomonas aeruginosa
	Other *Pseudomonas* sp
Anaerobes	*Bacteroides* sp (*B. fragilis*)
	Fusobacterium sp
Other	*Haemophilus influenzae* (coccobacillus)

Gram-Positive Baccili (GPB)	
Anaerobes	*Lactobacillus* sp
	Eubacterium sp
	Clostridium sp (spores)
	Bifidobacterium sp
	Actinomyces sp (branching, filamentous)
	Propionibacterium acnes
Bacillus sp	*B. cereus*, *B. subtilis* (large with spores)
Branching, beaded; partial acid-fast positive	*Nocardia* sp
CSF, blood	*Listeria monocytogenes*
Rapidly growing mycobacteria	*M. fortuitum*
	M. chelonei
Vaginal flora, rarely blood	*Lactobacillus* sp
Often blood culture contaminants	Diphtheroids (may be *Corynebacterium* sp)
Resistant to many agents except vancomycin	*C. jeikeium*
Other	*Actinomyces* sp (branching, beaded)

Gram-Negative Cocci (GNC)	
Diplococci, pairs	*Capnocytophaga* sp
	Fusobacterium sp (fusiform)
	Moraxella catarrhalis
	Neisseria meningitidis
	Neisseria gonorrhoeae
Coccobacilli	*Acinetobacter* sp
Anaerobes	*Veillonella* sp

Gram-Positive Cocci (GPC)	
Catalase-negative	*Streptococcus* sp (chains)
	Micrococcus sp (usually insignificant)
Catalase-positive	*Staphylococcus* sp (pairs, chains, clusters)
Coagulase-negative	Coagulase-negative staphylococci (CNS)
Bloods	*S. epidermidis* or CNS
Urine	*S. saprophyticus* (CNS)
Coagulase-positive	*S. aureus*
Anaerobes	*Peptostreptococcus* sp

KEY CHARACTERISTICS OF SELECTED BACTERIA *(Continued)*

Fungi

Molds

Sparsely septate hyphae	Zygomycetes (eg, *Rhizopus* sp and *Mucor*)
Septate hyphae brown pigment	Phaeohyphomycetes, for example, *Alternaria* sp *Bipolaris* sp *Curvularia* sp *Exserohilum* sp
Nonpigmented (hyaline)	Hyalophomycetes, for example *Aspergillus* sp (*A. fumigatus, A. flavus*) Dermatophytes *Fusarium* sp *Paecilomyces* sp *Penicillium* sp
Thermally dimorphic (yeast in tissue; mold *in vitro*)	*Blastomyces dermatitidis* *Coccidioides immitis* *Histoplasma capsulatum* (slow growing) *Paracoccidioides brasilliensis* *Sporothrix schenckii*
Yeast	*Candida* sp (germ tube positive = *C. albicans* *Cryptococcus* sp (no pseudohyphae) *C. neoformans* *Rhodotorula, Saccharomyces* sp *Torulopsis glabrata* *Trichosporon* sp

Virus	Influenza Hepatitis A, B, C, D Human immunodeficiency virus Rubella Herpes Cytomegalovirus Respiratory syncytial virus Epstein-Barr
Chlamydiae	*Chlamydia trachomatis* *Chlamydia pneumoniae* (TWAR) *Chlamydia psittaci*
Rickettsiae	
Ureaplasma	
Mycoplasma	*Mycoplasma pneumoniae* *Mycoplasma hominis*
Spirochetes	*Treponema pallidum* *Borrelia burgdorferi*
Mycobacteria	*Mycobacterium tuberculosis* *Mycobacterium intracellulare*

Most Common Blood Culture Contaminants

Alpha-hemolytic streptococci
Bacillus sp
Coagulase-negative staphylococci
Diphtheroids
Lactobacilli
Micrococcus sp
Propionibacterium sp

*May be lactose-negative.
†May produce red pigment and appear lactose-positive initially.
‡May be either bacillary or coccoid.

ANIMAL AND HUMAN BITES GUIDELINES

Wound Management

Irrigation: Critically important; irrigate all penetration wounds using 20 mL syringe, 19 gauge needle and >250 mL 1% povidone iodine solution. This method will reduce wound infection by a factor of 20. When there is high risk of rabies, use viricidal 1% benzalkonium chloride in addition to the 1% povidone iodine. Irrigate wound with normal saline after antiseptic irrigation.

Debridement: Remove all crushed or devitalized tissue remaining after irrigation; minimize removal on face and over thin skin areas or anywhere you would create a worse situation than the bite itself already has; do not extend puncture wounds surgically — rather, manage them with irrigation and antibiotics.

Suturing: Close most dog bites if <8 hours (<12 hours on face); do not routinely close puncture wounds, or deep or severe bites on the hands or feet, as these are at highest risk for infection. Cat and human bites should not be sutured unless cosmetically important. Wound edge freshening, where feasible, reduces infection; minimize sutures in the wound and use monofilament on the surface.

Immobilization: Critical in all hand wounds; important for infected extremities.

Hospitalization/I.V. Antibiotics: Admit for I.V. antibiotics all significant human bites to the hand, especially closed fist injuries, and bites involving penetration of the bone or joint (a high index of suspicion is needed). Consider I.V. antibiotics for significant established wound infections with cellulitis or lymphangitis, any infected bite on the hand, any infected cat bite, and any infection in an immunocompromised or asplenic patient. Outpatient treatment with I.V. antibiotics may be possible in selected cases by consulting with infectious disease.

Laboratory Assessment

Gram's Stain: Not useful prior to onset of clinically apparent infection; examination of purulent material may show a predominant organism in established infection, aiding antibiotic selection; not warranted unless results will change your treatment.

Culture: Not useful or cost effective prior to onset of clinically apparent infection.

X-Ray: Whenever you suspect bony involvement, especially in craniofacial dog bites in very small children or severe bite/crush in an extremity; cat bites with their long needle like teeth may cause osteomyelitis or a septic joint, especially in the hand or wrist.

Immunizations

Tetanus: All bite wounds are contaminated. If not immunized in last 5 years, or if not current in a child, give DPT, DT, Td, or TT as indicated. For absent or incomplete primary immunization, give 250 units tetanus immune globulin (TIG) in addition.

Rabies: In the U.S. 30,000 persons are treated each year in an attempt to prevent 1-5 cases. Domestic animals should be quarantined for 10 days to prove need for prophylaxis. High risk animal bites (85% of cases = bat, skunk, raccoon) usually receive treatment consisting of:

- human rabies immune globulin (HRIG): 20 units/kg I.M. (unless previously immunized with HDCV)
- human diploid cell vaccine (HDCV): 1 mL I.M. on days 0, 3, 7, 14, and 28 (unless previously immunized with HDCV - then give only first 2 doses)

Consult with Infectious Disease before ordering rabies prophylaxis.

Bite Wounds and Prophylactic Antibiotics

Parenteral vs Oral: If warranted, consider an initial I.V. dose to rapidly establish effective serum levels, especially if high risk, delayed treatment, or if patient reliability is poor.

Dog Bite:

1. Rarely get infected (~5%)
2. Infecting organisms: Coagulase-negative staph, coagulase-positive staph, alpha strep, diphtheroids, beta strep, *Pseudomonas aeruginosa*, gamma strep, *Pasteurella multocida*
3. Prophylactic antibiotics are seldom indicated. Consider for high risk wounds such as distal extremity puncture wounds, severe crush injury, bites occurring in cosmetically sensitive areas (eg, face), or in immuno-compromised or asplenic patients.

Cat Bite:

1. Often get infected (~25% to 50%)
2. Infecting organisms: *Pasteurella multocida* (first 24 hours), coagulase-positive staph, anaerobic cocci (after first 24 hours)
3. Prophylactic antibiotics are indicated in all cases.

ANIMAL AND HUMAN BITES GUIDELINES *(Continued)*

Human Bite:

1. Intermediate infection rate (~15% to 20%)
2. Infecting organisms: Coagulase-positive staph, alpha, beta, gamma strep, *Haemophilus*, *Eikenella corrodens*, anaerobic streptococci, *Fusobacterium*, *Veillonella*, bacteroides.
3. Prophylactic antibiotics are indicated in almost all cases except superficial injuries.

See attached table for prophylactic antibiotic summary.

Bite Wound Antibiotic Regimens

	Dog Bite	Cat Bite	Human Bite
Prophylactic Antibiotics			
Prophylaxis	No routine prophylaxis, consider if involves face or hand, or immunosuppressed or asplenic patients	Routine prophylaxis	Routine prophylaxis
Prophylactic antibiotic	Amoxicillin	Amoxicillin	Amoxicillin
Penicillin allergy	Doxycycline if >10 y or co-trimoxazole	Doxycycline if >10 y or co-trimoxazole	Doxycycline if >10 y or erythromycin and cephalexin*
Outpatient Oral Antibiotic Treatment (mild to moderate infection)			
Established infection	Amoxicillin and clavulanic acid	Amoxicillin and clavulanic acid	Amoxicillin and clavulanic acid
Penicillin allergy (mild infection only)	Doxycycline if >10 y	Doxycycline if >10 y	Cephalexin* or clindamycin
Outpatient Parenteral Antibiotic Treatment (moderate infections – single drug regimens)			
	Ceftriaxone	Ceftriaxone	Cefotetan
Inpatient Parenteral Antibiotic Treatment			
Established infection	Ampicillin + cefazolin	Ampicillin + cefazolin	Ampicillin + clindamycin
Penicillin allergy	Cefazolin*	Ceftriaxone*	Cefotetan* or imipenem
Duration of Prophylactic and Treatment Regimens			
Prophylaxis: 5 days			
Treatment: 10-14 days			

*Contraindicated if history of immediate hypersensitivity reaction (anaphylaxis) to penicillin.

ANTIBIOTIC TREATMENT OF ADULTS WITH INFECTIVE ENDOCARDITIS

Table 1. Suggested Regimens for Therapy of Native Valve Endocarditis Due to Penicillin-Susceptible Viridans Streptococci and *Streptococcus bovis* (Minimum Inhibitory Concentration ≤0.1 µg/mL)*

Antibiotic	Dosage and Route	Duration (wk)	Comments
Aqueous crystalline penicillin G sodium or	12-18 million units/24 h I.V. either continuously or in 6 equally divided doses	4	Preferred in most patients older than 65 y and in those with impairment of the eighth nerve or renal function
Ceftriaxone sodium	2 g once daily I.V. or I.M.†	4	
Aqueous crystalline penicillin G sodium	12-18 million units/24 h I.V. either continuously or in 6 equally divided doses	2	When obtained 1 hour after a 20- to 30-minute I.V. infusion or I.M. injection, serum concentration of gentamicin of approximately 3 µg/mL is desirable; trough concentration should be <1 µg/mL
With gentamicin sulfate‡	1 mg/kg I.M. or I.V. every 8 hours	2	
Vancomycin hydrochloride§	30 mg/kg/24 h I.V. in 2 equally divided doses, not to exceed 2 g/24 h unless serum levels are monitored	4	Vancomycin therapy is recommended for patients allergic to β-lactams; peak serum concentrations of vancomycin should be obtained 1 h after completion of the infusion and should be in the range of 30-45 µg/mL for twice-daily dosing

*Dosages recommended are for patients with normal renal function. For nutritionally variant streptococci, see Table 3. I.V. indicates intravenous; I.M., intramuscular.

†Patients should be informed that I.M. injection of ceftriaxone is painful.

‡Dosing of gentamicin on a mg/kg basis will produce higher serum concentrations in obese patients that in lean patients. Therefore, in obese patients, dosing should be based on ideal body weight. (Ideal body weight for men is 50 kg + 2.3 kg per inch over 5 feet, and ideal body weight for women is 45.5 kg + 2.3 kg per inch over 5 feet.) Relative contraindications to the use of gentamicin are age >65 years, renal impairment, or impairment of the eighth nerve. Other potentially nephrotoxic agents (eg, nonsteroidal anti-inflammatory drugs) should be used cautiously in patients receiving gentamicin.

§Vancomycin dosage should be reduced in patients with impaired renal function. Vancomycin given on a mg/kg basis will produce higher serum concentrations in obese patients than in lean patients. Therefore, in obese patients, dosing should be based on ideal body weight. Each dose of vancomycin should be infused over at least 1 h to reduce the risk of the histamine-release "red man" syndrome.

Table 2. Therapy for Native Valve Endocarditis Due to Strains of Viridans Streptococci and *Streptococcus bovis* Relatively Resistant to Penicillin G (Minimum Inhibitory Concentration >0.1 µg/mL and <0.5 µg/mL)*

Antibiotic	Dosage and Route	Duration (wk)	Comments
Aqueous crystalline penicillin G sodium	18 million units/24 h I.V. either continuously or in 6 equally divided doses	4	Cefazolin or other first-generation cephalosporins may be substituted for penicillin in patients whose penicillin hypersensitivity is not of the immediate type.
With gentamicin sulfate†	1 mg/kg I.M. or I.V. every 8 h	2	
Vancomycin hydrochloride§	30 mg/kg/24 h I.V. in 2 equally divided doses, not to exceed 2 g/24 h unless serum levels are monitored	4	Vancomycin therapy is recommended for patients allergic to β-lactams

*Dosages recommended are for patients with normal renal function. I.V. indicates intravenous; I.M., intramuscular.

†For specific dosing adjustment and issues concerning gentamicin (obese patients, relative contraindications), see Table 1 footnotes.

‡For specific dosing adjustment and issues concerning vancomycin (obese patients, length of infusion), see Table 1 footnotes.

ANTIBIOTIC TREATMENT OF ADULTS WITH INFECTIVE ENDOCARDITIS *(Continued)*

Table 3. Standard Therapy for Endocarditis Due to Enterococci*

Antibiotic	Dosage and Route	Duration (wk)	Comments
Aqueous crystalline penicillin G sodium	18-30 million units/24 h I.V. either continuously or in 6 equally divided doses	4-6	4-week therapy recommended for patients with symptoms <3 months in duration; 6-week therapy recommended for patients with symptoms >3 months in duration.
With gentamicin sulfate†	1 mg/kg I.M. or I.V. every 8 h	4-6	
Ampicillin sodium	12 g/24 h I.V. either continuously or in 6 equally divided doses	4-6	
With gentamicin sulfate†	1 mg/kg I.M. or I.V. every 8 hours	4-6	
Vancomycin hydrochloride†‡	30 mg/kg/24 h I.V. in 2 equally divided doses, not to exceed 2 g/24 h unless serum levels are monitored	4-6	Vancomycin therapy is recommended for patients allergic to β-lactams; cephalosporins are not acceptable alternatives for patients allergic to penicillin
With gentamicin sulfate†	1 mg/kg I.M. or I.V. every 8 h	4-6	

*All enterococci causing endocarditis must be tested for antimicrobial susceptibility in order to select optimal therapy. This table is for endocarditis due to gentamicin- or vancomycin-susceptible enterococci, viridans streptococci with a minimum inhibitory concentration of >0.5 µg/mL, nutritionally variant viridans streptococci, or prosthetic valve endocarditis caused by viridans streptococci or *Streptococcus bovis*. Antibiotic dosages are for patients with normal renal function. I.V. indicates intravenous; I.M., intramuscular.

†For specific dosing adjustment and issues concerning gentamicin (obese patients, relative contraindications), see Table 1 footnotes.

‡For specific dosing adjustment and issues concerning vancomycin (obese patients, length of infusion), see Table 1 footnotes.

Table 4. Therapy for Endocarditis Due to *Staphylococcus* in the Absence of Prosthetic Material*

Antibiotic	Dosage and Route	Duration	Comments
Methicillin-Susceptible Staphylococci			
Regimens for non-β-lactam-allergic patients			
Nafcillin sodium or oxacillin sodium	2 g I.V. every 4 h	4-6 wk	Benefit of additional aminoglycosides has not been established
With optional addition of gentamicin sulfate†	1 mg/kg I.M. or I.V. every 8 h	3-5 d	
Regimens for β-lactam-allergic patients			
Cefazolin (or other first-generation cephalosporins in equivalent dosages)	2 g I.V. every 8 h	4-6 wk	Cephalosporins should be avoided in patients with immediate-type hypersensitivity to penicillin
With optional addition of gentamicin†	1 mg/kg I.M. or I.V. every 8 hours	3-5 d	
Vancomycin hydrochloride‡	30 mg/kg/24 h I.V. in 2 equally divided doses, not to exceed 2 g/24 h unless serum levels are monitored	4-6 wk	Recommended for patients allergic to penicillin
Methicillin-Resistant Staphylococci			
Vancomycin hydrochloride‡	30 mg/kg/24 h I.V. in 2 equally divided doses; not to exceed 2 g/24 h unless serum levels are monitored	4-6 wk	

*For treatment of endocarditis due to penicillin-susceptible staphylococci (minimum inhibitory concentration ≤0.1 µg/mL), aqueous crystalline penicillin G sodium (Table 1, first regimen) can be used for 4-6 weeks instead of nafcillin or oxacillin. Shorter antibiotic courses have been effective in some drug addicts with right-sided endocarditis due to *Staphylococcus aureus*. I.V. indicates intravenous; I.M., intramuscular.

†For specific dosing adjustment and issues concerning gentamicin (obese patients, relative contraindications), see Table 1 footnotes.

‡For specific dosing adjustment and issues concerning vancomycin (obese patients, length of infusion), see Table 1 footnotes.

Table 5. Treatment of Staphylococcal Endocarditis in the Presence of a Prosthetic Valve or Other Prosthetic Material*

Antibiotic	Dosage and Route	Duration (wk)	Comments
Regimen for Methicillin-Resistant Staphylococci			
Vancomycin hydrochloride†	30 mg/kg/24 h I.V. in 2 or 4 equally divided doses, not to exceed 2 g/24 h unless serum levels are monitored	≥6	
With rifampin‡	300 mg orally every 8 h	≥6	Rifampin increases the amount of warfarin sodium required for antithrombotic therapy.
And with gentamicin sulfate§¶	1 mg/kg I.M. or I.V. every 8 h	2	
Regimen for Methicillin-Susceptible Staphylococci			
Nafcillin sodium or oxacillin sodium†	2 g I.V. every 4 h	≥6	First-generation cephalosporins or vancomycin should be used in patients allergic to β-lactam. Cephalosporins should be avoided in patients with immediate-type hypersensitivity to penicillin or with methicillin-resistant staphylococci.
With rifampin‡	300 mg orally every 8 h	≥6	
And with gentamicin sulfate§¶	1 mg/kg I.M. or I.V. every 8 h	2	

*Dosages recommended are for patients with normal renal function. I.V. indicates intravenous; I.M., intramuscular.

†For specific dosing adjustment and issues concerning gentamicin (obese patients, relative contraindications), see Table 1 footnotes.

‡Rifampin plays a unique role in the eradication of staphylococcal infection involving prosthetic material; combination therapy is essential to prevent emergence of rifampin resistance.

§For a specific dosing adjustment and issues concerning gentamicin (obese patients, relative contraindications), see Table 1 footnotes.

¶Use during initial 2 weeks.

Table 6. Therapy for Endocarditis Due to HACEK Microorganisms (*Haemophilus parainfluenzae, Haemophilus aphrophilus, Actinobacillus actinomycetemcomitans, Cardiobacterium hominis, Eikenella corrodens,* and *Kingella kingae*)*

Antibiotic	Dosage and Route	Duration (wk)	Comments
Ceftriaxone sodium†	2 g once daily I.V. or I.M.†	4	Cefotaxime sodium or other third-generation cephalosporins may be substituted
Ampicillin sodium‡	12 g/24 h I.V. either continuously or in 6 equally divided doses	4	
With gentamicin sulfate§	1 mg/kg I.M. or I.V. every 6 h	4	

*Antibiotic dosages are for patients with normal renal function. I.V. indicates intravenous; I.M. intramuscular.

†Patients should be informed that I.M. injection of ceftriaxone is painful.

‡Ampicillin should not be used if laboratory tests show β-lactamase production.

§For specific dosing adjustment and issues concerning gentamicin (obese patients, relative contraindications), see Table 1 footnotes.

Note: Tables 1-6 are from Wilson WR, Karchmer AW, Dajani AS, et al, "Antibiotic Treatment of Adults With Infective Endocarditis Due to Streptococci, Enterococci, Staphylococci, and HACEK Microorganisms," *JAMA*, 1995, 274(21):1706-13, with permission.

ANTIMICROBIAL DRUGS OF CHOICE

The following table lists the antimicrobial drugs of choice for various infecting organisms. This table is reprinted with permission from *The Medical Letter*, 1998, 40(1023): 37-42. Users should not assume that all antibiotics which are appropriate for a given organism are listed or that those not listed are inappropriate. The infection caused by the organism may encompass varying degrees of severity, and since the antibiotics listed may not be appropriate for the differing degrees of severity, or because of other patient-related factors, it cannot be assumed that the antibiotics listed for any specific organism are interchangeable. This table should not be used by itself without first referring to *The Medical Letter*, an infectious disease manual, or the infectious disease department. Therefore, only use this table as a tool for obtaining more information about the therapies available.

Infecting Organism	Drug of First Choice	Alternative Drugs
Gram-Positive Cocci		
Enterococcus[1]		
endocarditis or other severe infection	Penicillin G or ampicillin + gentamicin or streptomycin	Vancomycin + gentamicin or streptomycin; quinupristin/dalfopristin[2]
uncomplicated urinary tract infection	Ampicillin or amoxicillin	Nitrofurantoin; a fluoroquinolone[3]; fosfomycin
Staphylococcus aureus or *epidermidis*		
nonpenicillinase-producing	Penicillin G or V[4]	A cephalosporin[5,6]; vancomycin; imipenem or meropenem; clindamycin; a fluoroquinolone[3]
penicillinase-producing	A penicillinase-resistant penicillin[7]	A cephalosporin[5,6]; vancomycin; amoxicillin/clavulanic acid; ticarcillin/clavulanic acid; piperacillin/tazobactam; ampicillin/sulbactam; imipenem or meropenem; clindamycin; a fluoroquinolone[3]
methicillin-resistant[8]	Vancomycin ± gentamicin ± rifampin	Trimethoprim-sulfamethoxazole; a fluoroquinolone[3]; minocycline[9]
Streptococcus pyogenes (group A) and groups C and G[10]	Penicillin G or V[4]	Clindamycin; erythromycin; a cephalosporin[5,6]; vancomycin; clarithromycin[11]; azithromycin
Streptococcus, group B	Penicillin G or ampicillin	A cephalosporin[5,6]; vancomycin; erythromycin
Streptococcus, viridans group[1]	Penicillin G ± gentamicin	A cephalosporin[5,6]; vancomycin
Streptococcus bovis[1]	Penicillin G	A cephalosporin[5,6]; vancomycin
Streptococcus, anaerobic or *Peptostreptococcus*	Penicillin G	Clindamycin; a cephalosporin[5,6]; vancomycin
Streptococcus pneumoniae[12] (pneumococcus), penicillin-susceptible (MIC <0.1 mcg/mL)	Penicillin G or V[4]	A cephalosporin[5,6]; erythromycin; azithromycin; clarithromycin[11]; a fluoroquinolone; meropenem; imipenem; trimethoprim-sulfamethoxazole; clindamycin; a tetracycline[9]
Penicillin-intermediate resistance (MIC 0.1-1 mcg/mL)	Penicillin G I.V. (12 million units/day for adults) or ceftriaxone or cefotaxime	Levofloxacin, grepafloxacin or trovafloxacin; vancomycin
Penicillin-high level resistance (MIC ≥2 mcg/mL)	Meningitis: Vancomycin + ceftriaxone or cefotaxime ± rifampin	Meropenem; imipenem
	Other infections: Vancomycin + ceftriaxone or cefotaxime; or levofloxacin, grepafloxacin, or trovafloxacin	Quinupristin/dalfopristin[2]
Gram-Negative Cocci		
Moraxella (Branhamella) catarrhalis	Trimethoprim-sulfamethoxazole	Amoxicillin/clavulanic acid; erythromycin; a tetracycline[9]; cefuroxime[5]; cefotaxime[5]; ceftizoxime[5]; ceftriaxone[5]; cefuroxime axetil[5]; cefixime[5]; cefpodoxime[5]; a fluoroquinolone[3]; clarithromycin[11]; azithromycin
Neisseria gonorrhoeae (gonococcus)[13]	Ceftriaxone[5] or cefixime[5] or ciprofloxacin[3] or ofloxacin[3]	Cefotaxime[5]; spectinomycin; penicillin G
Neisseria meningitidis[14] (meningococcus)	Penicillin G	Cefotaxime[5]; ceftizoxime[5]; ceftriaxone[5]; chloramphenicol[15]; a sulfonamide[16]; a fluoroquinolone[3]
Gram-Positive Bacilli		
Bacillus anthracis (anthrax)	Penicillin G	Erythromycin; a tetracycline[9]
Bacillus cereus, subtilis	Vancomycin	Imipenem or meropenem; clindamycin
Clostridium perfringens[17]	Penicillin G	Clindamycin; metronidazole; imipenem or meropenem; chloramphenicol[15]
Clostridium tetani[18]	Penicillin G	A tetracycline[9]
Clostridium difficile[19]	Metronidazole	Vancomycin (oral)

Infecting Organism	Drug of First Choice	Alternative Drugs
Corynebacterium diphtheriae[20]	Erythromycin	Penicillin G
Corynebacterium, JK group	Vancomycin	Penicillin G + gentamicin; erythromycin
*Erysipelothrix rhusiopethiae	Penicillin G	Erythromycin, a cephalosporin[5,6]; a fluoroquinolone[3]
Listeria monocytogenes	Ampicillin ± gentamicin	Trimethoprim-sulfamethoxazole
Enteric Gram-Negative Bacilli		
*Bacteroides	Metronidazole or clindamycin	Imipenem or meropenem; amoxicillin/clavulanic acid; ticarcillin/clavulanic acid; piperacillin/tazobactam; cefoxitin[5]; cefotetan[5]; ampicillin/sulbactam; chloramphenicol[15]; cefmetazole[5]; trovafloxacin; penicillin G
*Campylobacter fetus	Imipenem or meropenem	Gentamicin
*Campylobacter jejuni	Fluoroquinolone[3] or erythromycin	A tetracycline[9]; gentamicin
*Citrobacter freundi	Imipenem or meropenem[21]	A fluoroquinolone[3]; amikacin; tetracycline[9]; trimethoprim-sulfamethoxazole; cefotaxime[5,21]; ceftizoxime[5,21]; ceftriaxone[5,21]; cefepime[5,21]; or ceftazidime[5,21]
*Enterobacter	Imipenem or meropenem[21]	Gentamicin, tobramycin, or amikacin; trimethoprim-sulfamethoxazole; ciprofloxacin[22]; ticarcillin[23]; mezlocillin[23] or piperacillin[23]; aztreonam[21]; cefotaxime[5,21]; ceftizoxime[5,21]; ceftriaxone[5,21]; cefepime[5,21]; or ceftazidime[5,21]
*Escherichia coli[24]	Cefotaxime, ceftizoxime, ceftriaxone, cefepime, or ceftazidime[5,21]	Ampicillin ± gentamicin, tobramycin or amikacin; carbenicillin[23]; ticarcillin[23]; mezlocillin[23] or piperacillin[23]; gentamicin, tobramycin, or amikacin; amoxicillin/clavulanic acid[21]; ticarcillin/clavulanic acid[23]; piperacillin/tazobactam[23]; ampicillin/sulbactam[21]; trimethoprim/sulfamethoxazole; imipenem or meropenem[21]; aztreonam[21]; fluoroquinolone[3]; another cephalosporin[5,6]
*Helicobacter pylori[25]	Tetracycline hydrochloride[9] + metronidazole + bismuth subsalicylate	Tetracycline hydrochloride + clarithromycin[11] + bismuth subsalicylate; amoxicillin + metronidazole + bismuth subsalicylate; amoxicillin + clarithromycin[11]
*Klebsiella pneumoniae[24]	Cefotaxime, ceftizoxime, ceftriaxone, cefepime, or ceftazidime[5,21]	Imipenem or meropenem[21]; gentamicin, tobramycin, or amikacin; amoxicillin/clavulanic acid[21]; ticarcillin/clavulanic acid[23]; piperacillin/tazobactam[23]; ampicillin/sulbactam[21]; trimethoprim-sulfamethoxazole; aztreonam[21]; a fluoroquinolone[3]; mezlocillin[23] or piperacillin[23]; another cephalosporin[5,6]
*Proteus mirabilis[24]	Ampicillin[26]	A cephalosporin[6,21]; ticarcillin[23]; mezlocillin[23] or piperacillin[23]; gentamicin, tobramycin, or amikacin; trimethoprim-sulfamethoxazole; imipenem or meropenem[21]; aztreonam[21]; a fluoroquinolone[3]; chloramphenicol[15]
Proteus, indole-positive (including Providencia rettgeri, Morganella morganii, and Proteus vulgaris)	Cefotaxime, ceftizoxime, ceftriaxone, cefepime, or ceftazidime[5,21]	Imipenem or meropenem[21]; gentamicin, tobramycin, or amikacin; carbenicillin[23]; ticarcillin[23]; mezlocillin[23] or piperacillin[23]; amoxicillin/clavulanic acid[21]; ticarcillin/clavulanic acid[23]; piperacillin/tazobactam[23]; ampicillin/sulbactam[21]; aztreonam[21]; trimethoprim-sulfamethoxazole; a fluoroquinolone[3]
*Providencia stuartii	Cefotaxime, ceftizoxime, ceftriaxone, cefepime, or ceftazidime[5,21]	Imipenem or meropenem[21]; ticarcillin/clavulanic acid[23]; piperacillin/tazobactam[23]; gentamicin, tobramycin, or amikacin; carbenicillin[23]; ticarcillin[23]; mezlocillin[23], or piperacillin[23]; aztreonam[21]; trimethoprim-sulfamethoxazole; fluoroquinolone[3]
*Salmonella typhi[27]	A fluoroquinolone[3] or ceftriaxone[6]	Chloramphenicol[15]; trimethoprim-sulfamethoxazole; ampicillin; amoxicillin
*other Salmonella[28]	Cefotaxime[5] or ceftriaxone[5] or a fluoroquinolone[3]	Ampicillin or amoxicillin; trimethoprim-sulfamethoxazole; chloramphenicol[15]
*Serratia	Cefotaxime, ceftizoxime, ceftriaxone, cefepime, or ceftazidime[5,29]	Gentamicin or amikacin; imipenem or meropenem[29]; aztreonam[29]; trimethoprim-sulfamethoxazole; carbenicillin[30]; ticarcillin[30]; mezlocillin[30] or piperacillin[30]; a fluoroquinolone[3]
*Shigella	A fluoroquinolone[3]	Azithromycin; trimethoprim-sulfamethoxazole; ampicillin; ceftriaxone[5]

ANTIMICROBIAL DRUGS OF CHOICE (Continued)

Infecting Organism	Drug of First Choice	Alternative Drugs
*Yersinia enterocolitica	Trimethoprim-sulfamethoxazole	A fluoroquinolone[3]; gentamicin, tobramycin, or amikacin; cefotaxime or ceftizoxime[5]
Other Gram-Negative Bacilli		
*Acinetobacter	Imipenem or meropenem[21]	Amikacin, tobramycin, or gentamicin; ciprofloxacin[22]; trimethoprim-sulfamethoxazole; ticarcillin[23], mezlocillin[23], or piperacillin[23]; ceftazidime[21]; minocycline[9]; doxycycline[9]
*Aeromonas	Trimethoprim-sulfamethoxazole	Gentamicin or tobramycin; imipenem; a fluoroquinolone[3]
Bartonella		
Agent of bacillary angiomatosis (*Bartonella henselae* or *quintana*)[31]	Erythromycin	Doxycycline[9]; azithromycin
Cat scratch bacillus (*Bartonella henselae*)[31,32]	Ciprofloxacin[22]	Trimethoprim-sulfamethoxazole; gentamicin; rifampin; azithromycin
Bordetella pertussis (whooping cough)	Erythromycin	Trimethoprim-sulfamethoxazole
*Brucella	A tetracycline[9] + streptomycin or gentamicin	A tetracycline[9] + rifampin; chloramphenicol[15] ± streptomycin; trimethoprim-sulfamethoxazole ± gentamicin; rifampin + a tetracycline[9]
*Burkholderia capacia	Trimethoprim-sulfamethoxazole	Ceftazidime[5]; chloramphenicol[15]
Calymmatobacterium granulomatis (granuloma inguinale)	Trimethoprim-sulfamethoxazole	Doxycycline[9] or ciprofloxacin ± gentamicin
Capnocytophaga canimorsus (DF-2)[33]	Penicillin G	Cefotaxime[5]; ceftizoxime[5]; ceftriaxone[5]; imipenem or meropenem; vancomycin; a fluoroquinolone[3]; clindamycin
*Eikenella corrodens	Ampicillin	An erythromycin; a tetracycline[9]; amoxicillin/clavulanic acid; ampicillin/sulbactam; ceftriaxone[5]
*Francisella tularensis (tularemia)	Streptomycin	Gentamicin; a tetracycline[9]; chloramphenicol[16]
*Fusobacterium	Penicillin G	Metronidazole; clindamycin; cefoxitin[5]; chloramphenicol[15]
Gardnerella vaginalis (bacterial vaginosis)	Oral metronidazole[34]	Topical clindamycin or metronidazole; oral clindamycin
*Haemophilus ducreyi (chancroid)	Azithromycin or ceftriaxone	Ciprofloxacin[22] or erythromycin
*Haemophilus influenzae		
meningitis, epiglottitis, arthritis, and other serious infections	Cefotaxime or ceftriaxone[5]	Cefuroxime[5] (but not for meningitis); chloramphenicol[15]; meropenem
upper respiratory infections and bronchitis	Trimethoprim-sulfamethoxazole	Cefuroxime[5]; amoxicillin/clavulanic acid; cefuroxime axetil[5]; cefpodoxime[5]; cefaclor[5]; cefotaxime[5]; ceftizoxime[5]; ceftriaxone[5]; cefixime[5]; a tetracycline[9]; clarithromycin[11]; azithromycin; a fluoroquinolone[3]; ampicillin or amoxicillin
Legionella species[35]	Erythromycin or clarithromycin[11] or azithromycin[11] or a fluoroquinolone[3] ± rifampin	Doxycycline[9] ± rifampin; trimethoprim-sulfamethoxazole
Leptotrichia buccalis	Penicillin G	A tetracycline[9]; clindamycin; erythromycin
Pasteurella multocida	Penicillin G	A tetracycline[9]; a cephalosporin[5,6]; amoxicillin/clavulanic acid; ampicillin/sulbactam
*Pseudomonas aeruginosa		
urinary tract infection	Ciprofloxacin[22]	Carbenicillin, ticarcillin, piperacillin, or mezlocillin; ceftazidime[5]; cefepime[5]; imipenem or meropenem; aztreonam; tobramycin; gentamicin; amikacin
other infections	Ticarcillin, mezlocillin, or piperacillin + tobramycin, gentamicin, or amikacin[36]	Ceftazidime[5], imipenem, meropenem, aztreonam, cefepime[5] + tobramycin, gentamicin, or amikacin; ciprofloxacin[22]; trovafloxacin[22]
Pseudomonas mallei (glanders)	Streptomycin + a tetracycline[9]	Streptomycin + chloramphenicol[15]
*Pseudomonas pseudomallei (melioidosis)	Ceftazidime[5]	Chloramphenicol[15] + doxycycline[9] + trimethoprim-sulfamethoxazole; amoxicillin/clavulanic acid; imipenem or meropenem
Spirillum minus (rat bite fever)	Penicillin G	A tetracycline[9]; streptomycin
*Stenotrophomonas maltophilia (Pseudomonas maltophilia)	Trimethoprim-sulfamethoxazole	Minocycline[9]; ceftazidime;[5] a fluoroquinolone[3]

Infecting Organism	Drug of First Choice	Alternative Drugs
Streptobacillus moniliformis (rat bite fever, Haverhill fever)	Penicillin G	A tetracycline[9]; streptomycin
Vibrio cholerae (cholera)[37]	A tetracycline[9]	A fluoroquinolone[3]; trimethoprim-sulfamethoxazole
Vibrio vulnificus	A tetracycline[9]	Cefotaxime[6]
Yersinia pestis (plague)	Streptomycin ± a tetracycline[9]	Chloramphenicol[15]; gentamicin; trimethoprim-sulfamethoxazole
Acid-Fast Bacilli		
*Mycobacterium tuberculosis	Isoniazid + rifampin + pyrazinamide ± ethambutol or streptomycin[15]	Ciprofloxacin, ofloxacin, or levofloxacin[22]; cycloserine[15]; capreomycin[15] or kanamycin[15] or amikacin[15]; ethionamide[15]; clofazimine[15]; aminosalicylic acid[15]
*Mycobacterium kansasii	Isoniazid + rifampin ± ethambutol or streptomycin[15]	Clarithromycin[11]; ethionamide[15]; cycloserine[15]
*Mycobacterium avium complex	Clarithromycin[11] or azithromycin + one or more of the following: ethambutol; rifabutin; ciprofloxacin[22]	Rifampin; amikacin[15]
prophylaxis	Clarithromycin[11]	Rifabutin
*Mycobacterium fortuitum complex	Amikacin + doxycycline[9]	Cefoxitin[5]; rifampin; a sulfonamide
Mycobacterium marinum (balnei)[38]	Minocycline[9]	Trimethoprim-sulfamethoxazole; rifampin; clarithromycin[11]; doxycycline[9]
Mycobacterium leprae (leprosy)	Dapsone + rifampin ± clofazimine	Minocycline[9]; ofloxacin[22,39]; sparfloxacin; clarithromycin[11,40]
Actinomycetes		
Actinomyces israelii (actinomycosis)	Penicillin G	A tetracycline[9]; erythromycin; clindamycin
Nocardia	Trimethoprim-sulfamethoxazole	Sulfisoxazole; amikacin[15]; a tetracycline[9]; imipenem or meropenem; cycloserine[15]
*Rhodococcus equi	Vancomycin ± a fluoroquinolone[3], rifampin, imipenem or meropenem or amikacin	Erythromycin
Tropheryma whippelii[41] (agent of Whipple's disease)	Trimethoprim-sulfamethoxazole	Penicillin G; a tetracycline[9]
Chlamydiae		
Chlamydia psittaci (psittacosis, ornithosis)	A tetracycline[9]	Chloramphenicol[15]
Chlamydia trachomatis		
(trachoma)	Azithromycin	A tetracycline[9] (topical plus oral); a sulfonamide (topical plus oral)
(inclusion conjunctivitis)	Erythromycin (oral or I.V.)	A sulfonamide
(pneumonia)	Erythromycin	A sulfonamide
(urethritis, cervicitis)	Azithromycin or doxycycline[9]	Erythromycin; ofloxacin[22]; amoxicillin
(lymphogranuloma venereum)	A tetracycline[9]	Erythromycin
Chlamydia pneumoniae (TWAR strain)	A tetracycline[9]	Erythromycin; clarithromycin[11]; azithromycin; a fluoroquinolone[22]
Ehrlichia		
Ehrlichia chaffeensis	A tetracycline[9]	Chloramphenicol[15]
Agent of human granulocytic ehrlichiosis[42]	A tetracycline[9]	
Mycoplasma		
Mycoplasma pneumoniae	Erythromycin or a tetracycline[9] or clarithromycin[11] or azithromycin	A fluoroquinolone[3]
Ureaplasma urealyticum	Erythromycin	A tetracycline[9]; clarithromycin[11]; azithromycin; ofloxacin[22]
Rickettsia — Rocky Mountain spotted fever, endemic typhus (murine), epidemic typhus (louse-borne), scrub typhus, trench fever, Q fever	A tetracycline[9]	Chloramphenicol[15]; a fluoroquinolone[3]
Spirochetes		
Borrelia burgdorferi (Lyme disease)[43]	Doxycycline[9] or amoxicillin or cefuroxime axetil[5]	Ceftriaxone[5]; cefotaxime[5]; penicillin G; azithromycin; clarithromycin[11]
Borrelia recurrentis (relapsing fever)	A tetracycline[9]	Penicillin G
Treponema pallidum (syphilis)	Penicillin G[4]	A tetracycline[9]; ceftriaxone[5]
Treponema pertenue (yaws)	Penicillin G	A tetracycline[9]

ANTIMICROBIAL DRUGS OF CHOICE *(Continued)*

*Resistance may be a problem; susceptibility tests should be performed.

1. Disk sensitivity testing may not provide adequate information; beta-lactamase assays, "E" tests, and dilution tests for susceptibility should be used in serious infections.

2. An investigational drug in the U.S.A. (*Synercid®*) available through Rhone-Poulenc Rorer (610-454-3071).

3. Among the fluoroquinolones, levofloxacin, sparfloxacin, grepafloxacin, and trovafloxacin have the greatest *in vitro* activity against *S. pneumoniae*, including penicillin and cephalosporin-resistant strains. Levofloxacin, sparfloxacin, grepafloxacin, and trovafloxacin also have good activity against many strains of *S. aureus*, but resistance has become frequent among methicillin-resistant strains. Ciprofloxacin and trovafloxacin have the greatest activity against *Pseudomonas aeruginosa*. Trovafloxacin is the most active against anaerobes. Sparfloxacin has a substantial incidence of photosensitivity reactions. For urinary tract infections, norfloxacin, lomefloxacin, or enoxacin can be used. Ciprofloxacin, ofloxacin, levofloxacin, and trovafloxacin are available for intravenous use. None of these agents are recommended for children or pregnant women.

4. Penicillin V (or amoxicillin) is preferred for oral treatment of infections caused by non-penicillinase-producing staphylococci and other gram-positive cocci. For initial therapy of severe infections, penicillin G, administered parenterally, is first choice. For somewhat longer action in less severe infections due to group A streptococci, pneumococci, or *Treponema pallidum*, procaine penicillin G, an intramuscular formulation, is given once or twice daily. Benzathine penicillin G, a slowly absorbed preparation, is usually given in a single monthly injection for prophylaxis of rheumatic fever, once for treatment of group A streptococcal pharyngitis and once or more for treatment of syphilis.

5. The cephalosporins have been used as alternatives to penicillin in patients allergic to penicillins, but such patients may also have allergic reactions to cephalosporins.

6. For parenteral treatment of staphylococcal or nonenterococcal streptococcal infections, a first-generation cephalosporin such as cephalothin or cefazolin can be used. For oral therapy, cephalexin or cephradine can be used. The second-generation cephalosporins cefamandole, cefprozil, cefuroxime axetil, cefonicid, cefotetan, cefmetazole, cefoxitin, and loracarbef are more active than the first-generation drugs against gram-negative bacteria. Cefuroxime is active against ampicillin-resistant strains of *H. influenzae*. Cefoxitin, cefotetan, and cefmetazole are the most active of the cephalosporins against *B. fragilis*, but cefotetan and cefmetazole have been associated with prothrombin deficiency. The third-generation cephalosporins cefotaxime, cefoperazone, ceftizoxime, ceftriaxone, and ceftazidime, and the fourth-generation cefepime have greater activity than the second-generation drugs against enteric gram-negative bacilli. Ceftazidime has poor activity against many gram-positive cocci and anaerobes, and ceftizoxime has poor activity against penicillin-resistant *S. pneumoniae* (Hess DW and Bonczar T, J *Antimicrob Chemother*, 1996, 38:293). Cefepime has *in vitro* activity against gram-positive organisms similar to cefotaxime and ceftriaxone and somewhat greater activity against enteric gram-negative bacilli. The activity of cefepime against *Pseudomonas aeruginosa* is similar to that of ceftazidime. Cefixime, cefpodoxime, and cefibuten are oral cephalosporins with more activity than second-generation cephalosporins against facultative gram-negative bacilli; they have no useful activity against anaerobes or *Pseudomonas aeruginosa* and cefixime and ceftibuten have no useful activity against staphylococci. With the exception of cefoperazone (which, like cefamandole, can cause bleeding), ceftazidime and cefepime, the activity of all currently available cephalosporins against *Pseudomonas aeruginosa* is poor or inconsistent.

7. For oral use against penicillinase-producing staphylococci, cloxacillin or dicloxacillin is preferred; for severe infections, a parenteral formulation of nafcillin or oxacillin should be used. Ampicillin, amoxicillin, bacampicillin, carbenicillin, ticarcillin, mezlocillin, and piperacillin are not effective against penicillinase-producing staphylococci. The combination of clavulanic acid with amoxicillin or ticarcillin, sulbactam with ampicillin, and tazobactam with piperacillin are active against these organisms.

8. Many strains of coagulase-positive staphylococci and coagulase-negative staphylococci are resistant to penicillinase-resistant penicillins; those strains are also resistant to cephalosporins, imipenem, and meropenem.

9. Tetracyclines are generally not recommended for pregnant women or children younger than 8 years old.

10. For serious soft-tissue infection due to group A streptococci, clindamycin may be more effective than penicillin. Group A streptococci may, however, be resistant to clindamycin; therefore, some *Medical Letter* consultants suggest using both clindamycin and penicillin to treat serious soft-tissue infections. Group A streptococci may also be resistant to erythromycin, azithromycin, and clarithromycin.

11. Not recommended for use in pregnancy.

12. Some strains of *S. pneumoniae* are resistant to erythromycin, clindamycin, trimethoprim-sulfamethoxazole, clarithromycin, azithromycin and chloramphenicol. Nearly all strains tested so far are susceptible to some of the newer fluoroquinolones (levofloxacin, sparfloxacin, grepafloxacin, and trovafloxacin) and quinupristin/dalfopristin.

13. Patients with gonorrhea should be treated presumptively for coinfection with *C. trachomatis* with azithromycin or doxycycline.

14. Rare strains of *N. meningitidis* are resistant or relatively resistant to penicillin. Rifampin or a fluoroquinolone is recommended for prophylaxis after close contact with infected patients.

15. Because of the possibility of serious adverse effects, this drug should be used only for severe infections when less hazardous drugs are ineffective.

16. Sulfonamide-resistant strains are frequent in the U.S.; sulfonamides should be used only when susceptibility is established by susceptibility tests.

17. Debridement is primary. Large doses of penicillin G are required. Hyperbaric oxygen therapy may be a useful adjunct to surgical debridement in management of the spreading, necrotic type.

18. For prophylaxis, a tetanus toxoid booster and, for some patients, tetanus immune globulin (human) are required.

19. In order to decrease the emergence of vancomycin-resistant enterococci in hospitals, many clinicians now recommend use of metronidazole first in treatment of most patients with *C. difficile* colitis, with oral vancomycin used only for seriously ill patients or those who do not respond to metronidazole (Wenisch C, *Clin Infect Dis*, 1996, 22:813).

20. Antitoxin is primary; antimicrobials are used only to halt further toxin production and to prevent the carrier state.

21. In severely ill patients, most *Medical Letter* consultants would add gentamicin, tobramycin, or amikacin.

22. Usually not recommended for use in children or pregnant women.

23. In severely ill patients, most *Medical Letter* consultants would add gentamicin, tobramycin, or amikacin (but see footnote 36).

24. For an acute, uncomplicated urinary tract infection, before the infecting organism is known, the drug of first choice is trimethoprim-sulfamethoxazole.

25. Eradication of *H. pylori* with various antibacterial combinations, given concurrently with an H₂-receptor blocker or proton pump inhibitor, has led to rapid healing of active peptic ulcers and low recurrence rates (*Medical Letter*, 1997, 39:1).

26. Large doses (6 g or more/day) are usually necessary for systemic infections. In severely ill patients, some *Medical Letter* consultants would add gentamicin, tobramycin, or amikacin.

27. A fluoroquinolone or amoxicillin is the drug of choice for *S. typhi* carriers.

28. Most cases of *Salmonella* gastroenteritis subside spontaneously without antimicrobial therapy.

29. In severely ill patients, most *Medical Letter* consultants would add gentamicin or amikacin.

30. In severely ill patients, most *Medical Letter* consultants would add gentamicin or amikacin (but see footnote 36).

31. Schwartzman W, *Annu Rev Med*, 1996, 47:365.
32. Role of antibiotics is not clear (Chia JKS, et al, *Clin Infect Dis*, 1998, 26:193).
33. Pera C, et al, *Clin Infect Dis*, 1998, 23:71.
34. Metronidazole is effective for bacterial vaginosis even though it is not usually active against *Gardnerella in vitro*.
35. Stout JE and Yu VL, *N Engl J Med*, 1997, 337:682.
36. Neither gentamicin, tobramycin, netilmicin, or amikacin should be mixed in the same bottle with carbenicillin, ticarcillin, mezlocillin, or piperacillin for intravenous administration. When used in high doses or in patients with renal impairment, these penicillins may inactivate the aminoglycosides.
37. Antibiotic therapy is an adjunct to and not a substitute for prompt fluid and electrolyte replacement.
38. Most infections are self-limited without drug treatment (American Thoracic Society, *Am H Respir Crit Care Med*, 1997, 156:S17.
39. Ji B, et al, *Antimicrob Agents Chemother*, 1997, 41:1953.
40. Gelber RH, Ji B, et al, *Antimicrob Agents Chemother*, 1997, 41:1618.
41. Durand DV, et al, *Medicine*, 1997, 76:170.
42. Jacobs RF and Schalzo GE, *J Pediatr*, 1997, 131:184.
43. For treatment of erythema migrans, facial nerve palsy, mild cardiac disease, and some cases of arthritis, oral therapy is satisfactory; for more serious neurologic or cardiac disease or arthritis, parenteral therapy with ceftriaxone, cefotaxime, or penicillin G is recommended (*Medical Letter*, 1997, 39:47).

ANTIRETROVIRAL THERAPY FOR HIV INFECTION

Report of the NIH Panel to Define Principles of Therapy of HIV Infection

GUIDELINES FOR THE USE OF ANTIRETROVIRAL AGENTS IN HIV-INFECTED ADULTS AND ADOLESCENTS

Adapted from *MMWR Morb Mortal Wkly Rep*, 1998, 47(RR-5)
and *JAMA*, 1998, 280:78-86.

Indications for Plasma HIV RNA Testing*

Clinical Indication	Information	Use
Syndrome consistent with acute HIV infection	Establishes diagnosis when HIV antibody test is negative or indeterminate	Diagnosis†
Initial evaluation of newly diagnosed HIV infection	Baseline viral load "set point"	Decision to start or defer therapy
Every 3-4 months in patients not on therapy	Changes in viral load	Decision to start therapy
4-8 weeks after initiation of antiretroviral therapy	Initial assessment of drug efficacy	Decision to continue or change therapy
3-4 months after start of therapy	Maximal effect of therapy	Decision to continue or change therapy
Every 3-4 months in patients on therapy	Durability of antiretroviral effect	Decision to continue or change therapy
Clinical event or significant decline in CD4+ T cells	Association with changing or stable viral load	Decision to continue, initiate, or change therapy

*Acute illness (eg, bacterial pneumonia, tuberculosis, HSV, PCP) and immunizations can cause increases in plasma HIV RNA for 2-4 weeks; viral load testing should not be performed during this time. Plasma HIV RNA results should usually be verified with a repeat determination before starting or making changes in therapy. HIV RNA should be measured using the same laboratory and the same assay.

†Diagnosis of HIV infection determined by HIV RNA testing should be confirmed by standard methods (eg, Western blot serology) performed 2-4 months after the initial indeterminate or negative test.

Risks and Benefits of Early Initiation of Antiretroviral Therapy in the Asymptomatic HIV-infected Patient

Potential Benefits

Control of viral replication and mutation; reduction of viral burden

Prevention of progressive immunodeficiency; potential maintenance or reconstitution of a normal immune system

Delayed progression to AIDS and prolongation of life

Decreased risk of selection of resistant virus

Decreased risk of drug toxicity

Potential Risks

Reduction in quality of life from adverse drug effects and inconvenience of current maximally suppressive regimens

Earlier development of drug resistance

Limitation in future choices of antiretroviral agents due to development of resistance

Unknown long-term toxicity of antiretroviral drugs

Unknown duration of effectiveness of current antiretroviral therapies

Indications for the Initiation of Antiretroviral Therapy in the Chronically HIV-Infected Patient

Clinical Category	CD4⁺ T-cell Count and HIV RNA	Recommendation
Symptomatic (ie, AIDS, thrush, unexplained fever)	Any value	Treat
Asymptomatic	CD4⁺ T cells <500/mm³ **or** HIV RNA >10,000 (bDNA) or >20,000 (RT-PCR)	Treatment should be offered. Strength of recommendation is based on prognosis for disease-free survival and willingness of the patient to accept therapy*
Asymptomatic	CD4⁺ T cells >500/mm³ **and** HIV RNA <10,000 (bDNA) or <20,000 (RT-PCR)	Many experts would delay therapy and observe; however, some experts would treat

*Some experts would observe patients whose CD4⁺ T-cell counts are between 350-500/mm³ and HIV RNA levels <10,000 (bDNA) or <20,000 (RT-PCR).

Rating System for Strength of Recommendation and Quality of Evidence Supporting the Recommendation

Category	Definition
Categories reflecting the strength of each recommendation	
A	Strong; should always be offered
B	Moderate; should usually be offered
C	Optional
D	Should generally not be offered
E	Should never be offered
Categories reflecting the quality of evidence supporting the recommendation	
I	At least one randomized trial with clinical endpoints
II	Clinical trials with laboratory endpoints
III	Expert opinion

ANTIRETROVIRAL THERAPY FOR HIV INFECTION *(Continued)*

Recommended Antiretroviral Agents for Treatment of Established HIV Infection

Preferred: Strong evidence of clinical benefit and/or sustained suppression of plasma viral load

One choice each from column A and column B. Drugs are listed in random, not priority, order:

Column A	Column B
Indinavir (AI)	ZDV + ddI (AI)
Nelfinavir (AII)	d4T + ddI (AII)
Ritonavir (AI)	ZDV + ddC (AI)
Saquinavir-SGC* (AII)	ZDV + 3TC§ (AI)
Ritonavir +	d4T + 3TC§ (AII)
Saquinavir-SGC or	Abacavir§§
HGC† (BII)	
Efavirenz•	
Amprenavir•	

Alternative: Less likely to provide sustained virus suppression

1 NNRTI (nevirapine)¶ + 2 NRTIs (Column B, above) (BII)

Saquinavir-HGC + 2 NRTIs (Column B, above) (BI)

Not generally recommended: Strong evidence of clinical benefit, but initial virus suppression is not sustained in most patients

2 NRTIs (Column B, above) (CI)

Not recommended:** Evidence against use, virologically undesirable, or overlapping toxicities

All monotherapies (DI)

d4T + ZDV (DI)

ddC + ddI†† (DII)

ddC + d4T†† (DII)

ddC + 3TC (DII)

---

*Virologic data and clinical experience with saquinavir-SGC are limited in comparison with other protease inhibitors.

†Use of ritonavir 400 mg bid with saquinavir soft-gel formulation (Fortovase™) 400 mg bid results in similar areas under the curve (AUC) of drug and antiretroviral activity as when using 400 mg bid of Invirase™ in combination with ritonavir. However, this combination with Fortovase™ has not been extensively studied and gastrointestinal toxicity may be greater when using Fortovase™.

§High-level resistance to 3TC develops within 2-4 weeks in partially suppressive regimens; optimal use is in three-drug antiretroviral combinations that reduce viral load to <500 copies/mL.

¶The only combination of 2 NRTIs + 1 NNRTI that has been shown to suppress viremia to undetectable levels in the majority of patients is ZDV + ddI + nevirapine. This combination was studied in antiretroviral-naive persons.

**ZDV monotherapy may be considered for prophylactic use in pregnant women who have low viral load and high CD4+T-cell counts to prevent perinatal transmission.

††This combination of NRTIs is not recommended based on lack of clinical data using the combination and/or overlapping toxicities.

•Not in original recommendations

§§May be added to a single drug in column B plus a choice from column A; not in original recommendations

GUIDELINES FOR THE USE OF ANTIRETROVIRAL AGENTS IN PEDIATRIC HIV INFECTION

Adapted from *MMWR Morb Mort Wkly Rep*, 1998, 47(RR-4).

1994 Revised Human Immunodeficiency Virus Pediatric Classification System: Immune Categories Based on Age-specific CD4+ T-lymphocyte Count and Percentage*

Immune Category	<12 (mo)		1-5 (y)		6-12 (y)	
	No./μL	%	No./μL	%	No./μL	%
Category 1 (no suppression)	≥1500	≥25	≥1000	≥25	≥500	≥25
Category 2 (moderate suppression)	750-1499	15-24	500-999	15-24	200-499	15-24
Category 3 (severe suppression)	<750	<15	<500	<15	<200	<15

*Modified from: CDC. 1994 Revised Classification System for Human Immunodeficiency Virus Infection in Children Less Than 13 Years of Age. *MMWR Morb Mort Wkly Rep*, 1994, 43(RR-12):1-10.

1994 Revised Human Immunodeficiency Virus Pediatric Classification System: Clinical Categories*

Category N: Not Symptomatic

Children who have no signs or symptoms considered to be the result of HIV infection or who have only **one** of the conditions listed in category A

Category A: Mildly Symptomatic

Children with **two** or more of the following conditions, but none of the conditions listed in categories B and C:

- Lymphadenopathy (≥0.5 cm at more than two sites; bilateral = one site)
- Hepatomegaly
- Splenomegaly
- Dermatitis
- Parotitis
- Recurrent or persistent upper respiratory infection, sinusitis, or otitis media

Category B: Moderately Symptomatic

Children who have symptomatic conditions other than those listed for category A or category C that are attributed to HIV infection. Examples of conditions in clinical category B include, but are not limited to, the following:

- Anemia (<8 g/dL), neutropenia (<1000/mm^3), or thrombocytopenia (<100,000/mm^3) persisting ≥30 days
- Bacterial meningitis, pneumonia, or sepsis (single episode)
- Candidiasis, oropharyngeal (ie, thrush) persisting for >2 months in children aged >6 months
- Cardiomyopathy
- Cytomegalovirus infection with onset before age 1 month
- Diarrhea, recurrent or chronic
- Hepatitis
- Herpes simplex virus (HSV) stomatitis, recurrent (ie, more than two episodes within 1 year)
- HSV bronchitis, pneumonitis, or esophagitis with onset before age 1 month
- Herpes zoster (ie, shingles) involving at least two distinct episodes or more than one dermatome
- Leiomyosarcoma
- Lymphoid interstitial pneumonia (LIP) or pulmonary lymphoid hyperplasia complex
- Nephropathy
- Nocardiosis
- Fever lasting >1 month
- Toxoplasmosis with onset before age 1 month
- Varicella, disseminated (ie, complicated chickenpox)

Category C: Severely Symptomatic

Children who have any condition listed in the 1987 surveillance case definition for acquired immunodeficiency syndrome, with the exception of LIP (which is a category B condition).

*Modified from: CDC. 1994 Revised Classification System for Human Immunodeficiency Virus Infection in Children Less Than 13 Years of Age. *MMWR Morb Mort Wkly Rep* 1994;43(RR-12):1-10.

ANTIRETROVIRAL THERAPY FOR HIV INFECTION *(Continued)*

Indications for Initiation of Antiretroviral Therapy in Children With Human Immunodeficiency Virus (HIV) Infection*

- Clinical symptoms associated with HIV infection (ie, clinical categories A, B, or C; see previous table)
- Evidence of immune suppression, indicated by CD4+T-lymphocyte absolute number or percentage (ie, immune category 2 or 3; see previous table)
- Age <12 months - regardless of clinical, immunologic, or virologic status
- For asymptomatic children ≥1 year of age with normal immune status, two options can be considered:

  - Preferred approach: Initiate therapy regardless of age or symptom status
  - Alternative approach: Defer treatment in situations in which the risk for clinical disease progression is low and other factors (eg, concern for the durability of response, safety, and adherence) favor postponing treatment. In such cases, the healthcare provider should regularly monitor virologic, immunologic, and clinical status. Factors to be considered in deciding to initiate therapy include the following:

    - High or increasing HIV RNA copy number
    - Rapidly declining CD4+ T-lymphocyte number or percentage to values approaching those indicative of moderate immune suppression (ie, immune category 2; see previous table)
    - Development of clinical symptoms

---

*Indications for initiation of antiretroviral therapy in postpubertal HIV-infected adolescents should follow the adult guidelines (Office of Public Health and Science, Department of Health and Human Services. Availability of report of NIH panel to define principles of therapy of HIV infection and guidelines for the use of antiretroviral agents in HIV-infected adults. Federal Register, 1997, 62:33417-8).

Recommended Antiretroviral Regimens for Initial Therapy for Human Immunodeficiency Virus (HIV) Infection in Children

Preferred Regimen

Evidence of clinical benefit and sustained suppression of HIV RNA in clinical trials in HIV-infected adults; clinical trials in HIV-infected children are ongoing

- One highly active protease inhibitor plus two nucleoside analogue reverse transcriptase inhibitors (NRTIs)

  - Preferred protease inhibitor for infants and children who cannot swallow pills or capsules: nelfinavir or ritonavir; alternative for children who can swallow pills or capsules: indinavir
  - Recommended dual NRTI combinations: the most data on use in children are available for the combinations of zidovudine (ZDV) and dideoxyinosine (ddI) and for ZDV and lamivudine (3TC); more limited data is available for the combinations of stavudine (d4T) and ddI, d4T and 3TC, and ZDV and zalcitabine (ddC)*

Alternative Regimen

Less likely to produce sustained HIV RNA suppression in infected adults; the combination of nevirapine, ZDV, and ddI produced substantial and sustained suppression of viral replication in two of six infants first treated at age <4 months†

- Nevirapine§ and two NRTIs

Secondary Alternative Regimen

Clinical benefit demonstrated in clinical trials involving infected adults and/or children, but initial viral suppression may not be sustained

- Two NRTIs

Not Recommended

Evidence against use because of overlapping toxicity and/or because use may be virologically undesirable

- Any monotherapy‡
- d4T and ZDV
- ddC and ddI
- ddC and d4T
- ddC and 3TC

---

*ddC is not available in a liquid preparation commercially, although a liquid formulation is available through a compassionate use program of the manufacturer (Hoffman-LaRoche Inc, Nutley, New Jersey). ZDV and ddC is a less preferred choice for use in combination with a protease inhibitor.

†Source: Luzuiraga K, Bryson Y, Krogstad P, et al. "Combination Treatment With Zidovudine, Didanosine, and Nevirapine in Infants With Human Immunodeficiency Virus Type 1 Infection." *N Engl J Med* 1997, 336:1343-9.

§A liquid preparation of nevirapine is not available commercially, but is available through a compassionate use program of the manufacturer (Boehringer Ingelheim Pharmaceuticals, Inc, Ridgefield, Connecticut).

‡Except for ZDV, chemoprophylaxis administered to HIV-exposed infants during the first 6 weeks of life to prevent perinatal HIV transmission; if an infant is identified as HIV-infected while receiving ZDV prophylaxis, therapy should be changed to a combination antiretroviral drug regimen.

Considerations for Changing Antiretroviral Therapy for Human Immunodeficiency Virus (HIV)-Infected Children

Virologic Considerations*

- Less than a minimally acceptable virologic response after 8-12 weeks of therapy; for children receiving antiretroviral therapy with two nucleoside analogue reverse transcriptase inhibitors (NRTIs) and a protease inhibitor, such a response is defined as a less than tenfold ($1.0 \log_{10}$) decrease from baseline HIV RNA levels; for children who are receiving less potent antiretroviral therapy (ie, dual NRTI combinations), an insufficient response is defined as a less than fivefold ($0.7 \log_{10}$) decrease in HIV RNA levels from baseline

- HIV RNA not suppressed to undetectable levels after 4-6 months of antiretroviral therapy†

- Repeated detection of HIV RNA in children who initially responded to antiretroviral therapy with undetectable levels‡

- A reproducible increase in HIV RNA copy number among children who have had a substantial HIV RNA response, but still have low levels of detectable HIV RNA; such an increase would warrant change in therapy if, after initiation of the therapeutic regimen, a greater than threefold ($0.5 \log_{10}$) increase in copy number for children ≥ 2 years of age and a greater than fivefold ($0.7 \log_{10}$) increase is observed for children <2 years of age

Immunologic Considerations*

- Change in immunologic classification; see 1994 Revised Human Immunodeficiency Virus Pediatric Classification System table§

- For children with CD4+ T-lymphocyte percentages of <15% (ie, those in immune category 3), a persistent decline of five percentiles or more in CD4+ cell percentage (eg, from 15% to 10%)

- A rapid and substantial decrease in absolute CD4+ T-lymphocyte count (eg, a >30% decline in <6 months)

Clinical Considerations

- Progressive neurodevelopmental deterioration

- Growth failure defined as persistent decline in weight-growth velocity despite adequate nutritional support and without other explanation

- Disease progression defined as advancement from one pediatric clinical category to another (eg, from clinical category A to clinical category B)**

*AT least two measurements (taken 1 week apart) should be performed before considering a change in therapy.

†The initial HIV RNA level of the child at the start of therapy and the level achieved with therapy should be considered when contemplating potential drug changes. For example, an immediate change in therapy may not be warranted if there is a sustained $1.5-2.0 \log_{10}$ decrease in HIV RNA copy number, even if RNA remains detectable at low levels.

‡More frequent evaluation of HIV RNA levels should be considered if the HIV RNA increase is limited (eg, if when using an HIV RNA assay with a lower limit of detection of 1000 copies/mL, there is a $\leq 0.7 \log_{10}$ increase from undetectable to approximately 5000 copies/mL in an infant <2 years of age.

§Minimal changes in CD4+ T-lymphocyte percentile that may result in change in immunologic category (eg, from 26% to 24%, or 16% to 14%) may not be as concerning as a rapid substantial change in CD4+ percentile within the same immunologic category (eg, a drop from 35% to 25%).

**In patients with stable immunologic and virologic parameters, progression from one clinical category to another may not represent an indication to change therapy. Thus, in patients whose disease progression is not associated with neurologic deterioration or growth failure, virologic and immunologic considerations are important in deciding whether to change therapy.

ANTIRETROVIRAL THERAPY FOR HIV INFECTION *(Continued)*

Guidelines for Changing an Antiretroviral Regimen for Suspected Drug Failure

- Criteria for changing therapy include a suboptimal reduction in plasma viremia after initiation of therapy, reappearance of viremia after suppression to undetectable, substantial increases in plasma viremia from the nadir of suppression, and declining CD4+ T-cell numbers. Refer to the more extensive discussion of these criteria in the previous table.

- When the decision to change therapy is based on viral load determination, it is preferable to confirm with a second viral load test.

- Distinguish between the need to change a regimen because of drug intolerance or inability to comply with the regimen versus failure to achieve the goal of sustained viral suppression; single agents can be changed or dose reduced in the event of drug intolerance.

- In general, do not change a single drug or add a single drug to a failing regimen; it is important to use at least two new drugs and preferably to use an entirely new regimen with at least three new drugs.

- Many patients have limited options for new regimens of desired potency; in some of these cases, it is rational to continue the prior regimen if partial viral suppression was achieved.

- In some cases, regimens identified as suboptimal for initial therapy are rational due to limitations imposed by toxicity, intolerance, or nonadherence. This especially applies in late-stage disease. For patients with no rational alternative options who have virologic failure with return of viral load to baseline (pretreatment levels) and a declining CD4+ T-cell count, discontinuation of antiretroviral therapy should be considered.

- Experience is limited with regimens using combinations of two protease inhibitors or combinations of protease inhibitors with nevirapine or delavirdine; for patients with limited options due to drug intolerance or suspected resistance, these regimens provide possible alternative treatment options.

- There is limited information about the value of restarting a drug that the patient has previously received. The experience with zidovudine is that resistant strains are often replaced with "wild-type" zidovudine sensitive strains when zidovudine treatment is stopped, but resistance recurs rapidly if zidovudine is restarted. Although preliminary evidence indicates that this occurs with indinavir, it is not known if similar problems apply to other nucleoside analogues, protease inhibitors, or NNRTIs, but a conservative stance is that they do.

- Avoid changing from ritonavir to indinavir or vice versa for drug failure, because high-level cross-resistance is likely.

- Avoid changing from nevirapine to delavirdine or vice versa for drug failure, because high-level cross-resistance is likely.

- The decision to change therapy and the choice of a new regimen require that the clinician have considerable expertise in the care of persons living with HIV infection. Physicians who are less experienced in the care of persons with HIV infection are strongly encouraged to obtain assistance through consultation with or referral to a clinician who has considerable expertise in the care of HIV-infected patients.

Possible Regimens for Patients Who Have Failed Antiretroviral Therapy: A Work in Progress*

Prior Regimen	New Regimen (not listed in priority order)
2 NRTIs +	2 new NRTIs +
Nelfinavir (NFV)	RTV; or IDV; or SQV + RTV; or NNRTI† + RTV; or NNRTI + IDV§
Ritonavir (RTV)	SQV + RTV§; NFV + NNRTI; or NFV + SQV
Indinavir (IDV)	SQV + RTV; NFV + NNRTI; or NFV + SQV
Saquinavir (SQV)	RTV + SQV; or NNRTI + IDV
2 NRTIs + NNRTI	2 new NRTIs + a protease inhibitor
2 NRTIs	2 new NRTIs + a protease inhibitor
	2 new NRTIs + RTV + SQV
	1 new NRTI + 1 NNRTI + a protease inhibitor
	2 protease inhibitors + NNRTI
1 NRTI	2 new NRTIs + a protease inhibitor
	2 new NRTIs + NNRTI
	1 new NRTI + 1 NNRTI + a protease inhibitor

*These alternative regimens have not been proven to be clinically effective and were arrived at through discussion by the panel of theoretically possible alternative treatments and the elimination of those alternatives with evidence of being ineffective. Clinical trials in this area are urgently needed.

†Of the two available NNRTIs, clinical trials support a preference for nevirapine over delavirdine based on results of viral load assays. These two agents have opposite effects on the CYP450 pathway, and this must be considered in combining these drugs with other agents.

§There are some clinical trials that have yielded viral burden data to support this recommendation.

Acute Retroviral Syndrome: Associated Signs and Symptoms and Expected Frequency

- Fever (96%)
- Lymphadenopathy (74%)
- Pharyngitis (70%)
- Rash (70%)
    - Erythematous maculopapular with lesions on face and trunk and sometimes extremities, including palms and soles
    - Mucocutaneous ulceration involving mouth, esophagus, or genitals
- Myalgia or arthralgia (54%)
- Diarrhea (32%)
- Headache (32%)
- Nausea and vomiting (27%)
- Hepatosplenomegaly (14%)
- Thrush (12%)
- Weight loss
- Neurologic symptoms (12%)
    - Meningoencephalitis or aseptic meningitis
    - Peripheral neuropathy or radiculopathy
    - Facial palsy
    - Guillain-Barré syndrome
    - Brachial neuritis
    - Cognitive impairment or psychosis

CLINICAL SYNDROMES ASSOCIATED WITH FOOD-BORNE DISEASES

Clinical Syndromes	Incubation Period (h)	Causes	Commonly Associated Vehicles
Nausea and vomiting	<1-6	*Staphylococcus aureus* (preformed toxins, A, B, C, D, E)	Ham, poultry, cream-filled pastries, potato and egg salad, mushrooms
		Bacillus cereus (emetic toxin)	Fried rice, pork
		Heavy metals (copper, tin, cadmium, zinc)	Acidic beverages
Histamine response and gastrointestinal (GI) tract	<1	Histamine (scombroid)	Fish (bluefish, bonito, mackerel, mahi-mahi, tuna)
Neurologic, including paresthesia and GI tract	0-6	Tetrodotoxin, ciguatera	Puffer fish
			Fish (amberjack, barracuda, grouper, snapper)
		Paralytic compounds	Shellfish (clams, mussels, oysters, scallops, other mollusks)
		Neurotoxic compounds	Shellfish
		Domoic acid	Mussels
		Monosodium glutamate	Chinese food
Neurologic and GI tract manifestations	0-2	Mushroom toxins (early onset)	Mushrooms
Moderate-to-severe abdominal cramps and watery diarrhea	8-16	*B. cereus* enterotoxin	Beef, pork, chicken, vanilla sauce
		Clostridium perfringens enterotoxin	Beef, poultry, gravy
	16-48	Caliciviruses	Shellfish, salads, ice
		Enterotoxigenic *Escherichia coli*	Fruits, vegetables
		Vibrio cholerae 01 and 0139	Shellfish
		V. cholerae non-01	Shellfish
Diarrhea, fever, abdominal cramps, blood and mucus in stools	16-72	*Salmonella*	Poultry, pork, eggs, dairy products, including ice cream, vegetables, fruit
		Shigella	Egg salad, vegetables
		Campylobacter jejuni	Poultry, raw milk
		Invasive *E. coli*	
		Yersinia enterocolitica	Pork chitterlings, tofu, raw milk
		Vibrio parahaemolyticus	Fish, shellfish
Bloody diarrhea, abdominal cramps	72-120	Enterohemorrhagic *E. coli*	Beef (hamburger), raw milk, roast beef, salami, salad dressings
Methemoglobin poisoning	6-12	Mushrooms (late onset)	Mushrooms
Hepatorenal failure	6-24	Mushrooms (late onset)	Mushrooms
Gastrointestinal then blurred vision, dry mouth, dysarthria, diplopia, descending paralysis	18-36	*Clostridium botulinum*	Canned vegetables, fruits and fish, salted fish, bottled garlic
Extraintestinal manifestations	Varied	Brainerd disease	Unpasteurized milk
		Brucella	Cheese, raw milk
		Group A *Streptococcus*	Egg and potato salad
		Listeria monocytogenes	Cheese, raw milk, hot dogs, cole slaw, cold cuts
		Trichinella spiralis	Pork
		Vibrio vulnificus	Shellfish

Adapted from "Report of the Committee on Infectious Diseases," *1997 Red Book*®, 24th ed.

COMMUNITY-ACQUIRED PNEUMONIA IN ADULTS

GUIDELINES FOR MANAGEMENT

Adapted from the Guidelines From the Infectious Diseases Society of America, *Clinical Infectious Diseases*, 1998, 26:811-38.

Algorithm

Patients with community-acquired pneumonia

Is the patient over 50 years of age? — **Yes** →

No ↓

Does the patient have a history of any of the following comorbid conditions?

Neoplastic disease
Congestive heart failure
Cerebrovascular disease
Renal disease
Liver disease

— **Yes** → Assign patient to risk class II-V based on prediction model scoring system

No ↓

Does the patient have any of the following abnormalities on physical examination?

Altered mental status
Pulse ≥125/minute
Respiratory rate ≥30/minute
Systolic blood pressure <90 mm Hg
Temperature <35° or ≥40° C

— **Yes** →

No ↓

Assign patient to risk class I

Stratification of Risk Score

Risk	Risk class	Based on
	I	Algorithm
Low	II	≤ 70 total points
	III	71-90 total points
Moderate	IV	91-130 total points
High	V	> 130 total points

COMMUNITY-ACQUIRED PNEUMONIA IN ADULTS *(Continued)*

The table below is the prediction model for identification of patient risk for persons with community-acquired pneumonia. This model may be used to help guide the initial decision on site of care; however, its use may not be appropriate for all patients with this illness and, therefore, should be applied in conjunction with physician judgment.

Scoring System

Patient Characteristic	Points Assigned[1]
Demographic factors	
Age: Male	age (in years)
Female	age (in years) -10
Nursing home resident	+10
Comorbid illnesses	
Neoplastic disease	+30
Liver disease	+20
Congestive heart failure	+10
Cerebrovascular disease	+10
Renal disease	+10
Physical examination findings	
Altered mental status	+20
Respiratory rate ≥30/minute	+20
Systolic blood pressure <90 mm Hg	+20
Temperature <35°C or ≥40°C	+15
Pulse ≥125/minute	+10
Laboratory findings	
pH <7.35	+30
BUN >10.7 mmol/L	+20
Sodium <130 mEq/L	+20
Glucose >13.9 mmol/L	+10
Hematocrit <30%	+10
PO$_2$ <60 mm Hg[2]	+10
Pleural effusion	+10

[1] A risk score (reset point score) for a given patient is obtained by summing the patient age in years (age -10 for females) and the points for each applicable patient characteristic.

[2] Oxygen saturation <90% also was considered normal.

Risk-Class Mortality Rates for Patients With Pneumonia

Risk Class	No. of Points	Validation Cohort		Recommendations for Site of Care
		No. of Patients	Mortality (%)	
I	No predictors	3,034	0.1	Outpatient
II	≤70	5,778	0.6	Outpatient
III	71-90	6,790	2.8	Inpatient (briefly)
IV	91-130	13,104	8.2	Inpatient
V	>130	9,333	29.2	Inpatient

Epidemiological and Underlying Conditions Related to Specific Pathogens in Selected Patients With Community-Acquired Pneumonia

Conditions	Commonly Encountered Pathogens
Alcoholism	*Streptococcus pneumoniae*, anaerobes, gram-negative bacilli
COPD/smoker	*S. pneumoniae, Haemophilus influenzae, Moraxella catarrhalis, Legionella* species
Nursing home residency	*S. pneumoniae*, gram-negative bacilli, *H. influenzae, Staphylococcus aureus*, anaerobes, *Chlamydia pneumoniae*
Poor dental hygiene	Anaerobes
Epidemic Legionnaires' disease	*Legionella* species
Exposure to bats or soil enriched with bird droppings	*Histoplasma capsulatum*
Exposure to birds	*Chlamydia psittaci*
Exposure to rabbits	*Francisella tularensis*
HIV infection (early stage)	*S. pneumoniae, H. influenzae, Mycobacterium tuberculosis*
Travel to the southwestern United States	*Coccidioides immiris*
Exposure to farm animals or parturient cats	*Caxiella burnetii**
Influenza active in community	Influenza, *S. pneumoniae, S. aureus, Streptococcus pyogenes, H. influenzae*
Suspected large-volume aspiration	Anaerobes, chemical pneumonitis
Structural disease of the lung (bronchiectasis or cystic fibrosis)	*Pseudomonas aeruginosa, Burkholderia (Pseudomonas) cepacia*, or *S. aureus*
Injection drug use	*S. aureus*, anaerobes, *M. tuberculosis*
Airway obstruction	Anaerobes

*Agent of Q fever
COPD = chronic obstructive pulmonary disease

COMMUNITY-ACQUIRED PNEUMONIA IN ADULTS *(Continued)*

Flow Chart Approach to Treating Outpatients and Inpatients with Community-Acquired Pneumonia

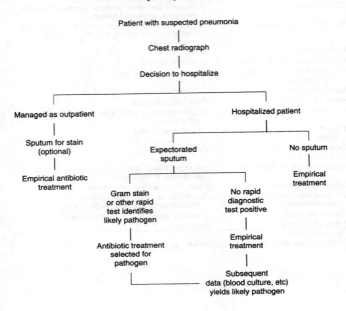

Community-Acquired Pneumonia

Possible reasons for failure of empirical treatment in patients with community-acquired pneumonia.

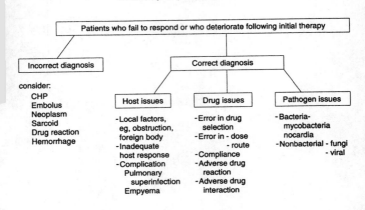

Treatment of Pneumonia According to Pathogen

Pathogen	Preferred Antimicrobial	Alternative Antimicrobial
Streptococcus pneumoniae		
Penicillin susceptible (MIC, <0.1 mcg/mL)	Penicillin G or penicillin V, amoxicillin	Cephalosporins,* macrolides,† clindamycin, fluoroquinolones,‡ doxycycline
Intermediately penicillin resistant (MIC, 0.1-1 mcg/mL)	Parenteral penicillin G, ceftriaxone or cefotaxime, amoxicillin, fluoroquinolones,‡ other agents based on *in vitro* susceptibility test results	Clindamycin, doxycycline, oral cephalosporins*
Highly penicillin-resistant□ (MIC, ≥2 mcg/mL)	Agents based on *in vitro* susceptibility results, fluoroquinolones,‡ vancomycin	
Empirical selection	Fluoroquinolones,‡ selection based on susceptibility test results in community§	Clindamycin, doxycycline, vancomycin
	Penicillin¶	Cephalosporins,* macrolides,† amoxicillin, clindamycin
Haemophilus influenzae	Second- or third-generation cephalosporins, doxycycline, beta-lactam - beta-lactamase inhibitor, fluoroquinolones‡	Azithromycin, TMP-SMZ
Moraxella catarrhalis	Second- or third-generation cephalosporins, TMP-SMZ, amoxicillin/clavulanate	Macrolides,† fluoroquinolones,‡ beta-lactam - beta-lactamase inhibitor
Anaerobes	Clindamycin, penicillin plus metronidazole, beta-lactam - beta-lactamase inhibitor	Penicillin G or penicillin V, ampicillin/amoxicillin with or without metronidazole
Staphylococcus aureus□		
Methicillin-susceptible	Nafcillin/oxacillin with or without rifampin or gentamicin□	Cefazolin or cefuroxime, vancomycin, clindamycin, TMP-SMZ, fluoroquinolones‡
Methicillin-resistant	Vancomycin with or without rifampin or gentamicin	Requires *in vitro* testing; TMP-SMZ
Enterobacteriaceae (coliforms: *Escherichia coli, Klebsiella, Proteus, Enterobacter*)□	Third-generation cephalosporin with or without an aminoglycoside, carbapenems**	Aztreonam, beta-lactam - beta-lactamase inhibitor, fluoroquinolones‡
Pseudomonas aeruginosa□	Aminoglycoside plus antipseudomonal beta-lactam: ticarcillin, piperacillin, mezlocillin, cefazidime, cefepime, aztreonam, or carbapenems**	Aminoglycoside plus ciprofloxacin, ciprofloxacin plus antipseudomonal beta-lactam
Legionella species	Macrolides† with or without rifampin, fluoroquinolones‡	Doxycycline with or without rifampin
Mycoplasma pneumoniae	Doxycycline, macrolides,† fluoroquinolones‡	
Chlamydia pneumoniae	Doxycycline, macrolides,† fluoroquinolones‡	
Chlamydia psittaci	Doxycycline	Erythromycin, chloramphenicol
Nocardia species	Sulfonamide with or without minocycline or amikacin, TMP-SMZ	Imipenem with or without amikacin, doxycycline, or minocycline
Coxiella burnetii#	Tetracycline	Chloramphenicol
Influenza A	Amantadine or rimantadine	
Hantavirus	None††	

Note: TMP-SMZ = trimethoprim-sulfamethoxazole

*Intravenous: Cefazolin, cefuroxime, cefotaxime, ceftriaxone; oral: cefpodoxime, cefprozil, cefuroxime

†Erythromycin, clarithromycin, or azithromycin

‡Levofloxacin, sparfloxacin, grepafloxacin, trovafloxacin, or another fluoroquinolone with enhanced activity against *S. pneumoniae*; ciprofloxacin is appropriate for *Legionella* species, fluoroquinolone-susceptible *S. aureus*, and most gram-negative bacilli.

□*In vitro* susceptibility tests are required for optimal treatment; for *Enterobacter* species, the preferred antibiotics are fluoroquinolones and carbapenems.

§High rates of high-level penicillin resistance, susceptibility of community strains unknown, and/or patient is seriously ill

¶Low rates of penicillin resistance in community and patient is at low risk for infection with resistant *S. pneumoniae*

**Imipenem and meropenem

#Agent of Q fever

††Provide supportive care

COMMUNITY-ACQUIRED PNEUMONIA IN ADULTS *(Continued)*

Empirical Antibiotic Selection for Patients With Community-Acquired Pneumonia

Outpatients
Generally preferred: Macrolides,* fluoroquinolones,† or doxycycline
Modifying factors
  Suspected penicillin-resistant *Streptococcus pneumoniae*: Fluoroquinolones†
  Young adult (>17-40 y): Doxycycline
  Hospitalized patients
    General medical ward
    Generally preferred: Beta-lactam‡ with or without a macrolide* or a fluoroquinolone† (alone)
  Alternatives: Cefuroxime with or without a macrolide* or azithromycin (alone)
Hospitalized in the intensive care unit for serious pneumonia
Generally preferred: Erythromycin, azithromycin, or a fluoroquinolone† plus cefotaxime, ceftriaxone, or a beta-lactam - beta-lactamase inhibitor¤
Modifying factors
  Structural disease of the lung: Antipseudomonal penicillin, a carbapenem, or cefepime plus a macrolide* or a fluoroquinolone† plus an aminoglycoside
  Penicillin allergy: A fluoroquinolone† with or without clindamycin
  Suspected aspiration: A fluoroquinolone plus either clindamycin or metronidazole or a beta-lactam - beta-lactamase inhibitor¤

*Azithromycin, clarithromycin, or erythromycin

†Levofloxacin, sparfloxacin, grepafloxacin, trovafloxacin, or another fluoroquinolone with enhanced activity against *S. pneumoniae*

‡Cefotaxime, ceftriaxone, or a beta-lactam - beta-lactamase inhibitor

¤Ampicillin/sulbactam, or ticarcillin/clavulanate, or piperacillin/tazobactam (for structural disease of the lung, ticarcillin/clavulanate or piperacillin)

MALARIA TREATMENT

Drug	Adult Dosage	Pediatric Dosage
All *Plasmodium* species except chloroquine-resistant *Plasmodium falciparum*		
Oral Drug of Choice		
Chloroquine phosphate	600 mg base (1 g), then 300 mg base (500 mg) 6 h later, and 300 mg base (500 mg) at 24 and 48 h	10 mg base/kg (max: 600 mg base), then 5 mg base/kg 6 h later (max: 300 mg base), and 5 mg base/kg/d at 24 and 48 h (max: 300 mg base)
Parenteral Drug of Choice		
Quinidine gluconate*	10 mg/kg loading dose, I.V. (max: 600 mg) during 1-2 h, then 0.02 mg/kg/min continuous infusion until oral therapy can be started	Same as adult
or		
Quinine dihydrochloride*†	600 mg in 300 mL of normal saline I.V. during 2-4 h; repeat every 8 h (max: 1800 mg/d) until oral therapy can be started	30 mg/kg/d; give ⅓ of daily dose over 2-4 h; repeat every 8 h until oral therapy can be started (max: 1800 mg/d)
***P. falciparum* acquired in areas of known chloroquine resistance**		
Oral Regimen of Choice‡		
Quinine sulfate§	650 mg 3 times/d for 3-7 d	30 mg/kg/d in 3 doses for 3-7 d
plus		
Tetracycline‖	250 mg 4 times/d for 7 d	5 mg/kg 4 times/d for 7 d (max: 250 mg 4 times/d)
Alternative Regimen		
Oral: Quinine sulfate	650 mg 3 times/d for 3-7 d	30 mg/kg/d in 3 doses for 3-7 d
Parenteral: Quinidine gluconate*	Same as above	Same as above
or		
Quinine dihydrochloride*†	Same as above	Same as above
plus		
Pyrimethamine-sulfadoxine (Fansidar®)¶	Single dose of 3 tablets on last day of quinine therapy	<1 y of age, single dose of ¼ tablet; 1-3 y of age, single dose of ½ tablet; 4-8 y of age, single dose of 1 tablet; 9-14 y of age, single dose of 2 tablets; >14 y of age, single dose of 3 tablets
or		
Mefloquine hydrochloride#**	Single dose of 15-25 mg/kg (max: 1250 mg)	15-25 mg/kg in a single dose (max: 1250 mg)
Prevention of relapses: *Plasmodium vivax* and *Plasmodium ovale* only		
Primaquine phosphate#	15 mg base (26.3 mg)/d for 14 d or 45 mg base (79 mg)/wk for 8 wk	0.3 mg base/kg/d for 14 d (max: 26.3 mg)

*Electrocardiogram monitoring is recommended to detect arrhythmias, widening QRS complex, or prolonged QT interval. Patients should also be monitored for hypotension. I.V. indicates intravenous.

†Not available in the United States.

‡The combination of quinine sulfate and tetracycline is the most efficacious regimen for all chloroquine-resistant *P. falciparum* infections.

§For treatment of *P. falciparum* infections acquired in Southeast Asia and possibility in other areas such as South America, quinine sulfate should be continued for 7 days.

‖Physicians must weigh the benefits of tetracycline therapy against the possibility of dental staining children younger than 8 years.

¶Use of Fansidar®, which contains 25 mg pyrimethamine and 500 mg sulfadoxine per tablet, is contraindicated in patients with a history of sulfonamide or pyrimethamine intolerance, in infants younger than 2 months and in pregnant women at term. Pregnant women should be administered chloroquine, or if chloroquine-resistant malaria is suspected, quinine or mefloquine. Resistance to pyrimethamine-sulfadoxine has been reported from Southeast Asia and the Amazon Basin, and therefore, this drug should not be used for treatment of malaria acquired in these areas.

#Mefloquine is not licensed by the Food and Drug Administration for children who weigh less than 15 kg, but recent Center for Disease Control and Prevention recommendations allow use of the drug to be considered in children without weight restrictions when travel to chloroquine-resistant *P. falciparum* areas cannot be avoided. Mefloquine is contraindicated for use by travelers with a known hypersensitivity to mefloquine, or for travelers with a history of epilepsy or severe psychiatric disorders. A review of available data suggests that mefloquine may be administered to persons concurrently receiving beta-blockers if they have no underlying arrhythmia. However, mefloquine is not recommended for persons with cardiac conduction abnormalities until additional data are available. Caution may be advised for persons involved in tasks requiring fine coordination and spatial discrimination, such as airline pilots. Quinidine or quinine may exacerbate the known side effects of mefloquine; patients not responding to mefloquine therapy or failing mefloquine prophylaxis should be monitored closely if they are treated with quinidine or quinine.

**For most patients, 15 mg/kg in a single dose is effective therapy, except for those who acquired infection in the areas of the Amazon basin, or the Thailand-Cambodian and Thailand-Myanmar borders (see ‡ footnote).

††Primaquine phosphate can cause hemolytic anemia in patients with glucose-6-phosphate dehydrogenase (G-6-PD) deficiency. A G-6-PD screen should be done before initiating treatment. Pregnant women should not be administered primaquine.

Adapted from "Report of the Committee on Infectious Diseases," *1997 Red Book®*, 24th ed.

RECOMMENDATIONS FOR PREVENTING THE SPREAD OF VANCOMYCIN RESISTANCE

Recommendations of the Hospital Infection Control Practices Advisory Committee (HICPAC)
(MMWR Morb Mortal Wkly Rep, 1995, 44(RR-12))

Prudent Vancomycin Use

Vancomycin use has been reported consistently as a risk factor for infection and colonization with VRE and may increase the possibility of the emergence of vancomycin-resistant *S. aureus* (VRSA) and/or vancomycin-resistant *S. epidermidis* (VRSE). Therefore, all hospitals and other healthcare delivery services, even those at which VRE have never been detected, should a) develop a comprehensive, antimicrobial-utilization plan to provide education for their medical staff (including medical students who rotate their training in different departments of the healthcare facility), b) oversee surgical prophylaxis, and c) develop guidelines for the proper use of vancomycin (as applicable to the institution).

Guideline development should be part of the hospital's quality-improvement program and should involve participation from the hospital's pharmacy and therapeutics committee; hospital epidemiologist; and infection-control, infectious-disease, medical, and surgical staffs. The guidelines should include the following considerations:

1. Situations in which the use of vancomycin is appropriate or acceptable

   - For treatment of serious infections caused by beta-lactam-resistant gram-positive microorganisms; vancomycin may be less rapidly bactericidal than are beta-lactam agents for beta-lactam-susceptible staphylococci

   - For treatment of infections caused by gram-positive microorganisms in patients who have serious allergies to beta-lactam antimicrobials

   - When antibiotic-associated colitis fails to respond to metronidazole therapy or is severe and potentially life-threatening

   - Prophylaxis, as recommended by the American Heart Association, for endocarditis following certain procedures in patients at high risk for endocarditis

   - Prophylaxis for major surgical procedures involving implantation of prosthetic materials or devices (eg, cardiac and vascular procedures and total hip replacement) at institutions that have a high rate of infections caused by MRSA or methicillin-resistant *S. epidermidis*. A single dose of vancomycin administered immediately before surgery is sufficient unless the procedure lasts >6 hours, in which case the dose should be repeated. Prophylaxis should be discontinued after a maximum of two doses.

2. Situations in which the use of vancomycin should be discouraged

   - Routine surgical prophylaxis other than in a patient who has a life-threatening allergy to beta-lactam antibiotics

   - Empiric antimicrobial therapy for a febrile neutropenic patient, unless initial evidence indicates that the patient has an infection caused by gram-positive microorganisms (eg, at an inflamed exit site of Hickman catheter) and the prevalence of infections caused by MRSA in the hospital is substantial

   - Treatment in response to a single blood culture positive for coagulase-negative *Staphylococcus*, if other blood cultures taken during the same time frame are negative (ie, if contamination of the blood culture is likely). Because contamination of blood cultures with skin flora (eg, *S. epidermidis*) could result in inappropriate administration of vancomycin, phlebotomists and other personnel who obtain blood cultures should be trained to minimize microbial contamination of specimens.

   - Continued empiric use for presumed infections in patients whose cultures are negative for beta-lactam-resistant gram-positive microorganisms

   - Systemic or local (eg, antibiotic lock) prophylaxis for infection or colonization of indwelling central or peripheral intravascular catheters

   - Selective decontamination of the digestive tract

   - Eradication of MRSA colonization

   - Primary treatment of antibiotic-associated colitis

   - Routine prophylaxis for very low-birthweight infants (ie, infants who weigh <1500 g)

   - Routine prophylaxis for patients on continuous ambulatory peritoneal dialysis or hemodialysis

- Treatment (chosen for dosing convenience) of infections caused by beta-lactam-sensitive gram-positive microorganisms in patients who have renal failure
- Use of vancomycin solution for topical application or irrigation

3. Enhancing compliance with recommendations

- Although several techniques may be useful, further study is required to determine the most effective methods for influencing the prescribing practices of physicians
- Key parameters of vancomycin use can be monitored through the hospital's quality assurance/improvement process or as part of the drug-utilization review of the Pharmacy and Therapeutics Committee and the medical staff

SUSPECTED ORGANISMS BY SITE OF INFECTION FOR EMPIRIC THERAPY

Urinary Tract

Community acquired — E. coli, other gram-negative rods, S. aureus, S. epidermidis, S. faecalis

Nosocomial — Resistant gram-negative rods, enterococci

Respiratory Tract

Pneumonia

Community acquired

normal adult — S. pneumoniae, virus, Mycoplasma (atypical)

normal child — S. pneumoniae, H. influenzae

aspiration — Aerobic and anaerobic mouth flora

alcoholic — S. pneumoniae, Klebsiella, anaerobes (below the belt)

COPD — S. pneumoniae, H. influenzae

Nosocomial

aspiration — Mouth anaerobes, gram-negative aerobic rods, S. aureus

neutropenic — Fungi, gram-negative aerobic rods, S. aureus

HIV-infected — Fungi, P. carinii, Legionella, Nocardia, S. pneumoniae

Epiglottis — H. influenzae

Acute sinusitis — S. pneumoniae, H. influenzae, M. catarrhalis (B. catarrhalis)

Chronic sinusitis — Anaerobes, S. aureus

Bronchitis, otitis — S. pneumoniae, H. influenzae, M. catarrhalis (B. catarrhalis)

Pharyngitis — Group A streptococci

Skin and Soft Tissue

Cellulitis — Group A streptococci, S. aureus

I.V. site — S. aureus, S. epidermidis

Surgical wound — S. aureus, gram-negative rods

Diabetic ulcer — S. aureus, gram-negative aerobic rods, anaerobes

Furuncle — S. aureus

Intra-abdominal — Anaerobes (B. fragilis), E. coli, enterococci

Cardiac

Endocarditis

subacute — S. viridans

acute

I.V. drug user — S. aureus, gram-negative aerobic rods, S. faecalis, fungi

prosthetic valve — S. epidermidis

Gastric

Gastroenteritis — Salmonella, Shigella, H. pylori, C. difficile, ameba, G. lamblia, viral, E. coli

Bone/Joint

Osteomyelitis/septic arthritis — S. aureus, gram-negative aerobic rods

Central Nervous System

Meningitis

<2 mo — E. coli, group B streptococci, Listeria

2 mo to 12 y — H. influenzae, S. pneumoniae, N. meningitidis

adult and nosocomial — S. pneumoniae, N. meningitidis, gram-negative aerobic rods

postneurosurgery — S. aureus, gram-negative rods

TREATMENT OF SEXUALLY TRANSMITTED DISEASES

Type or Stage	Drug of Choice	Dosage	Alternatives
CHLAMYDIA TRACHOMATIS			
Urethritis, cervicitis, conjunctivitis, or proctitis (except lymphogranuloma venereum)			
	Azithromycin or	1 g oral once	Ofloxacin[2] 300 mg oral bid x 7 d; erythromycin 500 mg oral qid x 7 d
	Doxycycline[1,2]	100 mg oral bid x 7 d	
Infection in pregnancy			
	Erythromycin[3]	500 mg oral qid x 7 d[4]	Amoxicillin 500 mg oral tid x 10 d; azithromycin[5] 1 g oral once
Neonatal			
Ophthalmia	Erythromycin	12.5 mg/kg oral or I.V. qid x 14 d	
Pneumonia	Erythromycin	12.5 mg/kg oral or I.V. qid x 14 d	Sulfisoxazole[6] 100 mg/kg/d oral or I.V. in divided doses x 14 d
Lymphogranuloma venereum			
	Doxycycline[1,2]	100 mg oral bid x 21 d	Erythromycin[3] 500 mg oral qid x 21 d
GONORRHEA[7]			
Urethral, cervical, rectal, or pharyngeal			
	Cefpodoxime 200 mg as a single dose; ceftriaxone	125 mg I.M. once	Cefixime 400 mg oral once; ciprofloxacin[2] 500 mg oral once; ofloxacin[2] 400 mg oral once; spectinomycin 2 g I.M. once[8]
Ophthalmia (adults)[9]			
	Ceftriaxone	1 g I.M. once, plus saline irrigation	
Bacteremia, arthritis, and disseminated[10,11]			
	Ceftriaxone	1 g I.V. daily x 7-10 days, or for 2-3 d, followed by cefixime 400 mg oral bid or ciprofloxacin 500 mg oral bid to complete 7-10 d total therapy	Ceftizoxime or cefotaxime, 1 g I.V. q8h for 2-3 days or until improved, followed by cefixime 400 mg oral bid or ciprofloxacin 500 mg oral bid to complete 7-10 d total therapy
Neonatal			
Ophthalmia	Cefotaxime or	25 mg/kg I.V. or I.M. q8-12h x 7 d, plus saline irrigation	Penicillin G[12] 100,000 units/kg/d I.V. in 4 doses x 7 d, plus saline irrigation
	Ceftriaxone	125 mg I.M. once, plus saline irrigation	
Bacteremia, arthritis, and disseminated	Cefotaxime	25-50 mg/kg I.V. q8-12h x 7-14 d	Penicillin G[12] 75,000-100,000 units/kg/d I.V. in 4 doses x 7-14 d
Children (<45 kg)			
Urogenital, rectal, and pharyngeal	Ceftriaxone	125 mg I.M. once	Spectinomycin[13] 40 mg/kg I.M. once; amoxicillin[12] 50 mg/kg oral once, plus probenecid 25 mg/kg (max: 1 g) oral once
Bacteremia, arthritis, and disseminated	Ceftriaxone or	50-100 mg/kg/d (max: 2 g) I.V. x 7-14 d	Penicillin G[12] 150,000-250,000 units/kg/d I.V. x 7-14 d
	Cefotaxime	50-200 mg/kg/d I.V. in 2-4 doses x 7-14 d	

TREATMENT OF SEXUALLY TRANSMITTED DISEASES
(Continued)

Type or Stage	Drug of Choice	Dosage	Alternatives
SEXUALLY ACQUIRED EPIDIDYMITIS			
	Ofloxacin	300 mg bid x 10 d	Ceftriaxone 250 mg I.M. once, followed by doxycycline[1] 100 mg oral bid x 10 d
PELVIC INFLAMMATORY DISEASE			
Hospitalized patients	Cefoxitin or	2 g I.V. q6h	Clindamycin 900 mg I.V. q8h plus gentamicin 2 mg/kg I.V. once, followed by gentamicin 1.5 mg/kg I.V. q8h until improved, followed by doxycycline 100 mg oral bid to complete 14 days[14]
	Cefotetan either one, plus	2 g I.V. q12h	
	Doxycycline[2] followed by	100 mg I.V. q12h, until improved	
	Doxycycline[2]	100 mg oral bid to complete 14 days	
Outpatients	Cefoxitin, plus	2 g I.M. once	Ofloxacin[2] 400 mg oral bid x 14 d, plus metronidazole 500 mg oral bid x 14 d or clindamycin 450 mg oral qid x 14 d
	Probenecid or	1 g oral once	
	Ceftriaxone, either one followed by	250 mg I.M. once	
	Doxycycline[2]	100 mg oral bid x 14 d	
VAGINAL INFECTION			
Trichomoniasis			
	Metronidazole[15]	2 g oral once	Metronidazole 375 mg or 500 mg oral bid x 7 d
Bacterial vaginosis			
	Metronidazole gel 0.75%	5 g intravaginally bid x 5 d	Metronidazole 500 mg oral bid x 7 d
Vulvovaginal candidiasis			
	Topical butoconazole, clotrimazole, miconazole, terconazole, or tioconazole[17]		Metronidazole 2 g oral once[16]; fluconazole 150 mg oral once
SYPHILIS			
Early (primary, secondary, or latent <1 y)			
	Penicillin G benzathine	2.4 million units I.M. once[18]	Doxycycline[2] 100 mg oral bid x 14 d
Late (more than 1 year's duration, cardiovascular, gumma, late-latent)			
	Penicillin G benzathine	2.4 million units I.M. weekly x 3 wk	Doxycycline[2] 100 mg oral bid x 4 wk
Neurosyphilis[19]			
	Penicillin G	2-4 million units I.V. q4h x 10-14 d	Penicillin G procaine 2.4 million units I.M. daily, plus probenecid 500 mg qid oral, both x 10-14 d
Congenital			
	Penicillin G or	50,000 units/kg I.M. or I.V. q8-12h for 10-14 d	
	Penicillin G procaine	50,000 units/kg I.M. daily for 10-14 d	
CHANCROID[20]			
	Erythromycin[3] or	500 mg oral qid x 7 d	Ciprofloxacin[2] 500 mg oral bid x 3 d
	Ceftriaxone or	250 mg I.M. once	
	Azithromycin	1 g oral once	

Type or Stage	Drug of Choice	Dosage	Alternatives
HERPES SIMPLEX			
First episode genital			
	Acyclovir	400 mg oral tid x 7-10 d	Acyclovir 200 mg oral 5 times/d x 7-10 d
First episode proctitis			
	Acyclovir	800 mg oral tid x 7-10 d	Acyclovir 400 mg oral 5 times/d x 7-10 d
Recurrent			
	Acyclovir[21]	400 mg oral tid x 5 d	
Severe (hospitalized patients)			
	Acyclovir	5 mg/kg I.V. q8h x 5-7 d	
Prevention of recurrence[22]			
	Acyclovir	400 mg oral bid	Acyclovir 200 mg oral 2-5 times/d

[1]Or tetracycline 500 mg oral qid or minocycline 100 mg oral bid.

[2]Contraindicated in pregnancy.

[3]Erythromycin estolate is contraindicated in pregnancy.

[4]In the presence of severe gastrointestinal intolerance, decrease to 250 mg qid and extend duration to 14 days.

[5]Safety in pregnancy not established.

[6]Only for infants older than 4 weeks.

[7]All patients should also receive a course of treatment effective for *Chlamydia*.

[8]Recommended only for use during pregnancy in patients allergic to beta-lactams. Not effective for pharyngeal infection.

[9]An oral fluoroquinolone, such as ciprofloxacin for 3-5 days, probably would also be effective, but experience is limited.

[10]If the infecting strain of *N. gonorrhoeae* has been tested and is known to be susceptible to penicillin or the tetracyclines, treatment may be changed to penicillin G 10 million units I.V. daily, amoxicillin 500 mg orally qid, doxycycline 100 mg orally bid, or tetracycline 500 mg orally qid.

[11]Endocarditis requires at least 3-4 weeks of parenteral therapy.

[12]If infecting strain of *N. gonorrhoeae* has been tested and is known to be susceptible.

[13]Not effective for pharyngeal infection.

[14]Or clindamycin 450 mg oral qid to complete 14 days.

[15]Metronidazole should be avoided during the first trimester of pregnancy; 2 g oral (single dose) may be given after the first trimester.

[16]Higher relapse rate, but useful for patients who may not comply with multiple-dose therapy.

[17]For preparations and dosage, see *The Medical Letter*, 36:81, 1994; avoid single-dose therapy.

[18]Some experts recommend repeating this regimen after 7 days, especially in patients with HIV infection.

[19]Patients allergic to penicillin should be desensitized.

[20]All regimens, especially single-dose ceftriaxone, are less effective in HIV-infected patients.

[21]Not highly effective for treatment of recurrences, but may help some patients if started early.

[22]Preventive treatment should be discontinued for 1-2 months once a year to reassess the frequency of recurrence.

TUBERCULOSIS TREATMENT GUIDELINES

Recommended Treatment Regimens for Drug-Susceptible Tuberculosis in Infants, Children, and Adolescents*

Infection or Disease Category	Regimen	Remarks
Asymptomatic infection (positive skin test, no disease):		If daily therapy is not possible, therapy twice a week may be used for 6-9 months. HIV-infected children should be treated for 12 months.
• Isoniazid-susceptible	6-9 months of isoniazid once a day	
• Isoniazid-resistant	6-9 months of rifampin once a day	
• Isoniazid-rifampin-resistant*	Consult a tuberculosis specialist	
Pulmonary	**6-Month Regimens** 2 months of isoniazid, rifampin, and pyrazinamide once a day, followed by 4 months of isoniazid and rifampin daily	If possible drug resistance is a concern (see text), another drug (ethambutol or streptomycin) is added to the initial drug therapy until drug susceptibilities are determined.
	or 2 months of isoniazid, rifampin, and pyrazinamide daily, followed by 4 months of isoniazid and rifampin twice a week	Drugs can be given 2 or 3 times per week under direct observation in the initial phase if nonadherence is likely.
	9-Month Alternative Regimens (for hilar adenopathy only) 9 months of isoniazid and rifampin once a day	Regimens consisting of 6 months of isoniazid and rifampin once a day, and 1 month of isoniazid and rifampin once a day, followed by 5 months of isoniazid and rifampin twice a week, have been successful in areas where drug resistance is rare.
	or 1 month of isoniazid and rifampin once a day, followed by 8 months of isoniazid and rifampin twice a week	
Extrapulmonary meningitis, disseminated (miliary), bone/joint disease	2 months of isoniazid, rifampin, pyrazinamide, and streptomycin once a day, followed by 10 months of isoniazid and rifampin once a day (12 months total)	Streptomycin is given with initial therapy until drug susceptibility is known.
	or 2 months of isoniazid, rifampin, pyrazinamide, and streptomycin once a day, followed by 10 months of isoniazid and rifampin twice a week (12 months total)	For patients who may have acquired tuberculosis in geographic areas where resistance to streptomycin is common, capreomycin (15-30 mg/kg/d) or kanamycin (15-30 mg/kg/d) may be used instead of streptomycin.
Other (eg, cervical lymphadenopathy)	Same as for pulmonary disease	See Pulmonary.

*Duration of therapy is longer in HIV-infected persons and additional drugs may be indicated.

Adapted from "Report of the Committee on Infectious Diseases," *1997 Red Book*®, 24th ed.

Commonly Used Drugs for the Treatment of Tuberculosis in Infants, Children, and Adolescents

Drugs	Dosage Forms	Daily Dose (mg/kg/d)	Twice a Week Dose (mg/kg per dose)	Maximum Dose	Adverse Reactions
Ethambutol	Tablets 100 mg 400 mg	15-25	50	2.5 g	Optic neuritis (usually reversible), decreased visual acuity, decreased red-green color discrimination, gastrointestinal disturbances, hypersensitivity
Isoniazid*	Scored tablets 100 mg 300 mg Syrup 10 mg/mL	10-15†	20-30	Daily, 300 mg Twice a week, 900 mg	Mild hepatic enzyme elevation, hepatitis,† peripheral neuritis, hypersensitivity
Pyrazinamide*	Scored tablets 500 mg	20-40	50	2 g	Hepatotoxicity, hyperuricemia
Rifampin*	Capsules 150 mg 300 mg Syrup formulated in syrup from capsules	10-20	10-20	600 mg	Orange discoloration of secretions/urine, staining contact lenses, vomiting, hepatitis, flu-like reaction, and thrombocytopenia; may render birth-control pills ineffective
Streptomycin (I.M. administration)	Vials 1 g 4 g	20-40	20-40	1 g	Auditory and vestibular toxicity, nephrotoxicity, rash

*Rifamate® is a capsule containing 150 mg of isoniazid and 300 mg of rifampin. Two capsules provide the usual adult (>50 kg body weight) daily doses of each drug. Rifater® is a capsule containing 50 mg of isoniazid, 120 mg of rifampin, and 300 mg of pyrazinamide.

†When isoniazid in a dosage exceeding 10 mg/kg/day is used in combination with rifampin, the incidence of hepatotoxicity may be increased.

Adapted from "Report of the Committee on Infectious Diseases," *1997 Red Book*®, 24th ed.

Rifampin is a bactericidal agent. It is metabolized by the liver and affects the pharmacokinetics of many other drugs, affecting their serum concentrations. Mycobacterium tuberculosis, initially resistant to rifampin, remains relatively uncommon in most areas of the United States. Rifampin is excreted in bile and urine and can cause orange urine, sweat and tears. It can also cause discoloration of soft contact lenses and render oral contraceptives ineffective. Hepatotoxicity occurs rarely. Blood dyscrasia accompanied by influenza-like symptoms can occur if doses are taken sporadically.

TUBERCULOSIS TREATMENT GUIDELINES *(Continued)*

Less Commonly Used Drugs for Treatment of Drug-Resistant Tuberculosis in Infants, Children, and Adolescents*

Drugs	Dosage Forms	Daily Dose (mg/kg/d)	Maximum Dose	Adverse Reactions
Capreomycin	Vials 1 g	15-30 (I.M. administration)	1 g	Ototoxicity, nephrotoxicity
Ciprofloxacin†	Tablets 250 mg 500 mg 750 mg	Adults 500-1500 mg total per day (twice a day)	1.5 g	Theoretical effect on growing cartilage, gastrointestinal tract disturbances, rash, headache
Cycloserine	Capsules 250 mg	10-20	1 g	Psychosis, personality changes, convulsions, rash
Ethionamide	Tablets 250 mg	15-20 given in 2 or 3 divided doses	1 g	Gastrointestinal tract disturbances, hepatotoxicity, hypersensitive reactions
Kanamycin	Vials 75 mg/2 mL 500 mg/2 mL 1 g/3 mL	15-30 (I.M. 1 g administration)	1 g	Auditory toxicity, nephrotoxicity, vestibular toxicity
Ofloxacin†	Tablets 200 mg 300 mg 400 mg	Adults 400-800 mg total per day (twice a day)	0.8 g	Theoretical effect on growing cartilage, gastrointestinal tract disturbances, rash, headache
Para-amino salicylic acid (PAS)	Tablets 500 mg	200-300 (3 or 4 times a day)	10 g	Gastrointestinal tract disturbances, hypersensitivity, hepatotoxicity

*These drugs should be used in consultation with a specialist in tuberculosis.

†Fluoroquinolones are not currently approved for use in persons younger than 18 years; their use in younger patients necessitates assessment of the potential risks and benefits (see Antimicrobials and Related Therapy).

Adapted from "Report of the Committee on Infectious Diseases," *1997 Red Book®*, 24th ed.

TB Drugs in Special Situations

Drug	Pregnancy	CNS TB Disease	Renal Insufficiency
Isoniazid	Safe	Good penetration	Normal clearance
Rifampin	Safe	Fair penetration Penetrates inflamed meninges (10% to 20%)	Normal clearance
Pyrazinamide	Avoid	Good penetration	Clearance reduced Decrease dose or prolong interval
Ethambutol	Safe	Penetrates inflamed meninges only (4% to 64%)	Clearance reduced Decrease dose or prolong interval
Streptomycin	Avoid	Penetrates inflamed meninges only	Clearance reduced Decrease dose or prolong interval
Capreomycin	Avoid	Penetrates inflamed meninges only	Clearance reduced Decrease dose or prolong interval
Kanamycin	Avoid	Penetrates inflamed meninges only	Clearance reduced Decrease dose or prolong interval
Ethionamide	Do not use	Good penetration	Normal clearance
Para-aminosalicylic acid	Safe	Penetrates inflamed meninges only (10% to 50%)	Incomplete data on clearance
Cycloserine	Avoid	Good penetration	Clearance reduced Decrease dose or prolong interval
Ciprofloxacin	Do not use	Fair penetration (5% to 10%) Penetrates inflamed meninges (50% to 90%)	Clearance reduced Decrease dose or prolong interval
Ofloxacin	Do not use	Fair penetration (5% to 10%) Penetrates inflamed meninges (50% to 90%)	Clearance reduced Decrease dose or prolong interval
Amikacin	Avoid	Penetrates inflamed meninges only	Clearance reduced Decrease dose or prolong interval
Clofazimine	Avoid	Penetration unknown	Clearance probably normal

Safe = The drug has not been demonstrated to have teratogenic effects.

Avoid = Data on the drug's safety are limited, or the drug is associated with mild malformations (as in the aminoglycosides).

Do not use = Studies show an association between the drug and premature labor, congenital malformations, or teratogenicity.

REFERENCE VALUES FOR ADULTS

Automated Chemistry (CHEMISTRY A)

Test	Values	Remarks
SERUM PLASMA		
Acetone	Negative	
Albumin	3.2-5 g/dL	
Alcohol, ethyl	Negative	
Aldolase	1.2-7.6 IU/L	
Ammonia	20-70 mcg/dL	Specimen to be placed on ice as soon as collected
Amylase	30-110 units/L	
Bilirubin, direct	0-0.3 mg/dL	
Bilirubin, total	0.1-1.2 mg/dL	
Calcium	8.6-10.3 mg/dL	
Calcium, ionized	2.24-2.46 mEq/L	
Chloride	95-108 mEq/L	
Cholesterol, total	≤220 mg/dL	Fasted blood required – normal value affected by dietary habits. This reference range is for a general adult population
HDL cholesterol	40-60 mg/dL	Fasted blood required – normal value affected by dietary habits
LDL cholesterol	65-170 mg/dL	LDLC calculated by Friewald formula... which has certain inaccuracies and is invalid at trig levels >300 mg/dL
CO_2	23-30 mEq/L	
Creatine kinase (CK) isoenzymes		
CK-BB	0%	
CK-MB (cardiac)	0%-3.9%	
CK-MM (muscle)	96%-100%	
CK-MB levels must be both ≥4% and 10 IU/L to meet diagnostic criteria for CK-MB positive result consistent with myocardial injury.		
Creatine phosphokinase (CPK)	8-150 IU/L	
Creatinine	0.5-1.4 mg/dL	
Ferritin	13-300 ng/mL	
Folate	3.6-20 ng/dL	
GGT (gamma-glutamyltranspeptidase)		
male	11-63 IU/L	
female	8-35 IU/L	
GLDH	To be determined	
Glucose (2-h postprandial)	Up to 140 mg/dL	
Glucose, fasting	60-110 mg/dL	
Glucose, nonfasting (2-h postprandial)	60-140 mg/dL	
Hemoglobin A_{1c}	8	
Hemoglobin, plasma free	<2.5 mg/100 mL	
Hemoglobin, total glycosylated (Hb A_1)	4%-8%	
Iron	65-150 mcg/dL	
Iron binding capacity, total (TIBC)	250-420 mcg/dL	
Lactic acid	0.7-2.1 mEq/L	Specimen to be kept on ice and sent to lab as soon as possible
Lactate dehydrogenase (LDH)	56-194 IU/L	
Lactate dehydrogenase (LDH) isoenzymes		
LD_1	20%-34%	
LD_2	29%-41%	
LD_3	15%-25%	
LD_4	1%-12%	
LD_5	1%-15%	
Flipped LD_1/LD_2 ratios (>1 may be consistent with myocardial injury) particularly when considered in combination with a recent CK-MB positive result		
Lipase	23-208 units/L	

Automated Chemistry (CHEMISTRY A) (continued)

Test	Values	Remarks
Magnesium	1.6-2.5 mg/dL	Increased by slight hemolysis
Osmolality	289-308 mOsm/kg	
Phosphatase, alkaline		
adults 25-60 y	33-131 IU/L	
adults 61 y or older	51-153 IU/L	
infancy-adolescence	Values range up to 3-5 times higher than adults	
Phosphate, inorganic	2.8-4.2 mg/dL	
Potassium	3.5-5.2 mEq/L	Increased by slight hemolysis
Prealbumin	>15 mg/dL	
Protein, total	6.5-7.9 g/dL	
SGOT (AST)	<35 IU/L (20-48)	
SGPT (ALT) (10-35)	<35 IU/L	
Sodium	134-149 mEq/L	
Transferrin	>200 mg/dL	
Triglycerides	45-155 mg/dL	Fasted blood required
Urea nitrogen (BUN)	7-20 mg/dL	
Uric acid		
male	2.0-8.0 mg/dL	
female	2.0-7.5 mg/dL	

CEREBROSPINAL FLUID

Glucose	50-70 mg/dL	
Protein		
adults and children	15-45 mg/dL	CSF obtained by lumbar puncture
newborn infants	60-90 mg/dL	

On CSF obtained by cisternal puncture: About 25 mg/dL
On CSF obtained by ventricular puncture: About 10 mg/dL
Note: Bloody specimen gives erroneously high value due to contamination with blood proteins

URINE

(24-hour specimen is required for all these tests unless specified)

Amylase	32-641 units/L	The value is in units/L and **not** calculated for total volume
Amylase, fluid (random samples)		Interpretation of value left for physician, depends on the nature of fluid
Calcium	Depends upon dietary intake	
Creatine		
male	150 mg/24 h	Higher value on children and during pregnancy
female	250 mg/24 h	
Creatinine	1000-2000 mg/24 h	
Creatinine clearance (endogenous)		
male	85-125 mL/min	A blood sample must accompany urine specimen
female	75-115 mL/min	
Glucose	1 g/24 h	
5-hydroxyindoleacetic acid	2-8 mg/24 h	
Iron	0.15 mg/24 h	Acid washed container required
Magnesium	146-209 mg/24 h	
Osmolality	500-800 mOsm/kg	With normal fluid intake
Oxalate	10-40 mg/24 h	
Phosphate	400-1300 mg/24 h	
Potassium	25-120 mEq/24 h	Varies with diet; the interpretation of urine electrolytes and osmolality should be left for the physician
Sodium	40-220 mEq/24 h	
Porphobilinogen, qualitative	Negative	
Porphyrins, qualitative	Negative	

REFERENCE VALUES FOR ADULTS (Continued)

Automated Chemistry (CHEMISTRY A) (continued)

Test	Values	Remarks
Proteins	0.05-0.1 g/24 h	
Salicylate	Negative	
Urea clearance	60-95 mL/min	A blood sample must accompany specimen
Urea N	10-40 g/24 h	Dependent on protein intake
Uric acid	250-750 mg/24 h	Dependent on diet and therapy
Urobilinogen	0.5-3.5 mg/24 h	For qualitative determination on random urine, send sample to urinalysis section in Hematology Lab
Xylose absorption test		
children	16%-33% of ingested xylose	
adults	>4 g in 5 h	
FECES		
Fat, 3-day collection	<5 g/d	Value depends on fat intake of 100 g/d for 3 days preceding and during collection
GASTRIC ACIDITY		
Acidity, total, 12 h	10-60 mEq/L	Titrated at pH 7

BLOOD GASES

	Arterial	Capillary	Venous
pH	7.35-7.45	7.35-7.45	7.32-7.42
pCO_2 (mm Hg)	35-45	35-45	38-52
pO_2 (mm Hg)	70-100	60-80	24-48
HCO_3 (mEq/L)	19-25	19-25	19-25
TCO_2 (mEq/L)	19-29	19-29	23-33
O_2 saturation (%)	90-95	90-95	40-70
Base excess (mEq/L)	-5 to +5	-5 to +5	-5 to +5

HEMATOLOGY

Complete Blood Count

Age	Hgb (g/dL)	Hct (%)	RBC (mill/mm³)	RDW
0-3 d	15.0-20.0	45-61	4.0-5.9	<18
1-2 wk	12.5-18.5	39-57	3.6-5.5	<17
1-6 mo	10.0-13.0	29-42	3.1-4.3	<16.5
7 mo to 2 y	10.5-13.0	33-38	3.7-4.9	<16
2-5 y	11.5-13.0	34-39	3.9-5.0	<15
5-8 y	11.5-14.5	35-42	4.0-4.9	<15
13-18 y	12.0-15.2	36-47	4.5-5.1	<14.5
Adult male	13.5-16.5	41-50	4.5-5.5	<14.5
Adult female	12.0-15.0	36-44	4.0-4.9	<14.5

Age	MCV (fL)	MCH (pg)	MCHC (%)	Plts (x 10³/mm³)
0-3 d	95-115	31-37	29-37	250-450
1-2 wk	86-110	28-36	28-38	250-450
1-6 mo	74-96	25-35	30-36	300-700
7 mo to 2 y	70-84	23-30	31-37	250-600
2-5 y	75-87	24-30	31-37	250-550
5-8 y	77-95	25-33	31-37	250-550
13-18 y	78-96	25-35	31-37	150-450
Adult male	80-100	26-34	31-37	150-450
Adult female	80-100	26-34	31-37	150-450

WBC and Diff

Age	WBC (x 10³/mm³)	Segs	Bands	Lymphs	Monos
0-3 d	9.0-35.0	32-62	10-18	19-29	5-7
1-2 wk	5.0-20.0	14-34	6-14	36-45	6-10
1-6 mo	6.0-17.5	13-33	4-12	41-71	4-7
7 mo to 2 y	6.0-17.0	15-35	5-11	45-76	3-6
2-5 y	5.5-15.5	23-45	5-11	35-65	3-6
5-8 y	5.0-14.5	32-54	5-11	28-48	3-6
13-18 y	4.5-13.0	34-64	5-11	25-45	3-6
Adults	4.5-11.0	35-66	5-11	24-44	3-6

Age	Eosinophils	Basophils	Atypical Lymphs	No. of NRBCs
0-3 d	0-2	0-1	0-8	0-2
1-2 wk	0-2	0-1	0-8	0
1-6 mo	0-3	0-1	0-8	0
7 mo to 2 y	0-3	0-1	0-8	0
2-5 y	0-3	0-1	0-8	0
5-8 y	0-3	0-1	0-8	0
13-18 y	0-3	0-1	0-8	0
Adults	0-3	0-1	0-8	0

Segs = segmented neutrophils
Bands = band neutrophils

Lymphs = lymphocytes
Monos = monocytes

Erythrocyte Sedimentation Rates and Reticulocyte Counts

Sedimentation rate, Westergren

Children 0-20 mm/hour
Adult male 0-15 mm/hour
Adult female 0-20 mm/hour

Sedimentation rate, Wintrobe

Children 0-13 mm/hour
Adult male 0-10 mm/hour
Adult female 0-15 mm/hour

Reticulocyte count

Newborns 2%-6%
1-6 mo 0%-2.8%
Adults 0.5%-1.5%

REFERENCE VALUES FOR CHILDREN

Chemistry

Albumin	0-1 y	2-4 g/dL
	1 y to adult	3.5-5.5 g/dL
Ammonia	Newborns	90-150 µg/dL
	Children	40-120 µg/dL
	Adults	18-54 µg/dL
Amylase	Newborns	0-60 units/L
	Adults	30-110 units/L
Bilirubin, conjugated, direct	Newborns	<1.5 mg/dL
	1 mo to adult	0-0.5 mg/dL
Bilirubin, total	0-3 d	2-10 mg/dL
	1 mo to adult	0-1.5 mg/dL
Bilirubin, unconjugated, indirect		0.6-10.5 mg/dL
Calcium	Newborns	7-12 mg/dL
	0-2 y	8.8-11.2 mg/dL
	2 y to adult	9-11 mg/dL
Calcium, ionized, whole blood		4.4-5.4 mg/dL
Carbon dioxide, total		23-33 mEq/L
Chloride		95-105 mEq/L
Cholesterol	Newborns	45-170 mg/dL
	0-1 y	65-175 mg/dL
	1-20 y	120-230 mg/dL
Creatinine	0-1 y	≤0.6 mg/dL
	1 y to adult	0.5-1.5 mg/dL
Glucose	Newborns	30-90 mg/dL
	0-2 y	60-105 mg/dL
	Children to adults	70-110 mg/dL
Iron	Newborns	110-270 µg/dL
	Infants	30-70 µg/dL
	Children	55-120 µg/dL
	Adults	70-180 µg/dL
Iron binding	Newborns	59-175 µg/dL
	Infants	100-400 µg/dL
	Adults	250-400 µg/dL
Lactic acid, lactate		2-20 mg/dL
Lead, whole blood		<30 µg/dL
Lipase	Children	20-140 units/L
	Adults	0-190 units/L
Magnesium		1.5-2.5 mEq/L
Osmolality, serum		275-296 mOsm/kg
Osmolality, urine		50-1400 mOsm/kg
Phosphorus	Newborns	4.2-9 mg/dL
	6 wk to ≤18 mo	3.8-6.7 mg/dL
	18 mo to 3 y	2.9-5.9 mg/dL
	3-15 y	3.6-5.6 mg/dL
	>15 y	2.5-5 mg/dL
Potassium, plasma	Newborns	4.5-7.2 mEq/L
	2 d to 3 mo	4-6.2 mEq/L
	3 mo to 1 y	3.7-5.6 mEq/L
	1-16 y	3.5-5 mEq/L
Protein, total	0-2 y	4.2-7.4 g/dL
	>2 y	6-8 g/dL
Sodium		136-145 mEq/L
Triglycerides	Infants	0-171 mg/dL
	Children	20-130 mg/dL
	Adults	30-200 mg/dL
Urea nitrogen, blood	0-2 y	4-15 mg/dL
	2 y to adult	5-20 mg/dL

Chemistry (continued)

Uric acid	Male	3-7 mg/dL
	Female	2-6 mg/dL

ENZYMES

Alanine aminotransferase (ALT)	0-2 mo	8-78 units/L
(SGPT)	>2 mo	8-36 units/L
Alkaline phosphatase (ALKP)	Newborns	60-130 units/L
	0-16 y	85-400 units/L
	>16 y	30-115 units/L
Aspartate aminotransferase (AST)	Infants	18-74 units/L
(SGOT)	Children	15-46 units/L
	Adults	5-35 units/L
Creatine kinase (CK)	Infants	20-200 units/L
	Children	10-90 units/L
	Adult male	0-206 units/L
	Adult female	0-175 units/L
Lactate dehydrogenase (LDH)	Newborns	290-501 units/L
	1 mo to 2 y	110-144 units/L
	>16 y	60-170 units/L

BLOOD GASES

	Arterial	Capillary	Venous
pH	7.35-7.45	7.35-7.45	7.32-7.42
pCO$_2$ (mm Hg)	35-45	35-45	38-52
pO$_2$ (mm Hg)	70-100	60-80	24-48
HCO$_3$ (mEq/L)	19-25	19-25	19-25
TCO$_2$ (mEq/L)	19-29	19-29	23-33
O$_2$ saturation (%)	90-95	90-95	40-70
Base excess (mEq/L)	-5 to +5	-5 to +5	-5 to +5

THYROID FUNCTION TESTS

T$_4$ (thyroxine)	1-7 d	10.1-20.9 µg/dL
	8-14 d	9.8-16.6 µg/dL
	1 mo to 1 y	5.5-16 µg/dL
	>1 y	4-12 µg/dL
FTI	1-3 d	9.3-26.6
	1-4 wks	7.6-20.8
	1-4 mo	7.4-17.9
	4-12 mo	5.1-14.5
	1-6 y	5.7-13.3
	>6 y	4.8-14
T$_3$ by RIA	Newborns	100-470 ng/dL
	1-5 y	100-260 ng/dL
	5-10 y	90-240 ng/dL
	10 y to adult	70-210 ng/dL
T$_3$ uptake		35%-45%
TSH	Cord	3-22 µU/mL
	1-3 d	<40 µU/mL
	3-7 d	<25 µU/mL
	>7 d	0-10 µU/mL

CALCULATIONS FOR TOTAL PARENTERAL NUTRITION THERAPY – ADULT PATIENTS

Condition	Calorie Requirement (kcal/kg/d)	Protein Requirement (g/kg/d)
Resting state (adult medical patient)	20-30	0.8-1
Uncomplicated postop patients	25-35	1-1.3
Depleted patients	30-40	1.3-1.7
Hypermetabolic patients (trauma, sepsis, burns)	35-45	1.5-2

1 g protein yields 4 kcal/g
1 g fat yields 9 kcal/g
1 g dextrose yields 3.4 kcal/g
1 g nitrogen = 6.25 g protein

Electrolytes Required/Day

	mEq/d
Sodium	60-120
Potassium	60-120
Chloride	100-150
Magnesium	10-24
Calcium	10-20
Phosphate	20-50 mmol/d
Sulfate	10-24
Acetate	60-150
Bicarbonate	Should not be added

Estimated Energy Requirements

Basal Energy Expenditure (BEE)	
Harris Benedict equation	
males	$BEE_{mal} = 66.67 + (13.75 \times kg) + (5 \times cm) - (6.76 \times y)$
females	$BEE_{fem} = 665.1 + (9.56 \times kg) + (1.85 \times cm) - (4.68 \times y)$
Total daily energy expenditure (TDE)	TDE = BEE × activity factor × injury factor
Activity factor	Confined to bed = 1.2
	Out of bed = 1.3
Injury factor	Surgery: Minor operations = 1-1.1 Major operations = 1.1-1.2
	Infection: Mild = 1-1.2 Moderate = 1.2-1.4 Severe = 1.4-1.6
	Skeletal trauma = 1.2-1.35
	Head injury (treated with corticosteroids) = 1.6
	Blunt trauma = 1.15-1.35
	Burns ≤20% body surface area (BSA) = 2 20%-30% BSA = 2-2.2 >30% BSA = 2.2

Estimated Fluid Requirements

30-35 mL/kg/d
or
mL/d = 1500 mL for first 20 kg of body weight + 20 mL/kg for body weight >20 kg

MEDIAN HEIGHTS AND WEIGHTS AND RECOMMENDED ENERGY INTAKE*

Age (y) or Condition	Weight (kg)	Weight (lb)	Height (cm)	Height (in)	REE† (kcal/d)	Multiples of REE	Average Energy Allowance (kcal)‡ /kg	Average Energy Allowance (kcal)‡ /d§
Infants								
0-0.5	6	13	60	24	320		108	650
0.5-1	9	20	71	28	500		98	850
Children								
1-3	13	29	90	35	740		102	1300
4-6	20	44	112	44	950		90	1800
7-10	28	62	132	52	1130		70	2000
Male								
11-14	45	99	157	62	1440	1.70	55	2500
15-18	66	145	176	69	1760	1.67	45	3000
19-24	72	160	177	70	1780	1.67	40	2900
25-50	79	174	176	70	1800	1.60	37	2900
51+	77	170	173	68	1530	1.50	30	2300
Female								
11-14	46	101	157	62	1310	1.67	47	2200
15-18	55	120	163	64	1370	1.60	40	2200
19-24	58	128	164	65	1350	1.60	38	2200
25-50	63	138	163	64	1380	1.55	36	2200
51+	65	143	160	63	1280	1.50	30	1900
Pregnant								+0
1st trimester								+300
2nd trimester								+300
3rd trimester								+300
Lactating								
1st 6 months								+500
2nd 6 months								+500

*From Recommended Dietary Allowances, 10th ed, Washington, DC: National Academy Press, 1989.
†Calculation based on FAO equations, then rounded.
‡In the range of light to moderate activity, the coefficient of variation is ±20%.
§Figure is rounded.

PEDIATRIC ALS ALGORITHMS

Bradycardia

Fig. 1: Pediatric bradycardia decision tree. ABCs indicates airway, breathing, and circulation; ALS, advanced life support; E.T., endotracheal; I.O., intraosseous; and I.V., intravenous.

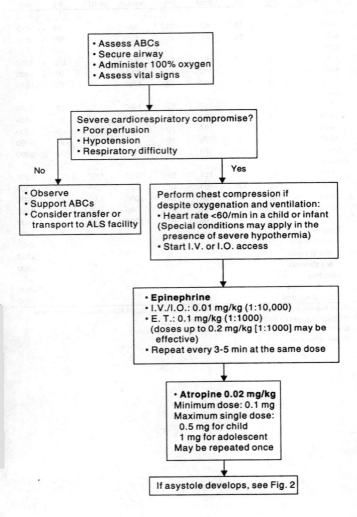

Asystole and Pulseless Arrest

Fig. 2: Pediatric asystole and pulseless arrest decision tree. CPR indicates cardiopulmonary resuscitation; E.T., endotracheal; I.O., intraosseous; and I.V., intravenous.

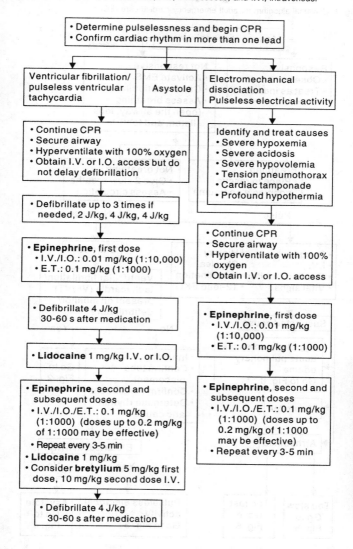

Used with permission: Emergency Cardiac Care Committee and Subcommittees, American Heart Association, "Guidelines for Cardiopulmonary Resuscitation and Emergency Care, IV: Pediatric Advanced Life Support," *JAMA*, 1992.

ADULT ACLS ALGORITHMS

Emergency Cardiac Care

Fig. 1: Universal algorithm for adult emergency cardiac care (ECC)

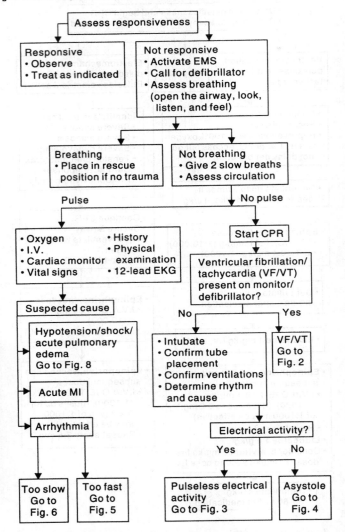

V. Fib and Pulseless V. Tach

Fig. 2: Adult algorithm for ventricular fibrillation and pulseless ventricular tachycardia (VF/VT)

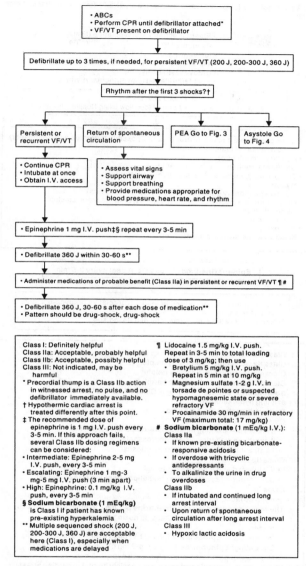

Used with permission: Emergency Cardiac Care Committee and Subcommittees, American Heart Association, "Guidelines for Cardiopulmonary Resuscitation and Emergency Care, III: Adult Advanced Cardiac Life Support," *JAMA*, 1992, 268:2199-241.

ADULT ACLS ALGORITHMS *(Continued)*

Pulseless Electrical Activity

Fig. 3: Adult algorithm for pulseless electrical activity (PEA) (electromechanical dissociation [EMD]).

PEA includes:
- Electromechanical dissociation (EMD)
- Pseudo-EMD
- Idioventricular rhythms
- Ventricular escape rhythms
- Bradyasystolic rhythms
- Postdefibrillation idioventricular rhythms

- Continue CPR
- Intubate at once
- Obtain I.V. access
- Assess blood flow using Doppler ultrasound

Consider possible causes (Parentheses = possible therapies and treatments)
- Hypovolemia (volume infusion)
- Hypoxia (ventilation)
- Cardiac tamponade (pericardiocentesis)
- Tension pneumothorax (needle decompression)
- Hypothermia
- Massive pulmonary embolism (surgery, **thrombolytics**)
- Drug overdoses such as tricyclics, digitalis, beta blockers, calcium channel blockers
- Hyperkalemia*
- Acidosis†
- Massive acute myocardial infarction

Epinephrine 1 mg I.V. push*‡, repeat every 3-5 min

- If absolute bradycardia (<60 beats/min) or relative bradycardia, give **atropine** 1 mg I.V.
- Repeat every 3-5 min up to a total of 0.04 mg/kg§

Class I: Definitely helpful
Class IIa: Acceptable, probably helpful
Class IIb: Acceptable, possibly helpful
Class III: Not indicated, may be harmful
* **Sodium bicarbonate** 1 mEq/kg is Class I if patient has known preexisting hyperkalemia
† **Sodium bicarbonate** 1 mEq/kg:
Class IIa
- If known pre-existing bicarbonate-responsive acidosis
- If overdose with tricyclic antidepressants
- To alkalinize the urine in drug overdoses
Class IIb
- If intubated and long arrest interval
- Upon return of spontaneous circulation after long arrest interval
Class III
- Hypoxic lactic acidosis
‡ The recommended dose of **epinephrine** is 1 mg I.V. push every 3-5 min. If this approach fails, several Class IIb dosing regimens can be considered.
- Intermediate: **Epinephrine** 2-5 mg I.V. push every 3-5 min
- Escalating: **Epinephrine** 1 mg-3 mg-5 mg I.V. push (3 min apart)
- High: **Epinephrine** 0.1 mg/kg I.V. push every 3-5 min
§ Shorter **atropine** dosing intervals are possibly helpful in cardiac arrest (Class IIb)

Used with permission: Emergency Cardiac Care Committee and Subcommittees, American Heart Association, "Guidelines for Cardiopulmonary Resuscitation and Emergency Care, III: Adult Advanced Cardiac Life Support," *JAMA*, 1992, 268:2199-241.

Asystole

Fig. 4: Adult asystole treatment algorithm.

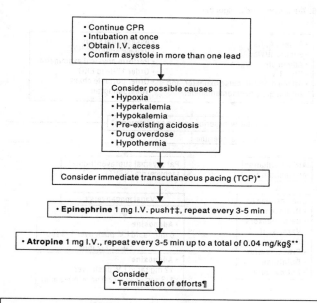

- Continue CPR
- Intubation at once
- Obtain I.V. access
- Confirm asystole in more than one lead

Consider possible causes
- Hypoxia
- Hyperkalemia
- Hypokalemia
- Pre-existing acidosis
- Drug overdose
- Hypothermia

Consider immediate transcutaneous pacing (TCP)*

- **Epinephrine** 1 mg I.V. push†‡, repeat every 3-5 min

- **Atropine** 1 mg I.V., repeat every 3-5 min up to a total of 0.04 mg/kg§**

Consider
- Termination of efforts¶

Class I: Definitely helpful
Class IIa: Acceptable, probably helpful
Class IIb: Acceptable, possibly helpful
Class III: Not indicated, may be harmful
* TCP is a Class IIb intervention. Lack of success may be due to delays in pacing. To be effective, TCP must be performed early, simultaneously with drugs. Evidence does not support routine use of TCP for asystole.
† The recommended dose of **epinephrine** is 1 mg I.V. push every 3-5 min. If this approach fails, several Class IIb dosing regimens can be considered:
- Intermediate: **Epinephrine** 2-5 mg I.V. push every 3-5 min
- Escalating: **Epinephrine** 1 mg-3 mg-5 mg I.V. push (3 min apart)
- High: **Epinephrine** 0.1 mg/kg I.V. push every 3-5 min
‡ Sodium bicarbonate 1 mEq/kg is Class I if patient has known pre-existing hyperkalemia

§ Shorter atropine dosing intervals are Class IIb in asystolic arrest
** Sodium bicarbonate 1 mEq/kg:
Class IIa
- If known pre-existing bicarbonate responsive acidosis
- If overdose with tricyclic antidepressants
- To alkalinize the urine in drug overdoses
Class IIb
- If intubated and continued long arrest interval
- Upon return of spontaneous circulation after long arrest interval
Class III
- Hypoxic lactic acidosis
¶ If patient remains in asystole or other agonal rhythm after successful intubation and initial medications and no reversible causes are identified, consider termination of resuscitative efforts by a physician. Consider interval since arrest.

Used with permission: Emergency Cardiac Care Committee and Subcommittees, American Heart Association, "Guidelines for Cardiopulmonary Resuscitation and Emergency Care, III: Adult Advanced Cardiac Life Support," *JAMA*, 1992, 268:2199-241.

ADULT ACLS ALGORITHMS *(Continued)*

Tachycardia

Fig. 5: Adult tachycardia algorithm.

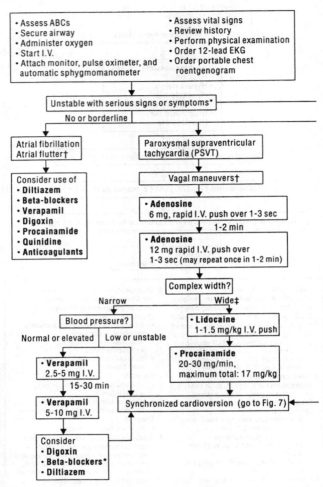

* Use extreme caution with beta-blockers after verapamil

Used with permission: Emergency Cardiac Care Committee and Subcommittees, American Heart Association, "Guidelines for Cardiopulmonary Resuscitation and Emergency Care, III: Adult Advanced Cardiac Life Support," *JAMA*, 1992, 268:2199-241.

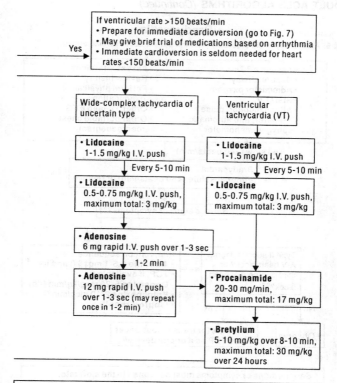

If ventricular rate >150 beats/min
- Prepare for immediate cardioversion (go to Fig. 7)
- May give brief trial of medications based on arrhythmia
- Immediate cardioversion is seldom needed for heart rates <150 beats/min

Yes →

Wide-complex tachycardia of uncertain type

- **Lidocaine**
  1-1.5 mg/kg I.V. push

  Every 5-10 min

- **Lidocaine**
  0.5-0.75 mg/kg I.V. push, maximum total: 3 mg/kg

- **Adenosine**
  6 mg rapid I.V. push over 1-3 sec

  1-2 min

- **Adenosine**
  12 mg rapid I.V. push over 1-3 sec (may repeat once in 1-2 min)

Ventricular tachycardia (VT)

- **Lidocaine**
  1-1.5 mg/kg I.V. push

  Every 5-10 min

- **Lidocaine**
  0.5-0.75 mg/kg I.V. push, maximum total: 3 mg/kg

- **Procainamide**
  20-30 mg/min, maximum total: 17 mg/kg

- **Bretylium**
  5-10 mg/kg over 8-10 min, maximum total: 30 mg/kg over 24 hours

** Unstable condition must be related to the tachycardia. Signs and symptoms may include chest pain, shortness of breath, decreased level of consciousness, low blood pressure (BP), shock, pulmonary congestion, congestive heart failure, acute myocardial infarction.

† Carotid sinus pressure is contraindicated in patients with carotid bruits; avoid ice water immersion in patients with ischemic heart disease.

‡ If the wide-complex tachycardia is known with certainty to be PSVT and BP is normal/elevated, sequence can include **verapamil**.

ADULT ACLS ALGORITHMS *(Continued)*

Bradycardia

Fig. 6: Adult bradycardia algorithm (with the patient not in cardiac arrest).

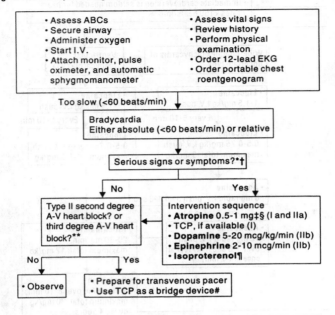

* Serious signs or symptoms must be related to the slow rate.
  Clinical manifestations include:
  Symptoms (chest pain, shortness of breath, decreased level of consciousness), and
  Signs (low BP, shock, pulmonary congestion, CHF, acute MI)
† Do not delay TCP while awaiting I.V. access or for **atropine** to take effect if patient is symptomatic.
‡ Denervated transplanted hearts will not respond to **atropine**. Go at once to pacing, **catecholamine** infusion, or both.
§ **Atropine** should be given in repeat doses in 3-5 min up to a total of 0.04 mg/kg. Consider shorter dosing intervals in severe clinical conditions. It has been suggested that atropine should be used with caution in atrioventricular (A-V) block at the His-Purkinje level (type II A-V block and new third degree block with wide QRS complexes) (Class IIb).
Never treat third degree heart block plus ventricular escape beats with **lidocaine.
¶ **Isoproterenol** should be used, if at all, with extreme caution. At low doses it is Class IIb (possibly helpful); at higher doses it is Class III (harmful).
# Verify patient tolerance and mechanical capture. Use analgesia and sedation as needed.

Electrical Conversion

Fig. 7: Adult electrical cardioversion algorithm (with the patient not in cardiac arrest).

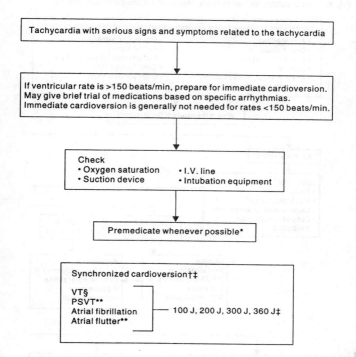

Tachycardia with serious signs and symptoms related to the tachycardia

If ventricular rate is >150 beats/min, prepare for immediate cardioversion.
May give brief trial of medications based on specific arrhythmias.
Immediate cardioversion is generally not needed for rates <150 beats/min.

Check
- Oxygen saturation
- Suction device
- I.V. line
- Intubation equipment

Premedicate whenever possible*

Synchronized cardioversion†‡

VT§
PSVT**
Atrial fibrillation
Atrial flutter** — 100 J, 200 J, 300 J, 360 J‡

* Effective regimens have included a sedative (eg, **diazepam, midazolam barbiturates, etomidate, ketamine, methohexital**) with or without an analgesic agent (eg, **fentanyl, morphine, meperidine**). Many experts recommend anesthesia if service is readily available.
† Note possible need to resynchronize after each cardioversion.
‡ If delays in synchronization occur and clinical conditions are critical, go to immediate unsynchronized shocks.
§ Treat polymorphic VT (irregular form and rate) like VF: 200 J, 200-300 J, 360 J.
** PSVT and atrial flutter often respond to lower energy levels (start with 50 J).

ADULT ACLS ALGORITHMS *(Continued)*

Hypotension, Shock

Fig. 8: Adult algorithm for hypotension, shock, and acute pulmonary edema.

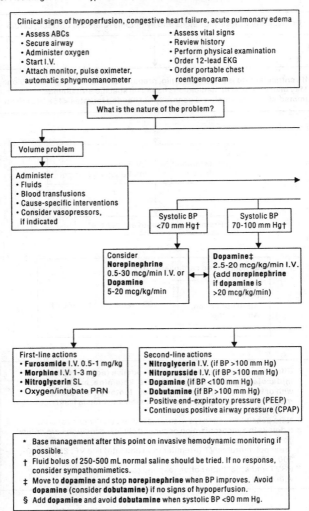

* Base management after this point on invasive hemodynamic monitoring if possible.
† Fluid bolus of 250-500 mL normal saline should be tried. If no response, consider sympathomimetics.
‡ Move to **dopamine** and stop **norepinephrine** when BP improves. Avoid **dopamine** (consider **dobutamine**) if no signs of hypoperfusion.
§ Add **dopamine** and avoid **dobutamine** when systolic BP <90 mm Hg.

Used with permission: Emergency Cardiac Care Committee and Subcommittees, American Heart Association, "Guidelines for Cardiopulmonary Resuscitation and Emergency Care, III: Adult Advanced Cardiac Life Support," *JAMA*, 1992, 268:2199-241.

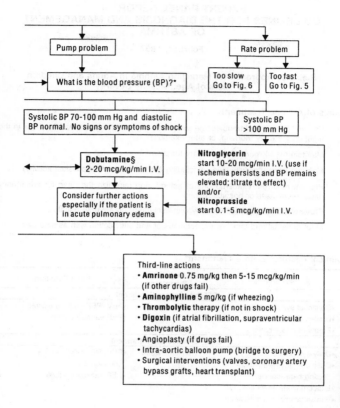

1455

ASTHMA

NATIONAL ASTHMA EDUCATION AND PREVENTION PROGRAM

EXPERT PANEL REPORT II:
GUIDELINES FOR THE DIAGNOSIS AND MANAGEMENT OF ASTHMA

February 1997

Stepwise Approach for Managing Asthma in Adults and Children >5 Years of Age: Classify Severity

Goals of Asthma Treatment

- Prevent chronic and troublesome symptoms (eg, coughing or breathlessness in the night, in the early morning, or after exertion)

- Maintain (near) "normal" pulmonary function

- Maintain normal activity levels (including exercise and other physical activity)

- Prevent recurrent exacerbations of asthma and minimize the need for emergency department visits or hospitalizations

- Provide optimal pharmacotherapy with minimal or no adverse effects

- Meet patients' and families' expectations of and satisfaction with asthma care

Clinical Features Before Treatment*

Symptoms**	Nighttime Symptoms	Lung Function
STEP 4: Severe Persistent		
•Continual symptoms •Limited physical activity •Frequent exacerbations	Frequent	•FEV_1/PEF ≤60% predicted •PEF variability >30%
STEP 3: Moderate Persistent		
•Daily symptoms •Daily use of inhaled short-acting beta$_2$-agonist •Exacerbations affect activity •Exacerbations ≥2 times/week; may last days	>1 time/week	•FEV_1/PEF >60% - 80% predicted •PEF variability >30%
STEP 2: Mild Persistent		
•Symptoms >2 times/week but <1 time/day •Exacerbations may affect activity	>2 times/month	•FEV_1/PEF ≥80% predicted •PEF variability 20% - 30%
STEP 1: Mild Intermittent		
•Symptoms ≤2 times/week •Asymptomatic and normal PEF between exacerbations •Exacerbations brief (from a few hours to a few days); intensity may vary	≤2 times/month	•FEV_1/PEF ≥80% predicted •PEF variability ≤20%

*The presence of one of the features of severity is sufficient to place a patient in that category. An individual should be assigned to the most severe grade in which any feature occurs. The characteristics noted in this figure are general and may overlap because asthma is highly variable. Furthermore, an individual's classification may change over time.

**Patients at any level of severity can have mild, moderate, or severe exacerbations. Some patients with intermittent asthma experience severe and life-threatening exacerbations separated by long periods of normal lung function and no symptoms.

Stepwise Approach for Managing Asthma in Adults and Children >5 Years of Age: Treatment

(Preferred treatments are in **bold** print)

Long-Term Control	Quick Relief	Education
STEP 4: Severe Persistent		
Daily medications: • **Anti-inflammatory: Inhaled corticosteroid (high dose)** AND • Long-acting bronchodilator: Either **long-acting inhaled beta$_2$-agonist**, sustained-release theophylline, or long-acting beta$_2$-agonist tablets AND • Corticosteroid tablets or syrup long term (2 mg/kg/day, generally do not exceed 60 mg per day).	• Short-acting bronchodilator: **Inhaled beta$_2$-agonists as needed** for symptoms. • Intensity of treatment will depend on severity of exacerbation; see "Managing Exacerbations" • Use of short-acting inhaled beta$_2$-agonists on a daily basis, or increasing use, indicates the need for additional long-term control therapy.	Steps 2 and 3 actions plus: • Refer to individual education/counseling
STEP 3: Moderate Persistent		
Daily medication: • Either — **Anti-inflammatory: Inhaled corticosteroid (medium dose)** OR — **Inhaled corticosteroid (low-medium dose)** and add a long-acting bronchodilator, especially for nighttime symptoms: Either **long-acting inhaled beta$_2$-agonist**, sustained-release theophylline, or long-acting beta$_2$-agonist tablets. • If needed — Anti-inflammatory: **Inhaled corticosteroids (medium-high dose)** AND — **Long-acting bronchodilator,** especially for nighttime symptoms; either **long-acting inhaled beta$_2$-agonist**, sustained-release theophylline, or long-acting beta$_2$-agonist tablets.	• Short-acting bronchodilator: **Inhaled beta$_2$-agonists as needed** for symptoms. • Intensity of treatment will depend on severity of exacerbation; see "Managing Exacerbations". • Use of short-acting inhaled beta$_2$-agonists on a daily basis, or increasing use, indicates the need for additional long-term control therapy.	Step 1 actions plus: • Teach self-monitoring • Refer to group education if available • Review and update self-management plan
STEP 2: Mild Persistent		
One daily medication: • **Anti-inflammatory: Either inhaled corticosteroid (low doses) or cromolyn or nedocromil** (children usually begin with a trial of cromolyn or nedocromil). • Sustained-release theophylline to serum concentration of 5-15 mcg/mL is an alternative, but not preferred, therapy. Zafirlukast or zileuton may also be considered for patients ≥12 years of age, although their position in therapy is not fully established.	• Short-acting bronchodilator: **Inhaled beta$_2$-agonists as needed** for symptoms. • Intensity of treatment will depend on severity of exacerbation; see "Managing Exacerbations." • Use of short-acting inhaled beta$_2$-agonists on a daily basis, or increasing use, indicates the need for additional long-term control therapy.	Step 1 actions plus: • Teach self-monitoring • Refer to group education if available • Review and update self-management plan
STEP 1: Mild Intermittent		
No daily medication needed.	• Short-acting bronchodilator: **Inhaled beta$_2$-agonists as needed** for symptoms. • Intensity of treatment will depend on severity of exacerbation; see "Managing Exacerbations" • Use of short-acting inhaled beta$_2$-agonists more than 2 times/week may indicate the need to initiate long-term control therapy	• Teach basic facts about asthma • Teach inhaler/spacer/holding chamber technique • Discuss roles of medications • Develop self-management plan • Develop action plan for when and how to take rescue actions, especially for patients with a history of severe exacerbations • Discuss appropriate environmental control measures to avoid exposure to known allergens and irritants

↓ **Step down**
Review treatment every 1-6 months; a gradual stepwise reduction in treatment may be possible.

↑**Step up**
If control is not maintained, consider step up. First, review patient medication technique, adherence, and environmental control (avoidance of allergens or other factors that contribute to asthma severity.)

ASTHMA *(Continued)*

Notes:

- **The stepwise approach presents general guidelines to assist clinical decision making; it is not intended to be a specific prescription. Asthma is highly variable; clinicians should tailor specific medication plans to the needs and circumstances of individual patients.**

- Gain control as quickly as possible; then decrease treatment to the least medication necessary to maintain control. Gaining control may be accomplished by either starting treatment at the step most appropriate to the initial severity of the condition or starting at a higher level of therapy (eg, a course of systemic corticosteroids or higher dose of inhaled corticosteroids).

- A rescue course of systemic corticosteroids may be needed at any time and at any step.

- Some patients with intermittent asthma experience severe and life-threatening exacerbations separated by long periods of normal lung function and no symptoms. This may be especially common with exacerbations provoked by respiratory infections. A short course of systemic corticosteroids is recommended.

- At each step, patients should control their environment to avoid or control factors that make their asthma worse (eg, allergens, irritants); this requires specific diagnosis and education.

Stepwise Approach for Managing Infants and Young Children (≤5 Years of Age) With Acute or Chronic Asthma Symptoms

Long-Term Control	Quick Relief
STEP 4: Severe Persistent	
Daily anti-inflammatory medicine • High-dose inhaled corticosteroid with spacer/holding chamber and face mask • If needed, add systemic corticosteroids 2 mg/kg/day and reduce to lowest daily or alternate-day dose that stabilizes symptoms	• Bronchodilator as needed for symptoms (see step 1) up to 3 times/day
STEP 3: Moderate Persistent	
Daily anti-inflammatory medication. Either: • Medium-dose inhaled corticosteroid with spacer/holding chamber and face mask OR Once control is established: • Medium-dose inhaled corticosteroid and nedocromil OR • Medium-dose inhaled corticosteroid and long-acting bronchodilator (theophylline)	• Bronchodilator as needed for symptoms (see step 1) up to 3 times/day
STEP 2: Mild Persistent	
Daily anti-inflammatory medication. Either: • Cromolyn (nebulizer is preferred; or MDI) or nedocromil (MDI only) tid-qid • Infants and young children usually begin with a trial of cromolyn or nedocromil OR • Low-dose inhaled corticosteroid with spacer/holding chamber and face mask	• Bronchodilator as needed for symptoms (see step 1)
STEP 1: Mild Intermittent	
No daily medication needed	• Bronchodilator as needed for symptoms <2 times/week. Intensity of treatment will depend upon severity of exacerbation (see "Managing Exacerbations"). Either: — Inhaled short-acting beta$_2$-agonist by nebulizer or face mask and spacer/holding chamber OR — Oral beta$_2$-agonist for symptoms • With viral respiratory infection: — Bronchodilator q4-6h up to 24 hours (longer with physician consult) but, in general, repeat no more than once every 6 weeks — Consider systemic corticosteroid if current exacerbation is severe OR Patient has history of previous severe exacerbations

↓ **Step Down**
Review treatment every 1-6 months. If control is sustained for at least 3 months, a gradual stepwise reduction in treatment may be possible.

↑ **Step Up**
If control is not achieved, consider step up. But first: review patient medication technique, adherence, and environmental control (avoidance of allergens or other precipitant factors)

Notes:

- **The stepwise approach presents guidelines to assist clinical decision making. Asthma is highly variable; clinicians should tailor specific medication plans to the needs and circumstances of individual patients.**

- Gain control as quickly as possible; then decrease treatment to the least medication necessary to maintain control. Gaining control may be accomplished by either starting treatment at the step most appropriate to the initial severity of their condition or by starting at a higher level of therapy (eg, a course of systemic corticosteroids or higher dose of inhaled corticosteroids).

- A rescue course of systemic corticosteroid (prednisolone) may be needed at any time and step.

- In general, use of short-acting beta$_2$-agonist on a daily basis indicates the need for additional long-term control therapy.

- It is important to remember that there are very few studies on asthma therapy for infants.

- Consultation with an asthma specialist is recommended for patients with moderate or severe persistent asthma in this age group. Consultation should be considered for all patients with mild persistent asthma.

ASTHMA *(Continued)*

Management of Asthma Exacerbations: Home Treatment*

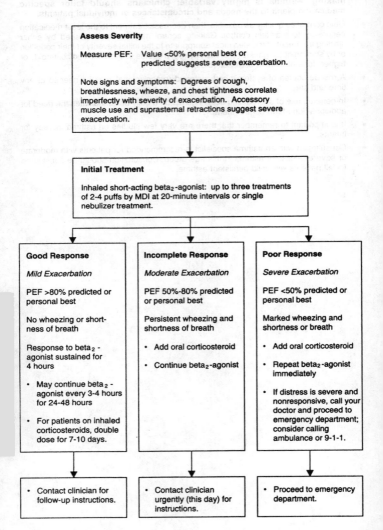

Assess Severity

Measure PEF: Value <50% personal best or predicted suggests severe exacerbation.

Note signs and symptoms: Degrees of cough, breathlessness, wheeze, and chest tightness correlate imperfectly with severity of exacerbation. Accessory muscle use and suprasternal retractions suggest severe exacerbation.

Initial Treatment

Inhaled short-acting beta$_2$-agonist: up to three treatments of 2-4 puffs by MDI at 20-minute intervals or single nebulizer treatment.

Good Response

Mild Exacerbation

PEF >80% predicted or personal best

No wheezing or shortness of breath

Response to beta$_2$-agonist sustained for 4 hours

- May continue beta$_2$-agonist every 3-4 hours for 24-48 hours

- For patients on inhaled corticosteroids, double dose for 7-10 days.

- Contact clinician for follow-up instructions.

Incomplete Response

Moderate Exacerbation

PEF 50%-80% predicted or personal best

Persistent wheezing and shortness of breath

- Add oral corticosteroid

- Continue beta$_2$-agonist

- Contact clinician urgently (this day) for instructions.

Poor Response

Severe Exacerbation

PEF <50% predicted or personal best

Marked wheezing and shortness or breath

- Add oral corticosteroid

- Repeat beta$_2$-agonist immediately

- If distress is severe and nonresponsive, call your doctor and proceed to emergency department; consider calling ambulance or 9-1-1.

- Proceed to emergency department.

*Patients at high risk of asthma-related death should receive immediate clinical attention after initial treatment. Additional therapy may be required.

Management of Asthma Exacerbations: Emergency Department and Hospital-Based Care

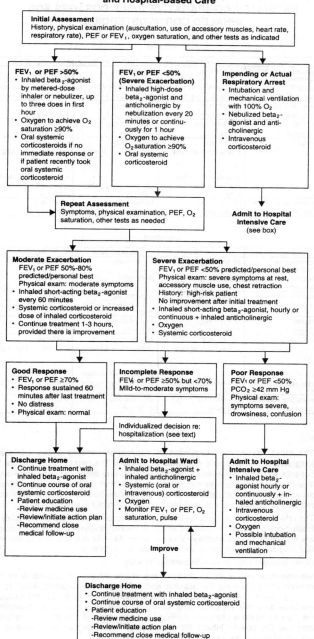

Initial Assessment
History, physical examination (auscultation, use of accessory muscles, heart rate, respiratory rate), PEF or FEV$_1$, oxygen saturation, and other tests as indicated

FEV$_1$ or PEF >50%
- Inhaled beta$_2$-agonist by metered-dose inhaler or nebulizer, up to three does in first hour
- Oxygen to achieve O$_2$ saturation ≥90%
- Oral systemic corticosteroids if no immediate response or if patient recently took oral systemic corticosteroid

FEV$_1$ or PEF <50% (Severe Exacerbation)
- Inhaled high-dose beta$_2$-agonist and anticholinergic by nebulization every 20 minutes or continuously for 1 hour
- Oxygen to achieve O$_2$ saturation ≥90%
- Oral systemic corticosteroid

Impending or Actual Respiratory Arrest
- Intubation and mechanical ventilation with 100% O$_2$
- Nebulized beta$_2$-agonist and anticholinergic
- Intravenous corticosteroid

Repeat Assessment
Symptoms, physical examination, PEF, O$_2$ saturation, other tests as needed

Admit to Hospital Intensive Care
(see box)

Moderate Exacerbation
FEV$_1$ or PEF 50%-80% predicted/personal best
Physical exam: moderate symptoms
- Inhaled short-acting beta$_2$-agonist every 60 minutes
- Systemic corticosteroid or increased dose of inhaled corticosteroid
- Continue treatment 1-3 hours, provided there is improvement

Severe Exacerbation
FEV$_1$ or PEF <50% predicted/personal best
Physical exam: severe symptoms at rest, accessory muscle use, chest retraction
History: high-risk patient
No improvement after initial treatment
- Inhaled short-acting beta$_2$-agonist, hourly or continuous + inhaled anticholinergic
- Oxygen
- Systemic corticosteroid

Good Response
- FEV$_1$ or PEF ≥70%
- Response sustained 60 minutes after last treatment
- No distress
- Physical exam: normal

Incomplete Response
FEV$_1$ or PEF ≥50% but <70%
Mild-to-moderate symptoms

Poor Response
FEV$_1$ or PEF <50%
PCO$_2$ ≥42 mm Hg
Physical exam: symptoms severe, drowsiness, confusion

Individualized decision re: hospitalization (see text)

Discharge Home
- Continue treatment with inhaled beta$_2$-agonist
- Continue course of oral systemic corticosteroid
- Patient education
  -Review medicine use
  -Review/initiate action plan
  -Recommend close medical follow-up

Admit to Hospital Ward
- Inhaled beta$_2$-agonist + inhaled anticholinergic
- Systemic (oral or intravenous) corticosteroid
- Oxygen
- Monitor FEV$_1$ or PEF, O$_2$ saturation, pulse

Admit to Hospital Intensive Care
- Inhaled beta$_2$-agonist hourly or continuously + inhaled anticholinergic
- Intravenous corticosteroid
- Oxygen
- Possible intubation and mechanical ventilation

Improve

Discharge Home
- Continue treatment with inhaled beta$_2$-agonist
- Continue course of oral systemic corticosteroid
- Patient education
  -Review medicine use
  -Review/initiate action plan
  -Recommend close medical follow-up

ASTHMA (Continued)

ESTIMATED COMPARATIVE DAILY DOSAGES FOR INHALED CORTICOSTEROIDS

Adults

Drug	Low Dose	Medium Dose	High Dose
Beclomethasone dipropionate	168-504 mcg	504-840 mcg	>840 mcg
42 mcg/puff	(4-12 puffs — 42 mcg)	(12-20 puffs — 42 mcg)	(>20 puffs — 42 mcg)
84 mcg/puff	(2-6 puffs — 84 mcg)	(6-10 puffs — 84 mcg)	(>10 puffs — 84 mcg)
Budesonide Turbuhaler	200-400 mcg	400-600 mcg	>600 mcg
200 mcg/dose	(1-2 inhalations)	(2-3 inhalations)	(>3 inhalations)
Flunisolide	500-1000 mcg	1000-2000 mcg	>2000 mcg
250 mcg/puff	(2-4 puffs)	(4-8 puffs)	(>8 puffs)
Fluticasone	88-264 mcg	264-660 mcg	>660 mcg
MDI: 44, 110, 220 mcg/puff	(2-6 puffs — 44 mcg)	(2-6 puffs — 110 mcg)	(>6 puffs — 110 mcg)
	or		or
	(2 puffs — 110 mcg)		(>3 puffs — 220 mcg)
DPI: 50, 100, 250 mcg/dose	(2-6 inhalations — 50 mcg)	(3-6 inhalations — 100 mcg)	(>6 inhalations — 100 mcg)
Triamcinolone acetonide	400-1000 mcg	1000-2000 mcg	>2000 mcg
100 mcg/puff	(4-10 puffs)	(10-20 puffs)	(>20 puffs)

Children

Drug	Low Dose	Medium Dose	High Dose
Beclomethasone dipropionate	84-336 mcg	336-672 mcg	>672 mcg
42 mcg/puff	(2-8 puffs)	(8-16 puffs)	(>16 puffs)
84 mcg/puff			
Budesonide Turbuhaler	100-200 mcg	200-400 mcg	>400 mcg
200 mcg/dose		(1-2 inhalations — 200 mcg)	(>2 inhalations — 200 mcg)
Flunisolide	500-750 mcg	1000-1250 mcg	>1250 mcg
250 mcg/puff	(2-3 puffs)	(4-5 puffs)	(>5 puffs)
Fluticasone	88-176 mcg	176-440 mcg	>440 mcg
MDI: 44, 110, 220 mcg/puff	(2-4 puffs — 44 mcg)	(4-10 puffs — 44 mcg)	(>4 puffs — 110 mcg)
		or	
		(2-4 puffs — 110 mcg)	
DPI: 50, 100, 250 mcg/dose	(2-4 inhalations — 50 mcg)	(2-4 inhalations — 100 mcg)	(>4 inhalations — 100 mcg)
Triamcinolone acetonide	400-800 mcg	800-1200 mcg	>1200 mcg
100 mcg/puff	(4-8 puffs)	(8-12 puffs)	(>12 puffs)

Notes:

- **The most important determinant of appropriate dosing is the clinician's judgment of the patient's response to therapy.** The clinician must monitor the patient's response on several clinical parameters and adjust the dose accordingly. The stepwise approach to therapy emphasizes that once control of asthma is achieved, the dose of mediation should be carefully titrated to the minimum dose required to maintain control, thus reducing the potential for adverse effect.

- The reference point for the range in the dosages for children is data on the safety on inhaled corticosteroids in children, which, in general, suggest that the dose ranges are equivalent to beclomethasone dipropionate 200-400 mcg/day (low dose), 400-800 mcg/day (medium dose), and >800 mcg/day (high dose).

- Some dosages may be outside package labeling.

- Metered-dose inhaler (MDI) dosages are expressed as the actuator dose (the amount of drug leaving the actuator and delivered to the patient), which is the labeling required in the United States. This is different from the dosage expressed as the valve dose (the amount of drug leaving the valve, all of which is not available to the patient), which is used in many European countries and in some of the scientific literature. Dry powder inhaler (DPI) doses (eg, Turbuhaler) are expressed as the amount of drug in the inhaler following activation.

ESTIMATED CLINICAL COMPARABILITY OF DOSES FOR INHALED CORTICOSTEROIDS

Data from *in vitro* and in clinical trials suggest that the different inhaled corticosteroid preparations are not equivalent on a per puff or microgram basis. However, it is not entirely clear what implications these differences have for dosing recommendations in clinical practice because there are few data directly comparing the preparations. Relative dosing for clinical comparability is affected by differences in topical potency, clinical effects at different doses, delivery device, and bioavailability. The Expert Panel developed recommended dose ranges for different preparations based on available data and the following assumptions and cautions about estimating relative doses needed to achieve comparable clinical effect.

- **Relative topical potency using human skin blanching**

  - The standard test for determining relative topical anti-inflammatory potency is the topical vasoconstriction (MacKenzie skin blanching) test.

  - The MacKenzie topical skin blanching test correlates with binding affinities and binding half-lives for human lung corticosteroid receptors (see table below) (Dahlberg, et al, 1984; Hogger and Rohdewald 1994).

  - The relationship between relative topical anti-inflammatory effect and clinical comparability in asthma management is not certain. However, recent clinical trials suggest that different in vitro measures of anti-inflammatory effect is not certain. However, recent clinical trials suggest that different in vitro measures of anti-inflammatory effect correlate with clinical efficacy (Barnes and Pedersen 1993; Johnson 1996; Kamada, et al, 1996; Ebden, et al, 1986; Leblanc, et al, 1994; Gustaffson, et al, 1993; Lundback, et al, 1993; Barnes, et al, 1993; Fabbri, et al, 1993; Langdon and Capsey, 1994; Ayres, et al, 1995; Rafferty, et al, 1985; Bjorkander, et al, 1982, Stiksa, et al, 1982; Willey, et al, 1982.)

Medication	Topical Potency (Skin Blanching)*	Corticosteroid Receptor Binding Half-Life	Receptor Binding Affinity
Beclomethasone dipropionate (BDP)	600	7.5 hours	13.5
Budesonide (BUD)	980	5.1 hours	9.4
Flunisolide (FLU)	330	3.5 hours	1.8
Fluticasone propionate (FP)	1200	10.5 hours	18.0
Triamcinolone acetonide (TAA)	330	3.9 hours	3.6

*Numbers are assigned in reference to dexamethasone, which has a value of "1" in the MacKenzie test.

- **Relative doses to achieve similar clinical effects**

  - Clinical effects are evaluated by a number of outcome parameters (eg, changes in spirometry, peak flow rates, symptom scores, quick-relief beta$_2$-agonist use, frequency of exacerbations, airway responsiveness).

  - The daily dose and duration of treatment may affect these outcome parameters differently (eg, symptoms and peak flow may improve at lower doses and over a shorter treatment time than bronchial reactivity) (van Essen-Zandvliet, et al, 1992; Haahtela, et al, 1991)

  - Delivery systems influence comparability. For example, the delivery device for budesonide (Turbuhaler) delivers approximately twice the amount of drug to the airway as the MDI, thus enhancing the clinical effect (Thorsson, et al, 1994); Agertoft and Pedersen, 1993).

  - Individual patients may respond differently to different preparations, as noted by clinical experience.

  - Clinical trials comparing effects in reducing symptoms and improving peak expiratory flow demonstrate:

  - BDP and BUD achieved comparable effects at similar microgram doses by MDI (Bjorkander, et al, 1982; Ebden, et al, 1986; Rafferty, et al, 1985).

  - BDP achieved effects similar to twice the dose of TAA on a microgram basis.

CONTRAST MEDIA REACTIONS, PREMEDICATION FOR PROPHYLAXIS

(American College of Radiology Guidelines for Use of Nonionic Contrast Media)

It is estimated that approximately 5% to 10% of patients will experience adverse reactions to administration of contrast dye (less for nonionic contrast). In approximately 1000-2000 administrations, a life-threatening reaction will occur.

A variety of premedication regimens have been proposed, both for pretreatment of "at risk" patients who require contrast media and before the routine administration of the intravenous high osmolar contrast media. Such regimens have been shown in clinical trials to decrease the frequency of all forms of contrast medium reactions. Pretreatment with a 2-dose regimen of methylprednisolone 32 mg, 12 and 2 hours prior to intravenous administration of HOCM (ionic), has been shown to decrease mild, moderate, and severe reactions in patients at increased risk and perhaps in patients without risk factors. Logistical and feasibility problems may preclude adequate premedication with this or any regimen for all patients. It is unclear at this time that steroid pretreatment prior to administration of ionic contrast media reduces the incidence of reactions to the same extent or less than that achieved with the use of nonionic contrast media alone. Information about the efficacy of nonionic contrast media combined with a premedication strategy, including steroids, is preliminary or not yet currently available. For high-risk patients (ie, previous contrast reactors), the combination of a pretreatment regimen with nonionic contrast media has empirical merit and may warrant consideration. Oral administration of steroids appears preferable to intravascular routes, and the drug may be prednisone or methylprednisolone. Supplemental administration of H_1 and H_2 antihistamine therapies, orally or intravenously, may reduce the frequency of urticaria, angioedema, and respiratory symptoms. Additionally, ephedrine administration has been suggested to decrease the frequency of contrast reactions, but caution is advised in patients with cardiac disease, hypertension, or hyperthyroidism. No premedication strategy should be a substitute for the ABC approach to preadministration preparedness listed above. Contrast reactions do occur despite any and all premedication prophylaxis. The incidence can be decreased, however, in some categories of "at risk" patients receiving high osmolar contrast media plus a medication regimen. For patients with previous contrast medium reactions, there is a slight chance that recurrence may be more severe or the same as the prior reaction, however, it is more likely that there will be no recurrence.

A general premedication regimen is

Methylprednisolone	32 mg orally at 12 and 2 hours prior to procedure
Diphenhydramine	50 mg orally 1 hour prior to the procedure

An alternative premedication regimen is

Prednisone	50 mg orally 13, 7, and 1 hour before the procedure
Diphenhydramine	50 mg orally 1 hour before the procedure
Ephedrine	25 mg orally 1 hour before the procedure (except when contraindicated)

Indication for nonionic contrast are

Previous reaction to contrast — premedicate*
Known allergy to iodine or shellfish
Asthma, especially if on medication
Myocardial instability or CHF
Risk for aspiration or severe nausea and vomiting
Difficulty communicating or inability to give history
Patients taking beta-blockers
Small children at risk for electrolyte imbalance or extravasation
Renal failure with diabetes, sickle cell disease, or myeloma
At physician or patient request

*Life-threatening reactions (throat swelling, laryngeal edema, etc), consider omitting the intravenous contrast.

DEPRESSION

Criteria for Major Depressive Episode

A. Five (or more) of the following symptoms have been present during the same 2-week period and represent a change from previous functioning; at least one of the symptoms is either (1) depressed mood or (2) loss of interest or pleasure.

1. Depressed mood most of the day, nearly every day

2. Marked diminished interest or pleasure in all, or almost all, activities

3. Significant weight loss (not dieting) or weight gain, or decrease or increase in appetite nearly every day

4. Insomnia or hypersomnia nearly every day

5. Psychomotor agitation or retardation nearly every day

6. Fatigue or loss of energy nearly every day

7. Feelings of worthlessness or excessive or inappropriate guilt (may be delusional) nearly every day

8. Diminished ability to think or concentrate, or indecisiveness

9. Recurrent thoughts of death, recurrent suicidal ideation without a specific plan, or a suicide attempt or a specific suicide plan

B. The symptoms cause clinically significant distress or impairment in social, occupational or other important areas of functioning.

C. The symptoms are not due to the direct physiologic effects of a substance or a general medical condition (eg, hypothyroidism).

Medications That May Precipitate Depression

Anti-inflammatory & analgesic agents	Indomethacin, pentazocine, phenacetin, phenylbutazone
Antimicrobial agents	Cycloserine, ethambutol, sulfonamides, select gram-negative antibiotics
Cardiovascular/antihypertensive agents	Clonidine, digitalis, diuretics, guanethidine, hydralazine, indapamide, methyldopa, prazocin, procainamide, propranolol, reserpine
CNS-agents	Alcohol, amantadine, amphetamine & derivatives, barbiturates, benzodiazepines, chloral hydrate, carbamazepine, cocaine, haloperidol, L-dopa, phenothiazines, succinimide derivatives
Hormonal agents	ACTH, corticosteroids, estrogen, melatonin, oral contraceptives, progesterone
Miscellaneous	Antineoplastic agents, cimetidine, disulfiram, organic pesticides, physostigmine

Medical Disorders & Psychiatric Disorders Associated With Depression

Endocrine diseases	Acromegaly, Addison's disease, Cushing's disease, diabetes mellitus, hyperparathyroidism, hypoparathyroidism, hyperthyroidism, hypothyroidism, insulinoma, pheochromocytoma, pituitary dysfunction
Deficiency states	Pernicious anemia, severe anemia, Wernicke's encephalopathy
Infections	Encephalitis, fungal infections, meningitis, neurosyphilis, influenza, mononucleosis, tuberculosis, AIDS
Collagen disorders	Rheumatoid arthritis
Systemic lupus erythematosus	
Metabolic disorders	Electrolyte imbalance, hypokalemia, hyponatremia, hepatic encephalopathy, Pick's disease, uremia, Wilson's disease
Cardiovascular disease	Cerebral arteriosclerosis, chronic bronchitis, congestive heart failure, emphysema, myocardial infarction, paroxysmal dysrhythmias, pneumonia
Neurologic disorders	Alzheimer's disease, amyotrophic lateral sclerosis, brain tumors, chronic pain syndrome, Cruetzfeld-Jakob disease, Huntington's disease, multiple sclerosis, myasthenia gravis, Parkinson's disease, poststroke, trauma (postconcussion)
Malignant disease	Breast, gastrointestinal, lung, pancreas, prostate
Psychiatric disorders	Alcoholism, anxiety disorders, eating disorders, schizophrenia

DEPRESSION *(Continued)*

Somatic Treatments of Depression in the Patient With Medical Illness

Condition	First Choice	Second-Line Options	Alternatives
Thyroid			
Hypothyroid	Thyroid (T)	T_4 or T_3 + antidepressant (SSRIs , TCAs, new generation agents)	ECT, other antidepressants psychostimulants
Hyperthyroid	Antidepressant and antihyperthyroid medications	Select a different group of antidepressants	
Diabetes mellitus	SSRIs, other new generation antidepressants	TCAs (second amine or low-dose tertiary amine) MAOIs	ECT, buspirone, psychostimulants, thyroid supplements, mood stabilizers
Cardiovascular disorders	SSRIs, bupropion	ECT, psychostimulants B-blockers, buspirone	ECT, TCAs, MAOIs, mood stabilizers
Renal disease	Fluoxetine, sertraline	TCAs, other new generation antidepressants, psychostimulants	ECT, anticonvulsants, lithium (if dialysis or CLOSELY monitored)
Hepatic disease (reduced dose ALL)	Sertraline	Other new generation antidepressants, TCAs-secondary amines	TCAs-tertiary amines
HIV	Bupropion, SSRIs, psychostimulants	TCAs	ECT
Transplant	**Closely monitor.** See cardiovascular, renal, liver, pulmonary, new antidepressant agents, TCAs-secondary amines		
Neurologic	Newer generation antidepressants, TCAs-secondary amines	Selegiline, anticonvulsants T	Bromocriptine
Malignancy	Newer generation antidepressants, TCAs-secondary amines psychostimulants	TCAs-tertiary amines of pain MAOIs	ECT
Respiratory	Activating antidepressants, buspirone		More sedating antidepressants, ECT
Gastrointestinal	TCAs-secondary amines, new generation antidepressants	TCAs-tertiary amines	ECT

DIABETES MELLITUS TREATMENT

INSULIN-DEPENDENT DIABETES MELLITUS

Treatment goals that emphasize glycemic control have been recommended by the American Diabetes Association (see table).

Glycemic Control for People With Diabetes

Biochemical Index	Nondiabetic	Goal	Action Suggested
Preprandial glucose	<115	80-120	<80 >140
Bedtime glucose (mg/dL)	<120	100-140	<100 >160
Hb A$_{1C}$ (%)	<8	<7	>8

These values are for nonpregnant individuals. Action suggested depends on individual patient circumstances, Hb A$_{1C}$ referenced to a nondiabetic range of 4% to 6% (mean 5%, SD 0.5%).

NONINSULIN-DEPENDENT DIABETES MELLITUS

Pharmacological Therapy of NIDDM - Consensus Statement

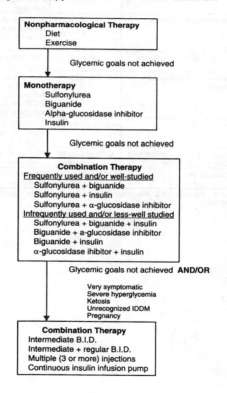

Nonpharmacological Therapy
Diet
Exercise

Glycemic goals not achieved

Monotherapy
Sulfonylurea
Biguanide
Alpha-glucosidase inhibitor
Insulin

Glycemic goals not achieved

Combination Therapy
Frequently used and/or well-studied
Sulfonylurea + biguanide
Sulfonylurea + insulin
Sulfonylurea + α-glucosidase inhibitor
Infrequently used and/or less-well studied
Sulfonylurea + biguanide + insulin
Biguanide + a-glucosidase inhibitor
Biguanide + insulin
α-glucosidase ihibitor + insulin

Glycemic goals not achieved **AND/OR**

Very symptomatic
Severe hyperglycemia
Ketosis
Unrecognized IDDM
Pregnancy

Combination Therapy
Intermediate B.I.D.
Intermediate + regular B.I.D.
Multiple (3 or more) injections
Continuous insulin infusion pump

EPILEPSY

Antiepileptic Drugs for Children and Adolescents by Seizure Type and Epilepsy Syndrome

Seizure Type or Epilepsy Syndrome	First Line Therapy	Alternatives
Partial seizures (with or without secondary generalization)	Carbamazepine	Valproate, phenytoin, gabapentin, lamotrigine, vigabatrin, phenobarbital, primidone; consider clonazepam, clorazepate, acetazolamide
Generalized tonic-clonic seizures	Valproate or carbamazepine	Phenytoin, phenobarbital, primidone; consider clonazepam
Childhood absence epilepsy		
Before 10 years of age	Ethosuximide or valproate	Methsuximide, acetazolamide, clonazepam, lamotrigine
After 10 years of age	Valproate	Ethosuximide, methsuximide, acetazolamide, clonazepam, lamotrigine; consider adding carbamazepine, phenytoin, or phenobarbital for generalized tonic-clonic seizures if valproate not tolerated
Juvenile myoclonic epilepsy	Valproate	Phenobarbital, primidone, clonazepam; consider carbamazepine, phenytoin, methsuximide, acetazolamide
Progressive myoclonic epilepsy	Valproate	Valproate plus clonazepam, phenobarbital
Lennox-Gastaut and related syndromes	Valproate	Clonazepam, phenobarbital, lamotrigine, ethosuximide, felbamate; consider methsuximide, ACTH or steroids, pyridoxine, ketogenic diet
Infantile spasms	ACTH or steroids	Valproate; consider clonazepam, vigabatrin (especially with tuberous sclerosis), pyridoxine
Benign epilepsy of childhood with centrotemporal spikes	Carbamazepine or valproate	Phenytoin; consider phenobarbital, primidone
Neonatal seizures	Phenobarbital	Phenytoin; consider clonazepam, primidone, valproate, pyridoxine

Adapted from Bourgeois BFD, "Antiepileptic Drugs in Pediatric Practice," *Epilepsia*, 1995, 36 (Suppl 2):S34-S45.

FEBRILE SEIZURES

A febrile seizure is defined as a seizure occurring for no reason other than an elevated temperature. It does not have an infectious or metabolic origin within the CNS (ie, it is not caused by meningitis or encephalitis). Fever is usually >102°F rectally, but the more rapid the rise in temperature, the more likely a febrile seizure may occur. About 4% of children develop febrile seizures at one time of their life, usually occurring between 3 months and 5 years of age with the majority occurring at 6 months to 3 years of age. There are 3 types of febrile seizures:

1. **Simple** febrile seizures are nonfocal febrile seizures of less than 15 minutes duration. They do not occur in multiples.

2. **Complex** febrile seizures are febrile seizures that are either focal, have a focal component, are longer than 15 minutes in duration, or are multiple febrile seizures that occur within 30 minutes.

3. **Febrile status epilepticus** is a febrile seizure that is a generalized tonic-clonic seizure lasting longer than 30 minutes.

Note: Febrile seizures should not be confused with true epileptic seizures associated with fever or "seizure with fever." "Seizure with fever" includes seizures associated with acute neurologic illnesses (ie, meningitis, encephalitis).

Long-term prophylaxis with phenobarbital may reduce the risk of subsequent febrile seizures. The 1980 NIH Consensus paper stated that after the first febrile seizure, long-term prophylaxis should be considered under any of the following:

1. Presence of abnormal neurological development or abnormal neurological exam

2. Febrile seizure was complex in nature: duration >15 minutes focal febrile seizure followed by transient or persistent neurological abnormalities

3. Positive family history of afebrile seizures (epilepsy)

Also consider long-term prophylaxis in certain cases if:

1. the child has multiple febrile seizures

2. the child is <12 months of age

Anticonvulsant prophylaxis is usually continued for 2 years or 1 year after the last seizure, whichever is longer. With the identification of phenobarbital's adverse effects on learning and cognitive function, many physicians will not start long-term phenobarbital prophylaxis after the first febrile seizure unless the patient has more than one of the above risk factors. Most physicians would start long-term prophylaxis if the patient has a second febrile seizure.

Daily administration of phenobarbital and therapeutic phenobarbital serum concentrations ≥15 mcg/mL decrease recurrence rates of febrile seizures. Valproic acid is also effective in preventing recurrences of febrile seizures, but is usually reserved for patients who have significant adverse effects to phenobarbital. The administration of rectal diazepam (as a solution or suppository) at the time of the febrile illness has been shown to be as effective as daily phenobarbital in preventing recurrences of febrile seizures. However, these rectal dosage forms are not available in the United States. Some centers in the USA are using the injectable form of diazepam rectally. The solution for injection is filtered prior to use if drawn from an ampul. A recent study suggests that oral diazepam, 0.33 mg/kg/dose given every 8 hours only when the child has a fever, may reduce the risk of recurrent febrile seizures (see Rosman, et al). **Note:** A more recent study by Uhari (1995) showed that lower doses of diazepam, 0.2 mg/kg/dose, were not effective.) Carbamazepine and phenytoin are not effective in preventing febrile seizures.

References

Berg AT, Shinnar S, Hauser WA, et al, "Predictors of Recurrent Febrile Seizures: A Meta-Analytic Review," *J Pediatr*, 1990, 116 (3):329-37.

Camfield PR, Camfield CS, Gordon K, et al, "Prevention of Recurrent Febrile Seizures," *J Pediatr*, 1995, 126 (6):929-30.

NIH Consensus Statement, "Febrile Seizures: A Consensus of Their Significance, Evaluation and Treatment," *Pediatrics*, 1980, 66 (6):1009-12.

Rosman NP, Colton T, Labazzo J, et al, "A Controlled Trial of Diazepam Administration During Febrile Illnesses to Prevent Recurrence of Febrile Seizures," *N Engl J Med*, 1993, 329 (2):79-84.

Uhari M, Rantala H, Vainionpaa L, et al, "Effects of Acetaminophen and of Low Intermittent Doses of Diazepam on Prevention of Recurrences of Febrile Seizures," *J Pediatr*, 1995, 126(6):991-5.

EPILEPSY *(Continued)*

CONVULSIVE STATUS EPILEPTICUS

Recommendations of the Epilepsy Foundation of America's Working Group on Status Epilepticus
(JAMA, 1993, 270:854-9)

Convulsive status epilepticus is an emergency that is associated with high morbidity and mortality. The outcome largely depends on etiology, but prompt and appropriate pharmacological therapy can reduce morbidity and mortality. Etiology varies in children and adults and reflects the distribution of disease in these age groups. Antiepileptic drug administration should be initiated whenever a seizure has lasted 10 minutes. Immediate concerns include supporting respiration, maintaining blood pressure, gaining intravenous access, and identifying and treating the underlying cause. Initial therapeutic and diagnostic measures are conducted simultaneously. The goal of therapy is rapid termination of clinical and electrical seizure activity; the longer a seizure continues, the greater the likelihood of an adverse outcome. Several drug protocols now in use will terminate status epilepticus. Common to all patients is the need for a clear plan, prompt administration of appropriate drugs in adequate doses, and attention to the possibility of apnea, hypoventilation, or other metabolic abnormalities.

Figure 1. Algorithm for the Initial Management of Status Epilepticus

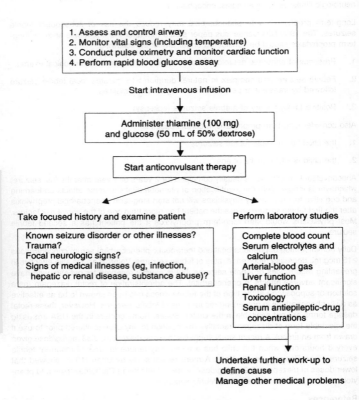

Adapted from Lowenstein A, "Current Concepts: Status Epilepticus," *N Engl J Med*, 1998, 338:970-6 with permission.

Figure 2. Antiepileptic Drug Therapy for Status Epilepticus

I.V. denotes intravenous and PE denoted phenytoin equivalents. The horizontal bars indicate the approximate duration of drug infusions.

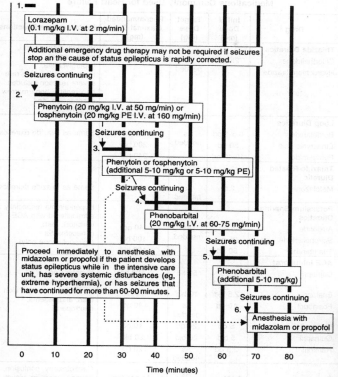

Adapted from Lowenstein A, "Current Concepts: Status Epilepticus," *N Engl J Med*, 1998, 338:970-6 with permission.

HEART FAILURE: MANAGEMENT OF PATIENTS WITH LEFT VENTRICULAR SYSTOLIC DYSFUNCTION

Adapted from U.S. Department of Health & Human Services, the Agency for Healthcare Policy and Research (ACHPR) Publication No. 94-0613, June, 1994

Medications Commonly Used for Heart Failure

Drug	Initial Dose (mg)	Target Dose (mg)	Recommended Maximal Dose (mg)	Major Adverse Reactions
Thiazide Diuretics				Postural hypotension, hypokalemia, hyperglycemia, hyperuricemia, rash; rare severe reaction includes pancreatitis, bone marrow suppression, and anaphylaxis
Chlorthalidone	25 qd	As needed	50 qd	
Hydrochlorothiazide				
Loop Diuretics				Same as thiazide diuretics
Bumetanide	0.5-1 qd	As needed	10 qd	
Ethacrynic acid	50 qd		200 bid	
Furosemide	10-40 qd		240 bid	
Thiazide-Related Diuretic				
Metolazone	2.5*	As needed	10 qd	Same as thiazide diuretics
Potassium-Sparing Diuretics				Hyperkalemia (especially if administered with ACE inhibitor), rash, gynecomastia (spironolactone only)
Amiloride	5 qd	As needed	40 qd	
Spironolactone	25 qd		100 bid	
Triamterene	50 qd		100 bid	
ACE Inhibitors†				Hypotension, hyperkalemia, renal insufficiency, cough, skin rash, angioedema, neutropenia
Captopril	6.25-12.5 tid	50 tid	100 tid	
Enalapril	2.5 bid	10 bid	20 bid	
Fosinopril	10 qd	As needed	40 qd	
Lisinopril	5 qd	20 qd	40 qd	
Quinapril	5 bid	20 bid	20 bid	
Ramipril	2.5 qd	As needed	20 qd	
Digoxin	0.125 qd	As needed	As needed	Cardiotoxicity, confusion, nausea, anorexia, visual disturbances
Hydralazine	10-25 tid	75 tid	100 tid	Headache, nausea, dizziness, tachycardia. lupus-like syndrome
Isosorbide dinitrate	10 tid	40 tid	80 tid	Headache, hypotension, flushing

*Given as a single test dose initially.

†ACE inhibitors which have FDA approval to treat CHF.

Note: ACE = angiotensin-converting enzyme.

HELICOBACTER PYLORI TREATMENT

Multiple Drug Regimens for the Treatment of *H. pylori* Infection

Drug	Dosages*	Duration of Therapy
Regimen 1†		
Bismuth subsalicylate (Pepto-Bismol®)	Two 262 mg tablets 4 times/day	2 weeks
plus		
Metronidazole (Flagyl®)	250 mg 3 or 4 times/day	2 weeks
plus		
Tetracycline (various) or amoxicillin (Amoxil®, others)	250-500 mg 4 times/day	2 weeks
plus		
Histamine H$_2$-receptor antagonist	Full dose‡ at bedtime	4-6 weeks
Regimen 2		
Metronidazole (Flagyl®)	500 mg 3 times/day	12-14 days
plus		
Amoxicillin (Amoxil®, others)	750 mg 3 times/day	12-14 days
plus		
Histamine H$_2$-receptor antagonist	Full dose† at bedtime	6-10 weeks
Regimen 3		
Bismuth subsalicylate (Pepto-Bismol®)	Two 262 mg tablets 4 times/day	2 weeks
plus		
Tetracycline (various)	500 mg 4 times/day	2 weeks
plus		
Clarithromycin (Biaxin™)	500 mg 3 times/day	2 weeks
plus		
Histamine H$_2$-receptor antagonist	Full dose† after evening meal	6 weeks
Regimen 4		
Omeprazole (Prilosec™)	20 mg twice daily	2 weeks
plus		
Amoxicillin (Amoxil®, others)	1 g twice daily or 500 mg 4 times/day	2 weeks
Regimen 5		
Omeprazole (Prilosec™)	20 mg twice daily	2 weeks
plus		
Clarithromycin (Biaxin™)	250 mg twice a day or 500 mg 2 or 3 times/day	2 weeks
or		
Lansoprazole (Prevacid®)	30 mg/day	
plus		
Amoxicillin (Amoxil®)	1 g twice daily	
plus		
Clarithromycin (Biaxin™)	500 mg twice daily	
Regimen 6		
Ranitidine bismuth citrate (Tritec™)	400 mg twice daily	4 weeks
plus		
Clarithromycin (Biaxin™)	500 mg 3 times/day	2 weeks

*All therapies are oral and begin concurrently.

†Marketed as Helidac®, a packet containing 262.4 mg bismuth subsalicylate, 250 mg metronidazole and 500 mg tetracycline; an H$_2$-antagonist must be purchased separately.

‡Full dose refers to the dosage used to treat acute ulcers, not to the maintenance dose.

HYPERGLYCEMIA- OR HYPOGLYCEMIA-CAUSING DRUGS

Hyperglycemia	Hypoglycemia	Hyperglycemia or Hypoglycemia
Caffeine	Anabolic steroids	Beta-blockers (also may mask symptoms of hypoglycemia)
Calcitonin	ACE inhibitors	Alcohol
Corticosteroids	Chloramphenicol	Lithium
Diltiazem	Clofibrate	Phenothiazines
Estrogens	Disopyramide	Rifampin
Isoniazid	MAO inhibitors	Octreotide
Morphine	Miconazole (oral form)	Fluoxetine
Nifedipine	Probenecid	
Nicotine	Pyridoxine	
Nicotinic acid	Salicylates	
Oral contraceptices	Sulfonamides	
Phenytoin	Tetracycline	
Sympathomimetic amines	Verapamil	
Theophylline	Warfarin	
Thiazide diuretics		
Thyroid products		

Adapted from American Association of Diabetes Educators, *A Core Curriculum for Diabetes Education*, 3rd ed, Vol 10, Chicago, IL: 1998, 338-41.

HYPERLIPIDEMIA

(*JAMA*, 1993, 269(23), 3015-23)

Risk Status Based on Presence of CHD Risk Factors Other Than Low-Density Lipoprotein Cholesterol*

Positive Risk Factors

Male ≥45 y

Female ≥55 y or premature menopause without estrogen replacement therapy

Family history of premature CHD (definite myocardial infarction or sudden death before 55 y of age in father or other male first-degree relative, or before 65 y of age in mother or other female first-degree relative)

Current cigarette smoking

Hypertension (blood pressure ≥140/90 mm Hg†, or taking antihypertensive medication)

Low HDL cholesterol (<35 mg/dL† [0.9 mmol/L])

Diabetes mellitus

Negative Risk Factor‡

High HDL cholesterol (≥60 mg/dL [1.6 mmol/L])

*High risk, defined as a net of two or more coronary heart disease (CHD) risk factors, leads to more vigorous intervention, shown in Figures 1 and 2. Age (defined differently for men and women) is treated as a risk factor because rates of CHD are higher in the elderly than in the young, and in men than in women of the same age. Obesity is not listed as a risk factor because it operates through other risk factors that are included (hypertension, hyperlipidemia, decreased high-density lipoprotein [HDL] cholesterol, and diabetes mellitus), but it should be considered a target for intervention. Physical inactivity is similarly not listed as a risk factor, but it too should be considered a target for intervention, and physical activity is recommended as desirable for everyone. High risk due to coronary or peripheral atherosclerosis is addressed directly in Figure 3.

†Confirmed by measurements on several occasions.

‡If the HDL cholesterol level is ≥60 mg/dL (1.6 mmol/L), subtract one risk factor (because high HDL cholesterol levels decrease CHD risk)

Initial Classification Based on Total Cholesterol and HDL Cholesterol Levels*

Cholesterol Level		Initial Classification
Total Cholesterol		
<200 mg/dL	(5.2 mmol/L)	Desirable blood cholesterol
200-239 mg/dL	(5.2-6.2 mmol/L)	Borderline-high blood cholesterol
≥240 mg/dL	(6.2 mmol/L)	High blood cholesterol
HDL Cholesterol		
<35 mg/dL	(0.9 mmol/L)	Low HDL cholesterol

*HDL indicated high-density lipoprotein.

HYPERLIPIDEMIA *(Continued)*

Summary of the Second Report of the National Cholesterol Education Program (NCEP) Expert Panel on Detection, Evaluation, and Treatment of High Blood Cholesterol in Adults (Adult Treatment Panel II)

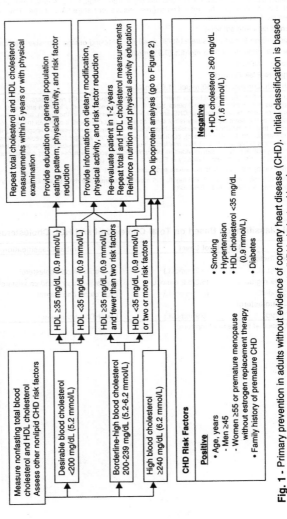

Fig. 1 – Primary prevention in adults without evidence of coronary heart disease (CHD). Initial classification is based on total cholesterol and high-density lipoprotein (HDL) cholesterol levels.

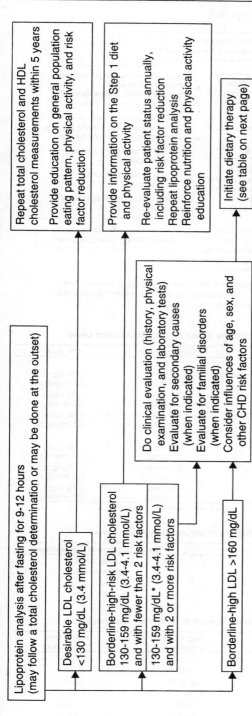

* On the basis of the average of two determinations. If the first two LDL cholesterol test results differ by more than 30 mg/dL (0.7 mmol/L), a third test result should be obtained within 1-8 weeks and the average value of the three tests used.

Fig. 2 - Primary prevention in adults **without** evidence of coronary heart disease (CHD). Subsequent classification is based on low-density lipoprotein (LDL) cholesterol level.

HYPERLIPIDEMIA *(Continued)*

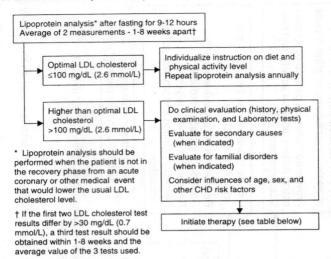

Fig. 3 - Secondary prevention in adults **with** evidence of coronary heart disease (CHD). Classification is based on low-density lipoprotein (LDL) cholesterol level.

Treatment Decisions Based on LDL Cholesterol Level*

Patient Category	Initiation Level	LDL Goal
Dietary Therapy		
Without CHD and with fewer than two risk factors	≥160 mg/dL (4.1 mmol/L)	<160 mg/dL (4.1 mmol/L)
Without CHD and with two or more risk factors	≥130 mg/dL (3.4 mmol/L)	<130 mg/dL (3.4 mmol/L)
With CHD	>100 mg/dL (2.6 mmol/L)	≤100 mg/dL (2.6 mmol/L)
Drug Treatment		
Without CHD and with fewer than two risk factors	≥190 mg/dL (4.9 mmol/L)	<160 mg/dL (4.1 mmol/L)
Without CHD and with two or more risk factors	≥160 mg/dL (4.1 mmol/L)	<130 mg/dL (3.4 mmol/L)
With CHD	≥130 mg/dL (3.4 mmol/L)	≤100 mg/dL (2.6 mmol/L)

*LDL: low-density lipoprotein; CHD: coronary heart disease

Classification of Serum Triglyceride Levels

Classification	Serum Triglyceride Concentration
Normal	≤200 mg/dL
Borderline-high	200-400 mg/dL
High	400-1000 mg/dL
Very high	>1000 mg/dL

NCEP Stepped Approach for Dietary Modification

Nutrient	Step 1 Diet (% total kcal)	Step 2 Diet (% total kcal)
Total fat	<30	<30
saturated	<10	<7
polyunsaturated	Up to 10	Up to 10
monounsaturated	10-15	10-15
Carbohydrates	50-60	50-60
Protein	10-20	10-20
Cholesterol	<300 mg/d	<200 mg/d
Total calories	qs to maintain desirable wt	qs to maintain desirable wt

HYPERTENSION

The Sixth Report of the Joint National Committee on Prevention, Detection, Evaluation, and Treatment of High Blood Pressure

Category	Systolic (mm Hg)		Diastolic (mm Hg)
Optimal	<120	and	<80
Normal	<130	and	<85
High normal	130-139	or	85-89
Hypertension†			
Stage 1	140-159	or	90-99
Stage 2	160-179	or	100-109
Stage 3	≥180	or	≥110

Not taking antihypertensive drugs and not acutely ill. When systolic and diastolic blood pressures fall into different categories, the higher category should be selected to classify the individual's blood pressure status. For example, 160/92 mm Hg should be classified as stage 2 hypertension, and 174/120 mm Hg should be classified as stage 3 hypertension. Isolated systolic hypertension is defined as SBP ≥140 mm Hg and DBP <90 mm Hg and staged appropriately (eg, 170/82 mm Hg is defined as stage 2 isolated systolic hypertension). In addition to classifying stages of hypertension on the basis of average blood pressure levels, the clinician should specify presence or absence of target-organ disease and additional risk factors. This specificity is important for risk classification and management.
Optimal blood pressure with respect to cardiovascular risk is <120/80 mm Hg. However, unusually low readings should be evaluated for clinical significance.

†Based on the average of two or more readings taken at each of two or more visits after an initial screening.

Age (y)	Girls' SBP/DBP		Boys' SBP/DBP	
	50th Percentile for Height	75th Percentile for Height	50th Percentile for Height	75th Percentile for Height
1	104/58	105/59	102/57	104/58
6	111/73	112/73	114/74	115/75
12	123/80	124/81	123/81	125/82
17	129/84	130/85	136/87	138/88

Adapted from the report by the NHBPEP Working Group on Hypertension Control in Children and Adolescents. SBP indicates systolic blood pressure; DBP, diastolic blood pressure.

Manifestations of Target-Organ Disease

Organ System	Manifestations
Cardiac	Clinical, electrocardiographic, or radiologic evidence of coronary artery disease; left ventricular hypertrophy or "strain" by electrocardiography or left ventricular hypertrophy by echocardiography; left ventricular dysfunction or cardiac failure
Cerebrovascular	Transient ischemic attack or stroke
Peripheral vascular	Absence of 1 or more major pulses in extremities (except for dorsalis pedis) with or without intermittent claudication; aneurysm
Renal	Serum creatinine ≥130 μmol/L (1.5 mg/dL); proteinuria (1+ or greater); microalbuminuria
Retinopathy	Hemorrhages or exudates, with or without papilledema

Recommendations for Follow-up Based on Initial Set of Blood Pressure Measurements for Adults

Initial Screening Blood Pressure (mm Hg)*		
Systolic	Diastolic	Follow-up Recommended†
<130	<85	Recheck in 2 years
130-139	85-89	Recheck in 1 year‡
140-159	90-99	Confirm within 2 months‡
160-179	100-109	Evaluate or refer to source of care within 1 months
≥180	≥110	Evaluate or refer to source of care immediately or within 1 week depending on clinical situation

*If the systolic and diastolic categories are different, follow recommendation for the shorter time follow-up (eg, 160/86 mm Hg should be evaluated or referred to source of care within 1 month).

†Provide advice about lifestyle modifications.

‡Modify the scheduling of follow-up according to reliable information about past blood pressure measurements, other cardiovascular risk factors, or target organ disease.

HYPERTENSION *(Continued)*

Major Risk Factors

Smoking
Dyslipidemia
Diabetes mellitus
Age >60 years
Sex (men and postmenopausal women)
Family history of cardiovascular disease; women <65 years or men <55 years

Target Organ Damage/Clinical Cardiovascular Disease

Heart diseases

- Left ventricular hypertrophy
- Angina/prior myocardial infarction
- Prior coronary revascularization
- Heart failure

Stroke or transient ischemic attack
Nephropathy
Peripheral arterial disease
Retinopathy

Blood Pressure Stages (mm Hg)	Risk Group A (No Risk Factors, No TOD/CCD)*	Risk Group B (At least 1 Risk Factor, Not Including Diabetes; No TOD/CCD)	Risk Group C (TOD/CCD and/or Diabetes, With or Without Other Risk Factors)
High-normal (130-139/85-89)	Lifestyle modification	Lifestyle modification	Drug therapy†
Stage 1 (140-159/90-99)	Lifestyle modification (up to 12 months)	Lifestyle modification‡ (up to 6 months)	Drug therapy
State 2 and 3 (≥160/≥100)	Drug therapy	Drug therapy	Drug therapy

For example, a patient with diabetes and a blood pressure of 142/94 mm Hg plus left ventricular hypertrophy should be classified as having stage 1 hypertension with target organ disease (left ventricular hypertrophy) and with another major risk factor (diabetes), this patient would be categorized as stage 1, Risk group C and recommended for immediate initiation of pharmacologic treatment.

*Lifestyle modification should be adjunctive therapy for all patients recommended for pharmacologic therapy. TOD/CCD indicates target organ disease/clinical cardiovascular disease

†For those with heart failure, renal insufficiency, or diabetes.

‡For patients with multiple risk factors, clinicians should consider drugs as initial therapy plus lifestyle modifications.

Risk Group A

Risk group A includes patients with high-normal blood pressure or state 1, 2, or 3 hypertension who do not have clinical cardiovascular disease, target organ damage, or other risk factors. Persons with stage 1 hypertension in risk group A are candidates for a longer trial (up to 1 year) of vigorous lifestyle modification with vigilant blood pressure monitoring. If goal blood pressure is not achieved, pharmacologic therapy should be added. For those with stage 2 or stage 3 hypertension, drug therapy is warranted.

Risk Group B

Risk group B includes patients with hypertension who do not have clinical cardiovascular disease or target organ damage, but have one or more of the risk factors shown in the table above but not diabetes mellitus. This group contains the large majority of patients with high blood pressure. If multiple risk factors are present, clinicians should consider antihypertensive drugs as initial therapy. Lifestyle modification and management of reversible risk factors should be strongly recommended.

Risk Group C

Risk group C includes patients with hypertension who have clinically manifested cardiovascular disease or target organ damage, as delineated in the above table. It is the clinical opinion of the JNC VI executive committee that some patients who have high-normal blood pressure as well as renal insufficiency, heart failure, or diabetes mellitus should be considered for prompt pharmacologic therapy. Appropriate lifestyle modifications always should be recommended as adjunct treatment.

- Lose weight if overweight.
- Limit alcohol intake to no more than 1 oz (30 mL) ethanol (eg, 24 oz [720 mL] beer, 10 oz [300 mL] wine, or 2 oz "60 mL" 100-proof whiskey) per day or 0.5 oz (15 mL) ethanol per day for women and lighter weight people.
- Increase aerobic physical activity (30-45 minutes most days of the week).
- Reduce sodium intake to no more than 100 mmol/day (2.4 g sodium or 6 g sodium chloride).
- Maintain adequate intake of dietary potassium (approximately 90 mmol/day).
- Maintain adequate intake of dietary calcium and magnesium for general health.
- Stop smoking and reduce intake of dietary saturated fat and cholesterol for overall cardiovascular health.

Indication	Drug Therapy
Compelling Indications Unless Contraindicated	
Diabetes mellitus (type 1) with proteinuria	ACE I
Heart failure	ACE I, diuretics
Isolated systolic hypertension (older patients)	Diuretics (preferred), CA (long-acting DHP)
Myocardial infarction	Beta-blockers (non-ISA), ACE I (with systolic dysfunction)
May Have Favorable Effects on Comorbid Conditions	
Angina	Beta-blockers, CA
Atrial tachycardia and fibrillation	Beta-blockers, CA (non-DHP)
Cyclosporine-induced hypertension (caution with the dose of cyclosporine)	CA
Diabetes mellitus (types 1 and 2) with proteinuria	ACE I (preferred), CA
Diabetes mellitus (type 2)	Low-dose diuretics
Dyslipidemia	Alpha-blockers
Essential tremor	Beta-blockers (non-CS)
Heart failure	Carvedilol, losartan potassium
Hyperthyroidism	Beta-blockers
Migraine	Beta-blockers (non-CS), CA (non-DHP)
Myocardial infarction	Diltiazem hydrochloride, verapamil hydrochloride
Osteoporosis	Thiazides
Preoperative hypertension	Beta-blockers
Prostatism (BPH)	Alpha-blockers
Renal insufficiency (caution in renovascular hypertension and creatinine ≥265.2 mmol/L [3 mg/dL])	ACE I
May Have Unfavorable Effects on Comorbid Conditions*	
Bronchospastic disease	Beta-blockers†
Depression	Beta-blockers, central alpha-agonists, reserpine†
Diabetes mellitus (types 1 and 2)	Beta-blockers, high-dose diuretics
Dyslipidemia	Beta-blockers (non-ISA), diuretics (high-dose)
Gout	Diuretics
2° or 3° heart block	Beta-blockers†, CA (non-DHP)†
Heart failure	Beta-blockers (except carvedilol), CA (except amlodipine besylate, felodipine)
Liver disease	Labetalol hydrochloride, methyldopa†
Peripheral vascular disease	Beta-blockers
Pregnancy	ACE I†, angiotensin II receptor blockers†
Renal insufficiency	Potassium-sparing agents
Renovascular disease	ACE I, angiotensin II receptor blockers

ACE I indicates angiotensin-converting enzyme inhibitors; BPH, benign prostatic hyperplasia; CA, calcium antagonists; DHP, dihydropyridine; ISA, intrinsic sympathomimetic activity; MI, myocardial infarction; and non-CS, noncardioselective.

Conditions and drugs are listed in alphabetical order.

*These drugs may be used with special monitoring unless contraindicated.

†Contraindicated.

1481

HYPERTENSION *(Continued)*

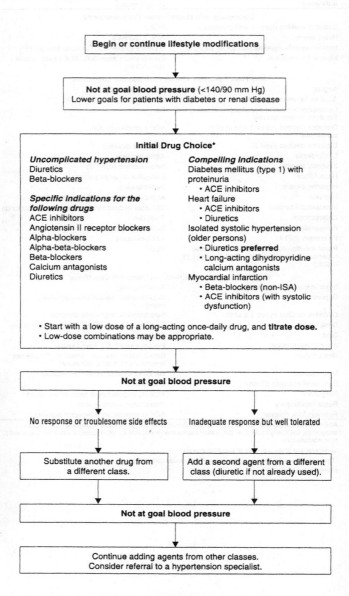

Begin or continue lifestyle modifications

Not at goal blood pressure (<140/90 mm Hg)
Lower goals for patients with diabetes or renal disease

Initial Drug Choice*

Uncomplicated hypertension
Diuretics
Beta-blockers

Specific Indications for the following drugs
ACE inhibitors
Angiotensin II receptor blockers
Alpha-blockers
Alpha-beta-blockers
Beta-blockers
Calcium antagonists
Diuretics

Compelling Indications
Diabetes mellitus (type 1) with proteinuria
• ACE inhibitors
Heart failure
• ACE inhibitors
• Diuretics
Isolated systolic hypertension (older persons)
• Diuretics **preferred**
• Long-acting dihydropyridine calcium antagonists
Myocardial infarction
• Beta-blockers (non-ISA)
• ACE inhibitors (with systolic dysfunction)

• Start with a low dose of a long-acting once-daily drug, and **titrate dose.**
• Low-dose combinations may be appropriate.

Not at goal blood pressure

No response or troublesome side effects

Inadequate response but well tolerated

Substitute another drug from a different class.

Add a second agent from a different class (diuretic if not already used).

Not at goal blood pressure

Continue adding agents from other classes.
Consider referral to a hypertension specialist.

* Unless contraindicated. ACE indicates angiotensin-converting enzyme; ISA, intrinsic sympathomimetic activity. Based on randomized controlled trials.

The report of the NHBPEP Working Group on High Blood Pressure in Pregnancy permits continuation of drug therapy in women with chronic hypertension (except for ACE inhibitors). In addition, angiotensin II receptor blockers should not be used during pregnancy. In women with chronic hypertension with diastolic levels of 100 mm Hg or greater (lower when end organ damage or underlying renal disease is present) and in women with acute hypertension when levels are 105 mm Hg or greater, the following agents are suggested.

Suggested Drug	Comments
Central alpha-agonists	Methyldopa (C) is the drug of choice recommended by the NHBPEP Working Group.
Beta-blockers	Atenolol (C) and metoprolol (C) appear to be safe and effective in late pregnancy. Labetalol (C) also appears to be effective (alpha- and beta-blockers).
Calcium antagonists	Potential synergism with magnesium sulfate may lead to precipitous hypotension. (C)
ACE inhibitors, angiotensin II receptor blockers	Fetal abnormalities, including death, can be caused, and these drugs should not be used in pregnancy. (D)
Diuretics	Diuretics (C) are recommended for chronic hypertension if prescribed before gestation or if patients appear to be salt-sensitive. They are not recommended in pre-eclampsia.
Direct vasodilators	Hydralazine (C) is the parenteral drug of choice based on its long history of safety and efficacy. (C)

Adapted from Sibai and Lindheimer. There are several other antihypertensive drugs for which there are very limited data. The U.S. Food and Drug Administration classifies pregnancy risk as follows: C, adverse effects in animals; no controlled trials in humans; use if risk appears justified; D, positive evidence of fetal risk. ACE indicates angiotensin-converting enzyme.

General Treatment Principles in the Treatment of Hypertensive Emergencies

Principle	Considerations
Admit the patient to the hospital, preferably in the intensive care unit. Monitor vital signs appropriately.	Establish intravenous access and place patient on a cardiac monitor. Place a femoral intra-arterial line and pulmonary arterial catheter, if indicated, to assess cardiopulmonary function and intravascular volume status.
Perform rapid but thorough history and physical examination.	Determine cause of, or precipitating factors to, hypertensive crisis if possible (remember to obtain a medication history including Rx, OTC, and illicit drugs). Obtain details regarding any prior history of hypertension (severity, duration, treatment), as well as other coexisting illnesses. Assess the extent of hypertensive end organ damage. Determine if a hypertensive urgency or emergency exists.
Determine goal blood pressure based on premorbid level, duration, severity and rapidity of increase of blood pressure, concomitant medical conditions, race, and age.	Acute decreases in blood pressure to normal or subnormal levels during the initial treatment period may reduce perfusion to the brain, heart, and kidneys, and must be avoided except in specific instances (ie, dissecting aortic aneurysm). Gradually establish a normal (or reasonable) blood pressure over the next 1-2 weeks.
Select an appropriate antihypertensive regimen depending on the individual patient and clinical setting.	Initiate a controlled decrease in blood pressure. Avoid concomitant administration of multiple agents that may cause precipitous falls in blood pressure. Select the agent with the best hemodynamic profile based on the primary treatment goal. Avoid diuretics and sodium restriction during the initial treatment period unless there is a clear clinical indication (ie, CHF, pulmonary edema). Avoid sedating antihypertensives in patients with hypertensive encephalopathy, CVA, or other CNS disorders in whom mental status must be monitored. Use caution with direct vasodilating agents that induce reflex tachycardia or increase cardiac output in patients with coronary heart disease, history of angina or myocardial infarction, or dissecting aortic aneurysm. Preferably choose an agent that does not adversely affect glomerular filtration rate or renal blood flow. Preferably choose agents that have favorable effects on cerebral blood flow and its autoregulation, especially patients with hypertensive encephalopathy or CVAs. Select the most efficacious agent with the fewest adverse effects based on the underlying cause of the hypertensive crisis and other individual patient factors.
Initiate a chronic antihypertensive regimen after the patient's blood pressure is stabilized	Begin oral antihypertensive therapy once goal blood pressure is achieved before gradually tapering parenteral medications. Select the best oral regimen based on cost, ease of administration, adverse effect profile, and concomitant medical conditions.

HYPERTENSION (Continued)

Oral Agents Used in the Treatment of Hypertensive Urgencies and Emergencies

Drug	Dose	Onset	Cautions
Captopril*	P.O.: 25 mg, repeat as required	15-30 min	Hypotension, renal failure in bilateral renal artery stenosis
Clonidine	P.O.: 0.1-0.2 mg, repeated every hour as needed to a total dose of 0.6 mg	30-60 min	Hypotension, drowsiness, dry mouth
Labetalol	P.O.: 200-400 mg, repeat every 2-3 h	30 min to 2 h	Bronchoconstriction, heart block, orthostatic hypotension

*There is no clearly defined clinical advantage in the use of sublingual over oral routes of administration with these agents.

Recommendations for the Use of Intravenous Antihypertensive Drugs in Selected Hypertensive Emergencies

Condition	Agent(s) of Choice	Agent(s) to Avoid or Use With Caution	General Treatment Principle
Hypertensive encephalopathy	Nitroprusside, labetalol, diazoxide	Methyldopa, reserpine	Avoid drugs with CNS sedating effects
Acute intracranial or subarachnoid hemorrhage	Nicardipine*, nitroprusside, trimethaphan	Beta-blockers	Careful titration with a short-acting agent
Cerebral infarction	Nicardipine*, nitroprusside, labetalol, trimethaphan	Beta-blockers, minoxidil, diazoxide	Careful titration with a short-acting agent. Avoid agents that may decrease cerebral blood flow.
Head trauma	Esmolol, labetalol	Methyldopa, reserpine, nitroprusside, nitroglycerin, hydralazine	Avoid drugs with CNS sedating effects, or those that may increase intracranial pressure
Acute myocardial infarction, myocardial ischemia	Nitroglycerin, nicardipine* (calcium channel blockers), labetalol	Hydralazine, diazoxide, minoxidil	Avoid drugs which cause reflex tachycardia and increased myocardial oxygen consumption
Acute pulmonary edema	Nitroprusside, nitroglycerin, loop diuretics	Beta-blockers (labetalol), minoxidil, methyldopa	Avoid drugs which may cause sodium and water retention and edema exacerbation
Renal dysfunction	Hydralazine, calcium channel blockers	Nitroprusside, ACE inhibitors, beta-blockers (labetalol)	Avoid drugs with increased toxicity in renal failure and those that may cause decreased renal blood flow.
Eclampsia	Hydralazine, labetalol, nitroprusside†	Trimethaphan, diuretics, diazoxide (diazoxide may cause cessation of labor)	Avoid drugs that may cause adverse fetal effects, compromise placental circulation, or decrease cardiac output.
Pheochromocytoma	Phentolamine, nitroprusside, beta-blockers (eg, esmolol) only after alpha blockade (phentolamine)	Beta-blockers in the absence of alpha blockade, methyldopa, minoxidil	Use drugs of proven efficacy and specificity. Unopposed beta blockade may exacerbate hypertension.
Dissecting aortic aneurysm	Nitroprusside and beta blockade, trimethaphan	Hydralazine, diazoxide, minoxidil	Avoid drugs which may increase cardiac output.
Postoperative hypertension	Nitroprusside, nicardipine*, labetalol	Trimethaphan	Avoid drugs which may exacerbate postoperative ileus.

*The use of nicardipine in these situations is by the recommendation of the author based on a review of the literature.

†Reserve nitroprusside for eclamptic patients with life-threatening hypertension unresponsive to other agents due to the potential risk to the fetus (cyanide and thiocyanate metabolites may cross the placenta).

Drug	Dose*	Onset of Action	Duration of Action	Adverse Effects†	Special Indications
Vasodilators					
Sodium nitroprusside	0.25-10 mcg/kg/min as I.V. infusion‡ (maximum dose for 10 minutes only)	Immediate	1-2 min	Nausea, vomiting, muscle twitching, sweating, thiocyanate and cyanide intoxication	Most hypertensive emergencies; caution with high intracranial pressure or azotemia
Nicardipine hydrochloride	5-15 mg/h I.V.	5-10 min	1-4 h	Tachycardia, headache, flushing, local phlebitis	Most hypertensive emergencies except acute heart failure; caution with coronary ischemia
Fenoldopam mesylate	0.1-0.3 mcg/kg/min I.V. infusion	<5 min	30 min	Tachycardia, headache, nausea, flushing	Most hypertensive emergencies; caution with glaucoma
Nitroglycerin	5-100 mcg/min as I.V. infusion‡	2-5 min	3-5 min	Headache, vomiting, methemoglobinemia, tolerance with prolonged use	Coronary ischemia
Enalaprilat	1.25-5 mg every 6 hours I.V.	15-30 min	6 h	Precipitous fall in pressure in high-renin states; response variable	Acute left ventricular failure; avoid in acute myocardial infarction
Hydralazine hydrochloride	10-20 mg I.V. 10-50 mg I.M.	10-20 min 20-30 min	3-8 h	Tachycardia, flushing, headache, vomiting, aggravation of angina	Eclampsia
Diazoxide	50-100 mg I.V. bolus repeated, or 15-30 mg/min infusion	2-4 min	6-12 h	Nausea, flushing, tachycardia, chest pain	Now obsolete; when no intensive monitoring available
Adrenergic Inhibitors					
Labetalol hydrochloride	20-80 mg I.V. bolus every 10 minutes; 0.5-2 mg/min I.V. infusion	5-10 min	3-6 h	Vomiting, scalp tingling, burning in throat, dizziness, nausea, heart block, orthostatic hypotension	Most hypertensive emergencies except acute heart failure
Esmolol hydrochloride	250-500 mcg/kg/min for 1 minute, then 50-100 mcg/kg/min for 4 minutes; may repeat sequence	1-2 min	10-20 min	Hypotension, nausea	Aortic dissection, perioperative
Phentolamine	5-15 mg I.V.	1-2 min	3-10 min	Tachycardia, flushing, headache	Catecholamine excess

I.V. indicates intravenous; I.M., intramuscular.

*These doses may vary from those in the *Physicians' Desk Reference* (51st edition).

†Hypotension may occur with all agents.

‡Require special delivery system.

MANAGEMENT OF OVERDOSAGES

Poison Control Center Antidote Chart

Antidote	Poison/Drug	Indications	Dosage	Comments
Acetylcysteine (Mucomyst®)	Acetaminophen	Unknown quantity ingested and <24 hours have elapsed since the time of ingestion or unable to obtain serum acetaminophen levels within 12 hours of ingestion. >7.5 g acetaminophen acutely ingested. Serum acetaminophen level >140 µg/mL at 4 hours postingestion. Ingested dose >140 mg/kg.	Dilute to 5% solutions with carbonated beverage, fruit juice, or water and administer orally. **Loading:** 140 mg/kg for 1 dose **Maintenance:** 70 mg/kg for 17 doses, starting 4 hours after the loading dose and given every 4 hours	SGOT, SGPT, bilirubin, prothrombin time, creatinine, BUN, blood sugar, and electrolytes should be obtained daily if a toxic serum acetaminophen level has been determined. **Note:** Activated charcoal has been shown to absorb acetylcysteine *in vitro* and may do so in patients. Serum acetaminophen levels may not peak until 4 hours postingestion, and therefore, serum levels should not be drawn earlier.
Amyl nitrate, sodium nitrate, sodium thiosulfate (cyanide antidote package)	Cyanide	Begin treatment at the first sign of toxicity if exposure is known or strongly expected.	Break ampul of amyl nitrate and allow patient to inhale for 15 seconds, then take away for 15 seconds. Use a fresh ampul every 3 minutes. Continue until injection of sodium nitrate (3% solution) 300 mg (0.15-0.33 mL/kg over 5 minutes in pediatric patients) can be injected at 2.5-5 mL/min. Then immediately inject 12.5 g 25% sodium thiosulfate, slow I.V. (1.65 mL/kg in children).	If symptoms return, treatment may be repeated at half the normal dosages. For pediatric dosing see package insert. Do **not** use methylene blue to reduce elevated methemoglobin levels. Oxygen therapy may be useful when combined with sodium thiosulfate therapy.
Antivenin (*Crotalidae*) polyvalent (equine origin)	Pit viper bites (rattlesnakes, cotton- mouths, copperheads)	Mild, moderate, or severe symptoms and history of envenomation by a pit viper **Mild:** Local swelling (progressive), pain, no systemic systems **Moderate:** Ecchymosis and swelling beyond the bite site, some systemic symptoms and/or lab changes **Severe:** Profound edema involving entire extremity, cyanosis, serious systemic involvement, significant lab changes	**Mild:** 3-5 vials of antivenin in 250-500 mL NS **Moderate:** 6-10 vials of antivenin in 500 mL NS **Severe:** Minimum of 10 vials of antivenin in 500-1000 mL NS Administer over 4-6 hours. Additional antivenin should be given on the basis of clinical response and continuing assessment of severity of the poisoning.	Draw blood for type and crossmatch, hematocrit, BUN, electrolytes, CBC, platelets, coagulation profile. Do **not** administer heparin for possible allergic reaction. A tetanus shot should also be given.

Poison Control Center Antidote Chart (continued)

Antidote	Poison/Drug	Indications	Dosage	Comments
Atropine	Organophosphate and carbamate insecticides, mushrooms containing muscarine (inocybe or clitocybe)	Myoclonic seizures, severe hallucinations, weakness, arrhythmias, excessive salivation, involuntary urination, and defecation	**Children:** I.V.: 0.05 mg/kg **Adults:** I.V.: 1-2 mg Repeat dosage every 10 minutes until patient is atropinized (normal pulse, dilated pupils, absence of rales, dry mouth)	Caution should be used in patients with narrow-angle glaucoma, cardiovascular disease, or pregnancy. Plasma and/or erythrocyte cholinesterase levels will be depressed from normal. Atropine should only be used when indicated; otherwise, use may result in anticholinergic poisoning. For organophosphate poisoning, large doses of atropine may be required.
Calcium EDTA (calcium disodium versenate)	Lead	Symptomatic patients or asymptomatic children with blood levels >50 µg/dL	50-75 mg/kg/day deep I.M. or slow I.V. infusion in 3-6 divided doses for up to 5 days	If urine flow is not established, hemodialysis must accompany calcium EDTA dosing. In most cases, the I.M. route is preferred.
Calcium gluconate	Hydrofluoric acid (HF), magnesium	Calcium gluconate gel 2.5% for dermal exposures of HF <20% concentration. S.C. injections of calcium gluconate for dermal exposures of HF in >20% concentration or failure to respond to calcium gluconate gel.	Massage 2.5% gel into exposed area for 15 minutes. Infiltrate each square centimeter of exposed area with 0.5 mL of 10% calcium gluconate S.C. using a 30-gauge needle. 1 mL/kg I.V. of a 10% solution for magnesium toxicity (intra-arterial injection).	Injections of calcium gluconate should not be used in digital area. With exposures to dilute concentrations of HF, symptoms may take several hours to develop. Calcium gluconate gel is not currently available. Contact your regional poison control center for compounding instructions.
Deferoxamine (Desferal®)	Iron	Serum iron >350 µg/dL. Inability to obtain serum iron in a reasonable time and patient is symptomatic.	**Mild symptoms:** I.M.: 10 mg/kg up to 1 g every 8 hours **Severe symptoms:** I.V.: 10-15 mg/kg/hour not to exceed 6 g in 24 hours; rates up to 35 mg/kg have been given.	Passing of vin rose-colored urine indicates free iron was present. Therapy should be discontinued when urine returns to normal color. Monitor for hypotension, especially when giving deferoxamine I.V.
Digoxin immune Fab (ovine), (Digibind®)	Digoxin, digitoxin, oleander, foxglove, lily-of-the-valley (?), red squill (?)	Life-threatening cardiac arrhythmias, progressive bradyarrhythmias, second or third degree heart block unresponsive to atropine, serum digoxin level >5 ng/mL, potassium levels >5 mEq/L, or ingestion >10 mg in adults (or 4 mg in children).	Multiply serum digoxin concentration at steady-state level by 5.6 and multiply the result by the patient's weight in kilograms, divide this by 1000 and divide the result by 0.6. This gives the dose in number of vials to use. For other dosing methods, see package insert.	Monitor potassium levels, continuous EKG. **Note:** Digibind® interferes with serum digoxin/digitoxin levels.

MANAGEMENT OF OVERDOSAGES *(Continued)*

Poison Control Center Antidote Chart *(continued)*

Antidote	Poison/Drug	Indications	Dosage	Comments
Dimercaprol (BAL in oil)	Arsenic, lead, mercury, gold, trivalent antimony, methyl bromide, methyl iodide	Any symptoms due to arsenic exposure. All patients with symptoms or asymptomatic children with blood levels >70 mcg/dL Any symptoms due to mercury and patient unable to take D-penicillamine.	3-5 mg/kg/dose deep I.M. every 4 hours until GI symptoms subside and patient switched to D-penicillamine. 3-5 mg/kg/dose deep I.M. every 4 hours for 2 days then every 4-12 hours for up to 7 additional days. 3-5 mg/kg/dose deep I.M. every 4 hours for 48 hours, then 3 mg/kg/dose every 6 hours, then 3 mg/kg/dose every 12 hours for 7 more days.	Patients receiving dimercaprol should be monitored for hypertension, tachycardia, hyperpyrexia, and urticaria. Used in conjunction with calcium EDTA in lead poisoning.
Ethanol	Ethylene glycol or methanol	Ethylene glycol or methanol blood levels >20 mg/dL. Blood levels not readily available and suspected ingestion of toxic amounts. Any symptomatic patient with a history of ethylene glycol or methanol ingestion.	**Loading dose:** I.V.: 7.5-10 mL/kg 10% ethanol in D_5W over 1 hour **Maintenance dose:** I.V.: 1.4 mL/kg/hour of 10% ethanol in D_5W. Maintain blood ethanol level of 100-200 mg/dL.	Monitor blood glucose, especially in children, as ethanol may cause hypoglycemia. Do not use 5% ethanol in D_5W as excessive amounts of fluid would be required to maintain adequate ethanol blood levels. If dialysis is performed, adjustment of ethanol dosing is required.
Flumazenil (Romazicon®)	Benzodiazepine	As adjunct to conventional management/ diagnosis of benzodiazepine overdose.	I.V.: 0.2 mg over 30 seconds; wait another 30 seconds, and then give an additional 0.3 mg over 30 seconds. Additional doses of 0.5 mg over 30 seconds at 1-minute intervals up to a cumulative dose of 3 mg.	Onset of reversal usually within 1-2 minutes. Contraindicated in patients with epilepsy, increased intracranial pressure, or coingestion of seizuregenic agents (ie, cyclic antidepressant).
Glucagon	Propranolol; Hypoglycemic agents	Propranolol-induced cardiac dysfunction. Treatment of hypoglycemia.	S.C., I.M., or I.V.: 0.5-1 mg May repeat after 15 minutes	Requires liver glycogen stores for hyperglycemic response. Intravenous glucose must also be given in treatment of hypoglycemia.
Leucovorin (citrovorum factor, folinic acid)	Methotrexate, trimethoprim, pyrimethamine, methanol, trimetrexate	Methotrexate-induced bone marrow depression (methotrexate serum level >1 x 10^{-5} mmol/L); may also be useful in pyrimethamine-trimethoprim bone marrow depression	Dose should be equal to or greater than the dose of methotrexate ingested. Usually 10-100 mg/m² is given I.V. or orally every 6 hours for 72 hours.	Most effective if given within 1 hour after exposure. May not be effective to prevent liver toxicity. Monitor methotrexate levels. May enhance the toxicity of fluorouracil.

Poison Control Center Antidote Chart *(continued)*

Antidote	Poison/Drug	Indications	Dosage	Comments
Methylene blue	Methemoglobin inducers (ie, nitrites, phenazopyridine)	Cyanosis Methemoglobin level >30% in an asymptomatic patient	I.V.: 1-2 mg/kg (0.1-0.2 mL/kg) per dose over 2-3 minutes. May repeat doses as needed clinically. Injection can be given as 1% solution or diluted in normal saline.	Treatment can result in falsely elevated methemoglobin levels when measured by a co-oximeter. Large doses (>15 mg/kg) may cause hemolysis.
Naloxone (Narcan®)	Opiates (eg, heroin, morphine, codeine)	Coma or respiratory depression from unknown cause or from opiate overdose	Give 0.4-2.0 mg I.V. bolus. Doses may be repeated if there is no response, up to 10 mg.	For prolonged intoxication, a continuous infusion may be used. See package insert for details or table previously presented in this text titled "Drugs to Be Utilized in the Toxic Patient With Altered Mental Status."
D-penicillamine (Cuprimine®)	Arsenic, lead, mercury	Following BAL therapy in symptomatic acutely poisoned patients Asymptomatic patients with excess lead burden Patient symptomatic from mercury exposure or excessive levels	100 mg/kg/day up to 2 g in 4 divided doses for 5 days 1-2 g/day in 4 divided doses for 5 days **Children:** 100 mg/kg/day up to 1 g/day in 4 divided doses. Given for 3-10 days. **Adults:** P.O.: 250 mg 4 times/day	Possible contraindication for patients with penicillin allergy. Monitor heavy metal levels daily in severely poisoned patients. Monitor CBC and renal function in patients receiving chronic D-penicillamine therapy. Dosages given are for short-term acute therapy only.
Physostigmine salicylate (Antilirium®)	Atropine and anticholinergic agents, cyclic antidepressants, intrathecal baclofen	Myoclonic seizures, severe arrhythmias Refractory seizures or arrhythmias unresponsive to conventional therapies	**Children:** Slow I.V. push: 0.5 mg. Repeat as required for life-threatening symptoms **Adults:** Slow I.V. push: 0.5-2 mg Same as above	Dramatic reversal of anticholinergic symptoms after I.V. use. Should not be used just to keep patient awake. **Contraindications:** Asthma, gangrene; physostigmine use in cyclic antidepressant-induced cardiac toxicity it controversial. **Extreme caution** is advised — should be considered only in the presence of life-threatening anticholinergic symptoms.
Pralidoxime (2-PAM, Protopam®)	Organophosphate, insecticides, tacrine	An adjunct to atropine therapy for treatment of profound muscle weakness, respiratory depression, muscle twitching	**Children:** 25-50 mg/kg in 250 mL saline over 30 minutes **Adults:** I.V.: 2 g at 0.5 g/minute or infused in 250 mL NS over 30 minutes	Most effective when used in initial 24-36 hours after the exposure. Dosage may be repeated in 1 hour followed by every 8 hours if indicated.
Phytonadione (vitamin K₁)	Coumarin derivatives, indandione derivatives	Large acute ingestion of warfarin rodenticides; chronic exposure or greater than normal prothrombin time	**Children:** I.M.: 1-5 mg. With severe toxicity, vitamin K₁ may be given I.V. **Adults:** I.M.: 10 mg	Vitamin K therapy is relatively contraindicated for patients with prosthetic heart valves unless toxicity is life-threatening.

MANAGEMENT OF OVERDOSAGES (Continued)

Poison Control Center Antidote Chart (continued)

Antidote	Poison/Drug	Indications	Dosage	Comments
Protamine sulfate	Heparin	Severe hemorrhage	Maximum rate of 5 mg/minute up to a total dose of 200 mg in 2 hours. 1 mg of protamine neutralizes 90 units of beef lung heparin or 115 units of pork intestinal heparin.	Monitor partial thromboplastin time or activated coagulation time. Effect may be immediate and can last for 2 hours. Monitor for hypotension.
Pyridoxine (vitamin B₆)	Isoniazid monomethyl-hydrazine-containing mushrooms (Gyromitra); acrylamide, hydrazine	Unknown overdose or ingested isoniazid (INH) amount >80 mg/kg	I.V. pyridoxine in the amount of INH ingested or 5 g if amount is unknown given over 30-60 minutes.	Cumulative dose of pyridoxine is arbitrarily limited to 40 g in adults and 20 g in children.
Succimer (Chemet®)	Lead, arsenic, mercury	Asymptomatic children with venous blood lead 45-69 μg/dL. Not FDA approved for adult lead exposure or other metals.	P.O.: 10 mg/kg or 350 mg/m² every 8 hours for 5 days. Reduce to 10 mg/kg or 350 mg/m² every 12 hours for an additional 2 weeks.	Monitor liver function; emits "rotten egg" sulfur odor.

From Rush Poison Control Center, Rush-Presbyterian-St Luke's Medical Center, Chicago, IL 60612.

TOXICOLOGY INFORMATION

Initial Stabilization of the Patients

The recommended treatment plan for the poisoned patient is not unlike general treatment plans taught in advanced cardiac life support (ACLS) or advanced trauma life support (ATLS) courses. In this manner, the initial approach to the poisoned patient should be essentially similar in every case, irrespective of the toxin ingested, just as the initial approach to the trauma patient is the same irrespective of the mechanism of injury. This approach, which can be termed as routine poison management, essentially includes the following aspects.

- Stabilization: ABCs (airway, breathing, circulation; administration of glucose, thiamine, oxygen, and naloxone)
- History, physical examination leading toward the identification of class of toxin (toxidrome recognition)
- Prevention of absorption (decontamination)
- Specific antidote, if available
- Removal of absorbed toxin (enhancing excretion)
- Support and monitoring for adverse effects

Drug	Effect	Comment
25-50 g **dextrose** (D₅₀W) intravenously to reverse the effects of drug-induced hypoglycemia (adult) 1 mL/kg D₅₀W diluted 1:1 (child)	This can be especially effective in patients with limited glycogen stores (ie, neonates and patients with cirrhosis)	Extravasation into the extremity of this hyperosmolar solution can cause Volkmann's contractures
50-100 mg intravenous **thiamine**	Prevent Wernicke's encephalopathy	A water-soluble vitamin with low toxicity; rare anaphylactoid reactions have been reported
Initial dosage of **naloxone** should be 2 mg in adult patients preferably by the intravenous route, although intramuscular, subcutaneous, intralingual, and endotracheal routes may also be utilized. Pediatric dose is 0.1 mg/kg from birth until 5 years of age	Specific opioid antagonist without any agent properties	It should be noted that some semisynthetic opiates (such as meperidine or propoxyphene) may require higher initial doses for reversal, so that a total dose of 6-10 mg is not unusual for the adults. If the patient responds to a bolus dose and then relapses to a lethargic or comatose state, a naloxone drip can be considered. This can be accomplished by administering two-thirds of the bolus dose that revives the patient per hour or injecting 4 mg naloxone in 1 L crystalloid solution and administering at a rate of 100 mL/hour 0.4 mg/ hour)
Oxygen, utilized in 100% concentration	Useful for carbon monoxide, hydrogen, sulfide, and asphyxiants	While oxygen is antidotal for carbon monoxide intoxication, the only relative toxic contraindication is in paraquat intoxication (in that it can promote pulmonary fibrosis)
Flumazenil	Benzodiazepine antagonist	Not routinely recommended due to increased risk of seizures

Laboratory Evaluation of Overdose

Unknown ingestion: Electrolytes, anion gap, serum osmolality, arterial blood gases, serum drug concentration
Known ingestion: Labs tailored to agent

TOXICOLOGY INFORMATION (Continued)

Toxins Affecting the Anion Gap

Drugs Causing Increased Anion Gap (>12 mEq/L)

Nonacidotic
- Carbenicillin
- Sodium salts

Metabolic Acidosis

Acetaminophen (ingestion >75-100 g)	Isoniazid
Acetazolamide	Ketamine
Amiloride	Ketoprofen
Ascorbic acid	Metaldehyde
Benzalkonium chloride	Metformin
Benzyl alcohol	Methanol
Beta-adrenergic drugs	Methenamine mandelate
Bialaphos	Monochloracetic acid
2-butanone	Nalidixic acid
Carbon monoxide	Naproxen
Centrimonium bromide	Niacin
Chloramphenicol	Papaverine
Colchicine	Paraldehyde
Cyanide	Pennyroyal oil
Dapsone	Pentachlorophenol
Dimethyl sulfate	Phenelzine
Dinitrophenol	Phenformin (off the market)
Endosulfan	Phenol
Epinephrine (I.V. overdose)	Phenylbutazone
Ethanol	Phosphoric acid
Ethylene dibromide	Potassium chloroplatinite
Ethylene glycol	Propylene glycol
Fenoprofen	Salicylates
Fluoroacetate	Sorbitol (I.V.)
Formaldehyde	Strychnine
Fructose (I.V.)	Surfactant herbicide
Glycol ethers	Tetracycline (outdated)
Hydrogen sulfide	Theophylline
Ibuprofen (ingestion >300 mg/kg)	Tienilic acid
Inorganic acid	Toluene
Iodine	Tranylcypromine
Iron	Vacor
	Verapamil

Drugs Causing Decreased Anion Gap (<6 mEq/L)

Acidosis

Ammonium chloride	Lithium
Bromide	Polymyxin B
Iodide	Tromethamine

Drugs Causing Increased Osmolar Gap

(by freezing-point depression, gap is >10 mOsm)

Ethanol*	Mannitol
Ethylene glycol*	Methanol*
Glycerol	Propylene glycol
Hypermagnesemia (>9.5 mEq/L)	Severe alcoholic ketoacidosis or lactic acidosis
Isopropanol* (acetone)	
Iodine (questionable)	Sorbitol*

*Toxins increasing both anion and osmolar gap.

Toxins Associated With Oxygen Saturation Gap

(>5% difference between measured and calculated value)

Carbon monoxide	Hydrogen sulfide (possible)
Cyanide (questionable)	Methemoglobin

Acetaminophen Toxicity

The Toxicology Laboratory is also very useful for determining levels of toxin in body fluids. Often these drug levels will guide therapy. For example, use of the Rumack-Matthew nomogram for acute acetaminophen poisoning can direct N-acetylcysteine therapy if the serum acetaminophen level falls above the treatment line.

Acetaminophen Toxicity Nomogram

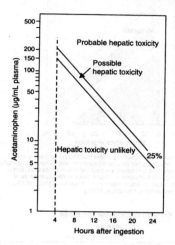

The Rumack-Matthew nomogram, relating expected severity of liver toxicity to serum acetaminophen concentrations.

From Smilkstein MJ, Bronstein AC, Linden C, et al, "Acetaminophen Overdose: A 48-Hour Intravenous N-Acetylcysteine Treatment Protocol," *Ann Emerg Med*, 1991, 20(10):1058, with permission.

Ibuprofen Toxicity Nomogram

Ibuprofen nomogram, (From Hall AH, Smolinske SC, Stover B, et al, "Ibuprofen Overdose in Adults," *J Toxicol Clin Toxicol*, 1992, 30:34.)

Serum Salicylate Intoxication

Similarly, the Done nomogram is somewhat useful in predicting salicylate toxicity in pediatric patients. Neither nomogram should be utilized with chronic ingestions. Recently, a nomogram has been devised for theophylline ingestion; see the following nomogram.

TOXICOLOGY INFORMATION *(Continued)*

Serum Salicylate Level and Severity of Intoxication
Single Dose Acute Ingestion Nomogram

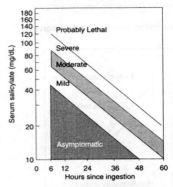

Done nomogram for salicylate poisoning. Note that this nomogram is not accurate for chronic ingestions nor for acute ingestions with enteric coated tabs. Clinical laboratory signs and symptoms are best indicators for assessments. (From Done AK, "Salicylate Intoxication: Significance of Measurements of Salicylate in Blood in Cases of Acute Ingestions," *Pediatrics*, 1960, 26:800; copyright American Academy of Pediatrics, 1960.)

Serum Theophylline Overdose
Nonsmokers

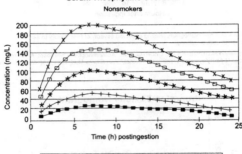

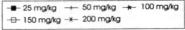

Serum Theophylline Overdose
Smokers and Children

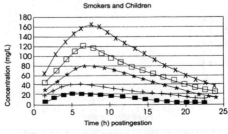

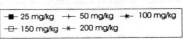

Nomogram for overdose of sustained-release theophylline in 1) nonsmoking adults, and 2) smokers and children. (Courtesy of Frank Paloucek, PharmD, College of Pharmacy, University of Illinois, Chicago.)

History and Physical Examination

While the history and physical examination is the cornerstone of clinical patient management, it takes on special meaning with regard to the toxic patient. While taking a history may be a more direct method of the determination of the toxin, quite often is is not reliable. Information obtained may prove minimal in some cases and could be considered partial or inaccurate in suicide gestures and addicts. A quick physical examination often leads to important clues about the nature of the toxin. These clues can be specific symptom complexes associated with certain toxins and can be referred to as "toxidromes".

Prevention of Absorption

Toxic substances can enter the body through the dermal, ocular, pulmonary, parenteral, and gastrointestinal routes. The basic principle of decontamination involves appropriate copious irrigation of the toxic substances relatable to the route of exposure. For example, with ocular exposure, this can be done with normal saline for 30-40 minutes through a Morgan therapeutic lens. With alkali exposures, the pH should be checked until the runoff of the solution is either neutral or slightly acidic. Skin decontamination involves removal of the toxin with nonabrasive soap. This should especially be considered for organophosphates, methylene chloride, dioxin, radiation, hydrocarbons, and herbicide exposure. Separate drainage areas should be obtained for the contaminated runoff.

Since >80% of incidents of accidental poisoning in children occur through the gastrointestinal tract, a thorough knowledge of gastric decontamination is essential. There are essentially four modes of gastric decontamination, of which three are physical removal (emesis, gastric lavage, and whole bowel irrigation). Activated charcoal associated with a cathartic is the fourth mode for preventing absorption.

Methods of Enhanced Elimination of Toxic Substances/Drugs

Emesis with Syrup of Ipecac

Indications

- Use within 1 hour of ingestion
- Hydrocarbons with "dangerous additives"
- Heavy metals
- Toxic insecticides

Contraindications

- Children <6 months of age
- Nontoxic ingestion
- Lack of gag reflex
- Caustic/corrosive ingestions
- Hemorrhagic diathesis
- Sharp object ingestion
- Prior vomiting
- Ingestion of pure petroleum distillate

Dose: + 15 mL H_2O

Children:	6-12 months:	10 mL
	1-5 years:	15 mL
	>5 years:	30 mL
Adults:		30 mL

Note: Ipecac use is becoming less frequently recommended since <30% of the stomach is usually emptied and its use may delay the use of activated charcoal.

Gastric Lavage

Indications

- Use within 1 hour of ingestion
- Comatose patient with significant ingestion without contraindications
- Failure to respond to ipecac
- Large quantities of toxins

Contraindications

- Seizures
- Nontoxic ingestion
- Significant hemorrhagic diathesis
- Caustic ingestions, hydrocarbons
- Usually unable to use large enough tube in children <12 years of age

Note: Lavage is not routinely recommended except for recent and very large ingestions of noncontraindicated toxins since it is believed to actually push a significant portion of drug into the intestine and may delay administration of activated charcoal.

Enhancement of Elimination

Only recently has this aspect of poison management received more than cursory attention in practice and in the literature. The standard practice for enhancement of elimination consisted primarily of forced diuresis in order to excrete the toxin. However, the past 10

TOXICOLOGY INFORMATION *(Continued)*

years experience has produced a radical change in the approach to this and therefore, a more focused methodology to eliminating absorbed toxins. Essentially, there are three methods by which absorbed toxins may be eliminated: recurrent adsorption with multiple dosings of activated charcoal, use of forced diuresis in combination with possible alkalinization of the urine, and use of dialysis or charcoal hemoperfusion.

Activated Charcoal Indications

Indications

- Single dose for agents known to be bound
- Multiple dose for drugs with favorable characteristics: Small volume of distribution (<1 L/kg), low plasma protein binding, biliary or gastric secretion, active metabolites that recirculate, drugs that exhibit a large free fraction (eg, dapsone, carbamazepine, digitalis, methotrexate, phenobarbital, salicylates, theophylline, tricyclic antidepressants), unchanged, lipophilic, long half-life

Recently, multiple dosing of activated charcoal ("pulse dosing") has been advocated as a method for removal of absorbed drug. This procedure has been demonstrated to be efficacious in drugs that re-enter the gastrointestinal tract through enterohepatic circulation (ie, digitoxin, carbamazepine, glutethimide) and with drugs that diffuse from the systemic circulation into the gastrointestinal tract due to formation of a concentration gradient ("the infinite sink" hypothesis).

Toxins Eliminated by Multiple Dosing of Activated Charcoal (MDAC)

Amitriptyline	Methotrexate
Amoxapine	Methyprylon
Baclofen (?)	Nadolol
Benzodiazepines (?)	Nortriptyline
Bupropion (?)	Phencyclidine
Carbamazepine*	Phenobarbital*
Chlordecone	Phenylbutazone
Cyclosporine	Phenytoin (?)
Dapsone	Piroxicam
Diazepam	Propoxyphene
Digoxin	Salicylates (?)*
Glutethimide	Theophylline*
Maprotiline	Valproic acid*
Meprobamate	

*Only agents routinely recommended for removal with MDAC.

Contraindications

- Absence of hypoactive bowel sounds
- Caustic ingestions
- Drugs without effect: Acids, alkalis, alcohols, boric acid, cyanide, iron, heavy metals, lithium, insecticides

Dose

Children and Adults: 50-100 g initially or 1 g/kg weight; repeat doses of 25 g or 0.5 g/kg every 2-4 hours

Most effective at 1-hour postingestion but can remove at >1-hour postingestion

Doses subsequent to first may be admixed with water rather than a cathartic such as sorbitol to avoid diarrhea and consequent electrolyte disturbances.

Whole Bowel Irrigation – propylene glycol based solutions

Initial dose of charcoal is necessary prior to use. Avoid pretreatment with ipecac.

Indications

- Iron, lead, lithium
- Agents not bound by charcoal
- Modified or sustained release dosage forms
- Body packers

Contraindications

- Bowel perforation
- Obstruction
- Ileus
- Gastrointestinal bleed

Dose

Maximum: 5-10 L
Toddlers/preschool: 250-500 mL/hour or 35 mL/kg

Adults: 1-2 L/hour

Terminate when rectal effluent = infusate = clear

Urinary Ion Trapping—to alkalinize the urine

Indications

* Salicylates
* Phenobarbital

Toxins Eliminated by Forced Saline Diuretics	Toxins Eliminated by Alkaline Diuresis
Bromidex	2,4-D chlorphenoxyacetic acid
Chromium	Fluoride
Cimetidine (?)	Isoniazid (?)
Cis-platinum	Mephobarbital
Cyclophosphamide	Methotrexate
Hydrazine	Phenobarbital
Iodide	Primidone
Iodine	Quinolones antibiotic
Isoniazid (?)	Salicylates
Lithium	Uranium
Methyl iodide	
Potassium chloroplatinite	
Thallium	

Dose

Sodium bicarbonate 1-2 mEq/kg every 3-4 hours or 100 mEq NaHCO$_3$ in 1 L D$_5$¼NS at 200 mL/hour (desired urine pH: 7.6-7.8)

A urine flow of 3-5 mL/kg/hour should be achieved with a combination of isotonic fluids or diuretics. Although several drugs can exhibit enhanced elimination through an acidic urine (quinine, amphetamines, PCP, nicotine, bismuth, ephedrine, flecainide), the practice of acidifying the urine should be discouraged in that it can produce metabolic acidosis and promote renal failure in the presence of rhabdomyolysis. **Note:** Use caution in alkalinizing urine of children to avoid fluid overdose.

Hemodialysis

Indications

Drugs with favorable characteristics

* Low molecular weight (<500 daltons)
* Ionically charged
* H$_2$O soluble
* Low plasma protein binding (<70%-80%)
* Small volume of distribution (<1 L/kg)
* Low tissue binding
* Methanol, ethylene glycol, boric acid

TOXICOLOGY INFORMATION *(Continued)*

Drugs and Toxins Removed by Hemodialysis

Acetaminophen
Acyclovir
Amanita phalloides (?)
Amantadine (?)
Ammonium chloride
Amphetamine
Anilines
Atenolol
Boric acid
Bromides
Bromisoval
Calcium
Captopril (?)
Carbromal
Carisoprodol
Chloral hydrate
Chlorpropamide
Chromium
Cimetidine (?)
Cyclophosphamide
Dapsone
Disopyramide
Enalapril (?)
Ethanol
Ethylene glycol
Famotidine (?)
Fluoride
Folic acid
Formaldehyde
Foscarnet sodium
Gabapentin
Glycol ethers
Hydrazine (?)
Hydrochlorothiazide

Iodides
Isoniazid
Isopropanol
Ketoprofen
Lithium
Magnesium
Meprobamate
Metal-chelate compounds
Metformin (?)
Methanol
Methaqualone
Methotrexate
Methyldopa
Methylprylone
Monochloroacetic acid
Nadolol
Oxalic acid
Paraldehyde
Phenelzine (?)
Phenobarbital
Phosphoric acid
Potassium
Procainamide
Quinidine
Ranitidine (?)
Rifabutin
Salicylates
Sotalol
Strychnine
Thallium
Theophylline
Thiocyanates
Tranylcypromine sulfate (?)
Verapamil (?)

Hemoperfusion

Indications

Drugs with favorable characteristics:

- Affinity for activated charcoal
- Tissue binding
- High rate of equilibration from peripheral tissues to blood

Examples: Barbiturates, carbamazepine, ethchlorvynol, methotrexate, phenytoin, theophylline

Drugs and Toxins Removed by Hemoperfusion (Charcoal)

Amanita phalloides (?)
Atenolol (?)
Bromisoval
Bromoethylbutyramide
Caffeine
Carbamazepine
Carbon tetrachloride (?)
Carbromal
Chloral hydrate (trichloroethanol)
Chloramphenicol
Chlorpropamide
Colchicine (?)
Creosote (?)
Dapsone
Diltiazem (?)
Disopyramide
Ethchlorvynol
Ethylene oxide
Glutethimide
Lindane

Meprobamate
Methaqualone
Methotrexate
Methsuximide
Methyprylon (?)
Metoprolol (?)
Nadolol (?)
Oxalic acid (?)
Paraquat
Phenelzine (?)
Phenobarbital
Phenytoin
Podophyllin (?)
Procainamide (?)
Quinidine (?)
Rifabutin (?)
Sotalol (?)
Thallium
Theophylline
Verapamil (?)

Exchange transfusion is another mode of extracorporeal removal of toxins that can be utilized in neonatal infant drug toxicity. It may be especially useful for barbiturate, iron, caffeine, sodium nitrite, or theophylline overdose.

TOXIDROMES

Management of Overdoses

Toxin	Vital Signs	Mental Status	Symptoms	Physical Exam	Laboratories
Acetaminophen	Normal	Normal	Anorexia, nausea, vomiting	RUQ tenderness, jaundice	Elevated LFTs
Cocaine	Hypertension, tachycardia, hyperthermia	Anxiety, agitation, delirium	Hallucinations	Mydriasis, tremor, diaphoresis, seizures, perforated nasal septum	EKG abnormalities, increased CPK
Cyclic antidepressants	Tachycardia, hypotension, hyperthermia	Decreased, including coma	Confusion, dizziness	Mydriasis, dry mucous membranes, distended bladder, decreased bowel sounds, flushed, seizures	Long QRS complex, cardiac dysrhythmias
Iron	Early: Normal; Late: Hypotension, tachycardia	Normal; lethargic if hypotensive	Nausea, vomiting, diarrhea, abdominal pain, hematemesis	Abdominal tenderness	Heme + stool and vomit, metabolic acidosis, EKG and x-ray findings, elevated serum iron (early); child: hyperglycemia, leukocytosis
Opioids	Hypotension, bradycardia, hypoventilation, hypothermia	Decreased, including coma	Intoxication	Miosis, absent bowel sounds	Abnormal ABGs
Salicylates	Hyperventilation, hyperthermia	Agitation; lethargy, including coma	Tinnitus, nausea, vomiting, confusion	Diaphoresis, tender abdomen	Anion gap metabolic acidosis, respiratory alkalosis, abnormal LFTs, and coagulation studies
Theophylline	Tachycardia, hypotension, hyperventilation, hyperthermia	Agitation, lethargy, including coma	Nausea, vomiting, diaphoresis, tremor, confusion	Seizures, arrhythmias	Hypokalemia, hyperglycemia, metabolic acidosis, abnormal EKG

TOXIDROMES (Continued)

Examples of Toxidromes

Toxidromes	Pattern	Example of Drugs	Treatment Approach
Anticholinergic	Fever, ileus, flushing, tachycardia, urinary retention, inability to sweat, visual blurring, and mydriasis. Central manifestations include myoclonus, choreoathetosis, toxic psychosis with lilliputian hallucinations, seizures, and coma.	Antihistamines Baclofen Benztropine Jimson weed Methylpyroline Phenothiazines Propantheline Tricyclic antidepressants	Physostigmine for life-threatening symptoms only; may predispose to arrhythmias*
Cholinergic	Characterized by salivation, lacrimation, urination, defecation, gastrointestinal cramps, and emesis ("sludge"). Bradycardia and bronchoconstriction may also be seen.	Carbamate Organophosphates Pilocarpine	• Atropine* • Pralidoxime for organophosphate insecticides*
Extrapyramidal	Choreoathetosis, hyperreflexia, trismus, opisthotonos, rigidity, and tremor	Haloperidol Phenothiazines	• Diphenhydramine • Benztropine
Hallucinogenic	Perceptual distortions, synthesis, depersonalization, and derealization	Amphetamines Cannabinoids Cocaine Indole alkaloids Phencyclidine	Benzodiazepine
Narcotic	Altered mental status, unresponsiveness, shallow respirations, slow respiratory rate or periodic breathing, miosis, bradycardia, hypothermia	Opiates Dextromethorphan Pentazocine Propoxyphene	Naloxone*

Examples of Toxidromes *(continued)*

Toxidromes	Pattern	Example of Drugs	Treatment Approach
Sedative/Hypnotic	Manifested by sedation with progressive deterioration of central nervous system function. Coma, stupor, confusion, apnea, delirium, or hallucinations may accompany this pattern.	Anticonvulsants Antipsychotics Barbiturates Benzodiazepines Ethanol Ethchlorvynol Fentanyl Glutethimide Meprobamate Methadone Methocarbamol Opiates Quinazolines Propoxyphene Tricyclic antidepressants	• Naloxone* • Flumazenil; usually not recommended due to increased risk of seizures* • Urinary alkalinization (barbiturates)
Seizuregenic	May mimic stimulant pattern with hyperthermia, hyperreflexia, and tremors being prominent signs	Anticholinergics Camphor Chlorinated hydrocarbons Cocaine Isoniazid Lidocaine Lindane Nicotine Phencyclidine Strychnine Xanthines	• Antiseizure medications • Pyridoxine for isoniazid* • Extracorporeal removal of drug (ie, lindane, camphor, xanthines) • Physostigmine for anticholinergic agents*

TOXIDROMES *(Continued)*

Examples of Toxidromes *(continued)*

Toxidromes	Pattern	Example of Drugs	Treatment Approach
Serotonin	Confusion, myoclonus, hyperreflexia, diaphoresis, tremor, facial flushing, diarrhea, fever, trismus	Clomipramine Fluoxetine Isoniazid L-tryptophan Paroxetine Phenelzine Sertraline Tranylcypromine Drug combinations include: • MAO inhibitors with L-tryptophan • Fluoxetine or meperidine • Fluoxetine with carbamazepine or sertraline • Clomipramine and meclobemide • Trazadol and buspirone • Paroxetine and dextromethorphan	Withdrawal of drug/benzodiazepine
Solvent	Lethargy, confusion, dizziness, headache, restlessness, incoordination, derealization, depersonalization	Acetone Chlorinated hydrocarbons Hydrocarbons Naphthalene Trichloroethane Toluene	Avoid catecholamines

Examples of Toxidromes (continued)

Toxidromes	Pattern	Example of Drugs	Treatment Approach
Stimulant	Restlessness, excessive speech and motor activity, tachycardia, tremor, and insomnia — may progress to seizure. Other effects noted include euphoria, mydriasis, anorexia, and paranoia.	Amphetamines Caffeine (xanthines) Cocaine Ephedrine/pseudoephedrine Methylphenidate Nicotine Phencyclidine	Benzodiazepines
Uncoupling of oxidative phosphylation	Hyperthermia, tachypnea, diaphoresis, metabolic acidosis (usually)	Aluminum phosphide Aspirin/Salicylates 2,4-Dichlorophenol Di-n-Butyl Phthalate Dinitrophenols Dinitro-o-cresols Hexachlorobutadiene Phosphorus Pentachlorophenol Tin (?) Zinc phosphide	Sodium bicarbonate to treat metabolic acidosis Patient cooling techniques Avoidance of atropine or salicylate agents Hemodialysis may be required for acidosis treatment

From Nice A, Leikin JB, Maturen A, et al. "Toxidrome Recognition to Improve Efficiency of Emergency Urine Drug Screens." *Ann Emerg Med*, 1988, 17:676-80.
*See the Poison Control Center Antidote Chart.

ADVERSE HEMATOLOGIC EFFECTS, DRUGS ASSOCIATED WITH

Drug	Red Cell Aplasia	Thrombo-cytopenia	Neutro-penia	Pancyto-penia	Hemolysis
Acetazolamide		+	+	+	
Allopurinol			+		
Amiodarone	+				
Amphotericin B				+	
Amrinone		++			
Asparaginase		+++	+++	+++	++
Barbiturates		+		+	
Benzocaine					++
Captopril			++		+
Carbamazepine		++	+		
Cephalosporins			+		++
Chloramphenicol		+	++	+++	
Chlordiazepoxide			+	+	
Chloroquine		+			
Chlorothiazides		++			
Chlorpropamide	+	++	+	++	+
Chlortetracycline				+	
Chlorthalidone			+		
Cimetidine		+	++	+	
Codeine		+			
Colchicine				+	
Cyclophosphamide		+++	+++	+++	+
Dapsone					+++
Desipramine		++			
Digitalis		+			
Digitoxin		++			
Erythromycin		+			
Estrogen		+		+	
Ethacrynic acid			+		
Fluorouracil		+++	+++	+++	+
Furosemide		+	+		
Gold salts	+	+++	+++	+++	
Heparin		++		+	
Ibuprofen			+		+
Imipramine			++		
Indomethacin		+	++	+	
Isoniazid		+		+	
Isosorbide dinitrate					+
Levodopa					++
Meperidine		+			
Meprobamate		+	+	+	
Methimazole			++		
Methyldopa		++			+++
Methotrexate		+++	+++	+++	++
Methylene blue					+
Metronidazole			+		
Nalidixic acid					+
Naproxen				+	
Nitrofurantoin			++		+
Nitroglycerine		+			
Penicillamine		++	+		
Penicillins		+	++	+	+++
Phenazopyridine					+++
Phenothiazines		+	++	+++	+
Phenylbutazone		+	++	+++	+
Phenytoin		++	++	++	+

Drug	Red Cell Aplasia	Thrombo-cytopenia	Neutro-penia	Pancyto-penia	Hemolysis
Potassium iodide		+			
Prednisone		+			
Primaquine					+++
Procainamide			+		
Procarbazine		+	++	++	+
Propylthiouracil		+	++	+	+
Quinidine		+++	+		
Quinine		+++	+		
Reserpine		+			
Rifampicin		++	+		+++
Spironolactone			+		
Streptomycin		+		+	
Sulfamethoxazole with trimethoprim			+		
Sulfonamides	+	++	++	++	++
Sulindac	+	+	+	+	
Tetracyclines		+			+
Thioridazine			++		
Tolbutamide		++	+	++	
Triamterene					+
Valproate	+				
Vancomycin			+		

+ = rare or single reports.

++ = occasional reports.

+++ = substantial number of reports.

Adapted from D'Arcy PF and Griffin JP, eds, *Iatrogenic Diseases*, New York, NY: Oxford University Press, 1986, 128-30.

BREAST-FEEDING AND DRUGS

Adapted from American Academy of Pediatrics Committee on Drugs:
"Transfer of Drugs and Other Chemicals Into Human Milk,"
Pediatrics, 1994, 93:137-50.

The following questions and options should be considered when prescribing drug therapy to lactating women (1) Is the drug therapy really necessary? Consultation between the pediatrician and the mother's physician can be most useful. (2) Use the safest drug, for example, acetaminophen rather than aspirin for analgesia. (3) If there is a possibility that a drug may present a risk to the infant, consideration should be given to measurement of blood concentrations in the nursing infant. (4) Drug exposure to the nursing infant may be minimized by having the mother take the medication just after she has breast-fed the infant and/or just before the infant is due to have a lengthy sleep period.

In tables 1-6, the fact that a pharmacologic or chemical agent does not appear on the lists is not meant to imply that it is not transferred into human milk or that it does not have an effect on the infant; it only indicates that there were no reports found in the literature.

Table 1. Drugs That Are Contraindicated During Breast-Feeding

Drug	Reason for Concern, Reported Sign or Symptom in Infant, or Effect on Lactation
Bromocriptine	Suppresses lactation; may be hazardous to the mother
Cocaine	Cocaine intoxication
Cyclophosphamide	Possible immune suppression; unknown effect on growth or association with carcinogenesis; neutropenia
Cyclosporine	Possible immune suppression; unknown effect on growth or association with carcinogenesis
Doxorubicin*	Possible immune suppression; unknown effect on growth or association with carcinogenesis
Ergotamine	Vomiting, diarrhea. convulsions (doses used in migraine medications)
Lithium	One-third to one-half therapeutic blood concentration in infants
Methotrexate	Possible immune suppression; unknown effect on growth or association with carcinogenesis; neutropenia
Phencyclidine (PCP)	Potent hallucinogen
Phenindone	Anticoagulant; increased prothrombin and partial thromboplastin time in one infant; not used in the United States

*Drug is concentrated in human milk

Table 2. Drugs of Abuse: Contraindicated During Breast-Feeding*

Amphetamine†	Marijuana
Cocaine	Nicotine (smoking)
Heroin	Phencyclidine

*The Committee on Drugs strongly believes that nursing mothers should not ingest any compounds listed in Table 2. Not only are they hazardous to the nursing infant, but they are also detrimental to the physical and emotional health of the mother. This list is obviously not complete; no drug of abuse should be ingested by nursing mothers even though adverse reports are not in the literature.

†Drug is concentrated in human milk

Table 3. Radioactive Compounds That Require Temporary Cessation of Breast-Feeding*

Drug	Recommended Time for Cessation of Breast-Feeding
Copper 64 (^{64}Cu)	Radioactivity in milk present at 50 h
Gallium 67 (^{67}Ga)	Radioactivity in milk present for 2 wk
Indium 111 (^{111}In)	Very small amount present at 20 h
Iodine 123 (^{123}I)	Radioactivity in milk present up to 36 h
Iodine 125 (^{125}I)	Radioactivity in milk present for 12 d
Iodine 131 (^{131}I)	Radioactivity in milk present 2-14 d, depending on study
Radioactive sodium	Radioactivity in milk present 96 h
Technetium-99m (^{99m}Tc), ^{99m}Rc macroaggregates, ^{99m}Tc O4	Radioactivity in milk present 15 h to 3 d

*Consult nuclear medicine physician before performing diagnostic study so that radionuclide that has shortest excretion time in breast milk can be used. Before study, the mother should pump her breast and store enough milk in freezer for feeding the infant; after study, the mother should pump her breast to maintain milk production but discard all milk pumped for the required time that radioactivity is present in milk. Milk samples can be screened by radiology departments for radioactivity before resumption of nursing.

Table 4. Drugs Whose Effect on Nursing Infants Is Unknown But May Be of Concern

Psychotropic drugs, the compounds listed under antianxiety, antidepressant, and antipsychotic categories, are of special concern when given to nursing mothers for long periods. Although there are no case reports of adverse effects in breast-feeding infants, these drugs do appear in human milk and thus conceivably after short-term and long-term central nervous system function.

Antianxiety	Antidepressant	Antipsychotic
Diazepam	Amitriptyline	Chlorpromazine
Lorazepam	Amoxapine	Chlorprothixene
Midazolam	Desipramine	Haloperidol
Perphenazine	Dothiepin	Mesoridazine
Prazepam*	Doxepin	
Quazepam	Fluoxetine	**Miscellaneous**
Temazepam	Fluvoxamine	Chloramphenicol
	Imipramine	Metoclopramide*
	Trazodone	Metronidazole
		Tinidazole

*Drug is concentrated in human milk

Table 5. Drugs That Have Been Associated With Significant Effects on Some Nursing Infants and Should Be Given to Nursing Mothers With Caution*

Drug	Reported Effect
Aspirin (salicylates)	Metabolic acidosis (one case)
Clemastine	Drowsiness, irritability, refusal to feed, high-pitched cry, neck stiffness (one case)
Mesalamine	Diarrhea (one case)
Phenobarbital	Sedation; infantile spasms after weaning from milk-containing phenobarbital, methemoglobinemia (one case)
Primidone	Sedation, feeding problems
Sulfasalazine (salicylazosulfapyridine)	Bloody diarrhea (one case)

*Measure blood concentration in the infant when possible.

BREAST-FEEDING AND DRUGS *(Continued)*

Table 6. Maternal Medication Usually Compatible With Breast-Feeding

Acebutolol
Acetaminophen
Acetazolamide
Acitretin
Acyclovir*
Alcohol (ethanol)
Allopurinol
Amoxicillin
Antimony
Atenolol
Atropine
Azapropazone (apazone)
Aztreonam
B_1 (thiamine)
B_6 (pyridoxine)
B_{12}
Baclofen
Barbiturate
Bendroflumethiazide
Bishydroxycoumarin
  (Dicumarol®)
Bromide
Butorphanol
Caffeine
Captopril
Carbamazepine
Carbimazole
Cascara
Cefadroxil
Cefazolin
Cefotaxime
Cefoxitin
Cefprozil
Ceftazidime
Ceftriaxone
Chloral hydrate
Chloroform
Chloroquine
Chlorothiazide
Chlorthalidone
Cimetidine*
Cisapride
Cisplatin
Clindamycin
Clogestone
Clomipramine
Codeine
Colchicine
Contraceptive pill with
  estrogen and
  progesterone
Cycloserine
D (vitamin)
Danthron
Dapsone

Dexbrompheniramine
  maleate with
  d-isoephedrine
Digoxin
Diltiazem
Dipyrone
Disopyramide
Domperidone
Dyphylline*
Enalapril
Erythromycin*
Estradiol
Ethambutol
Ethanol
Ethosuximide
Fentanyl
Flecainide
Flufenamic acid
Fluorescein
Folic acid
Gold salts
Halothane
Hydralazine
Hydrochlorothiazide
Hydroxychloroquine*
Ibuprofen
Indomethacin
Iodides
Iodine
Iodine (povidone-iodine/
  vaginal douche)
Iopanoic acid
Isoniazid
K_1 (vitamin)
Kanamycin
Ketorolac
Labetalol
Levonorgestrel
Lidocaine
Loperamide
Magnesium sulfate
Medroxyprogesterone
Mefenamic acid
Methadone
Methimazole (active
  metabolite of carbi-
  mazole)
Methocarbamol
Methyldopa
Methprylon
Metoprolol*
Metrizamide
Mexiletine
Minoxidil

Morphine
Moxalactam
Nadolol*
Nalidixic acid
Naproxen
Nefopam
Nifedipine
Nitrofurantoin
Norethynodrel
Norsteroids
Noscapine
Oxprenolol
Phenylbutazone
Phenytoin
Piroxicam
Prednisone
Procainamide
Progesterone
Propoxyphene
Propranolol
Propylthiouracil
Pseudoephedrine*
Pyridostigmine
Pyrimethamine
Quinidine
Quinine
Riboflavin
Rifampin
Scopolamine
Secobarbital
Senna
Sotalol
Spironolactone
Streptomycin
Sulbactam
Sulfapyridine
Sulfisoxazole
Suprofen
Terbutaline
Tetracycline
Theophylline
Thiopental
Thiouracil
Ticarcillin
Timolol
Tolbutamide
Tolmetin
Trimethoprim and sulfa-
  methoxazole
Triprolidine
Valproic acid
Verapamil
Warfarin
Zolpidem

*Drug is concentrated in human milk.

Antimicrobial Agents Taken by Mothers That Are Not Compatible With Breast-Feeding or Are Cause for Concern

Maternal Antimicrobial Agent	Reported Sign or Symptom in Infant or Possible Cause for Concern	Committee on Drugs Evaluation
Chloramphenicol	Possible idiosyncratic bone marrow suppression	Unknown effect
Metronidazole	*In vitro* mutagen; may discontinue breast-feeding 12-24 hours to allow excretion of dose when single-dose therapy is given to mother	Unknown effect
Ciprofloxacin	Theoretically may affect cartilage development of weight-bearing joints; case report of pseudomembranous colitis in a 2-month old nursing infant	Not evaluated
Norfloxacin, ofloxacin, lomefloxacin, cinoxacin, enoxacin	Theoretically may affect cartilage development of weight-bearing joints	Not evaluated
Isoniazid	None; acetyl metabolite also secreted; may be hepatotoxic	Usually compatible with breast-feeding
Nalidixic acid	Hemolysis in infant with G-6-PD* deficiency	Usually compatible with breast-feeding
Nitrofurantoin	Hemolysis in infant with G-6-PD* deficiency	Usually compatible with breast-feeding
Sulfapyridine	Caution in infant with jaundice or G-6-PD* deficiency, and in ill, stressed, or premature infant	Usually compatible with breast-feeding
Sulfisoxazole	Caution in infant with jaundice or G-6-PD* deficiency, and in ill, stressed, or premature infant	Usually compatible with breast-feeding

*Glucose-6-phosphate dehydrogenase.

Adapted from the *1997 Red Book - Report of the Committee on Infectious Diseases*, 24th ed.

Antimicrobial Agents Listed by the American Academy of Pediatrics (AAP) Committee on Drugs as Usually Compatible With Breast-Feeding*

Acyclovir	Dapsone†‡
Amoxicillin	Erythromycin§
Aztreonam	Kanamycin
Cefadaroxil	Moxalactam
Cefazolin	Pyrimethamine
Cefotaxime	Quinine
Cefoxitin	Rifampin
Ceprozil	Streptomycin
Ceftazidime	Sulbactam
Ceftriaxone	Tetracycline‡¶
Chloroquine	Ticarcillin
Clindamycin	Trimethoprim-sulfamethoxazole

*American Academy of Pediatrics Committee on Drugs, The Transfer of Drugs and Other Chemicals Into Human Milk, *Pediatrics*, 1994, 93:137-50.

†Sulfonamide detected in infant's urine.

‡While not listed as such by the Committee on Drugs, some experts recommend that the drug should be avoided in lactating women.

§Concentrated in human milk.

¶Negligible absorption by infant.

Adapted from the *1997 Red Book - Report of the Committee on Infectious Diseases*, 24th ed.

DISCOLORATION OF FECES DUE TO DRUGS

Black
Acetazolamide
Aluminum hydroxide
Aminophylline
Amphetamine
Amphotericin B
Bismuth salts
Chlorpropamide
Clindamycin
Corticosteroids
Cyclophosphamide
Cytarabine
Digitalis
Ethacrynic acid
Ferrous salts
Fluorouracil
Hydralazine
Hydrocortisone
Iodide-containing drugs
Melphalan

Methotrexate
Methylprednisolone
Phenylephrine
Potassium salts
Prednisolone
Procarbazine
Sulfonamides
Tetracycline
Theophylline
Thiotepa
Triamcinolone
Warfarin

Blue
Chloramphenicol
Methylene blue

Green
Indomethacin
Medroxyprogesterone

Yellow/Yellow-Green
Senna

Orange-Red
Phenazopyridine
Rifampin

Pink/Red
Anticoagulants
Aspirin
Barium
Heparin
Oxyphenbutazone
Phenylbutazone
Tetracycline syrup

White/Speckling
Antibiotics (oral)
Barium

DISCOLORATION OF URINE DUE TO DRUGS

Black/Brown/Dark
Cascara
Chloroquine
Ferrous salts
Metronidazole
Nitrofurantoin
Quinine
Senna

Blue
Triamterene

Blue-Green
Amitriptyline
Methylene blue

Orange/Yellow
Heparin
Phenazopyridine
Rifampin
Sulfasalazine
Warfarin

Red/Pink
Daunorubicin

Doxorubicin
Heparin
Ibuprofen
Oxyphenbutazone
Phenylbutazone
Phenytoin
Rifampin
Senna

FEVER DUE TO DRUGS

Most Common
Cephalosporins
Iodides
Isoniazid
Methyldopa
Penicillins
Phenytoin
Procainamide
Quinidine
Streptomycin
Sulfas
Vancomycin

Allopurinol
Antihistamines
Azathioprine
Barbiturates
Bleomycin
Carbamazepine
Cimetidine
Cisplatin
Clofibrate
Colistimethate
Diazoxide
Folic acid

Less Common
Hydralazine
Hydroxyurea
Ibuprofen
Mercaptopurine
Nitrofurantoin
Para-aminosalicylic acid
Pentazocine
Procarbazine
Propylthiouracil
Sulindac
Streptozocin
Triamterene

Drug Intell Clin Pharm, Table 2, "Drugs Implicated in Causing a Fever," 1986, 20:416.

DRUGS IN PREGNANCY

MEDICATIONS KNOWN TO BE TERATOGENS

Alcohol
Androgens
Anticonvulsants
Antineoplastics
Diethylstilbestrol
Isotretinoin

Iodides
Live vaccines
Misoprostol
Tetracycline
Thalidomide
Warfarin

MEDICATIONS SUSPECTED TO BE TERATOGENS

Antithyroid drugs
Benzodiazepines
Estrogens
Fluoroquinolones

Lithium
Oral hypoglycemic drugs
Progestogens
Tricyclic antidepressants

MEDICATIONS WITH NO KNOWN ADVERSE EFFECTS IN PREGNANCY*

Acetaminophen
Cephalosporins
Corticosteroids
Docusate sodium
Erythromycin

Multiple vitamins
Narcotic analgesics
Penicillins
Phenothiazines
Thyroid hormones

*These drugs appear to have minimal risk when used judiciously in usual doses under the supervision of a medical professional.

Adapted from DiPiro JT, Talbert RL, Hayes PE, et al, "Therapeutic Considerations During Pregnancy and Lactation," *Pharmacotherapy: A Pathophysiologic Approach*, 2nd ed, New York, NY: Elsevier, 1992.

LABORATORY DETECTION OF DRUGS

Agent	Time Detectable in Urine*
Alcohol	12-24 h
Amobarbital	2-4 d
Amphetamine	2-4 d
Butalbital	2-4 d
Cannabinoids	
Occasional use	2-7 d
Regular use	30 d
Cocaine (benzoylecgonine)	12-72 h
Codeine	2-4 d
Chlordiazepoxide	30 d
Diazepam	30 d
Dilaudid®	2-4 d
Ethanol	12-24 h
Heroin (morphine)	2-4 d
Hydromorphone	2-4 d
Librium®	30 d
Marijuana	
Occasional use	2-7 d
Regular use	30 d
Methamphetamine	2-4 d
Methaqualone	2-4 d
Morphine	2-4 d
Pentobarbital	2-4 d
Phencyclidine (PCP)	
Occasional use	2-7 d
Regular use	30 d
Phenobarbital	30 d
Quaalude®	2-4 d
Secobarbital	2-4 d
Valium®	30 d

Chang JY, "Drug Testing and Interpretation of Results," *Pharmchem Newsletter*, 1989, 17:1.

*The periods of detection for the various abused drugs listed above should be taken as estimates since the actual figures will vary due to metabolism, user, laboratory, and excretion.

LOW POTASSIUM DIET

Potassium is a mineral found in most all foods except sugar and lard. It plays a role in maintaining normal muscle activity and helps to keep body fluids in balance. Too much potassium in the blood can lead to changes in heartbeat and can lead to muscle weakness. The kidneys normally help to keep blood potassium controlled, but in kidney disease or when certain drugs are taken, dietary potassium must be limited to maintain a normal level of potassium in the blood.

The following guideline includes 2-3 g of potassium per day.

1. **Milk Group:** Limit to one cup serving of milk or milk product (yogurt, cottage cheese, ice cream, pudding).

2. **Fruit Group:** Limit to two servings daily from the low potassium choices. Watch serving sizes. Avoid the high potassium choices.

> **Low Potassium**
> Apple, 1 small
> Apple juice, applesauce ½ cup
> Apricot, 1 medium or ½ cup canned in syrup
> Blueberries, ½ cup
> Cherries, canned in syrup ⅓ cup
> Cranberries, cranberry juice ½ cup
> Fruit cocktail, canned in syrup ½ cup
> Grapes, 10 fresh
> Lemon, lime 1 fresh
> Mandarin orange, canned in syrup ½ cup
> Nectar: apricot, pear, peach ½ cup
> Peach, 1 small or ½ cup canned with syrup
> Pear, 1 small or ½ cup canned with syrup
> Pineapple, ½ cup raw or canned with syrup
> Plums, 1 small or ½ cup canned with syrup
> Tangerine, 1 small
> Watermelon, ½ cup
>
> **High Potassium**
> Avocado
> Banana
> Cantaloupe
> Cherries, fresh
> Dried fruits
> Grapefruit, fresh and juice
> Honeydew melon
> Kiwi
> Mango
> Nectarine
> Orange, fresh and juice
> Papaya
> Prunes, prune juice
> Raisins

3. Avoid use of the following salt substitutes due to their high potassium contents: Adolph's, Lawry's Season Salt Substitute, No Salt, Morton Season Salt Free, Nu Salt, Papa Dash, and Morton Lite Salt.

ORAL DOSAGES THAT SHOULD NOT BE CRUSHED

There are a variety of reasons for crushing tablets or capsule contents prior to administering to the patient. Patients may have nasogastric tubes which do not permit the administration of tablets or capsules; an oral solution for a particular medication may not be available from the manufacturer or readily prepared by pharmacy; patients may have difficulty swallowing capsules or tablets; or mixing of powdered medication with food or drink may make the drug more palatable.

Generally, medications which should not be crushed fall into one of the following categories:

- **Extended-Release Products**. The formulation of some tablets is specialized as to allow the medication within it to be slowly released into the body. This is sometimes accomplished by centering the drug within the core of the tablet, with a subsequent shedding of multiple layers around the core. Wax melts in the GI tract. Slow-K® is an example of this. Capsules may contain beads which have multiple layers which are slowly dissolved with time.

- **Medications Which Are Irritating to the Stomach**. Tablets which are irritating to the stomach may be enteric coated which delays release of the drug until the time when it reaches the small intestine. Enteric-coated aspirin is an example of this.

- **Foul Tasting Medication**. Some drugs are quite unpleasant in their taste and the manufacturer, to increase their palatability will coat the tablet in a sugar coating. By crushing the tablet, this sugar coating is lost and the patient tastes the unpleasant tasting medication.

- **Sublingual Medication**. Medication intended for use under the tongue should not be crushed. While it appears to be obvious, it is not always easy to determine if a medication is to be used sublingually. Sublingual medications should indicate on the package that they are intended for sublingual use.

- **Effervescent Tablets**. These are tablets which, when dropped into a liquid, quickly dissolve to yield a solution. Many effervescent tablets, when crushed, lose their ability to quickly dissolve.

Recommendations

1. It is not advisable to crush certain medications.

2. Consult individual monographs prior to crushing capsule or tablet.

3. If crushing a tablet or capsule is contraindicated, consult with your pharmacist to determine whether an oral solution exists or can be compounded.

4. Refer to individual drug monograph for crushing information.

Summary of Drug Formulations That Preclude Crushing

Type	Reason(s) for the Formulation
Enteric-coated	Designed to pass through the stomach intact with drug released in the intestines to: • prevent destruction of drug by stomach acids • prevent stomach irritation • delay onset of action
Extended release	Designed to release drug over an extended period of time. Such products include: • multiple layered tablets releasing drug as each layer is dissolved • mixed release pellets that dissolve at different time intervals • special matrixes that are themselves inert but slowly release drug from the matrix
Sublingual buccal	Designed to dissolve quickly in oral fluids for rapid absorption by the abundant blood supply of the mouth
Miscellaneous	Drugs that: • produce oral mucosa irritation • are extremely bitter • contain dyes or inherently could stain teeth and mucosal tissue

OVER-THE-COUNTER PRODUCTS*

Generic Name	Brand Name	Comments
Analgesics		
Acetaminophen and aspirin	Excedrin® Extra Strength Tablet; Gelpirin® Geltabs; Goody's® Headache Powders	Relief of mild to moderate pain or fever; avoid alcoholic beverages; take with food or a full glass of water
Acetaminophen and diphenhydramine	Arthritis Foundation® NightTime Max Strength Caplet; Excedrin P.M.®; Legatrin PM® Caplet; Midol® PM Caplet	Relief of mild to moderate pain or sinus headache
Acetaminophen and phenyltoloxamine	Percogesic® Tablet	Relief of mild to moderate pain
Capsaicin	Capsin®; Capzasin-P®; No Pain-HP®; R-Gel®; Zostrix®; Zostrix®-HP	FDA approved for the topical treatment of pain associated with postherpetic neuralgia, rheumatoid arthritis, osteoarthritis, diabetic neuropathy, and postsurgical pain. Unlabeled use: Treatment of pain associated with psoriasis, chronic neuralgias unresponsive to other forms of therapy, and intractable pruritis.
Choline salicylate	Arthropan®	Temporary relief of pain of rheumatoid arthritis, rheumatic fever, osteoarthritis, and other conditions for which oral salicylates are recommended; useful in patients in which there is difficulty in administering doses in a tablet or capsule dosage form because of the liquid dosage form
Triethanolamine salicylate	Myoflex® Cream; Sportscreme®	Relief of pain of muscular aches, rheumatism, neuralgia, sprains, arthritis on intact skin
Antacids, Antiflatulents, or Antiemetics		
Aluminum carbonate	Basaljel®	Hyperacidity; hyperphosphatemia
Aluminum hydroxide and magnesium carbonate	Gaviscon® Liquid	Temporary relief of symptoms associated with gastric acidity
Aluminum hydroxide and magnesium hydroxide	Aludrox®; Maalox® Plus; Maalox® Therapeutic Concentrate	Antacid; used to treat hyperphosphatemia in renal failure
Aluminum hydroxide and magnesium trisilicate	Gaviscon®-2 Tablet; Gaviscon® Tablet	Temporary relief of hyperacidity
Aluminum hydroxide, magnesium hydroxide, and simethicone	Di-Gel®; Gas-Ban DS®; Gelusil®; Maalox® Plus; Magalox Plus®; Mylanta®-II; Mylanta®	Temporary relief of hyperacidity associated with gas; may be used for indications associated with other antacids
Calcium carbonate and magnesium carbonate	Mylanta® Gelcaps®	Relief of hyperacidity
Calcium carbonate and simethicone	Titralac® Plus Liquid	Relief of acid indigestion, heartburn, peptic esophagitis, hiatal hernia, and gas
Cyclizine	Marezine®	Prevention and treatment of nausea, vomiting, and vertigo associated with motion sickness; control of postoperative nausea and vomiting
Dihydroxyaluminum sodium carbonate	Rolaids® Chewable Tablet	Symptomatic relief of upset stomach associated with hyperacidity
Dimenhydrinate	Calm-X® Oral; Dimetabs® Oral; Dramamine® Oral; Marmine® Oral; Tega-Vert® Oral; TripTone® Caplets®	Treatment and prevention of nausea, vertigo, and vomiting associated with motion sickness
Magaldrate and simethicone	Riopan Plus ®	Relief of hyperacidity associated with peptic ulcer, gastritis, peptic esophagitis, and hiatal hernia

OVER-THE-COUNTER PRODUCTS* *(Continued)*

Generic Name	Brand Name	Comments
Phosphorated carbohydrate solution	Emecheck® Liquid; Emetrol® Liquid; Naus-A-Way® Liquid; Nausetrol® Liquid	Relief of nausea associated with upset stomach that occurs with intestinal flu, pregnancy, food indescretions, and emotional upsets
Simethicone	Degas®; Flatulex®; Gas-X®; Maalox Anti-Gas®; Mylanta Gas®; Mylicon®; Phazyme®; Silain®; Ovol® (Canadian)	Relieves flatulence and functional gastric bloating, and postoperative gas pains
Antidiarrheals and Laxatives		
Attapulgite	Children's Kaopectate®; Diasorb®; Kaopectate® Advanced Formula; Kaopectate® Maximum Strength Caplets; Rheaban®	Symptomatic treatment of diarrhea
Bisacodyl	Bisac-Evac®; Bisacodyl Uniserts®; Bisco-Lax®; Carter's Little Pills®; Clysodrast®; Dacodyl®; Deficol®; Dulcolax®; Fleet® Laxative; Theralax®	Treatment of constipation; colonic evacuation prior to procedures or examination
Calcium polycarbophil	Equalactin® Chewable Tablet; Fiberall® Chewable Tablet; FiberCon® Tablet; Fiber-Lax® Tablet; Mitrolan® Chewable Tablet	Treatment of constipation or diarrhea by restoring a more normal moisture level and providing bulk in the patient's intestinal tract; calcium polycarbophil is supplied as the approved substitute whenever a bulk-forming laxative is ordered in a tablet, capsule, wafer, or other oral solid dosage form
Castor oil	Alphamul®; Emulsoil®; Fleet® Flavored Castor Oil; Neoloid®; Purge®	Preparation for rectal or bowel examination or surgery; rarely used to relieve constipation; also applied to skin as emollient and protectant
Docusate and casanthranol	Dialose® Plus Capsule; Diocto C®; Diocto-K Plus®; Dioctolose Plus®; Disanthrol®; DSMC Plus®; D-S-S Plus®; Genasoft® Plus; Peri-Colace®; Pro-Sof® Plus; Regulace®; Silace-C®	Treatment of constipation generally associated with dry, hard stools and decreased intestinal motility
Glycerin	Fleet® Babylax® Rectal; Sani-Supp® Suppository	Constipation
Kaolin and pectin	Kaodene®; Kao-Spen®; Kapectolin®	Treatment of uncomplicated diarrhea
Lactase enzyme	Dairy Ease®; Lactaid®; Lactrase®	Helps to digest lactose in milk for patients with lactose intolerance; may be administered with meals
Magnesium hydroxide and mineral oil emulsion	Haley's M-O® Oral Suspension	Short-term treatment of occasional constipation
Malt soup extract	Maltsuprex®	Short-term treatment of constipation
Methylcellulose	Citrucel® Powder	Adjunct in treatment of constipation
Mineral oil	Fleet® Mineral Oil Enema; Kondremul®; Milkinol®; Neo-Cultol®; Zymenol®	Temporary relief of constipation; relieve fecal impaction; preparation for bowel studies or surgery
Senna	Black Draught®; Senexon®; Senna-Gen®; Senokot®; Senolax®; X-Prep® Liquid	Short-term treatment of constipation; evacuate the colon for bowel or rectal examinations; liquid may be administered with fruit juice or milk to mask taste
Sodium phosphate	Fleet® Enema; Fleet® Phospho®-Soda	Short-term treatment of constipation; evacuation of the colon for rectal and bowel exams; source of sodium and phosphorus; treatment and prevention of hypophosphatemia
Asthma		
Aminophylline, amobarbital, and ephedrine	Amesec® Capsules	Symptomatic relief of asthma; should be administered with water 1 hour before or 2 hours after meals

Generic Name	Brand Name	Comments
Cough/Cold or Allergy		
Acetaminophen and dextromethorphan	Bayer® Select® Chest Cold Caplets; Drixoral® Cough & Sore Throat Liquid Caps	Treat mild to moderate pain; symptomatic relief of coughs caused by minor viral upper respiratory tract infections or inhaled irritants; most effective for a chronic nonproductive cough
Acetaminophen and pseudoephedrine	Allerest® No Drowsiness; Bayer® Select Head Cold Caplets; Coldrine®; Dristan® Cold Caplets; Dynafed®, Maximum Strength; Ornex® No Drowsiness; Sinarest®, No Drowsiness; Sine-Aid®, Maximum Strength; Sine-Off® Maximum Strength No Drowsiness Formula; Sinus Excedrin® Extra Strength; Sinus-Relief®; Sinutab® Without Drowsiness; Tylenol® Sinus, Maximum Strength	Temporary relief of sinus symptoms with no drowsiness
Acetaminophen, chlorpheniramine, and pseudoephedrine	Alka-Seltzer® Plus Cold Liqui-Gels Capsules; Aspirin-Free Bayer® Select® Allergy Sinus Caplets; Co-Hist®; Sinutab® Tablet	Temporary relief of sinus symptoms
Acetaminophen, dextromethorphan, and pseudoephedrine	Alka-Seltzer® Plus Flu & Body Aches Non-Drowsy Liqui-Gels; Comtrex® Maximum Strength Non-Drowsy; Sudafed® Severe Cold; Theraflu Non-Drowsy Formula Maximum Strength; Tylenol® Cold No Drowsiness; Tylenol® Flu Maximum Strength	Relief of cold and flu symptoms with no drowsiness
Brompheniramine	Bromarest®; Brombay®; Bromphen®; Brotane®; Chlorphed®; Cophene-B®; Diamine T.D.®; Dimetane® Extentabs®; Nasahist B®; ND-Stat®; Oraminic ® II; Sinusol-B®; Veltane®	Treatment of seasonal and perennial allergic rhinitis and other allergic symptoms including urticaria
Brompheniramine and phenylephrine	Dimetane® Decongestant Elixir	Temporary relief of symptoms of seasonal and perennial allergic rhinitis, and vasomotor rhinitis, including nasal obstruction
Brompheniramine and phenylpropanolamine	Bromalate® Elixir; Bromanate® Elixir; Bromatapp®; Bromphen® Tablet; Cold & Allergy® Elixir; Dimaphen® Tablet; Dimaphen® Elixir; Dimetapp® 4-Hour Liqui-Gel Capsule; Dimetapp® Elixir; Dimetapp® Tablet; Dimetapp® Extentabs®; Genatap® Elixir; Myphetapp®; Tamine®; Vicks® DayQuil® Allergy Relief 4 Hour Tablet	Temporary relief of nasal congestion, runny nose, sneezing, and itchy, watery eyes
Brompheniramine and pseudoephedrine	Brofed® Elixir; Bromfed® Syrup; Bromfed® Tablet; Bromfenex® PD; Drixoral® Syrup	Temporary relief of symptoms of seasonal and perennial allergic rhinitis, and vasomotor rhinitis, including nasal obstruction
Chlorpheniramine	Aller-Chlor®; AL-R®; Chlo-Amine®; Chlorate®; Chlor-Pro®; Chlor-Trimeton®; Kloromin®; Phenetron®; Telechlor®; Teldrin®	Relief of perennial and seasonal allergic rhinitis and other allergic symptoms including urticaria
Chlorpheniramine and acetaminophen	Coricidin® Tablet	Symptomatic relief of congestion, headache, aches, and pains of colds and flu
Chlorpheniramine and phenylephrine	Dallergy-D® Syrup; Ed A-Hist® Liquid; Histatab® Plus Tablet; Histor-D® Syrup; Novahistine® Elixir; Rolatuss® Plain Liquid; Ru-Tuss® Liquid	Temporary relief of nasal congestion and eustachian tube congestion as well as runny nose, sneezing, itching of nose or throat, itchy and watery eyes
Chlorpheniramine and phenylpropanolamine	Allerest® 12 Hour Capsule; A.R.M.® Caplet; Chlor-Rest® Tablet; Demazin® Syrup; Genamin® Cold Syrup; Ornade® Spansule®; Parhist SR®; Resaid®; Rescon Liquid; Silaminic® Cold Syrup; Temazin® Cold Syrup; Thera-Hist® Syrup; Triaminic® Cold Tablet; Triaminic® Allergy Tablet; Triaminic® Syrup; Tri-Nefrin® Extra Strength Tablet; Triphenyl® Syrup	Symptomatic relief of nasal congestion, runny nose, sneezing, itchy nose or throat, and itchy or watery eyes due to the common cold or allergic rhinitis
Chlorpheniramine and pseudoephedrine	Allerest® Maximum Strength; Anamine® Syrup; Anaplex® Liquid; Chlorafed® Liquid; Chlor-Trimeton® 4-Hour Relief Tablet; Co-Pyronil® 2 Pulvules®; Deconamine® SR; Deconamine® Syrup ; Deconamine® Tablet; Fedahist® Tablet; Hayfebrol® Liquid; Histalet® Syrup; Klerist-D® Tablet; Pseudo-Gest Plus® Tablet; Rhinosyn® Liquid; Rhinosyn-PD® Liquid; Ryna® Liquid; Sudafed Plus® Tablet	Relief of nasal congestion associated with the common cold, hay fever, and other allergies, sinusitis, eustachian tube blockage, and vasomotor and allergic rhinitis

OVER-THE-COUNTER PRODUCTS* *(Continued)*

Generic Name	Brand Name	Comments
Chlorpheniramine, phenylephrine, and dextromethorphan	Cerose-DM® Liquid	Temporary relief of cough due to minor throat and bronchial irritation; relief of nasal congestion, runny nose, and sneezing
Chlorpheniramine, phenylephrine, and phenylpropanolamine	Hista-Vadrin® Tablet	Symptomatic relief of rhinitis and nasal congestion due to colds or allergy
Chlorpheniramine, phenylephrine, and phenyltoloxamine	Comhist® Tablet; Comhist® LA Capsule	Symptomatic relief of rhinitis and nasal congestion due to colds or allergy
Chlorpheniramine, phenylpropanolamine, and acetaminophen	BQ® Tablet; Congestant D®; Coricidin D®; Dapacin® Cold Capsule; Duadacin® Capsule; Tylenol® Cold Effervescent Medication Tablet	Symptomatic relief of nasal congestion and headache from colds/sinus congestion
Chlorpheniramine, phenylpropanolamine, and dextromethorphan	Triaminicol® Multi-Symptom Cold Syrup	Relief of runny nose, sneezing with cough suppressant; promotes nasal and sinus drainage
Clemastine and phenylpropanolamine	Tavist-D®	Symptomatic relief of allergic rhinitis; pruritus of the eyes, nose, or throat; lacrimation and nasal congestion
Dexbrompheniramine and pseudoephedrine	Disobrom®; Disophrol® Chronotabs®; Disophrol® Tablet; Drixomed®; Drixoral®; Histrodrix®; Resporal®	Relief of symptoms of upper respiratory mucosal congestion in seasonal and perennial nasal allergies, acute rhinitis, rhinosinusitis, and eustachian tube blockage
Dextromethorphan	Benylin DM®; Children's Hold®; Creo-Terpin®; Delsym®; Drixoral® Cough Liquid Caps; Hold® DM; Pertussin® CS; Pertussin® ES; Robitussin® Cough Calmers; Robitussin® Pediatric; Scot-Tussin DM® Cough Chasers; Silphen DM®; St. Joseph® Cough Suppressant; Sucrets® Cough Calmers; Suppress®; Trocal®; Vicks Formula 44®; Vicks Formula 44® Pediatric Formula	Symptomatic relief of coughs caused by minor viral upper respiratory tract infections or inhaled irritants; most effective for a chronic nonproductive cough
Diphenhydramine and pseudoephedrine	Actifed® Allergy Tablet (Night); Banophen® Decongestant Capsule; Benadryl® Decongestant Allergy Tablet	Relief of symptoms of upper respiratory mucosal congestion in seasonal and perennial nasal allergies, acute rhinitis, rhinosinusitis, and eustachian tube blockage
Guaifenesin and phenylpropanolamine	Ami-Tex LA®; Coldlac-LA®; Conex®; Contuss® XT; Dura-Vent®; Entex® LA; Genagesic®; Genamin® Expectorant; Guaifenex® PPA 75; Guaipax®; Myminic® Expectorant; Naldecon-EX® Children's Syrup; Nolex® LA; Partuss® LA; Phenylfenesin® L.A.; Profen® II; Profen® LA; Rymed-TR®; Silaminic® Expectorant; Sildicon-E®; Snaplets-EX®; Triaminic® Expectorant; Tri-Clear® Expectorant; Triphenyl® Expectorant; ULR-LA®; Vicks® DayQuil® Sinus Pressure & Congestion Relief	Relief of respiratory conditions where tenacious mucous plugs and congestion complicate the problem
Guaifenesin and pseudoephedrine	Congess® Jr; Congess® Sr; Congestac®; Deconsal® II; Defen-LA®; Entex® PSE; Eudal-SR®; Fedahist® Expectorant; Fedahist® Expectorant Pediatric; Glycofed®; Guaifed®; Guaifed-PD®; Guaifenex® PSE; GuaiMAX-D®; Guaitab®; Guaivent®; Guai-Vent/PSE®; Guiatuss® PE; Halotussin® PE; Histalet® X; Nasabid®; Respa-1st®; Respaire-60® SR; Respaire-120® SR; Robitussin-PE®; Robitussin® Severe Congestion Liqui-Gels; Ru-Tuss® DE; Rymed®; Sinufed® Timecelles®; Touro® LA; Tuss-LA®; V-Dec-M®; Versacaps®; Zephrex®; Zephrex® LA	Enhances output of respiratory tract fluid and reduces mucosal congestion and edema in nasal passage
Guaifenesin, phenylpropanolamine, and dextromethorphan	Anatuss®; Guiatuss CF®; Naldecon DX Adult Liquid; Profen II DM®; Robafen® CF; Robitussin-CF®; Siltussin-CF®	Relief of nasal congestion and cough
Guaifenesin, phenylpropanolamine, and phenylephrine	Coldloc®; Contuss®, Dura-Gest®, Enomine®; Entex®; Guaifenex®; Guiatex®	Relief of nasal congestion, running nose, sneezing, itching of nose, throat, and watery eyes

Generic Name	Brand Name	Comments
Guaifenesin, pseudoephedrine, and dextromethorphan	Anatuss® DM; Dimacol® Caplets; Rhinosyn-X® Liquid; Ru-Tuss® Expectorant; Sudafed® Cold & Cough Liquid Caps	Relief of nasal congestion and cough
Oxymetazoline	Afrin® Children's Nose Drops; Afrin® Nasal Solution; Allerest® 12 Hour Nasal Solution; Chlorphed®-LA Nasal Solution; Dristan® Long Lasting Nasal Solution; Drixoral® Nasal (Canadian); Duramist® Plus®; Duration® Nasal Solution; Neo-Synephrine® 12-Hour Nasal Solution; Nostrilla®; NTZ® Long Acting Nasal Solution; OcuClear® Ophthalmic; Sinarest® 12 Hour Nasal Solution; Sinex® Long-Acting; Twice-A-Day® Nasal; Visine® L.R. Ophthalmic; 4-Way® Long Acting Nasal Solution	Symptomatic relief of nasal mucosal congestion and adjunctive therapy of middle ear infections associated with acute or chronic rhinitis, the common cold, sinusitis, hay fever, or other allergies; relief of redness of eye due to minor eye irritations
Phenindamine	Nolahist®	Treatment of perennial and seasonal allergic rhinitis and chronic urticaria
Phenyltoloxamine, phenylpropanolamine, and acetaminophen	Sinubid® Tablet	Intermittent symptomatic treatment of nasal congestion in sinus or other frontal headache; treatment of allergic rhinitis, vasomotor rhinitis, coryza; treatment of facial pain and pressure of acute and chronic sinusitis
Propylhexedrine	Benzedrex® Inhaler	Topical nasal decongestant
Pseudoephedrine and dextromethorphan	Drixoral® Cough & Congestion Liquid Caps; Vicks® 44D Cough & Head Congestion Capsule; Vicks® 44D Non-Drowsy Cold & Cough Liqui-Caps	Temporary symptomatic relief of nasal congestion due to the common cold, upper respiratory allergies, and sinusitis; promotes nasal or sinus drainage; symptomatic relief of coughs caused by minor viral upper respiratory tract infections or inhaled irritants; most effective for a chronic nonproductive cough
Pseudoephedrine and ibuprofen	Advil® Cold & Sinus Caplets; Dimetapp® Sinus Caplets; Dristan® Sinus Caplets; Motrin® IB Sinus Caplets; Sine-Aid® IB Caplets	Temporary symptomatic relief of nasal congestion due to the common cold, upper respiratory allergies, and sinusitis; promotes nasal or sinus drainage; relief of sinus headaches and pains
Terpin hydrate		Symptomatic relief of cough; contains 42% ethyl alcohol
Triprolidine and pseudoephedrine	Actagen® Syrup; Actagen® Tablet; Allercon® Tablet; Allerfrin® Syrup; Allerfrin® Tablet; Allerphed Syrup; Aprodine® Syrup; Aprodine® Tablet; Cenafed® Plus Tablet; Genac® Tablet; Silafed® Syrup; Triofed® Syrup; Triposed® Syrup; Triposed® Tablet	Temporary relief of nasal congestion; decongest sinus openings, runny nose, sneezing, itching of nose or throat, and itchy watery eyes due to common cold, hay fever, or other upper respiratory allergies; may cause drowsiness
Xylometazoline	Otrivin® Nasal	Symptomatic relief of nasal and nasopharyngeal mucosal congestion; use with caution in patients with hypertension, diabetes, cardiovascular or coronary artery disease; do not use for more than 4 days
Dermatologics		
Aluminum sulfate and calcium acetate	Bluboro®; Boropak®; Domeboro® Topical; Pedi-Boro®	Astringent wet dressing for relief of inflammatory conditions of the skin and used to reduce weeping that may occur in dermatitis
Bacitracin, neomycin, polymyxin B, and lidocaine	Clomycin®	Prevent and treat susceptible superficial topical infections
Benzoic acid and salicylic acid	Whitfield's Ointment	Treatment of athlete's foot and ringworm of the scalp

OVER-THE-COUNTER PRODUCTS* (Continued)

Generic Name	Brand Name	Comments
Benzoin	AeroZoin®; TinBen®; TinCoBen®	Protective application for irritations of the skin; sometimes used in boiling water as steam inhalants for their expectorant and soothing action
Benzoyl peroxide	Advanced Formula Oxy® Sensitive Gel; Ambi 10®; Ben-Aqua®; Benoxyl®; Benzac AC® Gel; Benzac AC® Wash; Benzac W® Gel; Benzac W® Wash; 5-Benzagel®; 10-Benzagel®; Benzashave® Cream; BlemErase® Lotion; Brevoxyl® Gel; Clear By Design® Gel; Clearsil® Maximum Strength; Del Aqua-5® Gel; Del Aqua-10® Gel; Desquam-E® Gel; Desquam-X® Gel; Desquam-X® Wash; Dryox® Gel; Dryox® Wash; Exact® Cream; Fostex® 10% BPO Gel; Fostex® 10% Wash; Fostex® Bar; Loroxide® Neutrogena® Acne Mask; Oxy-5® Advanced Formula for Sensitive Skin; Oxy-5® Tinted; Oxy-10® Advanced Formula for Sensitive Skin; Oxy 10® Wash; PanOxyl®-AQ; PanOxyl® Bar; Perfectoderm® Gel; Peroxin A5®; Peroxin A10®; Persa-Gel®; Theroxide® Wash; Vanoxide®	Adjunctive treatment of mild to moderate acne vulgaris acne rosacea
Camphor and phenol	Campho-Phenique® Liquid	Relief of pain and for minor infections
Camphor, menthol, and phenol	Sarna Topical Lotion	Relief of dry, itching skin
Chlorophyll	Chloresium®; Derifil®; Nullo®; PALS®	Topically promotes normal healing; relief of pain and inflammation; reduce malodors in wounds, burns, surface ulcers, abrasions, and skin irritations; used orally to control fecal and urinary odors in colostomy, ileostomy, or incontinence
Chloroxine	Capitrol® Shampoo	Treatment of dandruff or seborrheic dermatitis of the scalp
Coal tar	AquaTar®; Denorex®; DHS® Tar; Duplex® T; Estar®; Fototar®; Neutrogena® T/Derm; Oxipor® VHC; Pentrax®; Polytar®; psoriGel®; T/Gel®; Zetar®	Topically for controlling dandruff, seborrheic dermatitis, or psoriasis
Coal tar and salicylic acid	X-seb® T Shampoo	Control seborrheal dermatitis, dandruff
Coal tar, lanolin, and mineral oil	Balnetar® Bath Oil	Control psoriasis, seborrheal dermatitis, atopic dermatitis, eczematoid dermatitis
Dibucaine	Nupercainal®	Fast, temporary relief of pain and itching due to hemorrhoids, minor burns, or other minor skin conditions (amide derivative local anesthetic)
Dibucaine and hydrocortisone	Corticaine® Topical Cream	Relief of the inflammatory and pruritic manifestations of corticosteroid-responsive dermatoses and for external anal itching
Glycerin, lanolin, and peanut oil	Massé® Breast Cream	Nipple care of pregnant and nursing women
Lactic acid and sodium-PCA	LactiCare® Lotion	Lubricate and moisturize the skin counteracting dryness and itching
Lactic acid with ammonium hydroxide	Lac-Hydrin® Lotion	Treatment of moderate to severe xerosis and ichthyosis vulgaris
Lanolin, cetyl alcohol, glycerin, and petrolatum	Lubriderm® Lotion	Treatment of dry skin
Malathion	Ovide™ Topical Lotion	Treatment of head lice and their ova
Merbromin	Mercurochrome® Topical Solution	Topical antiseptic
Methoxycinnamate and oxybenzone	PreSun® 29; Ti-Screen®	Reduce the chance of premature aging of the skin and skin cancer from overexposure to the sun

Generic Name	Brand Name	Comments
Methylbenzethonium chloride	Diaparene®; Puri-Clens™; Sween Cream®	Treatment of diaper rash and ammonia dermatitis
Nonoxynol 9	Because®; Delfen®; Emko®; Encare®; Gynol II®; Intercept™; Koromex®; Ramses®; Semicid®; Shur-Seal®	Spermatocide in contraception
Parachlorometaxylenol	Metasep®	Aid in relief of dandruff and associated conditions
Povidone-iodine	ACU-dyne®; Aerodine®; Betadine®; Betadine® 5% Sterile Ophthalmic Prep Solution; Betagen®; Biodine; Efodine®; Iodex®; Iodex-p®; Isodine®; Mallisol®; Massengil® Medicated Douche w/ Cepticin; Minidyne®; Operand®; Polydine®; Summer's Eve® Medicated Douche; Yeast-Gard® Medicated Douche	External antiseptic with broad microbicidal spectrum against bacteria, fungi, viruses, protozoa, and yeasts
Pyrithione zinc	DHS Zinc®; Head & Shoulders® Shampoo; Sebulon®; Theraplex Z®; Zincon® Shampoo; ZNP® Bar	Relief of itching, irritation, and scalp flaking associated with dandruff and/or seborrheal dermatitis of the scalp
Salicylic acid	Acnex® (Canadian); Acnomel® (Canadian); Clear Away® Disc; Compound W®; Dr Scholl's® Disk; Dr Scholl's® Wart Remover; DuoFilm®; DuoPlant® Gel; Freezone® Solution; Gordofilm® Liquid; Mediplast® Plaster; Mosco® Liquid; Occlusal-HP Liquid; Off-Ezy® Wart Remover; Panscol®; Psor-a-set® Soap; P&S® Shampoo; Sal-Acid® Plaster; Salactic® Film; Sal-Plant® Gel; Trans-Planta® (Canadian); Trans-Ver-Sal® (Canadian); Trans-Ver-Sal® AdultPatch; Trans-Ver-Sal® PediaPatch; Trans-Ver-Sal® PlantarPatch; Wart-Off®;	Topically used for its keratolytic effect in controlling seborrheic dermatitis or psoriasis of body and scalp, dandruff, and other scaling dermatoses; remove warts, corns, and calluses
Salicylic acid and lactic acid	Duofilm® Solution	Treatment of benign epithelial tumors such as warts
Salicylic acid and propylene glycol	Keralyt® Gel	Removal of excessive keratin in hyperkeratotic skin disorders, including various ichthyosis, keratosis palmaris and plantaris, and psoriasis; may be used to remove excessive keratin in dorsal and plantar hyperkeratotic lesions
Sulfur and salicylic acid	Aveeno® Cleansing Bar; Fostex®; Pernox®; SAStid® Plain Therapeutic Shampoo and Acne Wash; Sebulex®	Therapeutic shampoo for dandruff and seborrheal dermatitis; acne skin cleanser
Thimerosal	Aeroaid®; Mersol®; Merthiolate®	Organomercurial antiseptic with sustained bacteriostatic and fungistatic activity
Triacetin	Fungoid®; Ony-Clear® Nail Aerosol	Fungistat for athlete's foot and other superficial fungal infections
Undecylenic acid and derivatives	Caldesene® Topical; Fungoid® AF Topical Solution; Pedi-Pro Topical	Treatment of athlete's foot, ringworm, prickly heat, jock itch, diaper rash, and other minor skin irritations
Vitamin A and vitamin D	A and D™ Ointment	Temporary relief of discomfort due to chapped skin, diaper rash, minor burns, abrasions, as well as irritations associated with ostomy skin care
Zinc oxide		Protective coating for mild skin irritations and abrasions; soothing and protective ointment to promote healing of chapped skin, diaper rash; if irritation develops, discontinue use and consult a physician; paste is easily removed with mineral oil; for external use only; do not use in eyes
Zinc oxide, cod liver oil, and talc	Desitin® Ointment	Relief of diaper rash, superficial wounds and burns, and other minor skin irritations; if condition persists, or if rash, irritation, or sensitivity develops, discontinue and contact physician; for external use only

OVER-THE-COUNTER PRODUCTS* *(Continued)*

Generic Name	Brand Name	Comments
Dietary Supplements		
Calcium citrate	Citracal®	Adjunct in prevention of postmenopausal osteoporosis; treatment and prevention of calcium depletion
Calcium lactate		Adjunct in prevention of postmenopausal osteoporosis; treatment and prevention of calcium depletion
Calcium phosphate, dibasic	Posture®	Adjunct in prevention of postmenopausal osteoporosis; treatment and prevention of calcium depletion
Ferrous salt and ascorbic acid	Ferancee®; Fero-Grad 500®; Ferromar®	Treatment of iron deficiency in nonpregnant or pregnant adults
Ferrous sulfate, ascorbic acid, and vitamin B complex	Iberet®-Liquid	Treatment of conditions of iron deficiency with an increased need for B complex vitamins and vitamin C; should be administered with water or juice on an empty stomach; may be administered with food to prevent irritation, however, not with cereals, dietary fiber, tea, coffee, eggs, or milk
Glucose, instant	B-D Glucose®; Glutose®; Insta-Glucose®	Management of hypoglycemia
Glucose polymers	Moducal®; Polycose®; Sumacal®	Supplies calories for those persons not able to meet the caloric requirement with usual food intake
Magnesium chloride	Slow-Mag®	Correct or prevent hypomagnesemia
Magnesium gluconate	Magonate®	Dietary supplement for treatment of magnesium deficiencies
Medium chain triglycerides	MCT Oil®	Dietary supplement for those who cannot digest long chain fats; malabsorption associated with disorders such as pancreatic insufficiency, bile salt deficiency, and bacterial overgrowth of the small bowel; induce ketosis as a prevention for seizures (akinetic, clonic, and petit mal)
Polysaccharide-iron complex	Hytinic®; Niferex®; Nu-Iron®	Prevention and treatment of iron deficiency anemias
Vitamin B complex	Apatate®; Gevrabon®; Lederplex®; Lipovite®; MegaB®; Megaton™; Mucoplex®; NeoVadrin® B Complex; Orexin®; Surbex®	Prevention and treatment of B complex vitamin deficiency
Vitamin B complex with vitamin C	Allbee® With C; Surbex-T® Filmtabs®; Surbex® With C Filmtabs®; Thera-Combex® H-P Kapseals®; Vicon-C®	Supportive nutritional supplementation in conditions in which water-soluble vitamins are required like GI disorders, chronic alcoholism, pregnancy, severe burns, and recovery from surgery
Vitamin B complex with vitamin C and folic acid	Berocca®; Folbesyn®; Nephrocaps®	Supportive nutritional supplementation in conditions in which water-soluble vitamins are required like GI disorders, chronic alcoholism, pregnancy, severe burns, and recovery from surgery
Zinc sulfate	Eye-Sed® Ophthalmic; Orazinc® Oral; Verazinc® Oral; Zincate® Oral	Zinc supplement (oral and parenteral); may improve wound healing in those who are deficient

Generic Name	Brand Name	Comments
Hemorrhoidal Preparations		
Pramoxine	Anusol® Ointment; Fleet® Pain Relief; Itch-X®; Phicon®; PrameGel®; Prax®; Proctofoam® NS; Tronolane®; Tronothane® HCl	Temporary relief of pain and itching associated with anogenital pruritus or irritation; treatment of dermatosis, minor burns, or hemorrhoids
Witch hazel	Tucks® Cream/Gel/Pads	After-stool wipe to remove most causes of local irritation; temporary management of vulvitis, pruritus ani, and vulva; help relieve the discomfort of simple hemorrhoids, anorectal surgical wounds, and episiotomies
Ophthalmics		
Artificial tears	Adsorbotear® Ophthalmic Solution; Akwa Tears® Solution; AquaSite® Ophthalmic Solution; Bion® Tears Solution; Comfort® Tears Solution; Dakrina® Ophthalmic Solution; Dry Eye® Therapy Solution; Dry Eyes® Solution; Dwelle® Ophthalmic Solution; Eye-Lube-A® Solution; HypoTears PF Solution; HypoTears Solution; Isopto® Plain Solution; Isopto® Tears Solution; Just Tears® Solution; Lacril® Ophthalmic Solution; Liquifilm® Tears Solution; Liquifilm® Forte Solution; LubriTears® Solution; Moisture® Ophthalmic Drops; Murine® Solution; Murocel® Ophthalmic Solution; Nature's Tears® Solution; Nu-Tears® Solution; Nu-Tears® II Solution; OcuCoat® Ophthalmic Solution; OcuCoat® PF Ophthalmic Solution; Puralube® Tears Solution; Refresh® Ophthalmic Solution; Refresh® Plus Ophthalmic Solution; Tear Drop® Solution; TearGard® Ophthalmic Solution; Teargen® Ophthalmic Solution; Tearisol® Solution; Tears Naturale® Free Solution; Tears Naturale® II Solution; Tears Naturale® Solution; Tears Plus® Solution; Tears Renewed® Solution; Ultra Tears® Solution; Viva-Drops® Solution	Ophthalmic lubricant; relief of dry eyes and eye irritation
Balanced salt solution	BSS® Ophthalmic	Intraocular irrigating solution; used to soothe and cleanse the eye in conjunction with hard contact lenses
Benzalkonium chloride	Benza®; Zephiran®	Surface antiseptic and germicidal preservative
Carboxymethylcellulose sodium	Cellufresh® Ophthalmic Solution; Celluvisc® Ophthalmic Solution	Preservative-free artificial tear substitute
Glycerin	Ophthalgan® Ophthalmic; Osmolglyn® Ophthalmic	Reduction of intraocular pressure; reduction of corneal edema; glycerin had been administered orally to reduce intracranial pressure
Naphazoline	AK-Con® Ophthalmic; Albalon® Liquifilm® Ophthalmic; Allerest® Eye Drops; Clear Eyes®; Comfort® Ophthalmic; Degest® 2 Ophthalmic; Estivin® II Ophthalmic; I-Naphline® Ophthalmic; Nafazair® Ophthalmic; Naphcon Forte® Ophthalmic; Naphcon® Ophthalmic; Nazil® Ofteno (Mexican); Opcon® Ophthalmic; Privine® Nasal; VasoClear® Ophthalmic; Vasocon Regular® Ophthalmic	Topical ocular vasoconstrictor; will temporarily relieve congestion, itching, and minor irritation; control hyperemia in patients with superficial corneal vascularity
Naphazoline and antazoline	Albalon-A® Ophthalmic Solution; Antazoline-V® Ophthalmic Solution; Vasocon-A® Ophthalmic Solution	Topical ocular congestion, irritation, and itching; use with caution in patients with cardiovascular disease
Naphazoline and pheniramine	Naphcon-A® Ophthalmic Solution	Topical ocular vasoconstrictor; use with caution in patients with cardiovascular disease
Phenylephrine and zinc sulfate	Optised® Ophthalmic; Phenylzin® Ophthalmic; Zincfrin® Ophthalmic	Soothe, moisturize, and remove redness due to minor eye irritation; discontinue use if ocular pain or visual changes are present after 3 days

OVER-THE-COUNTER PRODUCTS* *(Continued)*

Generic Name	Brand Name	Comments
Tetrahydrozoline	Collyrium Fresh® Ophthalmic; Eyesine® Ophthalmic; Geneye® Ophthalmic; Mallazine® Eye Drops; Murine® Plus Ophthalmic; Optigene® Ophthalmic; Tetrasine® Extra Ophthalmic; Tetrasine® Ophthalmic; Tyzine® Nasal; Visine® Extra Ophthalmic	Symptomatic relief of nasal congestion and conjunctival congestion
Oral		
Benzocaine, gelatin, pectin, and sodium carboxymethylcellulose	Orabase® With Benzocaine Paste	Topical anesthetic and emollient for oral lesions
Cetylpyridinium	Ceepryn®; Cëpacol® Troches	Temporary relief of sore throat
Cetylpyridinium and benzocaine	Cëpacol® Anesthetic Troches	Symptomatic relief of sore throat
Gelatin, pectin, and methylcellulose	Orabase® Plain	Temporary relief from minor oral irritations
Phenol	Baker's P&S Topical; Cepastat® Chloraseptic® Oral; Ulcerease®	Relief of sore throat pain and mouth, gum, and throat irritations
Saliva substitute	Moi-Stir®; Orex®; Xero-Lube®	Relief of dry mouth and throat in xerostomia
Otic		
Boric acid	Borofax® Topical; Dri-Ear® Otic; Swim-Ear® Otic	Ophthalmic: Mild antiseptic used for inflamed eyelids. Otic: Prophylaxis of swimmer's ear. Topical ointment: Temporary relief of chapped, chafed, or dry skin; diaper rash; abrasions; minor burns; sunburn; insect bites; and other skin irritations.
Miscellaneous or Multiple Use		
Sodium chloride	Adsorbonac® Ophthalmic; Afrin® Saline Mist; AK-NaCl®; Ayr® Saline; Breathe Free®; Dristan® Saline Spray; HuMist® Nasal Mist; Muro 128® Ophthalmic; Muroptic-5®; NaSal™; Nasal Moist®; Ocean Nasal Mist; Pretz®; SalineX®; SeaMist®	Prevention of muscle cramps and heat prostration; restoration of sodium ion in hyponatremia; induce abortion; restore moisture to nasal membranes; GU irrigant; reduction of corneal edema; source of electrolytes and water for expansion of the extracellular fluid compartment

TYRAMINE CONTENT OF FOODS

Food	Allowed	Minimize Intake	Not Allowed
Beverages	Milk, decaffeinated coffee, tea, soda	Chocolate beverage, caffeine-containing drinks, clear spirits	Acidophilus milk, beer, ale, wine, malted beverages
Breads/cereals	All except those containing cheese	None	Cheese bread and crackers
Dairy products	Cottage cheese, farmers or pot cheese, cream cheese, ricotta cheese, all milk, eggs, ice cream, pudding (except chocolate)	Yogurt (limit to 4 oz per day)	All other cheeses (aged cheese, American, Camembert, cheddar, Gouda, gruyere, mozzarella, parmesan, provolone, romano, Roquefort, stilton
Meat, fish, and poultry	All fresh or frozen	Aged meats, hot dogs, canned fish and meat	Chicken and beef liver, dried and pickled fish, summer or dry sausage, pepperoni, dried meats, meat extracts, bologna, liverwurst
Starches — potatoes/rice	All	None	Soybean (including paste)
Vegetables	All fresh, frozen, canned, or dried vegetable juices except those not allowed	Chili peppers, Chinese pea pods	Fava beans, sauerkraut, pickles, olives, Italian broad beans
Fruit	Fresh, frozen, or canned fruits and fruit juices	Avocado, banana, raspberries, figs	Banana peel extract
Soups	All soups not listed to limit or avoid	Commercially canned soups	Soups which contain broad beans, fava beans, cheese, beer, wine, any made with flavor cubes or meat extract, miso soup
Fats	All except fermented	Sour cream	Packaged gravy
Sweets	Sugar, hard candy, honey, molasses, syrups	Chocolate candies	None
Desserts	Cakes, cookies, gelatin, pastries, sherbets, sorbets	Chocolate desserts	Cheese-filled desserts
Miscellaneous	Salt, nuts, spices, herbs, flavorings, Worcestershire sauce	Soy sauce, peanuts	Brewer's yeast, yeast concentrates, all aged and fermented products, monosodium glutamate, vitamins with Brewer's yeast

VITAMIN K CONTENT IN SELECTED FOODS

The following lists describe the relative amounts of vitamin K in selected foods. The abbreviations for vitamin K is "H" for high amounts, "M" for medium amounts, and "L" for low amounts.

Foods*	Portion Size†	Vitamin K Content
Coffee brewed	10 cups	L
Cola, regular and diet	3½ fl oz	L
Fruit juices, assorted types	3½ fl oz	L
Milk	3½ fl oz	L
Tea, black, brewed	3½ fl oz	L
Bread, assorted types	4 slices	L
Cereal, assorted types	3½ oz	L
Flour, assorted types	1 cup	L
Oatmeal, instant, dry	1 cup	L
Rice, white	½ cup	L
Spaghetti, dry	3½ oz	L
Butter	6 Tbsp	L
Cheddar cheese	3½ oz	L
Eggs	2 large	L
Margarine	7 Tbsp	M
Mayonnaise	7 Tbsp	H
Oils		
Canola, salad, soybean	7 Tbsp	H
Olive	7 Tbsp	M
Corn, peanut, safflower, sesame, sunflower	7 Tbsp	L
Sour cream	8 Tbsp	L
Yogurt	3½ oz	L
Apple	1 medium	L
Banana	1 medium	L
Blueberries	⅔ cup	L
Cantaloupe pieces	⅔ cup	L
Grapes	1 cup	L
Grapefruit	½ medium	L
Lemon	2 medium	L
Orange	1 medium	L
Peach	1 medium	L
Abalone	3½ oz	L
Beef, ground	3½ oz	L
Chicken	3½ oz	L
Mackerel	3½ oz	L
Meatloaf	3½ oz	L
Pork, meat	3½ oz	L
Tuna	3½ oz	L
Turkey, meat	3½ oz	L
Asparagus, raw	7 spears	M
Avocado, peeled	1 small	M
Beans, pod, raw	1 cup	M
Broccoli, raw and cooked	½ cup	H
Brussel sprout, sprout and top leaf	5 sprouts	H
Cabbage, raw	1½ cups shredded	H
Cabbage, red, raw	1½ cups shredded	M
Carrot	⅔ cup	L
Cauliflower	1 cup	L
Celery	2½ stalks	L
Coleslaw	¾ cup	M
Collard greens	½ cup chopped	H
Cucumber peel, raw	1 cup	H
Cucumber, peel removed	1 cup	L

Foods*	Portion Size†	Vitamin K Content
Eggplant	1¼ cups pieces	L
Endive, raw	2 cups chopped	H
Green scallion, raw	⅔ cup chopped	H
Kale, raw leaf	¾ cup	H
Lettuce, raw, heading, bib, red leaf	1¾ cups shredded	H
Mushroom	1½ cups	L
Mustard greens, raw	1½ cups	H
Onion, white	⅔ cup chopped	L
Parsley, raw and cooked	1½ cups chopped	H
Peas, green, cooked	⅔ cup	M
Pepper, green, raw	1 cup chopped	L
Potato	1 medium	L
Pumpkin	½ cup	L
Spinach, raw leaf	1½ cups	H
Tomato	1 medium	L
Turnip greens, raw	1½ cups chopped	H
Watercress, raw	3 cups chopped	H
Honey	5 Tbsp	L
Jell-O® Gelatin	⅓ cup	L
Peanut butter	6 Tbsp	L
Pickle, dill	1 medium	M
Sauerkraut	1 cup	M
Soybean, dry	½ cup	M

*This list is a partial listing of foods. For more complete information, refer to references 1-2.

†Portions in chart are calculated from estimated portions provided in reference 4.

References

Booth SL, Sadowski JA, Weihrauch JL, et al, "Vitamin K₁ (Phylloquinone) Content of Foods a Provisional Table," *J Food Comp Anal*, 1993, 6:109-20.

Ferland G, MacDonald DL, and Sadowski JA, "Development of a Diet Low in Vitamin K₁ (Phylloquinone)," *J Am Diet Assoc*, 1992, 92, 593-7.

Hogan RP, "Hemorrhagic Diathesis Caused by Drinking an Herbal Tea," *JAMA*, 1983, 249:2679-80.

Pennington JA, *Bowes and Church's Food Values of Portions Commonly Used*, 15th ed, JP Lippincott Co, 1985.

THERAPEUTIC CATEGORY & KEY WORD INDEX

ANTI-INFLAMMATORY AGENT, INHALANT

ANTI-INFLAMMATORY AGENT, LOCALLY APPLIED

ANTI-INFLAMMATORY AGENT, OPHTHALMIC

ANTI-INFLAMMATORY AGENT, RECTAL

ANTILIPEMIC AGENT

ANTIMALARIAL AGENT

ANTIMANIC AGENT

ANTIMETABOLITE

ANTIMIGRAINE AGENT

(Continued)

ANTITHYROID AGENT

ANTITOXIN

ANTITUBERCULAR AGENT

ANTITUSSIVE

ANTITUSSIVE/DECONGESTANT

ANTITUSSIVE/DECONGESTANT/EXPECTORANT

ANTITUSSIVE/EXPECTORANT

ANTIVIRAL AGENT

ANTIVIRAL AGENT, INHALATION THERAPY

ANTIVIRAL AGENT, OPHTHALMIC

ANTIVIRAL AGENT, ORAL

ANTIVIRAL AGENT, PARENTERAL

ANTIVIRAL AGENT, TOPICAL

AROMATASE INHIBITOR

BARBITURATE

BENZODIAZEPINE
(Continued)

CONTROLLED SUBSTANCE IV

CONTROLLED SUBSTANCE V

CORTICOSTEROID

CORTICOSTEROID, ADRENAL

CORTICOSTEROID, INHALANT

CORTICOSTEROID, INTRANASAL

CORTICOSTEROID, OPHTHALMIC

(Continued)

NOTES:

Other titles offered by Lexi-Comp . . .

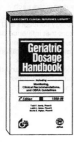

DRUG INFORMATION HANDBOOK FOR PHYSICIAN ASSISTANTS
1999-2000

by Michael J. Rudzinski, RPA-C, RPh; J. Fred Bennes, RPA, RPh

This comprehensive and easy-to-use handbook covers over 3,600 drugs and also includes monographs on commonly used herbal products. There are up to 24 key fields of information per monograph, such as; Pediatric and adult dosing with adjustments for renal/hepatic impairment, Labeled and unlabeled uses, Pregnancy & breast-feeding precautions, and Special PA issues. Brand (U.S. and Canadian) and generic names listed alphabetically for rapid access. It is fully cross-referenced by page number and includes alphabetical & pharmacologic indices.

DRUG INFORMATION HANDBOOK FOR ONCOLOGY *1999-2000*

by Dominic A. Solimando, Jr, MA; Linda R. Bressler, PharmD, BCOP; Polly E. Kintzel, PharmD, BCPS, BCOP; Mark C. Geraci, PharmD, BCOP

This comprehensive and easy-to-use oncology handbook was designed specifically to meet the needs of anyone who provides, prescribes, or administers therapy to cancer patients.

Presented in a concise and uniform format, this book contains the most comprehensive collection of oncology-related drug information available. Organized like a dictionary for ease of use, drugs can be found by looking up the *brand or generic name!*

This book contains 253 monographs, including over 1100 Antineoplastic Agents and Ancillary Medications.

Also containing up to 33 fields of information per monograph including: Use, U.S. Investigational, Bone Marrow/Blood Cell Transplantation, Vesicant, Emetic Potential. A Special Topics Section, Appendix, and Therapeutic Category & Key Word Index are valuable features to this book as well.

DRUG INFORMATION HANDBOOK FOR PSYCHIATRY *1999-2000*

by Matthew A. Fuller, PharmD; Martha Sajatovic, MD

The source for comprehensive and clinically relevant drug information for the mental health professional. Alphabetically arranged by generic and brand name for ease-of-use. Containing monographs on 1,063 generic drugs and up to 34 key fields of information including; effect on mental status and effect on psychiatric treatment.

A special topics/issues section includes; psychiatric assessment, overview of selected major psychiatric disorders, clinical issues in the use of major classes of psychotropic medications, psychiatric emergencies, special populations, diagnostic and statistical manual of mental disorders (DSM-IV), and suggested reading. Also contains a valuable appendix section as well as a therapeutic category index and a alphabetical index.

To order call toll free: 1-800-837-LEXI (5394)

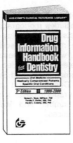
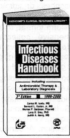

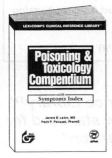

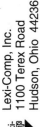

Thank you for purchasing Lexi-Comp's _Drug Information Handbook_

Return this postage-paid card so we can keep you up-to-date on all the latest products, promotions and upgrades.

☒ Please put me on your "Mailing List".

☒ Please put me on your "Standing Order List" to automatically receive the new edition each year.

Please print name of book

_____

☒ **Please send me information on quantity discounts.**

Name (First) _____ (Last) _____

Title _____

Company _____

Address _____

City _____ State/Province _____

Zip/Postal Code _____ Country _____

t: (___) _____ Fax: (___) _____

ess _____

OTHER AREAS OF INTEREST:

☐ Anesthesiology & Critical Care
☐ Diagnostic Procedures
☐ Laboratory Tests
☐ Drug Information for Allied Health
☐ Drug Information for Cardiology*
☐ Drug Information for Dentistry
☐ Drug Information for Nursing
☐ Drug Information for Psychiatry
☐ Drug-Induced Nutrient Depletion

☐ Geriatric Dosage
☐ Natural Products Information*
☐ Drug Information for Oncology
☐ Natural Therapeutics*
☐ Infectious Diseases
☐ Drug Information for Physician Assistants
☐ Pediatric Dosage
☐ Poisoning & Toxicology
☐ Drug Information for Advanced Practice Nursing*
☐ Drug Information for the Criminal Justice Professional

* 1999 targeted release

ALSO INTERESTED IN THE FOLLOWING:

☐ Lexi-Comp's Formulary/Lab Custom Publishing Service
☐ Lexi-Comp's Clinical Reference Library™ on CD-ROM
  (___ Academic ___ Personal ___ Institutional)
☐ Lexi-Comp's CRL™ on a hand-held device